BUSINESS
LAW
TEXT AND CASES

FOURTH EDITION

BUSINESS
LAW
TEXT AND CASES

FOURTH EDITION

Rate A. Howell
The Ohio State University

John R. Allison
University of Texas, Austin

Robert A. Prentice
University of Texas, Austin

The Dryden Press
Chicago   New York   San Francisco   Philadelphia   Montreal   Toronto
London   Sydney   Tokyo

Acquisitions Editor: Michael Reynolds
Developmental Editor: Deborah Acker
Project Editor: Holly Crawford
Design Supervisor: Jeanne Calabrese
Production Supervisor: Diane Tenzi
Permissions Editor: Doris Milligan
Director of Editing, Design, and Production: Jane Perkins
Text Designer: Hunter Graphics
Cover Design: Vargas/Williams Design
Copy Editor: Charlene Posner
Indexer: Richard Ruane, Little Chicago Editorial Services
Compositor: G & S Typesetters, Inc.
Text Type: 10/12 ITC Garamond Book

Library of Congress Cataloging-in-Publication Data

Howell, Rate A.
  Business law.

  Includes bibliographical references and index.
  1. Commercial law—United States—Cases.
I. Allison, John Robert, 1948–   .   II. Prentice,
Robert A., 1950–   .   III. Title.
KF888.H68   1988   346.73'07   87-5060
ISBN 0-03-011539-6   347.3067

Printed in the United States of America
 89-039-98765432

Address orders:
111 Fifth Avenue
New York, NY 10003

Address editorial correspondence:
One Salt Creek Lane
Hinsdale, IL 60521-2902

The Dryden Press
Holt, Rinehart and Winston
Saunders College Publishing

PREFACE

We have had but one goal in preparing the fourth edition of *Business Law: Text and Cases:* to make the text a more useful vehicle for the study of Business Law by future business managers at both graduate and undergraduate levels in our colleges and universities. In striving to attain this goal, we rejected the temptation merely to fine-tune the prior edition and have developed a number of new features which will be highlighted later in the preface.

This edition, nonetheless, retains the basic strengths of earlier editions, which can be described as follows:

First, we have continued to use a lucid, conversational writing style. In addition, we have tried to illuminate legal principles by frequent use of examples to show how these rules apply to "real world" situations.

Second, illustrative court cases are interspersed throughout the text materials, rather than relegated to chapter ends. As in previous editions, each case begins with a presentation of the facts by the authors so that students will not be confused by the sometimes difficult terminology used by higher courts in summarizing the proceedings of the lower courts. The opinions of the higher courts, on the other hand, are carefully edited but retain the courts' own language. This approach ensures that the students first have a clear idea of the controversy and then gives them a feel for the way the court resolved it. It allows students to see how the court weighed conflicting evidence in deciding what the facts were, how it viewed particular facts as relevant or irrelevant to the issues at hand, and how it selected the legal principles that it felt to be dispositive of those issues.

Third, the text continues to be essentially a traditional one, rather than an environmental one. In other words, despite a rather full discussion of the legal system in Part I and of several regulatory topics in Part VIII, most of the text is again devoted to such subjects as contracts, agency, sales, commercial paper, property, and business organizations.

This fourth edition benefits from numerous additions and changes that we feel enhance the widely acclaimed qualities of prior editions. The most significant of these is the addition of Professor Robert Prentice of the University of Texas at Austin as a coauthor. Although still at an early stage of his career, he has already received national recognition for his teaching, research, and writing. Because Professor Prentice's primary area of responsibility for this edition has been Part I, "The Legal Environment of Business," this part now provides a fresh, up-to-date introduction to those aspects of our legal system that cut across all areas of law and it establishes a vital foundation for understanding the substantive subjects that follow. These introductory topics include such matters as the roles of the state and federal court systems, and an examination of the theoretical foundations and practical applications of the various sources of law.

CHANGES IN THIS EDITION

- A new chapter on Business Ethics, Corporate Social Responsibility, and the Law (Chapter 9).

- A new chapter on Employment Law (Chapter 49).

- A new chapter on Dispute Resolution (Chapter 3).

- Two new appendixes: The Model Business Corporation Act and The Constitution of the United States.

- The addition of a substantial number of new cases throughout all parts of the text, many of which are 1985 and 1986 decisions. Concentration of these cases is especially high in the chapters on Court Systems, Dispute Resolution, Torts, Constitutional Law, Agency, Partnerships, and Corporations.

- Enhancement of instructional aids: opening outlines and concluding summaries have been added to all chapters.

- Realignment of the agency chapters to form a separate part of the text. Additionally, at the suggestion of reviewers, these chapters have been advanced to Part III in recognition of the frequent inclusion of the subject of agency in the beginning Business Law course.

- Particularly heavy rewriting of the chapters on Torts, Constitutional Law, Products Liability, Bankruptcy, Real Property, and Business Organizations.

- An updating of the chapter on Bankruptcy (Chapter 30) to reflect, among other things, recent changes Congress has made in regard to the kinds of debts that are not dischargeable in bankruptcy proceedings, as well as the increased importance of reorganization proceedings and the public policy questions they raise.

- A rewriting and combining of the materials on Personal Property and Bailments into a single chapter (Chapter 43), together with the inclusion of many new cases in these areas.

- Combination of the prior chapters on Contractual Capacity and Reality of Consent into a single chapter, Voidable Contracts (Chapter 14).

- Combination of the prior chapters on Common Law and Statutory Law into a single chapter (Chapter 4).

- Expanded treatment, in the chapters on Corporation Law, of stockholders' derivative suits, mergers, and takeovers as a consequence of increasing activity in these areas.

- Consolidation and treatment of the special sales law rules applicable to the formation and enforceability of sales contracts concurrently with discussion of the common-law rules applicable to ordinary contracts in Part II, "Principles of Contract Law."

ANCILLARY MATERIALS

Business Law: Text and Cases, fourth edition, is supported by a comprehensive ancillary package which includes an *Instructor's Manual and Transparency Masters,* a *Test Bank,* a set of preprinted tests, a *Computerized Test Bank,* and a *Study Guide.*

Each instructor has his or her own unique approach to the teaching of Business Law. Our *Instructor's Manual* is a tool that assists the instructor in integrating his or her style with the approach taken by the book. Each chapter begins with helpful authors' suggestions for teaching the chapter. Chapter outlines have been added to assist the instructor in organizing lecture notes. Succinct case briefs are included for each case in the book. We have also added an annotated list of additional cases so that the instructor can easily supplement the cases found in the text. Each chapter in the *Instructor's Manual* ends with answers to end-of-chapter questions and problems.

The *Test Bank* contains over 2,000 multiple-choice and true-false questions. We have added numerous essay questions for the instructor to choose from.

To make it easier for the instructor to give exams and quizzes, we have added preprinted tests to the ancillary package. The preprinted tests have been organized into logical chapter groupings using questions drawn directly from the *Test Bank.* There are two versions of every test.

A *Computerized Test Bank* is also available for this edition for use on IBM PC® or Apple II®.

A comprehensive *Study Guide* provides additional review and reinforcement of all topics covered in the text. Each chapter of the guide, which has traditionally been well received by students and instructors, begins with a chapter summary. The key term and matching exercises also provide an excellent review for students. The purpose of these two sections is to test the student's basic mastery of the concepts, laws, and rulings discussed in the text. Multiple-choice and true-false questions are provided, as well as case analysis problems which provide fact-patterns to which the student is asked to respond. All three types of questions will test the student's comprehension of the material in an examination setting. The questions are similar in format and type to those included in the *Test Bank.*

Another feature of the *Study Guide* is the inclusion of legal forms. We include these forms to give the student a good idea of how legal concepts are employed in the business world.

ACKNOWLEDGMENTS

As with any major undertaking, this text owes its existence to the efforts of many individuals. We wish to thank Louis Rodriquez at Arkansas State University for his preparation of the *Test Bank*, Carol D. Rasnic at Virginia Commonwealth University for the *Study Guide*, and the many reviewers who read the manuscript for this edition and provided valuable suggestions. They are Barry J. Baroni (University of New Orleans), Raymond A. Catazano (Nassau Community College), Bryce Denny (Austin College), Carol D. Rasnic (Virginia Commonwealth University), Daniel L. Reynolds (Middle Tennessee State University), Donald E. Sanders (Southwest Texas State University), Gabe Sanders (Jersey City State College), and Robert J. Senn (Shippensburg University).

We also wish to thank our editors at The Dryden Press, Mike Reynolds, Debby Acker, Holly Crawford, and Charlene Posner, for their commitment to excellence.

Finally, we are grateful to our students for keeping us fresh and fully challenged, and to our families for their continued support.

Rate A. Howell, *Columbus, Ohio*
John R. Allison, *Austin, Texas*
Robert A. Prentice, *Austin, Texas*

CONTENTS

Part I

THE LEGAL ENVIRONMENT OF BUSINESS

Part I of this text consists of nine chapters that are devoted to matters that cut across or substantially affect all areas of law. Its purpose is to lay the groundwork for an understanding of the somewhat narrower substantive bodies of law, such as the law of contracts and corporation law, that are covered in the parts of the text that follow.

These introductory matters are largely concerned with structures, processes, and analyses—the structure of our existing laws and court systems, the legal processes by which laws are made and applied to actual controversies, and analysis of the historical reasons responsible for these structures and processes.

Chapter 1 examines the nature and purpose of legal rules—the special characteristics that set these rules apart from other societal rules and the characteristics which these rules must possess if they are to remain an effective part of the legal system.

Chapter 2 provides familiarity with the structure and jurisdiction of the federal and state courts, while Chapter 3 examines the roles of the trial and appellate courts in the resolution of real controversies. We examine these "adjudicatory processes" of the law in these chapters so that actual court cases can be utilized in the text as early and effectively as possible.

Chapters 4 through 6 deal with "lawmaking processes"—the ways in which rules become rules of law. Chapter 4 describes the making of common law by the courts and statutory law by the legislatures; Chapter 5 discusses the application of constitutional principles by the courts; and Chapter 6 addresses the formulation of rules and regulations by administrative agencies.

Chapter 7 examines the most common types of torts, or civil wrongs, which are those kinds of wrongful conduct (such as negligence or assault and battery) that may be encountered in both business and nonbusiness settings. Chapter 8 focuses on business torts and crimes. Tort actions arising out of the sale of defective products are discussed in Chapter 22 in Part IV.

Chapter 9 concludes Part I with an examination of the ethical questions that pervade the legal system. It pays particular attention to the issue of the social responsibility of corporations.

Chapter 1

NATURE AND SOURCES OF LAW

A. P. Herbert once wrote: "The general mass, if they consider the law at all, regard it as they regard some monster in the zoo. It is odd, it is extraordinary; but there it is, they have known it all their lives, they suppose that there must be some good reason for it, and accept it as inevitable and natural." [1]

While the law is not nearly as odd or extraordinary as many persons believe, it is undeniably "there"—an integral part of the environment that has been a source of great interest, even fascination, for centuries.

Considering the pervasiveness of the law, this is hardly surprising. Almost all human activity is affected by it in one manner or another, and this alone is adequate explanation for such widespread interest. Certainly, anyone contemplating a business transaction of any magnitude today realizes that he or she must consider not only the physical and financial effort it will entail but—to some extent, at least—the legal ramifications as well. And beyond the practical effect law has on individual conduct in specific situations, it possesses additional characteristics that make its study uniquely rewarding.

First, while the law is by no means an occult language understood only by lawyers, it clearly is a subject that is *academically stimulating*. For students to get any real benefit from a course in law, they must at the very least learn to recognize precise legal issues, understand the reasoning of the courts as set forth in their decisions, and subject this reasoning to critical analysis. These activities involve varying degrees of mental exercise; and while this is not always pleasurable, it fosters a degree of mental discipline that is not easily acquired elsewhere.

Second, students should have the opportunity to consider the law as a *societal institution*—to see how it has affected conduct and thought and how it has been influenced by them in return. Whatever the law is, it certainly is not static, and it certainly does not exist in a vacuum.

This approach, which emphasizes the impact of social and economic changes on the law, gives the subject a liberal arts flavor. When viewed in this light, the law and its processes become rewarding to anyone having even a passing interest in economics, sociology, and political science.

A GLIMPSE OF THINGS TO COME

There is always some disagreement as to the proper objectives of introductory business law courses. It is not surprising that teachers, lawyers, and businessmen, for example, hold varying views about which aspects of the law will provide the most lasting benefits to students. Upon closer examination, however, most of these differences are seen to be minor, relating only to which topics should receive the most emphasis. There is general agreement as to the substantive matters that ought to be presented, in both the environmental and traditional arenas. [2]

Certain environmental matters—such as the workings of the judicial processes, the nature of statutory and common law, and the sweeping subject of constitutional law—are so basic to an understanding of our legal system as to require extended treatment. Before proceeding to these matters, however, we devote the remainder of this chapter to some preliminary aspects of the law—including its nature, sources, purposes, and classifications.

WHAT IS LAW?

Ever since the law began to take form, scholars have spent impressive amounts of time and thought analyzing its purposes and defining what it is and what it ought to be—in short, fitting it into a philosophical scheme of one form or another. While space does not permit inclusion of even the major essays in which these philosophers defend their respective views,

---

[1] *Uncommon Law,* 1936. Reprinted by permission of Lady Herbert.

[2] The reader should refer to the preface for a fuller description of the environmental approach.

their conclusions provide us with useful observations about the nature of law. Consider, for example, the following:

> We have been told by Plato that law is a form of social control, an instrument of the good life, the way to the discovery of reality, the true reality of the social structure; by Aristotle that it is a rule of conduct, a contract, an ideal of reason, a rule of decision, a form of order; by Cicero that it is the agreement of reason and nature, the distinction between the just and the unjust, a command or prohibition; by Aquinas that it is an ordinance of reason for the common good, made by him who has care of the community, and promulgated [thereby]; by Bacon that certainty is the prime necessity of law; by Hobbes that law is the command of the sovereign; by Spinoza that it is a plan of life; by Leibniz that its character is determined by the structure of society; by Locke that it is a norm established by the commonwealth; by Hume that it is a body of precepts; by Kant that it is a harmonizing of wills by means of universal rules in the interests of freedom; by Fichte that it is a relation between human beings; by Hegel that it is an unfolding or realizing of the idea of right.[3]

While these early writers substantially agree as to the general *purpose* of law—the insuring of orderliness to all human activity—their *definitions* of the term vary considerably. Today there is still no definition of *law* that has universal approval, even in legal circles—a fact that is no doubt attributable to its inherent breadth.[4]

Two Current Views

At the risk of oversimplification, it can be said that two major approaches to the law exist today. The **traditional approach to law** views the law as consisting of the rules that are in effect within a state or nation at a given time. This is very likely what practicing attorneys have in mind when they speak about the law, and it is a perfectly respectable view. Witness the following definition adopted by the American Law Institute: "[Law] is the body of principles, standards and rules which the courts . . . apply in the decision of controversies brought before them."[5]

The **environmental approach to law** sees the law in a broader light: the *processes by which the rules and principles are formulated* (rather than the rules and principles themselves) constitute the major element of law. Because law is necessitated solely by human activity, environmentalists contend that the ever-changing problems resulting from this activity and *the ways in which the law attempts to solve them* must receive primary emphasis if one is to gain a proper insight into the subject.

The following definition expresses this view: *"Law is a dynamic process, a system of regularized, institutionalized procedures for the orderly decision of social questions, including the settlement of disputes."*[6] Since Part I of this text is concerned primarily with the environmental aspects of law, we will adopt this definition for our purposes.

REQUISITES OF A LEGAL SYSTEM

In order for a legal system to function properly, particularly within a democratic government such as ours, it must command the respect of the great majority of people governed by it. In order

---

[3] Huntington Cairns, *Legal Philosophy from Plato to Hegel* (Baltimore: Johns Hopkins University Press, 1949).

[4] Consider, for example, just these few widely varying matters with which the law must deal: (1) the standards of care required of a surgeon in the operating room, (2) the determination of whether an "exclusive-dealing" provision in a motion picture distributor's contracts constitutes an unfair method of competition under federal law, and (3) the propriety of a witness's testimony when it is challenged as constituting "hearsay" under the rules of evidence.

[5] *Restatement, Conflict of Laws 2d,* §4. American Law Institute Publishers. Copyright 1971. Reprinted with the permission of The American Law Institute.

[6] James L. Houghteling, Jr., *The Dynamics of Law* (New York: Harcourt Brace Jovanovich, 1963).

to do so, the legal rules which compose it must, as a practical matter, possess certain characteristics. They must be (1) relatively certain, (2) relatively flexible, (3) known or knowable, and (4) apparently reasonable.

In the following chapters we consider these requirements more fully and determine the extent to which our legal system satisfies them. For the moment, we give brief descriptions of each of the four.

Certainty

One essential element of a stable society is reasonable certainty about its laws, not only at a given moment but over long periods of time. Many of our activities, particularly business activities, are based on the assumption that legal principles will remain stable into the foreseeable future. If this were not so, chaos would result. For example, no television network would enter into a contract with a professional football league, under which it is to pay millions of dollars for the right to televise league games, if it were not reasonably sure that the law would compel the league to live up to its contractual obligations or to pay damages if it did not. And no lawyer would advise a client on a contemplated course of action without similar assurances.

Because of these considerations, the courts (and to a lesser extent the legislatures) are generally reluctant to overturn principles that have been part of the law for any appreciable length of time.[7]

Flexibility

In any nation, particularly a highly industrialized one such as the United States, societal changes occur with accelerating (almost dismaying) ra-

pidity. Each change presents new legal problems that must be resolved without undue delay. This necessity was recognized by Justice Cardozo when he wrote that "the law, like the traveler, must be ready for the morrow."[8]

Some problems are simply the result of scientific and technological advances. Prior to Orville and Wilbur Wright's day, for example, it was a well-established principle that landowners had unlimited rights to the airspace above their property, any invasion of which constituted a *trespass*—a wrongful entry. But when the courts became convinced that the flying machine was here to stay, the utter impracticality of this view became apparent and owners' rights were subsequently limited to a "reasonable use" of their airspace.

Other novel problems result from changing methods of doing business or from shifting attitudes and moral views. Recent examples of the former are the proliferating use of the business franchise and of the general credit card. Attitudinal changes involve such questions as the proper ends of government, the propriety of Sunday sales, and the circumstances in which abortions should be permitted.

Some of these problems, of course, require solutions that are more political than legal in nature. This is particularly true where large numbers of the citizenry are faced with a common problem, such as the inability of many elderly persons to pay for proper health care, and where the alleviation of the problem may well be thought to constitute a legitimate function of either the state or federal government. The passage by Congress of the so-called Medicare Act of 1964 is an example of an attempted solution at the federal level of this particular problem.

Regardless of political considerations, however, the fact remains that there are many problems (particularly those involving disputes be-

---

[7] This is not to say, of course, that the law is static. Many areas of American law are dramatically different than they were fifty, or even twenty-five years ago. However, most of these changes resulted from a series of modifications of existing principles rather than from an abrupt reversal of them. The *Soldano v. O'Daniels* case later in this chapter illustrates one such modification.

[8] Benjamin N. Cardozo, *The Growth of the Law* (New Haven: Yale University Press, 1924), pp. 19–20.

tween individuals) which can be settled only through the judicial processes—that is, by one of the parties instituting legal action against the other. The duty to arrive at a final solution in all such cases falls squarely upon the courts, no matter how novel or varied the issues. It is to their credit, but it is also their curse, that Americans increasingly turn to them for dispute resolution, and not to the churches, schools, or other institutions that are available.

Knowability

One of the basic assumptions underlying a democracy—and, in fact, almost every form of government—is that the great majority of its citizens are going to obey its laws voluntarily. It hardly need be said that obedience requires a certain knowledge of the rules, or at least a reasonable means of acquiring this knowledge, on the part of the governed. No one, not even a lawyer, "knows" all the law or all the rules that make up a single branch of law; that could never be required. But it is necessary for persons who need legal advice to have access to experts on the rules—lawyers. It is equally necessary that the law be in such form that lawyers can determine their clients' positions with reasonable certainty in order to recommend the most advantageous courses of action.

Reasonableness

Most citizens abide by the law. Many do so even when they are not in sympathy with a particular rule, out of a sense of responsibility, a feeling that it is their civic duty, like it or not; others, no doubt, do so simply through fear of getting caught if they don't. But by and large the rules have to appear reasonable to the great majority of the people if they are going to be obeyed for long. The so-called Prohibition Amendment, which met with such wholesale violation that it was repealed in 1933, is the classic example of a rule lacking widespread acceptance. Closely allied with the idea of reasonableness is the requirement that the rules reflect, and adapt to,

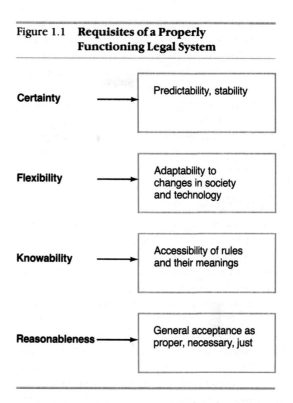

Figure 1.1   **Requisites of a Properly Functioning Legal System**

Certainty ⟶	Predictability, stability
Flexibility ⟶	Adaptability to changes in society and technology
Knowability ⟶	Accessibility of rules and their meanings
Reasonableness ⟶	General acceptance as proper, necessary, just

changing views of morality and justice. Figure 1.1 summarizes the qualities a legal system must possess to function properly.

SOME CLASSIFICATIONS OF LAW

While the lawmaking and adjudicatory processes are the major concern in Part I, the products that result from the law-making process—the rules themselves and the bodies of law which they make up—must not be overlooked. At the outset, particularly, it is useful to recognize some of the more important *classifications of law.*

Subject-matter Classification

One way of classifying all the law in the United States is on the basis of the *subject matter* to which it relates. Fifteen or twenty branches or subjects are of particular importance, among them:

- Administrative law
- Agency
- Commercial paper
- Constitutional law
- Contracts
- Corporation law
- Criminal law
- Domestic relations
- Evidence
- Partnerships
- Personal property
- Real property
- Sales
- Taxation
- Torts
- Wills and estates

Two observations can be made about this classification.

1. The subjects of agency, contracts, and torts are essentially *common law* in nature, while the subjects of corporation law, criminal law, sales, and taxation are governed by *statute.* Most of the remaining subjects, particularly evidence and property, are mixed in nature.

2. Several of these subjects obviously have a much closer relationship to the world of business than the others; these are the topics that fall within the usual business law or legal environment courses of a business school curriculum. Agency, contracts, corporation law, and sales are typical examples.

Federal and State Law

Another way of categorizing all law in this country is on the basis of the governmental unit from which it arises. On this basis, all law may be said to be either *federal law* or *state law.* While there are some very important areas of federal law, as we shall see later, the great bulk of our law is state (or "local") law. Virtually all the subjects in the preceding list, for example, are within the jurisdiction of the individual states. Thus it is correct to say that there are fifty bodies of contract law in the United States, fifty bodies of corporation law, and so on. But this is not as bewildering as it appears, because the rules that constitute a given branch of law in each state substantially parallel those that exist in the other states—particularly in regard to common-law subjects.

Common Law (Case Law) and Statutory Law

The term **common law** has several different meanings. It sometimes is used to refer only to the judge-made rules in effect in England at an early time—the "ancient unwritten law of England." It sometimes is also used to refer only to those judge-made rules of England that were subsequently adopted by the states in this country. In this text, however, we define the term more broadly to mean *all the rules and principles currently existing in any state, regardless of their historical origin, that result from judicial decisions in those areas of law where legislatures have not enacted comprehensive statutes.* This type of law, examined further in Chapter 4, is frequently referred to as case law, judge-made law, or unwritten law.

The term **statutory law,** by contrast, is generally used to refer to the state and federal *statutes* in effect at a given time—that is, rules which have been formally adopted by legislative bodies rather than by the courts. When *statutory law* is used in contrast to *common law,* it also comprises state and federal constitutions, municipal

Figure 1.2   Major Differences between Common and Statutory Law

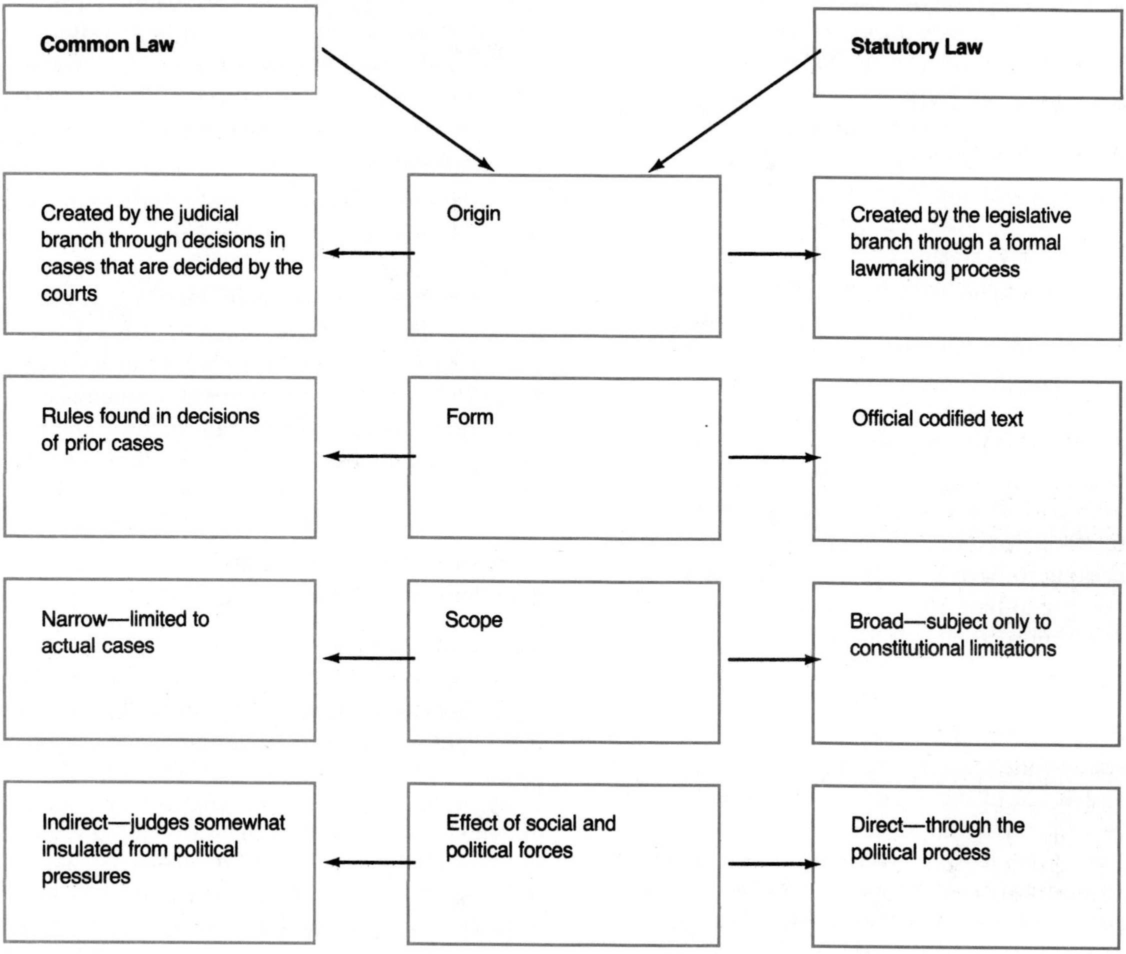

Common Law		Statutory Law
Created by the judicial branch through decisions in cases that are decided by the courts	**Origin**	Created by the legislative branch through a formal lawmaking process
Rules found in decisions of prior cases	**Form**	Official codified text
Narrow—limited to actual cases	**Scope**	Broad—subject only to constitutional limitations
Indirect—judges somewhat insulated from political pressures	**Effect of social and political forces**	Direct—through the political process

ordinances, and even treaties. Statutory law is frequently referred to as written law in the sense that once a statute or constitutional provision is adopted, its exact wording is set forth in the final text as passed—though the precise meaning, we should recall, is still subject to interpretation by the courts. (The subjects of statutory law and judicial interpretations are also covered in Chapter 4.) Figure 1.2 summarizes the major distinctions between common law and statutory law.

Civil and Criminal Law

Civil Law: The most common types of controversies are civil actions—that is, actions in which the parties bringing the suits (the **plaintiffs**) are seeking to enforce private obligations or duties against the other parties (the **defendants**). **Civil laws,** then, are all those laws which spell out the rights and duties existing between individuals (including, of course, business enterprises). Contract law, tort law, and sales law all fall within the civil category.

The usual remedy which the plaintiff is seeking in a civil suit is *damages*—a sum of money roughly equivalent to the loss which he or she has suffered as a result of the defendant's wrong. Thus if the X Company reneges on its contract to sell 10,000 bushels of corn to the Y Company for $22,500, with the result that the Y Company has to pay a third party $25,000 for the same quantity, the Y Company is entitled to $2,500 damages plus incidental damages, if any (such as additional storage or trucking costs resulting from the X Company's breach of contract). Another civil remedy is the *injunction,* a court decree ordering the defendant either to perform a particular act which he or she has the legal duty to perform, or to refrain from performing a particular act which he or she has no right to perform. In any event, in a civil suit the plaintiff is simply seeking to have an injury redressed rather than seeking to have the defendant punished by the imposition of a fine or by imprisonment.

Criminal Law: Criminal law, in contrast to civil law, comprises those statutes by which a state or the federal government prohibits specified kinds of conduct, and which additionally provide for the imposition of *fines or imprisonment* upon persons convicted of violating them. Criminal suits are always brought by the government whose law has allegedly been violated.

While any incursion into the vast area of criminal law is essentially outside the scope of this text, three observations are nonetheless in order.

1. In enacting criminal statutes, a state is saying that there are certain activities so inherently inimical to the public good that they must be flatly prohibited. Such statutes, then, provide the minimum standards of conduct to which all persons must adhere. There are other standards of conduct above this level which the law also requires in certain situations, but one who fails to meet these higher standards is normally liable

only in a civil action to the person who suffers a loss as a consequence of this wrong. To illustrate: X acts in a negligent (careless) manner and injures Y while doing so. While Y is entitled to recover damages from X in a civil suit because of the wrong that has occurred, the wrong is not of such a nature that the state could bring a criminal action against X.[9]

2. In addition to the nature of the liability that is imposed, criminal suits also differ from civil suits in another significant respect. In a criminal action (which is always brought by the state) it is necessary that the state's case be proved "beyond a reasonable doubt," whereas in civil actions the plaintiff—the person bringing the suit—need prove his or her allegations only by "a preponderance of the evidence." If the defendant—the accused—is able to raise *some* doubts regarding questions of fact (for example, was the defendant the driver or a passenger in a car causing the death of a pedestrian), the evidence in a criminal action may leave enough doubt in the jury's mind that it must return a verdict in favor of the defendant. The same evidence in a civil suit, however, might support a verdict in favor of the plaintiff, because of the lesser burden of proof.

3. Except for the most serious crime of treason, crimes are either *felonies* or *misdemeanors,* depending upon the severity of the penalty which the statute prescribes. The definition of **felony** differs somewhat from state to state, but it is usually defined as any crime where the punishment is either death or imprisonment in a state penitentiary, as in the cases of murder, arson, or rape. **Misdemeanors** are all crimes carrying lesser penalties—for example, petit larceny and disorderly conduct. Figure 1.3 outlines major differences between civil and criminal law.

---

[9]Some wrongful acts are of a dual nature, subjecting the wrongdoer to both criminal and civil penalties. For example, if X steals Y's car, the state could bring a criminal action against X, and Y could also bring a civil action to recover damages arising from the theft.

Figure 1.3   **Major Differences between Civil and Criminal Law**

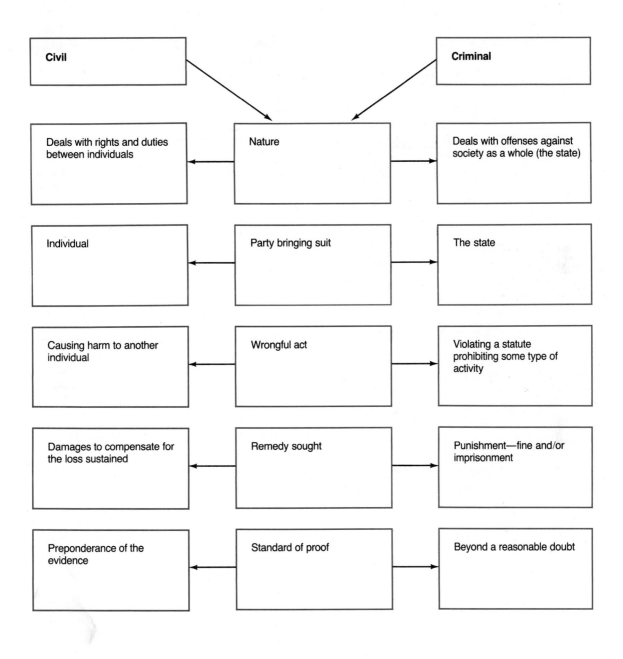

Public and Private Law

Some branches of law deal more directly with the relationship that exists between the government and the individual than do others. On the basis of the degree to which this relationship is involved, law is occasionally classified as public law or private law.

When an area of law is directly concerned with the government-individual relationship, it falls within the *public law* designation. Subjects that are most clearly of this nature are criminal law, constitutional law, and administrative law. Since *criminal laws* consist of acts that are prohibited by a government itself, the violation of which is a "wrong against the state," such laws more directly affect the government-individual relationship than do any of the other laws. To the extent that our federal Constitution contains provisions substantially guaranteeing that certain rights of the individual cannot be invaded by federal and state government activities, the subject of *constitutional law* falls within the same category. *Administrative law*—comprising the principles that govern the procedures and activities of government boards and commissions—is of similar nature, in that such agencies are also concerned with the enforcement of certain state and federal statutes (and regulations promulgated thereunder) against individual citizens.

Other areas of law, which are primarily concerned with the creation and enforcement of the rights of one individual against another, fall within the *private law* category. While a state is indeed concerned that all its laws be properly enforced, even when individuals' rights alone are being adjudicated, the concern in these areas is distinctly secondary to the interests of the litigants themselves.

LEGAL MISCONCEPTIONS

Before proceeding to the more substantive areas of law, we will reflect briefly on some widely held misconceptions about our legal system.

The Myth of the One Right Answer

It is widely believed that there is one "correct" legal answer to any legal controversy. This is true in a good many situations but certainly not as often as many persons believe. The chief reasons for divergent legal opinions are quite explainable.

1. Many rules are expressed in rather general terms so as to fit varying situations. Consequently, they afford the courts considerable latitude in deciding how they should be applied to specific situations.

2. The ultimate legal processes are in the hands of people, the judges, whose application of rules is always subject, to some extent, to their individual economic and political philosophies and personal moral beliefs. The law, therefore, is not an exact science and never will be.[10]

3. The nature of most legal problems is such that something can be said in behalf of both litigants. The ordinary controversy does not present a clear-cut case of a "good" person suing a "bad" one. In some cases, each party has acted in good faith; in others, each is guilty of some degree of wrong. Additionally, there are some "legal collision" situations, where one general principle of law may lead to one result while a second will lead to a different result. In such instances each principle will probably have to undergo some modification when applied to particular cases, with results that are not always harmonious.

The Myth of the Expensive Lawyer

The belief is sometimes expressed, usually with great feeling, that an individual or firm who is financially able to employ top-flight legal coun-

---

[10] It is sometimes said that the law is a "social science." While some view this term skeptically, in that it seems to ascribe to social studies the precision of the physical sciences, the label is perhaps acceptable in the sense that the rules of law attempt to describe and regulate all human activities.

sel is virtually "above the law." While it is undeniably true that a person who employs a competent lawyer will in general experience fewer
legal problems than would otherwise be the
case, this does not support the broad proposition that such a person can flout our legal rules at
will. The average attorney is competent enough
that his or her client will fare well under the law
when the rules support the client; when the
rules do not, the client will usually incur liability
under them, no matter how skilled the counsel
may be. (The conviction of a number of President Nixon's aides on obstruction of justice
charges growing out of the Watergate affair and
the bribery convictions of several Congressmen
in the FBI-conducted "Abscam" operation in
1981 are two of the more notable examples in
support of the latter proposition.)

The Myth of Judicial Eccentricity

The feeling is sometimes expressed that the law
is not based on common sense—that its rules
are so esoteric and arbitrary, and the judges and
lawyers so preoccupied with them, that the results are not in keeping with reality or with what
a reasonable person would expect. This indictment, in very large measure, is false. Cases invariably present practical problems for the courts,
and the courts keep the practical considerations
in mind in choosing the rules that apply.

Take, for example, this situation. C, a contractor, agrees to build a house according to certain
specifications for O, the owner, for $60,000.
When the house is completed, by which time O
has paid $36,000, O discovers that the family
room is 10 inches shorter than the plans specified. O refuses to make further payments for this
reason, whereupon C brings suit to recover the
balance of $24,000.

Now, as far as contract law is concerned, the
principle is well established that a person who
breaches a contract is not permitted to recover
anything from the other party. The question here
is: Should that rule be applicable to this specific
situation, where that would mean that C would

not recover any of the balance? The practical
person might well say, "I wouldn't think so—
where the defect is so slight, it would seem unfair for C to suffer a loss of $24,000." The law
reaches the same conclusion; under a view
known as the *doctrine of substantial performance*, a person in C's position is usually permitted to recover most of the unpaid balance (even
though he did, technically, breach the contract).

The foregoing does not mean, of course, that
the law is perfect or that startling or unfair decisions never occur. They do. But by and large the
unreasonable result occurs with much less frequency than reports in the news media would
indicate; and even in such cases, the possibility
usually exists that an appellate court will subsequently repair much of the damage.

LAW, JUSTICE, AND MORALS

Law and Justice

There is a close relationship between law and
justice, but the terms are not equivalent. Most
results of the application of legal rules are
"just"—fair and reasonable. Where this is not so
to any degree, the rules are usually changed. Yet
it must be recognized that results occasionally
"aren't fair." Without attempting to defend the
law in all such instances, some cautions should
nevertheless be voiced.

First, there is never complete agreement as to
what is just; there are always some decisions that
are just to some people but not to others. And
even if there were unanimity of opinion—a perfect justice, so to speak—the **fact-patterns** presented by some cases are such that it is simply
impossible to attain this end.[11]

In some situations, for example, a legal controversy may arise between two honest persons

---

[11] *Fact-pattern* refers to the proven acts of each party that
have led up to a particular controversy, together with the
circumstances surrounding such acts. The facts of a case are
usually determined by the jury but occasionally by the court,
that is, the judge.

who dealt with each other in good faith, as sometimes occurs in the area of "mutual mistake." Take this case: P contracts to sell land to G for $40,000, both parties mistakenly believing that a General Motors plant will be built on adjoining land. When G learns that the plant will not be built, he refuses to go through with the deal. If a court rules that the mistake frees G of his contractual obligations, the result might be quite unjust as far as P is concerned. And if it rules otherwise, the decision might seem quite unfair to G. Yet a decision must be made, one way or the other.

Second, in some instances it is fairly clear who is right and who is wrong, but the situation has progressed to the point where it is impossible, either physically or legally, to put the "good" person back into the original position. These "bad check" cases will illustrate: A buys a TV set from Z, giving Z her personal check in payment. If the check bounces, it is clear that Z should be allowed to recover the set. But what if the TV has been destroyed by fire while in A's hands? Here the most the law can do is give Z a *judgment* against A—an order requiring A to pay a sum of money to Z equal to the amount of the check, which A may or may not be financially able to do. Or suppose that A had resold the TV to X before Z learned that the check had bounced. Would it not be unfair to permit Z to retake the set from X, an innocent third party?

Because of these considerations, and others to be discussed later, the most the law can seek to accomplish is *substantial* justice in the greatest possible number of cases that come before it.

Law and Morals

Although the terms *law* and *morals* are not synonymous, legal standards and moral standards parallel one another more closely than many people believe. For example, criminal statutes prohibit certain kinds of conduct that are clearly "morally wrong"—murder, theft, arson, and the like. And other rules of law impose civil liability for similar kinds of conduct which, though not crimes, are also generally felt to be wrongful in

nature—such as negligence, breach of contract, and fraud. To illustrate: S, in negotiating the sale of a race horse to B, tells B that the horse has run an eighth of a mile in fifteen seconds on several occasions within the past month. In fact, the animal has never been clocked under eighteen seconds, and S knows this. B, believing the statement to be true, purchases the horse. In such a case S's intentional misstatement constitutes the tort of *fraud,* and B—assuming he can prove these facts in a legal action brought against S— has the right to set aside the transaction, returning the horse and recovering the price he has paid.

Why, then, are the terms *law* and *morals* not precisely synonymous? First, there are some situations where moral standards are higher than those imposed by law. For example, a person who has promised to keep an offer open for a stated period of time generally has the legal right to withdraw the offer before the given time has elapsed (for reasons appearing in a later chapter). Yet many persons who make such offers feel morally compelled to keep their offers open as promised, even though the law does not require this. Second, sometimes the law imposes higher standards than do our morals. For example, few religions or philosophies feature the 55-mile-per-hour speed limit as a major tenet, yet it is illegal to drive faster. Third, many rules of law and court decisions are based upon statutory or practical requirements that have little or no relationship to moral considerations. For example, in the area of minors' contracts, we see later that most courts feel, on balance, that it is sound public policy to permit minors to disaffirm (cancel) their contracts until they reach the age of majority, even though the contracts were otherwise perfectly valid and even though the persons with whom they dealt did not overreach or take advantage of them in any way. These observations notwithstanding, a society's moral standards will always heavily influence its legal standards.

The interplay between law and morality is illustrated in the following case. Because the study of law involves to a very great extent the ability to reason from cases, students must have some familiarity with court procedures and jurisdiction. For this reason, major emphasis on cases will begin in the following chapter. The case below is our first, and therefore requires a few prefatory comments:

1. This is a **wrongful death** action authorized by statute to allow close relatives of deceased persons to sue those whose wrongful acts have caused a death. Absent such statutes, we could be held liable for carelessly or intentionally injuring someone, but could escape civil liability if we killed them.

2. In a civil case, the jury is normally the "judge of the *facts.*" The trial judge decides the *law.* However, a judge, for reasons of judicial efficiency, can grant a summary judgment, terminating the case before it is ever tried. This can happen in two instances. First, summary judgment can be granted a defendant when plaintiff's legal theory is so defective that even if plaintiff proves all facts alleged, recovery should still be denied. Second, summary judgment is appropriately granted if the evidence in the case so clearly indicates that factually one side or the other is entitled to prevail that a trial would be a waste of time. Only if the judge can conclude that there is "no genuine issue of material fact" should a summary judgment be granted on this ground. The following case involves a summary judgment granted on the former basis.

3. If a trial court does grant a summary judgment motion, the losing party can always seek review in an appellate court. If the appellate court finds that the ruling was in error, the case will be returned to the trial court with instructions for a jury trial on the issue.

Soldano v. O'Daniels
California Court of Appeal, 190 Cal. Rptr. 310 (1983)

On August 9, 1977, Villanueva pulled a gun and threatened the life of Soldano at Happy Jack's Saloon. A patron of Happy Jack's ran across the street to the Circle Inn and informed the bartender of the threat, asking the bartender either to call the police or allow him to use the phone to call the police. The bartender refused both requests. Soon thereafter, Villanueva shot Soldano to death. The plaintiff in this wrongful death action is Soldano's child. Defendants are the bartender and his employer. The trial judge dismissed the claim upon defendants' motion for summary judgment. Plaintiff appeals.

Andreen, Associate Justice:

Does a business establishment incur liability for wrongful death if it denies use of its telephone to a good samaritan who explains an emergency situation occurring without and wishes to call the police?

. . . There is a distinction, well rooted in the common law, between action and inaction. It has found its way into the prestigious Restatement Second of Torts, which provides in section 314:

The fact that the actor realizes or should realize that action on his part is necessary for another's aid or protection does not of itself impose upon him a duty to take such action.

The distinction between malfeasance and nonfeasance, between active misconduct working positive injury and failure to act to prevent mischief not brought on by the defendant, is founded on "that attitude of extreme individualism so typical of anglo-saxon legal thought." (Bohlen, *The Moral Duty to Aid Others as a Basis of Tort Liability*, part I (1908) 56 U.Pa.L.Rev. 217, 219-220.)

Defendant argues that the request that its employee call the police [or assist the patron from Happy Jack's] is a request that it *do* something. He points to the established rule that one who has not created a peril ordinarily does not have a duty to take affirmative action to assist an imperiled person. . . .

The refusal of the law to recognize the moral obligation of one to aid another when he is in peril and when such aid may be given without danger and at little cost in effort has been roundly criticized. Prosser describes the case law sanctioning such inaction as a "refus[al] to recognize the moral obligation of common decency and common humanity" and characterizes some of these decisions as "revolting to any moral sense." (Prosser, *Law of Torts* (4th ed. 1971) §56.)

As noted in *Tarasoff v. Regents of University of California*, 131 Cal. Rptr. 14 (1976), the courts have increased the instances in which affirmative duties are imposed not by direct rejection of the common law rule, but by expanding the list of special relationships which will justify departure from that rule. . . . In *Tarasoff*, a therapist was told by his patient that he intended to kill Tatiana Tarasoff. The therapist and his supervisors predicted the patient presented a serious danger of violence. In fact he did, for he carried out his threat. The court held the patient-therapist relationship was enough to create a duty to exercise reasonable care to protect others from the foreseeable result of the patient's illness.

. . . Here there was no special relationship between the defendant and the deceased. But this does not end the matter.

It is time to re-examine the common law rule of nonliability for nonfeasance in the special circumstances of the instant case.

Besides well-publicized actions taken to increase the severity of punishments for criminal offenses, the Legislature has expressed a social imperative to diminish criminal action. [The court then referred to laws passed to compensate citizens for injuries sustained in crime suppression efforts, to make it a misdemeanor to refuse to relinquish a party line when informed that it is needed to call the police, and to establish an emergency '911' telephone system.]

The above statutes . . . demonstrate that "that attitude of extreme individualism so typical of anglo-saxon legal thought" may need limited re-examination in light of current societal conditions and the facts of this case to determine whether the defendant owed a duty to the deceased to permit the use of the telephone. . . .

As the Supreme Court has noted, the reluctance of the law to impose liability for nonfeasance, as distinguished from misfeasance, is in part due to the difficulties in setting standards and of making rules workable [citing *Tarasoff*].

Many citizens simply "don't want to get involved." No rule should be adopted which would require a citizen to open up his or her house to a stranger so that the latter may use the telephone to call for emergency assistance. As Mrs. Alexander in Anthony Burgess' *A Clockwork Orange* learned to her horror, such an action may be fraught with danger. It does not follow, however, that use of a telephone in a public portion of a business should be refused for a legitimate emergency call. Imposing liability for such a refusal would not subject innocent citizens to possible attack by the "good samaritan," for it would be limited to an establishment open to the public during times when it is open to business, and to places within the establishment ordinarily accessible to the public.

. . . We conclude that the bartender owed a duty to the plaintiff's decedent to permit the patron from Happy Jack's to place a call to the police or to place the call himself.

It bears emphasizing that the duty in this case does not require that one must go to the aid of another. That is not the issue here. The employee was not the good samaritan intent on aiding another. The patron was.

It would not be appropriate to await legislative action in this area. The rule was fashioned in the common law tradition, as were the exceptions to the rule. . . . The courts have a special responsibility to reshape, refine and guide legal doctrine they have created.

The words of the Supreme Court [in *Rodriguez v. Bethlehem Steel Corp.*, 115 Cal. Rptr. 765 (1974)] on the role of the courts in a common law system are well suited to our obligation here:

The inherent capacity of the common law for growth and change is its most significant feature. Its development has been determined by the social needs of the community which it serves. It is constantly expanding and developing in keeping with advancing civilization and the new conditions and progress of society, and adapting itself to the gradual change of trade, commerce, arts, inventions, and the needs of the country. . . .

In short, as the United States Supreme Court has aptly said, "This flexibility and capacity for growth and adaptation is the peculiar boast and excellence of the common law." [Citation omitted].

The possible imposition of liability on the defendant in this case is not a global change in the law. It is but a slight departure from the "morally questionable" rule of nonliability for inaction absent a special relationship. It is a logical extension of Restatement section 327 which imposes liability for negligent interference with a third person who the defendant knows is attempting to render necessary aid. However small it may be, it is a step which should be taken.

We conclude there are sufficient justiciable issues to permit the case to go to trial and therefore reverse.

Comment:

1. As this is our first case, a few comments about the mechanics of case reporting are in order:

    a. The opinion, written by Justice Andreen, is that of an intermediate appellate court in a state system. It hears appeals from California state trial courts, and its decisions can be appealed to the California State Supreme Court.

    b. The ellipsis points (. . .) appearing in the opinion indicate portions that have been deleted by the authors of this text. Deletions are made to eliminate redundancy or exclude issues irrelevant to points that the case has been selected to illustrate.

    c. When a general principle of law is stated in a decision, the court will frequently *cite* (refer to) earlier cases in which that principle has been established. Here, for example, the court has referred to *Tarasoff v. Regents of University of California* for such a purpose. To facilitate the reading of opinions, the authors have generally omitted such references except where the cited case is heavily relied upon to support the decision.

2. In regard to substantive matters presented by this case, the following can be noted.

    a. If a trial jury finds the bartender to have refused to act, as alleged, then he will be liable to plaintiff and so will his employer under *agency law.* While that subject is essentially outside the scope of this chapter, one of its principles imposes liability on an employer for the torts (wrongs) committed by employees if they were "carrying on the employer's business at the time." (This specific question is considered in detail in Chapter 19).

    b. If the jury finds the bartender liable and the employer pays the entire judgment to the plaintiff, the employer will have the legal right to seek reimbursement from the bartender. As a practical matter, however, employers seldom exercise this right.

3. A word of caution: It is imperative for readers to acquire the ability *to determine the precise issue of a case,* so they will not leap to unwarranted general conclusions. Could we say, for example, that the instant case establishes the principle that upon seeing one person attack another with a knife a bystander has the legal duty to personally intervene to save the victim? Not at all. This court was very careful in stating the issue narrowly, and emphasizing that it was only creating a small exception to the traditional rule.

CHOOSING AND USING LAWYERS

Choosing a lawyer can be as important as choosing one's clergyman, banker, or doctor . . . and more difficult.

Individuals

Individuals frequently require a lawyer's services for their business matters as well as for their personal affairs. As sole proprietors of, or partners in a business enterprise, individuals facing (or seeking to avoid) legal problems must select an attorney. This is no easy task.

Now that the Supreme Court has made advertising by lawyers permissible,[12] at least a little more information about attorneys is publicly available than was formerly the case. Still, much investigation and consultation may be required before a selection is made.

If friends or business associates have had similar problems in the past, their advice may be particularly helpful. If their experience with a specific attorney was quite favorable, that attorney can be contacted. Professionals in the area of concern are also valuable resources. For example, if the legal problem is financial in nature, an individual's banker might provide valuable insight regarding lawyers with experience in that type of case. A call to a nearby law school permits consultation with a professor who specializes in the problem area and will probably know local attorneys who practice that type of law. A trip to a library to consult the *Martindale-*

---

[12] *Bates v. State Bar of Ariz.,* 433 U.S. 350 (1977).

Hubbell Law Directory, which gives significant background information on attorneys and their specialties (and even rates them), can be beneficial. Finally, the Yellow Pages will list the local attorneys and contain the number of a lawyers' referral service sponsored by the local bar association.

An individual consulting an attorney must not be hesitant to ask questions, including: How much will I be charged for an initial consultation? Do you frequently handle this type of case? Will my case receive the attention of an experienced lawyer in the firm? How will the fee be structured? How much is your representation likely to cost for the total case?

The matter of fees is a delicate subject, but the client should demand that all specifics be spelled out before hiring an attorney. For many types of cases, lawyers work for an *hourly fee.* The rate charged varies with the geographic area, type of firm, and type of case. Unless the client investigates thoroughly, "comparison shopping" will be impossible. Some types of cases, particularly plaintiffs' personal injury cases, are handled on a *contingency fee* basis. That is, the lawyer's compensation is a percentage of the plaintiff's recovery, *if any.* No recovery usually means no fee for the attorney. Sometimes contingency fees are set on a sliding scale where the attorney receives an agreed percentage if the case is settled out of court, a larger percentage if the case is settled after suit is filed, and a still larger percentage (sometimes as high as 50 percent) if the case must be tried.

Once a relationship is established, clients must be completely open with their attorneys. Only if attorneys are given all relevant information by their clients can they provide effective counsel. Clients should trust their lawyers absent specific evidence of unethical practices, overbilling, or the like. The attorneys are being paid to provide advice, and that advice should normally be trusted just as a patient trusts a surgeon's advice. However, clients should always remember that it is *their case* that is the basis of the relationship. The attorney works for and is paid by the client, not vice versa. Matters of strategy are in the attorney's discretion, but the client has the ultimate choice of whether to file suit, whether to accept a settlement offer, and whether to take an appeal. An attorney who refuses to follow a client's instructions should be discharged.

Corporations

Corporations are even more dependent on attorneys than individual businesspersons. As fictional entities, corporations must appear in court through a lawyer. That is, while individuals have the right (although it is not usually the sensible thing to do) to represent themselves in court, corporations do not. Corporations normally must appear through a licensed attorney. Not even the president of the corporation can represent it in court if the president is not an attorney.

Many corporations have "in-house" counsel—lawyers who work for the corporation full time. Other corporations farm out all their legal work to law firms which represent a number of other clients as well. Many larger corporations combine these approaches, with routine matters handled by in-house counsel and litigation and specialty matters handled by outside counsel.

The high cost of litigation, particularly attorneys' fees, is a major concern for corporations. The average manufacturing company spends about 1 percent of its revenues on legal services. Some corporations have reacted to this problem by increasing their reliance on in-house counsel. Others have put their legal business up for competitive bid by local law firms. Still others have instituted "legal audits" in which experienced attorneys evaluate a company's practices in order to detect potential legal troublespots. These troublespots might not be illegal practices, only activities which might invite litigation or inhibit success should litigation ensue. Such "preventive law" is being hailed, much as is preventive medicine. A lawyer who can keep the client out of court altogether is every bit as valuable as a lawyer who can win a case in court.

Corporations, like individuals, must cooperate with their attorneys. Obviously corporations can act only through their employees. Those employees must also be open and cooperative. The Supreme Court has recognized this, holding that the attorney-client privilege attaches to communications made by corporate employees to the corporation's attorneys.[13]

SUMMARY

The law pervades our lives, both business and personal. Philosophers have characterized the law in an endless variety of ways, but two major approaches are the "traditional" and the "environmental." The former sees the law as a set of rules and standards which the courts use to resolve cases; the latter views the law more as a dynamic process for resolution of social questions.

An effective legal system must provide certainty, yet be flexible so it can adjust to changed circumstances. It must be knowable so that people realize what is generally expected of them, and it must generally be considered reasonable.

Our multifaceted law can be classified in many ways. Each law will fit into a particular subject-matter category—contract law, corporate law, tax law, and the like. At the same time it will be either a federal or a state law, a court-made rule or a statute, a civil or a criminal law, and a public or a private law. As in any field of study, mastery of the proper labels for concepts can facilitate understanding.

The untutored are likely to have various misconceptions about how the legal system operates. Because the law has so many human factors, there is no one right answer to legal questions. Witnesses perceive "facts" in different ways. Lawyers will view "the law" in various ways, depending on policy considerations and their own feelings of justice. You cannot simply feed the facts and the law into a computer and produce *the* right answer. Although it is generally helpful to have as much money as possible when facing a legal struggle, the ability to hire the best lawyers does not guarantee anyone absolute immunity from the restraints and punishments of the law. Finally, although judges do not always make the best decisions, their conclusions are seldom based on pure whim. Many judicial actions which seem ludicrous when summarized in the newspaper, are really quite reasonable when understood in context.

The purpose of law is to produce justice. Unfortunately, this is an amorphous concept. Because not all people can agree on what is just, not everyone will be able to agree on whether our law is producing justice. The law is heavily influenced by society's moral convictions, though practical considerations cannot be ignored in making legal rules.

Finally, hiring a lawyer is likely to be a difficult task for individuals and corporations alike. Substantial investigation and careful reflection are advised.

KEY TERMS

Traditional approach to law
Environmental approach to law
Common law
Statutory law
Plaintiff
Defendant
Civil law
Criminal law
Felony
Misdemeanor
Fact-pattern
Wrongful death

QUESTIONS AND PROBLEMS

1. In two cases reaching the U.S. Supreme Court in 1985, the United States—through action by the Solicitor General—asked the court to over-

---

[13] *Upjohn Co. v. United States,* 449 U.S. 383 (1981).

rule its controversial 1973 decision in *Roe v. Wade,* 410 U.S. 113. (In that case the court held that a Texas statute making it a crime for anyone to have an abortion within the state except where the abortion was done "upon medical advice for the purpose of saving the mother's life" violated the Due Process clause of the U.S. Constitution). In effect, this controversial ruling "legalized" abortion to the extent that it gave pregnant women the absolute right to an abortion during the first trimester of their pregnancies, if they so desired.

Leaving aside the precise constitutional question that is raised, do you generally agree with the 1985 position of the United States? In other words, do you feel—because of religious beliefs or moral principles—that a duly-enacted state "anti-abortion" statute (such as the Texas statute), ought not be set aside by the federal courts in the absence of a federal statute mandating such a result? Discuss.

2. While there is no universal agreement as to what law is when viewed in the abstract, there seems to be substantial agreement among philosophers as to what the *primary purpose* of law is.

    a. How would you describe this purpose?
    b. Identify the specific passage or clause in each of the philosophers' quoted observations that substantiates your conclusion.

3. Briefly summarize the main factors that require a nation's legal rules to be flexible and somewhat changing.

4. If X and Y make a contract and X later refuses to go through with the deal, having no reason to do so, we say that X's conduct is a *wrong* but it is not a *crime.* Why is it not a crime?

5. For some years the Washington Interscholastic Activities Association had a rule that prohibited girls from participating on high school football teams in the state. When this rule was challenged by parents of two girls who wanted to go out for football, the Supreme Court of Washington had to decide whether the rule violated the state constitution (*Darrin v. Gould,*

540 P.2d 882, 1975). Leaving aside the precise legal question that was posed, do you think that such a rule is a good one? Discuss.

6. In 1884 a ship sank 1600 miles from shore. Dudley, Stephens, Brooks, and a 17-year-old boy, Richard Parker, scrambled into a life boat with only two pounds of turnips to eat and no fresh water. They caught a turtle, but by their 12th day in the raft the provisions were completely consumed. Soon thereafter Dudley and Stephens proposed killing the boy for food, but Brooks resisted the idea. Finally, on the 20th day following the shipwreck as the boy lay almost dead, Dudley and Stephens slit his throat and Brooks then joined them in eating him. Four days later a passing ship picked up the three survivors. They were returned to England where Dudley and Stephens were charged with murder. Assume that you are the judge in this case. Assume further that the evidence shows (a) all four men would have been dead by the 24th day had Parker not been eaten and (b) the mandatory penalty for murder is death. What will you do? (*Regina v. Dudley & Stephens,* [1884] L.R., Q.B. 61.)

7. A minor child and its mother brought a paternity action against defendant. Defendant admitted that he was the father of the child and agreed to pay child support, but filed a counterclaim against the mother claiming (a) she had falsely represented that she was taking birth control pills, (b) defendant had engaged in sexual intercourse with her in reliance upon the misrepresentation, and (c) as a direct result of the birth he had been injured in the form of mental agony and distress and creation of an obligation to support the child financially. The mother moved to dismiss the counterclaim, arguing that even if the facts alleged by defendant were true, he should not be allowed to recover money damages. Discuss. (*Lasher v. Kleinberg,* 164 Cal. Rptr. 618, Cal. App. 1980.)

8. A wooden bridge crossing a canal ditch was destroyed by a fire of unknown origin one afternoon. McCarthy soon learned of the fire; he attempted to contact the County Commissioners but failed. Simpson also learned of the fire and told another traveler, Ramos, that he would notify somebody about the fire, but he did not do so. At 6:30 the next morning Roberson drove off the bridge in the dark and was killed. There were no barricades or any type of warning devices at the site of the burned-out bridge. Roberson's wife brought a wrongful death action against McCarthy and Simpson. Should she prevail? Discuss. (*Roberson v. McCarthy,* 620 S.W.2d 912, Tex. Civ. App. 1981.)

Chapter 2

COURT SYSTEMS, JURISDICTION, AND FUNCTIONS

Figure 2.1   **The Process of Adjudication**

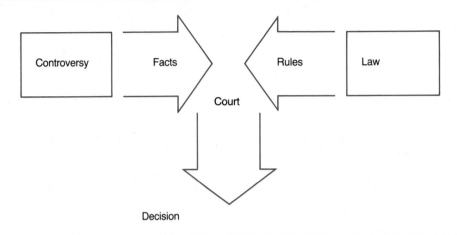

Legal rules and principles take on vitality and meaning only when they are applied to real-life controversies between real persons, when the rules are *applied to facts*—when, for example, a particular plaintiff is successful or unsuccessful in his or her attempt to recover a specific piece of land from a particular defendant, or where one company is successful or unsuccessful in recovering damages from another company as a result of an alleged breach of contract on the latter company's part. But the fitting of rules to facts—the settling of legal controversies—does not occur automatically. This process, which we call the process of **adjudication,** has to be in somebody's hands; that "somebody" is the state and federal courts that hear the thousands of cases that arise every year.[1] As Figure 2.1 indicates, rules and facts come together in the adjudication process, leading to a decision.

The primary reason, then, for looking at the courts and the work that they do is to gain an overall awareness of this important legal process. There is, however, another reason for doing so. In the following chapters many actual cases are presented. The reader is given the basic facts of a particular controversy, the judgment entered by the trial court on the basis of those facts, and excerpts of the appellate court's decision in affirming or reversing the trial court's judgment. Obviously, some familiarity with court systems and the judicial process will facilitate one's understanding of the legal significance of each step in these proceedings.

In this chapter, then, we take a brief look at the state and federal court systems, and at some problems of jurisdiction arising thereunder. In Chapter 3, we will first examine methods of dispute resolution other than formal litigation. Then we will examine the litigation process, focusing on the functions of the trial and appellate courts.

COURT SYSTEMS

As a result of our federal system of government, we live under two distinct, and essentially separate, sovereign types of government—the state governments and the federal government. Each

---

[1] In addition to the state and federal trial courts, many administrative agencies (such as the Federal Trade Commission) also hear certain kinds of controversies—usually those in which the agency is contending that a company has violated the agency's own rules or regulations. (The general subject of administrative agencies, including the role that they play in the adjudicatory process, is covered in Chapter 6.)

has its own laws and its own court system. For this reason, it is necessary to examine both systems in order to acquire an adequate knowledge of the court structures within which controversies are settled.

The Typical State System

While court systems vary somewhat from state to state, most state courts fall into three general categories. In ascending order, they are (1) courts of limited jurisdiction, (2) general trial courts, and (3) appellate courts (which frequently exist at two levels).

Courts of Limited Jurisdiction: In every state some trial courts are **courts of limited jurisdiction;** that is, they are limited as to the kinds of cases they can hear.[2] These courts include justice of the peace courts, municipal courts, traffic courts, probate courts, and domestic relations courts. While such courts actually decide a majority of the cases that come to trial, for the most part we are going to eliminate them from further consideration because they are not courts of general jurisdiction. Many of them deal with minor matters, such as the handling of small claims and traffic violations. Others (such as the probate courts) deal with much more substantial matters in terms of the amount of money involved; but even these courts are limited to cases of *very specialized subject matter.*

General Trial Courts: The most important cases involving state law, and the ones we will be most concerned with hereafter, commence in the **general trial courts.** These are courts of "general jurisdiction"; they are empowered to hear all cases except those expressly assigned by statute to the "minor" courts discussed above. Virtually all important cases involving contract law, criminal law, and corporation law, for ex-

ample, originate in the general trial courts.[3] In some states these courts are called "district courts," in others "common pleas courts," and in still others "superior courts" (the latter being something of a misnomer). Whatever the specific name, such a court normally exists in every county of every state. It is in these courts that trial by jury is generally available.

Appellate Courts: All states have one or more **appellate courts,** which hear appeals from judgments entered by the courts below. In many states there is only one such court, usually called the "supreme court," but in the more populous states there is a layer of appellate courts interposed between the trial courts and the supreme court. Such courts decide legal questions; they do not hear testimony of witnesses or otherwise entertain new evidence.

The Federal Court System

Article III, Section 1 of the U.S. Constitution provides that "the judicial power of the United States shall be vested in one Supreme Court, and in such inferior courts as the Congress may from time to time ordain and establish." The numerous federal courts that exist today by virtue of this section can, at the risk of oversimplification, be placed into three main categories similar to those of the state courts: (1) specialized courts, (2) general trial courts (district courts), and (3) appellate courts—the courts of appeal and the Supreme Court.

Specialized U.S. Courts: Some federal courts have limited jurisdiction, such as the U.S. Tax Court, the U.S. Court of Military Appeals, and the recently created U.S. Claims Court. While these courts frequently deal with important matters, we are eliminating them from further considera-

---

[2] *Jurisdiction* means the legal power to act; *jurisdiction of a court* refers to the types of disputes that a particular court is empowered to hear and decide.

[3] These courts may occasionally be referred to hereafter simply as *state trial courts,* to distinguish them from federal trial courts. When this is done, reference is being made to the trial courts of *general jurisdiction* rather than to the minor trial courts.

tion (as we did the similar state courts) because of their specialized nature.

General Trial Courts: The basic courts having general jurisdiction within the federal system are the *U.S. district courts,* sometimes called federal trial courts. Most federal cases originate in these courts.

Congress has created ninety-four judicial districts, each of which contains one federal district court. The federal districts, with the exceptions noted above, essentially are based upon state lines. The less populated states have only one federal district court within their boundaries, while most of the remaining states have two. Every square foot of land in this country and its territories is, geographically speaking, within the jurisdiction of one U.S. district court.

The Appellate Courts: Above the district courts are two levels of *federal appellate courts*—the U.S. courts of appeal and, above them, the U.S. Supreme Court. There are thirteen U.S. courts of appeal. Eleven of these, located in "circuits" across the country, have jurisdiction to hear appeals from the district courts located in the states within their respective boundaries. For example, the U.S. Court of Appeals for the Ninth Circuit in San Francisco hears appeals from decisions of district courts within the states of Alaska, Arizona, California, Hawaii, Idaho, Montana, Nevada, Oregon, and Washington. Each of these eleven appellate courts also hears appeals from the rulings of federal administrative agencies.

The jurisdiction of the remaining two courts of appeal is somewhat different from that of the others. The U.S. Court of Appeals for the District of Columbia hears appeals from the federal district court located in the District, as well as appeals from rulings of federal agencies that are issued there. The other appellate court is the U.S. Court of Appeals for the Federal Circuit, which hears all patent appeals from Patent and Trademark Office boards throughout the country and appeals from decisions of the new U.S. Claims Court, which is the trial court in which most

monetary claims against the federal government originate.

Appeals from judgments of the U.S. courts of appeal, like appeals from judgments of the state supreme courts that present federal questions, can be taken to the U.S. Supreme Court. That court, however, actually hears only a small percentage of such appeals, because review by the highest court is usually not a "matter of right"— that is, the U.S. Supreme Court usually has no legal obligation to review the judgment.[4] Rather, parties who seek a review normally must petition the Supreme Court for a *writ of certiorari,* and the court has absolute discretion in deciding which of these cases are sufficiently important to warrant the granting of certiorari.[5] In most instances certiorari is denied; in a typical year the Court hears only about 155 of the approximately 5,500 appeals that are made.

Some Observations

The typical state court system and the federal system can be diagrammed as in Figure 2.2. Several general comments can be made about this diagram.

1. The basic trial courts are the U.S. district courts and the state general trial courts; all courts above this level are appellate courts.

2. Trial courts must settle questions of both *fact* and *law,* while appellate courts rule on questions of law only. Questions of fact are "what happened" questions: for instance, did the defendant corporations expressly or implicitly agree not to sell goods to the plaintiff? Questions of law, by contrast, are "what is the rule applicable to the facts?" (Much more is said about the fact/law distinction in the next chapter.)

---

[4] Appeal as a matter of right does exist in very limited kinds of cases. For example, the U.S. Supreme Court *must* hear appeals in cases in which a state supreme court has ruled a federal statute to be unconstitutional, and cases in which a federal court of appeals has invalidated a state statute on the ground that it violated a provision of the U.S. Constitution.

[5] A *writ of certiorari* is an order of a higher court requiring a lower court to forward to it the records and proceedings of a particular case.

Figure 2.2   **The Federal and State Court Systems**

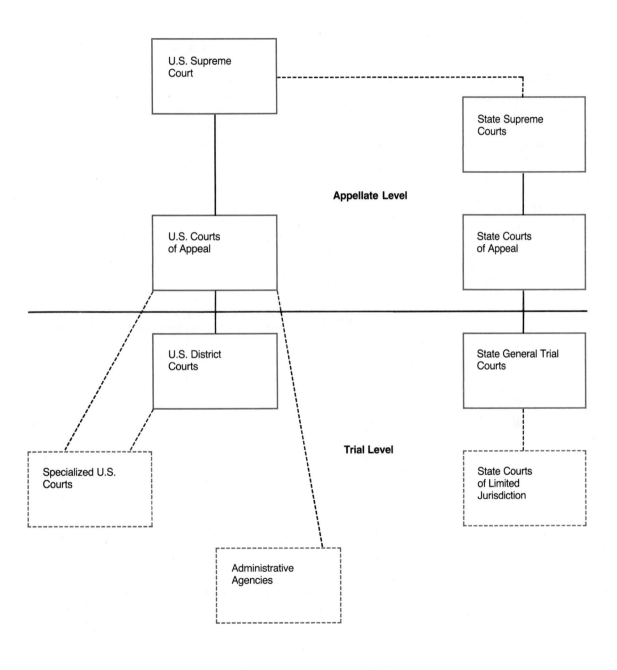

3. While a majority of the decisions of the trial courts are not appealed, a good many are. Hereafter we are concerned primarily with the *decisions of the appellate courts.* There are several basic reasons for this. First, state trial courts usually enter a judgment without writing a formal opinion as to their reasoning; and, even if there is such an opinion, it is normally not reported (published). Appellate courts, on the other hand, normally do write opinions which are reported, and access to them is available to anyone wishing to look up the rulings of law involved. Second, appellate courts have more opportunity to delineate the legal issues in their opinions for the benefit of lawyers and others who may read them. Third, if the appellate court disagrees with the result reached by the trial court, the appellate court's decision is, of course, controlling.

4. Once a case is initiated within a given court system, it will normally stay within that system until a final judgment is reached. Thus, if a case is properly commenced in a state court of general jurisdiction, any appeal from the trial court's judgment must be made to the next higher state court rather than to a federal appellate court. And if a case reaches the highest court in the state, its judgment is final. In other words, on matters of state law, state supreme courts are indeed supreme.[6] However, should a state supreme court rule on a case that turns on interpretation of a federal statute or a provision of the U.S. Constitution, an appeal could be taken to the U.S. Supreme Court which has the final word on matters of *federal* law.

5. With regard to the "title" of an appealed case, the state and federal courts follow somewhat different rules. In most state courts, the original plaintiff's name appears first—just as it did in the trial court. Suppose, for example, that Pink (plaintiff) sues Doe (defendant) in a state trial court, where the case is obviously *Pink v. Doe.* If the judgment of the trial court is appealed, the rule followed by most state courts is that the title of the case remains *Pink v. Doe* in the appellate courts, no matter which party is the *appellant* (the one bringing the appeal). In the federal courts, on the other hand, the appellant's name appears first. Under this rule, if Doe (defendant) loses in a U.S. district court and appeals to a U.S. court of appeals, the title of the case will be *Doe v. Pink* in the higher court. For this reason, when one sees a case in a federal appellate court so entitled, one cannot assume that Doe was the party who originated the action in the trial court. That determination must be made by referring to the facts of the case as set forth in the decision of the appellate court.

PROBLEMS OF JURISDICTION

In order for a court to settle a particular controversy, it is necessary for it to have "jurisdiction over the case."[7] This means that it must have **jurisdiction** of both the *subject matter* involved in the suit and, in most cases, jurisdiction of the *person* (the individual or company) against whom the suit is being brought. If a trial court should enter a judgment in a particular case and, on appeal, the higher court finds that either of these kinds of jurisdiction was lacking, the judgment of the trial court is void—of no effect whatever.

Subject Matter Jurisdiction

As we have already seen, some courts—such as a state probate court or the Federal Tax Court—are considerably limited as to the type of cases they can hear. Within a given court system, then, the subject matter jurisdiction of the several courts is essentially clear. Lines of demarcation between the general trial courts of the state sys-

---

[6] The normal terminology is being used here. In a few states, however, the "supreme court" label is given to an intermediate appellate court, with the highest court in the state bearing some other name. The court of last resort in the state of New York, for example, is the Court of Appeals of New York.

[7] As earlier, *jurisdiction* means the legal power to act, especially to hear and decide controversies.

tems and those of the federal system are less clear and require some explanation.

Subject Matter: State versus Federal Jurisdiction

Federal courts' subject matter jurisdiction is limited to the types of cases the Constitution provides they can hear. Most of the 75,000 or so cases filed each year in federal district court fall into one of two categories, "federal question" and "diversity of citizenship."

Federal Questions: A **federal question** exists in any suit where the plaintiff's claim is based in whole or in essential part upon a *federal statute* or upon a provision of the *U.S. Constitution* or a *U.S. treaty.* Thus, if a group of environmentally concerned citizens sued a corporation alleging that it was polluting in violation of the federal Clean Water Act, federal subject matter jurisdiction would exist, regardless of the amount in dispute.

Diversity of Citizenship: A federal court may hear a case based on *state* law if (a) plaintiff and defendant are citizens of different states,[8] and (b) the amount in controversy exceeds $10,000. A suit between citizens of different states involving less than $10,000 must be filed in a state trial court. The rationale for federal diversity jurisdiction has been succinctly stated as follows: "Diversity jurisdiction was created to alleviate fears that an out-of-state litigant might be subject to local bias in the courts of the state where his adversary resided, and to afford suitors the opportunity, at their option, to assert their rights in the federal rather than the state courts."[9]

Regardless of whether these fears of local bias are the motivation, a substantial portion of the cases filed in federal district courts each year are diversity cases. Many are as simple as an Oklahoma citizen injured in an auto accident caused by a Colorado citizen suing for $15,000 to cover medical bills and pain and suffering. Whether Colorado state law or Oklahoma state law would apply is a matter we shall address presently, but it is clear that in diversity cases federal courts must apply state substantive law (though they will apply their own procedural rules). It should also be clear that if both plaintiff and defendant were citizens of Oklahoma at the time suit was filed, or if the amount in controversy were only $5,000, there would be no federal subject matter jurisdiction.

Concurrent State Jurisdiction: A basic state trial court is a court of general jurisdiction which is *presumed* to have subject matter jurisdiction over the cases filed in it until the defendant can overcome the presumption. Most of the 25 million or so nontraffic cases filed in state courts each year could not have been filed in federal courts. However, many of them could have been because state courts have **concurrent jurisdiction** over most federal cases. That is to say, state courts can hear diversity cases involving more than $10,000 and can even hear federal question cases involving federal laws and the U.S. Constitution. There are, however, a few exceptions to this general rule—cases where the Constitution or federal statutes have given **exclusive jurisdiction** to the federal courts. Examples of this exclusive federal jurisdiction include federal criminal cases, patent, trademark, and copyright cases, bankruptcy cases, and certain federal securities law cases.

Removal: Because of concurrent jurisdiction, a plaintiff with a federal question or diversity case involving more than $10,000 may choose between filing it in federal court or in state court. Usually federal court is chosen, but considerations of court congestion, familiarity with procedures, or judges' philosophies might lead a plaintiff's lawyer to choose state court.

---

[8] For diversity of citizenship purposes, a corporation is a citizen of both the state in which it is incorporated and, if different, the state in which it has its principal place of business.

[9] 36 C.J.S., Federal Courts, §55, Copyright 1960 by West Publishing Co.

The fact that a case with federal court potential is filed in state court does not mean that it will stay there, because defendants usually have the **right of removal;** that is to say, they have the right to have a case with federal subject matter jurisdiction transferred from the state court in which it was filed to the federal district court having jurisdiction over that geographic area.

The right of removal exists in every federal question case. Part of the rationale is that the defendant is entitled to have a federal question determined by a federal court, which presumably is more expert in such matters. A defendant in a diversity case who is sued in state court in the plaintiff's state has the right to remove the suit to federal court in the plaintiff's state on the theory that a federal court is less likely to be biased against an out-of-state defendant than is a state court. On the other hand, a defendant sued in diversity in a state court in his own state cannot remove to federal district court because that defendant need not worry about being discriminated against by his own state's judge.

Jurisdiction of the Person

A court does not have the power to hear a case simply because its subject matter, the general nature of the proceeding, falls within its jurisdiction. A second type of jurisdiction—jurisdiction over *the person of the defendant* (or, in some cases, property of the defendant)—must also be present. In other words, while subject matter rules determine the court system that may hear a case, jurisdiction of person rules determine the *particular trial court* within that system where the case must be commenced. In this regard, a distinction between actions *in personam* and actions *in rem* must be noted.

Actions *in Rem*:   In some actions the plaintiff is seeking merely to enforce a right against certain *property* that is owned by the defendant or in which the defendant claims an interest. Such suits are **actions *in rem*,** and can be brought in any court within whose territorial jurisdiction the property—the *res,* or thing—is located.

The typical case is the mortgage foreclosure action, which can be illustrated as follows. X, a Missouri resident, owns an apartment building in Iowa with a $35,000 mortgage on it held by an Iowa bank. If X defaults on the mortgage payments, the bank can bring a mortgage foreclosure action in Iowa in the state district court of the county where the building is located. (Under the laws of most states relating to such actions, the bank need only publish notices of the suit in a newspaper in order to bring X's interest in the property within the jurisdiction of the court, in which case service upon X is said to be made "by publication," as distinguished from "personal service.")

The general notion in an *in rem* case is that if a defendant is going to claim an interest in a certain parcel of real estate, it is not unfair to make that defendant go where the real estate is located to defend a lawsuit. This is fairly straightforward. The more difficult questions tend to involve *in personam* actions.

Actions *in Personam*:   The great majority of civil actions are *in personam*—that is, actions in which the plaintiff is seeking to hold the defendant liable on a personal obligation. Three common examples would be: P sues D to recover damages (that is, a sum of money) arising out of a breach of contract by D, P sues to recover damages for personal injuries sustained in an accident caused by D, and P sues to recover a debt owed by D's Company.

Assume that plaintiff lives in Wisconsin and wishes to file suit there. For purposes of discussion we shall concentrate on state court, although the rules are basically the same for federal court. Traditionally, plaintiff could establish personal jurisdiction in one of three ways. First, if plaintiff can demonstrate that defendant is also a citizen of Wisconsin, then personal jurisdiction over defendant would exist.

But assume that defendant lives in Tennessee, and the lawsuit arises out of an accident that defendant caused while driving through Wisconsin on a vacation. Defendant is now back in Tennessee. A second method of establishing personal jurisdiction in Wisconsin is to serve defendant with a *summons* (which shall be explained in some detail in the next chapter) when defendant returns to Wisconsin. However, a defendant who knows that a potential lawsuit awaits in Wisconsin is likely to avoid the state altogether. The third traditional method to establish personal jurisdiction is to induce the defendant to consent to appear in the Wisconsin court. Obviously, few out-of-state defendants are so cooperative.

Thus, under these traditional methods of securing personal jurisdiction, our plaintiff is forced to go to Tennessee to file suit. This scarcely seems fair since the accident did take place in Wisconsin. The legislature of Wisconsin, and those of all other states, decided they were not adequately protecting the interests of their citizens against wrongs done by citizens of foreign states. Therefore, they passed **long-arm statutes** that authorize the "long arm of the law" emanating from the courts of Wisconsin to reach out to Tennessee to bring defendant back to Wisconsin to defend the suit. Most long-arm statutes provide that if a person does certain acts in a state, such as conduct business, enter into a contract, own real estate, drive a car, or actively

solicit sales, the law presumes that such person consents to be sued in the state in litigation arising out of those actions. Because our Tennessee defendant used Wisconsin roads and arguably committed a tortious act (negligent driving) in Wisconsin, the long-arm statute is satisfied.

However, in every instance in which a plaintiff attempts to invoke a long-arm statute to secure personal jurisdiction over an out-of-state citizen, two requirements must be met. First, plaintiff must demonstrate that defendant committed one of the acts listed in the long-arm statute.[10] Second, plaintiff must demonstrate that it is constitutional—i.e., consistent with our due process notions of fair play and justice—to make defendant come to plaintiff's jurisdiction to defend.

The following case illustrates the Supreme Court's view of how many contacts a defendant must have with a particular state before it is fair to make the defendant appear in that state to defend a lawsuit.

---

[10] Some states have omitted a listing of specific acts and simply make clear their intent to exercise personal jurisdiction over foreign citizens whenever it is constitutional to do so.

Helicopteros Nacionales de Colombia v. Hall
United States Supreme Court, 466 U.S. 408 (1984)

Petitioner "Helicol", a Colombian corporation, entered into a contract to provide helicopter transportation for Consorcio/WSH, a Peruvian consortium and the alter ego of a joint venture headquartered in Houston, Texas, during the consortium's construction of a pipeline in Peru. One of the helicopters crashed in Peru, killing four United States citizens. Respondents, survivors and representatives of the four decedents, filed this suit in Texas state court in Houston.

At the request of Consorcio/WSH, Helicol's chief executive officer had flown to Houston to negotiate the contract; the agreement was signed in Peru. During the years 1970–77, Helicol also purchased helicopters, spare parts, and accessories for more than $4,000,000 from a Fort Worth company. Helicol had sent prospective pilots to Fort Worth for training and to ferry the helicopters back to South America, and sent some management and maintenance personnel there for technical consultation also. Helicol received into its New York and

Florida bank accounts over $5,000,000 in payments from Consor-
cio/WSH drawn on a Houston bank.

On the other hand, Helicol has never been authorized to do business in Texas, and never had an agent for service of process there. Nor
has it ever performed helicopter operations, sold products, solicited
business, signed contracts, based employees, recruited employees,
owned property, maintained an office or records, or had shareholders in Texas.

Helicol filed a special appearance[a] in the trial court and moved to
dismiss for lack of personal jurisdiction. The trial court denied the
motion and, after a jury trial, entered a $1,141,200 judgment against
Helicol. The Texas Court of Civil Appeals reversed for lack of personal
jurisdiction, but the Texas Supreme Court later reinstated the verdict.
Helicol then appealed to the U.S. Supreme Court.

Blackmun, Justice:

[T]he Texas Supreme Court first held that the State's long-arm statute reaches
as far as the Due Process Clause of the Fourteenth Amendment permits. Thus,
the only question remaining for the court to decide was whether it was
consistent with the Due Process Clause for Texas courts to assert *in personam* jurisdiction over Helicol.

The Due Process Clause of the Fourteenth Amendment operates to limit
the power of a State to assert *in personam* jurisdiction over a nonresident
defendant. Due process requirements are satisfied when *in personam* jurisdiction is asserted over a nonresident corporate defendant that has "certain
minimum contacts with [the forum] such that the maintenance of the suit
does not offend 'traditional notions of fair play and substantial justice.'"
International Shoe Co. v. Washington, 326 U.S. 310 (1945). When a controversy is related to or "arises out of" a defendant's contacts with the forum, the
Court has said that a "relationship among the defendant, the forum, and the
litigation" is the essential foundation of *in personam* jurisdiction. *Shaffer v.
Heitner,* 433 U.S. 186 (1977).

Even when the cause of action does not arise out of or relate to the foreign
corporation's activities in the forum State, due process is not offended by a
State's subjecting the corporation to its *in personam* jurisdiction when there
are sufficient contacts between the State and the foreign corporation. *Perkins
v. Benguet Consolidated Mining Co.*, 342 U.S. 437 (1952). In *Perkins,* the
Court addressed a situation in which state courts had asserted general jurisdiction over a defendant foreign corporation. During the Japanese occupation of the Philippine Islands, the president and general manager of a Philippine mining corporation maintained an office in Ohio from which he
conducted activities on behalf of the company. He kept company files and
held directors' meetings in the office, carried on correspondence relating to

---

[a]In a special appearance, defendant comes into the state only to contest existence of personal
jurisdiction in the litigation and while there cannot be served summons in the traditional way.

the business, distributed salary checks drawn on two active Ohio bank accounts, engaged an Ohio bank to act as transfer agent, and supervised policies dealing with the rehabilitation of the corporation's properties in the Philippines. In short, the foreign corporation, through its president, "ha[d] been carrying on in Ohio a continuous and systematic, but limited, part of its general business," and the exercise of general jurisdiction over the Philippine corporation by an Ohio court was "reasonable and just."

All parties to the present case concede that respondents' claims against Helicol did not "arise out of," and are not related to, Helicol's activities within Texas. We thus must explore the nature of Helicol's contacts with the State of Texas to determine whether they constitute the kind of continuous and systematic general business contacts the Court found to exist in *Perkins.* We hold that they do not.

It is undisputed that Helicol does not have a place of business in Texas and never has been licensed to do business in the State. Basically, Helicol's contacts with Texas consisted of sending its chief executive officer to Houston for a contract-negotiation session; accepting into its New York bank account checks payable on a Houston bank; purchasing helicopters, equipment, and training services from Bell Helicopter for substantial sums; and sending personnel to Bell's facilities in Fort Worth for training.

The one trip to Houston by Helicol's chief executive officer for the purpose of negotiating the transportation-services contract with Consorcio/WSH cannot be described or regarded as a contact of a "continuous and systematic" nature, and thus cannot support an assertion of *in personam* jurisdiction over Helicol by a Texas court. Similarly, Helicol's acceptance from Consorcio/WSH of checks drawn on a Texas bank is of negligible significance. Common sense and everyday experience suggest that, absent unusual circumstances, the bank on which a check is drawn is generally of little consequence to the payee and is a matter left to the discretion of the drawer. Such unilateral activity of another party or a third person is not an appropriate consideration when determining whether a defendant has sufficient contacts with a forum State to justify an assertion of jurisdiction.

The Texas Supreme Court focused on the purchases and related training trips in finding contacts sufficient to support an assertion of jurisdiction. We do not agree with that assessment, for the Court's opinion in *Rosenberg Bros. & Co. v. Curtis Brown Co.*, 260 U.S. 516 (1923) makes clear that purchases and related trips, standing alone, are not a sufficient basis for a State's assertion of jurisdiction.

Nor can we conclude that the fact that Helicol sent personnel into Texas for training in connection with the purchase of helicopters and equipment in that State in any way enhanced the nature of Helicol's contacts with Texas. The brief presence of Helicol employees in Texas for the purpose of attending the training sessions is no more a significant contact than were the trips to New York made by the buyer for the [defendant] retail store in *Rosenberg.*

[Reversed.]

Comment: To reiterate, the concept of *in personam* jurisdiction is geographical in nature, and in the United States is inevitably linked to state boundaries. The court asks: Is it fair to make this defendant come to this state to defend? The result in *Hall* would probably have been the same had Helicol been from Oklahoma rather than Colombia. Also, the result would have been the same had the case been filed in *federal* district court in Houston rather than in state district court. Geographically, it is no less burdensome for Helicol to come to Houston to defend in federal court than in state court. A federal court usually uses the long-arm statute of the state in which it sits to determine personal jurisdiction.

Also note that had the president of Helicol caused an auto accident while in Houston negotiating the contract, he probably would have had to return to defend a subsequent lawsuit by the injured party because the suit arose out of the contact with Texas.

To make one last point, return to our hypothetical of the Tennesseean who caused an accident in Wisconsin. The statutory and constitutional prerequisites for assertion of long-arm jurisdiction by the Wisconsin courts appear to be met. What happens if defendant simply ignores the lawsuit, assuming that the Wisconsin courts cannot touch him? Defendant is wrong. Defendant's failure to appear will lead to a default judgment being rendered against him. In most instances, plaintiff can take that Wisconsin judgment and have it enforced by Tennessee courts just as though it had been rendered by them. Under the Full Faith and Credit Clause of the Constitution, Tennessee courts will honor and enforce most judgments from Wisconsin and other states.

Additional Concerns

Venue: That a court has subject matter and personal jurisdiction does not always end the inquiry. In our Wisconsin accident hypothetical, for example, every trial court in every county in Wisconsin would have had subject matter and personal jurisdiction over the defendant. But should the case be filed in southern Wisconsin or northern Wisconsin? **Venue** statutes answer this question. Most states provide that venue is available in the county where the defendant resides or where the cause of action arose. In our hypothetical, then, a plaintiff filing in state court should file in the county where the accident occurred.

Forum Non Conveniens: A court with both subject matter and personal jurisdiction may decline to exercise them if another court, more conveniently connected to the suit, also has both types of jurisdiction. Under the doctrine of ***forum non conveniens,*** the court may choose to transfer the suit or even dismiss it, forcing plaintiff to file in the more convenient court.

For example, in one case arising out of a defendant's agent carelessly causing a fire in the plaintiff's warehouse in Virginia, plaintiff sued 400 miles away in New York City where the state court had subject matter jurisdiction over the simple tort case and personal jurisdiction because of defendant corporation's many business contacts in New York. However, the New York court declined to exercise its jurisdiction on grounds that the suit was more conveniently brought in Virginia where plaintiff and all witnesses were located and where the accident had occurred. The only justification plaintiff gave for filing in New York—that a New York jury was likely to give a bigger verdict—was inadequate.[11]

In determining the most convenient forum, courts will consider private interest factors such as ease of access to sources of proof, costs of obtaining witnesses' attendance, the possibility of a view of the site of the accident, and the convenience of the parties. Public factors to be considered include the imposition of jury service on residents of the community, the congestion of court dockets, and the interest in having local controversies decided at home.

---

[11] *Gulf Oil Corp. v. Gilbert,* 330 U.S. 401 (1947).

A U.S. court of appeals recently affirmed, on *forum non conveniens* grounds, the transfer of litigation against Union Carbide arising out of the Bhopal tragedy in India from a federal district court in New York to India. It did so only after the trial judge convinced himself that Indian courts could provide substantial justice. The transfer was conditioned on Union Carbide's consent to the jurisdiction of the Indian courts and waiver of any statute of limitations defense.[12]

Conflict of Laws: Assume D Corporation, formed in Delaware with its principal place of business in Colorado, hires P from California to do subcontracting work on D's condominiums in New Mexico. The contract is negotiated in California, Colorado, and New Mexico before being signed in Colorado. When New Mexico officials ordered P to stop work because he did not have a license to do such work in New Mexico, D fired him. P sued in Colorado to recover for the work he had done before being stopped. Several states' laws are potentially applicable to this case. If they all lead to the same result, it does not matter which state's rules are applied. However, in this case, New Mexico law bars P from recovery because he had no license. Colorado and California law would allow him to recover despite the lack of a license. There is a "conflict of laws." To determine which state's laws to apply, we must resort to what are known as "choice of law" rules which are designed to prevent a plaintiff with multiple jurisdictions to choose from (because all have subject matter and personal jurisdiction) from "forum shopping" for the jurisdiction with the laws most favorable to him or her.

Contract cases: If the parties stipulate in the contract that, for example, "California law will govern any disputes arising out of this contract," the courts will normally respect that choice if it was fairly bargained for and California has at least a passing connection to the parties or the transaction.

Absent a choice by the parties, the traditional view was to apply the law of the state in which the contract was made to any litigation about the validity of the contract, and to apply the law of the state in which the contract was to be performed to any litigation about the performance of the contract. The strong modern trend, however, is to use an "interest" analysis.

Section six of the Restatement (Second) on Choice of Law suggests that the Colorado courts in our example should consider the following interests in deciding which state's rules to apply: (a) the needs of the interstate and international systems; (b) the relevant policies of the forum (Colorado); (c) the relevant policies of other interested states; (d) the protection of justified expectations (i.e., which state's laws did the parties assume would apply); (e) the basic policies underlying the particular field of law; (f) certainty, predictability, and uniformity of result; and (g) ease in the determination and application of the law to be applied.

In contract cases specifically, the Restatement suggests in §188 that the law of the state with the "most significant relationship" to the parties and the transaction under the principles of §6 should be applied. Factors to consider in applying the §6 principles to a contract case include: (a) the place of contracting; (b) the place of negotiation; (c) the place of performance; (d) the location of the subject matter of the contract; and (e) the domicile, residence, nationality, place of incorporation, and place of business of the parties.

In the factual situation outlined above, the Colorado Supreme Court applied New Mexico's law, reasoning that New Mexico's interest in protecting its citizens from substandard construction by unlicensed subcontractors outweighed Colorado's interest in validating agreements and protecting parties' expectations.[13]

---

[12] *In re Union Carbide Corp. Gas Plant Disaster at Bhopal, India in Dec. 1984,* __F.2d__ (2d. Cir. 1987).

[13] *Wood Bros. Homes, Inc. v. Walker Adjustment Bureau,* 601 P.2d 1369 (Colo. 1979).

Tort cases: Assume that a husband and wife from New Mexico are killed when a plane the husband is piloting crashes in Texas. The parties intended to return to New Mexico and had no other contacts with Texas. The estate of the wife filed suit against the husband's estate in state court in Texas. Texas' doctrine of interspousal immunity would not allow the suit. New Mexico has no such doctrine; its law would allow the suit. Which state's law should apply? The traditional view is to apply the law of the place of the tort— Texas. But why would Texas courts care whether or not a New Mexico wife can recover from a New Mexico husband? Again, the strong modern trend is to move away from an automatic choice of the law of the place of the tort to an interest analysis. The Restatement's §144 suggests that the following factors should be considered in deciding which state has the "most significant relationship" to the occurrence and the parties for purposes of applying §6's principles: (a) the place where the injury occurred; (b) the place where the conduct causing the injury occurred; (c) the domicile, residence, nationality, place of incorporation and place of business of the parties; and (d) the place where the relationship, if any, between the parties is centered. In this case, New Mexico law was applied.[14]

LAW, EQUITY, AND REMEDIES

In the next chapter we will examine the major steps in the process of adjudication, paying particular attention to the roles played by the trial and appellate courts in that process. We will see that in all legal controversies the plaintiff is asking for a **remedy**—an order addressed to the defendant, requiring that person to do (or not to do) a particular act. A remedy, then, is "the means by which a plaintiff's right is enforced, or the violation of a right is prevented, redressed, or compensated."[15] All remedies are either

"legal" or "equitable" in nature, a fact that can be explained only by a brief glimpse at the development of the early court systems in England.

Courts of Law

After the Norman conquest of England some nine hundred years ago, a nationwide system of courts was established. This was accomplished when the first Norman kings designated individuals throughout the country to be their personal representatives in the settling of certain kinds of legal controversies.

These early courts, which were called royal courts or king's courts, *were sharply limited as to the kinds of remedies they could grant.* Essentially, they could grant relief only in cases where the plaintiff was asking for (1) money damages, (2) the possession of real estate, or (3) the possession of personal property.

In settling the disputes within their limited jurisdiction, the courts made up their own rules as they went along, based largely on the customs and moral standards then prevailing, plus their own ideas of what kinds of conduct were "just" in particular situations. The formulation of rules in this manner, a process that continues today in some branches of law, gave birth to the common law. The courts ultimately became **courts of law,** and the remedies which they granted in the three types of controversies that they could hear were *remedies at law.*

Courts of Equity

While this system introduced a uniformity to the settling of disputes, controversies began to arise when plaintiffs sought remedies *other than those that the courts of law could grant.* Rebuffed by these courts, they frequently petitioned the king for relief. Most of the petitions were ruled on by the king's secretary, the chancellor, who granted relief when he thought the plaintiff's claim was a fair one. Out of the rulings of successive chancellors arose a new body of "chancery" rules and remedies for cases outside the jurisdiction of the courts of law.

---

[14] *Robertson v. McKnight,* 609 S.W.2d 534 (Tex. 1980).

[15] *Black's Law Dictionary,* Fifth Edition, Copyright 1979 by West Publishing Co.

Finally, a system of chancery courts, known as **courts of equity,** evolved. Thus it was that two systems of courts (each with different judges) and two bodies of rules—law and equity— existed concurrently. A plaintiff wanting a legal remedy brought an **action at law** in a court of law; a plaintiff wanting some other relief brought an **action in equity** in an equity court.

The two primary remedies that a court of equity could grant were the *injunction* and the *decree of specific performance.*

The Injunction: If a plaintiff brought an ac- tion in a king's court asking that the defendant be ordered to refrain from doing a particular act, his request had to be denied. For example: if P asked the court to order D to stop grazing cattle on land belonging to P, the court could only grant damages for the past injury done to the land; it did not have the power to prevent such tres- passes in the future. In such a case, P's only hope was that the chancellor, whose power to grant relief was not so circumscribed, would feel that his request was justified and would order the defendant to stop performing the wrongful act—an order that today is called the **injunc- tion.** (In later years, as courts of equity became established, actions for injunctive relief were commenced directly in those courts.)

The Decree of Specific Performance: The foregoing is also applicable to cases in which a plaintiff was asking for a **decree of specific per- formance**—an order commanding the defen- dant to live up to the terms of a contract made with the plaintiff. Courts of law could not do this; all they could do was order the defendant to pay the plaintiff a sum of money (damages) to com- pensate the plaintiff for losses suffered as a result of the breach of contract. Courts of equity, on the other hand, were empowered to issue a de- cree of specific performance when they felt that awarding damages would be an inadequate rem- edy—that is, in those exceptional situations where a sum of money would not, in their opin- ion, adequately recompense the plaintiff for the loss of services promised by the defendant or for

the property the defendant had contracted to convey. (The awarding of damages, however, is the normal remedy in breach of contract suits. Only in exceptional cases, involving highly unique services or property, is specific perfor- mance granted.)[16]

The Present Scene

While the distinction between legal and equi- table remedies as diagrammed in Figure 2.3 per- sists today, there has been a fusion of law and equity courts in virtually all states. This means that separate courts of law and equity, as such, have been eliminated. Instead, the basic trial courts in the state and federal systems are em- powered to hear both legal and equitable actions.

Today, the basic distinctions between the two kinds of actions are these:

1. Whether an action is one at law or in equity depends solely upon the *nature of the remedy* that the plaintiff is seeking.

2. There is *no jury* in an equitable action. Ques- tions of both fact and law are decided by the court, that is, the trial judge.

3. Proceedings in equitable actions are *less for- mal* than those at law, particularly in regard to the order in which witnesses' testimony can be presented and the determination of admissibility of their evidence.

SUMMARY

Both the state and the federal court systems are organized similarly. At the first level are general trial courts, supplemented by specialized courts of limited jurisdiction. Appeals from the judg- ments of these courts are heard by appellate courts. In some states and in the federal system,

---

[16] Other common equitable actions, in addition to those ask- ing for injunctions and decrees of specific performance, are (1) divorce actions, (2) mortgage foreclosure suits, and (3) actions for an accounting, brought by one member of a partnership against another.

Figure 2.3   Major Differences between Law and Equity

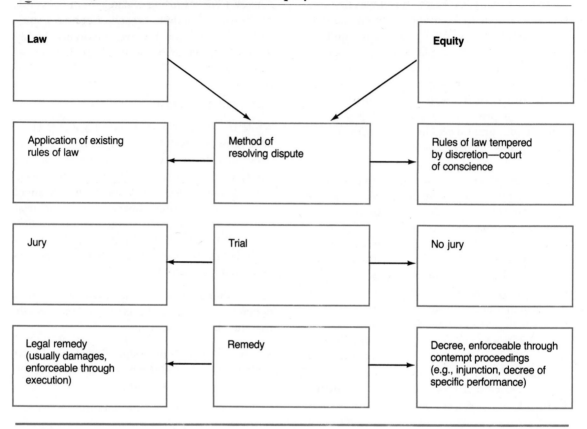

there is an intermediate appellate court as well as a supreme court for a final appeal.

Federal courts can hear only the types of cases specified in the Constitution, primarily cases turning on federal questions and cases where a citizen of one state is suing the citizen of another for more than $10,000. State trial courts can hear just about any type of case, except for a few categories specifically limited for exclusive federal jurisdiction. However, if a case with federal subject matter jurisdiction potential is filed in state court, it might not stay there; the defendant may remove it to federal court.

Every court must have subject matter jurisdiction. Personal jurisdiction over the defendant is also a prerequisite to a valid judgment. Courts frequently use the long-arm statute of their state to establish personal jurisdiction over defendants from other states, consistent with due process, of course. The establishment of subject matter and personal jurisdiction does not end the inquiry as to where a case will be tried— matters of venue and *forum non conveniens* must also be considered. A court deciding a case that has contacts with many states will have to use choice of law rules to determine which state's law to apply.

Historically, common law courts were divided into courts of law, which rendered mostly damage judgments, and courts of equity, which could grant more varied forms of relief. Though there are no longer two separate court systems, the procedures in a court may vary depending on whether the plaintiff asks for damages or injunctive relief.

KEY TERMS

Adjudication
Courts of limited jurisdiction
General trial courts
Appellate courts
Jurisdiction
Federal question
Concurrent jurisdiction
Exclusive jurisdiction
Right of removal
Action *in rem*
Action *in personam*
Long-arm statutes
Venue
Forum non conveniens
Remedy
Courts of law
Courts of equity
Action at law
Action in equity
Injunction
Decree of specific performance

QUESTIONS AND PROBLEMS

1. Gatch was an employee of a radio station (Arrow Broadcasting) who brought suit against Hennepin Broadcasting to recover $8,000 damages, alleging that Hennepin interfered with his contract with Arrow, and that this interference constituted a wrong under Minnesota law. (Gatch was a Minnesota resident, and Hennepin was a Minnesota corporation.) When Gatch filed this suit in a Minnesota state court, Hennepin asked that it be removed to the federal courts, claiming that a *federal question* was presented in view of the fact that Hennepin was subject to the rules and regulations of the Federal Communications Commission. Do you agree that this fact raises a federal question? Why or why not? (*Gatch v. Hennepin Broadcasting,* 349 F.Supp. 1180, 1972.)

2. Rate, a Georgia lawyer, is owed $18,250 in legal fees by Jackson, a Florida resident. Although Rate could have brought suit to recover the debt in a federal court in Florida on grounds of diversity of citizenship, he chose, instead, to file his suit in a Florida court in the county in which Jackson lives. If Jackson now asks that the suit be transferred to the federal courts, will his request have to be granted? Explain.

3. While walking across Gomez's property one evening, North is injured when he falls into an unguarded excavation. When North brings a negligence action against Gomez in the proper state court to recover damages, that court applies the rule that a trespasser cannot hold a landowner liable even if he is guilty of negligence, and dismisses the action. North appeals the decision to the state supreme court, which affirms the rule of nonliability. In this case, is the ruling of the state supreme court final? (If North were to appeal to the U.S. Supreme Court, would it refuse to consider the case?) Why or why not?

4. Ezra and Sharon Kulko, New York residents, were married in 1959 in California while Ezra was on a three-day stopover en route from a military base in Texas to a tour of duty in Korea. After his military duty was over he rejoined his wife in New York, where she had lived after the marriage. In 1972 the Kulkos separated, and a separation agreement was entered into obligating him to pay his wife $3,000 a year in support money to cover vacation periods when their children would be living with her.

Thereafter Mrs. Kulko got a divorce in Haiti, with the divorce decree incorporating the terms of the separation agreement. She then moved to California, and in 1975 brought action in a California court against Kulko asking that court to modify the divorce decree by awarding her full custody of the children and by increasing Kulko's support payments.

When Kulko received a summons in New York (apparently by registered mail), he made a special appearance in the California court contending that the California courts had no jurisdiction over him. The California trial court held that it *did* have jurisdiction, ruling that there were sufficient contacts between Kulko and the state of California to permit the suit to be brought in California. (These contacts were (a) Kulko's consent that their daughter spend nine months a year with her mother in California, and (b) the financial benefit Kulko received by not having to support the daughter while she was in California.) The California Supreme Court agreed with the trial court, and Kulko appealed that ruling to the U.S. Supreme Court. Do you agree with the California courts that Kulko's contacts were sufficient to permit the suit to be heard in that state? Why or why not? (*Kulko v. Superior Court of California,* 436 U.S. 84, 1978.)

5. Plaintiffs bought an Audi automobile in New York. Later, while moving to Arizona they were involved in a serious collision in Oklahoma when the Audi caught fire after being struck from behind. Filing in Oklahoma, plaintiffs sued the New York retailer from whom they had purchased the car and the wholesaler who had provided the car to the retailer. These defendants claimed that because they only sold cars in New York, an Oklahoma court had no personal jurisdiction over them. Does the Oklahoma long-arm statute reach this far? Discuss. (*World-Wide Volkswagen Corp. v. Woodson,* 444 U.S. 286, 1981.)

6. Plaintiff corporation, incorporated in Michigan, hired defendant from Florida to operate a helicopter to spray agricultural chemicals on fields in Ohio. In a contract written and signed by plaintiff in Michigan and later signed by defendant in Florida, defendant agreed that if he left plaintiff's employ he would not enter into a competing business. After two years, defendant left plaintiff's employ and did begin a competing business in Ohio. Plaintiff sued in Ohio to enforce the covenant not to compete. Such a covenant is void under Michigan law, but enforceable if reasonable under the laws of Florida and Ohio. Which state's law should be applied by the Ohio court? Discuss. (*S&S Chopper Service, Inc. v. Scripter,* 394 N.E.2d 1011, Ohio App. 1977.)

7. Defendant airline, a Delaware corporation headquartered in New York, invited several Texas travel agents to take an expense paid vacation to Mexico. While in Mexico, one of the travel agents was killed by unknown assailants. His wife, plaintiff, sued the airline in Texas, claiming that its Texas employees knew at the time of the invitation that portions of Mexico near the trip site were overrun with bands of armed guerrillas, yet they negligently failed to take precautions for the safety of her husband. Mexico's law would allow recovery on plaintiff's theory; Texas law would not. Which law should apply? Discuss. (*Semmelroth v. American Airlines,* 448 F.Supp. 730, E.D.Ill. 1978.)

8. Durant was left paralyzed from the waist down when his tractor struck defendant's guide wire. Durant sued defendant on a theory of negligent maintenance, filing the suit in Lee County, South Carolina. Defendant filed a motion to change the suit's venue to Sumter County on grounds of convenience to witnesses. Nine of defendant's employees, who would also be witnesses, filed affidavits stating that they would have to travel 23 miles to the Lee County Courthouse. Plaintiff responded with an affidavit indicating that because of his paralysis he was difficult to move, and that the Lee County rescue squad had agreed to transport him to and from the Lee County Courthouse but no further. Should the court grant the motion to change venue on *forum non conveniens* grounds? Discuss. See *Durant v. Black River Electric Cooperative, Inc.,* 248 S.E.2d 264 (S.C. 1978).

Chapter 3

DISPUTE RESOLUTION

Many American novels, movies, and television programs feature courtroom scenes to produce dramatic tension for the readers and viewers. This is appropriate, because courtroom battles can produce high drama. Nothing quite matches the tension which litigants and attorneys feel when a jury verdict is about to be announced in open court.

This chapter will examine the litigation process, from the initiation of a civil suit through the trial process all the way to final appeal. After this examination, you will be better able to appreciate the context in which these few dramatic moments occur. You will also understand that litigation can be extremely complicated, expensive, and time-consuming. Indeed, litigation is usually something to be avoided. But when you cannot avoid litigation, it pays to understand the process.

ALTERNATIVE METHODS OF DISPUTE RESOLUTION

Before we trace the life of the typical lawsuit from its inception to final judgment, it should be remembered that litigation is by no means the only method of resolving disputes. In fact, there are certain disputes—or types of disputes—that the courts are not well equipped to settle. Sometimes, for example, there is the problem of very large numbers of persons injured by the single wrong of a single defendant, or injured by a single type of conduct on the part of a very few defendants, as exemplified by the thousands of asbestos industry claims outstanding in the mid-1980s.[1] In other cases the nature of the problem is such that it requires an expertise that the courts cannot be expected to possess, such as the renegotiation of detailed collective bargaining agreements. And in the area of consumer law, a dispute over a poorly working television set, or even an automobile, for instance, may not justify the cost of court action (although the limited jurisdiction small claims courts are often a useful forum in this area). For these reasons we briefly note some of the alternative means of dispute resolution.

The Simple Out-of-Court Settlement

Most disputes are settled either by compromise or by one party giving up. The simplest compromise occurs where creditors accept smaller sums and debtors pay larger sums than either thinks is due. Or a contractor may agree to a modification in building plans in return for the building owner's agreement to a two-month extension for completion. In other instances one party may choose to forgo legal proceedings in order to preserve the other's goodwill, especially where the latter is a valued customer. Or one party may decide that pursuing any kind of remedy isn't worth the wear and tear, and he or she simply accepts the loss.

Arbitration Agreements

Another method of settling a dispute is through an *arbitration agreement,* a procedure that is being used increasingly in the business world today.[2] In these agreements, the parties to a dispute agree that it will be submitted to one or more arbitrators of their choice and that the arbitrator's decision will be binding.

Compared to litigation, voluntary arbitration has several advantages: (1) disputes can be settled more quickly, (2) arbitrators can be chosen

---

[1] Although plaintiffs normally sue only on their own behalf, the federal and state courts have a procedural device known as a "class action" whereby a single plaintiff can represent (and bind in litigation) an entire class of plaintiffs—sometimes numbering in the tens of thousands. To be allowed to represent an entire class, a plaintiff must convince the court of a number of facts, including that there are questions of law and fact common to all potential class members, that the class is numerically too large to allow all members to participate actively in the trial, and that the plaintiff and his or her attorneys can ably represent the interests of the class without conflict of interest.

[2] The American Arbitration Association is now providing arbitrators to settle some 45,000 disputes each year, and the federal courts are experimenting with court-annexed arbitration panels of three volunteer lawyers who decide relatively small civil cases (e.g., under $75,000).

who have special expertise in the particular business practices that are the subject of the controversy, (3) the proceedings are relatively informal, and (4) the cost is ordinarily less than if the cases go to court.

Generally, there are two kinds of arbitration agreements: agreements to submit and submission agreements. *Agreements to submit* are usually part of a larger contract (such as a collective bargaining agreement) and provide that future disputes arising out of the contract will be submitted to arbitration. *Submission agreements* are agreements to submit existing disputes to arbitration.

While the legal validity of arbitration agreements used to be subject to considerable doubt, most of this has been resolved. A federal statute, for example, now makes such written agreements involving interstate commerce "valid, irrevocable, and enforceable, save on such grounds as exist at law or in equity for the revocation of any contract." That law is applied in the following case.

Southland Corporation v. Keating
U.S. Supreme Court, 465 U.S. 1 (1984)

Appellant Southland Corp. is the owner and franchisor of 7-11 convenience stores; appellees are 7-11 franchisees. Each franchise agreement contains a clause requiring arbitration of any controversy or claim arising out of or relating to the agreement. Appellees sued appellant in state court in California, alleging various state common law claims such as fraud and breach of contract, and violation of the disclosure requirements of the California Franchise Investment Law. After the actions were consolidated, appellant moved to compel arbitration of the claims pursuant to the terms of the contract.

After certain rulings and appeals, the California Supreme Court held that claims arising under the California Franchise Investment Law are not arbitrable. It interpreted §31512 of that law—which renders void any provision purporting to bind a franchisee to waive compliance with any provision of that law—to require judicial consideration of claims brought under that statute, and held that the state statute did not contravene the United States Arbitration Act. Southland appealed.

Burger, Chief Justice:

The California Franchise Investment Law provides:

"Any condition, stipulation or provision purporting to bind any person acquiring any franchise to waive compliance with any provision of this law or any rule or order hereunder is void." Cal. Corp. Code §31512 (West 1977).

The California Supreme Court interpreted this statute to require judicial consideration of claims brought under the State statute and accordingly refused to enforce the parties' contract to arbitrate such claims. So interpreted the California Franchise Investment Law directly conflicts with §2 of the Federal Arbitration Act and violates the Supremacy Clause.

In enacting §2 of the federal Act, Congress declared a national policy favoring arbitration and withdrew the power of the states to require a judicial forum for the resolution of claims which the contracting parties agreed to resolve by arbitration. The Federal Arbitration Act provides:

"A written provision in any maritime transaction or a contract evidencing a transaction involving commerce to settle by arbitration a controversy thereafter arising out of such contract or transaction, or the refusal to perform the whole or any part thereof, or an agreement in writing to submit to arbitration an existing controversy arising out of such a contract, transaction, or refusal, shall be valid, irrevocable, and enforceable, save upon such grounds as exist at law or in equity for the revocation of any contract." 9 U.S.C. §2 (1976).

Congress has thus mandated the enforcement of arbitration agreements.

We discern only two limitations on the enforceability of arbitration provisions governed by the Federal Arbitration Act: they must be part of a written maritime contract or a contract "evidencing a transaction involving commerce" and such clauses may be revoked upon "grounds as exist at law or in equity for the revocation of any contract." We see nothing in the Act indicating that the broad principle of enforceability is subject to any additional limitations under State law. . . .

Although the legislative history is not without ambiguities, there are strong indications that Congress had in mind something more than making arbitration agreements enforceable only in the federal courts. The House Report plainly suggests the more comprehensive objectives:

"The purpose of this bill is to make valid and enforceable agreements for arbitration contained in contracts involving interstate commerce or within the jurisdiction or admiralty, or which may be the subject of litigation in the Federal courts." H. R. Rep. No. 96, 68th Cong., 1st Sess. 1 (1924) (Emphasis added.)

This broader purpose can also be inferred from the reality that Congress would be less likely to address a problem whose impact was confined to federal courts than a problem of large significance in the field of commerce. The Arbitration Act sought to "overcome the rule of equity, that equity will not specifically enforce any arbitration agreement." Hearing on S. 4214 Before a Subcomm. of the Senate Comm. on the Judiciary, 67th Cong., 4th Sess. 6 (1923) ("Senate Hearing") (remarks of Sen. Walsh). The House Report accompanying the bill stated:

"[t]he need for the law arises from . . . the jealousy of the English courts for their own jurisdiction. . . . This jealousy survived for so lon[g] a period that the principle became firmly embedded in the English common law and was adopted with it by the American courts. The courts have felt that the precedent was too strongly fixed to be overturned without legislative enactment. . . ." H. R. Rep. No. 96, supra, 1-2 (1924).

Surely this makes clear that the House Report contemplated a broad reach of the Act, unencumbered by state law constraints. As was stated in *Metro Industrial Painting Corp.* v. *Terminal Construction Corp.,* 287 F. 2d 382, 387 (CA2 1961) (Lumbard, Chief Judge, concurring), "the purpose of the act was to assure those who desired arbitration and whose contracts related to interstate commerce that their expectations would not be undermined by federal judges, or . . . by state courts or legislatures." Congress also showed its awareness of the widespread unwillingness of state courts to enforce arbitration agreements, *e.g.,* Senate Hearing, *supra,* at 8, and that such courts were bound by state laws inadequately providing for

"technical arbitration by which, if you agree to arbitrate under the method provided by the statute, you have an arbitration by statute[;] but [the statutes] ha[d] nothing to do with validating the contract to arbitrate." Ibid.

The problems Congress faced were therefore twofold: the old common law hostility toward arbitration, and the failure of state arbitration statutes to mandate enforcement of arbitration agreements. To confine the scope of the Act to arbitrations sought to be enforced in federal courts would frustrate what we believe Congress intended to be a broad enactment appropriate in scope to meet the large problems Congress was addressing.

. . . We are unwilling to attribute to Congress the intent, in drawing on the comprehensive powers of the Commerce Clause, to create a right to enforce an arbitration contract and yet make the right dependent for its enforcement on the particular forum in which it is asserted. And since the overwhelming proportion of all civil litigation in this country is in the state courts, we cannot believe Congress intended to limit the Arbitration Act to disputes subject only to *federal* court jurisdiction. Such an interpretation would frustrate Congressional intent to place "[a]n arbitration agreement . . . upon the same footing as other contracts, where it belongs." H. R. Rep. No. 96, *supra,* 1.

In creating a substantive rule applicable in state as well as federal courts, Congress intended to foreclose state legislative attempts to undercut the enforceability of arbitration agreements. We hold that §31512 of the California Franchise Investment Law violates the Supremacy Clause.

[Reversed.]

Mediation

Mediation is a method of resolving a dispute by bringing in a third party, the *mediator,* whose role is largely to narrow the issues, facilitate communication between the parties, and suggest possible compromises. Mediation thus differs from arbitration largely in the fact that while a mediator may make recommendations at various stages of the negotiations, he or she cannot impose a final settlement that is binding upon the parties.

While mediation can be useful in virtually any kind of dispute, it has traditionally been used most often in settling international disputes and, in the United States, in the labor-management area. In that regard, mention should be made of the Federal Mediation and Conciliation Service, a federal agency whose primary role is to facilitate the negotiation of collective bargaining agreements between unions and companies in interstate commerce.

Recent Developments

In recent years several additional methods of dispute resolution have been increasingly successful. Two of these merit special mention.

The *Magnuson-Moss Warranty Act,* a federal statute passed in 1975, facilitates the settlement of disputes between the buyers of *consumer products*—such as television sets and automobiles—and their manufacturers. It does this, first, by encouraging manufacturers to set up "informal dispute settlement mechanisms" within their companies to handle customer complaints.

Where a manufacturer has created such an office, consumers must use the informal procedures afforded by that office in order to settle their disputes before they can resort to court action. Secondly, where the informal procedures prove unsuccessful, both the Federal Trade Commission and the attorney general may seek injunctions against any manufacturer who has been found to violate any provision of the act.[3]

Another innovative method for settling commercial disputes is the *minitrial.* In this process, lawyers for corporations in a dispute present summaries of their respective companies' positions to a neutral advisor (with top executives of the firms usually present). The basic purpose of the advisor is to narrow the issues and to advise the parties how a court would probably rule on them in the event of litigation. After the minitrial, the executives meet (without the presence of their lawyers) in an effort to negotiate a settlement—an effort that has proved to be successful in a high percentage of cases.

A chief advantage of the minitrial is the speed with which disputes are settled, with the resultant cost savings to the parties; the typical minitrial is completed the same day it begins. Additionally, the process exposes executives of each company to the claims of its antagonist, and also gives the executives a greater hand in reaching a settlement than if the case had gone to trial. One of the most publicized controversies involving use of the minitrial was a three-way dispute between the National Aeronautics and Space Administration (NASA), a consortium of companies called the Space Communications Company (a prime contractor for construction of a $1.5 billion satellite system for NASA), and TRW, Inc., a prime subcontractor on the project, who contended it was entitled to an additional $100 million for the construction of certain components of the system. After three years of pretrial litigation—with no settlement yet in sight—the parties reached an agreement after a minitrial that lasted less than a month (with an estimated savings of over $1 million in additional legal fees). Two hundred major corporations have recently pledged to try the minitrial or other forms of alternative dispute resolution.

Settlement by Litigation

Despite the increasing settlement of disputes by the above processes, thousands of cases *are* initiated in the courts every year. It is only through the adjudication of these controversies by the courts that the implementation of the rules of law really takes place.[4]

While the trial and appellate courts are both concerned with the same general goal, the orderly settling of legal disputes, their basic responsibilities differ to a significant degree. As was noted earlier, the trial courts must decide the disputed questions of fact and then select the rules of law that are applicable.[5] The appellate courts, by contrast, are concerned exclusively with settling questions of law. They decide whether the rulings of the trial court, about which the appellant is complaining, were correct. With these observations before us, we now examine the processes by which the two levels of courts perform their duties.

THE TRIAL COURTS: PRETRIAL PROCEEDINGS

Pretrial proceedings consist of two stages, the **pleading stage** and the **discovery stage.** We now look at each of these steps briefly.

---

[3] The Magnuson-Moss Warranty Act is discussed further in Chapter 22.

[4] Again, a reminder that the settlement of controversies by *administrative agencies* is examined in Chapter 6.

[5] While the rulings of the trial courts are appealable, the importance of their work can hardly be overstated. It is on their determination of the facts that the precise legal issues are framed, and most of their decisions are final. (That is, a majority of the judgments of the trial courts are not, in fact, appealed.)

The Pleading Stage

The typical suit is commenced by the plaintiff, through an attorney, filing a **complaint** (or petition) with the court having jurisdiction of the case. At the same time, the plaintiff asks the court to issue a summons to the defendant, notifying that person that a complaint is on file. In most instances, service of process is accomplished by a law officer's hand delivering the summons to the defendant. However, when this cannot be reasonably accomplished, most states provide for service by registered mail or by leaving the summons at the defendant's usual place of business or home. Even service by publication in local newspapers is sometimes allowed. Service on a corporate defendant must be in accordance with strict rules. Many jurisdictions follow the Model Business Corporation Act which requires every corporation doing business in a state to maintain a registered agent for purposes of receiving service of process. That agent's address is on file in the Secretary of State's office. If a corporation fails to appoint a registered agent or if the agent cannot be found, service upon the Secretary of State is effective against the corporation.

After receiving the summons, the defendant has a prescribed period of time in which to file a response of some sort, normally an **answer,** to the complaint. After that has been done, the plaintiff can file a **reply** to the answer. The complaint, answer, and reply make up the *pleadings* of a case, the main purpose of which is to permit the court and the parties to ascertain the actual points in issue.

The Complaint: The complaint briefly sets forth the plaintiff's version of the facts and ends with a "prayer" (request) for a certain remedy based on those facts. Its primary purpose is to notify the defendant that a claim is being asserted against him or her based on certain *allegations* of fact.

The Answer: The defendant usually responds to the complaint by filing an *answer* (or, in circumstances to be noted later, a "motion to dismiss"). In the typical case the defendant will disagree with one or more allegations of fact set forth in the complaint, and the answer will indicate the specific points of disagreement. For example, three allegations in a complaint growing out of an automobile accident may be (1) that the defendant was the driver of a car that collided with the plaintiff's on a certain date, (2) that defendant's car was to the left of the center line at the time of impact, and (3) that defendant was driving negligently at the time. Depending upon the particular circumstances, the defendant might deny the first allegation (on which the others are obviously based), claiming that he or she was merely a passenger in the car, which was being driven by someone else. Or the defendant might admit allegations (1) and (2) but deny allegation (3), claiming that he or she was directed to drive left of center by a police officer who was investigating a prior accident at the scene. In either event, the answer would raise *questions of fact,* which would have to be settled at the trial.

The answer also permits the defendant to raise *affirmative defenses*—legal points that will absolve the defendant of liability even if his or her version of the facts is proved wrong. For example, the defendant in the above case may deny that he or she was driving negligently, and, in addition, may allege that plaintiff was guilty of *contributory negligence;* if this is true, it may free defendant of liability under the law of some states even if it is later established in the trial court that he or she was driving in a negligent manner at the time of the accident.

Additionally, an answer may be accompanied by a **counterclaim** which, in an auto accident case, might contend that the plaintiff was the real cause of the accident and that the defendant was injured also. In the same proceeding the jury would decide whether plaintiff or defendant was at fault, and who could recover from whom. Many a plaintiff has regretted instigating litigation after a jury resolved all issues in favor of the defendant's counterclaim.

Motion to Dismiss: If a defendant contends that he or she is not legally liable even if the plaintiff's allegations of fact are true, defendant will file a **motion to dismiss** instead of an answer. Technically this is called a "motion to dismiss" for the reason that the complaint states no cause of action: the complaint fails to state a legally recognizable claim. For example, if the D Company, a retailer, cut down two trees in front of its place of business in spite of protests from P, a neighboring retailer, and if P sued the D Company to recover damages, the D Company might well file such a motion in response to P's complaint. In such a case, assuming that the felling of the trees did not violate any municipal ordinance or rule of the local planning commission, the D Company had a perfect right to remove the trees; thus the motion to dismiss will be "sustained" by the court and the suit will be ended at that point. (A trial court's ruling on such a motion, however, may always be appealed to a higher court. If such court rules that a motion to dismiss should have been overruled rather than sustained, then the case will be sent back to the trial court for further proceedings.)[6]

By filing a motion to dismiss on the grounds that no cause of action is stated, the defendant does not admit that the plaintiff's version of the facts is correct. Rather, he or she is simply saying that even if the facts are as stated, plaintiff has no basis under the law for bringing the suit. Thus, if the motion is overruled, the defendant is permitted to raise questions of fact during the trial.

If the defendant files nothing within the prescribed time (20 days in the federal courts) after being served with a summons, the court may enter a **default judgment** against defendant. In essence, a default judgment determines that defendant has waived the right to contest liability.

The court then proceeds to hold a hearing on damages to determine how much plaintiff is entitled to recover.

The Reply: If the defendant raises new matter—additional facts—in his or her answer, then the plaintiff must file a reply. In this pleading plaintiff will either deny or admit the new facts alleged in the answer.

The Discovery Stage

In early years, cases moved directly from the pleading stage to the trial stage. This meant that each party, going into the trial, had little information as to the specific evidence that the other party would rely on in presenting his case. Trial proceedings, as a result, often became what was commonly described as a "cat and mouse" game, with the parties often bringing in evidence that surprised their opponents.

The undesirability of these proceedings was finally perceived by lawyers and judges, with the result that the Federal Rules of Civil Procedure, adopted in 1938, provided means (called "discovery proceedings") by which much of the evidence that each party was going to rely on in proving his or her version of the facts would be fully disclosed to the other party before the case came on for trial. The most common discovery tools recognized by these federal rules, which have now been essentially adopted by the states, are *depositions, interrogatories,* and *requests for production of documents.*

A deposition is testimony of a witness that is taken outside of court. Such testimony is given under oath, and both parties to the case must be notified so that they can be present when the testimony is given, and thus have the opportunity to cross-examine the witness.

Interrogatories are written questions submitted by one party to the other, which must be answered under oath. Use of this device is a primary way by which the questioning party may gain access to evidence that otherwise would be solely in the possession of his or her adversary.

---

[6] The terminology used in referring to this particular type of "motion to dismiss" follows the rules of civil procedure that have, in recent years, been adopted by many states. The earlier name for this same pleading device—the "demurrer"—continues to be used in a number of states, however. In such states, what has been said here in regard to the motion to dismiss applies with equal force to the demurrer.

A demand for documents permits a party to gain access to those kinds of evidence—such as business records, letters, and hospital bills—which are in the possession of the other party. Under modern rules of civil procedure the party seeking the documents has the right to obtain them for purposes of inspection and copying.

A party that refuses to comply in good faith with legitimate discovery requests faces court sanctions up to and including summary judgment. For example, in 1984 when a federal judge decided that Piper Aircraft Corp. had destroyed large amounts of evidence pertaining to the safety of its Cheyenne aircraft, one of which had crashed killing plaintiffs' relatives, he held that Piper had forfeited the right to defend the suit and entered judgment against it on the issue of liability. Piper was allowed to present evidence on the issue of damages.[7]

---

[7] *Carlucci v. Piper Aircraft Corp.,* 102 F.R.D. 472 (S.D. Fla. 1984).

Summary Judgment

At or near the end of discovery, one party or the other (and occasionally both) may file a motion for **summary judgment** as to one or more of the issues in the lawsuit. In filing such a motion a party is arguing to the judge, in essence, that the evidence adduced by discovery makes it so clear that the moving party is legally entitled to prevail that a trial would be a waste of time. A judge should grant such a motion only if a thorough review of the evidence obtained through discovery indicates that there is "no genuine issue as to any material fact"—that is, that there is no real question as to any important factual matter.

Judges have traditionally been reluctant to grant summary judgment motions, especially when plaintiffs had properly requested jury trials. In the following case, a federal court takes an aggressive stance regarding use of the summary judgment motion, which is authorized by Federal Rule of Civil Procedure #56.

Fontenot v. Upjohn Company
U.S. Fifth Circuit Court of Appeals, 780 F.2d 1190 (1986)

On December 20, 1983, plaintiff Fontenot, a mother of two children with heart valve problems, sued defendant Upjohn, which allegedly manufactured a drug which plaintiff claimed caused her childrens' heart defects. Upjohn served interrogatories asking plaintiff to list every witness whom she might call to support her claim that her childrens' heart defects were caused by the drug named in her complaint and to list any experts she had consulted. In her answers, filed ten months after the suit was initiated, plaintiff replied: "Unknown at the present time. However, these experts will be developed by the plaintiff prior to trial and information regarding these experts will be supplied to defendant as developed."

Soon thereafter, Upjohn filed a motion for summary judgment on the issue of causation, though it did not supply any affidavits or evidentiary material to negate the possibility that heart defects might be caused by the named drug (progesterone). Fourteen months after the lawsuit was filed plaintiff responded to the summary judgment

motion, again offering no evidence on causation, saying, "The question of causation by its very nature, addresses itself to the merits of the case, and is not a proper reason for the granting of a motion for summary judgment." The trial court did grant defendant's motion, and plaintiff appealed.

Rubin, Circuit Judge:

The principal function of the motion for summary judgment is to show that, in the absence of factual disputes, one or more of the essential elements of a claim or defense before the court is not in doubt and that, as a result, judgment should be entered on the basis of purely legal considerations. Summary judgment must, therefore, be rendered when the material offered in support of and in opposition to the motion "show that there is no genuine issue as to any material fact and that the moving party is entitled to a judgment as a matter of law." [Federal Rule of Civil Procedure 56(c).] In products liability cases in Louisiana, the plaintiff bears the burden of proving a causal connection between use of the product and the injury for which she seeks redress.

If the moving party can show that there is no evidence whatever to establish one or more essential elements of a claim on which the opposing party has the burden of proof, trial would be a bootless exercise, fated for an inevitable result but at continued expense for the parties, the preemption of a trial date that might have been used for other litigants waiting impatiently in the judicial queue, and a burden on the court and the taxpayers. Aside from counsel's fees, which this court has frequently fixed at rates of $100 per hour or more, a Rand Corporation study has estimated the public cost of the average jury trial in federal court to be over $7000. Hence, every hour of litigation is costly both to the parties and the taxpayers, and the expense should not be incurred needlessly.

If a party who does not have the burden of proof at trial has access to evidentiary materials that disprove the facts necessary to establish the opposing party's position, he should adduce them in one of the fashions mentioned by Rule 56: affidavit, deposition, or testimony, when permitted. If, however, it is evident that the party seeking summary judgment against one who bears the proof burden has no access to evidence of disproof, and ample time has been allowed for discovery, he should be permitted, as Upjohn did here, to rely upon the complete absence of proof of an essential element of the other party's case.

The district court should view such a motion critically to determine whether either inference or circumstantial evidence might suffice to create the existence of a factual dispute about the claims. The party opposing a motion supported by affidavits cannot discharge his burden by alleging legal conclusions. There is no sound reason why conclusory allegations should suffice to require a trial when there is no evidence to support them even if the movant lacks contrary evidence. Absent evidence, direct, circumstantial, or inferential, that would create a genuine issue of fact, and absent any suggestion concerning the utility of additional time for further discovery, the motion should be granted.

[The court then disagreed with the District of Columbia Circuit Court's decision in *Catrett v. Johns-Manville Sales Corp.,* 756 F.2d 181 (D.C. Cir. 1985), which held that until the movant produced evidence the opposing party was under no duty to counter the motion with evidence of its own.]

Summary judgment is not a "peculiar procedural shortcut," but an integral part of the "framework of the Rules, closely related to other provisions which are similarly intended to permit the early elimination of claims and defenses that the proponent cannot support." [Schwarzer, Summary Judgment Under the Federal Rules, 99 F.R.D. 465 (1984).] Summary judgment reinforces the purpose of the Rules to achieve the just, speedy, and inexpensive determination of actions, and, when appropriate, affords a merciful end to litigation that would otherwise be lengthy and expensive. Courts have been, as Judge William W. Schwarzer has said, ambivalent toward summary judgment, sometimes because of the "suspicion that [trial] judges, intent on controlling their dockets, may use summary judgment as a 'catch penny contrivance to take unwary litigants into its toils and deprive them of a trial.'" "Public demand for greater efficiency and economy, which is served by early disposition of baseless claims and defenses, is insistent and well-founded and has led to widespread efforts to find alternative means of dispute resolution. Proper use of Rule 56 is one way in which the judicial system can respond to that demand consistent with justice." [Schwarzer, at 467.] When everything that can be adduced at trial is before the judge on motion and the parties, while urging conflicting ultimate facts or conclusions, have no evidentiary disputes, a trial serves no useful purpose.

[Affirmed.]

Note that the Supreme Court has agreed with the *Fontenot* ruling. A Court of Appeals decision mentioned and rejected in *Fontenot* was reversed by the Supreme Court in 1986. The Court seemingly encouraged trial judges to use the summary judgment device, stating: "Summary judgment procedure is properly regarded not as a disfavored procedural shortcut, but rather as an integral part of the Federal Rules as a whole, which are designed 'to secure the just, speedy and inexpensive determination of every action.'" *Celotex Corp. v. Catrett,* 54 U.S.L.W. 4775 (1986).

THE TRIAL COURTS: TRIAL PROCEEDINGS

The Trial Stage

Unless a controversy is settled by a judgment on the pleadings (such as the granting of a motion to dismiss), or unless the parties settle out of court, a case will eventually come on for trial. In the **trial stage** a jury may be impaneled, evidence presented, a verdict returned, and a judgment entered in favor of one of the parties.

Impaneling a Jury: In any civil action in which the plaintiff is asking for a remedy at law, questions of fact are often resolved by a jury. However, a jury can be "waived" (dispensed with) if this is agreeable to both parties. In such instances the court decides questions of both fact and law. While waiver of a jury is increasingly common in civil actions today, there are still many actions where at least one of the parties demands a jury trial. The remainder of this discussion thus assumes the presence of a jury.

The names of prospective jurors are drawn from a list of those who have been selected for possible duty during the term. Each prospective juror is questioned in an effort to make sure that the jury will be as impartial as possible. If questioning indicates that a particular person would probably not be capable of such impartiality, he or she can be *challenged for cause.* Prospective jurors can be challenged, for example, if it is shown that they have a close friendship with one of the parties or the party's attorney, a financial interest in the case, or a bias resulting from any other aspect of the action. Any prospective juror disqualified for cause is excused, and another takes his or her place and is questioned in like fashion. This preliminary examination of prospective jurors is called the *voir dire* examination.

When there are no more challenges for cause, the attorney for each party has a limited number of **peremptory challenges.** Such challenges permit the attorney to have a juror removed arbitrarily, without assigning a reason for doing so. Once the number of prospective jurors who have survived both kinds of challenges reaches the number required by law to hear the case, they are sworn in and the case proceeds. (Traditionally the number of jurors has been twelve, but in recent years many states have reduced the number to eight, or even fewer, in civil actions.)

Order of Presentation of Proof: After the opening statements, the case is presented by the plaintiff, who has the "burden of proof" (the duty to prove the facts alleged in the complaint). The plaintiff attempts to meet this burden by calling witnesses whose testimony supports his or her version of the facts.

After each of the plaintiff's witnesses is examined by the plaintiff's attorney (direct ex-

amination), the defendant's attorney can cross-examine the witness for the purpose of discrediting the person's testimony on as many points as possible. For example, a cross-examination might divulge (1) that pertinent facts in the direct examination were omitted, (2) that a witness's powers of observation were poor, or (3) that the witness stood to benefit financially if the plaintiff won a judgment.

The Rules of Evidence: Before proceeding to the next steps in the trial of a case, a brief mention of *evidence* is necessary. As a practical matter, one of the most crucial steps in a lawsuit is the establishment of the facts—a final determination as to what actually happened. An early English judge said, "Without a known fact, it is impossible to know the law on that fact."[8] And unless a litigant can convince the jury that his or her version of the facts is correct, the case may very well collapse at the outset.

Because the findings of fact play such an important role in the outcome of a case, it is imperative that the jury determine the facts on the basis of the most reliable testimony possible—testimony that is relevant, unbiased, and based on direct observations of the witnesses. *The primary purpose of the rules of evidence is to exclude testimony that lacks these characteristics.* (With an exception to be noted later, the jury's findings of fact are conclusive. This means that an appellate court, in determining the propriety of a rule of law applied by a lower court, must normally accept the jury's version of the facts as being correct.)

While the **rules of evidence** are so numerous and so complex as to preclude any balanced survey of the subject here, it is possible to examine briefly three of the most common kinds of testimony that the rules ordinarily remove from the jury's consideration—assuming that timely objection to such testimony is made by counsel during the trial proceedings. That is, if improper testimony is elicited from a witness by the at-

---

[8] C. J. Vaughan, *Bushel's Case,* Jones (T.), 1670.

torney for one of the parties, and the opposing counsel does *not* make a formal challenge by "objecting" to it at that time, such testimony is normally permitted to become part of the record.[9]

Irrelevant Testimony: If a witness is asked a question that can have no possible bearing on the facts in issue, the opposing counsel may enter an objection on the basis that the answer would be "irrelevant." In a personal injury suit, for example, such matters as the defendant's religious beliefs, or the fact that he was convicted of a charge of negligent driving several years earlier, would have no bearing on the instant case. Objections to such testimony would be "sustained" by the court.

Hearsay: It is essential that the jury have before it direct evidence—testimony based on the witnesses' *personal knowledge and observation* of facts and circumstances surrounding the issues being litigated. Evidence not of this type is called **hearsay** and is usually excluded. Thus if an issue in a particular case is whether a trucker delivered a shipment of goods to the X Company on a certain day, witness W (a jogger in the vicinity at the time) could testify that he saw packages being unloaded from a truck on the day in question. But neither W nor any other witness would be allowed to testify that he was *told by a third party* (Z) that Z saw goods being unloaded on the day in question.[10]

There are, however, many exceptions to the hearsay rule; that is, many admissions of out-of-court statements where experience has shown the statements to be generally reliable, and where there is a "necessity" for admission of the statement. For example, *business records* may usually be introduced in evidence by the person having custody of such records if the record was made "in the usual course of business," and if the record was made at or near the time of the act or transaction which it records.

Opinion: Sometimes a witness is asked for, or volunteers, information about a matter he or she believes to be true but of which the person actually has no personal knowledge. Such testimony, calling for the **opinion** of the witness, is normally excluded. For example, a witness could testify that the defendant's car was weaving back and forth on a highway, but if he further testified—on the basis of that observation alone— that the defendant was "obviously drunk," a motion to strike that part of the testimony would be sustained. Not only does the witness lack personal knowledge as to the *cause* of the defendant's erratic behavior, but the statement also constitutes a "conclusion of fact"—an inference that the jury, rather than a witness, is to draw from the evidence presented.

Opinion testimony is not always excluded. On technical matters that lie outside the knowledge of ordinary jurors it is frequently necessary that qualified experts be permitted to state their opinions as an aid to the jury's determination of the probable facts. Thus a physician may give an opinion as to the cause of a death or an engineer as to the cause of a bridge collapsing. And, additionally, courts have discretion to permit opinions of lay witnesses (nonexperts) on a number of issues—the speed of a car or a third party's emotions at a particular time, for instance.

Motion for a Directed Verdict: After all the plaintiff's evidence has been presented, it is likely that the defendant's attorney will make a *motion for a directed verdict.* By doing so, the attorney is contending that plaintiff has failed to

---

[9] Actions brought in the federal courts are governed by the Federal Rules of Evidence which Congress adopted in 1975. The rules of evidence that are applicable to actions in state courts are adopted by the various state supreme courts, and the rules vary somewhat from state to state. However, the federal rules are generally acknowledged as representing the most "modern view" of evidentiary rules and are increasingly being adopted by the state courts.

[10] Hearsay is essentially defined as any assertion (either orally or written) made by a person who is not in court and not subject to cross-examination when the said assertion is offered to prove the fact asserted. Thus the hearsay rule excludes many kinds of offered testimony in addition to what witnesses were told by others, such as statements in newspapers and books (unless they are "learned treatises") and those made by television newscasters.

prove his or her case—that is, either plaintiff has failed to introduce evidence tending to prove one or more allegations of fact necessary to the case, or the evidence on such points was too weak to present a jury question. Such a motion asks the judge to rule on a factual question *as a matter of law,* and can be granted only if the judge is convinced that the evidence is so clearly in defendant's favor that "reasonable minds could not differ" on the matter. As with summary judgment motions, judges are reluctant to terminate litigation through a directed verdict motion, especially because by this stage of the proceedings the jury has invested a lot of time and effort.

If the defendant's directed verdict motion is denied, then the defendant will present its case through witnesses, depositions, and documents. At the close of defendant's case, both parties will likely make motions for directed verdicts but, again, these are usually denied because the evidence is not that conclusive. Questions of fact usually remain and should be determined by the jury.

Instructions: When a case is submitted to the jury, the court instructs it about the law applicable to the various findings of fact which it might make. While the jurors are the "judges of the facts," they must make their determination within a legal framework provided by the judge. The **instructions** will cover such matters as the jury's responsibilities (e.g., "All parties are equal before the law; a corporation is entitled to the same fair treatment as an individual"); matters of evidence (e.g., "You must decide the case based on the weight of the evidence, not the number of witnesses each side presented; you are entitled to believe a single witness who, though outnumbered by contrary witnesses, appeared accurate and reliable in his testimony"); and substantive rules of law (e.g., "Negligence is the failure to use ordinary care a reasonable person would have exercised under like circumstances").

After the Verdict: After the jury has returned its verdict, the court enters a judgment in conformity with it. Thereafter, the party against whom the judgment was entered may make one of two common types of motions. The first is a **motion for a new trial,** which basically argues that a new trial is in order because of a serious legal error which the judge made during the first one. The second is a motion for **judgment notwithstanding the verdict** (also known by its Latin term judgment *non obstante veredicto,* or simply JNOV), which may challenge the jury's conclusion on the facts. Only if the judge concludes that, yes, he or she made a serious legal error, or that no reasonable mind could agree with the jury's factual findings will such motions be granted. The process of litigation is illustrated in Figure 3.1.

THE APPELLATE COURTS

An Overview

The work of the higher courts in ruling on appeals differs considerably from that of the trial courts.[11] In the first place, appellate courts are concerned only with *questions of law*—that is, whether the rulings of the trial court, of which the appellant complains, were legally correct. Second, intermediate appellate courts are normally comprised of three judges, and the highest court in a state usually has five or seven justices. This obviously brings to bear *more judicial experience* on the points in issue than can be afforded by the single trial judge. Third, since only questions of law are in issue, there is *no reintroduction of evidence and thus no jury.* The questions of law are settled on the basis of the record in the lower court, together with consideration of the opposing parties' briefs (written arguments) and oral arguments as to the correctness of the rulings in question. As a result, unlike the rulings of the trial court, which must be made during "the heat of battle," the decisions of the appellate courts can be made in a detached and unhurried manner.

---

[11] All appellate courts have *some* "original jurisdiction"; that is, certain exceptional cases can be properly commenced in them. However, we are not here concerned with the work of the appellate courts in such situations.

Figure 3.1   Litigation Flow Chart

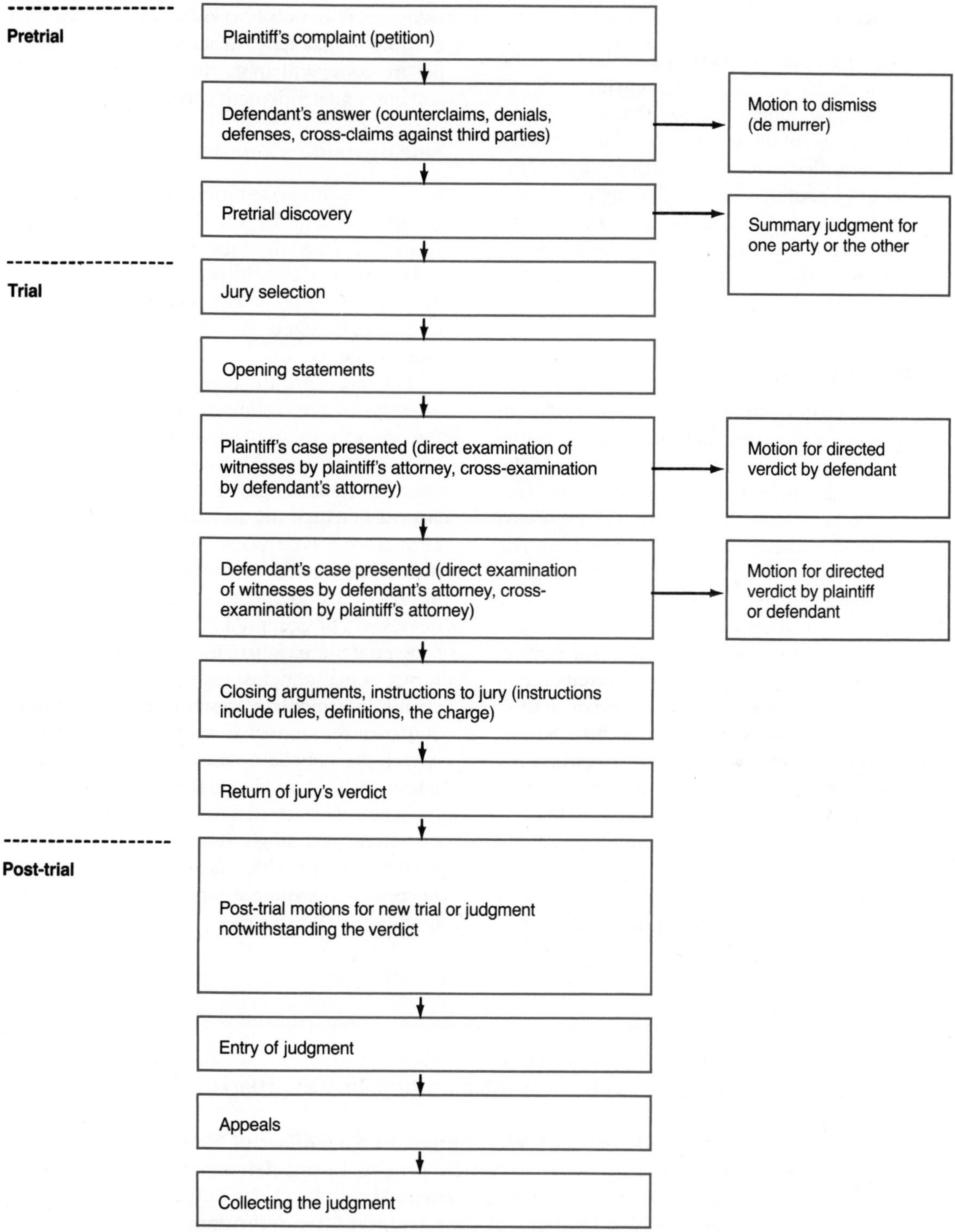

Pretrial

Plaintiff's complaint (petition)

↓

Defendant's answer (counterclaims, denials, defenses, cross-claims against third parties) → Motion to dismiss (de murrer)

↓

Pretrial discovery → Summary judgment for one party or the other

Trial

Jury selection

↓

Opening statements

↓

Plaintiff's case presented (direct examination of witnesses by plaintiff's attorney, cross-examination by defendant's attorney) → Motion for directed verdict by defendant

↓

Defendant's case presented (direct examination of witnesses by defendant's attorney, cross-examination by plaintiff's attorney) → Motion for directed verdict by plaintiff or defendant

↓

Closing arguments, instructions to jury (instructions include rules, definitions, the charge)

↓

Return of jury's verdict

↓

Post-trial

Post-trial motions for new trial or judgment notwithstanding the verdict

↓

Entry of judgment

↓

Appeals

↓

Collecting the judgment

Questions of Law

A great number of questions of law will be brought out by the cases in the remainder of this text. For now, suffice it to say that some of the most common of them arise where the appellant is claiming that errors were made by the trial court in (1) admitting or excluding testimony, (2) ruling on motions, particularly on motions for a directed verdict, (3) stating the law in instructions to the jury, and (4) interpreting state or federal statutes.

Effect of Error

If the appellate court is of the opinion that an alleged error did occur and that it conceivably could have affected the outcome of the case, the lower court's judgment will be reversed (set aside), and normally the case will be *remanded* (sent back) to the trial court for a new trial. The reason for remanding is that most errors are of such a nature that the higher court cannot be positive the verdict or judgment would have gone for the other party had the error not occurred. For example, if it were determined that the trial court erred in admitting hearsay testimony of one witness, it is *possible* that the verdict and judgment would still have been entered for the same party who won in the lower court even if the testimony had been excluded.

Some judgments, however, are reversed outright, with no further proceedings being necessary. This is particularly true where the rule of law that the trial court has applied to the established facts is simply contrary to the law then existing in that state. In such a situation the appellate court will apply the correct rule of law and enter final judgment accordingly.

Setting Aside a Verdict

Appellate courts commonly set aside judgments on grounds that the trial judge made a critical *legal* error in admitting evidence, ruling on motions, or instructing the jury. Much less often will they set aside a judgment because the jury erred in finding the facts, though they are frequently asked to do so.

The jurors are the designated finders of fact. They heard the testimony in person. They had the opportunity to observe the witnesses while they testified and to observe important details (such as body language or coaching from the attorney) which the appellate court cannot discern from a cold transcript of testimony. The jurors are trusted to resolve conflicts of testimony. Their judgments as to credibility of witnesses will be accepted.

Even if the appellate judges disagree with the jury's factual conclusions, they will uphold the verdict if the record contains *any substantial evidence* to support it. Only in rare instances where the appellate court can confidently say that there is no substantial evidence to support the jury's verdict will it be set aside. The credible testimony of a single witness, even one of the parties, can provide the substantial evidence necessary to sustain a jury's verdict, as the following case illustrates.

Batchoff v. Craney
Supreme Court of Montana, 172 P.2d 308 (1946)

D. A. (Jim) Batchoff was injured in November of 1940 when he was thrown from a car in which he was being driven from Billings to Butte, Montana. The car was owned by Craney, the defendant, and was being driven by Baily Stortz, a friend of the defendant.

Batchoff brought this action against Craney to recover damages, alleging (1) that Stortz was guilty of gross negligence in the operation of the vehicle, and (2) that Stortz was an agent of defendant Craney while making the drive to Butte. Defendant contended, on the other hand, that Stortz was acting as an agent of U.S. Senator Burton K. Wheeler at the time of the accident.

At the trial, plaintiff testified that he was at the Northern Pacific depot in Billings on the morning of November 2, waiting for the train to Butte, when he ran into the defendant, who said, "Oh, hell, Jim, stay here and miss this train. Senator and Mrs. Wheeler and Baily Stortz [Wheeler's secretary] are getting off of this train. . . . I am going to leave my automobile with Baily to drive it back to Butte and you can ride along with him." (Defendant himself was remaining in Billings.)

Later in the day plaintiff and Stortz set out for Butte in defendant's car, with Stortz driving. Plaintiff further testified that Stortz drove the car from seventy to seventy-five miles per hour; that he complained of the excessive speed but, instead of slowing down, the speed was increased to eighty-five miles per hour; there were wet spots in the road; the car hit a wet spot, skidded around several times; a door of the car swung open and plaintiff was thrown from the car into a borrow pit and the car followed and struck him, rendering him unconscious and causing the injuries complained of.

The jury accepted plaintiff's version of the facts and returned a verdict in his favor for $10,000. On appeal, the primary contention of the defendant was that the jury's verdict was unsupported by the evidence, and ought to be set aside for this reason.

In support of this contention, defendant argued that the jury should not have believed plaintiff's testimony that defendant offered plaintiff the ride, in view of the fact that defendant's witnesses testified that defendant had in fact *lent his car to Senator Wheeler* for the day, and in view of the fact that plaintiff, in an earlier proceeding before the State Industrial Accident Board, *had testified that it was Stortz, rather than the defendant, who had offered him the ride.*

(We shall now see, in the following opinion, how the Montana Supreme Court went about the job of determining whether the defendant-appellant's allegation of error was well-founded.)

Angstmann, Justice:

. . . Defendant produced witnesses who testified that he lent his car to Senator Wheeler for his use in and around Billings, and that Stortz was acting as agent of Senator Wheeler in returning the car to Butte when the accident occurred. In other words, the evidence was in sharp conflict if it can be said that the testimony of plaintiff is worthy of belief. *Whether his testimony was worthy of belief was for the jury to determine.* [Emphasis added.]

Thus in *Wallace v. Wallace,* 279 P. 374, this court said,

A jury may believe the testimony of one witness and disbelieve that of another, or any numbers of others, and the determination of the jury in this regard is final; having spoken, this court must assume that the facts are as stated by the witnesses, believed by the jury, and claimed by the prevailing party. The preponderance of the evidence may be established by a single witness as against a greater number of witnesses who testify to the contrary.

It follows that whenever there is a conflict in the evidence, this court may only review the testimony for the purpose of determining whether or not there is any substantial evidence in the record to support the verdict of the jury, and must accept the evidence there found as true, unless that evidence is so inherently impossible or improbable as not to be entitled to belief; and, where a verdict is based upon substantial evidence which, from any point of view, could have been accepted by the jury as credible, it is binding upon this court, although it may appear inherently weak.

[The court then ruled, in regard to the statements made by plaintiff before the Industrial Accident Board, that such statements could not be used as substantive evidence by the jury. At the most, the court said, such statements could cause the jury to question plaintiff's testimony in the trial court, and if it chose to accept his testimony despite the contradictory statements made earlier, it could do so. On this aspect of the case, the court quoted an opinion in *State v. Peterson,* 59 P.2d 61, as follows:]

A witness false in one part of his testimony is to be distrusted in others, and a witness may be impeached [by showing] . . . that he has made at other times statements inconsistent with his present testimony; but while proof of . . . inconsistent statements at other times . . . may discredit the witness, such proof goes only to the credibility of the witness, of which the jury remains the sole judge, as well as the weight to be given thereto.

It follows that, although the jury may reject the false testimony and assume, regarding the rest of it, an attitude of distrust, the jurors may render a verdict based upon the testimony of such witness if after examination they find it worthy of belief.

[In the instant case] there is nothing inherently incredible or improbable in plaintiff's version of what happened. . . .

Judgment affirmed.

Comment: When the owner of an automobile permits another person to drive it, and the driver injures a third party as a result of operating it negligently, the owner is *not necessarily* liable to the injured party. Under the law of Montana and many other states, the injured party must ordinarily prove that the driver was an *agent* of the owner of the automobile at the time of the accident in order to recover a judgment against the owner.

That is why, in the instant case, defendant Craney would have escaped liability if the jury had accepted the testimony of his witnesses to the effect that Craney had actually lent his car to Senator Wheeler for the day (and that Stortz, without Craney's knowledge, offered plaintiff the ride). In such a situation, Stortz would have been Wheeler's agent, rather than Craney's. As we know now, the jury rejected this version of the facts in returning a verdict for plaintiff.

Enforcement of Judgment

If a verdict for the plaintiff survives the appellate process (or if no appeal was ever taken), plaintiff may still have to worry about enforcing the judgment. If the defendant is wealthy, well-insured, or a large corporation, enforcement of the judgment will probably present no major obstacles.

If the defendant refuses to pay a valid judgment, the plaintiff will ask the court to issue a **writ of execution** by which a law enforcement official seizes defendant's nonexempt property and sells it at auction until enough money is raised to satisfy the judgment. Another procedure is a **writ of garnishment,** whereby the court orders a third party holding property belonging to the defendant (typically a bank with a savings account belonging to defendant) to deliver the property to the plaintiff in satisfaction of the judgment. Some states even allow garnishment of wages—a court order to defendant's employer to pay a specified percentage of defendant's wages to plaintiff every month until the judgment is satisfied. As we shall see in Chapter 51, there are legal limits on garnishment of wages.

ANALYSIS OF THE ADJUDICATIVE PROCESS

A good many criticisms are made of the manner in which controversies are settled under our present legal system. Many of these have to do with the general nature of the "adversary system," the role of the jury, and the selection and performance of judges.

The Adversary System

Most legal disputes are settled through *adversary proceedings,* where the parties meet face to face (legally speaking) with each permitted to contest the allegations of fact and points of law raised by the other. The attorney for each party determines how to prove that his or her client's version of the facts is correct, and each researches the law to find legal principles upon which to base the client's case. The parties themselves thus frame the issues, and the judge simply rules on the issues that are presented.

It is sometimes said that the adversary system puts an undue premium on the relative effectiveness of the competing attorneys and too greatly limits the trial judge's role in the outcome of the case. Overall, these criticisms are probably not as valid as they seem.

In the first place, the skill of the competing lawyers is usually equal enough for each party to be able to introduce the evidence and to present rules of law in support of his or her position. Additionally, the rules of procedure and evidence, and the normal desire of the trial judge to see that each party has a fair opportunity to "have a say," place certain limits on the practical advantage that one party might have in a case where his or her counsel is markedly more able than the other litigant's counsel.

The Role of the Jury

Many weaknesses, real or imagined, are attributed to the jury's role in the adjudicative processes, including the following: (1) jurors cannot understand the complex issues that are presented; (2) jurors are too likely to be influenced by the personalities of the attorneys rather than by objective considerations; and (3) given the rules of law applying to the various alternative findings that they may return, juries frequently ignore (or overemphasize) evidence in order to bring in a verdict in favor of a party for whom they have sympathy or against a party for whom they have animosity. In recent years juries have received severe criticism for the large size of the monetary awards they have granted personal injury plaintiffs, especially in products liability cases.

Supporters of the jury system, on the other hand, feel that most of these criticisms are not, in general, supported by the facts. First, in many cases there are only one or two controlling issues, and these are quite understandable to the average person. Second, verdicts can be set aside if they are clearly based on "passion or prejudice," in addition to the other grounds mentioned earlier. Third, there is substantial evidence that most jurors take their duties seriously and try to perform them conscientiously.

Performance of the Judges

The overall performance of a legal system obviously depends to a great extent upon the character and competence of its judges. For this reason, particularly, it is distressing to note that the judges of this country have, as a class, come in for rather heavy criticism over the years. While some of this criticism may be unjustified, there is considerable evidence that the performance of a significant percentage of our judges (though certainly not a majority) can be characterized as barely adequate, or worse.

Three factors are chiefly responsible. First, judges' salaries are often lower than the income that can be earned in private practice by attorneys. Second, in the United States, persons who aspire to a career in the judiciary are not required to take special training or to go through an apprenticeship of a year or two on an appeals court, as is the case in many countries. And, third, the judges of our state courts have traditionally been elected. This has frequently resulted in the nomination of candidates by the political parties on the basis of their party service and loyalty, rather than on ability and experience. And, once elected, incumbent judges have not easily been dislodged even when their performance has been mediocre or worse.

In recent years, in an effort to alleviate the shortcomings resulting from the election of judges, over thirty states and the District of Columbia have adopted some form of "merit plan" selection of judges. While these plans vary to some extent, they all are based on the idea that when a judicial vacancy occurs, a judicial nominating commission develops a list of three to five persons whom they feel to be the best qualified for the job. (These commissions are nonpartisan in nature, and are usually composed equally of lawyers and nonlawyers.) The list of names is submitted to the governor, who selects one person to fill the vacancy. Thereafter, appointees must indicate before their terms of office expire whether they wish to stand for another term. If so, the appointee runs unopposed in the next general election, with the voters simply indicating whether they are satisfied with the performance rendered during the first term of office. If the appointee loses on this vote, the appointive process then begins anew.

SUMMARY

Perhaps because of the time and expense involved in litigation, there has been a trend in recent years toward alternative methods of dispute resolution, including arbitration, mediation, and minitrials.

When a trial does take place, it is preceded by the pleadings phase of litigation in which the parties set forth their claims on paper, and the discovery phase where investigation will disclose which of the claims can be sustained by proof. A jury trial is a complicated process that includes impaneling a jury, presenting proof in accordance with the rules of evidence, various motions made by the parties, instructions by the judge to the jury, and finally, deliberation by the jury. A party unhappy with the jury's verdict may appeal. Appellate courts will reverse a case if they find the judge made a critical legal error or that the jury's verdict was not based on any substantial evidence whatsoever. Or they may send the case back to the trial court with instructions for a new trial.

Our system of justice is as controversial as it is important. Reforms of the adversary system, the jury system, and our methods of selecting judges are constantly being debated.

KEY TERMS

Mediation
Pleading stage
Discovery stage

Complaint
Answer
Default judgment
Reply
Counterclaim
Motion to dismiss
Summary judgment
Trial stage
Peremptory challenge
Rules of evidence
Hearsay
Opinion (testimony)
Instructions
Motion for a new trial
Judgment notwithstanding the verdict
Writ of execution
Writ of garnishment

QUESTIONS AND PROBLEMS

1. After ten years of litigation, a federal antitrust case was submitted to a formally summoned jury. However, the attorneys were given only a half-day in which to present their case and the decision of the jury was not binding. Why would such a procedure be undertaken?

2. Wydel Associates, a partnership, sued Thermasol, Ltd. on a breach of contract claim. Thermasol moved to dismiss the lawsuit because the contract contained a clause stating that any dispute should be arbitrated in New York rather than litigated. Wydel argued that the arbitration clause was not binding because the law of the state in which its partnership was formed provided that any partnership agreement to submit a claim to arbitration must be signed by *all* the partners. This contract had been signed by only one Wydel partner. Should the court dismiss the suit? *Wydel Associates v. Thermasol Ltd.,* 452 F.Supp. 739 (W.D.Tex. 1978).

3. The Brockton Bank sued First United, a broker-dealer, after defendant induced the bank to purchase a 90-day $1,000,000 CD from a bank (Penn Square) which failed. In discovery, Brockton sought to determine how much research

First United had done before making the recommendation to purchase. Four times during discovery defendant made untimely and only partial responses to court orders to produce documents. After arguing unsuccessfully for months that certain documents should be protected from discovery, defendant claimed that the documents had been discarded long before. Suspecting the documents had been destroyed, the trial judge ordered defendant's president to appear in court. The president did not appear, his attorney stating, "My client chooses not to obey." What should the court do? *See Brockton Sav. Bank v. Peat, Marwick & Mitchell,* 771 F.2d 5 (1st Cir. 1985).

4. In a report on plaintiff's business, defendant television station reported "[w]e spoke to Judge Rissman . . . he says they've [customers of plaintiff] got a good case." Plaintiff sued for defamation, claiming that this conversation never took place. Defendant moved to dismiss the suit on grounds that the conversation did take place and that it was just one man's opinion, anyway. Should the court dismiss? *See Action Repair, Inc. v. American Broadcasting Co.,* 776 F.2d 143 (7th Cir. 1985).

5. Defendant company built a swimming pool for Denault. On January 9, 1978, defendant's president was served with a summons in a lawsuit filed by Denault. Denault claimed defendant's sloppy building of the pool forced her to make $2000 in repairs. Under the court rules, an answer was due from defendant on January 29. Defendant tried to answer on January 31, but the court refused to accept the filing because it was untimely. The court entered a default judgment against defendant and set a hearing to establish damages. Defendant moved to set aside the default judgment on grounds of "excusable neglect", pointing out that its president had received two summons in the same week and thought Denault's had been served at the same time as the other summons, on January 13. Should the judge set aside the default judgment?

See Denault v. Holloway Builders, Inc., 248 S.E.2d 265 (S.C. 1978).

6. Under a kickback scheme devised by Moore, a purchasing agent, one of the bidders on a construction project submitted several price sheets; the purchasing agent read that bidder's price list last, choosing the highest one that was still low enough to get the bid. On discovering the extra sheets, Moore's secretary, Marren, exclaimed: "I've found the evidence I've been waiting for for a long time!" Marszalek overheard this statement. At Moore's criminal trial, Marszalek was asked about this statement because Marren died before trial. Should Marszalek be allowed to testify about the statement? *See U.S. v. Moore,* 791 F.2d 566 (7th Cir. 1986).

7. Plaintiff stored almost a million dollars worth of cotton bales in defendant's bonded warehouse. Defendant discovered that the warehouse's sprinkler system was broken, but he did not repair it or post a guard. That night a fire destroyed the warehouse. Plaintiff sued defendant, who counterclaimed, arguing that plaintiff was responsible for starting the fire because it had possibly delivered a "hot bale," one containing a latent ember, in its last delivery three weeks before. Plaintiff moved for summary judgment on defendant's counterclaim, offering the affidavits of four qualified experts who stated that it was their opinion the fire did not occur as a result of a "hot bale." In opposition to the motion, defendant offered the affidavit of one ex-

pert who stated: "It is my opinion that a potential cause of this fire was a smoldering bale" and "a fire packed bale could have caused the fire." Should the court grant summary judgment? Discuss. (*Coats & Clark, Inc. v. Gay,* 755 F.2d 1506, 11th Cir. 1985.)

8. A plane owned by Douglas landed at the Los Angeles airport and received permission from the tower to enter runway 22. Due to the shape of his plane, the Douglas pilot was not in a position to see clearly ahead, so he zigzagged the plane at 15° angles as he taxied to improve his forward vision. However, the plane collided with a P-51 owned by the government which was parked along the side of runway 22. The pilot of the government plane, which was painted a brown camouflaged, Army color, said after the accident: "I am sorry. I had no business being there. I have been here for about ten minutes. I called for a truck and they haven't come after me yet." The government sued Douglas for negligence; Douglas raised a contributory negligence defense. At the close of the evidence, the government moved for a directed verdict in its favor on the questions of respective negligence. The judge denied the motions, and the jury found for Douglas. On appeal, the government argued that the judge erred in failing to grant its directed verdict motions. Discuss. See *U.S. v. Douglas Aircraft Co.,* 169 F.2d 755 (9th Cir. 1948).

Chapter 4

COMMON AND STATUTORY LAW

There are several basic processes by which law is made: (1) the formulation of rules by the courts—the judges—in deciding cases coming before them in those areas of law where no statutes apply; (2) the enactment and interpretation of statutes; (3) the interpretation and application of constitutional provisions; and (4) the promulgation of rules and regulations by administrative agencies. In this chapter we examine the first and second of these lawmaking processes. First, we show how *common law* (or case law) is formed by the courts. Then we turn our attention to the enactment and interpretation of statutory law.

ORIGIN OF COMMON LAW

As we described in Chapter 2, the early king's courts in England largely made up the law on a case-by-case basis. If, for example, a plaintiff asked for damages for breach of contract in a situation where the defendant denied that a contract ever existed, the court had to spell out the nature of a contract—that is, specify the minimum elements which the court felt must exist in order for it to impose contractual liability on the defendant. Similarly, if a defendant admitted making the contract in question but sought to escape liability for reasons of illness or military service, the court had to decide what kinds of defenses ought to be legally recognizable—defenses that should free the defendant from his or her contractual obligations.

Over a period of time, then, as more and more cases were settled, a rudimentary body of contract law came into being. Thereafter, when other cases arose involving contractual matters, the courts quite naturally looked to the earlier cases to see what principles of law had been established. The same procedure was followed in many other branches of law, and the legal rules that arose in this manner constituted the common law, or **case law,** of England.

The common law rules that had developed in England became the law of our early colonies.

And, when those colonies achieved statehood, they adopted those rules as a major part of their respective bodies of law. As the territories became states, they followed suit so that at one time the major portion of the law of all states (with the exception of Louisiana) was common law in nature.[1]

The Current Scene

Gradually, the state legislatures began to pass increasing numbers of statutes, with the result that today most branches of the law are statutory in nature. For example, all states now have comprehensive statutes governing the areas of corporation law, criminal law, tax law, municipal corporations, and commercial law. Some of these statutes have been based largely on the common-law principles that were in effect earlier. Others, however, have been passed to create bodies of rules that did not exist previously, or that expressly overrule common-law principles.

Despite the ever increasing amount of statutory law in this country (which we examine in some detail later in this chapter), *several branches of law today are still essentially common-law in nature in forty-nine of our states*—particularly the subjects of *contracts, torts,* and *agency.* In these areas, where the legislatures have not seen fit to enact comprehensive statutes, the courts still settle controversies on the basis of **judge-made** or **case law**—the rules formulated by the courts in deciding earlier cases over the years, as illustrated in Figure 4.1. (While many of these rules had their origin in England, as has been indicated, our definition of common law also includes those additional rules that have originated in the state courts in this country.)

In deciding each case, judges bear the twin burden of attempting to provide "justice" for the

---

[1] Louisiana continues to be governed by the *civil-law* (as distinguished from common-law) system of law. Under such a system, adopted by most European countries, virtually all law is "codified"—that is, statutory.

Figure 4.1   Common Law

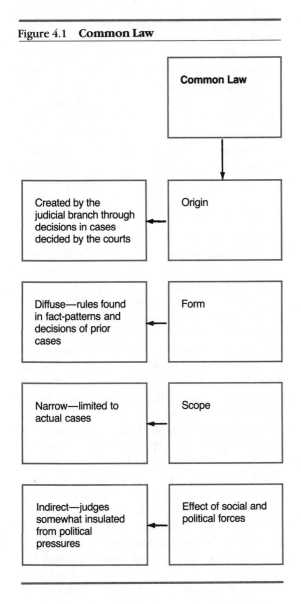

customs, morals, and forms of conduct that are generally prevailing in the community at the time of decision. There is no doubt that occasionally the judge's personal feelings as to what kinds of conduct are just and fair, what rule would best serve societal interests, and simply what is "right or wrong" enter the picture.

Role of the Judge

Benjamin N. Cardozo, an associate justice of the U.S. Supreme Court, contended that four "directive forces" shaped the law, and especially the common law, as follows: (1) philosophy (logic); (2) history; (3) custom; and (4) social welfare (or sociology).

In his lecture on the role of philosophy in the law, Cardozo briefly commented on the special tasks of the judge in interpreting statutes and constitutions, and then continued:

> We reach the land of mystery when constitution and statute are silent, and the judge must look to the common law for the rule that fits the case. . . . The first thing he does is to compare the case before him with the precedents, whether stored in his mind or hidden in the books. . . . Back of precedents are the basic juridical conceptions which are the postulates of judicial reasoning, and farther back are the habits of life, the institutions of society, in which those conceptions had their origin, and which, by a process of interaction, they have modified in turn. . . . If [precedents] are plain and to the point, there may be need of nothing more. *Stare decisis* is at least the everyday working rule of the law. . . .[2]

Early in that same lecture, however, Cardozo cautioned that the finding of precedent was only part of the judge's job, and indicated how the law

case at hand while at the same time setting a precedent that will serve the greater interests of society when applied in future cases. The common law rules, like legislative statutes, must serve public policy interests—the "community common sense and common conscience." Therefore, courts have laid great stress on the

---

[2]*Stare decisis* means, literally, "to stand by decisions." The concept is revisited later in this chapter.

must grow beyond the early precedents, in these words:

> The rules and principles of case law have never been treated as final truths, but as working hypotheses, continually retested in those great laboratories of the law, the courts of justice. . . . In [the] perpetual flux [of the law,] the problem which confronts the judge is in reality a twofold one: he first must extract from the precedents the underlying principle, the *ratio decidendi* [the ground of decision]; he must then determine the path or direction along which the principle is to move and develop, if it is not to wither and die. . . .
>
> The directive force of a principle may be exerted along the line of logical progression; this I will call the rule of analogy or the method of philosophy; along the line of historical development; this I will call the method of evolution; along the line of the customs of the community; this I will call the method of tradition; along the lines of justice, morals and social welfare, the *mores* of the day; and this I will call the method of sociology. . . .[3]

COMMON LAW—THE DOCTRINE OF *STARE DECISIS*

The heart of the common-law process lies in the inclination of the courts generally to follow precedent—to stand by existing decisions. This policy, as we were told by Cardozo, is referred to as the doctrine of ***stare decisis***. Under this approach, when the fact-pattern of a particular controversy is established, the attorneys for both parties search for earlier cases involving

---

[3] Benjamin N. Cardozo, *The Nature of the Judicial Process* (1921). Excerpts are used by permission of the Yale University Press.

similar fact-patterns in an effort to determine whether applicable principles of law have been established. If this research produces a number of similar cases (or even one) within the state where a rule has been applied by the appellate courts, the trial court will ordinarily feel constrained to follow the same rule in settling the current controversy. (But, as we will see later, this does not mean that the courts are reluctant to abandon a precedent if it produces clear injustice under "contemporary conditions.")

Types of Precedent

Authority originating in courts above the trial court in the appellate chain is called **mandatory authority.** The judge must follow it. Thus, a state trial judge in Ohio will follow the rulings of Ohio's intermediate appellate courts which will in turn follow the precedents established by the Ohio Supreme Court. In matters of federal law, the Ohio Supreme Court will follow the holdings of the United States Supreme Court. A judge who does not follow mandatory authority is not impeached or shot at dawn, but certainly runs a strong risk of reversal.

So strong is the hold of mandatory authority that judges will usually follow it even though they violently disagree with its reasoning and result. The following case illustrates this fact. The case involves a claim of *negligence,* which we shall study in detail in Chapter 7. It means simply that the defendant was more careless than a reasonable person would have been under the circumstances and should be liable for injuries which result. The case also involves a defense of governmental immunity, which stems from the ancient English doctrine that the King (or in this case the government) "can do no wrong" and therefore cannot be sued absent his consent. The decision is by a Michigan intermediate appellate court, sitting between the trial court and the Michigan Supreme Court in the appellate chain.

Edwards v. Clinton Valley Center
Court of Appeals of Michigan, 360 N.W.2d 606 (1984)

Plaintiff is the estate of Jean Edwards, who was fatally stabbed by a former mental patient. Defendant is a government mental hospital that refused to admit the killer after she was brought to the facility by police when she threatened to "kill someone." Plaintiff alleges that defendant's refusal to admit the killer was negligent. The trial judge dismissed the suit on a purely legal ground—governmental immunity. Plaintiff appealed.

Bronson, Presiding Judge:

Under the rule of stare decisis, this Court is bound to follow decisions of the Michigan Supreme Court, even if we disagree with them. The rule of stare decisis, founded on considerations of expediency and sound principles of public policy, operates to preserve harmony, certainty, and stability in the law. However, the rule "was never intended to perpetuate error or to prevent the consideration of rules of law to be applied to the ever-changing business, economic, and political life of a community". *Parker v. Port Huron Hospital,* 105 N.W.2d 1 (1960).

In *Perry v. Kalamazoo State Hospital,* 273 N.W.2d 421 (1978), the majority of the Supreme Court held that governmental immunity for tort liability extends to the day-to-day care public mental hospitals provide. An attempt to distinguish the instant case from *Perry* could not possibly withstand logical or honest analysis. As a member of the Court of Appeals, I am obligated to follow the decisions of our higher court. For that reason, and that reason alone, the order of summary judgment is affirmed.

I feel compelled, however, to register my fundamental disagreement with the result adopted by the *Perry* majority. I am much more inclined to follow the narrow interpretation of governmental immunity advanced by the dissenters, because the operation of a mental hospital is not an activity which can be done only by the government, it is not a governmental function within the meaning of [the Michigan statute establishing governmental immunity], and, therefore, a mental hospital should not be immune from liability for its torts.

If ever a factual situation invited reconsideration of the wisdom of a broad interpretation of what is, in the first place, an archaic doctrine, it is presented in the instant case. The Pontiac police bring Wilma Gilmore to the state-operated Clinton Valley Center. Gilmore threatens to kill someone. Gilmore had been previously institutionalized at the center. The center refuses to admit Gilmore. Four days later, Gilmore once again goes to the police and repeats her homicidal threats. She is told to leave. Two days later, Gilmore enters the apartment of Jean Edwards and fatally stabs her in the arms, throat, and abdomen. Of note is that nowhere in the record does the center offer a reason for its refusal to admit Gilmore.

I fail to see how summarily relieving the hospital of responsibility for such obvious gross negligence, without requiring of it even the slightest explanation, serves any viable public interest or protects the people of our state. Instead, it harshly imposes the entire risk of the center's negligence on Jean Edwards and her family. The time has come for either the Legislature or our Supreme Court to preserve and promote justice by modifying the doctrine of governmental immunity.

Affirmed.

What if a trial judge searches the law books and discovers that there is no precedent in the state on the legal question presented? In such a case, the judge may examine the decisions of courts of other states. For example, assume a state trial judge in Oregon is faced with the question of whether a landlord who did not attempt to lease an apartment after a tenant moved out in the middle of a lease should be barred from suing the tenant for damages. There are no Oregon cases addressing the issue, and the only case "on point" was rendered by the Alabama Supreme Court. Must the Oregon judge follow the Alabama precedent? No. Because the Oregon judge's decision cannot be appealed to the Alabama Supreme Court, the latter's rulings are not mandatory authority.

The Alabama decision would constitute **persuasive authority.** That is, the Oregon judge can examine the Alabama decision and, upon finding it persuasive, may choose to follow it. However, if the judge finds the decision not to be persuasive, the judge need not apply its rationale in Oregon.

What if there are two existing precedents, that of the Alabama Supreme Court and one from the North Dakota Supreme Court, that reach diametrically opposed results on the same issue? Again, they are both only persuasive authority for the Oregon judge who can examine them and follow the one that seems more reasonable. Of course, the judge can also reject both persuasive precedents and create yet a third approach to the issue. Despite the importance of stability to the law, the majesty of the common law lies in its flexibility and adaptability. Though judges revere stability, they will change a rule when they become convinced that it was wrongly established and never served society's interests, or that while it was a good rule when established, changing social, moral, economic, or technological factors have rendered it outmoded. If no valid reason supports a common-law rule, no matter how long it has been established, the judges should and usually will change it.

Sometimes common law rules change slowly. Exceptions or qualifications to the rule will slowly appear in the case law. Most of the history of the common law is of a slow evolution as the law keeps pace with a changing society. Refer back to *Soldano v. O'Daniels* in Chapter 1. That case not only illustrates a minor change in the slow evolution of the law regarding our duties to our fellow man, it contains some eloquent language extolling the virtues of our flexible common law.

Sometimes the law will change dramatically, as when modern judges decide an established rule no longer serves society and must be scrapped. The very judges who ignore the stability and predictability benefits of *stare decisis* as they throw out the old rule, then invoke them in protection of the new rule as the following case illustrates.

Clark v. Snapper Power Equipment, Inc.
Supreme Court of Ohio, 488 N.E.2d 138 (1986)

Five-year-old Paul Clark was injured by a power lawnmower being driven by his father. Ohio law allowed Paul, through his mother, to sue. Paul named the manufacturer of the lawnmower, his father Alan Clark, and his father's insurance company, Auto-Owners Mutual, as defendants. The trial court dismissed the father and his insurer, holding that the doctrine of parental immunity (which absolutely bars children from suing their parents in most cases) precludes this action. The intermediate appellate court affirmed. Paul appealed.

Celebrezze, Chief Justice:

The only issue to be decided is whether the doctrine of parental immunity is a bar to this action.

In reaching the conclusion to dismiss the suit against Alan Clark and Auto-Owners, the lower courts relied on our decision in *Teramano v. Teramano* (1966) 216 N.E.2d 375. In that case, this court held that "[a] parent is immune from suit by his unemancipated child for tort unless facts of the case are sufficient to show abandonment of the parental relationship."

However, in the more recent case of *Kirchner v. Crystal* (1984), 474 N.E.2d 275, this court expressly overruled its earlier decision in *Teramano*. *Kirchner* held that "[t]he doctrine of parental immunity is hereby abolished without reservation."

Justice A. W. Sweeney's majority opinion noted that parental immunity had been previously justified on four basic public policy justifications:

". . . [F]irst, the doctrine will preserve the domestic peace, harmony and tranquility of the family unit; second, the doctrine inhibits possible interference with parental discipline and control; third, the doctrine hinders the potential depletion of the family funds or exchequer; and fourth, the doctrine prevents the possibility of fraud and collusion."

Nevertheless, a majority of this court concluded that the ". . . traditional justifications posited in favor of the parental immunity doctrine . . ." no longer outweighed the desirability of providing ". . . the innocent victims of tortious conduct the forum they deserve in attempting to redress their claims."

More recently the court was again called upon to consider the viability of the doctrine of parental immunity in *Shearer v. Shearer* (1985), 480 N.E.2d 388. Judge Grey correctly noted in his majority opinion that "[t]here is no question that courts should avoid rules which can interrupt family harmony or usurp parental authority." However, the consensus of the court was that empirical data did not support a conclusion that abrogation of the doctrine had led to problems or the disintegration of the family. Thus, the court reaffirmed the holding of *Kirchner v. Crystal* which had abolished parental tort immunity.

For the third time in the past year we are called upon to reexamine the merits of this legal debate.

It is the policy of courts to stand by precedent and not to disturb a point once settled. The doctrine of *stare decisis* is one of policy which recognizes that security and certainty require that an established legal decision be recognized and followed in subsequent cases where the question of law is again in controversy.

Ohio's judiciary, lawyers, insurers and its citizenry have a right to rely on the previous holdings which abolished parental immunity. Their reasonable expectations would be thwarted if this court failed to apply a settled principle of law to all future cases where facts are substantially the same.

Departure from controlling authorities should be reserved for those instances where it is necessary to discard old ideas which are no longer beneficial and where it is wise to formulate new concepts to remedy continued injustice. Particularly instructive to this case is Justice William O. Douglas' apt observation that ". . . there will be no equal justice under law if a negligence rule is applied in the morning but not in the afternoon." Douglas, *Stare Decisis* (1949), 49 Colum. L. Rev. 735, 736.

Reversed and remanded to the trial court for further proceedings.

A PROFILE OF OUR FEDERAL AND STATE STATUTORY LAW

While a significant portion of our law is still common law in nature, most of our federal and state law today results from the enactment of **statutes** by legislative bodies. These are the formally adopted rules that constitute our *statutory law,* the second of the major sources of law.[4] All states, for example, have comprehensive statutes governing such subjects as banking law, criminal law, education, consumer sales, and motor vehicle law.

Similarly, at the federal level, sweeping statutes in the areas of antitrust law, labor law, food and drug regulation, and securities law have long been in effect. Newer (and usually narrower) statutes are added every year, including, for example, the Consumer Product Safety Act of 1972, the Bankruptcy Reform Act of 1978, and the Trademark Counterfeiting Act of 1984. Figure 4.2 summarizes the origin, form, scope, and effect of statutory law.

In this section our first objectives are to examine the reasons for the existence of statutory law, to become acquainted with the basic rules that delineate the jurisdictions of the federal and state governments, and to note the contrasts between statutory and common law. We then turn our attention to the closely related area of statutory interpretation—the process by which the courts spell out the precise meaning of statutes that are applicable to the particular cases coming before them—and conclude with a summary of selected state statutes that are of special significance to the business community.[5] As a backdrop for a better understanding of the issues that are addressed in this chapter, however, a brief

---

[4] The term "statutory law," when broadly used in contrast to "common law," includes not only laws passed by legislative bodies but, additionally, U.S. treaties, the federal and state constitutions, and municipal ordinances. In this chapter, however, the term is used in its more customary sense, referring only to acts of the state legislatures and of Congress.

[5] Selected federal statutes are discussed in Chapters 46–51.

Figure 4.2   Statutory Law

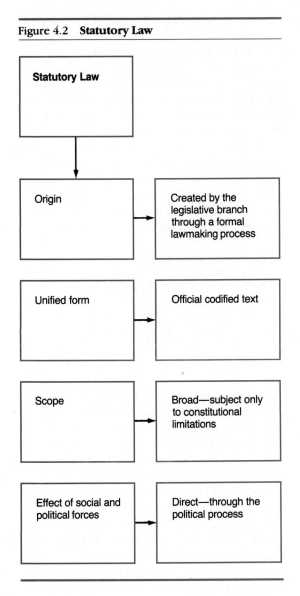

Statutory Law	
Origin	Created by the legislative branch through a formal lawmaking process
Unified form	Official codified text
Scope	Broad—subject only to constitutional limitations
Effect of social and political forces	Direct—through the political process

description of the vast scope of our statutory law is first in order.

STATUTORY LAW— THE RATIONALE

There are many reasons for the existence of statutory law, three of which deserve special mention. First, one of the primary functions of any legislative body is to adopt measures having to do with the *structure and day-to-day operation* of the government of which it is a part. Thus many federal statutes are of the "nuts and bolts" variety relating to such matters as the operation of the federal court system, the Internal Revenue Service, and the administration and employment rules of the U.S. Civil Service Commission. In similar vein, many state statutes relate to such matters as the property tax laws, the operation of school systems, and the setting forth of powers of municipalities within their borders.

Second, many activities are of such a nature that *they can hardly be regulated by common-law principles* and the judicial processes. In the area of criminal law, for example, it is absolutely essential for the general populace to know what acts are punishable by fine and imprisonment; the only sure way to set forth the elements of specific crimes is through the enactment of federal and state criminal statutes. Similarly, the activities of corporations are so complex and so varied that they do not lend themselves to judicial regulation. Few judges, for example, have either the expertise to deal with such questions as the conditions under which the payment of corporate dividends should be permitted or the time to deal with the spelling out of such conditions on a case-by-case basis. Thus the only practical way to deal with these and other problems is by the drafting of detailed statutes which, in total, make up the comprehensive corporation laws of the states.

The third function of a legislature is to change expressly (or even overrule) common-law rules where it believes such modifications are necessary, and—even more commonly—to enact statutes to *remedy new problems* to which common-law rules do not apply. Thus a state legislature might pass a statute making nonprofit corporations (such as hospitals) liable for the wrongs of their employees to the same extent as are profit-making corporations, thereby reversing the early common-law rule of nonliability for such employers. Or a legislature, aware of increasing purchases of its farmlands by foreign citizens—a situation not covered by common-law rules—might react to this perceived evil by passing a statute placing limits on the number of acres aliens may own or inherit. (Over twenty states today have such statutes, and approximately ten have passed laws that prohibit aliens who live outside the U.S. from owning *any* farmlands within these states' borders.)

LIMITATIONS ON LEGISLATIVE BODIES

Procedural Requirements

All state constitutions (and, to a lesser extent, the federal Constitution) contain provisions about the manner in which statutes shall be enacted. As a general rule, acts that do not conform to these requirements are void. For example, virtually all state constitutions provide that revenue bills "shall originate in the House of Representatives," a requirement that also appears in the federal Constitution. There are three other requirements that normally appear in state constitutions: (1) restricting the enactment of "special" or "local" laws,[6] (2) requiring that the subject of every act be set forth in its title, and (3) prohibiting a statute from embracing more than one subject. Additionally, all constitutions prescribe certain formalities in regard to the enactment processes themselves, such as specific limitations on the time and place of the introduction of bills, limitations on the amendment of bills, and the requirement that bills have three separate readings before final passage.

These kinds of provisions, while appearing to be unduly technical, actually serve meritorious purposes. For example, while legislatures normally strive to pass statutes of general application, it is necessary that some laws operate only upon certain classes of persons or in certain localities of a state. Such special or local laws are valid only if the basis of their classification is reasonable; two of the purposes of the constitutional provisions mentioned above are to insure such reasonableness and to guarantee that the classes of persons covered be given notice of the consideration of the bill prior to its passage. Similarly, the purpose of requiring that the subject of an act be expressed in its title is to insure that legislators voting on a bill are fully apprised as to its subject, thereby guarding against the enactment of "surprise" legislation. And the purpose of the requirement that a bill contain one subject is to prevent the passage of omnibus bills (those that bring together entirely unrelated, or incongruous, matters).

Requirement of Certainty

All statutes are subject to the general principle of constitutional law that they be "reasonably definite and certain." While the Constitution itself does not expressly contain such a provision, the courts have long taken the view that if the wording of a statute is such that persons of ordinary intelligence cannot understand its meaning, then the statute violates the due process clause of the Constitution and is thus invalid.[7] In such instances, it is said that the statute is "unconstitutionally vague."

As a practical matter, the majority of statutes that are challenged on the ground of vagueness or uncertainty are upheld by the courts. This is because most statutes are, in fact, drafted carefully and because the courts are extremely reluctant to declare a statute unconstitutional if they can avoid doing so. Thus, if the wording of a statute is subject to two possible but conflicting interpretations, one of which satisfies constitutional requirements and the other of which does not, the former interpretation will be accepted by the courts if they can reasonably do so.

An application of the vagueness analysis in a criminal case occurred in *Kolender v. Lawson,* 461 U.S. 352 (1983), where the U.S. Supreme Court struck down, on the ground of vagueness, a California statute that required persons who

---

[6] "A special or local law is one that, because of its restrictions, can operate on or affect only a portion of the citizens, or a fraction of the property embraced within a classification created thereby." 82 C.J.S., Statutes, §14, copyright © 1953 by West Publishing Co.

[7] *State v. Jay J. Garfield Bldg. Co.,* 3 P.2d 983 (1931).

loitered or wandered on the streets to provide "credible and reliable" identification and to account for their presence when requested to do so by a peace officer. The court, speaking through Justice Sandra Day O'Connor, said "It is clear that the full discretion accorded to the police whether the suspect has provided a 'credible and reliable' identification necessarily entrusts lawmaking to the moment-to-moment

judgment of the policeman on his beat," and "furnishes a convenient tool for harsh and discriminatory enforcement by local prosecuting officials against particular groups deemed to merit their displeasure."

In a case involving regulation of business, rather than criminal charges, the courts will not be as demanding in applying the vagueness test, as the next case illustrates.

U.S. v. Sun and Sand Imports, Ltd., Inc.
U.S. Second Circuit Court of Appeals, 725 F.2d 184 (1984)

The Consumer Products Safety Commission (CPSC) issued an administrative complaint charging that Sun and Sand Imports had imported and transported in interstate commerce flammable children's sleepwear in violation of the Flammable Fabrics Act (FFA). The garments in question are sold in sizes which fit infants and toddlers, are made of soft stretchable fabric with no trim, have attached feet and a front zipper running from neck to crotch, and are, admittedly, made of flammable fabric. The trial judge enjoined importation of the garments pending conclusion of CPSC administrative proceedings.

Sun and Sand appealed, arguing that the regulatory definition of sleepwear is void for vagueness under the due process clause of the Fifth Amendment.

Timbers, Circuit Judge:

Children's sleepwear is defined in a regulation promulgated under the FFA as

> *"any product of wearing apparel up to and including size 6X, such as nightgowns, pajamas, or similar or related items, such as robes, intended to be worn primarily for sleeping or activities relating to sleeping. Diapers and underwear are excluded from this definition."*

In addition, the CPSC uses the following factors to determine whether an item of children's clothing is sleepwear within the meaning of the regulation: the nature of the product and its suitability for use by children for sleeping or activities related to sleeping; the manner in which the product is distributed and promoted; and the likelihood that the product will be used by children primarily for sleeping or activities related to sleeping in a substantial number of cases.

Before turning to the merits of Sun and Sand's vagueness challenge, we must determine what standard to apply. A provision is void for vagueness if it is so vague that it gives no warning to the challenger that his conduct is prohibited. In *Village of Hoffman Estates v. The Flipside, Hoffman Estates, Inc.,* 455 U.S. 489 (1982), the Supreme Court held that a more relaxed standard is to be applied to economic regulations which do not implicate fundamental rights and provide only for civil penalties. The instant case involves an economic regulation. Sun and Sand argues that the more restrictive standard should apply because the FFA provides criminal penalties for willful violations. The critical distinction is that criminal penalties are imposed only for *willful* violations of the FFA. A scienter requirement may mitigate the vagueness of a law.[a] Moreover, the CPSC here sought only a cease and desist order. Sun and Sand remains free to assert a vagueness defense in any criminal action which may ensue.

We hold that the definition of children's sleepwear set forth in the regulation promulgated under the FFA is sufficiently specific. Moreover, the CPSC's criteria for determining whether an article of clothing is primarily sleepwear provide guidance to the manufacturer, as do the examples provided by the cease and desist orders published in the Federal Register. In addition, the agency is willing to give pre-enforcement advice to manufacturers concerned with the applicability of the FFA to their products. We find these factors persuasive. We decline Sun and Sand's invitation to require an unworkable level of specificity. In *Boyce Motor Lines, Inc. v. United States,* 342 U.S. 337, 340 (1952), the Supreme Courts recognized that because "few words possess the precision of mathematical symbols, most statutes must deal with untold and unforeseen variations in factual situations, and the practical necessities of discharging the business of government inevitably limit the specificity with which legislators can spell out prohibitions."

Sun and Sand focuses upon a 1978 memorandum by a compliance officer to the CPSC stating that "[d]ifferences between CPSC and firms regarding particular garments may then be litigated, as necessary, to resolve differences of opinion as to the intended use of the garments and to establish case precedence." Statutes and regulations, however, are not impermissibly vague simply because it may be difficult to determine whether marginal cases fall within their scope. *United States v. National Dairy Products Corp.,* 372 U.S. 29, 32 (1963). The burden upon a manufacturer of defending a cease and desist proceeding in a marginal case does not render the standard vague. It is not unfair to require that "one who deliberately goes perilously close to an area of proscribed conduct shall take the risk that he may cross the line." *Boyce Motor Lines, supra.* Only a reasonable degree of certainty is necessary. We hold that that requirement has been complied with here.

[The court then concluded that the trial court had properly held Sun and Sand's products to be within the statute because, *inter alia:* (1) they had the same characteristics as infant sleepwear, especially the attached feet; (2) Sun and Sand does not promote them as playwear; (3) customers in several stores were shown Sun and Sand's garments when they asked for sleepwear; (4) Sun and Sand's garments were intermingled with sleepwear in many stores; and (5) the garments bore a "striking similarity" to classic sleepwear garments.]

Affirmed.

---

[a] "Scienter" indicates an intent to do evil.

STATUTORY LAW AND COMMON LAW—A CONTRAST

Statutory law and common law differ in several significant respects. The most obvious of these are the *processes* by which each comes into being and the *form* of each after it becomes operative.

Processes and Form

Legislative acts become law only after passing through certain formal steps in both houses of the state legislatures (or of Congress) and, normally, by subsequent approval of the governor (or the president). The usual steps are (1) introduction of a bill in the house or senate by one or more members of that body; (2) referral of the bill to the appropriate legislative committee, where hearings are held; (3) approval of the bill by that committee and perhaps others; (4) approval of the bill by the house and senate after full debate; and (5) signing of the bill by the executive (or overriding an executive veto). At each of these stages the opponents of the bill are given considerable opportunity to raise objections, with the result that the bill may be voted down or may pass only after being substantially amended. *Common-law rules,* by contrast, are creatures of the judicial branch of government; they are adopted by the courts for settling controversies in those areas of law where the legislature has not spoken.

In addition to these obvious contrasts between the two types of law, there are others that are equally significant. We note these briefly.

Social and Political Forces

The social and political forces within a state have a greater and more evident impact on statutory law than on common law. Judges are somewhat more insulated from such pressures than are legislatures. Additionally, the steps required in the enactment of statutes enable representatives of vocal special-interest groups (who are frequently at odds with one another) to attract considerable publicity to their causes. And, of course, the raw political power that each is able to exert upon the legislators plays a significant, though not always controlling, part in the final disposition of a bill.

In addition to the political and financial pressures that have always been brought to bear by lobbyists, the last few years have seen an enormous increase in the activities of political action committees, or PACs. Where lobbyists' activities are directed toward the swaying of votes of *incumbent* lawmakers, the basic thrust of the PACs is in a different direction—the raising of funds *to elect* candidates who will support their particular causes after they are in office. A hint of the power of PACs can be gained from just three statistics: (1) spending by PACs for the 1986 elections was estimated to be over $120 million; (2) over three thousand PACs are registered with the Federal Elections Committee; and (3) estimates that the nation's two largest PACs—the National Congressional Club and the National Conservative Action Committee—alone raise over $15 million a year in support of conservative causes.

Legislative Options

While judges are required to settle controversies that come before them, legislatures generally have no duty to enact legislation. Thus legislatures have the option of refraining from the passage of laws where there is little public sentiment for them or where competing groups are so powerful that inaction is, politically, the better part of valor.

Legislative Scope

Subject only to the relatively few constitutional limitations placed upon it, the legislative power to act is very broad. Thus legislatures are not only free to enact statutes where case law is nonexistent, but they also can pass statutes that expressly overrule common-law principles. Examples of the latter are those statutes involving the legality of married women's contracts. Under English and early American common law, it was firmly established that married women lacked the capacity—the legal ability—to contract, and thus any agreements they entered into while married had no effect. Today, all states have enacted statutes that generally confer upon married women the same rights to contract as those enjoyed by other citizens.

As for jurisdictional scope, legislatures have the power to pass broad statutes encompassing all aspects of a given subject, whereas the courts can "make law" only in deciding the cases that come before them. Every state, for example, has comprehensive corporation acts, in which virtually all aspects of corporate activities, from incorporation procedures to dissolution procedures, are specified in detail. Similarly, every state has an all-encompassing criminal code, within which the criminal offenses in the state are defined.

STATUTORY INTERPRETATION

We have seen that legislative bodies make law whenever they enact statutes. By doing so, they formally state what kinds of conduct they are requiring or prohibiting in specified situations and what results they expect from the passage of these laws on the rights and duties of affected parties.

But the true scope and meaning of a particular statute is never known with precision until it is formally construed by the courts in settling actual disputes arising under it. This searching for legislative intent, which usually necessitates a *statutory interpretation,* is thus another major source of our law. **Interpretation** is the process by which a court determines the precise legal meaning of a statute as it applies to a particular controversy.

Interpretation: A Necessary Evil?

Whenever a dispute arises where either of the parties is basing his or her case upon the wording of a particular statute, one might think that the court's job would be mechanical in nature; that is, once the facts were established, a careful reading of the statute would make it clear what

result the legislature intended in such a situation. While this is often true, there are many instances in which it is not.

To bring the nature of the problem into sharper focus, consider the following situation. X flies a stolen airplane from one state to another and is convicted under a U.S. statute that makes the interstate movement of stolen motor vehicles a federal crime. In this statute, a motor vehicle is defined as "an automobile, automobile truck, automobile wagon, motorcycle, or any other self-propelled vehicle not designed for running on rails." Is an airplane a "motor vehicle" under this law? The problem is that the words of the statute are broad enough to embrace aircraft if they are given a literal interpretation; yet it is at least arguable that Congress did not really intend such a result. (The U.S. Supreme Court answered no to the question, with Justice Holmes saying that the term *vehicle* is "commonly understood as something that moves or runs on land, not something which flies in the air"—though he did admit that "etymologically the term might be considered broad enough to cover a conveyance propelled in the air.")[8]

The Plain-Meaning Rule

The primary source of legislative intent is, of course, the language that makes up the statute itself. In the relatively rare case where a court feels that the wording of an act is so clear as to dictate but one result, and that the result is not "patently absurd," the consideration of other factors is unnecessary. If, for example, a state statute provides that "every applicant for examination and registration as a pharmacist shall be a citizen of the United States," a state pharmacy board would have to refuse to process the application of an alien even though he or she may have *applied for* U.S. citizenship as of the date of the pharmaceutical examination.[9] In cases of this

---

[8]*McBoyle v. United States,* 283 U.S. 25 (1931).

[9]*State v. Dame,* Supreme Court of Wyoming, 249 P.2d 156 (1952).

sort (and occasionally in others where the language is somewhat less precise) the courts say that the statute possesses a **plain meaning** and that interpretation is thus unnecessary.

Aids to Interpretation

Most statutes, however, do not easily lend themselves to the plain-meaning rule. This is true (1) because laws are usually drafted so as to contain an element of "deliberate imprecision," the legislature intending thereby to afford the courts some latitude in their application, and (2) because very few words (even in statutes that are highly restricted in scope) are susceptible to but one meaning. Thus in the majority of cases the courts recognize that some degree of *interpretation* is necessary and that a consideration of factors beyond the express language of a particular clause is advisable, if not mandatory, in determining the precise legislative intent. Even when purporting to apply the plain-meaning rule, most courts bolster their conclusion with various aids to interpretation.

For example, the court will examine the law's **textual context,** which involves reading the statute as a whole rather than concentrating solely upon the language of the disputed clause. The title of the act might give some indication of how the legislature meant a particular clause contained in it to be interpreted. Similarly, use of the same words in different sections of the act can indicate how the legislature meant them to be taken in the disputed clause. Rules of grammar and punctuation supplement this examination, and occasionally the dictionary is consulted to determine how the words are used in ordinary life.

The court will also examine the purpose for which the law was enacted. If, for example, the law was passed to fight organized crime, the courts will construe ambiguous portions to help achieve that purpose. This is sometimes called the **circumstantial context** or "purpose rule."

Legislative history can be particularly important. What did the legislators say as they debated the bill that eventually was passed? Their comments, particularly those of its sponsors, may be enlightening.

Also, courts will give weight to prior *judicial interpretations* of the statute's meaning. This is appropriate simply on *stare decisis* grounds. More to the point, if a particular statute has been interpreted consistently by the courts for many years and Congress has never amended the provision in question although it has, perhaps, made changes in others in that statute, the courts sometimes assume Congress has implicitly approved the long-standing interpretation.

No matter which aids to interpretation the courts invoke, their guiding star in the process of interpretation is one thing only—*legislative intent.* The courts' task is not to interpret the statute to mean what they think it should say. It is not to interpret the statute to improve on what the legislature said. The courts' only duty is to discover the legislative intent and to interpret the law in a manner consistent with that intent. Sometimes this can be a distasteful task.

For example, the following case involves interpretation of the Racketeering Influenced Corrupt Organizations Act (RICO). There is no doubt that the act was aimed primarily at the infiltration of legitimate business by organized crime. Yet, its civil provisions, studies showed, were used in over 90 percent of the cases not against "mobsters" but against ordinary businesses, including stock brokers such as Merrill Lynch and Dean Witter, CPA firms such as Arthur Andersen and Peat Marwick, banks such as Citibank and Continental Illinois, and manufacturing companies such as Boeing and Miller Brewing. To slow down the spate of RICO lawsuits, some courts interpreted RICO's provisions to require that plaintiffs show that defendants had been *convicted* of certain specified "racketeering acts." The Supreme Court was called upon to resolve the meaning of the act. As you read the opinion, note which aids to interpretation the Court uses.

Sedima v. Imrex Co., Inc.
U.S. Supreme Court, 105 S.Ct. 3275 (1985)

Plaintiff Sedima entered into a joint venture with defendant Imrex Co. to provide electronic components to a Belgian firm. The buyer was to order parts through Sedima; Imrex was to obtain the parts in America and ship them to Europe. Sedima and Imrex were to split the net proceeds. After Imrex filled $8,000,000 in orders, Sedima became convinced that Imrex was inflating bills, cheating Sedima out of a portion of its proceeds by collecting for nonexistent expenses.

Sedima sued Imrex and two of its officers under the Racketeering Influenced and Corrupt Organizations Act (RICO). It contains both criminal provisions and the civil provisions which Sedima invoked. Sedima claimed that Imrex had by its presentation of inflated, fraudulent bills committed mail and wire fraud, which are "racketeering" acts within the meaning of RICO.

The trial court dismissed the RICO claims, and the Court of Appeals affirmed for the reason, among others, that the complaint was defective for failing to allege that defendants had been convicted of mail and wire fraud. Sedima appealed.

White, Justice:

RICO takes aim at "racketeering activity," which it defines as any act "chargeable" under several generically described state criminal laws, any act "indictable" under numerous specific federal criminal provisions, including mail and wire fraud, and any "offense" involving bankruptcy or securities fraud or drug-related activity that is "punishable" under federal law. Section 1962, entitled "Prohibited Activities," outlaws the use of income derived from a "pattern of racketeering activity" to acquire an interest in or establish an enterprise engaged in or affecting interstate commerce; the acquisition or maintenance of any interest in an enterprise "through a pattern of racketeering activity"; conducting or participating in the conduct of an enterprise through a pattern of racketeering activity; and conspiring to violate any of these provisions.

Congress provided criminal penalties. In addition, it set out a far-reaching civil enforcement scheme, §1964, including the following provision for private suits:

"Any person injured in his business or property by reason of a violation of section 1962 of this chapter may sue therefor in any appropriate United States district court and shall recover threefold the damages he sustains and the cost of the suit, including a reasonable attorney's fee." §1964(c).

The Court of Appeals found the complaint defective for not alleging that the defendants had already been criminally convicted of the predicate acts of mail and wire fraud, or of a RICO violation. This element of the civil cause of action was inferred from §1964(c)'s reference to a "violation" of §1962, the court also observing that its prior conviction requirement would avoid serious constitutional difficulties, the danger of unfair stigmatization, and problems regarding the standard by which the predicate acts were to be proved. . . .

As a preliminary matter, it is worth briefly reviewing the legislative history of the private treble damages action. The civil remedies in the bill passed by the Senate, S. 30, were limited to injunctive actions by the United States. . . .

During hearings on S. 30 before the House Judiciary Committee, Representative Steiger proposed the addition of a private treble damages action "similar to the private damage remedy found in the antitrust laws. . . . [T]hose who have been wronged by organized crime should at least be given access to a legal remedy. In addition, the availability of such a remedy would enhance the effectiveness of [RICO's] prohibitions." The American Bar Association also proposed an amendment "based upon the concept of Section 4 of the Clayton Act."

Over the dissent of three members, who feared the treble damages provision would be used for malicious harassment of business competitors, the Committee approved the amendment. . . .

The Senate did not seek a conference and adopted the bill as amended in the House. The treble damages provision had been drawn to its attention while the legislation was still in the House, and had received the endorsement of Senator McClellan, the sponsor of S. 30, who was of the view that the provision would be "a major new tool in extirpating the baneful influence of organized crime in our economic life."

The language of RICO gives no obvious indication that a civil action can proceed only after a criminal conviction. The word "conviction" does not appear in any relevant portion of the statute. To the contrary, the predicate acts involve conduct that is "chargeable" or "indictable," and "offense[s]" that are "punishable," under various criminal statutes. As defined in the statute, racketeering activity consists not of acts for which the defendant has been convicted, but of acts for which he could be. Thus, a prior conviction requirement cannot be found in the definition of "racketeering activity." Nor can it be found in §1962, which sets out the statute's substantive provisions. Indeed, if either §1961 or §1962 did contain such a requirement, a prior conviction would also be a prerequisite, nonsensically, for a criminal prosecution, or for a civil action by the government to enjoin violations that had not yet occurred.

The Court of Appeals purported to discover its prior conviction requirement in the term "violation" in §1964(c). However, even if that term were read to refer to a criminal conviction, it would require a conviction under RICO, not of the predicate offenses. That aside, the term "violation" does not imply a criminal conviction. It refers only to a failure to adhere to legal requirements. This is its indisputable meaning elsewhere in the statute. Section 1962 renders certain conduct "unlawful"; §1963 and §1964 impose consequences, criminal and civil, for "violations" of §1962. We should not lightly infer that Congress intended the term to have wholly different meanings in neighboring subsections.

The legislative history also undercuts the reading of the court below. The clearest current in that history is the reliance on the Clayton Act model, under which private and governmental actions are entirely distinct. The only specific reference in the legislative history to prior convictions of which we are aware is an objection that the treble damages provision is too broad precisely because "there need *not* be a conviction under any of these laws for it to be racketeering." 116 Cong. Rec. 35342 (1970) (emphasis added). The history is otherwise silent on this point and contains nothing to contradict the import of the language appearing in the statute. Had Congress intended to impose this novel requirement, there would have been at least some mention of it in the legislative history, even if not in the statute.

The Court of Appeals was of the view that its narrow construction of the statute was essential to avoid intolerable practical consequences. First, without a prior conviction to rely on, the plaintiff would have to prove commission of the predicate acts beyond a reasonable doubt. This would require instructing the jury as to different standards of proof for different aspects of the case.

We are not at all convinced that the predicate acts must be established beyond a reasonable doubt in a proceeding under §1964(c). . . . But we need not decide the standard of proof issue today. For even if the stricter standard is applicable to a portion of the plaintiff's proof, the resulting logistical difficulties, which are accepted in other contexts, would not be so great as to require invention of a requirement that cannot be found in the statute and that Congress, as even the Court of Appeals had to concede, did not envision.

The court below also feared that any other construction would raise severe constitutional questions, as it "would provide civil remedies for offenses criminal in nature, stigmatize defendants with the appellation 'racketeer,' authorize the award of damages which are clearly punitive, including attorney's fees, and constitute a civil remedy aimed in part to avoid the constitutional protections of the criminal law." We do not view the statute as being so close to the constitutional edge. The fact that conduct can result in both criminal liability and treble damages does not mean that there is not a bona fide civil action. The familiar provisions for both criminal liability and treble damages under the antitrust laws indicate as much. As for stigma, a civil RICO proceeding leaves no greater stain than do a number of other civil proceedings.

Finally, we note that a prior conviction requirement would be inconsistent with Congress' underlying policy concerns. Such a rule would severely handicap potential plaintiffs. A guilty party may escape conviction for any number of reasons—not least among them the possibility that the Government itself may choose to pursue only civil remedies. Private attorney general provisions such as §1964(c) are in part designed to fill prosecutorial gaps. This purpose would be largely defeated, and the need for treble damages as an incentive to litigate unjustified, if private suits could be maintained only against those already brought to justice.

[The Court then rejected another of the lower courts' grounds for dismissal, by refusing to interpret RICO to require that plaintiff allege a "racketeering injury"—an injury "caused by an activity which RICO was designed to deter." The Court held that allegations of injury stemming from the predicate acts themselves, in this case mail and wire fraud, are sufficient.]

Underlying the Court of Appeals' holding was its distress at the "extraordinary, if not outrageous," uses to which civil RICO has been put. Instead of being used against mobsters and organized criminals, it has become a tool for everyday fraud cases brought against "respected and legitimate 'enterprises.'" Yet Congress wanted to reach both "legitimate" and "illegitimate" enterprises. The former enjoy neither an inherent incapacity for criminal activity nor immunity from its consequences. The fact that §1964(c) is used against respected businesses allegedly engaged in a pattern of specifically identified criminal conduct is hardly a sufficient reason for assuming that the provision is being misconstrued.

It is true that private civil actions under the statute are being brought almost solely against such defendants, rather than against the archetypal, intimidating mobster. Yet this defect—if defect it is—is inherent in the statute as written, and its correction must lie with Congress. It is not for the judiciary to eliminate the private action in situations where Congress has provided it simply because plaintiffs are not taking advantage of it in its more difficult applications.

[Reversed.]

SELECTED STATE STATUTES

Before leaving the subject of statutory law, several widely adopted state statutes deserve special mention. (All of these statutes are discussed in considerable detail in later chapters.)

The Uniform Commercial Code

The **Uniform Commercial Code** is especially significant to businesspersons (1) because it is a dramatic illustration of one way changes in law can occur in response to shortcomings that exist in prior law; (2) because the statute governs eight commercial law subjects; and (3) because it has been adopted by all states except Louisiana, which has adopted Articles 1, 3, 4, and 5 only. To see what the code is and why it came about, a brief look at the past is necessary.

Historical Background: By the beginning of this century there was a tremendous volume of interstate commercial activity. The commercial laws of the individual states, however, varied widely, causing substantial planning problems for merchants engaged in interstate commerce. Unfortunately, early efforts to achieve some level of uniformity in state commercial laws failed.

However, in 1941 the National Conference of Commissioners on Uniform State Laws and the American Law Institute joined forces in an effort to draft a single "modern, comprehensive, commercial code, applicable throughout the country," covering eight areas of commercial law. The code was first adopted by Pennsylvania, in 1953. A 1962 official edition, containing some minor changes, was subsequently published, and it is this version (with again minor changes made in 1972) that forty-nine of the states have since adopted.

Coverage: The code, commonly referred to as the UCC, consists of ten articles, or chapters. The eight substantive areas of law covered by the code are found in Articles 2 through 9. (Article 1 covers only introductory matters. Article 10 simply lists the section numbers of prior statutes of the adopting state, which heretofore covered those areas of law encompassed by the code and which are expressly repealed to eliminate statutory conflict.) From the business student's standpoint, the two most important chapters of the code are Articles 2 and 3.

Article 2, Sales, consists of 104 sections that govern virtually all aspects of the law of sales. This article supplants the sales law that was in effect prior to the adoption of the code, which in most states was the old Uniform Sales Act.

Article 3, Commercial Paper, supplants the earlier Uniform Negotiable Instruments Law, which had at one time been adopted in all the states. Its eighty sections govern such matters as the rights and obligations of the makers of notes and the drawers of checks and drafts, and the rights and duties of holders and indorsers of all types of negotiable instruments.

Articles 4 through 8 deal with more specialized situations, such as the duties that exist between depositary and collecting banks and the resolution of problems resulting from the issuance and transfer of bills of lading and other documents of title. Article 9 is a lengthy chapter covering all kinds of secured transactions that were formerly governed by separate—and frequently dissimilar—state statutes on chattel mortgages, conditional sales, and other devices by which a creditor might seek to retain a security interest in goods that were physically in the possession of a debtor. (The subjects of sales and commercial paper are covered in Part IV, and secured transactions in Part V.)

Deceptive Trade Practices Acts

Most states have **deceptive trade practices acts** which specifically forbid specified kinds of business conduct. The typical deceptive trade practices act, for example, prohibits merchants from "passing off" (representing and selling) their goods or services as those of another; from representing goods as being new if they are reclaimed, used, or secondhand; and from disparaging the goods or services of competitors by false representations of fact in regard to such goods or services. Additionally, the typical statute also prohibits such practices as "advertising goods or services with the intent not to sell them as advertised," and the making of "false statements of fact concerning the reasons for, or the amounts of, price reductions."

Business Organization Acts

All states have comprehensive statutes which control the formation, operation, and dissolution of various forms of business organizations. These will be studied in some detail in Part VI of this text. For now it is sufficient to make just a few observations about these state laws. In the area of partnerships there is great uniformity in the law from state to state because virtually all states have adopted versions of the Uniform Partnership Act (UPA). The UPA has successfully accomplished the uniformity for partnership law which the UCC was supposed to create for commercial transactions.

There is less uniformity regarding the forming and operating of limited partnerships because the individual states have varied a little more in how strictly they adopted the Uniform Limited Partnership Act (ULPA) and because in 1976 dissatisfaction with the ULPA led to promulgation of the Revised Uniform Limited Partnership Act (RULPA) which many states adopted in whole or in part. Things became even more complicated in 1985 when a new version of RULPA was made available for the state legislatures to adopt if they wished. Nonetheless, generally speaking there is substantial uniformity across the United States in limited partnership law.

However, there is even less uniformity in the states' laws concerning corporations. For one thing, many states pattern their laws after the Model Business Corporation Act (MBCA). Because it is not a *uniform* act, but only a *model* act, the states which chose to pattern their corporate codes after the MBCA felt free to make substantial changes. Second, the MBCA has been revised many times over the years, and in 1985 a Revised Model Business Corporation Act (RMBCA) was issued. Finally, many states pattern their corporate codes not upon some version of the MBCA but upon the Delaware Corporate Code. Delaware is the leading jurisdiction in the country in the corporate law area.

SUMMARY

Judge-made or common law is not as pervasive in the American legal system as it once was, but it still dominates several important subject areas. As cases in these areas are decided over the years, a substantial body of precedent builds up. A judge who finds relevant decisions from courts above him or her in the appellate chain should follow that mandatory authority. If the only existing precedents come from courts that could not review the judge's decision, they need only be followed if the judge finds them persuasive.

The heart of the common law is the doctrine of *stare decisis,* which provides that relevant precedents from earlier cases should normally be followed so that the law will have stability and predictability. However, the common law is also flexible; it can be adapted to changing societal conditions. Therefore, if the policy reasons underlying a particular common law rule have evaporated, that rule can be changed. The need to correct an injustice outweighs the need for stability.

In recent years statutory law has become increasingly dominant in most areas of our legal system. The Constitution specifies the areas in which the federal Congress can legislate, and reserves the other areas for the states. If the proper procedures are followed and the laws passed are not so vague that citizens are unable to conform their actions to the law's requirements, the courts will enforce those laws. The courts may also be required to interpret the laws, for a legislature can never foresee all the circumstances that might arise. Then the courts must discover the legislative intent and construe the laws in such a way as to attain the legislative purpose. To achieve this the court will use various analytic techniques, including a close examination of the textual context, the stated purpose of the law, and its legislative history.

KEY TERMS

Case law
Stare decisis
Mandatory authority
Persuasive authority
Statute
Interpretation
Plain-meaning rule
Textual context
Circumstantial context
Legislative history
Uniform Commercial Code
Deceptive trade practices acts

QUESTIONS AND PROBLEMS

1. Dissenting in *Taylor v. Allen,* 151 La. 82 (1921), Justice O'Neill wrote: "I have heard that lawyers in one of the Western states [say that a] precedent is a 'goose case.' The expression arose from the perplexity of a so-called 'case lawyer,' who was unprepared to advise his client whether he was liable in damages because his geese had trespassed on his neighbor's lawn. The lawyer said he had found several cases where the owners were held liable because their horses, cows, sheep, goats, or dogs had committed acts of trespass; but he could not find a 'goose case.' The distinction which he observed was that his 'goose case' was not 'on all fours.'" Explain what constitutes a "goose case." How does one avoid the problems of the perplexed lawyer in Justice O'Neill's story?

2. Maddux was injured when the car she was riding in was struck by a car driven by Donaldson, and, almost immediately thereafter, by a second car driven by Bryie. When Maddux sued the two negligent drivers, the facts of the case were such that it was impossible to determine which of her injuries were caused by the first collision and which by the second collision. At the time of the suit, the Michigan common-law rule was that, in such a case, neither defendant could be held liable for any damages; accordingly, the trial court dismissed Maddux's action. She then appealed to the Supreme Court of Michigan, claiming that the rule of non-recovery was too unfair to an injured plaintiff. Do you agree with this contention? If so, what do you think a better rule would be? (*Maddux v. Donaldson*, 108 N.W.2d 33, 1961.)

3. In a number of cases, the supreme court of State X had adopted the rule that a seller of land who overstated the *value of the land* to a prospective buyer was not guilty of fraud, even if he knew that the true market value of the land was much lower than the figure that he stated to the buyer. (In these cases, the reasoning of the court was that the value of any property is merely a matter of opinion, and that the buyer should realize this.) After this rule is adopted, a new case reaches the supreme court in which the buyer of land claims that the seller was guilty of fraud when he—the seller—intentionally misrepresented the *rental value* of the property (seller told buyer, an out-of-state resident who had never seen the land, that "it can readily be rented for $100 a month," a statement that proved to be false). If the supreme court felt that the seller in such a case should be made to pay damages on the theory that he *was* guilty of fraud, would the court have to overrule the prior decisions, or do you think the facts of the new case are sufficiently different to permit the court

simply to apply a different rule to it? Explain your reasoning. (*Cahill v. Readon*, 273 P. 653, 1928.)

4. A student demonstrator and four labor pickets were convicted in the Hamilton County Municipal Court, Ohio, of violating a Cincinnati ordinance making it a criminal offense for three or more persons to assemble on a sidewalk "and there conduct themselves in a manner annoying to persons passing by." On appeal to the U.S. Supreme Court the five contended that the ordinance was unconstitutionally vague (that it was so vague that it violated the due process clause). Do you agree with this contention? Discuss. (*Coates v. Cincinnati*, 402 U.S. 611, 1971.)

5. The City of Petersburg had maintained a cemetery for over 100 years when it decided to move some of the bodies onto a 1.1 acre tract adjacent to the cemetery so that a road running in front of the cemetery could be widened. The Temples owned a home directly across the street from the 1.1 acre tract. They sued to prevent the bodies from being moved onto the tract, citing a state statute which said: "No cemetery shall be hereafter established within the corporate limits of any town; nor shall any cemetery be established within 250 yards of any residence without the consent of the owner of such residence." Does the City need the Temples' permission? Discuss. (*Temple v. City of Petersburg*, 29 S.E.2d 357, Va. 1944.)

6. Johnson, a teen-aged boy living in North Carolina, owned a motorcycle. After the motorcycle's original headlight became very weak, he and a friend taped a five-cell flashlight to the handlebars and that evening, with both boys on the motorcycle, they had a collision with an automobile. In ensuing litigation, the car owner pointed out that a North Carolina statute required every motorcycle to have a "headlamp," and he contended that the flashlight was not a headlamp. If you were a judge on the North Carolina Supreme Court hearing the case on appeal, what steps would you take in deciding whether the flashlight was a headlamp under the statute? What result? (*Bigelow v. Johnson,* 277 S.E.2d 347, 1981.)

7. In 1885 Congress passed a statute which provided: "[I]t shall be unlawful for any person, company, partnership, or corporation, in any manner whatsoever, to prepay the transportation, or in any way assist or encourage the importation or migration of any alien or aliens . . . into the United States . . . under contract or agreement . . . made previous to the importation or migration of such alien or aliens, . . . to perform labor or service of any kind in the United States." In 1887 the Holy Trinity Church of New York City made a contract with Warren, a pastor then living in England, under the terms of which he was employed to serve as its pastor. Pursuant to that contract, Warren immigrated to the United States and assumed his pastoral duties. The church was soon charged with violating the quoted statute. Did Congress intend the statute to cover this case? Discuss. (*Holy Trinity Church v. U.S.,* 143 U.S. 457, 1892.)

8. A city ordinance required that operators of coin-operated amusement machines be licensed, and provided that the chief of police was to determine whether an applicant has any "connections with criminal elements." The city manager, after receiving the report of the chief of police and reports from the building inspector and the city planner, would then decide whether to issue the license. (If the application were denied, the applicant could then petition the city council for a license.) In a legal case brought by a rejected applicant, the contention was made that the licensing ordinance was *unconstitutionally vague* because of the "connections with criminal elements" language. Do you think this contention is correct? Why or why not? (*City of Mesquite v. Aladdin's Castle, Inc.,* 102 S.Ct. 1070, 1982.)

Chapter 5

CONSTITUTIONAL LAW

The most important document in the United States, and, arguably, in the world, is the United States Constitution. This wonderful document is the foundation of our democratic system of government and the basis of our many freedoms. Though drafted in a simpler time, the Constitution has evolved over the past 200 years to keep pace with changes in American society. Partly through amendment, more importantly through flexible Supreme Court interpretations, the Constitution has remained as vital and timely a document as it was when originally written.

Very few areas of the law can be studied without reference to the Constitution. For example, the American court systems discussed in Chapter 2 are based on an organizational plan set out in the Constitution. The power of a court to exert personal jurisdiction over a defendant, also discussed in Chapter 2, is constrained by the Constitution's due process provisions.

The focus of this chapter will be on three major functions of the U.S. Constitution:

1. It prescribes the organization of the federal government, in addition to its jurisdiction.

2. It sets forth the authority of the legislative, executive, and judicial branches of that government.

3. It protects basic rights of individuals and businesses from governmental interference.

ORGANIZATION AND JURISDICTION

One major function of the Constitution is to establish the organization and jurisdiction of the federal government. In so doing, the Constitution also establishes the role of state and local governments in our dual system of sovereignty. Fifty-one primary governments exist in America—the federal government and the fifty state governments. To prevent overlapping areas of authority, the Constitution enumerates many significant federal powers, which are referred to as **delegated powers** (or "enumerated powers"). All other powers (**reserved powers**) rest in the state governments.

Article I, Section 8 of the Constitution spells out the powers of the U.S. Congress, the most important of which include the power

To lay and collect Taxes, Duties, Imposts and Excises, to pay the Debts and provide for the common Defense and general Welfare of the United States; . . .

To borrow Money on the Credit of the United States;

To regulate Commerce with foreign Nations, and among the several States, and with the Indian Tribes;

To establish an uniform Rule of Naturalization, and uniform Laws on the subject of Bankruptcies throughout the United States;

To coin Money, regulate the Value thereof, and of foreign Coin, and fix the Standard of Weights and Measures; . . .

To establish Post Offices and post Roads;

To promote the Progress of Science and useful Arts, by securing for limited Times to Authors and Inventors the exclusive right to their respective Writings and Discoveries;

To constitute Tribunals inferior to the Supreme Court; . . .

To declare War, grant Letters of Marque and Reprisal, and make Rules concerning Captures on Land and Water;

To raise and support Armies, but no Appropriation of Money to that Use shall be for a longer Term than two Years;

To provide and maintain a Navy;

To make Rules for the Government and Regulation of the land and naval forces;

To provide for calling forth the Militia to execute the Laws of the Union, suppress Insurrections and repel Invasions;

To provide for organizing, arming, and disciplining the Militia, and . . .

To make all Laws which shall be necessary and proper for carrying into Execution the foregoing Powers, and all other Powers vested by this Constitution in the Government of the United States, or in any Department or Officer thereof.

State Police Power

By and large, the lines of demarcation between the authority of the federal and state governments are quite clear. Most of the powers delegated to the federal government under Section 8—such as the power to operate post offices and to maintain the various armed forces—involve such clearcut activities that no state could claim to possess any regulatory powers over them.

By the same token, the powers reserved to the states are also, in general, clearly established. Virtually all of the powers of a given state spring from the **state police power**—a term referring to the state's inherent authority to regulate the health, safety, morals, and general welfare of its people. Statutes relating to the operation of motor vehicles, the manufacture and sale of intoxicating liquors, and the regulation of crime obviously fall within the police power, since they are directly involved with matters of health, safety, and morals. Typical statutes based upon the "general welfare" component of the police power are those that regulate such matters as marriage and divorce, the inheritance of property, and the landlord-tenant relationship. (The power to enact zoning laws also falls within the police power category, but the legislatures normally delegate this power to their cities; thus most zoning regulations are, in fact, found in municipal ordinances and regulations of municipal zoning commissions.)

The Commerce Clause

Although in most areas there is a clear delineation between the powers of the federal government on the one hand and the state governments on the other, one problem area exists—that of regulation of commerce. Federal regulation of commercial activity is nearly unlimited, yet the states also have a substantial role to play. Seldom does a year go by in which the Supreme Court does not decide an important case bearing on the respective spheres of authority to regulate commerce.

Federal Regulation of Interstate Commerce: Although early Supreme Court decisions gave a constricted interpretation of congressional power to regulate interstate commerce, more recent decisions have read Article I, Section 8's grant of power "to regulate Commerce with foreign Nations, and among the several States" very broadly.

If Congress detects a problem, even a problem which is not primarily economic in nature such as racial discrimination, and legislates a solution under the commerce clause, the Supreme Court usually asks only two questions: (1) Did the regulated activity have "any appreciable effect" on interstate commerce? (2) Was the solution Congress selected reasonable and appropriate under the circumstances? The Court tends not to be too searching with either inquiry.

"Commerce" includes such activity as transportation, manufacturing, and sales efforts. Because Congress can reach any intrastate commercial activity which *affects* interstate commerce, few local businesses can escape the reach of the federal government. For example, in *Wickard v. Filburn,* 317 U.S. 111 (1942), an Ohio farmer was limited by federal law to raising 11.1 acres of wheat. Farmer Filburn ignored the limitation and planted 23 acres. He fought a penalty assessed by the government by arguing that because he used much of the wheat he grew right on his own farm and sold the rest at an elevator a few miles away, he was not engaged in interstate commerce. But the Supreme Court held that the power to regulate interstate commerce includes the power to regulate prices. The purpose of the law in question was to support agricultural prices by limiting production. If all small farmers such as Filburn were viewed as beyond the reach of the act, the supply of wheat would no doubt increase and appreciably *affect* the price of wheat selling in interstate commerce. Congressional authority extended to Filburn.

In *Heart of Atlanta Motel v. United States,* 379 U.S. 241 (1964), the Supreme Court held that a motel in Atlanta, Georgia was subject to the Civil Rights Act of 1964, a federal statute prohibiting discrimination in places of public accommodation, even though all of its operations were conducted solely within the state and all of its employees were Georgia citizens. The court ruled, first, that the movement of persons from state to state constituted "commerce," and, second, that the motel's operations substantially affected interstate commerce in view of the fact that three-fourths of its clients were interstate travelers.

More recently, in *McLain v. Real Estate Board of New Orleans,* 444 U.S. 232 (1980), a question arose whether a number of New Orleans real estate firms and trade associations had violated the federal antitrust laws by entering into several price-fixing contracts. The lower courts dismissed the action, ruling that defendants' actions, which involved sales of land in New Orleans, were "purely local" in nature and thus not subject to federal law. The Supreme Court reversed, finding that the indirect effects of the defendants' activities were sufficiently related to interstate commerce to justify application of federal law. This finding of sufficient effect—a "not insubstantial effect"—was based primarily on the fact that (1) significant amounts of money lent by local banks to finance real estate purchases came from out-of-state banks, and (2) most of the mortgages taken by the local banks were "physically traded" by them to financial institutions in other states.

Although there are very few businesses today whose activities are so completely local (intrastate) in nature as to be outside the power of Congress to regulate, many federal statutes exempt certain companies from compliance—for example, those having assets of less than $5 million, or fewer than ten employees.

State Regulation of Interstate Commerce: Underlying the dominant federal role in regulation of commerce was the framers' "conviction that in order to succeed, the new Union would have to avoid tendencies toward economic Balkanization that had plagued relations among the Colonies and later among the States under the Articles of Confederation."[1] This does not mean, however, that the states have no role in regulating commerce. Obviously, their police powers give the states a very strong reason to protect the health, safety, and welfare of their citizens threatened by commercial activity originating both within and without the particular state's boundaries.

In fact, the states play a large role in the regulation of commercial activity, intrastate and interstate, in today's economy. However, because of the dominant federal role and the need for a smooth interstate flow of goods and services, there are three limitations on state regulation of commerce. First, a state cannot contradict a valid federal law regulating commerce. Second, a state cannot discriminate against interstate commerce. And, third, a state may not unduly burden the flow of interstate commerce.

Preemption: The federal government's authority to regulate interstate commerce is paramount. Because the Constitution's "Supremacy Clause" found in Article VI, Section I makes the Constitution and federal laws "the supreme law of the land," any state law that on its face contra-

---

[1] *Wardair Canada, Inc. v. Florida Dept. of Revenue,* 106 S.Ct. 2369 (1986), quoting *Hughes v. Oklahoma,* 441 U.S. 322 (1979).

dicts a federal law is automatically invalid. Any time it is impossible to comply with both a federal law and a state law, the state law must fall.

Furthermore, any time a state law undermines the objective of a federal law, it is invalid under the Supremacy Clause. For example, in *City of Burbank v. Lockheed Air Terminal, Inc.,* 411 U.S. 624 (1973), a city ordinance banned jet aircraft from taking off from a local airport between 11 p.m. and 7 a.m. Although the ordinance did not directly contradict a federal law, it conflicted with the purpose of the Federal Aeronautics Act by impeding the ability of the FAA to control air traffic flow.

On occasion, federal regulation of an area of commerce is so extensive that the courts conclude Congress has "occupied the field," leaving no room for state regulation. Sometimes Congress makes clear its intent to preempt state regulation, but many times the courts must decide whether such an intent should be inferred from congressional action. Obviously, the more comprehensive the federal scheme of regulation, the more likely it is that preemption will be inferred. To the extent that national uniformity is necessary for an effective regulatory scheme —as with air traffic control—the more likely preemption will be found. However, congressional *intent* to occupy the field, whether express or implied, is the key.

Discrimination: Even in an area where there is no federal regulation or where existing federal regulation is not so extensive as to preempt concurrent state regulation, the states may not discriminate against interstate commerce. They may not, for example, shelter their own industries from competition emanating from other states. While they may act to preserve their own natural resources, they may not do so by discriminating against out-of-state buyers. Nor may they require that business operations that could be more efficiently conducted elsewhere take place in-state. For example, a state could not require that shellfish caught off its shores be processed in-state before being shipped elsewhere for sale.

It would be a rare case indeed where a state could produce a sufficiently important state interest to justify discrimination against interstate commerce. Almost always the interest could be attained by less restrictive means which do not discriminate in this way. A leading case in this area is *Hunt v. Washington State Apple Advertising Commission,* 432 U.S. 333 (1977), which involved a North Carolina regulation, unique in the fifty states, that required all closed containers of apples shipped into the state to display the applicable USDA grade; state grades were expressly prohibited. For many years, all apples shipped from the state of Washington had a state grade; these grades were in all cases equal or superior to comparable USDA grades. The North Carolina law would have required repackaging or obliteration of labels for Washington apples that happened to end up in North Carolina. The Supreme Court found that although matters of health and consumer protection are naturally of legitimate state concern, the superiority of the Washington grade made those concerns irrelevant in this case. Rather, it appeared that the state of North Carolina was attempting to advance its own apple industry at the expense of the Washington apple growers who had gained a competitive and economic advantage through an expensive inspection and grading system.

Unduly Burdensome: Even if a state regulation of commerce is applied in an even-handed fashion, governing in-state and out-of-state businesses alike, it may be invalid if it unduly burdens the flow of interstate commerce. To be sustained, such a regulation must further a legitimate state interest, and that interest must outweigh the regulation's burden on interstate commerce. For example, a state requirement that cattle imported from other states be certified as free from certain types of diseases would be upheld so long as in-state cattle were required to meet the same standards in the interests of public health.

On the other hand, in *Kassell v. Consolidated Freightways Corp.,* 450 U.S. 662 (1981), the Supreme Court addressed an Iowa law which prohibited the use of 65-foot double-trailer trucks within its borders, while allowing 55-foot single trailers and 60-foot double trailers. States around Iowa all allowed 65-foot double trailers, but Iowa claimed the law was a safety measure. Statistics showed, however, that accidents were a function of mileage rather than truck size. Iowa's law actually worked against safety interests by requiring use of smaller trucks which

would have to drive more miles to deliver the same load. It surely burdened the flow of interstate commerce by requiring 65-foot double trailers either to go around Iowa or unload onto smaller trucks when reaching the Iowa border. Exceptions in the law made it appear that Iowa was trying to gain the benefits of large trucks while shunting to neighboring states the costs associated with their use. The law was invalidated.

The following case involves a recent application of the prohibitions against the undue burdening of interstate commerce.

Brown-Forman Distillers Corp. v. New York State Liquor Authority
U.S. Supreme Court, 106 S.Ct. 2080 (1986)

New York's Alcoholic Beverage Control Law (ABC Law) provided that a distiller, licensed to do business in the State, could not sell its products to wholesalers within the State except in accordance with a monthly price schedule previously filed with the State Liquor Control Authority, and required that the distiller include with the schedule an affirmation that the prices in the schedule were no higher than the lowest prices that the distiller would charge wholesalers anywhere else in the United States during the month. The Liquor Authority (appellee) determined that the ABC Law prohibited Brown-Forman (appellant) from offering certain promotional allowances (based on past purchases and projections of future purchases) to wholesalers in the State, and that the payment of the allowances to wholesalers in other States lowered the "effective price" of appellant's products in violation of the affirmation provision of the ABC law. Appellee instituted license revocation procedures and appellant sought court review. The New York trial and appellate courts found no violation of the Commerce Clause arising from the ABC law. The distiller appealed.

Marshall, Justice:

This Court has adopted what amounts to a two-tiered approach in analyzing state economic regulation under the Commerce Clause. When a state statute directly regulates or discriminates against interstate commerce, or when its effect is to favor in-state economic interests over out-of-state interests, we have generally struck down the statute without further inquiry. *See, e.g., Philadelphia v. New Jersey,* 437 U.S. 617 (1978). When, however, a statute has only indirect effects on interstate commerce and regulates evenhandedly, we have examined whether the State's interest is legitimate and whether the burden on interstate commerce clearly exceeds the local benefits. *Pike v. Bruce Church, Inc.,* 397 U.S. 137 (1970). We have also recognized that there is no clear line separating the category of state regulation that is virtually *per se* invalid under the Commerce Clause, and the category subject to the *Pike v. Bruce Church* balancing approach. In either situation the critical consideration is the overall effect of the statute on both local and interstate activity.

Appellant does not dispute that New York's affirmation law regulates all distillers of intoxicating liquors evenhandedly, or that the State's asserted interest—to assure the lowest possible prices for its residents—is legitimate. Appellant contends that these factors are irrelevant, however, because the lowest-price affirmation provision of the ABC Law falls within that category of direct regulations of interstate commerce that the Commerce Clause wholly forbids. This is so, appellant contends, because the ABC Law effectively regulates the price at which liquor is sold in other States. Appellant contends that this constitutes direct regulation of interstate commerce. The law also disadvantages consumers in other States, according to appellant, and is therefore the sort of "simple economic protectionism" that this Court has routinely forbidden.

If appellant has correctly characterized the effect of the New York lowest-price affirmation law, that law violates the Commerce Clause. While a State may seek lower prices for its consumers, it may not insist that producers or consumers in other States surrender whatever competitive advantages they may possess. Economic protectionism is not limited to attempts to convey advantages on local merchants; it may include attempts to give local consumers an advantage over consumers in other States. The mere fact that the effects of New York's ABC Law are triggered only by sales of liquor within the State of New York therefore does not validate the law if it regulates the out-of-state transactions of distillers who sell in-state. Our inquiry, then, must center on whether New York's affirmation law regulates commerce in other States.

We agree with appellants that a "prospective" statute such as New York's liquor affirmation statute, regulates out-of-state transactions in violation of the Commerce Clause. Once a distiller has posted prices in New York, it is not free to change its prices elsewhere in the United States during the relevant month. Forcing a merchant to seek regulatory approval in one State before undertaking a transaction in another directly regulates interstate commerce. That the ABC Law is addressed only to sales of liquor in New York is irrelevant if the "practical effect" of the law is to control liquor prices in other States.

Moreover, the proliferation of state affirmation laws has greatly multiplied the likelihood that a seller will be subjected to inconsistent obligations in different States. The ease with which New York's lowest-price regulation can interfere with a distiller's operations in other States is aptly demonstrated by the controversy that gave rise to this lawsuit. By defining the "effective price" of liquor differently than other States, New York can effectively force appellant to abandon its promotional allowance program in States in which that program is legal, or force those other States to alter their own regulatory schemes in order to permit appellant to lower its New York prices without violating the affirmation laws of those States. Thus New York has "project[ed] its legislation" into other States, and directly regulated commerce therein.

[Reversed.]

Other State Limitations

At this point, two other constitutional limitations on the discretion of states are appropriately mentioned—the Full Faith and Credit Clause, and the Contract Clause.

Full Faith and Credit: Section 1 of Article IV of the Constitution provides in part that "Full faith and credit shall be given in each State to the public acts, records, and judicial proceedings of every other State." The import of the **Full Faith and Credit Clause** is quite clear: the courts of one state must recognize judgments and other public actions of its sister states. Thus a business firm that obtains a valid judgment against a debtor in one state may enforce that judgment in the courts of any other state in which that debtor's property may be located. The Full Faith and Credit Clause is, however, subject to a number of limitations. For example, if the court that entered the judgment originally did not have jurisdiction of the defendant, the courts of other states will not recognize the judgment. And the courts in a state in which a foreign judgment is sought to be enforced will not enforce that judgment if it violates the public policy of that state.

Contract Clause: Article I, Section 10 of the Constitution provides that "No State shall . . . pass any . . . Law impairing the Obligation of Contracts. . . ." This clause does not apply to the federal government, only to the acts of state legislatures. The thrust of the statute is to prevent states from changing the terms of *existing* contracts by passage of subsequent legislation.

The Contract Clause has undergone several vacillations in Supreme Court interpretation. At the moment, it appears that the proper application of the clause depends on whether a private contract or a public contract is at issue. If a private contract (one not involving the state as a party) is impaired by state legislation, the Contract Clause is violated unless the legislation (1) serves an important and legitimate public interest, (2) is necessary for the achievement of the public interest, and (3) is a reasonable impairment of the contract.

For example, in *Exxon Corporation v. Eagerton,* 462 U.S. 176 (1983), Exxon had for years paid a severance tax on oil and gas it drilled in Alabama. Under its sales contracts, it was able to pass on any tax increase to purchasers. When Alabama raised the severance tax and forbade producers of oil and gas from passing on the increase to purchasers, Exxon challenged the law as violative of the Contract Clause. The Supreme Court rejected Exxon's claim, stressing that the law was not aimed at impairing a specific, existing contract, but was instead a generally applicable rule of conduct designed to advance a broad societal interest (protecting consumers from excessive prices) that applied to all oil and gas producers regardless of whether they happened to be parties to contracts such as Exxon's.

The Supreme Court appears to give less deference to legislation which impairs public contracts, perhaps because the legislature's own self-interest is at stake. The key in such a case is whether the legislative modification is both reasonable and necessary to an important state purpose. For example, in *United States Trust Co. v. New Jersey,* 431 U.S. 1 (1977), the Court invalidated New York and New Jersey statutes whose sole effect was to repeal a covenant that the two states had entered into with the holders of bonds issued by The Port Authority of New York and New Jersey.

LEGISLATIVE, EXECUTIVE, AND JUDICIAL AUTHORITY

The framers of the Constitution, drawing upon the ideas of Blackstone and Montesquieu, thought it imperative that the powers of the legislative, executive, and judicial branches be essentially separate from one another. This separation of powers is substantially brought about under the Constitution; and, by and large, the jurisdiction of each branch is clearly spelled out. Nonetheless, there are overlapping and gray areas. The executive branch has administrative law judges who perform essentially ministerial functions. The legislature has numerous investigative powers typically considered executive in nature. The judiciary clearly makes "law" through its interpretation of constitutional and statutory provisions. These are but a few examples of the exceptions to the separation of powers doctrine. Some of the overlaps cause legal problems.

Legislative Branch

Earlier in this chapter we saw that Article I, Section 8 of the Constitution enumerates the primary congressional powers. The ultimate source of congressional authority is in the specific provisions of the Constitution. Only in the realm of foreign affairs has the notion that the government has inherent power, independent of the Constitution, gained any currency.

Congress is composed of but 535 members who must cope with the most difficult and complex of problems. As we shall see in the next chapter, the courts have long recognized that the complexities of modern society require that Congress be allowed to delegate its legislative power to administrative agencies. Although that power to delegate, for very practical reasons, is construed broadly, the doctrine of separation of powers does impose some limitations.

For example, in *Bowsher v. Synar,* 106 S.Ct. 3181 (1986), the Supreme Court faced a legal challenge to the Balanced Budget and Emergency Deficit Control Act of 1985 ("Gramm-Rudman"), which established an automatic deficit reduction process. In the Act, Congress set a "maximum deficit amount" for each of the fiscal years 1986 through 1991. Each year the Directors of the Office of Management and Budget (OMB) and the Congressional Budget Office (CBO) were to estimate the amount of the deficit of the upcoming year. They then were to calculate program-by-program reductions necessary to achieve the target deficits and report to the Comptroller General who was required to issue his own report to the President who must issue a "sequestration" order containing the budget reductions specified by the Comptroller General. The Court found that this delegation of power to the Comptroller General violated the constitutionally requisite separation of powers. The powers conferred on the Comptroller General, the Court held, cannot constitutionally be exercised by an officer removable by Congress because they are executive-type powers.

Judicial Branch

Because there is very little federal "common law," the federal courts "make law" primarily through the interpretation of statutory and constitutional provisions. Atop the federal judiciary, of course, is the United States Supreme Court, the most powerful court in the world.

The Supreme Court's power to reverse the decisions of lower federal courts has always been accepted. What was not clear, at least early in the days of the Republic, was the question of which branch of government would reign supreme regarding Constitutional issues. The Constitution itself does not expressly grant authority to determine challenges to the constitutionality of actions of the legislature or the executive. However, in *Marbury v. Madison,* 5 U.S. 137 (1805), the Supreme Court assumed the power of **judicial review.** Under the doctrine of judicial review, the federal courts have the final say in whether the Constitution has been violated by a congressional law or an executive action.

Not long after *Marbury v. Madison,* the Supreme Court also assumed the power to review the decisions of state courts in both civil and criminal cases in which federal constitutional issues were at stake. The Supreme Court is truly the final arbiter of the meaning of the Constitution. It is no exaggeration to state that "the Constitution means what the Supreme Court says it means."

Executive Branch

The Executive Branch of the federal government contains a plethora of powers. Enforcement of the laws passed by Congress is no doubt the executive branch's chief responsibility. A variety of investigative and even quasi-judicial powers are brought to bear in accomplishing the task. Through **executive orders** the executive branch makes law. Sometimes these orders only direct the manner in which acts of Congress shall be implemented; sometimes, when issued in the absence of congressional authority, they may be subject to court challenge.

Although the President, as head of the executive branch, is correctly termed the most powerful person in the world, our constitutional system insists that any actions of the executive branch be authorized either by the Constitution or by congressional action. If unauthorized actions occur, the doctrine of judicial review may be invoked, as the following landmark case illustrates.

Youngstown Sheet and Tube Co. v. Sawyer
U.S. Supreme Court, 72 S.Ct. 863 (1952)

In the latter part of 1951 a dispute arose between the nation's major steel mills and their employees over terms and conditions to be included in their new collective bargaining agreement. Lengthy negotiations proved fruitless, and the employees' representative, United Steelworkers of America, C.I.O., gave notice of an intent to strike when the existing bargaining agreements expired on December 31.

The Federal Mediation and Conciliation Service then intervened in an effort to get labor and management to agree. When this and other efforts were unsuccessful, President Truman issued Executive Order No. 10340, which directed the secretary of commerce to take possession of most of the country's steel mills and keep them running. The indispensability of steel as a component of substantially all weapons and other war materials then being used by the armed forces in Korea led the president to believe that the work stoppage would immediately jeopardize the nation's national defense and that government

seizure of the mills was necessary in order to insure the continued availability of steel.

The secretary of commerce immediately issued his own orders, calling upon the presidents of the various seized companies to serve as operating managers for the United States. They were directed to carry on their activities in accordance with regulations and directions of the secretary. The next morning the president sent a message to Congress reporting his action. He sent another message twelve days later, and Congress took no action thereon.

Obeying the secretary's orders under protest, the companies brought proceedings against him in the U.S. district court. Their complaints charged that the seizure was not authorized by an act of Congress or by any constitutional provisions. The district court was asked to declare the orders of the president and the secretary invalid and to issue preliminary and permanent injunctions restraining their enforcement. Opposing the motion for preliminary injunction, the United States asserted that a strike disrupting steel production for even a brief period would so endanger the well-being and safety of the nation that the president had "inherent power" to do what he had done—power "supported by the Constitution, by historical precedent, and by court decisions."

The district court held against the government on all points and issued a preliminary injunction restraining the secretary from "continuing the seizure and possession of the plants . . . and from acting under the purported authority of Executive Order No. 10340." On the same day, April 30, the U.S. Court of Appeals stayed the injunction, and the U.S. Supreme Court "granted certiorari" (agreed to review the lower court's proceedings).

Black, Justice:

. . . We are asked to decide whether the President was acting within his constitutional power when he issued an order directing the Secretary of Commerce to take possession of and operate most of the Nation's steel mills. . . .

Two crucial issues have developed: First. Should final determination of the constitutional validity of the President's order be made in this case which has proceeded no further than the preliminary injunction stage? Second. If so, is the seizure order within the constitutional power of the President?

I

[In regard to the first question, the Court ruled that under the compelling circumstances that existed, an inquiry into the constitutional questions at this stage was proper. The Court then addressed itself to the second question.]

II

The President's power, if any, to issue the order must stem either from an act of Congress or from the Constitution itself. [Emphasis added.] There is no statute that expressly authorizes the President to take possession of property as he did here. Nor is there any act of Congress to which our attention has been directed from which such a power can fairly be implied. Indeed, we do not understand the Government to rely on statutory authorization for this seizure. There are two statutes which do authorize the President to take both personal and real property under certain conditions [the Selective Service Act of 1948 and the Defense Production Act of 1950]. However, the Government admits that these conditions were not met and that the President's order was not rooted in either of the statutes. The Government refers to the seizure provisions of one of these statutes [§201(b) of the Defense Production Act] as "much too cumbersome, involved, and time-consuming for the crisis which was at hand."

Moreover, the use of the seizure technique to solve labor disputes in order to prevent work stoppages *was not only unauthorized by any congressional enactment; prior to this controversy, Congress had refused to adopt that method of settling labor disputes.* [Emphasis added.] When the Taft-Hartley Act was under consideration in 1947, Congress rejected an amendment which would have authorized such governmental seizures in cases of emergency. *It is clear that if the President had authority to issue the order he did, it must be found in some provisions of the Constitution.* [Emphasis added.] And it is not claimed that express constitutional language grants this power to the President. The contention is that presidential power should be implied from the aggregate of his powers under the Constitution. Particular reliance is placed on provisions in Article II which say that "the executive Power shall be fully executed"; and that he "shall be Commander in Chief of the Army and Navy of the United States."

The order cannot properly be sustained as an exercise of the President's military power as Commander in Chief of the Armed Forces. The Government attempts to do so by citing a number of cases upholding broad powers in military commanders engaged in day-to-day fighting in a theater of war. Such cases need not concern us here. *Even though "theater of war" be an expanding concept, we cannot with faithfulness to our constitutional system hold that the Commander in Chief of the Armed Forces has the ultimate power as such to take possession of private property in order to keep labor disputes from stopping production. This is a job for the Nation's lawmakers, not for its military authorities.* [Emphasis added.]

Nor can the seizure order be sustained because of the several constitutional provisions that grant executive power to the President. In the framework of our Constitution, the President's power to see that the laws are faithfully executed refutes the idea that he is to be a lawmaker. The Constitution limits his functions in the lawmaking process to the recommending of laws he thinks wise and the vetoing of laws he thinks bad. And the Constitution is neither silent nor equivocal about who shall make laws which the President is to execute. The first section of the first article says that "All legislative powers herein granted shall be vested in a Congress of the United States. . . ." After granting many powers to the Congress, Article I goes on to provide that Congress may "make all Laws which shall be necessary and proper for carrying into Execution the foregoing Powers and all other Powers vested by this Constitution in the Government of the United States, or in any Department or Officer thereof."

The President's order does not direct that a congressional policy be executed in a manner prescribed by Congress—it directs that a presidential policy be executed in a manner prescribed by the President. [Emphasis added.] The preamble of the order itself, like that of many statutes, sets out reasons why the President believes certain policies should be adopted, proclaims these policies as rules of conduct to be followed, and again, like a statute, authorizes a government official to promulgate additional rules and regulations consistent with the policy proclaimed and needed to carry that policy into execution. The power of Congress to adopt such public policies as those proclaimed by the order is beyond question. It can authorize the taking of private property for public use. It can make laws regulating the relationships between employers and employees, prescribing rules designed to settle labor disputes, and fixing wages and working conditions in certain fields of our economy. *The Constitution did not subject this law-making power of Congress to presidential or military supervision or control.* [Emphasis added.]

It is said that other Presidents without congressional authority have taken possession of private business enterprises in order to settle labor disputes. But even if this be true, Congress has not thereby lost its exclusive constitutional authority to make laws necessary and proper to carry out the powers vested by the Constitution "in the Government of the United States, or in any Department or Officer thereof."

The founders of this Nation entrusted the law-making power to the Congress alone in both good and bad times. It would do no good to recall the historical events, the fears of power and the hopes for freedom that lay behind their choice. Such a review would but confirm our holding that this seizure order cannot stand.

The judgment of the District Court is affirmed.

As much as anything else, the decision in *Youngstown Sheet and Tube Co. v. Sawyer* illustrates the widespread acceptance of the doctrine of judicial review. Although President Truman violently disagreed with the Supreme Court's interpretation of his authority in such a critical matter, he promptly and without question complied with the Court's decision.

A more recent illustration of the limitations of presidential power under the Constitution occurred in *United States v. Nixon,* 418 U.S. 683 (1974), which arose out of a criminal action against several of President Nixon's staff members as a result of their alleged obstruction of justice activities in the "Watergate coverup." When the U.S. district court hearing the criminal case demanded—at the request of the special prosecutor—that President Nixon produce tapes and documents involving specified communications between him and his staff members, he refused to do so on the ground that the doctrine of executive privilege immunized the office of the presidency against such orders from the judicial branch of government. When the case reached the Supreme Court, it unanimously held that the judiciary, not the president, was the constitutional arbiter authorized to determine the legitimate scope of executive privilege.

Turning to the specific question, the Court ruled that "neither the doctrine of separation of powers nor the need of confidentiality of high-level communications" could insulate the presidency from the demands for tapes and documents where (1) the communications did not involve diplomatic or national security matters, and (2) the demands were necessary to an important governmental process, in this case the prosecution of important criminal cases in the courts. Accordingly, the request for the materials was upheld, and Mr. Nixon acceded to it although he must have known that the incriminating evidence on the tapes would spell the end of his presidency.

BASIC RIGHTS

The Constitution contains numerous limitations on the powers of the federal and state governments to restrict the freedoms of individuals and businesses. Many of our basic rights are guaranteed in the Bill of Rights—the first ten amendments to the Constitution. Others are found in the body of the original Constitution itself or in subsequent amendments such as the post-Civil War amendments freeing the slaves and protecting all citizens from unequal treatment by state governments.

Before we examine some of the more important freedoms which the Constitution protects, a couple of preliminary observations should be made. First, the Bill of Rights applies only to the *federal* government, not to the state and local governments. Nothing in the Constitution specifically prohibits the states from infringing, for example, on freedom of speech. However, through the **doctrine of incorporation**—which is well established but nonetheless controversial—the Supreme Court has extended virtually all of the important provisions of the Bill of Rights (freedom of speech, freedom of press, freedom of religion, right to counsel, privilege against self-incrimination, right against unreasonable search and seizure, and others) to the states. The Fourteenth Amendment to the Constitution does apply to the states, and it provides that they may not deprive citizens of **due process of law.** The Supreme Court has broadly construed the concept of due process to include "principles of justice so rooted in the tradition and conscience of our people as to be ranked as fundamental" and thus "implicit in the concept of ordered liberty." [2] Most of the rights protected from federal infringement by the Bill of Rights have been deemed part of this "concept of ordered liberty" and therefore protected from infringement by state and local government.

Second, the prohibitions on infringements of individual rights in the Constitution apply to governmental bodies, but not to private individuals. On its face, nothing in the Constitution would prevent a private employer from denying its employees any or all constitutional rights. However, constitutional protections apply to any "state action," a concept that has been interpreted to cover the actions of private individuals and businesses where the state compelled or sig-

---

[2] *Palko v. Connecticut,* 302 U.S. 319 (1937).

nificantly participated in the private conduct. For example, in *Burton v. Wilmington Parking Authority,* 365 U.S. 715 (1961), the discriminatory actions of a restaurant which operated as an "integral part" of a public parking building in which it was located were held to be "state actions" and therefore prohibited by the Fourteenth Amendment's equal protection provisions.

Further, as noted earlier, Congress has broad powers under the Commerce Clause to legislate civil rights protections. The *Heart of Atlanta Motel* case upheld such legislation.

Privileges and Immunities

Section 2 of Article IV of the Constitution provides, in part, that "The citizens of each State shall be entitled to all privileges and immunities of the several states." The basic import of the **Privileges and Immunities Clause** is that, in general, a state cannot discriminate against citizens of another state solely because of their foreign citizenship. Thus a state cannot prohibit travel by nonresidents within its borders, nor can a state deny nonresident plaintiffs access to its court system.

The Privileges and Immunities Clause is, however, subject to many judicially imposed limitations. For example, a state law may—within reasonable limits—subject nonresidents to certain limitations if the law involves protection of a matter of "legitimate local interest." Therefore a state statute may provide that in letting contracts for the construction of public buildings, preference may be given to raw materials or products produced within that state. Similarly, because state universities are essentially supported by taxation of residents, and also because of the interest that residents have in such schools, the charging of higher tuition for nonresident students does not violate the Privileges and Immunities Clause.[3] And since corporations are *not* "citizens" within the meaning of this clause, nonresident corporations can be subject to higher tax rates than those applicable to domestic corporations. (Such rates cannot, however, be so high as to be "confiscatory" in nature—that is, enacted largely as a punishment for the privilege of doing business—or be so onerous as to effectively exclude nonresidents from doing business within the state, for such taxation would likely violate both the Due Process and Commerce Clauses of the Constitution.)

In the following case, the U.S. Supreme Court was called upon to determine whether an Alaskan statute violated the Privileges and Immunities Clause.

---

[3] *Johns v. Redeker,* 406 F.2d 878 (1969). (The U.S. Supreme Court let this decision stand by denying certiorari.)

Hicklin v. Orbeck
U.S. Supreme Court, 437 U.S. 518 (1978)

Alaska passed a statute in 1972 (known as "Alaska Hire") for the avowed purpose of reducing unemployment within the state. The key provision of the statute required all employers engaged in specific lines of work to hire qualified Alaskan residents in preference to nonresidents. The types of employment covered by the act were, for the most part, activities relating to "oil and gas leases, and easements or right-of-way permits for oil or gas pipeline purposes." To implement the act, persons who had resided in the state for a minimum

period of one year were furnished "resident cards" as proof of their preferred status.

Hicklin and others, plaintiffs, were nonresidents who had worked on the Trans-Alaska pipeline for short periods until late 1975, when the act was first enforced. In 1976, when plaintiffs were refused employment on the pipeline, they brought this action against Orbeck, the state official charged with enforcement of Alaska Hire, contending that the act violated the Privileges and Immunities Clause. The Supreme Court of Alaska, by a vote of three to two, held that the law was constitutional. Plaintiffs appealed.

Brennan, Justice:

. . . The Privileges and Immunities Clause . . . establishes a norm of comity that is to prevail among the States with respect to their treatment of each other's residents. . . . Appellants' appeal to the protection of this Clause is strongly supported by this Court's decisions holding violative of the Clause state discrimination against nonresidents seeking to ply their trade, practice their occupation, or pursue a common calling within the State. For example, in [an early case this Court] . . . recognized that a resident of one State is constitutionally entitled to travel to another State for purposes of employment free from discriminatory restrictions in favor of state residents imposed by the other State.

Again, [in] *Toomer v. Witsell,* 334 U.S. 385 (1948), the leading exposition of the limitations the Clause places on a State's power to bias employment opportunities in favor of its own residents, [this Court] invalidated a South Carolina statute that required nonresidents to pay a fee 100 times greater than that paid by residents for a license to shrimp commercially in the three-mile maritime belt off the coast of that state. The Court reasoned that although the Privileges and Immunities Clause "does not preclude disparity of treatment in the many situations where there are perfectly valid independent reasons for it, it does bar discrimination against citizens of other States where there is no substantial reason for the discrimination beyond the mere fact that they are citizens of other States." A "substantial reason for the discrimination" would not exist, the Court explained, "unless there is something to indicate that noncitizens constitute a peculiar source of the evil at which the statute is aimed." . . .

Even assuming that a State may validly attempt to alleviate its unemployment problem by requiring private employers within the State to discriminate against nonresidents—an assumption made at least dubious [by prior cases]—it is clear under the *Toomer* analysis that Alaska Hire's discrimination against nonresidents cannot withstand scrutiny under the Privileges and Immunities Clause. For although the Statute may not violate the Clause if the State shows [in the words of *Toomer*] "something to indicate that noncitizens constitute a peculiar source of evil," *certainly no showing was made on this record that nonresidents were a peculiar source of the evil [that] Alaska*

Hire was enacted to remedy, namely, Alaska's uniquely high unemployment. [Emphasis added.] What evidence the record does contain indicates that the major cause of Alaska's high unemployment was not the influx of nonresidents seeking employment, but rather the fact that a substantial number of Alaska's jobless residents—especially the unemployed Eskimo and Indian residents—were unable to secure employment either because of their lack of education and job training or because of their geographical remoteness from job opportunities. The employment of nonresidents threatened to deny jobs to Alaska residents only to the extent that jobs for which untrained residents were being prepared might be filled by nonresidents before the residents' training was completed.

Moreover, even if the State's showing is accepted as sufficient to indicate that nonresidents were "a peculiar source of evil," *Toomer* compels the conclusion that Alaska Hire nevertheless fails to pass constitutional muster, [because] the discrimination the Act works against nonresidents does not bear a substantial relationship to the particular "evil" they are said to present. Alaska Hire simply grants all Alaskans, regardless of their employment status, education, or training, a flat employment preference for all jobs covered by the Act. A highly skilled and educated resident who has never been unemployed is entitled to precisely the same preferential treatment as the unskilled, habitually unemployed Arctic Eskimo enrolled in a job-training program. If Alaska is to attempt to ease its unemployment problem by forcing employers within the State to discriminate against nonresidents—again, a policy which [itself] may present serious constitutional questions—the means by which it does so must be more closely tailored to aid the unemployed the Act is intended to benefit. Even if a statute granting an employment preference to unemployed residents or to residents enrolled in job-training programs might be permissible, Alaska Hire's across-the-board grant of a job preference to all Alaskan residents clearly is not. . . . [For these reasons,] Alaska Hire cannot withstand constitutional scrutiny.

Judgment reversed.

Freedom of Religion

The First Amendment contains two clauses protecting freedom of religion. It provides that "Congress shall make no law [1] respecting an establishment of religion, or [2] prohibiting the free exercise thereof." Although the Establishment and Free Exercise Clauses overlap (and sometimes even conflict), they clearly create two separate guarantees. Both guarantees provide that the government's role is to be one of "benevolent neutrality," neither advancing nor inhibiting religion.

Establishment Clause: A large part of the metaphorical "wall" between church and state arises from the **Establishment Clause,** which prohibits the government from establishing a state religion and, according to the Supreme Court, from financially supporting religion, becoming actively involved in religion, or favoring one religion over another.

The most controversial manifestation of the Supreme Court's view of the Establishment Clause is probably the "school prayer" case, *Engel v. Vitale,* 370 U.S. 421 (1962). The New York State Board of Regents had written a nondenominational prayer to be recited by students in school on a voluntary basis. The Supreme Court found an Establishment Clause violation, saying, in part, that "the constitutional prohibition against laws respecting an establishment of a religion must at least mean that in this country it is no part of the business of government to compose official prayers for any group of the American people to recite as a part of a religious program carried on by any government."

An attempt to circumvent *Engel v. Vitale* by institution of a "moment of silence" in the public schools "for meditation or voluntary prayer" was declared unconstitutional in the recent case, *Wallace v. Jaffree,* 105 S.Ct. 2479 (1985). The legislative history of the law in question made it clear that its primary purpose was to promote religion.

When a state or federal law is challenged as violative of the Establishment Clause, it will be evaluated by a three-pronged test. First, the court will ask whether the law has a secular (nonreligious) purpose. If there is no such purpose, the law is invalid. Even if the law has a secular purpose, the court will ask, second, whether its *primary* purpose is to advance or inhibit religion. If the answer is in the affirmative, the law is unconstitutional. If the answer is in the negative, the court will ask, third, whether the law fosters excessive government entanglement with religion. Such entanglement might include government evaluation of religious practices, extensive government involvement in church finances and operations, or government attempts to classify what is religious and what is not. Presence of such entanglement obviously indicates an Establishment Clause violation.

A recent Establishment Clause case worth mentioning is *Estate of Thornton v. Caldor, Inc.,* 105 S.Ct. 2914 (1985), which involved a Connecticut statute guaranteeing every employee who "states that a particular day of the week is observed as his Sabbath," the right not to work on his chosen day. Because the law gave an absolute preference to the worker's religious practice, no matter how severe the hardship to the employer, the Court held that its primary purpose was to advance religion. Federal law validly requires that employers subject to Title VII, discussed in our later chapter on employment law, make "reasonable accommodations" for the religious practices of employees. But an absolute preference is invalid.

Finally, although the trend across the country is for states to repeal so-called **blue laws**—statutes and ordinances that limit or prohibit the carrying on of specified business activities on Sunday—such laws are generally upheld in the courts on the ground that the primary purpose of such statutes is the furtherance of legitimate social or economic ends, which affect religious beliefs and practices only incidentally. The case of *Braunfeld v. Brown,* 366 U.S. 599 (1961), is an example of such a view. There a Pennsylvania statute prohibited the retail sale of clothing and home furnishings, among other items, on Sundays. Its constitutionality was challenged by members of the Orthodox Jewish faith whose beliefs required them to abstain from all work and trade from Friday nights until Saturday nights, and who, therefore, customarily opened their stores on Sundays. The U.S. Supreme Court, in upholding the statute, said,

> If the purpose or effect of a law is to impede the observance of one or all religions or is to discriminate invidiously between religions, that law is constitutionally invalid. . . . But if the State regulates conduct by enacting a general law within its power, the purpose and effect of which is to advance the State's secular [nonreligious] goals, the statute is valid despite its indirect burden on religious observances. . . . We cannot find a State without power to provide a weekly respite from all labor and, at the same time, to set aside one day of the week apart from the others as a day of rest, repose, recreation and tranquility. . . .

Free Exercise Clause: The general thrust of this clause is to guarantee to all persons the right of religious belief and the freedom to practice their beliefs without governmental interference. The government may not single out any particular religion for discrimination. In order to claim the protection of the Free Exercise Clause, a plaintiff must normally prove that he is a sincere adherent of an established religion and that a fundamental tenet of that religion is at stake in the case. These requirements weed out spurious, insincere, and trivial claims.

Under the Free Exercise Clause, plaintiffs, frequently belonging to religious minorities, have paved the way for the religious freedoms we all enjoy. For example, in *West Virginia State Board of Education v. Barnette,* 319 U.S. 624 (1943), the Supreme Court held that a board of education requirement that students salute the flag and say the pledge of allegiance was unconstitutional as applied to plaintiff Jehovah's Witnesses. The court said: "If there is any fixed star in our constitutional constellation, it is that no official, high or petty, can prescribe what shall be orthodox in politics, nationalism, religion, or other matters of opinion, or force citizens to confess by word or act their faith therein. If there are any circumstances which permit an exception, they do not now occur to us."

In order to overcome the very important interest in free exercise of religious beliefs, the government must demonstrate that an unusually important interest is at stake (denominated in various cases "compelling," "of the highest order," or "overriding") and that granting an exemption to plaintiff will do substantial harm to that interest. The government has succeeded in cases requiring vaccinations for children against their parents' religious objections in furtherance of public health, in cases requiring medical treatment for children over their parents' objections where such treatment was necessary to save the child's life, and in cases banning the handling of poisonous snakes in religious services.

Freedom of Speech

None of the many rights Americans enjoy is protected more than freedom of speech. The First Amendment provides that "Congress shall make no law . . . abridging the freedom of speech." Un-

like citizens in so many other countries, we may freely criticize public officials and the laws of our government.

The Free Speech Clause protects messages that are both oral and written. It protects symbolic action, such as picketing and the wearing of black armbands (although conduct is frequently given slightly less protection than true speech). The First Amendment even protects the giving of money to political campaigns as a form of speech.

Implicit in the freedom to speak is the freedom not to speak in favor of causes we do not support. In the recent *Pacific Gas & Electric Co. v. Public Utilities Commission of California,* 106 S.Ct. 903 (1986), the Supreme Court overturned on free speech grounds a California Public Utilities Commission order which required a privately owned utility to include in its billing envelopes speech of a consumer group with which the utility disagreed. The court found that the order impermissibly burdened the utility's freedom not to speak which is protected because all speech inherently involves choices of what to say and what to leave unsaid.

Scope of Protection: Of course, like our other freedoms, the freedom of speech is not absolute. In the famous words of Justice Holmes, one is not free to yell "Fire" in a crowded theatre. Among the relatively few types of speech that are not protected by the First Amendment are obscenity, defamatory statements, and so-called "fighting words." Obscene speech is viewed as having no true value in a democratic society.

Defamatory statements, which by definition are untrue statements which injure another's reputation, similarly have nothing to contribute to a public debate of the issues in a free society. The impact of the freedom of speech on the tort of defamation is discussed in Chapter 7. "Fighting words" are epithets which by their nature are likely to lead to an outbreak of violence. Their minimal social value is viewed as outweighed by the danger to society. However, the "fighting words" exception is narrowly construed. As the Supreme Court said in *Cox v. Louisiana,* 379 U.S. 536 (1965), "Mere expression of unpopular views cannot be held to be a breach of peace." Sometimes the government has an obligation to provide protection for the speakers for unpopular positions.

Speech which is critical of the government, no matter how disrespectful or "unpatriotic," is amply protected by the Free Speech Clause. All such views contribute to the marketplace of ideas in a free society. Many prior Supreme Court cases have allowed the government to penalize speech that advocates the use of force or violation of the law. However, in *Brandenburg v. Ohio,* 395 U.S. 444 (1969), the Court held that even speech calling for the overthrow of the government or other illegal action is protected unless it is "directed to inciting or producing *imminent* lawless action and is *likely* to incite or produce such action."

Although the government cannot regulate the content of our speech, it can impose reasonable **time, place, and manner** restrictions on that speech. A city cannot tell the Ku Klux Klan it can never hold a rally, but it can prohibit the Klan from holding a rally in a hospital zone at 2:00 a.m.

Commercial Speech: In recent years the Supreme Court has decided that **commercial speech**—speech intended primarily to propose a commercial transaction—is protected by the First Amendment, though not quite to the extent that political speech is protected. Thus, in *Virginia Board of Pharmacy v. Virginia Citizens Consumers Council,* 425 U.S. 748 (1976), the Supreme Court struck down a ban on advertising the prices of over-the-counter drugs. Absolute prohibitions on advertising by lawyers were invalidated in *Bates v. Arizona State Bar,* 433 U.S. 350 (1977). Prohibitions on the posting of "for sale" signs on real estate were found violative of the Free Speech Clause in *Linmark Associates, Inc. v. Township of Willingboro,* 431 U.S. 85 (1977), though they had the purpose of preventing "white flight" from racially integrated neighborhoods.

According to the Supreme Court, commercial speech is protectable primarily because of the informational value it has for the listener (or reader). Drug consumers in the *Virginia Pharmacy* case could not learn, before the advertising ban was struck down, that variations of price of up to 600 percent existed commonly among competing stores. Information about the prices lawyers charge was viewed as valuable consumer information in *Bates.* Obviously, false advertising carries no informational value to the listener and is therefore unprotected by the First Amendment. The same may be said for speech proposing illegal transactions.

Truthful commercial speech, the Supreme Court has held, cannot be prohibited unless (1) a substantial government interest is served by the restriction, (2) the restriction directly advances that government interest, and (3) the restriction is no more extensive than necessary to serve that interest.

Corporate Speech: The First Amendment does not protect only the speech of individuals. It also protects the speech of corporations, though perhaps not to as great a degree. Like commercial speech, corporate speech is protected because of the informational value it carries. Whether commercial or political in nature, the speech of a corporation adds to the public pool of information and to the public debate on issues of importance. Thus, in *First National Bank of Boston v. Bellotti,* 435 U.S. 765 (1978), the Supreme Court struck down a state criminal statute which prohibited expenditures by business corporations for the purpose of influencing the vote on state referendum proposals not "materially affecting" any of the business of the corporation, noting: "The inherent worth of the speech in terms of its capacity for informing the public does not depend upon the identity of its source, whether corporation, association, union, or individual."

The Shopping Center Issue: In recent years a number of cases have arisen involving the constitutionality of regulations of privately-owned shopping centers and malls, which typically prohibit "soliciting, speech-making and the seeking of signatures on petitions" on their premises. Prior to 1972, the Supreme Court held that because they were open to the public, shopping malls were the "functional equivalent" of public property and therefore the actions of the mall owners constituted "state action" governed by the Constitution (i.e., the Free Speech Clause of the First Amendment as incorporated into the Fourteenth Amendment's Due Process Clause). However, in *Hudgens v. N.L.R.B.,* 424 U.S. 507 (1976), the Supreme Court expressly overruled the pre-1972 cases, holding that the actions of the owners of shopping malls were not state action and therefore not restricted by the U.S. Constitution.

In a later case, *PruneYard Shopping Center v. Robins,* 447 U.S. 74 (1980), where a group of high school students set up a card table in a shopping center's central area and asked passersby to sign petitions opposing a United Nations resolution against Zionism, the Supreme Court agreed with the California Supreme Court that PruneYard regulation's banning the activity violated the California Constitution. *PruneYard* thus indicated that even though shopping mall owners do not violate the U.S. Constitution, they still must comply with state constitutional restrictions. A few other states have interpreted their constitutions as broadly as California's was construed in *PruneYard.*

Equal Protection

The Fourteenth Amendment was passed in 1868, shortly after the Civil War. It states, in part, that "No State shall . . . deny to any person within its jurisdiction the equal protection of the laws." Although no provision of the Constitution explicitly mentions equal protection in connection with the *federal* government, the concept has been held to be implicit in the Fifth Amendment's Due Process Clause. Thus, no government, state or federal, may deny individuals or companies equal protection of the laws.

Because virtually every law and regulation involves distinctions and differences—e.g., applying to some industries, but not to others; applying to larger companies, but not to smaller ones; giving benefits to older people, but not to younger ones—many legal questions involving the **Equal Protection Clause** arise. The Supreme Court has used different formulations to gauge the legality of different types of distinctions. Three major types of distinctions that we shall discuss are (1) those involved in economic and social regulation, (2) those based on "suspect criteria", and (3) those involving gender discrimination.

Economic and Social Regulations: The Supreme Court realizes that legislatures must make distinctions in passing economic and social legislation. Only the poor need welfare; the rich do not. Some industries will cause pollution; others do not. Some jobs will imperil the safety of workers; others will not. Therefore, the Supreme Court uses a fairly lax standard for economic and social legislation when equal protection challenges are raised. If the distinction at issue bears a "rational relationship to a legitimate government interest," it will be sustained. Only if no reasonable state of facts can be conceived of to justify it, and it is clearly a display of arbitrary power and not a matter of judgment, will such a distinction be invalidated on equal protection grounds.

To decide that the "rational relationship" test applies is almost to decide the case. There is such a strong presumption of reasonableness that discriminations in economic and social legislation are almost always upheld. Distinctions need not be drawn with "mathematical nicety" nor must a legislature attack all aspects of a problem at once. Thus, a law requiring operators of "flea markets" who leased space to persons wishing to sell automobiles to have a type of license that persons who leased land to regular car dealers need not have, constituted permissible discrimination. The state has a legitimate interest in preventing fraud, and it is rational to presume that fraud will be a bigger problem in a "flea market" than in a stationary car dealership which will likely be there when a defrauded customer goes back to complain.[4] Similarly, in *Minnesota Clover Leaf Creamery Co.,* 449 U.S. 456 (1981), a Minnesota statute which banned the retail sale of milk in nonreturnable, nonrefillable plastic containers, but which permitted such sale in paperboard containers was sustained. Whether or not elimination of the plastic milk jug would in fact encourage the use of environmentally superior containers was not the issue, the Supreme Court held. "The Equal Protection Clause is satisfied by our conclusion that the Minnesota legislature could rationally have decided" that it would.

However, this is not to say that challenges under the rational relationship test are never successful. In *City of Cleburne v. Cleburne Living Center,* 105 S.Ct. 3249 (1985), for example, plaintiffs wished to establish a closely supervised and highly regulated home for the mentally retarded in Cleburne. The city required a special use permit for "homes for the lunatic" and denied plaintiff's request. The Court found that the denial was not based on any valid concern for public safety, but on an irrational prejudice against the retarded, and sustained plaintiffs' equal protection claim.

Suspect Criteria: If a law discriminates against "discrete and insular minorities", it utilizes "suspect criteria" under the Equal Protection Clause and is very much subject to challenge. Suspect criteria naturally include classifications based on race, but persons of Mexican ancestry and occasionally aliens have been protected also.

A law is also highly suspect if it discriminates among people regarding the exercise of certain "fundamental rights" (including freedom of association, right to travel interstate, right of privacy, right to vote, and freedom of speech).

Such laws undergo "strict scrutiny" and will be invalidated under the equal protection concept unless the challenged distinctions serve a *compelling state interest.* This is a very difficult test to meet, and almost always leads to invalidation of the discrimination. In *Korematsu v. United States,* 323 U.S. 214 (1944), the Supreme Court found a compelling government interest in the need for war-time national security, and therefore upheld discrimination against persons of Japanese ancestry in the form of relocation away from the West Coast and internment in prisonlike camps. History shows that this relocation was based on fear and prejudice rather than any real danger to security. The Supreme Court will henceforth be very careful before it finds that an interest justifies racial discrimination.

For example, in *Palmore v. Sidoti,* 466 U.S. 429 (1984), the Court invalidated the action of a trial judge who took a child away from its mother, who was white, because she married a black man. The Court held that the trial court's decision to shield the child from "the reality of private biases" was an insufficient justification for a racial classification. Only in the area of "affirmative action," which we discuss later in the chapter on employment law, has the Supreme Court found interests (e.g., remedying past intentional discrimination, achieving diversity in college admissions) sufficient to justify a race-based classification. Occasionally the courts find government interests sufficient to justify a classification that discriminates in matters of fundamental rights, but this is also relatively rare.

If a classification is neutral on its face and in its administration, yet unintentionally produces a racially disproportionate impact (e.g., a verbal job test is failed in disproportionately high percentages by blacks), *de facto* **discrimination** exists. However, *de facto* discrimination is judged by the relatively lax "rational relationship" test, rather than by the "strict scrutiny" applied to intentional racial classifications.

The following case involves strict scrutiny of a classification which discriminates against a fundamental right—the right to travel.

---

[4] *North Dixie Theatre, Inc. v. McCullion,* 613 F.Supp. 1339 (S.D. Ohio 1985).

Attorney General of New York v. Soto-Lopez
U.S. Supreme Court, 106 S.Ct. 2317 (1986)

The New York Constitution and Civil Service Law grant a civil service employment preference, in the form of points added to examination scores, to New York residents who are honorably discharged veterans of the Armed Forces, served during time of war, and were New York residents when they entered military service. Appellee Army veterans, long-time New York residents, passed the New York City civil service examinations but were denied the veterans' preference because they were not New York residents when they joined the Army. They then brought this action in federal district court, alleging that the requirement that they had to have been New York residents when they joined the military violated the Equal Protection Clause of the Fourteenth Amendment and their constitutional right to travel. The district court dismissed the suit. The court of appeals reversed. The New York Attorney General (appellant) appealed the case to the Supreme Court.

Brennan, Justice:

"[F]reedom to travel throughout the United States has long been recognized as a basic right under the Constitution." *Dunn v. Blumstein,* 405 U.S. 330 (1978). And, it is clear that the freedom to travel includes the "freedom to enter and abide in any State in the Union." *Id.* The textual source of the constitutional right to travel, or, more precisely, the right of free interstate migration, though, has proven elusive. It has been variously assigned to the Privileges and Immunities Clause of Art. IV, to the Commerce Clause, and to the Privileges and Immunities Clause of the Fourteenth Amendment. The right has also been inferred from the federal structure of government adopted by our Constitution. Whatever its origin, the right to migrate is firmly established and has been repeatedly recognized by our cases.

A state law implicates the right to travel when it actually deters such travel, when impeding travel is its primary objective, or when it uses "any classification which serves to penalize the exercise of that right." *Dunn.* Because the creation of different classes of residents raises equal protection concerns, we have also relied upon the Equal Protection Clause in these cases. Whenever a state law infringes a constitutionally protected right, we undertake intensified equal protection scrutiny of that law. Thus, in several cases, we asked expressly whether the distinction drawn by the State between older and newer residents burdens the right to migrate. Where we found such a burden, we required the State to come forward with a compelling justification. In other cases, where we concluded that the contested classifications did not survive even rational basis scrutiny, we had no occasion to inquire whether enhanced scrutiny was appropriate. The analysis in all of these cases, however, is informed by the same guiding principle—the right to migrate protects residents of a State from being disadvantaged, or from being treated differently, simply because of the timing of their migration, from other similarly situated residents.

New York offers four interests in justification of its fixed point residence requirement: (1) the encouragement of New York residents to join the armed services; (2) the compensation of residents for service in time of war by helping those veterans reestablish themselves upon coming home; (3) the inducement of veterans to return to New York after wartime service; and (4) the employment of a "uniquely valuable class of public servants" who possess useful experience acquired through their military service. All four justifications fail to withstand heightened scrutiny on a common ground—each of the State's asserted interests could be promoted fully by granting bonus points to *all* otherwise qualified veterans. New York residents would still be encouraged to join the services. Veterans who served in time of war would be compensated. And, both former New Yorkers and prior residents of other States would be drawn to New York after serving the Nation, thus providing the State with an even larger pool of potentially valuable public servants.

As we held in *Dunn:* "[I]f there are other, reasonable ways to achieve [a compelling state purpose] with a lesser burden on constitutionally protected activity, a State may not choose the way of greater interference. If it acts at all, it must choose 'less drastic means.'" Compensating veterans for their past sacrifices by providing them with advantages over nonveteran citizens is a long-standing policy of our Federal and State Governments. Nonetheless, this policy, even if deemed compelling, does not support a distinction between resident veterans based on their residence when they joined the military. "Permissible discriminations between persons" must be correlated to "their *relevant* characteristics." *Zobel v. Williams,* 457 U.S. 55, 70 (1982) (Brennan, concurring). Because prior residence has only a tenuous relation, if any, to the benefit New York receives from all armed forces personnel, the goal of rewarding military service offers no support for New York's fixed point residence requirement.

[Affirmed.]

Gender Discrimination: Although the Supreme Court has not been completely consistent, it has tended to treat gender as a "quasi-suspect" classification. It has not required the demonstration of a compelling government interest to justify a gender-based classification. Instead, the government must prove that the classification bears a "*substantial* relationship to an *important* government interest." Thus, this is a middle-tier test, stricter than the mere rational relationship test, but not requiring the strict scrutiny of a racial classification.

An interesting case is *Michael M. v. Superior Court of Sonoma County,* 450 U.S. 464 (1981), wherein the Supreme Court upheld a California statutory rape law which defined unlawful sexual intercourse as "an act of sexual intercourse accomplished with a female not the wife of the perpetrator, where the female is under the age of 18 years," thus making men alone criminally liable. The law was justified, the Court held, because (1) the state has a strong interest in preventing illegitimate teenage pregnancies; (2) the law protects women from sexual intercourse and pregnancy at a time when its physical, emotional, and psychological consequences are particularly severe; (3) virtually all of the significant and identifiable consequences of teenage pregnancy fall on women; and (4) the law would have no deterrent impact if women failed to report violations for fear of facing criminal sanctions themselves.

And in *Arizona v. Norris,* 463 U.S. 1073 (1983), the Supreme Court struck down an Arizona state employees' retirement plan which paid women smaller monthly benefits than men because actuarial tables predicted that the average woman would live longer than the average man. The plan was deemed unfair to the plaintiff who could not count on living as long as the "average" female.

The most controversial topic in the realm of gender discrimination law today is whether women doing jobs that are different than those done by men but of *comparable worth* to the employer should be paid the same as the men. This issue is addressed in our chapter on employment law.

Due Process of Law

The Fifth Amendment, applicable to the federal government, provides in part that "No person shall . . . be deprived of life, liberty, or property without due process of law." The Fourteenth Amendment contains a clause imposing the same limitation upon state action. As interpreted by the courts, the concept of due process can be divided into two separate but related doctrines: substantive due process and procedural due process.

Substantive Due Process: At one time the doctrine of **substantive due process** was a strong bastion protecting businesses from government regulation in the form of social and eco-

nomic reform. In one leading case, a law limiting the number of hours bakers could work was found violative of substantive due process because it unreasonably interfered with "the freedom of master and employee to contract in relation to their employment." Today, however, this doctrine which once invalidated an entire range of social legislation has a completely different status.

Economic and Social Legislation: In matters of economic and social legislation, the doctrine of substantive due process has been completely eviscerated as a protective device for business. When such a law is challenged today, the courts simply ask whether it can be viewed as "arbitrary or irrational." The courts presume such laws to be valid, and will uphold them unless no reasonable state of facts can be conceived to support them. Indeed, the courts virtually rubberstamp legislative judgments in this area.

In *Duke Power Co. v. Carolina Environmental Study Group, Inc.,* 438 U.S. 59 (1978), for example, the Supreme Court addressed a substantive due process challenge to the Price-Anderson Act, which placed a statutory limit of $560 million on the liability of nuclear power plant licensees. Although the trial court found the limitation unconstitutional, as not rationally related to potential losses and as tending to encourage irresponsibility in safety matters, the Supreme Court reversed because it deemed the act not "arbitrary or irrational." The Court found the risk of accident "exceedingly small" and noted that Congress had indicated a willingness to appropriate public funds if losses exceeded $560 million. This was a standard piece of economic legislation that should be presumed valid.

Individual Rights: In recent years the doctrine of substantive due process has been used more to protect valuable individual rights than as a shield for business. Although development in this area has been piecemeal on a case-by-case basis, substantive due process has been used to protect the right of privacy in matters of birth control, the right of personal autonomy in abortion cases, family rights when zoning restrictions have prohibited related persons from living together, and the right to reasonably safe conditions, freedom from bodily restraint, and minimally adequate training for the mentally ill.

Procedural Due Process: The primary purpose of the doctrine of **procedural due process** is to prevent the federal and state governments from depriving individuals of certain basic rights in an unfair or arbitrary manner. While life, liberty, and property can be taken in certain circumstances, the main thrust of the Due Process Clause—and the case law that has resulted under it—is that such deprivation should occur only by virtue of judicially acceptable proceedings. The underlying philosophy is aptly summed up in this statement:

> "Due process of law" implies at least a conformity with natural and inherent principles of justice, and forbids that one man's property, or right to property, shall be taken for the benefit of another, or for the benefit of the state, without compensation, and that no one shall be condemned in his person or property without an opportunity of being heard in his own defense."[5]

The guarantee springing from procedural due process extends to both criminal and civil proceedings. In criminal proceedings, the courts are especially solicitous of the rights of a defendant facing a deprivation of liberty. Key concerns include adequacy of notice of the charges, representation by counsel, fair selection of the jury, the ability to confront and cross-examine witnesses and to present evidence, and the impartiality of the judge. The statute under which a criminal charge is brought must also not be so vague as to fail to prescribe a "reasonable standard of guilt." In *City of Columbus v. Thomp-*

son, 25 Ohio St.2d 25 (1971), the defendant was charged under a municipal "suspicious person" ordinance, which defined a suspicious person as one "who wanders about the streets or other public ways or who is found abroad at late or unusual hours of the night without any visible or lawful business and who does not give satisfactory account of himself." The Ohio Supreme Court held the ordinance violated procedural due process by leaving the public "uncertain as to the conduct it prohibits" and leaving "judges and jurors free to decide, without any legally fixed standards, what is prohibited and what is not in each particular case."

Standards need not be so stringent when property, rather than life or liberty are at stake. Still, in our civilized society the basic rights to notice, hearing,[6] and an impartial decisionmaker are valued. In a recent civil case, for example, the Supreme Court held that an insurance company's due process rights were violated by a decision of the Alabama Supreme Court which adopted a new theory of recovery at the same time that it sustained a very large punitive damages verdict against the company. The judge who wrote the opinion, it turned out, was a plaintiff in two similar cases and would directly benefit from the decision. The Supreme Court wrote that it violates the Due Process Clause "to subject [a person's] liberty or property to the judgment of a court the judge of which has a direct, personal, substantial, pecuniary interest in reaching a conclusion against him in his case."[7]

Many due process cases involve actions of government agencies which adversely affect the economic interests of individuals and companies. An illustrative case appears in the next chapter on administrative law. In these and other procedural due process cases, the proper ap-

---

[5] *Holden v. Hardy,* 169 U.S. 366 (1898).

[6] The matter of a fair opportunity to be heard under the Due Process Clause was the key issue in *Helicopteros Nacionales de Colombia v. Hall* in Chapter 2.

[7] *Aetna Life Ins. Co. v. Lavoie,* 106 S.Ct. 1580 (1986).

proach is first to determine whether plaintiff has a protectable life, liberty, or property interest at stake. If so, then the court must ask how much "process is due" under all the circumstances.

The more serious the potential deprivation, the more elaborate the protections the courts will require. The following case is a recent Supreme Court pronouncement on the matter.

Cleveland Board of Education v. Loudermill
U.S. Supreme Court, 105 S.Ct. 1487 (1985)

The Cleveland Board of Education informed Loudermill, a security guard, that his employment was being terminated because he had lied on his employment application about a 1968 grand larceny conviction. Loudermill was not afforded an opportunity to respond to the charge of dishonesty or to challenge his dismissal. He did file an appeal with the Cleveland Civil Service Commission which appointed a referee who eventually held a hearing. Loudermill argued that he didn't state on the employment application that he had been convicted of a felony because he thought the 1968 conviction was a misdemeanor. The referee recommended reinstatement. But, after oral argument, the Commission upheld the dismissal.

The Cleveland Board also fired Donnelly, a bus mechanic, because he had failed an eye examination. He was offered a chance to retake the exam, but did not do so. Like Loudermill, Donnelly appealed to the Civil Service Commission, which ordered Donnelly reinstated, though without back pay. The procedures before the Civil Service Commission for both Loudermill and Donnelly took around a year to run their course.

Both Loudermill and Donnelly challenged the constitutionality of the dismissal procedures in federal district court. The trial court ruled against them. The court of appeals reversed, finding that both men had been denied due process. The Cleveland Board of Education (petitioner) brought the case before the Supreme Court.

White, Justice:

Respondents' federal constitutional claim depends on their having had a property right in continued employment. If they did, the State could not deprive them of this property without due process. Property interests are not created by the Constitution, "they are created and their dimensions are defined by existing rules or understandings that stem from an independent source such as state law. . . ." *Board of Regents v. Roth,* 408 U.S. 564 (1972). The Ohio statute plainly creates such an interest. Respondents were "classified civil service employees," Ohio Rev. Code Ann. §124.11 (1984), entitled to retain their positions "during good behavior and efficient service," who could not be dismissed "except . . . for . . . misfeasance, malfeasance, or nonfeasance in office," §124.34. . . .

[T]he Due Process Clause provides that certain substantive rights—life, liberty, and property—cannot be deprived except pursuant to constitutionally adequate procedures. Once it is determined that the Due Process Clause applies, "the question remains what process is due." *Morrissey v. Brewer,* 408 U.S. 471 (1972).

An essential principle of due process is that a deprivation of life, liberty, or property "be preceded by notice and opportunity for hearing appropriate to the nature of the case." *Mullane v. Central Hanover Bank & Trust Co.,* 339 U.S. 306 (1950). This principle requires "some kind of hearing" prior to the discharge of an employee who has a constitutionally protected property interest in his employment.

The need for some form of pretermination hearing is evident from a balancing of the competing interests at stake. These are the private interest in retaining employment, the government interest in the expeditious removal of unsatisfactory employees and the avoidance of administrative burdens, and the risk of an erroneous termination.

First, the significance of the private interest in retaining employment cannot be gainsaid. We have frequently recognized the severity of depriving a person of the means of livelihood.

Second, some opportunity for the employee to present his side of the case is recurringly of obvious value in reaching an accurate decision. Dismissals for cause will often involve factual disputes. Even where the facts are clear, the appropriateness or necessity of the discharge may not be; in such cases, the only meaningful opportunity to invoke the discretion of the decision-maker is likely to be before the termination takes effect.

The cases before us illustrate these considerations. Both respondents had plausible arguments to make that might have prevented their discharge. The fact that the Commission saw fit to reinstate Donnelly suggests that an error might have been avoided had he been provided an opportunity to make his case to the Board. As for Loudermill, given the Commission's ruling we cannot say that the discharge was a mistake. Nonetheless, in light of the referee's recommendation, neither can we say that a fully informed decision-maker might not have exercised its discretion and decided not to dismiss him, notwithstanding its authority to do so.

The governmental interest in immediate termination does not outweigh these interests. Affording the employee an opportunity to respond prior to termination would impose neither a significant administrative burden nor intolerable delays. Furthermore, the employer shares the employee's interest in avoiding disruption and erroneous decisions; and until the matter is settled, the employer would continue to receive the benefit of the employee's labors. It is preferable to keep a qualified employee on than to train a new one. A governmental employer also has an interest in keeping citizens usefully employed rather than taking the possibly erroneous and counterproductive step of forcing its employees onto the welfare rolls. Finally, in those situations where the employer perceives a significant hazard in keeping the employee on the job, it can avoid the problem by suspending with pay.

The foregoing considerations indicate that the pretermination "hearing," though necessary, need not be elaborate. We have pointed out that "[t]he formality and procedural requisites for the hearing can vary, depending upon the importance of the interests involved, and the nature of the subsequent proceedings." *Boddie v. Connecticut,* 401 U.S. 371 (1971).

The essential requirements of due process, and all that respondents seek or the Court of Appeals required, are notice and an opportunity to respond. The opportunity to present reasons, either in person or in writing, why proposed action should not be taken is a fundamental due process requirement. The tenured public employee is entitled to oral or written notice of the charges against him, an explanation of the employer's evidence, and an opportunity to present his side of the story. To require more than this prior to termination would intrude to an unwarranted extent on the government's interest in quickly removing an unsatisfactory employee.

We conclude that all the process that is due is provided by a pretermination opportunity to respond, coupled with post-termination administrative procedures as provided by the Ohio statute.

[Affirmed.]

SUMMARY

Our magnificent Constitution performs many functions. It prevents the undue concentration of power by dividing the authority of the government both vertically and horizontally. Vertically, the federal government is supreme, but is limited to certain enumerated powers set out in the Constitution. All other powers are reserved to the states and their subordinate units of government.

Horizontally, the vast authority of the federal government is separated into the legislative, executive, and judicial branches of government. A system of checks and balances prevents undue influence of any one branch. Although the President of the United States is probably the most powerful person in the world, executive authority to act must be rooted in the Constitution or in congressional acts. If the president acts without authority, or if Congress passes acts inconsistent with the Constitution, the judiciary, pursuant to the doctrine of judicial review, will

rein them in. The Constitution, after all, means what the Supreme Court says it means.

The Constitution also protects businesses and individuals from undue government encroachment. We enjoy more freedoms than citizens of any other country, including freedom of religion, freedom of speech, equal protection under the law, and due process of law.

KEY TERMS

Delegated powers
Reserved powers
State police power
Full Faith and Credit Clause
Judicial review
Executive orders
Doctrine of incorporation
Due process of law
Privileges and Immunities Clause
Establishment Clause

Blue laws
Free Speech Clause
Time, place, and manner restrictions
Commercial speech
Equal Protection Clause
De facto **discrimination**
Substantive due process
Procedural due process

QUESTIONS AND PROBLEMS

1. The Montana Fish and Game Commission adopted a regulation in 1976 that set the price of combination hunting licenses at $30 for residents and $225 for nonresidents. (A combination license permitted the taking of one elk, one deer, one black bear, and a specified number of game birds.) This regulation was challenged by nonresident hunters, who contended that it violated the Privileges and Immunities Clause of the U.S. Constitution. The State of Montana contended, among other things, that the interest of Montana residents in the wildlife within its borders was a matter of state protection, and that this interest was substantial enough to justify the regulation. Do you think the U.S. Supreme Court agreed with this defense? Why or why not? (*Baldwin v. Fish and Game Commission of Montana,* 436 U.S. 371, 1978.)

2. The aviation commissioner for the City of Chicago adopted regulations which severely restricted the distribution of literature and solicitation of contributions at city airports. Among other things, the regulations (a) provided that persons who wished to do these things had to register with airport officials daily between 9:00 and 9:30 a.m.; (b) provided that distribution and solicitation could be carried on only in specified public areas of the airports; and (c) prohibited the solicitation by more than one person from each group at a time. These regulations were challenged by a religious group on the ground that they violated the free speech guarantee of the Constitution. Which, if any, of the above regulations do you feel did violate that clause?

Explain. (*International Society for Krishna Consciousness, Inc. v. Rockford,* 585 F.2d 263, 1978.)

3. An Illinois criminal statute provided that violators would be subject to a fine and imprisonment for a specified period of time. It also provided that if a convicted person had no money to pay the fine, he or she was required to stay in prison for a longer time in order to "work off" the fine. Do you think that this statute might violate the Equal Protection Clause? Explain. (*Williams v. Illinois,* 399 U.S. 235, 1970.)

4. A national bank in Ohio was charged with violating a federal criminal law that prohibited national banks from making loans to political candidates who were running for office in specified elections. At the trial, the bank contended that the federal law violated the Equal Protection Clause of the Constitution in that it applied to national banks and not to a number of other lending institutions. What additional factors, if any, would you want to examine in order to determine whether the bank's contention is correct? What result? (*U.S. v. First National Bank,* 329 F.Supp. 1251, 1971.)

5. An Arizona Motor Vehicle Safety Responsibility law provided for the suspension of a driver's license when a judgment for personal injuries was enforced against the driver, and where the judgment was not satisfied (paid). The law also provided that even if the driver went into bankruptcy, the discharge in bankruptcy did not relieve the driver from the license suspension. A driver challenged this statute under the Supremacy Clause of the federal Constitution, contending that the statute was contrary to certain provisions of the National Bankruptcy Act. (The Supremacy Clause provides, in effect, that state statutes that conflict with federal statutes are unconstitutional.) The State of Arizona argued that even if there were a conflict, it was justified for the reason that the purpose of the statute was "the protection of the public using the highways from financial hardship that may result from the use of automobiles by financially irresponsible persons," and that this purpose was clearly within the police power of the state. Does this argument save the statute? Why or why not? (*Perez v. Campbell,* 91 S.Ct. 1704, 1971.)

6. A motorist was convicted of two traffic offenses in a mayor's court, and the convictions were affirmed by the state's supreme court. He appealed this judgment to the U.S. Supreme Court. He contended that he had been denied a trial before "a disinterested and impartial judicial officer as guaranteed by the Due Process clause," in view of the fact that a major part of the village's income was derived from the fines, costs, and fees imposed by the mayor's court. Do you believe that the appellant's contention is valid? Explain. (*Ward v. Village of Monroeville,* 34 L.Ed.2d 265, 1972.)

7. Ewing enrolled in a 6-year program of study at the University of Michigan which awarded an undergraduate degree and a medical degree upon successful completion of the program. To qualify for the final two years of the program a student must pass an examination known as NBME Part I. Ewing, after an undistinguished academic career, was dismissed from the university when he failed this examination with the lowest score recorded in the history of the program. He sued, seeking readmission to the program and an opportunity to retake the exam on the ground, *inter alia,* that he had a property interest in the program and that his dismissal was arbitrary and capricious in violation of due process. Evidence showed that academic authorities had given careful consideration to their decision to dismiss Ewing, but that all other students in the program who had failed NMBE Part I had been allowed to retake it, some as many as four times. Should Ewing's due process claim prevail? Discuss. (*Regents of the University of Michigan v. Ewing,* 106 S.Ct. 507, 1986.)

8. Bhatia, a devout member of the well-established Sikh religion, refused, on religious grounds, to shave. The Sikh religion forbids its adherents to cut or shave any body hair. Bhatia's employer, Chevron, required shaving of all employees in Bhatia's job description so that an airtight seal could be obtained with the respirator required of machinists. When Bhatia refused to shave, Chevron offered him a number of lower paying jobs. He took one of the jobs, paying 17 percent less than his prior position. He then sued, claiming that Chevron had violated Title VII of the Civil Rights Act of 1964, under which Congress requires employers not to discriminate on the basis of race, religion, and other grounds. Should Bhatia succeed? Discuss. (*Bhatia v. Chevron,* 734 F.2d 1382, 9th Cir. 1984.)

Chapter 6

LAWMAKING BY ADMINISTRATIVE AGENCIES

In the preceding chapters we have examined the major processes by which law is made—the formulation of common-law rules by the courts, the enactment of statutes by the legislative bodies, and the interpretation of statutes by the courts. But this examination does not present the total lawmaking picture. **Administrative agencies**—the hundreds of boards and commissions existing at all levels of government—also "make law" by their continual promulgation of rules and regulations.[1]

The number of administrative agencies has grown so rapidly in the last forty years that the practical impact of local, state, and federal agencies on the day-to-day activities of individuals and businesses is today probably at least as great as that of legislatures and courts. Every day, boards and commissions across the country engage in such traditional functions as assessing properties for tax purposes, granting licenses and business permits, and regulating rates charged in the transportation and public utility industries—actions that affect millions of Americans. And, more recently, newer agencies such as the Environmental Protection Agency (EPA), Occupational Safety and Health Administration (OSHA), and the National Highway Traffic and Safety Administration (NHTSA) have spawned regulations having broad impact on the nation's businesses. The automobile industry has especially felt the brunt of many regulations (for better or for worse), with the result that the size and power—not to mention cost—of the cars we drive today are substantially mandated by federal regulation. Justice Jackson was right when he wrote in *FTC v. Ruberoid Co.,* 343 U.S. 470 (1952):

> The rise of administrative bodies probably has been the most significant legal trend of the last century and perhaps more values today are affected by their decisions than by those of all the courts, review of admin-

istrative decisions apart. They also have begun to have important consequences on personal rights. . . . They have become a veritable fourth branch of the Government, which has deranged our three-branch legal theories as much as the concept of a fourth dimension unsettles our three-dimensional thinking.

RISE OF THE ADMINISTRATIVE AGENCY

At the risk of oversimplification, we can say that two major factors are responsible for the dramatic growth of the administrative agency in recent years. First was a change in attitude toward government regulation of business. Until about 1880 the basic attitude of the state and federal governments toward business firms was that of "hands-off"—a philosophy frequently characterized by the *laissez-faire* label. The theory was that trade and commerce could best thrive in an environment free of government controls. By the end of the nineteenth century, however, various monopolistic practices had begun to surface. The passage of the Sherman Act in 1890 reflected the growing idea that a certain amount of government regulation of business was necessary to preserve minimum levels of competition.

A second, and perhaps even more powerful, reason for the emergence of the modern administrative agency is that as our nation grew and became more industrialized, many complex problems sprang up that did not easily lend themselves to traditional types of regulation. Some were posed by technological advances such as the greatly increased generation and distribution of electrical power and the rapid growth of the airline industry. Others resulted from changes in social and economic conditions, particularly the rise of the giant manufacturers and the new methods by which they marketed their products on a national basis. The solution of these problems required expertise and enormous amounts of time for continuous regulation, which the courts and the legislatures simply did not possess. Faced with this situation,

---

[1] The specific activities of certain federal agencies, such as the Federal Trade Commission, are examined in more detail in Part VIII.

the legislative bodies sought new ways to regulate business (and to implement nonbusiness government programs, such as social security) that would be more workable.

THE AGENCY—AN OVERVIEW

In order to understand the basic workings of administrative agencies and the nature of the legal problems we will discuss later, it will be helpful to see how the typical agency is created and how it receives its powers. For this purpose, the Federal Trade Commission provides a good example.

By the turn of the century, it was apparent that some firms in interstate commerce were engaging in practices that, while not violating the Sherman Act, were nonetheless felt to be of an undesirable nature. While persons who were injured by these practices were sometimes able to obtain relief in the courts, the relief was sporadic and there was no single body that could maintain surveillance of these practices on a continuing basis.

Accordingly, in 1914 Congress passed the Federal Trade Commission Act, which created the *Federal Trade Commission* (*FTC*) and authorized it (among other things) to determine what constituted "unfair methods of competition" in interstate commerce. Not only could the commission issue regulations defining and prohibiting such practices but, additionally, it could take action against companies that it believed to be violating such regulations. While the commission's regulations are not *statutes,* they are nonetheless *legal rules* in that they impose certain limits upon the activities of firms engaged in interstate commerce.

LEGISLATIVE DELEGATION OF LAWMAKING POWER

The administrative agency sits somewhat uncomfortably in our tripartite (legislative-executive-judicial) system of government. An agency which is technically part of the executive branch or perhaps an "independent regulatory agency" may exert powers which entail adjudication and rulemaking as well as traditional executive functions such as investigation and enforcement. A constitutional problem arises because the Constitution in Article I, Section 1 clearly vests all legislative powers in the Congress and does not provide for delegation of those powers. Therefore, rules and regulations that have been promulgated by agencies, and that have the force and effect of law, have been challenged as resulting from an unconstitutional delegation of legislative power.

Only in a couple of cases decided during the 1930s, in which the Supreme Court found "delegation running riot," have such challenges succeeded. The courts are well aware of the very practical need for administrative agencies which was described earlier in this chapter. Therefore, they will uphold any agency ruling, regulation, or act which is within standards set forth in an enabling act *if* that act contains "reasonable standards" to guide the agency. What are reasonable standards? Courts have upheld as constitutional delegations of power "to promulgate regulations fixing prices of commodities," to institute rent controls on real property anywhere in the nation under specified circumstances, even "to issue such orders and regulations as he [the President] deems appropriate to stabilize prices, rents, wages and salaries." Indeed, the doctrine of unconstitutional delegation of legislative power appears moribund at the federal level, though it still has some vitality in litigation involving state agencies.[2]

FUNCTIONS AND POWERS

Ministerial and Discretionary Powers

Before addressing the legal questions that are presented when agencies' rules or orders are appealed to the courts, we will briefly look at

---

[2] E.g., *State v. Marana Plantations, Inc.,* 252 P.2d 87 (1953) where the power to "regulate sanitary policies in the interests of public health" was deemed too vague.

the nature of agency activities. The activities of these government boards and commissions vary widely. The functions and powers of some agencies are only **ministerial**—concerned with routinely carrying out duties imposed by law. Boards that issue and renew drivers' licenses fall within this category, as do the many social security offices that give information or advice to persons filing for social security benefits.

But most agencies also possess broad **discretionary powers**—powers that require the exercise of judgment and discretion in carrying out their duties. Again there is variety in the specific powers of these agencies. Some agencies' discretionary power is largely **investigative** in nature. Two examples are the authority granted to the Internal Revenue Service to inquire into the legality of deductions on taxpayers' returns and the authority of some commissions to make investigations for the purpose of recommending needed statutes to legislatures. Other agencies have largely **rulemaking powers,** with perhaps some investigative but little **adjudicatory power** (enforcement power).

But most "full-fledged" federal agencies, such as the Federal Trade Commission and the National Labor Relations Board, possess all three types of power—investigative, rulemaking, and adjudicative. Thus, typically, a board will conduct investigations to determine if conditions warrant the issuance of rules to require (or prohibit) certain kinds of conduct; then it will draw up the regulations and thereafter take action against individuals or firms showing evidence of violating them. In drawing up the rules the board acts quasi-legislatively, and in enforcing them it acts quasi-judicially.

The Investigative Power

Agencies frequently hold hearings before drafting regulations, and the investigative powers they possess in connection with such hearings are largely determined by the statutes by which they are created. Normally, agencies can order the production of accounts and records relative to the problem being studied and can **subpoena** witnesses and examine them under oath. More disruptive to businesses are the powers most major agencies have to investigate whether statutes they are charged with enforcing and rules they have promulgated are being violated. The two most intrusive forms of investigative power are the subpoena and the physical search and seizure.

Subpoena Power: In the exercise of its adjudicatory powers, which are soon to be discussed, agencies may issue subpoenas *ad testificandum,* which are writs ordering a witness into court (in this case before the Administrative Law Judge (ALJ)).

In any sort of investigation, agencies may issue subpoenas *duces tecum,* which are writs ordering the production of books, papers, records, and documents. Agency authority is construed very broadly in this area. According to *United States v. Powell,*[3] an agency must demonstrate that (1) the investigation will be conducted for a legitimate purpose, (2) the inquiry is relevant to the purpose, (3) the information sought is not already possessed by the agency, and (4) the administrative steps required by law have been followed. "Probable cause" in the criminal sense need not be shown.

Once the agency has established an apparently valid purpose for the investigation, the burden shifts to the company or individual being investigated to show that the purpose is illegitimate (e.g., undertaken for harassment). The following case illustrates the difficulty that the target of a federal agency's investigation can have in attempting to block enforcement of such a subpoena.

---

[3] 379 U.S. 48 (1964).

EEOC v. Peat, Marwick, Mitchell and Co.
U.S. Eighth Circuit Court of Appeals, 775 F.2d 928 (1985)

In May of 1982, the Equal Employment Opportunity Commission (EEOC) began investigating the retirement practices and policies of Peat, Marwick, Mitchell & Co. (PM) in an effort to determine whether those policies violated the Age Discrimination in Employment Act (ADEA). In accordance with its statutory investigative powers, the EEOC subpoenaed from PM documents bearing upon the relationship of members to the firm and documents relating to PM's retirement practices and policies.

PM refused to comply with the subpoena, so the EEOC initiated this enforcement proceeding in the district court. The district court ordered enforcement of the subpoena, and PM appealed.

Fagg, Circuit Judge:

PM's primary argument on appeal is that the subpoena should not be enforced because the EEOC's investigation is not for a legitimate purpose authorized by Congress. The ADEA prohibits discrimination by an employer against an employee or prospective employee on the basis of age. PM contends that its partners are not employees under the ADEA but rather they fall within the definition provided for employers in the Act. Thus, according to PM, the EEOC's investigation of the relationship of PM partners as employers, to the firm and to each other and its investigation of the retirement practices and policies of the partnership is not for a legitimate purpose authorized by Congress.

EEOC maintains that it has subpoenaed the records of PM in an effort to determine whether individuals that PM classifies as "partners" fall within the definition of "employees" for purposes of the ADEA.

Congress has established the EEOC as the administrative body empowered to investigate violations of the ADEA and has given the EEOC subpoena power in order to carry out its investigations. The authority to investigate violations includes the authority to investigate coverage under the statute. *Donovan v. Shaw,* 668 F.2d 985 (8th Cir. 1982). It can no longer be disputed that "a subpoena enforcement proceeding is not the proper forum in which to litigate the question of coverage under a particular federal statute." *Id.* The initial determination of the coverage question is left to the administrative agency seeking enforcement of the subpoena. Often a coverage question cannot be resolved until the administrative agency has had an opportunity to examine the subpoenaed records.

"The showing of reasonable cause required to support an application for enforcement of a subpoena duces tecum 'is satisfied . . . by the court's determination that the investigation is authorized by Congress, is for a purpose

Congress can order, and the documents sought are relevant to the inquiry.'" *Donovan,* 668 F.2d at 989. *See also United States v. Powell,* 379 U.S. 48 (1964). The EEOC's investigation of PM is in an effort to determine whether PM's retirement practices and policies discriminate against individuals classified as employees for purposes of the ADEA. Thus, EEOC's investigation is for a legitimate purpose authorized by Congress. PM has not questioned the relevancy of the documents subpoenaed by the EEOC to a determination of this question.

PM also argues that the district court committed error in enforcing the subpoena because it is abusive, unreasonable, not in good faith, and violative of the constitutional rights of PM and its members. In this regard, PM argues that the EEOC has never made or attempted to make a showing that PM's partners may in fact be employees for purposes of the ADEA, or that it has reason to believe that PM's retirement practices and policies may be violative of the ADEA.

The EEOC is not required to make such a showing. As previously indicated, the EEOC must show that its investigation is for a legitimate purpose authorized by Congress and that the documents subpoenaed are relevant to its inquiry. If this demonstration is made, the EEOC is entitled to the documents subpoenaed unless PM demonstrates that judicial enforcement of the subpoena would amount to an abuse of the court's process. PM has presented no evidence of bad faith or an abuse of the court's process by the EEOC.

We affirm.

Search and Seizure: Many agencies attempt to carry out actual on-site searches in investigating matters under their jurisdiction. From city health inspectors checking a restaurant's kitchen to OSHA investigating trenches at a work site to federal mine safety inspectors probing underground coal mines, such investigations are a frequent, and, for the investigated company, troublesome occurrence. Should companies be protected from unreasonable searches and seizures? Does a federal agency need a warrant to effectuate a search? If so, what must the agency demonstrate in order to obtain such a warrant legally? These questions were answered by the Supreme Court in the following landmark case.

Marshall v. Barlow's, Inc.
U.S. Supreme Court, 436 U.S. 307 (1978)

An OSHA inspector entered the customer service area of Barlow's, Inc., an electrical and plumbing installation business, and informed its president, Mr. Barlow, that he wished to conduct a search of the working areas of the business. Barlow asked whether there had been any complaints about his company. The inspector replied no, but that Barlow's, Inc. had simply turned up in the agency's selection process.

Because the inspector had no warrant, Barlow refused to allow him to inspect the nonpublic area of the business. Later the Secretary of Labor filed a suit in federal district court, seeking an order compelling Barlow to admit the inspector. Such an order was issued, but Barlow refused to comply. Barlow then filed this suit, raising his Fourth Amendment rights and seeking an injunction against warrantless searches. A three-judge federal district court found that a warrant was required, and held unconstitutional OSHA regulations allowing a warrantless search. The Secretary appealed.

White, Justice:

The Secretary urges that warrantless inspections to enforce OSHA are reasonable within the meaning of the Fourth Amendment. Regretfully, we are unable to agree.

The Warrant Clause of the Fourth Amendment protects commercial buildings as well as private homes. To hold otherwise would belie the origin of that Amendment, and the American colonial experience. The general warrant was a recurring point of contention in the colonies immediately preceding the Revolution. The particular offensiveness it engendered was acutely felt by the merchants and businessmen whose premises and products were inspected for compliance with the several Parliamentary revenue measures that most irritated the colonists.

This Court has already held that warrantless searches are generally unreasonable, and that this rule applies to commercial premises as well as homes. These same cases also held that the Fourth Amendment prohibition against unreasonable searches protects against warrantless intrusions during civil as well as criminal investigations.

The Secretary submits that warrantless inspections are essential to the proper enforcement of OSHA because they afford the opportunity to inspect without prior notice and hence to preserve the advantages of surprise. To the suggestion that warrants may be issued *ex parte* [without notice to the business to be inspected] and executed without delay and without prior notice, thereby preserving the element of surprise, the Secretary expresses concern for the administrative strain that would be experienced by the inspection system, and by the courts, should *ex parte* warrants issued in advance become standard practice.

We are unconvinced, however, that requiring warrants to inspect will impose serious burdens on the inspection system or the courts, will prevent inspections necessary to enforce the statute, or will make them less effective. In the first place, the great majority of businessmen can be expected in normal course to consent to inspection without warrant; the Secretary has not brought to this Court's attention any widespread pattern of refusal. Nor is it immediately apparent why the advantages of surprise would be lost if, after being refused entry, procedures were available for the Secretary to seek an *ex parte* warrant and to reappear at the premises without further notice to the establishment being inspected.

Whether the Secretary proceeds to secure a warrant or other process, with or without prior notice, his entitlement to inspect will not depend on his demonstrating probable cause to believe that conditions in violation of OSHA exist on the premises. Probable cause in the criminal law sense is not required. For purposes of an administrative search such as this, probable cause justifying the issuance of a warrant may be based not only on specific evidence of an existing violation but also on a showing that "reasonable legislative or administrative standards for conducting an . . . inspection are satisfied with respect to a particular [establishment.]" *Camara v. Municipal Court,* 387 U.S. 523 (1967). A warrant showing that a specific business has been chosen for an OSHA search on the basis of a general administrative plan for the enforcement of the Act derived from neutral sources such as, for example, dispersion of employees in various types of industries across a given area, and the desired frequency of searches in any of the lesser divisions of the area, would protect an employer's Fourth Amendment rights. We doubt that the consumption of enforcement energies in the obtaining of such warrants will exceed manageable proportions.

Nor do we agree that the incremental protections afforded the employer's privacy by a warrant are so marginal that they fail to justify the administrative burdens that may be entailed. The authority to make warrantless searches devolves almost unbridled discretion upon executive and administrative officers, particularly those in the field, as to when to search and whom to search. A warrant, by contrast, would provide assurances from a neutral officer that the inspection is reasonable under the Constitution, is authorized by statute, and is pursuant to an administrative plan containing specific neutral criteria. Also, a warrant would then and there advise the owner of the scope and objects of the search, beyond which limits the inspector is not expected to proceed.

[Affirmed.]

Comment: There are several exceptions to the *Barlow* rule under which agencies may carry out warrantless searches. One important exception is for industries which are so pervasively regulated that they have little or no reasonable expectation of privacy. This exception has been used to allow inspection of stone quarries under the Federal Mines Safety Act[4] and of day care centers under the California Health and Safety Code.[5]

Another exception is the "open field" exception, allowing searches of areas which are so open to plain view that no reasonable expectation of privacy exists. In one recent case, the Supreme Court approved a warrantless EPA search carried out with a commercial aerial photographer by flying over a 2,000-acre chemical plant consisting of numerous covered buildings with outdoor manufacturing equipment and piping conduits. Though the company had substantial ground-level security, the Court concluded that the plant was more like an open field than it was like "curtilage"—open space in the immediate vicinity of a dwelling, such as a yard. The Court

[4] *Donovan v. Dewey,* 452 U.S. 594 (1981).

[5] *Rush v. Obledo,* 756 F.2d 713 (9th Cir. 1985).

noted that a commercial property owner has to expect less privacy than a homeowner so that, correspondingly, the government's latitude to conduct warrantless searches is greater.[6]

Rulemaking

Much of the legislative-type activity of federal agencies is carried out through their rulemaking function. Sometimes Congress spells out the procedures for rulemaking by a particular agency in that agency's enabling statute. Sometimes the agency is left to follow the Administrative Procedure Act (APA), which the more specific statutes normally follow anyway. The APA provides a comprehensive set of procedural guidelines for a variety of agency activities. In the rulemaking area, the APA provides for two basic types— informal and formal. A third type, called hybrid rulemaking, has also developed.

Informal Rulemaking: Sometimes Congress will authorize informal rulemaking. To properly promulgate a rule under these procedures, the agency usually publishes a notice of the proposed rule in the Federal Register. There follows a comment period, typically of 30 days, in which any interested citizen or company may send written comments to the agency regarding the rule. Such comments might argue that the rule is unnecessary, unduly burdensome to business, does not go far enough to remedy the problem, goes too far, and the like. The agency is then supposed to digest and react to the comments, perhaps by altering or even scrapping the proposed rule. Normally the rule is modestly altered, and then published in final form in the Federal Register. At that point, it becomes effective. Ultimately it will be codified in the Code of Federal Regulations along with the rules of all other federal administrative agencies.

Formal Rulemaking: Formal rulemaking also involves "notice and comment," but supplements these with formal hearings at which wit-

nesses testify and are cross-examined by interested parties. Transcripts of the testimony are preserved and become part of the public record. Formal rulemaking can be very expensive and time-consuming, but theoretically leads to especially well-considered results.

Hybrid Rulemaking: Hybrid rulemaking closely resembles formal rulemaking, except that there is no right to cross-examine the agency's expert witnesses, and, as we shall soon see, a different standard of review is applied by the courts if the rulemaking procedure is challenged.

Judicial Review of Rulemaking: Naturally some parties are likely to be aggrieved by promulgation of rules that affect them adversely. Few important rules are issued without a subsequent court challenge. Courts will invalidate rules issued pursuant to an unconstitutional delegation of legislative power (as noted above, an extremely rare occurrence) and rules that are unconstitutional (perhaps because they discriminate on the basis of race in violation of equal protection principles).

Courts will also invalidate rules not issued in accordance with applicable procedural standards. For example, if an agency engaged in informal rulemaking fails to publish a proposed version of the rule in the Federal Register so that comments may be received, the rule will likely be invalidated if challenged. The courts will countenance minor deviations from APA procedures, but major ones are risky. In particularly sensitive areas, such as rules governing nuclear power plants, some courts have required more elaborate procedures than those specified in the APA's formal rulemaking sections. However, the Supreme Court, in *Vermont Yankee Nuclear Power Corp. v. Natural Resources Defense Council,*[7] held that courts could not legally require these extra procedures.

Standards of Review: In issuing rules, an agency will have to make several types of deci-

---

[6]*Dow Chemical Co. v. U.S.,* 106 S.Ct. 1819 (1986).

[7]435 U.S. 519 (1978).

sions. One type of decision will likely turn on a pure **question of law** regarding its powers and the scope of its charge under a law passed by Congress. Courts are experts on the law. Therefore, they have the authority to substitute their interpretations for the meaning of laws passed by Congress for the interpretations made by the agency. Nonetheless, the Supreme Court has concluded that it makes sense to give deference to the expertise developed by the agency, noting:

> When a court reviews an agency's construction of the statute which it administers, it is confronted with two questions. First, always, is the question whether Congress has spoken to the precise question at issue. If the intent of Congress is clear, that is the end of the matter; for the court, as well as the agency, must give effect to the unambiguously expressed intent of Congress. If, however, the court determines Congress has not directly addressed the precise question at issue, the court does not simply impose its own construction on the statute, as would be necessary in the absence of an administrative interpretation. Rather, if the statute is silent or ambiguous with respect to the specific issue, the question for the court is whether the agency's answer is based on a permissible construction of the statute. . . .

> We have long recognized that considerable weight should be accorded to an executive department's construction of a

statutory scheme it is entrusted to administer, and the principles of deference to administrative interpretations.[8]

An agency issuing rules must also make decisions as to facts and policy. Two tests predominate review of these types of decisions. The "arbitrary and capricious" test assumes the correctness of an agency's decision, placing the burden on any challenger to prove that the decision was not simply erroneous but so far off the mark as to be arbitrary and capricious. The "substantial evidence" test requires that an agency's decision be based not just on a scintilla of evidence, but on such relevant evidence as a reasonable mind might accept as adequate to support a conclusion.

The "arbitrary and capricious" test is usually used to judge any policy decision by an agency. Findings of fact made pursuant to formal rulemaking are judged by the "substantial evidence" test. Factual determinations made in informal rulemaking are gauged by the "arbitrary and capricious" test unless an agency's authorizing act calls for use of the "substantial evidence" test. Many courts have noted that there is little practical difference in how the two tests are usually applied. Both require court deference to agency decision making, but the following case shows that such deference is not unlimited.

---

[8] *Chevron U.S.A., Inc. v. Natural Resources Defense Council,* 467 U.S. 837 (1984).

Motor Vehicle Manufacturers Ass'n v. State Farm Mutual Auto. Ins. Co.
U.S. Supreme Court, 463 U.S. 29 (1983)

To improve highway safety, Congress passed the National Traffic and Motor Vehicle Safety Act of 1966, which directs the Secretary of Transportation or a delegee to issue motor vehicle safety standards. In 1967, the Secretary's delegee, the National Highway Traffic Safety Administration (NHTSA) issued Standard 208 which required installa-

tion of seatbelts in all new automobiles. Because usage by consumers was quite low, NHTSA studied passive restraints in the form of automatic seatbelts and airbags, which it estimated could prevent approximately 12,000 deaths and over 100,000 serious injuries annually. Deadlines for implementation of the passive restraint systems were repeatedly extended until, in 1977, the Secretary promulgated Modified Standard 208, which ordered a phase in on all new cars to take place between 1982 and 1984. The Secretary assumed that 60 percent of new cars would have airbags and 40 percent would have automatic seatbelts.

However, it soon became apparent that 99 percent of American cars would have *detachable* seatbelts. In light of this fact and of economic difficulties in the auto industry, the Secretary began in 1981 to reconsider the passive restraint requirement of Modified Standard 208 and ultimately rescinded it.

State Farm Mutual and other insurance companies sued for review of the rescission order. The federal district court and court of appeals held the rescission to be arbitrary and capricious in violation of law. The petitioner Motor Vehicle Manufacturers Association brought the case to the Supreme Court.

White, Justice:

Both the Motor Vehicle Safety Act and the 1974 Amendments concerning occupant crash protection standards indicate that motor vehicle safety standards are to be promulgated under the informal rulemaking procedures of §553 of the Administrative Procedure Act. The agency's action in promulgating such standards therefore may be set aside only if found to be "arbitrary, capricious, an abuse of discretion, or otherwise not in accordance with law." We believe that the rescission or modification of an occupant protection standard is subject to the same test.

The Department of Transportation argues that under this standard, a reviewing court may not set aside an agency rule that is rational, based on consideration of the relevant factors and within the scope of the authority delegated to the agency by the statute. We do not disagree with this formulation. The scope of review under the "arbitrary and capricious" standard is narrow and a court is not to substitute its judgment for that of the agency. Nevertheless, the agency must examine the relevant data and articulate a satisfactory explanation for its action including a "rational connection between the facts found and the choice made." *Burlington Truck Lines v. U.S.*, 371 U.S. 156 (1962). In reviewing that explanation, we must "consider whether the decision was based on a consideration of relevant factors and whether there has been a clear error of judgment." *Bowman Transp. Inc. v. Arkansas-Best Freight System, Inc.*, 419 U.S. 281 (1974). Normally, an agency rule would be arbitrary and capricious if the agency has relied on factors which Congress has not intended it to consider, entirely failed to consider an important aspect of the problem, offered an explanation for its decision that runs counter to the evidence before the agency, or is so implausible that it could not be ascribed to a difference in view or the product of agency expertise. The reviewing court should not attempt itself to make up for such deficiencies: "We may not supply a reasoned basis for the agency's action that the agency itself has not given." *SEC v. Chenery Corp.,* 332 U.S. 194 (1947). We will, however, uphold a decision of less than ideal clarity if the agency's path may reasonably be discerned." *Bowman Transp.*

The ultimate question before us is whether NHTSA's rescission of the passive restraint requirement of Standard 208 was arbitrary and capricious. We conclude, as did the Court of Appeals, that it was. We also conclude, but for somewhat different reasons, that further consideration of the issue by the agency is therefore required. We deal separately with . . . airbags and seatbelts.

The first and most obvious reason for finding rescission arbitrary and capricious is that NHTSA apparently gave no consideration whatever to modifying the Standard to require that airbag technology be utilized. Not one sentence of its rulemaking statement discusses the airbags-only option. [W]hat we said in *Burlington Truck Lines v. United States,* 371 U.S., at 167, is apropos here:

There are no findings and no analysis here to justify the choice made, no indication of the basis on which the [agency] exercised its expert discretion. We are not prepared to and the Administrative Procedures Act will not permit us to accept such . . . practice. . . . Expert discretion is the lifeblood of the administrative process, but "unless we make the requirements for administrative action strict and demanding, expertise, the strength of modern government, can become a monster which rules with no practical limits on its discretion." New York v. United States, *342 U.S. 882.*

We have frequently reiterated that an agency must cogently explain why it has exercised its discretion in a given manner. [T]he airbag is more than a policy alternative to the passive restraint standard; it is a technological alternative within the ambit of the existing standard. We hold only that given the judgment made in 1977 that airbags are an effective and cost-beneficial life-saving technology, the mandatory passive-restraint rule may not be abandoned without any consideration whatsoever of an airbags-only requirement.

Although the issue is closer, we also find that the agency was too quick to dismiss the safety benefits of automatic seatbelts. NHTSA's critical finding was that, in light of the industry's plans to install readily detachable passive belts, it could not reliably predict "even a 5 percentage point increase as the minimum level of expected usage increase." The Court of Appeals rejected this finding because there is "not one iota" of evidence that Modified Standard 208 will fail to increase nationwide seatbelt use by at least 13 percentage points, the level of increased usage necessary for the standard to justify its cost.

Recognizing that policymaking in a complex society must account for uncertainty . . . does not imply that it is sufficient for an agency to merely recite the terms "substantial uncertainty" as a justification for its actions. The agency must explain the evidence which is available and must offer a "rational connection between the facts found and the choice made." *Burlington Truck Lines.* Generally, one aspect of that explanation would be a justification for rescinding the regulation before engaging in a search for further evidence.

The agency is correct to look at the costs as well as the benefits of Standard 208 [but i]n reaching its judgment, NHTSA should bear in mind that Congress intended safety to be the preeminent factor under the Act.

The agency also failed to articulate a basis for not requiring nondetachable belts under Standard 208. By failing to analyze the continuous seatbelt in its own right, the agency has failed to offer the rational connection between facts and judgment required to pass muster under the arbitrary and capricious standard. We agree with the Court of Appeals that NHTSA did not suggest that the emergency release mechanisms used in nondetachable belts are any less effective for emergency egress than the buckle release system used in detachable belts.

"An agency's view of what is in the public interest may change, either with or without a change in circumstances. But an agency changing its course must supply a reasoned analysis. . . ." *Greater Boston Television Corp. v. FCC,* 444 F.2d 841 (CADC).

[Remand to Court of Appeals with directions to remand to NHTSA for further consideration consistent with this opinion.]

Adjudication

Most major federal agencies also exercise substantial powers of adjudication. That is, they not only issue rules and investigate to uncover violations, they may also charge alleged violators and try them to determine whether or not a violation has actually occurred.

Because the agency is acting as legislator, policeman, prosecutor *and* judge and jury, care must be taken to avoid abuse. For that reason, the APA and the courts demand that fairly formal procedural requirements be followed.

Over the years, procedures have evolved such that a person or company brought before an administrative agency for adjudication of a charged violation will usually have the right to notice, the right to counsel, the right to present evidence, and the right to confront and cross-examine adverse witnesses.

A jury trial is not allowed, but the case is heard by an Administrative Law Judge (ALJ), who is the finder of fact in the first instance. Although the 1000 plus ALJs in the federal system are employees of the agencies whose cases they hear, they cannot be disciplined except for good cause as determined by the federal Merit System Protection Board. Thus, the ALJs exercise substantial autonomy and are seldom puppets of the agency employing them.

Under the APA, all ALJ decisions are reviewable by the employing agency, which hears the case basically *de novo;* that is, the agency has full power to decide the case as if it had heard it first without the ALJ. Although agencies normally adopt the findings of the ALJ, they may utterly disregard the ALJ's findings. However, the ALJ's decision becomes part of the court record if the agency decision is challenged in litigation.

Adjudication is a very influential process. Not only are findings of fact required (e.g., Did the employer consult the union before deciding to move the plant?), but the ALJ and the agency must also interpret the applicable law (e.g., Is the employer required to consult the union before deciding to move the plant?). During the Reagan administration, the NLRB largely rewrote American labor policy through the process of adjudication. Though done piecemeal through several decisions involving unfair labor practice charges, the change in the law was as complete as if major rulemaking had been undertaken.

The quasi-judicial powers of major federal agencies are so significant that such decisions are normally reviewed directly by the Circuit Courts of Appeal. Other types of decisions—such as the decision to issue a subpoena or to promulgate a new rule—are normally reviewed

Figure 6.1 The Administrative Law Process

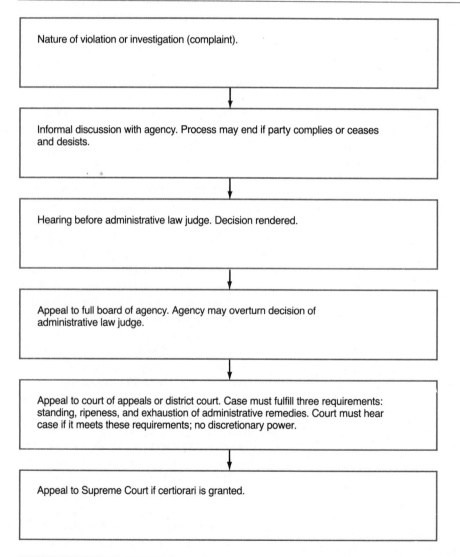

Nature of violation or investigation (complaint).

Informal discussion with agency. Process may end if party complies or ceases and desists.

Hearing before administrative law judge. Decision rendered.

Appeal to full board of agency. Agency may overturn decision of administrative law judge.

Appeal to court of appeals or district court. Case must fulfill three requirements: standing, ripeness, and exhaustion of administrative remedies. Court must hear case if it meets these requirements; no discretionary power.

Appeal to Supreme Court if certiorari is granted.

in the first instance by federal district courts. (Figure 6.1 helps illustrate the adjudicatory process of a federal agency.)

PROCEDURAL DUE PROCESS

Obviously a variety of agency actions can have an adverse impact on the status of individuals and companies. The Fifth Amendment to the Constitution prohibits the taking of life, liberty, or property, without due process of law. The right to due process protects us from the arbi-

trary actions of both state and federal agencies.

Exactly when we are entitled to due process, and how much process is due us are questions that the courts continually struggle to resolve. A leading due process case was discussed in the preceding chapter, *Cleveland Board of Education v. Loudermill.* Both *Loudermill* and another very persuasive Supreme Court case, *Mathews v. Eldridge,* 424 U.S. 319 (1976), are discussed and applied in the following case involving a due process challenge to an agency action.

Southern Ohio Coal Co. v. Donovan
U.S. Sixth Circuit Court of Appeals, 774 F.2d 693 (1985)

The Federal Mine Safety and Health Review Commission ("Commission"), a branch of the Department of Labor headed by Secretary Donovan, is charged with enforcing the Federal Mine Safety and Health Act of 1977. That act prohibits the discharge of employees in a manner that would discriminate against them for having asserted their safety rights under the Act. Upon a miner's timely complaint of unlawful discrimination, the Secretary must commence an investigation within 15 days. If the Secretary finds the complaint was not frivolously brought, the Commission "on an expedited basis *shall order* the immediate reinstatement of the miner pending final order on the complaint."

To implement this statutory scheme, the Commission promulgated Rule 44, which states that the Secretary's application must state his finding that the complaint was not frivolous, and must be accompanied by a copy of the miner's complaint. The application is to be examined on an expedited basis by an ALJ, and "if it appears that the Secretary's finding is supported by the application and accompanying documents, an order of temporary reinstatement shall be immediately issued." If such an order is issued, the mine operator may request a hearing before an ALJ, which must be held within five days of the request, to determine whether the complaint was "frivolously brought." Any arguments made to the ALJ may also be made to the Commission in a request for relief from the temporary reinstatement. Decisions of the ALJ and Commission are reviewable in the federal court of appeals.

Appellant Southern Ohio Coal Co. (SOCCO) was ordered by the ALJ to reinstate an employee it had fired for alleged excessive absenteeism. The employee had earlier complained to company officials

about unsafe methane levels in SOCCO's mines. SOCCO sought review of the ALJ's order. A federal district judge declared Rule 44 unconstitutional. Donovan appealed, raising several issues. Only SOCCO's claim regarding violation of due process is discussed in the portion of the opinion appearing below.

Wellford, Circuit Judge:

Whether the Commission's Rule 44 violates a mine operator's due process rights by failing to provide for a pre-deprivation hearing is at the heart of these controversies. Neither party questions that the mine operators are due some process under the Constitution when a miner claims the opportunity for immediate reinstatement. The Secretary, however, claims that a post-deprivation hearing is sufficient process in light of the (allegedly) overriding governmental interests involved. The mine operators, on the other hand, claim that a post-deprivation hearing is insufficient to protect their Constitutional rights and that a pre-deprivation hearing is mandated, because they could be compelled to make substantial payments before a decision is made initially as to the potential merit of a claim, and because they could be compelled to reinstate a person who is a danger to himself or to others.

Mathews v. Eldridge, 424 U.S. 319 (1976), requires a court to consider three factors to determine whether a particular procedure comports with the requirements of due process:

1. The private interests that will be affected by the official action in question;

2. The risk of an erroneous deprivation of such interests through the procedures involved and the probable value of additional or substitute procedural safeguards; and

3. The government's interest, including the function involved and the fiscal and administrative burdens that the additional or substitute procedural requirement would entail.

The final *Eldridge* factor is met in the instant case. Currently the Secretary is required to give the mine operator a hearing within five days of the temporary reinstatement order. What the mine operators would have this Court require is a pre-deprivation hearing—in other words, the Secretary would have to reverse the order of its procedures and hold a hearing before granting temporary reinstatement. Thus, there would be absolutely no additional fiscal or administrative burdens in granting the operators' desired pre-deprivation hearing.

The first and second factors, however, are not as easily answered as the third. On the first factor, the Secretary correctly notes that "[t]he usual rule has been '[w]here only property rights are involved, mere postponement of the judicial enquiry is not a denial of due process, if the opportunity given for ultimate judicial determination of liability is adequate.'" *Mitchell v. W. T. Grant Co.,* 416 U.S. 600 (1974). Were the employer permitted in all cases to provide merely economic reinstatement rather than normally being required to provide actual physical reinstatement, the Secretary's argument would be more persuasive.

The district court found "compelling" the mine operator's interest in "not being required to employ in a sensitive position a man whom it has discharged."

Prolonged retention of a disruptive or otherwise unsatisfactory employee can adversely affect discipline and morale in the work place, foster disharmony, and ultimately impair the efficiency of an office or agency.

This factor is particularly important when, as here, the order does not expire by its own terms at any specific time after it issues. Although an operator is given an opportunity to present evidence on its own behalf within five days of the reinstatement, the hearing focuses on whether the miner's complaint was frivolously brought, not whether the complaint is meritorious.

The reliability (or unreliability) of the initial procedures leading to an imposition of temporary reinstatement is perhaps a significant weakness in the administrative scheme under scrutiny. All the Secretary need do to force the mine operator to reinstate the discharged miner is find "minimal supporting evidence" in favor of the complainant. As long as the Secretary finds that the complaint was not "frivolously brought," then the Secretary makes an application for temporary reinstatement. The application itself consists only of the miner's complaint, an affidavit setting forth the Secretary's reasons for his finding that the complaint was not frivolously brought, and proof of service on the operator. The application permits no input from the employer. . . .

. . . [T]he Supreme Court's most recent pronouncement concerning due process requirements, *Cleveland Board of Education v. Loudermill,* 105 S.Ct. 1487 (1985), strongly supports the mine operators' arguments that the Secretary should provide them at least some kind of *pre-deprivation* hearing:

Some opportunity for the employee to present his side of these cases is recurringly of obvious value in reaching an accurate decision. Dismissal for cause will often involve factual disputes. Even where the facts are clear, the appropriateness or necessity of the discharge may not be; in such cases, the only meaningful opportunity to invoke the discretion of the decision maker is likely to be before the termination takes effect.

This language is equally applicable to the employer situations in which the issue presented is the issue of forced reinstatement rather than the other side of the coin, employee termination. We believe this rationale meets the second factor set out in *Mathews v. Eldridge.* While something less "than a *full* evidentiary hearing is sufficient prior to adverse administrative action," the employers here must be afforded a minimal opportunity to present their side of the dispute before temporary reinstatement is forced upon them. Since the Secretary's Rule 44 fails to insure any reasonable opportunity for at least some minimal pre-deprivation hearing, we hold that it violates the mine operators' due process rights.

[Affirmed.]

RECENT DEVELOPMENTS

The federal administrative process has been closely scrutinized from several angles in recent years. In order to make federal agencies more open to public view and more responsive to the needs of constituents and to fiscal and economic concerns, many changes have been made.

Freedom of Information Act

The Freedom of Information Act of 1966, with significant amendments in 1974, is codified as section 552 of the Administrative Procedure Act. Prior to its enactment it was extremely difficult for a private citizen to obtain and examine government-held documents. The agency from which the information was requested could deny the applicant on the grounds that he or she was not properly and directly concerned or that the requested information should not be disclosed because to do so would not be in the public interest. Under FOIA, any person may reasonably describe what information is sought and the burden for withholding information is on the agency. A response is required of the agency within ten working days after receipt of a request, and denial by the agency may be appealed by means of an expeditable federal district court action. There are, of course, exemptions—nine specific areas to which the disclosure requirements do not apply. That is, if the information concerns certain matters, the agency is not required to comply with the request. The nine exemptions apply to matters that are:

1. Secret in the interest of national defense or foreign policy

2. Related solely to internal personnel rules and practices of an agency

3. Exempted from disclosure by statute

4. Trade secrets and commercial or financial information obtained from a person and privileged or confidential

5. Inter-agency or intra-agency memoranda or letters

6. Personnel and medical files, the disclosure of which would constitute an invasion of personal privacy

7. Certain investigatory records compiled for law enforcement purposes

8. Related to the regulation or supervision of financial institutions

9. Geological and geophysical information and data, including maps concerning wells

With regard to the exemptions, Chief Judge Bazelon had this to say in *Soucie v. David,* 448 F.2d 1067 (D.C.Cir. 1971):

> The touchstone of any proceedings under the Act must be the clear legislative intent to assure public access to all governmental records whose disclosure would not significantly harm specific governmental interests. The policy of the Act requires that the disclosure requirements be construed broadly, the exemptions narrowly.

The Privacy Act

The Federal Privacy Act of 1974 seeks to protect individuals from unnecessary disclosures of facts about them from files held by federal agencies. Though the need of federal agencies for information is recognized through a large series of exceptions and qualifications, the general thrust of the Privacy Act is to prohibit federal agencies from disclosing information from their files about an individual without that individual's written consent. Federal agencies are specifically forbidden from selling or renting an individual's name and address, unless authorized by another law.

The Government in the Sunshine Act

A further effort to open up the government is provided by the 1976 Government in the Sunshine Act, codified as section 552b of the Administrative Procedure Act. The purpose of the Act is to assure that ". . . every portion of every meeting of an agency shall be open to public observation." There are, however, exceptions to the open meeting requirement. If the meeting qualifies for one of ten specified exemptions and the agency by majority vote decides to do so, the meeting may be closed to the public. The exemptions of the Act are similar to the nine provided for in the FOIA but are not identical.

At the state level, most have passed some form of open meetings laws. There is considerable diversity, but the common purpose is to permit the public to view the decision-making process at all stages.

The Regulatory Flexibility Act

We are all presumed to know the law, and when final versions of rules are published in the Federal Register, legally speaking, we are all put on notice of their existence. Congress realized, however, that as a practical matter many persons, especially small businesses, do not closely follow proposed and final rules printed in the Federal Register. Therefore, Congress passed the Regulatory Flexibility Act in 1980. Among other provisions, the RFA requires most federal agencies to transmit to the Small Business Administration on a semiannual basis agendas briefly describing areas in which they may propose rules having a substantial impact on small entities (including small businesses, small governmental units, and nonprofit organizations). In this way the small businesses may be on the lookout for potential changes. Also, when any rule is promulgated which will have a significant economic impact on a substantial number of small entities, the agency proposing the rule must give notice not only through the Federal Register but also through publications of general notice likely to be obtained by small entities, such as trade journals.

Office of Management and Budget

For purposes of fiscal restraint, President Reagan placed substantial control over the process of administrative rulemaking in the Office of Management and Budget (OMB). First, through Executive Order #12,291, executive agencies (not independent regulatory agencies such as the FTC) are required to conduct cost-benefit, least-cost analyses on every proposed rule change which would have an impact on the economy of more than $100 million. Furthermore, the agency must submit the rule for OMB review before asking for public comment and again at the end of the comment process.

Later, in Executive Order #12,498, an "early warning" for OMB was installed. Now, as soon as agencies even contemplate issuing an important rule, they must obtain OMB approval before taking any significant steps toward implementation.

Although OMB theoretically makes only recommendations and suggestions in the rulemaking process, functionally OMB has become a clearinghouse with substantial influence. Few proposed agency rules survive strong OMB opposition.

Deregulation

The economic efficiency of many programs of federal regulation is easily questioned. Furthermore, the paperwork burden on many companies attempting to comply with complex federal regulatory schemes can be overwhelming. For these and other reasons, the Carter administration commenced, and the Reagan administration attempted to accelerate the "deregulation" of the economy.

Efforts at deregulation can be seen in the introduction of free competition in ratemaking for the airline industry, the abolishment of the Civil Aeronautics Board (CAB), the proposition to terminate the Interstate Commerce Commission (ICC), and the adoption of a less aggressive attitude at agencies such as OSHA, the CPSC, and the EPA.

The advantages and disadvantages of deregulation will be debated for years. Proponents point to the cost savings and the general fare reductions which have occurred in the airline industry through introduction of free competition and elimination of government rate-setting. Opponents point to a recent rise in injuries from products and in the workplace, the provinces of OSHA and the CPSC, and to alleged increases in various types of pollution due to EPA inactivity. Neither increases in regulation nor decreases in regulation (as the *Motor Vehicle Manufacturers Ass'n v. State Farm Mutual Auto Ins. Co.* case shows) come without cost. To a large extent, the positions taken on the deregulation debate are determined by political philosophies and "whose ox is being gored."

SUMMARY

In terms of their influence on America's economy and society, administrative agencies truly constitute a "fourth branch of government."

Increased complexity in our economy and society means that our legislatures, state and federal, cannot give personal attention to even a fraction of the problems demanding government attention. Therefore, substantial legislative power is delegated to administrative agencies, sometimes under only the vaguest of guidelines.

Major federal agencies possess both ministerial and discretionary powers. The discretionary powers include those to investigate (as the executive branch does), to make rules (as the legislative branch does), and to adjudicate alleged violations (as the judicial branch does). The courts may review virtually all agency actions.

To be valid, agency rules must be promulgated in accordance with a constitutional delegation of authority, pursuant to proper procedures, in accordance with constitutional strictures—especially those of due process—and must not be arbitrary and capricious.

The power of administrative agencies is very controversial. In recent years the federal government especially has attempted to make administrative procedures more open to public scrutiny and to streamline them so they will be less burdensome for the regulated parties.

KEY TERMS

Administrative agency
Ministerial powers
Discretionary powers
Investigative powers
Rulemaking powers
Adjudicatory powers
Subpoena
Question of law

QUESTIONS AND PROBLEMS

1. Louisiana passed a statute to regulate commercial marine diving. Among other things, the statute created a Licensing Board, which thereafter promulgated rules and regulations relative to the qualifications of apprentice, journeyman, and master marine divers. One regulation provided that a person could be licensed as a master marine diver only if he had "continuously worked for a period of five years under supervision of a master marine diver." Under this regulation, the board refused to license a diver (as a master marine diver) who had had several years' diving experience in the U.S. Navy, and who had also had about eight years' commercial diving experience in Louisiana (but not under supervision of a master marine diver). The diver challenged the board's action, contending that the statute was an unconstitutional delegation of legislative authority in view of the fact that it permitted the board to set licensing qualifications without containing any statutory limitations on it, or any standards to which the board should look in setting its qualifications. Do you agree with this contention? Why or why not? (*Banjavich v. Louisiana Licensing Board of Marine Divers,* 111 So.2d 505, 1959.)

2. The U.S. Department of Energy (DOE) issued a subpoena for Phoenix Petroleum Company records during the course of an investigation to determine whether Phoenix had illegally sold crude oil. Phoenix moved to quash the subpoena, claiming DOE was on a "fishing expedition." DOE proved the subpoenaed items were reasonably relevant to the purpose of the investigation, but admitted that it could not establish probable cause to believe a violation had taken place. Should the subpoena be quashed by the court? Discuss. (*U.S. v. Phoenix Petroleum Co.,* 571 F.Supp. 16, S.D.Tex. 1982.)

3. Biswell, a pawnshop operator who was federally licensed to deal in sporting weapons, was visited one afternoon by a policeman and a Federal Treasury agent who requested entry into a locked gun storeroom. They had no search warrant, but showed Biswell a section of the Gun Control Act of 1968 which authorized warrantless entry of the premises of gun dealers. Biswell then allowed a search which turned up two sawed-off rifles and led to Biswell's conviction for dealing in firearms without having paid a required special occupational tax. On appeal, Biswell challenged the constitutionality of the warrantless search. Discuss. (*U.S. v. Biswell,* 406 U.S. 311, 1972.)

4. The Federal Trade Commission Act authorizes the Federal Trade Commission to determine what kinds of business practices constitute "unfair methods of competition, and deceptive or unfair practices," and to prohibit such practices. Traditionally, when such a practice has been found to exist, the FTC has simply ordered the offending company to stop the practice. In 1975, however, when the FTC ruled that Listerine ads had—for many years—falsely stated that Listerine was "effective in preventing and curing colds and sore throats," the FTC ordered the manufacturer to stop such advertising, and, in addition, it ordered the manufacturer to insert in *future* advertising the statement that Listerine would *not* prevent or cure colds and sore throats. The manufacturer then asked the federal courts to rule that the FTC did not have the power, under the Federal Trade Commission Act, to issue such an order (known as "corrective advertising"). Do you think the manufacturer's argument is a good one? Why or why not? (*Warner-Lambert v. FTC,* 562 F.2d 749, 1977.)

5. A New Jersey statute provided that every taxicab owner who wished to operate in a city within the state had to obtain consent of the "governing body" of the municipality. The statute also provided that the governing body could "make and enforce" ordinances to "license and regulate" all vehicles used as taxis. Under this law a New Jersey city passed an ordinance that set a flat rate taxicab fare of $1.15 for all trips made within the city, regardless of the miles involved. A taxicab owner who wanted to charge $1.50 for some trips attacked this ordinance on the ground that the statute did *not,* expressly or impliedly, give to cities the power to set taxi fares. (I.e., the gist of the attack was that legislatures could not delegate *ratemaking* powers to municipalities.) What was the result? Discuss. (*Yellow Cab Corp. v. Clifton City Council,* 308 A.2d 60, 1973.)

6. One section of an Oklahoma law provided that no person shall "knowingly sell" alcoholic beverages to a minor. Certain penalties were provided for, in the event of violations. Another section of the law authorized the Oklahoma Beverage Control Board to promulgate rules and regulations to carry out the act. The board then adopted a rule that, in essence, provided that any liquor license could be revoked if the licensee sold liquor to a minor, even if he did *not* know the buyer was a minor. When the license of a liquor retailer, Wray, was revoked by the board as a result of his sale of liquor to a person who he did not know was a minor, he contended in the Oklahoma courts that the rule of the board was invalid because it conflicted with the quoted statute. Do you agree with this argument? Discuss. (*Wray v. Oklahoma Alcoholic Beverage Control Board,* 442 P.2d 309, 1968.)

7. A Pueblo, Colorado, police officer violated the Pueblo City Code by removing his personnel file from the city personnel office without permission of the city Civil Service Commission. The commission viewed the officer's conduct as a form of theft, and therefore discharged him. He appealed this ruling to a Colorado court, con-

tending that the action of the commission was capricious and arbitrary—unreasonably harsh in view of the offense. If you were on the court, would you agree? Explain. (*Bennett v. Price,* 446 P.2d 419, 1968.)

8. The West Virginia Human Rights Act created a Human Rights Commission. The statute provided that "the commission shall encourage and endeavor to bring about mutual understanding and respect among all racial, religious and ethnic groups within the state and shall strive to eliminate all discrimination in employment and places of public accommodation by virtue of race, creed or religious belief." A later statute further listed certain specific discriminatory practices that were unlawful, including the refusal to rent property to minority group members. Thereafter the Human Rights Commission found a Mrs. Pauley guilty of such a violation. In addition to ordering her to stop the practice, the commission fined her $600. (Neither statute mentioned fines, nor the right of the commission to levy them.) When Mrs. Pauley appealed the ruling, the trial court agreed that the commission had neither the express nor the implied authority to fine violators. The commission appealed to the West Virginia Court of Appeals. What result? Explain. (*State Human Rights Commission v. Pauley,* 212 S.E.2d 77, 1968.)

Chapter 7

TORTS

Our primary concern in Part I of this text has been to familiarize the student with the aspects of our legal system that are common to all branches of law. Thus we have examined the nature and sources of law generally and the processes by which rules of law are formulated, paying little or no attention to such specific subjects as contracts, sales, or agency. (The only deviation from this approach occurred in Chapter 5, where the subject of constitutional law was given special treatment because of the inherently supreme position it occupies.) We now want to discuss one other branch of law that merits special consideration—**torts** ("civil wrongs"). We will treat the subject generally in this chapter, and specifically with respect to business in Chapter 8.

A PREFACE

Two areas of law, criminal law and contract law, developed at an early time in England. While both were intended to eliminate, insofar as possible, various kinds of wrongful conduct, each was concerned with markedly different wrongs. The major purposes of criminal law were to define *wrongs against the state*—types of conduct so inherently undesirable that they were flatly prohibited—and to permit the state to punish those who committed such acts by the imposition of fines or imprisonment. The major purposes of contract law, on the other hand, were (1) to spell out the nature of the rights and duties springing from *private agreements between individuals,* and (2) in the event that one party failed to live up to these duties, to compensate the innocent party for the loss resulting from the other's breach of contract.

While criminal law and contract law were in their initial stages of development, it became apparent that neither one afforded protection to the large numbers of persons who suffered losses resulting from other kinds of conduct equally unjustifiable from a social standpoint—acts of carelessness, deception, and the like. Faced with this situation, the courts at an early

time began to recognize and define other "legal wrongs" besides crimes and breaches of contract—and began to permit persons who were injured thereby to bring civil actions to recover damages against those who committed them. Acts that came to be recognized as wrongs under these rules, which were formulated by judges over the years on a case-by-case basis, acquired the name of *torts* (the French word for "*wrongs*").

Because tort law applies to such a wide range of activities, any introductory definition of tort must necessarily be framed in general terms—as, for example, "any wrong excluding breaches of contract and crimes," or "any noncontractual civil wrong committed upon the person or property of another." While such definitions are of little aid in illustrating the specific kinds of torts that are recognized, they do, at least, reflect the historical lines of demarcation between breaches of contract, crimes, and torts.[1]

SCOPE AND COMPLEXITY OF TORT LAW

As our society has become increasingly industrialized and complex, with many relationships existing among individuals that were perhaps unthought of fifty years ago, the legal duties owed by one member of society to others have become considerably more numerous and varied. As a result, tort law encompasses such a wide range of human conduct that the breaches of some duties have little in common with others. For example, some actions are considered tortious (wrongful) only when the actor intended to cause an injury, while in other actions—especially those involving negligence—the actor's intentions are immaterial. Similarly, in some tort actions the plaintiff is required to

---

[1] As indicated by these definitions, torts and crimes are essentially two different kinds of wrongs—the first a wrong against the individual and the second a wrong against the state. However, as we will see, in many situations a single wrongful act can constitute both a tort and a crime.

show physical injury to his or her property as a result of the defendant's misconduct, while in other actions such a showing is not required. In the latter situations other kinds of legal injury are recognized, such as damages to reputation or mental suffering.

A somewhat clearer picture of the broad sweep of tort law can be gained from the realization that the rules making up this area of law must deal with such diverse matters as the care required of a surgeon in the operating room, the circumstances in which a contracting party has a legal obligation to inform the other party of facts which he or she knows that the other party does not possess, and the determination of the kinds of business information (trade secrets) that are entitled to protection against theft by competitors.

The courts clearly engage in some degree of social engineering as they shape the common law of torts. Common to all successful tort actions are the twin concepts of *interest* and *duty*. Each time a court allows tort recovery, it is saying that the plaintiff has an interest (for example, in bodily integrity, in enjoying the benefits of private property, in a good reputation) sufficiently important for the law to furnish protection, and that, correspondingly, in a civilized society the defendant has a duty (for example, not to strike the plaintiff, not to steal plaintiff's property, not to falsely injure plaintiff's reputation) that was breached. As society evolves technologically, morally, philosophically, and otherwise, tort law will evolve also. For example, one hundred years ago, Americans had very little privacy. However, as increased wealth has allowed us to purchase and enjoy privacy, most of us have come to value privacy very much. In recent years most courts have come to recognize privacy as an interest worth protecting and, as we shall see, have imposed a duty on others not to invade our privacy.

The law of torts is so broad and so pervasive that it cannot be treated in a single chapter. This chapter focuses on the law of negligence and on certain intentional torts. A number of torts of specific concern to business are discussed in Chapter 8. Lawsuits arising out of the sale of defective products are also primarily tort related; they are discussed in Chapter 22. While these three chapters are devoted almost solely to tort law, the subject will make appearances in several other chapters.[2]

This chapter begins with a treatment of negligence law, and then examines several important intentional torts.

NEGLIGENCE

Negligence, to oversimplify, is carelessness. The courts long ago decided that our interests in economic well-being and personal safety are sufficiently important to be protected from the careless acts of others. Correspondingly, each of us has a duty as we live our lives and carry on our professions to exercise care so as not to carelessly injure others. Even though we may not intend to injure, the harm is just as real to the victim who is struck by the careless driver, burned by the carelessly designed product, crippled by the careless surgeon, or ruined financially by embezzlement that an accountant carelessly failed to detect.

The negligence cause of action is the most important method of redress existing today for persons injured accidentally. The newspapers are filled with accounts of negligence actions involving asbestos exposure, Agent Orange, Union Carbide's Bhopal disaster in India, and the like. Whether a plaintiff was injured by a careless driver, a careless product designer, a careless surgeon, or a careless accountant, the same basic elements must be proved to establish a right of recovery: (1) that defendant owed plaintiff a *duty* of due care; (2) that defendant *breached* that duty of due care; (3) that defendant's breach *proximately caused* the injury; and (4) that plaintiff suffered *injury*.

---

[2] For example, Chapter 19 (liability of parties in an agency relationship), Chapter 40 (legal liability of accountants), and Chapter 51 (consumer transactions and the law).

Duty

Few concepts are more fraught with difficulty than that of "duty" in the negligence cause of action. As a general rule, it may be said that we each owe a duty to every person whom we can *reasonably foresee* might be injured by our carelessness. If we drive down the street carelessly, pedestrians and other drivers are within the class of foreseeable plaintiffs whom we might injure. That we do not know the exact names of our prospective victims is unimportant.

To quickly illustrate, in *Burke v. Pan American World Airways, Inc.,*[3] plaintiff sued defendants allegedly responsible for a terrible plane collision in the Canary Islands, claiming that she, though in California at the time, felt as though she were being "split in two" and felt an emptiness "like a black hole" at the exact instant of the crash. Plaintiff claimed that in that instant she knew that something terrible had happened to her identical twin sister who was, in fact, killed in the collision. Plaintiff was prepared to document the phenomenon of "extrasensory empathy" between some pairs of identical twins. Even assuming plaintiff could establish the point, the court dismissed the suit. When a plane crashes because of an airline's negligence, its passengers are certainly foreseeable plaintiffs, as are any persons on the ground hit by falling wreckage. However, Burke's injuries were too bizarre to be reasonably foreseeable, even if she did sustain them. The defendants owed no legal duty to plaintiff.

---

[3] 484 F.Supp. 850 (S.D.N.Y. 1980).

Though foreseeability is a very important consideration in establishing the parameters of a careless actor's duty, it is not the only one. The California courts, which have extended the notion of duty about as far as any jurisdiction, have taken into account such factors as:

> . . . the foreseeability of harm to the plaintiff, the degree of certainty that the plaintiff suffered injury, the closeness of the connection between the defendant's conduct and the injury suffered, the moral blame attached to the defendant's conduct, the policy of preventing future harm, the extent of the burden to the defendant and consequences to the community of imposing a duty to exercise care with resulting liability, and the availability, cost, and prevalence of insurance for the risk involved.[4]

Indeed, these are the factors the court used in *Soldano v. O'Daniels,* a case discussed in Chapter 1, to impose a duty not to interfere with a Good Samaritan's attempt to aid a victim in distress.[5]

The following case is just one illustration of a court's struggle to meld foreseeability and public policy factors to produce a proper scope of duty.

---

[4] *Rowland v. Christian,* 70 Cal. Rptr. 97 (1968).

[5] Students should also consult *H. Rosenblum, Inc. v. Adler* in Chapter 40 regarding the duty accountants owe to foreseeable plaintiffs injured by the accountants' professional negligence.

Otis Engineering Corp. v. Clark
Texas Supreme Court, 668 S.W.2d 307 (1983)

Matheson, an employee of defendant Otis Engineering Corporation, had a history of being intoxicated on the job. One night he was particularly intoxicated and his fellow employees believed he should be removed from the machines. Roy, Matheson's supervisor, suggested

that Matheson go home, escorted him to the company parking lot, and asked him if he could make it home. Matheson answered that he could, but thirty minutes later and some three miles away he caused an accident killing the wives of plaintiffs Larry and Clifford Clark.

The Clarks sued Otis in a wrongful death action, but the trial court dismissed the suit holding that Otis could not be liable because Matheson was not acting within the scope of his employment at the time of the accident. The intermediate court of appeals reversed, and Otis appealed to the Texas Supreme Court.

Kilgarlin, Justice:

The Clarks contend that under the facts in this case Otis sent home, in the middle of his shift, an employee whom it knew to be intoxicated. They aver this was an affirmative act which imposed a duty on Otis to act in a non-negligent manner.

In order to establish tort liability, a plaintiff must initially prove the existence and breach of a duty owed to him by the defendant. As a general rule, one person is under no duty to control the conduct of another, *Restatement (Second) of Torts* §315 (1965), even if he has the practical ability to exercise such control. Yet, certain relationships do impose, as a matter of law, certain duties upon parties. For instance, the master-servant relationship may give rise to a duty on the part of the master to control the conduct of his servants outside the scope of employment. This duty, however, is a narrow one. Ordinarily, the employer is liable only for the off-duty torts of his employees which are committed on the employer's premises or with the employer's chattels.

Though the decisional law of this State has yet to address the precise issues presented by this case, factors which should be considered in determining whether the law should impose a duty are the risk, foreseeability, and likelihood of injury weighed against the social utility of the actor's conduct, the magnitude of the burden of guarding against the injury and consequences of placing that burden on the employer.

While a person is generally under no legal duty to come to the aid of another in distress, he is under a duty to avoid any affirmative act which might worsen the situation. One who voluntarily enters an affirmative course of action affecting the interests of another is regarded as assuming a duty to act and must do so with reasonable care.

Otis contends that, at worst, its conduct amounted to nonfeasance and under established law it owed no duty to the Clarks' respective wives. Traditional tort analysis has long drawn a distinction between action and inaction in defining the scope of duty. However, although courts have been slow to recognize liability for nonfeasance, "[d]uring the last century, liability for 'nonfeasance' has been extended still further to a limited group of relations, in which custom, public sentiment and views of social policy have led the courts to find a duty of affirmative action." W. Prosser, *The Law of Torts* at 339. Be that as it may, we do not view this as a case of employer nonfeasance.

What we must decide is if changing social standards and increasing complexities of human relationships in today's society justify imposing a duty upon an employer to act reasonably when he exercises control over his servants. Even though courts have been reluctant to hold an employer liable for the off-duty torts of an employee, "[a]s between an entirely innocent plaintiff and a defendant who admittedly has departed from the social standard of conduct, if only toward one individual, who should bear the loss?" W. Prosser, *supra*, at 257. Dean Prosser additionally observed that "[t]here is nothing sacred about 'duty,' which is nothing more than a word, and a very indefinite one, with which we state our conclusion."

During this year, we have taken a step toward changing our concept of duty in premises cases. In *Corbin v. Safeway Stores, Inc.*, 648 S.W.2d 292 (Tex. 1983), we held that a store owner has a duty to guard against slips and falls if he has actual or constructive knowledge of a dangerous condition and it is foreseeable a fall would occur. Following *Corbin*, why should we be reluctant to impose a duty on Otis? As Dean Prosser has observed, "[c]hanging social conditions lead constantly to the recognition of new duties. No better general statement can be made than the courts will find a duty where, in general, reasonable men would recognize and agree that it exists."

Therefore, the standard of duty that we now adopt for this and all other cases currently in the judicial process, is: when, because of an employee's incapacity, an employer exercises control over the employee, the employer has a duty to take such action as a reasonably prudent employer under the same or similar circumstances would take to prevent the employee from causing an unreasonable risk of harm to others. The duty of the employer is not an absolute duty to insure safety, but requires only reasonable care.

Therefore, the trier of fact in this case should be left free to decide whether Otis acted as a reasonable and prudent employer considering the following factors: the availability of the nurses' aid station [on the plant premises], a possible phone call to Mrs. Matheson, having another employee drive Matheson home, dismissing Matheson early rather than terminating his employment, and the foreseeable consequences of Matheson's driving upon a public street in his stuperous condition.

[Affirm judgment of court of appeals and remand to trial court.]

Duty of Landowners: A recurring problem in establishing the nature of a duty exists regarding the responsibility of owners or occupiers of land. How much of a duty they owe to visitors to their land has traditionally turned on whether the visitor was a trespasser (one who enters the land with no right to do so), a licensee (one who has a right to come onto the property for self-benefit, such as a door-to-door salesman or a neighbor dropping in uninvited), or an invitee (one invited by the owner or occupier or who enters for the benefit of the owner or occupier, such as a customer at a store). The following case discusses the duties owed under the traditional rule, and also examines a new trend toward breaking down the traditional categories and simply utilizing a foreseeability standard for all visitors to land. The traditional rule is still the majority rule, but cases such as this are eroding it.

Ouellette v. Blanchard
New Hampshire Supreme Court, 364 A.2d 631 (1976)

Defendant Blanchard, with a permit, was burning rubbish in an unsupervised fire on his premises. Plaintiff Jaye Ouellette, then ten years old, went onto the property with other children and with them threw sand on the fire. Jaye stepped on some hot coals and fell forward on her hands burning both her feet and hands. She and her father brought this negligence suit. At the close of plaintiffs' opening statement, defendant moved for judgment on grounds that Jaye was a trespasser to whom defendant owed no duty, or at best a licensee to whom he owed no duty of care regarding hazards known to her. The trial court denied the motion and transferred the question of law to the State Supreme Court.

Griffith, Justice:

The three-pronged classification of entrants on land was born judicially in the nineteenth century. In the initial rigid classifications all entrants without the consent of the landowner were *trespassers* as a matter of law and the landowner's liability was limited to intentional injuries. An entrant on land with the permission of the owner but for the entrant's purposes was a *licensee* and entitled only to a warning of hidden dangers. An *invitee* was an entrant on the property for the transaction of business with the occupier and as to him the ordinary rules of negligence were applicable to the occupier.

Whatever its origin, the original rigid classifications and harsh results have been subjected in the passage of time to the twin forces of the industrial age and the development of negligence law. The result has been a refining and erosion of the original rules with exceptions and distinctions piercing the landowners' cloak of immunity.

Rather than continue to embroider the garment when the basic fabric has worn out, many courts have now refused to predicate a landowner's liability solely on the status of the entrant. The California Supreme Court became the first American court to abolish the traditional status distinctions in *Rowland v. Christian,* 70 Cal. Rptr. 97 (1968). Substituting a test of reasonable care under all the circumstances the court observed, "[c]omplexity can be borne and confusion remedied when the underlying principles governing liability are based upon proper considerations. Whatever may have been the historical justifications for the common law distinctions, it is clear that those distinctions are not justified in the light of our modern society and that the complexity and confusion which has arisen is not due to difficulty in applying the original common law rules . . . but is due to the attempts to apply just rules in our modern society within the ancient terminology."

The *Rowland* rationale and result have been adopted entirely by a number of jurisdictions. However, a few courts have contented themselves with abolishing the distinction between invitees and licensees but have retained the trespasser classification. We are not disposed to limit our holding to abolishment of two-thirds of the trichotomy and to retain the category of trespassers as a legal area of immunity.

Whatever the social and policy considerations that led to the judicial creation of the invitee, licensee and trespasser immunities they no longer retain their viability under modern conditions and it is fitting and proper that they be laid to judicial rest.

Accordingly, we hold that henceforth in New Hampshire owners and occupiers of land shall be governed by the test of reasonable care under all the circumstances in the maintenance and operation of their property. The character of and circumstances surrounding the intrusion will be relevant and important in determining the standard of care applicable to the landowner. When the intrusion is not foreseeable or is against the will of the landowner, many intruders will be denied recovery as a matter of law. In other words, a landowner cannot be expected to maintain his premises in a safe condition for a wandering tramp or a person who enters against the known wishes of the landowner. Essentially the traditional tort test of foreseeability determines the liability or nonliability of the landowner in these cases. "If the defendant could not reasonably foresee any injury as the result of his act, or if his conduct was reasonable in the light of what he could anticipate, there is no negligence, and no liability." W. Prosser, *Law of Torts* §43 (4th ed. 1971).

In the present case, the jury may properly consider the activity being carried on by the defendant and the foreseeability of children intruding and being injured in determining whether the defendant acted as a reasonably prudent person in the operation of his property. In our opinion, this provides the triers of fact with a simpler and more exact guideline than to require them to first label the status of the plaintiff and then apply the various standards applicable to the found status.

Defendant's exception overruled; remanded.

Breach

To be liable for negligence, a defendant must have *breached* an existing duty. A breach occurs when defendant fails to exercise the same care as a "reasonable person under similar circumstances" would have exercised. This hypothetical "reasonable person" or "reasonable man"

standard can be fairly strict because of a jury's tendency, confronted with a seriously injured plaintiff, to use 20-20 hindsight:

> [The reasonable man] is one who invariably looks where he is going and is careful to examine the immediate foreground before he executes a leap or bound; who nei-

ther star-gazes nor is lost in meditation when approaching trap doors or the margin of a dock; . . . who never mounts a moving omnibus, and does not alight from any car while the train is still in motion . . . and who informs himself of the history and habits of a dog before administering a caress.[6]

All the Circumstances: Whether or not a defendant's conduct met the "reasonable person" standard of care should be examined in light of all the circumstances of the case. Emergency conditions, for example, may be considered. Normally it would be a clear breach of due care to abandon a moving vehicle, but if a cab driver does so because a robber in his back seat has pulled a gun, a jury might determine that, under all the circumstances, there was no breach of due care so as to render the cab company liable to a pedestrian who was struck by the driverless cab.[7] An unexpected bee sting might cause a bus driver unavoidably to lose control of a bus, though he was a most careful driver.[8] The doctrine of "unavoidable accident" excuses liability in such cases.

The custom of others in the community or of other companies in the industry may also shed light on the proper standard of due care. If the defendant has acted in the same manner as most others in the same situation, it is difficult to conclude that a reasonable person standard was breached. However, custom is not always binding. In one famous case, barges were lost at sea because the tugs towing them had no radio sets to listen to weather reports that would have warned them to take shelter from an approaching storm. That few tug companies used the radio sets was not proof that the "reasonable person" standard was met, because "a whole calling may have unduly lagged in the adoption of new and available devices."[9]

Conduct of Others: Traditionally the courts allowed us to assume that other members of society would act carefully and lawfully. In other words, we had no duty to anticipate the negligent or criminal acts of others. However, increasingly courts and juries are concluding that such acts can and must be anticipated in certain circumstances. Thus, operators of a motel located in a high crime area that has itself been the scene of criminal acts in the past may be held to have breached a duty of due care by not providing adequate security for guests who are victimized by crime.[10] Though some courts refuse to impose a duty in such circumstances, providing adequate security is increasingly a concern for motel owners, common carriers, store owners, concert promoters, and even universities.

Negligence *Per Se:* Though the standard of care to which a defendant will be held in a negligence case is usually formulated by the jury's assessment of what a reasonable person would have done, in some cases the conduct is measured in accordance with legislatively-imposed standards. One example is a "dramshop" act which many states have passed making it illegal to sell liquor to an intoxicated person. Another is the 55-mile-per-hour speed limit.

Most courts have held that if a defendant violates such a statute, it is negligence *per se.*[11] That is, if the plaintiff can show that he or she is within the class of persons that the statute was meant to protect and the harm sustained was the type the statute was meant to prevent, then the issue of

---

[6] A. P. Herbert, *Uncommon Law: Fardell v. Potts.* Reprinted by permission of Lady Herbert.

[7] *Cordas v. Peerless Transp. Co.*, 27 N.Y.S.2d 198 (N.Y. 1941).

[8] *Schultz v. Cheney School District,* 371 P.2d 59 (Wash. 1962).

[9] *The T. J. Hooper,* 60 F.2d 737 (2d Cir. 1932).

[10] *Garzilli v. Howard Johnson's Motor Lodges, Inc.,* 419 F.Supp. 1210 (E.D.N.Y. 1976) (the "Connie Francis case").

[11] And, of course, if a plaintiff violates such a statute it is contributory negligence *per se.* This is a concept we shall address directly under the topic of "defenses."

breach of due care is conclusively resolved against the defendant. The jury can be instructed that the defendant has breached the duty of due care. Lack of damages or proximate causation still might prevent recovery.

In one recent case, a small girl was abducted from the street in front of the building in which she lived, taken across the street to an open, vacant apartment, and assaulted. The girl sued the owners of the apartment building in which the assault occurred for not having locks on the doors, in violation of a city ordinance, and thereby providing a tempting location for the crime. Emphasizing that the ordinance was intended to provide security against crime by requiring all vacant apartments to be secured, the court found negligence *per se* in its violation.[12]

Many courts do not go quite so far, holding only that violation of a statute is one factor the jury can consider among all others in deciding whether defendant breached the duty of due care.

Proximate Cause

After proving existence and breach of a duty of due care, the plaintiff in a negligence action must demonstrate that the breach proximately caused plaintiff's alleged injuries. There are many different labels and many different approaches to the proximate cause concept. Fundamentally, **proximate cause** means direct cause—that there is a direct causal connection between defendant's act of carelessness and plaintiff's injury—but it is more complicated than that.

Many courts speak in terms of two requirements being necessary to establish "legal cause" in each case. First, they require *causation in fact.* This is sometimes termed "but for" causation; that is, can we say that "but for" the defendant's act the injuries would not have taken place. For example, assume that Jill is driving her car at 40 miles per hour on a street where the speed limit is 30 miles per hour when a small child darts into the street from between two cars and is hit by Jill's car. Assume further that the child was so close to Jill's car when he darted into the street that even had Jill been driving 30 miles per hour, or even 20, she could not have avoided striking the child. In such a case we cannot say that "but for" Jill's speeding the accident would not have happened. Jill's careless speeding was not a proximate cause of the accident and Jill would not be liable.

"But for" causation is insufficient in and of itself, however. Almost every act has consequences which ripple through society, and every incident has several causes. Perhaps "but for" your carelessly running a stop sign, ambulance driver A would never have met nurse B and had child C who at the age of 14 murdered D. May D's family sue you? Obviously not. For policy reasons, we must limit the liability stemming from our actions in some fashion.

Most courts return to the notion of *foreseeability* in establishing the second element of legal causation. Factual causation ("but for") plus foreseeability will establish proximate or legal causation. Because foreseeability is an important factor in the establishment of both duty and proximate cause, court discussions of the two concepts tend to overlap.

The most famous tort case of all time is perhaps *Palsgraf v. Long Island R.R.*,[13] in which railway employees carelessly pushed a passenger who was trying to board a train. This caused him to drop a package he was carrying which, it turned out, contained fireworks which exploded beneath the wheels of the train. The force of the concussion knocked over a scale at the far end of the train station, injuring Mrs. Palsgraf. Injury to the boarding passenger and his property was a foreseeable result of the negligence of the railroad employees. They owed a duty of care to him and any injuries to him

---

[12] *Nixon v. Mr. Property Management Co.*, 690 S.W.2d 546 (Tex. 1985).

[13] 162 N.E. 99 (N.Y. 1928).

would have been proximately caused by their actions. However, the court found the injury to Mrs. Palsgraf unforeseeable. The duty owed to the boarding passenger did not protect her.

The *Palsgraf* dissent argued that every person owes to the world a duty to refrain from careless acts, and that we should be liable for all injuries flowing directly from our negligence, regardless of foreseeability. The dissenters felt the wrongdoer should be liable for all "proximate consequences," even where they consist of injuries to persons outside the foreseeable radius of danger.

Generally speaking, the "foreseeability" test of *Palsgraf* holds sway in our law today, but the "direct consequences" view of the dissent is frequently applied in various circumstances. For example, if we carelessly injure a person who turns out to be a hemophiliac, who then bleeds to death when most persons would not have, we are still liable for the death. Courts say that we must take our victims as we find them. Though it might not be reasonably foreseeable to us that our victim would be a hemophiliac, his death is a direct result of our carelessness.

Independent Intervening Cause: Especially in terms of foreseeability, the concept of **independent intervening cause** is important. Such a cause is one that emanates from a third party or source to disrupt the causal connection between the defendant's careless act and plaintiff's injury. Assume that Sue is driving down the street when she comes upon an intersection that is blocked by an accident caused by Joe's having run a stop sign. Sue turns her car around and while driving away is hit by a tree that is blown down by a strong breeze. Sue can argue that "but for" Joe's carelessness the intersection would not have been blocked and she would have been several miles away from the tree at the time it blew over. But should we hold Joe liable for Sue's injury? No, because the tree's falling is an independent, intervening cause that breaks up the causal chain between Joe's careless driving and Sue's injury. The key, again, is foreseeability. An intervening cause that can reasonably be foreseen by the defendant is usually insufficient to break the causal chain, as the following case illustrates.

Anglin v. Florida Department of Transportation
Florida Court of Appeals, 472 So.2d 784 (1985)

Plaintiff Anglin, her husband, and her brother were traveling in a pickup truck on a rural road when they unexpectedly hit an accumulation of water that covered both lanes of travel and was approximately six inches deep. The truck motor was doused with water and died. The Anglins attempted to start the motor by pushing the truck down the road and then "popping" the clutch. Approximately fifteen minutes later, while they were still trying this procedure, DuBose passed the Anglin truck heading in the opposite direction. He turned his car around, intending to give the Anglins a push. Unfortunately, DuBose failed to see the truck in time, hit his brakes, slid into the rear of the truck, and pinned the plaintiff between the two vehicles causing injury which resulted in the amputation of both her legs.

Plaintiff sued the Florida Department of Transportation and Seaboard Coastline Railroad Company, alleging negligence in the design and maintenance of the road and adjacent railroad tracks by allowing

accumulations of water on the roadway. The trial judge entered summary judgment for defendants, ruling as a matter of law that DuBose's actions were an independent intervening cause unforeseeable to defendants, thereby breaking the chain of causation between their alleged negligence and plaintiff's injury. Plaintiff appealed.

Zehmer, Judge:

As a general rule, a tort feasor is liable for all damages proximately caused by his negligence. The term "proximate cause" (or "legal cause," in the language of the standard jury instructions) consists of two essential elements: (1) causation in fact, and (2) foreseeability. Causation in fact is often characterized in terms of a "but for" test, i.e., *but for* the defendant's negligence, the resulting damage would not have occurred. In the present case, there is no question as to causation in fact because "but for" the defendants' alleged negligence in causing the pooling of water on the highway, there would have been no accidental stopping of plaintiff's truck and resulting injury.

The second element of proximate cause, foreseeability, is, unlike causation in fact, a concept established through considerations of public policy and fairness whereby a defendant whose conduct factually "caused" damages may nevertheless be relieved of liability for those damages. Thus, proximate cause may be found lacking where the type of damage or injury that occurred is not within the scope of danger or risk created by the defendant's negligence and, thus, not a reasonably foreseeable result thereof. It is not necessary, however, that the defendants "be able to foresee the exact nature and extent of the injuries or the precise manner in which the injuries occur"; all that is necessary to liability is that "the tort feasor be able to foresee that *some* injury will likely result in *some* manner as a consequence of his negligent acts." *Crislip v. Holland,* 401 So.2d 1115 (Fla. 4th DCA 1984).

In the instant case, it cannot be said as a matter of law that an injury to plaintiff was not within the scope of danger or risk arising out of the alleged negligence. In the field of human experience, one should expect that negligently permitting a pool of water on an open highway would likely pose a substantial hazard to motorists because a vehicle crashing unexpectedly into water is likely to experience a stalled motor or other difficulty causing the vehicle to stop on the highway, thereby subjecting its occupants to the risk of injury from collision by other cars.

Proximate cause may be found lacking, however, where an unforeseeable force or action occurring independently of the original negligence causes the injury or damage. This force or action is commonly referred to as an "independent, efficient intervening cause." *Gibson v. Avis Rent-A-Car System, Inc.,* 386 So.2d 520 (Fla. 1980). For the original negligent actor to be relieved of liability under this doctrine, however, the intervening cause must be "efficient," i.e., truly independent of and not "set in motion" by the original negligence.

The trial court correctly characterized Mr. DuBose's negligent operation of his car as an independent intervening cause. The negligent pooling of water did not cause Mr. DuBose to negligently operate his vehicle into collision with plaintiffs. The trial court erred, however, in ruling as *a matter of law* that such intervening cause warranted entry of summary judgment for defendants. If an intervening cause is reasonably foreseeable, the negligent defendants may be held liable. Whether an intervening cause is foreseeable is ordinarily for the trier of fact to decide. The plaintiffs' exposure to danger was created by defendants' negligence, and the fact that a collision might occur while plaintiffs were extricating themselves from such danger up to fifteen minutes later presents a jury issue on foreseeability.

Reversed and remanded.

Injury

As the final element of a negligence cause of action, plaintiff must prove injury. The injury may be physical (such as broken bones suffered in a car accident) or economic (such as the loss of a building in a fire carelessly set). Damage for emotional distress may also be recovered, but recovery for this type of injury has been troublesome. Courts originally refused to allow recovery for emotional injury on the grounds that such damages were intangible and too easily faked. Over the years, the courts have slowly changed their view as psychiatric testimony regarding the actual existence of emotional distress has become more dependable.

At first, courts allowed recovery for negligently caused emotional distress where the plaintiff also sustained a physical injury in the accident. It was easier to believe that the plaintiff suffered emotional distress if there were accompanying physical injuries. Later courts also awarded recovery to plaintiffs who were not physically injured, but were in the "zone of danger." Thus, a pedestrian who was narrowly missed by an automobile which ran down a fellow pedestrian could sue the careless driver for emotional damages.

Because application of the "zone of danger" test leads sometimes to rather arbitrary distinctions, many courts have taken an additional step by allowing "bystander recovery." Thus, according to the leading case,[14] a parent who sees or hears an accident killing the parent's child can recover for emotional distress though not within the zone of danger. Three factors to be weighed in deciding whether to allow recovery are: (1) whether plaintiff was located near the scene of the accident; (2) whether the emotional shock resulted from a contemporaneous perception of the accident, as opposed to hearing about it later; and (3) whether the plaintiff and the victim were closely related. Many courts have rejected bystander recovery, which obviously entails an extension of the concept of duty. But the modern trend is to recognize that if an actor's carelessness causes an injury which kills or seriously injures someone, the victim's loved ones are almost certain to suffer emotional trauma.

Punitive damages, also known as exemplary damages, are not recoverable in mere negligence cases. These are monetary damages, over and above the sums necessary to compensate for plaintiff's injuries, which are assessed against the defendant to punish for wrongdoing and to deter defendant and others from engaging in such wrongful conduct. A defendant in a negligence action is guilty of mere carelessness, so punitive damages are viewed as inappropriate. However, punitive damages are available to plaintiffs in-

---

[14]*Dillon v. Legg,* 69 Cal. Rptr. 72 (1958).

jured by the intentional torts which we will discuss later in the chapter.

Defenses

Even if the plaintiff establishes all four elements of a negligence cause of action, the defendant may avert or reduce recovery by establishing certain defenses.

Contributory Fault: If the plaintiff is guilty of fault which contributed to the accident, a defense may exist. Under the old system of **contributory negligence,** a plaintiff who was guilty of carelessness which contributed in any material way to the accident was barred from recovery altogether. Even if the jury concluded that plaintiff was 1 percent at fault and defendant 99 percent, plaintiff could recover nothing, no matter how serious the injuries were.

Because of the harshness of the contributory negligence system, most jurisdictions have replaced it with a system of **comparative negligence.** Comparative negligence or comparative fault systems vary widely from jurisdiction to jurisdiction, so it is difficult to generalize. Some states have "pure" comparative negligence systems under which, no matter how great a share of the fault is attributable to plaintiff, plaintiff still is entitled to recover the portion of damages caused by defendant's carelessness. For example, let's assume that in a case arising out of an auto collision between P and D, a jury assesses P's damages at $100,000 and finds P 40 percent at fault and D 60 percent at fault. Rather than being barred from recovery as in a contributory negligence system, P would recover $60,000—that portion of the damages caused by D's fault. Indeed, in a pure system, even if P is found 99 percent at fault and D 1 percent, P would still recover $1,000. That P is many times more at fault than D does not bar recovery for that portion of the loss caused by D's carelessness.

Most jurisdictions have not adopted a pure comparative negligence system. Many allow a plaintiff to recover whatever percentage of damages were caused by defendant, unless plaintiff's share of the fault is assessed at 51 percent or higher. If plaintiff's fault exceeds 50 percent, recovery is barred altogether on the theory that plaintiff should recover nothing if he or she is more at fault than defendant. Other states set 49 percent as the cap, not allowing recovery to a plaintiff found 50 percent or more at fault.

As stated, these basic approaches vary from state to state, as do treatments of some more complex problems, including how to handle multiple plaintiffs and multiple defendants, how to handle counterclaims, how to reconcile negligence claims accompanied by strict liability claims not dependent on fault, and whether to differentiate between various types of plaintiff misconduct such as simple carelessness (not paying attention), product misuse (using a product for an unintended purpose), and assumption of risk (knowingly undertaking a dangerous risk).

Statute of Limitations: In negligence, as in other causes of action, every state has a **statute of limitations** within which the suit must be filed or forever barred. A typical tort statute of limitations is two years. Thus, a plaintiff injured by defendant's negligence must file suit within two years of the occurrence. Occasionally a plaintiff may not even know of the injury until more than two years after the occurrence, for example, when carelessly designed drugs with side effects which will not show up for years are sold. Most states have applied tolling devices which provide that in such a case the statute of limitations is tolled; that is, will not begin to run, until the plaintiff knows or should know of the injury. In response to the medical malpractice and products liability "crises," several states have passed statutes of "repose" which bar certain actions after, say 15 years, whether the injuries sustained were discoverable or not during that period.

No Fault Systems

Negligence has been eliminated as a basis for lawsuits in at least two contexts which should be mentioned here. Every state has a *workers' com-*

pensation system which allows injured employees to recover benefits from their employers when injured on the job. The employee can recover regardless of the presence of employer fault, but forfeits the right to sue the employer even if the employer has been careless. This topic is covered in more detail in Chapter 49.

Several states have enacted "no fault" automobile statutes. The thrust of these statutes is to reduce litigation by allowing persons who suffer only minor injuries in car accidents to recover only from their own insurance company. Though these laws vary widely from jurisdiction to jurisdiction, in most the plaintiffs' losses must exceed a certain statutory threshhold before resort to litigation is allowed.

MAJOR INTENTIONAL TORTS

Assault and Battery

Assault and battery are similar torts which may be treated together. Although modern courts and statutes frequently use the two terms interchangeably, technically a **battery** is a rude, inordinate contact with the person of another. An **assault,** basically, is any act which creates an apprehension of an imminent battery. That we can sue for assault and battery protects our personal dignity from intrusions of the mind (assault) and body (battery). The courts long ago concluded that we have a legitimate interest in being protected from offensive bodily contacts and fear of them.

Elements: One way to formulate the basic elements of the torts of assault and battery is to require plaintiff to prove: (1) defendant's affirmative conduct, (2) intent, and (3) plaintiff's injury.

Affirmative Conduct and Intent: If Sue is carefully driving down the street and is hit by a car that runs a red light and as a result Sue's car is pushed into a pedestrian, Sue has not committed assault or battery. Though the pedestrian has sustained both apprehension (assuming she saw the accident as it happened) and rude contact, Sue committed no affirmative act which caused the injuries. The driver of the car that ran the red light did commit an affirmative act that was tortious, but that act was negligence, not assault or battery. On the other hand, if, while driving down the street, Sue spotted an enemy and deliberately ran down that person in a crosswalk, an assault and battery would have occurred.

The intent required for both assault and battery is the intent either to create an offensive contact to plaintiff's body or the apprehension of it in plaintiff. Furthermore, a person is presumed to intend the natural consequences of his or her actions. Thus, if A points an unloaded gun at B and utters threats to use it, an assault occurs if B did not know the gun was unloaded even if A's intent is simply to play a harmless prank. The natural consequences of A's act of pointing the gun is to create an apprehension in B.

Under the *doctrine of transferred intent,* if Sam shoots at Bill, but Bill ducks and the bullet hits Carlos, Carlos has an assault (assuming he saw the incident happening) and battery claim against Sam even if he is Sam's best friend and Sam wouldn't intentionally hurt him for the world. The law transfers the intent Sam had to injure Bill to Carlos.

Injury: If plaintiff seeks to establish an assault, the injury sustained must be in the nature of an apprehension of imminent bodily contact of an offensive nature. A threat of future contact or a threat by a defendant far away is insufficient. Threats or even attempts at violence which the intended victim does not know about until much later do not create the requisite apprehension, as where D shoots at and misses P from so far away that P never realizes the shot was fired. Usually plaintiff's reactions are judged by what would have caused apprehension in a reasonable person, but if defendant knows that plaintiff is an unusually sensitive person and threatens contacts which plaintiff finds offensive though most persons would not, an assault occurs.

If plaintiff sues for battery, the injury that must be demonstrated is an offensive contact. Being struck with a fist, a knife, or a bullet obviously satisfies the requirement. So does being spat upon, poisoned, and having one's clothes ripped or cane knocked away.

The following case illustrates the concept of assault.

Western Union Telegraph Co. v. Hill
Court of Appeals of Alabama, 150 So. 709 (1933)

Plaintiff, Mr. Hill, owned a business in Huntsville, Alabama. He had a contract with Western Union under which it was to regulate and keep in repair an electric clock in plaintiff's office. When the clock needed attention, plaintiff was to notify Western Union's office manager in Huntsville, Sapp, who in turn would contact a repairman to do the work.

One day Mrs. Hill told Sapp over the phone that the clock needed repair. When the repairman failed to show up, she took the clock to the Western Union office herself. There she found Sapp in charge, sitting behind a four-foot counter that separated him and the telegraph operators from the public.

Sapp rose as Mrs. Hill entered, and from his side of the counter asked what he could do for her. (He testified at the trial that he had just finished "two or three drinks," and that he was feeling "good and amiable.") Mrs. Hill produced the clock and asked when he was going to fix it. Sapp looked at her for a minute or two and said: "If you will come back here and let me love and pet you, I will fix your clock." He then reached forward in an effort to grasp Mrs. Hill's arm, but she jumped back out of the way, and no physical contact occurred.

In this action by Mr. Hill, alleging an assault upon his wife, there was conflicting evidence as to whether Sapp would have been physically able to touch Mrs. Hill—because of the width of the counter separating them—even if she had not moved back. The trial court left this question to the jury, and it returned a verdict in Mr. Hill's favor against Sapp and Western Union. (That is, the jury found that a physical touching was possible, substantiating her claim of reasonable apprehension, and that an assault had thus occurred.) Judgment was for plaintiff, and Western Union appealed.

Samford, Judge:

. . . The first question that addresses itself to us is, Was there such an assault as will justify an action for damages? . . .

In this state an assault and battery is: "Any touching by one person of the person of another in rudeness or in anger."

While every battery [ordinarily] includes an assault, an assault does not necessarily require a battery to complete it. What it does take to constitute an assault is an unlawful attempt to commit a battery, incomplete by reason of some intervening cause; or, to state it differently, to constitute an actionable assault there must be an intentional, unlawful, offer to touch the person of another in a rude or angry manner under such circumstances as to create in the mind of the party alleging the assault a well-founded fear of an imminent battery, coupled with the apparent present ability to effectuate the attempt, if not prevented. . . .

[The court then summarized the conflicting evidence as follows:] The counter [according to defendants' testimony] was four feet and two inches high, and so wide that Sapp, standing on the floor, leaning against the counter and stretching his arm and hand to full length [could barely touch] the outer edge of the counter. The photographs in evidence show that the counter was as high as Sapp's armpits. [Additionally,] the physical surroundings as evidenced by the photographs [tend to show that] Sapp could not have touched plaintiff's wife across that counter even if he had reached his hand in her direction, unless she was leaning against the counter. . . . However, there was testimony tending to prove that, notwithstanding the width of the counter and the height of Sapp, Sapp could have reached from six to eighteen inches beyond the counter in an effort to place his hand on Mrs. Hill. This evidence [when considered with her testimony as to her feeling of fear] presents a question for the jury. This was the view taken by the trial judge, and in the several rulings bearing on this question there is no error. . . .

[The trial court's definition of assault, and the verdict in favor of plaintiff, were thus upheld. However, the judgment was reversed and the case remanded for further proceedings because the trial court's instruction on another aspect of the case was held to be erroneous.]

Defenses: In addition to the statute of limitations, which typically is two years in such cases, the two primary defenses to assault and battery are **consent** and **self-defense.** A plaintiff who has consented to offensive contacts and the threat of them cannot sue for assault and battery. Thus, a boxer who steps into the ring or the quarterback who steps onto the football field consents to the normal contacts that go with the rules of the game. However, if a football player is forearmed from behind by an opposing player after the play was over, he might have a good battery claim because his consent does not extend to this contact outside the rules of the game any more than it would extend to being shot by an opponent.[15]

Consent cannot be procured by fraud, nor can it be ill-informed. Thus, if M procures F's consent to sexual intercourse by hiding the fact that he has herpes, her consent to the intercourse does not constitute consent to the harmful contact with the disease. She may sue for battery.[16] Doctors performing surgery must be very careful to fully inform their patients regarding the

---

[15]*Hackbart v. Cincinnati Bengals,* 601 F.2d 516 (10th Cir. 1979).

[16]*Long v. Adams,* 333 S.E.2d 852 (Ga. App. 1985).

contacts that will take place during the surgery in order to avoid liability for battery. Consent to an appendectomy does not extend to removal of some of the reproductive organs even though it may be the doctor's best medical judgment that they should be removed.

Self-defense creates a well-recognized privilege to assault and battery. Though the courts do not require "detached reflection in the presence of an uplifted knife,"[17] the general rule permits only that degree of force reasonable under the circumstances. One is seldom privileged to shoot an assailant in the back once that assailant is clearly fleeing and poses no further threat. In some cases, retreat might even be required as preferable to deadly force. Violence is also allowed in defense of others, and even in defense of property, although obviously a lesser degree of force will be viewed as "reasonable" in defense of property.

Defamation

Long ago the courts decided that we have a legitimate interest in preserving our good reputation in the community. Those who damage our reputation by spreading falsehoods commit the tort of **defamation** and may be liable in damages. Though defamation has historic common law roots, its development in recent years has been strongly influenced by a series of Supreme Court decisions which have molded the tort in accordance with First Amendment principles.

Libel versus Slander: Defamation takes two basic forms. **Libel** is written defamation; **slander** is oral. Television and radio broadcasts have generally been categorized as libel. The distinction is important because, traditionally, libel, perhaps because of its more permanent form, was considered more damaging than slander. At common law, a person who proved libel was able to recover damages without any proof of special damages; that is, the very proof that something potentially damaging to the reputation was cir-

culated in public led the court to presume injury. The jury could assess damages without evidence of any specific loss.

Slander, on the other hand, required proof of special damages. Generally, a plaintiff had to prove some sort of economic loss stemming from the damage to reputation. Once that was proved, plaintiff could recover for all sorts of injuries, including humiliation, loss of friendship, and the like. However, in four special categories known as slander *per se,* no special damages needed to be proved. These categories were imputation of serious crime, of loathsome disease, of incompetence in plaintiff's profession, and of unchastity in women.

However, as we shall see, the Supreme Court's First Amendment decisions have had an impact on this traditional distinction.

Elements: In a defamation case, plaintiff must generally establish four elements in order to prevail: (1) that a matter defamatory of plaintiff, (2) and untrue, (3) was communicated by defendant, (4) to plaintiff's injury. Questions of defendant's fault, as we shall see, also arise.

Matter Defamatory of Plaintiff: To be defamatory, a statement must be of such a nature as to tend to lower plaintiff's esteem in the eyes of others. An infinite variety of statements have been held defamatory, but if defendant falsely tells others that plaintiff is a thief, a bankrupt, a nazi, a communist, or a homosexual, it is likely that plaintiff's esteem in the eyes of others will be lowered. Though most defamation actions are brought by individuals, they can also be brought by corporations and other organizations. Assume, for example, Joe bought a car from Sam's Cars, Inc., but chose one with too small an engine. Because Joe doesn't like the car he paints lemons all over it and a sign saying "I bought this lemon at Sam's Cars." As Joe drives around town he is probably defaming Sam's Cars.

The defamatory statement must be one that the readers or hearers will associate with plaintiff. Though not mentioned by name, a person who is obviously referred to in a disparaging way

---

[17]*Brown v. U.S.*, 256 U.S. 335 (1921).

in a "novel" that is closely based on reality may have a claim against the author. So may a member of a small group when defendant defames the entire group (e.g., "All the male clerks at this store have AIDS") though plaintiff is not mentioned by name. When larger groups are referred to (e.g., "All Republicans are fascists"), the courts hesitate to allow recovery.

Untrue: To be defamatory, a statement must not only tend to lower plaintiff's esteem in the eyes of others, it must be untrue. The question may be: Who has the burden of proving truthfulness or falsity? The common law presumed that everyone was a good person; therefore, if plaintiff proved that a statement tending to defame him had been published by defendant, the burden of proof was on defendant to prove the truthfulness of the statement. Truth, in other words, was an absolute *defense* to a defamation claim.

A recent Supreme Court case redistributed this burden of proof, at least in some cases, on First Amendment grounds. In *Philadelphia Newspapers, Inc. v. Hepps,*[18] the Court held that if the plaintiff is a public figure (such as a famous actress or athlete), a public official (such as a governor), or a "limited" public figure (a private citizen caught up in a public controversy, such as a businessman whose name appears in a newspaper article about the Mafia), free speech concerns require that the plaintiff be given the burden of proof to demonstrate falsity. The common law presumption that defamatory speech is false was rejected, at least when the defendant is a member of the media. The implications for a nonmedia defendant, or a case involving a private plaintiff not involved in any public controversy are unclear.

Communication: To be defamatory, a statement must be "published" or communicated by the defendant—that is, overheard or read by a third party. If Joe and Kim are standing alone in a field miles from anyone else, Joe can say all the nasty things he wants to Kim without committing defamation. Kim's reputation in the community cannot be hurt if no one else hears the statements. If Kim goes back into town and repeats the statements for others, it is Kim doing the communicating, not Joe.[19]

Injury: As noted earlier, the traditional common law rule presumed damages in libel and the four special types of slander. If a false statement tending to lower plaintiff's esteem in the eyes of others appeared in a local newspaper, it was sensible to presume that persons read it and that their impressions of plaintiff were adversely affected. Injury was presumed, and it made no difference that defendant did not intend to injure plaintiff.

Supreme Court interpretations of the First Amendment have had a big impact on this area. Injury can no longer be presumed unless, in some cases at least, plaintiff proves some fault on defendant's part. The law is still developing, but can be summarized by placing the cases into four categories.

1. A statement about a *public official or figure* involved in a *public* controversy. For example, assume a false statement is made concerning how a chief of police handles a significant law enforcement issue. To recover, plaintiff must prove actual malice on defendant's part. That is, plaintiff must prove that defendant knew or should have known that the statements were false. Good faith mistake is a defense. Plaintiff cannot recover punitive damages absent establishing malice.

2. A statement about a *public official or figure,* but involving a *private* matter. For example, assume a newspaper runs an untrue story about a famous actress being intoxicated in a restaurant. Again, plaintiff must prove malice to establish liability and, quite likely, to recover punitive damages.

---

[18] 106 S.Ct. 1558 (1986).

[19] This is not to rule out a possible, but probably weak, claim for intentional infliction of emotional distress in this scenario.

3. A statement about a *private figure* involved in a *public* controversy. For example, assume a newspaper makes a false statement about a lawyer representing a client in a controversial case. In such a case, plaintiff need not prove actual malice to establish liability, but must do so to recover punitive damages.

4. A statement about a *private figure* involved in a *private* matter. For example, assume that a credit reporting agency falsely reports to its clients that plaintiff has taken bankruptcy. Because no public interest such as encouraging freedom of the press regarding matters of societal importance is involved, the state's interest in compensating for injured reputations is of paramount importance. Plaintiff need not prove actual malice to establish liability or to collect punitive damages.

Defenses: Several noteworthy defenses are available in defamation cases.

Statute of Limitations: In most jurisdictions, the statute of limitations for defamation cases is one year, only half the two-year statute of limitations typically found for other types of tort claims.

Absolute Privilege: To encourage certain types of activity, the courts have created an absolute privilege for the potential defendant in several contexts. That is, even if the plaintiff could prove all the elements of defamation discussed above, no liability would attach. The two most important of these are the privileges for judicial and legislative proceedings. To encourage judges to judge, witnesses to testify, lawyers to advocate, and legislators to aggressively debate the issues, all are protected absolutely when involved in their respective activities. Note, however, that the absolute privilege is narrow in scope. An attorney who wrote a book about a case after the trial was over or a legislator making statements not while debating a bill but while campaigning would not be protected.

Qualified Privileges: There are also several qualified privileges where the defendant will be protected if he or she acted in *good faith;* that is, malice must be proved as a prerequisite for recovery. The primary example of this—when the plaintiff is a public figure or public official—has already been discussed. Others include, according to some jurisdictions, communications to those who can act in the public interest (for example, complaints to a school board about a teacher) and fair comment on matters of public interest by news commentators.

Many states have provided a business-related good faith privilege for those who traffic in commercially useful information such as credit reports and employee references. Thus, in many jurisdictions, a job applicant's former employer is protected if he tells the applicant's prospective employer that "We think she stole from us." Plaintiff would have to prove malice to prevail. Note, however, that *Dun & Bradstreet, Inc. v. Greenmoss Builders,* 105 S.Ct. 2939 (1985) makes it clear that this privilege is not constitutionally mandated.

Opinion: Under the First Amendment, there is no such thing as a false idea. We are all entitled to our opinions. Thus, "I think Joe is a jerk" is not actionable. Neither is: "I just don't trust Joe; he looks sneaky to me." On the other hand, "I think Joe is a crook, and if you knew what I know, you would think so, too" is actionable if false, because it implies an underlying *factual* basis for the statement.

Injurious Falsehood: Closely allied to defamation (and perhaps equally as closely connected to the business torts discussed in Chapter 8) is the tort of **injurious falsehood,** also known as "disparagement," "slander of goods," and "trade libel." The elements are generally the same as for traditional defamation, but the subject matter relates not to an individual's reputation, but to plaintiff's title to property or to the quality or conduct of plaintiff's business. The tort is aimed at protecting economic interests and would allow suit against a defendant who, for example, falsely stated that plaintiff's business was no longer in existence.

False Imprisonment

The privilege to come and go as we please is important in our society. The courts protect that interest by recognizing the right to sue for the tort of **false imprisonment** when persons are unlawfully confined or restrained without their consent. If the defendant purports to arrest plaintiff as well, the nearly identical claim of **false arrest** is applicable.

Elements: To prove a false imprisonment claim, plaintiff must usually prove that defendant: (1) confined or restrained plaintiff, (2) with intent, (3) without plaintiff's consent, (4) thereby injuring plaintiff.

Confinement: False imprisonment can occur when plaintiff is confined in a room, a building, a car, or even a boat. It can even occur in the wide open spaces if plaintiff is held in one spot against his or her will by force or threat. If defendant blocks one exit to a room, but another is available to plaintiff, the confinement requirement is not met.

Intent: If someone accidentally locks another in a room, perhaps negligence is involved, but not false imprisonment. False imprisonment requires a wrongful intent on the defendant's part. As with assault and battery, an intent to injure will suffice, as well as an intent to confine. If defendant stands outside plaintiff's house with a gun, issuing threats of bodily injury should plaintiff emerge, the intent requirement is met. Though defendant would like nothing better than for plaintiff to come out of the house, the natural consequence of defendant's actions is to force plaintiff to remain in the house.

Against Consent: The same force and threats of force that create an assault may force a person to remain in one place against his or her will. A large man could easily intimidate a small person into staying involuntarily in one place. However, if plaintiff stays in one place as an accommodation or to clear up an accusation with police, there is no involuntary confinement. If, for example, a store clerk told a customer only: "We believe you have stolen from the cash register and have called the police," and the customer voluntarily stayed in the store to give her side of the story—there would be no false imprisonment.

Injury: The injury necessary for a valid false imprisonment claim arises automatically from the confinement, even if it is brief. A restraint of hours or days is not required for the necessary injury to occur. However, since the injury is somewhat mental in nature, it will not occur if plaintiff is unaware of the confinement. Thus, if plaintiff sleeps through a confinement, there would be no cognizable injury. But if plaintiff knows of the confinement, actual and punitive damages are available.

Defenses: In addition to the statute of limitations (typically two years), the defendant's best chance in a false imprisonment case is to prove legal right. Obviously, police officers in possession of probable cause have the right to detain or confine suspects.

Many false imprisonment claims involve shopkeepers. Shoplifting, unfortunately, is a problem of epidemic proportions in the United States. When a shopkeeper detains a suspected shoplifter and presses charges, any number of things can prevent a conviction from being obtained, including prosecutorial or police error, or the failure of a witness to appear. At common law, even a well-founded belief by a shopkeeper that a theft had occurred frequently would not prevent the success of a later false imprisonment claim if, for whatever reason, no criminal conviction was obtained. However, many state legislatures have acted to protect shopkeepers with legislation such as that discussed in the following case.

Jacques v. Sears, Roebuck & Company
Court of Appeals of New York, 285 N.E.2d 871 (1972)

In May of 1966 the plaintiff, Jacques, a self-employed carpenter, entered a Sears store in Syracuse to purchase business supplies. He picked up nineteen reflectorized letters and numbers costing ten cents apiece and put them in his pants pocket. He then selected a mailbox and had two extra keys made. He paid for the mailbox and keys, but left the store without paying for the letters and numbers. At the time he had over $600 in cash and a $400 check in his wallet.

A Sears security officer, Varisco, had observed Jacques putting the items in his pocket and leaving the store without paying for them. As Jacques approached his car in the store parking lot, Varisco stopped him and told him that he was under arrest. Varisco took Jacques back to a security office, where he filled out a questionnaire in which he admitted having taken the letters without paying for them. He said he wished then to pay for the letters; that he was "sorry about the whole thing"; and that he "would never do anything like this again."

Sears' security officers called the Syracuse police, who arrived soon after the detention began. With the security officers accompanying them, the police took Jacques to police headquarters, booked him, and later released him on bail. Two days later he appeared in police court and stated that he was guilty of petit larceny. The court, however, refused to accept the plea and advised him to get a lawyer. The charge of petit larceny was subsequently dismissed on recommendation of the district attorney because of "lack of proof of intent."

Jacques then brought this action for damages against Sears, alleging false imprisonment and false arrest. Sears contended that its detention of Jacques was "reasonable," and thus lawful under New York's "antishoplifting statute" (the text of which appears in the decision below). The trial court disagreed with Sears' interpretation of the statute, and entered a judgment of $1600 in favor of Jacques, the amount of the jury's verdict.

Sears appealed to an intermediate court, which reversed the judgment and dismissed the action. Jacques appealed to New York's highest court, contending (1) that the statute afforded a defense against a reasonable detention, but not against any arrest; or, in the alternative, (2) that the statute afforded a defense only against arrests resulting in convictions.

Breitel, Judge:

. . . Section 218 of the General Business Law . . . provides merchants a defense in various types of actions, including arrests for false arrest: "Defense of lawful detention. In any action for false arrest, false imprisonment, (or) unlawful detention . . . brought by any person by reason of having been detained on or in the immediate vicinity of the premises of a retail mercantile establishment for the purpose of investigation or questioning as to the ownership of any merchandise, it shall be a defense to such action that the person was detained in a reasonable manner and for not more than a reasonable time to permit such investigation or questioning by a peace officer or by the owner of the retail mercantile establishment, his authorized employee or agent, and that such peace officer, owner, employee or agent had reasonable grounds to believe that the person so detained was committing or attempting to commit larceny on such premises of such merchandise. . . ."

[This] section has been interpreted [under the case law of this state] to make "reasonable detention" a defense in an action against a merchant for false arrest, thus wiping out plaintiff's asserted distinction between "arrest" and "detention." [The court then cited a number of other legal authorities to support its conclusion that "the words 'arrest' and 'detention' have traditionally been used interchangeably." It then turned to appellant's second contention, in the following paragraphs.]

The legislative history [of this statute] indicates a purpose to protect merchants from false arrest suits even where the criminal actions are eventually dismissed. The Governor's memorandum [in N.Y. Legis. Annual, 1960] stated in part: "The sponsors of this measure urge that it will reduce . . . costs by helping to overcome the extreme reluctance with which merchants now attempt to interfere with or apprehend shop-lifters. This reluctance is apparently caused by the vulnerability of merchants to suits for false arrest in the event of dismissal of the criminal case against a shop-lifter." . . .

The general rule is that a private arrest is invalid unless the person arrested has in fact committed the crime for which the arrest was made. In effect, Section 218 *carves out an exception* for merchants detaining or arresting shoplifters. [Emphasis added.]

Anti-shoplifting statutes in other states with provisions similar to Section 218 have been interpreted to provide merchants with immunity from civil liability for false arrest where there were reasonable grounds for the arrest, but no criminal convictions resulted. [Here a number of cases were cited.]

In this case, there was overwhelming evidence supporting the finding of reasonable detention, from the initial arrest to the arrival of police. Plaintiff admitted immediately upon being stopped or arrested in the parking lot that he had taken Sears' goods and carried them out of the store in his pocket without paying for them. He repeated the admission in his own handwriting when he filled out the written questionnaire in the security office. At no time did he offer any exculpatory explanation. Then, two days later he confessed guilt before a judge of the police court.

It makes no difference that subjectively a plaintiff may not have had the requisite intent to commit a crime. Thus, it is assumed, as he describes it, that the letters were put in his pocket to facilitate carrying other bulky items, handicapped as he was by having only three fingers on one hand, and that leaving the store without paying for them was done inadvertently. . . . The point is that even he thought he had committed a crime, and the objective facts established as much. Certainly [under these circumstances] the store detective is not required to probe further the nature of the intent before making a formal arrest. . . .

Similarly, defendants are not liable for the period after the police took plaintiff into custody. . . . Under the circumstances Sears was justified in handing plaintiff over to the police. [Section 218 impliedly permits] the turning over of the suspect to the police under reasonable circumstances and the execution of an information or complaint necessary for his initial arraignment. Of course, the limitation that detention to qualify under the statute must be "on or in the immediate vicinity of the premises" does not apply to custody by the police. . . .

The order of dismissal is affirmed.

Trespass

We work hard for our money, and when we spend it on property we should have the right to use that property without interference from others. When others infringe on our right to use real property—land and those things attached to it, such as houses—the tort of **trespass** to real property is committed. The tort has a convoluted common-law history that protects property owners from innocent as well as mean-spirited invasions of the right to use real property.

Elements: Generally speaking, to prevail in a trespass case plaintiff must establish the following elements: (1) affirmative conduct by defendant; (2) with intent to enter onto realty in the possession of another; and (3) resulting in actual entry.

Affirmative Conduct: If Joe is driving down the street when Alan runs a stop sign with his car, smashes into Joe, and pushes Joe up onto Ed's lawn, no trespass has been committed by Joe. He invaded Ed's real property, but not through any affirmative act of his own.

Intent: Unlike most other intentional torts, the intent element of a trespass cause of action requires only that plaintiff demonstrate that de-

fendant intended to enter the place he did, which place belonged to plaintiff. No intent to do harm is required. Thus, if Cindy walks across Ann's land believing that she is walking across her own or across land belonging to her friend Sally who has given her permission to cross it, Cindy commits a trespass actionable by Ann. Cindy's good faith is no defense. On the other hand, if Mark has a heart attack and dies instantly while driving down the street, and his car runs onto Ed's lawn, the affirmative conduct element is arguably not met and certainly the intent element is missing. The same may be said of a person who, driving too fast on slick streets, loses control of the car and winds up on someone's lawn. The intent element is missing.

Actual entry: Entry is required for completion of the tort, but *usually* no real injury. Damage is presumed from the fact of entry, even if the only injury is trampled blades of grass. A judgment in the form of nominal damages of a dollar or so would still be warranted. According to most courts, the invasion need only be slight, including throwing a rock onto plaintiff's property, shooting a bullet over it, or tunnelling under it. Some courts refuse to recognize injury where the invasion is truly minor, such as where A's tree limb grows so far that it extends over B's property line.

The court must sometimes balance competing interests. For example, in *Bradley v. American Smelting and Refining Co.*, 709 P.2d 782 (Wash. 1985), defendant operated a copper smelter which emitted particulate matter, including arsenic, cadmium, and other metals. Though indetectable by human senses, this matter did sometimes settle on plaintiff's property. The court felt constrained to create an exception to the general rule that any entry constitutes an injury, stating:

> When [airborne] particles or substance accumulates on the land and does not pass away, then a trespass has occurred. While at common law any trespass entitled a landowner to recover nominal and punitive damages for the invasion of his property, such a rule is not appropriate under the circumstances before us. No useful purpose would be served by sanctioning actions in trespass by every landowner within a hundred miles of a manufacturing plant. Manufacturers would be harassed and the litigious few would cause the escalation of costs to the detriment of the many. . . . The plaintiff who cannot show actual and substantial damages should be subject to dismissal.

The trespassory entry is an affront to the use of the property. Therefore, the cause of action is normally recognized as belonging to the possessor of the land. Thus, if T were renting a farm from L, and X trespassed on the farm, T would normally have the right to sue for trespass rather than L.

Defenses: In addition to the typical two-year statute of limitations (which is extended if the trespass is a continuing one, as where the trespasser has erected a small building on the plaintiff's property), the main defenses to a trespass cause of action are *consent* and *legal right.* Thus, a tenant has the landlord's consent, pursuant to a lease, to remain on the landlord's property. However, if the tenant stays beyond the term of the lease and refuses to leave, a trespass is committed because consent has expired.

A legal right might arise from, for example, an *easement,* which is a right to use someone's property for a limited purpose. Thus, if M's land is between N's land and a major highway, N might negotiate an easement from M, paying M a sum of money in exchange for the limited right to travel over M's land going to and from the highway.

OTHER INTENTIONAL TORTS

Invasion of Privacy

Slowly over the past 75 years or so, the courts have begun to recognize privacy as an interest worthy of legal protection. Today, many jurisdictions have recognized one or more of the following varieties of tort which come under the umbrella of **invasion of privacy.**

Intrusion: Intrusion occurs whenever a defendant intrudes into an area where a plaintiff has a reasonable expectation of privacy. Secretly placing a microphone under plaintiff's bed in order to overhear the goings on would be a classic example. A leading case involved an auto manufacturer's wiretapping and eavesdropping on Ralph Nader's activities.[20]

Disclosure of Embarrassing Private Facts: Where no justification exists, it may be actionable to disclose to the public facts which plaintiff finds embarrassing or offensive. Because they are "true," the disclosures do not constitute defamation; they may be more akin to blackmail. However, a newsworthiness defense exists, at least for the media. In one case, a woman sued for the embarrassment she was caused by a newspaper's disclosing that her husband was killed in a fire in a motel while accompanied by

---

[20] *Nader v. General Motors Corp.*, 255 N.E.2d 765 (N.Y. 1970).

another woman. The court held that fires are newsworthy events and the newspaper could not be liable for accurately reporting the names of the victims.[21]

False Light: Very similar to the tort of defamation, the action for "false light" privacy renders liable a defendant who makes statements or does acts which place the plaintiff in a false light in the public eye. While usually these statements or actions would injure plaintiff's reputation and also be actionable as defamation, occasionally they might involve statements that plaintiff had done many wonderful things which in fact he had not. An attraction of this tort is that it frequently has a two-year statute of limitations, longer than the one-year statutes typical for defamation.

Appropriation of Name or Likeness: This final type of privacy tort protects the economic interests that persons have in the potential exploitation of their names and faces. Thus, if a company uses the name or picture of a famous actress in its advertising campaign without her permission, it has appropriated her name or likeness to her economic detriment. The company should have acquired her consent and paid her for such use.

Intentional Infliction of Mental Distress

As noted earlier, because emotional injuries are difficult to prove and to value, courts have traditionally been reluctant to allow recovery for them. But just as they are now allowed in suitable cases of negligence, they are also allowed when intentionally caused. The turning point may have been cases like *Wilkinson v. Downtin,*[22] where, as a practical joke, defendant called plaintiff, a woman whose mental state was somewhat suspect anyway, and told her that her husband had been in a serious accident. This so upset plaintiff that she had to be hospitalized. Recovery for her emotional distress was allowed.

The requisite elements of proof for the tort of **intentional infliction of mental distress** are generally formulated as follows. First, that defendant is guilty of extreme and outrageous conduct. Mere insults are usually insufficient as are profanity and other abuses of a relatively minor nature. Second, defendant must have intended to cause plaintiff severe emotional distress. Again, defendant will be presumed to intend the natural consequences of his or her actions. And a defendant who is aware of a particular plaintiff's susceptibilities to mental distress will be judged accordingly. Finally, plaintiff must actually suffer such severe distress. Physical consequences are not required, but their presence does assist in establishing proof of severe emotional anguish.

Today, such suits frequently involve attempts by collection agencies to force debtors to pay bills. Thus, in *Turman v. Central Billing, Inc.,* 568 P.2d 1382 (1977), the collection agency was held liable to Turman, who was blind, when it badgered her in trying to collect a small debt assigned to it for collection, even after it knew that she and the creditor had come to a satisfactory settlement. This harassment, which resulted in plaintiff's hospitalization for anxiety and severe stress, was carried out by repeated phone calls—sometimes twice a day—in which defendant's agent "shouted" at her, used profanity, told her several times that her husband would lose his job and house if she didn't pay, and called her "scum" and a "deadbeat."

Fraud

The essence of the tort of *fraud* is the intentional misleading of one person by another, which results in a loss to the deceived party. Because many kinds of fraudulent conduct occur where the sole purpose of the wrongdoer is to cause the innocent party to enter a contract which that person otherwise would not make,

---

[21] *Fry v. Ionia Sentinel Standard,* 300 N.W.2d 687 (Mich. App. 1980).

[22] [1897] 2 Q.B.D. 57.

full consideration of this subject is undertaken in Chapter 13.

Conversion and Trespass to Personal Property

The tort of **conversion** renders actionable certain invasion of personal property interests, just as trespass protects real property interests. Conversion remedies invasions so serious that they justify forcing defendant to compensate plaintiff for the reasonable value of the item involved. An example would be defendant's theft of plaintiff's automobile. A tort which generally covers more minor invasions of personal property rights is frequently called trespass to real property. This tort would remedy, for example, defendant's minor vandalism of plaintiff's car.

Nuisance

Like trespass to real property, the tort of **nuisance** protects the enjoyment of such property. Frequently nuisance is used to compensate an intangible disruption of the enjoyment of property, as where plaintiff is injured by defendant's invasion through light (erection of tall light poles), vibrations (blasting with dynamite), or smells (pig farming). The courts will consider such factors as the type of neighborhood, the nature of the wrong, its proximity to the plaintiff, its frequency or continuity, and the nature and extent of the injury in deciding whether an actionable nuisance exists.

SPECIAL PROBLEMS

Business Torts

Some torts, such as the theft of trade secrets and the unjustified interference with business contracts, are so peculiarly related to the commercial world that they are called *business torts*. Because of the special issues that these kinds of torts present—and also because of their obvious importance to businesspersons—they will be considered at length in the next chapter.

Employers' Liability

Ordinarily, the application of the principles of tort law results in the imposition of liability upon the wrongdoer alone. There is one major exception, however, which springs from the principles comprising our master-servant law and our law of agency.

Under these principles, an employer is uniformly held liable for the torts of employees if the employees are acting "within the scope of their employment" at the time of the injury. Thus, if T, a truckdriver employed by the D Furniture Company, negligently injures P while delivering a piece of furniture to a customer's home, P has a cause of action against both T and the D Company, as illustrated in Figure 7.1.

Ordinarily, in such a case, P brings just one action against both defendants; if he is successful in proving the facts as alleged, he obtains a "joint and several" judgment against T and the D Company. This means that if he is awarded a judgment of $4,000, he can enforce the judgment against the assets of either party, or of both, until that sum is recovered. (The "scope of employment" problem is covered further in Chapters 18 and 19.)

Joint and Several Liability

When two defendants' actions together contribute to a plaintiff's injury, they are frequently held jointly and severally liable. The "joint" portion of this liability means that each defendant may be held responsible for the entire loss caused to plaintiff. Thus, theoretically one defendant who is only 10 percent at fault might have to pay also for the 90 percent fault of another defendant, especially if the latter defendant is judgment-proof. The relatively harsh result which this can have for "deep pocket" defendants is a major cause of criticism of our present tort system.

Statutory Reforms

Increases in the number of tort suits filed, the size of judgments and, consequently, insurance rates have become a major topic of discus-

Figure 7.1   Employer's Liability for Employee's Tort

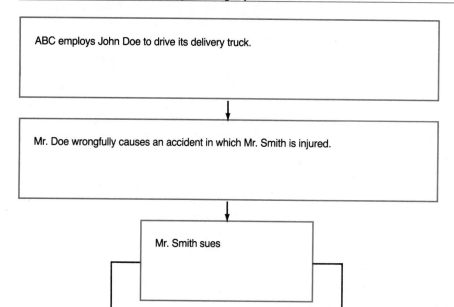

sion in both the federal and state legislatures. As this chapter is written both state and federal legislative reforms to limit tort recoveries are being debated and passed across the country. Though the ultimate impact of this wave of legislation cannot yet be gauged, it thus far has concentrated on such matters as medical malpractice and products liability suits, punitive damages, damages for emotional distress, and statutes of limitation.

SUMMARY

Tort law is, to a great extent, social engineering by the courts. As society evolves, the courts' concepts of what interests we have that are worth protecting also evolves. The courts impose duties on us not to injure the protectable interests of others.

The leading remedy for accidental injury in this country is the negligence cause of action. Existence of a duty and proximate causation, both of which turn largely on the notion of foreseeability, are the key elements for a plaintiff's recovery. A plaintiff's own carelessness can lead to reduction or a bar altogether on recovery.

Among intentional torts, assault and battery protect invasions of our mind and body, defamation protects our good reputation in the community, false imprisonment protects the right to come and go as we please, and trespass protects our right to enjoyment of our real property. To successfully pursue each tort, the plaintiff must prove a variety of specified elements. Each tort involves an intentional act by the defendant. Each has a variety of defenses ranging from self-defense for assault and battery, to absolute and qualified privileges for defamation, to consent and legal right for false imprisonment and trespass.

Intentional torts which are also worth noting include the four varieties of invasion of privacy tort, intentional infliction of emotional distress (which has been often used successfully against aggressive collection agencies), fraud, conversion, and nuisance (which involves lesser invasions of real property than does trespass).

Employers are liable for the torts of their employees committed within the scope of authority. And joint tortfeasors are each potentially liable for the entire judgment awarded plaintiff (though plaintiff cannot have a double recovery). Rapid change in the tort system and escalating monetary awards have led many legislatures to consider strong measures to reform American tort law. We are just now starting to see many of these changes.

KEY TERMS

Torts
Negligence
Proximate cause
Independent intervening cause
Contributory negligence
Comparative negligence
Statute of limitations
Battery
Assault
Consent
Self-defense
Defamation
Libel
Slander
Injurious falsehood
False imprisonment
False arrest
Trespass
Invasion of privacy

Intentional infliction of mental distress
Conversion
Nuisance

QUESTIONS AND PROBLEMS

1. For two years Lee was the patient of Milano, a psychiatrist. Lee was diagnosed as having an adjustment reaction to adolescence. He related many fantasies to Milano about being a hero or an important villain, or using a knife to threaten those who frightened him. At a session he showed a knife to Milano. Lee also related certain alleged sexual experiences with Kim, his next door neighbor. He was emotionally involved, possessive, and had fired a BB gun at a car occupied by Kim and her boyfriend as they drove away on a date. Later, Lee murdered Kim with a knife. Kim's family sued Milano in negligence for not having warned them of the danger from Lee. Should Milano be liable? Discuss. (*McIntosh v. Milano,* 403 A.2d 500, N.J. 1979.)

2. KHJ radio gave away money to listeners who could find deejay "The Real Don Steele" who traveled around town in a van. Two cars of teenagers arrived at one location to discover a prize had already been given away. Without knowledge of each other, they each decided to follow Steele to his next location in order to be the first to arrive. For the next few miles they jockeyed for position at speeds of up to 80 mph. The radio then announced that Steele was headed for Thousand Oaks off a certain ramp. When Steele took that exit off the freeway, the teenagers followed. In so doing, one of their cars carelessly forced Weirum's car onto the center divider where it overturned and Weirum was killed. His family sued KHJ for negligence. Should they be allowed to recover? Discuss. (*Weirum v. RKO General, Inc.*, 539 P.2d 36, Cal. 1975.)

3. Charles and Carolyn needed to repair and clean a well on their property. Charles entered the well and placed a gasoline-powered pump directly above it to remove water. This was a bad idea because all of the carbon monoxide from the engine seeped into the well. When Charles did not respond to Carolyn's calls, she asked her neighbor Bob for help. Bob entered the well to help Charles, but was overcome by fumes himself and died. Bob's family sued Carolyn and Charles' estate for negligence. Should the family recover? Discuss. (*Lowrey v. Horvath,* 689 S.W.2d 625, Mo. 1985.)

4. Two children, Lisa and Deborah, were standing alongside a highway when Lisa was struck by Burd's carelessly driven car. Deborah was barely missed. JoAnne, the girls' mother, saw the whole incident from her front porch. When Lisa, Deborah, and JoAnne sue Burd for the emotional distress caused by his careless driving, who will be allowed to recover? (*Sinn v. Burd,* 404 A.2d 672, Pa. 1979.)

5. Bruno was an insurance agent. He was not a doctor nor authorized to make medical examinations. Nonetheless, when he learned that another agent had sold insurance to Mrs. Bowman, he appeared at her door with a black bag and told her he was a doctor who had to perform a physical examination in order for the insurance application to be approved. He then, in the words of the court, "made the type of intimate examination which would have been proper enough if he had been authorized to make an examination for the presence of a hernia." Mrs. Bowman ultimately sued Bruno's company for battery. The company raised the defense of consent, pointing out that no force was involved. Is this a good defense? Discuss. (*Bowman v. Home Life Ins. Co. of America,* 243 F.2d 331, 3d Cir. 1957.)

6. In a review of plaintiff's restaurant, defendant newspaper columnist referred to the sauce on the duck as "yellow death on duck" and the poached trout as something which should be renamed "trout à la green plague." Plaintiff sued for defamation, proving that most persons very much liked both dishes. Does plaintiff have a strong defamation claim? Discuss. (*Mashburn v. Collins,* 355 So.2d 879, La. 1977.)

7. National Bond Co. sent two of its employees to repossess Whithorn's car when Whithorn got behind in his payments. The two repossessors located Whithorn while he was driving his car. They asked him to stop, which he did, but he refused to abandon the car to them. They called a wrecker and ordered the driver to hook Whithorn's car and move it down the street while Whithorn was still in it. Whithorn started the car and tried to escape, but the wrecker lifted the car off the road and progressed 75 to 100 feet before Whithorn managed to stall the wrecker. Whithorn claimed that this incident amounted to a false imprisonment and sued National Bond Co. Does Whithorn have a valid claim? Discuss. (*National Bond Co. v. Whithorn,* 123 S.W.2d 263, Ky. 1939.)

8. Defendant is a crop duster who became confused and flew over plaintiff's land, spraying poison on plaintiff's crop. Defendant thought he was spraying the land he had been hired to spray, which was adjacent to plaintiff's land. Plaintiff sued defendant in trespass. Does plaintiff have a good claim? Discuss. (*Schronk v. Gilliam,* 380 S.W.2d 743, Tex. Civ. App. 1964.)

9. In 1955, plaintiff was 17 years old. He was convicted of being involved in a hit-and-run accident which killed a Las Vegas policeman. In 1978, in an article about police officers who had died in the line of duty, defendant newspaper mentioned plaintiff's 1955 conviction and his conviction two years later for possession of marijuana. Plaintiff sued the newspaper for disclosure of embarrassing private facts. Should plaintiff prevail? Discuss. (*Montesano v. Donrey Media Group,* 668 P.2d 1081, Nev. 1983.)

10. Defendant credit company called plaintiff and, in order to obtain the address of her son for collection purposes, told her that her grandchild had been in a car accident and defendant needed her son's address. When this turned out to be false, plaintiff sued for infliction of emotional distress. Does she have a good claim? Discuss. (*Ford Motor Credit Co. v. Sheehan,* 373 So.2d 956, Fla. App. 1979.)

Chapter 8

Business Torts and Crimes

Some kinds of wrongful conduct are so closely related to the business world that they deserve special mention. In this chapter we will first examine the most common **business torts** (or "competitive torts," as they are sometimes called). These torts include wrongful interference with business rights that are recognized under common law principles, as well as injuries to business interests that could be characterized as "intellectual property" torts, including trademark, patent, and copyright infringement. The remainder of the chapter is devoted to the most common kinds of **business crimes**—wrongs committed by (or against) business firms that violate specific criminal statutes, and which thus subject the wrongdoer to both civil and criminal liability, such as the imposition of fines or imprisonment.

SELECTED BUSINESS TORTS

Certain kinds of business interests and rights have been recognized and protected by common law rules since very early times. Many of these interests receive supplemental, and sometimes primary, protection from state, and especially federal, statutes. In the first half of this chapter we will examine some of the most common wrongful invasions of these interests, i.e., business torts, including (1) interference with existing and prospective contractual and business relationships, (2) trademark infringement, (3) misuse of trade secrets, (4) patent infringement, and (5) copyright infringement.

Interference with Business Conduct

Beginning with the decision in an English case in 1853 in which an opera singer was induced by defendant theater owner to breach her contract to sing at plaintiff's theater and appear at defendant's instead,[1] the courts have recognized the general principle that a third party who wrongfully interferes with an existing contract has committed a tort. Indeed, the concept has been stretched to hold defendants liable for interfering with contracts which did not yet exist but were reasonably certain to be entered into, and with business relationships in general.

A typical example of **interference with business conduct** involved a salesman who followed customers away from his former employer's premises and convinced them to rescind their contracts with that business and purchase less expensive property from him.[2] Although his former employer's customers had the right under federal law to rescind their contracts within three days, the salesman was found civilly liable. Though there was no interference with an existing contract, there was interference with a prospective advantage flowing from an advantageous business relationship.

Elements of Tort: In a tortious interference case, plaintiff must prove: (1) the defendant acted intentionally to interfere with a known contract or business relationship or with one that was reasonably certain to occur; (2) defendant caused harm in so interfering; and (3) defendant acted in pursuit of an improper purpose or through improper means. No liability will attach if defendant's interference was not improper in the eyes of the law but was, instead, legally justified. Unfortunately, the law is somewhat muddled as to the line between acts that are justified and those that are unjustified and improper.

Defense of Justification: A defendant using improper means to induce a breach of contract or to interfere with a business relationship will likely be held liable. For example, as part of a campaign to terrorize Vietnamese fishermen competing with American fishermen in Gal-

---

[1] *Lumley v. Gye,* 2 E1 & B1 216.

[2] *Azar v. Lehigh Corp.,* 364 So.2d 860 (Fla. App. 1978).

veston Bay, the Ku Klux Klan told one man who leased his docks to the Vietnamese: "watch your boats—they're easy to burn," and sent a card to a woman who also leased her docks which said: "You have been paid a 'friendly visit' do you want the next one to be a 'real one.'" The court deemed this sufficient to establish an action for tortious interference with contractual relationships.[3]

Even if the means used are proper, such as simply opening up a competing business, the tort will be established if the purpose was improper. In one famous case,[4] the defendant opened up a competing barbershop not to make money, but as part of a malicious scheme to injure plaintiff by destroying his barbershop's business. "To call such conduct competition is a perversion of terms," the court said in allowing recovery for interference with business conduct.

Justification for a defendant's interference may be found if it is aimed at protecting a third person's legitimate interests, such as where a mother attempted to convince her child's school to exclude a diseased person,[5] or at protecting the public interest in general. Furthermore, the defendant can claim justification for interference in order to protect its own existing contractual or property interest. Two examples can help illustrate the general kinds of interests that are often held to justify interference.

Case 1:   P gets a new car franchise from D, an auto manufacturer. Later P makes a contract with X, a motorcycle wholesaler, under the terms of which X is permitted to sell motorcycles in a limited area in P's showroom. D subsequently causes P to break the contract with X because of complaints from new car buyers about dirt and noise associated with X's operation. Even if the contract between P and X did not violate any term of the franchise agreement, D's interest in the proper conduct of the new car dealership would probably justify its conduct (thus affording it a defense in any interference action brought either by P or X).

Case 2:   A bank made a contract with a city, under which the city agreed to vacate (close) a street so that the bank could greatly expand its facilities. When a neighboring savings and loan company induced the city to cancel the contract, the bank sued the savings and loan for damages. The court ruled in favor of the savings and loan, finding that its primary purpose in preventing the closing was "to preserve an unimpaired visibility of its premises." Because it was found that the threatened impairment might substantially affect the savings and loan company's business, and the bank was still able to make a reasonable expansion despite the cancellation of the closing, the savings and loan company's interest was held to outweigh the contractual right of the bank.[6] Thus the bank's only cause of action would be against the city, on the breach of contract theory.

While the defendant may act to protect *existing* economic interests, it is usually improper to induce a third party to breach a contract with plaintiff solely to gain new customers. The right to engage in free competition does not go quite that far. However, the courts will grant a defendant more leeway in terms of seeking new customers or contracts if plaintiff's interest has not itself been reduced to a binding contract but is only prospective in nature. For example, where plaintiff's contract is terminable-at-will by both parties, some courts find that the privilege of competition allows defendant to vie for the plaintiff's business with the third party by fair means.

The competition privilege was raised as a defense in the following case.

---

[3] *Vietnamese Fishermen's Ass'n v. Knights of the Ku Klux Klan,* 518 F. Supp. 993 (N.D.Tex. 1981).

[4] *Tuttle v. Buck,* 107 Minn. 145, 119 N.W. 946 (1909).

[5] *Legris v. Marcotte,* 129 Ill. App. 67 (1906).

[6] *Arlington Heights National Bank v. Arlington Heights Federal Savings and Loan Association,* 229 N.E. 2d 514 (1967).

Leonard Duckworth, Inc. v. Michael L. Field & Co.
U.S. Court of Appeals, Fifth Circuit, 516 F.2d 952 (1975)

Plaintiff Leonard Duckworth, Inc., is a real estate sales corporation. It brought together a potential seller (Chase Manhattan Bank) and a potential buyer (Michael L. Field & Co.). During negotiations, there were two written drafts of a sales contract signed by all three parties. In each, the seller was required to pay a commission to plaintiff. In September of 1972, Chase rejected Field's offer, but stated that it might accept it if it were resubmitted at the first of the year after certain changes in Chase's personnel. Plaintiff did contact Chase in January 1973 to help secure financing.

In February 1973, Field initiated direct negotiations with Chase without going through plaintiff. These negotiations led to acceptance of Field's offer to buy. Before execution of the contract, plaintiff learned of the negotiations and asserted a right to a commission. Field denied this, and at Chase's urging, inserted a clause into the final contract in which Field agreed to indemnify Chase for any commission that plaintiff might assert against it.

Plaintiff sued Field for interfering with plaintiff's reasonable expectancy of a real estate commission. The jury found that Field induced Chase to circumvent plaintiff in order to avoid paying a commission. A judgment of $113,250 was entered against Field and this appeal followed.

Skelton, Judge:

. . . Texas law permits a cause of action for interference with reasonably probable future contractual relations. The law was expressed as follows:

> *Texas courts recognize a cause of action for improper interference with contractual relationships, and the unenforceability of the contract is usually no defense to an action for tortious interference with its performance. Our courts have also recognized a cause of action for tortious and wrongful interference with advantageous business relationships. It need not be absolutely certain that the prospective contract would have been made were it not for such interference. A reasonable assurance thereof in view of all the circumstances is generally sufficient. But where there is no contract, as here, a party does not have a right to be free from competition, but instead merely has* the right to be free from malicious interference with the right to conduct negotiations that have a reasonable probability of resulting in a contract. *[Emphasis supplied.]* [Martin v. Phillips Petroleum Co., *455 S.W.2d 429, 435 (Tex. Civ. App. 1970).]*

In the case of *Glenn Point Park College,* 441 Pa. 474, 272 A.2d 895 (1971) the elements of the tort of wrongful interference with a prospective contract right are clearly enumerated: (1) there was a "reasonable probability" that [plaintiff] would have entered into a contractual relationship; (2) defendant acted maliciously by intentionally preventing the relationship from occurring with the purpose of harming plaintiff; (3) the defendant was not privileged or justified; and (4) actual harm or damage occurred as a result.

It is apparent that at the time the alleged interference occurred there was a reasonable certainty that Chase would have entered into a three party contract with the plaintiff and defendant for the sale of [the land] under which plaintiff would have been due a broker's commission. . . .

The requirement of malice in the context of the tort of malicious interference means an unlawful act done intentionally and without just cause or excuse. Under the evidence presented in the instant case, legal malice on the part of defendant Field Co. appears to be present. Notwithstanding knowledge of the extent of plaintiff's involvement in the continuing negotiations and the reasonable expectation of a real estate commission upon the execution of a purchase contract, defendant initiated surreptitious direct dealings with Chase. . . .

Defendant's malicious interference in plaintiff's reasonable expectancy could be excused if it were privileged or resulting from legitimate business considerations. The most frequently articulated privilege that is asserted to defend against the tort of wrongful interference is that of reasonable competition in the solicitation of contracts. This privilege however is limited to what is considered within the realm of "fair play." In view of the surreptitious negotiations, the proposed indemnity clause protecting the seller explicitly from plaintiff's claim for commissions and the defendant's apparent motive to prevent plaintiff from receiving the reasonably expected commissions, defendant's acts cannot be considered as protected by the same privilege afforded competitors who are fairly and honestly vying for competitive advantage. These acts can only be termed sharp, overreaching, and beyond the pale of "fair play" and should not be privileged.

[Affirmed.]

In one of the most controversial cases in recent legal history, Pennzoil sued Texaco for intentional interference with contract rights when Texaco bought control of Getty Oil after Pennzoil believed it had a contract to acquire Getty. A jury awarded Pennzoil the largest judgment in American legal history— $11.1 billion in compensatory and punitive damages. (That judgment is being appealed as this chapter is written in early 1987.)

Manager's Privilege: When a corporation breaches a contract, the other party will frequently not only sue the corporation for breach of contract but also sue the corporate officers who made the decision to breach on a tortious interference claim. The corporate officers are usually protected from liability by a doctrine called the "manager's privilege" if their decision to have the corporation breach the contract was based solely or essentially on the best interests of the corporation. Such would be the case where it would be far more advisable for a corporation to pay damages resulting from a breach of contract than to live up to a contract that might be financially disastrous. On the other hand, if the officer is acting primarily to further his or her own personal interests, tort liability will be imposed.

The following case raises the question of what rules should apply when the adviser is acting partially for the benefit of the corporation and partially for his or her personal gain.

Los Angeles Airways, Inc., v. Davis
U.S. Court of Appeals, Ninth Circuit, 687 F.2d 321 (1982)

Los Angeles Airways (LAA) had a contract with Summa Corporation and Hughes Air Corporation (HAC), two companies owned by the late Howard Hughes, under the terms of which the companies agreed to purchase all of LAA's assets. The contract was subsequently breached by Summa and HAC, an action taken upon the recommendation of Davis, the defendant, who was an attorney for Summa, HAC, and Hughes, and also a director of Summa and HAC.

LAA, plaintiff, alleged that Davis had two motives in bringing about the breach of contract: (1) to force LAA into bankruptcy, with the result that Summa and HAC could acquire its assets at bargain prices, and (2) to undermine the position of Robert Maheu, chief executive officer of Hughes' Nevada operations, so that Davis's position in the Hughes empire might thereby be enhanced. (This latter claim was based upon statements made in depositions of Davis, Maheu, and two other Hughes executives, and upon 41 exhibits filed by plaintiff.)

The trial court ruled that Davis's recommendation was privileged, even though motivated in part by a desire for personal gain. It thus entered summary judgment for defendant, and LAA appealed.

Reinhardt, Judge:

. . . The existence and scope of the privilege to induce a breach of contract must be determined by reference to the societal interests which it is designed to protect. The privilege exists whenever a person induces a breach of contract through lawful means in order to protect an interest that has a greater social value than the mere stability of the particular contract in question. The privilege is designed in part to protect the important interests served by the confidential relationship between a fiduciary and his principal.

[The court here said that Davis had the defense of qualified privilege, regardless of whether he was acting in his capacity as a director of the companies or as an attorney, when making the recommendation. If made in the first capacity, he possessed a "manager's privilege" to counsel his employer to breach a contract that he reasonably believed to be harmful to the employer's best interests. And if the statement were made in Davis's capacity as attorney, he would possess a similar privilege. The court then continued:]

The protection of the privilege may be lost if the advisor acts with improper intent. In determining whether an advisor's intent will result in the loss of the privilege, it is necessary to evaluate his intent in light of the societal interests which the privilege is designed to promote. . . . [It is true that the rule is] well established that a person is not justified in inducing a breach of contract simply because he is in competition with one of the parties to the contract and seeks to further his own economic advantage at the expense of the other. [The court then observed that, in some cases, the question of whether the actions of the agent were taken solely to further his own interests, rather than for the partial benefit of the principal, should be left to a jury. The court continued:]

[But] in this case LAA [admits] that Davis's advice was intended, among other things, to secure a benefit for Hughes: the acquisition of LAA at a "distress price." . . .

We conclude that where, as here, an advisor is motivated in part by a desire to benefit his principal, his conduct in inducing a breach of contract should be privileged. . . . We believe that advice by an agent to a principal is rarely, if ever, purely motivated by a desire to benefit only the principal. An agent naturally hopes that by providing beneficial advice to his principal, the agent will benefit indirectly by gaining the further trust and confidence of his principal. If the protection of the privilege were denied every time that an advisor acted with such mixed motive, the privilege would be greatly diminished and the societal interests it was designed to promote would be frustrated. . . .

Although we do not reach the question, we also seriously doubt that a desire to advance one's own career with an employer, even at the expense of a fellow employee's, would in any event constitute the type of motivation that causes loss of the privilege.

Judgment affirmed.

Trademark Infringement

A **trademark** is any distinctive word, symbol, device, or design adopted for the purpose of identifying the origin of goods being offered for sale. The tort of infringement, therefore, occurs when a competitor of the owner of the trademark uses a mark so similar to the owned trademark that purchasers of the competitor's goods are misled as to the origin of the goods which they are purchasing. In other words, a deception is accomplished that permits the competitor (typically a manufacturer) to "cash in" on the reputation and goodwill of the trademark owner (who is, typically, another manufacturer).

While the early trademark rules were exclusively common law in nature, the basis of most of our trademark law today is the Lanham Act—a federal statute passed in 1946. Nevertheless, case law remains a significant element of trademark law because certain aspects of this area of law are still governed by common-law principles, and also because a large body of case law has grown up as the courts have interpreted key provisions of the act on a case-by-case basis.

The act also governs other marks, such as **service marks**—used to identify the origin of services (for example "Budget," as applied to the car rental business) and certification marks—used by persons who do not own the marks, but who are authorized to indicate that their products are approved by the owner of such marks (for example, the "Good Housekeeping Seal of Approval"). We will limit our discussion here to consideration of only those principles of law having special applicability to the tort of trademark infringement.

Registration: Under the act, trademarks may be registered on a Principal Register if certain conditions are met. One applying for registration must show (1) ownership of the mark; (2) that the mark is affixed to or applies to his or her goods ("vendible commodities"); and (3) that the applicant has used the mark prior to the time of application. Additionally, the applicant must certify that, to his or her knowledge, neither the mark nor a similar mark is used by anyone else in connection with a competing product.

Registration on the Principal Register gives constructive notice to the world of the registrant's mark. The Bureau of Customs will thereafter protect the registrant's mark against infringing imports, and after five years of use the mark becomes "incontestable" subject to certain limits.

Certain kinds of marks are generally not registrable—the most important of which are those that are merely descriptive or geographic in nature, or are persons' surnames. Thus a term that merely describes a general kind of good, which is called a **generic term** (such as aspirin), cannot be registered under any circumstances. And other descriptive terms ("tender" steak), geographical terms ("Nebraska" butter), and surnames ("Henderson" hats) cannot be registered unless they have acquired a "secondary meaning" (a concept discussed later).

In *Zatrains, Inc., v. Oak Grove Smokehouse, Inc.*, 698 F.2d 786 (1983), where a primary question was whether Zatrains' trademark of "FISH FRI" batters was so descriptive of batters generally that it could not be protected against use of the mark "FISH FRY" batters by defendant Oak Grove, the higher court illustrated the applicable principles, as follows:

Courts and commentators have traditionally divided potential trademarks into four categories. A potential trademark may be classified as (1) generic, (2) descriptive, (3) suggestive, or (4) arbitrary or fanciful. These categories, like the tones in a spectrum, tend to blur at the edges and merge together. . . .

A *generic* term is the name of a particular genus or class of which an individual article or service is but a member. A generic term connotes the basic nature of articles or services rather than the more individualized characteristics of a particular product. Generic terms can never attain trademark protection. Furthermore, if at any time a registered trademark becomes generic as to a particular product or service, the mark's registration is subject to cancellation [under the Lanham Act]. Such terms as aspirin and cellophane have been held generic and therefore unprotectable as trademarks.

A *descriptive* term identifies a characteristic or quality of an article or service, such as its color, odor, function, dimensions, or ingredients. Descriptive terms ordinarily are not protectable as trademarks; they may become valid marks, however, by acquiring a secondary meaning in the minds of the consuming public. . . . [An] example of a descriptive mark would be . . . "Vision Center" in reference to a business offering optical goods and services. . . .

A *suggestive* term suggests, rather than describes, some particular characteristic of the goods or services to which it applies and requires the consumer to exercise the imagination in order to draw a conclusion as to the nature of the goods and services. A suggestive mark is protected without the necessity for proof of secondary meaning. The term "Coppertone" has been held suggestive in regard to sun tanning products.

Arbitrary or *fanciful* terms bear no relationship to the products or services to which they are applied. Like suggestive terms, [these] marks are protectable without proof of secondary meaning. The term "Kodak" is properly classified as a fanciful term for photographic supplies, and

"Ivory" is an arbitrary term as applied to soap.[7]

Secondary Meaning Concept: If a trademark is unregistrable because it is essentially descriptive or geographic, or is a surname, the mark may still be registered if the owner can prove that an appreciable number of purchasers within the applicable market do, in fact, associate the mark with the owner (as distinguished from the term's more general meaning). In such a case the mark is said to have acquired a **secondary meaning**—a name that is a misnomer, in view of the fact that such proof indicates the mark has, in fact, a strong meaning.[8] Waltham (watches) and Bavarian (beer) are examples of geographic names registered under the secondary meaning concept, and Safeway (food products) is a descriptive name that achieved registration under the same concept.

Element of Confusion: In most infringement actions the plaintiff mark owner has the burden of proving that defendant's mark is so similar to plaintiff's that defendant's use will produce a "likelihood of confusion" in buyers' minds as to the true origin of the goods or services. Whether such likelihood exists is a question of fact in any particular case, and is determined by such factors as similarity of design of the marks, similarity of product, proof of confusion among actual buyers, and marketing surveys of prospective purchasers showing an appreciable misassociation of defendant's mark with plaintiff's product. On the basis of these factors, for example, Rotary De-Rooting was held to be a mark so similar to Roto-Rooter that the owner of Roto-Rooter was successful in recovering damages from the owner of Rotary De-Rooting.[9] But if the products are substantially dissimilar, even identical marks may not cause confusion. Thus, where a clothing manufacturer had purchased the right to use the mark "Here's Johnny," a court held that the use of that mark by a manufacturer of portable toilets was not likely to cause purchasers of the toilets to associate them with the producer of the suits.[10]

---

[7] On this aspect of the case, the court held that FISH FRI was essentially descriptive (but, on the basis of other evidence, nonetheless protectable under the secondary meaning concept).

[8] With the exception of generic marks, marks which do not acquire a secondary meaning (or which cannot be registered on the Principal Register for any other reason) can gain some protection by being registered on a Supplemental Register.

[9] *Roto-Rooter Corp. v. O'Neal,* 513 F.2d 44, 1975.

[10] *Carson v. Here's Johnny Portable Toilets, Inc.,* 698 F.2d 831 (1983). Although plaintiff suit manufacturer was unsuccessful in the infringement aspect of the case, plaintiff Johnny Carson was granted an injunction restraining defendant company from further use of the mark on the invasion of privacy theory.

Universal City Studios, Inc. v. Nintendo Co., Ltd.
U.S. Court of Appeals, Second Circuit, 746 F.2d 112 (1984)

Plaintiff Universal claims ownership of the trademark in the name, character, and story of "King Kong," which should need no introduction. Defendant Nintendo manufactures and sells a video game known as "Donkey Kong," which requires a player to maneuver a computerized man named Mario up a set of girders, ladders, and elevators to save a blond pigtailed woman from the clutches of a malevolent, yet humorous gorilla, while simultaneously avoiding a

series of objects hurled at him by the impish ape. Nine months after defendant began marketing Donkey Kong, plaintiff filed this action claiming, among other things, trademark infringement.

After extensive discovery, the trial judge granted summary judgment to defendant on several grounds, including that as a matter of law consumers were unlikely to confuse Donkey Kong and King Kong. Plaintiff appealed.

Meskill, Circuit Judge:

. . . "It is well settled that the crucial issue in an action for trademark infringement or unfair competition is whether there is any likelihood that an appreciable number of ordinarily prudent purchasers are likely to be misled, or indeed simply confused, as to the source of the goods in question." *Mushroom Makers, Inc. v. R. G. Barry Corp.,* 580 F.2d 44 (2d Cir. 1978). The factors enumerated in *Polaroid Corp. v. Polaroid Electronics Corp.*, 287 F.2d 492 (2d Cir. 1961) are utilized and balanced to determine the likelihood of confusion:

Where the products are different, the prior owner's chance of success is a function of many variables: the strength of his mark, the degree of similarity between the two marks, the proximity of the products, the likelihood that the prior owner will bridge the gap, actual confusion, and the reciprocal of defendant's good faith in adopting its own mark, the quality of defendant's product, and the sophistication of the buyers. Even this extensive catalogue does not exhaust the possibilities—the court may have to take still other variables into account.

. . . The district court conducted a visual inspection of both the Donkey Kong game and the King Kong movies and stated that the differences between them were "great." It found the Donkey Kong game "comical" and the Donkey Kong gorilla character "farcical, childlike and nonsexual." In contrast, the court described the King Kong character and story as "a ferocious gorilla in quest of a beautiful woman." The court summarized that "Donkey Kong . . . creates a totally different concept and feel from the drama of King Kong" and that "at best, Donkey Kong is a parody of King Kong." Indeed, the fact that Donkey Kong so obviously parodies the King Kong theme strongly contributes to dispelling confusion on the part of customers. . . .

We agree with the district court that the two characters and stories are so different that no question of fact was presented on the likelihood of consumer confusion. The two properties have nothing in common but a gorilla, a captive woman, a male rescuer and a building scenario. Universal has not introduced any evidence indicating actual consumer confusion. Where, as here, the two properties are so different, Universal's claim cannot stand without some indication of actual confusion or a "survey of consumer attitudes under actual market conditions." *Mattel, Inc. v. Azrak-Hamway International, Inc.*, 724 F.2d 357 (2d Cir. 1983).

Universal points to the similarity of the two names, claiming that the use of the word "Kong" raises a question of fact on the likelihood of confusion. We disagree. In order to determine if confusion is likely, each trademark must be compared in its entirety; juxtaposing fragments of each mark does not demonstrate whether the marks as a whole are confusingly similar. The "Kong" and "King Kong" names are widely used by the general public and are associated with apes and other objects of enormous proportions. Nintendo's use of the prefix "Donkey" has no similarity in meaning or sound with the word "King." When taken as a whole, we find as a matter of law that "Donkey Kong" does not evoke or suggest the name "King Kong."

[Affirmed.]

Remedies: Where likelihood of confusion is established, the plaintiff's usual remedies under the Lanham Act or common-law principles are the *injunction* and *damages.* The injunction is an order prohibiting defendant's further use of the mark, and damages is a recovery of money to compensate plaintiff for the monetary injury (if any) which he or she has sustained as a result of the infringement.

Because of a tremendous increase in the trafficking of counterfeit designer goods, Congress passed the Trademark Counterfeiting Act of 1984 which provides escalating *criminal* penalties for multiple offenders. For example, a second offender, if an individual, can be fined up to $1,000,000 and/or imprisoned for up to 15 years.

Misuse of Trade Secrets

By means of industrial sabotage and the hiring of competitors' employees, companies acquire billions of dollars of confidential information each year. If patent law does not apply, only trade secret law can protect the information. "The maintenance of commercial ethics and the encouragement of innovation are the broadly stated policies behind trade secret law." [11]

A **trade secret** is "any formula, pattern, device or compilation of information which is used in one's business, and which gives him an opportunity to obtain an advantage over competitors who do not know or use it." [12] Examples of protectable trade secrets include customer lists, manufacturing processes, chemical formulas, marketing techniques, raw materials sources, and computer software.

Elements of the Tort: Simple concepts of fairness suggest that a company that has acquired information or developed processes as a result of its own efforts—information or processes not generally known to others—ought to be protected from the wrongful use of such information or processes by its competitors. To successfully bring a trade secret claim, a plaintiff must prove: (1) existence and ownership of a trade secret; (2) defendant's acquisition of the trade secret by wrongful or improper means; and (3) use or disclosure of the trade secret to the injury of plaintiff.

In any trade secret case, two issues are paramount: (1) whether the processes or information which the plaintiff is seeking to protect against the defendant's continued use are "secret" in the eyes of the law, and (2) if so, whether the defendant acquired the information by "wrongful means."

Secrecy: To be protected, information must be kept reasonably (not absolutely) secret by its owner. Thus, if a defendant has acquired information that was freely circulated by the plaintiff

---

[11] *Kewanee Oil Co. v. Bicron Corp.*, 416 U.S. 460 (1973).

[12] *Restatement of Torts* §757 comment b (1939).

company among its employees, customers, or suppliers, plaintiff company's action for damages will probably be dismissed. In contrast, protection will be afforded where a company gives secret information only to a small number of employees on a "need to know" basis, under clear instructions not to disclose it to others. If an employee breaches this trust by passing it to a competitor, it remains a trade secret and the competitor's use of it subjects the competitor to tort liability.

The Wrongful Acquisition Requirement: Even if information qualifies as a trade secret, its use by a competitor is normally lawful if the competitor has discovered the secret by means that are "not improper." Thus if the X Company discovers a manufacturing process by independent research, or even by means of "reverse engineering"—disassembling a product of the Y Company which it has lawfully purchased—the subsequent use of the process by the X Company is generally lawful.

Historically, acquisition was considered to be improper only when it was illegal (e.g., acquisition by trespass, theft, or wiretapping) or involved breach of a confidential relationship (e.g., bribery of an employee of the owners). More recently, courts have broadened the improper means concept to include methods which "fall below the generally accepted standards of commercial morality, even though not illegal." [13]

Patent Infringement

To encourage creation and disclosure of inventions, the Constitution authorizes the federal government to grant **patents** to inventors ("patentees"). In exchange for disclosing the

invention, the inventor patentee receives a 17-year (14 years in the case of design patents) exclusive right to make, use, or sell the patented item. The 17-year patent is nonrenewable; after expiration of the period the item goes into the public domain and may be made, used, or sold by anyone.

Subject Matter: Items that may be patented include (1) processes, (2) machines, (3) manufactures (e.g., products), (4) compositions of matter (e.g., new arrangements of elements as in metal alloys), and (5) any improvement upon the first four categories. In addition, design patents for ornamental designs have been granted, as have patents on new varieties of asexually reproducing plants which have been modified by humans and do not naturally occur in nature. In *Diamond v. Chakrabarty,* [14] the Supreme Court even found a new life form (a laboratory-created bacterium for "eating" oil spills) to be patentable.

On the other hand, one cannot patent (1) printed matter, (2) naturally occurring substances, (3) methods of doing business, (4) ideas (e.g., $E = MC^2$), or (5) scientific principles (e.g., chemical formulas). This list is nonexclusive, but the idea is that the patentee must create, not find; invent, not merely discover.

Patentability: If it fits into a proper subject matter category, an item may be patented if it meets three main tests: utility, novelty, and nonobviousness. An item has *utility* if it produces a direct benefit to mankind. It does not if it is dangerous, immoral, or merely a matter of curiosity. The *novelty* test is met if the item is distinctive from what was present in the prior state of the art. Prior patents, public use or sale, and written descriptions of the item can destroy novelty. *Nonobviousness* is also decided in light of the prior state of the art. If the item could easily have been produced by someone with normal skill in

---

[13] *E.I. duPont de Nemours & Co., Inc. v. Christopher* 431 F.2d 1012 (5th Cir. 1970), where duPont recovered damages from a company that had acquired its secret method of producing methanol by means of aerial photographs of a duPont plant under construction. Apparently companies need not use antiaircraft guns to keep their secrets; only "reasonable" efforts are required.

[14] 447 U.S. 303 (1980).

the area, or if it is an obvious next step from prior inventions, the nonobviousness test is not met. If a product is immediately a tremendous success or if it fills a long-felt need in the marketplace, there is a presumption of nonobviousness.

In practice, these tests are somewhat vague. For that reason, although the Patent Office grants about 60 percent of the patent applications, when these applications are challenged by alleged infringers, about 60 percent of issued patents are invalidated by the courts.

Patent Procedure: A patent application must be filed in the name of the inventor at the U.S. Patent and Trademark Office in Arlington, Virginia. The application must include a *specification* (a precise description of the item so that one skilled in the art could make use of it), and *claims* (a description of precisely what makes the item patentable—e.g., useful, novel, and nonobvious). The Patent Office will examine the application and search for previous patents on the same item. If the application is denied, it may be amended, and frequently substantial negotiation occurs between the applicant and the Patent Office. Decisions can be appealed administratively and, ultimately, to the courts.

Patent procedure is time consuming and expensive. It is also very complicated, and an inventor would be wise to hire an attorney who specializes in patent law.

Once the application is filed, the patentee can place "Patent Pending" on his products for which the patent is sought. This has no legal effect because the patent is not effective until issued by the Patent Office. However, it puts others on notice of the claim, and if the patent is ultimately granted they can be sued for infringements occurring during the patent pending stage.

Ownership: The patentee can sell his title to the patent to a third party. The patentee can also retain the title, but grant a license under which a third party can use the patented item in exchange for payment of a royalty to the patentee.

Assignments of title must be filed in the Patent Office.

Employees should be aware of the **shop right doctrine.** If an employee is hired for creative or inventive work, and invents something on company time while using company resources, the patent belongs to the company. The company will file the application in the employee's name, but the company will own it. Even if the employee was not hired for creative or inventive work, if he or she invents something on company time using company resources, the company will be granted a nonexclusive license to use the patented item without payment of a royalty. Of course, many employers have their employees sign agreements to assign title to all patents generated on company time to the employer.

Infringement: A person infringes a valid patent by using a device which meets the *doctrine of equivalents,* which provides that one device infringes on another if they do the "same work in substantially the same way and accomplish substantially the same result" even though they differ in name, form, or shape.[15]

Defenses: An alleged misuser may raise a number of defenses. First, of course, the misuser may claim that his or her device did not meet the doctrine of equivalents. Second, the misuser may challenge the validity of the patent by arguing that it flunks one or more of the tests of novelty, utility, and nonobviousness or that it is not the type of subject matter that may be properly patented. Third, the misuser may claim that the patentee *forfeited* the patent by not filing an application within one year after the invention was in public use, or should have the patent revoked because he or she breached the *duty of candor,* a duty the law imposes to disclose everything the patentee knows about previous inventions and other facts which might bear on

---

[15]*Autogyro Co. of America v. U.S.,* 384 F.2d 391 (Ct. Cl. 1967).

patentability. Finally, the infringer might argue that the patent should be revoked because of *patent misuse,* which occurs when the patentee abuses the patent, frequently in violation of antitrust laws, in order to gain more rights than the patent legally confers. For example, if the patentee agrees to grant a license to use a patented machine only if the licensee agrees to buy certain nonpatented items, this may be a "tying" arrangement which violates Section three of the Clayton Act.

Remedies: A patentee who successfully sues for infringement can obtain an injunction, damages of no less than a reasonable royalty rate (and perhaps trebled in the court's discretion where plaintiff was damaged to a greater extent than the demonstrated royalty rate), and in exceptional cases, attorneys' fees.

Copyright Infringement

To reward and stimulate intellectual endeavors, federal **copyright** law grants authors protection for the *expression* of their ideas, though not for the ideas themselves. Under the Copyright Act of 1976, all copyrightable works created after January 1, 1978, receive protection for the life of the author plus fifty years after his or her death.

During that period, the owner of the copyright has the exclusive right to produce the work in any medium, to control derivative works, to distribute copies of the work, to perform the work in public, and to display the work in public.

Subject Matter: Copyrights protect literary works (books, newspapers, magazines), works of a musical, dramatic, graphic, choreographic, or audiovisual nature, and sound recordings. This list is non-exclusive; the law is meant to protect any "original works of authorship." Computer programs, jewelry designs, and speeches reduced to writing have been protected.

Copyrightability: There are three basic elements of copyrightability. First, the work must

be *fixed* in some *tangible medium of expression.* When a book is written, a song is recorded, a picture is painted, or a choreography is filmed, this requirement is met. Until tangibly fixed, a mere idea is unprotected.

The work must be *creative,* at least to some degree. This requirement is loosely applied in most cases. Some courts require a "modicum of creative work," while others only seek to insure that the author put some effort or "sweat" into the work. Photographs of real life scenes (such as the fortuitous Zapruder film of the Kennedy assassination) are clearly copyrightable, as are compilations of facts and directories, though little creative thought is involved.

Most important, the work must be *original.* This does not require novelty, only that the work not be copied from someone else. A person who had never seen the novel *Moby Dick* but wrote a nearly identical book independently could successfully copyright it.

Copyright Procedure: Securing a copyright is much easier than securing a patent; the process is virtually self-executing. Copyright protection for a published work is obtained if each copy of the work contains (1) a copyright notice (e.g., the word "copyright," the abbreviation "Copr.," or the symbol ©), (2) the date of first publication, and (3) the name of the copyright owner.

The copyright owner should also file a simple application with the Copyright Office in Washington, D.C., including two copies of the work for deposit in the Library of Congress. Failure to register with the Copyright Office and deposit the copies does not invalidate the copyright. However, these steps must be carried out before the copyright holder can sue for infringement. Also, failure to register and deposit copies waives the right to statutory penalties and attorneys' fees in the event of a successful infringement suit, at least as to those who infringed before registration finally occurred.

Infringement: If a plaintiff proves (even by circumstantial evidence) that a defendant had *access* to plaintiff's work, and that defendant's work bears a *substantial similarity* to plaintiff's copyrighted work (or a part of it), a claim for infringement is established. Plaintiff need not prove intent; an innocent infringement is actionable. For example, in *Bright Tunes Music Corp. v. Harrisongs Music, Ltd.*,[16] the judge did not believe that former Beatle George Harrison intentionally copied an earlier song, "He's So Fine," when he composed "My Sweet Lord." Nonetheless, Harrison had access to the earlier song (which was widely played on popular radio), and his song was substantially similar. Harrison was held to have infringed the owner's copyright.

Fair Use Doctrine: An important, but rather vague, part of copyright law is the *Fair Use Doctrine.* Section 107 of the Copyright Act of 1976 states:

[T]he fair use of a copyrighted work, including such use by reproduction in copies or phonorecords or by any other means specified by [§106], for purposes such as criticism, comment, newsreporting, teaching (including multiple copies for classroom use), scholarship, or research, is not an infringement of copyright. In determining whether the use made of a work in any particular case is a fair use the factors to be considered shall include—

  1. the purpose and character of the use, including whether such use is of a commercial nature or is for nonprofit educational purposes;

  2. the nature of the copyrighted work;

  3. the amount and substantiality of the portion used in relation to the copyrighted work as a whole; and

  4. the effect of the use upon the potential market for or value of the copyrighted work.

Although the applications of this doctrine are shadowy at best, the Copyright Office has issued supplemental guidelines dealing with photocopies, and obviously copies used for literary criticism, classroom teaching, and parody fare better than those used for commercial purposes.

Remedies: A successful plaintiff in a copyright infringement action usually receives actual damages plus defendant's profits to the extent they were not calculated into the damage award. Most plaintiffs can waive these damages and receive instead "statutory damages" in lieu of regular damages. Statutory damages are awarded in an amount the court finds "just," with the normal range being between $250 and $10,000, although innocent infringers may have their penalty reduced to $100 and flagrant infringers can be assessed as much as $50,000. Injunctive relief, costs, and reasonable attorneys' fees in the discretion of the court are also available.

Copyright infringement can also constitute a federal misdemeanor punishable by fines of up to $10,000 and/or one year in jail.

Unfair Competition

The term **unfair competition** is an imprecise one. In its broadest sense, it covers all tortious business conduct. In its most common usage, however, the term refers only to those business practices that are based on *deception.* (Thus, of the torts discussed above, only trademark infringement would fall within the unfair competition category.)

In addition to trademark infringement, unfair competition includes any deceptive use by one person of the copyright or patent rights of another. It also embraces many other common-law torts, such as falsely inducing consumers to believe a product is endorsed by another, and "palming off." Palming off refers to any word or deed causing purchasers to be misled as to a product's source. It thus includes not only trademark infringement, but all other means of source-deception as well.

---

[16] 420 F. Supp. 177 (S.D.N.Y. 1977).

These torts are today often prohibited by state **deceptive trade practices acts.**[17] Other types of unfair competition that are usually prohibited by such statutes are the advertising of goods or services with the intent not to sell them upon the advertised terms, representing goods as new when they are used or second-hand, and disparagement—making false statements of fact about competitors' goods or services.

BUSINESS CRIMES

As we have noted, *crimes* are wrongs that violate state or federal statutes which not only prohibit specific acts, but which additionally impose fines or prison sentences upon violators. Because crimes are thus "wrongs against the state," the plaintiff in any criminal action is the government whose law has allegedly been violated be it local or federal. Additionally, where criminal conduct causes a physical or financial injury, as is usually the case, a civil suit can be brought by the injured party against the wrongdoer to recover damages. Thus a single wrongful act can be the basis for two lawsuits, as illustrated in Figure 8.1. (In practice, however, the injured parties often do not bring suit, either because the costs would exceed the possible recovery or because the wrongdoer is financially unable to pay a judgment even if one were obtained.)

In the remainder of this chapter we will note the special characteristics of criminal law generally, and then examine the most common types of business crimes—criminal acts that are most often committed by, or against, business firms. (While it is impossible even to assess roughly the cost of business crimes, some idea of the immensity of the problem can be gained from estimates indicating that shoplifting causes losses to businesses of approximately $20 billion a year, and that computer crime is responsible for additional losses of over $40 billion annually.)

---

[17] In states having such statutes, the wrongs are thus statutory torts (rather than common-law torts).

Figure 8.1   A Single Act as Both Tort and Crime

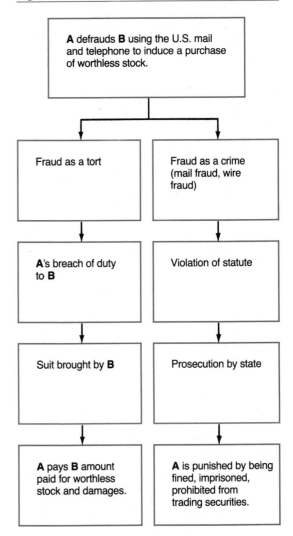

Criminal Law Principles

In addition to the fact that criminal actions are brought by the state, criminal law has other special characteristics that distinguish it from civil law proceedings. In general, these special characteristics are as applicable to business crimes as they are to nonbusiness crimes such as murder, burglary, and rape.

The Grand Jury: One of the first steps in a serious criminal action is usually the prosecutor's presentation of evidence to a grand jury, whose purpose is to decide whether there is "probable cause" for believing that the defendant has committed the crime of which he or she is accused. If no such cause is found, the proceedings are ended. On the other hand, if probable cause *is* found, an indictment (a formal written accusation on behalf of the state) is handed down and the case proceeds in the appropriate state or federal court. It is there that the trial jury will make the actual determination of guilt or innocence. The action before the grand jury is thus in the nature of a preliminary hearing (but one that is, nonetheless, of critical importance insofar as the defendant is concerned).

Degree of Proof: In criminal actions, where fact determinations are usually made by juries, the state must prove "beyond a reasonable doubt" that the defendant did, in fact, commit the acts of which he or she is accused. By contrast, in a civil action the plaintiff needs to prove his or her allegations only by a "preponderance of the evidence"—evidence that convinces the jury that the plaintiff's version of the facts is more believable than the defendant's version. Thus a specific criminal action might fail against a defendant, while a civil suit brought against him based on the same evidence may result in a judgment in favor of the plaintiff, the party injured by the wrong.

Criminal Intent: One of the required elements of most crimes is that of *wrongful intent* on the part of the defendant.[18] In such instances, the performance of the prohibited acts without such intent does not constitute a crime. For example, in the case of *Jacques v. Sears, Roebuck & Company* in Chapter 7 the criminal action that preceded the civil suit was dismissed because the applicable petit larceny statute defined that crime as "the taking [of property] with the intent to deprive the owner [of such property]," and the court hearing the criminal action determined that Jacques' failure to pay for the items in his pocket was an inadvertent (forgetful) taking rather than a willful taking.

Because a person's actual intent can rarely be known with absolute certainty, juries may often presume a criminal intent on the part of the defendant based on the established facts. Thus a jury may presume that an armed prowler apprehended in a house at night entered the house "with the intention of committing a felony," one of the usual statutory elements of the crime of burglary. And, where a corporation is charged with a crime requiring wrongful intent, and where the jury finds that the corporate directors or agents possessed the required intent, then this wrongful intent is imputed to—i.e., legally chargeable to—the corporation, with the result that the intent element of the crime is now established.

White-Collar Crime

The term **white-collar crime** originally referred only to crimes committed against business firms, usually by their employees, through the use of nonphysical, nonviolent means. In this sense, such crime consisted essentially of *embezzlement,* the taking of an employer's funds by an employee entrusted with such funds, and *theft,* the wrongful taking of any other property of the employer. Today, however, the term has almost universally been broadened to refer to all nonviolent criminal acts committed *by* business firms as well as *against* business firms. Used in this broader sense, white-collar crime embraces a very wide spectrum of business misconduct, covering such diverse wrongs as the practicing of fraud on insurance companies, securities fraud, obtaining property through misuse of credit cards, and even income tax evasion. The term also includes computer fraud, a topic warranting special attention at the end of this chap-

---

[18] Such crimes are *malum in se*—morally wrong. Crimes not requiring such intent—such as failure to obey a traffic light—are *malum prohibitum.*

ter. (Securities fraud is covered in detail in Chapter 50.)

In the following section, we will examine some of the most common business-related actions that violate federal or state criminal statutes—most of which fall under the "white-collar" heading.

SELECTED FEDERAL CRIMES

Mail Fraud

Prohibitions, Generally: Operation of the U.S. Postal Service is governed by a very large number of rules found in Title 39 of the U.S. Code. These rules, among other things, contain a list of "nonmailable" materials, and Title 18 of the code imposes criminal penalties on persons mailing such materials. For example, the mailing of firearms and poisonous drugs is generally prohibited, as is the sending of matter that could be interpreted by the addressee as "a bill, invoice, or statement of account due"—a notice legally requiring a response on the addressee's part—when, in fact, the matter is "a solicitation for the order [of] the addressee of goods and services" which the sender is trying to sell.

Even more important are the rules of 39 U.S.C. §3005, which, in part, prohibit any person from engaging "in a scheme or device for obtaining money or property through the mails by means of false representations," and also from engaging in the conduct of a "lottery . . . or a scheme for the distribution of money . . . by lottery, chance, or drawing of any kind. . . ."

Misrepresentation—Fraud: Fraud—a subject examined more fully in Part II—consists essentially of any word or deed by which one party intentionally deceives another, and which results in a loss to the deceived party. Obviously, the main thrust of the "false representation" section quoted above is to reduce, as much as possible, those fraudulent schemes which are carried on through the use of the mails. Under Title 18 of the code, criminal penalties have been imposed upon persons and firms engaged in a wide range of activities involving fraudulent representations: using the mails to advertise such articles as hair-growing products that proved to be worthless; retrofit carburetors that totally failed to improve automobile fuel economy; and false identification cards which the sellers knew were ordered by purchasers for the purpose of deceiving third parties. Similarly, schemes for the operation of "mail-order" schools, where degrees or diplomas are awarded "without requiring evidence of education or experience entitled thereto," and where the operators know such documents are likely to be used by purchasers to misrepresent their qualifications to prospective employers, violate these sections of the law.[19]

Antitrust Crimes

Many of our antitrust laws—a subject discussed more fully in Chapters 47 and 48—are non-criminal in nature. This means that parties who violate such laws, such as by engaging in price discrimination in violation of the Robinson-Patman Act, are subject to the remedies of injunction and damages in the civil actions brought against them, but are not subject to the imposition of fines or imprisonment.

Some antitrust laws, however, provide for the imposition of both civil and criminal liability. Chief among these are those provisions of the Sherman Act, a federal statute, providing that corporations which violate Section 1 by making contracts that unreasonably restrain trade, or which violate Section 2 by monopolizing or attempting to monopolize an industry, may be fined as much as $1 million, and further providing that individuals who violate either of these sections are subject to fines of $100,000 or three years' imprisonment or both. In this regard, two additional facts should be noted: (1) that treble damages may be recovered by firms that

---

[19]*National College of Arts and Sciences* (1981), PS Docket No. 11/64.

have suffered injuries as a result of violations of the Sherman Act, and (2) that, in practice, civil actions brought under the antitrust laws are far more common than criminal actions, because the federal government usually brings criminal actions only in cases of flagrant violations of these acts.

RICO

The Racketeering Influenced and Corrupt Organizations Act (RICO) is presently a very significant criminal statute. The act's aim is to blunt organized crime's intrusion into legitimate business. The act has civil provisions which have been broadly construed and applied primarily to "normal" business defendants rather than mobsters. An important Supreme Court case, *Sedima v. Imrex Co., Inc.*, seen earlier in Chapter 4,[20] discussed the fact that the civil side of RICO

seems to have gotten a little out of control. As of this writing, Congress is considering amending RICO to reduce its harsh impact on "normal" businesses.

RICO also has a criminal side which, fortunately, has been applied primarily to fairly hard-core criminal activity. The elements a prosecutor must prove in a criminal RICO case are: (1) the defendant engaged in an enterprise, (2) the enterprise affected interstate commerce, (3) the enterprise's affairs were conducted through racketeering activity, and (4) the conduct of those affairs involved two or more of the racketeering offenses set forth in the statute.[21]

Prosecutors have secured RICO criminal convictions in cases involving marijuana smuggling, kickbacks to judges, extortion of "protection money" by police officers, loansharking, gambling, and the like. The following case is illustrative.

---

[20] See also the discussion of civil RICO's application to securities law specifically in Chapter 50.

[21] *U.S. v. Qaoud,* 777 F.2d 1105 (6th Cir. 1985).

United States v. LeRoy
U.S. Court of Appeals, Second Circuit, 687 F.2d 610 (1982)

Defendant LeRoy was vice-president and later business manager of Local 214 of the Laborers International Union. During his terms, LeRoy was placed on the payroll of several contractors hiring Local 214's members. LeRoy did no work but received compensation so the contractors could "keep peace with the laborers." LeRoy also bought gasoline and had his brakes fixed and in so doing had the union pay the bills and then "reimburse" him as though he had paid them. LeRoy appeals his conviction of one count of conspiracy to violate §1962(c) of RICO, in violation of §1962(d).

Moore, Circuit Judge:

Pursuant to §1962(c), it is unlawful "for any person employed by or associated with any enterprise engaged in, or the activities of which affect, interstate or foreign commerce, to conduct or participate, directly or indirectly, in the conduct of such enterprise's affairs through a pattern of racketeering activity. . . ." Unions are expressly included within the term "enterprise."

LeRoy concedes that the Government conclusively proved the existence of an enterprise affecting interstate commerce—namely Local 214. He also admits that the Government demonstrated LeRoy's, as well as his co-conspirators', association with the union. LeRoy contends, however, that the Government failed to show that he participated in the conduct of the union's affairs or that his activities constituted a "pattern" of racketeering activity.

Specifically, LeRoy alleges that the Government proved at most illegal conduct committed in furtherance of LeRoy's personal interest, but not in the conduct of the union's business. Accordingly, LeRoy argues, his actions fall beyond the purview of the statute. We find no merit to LeRoy's contention and conclude that his actions took place in the conduct of Local 214's affairs and thus, within the scope of RICO. . . . [W]hile RICO does not specify the degree of interrelationship between the pattern of racketeering and the conduct of the enterprise's affairs, the Act also does not require that predicate acts be in furtherance of the enterprise.

The evidence in this case demonstrates that LeRoy accepted unearned wages while he served as vice-president of Local 214 from various contractors who testified that they paid him in order to preserve union peace, in violation of the Taft-Hartley Act, and later used his position as business manager to obtain payments from the union treasury for expenses not properly incurred, in violation of the Landrum-Griffin Act. These violations of the Landrum-Griffin and Taft-Hartley Acts were the predicate offenses forming the pattern of racketeering. LeRoy was able to commit these predicate offenses solely by virtue of his positions in Local 214, since the predicate acts were inextricably tied to LeRoy's role as a union official.

We also reject LeRoy's argument that the Government failed to prove that his participation in the union's affairs was "through a pattern of racketeering activity." A "pattern of racketeering activity" is established by proof of the commission of at least two "acts of racketeering" within a ten-year period. Moreover, a violation of either the Landrum-Griffin Act or the Taft-Hartley Act constitutes an act of racketeering. Since the evidence demonstrates that LeRoy violated the provisions of these acts on more than two occasions, the Government clearly proved a pattern of racketeering activity.

[Affirmed.]

Other Federal Crimes

There are many additional business-related acts that constitute federal crimes. For example, in the area of bankruptcy, covered in Chapter 30, the federal Bankruptcy Reform Act of 1978 makes it a crime for a debtor to willfully transfer property to a confederate before bankruptcy proceedings for the purpose of defrauding creditors, to conceal his or her assets during bankruptcy proceedings, and to give false testimony under oath during such proceedings.

Additionally, a number of federal statutes impose criminal liability on persons and firms who offer bribes and kickbacks to federal officials for the purpose of obtaining business advantages. Similarly, bribery of officials of foreign governments for the purpose of obtaining the sale of goods or services to those governments is a crime under the Foreign Corrupt Practices Act of 1977—an act passed after testimony in Congress divulged widespread use of such bribery by a number of U.S. firms in the late 1960s and early 1970s.[22] Any firm that violates this act can be fined up to $1 million, and officers and directors of such firms may be fined up to $10,000 or imprisoned for up to five years or both.

SELECTED STATE CRIMES

As might be imagined, there are so many criminal statutes in the various states—even when one's inquiry is limited to statutes relating to business offenses alone—that a comprehensive treatment of the subject is well beyond the scope of this chapter. Nonetheless, there are a number of major areas of business misconduct that are treated so uniformly by the various states' criminal laws that one can gain a "feel" for such laws by examining a few of these areas.

Larceny, False Pretenses, and Theft

Larceny is generally defined as the wrongful and fraudulent taking by one person of the personal property of another, with the intent on the part of the taker of converting the property to his or her own use. In addition to simple larceny statutes, some states have larceny by trick statutes or **false pretenses statutes** that generally prohibit the obtaining of another's money or property by deception, by trick, or by some other fraudulent ruse. Examples of such conduct are the filing of false claims with insurance companies and the taking of buyers' money for goods

or services with no intent of delivering such goods or services. Additionally, the sales in recent years by "investment firms" of investors' rights to participate in federally operated lotteries of oil lands, with investors being assured that their chances of selection are 1 in 4 (when in reality the chance is 1 in 1,000), clearly fall within the purview of these statutes. Violations of such statutes are usually misdemeanors when the money or value of the property is under a specific sum (such as $150), and felonies if the value is $150 or above.

More modern statutes in some states include all of these kinds of misconduct, plus some others, within a single statute. The Ohio statute, for example, is simply entitled "Theft," and provides, in material part, that:

(A) No person, with purpose to deprive the owner of property or services, shall knowingly obtain or exert control over either [property or services]:

(1) Without the consent of the owner or person authorized to give consent;

(2) Beyond the scope of the express or implied consent of the owner . . . ;

(3) By deception;

(4) By threat.[23]

Specialized Statutes

The obtaining of money or property by the giving of a bad check would seemingly fall within the general larceny and theft statutes. Nonetheless, all states have specific statutes relating to the issuance of bad checks, which generally impose criminal liability on persons who, with intent to defraud, issue or transfer checks or other negotiable instruments knowing that they will be dishonored. Such knowledge is presumed to exist, under the typical statute, if the drawer had no account with the drawee bank when the

---

[22] Two of the most publicized instances involved bribes of $1.6 million paid by McDonnell-Douglas Corporation to Pakistani agents in 1973 to induce the purchase of DC10 aircraft by Pakistani International Airlines, and alleged bribes of $2 million paid by Lockheed Aircraft Company in 1972 to Japanese officials. Criminal actions based on general "criminal fraud" statutes resulted in the payment of fines of over $1 million by McDonnell-Douglas, and of a similar sum by Lockheed.

[23] Ohio Revised Code §2913.02.

check was issued, or if the check was refused payment because of insufficient funds in the drawer's account when it was presented to the bank for payment. Similarly, most states have separate statutes relating to a number of other special offenses, such as the setting back of automobile odometers with the intent to defraud and the knowing delivery of "short weights"— the charging of buyers for quantities of goods that are greater than the quantities that were actually delivered.

CORPORATE CRIMINAL LIABILITY

Corporations

Until relatively recently, it was very rare for a corporation, which is after all a fictional entity, to be indicted for or convicted of a crime. But that has changed. Between 1976 and 1979, 574 corporations were convicted of federal crimes. And state courts are increasingly convicting corporations of crimes where there is an indication that the state legislature intended corporations to be covered by the criminal statutes.

The basic rule is that corporations can be held criminally liable for any acts performed by an employee (no matter how far down the corporate ladder) if that employee is acting within the scope of his or her authority. The basic idea is that the corporation receives the benefit when the agent acts properly, and must bear the responsibility when the agent errs. This is embodied in the *respondeat superior* doctrine.[24] The corporation can even be held liable when the agent is violating company policy or disobeying a specific order from a superior.

Corporations can also be convicted of crimes which have as an element of liability that the wrongdoer had specific criminal intent to do wrong. The intent of the employee will be im-

puted to the corporation so long as the employee was acting to benefit the corporation (and the corporation itself was not the victim of the crime).

Corporations have been indicted for homicide and a wide variety of lesser offenses. In 1985 indictments for health and safety violations arising out of toxic waste disposal, failure to remove asbestos from buildings, and construction-site accidents multiplied dramatically.

Corporate Officials

The increase in criminal indictments of corporations has been matched by an increase for corporate officials as well. Corporate officers will definitely be held liable for criminal acts they participate in or authorize. In addition, they will be held liable for acts which they aid and abet through any significant assistance or encouragement. Some courts find sufficient encouragement in mere acquiescence of a superior (which might signal tacit approval to a subordinate) and even in failure to stop criminal activity the official knows about. In rare instances corporate officers have been held criminally liable on a strict liability basis because they failed to control the criminal acts of subordinates (even where they had been assured that the criminal acts had been stopped).[25]

Indicative of the recent trend toward increased liability is *People v. O'Neil*,[26] in which a jury convicted three corporate officials of *murder* in the deaths of employees exposed to cyanide gas in the work place.

COMPUTER CRIME

The explosive growth in the use of computers in the business world the last several years has brought with it a corresponding flood of com-

---

[24] This doctrine is discussed in detail in Chapter 19.

[25] *U.S. v. Park,* 421 U.S. 658 (1975).

[26] No. 83C-11091 (Cook County, Ill. Circuit Court 1985) (on appeal).

puter misuse. We will briefly note some general characteristics of this kind of misuse, and then focus our attention on present-day computer law.

An Overview:

At some risk of oversimplification, these introductory observations can be made about the broad area of computer fraud and computer crime:

1. The traditional (precomputer) state and federal laws applicable to such crimes as trespass and larceny have lagged far behind the development of computer technology itself, and thus behind the kinds of wrongs that this technology makes possible today. In other words, the kinds of misconduct that are made possible by computer use often do not constitute crimes under traditional laws.

For example, one court held that a city employee's use of the city's computer facilities in his private sales venture could not support a theft conviction absent any evidence that the city was deprived of any part of value or use of the computer.[27] Use of a computer has not been deemed "property" within traditional theft statutes.[28]

2. While computer wrongs can be perpetrated through a wide variety of activities, these wrongs generally fall into three broad categories: simple unauthorized access, theft of information, and theft of funds.

Among schemes that have been subjects of litigation are: (1) stealing a competitor's computer program, (2) paying an accomplice to delete adverse information and insert favorable false information into the defendant's credit file, (3) a bank president's having his account computer coded so that his checks would be removed and held rather than posted so he could

later remove the actual checks without their being debited, and (4) creating a false vendor code in the defendant's sister's name so that the company computer would send checks supposed to go to Whirlpool Corporation to her account instead.

3. The vast majority of detected cases of computer misconduct do not ever get into court. This is largely true because (1) companies understandably do not want publicity about the inadequacy of their computer controls, and (2) financial institutions, such as banks and savings and loan companies, fear that reports of large losses of funds, even when insured, are likely to cause depositors to withdraw their funds in the interest of safety.

It is because of this relative dearth of civil and criminal actions that estimates of losses resulting from computer fraud based on court records are in the range of $350 to $500 million per year, while estimates of actual losses are as high as $35 to $40 billion a year (the latter figures including, in addition to thefts of funds, losses of computer programs and data, losses of trade secrets, and damage done to computer hardware).

Current State of the Law

Federal Law: There have been convictions for computer crimes under traditional federal statutes. For example, convictions have been obtained under federal statutes dealing with wire fraud, theft, and misappropriation. Nonetheless, the Congress has deemed it wise to enact statutes that deal directly with the problem, though no comprehensive statute exists.

The Access Device and Computer Fraud and Abuse Act of 1984 outlaws (1) obtaining classified information from a computer without authorization and with intent or reason to believe that it is to be used to injure the United States; (2) obtaining from a computer without authorization information that is protected by the Right to Financial Privacy Act or contained in

---

[27] *State v. McGraw,* 480 N.E.2d 552 (Ind. 1985).

[28] *People v. Weg,* 113 Misc.2d 1017, 450 N.Y.S.2d 957 (Crim. Ct. 1982).

the consumer files of a credit reporting agency; and (3) interfering with the operation of a government computer.

The Comprehensive Crime Control Act of 1984 contained a section on the use of computers in credit card fraud, and established penalties for violation. The Computer Fraud and Abuse Act of 1986 established three federal crimes for computer fraud, destruction, and password trafficking.

State Law: At least 45 states have passed laws dealing with computer crime. Most of the statutes comprehensively address the problem, outlawing (1) computer trespass (unauthorized access), (2) damage to computers or software, (3) theft or misappropriation of computer services, and (4) unauthorized obtaining or disseminating of information via computer.

Many states have also addressed the problem of credit card fraud, including that facilitated by use of computers.

There is every reason to believe that legislative attempts to deal with computer crime will continue to expand as the amount of computer crime continues to escalate.

SUMMARY

Businesses have a strong and legally protectable interest in free and fair competition, and in their intellectual property. The courts will protect against unfair interference not only with existing contractual and business relationships, but also, under proper circumstances, with prospective relationships. The key is frequently whether the defendant is acting with an improper purpose or in an improper manner.

The law protects properly registered trademarks so that producers can enjoy the reputations they have established and consumers are not misled as to the source of the products and services they purchase. To encourage creativity and inventiveness, the law protects intellectual property through patents and copyrights. And it

prohibits the theft of trade secrets—the confidential bits of information that can give a business a competitive advantage.

The law of business torts, summarized above, is complemented by the law of business crimes. Full-scale criminal processes can be applied to white-collar criminal charges as well as to regular street crime. Mail fraud, wire fraud, and antitrust violations are leading examples of federal crimes found in the business setting. The Racketeering Influenced and Corrupt Organization Act (RICO) is designed to attack businesses engaged in hard-core criminal activities. Important state criminal statutes include those outlawing larceny, regular theft, theft by false pretenses, and "hot" check writing.

Courts and legislatures are increasingly disposed to impose criminal liability on corporations whose agents violate the law. The agents themselves are, of course, also criminally responsible for their misdeeds.

Computer crime has become such an explosive problem that both the federal government and most state governments are passing special criminal statutes to deal with such problems as unauthorized access, theft of information, and improper transfer of money.

KEY TERMS

Business torts
Business crimes
Interference with business conduct
Justification
Trademark
Service marks
Generic term
Secondary meaning
Trade secret
Patent
Shop right doctrine
Copyright
Unfair competition
Deceptive trade practices acts

White-collar crime
False pretenses statutes

QUESTIONS AND PROBLEMS

1. Perfect Subscription Co. (Perfect) solicited magazine subscriptions by phone. It had twenty to thirty supervisors who recruited large numbers of telephone sales representatives ("reps") to conduct the business. These supervisors and reps over the years had collected lists of magazine "expires"—names of persons whose subscriptions had expired, and who were contacted by phone to renew their subscriptions. These lists of expires were obtained by the supervisors, by requesting such information from magazine publishers, and by the reps, who kept updating the lists they were furnished.

Kavaler, a vice president of Perfect, quit his job and formed his own subscription company. After he began collecting lists of expires by contacting the supervisors and reps of his old company (Perfect), Perfect brought an action seeking an injunction barring Kavaler from such contacts on the theory that the lists were trade secrets.

    a. During the trial, Kavaler introduced evidence showing that magazines often gave lists of expires to any company asking for them, and also that lists were sometimes exchanged between sales reps of competing companies. Do you think this evidence should cause the court to reject Perfect's contention that the lists were trade secrets? Discuss.

    b. If Kavaler had solicited these lists while still an officer of Perfect, do you think a court might be more likely to issue an injunction than in the instant fact-pattern? If so, on what theory might it be issued? (*Perfect Subscription Co. v. Kavaler,* 427 F. Supp. 1289, 1977.)

2. Plaintiff Walner purchased an ice cream parlor franchise from defendant Baskin-Robbins, Inc. The franchise agreement contained language requiring defendant's approval before the franchise could be sold. Two years later Walner contracted to sell the franchise to Garapet at a substantial profit, but Baskin-Robbins refused to grant permission for the sale. Walner sued for tortious interference with his right to contract with Garapet. Discuss. (*Walner v. Baskin-Robbins Ice Cream Co.,* 514 F. Supp. 1028, N.D.Tex. 1981.)

3. A trademark applicant wishes to mark the word "Bundt" in connection with one of its cake pans. Is this term suitable for trademark registration? Discuss. (*In re Northland Aluminum Products, Inc.,* 777 F.2d 1556, Fed. Cir. 1985.)

4. Miller Brewing Company purchased the trademark *Lite* and used this name on its labels for beer that was lower in calories than its regular beer. When a competitor, G. Heileman Brewing Company, started marketing a reduced-calorie beer that it labeled as "light beer," Miller brought a trademark infringement action against Heileman. At the trial, Heileman introduced evidence that the term "light" beer had been used for many years in the beer industry to refer to beers having certain flavors, bodies, or reduced alcoholic contents. On that basis, Heileman contended that "light" was, essentially, a generic term, and thus could not be the proper subject of a trademark. The trial court rejected this argument, and issued an injunction prohibiting further use of "light" by Heileman. On appeal, do you think the court should accept Heileman's argument? Discuss why, or why not. (*Miller Brewing Company v. G. Heileman Brewing Company,* 561 F.2d 75, 1977.)

5. The Dallas Cowboys Cheerleaders, Inc. (DCC) obtained a trademark on their "distinctive" uniform of white boots, blue blouse, and white starstudded vests and belt. Thereafter a film producer, Pussycat Cinema, Ltd. (PC), produced a film (*Debby Does Dallas*) which the trial court found to be "sexually depraved," and in which the cheerleading group wore a uniform "strikingly similar" to that of the DCC uniform. DCC then asked for an injunction based on trademark infringement, prohibiting showings of the film until the uniform was changed, contending that the PC uniform would likely be associated in viewers' minds with the DCC, and thus impugn and injure DCC's business reputation. In the trial court, PC contended (a) that the uniform was a purely functional design—as distinguished from an arbitrary design—and thus could not be trademarked, and (b) that, in any event, viewers of the film would not associate it with the DCC. How do you think the court should rule on these defenses? Explain. (*Dallas Cowboys Cheerleaders, Inc., v. Pussycat Cinema, Ltd.*, 604 F.2d 200, 1979.)

6. Three farmers, including McClung, entered into a number of contracts with French, under the terms of which French agreed to buy quantities of corn at varying prices somewhat above the going market prices (which were in the $1.60 per bushel range). The farmers made these contracts only after French showed them documents indicating he was a bonded grain dealer, and told them the reason he was paying the relatively high prices was that he had a large contract to sell corn to a feedlot at a price of $1.90 per bushel. In fact, French was not a bonded dealer, and did not have the large contract he described. McClung delivered several quantities of corn to French, and was paid for the first load or two, but not for the last thirteen loads (having a price of $22,900).

The State of Nebraska then brought a criminal action against French charging him with obtaining property under false pretenses. French admitted breaching the contracts, but claimed it was not proven that he made the contracts "with the intent to defraud," a necessary element of the crime. The jury in the trial court *inferred* an intent to defraud, based on the two misrepresentations French made to the farmers. Do you think the jury's inference as to French's intent was proper in this situation? Why or why not? (*Nebraska v. French,* 291 N.W.2d 248, 1980.)

7. Plaintiff Hustler Magazine printed a parody of an advertisement for Campari liquor which prominently displayed a photograph of Jerry Falwell. Entitled "Jerry Falwell talks about his first time," the parody patterns itself on the genuine Campari ads, which consist of interviews with famous persons about their "first time" with Campari. In Hustler's version, Falwell's first time involves not only Campari but an outright sexual experience—with his mother and in an outhouse—and the "interview" is replete with scatalogical attempts at humor. A purported disclaimer in small print read: "AD PARODY—NOT TO BE TAKEN SERIOUSLY." Falwell claimed outrage, and used the ad, which Hustler had copyrighted, as the basis for fundraising campaigns to raise legal funds and to battle the pornographers on behalf of the Moral Majority and the Old Time Gospel Hour. He raised hundreds of thousands of dollars. Hustler sued Falwell for trademark infringement—unauthorized use of the ad. Falwell claimed "fair use" in that he needed to send his followers a copy to give them information necessary to rebut the statements it contained. Hustler claimed the ad is clearly a parody, no one believed it was true, so there was nothing to rebut. A Falwell employee admitted that sending out copies of the ad was part of a "marketing approach" to fundraising. Is this fair use? Discuss. (*Hustler Magazine, Inc., v. Moral Majority, Inc.*, 796 F. 2d 1158, 9th Cir. 1986.)

8. By combining plastic support blocks on pontoons, spaced I-beams, and separate bouyant chambers, Rivet created a machine which could carry heavy loads across stump-filled marshes for extended periods. All three devices had been used before, but never in combination. Rivet's machine, which he patented, was significantly more efficient than any previous machine. Later, a former employee began making a similar machine. In a patent infringement suit, the defendant claimed Rivet's patent was invalid because the invention lacked novelty and nonobviousness. Discuss. (*Kori v. Wilco Marsh Buggies and Draglines, Inc.*, 708 F.2d 151, 5th Cir. 1983.)

Chapter 9

BUSINESS ETHICS, CORPORATE SOCIAL RESPONSIBILITY, AND THE LAW

INTRODUCTION

The study of an introductory chapter on Business Ethics will not make you a philosopher. Neither will the completion of this course qualify you for the bar. That is not our purpose. Our purpose is to involve you in a conscientious exploration of the subject matter that will help you to become mature and thoughtful in dealing with the ethical issues that will occur inevitably in a business career.

We will begin by addressing the fundamental concepts. What is ethics? Why be ethical? We will find that Business Ethics consists of the application of moral principles to people in a business setting, and that business people (managers and employees) and business entities like corporations (artificial or legal persons) do have moral responsibilities.

We will distinguish moral from legal and other responsibilities, and then, turning to a focus on business entities, examine the issue of corporate moral responsibility. Some writers and critics maintain that only the people within these firms can have such responsibilities, not the firms themselves. We will explore both sides of that question. Further, we will clarify the distinction between moral responsibility (the obligation to observe fundamental moral duties) and social responsibility (the obligation to go beyond the minimum and address "community" needs).

Moral standards, sometimes expressed as abstract principles (treat others as you would be treated) are more often expressed as plain-spoken norms of conduct (do not tell a lie). We will examine five fundamental moral norms that we characterize as the *moral minimum*. These basic components of moral behavior are honesty, promise-keeping, loyalty, fairness, and doing no harm. They are spoken of as *prima facie* moral duties, or, to phrase the matter more simply, they are to be strictly observed unless the *prima facie* duties are in conflict or unless there is an excusing condition.

We will clarify the position that business firms are morally entitled to take in the formulation of public policy, invoking the social responsibility of business beyond the moral minimum. We will illustrate the operation of these ethical concepts with examples taken from the daily experiences of ordinary business people. We will show that rational people have to be sensitive to many conflicting demands and uncertain situations. We will look at the question, should a corporation donate money to charity when the money could otherwise be returned to shareholders as dividends? Beyond that, there is nearly unanimous agreement that the air and water should be at least clean enough to protect public health, and that cars should be safe enough to minimize injury and loss of human life, but how clean is clean enough, and how safe is safe enough? Rational people can differ in their views on these matters, and sufficient facts are not always available. With limited resources and often inadequate information, how should business people and business firms address issues of public policy and the common good?

We will not be able to answer satisfactorily all the questions we raise, but, remember, that is not our objective. The answers are not in any text. At the very best our discussion can provide a starting point, but, as we will emphasize many times, you must face the responsibility for your own moral choices.

This chapter will begin the process of acquainting you with the language of ethics, with some famous philosophers and their contributions to moral theory, and with an approach to moral reasoning. Our approach, you will find, is simple and straightforward, and has application to legal analysis as well. We will develop it in more detail later, but the four basic components are as follows: (1) recognizing the issue, (2) selecting the appropriate moral principle (a moral standard that is basic and comprehensive) or norm (a moral standard that indicates how one should act), (3) applying the principle or norm rationally and objectively to the facts that are relevant to this issue, and (4) making a decision.

The challenge of these materials is one that cannot be avoided in the career of a business person, a challenge you cannot fail to take. If you meet this challenge be assured that it will place your conduct above the "bottom line."

ETHICS: THE RELATIONSHIP OF BUSINESS ETHICS TO THE WHOLE

The word **ethics** refers to the study of morality, moral standards, moral values, and moral judgments. It is also understood to be synonymous with the word **morality**, meaning right or good, and it is in this informal sense that we will use these words. Ethical or moral conduct, then, consists of acting in ways that are prompted by motives and supported by reasons that are calculated to produce "right" or fair treatment of others and the "good" life. Business Ethics is an integral component of the main stream of ethical concerns. It has a special application to issues confronting people in business, but it attaches no different or special rules to business people only. It builds on the ethics of everyday life.

Our first exposure to morality is in the home. Parents and relatives, and in later years, friends, teachers, and many others, condition or influence our behavior through verbal and nonverbal communications—don't push your brother, never tell a fib, share that candy with your friend. As we mature we learn the reasons supporting these admonitions, and we learn to act "instinctively" or "spontaneously" because we have internalized these lessons. In a sense we become the modern version of Aristotle's virtuous Athenian. Ideally speaking, the thought and knowledge of a virtuous person will be transformed smoothly into decisive action. On most occasions, a person will not have to ponder or reflect upon the proper course of conduct; neither doubt nor weakness of resolve intrudes. A person knows without question that it is wrong to lie to a customer about the qualities of a product, or to discriminate against a minority job prospect on the basis of race. The really tough ethical issues, however, the ones that challenge our in-

sight and our level of maturity, commitment, and creativity, are scarcely ever as clear-cut as these.

As we develop in our recognition of moral problems and our appreciation of the ways in which they touch so many other people and so many areas of our personal and business lives, we need a deeper understanding of ethics. A study of moral theory reveals a rational and coherent system of values and principles that makes civilization possible. This study advances our understanding of the system, of how its principles and values fit together, and why it makes a difference. The system encompasses the character of our society as a whole, the **ethos**, just as it does our individual character, our intentions, motives, actions, and inactions. In the fullest development, the mature moral person will define right action

> . . . in terms of universal principles chosen because of their logical comprehensiveness, their universality, and their consistency. These ethical principles are not concrete like the ten commandments but abstract universal principles dealing with justice, society's welfare, the equality of human rights, respect for the dignity of individual human beings, and with the idea that persons are ends in themselves and must be treated as such. The person's reasons for doing right are based on a commitment to these moral principles, and the person sees them as the criteria for evaluating all other moral rules and arrangements including democratic consensus.[1]

With this more sophisticated level of ethics in mind, we return to the moral questions referred to above—lying and racial discrimination. Of course it is wrong to lie to a customer about the quality of a product, but what latitude or range

---

[1] Lawrence Kohlberg, "Moral Stages and Moralization: The Cognitive-Developmental Approach," in Manuel Velasquez, *Business Ethics: Concepts and Cases* (Englewood Cliffs, N.J.: Prentice-Hall, 1982), 20–23.

of discretion does a salesperson have in extolling the features of a consumer good or service? Must every shortcoming of the item be revealed? May the sales-pitch be couched in vague, laudatory terms or must all responses be factual, precise, to-the-point? Must the salesperson be concerned about the customer's real need for such an item, or is the customer's apparent willingness to purchase the only thing that should concern the salesperson? Must there be a regard for the customer's susceptibility to promotional and advertising campaigns? In other words, there is a realm of ethical considerations beyond the obvious that are persistent and difficult to resolve. Perhaps their individual significance is not that of a blatant falsehood, but if you can imagine the various circumstances in which millions of business transactions are concluded in the United States in a single day, you will better appreciate the moral significance of dealing with less-than-headline-making issues. You will have the opportunity to pursue this matter further in Chapter 22, "Sales: Warranties and Products Liability," by examining the degree of flexibility that sellers are allowed in commending or "puffing" their products.

Reflect for a moment now on the matter of racial discrimination. Fair treatment on the personal level and social justice on the state and national level are issues that people can subscribe to in principle. In fact we scarcely need a Constitution or Civil Rights Act to remind us of the moral compulsion to treat others as unique human beings, as ends-in-themselves rather than objects. But in actual practice, there is very little accord in how to accomplish this ideal. Quite aside from constitutional and statutory requirements and prohibitions, are race-conscious affirmative action plans that deal with recruitment, hiring, compensation, promotion, and lay-offs morally superior to employment policies that are color-blind? What are the relevant considerations? Does the moral legitimacy of race-conscious plans depend upon actual proof of past discrimination by an employer? And what of

the nonminority laborers who are also minimally qualified for the job and whose needs and expectations are equal to those of minorities? Should they be bypassed even though they are not personally responsible for past or historical discrimination by the employer?

On these tough issues of fair treatment and social justice there is no wide consensus. The problems are so longstanding and peoples' attitudes so divergent, it takes the political system longer than many would like to come up with workable programs. With issues that tax our moral resolve, we can only identify with the moral point of view, an attitude that demands tolerance and regard for the opposing, rational position as much as it does commitment and a relentless pursuit of the ethical ideal.

As you examine the materials in Chapter 49, Employment Law, you will find that the U.S. Supreme Court ruled unconstitutional in *Wygant v. Jackson Board of Education,* 54 U.S.L.W. 4479 (1986), the layoff of more experienced white teachers under an affirmative action plan that maintained a racial balance between blacks and whites. The Court did *not* address the morality of the plan; that is *not* its role. However, if the justification of the plan had been stronger than merely alleviating some generalized societal discrimination or providing role models for minority students, the Court's constitutional decision might have been to enforce the racial balance. Do these or other reasons affect your view of the morality of the Jackson affirmative action plan?

You will notice that while our examples have a decided business and employment flavor, they are really not different from the kind of problems that are typically encountered by people in our society. There are no special ethical principles that apply to business situations only and that are different in kind or in degree from those that apply to everything else. The reason should be plain. Business is simply another human endeavor, an enterprise fraught with all the potential for good and evil that is inherent in other such undertakings. It is an integral component of our social system and the ethical standards we apply to one, we apply to others as well.

MORAL RESPONSIBILITIES DISTINGUISHED FROM LEGAL RESPONSIBILITIES

We have established that people in business do have moral responsibilities, and we want to distinguish them now from legal responsibilities. The determinative factor in this analysis is the *source of authority* that one can turn to in resolving legal and moral issues. Legal authority is external; you have to search "outside yourself." Moral authority is internal. As we described in the previous section, a person begins to absorb moral injunctions (do's and don'ts) almost from the moment of birth. Later on in life that is reinforced by the intellectual process of giving rational support and justification for one's conduct.

The law advances a definitive authority for resolving legal disputes and an enforcement mechanism as well—the U.S. Constitution; treatises; federal, state, and local statutes that are consistent with the Constitution; judicial decisions; and administrative rules at all levels document this reality. Legal authority may be complex, even murky, but it is always there. In the realm of morality, however, you can never get off the hook by referring to outside authority. One's only human source of authority is one's rational processes, clear and objective thinking about the dignity, worth, and integrity of people around you and your impact on their lives. How should other people be treated? This is one of the fundamental questions of ethics, and you can see that it is an important one because your behavior towards others is the key to your expectations of treatment in return. Even when one derives his or her basic moral standards from religion, thus referring to a higher authority, conformity with those standards involves an individual choice—an exercise of the will.

People in business, as in other walks of life, have been influenced by the concept of reciprocal treatment. Enshrined in **The Golden Rule,** it is a centuries-old source of guidance throughout the world. It underlines an important element of harmony between the spheres of religion and philosophy, each of which has its version, although in terms of authority, one entails a matter of faith and addresses a spiritual source while the other is rooted in the rational domain. Respect for the autonomy, freedom, and integrity of the individual is at the core of both.

The wisdom embodied in The Golden Rule inspired the great German philosopher Immanuel Kant to urge that every person be treated as an end, that is, as a unique, special person, rather than as a means-to-an-end. He further wrote of the necessity to act upon reasons that can be applied uniformly towards all others throughout the world. As we noted earlier, such treatment of others is the key to one's expectations of treatment in return. It is not permitted to make a special exception of yourself because the rule of conduct you apply to others is reciprocal. It is the one you should expect to be applied to you as well.

Other important philosophers, Jeremy Bentham and John Stuart Mill, for example, advanced **Utilitarianism,** an ethical theory that is committed solely to the purpose of promoting "the greatest good for the greatest number." Unlike the rule-based theory of Immanuel Kant, Utilitarianism permits all conduct that will serve the objective of maximizing the social good or utility. Both of these rather different philosophical approaches are used extensively as the basis for public and private decision making.

Finally, remember that the law can prohibit or forbid the conduct which is worst in us, but it cannot compel the performance of that which is best in us. That is a role reserved for ourselves, a mission of excellence that brings our full potential into harmony with our social ideals.

THE MORAL RESPONSIBILITY OF BUSINESS PERSONS: NATURAL PERSONS AND ARTIFICIAL PERSONS

There is near unanimous agreement that natural persons engaged in business—from the most recently employed laborer to a member of the board of directors—have moral responsibilities. In a later section, we will be as specific as we can be in explaining what those responsibilities are, but first we want to address the question, "Can corporations have moral responsibilities?" We believe the answer to this is "Yes," and we offer the following explanation of this view.

The most widely advanced view that corporations *cannot* have moral obligations is that of philosopher John Ladd who regards corporations as purely formal organizations analogous to programmable robots or machines.[2] Machines have neither freedom nor intention, and neither does a corporation which is bound by a state charter, organizational tables, channels of communication, authority, and internal responsibility, and by impersonal by-laws and operating procedures. The human cogs in this corporate machine are role-players. Beyond that they are replaceable. Rule-governed activities and impersonal operating procedures preclude the application, or even the hint, of moral responsibility.

Ladd's description, however, is thought by many people to be an inadequate way of viewing corporations and how they operate. Beginning with the observation that corporations are indeed artificial, not natural persons, we are reminded of the definition inscribed by Chief Justice John Marshall in the famous *Dartmouth College* case:

"A corporation is an artificial being, invisible, intangible, and existing only in contemplation of law. Being the mere creature of law, it possesses only those properties which the charter of creation confers upon it, either expressly, or as incidental to its very existence. These are such as are supposed best calculated to effect the object for which it was created."[3]

However, the fact that corporations are legal persons, "creatures" of the state, is not a sufficient reason to regard them as moral persons with moral responsibilities. State corporation laws generally permit one or more incorporators to bring the corporate entity into existence in agreement with the terms and conditions prescribed by the law. The articles of incorporation will describe the purposes and structure of the corporation, while the charter or certificate of incorporation represents the permission given by the state to conduct business in the corporate form. These documents—the articles, the charter, and later the by-laws which govern the day-to-day operations of the firm—are lifeless pieces of paper. They do not impart autonomy, independence of thought, or spontaneity to the corporate person. Corporations must be given life and vitality by the people who operate them. These employees are, of course, morally responsible for their own conduct. That can never be erased by joining anything, be it a club, fraternity, political party, or business organization. Over and beyond the personal moral responsibility of employees, however, is the **moral responsibility of the corporation** for the collective behavior of the corporate entity.

Organizational theory points to the phenomenon that group dynamics transcend individual behavior. We sometimes simply get caught up "in the spirit of things" and act as we never would have acted alone. In the corporate setting, the corporation as a principal can act only through the people it employs. This individual behavior, which is inspired and motivated by corporate purposes, is a necessary precondition to corporate action. It is frequently structured in

---

[2]John Ladd, "Morality and the Ideal of Rationality in Formal Organizations," *Monist* 54 (1970): 488–516.

[3]4 Wheat (17 U.S.) 518 (1819).

such a way that one committee or subgroup within the whole is never completely aware of or responsible for the total scene. Sometimes the left hand really doesn't know what the right hand is doing, or failing to do. Those at the top tend to give orders and seek results, but deny responsibility for outcomes they did not intend. Those at the bottom carry out the orders and deny responsibility for harmful consequences because they did not make policy and they intended no harm. This explains, in part at least, how the Pinto was built, a process that Lee Iacocca describes in his autobiography as bad management and for which he shares responsibility.[4] Such projects, and even much smaller and more routine ones, seem to exhibit their own momentum. As a rule, most actions and inactions of large corporations cannot be tallied as the sum of individual actions, and as a result, individuals escape moral accountability. Yet the corporation's moral position is derived from the morally charged acts and omissions of its employees.

In summary, the corporate charter authorizes intentional actions by agents or employees to achieve its stated purposes. These individual, intentional actions become, in a sense, anonymous as they are submerged in the processes of interpretation, modification, and implementation by other individuals and by groups and committees within the corporate structure. While individual conduct (action and inaction) is *necessary* for corporate action, only the totality of this process is *necessary* and *sufficient* for corporate action. This totality is not again reducible to individual action. It is corporate conduct, something more than the action and inaction of its agents and employees, and must be evaluated accordingly.

Having established, first, by general agreement, that people in business have the same kind of moral responsibilities that everyone else does, and, second, by examining the dynamics of

group action, that corporations have moral responsibilities, the question must now be raised, what are those moral responsibilities? The importance of this matter deserves special attention. We want to discuss it generally now and in later parts of the chapter return to the various components of moral responsibility in more detail.

THE COMPONENTS OF MORAL RESPONSIBILITY

Both business people and corporations have the following *prima facie* moral duties or obligations. Since rational persons act knowingly and freely, violation of these duties raises the presumption of a moral wrong.

1. Honesty (truthfulness): Lying is understood to consist of deliberate false statements that are intended to deceive others or are foreseen to be likely to deceive others.

2. Promise-keeping (abiding by agreements): Freedom to make promises entails the obligation to keep them. Freedom of contract, for example, does *not* mean that you are free to disregard contractual terms and obligations.

3. Loyalty (fidelity): A person who has placed faith and confidence in you is entitled to a comparable degree of fidelity in return.

4. Fairness (justice): Justice seeks reciprocity, i.e., treatment as you would be treated in return. It is an attempt to balance the distribution of tangible goods (wealth) and intangible goods (freedom, equality).

5. Doing no harm: This duty means causing no foreseeable harm through intentional, reckless, or negligent conduct.

We call these duties the **moral minimum.** There may be other, perhaps more comprehensive and detailed enumerations, but this captures the essence of the moral duties that business persons share with everyone else. These

---

[4] Lee Iacocca with William Novak, *Iacocca: An Autobiography* (New York: Bantam, 1984), 162.

duties bind the fabric of our civilization, make social life and personal relationships possible, and reinforce commercial and market operations as well.

Imagine, if you can, life in a world where these fundamental moral obligations were not operative. How would you survive in a setting where no one was obliged to tell the truth, promises were not kept, and treachery was the order of the day? Where injustice rules relationships and harmful actions are the norm, social life can no longer function.

In speaking of these duties as *prima facie,* we mean that they do not require justification. They are, in themselves, intrinsically right and good. You do not have to explain why you are telling the truth or keeping a promise. You do not have to explain or apologize for being loyal or fair or for doing no harm. In fact, the opposite of that is true!

Each of these duties has a dark side, a wrong-making feature. Lying has to be explained, not truthfulness. Breach of agreement requires justification, not promise-keeping. And it is the same with the other duties as well. Reasons must be advanced for being disloyal, unfair, and injurious. Bear in mind that the moral wrong involved here is "self-caused." The finger of blame is upon the actor; it cannot be pointed at anyone else. Later in the chapter we will turn our focus from the actor's responsibility for self-caused wrong to the duty of correcting someone else's wrong, that is, the duty of doing good or going-to-the-rescue.

No single case can quite illustrate all of the components of the Moral Minimum, but *Francis v. United Jersey Bank,* found in Chapter 38, will be helpful in demonstrating how moral principles support legal ones. In that case, a corporate director failed to stop two corporate managers (her sons) from "looting" the company treasury. Directors are responsible for the overall management of corporations. They are expected to be loyal and obedient to the shareholders and to exercise due care in making business decisions. Review the facts of the *United Jersey Bank* case and judge for yourself whether the director's conduct met the minimum that one might expect in terms of promise-keeping, fidelity, fairness, and doing no harm.

Moral Dilemmas

On some occasions *prima facie* duties may conflict. You know the familiar phrase for such a dilemma: "Caught between a rock and a hard place." Human experience counsels us that we will be confronted by these anxiety-producing situations at various times in our lives. How can one do right by two distinct duties that are mutually exclusive?

There is no easy way out. These challenges to our integrity and our resolve can only be met by looking deeply into our sense of value. What is really more important when duties conflict? Loyalty to a family member or friend, or truthfulness to an employer? Keeping promises to those you have entered a contract with, or doing no harm to innocent parties? Answers will not come easily, but you cannot avoid a choice because even indecision is a decision. There may not be a "nice" way out, and the anxieties that accompany these choices are not made easier by the knowledge that, whichever side you favor, you will bear the blame for the one you did not. Compromise is sometimes a possibility. However unsatisfactory it may be, it is an attempt to preserve the essence of both obligations. Sometimes it is not available, and the consequences of a divisive choice must be accepted.

In *Edwards v. Clinton Valley Center* (Chapter 4), you observed that a moral wrong—the negligent or even reckless refusal by employees of a state-operated mental hospital to admit an extremely dangerous homicidal maniac, leading to the death of an innocent person—was found not to constitute a legal wrong. What was the reason for this outcome? There is no assurance that the law will penalize every moral wrong, but why not? Is there a **moral dilemma** involved, that is, is the court recognizing the value of some more important moral duty that counts in favor of the defendant? Negligence or recklessness might be justified if it were necessary to prevent a more serious wrong, but is that principle operating in this case? In your view, was the court justified in letting the defendant off the hook for the behavior of its employees?

Excusing Conditions

Some reasons will be sufficient to justify *prima facie* wrong conduct. Lying, for example, is *prima facie* or intrinsically wrong but not absolutely or conclusively wrong. **Excusing** (or extenuating) **conditions** may be present. In some business transactions you will study later, one of the parties may be coerced into lying. In this situation, we might not characterize the falsehood as a lie because it was not spoken voluntarily, or we may find that a lie, compelled by some external force, is justified under the circumstances. Comparable reasons may be advanced for other violations of these *prima facie* duties, but the violation is presumptively wrong until it is explained or justified.

Not every falsehood or broken promise, nor every infidelity, injustice, or harm carries equal moral fault. Conduct that is morally blameworthy on the surface may be justified or excused by appropriate reasons. We say that a person is morally responsible for an act or omission only if that person *knowingly* and *freely* acted or failed to act in a particular way. Knowledge and freedom, then, are necessary preconditions of morally responsible conduct. Conditions or events that intrude upon these elements may reduce the degree of moral responsibility or totally remove it.

Excusing conditions may be characterized as those which (1) preclude the possibility of action, (2) preclude or diminish the necessary knowledge, or (3) preclude or diminish the necessary freedom. Illustrative of the first category are occasions where the act is impossible to perform, because one does not have the ability or opportunity, or because circumstances are simply beyond one's control. Hunger in America and throughout the world, for example, is a problem that no single person has the ability to resolve. If that person could contribute in some way and fails to do so, however, he or she should

be judged accordingly. Second, excusable ignorance of the act or omission may explain it or reduce the person's responsibility. You cannot be held responsible for failing to know something that you cannot be expected to know, for example, for failing to know all of the side effects of a fully tested pharmaceutical product. On the other hand, you or your firm may be held *legally* responsible on the basis of strict, without-fault liability. Finally, whether one approaches this from the individual or business perspective, there may be no free or rational alternatives to a particular action, for example, a limited amount of environmental pollution in the production of wheat, textiles, or steel. With regard to other individual or corporate conduct, there may be a lack of control brought on by some internal or external coercion.

THE SOCIAL RESPONSIBILITY OF BUSINESS

Regarding the social responsibility of business—business people, business firms, and particularly, corporations—the principal question is "What are those responsibilities?" Milton Freidman, a Nobel laureate in economics and a widely noted spokesman on this matter, does not challenge the assertion that managers and employees have social responsibilities. He does assert, however, that this responsibility consists entirely of making as much money as possible for the shareholders within the limits of the law, customary ethical practices, and open and free competition without fraud and deceit.

We have already examined the concept of corporate moral responsibility, and it is fair to say that Friedman does not subscribe to that view. The ethics he contends for are those of natural persons, referring of course to the ethics of managers and employees in a corporate setting. The possible inadequacy of Friedman's assessment, however, as with Ladd's, is its failure to deal with the problem of moral accountability, that is, it does not confront the frequent impossibility of redescribing group dynamics or organizational behavior as specific, individual action and holding the proper person morally accountable.

Our present inquiry begins with a distinction between the moral minimum and social responsibility. The distinction is not an absolute one. It is simply a matter of emphasis and illustration; it is not a difference in the nature or quality of the responsibility.

We have used the phrase *moral minimum* to convey the fundamentals, though some speak of this minimum as a floor or bottom line. These duties are compelled, not discretionary, and they have something of a negative cast—thou shall not lie, steal, treat others with ingratitude or unfairly, or do harm. They extend to some degree to all those individuals touched by corporate operations—customers, suppliers, shareholders, and employees. When someone violates one of these minimal obligations, we say that person is morally responsible for *self-caused harm.*

Social responsibility moves in focus from the realm of negative injunctions, of doing no wrong, to the affirmative position of doing good and of improving the well-being of those around you and of society. It may be described as going-to-the-rescue, that is, curing or correcting the harm caused by other people, not by yourself. This sense of being responsible is limited by our capacity to do good works and by other factors that we will discuss.

Social responsibility is influenced by and infused with moral concerns. As we have related before, moral considerations bind together the fabric of our society. Social responsibility contributes to this process as well, and it goes beyond the minimum. Moreover, it is coherent, selective, and focused. Under the customary usage of the term "social responsibility," a single firm should not be expected to do good works indiscriminately, but it should make a positive contribution to the common good or general welfare and participate in the process of achieving social justice.

Friedman interprets social responsibility quite narrowly and advances some persuasive

reasons supporting his position. He regards management as loyal agents of the shareholders/owners—the **agents-of-capital** concept. We will examine the position and contrast it with one we call the **agents-of-society** view. Then we will critique these positions and present an alternative model for consideration.

The Agents-of-Capital View

Milton Friedman proceeds on the view that management occupies an agency relationship with the owners or shareholders of a business and should act at all times to enhance or maximize the economic well-being of the owners. Corporate managers are free to devote their own time and money to whatever pursuits they deem morally or socially appropriate, but to divert corporate resources to such projects amounts to disloyalty and a breach in the fiduciary relationship with shareholders. Friedman finds the social responsibility movement to be something akin to theft of "someone else's money," and at the core a "fundamentally subversive doctrine." The proper role and function of government is to attend to matters of the common good and social justice. Corporate managers are not by training or otherwise equipped to do that, and even if they were, it would be intolerable in a democracy for unelected, unaccountable "civil servants" to be charged with that responsibility. While government might be slow and unresponsive in addressing current social problems, the insistence that this gap be filled by corporate action is no more than an acknowledgment of defeat by social responsibility proponents who "have failed to persuade a majority of their fellow citizens to be of like mind and [who] are seeking to attain by undemocratic procedures what they cannot attain by democratic procedures."[5]

Friedman gives corporate managers clear objectives in urging them to maximize profits within the boundaries of the law. When he speaks of observing "ethical custom," he is much

---

[5] *New York Times,* September 12, 1962, sect. 6, 122.

less clear, but it is at least plausible that he means something like the moral minimum because the behavior it requires supports free market operations. He does not intend to encourage managers to spend corporate time and effort "jousting windmills" in do-good, Don Quixote–like efforts.

Finally, Friedman's agents-of-capital view gives corporations no moral recognition. This view does not take group dynamics into account. It is, after all, generally acknowledged that group action and inaction may be qualitatively different from individual action. Since responsibility for corporate decisions cannot be conclusively traced to one individual or the other, moral assessment of corporate conduct is impossible under Friedman's view. We know that corporate action affects the lives of people in ways that can be described as good or bad, right or wrong, so how is it to be evaluated except in moral terms? Friedman's model of corporate conduct does not answer this question.

The Agents-of-Society View

In a speech to the Harvard Business School in 1969, Henry Ford II stated: "The terms of the contract between industry and society are changing. . . . Now we are being asked to serve a wider range of human values and to accept an obligation to members of the public with whom we have no commercial transactions." His words were foreshadowed by those of his grandfather some two generations earlier. "For a long time people believed that the only purpose of industry is to make a profit. They were wrong. Its purpose is to serve the general welfare."

Moral philosopher Thomas Donaldson, inquiring into the moral and social basis of "productive organizations," attempts to sharpen and clarify the "social contract" spoken of by the Fords. His pursuit leads him to hypothesize the existence of a "state of individual production," that is, a society in which individuals work and produce alone, not in the corporate form. A society such as this, composed of rational persons, would charter or permit the existence of corporations only if the benefits to consumers and employees outweighed the losses or drawbacks. Donaldson finds it imperative that corporations observe certain minimum standards of justice, for example, respect for workers as human beings, the avoidance of deception and fraud, the avoidance of any practice that systematically worsens the situation of any group in society.

Contrary to the Friedman view, corporations do indeed have a moral basis under the "social contract." Managers are not given a mission as explicit as profit maximization, but they are charged with obligations to improve efficiency, stabilize output, and increase income potential while minimizing the abuse of corporate power and the loss of employee pride and identification with the work product. Donaldson's mandate to executives is significantly broader than the one issued by Friedman. Managers are to be guided by community or social expectations fostered by implicit moral obligations. Within these constraints, managers are free to maximize profits. Operating under the Friedman approach, managers would observe these constraints only if, through some sort of enlightened self-interest, they happened to coincide with profit maximization, if they were enacted into law, or if they fell within the range of "customary ethics."

Finally, however, Donaldson does not acknowledge the moral status of corporate *owners.* In his discussion of the "social contract," he gives no explicit recognition that *shareholders* are entitled to any moral rights. His emphasis on the moral rights and moral status of consumers and employees may be laudable, but what about those who venture capital? In addition to the normal market risks they bear, corporate shareholders (owners) are apparently treated as moral nonpersons under Donaldson's "agents-of-society" model for corporate behavior.

A Concluding Note on Friedman and Donaldson

Friedman sees no moral status for corporations while Donaldson finds one at the very core of the "social contract." In most ways these writers could not be farther apart, yet there are many positions one could take in between and some, of course, on the outer extremes.

Whatever you think of these positions, remember that both Friedman and Donaldson have shared their vision with you. If their insights serve no more than as a starting point, that is still a lot. It is now a matter of bringing your own creative processes to the forefront and dealing with the inadequacies as you see them.

THE CORPORATE CITIZENSHIP MODEL (CCM)

The following alternative model of corporate responsibility responds to the most crucial concerns that have been expressed about the Friedman and Donaldson positions, and goes on to mark out roles that business people and business corporations might play in the public policy or lawmaking arena. Remember Friedman's point that profit-making activities should be confined within the limits of the law established by our democratic institutions. He makes a persuasive case for elected, not self-appointed, civil servants, and that lesson should not be forgotten. On the other hand, Friedman did not give any guidance on the nature or substance of the laws that we are to be governed by, nor the role of business people in contributing to the policy-making process. From Donaldson you gain a fairly clear picture of the moral principles he expects to have embodied in the law, but again no clear role for the business person in this process, and no apparent concern for the moral status of corporate shareholders. An alternative, here called the **Corporate Citizenship Model,** will be more comprehensive than those of Friedman and Donaldson, and will deal with these problems explicitly. Its major components follow.

The Moral Minimum

The moral minimum is regarded as a floor, a level beneath which all personal, business, and corporate conduct should be morally condemned. As with any standard of conduct—moral, legal, or professional—one may experience conflicting duties and lack of clarity at the extremes, but these are problems that the rational process cannot entirely eliminate, though it is the function of ethical studies to help us deal with them.

Something like the moral minimum may be implicit in Friedman's "ethical custom," but there is really no way to know. It deserves to be expressed, however, because in its absence market operations, contracts, and agency relationships—in a word, the economy—would collapse. Donaldson is likewise silent on the matter, but in view of the fact that his social contract builds morality into the existence and structure of all "productive associations," it is logical to infer that he would endorse something like the moral minimum as well.

Moral Status of Corporations

Another facet of this alternative model is the recognition of the moral status of corporations. Donaldson writes it into the social contract, while Friedman regards it as nonsense. Artificial responsibilities are the best that can be mustered for artificial persons, in his view, and that is meaningless.

The Corporate Citizenship Model takes a different approach for reasons we will briefly review. Everyone agrees that individual actions are morally significant, that natural persons are moral agents. Individual action is *necessary* for corporate action, but only group action is *sufficient* to totally account for it. As observed earlier, when individuals act collectively, the "group dynamic" is often truly different from or greater than that of the individual, segmented parts of the whole. Unscrambling an egg can frequently be easier than reassigning or redistributing to individuals the moral responsibility for group or corporate conduct. Consequently, the Corporate Citizenship Model includes corporate moral status that is derived from the collective acts and omissions of morally responsible employees. By recognizing the reality of group behavior, this model permits the full spectrum of business conduct (personal and corporate) to be accounted for, evaluated, and judged on rational standards that are consistent and appropriate for all morally significant endeavors.

The Social Responsibility of Business beyond the Moral Minimum

An examination of the moral minimum reveals the absence of any positive command to do good. Earlier, you will recall, we observed a distinction between the moral minimum and social responsibility and related that the "line" was for the sake of illustration and emphasis. It did not signal a difference in worth or importance between the obligation to do good and the obligation to observe the moral minimum or prevent self-caused moral wrongs. We do find, however, substantial reasons for applying this obligation with less force, or to a lesser degree, in a context where we are asking business persons or corporations to cure or correct the wrongs caused by other people.

As Milton Friedman made clear, corporate owners have distinct and legitimate profit expectations that follow from the nature of their risk. Employees benefit from this venture, as do consumers, suppliers, and the public generally. Donaldson's failure to account for shareholders' legitimate profit expectations and to acknowledge the reciprocal nature of moral rights and responsibilities must be dealt with. Any workable theory of social responsibility must include these expectations.

In exploring further the Corporate Citizenship Model, first consider the nature of the obligation to do good or to go to the rescue. Philosophers speak of this obligation as *beneficence.* It is more than the "flip side" of doing no harm because it involves an affirmative effort rather than mere restraint, and it is focused on harm caused by other people, not by oneself. As a rule, beneficence requires one to go "out of the way" to accomplish some worthwhile purpose.

How far "out of the way," then, must one go in order to satisfy the duty of rescue? You will recall the discussion of excusing conditions and the observation that knowledge and freedom are necessary preconditions for morally responsible conduct. The Corporate Citizenship Model begins with the logic that a single person cannot save the world. Beyond that, there is wide agreement on the concept of a rational balance between social *needs* and a person's *ability* to respond to those needs. No one would expect a nonswimmer to jump into deep water to save a drowning man, nor for a person to spend one's self into bankruptcy to support the United Fund or a minority college foundation. The common-sense approach to such matters has long been as follows: (1) assess the worth of alternative demands, (2) evaluate the nature of the needs and the urgency of each, (3) commit to these needs the energies and resources one has available in an efficient and orderly manner.

A person's energies and resources can be considered "available" for rescue efforts only to the extent that more fundamental demands have been taken care of first. Obligations to family, friends, and employer will be ranked ahead of the demands made by community projects—soliciting funds for muscular dystrophy, coaching a little league team, being a girl scout troop leader. This is not to say, however, that family or other obligations will preclude the exercise of social responsibilities. Even at the risk of making sacrifices in our personal and family life, we have an obligation to contribute something to the well-being of the community. Usually we are pressed in meeting all these demands. It requires a delicate and sometimes tight balance but it does not go so far as to require us to jeopardize the life, health, safety, or well-being of family and friends.

In like manner, corporations should be led to discharge their social responsibilities. With appropriate adjustment, these considerations are valid for artificial as well as natural persons. While not all corporations are large and powerful, or multinational in their dimensions, all of them have in common the collective mentality that we explored earlier. This moral personhood, derived from that of its employees, should be shaped along the lines found to be appropriate for individuals.

Economic, Legal, and Moral Restraints on Rescue: Shareholders have legitimate economic, legal, and moral claims upon corporate managers. If one can generalize regarding the economic expectations of shareholders as a group, it is probably fair to say that they are motivated by a variety of objectives including short-term income maximization, risk spreading through diversification, long-term growth in stock value, tax considerations, and so on. It follows, then, that the command issued by shareholders to management is far less precise than that envisioned by Friedman. Though none of these investment alternatives tolerate corporate waste or giveaways, managers find it impossible to cater to the interests of everyone. On the other hand, all of these investors venture their capital with full knowledge that corporations do indeed engage in neighborhood, community, and social improvement projects. From the dedication of land for parks and recreation to the funding of national environmental groups, from donations to high school band projects to subsidy of the arts, corporate giving remains an important source of creative ideas and talent, as well as financial assistance, for worthy social projects.

This is not evidence that corporate support of such efforts is motivated solely by ethical ideals. Some of it is obviously self-promotional. If the inspiration was purely doing good, such efforts might well be anonymous, but like much other human conduct it is diverse and multifaceted in its objectives. Good impulses, however, are no less morally significant because they are calculated ones, and corporate conduct along these lines is ample and fair warning to investors to reduce their profit-maximizing expectations—not every corporate effort is directly bent on producing maximum returns.

On the assumption that the long-standing record of corporate support for social projects is sufficient to modify an investor's profit expectations, it remains to be seen whether or not such conduct is justified. That is, why aren't investors entitled to a full return, undiminished by corporate giving and other such projects that are not 100 percent profit oriented?

From the legal perspective it should be noted that agents operate under a duty to obey all reasonable directions of the principal (employer), but this legal duty is subject to an important qualification. Comment a of the *Restatement (Second) of Agency,* section 385 (1), reads as follows:

> In determining whether or not the orders of the principal to the agent are reasonable . . . *business or professional ethics* . . . are considered. In no event would it be implied that an agent has a duty to perform acts which . . . are *illegal or unethical* . . . [Emphasis added.]

The inference is clear and compelling—the law does not command one to abdicate moral responsibility in the performance of managerial functions. However, there may be a personal price to pay for the exercise of one's conscience because not all areas of the law have developed with equal moral sensitivity. In recent years employees have gained some important legal protections, but it is still the rule in many states that an employee may be fired "at will" when the directions of his or her conscience lead to conduct that the employer perceives as disloyal (for example, whistleblowing or going public with information that is intended by the employee to prevent harm or to advance the public good). This rule applies unless the employee is protected by an individual employment contract or union-management collective bargaining agreement, or unless the particular state is one of those that has legislatively or judicially given greater protection in recent years. One can be certain, however, that judges weigh and evaluate the demands of loyalty versus those of doing no harm or doing good; the fact that outcomes are diverse is indicative of the difficulty of these issues and *not* that the courts are insensitive to them. There can be no certain legal vindication of one's moral position. Decisions under conditions of uncertainty, however, are not new to business persons. In a real sense, they "come with the territory."

The Kew Gardens Principles of Rescue: Need, Ability, Proximity, Last Resort

Twenty years ago a woman by the name of Kitty Genovese was murdered by an assailant who stabbed her to death on the streets of the Kew Gardens section of New York City. Thirty-eight people watched from the safety of their homes and apartments; no one went to her assistance or phoned the police.

In the wake of this event, and moved by the shock of seeing fellow-Americans doing nothing in the face of adversity, Yale law professor John Simon, and two Yale theologians, Charles Powers and Jon Gunnemann, formulated a set of principles for individual and for corporate rescue efforts—the **Kew Gardens Principles of Rescue.**[6] Briefly, these principles are as follows:

1. *NEED*—Need increases responsibility even though the need has been caused by someone else, or even by an Act of God (for example, corporate giving to the Red Cross or local emergency relief groups in times of flood or natural disaster). The need of those injured by wrongful acts of others, e.g., crime victims or battered women and children, is within the range of corporate rescue as well.

2. *ABILITY*—Even though shareholders have no reason to expect pure profit maximization, they do have legitimate economic claims that cannot be ignored. The obligation to act responsibly, and within an area of competence, in the process of building a better community and a better society is offset to an extent by other valid demands made upon the corporation. Not any single corporation (nor all of them together) has the ability to cure society's systemic ills—crime, poverty, unemployment, inflation, pollution, dis-

ease. However, guided by their areas of experience and competence, corporations can participate in the process of improving the quality of life without jeopardizing or sacrificing their principal economic function, that is, producing quality goods and services at competitive prices. Milton Friedman's doomsday scenario of managers spending "someone else's money" and bankrupting the firm is scarcely credible.

3. *PROXIMITY*—Notice or knowledge of a social need is normally imparted by nearness or proximity. Physical or spacial proximity alone is not the key, however. Awareness of a social problem by employees is attributable to the corporation, and the obligation to respond or rescue is a product of the severity or degree of need, the firm's ability, and awareness of that need. A failure of awareness or knowledge of the need *may or may not* be excusable.

4. *LAST RESORT*—The rescue operation may indeed be more appropriate for some other social institution. Milton Friedman warned that self-appointed civil servants posed a threat to our democratic institutions, and there is a core of truth to that proposition. But the "last resort" concept focuses on a range of potential projects that are worthwhile but perhaps not affordable with limited tax dollars, not priority items, or projects that the government has encouraged the private sector to respond to. After all, the government cannot be expected to do everything, and a corporation's resolve to address social issues does not necessarily spell sedition or self-aggrandizement. *It simply amounts to doing the right thing when the job needs to be done and no one else is doing it.*

Each of the components of the Kew Gardens Principles is implicit in the previous section entitled "Excusing Conditions," but bringing them to the forefront and supplying more detailed reasons for their application enhances the Corporate Citizenship Model by responding to Friedman's objections as well as to Donaldson's failure to acknowledge the legitimate expectations of corporate owners.

---

[6] John Simon, Charles Powers, and Jon Gunnemann, *The Ethical Investor* (New Haven, Conn.: Yale University Press, 1972), 22–25.

In order to become a little more familiar with the Corporate Citizenship Model in operation, try applying it to *Soldano v. O'Daniels* in Chapter 1. How great was the *need* of Soldano? Was O'Daniels *able* to meet that need without unreasonable sacrifice? Was the need *proximate,* that is, was O'Daniels sufficiently aware of the need? Was there anyone else to give Soldano a helping hand, or was O'Daniels the *last resort?*

You might also look ahead to Chapter 38, "Corporations: Rights and Liabilities of Shareholders and Managers," and engage in the same exercise with *Shlensky v. Wrigley.* In that case the Chicago Cubs were sued by a minority shareholder who claimed that the Board of Directors of the team, led by Phil Wrigley, was sacrificing profits by playing daytime baseball only. By refusing to install lights at Wrigley Field, the club president (Wrigley) was allegedly showing more concern about the deteriorating effects lights would have on the surrounding neighborhood than he was about financially benefiting the Cubs. After examining the case, determine for yourself whether or not the rescue principles are applicable. Consider, as well, whether certain components of the moral minimum, e.g., fairness and doing no harm, may be even more appropriate than the rescue principles.

The Public Policy Role of Business: The final segment of the Corporate Citizenship Model addresses the moral or ethical role of business people and corporations in the formulation of public policy. In its broadest reach, this would call for an examination of such policy-related activities as lobbying, testimony before federal, state, and local legislative bodies, public image advertising, contributions to candidates by corporate political action committees, personal contributions of time or money to political campaigns, and other related activities.

Friedman's agents-of-capital model did not specifically address the role of business in formulating public policy, nor did it suggest an ethical basis for the substance of that policy. From numerous other sources, however, it is clear that Friedman is generally supportive of public policies that enhance the free market and that favor efficient, productivity-oriented market solutions to social problems over regulatory or administrative solutions. With regard to the role of business people in advancing these policies, he, and Donaldson as well, would likely encourage them to use all legal and constitutional means of making their voices heard.

Donaldson's agents-of-society theory is also strongly supportive of efficient business operation, but he is willing to sacrifice a certain unspecified amount of efficiency in order to bring minimum standards of justice to the workplace, such as respect for workers as human beings, avoidance of practices that systematically worsen the situation of a group, and advancement of employees' sense of pride and self-fulfillment in their work. Milton Friedman would not necessarily oppose these objectives, but they are not explicit values in his formulation, so one would judge that he attaches a lesser degree of importance to them.

Both these men are recorded in opposition to "fraud and deception," an embryonic version of the moral minimum. The basis for this inference is more clearly to be found in Donaldson than in Friedman, but Friedman undoubtedly would acknowledge the necessity of *some* moral formulation supportive of contracts and free market operations. Otherwise it would be impossible to conduct economic activities.

Building upon this broad spectrum of agreement, and upon the elements of the Corporate Citizenship Model that have already been discussed, the Corporate Citizenship Model would include the following guidelines for the **public policy role of business:**

1. *THE MORAL MINIMUM.* This concept is at the very core of the Corporate Citizen Model, and is the touchstone for all business efforts to influence the substance of our nation's public policy. Neither the market, nor the society which nurtures it, nor other moral and social ideals which bind our nation together, can survive unless the norms of honesty, promise-keeping, loyalty, fairness, and doing no harm infuse our public policy.

2. *THE PRIORITY OF SOCIAL JUSTICE AND THE PUBLIC GOOD.* Just as the Rescue Principles were a deliberative balance that focused on correcting the harm caused by others, and not self-serving, so also must businesses' public policy input be balanced and not self-serving. The balance it must seek conditions and qualifies efficiency (profit and wealth-producing measures) with a concern for social justice and the public good. That is, it must be recognized that certain values—social justice and the common good—are more important than those that merely produce more profit *if* and *when* these objectives are in conflict.

It is not morally wrong to support efficiency or wealth-producing measures. In fact such measures are desirable because they strengthen and reinforce social justice and the common good. For example, it is easier to gain a wide consensus favoring welfare distribution laws, or favoring strong environmental protection laws, during good economic times (low unemployment, high profits) than in bad. Under the Corporate Citizenship Model, the efficiency-orientation is unjustified, however, when wealth production is elevated beyond its supportive, supplementary role and becomes an end in itself.

In summary terms, the Corporate Citizenship Model, as it relates to the public policy role of business, evaluates business input first on the basis of the moral minimum, and, beyond the minimum, places greater weight or value on the common good and social justice than on efficiency *when these interests are in conflict.* For example, some readily marketable but harmful products should not be produced in the interest of public health. When efficiency and social justice are in harmony, our public policy should promote the common good in the most efficient way.

MORAL REASONING

Clear thinking about moral problems, like clear thinking about other problems, can frequently bring a swift and decisive conclusion to a confusing matter. It cannot resolve all disputes, however, because some of them bring into conflict deep-seated social, cultural, or religious values that are apparently irreconcilable. This is the realm of ethical relativity, and not much more can be said about it beyond the observation that it is conceivable that two opposing ethical propositions could be equally valid. This is a serious concern for managers of multinational firms. It calls for much tolerance and for respect for the other person's point of view.

On a different level, however, rational thinking about the facts that are relevant to a particular issue can bring you to a valid, objective conclusion if you proceed from a sound moral principle or norm. It all begins, of course, with the recognition of moral issues. As a rule, the most blatant examples of wrong conduct are the easiest to recognize and evaluate. It is the subtler things that present the most difficulty. For example, what counts as sexual harassment? The promise by a foreman of job security and promotion in return for sexual favors would surely count, but what about flirting, sexual innuendo, smutty jokes, and a generally patronizing manner? Some people would think nothing of these situations, while those who did might be viewed by their peers, or some of their peers, as overly sensitive and even self-righteous.

Perhaps the best test to determine whether suspect conduct is morally offensive is for a person to ask how he or she would like to be treated in return. This is certainly not a foolproof test because of the different cultures and conditioning we experience during our lifetime. Women and men are socialized differently, and that is true on an individual and group level not only with regard to the sexes, but on the basis of race, religion, and national origin. We can only say that while the test is not perfect, it is a starting point, and one that you may be able to improve upon.

Issue recognition, however, is only the first step. At the second stage, an appropriate moral standard, that is, a general moral principle or specific norm of conduct, must be chosen or formulated. It must include proper regard for the problem of dilemmas (competing or divergent moral duties) and for excusing conditions. For example, if the issue is sexual harassment in the workplace, the moral standard may be a general principle (treat others as yourself) or a specific norm (do no harm). We could introduce a dilemma if the supervisor thought patronizing treatment was a necessary means of gaining top efficiency for the employer, and we could introduce the possibility of an excusing condition if the supervisor was simply not morally sophisticated or astute enough to realize that there was a problem. In any event, the moral standard must be comprehensive enough to deal with the relevant facts and sharp enough to operate as a decision tool.

The third stage of this **moral reasoning** format is the logical and thoughtful application of the moral standard to the facts. This cannot be taught in a paragraph, nor even in a course. One wonders if even a lifetime is enough. It takes practice, patience, and resolve. The rational process does not always deliver easy outcomes, and sometimes the ones that are delivered are inconclusive. The fourth stage, and the principal objective, is to arrive at an outcome that is sound, thoughtfully reasoned, and conclusive.

Memorizing this decision format will not help very much, but if one becomes skilled in using it in daily practice, he or she will find its application extends to other disciplines, including law. As you pursue your study of law, you will examine a number of appellate court cases in chapters to come. While the perspective in the present chapter has been that of ethics, you will find this decision format readily adaptable to analyzing the legal problems presented in these cases:

1. Examine the facts and pick out the issue or issues;

2. Find the legal authority (constitutional provision, statute, or previous court decision);

3. Examine and critique the judge's logical or reasoning process; and

4. Test the conclusion for soundness and validity.

SUMMARY

In this chapter, we have shown, first, that business, like other human endeavors, is to be evaluated by the same moral standard that is applied throughout our society, and that this moral standard depends on an individual exercise of free will. Next, we gave as a reason for attributing moral responsibility to corporations that these "artificial" persons engage in group behavior that cannot be ascribed to individual employees.

The following step was to describe the *moral minimum,* the level of ethical behavior that is expected of everyone both professionally and personally. Then we examined the contrasting corporate social responsibility models of Milton Friedman and Tom Donaldson, and offered the Corporate Citizenship Model for your evaluation. The Corporate Citizenship Model encompassed the moral minimum, the moral status of corporations, and the social responsibility of business beyond the moral minimum. Within the concept of social responsibility, we supplied guidelines for business people in going-to-the-rescue and in fulfilling a public policy role.

The chapter concluded with a suggested format for the process of moral reasoning and with the recommendation of extending this reasoning process into your study of law.

KEY TERMS

Ethics
Morality
Ethos
The Golden Rule
Utilitarianism
Moral responsibility of corporations
Moral minimum
Moral dilemmas
Excusing conditions

Agents of capital
Agents of society
Corporate Citizenship Model
Kew Gardens Principles of Rescue
Public policy role of business
Moral reasoning

QUESTIONS AND PROBLEMS

1. What is meant by the observation that the violation of a moral duty, for example, one of the duties enumerated in the moral minimum, is *prima facie* wrong?

2. What are the presuppositions of morally responsible action, that is, what conditions must be present and operative regarding a person's conduct before we will attach moral fault or blame to the outcome?

3. How does observance of the moral minimum support market operations?

4. Why does Milton Friedman insist that corporate social responsibility is a "fundamentally subversive doctrine?"

5. How can it be said that corporations have moral responsibilities beyond those of its managers or executives?

6. What is the agents-of-society view of corporate social responsibility?

7. In what significant way does the moral obligation to go-to-the-rescue, i.e., the obligation of beneficence or of doing good, differ from the moral obligations embodied in the moral minimum?

8. Are employers legally and/or morally obligated to protect the jobs of "whistleblowers?"

9. Briefly, what are the Kew Gardens Principles, and how do they operate in corporate going-to-the-rescue situations?

10. In a public policy role, by what standards should business people and business corporations be guided?

A Transitional Note

AN ENVIRONMENTAL-TRADITIONAL BRIDGE

In Part I we took a sweeping look at the aspects of our legal system that are common to all branches of law: the sources of our legal rules, the primary law-making processes, and the manner in which rules of law are generally implemented by the courts. This *environmental* approach is clearly valuable in that it familiarizes us with the general workings of our legal system.

However, the various branches of law that directly control all the legal aspects of business transactions—such as contracts, sales, and corporation dealings—are composed entirely of substantive rules. These are the currently existing rules or principles that define and recognize the specific rights and duties flowing from the many diverse business (and nonbusiness) relationships and transactions existing in modern society.

It is imperative, then, that we devote the rest of this text to these basic rules and principles—a modest change of approach which is often characterized as *traditional* (rule-oriented) in nature.

CONTRACT LAW—SPECIAL CHARACTERISTICS

Contract law, which will be considered in Part II, possesses several characteristics that make it the natural starting point for an examination of the other commercial law subjects. First is its all-pervasiveness, as a practical matter, in the average person's everyday activities. When a person buys a newspaper, leaves a car at a parking lot, or even purchases a ticket to an athletic event, a contract of some sort has been entered into. When someone borrows money, or asks a painter to paint a house, or insures a car, a contract has again certainly been made—a more complex one than in the prior cases. And the retailer (whether an individual running a corner store or a multimillion dollar corporation) has to make countless contracts of an infinite variety. The retailer must buy or lease office equipment, make agreements with employees, secure heat and light, and buy from suppliers most of the goods that stock the shelves. The formation of a partnership requires some kind of contract between the partners, and the formation of a corporation requires making two contracts (using the term broadly), one between the incorporators and the state and the other among the incorporators themselves.

Second, and equally important from the academic standpoint, is that the basic principles of contract law are the underpinning of the more specialized business-related subjects, such as sales and commercial paper. For example, the entire law of sales is applicable only to situations in which *sales contracts* have first been entered into; it is only where such contracts between sellers and buyers are found to exist that the more specialized rules of sales law—having to do with the buyers' and sellers' further obligations—are applicable.

The subject of contracts possesses yet a third virtue. Since it is essentially common-law in nature, the controversies that are presented usually require the courts to examine earlier decisions handed down in cases involving similar fact-patterns. Thus the doctrine of *stare decisis* is illuminated; and an allied question—whether today's conditions have so changed as to justify a repudiation of the earlier decisions—affords an opportunity to analyze more fully the process of judicial reasoning.

CONTRACT LAW AND SALES LAW—A SPECIAL RELATIONSHIP

By and large, the subjects of contracts and sales can be treated separately—for two reasons:

1. Sales law is applicable only to those contracts calling for the sale of tangible articles of personal property—goods such as automobiles, machine tools, grain, and items of clothing. Contract law, on the other hand, is applicable to virtually all other kinds of agreements—including leases, employment contracts, and real estate sales contracts.

2. As we have seen, our contract law is composed of common-law rules, while sales is a statutory subject.

At this point, one might conclude that the subject matter covered by the two branches of law is so dissimilar that a study of the law of contracts would require no reference to the law of sales. In fact, such references are occasionally made, and experience has convinced us that potential confusion can be eliminated by realizing the need for this at the very outset.

First, of all the contracts that are entered into, a substantial number *are* sales contracts. And even more importantly, while the basic principles of sales law found in Article 2 of the Uniform Commercial Code are essentially consistent with those of contract law, several rules of sales law differ from well-established principles of contract law. *The most important of these UCC modifications will be noted at appropriate points in Part II.* Sales law will be treated comprehensively in Part IV.

Part II

PRINCIPLES OF CONTRACT LAW

Part II is devoted entirely to the subject of contract law. Here we will be primarily focusing on the basic rules that make up this subject—an approach that is somewhat more traditional than the one taken in Part I (as explained in the "Transitional Note"). However, to preserve an analytical flavor to our treatment of the subject, the reasons underlying the rules are also given substantial attention.

Chapter 10 presents a brief description of the major classes of contracts recognized by the law. This presentation not only creates an awareness of the diversity of the subject, but also permits an identification of the conceptual principles applicable to all kinds of contracts.

Chapters 11 through 13 are devoted to the heart of contract law—examination of the basic elements that must generally be present in order for an agreement to rise to the level of an enforceable contract. In these chapters, then, we will examine the judicially imposed requirements applicable to the *agreement* (offer and acceptance); *consideration;* and the requirement of a *lawful objective.*

The next chapters deal with somewhat tangential matters, but ones of great significance in those situations where they apply. Thus Chapter 14 explores the circumstances in which the courts may free a person from his or her contractual obligations on the ground of minority, or upon proof of fraud, duress, or mistake of fact. Chapter 15 examines those kinds of contracts which are generally required by law to be in writing, and the rights of third parties are discussed in Chapter 16.

Chapter 17, the concluding chapter of Part II, is largely concerned with two subjects—performance and excuses for nonperformance. The first covers the level of performance that the law requires of a contracting party, while the second sets forth the circumstances in which a party may be legally freed of his or her contractual duties even in the absence of fraud, duress, or mistake of fact.

Chapter 10

NATURE AND CLASSIFICATION OF CONTRACTS

A PERSPECTIVE

We noted earlier that the great majority of people live within the law, routinely respecting the rights of others and meeting the numerous obligations imposed by the law without being threatened by legal action. Happily, the same is true about duties that result from making contracts; most persons fulfill their contractual obligations voluntarily. Thus in the area of contracts, as in the other branches of the law, the legal disputes that do arise—particularly those that find their way into the courts—are the exception rather than the rule.

Despite the foregoing, a substantial number of cases involving contract law *do* have to be settled by the courts every year, and these cases most clearly bring into focus the principles of contract law. It is one thing to get a general idea about a principle that is stated in the abstract; it is quite another to see the practical results of its application to a concrete situation. It is at the latter stage that a principle or theory takes on real life; thus this examination of the principles of contract law will be interspersed with a number of selected cases.

CLASSIFICATION OF CONTRACTS

The following chapters look at the "heart" of contract law—the various elements that the courts require to be present in order for a contract to exist. Before proceeding to these basic matters, however, one should realize that the law recognizes many different kinds of contracts, each bearing a generally accepted label. Thus a court may refer to a contract as being "voidable" in one case, "executory" in another, and "bilateral" in a third. For this reason alone an early exposure to the most common types of contracts is useful. But even more important is the fact that a comparison of types of contracts that appear at first glance to be dissimilar in nature frequently brings to light certain commonly shared elements.

Nature of a Contract

A contract is a special sort of agreement—one that the law will enforce in some manner in the event of a breach. As will be seen in the following chapter, some agreements are not enforceable because their terms are too indefinite, or they are entered into in jest, or they involve obligations that are essentially social in nature. (Examples of the latter are making a date or a luncheon appointment.) Even seriously intended, definite business agreements, however, are generally not enforceable unless three additional elements are present—what the courts refer to as consideration, capacity, and legality. (Generally, the law does not require contracts to be in writing. Exceptions are noted in Chapter 15.)

A comprehensive definition of *contract* cannot be attempted until these four elements have been examined in some detail. But for the limited purpose of this chapter—to convey a general idea of what is being classified—*a contract is an agreement that a court will enforce.*[1]

Bilateral and Unilateral Contracts

Most contracts consist of the exchange of mutual promises, the actual performance of which is to occur at some later time. When a manufacturer enters into a contract in May with a supplier, calling for the supplier to deliver 10,000 steel wheels during September at a specified price, each party has promised the other to perform one or more acts at a subsequent time. Such contracts, consisting of "a promise for a promise," are **bilateral contracts.**

The same terminology applies to offers (proposals) that precede the making of a contract. If the terms of an offer indicate that all the offeror

---

[1] A more technical definition is the following: "A contract is a promise or set of promises for the breach of which the law gives a remedy, or the performance of which the law in some way recognizes as a duty." *Restatement, Contracts 2d,* §1. Copyright, 1979. Reprinted with permission of the American Law Institute.

wants at the present time from the offeree is a return promise—rather than the immediate performance of an act—then the proposal can be called a **bilateral offer.**[2] Thus, if a professional football club sends a contract to one of its players in June, offering him $80,000 for the coming season, it is clear that all the club presently wants is the player's promise to render his services at a later time. Such an offer is bilateral; and if the player accepts it by signing and returning the contract, a bilateral contract has been formed.

Some offers, called **unilateral offers,** are phrased in such a way that they can be accepted only by the performance of a particular act. An example of such an offer would be the promise by a TV station to pay $5,000 to the first person who brings to its executive offices any piece of a fallen satellite, such as "Skylab." This offer can only be accepted by the actual physical production of a portion of the designated satellite, at

which time a **unilateral contract** is formed; a promise by an offeree that he or she will bring in the item later does not result in the formation of a contract.[3]

True unilateral offers occur rather rarely. And, in cases where there is doubt as to the type of offer made, the courts generally construe them to be bilateral in nature—a view that is usually in keeping with the reasonable expectation of the offeree. One type of unilateral offer, however, *is* made frequently in the real world—the promise by a seller of property to pay a real estate agent a commission when the agent finds a buyer for it. The following case involves such a promise, which comes into being when the seller signs a "listing contract." In the court's decision, attention is focused upon the exact nature of the "act" that such an offer legally requires.

---

[2] The *offeror* is the person making the proposal; the *offeree* is the one to whom it is made.

[3] Under sales law, the distinction between bilateral and unilateral offers is blurred in one limited situation. The section of Article 2 of the UCC responsible for this result will be discussed in the next chapter, where the primary focus is on offer/acceptance rules.

Judd Realty, Inc. v. Tedesco
Supreme Court of Rhode Island, 400 A.2d 952 (1979)

Frank Tedesco, defendant, wanted to sell a lot that he owned in Johnston, Rhode Island. On November 18, 1973, he listed the property with Judd Realty, plaintiff, giving it the exclusive right to sell the property for a period of six months—i.e., until the following May 18th. The stated price was $25,000. The "listing contract" signed by Tedesco contained this standard provision: "Should a purchaser be found during the life of this agreement by me, or by you . . . I will pay you a commission of 8 percent of the price received."

About a week before the listing contract expired, plaintiff's president told defendant that she had a buyer for his property. A day or two later she had the prospective purchaser sign the customary "purchase and sale agreement," which was an offer by him to buy the property for $25,000. On May 15, two days before the listing contract expired, plaintiff's president took this offer and a $1,000 check drawn

by the prospective purchaser to Tedesco. He told her then that he had decided not to sell. When he subsequently continued in his refusal to accept the offer to purchase, plaintiff brought this action to recover its commission.

The plaintiff claimed that it had produced a "purchaser" within the meaning of that term in the listing contract, even though no sale actually took place. Defendant, in support of the opposite view, contended that the term purchaser was an ambiguous one, in which case the court should follow the rule that the contract be construed against the drafter, the plaintiff. The trial court accepted defendant's contention, and thus ruled that the term "purchaser" meant "someone who actually purchases the property." On this basis it ruled there was no purchaser, and dismissed the complaint. Plaintiff appealed.

The higher court disagreed with the lower court's interpretation, saying that "It is well settled in Rhode Island that a broker has sufficiently performed, and is entitled to compensation under, a brokerage contract when the broker has produced a prospective purchaser who is ready, willing, and able to purchase at the price and terms of the seller." It thus reversed the judgment of the lower court and entered judgment for plaintiff. In that part of its decision appearing below, the higher court emphasized that the contract ultimately formed between plaintiff and defendant was *unilateral* in nature.

Weisberger, Justice:

. . . Williston distinguishes unilateral and bilateral contracts as follows: "An offer for a unilateral contract generally requires an *act* on the part of the offeree to make a binding contract. This act is consideration for the promise contained in the offer, and [the performance of the act] without more will create a contract. . . . On the other hand, an offer for a bilateral contract requires a *promise* from the offeree in order that there may be a binding contract." [Emphasis added.] 1 Williston, *Contracts* §65, Third Edition.

Corbin also contrasts unilateral contracts with bilateral contracts in respect to brokerage agreements:

"The most commonly recurring case is one in which the owner employs a broker to find a purchaser able and willing to buy, on terms stated in advance by the owner, and in which the owner promises to pay a specified commission for the service. This is an offer by the owner, the [acceptance of which occurs] by the actual rendition of the requested service [by the broker]. Here the only contemplated contract between the owner and the broker is a unilateral contract—a promise to pay a commission for services rendered [i.e., the production of a buyer].

Cases are very numerous in which the owner, after the broker has fully performed the requested service, fails to make conveyance [of the property] to the purchaser, and refuses to pay the commission. Such a refusal is not the revocation of an offer; it is the breach of the fully consummated unilateral contract to pay for services rendered. If the requested service is merely the production of a purchaser able and willing to buy on definitely stated terms, the broker has a right to his commission even though the owner at once refuses to accept the purchaser's offer." *[Emphasis added.] 1 Corbin,* Contracts §50 (1963). . . .

We conclude that the trial justice erred as a matter of law in construing the word "purchaser" in the brokerage agreement to mean "someone who actually purchases the property." . . .

Judgment reversed.

Comment: While the *broker* had a cause of action against Tedesco, the *prospective purchaser* in this case does not. As a general rule, a person who lists property for sale has a perfect legal right—insofar as prospective purchasers are concerned—to reject all purchase offers (as long as the rejection is not based on the purchaser's race, color, religion, or national origin).

Express, Implied, and Quasi-Contracts

As has been indicated, the essence of a contract is an agreement (an understanding) that has been arrived at in some fashion. If the intentions of the parties are stated fully and in explicit terms, either orally or in writing, they constitute an **express contract.** The typical real estate lease and construction contract are examples of contracts normally falling within this category.

Express contracts are frequently in writing and of considerable length, but this is not necessarily so. If B orally offers to sell his used car to W for $1,000 cash, and W answers, "I accept," an express contract has been formed. The communications between B and W, while extremely brief, are themselves sufficient to indicate the obligations of each.

An **implied contract** is one in which the promises (intentions) of the parties have to be inferred in large part from the facts of their conduct and from the circumstances in which it took place. It is reasonable to infer, for example, that a person who is getting a haircut in a barbershop actually desires the service and is willing to pay for it. If the patron does not pay voluntarily, a court will have no hesitation in saying that by his conduct the patron had made an implied promise to pay a reasonable price, and will hold him liable on this obligation.

The words and conduct test is a good starting point in distinguishing between the two kinds of agreement, but it is also somewhat of an oversimplification. This is primarily so because some agreements are reached through the use of words and conduct both—especially in the case where one person requests a service from another without specifying a price that he or she is willing to pay for it. For example, if T asks J to keep his lawn mowed during the two months that T will be in Europe, and if J performs the requested service, T's request for the service carries with it in the eyes of the law an implied promise that he will pay J the "reasonable value" of his services. Thus the contract that has been formed upon J's completion of the work is an implied contract, even though T requested the service expressly. *(Constructed-Contract)*

A **quasi-contract**, in contrast to the express and implied contracts, exists only in those exceptional circumstances where a court feels compelled to impose an obligation upon one person even though he or she had no intention of making a contract at all. The classic illustration is that of a doctor who renders first aid to an unconscious man and later sends a bill for his services. It is perfectly obvious that the patient neither expressly nor impliedly promised to pay for the services when they were rendered; yet to permit him to escape liability entirely on the grounds that a contract was not formed would be to let him get something for nothing—a result the law generally abhors. To solve this dilemma, the courts pretend that a contract was formed and impose a quasi-contractual obligation on the person receiving the service.[4]

A quasi-contractual obligation is imposed only in circumstances where the failure to impose such an obligation would result in one party receiving an "unjust enrichment"—a benefit which, on the grounds of fairness alone, he or she ought to pay for. Suppose, for example, that A plants and cultivates crops on land belonging to B, without B's knowledge. In such a case, B, upon learning the facts, is entitled to bring a *quantum meruit* action to recover from A the reasonable value of the benefit (the profit which A made as a result of the use of the land), for otherwise A would be unjustly enriched.[5]

Two limitations on the quasi-contractual principle should be noted.

1. It cannot be invoked by one who has conferred a benefit unnecessarily or as a result of

negligence or other misconduct. Thus, suppose that the X Company contracts to blacktop Y's driveway at 540 Fox Lane for $900, and the company's employees instead mistakenly blacktop the driveway of Y's neighbor, Z, at 546 Fox Lane, in Z's absence. In such a situation Z has no liability to the X Company, since his retention of the blacktop, while a benefit to him, is not an unjust benefit or an unjust retention under the circumstances.

2. Quasi-contracts are contracts in fiction only, since they are not based upon a genuine agreement between the parties. Thus they are not "true" contracts; and except for the limited mention given them in this chapter, they will not be considered in the rest of the chapters on contracts.

In the first of the following two cases, a state supreme court sets forth the general rules as to the nature and legal effects of implied contracts. The second presents a situation where a recovery of money by the plaintiffs under the quasi-contract principle might be proper.

---

[4] The technical name for implied contracts is *contracts implied in fact,* and for quasi-contracts *contracts implied in law.* We are using the less formal labels of "implied" and "quasi" for purposes of simplicity.

[5] *Quantum meruit* means, literally, "as much as is deserved."

Carroll v. Lee
Supreme Court of Arizona, 712 P.2d 923 (1986)

Judy Carroll lived with Paul Lee for fourteen years. Ultimately they settled in Ajo, Arizona, where Paul operated an automobile repair shop. Although Judy used the name Lee during this time, the couple did not marry or ever seriously consider marriage. In 1982 they "went their separate ways."

Prior to the relationship little personal property was owned by either party, and neither owned any real property (i.e., land). During the course of the relationship the couple jointly acquired three parcels of land, several antique or restored automobiles, a mobile home, and various other items of personal property. The real property was titled to the couple in one of three ways. Title was held either (1) as joint tenants with the right of survivorship, (2) as husband and wife, or (3) as husband and wife as joint tenants with the right of survi-

vorship. (The mobile home and some of the automobiles were titled to Paul T. Lee and Judy Lee, with other automobiles titled to Paul T. Lee alone.)

During the time the couple lived together Paul supplied virtually all of the money used to pay their living expenses, while Judy "kept the house" by cleaning, cooking, doing laundry, and working in the yard. After the couple split up Judy filed this partition action claiming a one-half interest in the jointly titled property listed above. (The fact that the properties were titled to both parties did not, in and of itself, convey a one-half interest to Judy. This was because Paul proved that the money used in purchasing them came from the operation of the repair shop, which he owned personally. In such a case, the rule in Arizona—and in most states—is that "where property is paid for by one party and title is taken in the name of that party and a second party who are not husband and wife, it is presumed that the property was taken for the benefit of the one paying for the property." Thus it was necessary for Judy to prove an agreement existed between them that they be co-owners, in order to rebut this presumption.)

The trial court ruled in favor of Judy, finding that an implied contract existed under which it was agreed that Paul and she would be co-owners of the property. (This finding was based on a 1984 case, *Cook v. Cook*, 691 P.2d 664, in which the Supreme Court of Arizona upheld an implied contract between an unmarried couple in circumstances similar to those presented by this case.) Paul appealed, and the court of appeals reversed the judgment (for reasons appearing below). Judy petitioned the Supreme Court of Arizona for review.

Gordon, Vice-Chief Justice:

. . . In *Cook v. Cook, supra,* [this court approved] an agreement between unmarried cohabitants to pool income, acquire assets, and share in the accumulations. We compiled basic concepts of contract law:

"The sine qua non [essential element] of any contract is the exchange of promises. From this exchange flows the obligation of one party to another. Although it is most apparent that two parties have exchanged promises when their words express a spoken or written statement of promissory intention, mutual promises need not be express in order to create an enforceable contract. Restatement (Second) of Contracts §4. *Indeed, a promise 'may be inferred wholly or partly from conduct,'* id., *and 'there is no distinction in the effect of the promise whether it is expressed in writing, or orally, or in acts, or partly in one of these ways and partly in others.'* id. §19. *Thus, two parties may by their course of conduct express their agreement, though no words are ever spoken. From their conduct alone the trier of fact can determine the existence of an agreement.* Restatement (Second) of Contracts §4."

The court of appeals [ruled that our decision in *Cook* was not applicable to the instant case because] "no evidence, in words or conduct, suggests mutual promises to contribute funds to a pool. . . ." [In other words, the court of appeals refused to apply the *Cook* rule because in that case both parties were earning income, while in the instant case Paul was the sole income producer. The supreme court disagreed with the court of appeals decision, and continued:]

In Arizona we recognize implied contracts, and there is no difference in legal effect between an express contract and an implied contract. An implied contract is one not created or evidenced by explicit agreement, but inferred by the law as a matter of reason and justice from the acts and conduct of the parties and circumstances surrounding their transaction. Furthermore, in this state monetary consideration is not always required as consideration. . . . Clearly a promise for a promise constitutes adequate consideration. . . .

We believe Judy proved the property requested to be partitioned was acquired through joint common effort and for a common purpose. It is not necessary for her to prove that she produced by her labor a part of the very money used to purchase the property. The parties had an *implied partnership or joint enterprise agreement* at the very least, based on the facts and circumstances presented. [Emphasis added.] Recovery for Judy should be allowed in accordance with these implied expectations. [The court here reviewed testimony by Paul in which he stated that it was his "preference" that Judy stay at home, cook meals, do washing and yardwork, and that she did, in fact, perform these services. This testimony ended with the following:]

Q. Did you ever intend that she be an owner with you at that time, at the time that you were acquiring these properties, that she be an owner of those properties at that time?

A. You mean a co-owner?

Q. Yes.

A. I suppose at the time I had it planned that way. [Emphasis added by the court.] . . .

the Intent

Judy's relevant testimony is as follows:

Q. All right. What type of an arrangement, if any, did you and Paul discuss about what he expected from your relationship in terms of contribution?

A. We didn't really discuss it. It just was there. He went to work. I stayed home and kept the house and, mostly because that's what he wanted me to do. [Emphasis added by the court.]

There was evidence from which the trial court could find the existence of an agreement for property to be acquired and owned jointly, as such was the method in which Paul took title in both the real and personal property. . . . Since Judy was a co-owner of the property under a contract theory, she had the right [under Arizona law] to seek partition and divide the jointly owned assets. . . .

We therefore vacate the opinion of the court of appeals and remand the case to the trial court for a redistribution of property not inconsistent with this opinion.

Comment: This case has been edited to emphasize the implied contract question. An additional question of equal importance was also presented: whether a finding that an implied contract existed even though the plaintiff's services were entirely of a "homemaking" nature, was contrary to public policy, on the ground that enforcement of such a contract might discourage marriage. The court of appeals, by refusing to apply the *Cook* rule, felt that the enforcement of such a contract would have that effect. The higher court, in a part of its decision omitted here, set forth reasons why enforcement of an implied contract in the circumstances presented here was *not* contrary to the public policy of the state.

Deskovick et al. v. Porzio
Superior Court of New Jersey, 187 A.2d 610 (1963)

Plaintiffs in this action are brothers, Michael and Peter Deskovick, Jr. Their father, Peter Deskovick, Sr., was hospitalized in 1958 until his death in 1959. During this period Michael paid the hospital and medical bills as they came in, under the impression that the father was financially unable to do so. (This impression was based on statements made by the senior Deskovick in which he indicated an apparently genuine fear that he would not be able to pay the expenses of the hospitalization.) After the father's death it was discovered that, in fact, his estate was adequate to cover all of the payments made by Michael. The plaintiffs thereupon brought this action against the executor of their father's estate, Porzio, to recover the amounts paid out.

In the trial court, plaintiffs proceeded on the theory that an *implied contract* existed between them and their father in the foregoing fact-pattern. (No mention of quasi-contractual liability was made.) While the evidence was somewhat conflicting as to whether Michael intended to be repaid out of his father's estate at the time he made the payments, the trial judge ruled as a matter of law that no such intention was present, and, for that reason, no implied contract had been formed. Accordingly, the court directed a verdict for the defendant. On appeal, plaintiffs contended for the first time that the estate should be liable on the theory of *quasi-contract*. (As a general rule, the parties cannot raise new issues on appeal. It does not appear why this was permitted in this case.)

Conford, Justice:

. . . If the question whether plaintiffs intended to be repaid at the time they advanced the monies in question were the sole material issue, we would conclude the trial court erred in taking the case out of the jury's hands [because of the conflicting evidence on that point]. However, . . . their intent to be repaid was immaterial in the factual situation presented, for the following reasons.

It is elementary that the assertion of a contract implied in fact [an "implied contract"] calls for the establishment of a consensual understanding as to compensation or reimbursement inferable from the circumstances under which one furnishes services or property and another accepts such advances. Here an essential for such a mutual understanding was absent *in that the decedent, on behalf of whom these advances were being made, was totally ignorant of the fact.* [Emphasis added.]

[After thus concluding that the proper reason why no implied contract was formed was because the father could not give his implied consent to his sons' actions when he was not aware of them, the appellate court turned to the question of whether recovery might be allowed under the quasi-contract theory, as follows:]

It is elementary that one who pays the debt of another as a volunteer, having no obligation or liability to pay nor any interest menaced by the continued existence of the debt, cannot recover therefor from the beneficiary. Nor can such a volunteer claim the benefit of the law of subrogation. If plaintiffs were mere volunteers, therefore, they would not, within these principles, be entitled to be subrogated to the creditor position of the hospitals and physicians whose bills they paid.

Notwithstanding the foregoing principles, however, we perceive in the evidence adduced at the trial, particularly in the version of the facts reflected in the deposition of Michael, adduced by defendant, a *quasi-contractual* basis of recovery which in our judgment ought to be submitted to a jury at a retrial of the case in the interests of substantial justice.

It is said that a "quasi-contractual obligation is one that is created by the law for reasons of justice, without any expression of assent. . . ." 1 *Corbin on Contracts* (1950), §19, p. 38; 1 *Williston, Contracts* (1957), §3A, p. 13. This concept rests "on the equitable principle that a person shall not be allowed to enrich himself unjustly at the expense of another, and on the principle that whatsoever it is certain that a man ought to do, that the law supposes him to have promised to do." The *Restatement of Restitution* (1937) undertakes to formulate a number of rules growing out of recognized principles of quasi-contract. Id., at p. 5 et seq. Section 26 (p. 116), entitled "Mistake in Making Gifts," reads: "(1) A person is entitled to restitution from another to whom gratuitously and induced thereto by a mistake of fact he has given money if the mistake (a) was caused by fraud or material misrepresentation. . . ." An innocent misrepresentation by the donee is within the rule. Id., comment, at p. 117. A "mistaken belief in the existence of facts which would create a moral obligation upon the donor to make a gift would ordinarily be a basic error" justifying restitution. Id., at p. 118. . . .

We think the foregoing authorities would apply in favor of sons, who, during their father's mortal illness, believing him without means of meeting medical and hospital bills as a result of what he had previously told them, and wishing to spare him the discomfort of concern over such expenses at such a time, themselves assumed and paid the obligations. The leaving by the father of an estate far more than sufficient to have met the expenditures would, in such circumstances, and absent others affecting the basic equitable situation presented, properly invoke the concept of a *quasi-contractual obligation* of reimbursement of the sons by the estate. [Emphasis added.] Such circumstances would take the payors out of the category of voluntary intermeddlers as to whom the policy of the law is to deny restitution or reimbursement. . . .

Judgment reversed and remanded.

Valid, Voidable, and Void Contracts

A **valid contract** is one in which all of the required elements are present. As a result, it is enforceable against both parties.

In some circumstances, one of the parties to a contract has the legal right to withdraw from it at a later time without liability. Such contracts are referred to as **voidable contracts.** Contracts in which fraud is present fall within this category, because the law permits the one who has been defrauded to set aside the contract. Minors' contracts are another common example of voidable contracts. (Because of their importance, voidable contracts are considered separately in Chapter 14.)

Courts occasionally designate a third type of contract as being *void.* Such contracts are those which, so far as the law is concerned, never existed at all. Contracts are usually void for either of two reasons: (1) one of the parties is wholly incompetent at the time of contracting (such as a person who has been legally declared insane) or (2) the purpose of the contract is totally illegal (such as an agreement calling for the commission of a crime). The designation **void contract** is admittedly self-contradictory—an improper combination of terms. Nevertheless, this label is used by the courts to distinguish such contracts from those which are merely voidable; and in that sense it is a useful term.

Another type of contract is referred to as being "unenforceable." An **unenforceable contract** was valid at the time it was made but was subsequently rendered unenforceable because of the application of some special rule of law. For example, if a debtor goes through bankruptcy proceedings, the debtor's nonexempt assets are distributed among creditors and the debtor ultimately receives a discharge in bankruptcy. Under bankruptcy law, this discharge prevents a creditor who was not paid in full from bringing legal action to recover the balance of the debt; thus the contract that created the indebtedness was rendered unenforceable by virtue of the discharge. Another example of an unenforceable contract is one that is held to be *unconscionable*—an agreement whose terms are so one-sided that a court will refuse to enforce it (see below). *One of the elements is missing.*

Negotiated Contracts and Contracts of Adhesion

The terms of many contracts are agreed upon only after a certain amount of bargaining, or "dickering," takes place between the parties. After one party makes an offer to the other, for example, the latter—the offeree—may indicate that he or she will accept only if a specified change is made in the terms of the offer. Or the offeree may respond with a counteroffer, a substantially different proposal from that of the original offer. Contracts that result from these kinds of exchanges are "negotiated contracts."

Contracts of adhesion, by contrast, are formed where one party—usually having greatly superior bargaining power than the other—prepares the terms of a proposed contract and presents it to the other party on a *take-it-or-leave-it basis.*

Examples of such "standard form" contracts are apartment leases, hospital admission forms, and sales contracts of new car dealers. While the terms of contracts of adhesion usually favor the parties who have prepared them, such contracts are generally enforceable unless the terms are so shockingly one-sided as to be, in the opinion of the courts, "unconscionable" in nature. (Unconscionable contracts are considered further in Chapter 13.)

Formal and Informal Contracts

Some specialized types of contracts are referred to as **formal contracts.** The term usually is used to refer to sealed contracts—ones that the parties have formalized either by making a physical impression on the paper on which the agreement was written or, in some instances, simply by having the word *seal* or the letters *L.S.* appear at the end of the document.[6]

The great majority of ordinary business contracts are not sealed and are therefore **informal contracts** (or "simple contracts"). Thus any unsealed contract can be referred to as "simple," even though it may be several pages long and contain complex provisions.

Executory and Executed Contracts *(has not been performed)*

Once a contract is formed, it is an **executory contract** until both parties have fully performed their obligations. When performance has taken place, the contract is said to be an **executed contract.** If one party has fully performed his or *has been performed* her part of the bargain but the other party has not, the contract is executed as to the former and executory as to the latter.

A NOTE ABOUT REMEDIES

This chapter and the following ones are primarily concerned with the general principles that guide the courts in determining (1) whether a

contract has been formed, and (2) if so, whether one of the parties has failed to live up to his or her part of the bargain. If the answers to both questions are affirmative, the next question is: What specific remedy will be afforded the party in whose favor judgment is given?

The subject of remedies was touched upon in Part I, where we traced the historical development of the branches of law and equity. There the emphasis was on remedies in general. Here we will focus briefly on the legal and equitable remedies most commonly sought in contract litigation.

Damages

In virtually all breach of contract actions, the injured party is entitled to the legal remedy of *damages,* sometimes called *money damages.* The law tries to put the successful plaintiff in the financial position that he or she would have occupied had there been no breach by the defendant. The usual (and frequently the only) way this can be done is by ordering the defendant to pay the plaintiff a sum of money.

The plaintiff generally is entitled to recover **compensatory damages**—a sum of money equal to the actual financial loss suffered as a direct result of the breach of contract. Thus, if a seller of corn reneges on his contract and the buyer has to pay an additional $1,500 to procure the same quantity of corn elsewhere, the buyer is entitled to recover at least this difference from the seller. In any event, the plaintiff is required to prove the damages with "reasonable certainty," the precise amount usually being determined by the jury.

Damages that are *speculative* (not within the contemplation of the parties when the contract was made) are not recoverable. In a leading English case on this point, a mill was shut down by a broken crankshaft. The owner of the mill delivered the shaft to defendant, a drayman, and paid him to transport it to another city, where it could be used as a model for a new shaft by the manufacturer. The defendant neglected to deliver the shaft for several days, as a consequence of which

---

[6]The letters stand for *Locus Sigilli,* meaning "the place for the seal."

(actual $ amt.)

there was a substantial delay before plaintiff received the new shaft. The milling company brought an action against the carrier to recover, among other things, the profits that it lost as a result of the shutdown of the mill. The higher court ruled that such profits were not recoverable, since a broken piece of machinery would not necessarily cause a mill to be shut down and since the defendant was not told that such was the case when he received the broken part.

The court said:

If the special circumstances [the possible closing down of the mill] under which the contract was made were communicated by the plaintiffs to the defendants, and thus known to both parties, the damages resulting from the breach of a contract, which they would reasonably contemplate, would be the amount of injury which would ordinarily follow from a breach of contract under these special circumstances so known and communicated. But, on the other hand, if these special circumstances were wholly unknown to the party breaking the contract, he at the most could only be supposed to have had in his contemplation the amount of injury which would arise generally, and in the great multitude of cases not affected by any special circumstances, from such a breach of contract.[7]

In the event a breach of contract results in no financial loss to the innocent party, that person is awarded **nominal damages**—a judgment of a trifling sum, such as a few cents or one dollar. While this may be of little consequence to the plaintiff, it establishes that the defendant's conduct was wrongful, and it permits the court to order the defendant to pay court costs.

Sometimes the parties will specify in the contract the amount of damages one party can recover in the event of a breach by the other. Such damages, called **liquidated damages,** are or-

dinarily given effect as long as the sum agreed upon appears to have been a reasonable attempt by the parties to estimate in advance what the actual loss would be in the event of a breach. On the other hand, if the court feels that the sum was clearly excessive under the circumstances, then it is termed a "penalty" and may be ignored. In such a case the plaintiff is entitled to receive actual damages only.

Specific Performance

In exceptional circumstances a plaintiff may be entitled to a **decree of specific performance**—an order requiring the defendant to perform his or her contractual obligations. When equity began to emerge some centuries ago, one basic idea was that a plaintiff seeking an equitable remedy had to prove that his remedy at law—usually damages—was inadequate. If the plaintiff was asking for specific performance, this requirement could ordinarily be met only if the person could show that the subject matter of the contract was unique. These basic requirements still exist today.

As a practical matter, the great majority of contracts do not involve unique subject matter, and specific performance is not generally granted. For example: Suppose that X has agreed to sell a hundred shares of General Motors stock to Y at a price of $80 per share, but X later refuses to transfer the shares. Because the stock is freely obtainable elsewhere, the remedy of damages is considered adequate, and a request by Y for the specific performance of the contract will thus be denied. On the other hand, if a contract calls for the sale of stock in a close corporation (one in which stock is held by a small number of people—usually family members), a decree of specific performance probably will be granted.

Contracts calling for the sale of real property constitute the one major type of contract in which specific performance *is* customarily granted. Thus, if S contracts to sell his farm to B for $150,000 and later refuses to convey the property, a court will order him to do so if B

---

[7]*Hadley v. Baxendale,* Court of Exchequer (1854).

requests such action. The theory is that each parcel of land is, of and by itself, necessarily unique—even though similar land may be available nearby.

In general, the law of sales parallels the principles set forth above—that is, a buyer of goods who is seeking a decree of specific performance against a defaulting seller must show that the goods are unique. In most sales contracts, such as those calling for the sale of a car or articles of furniture, this showing cannot be made and the buyer is entitled to recover damages only. Some exceptional contracts do meet the test of uniqueness—for example, the sale of family heirlooms, of a race horse with an exceptional reputation, or of a work of art by a famous artist. In these instances the award of damages clearly would not be adequate, and the purchaser is thus entitled to receive the particular thing itself.[8]

Injunction

Another equitable remedy that may be granted in exceptional circumstances is the **injunction**—a court order that forbids the defendant to do certain specified acts. The seller of a business, for example, may promise the buyer that he will not engage in a competing business in the surrounding area for a specified period of time. As will be seen in Chapter 13, such promises are frequently enforceable; thus, if the seller violates the promise, the buyer is entitled to injunctive relief—an order restraining the seller from competing in violation of the terms of the agreement. Similarly, employment contracts frequently contain express promises on the part of employees that they will not work for a competing employer during the existence of the contract and, perhaps, for a year or two thereafter. Such promises can ordinarily be enforced against the employee, if necessary, by granting an injunction to the employer.

An injunction against an employee may also be granted where the employee contracts to work for a certain period of time, and later quits before that time is up. If this is not done with the employer's permission, it may ask a court for an injunction restraining the employee from taking other employment for the balance of the contract period. For example, in 1979, when the New England Patriots' coach, Chuck Fairbanks, was contacted by the University of Colorado in an effort to get him to jump his Patriots' contract with four years remaining on it, the Patriots were successful in getting a court order that prohibited the university from further efforts to get Fairbanks to sign a contract with it.[9] (In a sequel to this suit, the professional team released Fairbanks when the Flatirons club, a Colorado boosters' group, reportedly paid the Patriots $200,000, and Fairbanks waived his rights to a substantial sum of deferred compensation that he was otherwise entitled to receive from the Patriots.)

Rescission *- Contract that is Void or Voidable Mutual Consent*

Once a contract is made, the parties may later mutually agree to rescind (cancel) it. We will use the term **rescission,** however, to refer to a ruling by a court—again acting as a court of equity—formally declaring that a contract is terminated. For example, if one party learns that he was induced to enter into a contract because of the other party's fraud, he can bring suit requesting the remedy of rescission rather than await action by the other party to enforce the contract against him.

SUMMARY

Contracts—agreements that courts will enforce—can be classified in several ways, depending upon the basis used. Sometimes the

---

[8] In the interest of accuracy, it should be noted that Sec. 2-716 of the Uniform Commercial Code authorizes the decree of specific performance in some circumstances even when the goods are not unique. Further consideration of this section appears in the sales chapters of Part IV.

---

[9] *New England Patriots Football Club v. University of Colorado,* 592 F.2d 1196 (1979).

primary focus is upon the nature of the acceptance which the offeror wants; if the offeror merely wants a return promise from the offeree (and if the offeree makes the requested promise), a bilateral contract is formed. On the other hand, if the offer is phrased in such a way that acceptance can only take place by the performance of a particular act, the performance of that act results in the formation of a unilateral contract. (One significance of this classification is that if the offeror clearly requests performance of an act, a promise by the offeree to perform the act later does not result in the formation of a contract.)

A second basis for classification depends upon the extent to which the parties have manifested their agreement. If the intentions (and obligations) of the parties are set forth clearly in the language used, the agreement is an express contract. By contrast, if the intentions of the parties have to be inferred from their conduct, or where the language used shows an agreement, but requires inferences to be made as to the parties' precise duties, the agreement is an implied contract.

A third basis for classification depends upon the extent to which a contract is enforceable. An agreement that is enforceable by both parties is a valid contract. A contract that one of the parties has a legal right to withdraw from is a voidable contract. And a contract which is so defective that it never existed in the law is a void contract. Other classifications are based upon such factors as the extent to which the terms of the contract were mutually bargained for, and the extent to which a contract has been performed.

On the subject of remedies, when one party breaches the contract the usual remedy of the other party is damages—the recovery of a sum of money to compensate him or her for the loss incurred as a result of the breach. In exceptional circumstances, however, the innocent party is entitled to the equitable remedies of specific performance or the injunction as a means of commanding, directly or indirectly, the other party's compliance with the contract.

KEY TERMS

Bilateral contract
Bilateral offer
Unilateral offer
Unilateral contract
Express contract
Implied contract
Quasi-contract
Valid contract
Voidable contract
Void contract
Unenforceable contract
Formal contract
Informal contract
Executory contract
Executed contract
Compensatory damages
Nominal damages
Liquidated damages
Decree of specific performance
Injunction
Rescission

QUESTIONS AND PROBLEMS

1. A corporation employed a contractor to build a barn. Later the contractor quit the job, leaving the subcontractor unpaid. A corporation officer then told the subcontractor to finish the job, and promised that the corporation would pay him for his time and materials. Later the subcontractor finished the job, but the corporation refused to pay the amount that the subcontractor demanded. (It was, however, willing to pay a lesser sum.) In the ensuing lawsuit the corporation contended that no contract had ever been entered into here; the subcontractor, on the other hand, argued that the corporation had made a unilateral offer which he, the subcontractor, had accepted by the act of completing the barn. Do you agree with the corporation that no contract of any kind was entered into here? Why or why not? (*Redd v. Woodford County Swine Breeders, Inc.,* 370 N.E.2d 152, 1977.)

2. The law of Ohio required boards of education to furnish transportation to all children who lived more than four miles from the nearest high school. When one board refused to furnish such transportation to one of its eligible students, the student's father drove him to and from school for the school year. When the father then sued the board to recover his driving expenses, the board contended that no contract of any kind ever existed between it and him, and that it thus had no liability. Do you think an implied contract existed here, under which the board should be liable? If not, could the father recover on the quasi-contract theory? Why or why not? (*Sommers v. Board of Education*, 148 N.E. 682, 1925.)

3. In the *Deskovick* case, it seems clear that no *implied contract* (as distinguished from a quasi-contract) ever was formed between the Deskovick sons and their father. Which of the specific elements necessary to the formation of an implied contract were lacking in this case?

4. Pendergast entered into a contract with the Oakwood Park Homes Corporation under the terms of which he agreed to buy a new home in a housing development that it was building. Later, Pendergast employed Callano to plant a substantial amount of shrubbery at the home. Callano planted the shrubbery, but soon thereafter Pendergast died and Oakwood Park Homes canceled its contract with him. Callano, having received nothing from Pendergast or his estate, brought action against Oakwood Park Homes to recover the value of the shrubbery on the quasi-contract theory, claiming that Oakwood Park Homes would be unjustly enriched if it were not held liable to him in this situation. Is Oakwood Park Homes liable on this theory? Explain. (*Callano v. Oakwood Park Homes Corp.*, 219 A.2d 332, 1966.)

5. A schoolteacher owned some land on Lake Michigan. The land was eroding, and the teacher talked to a contractor about having a retaining wall built, but she never told him to go ahead with the job. Nevertheless, the contractor later built the wall without her knowledge. She refused to pay him for the job, whereupon he sued her—on the quasi-contract theory—to recover the reasonable value of the wall. Do you think she should be liable on this theory? What arguments can be made for, and against, recovery by the contractor on this theory? (*Dunnebacke Co. v. Pittman and Gilligan*, 257 N.W.30, 1934.)

6. B contracts in writing to buy S's home for $85,000. S later refuses to go through with the deal, whereupon B brings an action asking for specific performance of the contract. At the trial, S's lawyer admits that S might be liable for damages for breach of contract, but he contends that a decree of specific performance—which would require S actually to deed the home to B—is unjustified in view of the fact that there is nothing physically unique about S's home or its location. Is such a contention correct? Explain.

7. Madison Square Garden (MSG) made a contract with a professional boxer, Primo Carnera, under which he agreed to fight the winner of a Schmeling-Stribling contest which was to take place at a future date. Carnera also promised not to fight Max Baer or Jack Sharkey before the Schmeling-Stribling contest took place. When Carnera violated this last clause by signing a contract to fight Sharkey *before* the Schmeling-Stribling fight occurred, MSG asked for an injunction prohibiting Carnera from going through with the Sharkey fight. Carnera's lawyers contended MSG was entitled to damages for breach of contract, but was not entitled to an injunction. Do you agree that an injunction was not a proper remedy in this case? Why or why not? (*Madison Square Garden, Inc., v. Carnera*, 52 F.2d 47, 1931.)

Chapter 11

THE AGREEMENT

The first and foremost element of any contract is an agreement—a reasonably definite understanding between two or more persons. It is for this reason that the liability or obligation resulting from the making of a contract (as distinguished from that imposed by the law of torts or the criminal law) is sometimes described as being "consensual" in nature.

The usual view taken by the law today is that if two or more persons, expressly or by implication, have reached a reasonably clear agreement as to what each party is to do, then that agreement shall be enforceable by the courts (assuming, of course, that the additional elements of consideration and legality are also present).[1] This means that if either party refuses to perform his or her part of the agreement without a lawful excuse, the other party is entitled to recover damages in a breach of contract action. On the other hand, if it is found that a legally sufficient agreement has *not* been formed, neither party has contractual liability to the other. In the latter situation, if a breach of contract action were brought by one party against the other based on the latter's refusal to perform, the court can dismiss the action without concerning itself about other contractual questions that may otherwise have been raised.

Because the word *agreement* encompasses a broad spectrum of situations where some kind of understanding has been reached (ranging from the extremely concise to the hopelessly vague), the courts are faced with the problem of deciding just what kinds of agreements are sufficiently definite to warrant judicial relief if they are breached. The universal approach to this problem is to break the agreement down into two parts—the offer and the acceptance. The inquiries then become whether either party made an *offer* to the other, and, if so, whether the offer was followed by an *acceptance.* Before considering the legal definitions of these terms, we will briefly mention the rules used by the courts to ascertain the intentions of the parties—with emphasis upon the applicability of these rules to the offer and acceptance.

INTENTION OF THE PARTIES

In cases where the parties disagree as to whether their communications constituted an offer and an acceptance, the court will frequently emphasize the principle that the *intention of the parties* is controlling. If the court finds that their intentions were the same (that there was a "meeting of minds," as it is sometimes phrased), then there is a contract.

One caution about this principle, however, should be noted. When the courts view the parties' communications for the purpose of determining whether their intentions were one and the same, it is the parties' *manifested* (or apparent) intentions that control, rather than their actual intentions.[2] For example, if X writes a letter to Y containing a proposal which meets the legal requirements of an offer, and if Y promptly accepts the offer in a return letter, there is a contract—even if X later claims to have had some mental reservations about the proposal, or says that he really did not intend his letter to be an offer. Thus when it is said that there must be a *meeting of minds* to have a contract, this means that there must only be a legal, or apparent, meeting of minds.

There are two compelling reasons for this view:

1. It is virtually impossible for a court to determine what a person's actual intent was at a specific moment.

---

[1] Surprisingly, this has not always been the case. Several centuries ago, the English courts would not enforce agreements (even though the intentions of the parties were quite clear) unless the most rigid formalities had been adhered to—which included not only reducing the agreement to writing but affixing the parties' seals to the document. (See Chapter 12 for a discussion of consideration and Chapter 13 for one of legality.)

[2] A person's manifested or apparent intent is frequently referred to by the courts as "objective" intent, while actual or secret intent is called "subjective" intent. Thus the test used by the courts that is described here is referred to as the "objective test."

2. It would be unfair to allow someone to indicate a particular intention to another person and then to come into court and claim that he or she did not mean what was apparently meant.

REQUIREMENTS OF THE OFFER

Inherent in the many definitions of the word **offer** is the idea that it is a proposal made by one person, called the offeror, to another, the offeree, indicating what the offeror will give in return for a specified promise or act on the part of the offeree. That is, the offeror must manifest a willingness to enter into a "contractual relationship" with the other party. Sometimes the manifestation is referred to as a "conditional statement" of what the offeror will do for the offeree. Used in this manner, the term *statement* is broad enough to include both *words* and *conduct* by which the offeror indicates a willingness to contract. Thus, if a person in a drugstore shows a magazine to the cashier and deposits $2.50 (the stated price) on the counter, it is perfectly clear that he or she has made an *offer to purchase* the item without speaking a word. Similarly, when a company delivers an unordered article of merchandise under circumstances which indicate to the recipient that a charge will be made for the article if it is accepted, the company's act constitutes an *offer to sell* the product at the stated price. Of course, the recipient of such unsolicited merchandise does not incur a duty to pay for it unless he or she actually uses it or otherwise indicates acceptance of the sender's offer.[3]

---

[3] If the unsolicited goods are sent *by mail,* ordinarily no duty to pay arises even if the recipient uses the goods. Sec. 3009 of Title 39 of the U.S. Code, the Postal Reorganization Act of 1970, provides in part that, except for "merchandise mailed by a charitable organization soliciting contributions," the mailing of any unsolicited merchandise "may be treated as a gift by the recipient, who shall have the right to retain, use, discard, or dispose of it in any manner he sees fit without any obligations whatsoever to the sender."

The courts have never tried to specify the exact language or the particular kinds of conduct that must exist in order for one person to make an offer to another, for any attempt to do so would be quite unrealistic in the "real world." What the courts have done, instead, is to formulate several general requirements that must be met in order for a particular communication (or act) to achieve the legal status of an offer. These requirements are (1) a manifestation of an intent to contract; (2) a reasonably definite indication of what the offeror and the offeree are to do; and (3) a communication of the proposal to the intended offeree.

The Intent to Contract

Some language is so tentative or exploratory in nature that it should be apparent that an immediate contract is not contemplated. Such communications do not constitute offers; they are designated **preliminary negotiations,** or "dickering." For example, the statement "I'd like to get $4,000 for this car" would normally fall into this category, as would a letter indicating "I will not sell my home for less than $56,000." If the addressee in either of these instances were to reply, "I accept your offer," a contract would not result since no offer was made in either case. Along similar lines, it is usually held that requests for information—called inquiries—do not manifest a genuine intent to contract, and consequently such questions do not constitute offers in most circumstances. Thus, if A writes B, "Would you rent your summer home for the month of June for $900?" and B replies, "Yes, I accept your offer," there is no contract. (The most that can be said in this situation is that B has now made an offer to A, and it will ripen into a contract only if A subsequently accepts it.)

The decision in the well-known case below helps show how the courts try to draw the lines between preliminary negotiations and offers in several common situations.

Richards v. Flowers et al.
District Court of Appeal, California, 14 Cal. Reptr. 228 (1961)

Mrs. Richards, plaintiff, wrote defendant Flowers on January 15, 1959, as follows: "We would be interested in buying your lot on Gravatt Drive in Oakland, California, if we can deal with you directly and not run through a realtor. If you are interested, please advise us by return mail the cash price you would expect to receive."

On January 19, 1959, Flowers replied: "Thank you for your inquiry regarding my lot on Gravatt Drive. As long as your offer would be in cash I see no reason why we could not deal directly on this matter. . . . Considering what I paid for the lot, and the taxes which I have paid I expect to receive $4,500 for this property. Please let me know what you decide."

On January 25, 1959, Mrs. Richards sent the following telegram to Flowers: "Have agreed to buy your lot on your terms will handle transactions through local title company who will contact you would greatly appreciate your sending us a copy of the contour map you referred to in your letter as we are desirous of building at once. . . ."

On February 5, 1959, Flowers entered into an agreement to sell the property to a third party, Mr. and Mrs. Sutton. Mrs. Richards, after learning of the Sutton transaction, called upon defendant to deliver his deed to her, claiming the above correspondence constituted a contract between him and her. Flowers refused to do so, denying that his letter of January 19 constituted an offer to sell, whereupon Mr. and Mrs. Richards commenced action, asking for specific performance of the alleged contract. (The Suttons intervened in this action to protect their interest by supporting Flowers' contention that a contract was not formed between him and plaintiffs.)

The trial court ruled that defendant's letter of January 19 did constitute an offer to sell, but it further ruled that plaintiff's telegram of January 25 was not a valid acceptance under a particular section of the California Code known as the "statute of frauds" (the provisions of which are not necessary to our consideration of this case). Accordingly the court entered judgment for the defendant. The Richardses appealed.

Shoemaker, Justice:

. . . Under the factual situation in the instant case, the interpretation of the series of communications between the parties is a matter of law and an appellate court is not bound by the trial court's determination. Respondent Flowers argues that the letter of January 19th merely invited an offer from appellants for the purchase of the property and that under no reasonable interpretation can this letter be construed as an offer. We agree with the respondent. Careful consideration of the letter does not convince us that the language therein used can reasonably be interpreted as a definite offer to sell the property to appellants. As pointed out in *Restatement of the Law, Contracts,* Section 25, comment a: "It is often difficult to draw an exact line between offers and negotiations preliminary thereto. It is common for one who wishes to make a bargain to try to induce the other party to the intended transaction to make the definite offer, he himself suggesting with more or less definiteness the nature of the contract he is willing to enter into. . . ." Under this approach, our letter seems rather clearly to fall within the category of mere preliminary negotiations. Particularly is this true in view of the fact that the letter was written directly in response to appellants' letter inquiring if they could deal directly with respondent and requesting him to suggest a sum at which he might be willing to sell. From the record, we do not accept the argument that respondent Flowers made a binding offer to sell the property merely because he chose to answer certain inquiries by the appellants. Further, the letter appears to us inconsistent with any intent on his part to make an offer to sell. In response to appellants' question, respondent stated that he would be willing to deal directly with them rather than through a realtor as long as their "offer would be in cash." We take this language to indicate that respondent anticipated a *future offer* from appellants but was making no offer himself. [Emphasis added.]

Appellants refer to the phrase that he would "expect to receive" $4,500 and contend this constitutes an offer to sell to them at this price. However, respondent was only expressing an indication of the lowest price which he was presently willing to consider. Particularly is this true inasmuch as respondent wrote only in response to an inquiry in which this wording was used. We conclude that respondent by his communication confined himself to answering the inquiries raised by appellants, but did not extend himself further and did not make an express offer to sell the property. We have before us a case involving a mere quotation of price and not an offer to sell at that price.

The cause, therefore, comes within the rule announced in such authorities as *Nebraska Seed Co. v. Harsh,* 1915, 152 N.W. 310, wherein the seller had written the buyer, enclosing a sample of millet seed and saying, "I want $2.25 per cwt. for this seed f.o.b. Lowell." The buyer telegraphed his acceptance. The court, in reversing a judgment for plaintiff buyer, stated: "In our opinion the letter of defendant cannot be fairly construed into an offer to sell to the plaintiff. After describing the seed, the writer says, 'I want $2.25 per cwt. for this seed f.o.b. Lowell.' He does not say, 'I offer to sell to you.' The language used is general, . . . and is not an offer by which he may be bound, if accepted, by any or all of the persons addressed"; and *Owen v. Tunison,* 1932, 158 A. 926, wherein the buyer had written the seller inquiring whether he would be willing to sell certain store property for $6,000. The seller replied: "Because of improvements which have been added and an expenditure of several thousand dollars it would not be possible for me to sell it unless I was to receive $16,000.00 cash. . . ." The court, in holding that the seller's reply did not constitute an offer, stated: "Defendant's letter . . . may have been written with the intent to open negotiations that might lead to a sale. It was not a proposal to sell." It would thus seem clear that respondent's quotation of the price which he would "expect to receive" cannot be viewed as an offer capable of acceptance. . . .

Since there was never an offer, hence never a contract between respondent Flowers and appellants, the judgment must be affirmed, and it becomes unnecessary to determine whether an appellant's purported acceptance complied with the statute of frauds or whether appellants failed to qualify for specific performance in any other regard.

Judgment affirmed.

Preliminary Negotiations: The descriptions of goods in *mail-order catalogues* are almost universally held by the courts to be preliminary negotiations rather than offers, even though the goods are described in detail and a specific price is set for each article. The same view is usually taken of *price quotations* that companies send out to their customers. Therefore, when one orders goods from a catalogue or in response to a quotation, the order does not constitute an acceptance. The placing of the order is instead an *offer to purchase* made by the buyer, which the firm may accept or reject as it pleases.

Advertisements: Advertisements are also usually considered to be preliminary negotiations, rather than offers to sell. The widely accepted general rule is that a store advertisement that merely names the company, describes the article to be sold, and gives the price of the article "constitutes nothing more than an invitation to patronize the store." And this is usually true even if the terms "offer" or "special offer" appear in the advertisement. (The historic rationale for the rule is based (1) on the fact that most advertisements are silent on other material matters, such as the available quantity and credit terms, and (2) on the traditional principle that sellers of goods have the right to choose the parties with whom they deal.) Thus, because the vast majority of advertisements fall within the general rule, a contract is normally *not* formed when a purchaser goes to the advertiser's store

and requests that an article be sold at the advertised price. Under this rule, such a request is an *offer to purchase* rather than an acceptance, which the advertiser may either accept or reject.[4]

Advertising Statutes: In an effort to limit abuses of the common-law rule by unscrupulous advertisers, virtually all states have enacted **advertising statutes** which generally provide for the imposition of civil or criminal liability upon businesspersons who refuse to sell goods or services in conformity with the terms of their advertisements. The usual provision of this type is found in the various state statutes which list a number of *deceptive trade practices,* among which is the "advertising of goods or services with the intent not to sell them as advertised." Under such a statute, the advertiser who refuses to sell on the terms of the advertisement thus runs the risk that a civil action for damages will be brought against him or her by the disappointed customer. Other states have special

---

[4] In the interest of accuracy, it should be noted that there are occasional decisions in which advertisements *have* been held to constitute offers. Most (but not all) of these exceptional cases involve advertisements containing unique statements from which the courts have inferred a genuine intent to contract on the part of the advertiser. (*Lefkowitz v. Great Minneapolis Surplus Store, Inc.*, 86 N.W.2d 689, 1957, is one such case.) Additionally, advertisements promising *rewards for information* leading to the apprehension of persons who have committed crimes are almost universally held to constitute offers; these decisions apparently are based on grounds of broad public policy.

"bait advertising" statutes which typically impose civil and criminal misdemeanor liability upon such advertisers. And in a few states such refusals to sell are covered by "false and misleading advertising" statutes (although generally such statutes simply prohibit the making of false or deceptive statements in advertisements about the goods or services that the advertiser is trying to sell).

Auctions: The placing of goods for sale at an *ordinary auction* does not constitute an offer to sell, and for this reason there is no obligation on the owner to sell the goods to the person who has made the highest bid—or to sell them at all. The bids of the prospective buyers are actually the offers; thus a particular bid does not ripen into a contract until it is accepted by the auctioneer, who is representing the owner. (A different situation is presented at auctions that have been announced as being "without reserve." In such instances the goods must be sold to the highest bidder.)

Up to this point, we have seen that the courts lay great stress on the actual language of a particular communication in determining whether it exhibited an intent to contract. Another factor the courts often have to consider is the background—the surrounding circumstances—in which the communication was made. Examination of the background sometimes makes it quite clear that an intent to contract was not present, even though the language taken by itself meets the requirements of an offer (as, for example, a statement made in jest or in anger).[5] Of course, it is always possible that a statement will actually

be made in jest (or in anger) under circumstances where this fact is *not* apparent to the offeree. Such a statement constitutes a valid offer and—if accepted—will impose contractual liability on the person making it.

Reasonable Definiteness

The requirement that the offer be *reasonably definite* is largely a practical one. The terms of an agreement have to be definite enough that a court can determine whether both parties lived up to their promises, in the event that a question of breach of contract arises. If the offer is too indefinite, the court is unable to do this.

As a general rule, then, a communication must cover *all major matters* affecting the proposed transaction in order to constitute an offer. If one or more of these is missing, the communication is merely a preliminary negotiation. Thus if S makes a written proposal to sell his farm Blackacre to B upon specified terms and conditions, "at a mutually agreeable price," and if B promptly sends an acceptance, there is no contract for the reason that S's proposal was not an offer. In a similar case, a company told an injured employee that it would "take care of him" and offer him "light work" when his doctor certified that he was capable of doing such a job. The company later refused to rehire him, and he sued to recover damages, alleging that this was a breach of contract. In ruling against the employee, the court said that since no specific position was mentioned, and there was no discussion of rates of pay or hours of employment, it had no way of determining the amount of the employee's loss. The statement of the company, in other words, was held to be too indefinite to constitute an offer.[6] Similarly, if X writes Y, "I will sell you my car for $1,000, credit terms to be arranged," and Y replies, "I accept," there is no contract. X's statement does not constitute an offer, since there is no way of knowing what

---

[5] A classic illustration is the case in which a $15 harness was stolen. The owner became angry, swore, and during the tirade made the statement that he would "give $100 to any man who will find out who the thief is." One of the persons who was present later gave the requested information and brought suit to recover the money, on the grounds that a contract had been formed. The higher court did not allow recovery, ruling that the quoted statement was not an offer under the circumstances. It was, instead, merely an "extravagant exclamation of an excited man." (*Higgins v. Lessig,* 49 Ill. App. 459, 1893.)

---

[6] *Laseter v. Pet Dairy Products Company,* 246 F.2d 747 (1957).

credit terms would be acceptable to her or whether any credit terms will ever be agreed on.

Despite the foregoing, the requirement of "reasonable definiteness" is, as the term itself indicates, relative rather than absolute. Thus it is not necessary that every detail be set forth in a contract, so long as there is agreement on major points. Where there is such agreement, missing terms about routine or mechanical matters may be supplied by the courts to "save" the contract;

they may say in regard to such matters that there was *implied agreement.* For example, if X agrees to do certain clean-up work around a construction site for Y for $1,000, neither party can successfully contend that the agreement was too vague simply because no time of performance was specified. In this situation, it is implied that X will have a reasonable time in which to perform.

The case below presents a typical "definiteness" problem in a modern-day setting.

Pyeatte v. Pyeatte
Court of Appeals of Arizona, Division 1, 661 P.2d 196 (1983)

Charles Pyeatte and Margrethe May Pyeatte were married in Tucson, Arizona, in 1972. At the time of the marriage both had received bachelor's degrees. In early 1974 the couple reached an agreement concerning postgraduate education for both of them. The undisputed terms of the agreement were, in Mrs. Pyeatte's words, that she "would put him through three years of law school without his having to work, and when he finished he would put me through my master's degree without my having to work."

Thereafter she supported herself and her husband while he attended law school in Tucson. After his graduation Charles went to work for a law firm in Prescott, Arizona. Because they realized that his salary would not at that time be sufficient to support the marriage and pay for her graduate work simultaneously, she agreed to defer her plans for "a year or two" (during which time she obtained part-time employment as a teacher).

In April, 1978, Charles told Margrethe he no longer wanted to be married, and in June she filed a petition for dissolution of the marriage. During the dissolution proceedings the trial court ruled that the above agreement constituted a reasonably definite and enforceable contract, and found that she had fully performed her part of the contract. The court also found that her husband had not performed his part of the contract, and that she had been damaged as a result of this failure to perform. Thus the court, in addition to granting a decree of dissolution, entered a judgment of $23,000 against Charles on the breach of contract theory (that amount based upon estimates of what her costs of obtaining a master's degree would be). Charles appealed this judgment.

On appeal, the primary questions were (1) whether the trial court was correct in ruling the agreement to be a valid contract, and (2) if

not, whether the award of damages should be, nonetheless, affirmed "as an equitable award of restitution on the basis of unjust enrichment" (on the quasi-contract theory).

Corcoran, Judge:

. . . Although the terms and requirements of an enforceable contract need not be stated in minute detail, it is fundamental that, in order to be binding, an agreement must be definite and certain so that the liability of the parties may be exactly fixed. Terms necessary for the required definiteness frequently include time of performance, place of performance, price or compensation, penalty provisions, and other material requirements of the agreement. . . .

Upon examining the parties' agreement in this instance, *it is readily apparent that a sufficient mutual understanding regarding critical provisions of their agreement did not exist.* [Emphasis added.] For example, no agreement was made regarding the time when appellee [Margrethe] would attend graduate school and appellant [Charles] would be required to assume their full support. Both parties concede that appellee could not have begun her master's program immediately after appellant's graduation because his beginning salary was not sufficient to provide both for her education and the couple's support. Appellee told appellant she was willing to wait a year or two until he "got on his feet" before starting her program. Nothing more definite than that was ever agreed upon. Furthermore, although appellee agreed to support appellant while he attended law school for three years, no corresponding time limitation was placed upon her within which to finish her education. Even if we assume that the agreement contemplated appellee's enrolling as a full-time student, the length of time necessary to complete a master's degree varies considerably depending upon the requirements of the particular program and the number of classes an individual elects to take at one time. Such a loosely worded agreement can hardly be said to have fixed appellant's liability with certainty.

The agreement lacks a number of other essential terms which prevent it from becoming binding. Appellee's place of education is not mentioned at all, yet there are master's programs available throughout the country. . . . Nor was there any agreement concerning the cost of the program to which appellee would be entitled under this agreement. There can be several thousand dollars' difference in tuition, fees, and other expenses between any two master's programs, depending upon resident status, public versus private institutions, and other factors. Appellant testified that at the time of the "contract" neither he nor his wife had any idea as to the specific dollar amounts that would be involved. . . .

We are aware of [the general legal concept that] contracts should be interpreted . . . in such a way as to uphold the contract [whenever possible]. The court's function, however, cannot be that of contract maker. Nor can the court create a contract simply to accomplish a purportedly good purpose. . . .

[After ruling that the trial court's award of damages on the breach of contract theory was erroneous, the court turned to appellee's claim based on quasi-contract as follows:] Appellee's last contention is that the trial court's award should be affirmed as an equitable award of restitution on the basis of unjust enrichment. She argues that appellant's education, which she subsidized and which he obtained through the exhaustion of community assets constitutes a benefit for which, in equity, he must make restitution.

[The court then ruled that the imposition of a quasi-contractual obligation against one spouse in favor of the other was not contrary to public policy, and continued:] The record shows that the appellee conferred benefits on appellant—financial subsidization of appellant's legal education—with . . . the expectation that she would be compensated therefor by his reciprocal efforts after his graduation and admission to the Bar. Appellant has left the marriage with the only valuable asset acquired during the marriage—his legal education and qualification to practice law. It would be inequitable to allow appellant to retain this benefit without making restitution to appellee. . . .

[The court then reversed the trial court's judgment, and remanded the case to that court for the purpose of determining the amount of recovery that appellee was entitled to, "the amount of the unjust enrichment." In order to determine that amount, the higher court instructed the trial court that "the award to appellee should be limited to the financial contribution by appellee for appellant's living expenses and direct educational expenses," whatever those expenses are found to be.]

Comment: In a number of states, the ex-spouse's recovery is determined by statute. For example, in *O'Brien v. O'Brien,* 489 N.E.2d 712 (1985), the New York Court of Appeals held that a professional license held by the defendant spouse (the right to practice medicine, in this instance) constituted "marital property" under the state's Domestic Relations Law, the value of which must be considered by a court in making an equitable distribution of the spouses' property. In such states the ex-spouse's recovery does not depend upon proof of an express or implied contract, or upon quasi-contract principles.

The Contract Law–Sales Law Relationship

In the transitional note preceding Part II, we noted that most contracts are governed by *contract law*—the common-law principles we are studying here. It was also noted, however, that an important class of contracts—sales contracts—are governed by *sales law,* which is essentially made up of the 100-odd sections that constitute Article 2 of the UCC. (Sales contracts are contracts calling for the sale of goods—tangible, movable property such as articles of clothing, automobiles, diesel oil and cold rolled steel sheets). Sales law is thus a statutory subject.

The great bulk of the provisions of Article 2 are designed to cover special problems relating to sales transactions, and these are examined in Chapters 20–23 in Part IV of this text. A number of the provisions of Article 2, however, contain rules applicable to the formation of sales contracts, and a few of these vary from (or are contrary to) the common-law principles that continue to apply to contracts generally. The section of Article 2 discussed below, Sec. 2-204, is one of these, and it is thus the first of a limited number of detours into the law of sales that will be made in Part II.

Definiteness of the Agreement: Sales Law

Among the most significant modifications of the common law achieved by the UCC is a general relaxation of the degree of definiteness required in the agreement. Several provisions indicate that the drafters of the UCC wanted to make the formation of binding contracts somewhat easier than under common law. They recognized that businesspersons frequently intend to enter into enforceable agreements in situations where it is impracticable to make those agreements as definite as required by common law.

A prime example of this approach is found in Sec. 2-204(3). This section broadly states that a sales contract is enforceable even if one or more terms are left open, so long as (1) the court feels that the parties *intended to make a binding contract* and (2) the agreement and the surrounding circumstances give the court a *reasonably certain basis for granting an appropriate remedy* (such as money damages). Of course, there is a line beyond which the courts will not go. For instance, the larger the number of undecided terms, the less likely it is that a court will find that the parties intended to be legally bound. For this reason, a seller and buyer who wish to make an agreement with one or more terms left for future determination would do well to state specifically whether they intend to be bound in the meantime.

In addition to Sec. 2-204, a number of other sections of the UCC deal with specific omissions or ambiguities often occurring in sales contracts. We will examine the most important of these "gap-fillers" here.

Open Price Provisions: In some circumstances a seller of goods may be primarily concerned with being assured of a market for the goods he or she is producing. Or perhaps a buyer wants a guaranteed supply of certain needed products. In either case, price may be of only secondary importance. Thus buyer and seller might draw up a contract for the sale and purchase of goods at a later date, with the contract providing that the price shall be agreed upon later. Or the contract may say nothing about price at all. (Open price terms may be especially desirable in a market where the going price is subject to daily or weekly fluctuation.)

At common law many courts refused to enforce either type of agreement because of its indefiniteness. Under Sec. 2-305 of the UCC, however, agreements of this nature are now enforceable if the court feels that the parties did intend to be bound by them. (Of course, if the evidence indicates that the agreement was merely tentative and the parties intended to be legally bound only if and when the price was ultimately set, there is no contract until that condition is met. The UCC cannot supply missing contractual intent.)

Whenever a court is called upon to enforce a contract in which the price (for one reason or another) was never actually set, and where it finds that the parties intended to be bound by the open price agreement, the court is faced with the task of providing a price term. Sec. 2-305 establishes a number of principles to guide the court in such a situation.

1. If the parties had expressly left the price *for later agreement* and then failed to agree, the price set by the court should be a "reasonable price at the time for delivery."

2. If the agreement had said *nothing at all about price,* and the price was never settled on, the method of determining it should depend on the circumstances. If the price had failed to be set through no fault of either party, the court should fix a "reasonable price at the time for delivery," as in item 1. But if the failure to set a price was caused by the fault of either party, the party not at fault can either treat the contract as cancelled or fix a "reasonable price" himself or herself. This price is binding and the court will uphold it, so long as it is found to be actually reasonable.

3. If the agreement had provided that the price was to be subsequently fixed *according to a definite standard set or recorded by a third party,* the rules for determining the unresolved price are exactly as they were in item 2. For example, the parties might have agreed that the contract price was to be the market price reported in a certain trade journal on a given date, but no such price was reported in the journal on that date. Or they might have agreed that an impartial third person was to set the price at a future date, but the third party later failed to do so. In either case, the price will be a "reasonable price at the time for delivery." This reasonable price will be set by the court if neither party was at fault; if one party caused the agreed upon method to fail, the other party may set a reasonable price.

4. If the parties had agreed that *one of them was to set the price* at a later time, the deciding party is obligated to set the price in good faith. Although *good faith* is defined differently for merchants and nonmerchants, the most compelling evidence of good or bad faith generally is whether the price fixed was a reasonable market price at that time.[7] If the party responsible for setting the price fails to do so or if he or she fixes a price in bad faith, the other party can either treat the contract as cancelled or set a reasonable price.

Open Time Provisions: The absence of a time provision does not cause a sales contract to be unenforceable. Sec. 2-309 states that, where a contract calls for some type of action by the *seller* (such as shipment or delivery) but does not specify the time for such action, a court may infer a "reasonable time" for performance. Of

applies to seller – selling date

---

[7] *Good faith* is generally defined in Sec. 1-201(19) of the UCC as "honesty in fact." In the case of a merchant, it is defined in Sec. 2-103(1)(b) as "honesty in fact *and* the observance of reasonable commercial standards of fair dealing in the trade." (Emphasis added.) Generally, the merchant definition will prevail, since open price terms are rare among nonmerchants.

course, a reasonable time in a given case depends on all the circumstances known to the parties. For instance, suppose that the parties did not set a specific time for delivery but that the seller knew the reason for the buyer's purchase and the use to which the buyer intended to put the goods. A reasonable time for delivery would certainly be soon enough for the buyer to put the goods to their intended use. (Similarly, contracts that are silent as to the time of the *buyer's* performance—that is, the time of payment—are governed by the rules of Sec. 2-310.)

pymt date
applies to Buyer

Open Delivery Provisions: A sales contract may also be enforceable even if certain delivery terms are to be decided at a later time. (We have already discussed the absence of a *delivery time.*) Another delivery term that might be absent is a provision for the *place of delivery.* Where the parties have not included this provision in their contract, Sec. 2-308 sets forth the following rules to serve as "gap-fillers."

1. The goods should be delivered to the buyer at the *seller's place of business.*

2. If the seller has no place of business, they should be delivered to the buyer at the *seller's residence.*

3. Where the contract refers to specifically identified goods, and both parties knew when making the contract that the goods were located at *some other place,* that place is where delivery should be made.

The UCC also attempts to account for other omitted details relating to delivery. For example, if the agreement contemplates shipping the goods but does not mention *shipping arrangements,* the seller has the right under Sec. 2-311 to specify these arrangements. (His or her actions are subject only to the limitation that they be in good faith and within limits set by commercial reasonableness). Another example is the situation where the contract fails to indicate whether the goods are to be delivered *all at once, or in several lots.* In such a case Sec. 2-307 obligates the seller to deliver them all at one time. However, there is one exception to this duty. If both parties, when making the contract, know that the circumstances are such that delivery in a single lot is not practicable, then the seller can deliver in several lots. (This would apply, for instance, to a situation where the quantity involved is so large that both parties realize that a single shipment is not feasible).

Open Payment Provisions: The foregoing discussion focuses on those provisions of the UCC which spell out the *seller's* obligations (as to points on which the contract is silent). Turning to the obligations of the *buyer,* his or her obligations are (1) to accept the goods (assuming they conform to the contract) and (2) to pay for them according to the terms of the contract. For example, the contract may grant a specific period of credit to the buyer; in such a case, of course, the seller cannot demand payment until the period has expired. As to contracts that are silent as to the time of payment, Sec. 2-310 fills such gap by providing, in general, that the buyer must pay for the goods at the time they are delivered. (In such cases, however, the buyer generally has the *right to inspect* the goods before making the payment—unless the contract provides otherwise—as in a cash on delivery (COD) contract.)[8]

Communication of the Offer

Returning to the subject of contract law (i.e., the common-law principles applicable to the formation of contracts), it is a primary rule that an offer has no effect until it has legally reached the offeree. This requirement of **communication** is based on the obvious proposition that an offeree cannot agree to a proposal before knowing about it. To illustrate: A city council, via a public advertisement, offers to pay $200 to the person or persons who apprehend an escaped criminal. If X captures the fugitive on his farm, only to learn of the offer later, his act does not

constitute an acceptance of the offer and he is not entitled to the reward under the principles of contract law. The relatively few cases that involve this kind of fact-pattern generally follow this view.[9]

The principle takes on broader scope—and is more difficult to apply—in situations where there has been clear-cut communication of some terms of the agreement but questionable communication of others. The so-called fine print cases illustrate the problem. For example, statements printed on the back of parking lot tickets frequently provide that "the company shall not be liable for loss of, or injury to, the automobile, regardless of cause," or words of similar import. The usual view is that such provisions have not been legally communicated to the owner of the car and that the owner is not bound by them unless they were actually brought to his or her attention when the contract was made.

One should not conclude, however, that an *actual* communication of terms is required in all cases. If a court feels that the offeror has made a reasonable effort, under the circumstances, to call the terms of the offer to the offeree's attention, then a legal communication has occurred. A subsequent acceptance of the offer would be binding on the offeree in such a case, even though he or she might not have been aware of all its terms.

The case of *Green's Executors v. Smith,* 131 S.E. 846 (1926) is particularly instructive. In that case Smith sent a folder to each of his garage patrons, which indicated on the cover, in large type, that "new storage rates" would be effective at a future date. Inside the folder various rates were set forth, followed by a "note" which provided, in effect, that commencing with the new rates, patrons would also accept all liability for injuries caused by Smith's drivers while taking the cars to and from patrons' homes. Subsequent litigation raised the question whether patrons

---

[8] The buyer's obligations, and the right of inspection, are discussed further in Chapter 23.

[9] There are exceptions, however, where recovery has been allowed on noncontract grounds (for example, public policy, inherent fairness, and the like).

were bound by the note even if they had not read it. The court held that they were not. Quoting from an earlier decision, the court said: "When an offer contains various terms, some of which do not appear on the face of the offer, the question whether the acceptor is bound by the terms depends on the circumstances. . . . The question arises when a person accepts a railroad or steamboat ticket, bill of lading, warehouse receipt, or other document containing conditions. *He is bound* by all the conditions whether he reads them or not *if he knows that the document contains conditions.* But he is *not bound* by conditions of which he is ignorant . . . *unless he knows that the writing contains terms or unless he ought to know that it*

contains terms, by reason of previous dealings, or by reason of the form, size, or character of the document." (Emphasis supplied by the court.) The court continued: "There was nothing on the face of the folder, nor in its form or character, to indicate that it contained [a liability change]. The paper only purported to contain a schedule of rates for services at plaintiff's garage, and defendant had no reason, on account of her previous dealings with plaintiff or otherwise, to know that plaintiff proposed . . . a new contract of such unusual terms."

The case below presents a communication of the offer problem in a much more modern setting.

Newman v. Schiff
U.S. Court of Appeals for the 8th Circuit, 778 F.2d 460 (1985)

Irwin Schiff, defendant, is a self-styled "tax rebel" who has made a career (and substantial profits) out of his tax protest activities. On February 7, 1983, Schiff appeared on CBS News Nightwatch in New York, a program with a viewer participation format. During the program he repeated his long-standing position that "there is nothing in the Internal Revenue Code which I have here, which says anybody is legally required to pay the (federal income) tax." After a number of viewers called in questioning this position, Schiff stated on the air: "If anybody calls this show—I have the Code—and cites any section of this Code that says an individual is required to file a tax return, I will pay them $100,000." A two-minute segment of the program, in which the reward proposal was made, was rebroadcast early the next day on the CBS Morning News.

Newman, plaintiff, is a St. Louis lawyer who saw the rebroadcast (but not the original broadcast). On February 9, a day after viewing the rebroadcast, Newman called the CBS Morning News and cited six sections of the Internal Revenue Code as authority for his position that individuals *are* legally required to pay federal income taxes. The same day he wrote a letter to CBS Morning News citing the same sections, and stated that the letter represented "performance of the consideration requested by Mr. Schiff in exchange for his promise to pay $100,000."

Some additional correspondence ensued between CBS, Schiff, and

Newman, which culminated in a letter from Schiff to Newman dated April 20, 1983. In that letter Schiff said, in part, "I did make an offer on the February 7, 1983, news." However, he went on to say that Newman had not properly accepted the offer, and was thus not entitled to the money. Newman then brought this action in federal district court to recover damages for breach of contract.

The court entered judgment for Schiff, ruling (1) that Schiff's offer remained open only until the conclusion of the live broadcast; (2) that the rebroadcast did not renew the offer, and (3) that Newman's acceptance was "untimely" (i.e., too late to result in the formation of a contract). Upon reconsideration of the case at Newman's request, the court ruled, in essence, that the offer *was* renewed when Schiff learned of the rebroadcast "and failed to object to it." The court concluded, however, that Newman's response to the renewed offer still was untimely. (While the court did not give a reason for this conclusion, it was apparently on the theory that Newman's phone call of February 9 was not an acceptance because it was directed to CBS rather than to Schiff, the offeror). Accordingly, the court affirmed its original judgment that no contract was formed; Newman appealed.

Bright, Senior Circuit Judge:

. . . Newman contends that the district court applied the wrong standard in judging the timeliness of his response to the rebroadcast. We do not [need to decide that issue], however, because we conclude that the district court erred by ruling that Schiff renewed his Nightwatch offer [by failing to disavow] the CBS Morning News rebroadcast. Consequently, we affirm the judgment of the district court on grounds that Newman did not accept Schiff's *initial and only offer* that had been made on the Nightwatch program. [Emphasis added.] . . .

The present case concerns a special type of offer: an offer of a reward [if a particular act is performed]. At least since the time of Lilli Carlill's unfortunate experience with the Carbolic Smoke Ball, courts have enforced public offers to pay rewards [if the offers have been legally communicated to the claimants]. . . . In that case, frequently excerpted and discussed in student law books, the Carbolic Smoke Ball Company advertised that it would pay a "100 £ reward" to anyone who contracted "the increasing epidemic of influenza, colds, or any disease caused by taking cold, after having used the Carbolic Smoke Ball three times daily for two weeks according to the printed directions supplied with each ball." Ms. Carlill, relying upon this promise, purchased and used a Carbolic Smoke Ball. It did not, however, prevent her from catching the flu. The court held that the advertised reward constituted a valid offer which Ms. Carlill had accepted, thereby entitling her to recover. . .[a]

---

[a] *Carlill v. Carbolic Smoke Ball Co.*, 1 Q.B. 256 (1892).

[The court here ruled that the legal principle relied upon by the trial court to find that the offer was renewed was not applicable to contract law, and thus should not have been invoked by that court. The court continued]: Schiff may have [impliedly] authorized CBS's act of rebroadcasting an excerpt of his Nightwatch interview, yet this did not give the rebroadcast legal effect as a renewed offer. The rebroadcast itself was not an offer, only a news report. Schiff's subsequent conduct and letter do not convert it into an offer. [After thus distinguishing this case from *Carlill,* the court concluded by saying:]

Schiff's claim that there is nothing in the Internal Revenue Code that requires an individual to file a federal income return demands comment. The kindest thing that can be said about Schiff's promotion of this idea is that he is grossly mistaken, or a mere pretender to knowledge in income taxation. We have nothing but praise for Mr. Newman's efforts which have helped bring this to light. Section 6012 of the Internal Revenue Code . . . provides that individuals having a gross income in excess of a certain amount "shall" file tax returns for the taxable year. Thus section 6012 requires certain individuals to file tax returns. . . . The district court stated that Schiff's argument is "blatant nonsense," [a ruling that] Schiff did not challenge . . . in his cross-appeal.

We affirm the judgment of the district court for the reasons discussed above.

Although Newman has not "won" his lawsuit in the traditional sense of recovering a reward that he sought, he has accomplished an important goal in the public interest of unmasking the "blatant nonsense" dispensed by Schiff. For that he deserves great commendation by the public. Perhaps now CBS and other communication media who have given Schiff's mistaken views widespread publicity will give John Newman equal time in the public interest.

Affirmed.

Comment: While television commercials that advertise goods or services as a general rule do not constitute legal offers, advertisements promising the payment of rewards for the production of certain information—such as information leading to the arrest and conviction of a person responsible for a particular crime—*are* generally held to constitute legal offers (if legally communicated). Thus the view of both the trial and appellate court that the February 7 telecast was an offer is not in conflict with, and does not change, the general rule as to advertisements of goods and services.

TERMINATION OF THE OFFER

Because of the rule that an offer can be accepted at any time before it is legally terminated, it becomes necessary to see what events will cause the offer to die. The rules in this area of the law are rather mechanical in their operation, and we need touch upon them but briefly.

Termination by Act of the Parties

Most offers are terminated by the conduct of the parties themselves by (1) revocation, (2) rejection, or (3) lapse of time.

Revocation: A **revocation** is a withdrawal of the offer by the offeror. Like the offer itself, it is effective only when it has been communicated to the offeree. The mere mailing of a revocation, in other words, ordinarily does not terminate the offer.[10]

The ordinary offer can be revoked at any time—assuming, of course, that it is communicated to the offeree before an acceptance has occurred. This is generally true even if the offeror had promised to keep the offer open a certain length of time. Thus, if X makes an offer to Y, stating that the offer will remain open thirty days, X can revoke it the very next day if he wishes. While this may seem unfair to Y, the reason for this view lies in the fact that Y has not given "consideration" (something of value) in return for X's promise to keep the offer open.

There are two notable exceptions to the general rule that an offer may be revoked at any time prior to its acceptance.

The Option: In an option (or option contract, as it is frequently called) the offeree—either at the request of the offeror or acting on his or her own initiative—does give the offeror some consideration (usually a sum of money) in return for the offeror's promise to keep the offer open. Once the consideration is accepted by the offeror, the offer cannot be revoked during the specified period of time.

Sales Law—The Firm Offer: The general rule and exception noted above apply with equal force to sales transactions. However, the UCC has added a second exception to the general rule by creating another type of irrevocable offer, referred to in Sec. 2-205 as a **firm offer.**

The following requirements must exist for an offer to be irrevocable under this section:

1. It must be an offer to buy or sell goods.

2. It must be made *by* a merchant—though not necessarily *to* a merchant. That is, only the offeror need be a merchant.

3. It must be written and signed by the offeror.

4. It must give assurance that it will be held open.

If all these requirements are met, the offer is irrevocable even if the offeree gives no consideration for the assurance that it will remain open.

The period of time during which the offeror cannot revoke the offer is the time stated in the offer so long as it does not exceed three months. If the offer contains an assurance that it will be held open but mentions no time period, it will be irrevocable for a reasonable time, again not exceeding three months. (The three-month limitation applies only where the offeree is relying on Sec. 2-205 to make the offer irrevocable. If he or she gives *consideration* for the offeror's assurance that the offer will remain open, an *option* exists, and the three-month limitation does not apply.)

Rejection: A **rejection** occurs when the offeree notifies the offeror that he or she does not intend to accept. Like the offer and the revocation, it takes effect only when it has been communicated (in this case, to the offeror). Thus, if an offeree mails a letter of rejection but changes his or her mind and telephones an acceptance before the letter arrives, there is a contract.

One form of rejection is the **counteroffer**—a proposal made by the offeree to the offeror that differs in any material respect from the terms of the original offer. Thus, if the price stated in an offer is $500, and the offeree replies, "I'll pay $400," the original offer is ended forever. A recent case, *Thurmond v. Weiser,* 699 S.W.2d 680 (1985), provides a further illustration. There the owner of a small Texas farm offered to sell it for $260,000. The buyer made a counter-offer of $250,000, which was rejected by the seller. Several negotiations ensued, which ended with the buyer sending a written "acceptance" of the $260,000 offer. The owner refused to convey

---

[10] However, one state—California—provides by statute that a revocation is effective when "dispatched" (when mailed, in this case).

the land, and in subsequent litigation it was held that there was no contract. The court ruled (1) that the original offer to sell for $260,000 was terminated by the buyer's counteroffer of $250,000, and (2) that because the seller did not renew her offer of $260,000 during the negotiations following the counteroffer, there was no outstanding offer capable of being accepted by the buyer.

A response in which the offeree deletes a term from, or adds a term to, the terms of the offer also constitutes a counteroffer. In the preceding case, for example, if the buyer had replied to the original offer, "Accept offer of $260,000; assume highway commission's proposed plan to relocate road on north side will be abandoned," the offer is again terminated.

Lapse of Time: If revocation and rejection were the only recognized means of terminating offers, many offers would remain open forever. To prevent such an unworkable result, a third method of termination is recognized—termination by the *passage of a reasonable length of time.*[11] What is reasonable depends on the circumstances of each case; thus it is virtually impossible to formulate general rules in this area of law.

What we will do instead is list the circumstances or factors that the courts consider in reaching an answer in a given case.

1. A circumstance of particular importance is the language used in the offer. Obviously, if an offeror states, "I must hear from you very soon," the time within which the offeree must accept is somewhat shorter than if such language were not used.

2. Another important circumstance is the means of communication used by the offeror. Sending the offer by telegram normally imports an urgency that the use of the mails does not.[12]

3. Yet another factor of special importance is based upon prevailing market conditions. If the price of a commodity is fluctuating rapidly, for example, a reasonable time might elapse within hours from the time the offer is received.

4. A final factor to be taken into consideration is the method by which the parties have done business in the past.

An offer in some circumstances may thus lapse soon after it has been made, while in other circumstances it may remain open weeks or even months. While there are surprisingly few cases in this area of law, *Ward v. Board of Education,* 173 N.E. 634 (1930) is one of them. In that case Ina Ward received an offer of employment for the following school year on June 18, and she mailed her acceptance on July 5. In subsequent litigation, the higher court stated the applicable rule as follows: "It is a primary rule that a party contracting by mail, as she did, when no time limit is made for the acceptance of the contract, shall have a reasonable time, acting with due diligence, within which to accept." Applying that rule, where Ms. Ward had no explanation for her delay other than the fact that she was hoping to hear from another school board, the court held that the offer had lapsed prior to July 5 and there was, therefore, no contract.

Termination by Operation of Law

The rule that a revocation must be communicated to the offeree in order for it to take effect is based on the grounds of both fairness and logic. In ordinary circumstances, it seems reasonable that the offeree ought to be legally able to accept

---

[11] A different rule applies to offers in which the offeree is given a *specific* period, such as five days, in which to accept. In such offers, the lapse of the stated period terminates the offer.

[12] Some courts, for example, adopt the general rule that an offer made via telegram lapses at the close of business hours on the day it is received. (This rule is not applicable, obviously, to offers that by their language expressly or impliedly grant a longer period of time.)

any offer until he or she has been put on notice that the offer has been terminated.

Certain exceptional events, however, will terminate an offer automatically—without notice to the offeree. These events fall into three categories: (1) death or adjudication of insanity of either party, (2) destruction of the subject matter of the contract, and (3) intervening illegality. The termination of an offer by any of these events is said to occur *by operation of law.*

To illustrate: On September 10, B offers a specific TV set to W for $525. On September 13, B dies. If W mails a letter of acceptance on September 14, there is no contract even if W is unaware of B's death. In the same example the result would be identical if, instead of B's death on September 13, the TV set were destroyed that day through no fault of B's. As another example, X offers to loan $1,000 to Y for one year with interest at the rate of 20 percent. Before the offer is accepted, a state statute takes effect which limits the rate of interest on that particular type of loan to 14 percent. The offer is terminated automatically. Figure 11.1 summarizes these methods of termination.

The various events that automatically terminate *unaccepted offers* generally do not terminate *existing contracts* (except those calling for the rendering of personal services, which we will discuss in Chapter 17). Thus, in the first example, if B's offer of September 10 had been accepted by W *before* B's death on September 13, B's estate would remain bound by the obligation to deliver the TV set.[13]

By the same token, the various terminations by operation of law do not generally apply to options (or option contracts). Thus, if B had promised on September 10 to keep his offer open for ten days, and if W had given B a sum of

money in return for this promise, B's death on September 13 would *not* terminate the offer.

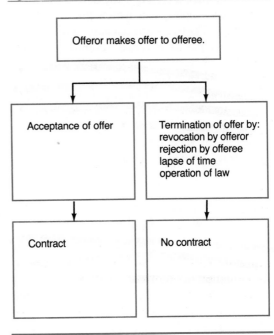

Figure 11.1   **Methods of Terminating an Offer**

PRELIMINARY CONSIDERATIONS OF THE ACCEPTANCE

An offer ripens into a contract if, and only if, it is accepted by the offeree. Remember that a bilateral offer is accepted by the offeree's making the return *promise* that the offeror has requested, while a unilateral offer is accepted only by the actual performance of the requested *act.*

In most situations the offeree's response to the offer is so clearly an acceptance or rejection of it that no misunderstanding between the parties arises. But in a few situations legal difficulties do crop up—as, for example, where the offeree "accepts" the offer but then adds new terms to it

---

[13] Whether the destruction of the TV on September 13 (instead of B's death) would free B's estate from the duty to deliver another set or would free W from the obligation to pay for the set is controlled by the law of sales, especially sections 2-509 and 2-613 of the Uniform Commercial Code. These sections are discussed in the sales chapters in Part IV.

or where the offeree's response is vague or indecisive. Another difficulty is the determination of the precise moment at which the acceptance becomes effective—specifically, whether the acceptance has to be actually communicated to the offeror before it becomes legally effective.

In the following discussion, emphasis is given to the acceptance of bilateral offers—those in which the offeror merely wants a return promise on the part of the offeree. Special problems raised by the acceptance of unilateral offers are considered later in the chapter.

REQUIREMENTS OF THE ACCEPTANCE

An acceptance is an expression on the part of the offeree by which he or she indicates a consent to be bound by the terms of the offer. Under general contract law, the acceptance must be a "mirror image" of the offer. Thus if a purported (intended) acceptance varies from the terms of the offer in any way—sometimes called a conditional acceptance—it ordinarily constitutes a counteroffer rather than an acceptance, as illustrated in Figure 11.2. (While an offeree usually states expressly that he or she is "accepting" the offer, it is not necessary that this particular term be used. Any language showing that the offeree is assenting to the proposal is sufficient.)

Regardless of the particular words used by the offeree in his or her response to the offer, the response must meet certain requirements in order to constitute an acceptance. Generally, an acceptance must be (1) unconditional, (2) unequivocal, and (3) legally communicated to the offeror or to the offeror's agent.

New Conditions

We have already seen that when an attempted acceptance changes the terms of the offer, it becomes a *counteroffer* and a rejection rather than an acceptance. The same is true when the attempted acceptance adds new terms or conditions to those of the offer.

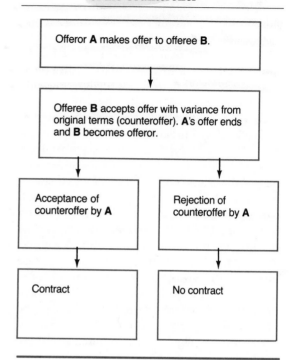

Figure 11.2 **Legal Ramifications of the Counteroffer**

Offeror **A** makes offer to offeree **B**.

Offeree **B** accepts offer with variance from original terms (counteroffer). **A**'s offer ends and **B** becomes offeror.

Acceptance of counteroffer by **A**

Rejection of counteroffer by **A**

Contract

No contract

Many times the changed or new terms are readily apparent—for example, where goods are offered at a price of $20 and the offeree replies that he will pay $15, or where the offeree replies, "I accept—deliver to Cody, Wyoming," when the offeror did not contemplate delivering the goods at all.

At other times the offeree's reply has to be scrutinized more carefully in order to determine its precise effect. To illustrate: Seller wrote Buyer, "I have about 80,000 feet of oak left yet, for which I will take $16 per M delivered on cars at Bridgewater 'log run.' I will take $8 per M for the mill culls I have at Bridgewater, as that is what it cost me, cut and deliver the same."

Buyer replied, in part, ". . . We will take your 4/4 oak at $16, mill culls out, delivered on cars at Bridgewater. We will handle all your mill culls, but not at the price you are asking. . . . We should be glad to handle yours at $4.50. . . . We will take the 80,000 feet and will depend on this. . . ."

Seller later refused to deliver either the lumber or the culls, contending that Buyer's reply did not constitute an acceptance. In ensuing litigation, the Supreme Court of North Carolina agreed with this contention.[14] In regard to the offer of the oak, the court held that Buyer's "acceptance" failed because of his addition of the

"4/4" dimension requirement—particularly where the evidence indicated that 4/4 oak was an entirely different article from that which Seller had on hand. (In regard to the mill culls, the court had no difficulty in holding that Buyer's response constituted a counteroffer because of the price discrepancy.)

The following case presents an intriguing situation in which both parties originally assumed, quite understandably, that an agreement had clearly been reached—until the sharp-eyed bus driver began to compare the language of the school board's "acceptance" with the language of his offer. At that point, the fun began.

_____

[14]*Morrison v. Parks*, 80 S.E. 85 (1913).

Lucier v. Town of Norfolk
Supreme Court of Errors of Connecticut, 122 A. 711 (1923)

Lucier, plaintiff, operated a school bus for the defendant town for the school years of 1915, 1916, 1918, and 1919. In the summer of 1920 plaintiff and defendant began negotiating a contract for the coming year.

After several communications between the parties, plaintiff was asked by the Norfolk Town School Committee to submit a bid covering the transportation of students for the 1920–1921 school year. On August 12, plaintiff submitted his bid, offering to provide transportation at "$175 per week each school week" for that year.

On August 17 the board passed the following resolution: "Voted to award the contract for transporting children to and from Gilbert school and to and from various points in town to Mr. E. A. Lucier for the sum of $35 per day." The next day, a member of the committee, one Stevens, told plaintiff that the board "had voted to award him the contract" and requested plaintiff to have his buses ready.

On the first day of school, September 7, plaintiff transported the students as agreed. On the evening of September 7 the board presented plaintiff with a formal contract for him to sign, the contract embodying the wording of the August 17 resolution. Plaintiff refused to sign the contract, on the ground that it was not in accordance with his bid for compensation at the rate of $175 per week, but at the rate of $35 per day instead. Thereupon defendant refused to employ plaintiff and awarded the transportation contract to a third party.

Plaintiff brought action to recover damages for breach of contract, alleging that a contract was formed on his terms and was breached by

defendant. (Specifically, plaintiff's argument was that his bid was accepted on August 18 when Stevens told him that the board "had voted to award him the contract.") Defendant contended that a contract was formed on *its* terms and that plaintiff was guilty of the breach. The trial court ruled that *no contract was formed in this situation* (but did award plaintiff $35 dollars, the reasonable value of his services performed on September 7). Plaintiff appealed.

Keeler, Justice:

. . . Summarily stated, the contentions of the plaintiff are: that the negotiations between him and the school board [resulted] in a contract express or implied, and the minds of the negotiating parties met; that Stevens, by reason of his position, had authority to make a contract binding the town; and that [plaintiff's bid, followed by Stevens' actions] resulted in a contract being formed. . . .

[Other] than as to the price to be fixed for the service, there is no dispute between the parties as to the terms submitted in the notice to bidders, and the plaintiff bid with reference to them, his offer conforming to these terms, the price for the service being the only open item in the transaction. The dispute turns upon the question of a rate per week as contrasted with a rate per day. The committee received from the plaintiff a bid of $175 per week; this undoubtedly meant to it the same as $35 per day, a result arrived at by a simple act of division of the larger number by five, the number of school days in the ordinary school week. It would seem that the committee were justified in reaching this conclusion, in that the plaintiff's pay in the contract for the year just past had been at a sum per day, and the notice for bids had called for a bid by the day. . . . When, therefore, the committee received a bid by the week they very naturally in their vote awarding the contract to the plaintiff substituted what they deemed an equivalent sum by the day, to accord with the requirement of the notice. This also was evidently the understanding of Stevens, when he afterward informed the plaintiff that the contract had been awarded to the latter. Subsequent events showed that this construction of his bid was not intended by the plaintiff, and that he intended to insist on the distinction between pay by the day and pay by the week, in that the latter afforded him compensation for work which would not in fact be required, when in any week a school day came upon a holiday.

In the pleadings, each side claimed the equivalence in fact and in effect of the expressions in the bid with those in the vote, each resolving the question of intent favorably to the contention by each, and each consequently claimed a contract which had been broken by the other party. *Both are wrong. It clearly appears from the facts found that the trial judge correctly found that there was no meeting of minds, and hence no contract. The plaintiff had the burden of establishing his construction of the claimed contract and has failed.* [Emphasis added.]

But the plaintiff further insists that he was in effect informed by Stevens that his bid had been accepted by the committee, that the latter was bound by

Stevens' statement, and that he [the plaintiff] acted in accordance with the information conveyed to him. Further, that Stevens was the agent of the committee, and had authority to bind it, and that the committee was so bound when Stevens told him that the contract had been awarded to him, which information was in his mind equivalent to a statement that his bid had been accepted in the form tendered. . . . So he says that whatever the committee really intended in the matter, it was bound by Stevens' statement that the contract had been awarded to him on the terms of his bid, even though the vote stated the price of the service at a sum differing therefrom. [The court rejected this contention of plaintiff, ruling that Stevens was simply informing plaintiff of the board's action so that he could get his equipment in readiness, and that Stevens did not intend—nor did he have the authority—to bind the board to anything other than the specific resolution as passed.]

Judgment affirmed.

A Note of Caution: In some situations the offeree's response does constitute an acceptance even though it contains one or more terms that were not set forth in the offer itself. This is true where a reasonable person, standing in the place of the offeree, would justifiably believe that the "new" terms were within the contemplation of, and were agreeable to, the offeror despite the failure to include them in the offer. Following are two illustrations.

1. For several years X has been buying goods from the Y Company, and it has always granted him ninety days' credit. If the Y Company offers a certain item to X for a price of "$500," and he replies by mail, "I accept on condition that I will have ninety days in which to pay," X's response very likely constitutes an acceptance. Under the circumstances—the manner in which they had been doing business in the past—X could assume that it was *implied* that the Y Company was granting him the usual credit.[15]

2. F offers to sell certain land to D for $55,000 cash. D replies by telegram, "I accept, assuming you will convey good title." This is an acceptance, even though F did not mention the quality of his title, because it is *implied* (under real property law) that a seller of land guarantees good or marketable title unless he or she indicates a contrary intention.

The purpose of the foregoing is simply to warn the student that it is possible for a term or condition to be literally new without necessarily being new in the legal sense. Thus, while the responses of the offerees in the preceding examples appear at first glance to constitute counteroffers, in the eyes of the law they add nothing new and therefore constitute valid acceptances.

New Conditions: Sales Law [16]

Under sales law, an acceptance may be effective (under limited circumstances) even though it contains terms that conflict with, or add to, the terms of the offer. A major reason for rejection of the mirror-image rule lies in the manner in which many kinds of sales contracts are entered

---

[15] The same result might obtain, even if there had been no past dealings between the two parties, if X could establish that the granting of credit was a widely accepted custom in the particular industry.

[16] Sec. 2-207 of the UCC, the basis of this discussion, is one of the most significant UCC sections relating to the acceptance of offers calling for the sale or purchase of goods. A limited number of other UCC provisions that also have application to the formation of sales contracts will, for ease of understanding, be considered together at the end of the chapter.

into. For example, commercial buyers often use their own printed forms in ordering goods from manufacturers or wholesalers, and the latter companies frequently use *their* forms in notifying buyers of their acceptance. As one would expect, the terms and conditions of the two forms are rarely identical, because the order forms used by buyers contain buyer-oriented terms, while forms used by sellers to acknowledge or accept orders contain seller-oriented terms.

While the great majority of such sales contracts are satisfactorily performed despite these variations, experience prior to adoption of the UCC showed that the common-law rule as applied to such "form-swapping" sometimes raised problems. The most common situation in which this was true occurred where, after a sales contract was apparently entered into, one of the parties decided to back out of the agreement before the goods were shipped.

To illustrate: Suppose that buyer B ordered a quantity of goods at a certain price from seller S, and that S sent B a form acknowledging the order and indicating that the goods would be shipped. S's form, however, *contained a clause excluding all warranties on the goods.* Later B notified S that he did not want the goods and would not go through with the deal, whereupon S sued B to recover damages for breach of contract. In such a case, under the common-law rule the court usually held that S's acknowledgment form—because of the warranty-exclusion clause—constituted a counteroffer rather than an acceptance. Thus no contract was ever formed, with the result that B had no liability to S. (Similarly, if it were S who reneged on the deal by refusing to ship the goods, he would have had no liability to B.)

The drafters of the UCC felt that application of the common-law rule to sales negotiations brought about undesirable results in this kind of situation, where the parties had, in fact, agreed on all major matters—the type and price of the goods, delivery dates, and so forth. In order to eliminate (or greatly reduce) such results, the drafters adopted Sec. 2-207.

Text of Sec. 2-207:   This section reads, in material part, as follows:

1. A definite and seasonable expression of acceptance or a written confirmation which is sent within a reasonable time *operates as an acceptance* even though it states terms *additional to or different from* those offered or agreed upon unless acceptance is expressly made conditional on assent to the additional or different terms.

2. The additional terms are to be construed as proposals for addition to the contract. *Between merchants, such terms become part of the contract unless:*
   a. the offer expressly limits acceptance to the terms of the offer;
   b. they materially alter it; or
   c. notification of objection to them . . .
is given within a reasonable time after notice of them is received. . . . [Emphasis added.]

Subsection 1—Is There a Contract? The primary import of this provision is that a seller's response to a buyer's order for goods which clearly indicates that the seller is accepting constitutes *an acceptance* even if it contains terms additional to or different from those found in the offer. Thus Sec. 2-207(1) expressly rejects the common-law view that was applied earlier.

We can illustrate the operation of subsection 1 by fleshing out the facts of the prior example as follows: Buyer B orders 2,000 A-20 widgets from seller S for $9,000, the price appearing in S's sales catalogue. S sends his acknowledgment form as follows: "Accept your sales order 1379; 2,000 A-20 widgets/ $9,000"; but on the back of the form is the new term "seller makes no warranties, express or implied, as to goods sold." *A contract now exists,* despite the new term in S's response. (In other words, under subsection 1 S's acknowledgment constitutes an acceptance rather than a counteroffer, with the result that if either party should subsequently refuse to perform, he or she is liable to the other party for damages for breach of contract.)[17]

Is the New Term Included in the Agreement? Now that a contract has been formed, the remaining question is whether the warranty exclusion clause has become a part of it. (If B notices the clause and agrees to it, then it is, of course, included.) But what about the usual case where B does not notice the clause, or, if he does notice it, he simply ignores it? In this situation, a distinction is made between terms that are "different from" those of the offer, and those which are "additional to" those of the offer.

Different Terms: If the term in the acceptance is different from (i.e., conflicts with) a term of the offer, the term does not become a part of the contract. Thus, in the above example, if B's order form had contained a clause setting forth certain warranties that were to be made by the seller (e.g., "seller warrants the widgets to be in conformity with U.S. Department of Defense specification #497 dated 6-15-85"), S's warranty exclusion clause would fail.

Additional Terms: As to any term in the acceptance that is an additional term—a term not in the offer—Sec. 2-207(2) provides that, *if both parties are merchants,* the term becomes a part of the contract without further assent on the part of the offeree unless (a) the offer stated that acceptance is limited to the terms of the offer itself; or (b) the term materially alters the contract, or (c) if the offeror objects to the new term within a reasonable time after receiving the offeree's acceptance.[18] Thus, in our example involving the widget purchase, if both B and S were merchants, and if B's order form made no reference to warranties, S's warranty-exclusion clause would automatically become part of the contract (unless barred by a, b, or c).

Cases in which the offeror is contending that he or she is not bound by the new term under exceptions a or c generally pose few problems for the courts. Both situations present simple questions of fact: as to (a), whether the offer did or did not provide that no changes in its terms could be made, and, as to (c), whether the offeror did or did not object to the new term within a reasonable time. If the answer to either of these questions is yes, the new term is excluded from the contract.

More difficult are the remaining cases, in which the offeror is contending that the new term or terms materially alter the contract—a question which the courts must answer upon the facts of the individual case, and which often depends on what is customary in a particular industry or between particular parties. Thus the thrust of subsection 2(b) is that the offeree is not allowed to slip anything important by the offeror. (Returning once more to our hypothetical case, a warranty-exclusion clause in most cases *is* held to be a material alteration. On that basis, it would not become a part of the contract between B and S). The case below is typical of those sales controversies in which the courts are called upon to apply the rules of Sec. 2-207.

---

[17] As the text of Sec. 2-207(1) indicates, there is one exception to this rule. If the offeree's response adds a new term and further indicates that he or she does not intend to be bound by the proposed agreement unless the offeror agrees to the new term, there is no contract at this point.

[18] Therefore, in determining whether there is a contract (under subsection 1), it is not necessary that the parties be merchants. But their status as merchants *is* important in determining whether the additional term becomes part of the contract. The reason for this is that the drafters of the UCC felt that additional terms should be included in the contract without express agreement only where the transaction is between two professionals.

Just Born, Inc. v. Stein, Hall & Co.
Court of Common Pleas of Pennsylvania,
59 Pa.D & C.2d 407 (1971)

On six occasions between May and September of 1967 the plaintiff, a candy manufacturer, ordered quantities of gelatin from defendant. The orders consisted of written purchase orders prepared by plaintiff, which specified the terms of the proposed agreement—such as quantity, price, and description of the goods. (Plaintiff's orders contained no provision as to how disputes arising out of the sales were to be handled.)

As each order was received, defendant sent plaintiff a "Sales Acknowledgment Agreement" and shipped the specified goods to plaintiff's plant. Each of defendant's acknowledgment forms contained, on its front side, the following paragraph under the heading "Arbitration Clause": "Any controversy or claim arising out of or relating to this agreement, or the breach thereof, shall be settled by arbitration in New York, N.Y., pursuant to the rules then obtaining, of the American Arbitration Association and the laws of New York. . . ."

Some time after all of the gelatin had been received, plaintiff filed suit in a state court in Pennsylvania to recover damages from defendant for breach of contract, alleging that the gelatin was not fit for its intended use. Defendant responded by contending that, according to their agreements, the dispute had to be resolved by arbitration proceedings, rather than in the courts. (The decision below is that of the trial court.)

Williams, Justice:

. . . The issue of whether the present dispute is subject to arbitration may be characterized as the "battle of [the] forms" . . .

Defendant contends that under the terms of the Uniform Commercial Code, §2-207, the "Sales Acknowledgment Agreements" were definite and seasonable acceptances of plaintiff's purchase orders and that the arbitration clause contained therein was an additional term which should be construed as having become part of the contracts. Plaintiff cites §2-207 for the opposite proposition, namely that the arbitration clause was an additional term which materially altered the offer to purchase the gelatin and thus did not become part of the contracts between plaintiff and defendant. [The court here quoted the text of Sec. 2-207, and continued]: Applying §2-207 to the facts of the case at bar, it is clear that a contract was formed by the exchange of forms between plaintiff and defendant, and that the arbitration clause contained in defendant's "Sales Acknowledgment Agreement" forms was an additional term. The Uniform Commercial Code, comment 2 to §2-207 provides:

Under this Article a proposed deal which in commercial understanding has in fact been closed is recognized as a contract. Therefore, any additional matter con-

tained in the confirmation or in the acceptance falls within subsection (2) and must be regarded as a proposal for an added term unless the acceptance is made conditional on the acceptance of the additional or different terms. . . .

[The court here observed that both parties were merchants, and that the arbitration clause thus automatically became a part of the contract under Sec. 2-207(2), unless it fell within one of the exceptions of that section. The court found that the clause was not barred by 2-207(2)(a), because plaintiff's orders did not expressly limit acceptance to their terms. The court also found that the clause was not barred by 2-207(2)(c), because plaintiff did not object to the clause in defendant's acceptances. The court then turned to the only remaining issue, whether the arbitration clause "materially altered" the contract, and was thus barred from becoming part of the contract by 2-207(2)(b). On this point the court said]:

The parties differ . . . as to whether the arbitration clause is a "material alteration" of the contract within the terms of subsection 2-207(2)(b). Defendant argues that the arbitration clause does not materially alter the contracts but merely sets forth the forum in which any disputes are to be decided without changing the substantive rights of either party with respect to the contracts. . . .

In *Application of Doughboy Industries,* 233 N.Y.S.2d 488 (1962), the New York court ruled that an arbitration clause contained in the seller's form but not in the buyer's form was a "material alteration" and under §2-207 did not become a part of the contract between the parties. In determining that the arbitration clause was a "material alteration," the New York court based its conclusion on the well-settled principle that in New York an agreement to arbitrate had to be clear and direct and could not depend upon implication, inveiglement or subtlety. Elaborating on this principle, the court held: "It follows then that the existence of an agreement to arbitrate should not depend solely upon the conflicting fine print of commercial forms which cross one another but never meet. . . ."

The Pennsylvania policy with regard to arbitration agreements is similar to the New York law relied upon by *Doughboy.* In *Scholler Bros., Inc. v. Hagen Corp.,* 158 Pa. Superior Ct. 170, (1945), it was held that:

[A]s an arbitration agreement bars recourse to the courts where arbitrators are named in advance at common law, . . . and even if not named in advance, the assent to relinquish a trial by jury is not to be found by mere implication. . . .

No technical or formal words are necessary to constitute a reference of a controversy to arbitration, but it must clearly appear that the intention of the parties was to submit their differences to a tribunal and to be bound by the decision reached by that body on deliberation.

Defendant wisely does not contend that there was actual assent or a meeting of the minds to include the arbitration clause in the present case, but urges that it be included by implication under §2-207 of the code.

In our opinion, *Doughboy* is a proper interpretation of §2-207 and is consistent with the principle of *Scholler* that an agreement to arbitrate is not to be found by implication. It should be noted that *Doughboy* has been uniformly followed in New York.

We conclude, therefore, that the arbitration clause contained in defendant's "Sales Acknowledgment Agreement" forms was an additional term which materially altered the offer and, as such, did not become a part of the contract between defendant and plaintiff. . . .

[As a result of the trial court's decision that the dispute did not have to be submitted to arbitration, the trial proceeded in that court.]

Unequivocal Assent

Returning to common-law principles an acceptance is an expression on the part of the offeree by which he or she indicates a consent to be bound by the terms of the offer. Under this definition, the courts require the "expression" be reasonably definite and unequivocal, and be manifested by some overt word or act. These requirements were developed, as a practical matter, to deal with the many situations where—from the language used by the offeree—his or her real intent is not at all clear; that is, the offeree's response is neither a clear-cut acceptance nor a flat rejection of the offer. At best, such responses cause initial delay and uncertainty between the parties as to whether a contract exists; at worst, litigation may ensue, with interpretation left to the courts.

To illustrate: X, in response to an advertisement placed by Y, sends a bid to Y offering to perform the described landscaping work for $23,000. Y replies by telegram: "Offer satisfies all requirements; will give it my prompt attention." Subsequently Y hires another landscaper to do the job, and, when X sues Y to recover damages for breach of contract, Y contends that his response did not constitute an acceptance of the offer. Applying the general rule to this case, Y's reply is too indefinite and tentative to satisfy the "unequivocal" requirement. Thus Y is correct in his contention that a contract was not formed.[19]

On the other hand, each case has to be decided on its own merits, including consideration of the circumstances surrounding the communications. Thus a different result might be reached in the foregoing example if the evidence indicated that X and Y had in the past considered such language to be binding.

Silence: As a general rule, there is no duty on the offeree to reply to an offer. Silence on the part of the offeree, therefore, *does not usually constitute an acceptance.* This is true even when the offer states, "If you do not reply within ten days, I shall conclude that you have accepted," or contains language of similar import. The reasons underlying this view are fairly obvious: (1) the view is consistent with the basic idea that any willingness to contract must be manifested in some fashion, and (2) it substantially prevents an offeree from being forced into a contract against his or her will.

In exceptional circumstances, however, the courts may find that the general rule is unfair to the offeror—that under the facts of the particular case, the offeree owed the offeror a *duty to reject* if he or she did not wish to be bound. In such cases, silence on the part of the offeree does constitute an acceptance.

While it is difficult to generalize about these exceptional situations, two types of case present little controversy.

---

[19] In a case of a similar nature, a school board advertised for bids for the construction of a school building. After fourteen bids were received, the board wired one contractor: "You are low bidder. Come on morning train." The board and the contractor were subsequently unable to agree to a formal contract, and litigation ensued. The Iowa Supreme Court ruled that the board's telegram did not of itself constitute an acceptance of the contractor's bid, saying that it indicated no more than a willingness on the part of the board to enter into contractual negotiations. (*Cedar Rapids Lumber Co. v. Fisher,* 105 N.W. 595, 1906.)

1. If an *offeree* initially indicates that silence on his or her part can be taken as acceptance, there is no reason why that person should not be bound by the statement. For example: "If you do not hear from me by March 1, you can conclude that we have a contract."

2. If a series of *past dealings* between the parties indicate that the parties consider silence to be an acceptance, it can be assumed by the offeror that this understanding continues until it is expressly changed. For example: a retail jewelry store has, over the years, received periodic shipments of both ordered and unordered jewelry from a large supplier; during this time, the retailer-buyer has always paid for any unordered goods not returned within two weeks. A failure by the retailer to reject a particular shipment, or to give notice of such rejection, within two weeks would very likely operate as an acceptance under the circumstances.

In both the preceding kinds of cases, the courts are likely to say that the offeror "had reason to understand" that silence on the part of the offeree was to be taken as a manifestation of assent, and that the offeree should have been well aware of this fact.

There is another, smaller group of cases in which it has been held that the offeror is justified in believing silence to be a manifestation of assent. These are situations in which a retail buyer gives a salesperson an order (offer) for certain goods, which the salesperson forwards to his or her company. If a reasonable period of time elapses without the company taking action, some courts hold that the buyer can justifiably view such silence as an acceptance of the offer and can hold the company liable for damages if it refuses to deliver the goods. Such courts reason that a company which sends salespeople out to solicit offers owes a duty to buyers to reject their offers within a reasonable time if it does not intend to accept them. (The same rule has sometimes been applied to mail-order houses when they have failed to reject buyers' orders within a reasonable time.)

When Does Acceptance Take Effect?

When the parties are negotiating orally—face to face or by telephone—any acceptance of a bilateral offer takes effect immediately. But when the parties are negotiating a contract through the mail or by telegram, there is necessarily a lapse of time between the moment the offeree starts a message of acceptance on its way to the offeror and the moment when it actually reaches him or her.

The Early Rule: When the offeror does not indicate how the offeree is to reply, the traditional rule was that the acceptance took effect upon dispatch—when sent—*if* the offeree used the same means of communication as that used by the offeror in extending the offer. For example, the acceptance of an offer sent by mail took effect the moment the offeree deposited the acceptance in the mail. Thus, under the "mailbox rule," if an acceptance is mailed at noon, there is a contract at that time even if the acceptance is delayed (or even lost) in the mail, or if the offeror attempted to revoke the offer by a telephone call to the offeree at any time after the acceptance was in the mail. On the other hand, if the offeree used a means of communication different from that used by the offeror, it was generally held that no contract was formed until the acceptance actually reached the offeror.

as long as "meeting of the mind" occurs

The Modern Rule: The rule applied by most courts today is the **reasonable medium rule.** Under this view, an acceptance takes effect upon dispatch as long as the medium chosen by the offeree is "reasonable, under the circumstances." Under this rule, then, a contract may be formed the moment the acceptance is dispatched even though the means selected by the offeree was different from that of the offeror. (Because the use of the mail is especially likely to be reasonable in such a case, the new rule—among other things—substantially broadens the applicability of the mailbox rule. But the new rule also applies, of course, to other kinds of acceptances, as, for example, a situation in which an offer is made by mail and accepted by telegram; normally a contract is formed in such a case the moment the offeree files his or her acceptance with the telegraph agent.)

How do the courts determine whether the medium chosen by the offeree was a reasonable one? In general, a medium is reasonable if (1) it was the same one used by the offeror; or (2) it was one customarily used in prior dealings between the parties; or (3) it was customarily used within the trade or industry in which the parties are doing business; or (4) it is one which is impliedly authorized by the language of the offer (for example, an acceptance by mail is probably reasonable in response to an offer by telegram if the offer indicated that there was no urgency about reaching an agreement).

Two further cases present additional facts:

Case 1: June 1—Y receives an offer in the mail from X.
June 2—X mails letter of revocation.
June 3—Y mails acceptance at 5 p.m.
June 4—Y receives the revocation.
June 5—X receives Y's acceptance.

Result: A contract was formed at 5 p.m. on June 3, since use of mail by Y was clearly reasonable. (Since a *revocation* is usually not effective until it is received, the letter that X mailed on June 2 had no effect until June 4, when Y received it. And by that time a contract had already been formed.)[20]

Case 2: June 1—Y receives an offer in the mail from X.
June 2—Y mails letter of rejection.
June 3—Y changes his mind and at 10 a.m. calls X on the telephone and

accepts the offer, telling X to disregard his letter of rejection.
June 4—X receives letter of rejection.

Result: A contract was formed at 10 a.m. on June 3, when Y gave X actual notice of acceptance. (Since a *rejection* is usually not effective until it is received, Y's letter of rejection had no effect on June 2. The offer was thus open on June 3, when Y accepted it.)

A necessary corollary of the reasonable medium rule is that acceptance by means of an *unreasonable medium* does not take effect upon dispatch. Nonetheless, such an acceptance still becomes effective when it actually reaches the offeror (assuming the offer has not been terminated in the meantime).

Some Words of Caution: Several observations about the reasonable medium rule are necessary.

1. Even if the offeree clearly uses a reasonable means of acceptance, he or she may still be faced with a problem in proving the actual time of dispatch. (In the next case, *Cushing v. Thomson,* the problem was resolved in the offeree's favor—although the decision was based upon evidence that was incomplete, to say the least.)

2. The rule does not apply to offers providing that the acceptance *must* be made by a particular medium; in such a case, the use of any other medium by the offeree constitutes a counteroffer rather than an acceptance. However, if the offer simply *suggests* a particular means of communication, an acceptance sent by a different means will become effective when it reaches the offeror—assuming that the offer has not been terminated prior to that time.

3. An offeror can always make it a condition of the offer that the acceptance must be actually received by him or her in order to take effect. In such instances, of course, the reasonable medium rule is inapplicable.

---

[20] As noted earlier, in California (and perhaps a few other states) a revocation is effective when mailed—here, on June 2. In such states there would be no contract.

Cushing v. Thomson
Supreme Court of New Hampshire, 386 A.2d 805 (1978)

An antinuclear protest group, the Clamshell Alliance, sent an application in March of 1978 to the New Hampshire Adjutant General's office, seeking permission to rent the national guard armory in Portsmouth the night of April 29. The alliance hoped to use the armory facilities for a dance it had scheduled on that date.

On March 31 the adjutant general mailed a "contract offer" to the alliance, agreeing to rent the armory upon specified terms. The offer required that a signed acceptance be returned to the adjutant general's office.

Cushing, a member of the alliance, received the offer at the alliance's office on Monday, April 3. That same day he signed it on behalf of the organization, put the acceptance in an envelope, and placed the letter in the office's "outbox."

At 6:30 in the evening of the next day, Tuesday, April 4, Cushing received a phone call from the adjutant general stating that he was withdrawing the offer on orders of Governor Meldrim Thomson. Cushing replied that he had already accepted the offer, but the adjutant general repeated the statement that the offer had been withdrawn. (The alliance's acceptance, postmarked April 5, reached the adjutant general's office on April 6.)

When the adjutant general continued in his refusal to give the alliance permission to use the armory, Cushing and other members of the organization brought suit against Governor Thomson and the adjutant general, seeking specific performance of the contract that had allegedly been formed. Defendants contended that there was no contract, claiming that they had revoked the offer prior to plaintiff's "acceptance." Although there was no direct evidence indicating the precise moment at which the outgoing mail was placed in the hands of the U.S. Postal Service, the trial court found that this had presumably occurred prior to the time of the attempted revocation on Tuesday evening. It thus ruled that a contract had been formed, and granted plaintiff a decree of specific performance. Defendants appealed.

Per Curiam:[a]

. . . The [primary] issue presented is whether the trial court erred in determining that a binding contract existed. Neither party challenges the applicable law. [The court quoted the rule from a prior New Hampshire decision as

---

[a] "Per curiam" is a phrase used to refer to an opinion of the whole court, as distinguished from an opinion written by any one judge.

follows:] "To establish a contract of this character, there must be an offer and an acceptance thereof in accordance with its terms. Where the parties to such a contract are at a distance from one another and the offer is sent by mail, the reply accepting the offer may be sent through the same medium, and the contract will be complete when the acceptance is mailed . . . and beyond the acceptor's control." Withdrawal of the offer is ineffectual once the offer has been accepted by posting in the mail.

The defendants argue, however, that there is no evidence to sustain a finding that plaintiff Cushing had accepted the adjutant general's offer before it was withdrawn. Such a finding is necessarily implied in the court's ruling that there was a binding contract. The implied finding must stand if there is any evidence to support it.

Plaintiffs introduced the sworn affidavit of Mr. Cushing in which he stated that on April 3 he executed the contract and placed it in the outbox for mailing. Moreover, plaintiff's counsel represented to the court that it was customary office practice for outgoing letters to be picked up from the outbox daily and put in the U.S. mail. No [other evidence bearing on this point] was submitted in this informal hearing, and . . . the court's order appears to be [based] in part . . . [on representations made by attorneys for both sides,] a procedure which was not objected to by the parties.

Thus the representation that it was customary office procedure for the letters to be sent out the same day that they are placed in the office outbox, supported the implied finding *that the completed contract was mailed before the attempted revocation [occurred].* [Emphasis added.] Because there is evidence to support it, . . . the trial court's finding that there was a binding contract . . . must stand.

Decree affirmed.

Acceptance of Unilateral Offers

Unilateral offers pose two unique problems insofar as offer and acceptance principles are concerned: (1) whether it is necessary for the offeree, having performed the requested act, to notify the offeror of that fact, and (2) whether the offeror has the right to revoke the offer after the offeree has commenced to perform but before the performance is completed.

Is Notice Required?   The general rule is that a unilateral offer is accepted the moment the offeree performs the requested act; giving notice that the act has taken place is usually not required. This rule does not apply, obviously, to offers that expressly request notification. In such

offers, a contract is not formed until the requisite notice is given.

Another type of case requiring notice involves those exceptional situations where the act is of such a nature that the offeror "has no adequate means of ascertaining with reasonable promptness and certainty" that the act has taken place.[21] The typical cases in this category are *contracts of guaranty*—those in which one person guarantees a loan made to another. For example: A, in Columbus, asks B, in Miami, to lend $1,000 to C, a Miami resident, A promising to pay the debt if C fails to do so. In this situation,

---

[21] *Restatement, Contracts 2d,* §54. Copyright 1979. Reprinted with permission of The American Law Institute.

most courts take the view that while a contract is formed between A and B the moment that B makes the loan, A's resulting obligation is discharged (terminated) if B fails to notify him within a reasonable time that the loan has been made.

When Can Revocation Be Made? Where the requested act will take a period of time for completion, the traditional rule has been that the offeror can revoke the offer at any time before full performance has taken place, even if the offeree has started to do the job. In such a case a contract is never formed. (However, under the quasi-contract theory, the offeree is ordinarily entitled to recover the reasonable value of his or her performance prior to the revocation. In the event that this partial performance is of no value to the offeror, the offeree will, of course, recover nothing.)

In recent years a growing number of courts have felt that the traditional view is unfair to the offeree in many circumstances, and they have abandoned it in favor of several other approaches. The most widely accepted of the newer views is that where the act is one that of necessity will take a period of time to complete, the *right of revocation is suspended* once the offeree starts to perform and remains suspended until the offeree has had a reasonable time to complete the act. This view is consistent with the traditional view to the extent that no contract is formed until the act has been completed, but it affords an interim protection to the offeree that the traditional view does not. Thus we have yet another illustration of the courts' freedom, within the framework of the common law, to modify those earlier principles whose application has brought about results of questionable merit.

Bilateral/Unilateral Contracts: Sales Law

Many sales contracts are clearly bilateral in nature. For example, a buyer on September 10 sends an order for goods at a specified price for November shipment, and the seller accepts the offer—i.e., promises to ship the goods as ordered—by mailing his or her acknowledgment to the buyer on September 16. Because Sec. 2-206 provides that "an offer to make a contract shall be construed as inviting acceptance in any manner and *by any medium reasonable in the circumstances,*" a bilateral contract is formed the moment the acceptance is deposited in the mail on the 16th (assuming the mail was a reasonable medium).

"Prompt Shipment" Offers: Prior to adoption of the UCC, if a buyer ordered goods using such terms as "prompt shipment," "for current shipment," or "ship at once," the offer was usually construed as being an offer for a unilateral contract. Under this common-law view, *actual shipment* was the only way in which the offer could be accepted; a *promise to ship* would not cause a contract to come into existence (a result that sometimes came as a surprise to one or both of the parties). Sec. 2-206(1) of the UCC rejects that view by providing that an offer containing such language shall be construed as inviting acceptance *either* by prompt shipment *or* by a prompt promise to ship. Therefore, an offeree's sending of a return promise to ship forms a bilateral contract in such circumstances (although prompt shipment must follow or the contract will be breached).[22] Sec. 2-206 thus blurs the common-law distinction between bilateral and unilateral offers by permitting the offeree, in this limited instance, a choice as to how his or her acceptance shall be made. The differences between common law and the UCC on this point are illustrated in Figure 11.3.

SUMMARY

The first element of a contract (excluding quasi-contracts) is an agreement—an offer followed by an acceptance. In order for a communication

---

[22] The buyer can still require acceptance of the offer only by the act of shipment itself, but he or she now must explicitly state this in the offer.

Figure 11.3   **Acceptance of a Unilateral Offer under Common-law and UCC Rules**

Common Law

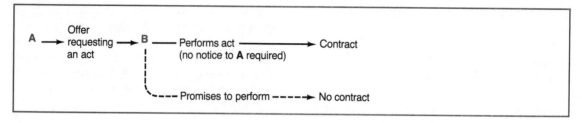

UCC 2-206

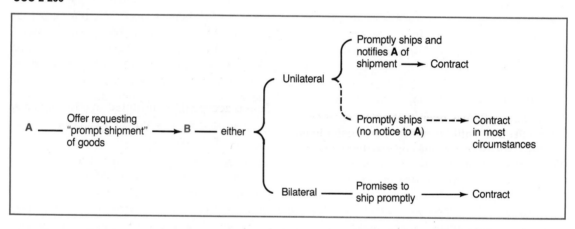

to constitute an offer, the courts require it to (1) manifest a genuine intent to contract, (2) be reasonably definite, and (3) be legally communicated to the offeree. Communications failing to meet requirement 1 constitute mere "preliminary negotiations." Insofar as requirement 2 is concerned, the common-law rules require that the offer (and thus the ensuing agreement) include all major obligations of the parties. Sales contracts, however, are governed by more liberal rules. Under the UCC, such contracts are enforceable even if they fail to state some of the terms of the agreement. (In such circumstances, the missing terms are supplied by applicable provisions of Article 2 of the UCC.)

Once an offer is made, it remains open until terminated by act of the parties or by operation of law. The most common acts of termination by the parties are revocation and rejection. If a revocation or rejection occurs, any subsequent acceptance is too late and does not result in the formation of a contract. Termination by operation of law—an automatic termination—results where any of the following conditions occur: (1) death or adjudication of insanity of either party, (2) destruction of the subject-matter of the contract, or (3) intervening illegality.

In order for a communication of the offeree to constitute an acceptance, it must show an unequivocal intent to accept and must be in conformity with all of the terms of the offer. If a new term is added, or a term of the offer is deleted, the offeree's communication is a counteroffer (and a rejection of the offer). Under sales law, however (Sec. 2-207 of the UCC), if the offeree's communication is a "definite" acceptance, it constitutes an acceptance even if it contains an additional term. And, in such a case, if both parties are merchants the additional term automatically becomes a part of the contract (with limited exceptions).

When the parties are not dealing face-to-face (or by telephone), the modern rule is that the acceptance of a bilateral offer is effective *when sent* if the offeree uses a reasonable medium of communication. In most situations the U.S. mail is a reasonable medium, and thus, in such cases (under the "mailbox rule") a contract is formed when the acceptance is placed in the mail—even if it is delayed in transmission, or never reaches the offeror. As to unilateral offers, the traditional rule has been that an acceptance is not effective until the offeree has completed performance of the requested act; thus a revocation before completion is effective. However, an increasing number of courts are taking the view that once the offeree has commenced performance the offeror's right to revoke is suspended until the offeree has had a reasonable time in which to complete the requested performance.

KEY TERMS

Offer
Preliminary negotiations
Advertising statutes
Communication (of offer)
Revocation
Firm Offer
Rejection
Counteroffer
Reasonable medium rule

QUESTIONS AND PROBLEMS

1. A construction company wished to submit a bid on the construction of a school. It showed a subcontractor the masonry requirements for the job, and asked the subcontractor to determine the lowest cost that it would do the work for. The subcontractor quoted a price, and the construction company replied, "Your bid is accepted. Come pick up the plans." Later, when the two companies tried to work out a written contract involving such matters as the manner of payment by the construction company, time for completion of the work, and bonding requirements, the construction company found that such an agreement could not be worked out, and it hired a different company to do the masonry work. The subcontractor then sued the construction company for damages, claiming that its quotation of a price for the job, followed by the construction company's statement that "your bid is accepted," constituted an offer and an acceptance even though no written agreement was ever entered into. Do you agree? Why or why not? (*Savoca Masonry Co. v. Homes & Son Construction Co., Inc.,* 542 P.2d 817, 1975.)

2. The board of directors of the American Bank Stationery Co. passed a resolution authorizing the sale of its stock "to such persons as may be selected by the President" at $50 a share. Later the president told all of the salesmen at a meeting that the stock was available to them. One of the salesmen, McGinn, told the president he would like to buy 100 shares at $50 each. Shortly thereafter, the president told him that this was too large a number, but he could have a smaller amount if he wished. (McGinn never asked for a smaller amount.) When the president ultimately refused to sell McGinn any stock at all, he sued the company for damages for breach of contract, contending that the company's resolution was an offer, and that his request for 100 shares was an acceptance. Is McGinn correct? Explain. (*McGinn v. American Bank Stationery Co.,* 195 A.2d 615, 1963.)

3. Blakeslee, who wished to buy some land owned by the Nelsons, wrote a letter to them asking if they would accept "$49,000 net" for the property. The Nelsons replied that they would "not sell for less than $56,000," whereupon Blakeslee wired back, "Accept your offer of $56,000 net." Does a contract now exist between the parties? Explain. (*Blakeslee v. Nelson,* 207 N.Y.S. 676, 1925.)

4. Petersen was employed as building construction manager for the Pilgrim Village Company under a contract which provided that he was to be paid a stated salary per year, and, in addition, was to receive "a share of the profits" of the operation while he remained in its employment. After several years on the job, during which time he received the stated salary, he asked for 10 percent of the profits made during that time, which he estimated to be $200,000. When the company refused that request, Petersen brought an action against it to recover "some share of the profits." At the trial, the company asked the court to rule that its promise as to the payment of profits was so vague and indefinite as to be unenforceable. How should the court rule? Explain. (*Petersen v. Pilgrim Village,* 42 N.W.2d 273, 1950.)

5. On June 1 X wrote a letter to Y offering to sell him a designated parcel of land in Salt Lake City for $75,000. The letter gave Y ten days in which to accept, and was received by Y on June 2. On June 9 Y heard over radio station KSL in Salt Lake that the city had reportedly purchased the land, but that two council members would neither confirm nor deny the report. Y, feeling he had no time to investigate this information, mailed a letter of acceptance that same day. Is there a contract between X and Y? What is the specific issue in this case?

6. The Gator Company, a Florida firm, offered to buy 100 tons of scrap metal from the Sooner Company, located in Norman, Oklahoma, at a specified price. The Sooner Company accepted this offer using one of its own forms, which contained this new term: "It is agreed that any disputes arising out of the performance of this contract will be governed by Oklahoma law." Later the Gator Company wanted to get out of the deal, and contended that the Sooner Company's "acceptance" was legally a counteroffer, and that thus a contract was never formed. Under sales law, Sec. 2-207 of the UCC:

    a. Is the Gator Company correct? Why or why not?
    b. If a contract were formed, do you think the Sooner Company's new term became a part of that contract? Why or why not?

7. Tayloe applied to an insurance company for a fire insurance policy on his home. The company forwarded Tayloe's application to Minor, its agent in Tayloe's area, with a letter telling Minor that he could go ahead and negotiate a policy with Tayloe. Minor then wrote Tayloe, saying that if he desired to effect the insurance coverage for which he had applied, "send me your check for $57 and the business is concluded." Tayloe received this offer on December 20 and deposited his check in the mail on December 21. On December 22, while Tayloe's check was in the mail, his residence burned down. Was an insurance contract between Tayloe and the company in effect at the time of the fire? Explain. (*Tayloe v. The Merchants Fire Insurance Company,* U.S.S.Ct., 9 Howard 390, 1850.)

Chapter 12

CONSIDERATION

An elusive thing called **consideration** is the second element ordinarily required in a contract. Generally, if an agreement lacks consideration, neither party can enforce it, even if it is in writing.[1] As a practical matter, consideration is present in most agreements; but since this is not always the case, we need a basic understanding of the *doctrine of consideration* in order to determine when an agreement is legally binding.

We mentioned this doctrine briefly in the preceding chapter. There we saw that an offeror who promises to keep an offer open a given number of days normally is allowed to revoke it before the specified time has elapsed. The promise is not binding because the offeror has received no consideration—something of value—from the offeree.[2] A similar situation is presented when one person promises a gift to another. Suppose, for example, that on December 1 an employer promises an employee that he will pay him a Christmas bonus of $100 on December 20, and the employee replies, "I accept." Assuming that the employment contract does not mention bonus payments, the employer in this situation ordinarily cannot be held liable for his promise, because the employee's acceptance did not obligate him to do anything in return for the bonus.

THE CONSIDERATION RATIONALE

These examples illustrate one of the basic ideas underlying the present-day requirement of consideration—that one party to an agreement should not be bound by it if the other party is not similarly bound. In neither of the preceding examples did the promisor receive anything of value from the promisee; as a result, neither promise was enforceable.[3] (A second major purpose of the consideration requirement—the prevention of exploitation of one contracting party by the other party—will be illustrated later in the chapter, in connection with the "pre-existing obligation" rule.)

Stating it positively, the concept of consideration requires that both parties to a contract shall have given and have received something as the "price" of their respective promises. For example: X promises to install a home air-conditioning unit for Y, and Y promises to pay X $1,100 for the job. Here the price X has received (in return for his promise to install the unit) is the right to a payment of $1,100 from Y when the job is done; similarly, the price Y has received (for her promise to pay the $1,100) is her right to have the unit installed.

Present-day concepts of consideration have resulted from a mixture of logic and historical accident. Thus we will first look briefly at the historical developments in this area of the law. Following this, the rest of the chapter will be divided into two parts—the first presenting the basic concepts and the second exploring some of the exceptional situations in which the courts have either modified these concepts or abandoned them altogether.

A Historical Note

Ever since the forerunners of our modern courts began to take shape centuries ago, they had to wrestle with the question of what agreements ought to be enforced. The problem existed in the countries that operated under the civil sys-

---

[1] From a technical standpoint, such agreements are not contracts. Nevertheless, courts and lawyers often refer to them as *unenforceable contracts*—indicating simply that neither party is bound by such agreements. (This use of the term "unenforceable" should not be confused with our earlier, stricter definition—a contract that was valid when made but that subsequently was rendered unenforceable by a change of law.)

[2] This should be distinguished, of course, from the situation where an *option contract* has been formed—that is, where the offeree has given the offeror something of value, usually a sum of money, in return for the promise to keep the offer open.

---

[3] This creates one of the relatively few areas in which established legal views part company with moral views. On moral grounds, most people believe (laudably) that they are obligated to live up to their promises regardless of whether they receive something in return, and most people act accordingly.

tem of law (the system of jurisprudence administered in the Roman empire and based strictly on codified law) as well as in the English-speaking nations that employed the common-law system.

Three basic periods stand out in the development of English and American law. The earliest English view, several centuries ago, was that contracts had to be "sealed" in order to be enforced. A **sealed contract** had to have a bit of wax affixed to it, on which the initials or other distinctive mark of each of the parties was imprinted. Contracts that lacked this formality were not legally recognized no matter how valid they were otherwise.

As trade and commerce began to grow in seventeenth-century England, it became increasingly apparent that the strict requirement of a seal often led to undesirable results. Thus a second era emerged; the courts began to enforce unsealed promises as well as sealed ones, as long as they were supported by what came to be called consideration.

This was the state of the English law at the time it was adopted by the United States. A third stage of development has now been reached in this country. Approximately forty states today take the view that virtually all promises must be supported by consideration in order to be enforceable, even if they are made under seal.[4]

THE BASIC CONCEPT OF CONSIDERATION

The courts agree substantially about the kinds of promises or acts constituting consideration in most situations. This is true because they have formulated, over the years, a number of definitions that have met with general approval. While these definitions or tests vary somewhat in de-

tail, they ordinarily lead to the same conclusions when applied to agreements where the question of consideration has been raised. To determine the technical and usual meaning of the term, we will examine these tests and see how they are applied to specific situations.

The Detriment Test

Whenever a promisee seeks to hold a promisor liable on his or her promise, and the latter claims nonliability on the ground that the promise was not supported by consideration, the courts usually inquire whether the promisee incurred a *detriment* under the contract. If so, they decide that consideration is present and the promise is enforceable.

People incur **legal detriments** when they do (or promise to do) something that they are not otherwise legally obligated to do, or when they refrain from doing (or promise to refrain from doing) something that they have a legal right to do. A few illustrations will simplify this idea.

1. Unilateral contract: X, a publisher, promises Y: "If you will lend $5,000 to my nephew for one year, I will run all your advertisements during that time at half the regular rate." Y makes the loan, but X refuses to provide advertising space at the reduced rate. If Y sues X to recover damages for breach of contract—that is, Y seeks to enforce X's promise—X is liable. Y's act of making the loan to the nephew constituted not only an acceptance of X's offer but a detriment to Y—the parting with something of value where he was not otherwise legally obligated to do so. Thus X's promise, supported by consideration, is enforceable against him.

2. Unilateral contract: A promises to pay C, his law partner, $750 if C will give up his part-time job in a dance band for the next nine months. C lives up to the terms of the offer, but A refuses to pay. If C brings suit to recover the $750, A is liable. Here again we have a unilateral contract, a promise in exchange for a negative act (or a forbearance)—the act of not playing in the

---

[4] Of these states, about half have reached this result by enacting statutes that expressly abolish the private seal. The other half have reached a similar result through judicial decisions. The eight or ten states that have not adopted the general rule continue to enforce all sealed promises, even when consideration is lacking.

band. C's refraining constituted both an acceptance of the offer and a legal detriment to him; thus, as in the prior case, we can see that A's promise was supported by consideration.

3. Bilateral contract: M and B enter into a contract in April under the terms of which M agrees to build a swimming pool for B in June, B promising to pay $2,500 in return. M later refuses to perform, and B sues him to recover damages for breach of contract. M is liable; that is, his promise is enforceable. The return promise made by B (to pay M $2,500) was a detriment to B; thus M's promise was supported by consideration.

A Variation of the Detriment Test: The courts of some states use the *detriment-benefit* test in determining whether consideration is present. Under this approach, consideration is present if the promisee has incurred a detriment, *or* the promisor has received a benefit. While this test, at first glance, appears to be substantially different from the detriment test, in reality it is not. This is because in virtually every instance where the courts have found that the promisor has received a benefit, the promisee has also incurred a detriment. Thus the same results are usually reached under either test.

Limitations on the Consideration Requirement: Neither the detriment test nor the detriment-benefit test provides the answer to every question in which the enforceability of a promise is raised. Conditions sometimes exist, for example, where the courts feel justified in enforcing a promise on the grounds of *promissory estoppel* when consideration is clearly lacking, and there are even rarer situations in which a promise may be enforced where consideration is lacking and the doctrine of promissory estoppel is inapplicable.[5] The detriment concept also has received criticism from several authorities;

and even the many courts that embrace it occasionally disagree on matters of interpretation and application. Nevertheless, the concept presents as simple a test as any yet devised, and the basic theory underlying it is generally accepted by courts and lawyers.

Identification of the Parties: The detriment test requires identification of the promisor and the promisee. In a unilateral contract this is easy to do, because there is only one promisor. In a bilateral contract, however, there are two promisors and two promisees (that is, each party is both promisor and promisee). In such a case, identification of the promisee—for the purposes of applying the test—must await the initiation of a lawsuit (or at least an examination of the two parties' situations in the event that a consideration question will be raised).

This can be illustrated by example 3 above. Because of the manner in which that case arose, the question presented was whether M's promise was enforceable. Thus, for the purpose of applying the test, B was the promisee. Suppose, however, that B (rather than M) had reneged on the contract, by informing M in May that he did not want the work done. If litigation then ensued, M would bring the action, attempting to enforce B's promise. B would thus be the promisor and M the promisee. In such a suit, B would be liable, because his promise to pay was supported by M's promise to build. By his promise, M had incurred a legally recognized detriment. (This manner of identifying the promisor and promisee should also make it clear that those terms are by no means synonymous with *offeror* and *offeree*. For example, when an offeree accepts an offer, he or she may make a return promise to the offeror. In regard to that promise, the offeree is the promisor.)

The Bargained-for Requirement: In order for a promisee's act (or promise) to constitute legal consideration, it must be the one asked for (expressly or impliedly) by the promisor. Con-

---

[5]The idea of promissory estoppel, and some of the other situations referred to here, will be examined later in this chapter.

sideration thus is "bargained for"—agreed to by both parties. Stating it another way, a promisee cannot unilaterally determine what promise or act constitutes consideration. Thus, if X promises to make a gift of $10 to Y on the following day, whereupon Y immediately purchases a shirt on the strength of the promise, Y's act of purchasing the shirt does not constitute the giving of consideration or the incurring of a detriment, and X's promise remains unenforceable. In such a case, the purchase constitutes nothing but mere reliance on the part of the promisee.

The following cases present typical situations in which the basic concepts are applied.

Hamer v. Sidway
Court of Appeals of New York, 27 N.E. 256 (1891)

William E. Story, Sr., promised to pay his nephew, William E. Story, II, $5,000 if he would refrain from drinking, using tobacco, swearing, and playing cards or billiards for money until he became twenty-one years of age. The nephew refrained from all the specified activities as he was requested to do, and on his twenty-first birthday he wrote his uncle a letter asking him for the money.

The uncle, in reply, assured the nephew, "You shall have the $5,000 as I promised you." The uncle went on, however, to explain that he had worked very hard to accumulate that sum of money and would pay it "when you are capable of taking care of it, and the sooner that time comes the better it will suit me."

Two years later the uncle died, without having made payment. The administrator of the uncle's estate, Sidway, refused to pay the $5,000, and suit was brought to recover that sum. (The plaintiff is Hamer, rather than the nephew, for the reason that at some time before litigation was begun the nephew had assigned—that is, sold—his rights against the estate to Hamer. Thus Hamer's right to recover is entirely dependent upon whether the nephew had a valid contractual claim against his uncle.)

The trial court ruled that the uncle's promise to pay the $5,000 was not supported by consideration on the part of the nephew (the promisee) and entered judgment for the defendant. The plaintiff appealed.

Parker, Justice:

. . . The defendant contends that the contract was without consideration to support it, and therefore invalid. He asserts that the promisee, by refraining from the use of liquor and tobacco, was not harmed, but benefited; that that which he did was best for him to do, . . . and insists that it follows that, *unless the promisor was benefited,* the contract was without consideration—a contention which, if well founded, would [inject into the law, in many cases, an element so difficult to measure that needless uncertainty would result].

[Emphasis added.] Such a rule could not be tolerated, and is without foundation in the law. . . .

Pollock, in his work on *Contracts,* page 166, says: "'Consideration' means not so much that one party is profiting as that the other abandons some legal right . . . as an inducement for the promise of the first." Now, applying this rule to the facts before us, the promisee used tobacco, occasionally drank liquor, and he had a legal right to do so. That right he abandoned for a period of years upon the strength of the promise of the [uncle] that for such forbearance he would give him $5,000. We need not speculate on the effort which may have been required to give up the use of those stimulants. *It is sufficient that he restricted his lawful freedom of action within certain prescribed limits upon the faith of his uncle's agreement,* and now, having fully performed the conditions imposed, *it is of no moment whether such performance actually proved a benefit to the promisor, and the court will not inquire into it;* . . . [Emphasis added.] Few cases have been found which may be said to be precisely in point, but such as have been, support the position we have taken. . . .

Judgment reversed.

Comment: Two consideration principles are underscored here, as a result of the higher court's rejection of the defenses raised by the uncle's estate. First, if a promisee incurs a detriment by waiving a legal right, the promisee has given consideration even though he or she may have received an incidental benefit at the same time. (Thus, the nephew gave consideration by giving up certain rights—such as the right to smoke—even though he may have also been physically benefited by this forbearance). Second, consideration exists if the promisee incurs a detriment. It is not a requirement that the promisor must also receive a benefit.

Lampley v. Celebrity Homes, Inc.
Colorado Court of Appeals, Division II, 594 P.2d 605 (1979)

Linda Lampley, plaintiff, began work at Celebrity Homes in Denver in May of 1975. On July 29 of that year Celebrity announced the initiation of a profit-sharing plan. Under that plan all employees were to receive bonuses if a certain "profit goal" were reached for the 1975 fiscal year—April 1, 1975, to March 31, 1976. (Linda was working under an at-will agreement—that is, both she and Celebrity could terminate the relationship at any time.)

Plaintiff's employment was terminated in January of 1976. At the end of March, 1976, the company announced that the profit goal had been reached, and it made its first distribution of profits in May, 1976. When plaintiff was excluded from this distribution, she brought this suit for the share allegedly due her.

In the trial court Celebrity argued that its promise to pay the bonus was a mere "gratuity" on its part, on the ground that there was no consideration on the employee's part to support its promise. The trial court rejected this contention and entered judgment for plaintiff. Celebrity appealed.

Kelly, Judge:

. . . In further support of its claim that the plan is not a binding contract, Celebrity contends that there was no consideration [given by plaintiff]. Benefit to the promisor or detriment to the promisee, however slight, can constitute consideration. The plan states as its objective:

"Our goal is. . . to produce added employee benefits gained through a higher quality of operation. Through teamwork in our day to day operation, we can achieve not only higher levels of profits, but also better performance for our customers, a better quality in design of products, fair treatment of customers, subcontractors, and suppliers."

This language indicates that the plan was established as an inducement to Celebrity's employees to remain in its employ and to perform more efficient and faithful service. Such result would be of obvious benefit to Celebrity, and thus consideration was present. . . . [The court also impliedly found a detriment on the part of the promise, as follows:]

Lampley, who was employed for an indefinite term, was not obligated to remain until 1976, and it can be inferred from the evidence in the record that she was induced to do so, in part at least, by the profit sharing offer made to her by Celebrity. Thus, this case can be distinguished from [those] which hold that there can be no recovery where the company gets no more service as a result of such a promise than it would if no such promise had been made. The memorandum of the profit sharing plan was an offer to add additional terms to the original employment contract, and Lampley's continued employment with Celebrity [until January 1976] was an acceptance of the offer and the consideration for the contract.

Judgment affirmed.

Performance of Preexisting Obligations

As a general rule, a promisee does not incur a detriment by performing, or promising to perform, an act that he or she was under a preexisting duty to perform. One can be under a **preexisting obligation** because of the general law of a state or the federal government, or because a prior contract has not yet been carried out.

Obligations Imposed by Law: The following is a simple illustration of an obligation imposed by law. X's store has been burglarized, and X promises a local policeman $75 if he uncovers, and turns over to the authorities, evidence establishing the identity of the culprit. If the policeman furnishes the requested information, he is not entitled to the reward. Under city ordinances and department regulations he already has a duty to do this; therefore it does not constitute a detriment to him.

Contractual Obligations: Greater difficulty is presented in situations where the preexisting obligation exists (or may exist) as the result of a prior contract between the parties. While such situations involve varying fact-patterns, the starting point can be illustrated as follows. D contracts to drill a seventy-foot well for G for $200. After he commences work, D complains that he is going to lose money on the job and may not finish it unless he gets more money. G then says, "All right. Finish up and I'll pay you $100 extra," and D completes the job. G now refuses to pay the additional $100, and D brings suit to hold G to his promise. In this situation most courts would rule that D's act of completing the well was simply the performance of his original obligation—that he incurred no detriment thereby, and cannot enforce G's promise to pay the additional money. Thus, as a general rule, a **modification contract**—a contract that alters the terms of an existing contract—*requires some new consideration in order to be enforceable.* (Consideration would have been present in the above case for example, had the modification contract required something extra of D— such as drilling the well to a depth of eighty feet.)

The primary rationale for the rule that performance of one's preexisting obligations does not constitute consideration is the prevention of coerced modification contracts. In other words, referring to the original example, the purpose is to prevent D—by threatening to stop work, or by actually stopping it—from enforcing the new promise made by G to pay more, in these circumstances.

Application of the preexisting obligation rule in most instances makes sense and brings about reasonable results. The following case is typical of those in which the rule prevents the enforceability of the modification contract. Following this case, a number of exceptions to the rule (and the reasoning underlying them) will be noted.

Quarture v. Allegheny County et al.
Superior Court of Pennsylvania, 14 A.2d 575 (1940)

Quarture, plaintiff, owned land in Pennsylvania. A portion of it was taken when the defendant county relocated and widened a state highway. Plaintiff needed legal help to recover damages from the county, and he employed a lawyer, Sniderman, to represent him in this effort.

A written contract was entered into, under the terms of which Sniderman was to "institute, conduct, superintend or prosecute to final determination, if necessary, a suit or suits, action or claim against the County of Allegheny on account of taking, injuring, and affecting (my, our) property in the relocation, widening, and opening of the State Highway known as Route No. 545." The contract further provided that Sniderman was to receive, as a fee for his services, "10 percent of all that might be recovered."

Sniderman represented plaintiff before the Board of Viewers of Allegheny County, and the board awarded plaintiff $1,650 damages. Plaintiff was dissatisfied with this amount and wished to appeal that award.

Subsequently, a new agreement was entered into between plaintiff and Sniderman. This agreement provided that Sniderman would appeal the case to the court of common pleas and that Quarture would pay him a fee of 33 percent of whatever recovery might be obtained on appeal.

Plaintiff, represented by Sniderman, then brought this action in the court of common pleas, appealing the award of the Board of Viewers, and the court awarded him a judgment of $2,961. At this point Sniderman filed a petition with the court, asking it to distribute to him 33 percent of the judgment—$987.

Quarture objected, contending that his promise to pay the larger percentage was not supported by consideration and that Sniderman was thus bound by his original contract (a fee of 10 percent). The court rejected this contention and awarded Sniderman $987. Plaintiff appealed.

Stadtfeld, Justice:

. . . Our first duty is to construe the original [contract]. What is meant by the terms "final determination?" . . . In the case of *Ex parte Russell,* 20 L.Ed. 632, it was said: "The final determination of a suit is the end of litigation therein. This cannot be said to have arrived as long as an appeal is pending."

The proceedings before the Board of Viewers cannot be considered as a "final determination," as their award is subject to appeal by either the owner of the property or by the municipality. If it were intended to provide for additional compensation in case of appeal from the award of viewers, it would have been a simple matter to have so provided in the contract. We cannot rewrite the contract; we must construe it as the parties have written it. . . .

The general principle is stated in *13 C.J. 351,* as follows: "A promise to do what the promisor is already bound to do cannot be a consideration, for if a person gets nothing in return for his promise but that to which he is already legally entitled, the consideration is unreal." Likewise, at p. 353: "The promise of a person to carry out a subsisting contract with the promisee or the performance of such contractual duty is clearly no consideration, as he is doing no more than he was already obliged to do, and hence has sustained no detriment, nor has the other party to the contract obtained any benefit. Thus a promise to pay additional compensation for the performance by the promisee of a contract which the promisee is already under obligation to the promisor to perform is without consideration."

There are many cases in which this rule of law is laid down or adhered to, but one that clearly sets out the reason for the rule is *Lingenfelder v. Wainwright Brewing Co.*, 15 S.W. 844. In that case, plaintiff, an architect engaged in erecting a brewery for defendant, refused to proceed with his contract upon discovering that a business rival had secured one of the sub-contracts. The company, being in great haste for the building, agreed to pay plaintiff additional compensation as an inducement to resume work. It was held that the new promise was void for want of consideration, the court saying:

It is urged upon us by plaintiff that this was a new contract. New in what? Plaintiff was bound by his contract to design and supervise this building. Under the new promise he was not to do any more or anything different. What benefit was to accrue to defendant? He was to receive the same service from plaintiff under the new [contract] that plaintiff was bound to render under the original contract. What loss, trouble, or inconvenience could result to plaintiff that he had not already assumed? No amount of metaphysical reasoning can change the plain fact that plaintiff took advantage of defendant's necessities, and extorted the promise of 5 percent on the refrigerator plant as the condition of his complying with his contract already entered into. . . . What we hold is that, when a party merely does what he has already obligated himself to do, he cannot demand an additional compensation therefor, and although by taking advantage of the necessities of his adversary he obtains a promise for more, the law will regard it as nudum pactum, *and will not lend its process to aid in the wrong. . . .*

While we do not question the value of the services rendered by Mr. Sniderman, we are nevertheless constrained by reason of our interpretation of the [first] agreement, *to limit the right of recovery to the amount stipulated therein [in view of the fact that the carrying on of the appeal was nothing more than what the first agreement required of him].* [Emphasis added.] It is unfortunate that [that] agreement did not stipulate additional compensation in case of an appeal.

Judgment reversed.

Exceptions to the Preexisting Obligation Rule

Generally, the preexisting obligation rule applies to both coerced promises and uncoerced promises. Thus if a party to a contract later makes a modification contract under which he or she agrees to pay a higher price for property or services to be received under the first contract, such party is not liable on the promise even if it was an entirely voluntary one on his or her part. Because the freeing of the promisor from liability on the second promise, when made voluntarily, is sometimes felt to be unfair to the promisee, the courts (or legislatures) of the various states have fashioned a number of exceptions that cause the voluntary modification contract to be enforceable. The exceptions noted below are often recognized (although the circumstances to which they apply are rather limited ones).

The Unforeseen Difficulties Exception: The **unforeseen difficulties rule** is most easily illustrated by reference to a leading case in which a builder, Schuck, contracted to dig a cellar under a portion of an existing house, to a depth of seven feet, for $1,500. (The contract was made after the parties examined an excavation across the street, where the soil appeared to be normal.) After commencing work, Schuck discovered that the ground below the three-foot level was "swamp-like, black muddy stuff," and that this condition would require the use of piling, which the parties did not contemplate under the contract. Thereupon the home owner, Linz, told Schuck to do whatever was necessary to dig a seven-foot cellar, adding that he would "pay him whatever additional cost" was involved. Schuck completed the job. In ensuing litigation, Linz denied that there was consideration on Schuck's part to support his promise to pay more than the

$1,500. The court rejected this contention and permitted Schuck to recover his additional costs.[6]

In reaching this conclusion, the court stated that, in its opinion, *the preexisting obligation rule should not be applied to a situation of this sort.* To support its reasoning the court relied upon these statements from a prior decision:

> It is entirely competent [legally possible] for the parties to a contract to modify or waive their rights under it and ingraft new terms upon it, and in such a case the promise of one party is the consideration for that of the other; but, where the promise to the one is simply a repetition of a subsisting legal promise, there can be no consideration for the promise of the other party, and there is no warrant for inferring that the parties have voluntarily rescinded or modified their contract. But where the party refusing to complete his contract does so by reason of some *unforeseen and substantial difficulties in the performance of the contract, which were not known or anticipated by the parties when the contract was entered into, and which cast upon him an additional burden not contemplated by the parties, and the opposite party promises him extra pay or benefits if he will complete his contract, and he so promises, the promise to pay is supported by a valid consideration.* [Emphasis added.] (*Bryant v. Lord,* 19 Minn. 396, 1872.)

Situations where the rule is applied are admittedly exceptional; the courts of a few jurisdictions do not recognize it at all. And, among courts that do, they have historically taken the

view that such circumstances as increased costs, unexpected labor difficulties, or loss of expected sources of materials do not fall within the unforeseen difficulties (or "unanticipated circumstances") rule. However, among such courts today there is a clear trend to recognize such circumstances as being within the rule if (1) the circumstance was truly unanticipated when the contract was made, and (2) the increased compensation is "fair and equitable under the circumstances"—i.e., the extra money promised is no more than a reasonable compensation to the promisee for the additional effort or costs he or she expended in finishing the job. To illustrate: C contracts to build a home for B for $95,000. After work is under way C is unable to get the Pella windows called for in the contract from his local supplier, because of a strike in the Pella plant. C learns, however, he can get the identical Pella windows from a distant supplier at a cost of $500 higher than he originally expected to pay for them. When C tells B this, B tells C to go ahead with the window installation and he will pay C the additional cost. If C completes the job, he is entitled to the extra $500.

The Written Modification Exception: A few states, notably California and New York, have adopted statutes providing that any *written* modification contract is binding, even if consideration is lacking. Had the earlier *Quarture* case arisen in such a state, and if Quarture's promise to pay Sniderman an increased fee of 33 percent of the final recovery had been in writing, Quarture would have been held liable for the larger amount.

The Mutual Rescission Exception: If the parties to the original contract expressly or impliedly rescind (cancel) it before it is fully performed, and enter into a new contract involving the same subject matter, the new contract is enforceable. To illustrate: C contracts to do certain work for B for $1,000. After C starts the job he complains on several occasions that he is going to lose money on the deal. B says that he will

---

[6] *Linz v. Schuck,* 67 Atl. 286 (1907). The facts of this case must be distinguished from those presented by the earlier well-drilling example. In that example, the well driller threatened to quit simply because he was losing money, not because of some unknown condition of the soil that required unanticipated efforts.

consider paying more, and suggests a new contract be made. C, with B's consent, then tears up the contract, and the parties make a new contract under which B agrees to pay C $1,200 for the job. When C finishes the work, he is entitled to the $1,200. The rationale is that the mutual cancellation of the first contract *freed* C of his preexisting duty to do the job, and when C later assumed the same obligation under the new agreement he thus incurred a new detriment sufficient to support B's promise to pay the larger sum. (While this view has been criticized by several authorities, it continues to be followed by most courts today.)

Modification Contracts: Sales Law

The drafters of the UCC felt that if the parties to a sales contract subsequently entered into a modification contract voluntarily, it should be binding upon the parties regardless of whether it is or is not supported by consideration. Accordingly, Sec. 2-209(1) rejects the general common-law rule by providing in part that "an agreement modifying a contract [for the sale of goods] needs no consideration to be binding." To illustrate: S and B have agreed that S will sell a certain quantity of goods (such as 10,000 gallons of fuel oil) to B at a certain price. S later finds that he is not going to be able to deliver by the agreed date. He contacts B, *who agrees to an extension of the time for delivery.* B subsequently has a change of heart and demands the goods on the original date. Under the UCC, *B is bound by the agreed-upon modification* even though S gave no additional consideration for the extension of time.[7]

Adequacy of Consideration

Whenever the enforceability of a promise is at issue, a finding that the promisee incurred a legally recognized detriment results in the promisor being bound by the contract. This is usually true even if the actual values of the promise and the detriment are unequal—as is reflected in the oft-repeated statement that "the law is not concerned with the **adequacy of consideration**." To illustrate: X contracts to sell an acreage in Montana to Y for $60,000. Y later discovers that the actual value of the land is under $30,000. Y is liable on his promise to pay $60,000, even though what he received was worth much less. Under the usual test, X incurred a detriment when he promised to convey the land—the surrender of his right to retain the property. The presence of this detriment constituted a consideration sufficient to support Y's promise to pay; and Y's claim of inadequacy is therefore of no relevance. The legal sufficiency of an act or promise, rather than its adequacy, is controlling.[8]

Mutuality of Obligation

The requirement of **mutuality of obligation** dictates that there must be consideration on the part of both parties to the contract. As we have indicated, in the typical bilateral contract each party's promise is supported by the promise of the other, and the requirement is met. If, however, in a particular case there is no mutuality because consideration is lacking on the part of one of the parties, neither party is bound by the agreement. Such an agreement is called an **illusory contract.** For example, A and B enter

---

[7]Although the modification agreement need not be supported by a new consideration, it must still meet two requirements that the UCC imposes on all contracts falling within its scope. First, the modification contract must be made in good faith—that is, it must not be a coerced modification. And, second, the contract must not be "unconscionable"—i.e., shockingly one-sided. (The subject of unconscionability is discussed further in Chapter 13).

[8]Adequacy of consideration is, however, inquired into by the courts in exceptional circumstances. They will, for example, refuse to issue a decree of specific performance against a promisor in a contract felt to be "unconscionable"—that is, where the value of the consideration given by the plaintiff-promisee is so grossly inadequate that enforcement of the contract would "shock the conscience and common sense of reasonable people." Additionally, the courts will refuse to enforce promises where the inadequacy of consideration suggests that the promisor has been the victim of fraud (a subject covered in some detail in Chapter 14).

into a written agreement under the terms of which A promises to employ B as his foreman for one year at a salary of $22,000 and B promises to work in that capacity for the specified time. The last paragraph of the agreement provides that "A reserves the right to cancel this contract at any time." Because A has thus not absolutely bound himself to employ B for the year, A has incurred no detriment (no unconditional obligation) by such a promise, with the result that B's promise to work for the year is not binding upon him. Thus, he can quit work at any time without liability to A. In such a case the requirement of mutuality of obligation has not been met, since A is said to have a "free way out" of the contract.

In the next case the right of cancellation was a restricted one. See if you agree with the distinction which the higher court makes between this kind of a clause, on the one hand, and one where the right to cancel is absolute, on the other.

Laclede Gas Company v. Amoco Oil Company
U.S. Court of Appeals, Eighth Circuit, 522 F.2d 33 (1975)

In 1970 a number of mobile home parks were being built by developers in Jefferson County, Missouri. At this time there were no natural gas mains serving these areas, so that persons living in them needed propane gas until the mains would be built.

In order to meet this demand, the Laclede Gas Company (Laclede) entered into a written contract with the American Oil Company (Amoco), under the terms of which Amoco would supply Laclede with propane for its customers living in the parks for a minimum period of one year. The contract contained a clause giving Laclede the right to cancel the agreement after one year upon 30 days written notice to Amoco, but it did not give Amoco any corresponding right to cancel the contract.

For several months Amoco made the required deliveries of propane to Laclede, but thereafter Amoco sent a letter to Laclede saying that it was "terminating" the contract. When Laclede brought this action to recover damages for breach of contract, Amoco contended that it was not bound by the contract because it lacked mutuality (that is, Amoco claimed that its promise to supply the propane was not supported by consideration on the part of Laclede because of the cancellation clause.) The trial court agreed with this contention, and Laclede appealed.

Ross, Judge:

. . . The [trial] court felt that Laclede's right to "arbitrarily cancel the agreement" . . . rendered the contract void "for lack of mutuality." We disagree with this conclusion. . . .

A bilateral contract is not rendered invalid and unenforceable merely because one party has the right to cancellation while the other does not.

There is no necessity that for each stipulation in a contract binding the one party there must be a corresponding stipulation binding the other.

The important question in the instant case is whether Laclede's right of cancellation rendered all its other promises in the agreement illusory, so that there was a complete [absence] of consideration. This would be the result had Laclede retained the right of immediate cancellation at any time for any reason.

However, in *1 Williston, Law of Contracts* §104, Professor Williston notes:

> *Since the courts do not favor arbitrary cancellation clauses, the tendency is to interpret even a slight restriction on the exercise of the right of cancellation as constituting such detriment as will satisfy the requirement of sufficient consideration; for example, where the reservation of right to cancel is for cause, . . . or after a definite period of notice, or upon the occurrence of some extrinsic event. . . .*

Professor Corbin agrees, and states simply that when one party has the power to cancel by notice given for some stated period of time, "the contract should never be held to be rendered invalid thereby for lack of mutuality or for lack of consideration." The law of Missouri appears to be in conformity with this general contract rule that a cancellation clause will invalidate a contract only if its exercise is *unrestricted.*

Here Laclede's right to terminate was neither arbitrary nor unrestricted. It was limited by the agreement in at least three ways. First, Laclede could not cancel until one year had passed after the first delivery of propane by Amoco. Second, any cancellation could be effective only on the anniversary date of the first delivery under the agreement. Third, Laclede had to give Amoco 30 days written notice of termination. These restrictions on Laclede's power to cancel clearly bring this case within the rule [and consideration on Laclede's part thus did exist]. . . .

Judgment reversed.

Requirements Contracts: Buyers and sellers of goods will sometimes enter into contracts where the quantity of the goods being sold—such as gasoline or coal—is not specified; rather, the quantity is to be determined by subsequent events. In some instances, the language of the contract is such that the buyer clearly has a "free way out"; that is, under the terms of the contract the buyer does not absolutely promise to buy any specific amount of goods. For example, S and B enter into a contract under the terms of which B promises to buy from S all the coal that he "might wish" over the next six months at a speci-fied price per ton, with S promising to sell such quantity. Because of the language used, either intentionally or accidentally, B has not bound himself to buy *any* quantity of coal at all; thus the contract is illusory, since B has incurred no detriment. Because mutuality of obligation is lacking, the result is that if B later desires some coal, he is free to buy it from whomever he chooses. Conversely, if B orders coal from S, S has no duty to supply it.

Application of the mutuality of obligation requirement to cases such as the above soon began to cast doubt on the validity of all sales contracts in which buyers did not absolutely commit themselves to purchase some specified minimum quantity of goods. Many contracts, for example, were phrased in such a manner that the quantity of goods the buyer was committed to purchase depended on his or her subsequent needs (whatever they might prove to be) rather than on an obligation to take a fixed number of units at the outset. For example: An ice company contracts to sell to an ice cream manufacturer "all the ice you will need in your business for the next two years" at a specified price per ton.

The courts recognized the practicality of such **requirements contracts** and wanted to enforce them if they could; but the theoretical difficulty was that these contracts did not, by their terms, absolutely bind the buyer to take even a single unit of the product or commodity in question.[9] The courts therefore sought a theory by which many of these contracts could be upheld without demolishing the concept of mutuality.

They accomplished this, in large measure, by adopting the following view. If the parties, by the language of the contract, indicate that the quantity of goods is to be dependent upon the *requirements of the buyer's business,* then the contract is not void for want of mutuality and both parties are bound by it. (The determination of the exact quantity of goods is simply postponed, of necessity, until expiration of the period in question.)[10] Under this theory, while the buyer might not require any of the item or commodity in question, consideration on the part of the buyer exists as follows. In the event that the buyer subsequently requires the product, he or she is obligated to buy it solely from the seller.

(That is, the buyer *gives up the right to buy it from others.*) Thus contracts such as the one in the ice case are generally binding on both parties.[11]

Output Contracts: Output contracts are essentially similar to and governed by the same principles as requirements contracts. A seller contracts to sell his or her entire output of a particular article, or of a particular plant, for a specified period of time to the buyer at a designated unit price. The implied promise of the seller (in the event he or she does produce the articles) not to sell them to anyone other than the buyer constitutes a detriment to the seller. And the promise of the buyer to purchase the output, in the event there is any, constitutes a corresponding detriment to the buyer. As a result, such contracts are usually enforceable.[12]

---

[9] Unlike the ice illustration, for example, it was often highly questionable whether the buyer would require any of the product at all, particularly where the period of time was a short one. (And even in the ice case it was possible that the buyer would go out of business the next day.)

[10] In other words, such contracts are to be distinguished from illusory contracts, in which the quantity is solely dependent upon the buyer's whim or will.

---

[11] This discussion simply sketches out the basic distinction between illusory and requirements contracts. There are many cases, however, where the courts have difficulty determining whether the contract falls into one category or the other. This is due largely to the fact that the language is frequently vague—terms much less rigid than *require* or *need* are commonly used. As one illustration, the courts by no means agree as to the effect of contracts in which the buyer promises to purchase all goods that he or she "wants" over a specified period. Many feel that this creates a requirements contract; others do not. Thus questions of interpretation arise. And in determining the effect of such terms, an examination of the surrounding circumstances—which differ from case to case—is always relevant. For these reasons, particularly, the results of some cases unquestionably conflict with others (and the student of the law just has to make the best of it).

[12] Sec. 2-306 of the UCC implicitly adopts the general principles stated above in regard to requirements and output contracts. It also tries to limit certain abuses that have occasionally cropped up. For example, a seller under an output contract might take advantage of the buyer by increasing his or her productive capacity far beyond anything the buyer could have anticipated on entering the contract. (A similar hardship can exist in a requirements contract when the buyer's requirements skyrocket far above what was reasonably contemplated by the seller or when the buyer shuts down operations solely for the purpose of escaping liability on the contract.) Sec. 2-306(1) tries to prevent such abuses by providing: *"A term which measures the quantity by the output of the seller or the requirements of the buyer means such actual output or requirements as may occur in good faith, except that no quantity unreasonably disproportionate to any stated estimate or in the absence of a stated estimate to any normal or otherwise comparable prior output or requirements may be tendered or demanded."*

Settlement of Debts

After a debt becomes due, sometimes the creditor and debtor enter into a *settlement agreement.* This occurs when the creditor, either on his or her own initiative or that of the debtor, promises to release the debtor of all further liability if the debtor pays a specified sum of money. If, after the specified sum is paid, the creditor seeks to recover the balance of the debt on the ground that the agreement lacked consideration on the part of the debtor, the success of the suit usually depends on whether the original debt was "unliquidated" or "liquidated."

Unliquidated Debts: An **unliquidated debt** is one where a genuine dispute exists between the debtor and creditor as to the amount of the indebtedness. *Compromise agreements as to such debts, if executed, are usually binding.* For example: C (creditor) claims that she is owed $150 by D (debtor) for work performed under a contract with D, and D contends that the job was to cost only $100. C then says, "I will settle for $120," and D pays her that sum in cash. If C later sues to recover the balance allegedly owing, *she will be unsuccessful* because her implied promise to release D is supported by D's payment of the $120. (The payment of $120 by D—a sum more than D admitted owing—constitutes consideration because D, by making the payment, thereby gave up the right to have a court rule on his contention that the debt was only $100. Since C's promise to release is thus supported by consideration, D has a good defense to C's suit to recover the balance.) In such a situation, the payment of the $120 by D and the acceptance of that sum by C is said to constitute an "accord and satisfaction"—a binding agreement of a type that will be discussed further in Chapter 17.

Payment by Check: The above rule—preventing a further recovery by the creditor—is also applicable to payments by check if the debtor indicates that the tendered payment is meant to be in full satisfaction of the indebtedness (rather than a partial payment.) For example: suppose that in the prior situation, before the parties had reached any agreement on the $120 figure, D simply mailed C a check for $120, bearing the inscription "payment in full." If C cashes the check, she is—because of the inscription—impliedly promising to free D of any balance. *This promise is binding on C* because D, the promisee-debtor, by making the payment again gave up his right to contend in court that the debt was only $100. (We are assuming that when C cashed the check she indorsed it "in blank"—that is, in the usual manner, simply by signing her name on the back of it.)[13]

Liquidated Debts: In **liquidated debts,** those in which there is *no dispute* as to the amount of the indebtedness, compromise agreements are less frequently binding. For example: A is owed $150 by B. The two parties agree about the amount of the debt and about its due date of June 1. On June 2, A agrees to accept $120 as payment in full, and B pays that sum in cash. A thereafter brings suit to recover the balance of $30, and B contends that A is bound by

---

[13] If the creditor endorses the check "without prejudice and under protest," or uses any similar language indicating that payment is being received under protest, a different issue is presented: whether the creditor may recover the alleged balance under Sec. 1-207 of the UCC. That section provides, in part, that "A party who with explicit reservation of rights . . . assents to performance in the manner demanded . . . by the other party does not prejudice the rights reserved." Of the state supreme courts that have ruled on the issue as of 1987, a clear majority have taken the view that this section is *not* applicable to "paid in full" checks. Thus most courts continue to apply the common-law rule to this situation, under which the creditor is again barred from recovery of any balance despite the fact that he or she endorsed "under protest." The courts of some states, however—notably those of New York—have ruled that Sec. 1-207 is applicable if the disputed debt arose out of a code-covered transaction, such as the sale of goods, in which case the creditor *can* recover the balance allegedly due. And the courts of at least one state, South Dakota, have ruled that the creditor who uses the "under protest" endorsement can recover the balance allegedly due in all cases. A particularly good review of the state of the law on this point is found in the decision of the Court of Appeals of Iowa in *RMP Industries, Ltd. v. Linen Center,* 386 N.W.2d 523 (1986).

the implied promise he made on June 2 to release him.

The common-law view here is that A's promise to release is *not binding, and he can therefore recover the balance of $30.* The reasoning is that the payment of $120 by B did not constitute a detriment to him, since it was less than what he admittedly owed. This rule is followed by the courts of most states even where the promise to release is in writing. (It should be noted, however, that a growing number of states have rejected the latter view by enacting statutes providing that all settlement agreements, *if in writing,* are binding upon the creditor even though consideration is absent. Typical of such statutes is Sec. 1541 of the California Civil Code, which reads as follows: "An obligation is extinguished by a release therefrom given to the debtor by the creditor upon a new consideration, or in writing, with or without new consideration.")

Payment by Check: The common-law view discussed above, permitting further recovery by the creditor in the liquidated debt situation, is also applied by the courts of most states where the compromise payment is made by check rather than in cash. Suppose, for example, that in the above case, where the debt was clearly $150, B sent A a check for $120 with the words "payment in full," and that A cashed it after endorsing it in blank. Even though A did not qualify his endorsement, the common-law view is that the payment of the $120 by B does not constitute the giving of consideration by B, and thus A is not bound by the implied promise to release which he made by cashing the check. Accordingly, A is *permitted to recover the balance,* just as in the case where payment was made in cash.[14] (Once more, a note of caution. In states having

the "written release" statute referred to above, the blank endorsement of the check by the creditor is often held to constitute a release "in writing." In such states a recovery by the creditor is thus barred.)

Composition Agreements: A different situation is presented when a debtor makes an agreement with two or more creditors, under the terms of which he or she agrees to pay each creditor who joins in the agreement a stated percentage of that person's claim, with the creditors agreeing in return to accept that percentage as full satisfaction of their claims. Such agreements, called **composition agreements** (or *creditors' composition agreements*), are ordinarily held to be binding on the participating creditors even though each of them receives a sum less than what was originally owed.

To illustrate: X owes Y $1,000 and Z $600. The three parties agree that X will pay each creditor 60 percent of the amount owed and that Y and Z will accept the 60 percent as payment in full. X then pays Y the $600 and Z the $360. If either Y or Z brings suit to recover an additional sum on the theory that his promise to release was not supported by X's payment of the lesser sum, the usual view is that the composition is binding; therefore, the creditor's suit will be dismissed. To reach this result, the courts of many states find consideration to be present in that the promise of each creditor to accept the smaller sum supports the promise of the other creditors to do likewise. Other courts reach the same result by simply ruling that such agreements are binding on the ground of public policy, without trying to find consideration.

Reliance and Moral Obligation

We have already seen that when a gift is promised to someone, the fact that the promisee spends money or incurs a debt on the strength of the promise does not constitute consideration, since the act was not bargained for. That is, *mere reliance* (the mere performance of an act by the

---

[14]Since the blank endorser under the general rule applicable to liquidated debts is permitted to recover the balance allegedly due, presumably the "under protest" endorser is similarly protected by the rule.

promisee that the promisor did not request or anticipate) usually is not consideration.

Furthermore, as a general rule, the *moral obligation* that results from making a promise is not sufficient to cause it to be enforceable. Neither are the motives or feelings of the promisor. Thus an uncle's promise to pay $500 to his niece "in consideration of the love and affection that I have for you" is not binding. Nor is a promise made "in consideration of your many acts of kindness over the years." These acts (commonly referred to as acts of past consideration), having been performed earlier and, presumably, without expectation of payment, have not been bargained for. Thus they do not make a promise enforceable.

SPECIAL SITUATIONS

Up to this point, we have emphasized the usual situations where the courts require consideration to be present in order for promises to be enforced. (Occasional references to minority views were made only for purposes of completeness.) In the remainder of this chapter, we will focus on three exceptional situations where promises can be enforced by the same courts when consideration clearly is not present. The three are promissory estoppel, promises to charitable institutions, and promises made after the statute of limitations has run.

Promissory Estoppel

While it is well established that a promise to make a gift is generally unenforceable by the promisee even where he or she has performed some act in reliance upon the promise, unusual circumstances exist where the application of this view brings about results that are grossly unfair to the promisee. In such circumstances, the courts occasionally will invoke the doctrine of **promissory estoppel** (or "justifiable reliance" theory, as it is often called) to enforce the promise.

The basic idea underlying this doctrine is that if the promisor makes a promise under circumstances in which he or she should realize that the promisee is almost certainly going to react to the promise in a particular way, and if the promisee does so react, thereby causing a substantial change in his or her position, *the promisor is bound by the promise even though consideration is lacking on the part of the promisee.* To illustrate: Tenant T leases a building from Landlord L from January 1, 1985, to December 31, 1986. In early December, 1986, T indicates that he is thinking of remodeling the premises and wants a renewal of the lease for another two years. L replies, "We'll get to work on a new lease soon. I don't know about two years, but you can count on one year for sure." T then spends $500 over the next few weeks in having the first-floor rooms painted, but the parties never execute a new lease. If L seeks to evict T in March 1987 on the ground that his promise to renew was not supported by consideration, he will probably be unsuccessful—that is, he will be held to his promise regarding the year 1987. In this case, where L should have realized the likelihood of T's conduct in consequence of his promise, L is said to be "estopped by his promise"; that is, he is barred by his promise from contending that the lack of consideration on T's part caused his promise to be unenforceable.

To illustrate further: "A has been employed by B for forty years. B promises to pay A a pension of $200 per month when A retires. A retires and forbears to work elsewhere for several years while B pays the pension. B's promise is binding." [15]

The following case presents yet another situation where resort to the estoppel doctrine seemed appropriate to the court.

---

[15] *Restatement, Contracts 2d.*, Section 90. Copyright 1973. Reprinted with permission of The American Law Institute. (The text of Section 90 itself appears in the decision in the next case.)

Hoffman v. Red Owl Stores, Inc.   — Promissory Estoppel
Supreme Court of Wisconsin, 133 N.W.2d 267 (1965)

In 1960 Hoffman, plaintiff, hoped to establish a Red Owl franchised grocery store in Wautoma, Wisconsin. During that year he and the divisional manager of Red Owl, Lukowitz, had numerous conversations in which general plans for Hoffman's becoming a franchisee were discussed. Early in 1961 Lukowitz advised Hoffman to buy a small grocery in order to gain experience in the grocery business before operating a Red Owl franchise in a larger community.

Acting on this suggestion, Hoffman bought a small grocery in Wautoma. Three months later Red Owl representatives found that the store was operating at a profit, at which time Hoffman told Lukowitz that he could raise $18,000 to invest in a franchise. Lukowitz then advised Hoffman to sell the store, assuring him that the company would find a larger store for him to operate elsewhere—that he would "be operating a Red Owl store in a new location by fall."

Relying on this promise, Hoffman sold the grocery and soon thereafter bought a lot in Chilton, Wisconsin (a site which the company had selected for a new store), making a $1,000 down payment on the lot. Hoffman then rented a home for his family in Chilton and, after being assured by Lukowitz that "everything was all set," made a second $1,000 payment on the lot.

In September 1961 Lukowitz told Hoffman that the only "hitch" in the plan was that he (Hoffman) would have to sell a bakery building he owned in Wautoma and that the proceeds of that sale would have to make up a part of the $18,000 he was to invest, thereby reducing the amount he would have to borrow. Hoffman sold the building for $10,000, incurring a loss thereon of $2,000.

About this time, Red Owl prepared a "Proposed Financing for an Agency Store" plan that required Hoffman to invest $24,100 rather than the original $18,000. After Hoffman came up with $24,100, by virtue of several new loans, Red Owl told him that another $2,000 would be necessary.

Hoffman refused to go along with this demand, negotiations were terminated, and the new store was never built. When Hoffman and his wife brought suit to recover damages for breach of contract, Red Owl defended on the ground that its promises were not supported by consideration on Hoffman's part (in view of the facts that no formal financing plan was ever agreed to by Hoffman and no franchise agreement obligations were undertaken by him). Hoffman contended that liability should nonetheless be imposed on the basis of promissory

estoppel; the trial court agreed, entering judgment in his favor. Red Owl appealed.

Currie, Chief Justice:

. . . Sec. 90 of Restatement, 1 Contracts, provides: "A promise which the promisor should reasonably expect to induce action or forbearance of a definite and substantial character on the part of the promisee and which does induce such action or forbearance is binding if injustice can be avoided only by enforcement of the promise."

[The Chief Justice then observed that the Wisconsin Supreme Court had never recognized the above rule, but continued:] Many courts of other jurisdictions have seen fit over the years to adopt the principle of promissory estoppel [embodied in Section 90], and the tendency in that direction continues. . . . The development of the law of promissory estoppel "is an attempt by the courts to keep the remedies abreast of increased moral consciousness of honesty and fair representations in all business dealings." *People's National Bank of Little Rock v. Linebarger Construction Co.*, 240 S.W.2d 12 (1951). . . .

Because we deem the doctrine of promissory estoppel, as stated in Section 90 of Restatement, 1 Contracts, [to be] one which supplies a needed tool which courts may employ in a proper case to prevent injustice, *we endorse and adopt it.* [Emphasis added.]

The record here discloses a number of promises and assurances given to Hoffman by Lukowitz in behalf of Red Owl, [and] upon which plaintiffs relied and acted upon to their detriment.

Foremost were the promises that for the sum of $18,000 Red Owl would establish Hoffman in a store, [and] in November, 1961, [the assurance] to Hoffman that if the $24,100 figure were increased by $2,000, the deal would go through. [In return,] Hoffman was induced to sell his grocery store fixtures and inventory in June, 1961, on the promise that he would be in his new store by fall. In November, plaintiffs sold their bakery building on the urging of defendants and on the assurance that this was the last step necessary to have the deal with Red Owl go through [and on which sale, incidentally, plaintiffs suffered the $2,000 loss earlier referred to].

We determine that there was ample evidence to sustain [the jury's finding that Hoffman relied on the promises of Red Owl], and that his reliance was in the exercise of ordinary care. . . .

[In regard to a contention by Red Owl that its promises were too vague and indefinite to be enforceable in this action, in view of the fact that the size, cost, and design of the proposed store building were never agreed upon, the court disagreed, saying:] We deem it would be a mistake to regard an action grounded on promissory estoppel as the [precise] equivalent of a breach of contract action. The third requirement [of promissory estoppel,] that the remedy can only be invoked where necessary to avoid injustice, is one that involves a policy decision by the court. Such a policy necessarily embraces an element of discretion.

> We conclude that injustice would result here if plaintiffs were not granted some relief because of the failure of defendants to keep their promises which induced plaintiffs to act to their detriment. . . .
>
> Judgment affirmed.

✓ Promises to Charitable Institutions

The law generally looks with favor upon charitable institutions, such as churches, hospitals, and colleges. One result of this policy is that many courts try to enforce promises to pay money to such institutions (1) by bending the rules to find that consideration exists, (2) by extending the doctrine of promissory estoppel, or (3) if neither of these views can be justified, simply on the ground of public policy.

In regard to the first situation, the language contained in many pledge agreements provides that the promise to pay is made "in consideration of the promises of others" to make similar gifts. If a person signs such a pledge, most courts will hold him or her liable if the promisee (the institution) can show that at least one other person signed a pledge containing the same language during the same campaign. The theory is that the promise of each promisor is supported by the promise of the other.

The imposition of liability by extending the doctrine of promissory estoppel beyond its normal bounds can be illustrated by the following: In March, X signs a "subscription agreement" promising to pay $1,000 to the Presbyterian Church on June 30. In May, the church purchases new robes for its choir, an expenditure based on the promise of the $1,000. Many courts will hold that X is liable on the ground of promissory estoppel (whereas, if the promisee had been someone other than a charitable organization, they would likely absolve X of liability on the ground that the purchase of the robes was an act of "mere reliance").

If the facts of a given case are such that neither of the above theories is applicable, many courts (though by no means all) will still enforce the promise on the grounds of public policy.

Promises Made Subsequent to the Running of a Statute of Limitations

All states have **statutes of limitations** limiting the time a creditor has in which to bring suit against the debtor after the debt becomes due.[16] If the specified period of time elapses without the initiation of legal proceedings by the creditor, the statute is said to have "run." While the running of a statute does not extinguish the debt, it does cause the contract to be unenforceable—that is, it prevents the creditor from successfully maintaining an action in court to collect the debt.

New Promise to Pay: To what extent is the situation altered if the debtor, after the statute has run, makes a new promise to pay the debt? One might conclude that such a promise is unenforceable, since there is clearly no consideration given by the creditor in return. This, however, is not the case. *In all states, either by statute or by judicial decision, such a promise, if in writing, is enforceable despite the absence of consideration.*[17] In such a case, the debt is said to have been "revived," and the creditor now has a new statutory period in which to bring suit. (If the new promise was to pay only a portion of the original indebtedness, such as

---

[16] These periods of time vary widely among the states, and there is no typical statute. As a general illustration, however, some states give the creditor three years on an oral contract and six years on a written one.

[17] This rule on the enforceability of promises to pay debts barred by the running of the statute of limitations was, at one time, generally applied to promises to repay debts that were made by debtors after they had gone through *bankruptcy proceedings.* However, under the federal Bankruptcy Reform Act of 1978, effective October 1, 1979, this is no longer true. Thus, today such a promise to repay a debt is not binding unless supported by consideration.

$200 of a $450 debt, the promise is binding only to the extent of that portion—in this case, $200.)

Part Payment or Acknowledgment: The debt is also revived if a part payment is made by the debtor after the statute has run. If, for example, a five-year statute had run on a $1,000 debt, and the debtor thereafter mailed a check for $50 to the creditor, the creditor now has an additional five years in which to commence legal action for the balance. A mere acknowledgment by the debtor that the debt exists will also revive the obligation to pay.

Imposition of liability in the above instances is based on the theory that the debtor has, by making the part payment or acknowledgment, *impliedly promised* to pay the remaining indebtedness. The debtor can escape the operation of this rule by advising the creditor, when making the payment or acknowledgment, that he or she *is not* making any promise as to payment of the balance.

SUMMARY

As a general rule, a party to a contract is not bound by his or her promises unless "consideration" is given by the other party in return for such promises. In the great majority of cases, if the first element of a contract—an offer and an acceptance—exists, consideration on the part of both parties is also present. In other words, the promises of one party support the promises of the other. In some instances, however, consideration is lacking on the part of one party; such party cannot, therefore, hold the other party to the contract. In any case where a promisor seeks to avoid liability on the ground that his or her promise was unsupported by consideration, then, the inquiry is as to the nature of consideration.

Under the usual test, consideration exists if the promisee has incurred a "detriment" under the contract. Because a detriment is the waiver—the giving up—of a legal right, the performance of an act which one is under a "preex-

isting obligation" to perform *does not constitute consideration.* Thus if a homeowner (H) contracts to pay a builder $20,000 for remodeling his home, and then promises to pay an additional $5,000 when the builder complains that he is going to lose money, the completion of the job by the builder is not consideration, and H is not bound to pay the additional amount.

In some instances, however, the courts have made exceptions to the rule. Additionally, the UCC expressly provides that modifications of sales contracts need not be supported by consideration if they are in writing. Insofar as requirements contracts are concerned, the general view is that such contracts are binding—i.e., supported by consideration—even though at the time of contracting the parties do not know what the buyer's needs will be (or whether there will be *any* need for such goods).

Applying the common-law rules to debt settlement agreements, a distinction is made between unliquidated and liquidated debts. If a debt is unliquidated (i.e., there is a genuine dispute as to the amount of debt), the acceptance by the creditor of the debtor's payment (under circumstances indicating it to be full payment) is binding upon the creditor. In such case, the creditor's express or implied promise to release is supported by consideration on the part of the debtor: the debtor's waiving of his or her right to contest the creditor's claim in court. If the debt is liquidated, however, the payment of a lesser sum than admittedly owing is not consideration, and thus the creditor is not bound by his or her promise to release. (In some states, however, the common-law rules have been modified by statute).

In limited situations the courts have dispensed with the consideration requirement. The most common of these are situations where (1) the promisee has justifiably relied on the promisor's promise, resulting in the promisor being held liable under the doctrine of promissory estoppel; (2) the promise is made to a charitable institution; and (3) a debtor, after the statute of limitations has run, makes a new promise to pay his or her debt.

KEY TERMS

Consideration

Sealed contract

Legal detriment

Preexisting obligation rule

Modification contract - new consideration required

Unforeseen difficulties rule

Adequacy of consideration

Mutuality of obligation

Illusory contract

Requirements contract - nonenforceable, its so vague

Output contract

Unliquidated debt

Liquidated debt

Composition agreement

Promissory estoppel p 290-1 Red Owl Store case

Statute of limitations

QUESTIONS AND PROBLEMS

1. Dr. Browning made a contract with Dr. Johnson, under which he was to sell his practice and equipment to Johnson for a specified price. Before the time for performance, Browning changed his mind and asked Johnson to relieve him of his obligation to sell. Thereafter a new contract was made, under the terms of which Browning promised to pay Johnson $40,000 in return for Johnson's cancellation of the first contract. Later Browning refused to pay the $40,000, contending that this promise of his was not supported by consideration on Johnson's part. Is Browning correct? If not, where is the consideration on Johnson's part? (*Browning v. Johnson,* 422 P.2d 319, 1967.)

2. Grombach was employed as a public relations representative for the Oerlikon Company. The written contract provided that Oerlikon had the right to cancel the contract by giving him written notice by May 1, 1953. If no such notice were given, the contract was to remain in effect for a specified number of additional years. On April 27, 1953, Oerlikon asked that its right of cancellation be extended to June 30 of that year, and Grombach agreed to this. On June 24

Oerlikon exercised its option and cancelled the contract. Thereafter Grombach sued for damages for breach of contract, contending that his promise to extend the right of cancellation until June 30 was not supported by consideration on the part of Oerlikon. Do you agree with this contention? Why or why not? (*Grombach v. Oerlikon Tool and Arms Corp. of America,* 276 F.2d 155, 1960.)

3. Vinson agreed to do a certain construction job for Leggett, the owner, for $3,950. After work was commenced, Vinson found out that he was going to lose money on the job. Leggett examined Vinson's bills for materials to date and said, "Go ahead and complete the work like we said and I will pay you an additional $1,000." Vinson then completed the job. Is Leggett bound by his promise? Explain. (*Leggett v. Vinson,* 124 So. 427, 1929.)

4. Scales owned and operated a retail gas station on property which he leased for five years from Lang. When Scales got behind on his rent payments, the president of the Hy-Test Corporation, whose products Scales sold, wrote a letter to Lang saying, "Don't worry about the rent; we will pay it if Scales does not." Is this promise binding on the Hy-Test company? Explain.

5. A Pontiac dealer sold a new car to Knoebel under a contract that obligated him to make specified monthly payments. When Knoebel fell behind in his payments, the dealer repossessed the car, which he had a right to do. On July 26 the dealer told Knoebel that if he would pay off the amount then due ($498.99) by August 10, he—the dealer—would return the car to him at that time. On August 7 Knoebel went to the dealer with the money, but the dealer had sold the car to a third party. When Knoebel sued the dealer for damages for breach of contract (for failure to hold the car for him), the dealer argued that his promise to hold the car was not supported by consideration on Knoebel's part. Is this argument correct? Why or why not? (*Knoebel v. Chief Pontiac, Inc.,* 294 P.2d 625, 1956.)

6. A New York girl and an Italian count were engaged to be married. A short time before the wedding date the girl's father promised, in effect, that if the marriage took place he would pay them $2,500 a year as long as his daughter lived. The marriage took place and payments were made for ten years. When the father discontinued the payments, suit was brought against him for damages for breach of contract. He defended on the ground that the couple already had a preexisting obligation to get married when he made the promise (as a result of their engagement contract) and that their act of marriage did not, therefore, constitute consideration on their part. Is his argument valid? Discuss. (*DiCicco v. Schweizer,* 117 N.E. 807, 1917.)

7. Walquist was struck by a car driven by Christensen. The parties were in dispute as to whether or not the accident was Christensen's fault; they were also in disagreement as to the extent of Walquist's injuries. In this setting, they made an agreement: Christensen paid Walquist $500, and Walquist in turn released him from all liability. Later, when it turned out that Walquist's doctor bills alone came to $700, he sued Christensen to recover an additional sum. Christensen used the settlement agreement as a defense, but Walquist contended that Christensen's payment of $500 was not a sufficient consideration to support his promise to release, in view of the facts that his damages were, in actuality, considerably greater than $500. Is Walquist right? Why or why not?

8. Mrs. Harmon was a long-time employee of the FoxLane Company. Her son's illness had caused her to consider retiring, but she was not sure she was financially able to do so. The president of the company told her, "Marie, I have tried to work something out for you. While I hope you can stay with us for two more years, I want you to know that upon your retirement—whenever it occurs—the company will pay you your present salary as long as you live." Two months later she retired, and the company made several monthly payments. When it then stopped the payments, she sued it for damages. The company contended that its promise was not supported by consideration on her part (i.e., the company did *not* say "Retire now and we will pay.") Was there consideration on Mrs. Harmon's part? If not, is there any principle under which she might recover? Explain.

Chapter 13

ILLEGALITY

The third element of a contract is *legality of purpose*—the attainment of an objective that is not prohibited by state or federal law. In this chapter we will examine some of the most common kinds of contracts that are ordinarily illegal under state law.[1] Within a given state, a contract is illegal because it is either (1) contrary to that state's statutes (including the regulations of its administrative agencies) or (2) contrary to the public policy of that state, as defined by its courts.

All states have criminal statutes (many of which, as we saw in Chapter 8, are directed towards various kinds of misconduct in the business world). Such statutes not only prohibit certain acts but, additionally, provide for the imposition of fines or imprisonment on persons who violate them. Any contract calling for the commission of a crime is clearly illegal. Many other statutes simply prohibit the performance of specified acts without imposing criminal penalties for violations. Contracts that call for the performance of these acts are also illegal. (An example of the latter is lending money under an agreement that obligates the borrower to pay interest at a rate in excess of that permitted by statute.)

Still other contracts are illegal simply because they call for the performance of an act that the courts feel has an adverse effect on the general public. (Examples of contracts contrary to public policy are those under which a person promises never to get married or never to engage in a certain profession.)

As a general rule, contracts that are illegal on either statutory or public policy grounds are not enforceable in court. This means that (1) in cases where the contract is entirely executory, neither party is bound by the agreement, and (2) in cases where one of the parties has performed his or her part of the bargain, such party cannot recover the consideration, or the value of the consideration, that has passed to the other party. (Exceptions to this general rule will be discussed later in the chapter.)

CONTRACTS CONTRARY TO STATUTE

Wagering Agreements

All states have statutes relating to **wagering agreements,** or gambling contracts. Under the general language of most of these statutes, making bets and operating games of chance are prohibited. Any obligations arising from these activities are *void* (nonexistent) in the eyes of the law, and thus completely unenforceable by the "winner."

Bets and Lotteries: In most instances wagering agreements are easily recognized. Simple bets on the outcome of athletic events and lotteries such as bingo (when played for money) are the most common of them. Definition of the term **lottery** is usually left to the courts; a typical one is "any scheme for the distribution of property by chance, among persons who have paid or agreed to pay a valuable consideration for the chance, whether called a lottery, a raffle, a gift enterprise, [or] some other name."[2] Regardless of the precise definition, any scheme must contain three elements to constitute a lottery: (1) a prize, (2) consideration given by the participant, and (3) chance.

Promotional schemes, such as supermarket drawings, are occasionally challenged on the grounds that they constitute lotteries. While it is difficult to state a general rule because of the many variations presented by such games, the courts tend to rule that a scheme that does not require a purchase of goods by the participant is not a lottery on the ground that the element of consideration is lacking. There are, however, cases to the contrary; in some promotional schemes it has been held that the purchase of a

---

[1] Certain federal statutes that have a bearing on the legality of contracts in interstate commerce will be covered in Part VIII.

[2] *Wishing Well Club v. City of Akron,* 112 N.E.2d 41 (1951).

stamp by a contestant who has entered a contest by mail constitutes consideration. And in *Seattle Times Company v. Tielsch,* 495 P.2d 1366 (1972), a somewhat similar situation, the court held that a football game forecasting contest (where contestants were to select winners of a number of games) was a lottery, the consideration consisting of the time spent by the participants in making their selections.

In recent years a growing number of state statutes have been liberalized to permit wagering and lottery activities within narrow limits. For example, so-called "friendly bets"—those defined as not producing substantial sources of income—are frequently exempted from the basic wagering statutes, as are some lotteries operated by religious or charitable organizations. Additionally, a few states have sanctioned state-operated lotteries by special statutes.

Insurance Contracts: Many contracts whose performance is dependent upon an element of chance are clearly not wagers. This is particularly true of **risk-shifting contracts** (as distinguished from **risk-creating contracts**). If a person insures a home against loss by fire, for example, the contract is perfectly legal even though it is not known at the time the policy is issued whether the insurer will have liability under it. The contract is legal despite this uncertainty because the owner had an "insurable interest" in the home prior to taking out the policy—that is, a financial loss would have resulted if a fire had occurred. Thus an insurance policy is simply a contract by which an existing risk is shifted to an insurance company for a consideration paid by the owner. By contrast, an insurance policy on a building which the insured does not own and in which he or she has no other financial interest is clearly a wager and is unenforceable.

Futures Contracts: Contracts calling for the sale of stock or commodities, while clearly lawful in the great majority of cases, sometimes present questions of legality in limited situations. A case in point is a **futures contract** in the commodity markets, under which a seller contracts to sell, at a specified price, a quantity of goods, such as corn or wheat, that he or she presently does not own, with delivery to be made at a designated time in the future. While this may constitute a wager under certain circumstances, such contracts are generally held to be lawful on one of two grounds.

1. Many futures contracts are merely hedging transactions, which the seller engages in simply as a means of protecting a legitimate business profit. These are clearly not wagers.

2. Other futures contracts are not considered to be wagering agreements as long as the parties, at the time of contracting, intend that an actual delivery of the commodity (or of a contract under which delivery can be obtained) will be made at the specified time. This intention is ordinarily presumed to be the case in the absence of evidence to the contrary.

Thus the only illegal futures contracts are those where evidence clearly proves that an actual delivery was never intended, with the parties merely "agreeing to settle on differences"—that is, betting on the direction the market price will move in the future.

Licensing Statutes

All states have **licensing statutes,** requiring that persons who engage in certain professions, trades, or businesses be licensed. Lawyers, physicians, real estate brokers, contractors, electricians, and vendors of milk and liquor are but a few examples of persons commonly subject to a wide variety of such statutes. In many instances, particularly those involving the professions, passing a comprehensive examination (along with proof of good moral character) is a condition of obtaining a license. In others, only proof of good moral character may be required.

To find out whether an unlicensed person can recover for services rendered under a contract, one must check the particular statute involved. Some licensing statutes expressly provide that recovery by unlicensed persons shall not be allowed (no matter how competent their work).[3] Others, however, are silent on the matter, in which case their underlying purposes must be determined. Most courts take the view in such instances that if the statute is *regulatory*—its purpose being the protection of the general public against unqualified persons—then the contract is illegal and recovery is denied. On the other hand, if the statute is felt to be merely *revenue-raising,* recovery is allowed.

The reasoning behind this distinction, of course, is that allowing recovery of a fee or commission by an unlicensed person in the first category would adversely affect public health and safety, while the enforcement of contracts in the second category does not have this result. Thus an unlicensed milk vendor who has sold and delivered a quantity of milk will ordinarily not be permitted to recover the purchase price from the buyer. Similarly, an unlicensed physician, real estate agent, or attorney will be denied his or her fee. On the other hand, a corporation that has merely failed to obtain a license to do business in a particular city is still permitted to enforce its contracts, because city licensing ordinances applicable to corporations are normally enacted for revenue-raising purposes.

The possibility that a regulatory statute might be passed for the protection of some persons, but not others, is presented in the case below.

---

[3] A provision that contracts made in violation of the statute shall be "void" usually, though not always, has this effect.

Bremmeyer v. Peter Kiewit Sons Company
Supreme Court of Washington, 585 P.2d 1174 (1978)

The State of Washington awarded Peter Kiewit a prime contract to construct several miles of Interstate 90. The highway right-of-way was overgrown, and needed to have the trees and debris cleared before construction could begin. For this purpose, Peter Kiewit subcontracted the necessary clearing operation to Bremmeyer. Under the subcontract, Bremmeyer agreed to pay Peter Kiewit $35,000 for the right to fall, yard, buck, load and haul to a mill all the merchantable timber within the right-of-way. (Bremmeyer was to keep the proceeds of the sale of the timber as his compensation.)

Bremmeyer paid the $35,000 and began clearing the right-of-way, but before he had finished the job the state terminated Peter Kiewit's prime contract. Peter Kiewit, in turn, cancelled Bremmeyer's subcontract. Peter Kiewit received $1,729,050 from the state for "cancellation costs," but offered to pay Bremmeyer only $38 for cancellation of the contract. Bremmeyer refused the $38 and brought this action to recover the value of the merchantable timber that was still uncut at the time of termination.

In defense, Peter Kiewit's primary argument was that a state statute, RCW 18.27, required contractors to be registered with the state, and that Bremmeyer's failure to register barred his recovery. The trial court, citing a 1973 Washington State case, agreed with this contention and summarily dismissed the action. Bremmeyer appealed.

Stafford, Justice:

. . . We first considered whether the legislature intended RCW 18.27 to bar actions by unregistered subcontractors against prime contractors in *Jeanneret v. Rees,* 511 P.2d 60 (1973). A majority of the court agreed the legislature intended to preclude such actions. [The court then went on to say, however, that it now felt that its decision in that case was based on too literal a reading of the statute, and thus was not necessarily controlling. The court continued:]

Continued reliance upon the literal expression of RCW 18.27 is particularly inappropriate in light of the legislature's amendment to the statute after our divided opinion in *Jeanneret.* . . . A new section now provides:

It is the purpose of this chapter to afford protection to the public from unreliable, fraudulent, financially irresponsible, or incompetent contractors. [Emphasis supplied by the court.]

In view of this newly declared statutory purpose and the minimal protections afforded the public by the statute, we are convinced the legislature did not intend to protect prime contractors from actions initiated by unregistered subcontractors. The statutory purpose clearly provides protection *to the public,* i.e., the customers of building contractors. In light of the amendment, and considering the judicial history of RCW 18.27, we do not believe the legislature also intended to protect contractors *from each other.* . . .

Our conclusion that the legislature did not intend to bar actions by unregistered subcontractors against prime contractors is also supported by the practicalities of the contracting trade. Members of the trade are in a more nearly equal bargaining position with respect to *each other.* Not only is information concerning financial responsibility and competence readily attainable within the trade, but each contractor is knowledgeable concerning the financial protections needed for any particular job involved. . . .

Judgment reversed, and case remanded for trial.

Sunday Contracts

At common law, contracts made on Sunday were perfectly legal. By the end of the 19th century, however, most states had enacted **Sunday statutes** which prohibited the transaction of various kinds of business on that day. (These statutes are still commonly referred to as blue-laws, named for the color of the paper they were printed on.) In recent years many states have repealed their statutes—largely as a result of political pressure by retailers' associations—and this trend is likely to continue. Nevertheless, because approximately fifteen states still have such statutes, a brief look at the Sunday laws is warranted.

It is difficult to summarize the kinds of contracts that are likely to be illegal on this ground, primarily because the statutes vary widely in scope. A few states, for example, have statutes that forbid carrying on "all secular labor and business on the Sabbath." Under such statutes, virtually all contracts made on a Sunday may be illegal and unenforceable (depending upon applicable judicial interpretations).

At the other extreme, some of the statutes merely prohibit the sale of certain kinds of goods on Sunday. Under these narrow statutes, all contracts made on Sunday (except those calling for the sale of the specified kinds of goods) are lawful.

The statutes of the remaining states fall between these extremes. These laws typically prohibit "common labor and the opening of a building for the transaction of business" on Sunday, "except in cases of work of necessity or charity," and follow with a number of activities that are expressly exempt from the operation of the law.

While the legal status of a particular Sunday contract can be determined only by resort to the applicable statute and case law, several generalizations can be made about the status of such contracts under the "middle ground" statutes referred to above.

1. The main thrust of such a statute is to prohibit Sunday sales of goods rather than to invalidate Sunday contracts generally. Thus such agreements as employment contracts and leases made on Sunday are probably lawful and enforceable.

2. Where a sale of goods in violation of the statute does occur, the transaction—if totally executed—will normally not be rescinded by a court despite its illegality. Thus, if B purchases a television set on Sunday from the S Company, with B making full payment and receiving possession on that day, neither he nor the S Company can subsequently rescind the agreement. On the other hand, if B contracts to buy the set on Sunday, with payment of the purchase price to be made later, B's executory promise to pay the price later is probably unenforceable on the ground of illegality. Some courts might even hold that B not only is free of the obligation to pay for the set but also can retain possession of it.

3. Particularly in regard to contracts other than those calling for the sale of goods, the tendency of the courts is to uphold Sunday contracts if it is reasonably possible to do so. Frequently they do this by ruling that the contract did not constitute the "transaction of business" within the intent of the statute or that it was "reasonably necessary" under the circumstances.

4. Usually, these statutes expressly provide that certain kinds of Sunday business activities are lawful. Such statutes, for example, often state that they are "not applicable to the providing of services or commodities incidental to" travel, sports events, recreation, and state and county fairs.

Usury

Partly as a result of religious views going back to early biblical statements, and partly because of the practical hardships resulting from high interest rates charged desperate borrowers, all states have statutes establishing the maximum rate of interest that can be charged on ordinary loans. Charging interest in excess of the permitted rate constitutes **usury.**

The interest ceilings that are imposed by the usury statutes vary from state to state. Traditionally the basic statutes have varied from 6 percent to 12 percent per annum. However, as a result of inflationary pressures in recent years, the basic statutes now generally range from 10 percent to 16 percent per annum.

More important, many kinds of loans are not governed by the basic state statutes. For example, most states put no limit on the rate of interest that can be charged on loans made to corporations. And, under federal regulations, national banks are permitted to charge interest rates that are usually in excess of those permitted by the state usury laws.

Additionally, all states in recent years—again, partly because of inflationary pressures—have adopted special statutes permitting higher rates of interest on other specified kinds of loans. For example, most state laws today provide that interest rates charged by issuers of bank credit cards (such as Visa and MasterCard), and by department stores on their revolving credit accounts, can be at an annual percentage rate of 18 percent. Similarly, home purchase and construction loans, car loans, and loans by credit unions may generally carry annual interest rates ranging from 18 to 25 percent.[4]

The basic statutes also vary widely insofar as the effect of usury is concerned. Many states permit the usurious lender to recover the principal and interest at the lawful rate, but not the excess interest. In such states the lender suffers no penalty. In others, the lender is permitted to recover the principal only, forfeiting all interest. And in three or four states, the lender forfeits both interest and principal.

It is thus clear that no determination can be made as to the legality or effect of a given loan without inspecting the statutes of the state in which the transaction took place.

Resale Price Maintenance Contracts

In earlier years, sellers of goods often inserted in their sales contracts provisions forbidding the buyer to resell the goods below a specified price. For example, a manufacturer might sell 1000 widgets to a retailer for $900 under a contract obligating the retailer to charge a minimum price of $1.50 each upon resale.

All such clauses—**resale price maintenance contract** provisions—in contracts that involve the sale of goods in interstate commerce are clearly illegal today. Such transactions come under the federal antitrust laws, and the U.S. Supreme Court has ruled that this kind of a provision in a contract unreasonably restrains trade—and is thus a violation of Section 1 of the Sherman Act. Therefore, in the above example—assuming that interstate commerce is involved—the retailer is free to sell the widgets at any price. Furthermore, the manufacturer in this situation might be subject to civil or criminal penalties

under the Sherman Act. Because of these rules, resale price maintenance contracts are seldom utilized today. Rather, the most the manufacturer can do in this regard is to specify a "suggested" resale price.

CONTRACTS CONTRARY TO PUBLIC POLICY

Contracts in Restraint of Trade ✓

Many contracts that unreasonably restrain trade or competition in interstate commerce are in violation of one or more federal statutes, such as the Sherman and Clayton acts.[5] Long before the enactment of these statutes, however, many other contracts in restraint of trade were illegal under the common law of the various states, and this continues to be the case today. Thus a contract that is not subject to the Sherman or Clayton acts may still result in such restraint of trade that courts will set it aside under common-law principles. These principles are briefly summarized here.

Contracts that contain **restrictive covenants** ✓ —promises by one party not to engage in a particular occupation or to operate a certain kind of business—compose one group of contracts that are in restraint of trade. However, such promises (sometimes called *covenants not to compete*) are not necessarily illegal.

Generally, covenants not to compete are lawful if two conditions are met. First, the covenant must be of an "ancillary" nature, and second, the restriction (the covenant) must be reasonable under the circumstances.

The Ancillary Requirement: An **ancillary covenant** is one that is a subsidiary or auxiliary part of a larger agreement. A common example of an ancillary covenant is that found in a contract calling for the *sale of a business,* where the contract contains a promise by the seller of the business not to engage in the same type of busi-

---

[4] It should also be noted that all states but one have adopted special statutes that expressly permit small loan companies, such as "personal loan companies," to charge rates of interest that are considerably higher than those of the general interest statutes. For example, a loan company that qualifies under such statutes may be allowed to charge interest at the rate of 3 percent *per month* on the first $150 of a loan, 2 percent per month on the amount from $151 to $300, and 1 percent on the balance. These statutes usually provide that if interest is charged in excess of the specified rates, the loan is void. In such a case, neither principal nor interest can be recovered.

---

[5] These acts, and other federal statutes of a similar nature, are examined in Part VIII.

ness within a prescribed geographical area for a certain length of time after the sale. Equally common are covenants in *employment contracts,* under which the employee promises not to compete with the business of his or her employer for a specified period of time after the employment is terminated. (Nonancillary promises, on the other hand, stand alone; they do *not* protect any existing, legally recognized interest such as that in the prior examples. These covenants—such as a promise by a father to pay $10,000 for the son's promise not to engage in medical practice—are generally considered to be an unreasonable restraint of trade in all circumstances, and thus illegal and unenforceable on public policy grounds.)

Reasonableness—Sale of Business Contracts: When a business is being sold, the interest to be protected relates to the goodwill of the business. A restrictive covenant on the part of the seller, in a particular case, is thus enforceable if its space and time limitations are no broader than are reasonably necessary to afford such protection. For example, a promise by the seller of a retail grocery in Kalispell, Montana, that he will not engage in the retail grocery business "within the City of Kalispell for the period of one year after the sale" is probably reasonable and thus lawful. Similarly, in *Gann v. Morris,* 596 P.2d 43 (1979), a promise by the seller of a silk-screening business in Tucson, Arizona, that he would not operate a competing business within a hundred-mile radius of Tucson for a specified period of time was held to be reasonable in view of the fact that at least one of the business's customers was located that distance away. Thus, in the above instances, if the seller should violate his or her promise, the purchaser of the business is entitled to an injunction against him or her. (On the other hand, if the restraint is found to be excessive—as would be the case if the seller of the grocery in Kalispell was prohibited from engaging in the grocery business "anywhere within the state of Montana" for one year—the restraint is illegal, and thus unenforceable by the buyer.)

Reasonableness—Employment Contracts: Restrictive covenants in employment contracts are reasonable (1) if the restriction is reasonably necessary to protect the employer, and (2) if the restriction is "not unreasonably excessive" as to the employee. Because of this second requirement, **geographical restraints** in employment contracts are more likely to be set aside by the courts than those in contracts where businesses are being sold. In other words, because such restraints may operate with particular harshness upon the employee insofar as his or her ability to make a living is concerned, they are scrutinized with particular care.[6] The following case is illustrative of this approach by the courts.

---

[6] In contrast to geographical restraints are those covenants under which the employee promises not "to contact or deal with persons who are customers of the employer at the time the employment relationship is terminated" for a stated period of time. Where the time period is found to be reasonable, these kinds of covenants are more likely to be enforced.

Slisz v. Munzenreider Corporation
Court of Appeals of Indiana, Fourth
District 411 N.E.2d 709 (1980)

After graduating from Ball State University, Dan Slisz went to work at a Muncie, Indiana, store owned by the Munzenreider Corporation, a company that operated several retail furniture stores in Indiana and others throughout the United States. After several promotions Slisz was made "managing partner" of United Freight Sales, Munzenreider's store in Bloomington, in 1975. At that time he signed an agreement with Munzenreider which contained, in addition to a compensation formula, two restrictive covenants.

Paragraph 11 provided essentially that as long as Slisz was an employee of the company he would not divulge to anyone, or use for his personal gain, any information or methods of operation acquired on the job, nor would he divulge names of past, present, or potential customers. Paragraph 12 read as follows:

> *The managing partner agrees that in the event of the termination of the partnership for any reason whatsoever, he will not for a period of two years from the date of such termination, then engage in or accept employment from or become affiliated with or connected with, directly or indirectly, or become interested in, directly or indirectly, in any way in any business within the counties of Monroe, Brown, Morgan, Owen, Greene and Lawrence, Indiana, similar or of a competitive nature to the business carried on by the partnership, or any other city or place wherein the partners operate a store or within thirty miles of said city where a store is maintained by the capital partners. . . .*

Because the Bloomington store started losing money in 1978, Munzenreider moved it to a new location in that city, replaced Slisz as manager, and offered him a job with one of its stores in South Dakota. Slisz declined the offer, left his employment with Munzenreider, and opened up his own retail furniture business, Warehouse Furniture Sales, at the same location in Bloomington that was occupied by United Freight Sales prior to its move.

Munzenreider Corporation then brought this action asking for an injunction against Slisz restraining him from continued operation of his business. The trial court granted a two-year injunction, and he appealed.

Miller, Judge:

. . . In light of the broad language utilized in the instant agreement—which purported in part to prohibit involvement in *any* city where Munzenreider operated a store, in any business "*similar or of a competitive nature to*" that carried on by the partnership—combined with the fact it does not appear Slisz possessed any trade secrets, customer lists, or other special or confidential information regarding Munzenreider's operation, we conclude this restrictive language is void, and that the trial court's injunction must accordingly be reversed. [Emphasis added by the court.] . . .

Consideration of [this] appeal must begin from the general proposition that restraints on competition between an employer and his former employee, similar to that in this case involving a "managing partner," are not favored by the law, but will nevertheless be enforced where 1) the restraint is reasonably necessary to protect the employer's business; 2) it is not unreasonably restrictive of the employee; and 3) the covenant is not antagonistic to the general public interest.

[Because of the onerous effects such restraints have on employees, in applying the foregoing test] many courts have held an employer must demonstrate some "special facts" giving his former employee a unique competitive advantage or ability to harm the employer before such employer is entitled to the protection of a noncompetitive covenant. . . . Those special facts may include (but are not limited to) such things as trade secrets known by the employee, the employee's "unique" services, confidential information (such as customer lists) known to him, or the existence of a confidential relationship. At the same time, the rule is generally stated that the mere fact that an employee has acquired skill and efficiency in the performance of the work as a result of his employment does not suffice to warrant the enforcement of a covenant on his part not to compete.

[The court here noted the geographical breadth of the covenant, as follows:] The covenant encompasses not only the City of Bloomington and Monroe County and various counties adjoining it, but indeed every city and a 30-mile radius around it in which Munzenreider operates a store, and apparently without regard to whether such city is in Monroe County, the State of Indiana, or even the entire United States. It seems evident, as our courts have held, that so geographically broad a covenant may be reasonable *only in very unusual circumstances,* such as where "trade secrets" are involved. [Emphasis added.] . . .

There was no evidence to support the allegations of Munzenreider that Slisz utilized or even had access to any confidential or secret information. [Neither was there evidence that Slisz was aware of, or took with him, customer lists or information on customer requirements.] It does not appear any similar evidence involving possible harm to "good will" was presented. [The most that can be said is that a witness for Munzenreider] testified that he believed Slisz might benefit from "confused customers" responding to Munzenreider's ads by going to Slisz's store at the former Munzenreider location. . . . There was no showing that Slisz was actively soliciting Munzenreider customers by, for example, advertising his former association with the corporation's stores. . . .

Munzenreider cites *Welcome Wagon, Inc. v. Haschert,* 127 N.E.2d 103, 1955, which held there was a protectible interest in the employer (Welcome Wagon) where its hostess, a woman . . . with a "personal following" and "extensive acquaintanceship" in her community, learned the novel and unique business methods of Welcome Wagon and then quit to establish her own similar operation in the same city, Kokomo, Indiana, using some of the same "sponsors." The special business methods included a national training program in New York . . . where she was instructed in Welcome Wagon's method of calling on brides, newlyweds and newcomers to the community. . . . We believe the situation in the instant case [does not resemble] the unusual facts of the Welcome Wagon case, since the evidence in the case at bar does not suggest Slisz possessed a particular following, unique skills, . . . or trade secrets. . . .

In short, it appears the agreement in question [merely tries to prevent Slisz] from using the general skills he has acquired during his employment in the operation of any similar business in a broad geographical area. . . . We hold the covenant to be unreasonable and unenforceable. . . .

Judgment reversed.

Will the Courts Rewrite the Contract? Where ancillary restraints are found to be unreasonably broad, the question arises whether the covenantee (the buyer of the business, or the employer in an employment situation) will be given any remedy at all. At the risk of overgeneralization, we can say that the courts of most states follow the traditional view, striking down the covenant entirely. Under this approach, the covenantor (the seller of the business, or the employee) may establish or reenter a competing business at any location, at any time. The courts of a number of states, however, will "reform" the covenant, determining for themselves what a reasonable limitation would be. In the case of an overly broad statewide prohibition, for example, such a court might prohibit commercial activity by the covenantor within specified counties.

Exculpatory Clauses

The law of torts imposes certain duties on all persons, one of which is to carry out one's activities in a reasonably careful manner. If a person violates this duty by performing an act carelessly, he or she is guilty of the tort of negligence and is answerable in damages to anyone who was injured thereby.

Businesspersons, and others, often try to avoid this potential liability through the use of **exculpatory clauses** that purport to excuse them from liability resulting from their own negligence. Such clauses are generally—though not always—held to be contrary to public policy, and thus *unenforceable* against the injured party.[7]

The Public Interest Inquiry: The legality of the exculpatory clause depends almost entirely upon the relative strength of the bargaining powers of the contracting parties. Where the party utilizing the clause has *vastly superior bargaining power* over the other, the clause is clearly void. Such disparity is normally found only in those contracts that "substantially affect the public interest"—in other words, in contracts of parties who furnish goods or services that are routinely used by companies and individuals in the carrying on of their everyday business or personal activities.

Such a contract "exhibits some or all of the following characteristics. It concerns a business of a type generally thought to be suitable for public recognition. The party seeking exculpation is engaged in performing a service of great importance to the public, which is often a matter of practical necessity for some member of the public who seeks it. The party holds himself out as willing to perform this service for any member of the public who seeks it . . . [and] as a result of the essential nature of the service . . . the party seeking exculpation possesses a decisive advantage of bargaining strength against any member of the public who seeks his service."[8] Under this approach, exculpatory clauses in contracts of public utilities, common carriers, and banks are void. Also usually included within the public service category are car repair shops,

---

of clause, not contravening public policy, is ordinarily lawful and binding. One example: a school district's form requiring parental permission for a student's attendance at a field day might provide "The district shall have no liability for injuries arising out of transportation of student to and from said location, other than those directly resulting from negligence of district-employed drivers."

[7] Some exculpatory clauses do *not* attempt to free a party from his or her negligence, but only from liability for injury caused by circumstances ouside his or her control; this kind

[8] *Tunkl v. Regents of the University of California,* 383 P.2d 441 (1963).

employers, and apartment owners. Thus all of the above kinds of parties can be held liable for injuries occasioned by their negligence. By contrast, exculpatory clauses in contracts of physical fitness establishments[9] and drag strip operators[10] have been held *not* to affect the public interest, with the result that the clauses do insulate the establishment owner from liability for injuries occasioned by ordinary negligence— assuming, of course, that they were legally communicated to the patron.

The decision in an early landmark case is particularly instructive on the public policy aspects of employment contracts.[11] A brakeman was employed by a railroad under a contract providing that he "took upon himself all risks incident to the position," and would not hold the company liable for any injury he might sustain as a result of accidents or collisions on the roads, "or which may result from defective machinery, or carelessness or misconduct of himself or any other employee and servant of the company."

The brakeman was subsequently killed in an accident caused by a defective switch, and his estate brought an action against the railroad to recover damages. Evidence at the trial indicated that the switch's defective condition was the result of negligence on the part of the railroad. The railroad contended that, even so, the quoted provision released it of liability. The trial court held that the provision was illegal on the ground that it was contrary to public policy, and entered judgment for the estate. The appellate court agreed, spelling out the public policy considerations in these words:

> It is an elementary principle in the law of contracts that the form of agreement and the convention of parties override the law.

---

[9] *Owen v. Vic Tanney Enterprises, Inc.*, 199 N.E.2d 280 (1964).

[10] *Winterstein v. Wilcom*, 293 A.2d 821 (1972).

[11] *Little Rock & Fort Smith Ry. Co. v. Eubanks*, 3 S.W. 808 (1886).

But the maxim is not of universal application. Parties are permitted, by contract, to make a law for themselves only in cases where their agreements do not violate the express provisions of any law, nor injuriously affect the interest of the public. . . . The law requires the master to furnish his servant with a reasonably safe place to work in, and with sound and suitable tools and appliances to do his work. If he can supply an unsafe machine, or defective instruments, and then excuse himself against the consequences of his own negligence by the terms of his contract with his servant, he is enabled to evade a most salutary rule.

[The defendant argues that this provision] is not against public policy, because it does not affect all society, but only the interest of the employed. But surely the state has an interest in the lives and limbs of all its citizens. Laborers for hire constitute a numerous and meritorious class in every community. And it is for the welfare of society that their employers shall not be permitted, under the guise of enforcing contract rights, to abdicate their duties to them. The consequence would be that every railroad company, and every owner of a factory, mill, or mine, would make it a condition precedent to the employment of labor, that the laborer should release all right of action for injuries sustained in the course of the service, whether by the employer's negligence or otherwise. The natural tendency of this would be to relax the employer's carefulness in those matters of which he has the ordering and control, such as the supplying of machinery and materials, and thus increase the perils of occupations which are hazardous even when well managed. And the final outcome would be to fill the country with disabled men and paupers, whose support would become a charge upon the counties or upon public charity.

Reasonableness is key by Bailment

✓**Bailment Contracts: Bailment contracts** are similar to leases and employment contracts in that they, too, are so widely used as to substantially affect the public interest. Accordingly, the status of exculpatory clauses in such contracts is essentially the same as those in leases and employment contracts—that is, highly suspect in the eyes of the law.

A *bailment* occurs when the owner of an article of personal property temporarily relinquishes the possession and control of it to another. The person who has parted with the possession is the *bailor,* and the one receiving it is the *bailee.* Typical bailments result from checking a coat at a nightclub, leaving a car at a garage for repairs, and storing goods at a warehouse.

Under general bailment law, a bailee is liable for any damages to, or loss of, the property that is the result of his or her negligence—the failure to use reasonable care under the circumstances. Bailees frequently attempt to escape this liability by the use of an exculpatory clause in the bailment contract. Companies operating parking lots, for example, customarily print on the back of identification tickets something like the following: "The company will endeavor to protect the property of its patrons, but it is agreed that it will not be liable for loss or damage to cars, accessories, or contents, from whatever cause arising."[12]

As suggested earlier, such a clause is *contrary to public policy*—at least to the extent that it purports to free the bailee from liability for loss caused by his or her negligence. The reasoning, of course, is analogous to that applied in the illustration involving the employment contract—specifically, that if such a clause were given effect, all bailees would utilize it, with a consequent lessening of care on their part. As a result,

such provisions do not prevent a bailor whose property is damaged while in the bailee's hands from bringing suit. If it is established that the loss was occasioned by negligence on the part of the bailee, the bailor can recover damages.[13]

Unconscionable Contracts ✓

As a general rule, the courts are not concerned with the fairness or unfairness of a particular contract. In other words, where competent parties have struck an agreement, it will normally be enforced even if it proves to be much more advantageous to one party than to the other. If, however, the terms of a particular contract are, in the opinion of the court, so grossly or so extremely unfair to one of the parties that they "shock one's conscience"—in which case it is said to be an **unconscionable contract**—the court will refuse to enforce the contract. (Such contracts usually involve a high pressure salesperson, a poor and often illiterate consumer, and a price for the goods or services being purchased that is greatly in excess of their market value.)

The doctrine of unconscionability has been recognized under common-law principles since very early days. However, its application was relatively limited until adoption of Sec. 2-302 of the UCC (which is discussed presently). Although that section is applicable only to sales contracts, its express recognition of the doctrine of unconscionability has, since its adoption, been the impetus for the courts of most states to increasingly recognize and apply the doctrine to disputes governed by common-law principles—i.e., to disputes not governed by the UCC.

---

[12] While leaving a car at a parking lot creates a bailor-bailee relationship under ordinary circumstances, this is not always true. Many courts, for example, rule that such a relationship is not created if the patron is permitted to keep the car keys, on the theory that the lot operator in such a case is not given control of the car.

[13] Clauses that place a *limit* on the bailee's liability, in the event of a loss, are viewed more favorably by the courts. Such provisions, if reasonable, are usually not considered to be illegal. Additionally, some bailees are expressly permitted by statute to limit their liability by contract. Under federal law, for example, common carriers in interstate commerce are permitted to do so within limits approved by the Interstate Commerce Commission; thus the limitations commonly found in bills of lading and other transportation contracts are generally enforceable.

(sales contract)

3 options under the UCC of a contract is unconscionable

One of the most illustrative cases in this area is *Williams v. Walker-Thomas Furniture Company,* 350 F.2d 445 (1965). There, a Mrs. Williams purchased some furniture in Washington, D.C., in 1957 on credit under a contract which contained the standard provision that the company would retain title to the goods until all monthly payments were made, and that the company could repossess in event of default. The contract also contained a clause that if Mrs. Williams purchased additional goods on credit, the company had the right to "credit pro-rata" her monthly payments against all such goods. She did, in fact, buy a number of additional items between 1957 and 1962, and the company, as permitted by the pro-rata clause, during that time had applied her payments so that a small balance remained due on all items, even those purchased in 1957 and 1958. In 1962, by which time Mrs. Williams had made payments of over $1,400, she was unable to make additional payments. When the company then sought to repossess all of the goods in her hands, the court refused repossession as to the first items that she had purchased. In part, the court said: "When a party of little bargaining power, and hence little real choice, signs a commercially unreasonable contract with little or no knowledge of its terms, it is hardly likely that his consent, or even an objective manifestation of consent, was ever given to all the terms. In such a case the usual rule that the terms of the agreement are not to be questioned should be abandoned, and the court should consider whether the terms of the contract are so unfair that enforcement should be withheld." (Although sales contracts were the subject of this action, the court applied common-law principles because Mrs. Williams' purchases were made before the UCC was in effect in the District of Columbia.)

Unconscionability: Sales Law

As indicated above, Sec. 2-302 of the UCC introduces the concept of unconscionability to the law of sales. Under this section, if a court as a matter of law finds a sales contract or any clause of the contract to be unconscionable at the time it was made, three options are available. The court (1) may refuse to enforce the contract, or (2) may enforce the remainder of the contract without the unconscionable clause, or (3) may limit the application of any unconscionable clause as to avoid any unreasonable result. This section does not define "unconscionability," apparently because the drafters of the UCC felt that the common-law meaning of the term is sufficiently well-understood as meaning a contract, or a clause in a contract, so unfair and so oppressively one-sided as to "shock the conscience" of the court.[14]

It appears from many of the recently decided cases that the principal beneficiaries of Sec. 2-302 will be consumers—that is, buyers of consumer goods such as furniture and television sets—and particularly such buyers who are economically or educationally disadvantaged. (Cases do exist in which unconscionability has been found to exist in a contract between two merchants, but they are rare.)

Many of the unconscionable contract cases

---

[14] Some state statutes furnish aid to the courts in determining whether a sales contract is unconscionable. §1345.03 of the Ohio Revised Code, for example, provides that in determining whether an act or practice is an unconscionable consumer sales practice, "the following circumstances shall be taken into consideration: (1) Whether the supplier has knowingly taken advantage of the inability of the consumer reasonably to protect his interests because of his physical or mental infirmities, ignorance, illiteracy, or inability to understand the language of an agreement; (2) Whether the supplier knew at the time the consumer transaction was entered into that the price was substantially in excess of the price at which similar property or services were readily obtainable in similar consumer transactions by like consumers; (3) Whether the supplier knew at the time the consumer transaction was entered into of the inability of the consumer to receive a substantial benefit from the subject of the consumer transaction; (4) Whether the supplier knew at the time the consumer transaction was entered into that there was no reasonable probability of payment of the obligation in full by the consumer; (5) Whether the supplier required the consumer to enter into a consumer transaction on terms the supplier knew were substantially one-sided in favor of the supplier; (6) Whether the supplier knowingly made a misleading statement of opinion on which the consumer was likely to rely to his detriment; (7) Whether the supplier has, without justification, refused to make a refund in cash or by check for a returned item that was purchased with cash or by check, unless the supplier had conspicuously posted in the establishment at the time of the sale a sign stating the supplier's refund policy."

have focused on specific clauses in the sales contract, rather than on the contract as a whole. For example, in several decisions the courts have refused to enforce clauses in consumer sales contracts that grant exclusive jurisdiction to a court far from the consumer's home, in the event any disputes arise out of the transaction. And in a few cases the courts have refused to enforce consumer sales contracts where the price alone was excessive—perhaps several times the market value of the goods.

While the terms of the typical unconscio-

nable contract are grossly one-sided in nature (as a result of the great disparity of the parties' bargaining powers), courts have sometimes found contracts to be unconscionable even in the absence of specific, oppressive clauses. The overall circumstances in these cases usually have not only included parties with grossly unequal bargaining power, but, additionally, the use of unscrupulous practices by the party possessing the superior power during the *contract-formation process*. The following case is one falling within this category.

Brooklyn Union Gas Co. v. Jimeniz
Civil Court of New York, 371 N.Y.S.2d 289 (1975)

Rafael Jimeniz, defendant, purchased a gas conversion burner from Brooklyn Union Gas Co., plaintiff. Defendant apparently owned a tenement house, and the gas burner was to be used in it. Plaintiff did not initiate the negotiations with defendant personally, but induced defendant's tenants to pressure him into making the purchase. The sales contract, written in English only, was presented to the defendant by an employee of plaintiff, David Mann. Defendant spoke and wrote Spanish fluently, but had very limited comprehension of English. When he requested an explanation of the contract, he was told to just "sign it." He admitted signing it, but testified that it never was explained to him. (Mann, plaintiff's employee, had had defendant sign the contract at the tenement rather than at plaintiff's main office, where a Spanish interpreter would have been available.)

The contract was signed on June 15, 1971. A month later defendant attempted to make the first payment, but he was told that he need not pay for another year. The contract he had signed did, in fact, provide for payments to be deferred for twelve months. After the year had passed, defendant began making payments in June, 1972, and he continued making them for the rest of the year. (For reasons not appearing in the record, no payments were made after 1972.)

In May of 1973 defendant complained to plaintiff that the unit was not functioning. Plaintiff's field repairmen found that a transformer was burned out, and they placed an order for the part with plaintiff's office. Soon thereafter, however, plaintiff discovered that defendant had made no payments past 1972, and plaintiff consequently took no further action to supply the part. When the unit never did get repaired, defendant refused to resume the making of payments. Plaintiff then brought this action to recover the balance of the purchase

price of the burner, and the trial court rendered the following decision.

Shilling, Justice:

. . . Under UCC Sec. 2-302 "If the court as a matter of law finds the contract or any clause of the contract to have been unconscionable at the time it was made the court may refuse to enforce the contract."

This is the situation here—the court finds, as a matter of law, that the contract introduced by plaintiff is unconscionable and, thereby, under the UCC, unenforceable in this forum. The Court of Appeals has made it plain in *Wilson Trading Corp. v. David Ferguson, Ltd.*, 23 N.Y.2d 398 (1968), that whether a contract or any clause of the contract is unconscionable is a matter for the court to decide against the background of the contract's commercial setting, purpose and effect. This court has the power and the discretion to determine whether a contract is unconscionable. . . .

An unconscionable sales contract contains procedural elements involving the contract formation process, including the use of high-pressure sales tactics, failure to describe terms of the contract, misrepresentation and fraud on the part of the seller, a refusal to bargain on certain critical terms, clauses hidden in fine print, and unequal bargaining power aggravated by the fact that the consumer, in many cases, can't speak English. . . . The term Caveat Emptor ["let the buyer beware"] has been eroded by the UCC; no longer can a seller hide behind it when acting in an unconscionable manner. . . . In making an agreement, the contracting parties create obligations as between themselves—the law of contracts generally contemplate[s] that the parties will meet each other on a footing of social and approximate economic equality. The basic test of unconscionability of a contract is whether under the circumstances existing at the time of the creation of the contract the parties were in equality to each other on all levels. The court can look into the contract to make its determination and ascertain how the contract was made and if the contract was one-sided.

The defendant, in this case, was not looking for any arrangement but was induced to enter into this agreement by the plaintiff. The plaintiff, through its agent, made no attempt to explain to the defendant directly or indirectly what was involved. High pressure sales tactics were used and a Spanish speaking interpreter was not provided by the plaintiff before the contract was signed. Apparent throughout the trial of this matter was that the defendant had a reasonable though limited comprehension of day to day English language usage. On technical or legal issues, however, he demonstrated an uncertainty with various terms and difficulty in expressing himself often found in people in this city for whom English remains a second language. . . . [A]n interpreter was used throughout this trial.

The doctrine of unconscionability is used by the courts to protect those who are unable to protect themselves and to prevent injustice, both in consumer and nonconsumer areas. Unequal bargaining powers and the absence of meaningful choice on the part of one of the parties, together with contract terms which unreasonably favor the other party, may spell out unconscionability. In this case, the defendant had a limited knowledge of the English language and no knowledge of the technical or legal tools of English. The plaintiff never provided an interpreter to explain the contract. The bargaining positions, therefore, were unequal. The defendant was and is, under these facts, unable to protect himself. Since he cannot protect himself, the court must protect him and thus this court declares the contract unconscionable and a nullity.

[Judgment for defendant.]

Other Illegal Contracts

Many other contracts are generally held to be contrary to public policy. Of these, one broad class deserves comment—contracts that "injure the public service." Promises to pay legislators money in return for their votes and similar promises to judges in return for favorable rulings are clearly injurious to the public and therefore illegal. On the other hand, **lobbying contracts,** under which a person is employed by a third party to influence a legislator's vote or an administrator's decision in the awarding of a contract, are not necessarily illegal. The legality of such contracts largely depends on the propriety of the means used by the lobbyist. If, for example, an engineer simply agrees, for a fee, to present to a lawmaker or administrator factual information tending to show the superiority of one product or material over another, the means are proper and the agreement is not contrary to public policy. A contract, however, that contemplates influencing a government official essentially by reliance on the lobbyist's long personal friendship with that person would be illegal.

In regard to **contingent fee contracts,** under which payment of the fee is conditional upon passage of a particular bill or awarding of a contract, many courts flatly deny the lobbyist recovery of his or her fee under any circumstances—on the ground that the tendency of such contracts to induce improper activities is, by itself, sufficient to cause them to be contrary to public policy. Other courts, in such cases, permit the lobbyist to recover if he or she can prove proper conduct—that is, conduct free of deception, undue pressure, and the like.

EFFECT OF ILLEGAL CONTRACTS

As noted early in the chapter, illegal contracts are generally unenforceable. This means that neither party to such a contract will be assisted by the courts in any way, regardless of the consequences to the parties involved. Thus, if S brings suit to recover the purchase price of a quantity of liquor that he has sold and delivered to B in violation of law, his action will be dismissed. Conversely, if B had paid the purchase price when the contract was made and S subsequently failed to deliver the liquor, any action brought by B to recover the price will also be unavailing.

Courts feel that such a hands-off policy is, in most cases, the best way to discourage the making of illegal contracts. There are exceptional situations, however, in which the courts feel that the results obtained under such a policy are so questionable as to warrant some measure of judicial relief. We will examine three of these situations.

Rights of Protected Parties

Some statutes have as their clear purpose the protection of a certain class of persons. Any contract made in violation of such a statute is enforceable by persons within that class, despite its illegality. For example: a Nebraska insurance company, not licensed to sell insurance in Colorado, issues a fire insurance policy on K's home in Denver. The home is destroyed by fire, and the company refuses to pay on the ground that the contract was illegal. The company is liable on its policy. It would be a ludicrous result if K, a person for whose benefit the licensing statutes were enacted, were to be denied recovery on the ground of illegality.

Parties Not Equally at Fault

In most illegal contracts the parties are equally at fault (or substantially equally at fault). In such instances when an action is brought to enforce the contract, the defendant may successfully assert the defense of *in pari delicto*—(literally, "at equal fault").

In some situations, however, the plaintiff may convince the court that he or she was *not* equally at fault with the defendant—i.e., that his or her guilt was substantially less than the defendant's. In such a case the plaintiff's action may be maintained. The exception applies particularly—but not exclusively—where the plaintiff was ignorant of essential facts when the contract was made, through no fault of his or her own. For example: X forges a warehouse receipt, which makes it appear that he is the owner of certain goods stored at a warehouse. X takes the receipt to a trucking company and employs it to pick up the goods at the warehouse and to deliver them

to his place of business. The trucking company does so, not knowing that X is not the owner of the goods. The company is entitled to receive its transportation charge from X, even though it was a participant in an illegal transaction. (The next case in the chapter presents a discussion as to the applicability of the *in pari delicto* defense in a modern-day setting.)

Severable Contracts

Sometimes a single contract turns out on analysis to be two separate agreements. This can be illustrated by a contract under which a retiring restaurant owner agrees to sell to a former competitor his "ten pinball machines for $50 and one electric broiler for $75." In such a contract, called a **severable contract,** the fact that one of the agreements may be illegal does not prevent the other from being enforced. Thus, if the sale of the pinball machines is prohibited by law, the seller is still under an obligation, enforceable in court, to deliver the broiler. However, most contracts that contain several promises on the part of both parties are not severable. The promises of the two parties usually are so interdependent that the court must rule that they resulted in the creation of a single, indivisible contract. In such cases, if any part of the contract is illegal, the entire agreement is unenforceable.

Bateman Eichler, Hill Richards, Inc. v. Berner
U.S. Supreme Court, 472 U.S. 299 (1985)

Berner and a number of other investors filed this damages action in a U.S. district court in California against three defendants: Bateman Eichler, Hill Richards, Inc., a San Francisco-based stock brokerage firm (hereafter referred to as Bateman Eichler); Charles Lazzaro, a broker employed by the firm; and Leslie Neadeau, president of T.O.N.M. Oil and Gas Exploration Corporation (TONM). The gist of the complaint was that Lazzaro and Neadeau, acting together, had violated the Securities and Exchange Act of 1934 and the Securities and Exchange Commission rule 10b-5 promulgated under that act by fraudulently inducing the plaintiffs to purchase large quantities of TONM stock by giving them inside information about TONM's operations, that the information was false and that Lazzaro and Neadeau knew it was false, and that plaintiffs suffered losses when the market price of the stock ultimately fell far below the prices which they paid for it.[a]

More specifically, the complaint alleged that Lazzaro told plaintiffs that he personally knew TONM insiders, and from them learned that vast amounts of gold had been discovered in Surinam; that the discovery was not publicly known; and that TONM had options to buy thousands of acres in the gold producing regions. The complaint further alleged that Lazzaro told them that TONM was negotiating with other companies to form a joint venture for mining the Surinamese gold; that all of this information was soon to be released; and that TONM stock, which was then selling from $1.50 to $3.00 a share, would increase in value from $10 to $15 a share shortly after the release, and "might increase to $100 a share" within a year. As to Neadeau, the complaint alleged that when plaintiffs contacted him to determine whether Lazzaro's tips were accurate, Neadeau—who, like Lazzaro, allegedly knew the information was essentially false—merely stated that the information "was not public knowledge"; that he could "neither confirm nor deny those claims"; and that Lazzaro was "a very trustworthy and a good man." (Neadeau stood to make secret profits from any advance in the price of the stock as the owner of 100,000 shares, and Lazzaro would have profited from such advance not only as the owner of a "large block" of the stock, but also on the taking of commissions on the sales of hundreds of thousands of shares owned by his clients).

The trial court dismissed the complaint, reasoning that "the trading [by the plaintiffs] on insider information is itself a violation of Rule 10b-5," and that the plaintiffs' complaint demonstrated that they themselves had "violated the particular [statute] under which recovery is sought."[b] Thus, the court concluded, plaintiffs were *in pari delicto* with Lazzaro and Neadeau and were "absolutely barred" from recovery. The Court of Appeals for the Ninth Circuit reversed, holding that the *in pari delicto* defense was not a bar to the action. Bateman Eichler appealed to the U.S. Supreme Court.

Brennan, Justice:

The question presented by this case is whether the common-law *in pari delicto* defense bars a private damages action under the federal securities

---

[a]Sec. 10(b) of the act provides that it is unlawful for any person to use any "manipulative or deceptive device" in connection with the sale or purchase of securities in violation of any Securities and Exchange Commission rule. SEC Rule 10b-5, in essence, makes it unlawful for any person, in connection with the sale or purchase of a security, to employ any scheme to defraud; to make any untrue statement of a material fact or fail to state a material fact; or to engage in any conduct which operates as a fraud upon any person.

[b]Under Sec. 16(b) of the act, "insiders" are defined as officers and directors of corporations, and owners of more than 10 percent of the shares of any class of a corporation's stock.

laws against corporate insiders and broker-dealers who fraudulently induce investors to purchase securities by misrepresenting that they are conveying material nonpublic information about the issuer. . . .

The lower courts [in a number of cited cases] have divided over the proper scope of the *in pari delicto* defense in securities litigation. [Accordingly,] we granted certiorari. . . .

The common-law defense at issue in this case derives from the Latin, *in pari delicto potior est condition defendentis:* "In a case of equal or mutual fault, the position of the [defending] party is the better one." The defense is grounded on two premises: first, that courts should not lend their good offices to mediating disputes among wrongdoers; and second, that denying judicial relief to an admitted wrongdoer is an effective means of deterring illegality. In its classic formulation, the *in pari delicto* defense was narrowly limited to situations where the plaintiff truly bore at least substantially equal responsibility for his injury, because "in cases where both parties are in delicto, concurring in an illegal act, it does not always follow that they stand in pari delicto; for there may be, and often are, very different degrees in their guilt." J. Story, *Equity Jurisprudence* (13th ed. 1886). . . . Notwithstanding [this traditional limitation,] many courts have given the *in pari delicto* defense a broad application to bar actions where plaintiffs simply have been involved generally "in the same sort of wrongdoing" as defendants. . . .

The District Court and Court of Appeals proceeded on the assumption that the respondents [plaintiff-investors] had violated §10(b) and Rule 10b-5, an assumption we accept for purposes of resolving the issue before us. Bateman Eichler contends that the respondents' *delictum* was substantially *par* to that of Lazzaro and Neadeau. . . .

We [do not agree] that an investor who engages in [trading on an inside tip] is necessarily as blameworthy as a corporate insider or broker-dealer who discloses the information for personal gain. Notwithstanding the broad reach of §10(b) and Rule 10b-5, there are important distinctions between the relative culpabilities of tippers, securities professionals, and tippees in these circumstances. The court has made it clear in recent [cases] that a tippee's use of material nonpublic information does not violate §10(b) and Rule 10b-5 unless the tippee owes a corresponding duty to disclose the information. That duty typically is "derivative from . . . the insider's duty." In other words, "the tippee's obligation has been viewed as arising from his role as a participant *after the fact* in the insider's breach of a fiduciary duty" toward corporate shareholders.[c] [Emphasis added.] In the context of insider trading, we do not believe that a person whose liability is solely derivative can be said to be as culpable as one whose breach of duty gave rise to that liability in the first place.

Moreover, insiders and broker-dealers who selectively disclose material nonpublic information commit a potentially broader range of violations than

---

[c] The quotations are from *Dirks v. SEC,* 463 U.S. 646, 1983 and *Chiarello v. U.S.*, 445 U.S. 222, 1980 respectively.

do tippees who trade on the basis of that information. A tippee trading on inside information will in many circumstances be guilty of fraud against individual shareholders, a violation for which the tipper shares responsibility. But the insider, in disclosing such information, also frequently breaches fiduciary duties toward the [issuing corporation] itself. And in cases where the tipper intentionally conveys false or materially incomplete information to the tippee, the tipper commits an additional violation: fraud against the tippee. . . .

There is certainly no basis for concluding at this stage of this litigation that the respondents were *in pari delicto* with Lazzaro and Neadeau. The allegations are that Lazzaro and Neadeau masterminded this scheme to manipulate the market in TONM securities for their own personal benefit, and that they used the purchasing respondents as unwitting dupes to inflate the price of TONM stock. . . .

[Turning from the question of the relative guilt of the parties, the court continued]: We also believe that denying the *in pari delicto* defense in such circumstances will best promote the primary objective of the federal securities laws—protection of the investing public and the national economy through the promotion of a high standard of business ethics . . . in every facet of the securities industry. . . . To begin with, barring private actions in cases such as this would inexorably result in a number of alleged fraudulent practices going undetected by the authorities and unremedied. The Securities and Exchange Commission has advised us that it "does not have the resources to police the industry sufficiently to ensure that false tipping does not occur or is consistently discovered," and that "without the tippees' assistance, the Commission could not effectively prosecute false tipping—a difficult practice to detect." . . . Moreover, we believe that deterrence of insider trading most frequently will be maximized by bringing enforcement pressures to bear on the sources of such information—corporate insiders and broker-dealers. . . .

Although situations might well arise in which the relative culpabilities of the tippee and his insider source merit a different mix of deterrent incentives, we therefore conclude that in tipper-tippee situations such as the one before us the factors discussed above preclude recognition of the *in pari delicto* defense. . . . [The case was, therefore, remanded to the trial court.]

Affirmed.

SUMMARY

A contract may be illegal either because it violates a statute (or administrative regulation), or because it is contrary to public policy. In either event such a contract is generally unenforceable. Contracts that are often prohibited by state statute are wagers, those calling for the performance of work by unlicensed persons, contracts entered into (or to be performed) on Sundays, and usurious contracts (those in which a lender charges a rate of interest in excess of that permitted by law). Not all of these contracts, however, are illegal in all states. And even in states where a particular contract is contrary to the letter of a statute, the courts have, in limited circumstances, held the contract to be outside the statute. For example, they usually permit an unlicensed person to recover the contract price of his or her services if the licensing statute was primarily a revenue-raising one (as distinguished from a statute having as its purpose the protection of the health or safety of the citizenry). And, as to Sunday contracts, two points are noteworthy: (1) the number of states retaining such statutes has declined in recent years (with only about 15 having them as of 1987), and (2) in such states the primary thrust of the statutes is the prohibition of retail sales.

The question of whether a particular contract, if enforced, would be injurious to the public at large is determined by the highest court in each state. If the contract is deemed injurious, enforceability is denied on the ground that the contract is contrary to public policy. Contracts that unreasonably restrain trade—being inimical to free and open competition—have long been held to fall within this category. Whether a particular restraint is unreasonable depends upon its purpose, and the scope of its time and space restrictions. Where the restraint is an ancillary part of a contract which itself is lawful, such as a promise by a seller of a business not to compete with the buyer, the restraint is lawful if the protection it affords the buyer is reasonable under the circumstances. Thus a promise by a seller of a single retail establishment not to engage in a similar business anywhere in the state would normally be unreasonably broad, and unenforceable. The test of reasonableness is also applied to restrictive covenants in employment contracts, but—as indicated in the Slisz case—such restrictions are subject to closer scrutiny by the courts than are those in sale of business cases.

Exculpatory clauses in contracts that purport to free one party from liability for loss caused by his or her negligence are also viewed with disfavor by the courts, especially where the company utilizing the clause provides a service

essential to the business world and which, therefore, possesses bargaining power superior to that of the other party. Unconscionable contracts are a third type of contract held to be contrary to public policy. Such contracts generally possess two characteristics: (1) terms that are shockingly one-sided, and (2) possession of greatly superior bargaining power by the party in whose favor the terms operate.

KEY TERMS

Wagering agreement
Lottery
Risk-shifting contract
Risk-creating contract
Futures contract
Licensing statutes
Sunday statutes
Usury
Resale price maintenance contract
Restrictive covenant
Ancillary covenant
Geographical restraints
Exculpatory clause
Bailment contract
Unconscionable contract
Lobbying contract
Contingent fee contract
Severable contract

QUESTIONS AND PROBLEMS

1. Wilson was a licensed Hawaii architect who rendered extensive professional services for the owner of a ranch. When he sought his $33,900 fee, the owner refused to pay because Wilson had failed to pay a $15 state "annual registration fee." Does this failure to pay render Wilson's contract illegal, as the ranch owner contends? Explain. (*Wilson v. Kealakekua Ranch, Ltd.*, 551 P.2d 525, 1976.)

2. Bonasera brought an action against Roffe to recover a real estate commission due him for finding a buyer for Roffe's property. Bonasera was not a licensed broker, and Roffe's defense was an Arizona statute providing that only licensed brokers could recover real estate commissions in that state. Bonasera contended that the statute was not applicable to him since he was not in the real estate business, his activity in this instance being but a "single, isolated transaction." Is the statute applicable to Bonasera? Explain. (*Bonasera v. Roffe*, 442 P.2d 165, 1968.)

3. A brewery rented a building "for use as a saloon" for a period of eight years. Five years later the state enacted a statute making the sale of liquor illegal. The brewing company claimed that passage of the statute freed it of its obligations under the lease for the three remaining years. Is this argument correct? Why or why not? (*Heart v. East Tennessee Brewing Co.*, 113 S.W. 364, 1908.)

4. What are resale price maintenance contracts, and why are they illegal today when used in interstate commerce?

5. Lally sold a barbershop located in Rockville, Connecticut, "together with all good will," to Mattis. The bill of sale contained a clause providing that Lally would not engage in the barbering business in any capacity for a period of five years "anywhere in the City of Rockville, or within a radius of one mile" of the shop's location on Market Street in Rockville. (The one-mile alternative was included because the shop was located only a quarter of a mile from the Rockville city limits.) After the sale, Lally operated a restaurant; but when this became unprofitable a year or two later, he opened a one-chair barbershop in his own home, three hundred yards from the shop Mattis had purchased. When Mattis' business fell off thereafter, he brought an action asking the court to enforce the restric-

tive clause in the contract. Lally contended that the clause in question constituted an unreasonable restraint of trade and was therefore unlawful. Is Lally's contention correct? Explain. (*Mattis v. Lally*, 82 A.2d 155, 1951.)

6. Soble, a lawyer, represented a client in a condemnation suit—a suit in which the client's land was being taken by the state. Soble employed an expert real estate appraiser, Laos, to testify in the suit as to the value of the property. The contract between Soble and Laos provided that Laos was to receive a fee of $1,500 if the court found the value of the property to be $200,000 or less, and $2,500 if the valuation were set at any amount above $200,000. In subsequent litigation, the question arose as to whether this contingent fee contract was contrary to public policy and thus illegal. On what basis could it be argued that the contract *was* illegal? Discuss. (*Laos v. Soble*, 503 P.2d 978, 1972.)

7. When Bova left her car at a parking lot operated by Constantine, she was given an identification ticket upon which was printed matter, which she did not read, as follows: "This station will endeavor to protect the property of its patrons but it is agreed that it will not be liable for loss or damage of cars, accessories or contents from whatever cause arising." When Bova returned, the car was not in the lot. It had been stolen, and, when found, was in need of repairs totaling $154. In an action brought against Constantine to recover this amount, he contended that the clause on the identification ticket freed him of all liability. Was the clause lawful, and thus a good defense to the suit? Explain. (*Agricultural Insurance Co. v. Constantine*, 58 N.E.2d 658, 1944.)

8. Describe three situations in which contracts may be enforceable even though they are illegal in some respect.

Chapter 14

VOIDABLE CONTRACTS

[margin note: legally set aside]

A **voidable contract** is a contract which may be avoided—that is, may be legally set aside—by one of the parties, even though the contract consists of a definite agreement, is supported by consideration, and has a lawful purpose. In this chapter we will examine the most common grounds for the avoidance (disaffirmance) of a contract: *lack of capacity,* and *lack of reality of consent.*

CAPACITY   *[margin note: legal ability to enter into a contract]*

The term **capacity** means the legal ability—the ability or "competence" in the eyes of the law—to perform a particular act. Within the context of this chapter, the particular act under consideration is the making of a binding contract.

A person's capacity to contract may be limited (or entirely lacking, in some instances) for any of three primary reasons: *minority, mental infirmity,* and *intoxication.* We will consider these subjects in order.[1]

MINORS

Centuries ago, the English courts became aware of the fact that many of the contracts entered into by young persons displayed a shocking lack of judgment; such persons assumed obligations and made purchases that they probably would not have had they possessed greater maturity and experience. The courts, desirous of "protecting the young from the consequences of their own folly," began to wrestle with the question of how this protection could best be brought about.

They initially approached the problem by devising what came to be known as the *harm-benefit test.* Under this view, the courts permitted persons who had entered into contracts while under the age of twenty-one to disaffirm them if they were shown to be harmful to these individuals. This approach was followed for a time in the United States. Its application, however, produced such conflict and uncertainty in the law that a new solution became necessary.

The Common-Law Rule

The U.S. courts finally adopted the sweeping rule that, virtually without exception, *all minors' contracts are voidable at their option.* The right thus given to minors to escape their contractual obligations is no longer dependent upon a showing that the contract is harmful or unwise, or that they have been taken advantage of in some way. To effect a disaffirmance of any contract, all the minor has to do is indicate to the other party his or her intention not to be bound by it. The disaffirmance can be express or implied, and the right to disaffirm continues until the minor reaches the age of majority, plus a "reasonable time thereafter."

Two Caveats: First, minors' contracts are *valid* when made; thus they are enforceable against the minor until a disaffirmance occurs. And, second, the right to disaffirm is entirely one-sided; because it is based solely on the fact of incompetence, the other party to the contract has no corresponding right to disaffirm.

Definition of Minority

At common law the age of majority was twenty-one, and as late as 1970 this view was followed by over half the states. Thus a **minor** (or "infant") was anyone who had not attained this age. Since that time, however, virtually all states by statute have reduced the age of majority to eighteen for most purposes, including that of making valid contracts.[2] Therefore, the discussion and

---

[1] Historically, there have been a number of additional classes of persons who possessed little or no capacity to contract: married women, convicted felons, aliens, American Indians, and unincorporated associations. Today, the legal capacity of some of these classes (e.g., married women, aliens, and felons) has generally been restored by statute or by judicial decision, and cases involving the others do not arise often. Thus we will not discuss these classes of persons in this chapter.

[2] These statutes almost uniformly confer upon eighteen-year-olds the rights to sue and be sued in their own names, to make wills, to marry without parental consent, and to choose their own domiciles; but generally they do not sanction the right to buy alcoholic beverages until the age of twenty-one is reached.

illustrations in this chapter assume that a minor is any natural person under the age of eighteen. The agreements of minors of "tender years"—children so young that their minds have not matured sufficiently to understand the meaning of contractual obligations—are void, rather than voidable. Because legal actions against this type of minor are virtually nonexistent, the rules considered below are those applicable to the contracts of "older minors"—typically, sixteen- and seventeen-year-olds.

We will now examine the results of the general rule permitting minors to disaffirm contracts at their option in three basic situations: (1) **ordinary contracts**—that is, contracts under which the goods or services being purchased are not necessities of life; (2) contracts for the purchase of "necessaries," and (3) contracts in which the minor has misrepresented his or her age.

Minors' Liability on Ordinary Contracts

Executory Contracts: *not completed* Few problems arise where the minor's repudiation occurs before either party has started to perform the obligations under the contract (that is, where the contract is still *executory*). Since the other party is caused little hardship in such a case, all states take the view that the disaffirmance entirely frees the minor of liability. For example, suppose that M, a minor, contracts on July 1 to buy a home stereo system from X for $1,200, the contract providing that the system will be delivered and the purchase price paid on July 15. If M notifies X on July 10 that he will not go through with the deal, the contract is at an end and X has no recourse against M. Similarly, if M contracts to paint Y's house for $400 and later refuses to do the job, the refusal absolves M of liability. If either X or Y were to bring suit against M to recover damages for breach of contract, the suit would be dismissed. *— contract not completed* *completed*

Executed Contracts: Surprising as it may seem, the same rule is also generally applied to executed contracts—those that have been fully

performed before the repudiation takes place. *however most states deduct for wear & tear of car* Thus, in virtually all states, a minor can purchase a car for cash, drive it until he or she becomes an adult, and still disaffirm the contract (assuming, as is usually the case, that the car is not a necessity of life).[3]

While virtually all courts agree as to the minor's *right to disaffirm* a contract in a situation such as the above, they do not agree about the *extent of the relief* that should be given to the minor in some circumstances. This can be illustrated by amplifying the facts about the car purchase. Suppose that the purchase price of the car was $2,800 and that the minor brings suit to recover that amount. At the trial, the seller offers evidence establishing that the value of the car at the time the minor offered to return it was $1,500. In such a case the seller can make at least two contentions: (1) that the minor should be charged with the benefit received—that is, the reasonable value of the use of the car prior to disaffirmance or (2) if this contention is rejected, that the minor should at least be charged with the depreciation of the car while it was in the minor's hands.

The Majority View: The courts of most states reject both contentions, permitting the minor to recover the full price of $2,800. Assuming that the automobile does not constitute a necessity, the majority rule is that the minor's only obligation is *to return the consideration if able to do so.* Under this view, the return of the car—even though it has greatly depreciated in value by reason of use or accident—entitles the minor to recover his or her *entire payment.* Furthermore, if the minor is unable to return the consideration, as would be the case if the car were stolen, the minor is still permitted to recover the $2,800 from the unfortunate seller. And regardless of whether the consideration has

NJ when minor completes contract is liable for contract

---

[3] Standard forms of many car dealers contain a statement that the buyer "hereby certifies that he or she is eighteen years of age, or over." The minor's right to disaffirm this kind of contract is discussed later under the "misrepresentation of age" section.

depreciated in value or cannot be returned, the minor is not charged with the benefit received from the possession and use of the consideration.

Freedom from liability would also exist if the minor had purchased the car on credit rather than for cash. In that case, if the minor disaffirmed the contract before paying off the balance, and if the seller then brought action to recover that balance, the minor would again be freed of all liability (subject, again, only to the obligation to return the car if he or she is able to do so).[4]

---

[4]A procedural note: as the above examples illustrate, minority cases ordinarily arise in one of two ways. In the first (and most common) situation the minor has paid *cash* for the goods or services, and, upon disaffirmance, the minor is the plaintiff seeking return of his or her payment. In the second case, where the minor purchases goods or services *on credit* and then disaffirms, the unpaid seller is the plaintiff, seeking to recover the contract price. Regardless of how the cases arise, the applicable minority rules apply with equal force. (That is, if under the applicable rules the minor in the first case is permitted to recover the full purchase price, he or she in the second case will be entirely freed of the obligation to pay for the goods.)

Some Other Views: The courts of a growing number of states, feeling that the majority view imposes unreasonable hardship on the other party to the contract, *do* impose liability on the minor under one of two theories. Some states hold the minor liable for the *reasonable value of the benefit* received prior to the disaffirmance, while others reach a similar result by holding the minor liable for the depreciation that has occurred to the goods while in his or her possession. Going back to the original illustration, where the minor had paid cash for the car, the courts of these states would permit the minor to recover the purchase price *minus* the value of the benefit (or depreciation), whatever the jury finds this to be.

The case below illustrates the broad protection the majority view affords the minor in a typical fact-pattern. (The rationale underlying this view follows the case.)

Halbman v. Lemke

Supreme Court of Wisconsin, 298 N.W.2d 562 (1980)

James Halbman, a minor, worked at a gas station in Greenfield, Wisconsin. During his employment he contracted to buy a 1968 Oldsmobile from Michael Lemke, the station manager, for $1,250. At the time the contract was made Halbman paid Lemke $1,000 cash and took possession of the car. (Title to the vehicle was retained by Lemke.) Under the contract Halbman agreed to pay $25 per week until the balance was paid off.

A little more than a month later, at which time Halbman had paid $1,100 of the price, a connecting rod in the engine broke. He took the car to a garage, where it was repaired at a cost of $637. Halbman did not pay the repair bill. Shortly thereafter Lemke endorsed the car's title over to Halbman, even though the full purchase price had not been paid, in an effort to avoid any liability for the operation and maintenance of the vehicle (including the repair bill). Halbman returned the title to Lemke, with a letter saying he was disaffirming the contract and demanding the return of the $1,100 he had paid. Lemke did not return the money and did not pay the bill. (The car remained in possession of the repair shop). Five months later, with the repair bill still unpaid, the garage removed the car's engine and transmission in satisfaction of the debt. The garage then towed the vehicle to the home of Halbman's father. While there it was subjected to vandalism which made the car "unsalvageable."

Halbman then brought this action to recover the $1,100 he had paid, and Lemke counterclaimed for $150, the amount still owing on the contract. The trial court granted judgment for Halbman, ruling that when a minor disaffirms a contract for the purchase of an item, his or her only obligation is to return the property remaining in his hands. The court of appeals affirmed, and Lemke petitioned the Supreme Court of Wisconsin for review.

[handwritten: exculatory Contract — minor didn't complete contract — can get out of contract not necessarily]

Callow, Justice:

. . . The sole issue before us is whether a minor, having disaffirmed a contract for the purchase of an item which is not a necessity and having tendered the property back to the vendor, must make restitution to the vendor for damage to the property prior to the disaffirmance. Lemke argues that he should be entitled to recover for the damage to the vehicle up to the time of disaffirmance, which he claims equals the amount of the repair bill.

Neither party challenges the absolute right of a minor to disaffirm a contract for the purchase of items which are not necessities. That right, variously known as the doctrine of incapacity or the "infancy doctrine," is one of the oldest and most venerable of our common-law traditions. Although the origins of the doctrine are somewhat obscure, it is generally recognized that its purpose is the protection of minors from foolishly squandering their wealth through improvident contracts with crafty adults who would take advantage of them in the marketplace. . . .

As a general rule, a minor who disaffirms a contract is entitled to recover all consideration he has conferred incident to the transaction. In return the minor is expected to restore as much of the consideration as, at the time of disaffirmance, remains in the minor's possession. The minor's right to disaffirm is not contingent upon the return of the property, however, as disaffirmance is permitted even where such return cannot be made. . . .

The law regarding the rights and responsibilities of the parties relative to the consideration exchanged on a disaffirmed contract is characterized by confusion, inconsistency, and a general lack of uniformity as jurisdictions attempt to reach a fair application of the infancy doctrine in today's marketplace. [The court then analyzed a number of cases which, Lemke contended, barred recovery by Halbman in this action. The court rejected the rules of those cases, saying]: Because these cases would at some point force the minor to bear the cost of the very improvidence from which the infancy doctrine is supposed to protect him, we cannot follow them.

As we noted in [a prior Wisconsin case], modifications of the rules governing the capacity of infants to contract are best left to the legislature. Until such changes are forthcoming, however, we hold that, absent misrepresentation or tortious damage to the property, a minor who disaffirms a contract for the purchase of an item which is not a necessity may recover his purchase price without liability for use, depreciation, damage, or other diminution in value. . . .

The decision of the court of appeals is affirmed.

Rationale: There is no question but that the majority rule, as applied to specific situations, frequently results in a severe financial loss to the party who has dealt with the minor. It is also possible that some young people, aware of the rule, enter into contracts with the intention of getting something for nothing. Nevertheless, most courts justify the occasional hardships that result under the majority rule by noting that "the primary purpose of the common-law rule is to afford protection to minors by discouraging others from contracting with them," and this rule no doubt tends to bring about such a result. Thus we have once again a situation where the rights of some individuals, under certain circumstances, must give way to the rights of others because of public policy considerations.

A competent person can, of course, ordinarily escape such hardships by refusing to deal with minors.[5] All persons are presumed to know the law, so that (in theory at least) one who deals with a minor is on notice that it is at his or her peril. A second solution for someone who wishes to make a sale is to refuse to deal with the minor and to contract instead with one of the minor's parents. In such a case the possibility of a disaffirmance is eliminated, since both parties to the contract are competent. A third solution, in situations where the competent party does not know whether the person with whom he or she is dealing is a minor, is to have that person make a statement, preferably in writing, that he or she is over the age of eighteen. (The protection af-

forded to the competent party by such a representation is considered later in the chapter.)

Ratification: Once a minor reaches the age of majority, he or she has the ability to ratify any contracts made earlier. A **ratification** occurs when the minor indicates to the other party, expressly or impliedly, the intent to be bound by the agreement. Thus, if a minor, after reaching the age of eighteen, promises that he or she will go through with the contract, an express ratification has taken place and the right of disaffirmance is lost forever. Similarly, if a minor has received an article, such as a typewriter, under a contract and continues to use it for more than a "reasonable time" after reaching the age of eighteen, an implied ratification has occurred. Another situation in which a ratification can take place involves purchases made under installment contracts. Suppose, for example, that a minor has purchased a motorcycle, agreeing to pay the seller $25 a month until the purchase price has been paid in full. If he continues to make payments for any length of time after reaching the age of eighteen, it is probable that such payments will be held to constitute a ratification of the contract. (It is obvious, then, that any young person should review all of his or her contracts upon becoming an adult, and refrain from any conduct that would indicate to the other party an intent to be bound by them if he or she wishes to set any of them aside.)

Minors' Liability on Contracts to Purchase "Necessaries"

When a minor purchases **necessaries** (goods that the law considers necessary to life or health), he or she incurs a greater liability than

---

[5]Some persons, such as common carriers, have a legal duty to deal with everyone who requests (and is able to pay for) their services. Disaffirmance against such persons is generally not permitted once the contract has been executed. Thus, a seventeen-year-old who purchases and uses an airline ticket is not permitted to recover his or her fare.

that imposed (by the majority rule) under contracts calling for the purchase of goods that are not necessities. The rule applicable to contracts calling for the purchase of "necessaries" is that the minor is liable to the other party for the *reasonable value of the goods actually used.* To illustrate: M, seventeen, buys a topcoat from C, contracting to pay the price of $150 one year later. At the end of that time, when the coat is completely worn out, C brings suit to recover the purchase price. If the court rules that the coat is a necessary, then it must determine what its reasonable value was at the time of the purchase, and M is liable to C in that amount. (In contrast, if the coat is held *not* to constitute a necessary, M is usually freed of all liability—as has been seen earlier.) This imposition of liability occurs only where the goods or services have been used by the minor; contracts calling for the purchase of necessaries can still be set aside as long as they are executory. Thus, if M contracts to purchase a coat from C, which is to be delivered one week later, he can set aside the contract without liability if he notifies C of his disaffirmance before the week is out—and indeed, even later as long as he does not use the coat.

What Constitutes a Necessary?   In answering the question of what constitutes a necessary, it is possible to draw a clear line in most cases. Mini-

mum amounts of food, clothing, and medical services are clearly necessary. So, too, is the rental of a house or apartment by a minor who is married. Many items, on the other hand, are clearly luxuries—such as TV sets, sporting goods, and dancing lessons, under most circumstances.[6]

Cars are generally held not to be necessaries, but there is disagreement in regard to cars (and other items) used by the minor in his or her work. Most courts continue to follow the older rule in this area, holding that such items do not constitute necessaries. Recent decisions, however, have increasingly taken the view that *property used by the minor for self-support does constitute a necessity.*

It should be noted that an item is a necessity only if it is actually needed at the time of purchase. Thus if a minor purchases an item that appears to be a necessity, such as an article of clothing, the minor still has no liability to the seller if he or she can prove that a parent or guardian was "willing and able" to furnish clothing of the type purchased under that particular contract.

The following case presents a problem typical of those arising in the "necessity" area.

[handwritten note in margin: your only means of getting to school—Court rules it is a car necessity]

---

[6]In determining whether a doubtful item is a necessary, the courts take into account the "station in life" occupied by the particular minor. Thus a fourth sport coat might be ruled a necessary for a minor who is a member of high society, while it would not be so ruled in regard to others.

Gastonia Personnel Corporation v. Rogers
Supreme Court of North Carolina, 172 S.E.2d 19 (1970)

Rogers was a minor who was studying civil engineering in a North Carolina college. When his wife became pregnant he had to quit school and go to work. In order to get suitable employment, Rogers signed a contract with an employment agency, Gastonia Personnel Corporation, the plaintiff. Under the terms of this agreement Rogers agreed to pay plaintiff a fee of $295 if it produced a "lead" that resulted in a job for him.

Soon thereafter one of plaintiff's personnel counselors put Rogers in touch with a Charlotte firm which hired him as a draftsman. Rogers

subsequently disaffirmed the contract with plaintiff on the ground of minority, and refused to pay its fee. Plaintiff then brought suit to recover the $295 or, in the alternative, the reasonable value of its services. Plaintiff's primary contention was that its services constituted a necessity, under the circumstances of the case. The trial court ruled as a matter of law that the services were not a necessity, and dismissed the action. Plaintiff appealed.

Bobbitt, Chief Justice:

. . . "By the fifteenth century it seems to have been well settled that an infant's bargain was [voidable] at his election, and also [well settled] that he was liable for necessaries." 2 *Williston, Contracts* §223 (1959). . . . In accordance with this ancient rule of the common law, this court has held an infant's contract, unless for "necessaries" or unless authorized by statute, is voidable by the infant, at his election, and may be disaffirmed during infancy or upon attaining the age of [majority]. . . .

In general, our prior decisions are to the effect that the "necessaries" of an infant, and his wife and child, include only such necessities of life as food, clothing, shelter, medical attention, and so forth. In our view, the concept of "necessaries" should be enlarged to include such articles of property and such services as are reasonably necessary to enable the infant to earn the money required to provide the necessities of life for himself and those who are legally dependent upon him. . . .

The evidence [shows] that defendant, when he contracted with plaintiff, . . . was married, a high school graduate, within "a quarter or 22 hours" of obtaining his degree in applied science, and capable of holding a [draftsman's] job at a starting annual salary of $4,784. To hold, as a matter of law, that such a person cannot obligate himself to pay for services rendered him in obtaining employment suitable to his ability, education, and specialized training, enabling him to provide the necessities of life for himself, his wife and his expected child, would place him and others similarly situated under a serious economic handicap.

In the effort to protect "older minors" from improvident or unfair contracts, the law should not deny to them the opportunities and right to obligate themselves for articles of property or services which are reasonably necessary to enable them to provide for the proper support of themselves and their dependents. The minor should be held liable for the reasonable value of articles of property or services received pursuant to such contract. Applying the foregoing legal principles, which modify the ancient rule of the common law, we hold that the evidence offered by plaintiff was sufficient for submission to the jury for its determination of issues substantially as indicated below.

To establish liability, plaintiff must satisfy the jury . . . that defendant's contract was an appropriate and reasonable means for defendant to obtain suitable employment. If this issue is answered in plaintiff's favor, plaintiff must then establish the reasonable value of the services received by defendant pursuant to the contract. Thus, plaintiff's recovery, if any, cannot exceed the reasonable value of its services. . . .

Judgment reversed, and case remanded.

Minors' Liability on Contracts Involving Misrepresentation of Age

We have assumed so far that the minor has not led the other party to believe that he or she is an adult. If such misrepresentation does occur, the minor is guilty of a kind of fraud, and the courts of most jurisdictions will deny the protection that otherwise would be given that person.

Some states have provided by statute that a minor who has misrepresented his or her age is liable on the contract exactly as if he or she were an adult. Most states, however, have left the matter up to the courts, and a spate of rules has resulted. Without attempting to consider all of them, we can make one or two generalizations.

First, where the minor repudiates the contract while it is entirely executory, most courts permit the disaffirmance just as if there had been no misrepresentation. Although this does not penalize the minor for wrongdoing, it also does not cause particular hardship to the other party in most instances.

Second, where a contract calling for the purchase of a nonnecessary item has been fully or partially executed before the attempted disaffirmance, many courts allow the disaffirmance *only if it will not cause a loss to the other party.*[7] Under this approach, each case is analyzed separately to determine the effect of the disaffirmance. Two illustrations follow.

1. M, a minor, purchases a car from C, a competent party, for $2,500 cash, after telling C that she is eighteen. A year later, just before becoming eighteen, M wishes to disaffirm; at this time the market value of the car is $1,400. Despite the misrepresentation, disaffirmance will be permitted. C, however, will be allowed to withhold from the $2,500 the amount of the depreciation, $1,100, which—added to the $1,400 car—will restore him to his original position. M's recovery is thus only $1,400.

2. M purchases a car from C under a contract providing, "Buyer certifies that he or she is eighteen years of age or older." The purchase price is $2,500, with $100 paid at the time of purchase and the balance of $2,400 payable in twenty-four monthly installments. Six months later, when the car is stolen, M notifies C that she wants to be relieved of the balance of the contract. Disaffirmance will probably not be allowed since this would cause a loss to C; thus a suit by C to recover the unpaid balance will be successful.[8]

The contract liability of minors regarding both executory and executed contracts is illustrated in Figure 14.1.

Contracts That Cannot Be Disaffirmed

Not all contracts can be disaffirmed on the ground of minority. For example, disaffirmance of marriage contracts and contracts of enlistment in the armed forces is not permitted on the ground of public policy. For certain other contracts, such as those approved by a court or those made with banks or insurance companies, the same result is generally brought about by statute. For example, a North Carolina statute authorizes banks "in respect to deposit accounts

[7] In cases of "necessary" contracts, the usual rule normally continues in effect—the minor is liable for the reasonable value of the articles actually used.

[8] This example is based on *Haydocy Pontiac, Inc. v. Lee,* 19 Ohio App.2d 217 (1969). The minor in this case was held to be "estopped" from disaffirming, in view of her misrepresentation; and she continued to be liable for the "fair value of the property."

Figure 14.1   **Contract Liability of Minors**

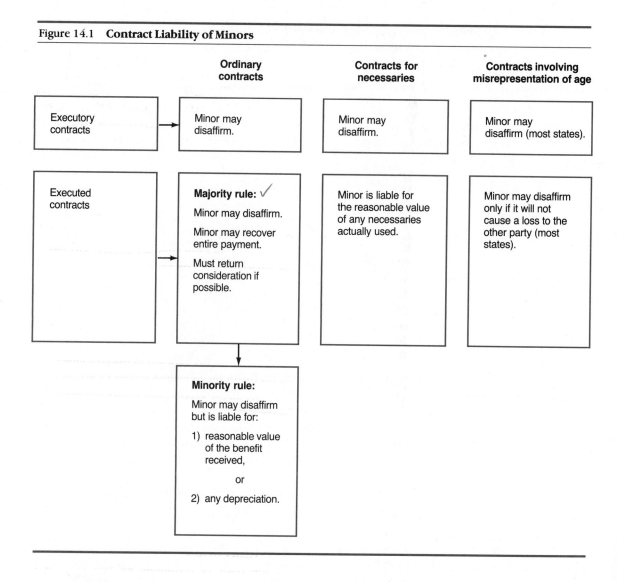

	Ordinary contracts	Contracts for necessaries	Contracts involving misrepresentation of age
Executory contracts	Minor may disaffirm.	Minor may disaffirm.	Minor may disaffirm (most states).
Executed contracts	**Majority rule:** ✓ Minor may disaffirm. Minor may recover entire payment. Must return consideration if possible.	Minor is liable for the reasonable value of any necessaries actually used.	Minor may disaffirm only if it will not cause a loss to the other party (most states).

Minority rule:

Minor may disaffirm but is liable for:

1) reasonable value of the benefit received,

or

2) any depreciation.

and the rental of safe deposit boxes" to deal with minors as if they were adults. And another North Carolina statute authorizes minors of fifteen and over to make life insurance contracts to the same extent as adults.

Torts and Crimes

The rules permitting minors to disaffirm most contracts do not apply to acts that are tortious or criminal in nature. Generally, minors are fully liable for any torts or crimes they commit (except, of course, minors of "tender years," such as two- or three-year-olds). Thus, if a minor drives a car negligently, anyone injured thereby can recover damages from him or her. Such liability cannot be disaffirmed. Similarly, if a minor operates a motor vehicle while intoxicated, the usual criminal penalties can be imposed (although in the criminal area, the penalties may be tempered under juvenile court procedures).

MENTALLY IMPAIRED AND INTOXICATED PERSONS

Mentally Impaired Persons

Persons with impaired mental capacity are, like minors, given substantial protection by the law insofar as their contractual obligations are concerned. We will briefly examine the general rules applicable to those falling within this broad category which includes the mentally retarded, the brain damaged, the senile, and persons suffering from mental illness. (In the law, the term "insane" is often broadly used to encompass all of the above classes, but sometimes is used more restrictively to refer only to the last class—persons of average intelligence who suffer periods of derangement that often vary widely as to intensity and duration.)[9]

Some mentally impaired persons are formally declared to be incompetent by a court after hearings and examination by psychologists or psychiatrists. After such declaration a guardian is appointed, any "contract" made by the impaired person after the adjudication is absolutely void—that is, creates no liability whatever, even if it is never disaffirmed by the incompetent person or the guardian. (However, if any goods or services furnished under the contracts were necessities not being furnished by the guardian, the impaired person would be liable for their fair market value under the quasi-contract theory.)

Many other persons who suffer from some degree of mental disability have never been the subject of incompetency proceedings. Such persons' contracts are not void, but voidable—i.e., they may be set aside by a court at the request of the impaired party after he or she regains full mental capacity, depending upon the circumstances existing at the time of contracting.

In any action in which the one claiming incompetence seeks to have the contract set aside (or "avoided"), the usual test that is applied presents a question of fact: was he or she capable of understanding the nature and effect of the particular agreement at the time that it was entered into? If the trier of fact finds such understanding was lacking, rescission of the contract will be allowed. In such an instance the impaired person is sometimes referred to as **insane in fact** in contrast to one "insane at law," the latter term referring to one **adjudicated insane.** On the other hand, if such understanding is found to have existed, the contracting party is bound by the contract to the same extent as any fully competent party. (Again, if rescission is allowed, liability for the fair market value of any necessities furnished under the contract would exist under the quasi-contract principle.)

Hanks v. NcNeill Coal Corporation, 168 P.2d 256 (1946), is typical of those controversies in which the evidence on the "understanding" issue was in sharp conflict. In that case Hanks, a farmer who had never been adjudicated insane, sold coal lands in Colorado to the coal company. At his death his executor sought to rescind the contract on the ground that Hanks was insane in fact—actually insane—at the time of the transaction. In support of this contention, the executor introduced evidence that in the months prior to the sale Hanks was increasingly interested in the "emotional type" of religion; was increasingly abusive to his family members; and manufactured a medicine for horses made of brick dust, burnt shoe leather, and pieces of ground glass. Despite this evidence, the court ruled Hanks to be sane with respect to the sale, on the basis of testimony by lawyers and a banker who had other dealings with him about the time of the sale, who testified that, as to business matters, he appeared to be "in grasp of his affairs" and "rational." In explaining its ruling, the court said: "One may have insane delusions regarding some matters and be insane on some subjects, yet [be] capable of transacting business concerning matters wherein such matters are not concerned, and such insanity does not make one incompetent to contract unless the subject matter of the contract is so connected with an insane delusion as to render the afflicted party

---

[9]In any event, the various terms or labels used in the law, such as those we mention here, are often somewhat different from, or less precise than, those used by the medical profession.

incapable of understanding the nature and effect of the agreement, or of acting rationally in the transaction."

Intoxicated Persons

People occasionally seek to escape liability under a contract on the ground that they were intoxicated when it was made. Success in doing so depends primarily on the degree of intoxication found to exist at that time. Disaffirmance is allowed only if a person can establish that he or she was so intoxicated as not to understand the nature of the purported agreement. Thus a question of fact is presented, for a lesser degree of intoxication is not grounds for disaffirmance.

If the required degree of intoxication is found to have existed, the intoxicated person's right to disaffirm, upon regaining sobriety, also substantially parallels that of a minor—again, however, with one basic exception. While we have seen that minors may, as a general rule, disaffirm contracts even though unable to return the consideration that they received, intoxicated persons are required by most courts to return the full consideration as a condition of disaffirmance in all cases (unless they are able to show fraud on the part of the other contracting party).

REALITY OF CONSENT

A contract that has been entered into between two persons having full capacity to contract, and which appears to be valid in all other respects, may still be unenforceable if it turns out that the apparent consent of one or both of the parties was, in fact, not genuine. Contracts that are tainted with *fraud, innocent misrepresentation, mistake, duress, or undue influence* can ordinarily be voided (set aside) by the innocent parties. In such instances the courts will allow rescission on the ground that there was "no reality of consent." That is, although it *appears* from the form of the contract alone that the consent of both parties was genuine (or "real"), in fact it was not.

Many areas of law are essentially made up of rules that discourage conduct that is deceitful or otherwise injurious to individuals or to society in general. Some types of conduct are felt to be so detrimental to a stable society that they are flatly prohibited, and punishment for violators is prescribed. From hence have our bodies of criminal law been built up.

In other areas of law rules have come about that attempt to insure at least some degree of care and fairness when private citizens have dealings with one another, and which grant civil remedies against persons who violate them. We have seen, for example, that tortious conduct causes the wrongdoer to answer in damages to the injured party. This continuing filament of thought, to the effect that a person should not be allowed to profit by conduct that is patently offensive, is woven into the law of contracts. It is most apparent in that part of law having to do with fraud and duress and, to a lesser extent, mistake and undue influence.

FRAUD

Leaving aside, for the moment, any attempt to define the term, the essence of **fraud** is deception—the intentional misleading of one person by another. Perhaps the most common type of fraud occurs when one person simply lies to another about a material fact, as a result of which a contract is made. Thus, if S, the owner of a current model car, tells B that he purchased it new six months ago, S knowing that it was in fact "second-hand" when he acquired it, S is guilty of fraud if B, believing this statement to be true, subsequently purchases the car. In this case, B—after learning the true facts—ordinarily can either rescind the contract and recover the purchase price or keep the car and recover damages from S.

Elements of Fraud

One person can mislead another in so many ways that the courts have been reluctant to fashion a hard and fast definition of fraud; any precise definition almost certainly could be circumvented by persons intent on getting around it.[10] Instead, the courts generally recognize that the various forms of deception they wish to forestall usually contain common elements. When a court is called upon to decide in a given case whether the conduct of one of the parties was fraudulent, its usual approach is to see if the required elements are present. If so, fraud has been established and the victim will be afforded relief.

To be successful in a fraud action, the plaintiff is required to show all of the following:

1. That defendant made a *misrepresentation of fact.*

2. That the statement was made with the *intent to deceive* (i.e., defendant knew or should have known the statement was false).

3. That plaintiff *reasonably relied* on the misrepresentation.

4. That plaintiff suffered an *injury* as a result.

Misrepresentation of Fact

Misrepresentation of fact (or *misstatement*) is broadly interpreted to include any word or conduct that causes the innocent person to reach an erroneous conclusion of fact. Thus a seller of apples who selects the best ones in a basket and puts them on top of others of inferior quality has, in the eyes of the law, made a "statement" to a prospective buyer that all the apples are of the same quality as those which are visible.

In order for a misstatement to be fraudulent, it must be a **statement of fact**—an actual event, circumstance, or occurrence. Statements about the age of a horse, the number of acres in a tract of land, and the net profit made by a business during a given year are all statements of fact—

that is, statements about a fact. If the innocent person can prove that the particular statement made to him or her was false, the first element of fraud has been established.

Predictions: Statements as to what will happen in the future are clearly not statements of fact and therefore are not fraudulent even if they turn out to be in error. Thus, if a seller of stock tells a buyer that the stock is "bound to double in value within six months," the buyer is not entitled to relief in the event the increase in value does not come about. The same is true when the seller of a motel states that "it will certainly net $14,000 in the coming year." The reason for the view that such statements do not constitute fraud, of course, is that no one can predict what will happen in the future, and a reasonable person would not put faith in such statements.[11]

Opinion: **Statements of opinion,** like predictions, are also distinguished from statements of fact. Contracts cannot be set aside on the ground of fraud simply because one of the parties, prior to making the contract, expressed an opinion that later turned out to be incorrect.

Most statements of opinion, in which the declarant is merely expressing personal feelings or judgments on a matter about which reasonable persons might have contrary views, are usually easy to recognize. For example, statements that "this is an excellent neighborhood in which to

---

[10] Some helpful definitions do exist, of course. One provides that fraud is "a false representation of a material fact made with knowledge of its falsity or culpable ignorance of its truth, with intention that it be acted upon by the party deceived and inducing him to contract to his injury." 17 C.J.S., *Contracts*, §153. Copyright 1963 by West Publishing Co.

[11] One important type of statement about a present or future event or condition *does* impose a legal obligation on the one making it if it proves to be false: statements that are "warranties"—guarantees as to existing fact or assurances about future performance of a product by the seller. For example: A manufacturer of house paint states on the cans that "this paint, when applied according to the manufacturer's instructions above, will not crack, fade, or peel within two years of its application." If the statement proves to be false, a buyer who has purchased the paint in reliance on the statement can recover damages. The recovery in such a case would be on *breach of warranty* rather than on fraud, except in the rare situation where the buyer can prove that the seller knew the representation to be false when he or she made it. (Most, but not all, warranties are governed by the *law of sales*. Specific questions about the definition and application of express and implied warranties in regard to the sale of goods require reference to Secs. 2-312, 313, 314, 315, and 316 of the UCC, discussed in detail in Chapter 22.)

raise children" or that "this painting will harmonize beautifully with the colors of your living room" involve conclusions with which others might disagree; thus they cannot be the basis of an action of fraud brought by one who relied upon them.

Other statements, however, are not so easily placed in the "opinion" or "fact" categories. A statement by the seller of a boat that it is "perfectly safe" or a statement by a home owner that "the foundation is sound" are closer to being statements of fact than the previous representations about the neighborhood and the painting. But there are varying degrees of safety and soundness, so these statements too can be held in given situations to constitute only expressions of opinion—particularly if the declarant and the innocent party were on a relatively equal basis insofar as their experience and general knowledge of the subject matter were concerned. (On the other hand, if the declarant is considerably more knowledgeable than the other party, such statements are likely to be viewed as statements of *fact,* and thus fraudulent if false. For example, in the case of *Groening v. Opsata,* 34 N.W.2d 560, 1948, it was held that a false statement by the seller of a summer home located on an eroding cliff on the shore of Lake Michigan that "it isn't too close [to the lake]" and that "there is nothing to fear, everything is all right" constituted fraud, in view of the fact that the seller was a builder of homes in the area.)

Value: Statements about an article's *value* have also caused difficulties. Nevertheless, the courts today adhere to the traditional view (in most circumstances) that the value of an article or piece of property is a matter of opinion rather than fact. Two practical reasons are the basis for this view: (1) an awareness that many types of property are prized by some people but are considered of little value by others, and (2) a recognition of the fact that sellers generally overvalue the things they are attempting to sell, and prospective buyers must accordingly place little or no reliance upon such statements.[12] Consequently, if a seller states that "this apartment building is easily worth $80,000," the buyer normally can not rescind the contract on the ground of fraud, even though he or she relied on the statement and can prove later that the actual market value of the building at the time of sale was nowhere near the stated figure and that the seller knew this at the time.

Again, the general rule is not followed when the declarant's experience and knowledge of the particular subject matter are *markedly superior* to those of the other party—especially if they are so great that the declarant is considered an "expert" in the eyes of the law. (In order to prevent such a person from taking grossly unfair advantage of those who are clearly less knowledgeable, his or her intentional misrepresentations *are* held to be fraudulent.)

The next case presents an allegation of fraud in a modern setting.

---

[12] Statements of gross overvaluation, like others that are grossly extravagant in nature ("this sport coat will wear like iron"), constitute mere "dealers' puffing."

Steinberg v. Chicago Medical School
Supreme Court of Illinois, 371 N.E.2d 634 (1977)

The Chicago Medical School, defendant, issued a bulletin for the 1974–1975 school year which stated that applicants would be selected "on the basis of academic achievement, Medical College Admission Test results, personal appraisals by a pre-professional advisory committee or individual instructors, and the personal inter-

view, if requested by the Committee on Admissions." Steinberg received a bulletin, applied for admission, and paid the required $15 application fee.

After his application was rejected, Steinberg learned that the defendant, in fact, used "nonacademic criteria" in admitting applicants, primarily the ability of the applicant or his family to pledge or make payments of large sums of money to the school. Steinberg then brought this action on behalf of all rejected applicants, claiming that defendant was guilty of fraud in failing to disclose such factors.

A number of issues were raised in the trial court. Two of these were (1) whether a contract was ever formed between the parties, and (2) if so, whether defendant's representations in its bulletin constituted fraud. The trial court ruled against plaintiff on all issues and dismissed the action. An intermediate court of appeals affirmed some rulings of the trial court but reversed others. Plaintiff appealed to the Supreme Court of Illinois. (Only those parts of the highest court's decision applicable to the two selected issues are set forth below).

Dooley, Justice:

. . . An offer [and] an acceptance . . . are basic ingredients of a contract. Steinberg alleges that he and [others] received a brochure describing the criteria that defendant would employ in evaluating applications. He urges that such constituted an invitation for an offer to apply, that the filing of the applications constituted an offer to have their credentials appraised under the terms described by defendant, and that defendant's voluntary reception of the application and fee constituted an acceptance, the final act necessary for the creation of a binding contract.

This situation is similar to that wherein a merchant advertises goods for sale at a fixed price. While the advertisement itself is [usually] not an offer to contract, it constitutes an invitation to deal on the terms described in the advertisement. . . . When the merchant takes the money [there is] an acceptance of the offer to purchase. [The court then agreed with Steinberg's contention that the defendant's receipt of his application and fee constituted an acceptance of his application offer, and that a contract was thus formed. The court next turned to the question of fraud.]

Count III alleges that, with intent to deceive and defraud plaintiffs, defendant stated in its catalogs it would use certain criteria to evaluate applications; that these representations were false in that applicants were selected primarily for monetary considerations; that plaintiffs relied on said representations and were each thereby induced to submit their applications and pay $15, [and that plaintiffs were damaged as a result].

These allegations support a cause of action for fraud. Misrepresentation of an existing material fact coupled with scienter [knowledge], deception, and injury are more than adequate. . . . Plaintiff's allegations of fraud meet the test of common-law fraud.

Not to be ignored is defendant's *modus operandi* as described in *De-Marco v. University of Health Sciences*, 352 N.E.2d 356 (1976):

> *An analysis of those exhibits shows that in 1970, at least 64 out of 83 entering students had pledges made in their behalves totalling $1,927,900. The pledges varied in amounts from $1400 to $100,000 and averaged $30,123. In 1971, at least 55 out of 83 students had pledges made in their behalves totalling $1,893,000. The pledges varied in amounts from $3000 to $100,000 and averaged $34,418. In 1972, at least 73 out of an entering class of 92 had contributions made in their behalves totalling $3,111,000. The pledges varied in amounts from $20,000 to $100,000 and averaged $42,603. In 1973, at least 78 out of 91 students had contributions made in their behalves totalling $3,749,000. The pledges varied in amounts from $10,000 to $100,000 and averaged $48,064. In addition, there were amounts pledged and partial payments made for students who did not enter or dropped out shortly after entering.*

It is immaterial here that the misrepresentation consisted of a statement in the medical school catalog, referring to future conduct, that "student's potential for the study and practice of medicine will be evaluated on the basis of academic achievement, Medical College Admission Test results, personal appraisals by a pre-professional advisory committee or individual instructors, and the personal interview, if requested by the Committee on Admissions." We concede the general rule denies recovery for fraud based on a false representation of intention or future conduct, but there is a recognized exception where the false promise or representation of future conduct is alleged to be the scheme employed to accomplish the fraud. Such is the situation here. . . .

[The higher court, disagreeing with the trial court, thus ruled that Steinberg's allegations, if true, did state a cause of action. It therefore remanded the case to the trial court for determination of the factual issues presented.]

Law: Under the early common-law rule of this country, *statements of law* made by lay persons were clearly held not to constitute statements of fact and thus could not be the basis for actions of fraud. If the seller of a vacant lot that carries a C-1 zoning classification assures the buyer that "this classification permits the erection of duplex rental units," a statement that the seller knows is not true, the buyer who purchases the property in reliance on the statement ordinarily cannot maintain an action for damages. The rule was based on two grounds: (1) the generally reasonable feeling that a statement made by a non-lawyer about a point of law should not be relied upon by the one to whom it is made, and (2) the somewhat more questionable maxim that "everyone is presumed to know the law."

While this is still the rule applied to most cases, it is subject to an increasing number of exceptions. One major exception comprises statements of law made by persons who—because of their professional or occupational status—can reasonably be expected to know the law relating to their specialty, even though they are not attorneys. Thus intentional misrepresentations of law by persons such as real estate brokers and bank cashiers as to legal matters within their particular specialties are frequently held to be fraudulent. (One aspect of question 4 in Questions and Problems presents an issue in this area.)

Silence, Generally: Because the essence of fraud is the affirmative misleading of one person by another, the general rule that mere silence does *not constitute fraud* (i.e., does not constitute a misrepresentation of fact) applies to most situations. This is because the majority of "silence" cases that reach the courts present fact-patterns in which the parties are dealing at arm's length,[13] because the parties possess roughly the same amount of experience and knowledge relating to the subject matter of the contract; and because, in many situations, the facts not disclosed could have been ascertained by the party claiming fraud if he or she had used reasonable diligence prior to entering into the contract. As a result of these considerations, the private seller of a used car who knows it has been involved in an accident is ordinarily not guilty of fraud if he or she fails to disclose this fact to the buyer.[14] Similarly, a tenant who is attempting to sublet an apartment with the owner's consent is not guilty of fraud for failing to tell a prospective renter that he or she has had numerous run-ins with the owner, and has generally found the owner a difficult person to deal with.

Silence and the Duty to Speak: There are, however, exceptional circumstances in which the withholding of information is so manifestly unfair that the silence will constitute fraud. To prevent unfairness of this degree, the courts say that, in such situations, a "duty to speak" existed. It is difficult to summarize the duty to speak categories with precision, because the silence cases involve such a wide variety of fact-patterns, and because the rules of the various states applicable to duty to speak situations are often couched in general terms (to give the courts substantial discretion in their application). Additionally, the law is continuing to evolve in this area, as the courts seek to raise moral standards in the marketplace by applying the rules to situations that were earlier outside their scope.

Despite these factors, several fairly well-defined situations do exist in which the courts generally agree that a duty to speak exists. (In such instances the courts often speak of "intentionally withheld information," of "concealment," and of silence as part of a "plan" to deceive.)

The first of these instances is the sale of property that contains a **latent defect** (or *hidden defect*)—one that a simple or casual inspection by a prospective purchaser ordinarily would not disclose. Common examples are a cracked motor block in an automobile and a termite infestation in a house. A property owner who has knowledge of such conditions is guilty of fraud if he or she does not apprise the prospective purchaser of them—assuming, of course, that the innocent purchaser subsequently enters into a contract to buy the property.

While the latent defect rule, abstractly stated, is highly commendable, the practical protection it affords is less than one might hope for. Frequently it is difficult for the buyer to prove that the defect actually existed at the time of purchase—particularly if a long period of time has elapsed before its discovery. And even if this hurdle is cleared, the buyer has to establish that the seller knew, or should have known, of the defect when the sale occurred. The seller's contention that he or she was honestly unaware of the defective condition is frequently accepted by a jury.[15]

A second duty to speak situation occurs where a **fiduciary relationship** exists—that is, where

---

[13] Parties are said to deal at "arm's length" when their relationship is such that neither party owes a duty to divulge information to the other party (as distinguished from such exceptional relationships as attorney-client and guardian-ward relationships.)

[14] Buyers can protect themselves in cases of this sort by asking if the car had ever been in an accident. If the seller answers falsely, he or she is clearly guilty of fraud. (And if the seller refuses to answer, the buyer is at least alerted to the fact that further inquiry should be made.)

[15] Normally the rule on hidden defects does not work in reverse. Thus, if the buyer possesses information about the property that causes its value to be higher than the seller believes it to be, the buyer does not have a duty to divulge this information to the seller (unless the buyer is an expert in the field by reason of training or experience).

one of the parties occupies a position of "trust and confidence" relative to the other. (This differs from the ordinary situation, where the parties are dealing "at arm's length.") For example, when a partnership is considering a land purchase, a partner who is part owner of the land under consideration has a duty to divulge his or her interest to the co-partner before the purchase is made. Similarly, a corporate officer who is purchasing stock from a shareholder has a duty to disclose any special facts of which he or she has knowledge, by virtue of that position, which would affect the value of the stock.

The third category comprises situations in which one party has **superior knowledge** about the subject matter of the contract as a result of his or her experience, training, or special relationship with the subject matter. In this type of circumstance the rule has obvious application where the silent party—the one possessing the superior knowledge—is an "expert" in the area, but it often applies to other parties as well. The rule commonly applied is that if one party has superior knowledge, *or* knowledge which is not within the reasonable reach of the other party (and which such party could not discover by the exercise of means open to both parties), there is a duty on the party possessing the knowledge to disclose it. Under this rule,

for example, a buyer of Oklahoma land who, by virtue of his employment with an oil company, learns of an oil "strike" on an adjacent ranch would be guilty of fraud if he did not disclose this information to the seller, a rancher. On the other hand, if the buyer was simply another ranch owner in the area, his or her nondisclosure of this information would probably not be fraudulent.

Outside of these situations, most courts take the view that neither party has a duty to volunteer information to the other, even though it might bear materially on the other's decision of whether to contract. Thus the seller of a trash collection business probably has no duty to tell a prospective purchaser of indications that the city is going to institute a collection service of its own—especially if this information is as available to the buyer as it is to the seller.[16]

In the case below the California court applied a rule that was, in essence, the superior knowledge rule, although it did not specifically label it as such.

---

[16]*Jappe v. Mandt,* 278 P.2d 940 (1955). (Although the buyer's action for damages based upon fraud failed, an action for rescission might have succeeded on the ground of "unilateral mistake"—a subject discussed later in the chapter—*if* the buyer had been able to show that the seller was aware of his ignorance about the proposed city action.)

Kallgren v. Steele
District Court of Appeal, 2nd District, California, 279 P.2d 1027 (1955)

Drapeau, Justice:

. . . Plaintiffs purchased from defendant Fred A. Steele and his wife a resort in the San Bernardino mountains, consisting of a store, gasoline and service equipment, and several cabins. These improvements were located on United States government land in the San Bernardino National Forest, and along the state highway. For many years the resort had been known as "Bear Creek Lodge."

The improvements had been built upon the government land, and maintained there under a special use permit from the federal forest service, with an annual rental of $150. The permit provided that it could be terminated at any time for any reason by the forest service.

The purchase price of the Lodge was $12,000, with $6,000 [paid] in cash, and the remainder [to be paid] in monthly installments of $100 or more.

At the time of the negotiations for the sale, the parties went to the office of the forest service and explained what they were doing. The forest service made no objection to the transfer of the permit to plaintiffs. Apparently the permit was continued in Mr. Steele's name until plaintiffs paid him the last installment on the purchase price.

Then the forest service notified plaintiffs that the permit would be revoked at the end of five years. The reasons given for this drastic action were that the store and cabins were too close to the state highway, that they were in very poor condition, and that they impaired scenic values.

This was the first time that plaintiffs learned that any part of Bear Creek Lodge was *within or too close to the state right of way.* Defendant, Mr. Steele, knew about it all the time, but said nothing about it to plaintiffs. And due to the location of the buildings on the side of a precipitous mountain canyon it is impossible to move them farther away from the state highway.

Thus the forest service put an end to all of plaintiffs' rights in and to Bear Creek Lodge, except salvage value of the buildings if the cost of removing them should possibly be less than what they can be sold for. . . .

Plaintiffs brought this action for damages from defendants for fraud in concealing the fact that the improvements were in part within the highway right of way. Findings in the Superior Court were for plaintiffs, with damages fixed at $6,369.00. Defendants appeal from the judgment.

Reading the record, it appears quite likely that none of the parties gave much consideration to what the forest service might or might not do about the permit, or that the improvements would ever have to be moved on account of the state right of way. Bear Creek Lodge had been there for thirty years, and the parties just went ahead, without realizing that the tenancy was subject to the whim of some government officer clothed with a little brief authority.

This case presents an interesting example of the exercise of bureaucratic powers. If the improvements were too close to the highway, if their condition was poor, and if they impaired scenic values, it would seem but fair that the forest service should have advised plaintiffs of the impending revocation of the permit. The forest service knew of the sale, and that plaintiffs were proposing to invest $12,000 in Bear Creek Lodge.

However, the function of evaluating testimony and determining the rights of litigants based upon such testimony is not committed to courts of review in California. It is without conflict in the record that Mr. Steele did not mention the fact that any part of the improvements were within the state right of way, although he knew about it; and it is without conflict that the buyers didn't know about it when they bought the property, and didn't find out about it until just before they made the last installment payment. . . .

Defendant contends that the rule of *caveat emptor* [let the buyer beware] is applicable in this case, *and that there was no duty on his part to divulge any information to the plaintiffs. This contention is untenable in the law of fraud.* [Emphasis added.]

Fraud may consist in the misrepresentation or concealment of material facts, and may be inferred from the circumstances and condition of the parties contracting.

Deceit [fraud] is the suppression of a fact, by one who is bound to disclose it, or who gives information of other facts which are likely to mislead for want of communication of that fact.

As was said in *Kuhn v. Gottfried,* 229 P.2d 137: "Concealment may constitute actionable fraud where the seller knows of facts which materially affect the desirability of the property, which he knows are unknown to the buyer." . . .

Judgment [for plaintiffs] affirmed.

Intent to Deceive

The second element of fraud is *knowledge of falsity* (or, as it is sometimes called, "scienter"). Thus the innocent party must ordinarily prove that the person making the statement knew, or should have known, that it was false at the time it was made. However, the knowledge of falsity requirement is also met if a person makes a statement "with a reckless disregard for the truth," even if the declarant did not actually know it was false. Thus, if the seller of a used car has no idea as to its mileage but nevertheless states that "it has not been driven more than 30,000 miles," the statement constitutes fraud if it is later proven that the true mileage materially exceeded that figure.

Reliance

The victim of a misrepresentation must show that he or she reasonably relied on the misstatement at the time of contracting. Sometimes this is not difficult to establish. The innocent party does not have to prove that the fact in regard to which the misrepresentation was made was the primary factor in inducing him or her to make the contract. It is sufficient that the misrepresentation involved a matter tending to influence the decision.

Reliance does not exist, of course, if the one accused of fraud can prove that the other party actually knew the true facts before making the contract. Also, a charge of fraud will fail if the victim's reliance was not reasonable under the circumstances. While the old rule of *caveat emptor* ("let the buyer beware") is much less significant than formerly, a buyer still cannot blindly accept everything he or she is told. For example, a buyer given an opportunity to view the property is presumed to observe any patent (obvious) defects that might exist. To illustrate—the seller of a used television set tells the buyer it "produces an excellent picture on all channels." If the buyer viewed the set in operation prior to the sale and complained of reception on one channel, that person could hardly contend after the sale that he had reasonably relied on the seller's representation.

Injury

The last element of a successful fraud action is a showing by the innocent party that he or she suffered an injury, usually an economic loss, as a result of the misrepresentation. In most cases proof of injury (or "damage") is the easiest of the fraud elements to prove. For example, in a typical case involving the sale of property, the buyer is able to show that the value of the property he or she received is substantially less than it would have been if the seller's representations had been true.

Remedies for Fraud

Once fraud is established, the defrauded party always has the right to rescind the contract. When such a person chooses the remedy of *rescission,* he or she must ordinarily return the consideration, if any, that was received from the other party. Rescission, then, is designed to restore the parties to their original positions.

In some instances the defrauded party may wish to keep the consideration, for example, a parcel of land, even though it had been misrepresented by the seller. In such a case the buyer may keep the consideration (i.e., "affirm the contract") and bring suit for *damages*—which in the usual situation is, at the minimum, the difference between the actual value of the property the buyer received, and the value it would have had if the representations had been true. (Additionally, because fraud is a tort, the innocent party may be awarded punitive damages as well.)

As a general rule, the defrauded party must elect either to rescind the contract or to recover damages. However, where the fraud involves the making of a sales contract, such an election need not be made. Sec. 2-721 of the UCC provides, in part, that where fraud is established, "Neither rescission nor a claim for rescission of the contract . . . shall bar or be . . . inconsistent with a claim for damages or other remedy." Thus in circumstances where a buyer or seller seeking rescission can show that he or she will suffer a loss notwithstanding the rescission, damages may also be recovered.

INNOCENT MISREPRESENTATION

If all the elements of fraud are present in a particular case, except that the person making the misstatement honestly (and reasonably) believed the statement to be true, that person is guilty of **innocent misrepresentation** rather than fraud. Under the rule of most states, the victim can rescind the contract on that ground, but is usually not given the alternative remedy of damages. Innocent misrepresentation and fraud are contrasted in Figure 14.2.

MISTAKE

Cases are continually arising where one of the parties to a contract attempts to have it set aside by the court on the ground that he or she was mistaken in some respect at the time the contract was made. Often the mistake involves opinion or judgment rather than fact, in which case no relief will be granted. For example, a person contracts to buy land for $30,000 thinking this is its true value. If its actual value proves to be much less, he or she has shown bad judgment and will not be permitted to rescind the contract. Similarly, if a person purchases stock in the belief that it will greatly increase in value in a short time, he or she obviously cannot have the contract set aside in the event that it does not perform as hoped. If rescission were permitted on grounds such as these, the basic value of all contracts would be destroyed.

However, in certain limited situations a plea of mistake will afford grounds for rescission of a contract, if the mistake was one of *fact.* The general rule is that if both parties were mistaken as to a material fact at the time of contracting, either party can rescind the agreement. On the other hand, if only one of the parties was mistaken, rescission will not be granted unless that person can show that the other party knew, or should have known, of the mistake at the time the contract was made. When both parties are mistaken, the mistake is a **bilateral mistake;** when only one is mistaken, it is a **unilateral mistake.**

Bilateral Mistake

The following examples illustrate the general principle that a contract can be set aside if there is a mutual mistake as to the *existence,* the *iden-*

Figure 14.2   Fraud and Innocent Misrepresentation

	Innocent Misrepresentation	Fraud
Elements	The representation must: 1. Be false 2. Concern a fact 3. Be material 4. Be relied upon	
	5. Be made with reasonable belief that it is true	5. Be made with knowledge of its falsity 6. Be made with the intent to deceive
Injury	None required	Financial loss as a result of the misrepresentation
Remedies	Rescission	Rescission, or retention of defective performance by fraud victim, *and* recovery of damages

tity, or the *character* of the subject matter of the contract.

1. B purchases S's summer home on April 10. Subsequently, B learns that, unknown to either party, the home was destroyed by fire on April 1. Since both parties entered into the contract under the mistaken assumption that the subject matter of the contract actually existed at that time, B can have the contract set aside.

2. P owns two properties outside Woodsfield, Ohio. G, after viewing both acreages, makes P a written offer to purchase one for $18,000. P accepts the offer. It later develops that G had one property in mind while P, after reading the description contained in G's offer, honestly and reasonably believed that G was referring to the other property. Either party can rescind the agreement, because there was a mutual mistake about the identity of the contract's subject matter.

3. C purchases a gemstone from D for $25. At the time of contracting, both parties believe the stone is a topaz. In fact, it turns out to be an uncut diamond worth $700. Since both parties were mistaken about the true character of the contract's subject matter, D can have the contract rescinded, thereby recovering the stone.

The principle is not applicable to situations where both parties realize that they are *in doubt* as to a particular matter, but enter into a contract nonetheless. Thus, in example 3 above, if neither C nor D had any idea what the stone was when they made the contract, D could not rescind the contract when the stone proved to be an uncut diamond (nor could C have rescinded had the stone turned out to be a worthless one). In such an instance both parties had, by contract, "assumed the risk" as to the stone's value.

With these general rules of law in mind let us examine the problem presented by the following case.

Beachcomber Coins, Inc. v. Boskett
Superior Court of New Jersey, Appellate
Division, 400 A.2d 78 (1979)

Boskett was a part-time dealer in coins in New Jersey. He owned a 1916 dime which bore the letter "D," indicating that it had been minted in Denver. Because of the rarity of such coins, their market value was greatly in excess of their monetary worth.

Beachcomber Coins, plaintiff, was interested in buying the coin, and one of its owners examined the coin to determine its genuineness. After an examination of forty-five minutes he was satisfied that the coin was, in fact, minted in Denver, and he purchased it on behalf of plaintiff for $500. Later plaintiff was advised by the American Numismatic Society that the "D" was a counterfeit. When Boskett, the seller, refused to take back the coin and refund the purchase price, plaintiff brought this action asking rescission of the contract.

The trial judge, sitting without a jury, found that there was a mutual mistake of fact (a mistake as to the coin's genuineness) that would ordinarily justify rescission of the contract. However, he further found that under customary coin dealing procedures a buyer of a coin who was permitted to examine it before purchase "assumed the risk" that it might be counterfeit. He therefore dismissed the action and plaintiff appealed.

Conford, Judge:

. . . The evidence and trial judge's findings establish this as a classic case [in which rescission should be allowed on the basis of] mutual mistake of fact. As a general rule, "where parties on entering into a transaction that affects their contractual relations are both under a mistake regarding a fact assumed by them as the basis on which they entered into the transaction, it is voidable by either party if enforcement of it would be materially more onerous to him than it would have been had the fact been as the parties believed it to be." *Restatement, Contracts,* §502 (1932). . . .

Moreover, [the *Restatement* provides that] "negligent failure of a party to know or discover the facts as to which both parties are under a mistake does not preclude rescission or reformation on account thereof." The law of New Jersey is in accord. . . .

Defendant's contention that plaintiff assumed the risk that the coin might be of greater or lesser value is not supported by the evidence. It is [true that] a party to a contract can assume the risk of being mistaken as to the value of the thing sold. The *Restatement* states the rule this way:

Where the parties know that there is doubt in regard to a certain matter and contract on that assumption, the contract is not rendered voidable because one is disappointed in the hope that the facts accord with his wishes. The risk of the existence of the doubtful fact is then assumed as one of the elements of the bargain.

However, for this rule to apply, the parties must be conscious that the pertinent fact may not be true and make their agreement at the risk of that possibility. [That rule is not applicable] in this case, because both parties were certain that the coin was genuine. . . .

[The court then turned to the trial judge's finding that it was customary in the coin dealing business for buyers of coins to assume the risk of genuineness. After examining the testimony on this point at the trial, the court concluded that it was too weak to support the finding of "custom and usage" under New Jersey law. The court thus reversed the judgment, and ordered rescission of the contract.]

Unilateral Mistake

Where only one party to a contract is mistaken about a material fact, rescission is ordinarily not allowed unless the mistake was (or should have been) apparent to the other party. Two examples follow.

1. B purchases a painting from S for $300; B believes it was painted by a well-known artist. B does not, however, disclose this belief to S. In fact, the painting is the work of an amateur and consequently worth no more than $50. Since only B was mistaken as to the identity of the artist, the mistake is unilateral and the contract cannot be rescinded. On the other hand, B would have been permitted to rescind if S had been aware of B's mistake and had not corrected it.

2. X furnishes three contractors with specifications for a building project and asks them to submit construction bids. C submits a bid for $48,000 and D submits one for $46,500. E's bid, because of an error in addition, is $27,000 rather than the intended $47,000. If X accepts E's bid, E can have the contract set aside if the jury finds (as is likely to be the case) either that X actually knew of the mistake when he accepted the bid or that he should have been aware of the mistake because of the wide discrepancy in the bids.

In most cases where the mistake is known to the other party, that party's failure to correct is not viewed as constituting fraud. Thus the mistaken party is ordinarily limited to the remedy of rescission. (This is not always true, however, because a case involving a failure to correct a known mistake might fall within one of the exceptional "duty to speak" categories discussed earlier. Since fraud does exist in such a case, the mistaken party may rescind *or* recover damages.)

Cautions

The "bilateral-unilateral mistake" rule of thumb, while widely followed, by no means settles all cases that arise in the general area of mistake. In the first place, there is some disagreement as to what constitutes a bilateral mistake. Many courts, for example, take the view that such a mistake exists only where the parties have arrived at their erroneous conclusions independently of one another, rather than one party simply relying on information supplied by the other.

Second, the courts will sometimes settle cases purely on "equitable principles"—the basis of overall fairness in particular situations—thereby giving little or no weight to the bilateral-unilateral factor. For example: X and Y make a contract on June 12, at which time X is mistaken as to a material fact. If X should notify Y of the mistake on June 14, at which time Y has neither commenced performance of the contract nor otherwise relied upon its existence, rescission is often allowed even if Y was totally ignorant of the mistake when the contract was made. And, third, a few states have statutes relating to contracts entered into under mistake of fact that sometimes permit rescission where common-law principles would not.

Additional Types of Mistake

Occasionally a mistake involves the provisions of the contract itself rather than the contract's subject matter. For example, an offeree might accept an offer that he or she has misread, only to learn later that the offer was in fact substantially different than it seemed. This is a unilateral mistake, and the offeree is bound by the resulting contract (unless the acceptance itself discloses the mistake to the offeror).

Mutual mistakes as to the value of an article being sold generally are held to constitute mistakes of opinion rather than fact, and rescission is not permitted in such cases. Thus, if B buys a painting from S for $10,000, both parties correctly believing that the artist was Andrew Wyeth, B obviously cannot have the contract set aside simply because he later learns that the painting's true value is only $5,000.

There is somewhat greater uncertainty insofar as mistakes of law are concerned. The courts at one time refused to permit rescission of contracts where a mistake of law existed, either bilateral or unilateral, on the theory that such a mistake was not a mistake of fact. (This idea was consistent with the view that a *misstatement of law* does not constitute a misstatement of fact, under the law of fraud.) Today, however, most courts treat *mistakes of law and fact* the same—that is, they will set aside contracts which both parties entered into under a mistake of law as well as those in which the mistake of one party was apparent to the other.

DURESS

Occasionally a person will seek to escape liability under a contract on the ground that he or she was forced to enter into it. Often the courts find that the "force" is insignificant in the eyes of the law, and the complaining party is held to the contract. For example, if a person enters into a contract simply because he or she knows that failure to do so will incur the wrath of some third person, such as his or her employer or spouse, relief will not be granted. If, on the other hand, the degree of compulsion is so great as to totally rob the person of free will, duress exists, and the contract can be rescinded.

One early definition of **duress** that still remains authoritative is the following:

(1) any wrongful act of one person that compels a manifestation of apparent assent by another to a transaction without his volition, or (2) any wrongful threat of one person by words or other conduct that induces another to enter into a transaction

under the influence of such fear as precludes him from exercising free will and judgment, if the threat was intended or should reasonably have been expected to operate as an inducement.[17]

A necessary element of duress is fear—a genuine and reasonable fear on the part of the victim that he or she will be subjected to an injurious, unlawful act by not acceding to the other party's demands. Thus, if a person signs a contract at gunpoint or after being physically beaten, duress exists, and the victim can escape liability on that ground. Duress also exists when a person makes a contract as a consequence of another person's threat of harm (for instance, kidnapping a child) if the contract is refused.

Generally, the innocent party must show that the act actually committed or threatened was a wrongful one. For instance, a contract entered into between a striking union and an employer cannot be set aside by the latter on the ground of duress if the strike was a lawful one—as, for example, if the strike occurred after an existing "no-strike" contract between union and employer had expired.

The threat of a criminal suit is generally held to constitute duress. For example: X proposes a contract to Y and tells him that if he refuses to sign the agreement, X will turn over evidence to the prosecuting attorney's office tending to prove that Y had embezzled money from his employer six weeks earlier. To prevent this, Y signs the contract. Y can have the contract rescinded on the ground of duress, because a threat to use the criminal machinery of the state for such a purpose is clearly wrongful—regardless of whether or not Y had actually committed the crime in question. Threat of a civil suit, on the other hand, usually does not constitute duress.

While a contract cannot be set aside simply because there is a disparity of bargaining power between the parties, the courts are beginning to accept the idea that *economic duress* (or business compulsion) can be grounds for the rescission of a contract in exceptional situations. The decision in the next case sets forth three requirements that ordinarily must be met in order for a plaintiff to be successful in a suit asking rescission on this ground.

---

[17] *Restatement, Contracts,* §492. Copyright 1932. Reprinted with the permission of The American Law Institute.

Totem Marine T. & B. v. Alyeska Pipeline
Supreme Court of Alaska, 584 P.2d 15 (1978)

Totem Marine Tug and Barge, Inc., entered into a contract with Alyeska Pipeline Services under which Totem was to transport large quantities of pipeline construction materials from Houston, Texas, to Alaska. After Totem began its performance, many problems arose. One major difficulty was the fact that the tonnages to be shipped were six times greater than Alyeska had indicated. Additionally, long delays occurred in getting Totem's vessels through the Panama Canal, which resulted from Alyeska's failure to furnish promised documents to Totem by specified dates. After these and other problems, Alyeska cancelled the contract without cause.

At the time of the wrongful termination, Alyeska owed Totem about $300,000. Officers of Alyeska at first promised that it would pay Totem invoices promptly, but later they told Totem that it would have

its money "in six to eight months." (Totem alleged that the delay in payment occurred after Alyeska learned through negotiations with Totem lawyers that Totem's creditors were pressing it for their payments, and that without immediate cash it would go into bankruptcy—allegations that Alyeska did not deny.)

After further negotiations, a settlement agreement was made in 1975, under which Alyeska paid Totem $97,000 in return for surrender of all claims against it. In early 1976 Totem brought this action to rescind the settlement agreement on the ground of economic duress, and to recover the balance allegedly due under the original contract. The trial court ruled as a matter of law that the circumstances under which the settlement occurred did not constitute duress, and dismissed the complaint. Totem appealed.

Burke, Justice:

. . . This court has not yet decided a case involving a claim of economic duress, or what is also called business compulsion. . . . [In recent cases] this concept has been broadened to include myriad forms of economic coercion which force a person to involuntarily enter into a particular transaction. . . .

There are various statements of what constitutes economic duress, but as noted by one commentator, "The history of generalization in the field offers no great encouragement for those who seek to summarize results in any single formula." Dawson, *Economic Duress,* 45 Mich.L.Rev. (1947). . . . [However, many states adopt the view that] duress exists where: (1) one party involuntarily accepted the terms of another, (2) circumstances permitted no other alternative, and (3) such circumstances were the result of coercive acts of the other party. . . .

One essential element of economic duress is that the plaintiff show that the other party, by wrongful acts or threats, intentionally caused him to enter into a particular transaction. . . . This requirement may be satisfied where the alleged wrongdoer's conduct is criminal or tortious, but an act or threat may also be wrongful if it is wrongful in the moral sense. . . .

Economic duress does not exist, however, merely because a person has been the victim of a wrongful act; in addition, the victim must have no choice but to agree to the other person's terms or face serious financial hardship. Thus, in order to avoid a contract, a party must also show that he had no reasonable alternative to agreeing to the other party's terms, or as it is often stated, that he had no adequate remedy if the threat were carried out. . . .

Turning to the instant case, we believe that Totem's allegations, if proved, would support a finding that it executed a release of its contract claims against Alyeska under economic duress. Totem has alleged that Alyeska deliberately withheld payment of an acknowledged debt, knowing that Totem had no choice but to accept an inadequate sum in settlement of that debt; that Totem was faced with impending bankruptcy; that Totem was unable to meet its pressing debts other than by accepting the immediate cash payment offered by Alyeska; and that through necessity, Totem thus involuntarily accepted an inadequate settlement offer from Alyeska and executed a release of all claims under the contract. If the release was in fact executed under these circumstances, we think that . . . this would constitute the type of wrongful conduct and lack of alternatives that would render the release voidable by Totem on the ground of economic duress. . . .

Reversed, and case remanded.

UNDUE INFLUENCE

There are some circumstances in which a person can escape contractual liability by proving that his or her consent was brought about by the **undue influence** of the other party to the contract. While many kinds of influence are perfectly lawful, influence is undue (excessive) where one party so dominates the will of the other that the latter's volition actually is destroyed. A common example occurs where one person, as the result of advanced age and physical deterioration, begins to rely more and more upon a younger, more energetic acquaintance or relative for advice until the point is reached where the older person's willpower and judgment are almost totally controlled by the dominant party. If the older, weaker person can show (1) that he or she was induced to enter into a particular contract by virtue of the dominant party's power and influence, rather than as the result of exercising his or her own volition, and (2) that the dominant party used this power to take advantage of him or her, undue influence is established and he or she is freed of liability on this ground.

A STATUTORY POSTSCRIPT

Many contracts are made in which one party, usually the buyer of household goods, is persuaded to contract by the high-pressure selling tactics of the other party. In such cases the victim is usually unable to prove that the seller was guilty of fraud, and, as a general rule, the courts take the view that high-pressure salesmanship does not constitute duress. Thus the common-law principles discussed in this chapter usually furnish little aid to the buyer who wishes to escape liability under the contract.

However, in a limited attempt to afford relief in some of these situations, over half the states have passed **home solicitation statutes,** and a good many cities in other states have adopted similar ordinances. While these statutes vary to some extent, particularly in regard to the exceptions that they contain, they essentially provide that contracts entered into as a result of home solicitations initiated by sellers—typically door-to-door salespersons—can be rescinded by the buyer simply giving notice by mail to the other party within three business days (the cooling-off period) after making the contract. Most of these statutes apply to all home solicitation contracts involving the sale of consumer goods or services in which the price is $25 or more—though some statutes apply only to contracts that would result in a lien attaching to a home owner's property, such as in home improvement sales. In any event, the right to rescind is automatic; that is, the buyer need not allege or prove fraud or duress. (In relatively recent years, the Federal Trade Commission has adopted a three-day cooling-off rule similar to the state statutes. This rule is of particular importance to buyers who have entered into home solicitation contracts in those states where special statutes have not been adopted—assuming, of course, that interstate commerce is involved.)

SUMMARY

A voidable contract is an agreement in which one of the parties possesses the legal right to have the contract set aside (i.e., avoided or disaffirmed). The two most common situations in which such a right exists are (1) where there is a lack of capacity, as in minors' contracts, and (2) where reality of consent is lacking, as in contracts tainted with fraud, mistake, or duress.

Minors generally have the right to disaffirm their contracts any time before reaching the age of majority—18 in most states—plus a reasonable time thereafter, even as to contracts that have been fully performed. In such a situation, the minor is required to return the consideration if able to do so. In situations where return of the consideration is not possible, disaffirmance is still generally allowed, in which case the entire loss is borne by the other party to the contract. Additionally, the right to disaffirm is a one-sided one, being possessed only by the minor.

Under the majority rule, where the minor is disaffirming an executed contract calling for the purchase of goods that are not a necessity of life, he or she can recover all of the contract price paid, without being charged with the reasonable value of the use of the goods while in his or her possession. However, where the contract is for the purchase of goods or services that qualify as necessities, the minor in all cases is liable for the reasonable value of the goods actually used, or the services received. And, in any case in which the minor, after reaching the age of majority, expressly or impliedly indicates that he or she will abide by it, the contract has been ratified and the right to disaffirm is lost. The rights of contracting parties who are under a mental disability, or who are intoxicated, generally parallel those of minors.

Even if both parties to a contract are competent, the contract can be set aside if tainted with fraud, innocent misrepresentation, or duress, and—in some circumstances—on the ground of mistake. The elements of fraud are (1) misrepresentation of a fact, (2) made with the intent to deceive (i.e., with knowledge of falsity), (3) reasonable reliance by the other party, and (4) injury to such party. A statement of opinion cannot normally be the basis for a fraud action unless the declarant—the one expressing the opinion—possesses a knowledge of the subject matter of the contract that is markedly superior to that of the other party. And silence does not constitute fraud, except in those limited circumstances in which the courts hold there was a "duty to speak." On the subject of mistake, the basic rule is that a contract can be rescinded only on the ground of mutual mistake of fact, or on the ground of unilateral mistake known to the other party. Duress—when one deprives a party of his or her free will to contract by committing (or threatening to commit) a wrongful act—is also a ground for the rescission of a contract.

KEY TERMS

Voidable contract
Capacity
Minor
Ordinary contract
Ratification
Necessaries
Insane in fact
Adjudicated insane
Fraud
Misrepresentation of fact
Statement of fact
Statement of opinion
Latent defect
Fiduciary relationship
Superior knowledge
Innocent misrepresentation
Bilateral mistake
Unilateral mistake
Duress
Undue influence
Home solicitation statutes

QUESTIONS AND PROBLEMS

1. McAllister, while a minor, purchased a car under circumstances in which it was clearly not a necessity, and gave the seller his promissory note in payment. The note obligated McAllister to make specified monthly payments beginning with the time of purchase. Just before reaching the age of majority, at which time McAllister had made no payments on the note, he lost posses-

sion of the car under circumstances which the trial court found to be "unknown." (It was clear, however, that the car was neither retained by McAllister nor returned to the seller.) Three years after McAllister reached the age of majority, at which time he had still made no payments, the seller sued him on the note, and McAllister then informed the seller that he was disaffirming the purchase and the note. The seller argued that McAllister's attempted disaffirmance was invalid since he waited so long to exercise this right. Is the seller correct? Explain. (*Warwick Municipal Employees Credit Union v. McAllister,* 293 A.2d 516, 1972.)

2. Ballinger and his wife, while minors, purchased a mobile home. In payment, they gave the seller of the home a promissory note which they signed as co-makers. Before reaching the age of majority they disaffirmed the contract and the note. The seller then brought suit against them to recover the reasonable value of the home, on the ground that it constituted a necessity of life. At the trial, the Ballingers introduced evidence showing that Ballinger's parents were more than willing to furnish them with living accommodations in their own home at the time they made the purchase, and thereafter. What bearing, if any, would this evidence have on the question whether the home constituted a necessity? Explain your reasoning. (*Ballinger v. Craig,* 121 N.E.2d 66, 1953.)

3. Robert Moore opened joint savings accounts in two banks, with the accounts listing a nephew and niece as co-depositors. These accounts, if valid, would result in the money in them passing to the nephew and niece as gifts upon Moore's death. After Moore died, other relatives brought a court action to set aside these joint accounts on the ground that Moore was incompetent to contract at the time that he established them. To support this contention, these relatives produced evidence that over a period of several weeks prior to the opening of the accounts Moore had often been found wandering on city streets late at night, not knowing where he was;

that on one occasion he tried to extinguish the cooking units on his electric stove by pouring water on them; that a neighbor stopped transacting business with him "because he acted so queerly"; and that he was once stopped on a street by a police officer because of "insufficient clothing." Do you think this evidence is sufficient to support the relatives' claim that Moore was incompetent when he made the transactions with the banks? Can you think of other evidence that might contradict this claim? Discuss. (*In re Moore's Estate,* 188 N.E.2d 221, 1962.)

4. Several employees of Empiregas, Inc., plaintiffs, had signed one-year employment contracts with that company over a period of many years. Each time that the employees objected to noncompetition clauses in the contracts they were told by supervisors not to worry about them, just "to sign." At the time of signing their most recent contracts the employees were told by their supervisor that "you know what we have always told you. (These contracts) are not worth a damn; it is just a piece of paper." The employees signed, and after they had fulfilled their contracts they sought employment with a competing firm. Empiregas wrote the competing firm that the employees could not be hired by it because of the noncompetition clauses in their contracts. Empiregas also threatened to sue the firm and employees if it hired them. When the firm decided not to employ them, the employees brought this action against Empiregas alleging that it had "fraudulently induced" them to sign the contracts. Two of Empiregas's defenses were that the statements were not fraudulent because (1) they were merely statements of opinion and (2) they were statements of law rather than fact. Do you agree with either defense? Why or why not? (*Empiregas, Inc. v. Hardy,* 487 So. 2d 244, 1985.)

5. Midwest Supply, a company in the business of preparing income tax returns, advertised "guaranteed accurate tax preparation." Waters, after reading the ad, contacted Midwest and was induced to apply for refunds that he was not legally entitled to. After Waters received the improper refunds, the Internal Revenue Service recovered the payments from him in addition to substantial penalties. Waters then sued Midwest to recover damages on the basis of fraud, alleging that (1) the statement in its ad was false; (2) the employees of Midwest had little or no training in accounting or income tax preparation; and (3) Midwest told its employees not to correct newswriters who described the employees as "specialists and tax experts." On these facts, is Midwest guilty of fraud? Discuss. (*Midwest Supply, Inc. v. Waters,* 510 P.2d 876, 1973.)

6. Whale applied for the position of rabbi with the Jewish Center of Sussex County, New Jersey. The application listed information regarding his education, ordination as a rabbi, and job experience from 1956 to 1977, all of which was true. The Jewish Center employed Whale, but soon thereafter brought action to rescind the contract on the ground of fraud, alleging that Whale failed to disclose the fact that he had earlier been convicted of the crime of using the mails to defraud. Whale defended on the ground that in his resumé accompanying the application he indicated that further information and references would be furnished on request, but that the center did not avail itself of this opportunity. Is Whale's defense good? Why or why not? (*Jewish Center of Sussex County v. Whale,* 397 A.2d 712, 1978.)

7. The seller of a building in Lusk, Wyoming, told an out-of-state buyer who had not seen the property that "it could readily be rented for $100 per month." The buyer, after making the contract, learned that the building had no rental value and that the seller knew this when he made his statement. When the buyer brought a fraud action against him, the seller contended that his statement was merely an expression of value, and thus a statement of opinion rather than one of fact. Rule on this defense, with reasons to support your ruling. (*Cahill v. Readon,* 273 P. 653, 1928.)

8. Black purchased two violins from White for $8,000, the bill of sale describing them as "one Joseph Guarnerius violin and one Stradivarius violin dated 1717." Unknown to either party, neither violin was made by Guarnerius or Stradivarius. Upon discovery of this fact, can Black set aside the purchase and recover payment? Explain.

9. The owner of a South Dakota ranch drove a prospective buyer around the property. He pointed out the boundaries of the ranch as clearly as possible, but because of the rough terrain it was not possible for the buyer to reach one or two parts of the property. Some time after the buyer purchased the land he wanted to set aside the contract on the ground of mistake, because he thought several strategically located acres were part of the ranch which, in fact, were not. The seller defended on the ground that at no time during the negotiations did the buyer indicate that he was expecting to get the acres in question, and that he (the seller) thus was not aware of the buyer's mistake of fact. Is this a good defense? Explain. (*Beatty v. DePue,* 103 N.W.2d 187, 1960.)

Chapter 15

CONTRACTS
IN WRITING

Many people have the idea that contracts are never enforceable unless they are in writing. Insofar as the law is concerned, however, most oral contracts are just as enforceable as written contracts *if their terms can be established in court.*[1] In this chapter we will examine the relatively few kinds of contracts that *are* required by law to be in writing; then we will consider general problems relating to written contracts. (In a situation where the law requires a contract to be in writing, any contract that does not meet that requirement—i.e., one that is entirely oral in nature, or that is written but ambiguous—is an "unenforceable" contract, rather than a "void" or "voidable" one. Thus, as the term indicates, neither party is bound by such a contract—with limited exceptions noted later).

THE STATUTE OF FRAUDS

In England, prior to the latter part of the seventeenth century, all oral contracts were enforceable as long as their existence and terms could be established. Under this approach, it became apparent that many unscrupulous plaintiffs were obtaining judgments against innocent defendants by the use of *perjured testimony*—false testimony given under oath. To illustrate: P claimed that D had breached a particular oral contract, a contract that D denied making. If P could induce his witnesses (usually by the payment of money) to falsely testify that they heard D agree to the alleged contract, and if D could neither refute such testimony by witnesses of his own nor otherwise prove that P's witnesses were lying, a judgment would ordinarily be

granted in favor of P.[2] To eliminate this and other kinds of fraud, Parliament in 1677 passed "An Act for the Prevention of Frauds and Perjuries"—or, as it is commonly called, the **Statute of Frauds.**

Section 4 of the statute provided, essentially, that five specified kinds of contracts had to be in writing in order to be enforceable, and Section 17 required a sixth type of contract to be in writing (with certain exceptions). In this country, virtually all the states have reenacted the provisions of Sections 4 and 17 with but slight variations. Thus, when the question arises of whether a given contract today has to be in writing under the statute of frauds, reference is being made to the *state statute* operating in the jurisdiction within which the contract was made.

The introductory language of the statute is this: "*No action shall be brought* [upon the following kinds of contracts] *unless the agreement upon which such action shall be brought, or some memorandum or note thereof, shall be in writing* and signed by the party sought to be charged therewith or some other person thereunto by him lawfully authorized." (Emphasis added.) Thus, properly speaking, it is not necessary for the contract itself to be in writing; a memorandum of the agreement may satisfy the statute. Nor is it necessary that both parties sign the writing; it is sufficient that it be signed by the party sought to be charged—the defendant, in most cases.

To illustrate the latter provision: S orally agrees to work as a secretary for D for three years, at a specified monthly salary. (This agreement, as we shall see later, falls within the statute of frauds because it cannot be performed within one year). A week after the agreement is made, D mails S a signed letter setting forth the terms agreed to earlier. In this situation, S can enforce the contract against D, but D cannot enforce it against S. In other words, S could recover dam-

---

[1] Many actions based on oral contracts that are otherwise valid are dismissed by the courts because their terms cannot be sufficiently established. For this reason, all contracts of any importance ought to be in writing, even when not required by law. The practical weakness of oral contracts is probably what gives rise to the popular misconception that oral contracts are never enforceable, a feeling expressed in a statement attributed to Sam Goldwyn, the movie magnate, that "oral contracts aren't worth the paper they're written on."

[2] D's situation was particularly difficult because, at the time we are speaking of, the parties to a civil suit were not permitted to testify in their own behalf; thus the testimony of their witnesses was all important.

ages from D if he discharged her without cause before the three years were up, but he could not recover damages from her if she quit the job a month after commencing work.

CONTRACTS THAT MUST BE IN WRITING

The typical statute today, closely following the language of Section 4 of the English act, requires the following kinds of contracts or promises to be in writing (or be evidenced by a written memorandum):

1. A contract calling for the sale of land or an interest therein.

2. A contract not to be performed within one year.

3. A promise by one person to pay the debt of another.

4. A promise made in consideration of marriage.

5. A promise by the administrator or executor of an estate to pay a debt of the estate out of his or her own funds.

Each of the above requirements raises questions of judicial interpretation—what is meant by *land,* by an *interest in land,* and so on. Only by examining these interpretations can one tell whether a particular contract falls within the statute or outside it. To illustrate: S, the owner of ten acres of land, orally contracts in July to sell the corn then growing on the land to B for $300. After the crop matures, S refuses to abide by the agreement, and B sues him to recover damages for breach of contract. S admits making the contract but pleads the statute of frauds as a defense; that is, S contends that the contract was required by the statute to be in writing. If the court rules that the growing crop constitutes land or an interest therein, the contract falls within the statute and S's defense will be sustained. On the other hand, if the court rules that the crop does *not* constitute land or an interest therein, the contract falls outside the statute and S is liable

for damages even though the contract was not in writing. We will now examine the kinds of contracts that are held to fall within the five categories, with particular emphasis on the first three.[3]

Contracts Calling for the Sale of Land

As a practical matter, the most important contracts required by the statute to be in writing are those calling for the sale of land—real estate. With an exception to be noted later, unwritten agreements of this kind are absolutely unenforceable. Thus, if X orally agrees to sell a farm to Y for a specified price, neither X nor Y can recover damages from the other if one of them refuses to go through with the deal. This is true even in the unlikely event that both parties admit in court that they made the contract.

In most cases it is easy to determine whether a contract does or does not involve the sale of land. Land, or *real property,* essentially consists of the earth's surface, vegetation, buildings, and other structures permanently attached to the soil. Growing crops, being physically attached to the ground, are also generally considered to be real property when sold in conjunction with the land. Thus, if S, by a written agreement, contracts to sell his farm to B for $50,000, B is entitled to receive any crops then growing on it, as well as the land itself—unless the contract provides otherwise. On the other hand, if S contracts merely to sell the crop to B—a situation alluded to earlier—the crop is considered *personal property* and the contract does not have to be in writing under the Statute of Frauds. (If, however, the price of the crop were $500 or more, the contract would then be required to be in writing under a special section of the Uniform Commercial Code, which will be discussed later in the chapter.)

---

[3] The parties to most oral business contracts do, in fact, perform their obligations in full, even though, because of the statute, they are not obliged to. The statute is important, then, in those relatively few situations where one of the parties decides to stand on his or her legal rights by refusing to perform under an oral—but otherwise valid—contract.

Interests in land include real estate mortgages and easements. A real estate **mortgage** is a conveyance of an interest in land by a debtor to a creditor as security for the debt. An **easement** is the right of one person to use or enjoy the land of another in a limited manner. Easements can be created in two general ways—expressly or by implication. If created in an express manner, the granting of the right must be evidenced by a writing—either specific language in a deed or a written contract in place of a deed. An easement created by implication, on the other hand, need not be evidenced by a writing. (One example of such an easement is an "implied easement of necessity." This is created when a landowner sells part of his or her property to another, the land being situated in such a way that the buyer has no access to it except by going across the seller's remaining land.) While real estate *leases* also convey interests in land and thus normally fall within the Statute of Frauds, most states have enacted special statutes providing that oral leases of a year's duration or less are valid.

Effect of Part Performance—Estoppel: In some circumstances the courts have generally felt that oral contracts ought to be enforceable even though they are not in writing. Accordingly, they have recognized limited exceptions to the rules embodied in the statute of frauds.

One of these exceptions involves oral contracts calling for the sale of land. Such contracts are generally held to be enforceable if the buyer, in reliance upon the oral contract, has (1) paid part of the purchase price, (2) taken possession of the land, and (3) added substantial improvements to it.[4] In these circumstances the courts will permit the buyer to enforce the contract for either of two reasons. (In regard to oral *leases* of land of over one year, requirement 1 is, of course, dispensed with.)

First, the actions of the buyer, in and of themselves, may be felt to be "referable" to the oral contract that the buyer alleges has been formed—that is, the buyer's actions are fairly good evidence that an oral contract has, in fact, been entered into. These are actions that a person would normally take only if he or she expected to become the owner of the land. The second reason often cited for permitting the buyer to enforce the oral contract is the doctrine of *promissory estoppel* (discussed in Chapter 12). The reasoning here is that where the seller of the land has permitted the buyer to take such actions, it would be manifestly unfair to permit the seller to evict the buyer on the ground that the contract was not in writing. In such a case, the courts are increasingly taking the view that the seller is estopped (i.e., prevented) from using the statute of frauds as a basis for having the oral contract set aside.

The case below presents two common questions: (1) Was a reasonably definite oral contract entered into? and (2) If so, was it saved by the part performance doctrine? (The second case in the chapter presents a situation in which the issue is whether the estoppel doctrine ought to be invoked.)

---

[4] Of course, if both parties have fully performed the contract, the statute is no longer relevant, and neither party can rescind it on the ground that it was originally required to be in writing.

L.U. Cattle Company v. Wilson
Colorado Court of Appeals, 714 P.2d 1344 (1986)

Prior to September of 1980 the L.U. Cattle Company had been conducting farming operations on some Colorado land it was leasing from the land's owners, the Wilsons. Because the existing lease expired on November 1, 1980, a representative of the company, Kroeger, met with the Wilsons in September for the purpose of entering into a

new lease. During the discussion the Wilsons told Kroeger that they wanted the company to plant alfalfa in the future, rather than corn, because this would produce more cash income out of which the company could make its rental payments. Kroeger said that if the acreage was to support alfalfa it had to be fertilized before planting, and, to maximize the efficiency of this plan, it would be necessary to plow and fertilize in the fall of 1980.

After a second meeting, Kroeger felt that as a result of these discussions an oral agreement had been reached for a lease that would be reduced to writing at a later date. Acting on this understanding, Kroeger prepared and mailed a memorandum to the Wilsons on October 4 expressing the terms of the parties' agreement. The last line of the memorandum read: "We will start plowing the last of the week." The Wilsons read and discussed the memorandum, but did not sign it or otherwise respond to it.

During the rest of October and early November the company plowed and fertilized the land, and Wilson was notified of this action. In late January of 1981 the company's owners were concerned that they had no written commitment from the Wilsons. On January 25 Kroeger expressed this concern to Wilson on the phone, who agreed to sign a lease. The next day Kroeger prepared a "Lease Agreement" which he signed on behalf of the company and mailed to the Wilsons. The Wilsons again did not respond to this document. Nothing further occurred until early March, when Wilson told Kroeger that he would not sign the agreement. Kroeger then removed certain equipment from the land and sent the Wilsons a bill for the cost of the fertilization. Wilson sent a check for the billed amount, but the company did not cash it. The cattle company then filed this suit asking for damages resulting from breach of the oral lease (including lost profits). The Wilsons defended on the ground that the contract was invalid under the statute of frauds.

The trial court found (1) that an oral lease had been entered into, and (2) that the company's actions in fertilizing the land constituted part performance of the agreement which "removed it from the statute of frauds"—i.e., which made the agreement enforceable. Accordingly, the court entered judgment for the company in the amount of $30,862. The Wilsons appealed, disputing both findings of fact.

Sternberg, Judge:

. . . The [first] question here is whether the parties reached an oral contract of lease. The validity of such a contract depends upon proof of a definite agreement as to the extent and bounds of the property leased; . . . a definite and agreed term; and . . . a definite and agreed price of rental, and the time and manner of payment. . . . The memorandum sufficiently indicates the property to be leased, the amount of the rental, and the term [duration] of the lease. [While the memorandum was silent as to the times that rental payments were to be paid,] testimony given by Kroeger, uncontested by lessors [the Wilsons] was sufficient to establish the inference that the parties had contemplated that payment would be made as it had been made under the [prior] lease.[a] Therefore, the trial court did not err in concluding that the parties had reached an [oral] lease.

The next question to be resolved concerns the enforceability of the lease. Colorado's statute of frauds provides that contracts for the leasing of lands for periods longer than a year, or notes or memoranda thereof, are void unless in writing and subscribed by the lessor. . . . Where there is part performance of such an oral contract, however, it may be enforceable notwithstanding these requirements.

Here, because lessors did not sign it, the October 4 memorandum was insufficient to remove the lease from the statute of frauds. The trial court, however, made no finding that it did. Rather, it found that the statute was overcome by virtue of lessee's [the company's] actions in plowing the land and in purchasing and applying fertilizer.

This case was presented, argued, and tried on the assumption that the doctrine of part performance is applicable in actions for damages at law. Such performance must be at least substantial part performance. It must be required by, and fairly referable to, no theory other than that of the alleged agreement. Further, the part performance must be known to the other party . . . at the time of its occurrence.

The evidence in this case established that the parties' agreement obligated lessee to plant alfalfa and that lessors were aware of the necessity for proceeding with field preparation in the fall of 1980. The October 4 memorandum expressly notified lessors of lessee's intent to do so, yet the lessors took no action indicating that they did not want lessee to proceed. Although lessors argue that lessee's actions [were referable to the earlier lease made with a prior owner of the land, rather than to the oral lease made by lessors,] there was sufficient evidence in the record from which the trial court could find that it was not. On the facts and circumstances of this case, the trial court did not err in concluding that lessee's actions constituted part performance sufficient to render the lease enforceable despite the statute of frauds. . . .

The judgment is affirmed.

---

[a] The prior lease was made with one Mason, from whom the Wilsons bought the land.

Contracts Not to Be Performed within One Year

The section of the statute requiring that *agreements not to be performed within one year of the making thereof* be in writing is based on the fact that disputes over the terms of long-term oral contracts are particularly likely to occur; witnesses die, the parties' memories become hazy, and so on. Despite the logic underlying this provision, it has posed numerous problems in practice.

In deciding whether a particular agreement falls within this section, the usual approach taken by the courts is to determine whether it was *possible,* under the terms of the contract in question, for the contract to have been fully performed within one year from the time it was made. If so, the contract is outside the statute and need not be in writing. (The fact that performance *actually* may have taken more than one year is immaterial.) For example: A, on June 1, 1985, orally agrees to work for B in a certain capacity at a salary of $2,000 per month "as long as you [B] shall live." In June 1987 B discharges A without cause, whereupon A brings suit to recover damages for breach of contract. As two years have elapsed since the making of the contract, B contends that the contract was within the statute and that A's action must therefore be dismissed. In this situation, B's contention is incorrect. Since it was possible that B might have died within the first year—in which case the contract would have been fully performed—the contract is outside the statute and A is entitled to damages.

An entirely different situation would be presented if, in the above example, A had contracted on June 1, 1985, to work for B "for the next two years." In this case, the contract would clearly have fallen within the statute. Thus, if B had discharged A without cause in February 1986, A could not recover damages. This contract falls within the statute because the agreement could not have been fully performed under any circumstances prior to May 31, 1987. True, it was again *possible* that B could have died within twelve months of June 1, 1985, but under the particular terms of the contract this event would not have caused the contract to be "fully performed" upon B's death. (Instead, B's death would have *excused* performance under the doctrine of impossibility; see Chapter 17 for a discussion of this doctrine.)

The courts have occasionally made exceptions to the requirement that "over one year" contracts must be in writing, where they feel that this is necessary to bring about just results (as they have done with most of the other statute of frauds categories). The case below is typical of those in which the exceptional result is largely based upon the principle of estoppel.

Harmon v. Tanner Motor Tours of Nevada, Ltd.
Supreme Court of Nevada, 377 P.2d 622 (1963)

This litigation came about as a result of a dispute over which one of two competing common carriers had the exclusive limousine ground transportation franchise for servicing the Las Vegas, Nevada, airport for a period of ten years. The carriers were Tanner Motor Lines, Ltd., plaintiff, and Las Vegas-Tonopah-Reno Stage Lines, Inc. (LTR), one of the defendants.

Five legal issues were involved, one of which had to do with the enforceability of an oral contract entered into between Tanner and the Board of Clark County Commissioners (Board), which was the governing authority of the Las Vegas airport. (Only that part of the fact-pattern and decision of the case relating to this issue is considered below.)

In late 1959 Tanner submitted a written bid for the limousine service, and that bid was *orally* accepted by the board members. Despite this acceptance, the board entered into a written contract in 1960 with the second carrier, LTR, giving it the exclusive transportation rights.

Tanner then brought this action against Harmon, a representative of the board, and LTR, defendants, asking for specific performance of its 1959 contract. The defendants contended, among other things, that that oral contract was unenforceable under the statute of frauds, because its performance was to take more than one year. The trial court ruled against the defendants on all points, and entered a decree of specific performance. (That is, the court ruled that Tanner's contract was valid and that he thus did possess the exclusive transportation rights, and it accordingly ordered the board to recognize these rights.) Defendants appealed.

Thompson, Justice:

. . . [The Nevada statute of frauds] provides that every agreement which, by its terms, is not to be performed within one year from the making thereof, shall be void, unless such agreement, or some note or memorandum thereof, expressing the consideration, be in writing and subscribed by the party charged therewith. The Tanner proposal which the board accepted was to provide limousine airport transportation service over a ten year period. It could not be performed within one year and is, therefore, squarely within the mentioned statute. [The court, however, continued:]

Following the acceptance of the Tanner bid, the board [orally] assured Tanner that a formal written agreement would be prepared for signature. *In reliance, Tanner continued to provide limousine service to the airport, paid $3,600 as the minimum guarantee for the ensuing year, and purchased two new 1960 limousines at the cost of about $9,000.* [Emphasis added].

We acknowledge the general rule that, in the absence of fraud, a promise to reduce an agreement to writing is not, standing alone, a basis for invoking an estoppel against raising the statute of frauds in defense [that is, such a promise alone does not make the oral agreement enforceable]. It is likewise true, as a general rule, that part performance of an agreement within the "one year provision" of the statute of frauds [does not alone make the oral agreement enforceable]. However, where both occur, i.e., a promise to reduce an agreement to writing *and* part performance, an *estoppel* is properly invoked [by the one seeking specific performance], and the main agreement [is enforceable]. We conclude, therefore, that the board cannot rely upon [the statute of frauds] as a defense to this action. . . . The lower court [did not err] in directing the board to execute a formal contract with Tanner and thereafter specifically perform the same. . . .

Affirmed.

Promises to Pay Debts of Another

The statute expressly provides that no action shall be brought "to charge the defendant upon any special promise to answer for the debt, default or miscarriage of another" unless the promise or some memorandum thereof is in writing. Such promises are most commonly found in "contracts of guaranty," two examples of which follow.

1. R says to D, "Furnish all the lumber to P that he needs to build his garage, and I will pay for it if he does not." D furnishes the lumber, but P is unable to pay; thereupon D sues R on his promise. R's promise falls within the statute; and since it was not in writing, he escapes liability. This is a typical contract by which one person guarantees the debt of another.

2. G owes H $600. J orally promises H that if she will not bring suit against G for one month, he (J) will pay the debt if G has not done so by that time. H refrains from bringing suit, and at the end of the month G still has not paid. If H now sues J on his promise, J will escape liability.

Some Notes of Caution: In practice, many difficulties have arisen in the interpretation and application of this provision of the statute. However, these observations can be made about the above examples:

1. Only secondary, or collateral, promises are subject to the statute. In example 1, if R had told D, "Furnish all the lumber that P needs and charge it to me," R's promise would have been enforceable even though it was made orally. The reason is that here R made a *primary* promise to pay—that is, the debt was his own, rather than P's, from the start. Thus R's promise was not "a promise to pay the debt of another."

2. Along similar lines, a promise is primary rather than secondary if the debtor is released from liability by the creditor. Redoing example 2, G again owes H $600. This time J orally tells H, "If you will free G, I'll pay the debt myself." H then expressly releases G. J is now liable on his promise, because when the release occurred, the debt became his alone; hence his promise to pay was primary rather than secondary.

3. Even if an oral promise is secondary and thus apparently within the statute, most courts recognize an exception to the rule of nonliability—when the promisor's *main purpose* in making the promise is to secure a benefit to himself (and where the benefit is thereafter actually received). To illustrate: X orally tells Y, "Furnish Z with all the fuel oil that he will need for heating his home this winter and I will pay you for it if Z does not." Y furnishes the oil, but Z never pays for it. If Y can show that Z was a valuable employee of X, and that X made the promise in order to prevent Z from leaving his employment for a job in Florida, Y can hold X liable on his promise. In such a case, under the "main purpose" exception, X is liable despite the statute.

Other Promises

Two categories of contracts—*promises made in consideration of marriage* and *executors' contracts*—are relatively insignificant today. However, they do fall within the statute. Thus, if A promises to pay B $5,000 when and if B marries C, A is liable only if his promise is in writing. The same is true in regard to prenuptial agreements, in which parties about to be married to each other expressly spell out their interests in the other's properties. Finally, if the administrator or executor of an estate promises personally to pay a debt of the deceased, the creditor can hold the promisor liable only if the promise is in writing.

CONTRACTS CALLING FOR SALE OF GOODS

Section 17 of the English Statute of Frauds provided, in essence, that contracts calling for the sale of goods at a price of ten pounds or more were unenforceable unless either (1) the buyer paid part of the purchase price, (2) the seller delivered and the buyer accepted part of the goods, or (3) the contract was in writing. A similar provision has found its way into the Uniform Commercial Code. Thus today in addition to the five classes of contracts dealt with in the typical state statute of frauds, there is another class of contracts that generally must be in writing.

The UCC Statute of Frauds

Section 2-201 of the code, known as the **UCC statute of frauds,** states that a contract for the sale of goods for a price of $500 or more must be in writing to be enforceable (with exceptions noted subsequently). To illustrate: B orally agrees to buy a used car from the S Company for $1,700, and an officer of the company orally agrees to this proposal. As long as nothing is put in writing, neither B nor the S Company is bound by the agreement.

As is true of other statute of frauds provisions applicable to nongoods transactions, the requirement of Sec. 2-201(1) can be satisfied either (1) by having the contract itself in writing, or (2) by having a subsequent written memorandum of the oral agreement. In either situation, *the writing must be signed by the party against whom enforcement is sought.*

The UCC Confirmation: The language of Sec. 2-201(1) in regard to enforceability parallels that of the basic statute of frauds. That is, if an oral sales contract is followed by a writing signed by only one of the parties, the signer is bound by the contract but the nonsigner is not. To eliminate this onesidedness in certain circumstances, subsection 2 of Sec. 2-201 provides another method (in addition to the two set forth above) for satisfying the writing requirement of subsection 1.

The kind of situation to which Sec. 2-201(2) may apply can be illustrated by this case. Suppose that two parties have orally agreed on a sale of goods. One of the parties then sends a signed letter or other written communication to the other party, saying: "This is to confirm that on June 20 we entered into an agreement for the sale of 175 men's suits on the following terms [the terms being stated in the letter]." If this is the only writing the parties make, the question is whether it can be used to satisfy the requirements of Sec. 2-201(1). If the sender breaches the contract, the letter can be used in a lawsuit by the recipient against the sender because the sender signed it. But if it is the recipient who breaches the contract, can the sender use the letter in his lawsuit to recover damages from the recipient, the nonsigner? In transactions not governed by the UCC, as we have seen, the answer is no. But as to sales of goods, however, (as in

the above example), the answer sometimes is yes.

Under Sec. 2-201(2), the **UCC confirmation rule,** a confirmation such as the above can be used by the sender against a nonsigning recipient if the following requirements are met:

1. The writing must be "sufficient against the sender." In other words, the *sender* must have *signed* the confirmation, and its contents must meet the relatively lenient sufficiency requirements discussed later in the chapter.

2. Both parties must be *merchants.*

3. The recipient must have had reason to know of the contents of the confirmation *but had not objected to it in writing within ten days after receiving it.*

UCC Exceptions

Section 2-201(3) defines three situations in which an oral contract, if proved, will be enforceable despite the total absence of a writing, even when it involves a sale of goods for a price of $500 or more. The first exception can be used only by a seller; the other two can be used by either a seller or a buyer.

1. If the oral contract is for goods to be specially manufactured for the particular buyer, it is enforceable against the buyer if two requirements are met:

   a. The goods must be of a type not suitable for sale to others in the ordinary course of the seller's business. For example: Suppose that C is an importer of small, foreign-made pickup trucks, and D is a manufacturer of campers that are mounted on pickups. C orally orders from D a number of campers made to fit the pickups imported by C (that is, they will fit no other pickups on the market). If C repudiates the bargain after the campers are made, D will be hard-pressed to sell them elsewhere. He might eventually be able to do so, but considerable effort would probably be required. Thus the goods cannot be sold in the ordinary course of his business.

   b. The seller must either have substantially started the manufacture of the goods, or have made commitments for procuring them, before he or she learned of the buyer's repudiation of the agreement.

2. If the defendant "admits in his pleading, testimony or otherwise in court that a contract for sale was made," it will be enforceable even though oral. (The common-law court decisions on this point are conflicting, most courts holding that such an admission does *not* remove the requirement of a writing. Thus the UCC exception represents a significant innovation in this regard.) Observe that not just any admission will suffice; the admission by the defendant must become part of official court records.

3. An oral agreement will be enforced to the extent that payment has been made and accepted or that the goods have been received and accepted. Suppose, for example, that X and Y have made an oral contract for Y to sell X twenty-five television sets at a price of $300 each. Before any of the sets are delivered, X makes a prepayment of $1,800, which Y accepts. Y then refuses to honor the contract. Even if Y were not bound by the contract, X could of course get her money back under the unjust enrichment theory (see Chapter 10). But under the UCC her part payment will make the contract partially enforceable, and she will be able to maintain a suit for breach of a contract obligation to deliver six of the twenty-five television sets. Similarly, if X has made no payment but Y has made a partial shipment which X has accepted, the oral contract is again partially enforceable. That is, if Y delivers and X accepts six television sets, and X then repudiates the agreement, Y can maintain a suit for breach of a contract obligation to pay $1,800.[5]

The rationale underlying these exceptions is entirely consistent with the purpose of the basic writing requirement of Sec. 2-201(1), which is to forestall the possibility of a party successfully maintaining a fabricated breach of contract suit by the use of perjured testimony. By providing these exceptions, the drafters of the UCC have recognized that, in cases falling within them, it is extremely unlikely that plaintiff's claim will be a complete fabrication. Therefore, because the original purpose for the writing requirement no longer exists in such instances, the oral agreements ought to be binding. Compliance with the statute of frauds under UCC 2-201 is summarized in Figure 15.1.

Modification Contracts

Under Section 2-209 of the UCC, agreements that modify existing sales contracts must be in writing in order to be enforceable in two situations:

1. The modification must be in writing if the original agreement had provided that it could be modified only by a writing.[6]

2. The modification must be in writing if the whole contract, *as modified,* is required to be in writing under the UCC statute of frauds (Sec. 2-201, discussed above).

Other Statutes Requiring a Writing

In addition to the basic statute of frauds and Sections 2-201 and 2-209 of the UCC, all states have additional statutes—usually narrow in scope—that require still other kinds of contracts to be in writing. For example, most states require real estate listing contracts to be in writing. Additionally, Sec. 8-319 of the UCC requires, in general, that contracts calling for the sale of

---

[5]Prior to enactment of the UCC, part performance of this type made the *entire contract* enforceable. Also, the statutory language in this exception does not address the situation in which the buyer has made a partial prepayment that cannot be allocated to a certain number of individual units of goods. For example, what if buyer makes and seller accepts a $1,000 down payment on a single $6,000 automobile? In the few cases involving this question since enactment of the UCC, most courts have applied the common-law rule and have held the entire contract to be enforceable despite the absence of a sufficient written document.

[6]Section 2-209(2) has an additional provision applicable to those sales contracts entered into between a merchant and a nonmerchant. In such a case, if the contract results from use of the *merchant's form* (with that form containing the requirement that any later modification had to be in writing), that requirement must itself be "separately signed" by the nonmerchant in order to be binding upon him or her.

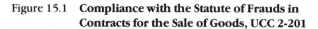

Figure 15.1   **Compliance with the Statute of Frauds in Contracts for the Sale of Goods, UCC 2-201**

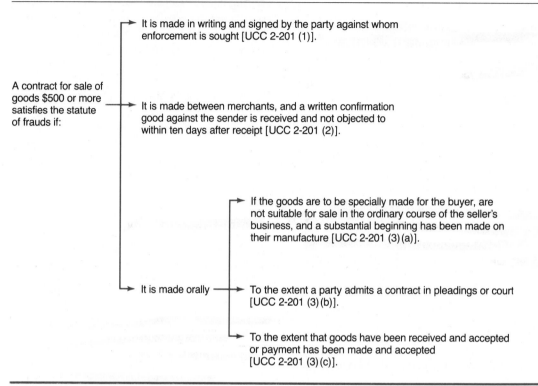

A contract for sale of goods $500 or more satisfies the statute of frauds if:

It is made in writing and signed by the party against whom enforcement is sought [UCC 2-201 (1)].

It is made between merchants, and a written confirmation good against the sender is received and not objected to within ten days after receipt [UCC 2-201 (2)].

If the goods are to be specially made for the buyer, are not suitable for sale in the ordinary course of the seller's business, and a substantial beginning has been made on their manufacture [UCC 2-201 (3)(a)].

It is made orally → To the extent a party admits a contract in pleadings or court [UCC 2-201 (3)(b)].

To the extent that goods have been received and accepted or payment has been made and accepted [UCC 2-201 (3)(c)].

securities (i.e., stocks and bonds) must be evidenced by a writing, and Sec. 9-203 of the UCC imposes the same requirement upon most "security agreements" governed by Article 9 (i.e., agreements that create security interests in favor of lenders of money or unpaid sellers of goods).

WHEN IS THE WRITING SUFFICIENT?

Contract Law

Whenever a party brings an action to enforce a written contract (or a memorandum thereof) that is not entirely complete, the defendant may contend that the writing does not "satisfy" the statute—that is, the writing is too indefinite to permit the court to interpret and enforce it. In such situations, the courts *generally require that the writing include at least the following*: (1) names of both parties, (2) the subject matter of the contract, (3) the consideration to be paid, and (4) any other terms that the court feels are material under the circumstances. Under this fairly strict approach, if any basic term is missing, the contract continues to be unenforceable.

This does not mean, however, that the writing must be in any particular form, or be complete in every detail. And because of the provision that a memorandum or note of the contract may satisfy the statute, it is entirely possible that an oral contract can be validated by the production in court of a confirming telegram, sales slip, check, invoice, or some other writing—assuming, of course, that it contains all the material terms of the agreement.

Additionally, it frequently happens that the contract is evidenced by two or more separate writings, none of which alone is sufficiently complete to satisfy the statute. In such cases the writings may be construed together, thus satisfying the memorandum requirement, if the writings clearly refer to one another (expressly or impliedly), or if they are physically attached to one another.

Sales Law

[handwritten: applies to Sales Only, commercial transaction buyer/selling of goods]

Contracts calling for the sale of goods are often made in the business world under circumstances where, because of the press of time or other factors, the parties put only the barest essentials of the agreement in writing. Recognizing this reality, Sec. 2-201 of the UCC has *greatly relaxed the requirements of the sufficiency of the writing.* For sales of goods, that section provides that the writing (whether the contract itself, or memorandum, or subsequent confirmation) merely has to be "sufficient to indicate that a contract for sale has been made between the parties." The only term that *must be included in the writing is the quantity.* Other terms that are orally agreed upon can be proved in court by oral testimony.[7] Terms that are not agreed upon at all can be supplied by Article 2 itself (as we saw in Chapter 11).

Cases have arisen presenting the question of whether a written "requirements contract" satisfies the quantity requirement of Sec. 2-201. For example, a seller might obligate himself or herself to sell and deliver "all of the 21 oz. plastic your plant can use" over a specified period of time at a specific unit price. In a case in which

such language was utilized, *Fortune Furniture Co. v. Mid-South Plastic Co.*, 310 So.2d 725 (1975), the Supreme Court of Mississippi—following the majority rule—held that this type of provision satisfied the requirement that the writing state a quantity.

THE PAROL EVIDENCE RULE

Whenever a contract (or a memorandum thereof) is reduced to writing, the writing ought to contain *all* the material terms of the agreement. This is true not only for contracts that fall within the statute of frauds, but for all other contracts where a writing is utilized as well. One reason for this, as to statute of frauds contracts, is to make sure that the writing meets the sufficiency requirement under the statute. An equally powerful reason lies in the **parol evidence rule.** This rule provides, in general, that when any contract has been reduced to writing, neither party can introduce "parol" (outside) evidence in court for the purpose of modifying or changing the terms of that contract. More specifically, the rule prohibits a party to a written contract from unilaterally introducing either oral or written statements or agreements made at (or prior to) the time the written contract was made which either conflict with, or add to, the terms of the written contract. (As to sales contracts, the UCC parol evidence rule of Sec. 2-202 is essentially the same as the common-law parol evidence rule, discussed above).

Exceptions

The courts feel that the parol evidence rule brings about clearly undesirable results in some circumstances; accordingly, they have recognized a number of exceptions to it. (In general, these exceptions apply both to cases governed by common-law principles and those governed by sales law). Following are the most important situations in which a party to a written contract *is* permitted to introduce parol evidence in subsequent legal proceedings:

---

[7] The oral testimony referred to here is intended to supplement an incomplete writing. If the writing does contain a particular term, oral testimony about anything supposedly agreed upon prior to execution of the writing is not admissable in court for the purpose of contradicting the clear terms of the writing. This is because of the UCC's "parol evidence rule," Sec. 2-202, which will be discussed subsequently.

1. The written contract itself appears to be incomplete.

2. The written contract is ambiguous, and the parol evidence tends to clear up the ambiguity.

3. The parol evidence shows that the contract was not a valid one, as, for example, that it was induced by fraud or duress on the part of the other party, or was formed under mutual mistake of fact.

4. The evidence shows that the contract was subject to a condition precedent—i.e., that the parties had agreed that a specified event had to occur before performance was due, and that the event had not occurred.

5. The evidence tends to prove that the parties made either an oral or written agreement that modified the written contract *after* the written contract had been entered into (and assuming, in the case of non-sales contracts, that the subsequent agreement was supported by consideration).

SUMMARY

Oral contracts are, as a general rule, enforceable if their terms can be proven in court. Under the typical state statute of frauds, however, five classes of contracts must generally be in writing (or be evidenced by a writing) in order to be enforceable. The most important of these are: (1) contracts to sell land or an interest in land; (2) contracts not to be performed within one year from the time they were made; and (3) promises to pay debts of another. In all of these cases, however, the courts have recognized exceptions to the rules—thus enforcing the oral contracts—in circumstances where they feel a refusal to enforce would be extremely unfair to one of the parties. In cases where oral contracts have been entered into which clearly fall within the statute, followed by a written confirmation of the contract, the party who has signed the confirmation is bound by the contract, but the other party is not.

Article 2 of the UCC provides a sixth type of contract that must generally be evidenced by a writing: contracts calling for the sale of goods where the price is $500 or more. The UCC statute of frauds substantially removes, as to sales contracts, the onesidedness that exists under the basic statute where one party has signed a written confirmation but the other party has not. This is achieved by Sec. 2-201(2), which provides that, if both parties are merchants, a written confirmation signed by one party and sent to the other party is binding upon the latter unless he or she objects to its terms within ten days of receiving it. Sec. 2-201(3) also specifies three exceptional situations in which oral contracts of $500 or more are valid even if not evidenced by a writing at all. If a contract falls within the basic statute, the written contract (or memorandum thereof) satisfies the statute only if it contains all the material terms of the agreement. By contrast, to satisfy the UCC requirement, the writing need only indicate that a sales contract has been entered into, and contain the quantity of the goods being sold.

Whenever a contract is in writing, whether or not it is required by law to be in writing, the *parol evidence rule* generally forbids either party from producing outside evidence in a later court action in an effort to change or add to the terms of the contract. The rule achieves this result by prohibiting the introduction of evidence showing that the parties, at or prior to the time of contracting, made oral or written promises in conflict with, or in addition to, the written terms. However, such evidence is allowed in some circumstances, as, for example, where the written contract is incomplete or ambiguous, or where the outside evidence shows that the contract itself was invalid.

KEY TERMS

Statute of frauds
Mortgage
Easement
UCC statute of frauds

UCC confirmation rule
Parol evidence rule

QUESTIONS AND PROBLEMS

1. Dr. Sahlin owned a summer cottage in New York. He told his nurse of many years that if she and her husband—the Strandbergs—would live at the cottage with him on the weekends, and care for him and keep the property in good repair, they would receive the property when he died. The couple rendered the specified services until the time of his death, a period of several years. (Among other things, Mr. Strandberg reconstructed the cottage by shingling it, painting and rewiring it, and putting in new footings and plumbing throughout.) Dr. Sahlin died without a will, and the executor of his estate refused to convey the property to them since there was nothing in writing evidencing the agreement. Do you think the various services the Strandbergs performed caused the contract to be enforceable? Why or why not? (*Strandberg v. Lawrence,* 216 N.Y.S.2d 973, 1961.)

2. Warner wished to build a lumber mill, which would require construction of a railroad switch and spur line from the Texas and Pacific Railroad's main line in Texas. In 1874, he entered into an oral contract with the railroad, under the terms of which he was to supply the ties and grade the ground for the switch, with the railroad promising to construct and maintain the switch and spur line "for Warner's benefit as long as Warner needed it." Warner built the mill, and the railroad built the spur line and switch and maintained service for several years. In 1887, however, the railroad tore up the switch and ties, leaving Warner without transportation facilities. When Warner sued to recover damages for breach of contract, the railroad contended that the oral agreement "was a contract not to be performed within one year" and within the statute of frauds, and therefore was not enforceable against it. Is the railroad's contention correct? Explain. (*Warner v. Texas and Pacific Ry.,* 164 U.S. 418, 1896.)

3. An automobile collision occurred between cars driven by Griffin and Martin. Immediately thereafter, Harris, a friend of Martin, arrived at the scene and orally promised Griffin that he would pay for the damage caused to Griffin's car if Griffin would not bring suit against Martin. Griffin refrained from bringing legal action against Martin and several months later brought suit against Harris to hold him liable on his agreement. Harris claimed that his promise was "a promise to pay the debt of another" and was thus unenforceable under the statute of frauds. Is Harris liable on his oral promise? Why or why not? (*Harris v. Griffin,* 83 So.2d 765, 1955.)

4. Wilson orally agreed to sell a thoroughbred horse, "Goal Line Stand," to Presti for $60,000. When Presti sent a check in payment, Wilson told him that he was going to hold the check for a month for tax purposes, rather than cash it immediately. (Possession of the horse was retained by Wilson.) Thereafter, while the check remained uncashed, a dispute arose between the parties. In subsequent litigation Wilson contended that the contract was unenforceable since it was only made orally; Presti, on the other hand, claimed that his giving of the check constituted payment, and that this made the oral contract enforceable. Is Presti's claim correct? Discuss. (*Presti v. Wilson,* 348 F.Supp. 543, 1972.)

5. The owner of a dairy company orally contracted to sell certain land to the Hancock Construction Company, but later refused to go through with the deal. When the construction company brought an action for specific performance (an action seeking the property), the dairy company defended on the ground that the contract was not in writing. The construction company pointed out, however, that after the contract was made it had engineering studies made of the property, and also had made application for a loan of over $292,000 in order to finance the purchase. The construction company then contended that these acts on its part constituted "part performance" of the contract, and thus made the oral contract enforceable. Is this contention correct? Why or why not? (*Hancock*

Construction Co. v. Kempton & Snedigar Dairy, 510 P.2d 752, 1973.)

6. Lang orally contracted to purchase $600 worth of calendars from a printer, who was to put the inscription "Lang's Cody Inn" on them. After the printer had completed the work, but before the calendars were delivered, Lang told him he would not go through with the deal. When the printer brought suit for the contract price, Lang defended on the ground that this was a contract calling for the sale of goods of over $500, and that the contract was thus unenforceable under Article 2 of the UCC since it was not in writing. Is this a good defense? Explain.

7. What is the parol evidence rule, and what are three important exceptions to it?

Chapter 16

RIGHTS OF
THIRD PARTIES

As a general rule, the rights created by the formation of a contract can be enforced only by the original parties to the agreement. A contract is essentially a private agreement affecting only the contracting parties themselves; both legal and practical difficulties would arise if a stranger to the contract (a **third party**) were permitted to enforce it. Suppose, for example, that X employed B to paint her house and that B subsequently refused to do the job. If Y, one of X's neighbors, were to bring suit against B to recover damages for breach of contract, it would be ludicrous if he were permitted to get a judgment. Since Y was not a party to the contract, he clearly had "no standing to sue," and his suit would be dismissed.

However, in certain exceptional circumstances a third party is permitted to enforce a contract made by others, particularly (1) where it appears, expressly or by necessary implication, that the parties to the contract intended that that person receive the benefit of the contract, or (2) where one of the parties, after making the contract, assigned (transferred) his or her rights to a third party. In the former situation the third party is called a *third-party beneficiary,* and in the latter he or she is designated an *assignee* of the contract.

THIRD-PARTY BENEFICIARIES

The law recognizes three kinds of beneficiaries—creditor, donee, and incidental. Generally, creditor and donee beneficiaries can enforce contracts made by others, while incidental beneficiaries cannot.

Creditor Beneficiaries

When a contract is made between two parties for the express benefit of a third person, the latter is said to be a **creditor beneficiary** if he or she had earlier furnished consideration to one of the contracting parties. To illustrate: A owes X $500. A later sells a piano to B, on the under-

standing that B, in return, is to pay off A's indebtedness to X. Here X is a creditor beneficiary of the contract between A and B, inasmuch as she originally gave consideration to A, which created the debt in her (X's) favor. Once A has delivered the piano, X is entitled to recover the $500 from B—by suit, if necessary.

Assumption of Mortgage: One typical situation involving a creditor beneficiary arises when mortgaged real estate is sold, with the purchaser agreeing to pay off the existing mortgage. For example: S owns a home subject to a $15,000 mortgage held by the Y Bank. S finds a buyer for the home, Z, who is willing to *assume the mortgage.* Thereupon S and Z enter into a contract, under the terms of which S agrees to convey the property to Z, and Z promises to pay S's existing indebtedness to the bank. The Y Bank now has become a creditor beneficiary of the contract between S and Z, since it originally gave consideration to S by making the loan, and it can hold Z liable on his promise to pay the indebtedness. (The assumption of the mortgage by Z does not by itself free S of his liability. Thus the bank can look to either party for payment in case Z defaults—unless it has expressly released S from his obligation.)

Donee Beneficiaries

Where a contract is made for the benefit of a third person who has not given consideration to either contracting party, that person is designated a **donee beneficiary** of the contract. To illustrate: P, an attorney, agrees to perform certain legal services for Q, with the understanding that Q will pay the $200 legal fee to R, P's son-in-law. Here P has made a gift of $200 to R, and R— the donee beneficiary of the contract—can enforce it against Q if Q refuses to pay him voluntarily.

Life Insurance Contracts: The most common type of contract involving donee beneficiaries is that of the ordinary life insurance policy. If

A insures his life with the B Insurance Company, and the policy expressly designates C as the beneficiary of the proceeds of that policy, C—the donee beneficiary—can enforce the contract against the company. The fact that C has not furnished consideration to the company is immaterial; it is sufficient that A, the insured, has done so by making his premium payments.

Incidental Beneficiaries 3ʳᵈ

An **incidental beneficiary** is a person whom the contracting parties did not intend to benefit by making the contract, but who nevertheless will benefit in some way if the contract is performed. Such a beneficiary, unlike a donee beneficiary, has no rights under the contract and thus is not entitled to enforce it. For example, a retail merchant in a college town would benefit from a contract between a construction firm and the university calling for the construction of a four-level parking facility on campus property just across the street from his (or her) store. However, if the builder breaches the contract with the university by refusing to go ahead with the project, the merchant cannot recover damages from the builder.

In determining whether a beneficiary is a donee beneficiary or an incidental beneficiary, the usual test is whether the contract was made primarily for his or her benefit. If so, the beneficiary is a donee beneficiary; if not, he or she is merely an incidental beneficiary. Two illustrations of the rule may be helpful.

1. A city makes a contract with the X Company, under the terms of which the company promises to supply heat to a public building. It fails to do so during a three-day period, and a visitor there contracts pneumonia as a result. The visitor probably cannot recover damages from the X Company.

2. T leases an apartment from L, with the contract providing that L will keep T's premises in good repair. L breaches this promise, as a consequence of which one of T's guests is injured.

Figure 16.1 **Assignment of Rights**

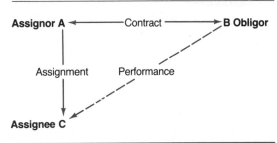

While there is diversity of opinion on this issue, a majority of courts take the view that the major purpose of the clause is to protect T only; thus the guest is ruled to be an incidental beneficiary and cannot recover damages from L.

ASSIGNMENTS

Assignment of Rights

All contracts create certain rights and duties. With exceptions to be noted later, the *rights* a person has acquired under a contract can be transferred, or *assigned,* by that person to a third party.[1] Suppose, for example, that A agrees to add a family room to B's home for $13,500 and that A performs the required work. A thereafter assigns his right to collect the $13,500 to C, in which case A is the **assignor** and C the **assignee.** C can now recover the $13,500 from B, just as A could have done had there been no assignment. The relationship among the parties to an assignment is set forth in Figure 16.1.

Status of the Assignee

Whenever an assignment takes place, the assignee acquires no greater rights than those pos-

---

[1] While a person's *duties* under a contract can also be transferred to a third party in some circumstances, such a transfer is a *delegation* rather than an *assignment.* The delegation of duties is discussed later in the chapter.

sessed by the assignor. Putting it another way, **the obligor** (the person with a duty to perform) can assert the same defenses (if any) against the assignee that he or she had against the assignor.

This can be easily illustrated by referring again to Figure 16.1. If B refuses to pay C and C brings suit against him on the contract, B can escape liability if he can prove that A breached his contract in some material way—by failing to complete the job, for example, or by using materials inferior to those required by the contract. In such a case C's only redress is the right to recover from A any consideration he had given to A in payment for the assignment.[2]

What Rights Can Be Assigned?

Occasionally, when an assignee requests the obligor to perform his or her part of the bargain, the obligor refuses to do so on the ground that the assigned right was of such a nature that it could not be legally transferred without his or her consent. Usually, this contention is not accepted by the courts; most contractual rights can be assigned without the obligor's consent. This is especially true where the assigned right was that of *collecting a debt.* The reasoning is that it is ordinarily no more difficult for a debtor

---

[2] The rule that the assignee of a simple contract acquires no greater rights than those possessed by the assignor does not apply when a particular kind of contract—a *negotiable instrument*—is utilized by the parties. Under the law of commercial paper (which will be discussed in Part IV) the purchaser of that special kind of instrument may qualify as a *holder in due course* of such instrument, in which case he or she can enforce the instrument against the obligor in certain situations where the seller of the instrument could not do so. In the above case, for example, if B's obligation were in the form of a negotiable promissory note, and if A negotiated the note to C, a holder in due course, *C is entitled to recover the amount of the note from B* even though A breached his contract with B. B's recourse is then to sue A for damages for breach of contract.

(obligor) to pay the assignee than to pay the assignor (the original creditor); hence the obligor has no cause to complain.

Some rights, however, *cannot* be assigned without the obligor's consent. Following are the most common of these situations:

1. The terms of the contract expressly prohibit assignment by one or both parties.

2. The contract is "personal" in nature; specifically, the right in question involves a substantial *personal relationship* between the original parties to the contract. If X, for example, agrees to be Y's secretary for one year, any assignment by Y of the right to X's services would be invalid unless X consented to it. In fact, many (perhaps most) employment contracts fall within this category.

3. The assignment would materially alter the duties of the obligor. For example: S, of Columbus, Ohio, agrees to sell certain goods to B, also of Columbus, with the contract providing that "S will deliver the goods to the buyer's place of business." If B assigned this contract to the X Company of Cheyenne, Wyoming, S's obligation would be drastically increased and he would not be bound by the assignment unless he consented to it.

Additionally, the assignment of some rights is prohibited by statute. For example, a federal law (31 U.S.C.A. §203) generally prohibits the assignment of claims against the federal government, and some state statutes prohibit the assignment of future wages by wage earners. When the assignment of rights is prohibited by statute, such rights cannot be assigned even with the obligor's consent.

The following case poses a question of assignability in a modern business setting.

Schupach v. McDonald's System, Inc.
Supreme Court of Nebraska, 264 N.W.2d 827 (1978)

McDonald's, defendant, is the corporation that grants all McDonald's fast food restaurant franchises. In 1959 defendant granted a franchise to a Mr. Copeland, giving him the right to own and operate McDonald's first store in the Omaha-Council Bluffs area. A few days later, in conformity with the negotiations leading up to the granting of the franchise, McDonald's sent a letter to Copeland giving him a "Right of First Refusal"—the right to be given first chance at owning any new stores that might subsequently be established in the area. In the next few years Copeland exercised this right and opened five additional stores in Omaha. In 1964 Copeland *sold and assigned all of his franchises* to Schupach, plaintiff, with McDonald's consent.

When McDonald's granted a franchise in the Omaha-Council Bluffs area in 1974 to a third party without first offering it to Schupach, he brought this action for damages resulting from establishment of the new franchise, claiming that the assignment of the franchises to him *also included the right of first refusal.*

A number of issues were raised in this litigation. Defendant contended, among other things, that the right it gave to Copeland was personal in nature, and thus was not transferable without its consent. Plaintiff alleged, on the other hand, that the right was not personal in nature, or, in the alternative, that its transfer was, in fact, agreed to by defendant.

On these issues the trial court ruled that the right was personal in nature. It also ruled, however, after analyzing voluminous correspondence between the parties, that defendant *had* consented to the transfer. It entered judgment for plaintiff, and defendant appealed. (Only that part of the higher court's opinion relating to these two issues appears below.)

White, Justice:

. . . McDonald's was founded in 1954 by Mr. Ray Kroc. Kroc licensed and later purchased the name of McDonald's [and all other rights relating thereto] from two brothers named McDonald, who were operating a hamburger restaurant in San Bernardino, California. In 1955 Kroc embarked on a plan to create a nationwide standardized system of fast-food restaurants. . . .

At the trial, Kroc testified about the image he sought to create with McDonald's. . . . He wanted to create "an image people would have confidence in. An image of cleanliness. An image where the parents would be glad to have the children come and/or have them work there."

Kroc testified that careful selection of franchisees was to be the key to success for McDonald's and the establishment of this image. . . . People were selected "who had a great deal of pride, and had an aptitude for serving the public, and had dedication."

Fred Turner, the current president of McDonald's, testified [in a similar vein]. . . . He stated that by 1957 it became apparent that McDonald's could only achieve its goal by careful selection of persons who would adhere to the company's high standards. He stated that an individual's managerial skills and abilities were a matter of prime importance in the selection process. . . .

Summarizing, the evidence is overwhelming, [and establishes the conclusion that] the Right of First Refusal was intended to be personal in nature, and was separately a grant independent of the terms of the franchise contract itself. [It also establishes the fact that] the grant depended upon the personal confidence that McDonald's placed in the grantee, and that to permit the assignability by the grantee without permission of McDonald's would serve to destroy the basic policy of control of the quality and confidence in performance in the event any new franchises were to be granted in the locality. . . .

[The court then reviewed the same correspondence which was examined by the trial court, and ruled that McDonald's had *not* given its permission to the transfer of the right. The judgment for plaintiff was therefore reversed.]

Form of the Assignment

As a general rule, no particular formalities need be observed in order for an assignment to be legally effective. Any words or conduct that indicate an intention on the part of the assignor to transfer his or her contractual rights are normally sufficient. Some assignments, however, are required by statute to be in writing. Thus the assignment of a contract that falls within the statute of frauds must be evidenced by a writing; similarly, under the statutes of most states, the assignment of one's rights to collect wages from an employer must also be in writing.

Absence of Consideration

Once a valid assignment has occurred, the assignee is entitled to enforce the contract against the obligor even if the assignee did not give consideration for the assignment to the assignor. The absence of consideration on the part of the assignee does have one significant effect, however; the assignor in such a case has the right to *rescind the assignment* at any time before the contract has been performed by the obligor,
without liability to the assignee. (It is assumed here that the assignment was not meant to be a *gift.* If it were, rescission of the assignment would not, of course, be permitted.)

Notice of Assignment

A valid assignment takes effect the moment it is made, regardless of whether the obligor is aware that the assignment has occurred. However, the assignee should give *immediate notice* to the obligor whenever an assignment is made, in order to protect the rights received under it.

A primary reason for giving notice is that an obligor who does not have notice of an assignment is free to go ahead and render performance to the assignor, thereby discharging his or her contractual duties. Suppose, for example, that X is owed $500 by Y and that X assigns the right to collect the debt to Z. If Y, not knowing of the assignment, pays the debt to X (assignor), Z has lost her right to collect the indebtedness from Y. Any other result would be patently unfair to Y. Z's only redress in such a case is to recover payment from X, who clearly has no right to retain the money.

Notice of assignment can also be important in a case where successive assignments occur. To illustrate: R owes money to S. S assigns his right to collect the debt to A on June 10, then assigns the same right to B on June 15, B not knowing of the prior assignment. Suppose that the first assignee, A, does not give notice of assignment to R until June 25, while the second assignee, B, gives notice on June 20. In such a situation, a number of courts—though not a majority—would rule that B is entitled to payment of the debt, rather than A; in other words, the assignee who first gives notice prevails. (In states adopting this minority view, A's only redress is to recover the consideration, if any, that he gave to S in exchange for the assignment.) The majority view is that A, the first assignee, collects, even if he did not give notice first.

DELEGATION OF DUTIES ✓

Our discussion so far has been directed to those cases in which contractual rights alone have been transferred, or assigned—in other words, to those common situations in which it is reasonably clear that the parties understood that the assignor alone would be the party who would perform the contract, as he or she originally contracted to do. In many circumstances, however, a **delegation of duties**—the transfer of one party's contractual duties to another—*is* intended as part of the assignment of rights, and in other circumstances a delegation of duties may occur without an assignment of rights. We will briefly examine these situations.

Delegation in Conjunction with an Assignment

If an assignment occurs in which the assigning party also delegates his or her contractual duties to the assignee, that party is the **delegant** (or assignor-delegant), and the party to whom the duties are transferred is the **delegate** (or assignee-delegate). The remaining party—the party to the original contract to whom the performance is owed—is the **obligee.** When a del-

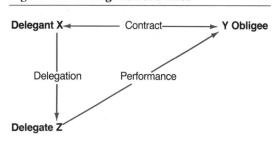

Figure 16.2 **Delegation of Duties**

egation occurs in conjunction with an assignment, the delegate usually (but not necessarily) expressly or impliedly promises that he or she will perform the delegant's duties under the contract. Assuming such a promise, the relationships are diagrammed in Figure 16.2.[3]

Obligations of the Parties: Where a delegation occurs, and where the delegate expressly or impliedly promises to perform the delegant's duties, the delegate assumes the primary responsibility for performance of those duties. The delegant, however, remains secondarily liable for performance of those duties. To illustrate: X contracts to put in a driveway for Y, and X then delegates the duty to Z. If Z fails to do the job, X must either perform the job or be liable to Y, the obligee, for damages for breach of contract. Thus, where the contract is never performed, the obligee has causes of action against both the delegate and delegant. In other words, a delegation of duties—even when consented to by the obligee—does not in and of itself free the delegant of liability.[4] (Thus, although a delegation is generally defined as a "transfer" of duties, this

---

[3]This discussion is based upon the assumption of a valid delegation—i.e., one in which the obligee has consented to the delegation, or in which the duty is of such nature that it can be delegated without the obligee's consent. (Nondelegable duties—those that cannot be assigned without the obligee's consent—will be examined later.)

[4]If, additionally, the obligee expressly or impliedly frees the delegant, then a *novation* exists which does discharge the delegant. See Chapter 17 for details.

term is not entirely accurate in view of the retention of secondary liability by the delegant.)

The above discussion has assumed that the delegate has promised, expressly or by clear implication, to perform the delegant's duties. In some situations, however, it is unclear whether the delegate has made an implied promise to perform. Going back to the driveway illustration, for example, the assignment document might state that X hereby assigns to Z "all of my rights and obligations under my contract with Y," or it may simply say that X hereby assigns to Z the "entire contract" that he (X) has with Y. In either case, if Z accepts the assignment of rights but neither expressly promises to perform the contract nor commences performance, is he or she liable to Y if the driveway is never built? While there is disagreement on this point, the trend among the courts of most states *is* to find an implied assumption of duties by Z in both cases—with Z thus incurring liability in case he or she fails to perform.

Delegation in Absence of Assignment—Subcontracts

A delegation of duties may be made without an assignment of the delegant's rights under his or her contract with the obligee. In such cases, where the delegate by contract promises to perform the delegant's duties, the general rule is that the delegate's only obligation is to the delegant. In the "real world" a delegation of duties in the absence of an assignment most often involves a partial delegation of duties. To illustrate: X, a builder, contracts to build a home for Y for $92,000. X then subcontracts the electrical work to the Z Company, an electrical firm. If the Z Company fails to do the work, or does it in an unacceptable manner, it is liable to X but not to Y. (Similarly, it should be noted in passing that if the Z Company *does* perform, it may look only to X, the delegant, for payment. In other words, in the usual situation, the subcontractor is neither a beneficiary nor an assignee of the contract between the prime contractor-delegant and the obligee.)

What Duties Are Delegable?

In exceptional circumstances the obligee, upon learning of the delegation, will notify the parties that he or she will not accept performance by the delegate. The general rule applicable to such a controversy is that any contractual duty may be delegated without the obligee's consent except (1) duties arising out of contracts which expressly prohibit delegation, and (2) contracts in which the obligee has a "substantial interest" in having the obligor-delegant perform personally.

Under the latter rule, contracts calling for the performance of *personal services*—such as those of a teacher, physician, or lawyer—are clearly nondelegable without the obligee's consent (even if the delegate is as professionally competent as the delegant). Most other contracts call for the performance of duties that are described as essentially *routine* in nature, such as the repair of a building, the sale of goods, or the overhaul of machinery, and these duties are generally held to be delegable. (This result is not as unfair to the objecting obligee as it might appear, because, as we noted earlier, he or she may hold the delegant liable if the delegate's performance is defective.)

SUMMARY

While contracts can normally be enforced only by the original contracting parties, some persons—called third parties—can enforce contracts made by others in certain circumstances. The major classes of third parties possessing this ability are beneficiaries and assignees. There are three types of beneficiaries: creditor, donee, and incidental beneficiaries. A creditor beneficiary is a third party to whom one of the contracting parties owes a debt, and who is to receive performance from the other contracting party as a means of extinguishing the debt. A donee beneficiary is a third party who, under the contract, is to receive performance from one of the contracting parties as a gift from the other contracting party. Creditor and donee beneficiaries are permitted to enforce the contracts because in both instances the contracts in question were made primarily for their benefit, i.e., the contracting parties had such beneficiaries in mind as persons who were to receive performance. By contrast, the incidental beneficiary is a person who might have some interest in seeing that the contract be performed, but was *not* a person for whose benefit the contract was made. Accordingly, incidental beneficiaries cannot enforce contracts made by others.

Assignees are persons to whom contractual rights have been assigned after the contract was entered into. As a general rule, one party to a contract may assign his or her rights under the contract without the consent of the other party, the "obligor." (There are, however, limited situations in which the obligor's consent is required.) Once an assignment has occurred, the assignee stands in the same position as the assignor; that is, if the assignor could have enforced the right against the obligor, the assignee has the same power. On the other hand, if the obligor had a valid defense against the assignor (such as breach of contract), the obligor can assert the same defense against the assignee.

In some situations a party to a contract may delegate his duties under the contract to a third party. (In such case, the person transferring his or her duties is the "delegant," the other party to the contract is the "obligee," and the person to whom the duties have been delegated is the "delegate.") Delegation of duties requires consent of the obligee if the contract was made primarily upon the personal qualities or skill of the delegant, but is not required if the performance owed by the delegant to the obligee is "routine in nature." In any event, once a valid delegation occurs the delegant remains secondarily liable to the obligee in the event the delegate fails to perform the contract (unless the obligee had expressly released the delegant).

KEY TERMS

Third party
Creditor beneficiary
Donee beneficiary
Incidental beneficiary
Assignor
Assignee
Obligor
Delegation of duties
Delegant
Delegate
Obligee

QUESTIONS AND PROBLEMS

1. An agency of the State of Washington operated a ferry system providing service between the mainland and offshore islands. The ferry employees were unionized, and they worked under a contract between the union and the state. Just before a Labor Day weekend the union called a strike, which was a breach of its contract. As a result, tourist travel to the islands was substantially cut, and resort owners located on the islands sued the union to recover damages for breach of contract. Should they be able to recover on the theory they were donee beneficiaries? Why or why not? (*Burke and Thomas v. International Organization of Masters,* 585 P.2d 152, 1978.)

2. An insurance company issued a policy of automobile liability insurance to Enos. While Enos was driving the car he had an accident that injured a passenger, Wagner. A doctor, Jones, treated her injuries. After being unable to recover his fee from Enos, Dr. Jones sued the insurance company to hold it liable. The company defended on the ground that he could not maintain the suit since he was not a party to the insurance contract. Is this a valid argument? Discuss. (*Franklin Casualty Insurance Co. v. Jones,* 362 P.2d 964, 1961.)

3. A labor union entered into a collective bargaining agreement with the Powder Power Tool Corporation, under which the company agreed to pay specified wages to various classes of its employees. When Springer, an employee and union member, was not paid the full wages to which he was entitled under the agreement, he brought action to recover the additional payments as specified. The company defended on the ground that Springer was not a party to the contract and thus could not maintain the action. Is the company correct? Explain. (*Springer v. Powder Power Tool Co.,* 348 P.2d 1112, 1960.)

4. The Brookfield Municipal Utility District (the District) made a contract with a land developer under the terms of which it agreed to furnish water and sewer service to a specific tract of land. A year later, after condominiums were built on the land, service was terminated. The condominium owners then sued the District for damages for breach of contract. The owners conceded they were not parties to the contract, but contended that they were beneficiaries of it, and thus entitled to sue. Is this a good argument? Why or why not? (*Greenway Park v. Brookfield Municipal Utility District,* 575 S.W.2d 90, 1978.)

5. Abramov, when leaving the employment of a partnership, signed a contract promising not to compete with the partnership for five years. Soon thereafter the partnership incorporated. Abramov later started a business in competition with the corporation, whereupon it brought action for an injunction ordering him to live up to the terms of the contract not to compete. The issue was whether the contract could be assigned by the partnership to the corporation without Abramov's consent. Decide, with reasons. (*Abramov v. Royal Dallas, Inc.,* 536 S.W.2d 388, 1976.)

6. Cullins worked for an insurance agency under an employment contract that prevented him from competing with that agency for a period of three years after leaving its employment. Later, another company, Smith, Bell and Hauck, Inc., purchased the insurance agency. When Cullins quit the agency and formed a new insurance firm, Smith, Bell and Hauck brought an action for an injunction ordering Cullins to live up

to his contract not to compete. When Cullins defended on the ground that Smith, Bell and Hauck were not parties to the contract, they contended that an implied assignment of the contract from the insurance agency had taken place and, as assignees, they were entitled to enforce that contract. Is this a good argument? Discuss. (*Smith, Bell and Hauck, Inc., v. Cullins,* 183 A.2d 528, 1962.)

7. Folquet was employed as a school bus driver by the Woodburn Public School District for a contract period of five years at a salary of $125 per school month. The contract required Folquet to furnish and maintain a bus at his own expense, to conduct himself in a proper and moral manner, and to be responsible for the conduct of the pupils while in the bus. Folquet died before the five years elapsed, and his son, an adult, was appointed administrator of his estate. When the son offered to drive the bus for the remainder of the contract, the district refused to let him do so. The son then brought suit to recover damages for breach of contract. The school district contended that the contract was of a personal nature and thus could not be delegated or assigned to any other driver without its consent. Is the school district's defense valid? Explain. (*Folquet v. Woodburn Public Schools,* 29 P.2d 554, 1934.)

8. A company assigned its accounts receivable to an insurance company and later assigned the same accounts to a bank. The bank gave notice of the assignment to the account debtors before the insurance company did. In subsequent litigation the issue was which of the two assignees was entitled to collect the accounts receivable. (*Boulevard National Bank of Miami v. Air Metals Industries, Inc.,* 176 So.2d 94, 1965.)

   a. If the majority rule were applied, who would win?

   b. If the minority rule were applied, who would win?

Chapter 17

DISCHARGE
OF CONTRACTS

Sooner or later all contractual obligations come to an end. When this occurs in a particular case, the contract is said to be *discharged.* What is meant by this is that the *duties* of the contracting parties have been discharged.

There are many ways in which a discharge, or termination, can come about. Most of these result from the conduct of the parties themselves, while others involve events completely outside the control of either party. One leading treatise on contract law recognizes at least twenty separate and distinct ways in which a person's contractual obligations can be discharged.[1] The most important of these are discharge by (1) operation of conditions; (2) performance; (3) breach by the other party; (4) circumstances excusing performance (impossibility, impracticability, and frustration); (5) agreement of the parties; and (6) operation of law.

DISCHARGE BY OPERATION OF CONDITIONS

Conditions, Generally

In many contracts the parties simply exchange mutual promises to perform specified duties, with neither promise being conditioned or qualified in any way. Once such a contract is formed, each party is said to have incurred a "duty of immediate performance"—even though the performance of one or both parties may not be due until some specified time in the future.

In some situations, however, the performance of the contemplated contract is beneficial to one or both of the parties only if a certain event occurs in the future. And in other situations a contract may be mutually beneficial to the parties when entered into, but would be of little benefit if some event should occur before the stated time of performance arrives.

In these situations the parties can achieve substantial protection by the use of conditions in their contract. The term **condition,** in its broadest sense, can be defined as an express or implied provision in a contract which, upon the occurrence or nonoccurrence of a specified event, either creates, suspends, or terminates the rights and duties of the contracting parties. (While this definition refers to a provision or clause in a contract creating the condition, the terms may also be used to refer to the event itself that is designated in such provision.)

The law recognizes three kinds of conditions—*conditions precedent, conditions subsequent,* and *conditions concurrent.* Each type of condition can be further classified as *express* or *implied.* (Our discussion initially will focus on the nature of express conditions, with consideration of implied conditions precedent and implied conditions subsequent being delayed until we reach the subjects of performance and impossibility, respectively.)

Conditions Precedent

A **condition precedent** is a clause in a contract which indicates that the promises made therein are not to be operative until a specified event occurs. For example, X makes this offer to Y: "If the city rezones your property at 540 Fox Lane from C-3 to C-1 within thirty days, I will pay you $18,000 cash for it." Y accepts the offer. While a contract has now been formed, it is clear that the specified event must occur before either party incurs "a duty of immediate performance." The act of rezoning, therefore, is a condition precedent. And, because the condition resulted from the language of the contract, rather than by implication, the rezoning constitutes an *express* condition precedent.[2]

---

[1] *Restatement, Contracts 2d,,* The American Law Institute, 1979.

[2] Conditions precedent can usually be identified by clauses containing the words *if, in the event,* or *when.* Thus the following language creates a condition precedent: "If X is able to obtain a building permit from the city within sixty days" (or "In the event X is able to obtain a building permit . . ."), "it is agreed that Y will construct a swimming pool for her, according to the attached specifications, for $9,000."

Discharge by Failure (or Nonoccurrence) of a Condition Precedent: Where a contract clearly creates a condition precedent, no "duty of immediate performance" arises until the specified event occurs. In the above case, then, should the rezoning not occur within the specified time, the condition is said to have "failed" and both parties are accordingly discharged of their obligations.

Conditions Subsequent

Occasionally both parties to a contract are willing to incur a duty of immediate performance, but want to be freed of their obligations if a particular circumstance arises before the performance date. The parties can achieve this protection by use of an express **condition subsequent**—a clause in a contract providing that upon the happening of a specified event, the contract shall be inoperative (or void).[3] For example: S owns a grocery store located near a private school, Y College. In April S contracts to sell the store to B for $32,000, the contract providing that the first payment of $8,000 is to be due the following July 1, with payments thereafter to be made in the amount of $200 per month. The contract contains this further provision: "In the event that Y College is permanently closed at the end of the present school year, this contract shall be null and void."

Discharge by Occurrence of Condition Subsequent: In the above illustration, B has incurred a duty of immediate performance, but the duty is discharged if the specified event—the closing of the college—occurs. Conditions precedent are contrasted to conditions subsequent in Figure 17.1.

Most conditions subsequent (as is true of conditions generally) are express rather than implied. They can ordinarily be recognized by language providing that the contract is to be void, inoperative, or canceled if a certain event occurs in the future. (The relatively few situations in which implied conditions subsequent exist will be discussed later in the chapter.)

Conditions Concurrent

Conditions concurrent exist when a contract expressly provides (or if one can reasonably infer from its terms) that the performances of the parties are to occur at the same time. A common example is a land sale contract which provides that the seller is to deliver the deed on payment of the purchase price. The duty of each party is thus conditioned on performance by the other. The seller has no duty to deliver the deed until the buyer pays (or tenders) the purchase price, and the buyer has no duty to pay until the seller delivers (or tenders) the deed.[4]

The legal consequences that result from the use of express conditions precedent and subsequent are clear, once either condition is proven to exist. It is, however, often a more difficult question whether the parties conditioned their obligations at all, and, if so, whether the condition in the particular case fell in the precedent or subsequent category. The following case highlights the impact that such a determination might have on the outcome of a particular controversy.

---

[3] Thus the essential difference in legal effect between the two basic kinds of conditions is that the occurrence of a condition precedent *imposes* a duty of immediate performance, while the occurrence of a condition subsequent *removes* such a duty.

---

[4] A tender is an *offer* to perform one's obligation.

Figure 17.1   **Conditions Precedent and Conditions Subsequent**

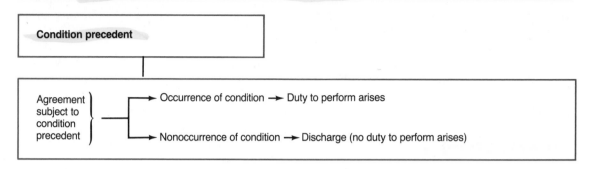
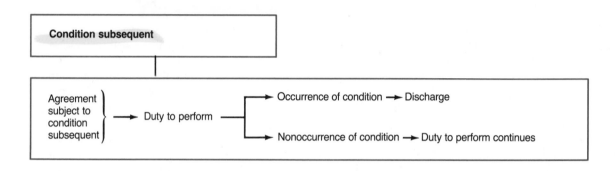

Rincones v. Windberg
Court of Appeals of Texas, Austin, 705 S.W.2d 846 (1986)

Rincones and Mena, plaintiffs, entered into a contract with Windberg, defendant, under which they were to "compile, research and edit material for academic and student services for a migrant program handbook." The contract was termed a "Consultant Agreement," and under it each plaintiff was to write specified chapters, for which Windberg would pay each $1,250 per chapter for their respective chapters.

The handbook was ultimately to be used by California authorities, and the parties were aware that the funds to pay plaintiffs would ultimately come from the State of California. *The consultant agreement, however, made no mention of Windberg's obligation to pay being contingent upon his receipt of funding by California.* Plaintiffs submitted the drafts of their respective chapters to Windberg, but he refused to pay for them because "the publication was not

accepted by California," and no funding from that state, therefore, was available for the project.

Plaintiffs then brought this action to recover the monies promised them. The primary question was whether Windberg's receipt of funding from California was a condition precedent to his obligations under the contract, as Windberg contended. The trial court found (1) that the contract was partly written and partly oral; (2) that, under the oral agreement and the circumstances surrounding it, the parties had agreed that the contract was contingent upon California's funding of the project; and (3) that California refused to fund the project. The court concluded that a "condition precedent" existed; that proof of the condition was not barred by the parol evidence rule; that the condition precedent had not been met; that the contract was of no further force and effect, and that Windberg thus had no liability under it.[a] The plaintiffs appealed.

Shannon, Chief Justice:

. . . The meaning of "condition precedent" in Texas jurisprudence is less than clear. For purposes of the parol evidence rule, however, we think that the definition from [a previous case] correctly states that a condition precedent is a condition "which postpones the effective date of the instrument until the happening of a contingency." . . . By way of contrast, a condition subsequent "is a condition referring to a future event, upon the happening of which the obligation no longer becomes binding upon the other party, if he chooses to avail himself of the condition." *Id.* [The court here noted that parol evidence of a condition precedent is admissible to vary or contradict a written contract, while parol evidence of a condition subsequent is not admissible.]

We now examine the record in an effort to determine whether the evidence supports the court's conclusion that funding from California was a condition precedent to the contract, or whether, to the contrary, the evidence shows an already effective and binding contract subject to a condition subsequent. The admissibility of the parol evidence turns on whether the contract was binding and effective from its inception, or whether it would become binding and effective only upon the occurrence of the contingency.

The evidence shows that all parties devoted substantial amounts of time and money attempting to perform their obligations under the Consultant Agreement. Appellants (plaintiffs) prepared and submitted a first draft of their manuscript, which Hardy [an associate of Windberg] took to California for revisions and recommendations. Thereafter, appellants worked on revisions and submitted a second draft for approval. Hardy, meanwhile, made several trips to California and spent $4,000 of her own money attempting to gain approval and receive funding from the state. All parties initially thought

---

[a] As was noted in Chapter 15, parol evidence showing a condition precedent is admissible under one of the exceptions to the parol evidence rule.

approval and funding for the project was certain, and performed under the contract accordingly. Only after several months had passed did they learn that political changes in California had placed their funding in jeopardy.

In our opinion the evidence shows that the parties understood that they had a binding and effective contract, and performed accordingly. The evidence is not [consistent] with a determination that the parties had agreed to postpone the effective date of the contract until the condition, funding from California, occurred. . . . [We conclude] that the parol payment condition [is a condition subsequent rather than a condition precedent.] As such, it is inconsistent with the terms of the written contract and is therefore inadmissible under the parol evidence rule. . . .

The judgment is reversed and the case is remanded to the trial court for new trial consistent with this opinion.

DISCHARGE BY PERFORMANCE

Most contracts are discharged by performance—by each party completely fulfilling his or her promises. In such cases, obviously, no legal problems exist. Nevertheless, the subject of performance merits special attention for several reasons.

In the first place, many cases arise in which the actual performance of a promisor is, to some extent, defective. Sometimes the performance falls far short of what was promised; other times it deviates from the terms of the contract in only minor respects. As one might expect, the legal consequences of a major breach of contract are more severe and far-reaching than those resulting from a minor breach.

Second, in some cases the courts must determine whether the defective performance constituted a breach of a condition or a mere breach of a promise. A breach of a condition, no matter how slight, usually frees the nondefaulting party, while a breach of a promise generally does not unless it is a material one.

Promises: Degree of Performance Required

Many agreements consist simply of the exchange of mutual promises, with neither party's obligations expressly conditioned in any way. In most of these contracts, however, it is usually apparent from their nature that one of the parties is to perform his or her part of the bargain before the other is obligated to do so. For example: If X contracts to landscape Y's new home for $1,500, it can reasonably be inferred that the work is to be done by X before he can demand payment of Y.[5] Thus, in general, when a promisor seeks to recover the contract price, that person must show that he or she has *fully performed* the promise in some cases or *substantially performed it* in others—depending on the nature of the obligation involved. If it is determined that this performance has met the applicable minimum standard, the promisor is entitled to recover the contract price minus damages (if any) suffered by the promisee. However, if the performance falls short of this minimum, the promisor's obligation has not been discharged, and he or she will recover little or nothing. (The rules determining the extent of recovery in each of these situations will be discussed immediately after the next case in the chapter.)

Total Performance: Some promises are of such a nature that they can be discharged only by complete performance. If a promisor's perfor-

---

[5] In this regard, it is sometimes said that the actual performance of one's promises constitutes an *implied* condition precedent that must be met by that person.

mance falls short of that called for under such a contract, even though the breach is minor, his or her obligation is not discharged. Suppose, for example, that B contracts in May to buy a car from S for $2,000—the contract providing that the price is to be paid in full by B on June 1, at which time S is to assign the car title to her. If, on June 1, B tenders S a check for $1,950, S has no obligation to transfer the title. A contract under which a seller of land is obligated to convey "merchantable title" falls into the same category; delivery of a deed conveying any interest or title less than that specified will not discharge the seller's obligation.

Substantial Performance: Many obligations are of such a nature that it is unlikely (indeed, not even to be expected, given the frailties of mankind) that a 100 percent performance will actually occur. The typical example involves a construction contract under which a builder agrees to build a home according to detailed plans and specifications. It is quite possible that the finished building will deviate from the specifications in one or more respects no matter how conscientious and able the builder is. In contracts of this sort, if the promisee-owner seeks to escape liability on the ground of nonperformance of the promisor-builder, it is ordinarily held that the promisor has sufficiently fulfilled the obligation if his or her performance, though imperfect, conformed to the terms of the contract in all major respects. This rule is known as the doctrine of **substantial performance.**

In order for the doctrine to be applicable, two requirements must ordinarily be met:

A. Performance must be "substantial"—that is, the omissions and deviations must be so slight in nature that they do not materially affect the usefulness of the building for the purposes for which it was intended.

B. The omissions or deviations must not have been occasioned by bad faith on the part of the builder. (This is ordinarily interpreted to mean that the omissions or deviations must not have been made knowingly by the builder.)

Using the illustration involving the construction of a house, let us examine three cases where the builder is bringing suit against the owner to recover the last payment of $5,000 called for under the contract and where the owner is refusing to pay on the ground of inadequate performance.

1. The owner proves that the following defects exist: (a) the plaster in all rooms is considerably softer than expected, because the builder used one bag of adamant for each hod of mortar instead of the two bags called for by the contract, and (b) water seepage in the basement is so great as to make the game room virtually unusable, as a result of the builder's failure to put a required sealant on the exterior of the basement walls. Here the defects are so material, and so affect the enjoyment and value of the home, that the builder has *not substantially performed* his obligations. Thus recovery will be denied, even if the breaches on the part of the builder are shown to be accidental rather than intentional.

2. The owner proves that the following defects exist: (a) the detached garage was given but one coat of paint rather than the two required; (b) the water pipes in the walls were made by the Cohoes Company rather than the Reading Company as was specified (though otherwise the two types of pipe are virtually identical); and (c) the wallboard installed in the attic is ⅛ inch sheeting instead of the ¼ inch that was called for. Here the defects are so slight in nature, even when taken in total, that the builder has substantially performed the contract and can thus probably recover under the doctrine.

3. Same facts as case 2, but, in addition, the owner can show that one or more of the deviations were *intentional;* for example, he produces evidence tending to prove that the builder ordered the installation of the substitute pipe and wallboard knowing that they were not in conformity with the contract. Here the deviations are willful (rather than the result of simple negligence); therefore the builder is guilty of bad faith and the doctrine is not applicable.

Obviously, the requirement that performance be "substantial" is a somewhat elastic one, and necessitates a comparison of the promisor's actual performance with that which the terms of the contract really required of him. The following case is typical of those presenting substantial performance problems.

Lane Wilson Company, Inc., v. Gregory
Court of Appeal of Louisiana, Second
Circuit, 322 So.2d 369 (1975)

Lane Wilson Company, plaintiff, contracted to build a swimming pool for Gregory, defendant, at Gregory's KOA Campground outside Monroe, Louisiana, for $12,000. Under the written agreement, the pool was to be thirty by sixty feet, with a depth varying from three feet to six feet. Later the parties orally modified their contract by agreeing that plaintiff would add a diving board and increase the depth of the pool to accommodate persons using the diving board. It was also orally agreed that a walkway around the pool would be enlarged, and a longer fence built than was originally contemplated. The cost of these modifications raised the contract price to $13,643.

During construction, defendant paid $8,400 on the contract. After the job was completed, however, he refused to pay the balance due because of various defects in the pool's construction (the most important of which are described in the appellate court's decision following). Plaintiff then brought this action to recover the balance allegedly due. The trial court held that plaintiff had *substantially performed* the contract, and that plaintiff was thus entitled to the balance of the contract price minus a credit of $300 to remedy one of the defects (the installation of a chlorinator). Defendant appealed.

Burgess, Judge:

. . . Defendant alleged [in his answer] that plaintiff had not constructed the pool according to the terms of the contract. . . . This appeal presents two issues. First, has plaintiff substantially performed the contract, thereby enabling him to recover the balance due on the contract price? Second, if plaintiff has substantially performed, are there any defects in the construction which entitle defendant to damages in an amount sufficient to remedy the faulty performance?

In *Airco Refrigeration Service, Inc., v. Fink,* 134 So.2d 880 (1961), the supreme court considered . . . the meaning of "substantial performance." The court stated:

The principal question presented in this case is whether or not there has been substantial performance so as to permit recovery on the contract. This is a question of fact. Among the factors to be considered are the extent of the defect or non-performance; the degree to which the purpose of the contract is defeated; the ease of correction, and the use or benefit to the defendant of the work performed.

In light of the factors enumerated above, we cannot say the trial court was manifestly erroneous in finding that plaintiff substantially performed the contract. Defendant contracted for a 30 by 60 foot swimming pool deep enough to accommodate persons using a diving board. The defects alleged by defendant are not such that defeat the purpose of the contract or prevent defendant from using the pool. In addition, the defects for which plaintiff may be held accountable are easily remedied.

[The court here examined all of the defects in the job in order to determine whether or not plaintiff had substantially performed the contract. The most important of these defects were described as follows:]

(a) Rather than measuring 30 by 60 feet as called for by the contract, the pool's measurements fluctuate from 59 feet six inches to 59 feet three and one-half inches in length, and from 29 feet one-half inch to 29 feet three and one-half inches in width.

(b) The walls of the pool are not vertical, but slope severely to form a bowl-shaped pool.

deviations

(c) Plaintiff installed only six water inlets as opposed to twelve water inlets called for by the contract; this deficiency coupled with the poor placement of the inlets results in insufficient water circulation in the pool.

(d) The pool is not ten feet deep as the parties allegedly agreed.

[The court here expressed its opinion as to the materiality of these defects as follows:]

(a) In the instant case we find the deviations in dimensions, which could be discovered only by measuring the pool, *in no way defeat the purpose of the contract.* [Emphasis added.] Plaintiff also testified the method of constructing the pool made it impossible to achieve perfect compliance with the exact measurements called for by the contract. Therefore, under the authority of [earlier cases in this state], we find the slight deviation in measurements did not constitute a breach of the contract.

(b) Defendant made no complaint about the shape of the pool walls until after suit was filed. The defect, if it be one at all, was apparent and defendant is held to have accepted same since he made no objection to the walls until suit was filed.

(c) The number of water inlets was changed at the suggestion of the supplier of the equipment because twelve water inlets would have lowered the water pressure and caused improper circulation in the pool. Defendant agreed to the change in plumbing and cannot now claim that change as a defect.

(d) Defendant failed to prove that the parties agreed to a ten-foot depth for the pool. We find the pool, as constructed, is deep enough to accommodate a diving board and, therefore, there is no defect in regard to the depth of the pool.

[On the basis of this analysis, the court agreed with the trial court that plaintiff had substantially performed the contract. The court then turned to the question of defendant's damages. On this point the court ruled that, in addition to the $300 damages (credit) allowed by the trial court, additional damages should have been allowed to compensate defendant for his removal of incorrect depth markers and the installation of new markers; for his removal of waste cement and cement forms; and to compensate defendant for 200 feet of pipe owned by him that plaintiff used in building the pool. The court summarized these adjustments as follows:]

Totalling the amounts listed above, we find defendant is entitled to $331.02 as damages to correct defects in plaintiff's performance, in addition to the $300 allowed by the trial court for the cost of an additional chlorinator which plaintiff admitted the pool needed.

For the reasons assigned the judgment in favor of plaintiff is amended to reduce the award from $4,943.36 to the sum of $4,612.34, and as amended is affirmed.

Substantial Performance—Amount of Recovery: As noted earlier, if the rule of substantial performance is applicable to a particular case, the promisor-plaintiff is entitled to recover *the contract price minus damages* (that is, the promisor may recover the amount that the promisee agreed to pay under the contract, minus damages—if any—which the promisee sustained as a result of the deviations). Since the damages are typically inconsequential, the promisor usually recovers a high percentage of the contract price. By contrast, where the doctrine is not applicable, the recovery may be little or nothing. The general rules for such situations can be summarized as follows:

1. Where the performance falls short of being substantial and the breach is intentional, the promisor receives nothing. The rationale, of course, is that an intentional wrongdoer should not be rewarded—particularly where the promisee has not received the performance he or she was entitled to. (The rule of nonrecovery also has an affirmative aspect—it strongly "persuades" the promisor to actually finish the job, since he or she will receive nothing otherwise.)

2. In the somewhat rarer case where the performance is not substantial but the breach is unintentional, recovery is allowed on the basis of quasi-contract. For example, if the promisor is permanently injured when only halfway through the job, he or she is entitled to receive the reasonable value of the benefit received by the promisee as a result of the partial performance.

3. If the performance is clearly substantial but the breach is willful, there are conflicting views. Some courts deny any recovery, regardless of other circumstances, embracing the principle that aid should never be given the intentional wrongdoer. Most courts, while endorsing this principle in the abstract, in practice allow the promisor to recover "the reasonable value of the benefit resulting from the performance, minus damages" (as distinguished from the "contract price, minus damages" recovery allowed in situations where the substantial performance requirements are met). Such a recovery is especially common where a failure to allow the promisor anything would result in the promisee being unjustly enriched—a result most likely to occur in cases where the performance is of such a nature that it cannot be returned by the promisee.

How much was the intend to willfully perform — up to what degree

Special Problems Relating to Performance

Personal Satisfaction Contracts: Under the ordinary contract, a person who has undertaken the performance of a job impliedly warrants only that he or she will perform in a "workmanlike manner," i.e., the performance will be free of material defect and of a quality ordinarily accepted in that line of work. If the performance meets this standard, he or she is entitled to recover the contract price even if the person for whom the work was done is not satisfied with it.

Some contracts, however, provide that "satisfaction is guaranteed," or contain other language of similar nature. In such cases, it is usually held that such satisfaction is a condition precedent that must be met in order for the promisor to recover under the contract; workmanlike performance alone will not suffice. In determining whether the condition has been met, the courts distinguish between two kinds of contracts: (1) those in which matters of personal taste, esthetics, or comfort are dominant considerations, and (2) those that entail work of mere "mechanical utility."

For contracts in the first category, the condition is fulfilled only if the *promisee is actually satisfied* with the performance that was rendered—no matter how peculiar or unreasonable that person's tastes may be. For example: X, an artist, contracts to paint a portrait of Y for $500 "that will meet with Y's complete satisfaction." When the portrait is completed, Y refuses to pay on the ground that he simply does not like it. If X brings suit to recover the $500, a question of fact is presented: Is Y's claim of dissatisfaction genuine? If the jury so finds, the condition has not been met and X is denied recovery. (Of course, if the jury finds that Y's claim of dissatisfaction is false—that is, he is actually satisfied and is simply using this claim as a ground to escape an otherwise valid contract—then the condition has been met and recovery is allowed.)

For contracts in the second category, where the performance involves work of mere mechanical fitness (or mechanical utility), an objective test is used. For example: M agrees to overhaul the diesel engine in T's tractor-trailer for $200, guaranteeing that T will be "fully satisfied" with the job. In this case, the condition precedent is met if the jury finds that *a reasonable person would have been satisfied* with M's job, even though T himself is dissatisfied.

Performance by an Agreed Time: If a contract does not provide a time by which performance is to be completed, the general rule is that each party has a reasonable time within which to perform his or her obligations. Whether the performance of a promisor in a given case took place within such a time is ordinarily a question for the jury. In practice this rule poses few problems and seems to produce acceptable results.

A more troublesome situation is presented by contracts that *do* contain a stated time of performance. For example: A printer agrees to print up 15,000 letterheads for a customer, with the contract specifying "delivery by April 10." If delivery is not made until April 14, and the customer refuses to accept the goods because of the late performance, the question for the jury is whether the stated time of performance legally constituted a condition precedent. If it did, the condition has obviously not been met and the customer has no obligation to accept the shipment.

The general rule is that such a provision, of and by itself, *does not create a condition precedent.* Under this view, it is sufficient if the performance occurs within a reasonable time after the date specified. Thus, in the preceding illustration, the customer is very likely obligated to accept the letterheads where delivery was only four days late.

In some situations, however, the parties clearly intend that performance must actually take place by the specified time in order for the promisor to recover from the other party. In such situations, *performance by the agreed-upon time does constitute a condition precedent.* The intention can be manifested in two ways: (1) by the express wording of the agreement itself and (2) by implication (reasonable inference from the nature and subject matter of the contract alone).[6] Two examples may be helpful.

---

[6]The latter possibility is eliminated in some jurisdictions. A number of states provide by statute that time is never of the essence unless the contract expressly indicates that it is.

1. P agrees to print up and deliver 15,000 letterheads to Q by April 10, the contract further providing that *time is of the essence.* By this clause, the parties have made the stated time of performance an express condition precedent. Thus, if P fails to deliver the letterheads until April 11, Q can refuse to accept the belated performance. P's failure to meet the condition frees Q of her obligations under the contract. Additionally, Q can recover damages from P in a breach of contract suit. (An alternative open to Q is to accept the late performance and "reserve her rights" against P—in which case she is entitled to an allowance against the purchase price to the extent that she has suffered damages as a result of the late performance.)

2. A chamber of commerce purchases fireworks for a Fourth of July celebration it is sponsoring, with the contract providing that "delivery is to be made prior to July 4th." The fireworks arrive too late on July 4th to be used. From the nature of the *subject matter alone* it can be inferred that the stated time is a condition precedent, and the late delivery obviously did not meet that condition. In such a case it is said that time was made a condition "by operation of law" (that is, without regard to other factors).

The courts are reluctant to rule—from the subject matter of the contract or from the nature of the contract alone—that time is of the essence. Limited instances in which such a ruling *may* be made, however (in addition to the rare case typified in example 2), are option contracts—where, for example, a seller of land contracts to keep an offer open ninety days—and contracts in which the value of the subject matter is fluctuating rapidly.

At one time, many courts ruled that time was presumed to be of the essence in sales contracts. Today, however, this is not the general rule. Thus, in most states, a late delivery does not free the buyer unless he or she can clearly prove that delivery by the date contained in the contract *was* material, and that the seller knew or should have been aware of the materiality.

DISCHARGE BY BREACH

Actual Breach

It would be contrary to common sense if a person who had materially breached a contract were nevertheless able to hold the other party liable on it, and the law does not tolerate such a result. As the preceding section on performance indicates, an **actual breach**—failure of the promisor to render performance that meets the minimum required by law (full performance in some cases and substantial performance in others)—ordinarily results in the other party's obligations being discharged. In such cases the promisor's breach operates as "an excuse for nonperformance" insofar as the other's obligation is concerned.

This principle has found its way into the law of sales. Thus, if Seller S on May 1 contracts to deliver a thousand gallons of crude oil to Buyer B on August 15, and on that date S delivers only two hundred gallons with no indication that the balance will be delivered shortly thereafter, B can cancel the entire contract, returning the oil already delivered (see Secs. 2-610 and 2-711 of the UCC).

Anticipatory Breach

If one contracting party indicates to the other, before the time of performance arrives, that he or she is not going to perform his or her part of the bargain, an **anticipatory breach** has occurred; in most cases this has the same effect as an actual breach. For example: In March, X contracts to put in a sewer line for a city, with the contract providing that the work will be commenced by June 1. On April 10, X tells the city that he will not do the job. The city can immediately hire a new contractor to do the work and can institute a suit for damages against X as soon as the damages can be ascertained, without waiting until June to do so. (Such action is not mandatory; the city may ignore the repudiation in the hope that X will have a change of heart and actually commence the work on schedule.)

The doctrine of anticipatory breach does not apply to promises to pay money debts, such as those found in promissory notes and bonds. To illustrate: S borrows $500 from T on February 1, giving T a promissory note in that amount due September 1. If S tells T on August 6 that he will not pay the debt, T must nevertheless wait until September 2 before bringing suit to recover the $500.

DISCHARGE BY LEGAL IMPOSSIBILITY

ex closing of house / houses etc. or house might fire before or

Between the time of contracting and the time of performance, some event may occur that will make the performance of the contract—for one party, at least—considerably more difficult or costly than originally expected. When this happens, a promisor may contend that the occurrence legally discharged his or her obligations under the contract—that is, it created a **legal impossibility**.[7] For example: A, an accountant for a large corporation who "moonlights" in his spare time, contracts in May to perform certain auditing services for B during the first three weeks of August, A's regularly scheduled vacation. In June A is transferred to a city five hundred miles away; as a result, he does not perform the promised services. If B were to seek damages for breach of contract, the issue presented would be whether A's transfer discharged his obligations under the contract.

In such a case, the courts resort to a two-step process. The first question to be decided is whether one of the parties had assumed the risk in some manner. For example, in the case above, a court might conclude—from a reading of the entire contract, or from testimony regarding the negotiations leading up to the contract—that B had, in fact, agreed that A need not perform if he were located. If so, B had assumed the risk, and A need not perform.

If no assumption of risk is apparent (as is often the case), the court must proceed to the second question: whether it can rule, on the basis of the circumstances under which the contract was made, that the contract necessarily contained an *implied condition subsequent.* In other words, in the case above, A would be excused from performing the contract only if he could convince the court that *he and B agreed by implication* that the contract would be voided if he were transferred before the date of performance.

In most cases of this sort, the promisor's contention that an implied condition subsequent existed is rejected by the courts. The usual view is that such possibilities should have been guarded against by an express condition in the contract. Thus, when a corporation promises to manufacture engines by a certain date under a contract containing no express conditions, the fact that it is unable to do so because of a strike at one of its plants is no legal excuse for its nonperformance of the contract. And when a contractor agrees to construct a building by a certain date, with a monetary penalty imposed for late completion, the law normally does not excuse late performance simply because unexpectedly bad weather delayed the work. Nor will a court normally free a builder from his obligations, in the absence of an express condition, merely because unexpectedly high labor or materials costs will cause him to suffer a loss if he is held to the contract.

Notwithstanding these generalizations, there *are* limited situations in which the defense of legal impossibility is accepted by the courts. We will discuss them briefly.

True Impossibility

Essentially, a contract is rendered impossible of performance only where the supervening event—the event occurring between the making of the contract and the time of performance—was unforeseeable at the time of contracting, and which creates an objective impossibility. An

---

[7]A related subject, the doctrine of commercial impracticability, will be discussed subsequently.

objective impossibility results in a situation where, as a result of the unanticipated occurrence, no one can perform the contract—that is, performance is physically impossible. By contrast, an occurrence that makes performance by the promisor, only, impossible (but does not make performance by others impossible) does not discharge the promisor's obligations. For example, the inability of a buyer of a condominium to make a cash payment of $10,000 at the time of closing, as required by the contract, is not excused because his or her business suffered a catastrophic loss just prior to that time. (The difference between the two types of impossibility is often summarized thus: where a promisor is claiming objective impossibility, he is saying "*No one* can perform," while in the subjective impossibility situation he is simply saying "*I* cannot perform.")

Up until recent years, implied conditions subsequent—i.e., conditions resulting in legal (objective) impossibility—have been recognized by the courts in only three situations: (1) in contracts calling for personal services, (2) where the subject matter of the contract is destroyed without the fault of either party, and (3) where the performance of the contract becomes illegal after the contract is formed.[8]

Personal Services: In contracts calling for the rendering of *personal services,* such as the ordinary employment contract, the death or incapacity of the promisor (employee) terminates the agreement. The same is true of contracts that contemplate a *personal relationship* between the promisor and the other party. In such cases the courts will accept the argument that the performer's promise was *subject to the implied condition* that his or her death prior to the time of performance (or illness at the time of performance) rendered the contract null and void.[9]

Destruction of the Subject Matter: The principle is well established that destruction of the subject matter of a contract without the fault of either party, before the time for performance, terminates the contract. Where such a situation occurs, the courts will accept the argument that the destruction *constituted an implied condition subsequent* and will rule, as in the personal service contracts, that a legal impossibility has occurred. For example: If C contracted in January to move D's house in March, the contract would be discharged if the house were destroyed by flood in February. In this regard, it can be said that the destruction of the subject matter of a contract by an act of God creates a legal impossibility. It should be noted, however, that it is the fact of destruction that discharges, rather than the cause (as long as the destruction is not at-

---

[8] The view is commonly held among lay persons, and sometimes finds its way into court decisions, that promisors are freed of their obligations by any "act of God," or "force majeure"—i.e., a force of nature of such degree that it could not be guarded against or prevented by any degree of care or diligence (such as an earthquake or unprecedented flood). This generalization is true when the subject matter of a contract is destroyed by such an occurrence, but it is not necessarily true in other cases. For example, the destruction of a partially completed building by a tornado may be accepted by a court as grounds for permitting the contractor additional time in which to complete the job, but, as a general rule, it does *not discharge* the contractor from the obligation to rebuild.

   Because of this rule, and because of uncertainty as to application of the act-of-God defense to other contracts, construction contracts (and many others) typically contain *express* conditions subsequent excusing delays in performance, or completely excusing performance, in the event of adverse weather conditions, strikes, and so forth. The following clause, in a maritime shipping contract, is typical. "FORCE MAJEURE: In the event of any strike, fire or other event falling within the term 'Force Majeure' preventing or delaying ship-

---

ment or delivery of the goods occurring prior to shipment or delivery and preventing or delaying reception of the goods by the buyer, then the contract period of shipment or delivery shall be extended by 30 days on telex request made within seven days of its occurrence. Should shipment or delivery of the goods continue to be prevented beyond 30 days, the unaffected party may cancel the unfulfilled balance of the contract. Should the contract thus be cancelled and/or performance be prevented during any extension to the shipment or delivery period *neither party shall have any claim against the other.*" [Emphasis added.]

[9] Note, however, that many obligations are not personal in nature. For example: If B contracts to sell his land to W for $30,000, and B thereafter dies, the agreement is not terminated. The reason is that B's estate, acting through the executor, is just as capable of delivering a deed to W as was B, had he lived. Nor would the contract be terminated if W rather than B had died. W's estate is just as capable of paying the $30,000 as W would have been, had he lived.

tributable to neglect or misconduct of the parties). To illustrate: X contracts with an investors' syndicate to drive its race car at the next Indianapolis 500, and the night before the race the car is destroyed by a fire set by an arsonist. Both parties are discharged from their obligations, although the arsonist's act is not an act of God.

Beyond cases such as the above, it is often difficult to determine what is meant by the "subject matter" of a contract; the term is often used by the courts to include not only the precise subject matter involved, but any other "thing" or property that performance of the contract necessarily depends on. For example, the X Company in January agrees to manufacture and deliver five hundred widgets to the Y Company in March. In February the X Company's only plant is destroyed by fire, with the result that the widgets cannot be manufactured. In this case the courts will ordinarily rule that the existence of the plant is so necessary to the fulfillment of the contract that its destruction excuses the X Company from its obligations. (Such a ruling would not be made, however, if the X Company operated several plants and if there was no indication in the contract, expressly or impliedly, that the parties intended for the widgets to come from the particular plant that was destroyed.)[10]

Subsequent Illegality: If, after a contract is made, its performance becomes illegal because of a change in the law (including a promulgation of an administrative agency's regulation), a legal impossibility is created. Thus if B in September contracts to sell fifty pinball machines to G in December, the parties' obligations would be discharged if a state statute prohibiting such a transaction took effect in November.

The case below raises a "destruction of the subject matter" issue in regard to the performance of a construction contract that contained no express conditions subsequent. (However, as noted earlier, the general subject of impossibility should also be considered with a related view, the doctrine of "commercial impracticability," which is discussed immediately after this case.)

---

[10] Special problems arise in the "destruction" cases involving *sales of goods.* Specific "risk of loss" rules in Article 2 of the UCC govern situations of this sort, and are considered in Chapter 21.

La Gasse Pool Construction Co. v. City of Fort Lauderdale
Florida District Court of Appeal, Fourth
District, 288 So.2d 273 (1974)

The La Gasse Company, plaintiff, made a contract with the City of Fort Lauderdale under which it was to repair and renovate one of the city's swimming pools for a specified price. One night, when the job was almost completed, vandals damaged the pool so badly that most of the work had to be redone.

When the city refused to pay more than the contract price, plaintiff brought this action to recover compensation for the additional work. The primary contention of plaintiff was that the damage to its work constituted a destruction of the subject matter of the contract, and that it was consequently discharged from any obligation to redo the work. Accordingly, plaintiff argued, when it did do the work over again it was entitled to additional compensation for its services.

The trial court rejected this contention, holding that plaintiff had the responsibility under the original contract to redo the work, and it entered judgment for defendant. Plaintiff appealed.

Downey, Judge:

. . . The question presented for decision is: Where the work done by a contractor, pursuant to a contract for the repair of an existing structure, is damaged during the course of the repair work, but the existing structure is not destroyed, upon whom does the loss fall where neither contractor nor the owner is at fault?

The general rule is that under an indivisible contract to build an entire structure, loss or damage thereto during construction falls upon the contractor, the theory being that the contractor obligated himself to build an entire structure, and absent a delivery thereof he has not performed his contract. If his work is damaged or destroyed during construction he is still able to perform by rebuilding the damaged or destroyed part; in other words, doing the work over again.

In the case of contracts to repair, renovate, or perform work on existing structures, the general rule is that total destruction of the structure . . . without fault of either the contractor or owner, excuses performance by the contractor and entitles him to recover the value of the work done. The rationale of this rule is that the contract has an implied condition that the structure will remain in existence so the contractor can render performance. Destruction of the structure makes performance impossible, and thereby excuses the contractor's nonperformance.

But where the building or structure to be repaired is *not destroyed,* [and] the contractor's work is damaged so that it must be redone, performance is still possible, and it is the contractor's responsibility to redo the work so as to complete the undertaking. [Emphasis added.] In other words, absent . . . some other reason for lawful nonperformance, the contractor must perform his contract. Any loss or damage to his work during the process of repairs which can be rectified is his responsibility. The reason for allowing recovery without full performance in the case of total destruction (i.e., impossibility of performance) is absent where the structure remains and simply requires duplicating the work. . . . Accordingly, the judgment for [defendant] is affirmed.

DISCHARGE BY COMMERCIAL IMPRACTICABILITY

Under the traditional views just discussed, most contracts did not present situations in which legal impossibility was recognized. Thus most contracting parties were not freed from their obligations even in cases where their performance was clearly made more difficult by events that occurred after the contracts were entered into. Today, however, courts are more likely to free contracting parties than was the case earlier, because of increasing recognition of the **doctrine of commercial impracticability.**

In the 1950s, when Article 2 of the UCC (Sales) was being written, its drafters felt that sellers of goods should be excused from their obligations in more situations than was the case under the impossibility doctrine. To achieve this, they adopted the doctrine of commercial impracticability (or, as it is sometimes called, the doctrine of commercial frustration).

Commercial Impracticability under the UCC

Section 2-615 of the UCC reads, in part, as follows: "Delay in delivery or nondelivery in whole or in part by a seller . . . is not a breach of his duty under a contract for sale if performance as agreed has been made impracticable by the occurrence of a contingency the non-occurrence of which was a basic assumption upon which the contract was made."

While a full discussion of the scope and ramifications of the commercial impracticability doctrine cannot be undertaken here, several of its basic characteristics can be noted. These characteristics are best explained in Comment 4 following Sec. 2-615, which reads as follows:

> Increased cost alone does not excuse performance unless the rise is due to some unforeseen contingency which alters the essential nature of the performance. Neither is a rise or a collapse in the market in itself a justification, for that is exactly the type of business risk which business contracts made at fixed prices are intended to cover. But a severe shortage of raw materials or of supplies due to a contingency such as war, embargo, local crop failure, unforeseen shutdown of major sources of supply or the like, which either causes a *marked increase in cost* or *altogether prevents the seller* from securing supplies necessary to his performance, is within the contemplation of this section." [Emphasis added.]

Thus this section clearly recognizes certain kinds of contingencies *in addition to* those constituting true impossibilities that may free the seller of his or her obligations under the contract. (In that regard, however, under both Comment 1 to Sec. 2-615 and the case law that has developed with respect to this section, the seller must show that the contingency was an unforeseeable one—that is, one that was not within the contemplation of the parties at the time of contracting.)

A second change brought about by the impracticability doctrine is its recognition that a "marked increase" in cost will free the seller, if caused by an unforeseen contingency. (By contrast, increased cost of performance alone is almost never recognized under the impossibility doctrine as a ground for excusing performance.) However, determination of what constitutes a marked increase in cost is left to the courts to decide on a case-by-case basis, and the courts have interpreted this term quite narrowly. That is, under the decisions, the courts have generally taken the view that the seller must prove that the cost of performance (as a result of the contingency) would at least be double or triple the original cost of performance. Thus the increased cost provision does not afford sellers relief in as many cases as would at first appear.[11]

After adoption of the UCC, the courts generally recognized commercial impracticability as an excuse for nonperformance in sales contracts only, continuing to require a showing of strict impossibility where other types of contracts were involved. Today, however, *there is a growing tendency among the courts to apply the commercial impracticability yardstick to all kinds of contracts.*

The Supreme Court of Alaska, in the case below, first speaks of impossibility in the true sense. But it also reflected the tendency noted above by buttressing its decision with references to the doctrine of commercial impracticability, even though the contract in question was not a sales contract.

---

[11] *Eastern Airlines, Inc. v. Gulf Oil Company,* in Chapter 23, is representative of such cases.

Northern Corporation v. Chugach Electric Association
Supreme Court of Alaska, 518 P.2d 76 (1974)

In August of 1966 the Northern Corporation, a contractor, entered into a contract with Chugach Electric Association. The contract called for Northern to install protective riprap on a dam owned by Chugach on Cooper Lake, Alaska, for $63,655. The job essentially involved the quarrying and transporting of large quantities of rock, and installing the rock on the upstream face of the dam.

The parties originally contemplated that the rock was to be drilled and shot at a designated quarry. However, when this rock was found to be unsuitable, the parties amended the contract in September so that Northern could use alternative quarry sites, and the contract price for the job was increased by $42,000. Northern then selected a site that was at the opposite end of the lake, intending to transport the rock across the lake on the ice during the winter of 1966–1967. The contract apparently did not specify a means of transportation, but at the time of the contract amendment Chugach sent Northern a letter authorizing transportation across the lake. Work commenced in the new quarry in October, and all of the required rock was drilled and shot by the end of that month.

During the following winter Northern commenced hauling operations, but had to stop them because two of its vehicles went through the ice; a loader sank, and a tractor was recovered. Northern then told Chugach that the ice was too unsafe for the job, but Chugach and its engineering firm insisted that the job be performed. Nevertheless, in March of 1967 Northern ceased operations, apparently with Chugach's approval.

After a long period of negotiations, Chugach advised Northern in January of 1968 that it would hold Northern liable for damages for breach of contract unless all rock was hauled by April 1. In late January, when ice conditions appeared to be much more favorable than the previous year, Northern started its hauling operation again. However, in February two half-loaded trucks broke through the ice, resulting in the deaths of the drivers and loss of the trucks. Northern then advised Chugach that it considered the contract "terminated for impossibility of performance."

Northern then brought this action against Chugach, asking for (1) a ruling that the contract was impossible of performance, and (2) damages equal to the costs which it incurred in attempting to perform the contract. Chugach counter-claimed, contending that performance was not impossible, and that it was thus entitled to damages incurred between the date of completion specified in the amended contract and the date of its termination by Northern. The trial court

discharged both parties on the ground of impossibility, and denied both parties' claims for damages. Both parties appealed.

In the Supreme Court of Alaska, four issues were raised. Only two of these are considered here.

Boochever, Justice:

. . . The issues on this appeal may be summarized as follows: . . .

1. Was the contract, as modified, impossible of performance?

2. If the modified contract was impossible of performance, is Northern entitled to reasonable costs in endeavoring to perform it? . . .

The focal question is whether the amended contract was impossible of performance. The September directive specified that the rock was to be transported "across Cooper Lake to the dam site when such lake is frozen to a sufficient depth to permit heavy vehicle traffic thereon," and the formal amendment specified that the hauling to the dam site would be done during the winter of 1966–1967. . . . [Despite the foregoing] Chugach contends . . . that Northern was nevertheless bound to perform [under the contract itself,] and that it could have used means other than hauling by truck across the ice to transport the rock. The answer to Chugach's contention is that, as the trial court found, the parties contemplated that the rock would be hauled by truck once the ice froze to a sufficient depth to support the weight of the vehicles. The specification of this particular method of performance presupposed the existence of ice frozen to the requisite depth. Since this expectation of the parties was never fulfilled, . . . *Northern's duty to perform was discharged by reason of impossibility.*

There is an additional reason for our holding that Northern's duty to perform was discharged by impossibility. It is true that in order for a defendant to prevail under the original common law doctrine of impossibility, he had to show [not only that he could not perform, but also] that no one else could have performed the contract. However, this harsh rule has gradually been eroded, and the Restatement of Contracts has departed from the early rule by recognizing the principle of "commercial impracticability." Under this doctrine, a party is discharged from his contract obligations, even if it is technically possible to perform them, *if the costs of performance would be so disproportionate to that reasonably contemplated by the parties as to make the contract totally impractical in a commercial sense. . . .* [Emphasis added.]

Removed from the strictures of the common law, "impossibility" in its modern context has become a coat of many colors, including among its hues the point argued here—namely, impossibility predicated upon commercial "impracticability." This concept—which finds expression both in case law and in other authorities—is predicated upon the assumption that in legal contemplation something is impracticable when it can only be done at an excessive and unreasonable cost. [The court here cited a California case in which the doctrine of commercial impracticability was applied, where the cost of the only alternative means of performance was ten times that of the means originally contemplated by the parties.] . . .

There is ample evidence to support [the trial court's findings that "the ice haul method of transporting riprap . . . was within the contemplation of the parties and was part of the basis of the agreement which ultimately resulted in the contract amendment,"] and that that method was not commercially feasible within the financial parameters of the contract. . . .

[The court then turned to the question of damages, and ruled that plaintiff *should* have been allowed damages to cover its costs incurred in attempting to perform the contract. It then set forth the rules that should be applied in determining this measure of damages.]

Judgment affirmed in part, reversed in part, and remanded.

Comment:

1. The court states that commercial impracticability is one form of impossibility. While this view blurs the line of demarcation that most courts have drawn between the two doctrines in the past, it is one that has had increasing acceptance in recent years.

2. In a subsequent rehearing, the Alaska Supreme Court modified its decision in this case. The modification, however, had only to do with a restating of the rules applicable to the determination of damages; the holding as to impossibility and commercial impracticability was thus unchanged.

DISCHARGE BY FRUSTRATION OF PURPOSE

Occasionally, after a contract is entered into, some event or condition will occur that clearly does not fall within the impossibility or commercial impracticability doctrines, yet one of the parties will argue that it so *frustrated the purposes of the contract* that its occurrence ought to free him nonetheless. (In other words, such a party is contending that the happening of the event caused the contract to become worthless to him.) To illustrate: D, a car dealer embark-

ing on an ambitious expansion program, makes a contract with C, a contractor, under the terms of which he is to pay C $250,000 for the construction of new showroom facilities. Shortly thereafter, because of an unanticipated national defense emergency, the federal government orders a 90 percent reduction in the production of new automobiles. D contends that this action constitutes grounds for cancelling its construction contract, since he will obviously have few new cars to sell.

Here the courts are on the horns of a dilemma. On the one hand, they understand that the virtual stoppage of new car production substantially eliminates the purpose for which the contract was made—and may even drive D into bankruptcy if he is held to its terms. On the other hand, the adoption of a general rule to the effect that contracts are discharged whenever the *purposes* of one of the parties cannot be attained as a result of unanticipated future occurrences would cast great uncertainty on the enforceability of almost all contracts.

While it is dangerous to generalize about the kinds of cases in which the doctrine of frustration may be accepted as grounds for avoiding contractual liability, it can safely be said that the courts—while giving the doctrine due consideration in their decisions—actually find it to be *inapplicable* in the great majority of cases. Thus, in the example above, D's contention that he was freed on the ground of frustration of purpose will probably (though not certainly) be rejected.

DISCHARGE BY PARTIES' AGREEMENT

Once a contract has been formed, it is always possible for the parties to make a new agreement that will discharge or modify the obligations of one or both parties under the original contract. The new agreement can take any of several forms, the most common of which are rescission, novation, and accord and satisfaction.

Rescission

A contract can always be canceled by mutual agreement. When this agreement occurs, the contract is *rescinded,* and the obligations of both parties are thereby discharged. An oral rescission agreement is generally valid and binding, even where the original contract was in writing—with one major exception. A rescission agreement must be in writing if it involves a retransfer of real property. (Additionally, under Sec. 2-209[2] of the UCC, modification or rescission of a written *sales contract* must be evidenced by a writing if the original contract so provides.)

Novation

A **novation** occurs when the party entitled to receive performance under a contract agrees to release the party who "owes" the performance and to permit a third party to take that person's place. It is simply a three-sided agreement that results in the substitution of one party for another. For example: X and Y have a contract. Later, they and Z agree that Z will perform X's obligations, with Y expressly releasing X from the original contract. X's obligations are now discharged. *usually no 3rd parties in Novation*

Accord and Satisfaction

After a contract has been formed, the parties may agree that one of them will accept, and the other will render, a performance different from what was originally called for. Such an agreement is an *accord.* Thus, if B owes W $1,800, and they subsequently agree that B will air-condition W's home in satisfaction of the debt, an accord exists. The reaching of an accord does not, of and by itself, terminate the existing obligation. To effect a discharge, a *satisfaction* must take place—the actual performance of the substituted obligation. Thus B's indebtedness is discharged by **accord and satisfaction** only when he completes the air-conditioning job. *similiar to barter*

DISCHARGE BY OPERATION OF LAW

In addition to the types of discharge already discussed, other events or conditions can bring about a *discharge by operation of law.* The most common of these are bankruptcy proceedings, the running of a statute of limitations, and the fraudulent alteration of a contract.

Bankruptcy Proceedings[12]

Bankruptcy actions today are governed by the federal Bankruptcy Reform Act of 1978. If an individual has been adjudged bankrupt after proper bankruptcy proceedings have taken place, he or she receives a *discharge in bankruptcy* from a court which covers most—but not all—of his or her debts. While the discharge technically does not extinguish the debts that are subject to it, it does so as a practical matter by prohibiting creditors from thereafter bringing court action against the debtor to recover any unpaid balance.

---

[12] The subject of bankruptcy is treated in Chapter 30.

Running of Statutes of Limitations

All states have statutes providing that after a certain amount of time has elapsed, a contract claim is barred. The time limits vary widely from one jurisdiction to another. In some states, for example, claimants are given three years in which to bring suit on oral contracts and five years on written ones; in others, the times vary from two to eight years on oral contracts and from three to fifteen years on written ones.

In any event, if a contract claimant lets the applicable time elapse without initiating legal proceedings, the statute of limitations has run and subsequent court action by that person is barred. The period of time begins the day after the cause of action accrues. Thus, if X promises to pay Y $500 on June 10, 1984, in a state having a three-year statute, the statute begins to run on June 11, with the result that Y has until June 10, 1987, to institute suit. (As in the case of a discharge in bankruptcy, the running of the statute does not extinguish the debt or claim itself; it simply prevents the claimant from subsequently bringing a legal action to recover the indebtedness.)

Alteration

The law generally strives to discourage dishonest conduct. Consistent with this policy is the rule that the fraudulent, material **alteration** of a written contract by one of the parties discharges the other party as a matter of law. Suppose, for example, that A makes a written contract with B under the terms of which he is to sell 1,000 gallons of paint to B at a specified price per gallon. If B subsequently changes the quantity to 1,200 gallons without A's knowledge, A is excused from delivering any paint at all, if that is his desire. (A also has the right to enforce the contract according to its original terms or as altered—that is, he can tender either 1,000 or 1,200 gallons to B and hold him liable for the quantity chosen.)

SUMMARY

In some situations a contracting party does not want to be obligated by the contract unless and until a certain event occurs. This protection can be achieved by use of an express condition precedent—a clause in the contract providing that performance is to occur only if the specified event occurs. In other circumstances a party might want the contract to be performed unless a certain event occurs within a stated time. In the latter case he or she may achieve protection by use of an express condition subsequent—a clause providing that if the specified event occurs, the contract shall be null and void.

In addition to *express* conditions, in some circumstances the law will recognize that the contract was subject to various *implied* conditions. Most contracts are of such a nature that the parties understood that one party (X) was to perform his part of the bargain (e.g., the painting of Y's house) before the other party (Y) had a duty to pay. In such instances, performance by X constitutes an implied condition to his recovery of the price.

In cases where the promisor's performance falls short of complete performance, he or she may still be able to recover under the doctrine of substantial performance. Under this doctrine, the promisor is entitled to receive the contract price minus damages to the promisee if (1) the defects in his or her performance were slight, and (2) the failure to perform completely was not due to bad faith—i.e., the deviations from 100 percent performance were not intentional.

As seen above, one's contractual obligations may be discharged by the failure of an express condition precedent to occur, the occurrence of an express condition subsequent, or by complete or substantial performance on his or her part. One's contractual obligations are also discharged by breach by the other party, or where a legal impossibility exists. Such an impossibility exists in situations where the courts can rule that, under the circumstances, the contract was subject to an *implied* condition subsequent. Implied conditions are found to exist in only three limited situations: (1) in contracts calling for performance of personal services, and where the promisor dies prior to the time of performance (or is incapacitated at that time); (2) where the subject-matter of the contract is destroyed without fault of either party prior to the time of performance; and (3) where performance becomes illegal prior to the time of performance. Because the impossibility view excuses a promisor only in limited circumstances, most courts today are applying the more liberal doctrine of commercial impracticability, instead—a doctrine first recognized under sales law, and one which frees the promisor in more circumstances than does the impossibility view.

KEY TERMS

Condition
Condition precedent
Condition subsequent
Conditions concurrent
Substantial performance
Actual breach
Anticipatory breach
Legal impossibility
Doctrine of commercial impracticability
Novation
Accord and satisfaction
Alteration

QUESTIONS AND PROBLEMS

1. Roper contracted in writing to buy a Wyoming ranch from Lewis for a specified price. At the same time that this contract was made Roper and Lewis also orally agreed, in rather general terms, that Lewis would also sell his 400 head of cattle and some ranch machinery to Roper. Later, when the cattle and machinery deal fell through, Roper brought court action asking for rescission of the ranch contract. Roper's contention was that performance of the cattle and machinery agreement was a *condition precedent* to his ob-

ligations under the ranch-purchase contract. Lewis disagreed, pointing out that (a) the written ranch contract did not mention the oral agreement, and (b) that, in fact, the parties never did come to specific terms as to the cattle and machinery prices. Would these factors cause the court to rule that performance of the cattle and machinery contract was *not* a condition precedent? Discuss. (*Lewis v. Roper*, 579 P.2d 434, 1978.)

2. Mr. and Mrs. Funk contracted to buy the Cox home in North Carolina. The contract provided that the contract was subject to the sale of the purchasers' present residence (the Funks' residence). When Cox later brought an action demanding that the Funks go through with the contract and pay the purchase price, the Funks stated that they had not yet been able to sell their residence. The Funks thus contended that the actual sale of their old residence was a *condition precedent* to their obligation to buy the Cox home, and since the condition had not occurred, they did not yet have the duty to pay for the Cox home. Is this a good argument? Why or why not? (*Cox v. Funk*, 255 S.E.2d 600, 1979.)

3. Cayias owned a pool hall business, which he operated in a leased building. Wishing to sell the business, he listed it with the Associated Investment Company, a broker, under a contract providing that if the company found a buyer at a price agreeable to him, he would pay the company a commission of 10 percent of the purchase price. The company found a buyer willing to pay $3,000, and Cayias and the buyer entered into a contract calling for the sale of the business at that price. The contract provided, however, that if the buyer was not able to obtain a new lease on the building at a monthly rental of $150, "then and in that event the agreement shall become null and void." The purchaser thereafter was apparently not able to get a lease from the owner of the building at this figure, so the sale of the business fell through. The company now sued Cayias, the seller, to recover its commission of $300. Cayias defended on the ground that (a) the quoted clause in the purchase agreement constituted a condition subsequent, and (b) since the condition (the inability of the buyer to get a lease) occurred with the result that the buyer was released, he (Cayias) was released from his obligation to pay a commission on the "sale." Rule on the correctness of Cayias' contention. (*Associated Investment Co. v. Cayias*, 185 P. 778, 1920.)

4. A contractor who built a country home for Kent for $77,000 sought to recover the unpaid balance of $3,400. Kent refused to make the final payment because the building contract required that all pipe in the home be of "Reading manufacture," and the pipe actually installed was made by a different manufacturer, the Cohoes Company. The contractor proved that the Cohoes pipe met all the specifications of the Reading pipe and that he was not aware of the Reading requirement in the contract when he installed the other pipe. On these facts, does the doctrine of substantial performance apply to the plaintiff, the contractor? Explain. (*Jacobs and Young, Inc. v. Kent,* 129 N.E. 889, 1921.)

5. The MTK Potato Company (the M Co.) contracted to buy a quantity of potatoes from the Tallackson Potato Company (the T Co.). Both companies were members of a potato "co-op." The contract provided a "payment schedule" under which the M Co. was to make its payments. Later the M Co. refused to go through with the deal, whereupon the T Co. sued it for damages for breach of contract. At the trial the M Co. tried to prove (a) that when the contract was made it was understood by the T Co., the seller, that the M Co. expected to get the money to pay for the potatoes from the co-op, and (b) that, in fact, the co-op had never made any payments of money to it, the M Co. While the M Co. admitted that its receipt of the money from the co-op was not a condition of the contract, it did argue that the failure of the co-op to pay it (M Co.) the necessary sums of money constituted an "impossibility and/or a commercial impracticability" that thus freed it from its contractual

obligations. Is this a good argument? Explain. (*Tallackson Potato Co. v. MTK Potato Co.,* 278 N.W.2d 417, 1979.)

6. A professional football player made a contract with Alabama Football, Inc. (Alabama), which at that time was a member of the World Football League. Under the contract Alabama agreed to pay the player a salary covering the years 1977, 1978, and 1979. Soon after the contract was made, the World Football League folded—ceased to exist. In subsequent litigation, Alabama contended that the failure of the league constituted a *legal impossibility* that freed Alabama of its obligations to the player. Should the court accept this argument? Discuss. (*Alabama Football, Inc. v. Wright,* 452 F.Supp. 182, 1977.)

7. The Republic Creosoting Company contracted to sell and deliver to the City of Minneapolis a quantity of paving blocks, with deliveries to be made in the first six months of 1920. The contract did not contain any clause excusing a late delivery in the event of a strike, a boxcar shortage, or similar events beyond the company's control. Because of a nationwide boxcar shortage, the company was unable to deliver the blocks at the agreed upon time. The city considered this a breach of contract and purchased the blocks from another supplier at a higher price. The city then brought suit against the company to recover damages for breach of contract, and the company defended on the ground that the nationwide boxcar shortage constituted a legal impossibility. Rule on the validity of this defense (a) on the ground of impossibility, and (b) on the ground of commercial impracticability. (*Minneapolis v. Republic Creosoting Co.,* 201 N.W. 414, 1924.)

8. One railroad (the lessor) leased part of its depot facilities in Milwaukee to another railroad (the lessee) under a long-term contract. Thereafter, with several years on the contract remaining, Amtrak was formed by an act of Congress that resulted, among other things, in the lessee's passenger service in the Milwaukee area being very substantially reduced. As a result, the lessee would have very little use for the depot facilities. When the lessor sued the lessee to recover $2 million rental fees for subsequent years, the lessee contended that the formation of Amtrak (and the sharp curtailment of its services) freed it from its remaining obligations under the *frustration of purpose* doctrine. The lessor contested this argument, and offered evidence to show (a) that when the contract was made the lessee was aware that Amtrak might come into existence; (b) that both parties realized that their need for the depot might be substantially cut; and (c) that the lessee, by joining Amtrak—which it was not required by law to do—was itself partly responsible for its cutback of services. Should this evidence convince the court to rule that the frustration of purpose doctrine is *not* applicable? (That is, should this evidence cause the court to rule that the lessee is still bound by the contract?) Why or why not? (*Chicago, M., St.P.&P.R. Co. v. Chicago & N.W.*, 203 N.W.2d 189, 1978.)

Part III

AGENCY

The law of agency deals with the various rights and responsibilities that exist when one person acts in a representative role for another. Because most of the world's work is done by persons acting as representatives, the law of agency is among the most fundamental of subject areas. Moreover, an understanding of the law of agency is essential to the study of business organizations which follows in Part VI. Chapter 18 focuses on the basic nature of the agency relationship, the methods by which such a relationship is created and terminated, and the duties of the principal and agent to one another. Chapter 19 then examines the duties and liabilities of the principal and agent to third parties.

The law of employment is very closely related to the law of agency, because many agents are also employees. Most of our present laws governing employment, however, are statutory in nature, and most create legal rights for employees that were not recognized by the common law of agency. For this reason we are deferring our discussion of employment law to Part VIII, Government Regulation of Business.

Chapter 18

AGENCY
Nature, Creation, Duties, and Termination

NATURE OF THE AGENCY RELATIONSHIP

In a legal context the term **agency** ordinarily describes a relationship in which two parties—the principal and the agent—agree that one will act as a representative of the other. The **principal** is the person who wishes to accomplish something, and the **agent** is the one employed to act in the principal's behalf to achieve it.

At one time or another, almost everyone has come into contact with the agency relationship. Anyone who has purchased merchandise at a retail store almost certainly has dealt with an agent—the salesclerk. Similarly, anyone who has ever held a job probably has served in some type of representative capacity for the employer.

The usefulness of the agency relationship in the business world is obvious. With few exceptions, no single individual is capable of performing every act required to run a business enterprise. Furthermore, many businesses are organized as corporations (see Chapter 36 for details), which by definition can act only by employing agents. As a result, most business transactions throughout the world are handled by agents.

The term *agency* is often used loosely to describe many different types of relationships in which one party acts in a representative capacity for another. *Principal* and *agent* are also sometimes used loosely to denote the parties to various types of arrangements. However, throughout our discussion these terms are used narrowly to describe a particular type of relationship. The **principal-agent relationship,** as we use it, means a relationship in which the parties have agreed that the agent is to represent the principal in negotiating and transacting business; that is, the agent is employed to make contracts or enter similar business transactions in behalf of the principal. The term will ordinarily be used in discussions of contractual liability.

Two similar relationships are the **master-servant relationship** (or *employer–employee*) and the **employer–independent contractor relationship.** In these arrangements the subor-dinate has been employed to perform *physical work* for his or her superior, and the matter in dispute usually concerns *tort liability.*[1] Of course, a person may be hired to represent the employer in commercial dealings and also to perform physical tasks. In such a case he or she is an agent with respect to the authority to transact business and either a servant or an independent contractor with respect to the performance of physical tasks. Although courts sometimes loosely use the term *agent* to describe someone who performs physical duties, again, to avoid confusion, the term is used here in its narrow sense.

Most of our discussion in these two chapters involves the principal-agent relationship; the master-servant and employer–independent contractor relationships are dealt with in the latter part of the next chapter.

CREATION OF THE AGENCY RELATIONSHIP

Necessary Elements

The agency relationship is *consensual*—that is, based on the agreement of the parties. Many times it is created by a legally enforceable employment contract between the principal and the agent. A legally binding contract is not essential, however. An agency relationship that gives the agent authority to represent the principal and bind him or her by the agent's actions can generally be established by any words or actions that indicate the parties' consent to the arrangement. Consideration is not required.

In fact, no formalities are required for the creation of an agency relationship in most circumstances. For example, it is not usually necessary to spell out the agent's authority in writing; oral authority is ordinarily sufficient. Exceptions do exist, however. The most common one oc-

---

[1] This statement is admittedly something of an oversimplification, because a few torts, such as fraud and slander, are not of a physical nature. Questions of liability for such torts may occur even if the subordinate's tasks are entirely nonphysical.

curs when an agent is granted authority to sell real estate. In a majority of states an agent can make a contract for the sale of real estate that will bind the principal only if the agent's authority is stated in writing.

Even though formalities are usually not required for the creation of an agency, it is certainly wise to express the extent of an agent's authority and any other relevant matters in writing. This precaution often prevents misunderstandings between the principal and agent or between the agent and third parties with whom he or she is dealing. The formal written authorization given by a principal to an agent is frequently referred to as a **power of attorney.** When a formal power of attorney is used, the agent is sometimes referred to as an **attorney-in-fact.** This is simply another term for an agent, and should not be confused with attorney-at-law (a lawyer). Courts generally scrutinize powers of attorney very carefully and interpret their language strictly.

In the following case, an agent learned the hard way about the rule that powers of attorney are interpreted very strictly, and found that good intentions are no substitute for authority.

King v. Bankerd
Court of Appeals of Maryland, 492 A.2d 608 (1985)

Howard R. Bankerd (Bankerd) and his wife Virginia owned, as "tenants by the entirety," a home in Montgomery County, Maryland. (A "tenancy by the entirety" is one type of joint ownership created by the marriage relationship in some states; see Chapter 41 for details.) They lived there until 1966 when Mrs. Bankerd moved out as a result of marital problems. Bankerd continued to live at the property until July, 1968, when he "left for the west." Mrs. Bankerd then resumed living on the property. For the next twelve years, Bankerd lived at various locations in Nevada, Colorado, and Washington, and made no payments on the mortgage, for taxes, or for the maintenance of the home.

Before Bankerd's departure, he executed a power of attorney to King, an attorney with whom he was acquainted. From 1971 to 1974, Bankerd did not communicate with King in any way. In 1975, however, King sent Bankerd a letter enclosing an updated power of attorney because the Washington Suburban Sanitary Commission was about to put a sewer adjacent to the property, and King believed the new power would be needed. This power of attorney, dated October 30, 1975, was executed by Bankerd and returned to King. It stated:

KNOW ALL MEN BY THESE PRESENTS, that I, Howard R. Bankerd, hereby make, constitute and appoint ARTHUR V. KING, my attorney for me, and in my name to convey, grant, bargain and/or sell the property designated in the Montgomery County land record as Lot 9 of an unrecorded subdivision as recorded in Liber 3027 at folio 293, situated at 14026 Travilah Road, Rockville, Maryland on such terms as to him may seem best, and in my name, to make, execute, acknowledge and deliver, good and sufficient deeds and conveyances for the same with or without cove-

*nants and warranties and generally to do and perform all things neces-
sary pertaining to the future transfer of said property, and generally to
do everything whatsoever necessary pertaining to the said property.*

After granting this power of attorney, Bankerd had no further communication with King until 1978.

Mrs. Bankerd, who had been living at and maintaining the property
since 1968, requested King in September 1977 to exercise the power
of attorney and to transfer Bankerd's interest in the property to her.
King was aware that Mrs. Bankerd was nearing retirement and that
she was "saddled" with a property she could neither sell nor mortgage because of her husband's legal interest in it. Consequently, King
made several attempts to find and communicate with Bankerd, but
was unsuccessful.

Mrs. Bankerd informed King that her husband had once attempted
to give the property away to a neighbor on the condition that the
neighbor assume the mortgage payments. As a result, King asserted
that he believed Bankerd "didn't give a damn" about the property, and
that given Bankerd's age (approximately sixty-nine years), King believed that Bankerd might even be deceased. King therefore conveyed Bankerd's interest in the property to Mrs. Bankerd by deed in
1978. Mrs. Bankerd paid no consideration for the transfer and King
received no compensation for executing the deed. Mrs. Bankerd then
sold the property to a third party for $62,500.

In 1981 Bankerd filed suit against King alleging that King had acted
negligently and had exceeded his authority as Bankerd's agent. The
trial court granted summary judgment to Bankerd against King and
awarded $13,555.05 in damages. The intermediate appellate court
affirmed, and King appealed to Maryland's highest court.

Cole, Judge:

The single issue presented in this case is whether a power of attorney authorizing the agent to "convey, grant, bargain and/or sell" the principal's property authorizes the agent to make a gratuitous transfer [i.e., a gift] of that
property. . . .

Broadly defined, a power of attorney is a written document by which one
party, as principal, appoints another as agent (attorney-in-fact) and confers
upon the latter the authority to perform certain specified acts or kinds of acts
on behalf of the principal. . . . Various rules govern the interpretation of
powers of attorney. . . . One well-settled rule is that powers of attorney are
strictly construed . . . and are held to grant only those powers which are
clearly delineated. . . .

Another accepted rule of construction is to discount or disregard all-
embracing expressions found in powers of attorney. Because powers of attorney are ordinarily very carefully drafted and scrutinized, courts give the
terms used a technical rather than a popular meaning. In addition, ambiguities in an instrument are resolved against the party who made it or

caused it to be made, because that party had the better opportunity to understand and explain his meaning. Finally, general words used in an instrument are restricted by the context in which they are used, and are construed accordingly. . . .

For the reasons below, we conclude that an agent holding a broad power of attorney lacks the power to make a gift of the principal's property, unless that power (1) is expressly conferred, (2) arises as a necessary implication from the conferred powers, or (3) is clearly intended by the parties, as evidenced by the surrounding facts and circumstances.

First, the power to make a gift of the principal's property is a power that is potentially hazardous to the principal's interests. Consequently, this power will not be lightly inferred from broad, all-encompassing grants of power to the agent. Accordingly, "the agent must be circumspect with regard to the powers created—or the lack of them."

Second, the main duty of an agent is loyalty to the interest of his principal. Thus, in exercising granted powers under a power of attorney, the attorney in fact is bound to act for the benefit of his principal and must avoid where possible that which is detrimental unless expressly authorized. It is difficult to imagine how a gift of the principal's real property would be to the benefit of the principal when the power of attorney does not authorize such a gift or the principal does not intend to authorize such a gift. In short, the agent is under a duty to serve his principal with only his principal's purposes in mind. Third, it would be most unusual for an owner of property to grant a power of attorney authorizing the attorney in fact to give his property away. If a person has decided to make a gift of property, he or she usually decides as to who is going to be the donee. . . .

The facts and surrounding circumstances presented in this case do not give rise to any fact or inference that King was authorized to make a gift of Bankerd's real property. In arguing that his conduct was reasonable under the circumstances, King points to his "beliefs" that Bankerd had abandoned the property, that Bankerd did not care about the property, and that Bankerd might be deceased. These arguments completely miss the mark. King's conduct could only be "reasonable" if Bankerd intended for King to give the property away. Although the facts and surrounding circumstances to which King points suggest reasons why he made the gift, they do not support an inference that Bankerd intended to authorize the gift.

Furthermore, the only evidence before the trial court that was relevant to this issue indicated that Bankerd did not intend to authorize King to give the subject property to Bankerd's wife or anyone else. In a letter Bankerd sent to King along with the executed power of attorney, Bankerd wrote that "[y]ou know if I outlive Va., (and I'm ornery enough) you would certainly have a job on that Travilah Road bit *if* you would accept it, that is." Nothing could more clearly belie an assertion that Bankerd authorized any gift of the property. Bankerd, by virtue of this correspondence, notified King that he clearly anticipated maintaining his interest in the property. Furthermore, King wrote Bankerd assuring him that if the latter executed the new power of attorney he would do nothing detrimental to Bankerd's interests. Certainly, had King believed that he was acquiring the authority to give away Bankerd's property, King would not have made this representation.

In sum, there is no genuine dispute as to any material fact. The trial court did not err in granting Bankerd's motion for summary judgment.

Judgment affirmed. [Note: Instead of suing his agent for damages, Bankerd could have sued to set aside the transfer of his interest to his wife, which, in turn, would have invalidated the transfer by her to the third party.]

Capacity

If an agent, acting in behalf of a principal, makes a properly authorized contract with a third party, the contract is viewed legally as being one between the principal and the third party; that is, it is the *principal's* contract, not the agent's. For this reason the principal's capacity to make contracts may be important in determining the validity of the contract in question. The minority, insanity, or other incapacity of the principal has the same effect on contracts made through an agent as it does on contracts made personally.

On the other hand, the agent's capacity is usually immaterial. The reason is the same—the contract made by the agent for the principal is the principal's contract. A minor, for example, can serve as an agent; his or her lack of contractual capacity ordinarily has no effect on a contract made in behalf of the principal.[2]

DUTIES OF PRINCIPAL AND AGENT

The principal-agent relationship is a **fiduciary relationship**—one of trust. Each party owes the other a duty to act with the utmost good faith. Each should be entirely open with the other, not keeping any information from the other that has any bearing on their arrangement.

We will now consider other duties, some of which are merely specific applications of the general fiduciary obligation.

Duties Owed by Principal to Agent

The primary duty owed by the principal to the agent is simply that of complying with the terms of their employment contract, if one exists. Failure of the principal to do so will render him or her liable to the agent for damages; if the breach is material, it will justify the agent in refusing to act for the principal any further. For example: P and A have agreed that A is to be paid a specified percentage of the sales she makes for P. If P refuses or fails to pay A, A can rightfully terminate their arrangement and hold P responsible for damages.

In addition, the principal is under a duty to reimburse the agent for any expenditures reasonably incurred by the agent in furthering the interests of the principal. For example, if P directs A to travel from Chicago to Los Angeles to transact business for P, but does not provide her with any funds for travel expenses, P will be under a duty when A returns to reimburse her for amounts she reasonably expended in making the trip, such as her round-trip air fare.

Duties Owed by Agent to Principal

Obedience: It is the duty of the agent to obey the clear instructions of the principal, so long as such instructions are legal. If the instructions are ambiguous, the agent cannot disregard them altogether, but he or she can fulfill the duty by acting in good faith and interpreting them in a manner that is reasonable under the circumstances.

---

[2] Of course, the agent's lack of contractual capacity has an effect on his or her own contract of employment with the principal, if one exists. The agent's capacity can also be important if for any reason the third party attempts to hold the agent personally responsible on a contract made with that party.

Figure 18.1   **Duties of Agents and Principals to Each Other**

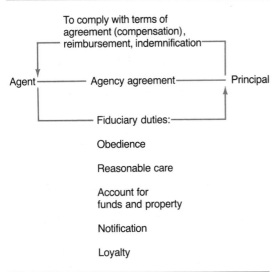

To comply with terms of agreement (compensation), reimbursement, indemnification

Agent ——— Agency agreement ——— Principal

Fiduciary duties:

Obedience

Reasonable care

Account for funds and property

Notification

Loyalty

Where the instructions are both legal and clear, the agent is justified in departing from them on only rare occasions. One such occasion is when an *emergency* occurs and following the principal's original instructions is not in that person's best interests. The agent should, of course, consult with the principal and obtain new instructions if possible. But if there is no opportunity to consult, the agent is justified in taking reasonable steps to protect the principal, even if it means deviating from prior instructions. Indeed, the agent may even be under a duty to depart from instructions if following them in the emergency can be considered so unreasonable as to be negligent. (The agent's authority to act in emergencies is discussed more fully in the next chapter.)

Reasonable Care: Unless special provisions in the agreement say otherwise, an agent is normally expected to exercise the degree of care and skill that is reasonable under the circumstances. In other words, the agent has a duty not to be negligent. For example, suppose that B has

funds which he wishes to lend to borrowers at current interest rates. He employs C to act in his behalf in locating the borrowers. C lends B's money to T without investigating T's credit rating and without obtaining from T any security for the loan. T turns out to be a notoriously bad credit risk and is actually insolvent at the time of the loan. If B is later unable to collect from T, C will probably be liable to B, because he failed to exercise reasonable care in making the loan.

Under some circumstances, an agent may be under a special duty to exercise more than an ordinary degree of care and skill. For example, if a person undertakes to serve in a capacity that necessarily involves the possession and exercise of a special skill, such as that of a lawyer or stockbroker, he or she is required to exercise the skill ordinarily possessed by competent persons pursuing that particular calling.

In any agency relationship, the principal and agent can by agreement change the agent's duty of care and skill, making it either stricter or more lenient.

Duty to Account: Unless principal and agent agree otherwise, it is the agent's duty to keep and make available to the principal an account of all the money or property received or paid out in behalf of the principal. In this regard, an agent should never mix his or her own money or property with that of the principal. The agent should, for example, set up a separate bank account for the principal's money. If the agent commingles (mixes) his or her own money or property with the principal's in such a way that it cannot be separated or identified, the principal can legally claim all of it.

Duty to Notify: Another important duty of the agent is to notify the principal of all relevant facts—just about any information having a bearing on the interests of the principal—as soon as reasonably possible after learning of them. For example, if A (the agent) discovers that one of P's (the principal's) creditors is about to foreclose a lien on P's property, A should promptly notify P. Or if A learns that one of P's important customers, who owes P a substantial amount of money, has just filed for bankruptcy, A should contact P as soon as possible.

Loyalty: Perhaps the most important duty owed by the agent to the principal is that of loyalty. Violation of this duty can occur in numerous ways. A few of the more significant actions constituting a breach of the duty are discussed below.

Quite obviously, the agent should not *compete* with the principal in the type of business he or she is conducting for the principal, unless the principal expressly gives consent. To illustrate: X, who owns a textile manufacturing business, employs Y to act as his sales agent. Y will be violating his duty of loyalty if, without X's consent, he acquires a personal interest in a textile manufacturing business that competes with X's.

The law presumes that a principal hires an agent to serve the principal's interests and not the personal interests of the agent. Thus the agent should avoid any existing or potential conflict of interest. For example, if B is hired to sell goods for R, he should not sell to himself. Or if he is hired to buy goods for R, he should not buy them from himself. It is difficult, if not impossible, for the agent to completely serve the principal's interests when his or her own personal interests become involved. Of course, such things can be done if the principal is fully informed and gives consent.

In a similar fashion, the agent should not further the interests of any third party in his or her dealings for the principal. The agent also should not work for two parties on opposite sides in a transaction unless both parties agree to it.

If the agent, in working for the principal, acquires knowledge of any *confidential information,* he or she should not disclose this information to outsiders without the principal's consent. To illustrate: G hires H, a lawyer, to represent G in defending a lawsuit filed against G by T. T alleges that his factory was damaged in a fire caused by certain chemicals, purchased by T from G, that were highly flammable and not labeled with an adequate warning. In order to properly defend G, H must learn the secret formulas and processes for producing the chemicals. After learning them, he should not disclose them to anyone without G's consent, either at that time or at any time in the future.

The following case illustrates the strictness of the duty of loyalty owed by an agent to the principal.

Girard v. Myers
Court of Appeals of Washington, 694 P.2d 678 (1985)

Michael Myers was a real estate developer and licensed salesman in the state of Washington. In 1974, he contracted to purchase a 290-acre tract of land known as the Pickering Farm. The purchase contract divided the land into seven parcels, and Myers then obtained groups of investors to purchase each parcel. Myers himself bought one 13.2-acre parcel out of the tract. As a condition of their participation, Myers required these investors to sign a document entitled "Trust and Resale Agreement." This agreement designated Myers as the exclusive sales agent for all of the investors in the event they later desired to resell their parcels, and also gave Myers a "right of first refusal." Under this right of first refusal, if a particular investor or

group of investors owning a parcel subsequently desired to resell the land to a third party, they first had to give Myers the opportunity to purchase it at the price offered by the third party, less an 11 percent discount. If Myers chose not to buy the parcel, the investor was obligated to pay Myers an 11 percent commission on the sale to the third party.

In early 1977, two investors, Butler and Kline, decided to sell one-half of their parcel to Girard. Myers indicated that he would refrain from exercising his right of first refusal only if Girard signed a Trust and Resale Agreement identical to that signed by the original investors. This was done and Girard made the purchase, with Myers receiving a sales commission from Butler and Kline.

Myers controlled three limited partnerships that engaged in real estate investment and development. In late 1977 and 1978, these partnerships acquired 51 acres next to the parcel owned by Girard. In 1979 Girard informed Myers that Girard wanted to transfer his land to a partnership that was being formed between Girard and John Sato. Girard also told Myers that Girard considered the Trust and Resale Agreement to be void and that he did not intend to honor it. Girard filed suit asking the court to declare the agreement void and unenforceable. Myers asserted a counterclaim for an 11 percent sales commission on the transfer.

The court ruled that the right of first refusal was unenforceable because it placed no time limit on Myers' exercise of the right and because its terms were too vague, and then held that the sales commission and price discount provisions were void because Myers' ownership and financial interests in the 13.2-acre and 51-acre parcels created an impermissible conflict of interest. Thus the trial court held for Girard and dismissed Myers' counterclaim for the sales commission, and Myers appealed. Only that portion of the appellate court's opinion dealing with the conflict of interest is presented below.

Scholfield, Chief Judge:

The trial court found that the 51 acres acquired by three limited partnerships . . . and the 13.2-acre parcel individually acquired by Myers were "actually or potentially competitive" with the Girard property. . . . Myers argues that his interest in and ownership of property adjacent to the Girard parcel did not violate his fiduciary duties as selling agent "because Girard knew before he purchased the property or signed the agreement that Myers both owned property and intended to remain involved in the coordinated development of the Pickering Farms parcels." He also argues that the Trust and Resale Agreement made the following disclosure:

(8) DISCLOSURE: Agent is in the business of selling and purchasing real property for its own account and as agent for other principals, disclosed and undisclosed. Owner has employed agent for the specific purposes set forth herein and no other

relationship of a legal, quasi-legal or of a fiduciary nature exists between the parties.

The record would support a finding Girard knew of Myers' ownership of the 13.2 acres. However, the record is clear that Myers acquired the 51 acres through the three limited partnerships after Girard signed the Trust and Resale Agreement.

Myers does not [challenge] the findings of fact in which the trial court found that the properties Myers owned or had substantial interest in were actually or potentially competitive with the Girard parcel. Thus, a conflict of interest is an established fact in this case. The only issue is whether Myers made a full and timely disclosure to Girard of all material facts regarding the conflict. [As stated by this court in a previous case]:

We begin with the fundamental rule that a real estate agent has the duty to exercise the utmost good faith and fidelity toward his principal in all matters falling within the scope of his employment. Such agent must exercise reasonable care, skill, and judgment in securing the best bargain possible, and must scrupulously avoid representing interests antagonistic to that of the principal without the explicit and fully informed consent of the principal. Further, the agent must make a full, fair, and timely disclosure to the principal of all facts within the agent's knowledge which are, or may be, material to the transaction and which might affect the principal's rights and interests or influence his actions. Consequently, a dual agency relationship is permissible when both parties have full knowledge of the facts and consent thereto. Before such consent can be held to exist, clear and express disclosure of the dual agency relation and the material circumstances that may influence the consent to the dual agency must be made.

A full and timely disclosure of the facts regarding the 51 acres could not have been made before Girard signed the Trust and Resale Agreement because those properties were not acquired until after the Trust and Resale Agreement was signed. If Myers desired to show that he had made a full disclosure to Girard when the 51 acres were acquired and that he had given Girard the option of either consenting to the conflict of interest or terminating the Trust and Resale Agreement, Myers had the burden of producing evidence on that issue. . . .

The record does not support Myers' argument that all material facts giving rise to the conflict of interest were fully disclosed to Girard. Myers' conflict was unusual in this case because he could profit personally by arranging sales of properties in which he had a personal interest and, at the same time, he could frustrate a sale by Girard to a prospective purchaser interested in both properties, through his claimed right of first refusal and an 11 percent discount. The findings of the trial court on the conflict issue are supported by substantial evidence. We conclude that Myers' claim for a commission should be denied because Myers breached his fiduciary duty as a selling agent.

TERMINATION OF THE AGENCY RELATIONSHIP

Like most private consensual arrangements, the agency relationship usually comes to an end at some point. Termination can occur because of something done by the parties themselves or by operation of law (something beyond their control). Our discussion focuses on the termination of the relationship between the principal and the agent, ignoring for the moment the effects of termination on third parties who might deal with the agent. (The circumstances under which third parties should be notified of the termination and the type of notice required are dealt with in the next chapter.)

Termination by Act of the Parties

Fulfillment of Purpose: Many times an agent is employed to accomplish a particular object, such as the sale of a tract of land belonging to the principal. When this object is accomplished and nothing else remains to be done, the agency relationship terminates.

Lapse of Time: If principal and agent have agreed originally that the arrangement will end at a certain time, the arrival of that time terminates their relationship. If nothing has been said as to the duration of the agency, and if nothing occurs to terminate it, the relationship is deemed to last for a period of time that is reasonable under the circumstances. This generally is a question of whether, after passage of a particular period of time, it is reasonable for the agent to believe that the principal still intends for him or her to act as earlier directed. Of course, if the principal *knows* that the agent is continuing to make efforts to perform, and if the principal does nothing about the situation, the agency relationship may remain alive for a period of time longer than would otherwise be held reasonable.

Occurrence of Specified Event: In a similar fashion, if the principal and agent have originally agreed that the agency, or some particular aspect

of it, will continue until a specified event occurs, the occurrence of the event results in termination. For example: P authorizes A to attempt to sell P's farm, Blackacre, for him "only until P returns from New York." When P returns, A's authority to sell Blackacre as P's agent comes to an end. An analogous situation occurs when principal and agent have agreed that the agency, or some aspect of it, will remain in existence only during the continuance of a stated condition. If the condition ceases to exist, the agent's authority terminates. For instance: X directs Y, X's credit manager, to extend $10,000 in credit to T, so long as T's inventory of goods on hand and his accounts receivable amount to $50,000 and his accounts payable do not exceed $25,000. If T's combined inventory and accounts receivable drop below $50,000, the agency terminates insofar as it relates to Y's authority to grant credit to T.

Mutual Agreement: Regardless of what the principal and agent have agreed to originally, they can agree at any time to end their relationship. It makes no difference whether the relationship has been based on a binding employment contract or whether no enforceable employment contract exists; their mutual agreement terminates the agency in either case. It is a basic rule of contract law that the parties can rescind (cancel) the contract by mutual agreement.

Act of One Party: Since the agency relationship is consensual, it can usually be terminated by either the principal or the agent if that person no longer wants to be a party to the arrangement. In most circumstances termination occurs simply by one party indicating to the other that he or she no longer desires to continue the relationship. This is true even if the parties had originally agreed that the agency was to be irrevocable.

If no binding employment contract exists between the two of them, the party terminating the agency normally does not incur any liability to the other by this action. If an enforceable employment contract does exist, one party may be justified in terminating it if the other has violated any of the duties owed under it. Of course, if there are no facts justifying termination, the party taking such action may be responsible to the other for any damages caused by the breach of contract. But the agency relationship is ended nevertheless.

One major exception exists to the ability of either party to terminate the relationship. If the agency is not just a simple one but instead is an **agency coupled with an interest** (that is, the agent has an interest in the subject matter of the agency), the principal cannot terminate the agent's authority without the agent's consent.[3] (Note, however, that an agent is not considered to have an interest in the subject matter simply because he or she expects to make a commission or profit from the activities as agent.) To illustrate: P borrows $5,000 from A. To secure the loan, P grants A a *security interest* (a property interest for the sole purpose of securing a debt) in P's inventory. As part of the agreement, P makes A his agent for the sale of the inventory in case P defaults on the loan. Since A has an interest in the subject matter of the agency (the inventory), the arrangement is an agency coupled with an interest, and P cannot terminate A's authority to sell without A's consent (unless, of course, P repays the loan, in which case A no longer has an interest in the subject matter).

The reason for the exception is that the agent is not really acting for the principal in this situation. By exercising this authority, the agent is acting in his or her own behalf to assert a personal interest.

Termination by Operation of Law

Death or Insanity: The death or insanity of the *agent* immediately terminates an agency re-

lationship. The death or insanity of the *principal* also terminates an agency relationship. In most cases the termination of an agency by the principal's death or insanity occurs immediately, regardless of whether the agent knows what has happened.

Bankruptcy: The insolvency or bankruptcy of the *agent* does not always terminate the agency, but will do so in those circumstances where it impairs the agent's ability to act for the principal. To illustrate: B is authorized by I, an investment house, to act as its agent in advising I's local clients about investments. If B becomes bankrupt, he will no longer be authorized to act for I. The reason is simple; the agent in this situation should realize that the principal probably would not want him to act in its behalf any longer if it knew the facts.

Suppose, however, that the *principal* becomes insolvent or bankrupt, and the agent knows about it. In this case the agent might no longer have authority to act for the principal— but only under circumstances where the agent ought to realize that the principal would no longer want such transactions to be conducted in his or her behalf. For example: P has authorized A to buy an expensive fur coat on credit for P. If P becomes bankrupt, this will probably terminate the agency when A learns of it. A should reasonably infer that under the circumstances P will no longer want him to make such a purchase. However, if A is P's housekeeper and has been authorized to buy groceries for P's household, P's bankruptcy probably will not extinguish that authority. The inference that A should reasonably draw when learning the facts is that P will want her to continue buying necessities such as food until informed otherwise. It is simply a matter of reasonableness.

Change of Law: If a change in the law makes the agency or the performance of the authorized act *illegal,* the agent's authority is ordinarily extinguished when he or she learns of the change. To illustrate: S is a salesperson for T, a toy manu-

---

[3]Considerable confusion and conflict exist in the law with regard to an agency coupled with an interest (also referred to as an "agency for security," a "power coupled with an interest," and a "power given for security"). We have therefore tried to keep our discussion simple enough to avoid these pitfalls.

facturer. If a federal agency determines that certain of T's toys are dangerous and bans them, S's authority to sell them to retailers probably will be terminated when she learns of the government ban. That is, upon learning the facts, S should reasonably assume that T will no longer want her to sell the banned items.

Even if the change in the law does not make the agency or the authorized act illegal, termination can still occur if the agent learns of the change and should reasonably expect that the principal will no longer want him or her to act in the manner previously authorized. For instance: A is authorized to purchase fabricated aluminum from a foreign supplier. The federal government imposes a new tariff on imported aluminum that results in substantially higher prices. It is likely that A's authority to buy foreign aluminum will be terminated when he learns of the change.

Loss or Destruction of Subject Matter: The loss or destruction of the subject matter of an agency relationship will terminate the agent's authority. If, for example, X employs Y to sell grain belonging to X that is being stored in a particular storage elevator, the destruction by fire of the elevator and the grain will ordinarily extinguish Y's authority.

Whether the agent's authority terminates automatically or only when he or she learns of the facts depends on the nature and terms of the original agreement between principal and agent. In the instant case, if, instead of a fire, X himself sells the grain to a buyer (which actually amounts to X revoking Y's authority), Y's authority may or may not be automatically terminated. If X has given Y *exclusive authority* to sell, that authority ends only if X notifies Y that he has sold the grain himself. On the other hand, if the authority is not exclusive and Y should realize that X may try to sell the grain himself, Y's authority will terminate when X sells the grain even if Y does not know of the sale.

If the subject matter of the agency (such as the grain) is not lost or destroyed but is merely damaged, Y's authority is terminated if the circumstances are such that Y ought to realize that X would not want the transaction to be carried out.

Miscellaneous Changes of Conditions: The various occurrences we have discussed that terminate an agency by operation of law are by no means an exclusive list. For instance, in some circumstances the outbreak of war, a sudden change in the market value of the subject matter of the agency, or an unexpected loss of some required qualification by the principal or the agent (such as a license) may terminate the agency. Again, if all the circumstances known to the agent are such that he or she, as a reasonable person, ought to realize that the principal would no longer wish him or her to continue in the endeavor, the authority is ended. The agent simply must act in a reasonable fashion until there is an opportunity to consult with the principal.

SUMMARY

The law of agency governs the rights and responsibilities created when one person acts in a representative role for another. When the subordinate transacts business in behalf of the superior, the relationship is usually referred to as that of principal and agent. When the subordinate performs physical tasks for the superior, or when there is any question regarding the superior's tort liability for the actions of the subordinate, the relationship is usually referred to as that of either master and servant or employer and independent contractor. In general, an agency relationship of any type is created by agreement. The agreement may be a legally enforceable employment contract, but it does not have to be. The principal-agent relationship is a fiduciary relationship in which each party owes the other a duty to act in the utmost good faith. The principal owes to the agent the duty to compensate, reimburse for necessary expenses, and comply with any other terms of their agreement. The agent owes to the principal the duty to obey instructions, act with reasonable care, account for the principal's funds or property in the agent's possession, notify the principal of any facts relating to the interests of the principal, and always act with loyalty to the principal's interests. The principal-agent relationship may be terminated by various acts of the parties themselves, or by operation of law.

KEY TERMS

Agency
Principal
Agent
Principal-agent relationship
Master-servant relationship
Employer–independent
  contractor relationship
Power of attorney
Attorney-in-fact
Fiduciary relationship
Agency coupled with an interest

QUESTIONS AND PROBLEMS

1. Explain the difference between attorney-in-fact and attorney-at-law.

2. What formalities are required for the creation of the principal-agent relationship?

3. Fortner, a minor, employed Jones, an adult, as his agent for the purpose of selling his motorcycle for $400. Jones sold the motorcycle to Todd for $400. Fortner later changed his mind and tried to disaffirm the sale. Todd claimed that Fortner could not do so because Jones was an adult. Is Todd's contention correct? Explain.

4. Pointer hired Anderson as his agent for the purpose of buying a thousand shares of stock in Zeta Co. Unknown to Pointer, Anderson owned a thousand shares of Zeta stock. Anderson sold his stock to Pointer at the current market price of $20 per share. When Pointer found this out, he demanded that Anderson take back the stock and refund the price. Is Anderson required to do so? Explain.

5. Carter promised to pay Hines a commission if he would sell a tract of land for Carter. Hines sold the land to Jackson, who had employed Hines to purchase land for him, also for a commission. When Carter learned of this dual arrangement, he refused to pay Hines the promised commission. Was Carter entitled to make such a refusal? Discuss.

6. Swenson instructed Thompson, his banker, to invest some money for him. Thompson purchased mining stock with the money. The stock proved to be virtually worthless. Swenson sued Thompson for his loss. Is Thompson liable? Discuss.

7. Clay was hired by Green to sell Green's boat for not less than $700, out of which Clay was to receive a 10 percent commission. Clay sold the boat for $800 and offered Green $630 in settlement ($700 less 10 percent). Green demanded an additional $90 as the amount due him. Was Green justified in claiming the additional money? Explain.

8. Harkins, a salesman for Watson, was paid a commission on sales made for Watson. Harkins took an order from Boswell for merchandise. Watson accepted the order and shipped the merchandise. In the meantime, Boswell changed his mind and repudiated the transaction, claiming he no longer needed the goods. When they arrived, he refused to accept or pay for them and shipped them back to Watson. Watson claimed that Harkins was not entitled to a commission because the sale had not been completed. Is Watson correct? Explain.

9. What is the meaning and significance of the phrase *agency coupled with an interest?*

10. When will an agent's bankruptcy terminate the agency relationship?

Chapter 19

AGENCY
Liability of
the Parties

We have already discussed the formation and termination of the agency relationship and the duties existing between the parties. Now we will focus our attention on the legal consequences of this relationship, primarily the *contractual liability* of those involved: principal, agent, and third parties. Near the end of the chapter we will deal with a superior's liability for the torts and crimes of his or her subordinates.

LIABILITY OF THE PRINCIPAL

The principal is, of course, liable to the agent if he or she breaches a valid employment contract with the agent or violates any other duty owing to the agent. However, the most important questions in this area relate to the principal's liability to the third parties with whom the agent has dealt. If A, acting in behalf of P, makes a contract with T, what is P's legal responsibility to T? If P does not perform as required in the contract, is P required by law to compensate T for T's losses resulting from P's breach?

The answers to these questions usually depend on the court's decision on another question: Was the agent acting within the scope of his or her *authority* in making this particular contract? We will now examine the approach taken by the courts in arriving at an answer.

The Agent's Authority to Act for the Principal

The fact that you have hired someone to act as your agent does not mean that the person can represent you in any way he or she sees fit. An agent ordinarily can act for the principal in such a way as to make the principal legally responsible only when he or she has **authority** to act that way. The agent's authority can be divided into two basic types: actual and apparent. **Actual authority** is the authority that the agent does, in fact, have. For convenience it can be further divided into *express authority* and *implied authority.* On the other hand, *apparent authority* is something of a contradiction in terms. It

describes a concept which, because of unusual circumstances giving rise to an appearance of authority, occasionally holds the principal responsible for certain of the agent's actions that were not really authorized at all.

Express Authority: **Express authority** is the most obvious and the most common type of authority—that which is directly granted by the principal to the agent. To illustrate: P authorizes A to sell P's farm for at least $25,000. If A sells the farm to T for $30,000, P is bound by the transaction and must honor it. The obvious reason is that A's actions are within the scope of his express authority. Conversely, under most circumstances, P will not be required to honor the transaction if A sells the farm for $20,000.

Implied Authority: As is the case with most business transactions, the principal and agent rarely, if ever, contemplate and provide for every possible event that might occur during the existence of their relationship. The law seeks to allow for this fact through the concept of implied authority. **Implied authority** is primarily a matter of what is *customary.* In other words, where the principal has said nothing about a particular aspect of the agent's authority, whether the agent has such authority normally depends on what type of authority a person in a similar position customarily has. Of course, the principal has the final word as to what authority the agent possesses and can grant more or less authority than such an agent usually has. The concept of implied authority serves only to fill in gaps where the principal has not spoken specifically on the subject but where it is reasonable to assume that the principal would have granted such authority if he or she had thought about it.

Many examples of implied authority can be found. For instance, unless the principal has given indications to the contrary, a traveling salesperson ordinarily has authority to take orders but not to make a binding contract to sell the principal's goods. He or she often will be in possession of samples but there usually is no implied authority to sell them. If, however, the salesperson is one who possesses goods *for immediate sale* (such as a salesclerk in a retail store or a door-to-door sales agent who actually carries the principal's merchandise), he or she ordinarily has authority to sell them and collect payment. But this type of agent still does not have implied authority to grant credit or accept payment from the customer for prior credit purchases. Such authority usually exists only if expressly given by the principal, because it is simply not customary for a salesperson to do these things.

Another common application of the concept of implied authority enables an agent to perform those acts which are merely incidental to the main purpose of the agency. (Some legal writers, in fact, use the term *incidental authority.*) Again, the key is what is customary. The rule regarding such authority is: *Unless the principal has indicated otherwise, his or her agent has implied authority to do those things which are reasonably and customarily necessary to enable that person to accomplish the overall purpose of the agency.*

To illustrate: O, the owner of a retail clothing store, hires M to act as manager of the store and gives M express authority to act in certain ways. For instance, M probably will be expressly authorized to purchase inventory and make sales. In addition, M will have implied authority to handle matters that are incidental to the main purpose of the agency. Thus, if the plumbing in the store begins to leak, M can hire a plumber, and O is bound to pay for the services. Similarly, unless instructed otherwise, M can hire an electrician to repair a short in the wiring or a janitorial service to clean the floors. He can also hire a salesclerk or other necessary assistants.

Of course, if the transaction is out of the ordinary or involves a substantial expenditure, the agent should first consult with the principal, because the agent's implied authority may not extend to such matters. Thus, if the electrician hired by M to repair a shorted wire informs him that the wiring in the building is badly worn and does not comply with city building code requirements, M should not act on his own to contract for the rewiring at a substantial cost. Instead he should consult with O before taking further action.

Interesting questions regarding an agent's authority are sometimes raised by the occurrence of an *emergency.* Although it is often said that the scope of an agent's implied authority is "expanded" in emergency situations, this is only sometimes true. If an emergency occurs and there is no opportunity to consult with the principal, the agent has implied authority to take steps that are reasonable and prudent under the circumstances—including actions that may be contrary to prior instructions by the principal.

To illustrate: A has been ordered by P to purchase badly needed raw materials from country X and to ship them through country Y, which has the nearest port facility where the goods can be loaded on vessels. A makes the purchase but then learns from a usually reliable source that a revolution is imminent in country Y and will probably break out while the goods are en route. Fearing that transportation may be impaired or that the goods may be seized by the revolutionaries, A attempts to contact P but is unable to do so. Since he knows that P needs the goods quickly, A arranges for shipment to another port through country Z. Shipment over the other route will be slightly more expensive and time-consuming but also presumably safe, and P will still receive the goods in time to meet his needs.

In this case, A was impliedly authorized to act as he did—even if no revolution actually occurred. What is important is that two elements were present: (1) A, the agent, was *unable to consult with his principal;* and (2) he acted *reasonably,* in light of all the knowledge available to him, to protect the interests of his principal.

Apparent Authority: Thus far we have dealt with situations where the agent has actual authority, either express or implied. Now we will examine the peculiar concept of **apparent**

authority (sometimes called **ostensible authority**). As we mentioned earlier, speaking of apparent authority as a specific type of authority is something of a contradiction, because the phrase describes a situation where the agent actually has no authority. If the agent acts outside the scope of his or her actual (express or implied) authority, the principal is normally not responsible on the unauthorized transaction. However, if the principal, *by his or her own conduct,* has led reasonable third parties to believe that the agent actually has such authority, the principal may be responsible. In discussing implied authority, we were concerned with what appeared reasonable to the *agent.* But for apparent authority, our concern is with the viewpoint of reasonable *third parties.* Obviously, some situations can fall within the scope of either implied or apparent authority. In such cases we usually speak in terms of implied authority; apparent authority is used as a basis for holding the principal responsible only where no express or implied authority is present.

The importance of apparent authority can be illustrated by two examples:

1. S, a salesman for R, has in his possession R's goods (not just samples). It is customary for an agent in S's position who is handling this type of goods to have authority to actually sell and collect payment for them. While making his rounds, S calls the home office. R tells him that he is afraid some of the items S has are defective and instructs him not to sell the goods in his possession but merely to take orders for a period of time. Contrary to instructions, S sells the goods. R is bound by the transactions and will be responsible to T, the buyer, if the goods actually are defective. It appears that R has acted in a reasonable fashion under the circumstances. However, by allowing S to have possession of the goods, he has led T to believe that S is authorized to sell—because it is *customary.* T has no way of knowing that S's actual authority has been expressly limited to something less than what is customary. The basis of R's liability is *not* S's implied authority, because S *knew* that he had no authority and was acting contrary to express instructions. Instead, the basis for R's liability is apparent authority—arising out of the fact that T has been misled by the *appearance of authority.*

2. When the agency is terminated, the agent's *actual authority* is also terminated. But this does not automatically dispose of the problem of *apparent authority.* It is sometimes necessary to notify third parties of the termination in order to keep the principal from being liable under the concept of apparent authority. As a general rule, where termination has occurred *as a matter of law* (see Chapter 18 for details), all authority ceases automatically and the principal is not responsible for the agent's further actions regardless of whether the third party has been notified.[1] Most problems involving termination and apparent authority arise when the agency has been ended *by act of the parties* (such as the principal firing the agent). Where termination is by act of the parties, the principal may still be bound by the agent's actions (because of apparent authority) unless and until the third party is notified of the termination. The principal must notify third parties with whom the agent has dealt in the past by letter, telegram, telephone, or some other method of *direct communication* if their identities are reasonably easy to ascertain. Regarding all other third parties, the principal can protect himself simply by giving *public notice.* An advertisement in a local newspaper is the most common form of such notice, but other methods may be sufficient if they are reasonable under the circumstances.

Ratification of Unauthorized Transactions

If an agent's action is not within the scope of his or her actual (express or implied) authority, and if the facts are such that no apparent authority is

---

[1] However, a few courts have held that where the agency is terminated by the principal's *death,* his or her estate can continue to be liable for the agent's actions, under the doctrine of apparent authority, until the third party learns of the death.

present, the principal generally is not liable to the third party for that action. Even in the absence of actual or apparent authority, however, the principal may become responsible if he or she *ratifies* (or *affirms*) the agent's unauthorized actions. An unauthorized act ratified by the principal is treated by the courts in the same manner as if it had been actually authorized from the beginning. The two forms of **ratification**—express and implied—are discussed below.

Express Ratification: If, upon learning of the agent's unauthorized dealings, the principal decides to honor the transaction, he or she can simply inform the agent, the third party, or someone else of that intention. In this situation an **express ratification** has obviously occurred.

Implied Ratification: Even if the principal has not expressly communicated the intent to ratify, the person can nevertheless be deemed to have done so if his or her words or conduct reasonably indicate that intent. *Inaction* and *silence* may even amount to ratification if, under the circumstances, a reasonable person would have voiced an objection to what the agent had done. The following five examples will help clarify the concept of **implied ratification.** For each example, no actual authority exists, and there are no facts present to indicate apparent authority.

Example 1.   A, who is a driver of a truck owned by P, enters into an unauthorized agreement with T, under which A is to haul T's goods on P's truck. Sometime later, while A is en route, T becomes concerned about the delay and calls P. Upon learning of the transaction, P does not repudiate it but instead assures T that "A is a good driver and the goods will be properly cared for." P has ratified the agreement.

Example 2.   Same facts as Example 1. This time, however, T does not call P. The goods arrive safely at their destination, and T sends a check for the shipping charges to P. This is when

P first learns of the transaction. If P cashes or deposits the check and uses the money, he will be deemed to have ratified the agreement. Even if he simply retains the check for an appreciable period of time and says nothing, he will probably be held to have ratified.

Example 3.   A makes an unauthorized contract to sell P's goods to T. Upon learning of the contract, P says nothing to A or T but assigns the right to receive payment for the goods to X. P has ratified the agreement.

Example 4.   Same facts as Example 3. This time, however, P does not assign the right to receive payment. Instead he ships the goods to T. P has ratified the agreement.

Example 5.   Same facts as Example 4, but the goods are shipped to T without P's knowledge. P then learns of the transaction, and when T does not make payment by the due date, P files suit against T to collect the purchase price. P has ratified the transaction. (P would not have ratified if he had filed suit to rescind the sale and get his goods back.)

Requirements for Ratification: Certain requirements must be present for ratification to occur. Following are the most important of them:

1. The courts generally hold that a principal can ratify only if the agent, in dealing with the third party, has indicated that he or she is acting *for a principal* and not in his or her own behalf.

2. At the time of ratification, the principal must have *known* or *had reason to know* of the essential facts about the transaction. What this means is that the principal must have had either actual knowledge of the relevant facts or sufficient knowledge so that it would have been easy to find out what the essential facts were. The requirement of knowledge is usually important when the third party tries to hold the principal liable by claiming that some words or actions of the principal had amounted to ratification.

3. Ratification must occur within a *reasonable time* after the principal learned of the transaction. What constitutes a reasonable time will, of course, depend on the facts of the particular case. However, a court will automatically rule that a reasonable time period has already expired, and thus that there can be no ratification, if there has been a fundamental change in the facts that had formed the basis of the transaction. An example would be damage to or destruction of the subject matter of the transaction. Similarly, the principal will not be permitted to ratify if the third party has already indicated a desire to withdraw from the transaction. The third party has the right to withdraw prior to ratification and, when he or she does so, any later attempt by the principal to ratify will be treated as being too late.

4. If the principal ratifies, he or she must ratify the *entire transaction* rather than ratifying that part which is to his or her advantage and re-

pudiating that which is to his or her disadvantage. For example, a principal ratifying a contract for the sale of goods to a third party is obligated on any warranties that accompany the goods.

5. The transaction obviously must be *legal,* and the principal must have the *capacity* required to be a party to the transaction.

6. If any *formalities* (such as a writing) would have been required for an original authorization, the same formalities must be met in ratifying the transaction. Of course, if formalities are required, the ratification will have to be express—it cannot be implied. Since most authorizations do not require any special formalities, this usually poses no problem.

The following two cases both deal with the question of apparent authority. The second case also involves the issue of ratification.

Industrial Molded Plastic Products, Inc., v. J. Gross & Son, Inc.
Superior Court of Pennsylvania, 398 A.2d 695 (1979)

Industrial Molded Plastic Products (Industrial) is in the business of manufacturing custom injection molded plastics by specification for various manufacturers. Industrial also manufactures various "fill-in" items during slack periods, such as electronic parts, industrial components, mirror clips, and plastic clothing clips. J. Gross & Sons (Gross) is a wholesaler to the retail clothing industry, selling mostly sewing thread, but also other items such as zippers, snaps, and clips.

Sometime in the fall of 1970, Stanley Waxman (Gross's president and sole stockholder) and his son Peter (a twenty-two-year-old salesman for Gross) appeared at the offices of Industrial's president, Judson T. Ulansey. They suggested to him that they might be able to market Industrial's plastic clothing clips in the retail clothing industry, in which they had an established sales force. At this initial meeting, there was no discussion of Peter Waxman's authority or lack thereof in the company. After this meeting, Stanley authorized Peter to purchase a "trial" amount of clips (not further specified) to test the market, but neither this authorization nor its limitation was communicated to Ulansey. All subsequent negotiations were between

Ulansey and Peter Waxman only. Deceiving both his father and Ulansey, Peter held himself out as vice-president of Gross, and on December 10, 1970, signed an agreement obligating Gross to purchase from Industrial five million plastic clothing clips during the calendar year of 1971, at a price of $7.50 per thousand units, delivery at Industrial's plant in Blooming Glen, Pennsylvania. Before the execution of this agreement, Ulansey telephoned Stanley Waxman, who told Ulansey that Peter could act on behalf of Gross. There was no discussion of the specific terms of the agreement, such as the quantity purchased.

Industrial immediately began production of the five million clips during "fill-in" time. As they were manufactured, they were warehoused in Industrial's plant as specified in the contract. In February 1971, Peter Waxman picked up and paid for 772,000 clips. Stanley Waxman, who had to sign Gross's check for payment, thought that this was the "trial amount" he had authorized Peter to buy. These were the only clips which Gross ever took into its possession. On numerous occasions during the year Ulansey urged Peter to pick up more of the clips, which were taking up more and more storage space at Industrial's plant as they were being manufactured. Peter told Ulansey that he was having difficulty selling the clips and that Gross had no warehousing capacity for the inventory that was being accumulated. At no time, however, did Peter repudiate the contract or request Industrial to halt production. By the end of 1971, production was completed and Industrial was warehousing 4,228,000 clips at its plant.

On January 19, 1972, Industrial sent Gross an invoice for the remaining clips of $31,506.45. However, Gross did not honor the invoice or pick up any more of the clips. Ulansey wrote to Stanley Waxman on February 7, 1972, requesting him to pick up the clips. Receiving no response, Ulansey wrote to Stanley Waxman again on February 23, 1972, threatening legal action if shipping instructions were not received by March 1, 1972. Finally, on March 30, 1972, Peter Waxman responded with a letter to Ulansey, which stated that Gross's failure to move the clips was due to a substantial decline in the clothing industry in 1971 and competition with new lower-cost methods of hanging and shipping clothes. The letter asked for Industrial's patience and predicted that it would take at least the rest of the year to market the clips successfully. At this point, Industrial sued. Stanley Waxman learned of the five-million clip contract for the first time when informed by his lawyer of the impending lawsuit. At this time, Peter began an extended (four years) leave of absence from Gross.

The trial court ruled in favor of Industrial, the plaintiff, but awarded damages of only $2,400. Both parties appealed, plaintiff claiming that it should be entitled to the entire contract price of over $31,000, and defendant claiming that it should not be liable at all.

Hoffman, Judge:

. . . Gross contends that it was not bound by the agreement to purchase the clips because Peter Waxman had no authority to sign the contract for Gross. However, Peter was an agent of Gross and did have express authority to purchase for Gross, as its president instructed him to purchase a "trial amount" of clips. A principal's limitation of his agent's authority in amount only, not communicated to the third party with whom the agent deals, does not so limit the principal's liability. Although the agent violates his instructions or exceeds the limits set to his authority, he will yet bind his principal to such third persons, if his acts are within the scope of the authority which the principal has caused or permitted him to possess. Such limitations will be binding [only] upon third persons *who know of them.*

An admitted agent is presumed to be acting within the scope of his authority where the act is legal and the third party has no notice of the agent's limitation. The third person must use reasonable diligence to ascertain the authority of the agent, but he is also entitled to rely upon the apparent authority of the agent when this is a reasonable interpretation of the manifestations of the principal.

Here, the limitation on Peter's authority was not communicated to Industrial. As Stanley Waxman brought Peter into the initial meeting soliciting business from Industrial, Ulansey could reasonably presume his authority to act for Gross in consummating the deal. Gross complains that Ulansey was not diligent in ascertaining Peter's authority, but in fact Ulansey telephoned Stanley Waxman precisely for the purpose of verifying Peter's authority. As Stanley said that Peter was authorized to act on behalf of Gross, the principal thus completed clothing the agent in apparent authority to bind the corporate entity on the agreement. If anybody was lacking in diligence, it was Stanley Waxman in not inquiring as to the amount of the contract Peter proposed to sign. Thus, we affirm the conclusion of the court below that Gross was bound by the agreement to purchase the clips.

[The court then held that the trial court had incorrectly computed damages, and that Industrial was entitled to the total contract price of $31,506.45 plus interest from the invoice date.]

City Electric v. Dean Evans Chrysler-Plymouth
Supreme Court of Utah, 672 P.2d 89 (1983)

Dave Sturgill was a salesman for Dean Evans Chrysler-Plymouth, a retail automobile dealership. Dean Evans was president of the firm, and Mike Evans was assistant secretary. Mike Evans was also a partner with Johnny Rider in another business, Johnny Rider's Backstage Restaurant. On one occasion, Mike Evans and Johnny Rider were discussing the remodeling of their restaurant. Sturgill happened to

be present during the discussion, and volunteered to contact City Electric, an electric materials supplier that Sturgill had previously worked for. Sturgill said that he might be able to get them a good price on the electrical materials they would need for the remodeling project. Sturgill called Don Hatch, a salesman for City Electric, and told Hatch that Sturgill was trying to do a favor for his boss (Mike Evans). Sturgill asked if City Electric would give Mike Evans a fair price, and if the restaurant could establish an account. Shortly after this conversation, and before City Electric had time to set up an account for the restaurant, Mike Evans told Sturgill that the materials should be purchased on the auto dealership's account with City Electric.

The next day, Sturgill again called Hatch and placed an order for materials, stating that the materials were to be charged to the account of Dean Evans Chrysler-Plymouth. Sturgill said that he was acting pursuant to Mike Evans's directions, but there was never any representation that the auto dealership owned or was affiliated with the restaurant. Hatch checked his firm's computer printouts of open accounts and found that the auto dealership did have such an account with City Electric. Hatch put this and several later orders on the account, and the materials were delivered to the restaurant. Several invoices were sent to the auto dealership, and two of them dated October 8 and 9, 1978, were paid in December, 1978. There was no evidence indicating who paid these two invoices in behalf of the auto dealership. Apparently, either Mike Evans or Sturgill paid the two invoices with company funds before the dealership's president, Dean Evans, discovered what had happened. Thereafter, the dealership refused to make any further payments, leaving an unpaid balance of $2,332.70. City Electric, plaintiff, filed suit against Dean Evans Chrysler-Plymouth, defendant, for this unpaid balance. The trial court held that both Mike Evans and Dave Sturgill had apparent authority to charge the orders to the dealerships account, and ruled in favor of plaintiff. Defendant appealed.

Howe, Justice:

It is well settled law that the apparent or ostensible authority of an agent can be inferred only from the acts and conduct of the principal. Where corporate liability is sought for acts of its agent under apparent authority, liability is premised upon the corporation's knowledge of and acquiescence in the conduct of its agent which has led third parties to rely upon the agent's actions. Nor is the authority of the agent "apparent" merely because it looks so to the person with whom he deals. It is the principal who must cause third parties to believe that the agent is clothed with apparent authority. (See *Forsyth v. Pendleton,* 617 P.2d 358 (Utah 1980), where the referral by seller to her attorney of a letter written to her by buyers constituted an act sufficient to clothe the attorney with apparent authority to act for seller.) It follows that one who deals exclusively with an agent has the responsibility to ascertain that agent's authority despite the agent's representations. Moreover, it has been held that apparent authority vanishes when the third party has actual knowledge of the real scope of the agent's authority. . . .

Under the applicable standard of review this Court will accord the findings of the trial court a presumption of validity and correctness so long as there is support for them in the evidence. That support is singularly absent in this case. . . . Sturgill's apparent authority was never established. His request for electrical materials for the remodeling of the restaurant fell wide of the mark of his scope of employment. . . . His own statement could not establish any authority in him.

Plaintiff's credit manager testified that all purchases made between October and December of 1978 were made out to Johnny Rider of the Backstage Restaurant and that none of the receipts was signed by anyone on behalf of the defendant. None of the materials was delivered to the defendant and most of them were picked up by workers involved with the remodeling. Hatch testified that Sturgill told him he was trying to do his boss (Mike Evans) a favor by getting him good prices. Hatch never talked to Mike, who he knew was a son of Dean Evans, and who he assumed had a management position with defendant. His only contact was with Sturgill, who he assumed had no management position with the defendant. Sturgill made no representation to Hatch that defendant owned the Backstage Restaurant and the only authority Hatch relied upon was Sturgill's telling him that Mike told Sturgill to call and arrange for the materials. When questioned whether he took credit information from Sturgill from which he could determine whether to extend credit, Hatch answered "No. I looked on our computer printout for addresses and open accounts, and Dean Evans Chrysler-Plymouth had an account with us." Hatch did not claim that plaintiff had an agreement with the defendant relating to the materials. Hatch's dealings were exclusively with Sturgill and on a matter unrelated to the business of the defendant. Whatever apparent authority Sturgill might have otherwise had vanished for that reason alone. Unless otherwise agreed, general expressions used in authorizing an agent are limited in application to acts done in connection with the act or business to which the authority primarily relates.

Plaintiff's argument that the contract was ratified by payments made of the October 8 and October 9 invoices fares no better. Plaintiff's exhibit offers no clue as to who paid them. A penciled notation "Paid in Dec 1978" does not rise to the level of ratification by defendant as required by law. Ratification is premised upon the knowledge of all material facts and upon an express or implied intention on the part of the principal to ratify. There is not a shred of evidence in the record that defendant paid the two mentioned invoices, nor is the court's statement that "everybody knew that Mike was connected" sufficient to impute knowledge of Sturgill's actions to the defendant, let alone an intent to subsequently ratify those actions.

The plaintiff failed to establish its case and it was error for the trial court to find in its favor. The judgment is reversed.

Importance of the Agent's Knowledge

In deciding the question of a principal's liability to a third party, sometimes a key issue is whether the principal has received notice of a particular fact. For example, P is obligated under a contract to make payment to T. T assigns her right to receive this payment to X, an assignee. Assuming that T's right is assignable, P is bound to honor the assignment and pay X instead of T only if he has received notice of the assignment. But what if P's agent, A, receives this notice rather than P himself? If A promptly relays the information to P, there is usually no problem. What happens, though, if A fails to do so and P, not knowing of the assignment, pays T instead of X? Is P liable to X because P's agent had received notice?

Ordinarily, in any case where notice to the principal is important, *notice to the agent is treated as notice to the principal if the agent's receipt of the notice is within the scope of his or her actual or apparent authority.* In other words, in such cases the law will treat the principal as if he or she had received notice even if the agent did not transmit it. Obviously, however, this does not apply where the third party who notifies the agent knows that the agent is acting adversely to the interests of the principal (as where the third party and the agent are conspiring to defraud the principal).

LIABILITY OF THE AGENT

When the agent is acting for the principal, the agent ordinarily incurs no personal responsibility if he or she acts in a proper fashion. However, circumstances do exist where the agent can become liable.

Breach of Duty

If the agent violates any of the duties owed to the principal, he or she naturally is liable for the damages caused by the breach. Where the duty which has been violated is that of loyalty, the penalties may be even more severe. A disloyal agent is not only responsible to the principal for any resulting loss sustained by the latter but also usually forfeits his or her right to be compensated for services rendered. Furthermore, the agent must turn over to the principal any profits made from his or her disloyal activity.

Exceeding Authority

The agent who exceeds his or her actual authority is personally responsible unless the principal ratifies the unauthorized actions. Whether this responsibility is to the principal or to the third party depends on the circumstances. If the agent exceeds his or her actual authority, but the principal is liable to a third party on the ground of apparent authority, the agent's liability is to the *principal.* On the other hand, if the agent exceeds his or her actual authority and the facts are such that the principal is not liable to a third party under apparent authority, then the agent's liability is to the *third party.*

Assuming Liability

If the agent personally assumes liability for a particular transaction, then he or she obviously is responsible. For instance: A is attempting to purchase goods for P on credit. T, the seller, is wary of P's credit rating and refuses to grant credit unless A also becomes obligated. A signs the agreement as P's agent and in his own individual capacity. A is in effect a *co-principal* and therefore personally liable to T if P defaults.

Nondisclosure of Principal

If the agent, in dealing with a third party, fails to disclose that he or she is *acting for a principal* or fails to disclose the *principal's identity,* the agent is personally responsible to the third party. Additionally, the agent will sometimes be liable if he or she acts for a nonexistent principal or for one not having legal capacity. (These subjects are dealt with specifically later in the chapter.)

Commission of a Tort

If the agent commits a *tort,* he or she is personally responsible to the injured party for the resulting harm. This is true regardless of whether the agent was working for the principal at the time. (Sometimes the principal also is responsible. This problem is discussed later in the chapter.)

LIABILITY OF THE THIRD PARTY

Relatively little need be said about the liability of the third party. Since that party is acting in his or her own behalf, he or she is personally responsible to the other party to the transaction. This ordinarily means that:

1. If the third party fails to live up to his or her part of the bargain, that person will be liable to the principal.

2. The third party owes no responsibility to the agent unless the agent has personally become a party to the transaction.

3. The third party is liable for his or her torts to any party injured as a result.

NONEXISTENT, PARTIALLY DISCLOSED, AND UNDISCLOSED PRINCIPALS

In discussing the principal-agent relationship we have thus far assumed that the principal exists when the agent executes the transaction in question and that both the existence and the identity of the principal are disclosed to the third party. This is usually, but not always, the case. The special problems that arise in connection with *nonexistent, partially disclosed,* and *undisclosed principals* are discussed below.

Nonexistent Principals

If an agent purports to act for a principal who does not exist at the time, the agent is usually liable to the third party. Of course, since there is no principal, the agent is not really an agent at all; he or she merely *claims* to be one.

While this situation does not occur frequently, it is by no means rare. A common instance of the

nonexistent principal is that of a person attempting to act for an organization that is not legally recognized as a separate entity. (A *legal entity* is an organization—such as a corporation—that is recognized by the law as having the rights and duties of a person, although it is not flesh and blood. It can, for example, make contracts, sue, and be sued in its own name.) Thus a member of an unincorporated association, such as a church, club, fraternity, or the like, may attempt to contract in behalf of the association. Since the "principal" is not legally recognized as one, the members who make the agreement are personally responsible. It is for this reason that many churches and other such organizations form corporations.

The contracts of *corporate promoters* (those who play a part in the initial organization of a corporation) have posed similar problems. Quite often, these people make various types of agreements before the proposed corporation is formed. They may, for example, enter contracts for the purpose of raising capital, purchasing a building site, or procuring the services of an attorney, an accountant, or other professionals. The liabilities of the promoter, of the corporation once it is formed, and of the third party are discussed in Chapter 36.

A similar situation occurs when a principal has existed but is now dead or lacks contractual capacity when the agent contracts with the third party. As we mentioned in Chapter 18, such an occurrence often terminates the agency, and the principal (or that person's estate) is not bound. If the agency is not terminated, the principal's status affects his or her own liability in the same way as if the principal had personally dealt with the third party.

Whether the *agent* is personally liable depends on the circumstances. If the principal is *dead* or has been *declared insane by a court* at the time of the transaction, the agent invariably is held personally liable to the third party. On the other hand, if, at the time the transaction is made, the principal is either a *minor* or *insane* (but not officially declared insane by a court), the agent is personally responsible to the third party in only two situations:

1. The agent is liable if he or she has made representations to the effect that the principal has contractual capacity. This is true even if the agent is honestly mistaken.

2. The agent who has made no such representations is still liable to the third party if he or she *knew or had reason to know* of the principal's lack of capacity *and* the third party's ignorance of the facts.

Partially Disclosed Principals

As we indicated earlier, an agent usually is responsible to the third party if the agent discloses the fact that he or she is acting for a principal but does not *identify* that person. If the agent acts with authority, the principal is also responsible and may be held liable when the third party learns his or her identity.[2] Since the third party knows that the agent is acting for someone else, the third party is, in turn, liable to the principal. In sum, the liability of the principal and the third party is the same as in the case of a completely disclosed principal. The only difference is that in the case of a **partially disclosed principal,** *the agent is also liable,* unless the agent and the third party agree otherwise.

Undisclosed Principals

Individuals and business organizations sometimes prefer not to have their connection with a transaction be known. If an agent acts in behalf of a principal but does not disclose to the third party the fact that he or she is representing another, it is said that the agent acts for an **undisclosed principal.** In other words, the third party, not knowing that a principal-agent rela-

tionship exists, thinks that the agent is dealing solely for himself.

In a case such as this, the agent is personally liable to the third party. If and when the principal makes himself known, that person is also liable to the third party if the agent acted within the scope of his authority. In such an event, the third party must *elect* whether to hold the agent or the principal responsible.[3]

Thus far we have focused on the liability of the undisclosed principal and the agent. But what about the liability of the *third party?* Since the *agent* is a party to the contract, he or she can enforce the agreement against the third party. Once revealed, the *principal* ordinarily can also enforce the agreement. In three situations, however, the third party can refuse to perform for the undisclosed principal and can continue to treat the agent as the sole party to whom he or she is obligated.

1. If the third party has already performed for the agent before the principal is revealed, the third party is not required to render a second performance.

2. If, prior to the transaction, the third party has indicated that he or she will not deal with the one who is the undisclosed principal, the third party is not required to perform for that principal. Similarly, the third party is not responsible to the undisclosed principal if the former has indicated beforehand or in the agreement that he or she will not deal with *anyone* other than the agent.

3. In all other situations the undisclosed principal is treated in much the same way as an *as-*

---

[2] There is conflict among the courts on whether the third party must make a choice (or *election*) between the agent and the principal in such a case or whether he or she can hold both of them responsible.

[3] Different jurisdictions apply different rules as to what constitutes an *election.* Demanding payment from the agent or the principal or even filing suit against one of them usually *is not* considered the third party's "point of no return." Obtaining satisfaction of the claim obviously *is* an election. However, courts differ on whether *obtaining a court judgment* (which has not yet been collected) constitutes an election. Of course, if the third party obtains a judgment against the agent before knowing the principal's identity, there is no binding election and the third party can still pursue the principal.

signee from the agent (see Chapter 16 for a discussion of assignees). He or she can demand performance from the third party only if the contract is of a type that can be assigned. Thus, if the contract calls for personal service by the agent or if the agent's personal credit standing, judgment, or skill played an important part in the third party's decision to deal with that individual, the third party cannot be forced to accept the undisclosed principal as a substitute.

TORT LIABILITY

Until now, our discussions of legal responsibility have focused almost exclusively on the parties' contractual liability. Now we will turn to their *tort liability.*

Circumstances in which the Superior Is Liable for the Subordinate's Torts

Obviously, if either the superior, the subordinate, or the third party personally commits a tort, that person is liable to the one injured by the wrongful act. If the *subordinate* commits a tort, the additional question often arises whether his or her *superior* is also liable to the injured third party. This is often important because ordinarily the superior is insured or otherwise more financially capable of paying damages.

If the superior personally is at fault, that person obviously is liable because he or she has committed a tort. This can be seen in the following situations:

1. If the superior *directs* the subordinate to commit the tort (or even if the superior *intends* that the tort be committed), he or she is responsible.

2. If the superior carelessly allows the subordinate to operate potentially dangerous equipment (such as an automobile or truck), even though he or she knows or should know that the subordinate is unqualified or incapable of handling it safely, the superior is responsible for any resulting harm. The phrase *negligent entrustment* is often used to describe this situation.

3. Similarly, the superior is held liable if he or she is negligent in *failing to properly supervise a subordinate.*

Most often, however, the superior has not directed or intended the commission of a tort and has no reason to suppose that he or she is creating a dangerous situation. Therefore, the third party usually seeks to impose **vicarious liability** (liability imposed not because of one's own wrong but solely because of the wrong of one's subordinate) on the superior. The imposition of liability on the superior for a tort committed by a subordinate is based on the doctrine of **respondeat superior** ("let the master answer").

The theoretical justification for holding the superior responsible is that he or she can treat the loss—or the premiums for liability insurance—as a cost of doing business. The cost is thus reflected in the price of his or her product, and the loss is ultimately spread over that segment of the population benefiting from that product.

When the superior is required to pay damages to a third party because of the tort of a subordinate, the superior usually has a legal right to recoup the loss from that subordinate. As a practical matter, this is an illusory right in many cases, because the subordinate frequently is unable to pay.

Of course, the superior is not always responsible for the torts of subordinates. In this regard, two issues must ordinarily be dealt with:

1. Was the relationship that of master-servant (i.e., employer–employee) or employer–independent contractor?

2. If a master-servant relationship existed, was the servant acting within the scope of his or her employment at the time of committing the alleged tort?

Master-Servant or Employer– Independent Contractor

Legal Significance of the Distinction: The imposition of vicarious liability often depends on the nature of the relationship involved. If it is found to be that of master and servant, the master is liable for a tort committed by his or her servant if it was committed in the scope of the servant's employment for the master.

On the other hand, if the relationship is found to be that of employer and independent contractor, the employer generally is not liable for a tort committed by the independent contractor. Those few instances in which the employer *is liable* for a tort are as follows.

1. If the task for which the independent contractor was hired is *inherently dangerous,* the employer will be responsible for harm to third parties caused by the dangerous character of the work. The employer's responsibility in such a case is based on the tort concept of *strict liability.* That is, the responsibility exists solely because of the nature of the activity, regardless of whether any negligence or other fault brought about the damage. Activities deemed to be inherently dangerous include blasting, using deadly chemicals, or working on buildings in populated areas where people must pass below the activity.

2. If the employer owes a *nondelegable duty,* he or she cannot escape ultimate responsibility for performing that duty by obtaining an independent contractor to perform it. Thus, if the independent contractor is negligent or commits some other tort in the performance of such a task, the employer is liable to the injured third party. Nondelegable duties are those duties owed to the public which courts feel to be of such importance that responsibility cannot be delegated. Examples are (a) a duty imposed by statute, such as the statutory duty of a railroad to keep highway crossings in a safe condition; (b) the duty of a city to keep its streets in a safe condition; (c) the duty of a landlord who has assumed responsibility for making repairs to the premises to see that those repairs are done safely; and (d) the duty of a business proprietor whose premises are open to the public to keep the premises in a reasonably safe condition.

Making the Distinction: The determination of whether a particular subordinate is a servant or an independent contractor depends essentially on the issue of *control.* If the superior has hired the subordinate merely to achieve a result and has left decisions regarding the method and manner of achieving that result up to the subordinate, the latter is an independent contractor. On the other hand, if the superior actually controls or has the right to control the method and manner of achieving the result, then the subordinate is a servant. Thus a construction contractor hired to erect a building is usually an independent contractor, while a secretary hired to type and take dictation is usually a servant.

However, the delineation is not always easy, and sometimes it produces problems of extreme conceptual difficulty. The most important question, of course, is whether the superior *controls or has the right to control the method and manner of doing the work.* Where the matter of control is not so obvious as to make the determination readily apparent, other factors can be taken into account. Some facts which would increase the likelihood of a subordinate being viewed as an independent contractor are: (1) the subordinate has his own independent business or profession; (2) the subordinate uses his own tools, equipment, or workplace to perform the task; (3) the subordinate is paid by the job, not by the hour, week, or month; (4) the subordinate has irregular hours; and (5) the subordinate is performing a task that is not part of the superior's regular business. None of these facts automatically makes a subordinate an independent contractor; each is simply a factor to be weighed along with all the other evidence.

In recent years, *franchising* has become a common method of doing business. In a franchise agreement, the *franchisor* owns and promotes a trademark. Agreements are made with *franchisees,* independent entrepreneurs who own and operate local outlets (such as fast-food restaurants). The franchising agreement will give the franchisee the right to use the franchisor's trademark and will place various restrictions on the way the local outlet is operated. The franchisee will be required to pay a royalty for his use of the trademark, which usually is a percentage of the franchisee's gross sales, and the franchisor usually promises to provide national advertising and various kinds of assistance. In the following case, the court considers the important question of whether a franchisee is an independent contractor or a servant of the franchisor.

Singleton v. International Dairy Queen, Inc.
Superior Court of Delaware, 332 A.2d 160 (1975)

Christine Singleton, nine years old, went to the local Dairy Queen store in Newark, Delaware. After purchasing ice cream, she started to leave. As she attempted to open the door, not by touching the glass but by pushing on a metal crossbar designed for the purpose, the bottom part of the door glass cracked and fell outward. Because of her forward motion, Christine fell through the door and onto the broken glass, suffering severe lacerations and other injuries.

In Christine's behalf, her father sued W. R. Hesseltine, the owner of the local Dairy Queen franchise, and International Dairy Queen, Inc., the franchisor. The franchisor (Dairy Queen) filed a motion for summary judgment prior to trial, claiming that the documentary evidence established as a matter of law that Hesseltine was an independent contractor. In other words, Dairy Queen asserted that there was no issue of fact as to its liability and that it should be dismissed from the case, because even if plaintiff proved that the franchisee had been negligent in not maintaining a safe premises (which almost certainly would be the case), Dairy Queen could not be held liable for that tort. Following is the trial court's decision in ruling upon Dairy Queen's motion.

Longobardi, Judge:

. . . [The court first noted that Hesseltine had recently remodeled the store and that, in connection with the remodeling project, Hesseltine's personal architect had based his plans and specifications on plans furnished by Dairy Queen. The use of Dairy Queen's plans was required by the franchise agreement.]

In addition to the requirement that any structure had to be built according to Dairy Queen's plans, the franchise agreement also contains the following pertinent conditions: (a) Dairy Queen imposes "rules and controls" for the "conduct of the Dairy Queen business"; (b) Dairy Queen has the right to inspect the premises; (c) The "mix" formulas are subject to Dairy Queen's regulation; (d) The franchise agreement cannot be assigned without prior approval; (e) Only the words "Dairy Queen" are to be displayed as the trade name of the store; (f) Dairy Queen reserves the right to inspect the premises for the purpose of quality control of the product "and the conditions of manufacture or sale thereof"; (g) Suppliers of "mix" have to be approved by Dairy Queen. All other products have to be purchased from Dairy Queen's approved suppliers; (h) Dairy Queen requires the store be kept in a "high state of repair"; (i) All employees have to wear uniforms approved by Dairy Queen; (j) All advertising cartons and containers used in the business must be marked to indicate they are being used under the authority of Dairy Queen; (k) Freezers must be purchased from "authorized" manufacturers; (l) Dairy Queen dictates portion control which can vary from time to time as they see fit; (m) All freezers used on the premises must have a name plate containing only the name "Dairy Queen"; (n) Dairy Queen reserves the right to dictate what additional items may be sold besides the dairy product from the freezer; (o) The franchisee must keep records and make monthly reports on the number of gallons of mix, from whom they were purchased and the date the mix was received; (p) Dairy Queen has the right to cancel the franchise agreement for many reasons, not the least of which is the franchisee's failure to meet the requirements proposed by Dairy Queen for the "physical properties"; (q) Dairy Queen renounces liability or responsibility for the "business operations" of the franchisee.

Private franchising, the multibillion dollar entrepreneurial goliath, thrives so long as it can maintain control of its service, product and trade name. The franchise agreement attests to the skill of corporate counsel in reserving as many rights as is possible to maintain control and to protect the product or service covered by the trademark. The necessity to maintain control for the purpose of protecting its product, service, know-how and name, however, may also result in a master-servant relationship wherein the franchisor becomes liable for the torts of the franchisee. [Other cases] have decided that when the control becomes excessive the borderline is breached and a master-servant relationship is created.

In the instant case, the control exercised by Dairy Queen appears to be excessive. When an entity can control the size, shape and appearance of its franchisor's establishment, impose the nationally known sign "Dairy Queen" as the only sign for the premises, require all containers to show the name of the parent company, dictate portion control, the size and shape of containers, the uniforms of the employees, subject the franchisor to the obligation to obey subsequent rules and regulations, reserve the right to inspect the premises . . . , name the suppliers and even dictate what else may be sold on the premises, there appears little else to establish agency. The very lifeblood of the agent is in the hands of the franchisor. What greater control can there be than portion control or the nebulously defined sanction of termination by the unilateral action of the franchisor? In addition, Hesseltine himself [said in his pretrial deposition that] Dairy Queen did control the day to day operations through their inspections. [The court then ruled that, in light of Hesseltine's testimony in his deposition as to Dairy Queen's control over him, which conflicted with the statement in the written franchise agreement that Dairy Queen had no such control, there was a fact issue as to the nature of their relationship.] . . .

The dispute is not resolved merely because the agreement says Dairy Queen is not responsible for the "business operations" of franchisee. The label by which parties to a relationship designate themselves is not controlling. In addition, the franchise agreement is so broadly drawn it requires additional discovery or testimony at trial to decide what the parties meant and understood by its terms. These are issues which are best resolved at trial during which the parties are given an opportunity for a full and rigorous examination of the facts.

In addition, there is a fact question as to Hesseltine's being an "apparent" servant of Dairy Queen. . . . [O]ne who represents . . . that another is his servant and causes a third person to justifiably and reasonably rely upon the care and skill of such apparent [servant] is subject to liability to the third person for harm caused by the lack of care or skill of the one appearing to be a servant as if he were such. [Thus, the court held that there were fact issues, to be decided at trial, as to both an "actual" and an "apparent" master-servant relationship.]

Defendant Dairy Queen's motion for summary judgment is denied.

Comment: Although one can only speculate, it is very likely that, after this decision, Dairy Queen either settled with the Singletons or was held liable along with Hesseltine after a trial.

Scope of Employment

If the subordinate is deemed to be a servant, the master is liable to third parties for those torts committed by the servant in the *scope of his or her employment* for the master. There exists no simple definition of the **scope of employment** (sometimes called *course of employment*) concept. Obviously, a servant is acting within the scope of employment while performing work that he or she has been *expressly directed to do by the master.* To illustrate: M has directed S to drive M's truck from New York to Albany via a certain route. While on that route, S drives negligently and injures T. M is liable to T.

In the absence of a specific directive given by the master, an act usually is in the scope of employment if it is *reasonably incidental to an activity that has been expressly directed.* Thus, in the above example, if S had stopped to buy gasoline and had negligently struck a parked car belonging to T, M would have been liable to T.

Deviations: The master sometimes can be held liable even though the servant has deviated from the authorized activity. The master's liability in such cases depends on the *degree* and *foreseeability* of the deviation. If the deviation is great, the master usually is not responsible. Suppose that S, in driving M's truck from New York to Albany, decides to go a hundred miles off his authorized route to visit an old friend. On the way there, S negligently collides with T. In this situation, M is not liable.

But what if S has been to see his friend and was returning to his authorized route when the collision occurred? Three different viewpoints have been taken by various courts. Where there has been more than a slight deviation from the scope of employment, as in this case, some courts have held that the reentry into the scope of employment occurs only when the servant has *actually returned to the authorized route or activity.* Others have held that there is reentry the moment that the servant, with an intent to serve the master's business, *begins to turn back toward the point of deviation.* However, a majority of courts have held that reentry occurs when the servant, with an intent to serve the master's business, *has turned back toward and come reasonably close to the point of deviation.*

If the deviation from the authorized route or activity is only slight, many courts have held that the servant is still within the scope of the employment if the type of deviation was *reasonably foreseeable* by the master. For example: While driving from New York to Albany, S stops at a roadside establishment to get something to eat or buy a pack of cigarettes. While pulling off the road, he negligently strikes a parked car. In this situation M is liable. Although buying

something to eat or smoke may not be necessary to drive a truck from New York to Albany (as is the purchase of gasoline) and although S was not really serving his master, the deviation was only slight and was of the type that any master should reasonably expect.

Many examples of the scope of employment issue—such as the next two cases—involve auto accidents (though certainly the issue is not limited to them). These two cases illustrate some typical problems in this area.

Lazar v. Thermal Equipment Corp.
Court of Appeals of California, 195 Cal. Rptr. 890 (1983)

Richard Lanno was employed as a project engineer for Thermal Equipment Co., which was a manufacturer of heating equipment and pressure vessels for the aerospace industry. In connection with his job, Lanno was sometimes required to proceed from his home directly to a job site in the mornings. In addition, he was constantly on call as a trouble-shooter, and, consequently, Thermal's customers occasionally called him at his home after hours and on weekends. In order to answer these calls, Lanno needed the company truck, in which he sometimes carried tools; if the truck was not at his home, he would stop at Thermal to pick up needed tools on the way to answer the call. To facilitate these duties, Thermal allowed Lanno to take the company truck home with him on a daily basis. Thermal provided Lanno with gasoline for the truck, and allowed him to use it for personal purposes.

On one occasion, Lanno finished work and left Thermal's business premises. Driving the company truck, he headed in a direction away from both the workplace and his home; Lanno testified that he planned to stop at a store, purchase something, and then go home. Before reaching the store, Lanno was involved in an accident with Lazar, who suffered bodily injury and damage to his car. Lazar filed suit against Thermal, claiming that Lanno had driven the truck negligently and that Lanno was within the scope of his employment at the time of the accident. The jury found that Lanno was not acting within the scope of his employment at the time of the accident, but the trial court granted Lazar's motion for judgment notwithstanding the verdict, holding that Lanno was within the scope of employment as a matter of law. The jury had found Lazar's damages to be $81,000, and the trial court rendered judgment for Lazar against Thermal in this amount. Thermal appealed.

Schauer, Presiding Judge:

Under the doctrine of respondeat superior, an employer is responsible for the torts of his employee if these torts are committed within the scope of employment. The "going and coming" rule acts to limit an employer's liability under respondeat superior. This rule deems an employee's actions to be outside the scope of employment when these actions occur while the employee is going to or returning from work. The "going and coming" rule, in turn, has been limited in recent years. Under the modern rule, if the employee's trip to or from work "involves an incidental benefit to the employer, not common to commute trips made by ordinary members of the work force," the "going and coming" rule will not apply. Thus in *Hinman v. Westinghouse Electric Co.*, 2 Cal.3d 956 (1970), it was held that the "going and coming" rule did not apply where the employer had made the commute part of the workday by compensating the employee for his travel time. Similarly, in *Huntsinger v. Glass Containers Corp.*, 22 Cal. App.3d 803 (1972), an employee was required to drive to and from work in order to have his vehicle available for company business. The court held that these circumstances, if confirmed by a jury, would support a finding that the employee's commute conferred an incidental benefit on the employer; a jury could therefore find that the commute fell within the scope of employment.

In the [present] case, the trial court was presented with uncontroverted evidence that Thermal derived a special benefit from Lanno's commute. This commute was made in the company vehicle, and an object of the commute was to transport the vehicle to Lanno's home where it would be ready for business use in case Lanno received emergency after-hours calls for repair from the employer's customers. In traveling to and from work, Lanno was thus acting in the scope of his employment, conferring a tangible benefit on his employer; the "going and coming" rule is thus inapplicable.

A further issue, however, is presented in this case. . . . Lanno decided that, before going home, he would stop at a shop and buy a certain, now forgotten, item. To further complicate the question, this shop and item were located in the opposite direction from Lanno's home. . . .

Categorization of an employee's action as within or outside the scope of employment . . . begins with a question of foreseeability. . . . Foreseeability as a test for respondeat superior merely means that in the context of the particular enterprise an employee's conduct is not so unusual or startling that it would seem unfair to include the loss resulting from it among other costs of the employer's business.

One traditional means of defining this foreseeability is seen in the distinction between minor "deviations" and substantial "departures" from the employer's business. The former are deemed foreseeable and remain within the scope of employment; the latter are unforeseeable and take the employee outside the scope of his employment.

Witkin [an authority on the law of agency] describes the traditional distinction as follows: "The question is often one of fact, and the rule now established is that only a substantial deviation or departure takes the employee outside the scope of his employment. If the main purpose of his activity is still the employer's business, it does not cease to be within the scope of the employment by reason of incidental personal acts, slight delays, or deflections from the most direct route. . . ."

In the [present] case, we are asked to decide whether Lanno's personal errand was a foreseeable deviation from the scope of his employment, or whether evidence or inferences therefrom have been presented which would lead a jury to believe that this errand was an unforeseeable, substantial departure from his duties. . . .

The evidence presented to the trial court was not controverted. Lanno testified that on the day of the accident he left work and headed away from his home, planning to buy an item and then return directly home. The evidence thus clearly showed that Lanno planned a minor errand to be carried out, broadly speaking, on the way home. Lanno further testified that this type of errand occurred with his employer's permission. No evidence was presented, nor could any inference be drawn from the evidence, showing that Lanno had any other object in mind that day than a brief stop at a store before going home.

The evidence, then, leads ineluctably to the conclusion that Lanno's errand was a minor deviation from his employer's business. While the specific act was one "strictly personal" to Lanno, it was "necessary to his convenience" under the standard [set forth in] *Alma W. v. Oakland Unified School Dist.*, 123 Cal. App.3d 133. While this standard was suggested for deviations "at work," we think it is applicable to deviations made on the way home, in the employer's vehicle, when the trip home benefits the employer. Here, it would have been unreasonable and inconvenient for Lanno to drive his truck home, stop there, then return to purchase the needed item, passing work on the way. The decision to stop to buy the item on the way home was one reasonably necessary to Lanno's comfort and convenience. For this reason the detour must be considered a minor deviation.

The detour was foreseeable for much the same reason. While a decision to stop at a party, or a bar, or to begin a vacation, might not have been foreseeable, we can think of no conduct more predictable than an employee's stopping at a store to purchase a few items on the way home. Where, as here, the trip home is made for the benefit of the employer, in the employer's vehicle, accidents occurring during such minor and foreseeable deviations become part of the "inevitable toll of a lawful enterprise." . . .

Finally, we note that Thermal makes much of the fact that Lanno was headed in the direction opposite his home at the time of the accident. . . . An employer's liability, however, should not turn simply on a point of the compass; the fact that the store Lanno decided to visit was to the north of his workplace, rather than to the south, is not the controlling factor in this case. Instead, the modern rationale for respondeat superior requires that liability be hinged on the foreseeability and substantiality of the employee's departure from his employer's business. Where, as here, the deviation is insubstantial and foreseeable, the doctrine of respondeat superior will apply.

The judgment is affirmed.

Comment: If the deviation had been substantial and unforeseeable, such as a two-hour stop at a bar, Lanno would have been outside the scope of his employment during the deviation. However, because the "coming and going" rule did not apply to this case, Lanno would have *re-entered* the scope of employment upon getting back into the truck and resuming the trip toward home.

Dinkins v. Farley
New York Supreme Court, Monroe
County, 434 N.Y.S.2d 325 (1980)

As part of its personnel policy, Xerox Corporation maintained a National Tuition Aid Program that provided financial assistance to employees taking advanced college courses. An employee's application to participate in the program had to be approved by the employee's immediate supervisor. The company provided tuition assistance only for those courses directly related to a present job or to a future job to which an employee might reasonably aspire at Xerox. Upon approval of the employee's application, Xerox advanced 100 percent of the tuition and lab fees and then deducted 35 percent of that amount from the employee's paychecks in installments. Thereafter, the employee was required to verify enrollment by submitting itemized receipts from the college, and later to verify successful completion of a course by submitting a grade report to Xerox within 30 days after the end of the semester. If a grade report for a course was not submitted to Xerox within 50 days after semester's end, the company initiated steps to collect the other 65 percent of course expenses from the employee. However, if the employee ultimately received an advanced degree as a result of his participation in the tuition aid program, Xerox would refund the 35 percent that had been paid by the employee. A course taken under the program was expected to be scheduled outside of working hours if possible; if this was not possible, the employee could have limited time off during the workday to attend classes, subject to approval by the employee's supervisor. Such time off had to be made up at another time decided by the supervisor. Xerox spent about $1,000,000 annually on the program, and at the time of this case over 6,000 of Xerox's employees had participated.

Victor Farley, an employee of Xerox, had a bachelor's degree in engineering and wished to take a linear systems course that would better prepare him for pursuing a master's degree in that field. His application for the tuition aid program was approved by Xerox and he enrolled in the course at the Rochester Institute of Technology. He usually got out of work at 4:20 or 4:30 p.m., and frequently was a few minutes late for the class, which began at 4:20. One afternoon as Victor was driving to class, he was involved in an automobile accident at an intersection on campus. The other driver, Diane Dinkins, sued both Victor and Xerox, claiming that Victor was guilty of negligence and that Xerox was also liable because Victor was acting within the scope of his employment at the time of the accident. Before trial, Xerox filed a motion for summary judgment on the ground that, as a matter of law, Victor was not acting within the scope of his employment when the accident occurred. Below is the opinion of the trial court on this issue.

Boehm, Justice:

Although Xerox subsidizes the outside education of an employee who successfully completes course work for a degree, this alone should not be controlling in creating a "scope of employment" status, at least while the course is still in progress, because failure to complete the course would make the employee responsible to pay the entire tuition. Thus, if tuition payments alone were the criterion by which scope of employment was determined, one would not know whether or not an employee was within the scope of his employment during the course year until his work had been graded at the end of the school year. Until that time an employee's status would be a contingent one, ripening only after the grades were issued. If, in the meantime, the employee had an accident driving to or from class, Xerox would not know whether it could be held responsible as his employer until the employee had passed or flunked.

Further, the purpose of Victor Farley in working toward a master's degree was predominantly personal. Although it may also serve a purpose of Xerox to have its employees better trained or more satisfied on the job by being promoted from within the organization, this purpose is subservient to the personal motive of Victor to better his own employment and economic status by obtaining a master's degree, a degree which would remain his and continue to benefit him even if he should no longer work for Xerox. . . .

No doubt there is a good business and policy reason for Xerox to subsidize the education of its employees within certain areas of value to Xerox, but it cannot be said that such a purpose is necessary or vital to its operation except insofar as ambitious, well-trained or satisfied employees are vital to any organization in the same way as healthy employees are. . . .

Further, it is undisputed that Xerox does not direct the number of times an employee must attend class nor whether he must attend at all. Hypothetically, if an employee were able to successfully complete a course by home study and never attend class, Xerox would still be obligated for 100 percent of the tuition. It is not going to and from class which determines whether an employee is reimbursed; it is whether he successfully completes his educational course.

If Xerox could be held liable in this case under respondeat superior, other circumstances come to mind which would also appear to impose liability upon it. For example, if Victor Farley carelessly handled volatile materials in a chemistry class and another student were injured or property were destroyed, Xerox could be held responsible. If Xerox is responsible for what an employee does on his way to class, why would it not be equally responsible for what an employee does in class? Or, if educational sabbaticals funded by scholarship grants under the same aid program were encouraged by Xerox, it could be responsible for injuries caused by one of its employees during such a sabbatical driving to or from class at a university hundreds of miles away from the plant. Or, if Xerox encouraged its employees to take paid leaves of absence to participate in worthwhile community organizations or projects, it could be responsible for injuries caused by an employee while so participating.

Other areas of liability come to mind. If Xerox encouraged noontime physical activity by its employees, such as jogging, would it be responsible for an injury caused to a pedestrian by one of its jogging employees in the area around Xerox Square? . . .

In none of these examples would an employee be acting in the scope of his employment as that term has been historically understood. Scope of employment "refers to those acts which are so closely connected with what the servant is employed to do, and so fairly and reasonably incidental to it, that they may be regarded as methods, even though quite improper ones, of carrying out the objectives of the employment." (Prosser, Law of Torts [4th ed], pp. 460–461.)

The Restatement of Agency sets forth the requirements as follows: *(1) Conduct of a servant is within the scope of employment if, but only if: (a) it is of the kind he is employed to perform; (b) it occurs substantially within the authorized time and space limits; (c) it is actuated . . . by a purpose to serve the master. . . .*

(2) Conduct of a servant is not within the scope of employment if it is different in kind from that authorized, far beyond the authorized time or space limits, or too little actuated by a purpose to serve the master.

Victor's activity at the time of the accident in driving to a course whose successful completion was of primary and direct benefit to him cannot be said to be in the scope of his employment. Taking the course was not "closely connected" with what he had been employed to do nor was it "fairly and reasonably incidental" to the carrying out of the objectives of his employment. It was "too little actuated by a purpose to serve the master"; his own purpose was clearly the prevailing one. Nor was Xerox exercising control over him, directly or indirectly, at the time. He was driving a car not owned by Xerox; he selected his own mode of transportation; he chose the course which he was attending, but he could have gone or not gone as he saw fit and if he failed to attend class after enrolling the jeopardy he suffered was not his job but only the tuition Xerox had advanced on his behalf. It is difficult to see how Xerox was in control or could have been in control of Victor when the accident happened.

The case of *Makoske v. Lombardy,* 47 A.D.2d 284, is not to the contrary for there the employees were required to attend the training session at Saratoga. They were obliged to go. They did not have the same option which Victor had. . . .

The motion of defendant Xerox Corporation is granted. [Thus, Xerox would not be liable even if Victor was found to have been guilty of negligence. The question of Victor's liability for negligence would be decided at trial, because genuine fact issues existed with regard to this question.]

Intentional Torts: Thus far we have assumed the tort to be that of *negligence* (simple carelessness). Most cases in fact are concerned with the servant's negligence. However, a servant's *intentional tort,* such as assault and battery, libel, slander, fraud, trespass, or the like, can also subject the master to liability. The test is the same. The master is liable if the servant was acting within the scope of his or her employment at the time. It should be emphasized, though, that a master is *less likely* to be responsible if the servant's tort was *intentional* rather than merely negligent. The reason is that when a servant intentionally commits a wrongful act, he or she is more likely to be motivated by personal reasons rather than by a desire to serve the master. Those cases where the master *has* been held liable for his or her servant's intentional torts usually fall within one of three broad categories.

1. *Where the tort occurs in a job in which force is a natural incident.* An example is a bouncer in a saloon, who is naturally expected to use force occasionally. But if *excessive* force is used, the master is liable.

2. *Where the servant is actually attempting to promote the master's business but does it in a wrongful manner.* For example, two competing tow truck drivers are attempting to beat each other to the scene of an accident to get the business for their respective masters. One intentionally runs the other off the road. The master of the one committing the tort is liable.

3. *Where the tort results from friction naturally brought about by the master's business.* For instance, the servant, who works for a building contractor, argues with an employee of a subcontractor about the method for laying a floor. They become angry, and the servant strikes

the other party. The building contractor, as master, is probably liable.

Concluding Note on Tort Liability

Two additional problems regarding a master's tort liability need to be discussed:

1. A minor is not necessarily the servant of his or her parents. Thus, in the absence of a special statute, the parent is not liable for the torts of a minor child unless the child was acting as a servant in the scope of employment for the parent. The parent can, of course, be held liable for his or her own wrongful act in negligently supervising the child. Also, several states have passed statutes making parents liable within set limits for intentional property damage caused by a minor child.

2. Although the subject of bailments is beyond the scope of this discussion, it should be mentioned that a bailee is not necessarily the servant of the bailor. A *bailment* occurs when the owner of an item of property (the bailor) turns over temporary custody (not ownership) of the item to the bailee for any reason. The bailor ordinarily is *not* liable to third parties for torts committed by the bailee while using the bailor's property. The bailor *is* liable, however, if he or she was negligent in entrusting the item to one whom he or she knew not to be qualified or capable of handling it safely. Otherwise, the bailor generally is liable only if the bailee was acting as the bailor's *servant* in the scope of employment at the time of the tort. Two exceptions exist with regard to *bailments of automobiles:*

  a. A few states follow the *family purpose doctrine.* Under that judge-made doctrine, a member of the family is treated as the servant of the head of the household when driving the family car, regardless of whether such a relationship actually existed.

b. A few states have passed *owner-consent statutes,* which hold the owner of an automobile liable to a third party injured by the negligence of anyone who is driving it with the consent of the owner. This liability exists regardless of any master-servant relationship and regardless of whether the owner was personally negligent.

CRIMINAL LIABILITY

As a general rule, a superior cannot be *criminally* prosecuted for a subordinate's wrongful act unless the superior expressly authorized it. Thus, if S, a subordinate, while acting within the scope of her employment, injures T, and T dies, S's superior can be held liable in a civil suit for damages but cannot be subjected to criminal liability. Any criminal responsibility rests on the shoulders of the subordinate. The rule exists because crimes ordinarily require intent, and the superior in this situation has no criminal intent.

Exceptions to the rule usually fall within one of two categories:

1. The statute making the particular act a crime may specifically provide for placing criminal responsibility on the superior. For example, the federal antitrust laws provide for criminal penalties to be levied against corporations, which can commit crimes only through their human agents.

2. A superior can sometimes be criminally prosecuted under statutes that do not require intent for a violation. A specific example is the offense of selling adulterated food under the federal Food, Drug, and Cosmetic Act. Other examples can be found in some state laws regulating liquor sales and the accuracy of weights of goods sold on that basis.

SUMMARY

The contractual liability of the principal to third parties for transactions made by the agent is dependent on the agent's authority. If the agent acted within the scope of his or her authority when executing the transaction, the resulting contract is the principal's contract and the principal is bound by it. An agent's authority may be express—that which is directly granted by the principal to the agent. It may also be implied—that which is customary for an agent in such a position, or which is reasonably incidental to the agent's express authority. Even if the agent has no express or implied authority, it is possible for the principal to be liable for the agent's actions on the grounds of apparent authority. Apparent authority exists when the principal, by his or her conduct, has misled a reasonably acting third party to believe that the agent had authority. In addition, it is possible for a principal to become liable to the third party by subsequently ratifying the agent's unauthorized transaction. When a principal's liability to a third party depends on whether the principal had notice or knowledge of particular facts, notice to the agent is treated as notice to the principal if receipt of such information was within the scope of the agent's actual or apparent authority.

The agent usually does not incur personal liability when acting in behalf of the principal. The agent can become liable, however, by breaching a duty to the principal, exceeding his or her authority, personally assuming liability, not fully disclosing to the third party that the agent is acting for a particular principal, or committing a tort against a third party.

When a subordinate commits a tort harming a third party, the subordinate clearly is legally responsible to the third party. The superior also can be liable to the third party if it is found that the subordinate was a servant rather than an independent contractor, and if the subordinate was acting within the scope of his or her employment when the tort was committed. A subordinate is a servant if the superior had the right to exercise detailed control over the method and manner by which the subordinate was to accomplish the task. A subordinate is an independent contractor if he or she was hired to accomplish a particular result, and the details of how to do it were within the subordinate's discretion.

KEY TERMS

Authority
Actual authority
Express authority
Implied authority
Apparent authority (or ostensible authority)
Ratification
Express ratification
Implied ratification
Nonexistent principal
Partially disclosed principal
Undisclosed principal
Vicarious liability
Respondeat superior
Scope of employment

QUESTIONS AND PROBLEMS

1. Simpson gave Ricks written authority to sell Simpson's residential lot for $5,000. Ricks procured a buyer willing to pay that price, made a contract with the buyer in Simpson's behalf, and executed a deed conveying the land to the buyer. When Simpson learned of Ricks's actions, he disavowed the transaction, claiming that Ricks had exceeded her authority. Is Simpson correct?

2. A check was made payable to Mrs. Robert Jenkins. Robert Jenkins endorsed his wife's name on the check and cashed it. The teller at the bank where he cashed the check watched Jenkins endorse his wife's name. Jenkins used the money to buy an outboard motor for his boat. Jenkins and his wife were having marital difficulties and separated shortly thereafter. When Mrs. Jenkins learned of her husband's actions in cashing the check, she sued the bank to recover the money that had been paid to her husband. Did she prevail?

3. Suppose that in Question 2, Mrs. Jenkins had been standing silently beside Mr. Jenkins at the time he endorsed her name in front of the teller. What would be the result if she later sued the bank? Discuss.

4. In 1959, Bert Bell, Commissioner of the National Football League (NFL), entered into an agreement with representatives of the NFL Players Association, which provided for certain pension benefits for players who had retired from the NFL prior to 1959. The bylaws of the NFL required any such agreement to be approved by the owners of at least ten of the twelve NFL teams. During negotiations leading to the agreement, Bell stated that he would resign if the agreement were not approved. The agreement was not approved and the pension benefits were not paid. Those players who would have received benefits under the agreement sued both the NFL and the players association, claiming that the NFL was bound by the agreement because Bell had acted with apparent authority. Should the players have won their lawsuit? Discuss. (*Soar v. National Football League Players Ass'n,* 438 F.Supp. 337, 1975.)

5. Roberts, a salesclerk in a jewelry store, wanted to take a short break. He asked Jones, the store janitor, to watch the store for a few minutes while he was gone. Jones, dressed in soiled work clothes, sold a silver tray priced at $300 to a customer for $250. Roberts returned shortly thereafter and learned what Jones had done. As soon as Roberts was able to contact the customer, he demanded the return of the tray or payment of the additional $50. Does the customer have to comply with the demand?

6. Suppose that in Question 5, Roberts had asked Richardson, the bookkeeper, to watch the store rather than the janitor. Would the result be any different in this case? Would it matter whether the buyer was a new customer or a regular customer who knew the store's employees? Discuss.

7. Rodriguez was a salesman at a retail carpet outlet owned by Carpet World, Inc. He usually was the only employee in the store, and the company's sales manager only made occasional visits to the store. Although he had no hiring authority, Rodriguez hired Amy Schoonover on a salary and commission basis. Amy worked for two months, earning salary and commissions of $714, but was never paid. Rodriguez disappeared, and Amy sued Carpet World for her unpaid compensation. Is Carpet World liable? Discuss. (*Schoonover v. Carpet World, Inc.*, 588 P.2d 729, 1978.)

8. Bruton lent a D-8 Caterpillar rent-free to David Eckvall, who wanted to clear some land owned by Eckvall. It was agreed that Eckvall would provide an operator and pay for fuel and routine maintenance. Nothing was said about major repairs. While Eckvall was using the Cat, it broke down. Without contacting Bruton, he took it to Automatic Welding & Supply (AWS), where extensive repairs were made at a cost of $2,340. When the repairs were almost completed, Bruton happened to come into the AWS shop on other business and saw his Cat. He spoke to an AWS mechanic and learned of the scope of the repairs, but nothing was said about cost. After the repairs were completed, the Cat was returned to Eckvall's property, where he used it for some time thereafter. AWS billed Bruton for the repairs. Bruton denied liability, and AWS sued. Is Bruton responsible for the $2,340? Discuss. (*Bruton v. Automatic Welding & Supply,* 513 P.2d 1122, 1973.)

9. Chipman, an employee at Barrickman's service station, was towing a disabled car for Barrickman. Estell, Chipman's girlfriend, was a passenger in the tow truck. She was just along for the ride, without Barrickman's knowledge. The tow truck was involved in an accident and Estell, who was injured, sued Chipman and Barrickman. The trial court dismissed the suit against Barrickman, because he had an official "no rider" rule, even though he didn't always enforce it. Estell appealed. How should the appellate court rule? Discuss. (*Estell v. Barrickman,* 571 S.W.2d 650, 1978.)

10. Hartford Ice Cream Co. manufactured ice cream. Son operated a grocery store, selling, among other items, Hartford's ice cream. Hartford delivered the ice cream to Son by truck, and the driver was instructed to collect the price on delivery. On one occasion, Son claimed that the ice cream being delivered had not been properly refrigerated, and he refused to accept or pay for it. The driver tried to take the money from Son's cash register, but Son managed to lock the register before this could be done. The driver then started to carry away the entire cash register, and a struggle for its possession developed. Although Son prevented the driver from removing the cash register, Son was severely beaten by him. Son sued both the driver and Hartford Ice Cream Co. for the damages caused by the beating. Is Hartford liable for the actions of the driver? Discuss. (*Son v. Hartford Ice Cream Co.*, 129 Atl. 778, 1925.)

Part IV

COMMERCIAL TRANSACTIONS

Part IV surveys the subjects of sales law and commercial paper. These areas of law govern two of the most important business activities that are carried on in our economic system—sales of personal property (such as television sets and machine tools) and the issuance of negotiable instruments (such as promissory notes and checks). Both of these subjects are governed by the Uniform Commercial Code (UCC); thus, unlike the common-law rules that make up the subject of contracts, the rules we will be considering throughout Part IV are entirely statutory in nature.

Chapters 20 through 23 are devoted to *sales law*—the examination and application of the rules of Article 2 of the UCC. The first of these chapters is concerned with defining "goods" and highlighting the essential elements of a sale, so that sales transactions can be distinguished from other transactions in goods (such as bailments) and from contracts calling for the performance of services.

Chapter 21 deals with the rules that determine when title and risk of loss pass from seller to buyer—the latter being of special significance in cases where the goods are damaged or lost before reaching the buyer's hands. Of even more importance in many cases are the areas of warranties and products liability (covered in Chapter 22), which together impose the basic liability that sellers of goods have for injuries caused by defective products. Chapter 23 concludes the subject of sales law by summarizing the rights that a buyer or seller has when the other party breaches a sales contract.

Commercial paper—governed by Article 3 of the UCC—is covered in Chapters 24 through 28. The special characteristics of negotiable instruments and the rules applicable to the negotiation (transfer) of such instruments are summarized in Chapters 24 and 25. The next two chapters deal with the subjects of holders in due course and defenses, and liability of the parties (i.e., the liability of makers, drawers, and endorsers of negotiable instruments). Chapter 28 concludes Part IV by examining the special rules applicable to checks and to the bank-depositor relationship.

Chapter 20

SALES
Introduction to
the Law of Sales

A college student purchases a stereo. A home owner buys several cans of house paint. A manufacturer of tires purchases raw rubber, sulphur, and other materials and ultimately sells tires to automobile owners. A mining company sells coal to an electric utility company. All of the above have at least two things in common. First, they are quite ordinary transactions, occurring countless numbers of times. Second, they involve sales of goods. Thus we can hardly question the relevance of studying the law of sales.

As is true of any area of the law, the principles governing sales of goods do not exist in a vacuum. Different areas of law frequently interact, and isolation is not often practicable. However, limitations must be placed on the scope of any discussion of legal principles. Otherwise, the discussion will be unstructured, unwieldy, and probably unusable. The chapters on the law of sales (Chapters 20 through 23) will be confined largely to those principles relating to the sales transaction itself, although closely related matters will occasionally be treated. For example, this first chapter briefly mentions *documents of title*. In most instances, however, related subjects are left for discussion elsewhere in the text.

HISTORICAL NOTE

Before discussing the law of sales as it is today, a brief historical digression is in order. All commercial law reflects to some extent the customs and traditions of business people. The influence of such customs on the law of sales is readily apparent from an examination of its origin. Most commercial trade in early England was conducted at "fairs," where merchants came together to buy and sell their goods. These merchants established their own courts at the fairs to settle disputes and enforce obligations among themselves. The *fair courts,* as they were called, developed a rather extensive body of rules, based in large part on commercial customs and practices existing at that time. This body of unofficial law was referred to as the **law merchant.**

The fair courts were not officially recognized by the king's courts until early in the seventeenth century. By the end of that century, the king's courts had absorbed the fair courts, and the law merchant melted into and became part of the common law. For many years thereafter, the law of sales and other areas of law which had originated with the law merchant were entirely judge-made.

The first attempt in the United States to codify the law of sales occurred with the drafting of the Uniform Sales Act in 1906, which was eventually enacted by the legislatures of thirty-six states. By the 1940s, lawmakers recognized that the Uniform Sales Act and other uniform laws were in need of substantial revision to reflect more modern commercial practices. The Uniform Commercial Code superseded the Uniform Sales Act and the other uniform laws and was eventually enacted in every state except Louisiana,[1] plus the District of Columbia and the Virgin Islands.

SCOPE OF ARTICLE 2 OF THE UCC

Article 2 of the UCC deals with the sale of goods. It forms the basis for most of the following discussion of the law of sales.

Sales

A **sale** is defined in Sec. 2-106 of the UCC as "the passing of title from the seller to the buyer for a price." Thus Article 2 does not apply to leases—such as the lease of an automobile—or to other types of bailments—such as the storage of furniture in a warehouse—because only temporary possession of the goods (rather than title) is

---

[1] Louisiana has enacted some parts of the UCC, but it has not enacted Article 2, which governs sales of goods.

transferred in these transactions.[2] Neither does Article 2 apply to gifts, because no price is paid. (The section on documents of title later in this chapter briefly discusses bailments, while Chapter 43 contains a more complete treatment of the subject. Gifts are also dealt with in Chapter 43.)

Goods

In the majority of cases there is no problem ascertaining whether the subject matter should be classified as **goods**. Occasionally, however, the term may present problems. Essentially, two requirements must be met before a particular item of property is classified as a good:

1. It must be *tangible.* In other words, it must have a physical existence. Thus intangible property such as a patent, copyright, trademark, investment security, or contract right would not come within the scope of Article 2.

2. It must be *movable.* This requirement obviously excludes real estate, which is tangible but not movable. (Of course, almost anything, even real estate, is capable of being moved, shovel by shovel, if enough effort is expended. But the word is intended reasonably rather than literally.)

Using these two requirements we can easily envision the wide variety of products that are classified as goods, from airplanes to toothpaste.

Should things that are attached to real estate be considered goods? Because of the movability requirement this question would involve considerable conceptual difficulty were it not for Sec. 2-107 of the UCC, which sets forth the following basic rules:

1. A contract for the sale of *minerals or a structure* (such as a building or its materials) is a contract for the sale of goods if they are to be severed from the land by the *seller.* If, however, they are to be severed from the land by the *buyer,* the transaction is a sale of real estate and is governed by the principles of real estate law rather than by the UCC. Two examples may be of some help. First, suppose that S and B agree that S will sell to B a quantity of gravel to be taken from beneath the surface of land owned by S. If their agreement states that S will dig and remove the gravel, the transaction is a sale of goods. If, on the other hand, B is to dig and remove the gravel, the transaction is a sale of real estate. Second, suppose that S and B agree that S will sell to B a storage building (or perhaps the lumber from the building) located on land owned by S. If their agreement indicates that B will remove the building from the land, the transaction is a sale of real estate. If removal is to be by S, it is a sale of goods.

2. A contract for the sale of *growing crops* or *timber* is a contract for the sale of goods, regardless of who is to sever them from the land.

3. A contract for the sale of *anything else attached to real estate* is a sale of goods if it can be severed *without material harm* to the real estate. This rule is, perhaps, not as important as the two rules just discussed, simply because most of the problems regarding things attached to real estate have involved minerals, structures, timber, or growing crops. Situations might exist, however, where this third rule would be pertinent. For example: X and Y agree that X will sell to Y a window air conditioner that is now attached to X's home. (We are assuming it is attached, for otherwise the question would never arise—it would obviously be a sale of goods.) The air conditioner is bolted to a metal shelf supported by braces that are secured to the side of the house by bolts. It is fairly evident that the air conditioner can be removed without material harm to the real estate. Suppose, however,

---

[2]Actually, Sec. 2-102 states that it applies to "transactions in goods." Therefore, one could argue that Article 2 is not limited to sales but includes all transactions in goods. However, the great majority of authorities agree that Article 2 applies only to sales. Even so, in a few cases the courts have applied the sections of Article 2 that deal with warranties (discussed in Chapter 22) to *leases* of goods.

that the subject of the sale is a floor furnace. In this case a gaping hole in the floor would result. This might be a material harm, causing the sale to be treated as a sale of real estate rather than goods.

The rules regarding sales of goods attached to real estate apply to those contracts under which the items are being sold apart from the land. However, if two parties agree that one will sell a tract of land to the other, including a building or some timber located on the land, the sale is treated as a sale of real estate.

The UCC also gives special attention to three other potential problems of classification. It provides that (1) unborn animals are goods; (2) money treated as a commodity, such as a rare coin, is a good (though money used as a medium of exchange is not); and (3) things that are specially manufactured for the buyer are goods. Although item 3 seems clear-cut, the framers of Article 2 felt that such a sale might be seen as predominantly a sale of services rather than goods and therefore stated it definitely.

Sales of services (such as employment contracts) are obviously not within the scope of Article 2. However, as we saw in item 3, goods and services sometimes are so entwined that classification is no easy task. For example, when a hospital supplies blood to a patient, is the hospital selling a good or supplying a service? The blood itself meets the UCC requirements for a good, but the courts have to determine if the predominant feature of the transaction as a whole (including the transfusion) is that of selling a good or supplying a service.[3] Some courts have held that it is a sale of goods within Article 2; other courts have held it is not. A number of states have passed specific statutes which provide that a blood transfusion is not a sale of goods. The same problem arises where a beautician applies hair dye to a customer in a beauty parlor, and again the court decisions are in conflict. Although the UCC makes no statement regarding blood transfusions or hair treatments, it does specifically provide in Sec. 2-314(1) that food sold in a restaurant is a sale of goods (at least as far as creation of the implied warranty of merchantability is concerned).

The two cases that follow involve the difficult problem of determining whether the law of sales is applicable to "mixed" transactions. The first of these presents a situation where some of the items being sold are clearly goods, but other items consist of intangibles. In the second case, the question is whether the contract was a sales contract or a contract calling for the expenditure of services.

---

[3] The issue in these cases has usually been whether a recipient of contaminated blood is protected by the *implied warranty of merchantability* (which will be discussed in Chapter 22). In those jurisdictions where the transaction is considered a service rather than a sale of goods, the injured party can recover damages only by proving that the hospital acted negligently.

De Filippo v. Ford Motor Co.
U.S. Court of Appeals for the Third Circuit, 516 F.2d 1313 (1975)

De Filippo and Fleishman, plaintiffs, became Ford dealers at Chestnut Motors, Inc., in West Philadelphia in 1969. Less than nine months later part of the facility, which had been leased from the previous dealer, was destroyed by fire. Plaintiffs and Ford discussed the possibility of plaintiffs acquiring another dealership in the city. On December 18, 1969, plaintiffs signed a contract under which they were

to purchase the assets, not including real estate, of Presidential Motors. They were to lease the real estate from Ford.

Certain provisions of the contract were more attractive than those for other dealers in the Philadelphia area. As a result, the other dealers protested to Ford. Ford, reconsidering the agreement with plaintiffs, refused to comply with some of its provisions. Plaintiffs then brought suit in a federal district court, charging a violation of federal antitrust laws (to be discussed in Part VIII) and breach of contract.

The district court held for plaintiffs on the antitrust issue and for defendant (Ford) on the breach of contract issue. The latter holding was because the court ruled that the contract *involved the sale of goods,* and, therefore, under one section of Article 2, the contract was not enforceable against Ford because Ford had never signed the contract. (The rule of this section, which generally provides that a sales contract having a price of $500 or more must be signed by the party against whom enforcement is sought—Ford, in this instance—was discussed earlier in Chapter 15.) Plaintiffs received a judgment for over $2.5 million on the antitrust issue, and defendant appealed.

The court of appeals reversed the antitrust decision of the lower court and upheld the breach of contract decision, thereby deciding completely against plaintiffs. That part of the court of appeals' opinion dealing with the breach of contract issue is reproduced below.

Aldisert, Chief Justice:

. . . Whether the December 18th instrument was subject to the UCC Statute of Frauds for the sale of goods, as the trial court concluded, depends on whether the subject matter of the sale falls within the contemplation of "goods" as that term is defined in UCC §2-105. Accordingly, our analysis begins with an examination of the documents involved in the December 18th transaction.

Accompanying the letter signed by plaintiffs were several exhibits, the principal one of which was entitled, "Assets to Be Sold and Computation Price." The document listed: parts and accessories, miscellaneous inventories, work in process, equipment, leasehold improvements, service vehicles, new vehicles, demonstrators, used vehicles, daily rental vehicles, leased vehicles, notes receivables, vehicle receivables, parts and service receivables, contracts covering services, and used car warranties. The exhibit also established a formula for deferring rent on the premises owned by Ford's subsidiary, Leaseco; specifically set forth a method for computing the cost of inventories; and provided: "The purchase price to be paid by the Buyer for the assets to be sold shall be the aggregate sum determined in accordance with the computations and the inventories to be made as specified herein, less $65,000."

. . . Although no [prior] Pennsylvania cases [deal with] the transfer of the assets of an automobile dealership, the Pennsylvania courts had held that the prior Sales Act governed the sale of a whole business. In addition, other jurisdictions have held that motor vehicles are "goods."

For their part, plaintiffs claim an analogue in *Field v. Golden Triangle Broadcasting, Inc.*, 305 A.2d 689 (1973). There, the Pennsylvania Supreme Court was concerned with an agreement for the sale of two radio stations, including FCC licenses and various physical assets. The seller sought to invoke those provisions of the UCC which allow a seller to demand adequate assurance of performance and, in the absence thereof, to suspend his performance. The court stated: "We do not believe that Article 2 of the UCC applies to the instant contract. Rather than being an agreement for the sale of 'goods,' this is a contract for the sale of the businesses of two radio stations, including their tangible and intangible assets, as a going concern."

We believe that *Field* offers plaintiffs little comfort. . . . The factual complex in *Field* is distinct from that in the instant case. There, only $30,000 of the total purchase price of $650,000—or 4.6 per cent—represented physical assets, including nonmovables such as towers and fences. This is to be contrasted with the proposed sale of Presidential Motors in which, we agree with Ford's assessment, the value of movables to be sold was well in excess of three times the value of assets not properly classified as "goods."

For the Statute of Frauds relating to the sale of goods to become applicable, we do not believe every asset subject to the sale must qualify under the "movable" test of UCC §2-105. *Rather than a view of mechanical technicality or of mathematical nicety, a view of the reasonable totality of the circumstances should control the characterization of the contract for sale. If, viewed as a whole, it can be concluded that the essential bulk of the assets to be transferred qualify as "goods," then it is appropriate to consider the transaction a "contract for the sale of goods."* [Emphasis added.] To insist that all assets qualify as "goods" would substantially thwart the intentions of the drafters of the Uniform Commercial Code; it would sanction the absurd. The agreement of sale and purchase could cover physical, movable assets, thus qualifying as "goods," as well as other assets—such as receivables from their particular lines—not so qualifying. But to segregate "goods" assets from "nongoods" assets, and to insist that the Statute of Frauds apply only to a portion of the contract, would be to make the contract divisible and impossible of performance within the intention of the parties.

We believe it preferable to utilize a rule of reasonable characterization of the transaction as a whole. Applying this rule to the facts before us and carefully examining the list of assets to be sold, we note that title to no real estate was to pass in the transaction, nor was any value assigned for good will or the value of the business as a going concern. Accordingly, we have no hesitation in agreeing with the district court's applying UCC §2-201 and its finding that the alleged contract was unenforceable for want of the signature of Ford Motor Company. . . .

The judgment of the district court will be reversed with a direction to enter judgment in favor of appellant Ford Motor Company.

Grossman v. Aerial Farm Service, Inc.
Court of Appeals of Minnesota, 384 N.W.2d 488 (1986)

Grossman owned a farm outside New Ulm, Minnesota, which he rented to the Suess Brothers for the planting of crops. The Suess Brothers contracted with Aerial Farm Service, Inc. (Farm Service) for the sale and application of "2, 4-D" herbicide on a section of the farm. Krause, an employee of Farm Service, sprayed the chemical on the crops. Unfortunately, the spray "drifted from its intended target" and damaged a stand of elm trees adjacent to the field. Grossman then brought this action for damages to his trees, alleging negligent application of the herbicide and breach of contract.

Because Grossman's suit was commenced more than two years after the application, the ultimate question was whether the transaction between the Suess Brothers and Farm Service was a contract for the performance of services, or the sale of goods. If it were a services contract, the action was barred by Minnesota's general two-year statute of limitations. On the other hand, if it were a sales contract, Grossman's action was maintainable under a four-year statute of limitations contained in Minnesota's version of the Uniform Commercial Code. The trial court ruled as a matter of law that the contract was one for services, and entered summary judgment for Farm Service. Grossman appealed.

Nierengarten, Judge:

. . . Grossman argues that the contract for the sale and application of the herbicide is within the coverage of the Uniform Commercial Code, thereby exempting his cause of action from the two-year limitations period of Minn. Stat. §541.07(8). If Grossman's action is within the coverage of the Uniform Commercial Code, he has four years from the date of injury to commence his lawsuit.

Article 2 of the Uniform Commercial Code applies only to transactions or sales of goods. But here, the contract contained both a sale of goods (herbicide) and rendition of services (aerial application of the herbicide).

We have, then, the question of the applicability of Article 2 of the Uniform Commerical Code to mixed goods and services contracts. Both parties agreed that determination of this issue could best be resolved by adopting the test applied in *Bonebrake v. Cox,* 499 F.2d 951 (8th Cir. 1974).

Bonebrake involved the issue of whether a contract dealing with the sale and installation of bowling equipment fell within the provisions of Article 2 of the Uniform Commercial Code. The *Bonebrake* court enumerated the following test to be applied in mixed goods and service contracts:

The test for inclusion or exclusion is not whether [the contracts] are mixed, but, granting that they are mixed, whether their predominant factor, their thrust, their purpose, reasonably stated, is the rendition of service, with goods incidentally involved (e.g., contract with artist for painting) or is a transaction of sale, with labor incidentally involved (e.g., installation of a water heater in a bathroom).

The trial court, applying the *Bonebrake* test, found as a matter of law that the dominant purpose and character of the contract between the Suess Brothers and the Aerial Farm Service was for services (the aerial application of the herbicide), and that sale of the herbicide was merely incidental to the essential service character of the contract, thereby excluding it from coverage of the Uniform Commercial Code.

[The court here rejected Grossman's argument that determination of the predominant purpose of a contract was a factual matter which should have been decided by the jury, rather than being disposed of by a summary judgment, saying]: There are no factual disputes here for the jury to consider, but only a question of whether the predominant purpose of the contract is for goods or services.

There are several methods by which the Suess Brothers could have applied the herbicide, including ground spraying through use of a tractor and trailer. They selected, however, a method of application which could only be performed by a contractor equipped to handle their specific request. By making such selection, the dominant purpose and character of the contract between the Suess Brothers and Farm Service became one for services and, as a result, the transaction did not fall within the scope of the Uniform Commercial Code, and the four-year statute of limitations of the code is not applicable. . . .

Affirmed.

Merchants

For the most part, Article 2 applies to all sales contracts, even those in which neither the seller nor the buyer is a merchant. However, a few provisions of Article 2 do require one or both of the parties to be merchants in order for such provisions to be applicable. For this reason, we will now examine the UCC definition of a **merchant.**

Most people who see the word *merchant* probably think of someone engaged in the retail grocery business, the retail clothing business, or similar endeavors. While such people (or corporations) are indeed merchants, the UCC definition includes many others as well.

Sec. 2-104 of the UCC details three different ways in which a person or organization can be considered a merchant.

1. One who "deals in goods of the kind" that are involved under the particular contract in question is a merchant; thus, not only retailers but also wholesalers and probably even manufacturers are merchants. A party is considered a merchant, however, only for the types of goods dealt with regularly in his or her business. That is, a merchant in one type of goods is not a merchant for all purposes. Thus a retail shoe seller is a merchant with respect to transactions involving the purchase or sale of shoes. But if that person buys a new car or sells a secondhand lawn mower, he or she is not a merchant in those transactions.

2. Even if a person does not regularly "deal" in a particular type of goods, he is nevertheless a merchant if he "by his occupation holds himself out as having knowledge or skill peculiar to the

practices or goods involved in the transaction." While most persons who fall within this provision are also merchants under the first provision by dealing in the particular goods, there are a few who do not really deal in goods but who are merchants within this second category. For example, if we assume that the word *deal* means "to buy and sell goods," a building contractor does not actually deal in goods. He buys building materials but does not resell them; instead he uses them in the performance of a service—constructing a building. However, he does, by his occupation, hold himself out as having "knowledge or skill peculiar to the practices or goods" involved in certain transactions and thereby is a merchant by definition. Of course, his status is irrelevant in any agreement to construct a building, because that agreement is essentially for services and not within the scope of Article 2. But his status as a merchant can be important with respect to a dispute arising from the sale contract between him and his materials supplier.

3. If a party is not a merchant under either of the first two categories, he or she may nevertheless be treated as one by *employing a merchant* to act in his or her behalf in a particular transaction. The UCC states that one is a merchant if one employs "an agent or broker or other intermediary who by his occupation holds himself out" as having knowledge or skill peculiar to the goods or practices involved in the transaction. Suppose, for example, that Smith, who does not regularly deal in grain, hires a professional grain broker to procure a large quantity of feed for Smith's cattle. In this situation Smith is considered a merchant.

The common thread running through all the above categories of merchants is the possession of or access to a degree of commercial expertise not found in a member of the general public. While the UCC usually treats merchants no differently from others, occasionally it applies different standards to them.

In the case that follows, the Supreme Court of Alabama deals with an issue that has posed a problem for several courts in recent years: Is a farmer who sells his crops a merchant?

Loeb & Company, Inc. v. Schreiner
Supreme Court of Alabama, 320 So.2d 199 (1975)

The plaintiff, Loeb and Company, Inc., marketed raw cotton. The defendant, Charles Schreiner, was a farmer who had grown cotton and other crops since 1963.

In April 1973 plaintiff and defendant entered into an oral contract for the sale of 150 bales of cotton. Shortly thereafter the price of cotton more than doubled, and defendant refused to sell his cotton to plaintiff.

Since this contract was for the sale of goods for a price of $500 or more, it was required to be in writing and signed by defendant. (This rule, it may be recalled, was discussed in Chapter 15.) However, according to Sec. 2-201(2) of the UCC, if both seller and buyer are merchants, a later written confirmation of their oral agreement will satisfy this requirement, even if only the sender signs it—so long as the recipient does not make written objection to the terms of the confirmation within ten days after receiving it. In this case plaintiff had sent a confirmation to defendant, and defendant had made no objection. There was no doubt that plaintiff was a merchant. Thus, if defendant was also a merchant, the confirmation could be used to satisfy the statute of frauds even though defendant signed nothing. If he was not a merchant, however, the confirmation would not be a sufficient writing and the contract would be unenforceable.

The trial court ruled that defendant was not a merchant and that the contract was unenforceable. Plaintiff appealed.

Almon, Justice:

. . . Only a few courts have considered the question of whether a farmer is a "merchant." In *Cook Grains v. Fallis,* 395 SW2d 555 (1965), the Arkansas Supreme Court held that a soybean farmer was not a merchant when he was merely trying to sell the commodities he had raised. The court stated that there was not

> . . . *a scintilla of evidence in the record, or proffered as evidence, that appellee is a dealer in goods of the kind or by his occupation holds himself out as having knowledge or a skill peculiar to the practices or goods involved in the transaction, and no such knowledge or skill can be attributed to him.*

In *Oloffson v. Coomer,* 296 NE2d 871 (1973), the Third Division of the Appellate Court of Illinois stated in dictum that a farmer in the business of growing grain was not a "merchant" with respect to the merchandising of grain. However, in *Campbell v. Yokel,* 313 NE2d 628 (1974), the Fifth District of the Appellate Court of Illinois dealt with a case that involved an action against some soybean farmers on an alleged breach of an oral contract for the sale of soybeans. The court held that the soybean farmers, who had grown and sold soybeans for several years were "merchants" when selling crops and were therefore barred by §2-201(2) from asserting the statute of frauds as a defense.

One court has suggested that whether or not a farmer is a "merchant" within the meaning of §2-104 should turn upon whether or not he has engaged in a particular type of sale in the past. In *Fear Ranches, Inc. v. Berry,* 470 F2d 905 (10th Cir. 1972), a breach of warranty case, the court held that where the defendant cattle farmers made a sale to a nonmeatpacker for resale when they had previously sold all of their cattle to meatpackers, they were not "merchants" with respect to the sale to the nonmeatpacker. The court felt that the sale of cattle for resale was a sale of a different type of goods and made up a different type of business than the sale of cattle to meatpackers.

We hold that in the instant case the appellee was not a "merchant" within the meaning of §2-104. We do not think the framers of the Uniform Commercial Code contemplated that a farmer should be included among those considered to be "merchants."

In order for a farmer to be included within the §2-104 definition of "merchants," he must do one of the following:

1. deal in goods of the kind;

2. *by his occupation* hold himself out as having knowledge or skill peculiar to the practices or goods involved in the transaction; or

3. employ an agent or broker or other intermediary who by his occupation holds himself out as having such knowledge or skill.

Since the farmer in the instant case did not qualify as a merchant under 3 above, he would have to qualify under 1 or 2. It is not sufficient under 2 that one hold himself out as having knowledge or skill peculiar to the practices or goods involved, he must *by his occupation* so hold himself out. Accordingly, a person cannot be considered a "merchant" simply because he is a braggart or has a high opinion of his knowledge in a particular area. We conclude that a farmer does not solely *by his occupation* hold himself out as being a professional cotton merchant.

The remaining thing which a farmer might do to be considered a merchant is to become a dealer in goods. Although there was evidence which indicated that the appellee here had a good deal of knowledge, this is not the test. There is not one shred of evidence that appellee ever sold anyone's cotton but his own. He was nothing more than an astute farmer selling his own product. We do not think this was sufficient to make him a dealer in goods.

The official comment to §2-104 states in part as follows:

> *This Article assumes that transactions between* professionals *in a given field require special and clear rules which may not apply to a* casual or inexperienced seller or buyer. *It thus adopts a policy of expressly stating rules applicable "between merchants" and "as against a merchant," wherever [such rules] are needed instead of making them depend upon the circumstances of each case as in the statutes cited above. This section lays the foundation of this policy by defining those who are to be regarded as professionals or "merchants" and by stating when a transaction is deemed to be "between merchants." [Emphasis added by the court.]*

Although a farmer might sell his cotton every year, we do not think that this should take him out of the category of a "casual seller" and place him in the category with "professionals."

If indeed the statute of frauds has, as claimed, permitted an injustice, it is a matter which addresses itself to the legislature.

The judgment is due to be and is hereby affirmed.

Comment: The view taken by the Supreme Court of Alabama, to the effect that a farmer who merely sells his or her own crops is not a merchant, represents what may be called the "traditional" view. However, more recently the courts of approximately half the states have taken the view that the issue should be settled on a case-by-case basis. Thus in *Nelson v. Union Equity Co-operative Exchange,* 548 S.W.2d 352 (1977), the Supreme Court of Texas held that a farmer was a merchant in wheat where, in addition to raising cattle and growing cotton, he regularly raised and sold wheat to grain companies. And in *Dotts v. Bennett,* 382 N.W.2d 85 (1986), the Supreme Court of Iowa upheld a jury verdict finding the defendant-farmer a merchant in hay as a result of periodic sales over a five-year period, even though he did not sell it on a regular basis, sold it only to other farmers, and received only 5 percent of his total income from such sales.

DOCUMENTS OF TITLE

When a sale of goods takes place, the seller may personally deliver the goods or the buyer may personally pick them up at the seller's place of business. It is more common, however, for the goods to be shipped to the buyer by way of a "carrier," such as a trucking, railway, or air cargo company. It is also quite common for a seller to store goods at a warehouse before selling them and for the buyer to pick them up there. In either case, whether the goods are shipped by a carrier or stored in a warehouse, the seller is turning over temporary possession of them to a third party. Such a transaction is called a *bailment.* The owner of the goods is sometimes called a *bailor,* and the party taking temporary possession is sometimes called a *bailee.* The above transactions are certainly not the only instances in which bailments occur, but they are two of the most frequent ones.

When an owner of goods parts with possession in such a manner, he or she is given a receipt for them. If the goods are being shipped and the bailee is a carrier, this receipt is a *bill of lading.*[4] Besides being a receipt for goods, it contains instructions to the carrier regarding destination and the like, as well as the terms of the shipping agreement. If the goods are being stored and the bailee is a warehouseman, the receipt is a *warehouse receipt.* It, too, contains the terms of the storage agreement. Both bills of lading and warehouse receipts are sometimes referred to as *documents of title,* because they provide evidence of title to goods.

Documents of title are governed by Article 7 of the UCC, and are of two basic types: negotiable and nonnegotiable.[5] A **negotiable document of title** is defined by Section 7-104 as one which by its terms specifies that the goods are to be delivered to "bearer" or to the "order" of a named person. Documents not meeting this requirement are **nonnegotiable documents of title**. Following are examples of document of title terms.

1. "Deliver to bearer" (the person who presents the document to the bailee). This is a negotiable document.

2. "Deliver to the order of Dan Owens" (that is, to Dan Owens or to anyone else to whom he has transferred the document by endorsing it). This is a negotiable document.

3. "Deliver to Dan Owens." This is a nonnegotiable document.

A negotiable document is actually more than a mere receipt for the goods and a contract for their carriage or storage. The person who is in legal possession of a negotiable document is entitled to the goods described therein (that is, legal possession of the document is tantamount to ownership of the goods). Thus whoever is in legal possession of a document stating that possession is to be made to "bearer" is entitled to the goods upon presentation of the document to the bailee. Similarly, if a document states that delivery is to be to the "order of Dan Owens," whoever is in legal possession of the document and presents it to the bailee is entitled to the goods if Dan Owens has properly endorsed it.

Legal possession of a nonnegotiable document, on the other hand, is not tantamount to ownership of the goods. Regardless of who presents the document to the bailee, that party will be governed by the instructions of the bailor. The bailee is under a duty to insure that he or she is delivering the goods to the party

---

[4] Technically, the bill of lading is called an *airbill* when air transportation is used.

[5] A negotiable bill of lading is sometimes called an *order bill* and a nonnegotiable one a *straight bill.*

who is supposed to receive them under the bailor's instructions. (The difference between a negotiable and a nonnegotiable document is somewhat akin to the difference between a five-dollar bill and a copy of a contract.)

SUMMARY

Sales law—Article 2 of the UCC—applies to sales of goods: items of tangible personal property, such as books, stereos, and structural steel plate. Contracts calling for the sale of land, or the transfer of intangible property (such as the assignment of contractual rights) are not, therefore, governed by Article 2. A sale is a transfer of title to goods from the seller to the buyer for a price. Contracts calling for the sale of growing crops and timber are sales of goods in all cases, but there are special rules for determining the status of sales of minerals, structures, and fixtures. If a sale contract is "mixed," covering goods and nongoods, the rule is that the contract is a sales contract if the bulk of the assets transferred qualify as goods, and is thus governed by Article 2.

As a general rule, sales law applies to sales by both merchants and nonmerchants. However, a few provisions of Article 2 apply only to sales by merchants, and others only to contracts where both parties are merchants. The courts of about half of the states take the view that a farmer is not a merchant, with the result that he or she is not subject to the special rules applicable to merchant sellers. An almost equal number of courts, however, hold the opposite view.

Sales of goods are frequently made by the transfer of a "document of title" from seller to buyer—e.g., a warehouse receipt or a bill of lading. If the document is "negotiable," the person who is in lawful possession of it is entitled to the goods; that is, such possession is tantamount to ownership of the goods. But if the instrument is nonnegotiable in form, the possessor's rights in the goods are subject to the party who originally delivered them to the warehouse or carrier.

KEY TERMS

Law merchant
Sale
Goods
Merchant
Document of title
Negotiable document of title
Nonnegotiable document of title

QUESTIONS AND PROBLEMS

1. What is the law merchant? What part did it play in the development of our modern law of sales?

2. Why does Article 2 of the UCC not apply to bailments and gifts?

3. Helvey filed suit against Wabash County REMC for breach of a contract to supply electricity to Helvey's furniture factory. During the course of the lawsuit the issue arose as to whether Article 2 of the UCC applied to the dispute. Discuss whether the contract between Helvey and Wabash is covered by Article 2. (*Helvey v. Wabash County REMC,* 278 N.E.2d 608, 1972.)

4. Ernst and Williams agreed to trade an airplane owned by Ernst for an undeveloped residential lot owned by Williams. A dispute arose as to the time, place, and manner of delivering the airplane. Is this dispute governed by the provisions of Article 2? Explain.

5. Hauter agreed to sell 1,500 shares of General Manufacturing Co. common stock to Rogers for $15,000. Later, several terms of the contract became the subject of disagreement between Hauter and Rogers. Hauter filed suit. Does Article 2 govern the transaction? Explain.

6. Playboy Clubs International, Inc., operates a number of hotels and nightclubs. Playboy bought fabrics from Loomskill, Inc., which it was going to have made into costumes for its employees by a third party. A dispute arose between

Playboy and Loomskill regarding the sale. Relevant to this dispute is a section in Article 2 which applies only if Playboy is considered a merchant. Does this section apply? Discuss. (*Playboy Clubs International, Inc., v. Loomskill,* 13 U.C.C. Rep. Serv. 765, 1974.)

7. *Loeb & Company, Inc. v. Schreiner* held that a farmer who sells his crops is not a merchant in those transactions. Argue the contrary position. Support your argument with references to the UCC and to statements made in the *Loeb* case itself.

8. Are there any circumstances in which a university might be considered a merchant? Discuss.

9. What part can documents of title play in a sale of goods? Explain.

10. How can one tell whether a document of title is negotiable or nonnegotiable? What is the basic difference between the rights of a person in legal possession of a negotiable document of title and the rights of a person in legal possession of a nonnegotiable document of title?

Chapter 21

SALES
Title, Risk of Loss,
and Insurable Interest

The ultimate objective of a sale of goods is to transfer from one party to another the rights and responsibilities that accompany ownership. After negotiation and formation of the sale contract, some amount of time will usually pass before this objective is realized. Time may be needed to produce, procure, or manufacture the goods, or simply to take them from inventory and ship them. And the buyer may not wish to receive the goods until some future date even if the seller is capable of immediate delivery.

Many events can occur during the lapse of time preceding the transfer of ownership. The goods may be destroyed by fire, flood, or other act of God. They may be lost or damaged in transit. The seller or buyer, or both, may attempt to obtain a casualty insurance policy on the goods. A government entity may levy a tax on them. During this lapse of time, then, the question often arises as to which of the contracting parties possesses various rights and is subject to various responsibilities regarding the goods.

In this chapter we will examine the rules of Article 2 of the UCC that spell out these rights and responsibilities. All of these rules, however, assume the existence of a valid sales contract (some aspects of which we touched upon in our study of contract law in Part II). For this reason, we begin this chapter with a further word about the rules applicable to the formation and interpretation of sales contracts.

THE SALES CONTRACT, REVISITED

In general, a sales contract must possess the same elements as any other contract; that is, there must be an agreement, consideration (in most instances), a lawful objective, and so forth. By and large, then, the rules of Article 2 applicable to the formation of a sales contract parallel the common-law rules. In Part II, however, we noted a number of sales law rules which *differ markedly* from the common-law principles. For review purposes, they are the following:

• The "open terms" provisions, Sec. 2-204 et seq. (Chapter 11, at p. 247 et seq.)

• The "firm offer" rule, Sec. 2-205. (Chapter 11, at p. 253.)

• The "new term in acceptance" rule, Sec. 2-207. (Chapter 11, at p. 259 et seq.)

• The acceptance of "prompt offers" rule, Sec. 2-206. (Chapter 11, at p. 269.)

• The "modification of contracts" rule, Sec. 2-209. (Chapter 12, at p. 294.)

• The UCC "Statute of Frauds" rule, Sec. 2-201. (Chapter 15 at p. 361 et seq.)[1]

Interpretation of the Sales Contract

The language used by parties to a contract is not always clear and precise. And even where it seems to be straightforward initially, doubt can later arise as to the meaning of a particular word or phrase. Therefore, the need frequently arises for court interpretation of an agreement.

The basic rules used by the courts for interpreting sales contracts are the same as those employed in interpreting other contracts. Since the purpose of interpretation is to determine the *intent* of the parties, the courts decide on the basis of the parties' outward manifestations (their words and conduct), along with the circumstances surrounding the transaction. The essential question is: What would a reasonable person mean in these circumstances by this word, this phrase, or this act?

For the purpose of interpretation, the UCC emphasizes the importance of course of performance, course of dealing, and usage of trade. While these tools were used by courts prior to adoption of the UCC, they have been defined more succinctly by the drafters of this statute.

Course of Performance: In Sec. 2-208(1), **course of performance** is defined in the following manner: "Where the contract for sale in-

---

[1] Additionally, a provision of Article 2 that substantially *parallels* its common-law counterpart—Sec. 2-302, applicable to unconscionable contracts—was examined in Chapter 13.

volves repeated occasions for performance by either party with knowledge of the nature of the performance and opportunity for objection to it by the other, any course of performance accepted or acquiesced in without objection shall be relevant to determine the meaning of the agreement." This aid to interpretation is based simply on how the parties themselves apparently understood the agreement *while they were in the process of performing it.*

Course of Dealing: Section 1-205 defines **course of dealing** as "a sequence of previous conduct between the parties to a transaction which is fairly to be regarded as establishing a common basis of understanding for interpreting their expressions and other conduct." In other words, if the parties in their *past dealings* have always attributed a particular meaning to certain words or actions, this fact may be used by the court to help ascertain what the parties mean in the present case.

Usage of Trade: The same section defines **usage of trade** as "any practice or method of dealing having such regularity of observance in a place, vocation or trade as to justify an expectation that it will be observed with respect to the transaction in question." Thus, if the parties haven't indicated otherwise by their words or conduct, they are treated as having implicitly consented to follow well-established customs of the locale or of the industry in which they are both involved.

Section 2-208(2) goes on to provide that, in any dispute involving a contract's meaning, the express terms of the agreement, and any applicable course of performance, course of dealing, and usage of trade shall be construed by the court, where it is reasonable to do so, "as consistent with each other." However, when such construction is not reasonable, "express terms shall control course of performance and course of performance shall control both course of dealing and usage of trade."

With these considerations in mind, we turn to the most common title, risk of loss, and insurable

interest problems arising out of sales contracts, and to the primary sections of Article 2 designed to resolve such controversies.

TITLE TO GOODS

Prior to enactment of the UCC, all issues of rights and responsibilities were decided by answering a single question: Who had "title" to the goods at the relevant point in time? This procedure often produced fair and logical results, but sometimes it gave rise to poor ones. Different situations can involve different policy considerations and should therefore not be governed by a single standard. Moreover, the courts were never able to develop an objective method of determining the location of title. For these reasons the UCC has abandoned the concept that title determines all questions of rights and responsibilities, and has adopted the approach of identifying specific problems and establishing rules for their solution that do not depend on who had title to the goods at a given time. *The location of title is thus unimportant in resolving most legal issues arising under the UCC.*

However, in some situations title is still a relevant consideration. A few UCC provisions, for example, do make specific mention of title to the goods. Furthermore, application of various laws other than the UCC can depend on the location of title. (For instance, the issue of title can determine the party upon whom certain tax liabilities rest.) These situations make it desirable to discuss specific UCC rules for locating title and a few special problems relating to title. Later in the chapter we will consider the UCC's treatment of two important and related legal problems—who bears the risk in case of casualty to the goods and who has sufficient interest in the goods to obtain insurance coverage.

Passage of Title

Under Sec. 2-105 of the UCC, goods must be *existing* before any interest in them can pass. Thus **future goods** (such as crops to be grown) can be the subject of a sale contract, but no title to them can pass to the buyer until they actually come into existence.

Other rules relating to passage of title are delineated in Sec. 2-401: ✳

1. Goods must be not only existing but also *identified* before title can pass to the buyer. Generally speaking, identification occurs when specific goods are designated as being the subject of the sale contract. Thus, if a seller has an inventory of lumber and agrees to sell a certain described quantity, no title can pass to the buyer until the specific lumber to be sold is marked, segregated, or otherwise identified. This does not mean that title always passes when the goods are identified; identification is simply a condition that must be met before title can pass.

2. Subject to the requirement of identification, title can pass to the buyer in any manner and on any conditions expressly agreed on by the parties.

3. If the parties do not expressly agree as to passage of title, when and where this occurs depends on how the goods are to be delivered. If they are to be shipped to the buyer, title passes to the buyer when the seller "completes his performance with reference to the physical delivery of the goods." In this regard, two situations are possible:

   a. The parties might make a *shipment contract.* Under this type of agreement, the seller is authorized or required to ship the goods to the buyer but is not obligated to see that they actually reach that person. The seller's only obligation is to deliver the goods to a carrier, such as a trucking company, at which time title passes to the buyer.
   b. On the other hand, the parties might make a *destination contract.* In this case the seller is obligated to see that the goods are actually delivered to the buyer. Title passes to the buyer only when that obligation is performed by tendering the goods at their destination. This is true whether the seller ships the goods by independent carrier or personally delivers them to the buyer. (Whether a contract is a shipment contract or a destination contract is usually determined by reference to its FOB terms. To illustrate: a contract is made between a seller in Dallas and a buyer in Miami. If the stated price is "$2,500 FOB Dallas," or "$2,500 FOB seller's plant," it is a shipment contract. On the other hand, if the price is "$2,500 FOB Miami," or "$2,500 FOB buyer's plant," it is a destination contract. In practice, shipment contracts are more common than destination contracts.)[2]

4. Sometimes the parties will agree that delivery to the buyer is to be accomplished *without physically moving the goods.* For example, the contract may require the buyer to pick up the goods at the seller's place of business or at a warehouse owned by a third party. In this situation, title passes at either of two different times, depending on whether a document of title is used.

   a. If the seller is required to deliver a document of title (such as a warehouse receipt) to the buyer, title passes *when the document is delivered.* Thus the buyer can have title to the goods even if he or she leaves them in the possession of the warehouseman for a time.
   b. If the seller is not required to furnish a document of title, passage of title occurs *when the sale contract is made*—if the goods are identified. If the goods are not identified at that time, title passes when identification does occur. (An example of the application of this rule is the situation where the buyer is to pick up the goods at the seller's premises.) These rules are illustrated in Figure 21.1.

Special Problems Regarding Title

Sales by Persons with Imperfect Title: A situation occasionally exists where a party with no title or with imperfect title sells goods to another. To illustrate: Suppose that S sells goods

---

[2] These terms, and other commercial shipping terms, are explained further in Chapter 23.

Figure 21.1 Passage of Title under UCC 2-401

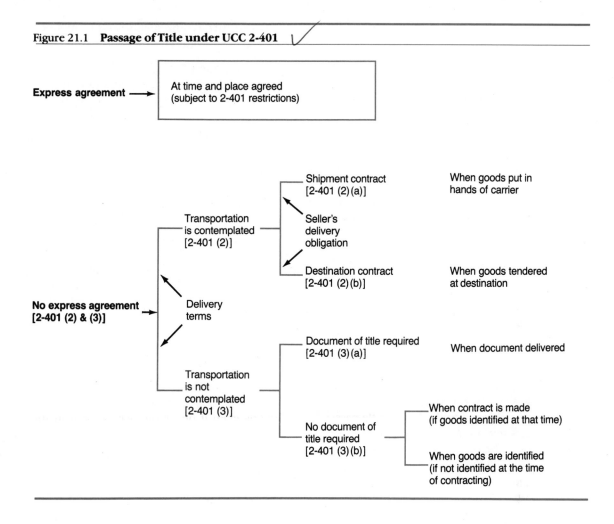

to B. O then appears on the scene and claims to be the true owner or to have some interest in the goods.[3] If O is correct, S will ultimately be responsible for any loss he has caused O or B. Often, however, the real dispute is between O and B over who has the greater right to the goods.

In attempting to resolve the conflict between O and B, UCC Sec. 2-403 focuses on the type of title held by S, distinguishing between a void and a voidable title. If S has a void title (which is actually no title at all), he cannot transfer any interest in the goods to B. The most common example of this situation is where S is a thief. If S has stolen goods from O and then sold them to B, O can reclaim the goods from B—even if B had no knowledge of the theft.

The result may be different if S has a **voidable title** at the time he sells to B. Here S actually has title, but O has the power to void S's title for some reason. Common examples are these:

---

[3] If O is a creditor of S and claims that the goods are the agreed-upon security for the debt, his right to the goods is governed by Article 9 of the UCC, dealing with secured transactions, which is the subject of Chapter 29. At this point we are not dealing with that situation.

1. S purchases the goods from O through fraud.

2. S purchases the goods from O in a "cash on delivery" transaction and pays with a check that bounces.

3. S is insolvent when he purchases the goods on credit from O. In this case, O's power to void S's title and reclaim the goods generally exists for only ten days after S receives the goods. However, under Sec. 2-702(2), if S has misrepresented his solvency to O in writing within three months before delivery, O's power to void S's title and reclaim the goods is not subject to the ten-day limitation.

4. S purchases the goods from O when O is a minor.

If O asserts his rights in any of the above situations while S still has the goods, no particular problems arise. Suppose, however, that S has already sold them to B. Can O reclaim the goods from B? The answer is yes, unless B is classified as a **bona fide purchaser** (BFP). Section 2-403(1) states that "a person with voidable title has power to transfer *good* title" to a BFP. (Emphasis added.) This represents an important exception to the general rule that a person can transfer no better title than he or she has.

A BFP is defined as a "good faith purchaser for value." Thus two requirements must be met before B can be considered a BFP.

1. B must have acted in "good faith." This essentially means that B purchased without notice of the facts that caused S's title to be voidable. ("Notice" means actual knowledge of such facts, or the possession of information that would have caused a reasonably prudent person to discover such facts.)

2. B must have given "value" for the goods, that is, "any consideration sufficient to support a simple contract." B meets the value requirement not only by giving S a usual form of consideration—such as payment in cash or by personal check—but also when B receives the goods in satisfaction of a preexisting claim against S. (However, an unreasonably small consideration might be evidence of bad faith on the part of the buyer.)[4]

The following case illustrates that under Sec. 2-403, a buyer cannot simply ignore suspicious circumstances and then claim to have purchased the goods without notice that the seller's title was voidable.

---

[4]The requirement of value is easier to satisfy for a BFP than for a holder in due course of a negotiable instrument (see Chapter 26 for details).

Landshire Food Service, Inc. v. Coghill
Missouri Court of Appeals, Eastern
District, 709 S.W.2d 509 (1986)

This was an action brought by Hyken and the company he owned, Landshire Food Service, Inc. (hereinafter collectively referred to as Hyken), to be declared the owner of a Rolls Royce Corniche automobile. Hyken had purchased the automobile from a man who had acquired it by giving a bad check to Coghill, the original owner (defendant).

The suit arose out of the following circumstances. In August of 1984 Coghill, an Illinois resident, sold his 1979 Rolls Royce to a person who claimed to be one Daniel Bellman. Bellman gave Coghill a

cashier's check in the amount of $94,000. Coghill dated and signed the Illinois Certificate of Title and filled in the name of "Executive Jet Leasing" on the transferee (buyer) line, as requested by Bellman. Coghill's bank later refused to credit his account because the check was "a forged instrument," and he reported the vehicle as stolen.

Early in September of 1984 Hyken, whose hobby was "trading" in expensive, imported cars, responded to an ad in a St. Louis newspaper for the sale of a 1980 Rolls Royce Corniche. Hyken met the alleged owner (hereinafter "Seller") at a hotel near the St. Louis airport. Hyken questioned Seller about the discrepancy between the year of the car in the newspaper ad (1980) and the actual year of the car (1979). Seller attributed the error to a newspaper misprint. Seller at this time was using defendant's name, Coghill, but later was identified as the same man who had represented himself as Bellman to Coghill. Seller was asking $62,000 for the car.

After inspecting the car, Hyken telephoned Schwartz, a dealer and appraiser of imported automobiles. In Schwarz's opinion, the asking price was at the low side of the fair market value, or "wholesale," and Hyken "could not go wrong" if he bought the car for that amount.

Hyken notified Seller that he intended to purchase the vehicle. When Hyken requested identification, Seller produced a New Hampshire State driver's license with a New Hampshire address, and an air carrier crew card with an Illinois address. Hyken did not question Seller about the disparity between the two addresses. Instead, he accepted Seller's explanation that he presently lived in Illinois but was in the process of relocating in the St. Louis area.

On September 4, 1984, Seller met at Hyken's office to complete the sale of the Rolls Royce. He had with him an Illinois Certificate of Title which was signed by J. A. Coghill as seller, dated August 25, 1984, and showed the transferee (buyer) as "Executive Jet Leasing." Seller explained that this assignment was an attempted transfer to his company which he had not completed on the advice of his accountants. Seller signed an affidavit stating that the first transferee had been inserted by mistake. Hyken confirmed that the serial number on the automobile matched the serial number on the title. Executive Jet Leasing was then crossed out and "Landshire Foods and B. J. Hyken" were written in as transferees. Hyken gave Seller a cashier's check for $58,500 and a check from Landshire Foods for $3,500. On September 17, Hyken registered the title and paid the sales tax. On October 2, the St. Louis County Police took possession of the vehicle at the request of the Illinois authorities, and placed it in a police garage.

In this action by Hyken to recover the car as its owner, the trial court ruled that he failed to qualify as a bona fide purchaser, and entered judgment for defendant, Coghill. Hyken appealed.

The court of appeals first noted that although Seller's completion and delivery of the certificate of title was in conformity with the

Missouri Motor Vehicle statutes, that fact alone did not convey good title to Hyken because Seller had only a voidable title. The higher court then discussed the bona fide purchaser issue in that part of its decision appearing below.

Crandall, Presiding Judge:

. . . The next issue is whether Hyken was a bona fide purchaser under the facts of this case. Where fraud in the original transfer is shown, a subsequent purchaser has the burden of proving that he was in fact a bona fide purchaser. This proof is necessary because, in Missouri, a certificate of title to a motor vehicle is not conclusive proof of the ownership of such vehicle (as explained earlier), but is only prima facie evidence of ownership capable of being rebutted by other evidence.

Case law has established the definition of a bona fide purchaser as one who pays valuable consideration, has no notice of the outstanding rights of others, and who acts in good faith. A buyer will not be protected where he is put on notice of the irregularities in a seller's title either by defects on the face of the certificate or by other circumstances. The requisite notice may be imparted to a prospective purchaser by actual or constructive notice of facts which would place a reasonably prudent person upon inquiry as to the title he is about to purchase.[a]

The trial court, as the trier of fact, was free to believe or to disbelieve any of the testimony. . . . If we view the question of whether Hyken met his burden of proving that he was a bona fide purchaser as one of fact, we must affirm the trial court's determination that he did not meet this burden.

In finding that Hyken was not a bona fide purchaser, the trial court focused on the issue of constructive notice. It considered the following evidence: Hyken's knowledge of a previous transaction, as evidenced by a prior assignment on the Illinois certificate of title; his failure to have Seller re-sign and re-date the certificate of title at the time of sale; his failure to question Seller about the two contradictory home addresses; his recognition that the asking price for the Rolls Royce was at the low end of fair market value; and his failure to verify the existence and status of Executive Jet Leasing, the prior transferee named on the title.

Considering the entire record, we find that there was substantial evidence from which the trial court reasonably could have concluded that the title on its face and the totality of the circumstances surrounding the sale were such that Hyken should have been placed on inquiry as to the title of the automobile. The trial court therefore did not err in holding that he was not a bona fide purchaser. . . .

Judgment of the trial court is affirmed.

---

[a]Constructive notice is information or knowledge of a fact imputed by law to a person (although he or she may not actually have it), because such person could have discovered the fact by the exercise of due diligence.

Entrustment to a Merchant: One additional situation exists in which a seller can transfer a better title to a buyer than the seller actually has. Under Sec. 2-403(2), if an owner entrusts possession of goods to a merchant who deals in goods of that kind, the merchant has the power to transfer good title to a "buyer in the ordinary course of business." Suppose that Owner O leaves her typewriter to be repaired by M, who is in the business of both repairing and selling typewriters. M then sells O's typewriter to a customer, D. If D purchases the typewriter in an ordinary way from M, and if D has no knowledge that the typewriter actually belongs to O, D has good title. O's only remedy is to sue M for damages; she cannot reclaim the typewriter from D.[5] The "entrustment" necessary to bring this rule into effect can also occur if a buyer allows a merchant-seller to remain in possession of the goods after the sale. An obvious purpose of the rule is to facilitate the free flow of trade by relieving ordinary customers from the necessity of inquiring into the status of the merchant's title.[6]

Rights of Seller's Creditors against Goods Sold: If a seller for some reason retains possession of the goods after they have been sold, his or her creditors can be misled by this fact. For example, a lender (a "new creditor") may make a loan to the seller, believing that the seller's assets are greater than they really are. Or a person who had a claim against the seller prior to the sale (an "existing creditor"), under the same erroneous belief, might fail to take timely protective measures that he or she would otherwise have taken.

Because of these possibilities, all states have **fraudulent conveyance statutes** which, while not entirely uniform, generally prescribe the cir-

cumstances in which the seller's retention of sold goods is fraudulent. When such retention in a particular case is found to be fraudulent, the applicable statute gives certain rights to the creditors insofar as the goods are concerned. The drafters of the UCC, wishing not to interfere with these rights that are created under the local law, achieved this purpose in Sec. 2-402. Section 2-402(2) provides, in essence, that if the seller's retention is "fraudulent under any rule of law of the state where the goods are situated," the seller's creditors *can treat the sale as being void* and the goods as being subject to their claims. Even "unsecured creditors" (those not having a lien on the specific goods) possess this power.[7]

The seller's retention of goods after the sale does not always constitute a fraud on creditors. Indeed, Sec. 2-402(2) states that *it is not fraud* for a seller to retain possession in good faith for a "commercially reasonable time." In other words, the retention must be for a legitimate purpose (such as making adjustments or repairs), and the seller must not keep the goods longer than is reasonably necessary to accomplish this purpose. If the criteria of good faith and a commercially reasonable time are met, the seller's unsecured creditors cannot void the sale.

Retention of possession is not the only way a seller can defraud his or her creditors. Sometimes the sale itself is fraudulent and can be voided by the creditors regardless of who has possession. For instance, a sale made for less than "fair consideration" (thereby depleting the seller's assets) is a fraud on the seller's creditors in either of the following two situations: (1) where the seller is *insolvent* (liabilities exceed assets) at the time of the sale or is made insolvent by the sale, or (2) where the evidence proves that the seller actually intended to hinder, delay, or defraud the creditors. These rules are intended to protect creditors from an attempt by the seller to conceal his or her assets

---

[5] D's purchase would not be in the "ordinary course of business," however, if he received the typewriter as security for or in satisfaction of a preexisting debt owed to him by M. D also would not be buying in the ordinary course of business if the typewriter was part of a bulk purchase of all or a substantial part of M's inventory.

[6] But even though D can acquire greater title in this situation than M had, D's title can be no better than O's.

---

[7] The rights of "secured" creditors will be discussed in Chapter 29.

through a sham transaction (usually with a friend or relative).

Bulk Transfers: Suppose that a merchant owing money to creditors sells his or her inventory to a third party. If the merchant uses the proceeds to pay the debts as they fall due, no problems arise. But what if he or she pockets the money and disappears, leaving the creditors unpaid? Can these creditors lay any claim to goods that are now in the buyer's hands? If the buyer has paid a fair consideration, the sale is not fraudulent under the rules just discussed.

In such a case, however, if the sale constitutes a "bulk transfer" (or bulk sale, as it is commonly called), the merchant's creditors may be protected by Article 6 of the UCC. The basic rules of that article are as follows:

1. A **bulk transfer** is any transfer (sale) "in bulk and not in the ordinary course of the transferor's business" of a major part of the inventory of an enterprise whose principal business is the sale of merchandise from inventory.

2. Before the bulk transfer takes place, the seller must furnish a list of his or her creditors to the buyer. Then the seller and buyer must prepare a list of the property to be sold. Finally, the buyer must notify the seller's creditors of the bulk sale at least *ten days* before taking possession of or paying for the goods (whichever occurs first). This notice enables creditors to take steps to protect themselves; for example, they can impound the proceeds of the sale if they deem it necessary.

3. If the buyer fails to comply with this advance notice requirement, the sale is ineffective against the seller's existing creditors. (Those who become creditors after the notice is given are not entitled to any notice.) That is, in seeking to obtain satisfaction of their claims, the seller's creditors can treat the goods as still belonging to the seller. For example, a creditor might obtain judgment against the seller and then levy execution on the goods (have them seized) even though they are in the buyer's hands. The creditor must do so, however, within *six months* after the buyer takes possession.

4. Even if a bulk transfer is ineffective because proper notice has not been given, the buyer can transfer good title to a BFP.

RISK OF LOSS

A warehouse fire damages thousands of dollars' worth of goods. A truck, train, ship, or airplane is involved in an accident that destroys a substantial quantity of goods. In these kinds of situations the question may arise as to who must bear the financial burden of the loss.

The **risk of loss** question is especially provocative when the goods are the subject of a sale contract at the time of damage or destruction. The risk that the goods will suffer some casualty initially rests on the seller, but ultimately it passes to the buyer. The crucial issue is whether the risk had passed from the seller to the buyer at the time of the loss. If it had not yet passed, the financial loss is borne by the seller. (Whether the seller in such a case also remains responsible to fulfill the contract with the buyer is a separate issue, to be discussed in Chapter 23.) If it had already passed, the buyer must bear the loss. This means that the buyer is obligated to pay for the goods if payment had not yet been made, and he or she is not entitled to a refund of any payment already made.

The existence of insurance coverage does not lessen the importance of this question; it simply means that the real issue is whose insurance company must bear the loss. Of course, insurance coverage may be inadequate or totally lacking in a given case. If the goods are damaged, lost, or destroyed while in possession of a bailee such as a carrier or warehouseman, the bailee will often be liable (see Chapter 43 for details). The risk of loss question in such a case is still important, however, because it determines whether the seller or buyer bears the burden of pursuing the bailee for a remedy.

As mentioned earlier in this chapter, risk of loss does not automatically pass with title. In resolving the problem of who bears the risk, the UCC differentiates between two situations: (1) where the contract has not been breached when the loss occurs, and (2) where there has been a breach at the time of the loss.

Risk of Loss Where the Contract Is Not Breached

The rules for placing the risk of loss in the ordinary situation are found in Sec. 2-509, as follows:

1. As was the case with passage of title, the parties can make any agreement regarding the time at which risk of loss passes from seller to buyer.

2. Where there is no agreement as to when the risk passes, the issue is based on *how the goods are to be delivered.* Where the sale contract requires or authorizes the seller to ship the goods by carrier, the timing of the passage of risk depends on the seller's obligation.

    a. If the parties have made a *shipment contract,* in which the seller's obligation is completed upon shipment of the goods, the risk of loss passes to the buyer under Sec. 2-509(1)(a) when the goods are "duly delivered" to the carrier by the seller. In most cases, a due delivery occurs when the seller *puts the goods in the possession of the carrier.* Any loss occurring thereafter falls on the buyer. (The basic shipment section, Sec. 2-504, also requires the seller (1) to make a reasonable transportation contract with the carrier, including delivery to the buyer of any documents necessary for the buyer to take possession of the goods, and (2) to promptly notify the buyer of the shipment—actions that are, in fact, usually performed by the seller as a matter of routine. However, that section goes on to provide that if the seller fails to perform either of these additional acts, the buyer may reject the shipment only if "material loss ensues"—a clause that most courts interpret as meaning "ensues *as a result of* such failure." Because most cases of loss or damage during shipment are caused by factors unrelated to the seller's nonperfor-

mance of either of these duties, the usual result is that the buyer must accept and pay for goods damaged or lost in the carrier's possession even in those cases where the seller fails to perform either of these additional duties.)

    b. If the parties have made a *destination contract,* in which the seller is obligated to see that the goods are actually delivered to the buyer, the risk of loss passes only upon fulfillment of that obligation *by the seller tendering the goods at their destination* under Sec. 2-509(1)(b).

    Generally, in 2a and 2b situations, the rules governing risk of loss essentially correspond to those governing passage of title—though differences in wording between the two sections occasionally give rise to a situation where title and risk of loss do not pass at exactly the same time.

3. Sometimes the goods at the time of sale are being held by a **bailee** and are to be delivered *without being moved.* For example, they might be stored in a warehouse, the buyer intending to pick them up there or perhaps to leave them in storage until they are resold to someone else. In such a case, the placing of the risk of loss hinges primarily on whether the bailee has issued a document of title (warehouse receipt) and, if so, what type of document it is. Under Sec. 2-509(2):

    a. If a *negotiable* document of title has been issued for the goods, the risk of loss passes to the buyer when he or she receives the document. Since the holder of a negotiable document generally has an automatic right to receive the goods, it is logical to place the risk of loss on that person.

    b. If a *nonnegotiable* document of title has been issued, the problem is different. A buyer with this kind of document is not as well protected as one who has a negotiable document. This person can, for example, lose his or her right to the goods to some third party, such as a creditor of the seller or a purchaser from the bailee. And the buyer does not actually have a right to the goods until he or she *notifies the* *bailee of the purchase.* (Indeed, the buyer does not have to accept a nonnegotiable document as performance by the seller; but if the buyer does not object, the seller can satisfy his or her performance requirements with such a document.) Logically, then, the buyer's receipt of a nonnegotiable document does not immediately shift the risk of loss to that person. In fact, the risk does not pass to the buyer until he or she has had a *reasonable amount of time* to present the document to the bailee and demand the goods; and, of course, the risk does not shift if the bailee refuses to honor the document.

c. When the bailee holds goods for which *no document of title* has been issued and the seller wishes to sell the goods without moving them, he or she can do so in either of two ways. First, the seller can give the buyer a writing that directs the bailee to deliver the goods to the buyer. Risk of loss in this instance is determined in the same way as if a nonnegotiable document of title had been issued. Second, the seller can obtain from the bailee an acknowledgment that the buyer is entitled to the goods. In this case, risk of loss passes to the buyer when the bailee acknowledges the buyer's right to possession.

4. Some situations are not covered by any of the foregoing rules. Two common examples are transactions in which the buyer picks up the goods at the seller's premises or in which the seller personally delivers the goods to the buyer (rather than shipping by independent carrier). In such cases, the time at which the risk of loss shifts to the buyer depends on whether the seller is a *merchant.* The rules set forth below are found in Sec. 2-509(3).

If the seller is a merchant, his or her responsibility is somewhat greater than that borne by the nonmerchant; thus the risk of loss does not pass from seller to buyer until the buyer *actually receives the goods.* If the seller is *not* a merchant, the risk of loss passes to the buyer when the seller "tenders" delivery. (The concept of *tender* is discussed in greater detail in Chapter 23, but it essentially means that the seller has placed at the buyer's disposal goods conforming to the contract requirements and has notified the buyer so as to enable that person to take possession.) Suppose, for example, that B purchases a new car from S, a dealer. S is supposed to install an AM-FM radio and speaker system before B takes possession of the car. S does the work and parks the car on his lot, then telephones B and informs her that the car is ready. Before B picks up the car, it is severely damaged by a hailstorm. S must bear the loss. *Since he is a merchant, the risk does not shift to B until the latter actually takes possession.* If S had been an individual selling his personal car, the loss would have been borne by B because risk of loss in that case would have passed to B *at the time of the tender*—the phone call from S prior to the storm.

The preceding points regarding risk of loss are capsulated in Figure 21.2.

The following case presents a typical situation in which determination of the time of passage of risk of loss becomes all important.

Lumber Sales, Inc. v. Brown
Court of Appeals of Tennessee, 469 S.W.2d 888 (1971)

Lumber Sales, Inc., plaintiff, contracted to sell and deliver five carloads of lumber to Brown, the defendant, under a destination contract. Brown received four carloads of lumber and paid for them. He refused to pay for the fifth carload, however, because it was appar-

Figure 21.2 **Risk of Loss**

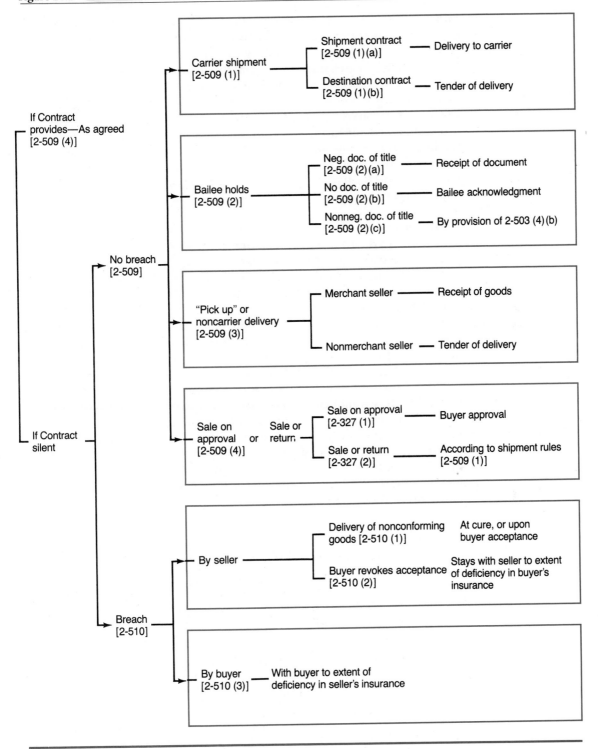

ently stolen before he was able to take possession of it. Plaintiff then brought this action to recover the purchase price of the fifth carload.

The pertinent facts surrounding the loss of the lumber were undisputed. The parties had agreed that the lumber was to be delivered at a railroad siding about one-half mile from defendant's place of business. It was known as a "team track," which means that it was available for use by several parties which, in this case, included defendant. Track location 609-A on this siding was a point where a loading platform was located.

During the early morning hours of November 27, 1968, the Louisville and Nashville Railroad (the carrier) placed a boxcar loaded with lumber consigned to the defendant on this siding at track location 609-A.

This boxcar was inspected by an employee of the carrier between 8:00 a.m. and 8:30 a.m. on November 27, at which time it was found loaded with cargo, and was so designated upon the carrier's records.

At 11:07 a.m. on November 27 the carrier notified one of defendant's employees that the carload of lumber had been delivered at track location 609-A.

At approximately 4:00 p.m. on that same day an employee of the carrier again inspected the boxcar, found one of the seals on it to be broken, and he resealed it at that time. (There was no evidence to show whether the car was still loaded at that time or not.)

The following day, November 28, was Thanksgiving Day, and there was no evidence that the carrier inspected the boxcar on that date. But on November 29 an employee of the carrier inspected the car between 8:00 a.m. and 8:30 a.m., and found it empty.

The trial court, on the above facts and additional evidence appearing below, held for plaintiff on the basis of its finding that the lumber had been delivered and the risk of loss had passed to defendant prior to the theft. Defendant appealed.

Puryear, Justice:

. . . From evidence in the record before us it is impossible to reach any logical conclusion as to what happened to the carload of lumber without indulging in speculation and conjecture; but the defendant earnestly insists that he did not unload it, and there is no evidence to the contrary.

The particular Code Section applicable here is Sub-section (1) of 2-509, as follows:

Risk of loss in the absence of breach.—*(1) Where the contract requires or authorizes the seller to ship the goods by carrier. . . (b) if it does require him to deliver them at a particular destination and the goods are there duly tendered while in the possession of the carrier, the risk of loss passes to the buyer when the goods are there duly so tendered as to enable the buyer to take delivery.*

The trial court held that the risk of loss in this case did, in fact, pass to the defendant buyer [at 11:07 a.m. on November 27].

Now let us further examine the evidence for the purpose of determining whether or not it preponderates against this conclusion of the trial Court.

There is competent evidence in the record which shows that on November 27 at 11:07 a.m. the carrier notified the defendant's employee, Mr. Caldwell, at defendant's business office, that the carload of lumber had been delivered at track location 609-A. Mr. Caldwell did not testify, so this evidence is uncontroverted.

There is no evidence in the record to the effect that the defendant declined to accept delivery at that time or asked for a postponement of such delivery until a later time.

The defendant testified that it would normally require about four or five hours for him and his employees to unload a carload of lumber and that on November 27 he and his employees were so busily engaged in other necessary work that he could not unload the lumber on that day and since the following day was Thanksgiving, he could not unload it until November 29, at which time, of course, the carrier found the car to be empty. . . .

One Kenneth E. Crye, freight agent of the carrier, Louisville and Nashville Railroad Company, testified that on Thanksgiving Day, November 28th, he saw what he believed to be a railroad car being unloaded at track location 609-A, but he could not identify the car or the persons whom he believed to be unloading it. He qualified this testimony by saying that he was not positive that the car was being unloaded, but there was some lumber and some kind of activity on the platform, none of which appeared to be unusual.

From evidence in the record, a trier of fact could logically form one of two inferences:

(1) That the lumber was either stolen or unloaded by mistake by someone other than the defendant at some time between 8:30 a.m. and 11:07 a.m. on November 27th; or (2) that it was stolen or unloaded at some time after 11:07 a.m. November 27th. . . .

If the first inference should be formed, then the issue should be found in favor of defendant [because the risk during that time was still with plaintiff-seller.] But if the second inference should be formed, then the issue should be found in favor of plaintiff if it could also be found that the loss occurred after defendant had sufficient time to protect himself against loss after notice of delivery.

We think the second inference is the more logical of the two, especially in view of the difference between the two intervals of time and also in view of Mr. Crye's testimony to the effect that on Thanksgiving Day, November 28th, he observed some activity at track location 609-A, which he believed to be unloading of a railroad car at that location.

Of course, we recognize and adhere to the rule that the burden of proof is upon plaintiff to prove delivery of the lumber and we are not required to indulge either of the above mentioned inferences because the trial Court . . . concluded that the plaintiff had successfully carried the burden of proof . . . and the evidence does not preponderate against that Court's conclusion.

Counsel for defendant argues that the lumber in question was not duly "*so tendered as to enable the buyer to take delivery*" as required by 2-509.

However, this argument seems to be based upon the premise that it was not convenient for the defendant to unload the lumber on November 27th, the day on which it was delivered at track location 609-A and defendant was duly notified of such delivery.

This was an ordinary business day and the time of 11:07 a.m. was a reasonable business hour. If it was not convenient with the defendant to unload the lumber within a few hours after being duly notified of delivery, then he should have protected himself against risk of loss by directing someone to guard the cargo against loss by theft and other hazards.

To hold that the seller or the carrier should, under the circumstances existing in a case of this kind, continue to protect the goods until such time as the buyer may find it convenient to unload them would impose an undue burden upon the seller or the carrier and unnecessarily obstruct the channels of commerce.

The language of Sub-section (1)(b) of 2-509 does not impose such a burden upon the seller, in the absence of some material breach of the contract for delivery, and we think a reasonable construction of such language only requires the seller to place the goods at the buyer's disposal so that he has access to them and may remove them from the carrier's conveyance without lawful obstruction, with the proviso, however, that due notice of such delivery be given to the buyer. . . .

[Affirmed.]

Effect of Breach on Risk of Loss

When one of the parties has breached the contract, that party sometimes is required to shoulder a risk that he or she otherwise would not have to bear. This risk is, of course, in addition to any damages that the party may have to pay. Section 2-510 sets forth three basic rules to cover such situations; rules 1 and 2 apply to breaches by the seller arising out of the delivery of nonconforming goods, while rule 3 applies to breaches by the buyer.

1. When a seller tenders or delivers goods that do not conform to the requirements of the contract, the buyer usually has a right to *reject* the goods. In such a case, the risk of loss does not pass to the buyer until the seller "cures" the defect or the buyer accepts the goods despite their nonconformity.[8] Suppose that S and B have made a shipment contract for the sale of some office furniture. The risk of loss in this situation ordinarily passes to the buyer when the goods are duly delivered to the carrier. However, in this case some of the furniture is improperly upholstered. On receiving and inspecting the furniture, B rejects the shipment. The risk remains with S until he reupholsters the defective pieces of furniture or substitutes good pieces for the bad ones. However, if B had accepted the shipment despite its defects, the risk would have passed to him on acceptance. In other words, if the nonconforming shipment is destroyed or damaged (through no fault of the buyer) prior to cure or acceptance, the loss falls on S.

---

[8] The circumstances under which the buyer can reject goods are discussed in Chapter 23. And, in speaking of cure, we are assuming here that the seller has a right to do so—which may or may not be the case. If the seller does not have the right, he or she cannot cure the defect and then force the buyer to take the goods. (The subject of cure is also treated more fully in Chapter 23.)

2. In some situations, a buyer who has accepted goods can *revoke the acceptance.* Suppose, for example, that B does not discover the defect until after he has accepted the shipment. (The circumstances in which B has a right to revoke his acceptance will be discussed in Chapter 23. Here, assume that B does have this right.) If B revokes his acceptance, the risk of loss is treated as having remained with S from the beginning. However, the risk borne by S is *only to the extent that B's insurance coverage is deficient.* Suppose, for example, that the value of the goods is $10,000 but that B has insurance coverage of only $5,000. If the goods are destroyed through no fault of either party (for example, by flood or fire), S will bear a loss of $5,000 and B's insurance company will bear the remaining $5,000 loss. If B had had no insurance, S would have borne the entire loss. If B's insurance had covered the entire loss, S would have borne none of it.

3. Situations 1 and 2 involved a breach by the *seller.* What effect does a breach by the *buyer* have on the risk of loss? Stated simply, a breach of the contract by the buyer immediately shifts the risk of loss to him or her. Of course, the risk shifts only if, before B's breach, specific goods had already been identified as the subject of the contract. For example, S might ship conforming goods and B might wrongfully reject them on their arrival. Or, after specific goods had been identified, but before shipment, B might notify S that he will not comply with the contract. In either case, the risk of loss immediately shifts to B even if it would not have passed until later had B not breached the contract. B must bear the risk, however, *only for a reasonable time thereafter* and *only to the extent that S's insurance coverage is deficient.*

In the case that follows, the issues are (a) whether the buyer breached, and (b) if so, how the rules summarized in 3 above would apply.

Multiplastics, Inc. v. Arch Industries, Inc.
Supreme Court of Connecticut, 348 A.2d 618 (1974)

The plaintiff, Multiplastics, Inc., brought this action to recover damages from the defendant, Arch Industries, Inc., for the breach of a contract to purchase 40,000 pounds of plastic pellets.

Plaintiff, a manufacturer of plastic resin pellets, agreed with defendant on June 30, 1971, to manufacture and deliver 40,000 pounds of brown polystyrene plastic pellets for nineteen cents a pound. The pellets were specially made for defendant, who agreed to accept delivery at the rate of 1,000 pounds per day after completion of production. Defendant's confirming order contained the notation, "Make and hold for release. Confirmation." Plaintiff produced the order of pellets within two weeks and requested release orders from defendant. Defendant refused to issue the release orders, citing labor difficulties and its vacation schedule. On August 18, 1971, plaintiff sent defendant the following letter:

Against P.O. 0946, we produced 40,000 lbs. of brown high impact styrene, and you have issued no releases. You indicated to us that you would be using 1,000 lbs. of each per day. We have warehoused these products for more than forty days, as we agreed to do. However, we cannot warehouse these products indefinitely, and request that you send us shipping instructions. We have done everything we agreed to do.

After August 18, 1971, plaintiff made numerous telephone calls to defendant to seek payment and delivery instructions. In response, beginning August 20, 1971, defendant agreed to release orders but in fact never did.

On September 22, 1971, plaintiff's plant, containing the pellets manufactured for defendant, was destroyed by fire. Plaintiff's fire insurance did not cover the loss of the pellets, and plaintiff brought action against defendant to recover the contract price.

The trial court concluded that (1) plaintiff had made a valid tender of delivery by its letter of August 18, 1971, and by its subsequent requests for delivery instructions; (2) defendant had repudiated and breached the contract by refusing to accept delivery on August 20, 1971; (3) the period from August 20, 1971, to September 22, 1971, was not a commercially unreasonable time for plaintiff to treat the risk of loss as resting on defendant under UCC Sec. 2-510(3); and (4) plaintiff was entitled to recover the contract price plus interest. Defendant appealed.

Bogdanski, Justice:

. . . [Section] 2-510, entitled "Effect of breach on risk of loss," reads, in pertinent part, as follows: "(3) Where the buyer as to conforming goods already identified to the contract for sale repudiates or is otherwise in breach before risk of their loss has passed to him, the seller may to the extent of any deficiency in his effective insurance coverage treat the risk of loss as resting on the buyer for a commercially reasonable time." The defendant contends that §2-510 is not applicable because its failure to issue delivery instructions did not constitute either a repudiation or a breach of the agreement. The defendant also argues that even if §2-510 were applicable, the period from August 20, 1971, to September 22, 1971, was not a commercially reasonable period of time within which to treat the risk of loss as resting on the buyer. . . .

The trial court's conclusion that the defendant was in breach is supported by its finding that the defendant agreed to accept delivery of the pellets at the rate of 1,000 pounds per day after completion of production. The defendant argues that since the confirming order instructed the [plaintiff] to "make and hold for release," the contract did not specify an exact delivery date. This argument fails, however, because nothing in the finding suggests that the notation in the confirming order was part of the agreement between the parties. Since, as the trial court found, the plaintiff made a proper tender of delivery, beginning with its letter of August 18, 1971, the plaintiff was entitled to acceptance of the goods and to payment according to the contract. . . .

The remaining question is whether, under §2-510(3), the period of time from August 20, 1971, the date of the breach, to September 22, 1971, the date of the fire, was a "commercially reasonable" period within which to treat the risk of loss as resting on the buyer. The trial court concluded that it was "not, on the facts in this case, a commercially unreasonable time," which we take to mean that it was a commercially reasonable period. The time limitation in §2-510(3) is designed to enable the seller to obtain the additional requisite insurance coverage. . . . [Under the particular facts of this case,] August 20 to September 22 was a commercially reasonable period within which to place the risk of loss on the defendant. As already stated, the trial court found that the defendant repeatedly agreed to transmit delivery instructions and that the pellets were specially made to fill the defendant's order. Under those circumstances, it was reasonable for the plaintiff to believe that the goods would soon be taken off its hands and so to forego procuring the needed insurance.

We consider it advisable to discuss one additional matter. The trial court concluded that "title" passed to the defendant, and the defendant attacks the conclusion on this appeal. The issue is immaterial to this case. [Section] 2-401 states: "Each provision of this article with regard to the rights, obligations and remedies of the seller, the buyer, purchasers or other third parties applies irrespective of title to the goods except where the provision refers to such title." As one student of the Uniform Commercial Code has written:

The single most important innovation of Article 2 is its restatement of . . . [the parties'] responsibilities in terms of operative facts rather than legal conclusions; where pre-Code law looked to "title" for the definition of rights and remedies, the Code looks to demonstrable realities such as custody, control and professional expertise. This shift in approach is central to the whole philosophy of Article 2. It means that disputes, as they arise, can focus, as does all of the modern law of contracts, upon actual provable circumstances, rather than upon a metaphysical concept of elastic and endlessly fluid dimensions. Peters, "Remedies for Breach of Contracts Relating to the Sale of Goods Under the Uniform Commercial Code: A Roadmap for Article Two." 73 Yale L.J. 199, 201. . . .

[Affirmed.]

INSURABLE INTEREST

Parties often obtain insurance coverage to protect themselves against the possibility that property in which they have an interest might be lost, damaged, or destroyed. An insurance policy is valid only if the party purchasing the protection has an **insurable interest.** Whether a party has this in a given situation is primarily a matter of insurance law rather than sales law. Article 2 of the UCC does, however, contain certain rules regarding insurable interest in goods.

Seller's insurable interest. So long as the seller has title to the goods, he or she obviously has an insurable interest. But even if title passes to the buyer, the seller continues to have an insurable interest—and can insure the goods—so long as he or she has a "security interest" (a lien or mortgage to secure payment) in the goods.

Buyer's insurable interest. The buyer obtains an insurable interest and can insure the goods as soon as they have been identified as the subject of the sale contract.

Under these rules, seller and buyer can both have an insurable interest in the same goods at the same time. Of course, even if a party has an insurable interest and obtains insurance coverage, that person has no right to recover from the insurance company unless he or she actually sustains a loss.

In the following case, the defendant, an insurance company, sought to be relieved of responsibility for the plaintiff's damaged airplane on the ground that plaintiff no longer had an insurable interest in the craft.

Bowman v. American Home Assurance Co.
Supreme Court of Nebraska, 213 N.W.2d 446 (1973)

This was an action by James Bowman, the owner of an airplane, against his insurance company to collect under the policy for damage done to the plane when it was involved in an accident. The insurance company refused to pay, claiming that a few days prior to the accident Bowman had sold the plane to a third party, Hemmer. Thus, the company contended, Bowman did not have an insurable interest in the plane, and thus no effective insurance coverage, at the time of the loss.

The salient facts were not in dispute. Bowman, plaintiff, was a partner in a firm in Fremont, Nebraska. The partnership purchased the twin-engine Cessna in 1969. Bowman obtained insurance on the plane, in his own name, from American Home Assurance Company, defendant. The insurance policy covered the period from December 23, 1969, through December 23, 1970.

In early December of 1970 Bowman and James Hemmer entered into negotiations for the sale of the plane to Hemmer. On December 12 Bowman contracted to sell the plane to Hemmer for $18,500, and Hemmer paid $15,000 down. Hemmer requested a bill of sale signed by both partners, to protect himself and to comply with the Federal Aviation Administration requirements for the transfer of ownership of an aircraft. (The bill of sale was to be delivered to Hemmer later.)

At the time of the trial Bowman and Hemmer both testified as to their understanding at the time of making the contract on December 12, 1970. Bowman testified that it was agreed that he was to remain the owner of the aircraft until "we were able to fill out the necessary paperwork." Hemmer similarly testified that he was to be the owner when he received the bill of sale. Bowman also testified that he told Hemmer that he would leave his insurance in effect until it expired on December 23, 1970, only 11 days later. Bowman retained possession of the plane.

On December 15, 3 days after making the contract, Hemmer asked Bowman for permission to use the plane on the following Friday and Saturday. Bowman and Hemmer specifically examined Bowman's insurance policy to determine whether it would provide coverage while Hemmer flew the plane. Bowman then gave Hemmer permission to fly the plane to Columbus, Nebraska, and thence to Mitchell, South Dakota, and return. On December 18, when Hemmer attempted to take off from Mitchell, the plane was extensively damaged when the tip of a wing caught in a snowbank.

In Bowman's action against the insurance company the jury, in response to two special interrogatories, found (1) that the seller had not completed physical delivery of the plane prior to the accident; and (2) that the parties had agreed that title was not to pass until the necessary paperwork was done, and that this paperwork had not been completed prior to the accident. On the basis of these facts, the trial court ruled that Bowman had an insurable interest in the plane at the time of the accident and entered judgment in his favor. The insurance company appealed.

White, Chief Justice:

. . . Hemmer testified that the Federal Aviation Administration regulations require that a registration certificate be in an aircraft before title to the plane can be transferred to a new owner, and that once the bill of sale is received, it is attached to a new registration application and sent to the Federal Aviation Administration. A pink copy of the new registration is placed in the aircraft to serve as a temporary registration. This paperwork had not been completed at the time of the loss because the bill of sale had not yet been received. The registration certificate in the aircraft at the time of the accident showed James Bowman as the owner.

The signature of Bowman's partner was obtained and the bill of sale was mailed to Hemmer on December 18, the day of the accident. Hemmer received the bill of sale on December 20. The bill of sale was in blank form and had not been filled out at the time Hemmer received it. It was understood that Hemmer was to fill out the necessary information on the bill of sale. Bowman filed an accident report after the accident and indicated he was the owner.

The controversy between the parties centers around two provisions of the Uniform Commercial Code. Section 2-501, UCC, provides in part: "(2) The seller retains an insurable interest in goods so long as title to or any security interest in the goods remains in him." . . .

Section 2-401, UCC, details the concept of passage of title: "(2) *Unless otherwise explicitly agreed* title passes to the buyer at the time and place at which the seller completes his performance with reference to the physical delivery of the goods, despite any reservation of a security interest and even though a document of title is to be delivered at a different time or place." . . . (Emphasis supplied.)

As section 2-501, UCC, provides, the seller has an insurable interest until the title passes to the buyer. Under section 2-401, UCC, title passes to the buyer (1) at the time and place where the seller completes his performance with reference to the physical delivery of the goods or (2) at any other time explicitly agreed to by the parties. As dictated by the Uniform Commercial Code, the trial court submitted two factual questions to the jury. First, whether the seller had completed physical delivery of goods. Second, whether there was an explicit agreement between the buyer and the seller as to the time when title was to pass. A jury finding in favor of the insured upon either of these factual issues supports the verdict. Where reasonable minds might draw different inferences or conclusions from the evidence, it is within the province of the jury to decide the issues of fact and the jury verdict will not be set aside unless it is clearly wrong.

There was substantial evidence from which the jury could have inferred that the seller had not completed physical delivery of the goods. The evidence shows that the buyer was only given limited use of the plane to make the trip to South Dakota. The buyer even asked the seller for permission to use the plane for this one trip. The seller had only granted a limited possession of the plane to the buyer, even though the buyer had possession of the plane for 3 days prior to the accident.

The jury could have also inferred from the evidence that the buyer and seller had an explicit agreement that title was to pass upon the completion of the "necessary paperwork." The code itself provides no definition of the term "explicit" as used in section 2-401, U.C.C. In *Harney v. Spellman,* 251 N.E.2d 265 (1969), the court defined "explicit" in reference to section 2-401, UCC, as follows: "The term 'explicit' means that which is so clearly stated or distinctly set forth that there is no doubt as to its meaning." . . .

Bowman testified that it was agreed that he was to remain the owner of the aircraft until "we were able to fill out the necessary paperwork." The only other testimony by Bowman on this subject was the testimony of Bowman on cross-examination that he thought a sale had occurred on December 12, 1970. On redirect, however, Bowman testified that he meant an agreement to sell the plane was entered into on December 12, 1970. The buyer testified numerous times that there was an agreement that he was to be the owner when he received the bill of sale. This was to allow the buyer to complete the Federal Aviation Administration requirements and make arrangements for insurance prior to the time he was to become the owner. From all this testimony the jury could infer that there was an explicit agreement. The credibility of the witnesses and weight to be given to their testimony are for the triers of fact. On the record as a whole, we cannot conclude that there was not sufficient evidence to support a jury finding that there was an explicit agreement as to the passage of title of the aircraft.

The evidence showed that the bill of sale sent to the buyer from the sellers on the day of the accident was not signed by both sellers until the day of the accident. The bill of sale was not received by the buyer until several days after the accident, and even at this time it remained in blank form. The parties knew that the buyer would fill in and complete the bill of sale after he received it. Thus, it is clear from the evidence that "completion of the necessary paperwork" involved more than the mere signing of the bill of sale by both sellers. It at least included receipt of the blank bill of sale by the buyer, but it could also have included the action of the buyer in filling out the necessary Federal Aviation Administration papers and completing the bill of sale. None of the above steps had been completed at the time of the accident, and therefore the time of the completion of the necessary paperwork had not occurred at the time of the accident.

In summary, the jury could reasonably have found from substantial evidence that either (1) the seller had not completed physical delivery of the goods under section 2-401, UCC, or (2) there was an explicit agreement for title to pass upon completion of the necessary paperwork which had not occurred at the time of the accident. Under either of these findings title had not passed to the buyer under section 2-401, UCC, and therefore under section 2-501, UCC, the sellers retained an insurable interest. For these reasons we affirm the judgment of the District Court.

Affirmed.

SALE ON APPROVAL AND SALE OR RETURN

Occasionally a seller and buyer agree that the buyer is to have a *right to return the goods to the seller* even though the goods conform to the sale contract. Such transactions possess certain unique characteristics warranting a separate discussion.

A sale of this type is either a **sale on approval** or a **sale or return.** Which of the two forms the transaction takes can always be expressly agreed upon by the parties. If the contract provides for a return of conforming goods but does *not* designate which form is intended, the UCC provides specific rules for classifying the arrangement. Section 2-326 states: "Unless otherwise agreed, if delivered goods may be returned by the buyer even though they conform to the contract, the transaction is (a) a 'sale on approval' if the goods are delivered primarily for *use,* and (b) a 'sale or return' if the goods are delivered primarily for *resale.*" (Emphasis added.) This is a common sense test. The purpose of a *sale on approval* is to allow the buyer who will be using the goods an opportunity to try them out before committing himself or herself to pay for them. The purpose of a *sale or return* is to allow the buyer of goods who intends to resell them to others an opportunity to return the unsold items.

In either type of transaction the sale contract can specify the period of time within which the buyer must make a decision. If no time is specified, the choice must be made within a *reasonable time.* Failure to decide within this time constitutes acceptance of the goods, and the buyer must pay for them.

In a sale on approval transaction, the buyer can express approval in several ways. For example, as we have already indicated, failure to express disapproval within the required time constitutes approval. Approval can also be given by any statements or actions signifying it. Of course, the buyer can make a *trial use* of the goods without implying approval—though the question sometimes arises as to whether a particular use is really just a trial. While this question must be answered on the basis of the facts of each case, the key is whether the use being made of the goods is consistent with the purpose of a trial.

Consequences of Approval and Return Sales

Under Sec. 2-327, the legal consequences of a sale on approval and a sale or return differ in several significant respects. The most important of these are the following:

1. In a sale on approval, no sale exists until the buyer accepts the goods by giving approval. Up to that time the arrangement is a bailment (the buyer being the bailee), with title and risk of loss *remaining with the seller* until the buyer gives approval.[9] By contrast, in a sale or return a valid

---

[9] Of course, if the goods are damaged, lost, or destroyed due to the buyer's negligence or intentional wrong, he or she is responsible regardless of where the risk of loss rests.

sale exists until the buyer returns the goods. Thus title and risk of loss *pass to the buyer* as in any other sale, and remain with him or her until the goods are actually returned to the seller.

2. In a sale on approval, if the goods are returned the seller bears the expense of such return (but if the buyer is a merchant, he or she must follow all reasonable instructions of the seller in making the return). On the other hand, under a sale or return the buyer bears the expense of returning the goods.[10]

3. The rights of creditors also differ with the nature of the transaction. In a sale on approval, the buyer is not the "owner" of the goods in his or her possession prior to approval. Consequently, until an approval occurs, the goods are subject to the claims of the seller's creditors and, with one exception discussed below, not to the claim of the buyer's creditors. By contrast, in a sale or return the buyer *is* the owner of the goods in his or her possession. Therefore, such goods are subject to claims of the buyer's creditors rather than the seller's creditors.

4. We noted earlier that the parties can agree as they wish on whether a particular arrangement permitting the return of conforming goods is a sale on approval or a sale or return. One important exception to this rule places significant constraints on that freedom. Under Sec. 2-326(3), if the buyer maintains a place of business where he or she deals in goods of the kind involved, and if that place of business is conducted under any

name other than that of the seller, then the goods in the buyer's possession "are deemed to be on sale or return." *In other words, in such a situation, the goods in the buyer's possession are subject to the claims of his or her creditors.*[11] This is true even though the parties had *agreed* that the arrangement was to be a consignment or a sale on approval, and even though the seller is still the owner of the goods. In order to protect creditors of the buyer, who might be misled by the buyer's possession, this section essentially provides that the agreement of the seller and buyer can simply be ignored. It will still be effective, however, in regard to the rights and obligations existing between the seller and buyer.

In this situation, certain measures are available to the seller to protect his or her ownership rights in the goods. In other words, even though the goods are reachable by the buyer's creditors, a cautious seller can take steps to see that his or her interest prevails. Section 2-326(3) spells out alternatives for the seller, the best of which is compliance with the provisions of Article 9 (secured transactions) with respect to obtaining a "security interest" in the goods and filing public notice of that interest with the appropriate state official. (See Chapter 29 for a detailed discussion of security interests.)

SUMMARY

In general, the rules applicable to the formation of sales contracts parallel common-law principles. However, in limited situations special sales law rules apply (which have been discussed in Chapter 11). In most circumstances it is immaterial at what moment title to the goods passed from seller to buyer. However, in cases where it is necessary to pinpoint the time of passage, Sec. 2-205 contains rules for making this determination.

---

[10] Somewhat akin to a sale on approval and a sale or return is the *sale on consignment.* In such a transaction, a seller (the consignor) delivers goods to another person (the consignee) for the purpose of having the consignee sell them on behalf of the consignor. In such a case the consignee is merely an agent of the consignor; both title and risk of loss *remain with the consignor* while the goods are in the consignee's hands. Any unsold goods are, of course, returned to the consignor. The sale on consignment differs from a sale on approval because the consignee does not have possession for the purpose of deciding whether he or she wishes to buy the goods. And it differs from a sale or return because in that transaction the buyer acquires title to the goods for the purpose of reselling them; by contrast, a consignee—being merely an agent of the consignor—does not acquire title to the goods.

---

[11] The exception does not apply if the buyer is an affiliate of the seller doing business under the seller's name. In this case the buyer's creditors should be aware of the seller's interest.

There are four situations relevant to the transfer of title which are governed by special code rules, rather than those in Sec. 2-205. Two of these situations are (1) sales by persons having voidable title, and (2) sales by merchants of goods entrusted to them. In these situations an innocent purchaser may receive better title than that possessed by the seller.

Where goods are lost or damaged before receipt by the buyer, it is necessary to determine whether the risk of loss had, or had not, passed from seller to buyer prior to the time of loss or damage. Where neither party has breached the contract, the rules of Sec. 2-509 determine the time of passage of risk. If the parties had made a shipment contract, risk of loss passes when the seller delivers the goods to the carrier. In a destination contract, by contrast, the risk does not pass until the goods have reached their destination and the seller has made a due tender there.

In other situations, where transportation of the goods is not contemplated, the goods at the time of contracting are usually in the possession of a bailee (a warehouse) or in possession of the seller. In the first situation, if the warehouse receipt is negotiable, the risk of loss passes to the buyer when he or she receives the receipt. (If it is nonnegotiable, risk of loss does not pass until the buyer notifies the warehouse of the purchase). In the second situation, where possession is in the seller, the risk of loss does not pass to the buyer until he or she receives the goods *if* the seller is a merchant. If the seller is not a merchant, the risk of loss passes when the seller has tendered delivery (which is usually at some time before the buyer receives the goods).

If one of the parties has breached the contract prior to the time of the loss or damage, special rules set forth in Sec. 2-510 determine the time that risk of loss passes. When one of the parties is attempting to hold his or her insurance company liable for the loss or damage to the goods, such party must show that he or she possessed an insurable interest in the goods at the time of loss or damage. Section 2-501 sets forth the circumstances in which the buyer may have an insurable interest, and those in which the seller may have such an interest.

Sales on approval and sale or return transactions are those in which the buyer has the right to return the goods even though they conform to the terms of the contract. In a sale on approval title and risk of loss remain with the seller until the buyer expressly or impliedly approves; by contrast, in a sale or return title and risk of loss pass to the buyer when he or she receives the goods (but reverts to the seller if the buyer returns them).

KEY TERMS

Course of performance
Course of dealing
Usage of trade
Future goods
Voidable title
Bona fide purchaser
Fraudulent conveyance statutes
Bulk transfers
Risk of loss
Bailee
Insurable interest
Sale on approval
Sale or return

QUESTIONS AND PROBLEMS

1. Briefly explain why the concept of *title* is not as important in the law of sales under the UCC as it was prior to enactment of the code.

2. In 1945, Lieber, then in the United States Army, was among the first soldiers to occupy Munich, Germany. There, he and some companions entered Adolph Hitler's apartment and removed various items of his personal belongings. Lieber brought his share, including Hitler's uniform jacket and cap and some of his decorations and personal jewelry, home to the U.S. after the war. In 1968 the collection was stolen by Lieber's chauffeur, who sold it to a New York dealer in historical Americana. The dealer sold it to the defendant, who purchased it in good faith. Through collectors' circles Lieber soon discovered the whereabouts of his stolen property. Lieber's demand for return of the property was refused, and he filed suit against defendant, seeking the return. Did Lieber or defendant prevail? Explain. (*Lieber v. Mohawk Arms, Inc.*, 64 Misc.2d 206, 1970.)

3. What is the distinction between void and voidable title under the UCC? Discuss.

4. A entrusted goods to B, who was a merchant in the business of selling such goods. B was not authorized to sell A's goods, but he did in fact sell them in his regular manner to C, who thought they belonged to B. C paid for the goods by paying a debt that B owed to X. A filed suit to reclaim the goods from C. Was A successful? Explain.

5. Briefly describe the purpose of the law concerning bulk transfers.

6. Williams owned a motorboat, which he stored in a hobby shop. He agreed to sell the boat to Sanders. After making the agreement, Williams and Sanders went to the hobby shop, where Williams told the person in charge that Sanders would pick up the boat. Arrangements for the pickup were made between Sanders and the person in charge of the shop. When Sanders later returned to pick up the boat, it was gone. Sanders refused to pay for the boat, and Williams sued Sanders for the purchase price. Did he win his suit? Explain.

7. Lair Co. sold a TV antenna on credit to Crump. The contract provided that Crump could not remove the antenna from his premises while the price remained unpaid. The antenna was delivered and installed by Lair Co. Later it was destroyed by fire, and Crump refused to continue paying for it. When Lair Co. sued for the price, Crump claimed that risk of loss had

not yet passed at the time of the fire. His reasoning was that, since the antenna was not shipped by carrier and not held by a bailee, risk would pass from Lair Co. (a merchant) to him only when he actually *received* the antenna. He argued that because of the restrictions placed upon his control of the antenna, Lair Co. technically had retained possession and he had not really received it. Who prevailed? Explain. (*Lair Distrib. Co. v. Crump,* 261 So.2d 904, 1972.)

8. X Company contracted to sell goods to Z Company. Both agreed that Z would pick up the goods at X's premises. The contract called for delivery "FOB purchaser's truck." X notified Z that the goods were ready for Z to pick up. Before Z called for them, however, they were destroyed. X Company sued for the purchase price. Did X win? Explain.

9. Shook bought electric cable from Graybar Electric Co. Shook was a contractor doing road work, and his place of operation continually changed. Graybar delivered the wrong cable to Shook, who promptly notified Graybar of the error and of the location where Graybar could pick up the cable. Graybar made no effort to take back the cable it had delivered, and after three months it was stolen. Graybar sued Shook to recover the purchase price for the cable. Did Graybar prevail? Explain. (*Graybar Elec. Co. v. Shook,* 195 S.E.2d 514, 1973.)

10. Scarola purchased goods from Pearsall, not knowing that Pearsall had stolen the goods. Scarola obtained an insurance policy on the goods, which were later destroyed by fire. When Scarola sought to recover their value from the insurance company, the company asserted that Scarola had no insurable interest in the goods. Scarola sued. Did he prevail against the insurance company? Discuss. (*Scarola v. Insurance Co. of North America,* 292 N.E.2d 776, 1972.)

Chapter 22

SALES
Warranties and
Products Liability

In recent years, courts have found themselves plagued with the problem of manufacturer liability, specifically the extent to which a manufacturer should be liable to a consumer who is injured by his product. To address this problem, various rules and legal theories for determining liability have been developed, and these make up the expanding area of law known as *products liability.* Since the 1960s, products liability has become one of the most rapidly changing areas in the history of English common law, its bias having undergone a dramatic shift away from the seller to favor, instead, the consumer. The pendulum has taken such a sudden swing that sellers' liability has emerged as one of the most controversial subjects in the business world today.

Under products liability law and sales law, three legal theories may be available to an injured consumer seeking redress: (1) warranty, (2) negligence, and (3) strict liability. The first is a contract theory and is governed by the UCC; the other two are tort theories. The elements of negligence have been discussed in Chapter 7 and will be applied here in the context of products liability. The principles of strict liability are taken from Section 402A of the American Law Institute's *Restatement (Second) of Torts.* Unlike the UCC, the *Restatement* is not a statute, but a model code of law whose recommendations have been adopted by courts of law in many states. Like the UCC, the strict liability theory applies primarily to transactions involving goods and not to those involving real estate or services.

✓ WARRANTY

A **warranty** is an assurance or guarantee that goods will conform to certain standards. If the standards are not met, the buyer can recover damages from the seller, under a breach of warranty theory.

Such has not always been the case, for though suits involving warranties date as far back as fourteenth century England, a recovery theory was slow in developing. *Caveat emptor* ("let the buyer beware") governed the state of law until recent times—here in America, until the beginning of the twentieth century. The concept of caveat emptor allowed the seller to escape liability altogether, in the absence of fraud.

With the growth of business and industry came a clear need to move away from laissez-faire values and to place legal strictures on sales transactions. Chains of distribution were widening the distance between manufacturers and ultimate consumers; and an increasing sophistication in product design made inspection for defects more difficult. As a result, courts came to recognize the existence of three types of warranties, discussed in the following pages: express warranties, implied warranties, and warranties of title.

✓ Express Warranties

Express warranties are those which originate from the words or actions of the seller. To create an express warranty, the seller does not have to use the word "warranty" or "guarantee," and the buyer does not have to show that the seller intended to make a warranty. Under Sec. 2-313 of the UCC, a seller can create an express warranty in three different ways: (1) by an affirmation of fact or a promise relating to the goods, (2) by a description of the goods, or (3) by providing a sample or model of the goods. Such representations by the seller create contractual obligations to the extent that they become "part of the basis of the bargain."

Affirmation of Fact or Promise: By making an affirmation of fact or a promise relating to the goods, the seller tacitly guarantees that the goods will conform to the specifics he sets forth. For example, the seller might claim, "This boat is equipped with a two-year-old, 100 horsepower engine that was overhauled last month." The statement contains several affirmations of fact: (1) the boat is equipped with an engine, (2) the engine is two years old, (3) it generates 100 horsepower, and (4) it was overhauled last month. The seller might further state, "I assure you that this boat will not stall when run in

his promise of future events — no guarentie warranty

choppy water." His affirmations concern past and present conditions; his promise, by contrast, relates to future events. Both affirmations and promises may create express warranties.

A seller's *commendation* or *expression of opinion* does not constitute an express warranty; neither does a statement that relates only to the *value* of the goods. Thus, the seller could claim that his boat was a "first class vessel, worth $25,000 at retail" without creating a warranty. The law is not so rigid as to disallow "puffing" of products; it assumes that a consumer can distinguish between sales talk and fact.

But at times the distinction between fact and opinion is not easy to make. Consider, for example, the following statement: "The steering mechanism on this boat has been thoroughly engineered." The claim is rather vague, and, as a descriptive phrase, "thoroughly engineered" may not be appreciably different from "first class." Yet the reference to engineering may create an impression of technological excellence in the mind of an unsophisticated buyer, and thus create a wrong impression.

In such cases, the courts tend to consider a number of factors, principally the buyer's frame of reference. If the buyer has limited knowledge of the goods involved, the statement from the seller is apt to be an affirmation of fact. If, however, the buyer is more knowledgeable than the seller, vague statements will be treated as mere expressions of opinion.

These additional generalizations can be made about the creation of express warranties: Statements which are specific and absolute are more readily construed as warranties than indefinite ones. Terms put in writing are more likely to create warranties than those given orally.

Description of Goods: A descriptive word or phrase used in a sale of goods may create an express warranty that the goods will conform to the description. The word "pitted" or "seedless" on a box of prunes or raisins warrants that the fruit will have no seeds. Recognized trade terms may also constitute descriptions. For example,

the term "Scotchguard," used in connection with furniture upholstery, describes fabric which has been treated to make it water and stain resistant. Goods described by trade terms are warranted to possess those characteristics generally associated with the terms in the trade or business involved.

Sample or Model: If the buyer receives a sample or model which establishes a *standard of quality* for the sale, a warranty exists that the goods will conform to the sample or model. A sample is a single item taken from the mass to be sold, whereas a model is used to represent the goods. In a sale of wheat, a sample of one bushel might be drawn from the thousand bushels to be sold. But when the item being sold has not yet been manufactured or is too difficult to transport, a model might be used instead.

breach of if Buyer depended oh sample color

While the UCC makes no distinction between express warranties arising out of sales by sample or by model, a sample is more likely to create such a warranty than a model. Since a sample is actually taken from the inventory to be sold, it is usually easier for the buyer to prove that a sample was intended to establish a standard of quality for the sale.

Basis of the Bargain: Under Sec. 2-313, an express warranty is created only if the affirmation or promise, description, model, or sample is "part of the basis of the bargain." Courts have applied this phrase to two types of circumstances: First is the case where the seller makes a statement about the goods, and circumstances indicate that both parties intended the statement to be a part of the agreement. This would certainly be true if the statement appeared in the sales contract itself, and would apply also where it is reasonably clear that the statement played a material part in the buyer's decision to purchase the goods. The second type of case involves statements of fact contained in a brochure, provided to the buyer by the seller. Under pre-Code law, the burden of proof was generally on the buyer to show that he had read the statement and relied on it. If reliance could not be shown, the buyer could not recover on the breach of warranty theory. By contrast, under the "basis of the bargain" language, courts *assume* that the statement became a part of the contract unless the seller can show "good reason" for the contrary (Sec. 2-313, comment 8).

A different question arises when, *after* the sale has been made, the buyer requests a promise from the seller that the goods meet certain standards. If given, does this promise become "part of the basis of the bargain"? Prior to the enactment of the UCC, the answer probably would have been *no;* today it is probably *yes.* Under Sec. 2-209(1), the seller's post-sale promise is a modification of the contract and becomes

an integral part of the agreement, even without additional consideration from the buyer.

A similar problem occurs sometimes in a sales negotiation, during which the seller makes statements that fail to appear in the written contract. Buyers who attempt to base a claim for breach of warranty on a recollection of oral statements are often thwarted by the *parol evidence rule* of UCC Sec. 2-202. Under this rule, if the court finds that the written form was intended as the final expression of the parties' agreement, any oral statement in contradiction of the written terms will not be admissible as evidence.

The following case illustrates how a company's advertising may expand the scope of an express warranty.

Community Television Services, Inc. v. Dresser Industries, Inc.
U.S. Court of Appeals, 8th Circuit, 586 F.2d 637 (1978)

In 1965, two television stations in South Dakota created a separate corporation, Community Television Services, Inc. (Community), for the purpose of constructing and operating a 2,000 foot tower that would broadcast signals for both stations. Community contracted with Dresser Industries, Inc. (Dresser), who designed, manufactured, and erected the tower for a price of $385,000. The tower was completed in 1969 and Community used it until 1975. During this time, Community regularly inspected and properly maintained the tower. On January 10 and 11, 1975, a severe winter blizzard occurred in the area where the tower was located. During the early morning hours of January 11, as the storm reached its height with wind speeds of up to eighty miles per hour near the top of the tower, the structure collapsed.

Dresser denied responsibility and Community sued in federal district court for breach of an express warranty. The verdict and judgment in the trial court were in favor of Community, the plaintiff, for damages of $1,274,631.60, and Dresser, the defendant, appealed.

Lay, Circuit Judge:

. . . Expert witnesses called by both sides differed in their opinions as to the cause of the collapse. Community's experts testified that they had eliminated metallurgical or mechanical failure or abnormal wind loading as the cause of collapse. They theorized that the cause was high winds setting up a phenomenon known as mechanical resonance. They concluded that because of the resonance, the tower members "were inadequate to support the load that they sustained." On the other hand, Dresser's experts testified that a combination of ice, snow and wind subjected the tower to a total force greater than the ultimate capacity of its structural elements. They theorized that a substantial accumulation of ice on the upper fourth of the tower enlarged the tower members to a greater load than their designed wind loading capacity. Community attempted to refute Dresser's ice theory by calling several witnesses who testified that they did not see any such ice on or near the area where the tower collapsed. In turn, Dresser countered Community's theory through expert testimony that relatively constant winds were necessary for resonance to begin, and the winds were gusty and varied in speed and direction at the time of collapse. Furthermore, Dresser argued that the warranty did not guarantee against mechanical resonance, and experts testified that its prevention was beyond the current state of the art.

The specifications incorporated in the sale contract included a specified "Design Wind Load," which set forth the tower's capacity to withstand wind velocity as measured in pounds of pressure per square foot against the flat surface of its members. The specification reads: "The tower shall be designed to resist a uniform wind load per drawing T-5172, sheet S-1, 60 psf on flats." The trial court instructed the jury that this specification constituted an express warranty that the structure would withstand wind exerting pressure of 60 pounds per square foot on the flat surfaces of the tower. Dresser's advertising materials and the testimony of experts at trial revealed that the wind velocity necessary to create 60 pounds of pressure on the flat surfaces of the tower would be approximately 120 miles per hour. The evidence showed that the wind loading specifications referred, at least in engineering parlance, to "a force caused by the wind that is introduced parallel to the ground . . . [which] would be tending to blow the structure over."

Dresser argues that the trial court erred in failing to direct a verdict on the express warranty claim or grant it judgment notwithstanding the verdict, because expert testimony that the tower met the design specification was uncontradicted. Community's own experts stated unequivocally that in their opinion the tower conformed in a mathematical or analytical sense to the 60 pounds per square foot wind loading specification. If the warranty may be restricted to the technical specification set forth in the written contract, we would find Dresser's argument convincing. However, we agree with Community that the warranty was amplified, in advertising materials Dresser gave to Community prior to purchase of the tower, to promise more than mere compliance with technical measurements. In an advertising catalog, Dresser made the following supplementary affirmation:

Wind force creates the most critical loads to which a tower is normally subjected. When ice forms on tower members thereby increasing the surface area resisting the passage of wind, the load is increased.

Properly designed towers will safely withstand the maximum wind velocities and ice loads to which they are likely to be subjected. Dresser-Ideco can make wind and ice load recommendations to you for your area based on U.S. Weather Bureau data.

In the winter, loaded with ice and hammered repeatedly with gale force winds, these towers absorb some of the roughest punishment that towers take anywhere in the country . . . yet continue to give dependable, uninterrupted service.

Although we agree with Dresser that a seller cannot be held to be the insurer of its product, Dresser nevertheless provided the catalog to Community to induce purchase of its product, and in the absence of clear affirmative proof to the contrary, the above affirmation must be considered part of the "basis of the bargain." Standing alone, the statements provide a warranty that Dresser's tower would be properly designed so as to safely withstand the maximum wind velocities and ice loads to which it would likely be subjected. Dresser did not indicate that this broad affirmation was superseded or cancelled by the technical specification in the contract. When the affirmation is read in tandem with the contract, as part of the "fabric" of the agreement of the parties, it enlarges the warranty created by the technical wind loading specification, giving evidence of its full intent and scope.

We find that the statements in the advertising catalog, which supplement the wind loading specification, could reasonably have been found by the jury to be an affirmation of fact or a promise concerning the actual durability or performance of the tower during the wind and ice storms to which it was likely to be subjected.

Although Dresser's defense was that the tower collapsed by reason of excessive loading due to ice on the tower members, no disclaimer or limitation of the warranty that a properly designed tower would safely withstand the maximum wind and ice loads to which it was likely to be subjected appeared in the advertising materials or the contract. Under the *integrated* warranty given, a purchaser could reasonably assume that the tower, if properly designed for its location, would withstand maximum wind speeds to which it was likely to be subjected, even if ice accumulated on the tower members. While the blizzard was a severe one, the evidence does not support the conclusion that the wind alone, or the combination of wind and ice which Dresser claimed caused the collapse, was not within the range of storm conditions to be reasonably contemplated for the tower's location. Breach of a warranty created by standards describing the specific capacity of goods is proved when the product is shown by direct or circumstantial evidence to have failed to perform reasonably and safely the function for which it was intended by the manufacturer. In view of the affirmation made in the catalog, there was sufficient evidence for the jury to reasonably find that the tower was not as durable as it was warranted to be.

[Affirmed.]

Implied Warranties ✓

An implied warranty is created through the mere act of selling and is imposed upon the seller by law. Its purpose is to protect consumers who suffer economic and commercial losses when products fail to serve their needs. Unlike with express warranties, specific representations about a product have not actually been made. The consumer has been guided, instead, by the belief that his purchase is suitable for its intended use. In Sec. 2-314 and Sec. 2-315, the UCC names two types of implied warranties: the implied warranty of merchantability and the implied warranty of fitness for a particular purpose.

Merchantability: The law injects into the sales contract a warranty that the goods are "merchantable," if the seller is a *merchant with respect to the type of goods being sold.* (When a student sells her 1980 VW to a neighbor, no implied warranty of merchantability exists because she is not a merchant in automobiles.)

"Merchantable" means essentially that the goods are *fit for the ordinary purpose for which such goods are used.* The warranty of merchantability requires, for example, that shoes have their heels attached well enough that they will not break off under normal use. The warranty does not require, however, that ordinary walking shoes be suitable for mountain climbing. To be merchantable, goods must also serve their ordinary purpose *safely.* A refrigerator that keeps food cold but that gives an electric shock when the handle is touched is not merchantable. This is not to say that the seller becomes an insurer against accident or malfunction; the purchaser is expected to maintain his goods against the attrition of use.

The **implied warranty of merchantability** also does not guarantee that goods will be of the highest quality available. They are required to be only of *average or medium grade,* in addition to being adequately packaged and labeled.

When applied to food, the implied warranty of merchantability can be related to *wholesomeness.* A tainted pork chop, for instance, is not merchantable. A number of cases decided prior to enactment of the UCC held that food purchased at a restaurant, hotel, or other such establishment carried no warranty because the sale involved a service rather than a product. The UCC, however, explicitly states that the implied warranty of merchantability extends to food sold at service establishments such as restaurants and hotels, whether the food is consumed on or off the premises.

Many cases alleging a breach of the implied warranty of merchantability have involved objects in food that caused harm to the consumer. Exceptional examples range from a mouse in a bottled soft drink to a screw in a slice of bread. In such cases the courts traditionally have distinguished between "foreign" and "natural" objects. They usually find that if the object is foreign to the mass (such as the mouse or screw mentioned above), the warranty of merchantability has been breached. If, on the other hand, the object is natural (such as a bone in a piece of fish), no breach of warranty has occurred.

A growing number of courts have rejected this approach and have based their decisions instead on the "reasonable expectation" of the consumer. The controlling factor in this approach is whether a consumer can reasonably expect the object in question to be in the food. A piece of chicken may be expected to contain a bone, but not when in a chicken sandwich; an olive may be expected to contain a pit, but not when a hole at the end indicates that it has been pitted. Bones and olive pits will not render food unmerchantable under the "foreign-natural object" test, *but may do so under the "reasonable expectation" test.* Thus, the results of a legal suit may vary considerably, depending on which approach is used. A famous case in this area follows.

Webster v. Blue Ship Tea Room, Inc.
Supreme Judicial Court of Massachusetts, 198 N.E.2d 309 (1964)

Plaintiff Webster, who was born and brought up in New England, ordered a cup of fish chowder while dining at defendant's "quaint" Boston restaurant. She choked on a fish bone contained in the soup, necessitating two esophagoscopies at the Massachusetts General Hospital. Plaintiff sued for breach of the implied warranty of merchantability. A jury returned a verdict for plaintiff. Defendant appealed the trial judge's refusal to direct a verdict for defendant.

Reardon, Justice:

We must decide whether a fish bone lurking in a fish chowder, about the ingredients of which there is no other complaint, constitutes a breach of implied warranty under applicable provisions of the Uniform Commercial Code. As the [trial] judge put it, "Was the fish chowder fit to be eaten and wholesome? Nobody is claiming that the fish itself wasn't wholesome. But the bone of contention here—I don't mean that for a pun—but was this fish bone a foreign substance that made the fish chowder unwholesome or not fit to be eaten?"

The plaintiff has vigorously reminded us of the high standards imposed by this court where the sale of food is involved.

The defendant asserts that here was a native New Englander eating fish chowder in a "quaint" Boston dining place where she had been before; that "[f]ish chowder, as it is served and enjoyed by New Englanders, is a hearty dish, originally designed to satisfy the appetites of our seamen and fishermen"; that "[t]his court knows well that we are not talking of some insipid broth as is customarily served to convalescents." We are asked to rule in such fashion that no chef is forced "to reduce the pieces of fish in the chowder to miniscule size in an effort to ascertain if they contained any pieces of bone." In so ruling, we are told (in the defendant's brief), "the court will not only uphold its reputation for legal knowedge and acumen, but will, as loyal sons of Massachusetts, save our world-reknowned fish chowder from degenerating into an insipid broth containing the mere essence of its former stature as a culinary masterpiece."

Chowder is an ancient fish dish preexisting even "the appetites of our seamen and fishermen." It was perhaps the common ancestor of the "more refined cream soups, purees, and bisques." Berolzheimer, The American Woman's Cook Book (Publisher's Guild, Inc., New York, 1941) p. 176. The all embracing Fannie Farmer states in a portion of her recipe, fish chowder is made with a "fish skinned, but head and tail left on. Cut off head and tail and remove fish from backbone. Cut fish in 2-inch pieces and set aside. Put head, tail, and backbone broken in pieces, in stewpan; add 2 cups cold water and bring slowly to boiling point."

Thus, we consider a dish which for many years, if well made, has been made generally as outlined above. It is not too much to say that a person sitting down in New England to consume a good New England fish chowder embarks on a gustatory adventure which may entail the removal of some fish bones from his bowl as he proceeds. We are not inclined to tamper with age old recipes by any amendment reflecting the plaintiff's view of the effect of the Uniform Commercial Code on them. We are aware of the heavy body of case law involving foreign substances in food, but we sense a strong distinction between them and those relative to unwholesomeness of the food itself, e.g., tainted mackerel, and a fishbone in fish chowder. We consider that the joys of life in New England include the ready availability of fresh fish chowder. We should be prepared to cope with the hazards of fish bones, the occasional presence of which in chowders is, it seems to us, to be anticipated, and which, in the light of a hallowed tradition, do not impair their fitness or merchantability.

Judgment for the defendant.

We include one more breach of implied warranty of merchantability case which, while not involving food, does involve a sticky issue that frequently arises in such litigation.

Mohasco Industries, Inc. v. Anderson Halverson Corp.
Supreme Court of Nevada, 520 P.2d 234 (1974)

Anderson Halverson Corp., owner of the Stardust Hotel in Las Vegas, Nevada, ordered carpeting to be manufactured by Mohasco and installed in the hotel lobby and casino showroom of the Stardust. After installation the buyer refused to pay, claiming that the carpet "shaded" excessively, giving it a mottled effect and the appearance of being water stained. Mohasco, plaintiff, sued Anderson Halverson, defendant, to recover the price of $18,242.50. The trial court held in favor of defendant, and plaintiff appealed.

Thompson, Justice:

. . . One Fritz Eden, an interior decorator selected and hired by Stardust, designed a pattern for the carpet to be used in the hotel lobby and casino showroom. A sample run of the chosen pattern was taken to the hotel by Eden, and was approved. Eden then specified the material and grade of carpet which the Stardust also approved. The Stardust then issued a detailed purchase order designating the type and length of yarn, weight per square yard, type of weave, color and pattern. No affirmation of fact or promise was made by any representative of . . . the seller to . . . the buyer. The carpet which was manufactured, delivered and installed was consistent with the sample and precisely conformed to the detailed purchase order. There were no manufacturing defects in the carpet.

Upon installation, however, the carpet did shade and, apparently, to a much greater extent than the Stardust or its representative had anticipated. It is clear from the testimony that "shading" is an inherent characteristic of all pile carpeting. When the tufts of the carpet are bent in different angles, the light reflection causes portions of the carpet to appear in different shades of the same color. The only explanation in the record for the "excessive shading" was that Fritz Eden, the decorator for Stardust, decided not to specify the more expensive "twist yarn." That type yarn causes the tufts to stick straight up (or at least tends to do so) thus aiding in the elimination of excessive shading.

The trial court found that the sale of the carpet was a sale by sample which was made a part of the basis of the bargain and created an express warranty that the carpet delivered for installation would conform to the sample. Moreover, [the trial court found] that the *express warranty was breached by the seller,* thus precluding its claim for relief. [Emphasis added.] . . .

That finding is clearly erroneous. The installed carpet conformed precisely to the description of the goods contained in the purchase order. Moreover, it conformed precisely to the sample which the buyer approved. Whether the sale be deemed a sale by description or by sample, in either event the express warranty of conformity was met. The seller delivered the very carpet which the buyer selected and ordered.

Although there is substantial evidence to support the trial court's finding that the installed carpet shaded excessively, that consequence may not be equated with a breach of an express warranty since the seller delivered and installed the very item which the buyer selected and ordered. Had the buyer, through its interior decorator, selected the more expensive carpet with "twist yarn," perhaps this controversy would not have arisen. The buyer, not the seller, must bear the consequence of that mistake.

[The court then turned to the implied warranty of merchantability question, as follows:] As already noted, the judgment below rests upon an erroneous finding that the seller breached an express warranty that the whole of the carpet would conform to the sample which the buyer had approved. The buyer suggests, however, that the judgment should be sustained in any event since it is otherwise clear that the seller breached the implied warrant[y] of merchantability. . . . We turn to consider this contention.

Unless excluded, or modified, a warranty of merchantability is implied in a contract if the seller is a merchant with respect to the goods in question. We have not, heretofore, had occasion to consider the impact, if any, of the implied warranty of merchantability upon a case where the goods are sold by sample or description and the buyer's specifications are so complete that it is reasonable to conclude that he had relied upon himself and not the seller with regard to the merchantability of the goods. . . .

It is apparent that in a case where the sample or description of the goods may, for some reason, result in an undesirable product, the seller is placed in a dilemma. In Hawkland, A Transactional Guide to the Uniform Commercial Code, Sec. 1.190206, at 65, the following example is given. Suppose a buyer provides his seller with minute specifications of the material, design and method of construction to be utilized in preparation of an order of shoes, and the seller delivers to the buyer shoes which exactly conform to the specifications. If the blueprints are in fact designs of defective shoes, the buyer should not be able to complain that the shoes are defective. For such an order might put the seller in the dilemma of being forced to breach either the express warranty of description or the implied warranty of merchantability.

The matter at hand is similar to the example just given. Although the carpet was not defective, it did shade excessively and was, in the view of the buyer, an undesirable product. Yet, it was the product which the buyer specified and ordered. The manufacturer-seller was not at liberty to add "twist yarn" and charge a higher price. The buyer relied upon its decorator, Fritz Eden, and the seller performed as directed. . . . *[W]e hold that the implied warranty of merchantability is limited by an express warranty of conformity to a precise description supplied by the buyer, and if the latter warranty is not breached, neither is the former.* [Emphasis added.] . . .

The judgment for [the buyer] is reversed, and since there is no dispute concerning the amount of the plaintiff's claim, the cause is remanded to the district court to enter judgment for the plaintiff against the said defendant for $18,242.50, together with appropriate interest and costs.

Fitness for a Particular Purpose: In Sec. 2-315, the UCC provides: "Where the seller at the time of contracting has reason to know any particular purpose for which the goods are required and that the buyer is relying on the seller's skill or judgment to furnish suitable goods, there is . . . an implied warranty that the goods shall be fit for such purpose" (hence the name **implied warranty of fitness for a particular purpose,** sometimes referred to as "warranty of fitness"). Note that the seller is not required to be a merchant, although merchants are defendants in the majority of cases.

Often the liability incurred by the seller under the implied warranty of fitness is greater than one incurred under the implied warranty of merchantability—a difference that can be best illustrated by a simple example: Suppose a buyer purchases an electric clock and discovers that its hands do not glow in the dark. The packaging carries no reference to visibility of the dial, neither does the instruction card. No breach of the implied warranty of merchantability exists here, for visibility of the dial under all conditions is not within the realm of a clock's "ordinary purpose." Yet the seller *may* be liable to the buyer for breach of the implied warranty of fitness for a particular purpose.

A close examination of facts is required to ascertain whether a warranty of fitness exists, because such a warranty arises only if the following conditions exist:

1. The seller had "reason to know" of the particular purpose for which the goods were purchased. This requirement is obviously met if the seller was *actually informed* of the intended purpose; but such knowledge does not have to be proven. The requirement is also met if the circumstances dictate that the seller, as a reasonable person, *should have known* that the buyer was purchasing the goods for a particular purpose.

2. The seller also had reason to know that the

buyer was relying on the seller's skill or judgment to furnish suitable goods. That is, the buyer must have relied on the seller's recommendation and the seller must have known or should have known of this dependence. If the buyer shows initiative by presenting brand names or introducing other specifications, recovery will be less likely.

3. Items 1 and 2 above must have existed at the time of contracting. If the seller learns the relevant facts only after the sale contract is made, a warranty does not exist.

These elements are applied in the following unique case.

Dempsey v. Rosenthal
Civil Court, City of New York, 448 N.Y.S.2d 441 (1983)

Plaintiff bought a poodle, Mr. Dunphy, from defendant for $541.25. Five days later, an inspection by a veterinarian disclosed that Mr. Dunphy had one undescended testicle. Plaintiff returned the dog and demanded a refund. Defendant refused. Plaintiff brought this suit in small claims court, claiming breach of the implied warranties of merchantability and fitness.

Saxe, Judge:

[The judge first found that Mr. Dunphy's condition breached the implied warranty of merchantability because a dog with an undescended testicle would not pass without complaint in the trade. Though fertile, the dog could pass the condition on to future generations. The judge then turned to the matter of implied warranty of fitness.]

The next issue to be resolved here is whether warranty of fitness for a particular purpose has been breached. [The UCC] makes it clear that the warranty of fitness for a particular purpose is narrow, more specific, and more precise than the warranty of merchantability which involves fitness for the *ordinary* purposes for which such goods are used. The following are the conditions that are not required by the implied warranty of merchantability but that must be present if a plaintiff is to recover on the basis of the implied warranty of fitness for a particular purpose:

1. The seller must have reason to know the buyer's particular purpose.

2. The seller must have reason to know that the buyer is relying on the seller's skill or judgment to furnish appropriate goods.

3. The buyer must, in fact, rely upon the seller's skill or judgment.

Nevertheless, I find that the warranty of fitness for a particular purpose has also been breached. Ms. Dempsey testified that she specified to [defendant's] salesperson that she wanted a dog that was suitable for breeding purposes.

Although this is disputed by the defendant, the credible testimony supports Ms. Dempsey's version of the event. Further, it is reasonable for a seller of a pedigree dog to assume that the buyer intends to breed it. But, it is undisputed by the experts here (for both sides) that Mr. Dunphy, with only one descended testicle, was as capable of siring a litter as a male dog with two viable and descended testicles. This, the defendant contends, compels a finding in its favor. I disagree. While it is true that Mr. Dunphy's fertility level may be unaffected, his stud value, because of this hereditary condition (which is likely to be passed on to future generations) is severely diminished.

The fact that Mr. Dunphy's testicle later descended and assumed the proper position is not relevant. "The parties were entitled to get what they bargained for at the time that they bargained for it. The right of the buyer to rescind must be determined as of the time the election to rescind was exercised. The parties' rights are not to be determined by subsequent events." *White Devon Farm v. Stahl,* 389 N.Y.S.2d 724 (Sup.Ct.N.Y.Co. 1976). *White Devon Farm* involved the "tale of a stud who was a dud." The court there held that the warranty of fitness for a particular purpose was breached despite the fact that the horse's fertility later rose and the stallion sired 27 live foals.

A judgment for the claimant in the amount of $541.25 shall be entered by the clerk.

Warranties of Title

In most sales of goods, a warranty as to the validity of the seller's title automatically exists. Section 2-312 of the UCC imposes two basic types of **warranty of title.** The first is a warranty that *the title conveyed shall be good and its tranfer rightful.* This warranty is obviously breached if the seller has stolen the goods from some third party and therefore has no title at all. Other breaches, however, are not so obvious. Suppose that A buys goods from B and then is approached by C who claims to be the rightful owner. Inquiries reveal that there is some basis for C's claim and that the matter can be resolved only through a lawsuit. Will A have to become involved in a lawsuit initiated by C to determine if she bought a good title from B? Or has B breached his warranty of title by conveying a "questionable" title? The answer is that A has the option of returning the goods to B and getting her money back or defending against C's claim. If A takes the latter route and wins the lawsuit, she can recover her legal expenses from B. If A loses the lawsuit, she can recover from B not only her legal expenses, but also the value of the goods lost to C.

The second type of title warranty is that *the goods shall be delivered free from any security interest or other lien or encumbrance of which the buyer at the time of contracting has no knowledge.* This warranty will be breached, for instance, if B sells mortgaged goods to A without telling A of the mortgage.

Warranties of title accompany a sale of goods unless the seller indicates by specific language that no such assurances are being made, or unless the circumstances indicate as much (for example, in a public sale of goods seized by the sheriff to satisfy a debt, rightful transfers of title are generally not guaranteed).

An additional obligation—not, strictly speaking, a warranty of title—is imposed upon some sellers by Sec. 2-312: Unless otherwise agreed, a seller who is a merchant in the type of goods involved is deemed to warrant *that the goods sold do not infringe upon the patent, copyright, or trademark of a third party.* If a claim of infringement is made by a third party against the buyer, the seller is responsible—unless, of course, the goods were manufactured according to the *buyer's specifications.*

Conflicting and Overlapping Warranties

Two or more warranties sometimes exist in a single sales transaction. For example, a machine might be warranted to perform certain functions and to last for a specified time. In addition to these express warranties, an implied warranty of merchantability or of fitness for a particular purpose, or both, might exist.

When more than one warranty is created in a given transaction, the buyer does not have to choose among them. The warranties are *cumulative,* such that the buyer can take advantage of *any* or *all* of them. According to Sec. 2-317, courts should interpret the warranties as being "consistent" whenever such an interpretation is reasonable. In the unusual event that two warranties are in conflict and cannot both be given effect, the court must attempt to determine the intent of the parties as to which warranty should prevail. Several rules offer guidance in determining intention:

1. Exact or technical specifications take precedence over inconsistent samples or models or general language of description.

2. A sample drawn from the goods to be sold takes precedence over inconsistent general language or description.

3. An express warranty, regardless of how it was created, takes precedence over the implied warranty of merchantability if the two are inconsistent. (An express warranty does not take precedence over the implied warranty of fitness for a particular purpose, although it is difficult to imagine a situation in which the two would be inconsistent.)

These rules are not absolute and can be disregarded by the court if they produce an unreasonable result.

Disclaimers (Excluding and Limiting Warranties)

As we have seen, a sales transaction can give rise to three types of warranties: express warranties, implied warranties, and warranties of title. But the creation of these warranties is by no means automatic. The UCC allows a seller to disavow the existence of warranties or to limit the circumstances in which liability will apply by including a **disclaimer** in the sales contract. Theoretically, disclaimers can be justified on the grounds that their use advances freedom of contract, permitting parties to bargain over contract terms and to allocate the risk of loss. Yet in reality, the arrangement tends to be one-sided: consumers usually are in no bargaining position and often do not read disclaimers when making a purchase. For this reason, courts may find a particular disclaimer *unconscionable* under UCC Sec. 2-302.

Disclaimers of Express Warranties: A seller who wishes to avoid liability on an express warranty obviously should not do anything to create a warranty in the first place (a highly impractical measure to take in making sales!). An alternative would be to include a disclaimer in the contract. However, if a warranty has actually become part of the contract, an attempt to disclaim liability will usually not be effective. Section 2-316(1) states that a disclaimer will be disregarded if it is inconsistent with the words or conduct that created the express warranty. Suppose that an express warranty has been created by a statement of the seller, by the use of a sample, or by a written description of the goods. Liability could not then be disclaimed by specifying: "These goods are sold without warranties." Such a statement would almost always be inconsistent with the words or conduct that created the warranty. In short, *it is extremely difficult for a seller to disclaim an express warranty which has become part of the contract.*

Disclaimers of Implied Warranties: Because the existence of an implied warranty de-

see page 1210 Modification
Exclusion of Warranties

pends on circumstances rather than on the precise words used by the seller, such a warranty is relatively easy to disclaim. The UCC permits disclaimers of implied warranties through (1) the use of language specified in Sec. 2-316 of the Code, (2) the buyer's examination of the goods, or (3) custom and usage.

Disclaimer by Language: In the case of the *warranty of merchantability,* the language used by the seller to disclaim liability does not have to be in writing. If written, however, the disclaimer must be "conspicuous" enough to be noticed by any reasonable person involved in the purchase. (A disclaimer printed in larger type or in a different color than the remainder of the document will probably be considered conspicuous.) In addition, the word "merchantability" must be used—unless the seller employs a phrase such as "with all faults" or "as is," language which serves to disclaim *both* or *either* of the implied warranties.

In the case of the *warranty of fitness for a particular purpose,* the disclaimer must be in writing and must be conspicuous. Yet the statement itself can be a general one, such as, "There are no warranties extending beyond the description on the face hereof." *ex - fire Extinguisher*

Disclaimer by Examination: If before making a contract, the buyer fully examines the goods (or a sample or model of them), or, on the other hand, deliberately refuses to examine them at all, no implied warranty exists for *reasonably apparent* defects. Yet if the buyer has no opportunity to examine the goods before contracting, the seller becomes liable for such defects.

When defects are hidden, the seller is always liable, unless it can be proved that the buyer had knowledge of the defects before contracting. It should be noted here that when deciding whether a defect is "reasonably apparent" or "hidden," a court will take into account the buyer's knowledge or skill. Such a factor obviously has a bearing on what an examination should have revealed to the buyer.

For example, in *Dempsey v. Rosenthal,* Mr. Dunphy's defective condition—the undescended testicle—was not readily observable. A manual manipulation of the scrotal area would have been the only means to verify the condition. The court found that Ms. Dempsey, the buyer, did not know this and should not be charged with knowledge of the fact. The type of examination that would be undertaken by the average buyer of a male puppy would not disclose the defective condition, so recovery was not barred by the inspection provisions of UCC 2-316.

Disclaimer by Custom or Usage: Implied warranties are sometimes excluded or modified by *trade usage* (industry-wide custom) or by a custom that has been established between the contracting parties. An industry-wide custom will have no effect, however, on a buyer who is not a member of the particular industry and is unaware of the custom.

Limitation on Damages: In contract cases, punitive damages traditionally have not been available to plaintiffs. For this reason, express and implied warranty suits usually involve two types of damages: basis-of-the-bargain damages (the value of the goods warranted less the value received) and consequential damages (personal and property damages proximately caused by the warranty breach, along with any indirect economic loss foreseeable by the defendant).[1]

The Code allows limitations to be placed by the seller on damages that may be recovered for a breach of warranty, but only to the extent that the limitation would not be unconscionable. For example, recovery may be limited to *liquidated damages*—that is, a specified amount to be paid in the event of a breach. A limitation may also be placed on the type of remedy available, guaranteeing, for example, only the replacement of the product without charge. (Note: If the limited

---

[1] In addition to damages, the buyer has an option to rescind the contract when a warranty has been breached, as we shall see in the next case, *Stream v. Sportscar Salon, Ltd.*

warranty is not honored, the limitation no longer applies and the buyer may claim all warranties and remedies available to him under the UCC.)

A number of disclaimer of warranty and limitation of damage issues are discussed in the following case.

Stream v. Sportscar Salon, Ltd.
Civil Court of the City of New York, 397 N.Y.S.2d 677 (1977)

Pursuant to a contract dated February 28, 1976, plaintiff Stream purchased from defendant Sportscar Salon, Ltd., an automobile which broke down on April 12, 1976, having been driven about 300 miles. Plaintiff had been adding oil, but the engine "seized" and was out of oil. The car was towed to defendant's premises. Defendant agreed to put another engine in the car. On April 20, plaintiff, after making reference to the defective engine and to other defects, notified defendant that he elected to "rescind" the sale and demanded return of the purchase price. The notice further stated that the plaintiff would consider "re-accepting" the car if it were repaired. Defendant worked on the car, and on May 1, 1976, plaintiff picked it up.

A few days later, the car broke down again. Plaintiff's mechanic examined the car and found its engine to be so defective as to be inoperable. The car was again towed to the defendant's premises. Plaintiff delivered the car's title to defendant and again notified defendant that he "elected to stand upon" the previous notice of rescission and demanded return of the purchase price. Defendant refused. The car, at time of trial, remained at defendant's lot. The following is the opinion of the trial judge.

Cohen, Judge:

[The judge found that the car clearly contained a defective engine. He then addressed the disclaimer issue.]

The Warranties Made and Their Breach

The contract of sale on defendant's form states in paragraph 7: "It is expressly agreed that there are no warranties, express or implied, made by either the dealer or the manufacturer on the motor vehicle, chassis or parts furnished hereunder." The bill of sale has stamped on it the statement "Limited Used Car Warranty" without further explanation. In another one of defendant's forms entitled "One Year Mechanical Guarantee" and signed by both parties, defendant "agrees that it will protect the purchaser from any cost of repairs other than normal maintenance and wear on the vehicle during the term of this guarantee for one repair or replacement on each of the specified parts, subject to the terms and conditions hereinafter set forth: A. Engine . . . This guarantee is only valid for a mechanical failure. This does not cover normal wear." While this paper further states that "You have the finest guarantee on your car that is offered anywhere in the world" and also states that this is defendant's "famous one-year mechanical guarantee on parts and labor. This guarantee guards you against unforseen (sic) costly repairs on your car for one full year," it contains many exclusions and conditions including one stating that the limit of liability for loss shall not exceed "either (1) the actual cash value of the vehicle at the time of loss or (2) the reasonable value of the repair or replacement including labor thereon" and another stating that defendant "assumes no liability whatsoever except for the terms of the guaranteed (sic) as expressly stated herein. Representatives or agents of Sportscar Salon, Ltd., are not authorized to amend or change either verbally or in writing the terms and conditions of this guarantee."

Defendant does not rely on the express denial of warranties as set forth in the contract of sale. It could hardly do so since the subsequent bill of sale it issued declares that there is a "Limited Used Car Warranty" and the "Guarantee" makes what defendant itself regards as certain warranties. Indeed, defendant's service manager in his testimony referred to warranties made with respect to the car. Considering the fact that these papers were forms prepared by defendant, any ambiguity concerning their interpretation must be construed against defendant and in favor of plaintiff. This is particularly true with respect to a "contract of adhesion" such as is involved here. The court finds, after consideration of the language used in the papers in question, which were prepared by defendant, that defendant warranted that the engine was not defective. See UCC 2-313.

Moreover, . . . the implied warranty of merchantability . . . is applicable unless excluded or modified in accordance with UCC 2-316. [The judge then quoted subsections 2 and 3 of UCC 2-316.]

There is no mention of the word "merchantability" in any of the papers involved in this case. Therefore, the implied warranty of merchantability remained in effect by virtue of subsection (2) unless subsection (3) came into effect. The phrases quoted in subsection (3) ["as is" and "with all faults"] were not used in the various papers involved, and while the contract of sale had an inconspicuous disclaimer of all warranties in paragraph 7, under the circumstances of this case, where the contract of sale was followed by the bill of sale and guarantee indicating that there were in fact some warranties, this disclaimer was ineffective. Accordingly, the implied warranty of merchantability is applicable to the sale of this car. [The Court then found that both the express warranty and the implied warranty of merchantability had been breached.]

The Recovery of the Purchase Price as a Remedy

Defendant contends that under no circumstances can plaintiff recover the purchase price. It contends that its obligation was limited to the repair and replacement of defective parts and that it satisfied this obligation by replacing the car's engine.

The buyer's remedies in general are set forth in UCC 2-711, which includes the following language which may be applicable to the situation presented in this case: "Where . . . the buyer . . . justifiably revokes acceptance with respect to any goods involved . . . the buyer may cancel and whether or not he has done so may in addition to recovering so much of the price as had been paid. . . ." However, in determining whether plaintiff is entitled to this relief—assuming a justifiable revocation of acceptance—consideration must be given to any attempt to limit or modify remedies in accordance with UCC 2-316(4) which states: "Remedies for breach of warranty can be limited in accordance with the provisions of this Article on liquidation or limitation of damages and on contractual modification of remedy (Sections 2-718 and 2-719)." [The court then quoted UCC 2-719(1) and (2).]

An examination of the language used in the express warranty reveals that while reference is made to "repairs" and "replacement," it is not "expressly agreed" that plaintiff's remedy was limited to repair and replacement. Indeed, the language used is in terms of limitation of "liability" rather than in terms of limitation of "remedies." As pointed out in Official Comment 2 to UCC 2-719:

> *Subsection (1)(b) creates a presumption that clauses prescribing remedies are cumulative rather than exclusive. If the parties intend the term to describe the sole remedy under the contract, this must be clearly expressed.*

Accordingly, the court concludes that the remedy of "repair and replacement" is not exclusive and that the remedy permitting the recovery of the purchase price is available to plaintiff.

Moreover, the court notes that in the beginning of the "Guarantee" there is a provision for "one repair or replacement" of the engine. In this case, there was a repair and replacement which still left the car with a defective engine. Even if the "Guarantee" were effective in limiting plaintiff's remedy to repair and replacement, under these circumstances such an exclusive or limited remedy failed "of its essential purpose," and under UCC 2-719(2) any "remedy may be had as provided under the Act." Indeed, under the circumstances of this case, if plaintiff's remedy were to be limited to "one repair or replacement" of the engine, such a limitation might very well be unconscionable. Further, even if the language of the "Guarantee" as well as in the contract of sale and bill of sale are regarded as ambiguous, this language appears in forms prepared by defendant and any such ambiguity is to be resolved against defendant.

Also, there is, in addition to the express warranty, the implied warranty of merchantability. Since there has been no mention of merchantability in the papers prepared by defendant, there may be no limit on the remedy available to plaintiff—who seeks to recover the purchase price—by reason of the breach of the implied warranty of merchantability.

Judgment is directed in favor of plaintiff against defendant for the sum of $2,688 with interest.

Defenses

The Privity Defense: As our discussion has borne out, disclaimers and limitation clauses often operate against full recovery by the buyer and so constitute a problem area in warranty law. Another difficulty standing in the way of the buyer's legal recourse against the manufacturer is the doctrine of privity.

Privity is a legal term for the direct relationship between buyer and seller. **Privity of contract** means relationship of contract: If A sells a yacht to B, and B sells it to C, there is privity of contract between A and B and between B and C, but *not* between A and C.

Because a warranty arises from the formation of a contract, privity of contract between the plaintiff and defendant always used to be required in order for the plaintiff to recover damages on the breach of warranty theory. Warranties did not "run with the goods" to subsequent purchasers and users.

In the early history of this country, when consumers bought their goods directly from artisans or local manufacturers, the privity requirement was not a hindrance to most breach of contract actions. In the decades which followed, however, it became more common for goods to travel through chains of distribution before reaching the ultimate consumer.

Under marketing conditions such as these, the requirement of privity had many burdensome effects on the consumer. One result was that the retailer (the only party with whom the consumer had privity) was often financially unable to compensate the consumer for losses, while at the same time the manufacturer and wholesaler escaped liability altogether. For these reasons, the privity requirement has been *greatly relaxed today and is in the process of being eliminated.* All parties in the chain of distribution are now usually responsible to the last buyer for failure of the goods to live up to the standards of any warranties.

A final problem with the privity requirement was that defects in goods sometimes affected persons other than the last purchaser; yet jeopardized nonpurchasers could not successfully sue anyone in the chain of distribution on the breach of warranty theory. Innocent bystanders, for example, might suffer injury without recourse, and so might those who borrowed the defective goods from the purchaser.

Section 2-318 of the UCC has somewhat alleviated this problem by extending warranty protection to (1) members of the buyer's family, (2) members of the buyer's household, and (3) guests in the buyer's home, "if it is reasonable to expect that such person may use, consume or be affected by the goods, and [such person] is injured [physically] by the breach of the warranty." As the language indicates, the extended protection applies only when defective goods have caused a *physical injury to the individual.*

In recent years the drafters of the UCC have proposed alternative versions of Sec. 2-318 to further relax the privity requirement—primarily by granting protection to *any* injured person who could reasonably have been expected to use, consume, or be affected by the goods. While few states have enacted these versions of Sec. 2-318 to date, the trend in most jurisdictions is toward a loosening of the privity requirement in breach of warranty actions.

Plaintiff Misconduct Defenses: When a plaintiff's carelessness contributes to a products-related accident, the defendant can use that carelessness as a defense in most jurisdictions. However, there is a wide variety of approaches throughout the states regarding how to treat the plaintiff misconduct defense.

In negligence cases, of course, a plaintiff's carelessness is simply compared to the defendant's in most jurisdictions. The plaintiff's own carelessness can reduce or even bar recovery totally. In warranty cases, many jurisdictions do not deal simply with "plaintiff carelessness," as a single category. Instead, they recognize several types of such carelessness, with different categories having different effects on liability.

One category is *simple plaintiff carelessness*—frequently described as the failure to detect or guard against a defect in a product. In many jurisdictions this carelessness is compared to the defendant's fault under the comparative negligence statute.

Another category of plaintiff misconduct is **product misuse,** which occurs when a plaintiff uses a product for a purpose which was unforeseeable to the manufacturer. For example, the plaintiff might use a pop bottle as a hammer or a lawn mower as a hedge trimmer. Only when such misuse was not reasonably foreseeable to the defendants does a defense exist. When misuse is foreseeable, the law may impose on defendants a duty to warn against the misuse, or perhaps even to install safety devices to guard against the misuse. In some jurisdictions, unforeseeable product misuse constitutes a complete defense to a warranty claim; in other jurisdictions, it is merely evidence of plaintiff misconduct to be compared to defendants' fault.

A third category of plaintiff misconduct is **assumption of risk,** which occurs when a plaintiff, having discovered a defect in the product and fully appreciating its danger, uses the product anyway. Thus, assume that Sally purchases an airplane. The sellers promise Sally that the plane will fly six hours on a full tank of fuel. However, Sally is later told by several pilots who have experience with this type of plane that it will not fly more than five hours on a full tank. Nonetheless, Sally attempts to fly six hours and a crash ensues. Many courts would hold that Sally voluntarily and knowingly assumed the risk of the product's danger. In many jurisdictions, recovery is barred completely on a warranty theory. In other jurisdictions, the plaintiff's assumption of risk is compared to the defendant's fault under a comparative negligence statute, with the result that a plaintiff may still recover something.

Treatment of the plaintiff misconduct defense in the warranty area is similar to its treatment in a strict liability claim. Later in the chapter we will address these defenses in the strict liability context, and include a case illustrating one approach, *Smith v. Goodyear Tire & Rubber Co.*

Statute of Limitations and Notice Requirements: Under UCC 2-725, an action for breach of any contract for sale must be commenced within four years after the cause of action accrues.[2] This statute of limitations provides a defense to many warranty actions, express and implied. The Code further provides that by agreement the parties may reduce the period of limitation to not less than one year, but may not extend it.

Some warranty actions are barred by a plaintiff's failure to comply with UCC 2-607(3) which imposes on the buyer a duty to notify the seller of a breach within a reasonable time after he or she discovers or should discover any breach, or be barred from any remedy. However, courts have been reluctant to allow this provision to bar recovery by consumers who suffered personal injuries due to a breach of warranty. Courts are inclined to construe a "reasonable time" as being a longer period in a personal injury case than in a suit brought for economic loss by a commercial purchaser.

NEGLIGENCE

Because the elements of negligence have been discussed at length in Chapter 7, our purpose here is simply to apply them to the area of products liability. Remember that in an action based on negligence, the defendant must have owed a duty to the plaintiff, and this duty must have been breached. Where a sales transaction is involved, the seller's duty to use reasonable care arises from the mere act of placing goods on the market. The economic benefit derived from a sale generates a responsibility to consumers; for the act of selling directly affects the interests of those who have no choice but to rely on the

---

[2] Under the UCC, the statute of limitations begins running at the time of the sale. In tort cases, however, the period runs from the time the defect was (or should have been) discovered and usually extends for up to two years, depending on the jurisdiction.

integrity of sellers. Privity of contract is no longer required in the usual negligence suit.

The manufacturer's liability for negligence is often predicated on negligent design or manufacture; in addition, *both* manufacturer and seller may be liable for failure to inspect or failure to adequately warn.

If the seller is a retailer, distributor, or wholesaler, he or she usually has no duty to inspect new goods, barring knowledge of defects. A duty to inspect does exist, however, when the seller is involved in the installation of goods (new or used) or in their preparation for eventual sale. Liability is imposed to the extent that defects are *reasonably apparent.* By the same token, a manufacturer is charged with taking reasonable measures to discover flaws created during the production process.

A *duty to warn* arises when a product's design (or its intended use) subjects the user to hazard or risk of injury. The danger in question need only be reasonably foreseeable—discoverable only within the limits of existing technology. Warnings given must be adequate in their specifics and must extend to all individuals whose harm is reasonably foreseeable. There is no duty to warn of obvious dangers—no duty, for example, to warn about fire on a box of matches.

Negligent manufacture is often cited in cases where defects are the result of oversight, human or mechanical error, or lack of judgment. For example, production line employees might not be properly trained, or materials selected for construction might not have sufficient strength to resist the stresses of normal use.

In contrast, actions based on charges of *negligent design* hold the manufacturer responsible for more than the exercise of care in production. In addition to warning about risks and hazards inherent in a design, the manufacturer is expected to design a product with optimal safety as the ideal, compromised only where the costs of improving design exceed the benefits derived therefrom. Under the rule adopted by most states, there is a duty to design products so that

accidents are unlikely to occur and so that injuries suffered will be minimal if an accident does occur. To illustrate: Say X is driving a car which explodes when struck in the rear by Y, who has negligently maneuvered his truck. X may recover from Y for initial injuries, and may possibly recover from the car's manufacturer for additional injuries resulting from the impact if, for example, the gas tank were located vulnerably close to the rear bumper.

Of course, it would be unreasonable to expect cars to be accident-proof in all situations. (If this were the law, some courts have observed, manufacturers would produce nothing but tanks.) In evaluating the adequacy of design standards, courts have considered such factors as the state of existing technology, the expectation of the ordinary consumer, the danger of a product in relation to its social utility, and compliance with government safety standards.

To conclude, the negligence theory became viable as an avenue of recovery to injured plaintiffs when the privity requirement was finally abandoned. This theory offers some advantages over the warranty theory, e.g., the buyer does not have to prove that a warranty existed, the buyer does not have to notify the seller within a reasonable time after discovering the defect, and disclaimers in the sales contract usually do not allow the seller to escape liability resulting from his or her negligence.

Yet certain disadvantages exist as well. A plaintiff must prove negligent conduct on the part of the manufacturer or seller, and proof of negligence is at times almost impossible to establish. Only in relatively rare cases have courts inferred negligence pursuant to the doctrine of **res ipsa loquitur** ("the thing speaks for itself").[3]

---

[3] The doctrine of *res ipsa loquitur* may presume negligence from the fact that the accident did indeed occur. A plaintiff who can show that (a) the defendant controlled the product, and (b) the defect would not normally occur absent negligence can benefit from *res ipsa loquitur's* presumption of negligence. The presumption would be applicable, for example, if a product exploded immediately upon being removed from a container which was sealed at the defendant's factory.

A second impediment to recovery under the negligence theory is that any type of plaintiff misconduct, even simple plaintiff carelessness will reduce or bar recovery.

STRICT LIABILITY

It has been felt in recent years that the negligence and warranty theories do not afford consumers as much protection as they ought, in fairness, to have. In many negligence actions, for example, the plaintiff is not able to prove specific acts of negligence on the part of the manufacturer, and some warranty actions are dismissed simply because the plaintiff failed to give the defendant notice of the breach within a specified period of time.

In recognition of such deficiencies, the courts have increasingly adopted the theory of **strict liability** by which manufacturers and sellers are held liable, irrespective of fault. Under this theory, a showing of negligence or intent to guarantee is not required, privity of contract is not necessary for recovery, disclaimers cannot bar recovery, and notifying the seller of the defect within a reasonable time is also not required. A purchaser who is injured by a product has a cause of action simply by showing (1) that the product was defective, (2) that the defect was the proximate cause of injury, and (3) that the defect caused the product to be unreasonably dangerous (see Figure 22.1 for a comparison of strict liability with negligence). Strict liability has been recognized and applied in at least two-thirds of the states in this country.

The revival of strict liability began in the early 1960s and has received such widespread approval that today it is one of the most common grounds for imposition of liability upon manufacturers and sellers. Indeed, its acceptance has imposed liability upon manufacturers to an extent unanticipated twenty years ago. According to one estimate, products liability (juries' verdicts plus the total of liability insurance premiums) cost American businesses over $100 billion in 1983.

One of the landmark cases continues to be *Greenman v. Yuba Power Products, Inc.*, 59 Cal.2d 57 (1963). Here the plaintiff purchased at retail a "shopsmith combination power saw and drill" manufactured by the defendant company, and received serious head injuries when a piece of wood flew out of the machine while he was using it. The Supreme Court of California conceded that the plaintiff's action might fail if based on warranty alone, because notice of the warranty breach had not been given. Yet the court held the manufacturer "strictly liable in tort" and spelled out this theory as follows: "A manufacturer is strictly liable in tort when an article he places on the market, knowing that it is to be used without inspection for defects, proves to have a defect that causes injury to a human being. Recognized first in the case of unwholesome food products, such liability has now been extended to a variety of other products that create as great or greater hazards if defective." The court then cited fourteen cases where similar results were reached, involving such defective products as automobiles, bottles, vaccines, and automobile tires.

Justification for the strict liability theory lies in the notion that merchants and manufacturers are better able to bear losses than injured consumers, and that in many cases, losses will be transferred to the buying public in the form of higher prices on products. Thus, society at large assumes the cost of damages suffered by a few— an arrangement which is perhaps more equitable in that it offers relief for those injured by defective products.

Proponents of strict liability argue, in addition, that eliminating the need to prove negligence in a tort action will make manufacturers and sellers more mindful of accident prevention. (The opposing view holds, on the other hand, that strict liability will ultimately inhibit the development of new products.)

Finally, there is an economic basis for adopting this liability theory: Because negligence is often difficult to prove, litigation becomes excessively costly. From an overall economic

Figure 22.1   Differences between Negligence and Strict Liability

	Negligence	Strict Liability
Principle	A test of whether reasonable care has been taken	A test of existence of defect
Application	Applies to virtually all goods and actions	Applies to products shown to have been dangerously defective in manufacture or design
Elements	Duty, breach, damages	Product defective in manufacture, design Defect caused product to be unreasonably dangerous Resulting injury
Defenses	Contributory or comparative negligence of plaintiff	Material alteration of product Unforeseeable misuse of product Unreasonable assumption of risk

standpoint, then, it can make sense to abandon proof of negligence in a products liability action.

Elements of Strict Liability

The elements of strict liability are recorded in Section 402 of the American Law Institute's *Restatement (Second) of Torts,* a summary and clarification of American common-law principles. Section 402A reads:

> **1.** One who sells any product in a defective condition unreasonably dangerous to the user or consumer or to his property is subject to liability for physical harm thereby caused to the ultimate user or consumer, or to his property, if
>
> > **a.** the seller is engaged in the business of selling such a product, and
> >
> > **b.** it is expected to and does reach the user or consumer without substantial change in the condition in which it is sold.
>
> **2.** The rule stated in Subsection (1) applies although
>
> > **a.** the seller has exercised all possible care in the preparation and sale of his product, and
> >
> > **b.** the user or consumer has not bought the product from or entered into any contractual relation with the seller.

Two points regarding Section 402A merit special emphasis. First, Subsection (1)(a) limits application of the strict liability theory to those engaged in the business of selling the products in question. Second, Subsection (2) makes it clear that negligence and privity are not issues under the strict liability theory.

Thus in certain respects, strict liability may be viewed as an extension of the implied warranty of merchantability, where the warranty theory was applied to foreign objects in food and drink. (Recall our discussion of the "reasonable expectation" and "foreign-natural object" tests.) Taken further, strict liability is applied in cases involving virtually all kinds of goods. Though there

is in fact some overlapping here with the warranty theory, actions based on strict liability are nevertheless considered to be actions in tort rather than under warranty.

The crux of a Section 402A action is the sale of a *defective product* which is *unreasonably dangerous* to the *user* or *consumer* or to his property. Section 402A covers only sales of products, not services. A product is defective if it is unreasonably dangerous because of a flaw in the product or a weakness in its design, or because adequate warning of risks and hazards related to the design has not been given.

A strict liability action differs from a negligence action in that the plaintiff need not prove the defect resulted from the defendant's failure to use reasonable care. Though in failure-to-warn cases the manufacturer will almost always be found negligent, the same cannot be said of resellers. New products packaged with inadequate warnings may be resold without subjecting middlemen and retailers to liability under the negligence theory; yet these very resellers could be held liable under Sec. 402A because no fault is required under the strict liability theory.

Defective conditions may result not only from flaws or harmful ingredients within the product, but also from foreign objects in its composition and defects in its container. In this regard, a product is not defective "when it is safe for normal handling or consumption." For example, beer consumed in moderate amounts is not harmful. If a student drinks too much beer, and then becomes ill, the seller is not liable.

To be safe, a product should be properly packaged and otherwise treated so that it will not deteriorate or be rendered dangerous within a reasonable period of time under normal conditions.

The question of what constitutes an "unreasonably" dangerous product is taken up in Sec. 402A, comments i and k. Presumably, certain products are reasonably dangerous or "unavoidably unsafe"—that is to say, existing technology and scientific knowledge are insufficient to produce a completely safe result. An example often cited is that of the rabies vaccine, which has dangerous side-effects but which is the only existing treatment against a deadly disease. Drugs sold under prescription and experimental treatments also fall within this category. Unavoidably unsafe products must be accompanied by instructions and warnings, so that the user can decide whether to undergo the risks involved. If the harmful consequences of using a product generally exceed the benefits and if safer alternatives are available, a product will be considered unreasonably unsafe. In defining what is meant by "unreasonably unsafe," Sec. 402A also considers the expectations of the ordinary consumer, stating: "The articles sold must be dangerous to an extent beyond that which would be contemplated by the ordinary consumer who purchases it, with the ordinary knowledge common to the community as to its characteristics. . . . Good butter is not unreasonably dangerous merely because, if such be the case, it deposits cholesterol in the arteries and leads to heart attacks; but bad butter, contaminated with poisonous fish oil, is unreasonably dangerous."

Another stipulation in Sec. 402A is that products must be in a defective condition when they leave the seller. The burden of proof lies with the plaintiff to show that the product was defective at the time of sale. Subsequent alteration or further processing may operate to relieve the seller of liability.

In addition, the plaintiff's injury must occur as a result of a defect in the product itself, rather than from conditions surrounding its use or consumption. For example, if a killer bee stings a longshoreman unloading crates of tropical fruit, the fruit company is not necessarily liable under Sec. 402A—first, because there is no proof that the bee was a stowaway in the fruit, and second, because there is no defect inherent in the fruit itself.

In the following case, the strict liability theory was invoked by a plaintiff in an unusual situation. Among other points, the case illustrates that while most courts find a product "unreasonably dangerous" only if it is more dangerous than the average consumer would expect, some jurisdictions judge design defects by a "risk/utility" test.

Patterson v. Rohm Gesellschaft
U.S. District Court, Northern District of
Texas, 608 F.Supp.1206 (1985)

This strict liability action involves a Rohm .38 caliber revolver, a "Saturday Night Special" manufactured by the defendant. The gun functions as it was intended, by firing a bullet with deadly force when the trigger is intentionally pulled. Unfortunately, the gun was used in a robbery and caused the death of the clerk at the grocery store being robbed. The plaintiff in this action is the mother of the robbery victim. The following is the trial judge's ruling on defendant's motion for summary judgment.

Buchmeyer, District Judge:

The Texas law of products liability controls this diversity case. Texas has adopted the *Restatement (Second) of Torts* §402A—which provides one who sells a product "in a defective condition unreasonably dangerous" is subject to liability for injuries caused by the product.

However, under Texas law, the manufacturer is not required to insure that its products are completely safe or that they will not cause injury to anyone. Instead, the manufacturer is liable for injuries resulting from a product only if that product is "defective"—*i.e.*, has a defect in the sense that something is wrong with it. This required defect may be one of three distinct types:

(i) The product may malfunction because of some manufacturing defect.

(ii) The product may be defective because it was sold without sufficient warning or instructions.

(iii) The product may be defective because its basic design is unsafe.

In cases involving the third type of defect, that of defective design, Texas uses the "risk/utility balancing test": whether the product is "unreasonably dangerous" in the sense that "the danger-in-fact associated with the use of the product outweighs the utility of the product." Typically, this requires the jury to weigh the risks involved in the defective product against the feasibility and cost of an improved design. For example, if placing the gasoline tank in the center of the car "would reduce the chances of fire in rear-end collisions without creating other risks, significantly reducing performance, or significantly increasing costs, then the risk of the rear-end design outweighs its utility, and the car is defective." Note, 97 *Harvard Law Review* 1912 (1984).

In this case, it is admitted that the Rohm .38 caliber revolver did not malfunction and that it did not lack any essential safety features. Nevertheless, the plaintiff's attorneys argue (i) that Texas law no longer requires a showing that the product is defective; (ii) that the word "defective" in §402A is merely synonymous with the phrase "unreasonably dangerous"; and (iii) that the jury may simply apply the "risk/utility test" to any product (whether or not it has a defect).

By this reasoning, the plaintiff's attorneys contend that a nondefective handgun will be "defective and unreasonably dangerous" if the jury determines that the risks of injury and death outweigh any utility a handgun may have. Specifically, they argue that:

> . . . *handgun use results in 22,000 deaths every year in the United States and that medical care for gunshot victims costs approximately $500 million each year. Although handguns constitute only thirty percent of all firearms sold in the United States, ninety percent of all cases of firearm misuse involve handguns. Most murders are sudden crimes of passion; without the ready availability of handguns, such crimes would be less likely. Proponents of manufacturers' liability further argue that handguns are almost useless for self-protection: a handgun is six times more likely to be used to kill a friend or relative than to repel a burglar, and a person who uses a handgun in self-defense is eight times more likely to be killed than one who quietly acquiesces. Thus, handguns, at least as distributed to the general public, are said to be defective."* Note, 97 Harvard Law Review *1912 (1984).*

Aside from the fact that contrary evidence can obviously be advanced to argue the "social utility" of handguns—and despite this Court's admiration for such a delightfully nonsensical claim: that a product which does not have a defect can nevertheless, under the law, be defective—the plaintiff's attorneys are simply wrong. Under Texas law, there can be no products liability recovery unless the product does have a defect. Without this essential predicate, that something is wrong with the product, the risk/utility balancing test does not even apply.

This is demonstrated by any of the Fifth Circuit cases which state the principles of Texas products liability law. For example, in *Syrie v. Knoll International,* 748 F.2d 304 (5th Cir. 1984), the court listed the four essential elements of a "strict liability cause of action"—and the very first one was "a product [that] is defective."

This established principle—that a manufacturer is liable only if there is a defect in its product—is not changed by the fact that there are, as plaintiff's attorneys argue, Fifth Circuit opinions which state that the words "defective" and "unreasonably dangerous" are *essentially* synonymous. This is, in fact, true in most design defect cases. However, even a cursory review of these cases demonstrates that, in each instance, the Fifth Circuit required the existence of a defect—either one arising in a product's design, or in its manufacture, or in its marketing—before there could be recovery under Texas products liability law.

In addition, the theory advanced by the plaintiff's attorneys perverts the very purpose of the "risk/utility balancing test." That test, itself, incorporates the idea that a defect is something that can be remedied or changed. Thus, in considering a design defect claim, the "very factors a jury is supposed to consider when weighing risk and utility includes the feasibility and cost of an improved design." Note, *supra.*

But here, the plaintiff's attorneys offer no alternatives and no safer designs for a handgun. Nor can they do so—because a gun, by its very nature, must be dangerous and must have the capacity to discharge a bullet with deadly force. Accordingly, by their unconventional application of the risk/utility test to a nondefective product, the plaintiff's attorneys simply want to eliminate handguns.

Moreover, if this unconventional theory were correct, then it should apply equally to other products besides handguns—to rifles, to shotguns, to switchblade and kitchen and Swiss Army knives, to axes, to whiskey, to automobiles, etc.—even though these products are not defective.

As an individual, I believe, very strongly, that handguns should be banned and that there should be stringent, effective control of other firearms. However, as a judge, I know full well that the question of whether handguns can be sold is a political one, not an issue of products liability law—and that this is a matter for the legislatures, not the courts.

Accordingly, this case is Dismissed.

Limitations and Defenses

As we have already observed, the advantages of the strict liability theory are heavily stacked in favor of the consumer. The focus is no longer on the conduct of the defendant, but on the product itself—a far more tangible target. However, the strict liability theory is not an answer to every plaintiff's prayer. Various limitations and defenses operate against him, a number of which are effective in some states but not in others.

Limitations: First is the requirement that the product undergo no material change in condition after leaving the defendant's hands. To date, cases litigated have involved only products which are expected to reach the consumer without further processing. The Institute has not issued guidelines to cover circumstances where products are expected to undergo substantial change before reaching the ultimate user.

Second, the plaintiff may find it difficult to prove that a product left the hands of the seller in a defective condition. Where the technology involved in production is complex, witnesses who can testify to defective manufacture may not be available. For this reason, failure-to-warn cases are more common than those alleging errors in the production process.

While strict liability makes recovery easier in certain respects, the requirement that a defective product be "unreasonably dangerous" precludes recovery in many instances. Damages resulting from the failure of a product to perform its ordinary purpose, for example, would not be covered under Sec. 402A. As a result, some states have eliminated the "unreasonably dangerous" requirement.

In addition, Sec. 402A limits recovery to users and consumers (including family members, guests, and employees of the purchaser; and individuals who prepare a product for consumption, who repair a product, and who passively enjoy the benefit of a product, as in the case of passengers on an airplane). Recovery is not always allowed to injured bystanders or others who are brought into contact with the defective product; courts differ on this point, depending on the state. Most states have extended application of the theory to anyone suffering reasonably foreseeable injury because of the defect (such as the driver of a car struck from behind by another vehicle whose brakes were defectively manufactured).

Finally, limitations may also be placed on the recovery of damages in strict liability cases. Plaintiffs can usually recover only for property damages and personal injuries, but not for basis-of-the-bargain damages. Punitive damages are available in some jurisdictions if the defendant evinces utter disregard for the safety of consumers and users of the product—but because of the success that plaintiffs have enjoyed recently (both in the number of recoveries and in the size of judgments obtained), approximately half the states have placed statutory limits on the consumer's right to sue and on the amounts that can be won in products liability cases.

Defenses: Though the privity requirement has been completely abolished under Sec. 402A(2)(b), not all jurisdictions conform with this position. Courts in certain states have retained the privity requirement for injured bystanders. Others have eliminated privity for personal injury claims, but have maintained the requirement where the losses incurred are economic—the basis for the distinction being that individuals are better able to bear economic losses than personal disasters which impair both health and earning capacity.

In some states the middleman is protected from Sec. 402A liability by stipulations that the manufacturer be included in the plaintiff's suit whenever possible, or that the manufacturer be sued instead of the middleman.

Plaintiff misconduct defenses are generally not available in strict liability cases. While simple plaintiff carelessness may absolve the defendant in a negligence suit, it will not do so in a Sec. 402A case. Thus a buyer's failure to inspect the goods or to discover a defect will not prevent recovery of damages. Even misuse of the goods usually will not prevent recovery if the misuse is one which the seller could have reasonably foreseen. Thus, the only defense clearly appropriate to a strict liability claim is *assumption of risk*—the doctrine preventing suit by the buyer who knew of the defect and the resulting danger, but who used the goods anyway. Comparative fault has also been applied in 402A cases by many states adopting this defense.

There has been tremendous variation among the states regarding application of the defenses of simple contributory negligence, unforeseeable product misuse, and knowing assumption of risk in strict liability cases. The following case illustrates one court's thinking on the matter.

Smith v. Goodyear Tire & Rubber Co.
U.S. District Court, District of Vermont, 600 F.Supp.1561 (1985)

Plaintiff Smith was injured in an automobile accident. He brought this action alleging negligence on the part of the driver, Young, in whose car Smith was riding at the time of the accident, and alleging a strict liability claim against defendant tire manufacturer, the Goodyear Tire & Rubber Company.

Defendants raised a "seat belt defense," asserting that their liability is reduced or completely erased by the fact that Smith was not wearing a seat belt although one was available to him, and that wearing it would have reduced, if not eliminated, his injuries. Plaintiff moved to strike this defense. The following is the trial judge's ruling on the plaintiff's motion.

Coffrin, Chief Judge:

Courts are divided on the issue of whether evidence regarding the nonuse of automobile seatbelts should be admissible in comparative negligence cases. Plaintiff relies heavily in his brief on the fact that regulations adopted pursuant to Vermont statutes, although they do require that pleasure cars be equipped with seat belts in their front seats, do not require that the seat belts be used. Plaintiff also points out that Vermont courts have never imposed such a duty.

Plaintiff asserts that courts' reluctance to "find a duty to buckle up" stems from a concern that requiring seat belt use would lead to a flood of litigation in which defendants would argue that, as a matter of law, any plaintiff who fails not only to use his seat belt but also to install an air bag in his car, to adjust his head rest, or, indeed, "to drive a Mack Truck" would be more vulnerable to injury and, thus, guilty of contributing to his own injury.

We are unpersuaded by such reasoning. First, admitting such evidence would not create a duty but would merely allow the jury to consider the information on the question of negligence. Second, the test of negligence would continue to be whether the person acted *reasonably under the circumstances presented.* We do not presume to decide whether or not Plaintiff's failure to fasten his seat belt in the instant case was reasonable. We do believe, however, that the arguments on both sides of the issue are such that a reasonable jury could decide either way. As stated by a New York court,

[T]he seat belt affords the automobile occupant an unusual and ordinarily un-available means by which he or she may minimize his or her damages prior to the accident. [T]he burden of buckling an available seat belt may, under the facts of the particular case, be found by the jury to be less than the likelihood of injury when multiplied by its accompanying severity. Spier v. Barker, *323 N.E.2d 164, 168 (Ct.App. 1974).*

We hold that the jury should be given the task of making this assessment.

. . . Comment (c) to §402A explains that the justification for this special doctrine of liability is "that the seller, by marketing his product for use and consumption, has undertaken and assumed a special responsibility. . . ." Comment (n) goes on to say that contributory negligence "is not a defense to strict liability when such negligence consists merely in a failure to discover the defect in the product, or to guard against the possibility of its existence." Instead, the Comment states, Plaintiff will be barred from recovery only if he "discovers the defect and is aware of the danger, and nevertheless proceeds unreasonably to make use of the product."

Even if Goodyear cannot prove the latter, however, we decline to follow the rigid requirements of Comment (n), and hold that Goodyear should be able to introduce evidence of Plaintiff's failure to use his seat belt as a defense to strict liability. Because Vermont follows the doctrine of comparative negligence, it need not be swayed by the "all or nothing" considerations present in the Comment to the Restatement or in contributory negligence jurisdictions. The purpose behind the strict liability doctrine is to hold certain sellers to a higher standard of care due to their assumption of a special responsibility. Our holding does not thwart that purpose, since Plaintiff still would not have to prove negligence on the part of Goodyear. Although we would be reluctant to completely excuse defendants simply because *some* of a plaintiff's injuries might have resulted from his own actions, it also does not seem fair to allow a negligent plaintiff, who may have contributed to as much as fifty percent of his injuries, to pay for none of them and to recover as much as a plaintiff who had taken all precautions reasonable under the circumstances.

There is a split of authority among other states on this issue. For the reasons stated above, we choose to follow the reasoning of many other comparative fault jurisdictions, and hold that juries may consider evidence of plaintiffs' negligence in assessing damages as to strict liability claims as well as to negligence claims.

Plaintiff's motion is Denied.

In conclusion, the strict liability doctrine favors plaintiffs in that it possesses most of the advantages of the warranty and negligence theories, namely: (1) few defenses against liability can be raised by the defendant, (2) disclaimers are ineffectual; (3) privity is not required; and (4) buyers must prove only that goods were *dangerously defective* when they left the seller's hands and that this defect caused the buyer's injury.

On the other hand, disadvantages to the plaintiff include (1) applicability of Sec. 402A only against sellers who are merchants; and (2) availability of damages only for physical injuries to person and property, and not for economic injuries.

FEDERAL CONSUMER LEGISLATION

Over the years Congress has enacted a number of federal regulatory laws dealing with the safety and quality of goods. For the most part these laws have focused solely on protecting ultimate consumers from physical harm, and until recently, they were enacted piecemeal and were rather narrow in scope. Examples include the Food, Drug and Cosmetic Act (1938), the Flammable Fabrics Act (1953), the Refrigerator Safety Act (1956), the Hazardous Substances Act (1960), and the Poison Prevention Packaging Act (1970).

Consumer Product Safety Act

In 1972 Congress enacted the Consumer Product Safety Act—the first law to deal with the safety of consumer products in general—and created a federal agency, the Consumer Product Safety Commission (CPSC), to administer it.[4]

This agency possesses broad powers and performs many functions, ranging from safety research and testing to preparing safety rules and standards for over 10,000 products. It has the power to ban or recall products and to require special labeling in certain circumstances. It can levy civil penalties on those who violate the Act and criminal penalties on those who willfully violate it. Yet despite the extensive range of its power, the CPSC has been criticized for not issuing enough standards to ensure the integrity of consumer products.

---

[4]Some consumer products are not covered by the Consumer Product Safety Act because they come under the aegis of other federal laws. The most important of these are food, drugs, and cosmetics, which are regulated by the Food and Drug Administration under the Food, Drug, and Cosmetic Act. Automobiles are also excluded because of coverage by other legislation.

Magnuson-Moss Warranty Act

In 1975 Congress passed the **Magnuson-Moss Warranty Act.** Like the federal legislation discussed above, this statute is consumer-oriented. It applies only to purchases by ultimate consumers for personal, family, or household purposes, not to transactions in commercial or industrial settings. The Warranty Act, which is usually enforced by the Federal Trade Commission (FTC), does not regulate the safety or quality of consumer goods. Instead it prevents deceptive warranty practices, makes consumer warranties easier to understand, and provides an effective means of enforcing warranty obligations. The federal Warranty Act is limited to consumer transactions, and it modifies the UCC warranty rules in some respects; in nonconsumer transactions, the UCC rules continue in effect.

The type of warranty to which the Act applies is much more narrowly defined than is an express warranty under the UCC. Specifically, it is (1) any *written* affirmation of fact made by a supplier to a purchaser relating to the quality or performance of a product and affirming that the product is defect-free or that it will meet a specified level of performance over a period of time; or (2) a written undertaking to "refund, repair, replace, or take other action" if a product fails to meet written specifications. Obviously express warranties which are not in writing, such as those created by verbal description or by sample, will continue to be governed solely by the UCC, even though a consumer transaction is involved.

The Warranty Act does not *require* anyone to give a warranty on consumer goods. It applies only if the seller *voluntarily chooses* to make an express written warranty (perhaps in an effort to render a product more competitive). When a written warranty is provided for a product costing $10 or more, it must be labeled as either "full" or "limited". When the cost of goods exceeds $15, the warranty must be contained in a single document, must be written in clear language, and must make a number of disclosures, including (1) a description of items covered and those excluded, along with specific service guarantees; (2) instructions on how to proceed in the event of product failure; (3) the identity of those to whom the warranty is extended; and (4) limitations on the warranty period.

Under a full warranty, the warrantor must assume certain minimum duties and obligations.[5] For instance, he must agree to *repair or replace* any malfunctioning or defective product within a "reasonable" time and without charge. If the warrantor makes a reasonable number of attempts to remedy the defect and is unable to do so, the consumer can choose to receive a *cash refund* or *replacement* of the product without charge. No *time limitation* can be placed on a full warranty; and consequential damages (such as for personal injury or property damage) can be disclaimed only if the limitation is *conspicuous.*

A written warranty which does not meet the minimum requirements must be designated conspicuously as a *limited warranty.* It may cover, for example, parts but not labor, or it may levy shipping and handling fees. If a time limit (such as twenty-four months) is all that prevents the warranty from being a full one, it can be designated as a "full twenty-four month warranty."

Since its purpose is to regulate *written* warranties, the Warranty Act generally does not concern the implied warranties of merchantability and fitness for a particular purpose. These are governed by the UCC; and as we have seen, the UCC allows implied warranties to be disclaimed. However, drafters of the Warranty Act saw fit to limit the use of disclaimers where written warranties are involved, because of certain abusive practices prevalent at the time: Sellers were providing limited express warranties in bold print and then disclaiming implied warranties, thus leaving the consumer with few rights while appearing to offer substantial protection.

For this reason, the Magnuson-Moss Act *prohibits a disclaimer of implied warranties* (1) when an express written warranty is given, whether full or limited, or (2) when a service contract is made with the consumer within ninety days after the sale.[6] If the written warranty specifies a *time* limitation, however, implied warranties may be suspended by a disclaimer, effective *after* the written warranty expires.

The Warranty Act is usually enforced by the FTC, but the Attorney General or an injured consumer can also initiate an action if informal procedures for settling disputes prove ineffective. Sellers are authorized to dictate the informal procedures by which a particular dispute is to be settled. If these procedures follow FTC guidelines, the consumer cannot resort to court action until all established means have been exhausted.

LEGISLATIVE LIMITATIONS ON PRODUCTS LIABILITY REVOLUTION

The past several years have witnessed a growing need for reform in the area of products liability law. While injured consumers have been well served, damage awards ranging into the millions of dollars have led to higher priced products and pushed the cost of insurance premiums beyond the pale. Some companies have ceased manufacturing certain products to avoid the threat of lawsuits; others have been reluctant to improve products, fearing that such refinements will be used as evidence of an older product's defectiveness. American business has also suffered a competitive disadvantage abroad: the expense of designing eminently safe products, coupled with insurance rates twenty times higher than those in Europe, have added signifi-

---

[5] Only the person who actually makes the written warranty—no one else in the chain of distribution—is responsible under the Warranty Act.

[6] Under a *service contract* the seller agrees to service and repair a product for a set period of time in return for a fixed fee.

cantly to the costs of production. The virtual "explosion" of products liability has raised a storm of protest among manufacturers and sellers, and at present, almost every state is considering tort reform.

Some states have already placed ceilings on damage awards in product liability suits. Others have enacted provisions which prohibit advances in technology from being used, with the benefit of hindsight, against manufacturers. More than one-third of the states have enacted **statutes of repose.** These provide a time period after which the manufacturer is not liable for injuries caused by a product, the statute of limitations notwithstanding. The periods range from five to twelve years and begin when a product is sold to an ultimate consumer (one who does not purchase for resale). The purpose of these provisions is to protect manufacturers from liability in situations where defects do not manifest themselves until many years after the product is sold.

While some maintain that optimal products liability law will eventually develop at the state level, the advantage of a comprehensive federal bill is clearly evident. Most manufacturers deal in interstate commerce and at present are subject to fifty different standards. For their own protection, manufacturers tend to follow the most rigorous of these standards, to their economic detriment.

Federal Products Liability Legislation

Though for years Congress has recognized the need for reformatory measures, a federal products liability bill has not been forthcoming. In 1982 the Reagan Administration endorsed the Kasten bill, known as the Product Liability Act. If passed, this Act would return tort law essentially to what it was in the early 1960s, before the resurgence of strict liability. The bill's underlying reformatory measure would be a reintroduction of the fault standard—that is, the requirement that a claimant prove negligence on the part of the defendant. There would be no liability for injuries resulting from an "unreason-

able or unforeseeable use or alteration of the product." Liability would be assessed only on manufacturers negligent in the "design, production, distribution or sale" of a product, if such a product were *unreasonably dangerous* and were the *proximate cause* of the plaintiff's injury.

The standards by which negligence would be measured are somewhat different under the Kasten bill than those discussed heretofore. A "reasonable prudence" test would be applied in design-defect and failure-to-warn suits, requiring that the manufacturer exercise the judgment of a "reasonably prudent person" in choosing a design and in providing warnings or instructions to prevent harm.[7]

A second test would be applied in cases involving a product's construction or manufacture. Here manufacturers would be bound by their *own* design specifications, performance standards, or formulae for production. They would be liable only for product *deviations* causing injury to the consumer. In other words, manufacturers would be free to set their own safety standards and to advertise these in marketing the product. High standards would yield higher priced goods, and less exacting standards would offer a savings to the consumer. The arrangement would promote consumer sovereignty, allowing buyers to assume a greater amount of risk in exchange for lower prices.

Under the Kasten bill, limits would be placed on pain-and-suffering awards and on punitive damages. The administration has proposed a $100,000 limit for each category (a figure which has not been well received among consumer groups, to say the least). Punitive damages are to be levied only where the manufacturer or seller has evinced reckless disregard for the safety of users. The amount would be determined by a judge; and only one punitive damage award would be granted for each instance of

---

[7] Middlemen would be evaluated for their inspection of products and for the adequacy of their instructions and warnings.

reckless conduct. In addition, the bill proposes to limit attorneys' fees, so that in cases taken on contingency, the attorney could receive no more than a certain percentage of the award. It also adopts the principle of comparative fault, referred to as "comparative responsibility."

The bill provides a two-year statute of limitations and a twenty-five-year statute of repose. It applies to cases where defective goods cause personal injury, property damage, and emotional suffering. (Commercial losses and basis-of-the-bargain damages are not covered.) While the bill, if enacted into law will not satisfy the interests of all labor and consumer groups, it will certainly bring uniformity to the area of products liability and will afford some relief to manufacturers from the excessive costs they have come to bear under the theory of strict liability.

SUMMARY

A plaintiff injured by a defective product has several possible legal theories to pursue. If the defendant, be it retailer, wholesaler, or manufacturer, made any representations or affirmations of fact regarding the product's performance, an express warranty theory is available if the promises were breached. Although salespersons are allowed to "puff" their product, specific promises made orally or in written "guarantees" or in product advertising may form the basis for an express warranty claim.

Even if the seller makes no representations about a product, the law implies a promise that the good is "merchantable"—of average quality acceptable in the trade of such goods—any time a merchant (one who makes a living selling such goods) sells a consumer a product. Additionally, if that merchant sells a good knowing that the purchaser needs it for a specific purpose and is relying on the seller's expertise to provide a product that can fulfill that purpose, a warranty of fitness for a particular purpose will be implied by the law.

Both implied warranties may be disclaimed, and recovery may be limited *if* UCC rules are strictly followed and the disclaimer or limitation is not "unconscionable."

A consumer injured by a defective product can recover against any parties the consumer can prove negligently designed, manufactured, tested, or marketed the product. Careless failure to warn of the unavoidable dangers of a product can also be grounds for suit.

Unlike the negligence theory, which focuses on the conduct of the defendant, the strict liability theory focuses only on the product. If the product is defective and unreasonably dangerous, defendants in the distribution chain (manufacturer-wholesaler-retailer) are liable for injuries caused by the defects, no matter how careful they were.

These remedies are supplemented by several federal statutes designed to protect the consumer, most importantly the Magnuson-Moss Act dealing with express warranties and the Consumer Product Safety Act.

Many believe the law of products liability has become so "pro-consumer" that drastic reforms are needed. Many state legislators have passed reform legislation which, for example, imposes "statutes of repose" to prevent recovery for injuries caused by old machines and limits on certain types of damage recoveries. As this chapter is written, Congress is considering federal legislation which would dramatically change the law that has evolved during the "consumer revolution" of the past twenty-five years.

KEY TERMS

Warranty
Express warranty
Implied warranty of merchantability
Implied warranty of fitness for a particular purpose
Warranty of title
Disclaimer
Privity of contract
Product misuse
Assumption of risk
Res ipsa loquitur

Strict liability
Magnuson-Moss Warranty Act
Statute of repose

QUESTIONS AND PROBLEMS

1. Arthur sold goods to Edward. The bill of sale stated that seller transferred all of his "right, title, and interest," that "no other title to his knowledge existed," and that the "bill of sale was the original evidence of title." After the sale, a third party asserted an interest in the goods, and Edward sued Arthur for breach of the warranty of title. Arthur contended that the contract's language constituted a disclaimer of the warranty of title. Is Arthur correct? Discuss.

2. Plaintiff purchased a 1970 Dodge from Norm's Auto Sales after being told by Boyd, a salesman, that the car had a rebuilt carburetor and was a "good runner." On the next day, plaintiff was seriously injured when the car went out of control and crashed into a tree because of a defect in the accelerator linkage. Plaintiff filed suit on an express warranty theory. Did the salesman's statements constitute an express warranty? Discuss. (*Crothers v. Cohen,* 384 N.W.2d 562, Minn.App. 1986.)

3. Walcott & Steele, Inc., sold seed to Carpenter. State law required the package label to give the percentage of germination. The label on the seed bought by Carpenter carried the required statement, but the seed did not perform at the listed percentage. Carpenter sued for breach of an express warranty, which he claimed was created by the statement regarding percentage of germination. Did Carpenter prevail? Discuss. (*Walcott & Steele, Inc. v. Carpenter,* 436 S.W.2d 820, 1969.)

4. Kassab, a cattle breeder, purchased feed which had been manufactured by Central Soya. The feed was intended for breeding cattle, but Central had accidentally included an ingredient that should be used only for beef cattle. After eating the feed, Kassab's cattle grew and prospered. Kassab was upset, however, when he discovered that the mistakenly included ingredient had caused his entire herd of prize breeding cattle to become sterile. He sued Central for breach of the implied warranty of merchantability. Central claimed that there was no such breach because the feed had made the cattle gain weight exactly as it was supposed to do. Is Central's contention correct? Explain. (*Kassab v. Central Soya,* 246 A.2d 848, 1968.)

5. Henningsen bought a new automobile from Bloomfield Motors, Inc. Only ten days after the purchase, when the Chrysler had only 468 miles on the odometer, something under the hood cracked and the car veered 90 degrees into a brick wall. Henningsen's wife was seriously injured. When Henningsen sued Bloomfield and Chrysler on an implied warranty of merchantability theory, they raised as a defense a clause in the purchase contract which provided that the manufacturer's "obligation under this warranty [is] limited to making good at its factory any part or parts thereof which shall, within 90 days after delivery of such vehicle to the original purchaser or before such vehicle has been driven 4,000 miles, whichever event shall first occur, be returned to it with transportation charges prepaid and which its examination shall disclose to its satisfaction to have been thus defective; this warranty being expressly in lieu of all other warranties expressed or implied." Does this disclaimer bar plaintiff's suit? Discuss. (*Henningsen v. Bloomfield Motors, Inc.*, 161 A.2d 69, N.J. 1960.)

6. Johnson, plaintiff, raised hogs. He needed ventilating fans for his hog barn. He told the supplier's representative of his needs. When asked, plaintiff told the representative that there were no unusual humidity or dust problems in the hog barn, but this was not accurate. Plaintiff was advised to purchase certain fans with "open" motors not sealed off from outside air. He bought them but they malfunctioned because of clogging from humidity and feed dust. Many hogs died; plaintiff sued the supplier and the manufacturer, among others, for breach of the implied warranty of fitness for a particular purpose. Should plaintiff prevail? Discuss. (*Johnson v. Lappo Lumber Co.*, 181 N.W.2d 316, Mich.App. 1970.)

7. Isaac J. Fraust, then 16 months old, choked while eating Peter Pan Creamy Peanut Butter spread on bread. As a result, Isaac suffered severe brain damage. Isaac's parents sued Peter Pan on a strict liability theory, claiming that the peanut butter was unsafe because it lacked a warning that it should not be fed to children under four years of age, that peanut butter presents a particular danger to children under four years because of its texture and consistency and the immature eating and swallowing abilities of young children, and that defendant targets young children in its advertising and marketing. Defendant moved for summary judgment contending peanut butter is not unreasonably dangerous as a matter of law. Discuss. (*Fraust v. Swift and Co.*, 610 F.Supp. 711, W.D.Pa. 1985.)

8. Laaperi bought a smoke detector from Sears and installed it in his bedroom. The detector was designed to be powered by AC (electrical) current. Six months later a fire broke out in the Laaperi home, killing three of Laaperi's children. The smoke detector did not sound an alarm on the night of the fire, because the fire started in a short circuit in an electrical cord. The smoke detector was connected to the circuit which shorted and cut off. Laaperi sued Sears claiming that it had breached a duty to warn him that the very short circuit which might ignite a fire in his home could, at the same time, incapacitate the smoke detector. Is this a viable theory? Discuss. (*Laaperi v. Sears, Roebuck & Co., Inc.*, 787 F.2d 726, 1st Cir. 1986.)

9. The Hauters, plaintiffs, purchased a "Golfing Gizmo" for their son from defendants. The device was designed to provide driving practice for novice golfers. On the package it said, "Completely safe ball will not hit player." But the Hauter's son, while using it as directed, was hit in the head by the ball and severely injured. Plaintiffs sued for breach of express and implied warranties, but defendants argued that their only obligation was to provide a device that was safe when the ball was hit "properly" and that a drawing on the package depicted a golfer hitting the ball "properly." Is this a good defense? Discuss. (*Hauter v. Zogarts,* 534 P.2d 377, Cal. 1975.)

10. Welch, plaintiff, bought a new Dodge station wagon from Fitzgerald-Hicks Dodge, Inc. (FHD). Over the next six months the car required a large number of repairs—"repairs too numerous to list," in the words of the higher court. While most repairs were satisfactory, the major continuing problem was a "shimmying" that could be felt when the car was driven. After many unsuccessful attempts by FHD to remedy that problem, plaintiff left the car with FHD with a letter stating that he was revoking his acceptance. Plaintiff then brought this action against FHD and Chrysler Corporation, the manufacturer, to recover the purchase price. Among the numerous issues at trial was the major question as to whether the shimmy caused the car to be unmerchantable. On that point plaintiff introduced evidence that the shimmy, while reduced, was still noticeable and bothersome; defendants, on the other hand, contended that, taken as a whole, the car was of such a nature that it would "pass without objection within the automobile industry." The jury found the car to be unmerchantable; on appeal, one of the questions was whether the jury's finding of unmerchantability was supported by the evidence (in view of evidence that all other aspects of the car were, by that time, satisfactory). Do you think the jury's verdict should be upheld? Discuss. (*Welch v. Fitzgerald-Hicks Dodge, Inc.*, 430 A.2d 144, 1981.)

Chapter 23

SALES
Performance
and Remedies

In this final chapter on the law of sales we will discuss two subject areas: (1) performance of the sale contract (the obligations of both seller and buyer that are necessary to fulfill their agreement) and (2) remedies (the various avenues available to a seller or buyer if the other fails to live up to the contract obligations).

PERFORMANCE OF THE SALE CONTRACT

Generally speaking, the seller's obligation is to deliver conforming goods, and the buyer's obligation is to accept and pay for them. In Chapter 22, we dealt with the standards that goods must meet in order to be "conforming." While supplying goods that conform to the contract and to any applicable implied warranties is a very basic part of the seller's obligation, *total performance* involves a number of other aspects as well. In addition, several problem areas in the buyer's basic obligations of acceptance and payment require a closer look. The most important thing to remember is that the performance obligations of seller and buyer are ultimately controlled by the agreement of the parties themselves. The primary purposes of the UCC provisions in this area are to help in interpreting the agreement and to establish rules on matters not covered by the agreement.

Seller's Obligations

Tender of Delivery: How does a seller deliver the goods? Must he or she actually put them into the buyer's hands? Has the seller performed the obligation if the buyer has changed his or her mind and refuses to take the goods? The answer to these questions is that the seller fully performs the delivery obligation by "tendering" delivery. According to Sec. 2-503(1), to make a **tender of delivery** the seller must "put and hold conforming goods at the buyer's disposition and give the buyer any notification reasonably necessary to enable him to take delivery." That is, the seller must keep the goods available for the period of time reasonably necessary to enable the buyer to take possession.

Tender must be made at a *reasonable hour.* Suppose, for example, that prices have risen since the making of the contract. The seller cannot perform by tendering delivery at three o'clock in the morning (unless the agreement so provided) in the hope that the buyer will reject the tender.

If the agreement makes no mention of the *place of delivery,* it should be at the seller's place of business or, if the seller has none, at his or her residence. However, if at the time the contract is made the goods are identified and both parties know that they are located at some other location, that place is the place of delivery.

Usually the parties will have agreed on the place of delivery, and most agreements fall within either of two categories:

1. The buyer agrees to pick up the goods at a particular place without the seller having any responsibility for moving them.

2. The seller undertakes responsibility for transporting the goods to the buyer.

The first category may involve an agreement that the buyer will call for the goods at the seller's premises. Or the goods may be in the possession of a bailee (such as a warehouseman), with the buyer being responsible for picking them up. Where the goods are held by a bailee, tender of delivery by the seller is a matter of paperwork. He or she must either deliver to the buyer a *negotiable document of title* (a warehouse receipt) or obtain the *bailee's acknowledgment* that the buyer is entitled to possession (see Chapter 20 for a discussion on documents of title). Delivery by the seller of a nonnegotiable document of title is a proper tender of delivery only if the buyer does not object. Similarly, a mere written direction to the bailee to hand the goods over to the buyer (with no acknowledgment by the bailee of the buyer's rights) is a sufficient tender only if the buyer does not object.

The second category of agreement, in which the seller ships the goods, is further divided into shipment contracts and destination contracts. In a *shipment contract* the seller performs his or her obligations by tendering delivery at the point of shipment. Sec. 2-504 provides that, unless otherwise agreed:

1. The seller must put the goods in the possession of a carrier (such as a trucking or railway company), and the choice of carrier must be reasonable under the circumstances. Further, the seller's contract with the carrier for transporting the goods must also be reasonable under the circumstances. (For example, a contract with the carrier that understates the value of the goods for insurance purposes is not considered reasonable.)

2. The seller must obtain and promptly deliver in proper form any document (such as a bill of lading) necessary for the buyer to take possession of the goods.

3. The seller must promptly notify the buyer of shipment.

If the seller fails to meet the above requirements, the buyer can reject delivery only if a material loss or delay resulted—unless the parties have agreed differently. For instance, they might agree that failure to give prompt notification is a ground for rejection regardless of the consequences of the failure.

The seller's obligation in a *destination contract* is not fulfilled until delivery is tendered at the destination. Since the seller's required performance extends to the buyer's doorstep, so to speak, special provisions regarding selection of a carrier are not needed for the buyer's protection. The general tender requirements already set forth are sufficient. At the point of destination, the seller must put and hold the goods at the buyer's disposition at a reasonable hour, for a reasonable period of time, and with proper notice. And, of course, the seller must furnish any

required documents. Figure 23.1 illustrates the above requirements.

Commercial Shipping Terms: Sales contracts frequently contain terms that have well-established meanings in the commercial world but that are somewhat mysterious to the newcomer. For example, the contract may include phrases such as *FOB Detroit* or *FAS vessel, New York.* These indicate the parties' agreement on particular terms of shipment and are treated as shipping terms even when they appear only in connection with the price ("2.00/lb. FOB seller's plant"). Some of the more common terms are defined below.

FOB ("free on board"). If the named location following the FOB designation is the point of shipment, the agreement is a *shipment contract.* If the vehicle of transportation at the point of shipment is also referred to, the seller must not only put the goods into the possession of a carrier but also bear the expense of loading them on board. An example is "FOB Car 235Y, Mo. Pac. R.R. Depot, Dallas." If the named location following the FOB designation is the destination, the agreement is a *destination contract.*

FAS ("free alongside" vessel). FAS, frequently found in sale contracts where the goods are to be transported by seagoing vessel, indicates that a *shipment contract* has been made. The seller performs by delivering the goods alongside (on the dock next to) the vessel on which they are to be loaded, but does not bear the expense of loading.

Ex-ship ("from the carrying vessel"). The phrase *ex-ship,* also a maritime term, is actually the reverse of FAS. It denotes a *destination contract* and indicates that the seller's obligation extends to unloading the goods at the port of destination.

CIF ("cost, insurance, and freight") and C & F ("cost and freight"). CIF and C & F are also found almost exclusively in maritime agreements. CIF indicates that the price paid by the buyer includes the cost of the goods, insurance

Figure 23.1 **Seller's Obligations**

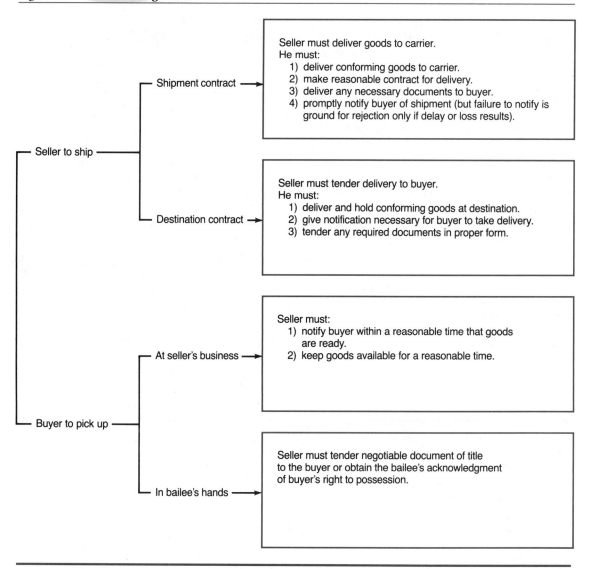

Seller must deliver goods to carrier.
He must:
1) deliver conforming goods to carrier.
2) make reasonable contract for delivery.
3) deliver any necessary documents to buyer.
4) promptly notify buyer of shipment (but failure to notify is ground for rejection only if delay or loss results).

Seller must tender delivery to buyer.
He must:
1) deliver and hold conforming goods at destination.
2) give notification necessary for buyer to take delivery.
3) tender any required documents in proper form.

Seller must:
1) notify buyer within a reasonable time that goods are ready.
2) keep goods available for a reasonable time.

Seller must tender negotiable document of title to the buyer or obtain the bailee's acknowledgment of buyer's right to possession.

Seller to ship — Shipment contract / Destination contract

Buyer to pick up — At seller's business / In bailee's hands

while they are in transit, and all freight charges. C & F means that the price includes the cost of the goods and freight charges but not insurance. Although the terms indicate that the agreement is a *shipment contract*, their inclusion means that the seller assumes obligations in addition to those of an ordinary shipment contract. The C & F term obligates the seller to see that the goods are loaded and to pay the freight charges. The CIF term further obligates the seller to obtain appropriate insurance coverage.

The Perfect Tender Rule: At common law there developed a doctrine known as the **perfect tender rule.** Under this rule, the seller's tender of delivery was required to conform in every detail to the terms of the agreement. In other words, the doctrine of substantial performance (discussed in Chapter 17) did not apply to contracts for the sale of goods. An extreme illustration of the perfect tender rule is found in *Filley v. Pope,* 115 U.S. 213 (1885). The seller agreed to sell pig iron to the buyer, the contract calling for shipment to New Orleans from Glasgow, Scotland. When the time for shipment arrived, no ships were available at Glasgow. The seller's factory in Scotland was halfway between the ports of Glasgow and Leith; and since vessels were available at Leith, he sent the iron to Leith for shipment. The buyer rejected the goods when they arrived. The Supreme Court held that the buyer was entitled to do so, because a contract calling for shipment from Glasgow is not fulfilled by a shipment from Leith even though no delay results.

UCC Sec. 2-601 essentially restates the perfect tender rule by providing that "if the goods or the tender of delivery fail in *any respect* to conform to the contract," the buyer is not obligated to accept them. (Emphasis added.)

Exceptions to the Perfect Tender Rule: The perfect tender rule is not as absolute as it might at first seem. The parties themelves can, of course, limit the rule by agreement. For example, they might agree that a delivery of defective goods cannot be rejected if the seller repairs or replaces the defective parts.[1]

Even though Sec. 2-601 makes the perfect tender rule seem rigid, several other provisions of the UCC significantly relax this strictness. The most important of these modifications are discussed below.

Cure: At common law the seller had only one chance to make a perfect tender. Somewhat more latitude is given the seller by Sec. 2-508 of the UCC. This section applies to the situation where the seller makes a tender of delivery that is deficient in some way but where the *time for performance has not yet expired.* In such a case, if the seller promptly notifies the buyer of an intention to "cure," he or she can then make a conforming delivery *before* expiration of the time for performance.

In certain unusual circumstances, Sec. 2-508 allows cure even after the agreed upon time for performance has expired. This can occur where the seller makes a tender of delivery that does not conform to the contract because he or she had *reasonable grounds to believe that the nonconforming tender would be acceptable.* For example, suppose that S is a distributor of petroleum products who supplies B's factory with machine lubricants. S and B have dealt with one another over a period of time, with each contract calling for delivery of Z brand oil. On several occasions in the past, when Z brand was unavailable, S substituted Y brand, which is equivalent to Z brand. On these occasions B did not object to the substitution. When the substitution occurred under the most recent contract, however, B rejected the oil, much to the surprise of S.[2] Since S had a reasonable basis for believing that the nonconforming delivery would be acceptable, he can make another tender of delivery if he promptly notifies B of his intention to do so. He must make the new tender within a reasonable time, which may extend beyond the contractual time for performance.

Installment contracts: An **installment contract** is defined in Sec. 2-612 as one requiring or authorizing the delivery of goods in separate lots to be separately accepted. A buyer can reject a particular installment only if the non-

---

[1] However, insofar as such a clause limits the application of an implied warranty, it must meet all the requirements of the UCC regarding disclaimers of warranty. In a consumer transaction it also must comply with the Magnuson-Moss Warranty Act.

[2] This situation involves a number of separate transactions rather than a single contract calling for delivery in several installments.

conformity *substantially impairs the value of that installment.* Furthermore, a nonconformity in a particular installment is a breach of the sale contract only if it substantially impairs the value of the *whole contract.* But if the buyer accepts the nonconforming installment without notifying the seller of cancellation, the contract is reinstated. This section of the UCC actually applies the doctrine of substantial performance to sale of goods contracts where delivery is in two or more separate lots.

Improper shipping arrangements: Remember that in a shipment contract the seller must (1) act appropriately in selecting and making a transportation contract with the carrier, (2) provide any documents necessary for the buyer to take possession of the goods, and (3) promptly notify the buyer of the shipment. However, failure by the seller to fulfill these obligations entitles the buyer to reject the delivery only if *material loss or delay* has resulted.

Substitute means of delivery: In some cases the parties specifically agree on the type of facilities to be used in loading, shipping, or unloading the goods. If, through no fault of either party, these agreed upon facilities become unavailable or impracticable, but a commercially reasonable substitute is available, the seller and buyer are required by Sec. 2-614 to use the substitute. (If the UCC had existed at the time of *Filley v. Pope,* the outcome of that case would have been different.)

Effect of Unforeseen Occurrences: The common-law rules applying to contracts in general also apply to sale of goods contracts unless they have been altered by the UCC. Thus, if the specific subject matter of the sale contract has been destroyed through no fault of either party, or if performance has become illegal because of a change in the law, both parties are excused from their contractual obligations.

Suppose that seller S and buyer B have contracted for the sale of one hundred head of cattle. If the cattle are damaged or destroyed

after risk of loss has passed to B (as would be the case in a shipment contract if the carrier is involved in an accident while transporting the cattle), then obviously S has already performed and B will have to pay for the goods. On the other hand, if a flash flood on S's land destroys the cattle *before* risk of loss has passed to B, then the financial loss will have to be borne by S, and B will not have to pay for the cattle.

If the destruction occurs before the risk of loss has passed, a further question remains: Is S excused from performing his part of the bargain? If the contract was for the sale of one hundred head of cattle but not necessarily the specific cattle that were destroyed, the answer is no. Not only has S suffered the loss but he also must still perform the contract by delivering one hundred head of cattle. But if the contract was for the sale of the specific cattle that were subsequently destroyed, S is excused from his obligation and is under no further duty to perform. This common-law rule is restated in UCC Sec. 2-613. (In addition to the basic rule covering cases of *total* destruction, Sec. 2-613 also covers cases where the loss is only *partial.* In such a situation B has a choice. He can treat the contract as canceled, thereby excusing both parties from their obligations. Or he can accept the goods in their damaged condition with an allowance deducted from the contract price.)

Commercial impracticability: The UCC also contains a provision, Sec. 2-615, to deal with certain types of unforeseen occurrences that do not result in damage to the specifically identified subject matter of the contract. If, because of unforeseen circumstances, delivery of the goods becomes "commercially impracticable," the parties are excused from their obligations. Of course, an increase in costs or change in the market price alone is not enough to relieve the seller of his or her responsibility; the existence of such risks is one of the main reasons for making binding contracts. But where the difficulty is of an *extraordinary* nature, such as the destruction of a source of supply that had been agreed upon or contemplated by both parties, the seller is excused. In such a case, however, the seller must have taken *all reasonable steps* to assure himself or herself that the source would not fail. The seller also is excused from delivering if a severe shortage of raw materials due to such events as war, embargo, or local crop failure causes a drastic increase in cost or completely prevents the seller from securing necessary supplies. A seller seeking to be excused because of commercial impracticability, however, must *promptly notify* the buyer of the problem.

Sometimes the commercial impracticability affects only *part* of the seller's capacity to perform. For instance, the unforeseen occurrence might result in a material delay or in a diminution of the quantity of available goods. Where the available quantity is diminished, Sec. 2-615 requires the seller to *allocate deliveries* among customers, including all customers then under contract and, if he or she chooses, regular customers not currently under contract. The seller must give *prompt notification* of either a delay or an allocation and, in the case of an allocation, must make an estimate of the quota available.

Buyer's Choices: When the buyer is notified of a significant delay or an allocation justified by commercial impracticability, he or she has a choice of cancelling the contract or keeping it in effect. To cancel, the buyer can either notify the seller or merely remain silent. However, if the seller's inability relates only to a particular delivery in an installment contract, the buyer can cancel the contract only if the value of the *whole contract* is substantially impaired. If the buyer has a right to cancel but wishes to keep the contract alive, he or she must give written notice to the seller indicating agreement to the delay or allocation. This notice by the buyer actually amounts to a modification of the contract and must be made within a reasonable time, not exceeding thirty days.

Although the doctrine of commercial impracticability is always important, it takes on added significance during times of economic uncertainty. The following case involves an attempt to escape from a contract which had been made less profitable by the energy crisis.

Eastern Airlines, Inc. v. Gulf Oil Co.
U.S. District Court, So. Dist. of Florida, 415 F.Supp. 429 (1975)

For a number of years Gulf Oil Co. had been a major supplier of the jet fuel used by Eastern Airlines to operate its fleet. The most recent contract between the two was made in 1972, and obligated Gulf to supply Eastern's fuel requirements at certain specified cities.

Since jet fuel is refined from crude oil, the cost of producing the fuel is directly affected by the price of crude. Although the price of crude oil produced in the United States was regulated by the federal government, this price had been increasing and was expected by Gulf and Eastern to continue rising. In addition, the percentage of oil imported into this country from foreign sources had been growing. The price of imported oil could not be regulated by the U.S. government and, therefore, was more subject to market fluctuations. Because of these factors, Gulf and Eastern included in their 1972 contract a clause which permitted Gulf to charge higher prices on future deliveries of jet fuel to Eastern as the price of crude oil increased. However, this "escalator" clause in their contract permitted a rise in

the jet fuel price only to the extent the government-regulated price of U.S.-produced oil increased.

After Gulf and Eastern made their agreement, the federal government partially decontrolled the price of domestically produced oil. In other words, the government removed the ceiling on the price of a portion of the oil produced in this country, thus permitting this price to rise to the world market level. Shortly thereafter, the foreign oil cartel, OPEC (Organization of Petroleum Exporting Countries), increased the price of its oil about 400 percent. This, of course, also caused the unregulated portion of U.S.-produced oil to rise dramatically. In producing jet fuel, Gulf was using some regulated domestic oil (on which there was a government-imposed price ceiling), some unregulated domestic oil, and some foreign oil. The escalator clause in the Gulf-Eastern contract *only* permitted jet fuel price increases in accordance with increases in the government-regulated price of domestic oil. Gulf ultimately found this clause to be quite inadequate to cover its increased costs of production.

In March, 1974, Gulf demanded that Eastern pay more for jet fuel then the escalator clause permitted, or Gulf would shut off Eastern's supply of fuel. Eastern refused to pay more and sued Gulf for breach of contract. Gulf defended on the ground that performance of the contract had become "commercially impracticable" and that it should therefore be excused from the contract as provided in UCC Sec. 2-615. The federal district court ruled as follows.

King, District Judge:

. . . Official Comments 4 and 8 to UCC §2-615 [prepared by the drafters of the Code] provide:

> *4. Increased cost alone does not excuse performance unless the rise in cost is due to some unforeseen contingency which alters the essential nature of the performance. Neither is a rise or a collapse in the market itself a justification, for that is exactly the type of business risk which business contracts made at fixed prices are intended to cover. But a severe shortage of raw materials, or of supplies due to a contingency such as war, embargo, local crop failure, unforeseen shutdown of major sources of supply or the like, which either causes a marked increase in cost or altogether prevents the seller from securing supplies necessary to his performance, is within the contemplation of this section. . . .*

> *8. The provisions of this section are made subject to assumption of greater liability by agreement and such agreement is to be found not only in the expressed terms of the contract but in the circumstances surrounding the contracting, in trade usage and the like. Thus the exemptions of this section do not apply when the contingency in question is sufficiently foreshadowed at the time of contracting to be included among the business risks which are fairly to be regarded as part of the dickered terms, either consciously or as a matter of reasonable, commercial interpretation from the circumstances. . . .*

In short, for UCC §2-615 to apply there must be a failure of a presupposed condition, which was an underlying assumption of the contract, which failure was unforeseeable, and the risk of which was not specifically allocated to the complaining party. The burden of proving each element of claimed commercial impracticability is on the party claiming excuse.

The modern UCC §2-615 doctrine of commercial impracticability has its roots in the common law doctrine[s] of frustration of [purpose and] impossibility and finds its most recognized illustrations in the so-called "Suez Cases," arising out of the various closings of the Suez Canal and the consequent increases in shipping costs around the Cape of Good Hope. Those cases offered little encouragement to those who would wield the sword of commercial impracticability. As a leading British case arising out of the 1957 Suez closure declared, the unforeseen cost increase that would excuse performance "must be more than merely onerous or expensive. It must be positively unjust to hold the parties bound." *Ocean Tramp Tankers v. V/O Sovfracht (The Eugenia),* 2 QB 226, 239 (1964). . . .

[R]ecent American cases similarly strictly construe the doctrine of commercial impracticability. For example, one case found no UCC defense, even though costs had doubled over the contract price. . . . Recently, the Seventh Circuit has stated: "The fact that performance has become economically burdensome or unattractive is not sufficient for performance to be excused. We will not allow a party to a contract to escape a bad bargain merely because it is burdensome. [T]he buyer has a right to rely on the party to the contract to supply him with goods regardless of what happens to the market price. That is the purpose for which such contracts are made." *Neal-Cooper Grain Co. v. Texas Gulf Sulfur Co.,* 508 F.2d 283 (7th Cir. 1974). . . .

With regard to Gulf's contention that the contract has become "commercially impracticable" within the meaning of UCC §2-615, because of the increase in market price of foreign crude oil and certain domestic crude oils, the court finds that the defense has not been proved. On this record the court cannot determine how much it costs Gulf to produce a gallon of jet fuel for sale to Eastern, whether Gulf loses money or makes a profit on its sale of jet fuel to Eastern, either now or at the inception of the contract, or at any time in between. Gulf's witnesses testified that they could not make such a computation. The party undertaking the burden of establishing "commercial impracticability" by reason of allegedly increased raw material costs undertakes the obligation of showing the extent to which he has suffered, or will suffer, losses in performing his contract. The record here does not substantiate Gulf's contention on this fundamental issue.

Gulf presented evidence tending to show that its "costs" of crude oil have increased dramatically over the past two years. However, the "costs" to which Gulf adverts are unlike any "costs" that might arguably afford ground for any of the relief sought here. Gulf's claimed "costs" of an average barrel of crude oil at Gulf's refineries (estimated by Gulf's witness Davis at about $10.00 currently, and about $9.50 during 1974) include *intracompany profits,* as the oil moved from Gulf's overseas and domestic production departments to its refining department. *The magnitude of that profit was not revealed.* . . . [Emphasis added.]

[T]hese are not the kinds of "costs" against which to measure hardship, real or imagined, under the Uniform Commercial Code. Under no theory of law can it be held that Gulf is guaranteed preservation of its intracompany profits, moving from the left hand to the right hand, as one Gulf witness so aptly put it. The burden is upon Gulf to show what its real costs are, not its "costs" inflated by its internal profits at various levels of the manufacturing process and located in various foreign countries.

No criticism is implied of Gulf's rational desire to maximize its profits and take every advantage available to it under the laws. However, these factors cannot be ignored in approaching Gulf's contention that it has been unduly burdened by crude oil price increases. No such hardship has been established. On the contrary, the record clearly establishes that 1973, the year in which the energy crisis began, was Gulf's best year ever, in which it recorded some $800 million in net profits after taxes. Gulf's 1974 year was more than 25% better than 1973's record: $1,065,000,000 profits were booked by Gulf in 1974 after paying all taxes.

For the foregoing reasons, Gulf's claim of hardship giving rise to "commercial impracticability" fails.

But even if Gulf had established great hardship under UCC §2-615, which it has not, Gulf would not prevail because the events associated with the so-called energy crisis were reasonably foreseeable at the time the contract was executed. If a contingency is foreseeable, it and its consequences are taken outside the scope of UCC §2-615, because the party disadvantaged by the contingency [could] have protected himself in his contract. . . .

The record is replete with evidence as to the volatility of the Middle East situation, the arbitrary power of host governments to control the foreign oil market, and repeated interruptions and interference with the normal commercial trade in crude oil. Even without the extensive evidence present in the record, the court would be justified in taking judicial notice of the fact that oil has been used as a political weapon with increasing success by the oil-producing nations for many years, and Gulf was well aware of and assumed the risk that the OPEC nations would do exactly what they have done.

With respect to Gulf's argument that [partial decontrol of domestic oil prices by the U.S. government] was not "foreseeable," the record shows that domestic crude oil prices were controlled at all material times, that Gulf foresaw that they might be decontrolled, and that Gulf was constantly urging to the Federal Government that they should be decontrolled. Government price regulations were confused, constantly changing, and uncertain during the period of the negotiation and execution of the contract. During that time frame, high ranking Gulf executives, including some of its trial witnesses, were in constant repeated contact with officials and agencies of the Federal Government regarding petroleum policies and were well able to protect themselves from any contingencies. . . .

Knowing all the facts, Gulf drafted the contract and tied the escalation clause to the [government-regulated price]. The court is of the view that it is bound thereby.

[Judgment for plaintiff Eastern; decree of specific performance issued against Gulf.]

Buyer's Obligations

When the seller has made a sufficient tender of delivery, the burden then falls on the buyer to perform his or her part of the contract.

Providing Facilities: Unless otherwise agreed, the buyer must furnish facilities that are reasonably suited for receipt of the goods.

Right of Inspection: Inspection of the goods by the buyer is a matter depending entirely upon the terms of the agreement. But if the parties have not limited inspection by their agreement, the buyer has a right to inspect the goods before accepting or paying for them—at any reasonable place and time and in any reasonable manner. When the goods are shipped to the buyer, inspection can occur after their arrival. Expenses of inspection must be borne by the buyer but can be recovered from the seller if the goods do not conform and are rejected.

Sometimes the parties' agreement obligates the buyer to make payment before inspecting the goods. For example, when a contract calls for COD ("collect on delivery"), there is no right of inspection before payment unless other terms of the contract expressly grant such a right. Contracts can also require "payment against documents," which means that, unless otherwise agreed, payment is due on receipt of the required documents of title regardless of when the goods themselves actually arrive. CIF and C & F contracts, for example, require payment on receipt of documents unless the parties have agreed to the contrary. Where a contract calls for payment before inspection, payment must be made unless the goods are so obviously nonconforming that inspection is not needed.

When payment is required before inspection, it does not constitute a final acceptance of the goods. Rejection of the goods can still occur if the buyer inspects after the required payment and finds that they are nonconforming.

Acceptance: When conforming goods have been properly tendered, the buyer's basic duty is to accept them, which means simply that the buyer takes the goods as his or her own. This **acceptance** can occur in three different ways:

1. The buyer can expressly indicate acceptance by words. For example, there is an acceptance if the buyer, after having had a reasonable opportunity to inspect, signifies to the seller either that the goods are conforming or that he or she will take them despite their nonconformity.

2. Acceptance also occurs if the buyer has had a reasonable opportunity to inspect the goods and has failed to reject them within a reasonable period of time.

3. The buyer accepts the goods by performing any act inconsistent with the seller's ownership. For example, using, consuming, or reselling the goods usually constitutes an acceptance. However, reasonable use or consumption for the sole purpose of testing is not an acceptance.

Partial Acceptance: If part of the goods are conforming and part are nonconforming, the buyer can make a partial acceptance; he or she cannot, however, accept less than a commercial unit. A *commercial unit* is defined in Sec. 2-105 as a unit of goods recognized in commercial practice as being a "single whole" for purposes of sale, the division of which materially impairs its value. It can be a single article (such as a machine), a set of articles (such as a suite of furniture or an assortment of suits in different sizes), a quantity (such as a bale, gross, or carload), or any other unit treated in use or in the relevant market as a single whole.

Payment: Seller and buyer can agree upon credit arrangements or agree that payment is due when the buyer receives a document of title, regardless of when the goods arrive. But if the parties do not expressly agree on a time for payment, *it is due when the buyer receives the goods.*

While the price is ordinarily payable in money, the parties can agree that some other medium of exchange (such as other commodities) will be used. In addition, the buyer can use any method of making payment that is generally acceptable in the commercial world (such as a check). But the seller can demand payment in *legal tender* (currency) if he or she desires. A seller who makes such a demand must allow the buyer a reasonable amount of time to obtain legal tender. If the buyer pays by check and the check is accepted by the seller, the buyer has performed the obligation of payment unless the check is dishonored (bounced) by the bank.

Some buyers pay with a *letter of credit* (used primarily in foreign commerce). The buyer obtains the letter of credit from his or her own bank, and the bank guarantees to the seller that payment will be made when the proper documents are tendered.

INTRODUCTION TO REMEDIES

Thus far we have focused our discussion on the performance of the sale contract by both parties. But suppose the contract is instead breached by one of the parties. What avenues are open to the other party?

Options in the Event of Anticipatory Repudiation

A breach of contract can occur at any stage in the transaction after the contract is made, even before the time for performance falls due. If, before time for performance, one party clearly communicates to the other the intention not to perform, that party has breached the contract by an **anticipatory repudiation.** In such an event, Sec. 2-610 provides that the "aggrieved party"—the party receiving the repudiation—has two options. First, the party may wait a reasonable length of time before resorting to any remedies, in the hope that the repudiating party will change his or her mind. In the alternative, the aggrieved party may treat the contract as having been breached, and immediately pursue the appropriate remedies. (And, in either case, the aggrieved party may suspend his or her performance.)

Sometimes there is not a clear-cut repudiation but the circumstances are such that one party has reasonable doubts about whether the other is going to perform. In such a case the party who has a reasonable basis for feeling insecure can demand in writing that the other party give *assurance of performance.* Adequate assurance of performance must then be given within a reasonable time (not exceeding thirty days) after receipt of the demand. Failure to give this assurance in response to a justified demand constitutes an anticipatory repudiation.

SELLER'S REMEDIES

The seller's remedies are set forth in Secs. 2-703 to 710 of the UCC. Under these sections, the remedies that are available to a seller in a particular situation depend on the circumstances existing at the time of the buyer's breach.

Where Buyer Breaches before Receiving the Goods

Following are the remedies for the seller where the buyer has repudiated or otherwise breached the contract before receiving the goods:

1. The seller can cancel the contract.

2. If the goods are in the seller's possession or control but have not yet been identified, he or she can take the steps necessary to identify them (separate them from inventory, tag or label them, and so on). If they are in an unfinished condition, the seller can complete their manufacture if it is reasonable to do so for the purpose of minimizing the loss—or cease manufacture and resell for scrap or salvage value.

3. The seller can *withhold delivery* of goods still in his or her hands, and in some cases even *stop delivery* where the goods have been shipped but have not yet been received by the buyer. Because of the burden to the carrier, seller can stop delivery only if a carload, truckload, planeload, or larger shipment is involved. (The only exception to this quantity requirement is where delivery is stopped because of the buyer's insolvency. In such a case, delivery can be stopped regardless of the quantity of goods involved.) Also, if the carrier has issued a *negotiable bill of lading* (see Chapter 20), the seller can stop delivery only by surrendering the document to the carrier. Thus stoppage in transit cannot occur if the seller has already sent a negotiable bill of lading to the buyer.

4. The seller can *resell* the goods in a commercially reasonable manner at either a private or public (auction) sale. If the resale is *private,* the buyer must be given prior notice of it; if it is *public,* the buyer must be given prior notice unless the goods are perishable or otherwise threaten to rapidly decline in value. A purchaser who buys in good faith at a resale takes the goods free of any rights of the original buyer even if the seller has not conducted the resale in a commercially reasonable manner. When the seller has resold the goods in a proper manner, the damages to which he or she is entitled include the amount by which the contract price exceeds the resale price plus incidental damages such as additional transportation and handling expenses.[3] Any expenses saved because of the buyer's breach are deducted from the seller's damages. If the seller *does not resell,* the damages are computed in either of two ways, depending on which is more advantageous to the seller: (a) the amount by which the contract price exceeds the market price at the time and place for tender (rather than the actual resale price), plus incidental damages, minus expenses saved; or (b) the profit that the seller would have made had the contract been performed, plus incidental damages, minus expenses saved.

5. Under some circumstances the seller can sue to recover the *purchase price* from the buyer, even though the buyer did not receive the goods. This can occur, for example, where (a) the

buyer legally accepted the goods while they were still in the seller's possession; (b) the seller shipped conforming goods that were lost or destroyed after risk of loss had passed to the buyer; or (c) the seller made reasonable but unsuccessful efforts to resell the goods at a reasonable price. If the seller receives a court judgment against the buyer for the purchase price, and then, because of changed conditions, is able to resell the goods before the buyer pays the judgment, the proceeds of the sale must be credited to the buyer. Payment of the judgment entitles the buyer to any of the goods not resold.

Where Buyer Breaches after Receiving the Goods

The seller's remedies where buyer's breach occurs after he or she receives the goods are:

1. If the buyer accepts the goods and does not pay for them, the seller can recover the purchase price plus any incidental damages resulting from the breach.

2. If the buyer wrongfully rejects or revokes acceptance and does not pay, the seller's remedies depend on *whether he or she retakes possession* of the goods. If possession is retaken, the remedies are basically the same as if the buyer had breached *before* receiving the goods. In addition to canceling the contract, the seller can resell the goods, keep them and recover damages, or recover the purchase price plus incidental damages if resale is impossible. If the seller does not retake possession, the remedies are the same as if the buyer had accepted the goods. In other words, the seller can recover the purchase price plus incidental damages.

The issue raised in the following case, where the buyer breached the contract while the goods were still in the seller's hands, is typical of those which necessitate interpretation of the code sections applicable to sellers' (and buyers') remedies.

---

[3]The seller is not accountable to the buyer for any profit made on the resale.

Luprofresh, Inc. v. Pabst Brewing Company
Superior Court of Delaware, New Castle
County, 505 A.2d 37 (1985)

Luprofresh, Inc., plaintiff, contracted to sell a quantity of hops to Pabst Brewing Company at a specified price. Luprofresh, after processing and storing the hops, notified Pabst that the hops were ready for delivery. Pabst replied with a letter saying it "accepted" the goods, but thereafter breached the contract by refusing to issue shipping orders. Luprofresh then brought this action to recover the purchase price of the hops from Pabst, defendant.

Defendant, in its pleadings, raised two defenses: (1) a claim that plaintiff's pricing policies (upon which the contract price was based) violated the federal antitrust laws, and (2) the contention that, under Article 2 of the UCC, plaintiff was entitled to recover the purchase price only after making a reasonable effort to resell the goods, and that plaintiff's pleadings did not allege such an effort was made.

The court ruled against defendant on both points. Accordingly, it entered a summary judgment (judgment on the pleadings) for plaintiff in the amount of the contract price. (Only that part of the trial court's decision relating to the UCC issue appears below.)

Taylor, Judge:

. . . [Plaintiff] contends that it is entitled to the full purchase price under the contract. Defendant contends that under [Section 2-709 of the UCC] the plaintiff cannot recover the contract price until it proves reasonable effort to resell the goods at a reasonable price, or that such effort would be unavailing.

UCC §2-709 permits the seller to recover the purchase price of goods which have been accepted by the buyer. Plaintiff contends that the hops were accepted by defendant, [pointing to] defendant's letter to plaintiff which states, "we have accepted the following lots (nos. and quantity specified)." A subsequent letter to Luprofresh requests "confirmation of the quantity of hops inventories owned by us and stored on your premises as of December 31, 1984."

UCC §2-606 provides that goods are accepted by the buyer when (1) after reasonable opportunity to inspect the goods, the buyer signifies to the seller that the goods are conforming, or (2) after such opportunity the buyer fails to reject the goods, or (3) the buyer does any act inconsistent with the seller's ownership. The letters from plaintiff referred to above are evidence of identification of specific goods and acceptance satisfying §2-606. Defendant has presented no [evidence] disputing this.

Defendant contends that any recovery by the seller is subject to the restriction that the seller must have made reasonable effort to resell the goods at a reasonable price. This contention is not supported by the language of §2-709, because it fails to differentiate between the Code provisions applicable to "goods accepted" and "goods identified." §2-709(1)(a) gives an unqualified right to the seller of "goods accepted" to recover the price. §2-709(1)(b) gives a conditional right to the seller to recover the price "if the seller is unable after reasonable effort to resell them at a reasonable price or the circumstances reasonably indicate that such effort will be unavailing." "Goods accepted" are specific goods which have been inspected by the buyer, or at least the buyer must have been afforded reasonable opportunity for such inspection. Hence, all "goods accepted" are "goods identified."

It is noted that subsection (2) [of §2-709] imposes the prerequisite to recovery of the purchase price that the seller "must hold for the buyer any goods which have been identified to the contract and are still in his control." That section does permit the seller to resell the goods, but since it uses the words "he may resell them at any time prior to collection of the judgment" *it does not mandate resale.* [Emphasis added.]

The status of "goods identified" is achieved by the unilateral action of the seller. The status of "goods accepted" requires that the buyer must have accepted the goods after inspection or waived his right of inspection . . . by inaction, in addition to the seller's action in identifying the goods. The draftsmen of §2-709 contemplated a different standard of recovery for the seller of "goods accepted" from that provided for the seller of "goods identified" [but not accepted]. The apparent objective of §2-709(1)(a) *was to afford a more direct remedy against the buyer who had "accepted" goods than it afforded against the buyer who has not "accepted" goods.* [Emphasis added.]

Based on the foregoing considerations, I find nothing in the portions of the UCC which have been cited which prevents plaintiff from recovering the purchase price. . . .

Judgment for plaintiff.

BUYER'S REMEDIES

The buyer's remedies are set forth in Secs. 2-711 to 2-718 of the UCC.

Where Seller Fails to Deliver

When the seller breaches the contract by failing to deliver the goods according to the contract, the following remedies are available to the buyer:

1. The buyer can cancel the contract, which relieves him or her of any contractual obligations.

2. The buyer can recover any prepayments made to the seller.

3. The buyer can **cover** (buy the goods elsewhere in a commercially reasonable manner) and receive damages. The damages include (a) the amount by which the cover price exceeds the contract price; (b) any incidental expenses—out-of-pocket costs such as additional transportation and handling expenses; and (c) any consequential losses, such as the buyer's lost profits, that should have been foreseen by the seller as resulting from the breach. Deducted from the buyer's damages, however, are any expenses saved because of the seller's breach. If the buyer does not wish to cover, he or she can receive the amount by which the market price exceeds the contract price, plus any incidental and consequential damages, minus any expenses saved. The market price is determined as of the time when the buyer learned of the breach and as of the place where delivery should have been tendered.

4. In most cases the buyer will be unable to recover the goods themselves from the seller and will have to be content with money damages. In certain circumstances, however, the buyer can obtain a court decree entitling him or her to possession of the particular goods contracted for. If the goods are *unique* (such as an heirloom), the buyer can recover them by obtaining a decree of *specific performance* (an order commanding the seller to live up to the agreement). Even if the goods are not unique, the buyer can recover them (a) where they have been specifically identified and (b) where the buyer has made reasonable but unsuccessful efforts to cover or where the circumstances reasonably indicate that such efforts would be fruitless (such as where the goods are in very short supply). The technical name for the buyer's recovery of goods in this type of situation is *replevin.*

Where Seller Delivers Nonconforming Goods

If the seller delivers goods that are defective or in some other way do not conform to the contract, the buyer must notify the seller within a reasonable time after discovering the nonconformity in order to be able to pursue available remedies. The buyer's remedies in this situation are:

1. The buyer can cancel the contract.

2. The buyer can recover any prepayments made to the seller.

3. The buyer can *reject* the delivery. Under the perfect tender rule, the buyer can usually reject if the tender or the goods fail in any respect to conform to the contract. Where the defects are of a type that can be discovered by reasonable in-spection, sometimes the buyer can reject only by specifying them in the notice to the seller. This duty to specify defects exists (a) where they can be cured if the seller learns of them promptly or (b) where the specification is requested by one merchant from another merchant.

4. If the buyer has already accepted delivery, however, he or she cannot thereafter reject it. Of course, acceptance is more than just receiving the goods; it means taking them as one's own. However, in a few circumstances the buyer can *revoke his or her acceptance.*

  a. An acceptance can be revoked only if the nonconformity *substantially impairs the value* to the buyer of the delivery or commercial unit in question. For example, a cracked engine block substantially impairs the value of a car, while a malfunctioning clock in the dashboard does not.

  b. Where the buyer *knew* of the nonconformity when accepting, he or she can revoke the acceptance only if it was made on the reasonable assumption that the nonconformity would be cured, but it has not been. On the other hand, where the buyer *did not know* of the nonconformity when accepting, he or she can revoke (1) if the acceptance had been made because of the difficulty of discovering the nonconformity at an earlier time or (2) because of the seller's assurances that there were no defects.

  c. Revocation of acceptance must occur within a reasonable time after the buyer discovers the basis for it and before any substantial change occurs in the condition of the goods (other than by their own defects).

5. The effect of a rejection or a revocation of acceptance is the same: the goods are not the buyer's and he or she does not have to pay for them. After a justified rejection or revocation the seller usually makes arrangements to take back the goods. The buyer must return the goods on request if the seller refunds any payments made on the price and reimburses the buyer for reasonable expenses incurred in inspecting, receiving, transporting, and caring for them. While in possession of the goods the buyer has certain rights and duties with respect to them:

a. The first duty is to follow all reasonable instructions given by the seller regarding the goods. A seller's instructions are unreasonable if he or she does not guarantee payment of expenses after the buyer has demanded it.

b. If the seller does not pick up the goods or give instructions as to their handling within a reasonable time, the buyer has three alternatives—storing the goods for the seller's account, reshipping them to the seller, or reselling them for the seller's account. (In unusual situations the buyer is actually under a *duty to try to resell the goods* for the seller when reasonable instructions are not given. This duty arises if the buyer is a merchant, the seller has no agent or place of business in the buyer's locality, and the goods are perishable or otherwise threaten to rapidly decline in value.) The buyer has a right to recover reasonable expenses in handling the goods in these situations, just as when following the seller's instructions. One note of caution: a buyer who resells goods without being entitled to do so has legally accepted them.

6. The buyer can cover if he or she wishes, and damages will be computed in the same manner as when the seller breaches by failing to deliver.

7. Finally, the buyer can *accept and keep the goods* despite their nonconformity and still recover all damages caused by the nonconformity. This is frequently the situation in *breach of warranty* cases where the product has already been used or consumed when the defect is discovered. The buyer's damages in such cases are the difference between the actual value of the goods and the value they would have had if they had conformed to the warranty, plus incidental and consequential damages. Consequential damages in a breach of warranty case include bodily injury and property damage caused by the breach and often constitute the largest portion of the buyer's damages. If the goods are not yet paid for, the purchase price is offset against the damages.

Both of the following cases have to do with buyers' remedies. In the first of these, the question is whether the buyer had the right to revoke his acceptance of the goods. The second case illustrates application of the rule that a plaintiff is allowed to recover only those damages which are the reasonably direct and foreseeable consequence of the defendant's breach of contract.

Vista Chevrolet, Inc. v. Lewis
Court of Appeals of Texas, Corpus Christi, 704 S.W.2d 363 (1985)

Lewis, plaintiff, purchased a new 1981 Chevrolet Monte Carlo automobile for his wife from Vista Chevrolet (Vista), defendant, in December of 1980. On March 3, 1981, Mrs. Lewis attempted to start the car after it had not been used over a weekend. When the car would not start she had to "jump start" it, and then drove it to Vista to have it repaired.

Subsequently, over a period of 16 months, Mrs. Lewis continued to experience the "exact same problem" ("it wouldn't start after it sat"), and the vehicle was returned to Vista to be repaired for the same problem on ten separate occasions. (During that same period the car failed to start "three or four" additional times, but it was not returned in these instances because Mrs. Lewis did not have time to take it in.)

When Vista's repeated attempts to correct the defect between March of 1981 and May of 1982 were unsuccessful, Mrs. Lewis contacted her attorney. On June 21, 1982, he wrote to Vista that Mr. Lewis was revoking his acceptance of the automobile, and demanded the return of the payments that had been made. When Vista refused to take the car back, Lewis brought this action against Vista to recover the payments, asserting that he had "properly exercised his right to revoke acceptance of said vehicle" pursuant to Sec. 2-608 of the UCC. Lewis also sought damages from Vista, alleging that it had made false representations about the vehicle at the time of purchase in violation of the Texas Deceptive Trade Practices Act (DTPA).

The trial court, based upon the jury's findings, rendered judgment on both the revocation of acceptance and the DTPA causes of action in favor of Lewis, and Vista appealed. (Only that part of the higher court's decision dealing with the revocation of acceptance issue is set forth below.)

Utter, Justice:

. . . The record shows (1) that, on March 3, 1981 (the date of the first occurrence of the problem), the automobile had been driven approximately 2,498 miles; (2) that, at the time of the alleged revocation of acceptance on June 21, 1982, the automobile had been driven approximately 22,232 miles; and (3) that, at the time of the trial (beginning February 27, 1984), the automobile had been driven approximately 40,000 miles. . . .

Appellant [Vista] asserts that there is no evidence or insufficient evidence in the record to show (1) that the claimed defect or nonconformity of the automobile substantially impaired the value of the automobile to appellee [Lewis], . . . and (3) that the revocation of acceptance occurred within a reasonable time after discovery of the claimed defect or nonconformity. . . .

Appellant argues that, since Mrs. Lewis had driven the automobile approximately 22,200 miles over a twenty month period before the alleged revocation of acceptance, the claimed defect or nonconformity could not have substantially impaired the value of the automobile to her. . . . The evidence reflects Mrs. Lewis' continued use of the automobile prior to the alleged revocation of acceptance was, at least in part, induced by the repeated representations by Vista Chevrolet that the claimed defect or nonconformity could be and had been repaired; whereas the evidence also shows that all of the repeated attempts to repair the problem with the automobile were unsuccessful.

The determination regarding whether the defect or nonconformity substantially impaired the value of the good to the buyer to justify revocation of acceptance is a fact issue for the trier of fact to determine. . . .

The mere fact that the continued use of a motor vehicle increases the mileage placed on the vehicle does not bar the buyer from revoking his acceptance of the vehicle for substantial impairment of the value of the vehicle to the buyer. . . . We hold that, under the facts of this case, there is evidence upon which the jury could have found that the claimed defect or nonconformity substantially impaired the value of the automobile to the appellee, especially when that defect or nonconformity remained uncorrected despite the seller's repeated repair attempts and assurances of correction. . . .

In regard to the reasonableness of notification requirement for revocation of acceptance, appellant argues that, considering (a) the length of time between the date of purchase and the date of the alleged revocation of acceptance and (b) the length of time during which appellee and Mrs. Lewis knew that the claimed defect or nonconformity existed, "it would seem that the timing was anything but reasonable."

It is a question of fact for the trier of fact to determine whether notice was made within a "reasonable time." A delay in making notice of revocation of acceptance of goods is justified where a seller makes repeated assurances that the defect or nonconformity will be cured, and attempts to do so. We conclude that, under the facts of this case, the jury could have found that appellee was reasonably justified in delaying his notice of revocation of acceptance of the automobile in view of Vista Chevrolet's repeated assurances that the defect or nonconformity would be cured and its unsuccessful attempts to do so. Consequently, we hold that there is sufficient evidence upon which the jury could have found that appellee notified Vista Chevrolet of its alleged revocation of acceptance within a "reasonable time."

[The higher court thus affirmed the trial court's judgment in favor of Lewis on the revocation of acceptance issue. However, that part of the trial court's judgment relating to Lewis's DTPA claim was reversed because the trial court's method of determining damages was erroneous. Accordingly, the case was remanded to the trial court for the sole purpose of having that court redetermine Lewis's damages in conformity with rules supplied by the higher court.][a]

---

[a]Most states today have special statutes—so-called "lemon laws"—that provide remedies to buyers of new cars additional to those of the UCC. These statutes are examined briefly at the end of the chapter.

Baden v. Curtiss Breeding Service
U.S. District Court, Montana, 380 F.Supp. 243 (1974)

Baden, a rancher, purchased bull semen from Curtiss Breeding Service for the purpose of artificial insemination. The semen was defective and no calves were born. Baden, plaintiff, sued Curtiss, defendant, for breach of warranty, contending that his consequential damages should include not only the value of the 1972 calf crop which was not born but also the 1974 calf crop that might have been expected from the calves born in 1972. The opinion of the trial court on this point appears below.

Smith, Justice:

. . . Under the code the rule with respect to consequential damage is: "All that is necessary, in order to charge the defendant with the particular loss, is that it is one that ordinarily follows the breach of such a contract in the usual course of events, or that reasonable men in the position of the parties would have foreseen as a probable result of breach." In the case of semen sold for artificial insemination, the seller knows that if the semen is defective the inseminated cow may not become pregnant and the capital investment devoted to that cow in that year may be totally unproductive. Certainly the loss of a calf or calves is one that ordinarily follows the use of defective semen and one which the parties would reasonably foresee. I have difficulty, however, in extending this foreseeability to the loss of the second calf crop, that is, the calves which would have been produced in 1974 by the 1972 calf crop had there been one.

When a rancher discovers that his cows are barren he may be expected to keep his capital, that is, the ranch, equipment and livestock, busy in what seems to him to be the most productive way. The fact that a calf crop is lost does not mean that the ranch operation stops. Replacements for the cow herd are bought and are bred and the operation continues. The capital is kept busy, and it appears to me that reasonable men in the position of the parties here would not foresee the loss of a second calf crop as a proximate result of the defective semen, nor do I think they would foresee that a plaintiff would so conduct his operation that a second calf crop actually raised necessarily would be of less value than the one which the plaintiff had hoped to raise. . . .

Many variables affect the commercial production of beef animals. Always present are the factors of the fertility of the heifer, the fertility of the bull, the efficacy of the breeding, the risks of calving, disease, and accident. These risks make the projection of the result of the breeding in any one season somewhat uncertain. But if projections are extended beyond the first calving and into the calving of the calves (a period of over two and one-half years from the first breeding), the effects of the variables are greatly magnified and the projection becomes more uncertain.

Any rule of damages which permits the recovery for losses beyond the first calf crop makes the selling defendant accept in some degree another variable, and that is the risk of the buying plaintiff's management.

Allowing recovery for consequential damages up to the first calf crop does permit plaintiffs to produce evidence to show the effect of the variables in the first year and does make defendant accept what may be inequities in the appraisal of those variables. It may seem arbitrary to hold that the uncertainties up to the first calf crop may be tolerated but that no matter what the proof is the uncertainties beyond that point will not be. At some point, however, the degree of uncertainty permitted becomes a question of law. The fact is that as to the first calf crop we deal with cows that were born and did live long enough to become fertile. In the case of the second calf crop we must project a supposititious calf into a period of supposititious fertility followed by a supposititiously successful breeding which is in turn followed by a supposititiously successful calving, and hence motherhood. In my opinion the need for these suppositions is sufficient to warrant a distinction between the loss of the first calf crop and the loss of the second and to permit the line to be drawn where I have drawn it.

[Judgment for plaintiff for damages caused by loss of 1972 calf crop only.]

Insolvency ✓

The insolvency of one party may affect the other's remedies. Suppose, for example, that the buyer has prepaid the purchase price and seller becomes insolvent before shipping the goods. If the goods have been identified to the contract, the buyer can compel the seller to turn them over to him or her in certain circumstances. (Sec. 2-502).

If the buyer becomes insolvent during the course of a transaction, under Sec. 2-702 the seller can refuse to deliver except for cash. Also—as noted earlier—if the goods have been shipped and are still in transit, the seller can usually stop delivery unless he or she has already forwarded a negotiable document of title to the buyer.

There are times, however, when the UCC, which is state law, will not prevail. A seller or buyer who becomes insolvent will often go into bankruptcy, a proceeding governed by federal law. Since the federal bankruptcy law prevails over state laws, the remedies granted in the UCC may have little practical significance in cases of insolvency.

Prior Agreement as to Remedies

The parties to a sale contract can provide in their agreement for remedies to be available in the event of breach. Under Sec. 2-718, they can agree on liquidated damages (the measure of damages to be payable in case of breach). Their provision must be reasonable, taking into account the anticipated or actual harm caused by the breach, the difficulties of proof of loss, and the inconvenience of otherwise obtaining an adequate remedy. If the contract sets an unreasonably large amount of liquidated damages, the amount will simply be ignored by the court.

More generally, Sec. 2-719 states that "the agreement may provide for remedies in addition to or in substitution for" those provided in the UCC. For example, the parties might agree that the buyer's only remedy for breach of warranty will be to bring the goods back to the seller for repairs. However, Sec. 2-719 also provides that if the clause limiting remedies "fails of its essential purpose," it will be ignored by a court and the remedies normally available under the UCC will apply. A remedy limitation "fails of its essential purpose" if circumstances cause the limitation to substantially deprive one party of the value of his or her bargain. Thus, in the example above, if the seller does not repair the defective item within a reasonable period of time, the limitation clause will be ineffective and the buyer can resort to whatever remedies the UCC gives him in the circumstances. Furthermore, a limitation of remedies will be ignored by a court if it is so unfair and represents such a gross abuse of bargaining power that it is deemed *unconscionable*. Section 2-719 provides that, in a sale of *consumer goods*, a clause which limits the availability of damages for *bodily injury* is *presumed* to be unconscionable. Even though a remedy limitation clause is different from a warranty disclaimer (as explained in Chapter 22), such a clause in a consumer transaction must comply with the Magnuson-Moss Warranty Act when applicable.

LEMON LAWS

Today, increasing numbers of car owners who experience problems similar to those in the case of *Vista Chevrolet, Inc. v. Lewis* are obtaining relief under special statutes applicable to motor vehicles, rather than bringing actions under the UCC. This results from the fact that by 1987 41 states had adopted such statutes, commonly called **lemon laws,** and this number will probably continue to grow in the immediate years ahead. While these laws vary in detail from state to state, in general they provide that (1) if a car under warranty possesses a defect which significantly affects its value or use, and (2) if the dealer is unable to fix the defect in four tries, the owner is entitled to a new car, a "buy-back" (an order requiring the manufacturer to refund the purchase price minus a per-mile depreciation charge), recovery of repair costs, or free replacement parts, depending upon the circumstances of the case.

Most lemon laws require that before the buyer is entitled to a buy-back, recovery of repair costs, or some other relief, he or she must go before an "appeal jury" which makes findings of fact relative to the buyer's claim, that is, as to the severity of the defects, and as to the extent of the dealer's correction of the defects. Arbitration is free to the buyer, and usually produces a decision within 40 to 60 days. (Among the major manufacturers, General Motors, American Motors, Honda, Nissan, Volkswagen, and Volvo have designated over 150 Better Business Bureaus to handle their disputes. Ford and Chrysler sponsor their own national mediation programs—Ford's panels are called Consumer Appeals Boards, and Chrysler's are Customer Satisfaction Boards. While mediation boards usually handle only warranty-related disputes, complaints involving out-of-warranty vehicles have sometimes been mediated.)

In general, appeal decisions are binding on the manufacturers but not on the car owners. Thus if a jury orders a buy-back, the manufacturer cannot appeal the decision to the courts, while a jury decision against the buyer is appealable. Although appeal juries have ordered manufacturers either to furnish new cars or make buy-backs in a number of cases, more often they have ordered manufacturers to make refunds of repair costs or to replace defective parts, such as transmissions and engines, with new components. (In a typical year, for example,

Better Business Bureaus hear approximately 25,000 cases, but award less than 4,000 buy-backs.)

SUMMARY

The basic obligation of the seller is to make a tender of delivery of the goods in conformity with the terms of the contract, and to keep the goods available for a period of time reasonably necessary for the buyer to take possession. If the seller has no responsibility for transporting the goods and they are in the possession of a bailee, the seller must deliver a negotiable document of title to the buyer or obtain the bailee's acknowledgment that the buyer is entitled to possession. If the seller does have responsibility for transporting the goods, under a shipment contract he or she must deliver the goods to a carrier, obtain and deliver any documents necessary for the buyer to take possession of the goods, and notify the buyer of the shipment. Under a destination contract, the seller is required to tender delivery of the goods at their destination.

Although Sec. 2-601 of the UCC adopts the common-law perfect tender rule, this rule is modified by other sections of the UCC. For example, if the seller's performance is deficient, he or she is permitted to "cure" by making a conforming delivery before expiration of the time for performance. (In some situations, cure may even be made after such time.) If, after a sales contract has been entered into, some unanticipated event occurs before the time of performance, the seller may be freed of his or her contractual obligations under the doctrine of commercial impracticability. Under that doctrine a late performance by the seller, or nondelivery in whole or in part, is excused if, because of an unforeseen circumstance, delivery of the goods becomes "commercially impracticable." While the determination of whether a contract has been rendered commercially impracticable is made on a case-by-case basis, in general delivery is impracticable if the unforeseen circumstance makes delivery impossible, or if it so alters the essential nature of the performance that it results in a very marked increase in the cost of performance (with the courts often requiring the seller to show that his or her costs of performance would be doubled or tripled before he or she is freed under this doctrine).

The buyer's basic obligation—to pay for the goods in conformity with the contract—is generally subject to the right of inspection. However, the right of inspection prior to payment is lost if the transaction is a COD one, or contains other terms extinguishing the right. If the buyer breaches the contract before receiving the goods, the *seller's* primary remedies are the right to cancel, to withhold or stop delivery, to resell the goods and recover resulting damages (or, in limited cases, to recover the price). If the buyer breaches after receiving the goods, the seller can recover the price. Also, if the seller reacquires possession, his or her remedies are the same as in the case where the buyer breaches before receiving the goods.

Turning to the *buyer's* remedies, if the seller breaches the contract by failing to deliver, the buyer's primary remedies are the right to cancel, to cover, and to recover damages if the cost of cover exceeds the contract price. If the seller breaches by delivering nonconforming goods, the buyer may cancel, and reject the delivery. And, if the buyer has accepted the goods prior to discovery of the nonconformity, the buyer may revoke his or her acceptance under limited conditions.

KEY TERMS

Tender of delivery
Perfect tender rule
Installment contract
Acceptance
Anticipatory repudiation
Cover
Lemon laws

QUESTIONS AND PROBLEMS

1. Explain the significance of the notation *FOB* as a shipping term.

2. Smith purchased a new car. Almost immediately after taking delivery he discovered that the car had a defective transmission, and he promptly took the car back to the dealer. When he told the dealer that he wanted to return the car and cancel the sale, the dealer offered to replace the transmission. Smith refused the dealer's offer of "cure," left the car with the dealer, and made no further payments. The dealer fixed the car, resold it, and sued Smith for damages. Did the dealer prevail? Discuss. (*Zabriskie Chevrolet, Inc. v. Smith,* 240 A.2d 195, 1968.)

3. After Gulf and Sylvan carried on a series of negotiations, they made a contract providing for delivery in three separate lots, to be separately accepted and evidenced by three separate purchase orders sent on the same date. No problems arose in the first two deliveries, but the buyer noticed a minor defect in the third delivery and rejected it, citing the perfect tender rule as his authority. Moreover, he claimed that the seller had breached the entire contract. Is he correct? Explain. (*Gulf Chemical & Metallurgical Corp. v. Sylvan Chemical Corp.,* 12 U.C.C. Rep. Serv. 117, 1973.)

4. What part does foreseeability play in commercial impracticability, according to UCC Sec. 2-615?

5. A dairy farm contracted with a public school district to supply the latter with half-pints of milk. Between the time of contracting and the time for performance, the price of raw milk rose 23 percent. Other increases in the market price had occurred in the past. The dairy filed suit for a declaratory judgment, asking the court to relieve it from its obligation to deliver the milk under Sec. 2-615. What was the result? Discuss. (*Maple Farms, Inc. v. City School Dist. of the City of Elmira,* 352 N.Y.S.2d 784, 1974.)

6. Eckerd purchased a new mobile home from Zippy Mobile Home Sales. After the purchase but before moving into the home, Eckerd discovered a slight leak in one of the plumbing fixtures. He moved into the mobile home and then repaired the leak. Shortly thereafter, Eckerd became dissatisfied with the home because it was not large enough for his family. He went to Zippy and indicated that he was rejecting the mobile home because of defective plumbing. Zippy's manager said that he could not reject because he had already accepted. Who is correct? Explain.

7. What is a commercial unit? Explain its importance.

8. Under their sale contract seller S was required to deliver goods to buyer B on October 25. On April 30, S called B and demanded more money for the goods. B refused, and S said, "Well, if that's the way you want it." On May 30, B filed suit against S for breach of contract. S contended that B was not entitled to file suit until after the date for performance, October 25. Is S correct? Explain.

9. Plymouth Chemical Co. used propane gas as an essential raw material in producing certain chemicals. It had a long-term supply contract for such gas with Commonwealth Gas Co. A shortage of propane gas occurred, and most suppliers were no longer committing themselves to long-term contracts. Commonwealth breached the contract, and Plymouth sued for specific performance. Commonwealth claimed that Plymouth should be allowed to sue for damages but not for specific performance. Is Commonwealth correct? Explain.

10. After Buyer's breach of contract, Seller resold the goods at a private sale but did not give prior notice of the sale. The resale netted Seller $1,000 less than he would have received under the contract with Buyer. Seller sued Buyer for the $1,000. Buyer claimed that Seller could not recover the $1,000 deficiency because he had not notified Buyer of the sale. Is Buyer correct? Explain.

Chapter 24

COMMERCIAL PAPER
Types, Parties, and
Basic Concepts

The term **commercial paper** refers to written promises or orders to pay sums of money and comprises such instruments as drafts, promissory notes, checks, and certificates of deposit. (The most common of these are notes and checks.) With the advent of "electronic banking" in recent years—such as the widespread use of automated teller machines and experimentation with point-of-sale terminals in retail stores—it has been predicted that some day we will live in an almost checkless society.[1] Despite these advances, however, the number of checks written in this country has actually continued to grow approximately 3 percent a year (with an estimated 45 billion checks having been written in 1987). Thus the present use of commercial paper in our credit-oriented society is of enormous significance, and will remain so well into the foreseeable future. A knowledge of the basic rules for dealing with this subject thus continues to be important to the businessperson.

DEVELOPMENT OF THE LAW

Commercial paper has been used for many centuries, probably as early as 1500 B.C., according to archeologists, who tell us that crude promissory notes existed in very early civilizations. By the thirteenth century, merchants in the Middle East were making significant use of both promissory notes and bills of exchange, and by the beginning of the seventeenth century both kinds of instruments were commonly used in England.

Because the early English courts refused to recognize commercial paper, the merchants created their own methods for enforcing rights arising from the use of these instruments. The rules they developed were enforced by traders at their "fair" or "borough" courts, and together they made up what is known as the *law merchant* (see Chapter 20 for details).

During the eighteenth and nineteenth centuries these principles were substantially recognized by English and American courts and became part of the common law of both countries. In 1896 the American Bar Association drafted the Uniform Negotiable Instruments Law (NIL) for state consideration, and by the early 1920s this act was adopted by all the states. This caused our negotiable instruments law to be "codified."

The Uniform Commercial Code

Today the old NIL has been superseded in all states by Article 3 of the Uniform Commercial Code, entitled "Commercial Paper." (Louisiana has not adopted the UCC in its entirety, but it has enacted Articles 1, 3, 4, and 5.) While the adoption of the UCC resulted in a substantial updating of the earlier rules to conform to modern-day practices, the most important provisions of Article 3 are not much different from those of the original NIL. In any event, legal questions growing out of the use of negotiable instruments today are governed almost entirely by Article 3 of the UCC—although references to Article 4 are also necessary if problems arise that deal with the relationship existing between the drawer of a check and the bank upon which it is written.[2]

PURPOSES OF COMMERCIAL PAPER

During the early part of the Middle Ages, merchants and traders had to carry gold and silver to

---

[1] More will be said about electronic banking in Chapter 28.

[2] A subcommittee of the Permanent Editorial Board of the UCC, a joint effort of the National Conference of Commissioners on Uniform State Laws and the American Law Institute, is currently drafting amendments to Articles 3 and 4 of the UCC. (These amendments will replace a now-abandoned proposal suggested by the board in 1983, the "Uniform New Payments Code," which would not only have amended Article 3 but, additionally, would have replaced Article 4 and the Electronic Funds Transfer Act in their entireties.) Because proposed amendments are typically in the drafting and comment stages for extended periods of time, it is unlikely that final changes will be submitted to the state legislatures for adoption before the early 1990s. Accordingly, these chapters on Commercial Paper are based on Articles 3 and 4 of the UCC currently in effect (i.e., the official 1978 text).

pay for the goods they purchased at the various international fairs. These precious metals were continually subject to loss or theft through the perils of travel.

To eliminate dangers of this sort, merchants began to deposit their gold and silver with bankers. When they needed funds to pay for goods they had purchased, they "drew" on them by giving the seller a written order addressed to the bank, telling it to deliver part of the gold or silver to the seller. These orders, called bills of exchange, were *substitutes for money*. Today, checks and the drafts and promissory notes that are payable on demand serve this same basic purpose.

The second major purpose of commercial paper is to serve as a *credit device*; this came about as a logical extension of its initial use as a money substitute. Soon after bills of exchange became established as substitutes for money, merchants who wished to purchase goods on credit discovered that sellers were sometimes willing to accept bills of exchange that were not payable until a stated time in the future—such as "ninety days after date." If the seller was satisfied as to the commercial reputation of the bill's drawer (the purchaser), he would take such an instrument (called a *time bill* or *draft*) and wait until the maturity date to collect it. In this way the seller-payee extended credit to the buyer-drawer.

Soon thereafter ways were devised by which payees could sell these instruments to third parties, usually banks, and receive immediate cash in return. Since the banks would then have to wait for the maturity dates before receiving payment, the payees would have to sell them the paper at a discount—that is, at perhaps 5 or 10 percent less than the face amount. This meant, in effect, that the purchasing banks were charging the sellers interest in advance as compensation for their role in the transaction.

Today, because of the widespread use of time notes and drafts, the credit aspect of commercial paper is as important to the business community as its "substitute for money" aspect.

TYPES OF COMMERCIAL PAPER

There are numerous ways to classify the basic types of commercial paper. Of these, the classification specified by Article 3 of the UCC probably merits top billing.

The UCC Classification

Section 3-104 specifies four types of instruments—drafts, checks, certificates of deposit, and notes.

Drafts: A **draft,** or bill of exchange, is an instrument whereby the party creating it (the *drawer*) orders another party (the *drawee*) to pay money to a third party (the *payee*). For example: X owes Y $100, and Y owes Z the same amount. Y signs a written order directing X to pay the $100 to Z and gives it to Z. Z presents the instrument to X, who then pays him. Here Y is the drawer, X the drawee, and Z the payee.

In order for a draft to work, one of two general conditions must exist. Either the drawee must owe the drawer a debt (in which case the drawer is simply telling the drawee to pay the debt or a portion of it to a third party) or some kind of agreement or relationship must exist between the parties under which the drawee has consented to the drawing of the draft. If neither of these conditions existed, the drawee would not obey the order to pay the amount of the draft to the payee or to any subsequent holder of the instrument.

When a draft is used in connection with a sale of goods, it is called a **sales draft** (an instrument that has largely supplanted the "trade acceptance" of earlier years). A sales draft is a draft drawn by the seller of goods on the purchaser of those goods, which is subsequently accepted (signed) by the purchaser. The purpose of the transaction is to enable the seller to raise money on the paper before the purchaser's obligation matures under the sales contract.

We can illustrate this usage by referring to the specimen sales draft reproduced here. The Knowles Corporation has sold goods to DMG

Draft   A *draft* is an instrument by which the party creating it, the drawer (Paul Psilos in the example below) orders another party, the drawee (the bank) to pay money to a third party, the payee (Russell Hahn).

$ 5,000.00   January 2   19 XX

Ninety (90) days after the above date   PAY TO THE ORDER OF

Russell Hahn

five thousand and no/100 --- DOLLARS
                                          WITH EXCHANGE

VALUE RECEIVED AND CHARGE TO ACCOUNT OF

TO   First National Bank of Chicago   *Paul D Psilos*

NO.   02683   Chicago, Illinois   Paul Psilos

STOCK FORM 990-8 BANKFORMS, INC.

Sales Draft   A *sales draft* is a draft or bill of exchange drawn by the seller of goods on the purchaser of those goods and accepted (signed) by the purchaser. The purpose of the transaction is to enable the seller to raise money on the paper before the purchaser's obligation matures under the sales contract.

Draft

Draft No. 1234   Date   January 2, 19XX

At   ***90 Days From Date***

Pay to the Order of   ***KNOWLES CORPORATION***

the sum of   Five Thousand and no/100ths ********************** Dollars $ 5,000.00

Value received and charge to the account of

                     DMG Imports   The Knowles Corporation

To   {   *Kane Knowles*
                     Evanston, Illinois   Authorized Signature

1-22-0018 (6/78)

ACCEPTED: DMG Imports   *Paul Psilos*

Imports. Because DMG Imports wishes to utilize a negotiable instrument rather than pay cash for the goods immediately, the Knowles Corporation (drawer) draws a draft on DMG Imports for the purchase price of the goods. The instrument orders DMG Imports to pay the stated sum to the order of the Knowles Corporation at a stated time in the future—in this case, ninety days after January 2. (The Knowles Corporation is thus both the drawer and the payee of the instrument.) It is then presented to an officer of DMG Imports—Paul Psilos, in this instance—who accepts it by affixing that company's name to it in the space at the left hand margin. The accep-

Drawer
Drawee

90 days after Jan 1987

[Handwritten: demanded Instrument becomes time Instrument when you date it]

Check   A *check* is the most common type of draft; it is an order (draft or bill of exchange) drawn on a bank and payable on demand.

[Handwritten: there is no form for a bill of exchange — can do it on a simple blank paper]

[Check image with handwritten annotations:]

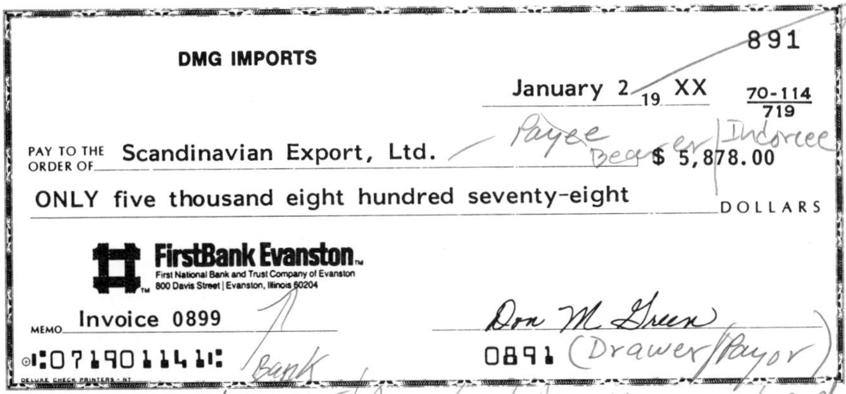

DMG IMPORTS   891

January 2 19 XX   70-114 / 719

PAY TO THE ORDER OF Scandinavian Export, Ltd. *[Payee / Bearer / Indorsee]* $ 5,878.00

ONLY five thousand eight hundred seventy-eight   DOLLARS

FirstBank Evanston
First National Bank and Trust Company of Evanston
800 Davis Street | Evanston, Illinois 60204

MEMO Invoice 0899   Don M. Green *[Drawer/Payor]*

⑆:071901141⑈ *[bank]*   0891

[Handwritten: drawer/Acceptor (when you accept and cash — primary party on instrument)]

[Handwritten: Payee (back of check) endorsement]

tance, which constitutes a promise by DMG Imports (the drawee-acceptor) to pay the instrument when it becomes due, is then returned to the Knowles Corporation. It can now negotiate the draft to a third party, usually the Knowles Corporation's bank, and receive cash immediately. Use of the instrument in this manner—by sellers of goods—explains why it is called a *sales* draft. (Other kinds of drafts are also frequently accepted by their drawees; these are discussed in Chapter 27.) Another frequently used draft is the *bank draft,* which is utilized when one bank draws on its funds in another bank.

Checks: A **check** is a particular type of draft. Under Sec. 3-104(2), it is by definition a "draft drawn on a bank [and] payable on demand." It is thus distinguished from demand drafts drawn on individuals, or on corporations that are not banks. Similarly, it is also distinguished from drafts drawn on banks, but which are payable at specific future dates. As one might guess, checks are by far the most commonly used form of drafts.

One particular form of check is the *cashier's check,* which is drawn by a bank on itself, payable on demand to a payee. Because this check is drawn by the bank ordering itself to pay, the bank must honor the check upon proper presentment. For this reason, in transactions involving the sale of property—where the owner-seller requires some form of guaranteed payment to accompany all offers to purchase—bidders commonly submit cashier's checks along with their bids.

Notes: A **note** is a promise by one party (the *maker*) to pay a sum of money to another party (the *payee*). Notes differ from drafts in two primary respects. They always contain promises to pay money (as distinguished from orders), and they have two parties—maker and payee—rather than three.

Because notes are used in a variety of transactions, they come in many different forms. For example, a note used in a real estate transaction secured by a mortgage on the property being purchased is a *real estate mortgage note.* A note containing a promise to make payments in specified installments, such as payments for a new car, is an *installment note.* And a note secured by personal property is a *collateral note.* While all

Promissory Note   A *promissory note* is an instrument by which the maker promises to pay a sum of money to another party (the payee).

$ 5,000.00 _____ , _____ 2 January _____ 19 XX

_____ Ninety (90) days _____ ~~CANCELLED~~ _____ after date ¹ _____ promise to pay to

the order of _____ James J. Walsh _____

Five thousand and no/100 _____ Dollars

at ___ twelve and one-half percent (12.5%) per annum
Value received.
No. ___083153___ Due _____   *[signature]*

Certificate of Deposit   A *certificate of deposit* is an instrument by which a bank acknowledges receipt of money and promises to return it at a later date or on demand. Certificates of deposit may be negotiable or nonnegotiable, depending upon their terms.

CERTIFICATE OF DEPOSIT NOT SUBJECT TO CHECK	AUTOMATICALLY RENEWABLE

Bank of Hinsdale
400 EAST OGDEN AVENUE · HINSDALE, ILLINOIS 60521

5740

2 January   19XX

Dawn M. Gerth   HAS DEPOSITED

five thousand and no/100 ------------------------- DOLLARS $ 5,000.00

Payable to the Registered Holder hereof in current funds upon the surrender of this Certificate properly endorsed _____ after date, or at any subsequent maturity date as herein-after provided.

It is understood and agreed that this Certificate shall be automatically renewed for an additional period of time equal to the original term hereof, dating from the first maturity date, unless the Registered Holder shall present this Certificate for payment at any maturity date, or 7 days thereafter, or unless the Bank shall prior to any maturity date, mail written notice to the Registered Holder, at the address appearing on the books of the Bank, of its decision to redeem this Certificate.

Interest at the rate of _____ % per annum shall be paid to the Registered Holder hereof _____ , but the rate of interest to be paid in future renewal periods shall be equal to the rate then in effect at this Bank for similarly issued certificates of deposit of like term and amount

This Certificate and the deposit which it evidences are subject to the Rules and Regulations of any Governmental Agency responsible for operating the Bank, including interest rate and other Rules and Regulations of the Bank in force from time to time. Current FDIC regulations require a substantial interest penalty if this deposit is withdrawn before maturity date.

ADDRESS 2683 Stewart Ave.
Evanston, IL   60201   ~~CANCELLED~~
SOCIAL SEC. NO. 000-00-0000

of these are *promissory notes* in a general sense, that term when used alone usually refers to the simplest kind of notes, those merely containing promises by one person to pay money to another.

Certificates of Deposit: A **certificate of deposit** is an acknowledgment by a bank of receipt of money with a return "promise" on the bank's part to repay it at a fixed future date or, in some instances, on demand.

✓ Promises to Pay and Orders to Pay

A second method of classifying commercial paper uses only two categories. All instruments involving the payment of money, regardless of their specialized names within the business community, contain one of two elements— *promises* to pay money or *orders* to pay money. Instruments containing promises to pay can be broadly classified as *notes* and those containing orders to pay as *drafts*. As already indicated, the

NOTE: Drafts are called Instruments

certificate of deposit is a special type of note, and the check is a special type of draft.

Demand and Time Instruments

A third method of classifying commercial paper is based solely on the time at which the instrument is payable. Instruments that are payable whenever the holder chooses to present them to the maker (in the case of a note) or to the drawee (in the case of a draft) are called **demand instruments** (or *sight instruments*). Those payable at a specific future date are **time instruments.** Notes, drafts, and certificates of deposit can be either demand or time instruments, while checks—by definition—must be payable on demand.

Negotiable and Nonnegotiable Instruments ✓

The term *commercial paper,* used in its broadest sense, embraces both negotiable paper and nonnegotiable paper. **Negotiable instruments** are those whose terms meet the requirements of negotiability appearing in Sec. 3-104 of the UCC, while **nonnegotiable instruments** do not meet such requirements. Thus, whether a particular instrument falls into the one category or the other depends entirely on its form and content.

In many instances the negotiable-nonnegotiable classification of commercial paper transcends all others in importance, for two primary reasons:

1. The rules of Article 3 of the UCC apply (with rare exception) only to instruments that meet the tests of negotiability. By contrast, nonnegotiable instruments are governed by the ordinary principles of contract law. In other words, the rights and liabilities of makers, drawers, and indorsers of negotiable instruments are controlled by one body of law, while those of parties to nonnegotiable instruments are governed by another.

2. It is possible under the rules of Article 3 for a holder of a negotiable instrument to enjoy a special status, that of a *holder in due course* (*HDC*). Such a holder takes the instrument free of many defenses that exist between its original parties. (*Defenses* are matters pleaded by defendants as a reason in law or fact why the plaintiff should not recover what he or she seeks.) The holder of a nonnegotiable instrument—such as a simple contract—on the other hand, can never qualify as an HDC. Such a holder takes it subject to these defenses.

While an examination of the precise rights of the HDC must await the subject of defenses in Chapter 26, the basic distinction between the status of such a holder and that of a mere assignee will be brought to light here.

ASSIGNEE VERSUS HOLDER IN DUE COURSE

Under contract law, the assignee of a simple contract acquires no better rights under the contract than those possessed by the assignor. For example: X contracts to buy a bulldozer from Y for $25,000 under an installment contract. After delivery, Y assigns the contract (the right to collect the price) to a third party, Z. If the machine proves defective, X can successfully assert this fact as a defense against Z, just as he could have asserted it against Y had there been no assignment. This means that the assignee, Z, is not entitled to a judgment against X. The same would be true if X had simply given Y a nonnegotiable note or draft in payment for the bulldozer; Z's rights would be no better than those possessed by Y.

On the other hand, if X had given Y a *negotiable* note, draft, or check in payment for the machine, and if Y had then transferred the instrument to Z under circumstances that qualified Z as a holder in due course, then Z would be entitled to recover the full amount of the instrument from X, despite the fact that Y had

Bank will not give out on two signatures rather not give out if odds are against getting money back

breached his contract with X by delivering a defective machine.

The above is a simple illustration of one of the basic commercial paper concepts—*that it is possible for a third party-HDC to acquire greater rights under a negotiable instrument than those possessed by the payee-transferor.* This does not mean, however, that the HDC is always legally entitled to payment from the primary party. Sometimes the primary party has available a "real" or "universal" defense, which he or she can successfully assert against any holder, even the HDC. And the holder-in-due-course doctrine itself has been sharply limited in recent years. (These limitations will be explained more fully in Chapter 26.)

PARTIES TO COMMERCIAL PAPER

We have already seen that notes have two original parties—the maker and the payee—while drafts and checks have three—the drawer, the drawee, and the payee. But after an instrument is issued, additional parties can become involved. (The liability incurred by each of these parties is spelled out in Chapter 27.)

The Acceptor

Frequently, after a draft is issued, it is presented by the payee (or a subsequent holder) to the drawee (the person to whom the order is addressed) for that person's *acceptance.* Under the UCC some types of drafts require a presentment, while for others the presentment is at the option of the holder. In any event, the drawee who "accepts" the draft is called the **acceptor** (or *drawee-acceptor*), and he or she becomes a primary party to the instrument. (As we have seen, an acceptance occurs when the drawee signs his or her name somewhere on the face of the instrument.) In this capacity, the acceptor's liability is roughly akin to that of the maker of a note.

Indorsers

Often the payee of a note or draft transfers it to a third party soon after acquiring it, instead of presenting it to the primary party for payment. When such a transfer occurs, the payee-transferor almost always "indorses" the instrument by signing his or her name on the back of it before delivering it to the third party; by so doing, the payee becomes an **indorser.** For example, if P, the payee, receives a check from D, P can indorse it to a third party, Z, in payment of a debt that P owes to Z (or for any other reason).

Indorsees

The **indorsee** is the person who receives an indorsed instrument; in the example above, the indorsee is Z. Z can indorse the instrument to another party, in which case Z also becomes an indorser.

The Bearer

From both a legal and a practical standpoint, the term *bearer* is of limited (though well-defined) significance. A **bearer** is any person who has physical possession of an instrument that legally qualifies as a *bearer instrument.* For example, if a note is expressly made "payable to bearer" or is simply payable to "cash," whoever possesses it is the bearer.

Another type of bearer instrument comes into existence when an instrument is originally payable to the order of a named person, and the named person indorses it by signing his or her name on the back. An indorsement such as this, called a *blank indorsement,* converts the paper into a bearer instrument; therefore, the subsequent taker of the instrument also is a bearer.

Holders

The term *holder* is broader in scope and of greater legal significance than the term *bearer.* Section 1-201(20) of the UCC defines a **holder** as a person who possesses a negotiable instrument which is either payable to the bearer or payable to such a person as the payee or in-dorsee. Thus the term includes not only persons possessing bearer instruments but also payees and indorsees possessing order instruments. To illustrate: X pays a utility bill by drawing a check "payable to the order of Columbia Gas of Ohio" and mailing it to that company. While Columbia Gas cannot be called a bearer (since the check is not payable to bearer), as payee it clearly quali-fies as a holder.

Holder in Due Course: Under Sec. 3-302, a **holder in due course** is a holder who has given value for the instrument, has acquired it before it was overdue, and has taken it in good faith. As indicated earlier, it is the HDC who is afforded most-favored status under the code.[3]

Ordinary Holder: A person who qualifies as a holder but does not meet all the HDC require-ments is called an **ordinary holder.** Unlike the HDC, an ordinary holder cannot enforce the in-strument against the primary party if the latter has a personal defense, such as fraud on the part of the payee. In other words, the ordinary holder takes the instrument subject to all defenses, much like the assignee of a nonnegotiable instru-ment. However, also like the assignee, the ordi-nary holder can enforce the instrument against the primary party if the latter has no defense available.

Holder through a Holder in Due Course: If a holder fails to qualify as an HDC, he or she can still enjoy the special rights of a holder in due course by showing that any prior holder qualified as an HDC. Such a person is called a *holder through a holder in due course.*

SUMMARY

The term commercial paper refers to written promises or orders to pay sums of money arising from the use of such instruments as drafts, checks, and promissory notes. These instru-ments may be either "negotiable" or "non-negotiable," depending upon their terms. The question of negotiability is of primary concern to a purchaser of such an instrument, for if the instrument is negotiable the purchaser may qualify as a holder in due course. In such a case he or she takes the instrument free of many de-fenses that might exist between the maker (or drawer) and the payee.

For an instrument to qualify as a negotiable instrument, it must meet the requirements of Sec. 3-104 of the UCC (which are discussed in the next chapter). The UCC recognizes four kinds of commercial paper: drafts, checks, notes, and certificates of deposit. Drafts and checks contain orders to pay money. The person to whom the order is addressed is the drawee, the person to whom the order is payable is the payee, and the person issuing the instrument is the drawer. In contrast to drafts, notes contain promises to pay, and have only two parties. The maker is the person making the promise to pay, and the payee is the person to whom the note is payable.

In many instances—usually after the instru-ment has been issued—two other classes of per-sons may become parties to it, the acceptor and the indorser. An acceptance occurs if the holder of a draft presents it to the drawee for his or her signature; by signing, the drawee becomes the acceptor (and is thus primarily liable on the instrument). The indorser, in most instances, is the owner of an instrument who signs his or her name on the back of it before delivering it to a third party, the indorsee.

Other persons recognized under Article 3 are the holder and the bearer. The holder is any per-son who possesses a negotiable instrument which is payable either to the bearer, to his or her order, or to the indorsee of such an instru-ment. A holder who meets certain requirements of Article 3 (also to be discussed in the next chapter) is a holder in due course; one not meet-ing these requirements is an ordinary holder.

---

[3]The precise rights of the holder in due course, ordinary holder, and holder through a holder in due course will be examined in Chapter 26.

KEY TERMS

Commercial paper
Draft
Sales draft
Check
Note
Certificate of deposit
Demand instrument
Time instrument
Negotiable instrument
Nonnegotiable instrument
Acceptor
Indorser
Indorsee
Bearer
Holder
Holder in due course
Ordinary holder

QUESTIONS AND PROBLEMS

1. X contracts to paint Y's house for $1,200 in June. On June 20, when X is half-way through with the job, Y is called to Europe on a business trip. Before leaving, Y makes out a promissory note for $1,200 that is payable July 15, and hands it to X. The next day X sells the note to a local bank for $1,100 (he "discounts" the note). In late July, when the bank demands payment from Y, Y refuses to pay the instrument because X never finished the job. If the note in question turns out to be nonnegotiable in form, what effect—if any—does this have upon Y's liability to the bank? Explain.

2. What were the major factors that were responsible for the creation of commercial paper in the Middle Ages?

3. Often the holder of a promissory note that is not due until some future date will "discount" it at a bank. What are the advantages to the holder, and to the bank, in doing this?

4. Tom is owed $1,000 by Dick, but he (Tom) in turn owes Harry $400. When Harry presses Tom for payment, Tom gives Harry this letter addressed to Dick: "Out of the $1,000 you owe me, please pay $400 of it to Harry as soon as he requests it." Does this letter look like a *draft*, or more like a *note?* What is the primary reason for your answer?

5. The Scarlet Corporation orders 10 snowmobiles from the Gray Company at a total cost of $12,000. If a *sales draft* were to be used here (instead of a cash payment by the Scarlet Corporation), who would be (a) the drawer, (b) the drawee, and (c) the acceptor?

6. X sells a used car to Y and takes a promissory note from Y in payment. When the note comes due Y is financially unable to pay it. X then brings suit on the note, and Y's only defense is that the note is *nonnegotiable* in form. (That is, there was nothing wrong with the car that he received.) If Y can clearly prove that the note *is* nonnegotiable, is his defense good? (That is, will the court dismiss the action?) Why or why not?

7. You see this statement in a text: "As a general rule, bearer instruments are governed by contract law, and order instruments by Article 3 of the UCC." Is this statement essentially true? Why or why not?

8. B is the maker of a negotiable promissory note, and he issues it to C. C later negotiates it to D. In such a situation, D may qualify as a *holder in due course,* or he may be only an *ordinary holder.* If D were forced to bring suit against B in an effort to obtain payment of the note, under what circumstances might D's success depend entirely upon whether he was the one type of holder or the other? Explain.

Chapter 25

COMMERCIAL PAPER
Negotiability
and Transfer

In many situations, whether an instrument is negotiable or nonnegotiable is of little importance. Suppose, for example, that P is willing to sell goods to M on credit, taking a promissory ninety-day note signed by M as evidence of the indebtedness. Suppose further that M's financial reputation is good, and that P is perfectly willing to hold the note himself until it matures. In these circumstances P might well be satisfied with a nonnegotiable note, for his chances of being paid on the due date, and his legal rights against M if payment is not made voluntarily, are about as good as those he would possess if the note were negotiable.

In many other circumstances, however, the negotiability or nonnegotiability of an instrument is of vital importance, for a number of reasons. First, as we briefly suggested in the preceding chapter, when legal problems arise as to the enforceability of the instrument, the rights and obligations of the parties are resolved under Article 3 of the UCC if the instrument is negotiable and under ordinary contract law if it is not. And since the holder-in-due-course concept is recognized only under Article 3, any person seeking to enforce the instrument under this concept must (among other things) show at the outset that the instrument meets the tests of negotiability.

In addition, as a practical matter, commercial paper cannot serve its "substitute for money" and "extension of credit" roles unless it is freely transferable (that is, unless prospective purchasers of the paper, especially financial institutions, are willing to accept it routinely). And, before such purchasers are willing to accept commercial paper, they not only want to be able to determine that the paper is negotiable in form but, additionally, that the seller/transferor has taken the steps necessary to insure that the transfer constitutes a "negotiation" of the paper as defined by Article 3 of the UCC.

In this chapter, then, we will discuss (1) the requirements of negotiability and (2) the rules applicable to the transfer of negotiable instruments.

REQUIREMENTS OF NEGOTIABILITY

Today the **requirements of negotiability** are expressly set forth in Sec. 3-104 of the UCC. Subsection 1 reads as follows:

> Any writing to be a negotiable instrument within this Article must (a) be signed by the maker or drawer; and (b) contain an unconditional promise or order to pay a sum certain in money and [must contain] no other promise, order, obligation, or power given by the maker or drawer except as authorized by this Article; and (c) be payable on demand or at a definite time; and (d) be payable to order or to bearer.

As a result of these requirements, the negotiability or nonnegotiability of an instrument is entirely dependent upon its *form* and *content.* Each of these requirements, together with later sections that help in the interpretation of Sec. 3-104, will now be examined.

The Writing and Signing Requirements

The Writing: Just as there is no such thing as "oral money," an oral promise or order to pay money obviously cannot serve as a substitute for it. Under contract law it is true that an oral promise to pay money can be enforced as long as its existence can be established in court. However, in the commercial world, where large numbers of promises and orders must be transferred daily, the need for such obligations to be evidenced in tangible written form becomes obvious. Under Sec. 1-201(46), this "writing" can be handwritten, printed, or typewritten, or it can consist of "any other intentional [method of] reduction to tangible form."

Normally, of course, the substance on which the writing appears is paper, but the UCC does not require this. Thus we occasionally read in the newspaper about the holder of a "check" written on a watermelon or some similar object who was able to obtain payment at the drawee bank upon physical presentment of the object. These cases, of course, are rarities; they do, however, bring a welcome degree of humor and ingenuity to the subject of commercial paper (though the bank officials involved might not entirely share this view).

The Signing: A negotiable instrument must be signed by the maker in the case of a note or by the drawer in the case of a draft. Ordinarily there is little trouble with this requirement, since such a party almost invariably affixes his or her signature (in longhand) to the instrument at the outset.

In some instances, however, questions do arise. Section 1-201(39) is designed to alleviate these by stating that the term *signed* means "any symbol executed or adopted by a party with [the] present intention to authenticate a writing." Thus a signing can occur through the use of one's initials, a rubber stamp, or some other type of "signature," such as the mark X, so long as it is made with the intention of giving assent to the writing's terms. (Problems that relate to forgeries and the unauthorized signing of principals' names by their agents are examined in Chapter 27.)

The Promise or Order Must Be Unconditional

In order for an instrument to be treated as a substitute for money or as a credit extension device, the holder wants assurance that no conditions will be imposed on the instrument's payment. Whether such conditions exist in a given case, thus causing the instrument to be non-negotiable, depends on the totality of the terms and provisions that make up the instrument.

An almost infinite variety of clauses or notations find their way into some instruments and raise legitimate questions as to whether they condition the basic promise or order to pay. We will consider here the most common of these.

Express Conditions: A small percentage of notes and drafts contain clauses that *expressly*

condition the primary promise or order to pay. Obviously these clauses destroy negotiability of the instrument at the outset. A note signed by M, maker, which is payable "upon the marriage of my daughter" or "on the date of the next Rose Bowl game," falls into this category, for it is expressly made payable upon an event that may never occur. Even if the event is very likely to occur (or does, in fact, occur subsequently), the instrument continues to be a nonnegotiable one.

Permitted Provisions: A more common situation is one where the basic obligation is itself unconditional but where the instrument contains language or clauses which will *possibly* condition the primary obligation—depending, of course, on how the clauses are legally interpreted.

Section 3-105 resolves many of these problems of interpretation. Subsection 1 contains eight express types of clauses or notations that may appear on the face of an instrument which do *not* condition the promise or order to pay. Thus any clause falling within this subsection does not destroy the negotiability of the instrument. For example, subsection 1 permits the maker or drawer to note on the face of the instrument its purpose ("January rent"), or the consideration received in exchange for the instrument ("Payment for 100 bushels wheat"). It also permits the maker or drawer to indicate that the instrument has arisen out of a separate agreement, if such is the case, or is secured by a mortgage on specified property. The UCC recognizes that these kinds of references should have no adverse legal or practical effect on the instrument's negotiability.

Subsections f and g under subsection 1 contain two "fund" provisions. Subsection f permits inclusion on the face of an instrument a clause which merely "indicates a particular account to be debited or any other fund from which *reimbursement* is to be made." Two examples: (1) D draws a check on which he writes the words, "Charge to petty cash"; and (2) the X Corporation, a manufacturer holding several construction contracts with the U.S. Navy, writes on an obligation, "Charge to Navy Contract SX-102." In both instances it is clear that the instruments pledge the general credit of the parties issuing them, and that the extra notations merely refer to funds (or assets) out of which the parties will reimburse themselves after they have paid the instruments. The instruments, therefore, remain negotiable.

Subsection g further provides that two kinds of instruments are negotiable even though they are *payable* out of a specified fund. The more important of these consists of instruments issued by a government, a governmental unit, or a governmental agency. Thus a state-issued bond, payable out of the revenue of that state's turnpike commission, is a negotiable instrument. (In other words, under subsection g the commission's promise to pay is not conditioned upon the existence of a fund at maturity sufficient to permit payment of the full face value of the bonds.) Governmental obligations are given this special treatment because government funds are almost always adequate to honor the obligations, while this is less likely to be the case where the maker is an ordinary corporation or an individual.[1]

＊Unpermitted Provisions: Subsection 2 of Sec. 3-105, in contrast to subsection 1, refers to two kinds of clauses or provisions that *do* destroy the negotiability of any note or draft.

"Subject To" Clauses: Instruments that contain language indicating that the promises or orders to pay are *subject to* some other agreement, such as a mortgage or a lease, are nonnegotiable. This results from subsection 2a, which provides that "A promise or order is not unconditional if the instrument states that it is subject to or governed by any other agreement." Prior to the adoption of the UCC, some courts took the view that the negotiability of an instrument that was subject to some other agreement depended upon the actual terms of that agreement. This meant that a prospective purchaser would have to search out that other agreement in order to know what the status of the instrument was—a most impractical requirement in the commercial world. Subsection 2a makes such instruments *nonnegotiable as a matter of law*—regardless of what the terms of the other agreement actually are. This subsection underscores the general idea that the negotiability or nonnegotiability of an instrument must be determinable from the face of the instrument alone.

＊*"Payable Out of Fund" Instruments:* The second kind of clause that destroys negotiability, found under subsection 2b, is that which makes the instrument *payable out of a specified fund* (with the two narrow exceptions noted in the discussion of Sec. 3-105(1)(g) above). Because the payment of such instruments is subject to the possibility that there may be no such fund in existence at maturity, the promise or order is obviously conditional in nature, and 2b expressly so provides. Thus if X in June promises to pay $5,000 to the order of Y on the following December 1 "out of the proceeds of the sale of my Ford Motor stock," the instrument is nonnegotiable when issued to Y, and remains nonnegotiable even if the stock is sold before December 1 for more than $5,000.[2]

The primary question in the following case is whether the promise of the maker of the note was unconditional under the rules discussed above.

---

[1] The second type of instrument that is negotiable, although payable out of a fund, consists of instruments payable out of the "entire assets of a partnership, unincorporated association, trust, or estate by or on behalf of which the instrument is issued."

[2] The "fund" rules of Sec. 3-105 can be summarized as follows: (1) An instrument that refers to a fund out of which reimbursement is to be made is negotiable. (2) An instrument that is payable out of a fund is nonnegotiable, except for instruments payable out of governmental funds and those payable out of the entire assets of a partnership, unincorporated association, trust, or estate.

* **Calfo v. D. C. Stewart Co.**   *Calfo - 3rd party; Stewart Co.*
Supreme Court of Utah, 717 P.2d 697 (1986)   *primary party*

D. C. Stewart Company (Stewart) owned the Astro Motel in Cedar City, Utah. It listed the motel for sale with C. J. Realty, and C. J. Realty obtained a Mr. and Mrs. Downward as potential buyers of the property. Stewart entered into a lease and purchase agreement with the Downwards on September 24, 1979, which gave the Downwards (lessees) an option to purchase the motel at a specified price until May 1, 1980.

Also, on September 24, Stewart executed a promissory note for $15,900 payable to C. J. Realty to secure the commission it would be entitled to if the lessees exercised their option to purchase. The note provided that it would be payable "upon final closing between . . . seller and . . . buyers, which shall be on or before May 1, 1980, when buyers exercise their option to purchase the Astro Motel. . . ."

On September 27 C. J. Realty sold the note to Calfo, plaintiff, for $12,720. After May 1, 1980, Calfo presented the note to Stewart for payment. Stewart refused to pay because the lessees did not exercise their option to purchase—i.e., the motel was never sold. Calfo then brought this action against Stewart, the maker, and C. J. Realty and an agent of C. J. Realty, the indorsers.

At the conclusion of the pleading stage, after a series of hearings, the trial court entered summary judgment in favor of Calfo, ruling (1) that the note was a negotiable instrument; (2) that Calfo was a holder in due course; and (3) that defendant Stewart, therefore, could not assert its defense of non-sale of the property against Calfo. Stewart appealed.

Zimmerman, Justice:

. . . Stewart argues that the trial court erred in finding the promissory note to be a negotiable instrument. To be negotiable under Section 3-104(1) of the Uniform Commercial Code, an instrument must meet four criteria. Specifically, it must (i) evidence a signature by the maker or drawer, (ii) contain an unconditional promise or order to pay a sum certain in money, (iii) be payable on demand or at a definite time, and (iv) be payable to order or to bearer. Stewart and Calfo agree that the note in question satisfied the first and fourth of these requirements. They disagree as to whether the second and third are met.

Although the second and third requirements of negotiability are separately stated, in fact they are closely related. Both focus on whether the instrument is a clear and unconditional promise to pay. These concerns are central to the whole concept of negotiable instruments, and that should be kept in mind in determining whether a document is entitled to be treated as a negotiable instrument under the Uniform Commercial Code. Two important functions of negotiable instruments are "to supplement the supply of currency" and to provide a present representation of "future payment of money." 1 W. Hawkland, *A Transactional Guide to the Uniform Commercial Code* §2.0304 (1964). . . . Because a negotiable instrument is a substitute for money or currency, both the promise to pay and the certainty of payment must be unequivocal.

For similar reasons, an instrument's negotiability must be determinable from what appears on its face and without reference to extrinsic facts. This requirement protects transferees from latent defenses to payment, *i.e.,* those defenses which are not readily apparent from the document. On the other hand, if the document evinces terms which should alert the transferee of possible defenses, then the transferee is not entitled to insulation from those apparent defenses. . . .

The present case involves a promissory note which is "due in full upon final closing between . . . seller and . . . buyers, which shall be on or before May 1, 1980, when buyers exercise their option to purchase the Astro Motel. . . ." In determining whether this promise to pay is conditional or indefinite, we are not aided by the trial court's summary finding that this is a "good note." The document specifically states that it is due only upon final closing "when buyers exercise their option to purchase." This language clearly places the holder on notice that the note will become due only upon a contingency which the holder cannot control, *i.e.*, the exercise by buyers of their option to purchase. As for definiteness, the date set forth, May 1, 1980, merely defines when the option to purchase expires, and does not establish a time as to when the note will certainly become due. On these facts *we find the note to be both conditional and indefinite on its face.* [Emphasis added.]

For the reasons stated, we hold that the promissory note sued upon is not a negotiable instrument and that judgment was improperly entered against Stewart. There appears to be no dispute in the record that the sale of the Astro Motel did not occur. Stewart's defenses of lack of consideration, non-maturity of the note, and failure of a condition precedent seem to be [valid]. We therefore remand the case for entry of a judgment in favor of Stewart, . . . and for such further proceedings against the other defendants as are . . . consistent with this opinion.[a]

---

[a]In the subsequent proceedings in the trial court, Calfo presumably recovered the amount he paid for the note, $12,720, from C. J. Realty, the indorser. This is because an indorser warrants to subsequent purchasers that there is no defense good against him (the indorser). Since Stewart did possess a defense—non-sale of the property—C. J. Realty's warranty to Calfo was breached.

Definite Promise or Order to Pay: Occasionally an instrument refers to the existence of a debt, but its language raises the question of whether the instrument really constitutes a promise or order that the debt be paid. For example, one person may hand to another a written IOU. A statement of this kind, or any other statement that merely acknowledges the existence of a debt, does not constitute a promise to pay, and the instrument thus fails to meet the requirements of negotiability.

Amount to Be Paid Must Be a Sum Certain in Money

If an instrument is to be a substitute for money and have an equivalent degree of acceptability, the necessity that the amount be a *sum certain* is obvious. This requirement of certainty is met if the holder can determine from the terms of the instrument itself the amount he or she is entitled to receive at maturity.

The UCC recognizes that some instruments contain provisions that at least raise the question of whether they violate this requirement, and Sec. 3-106 is meant to "save" the negotiability of many of these instruments by providing that

> the sum payable is a sum certain even though it is to be paid (a) with stated interest or by stated installments; or (b) with stated different rates of interest before and after default or a specified date; or (c) with a stated discount or addition if paid before or after the date fixed for payment; or (d) with exchange or less exchange, whether at a fixed rate or at the current rate; or (e) with costs of collection or an attorney's fee or both upon default.

Subsections a, b, c, and e are self-explanatory. Subsection d refers to instruments that are payable in foreign currency. The holder of this kind of instrument may want payment in his or her own country's currency, which requires application of the exchange rate in effect between the two countries. Such instruments, whether payable at fixed exchange rates or at "current rates," are deemed by subsection d to meet the "sum certain" requirement.

Payment to Be Made Only in Money: Instruments must be payable only in *money*. Thus,

any contract that requires the obligor to perform an act other than, or in addition to, the payment of money is nonnegotiable (with exceptions noted later in the chapter).[3] Three examples of such contracts are: (1) M, in return for a loan, promises to deliver "sixty bushels of U.S. #1 blackeye peas ninety days after date"; (2) M signs a note that obligates him to pay at maturity $1,000 *and* to deliver to the holder at that time sixty bushels of U.S. #1 blackeye peas; and (3) M signs a note that obligates him to pay $1,000 *or* to deliver the peas at maturity.

Money is defined in Sec. 1-201(24) as a "medium of exchange authorized or adopted by a domestic or foreign government as a part of its currency." It thus follows that any instrument payable in the currency of a recognized government is payable in money regardless of where the instrument is to be paid. In that regard, Sec. 3-107(2) provides that an instrument payable in this country whose amount is stated in a foreign currency (such as 2,000 German marks) can be satisfied by the payment of an equivalent number of American dollars at the due date, unless the instrument *expressly* requires payment in marks. In either event the instrument is negotiable. In no case, however, can the instrument be payable in something other than money. To illustrate:

1. An instrument drafted in Mexico City and payable in Austin, Texas, expressly calls for payment in ten thousand Mexican pesos. The instrument is payable in money.

2. An instrument payable in U.S. government bonds is not negotiable, since government bonds are not a medium of exchange recognized by the U.S. government.

---

[3] However, contracts that require the *delivery of goods* at a future date often do possess the quality of negotiability. While bills of lading and warehouse receipts fail to qualify as negotiable instruments under Article 3 of the UCC, because they do not contain promises to pay money, they do qualify as negotiable documents of title under Article 7 of the code.

Payable on Demand or at a Definite Time

Under Sec. 3-108, to be negotiable an instrument must be either payable on demand or at a definite time. This requirement recognizes that the holder of an instrument wants to know with certainty when he or she will be entitled to payment. Any appreciable uncertainty as to time of payment makes the instrument commercially unacceptable and defeats the concept that a negotiable instrument is a substitute for money.

Instruments payable *on demand* (called **demand instruments**) include (1) those which are expressly so payable; (2) those whose terms make the instrument payable "at sight" or "on presentation" by the holder; or (3) those in which no time for payment is stated, as, for example, the following: "I promise to pay to the order of P one hundred dollars. (signed) M."

Instruments that are not payable on demand, called **time instruments,** must be payable at a definite time in order to be negotiable. When issuing this kind of note or draft, the maker or drawer usually wants assurance that there will be no obligation to pay until the specified time period has elapsed. The terms clearly indicate a definite future time for payment, such as "payable one year from date" or "payable July 1, 1990."

While no problems of negotiability are presented by these kinds of instruments, problems do arise when the note or draft contains additional terms that apparently conflict with the definite time requirement. Section 3-109 clears up most of these problem situations, as follows:

(1) An instrument is payable at a definite time if by its terms it is payable (a) on or before a stated date or at a fixed period after a stated date; or (b) at a fixed price after sight; or (c) at a definite time subject to any acceleration; or (d) at a definite time subject to extension at the option of the holder, or to extension to a further definite time at the option of the maker or acceptor or automatically upon or after a specified act or event.

(2) An instrument which by its terms is otherwise payable only upon an act or event uncertain as to time of occurrence is not payable at a definite time even though the act or event has occurred.

We will now briefly examine subsections a and b of Sec. 3-109(1), together with a case that involves an interpretation of these provisions. Following the case we will return to the "acceleration" and "extension" provisions of subsections c and d.

Subsections 1a and 1b: Subsections a and b of Sec. 3-109(1) are virtually self-explanatory. An instrument payable on or before a specified date gives the maker, drawer, or acceptor the option of paying before the stated maturity date if he or she wishes. Subsection 1a simply points out that such uncertainty does not violate the definite time requirement. Subsection 1b refers to a common provision in drafts that they are payable a specified time (frequently sixty or ninety days) "after sight." That is, the time period does not begin to run until "sight" (the moment the draft is accepted by the drawee) occurs. Although the time at which the acceptance will occur is unknown when the instrument is first issued, this subsection provides that the instrument nonetheless meets the definite time requirement.

In the following case the primary question is: "When is the instrument due?" rather than "Is the instrument negotiable?" The case is nonetheless useful, because in answering the primary question the higher court clearly implied that the note did qualify as a negotiable instrument under the code.

Ferri v. Sylvia
Supreme Court of Rhode Island, 214 A.2d 470 (1965)

Mr. and Mrs. Sylvia, the defendants, signed a promissory note payable to Maria Ferri, plaintiff. Under the terms of the note, dated May 25, 1963, the Sylvias promised to pay plaintiff $3,000 "within ten (10) years after date." At some unspecified time thereafter, but long before the ten years had elapsed, plaintiff brought action to recover on the note. The Sylvias defended on the ground that the instrument had not yet matured.

The trial court ruled that the maturity date was "uncertain" and therefore admitted oral testimony by both parties "as to their intentions and prior agreements." On the basis of that testimony the court ruled that plaintiff had the right to demand payment at any time after May 25, 1963. Judgment was thus entered for plaintiff, and defendants appealed.

Joslin, Justice:

. . . The question is whether the note is payable at a fixed . . . time. If the phrase, "within ten (10) years after date" lacks explicitness or is ambiguous, then clearly parol [oral] evidence was admissible for the purpose of ascertaining the intention of the parties. . . . While the trial justice in admitting and accepting the extrinsic evidence apparently relied on [this principle], it is not applicable because the payment provisions of the note are not uncertain nor are they incomplete.

[Under] the law merchant it was generally settled that a promissory note or a bill of exchange payable "on or before" a specified date fixed with certainty the time of payment. The same rule has been fixed by statute first under the Negotiable Instruments Law, . . . and now pursuant to the Uniform Commercial Code. The Code in Sec. 6A-3-109(1) reads as follows: "An instrument is payable at a definite time if by its terms it is payable (a) on or before a stated date. . . ."

The courts in the cases we cite were primarily concerned with whether a provision for payment "on or before" a specified date impaired the negotiability of an instrument. Collaterally, of course, they necessarily considered whether such an instrument was payable at a [definite] time, for unless it was, an essential prerequisite to negotiability was lacking.

They said that the legal rights of the holder of an "on or before" instrument were clearly fixed and entitled him to payment upon an event that was certain to come, even though the maker might be privileged to pay sooner if he so elected. They held, therefore, that the due date of such an instrument was fixed with certainty and that its negotiability was unaffected *by the privilege given the maker* to accelerate payment. [Emphasis added.] . . .

Judge Cooley in *Mattison v. Marks* [cited earlier], observing that notes of this kind were common in commercial transactions, said:

It seems certain to us that this note is payable at a time certain. It is payable certainly, and at all events, on a day particularly named; and at that time, and not before, *payment might be enforced against the maker. . . . True, the maker may pay sooner if he shall choose, but this option, if exercised, would be a payment in advance of the legal liability, and nothing more. [Emphasis added.]*

On principle no valid distinction can be drawn between an instrument payable "on or before" a fixed date and one which calls for payment "within" a stipulated period. This was the holding of *Leader v. Plante,* 95 Me. 339, where the court said: "'Within' a certain period, 'on or before' a day named and 'at or before' a certain day, are equivalent terms and the rules of construction apply to each alike." . . .

For the foregoing reasons it is clear that the parties unequivocally agreed that the plaintiff could not demand payment of the note until the expiration of the ten-year period. It is likewise clear that any prior . . . oral agreements of the parties relevant to its due date were so merged and integrated with the writing as to prevent its being explained or supplemented by parol evidence. . . .

Judgment reversed.

Acceleration Clauses: Instruments due at a fixed future date sometimes have **acceleration clauses** providing that the date of maturity shall be *moved ahead* if a specified event occurs prior to the stated due date. An instrument issued this year with a maturity date two years hence might contain, for example, either of these acceleration clauses: (1) "This instrument shall become immediately due and payable upon the maker's (or acceptor's) bankruptcy"; or (2) for a note payable in monthly installments, "If any installment is not paid when due, the entire instrument is due and payable."

Under Sec. 3-109(1)(c) all instruments with acceleration clauses meet the definite time test, even if the events upon which the acceleration is based are to some extent within the holder's control. To illustrate: "Should the holder deem himself insecure at any time prior to the maturity date, he can demand payment at such time and the entire instrument shall thereupon immediately become due and payable." However,

the right of the holder to accelerate an instrument containing a clause such as this is subject to the good faith requirement contained in Sec. 1-208—that the clause "shall be construed to mean that he shall have the power [to accelerate] only if he in good faith believes that the prospect of payment or performance is impaired."

Extension Clauses: **Extension clauses** are the reverse of acceleration clauses; that is, they appear in notes or drafts having a fixed future maturity date and provide that, under certain circumstances, the date shall be *extended further.* Before enactment of the UCC this kind of clause posed a number of questions for the courts about their effect on negotiability. Virtually all these questions have been eliminated by UCC Sec. 3-109(1)(d), which provides that an instrument is negotiable if by its terms it is payable "at a definite time subject to extension at the option of the holder, or to extension to a further definite time at the option of the maker or acceptor or automatically upon or after a specified event."

Thus extension clauses that give the *obligor* (maker or acceptor) the right to extend the time of payment meet the definite time test only if they contain a new fixed maturity date. (The same is true for clauses that extend the time of payment automatically on the occurrence of a specified event.) On the other hand, clauses giving the *holder* the right to extend the time of payment need not contain a new fixed maturity date.

This distinction is logical. If the obligor had the right to extend payment without limit, neither the holder nor any potential purchaser could determine with certainty when he or she would have the right to be paid. But when the holder has the option, he or she is free to demand payment at the maturity date or at any time thereafter. (Actually, the holder of any instrument is free to postpone the time of payment even if no extension clause appears.)

We can illustrate the primary effects of subsection d as follows:

1. "It is expressly agreed that the holder of this note at the date of maturity can extend the time of payment until the following Thanksgiving or even later if she wishes." *Result:* Negotiability is not destroyed, even though it is not known how long the extension will be, since the option is solely that of the holder.

2. "The maker has the unconditional right to postpone the time of payment of this note beyond its November 1, 1988, maturity date, but for no longer than a reasonable time after such date." *Result:* The definite time requirement is not met and the negotiability of the instrument is thus destroyed, since the right to extend is the maker's and since no further definite time is contained in the extension clause.

Payable upon Happening of Specified Event:
An instrument that is payable upon the happen-

ing of an event that may never occur (such as "upon the marriage of my daughter") is nonnegotiable for the reason that the promise or order to pay is clearly *conditional* in nature. The instrument remains nonnegotiable even if the event subsequently does occur (although it would, of course, become *payable* at that time.)

[handwritten: "subject to clause"]

Section 3-109(2) goes one step further by providing that "an instrument which by its terms is . . . payable only upon an act or event uncertain as to time of occurrence is not payable at a definite time even though the act or event has occurred." To illustrate: A draft is payable "upon the death of X." Even though X's death is an event that is certain to happen, the draft is nonnegotiable when issued, and remains nonnegotiable even after X's death. (As in the prior example, the draft would, however, become *payable* at that time.)

Payable to Order or to Bearer

It is fundamental to the concept of negotiability that the instrument contain language clearly indicating that the maker or drawer intends it to be fully capable of being transferred to some person or persons other than the one to whom it was originally issued. This is why Sec. 3-104(1)(d) states that the instrument must "be payable to order or to bearer." *Order* and *bearer* are frequently referred to as the "words of negotiability" (although any other words indicating a similar intention will also meet this requirement of the code).[4]

Order Instruments: Section 3-110 defines **order instrument** and helps interpret Sec. 3-104(1)(d). Essentially Sec. 3-110(1) provides that "an instrument is payable to order when by its terms it is payable to the order or assigns of

---

[4] We are here concerned with the order-bearer requirement only as it affects *negotiability* of an instrument, but the requirement also affects the manner in which instruments are to be *transferred.* As we will see later in the chapter, a bearer instrument can be "negotiated" to a third party without being indorsed by the transferor, while an indorsement is essential for order instruments.

any person therein specified with reasonable certainty, or to him or his order."[5] Additionally, the instrument can be payable "to the order of (a) the maker or drawer; or (b) the drawee; or (c) a payee who is not maker, drawer, or drawee; or (d) two or more payees together or in the alternative; or (e) an estate, trust or funds . . . ; or (f) an office or an officer by his title as such . . . ; or (g) a partnership or unincorporated association. . . ."

The requirements of the order instrument are met by such language as "pay to the order of Jennifer Howell" and "pay to Melanie Howell or order." However, an instrument "payable to Carolyn Howell" is not an order instrument, and therefore is nonnegotiable.

---

[5] *Assigns* simply means all third parties to whom the instrument might subsequently be transferred.

Bearer Instruments: A note or draft that fails to qualify as an order instrument is nonetheless negotiable if it is payable to the *bearer.* Section 3-111 provides that "an instrument is payable to bearer when by its terms it is payable to (a) bearer or the order of bearer; or (b) a specified person or bearer; or (c) 'cash' or the order of 'cash,' or any other indication which does not purport to designate a specific payee."

Under this section the following all qualify as **bearer instruments:** "payable to bearer," "payable to the order of bearer," and "payable to X or bearer." However, an instrument that is payable only to a specified person ("payable to X") is not payable to bearer and hence is nonnegotiable.

The following case presents the general question of whether postal money orders meet the tests of negotiability.

United States v. The First National Bank of Boston
U.S. District Court, District of Massachusetts,
263 F.Supp. 298 (1967)

Joseph MacDonald stole sixty-three domestic money order blanks and an "all purpose dating stamp" from two post offices. Thereafter he completed the money orders so that they were payable to a fictitious person, wrote in a fictitious initial of a supposed employee of one of the post offices, and impressed the mark of the stolen validating dating stamp on the instruments.

On the back of each money order appeared the following:

PAYEE MUST ENDORSE BELOW ON LINE MARKED 'PAYEE.'

OWNERSHIP OF THIS ORDER MAY BE TRANSFERRED TO ANOTHER PERSON OR FIRM IF THE PAYEE WILL WRITE THE NAME OF SUCH PERSON OR FIRM ON THE LINE MARKED 'PAY TO' BEFORE WRITING HIS OWN NAME ON THE SECOND LINE. MORE THAN ONE INDORSEMENT IS PROHIBITED BY LAW. BANK STAMPS ARE NOT REGARDED AS INDORSEMENTS.

PAY TO————————————————————————

————————————————————————————

THIS ORDER BECOMES INVALID AFTER **20** YEARS. THEREAFTER NO CLAIM FOR PAYMENT WILL BE CONSIDERED.

A number of the money orders were indorsed to the First National Bank, defendant, and were honored by it. The bank presented the orders to the United States and was paid the full amount of $100 for each of the money orders. The United States, after learning the facts, brought action against the defendant bank to recover the amount of money it had paid out to that bank.

The bank relied on two defenses. First, it contended that the money orders qualified as negotiable instruments, in which case it had no liability because of the applicability of Sec. 3-418 of the UCC. Second, the bank contended that even if the money orders were nonnegotiable, it should not have liability to the government "on grounds of public policy." (Only that part of the trial court's decision relating to the first defense is set forth below.)

Wyzanski, Chief Justice:

This case . . . presents . . . the question whether when a stolen postal domestic money order . . . is bought by a good faith indorsee [the defendant bank], and that indorsee has received payment from the United States, the United States may recover back its payment from the indorsee. . . .

[The] broadest contention [of defendant bank] is that today the postal domestic money order. . . . is a negotiable instrument within the meaning of the Uniform Commercial Code and that it is therefore proper to apply to it Sec. 3-418 of the Code which provides that "payment . . . of any instrument is final in favor of a holder in due course, or a person who has in good faith changed his position in reliance on the payment. . . ."

There is difficulty in sustaining this broad contention. [It is true that the money order meets the requirement that it be "payable to order or bearer," in view of the fact that the] order states that "ownership . . . may be transferred to another person or firm" [by indorsement]. However, the money order adds . . . that "More than one indorsement is prohibited by law."

Such a restriction is contrary to §3-301 of the Uniform Commercial Code, which provides that "the holder of an instrument whether or not he is the owner *may transfer and negotiate it,*" and is out of harmony with §3-206(1), which provides that "No restrictive indorsement prevents further transfer or negotiation of the instrument." *Thus it cannot be said that in all respects a postal domestic money order is like the ordinary negotiable instrument covered by modern codes and statutes.* [Emphasis added.]

[The court thus rejected the bank's contention that the money orders were negotiable instruments. However, in the remaining part of its decision the court accepted the second defense of the bank, citing three "policy considerations" which it felt should prevent the United States from recovering from an innocent bank in these circumstances. Accordingly, judgment was entered in favor of defendant bank.]

Terms and Omissions Not ✳
Affecting Negotiability

The negotiability of most instruments is settled by reference to the basic sections we have examined. Occasionally, however, instruments present special problems—sometimes because they contain terms not covered by the preceding sections, sometimes because terms are omitted that normally are present, and sometimes because they contain provisions that are in apparent conflict. Sections 3-112 through 3-118 are designed to resolve most peripheral problems of this sort. We will discuss below the more important of these rules.

Section 3-112—Omissions: Section 3-112 provides in part that the negotiability of an instrument is not affected by "the omission of a statement of any consideration, or of the place where the instrument is drawn or payable." This provision rejects the possible view that such omissions cause an instrument to be incomplete and therefore nonnegotiable. (Along similar lines, Sec. 3-114 states that the negotiability of an instrument is not destroyed simply because the date of issue does not appear—unless, of course, the date of maturity is tied to the date of issue, as when an undated note is "payable sixty days after date.")

Section 3-112—Additional Powers and Promises: We have seen that under Sec. 3-104(1)(b) any instrument containing a promise or order *in addition to* the "promise or order to pay a sum certain in money" causes the instrument to be nonnegotiable "except as authorized by this Article." Several of these additional promises are expressly authorized by subsections b and c of Sec. 3-112.

Subsection b states that the negotiability of an instrument is not affected by a statement that collateral has been given as security for the obligation. Nor is it affected by a promise on the part of the maker, drawer, or acceptor to *maintain,* to *protect,* or to *give additional collateral* in specified circumstances. To illustrate: The maker of a time note has given the payee a warehouse receipt for six hundred bags of beans in the X Warehouse as security. The note further provides that "if a decline in the market value of this collateral should cause the holder of this instrument to deem himself insecure, the maker shall deliver additional collateral upon demand." This note is negotiable.

The reason why Sec. 3-112 provides that the stipulations noted above do not destroy negotiability lies in the fact that the stipulations actually *enhance* the value of the basic obligation, rather than limiting or conditioning it. Thus the instruments are more freely acceptable in commerce and even better able to fulfill their role as substitutes for money or as credit instruments than would be the case if the clauses were absent.

TRANSFER ✳

Commercial paper is designed primarily for the purpose of circulating freely in the business world, as was noted earlier. In the remainder of this chapter, then, we will look at the various ways such paper can be transferred from one holder to another, and at the basic UCC rules that apply to such transfers.

ASSIGNMENT AND NEGOTIATION

A negotiable instrument has no legal significance of and by itself. In other words, its legal life does not begin until it is issued by the maker or drawer to the first holder.[6] After it has been issued to that person, it can be further transferred by him or her in one of two ways—by *negotiation* or by *assignment.*[7] While we shall

---

[6] *Issue* is defined in Sec. 3-102(1)(a) as "the first delivery of an instrument to a holder."

[7] By contrast, the transfer of a nonnegotiable instrument *always* constitutes an assignment, no matter how the transfer is effected. This is because the negotiation provisions of Article 3 apply only to *negotiable instruments* (as is true of all other provisions of that article).

be concerned in this chapter primarily with the legal requirements of a negotiation and the significant rights and duties that flow from it, it is first necessary to distinguish between the two kinds of transfers.

If a payee or other holder of an instrument transfers it to a third party in such a manner that the transfer qualifies as a negotiation under the UCC, the transferee is by definition a holder of the instrument. This makes it possible for the transferee to qualify as a holder in due course (HDC) if he or she meets the other HDC requirements of Article 3. As an HDC the person can acquire *greater rights* under the instrument than those possessed by the transferor, as indicated earlier.

Assignment

If the transfer fails to qualify as a negotiation, it is merely an **assignment,** and the transferee is an *assignee* rather than a holder. As such, his or her status is governed by the common-law contract rules discussed in Chapter 16, under which the transferee's rights cannot be greater than those of the transferor. Obviously, then, the purchaser of a negotiable instrument will almost always want to be sure that the transfer qualifies as a negotiation rather than an assignment.

Negotiation

The definition of **negotiation** and the requirements that must be met in order for the transfer of a particular instrument to qualify as a negotiation are found in Sec. 3-202(1): "Negotiation is the transfer of an instrument in such form that the transferee becomes a holder. If the instrument is payable to order it is negotiated by delivery with any necessary indorsement; if payable to bearer, it is negotiated by delivery [alone]." [8]

---

[8] The issuance of an instrument to the payee technically constitutes a negotiation in view of the fact that the payee (as seen in Chapter 24) is one of the persons who qualifies as a holder under Sec. 1-201(20). However, in actual practice *negotiation* refers only to transfers that occur after an instrument has been issued.

The requirements that must be met, then, in order for a particular transfer to qualify as a negotiation depend entirely upon the form of the instrument at the time of transfer. Before we examine the various kinds of indorsements that can be used, we will illustrate the basic delivery-indorsement requirements.

1. M issues two notes to X, one "payable to bearer" and the other "payable to cash." Because both notes are obviously bearer instruments, X can further negotiate either or both of them to a subsequent purchaser, Y, simply by handing them or mailing them to Y without an indorsement of any kind. (In practice, the purchaser of a bearer instrument normally requests the transferor to indorse it, but the indorsement is not required by the UCC.)

2. Same facts as for example 1, except that the two bearer notes are stolen from X's home by a thief, T. Because *delivery* means a voluntary delivery by the transferor, T's acquisition of the notes in this manner does not constitute a delivery; hence, no negotiation has occurred. However, a further delivery of either note by T to a third party does constitute a negotiation. This points up one of the dangers arising from the use of a bearer instrument. While a thief (or a finder) does not acquire title to the instrument by virtue of the theft (or finding), he or she can *transfer title* to a subsequent innocent purchaser. In such a case, the original owner, X, has lost all rights to the instrument itself.

3. D draws a check that is "payable to the order of P" and mails it to P. P writes her name on the back of the check (an indorsement) and transfers it to her grocer, G, in payment for groceries. The transfer from P to G constitutes a negotiation of this order instrument, since indorsement and delivery have both occurred. However, if P had delivered the instrument without indorsement, it would not constitute a negotiation. (G's rights in such a case will be discussed near the end of this chapter.)

4. B draws a check that is "payable to the order of C" and mails it to C. T, a thief, steals the check, signs C's name on the back, and delivers it to R, a retailer, in payment for liquor. The transfer from T to R is not a negotiation (nor is it even an assignment) because a forged "indorsement" is no indorsement. Nor would a further transfer by R constitute a negotiation; no one can qualify as a holder under a forged indorsement on an order instrument.

BLANK, SPECIAL, QUALIFIED, AND RESTRICTIVE INDORSEMENTS

Essentially there are four kinds of indorsements: blank, special, qualified, and restrictive.

Blank Indorsements

Under Sec. 3-204(1) a **blank indorsement** is one that specifies no particular indorsee; ordinarily it consists only of the name of the payee. If a check is payable "to the order of Mary Glenn," she can indorse it *in blank* by simply writing or stamping her name on the back of the instrument.[9]

A blank indorsement converts an order instrument into a bearer instrument. If Mary Glenn delivers the check to Mark Rhee after indorsing it in blank, Rhee can further negotiate the check by delivery only. A blank indorsement makes the instrument virtually as transferable as cash, and for that reason the instrument should ordinarily be indorsed only at the time it is actually delivered to the transferee.

A person who receives an instrument bearing a

blank indorsement can protect himself or herself against the possibility of loss of title through subsequent negotiation by a thief. Section 3-204(3) provides that a "holder may convert a blank indorsement into a special indorsement by writing over the signature of the indorser in blank any contract consistent with the character of the indorsement." Thus, where the instrument was indorsed "Mary Glenn" and delivered to Mark Rhee, he can write above the Glenn signature "pay to the order of Mark Rhee." The instrument is now "indorsed specially" and cannot be negotiated further without Rhee's indorsement. (Special indorsements will be discussed later in the chapter.)

Effect of Indorsement: A blank indorsement has three effects (in addition to converting the instrument into a bearer instrument):

1. It transfers title to the instrument to the indorsee on delivery. (validity of check)

2. It extends certain warranties to the indorsee and all subsequent holders.

3. It imposes a legal obligation on the indorser to pay the amount of the instrument to the person holding it at maturity if the maker, acceptor, or drawee does not pay (and if certain other conditions are met). This obligation is sometimes called the "conditional" or "secondary" liability of the blank indorser.[10]

The following case involves the negotiation of a note by a hospital—through the use of a blank indorsement—to a bank, and a subsequent retransfer of the instrument by the bank back to the hospital. (Following this case, the examination of other types of indorsements is resumed.)

---

[9] Indorsements are ordinarily written on the instrument itself. However, under Sec. 3-202(2), if there are so many indorsements on the back of an instrument that there is no room for more, subsequent indorsements can be written "on a paper so firmly affixed thereto as to become a part thereof." Such a paper, called an *allonge*, must be firmly pasted or stapled to the instrument; attachment by paper clip alone will not suffice.

---

[10] The warranty and conditional liabilities mentioned here arise from Secs. 3-417(1) and 3-414(1) respectively. Their nature and extent are covered in Chapter 27.

Westerly Hospital v. Higgins ⁎
Supreme Court of Rhode Island, 256 A.2d 506 (1969)

[handwritten: whether or not negotiable and Could 3ʳᵈ party bring suit]

Mr. Higgins, in consideration for services rendered by the plaintiff hospital in connection with the birth of a child to his wife, executed a promissory note payable to the order of the hospital. The note, co-signed by Mrs. Higgins, was payable in eighteen monthly installments.

An authorized officer of the hospital indorsed the note by blank indorsement and negotiated it to the <u>Industrial National Bank</u> (here- *[handwritten: 3ʳᵈ party]* after referred to as Industrial), with the hospital receiving cash in return. The indorsement contained a clause under which the hospital guaranteed payment of principal and interest in the event that the maker, Higgins, should default on the obligation.

Higgins made only the three initial payments to Industrial. As a result of this default the hospital paid Industrial the balance due, as it was obligated to do by the guarantee clause. Industrial then redelivered the note to the hospital, which subsequently brought action against Higgins to recover the balance.

At the trial Higgins contended that the redelivery of the note by Industrial to the hospital did not constitute a negotiation, that the hospital was therefore not a holder of the instrument, and that it consequently could not bring this suit. These contentions were based on evidence indicating that (1) at the time Industrial redelivered the note one of its employees indorsed the instrument on Industrial's behalf, and (2) such indorsement was invalid because the employee possessed no authority to make the indorsement.

The trial court, for reasons appearing in the following decision, rejected Higgins' contentions and entered judgment for the plaintiff hospital. Higgins appealed.

Roberts, Chief Justice:

. . . The defendant contends that the trial justice's ruling granting . . . judgment to plaintiff was error because a genuine issue existed as to whether Westerly Hospital *or Industrial* was in fact the proper party to bring the instant action on the note. We cannot agree with this contention. . . .

The face of the instrument reveals that Westerly Hospital was the payee of the note made by defendant and his wife as co-makers. It further discloses that an indorsement of guarantee was executed in blank [by the] plaintiff hospital. The note was then delivered to Industrial [which then became a holder of the instrument]. . . . Thereafter, when defendant defaulted, Industrial redelivered the note to plaintiff in return for the payment of the remaining amount of defendant's obligation that had been guaranteed by plaintiff hospital, [and it is the validity of this second transfer that is at issue here].

The defendant argues that this delivery of the note [by Industrial] back to plaintiff was not sufficient to constitute a negotiation [for the reason that the representative of Industrial who indorsed the instrument on Industrial's behalf did not possess the authority to do so]. Thus, according to defendant, . . . Westerly Hospital was precluded from becoming a holder of the instrument, . . . and Industrial was the proper party to bring the action on this note [rather than the hospital].

However, [Sec. 3-204] of the Uniform Commercial Code states, in pertinent part, that "An instrument payable to order and indorsed in blank becomes payable to bearer and may be negotiated by delivery alone until specially indorsed." Here Westerly Hospital as payee of the note caused its indorsement to appear thereon without specifying to whom or to whose order the instrument was payable. Instead, a blank indorsement, one specifying no particular indorsee, was made. The legal effect of such an indorsement and delivery was to authorize Industrial as the transferee and holder of the note *to further negotiate the note without indorsement but by mere delivery alone. It is clear that any attempt on its part to achieve negotiation by indorsing the note to plaintiff would have been mere surplusage.* [Emphasis added.]

In our opinion, then, the redelivery of the note in question by Industrial to Westerly Hospital accomplished a negotiation of the instrument, and the fact that a purported special indorsement to Westerly Hospital was not legally executed is of no consequence and does not affect plaintiff's status as the holder of the note. It is our conclusion that in these circumstances [the ruling of the trial court was correct].

Judgment affirmed.

Special Indorsements

Under Sec. 3-204(1), a **special indorsement** "specifies the person to whom or to whose order it makes the instrument payable." To illustrate: A check is payable to the order of P, and he indorses it, "Pay to the order of X, (signed) P." An instrument indorsed in this manner remains an order instrument, and X's indorsement will be necessary for a further negotiation to occur. An indorsement need not, however, include words of negotiability; an indorsement "Pay to X (signed) P" has the same legal effect as "Pay to the order of X, (signed) P."

A special indorsement on a bearer instrument converts it into an order instrument. To illustrate: A note is "payable to bearer." The first holder, H, indorses it, "Pay to the order of X, (signed) H" and then delivers it to X. X's indorsement is now necessary for a further negotiation of the instrument. However, if X indorses it in blank, it is now reconverted to a bearer instrument.

The primary effect of a special indorsement, then, is that it requires the indorsement of the special indorsee before it can be negotiated further.

Qualified Indorsements

Blank and special indorsements are "unqualified" indorsements for the reason that indorsers who use them incur what is called conditional liability on the instruments negotiated in this manner. Specifically, such indorsers are promising to pay the instruments themselves if the

Figure 25.1 Blank, Special, and Qualified Indorsements

Blank

Peter Payee

Effects:
1. Transfers title
2. Extends warranties
3. Sets "conditional" liability

Also—converts order paper to bearer paper.

Special

Pay to John Doe
Peter Payee

Effect:
   Same as blank

But—allows order paper to remain order paper.

Qualified

Without recourse
Peter Payee

Effects:
   1. Transfers title
   2. Extends warranties

No conditional liability.

holder is unable to obtain payment from the maker, acceptor, or drawee at maturity. A blank or special indorser, then, is actually guaranteeing payment of the instrument in addition to transferring title to it.

A **qualified indorsement,** by contrast, is one whose wording indicates that the indorser is not guaranteeing payment of the instrument. The usual qualified indorsement is "without recourse, (signed) X," and the precise effect is illustrated as follows: P receives a check in the mail, drawn on an out-of-town bank and payable to his order. He indorses it "without recourse, (signed) P" and negotiates it to H. H deposits the check in his account at a local bank, but a week later the bank returns it to him because the

drawer did not have sufficient funds in his account. Because P indorsed the instrument qualifiedly, H cannot recover the amount of the dishonored check from him.

Except for eliminating the conditional liability of the indorser, a qualified indorsement has the same general effect as an unqualified (blank or special) indorsement. "Without recourse" indorsements thus transfer title to the indorsee, permitting further negotiation of the instrument. They also impose a warranty liability on the indorser that is quite similar to the liability of the blank and special indorsers (see Chapter 27 for details).

The effects of blank, special, and qualified indorsements are illustrated in Figure 25.1.

Restrictive Indorsements

It is difficult to make broad generalizations about **restrictive indorsements,** because the UCC recognizes four distinctly separate kinds. Nonetheless, two observations do apply to all of them:

1. Under Sec. 3-206(1) restrictive indorsements are similar to the other indorsements discussed in this chapter in that they do not (despite their name) restrict the further negotiation of any instrument so indorsed.

2. They differ from the other indorsements by restricting the rights of the indorsee in order to give certain protection to the indorser.

According to Sec. 3-205:

> An indorsement is restrictive which either (a) is conditional; or (b) purports to prohibit further transfer of the instrument; or (c) includes the words "for collection," "for deposit," "pay any bank," or like terms signifying a purpose of deposit or collection; or (d) otherwise states that it is for the benefit or use of the indorser or of another person.

Conditional Indorsements: As the name indicates, a **conditional indorsement** is an order to pay the instrument only if a specified event occurs. As such, the indorsement imposes a condition on the indorsee's right to collect the proceeds of the instrument. This kind of indorsement is not common, but it is useful in certain situations, particularly when combined with a special indorsement. To illustrate: "Pay to the order of Karen R. Jones upon her delivery to me of one hundred shares of AT&T stock as per our agreement of last November. (Signed) Paul Miller."

Such an indorsement has three basic effects:

1. It does not prohibit further negotiation of the instrument, regardless of whether the condition has or has not occurred.

2. Until the stated condition does occur, however, neither the restrictive indorsee nor any

subsequent holder has the right to enforce the instrument.

3. In the event that a holder does receive payment from the maker (or drawee) when the condition has not yet occurred, both the maker (or drawee) and the holder remain liable to the restrictive endorser for the amount of the instrument.

Special Bank Rules: Because of the large volume of commercial paper handled in the bank collection process, certain banks in that process are permitted to disregard any restrictive indorsements (including, of course, conditional indorsements). This result flows from Sec. 3-206(2), which provides that "an intermediary bank, or a payor bank which is not the depositary bank, is neither given notice nor otherwise affected by a restrictive indorsement of any person excepting the bank's immediate transferor or the person presenting for payment." To illustrate: D, in Worthington, Ohio, draws a check on his Worthington bank and mails it to P, payee, in Bozeman, Montana. P indorses it conditionally and cashes it at his Bozeman bank. The check, now in the bank collection process, is forwarded to a Billings bank, thence to a Chicago bank, and ultimately to the drawee bank in Worthington. Under Sec. 3-206, the Worthington bank may honor the instrument even if the condition specified in the indorsement has not occurred. Neither that bank nor the Billings or Chicago banks could be held liable to the restrictive indorser in such a situation.[11]

Indorsements Purporting to Prohibit Further Negotiation: Section 3-205(b) refers to indorsements that intend to prohibit further negotiation—for example, "Pay to the order of X only, (signed) P." Under pre-UCC law such an

---

[11] Here the Bozeman bank is the "depositary bank"—the first bank to which an item is transferred for collection, under Sec. 4-105(a). The Billings and Chicago banks are "intermediary banks," and the Worthington bank the "payor" (and drawee) bank.

indorsement terminated negotiability of the instrument, and no subsequent purchaser could qualify as a holder. While this kind of indorsement is rarely used today, the drafters of the UCC reversed the common-law view. Section 3-206(1) provides expressly that "no restrictive indorsement prevents further transfer or negotiation of the instrument." A "pay to X only" or "pay to the order of X only" indorsement thus has the same legal effect as a special indorsement, and an instrument indorsed in this manner can be further negotiated by X upon proper indorsement and delivery by him or her.

"For Collection" and "For Deposit" Indorsements:

Indorsements for collection and for deposit are by far the most commonly used types of restrictive indorsements. Instruments indorsed in either way are almost always put directly into the bank collection process. Under Sec. 3-206(3), in such situations any depositary bank receiving the instrument is responsible for acting consistently with the terms of the indorsement, which ordinarily means that it must credit the restrictive indorser's account.

The protection afforded to the restrictive indorser is best illustrated by a situation where the transferee–depositary bank fails to live up to the duty imposed by Sec. 3-206: D draws and delivers a check payable to P. P indorses the check, "For deposit, (signed) P" and gives the check to his accountant, A, to deposit in P's bank. P's bank gives A cash for the check (or credits A's account), and the cash is not in fact turned over to P (or the funds in A's account are not subsequently made available to P). P can now maintain an *action of conversion* against the bank, and the bank will be liable because it clearly has acted inconsistently with the terms of the restrictive indorsement.

Special Bank Rules: As indicated in the discussion of conditional indorsements, drawee and intermediary banks holding restrictively indorsed paper do not have the responsibility that is imposed on depositary banks. Thus, under Sec. 3-206(2), drawee and intermediary banks in possession of instruments indorsed "for collection" or "for deposit" are neither given notice of nor affected by such indorsements. In other words, these banks cannot be held liable to the restrictive indorser if the restrictive indorsee—depositary bank fails to act consistently with the terms of the indorsements.

A similar type of restrictive indorsement is the *pay any bank or banker indorsement.* This is expressly deemed a restrictive indorsement under Sec. 3-206(3), and the rules applicable to it are the same as those for the other types of restrictive indorsements discussed in this section.

Trust Indorsements: The fourth type of restrictive indorsement is one which by its terms shows an intent to benefit the indorser or some third party; it is frequently referred to as a **trust indorsement** or *agency indorsement.* For example: "Pay to A as agent of P, (signed) P," and "Pay to A in trust for B, (signed) P." In these situations, two results flow from the indorsements. (1) When the restrictive indorsee, A, receives payment of the instrument, he holds the proceeds in trust for the named beneficiary. (2) Any subsequent purchaser of the instrument takes it free of the restriction, and thus qualifies as an HDC unless he or she has actual knowledge that A's negotiation of the instrument is a breach of A's fiduciary duty.

The following case serves notice on bank officers of the unfortunate circumstances that may befall a bank when an employee takes an instrument without noticing that it has been restrictively indorsed.

In re Quantum Development Corp.; American Fidelity Fire Ins. Co. v. Joy; Lang v. Bank of Nova Scotia
U.S. District Court, Virgin Islands, District of
St. Croix, 397 F.Supp. 329 (1975)

American Fidelity Fire Insurance Company, plaintiff, was a surety of the Quantum Development Corporation. (A *surety* is a person or firm who has made himself or itself responsible for the debts or other obligations of another.)

Quantum Development went into bankruptcy in March of 1973. Soon thereafter American Fidelity, responding to its obligations as surety, delivered a certified check in the amount of $84,858 to the clerk of the bankruptcy court, who delivered the check to Charles Joy, the receiver of the bankrupt firm. The check was made payable to "Charles R. Joy, Receiver," and the bankruptcy judge ordered Joy to put the bulk of the money into certificates of deposit in Quantum Development's name, and the balance into a checking account for Quantum Development.

Joy took the check to Chandler, the manager of a branch of the Bank of Nova Scotia (BNS), and purchased $75,000 worth of certificates of deposit with the check. The balance of approximately $9,000 was placed in a checking account in Joy's name. Although Joy indorsed the check "For Deposit in Quantum Acct. Quantum Bankruptcy, Charles R. Joy," the bank made out the CDs in the name of Joy personally.

Six months later, when the CDs matured, Joy cashed them at the bank and vanished with the money. Thereafter American Fidelity brought this action against BNS to recover the value of the CDs. (The decision below is that of the trial court.)

Young, Justice:

. . . As heretofore noted, the check which Joy presented to Mr. Chandler was payable to "Charles R. Joy, Receiver," and bore on the back the indorsement "For Deposit in Quantum Acct. Quantum Bankruptcy, Charles R. Joy." A perusal of §3-205 of the Uniform Commercial Code, intended to provide a functional definition of the term "restrictive indorsement," leaves little doubt that the foregoing fits within the prescription:

"An indorsement is restrictive which either . . . (c) includes the words 'for collection,' 'for deposit,' 'pay any bank,' or like terms signifying a purpose of deposit or collection; or (d) otherwise states that it is for the benefit or use of the indorser or of another person."

The indorsement clearly indicates that it was for the benefit or use of the Quantum bankruptcy estate.

The recognized purpose of a restrictive indorsement *is to restrict the use to which the indorsee may put the proceeds of the instrument when a party pays them to the indorsee.* [Emphasis added.] [Although] no section of the UCC specifically requires an indorsee-bank to examine the restriction and to ensure that its payment is not inconsistent therewith, . . . such duty and resulting liability for the failure to carry out such duty can be fairly inferred from a number of Code sections.

Section 3-206(2), for example, permits an intermediary bank, or a payor bank *which is not the depositary bank,* to disregard any restrictive indorsement except that of the bank's immediate transferor. . . . [But] it is clear under the facts of the instant case [that] BNS stands in the position of the depositary bank rather than an intermediary bank. Thus, at least by negative implication, . . . the Code provides a remedy in conversion against a *depositary bank* which fails to pay or apply the proceeds in accordance with the terms of a restrictive indorsement. [Emphasis added.]

By his own admission, Mr. Chandler never examined the indorsement on the check, which indorsement was made in his presence. Instead, he merely instructed his secretary to make out the CDs in accordance with Mr. Joy's wishes. Certainly, such actions on the part of BNS's branch manager do not comport with reasonable commercial standards. The very least Chandler could have done was to ensure that the inscription on the CDs corresponded to that on the original check. Although he noticed that the check was made out to Joy in his representative capacity, Chandler made no effort to ascertain for whom Joy was a receiver. . . .

Ignoring the restrictive indorsement inscribed on the back of a check in the substantial amount of over $84,000, the bank proceeded to issue to Mr. Joy in his personal and individual capacity the CDs in the amount of $25,000 each. Although the bank officials in no way participated in the extreme breach of trust of which Mr. Joy was guilty, their placing the CDs in Joy's individual name provided the opportunity and encouragement which Joy may have needed to perpetuate his scheme. . . .

Judgment for the plaintiff to be paid by the defendant BNS for the sum of $77,664.54 plus interest.

MISCELLANEOUS NEGOTIATION PROBLEMS

We conclude this chapter with a discussion of several peripheral problems not covered by the general rules of negotiation.

Multiple Payees

Under Sec. 3-116(a), instruments are sometimes payable to two or more *alternative* persons ("pay to the order of A or B"). Negotiation of such an instrument requires only the indorse-ment of either of the payees. On the other hand, under Sec. 3-116(b), if the instrument is payable to the parties *jointly* ("pay to A and B"), then both indorsements are required for a further negotiation of the instrument.

Correction of Names

Section 3-203 is self-explanatory; it provides that "where an instrument is made payable to a person under a misspelled name or [a name] other than his own, he may indorse in that name or his own or both; but signature in both names may be required by a person paying or giving value for the instrument."

Transfer of Unindorsed Order Paper

If an order instrument is transferred without the indorsement of the payee, the transferee is not a holder of the instrument and therefore cannot negotiate it. He or she does, however, have the right (by legal action, if necessary) to require the transferor to indorse the instrument. Upon receiving the indorsement the transferee qualifies as a holder.

There is one exception to the rule that the transferee of an unindorsed order paper cannot negotiate the instrument further. Sec. 4-205 permits a depositary bank that received such a check either to supply its customer's indorsement or simply to note on the instrument that it has credited the check to its customer-depositor's account. In either case the bank is a holder and can negotiate the instrument further.

The following case shows how well this exception worked out for the defendant, the depositary bank.

Cole v. First National Bank of Gillette
Supreme Court of Wyoming, 433 P.2d 837 (1967)

Clarence and Wilma Cole, plaintiffs, purchased a home from Wyoming Homes of Gillette, Wyoming. As a down payment on the contract Mrs. Cole gave a Wyoming Homes salesman a $4,000 check. The check was drawn by Buffalo Auto Supply (a company owned by the Coles) on that company's account in the First National Bank of Buffalo, Wyoming, and it was payable to the order of Wyoming Homes.

The salesman took the check to the First National Bank of Gillette and, without indorsing it, deposited it in the Wyoming Homes account with that bank.

The Gillette bank stamped the check "First National Bank, Gillette, Wyoming, For Deposit Only" and put it into the bank collection process. The check reached the drawee bank in Buffalo, and the $4,000 was duly charged to the Buffalo Auto Supply account. Thereafter the Coles claimed that Wyoming Homes (1) had failed to give consideration and (2) was guilty of fraud in the sale of the home.

The Coles brought action against the First National Bank of Gillette to recover the $4,000 on the theory that it was merely a transferee of the check and had only the rights of the transferor, Wyoming Homes, in view of the fact Wyoming Homes did not indorse the check on depositing it in the Gillette bank. As a result, the Coles contended that the Gillette bank was not a holder in due course, or even a holder of the check as defined by the UCC, and that the bank thus took the check subject to the defenses of failure of consideration and fraud.

The trial court rejected plaintiffs' contentions and entered summary judgment for the defendant. The Coles appealed, claiming that the Supreme Court of Wyoming should, as a matter of law, reverse that judgment.

Harnsberger, Chief Justice:

. . . Appellants' first argument is that under [a number of cited sections of the UCC] the appellee owned merely an equitable title to the check which was subject to all defenses available to its maker.

In the view we take, only [Wyoming Statute] §34-4-205 is of importance [in this case.] . . . Section 34-4-205 clearly authorized the Gillette bank, as the depositary bank taking the check for collection, *to place a statement on the check to the effect that the item was credited to the account of a customer, which statement is said to be as effective as the customer's endorsement.* [Emphasis added.] This was done. The section is as follows:

(1) A depositary bank which has taken an item for collection may supply any indorsement of the customer which is necessary to title unless the item contains the words "payee's endorsement required" or the like. In the absence of such a requirement a statement placed on the item by the depositary bank to the effect that the item was deposited by a customer or credited to his account is effective as the customer's indorsement.

(2) An intermediary bank, or payor bank which is not a depositary, is neither given notice nor otherwise affected by a restrictive indorsement of any person except the bank's immediate transferor.

Any question as to whether Wyoming Homes was such a "customer" within the meaning of §34-4-205 is answered by §34-4-104(e), W. S. 1957 (1965 Cum. Supp.), reading, " 'Customer' means any person having an account with a bank or for whom a bank has agreed to collect items and includes a bank carrying an account with another bank."

It follows that the Gillette bank having credited the amount of the check to the account of its payee and a final settlement of the item having been made, the bank did not step into the shoes of the payee or become subject to any equities between the check's maker or its payee. *Thus matters of possible failure of consideration or of fraud relate solely to matters between the Coles and Wyoming Homes, to which transactions the appellee was not a party.* [Emphasis added.]

The judgment of the trial court is affirmed.

Rescission of Indorsements

Sometimes the indorsement and delivery of an instrument are made under circumstances in which the indorser, under ordinary contract law, has the right to rescind the transaction. The most common situations are those where: (1) the indorser is a minor, (2) the indorsement and subsequent delivery are brought about by fraud or duress on the part of the indorsee, and (3) the negotiation is part of an illegal transaction. Under Sec. 3-207:

1. Such negotiations are "effective" (that is, the indorsee qualifies as a holder and thus is capable of negotiating the instrument further).

2. However, until the instrument is negotiated to a party who qualifies as an HDC, the indorser can rescind the indorsement. To illustrate:

   a. P, a minor, indorses a note to H, the holder. As long as the note remains in H's hands, P can rescind the indorsement and recover the instrument.

   b. P indorses a note to H as a result of fraud

practiced on him by H. After H negotiates the instrument to X (holder 2), P seeks to disaffirm the indorsement and recover the note from X. If X qualifies as an HDC of the instrument (under rules examined in the next chapter), P cannot set aside the negotiation.

The Fictitious Payee Problem

The **fictitious payee** situation most often occurs where a dishonest employee, usually someone in charge of payrolls or payment of bills, draws a company check payable to the order of a nonexistent person or to the order of an actual person who is not entitled to payment. Following are three cases that illustrate situations to which the "fictitious payee" rule of Article 3 apply (with the results of that rule explained immediately thereafter.)

Case 1: The D Company has fifty employees. B, the company's bookkeeper, has authority to issue checks in the corporate name to pay bills and the payroll for the firm's employees. B issues a check to P, who is neither a creditor nor an employee of the company. The check is drawn on the X Bank, where the company has its checking account. After drawing the check, *B indorses P's name on the back* and cashes it at some other local bank. The X Bank (drawee) receives the check through the collection process and charges the D Company's account.

Case 2: The same situation as for Case 1, except that B prepares checks for T, the company's treasurer, to sign. B drafts a check drawn on the X Bank payable to P (an accomplice of B) and puts the check, among others, on T's desk for his signature. T signs the check in the corporate name, believing P to be a creditor of the firm. B takes the check to P after T has signed it; P then indorses it and cashes it at a local bank. The X Bank (drawee) receives the check through the collection process and charges the D Company's account.

Case 3: The same situation as for Case 2, except that B, after receiving the signed check pay-

able to the order of P, indorses P's name on the back and transfers it to a third party, H, instead of delivering it to P. H, an innocent purchaser, presents the check to the X Bank for payment but finds that payment has been stopped by the D Company, which had discovered what B had done.

Suppose, in Cases 1 and 2, that the D Company after learning the facts sues the X Bank to recover the amount of the checks on the theory that the indorsements were forgeries. And, in Case 3, suppose that H sues the D Company (drawer) on the check, and the D Company defends on the ground that the indorsement of P was a forgery. Under Sec. 3-405, *the D Company loses in all three of these situations.*

In Case 1, where B had the authority to sign checks in the corporate name and did so knowing that P was not entitled to payment, Sec. 3-405(1)(b) applies. It provides that "the indorsement by any person in the name of a named payee *is effective* if a person signing as or on behalf of a maker or drawer *intends the payee to have no interest in the instrument.*" (Emphasis added.) Thus the signing of P's name by B is an effective indorsement rather than a forgery. Consequently, the bank effectively obeyed the D Company's order to pay, and it was therefore entitled to charge the company's account.

The same is true in Case 2, where B supplied the D Company's treasurer with the checks payable to the order of P. This is because Sec. 3-405(1)(c) provides that "the indorsement by any person in the name of a named payee *is effective* if an agent or employee of the maker or drawer *has supplied him with* the name of the payee intending the latter to have no such interest." (Emphasis added). Thus the X Bank again had the right to charge the company's account with the check—assuming, of course, that the bank had no knowledge of B's misconduct.

In Case 3, for the same reason, the holder of the check, H, can enforce the check against the D Company. (As will be seen in Chapter 28, the fact that the D Company stopped payment on the check does not necessarily insulate it against liability to the holder of the check. A stop payment order simply prevents the holder from receiving payment on presenting the check to the drawee bank; a subsequent lawsuit by the holder against the drawee is what determines the liability or nonliability of the drawer.)

SUMMARY

The negotiability or nonnegotiability of an instrument is determined entirely by its form and content. Under Sec. 3-104, to be negotiable an instrument must (1) be signed by the maker or drawer; (2) contain an unconditional order or promise to pay a sum certain in money; (3) be payable on demand or at a definite time; and (4) be payable to order or to bearer. Subsequent sections of Article 3 clarify these requirements. The "unconditional" requirement means that the promise or order must be absolute, rather than one payable only in certain circumstances. Two types of provisions generally condition an order or promise, and thus cause the instrument to be nonnegotiable: (1) provisions stating that payment is to be out of a specified fund, and (2) promises stating that the instrument is "subject to" another agreement. With respect to the time of payment requirements, an instrument is payable on demand if it so provides, or if it contains no time of payment. An instrument is payable at a definite time if payable at a specified future date, or at such a date with an acceleration clause providing for an earlier maturity date if a certain event occurs. Instruments payable "on or before" a specified date also meet the definite time requirement. An instrument payable "to X" is not negotiable, because it is neither a bearer nor an order instrument.

Turning to the question of transfer, a bearer instrument may be negotiated by delivery only, but an order instrument requires an indorsement in addition to delivery. If a transfer does not meet the "negotiation" requirements the transferee is merely an assignee of the transferor's rights, and the transferee cannot achieve the favored holder-in-due-course status.

There are four kinds of indorsements: blank, special, qualified, and restrictive. A blank indorsement converts an order instrument into a bearer instrument. Blank and special indorsements have three additional consequences. First, they transfer title to the indorsee when accompanied by delivery of the instrument. Second, such indorsers extend certain warranties, or guarantees, to the indorsee and to all subsequent holders. Third, such indorsers have the legal obligation to pay the instrument at maturity if the maker, acceptor, or drawee dishonors it. A qualified ("without recourse") indorsement has the same consequences as blank and special indorsements except that such an indorser does *not* have the legal obligation to pay the instrument if it is dishonored.

Restrictive indorsements are of four types. They do *not* prohibit further negotiation, but, in general, do restrict the rights of the indorsee in order to give certain protection to the indorser relative to the proceeds of the instrument upon its payment. A forged indorsement necessary to the negotiation of an order instrument is void. Thus if a payee's indorsement is forged and the instrument thereafter transferred, no negotiation has occurred and the transferee is neither a holder of the instrument nor entitled to payment of the instrument.

KEY TERMS

Requirements of negotiability
Demand instrument
Time instrument
Acceleration clause
Extension clause
Order instrument
Bearer instrument
Assignment
Negotiation
Blank indorsement
Special indorsement
Qualified indorsement
Restrictive indorsement
Conditional indorsement
Trust indorsement
Fictitious payee

QUESTIONS AND PROBLEMS

1. Sain Builders gave a $4,000 promissory note to Samuel Feinberg, with whom it had an existing contract. Feinberg later negotiated the note to D'Andrea. The note contained a clear-cut promise to pay, and was negotiable in all other respects, but in the lower left hand corner Sain Builders had written in the words "as per contract." Does this inscription destroy negotiability of the instrument? Why or why not? (*D'Andrea v. Feinberg*, 256 N.Y.S.2d 504, 1965.)

2. A law firm performed legal services for a client. Later the client wrote this letter: "I agree to pay to your firm as attorney's fees for representing me in obtaining property settlement agreement and tax advice, the sum of $2,760, payable at the rate of $230 per month for twelve (12) months beginning January 1, 1970. (Signed) Barbara Hall Lodge." Is this written promise a negotiable instrument? Why or why not? (*Hall v. Westmoreland et al.*, 182 S.E.2d 539, 1971.)

3. Following is a promissory note, written entirely in longhand: "I, the undersigned, hereby promise to pay to the order of Kevin Smith or bearer on January 2, 1987, one hundred dollars. Should I become bankrupt at any time, the entire sum shall be immediately due and payable upon demand of the holder. (Signed) Mark Gibson."
    a. Is this instrument payable to order or to bearer? Explain.
    b. Does the acceleration clause destroy negotiability of the instrument? Explain.

4. Holly Hill Acres, Ltd., executed a promissory note and a mortgage securing it and delivered both instruments to the payee, Rogers and Blythe. Part of the note read as follows: "This note with interest is secured by a mortgage on real estate . . . made by the maker hereof in favor of the said payee, and shall be construed and enforced according to the laws of the State of Florida. The terms of said mortgage are by this reference made a part hereof." Does this writing affect the negotiability of the note? Why or why not? (*Holly Hill Acres, Ltd. v. Charter Bank of Gainesville,* 17 UCC Rep. 144, 1975.)

5. M is the maker of a note "payable on or before June 1, 1987."
    a. Does this clause give the *maker* the right to pay the instrument before the due date, or does it give the *holder* the right to demand payment before the due date? What is the basis for your answer?
    b. Does the clause destroy the negotiability of the note? Explain.

6. The X Corporation issues a check "payable to the order of Ron St. Pierre." St. Pierre indorses the instrument in blank ("Ron St. Pierre") and negotiates it to the Y Company. Before the Y Company has time to indorse the check it is stolen by Z and transferred to H, who has no knowledge of the theft. The X Corporation then learns of the theft and stops payment on the check. In a subsequent suit brought by H against the X Corporation to recover the amount of the instrument, the X Corporation contends that H is not a holder of the instrument since the Y Company had not indorsed it. Is this contention correct? Why or why not?

7. D draws a draft payable to the order of P. P indorses it to A as follows: "Pay to A without recourse, (signed) P." A indorses the instrument to B as follows: "Pay to B upon her delivery of her 1980 Citation, (signed) A." B indorses the instrument, "Pay to the order of C, (signed) B," and gives it to C.
    a. Classify each of the above indorsements.
    b. Since P indorsed the instrument "Pay to A . . ." instead of "Pay to the order of A . . . ," does this mean that A's subsequent transfer of it to B is not a negotiation? Explain.
    c. Which of the transferees (A, B, or C)—if any—qualify as holders?

8. The D Company purchases its oil from a jobber, the P Company. In payment for its December purchases of oil the D Company sent a check to the P Company for $975, the check being payable "to the order of the P Company." An authorized employee of the P Company indorsed the check, by rubber stamp, "Pay to the order of Gulf Oil, the P Company." X, a janitor of the P Company, stole the check and forged this indorsement on it: "Gulf Oil, by John Andrews, assistant treasurer." If this instrument should later be cashed by a bank under circumstances in which it had no reason to suspect the forged indorsement, would the bank be a holder of it? Why or why not?

9. A check is drawn payable to the order of Chauncey Ricks, who is a minor. Chauncey indorses the check to X, and X in turn indorses it to Y. Y later learns that Chauncey is a minor, and also that he has disaffirmed the contract in payment for which he had negotiated the check to X. Does the fact that Chauncey disaffirmed his contract with X prevent Y from qualifying as a holder of the instrument? Why or why not?

10. The Soong Company of San Francisco draws a $1,500 check on its local bank payable to the order of the West Company of Baltimore, and mails it to the West Company. An officer of the West Company, which is in the process of liquidation, indorses the check under court order: "Pay to John Chandler, trustee of the X Company, (signed) the West Company." Chandler cashes the check at a Baltimore bank, which gives him cash for it. The bank then sends it to the San Francisco bank via a Chicago bank. If Chandler fails to turn the $1,500 over to the West Company, and if a new trustee is appointed, does the new trustee have any right to hold either the Baltimore bank or the Chicago bank liable for the amount of the instrument? Explain.

Chapter 26

COMMERCIAL PAPER
Holders in
Due Course
and Defenses

Under ordinary contract law the assignment of a contractual (nonnegotiable) right passes to the assignee the same rights possessed by the assignor—no more and no less. The assignee thus takes the right or claim *subject to* all defenses that might exist between the original parties to the contract, regardless of whether the assignee knows of them at the time of acquiring the right. As a result, contractual claims are not transferred in large numbers in the business community, for most prospective assignees will purchase a claim only after satisfying themselves that the original obligor on the contract does not have a defense against it. This is usually a time-consuming process and often an impossible one.

The purchasers of negotiable instruments, by contrast, acquire them *free* of many defenses that exist between the original parties to the instrument if such purchasers qualify as "holders in due course" of the instruments. In fact, a major purpose of Article 3 of the UCC is to facilitate the negotiation of commercial paper by (1) spelling out the requirements that must be met by the purchaser of a negotiable instrument in order for that person to acquire the most favored status of a holder in due course (HDC), and (2) identifying the specific kinds of defenses that are cut off when a purchaser of the instrument attains this status.

In this chapter we will discuss, first, the holder in due course, and, second, the subject of defenses.

HOLDERS IN DUE COURSE

Holder in Due Course Status

It is helpful, at the outset, to understand the typical situation in which an HDC acquires greater rights than those possessed by his or her transferor. Suppose, for example, that M, a building contractor, has contracted to purchase certain plumbing fixtures from the P Company, a plumbing supply firm, for $2,250. M makes a negotiable promissory note for that amount, due sixty days later, and gives it to the P Company. After receiving the note, P Company negotiates it immediately to the B Bank, receiving cash in return (probably something less than $2,250). When the note comes due, M refuses to pay it because many of the fixtures delivered by the P Company are defective. In this situation the B Bank—if it qualifies as an HDC—*is entitled to a judgment against M for the full $2,250, even though its transferor, the P Company, probably would have recovered nothing from M* had it held the instrument itself until maturity.

The bank is entitled to a judgment in full because M's defense—breach of contract on the part of the payee—is one of the defenses that are cut off by negotiation of the instrument to an HDC. (Such defenses, often called "personal" defenses, will be discussed along with "real" defenses later in the chapter). Two further observations about HDCs and other holders should be made.

Status of the Ordinary Holder: In some situations a holder is entitled to payment of the instrument even though he or she is an ordinary holder (one who does *not* qualify as an HDC). In the above illustration, for example, if the plumbing fixtures that were delivered by the P Company to M were not defective in any way—in which case M possesses no defense against the P Company—the B Bank is entitled to recover the full $2,250 from M even if it did not meet the HDC requirements of the code. Thus the favored status of the HDC ordinarily is of significance only in those situations in which the primary party possesses a personal defense against the payee.

Limitations on the Holder in Due Course: Despite the favorable position that the HDC usually occupies, even holders in due course do not *always* prevail against the obligor. In the first place, if the obligor has a "real" defense—such as forgery—he or she may assert this defense against *all* holders. Second, and perhaps more important, *several recently enacted consumer protection statutes and orders of regulatory* *agencies have cut down the right of holders in due course by permitting obligors to assert personal defenses against them in certain situations.* (These limitations on the holder in due course doctrine will be discussed later in the chapter.)

Holder in Due Course Requirements

Section 3-302 of the UCC is the definitive **holder in due course** section, containing the three basic requirements for HDC status. According to Sec. 3-302(1): "A holder in due course is a holder who takes the instrument (a) for value; and (b) in good faith; and (c) without notice that it is overdue or has been dishonored or of any defense against or claim to it on the part of any person." The major purpose of these requirements is to define the kind of person who deserves, as a matter of policy, to take the instrument free of certain defenses (such as breach of contract by the payee). Some purchasers of instruments are denied this favored treatment, for example, because they either knew or should have known of an existing defense at the time of purchase.

Before examining each of the requirements, we should remember that a person seeking HDC status must first qualify as a *holder,* defined by Sec. 1-201(20) as "a person who is in possession of . . . an instrument . . . drawn, issued or indorsed to him or to his order or to bearer or in blank." A transferee who acquires an instrument other than by issue or negotiation thus ordinarily fails to qualify as an HDC at the outset, regardless of the other circumstances under which the acquisition took place.

Value: The term **value** is defined in Sec. 3-303, which states that a holder (usually a purchaser) has given value (1) to the extent that the agreed-upon consideration has been performed (by him or her) or to the extent that he or she acquires a security interest in or a lien on the instrument other than by legal process, or (2) when he or she takes the instrument in payment of, or as security for, an antecedent claim against any person, whether or not the claim is due, or (3) when he or she gives a negotiable instrument in payment for it. The reasoning underlying the value requirement is that if a person receives a note or a check without having given value for it, he or she obviously will suffer no out-of-pocket loss by being unable to recover from the primary party in the event that the latter has a personal defense available.

The following examples most easily illustrate the basic import of Sec. 3-303.

1. P, the payee of an out-of-town check, cashes it at his own bank. The bank, by giving P cash, has obviously given value.

2. P, a retailer, is the payee of a $900 note issued by M. P makes a contract with a third party, H, under which H is to deliver thirty cameras to P in exchange for the note. Before the delivery date P runs into financial difficulties, and H, fearing that the note might be attached by P's creditors, demands that it be negotiated to him immediately. P delivers the note to H, and H later delivers the cameras. H is a holder for value, since he performed the agreed-upon consideration by delivering the cameras. H is entitled to enforce the instrument against the maker, M, at maturity even if M has a personal defense against P.

3. Same facts as 2, above, except that after H received the note, he delivered only twenty cameras, at which time H learned that M had a defense against P. Here H would be accorded HDC status only to the extent of $600 (the extent to which the "agreed-upon consideration has been performed").

4. Same facts as 2, above, except that after H received the note he failed to deliver any of the cameras before learning of M's defense against P. Here H has not given value for the instrument (that is, H's original *promise* to deliver the cameras does not constitute value). This illustration points up the fact that the term *value* in Article 3 of the UCC is not synonymous with *consideration* under contract law; that is, while a promise to perform an act constitutes consideration, it does *not* constitute value.

Good Faith: The requirement that one must take the instrument in good faith in order to qualify as an HDC is contained in Sec. 3-302(b). **Good faith** is defined (not too helpfully) in Sec. 1-201(19) as "honesty in fact in the conduct or transaction."

The wide-ranging circumstances in which a maker, acceptor, or drawer of an instrument can at least argue that the plaintiff-holder did not take the instrument in good faith make it difficult to accurately explain this term.[1] In some situations, for example, a purchaser might take an instrument under circumstances that are somewhat suspicious but of such a minor nature that he or she honestly does not believe the instrument is defective. Under these circumstances the purchaser might well satisfy the good faith requirement. At the other extreme, the circumstances under which a person acquires an instrument might be so unusual that it is quite clear he

or she is not acting honestly in the transaction and hence is guilty of bad faith. An example of the latter is if a buyer of a $1,500 instrument purchases it from the payee for $500 in cash, a grossly inadequate consideration.

In most cases the good faith requirement and the requirement that a holder take an instrument "without notice of a defense" overlap. That is, if a court in a particular case finds the holder to be barred from holder in due course status because the instrument was acquired under circumstances in which he or she should have known of an existing defense, such holder also often has taken the instrument in bad faith. Conversely, if a court rules that the holder did *not* have reason to know of an existing defense when he or she acquired the instrument, such holder is also usually found to have taken the instrument in good faith.

Be that as it may, the UCC treats the two as separate requirements and, as the next case illustrates, so do many defendants when presenting reasons why the plaintiff is not an HDC. (This case also illustrates how a principle known as the "close connection" doctrine may lead to a finding that the holder of an instrument did not take it in good faith.)

---

[1] Partly as a result of this difficulty, the courts frequently attack the question from the other side by determining if the purchaser took the instrument in *bad faith*—a standard that is somewhat easier to apply. Either way, however, the test is subjective, asking, "Did the purchaser take the instrument honestly?" rather than "Did the purchaser act with the care of the reasonable, prudent person?" (This test is sometimes referred to as the "pure heart, empty head" concept.)

Arcanum National Bank v. Hessler
Supreme Court of Ohio, 433 N.E.2d 204 (1982)

Hessler was in the hog raising business. For several years prior to 1977 he had an arrangement with John Smith Grain Co. under which either that company or J & J Farms, Inc., would sell hogs to Hessler, with the grain company requiring Hessler to sign promissory notes payable to the grain company to cover each delivery of hogs. The grain company would then sell the notes to Arcanum National Bank (the bank), plaintiff, which would credit the grain company with the amount of each note and open a commercial loan account for Hessler for said amount.

On January 4, 1977, Hessler signed a $16,800 promissory note payable to the grain company for hogs delivered on that date, and the grain company negotiated the note to the bank. Hessler then learned that the hogs delivered by J & J Farms, Inc., had previously been mortgaged to a third party. Therefore, because Hessler did not have clear title to the hogs, he refused to pay the note to the bank at maturity. (That is, Hessler had the defense of failure of consideration.)

In the bank's suit on the note, Hessler contended that the bank was not an HDC because the bank (1) took the note with notice of the defense, and (2) did not take the note in good faith. The trial court ruled against Hessler on both points because there was no proof that officers of the bank had actual knowledge of the mortgage, and entered judgment for the bank. Hessler appealed.

The Supreme Court of Ohio reversed, agreeing with Hessler that the bank did have notice of the defense, and did not take in good faith. (Only that part of the higher court's opinion dealing with the good faith issue appears below.)

Krupansky, Justice:

The sole issue in this case is whether appellee [the bank] is a holder in due course who takes the note free from appellant's [Hessler's] defense of want of consideration.[a]

In a suit by the holder of a note against the maker, the holder obtains a great advantage if granted the status of holder in due course. Article 3 of the UCC provides that a holder in due course takes the instrument free from most defenses and claims. One such defense which is of no avail when raised against a holder in due course is want of consideration, the defense raised by appellant.

Whether one is a holder in due course is an issue which does not arise unless it is shown that a defense exists. Once it is established a defense exists, the holder has the full burden of proving holder in due course status in all respects. . . .

Appellant . . . contends, in essence, appellee bank failed in its burden of proving holder in due course status because appellee failed to establish it took the note in good faith as required [by Sec. 3-302 of the UCC].

"Good faith" is defined as "honesty in fact in the conduct or transaction concerned" [UCC Sec. 1-201(19)]. Under the "close connectedness" doctrine . . . a transferee does not take an instrument in good faith when the transferee is so closely connected with the transferor that the transferee may be charged with knowledge of an infirmity in the underlying transaction. The rationale for the close connectedness doctrine was enunciated in [*Unico v. Owen*, 232 A.2d 405, 1967] as follows:

> *In the field of negotiable instruments, good faith is a broad concept. The basic philosophy of the holder in due course status is to encourage free negotiability of commercial paper by removing certain anxieties of one who takes the paper as an*

---

[a] The court referred to the defense as "want of consideration" at times, and "failure of consideration" at others.

innocent purchaser knowing no reason why the paper is not sound as its face would indicate. It would seem to follow, therefore, that the more the holder knows about the underlying transaction, and particularly the more he controls or participates or becomes involved in it, the less he fits the role of a good faith purchaser for value; the closer his relationship to the underlying agreement which is the source of the note, the less need there is for giving him the tension-free rights considered necessary in a fast-moving, credit-extending world.

Soon after the decision in *Unico* was reached, the close connectedness doctrine was adopted by Ohio courts [in *American Plan v. Woods,* 240 N.E.2d, 1968, where it was said]: "A transferee of a negotiable note does not take in good faith and is not a holder in due course of a note given in the sale of consumer goods where the transferee is a finance company involved with the seller of the goods, and which has a pervasive knowledge of factors relating to the terms of the sale". . . .

According to White and Summers, noted authorities on the Uniform Commercial Code, the following five factors are indicative of a close connection between the transferee and transferor:

(1) Drafting by the transferee of forms for the transferor; (2) approval or establishment . . . of the transferor's procedures by the transferee (e.g., setting the interest rate, approval of a referral sales plan); (3) an independent check by the transferee on the credit of the debtor . . . ; (4) heavy reliance by the transferor upon the transferee (e.g., transfer by the transferor of all or a substantial part of his paper to the transferee); and (5) common or connected ownership or management of the transferor and transferee. *White & Summers, Uniform Commercial Code* 481 (1972).

An analysis of the above factors [in this case] reveals an unusually close relationship between appellee bank (the transferee), the John Smith Grain Company (the transferor-payee) and J & J Farms, Inc.

Appellee bank provided John Smith Grain Company with the forms used in the transaction and supplied the interest rate to be charged. At the time of purchase of the first note, appellee bank ran an independent credit check on the appellant. There is evidence of a heavy reliance by John Smith Grain Company upon appellee bank insofar as it was customary for the grain company to transfer substantially all of its commercial paper to appellee bank. There was not only a common director of appellee and John Smith Grain Company, but also common directors or management between John Smith Grain Company and J & J Farms. . . .

The facts indicate appellee bank . . . had reason to know . . . that there was no consideration given by the John Smith Grain Company for the note. [The court reached this conclusion by noting (1) that one North, an officer and director of both the grain company and J & J Farms, had actual knowledge that the hogs had been mortgaged by J & J Farms prior to their sale to Hessler, appellant; (2) that North's knowledge was thus imputed to the grain company, the payee-transferor, and (3) that this knowledge was also imputed to the bank, the transferee, because the president of the grain company was also a director of the bank. The court buttressed this last conclusion by further noting that a vice-president of the bank had been meeting with officers of the grain company several times a week prior to the Hessler transaction to advise them in making business decisions to alleviate the grain company's financial difficulties.]

[Although] one cannot conclude with absolute certainty that appellee bank had actual knowledge of the failure of consideration, . . . we find that the relationship between appellee bank and John Smith Grain Company was so entwined that it was error for the trial court not to apply the doctrine of close connectedness. . . . We can reach only one conclusion, viz., appellee bank did not take the note in good faith. . . .

Judgment reversed.

The Taking "Without Notice" Requirement:
Section 3-302(1)(c) provides that, to be an HDC, a holder must take the instrument "without notice that it is overdue or has been dishonored [and without notice] of any defense against it or claim to it on the part of any person." The basic thrust of this section is that a holder should not receive the protection afforded an HDC if he or she acquires an instrument knowing that something is wrong with it.

Under Sec. 1-201(25) of the UCC, a person has notice of a fact when he or she has actual knowledge of it, or from the circumstances "has reason to know" of such fact. Thus if H acquires an instrument knowing that the payee has breached his or her contract with the maker or drawer, or under circumstances where a prudent person would reasonably suspect such a breach (although H did not have such suspicion), H is not an HDC.

Section 3-304 is an aid to the interpretation of the "without notice" requirement. Because of its length, the application of only a few of its salient provisions are summarized here. (The section can be read in its entirety in Appendix A.)

Notice That Paper Is Overdue or Has Been Dishonored: As we saw in Chapter 24, all negotiable instruments are either time or demand instruments. Those bearing a fixed future date of maturity, such as "payable July 1, 1991," are time instruments; those stating that they are payable on demand or having no stated maturity date are demand instruments.

A person who purchases a *time instrument* even one day after its stated maturity date takes it with notice that it is overdue. Thus, if a note payable on September 1 is acquired by H on September 2, H does not qualify as an HDC. Section 3-304(3) provides in part that "the purchaser has notice that an instrument is overdue if he has reason to know (a) that any part of the principal amount is overdue or that there is an uncured default in payment of another instrument of the same series." And the purchaser has such notice here because the instrument carried its maturity date on its face.

The question as to when *demand* instruments are overdue has caused difficulties because such instruments do not, of course, contain a stated maturity date. The primary rule of Sec. 3-304(3)(c) is that a purchaser takes a demand instrument with notice that it is overdue if he or she acquires it more than a "reasonable time after its issue."

What Is a Reasonable Time? The above section contains the only UCC provision that specifically defines a reasonable time, and it applies only to checks; as to checks drawn and payable in the United States, a reasonable time "is presumed to be 30 days." Thus if D draws and issues a check on June 1 payable to the order of P, and the check is negotiated to H on July 15, H is not an HDC in most circumstances. (The thirty-day limit is not absolute, however; rather, thirty days is "presumed" to be the deadline. In exceptional circumstances, then, a person might acquire a check beyond that limit and still qualify as an HDC.)

As to other instruments—demand notes and sight drafts—the question of reasonable time is left to the courts. Because these instruments are often held for longer periods of time than are checks, a person may well take such an instrument two or three months (or even longer) after its issue, and still qualify as an HDC. In determining what is a reasonable time in a given case, the courts take into account business and community customs, and other circumstances (e.g., interest-bearing notes circulate longer than noninterest-bearing ones, and a reasonable time is generally longer in rural areas than when the parties are residents of larger cities).

Notice of Claim or Defense: Section 3-304(1) reads in part as follows:

> The purchaser has notice of a claim or defense if (a) the instrument is so incomplete, bears such visible evidence of forgery or alteration, or is otherwise so irregular as to call into question its validity, terms or ownership or to create an ambiguity as to the party to pay; or (b) the purchaser has notice that the obligation of any party is voidable in whole or in part, or that all parties have been discharged.

Subsection a addresses itself to situations where some unusual aspect about the face of the instrument itself should indicate to a reasonable person that a defense very likely exists. Under this section, the fact that an instrument is incomplete to *some* extent or bears *some* evidence of a possible forgery or alteration does not necessarily prevent the holder from qualifying as an HDC. Rather, the disqualification occurs only where the irregularity is one that is so material as to call into question the instrument's validity, terms, or ownership.

Missing Terms: On the subject of incompleteness, it is well established that any third party who acquires an instrument so incomplete

that one of the requirements of negotiability is missing is not an HDC. Thus, if H takes a check from P, payee, the amount of which is entirely blank, H does not qualify as an HDC since the instrument was not negotiable at the time she acquired it. Similarly, if H takes an instrument "payable twenty _____ after date," she is not an HDC.[2]

On the other hand, an instrument that is incomplete in only a minor respect is not considered so irregular as to prevent a purchaser from attaining HDC status. For example: A note is complete in all respects except that it contains this clause: "Payable at _____." Here the purchaser qualifies as an HDC because the place where an instrument is payable is not a required element of negotiability; thus the fact that this particular blank is not filled in does not of itself cause a reasonable person to question the instrument's validity. The same is true of a check that does not bear its date of issue; this alone is not a disqualifying irregularity.

Altered Terms: This approach also applies to altered terms in an instrument. Unexplained alterations that are both material and apparent (such as a line drawn through the original payee's name, with a second name substituted for it) will disqualify a taker from HDC status. But alterations so skillfully done that they are not readily apparent will not keep the instrument taker from qualifying as a HDC. Similarly, an instrument bearing some evidence of erasure and subsequent correction of a necessary element will not necessarily put a purchaser on notice of a defense; for example, the purchaser might have inquired about the erasure and received an adequate explanation of it. Thus any case arising under this section, like those dealing with the question of when a demand instrument is overdue, must also be settled on the basis of its own facts.

---

[2] If, in either of these cases, H completes the instrument and negotiates it to X, another holder, X probably will qualify as an HDC if he meets the other requirements. X's rights in these circumstances are discussed in the next chapter.

The gist of Sec. 3-304(1), then, is that a person who purchases an instrument knowing of a defense—or having reason to know of it because of the instrument's irregular, missing, or altered terms—is not a holder in due course.

In the next case it may be argued that the plaintiffs did not actually know that a defense (breach of contract) existed before they purchased the instrument. But let us see what other information the plaintiffs did possess at that time, and how the court viewed the effect of that information.

Salter v. Vanotti
Colorado Court of Civil Appeals, Div. III, 599 P.2d 962 (1979)

Mr. and Mrs. Vanotti, defendants, signed an agreement to purchase a lot in an Arizona development from Cochise College Park, Inc. (Cochise), the developer of the area. As part of the transaction the Vanottis signed a negotiable promissory note (payable to Cochise) in the amount of $4,392, payable in monthly installments. Cochise thereafter negotiated the note to the Salters, plaintiffs.

The Vanottis made three monthly payments on the note, after which time they visited the property and found that it was not as Cochise had represented it to be. The Vanottis then demanded the return of their payments under a "money back guarantee" contained in the contract, but Cochise refused this demand.

In this action by the Salters to recover the unpaid balance of the note, the Vanottis alleged that they had several defenses against Cochise, and they further alleged that the Salters were not holders in due course of the note. On this basis the Vanottis claimed that they could assert their defenses against the Salters.

The trial court agreed that the Vanottis' defenses against Cochise were valid, and also agreed that the Salters were not holders in due course (for reasons appearing in the decision below). Accordingly, it dismissed the action. Plaintiffs appealed.

Silverstein, Chief Judge:

. . . The trial court found that defendants had three defenses: (1) that defendants had attempted to exercise their rights under the money back guarantee, as provided in the Property Report, and that the attempt was not honored by Cochise; (2) that defendants did not receive a copy of the Property Report prior to, or at the time they entered into the agreement as required by [federal law], and (3) that the contract had been breached [by Cochise] by failure to deliver a deed after three payments had been made. . . .

The primary issue on appeal is whether plaintiffs are holders in due course of the note. Under the Uniform Commercial Code a holder in due course must, [among other requirements,] take the instrument . . . without notice . . . of any defense against or claim to it on the part of any person. §3-302. "The purchaser of an instrument has notice of a claim or defense if (b) the purchaser has notice that the obligation of any party is voidable in whole or in part. . . ." §3-304. And, "a person has 'notice' of a fact when (c) from all the facts and circumstances known to him at the time in question he has reason to know that it exists." §1-201(25).

The significant "facts and circumstances" are these: Prior to purchasing the defendants' note, plaintiffs had bought seven similar notes from Cochise, and bought three more simultaneously with the purchase of defendants' note; at the time the note was delivered to plaintiffs, they also received the additional documents which set forth defendants' rights under the contract, and one of plaintiffs [admitted] "I had all the supporting documents." . . .

Here plaintiffs knew, from the documents delivered with the note, that defendants had a right to rescind the contract within six months from the date of the contract, that apparently defendants had not received a copy of the Property Report, and that defendants were entitled to a deed after making three monthly payments on the note. Plaintiffs further knew that they were not in a position to deliver such a deed, since only a photocopy was forwarded to them, [and yet] took no steps to investigate these facts. . . . The protection afforded a holder in due course cannot be used to shield one who simply refuses to investigate when the facts known to him suggest an irregularity concerning the commercial paper he purchases. This is especially so where, as here, the note was not purchased for value, but was discounted forty percent. . . .

[And, in regard to plaintiffs' claim that they took the instrument in good faith,] under the UCC if a holder takes an instrument with notice "that the obligation of any party is voidable in whole or in part," §3-304, that notice is sufficient to prevent the holder from qualifying as a holder in due course, regardless of good or bad faith. And, since plaintiffs had such notice they were not holders in due course, and thus, held the note subject to any valid defenses.

Judgment affirmed.

Related Holder in Due Course Matters

Holder through a Holder in Due Course: Any taker of an instrument who does not meet all the requirements for a holder in due course is called an *ordinary holder* (or sometimes a *mere holder*). This person takes the instrument subject to all outstanding defenses—that is, like an assignee of a nonnegotiable instrument, the ordinary holder acquires only the rights of prior parties, no greater ones.

However, if an ordinary holder takes an instrument from someone who is an HDC, or takes an instrument where *any* prior party qualified as an HDC, he or she is now a "holder with all the rights of an HDC."[3] Thus if H purchases a note that is clearly overdue, or receives it as a gift, he can still enforce the instrument against the maker, even though the maker has a defense, if H can show that any prior holder met the requirements of an HDC.

---

[3] This results from Sec. 3-201(1), which provides that "the transfer of an instrument vests in the transferee such rights as the transferor has therein." This section, based on assignment law, is referred to as the *shelter provision* of the code.

One exception to the above does exist, however. If a purchaser of an instrument negotiates it to a subsequent holder and ultimately repurchases it from either that holder or a later holder, his or her status is determined at the time of first acquiring it. To illustrate: H purchases an instrument, failing to qualify as an HDC for some reason. Later she negotiates the instrument to a holder who does qualify as an HDC. If H reacquires the instrument subsequently, she is not accorded "holder with the rights of an HDC" status. In other words, H cannot improve her position by reacquiring from an HDC.

The Payee as a Holder in Due Course: Before adoption of the UCC, some courts took the view that the payee of an instrument was not a "holder," and thus could not qualify as an HDC even though he or she gave value for the instrument, purchased it before it was overdue, and took it without notice of any defense against, or claim to the instrument. Other courts disagreed. Section 3-302(2) of the UCC has resolved this conflict by flatly providing that "a payee may be a holder in due course" (assuming, of course that he or she meets the three basic HDC requirements).

As a practical matter, a payee who has fully performed his or her contract with the maker or drawer of an instrument ordinarily qualifies as an HDC, because in most such instances the payee has given value for the instrument, the maker or drawer possesses no defense, and the payee takes the instrument before it is overdue. In such cases the payee is clearly entitled to payment. On the other hand, if the maker or drawer *does* possess a defense, the payee ordinarily is not an HDC because a defense usually arises out of some default or misconduct on the part of the payee—such as breach of contract, or the perpetration of fraud upon the maker or drawer— of which the payee necessarily has notice. Thus, in an action by the payee in such a case, the maker or drawer may successfully assert the defense.

DEFENSES

Earlier in the chapter we mentioned the two general classes of defenses, using the terms *personal* and *real.* While the UCC refers to these classes as *limited* and *universal,* we will use the older terms, personal and real, because they continue in widespread use today.

Personal defenses, under the UCC, can be asserted only against ordinary holders; generally they cannot be asserted against an HDC or against a holder with all the rights of an HDC. In fact, it is the cutting off of these defenses that gives the HDC his or her status as a favored holder.

Real defenses can be asserted against all holders, including HDCs and holders with all the rights of an HDC.[4] A defendant-maker who has available a real defense is under no liability to the plaintiff even if the latter is an HDC. This is why HDCs are not always entitled to judgments in actions brought against makers, acceptors, or drawers of negotiable instruments.

Personal Defenses

Section 3-306 of the UCC lists all the **personal defenses** (or *limited defenses*)—those that are ordinarily assertable only against ordinary holders. The major part of that section follows:

> Unless he has the rights of a holder in due course, any person takes the instrument subject to (a) all valid claims to it on the part of any person; and (b) all defenses of any party which would be available in an action on a simple contract; and (c) the defenses of want or failure of consideration, nonperformance of any condition precedent, non-delivery, or delivery for a special purpose; and (d) the defense that he or a person through whom he holds the instrument acquired it by theft, or that payment or satisfaction to such holder would

---

[4] Throughout this chapter, when we refer to the rights of an HDC, we will assume that whatever is said applies equally to holders with all the rights of an HDC.

be inconsistent with the terms of a restrictive indorsement.

We will now examine the most common kinds of personal defenses under this section.

Breach of Contract: *Breach of contract* (or "failure of consideration") is the most common defense falling within the provision of Sec. 3-306(b). Many instruments are issued to payees in payment for goods (or services) that the payees are obligated to deliver (or perform) under contracts with the makers or drawers of the instruments. If the contract is breached by the payee, the maker of the note can refuse to pay it, and the drawer of a check can stop payment on it, claiming that the failure of the payee to perform the contract relieves him or her of liability.

The case of *Salter v. Vanotti*, earlier in the chapter, illustrates these rules. In that case the seller of land (Cochise) breached its contract with the buyers (the Vanottis) in at least two respects: (1) by failing to permit them to cancel the purchase, as the contract provided, if they were not satisfied with the land; and (2) by failing to deliver a deed to them after they had made three monthly payments. Those breaches afforded the Vanottis their personal defenses (which defeated the action brought by the Salters, who were not holders in due course).

Breach of warranty—a form of breach of contract—occurs when a seller of goods makes an express or implied statement or promise about the goods, and the goods do not conform to the statement or promise. For example, under sales law a merchant seller impliedly warrants that the goods are merchantable. If the buyer pays for the goods by giving the seller a negotiable note and later finds that the goods are not merchantable (do not perform in the expected manner), the buyer may assert the defense of breach of warranty against any holder of the note who is not an HDC.

A typical breach of warranty case is that of *United Securities Corp. v. Bruton*, 213 A.2d 892 (1965). Bruton purchased two wigs from a retailer, giving the retailer her promissory note in payment. The retailer-payee negotiated the note to United Securities. When United Securities presented the note to Bruton for payment, she refused to pay because the wigs were clearly defective—i.e., unmerchantable. In the ensuing lawsuit, Bruton was permitted to assert her defense of breach of warranty against United Securities (which did not qualify as an HDC of the note).

Lack of Consideration: *Lack (or want) of consideration* (as we saw in Chapter 12) exists in a commercial paper context where a maker or drawer of an instrument issues it to the payee in any case where the payee does not give consideration under ordinary contract law principles. In such situations "want of consideration" can be asserted by the maker or drawer against an ordinary holder. To illustrate: D, a distant relative of P, drafts a check and makes a gift of it to P so that P can attend college. P negotiates the check to H. P does not go to college, and D, in disgust, stops payment on the check. If H sues D on the instrument, D can successfully assert the defense of want of consideration—but only if H fails to qualify as an HDC.

Fraud in the Inducement: Two kinds of fraud are recognized in the area of commercial paper; one creates a personal defense and the other a real defense. **Fraud in the inducement** falls into the personal category. It arises where a person who signs a negotiable instrument (knowing it to be such) has been induced to sign by some intentional misrepresentation of the other party. For example: B agrees to purchase S's year-old car for $7,500 after being assured by S that the car is a demonstrator that S had purchased just six months earlier from a new car dealer. At the time of purchase B gives S $1,500 in cash and a promissory note for the balance of $6,000. Soon thereafter B learns that S had actually purchased the car from a private owner, a farmer, who in fact had driven it extensively before selling it to S. S's intentional misrepresentation constitutes fraud in the inducement, and

B can assert this defense against S and against any subsequent holder who does not qualify as an HDC.

Illegality: Like the general defense of fraud, some types of *illegality* constitute personal defenses and others constitute real defenses. This is so because although certain transactions are illegal (prohibited) under state statutes or ordinances, the applicable statutes do not always provide that the prohibited transactions are void. If a statute voids the transaction, the defense is real; if it does not, the defense is merely personal. To illustrate: A retailer sells goods to D on a Sunday in violation of a state statute prohibiting the sale of goods by merchants on that day. However, the statute does not provide that such sales, or the contracts or papers connected with them, are void. The next day the retailer negotiates the check to H, who subsequently learns that D, the buyer-drawer, has stopped payment on it. Here D can assert the defense of illegality against H only if H is an ordinary holder. (Illegality as a real defense is discussed later in the chapter.)

Unauthorized Completion: Although it is ordinarily a bad practice, the maker or drawer of an instrument sometimes signs it while it is incomplete in some respect (for example, leaving blank the amount or the payee's name). He or she usually gives it to a third party—often an employee but sometimes the payee—with instructions as to how the blank should be filled in (such as, "fill in the amount for no more than $400"). The instrument is then completed contrary to instructions and later is acquired by a subsequent holder. If the latter fails to qualify as an HDC, the maker or drawer usually can assert the defense of **unauthorized completion** and avoid liability. However, under Sec. 3-407(3), if the subsequent holder does qualify as an HDC (by taking the instrument without knowledge of the wrongful completion and by meeting the other HDC requirements), he or she can enforce the instrument as completed. Thus, where the maximum authorized amount is $400, if the third party completes the instrument to read $1,000, a subsequent HDC can recover the full $1,000 from the maker or drawer. Therein lies the danger in signing an incomplete instrument.

Nondelivery of an Instrument: Sometimes an instrument finds its way into the hands of a subsequent holder through loss or theft. In such a case the maker or drawer of the instrument has available the defense of *nondelivery*. To illustrate: M is the maker of a bearer instrument that is stolen from her home by X and negotiated to H. If H is merely an ordinary holder, he takes the instrument subject to the defense of nondelivery and therefore cannot enforce it against M.

The case below involves a claim by the payee of a note against the maker's estate. The primary question was whether the estate's defense of nondelivery was a valid one.

Matter of Estate of Balkus
Court of Appeals of Wisconsin, 381 N.W.2d 593 (1985)

James Balkus died on December 4, 1983, leaving no will. A few days after his death his sister, Ann Vesely, examined his personal effects and found, among other things, two promissory notes in the amount of $6,000 each. The notes were payable to her order, and Balkus was the maker of both instruments.

When the administrator of Balkus's estate refused to pay the amount of the notes to Vesely, she filed a claim against Balkus's estate in the

amount of $12,000. The circuit court ruled that Vesely was not a holder in due course of the notes, and thus held that the estate's defense of nondelivery was assertable against her. Judgment was accordingly entered for the estate, and Vesely appealed.

On appeal, Vesely's primary argument was that the estate did *not* possess the defense of nondelivery because there had been a "constructive delivery" of the instruments to her—that is, a delivery in the eyes of the law, although not a physical delivery. (If the estate did not possess such defense, Vesely contended that she, as payee, was entitled to payment even if she did not qualify as a holder in due course.)

Nettesheim, Judge:

. . . We now look to the defense of nondelivery asserted by the personal representative [the administrator of the estate]. It is undisputed that Balkus did not physically deliver the notes to Vesely. She argues, however, that a letter she received from Balkus in August 1974 constituted constructive delivery of the notes. The letter, in pertinent part, stated:

Also you will get & shall I say I will bequeath to you all my other junk in my apt. such as tools, radios, TV sets, clothing, clothes and also the money I owe you. I have . . . government bonds made out in your name & the banker told me, nobody could take it away from you. I also have 2 . . . notes made out to you for the amount of money I borrowed from you in 1961 and 1962. That should take care of the interest I was supposed to pay you but I didn't.

The trial court found that Balkus retained dominion and control of the notes, and that he "simply never gave up ownership." These findings are not . . . erroneous.

The general rule is that a promissory note has no effect unless it is delivered. The UCC defines delivery of an instrument as the "voluntary transfer of possession." Sec. 1-201(14). A constructive delivery may be sufficient. [*Casto v. Martin,* 230 S.E.2d 722, 1976.] A constructive delivery occurs only when the maker indicates an intention to make the instrument an enforceable obligation against him or her by surrendering control over it and intentionally placing it under the power of the payee or a third person.

Balkus never surrendered control nor transferred possession of the note. It is undisputed that the notes were found in Balkus's possessions after his death. The notes were never placed under the control of Vesely or any other third party. We therefore reject Vesely's argument that the letter served as constructive delivery of the notes. . . .

Judgment affirmed.

Prior Payment: When a note or draft is paid by the maker or acceptor, it is routinely surrendered to that person, regardless of whether it is paid at or before maturity. Either way the instrument normally stops circulating. However, the maker or acceptor may neglect to ask for the return of the instrument, or, after its return, it may be stolen. If payment of the instrument occurred before maturity, and if the instrument bears no notation of payment, it is possible that it will get into the hands of an innocent third party. When that holder demands payment at maturity, the maker or acceptor has available the defense of *prior payment* or *payment before maturity* and is therefore not liable if the holder fails to qualify as an HDC. (If the holder is an HDC, the maker or acceptor must pay a second time.)

Incapacity (except Minority): As seen in Chapter 14, the law recognizes various types and degrees of incapacity. However, unless a maker's or drawer's incapacity is so extreme that under local law the contract or instrument is completely nullified, the defense of *incapacity* is only personal—except in the case of a minor (discussed later in the chapter).

Duress: Similarly, there are varying degrees of duress under the law, most of which are merely personal in nature. Thus if a person signs an instrument under a vague threat or through fear of economic retaliation, the defense is only personal in nature. (Duress as a real defense is also discussed later in the chapter.)

Real Defenses

Real defenses (or *universal defenses*) are defenses that can be successfully asserted against all holders, including holders in due course. We will now describe the more common types of real defenses, including the offshoots of some of the personal defenses already discussed.

Forgery: A fundamental legal principle of commercial paper, appearing in Sec. 3-401(1), is that a person cannot be held liable on an instrument unless his or her name appears on it. In the case of **forgery** the person's name does appear, probably as maker or drawer, but it is signed by another person who has no authority to do so. (An unauthorized signature of indorsement is defined in Sec. 1-201(43) as "one made without

actual, implied, or apparent authority and includes a forgery.")

The "pure" forgery case occurs where a person who has no authority from (and usually no relationship with) the purported drawer or maker simply commits a criminal act by signing the latter's name to an instrument. For example: A thief steals a book of personalized checks belonging to D. The thief drafts a check and signs D's name as drawer. In this case D has no liability to any holder of the instrument. Section 3-404(1) provides that "any unauthorized signature is *wholly inoperative* as that of the person whose name is signed unless he ratifies it or is precluded from denying it." (Emphasis added.) *Ratification* consists of any conduct on the part of the person whose name has been signed without authority which indicates to third parties that he or she will assume liability on the instrument despite the unauthorized signing. It occurs rarely; and when it does, it is usually in a situation where a principal-agent relationship exists between the purported drawer and the forger.[5]

A situation related to forgery exists when an agent exceeds his or her authority by signing the principal's name on an instrument as drawer or maker. If the principal can show that the agent had no express, implied, or apparent authority to sign, and if the principal does not subsequently ratify the signature, he or she can assert the defense of *unauthorized signing* against any holder, even an HDC. (See Chapter 19 for a treatment of the rules which the courts use in determining whether express, implied, or apparent authority exists.)

Fraud in the Execution: Unlike fraud in the inducement, in the case of **fraud in the execution** a person is caused to sign a negotiable instrument under circumstances in which he or she honestly and reasonably believes it to be

---

[5]Under Sec. 3-404(1), the primary situation in which a drawer of an instrument may be precluded from asserting the defense of forgery is where he or she is guilty of negligence that contributed to the forgery. This topic will be discussed in Chapter 28.

something other than a negotiable instrument, as, for example, a lease or receipt of some kind.

This commonly occurs when an experienced, high-pressure salesperson talks a home owner who has little education (or perhaps who is even illiterate) into signing a promissory note by telling him or her that it is only a request for an estimate or an application of some kind. The salesman's company then negotiates the instrument to a holder. Here the home owner-maker has a real defense, good against any holder, if the following conditions are met. The maker must show not only that he or she honestly believed the signing was for something other than a negotiable instrument but also that he or she was not guilty of negligence under the circumstances in failing to realize that the document was a negotiable instrument. The phrase *under the circumstances* takes into account such factors as the signer's age, experience, and schooling. Thus the maker who is very inexperienced in the business world, or is aged, or has failing eyesight may have a real defense, while such a defense would not exist if he or she were a businessperson who hurriedly signed the note after a cursory look (or perhaps without reading it at all) simply because in a rush to attend a meeting.

Material Alteration: Section 3-407, entitled "Alteration," covers two essentially different situations—alteration of a completed instrument and completion of a blank instrument contrary to instructions. (The latter topic was discussed earlier, under "Personal Defenses.")

Alteration of a Completed Instrument: Sometimes, after a completed instrument is issued by the maker, one or more of the terms are changed without his or her knowledge by a holder, and the instrument is thereafter negotiated to a subsequent holder. The issue is thus raised whether the last holder can recover on the instrument—and, if so, to what extent. The answer to these questions depends on two factors: (1) whether the alteration was material and (2) whether the holder qualifies as an HDC.

Section 3-407 essentially defines a material alteration as one that changes the contract of the parties in any respect. A change in the amount of the instrument even by the addition of one cent, or an advance of the date of payment even by one day, is thus material. On the other hand, a correction of the spelling of the payee's name or the addition of the address of the maker would not be material. (If the alteration is not material, all holders are entitled to enforce the instrument as it was originally drawn.)

If the alteration *is* material, the holder's rights depend on whether he or she is an HDC. It is possible to be an HDC when the alteration is so skillfully done that it is not readily apparent to the subsequent purchaser.

Under Sec. 3-407(3), an HDC can enforce the instrument according to its "original tenor"—that is, as originally drawn. To illustrate: M is the maker of a note payable to the order of P in the amount of $1,000. P alters the amount to read $3,000 and negotiates the instrument to H, an HDC. At maturity, H is entitled to recover $1,000. (Since H cannot recover the balance of $2,000 from M, it is said that the defense of material alteration is a defense "to the extent of the alteration.") If, on the other hand, H is not an HDC, he recovers nothing. This is so because a material alteration that is also fraudulent—as is usually the case—is a complete defense against an ordinary holder. (See Figure 26.1.) In the unlikely event that the alteration is not fraudulent, the ordinary holder—like the HDC—is entitled to enforce the instrument according to its original tenor.

Other Real Defenses:

Illegality: As we indicated in the section on personal defenses, some kinds of transactions are not only prohibited by statute but expressly made *void* or *void ab initio* (from the beginning). The defense of *illegality* in these situations is a real defense, assertable against both ordinary holders and HDCs. In a number of states, for example, checks and notes given

Figure 26.1 **Material Alteration**

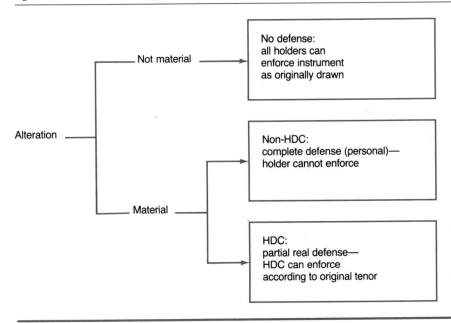

in payment of gambling debts fall into this category.

The next case illustrates the fact that while crime does not pay, it frequently provides the innocent drawer of a check with a most welcome real defense.

Commercial Bank & Trust Co. v. Middle Georgia Livestock Sales
Georgia Court of Appeals, 182 S.E.2d 533 (1971)

Middle Georgia Livestock Sales (MGLS) bought some cattle at an auction and gave the seller its check in payment. Soon thereafter MGLS discovered that the seller had stolen the cattle, and that it therefore had not acquired title to them. MGLS accordingly stopped payment on the check—that is, it ordered the drawee bank not to honor it when it was presented for payment.

Without knowledge of these facts another bank, the Commercial Bank and Trust Company, cashed the check for the seller-thief, and routinely presented it for collection to the drawee bank. That bank, because of the stop payment order, refused to pay it and returned the check to Commercial. Commercial then brought this action against MGLS, the drawer, who claimed that it possessed a real defense.

The trial court granted judgment for the plaintiff, and MGLS appealed.

Been, Justice:

. . . The sole question in this case is *whether a holder in due course for value of a check given by an innocent [drawer] for the purchase of cattle which turned out to be stolen may recover the value of such check from the [drawer].* [Emphasis added.] This in turn involves a construction of the controlling section of the Uniform Commercial Code, §3-305(2)(b) providing that a holder in due course takes the instrument free from defenses of any party thereto with whom it has not dealt except "such other incapacity, or duress, or illegality of the transaction as renders the obligation of the party a nullity."

Under the Commercial Code "a holder in due course is subject to the defense of illegality when under the applicable local law such illegality makes the obligation of the defending party a nullity or void, but he is not subject to the defense when the illegality makes the obligation merely voidable." Anderson's Commercial Code, vol. 1, §3-305:14, p. 607.

This means that the illegality is considered as of statutory origin and its "existence and effect is left to the law of each state. If under the local law the effect is to render the obligation of the instrument entirely null and void, the defense may be asserted against a holder in due course. If the effect is merely to render the obligation voidable at the election of the obligor, the defense is cut off." . . .

In *Pac. Nat. Bk. v. Hernreich* (398 S.W.2d 221) the court held that the instruments must be not merely unenforceable but void *ab initio* under applicable state law to present a defense against a holder in due course. The case then turns on the question of whether the sale of stolen [cattle], presuming the seller possessed guilty knowledge of the fact but the buyer did not, represents an "illegal consideration" so as to render it absolutely void. "A contract to do an immoral or illegal thing is void." Code §20-501. A sale of stolen goods, although to a bona fide purchaser for value, cannot transfer any lawful interest in the property and does not divest the title of the true owner.

Knowingly disposing of stolen property is, like the actual asportation, a type of theft and a statutory offense. Being prohibited by statute, it is an illegal transaction within the meaning of Code Ann. 109A-3-305(2)(b) supra, which under the Uniform Commercial Code leaves the determination of what transactions are illegal to be decided under the statute law of the forum. This accords with decisions of our courts. In *Smith v. Wood*, 36 S.E. 649, it was held: "A note given for something . . . which the law absolutely prohibits and makes penal is based upon an illegal consideration, and is consequently void in the hands of any holder thereof. The thing for which the note is given is outlawed, and the note standing upon such a foundation is outlawed also." [In accord is] *Johnston Bros. & Co. v. McConnell*, 65 Ga. 189, dealing with a sale of fertilizer prohibited by statute, and holding that contracts for the sale of articles prohibited by statute are not only void as between the parties themselves but gather no vitality by being put in circulation. "To hold otherwise would be to have them transferred as soon as executed, enabling parties claiming to be innocent, and perhaps really so, to collect money upon a consideration the foundation of which would have its existence in the positive violation of a criminal law."

It follows that the note is unenforceable even in the hands of a holder in due course, and the trial court erred in granting summary judgment for the plaintiff. [Emphasis added.]

Judgment reversed.

Incapacity of a Minor or Insane Person: When the maker or drawer of an instrument is a minor, he or she may escape liability on the ground of *incapacity*. Whether this defense is real or personal depends upon applicable state law (and as we saw in Chapter 14, state laws differ in their treatment of minors' rights). Still, the defense of *minority* is in most states a real defense. Under this view, if it is asserted by the maker or drawer of an instrument—even against an HDC—the holder recovers nothing. Similarly, if a person signs a note or draft after having been adjudicated insane by a court, his or her defense is also real, the instrument being void *ab initio.*

Extreme Duress: Most kinds of duress constitute only personal defenses. *Extreme duress,* however, is another matter; it exists where the force or threat of force is so overwhelming that the victim is entirely deprived of his or her will. A real defense exists, for example, if a person signs an instrument at gunpoint.

Discharge in Bankruptcy: In some situations the general defense of *discharge* is available to one of the parties to an instrument; yet the instrument can still circulate, and an HDC can still take it free of the defense. One kind of discharge, however, is always a real defense: the *discharge in bankruptcy.* The person who has been discharged under bankruptcy proceedings has no further liability on any outstanding instrument, even if it is held by an HDC.

Lack of Title: When a party to an instrument is being sued, he or she may be able to prove that the plaintiff is not even a holder. This defense obviously rules out any recovery by the plaintiff. Thus, if an instrument is payable to the order of P, and P's indorsement in blank is forged, no subsequent purchaser qualifies as a holder; nor can such a purchaser recover anything from the instrument's maker or drawer. Where lack of title is established, the plaintiff simply has no standing to sue; that is, the plaintiff is not the owner of the instrument that he or she is attempting to enforce.

LIMITATIONS ON HOLDER IN DUE COURSE DOCTRINE

The basic holder in due course concept, which permits an HDC to take an instrument free of all personal defenses, is a necessity if commercial paper is to circulate freely. In certain situations, however, the HDC doctrine has brought about results that have been the subject of increasing scrutiny and dissatisfaction. A typical example is the situation where a person purchases a consumer good, such as a television set, from a retailer and gives the retailer an installment note in payment for it. The retailer then negotiates the instrument to a third party (usually a lending institution), who probably qualifies as an HDC. In such a case, if the television does not work properly (or even if it is never delivered), *the buyer remains fully liable to the HDC.* The buyer's only recourse is to harass the retailer until he or she delivers a workable set or to recover damages for breach of contract—certainly an unsatisfactory solution for the buyer. In recent years two general kinds of limitations on the HDC doctrine have come into existence in an effort to give the purchaser of consumer goods some relief.

State Statutes

Some state legislatures have enacted statutes that give the consumer a measure of protection in situations such as the one described above. Because of their diversity, these statutes can only be summarized briefly.

A few states have adopted the Uniform Consumer Credit Code (not to be confused with the UCC), which prohibits a seller of consumer goods from taking a negotiable instrument—other than a check—as evidence of the buyer's obligation. Some other states have enacted legislation that flatly abolishes the HDC doctrine in many situations. And a number of states have legislation requiring instruments that evidence consumer indebtedness to bear the words "consumer paper," and providing further that such instruments are nonnegotiable.

The Federal Trade Commission Rule

The statutes mentioned above have brought about consumer protection that varies from state to state, and in some states they give less protection than was originally expected. For that reason, the Federal Trade Commission (FTC) promulgated a "Rule to Preserve Buyers' Claims and Defenses in Consumer Installment Sales." This rule, usually referred to as the **FTC holder in due course rule,** took effect in 1976.

In general, the FTC rule applies to two situations: (1) where a buyer of consumer goods executes a sales contract that includes giving a promissory note to the seller, and (2) where a seller of consumer goods arranges for a direct loan by a third party—usually a bank or other commercial lending institution—to the customer in order for the sale to be made.

In regard to the first situation, the rule provides in part:

In connection with any sale or lease of goods or services to consumers, in or affecting [interstate] commerce . . . it is an unfair or deceptive trade practice . . . for a seller, directly or indirectly to (a) *Take or receive a consumer credit contract which fails to contain* the following provisions in at least ten point, bold face type:

NOTICE
ANY HOLDER OF THIS CONSUMER CREDIT CONTRACT IS SUBJECT TO ALL CLAIMS AND DEFENSES WHICH THE DEBTOR COULD ASSERT AGAINST THE SELLER OF GOODS OR SERVICES OBTAINED PURSUANT HERETO OR WITH THE PROCEEDS HEREOF. RECOVERY HEREUNDER BY THE DEBTOR SHALL NOT EXCEED AMOUNTS PAID BY THE DEBTOR HEREUNDER.[6]

In regard to the direct loan by a third party situation, the rule provides in part:

In connection with any sale or lease of goods or services to consumers, in or affecting [interstate] commerce . . . it is an unfair or deceptive trade practice . . . for a seller, directly or indirectly to (b) accept, as full or partial payment for such sale or lease, the proceeds of any purchase money loan . . . unless any consumer credit contract made in connection with such purchase money loan *contains the following provision* in at least ten point, bold face type:

NOTICE
ANY HOLDER OF THIS CONSUMER CREDIT CONTRACT IS SUBJECT TO ALL CLAIMS AND DEFENSES WHICH THE DEBTOR COULD ASSERT AGAINST THE SELLER OF GOODS AND SERVICES OBTAINED WITH THE PROCEEDS HEREOF. RECOVERY HERE-

---

[6]The failure by a seller who is a "dealer" to include the required notice in each consumer credit contract subjects that person to a possible fine of up to $10,000 and to possible liability in a civil suit brought by the customer to recover damages incurred as a result of such failure.

UNDER BY THE DEBTOR SHALL NOT EXCEED
AMOUNTS PAID BY THE DEBTOR HEREUNDER.

While the FTC rule permitting assertion of defense has widespread applicability, it does not, by any means, bring about the death of the HDC doctrine. For example, the rule does not apply to contracts of commercial buyers (as distinguished from consumer buyers), and commercial contracts account for a great deal of commercial paper activity. Additionally, the rule applies only to consumer purchases on credit; thus purchases in which checks are given in full payment are not subject to it. Finally, the rule permits the assertion of only those personal defenses which the purchaser could assert against the seller of the goods (such as fraud or breach of contract).

SUMMARY

The primary attribute of the holder in due course (HDC) is that such a holder takes the instrument free of "personal" defenses existing between prior parties. (Ordinary holders, by contrast, take the instrument subject to such defenses.) A holder, to qualify as an HDC, must take the instrument (1) for value, (2) in good faith, and (3) without notice that it is overdue or has been dishonored, or that a defense against or a claim to the instrument exists. These requirements of Sec. 3-302 are explained in succeeding sections of Article 3.

The purpose of the value requirement is obvious; if a holder receives an instrument as a gift he or she does not need the protection given to a third party who has given value for it. Similarly, a holder should not be afforded HDC protection if he or she knows or should know of an existing claim to, or defense against, the instrument. This latter requirement essentially overlaps the good faith requirement, because a holder who knows or should know of a claim or defense would often also be a taker in bad faith.

In regard to the overdue requirement, there are three basic rules. (1) A note or draft with a fixed maturity date is overdue the day after such date. (2) Demand instruments become due a reasonable time after issue which (except for checks) varies from case to case. (3) Under Article 3, a reasonable time after issue is presumed to be no more than thirty days after issue.

An HDC, as indicated, takes an instrument free of personal ("limited") defenses. The most common of these are (1) breach of contract, (2) fraud in the inducement, and (3) unauthorized completion. Breach of contract exists where the payee of the instrument fails to perform the contract he or she had with the maker or drawer. Fraud in the inducement occurs where one person is induced to enter into a contract as a result of intentional misrepresentations by the other party, and as part of the transaction the victim of the fraud gives the defrauding party a note, draft or check in payment. The defense of unauthorized completion arises where a maker or drawer either entrusts an incomplete instrument to another, or issues such an instrument to the payee, and that party completes the instrument contrary to the instructions of the maker or drawer. While the maker or drawer cannot assert personal defenses against an HDC, he or she can assert them against ordinary holders.

Real ("universal") defenses are those possessed by the maker or drawer which free them of liability to HDCs as well as to ordinary holders. While real defenses are less common than personal defenses, the most representative of these are forgery, material alteration, and some types of illegality. Forgery is the signing of a maker or drawer's name by a party having no authority to do so. Such a signature is void. Material alteration occurs where a maker or drawer issues a completed instrument, and an essential term—usually the amount—is subsequently changed without his or her consent. (If a later purchaser qualifies as an HDC, such purchaser is entitled to payment according to the original terms of the instrument). Illegality constitutes a real defense, rather than a personal defense, if an instrument is given in payment for the commission of a criminal act, or in connection with any other transaction which is not only prohibited by law but which is expressly made void under the law.

In recent years the holder in due course concept has been increasingly viewed as bringing about unfair results in some cases. This is especially true in the situation where a buyer of consumer goods gives a negotiable instrument in payment for them, and subsequently is obligated to pay a holder in due course the full amount of the instrument even if the goods prove to be defective, or are never received by the buyer. To provide the buyer protection in such a case, two major limitations on the HDC doctrine now exist. First, some states have adopted statutes prohibiting sellers of consumer goods from accepting negotiable instruments (except checks) in payment for such goods. And, second, the Federal Trade Commission has adopted a rule which provides, in general, that any credit contract received by a seller or lessor of consumer goods (or by a party supplying credit for such a sale or lease) must provide that any holder of the contract is subject to all claims and defenses which the buyer or lessee possesses against the seller or lessor.

KEY TERMS

Holder in due course
Value
Good faith
Personal defense
Fraud in the inducement
Unauthorized completion
Real defense
Forgery
Fraud in the execution
FTC holder in due course rule

QUESTIONS AND PROBLEMS

1. Willman was the maker of several notes payable to the order of a designated payee, and he issued them to the payee. Later the payee wanted to borrow money from Wood, and in order to get the loan the payee had to pledge the notes (deliver them) to Wood as security for the loan. The amount of the loan was substantially less than the total amount of the notes.

In subsequent litigation by Wood against Willman, the maker of the notes, the question arose whether Wood was a holder in due course to the full extent of the notes or only to the extent of the amount of the loan which Wood had made to the payee. How would you rule on this issue? What is your reason? (*Wood v. Willman,* 423 P.2d 82, 1967).

2. On July 1, M signs a note, as maker, in the amount of $1,000, payable ninety days after date. He issues it to P, payee, in payment for the purchase of P's motorcycle. One month later P, needing cash to pay a debt, negotiates the note to H, who pays P $600 cash and agrees orally to pay an additional $400 within thirty days. Before the thirty days are up, H learns that M has rescinded the motorcycle purchase, claiming that the motorcycle has serious engine problems and that P knew this at the time of the sale.

    a. In this situation does H qualify as a holder in due course under the UCC? Explain.

    b. Assuming, for the sake of argument, that H is a holder in due course, to what extent (if any) can M assert as a defense his claim that the motorcycle was defective at the time of the sale? Explain.

3. A demand note, dated June 1, is issued to P on that date. On June 15, P demands payment from M, the maker, and payment is refused. On June 20, P negotiates the instrument to S. Later, S sues M on the note, and M proves that S knew, or had reason to know, of the dishonor at the time he acquired the instrument. S contends he still qualifies as an HDC since he clearly acquired the instrument within a reasonable time of its issue. Is S correct? Explain.

4. Cey makes out a promissory note payable to the order of the Griffey Corporation, and issues it to the corporation in payment for work to be done by it later. The Griffey Corporation negotiates the note for value to Concepcion, who qualifies as a holder in due course. Thereafter

Concepcion becomes indebted to the Griffey Corporation, and in payment of this debt he negotiates the instrument back to the Griffey Corporation. When the note matures Cey (maker) refuses to pay the Griffey Corporation for the reason that the Griffey Corporation never did the work that it contracted to do for Cey in the first place.

    a. Was the Griffey Corporation an HDC when it first received the note? Explain.

    b. Does the Griffey Corporation have all the rights of an HDC in view of the fact that it acquired the note from Concepcion, who *was* an HDC? Why or why not?

5. A corporation borrowed $25,000 from a bank, with the corporation giving its promissory note to the bank as evidence of the debt. As a part of the deal, the bank demanded that four individuals—including Rochman—indorse the instrument as accommodation indorsers, who would thereby guarantee payment by the corporation. Rochman told the bank that he would indorse the note only if Raymond D'Onofrio would also indorse it, and the bank agreed to this condition. Rochman then indorsed the note, but the bank never did get D'Onofrio's indorsement. When the maker of the note (the corporation) later defaulted, the bank sued Rochman as indorser. Assuming that the bank is not an HDC, can Rochman successfully assert his defense against the bank that his liability was conditioned upon D'Onofrio's indorsement? Explain. (*Long Island Trust Company v. International Institute for Packaging Education, Ltd.*, 344 N.E.2d 377, 1976.)

6. A salesman for a corporation demonstrated a water softening device to the Hutchinsons. Before leaving, the salesman asked them to sign a form so that he could show it to his employer as proof that he had made the demonstration. The Hutchinsons signed, and later learned that they had actually signed a promissory note. The note was subsequently negotiated to a bank, which qualified as an HDC. When the bank sued the Hutchinsons after the note came due, they claimed that they had a real defense in view of the fact that they honestly did not think they were signing a promissory note. The bank sought to overcome that defense by producing evidence that showed the Hutchinsons were intelligent people, and could easily have discovered the true nature of the instrument if they had just read it. If this evidence is true, what effect—if any—does it have upon the Hutchinson's defense? Explain. (*Reading Trust Co. v. Hutchinson,* Court of Common Pleas of Pennsylvania, 1964.)

7. D, drawer, signs a check in blank for her son since she is going to be out of town for two weeks; she authorizes him to fill in an amount "not over $200." D's son loses the check before he has had a chance to complete it. F, finder, fills in his own name as payee and $400 as the amount. F then negotiates the instrument to H, who pays him $350 for it. D's son notifies D that he has lost the check, and D immediately stops payment. H now wishes to enforce the check against D.

    a. What is the name of D's defense?

    b. If H does not qualify as a holder in due course, is he entitled to recover $200, $400, or nothing from D? Explain.

8. M issues a promissory note to P for $500. P alters the amount of the note to $5,000 and negotiates it to H. At the date of maturity H demands payment of $5,000 from M, and M refuses to pay H anything. If H is a holder in due course, is he entitled to receive $500, $5,000, or nothing from M? Explain.

Chapter 27

COMMERCIAL PAPER
Liability of
the Parties

All parties to commercial paper fall into one of two categories, as was noted in Chapter 24. Makers of notes and acceptors of drafts are **primary parties,** and all others are **secondary parties.**

As a general rule, a primary party is absolutely liable on the instrument, while a secondary party is only conditionally liable on it. Before we examine the ramifications of this rule, and its exceptions, it is necessary to see how a person may become a "party" in the first place.

THE SIGNING REQUIREMENT

Section 3-401(1) of the UCC provides that "no person is liable on an instrument unless his signature appears thereon." (That section goes on to define a signature as "the use of any name . . . upon an instrument, or any word or mark used in lieu of a written signature.") A signature may be made personally, or by an authorized agent.

Signing by an Agent

In most instances the maker, acceptor, drawer, or indorser does in fact personally sign the instrument, in which instances no problems arise under the above section. However, in cases where the instrument is signed by an agent or other representative, two related problems may arise. The first involves the liability of the principal (the person whom the agent is representing, and whose name is signed to the instrument), and the second involves the personal liability of the agent or representative himself. These problems—or potential problems—take on added significance when one realizes that all commercial paper issued by corporations necessarily involves corporate names being signed by agents, because all corporate activity can be carried on *only* through the actions of agents and employees.

Signature by Authorized Agent: Section 3-403 provides that the authority of the agent may be established "as in any other cases of represen-

tation"—i.e., under the ordinary principles of agency law.[1] Thus if the treasurer of the X Company has express or implied authority to issue promissory notes in the name of the corporation, the corporation alone would be liable as the maker of a note signed "The X Company, by R. J. Thomas, Treasurer."

Liability of Agent—Improper Signature: Occasionally a signature on an instrument contains the name of both principal and agent, but fails to indicate that the agent signed in a representative capacity. (In the above example, the names of the makers may thus appear as "The X Company" and "R. J. Thomas.") Or the signature may not contain the name of the principal, but does show that the agent signed in a representative capacity ("R. J. Thomas, Treasurer").

Section 3-403(2)(b) applies to both of these situations. It provides that "except as otherwise established between the immediate parties, the representative (agent) is personally obligated on the instrument." Thus if the agent is being sued by a third-party holder—someone to whom the instrument has been negotiated—*the agent is personally liable.* (On the other hand, if the agent is being sued by the *payee,* the agent is permitted to introduce evidence showing that he or she actually signed in a representative capacity, and that the payee knew this to be the case. In such a case the agent is not liable.)

Signature by Unauthorized Agent: If an agent executes an instrument in the name of a principal that the agent has absolutely no authority to make, the named principal has no liability on the instrument. Section 3-304(1) provides, in part, that "Any unauthorized signature is wholly inoperative as that of the person whose name is signed. . . ." In effect, therefore, the unauthorized signature is a forgery. *The agent, however, is personally liable on the instru-*

---

[1] For a discussion of the different kinds of authority an agent might possess, see Chapters 18 and 19.

ment. This results from additional language in that section which provides that an unauthorized signature "*operates as the signature of the unauthorized signer* in favor of any person who in good faith pays the instrument or takes it for value." (Emphasis added.)

In the following case the holder of a number of corporate checks brought action against the corporation's president in an effort to hold him personally liable on them. The president clearly had the authority to draw the checks, but he failed to indicate that he was signing in a representative capacity. As you read the case, note the factors to which the court looked *in addition to the form of the signature* in determining whether the president was personally liable on the checks. (While courts often consider such factors in the case of payroll checks, the type of check involved here, they are less likely to do so in regard to other instruments.)

Pollin v. Mindy Mfg. Co. and Apfelbaum
Superior Court of Pennsylvania, 236 A.2d 542 (1967)

In September 1966 the Mindy Mfg. Co. issued to its employees payroll checks that were drawn on the Continental Bank and Trust Co. of Norristown, Pennsylvania. Thirty-six employees indorsed their checks to Pollin, who operated a check cashing business. Payment on these checks was refused by the drawee bank (Continental) because Mindy did not have sufficient funds in its account. These checks were returned to Pollin, who then brought suit against Mindy and Robert Apfelbaum, Mindy's president.

**Each check was "boldly imprinted" at the top: "Mindy Mfg. Co.";
each clearly stated that it was a payroll check; and "Mindy Mfg. Co."
was also imprinted in the lower right-hand corner of each check, with two blank lines appearing below it. Apfelbaum had simply signed his name on one of the blank lines, *without indicating his position or his capacity in any way*. It was on this basis that the trial court ruled Apfelbaum to be personally liable.**

The trial court entered judgments against both the Mindy company and Apfelbaum. Apfelbaum appealed this judgment, claiming that he signed only in a *representative capacity* and thus could not be held personally liable on the checks.

Montgomery, Justice:

. . . Judgment against [Apfelbaum] was entered by the lower court on the authority of Section 3-403 of the Uniform Commercial Code . . . which provides, "An authorized representative who signs his name to an instrument . . . (b) except as otherwise established between the immediate parties, is personally obligated if the instrument names the person represented but *does not show that the representative signed in a representative capacity* . . . ," and our decision is thereunder. [Emphasis added.]

The issue before us, therefore, is whether a third party to the original transaction, the endorsee in the present case, may recover against one who affixes his name to a check in the place where a [drawer] usually signs without indicating he is signing in a representative capacity, without giving consideration to other parts of the instrument or extrinsic evidence. This appears to be a novel question under the Uniform Commercial Code.

If this were an action brought by the payee, parol [oral] evidence would be permitted to establish the capacity of the person affixing his signature under Section 3-403 previously recited and our decisions in *Bell v. Dornan* and *Pittsburgh National Bank v. Kemilworth Restaurant.*

However, since this is an action brought by a third party our initial inquiry must be for the purpose of determining whether *the instrument* indicates the capacity of appellant as signer. Admittedly, the instrument fails to show the office held by appellant. However, we do not think this is a complete answer to our problem, since the Code imposes liability on the individual only ". . . if the instrument . . . does not show that the representative signed in a representative capacity. . . ." *This implies that the instrument must be considered in its entirety.* [Emphasis added.]

Although Section 3-401(2) of the Code provides that "A signature is made by use of any name, including any trade or assumed name, upon an instrument, or by any word or mark used in lieu of a written signature," which would be broad enough to include the printed name of a corporation, we do not believe that a check showing two lines under the imprinted corporate name indicating the [place for the] signature of one or more corporate officers would be accepted by any reasonably prudent person as a fully executed check of the corporation. It is common to expect that a corporate name placed upon a negotiable instrument in order to bind the corporation as [drawer], especially when printed on the instrument, will be accompanied by the signatures of officers authorized by the by-laws to sign the instrument. While we do not rule out the possibility of a printed name being established as an acceptable signature, we hold that such a situation is uncommon, and in the present case the two lines under the printed name dictate against a valid corporate signature [in the absence of a signature by an officer].

Next we must give consideration to the distinction between a check and a note. A check is an order of a depositor on a bank in the nature of a draft drawn on the bank and payable on demand. It is revokable until paid or accepted for payment. A note is an irrevocable promise to pay on the part of the maker. The [drawer] of a check impliedly engages not only that it will be paid, but that he will have sufficient funds in the bank to meet it. In the present instance the checks clearly showed that they were payable from a special account set up by the corporate defendant for the purpose of paying its employees. This information disclosed by the instrument of itself *would refute any contention* that the appellant intended to make the instrument *his own order* on the named bank to pay money to the payee. [Emphasis added.] The money was payable from the account of the corporation, over which appellant as an individual had no control.

> Considering the instrument as a whole we conclude that it sufficiently discloses that appellant signed it in a representative capacity. . . .
> Judgment reversed and entered for appellant-defendant.

LIABILITY OF PRIMARY PARTIES

For the remainder of this chapter we will make two assumptions: (1) that the party whose liability is being examined signed the instrument personally, and (2) that such party does not have an assertable defense against the holder. On this basis we will first examine the liability of *primary parties* (makers of notes and acceptors of drafts).

Liability of the Maker

Contractual Liability: The maker of a note is *primarily* (absolutely) *liable* on it. That is, the party has the duty to pay the instrument at its maturity date even if the holder does not demand payment at that time. Section 3-413(1) provides that "the maker or acceptor engages [promises] that he will pay the instrument according to its tenor at the time of his engagement or as completed pursuant to Section 3-115 on incomplete instruments."

Furthermore, the maker—unlike the indorser—*is not discharged in any way by the fact that the instrument is presented for payment late;* even if a note is presented for payment many months or even years after its due date, the maker remains fully liable on it (until the statute of limitations has run).

There is, however, one limited exception to this rule. Under Sec. 3-502(1)(b), where a note is payable at a specified bank, and where presentment is not made at maturity, and where the bank becomes insolvent after the maturity date but before presentment for payment actually occurs—with the result that the maker is "deprived of funds" during the delay—the maker "may discharge his liability by written assignment to the holder of his rights against . . . the

payor bank in respect [to] such funds." To illustrate: A note is made payable at the X Bank on March 1, at which time the maker has sufficient funds on deposit to meet the note. Presentment is not made on March 1 as required by the UCC.[2] On March 10 the bank fails. Presentment is finally made by the holder on March 11, at which time, of course, he does not obtain payment, because the bank has closed. In this case the maker can *assign his rights against the funds in the bank* (to the extent of the amount of the note) to the holder and *thereby be discharged* of further liability. Thus, if the bank does not pay out a hundred cents on the dollar and the account is not covered by federal deposit insurance, the loss falls on the holder because of the late presentment.

Liability on Admissions: By signing a promissory note, the maker *admits* (guarantees) certain facts. Section 3-413(3) provides in part that the maker "admits against all subsequent parties . . . the existence of the payee and his then capacity [capacity at the time of signing the note] to indorse." Thus, if a payee who is a minor negotiates an instrument to a holder and subsequently recovers the instrument by disaffirming his or her indorsement, the holder can recover from the maker any damages incurred as a result of the rescission.

Liability of the Acceptor

As we saw in Chapter 24, time drafts are frequently presented to the drawee prior to matu-

---

[2]Presentment here is due on March 1 because, under a rule to be examined later, an instrument that is payable at a fixed future date must ordinarily be presented for payment *on that date.*

rity for his or her *acceptance.* Under the UCC, in some instances presentment for acceptance is mandatory while in others it is optional. In any event, when the drawee accepts the instrument he or she becomes liable on it for the first time.[3]

Once an acceptance occurs, the liability of the drawee-acceptor is virtually identical to that of the maker of a note. Under Sec. 3-413(3), by accepting, he or she admits the existence of the payee and that person's then capacity to indorse. More important, under Sec. 3-413(1) the drawee-acceptor promises to pay the instrument at its maturity date. Again the obligation to pay is not cut off or diminished by a late presentment for payment.[4] The only exception to this rule of continuing liability arises in the same circumstances as those connected with the liability of the maker of a note—where the draft is payable at a bank and where that bank becomes insolvent between the time presentment should have been made under the code and the time it actually was made. In such a situation, the acceptor can discharge his or her liability to the holder by giving that person an assignment of funds, just as the maker of a note can do in similar circumstances.

Two further observations regarding acceptances are needed:

1. Until a draft is accepted, the drawee has no liability on the instrument to the payee or to any other holder. As we will see later in this chapter, the drawee usually owes the *drawer* a legal duty to accept the instrument, but does not owe such a duty to any *holder* of the draft. Thus if a holder presents the draft for acceptance and the drawee refuses to accept, the holder cannot bring action against the drawee (although he or she can bring action against the drawer, who is a secondary party).

2. As a general rule, a refusal by the drawee to accept a draft that is properly presented constitutes a dishonor of the instrument, which triggers the liability of secondary parties on the instrument—the drawer and all indorsers except those indorsing "without recourse" (that is, without guaranteeing payment). The precise elements and ramifications of a dishonor will be examined later in this chapter.

PROMISSORY LIABILITY OF SECONDARY PARTIES, GENERALLY

Secondary parties are *drawers* of drafts and checks and *indorsers* of all instruments. The liability of these parties is often significantly less than that of primary parties.

Primary parties *absolutely promise* to pay the instruments they have signed. Secondary parties promise to pay *only if certain conditions are met:* (1) due presentment, (2) dishonor, and (3) notice of dishonor. Essentially, the secondary party (except for the "without recourse" indorser) is saying, "I will pay this instrument to anyone holding it *if* it is presented to the primary party (or the drawee), and *if* he or she dishonors it (usually by failing to pay), and *if* I am given notice of the dishonor." These conditions, unless waived, must be met in order for the secondary party to be held on his or her **promissory liability**—or "contractual liability," as it is often called.[5] (These conditions need not be met, however, if a person is seeking to hold the secondary party liable on his or her *warranty* liability, an area we will examine later in this chapter.)

---

[3] While acceptance does not take place in the case of checks, they can be "certified," an act that is similar to acceptance (see Chapter 28 for details).

[4] The primary rules prescribing the various times at which presentments for acceptance or payment should be made are discussed later in the chapter.

---

[5] Some drafts provide that the drawer waives presentment, dishonor, and notice of dishonor. This discussion, however, assumes that no such waiver exists. (Also, under Sec. 3-511, delay in presentment and notice of dishonor are excused in certain circumstances.)

PROMISSORY LIABILITY OF DRAWERS

All drawers, like makers and acceptors, admit the existence of the payee and his or her then capacity to indorse. Of more importance, however, is the drawer's promissory liability.

Under Sec. 3-413(2), a drawer promises that "upon dishonor of the draft and any necessary notice of dishonor . . . he will pay the amount of the draft to the holder or to any indorser who takes it up." Thus the drawer's contractual liability is conditioned upon the events of dishonor and the notice of dishonor. We will examine these conditions here.

Dishonor of Drafts

While checks and promissory notes require only one kind of presentment, presentment for payment, drafts often involve two presentments—*presentment for acceptance* and, later, *presentment for payment.* Insofar as drafts are concerned, then, a dishonor can occur either by the refusal of the drawee to accept or the refusal to pay.

Dishonor by Nonacceptance: Under Sec. 3-501(1)(a), presentment for acceptance is required in three situations. This section provides that, unless excused, presentment for acceptance is necessary to charge the drawer and indorsers (1) "where the draft so provides," (2) where it "is payable elsewhere than at the residence or place of business of the drawee," or (3) where its "date of payment depends upon such presentment." This section also provides that "the holder may *at his option* present for acceptance any other draft payable at a stated date"—that is, "time" drafts. Any refusal by the drawee to accept a draft that is properly presented for acceptance, regardless of whether presentment is required or optional, *constitutes a dishonor* that triggers the liability of the drawer and indorsers (assuming that any necessary notice of dishonor is also given).

Dishonor by Nonpayment: After an acceptance occurs, as well as in any case where an optional presentment for acceptance is dispensed with by the holder, a *presentment for payment,* at maturity, is required in order to fix the liability of the drawer—and indorsers, as well. (Until such presentment is made by the holder no dishonor has occurred, and the secondary parties' liability is not fixed.) Once a proper presentment for payment is made, however, a refusal by the drawee to make payment does constitute a dishonor.

Effect of Late Presentment: Section 3-503 brings together the rules that set the time limits within which presentment for acceptance and payment are to be made. Insofar as drafts are concerned, the rules for *presentment for payment* are as follows:

1. Where a draft is payable at a fixed future date, presentment is due on that date.

2. As to other drafts, presentment must be made within a "reasonable time" after the secondary party became a party; in other words, where the drawer's liability is concerned, within a reasonable time after the draft is issued. Generally, under Sec. 3-503 a reasonable time in regard to such a draft is determined "by any usage of banking or trade, and the facts of the particular case." However, in the case of an uncertified check that section provides that it is "presumed" that 30 days after issuance is a reasonable time for presentment insofar as the drawer is concerned (but a shorter time applies to indorsers, as will be seen subsequently).

Drawer's Liability Contrasted with Indorser's Liability: While drawers and indorsers are both secondary parties, their liabilities differ in one significant respect. While a late presentment automatically frees indorsers of their secondary liability, such a presentment does not free the drawer except in the rare case where the drawee becomes insolvent during the delay in presentment. To illustrate, using the check as an example: D issues a check to P on June 10, and P indorses it to H on June 22. H presents the check to the drawee bank for payment on July 18, at which time the bank dishonors it because of a computer error showing insufficient funds in D's account. H gives immediate notice of dishonor to D. Although the presentment on July 18 was late—i.e., more than 30 days after its June 10 issuance—D remains liable on the instrument because the drawee bank did not fail after the 30 days had elapsed. (Because the "time of presentment" rules are thus of more significance to indorsers than to drawers, a fuller discussion of these rules appears in the "Liability of Indorsers" section later in this chapter.)

Notice of Dishonor

When a dishonor occurs, notice of dishonor must generally be given to fix the drawer's liability. Section 3-508 provides that such notice may either be sent by mail or given orally. This section also provides that where the party giving notice is a bank, notice must be given "before its midnight deadline"—that is, by midnight of the next business day following the dishonor. Where the party giving notice is not a bank, notice must be given by midnight of the third business day following dishonor. (Under Sec. 3-511, however, notice of dishonor may be waived or excused; the most common situation in which notice is dispensed with is in the case where dishonor of a check occurs as a result of a stop-payment order issued to the drawee bank by the drawer; in such a case the drawer is obviously aware that the dishonor will be made.)

PROMISSORY (CONDITIONAL) LIABILITY OF INDORSERS

Unqualified indorsers have two kinds of liability—*conditional liability* and *warranty liability.* Qualified ("without recourse") indorsers, on the other hand, incur warranty liability only. These two general kinds of liability will be discussed in order.

Conditions: Presentment, Dishonor, and Notice

All unqualified indorsers promise that they will pay the instrument themselves if (1) the instrument is properly presented for acceptance or payment, (2) the instrument is dishonored, and (3) a proper notice of dishonor is given them. Thus the conditional liability of the indorser and drawer is the same in this respect: neither party incurs such liability until the specified conditions have occurred. There remains, however, the significant difference—noted earlier—that a *late* presentment frees the indorsers of their conditional liability in all cases, while this is not true of drawers.[6]

How Presentments Are Made: Under Sec. 3-504(1), presentment is a demand for acceptance or payment made upon the maker, acceptor, drawee, or other payor by or on behalf of the holder. It can be made by mail (in which case the time of presentment is the time at which it is received); through a clearing house; at the place specified in the instrument; or, if no place is specified, at the place of business or at the residence of the maker. (In the latter case, if neither the maker "nor anyone authorized to act for him is accessible" at such place, then presentment is excused.) The importance of these rules is that if an attempted presentment is made in any manner other than these authorized ways, a refusal of the maker, acceptor, or drawee at that time does not constitute a dishonor.

Time of Presentment: As indicated, a required presentment must be made not only in a proper manner but also at a *proper time* if indorsers are to be held on their conditional lia-

---

[6] Throughout this section it is assumed that the requirements of dishonor and notice of dishonor are not waived. In some situations, however, the purchaser of an instrument will not take it unless the transferor's indorsement provides that "presentment, dishonor, and notice of dishonor are hereby waived" (by the indorser). In such cases the discussion is inapplicable.

bility. What is a proper time depends upon the type of presentment (presentment for acceptance or presentment for payment) and the time at which the instrument is payable.

Section 3-503(1) sets forth the rules for determining the times at which *all* presentments must be made. In the interest of brevity, we will concern ourselves only with those parts of this section that apply to presentments for payment. (This section appears in full in Article 3, Part Five of Appendix A.)

The two basic rules are provided by subsections c and e of Sec. 3-501(1). In essence, they are as follows:

1. If an instrument is payable at a specified time (for instance, "November 20, 1991"), presentment must be made *on that date* if secondary parties are to be held liable in the event of a dishonor.

2. As to all other instruments—demand notes, demand drafts, and checks—presentment must be made *within a reasonable time after the secondary party signed the instrument.*

As was indicated earlier, Sec. 3-503(2) goes on to indicate the factors to be taken into account in determining what is a reasonable time for various instruments, and provides that in regard to uncertified checks drawn and payable in the United States a reasonable time with respect to the *drawer* is presumed to be thirty days after its date or issue, whichever is later. Additionally, that section provides that with respect to the liability of an *indorser* of such a check a reasonable time is presumed to be "seven days after his indorsement."

We will now examine several of the more common fact-patterns to which these rules apply.

1. *Promissory note, payable at a fixed future date.* On March 3, M signs a note as maker and issues it to P, payee. The note is payable the following *September 5th.* P indorses the instrument in blank later in March and negotiates it to H. H presents the note to M for payment on September 10, and it is dishonored (that is, M

simply does not pay it). Here H cannot hold the indorser, P, liable because presentment was five days late.

2. *Promissory note, payable on demand.* On February 2, M signs a note as maker and issues it to P, payee. The note is payable "on demand." On March 2, P indorses the instrument with a blank indorsement and negotiates it to H. On May 20, H presents the note to M for payment, and it is dishonored. H now brings action against P on her indorsement. Since the note is a demand note and thus governed by Sec. 3-503(1)(e), H—in order to hold P liable—must show that his presentment on May 20 was *within a reasonable time after P indorsed the instrument.* (As indicated earlier, a reasonable time as to demand notes and drafts "is determined by the nature of the instrument, any usage of banking or trade, and the facts of the particular case." Under this clause, for example, it is generally held that an interest-bearing demand note can be presented somewhat later than one bearing no interest, and that a reasonable time for presentment in rural communities is somewhat longer than when the parties are in urban areas.)

3. *Regular (uncertified) check.* D draws a check on his account in the B Bank payable to the order of P on April 6, and he issues it to P on that date. P, by a blank indorsement, negotiates the check to X on April 15, and X, by blank indorsement, negotiates it to H on April 20. On April 26, H presents the check to the drawee, the B Bank, and payment is refused for some reason; H then gives immediate notice of the dishonor to both indorsers, P and X. Under the "seven day" rule of Sec. 3-503(2) that applies to indorsers of ordinary checks, the last indorser (X) is liable to H, but the prior indorser, P, is not. Since P indorsed on April 15, he could be held on his conditional liability only if the check were presented to the drawee bank, or at least put into the bank collection process, within seven days—by April 22. In this case presentment on April 26 was late as to P but effective as to X, since the presentment *was* within seven days of X's becoming an indorser. (And if action were brought by H against D, drawer, as well, obviously the presentment *as to him* would be timely, since it would conform to the "within thirty days of issue" rule applicable to drawers.)

Notice of Dishonor and Protest: When a dishonor occurs, either by a refusal to accept or by nonpayment, any indorser is freed of conditional liability unless he or she is given a *notice of dishonor* within the time specified by Sec. 3-508. That section provides in part, as noted earlier, that "any necessary notice must be given by a bank before its midnight deadline, and *by any other person before midnight of the third business day after dishonor.*" (Emphasis added.)[7] The indorser receiving the notice then has the same prescribed time in which to give notice to his or her immediate indorser, if any.

Under Sec. 3-509, in some situations a *protest* (a formal, notarized notice of dishonor) can be made. Protest is required only where the dishonored instrument is drawn in or payable in a foreign country. As to other instruments, use of protest in lieu of ordinary notice of dishonor is optional.

---

[7] The midnight deadline rule requires that if payment cannot be made because of insufficient funds or because of a stop payment order has been issued, the drawee bank must give notice to its transferor no later than *midnight of the next business day.* If that transferor is also a bank, it must in turn give notice by midnight of the day following its receipt of the original notice.

When Presentment Is Excused or Delay Permitted: Section 3-511(1) provides: "Delay in presentment, protest or notice of dishonor is excused when the party is without notice that it is due or when the delay is caused by circumstances beyond his control and he exercises reasonable diligence after the cause of the delay ceases to operate." The phrase *without notice that it is due* has particular application to an instrument containing an acceleration clause. It is entirely possible that a holder will take an instrument *after* the time of payment has been accelerated but having no knowledge of the acceleration at the time of taking it. The phrase *circumstances beyond his control* excuses delay in presentment or in notice of dishonor when the delay is caused by such things as extreme weather conditions or the emergency closing of businesses in a certain area by act of the governor of the involved state.

Additionally, Sec. 3-511(2) provides that presentment or notice of dishonor is entirely excused if the party to be charged (1) has waived presentment or notice; (2) has personally dishonored or stopped payment on the instrument; or (3) "if by reasonable diligence the presentment . . . cannot be made, or the notice given."

The fact-pattern of the following case is typical of those in which the courts are required to determine whether or not the holder exercised "reasonable diligence" in trying to make presentment.

Gaffin v. Heymann
Supreme Court of Rhode Island, 428 A.2d 1066 (1981)

In 1967 Gaffin (plaintiff) loaned $10,000 to Michael Heymann so he and a friend could open a travel agency. Later, the business failed and Gaffin told Heymann he wanted the loan repaid.

A series of negotiations between plaintiff, Michael Heymann, and Michael Heymann's father, Paul Heymann (defendant), then ensued. As a result of these discussions, plaintiff finally agreed to accept two promissory notes payable to his order in the amounts of $8,000 and

$2,000 signed by Michael Heymann as maker, on condition that Paul Heymann would also be a party to the $8,000 note.

Accordingly, Michael Heymann delivered the notes to plaintiff in March 1968. The $8,000 note—the one involved in this litigation—had a maturity date of March 10, 1973. *Michael Heymann was the maker of this interest-bearing note, and the instrument bore the signature of Paul Heymann on the back.*

Over the next year or two several interest payments were missed. For reasons appearing in the decision below, plaintiff was unable to locate Michael Heymann in order to collect the payments, and he was also unable to present the note to Michael Heymann for payment on March 10, 1973. Plaintiff then brought this action to recover the amount of the note from defendant.

At the trial, defendant raised two primary issues: (1) whether he was a comaker of the note, as plaintiff contended, or an indorser; and (2) if he was an indorser, whether he was excused from liability because of plaintiff's failure to present the note to the maker at maturity. The trial court ruled that defendant was legally a *comaker* of the note, in view of plaintiff's refusal to accept the note unless signed by defendant. Accordingly, judgment was entered for plaintiff.

In the appellate court defendant raised the same issues as those presented in the trial court. As to the first issue, the appellate court accepted defendant's argument that he was an *indorser* of the instrument, rather than a comaker. This ruling was reached on the basis of Sec. 3-402 of the UCC, which provides that "unless the instrument clearly indicates that a signature is made in some other capacity, it is an indorsement."

The appellate court then turned to the second issue, whether defendant, as indorser, was released of liability by plaintiff's failure to present the note to the maker at maturity. The part of the opinion dealing with this issue appears below.

Kelleher, Justice:

. . . An indorser's liability attaches only after presentment and demand has been made on the maker, in this instance, Michael. After the maker has dishonored the note, the indorser is required to pay the instrument according to the tenor at the time he signed it. *Unless excused,* failure to make presentment to the maker will act to discharge the indorser. [Emphasis added.] Heymann [defendant] argues that since Gaffin [plaintiff] has acknowledged he did not present the note to Michael when due, he has been discharged of his obligation to pay. Gaffin has countered this contention by claiming that presentment was waived by Michael.

[The court here quoted Sec. 3-511, as follows: "Presentment or notice of protest . . . is entirely excused when . . . (c) by reasonable diligence, the presentment or notice of protest cannot be made or the notice given." The court then continued:]

Once Michael delivered the note to Gaffin, he left Massachusetts to live in Rhode Island. After living in Rhode Island for an indeterminate period, he traveled abroad. Heymann told the trial justice that although he had spoken frequently to Michael on the phone since his return to the United States, he was unaware of Michael's address or place of employment. According to his father, Michael, at the time of trial, was residing somewhere in Connecticut.

In ruling that Gaffin had exercised reasonable diligence in attempting to locate Michael, the trial justice noted that Michael had not responded to mail addressed to him at his last-known address, and had not responded to phone messages left at his father's residence. Although these attempts to reach Michael occurred prior to the due date of the note, the trial justice implied that had Gaffin made further efforts after March 10, 1973, they too would have failed. In view of the fact that Heymann was aware that Gaffin had attempted to contact Michael and that these attempts had been unsuccessful, there would be little to be gained by requiring Gaffin to continue his attempts ad infinitum. This is particularly true when the indorser is in a better position to know the location of the maker than is the payee of the note. Hence, we [agree with the trial court's] finding that Gaffin had indeed exercised due diligence in attempting to locate Michael. [Accordingly, the court said, presentment was excused under Sec. 3-511, and defendant was thus liable as indorser.]

Judgment affirmed in part, reversed in part, and case remanded.

Comment: Although both courts held defendant liable for the face amount of the note (on different theories), the case was remanded to the trial court under instructions to recompute the amount of interest due.

WARRANTY LIABILITY OF INDORSERS

Every indorser makes certain warranties (or guarantees) about the instrument he or she is negotiating. This creates a **warranty liability,** which is sometimes called the unconditional liability of secondary parties, meaning that the liability is *not* conditioned upon proper presentment, dishonor, and notice of dishonor.

Unqualified Indorsers

The warranties made by all unqualified indorsers are set forth below. (With an exception to be noted later, the same warranties are also made by qualified indorsers.)

Section 3-417(2) provides in part that a person who negotiates an instrument by indorsement and who receives consideration for it makes five warranties to the indorsee and subsequent holders.[8] Under this section the indorser essentially warrants that:

1. He or she has good title to the instrument.

2. All signatures are genuine or authorized.

3. The instrument has not been materially altered.

4. No defense of any party is good against him or her (the indorser).

---

[8]The liability of a person who negotiates an instrument *by delivery only* (without indorsing it) is discussed later in the chapter.

5. He or she has no knowledge of any insolvency proceeding instituted against the maker, acceptor, or drawer of an unaccepted instrument.

The first four of these warranties are illustrated below. The fifth is rarely encountered.

A breach of *warranty of title* often involves a forged indorsement. For example: D draws and issues an instrument payable to the order of P. The instrument is stolen from P, and the thief forges P's indorsement on the back of it. He then sells the instrument to A, an innocent purchaser, who by blank indorsement, negotiates the instrument to B. B presents the instrument for payment, but payment is refused because the maker, acceptor, or drawee has learned that P's indorsement is a forgery. Because of the forged indorsement of P, B has not acquired title to the instrument and cannot hold the maker (or acceptor or drawee, in the case of a draft or check) liable on it. However, he can hold A liable on the warranty of title theory, because A did not have title either, because of the forged indorsement. A is liable on this warranty even if he had no reason to suspect the forgery and (as is true of all other warranties) even if the presentment for payment by B to the primary party was late.

The warranty that *all signatures are genuine or authorized* is almost self-explanatory. Suppose, for example, that P received a note of which M was the apparent maker. P later indorsed the note to H, and H recovered nothing from M because M was able to prove that her signature on the note was a forgery. (It may take a lawsuit against M to establish the fact of the forgery, or evidence of the forgery may be so convincing that H foregoes a lawsuit against M.) H can now hold P, the indorser, on his warranty that all signatures on the instrument at the time of the indorsement were genuine. Again, H need not show that P knew of the forgery when he indorsed; it is the fact of the forgery that is controlling.

We discussed the defense of *material alteration* in Chapter 26, where we saw that a maker or acceptor might escape liability on an instrument by showing that it was materially altered after he or she had made (or accepted) it. The ordinary holder who presents for payment in this situation will probably recover nothing from the maker or acceptor, and an HDC may make only a partial recovery (especially if the alteration involved a raising of the amount of the instrument.) However, either holder can hold any indorser liable on the breach of warranty theory and thereby recover whatever loss he or she sustained—assuming, of course, that the alteration occurred prior to the indorsement.

The warranty that *no defense is good against the indorser* refers to any kinds of defenses that do not fall within the first three subsections of Sec. 3-417(2)—as, for example, the defense of illegality. To illustrate: After a Saturday night poker game A ends up owing B $175; A gives B a check for that amount in payment. The following Monday A learns from a lawyer friend that gambling debts are totally unenforceable in his state, so he stops payment on the check. In the meantime B has indorsed the check to C. In this situation, after being refused payment by the drawee bank, C can hold B (the indorser) liable for breach of the warranty that no defense existed against him.

Qualified Indorsers

The warranty liability of the person who indorses "without recourse" is exactly the same as that of the unqualified indorser—with one exception. While the unqualified indorser flatly guarantees that no defense of any party is good against him or her, the qualified indorser warrants only that he or she "has no knowledge of such a defense"—Sec. 3-417(3). Thus, if a check were given in payment of a totally illegal obligation and subsequently a party indorsed the instrument "without recourse," that indorser would not be liable upon dishonor unless it were established that he or she *knew of the defense* at the time of indorsement.

However, this warranty applies only to defenses falling within subsection d. Thus, if the qualified indorser were being sued for breach of the warranty that all signatures were genuine, for example, the indorser would be liable if the drawer's or maker's signature were a forgery, even if he or she did not know of the forgery.

The next case shows particularly well how the application of Sec. 3-417(3) works out in real life.

Fair Finance Co. v. Fourco, Inc.
Court of Appeals of Ohio, 237 N.E.2d 406 (1968)

Fourco, defendant, sold goods to a buyer and had the buyer, in payment thereof, sign a promissory note payable to the order of Fourco. (For this reason, Fourco is usually referred to in the decision as the vendor-payee.)

Fourco indorsed the note "without recourse" and negotiated it to Fair Finance, plaintiff. When plaintiff sought payment from the maker (the buyer of the goods), it was discovered that the defendant (the payee and qualified indorser) had computed the interest at too high a rate in determining the face amount of the note. The maker was thus obligated to pay the plaintiff only the corrected amount due, and plaintiff then sought recovery of the balance from the defendant, the qualified indorser.

The lower court found that defendant had no notice of the fact that the interest provided for in its note was usurious (in excess of that permitted by Ohio law). In view of this fact, the court ruled that the defendant, having transferred the instrument by qualified indorsement, was not liable to plaintiff for the balance of the interest. Plaintiff appealed.

Hunsicker, Justice:

. . . Is this, then, a matter which is provided for in the Uniform Commercial Code?

Section 1303.53, Revised Code (U.C.C. 3-417), says in part:

(B) Any person who transfers an instrument and receives consideration warrants to his transferee and if the transfer is by indorsement to any subsequent holder who takes the instrument in good faith that: . . . (4) no defense of any party is good against him; and

(C) By transferring "without recourse" the transferor limits the obligation stated in division (B)(4). . . . to a warranty that he has no knowledge of such a defense. . . .

Fair Finance Company admits that Fourco, Inc., had no [actual] knowledge of the defense of improper computation until after an attempt to obtain payment by court action against the maker was instituted. There is no claim of fraud in the sale and purchase of this promissory note. Counsel for the Fair Finance Company, in their statements to the trial court and to this court, [however,] said: "We do claim unintentional misrepresentation." [Fair Finance's claim] of misrepresentation arises from the fact that interest on the note was [accidentally] calculated by the vendor, Fourco, Inc., at the beginning of the interest period and taken in advance instead of at the end of the interest period.

Is the claim of "unintentional misrepresentation" such that it is exempt from the provisions of Section 1303.53(B)(4) and (C), Revised Code, set out above? We find no reported cases in Ohio, or elsewhere, interpreting this section of the Uniform Commercial Code. Counsel have cited several cases from other jurisdictions which bear on the question, [but these] were decided prior to the adoption of the Uniform Commercial Code. . . .

The vendor in the instant case, Fourco, Inc., used its own printed note to obtain the written promise of the maker. The terms of that note concerning the computation of interest were its handiwork. The computation of interest was not made by the maker but by the vendor of the note who now wishes, because of its own error and improper computation of interest, to be relieved of liability because of the indorsement, "without recourse." Is this such a lack of knowledge of a defense as releases the vendor-indorser from liability? *We think it is not,* for we believe that where an indorsement of a promissory note "without recourse" is made by a vendor-payee, who computes the interest incorrectly in determining the face value of that note at the time of sale, and where the form of note and terms thereof are those of the vendor-payee, *such vendor-payee has knowledge of that wrongful computation, and the defense arising therefrom, within the terms of Section 1303.53(C). Revised Code.* [Emphasis added.]

It is the conclusion of this court that the judgment must be reversed, and, as there is no dispute as to the facts, final judgment shall be ordered entered herein for the appellant, Fair Finance Company, for the amount admitted by the parties hereto as being the improper computation of interest by Fourco, Inc.

Judgment is reversed.

SELECTED TRANSFEROR-INDORSER PROBLEMS

Liability of Transferor without Indorsement

A person who negotiates a bearer instrument by mere delivery (that is, without indorsing it) has no conditional liability on the instrument. If the primary party is unable to pay the instrument at maturity, the transferor is not liable to the holder.

However, a transferor by mere delivery does have the same warranty liability as an unqualified indorser, with one important exception. While the warranties of indorsers run to all subsequent holders of the instrument, the warranties of the person who transfers without indorsement run only to his or her *immediate transferee.* To illustrate: P receives a bearer note of which M is apparently the maker. P negotiates the note to X by delivery only, and X in turn negotiates it by delivery only to H. If M's signature turns out to be a forgery, H can hold X, his immediate transferor, liable on his warranty that all signatures are genuine, but he cannot hold P, the prior transferor. (Of course, if X has to pay damages to H arising out of the breach of his warranty, X can then hold P because P's warranty did run to him.)

Order of Indorsers' Liability

Where two or more indorsements appear on an instrument, it is presumed, under Sec. 3-414(2), that the indorsers are liable in the order in which their signatures appear. For instance, a note is indorsed by X, and the names of Y and Z appear successively below her indorsement. If Z is held liable to the holder, H, following a dishonor, Z can proceed against Y and Y against X. X will then be limited to an attempt to recover the amount of the instrument from the maker.[9]

While the holder of a dishonored instrument usually seeks to hold the last indorser liable, the holder is not limited to such a proceeding. For example, in the above case, if, upon dishonor, H *gives proper notice* to X, Y, and Z, he can then "skip" Y and Z if he wishes and bring suit directly against X, the first indorser.

Liability of Accommodation Indorsers

Sometimes a person will indorse an instrument merely for the purpose of lending his or her credit to the instrument. Such a person is an **accommodation indorser.** To illustrate: P is the holder of a check of which she is the payee, and she wishes to cash it at a bank where she is unknown. At the bank's suggestion P asks A, an acquaintance who is a local merchant and depositor at the bank, to indorse the check along with her. A does so, becoming an accommodation indorser; the bank then cashes the check, giving the amount of the instrument to P in cash. (In this case, P is known as the *accommodated party.*)

In general, an accommodation indorser has the same liability to subsequent holders as does any other indorser. The accommodation indorser has both conditional and warranty liability to any subsequent holder (including a holder who knew that he or she was signing merely as an accommodation indorser). Once there is a dishonor of the instrument and proper notice is given to the accommodation indorser, that person is immediately liable to the holder. That is, the holder does not have to bring suit against the primary party in an effort to obtain payment before initiating action against the accommodation indorser.

DISCHARGE OF THE PARTIES

Examination of the rules regarding the liability of secondary parties has already presented several situations in which these parties are discharged—such as failure to make a required presentment or failure to give a notice of dishonor. Now we will briefly describe additional ways in which parties to commercial paper can be discharged.

Discharge by Payment

The vast majority of negotiable instruments are discharged by payment. Under Secs. 3-601(1)(a) and 3-603, payment in good faith to the holder by a primary party or by the drawee of an unaccepted draft or check usually discharges all parties on the instrument. Payment by any other party, such as an indorser, only discharges the indorser and subsequent parties on the instrument. In such a case, the party making payment can still seek recovery from prior parties on the instrument.

If a payment is less than the amount owed, the party making the payment is discharged only to the extent of the payment, as determined by the rules of debt settlement (see Chapter 12). Under Sec. 3-604, if a party tenders payment, but it is refused, the party is not discharged from liability.

---

[9] It is only *presumed* that the indorsers are liable in the order in which their signatures appear; a contrary agreement may exist among the indorsers. In the example above, X will not be liable to Y if she can prove that such an agreement existed between her and Y at the time of her indorsement.

However, the holder cannot later recover interest from the time of the tender; nor can he or she recover legal costs or attorney's fees.

Alteration

Under Sec. 3-407, alteration of an instrument by a holder discharges any party whose obligation is affected by the alteration, except that a holder in due course can enforce the instrument according to its original terms.

Cancellation and Renunciation

Section 3-605(1)(a) reads as follows: "(1) The holder of an instrument may even without consideration discharge any party (a) in any manner apparent on the face of the instrument or the indorsement, as by intentionally cancelling the instrument or the party's signature by destruction or mutilation, or by striking out the party's signature." To illustrate: Marking an instrument "paid" constitutes a cancellation of the instrument itself, as does intentional destruction or mutilation of it. Similarly, striking out a party's indorsement cancels that party's liability (but not the liability of prior parties). Under Sec. 3-605(1)(b), *renunciation* occurs when a holder gives up his or her rights against a party to the instrument in a particular way—either by renouncing them in a signed writing given to such party or by surrendering the instrument to that party.

Discharge of a Prior Party

As a general rule, the intentional cancellation of an instrument discharges all parties to it. Additionally, the discharge of a *particular party* by cancellation or renunciation normally discharges that party and all subsequent parties. These results flow from Sec. 3-606, which provides in part that "the holder discharges any party to the instrument" when he or she "releases or agrees not to sue any person whom [that] party has a right of recourse against." To illustrate: A note bears three indorsements: X, Y,

and Z, in that order. If the holder, H, gives a valid release to the first indorser, X, both subsequent indorsers, Y and Z, are thereby discharged. It is possible, however, for H in such a situation to release X but to expressly "reserve his rights" against Y and Z. If this occurs, and if H later collects the amount of the instrument from either Y or Z, then that party still retains the right of recourse against X, the first indorser. Thus H's release of X, where he reserves his rights against subsequent indorsers, does not insulate X from liability to the subsequent indorsers.

Discharge by Reacquisition

If a person acquires an instrument that he or she had held at a prior time, all intervening indorsers are discharged as against the reacquiring party and as against subsequent holders who do not qualify as holders in due course. To illustrate: P indorses a note to A, and A indorses it to B. If P reacquires the note, indorsers A and B are freed of all liability to P. And if P thereafter recirculates the instrument, A and B will have liability to subsequent holders only if such holders are HDCs.

SUMMARY

The primary parties to commercial paper are the makers of notes and acceptors of drafts. Both such parties admit (guarantee) the existence of the payee, and the payee's capacity to indorse. Of much more importance, however, is the promissory liability of makers and acceptors. Assuming they have no defenses against the holder of an instrument, their promises to pay are absolute—i.e., their liability is not extinguished by a late presentment for payment. To this there is one limited exception: if an instrument is payable at a designated bank, and if the bank fails between the time presentment should have been made and the time of the late presentment, the maker or acceptor may discharge his or her liability by giving the holder an assignment of his or her rights against the bank in respect to the funds held in the bank for payment.

Secondary parties are drawers of drafts and checks, and indorsers of all instruments. Such parties, like makers and acceptors, make certain guarantees about the instrument, and also have promissory liability. This promissory liability, however, unlike that of makers and acceptors, is conditional in nature; that is, they promise to pay the holder the amount of the instrument only upon the occurrence of three events: (1) a presentment for payment to the maker or drawee-acceptor; (2) a dishonor by such party; and (3) receipt of notice of dishonor. In that regard, however, the promissory liability of the drawer differs markedly from that of an indorser. While it is true that the drawer cannot be held liable until the three specified events occur, a late presentment—followed by dishonor and notice of dishonor—does not discharge the drawer from his or her promissory liability (except in the rare case where the drawee fails prior to the time of the late presentment). By contrast, assuming there is no waiver of presentment, dishonor, and notice, a late presentment automatically frees the indorser of his or her promissory liability.

Turning to the subject of warranty liability, the UCC provides that all persons who negotiate an instrument by indorsement (and who receive consideration for the indorsement) make four primary warranties to the indorsee and to all subsequent holders. Such indorsers warrant that (1) he or she has good title to the instrument; (2) all signatures and indorsements on the instrument at the time of indorsement are genuine or authorized; (3) the instrument has not been materially altered; and (4) no defense of any party is good against him or her (the indorser). If there is a breach of any of these guarantees resulting in failure of the indorsee or subsequent holder to obtain payment from the maker or drawee-acceptor, the indorser is liable in damages to such person. The warranty liability of the qualified ("without recourse") indorser is the same as that of the unqualified indorser, except that, as to warranty 4, the warranty is that he or she has *no knowledge* of any existing defenses.

Finally, the warranty liability of an indorser, unlike his or her promissory liability, is not extinguished by a late presentment for payment.

KEY TERMS

Primary parties
Secondary parties
Promissory liability
Warranty liability
Accommodation indorser

QUESTIONS AND PROBLEMS

1. A promissory note was signed by three makers, as follows: "Leo Palmer; George Johnson, Secy; Hubert Alligood." All three men were officers of a corporation for whose benefit the note was issued, but the name of the corporation did not appear anywhere on the instrument. When the instrument was not paid at maturity, the payee-holder brought suit against Johnson personally. As a defense, Johnson offered evidence showing that the plaintiff knew, when he received the instrument, that Johnson was simply signing as a representative of the corporation. Should this evidence be allowed? Why or why not? (*Kramer v. Johnson,* 176 S.E.2d 108, 1970.)

2. A promissory note was issued by the Gold Company, payable to the order of X, and bears the following signatures as makers: (a) "The Gold Company, by George Blue, President," and (b) "Derek Vance." The note was subsequently negotiated by X to the Last National Bank. When the note was not paid at maturity, the bank sought to hold Vance personally liable on it. At the trial, Vance offered evidence showing that the payee, X, knew that he (Vance) was secretary-treasurer of the Gold Company, and that he also knew that Vance was simply signing as a representative of the company. Should this evidence be admitted? Explain why or why not.

3. As part of a real estate transaction, a $20,000 check was issued by Francis Kirby, of which he was the drawer. When difficulties about the transaction arose later, the holder of the check telephoned the drawee bank to find out whether Kirby had sufficient funds in his account to cover the check. A bookkeeper of the bank replied that the funds were insufficient. In subsequent litigation, the question arose as to whether the holder's inquiry to the bank constituted a valid "presentment for payment" under the UCC. Do you think the telephone call was a valid presentment? Why or why not? (*Kirby v. Bergfield,* 182 N.W.2d 205, 1970.)

4. Lucile Fisher was an accommodation indorser of a check that was drawn on a Missouri bank. The check was cashed by the payee at the Nevada State Bank (which was also Fisher's bank). The check was put in the channels of collection by the Nevada State Bank, but was "lost in transit" for almost three months before it finally reached the drawee bank in Missouri. At this time the instrument was dishonored by the drawee bank because of insufficient funds in the drawer's account. The drawee bank promptly returned the check to the Nevada State Bank, which gave Fisher notice of dishonor the next day. When the Nevada State Bank sought to hold Fisher liable as indorser, she contended that she was freed of liability in view of the fact that ninety days had elapsed between the time she indorsed the check and the time she was given notice of dishonor by the Nevada State Bank. Do you agree with this contention? Explain. (*Nevada State Bank v. Fisher,* 565 P.2d 332, 1977.)

5. M was the maker of a $5,000 note issued in 1985, due "June 1, 1987." The note was payable at the XYZ Bank. The holder of the note presented it for payment on June 1, 1987, only to learn for the first time that the bank had failed three months earlier. In a suit by the holder against M, M proved that he lost 50 percent of his money that was in the bank when it failed—assuming that for some reason federal deposit insurance did not cover the loss—and he argues that he is thus liable to the holder only in the amount of $2,500. Is M correct? Why or why not?

6. A corporation issues a note payable to the order of X. The note is stolen from X, and the thief forges X's indorsement on the back. The thief transfers the note to Y, an innocent purchaser, who indorses it "without recourse, Y" and transfers it to Z. The corporation refuses to pay the note after learning of the forgery of X's name, whereupon Z sues Y, the qualified indorser, claiming breach of warranty of title. Y claims he is not liable because he had no knowledge of the forgery whatever. Is this a good defense? Why or why not?

7. D draws a check "payable to bearer" and issues it to X. X negotiates it to H the next day by delivery only (without indorsing it) and H immediately presents the check to the drawee bank for payment. If the check is dishonored because of insufficient funds and if H gives X prompt notice of the dishonor, is X liable to H? Explain.

8. A note held by H bears the successive indorsements of Alpha (payee), Bravo, and Charlie. The note is not paid at maturity, whereupon H talks his old friend Bravo into taking up the instrument (Bravo pays the full amount of the note to H, who returns it to Bravo). What effect, if any, does this have on the liability of (a) the maker, (b) Alpha, and (c) Charlie?

Chapter 28

COMMERCIAL PAPER
Checks and the Bank-Depositor Relationship

While checks are simply one type of commercial paper, they do possess certain characteristics that set them apart from promissory notes and drafts. Although some of these special aspects have been discussed in prior chapters, others have not. In this chapter we will first summarize the special attributes of checks and then examine the legal relationship existing between the drawer of a check and the **drawee bank** (the bank on which the check is drawn).[1] A brief look at the subject of electronic banking and the basic federal law applicable to its various facets—the Electronic Funds Transfer Act—concludes the chapter.

CHECKS

Under Sec. 3-104 of the UCC, a check is by definition "a draft drawn on a bank payable on demand." (The *demand* requirement thus means that a "postdated check"—for instance, one issued to the payee on March 10 but dated April 5—is, technically speaking, a draft rather than a check. The primary consequence of postdating is that the drawee bank should not honor the instrument until the specified date arrives.)

Checks generally have a shorter life than other instruments and thus circulate more quickly than ordinary drafts and promissory notes. This is reflected in Sec. 3-503, which provides that (1) for the drawer of a check, it is presumed that a reasonable time for presentment is to be no more than thirty days after issue, and (2) for an indorser, presumably only seven days after the indorsement.

In regard to the thirty-day provision, the general rule for drawers of drafts—that a late presentment excuses them of liability only if they have suffered a loss as a result of the delay—

is illustrated as it specifically applies to checks: D draws and issues a check to P on March 1; after several negotiations the check is presented by H, the last holder, to the drawee bank on June 18. Payment is refused at that time (perhaps because D has insufficient funds in her account or because a creditor of D, through legal proceedings, has attached D's funds in the bank). In this case, though presentment has been made more than two months after the thirty-day deadline (March 31), D remains fully liable to H on the instrument *unless* the drawee bank failed after March 31 and before the late presentment on June 18. In that limited situation D can discharge her liability by giving an assignment of funds to H in the amount of the instrument, in the same manner that the maker of a note payable at a bank can—see Chapter 27.

A Check Is Not an Assignment of Funds

As a practical matter, checks are drawn (and received by the payee and subsequent holders) on the assumption that the drawer has funds in his or her account at the drawee bank sufficient to pay the instrument when it is presented. In the great majority of instances this is, in fact, the case. Federal Reserve Board figures indicate that of every thousand checks drawn, only six or seven are dishonored because of insufficient funds.

Despite the likelihood that a given check will actually be honored, under Sec. 3-409 the issuance of a check does not constitute an "assignment of funds" in the drawee bank. Until final payment is made by the drawee bank, the issuance and circulation of the instrument have no effect on the funds in the drawer's account; nor do they discharge the underlying debt in payment for which it was issued.

Thus, while a check may be accepted by the payee in payment of a debt owed by the drawer, and while the payee may even give the drawer a receipt marked "paid in full," the receipt is conditional upon the check actually being honored by the drawee bank when presented. The same thing is true for bank credits. Thus where a

---

[1] As indicated in Chapter 24, proposed amendments to Articles 3 and 4 of the UCC which may effect some changes in the bank-depositor relationship are in the drafting stage. Because neither the final text nor ultimate disposition of these amendments can be predicted, this chapter is based on the present form of Articles 3 and 4.

payee deposits a check in his or her account in a bank (the depositary bank) and receives credit for the deposit, and that bank forwards the check to an intermediary bank which credits the depositary bank's account, the entire process is reversed if the drawee bank dishonors the check. That is, the check is returned to the payee through the same channels, each bank charging its transferor bank with the amount of the instrument. Ultimately the check is returned to the depositary bank, which charges the account of its depositor, the payee, with the amount of the check and returns it to him or her. The payee can then sue the drawer on the check or on the underlying debt itself.

Certification of Checks

In our discussion of drafts we noted that checks (unlike many drafts) are not presented for acceptance. However, they are occasionally presented to the drawee bank for *certification;* if certification is made, the bank's liability is the same as that of the acceptor of a draft.

One of the most common uses of a **certified check** is where a seller of goods, such as a used car dealer, is selling to a buyer with whom he or she has had no business dealings. In such a case the seller will probably want the buyer to have his or her personal check certified before taking it in payment. From a practical standpoint the primary result of certification is that the seller no longer has to worry that the check will be dishonored because of insufficient funds. Frequently, certified checks are required by law from purchasers of real estate at sheriff's sales, and occasionally they are required from persons who are paying fees owed to a state or state agency.

Mechanics and Effect: In the absence of a special agreement, a bank has no legal duty to certify a check drawn on it; its only duty is to pay the holder in conformity with the terms of the instrument. A bank that accedes to a request for certification does so by stamping the word *certified* on the face of the check, together with the

name of the bank and the date, and including the handwritten signature or initials of the officer making the certification. At that time the bank charges the drawer's account with the amount of the check and transfers the funds to its certified check account.

Certification has three basic effects:

1. The certifying bank is now primarily liable on the instrument (it absolutely promises to pay the instrument when it is presented for payment).

2. The certification of a check at the request of a holder discharges the drawer and any indorsers who indorsed prior to certification. To illustrate: A check drawn by D is issued to P; P indorses it to H, and H obtains certification from the drawee bank. At this point D (the drawer) and P (the indorser) are released of all liability on the instrument. On the other hand, if the *drawer* requests the certification, he or she remains secondarily liable; that is, in the unlikely event that the certifying bank subsequently cannot or will not honor the check when it is presented for payment, the drawer is liable to the holder. (While it is unlikely that any indorsements will appear on the instrument when certification is requested by the drawer, if there are any, the same rule applies to the indorsers; like the drawer, they are not released of secondary liability by the certification.)

3. Once a check is certified, the drawer no longer has the right to stop payment on it. This is true no matter who obtained the certification. (UCC Sec. 4-403, comment 5.)

Revocation of Certification: Under pre-UCC law a bank had the right to revoke a certification (sometimes called the right to "uncertify") if it could show that certification was obtained by fraud or made under a mistake of fact on its part—provided that the holder at the time of revocation had not substantially changed his or her position in reliance on the certification. This is still the general rule today, with one modification. Because Sec. 3-418 provides that "payment or acceptance of any instrument is final in favor of a holder in due course," it is probable that revocation cannot be made if the holder at the time of attempted revocation qualifies as an HDC, regardless of whether that person had changed his or her position subsequent to the certification.

THE BANK-DEPOSITOR RELATIONSHIP

A bank may be liable to a depositor or a depositor liable to a bank solely through Article 3 of the UCC (dealing with commercial paper). However, the bank-depositor relationship is a broad one; thus many of the general rights and duties of the two parties spring from several sources in addition to that article. These sources include the following:

1. A *creditor-debtor relationship* exists between the depositor and the drawee bank, and sometimes the bank's obligations are essentially those of debtors generally.

2. In some transactions a *principal-agent relationship* exists between the depositor and the bank, and in these situations the bank has the same obligations as those imposed on all agents— for example, the duty to use reasonable care and the duty not to profit at the principal's expense.

3. In many situations involving controversies between the depositor and the bank, specific sections of Article 4 of the UCC (dealing with bank deposits and collections) enter the picture.

We begin our discussion by stating the primary duties of a bank. We will then examine some specific situations that commonly cause bank-depositor controversies.

The Bank's Duties

Duty to Honor Orders: The drawee bank is generally obligated to honor checks drawn by the depositor so long as he or she has sufficient funds in the account and has not stopped pay-

ment.[2] The bank's failure to honor a check usually makes it liable to the depositor, under ordinary breach of contract principles, for damages resulting from the refusal to pay. (As we will see in more detail later, the bank also is obligated to obey the stop payment orders of its drawers.)

Stale Checks: The duty to honor checks is not absolute, however. For example, the bank obviously does not have to honor checks if there are not sufficient funds in the drawer's account. The bank also does not have to honor **stale checks.** UCC Sec. 4-404 provides that "a bank is under no obligation to a customer having a checking account to pay a check, other than a certified check, which is presented more than six months after its date, but it may charge its customer's account for a payment made thereafter in good faith." This section suggests that a drawee bank presented with a check beyond the six-month time limit should secure a confirmation from the drawer before honoring it; failure to do so raises at least the possibility that the bank might not be able to show "good faith" in making the payment. (But see the *Granite Equipment Leasing Corp.* case later in the chapter for a fuller discussion of the good faith requirement.)

Duty to Pay after Death of Drawer: While the general rule under common law is that the death of a principal automatically terminates the authority of the agent to act on his or her behalf, the drafters of the UCC have taken a different position on checks. Section 4-405 provides in essence that the death of a customer (drawer) does not revoke the bank's authority to pay that customer's checks "until the bank knows of the fact of death . . . and has reasonable opportunity to act on it." Since the bank might not actually know of a customer's death for a long time after

---

[2] A bank can, if it wishes, honor a drawer's check even if there are insufficient funds in the drawer's account. In such a case an *overdraft* is created, and the bank has the right to recover from the drawer the amount of the overdraft.

it has occurred (possibly weeks or even months), if it honors any of the customer's checks during this period, it is generally not liable to the drawer's estate for funds so paid out.

A second provision of Sec. 4-405 pertains to a different situation—where the bank does receive notice of the drawer's death soon after it has occurred. In this case the drawee bank still has the right to honor checks for a limited time. Section 4-405(2) provides: "Even with knowledge [of death] a bank may for ten days after the date of death pay or certify checks drawn on or prior to that date unless ordered to stop payment by a person claiming an interest in the account."

Duty to Pay on Only Genuine or Authorized Signatures: As we will see in more detail later in the chapter, a drawee bank that honors a check bearing a forged drawer's signature cannot legally charge the purported drawer's account even if the bank did not know of the forgery when it honored the instrument. Thus, if D's signature is forged to a check drawn on the X Bank, and that bank subsequently honors the instrument by paying a holder and charging D's account, D, upon discovery of the forgery, can require the bank to recredit her account in the amount of the instrument.

Duty to Use Reasonable Care as Agent: A bank has the duty to use reasonable care in handling commercial paper when acting as an agent for a depositor. This relationship is usually created when a bank's customer deposits in his or her own account a check drawn by a third party (often on some other bank). In such a case, under Sec. 4-201(1), it is presumed that the bank receiving the check is taking it simply as agent for its depositor rather than purchasing it outright—and this presumption continues even if the bank permits the depositor to make immediate withdrawals against it. As a result of this relationship, the bank owes the depositor (among other things) the duty to use reasonable care in handling and forwarding the instrument through the bank collection process.

The following case invited a Pennsylvania appellate court to make forays into such varied but related matters as the law of bailments, the legality of "exculpatory clauses" in general, and the great public necessity for competent (nonnegligent) banking services.

Phillips Home Furnishings, Inc. v. Continental Bank
Superior Court of Pennsylvania, 331 A.2d 845 (1974)

On the evening of June 16, 1973, Max Shectman prepared a bank deposit of $5,669 in receipts from his business, Phillips Home Furnishings, Inc. He then picked up his wife at her place of employment and proceeded to an office of Continental Bank, where he had done his banking for thirty years. Upon arriving at the bank, he placed his deposit in the bank's night depository safe in the wall of the bank building and returned home. Five days later, having received no confirmation of his deposit, Shectman phoned the bank, only to learn that it had no record of the deposit and no explanation of what might have happened to it. (At the subsequent trial, the two employees who had opened the safe the morning after the deposit was made filed affidavits in which they stated that no bag belonging to Shectman was found).

When Shectman made further inquiries of the bank, one of its officers showed him a copy of the "night depository agreement" he had signed a year earlier. That agreement stated in part:

Bank grants to the undersigned the privilege of using the Night Depository gratuitously and solely as an accommodation to the undersigned; and the exercise of the privilege by the undersigned will be at the sole risk of the undersigned. Bank will employ such safeguards . . . as it deems proper, [but] without any liability to the undersigned for their sufficiency. . . . Bank shall be under no liability with respect to anything placed in the Night Depository, except for the amount of cash and checks actually taken into its possession upon opening the Night Depository Safe.

The bank, relying upon this agreement, refused to credit Shectman's account. He then brought action to recover damages for the bank's failure to credit the amount. The lower court found the night depository agreement to be legal and binding, and it entered judgment for the bank. Shectman appealed.

Jacobs, Justice:

. . . The first issue thus presented is whether a bank may contractually absolve itself from all liability in connection with the use of a night depository facility, so that its customers are required to use the facility at their own risk. Other courts which have examined this question have concluded that there is nothing inherently wrong with permitting a bank to make its Night Depository Service available under terms and conditions which place the risk of loss on the customer. The courts in these cases find no reason in law or social policy why a bank cannot make the facility available on those terms and conditions mutually agreed upon.

In Pennsylvania, however, the rule has developed . . . that the bailor-bailee relationship is one in which the law will protect the former party from attempts by the latter to exculpate himself from the consequences of his own negligence. This rule is particularly applicable here because neither party disputes that the relationship was one of bailment. . . . In *Downs v. Sley System Garages*, 194 A. 772, we stated the "well-recognized rule . . . that a bailee cannot relieve himself of a liability for his own negligence." . . .

We, however, will not rest our decision upon so thin a reed, because we find a much stronger foundation in the bank-customer relationship and the public policy which encircles it and similar relationships.

[The court then conceded that exculpatory clauses were lawful in certain circumstances, and continued:] However, the law also recognized that lying behind these contracts is a residuum of public policy which is antagonistic to carte blanche exculpation from liability, . . . and thus developed the rule that these provisions would be strictly construed . . . against the party seeking their protection. . . . Where a disparity of bargaining power has grown out of economic necessity for certain goods or services or from a monopolistic position of a seller, courts have found exculpatory clauses inimical to the public interest. Where an agreement does not represent a free choice on the part of the plaintiff, where he is forced to accept the clause by the necessities of his situation, *courts have refused to enforce such agreements as contrary to public policy.* [Emphasis added.] . . .

In Pennsylvania, both the courts and the legislature have implicitly agreed that the public necessity for banking services belies the concept that the bank-customer relationship is one of equal parties evenly bargaining. [The court then noted that the position of banks was similar to that of common carriers and cited Pennsylvania cases in which it was held: "This court has consistently decided that it is against public policy to permit a common carrier to limit its liability for its own negligence." The court also noted that Sec. 4-103 of the UCC prevents a bank from disclaiming or limiting its liability for lack of good faith or failure to exercise ordinary care in connection with bank deposits and collections.]

We, therefore, . . . hold that a bank cannot contractually exculpate itself from the consequences of its own negligence or lack of good faith in the performance of any of its banking functions. We find the public need for professional and competent banking services too great, and the legitimate and justifiable reliance upon the integrity and safety of financial institutions too strong, to permit a bank to contract away its liability [in the manner attempted here].

[The court then reversed the judgment of the lower court and remanded the case with instructions that further evidence be considered bearing on the question of whether the bank was in fact guilty of negligence.]

The Depositor's Duties

The depositor has the general obligation to keep sufficient funds in his or her checking account to permit the bank to honor all checks drawn on the account. In this respect the drawer of a check has a greater potential liability than the drawer of a draft. The drawer of a draft is liable only in a civil action to the holder of a draft where it is not paid by the drawee at maturity. The drawer of a check, however, has not only civil liability but also criminal liability for writing a "bad" check (if it is proved that the drawer issued the check with the intent to defraud). Under the statutes of many states there is a presumption of intent to defraud if the drawer does not "make good" to the holder of the check within a specified number of days after the dishonor occurs. Finally, as we will see in more detail later in the chapter, a depositor owes his or her bank the general duty to report forgeries and alterations within a reasonable length of time after he or she knows, or should know, of them.

SELECTED BANK-DEPOSITOR PROBLEMS

Stop Payment Orders

As we have indicated, it is possible for the drawer of a check to countermand the order contained in it by issuing the drawee bank a **stop payment order.** The purpose of this, of course, is to prevent the payee or other holder from receiving immediate payment from the bank. Usually the stop payment order is given only after the drawer discovers some default on the part of the payee (such as fraud or the delivery of defective goods under a sales contract) or after the check has been lost.[3] The order is binding for only a limited time period. Section 4-403(2) provides that "an oral order is binding upon the bank only for fourteen calendar days unless confirmed in writing within that period. A written order is effective for only six months unless renewed in writing."

1. What is the effect of such an order on the drawer?

2. What is the bank's liability in the event that it fails to obey the order?

Effect of Stop Payment Order on Drawer: Assuming that a stop payment order is given in time to permit the bank to act on it, the immediate effect is that the holder of the check fails to obtain payment when he or she presents it to the drawee bank. This does not necessarily mean, however, that the drawer is freed of liability on the instrument.

If the payee, after being refused payment, brings suit against the drawer, he or she may be above to prove that the drawer had no legal grounds for stopping payment; that is, the court may determine that the drawer had no assertable defense against the payee. In such case the payee is entitled to recover the amount of the instrument in full. The drawer also might have liability in a situation where he or she does in fact have a personal defense against the payee but where the holder who was refused payment qualifies as an HDC. In a suit against the drawer such a holder would also be entitled to full payment of the instrument.

Even in these instances the stop payment order is of some benefit to the drawer, for it at least assures him or her of the right to present, in a court proceeding, any reason for believing that the holder is not entitled to payment. And, of course, in many such proceedings the drawer can prove an assertable defense and escape all liability to the holder-plaintiff.

Bank's Liability for Disobeying Stop Payment Order: If the drawee bank honors a check after a valid stop payment order has been issued against it, the bank is liable to the drawer for any loss he or she suffers by reason of the wrongful payment. However, if the drawer has to bring legal action against the bank in order to have the account recredited in the amount of the check, he or she has the burden of proving the amount of loss.

Often it is not difficult for the drawer to prove that he or she suffered a loss. Such is the case where the payee obtained payment and the drawer is able to establish clearly that he or she had either a personal or real defense that could have been asserted against the payee. In this situation, if the stop payment order had been obeyed by the bank, it is obvious that the payee would never have been able to enforce the instrument against the drawer. The result is that the bank must recredit the drawer's account in the amount of the check.[4]

In some situations, however, the bank may be able to show that the drawer did *not* suffer a loss as a result of its failure to honor the stop payment order. Such is the case where, in the suit by the drawer against the bank, the facts are that the drawer did not have a defense of any kind against the payee. In this situation no loss was incurred by the drawer, because even if the stop payment order had been obeyed by the bank, the payee would still have been entitled to payment on the check (by legal action against the drawer, if necessary). The payee therefore had the right to the proceeds of the check in any event, and the drawer's suit against the bank will thus fail. The same result will occur (in the suit by the drawer against the bank) if it is determined that although the drawer had a personal defense against the payee, the person who obtained pay-

---

[3]We are speaking throughout this section of *uncertified checks*. Once a check has been certified, at the request of either the drawer or a holder, no stop payment order can thereafter be effective.

[4]Written stop payment orders sometimes contain clauses to the effect that the drawer agrees not to hold the drawee bank liable if it should honor the check "through inadvertence or oversight." Such disclaimers are generally invalid. Section 4-103(1) provides in part that "no agreement can disclaim a bank's responsibility for its own lack of good faith or failure to exercise ordinary care" in a particular transaction.

Figure 28.1 Bank's Liability for Disobeying Stop Order

Example 1.

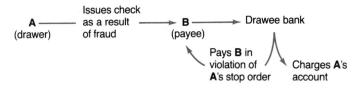

Bank need not recredit **A**'s account.
Fraud is a personal defense
and not good against HDC; therefore,
A has suffered no loss.

Example 2.

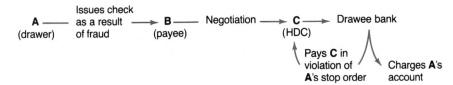

Bank must recredit **A**'s account.
A has a defense that
is good against **B**; therefore **A**
has suffered a loss. Bank would be subrogated to **A**'s rights against **B** [UCC Sec. 4-407 (c)].

ment was a holder in due course—someone to whom the payee had negotiated the instrument and who met all the HDC requirements. These rules are illustrated in Figure 28.1.

The following case is particularly instructive in that it raises two important questions: (1) Is a bank generally free to honor a check after a stop payment order has expired, and (2) if so, does it have this right even when the check is presented several months after the expiration?

Granite Equipment Leasing Corp. v. Hempstead Bank
New York Supreme Court, Nassau
County, 326 N.Y.S.2d 881 (1971)

Granite Equipment Leasing Corp. kept a checking account with Hempstead Bank. On October 10, 1968, Granite drew a check payable to Overseas Equipment Co., Inc. After Overseas advised that the check had not been received, Granite wrote the bank on October 15, 1968, to *stop payment* on it. On that same day Granite authorized the bank to

wire the funds to the payee in the same amount as the stopped check, and the bank did so. Granite did not renew its stop payment order. On November 10, 1969, without notice or inquiry to Granite, the bank accepted the check on which payment had been stopped the year before, paid the indicated funds to a collecting bank, and charged Granite's account.

Granite then sought to recover the amount of the check from the defendant, Hempstead Bank. The bank defended on the ground that, under UCC Sec. 4-403, the stop payment order had expired for want of renewal and that, acting in good faith, it was entitled under UCC Sec. 4-404 to pay the stale check.

Harnett, Justice (of the trial court):

. . . Under the Uniform Commercial Code, does a bank have a duty of inquiry before paying a stale check? Does it matter that the stale check had been previously stopped under a stop payment order which expired for lack of renewal? So this case goes.

[The court here stated the facts, and continued:]

There is no doubt the check is stale. There is no doubt the stop payment order was properly given at the outset, and that it was never renewed. Granite essentially maintains the bank had a duty to inquire into the circumstances of that stale check, and should not have paid in face of a known lapsed stop order without consulting its depositor.

The UCC, which became effective in New York on September 27, 1964, provides that:

(1) A customer may by order to his bank stop payment of any item payable for his account . . . (2) . . . A written [stop] order is effective for only six months unless renewed in writing. UCC Sec. 4-403.

The Official Comment to UCC Sec. 4-403 notes that:

the purpose of the [six-month limit] is, of course, to facilitate stopping payment by clearing the records of the drawee of accumulated unrevoked stop orders, as where the drawer has found a lost instrument or has settled his controversy with the payee, but has failed to notify the drawee. . . .

. . . Granite cannot be permitted to predicate liability on the part of the bank on its failure to inquire about and find a stop payment order which had become terminated in default of renewal. *Feller v. Manufacturers Trust Co.,* 4 NY2d 951, held that a drawee bank was not liable to a drawer for payment of a check two months after expiration of a stop payment order which had not been renewed. See also, *William Savage, Inc. v. Manufacturers Trust Co.,* 20 Misc2d 114, holding a bank not liable for payment on an eleven month old check after expiration of a stop payment order.

Neither may Granite predicate a claim of liability upon the bank's payment of a stale check. The legal principles applicable to this circumstance are codified in UCC Sec. 4-404, which provides that:

a bank is under no obligation . . . to pay a check, other than a certified check, which is presented more than six months after its date, but it may charge its customer's account for a payment made thereafter in good faith. *[Emphasis supplied.]*

[After overruling a cited case, the court continued:] There is no obligation under the statute on the bank to search its records to discover old lapsed stop payment orders. The bank does not have to pay a stale check, but it may pay one in "good faith." Significantly, UCC Sec. 1-201(19) defines "good faith" as "honesty in fact in the conduct or transaction concerned." In the absence of any facts which could justify a finding of dishonesty, bad faith, recklessness, or lack of ordinary care, in the fact of circumstances actually known, or which should have been known, the bank is not liable to Granite for its payment of the check drawn to Overseas.

One statute invalidates stop payment orders not renewed within six months. Another statute allows payment in good faith of stale checks. Granite cannot combine the two statutes to reach a synergistic result not contemplated by either separately.

Granite's complete remedy lies in its pending Florida action against Overseas to recover the extra payment.

Judgment in favor of defendant dismissing the complaint.

Payment on a Forged Indorsement

If a drawee bank honors a depositor's check that bears a *forged indorsement,* the bank must recredit the drawer's account upon his or her discovery and notification of the forgery. To illustrate: D draws a check on the X Bank payable to the order of P. The check is stolen from P by T, and T forges P's indorsement on the back of the instrument. Thereafter T negotiates the instrument to Y, and Y obtains payment from the X Bank, which has no knowledge of the forgery. The bank then charges D's account and returns the check to D at the end of the month along with D's other cancelled checks. If D later learns of the forged indorsement and notifies the bank within a reasonable time after this discovery, *the bank must recredit D's account in the amount of the check*; the bank in this case has obviously paid out the money to a person who was not the holder of the instrument. Usually the bank will recredit the account voluntarily; but if it does not, under Sec. 3-419(1) and (2) the drawer can bring an action of conversion against it to recover the amount of the check.

Bank's Rights against Surrendering Party: Since it is the bank rather than the drawer who initially suffers the loss in the case of a forged indorsement, the question arises whether the bank can recover payment from the person who surrendered the check to it for payment (Y in the above illustration). The general rule is that the bank can recover, even if the persons who surrendered the instrument for payment did not know of the forgery. Section 4-207(1)(a) provides that a customer "who obtains payment or acceptance of an item . . . warrants to the payor bank . . . that (a) he has good title to the item." Obviously, a person who surrenders an instrument for payment with a forged indorsement does not have title, so he or she is liable to the drawee bank in the amount of the check on the breach of warranty theory. (After making good to the bank, the person who surrendered the instrument can, of course, proceed against the forger, if that individual can be found.)

Payment on a Forged Drawer's Signature

A somewhat different situation is presented when the drawee bank honors a check on which the *drawer's signature* is a forgery. To illustrate: F, forger, draws a check on the Z Bank payable to the order of himself and forging the signature of G, one of the bank's depositors, as the drawer. F indorses the check to H, and H presents the check to the X Bank for payment. The X Bank, not knowing of the forgery, honors the instrument and charges G's account. At the end of the month the forged check is returned to G along with his other cancelled checks.

At this point, assuming that the forgery had occurred without any negligence on the part of G and that G has promptly notified the bank of the forgery, the bank must *recredit G's account in the amount of the check.* This is true because (1) a forged signature is wholly inoperative and (2) a drawee bank is presumed to know the signatures of its depositors. (The latter is based in part on the fact that when a depositor opens a checking account, he or she signs a signature card that is held by the bank and that can be used to determine whether the checks subsequently presented to the bank in the depositor's name are genuine.)

Negligent Drawer: The rule that the drawee bank is liable to its depositor in the case of forgery does not apply if the bank can show that the drawer was guilty of negligence that substantially contributed to the forgery.

Two primary situations exist in which negligence on the part of the drawer may be found to exist:

1. If the drawer (usually a corporation in this instance) signs its checks by means of a mechanical check writer, it may be shown that the drawer failed to use reasonable care in preventing unauthorized persons from gaining access to the machine. For example, if the device is left in an area where it is readily accessible to a large number of employees and the forgery is made by one of these employees, the drawer cannot require the bank to recredit its account.

2. It has long been established that a customer owes to the drawee bank the duty of examining his or her cancelled checks within a reasonable time after they have been returned to discover if any of the signatures are forgeries. If the person fails to do so, he or she may well be barred from holding the bank liable. This is especially true where a series of forgeries occurs after the initial one that went undetected.

Section 4-406(1) contains the basic provision requiring the drawer to "exercise reasonable care and promptness" in examining checks and statements. Section 4-406(2) sets forth specific rules that apply to various "failure to examine" situations. Because these subsections are difficult to understand in the abstract, we will present a hypothetical case along with the appropriate rules:

February 2—D, drawer, receives thirty cancelled checks from the drawee bank that have been charged against his account during the month of January. His signature has been forged on one check by E, an employee of D's who has access to D's printed check forms.

February 10—E forges another check and cashes it at the drawee bank.

March 2—this check is returned to D with others honored by the bank during February.

March 3 to March 31—E forges and cashes five more checks; these are also charged to D's account.

April 2—D receives all cancelled checks for the month of March, including the five forged checks.

On April 5, *D for the first time examines all the checks returned to him in February, March, and April.* He discovers the seven forgeries and immediately notifies the bank of them; later he asks the bank to recredit his account for all the forged checks. The bank refuses to do so, contending that it has no liability in view of D's failure to discover the first forgeries promptly.

In this situation D can probably hold the bank liable for the first two checks but not for the following five. Section 4-406(2)(b) states in essence that when a forged check is returned to the depositor and that person does not discover it within *fourteen days from the time of return,* he or she is "precluded from asserting" any *subsequent* forgeries against the bank that are forged "by the same wrongdoer." Thus, since the first forged check was returned to D on February 2, he had until February 16 to give the bank notice in order to protect himself against subsequent forgeries. Since he did not meet this deadline, the liability for the forged checks that were honored after that date is shifted from the bank to D.[5]

Bank's Rights against Surrendering Party: As seen earlier, if the drawer promptly examines his or her cancelled checks for forgeries and notifies the drawee bank of them, the bank rather than the drawer suffers the loss. The question then arises (as it did in the forged indorsement case) as to whether the bank can recover the amount of the check from the person who surrendered it for payment. The rule here (unlike that involving the forged indorsement) is that if the person did not know of the forged drawer's signature when receiving payment, the bank *cannot* hold him or her liable. Under Sec. 4-207(1)(b), a person who surrenders an instrument for payment guarantees to the drawee bank only that "he has *no knowledge* that the signature of the . . . drawer is unauthorized." (Emphasis added.) Thus, unless the bank can prove such knowledge, its only recourse is an action against the forger (if that person can be identified and located).

Payment on an Altered Check

While it happens rather rarely, it is possible that the amount of a check will be raised and the instrument will be presented to the drawee bank and paid in its altered form. To illustrate: N draws a check for $75, and P (payee) or a subsequent holder alters the amount—both figures and words—to $175. If the bank charges N's account with the full $175, N can recover from the bank the amount of the alteration—$100. The general rule is that the drawee bank can charge the drawer's account only with the original amount of the check.

The exception to this rule is similar to that involving the forged drawer's signature. If the drawee bank can establish negligence on the part of the drawer that substantially contributed to the alteration, then the drawer is barred from recovering the difference. Two common kinds of negligence follow:

1. One kind of negligence occurs where a drawer drafts an instrument so carelessly that it invites alteration. For example, the amount might be written in such a way that there is ample space to insert a digit before (or after) it. Or the place where the amount is to appear in words is left entirely blank.

2. Another kind of negligence occurs where the drawer does not inspect his or her cancelled checks within a reasonable time after they are returned and thus fails to give the bank the notice of alteration that it is entitled to receive. Under Sec. 4-406(1), (2), and (3), the drawer in this situation is barred from asserting the fact of alteration against the drawee bank—in the same circumstances and to the same extent as the drawer who negligently failed to detect forged signatures on his or her cancelled checks.

Bank's Rights against Surrendering Party: We have seen that where no negligence exists on the part of the drawer, the loss (the amount of

---

[5] As to the first two checks, since they had already been paid by the drawee bank before the February 16 deadline, it is probable that the bank could not shift its loss to the drawer—though Sec. 4-406(2)(a) keeps this possibility open in exceptional circumstances.

the alteration) is borne by the drawee bank. However, as a general rule, the bank is entitled to recover that loss from the person who surrendered the instrument for payment. Section 4-207(1)(c) provides that, with limited exceptions, a customer who obtains payment of an item warrants to the payor bank "that the item has not been materially altered." Thus the person who surrenders the check is usually liable on the breach of warranty theory even if he or she did not know of the alteration at the time of obtaining payment.

ELECTRONIC BANKING

Developments in computer technology have brought about a significant (and growing) phenomenon in recent years—the transfer of funds from one account to another electronically. As electronic fund transfers (**electronic banking**) increase in the years ahead, the use of checks will correspondingly decrease, and the rules applicable to electronic fund transfers will be of increasing importance insofar as the bank-depositor relationship is concerned. We will here note the most important developments in the area of electronic funds transfers and briefly summarize the basic federal law applicable to these transfers.

Types of Transfers

Automated Teller Machines: It is estimated that roughly half of the adults in the larger cities of the United States today have coded bank cards that enable them to use automated teller machines (ATMs). In these cities—and smaller ones, too—bank customers are becoming increasingly accustomed to using ATMs for such routine tasks as making withdrawals from checking accounts, making deposits in checking accounts, and transferring funds between savings and checking accounts. (The use of these "electronic branches" is not only a convenience to bank customers, but also constitutes an effort by banks to rein in their costs by reducing person-

nel and traditional branches. For example, Bank-America closed 120 of its branch offices in California in 1984, thereby reducing its work force by approximately 4,000.)

Point of Sale Terminals: Point of sale transfers occur when a customer in a retail store, after making a purchase, gives a bank card to the sales clerk, who passes it through a "reading machine" attached to the cash register. The customer then punches in his or her personal identification number (the same number used for entry to ATMs) on a keyboard. The cash register electronically charges the customer's account at the bank with the amount of the purchase, and electronically credits the store's account in the same amount. The transaction is verified by a "processing center," thus enabling the store to give the customer a receipt. (Point of sale transactions, if widely accepted, would be *the* single largest step towards our becoming a checkless society. However, point of sale purchasing has largely been carried on in only a few parts of the country since its introduction in 1984. And, on the basis of this use, customer acceptance of point of sale to date has been considerably less than originally expected.)

Home Shopping and Banking: What is sometimes called the ultimate step in electronic banking is home shopping and banking. This development, involving a "home information service" consisting of a television set and a personal computer, permits customers to pay bills, make purchases from cooperating retailers, and conduct most of their banking transactions from their own homes. The relevant fund transfers in all of these transactions would, again, be done electronically. (For example, in regard to home purchases, the amount of purchase is automatically charged to the buyer's bank account, and automatically credited to the seller's account.) This latest step in electronic banking is presently in a formative stage; for example, a consortium of six Ohio banks began operating a home information and banking service in mid-1984 on a test basis in selected areas of the state. (While early predictions were that 30% of U.S. households would have some form of home banking by 1988, that figure has recently been scaled back to 10%. Thus, because of such factors as cost and the "de-personalizing" of retail shopping, the ultimate impact of this development—like point of sale—remains to be seen.)

Electronic Funds Transfer Act

Electronic banking—even the simple use of ATMs—has carried with it a number of side effects. The stop payment order, for example, is eliminated (except for preauthorized transfers), and so is **float**—the period between the time a check is issued and the time it is charged to the drawer's account by the drawee bank.[6] More important, because electronic banking radically alters the way in which the bank and its customers have been doing business, it also creates potential new problems for both parties, including the unauthorized transfer of funds, the lack of documents (such as cancelled checks and deposit slips) in the customer's hands in order to prove alleged bank errors, and liabilities of the parties in case the customer's debit card is lost or stolen.

Anticipating these kinds of problems, Congress passed the **Electronic Funds Transfer Act** in 1978 (15 U.S.C. §1693). First, the act defines an electronic transfer of funds as "any transfer of funds, other than by check, draft, or similar paper instrument, which is initiated through an electronic terminal, telephone instrument, computer, or magnetic tape so as to order, instruct or authorize a financial institution to debit or credit an account." The act then requires financial institutions to give disclosure statements to the "consumer" (the institution's customers) that describe the consumers' rights and duties; requires the institutions to keep written documentation of all electronic fund transfers; provides methods of dispute resolution; and spells

out the consumers' and institutions' liabilities. We will examine these matters briefly.

Disclosure Statements: The law requires the institution to provide a **disclosure statement** indicating to the consumer—in "readily understandable language"—such matters as the types of transfers that can be made through its transfer mechanisms; the telephone number and address of the person or office of the institution who should be contacted in the event that the consumer believes an error has been made; the consumer's right to stop payment of a preauthorized fund transfer; and the parties' rights, duties, and liabilities in the case of a breach of duty.

Documentation: The law obligates the institution to keep written documentation of all electronic funds transfers. This documentation must show the amount of the transfer, the number of the account being charged, the date of transfer, the identity of the party receiving the transfer, and the terminal location used in making the transfer. Additionally, the institution must send periodic statements to the customer summarizing the transfers made during the prior period.

Dispute Resolution: If a consumer believes that an error has been made by the institution, he or she must give notice of the alleged error to the person or office named in the periodic statement within sixty days of receipt of the institution's statement. The notice can be made either orally or in writing, but it must indicate the account number of the consumer (or information which will enable the institution to determine the number); indicate the consumer's belief that the account contains an error, and the amount of the error; and set forth (where applicable) the "reasons for the consumer's belief" that the error has occurred.

When a notice of error is received by a financial institution, it must "investigate the alleged error, determine whether an error has occurred, and report or mail the results of such investi-

---

[6]A *preauthorized transfer* is a statement in writing by the customer authorizing in advance certain electronic transfers that the institution may automatically make in the future.

gation and determination within ten business days." If the institution determines that the error did occur, it must correct the error within one business day. If the institution determines that the error did not occur, it must deliver to the consumer an explanation of such determination within three business days after the conclusion of its investigation.

As an alternative to the above procedures, the institution, upon receipt of a notice of error, may within ten days "provisionally recredit" the consumer's account with the amount of the alleged error. In such case, it then has forty-five days in which to make its investigation and determination. The act goes on to provide that the consumer may recover *treble damages* from the institution if it "knowingly and willfully" concluded that the consumer's account was not in error when such conclusion could not reasonably have been made, or, in regard to the alternative procedure, if the institution did not recredit the consumer's account within the ten day period and if (1) the institution did not make a good faith investigation of the alleged error, or (2) did not have a reasonable basis for believing that the account was not in error.

Consumer Liability: The act requires financial institutions to furnish to consumers wishing to make electronic transfers a "means of access"—usually a personal bank card—by which the consumer can request fund transfers. There are several rules as to the consumer's liability for unauthorized transfers made as a result of loss or theft of the card. The basic rule is that the consumer has the duty to notify the institution when he or she knows of the loss or theft of the card, in which case the consumer's liability is *limited to $50* (that is, $50 or the actual amount of the unauthorized transfers, whichever is less).

If the consumer fails to give notice to the institution within two business days after learning of the loss or theft, the ceiling on the consumer's liability is *raised to $500* (that is, $500 or the actual amount of the unauthorized transfers, whichever is less). And the consumer is liable for the *total amount* of the unauthorized

transfers if he or she fails to give notice of such transfers within sixty days of receiving the institution's first periodic statement that reflects the transfers. In extenuating circumstances—for example, where the consumer is away on "extended travel" or is hospitalized—the sixty-day provision is replaced by the duty to give notice "within a reasonable time, under the circumstances."

The Institution's Liability: The act has a number of provisions imposing *civil liability* upon financial institutions for damages the consumer suffers as a result of the institutions' breaches of duty, such as failure to make authorized transfers and failure to make a transfer on the erroneous ground that there were insufficient funds in the consumer's account to permit the transfer. Generally, the institutions' liability for breach of a duty is limited to actual damages incurred by the consumer; however, greater damages are sometimes allowed where bad faith on the part of the institution is shown. (The act also specifies situations in which class actions can be brought.)

Criminal liability is imposed by the act upon any person (including the consumer as well as the institution) who "knowingly and willfully" gives false information or fails to provide information required by the act. The liability for these violations is a fine of up to $5,000 or imprisonment for not more than a year, or both. And stiffer criminal penalties are provided for other specified wrongs affecting interstate commerce—such as knowingly using forged, fictitious, or lost **debit instruments** (usually personal bank cards); knowingly transporting such instruments in interstate commerce; and knowingly furnishing money, property, or services to another through the use of such instruments.

SUMMARY

Checks are governed in some instances by special rules of Article 3 of the UCC, and, additionally, the bank-depositor relationship is governed by special rules in both Articles 3 and 4. A check is, by definition, "a draft drawn on a bank payable on demand." The issuance of a check does not, in and of itself, result in an assignment of funds to the payee or to a subsequent holder; this occurs only after the instrument is honored by the drawee bank. A bank has no duty to certify a check, either at the request of the drawer or of a holder. If it does certify, however, the bank becomes primarily liable on the instrument (much like the acceptor of a draft). A certification at the request of a holder of the instrument discharges the drawer from liability, but a certification at the request of the drawer does not have this effect.

One of the primary duties owed by a bank to its depositor is to honor checks drawn by the depositor if there are sufficient funds in his or her account at presentment. If a check is stale— more than six months old at the time of presentment—the bank has no duty to honor it. It may, however, honor a stale check if it wishes, without liability to the drawer, unless its payment was made in bad faith.

There are limited situations where special bank-depositor rules apply; for example, the issuance of stop payment orders. A drawer may stop payment on his or her check by giving the drawee bank such an order. An oral order is effective for 14 days, while a written one is effective for six months. If a bank disobeys a stop payment order by paying the instrument, it is liable to the drawer for any loss resulting from its failure to observe the order. A second example involves payment by a drawee bank of a check drawn by a depositor which—unknown to the bank at the time of payment—bore the forged indorsement of a party whose indorsement was necessary for the negotiation of the instrument. In such a case the bank, having made payment to a person who did not have title, must credit the drawer's account with the amount of the check. The bank—assuming it was not guilty of negligence in failing to know of the forged indorsement—may then recover the amount of the check from the surrendering party (the party to whom it made payment).

A different situation exists when a drawee bank honors an instrument bearing the forged signature of the drawer (its depositor). The bank must again credit the drawer's account, assuming the drawer was not negligent in the transaction, but in this situation the bank can *not* recover from the surrendering party (unless he or she knew of the forgery when receiving payment).

A drawer may be negligent if a cancelled check bearing the drawer's forged signature is returned by the bank (together with all other cancelled checks for that period), and he or she does not notify the drawee bank of the forgery within 14 days of the time the checks were returned. In such case, the drawer can *not* require the drawee bank to credit his account with the amount of any additional checks (forged by the same person) which the bank honors between the expiration of the 14-day period and the time that the drawer does ultimately give the bank notice of the first forgery.

Transfers of funds via the use of electronic devices (i.e., "electronic banking") are governed by the federal Electronic Funds Transfer Act, rather than by Articles 3 and 4 of the UCC.

KEY TERMS

Drawee bank
Certified check
Stale check
Stop payment order
Electronic banking
Point of sale transfers
Float
Electronic Funds Transfer Act
Disclosure statement
Debit instruments

QUESTIONS AND PROBLEMS

1. On July 1, D draws a check payable to the order of P and issues it to P. P forgets about the check until August 10, at which time she presents it to the drawee bank for payment. Under what circumstances might D's liability be reduced as a result of the late presentment? What is D's only obligation in such circumstances?

2. What are the three basic effects of certifying a check?

3. You are manager of a branch bank, and one of your tellers comes to you with a check that an apparent holder wishes to have cashed. The check is drawn by one of your depositors, but it is seven months old. What are your bank's rights and duties in regard to this check?

4. On June 10, D (drawer) issues an oral stop payment order on a particular check to his drawee bank, just before leaving town for a short vacation. When he returns at noon on June 20, he goes to the bank and signs a written stop payment order. It turns out, however, that the bank had already honored the check at 10 A.M. that day. The bank now wishes to charge D's account with the amount of the check, in view of the fact that it had honored the check before the written order was issued. Can the bank charge D's account in these circumstances? Explain.

5. D issues a valid stop payment order, but the drawee bank, without excuse, fails to obey the order and charges D's account with the amount of the check. D sues the bank to force it to credit her account in the amount of the check. The bank can totally escape liability to D if it proves that she suffered no loss as a result of its failure to obey the stop payment order. What are the circumstances under which the bank can prove this?

6. D issues a check payable to the order of P. A few days later the drawee bank cashes the check at the request of H (who surrenders it to the bank). The instrument apparently bears the blank indorsement of P, the payee, at the time of surrender. The bank later learns, however, that P's indorsement is a forgery, so it credits D's account as required by law and now seeks to recover the amount of the check from H. H defends on the ground that he neither knew nor had reason to know that the indorsement was forged. Is H's defense valid? Explain.

7. D issues a check payable to the order of P. One week later the drawee bank cashes the check at the request of H, the surrenderer. At the time of the surrender the amount of the check was "$700," and that is the amount that the drawee bank gave to H when he cashed it. Later the bank learns that the original amount of the check was *$100,* and that P apparently was the party who made the alteration. The bank, having no reason to suspect the alteration, now seeks the $600 difference from H; H contends that he, too, was innocent of the alteration. Is H's defense good? Why or why not?

8. The general rule is that a drawer's account cannot be charged with checks that are proved to be forgeries, unless the drawer has been guilty of negligence that contributed to the forgeries. Give examples of the two general types of misconduct on the part of the drawer that may constitute such negligence.

Part V

SECURED TRANSACTIONS AND BANKRUPTCY

In today's world, credit is an integral part of our business and personal lives. As a result, legal principles establishing the rights and duties of debtors and creditors are an important part of our law.

In Part V we deal with two major areas of debtor-creditor law: secured transactions and bankruptcy. In Chapter 29, "Secured Transactions," we focus on the rights and responsibilities of the debtor and creditor when items of personal property (inventory, equipment, consumer goods, or intangibles) belonging to the debtor are used as security for the creditor's claim. In Chapter 30, "Bankruptcy," we first survey the various methods for dealing with unpaid debts, and then focus on bankruptcy proceedings under federal law.

653

Chapter 29

SECURED TRANSACTIONS

A very large part of the business that is carried on in this country is done "on credit." While there are many types of transactions in which credit is extended by one person or firm to another, probably the two most common of these arise from sales of goods (in which the buyer promises to pay the purchase price in installments) and loans of money. In these transactions a *debtor-creditor* relationship results, with the buyer (or borrower) being the debtor, and the seller (or lender) being the creditor.

Sometimes a seller or lender is willing to extend credit without receiving any security from the debtor. Such transactions frequently occur at the retail sale level where, for example, a department store will sell a modestly priced article to a buyer who is permitted to charge it to his or her credit card account without executing a security agreement. Unsecured credit may also be extended by wholesalers and manufacturers, and by lenders, especially to debtors who have established a good credit record with the creditor as a result of past dealings.

In all unsecured credit cases, once the creditor delivers the goods or makes the loan to the debtor he or she has lost all rights to the goods or money. This means that if the debtor subsequently defaults, the creditor cannot immediately claim or attach any specific goods or money in the debtor's possession. Instead, he or she is initially limited to bringing an action to recover the amount of the indebtedness. After getting a judgment in such a suit the creditor has the right to have any unencumbered property then in the debtor's possession sold under court order to satisfy the debt.[1] However, it may be that these limited assets will have to be shared with other judgment creditors—or worse still, it may be that the debtor may not own any property at all by the time the judgment is obtained, or that the debtor has even become bankrupt by this time. ***Thus an unsecured creditor runs a distinct risk that he or she may recover little or nothing from the debtor.***[2]

SECURED CREDIT TRANSACTIONS

To minimize the above risks, many sellers and lenders routinely require the debtor to enter into a *security agreement* at the time credit is extended—an agreement by which the debtor conveys to the creditor a legally recognized interest in specific personal property owned by the debtor. Once such an interest is created, the creditor has the right to have the specific property sold if the debtor defaults on the payments, and to receive as much of the proceeds of the sale as is necessary to pay off the debt. (If the proceeds are not sufficient to pay the total indebtedness, the creditor then has an *unsecured* claim as to the unpaid balance.)

The dual purpose of a **secured transaction,** then, is to give to the creditor (1) a *specific interest* in the debtor's property that is covered by the security agreement, and (2) a *priority claim* in that property against other creditors who may seek to have the property sold in satisfaction of their claims. This priority, usually obtained by giving notice to all other creditors and third parties who may subsequently become creditors, is called "perfection." (The subject of perfection will be discussed in more detail later in the chapter.)

To illustrate a secured transaction situation: R, an office supply retailer, needs to restock her inventory of electronic word processors, but does not want to pay cash for them. R finds a wholesaler, W, who is able to make immediate delivery of the kind of processor that R wants,

---

[1] Unencumbered property is that which the debtor owns outright—that is, free of any security interest, mortgage, or other lien of a third party.

[2] By contrast, a secured creditor's interest in specific collateral, if "perfected," *is* protected against the claims of judgment creditors. And, if the debtor becomes bankrupt, the security interest survives bankruptcy proceedings—i.e., the collateral cannot be sold by the trustee in bankruptcy for the benefit of unsecured creditors.

and W is willing to sell the goods on credit. R and W therefore sign a security agreement under the terms of which W agrees to sell the word processors to R, with R paying 10 percent down and promising to pay the balance in monthly installments. The agreement describes the goods being sold, and further provides that W is retaining a security interest in them until the total price is paid. At this point a debtor-creditor relationship has been created. W, the secured party, has the inventory collateral of R as security for the debt. W now files a financing statement to give notice to all others of his security interest in the collateral. If R subsequently defaults, W can repossess the remaining inventory to satisfy the debt. Furthermore, assuming that W's filing has given him priority, the collateral will go first to pay off R's debt with W, with only the remaining collateral being available to other creditors.

PRE-UCC SECURED TRANSACTIONS LAW

Before adoption of the UCC, the law on secured transactions was concerned primarily with the person who had "title" to the property and the "form" of the transaction. A separate body of law and a separate terminology existed for each form used. To determine the rights of the creditor, the debtor, and third parties, one had to know what type of security device had been used. (The most common of such devices were the conditional sales contract, the chattel mortgage, the trust receipt, and the pledge; other devices were the factor lien and the assignment of account.) To add to the complexity, notices given to third parties about the outstanding security interests varied widely insofar as their effect upon the parties' priorities were concerned. The laws also varied as to the circumstances under which the creditor had to resell repossessed collateral, and those under which the creditor could keep it in satisfaction of the debt.

Because of the complexity and conflict that existed in pre-UCC secured transaction law,

the basic goals which the drafters of the UCC sought to accomplish were clear—simplicity and uniformity.▪

ARTICLE 9 TERMINOLOGY

Under Article 9 of the UCC the various forms of the security transaction were abandoned, and a simple terminology was created. The same terms now appear in security agreements, financing statements, and any other such documents. Following are the terms needed for an understanding of the basic concepts of secured transactions law. (These definitions come from Sec. 9-105, except where noted otherwise.)[3]

● *Secured party.* A **secured party** is a lender, seller, or other person in whose favor a security interest exists—including a person to whom accounts or chattel paper have been sold. This person was formerly referred to as a chattel mortgagee, conditional seller, entruster, factor, or assignee of accounts.

● *Debtor.* A **debtor** is a person who owes payment or other performance of the obligation that is secured, regardless of whether he or she owns or has rights in the collateral, and includes the seller of accounts or chattel paper. Formerly this person was referred to as a chattel mortgagor, conditional buyer, trustee, borrower, or assignor of accounts.

● *Security interest.* Under Sec. 1-201(37), a **security interest** is an interest in personal property or fixtures that secures payment or performance of an obligation—that is, the interest granted the secured party. Formerly this term was referred to as the "lien" in a chattel mortgage, the "title" in a conditional sales contract, the "security interest" in a trust receipt, and the "sale" or "transfer" in an assignment of accounts.

---

[3] All sections cited in this chapter with a "Sec. 9" prefix are sections in Article 9, which has been adopted with but minor variations in all states except Louisiana.

- *Security agreement.* A **security agreement** is a security arrangement between the debtor and the secured party—the agreement that creates the security interest. Formerly this agreement was referred to as a chattel mortgage, conditional sales contract, trust receipt, factoring agreement, or assignment contract.

- *Collateral.* **Collateral** is the property subject to a security interest, and includes accounts and chattel paper that have been sold.

- *Perfection.* **Perfection** is the taking, by a secured creditor, of those steps which are required under the UCC in order for his or her security interest to be valid as against other creditors.

- *Financing statement.* Under Secs. 9-401 and 9-402, the **financing statement** is the instrument filed to give public notice of the security interest in the collateral.

Following is an illustration of the basic concepts using this terminology. The *secured party* and *debtor* usually enter into a *security agreement* by which the secured party receives a *security interest* in one or more pieces of the debtor's collateral, to be available in the event of the debtor's default. To gain priority over others who may also want a security interest in this same collateral, the secured party files a *financing statement* as notice of his or her claim. The secured interest is now *perfected.* (While the usual security device is expressly labelled "security agreement" to conform to this terminology, older forms creating security interests—the chattel mortgage or conditional sale—are still used occasionally. In such cases these devices, too, are treated today as ordinary security agreements.)

SCOPE OF ARTICLE 9

Article 9 covers agreements that create security interests in *personal* property. Therefore, security agreements applicable to interests in *real* property, such as those created by the mortgage

of a farm or a home, are not governed by this article.[4]

Many times personal property that is subject to a security interest has a tangible existence as **goods.** Typical examples of goods are automobiles, cattle, grain, and television sets. In addition to goods, however, security interests are also commonly created in certain kinds of personal property that have no physical substance. These kinds of property, consisting of rights and interests, are properly termed "intangibles." Because some of these kinds of property, however, possess certain characteristics similar to goods, it is useful to label these as "quasi-tangibles," and the remainder as "intangibles" (or "pure intangibles"). These three categories of property—goods, quasi-tangibles, and intangibles—may be further classified as indicated below.

Tangible Collateral ("Goods")

Under Sec. 9-109, there are four kinds of goods, as follows:

- *Consumer goods.* Goods are consumer goods if they are used or bought for use primarily for personal, family, or household purposes.

- *Equipment.* Goods are equipment if they are used or bought for use primarily in business (including farming or a profession).

- *Farm products.* Goods are farm products if they are crops or livestock or supplies used or produced in farming operations, or products of crops or livestock in their unmanufactured state (such as eggs, milk, or sap used in the production of maple syrup), and if they are in the pos-

---

[4]Some security interests in personal property fall outside the scope of Article 9. For example, under special statutes an auto mechanic usually obtains a lien on a car while it is in his or her possession, and under Article 2 of the UCC an unpaid seller of goods may have an interest in the goods while they are en route to the buyer. Such interests are governed by the special statutes that create them. Additionally, security interests in aircraft and maritime vessels are generally governed by specific federal statutes.

session of a debtor engaged in raising, fattening, grazing, or other farm operations.

• *Inventory.* Goods are inventory if they are held by the debtor for the purpose of sale or lease to others in the ordinary course of the debtor's business. Also included in the inventory category are goods to be furnished by the debtor to others under service contracts, raw materials, work in process in the hands of a manufacturer, and materials used or consumed in a business. The last category is broad enough to include such items as duplication paper and related supplies of a bank, and the law books in an attorney's office.

A UCC drafters' comment to Sec. 9-109 states that the above classes of goods are "mutually exclusive"; a particular item of property cannot fall into two categories at the same time. However, a particular item of property may fall into different classes at different times. For example, a sofa on the floor of a furniture store is inventory, but is consumer goods when subsequently delivered to a buyer's home.

In addition to the four classifications of goods noted above, Article 9 also covers security interests in another kind of tangible property, *fixtures.* As we will see in Chapter 41, **fixtures** begin life as items of personal property but are subsequently attached to real estate—land and buildings—in such a manner that they become a part of that real estate.[5] To illustrate: M, a manufacturer, purchases an industrial electric motor on credit from the inventory of W, a wholesaler. The motor is delivered to M's factory, where it is permanently bolted to a concrete bed in the building. (Under special rules discussed later, a security interest in the motor given by M to W at the time of the purchase may continue to exist even though the motor has been converted from personal to real property.)

---

[5] This is not true, however, in the case of ordinary building supplies, such as lumber that is used in building a house. In this case the lumber is not a fixture, and any security interest is lost when it becomes a part of the building.

Quasi-Tangible Collateral

Quasi-tangible collateral that may be the subject of a security interest can best be described as rights that are created by (in addition to being evidenced by) pieces of paper—written documents such as promissory notes and bills of lading. Under Sec. 9-102, the types of personal property falling within this category are "documents of title," "instruments," and "chattel paper." Quasi-tangible collateral is similar to tangible collateral in that both types of collateral can be "pledged"—i.e., physically delivered to the creditor. (Pledges, and the related subject of perfection by delivery, are considered later in the chapter.)

Documents of Title: Under Sec. 1-201(15) of the UCC, **documents of title** include bills of lading, dock warrants, dock receipts, warehouse receipts, or any other orders for delivery of goods, and any other documents which in the regular course of business or financing are treated as adequate evidence that the person in possession is entitled to receive, hold, and dispose of them and the goods they cover. (In passing, it may be noted that documents may be either "negotiable" or "nonnegotiable," depending upon whether their specific terms meet the requirements of negotiability set forth in Sec. 7-104 of the UCC. Because security interests in negotiable documents are more common than those in nonnegotiable ones, our subsequent references to documents will focus on the rules applicable to negotiable documents.)

Instruments: Under Sec. 9-105(1)(i), the term **instrument** essentially refers to two interests: *negotiable instruments and securities.* A negotiable instrument is a promissory note, check, or any other written promise or order to pay money whose terms meet the requirements of negotiability set forth in Sec. 3-104 of the UCC. (See Chapter 25 for details.) Security refers to corporate stocks and bonds.

Chattel Paper: Under Sec. 9-105(1)(b), **chattel paper** means a writing or writings that evidence both a monetary obligation *and* a security interest in goods. For the most part, the term refers to promissory notes which not only contain the usual promise to pay a sum of money at a stated future time but, additionally, contain language that conveys to the holder of the note a security interest. To illustrate: F, a farmer, purchases a tractor from an implement dealer under a conditional sales contract. The contract (note) that F signs contains the usual promise that he will pay the stated contract price in specified monthly installments, and the contract further provides that the dealer-seller shall retain a security interest in the tractor until the note is paid in full. If the implement dealer thereafter borrows money from a bank and assigns (transfers) the contract to the bank as security for that loan, the contract in that situation constitutes chattel paper, with the dealer being the debtor and the bank the secured party. By contrast, if F had originally given a simple promissory note to the dealer—a promise to pay the purchase price of the tractor in stated installments *without* any security provision—the note would be a negotiable instrument falling within the instruments category rather than the chattel paper category.

Intangible Collateral

Those types of personal property interests that do not possess the characteristics of goods or quasi-tangibles are **intangible collateral.** Such interests are either *accounts* or *general intangibles.*

Accounts: Under Sec. 9-106, an **account** is any right to payment for goods sold or leased, or for services rendered, which is not evidenced by an instrument or chattel paper. Generally, the term refers to *accounts receivable.*

General Intangibles: General Intangibles is a catch-all category, which is defined under Sec. 9-106 as consisting of any personal property ("including things in action"—rights to collect money or property) *other than* goods, accounts, chattel paper, documents, instruments, and money. Typical examples are literary rights, trademarks, patents, copyrights, and the like.

The case below presents one situation in which a determination of the type of collateral is necessary in order to decide the validity of a secured creditor's claim to the proceeds of that collateral.

In re K. L. Smith Enterprises, Ltd.
United States Bankruptcy Court,
D. Colo., 28 UCC Rep. 534 (1980)

K. L. Smith Enterprises operated a large-scale egg production business in Colorado. It housed thousands of laying hens in unique, semi-automated "egg production units" that permitted the efficient collection, sizing, and packaging of large quantities of eggs daily.

In November 1976 the United Bank of Denver loaned $2,400,000 to Smith Enterprises. In connection with the loan, Smith Enterprises executed two security agreements granting the bank security interests in all of its *inventory, accounts, contract rights, equipment, and machinery,* and in *"the proceeds therefrom"*—that is, in the

money received by Smith Enterprises from the sale of any of the designated assets.[a]

In November 1979 Smith Enterprises sold $40,000 worth of eggs to Safeway Stores, Inc., its principal customer for many years. That same month it also sold a quantity of eggs to Gonzales, one of its occasional customers, and in December it sold 120,000 hens to the Campbell Soup Company. The sale to Safeway was "on account"—an account receivable was created on Smith Enterprises' books—and the sale of eggs to Gonzales was a cash transaction. It is not clear whether the sale of the hens to Campbell was on account or for cash.

Shortly thereafter Smith Enterprises went into bankruptcy. In those proceedings the United Bank of Denver claimed that it had a valid security interest in the eggs and chickens, and thus in the proceeds thereof. In response, Smith Enterprises (plaintiff in this action) filed a complaint disputing the bank's claim to the eggs, chickens, and the "cash collateral" in Smith Enterprises' possession at the time of bankruptcy. (In the decision below, Smith Enterprises is referred to as "the debtor.")

Keller, Bankruptcy Judge:

This matter came before the court upon the complaint of the Debtor to determine the nature, extent, and validity of a claimed lien by the United Bank of Denver in certain property and certain cash. . . .

The Bank contends that the eggs are inventory within the meaning of its security instruments, and that the chickens may be inventory or may in fact be equipment. It asserts that it, therefore, had a valid security interest in [the] chickens and eggs. Notwithstanding the status of the chickens and eggs, it asserts a security interest in all of the sales to Safeway, which it claims to have been pursuant to contract; the sale to Mr. Gonzales, likewise asserted to have been pursuant to contract; and the sale of the chickens to Campbell Soup Company, which the Bank suggests may have been pursuant to contract as well. The Bank further claims a security interest in the accounts receivable as of the date of the filing of the petition, thus concluding that all of the cash in the Debtor's possession is "cash collateral," to which the Bank's security interest extends.

The Debtor asserts that the chickens and eggs are "farm products" as that term is used in the Colorado version of the Uniform Commercial Code. [§4-9-109.] That section describes farm products as:

"crops or livestock or supplies used or produced in farming operations or if they are products of crops or livestock in their unmanufactured states (such as ginned cotton, wool-clip, maple syrup, milk, and eggs), and if they are in the possession of a debtor engaged in raising, fattening, grazing, or other farming operations. If goods are farm products they are neither equipment nor inventory."

---

[a] The subject of "proceeds" will be discussed further under the topic of perfection.

It would thus seem that if eggs are products of "livestock," the hens them-selves must be "livestock" within the meaning of that section. There does at least seem to be a biological connection. . . . The Bank has not disavowed this connection but asserts that in the operation such as this, where the sole business is the production of eggs, the eggs lose their characteristic as farm products and instead become inventory in the operation of a business. Great emphasis is placed by the Bank on the fact that there are no residents on the property of the Debtor and that while certain wheat was grown on adjacent land owned by the Debtor, it was not harvested. The Official Comment to UCC §9-109 states:

"Products of crops or livestock, even though they remain in the possession of a person engaged in farming operations, lose their status as farm products if they are subjected to a manufacturing process. What is and what is not a manufacturing operation is not determined by this Article. At one end of the scale some processes are so closely connected with farming—such as pasteurizing milk or boiling sap to produce maple syrup or maple sugar—that they would not rank as manufacturing. On the other hand an extensive canning operation would be manufacturing. The line is one for the courts to draw. After farm products have been subjected to a manufacturing operation, they become inventory if held for sale."

[The court then rejected the bank's contention that the debtor's actions of washing, candling, and packaging the eggs constituted a "manufacturing pro-cess," in these words:] The pasteurization of milk or the boiling of sap seem to the court to be even more significant treatment of raw product than does the washing, candling, and spraying with oil of eggs. At the very least, they are in the same category, and the internal structure of the egg is not changed. The packaging of eggs in cartons does not seem to this court to be analogous to the "extensive canning operations" characterized by the Official Comment. Nearly all farm products must be packaged in some way for delivery to the farmer's customer. The facts that the packaging is done in the customer's package to eliminate a step in handling or that the operation is highly mecha-nized, do not seem to this court to disqualify the operation from the normal farm category. The language of the Code seems reasonably specific in its determination of what are farm products and does not appear to distinguish between the methods of producing the same product. The Bank's refreshing view that only conventional farming techniques which are unmechanized, unsophisticated, and labor intensive can produce farm products is unper-suasive. It is somewhat interesting to note that the loan at the Bank was made through its agricultural loans department.

The cases have uniformly found cattle feeding operations to be "farms" for the purposes of UCC §9-109, although they are not farms in the traditional sense. [The court then conceded that the term "farm" as used in some statutes might be subject to varying interpretations. But the court ruled that such was not the case here, saying:]

The construction of this [particular] statute, however, compels the conclu-sion that chickens are livestock and eggs are products of livestock. The statutory language is simply too clear [to permit the court to accept the bank's view that only conventional, unmechanized farming techniques can produce farm products]. More importantly, the purposes of the Code could be badly abused [by excessive interpretation]. The Code was designed to provide a simple public explanation of claimed security interests so that the public might know under what conditions they were dealing with a debtor. To strain the statutory construction as sought by the Bank would seriously impair the public notice features which are the hallmark of the Uniform Commercial Code.

[Because of the court's conclusion that the chickens and eggs were farm products rather than inventory, the bank's contention that it had a security interest in the proceeds of the sale of those products necessarily failed. Accordingly, judgment was for Smith Enterprises.]

ATTACHMENT (CREATION) OF A SECURITY INTEREST

Under Sec. 9-203, in order for the businessperson to be sure of having an **attachment**, i.e., an enforceable security interest that attaches to the collateral, three conditions must be met:

1. There must be a *security agreement* entered into which describes the collateral. This agreement must be in writing and signed by the debtor, with one exception: where the collateral is put in the possession of the secured party. Such delivery of possession, called a "pledge," can occur only where the collateral consists of goods (such as jewelry, cattle, or furniture) or quasi-tangibles (such as warehouse receipts or negotiable instruments). Because intangibles are incapable of physical delivery, security agreements creating interests in intangibles must always be in writing.

2. The secured party must give *value* to the debtor. In most instances this consists of a delivery of goods by the secured party to the debtor, or of the advancing of money by the secured party. However, under Sec. 1-201(44) of the UCC a person also gives value for rights in collateral if he or she acquires them (a) as security for a preexisting claim, or (b) in return for a binding commitment to extend credit in the future, or (c) in return for any consideration sufficient to support a simple contract.

3. The debtor must have *rights* (any current or future legally recognized interest) in the collateral. Obviously, if the debtor did not possess any such right, he or she could not convey a right to the secured party.

The following case illustrates the importance of these three requirements as applied to a real-life controversy.

M. Rutkin Electric Supply Co. Inc. v. Burdette Electric, Inc.
Superior Court of New Jersey (Chancery Division), 237 A.2d 500 (1967)

Burdette Electric, Inc. (defendant), was adjudicated an insolvent corporation on June 26, 1964, and a receiver was appointed. Most of the corporation's assets consisted of accounts receivable—sums of money

owed by customers for goods that Burdette had delivered to them prior to its bankruptcy.

Among the accounts receivable held by Burdette was one owed by B. J. Builders, Inc. During the bankruptcy proceedings a third party, Milton Rabin (plaintiff) claimed that this account receivable had been assigned by Burdette to him prior to Burdette's bankruptcy, the assignment allegedly having been made because of certain advances of money Rabin had made to Burdette at an earlier time. *In this action Rabin now claims an enforceable security interest in the account receivable.*

At the trial Rabin, in support of his claim, proved that a financing statement had been signed by Burdette in early 1964, and that he had filed this statement with the Secretary of State on March 6, 1964.[a] Accordingly, at the trial, Rabin was instructed to produce a security agreement in support of this transaction. When he failed to do so, the lower court concluded (1) that no written security agreement was ever executed by Burdette, and (2) that such an agreement was a necessary element in the creation of a security interest in favor of Rabin. Accordingly, the court dismissed Rabin's action, and he appealed.

Mintz, Justice:

. . . The debtor, Burdette Electric, had rights in the collateral, and Rabin, the alleged secured party, advanced value. But, as noted earlier, Rabin has failed to produce a written security agreement to document his acquisition of a security interest in the B. J. Builders account receivable. Thus Rabin's claim fails unless he can prove the existence of some form of enforceable "agreement" which provides that his security interest in the account receivable be created. . . .

New Jersey Study Comment, Note 2, to UCC §9-204 indicates that in order to ascertain whether an "agreement" to attach a security interest has legal sufficiency . . . Chapter 9's statute of frauds must also be considered. The Study Comment reads:

The requirement that there must be an agreement must be read not only *in connection with §1-201(3), but also in connection with §9-203 which requires that the security agreement be written (see Comments, §9-203) unless the collateral is in the possession of the secured party. . . .*

Accordingly, in order for an "agreement" to arise, signifying the creation of an enforceable security interest, *either the collateral must be in the possession of the secured party or the debtor must have signed a security agreement which contains a description of the collateral.* [Emphasis added.] An ac-

---

[a] As will be seen later, such a filing would perfect the security interest—i.e., make it effective against the claims of third parties—*if* it had been preceded by the making of a valid *security agreement.*

count receivable is an intangible and as such cannot be "possessed" within the meaning of the Code.

Hence, "possession" is unavailable to Rabin as a means of signifying an agreement with the insolvent that the security interest attach. A security interest in an account receivable must be evidenced by a security agreement signed by the debtor and containing a description of the collateral. . . . In the instant situation, since Rabin can proffer no writing signed by the debtor giving, even sketchily, the terms of the security agreement, it is unenforceable. The financing statement signed by the parties and duly filed with the Secretary of State is no substitute for a security agreement. It alone did not create a security interest. It was but notice that one was claimed. . . .

Hence, the alleged assignee Rabin has no enforceable security interest in the account receivable in question and the same is vested in the receiver. Rabin's claim that he holds a security interest through an assignment is unsubstantial and only colorable [having the mere appearance of reality] at best. . . .

Judgment for defendant affirmed.

PERFECTION OF THE SECURITY INTEREST

Under Sec. 9-201, the security agreement binds the debtor and secured party the moment that it attaches, without the taking of any additional steps by the secured party. In general, however, *the agreement does not protect the creditor against the rights of third parties until the agreement is perfected.* To illustrate: A loans B $500 and takes a security interest in a prize bull belonging to B. A does not perfect the security interest (that is, he neither files a financing statement nor takes possession of the bull). Later a third party, the X Bank, loans B $1,000, the bank also taking a security interest in the bull. The X Bank then perfects by duly filing its financing statement. If B thereafter defaults on both loans, under Sec. 9-312 X Bank's perfected security interest will prevail over A's unperfected interest even though A's security interest was created first.[6]

In order for the secured party to obtain *maximum protection against third parties* who may subsequently claim an interest in the collateral—such as the debtor's other secured and unsecured creditors, persons who may have purchased collateral from the debtor, and against a trustee in bankruptcy in case the debtor becomes bankrupt—*the secured party must perfect his or her interest.* Not only does perfection usually give the secured party a protected interest in the collateral, but it also usually gives him or her a protected interest in the *proceeds* of the collateral in case the debtor sells it. Under Sec. 9-306, proceeds is defined as "whatever is received when collateral . . . is sold . . . or otherwise disposed of," and usually consists of cash and checks which the debtor has received upon

---

[6]In addition to the priority gained under Sec. 9-312 by a subsequent third party who perfects his or her interest, as in the case of the X Bank above, there are a number of other

third parties whose interests in the collateral also supersede those of the unperfected creditor under Sec. 9-301. (Additionally, as will be seen later, the rights of third parties in some situations even take precedence over perfected interests; obviously, the rights of these parties also prevail over unperfected interests.) As a result of these rules, it can be said that an unperfected interest generally affords *no protection against any third party* except a subsequent secured party who also fails to perfect his or her interest.

sale of the collateral. The right to proceeds is especially important in situations where the collateral cannot be traced, or is in the possession of a third party who, under special UCC provisions noted later, takes the collateral free from the secured party's interest even though perfection has occurred. (The security agreement and financing statement usually expressly provide that the agreement covers proceeds. However, the secured party's right to proceeds exists *even in the absence of such a provision* unless the security agreement—or a subsequent agreement between the secured party and the debtor—provides otherwise. Sec. 9-306[2].)

Methods of Perfection, Generally

The secured party may perfect his or her interest in one of three ways, depending on the type of collateral that is involved. In many situations the secured party has a choice of means of perfection, while in others there is only one method that can be used. Except where the collateral consists of goods which are covered by certificates of title under state law (such as motor vehicles) and fixtures, the three methods of perfection are the following:[7]

1. *Perfection by filing.* As a general rule, perfection requires the creditor to file a financing statement at a designated location specified by the code. (As noted earlier, a financing statement is a document that evidences the secured party's interest and contains a description of the collateral covered by the security agreement.) **Filing** is the most commonly used method of perfection, and is the *only* way that perfection can occur where the collateral consists of intangibles. Because filing is the customary way of achieving perfection, it will be discussed more fully later in this chapter.

2. *Perfection by possession.* Section 9-305 provides, in part, that "a security interest in . . . goods, instruments . . . money, negotiable docu-

ments or chattel paper may be perfected by the secured party's taking possession of the collateral." In other words, such a transfer of possession of the collateral to the secured party (a transfer often called a "pledge") can occur only where the collateral consists of money, goods (such as jewelry) or quasi-tangibles (such as promissory notes or shares of stock).

Two special rules in regard to this kind of perfection of interests in quasi-tangible collateral should be noted. Both of these rules are found in Section 9-304(1).

A. If the collateral consists of negotiable instruments (or of money), possession is the *only* means of perfection; filing will not suffice.

B. If the collateral consists of chattel paper or negotiable documents of title, perfection by filing is permitted. However, Sections 9-308 and 9-309 provide, in general, that security interests in such types of collateral that have been perfected by filing *lose their priority* to good faith purchasers of the collateral. Thus, in order for a party who has a security interest in either chattel paper or negotiable documents of title to receive maximum protection—that is, to insure that the collateral will not be subsequently sold to a good faith purchaser—the secured party *should perfect by taking possession.*

While many kinds of collateral are too bulky for a transfer of possession, and others will not be transferred because the debtor needs to use them in his or her business—as in the case of plant machinery—the pledge, where feasible, does possess two significant advantages over the other kinds of perfection. First, it obviates the need for the security agreement to be in writing (though, in practice, a written agreement is still advisable). And, second, as indicated above, it reduces the possibility that third parties will subsequently acquire or claim interests in the collateral.

3. *Automatic perfection.* Occasionally an interest is perfected by mere attachment—that is, automatically—at the moment that the security interest is created. Such attachment, called **automatic perfection,** is applicable only where

---

[7] The special rules applicable to motor vehicles and fixtures are discussed subsequently.

the collateral consists of *consumer goods* being purchased by the debtor. It exists in two common situations: (a) where the creditor (usually a retailer) sells the goods on credit and takes a security interest in return, or (b) where the creditor (usually a bank or finance company) loans money to the debtor for the purpose of buying the goods, and takes a security interest in return. To illustrate: B buys a washer and dryer on credit from the S Company under a conditional sale agreement (an agreement under which title to the goods is retained by the S Company until the price is paid in full). Under Sec. 9-302(1)(d) the interest of the S Company—called a **purchase money security interest**—is perfected even though it does not file a financing statement, and even though it does not have possession of the goods. Similarly, if B borrows the money to buy the appliances from a finance company, with that company taking a security interest in the goods when purchased, the finance company has a perfected, purchase money security interest in the washer and dryer when B buys them.[8] (The reason for the automatic perfection rule is one of practicality—the fact that secured sales of consumer goods are made in such large numbers by retailers that the filing requirement would place an undue burden upon such sellers.)

While automatic perfection does away with the necessity of filing a financing statement, it should be noted that the security agreement itself *must be in writing;* otherwise there is no attachment to which the perfection can relate.

Perfection: Motor Vehicles and Fixtures

Motor Vehicles: Under Sec. 9-302(3), the usual methods of perfection are not applicable to security interests in collateral which are subject to state certificate of title laws—motor vehicles, boats, and motor homes. Security interests in such goods can be perfected only by compliance with the applicable state statute. In regard to automobiles (and to the other goods in this category), what this means is that—under the law of most states—a security interest can be perfected *only by the notation of such interest on the certificate of title covering the vehicle subject to the interest.* Generally, if such notation is not made, a good faith purchaser of the automobile takes it free of the interest. (In regard to the relatively few states that do not utilize title registration of such vehicles, an examination of the special statutes of such states must be made to determine the priority of conflicting interests.)

Fixtures: Prior to the adoption of the UCC a number of varying priority rules caused difficulty in the case where fixtures were added to real estate. In one of the most common controversies, land and a building thereon would be subject to a real estate mortgage, and thereafter the owner (the person buying the real estate under the mortgage) would purchase an item of personal property—such as a furnace—on credit and install it in his or her home on the land. If the seller of the furnace took a purchase money security interest from the buyer-homeowner, controversies between the holder of the mortgage

---

[8] An entirely different situation exists where a purchaser buys consumer goods (such as a washer or dryer) and pays cash for them, and subsequently uses such goods as collateral for a loan. Prior to 1984 these were very common transactions; typically, a person who wanted to borrow money from a lender—usually a small loan company, but sometimes a savings and loan association or a bank—would be asked to check a box in the lender's loan form which gave to the lender a blanket security interest in all of the borrower's household goods. In hearings before the Federal Trade Commission (FTC) in the early 1980s, voluminous testimony was given indicating that the use of such devices ("non purchase money interests") was attended by a variety of evils. Chief among these were (1) the fact that lenders often used these devices to continually threaten defaulting borrowers with repossession, causing borrowers "mental and psychological" injury; and (2) the fact that in cases where repossession actually occurred, the price of the goods obtained by the lender upon resale was usually so low that the borrower's obligation to the lender was actually reduced very little by the resale. Accordingly, the FTC included in Part VI of its Credit Practices Rule (adopted in 1984 and effective March 1, 1985) a rule that, in general, *prohibits lenders in interstate commerce from taking non–purchase money security interests in household goods.* Two observations about the rule: (1) the term "household goods" excludes specified nonnecessities, such as jewelry and works of art; and (2) the rule does not, of course, have application to, or impose limitations upon the use of, *purchase money* security interests in household goods.

on the real estate and the seller of the fixture often arose.

The rule applied to this situation, Sec. 9-313 (4)(a), is that the purchase money security interest (the interest of the seller of the furnace) has priority over the real estate mortgage, provided that the purchase money security interest is properly filed before the good (the furnace) becomes a fixture—that is, becomes attached to the real estate—or within ten days thereafter. However, a different provision of Sec. 9-313 applies to the case where the home is *under construction,* with a construction mortgage being recorded before installation of the fixture. In that situation the purchase money security interest is subordinate to the construction mortgage. (Additionally, it should be noted that not all states have adopted these particular sections; in such states the applicable statutes may bring about different results.)

Filing Requirements, Generally

The Financing Statement: Where perfection is made by the filing of a financing statement, as is usually the case, the requirements of Sec. 9-402 must be met. That section initially provides that "A financing statement is sufficient if it gives the names of the debtor and the secured party, is signed by the debtor, gives an address of the secured party from which information concerning the security interest may be obtained, gives a mailing address of the debtor and contains a statement indicating the types, or describing the items, of collateral." The section goes on to provide that additional information is needed for some types of collateral, so that a reading of the full section is necessary to determine the sufficiency of a financing statement in a given situation.

Section 9-402 also provides that a separate document or a copy of the security agreement properly filed is itself sufficient as a financing statement if it meets certain requirements:

1. The document or agreement must be signed by the debtor.

2. It must contain the names and addresses of both the debtor and the secured party.

3. It must contain a description of the type or types of collateral. Under Sec. 9-402(1), when the collateral of the security interest is crops, timber to be cut, minerals, accounts under Sec. 9-103(5), or goods that are to become fixtures, additional requirements must be met.

Place of Filing: In all cases where filing is utilized, the place for doing so depends on the classification of the collateral. In that regard, however, determination of the status of the debtor is not sufficient for a proper classification of the collateral. Rather, the determination depends on how the collateral is used by the debtor. For example, a refrigerator is a *consumer good* if it is sold to a housekeeper, *inventory* if it is in the hands of a merchant selling appliances, *equipment* if it is used by a doctor for storing drugs in his or her office, and *farm equipment* if it is used to store eggs for resale.

Most states have two locations for filing—a *central* one (usually with the secretary of state) and a *local* one (usually with a county clerk). While the states have adopted somewhat varying location rules, most have adopted that version of Sec. 9-401(1) providing, essentially, that where the collateral is *farm equipment, farm products, or consumer goods,* filing is to be at a designated office in the county of the *debtor's residence* (or, if the debtor is not a resident of the state, then at a designated office in the county where the goods are kept). In other words, there is local filing for these kinds of security.

Where the collateral is *timber to be cut, minerals* (including oil and gas), *crops, or fixtures,* local filing is again usually proper—but, in these instances, "in the office where a mortgage on the real estate would be . . . recorded"—in such office in the county *where the land is located.*[9]

---

[9] Many states require an additional filing (dual filing) in the case of some of these kinds of collateral, especially fixtures.

Filings covering all other kinds of collateral, with minor exception, are to be made centrally—in the office of the secretary of state of the appropriate state. (That state is usually the state of the debtor's residence, or, in the case of a business firm, a state in which it has a place of business.)

Duration of Filing: Under Sec. 9-403(2), a filed financing statement is effective for five years from the date of filing. After this period, under Sec. 9-403(3), the security interest generally becomes unperfected unless the secured party files a *continuation statement* within six months prior to the expiration date. This continuation, good for five more years, can again be continued using the same procedure. Thus the secured party can continue the perfected interest indefinitely.

Collateral Moved to Another State

There is always the possibility that collateral subject to a perfected security interest will be moved out of the state in which the perfection was made. Such movement may or may not have been contemplated by the parties, and it may or may not be a violation of the terms of the security agreement. In any event, the creditor needs to know what steps must be taken in order to keep his or her interest protected.

General Rule: The perfection of security interests in "multiple state transactions" is governed by Sec. 9-103. In regard to most kinds of collateral ("documents, instruments, and ordinary goods"), Sec. 9-103(1)(d) provides that the perfected creditor has *four months after the collateral has entered another state in which to reperfect.* If reperfection is made within that time, the security interest shall be "deemed to be perfected continuously" under Sec. 9-303(2). Thus if collateral is moved to a new state on March 1, and the creditor refiles there on May 10, his or her interest is generally protected as against any claimants in the state whose claim attached between those dates. On the other hand, if no reperfection is made within the four-

month period, the creditor's interest is *unperfected beginning with the time that the collateral entered the state.* In other words, where there is no new perfection within the four-month period, the creditor is not protected by the four-month grace period.

Special Rules—Motor Vehicles: In cases where the collateral consists of accounts, general intangibles, chattel paper, and minerals, special rules apply. (Sec. 9-103[2][3][4] and [5].) Because of the complexity of these rules, the resolution of multistate disputes involving interests in these kinds of collateral can be achieved only by a careful reading of these express provisions and the case law developed under them.

Motor vehicles (and other goods covered by state certificate of title laws) are expressly exempted from the basic filing requirements of Article 9. As to security interests in such collateral as automobiles, then, perfection can be made only pursuant to the applicable state law. The rules here are complicated by the fact that while most states have certificate of title laws, some do not. Additionally, while the laws of most of the states having certificate of title laws provide that a notification of the security interest on the certificate of title is the only means of perfection, the laws of some title states do not so provide. Despite these variations, the rules applicable to two of the most common situations are clear:

1. Where a security interest exists in an automobile (or similar "certificate collateral") in a title state, and where the interest is duly noted on the certificate of title as required by the law of that state, the perfection continues after the automobile is removed to another title state *until it is registered* in the new state—the general four-month rule is inapplicable. Thus the secured party is protected against anyone who purchases the car in the new state prior to the new registration. Additionally, because a new registration normally requires the surrender of the old certificate of title, and the secured party is normally the holder of that certificate, the secured party usually can require that the security

interest also be noted on the new certificate of title.

2. Where a security interest exists in an automobile in a non-certificate of title state, and where the interest is perfected by a filing of a financing statement under the basic filing section of Article 9, the security interest is generally protected when the automobile is moved to a new state *for four months* after it is brought into such state.

LIMITATIONS ON PERFECTION

There are limited situations in which certain third parties acquire the collateral *free of* the security interest, even though the interest has been perfected. Following are the primary situations in which these third parties prevail.

Buyers in the Ordinary Course of Business

Section 9-307(1) provides that "a buyer [of goods] in the ordinary course of business . . . takes free of a security interest created by his seller even though the security interest is perfected and even though the buyer knows of its existence." The rationale for this is that the ordinary person who purchases goods from a merchant should not be required to find out if there is an outstanding security interest covering the merchant's inventory. The key words identifying the buyer in this case, a **buyer in the ordinary course of business,** mean that he or she made the purchase in the ordinary course of the debtor's business—that is, that the collateral purchased was of a type which the debtor normally sold (customarily meaning inventory).

To illustrate: M, a merchant in the appliance business, seeks a loan from B Bank, putting up his inventory of refrigerators, stoves, freezers, and other appliances as security for the loan. B Bank perfects its security interest by filing a financing statement centrally with the secretary of state. A week later, C, a consumer, purchases a freezer from M for cash. Since C has purchased in the ordinary course of the seller's business, *he takes the property free of B Bank's security interest.*

There are two limitations upon the ordinary course of business rule. First, the rule does not apply to the buyer who not only knows of the existence of the security interest, but also knows that the sale of the goods was a *violation* of the security agreement (a situation that rarely exists). Second, the buyer of *farm products* from a farmer takes the goods subject to the security interest, even if the buyer knows nothing about the existence of a security agreement.

Buyers Not in the Ordinary Course of Business

A second class of buyer who receives protection in some circumstances against a perfected security interest is the buyer who buys consumer goods not in the ordinary course of business, sometimes referred to as "the next-door neighbor buyer." This priority arises under Sec. 9-307(2), which applies to the situation where consumer goods are sold (usually by a retailer) subject to a purchase money security interest in favor of the seller, in which case—as we saw earlier—perfection is automatic. That section provides, in effect, that if the consumer-buyer (the debtor) resells the goods to a third party not in the ordinary course of business, the third party takes the goods *free of the perfected security interest* if the following conditions are met:

1. The buyer must buy without knowledge of the security interest.

2. He or she must give value for the goods.

3. The purchase must be for the buyer's own personal, family, or household purposes.

4. The purchase must take place before the secured party files a financing statement—a condition that is normally easy to meet, since the secured party in such a case usually does not file at all.

To illustrate: M, a merchant in the appliance business, sells a freezer out of his inventory to C, a consumer, under a conditional sales contract, because C cannot pay the full purchase price. Since this is a purchase money security interest in consumer goods, M makes no filing. C takes the freezer home but decides he does not like it and sells it to his friend, F, who purchases the freezer for his own use without knowledge of M's security interest. If C defaults, M will lose his security interest in the freezer and become a general creditor of C, since F has met the UCC requirements.

Buyers of Chattel Paper, Negotiable Instruments, and Negotiable Documents

Under Article 3 of the UCC, "Commercial Paper," good faith purchasers of negotiable instruments who give value for such instruments generally take the instruments free of claims asserted by prior parties. This same general concept is recognized under Sections 9-308 and 9-309 of the UCC.

Section 9-308 provides, in part, that "a purchaser of chattel paper . . . who gives new value and takes possession of it in the ordinary course of his business *has priority over a security interest in the chattel paper* . . . which is perfected [by filing]." (Emphasis added.) Thus, if a perfected creditor does not take possession of the chattel paper, a person who buys the paper from the debtor in good faith generally takes it free of the perfected interest.

The most common situation (but by no means the only one) to which this section is applicable is the case where a dealer, usually a retailer, sells goods (for example, furniture) on credit to a consumer, the debtor, with the dealer taking a chattel paper (usually a promissory note coupled with a security interest in favor of the dealer) from the consumer-debtor. The dealer then subsequently assigns the paper to a financial institution, usually a bank, as security for a loan made

by the bank to the dealer.[10] In such a case, if the bank perfects by filing only, leaving possession of the paper in the dealer, a person who purchases the paper from the dealer in good faith—that is, without knowledge of the security interest of the bank—and for value takes the chattel paper free of the bank's perfected interest.

Along similar lines, Sec. 9-309 provides, in essence, that a holder in due course of a negotiable instrument, and a holder to whom a negotiable document of title has been duly negotiated, *takes priority over* an earlier security interest in such instrument or document even though the security interest is a perfected one. Further, that section provides that the filing of a security interest in a negotiable instrument or negotiable document (by the original secured party) does not constitute notice of the security interest to such holders.

Other Protected Parties

In addition to buyers of collateral discussed above, there are other third parties whose interests in the collateral (usually arising under other statutes) are excluded from operation of Article 9 by Sec. 9-104. Such interests thus have priority over interests perfected under Article 9. Some of these interests, for example, are those arising under statutes of the United States, landlord liens, and liens "given by statute . . . for services or materials. . . ." To illustrate an interest in the latter category: M, a mechanic, repairs an automobile owned by O that is subject to a security interest in favor of a bank. Under the typical state

---

[10] In the general situation presented here (especially common in the furniture industry), the consumer-debtor is not notified of the assignment to the bank. Thus, in the usual case where the dealer retains possession of the paper *instead of selling it* to a third party, the consumer-debtor continues to make monthly payments to the dealer, and the dealer remits them to the bank. The transaction is referred to as *non-notification* (or *indirect collection*), as distinguished from the case of *notification* (or *direct collection*), where the consumer-debtor is notified of the assignment and makes payments directly to the bank. In the case of direct notification, common in the automobile industry, possession of the paper is normally transferred to the bank, the secured party.

statute M possesses an *artisan's lien*—the right to retain possession of the car until he or she is paid for the repair work. Generally, under such a lien the mechanic's right to retain possession may be successfully asserted against the bank.

PERFECTION AND THE FLOATING LIEN CONCEPT

Section 9-204 of the UCC permits the security agreement to include a clause providing that the obligation covered by the agreement is also secured by any collateral that may subsequently be acquired by the debtor. Such a provision, called an **after-acquired property clause,** permits the secured creditor to have a **"floating lien"**—a lien on changing or shifting assets of the debtor. This clause is most often used to cover inventories of the debtor, where goods are continuously being sold and restocked by the debtor, but sometimes covers non-inventory assets of the debtor (such as plant machinery).

Section 9-204 also permits the security agreement to contain a **future advances clause,** which is a clause providing that the debtor's collateral shall also be security for any extensions of credit (advances) which the creditor may make in the future. The following example illustrates the extensive protection that is afforded a secured party who utilizes both the after-acquired property and future advances clauses.

April 2—D borrows money from X (creditor #1) under a security agreement that gives X a security interest in all of the equipment in D's plant. The agreement contains an after-acquired property clause and also a future advances clause. X perfects the same day by filing a financing statement centrally.

June 1—D purchases a new piece of equipment for $50,000, and pays cash for it.

June 15—D decides to replenish his raw material inventory. He does this by getting a loan from Y (creditor #2) for $25,000, putting up his new piece of equipment as security for the loan.

June 16—Y perfects by filing a financing statement centrally.

June 30—D needs additional funds to meet his payroll, and approaches X (creditor #1) for a $20,000 loan for this purpose. X makes the loan.

September 1—D's business is hit by a recession, with the result that D is in default to both X and Y.

In this situation, X's interest in the new piece of equipment has priority over Y's interest, for either of two reasons:

1. If D owes any balance on the original debt incurred April 2, X has a protected security interest in the new equipment by virtue of the after-acquired property clause. Thus, the new equipment can be acquired by X as satisfaction for that debt.[11]

2. If D's indebtedness arises out of the advance made to him by X on June 30, X again has priority even though Y's security interest was perfected prior to that advance. This results from the future advances clause, which causes the June 30 advance *to date back to the April 2 perfection.*

PROCEEDS AND COMMINGLING

The secured party's right to proceeds is extremely important when the debtor sells the collateral to a third party under circumstances in which the secured party loses his or her interest in the collateral. In such a case, any payments (or proceeds) made by the third party to the debtor can be claimed by the secured party in satisfaction of the debt. Under Secs. 9-203 and 306, this right of the secured party is automatic unless the parties agree otherwise, and it is usually continuous in duration until the debt is paid.

---

[11] The usual priority afforded by an after-acquired property clause may be lost in circumstances where the second creditor's interest is a "purchase money security interest." The special rules applicable to such interests are examined later in the chapter.

In certain business operations, goods under a perfected security interest are commingled with other goods and become part of the product or mass. What then happens to the security interest? Section 9-315(1) provides that the security interest *continues* in the product or mass if the goods lose their identity in processing or manufacturing, or if the financing statement covering the original goods also covers the product into which the goods have been manufactured or processed. Under Sec. 9-315(2), in the same situation, if more than one security interest attaches to the product or mass, they all rank equally according to the cost ratio of their contribution to the total.

The rules relating to after-acquired property, future advances, commingled or processed goods, and proceeds also make it possible for the lien to float on a *shifting stock* of goods. Under Sec. 9-205, the lien can start with raw materials and pass to work in process, to finished inventory, to accounts receivable or chattel paper, and to any cash proceeds under a single perfected security interest.

PRIORITIES BETWEEN CREDITORS

Earlier, in the section entitled "Limitations on Perfection," we saw that certain *buyers of the collateral* took it free of a perfected security interest. In other words, in a contest between the perfected creditor and a buyer of the collateral, the buyer's interest (in limited circumstances) had priority over that of the creditor.

Here we will examine the rules applicable to even more common controversies—those in which both of the competing parties are *creditors of the debtor* (with both parties' interests arising under Article 9).

Unperfected Security Interests

The basic priority section is Sec. 9-312, and most of the provisions found there deal with priorities between perfected creditors—situations in which both of the claimants to the collateral hold perfected security interests. Before we turn to an examination of these important rules, however, two introductory rules involving priorities relative to *unperfected* interests should be kept in mind.

First, in contests between two secured but unperfected creditors, under Sec. 9-312(5)(b) the creditor's interest that attached first—was created first—takes priority over the other.[12] (It should also be kept in mind, however, that should the debtor go into bankruptcy both unperfected interests are lost, with the unperfected creditors simply sharing in the bankrupt's assets along with his or her unsecured creditors.)

Second, in a contest between an unperfected creditor and a perfected creditor, the perfected creditor's interest, of course, has priority over the unperfected interest—Sec. 9-301(1)(a). And this priority exists even if the unperfected creditor's interest had attached first, and even if the perfected creditor knew of the unperfected interest before he or she perfected.

Perfected Security Interests

Subject to special rules noted later, the basic priority rule applicable to controversies between perfected creditors is that *conflicting security interests rank according to priority in time of filing or perfection, whichever is earlier.* (Sec. 9-312[5][a].) The following example illustrates the rule.

June 1—Bank A agrees to loan $4,000 to D, with the actual advance of the money to be made when subsequently requested by D. D signs a security agreement giving the bank a security interest in his Audemars Piguet watch, valued at $9,000. D retains possession of the watch.

June 2—Bank A files its financing statement.

June 5—D borrows $6,000 from bank B, signing

---

[12] This situation does not get into the courts often, because in "real life" when it appears that there is going to be a controversy between two unperfected creditors, one or both of the creditors perfect before litigation begins.

a security agreement that gives the bank a security interest in the same watch. Bank B, after advancing the money, perfects by filing its financing statement immediately.

June 7—Bank A advances the $4,000 to D.

If D defaults on both loans, *bank A's interest has priority over that of bank B,* even though bank B's perfection occurred first.[13] The rationale for the rule, as applied to this situation, is that bank B would have known of bank A's agreement had it checked the appropriate filing system before making its loan.

Two words of caution about the basic rule must be made. First, the "first filing" part of the rule grants priority to such filer over a subsequently perfected interest only in those cases where a security agreement and filing occur at a given time, with the actual advance being made by the filing party at a later date (as in the example above). In the much more common case, where both the first and second creditors immediately advance funds upon the debtor's signing of their respective security agreements, the creditor who *perfects first* prevails. To illustrate: X borrows $1,000 from A on June 1, and signs a security agreement on that date giving A a security interest in certain collateral. X then borrows $2,000 from B on June 15, giving B a security interest in the same collateral. If B perfects by filing before A does, B's interest has priority over A's.

Second, the basic rule *does not always* give the party who files first or perfects first protection against subsequent creditors who possess purchase money security interests in the collateral (as indicated in the following discussion).

---

[13] Bank B's perfection occurred on June 5, and bank A's perfection did not occur until June 7. Bank A's filing on June 2 did not constitute a perfection, because its interest had not even attached since it had not yet given value.

SPECIAL RULES APPLICABLE TO PURCHASE MONEY SECURITY INTERESTS

Section 9-312 contains a number of special rules that bring about results different from those obtained under the general rule discussed above. Of these, two that grant special priority to holders of purchase money security interests in limited circumstances merit attention.

Purchase Money Security Interests in Noninventory Collateral

Section 9-312(4) provides that "a purchase money security interest in collateral other than inventory has priority over a conflicting interest in the same collateral . . . if the purchase money security interest is perfected at the time the debtor receives possession of the collateral, or within ten days thereafter." This priority is sometimes referred to as the "super priority" of a purchase money security holder, because his or her interest takes precedence over the person who holds the conflicting interest in the collateral even if that person's interest was perfected prior to the creation of the purchase money interest.

One situation (among several) to which this rule applies is the following: M, a manufacturer, borrows money from bank A, under a written agreement providing that the bank shall have a security interest in the M Company's present and future plant machinery. The bank duly files a financing statement that includes the after-acquired property clause. Thereafter, M buys additional machinery on credit from the XYZ Corporation (a tool and die company) under a security agreement conveying an interest in the additional machinery to the XYZ Corporation. The XYZ Corporation, the purchase money security interest holder, delivers the additional machinery to the M Company and files its financing statement within ten days of delivery. The XYZ Corporation's purchase money security interest in the additional machinery has priority over that of the bank's interest.

Purchase Money Security Interests in Inventories

Purchase money security holders also have "super priority" over existing perfected holders of interests in inventory, but under more limited circumstances. Section 9-312(3)(b) provides, in part, that a perfected purchase money security interest *in inventory* has priority over a conflicting interest in the same inventory if two basic requirements are met: (1) the purchase money security interest must be perfected by the time that the debtor receives the inventory being purchased, and (2) if the holder of the conflicting interest in the inventory has perfected by filing only, the purchase money secured party must give written notification to such holder before the purchase money secured party files his or her financing statement, such notification stating that the purchase money secured party has or expects to acquire a purchase money interest in the debtor's inventory, describing such inventory by item or type. Once this notification is received by the holder of the conflicting interest, it is good for a period of five years.

Again, a note of caution: as to any priority controversies presenting facts that do not clearly fall within the general rule of Sec. 9-312(5) or within the special rules of Sec. 9-312(3)(b) applicable to purchase money security interests, other sections of Sec. 9-312 may apply. (Additionally, the status of perfected security interests in crops is governed by Sec. 9-312[2], a section whose complexity also precludes its treatment in an introductory chapter such as this.)

Both of the next two cases present priority issues in controversies between perfected creditors.

Kimbrell's Furniture Co., Inc. v. Friedman
Supreme Court of South Carolina, 198 S.E.2d 803 (1973)

This suit deals with two separate purchases made from the plaintiff, Kimbrell's Furniture Company—a new television set by Charlie O'Neal on July 11, 1972, and a tape player by his wife on July 15, 1972. Each purchase was on credit, and in each instance there was executed, as security, a conditional sale contract, designated a *purchase money security agreement*. On the same day of each purchase, O'Neal took the items to defendant, Friedman, a pawnbroker doing business as Bonded Loan, and *pledged* them as security for a loan— the television for a loan of $30 and the tape player for a loan of $25.

Kimbrell's did not record any financing statement or notice of these security agreements. O'Neal thereafter failed to make his required monthly payments to Kimbrell's, whereupon Kimbrell's brought this action to recover possession of the goods.

Bonded Loan, which held possession of the television set and tape player as security for its loan, contended that its lien had priority over Kimbrell's unrecorded security interest. The lower court sustained this contention, and Kimbrell's appealed.

The question to be decided was the following: Is a conditional seller of consumer goods required to file a financing statement in

order to perfect his or her security interest as against a pawnbroker who subsequently takes possession of such goods as security for a loan?

Lewis, Justice:

. . . Prior to the adoption of the Uniform Commercial Code (UCC), . . . purchase money security interests, including conditional sales contracts for consumer goods, were required to be recorded in order to perfect such security interests against subsequent creditors, including pawnbrokers.

. . . However, insofar as it applied to the perfection of security interests in consumer goods, this rule has been repealed by the UCC and the provisions of the latter are controlling in the determination of the present question.

Goods are classified or defined for purposes of secured transactions under §10.9-109. Subsection 1 defines "consumer goods" as those "used or bought for use primarily for personal, family or household purposes." The property here involved was a television set and tape player. They are normally used for personal, family or household purposes and the purchasers warranted that such was the intended use. It is undisputed in this case that the collateral involved was consumer goods within the meaning of the foregoing statutory definition.

Kimbrell clearly held a *purchase money security interest* in the consumer goods sold to the O'Neals and, by them, subsequently pledged to Bonded Loan. Section 10.9-107(a).

When filing is required to perfect a security interest, the UCC requires that a document designated as a financing statement (§10.9-402) must be filed. Section 10.9-302. Contrary to the prior provisions of §60-101, supra, the UCC does not require filing in order to perfect a purchase money security interest in consumer goods. Pertinent here, §10.9-302(1)(d) provides:

(1) A financing statement must be filed to perfect all security interests except the following: . . . (d) a purchase money security interest in consumer goods; . . .

Since filing was not necessary, the security interest of Kimbrell attached and was perfected *when the debtors executed the purchase money security agreements and took possession of the property.* Sections 10.9-204, 10.9-303(1). [Emphasis added.] Therefore, Kimbrell's security interest has priority over the security interest of Bonded Loan by virtue of §10.9-312(4), which provides:

(4) A purchase money security interest in collateral other than inventory has priority over a conflicting security interest in the same collateral if the purchase money security interest is perfected at the time the debtor receives possession of the collateral or within ten days thereafter.

This result is consistent with and confirmed by the residual priority rule of 10.9-312(5)(b) providing for priority between conflicting security interests in the same collateral ". . . in the order of perfection unless both are perfected by filing. . . ."

Bonded Loan, however, alleges that its interest takes priority over the security interest of Kimbrell by virtue of §10.9-307(1), which is as follows:

(1) A buyer in ordinary course of business (subsection (9) of Section 10.1-201) other than a person buying farm products from a person engaged in farming operations takes free of a security interest created by his seller even though the security interest is perfected and even though a buyer knows of its existence.

The above section affords Bonded Loan no relief. It was not a buyer in the ordinary course of business so as to take free of the security interest of Kimbrell. A buyer in the ordinary course of business is defined in subsection (9) of §10.1-201 as follows:

"Buyer in ordinary course of business" means a person who in good faith and without knowledge that the sale to him is in violation of the ownership rights or security interest of a third party in the goods buys in ordinary course from a person in the business of selling goods of that kind. . . .

In the Reporter's Comments to §10.9-307(1), supra, Dean Robert W. Foster points out that, under the foregoing definition, a buyer in ordinary course of business "must be 'without knowledge that the sale to him is in violation of the ownership rights or security interest of a third party . . .' *and* the seller must be a 'person in the business of selling goods of that kind. . . .' Thus subsection (1) (of §10.9-307) is limited to the *buyer out of inventory* who may know of the inventory financer's security interest but does not know that the sale to him is unauthorized." [Emphasis added.]

Therefore, Bonded Loan could not have been a buyer in the ordinary course of business when O'Neal pledged the property to it, because O'Neal was not "a person in the business of selling goods of that kind."

The judgment of the lower court is accordingly reversed and the cause remanded for entry of judgment in favor of plaintiff, Kimbrell's Furniture Company, Inc., in accordance with the views herein.

In re Ultra Precision Industries, Inc.
U.S. Court of Appeals for the Ninth Circuit, 503 F.2d 414 (1974)

This is a controversy between two creditors of Ultra Precision Industries, Inc. (Ultra): the National Acceptance Company of California (National) and the Community Bank (the bank).

Ultra, a California manufacturer, borrowed $692,000 from National in early March 1967. As security for the loan, Ultra gave National a "chattel mortgage security agreement" giving National a security interest in specifically described equipment owned by Ultra and used in Ultra's plant. The agreement and the financing statement signed by Ultra contained the usual after-acquired property clause. National perfected its security interest by filing the financing statement.

Thereafter Ultra ordered two Rigid Hydro Copy Profiling machines from the Wolf Machinery Company (Wolf). Because of the complexity of the machines, it was agreed between Ultra and Wolf that Ultra would be given an opportunity to test them in their operations for a reasonable time, and that arrangements satisfactory to Ultra for outside financing was a condition precedent to the ultimate purchase of the machines.[a]

The machines were delivered to Ultra on April 30 and June 20, 1968. Satisfactory testing was accomplished, outside financing was obtained, and on *July 31, 1968,* Ultra and Wolf executed a "purchase money security interest conditional sales agreement" covering the sale of the machines by Wolf to Ultra. Wolf, in consideration of a payment of $128,122, then assigned the security interest agreement to the Community Bank. The bank perfected this interest by filing a financing statement on *August 5, 1968.*

Ultra subsequently defaulted on its obligations to National and to the bank, and then became bankrupt. The trial court ruled that the purchase money security interest held by the bank took priority over National's interest in the machinery, and National appealed.

East, Senior District Judge:

The priorities among the . . . security interests involved are determined by the application of §9312(4), which reads:

A purchase money security interest in collateral other than inventory has priority over a conflicting security interest in the same collateral if the purchase money security interest is perfected at the time the debtor receives possession of the collateral or within 10 days thereafter. *[Emphasis added by the court.]*

The sole issue presented by the facts and the contentions of the parties on appeal is: On what date did Ultra become "the debtor [receiving] possession of the collateral [the machines]" within the meaning of §9312(4)?

Briefly stated, National contends that Ultra was its "debtor" in "possession of the collateral" at the moment it received physical delivery of the . . . machines, without regard to any agreement to the contrary between Wolf and Ultra as to the terms and conditions of the ultimate sale and purchase of the machines; hence, the machines were within the grasp of the after-acquired property clause. Since the security interest agreement held by Bank was not perfected within ten days "thereafter" as commanded by §9312(4), the interests are unenforceable [National contends] as against National's perfected interest.

Bank . . . contends that Ultra did not become a "debtor" in "possession of the collateral" [when the machines were physically delivered to Ultra, but,

---

[a]A third machine was purchased subsequently under an agreement identical to the first agreement. Because the financing of that machine was with a different finance company, and subsequently involved an assignment and reassignment of the claim, consideration of this purchase is omitted in the interest of simplicity.

rather, that Ultra became a debtor only after] the terms and conditions of the proposed sales and purchases thereof had been met and the Security Interest Agreement had been executed and delivered. We subscribe to that contention.

Section 9105(1) of the Code provides:

(1) In this division unless the context otherwise requires: (d) 'Debtor' means the person who owes payment or other performance of the obligation secured. . . .

National urges that the term "debtor" as used in §9312(4) means the debtor under its "conflicting security interest." Such an interpretation does violence to the clear language of the section. . . . To us, the word "debtor" in §9312(4) means the debtor of the seller or holder of the "purchase money security interest in collateral (the thing sold)."

It is manifest that Ultra was not a "debtor" of Wolf and did not owe payment or other performance of the obligation secured unto Wolf until the moment of the execution and delivery of the Security Interest Agreement on July 31, 1968. . . . Suffice to say that prior to that date (a) Wolf held no definitive security interest in the machines which could be perfected by the filing of a Financing Statement, and (b) Ultra held no assignable legal interest in the machines which could fall into the grasp of National's after-acquired property clause.

We hold that Ultra became the purchase money security interest "debtor [receiving] possession of the collateral" . . . at the instant of the execution and delivery of the Security Interest Agreement [on July 31, 1968] *and not before*; and, further, that since . . . the Security Interest Agreement [was] timely perfected [by the bank's filing on August 5, 1968] the security interest of the bank is prior and superior to the conflicting interest held by National. [Emphasis added] . . .

Affirmed.

RIGHTS AND DUTIES PRIOR TO TERMINATION

The security agreement determines most of the rights and duties of the debtor and secured party. However, other rights and duties are imposed by the UCC, some of which are applied in the absence of a security agreement.

Release, Assignment, and Amendment

Under Sec. 9-406, the secured party of record can release all or part of any collateral described in the filed financing statement, thereby ending his or her security interest in the described collateral. Under Sec. 9-405, the secured party can also assign all or part of the security interest to an assignee, who, in order to become the secured party of record, must file either by a disclosure method provided for in the code (such as a notation on the front or back of the financing statement) or by a separate written statement of assignment.

If the debtor and secured party so agree, under Sec. 9-402, the financing statement can be amended (for example, to add new collateral to the security interest). But the filed amendment must be signed by both the debtor and the secured party. This amendment does not extend the time period of the perfection unless collateral is added; in such a case, the perfection for the new collateral applies from the date of filing the amendment.

The debtor's signature is needed for (1) the security agreement, (2) the original financing statement, and (3) amendments to the financing statements. All other documents can be filed with only the signature of the secured party.

Information Requests by Secured Parties

In most states the filing officer must furnish specified information on request to certain parties. For example, under Sec. 9-407(1), the person filing any of the above statements can furnish the filing officer with a duplicate and request that the officer note on such copy the file number, date, and hour of the original filing. The filing officer must send this copy to the person making the request, without charge.

Frequently, prospective secured parties request of the filing officer a certificate giving information on possible perfected financing statements with respect to a named debtor. Under Sec. 9-407(2), if so requested, the filing officer must furnish a copy of any filed financing statement or assignment. Given the priorities of secured interests and the attachment of security interest under the concept of the floating lien, businesspersons ought to request such information before advancing credit to debtors.

Security Party in Possession of the Collateral

Section 9-207 provides that generally a secured party in possession of the collateral must use reasonable care in the custody and preservation of it and is subject to liability by the debtor for any failure to do so (although he or she does not lose the security interest thereby). The secured party can use or operate the collateral as permitted in the security agreement or to preserve its value. Should the collateral increase in value or profits be derived from it, the secured party can hold these increases as additional security unless they are in the form of money. Any increase in

money must be either remitted to the debtor or applied to reduction of the secured obligation.

Under the same section, the secured party must keep the collateral identifiable (except that when the collateral is fungible, it can be commingled with like goods). He or she can repledge the collateral, but this must be done on terms that do not impair the debtor's right to redeem it upon paying the debt.

Again under the same section, unless the security agreement provides to the contrary, the debtor is responsible for all reasonable charges incurred in the custody, preservation, and operation of the collateral possessed by the secured party. These charges include insurance, taxes, storage, and the like.

Debtor's Right to Request Status of Debt

Under Sec. 9-208, the debtor can sign a statement indicating what he or she believes to be the aggregate amount of the unpaid indebtedness as of a specific date (and, under certain circumstances, including a list of collateral covered by the security agreement) with the request that the secured party approve or correct the statement. The secured party, unless he or she has a reasonable excuse, must comply with the request within two weeks of receipt or be liable for any loss caused to the debtor by such failure. Since the debtor could become a nuisance by making numerous and continuous requests to the secured party, he or she is entitled to make such a request without charge only once every six months. For each additional request made during this period, the secured party can require payment of a fee not exceeding $10.

DEFAULT OF THE DEBTOR

In general, under Sec. 9-501, when the debtor is in default, the secured party can reduce his or her claim to judgment, foreclose, or otherwise enforce the security interest by any available judicial procedure. Under Sec. 9-503, unless otherwise agreed, the secured party also has the right to take possession of the collateral on default. This can be done without judicial process only if no breach of the peace occurs. Thus the creditor should not attempt to break into the debtor's home or take the collateral by force. If force is used, the debtor can file criminal charges against the secured party and can bring an action in tort for any damages he or she sustains. Although Section 9-503, the so-called "self-help" section on repossession, has been challenged by debtors in numerous cases on the ground that repossession without judicial process is a violation of the Due Process clause of the U.S. Constitution, the

highest courts of most states have ruled that the section is constitutional.[14]

The following case presents a typical situation in which the constitutionality of Section 9-503 is challenged. The case also presents a further question: If the collateral is in the possession of a third party who himself or herself possesses a mechanic's lien in the collateral, can the secured property pay off the lien holder and thus gain possession of the collateral?

---

[14] The basis for this view is that the act of repossession—the "taking" of the property—is not state action, and is therefore not a taking that is subject to the due process clause of the Constitution. (As of mid-1987 the U.S. Supreme Court has not taken a position on the issue.)

Hunt v. Marine Midland Bank-Central
Supreme Court, Onondoga County, 363 N.Y.S.2d 222 (1974)

Hunt, the plaintiff-debtor, purchased a 1973 Lincoln Mark IV on April 24, 1973, from codefendant Heritage Lincoln Mercury, Inc., and financed the automobile through codefendant Marine Midland Bank-Central on a retail installment contract (the security agreement under which the bank was the secured party). Payment was to be made over a thirty-six-month period beginning in June. Plaintiff made the June and July payments, but for a period of time she was in default for her August and September payments. On October 1, 1973, plaintiff made the August payment but did not pay the late charge, and did not make the September payment.

On October 2, 1973, the bank learned that plaintiff had returned the car to the Heritage dealership in August for repairs and that Heritage still had possession, claiming a mechanic's lien on the car for nonpayment of the repair bill. The bank, determining that its security was in jeopardy, *paid off the lien and took possession of the car* pursuant to the terms of the security agreement and Sec. 9-503.

Although plaintiff did make the September payment on October 4, she did not make any further payments during the month for her October obligation. Thus the bank, pursuant to the terms of the security agreement, sold the car in late October. From the proceeds of the sale it deducted costs and the balance due on the security agreement, including the repair charges by Heritage. A deficiency apparently existed, and plaintiff was asked to pay the balance. She refused and instead *sued the codefendants* on the alternate theories of conversion and violation of her constitutional right of due process, based on the manner of repossession.

Specifically, plaintiff contended that the self-help repossession procedures of Sec. 9-503 are unconstitutional, because they violate the due process clause of the federal Constitution and the state constitutions in that they do not require notice and an opportunity to be heard prior to taking the collateral in question. Marine Midland contended that under the terms of the installment contract it had the right to repossess the vehicle without judicial process as long as it was done peacefully. It further contended that under Sec. 9-503 it had the right to take possession in the event of default, especially where (as here) the security agreement provided for such procedure.

Aloi, Justice:

. . . Although plaintiff "owned" the goods which she had purchased under the installment sales contract, her title [as] vendee-debtor was encumbered [since] she had both title and possession of the goods *subject to* her contractual obligation to continue to make timely installment payments. Defendant, Marine Midland, as the vendor-creditor, also had an interest in the property in the form of a vendor's lien to secure the unpaid balance of the purchase price. This Court realizes that *both* the seller and buyer had current, real interests in the property. Resolution of the due process question must take account not only of the interests of the buyer of the property but those of the seller as well.

In striving for a constitutional accommodation of the respective rights and interests of both buyer and seller, this Court stands prepared to protect the buyer's possessory interest to use and enjoy her automobile and the seller's right in being timely paid in accordance with the contract or repossessing the goods for the purpose of foreclosing its lien and recovering the unpaid balance.

Plaintiff has asserted that the "self-help" remedy under Section 9-503 of the UCC is unconstitutional under the rationale of *Sniadach v. Family Finance Corp.*, 395 U.S. 337, and *Fuentes v. Shevin,* 407 U.S. 67. This Court acknowledges the distinction made by many commentators between "self-help repossession" when authorized by a private contract establishing a security interest, and replevin prior to a taking, even though both involve a "taking" of the debtor's property before any judicial determination of the validity of the taking.

In a recent case similar to the one at bar, the court held that "an agreement entered into in compliance with Section 9-503 of the Uniform Commercial Code must be held to be legal [i.e. in conformity with the due process clause] especially where the debtor has expressly authorized the 'self-help' provisions of the contract. [Furthermore] such an agreement cannot be held to be unconscionable when such terms are expressly authorized by statute." *Frost v. Mohawk National Bank,* 347 N.Y.S.2d 246 (1973).

Plaintiff has contended that since Marine Midland accepted certain payments after the 7th of each month, it established a "course of conduct" which precluded it from demanding timely payment each month. This Court rejects this contention on the basis that a clear precedent for late payment was never clearly established nor did Marine Midland ever *intend* to waive its right to repossess despite accepting payment after the 7th of the month.

Heritage has asserted that under existing case and statutory law its lien was lawful and its transfer to Marine Midland was a valid exercise of its rights and obligations pursuant to Section 184 of the Lien Law, which reads in part:

A person keeping a garage, hangar or place for the storage, maintenance, keeping or repair of motor vehicles . . . and in connection therewith stores, maintains, keeps or repairs any motor vehicle . . . has a lien upon such motor vehicle . . . or the sum due for such . . . at any time it may be lawfully in his possession until such sum is paid.

Heritage therefore had a lawful lien on the automobile in question. Upon demand by Marine Midland of the automobile, because of the default in payment by the plaintiff, and upon the tender of a sum of money sufficient to satisfy the lien then in effect, Heritage had no choice but to transfer the automobile to a prior secured party who had the right to possession thereof. In *Kaufman v. Simons Motor Sales, Inc.*, 184 N.Y. 739 (1933), the court held that the assignee of a contract of sale has a right to take possession of the property upon the default of payment by the buyer.

Accordingly, it is the decision of this Court that defendants' motions for summary judgment dismissing plaintiff's complaint be granted. . . .

Duty to Assemble Collateral

Under Sec. 9-503, if the security agreement so provides, the secured party can require the debtor to assemble the collateral upon default and to make it available at a location reasonably convenient to both. If it is impractical to move the collateral or it is too expensive to store, the secured party has the right to render the collateral unusable to the debtor and, following the proper procedure, to dispose of it on the debtor's premises.

Disposal of Collateral

Under Sec. 9-504(1), once the secured party obtains possession, he or she generally has the right to sell, lease, or otherwise dispose of the collateral in its then existing condition or following any commercially reasonable preparation or process. Under 9-507(2), if the secured party sells the collateral, the sale must be handled in a "commercially reasonable manner." Although this is not expressly defined, the code does mention certain actions as being commercially reasonable. Sales made through such actions, or made otherwise and in good faith, are usually held to constitute compliance.

Under Sec. 9-504(3), the collateral can be disposed of at either a public or private sale if done in a commercially reasonable manner. Unless the collateral is perishable, threatens to decline quickly in value, or is of a type customarily sold in a recognized market, the secured party must give the debtor reasonable notice of the time and place of the sale (unless the debtor, after default, signed a statement renouncing or modifying this right to notification). No additional notification need be sent in the case of consumer goods, but in other cases notice must also be sent to any other secured creditor from whom the secured party has received written notice of a claim of an interest in the collateral. (Failure of the secured party to give such notice makes him or her liable for any ensuing loss.) The secured party can buy at *any* public sale—and at a private sale if the collateral customarily is sold in a recognized market or is of a type that is the subject of a widely distributed standard price quotation. (Under Sec. 9-501[3][b], these provisions cannot be waived or varied.)

Under Sec. 9-504(4), when collateral is disposed of by a secured party after default of the debtor, a purchaser for value receives all the debtor's rights in the collateral free from the security interest and subordinate interests and liens. This is true even if the secured party failed to comply with the requirements of disposal under the code or under judicial proceedings, so long as the purchaser bought in good faith, and, at a public sale, had no knowledge of such interests or rights.

Section 9-505 provides that, except where the defaulting debtor has paid 60 percent of an obligation involving consumer goods, the secured party, upon obtaining possession of the goods, can *retain the collateral* in satisfaction of the secured obligation. However, to do so, the secured party must send written notice of such intention to the debtor and (except in the case of consumer goods) to any other secured party from whom written notice of a claim of an interest in the collateral has been received before such notification is sent to the debtor. If no objection is received from such parties within twenty-one days after notice is sent, the secured party can retain the collateral. But if any timely objection is received, the collateral must be disposed of in compliance with Sec. 9-504.

Section 9-505(1) provides that in the case of consumer goods, where the debtor has paid 60 percent or more of the obligation prior to default, the secured party must *dispose of the collateral* as previously discussed (in Sec. 9-504) within ninety days after taking possession—unless the debtor has signed a statement renouncing all rights in the collateral. Under Sec. 9-507(1), should the secured party fail to do so within this period, the debtor can recover an amount "not less than the credit service charge

plus 10 percent of the principal amount of the debt or the time price differential plus 10 percent of the cash price." The secured party may thus suffer a loss by waiting too long to dispose of the collateral in this situation.

Application of Proceeds

The proceeds of the sale are, under Sec. 9-504(1), applied first to the expenses incurred by the secured party in retaking, holding, and selling or leasing the collateral—including reasonable attorney's fees if the security agreement so provides. After these expenses are deducted, the remaining proceeds are applied to the indebtedness of the secured party. If any proceeds are then left, subordinate security interests, if any, are to be satisfied if the subordinate interest holders have made written demand for payment before the proceeds were distributed. (Of course, the secured party can demand that these holders give reasonable proof of their claims.) Thus, even if a businessperson's security interest is second in priority, it is still possible for that person to receive part of the proceeds in satisfaction of the claim by following the UCC procedure.

As a general rule, under Sec. 9-504(2), if any surplus is left after the expenses have been paid and the indebtedness and subordinate security interests have been satisfied, it goes to the debtor. Furthermore, under Sec. 9-501(3)(a), the duty to account to the debtor for this surplus cannot be waived or varied by agreement. Should the proceeds not cover the expenses and the indebtedness to the secured party, under Sec. 9-504(2), the debtor is liable for the deficiency unless otherwise agreed. If the collateral involves the sale of accounts or chattel paper, the rules regarding distribution of surplus and deficiency apply only if they are provided for in the security agreement.

Redemption of Collateral

Section 9-506 provides that the debtor (or any other subordinate secured party) can redeem the collateral at any time before the primary secured party has disposed of (or contracted to dispose of) it, unless he or she has waived the right of redemption in writing after the default. The redemption is accomplished by tendering payment of all obligations secured by the collateral as well as all reasonable costs incurred by the secured party. Under Sec. 9-501(3)(d), a sale of part of the collateral does not remove the right of redemption for any collateral left in the hands of the secured party, and this right can be waived only in the manner indicated here.

TERMINATION

The ultimate goal of the parties is to have the debt paid and the security interest terminated, particularly where it has been perfected by a filing. To accomplish this, when the debt is paid, the secured party files a *termination statement* with the officer with whom the financing statement was filed.

Under Sec. 9-404, if the financing statement covers consumer goods, the secured party must file the termination statement within one month after the secured obligation is no longer outstanding; however, if the debtor demands the statement in writing, it must be filed within ten days after the obligation is no longer outstanding. Thus filing of a termination statement in the case of consumer goods is required even if no demand is made for it by the debtor. In all other cases the secured party must file or furnish the debtor with a termination statement within ten days after written demand is made by the debtor. If the secured party fails to file or furnish the statement to the debtor, he or she is liable to that person for $100 and for any loss caused to the debtor by such failure.

SUMMARY

The purposes of a secured transaction are twofold: (1) to give to a creditor a legally recognized interest in specific property of the debtor, and (2) to give such creditor a priority claim in that property against other creditors who may seek to have the debtor's assets sold in satisfaction of their claims. Secured transactions are governed by Article 9 of the UCC. Under the terminology of that article, the creditor is the secured party, the one owing the debt is the debtor, the interest of the creditor is a security interest, and the property subject to the interest is the collateral.

Secured transactions law applies only to secured interests in personal property. Such property may be classified as goods, quasi-tangibles, and pure intangibles. Goods consists of tangible personal property, such as cattle, automobiles, and jewelry. Quasi-tangibles ordinarily consist of documents of title (such as warehouse receipts) and commercial paper (such as checks and notes). Pure intangibles is the name given to ordinary contractual rights and patent rights.

A security interest attaches (i.e., is created) by means of a security agreement between the secured party and the debtor. This agreement must be in writing unless the secured party takes possession of the collateral. (Since it is not possible for the creditor to take possession of an intangible, security agreements in intangibles must be in writing). After a security agreement is made, the secured party will ordinarily "perfect" the interest so that it will have maximum protection against claims of other parties to the collateral. (If there is no perfection, the secured party loses his or her interest to a party having a perfected interest in the same collateral; the secured party also loses the interest if the debtor goes into bankruptcy). Perfection is usually achieved by the filing of a financing statement by the creditor (at a designated office specified by the provisions of Article 9). Perfection may be achieved, however, by the secured creditor's taking possession of the collateral, and in some instances involving the sale of consumer goods on credit, perfection is automatic. There are special filing rules as to motor vehicles, fixtures, and to collateral moved to another state.

While a perfected interest is generally valid against all third parties, there are exceptions to this rule. A perfected creditor's interest, for example, is lost if the debtor sells the collateral to a buyer in the ordinary course of the debtor's business. Additionally, such interest is lost to a buyer *not* in the ordinary course of business under certain circumstances, and, where the collateral consists of negotiable instruments left in the debtor's possession, the creditor's interest is lost to a party who purchases them in good faith and for value.

A security agreement may cover a certain type of property (such as machinery or inventory) and such type of property as the debtor may acquire in the future. This protection can be achieved by use of an "after-acquired property" clause in the security agreement. However, this protection might be lost to the unpaid seller of such additional property who himself may have a purchase-money security in that property. A perfected security interest has priority over a nonperfected interest in the same property. Where there are two or more perfected interests in the same property, the rule is that the interests rank "according to priority in filing or perfection, whichever is earlier." The rights and duties of the parties prior to termination of the interest generally are spelled out in the security agreement. In the event of a default by the debtor, the creditor's remedies are set forth in Sec. 9-501 of the UCC.

KEY TERMS

Secured transaction
Secured party
Debtor
Security interest
Security agreement
Collateral
Perfection
Financing statement
Goods
Fixtures
Quasi-tangible collateral
Documents of title
Instrument
Chattel paper
Intangible collateral
Account
General intangibles
Attachment
Filing
Automatic perfection
Purchase money security interest
Buyer in the ordinary course of business
Floating lien
After-acquired property clause
Future advances clause

QUESTIONS AND PROBLEMS

1. Rike-Kumler, a jeweler, sold a $1,237 diamond ring to Nicolosi which he was going to give to his fiancée. Nicolosi made a down payment and executed a purchase money security agreement to Rike-Kumler for the unpaid balance. Rike-Kumler did not file a financing statement. Nicolosi gave the ring to his fiancée, and later went into bankruptcy. His fiancée called off the engagement and delivered the ring to the trustee in bankruptcy. Rike-Kumler then claimed a protected purchase money security interest in the ring, as against the trustee's claim. At the trial, the trustee in bankruptcy contended that the ring was not a "consumer good," because Nicolosi did not intend to wear it himself. Do you think that the ring was a consumer good? Why or why not? In regard to Rike-Kumler's claim, what difference does it make whether the ring is or is not a consumer good? Explain. (*In re Nicolosi,* 4 UCC Rptr. 111, 1966.)

2. A, a furniture dealer, purchased a large number of sofas from W, a furniture wholesaler, signing a security agreement for the purchase price. A sold one of the sofas to B for $150, with B paying $100 down and signing a security agreement for the balance.

> **a.** How is an enforceable security interest created in this collateral by W? By A?
> **b.** What is the classification of collateral as between W and A? Between A and B? Where would each security interest be properly perfected?
> **c.** Suppose that, with both security interests in existence, A is in default to W. Assuming W's interest is properly perfected, does W have any rights in the sofa purchased by B? Why or why not?

3. A loan's collateral is a refrigerator. How would you, as the secured party, properly perfect your security interest in it under the following circumstances?

    a. You are a wholesaler and the refrigerator is part of a 250-appliance installment sale to a retailer.

    b. You are a retailer and sell the refrigerator, on an installment purchase plan, to a customer, for use in the customer's home.

    c. You are a retailer and sell the refrigerator, on an installment contract, to a farmer for use in storing eggs until they can be marketed.

4. Weiss and Bostron (W&B), engaged in a joint venture, borrowed money from a bank in Brush, Colorado, to buy some cattle. Weiss gave the bank a purchase money security interest in the cattle under a security agreement. After buying the cattle he bought feed on credit from the Colorado High Plains Agricultural Credit Corporation (CHPACC), giving that corporation a security interest in "all feed now or hereafter acquired," and in the "proceeds" of the feed. The cattle consumed the feed and were subsequently sold at a loss.

The sale of the cattle did not bring enough to pay off the full amount of the debt owed the bank, so the bank sued W&B for the balance due it. At this point the seller of the feed, CHPACC, intervened, claiming that any money the bank was able to recover from W&B was subject to its security under the proceeds clause of its security agreement. In other words, CHPACC claimed that since it would have priority in the proceeds of the feed if the feed were sold instead of being eaten by the cattle, it thus had a priority in the proceeds of the cattle sale, giving it priority over any money that might be recovered by the bank from W&B. The bank, by contrast, argued that once the feed was eaten, it lost its identity and that the proceeds sought to be recovered by CHPACC were also lost. Which of these arguments is the better? Explain. (*First National Bank of Brush v. Bostron,* 564 P.2d 964, 1977.)

5. CS, a college student, needed $5,000 to start up a small business. On October 10 the ABC Bank agreed to loan him that amount, the ad-

vance of which would not occur until he notified the bank that the money was needed. On that same date CS signed a security agreement giving the bank a security interest in specified jewelry CS had just inherited. The bank perfected by filing a financing statement the same day.

On October 20 CS needed additional money for his project, so he borrowed another $5,000 from a second bank, the XYZ bank. CS signed a security agreement in favor of the XYZ Bank giving it a secured interest in the same jewelry. Because the bank had had difficulties with student loans before, it took possession of the jewelry with CS's permission and without knowledge of the ABC Bank's interest.

On November 1 the ABC Bank, at CS's request, advanced him the $5,000 it had earlier agreed to make available. Thereafter CS defaulted on both loans, and each bank claimed that its interest in the jewelry had priority over the interest of the other bank. Which bank wins? Explain.

6. A secured party has this problem: Four and a half years ago he properly created a security interest in the collateral of a debtor and filed a financing statement. The debtor now is unable to repay the loan. The secured party feels that, given more time, the debtor will be able to pay the balance due. However, another secured party whose filing came after his is in the same position. The collateral is sufficient to satisfy the remaining balance of either loan, but not both. What would you advise the first secured party to do to protect his interest in the collateral?

7. Rompon borrowed money from a bank in order to buy a mobile home. He gave a purchase money security interest in the mobile home to the bank, which perfected its interest by having a notation of such interest made on the Florida certificate of title covering the home, as required by the Florida certificate of title law. Thereafter Rompon moved the home to a trailer park, where its wheels were removed, the home was physically attached to the real estate, and hookups were made to underground facilities. Later the land to which the mobile home was attached was sold at a sheriff's sale to Langelier and Corbeil.

The bank then sought to foreclose on its lien (that is, to have the home sold) and to receive the proceeds of the sale free of any interest that Langelier and Corbeil might have in the home or its proceeds. The trial court ruled that the mobile home had become a "fixture" within the meaning of Article 9 of the UCC, and that since the bank's interest was not perfected as required by Sec. 9-401, the bank's interest was *subordinate to* the rights of Langelier and Corbeil. Was the judge correct? Why or why not? (*Barnett*

Bank of Clearwater N.A. v. Rompon, 377 So.2d 981, 1979.)

8. You are a debtor who has a number of security agreements with a single secured party. You have put up numerous pieces of collateral as security for these loans, and you are no longer sure of the balance on any of them. You think some of the loans have been paid off, and you do not know which pieces of collateral are still subject to the remaining loans. You have called the secured party but have not yet received a satisfactory response. Is there anything you can legally do to get the information you want? Explain.

Chapter 30

BANKRUPTCY

OVERVIEW OF DEBTOR-CREDITOR RELATIONS

The treatment of debtors has varied greatly over the years. During certain early periods, debtors were forced to become servants of their creditors, were thrown into prison, or even had body parts removed for failure to pay a debt. History finally demonstrated to both creditors and society that very little was accomplished by such methods. In seeking more humane solutions, the general problem has been how to balance the creditor's rights with the debtor's desire for relief from debts.

Numerous devices have been developed through the years for resolving debtor-creditor disputes. In this chapter we will deal primarily with one such procedure—*bankruptcy under federal law.* However, many of the other methods available under state common-law principles, state statutes, and private agreements may actually be preferable to bankruptcy when it is possible to use them. Bankruptcy, therefore, is generally viewed as an avenue of last resort. Before we turn to a detailed examination of the federal bankruptcy law, we first will survey some of the alternatives.

Alternatives to Bankruptcy

Although time and space do not permit a detailed analysis of each method of debt resolution, the following methods are frequently used when a debtor cannot pay his or her obligation: (1) foreclosure on a real estate mortgage, (2) enforcement of a secured transaction (Article 9 of the UCC), (3) enforcement of an artisan's lien, (4) enforcement of a mechanic's lien, (5) writ of execution on a judgment, (6) garnishment, (7) attachment, (8) receivership, (9) cancelling a fraudulent conveyance, (10) composition of creditors, (11) assignment for the benefit of creditors, and (12) creditors' committees.

Foreclosure on a Real Estate Mortgage:

When a mortgagor (debtor) defaults under the terms of a mortgage agreement, the mortgagee (creditor) has the right to declare the entire mortgage debt due and enforce his or her rights through a remedy called **foreclosure.** In most states the mortgagee is required to sell the mortgaged real estate (even if it is the person's homestead) under the direction of the court, using the proceeds to pay the foreclosure costs and the balance of the debt. If any proceeds are left over, the surplus goes to the mortgagor. If the proceeds are insufficient to cover the costs of foreclosure and the remaining indebtedness, the mortgagor is liable to the mortgagee for the unpaid balance of the debt. However, before the actual foreclosure sale and for a certain period of time thereafter (set by state statute), the mortgagor can *redeem* the property by full payment of costs, indebtedness, and interest.

Enforcement of a Secured Transaction:

As we saw in the last chapter, under Article 9 of the UCC, when a debtor defaults on the security agreement made with a secured party (the creditor), the collateral (personal property) that is the subject of the security agreement can be used to satisfy the debt. The secured party can retain possession of the collateral or take it from the debtor, either by court order or without court action if it can be accomplished peaceably. He or she can then either (1) *keep the collateral* in satisfaction of the debt by giving proper notice to the debtor of such intention (assuming the debtor does not object), or (2) *sell the collateral* through a "commercially reasonable" process. The secured party must always sell the collateral if proper objection is made by the debtor to the party keeping it or if the collateral is classified as "consumer goods" and the debtor has paid 60 percent or more of the debt.

If the collateral is kept by the secured party, the debt is discharged. If the collateral is sold and the proceeds are insufficient to pay the debt and the costs of enforcing the security interest, the secured party is usually entitled to seek a deficiency judgment for the balance. The debtor can redeem the collateral at any time until its sale or disposal.

Enforcement of an Artisan's Lien: The **artisan's lien,** a possessory lien given to creditors who perform services on personal property or take care of goods entrusted to them, was developed at common law. If the debtor does not pay for the services, the creditor is permitted to obtain a judgment and/or foreclose and sell the property in satisfaction of the debt. Any proceeds remaining from the sale of the property after paying the debt and costs of sale must be returned to the debtor. In order to exercise this lien, the creditor must have retained possession of the property and must not have agreed to provide the services on credit. Many states have passed statutes governing the procedures to be followed in enforcing such a lien. If the creditor operates a warehouse and the claim arises from unpaid storage charges, the procedures which must be followed are set forth in Article 7 of the Uniform Commercial Code.

Enforcement of a Mechanic's Lien: Certain other liens have been made available to creditors by state statutes. One of the most common is the **mechanic's lien**—a lien against real estate for labor, services, or materials used in improving the realty. When the labor or materials are furnished, a debt is incurred. To make the real property itself security for the debt, the creditor must file a notice of lien in a manner provided by statute. To be effective, it usually must be filed within a specified period (usually 60 to 120 days) after the last materials or labor were furnished. If the notice is properly filed and the debt is not paid, the creditor can foreclose and sell the realty in satisfaction of the debt. (This is similar to a foreclosure of a real estate mortgage.)

Writ of Execution on a Judgment: Once a debt becomes overdue, a creditor can file suit for payment in a court of law and, if successful, be awarded a "judgment." If the judgment is not satisfied by the debtor, the creditor has the right to go back to court and obtain a **writ of execution.** The writ, issued by the clerk of the court, directs the sheriff or other officer to levy upon (seize) and sell any of the debtor's *nonexempt property* within the court's jurisdiction. The judgment is paid from the proceeds of the sale, and any balance is returned to the debtor. One limitation on the writ is that it can be levied only on nonexempt property. That is, exempt property, such as the debtor's homestead, cannot be taken to satisfy the judgment.

Garnishment: Another limitation of the writ of execution is that it usually cannot reach debts owed to the judgment debtor by third parties or the debtor's interests in personal property legally possessed by third parties. However, the law does permit the creditor (using the proper court procedure) to require these persons to turn over to the court or sheriff money owed or property belonging to the debtor. This method of satisfying a judgment is called **garnishment;** the third party, called the *garnishee,* is legally bound by the court order. The most common types of "property" garnished are wages and bank accounts. The federal Consumer Credit Protection Act limits garnishment of a debtor's current wages to 25 percent of take-home pay, and prohibits the debtor's employer from discharging him or her because of a single garnishment order. Some state laws place greater restrictions on garnishment of wages.

Attachment: The seizing of a debtor's property under a court order, known as *attachment,* is a statutory remedy and can be exercised only in strict accordance with the provisions of the particular state statutes. It is available to a creditor even *before* a judgment has been rendered, under some statutes. Statutory grounds for attachment prior to judgment are limited, usually including situations where the debtor is unavailable to be served with a summons or where there is a reasonable belief that the debtor may conceal or remove property from the jurisdiction of the court before the creditor can obtain a judgment.

To employ attachment as a remedy, the creditor must file with the court an affidavit attesting to the debtor's default and the legal reasons why attachment is sought. Additionally, the creditor must post a bond sufficient to cover at least the value of the debtor's property, the value of the loss of use of the goods suffered by the debtor (if any), and court costs in case the creditor loses the suit. The court then issues a *writ of attachment,* directing the sheriff or other officer to seize nonexempt property sufficient to satisfy the creditor's claim. If the creditor's suit against the debtor is successful, the property seized can then be sold to satisfy the judgment.

Receivership: Attachment may prove inadequate to protect creditors while they pursue their claims if the debtor's property requires care (such as crops, livestock, etc.). In such cases, on essentially the same grounds as for attachment, the court may appoint a *receiver* to care for and preserve the property pending the outcome of the lawsuit in which one or more creditors are seeking to collect unpaid debts. It is then said that the debtor's property is placed in **receivership.** The object of receivership is to prevent a debtor from "wasting" assets while being pursued by creditors. Receivership may also be the appropriate protective device where the debtor has a going business and where creditors can convince the court that it is being grossly mismanaged.

Cancelling a Fraudulent Conveyance: A debtor may transfer property to a third party by gift or contract under circumstances in which his or her creditors are defrauded. If such fraud can be established, any creditor can have the conveyance (transfer) set aside and the property made subject to his or her claim—even if the property is in the hands of a third party.

The fraud necessary to have a conveyance set aside can be either fraud in fact or fraud implied in law. **Fraud in fact** occurs when a debtor transfers property with the specific intent of defrauding his or her creditors. A creditor will usually encounter difficulty in having a conveyance voided on this ground, simply because of the inherent problems in proving fraudulent intent.

The creditor's chances of proving this intent will, however, be somewhat greater if the transfer was to the debtor's spouse or other relative. In addition, it is often the case that the debtor actually had no such fraudulent intent, but the creditor is harmed nevertheless.

To assist the creditor, most states have enacted laws (such as the Uniform Fraudulent Conveyance Act) which create a *presumption* of fraud under certain circumstances. This means that, in some situations, the burden of proof shifts to the debtor. If the debtor fails to prove the absence of fraud, there is **fraud implied in law** and the transfer is voided. Generally speaking, these statutes create a presumption of fraud whenever a debtor transfers property without receiving "fair consideration" in return and the debtor has insufficient assets remaining to satisfy creditors.

Composition of Creditors: Sometimes a debtor or his or her creditors recognize early (before bankruptcy) that the debtor is in financial difficulty. Instead of pursuing remedies under bankruptcy, the debtor and creditors make a *contract* to resolve the debts. The contract—referred to as a **composition of creditors**—calls for the debtor's immediate payment of a sum less than that owed and for the creditor's immediate discharge of the debt. This payment can be made from any of the debtor's assets, including exempt property. Such contracts are held to be binding by the courts. The advantage of an immediate payment and minimum costs makes the composition attractive to creditors. Whether the composition agreement is binding on nonparticipating creditors depends on state law. At common law the agreement was not binding on these creditors.

Assignment for the Benefit of Creditors: Under common-law principles and, in some states, under statute, an **assignment for the benefit of creditors** is available as an alternative to bankruptcy. In such an arrangement, the debtor voluntarily transfers title to some or all assets to a "trustee" or "assignee" for the creditors' benefit. By such a transfer, the debtor irrevocably gives up any claim to or control over the property. The trustee or assignee liquidates (sells) the property and makes payment to the creditors on a pro rata basis.

Creditors can either accept or reject the partial payment. One accepting such a payment is in effect releasing the balance of his or her claim. In most states, creditors who do not participate in the assignment cannot reach the assets that have been so assigned. They do, however, have rights to any surplus remaining after participating creditors have been paid, any nonexempt property not assigned, and any nonexempt property acquired after the assignment. Nonparticipating creditors may also be able to force the debtor into bankruptcy.

Creditors' Committees: Sometimes creditors have reason to doubt the debtor's ability to manage his or her business affairs. Poor management often results in increased indebtedness and eventual failure of the debtor's business. In this situation, the debtor may agree to a payment plan satisfactory to the creditors. To be sure that the plan will not be altered, the debtor also agrees to submit his or her business and financial affairs to the control of a committee appointed by the creditors—a **creditors' committee.** This committee will virtually control the debtor's business operations until the debts are paid.

BANKRUPTCY PROCEEDINGS

History of Bankruptcy Statutes

Bankruptcy as a legal device was initially applied only to commercial business failures. The first Bankruptcy Act in England was adopted in 1542 and applied only to traders or merchants who were unable to pay their debts. It was not until 1861 that bankruptcy was extended to other types of debtors.

The founders of the United States were well acquainted with the problems of debtors. In drafting the U.S. Constitution they stated in Article I, Section 8, clause 4: "The Congress shall have the power . . . to establish . . . uniform laws on the subject of bankruptcies throughout the United States."

Despite the fact that some of the colonies were founded by debtors formerly imprisoned in England, U.S. bankruptcy laws had a shaky beginning. The first act was not passed until 1800, and it applied only to traders. This act was short-lived, being repealed three years later. The next act came in 1841, and although it extended beyond traders, it was repealed two years later. In 1867, Congress passed another bankruptcy act; this one was repealed in 1878. For the next twenty years Congress did not pass any bankruptcy acts, and various states took the opportunity to pass different types of insolvency laws. Finally, in 1898, Congress passed the Bankruptcy Act, which was substantially revised in 1938.

Bankruptcy Proceedings Today

After several years of consideration, Congress passed a new federal bankruptcy law in 1978. This law, referred to either as the Bankruptcy Reform Act or the Bankruptcy Code, made many changes in the rules governing bankruptcy proceedings. Perhaps because it contained so many changes, the Code was controversial from the beginning, some critics claiming that it treated debtors too leniently. Consequently, the Code was amended substantially in 1984. In our discussion, references to the 1978 Code includes these amendments.

Prior to 1978, the handling of bankruptcy cases was the responsibility of the federal district courts. In most cases, however, the judges of these courts delegated this responsibility to "bankruptcy referees," who were technically not federal judges but who performed many of the same functions. The 1978 Code established a set of bankruptcy courts, with one such court in each federal district. The judges of these bankruptcy courts are appointed for fourteen-year terms by the U.S. Court of Appeals for the circuit within which the bankruptcy court is located.

Bankruptcy courts hear and decide all of the issues directly involving the bankruptcy proceeding itself, but related nonbankruptcy matters, such as a tort claim by or against the debtor, are decided by the federal district court. An appeal from a decision of the bankruptcy court is heard by the federal district court.

As we noted earlier, bankruptcy is a solution of last resort. Despite this fact, thousands of cases are filed each year under the federal bankruptcy law. The large number of cases is not, however, the only reason for the importance of modern bankruptcy law. Many people have their only direct exposure to our legal system in bankruptcy proceedings. In bankruptcy court debtors and creditors alike find final, if not totally satisfactory, conclusions to disputes that may have seemed endless. In bankruptcy court businesses of all sizes are liquidated or rehabilitated, often affecting the livelihoods of many employees, the security of suppliers and customers, and even the economies of local communities.

The 1978 Code provides for three different kinds of proceedings: (1) Liquidation; (2) Reorganization; and (3) Adjustment of the Debts of an Individual with Regular Income. Our discussion focuses primarily on the liquidation proceeding, often referred to as "straight bankruptcy," because it is the most common type. We will, however, devote some attention to the other two types of proceedings at the end of this chapter. It should also be noted that the new bankruptcy law contains a special section dealing with the rehabilitation of bankrupt *municipalities,* which is beyond the scope of our discussion.

LIQUIDATION PROCEEDINGS

Stated very generally, the object of a **liquidation proceeding** under Chapter 7 of the Bankruptcy Act is to sell the debtor's assets, pay off creditors insofar as it is possible to do so, and legally discharge the debtor from further responsibility.

Commencement of the Proceedings

A liquidation proceeding will be either a *voluntary case,* commenced by the debtor, or an *involuntary case,* commenced by creditors.

Voluntary Case: The filing of a **voluntary case** automatically subjects the debtor and its property to the jurisdiction and supervision of the Bankruptcy Court. Any debtor, whether an individual, a partnership, or a corporation, may file a petition for voluntary bankruptcy, with the following exceptions: (1) banks, (2) savings and loan associations, (3) credit unions, (4) insurance companies, (5) railroads, and (6) governmental bodies. These exempted organizations are covered by special statutes and their liquidation is supervised by particular regulatory agencies.

A debtor does *not* have to be insolvent in order to file a petition for voluntary bankruptcy, but as a practical matter it is usually insolvency that prompts such a petition.[1] In addition, a husband and wife may file a joint case if both consent.

Involuntary Case: The types of organizations which are not permitted to file a voluntary liquidation case also cannot be subjected to an **involuntary case.** In addition to these exemptions, creditors also cannot file an involuntary case against *farmers*[2] or *nonprofit corporations.*

If the debtor has twelve or more creditors, at least three must join in filing the case. If there are

---

[1] Insolvency is defined in the federal bankruptcy law as the financial condition of a debtor whose debts exceed the fair market value of assets. The definition of insolvency under state law, as set forth in UCC Sec. 1-201(23), is broader. It states that a debtor is insolvent in the above situation *or* when the debtor "fails to pay his debts in the ordinary course of business or cannot pay his debts as they become due."

[2] Farmers are defined as persons (which includes individuals, partnerships, or corporations) who received more than 80 percent of their gross income during the preceding taxable year from farming operations owned and operated by them. "Farming operations" includes growing crops, dairy farming, and raising livestock or poultry.

fewer than twelve creditors, the involuntary case may be filed by one or more of them. Regardless of the number of creditors, those filing the petition must have noncontingent unsecured claims against the debtor totalling at least $5,000.

The debtor and its property automatically become subject to the jurisdiction and supervision of the bankruptcy court if the involuntary petition is not challenged. However, if the debtor contests the creditors' petition, they must prove either (1) that the debtor has not been paying debts as they became due or (2) that the debtor's property has been placed in a receivership or an assignment for the benefit of creditors within 120 days before the involuntary petition was filed. If the filing creditors prove either of the above, the debtor and its property are then under the supervision of the court. If no such proof is made, the petition is dismissed.

Automatic Stay: As soon as the petition is filed in either a voluntary or involuntary case, an **automatic stay** is in operation. The automatic stay puts creditors' claims "on hold" until they are dealt with in the bankruptcy proceeding, and prevents creditors from taking action against the debtor. A *secured creditor,* however, may petition the bankruptcy court and receive protection against the loss of its security. The court-ordered protection for secured creditors may take the form of cash payments from the debtor, substitute collateral, or an express exemption from the automatic stay permitting foreclosure of the security interest.

The Trustee

After the debtor becomes subject to the bankruptcy proceeding, the court must appoint an **interim trustee** to take over the debtor's property or business. Within a relatively short time thereafter, a **permanent trustee** will take over. This trustee is usually elected by the creditors, but if they do not do so, the interim trustee receives permanent status.

The trustee is an individual or corporation who, under the court's supervision, administers and represents the *debtor's estate.* (Which property is included within the debtor's estate is discussed later.) The basic duties of the trustee are to: (1) investigate the financial affairs of the debtor; (2) collect assets and claims owned by the debtor; (3) temporarily operate the debtor's business if necessary; (4) reduce the debtor's assets to cash; (5) receive and examine the claims of creditors, and challenge in bankruptcy court any claim which the trustee feels to be questionable; (6) oppose the debtor's discharge from its obligations when the trustee feels that there are legal reasons why the debtor should not be discharged; (7) render a detailed accounting to the court of all assets received and the disposition made of them; and (8) make a final report to the court when administration of the debtor's estate is completed. To fulfill these duties as representative of the debtor's estate, the trustee has the power to sue and be sued in that capacity and to employ accountants, attorneys, appraisers, auctioneers, and other professionals.

If they wish, unsecured creditors may elect a creditors' committee of three to eleven members for the purpose of consulting with the trustee. This committee may make recommendations to the trustee regarding the latter's duties and may submit questions to the court concerning administration of the debtor's estate.

Creditors' Meetings

Within a reasonable time after commencement of the case, the bankruptcy court must call a meeting of unsecured creditors. The debtor will have already supplied the court with a list of creditors, so that they may be notified of the meeting. The judge of the bankruptcy court is not permitted to attend a creditors' meeting.

At the first meeting, creditors will ordinarily elect the trustee. In order for such election to be possible, at least 20 percent of the total amount of unsecured claims which have been filed and allowed must be represented at the meeting. A trustee is elected by receiving the votes of creditors holding a majority, in amount, of unsecured claims represented at the meeting.

The other major item of business at the first creditors' meeting is an *examination of the debtor.* The debtor, under oath, will be questioned by the creditors and the trustee concerning (1) the debtor's assets, and (2) matters relevant to whether the debtor will be entitled to a discharge.

If necessary, other creditors' meetings may be held. For instance, the trustee might resign or die and creditors would have to meet for the election of a successor trustee.

Duties of the Debtor

The bankruptcy law imposes the following duties on the debtor: (1) within a reasonable time after commencement of the proceedings, file with the court a list of creditors, a schedule of assets and liabilities, and a statement of financial affairs; (2) cooperate and respond truthfully during the examination conducted at the first creditors' meeting; (3) surrender to the trustee all property to be included in the debtor's estate, as well as all documents, books, and records pertaining to this property; (4) cooperate with the trustee in whatever way necessary to enable the trustee to perform his or her duties; and (5) appear at the hearing conducted by the court concerning whether the debtor should be discharged.

A debtor who fails to fulfill any of these duties may be denied a discharge from liabilities.

The Debtor's Estate

Types of Property: The property owned by the debtor which becomes subject to the bankruptcy proceeding, ultimately to be sold by the trustee, is the **debtor's estate.** This includes all tangible and intangible property interests of any kind, unless specifically exempted. For example, the estate could consist of consumer goods, inventory, equipment, any of the various types of interests in real estate, patent rights, trademarks, copyrights, accounts receivable, and various contract rights.

After-Acquired Property: In addition to property owned at the time the bankruptcy petition (either voluntary or involuntary) was filed, the debtor's estate also includes after-acquired property under some circumstances. Specifically, the estate includes any type of property which the debtor acquires, or becomes entitled to acquire, within 180 days after the petition filing date (1) by inheritance, (2) as a beneficiary of a life insurance policy, or (3) as a result of a divorce decree or a property settlement agreement with the debtor's spouse. And, of course, if a particular item of property is part of the estate, any proceeds, income, production, or offspring from it will also be part of the estate. However, the debtor's earnings from his or her own labor or personal service after the filing date are *not* included in the estate.

Exemptions: A debtor who is an individual (rather than a partnership or corporation) may claim certain **exemptions.** This means that certain types of property are *exempt* and are not included in the debtor's estate. The debtor may keep such property and still receive a discharge from liabilities at the close of the proceedings. Every state has exemption statutes setting forth the types of property which are exempt from seizure under a writ of execution. Before passage of the new bankruptcy law, the debtor's exempt property in a federal bankruptcy case was determined solely by the exemption statutes of the state where he or she lived. The 1978 Bankruptcy Code, however, includes for the first time a list of federal exemptions which are available to the debtor in bankruptcy regardless of the state of domicile.

Under the 1978 Code the debtor may claim the following exemptions (and *each* spouse may claim them in a joint case): (1) the debtor's interest in a homestead used as a residence, up to a value of $7,500; (2) the debtor's interest in a motor vehicle, up to $1,200; (3) the debtor's interest, up to $200 *per item,* in household furnishings, appliances, wearing apparel, animals, crops, or musical instruments which are owned primarily for personal, family, or household (nonbusiness) uses, subject to a total of $4,000 for all such items; (4) the debtor's interest in jewelry, up to a total of $500, which is owned primarily for personal, family, or household uses; (5) the debtor's interest in any kind of property, up to a limit of $400; (6) any unused portion of the $7,500 homestead exemption, subject to a limit of $3,750; (7) the debtor's interest in implements, tools, or professional books used in his or her trade; (8) any unmatured life insurance policies owned by the debtor (except for credit life policies); (9) professionally prescribed health aids; (10) the debtor's right to receive various government benefits, such as unemployment compensation, social security, and veteran's benefits; (11) the debtor's right to receive various private benefits, such as alimony, child support, and pension payments, to the extent reasonably necessary for support of the debtor or the debtor's dependents; and (12) the right to receive damage awards for bodily injury.

Unfortunately, the 1978 Code has not brought about a great deal of national uniformity in the exemptions given to bankrupt debtors, for two reasons. First, the Code also includes a provision permitting the debtor to choose either the federal exemptions or those of the state where the debtor lives.[3] Because some state exemption laws are more advantageous than the federal exemptions for certain debtors, disparate state exemption laws continue to be important in federal bankruptcy cases. Second, Congress further stated in the 1978 Code that any state legislature can prohibit debtors in that state from using the federal exemptions in a bankruptcy case. The legislatures in a majority of states have done so; in these states, bankrupt debtors must use the state exemptions.

Even though bankruptcy proceedings are governed by federal law, the ownership interests of a bankrupt debtor in particular items of property ordinarily are determined by *state* law. On the other hand, as we will see in the following case, if a principle of state law conflicts with the overall purposes of the Bankruptcy Code, the state rule will not be applied.

---

[3] The debtor must choose one or the other, as a whole; there cannot be a selection of some exemptions from the federal law and some from a state law.

Mickelson v. Detlefsen
U.S. District Court, District of Minnesota, 466 F.Supp. 161 (1979)

In 1966 Gustav Detlefsen executed a will which would establish a trust to provide his wife with income during her life. Upon her death the principal of the trust was to be distributed to Gustav's living descendants. Gustav died in Chicago in 1974 and his will was probated in Illinois. His wife, Elsa, received income from the trust until her death in December 1976.

At the time of Elsa's death, Guy Detlefsen was Gustav's and Elsa's only living child and, therefore, was entitled to the trust principal. However, Guy Detlefsen had become subject to federal bankruptcy proceedings in Minnesota about six weeks before his mother died. After her death, Guy filed in an Illinois court a disclaimer of any interest in his father's will. The effect of this disclaimer, which complied with Illinois law, would be to make Guy's children entitled to the trust principal. At the time, the principal was in the form of cash and securities and was being held by a securities dealer.

Mickelson, the trustee in Guy's bankruptcy case, sued Guy and the securities dealer, asking the court to rule that the trust principal was part of the bankrupt debtor's estate. The bankruptcy court held for the trustee, and Guy appealed to a U.S. district court.

MacLaughlin, Judge:

. . . The law of the states plays an integral role in bankruptcy proceedings. In the Bankruptcy Act, for example, Congress grants the bankrupt the exemptions permitted by state law. More relevant, state law helps define the property of the bankrupt. . . . But although state law thus plays an important definitional part in bankruptcy proceedings, it remains subordinate to the federal policies that inhere in the Bankruptcy Act. . . . A principal purpose of the Bankruptcy Act is to marshal the bankrupt's assets and distribute them ratably to creditors.

Bequeathed property must "vest in the bankrupt within [180 days] after bankruptcy" [to be included in the bankrupt debtor's estate.] The bankrupt's interest in the trust proceeds was defined at the time of his mother's death, which was within two months of the date he filed for bankruptcy. Under Illinois law, however, because of the disclaimer, the interest never vested in the bankrupt. . . .

The bankrupt contends that disclaimers as authorized by state law mesh with the policies of the Bankruptcy Act. He argues that no proof exists that his creditors in extending credit relied on his expectancy in the trust. . . . The absence of reliance, however, does not inexorably align Illinois and federal law. The bankrupt argues that no federal policy is frustrated because the disclaimer prevents him as well as his creditors from receiving the trust proceeds. But the argument ignores the exercise of choice by the bankrupt as to the proper recipient of his windfall: whether the windfall of bequest should devolve to the bankrupt's creditors or the beneficiaries of his disclaimer. Congress . . . has asserted its prerogative and taken the choice from the bankrupt. If the windfall occurs within [180 days] of the bankruptcy, it is within reach of the trustee. If the windfall occurs more than [180 days] after bankruptcy, it is beyond the trustee's reach.

To permit the bankrupt to exercise the choice made available by state law would render [a portion of the federal bankruptcy law] largely nugatory. The common law recognized the right of a testamentary beneficiary [a beneficiary under a will] to disclaim his inheritance, and some statutes grant an heir [when there is no will] an equivalent right. . . . Thus, the law in a number of states would permit individuals who have filed for bankruptcy to divert legacies from creditors to persons with whom the bankrupt is usually on more amiable terms. The supremacy clause [of the U.S. Constitution] requires that such laws yield to apparent congressional intent.

In the instant case, the bankrupt's interest in the trust proceeds became fixed and determined at the time of his mother's death. . . . The bankrupt's disclaimer of the interest is [void]. [The principal of the trust, therefore, is part of the debtor's estate subject to the claims of his creditors.]

Affirmed.

Voidable Transfers

In a number of circumstances, the trustee has the power to sue and restore to the debtor's estate property or funds which the debtor (or someone acting in the debtor's behalf) had transferred to some third party. These situations, called **voidable transfers,** are as follows:

1. The trustee generally may cancel any transfer of property of the debtor's estate which was made *after* the debtor became subject to the bankruptcy proceeding. The trustee must exercise this power within two years after the transfer was made, or before the bankruptcy case is concluded, whichever occurs first.

2. The trustee may cancel any *fraudulent transfer* made by the debtor within one year prior to the filing of the bankruptcy petition. This power of the trustee applies to both *fraud in fact* and *fraud implied in law,* as discussed earlier in the chapter. It will be remembered that insolvency is an element of fraud implied in law. In determining the fair value of assets for this purpose under the bankruptcy law, exempt property and the property transferred in the particular transaction being challenged are not included.

3. The trustee has the power to cancel a property transfer on any ground that the debtor could have used, such as fraud, mistake, duress, undue influence, incapacity, or failure of consideration.

Voidable Preferences

One of the fundamental objectives of the bankruptcy law is to insure equal treatment of most types of unsecured creditors. The primary reason why we are so concerned with equal treatment of creditors, of course, is that a bankrupt debtor's assets are usually sufficient to pay only a fraction of creditors' total claims. As a result of this concern, the trustee has the power to cancel any transfer by the debtor to a creditor which amounted to a **preference.** A preference is essentially a transfer of property or money, in payment of an existing debt, which causes that creditor to receive more of the debtor's estate than he or she would be entitled to receive in the bankruptcy proceeding.

General Rules for Cancelling Preferences: In the ordinary situation, a preferential transfer to a creditor can be cancelled by the trustee, and the property or funds returned to the debtor's estate, if (1) it occurred within *90 days* prior to the filing of the bankruptcy petition, and (2) the debtor was *insolvent* at the time of the transfer. In this situation, however, insolvency is *presumed.* In other words, if a creditor has received a preferential transfer within the 90-day period prior to the filing of the bankruptcy petition, that creditor must prove that the debtor was *not* insolvent.

Insiders: If the creditor receiving the preference was an **insider,** the trustee's power of cancellation extends to any such transfer made within *one year* before the bankruptcy petition was filed. In general, an insider is an individual or business firm which had a close relationship with the debtor at the time of the transfer. Examples would include a relative or partner of the debtor, a corporation of which the debtor was a director or officer, or a director or officer of a corporate debtor. In such a case, however, the presumption of insolvency only applies to the

Figure 30.1   **Trustee's Recovery of Voidable Preference**

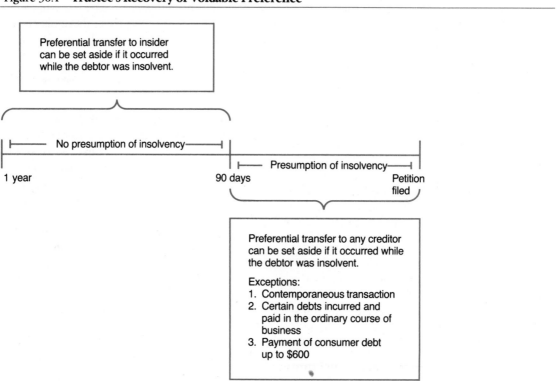

90 days prior to the petition filing. Therefore, if the preference being challenged by the trustee had taken place more than 90 days but less than a year before the petition filing, the trustee must prove that the debtor was insolvent. Figure 30.1 illustrates the rules for cancelling preferences to insiders and other creditors.

Exceptions: In certain circumstances, a payment or transfer to a creditor cannot be cancelled even though it meets the basic requirements of a voidable preference. Two of the most important exceptions are:

1. A transaction which involved a "contemporaneous" (that is, within a very short period of time) exchange between debtor and creditor cannot be cancelled by the trustee. For example,

the debtor may have bought goods from the creditor and either paid for them immediately or within a few days. This type of transaction is treated differently than one in which the debtor was paying off a debt which had existed for some time. Such a contemporaneous exchange will be left standing even though it occurred during the 90-day period prior to the filing date.

2. Even though there is no contemporaneous exchange, a payment or transfer to a creditor within the 90-day period will not be cancelled if (1) the particular debt had been incurred by the debtor in the ordinary course of business, (2) the payment was made in the ordinary course of the debtor's business, and (3) the payment was made according to ordinary business terms. An example would be the debtor's payment, during the 90-day period, of the previous month's utility bill.

3. A debtor's repayment during the 90-day period of up to $600 in *consumer debt* is not treated as a voidable preference.

Voidable preferences can occur in an almost infinite variety of circumstances. The following case illustrates one such situation, and also shows one of the many reasons why it is so important for a creditor to obtain and perfect a security interest whenever possible.

In re A. J. Nichols, Ltd.
U.S. Bankruptcy Court, N.D. Georgia, 21 Bankr. Rptr. 612 (1982)

G. A. Gertmenian & Sons was a wholesale dealer in oriental rugs who supplied them to A. J. Nichols, Ltd., under an arrangement giving Nichols the right to return unsold rugs to Gertmenian. As we saw in Chapter 21 concerning sales of goods, a "sale or return" is a sale transaction in which the buyer has a right to return the items to the seller within an agreed time period. A true sale or return actually transfers title to the buyer until a particular article is returned. In contrast, a "sale on approval" is a transaction in which the buyer has an agreed period of time to decide whether to keep the goods, with no title passing until the expiration of that time or until the buyer affirmatively indicates a desire to keep them. In other words, a sale on approval is a "consignment," the supplier being the "consignor" and the one holding them being the "consignee." A consignee is merely an agent for the purpose of selling the principal's goods, and owns no interest in them. When a right of return exists and the parties have not specified whether it is a sale or return or a sale on approval, the UCC provides that it usually is a sale or return if the goods are taken by the buyer for the purpose of resale, and a sale on approval if they are taken by the buyer for the purpose of use.

Under this arrangement with Gertmenian, Nichols was holding 45 oriental rugs having a wholesale value of $29,505. Gertmenian did not take a security interest in the rugs. Nichols returned the rugs to Gertmenian, and five weeks after the return Nichols filed a petition for voluntary liquidation under Chapter 7 of the Bankruptcy Code. Loeb (plaintiff), the bankruptcy trustee, claimed that Nichols' return of the rugs to Gertmenian was a voidable preference and filed a complaint against Gertmenian (defendant) seeking to have the value of the rugs restored to the bankrupt debtor's estate.

Drake, Bankruptcy Judge:

Section 547(b) of the Bankruptcy Code provides in relevant part:

Except, as provided in subsection (c) of this section, the trustee may avoid any transfer of property of the debtor

(1) to or for the benefit of a creditor;

(2) for or on account of an antecedent debt owed by the debtor before such transfer was made;

(3) made while the debtor was insolvent;

(4) made. . . on or within 90 days before the date of the filing of the petition; and

(5) that enabled such creditor to receive more than such creditor would receive if (A) the case were a case under Chapter 7 of this title; (B) the transfer had not been made; and (C) such creditor received payment of such debt to the extent provided by the provisions of this title.

The plaintiff relies on the above section of the Bankruptcy Code and asserts that the transfer in question satisfies each and every provision of §547(b) of the Bankruptcy Code, thus making the transfer a voidable preference. The defendant contends that no property of the debtor was transferred and that the elements set forth in §547(b)(2), (3), and (5) have not been satisfied. The plaintiff has the burden of proof on each of the elements of §547(b).

The threshold requirement of §547(b) is that there must be a transfer of property of the debtor in order for there to be a voidable preference. "Transfer" is defined in [the Bankruptcy Code] as every mode of parting with property or with an interest in property. The term "property of the debtor" is not defined in the Bankruptcy Code, but it has been held that a preference may exist "where property in which a debtor has any interest is transferred out of his estate." *In re Lucasa International,* 8 B.C.D. 444 (1981).

Georgia Code §109A-2-326(2) and (3) [i.e., §2-326 of Georgia's Uniform Commercial Code] state that goods delivered primarily for resale, as were the rugs in the instant case, are deemed to be "on sale or return." It is clear that at the time of the transfer of the rugs, since these goods were subject to the claims of the debtor's creditors, some property interest did exist in the debtor concerning said rugs. . . .

Moreover, the debtor in this case had more than just a possessory interest in the rugs. These rugs were in the possession of the debtor on a "consignment" or "sale or return" basis. Under [the U.C.C., as enacted in Georgia], goods held on a sale or return basis are subject to the claims of a buyer's creditor while in the buyer's possession, [subject to three exceptions]. [U.C.C. §2-326(3)] . . . provides three exceptions to the general rule that delivery of goods to a person for sale in the ordinary course of business is deemed to be a sale or return even though the agreement (1) purports to reserve title to the person making delivery until payment or resale or (2) uses such words as "on consignment."

The first exception requires compliance with "an applicable law providing for consignor's interest or the like to be evidenced by a sign." The debtor never posted such signs. The second exception exists if the consignor can show that the consignee is generally known by his creditors to be substantially engaged in selling the goods of others. The burden of proof is on the defendant. . . . The evidence before the Court shows that the debtor's creditors did not have actual knowledge that the goods sold by the debtor were on consignment, as required by [Georgia law]. The final exception to [U.C.C. §2-326] is that the consignor meet the filing requirements of Article 9 of the Georgia U.C.C. provisions [for perfection of a security interest]. There is no dispute that the defendant did not file a financing statement in the instant case.

Therefore, as the above discussion indicates, the defendant has failed to meet any of the [exceptions] that would result in the defendant's being deemed a consignor of the rugs which the debtor returned to the defendant. Accordingly, the Court finds that the relationship between the defendant and the debtor is not that of a consignor and consignee, but finds instead that the transaction which the parties entered into was a sale or return. It follows from this determination that the [return] of certain rugs from the debtor to the defendant was a transfer of the debtor's property under §547(b) [of the Bankruptcy Code]. . . .

Once the threshold requirement of transfer of the debtor's property has been met, the trustee must prove the five elements of §547(b) [of the Bankruptcy Code]. The first requirement is that the transfer be to or for the benefit of a creditor. Under [the Bankruptcy Code] a "creditor" is an "entity that has a claim against the debtor that arose at the time of or before the order for relief concerning the debtor." A "claim" is "a right to payment or a right to an equitable remedy." The Court finds that prior to the transfer, the defendant, whether a consignor or a seller on a sale or return basis, had a right to either payment for the rugs or the right to an equitable remedy for the return of the rugs. Thus it is clear that the defendant had a claim against the debtor and that the defendant was a creditor within the [meaning] of the Bankruptcy Code. For this reason, the Court finds that the transfer was to or for the benefit of a creditor.

By virtue of the same analysis in which this Court determined the defendant was a creditor of Nichols, the Court also finds that the transfer was "for or on account of an antecedent debt owed by the debtor before such transfer was made. . . ."

The third requirement to be shown by the plaintiff is that the transfer must be made while the debtor was insolvent. Under §547(f), there is a presumption that for ninety days preceding the filing of the debtor's petition, the debtor is insolvent. This places the burden of going forward with the evidence of the debtor's solvency on the defendant. The Court finds that the defendant has failed to overcome the presumption of insolvency. Moreover, the trustee has proven the insolvency of the debtor. The evidence showed that a $50,000 claim against an officer of the debtor, who left in 1979 with $50,000 of the debtor's assets, was scheduled as an asset of the debtor. As the claim was shown to have no prospect of collection, the debtor's schedules are not a fair indication of the debtor's solvency. This Court finds that the debtor was insolvent at the time of the transfer of the property.

It is undisputed by the parties that the property was transferred from the debtor to the defendant within ninety days of the filing of the petition.

Finally, the plaintiff must show that this transfer enabled the creditor to receive more than the creditor would have received if the transfer had not been made and the defendant had received payment of its claim to the extent provided by the provisions of the Bankruptcy Code. Because this transfer allowed the defendant to recover the entire amount of his claim and because the defendant did not have a perfected security interest nor a true consignment, the Court finds that the creditor received more than it would have under a Chapter 7 liquidation if this transfer had not been made.

Therefore, the Court finds that the plaintiff has carried the burden of proof with respect to each element of §547(b) and that the transfer of forty-five rugs from the debtor to the defendant was a voidable preference. Judgment is granted in favor of the plaintiff in the amount of $29,505.00.

Comment: In 1984 Congress amended the Bankruptcy Code section relating to voidable preferences by changing the language "transfer of property" to "transfer of an interest," thus expressly agreeing with this court's conclusion that in a sale or return arrangement the buyer's return of the goods is covered by the voidable preference provision.

Claims

As a general rule, any legal obligation of the debtor gives rise to a claim against the debtor's estate in the bankruptcy proceeding. There are, however, several special situations we should mention.

1. If the claim is *contingent* on the happening or nonhappening of some future event or, if its *amount is in dispute*, the bankruptcy court has the power to make an estimate of the claim's value.

2. If the claim against the debtor is for breach of contract, it will include any damages which accrued prior to the filing of the bankruptcy petition, and also those damages attributable to the debtor's failure to perform any future obligations under the contract. Of course, this is no different from an ordinary breach of contract claim when bankruptcy is not involved. However, under the bankruptcy law, if the claim arises out of an *employment contract* or a *real estate lease,* limits are placed on a claim for damages relating to future nonperformance. In the case of an employment contract, such damages are limited to a term of *one year* from the filing

date or the date the contract was repudiated, whichever is earlier. In the case of a real estate lease, damages are limited to either *one year* or *15 percent* of the remaining term of the lease, whichever is greater, up to a maximum of *three years.* The starting point for measuring this time is the same as for employment contracts. The reason for these limits is that contracts of these two types are frequently long-term ones, and the farther in the future we try to compute damages, the more speculative they get.

3. A creditor who has received a voidable transfer or preference may not assert a claim of any kind until the wrongfully received property or funds are returned to the debtor's estate.

Subject to the above limitations, any claim filed with the bankruptcy court is allowed unless it is contested by an interested party, such as the trustee, debtor, or another creditor. If challenged, the court will rule on the claim's validity after pertinent evidence is presented at a hearing held for that purpose. In this regard, claims against the debtor's estate will be subject to any defenses that the debtor could have asserted had there been no bankruptcy. The fact that a claim is allowed, of course, does not mean that the particular creditor will be paid in full; it just means that the creditor has the hope of receiving *something.*

Distribution of Debtor's Estate

A secured creditor—one having a security interest or lien in a specific item of property—can proceed directly against that property for satisfaction of his or her claim. This is true even though the debtor is or is about to become subject to a bankruptcy proceeding. In a sense, then, **secured creditors** have priority over all classes of unsecured creditors (usually referred to as **general creditors**). However, if a portion of a secured creditor's claim is not secured, that portion is treated like any other unsecured claim.

When the trustee has gathered all the assets of the debtor's estate and reduced them to cash, these proceeds will be distributed to unsecured creditors. There are certain unsecured claims which are given priority in this distribution. These claims are paid in full *in the order of their priority,* assuming there are sufficient proceeds available. The following six classes of debts are listed in order of priority. Each class must be fully paid before the next is entitled to anything. If the available funds are insufficient to satisfy all creditors within a class, payment to creditors in that class is made in proportion to the amounts of their claims.

1. First to be paid are all costs and expenses involved in the administration of the bankruptcy proceeding, such as an auctioneer's commission, the trustee's fee, and accountants' and attorneys' fees.

2. If the proceeding is an *involuntary* one, the second priority is any expense incurred in the ordinary course of the debtor's business or financial affairs *after* commencement of the case but *before* appointment of the trustee.

3. Next is any claim for wages, salaries, or commissions earned by an individual within 90 days before the filing of the petition or the cessation of the debtor's business, whichever occurs first. This priority, however, is limited to $2,000 per individual.

4. The fourth priority is any claim for contributions to an employee benefit plan arising from services performed within 180 days before filing or business cessation. Again the limit is $2,000 per individual. However, a particular individual cannot receive more than $2,000 under the third and fourth priorities combined.

5. Next are claims of individuals, up to $900 per person, for deposits made on consumer goods or services that were not received.

6. Claims of governmental units for various kinds of taxes, subject to time limits that differ depending on the type of tax, are the last priority.

If all priority claims are paid and funds still remain, general creditors are paid in proportion to the amounts of their claims. Any portion of a priority claim that was beyond the limits of the priority is treated as a general claim. An example would be the amount by which an individual's wage claim exceeded $2,000. Figure 30.2 outlines the process of distributing the debtor's estate.

Discharge

After the debtor's estate has been liquidated and distributed to creditors, the bankruptcy court will conduct a hearing to determine whether the debtor should be discharged from liability for remaining obligations.

Grounds for Refusal of Discharge: Under certain circumstances the court will refuse to grant the debtor a **discharge.** These are as follows:

1. Only an *individual* can receive a discharge in a liquidation proceeding. For a corporation to receive a discharge it must go through a reorganization proceeding (discussed later in the chapter), or be dissolved in accordance with state corporation statutes.

2. A debtor will be denied a discharge if he or she had previously received such a discharge within *six years* before the present bankruptcy petition was filed.

3. The debtor will be denied a discharge if he or she has committed any of the following acts: (a) intentionally concealed or transferred assets for the purpose of evading creditors, within one year before the filing of the petition or during the bankruptcy proceedings; (b) concealed, de-

Figure 30.2   Distribution of Debtor's Estate

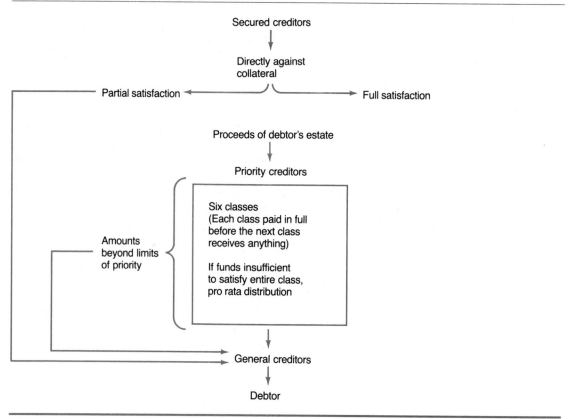

stroyed, falsified, or failed to keep business or financial records unless there was reasonable justification for such action or failure; (c) failed to adequately explain any loss of assets; (d) refused to obey a lawful court order or to answer a material court-approved question in connection with the bankruptcy case; or (e) made any fraudulent statement or claim in connection with the bankruptcy case.

4. If a discharge has been granted, the court may revoke it within one year if it is discovered that the debtor had not acted honestly in connection with the bankruptcy proceeding.

In the following case, creditors of the bankrupt debtor claimed that the debtor should not be discharged from his obligations because he had demonstrated an actual intent to defraud his creditors and had failed to explain satisfactorily the absence of certain assets. The case demonstrates the importance of looking at a debtor's overall pattern of conduct when determining whether he or she has acted fraudulently.

In re Hugh Reed
U.S. Court of Appeals for the Fifth Circuit, 700 F.2d 986 (1983)

Hugh Reed, as a sole proprietor, opened a retail clothing shop using the trade name, Reed's Men's Wear. He financed the venture in part by obtaining a $150,000 bank loan guaranteed by the federal Small Business Administration (SBA). Three months later the same bank gave Reed an additional $50,000 line of credit, and the SBA agreed to subordinate the original loan to this line of credit. The store showed a profit for the first nine months of operation in 1977, but began to lose money in 1978. By February 1979, Reed knew that his business was insolvent. He reached an agreement with the bank, the SBA, and his major trade creditors under which he turned over management of the store to a consulting firm for the remainder of 1979 and the creditors postponed collection efforts until January 1980. The business continued to fail, however, and on December 21, 1979, Reed and his wife filed for bankruptcy under Chapter 7 of the Code.

In the liquidation proceeding, the evidence showed that from 1977 to 1979, in addition to operating Reed's Men's Wear, Reed traveled extensively as a sales representative for Scully Leather, Inc. In 1977, he worked in his store about 75 percent of the time and traveled for Scully about 25 percent. In 1978 he divided his time evenly, but by 1979 he was traveling for Scully about 60 percent of the time. In December 1978 he set up Reyata Corporation, wholly owned by himself, to receive sales commissions from Scully. In 1979, Scully paid Reyata $15,000 per month. The bankruptcy judge found that Reyata was simply Reed's alter ego and refused to treat it as a separate entity.

Reed also collected antiques, gold coins, and guns, and made various other investments. In a financial statement filed with the SBA in April 1979, Reed valued his gun collection at $20,000 and his antiques at $3,000. During the period of September through December 1979, he added substantially to these collections. Part of the money used to do so was borrowed by Reyata Corp. Included in these purchases were three separate transactions in October and November in which he paid $22,115 for a collection of South African gold Krugerrands and Mexican 50-peso pieces. In November, one month before filing for bankruptcy, Reed paid $15,000 for a one-third interest in a business known as Triple BS Corporation. (In a footnote, the court said, "The significance of the initials is not elucidated in the record.")

In October 1979 Reed opened a separate bank account without the knowledge of his creditors, and until the store closed in mid-December he deposited the store's daily receipts in this account. In late November, Reed used the account to repay the loan that Reyata had obtained to purchase antiques, guns, and foreign currency.

Around the same time Reed began selling his personal assets. In several transactions he sold all of his antiques to friends and acquaintances for $8,500. Although their fair market value was not established, these items had been recently purchased by Reed for $14,000. On December 10 he sold his gold coins through a broker for $19,500, their approximate market value. On December 11 he sold to one of the same friends both the gun collection and the one-third interest in Triple BS Corporation for $5,000 each. Again, no market value for these items was established, but Reed had purchased the stock in Triple BS only one month earlier for $15,000. Reed used the $38,000 received from all of these sales of personal assets to reduce the two mortgages on his home.

Based on these facts, and also on Reed's failure to account for over $19,000 in cash, the bankruptcy court denied Reed's discharge. The federal district court affirmed this judgment, and Reed appealed to the U.S. court of appeals.

Rubin, Circuit Judge:

The Bankruptcy Code provides that a debtor may be denied discharge if he has transferred property "with intent to hinder, delay, or defraud a creditor," or has "failed to explain satisfactorily . . . any loss of assets." Reed was denied discharge on both bases. Though either would suffice, we [will] review [both].

In considering the effect of Reed's transfers of assets, we distinguish, as did the careful opinion of the bankruptcy court, the debtor's entitlement to the exemption of property from the claims of his creditors and his right to a discharge from his debts. The Bankruptcy Code allows a debtor to retain property exempt either (1) under the provisions of the Bankruptcy Code, if not forbidden by state law, or (2) under the provisions of state law and federal law other than the minimum allowances in the Bankruptcy Code. . . .

The Code adopts the position that the conversion of nonexempt to exempt property, without more, will not deprive the debtor of the exemption to which he would otherwise be entitled. . . . The result which would occur if debtors were not allowed to convert property into allowable exempt property would be extremely harsh, especially in those jurisdictions where the exemption allowance is minimal. [However, this general approval by Congress of a debtor's conversion of nonexempt to exempt property is restricted if there is] extrinsic evidence of actual intent to defraud. . . .

Reed elected to claim his exemptions under state law. The bankruptcy judge, therefore, referred to Texas law to determine both what property was exempt and whether the exemption was defeated by the eleventh-hour conversion. Texas constitutional and statutory protection of the homestead is absolute, and the bankruptcy judge interpreted Texas law to allow the exemption in full regardless of Reed's intent. . . . The allowance of the exemption is not challenged [by Reed's creditors]. . . .

While the Code requires that, when the debtor claims a state-created exemption, the scope of the claim is determined by state law, it sets separate standards for determining whether the debtor shall be denied a discharge. The debtor's entitlement to a discharge must, therefore, be determined by federal, not state, law. In this respect, §727(a)(2) [of the Bankruptcy Code] is absolute: the discharge shall be denied a debtor who has transferred property with intent to defraud his creditors. . . . As noted above, mere conversion [of nonexempt to exempt property] is not to be considered fraudulent unless other evidence proves actual intent to defraud creditors. While pre-bankruptcy conversion of nonexempt into exempt assets is frequently motivated by the intent to put those assets beyond the reach of creditors, which is, after all, the function of an exemption, evidence of actual intent to defraud creditors is required to support a finding sufficient to deny a discharge. For example, evidence that the debtor, on the eve of bankruptcy, borrowed money that was then converted into exempt assets would suffice to support a finding of actual intent to defraud. . . .

The evidence amply supports the bankruptcy court's finding that Reed had an actual intent to defraud. Reed's whole pattern of conduct evinces that intent. . . . His rapid conversion of nonexempt assets to extinguish one home mortgage and to reduce another four months before bankruptcy, after arranging with his creditors to be free of payment obligations until the following year, speaks for itself as a transfer of property in fraud of creditors. His diversion of the daily receipts of Reed's Men's Wear into an account unknown to his creditors and management consultant and his subsequent use of the receipts to repay a loan that had been a vehicle for this conversion confirm his fraudulent motivation. . . .

Reed asserts that denial of a discharge makes the exemption meaningless. This is but fulmination. Reed may retain his home, mortgages substantially reduced, free of claims by his creditors. In light of the ample evidence, aside from the conversion itself, that Reed had an actual intent to defraud his creditors, he simply is not entitled to a discharge despite the fact that a generous state law may protect his exemption. . . .

[With respect to the separate ground for denying Reed a discharge, that he failed to satisfactorily explain the disappearance of $19,586.83,] Reed could only respond that he had many business and household expenses which he paid for in cash as they arose, and that he had lost an unspecified amount of cash gambling in Las Vegas. We [agree with] the bankruptcy judge's finding that this did not constitute a satisfactory explanation. . . .

For these reasons, the judgment [denying Reed a discharge from his debts] is affirmed. [The lower courts had also found that Reed's wife, Sharon, *should* be permitted a discharge because she did not have sufficient knowledge of Reed's activities to demonstrate actual fraudulent intent. The Court of Appeals felt that there was a very close question on this point, but affirmed the judgment granting Sharon Reed a discharge because the decision of the lower courts was not clearly erroneous.]

Nondischargeable Debts: Even if the debtor is granted a general discharge from obligations, there nevertheless are a few types of claims for which he or she will continue to be liable. These **nondischargeable debts** are as follows:

1. Obligations for payment of taxes are not discharged if (a) the particular tax was entitled to a priority in the distribution of the debtor's estate, but was not paid; or (b) a tax return had been required but was not properly filed; or (c) the debtor had willfully attempted to evade the particular tax.

2. Claims arising out of the debtor's fraud, embezzlement, or larceny are not discharged.

3. The debtor is not excused from liability for a willful and malicious tort.

4. Claims for alimony and child support are not discharged.

5. The debtor is not discharged from a claim that he or she failed to list in the bankruptcy case if this failure caused the creditor not to assert the claim in time for it to be allowed.

6. An obligation for a student loan is not discharged if it became due and payable less than five years prior to the filing of the petition.

7. Any judgments or awards of damages resulting from the debtor's operation of a motor vehicle while legally intoxicated are not dischargeable.

8. Primarily because of credit card abuse by debtors shortly before filing for bankruptcy, two types of *consumer debts* have been made nondischargeable: (a) debts of more than $500 to a particular creditor for *luxury goods or services,* if incurred within 40 days of the order for relief (i.e., the petition); and (b) cash advances totalling more than $1,000 obtained by using a credit card or other open-ended consumer credit arrangement, if incurred within 20 days of the order for relief.

Reaffirmation

Prior to the 1978 Code, a debtor could renew his or her obligation on a debt that had been discharged in bankruptcy simply by expressing a willingness to be bound. This **reaffirmation** required no new consideration by the creditor, but some states did require it to be in writing.

During the course of revising the bankruptcy law, Congress found that many of these reaffirmations were obtained by creditors through the use of coercion or deception. As a result, the new law places significant constraints on the making of a reaffirmation. Specifically, a reaffirmation is not valid unless (1) the bankruptcy court conducted a hearing at which the debtor was fully informed of the consequences of his or her action, and (2) the agreement to reaffirm was made *before* the debtor's discharge. In addition, the debtor can rescind the reaffirmation within 30 days after it is made.

BUSINESS REORGANIZATION

If it is felt that reorganization and continuance of a business is feasible and is preferable to liquidation, a petition for reorganization may be filed under Chapter 11 of the 1978 Bankruptcy Code. The reorganization procedure is intended for use by *businesses,* but it does not matter whether the owner of the business is an individual, partnership, or corporation. A **reorganization case** can be either voluntary or involuntary, and the requirements for filing an involuntary case are the same as for a liquidation proceeding. In general, the types of debtors exempted from reorganization proceedings are the same as those exempted from liquidation proceedings. The major difference in coverage is that a railroad *can* be a debtor in a reorganization proceeding. The most important aspects of a reorganization case are summarized below.

1. As soon as the petition is filed, an *automatic stay* is in operation just as in a liquidation proceeding. The automatic stay is even more important in a reorganization proceeding, because without such a stay the debtor often would find it impossible to continue operating its business.

2. There may or may not be a trustee in a reorganization case. If a trustee is appointed, he or she will take over and will have basically the same duties and powers as in a liquidation case. Essentially, the court will appoint a trustee if requested by an interested party (such as a creditor) and if it appears that such an appointment would be in the best interests of all parties involved. Obviously a trustee will be appointed if the court feels there is a possibility of the debtor's business being mismanaged or assets being wasted or concealed. If a trustee is not appointed, the debtor remains in possession and control of the business. In this situation, the debtor is called the **debtor-in-possession,** and has all the powers of a trustee.

3. After commencement of the case, the court must appoint a committee of unsecured creditors. If necessary, the court may appoint other creditors' committees to represent the special interests of particular types of creditors. A committee of shareholders may also be appointed to oversee the interests of that group, if the debtor is a corporation.

4. The creditors' and shareholders' committees, and the trustee, if one was appointed, will investigate the business and financial affairs of the debtor. A *reorganization plan* will then be prepared and filed with the bankruptcy court. This plan must divide creditors' claims and shareholders' interests into classes according to their type. For instance, claims of employees, secured creditors, bondholders, real estate mortgage holders, and government units might be segregated into different classes. The plan must indicate how claims within each class are going to be handled and to what extent each class will receive less than full payment. Treatment of claims within each class must be equal.

5. The court will "confirm" (approve) the reorganization plan if (a) each class has approved the plan and (b) the court rules that the plan is "fair and equitable" to all classes. A plan is deemed to be accepted by a class of creditors if it received favorable votes from those representing at least two-thirds of the amount of claims and more than half of the number of creditors within that class. Acceptance by a class of shareholders requires an affirmative vote by those representing at least two-thirds of the shares in that class. If the parties are unable to produce an acceptable plan or if the plan subsequently does not work as expected, the court may either dismiss the case or convert it into a liquidation proceeding.

6. After the plan has been confirmed, the debtor is discharged from those claims not provided for in the plan. However, the types of claims that are not discharged in a liquidation case are also not discharged in a reorganization case.

Policy Issues in Reorganizations

The attempt by bankruptcy laws to achieve equity among debtors and creditors has always raised questions of ethics and public policy. Indeed, the provisions of the Bankruptcy Code dealing with voidable preferences, refusal of discharge, and nondischargeable debts have ethical and policy questions at their core. The fact that the 1978 Code no longer requires that a debtor be insolvent to file a voluntary case has made these ethical questions even more important: If it is in the best interest of society to provide relief to an insolvent debtor, how far should public policy go in letting a debtor start afresh when that debtor is financially beleaguered but not insolvent?

Since the enactment of the 1978 Code, ethical and policy questions have arisen with increasing frequency in business reorganization cases under Chapter 11 of the Code. Again, there is no insolvency requirement, and the ultimate objective of a reorganization is to permit the debtor to continue as a viable entity. Although the reorganization provisions of Chapter 11 pursue worthwhile goals, the process of reorganization does present opportunities for abuse. As we mentioned previously, if a trustee is not appointed in a reorganization proceeding, the debtor becomes a so-called *debtor-in-possession,* with all the powers of a trustee. Although the exercise of such power obviously is under the supervision of the bankruptcy court, creditors, employee unions, and other groups often are understandably concerned about the actions of the debtor-in-possession.

One of the most important powers of the debtor-in-possession, like a trustee, is the power to *cancel executory contracts.* For a time, there was a question whether a debtor-in-possession could cancel a collective bargaining agreement covering its unionized employees. Unions claimed that a debtor-in-possession should not have the power to cancel collective bargaining agreements because an employer could then use a Chapter 11 reorganization as a "union busting" device. The Supreme Court ruled, however, in *NLRB v. Bildisco & Bildisco,* 104 S.Ct. 1188 (1984), that collective bargaining agreements, like other contracts, can be cancelled by the debtor-in-possession when cancellation is in the best interests of a successful reorganization. Shortly thereafter, Congress amended the law so as to place restrictions on this power. Specifically, Congress provided that the debtor-in-possession (i.e., the employer) must first propose reasonable modifications to the existing union contract. If the union rejects these proposed modifications, the Bankruptcy Court then conducts a hearing to determine whether the union has "good cause" for the rejection. A union has good cause for rejecting the proposed modifications if the employer has failed to prove

that the contract changes are "fair and equitable" to all parties and necessary for the company's survival. If it is found that the union does have good cause, the burden is then upon the employer to make further proposals. If the court finds that the union did not have good cause for rejecting a particular proposal for modifying the collective bargaining agreement, the employer then has the power to cancel the agreement and set new employment terms unilaterally. An example of the application of these new provisions is found in *Wheeling-Pittsburgh Steel Corp. v. United Steelworkers of America,* 791 F.2d 1074 (3d Cir. 1986), in which the court concluded that the union had good cause for rejection primarily because the employer based its proposals on a "worst case scenario" that required a one-third wage cut for five years and did not include a "snap back" provision that would increase workers' wages and benefits if the company performed better than expected.

Reorganizations have also raised various ethical and policy questions in other situations. Suppose, for example, that a large, profitable company is faced with a great many claims for injuries allegedly arising from products made by the company. A large number of claims have already been filed, and many others are anticipated in the future, making it necessary for the company to set aside extremely large reserves to cover contingent liabilities. Can the company use a Chapter 11 reorganization proceeding to obtain settlements of these claims in an organized, hopefully uniform fashion? This is the question faced by the court in the following case.

In re Johns-Manville Corporation
U.S. Bankruptcy Court, S.D. New York, 36 Bankr. Rptr. 727 (1984)

Johns-Manville Corp. (Manville) was a large, highly successful manufacturing enterprise. It and several other companies were major producers of several products, such as insulation, that contained asbestos. After many people who had been exposed to asbestos for

lengthy periods of time developed very serious diseases such as asbestosis and lung cancer, large numbers of lawsuits began to be filed against asbestos producers.

Manville filed a petition for reorganization under Chapter 11 of the Bankruptcy Code, claiming that such filing was made necessary by the "uncontrolled proliferation" of asbestos-related lawsuits. At the time of the court's initial decision in the reorganization case, over 16,000 such suits had been filed against Manville. The company stated that its problems were compounded by the "crushing economic burden to be suffered by it over the next 20–30 years by the filing of an even more staggering number of suits by those who had been exposed but who will not manifest the asbestos-related diseases until some time during this future period." In addition, Manville showed that the insurance industry had generally disavowed coverage for asbestos-related claims under products liability insurance policies carried by the company. The question of insurance coverage had been tied up in state court litigation in California for several years.

Several different groups of creditors and asbestos-lawsuit plaintiffs challenged Manville's reorganization petition as inappropriate, and asked that it be dismissed. These groups contended that Manville was a healthy company and was misusing the Bankruptcy Code by attempting to use a reorganization proceeding to resolve products liability claims. The opinion of the Bankruptcy Court follows.

Lifland, Bankruptcy Judge:

Clearly, Manville meets the requirements . . . for debtors under all chapters of the Code in that it is domiciled and has its place of business in the United States. . . . In addition, Manville meets the eligibility requirements applicable to Chapter 11 debtors. . . . Moreover, it should also be noted that neither Section 109 [containing eligibility requirements] nor any other provision relating to voluntary petitions by companies contains any insolvency requirement. . . . This is in striking contrast to the requirement of insolvency . . . with regard to the commencement of involuntary cases. . . .

The filing of a Chapter 11 case creates an estate for the benefit of all creditors and equity holders of the debtor wherein all constituencies may voice their interests and bargain for their best possible treatment. . . .

A principal goal of the Bankruptcy Code is to provide open access to the bankruptcy process. . . . [According to congressional reports,] the rationale behind this "open access" policy is to provide access to bankruptcy relief which is as "open" as "access to the credit economy." Thus, Congress intended that "there should be no legal barriers to voluntary petitions." Another major goal of the Code, that of "rehabilitation of debtors," requires that relief for debtors must be "timely." Congress declared that it is essential to both the open access and rehabilitation goals that

[i]nitiating relief should not be a death knell. The process should encourage resort to it, by debtors and creditors, that cuts short the dissipation of assets and the

accumulation of debts. Belated commencement of a case may kill an opportunity for reorganization or arrangement.

Accordingly, the drafters of the Code envisioned that a financially beleaguered debtor with real debt and real creditors should not be required to wait until the economic situation is beyond repair in order to file a reorganization petition. The congressional purpose in enacting the Code was to encourage resort to the bankruptcy process. This philosophy not only comports with the elimination of an insolvency requirement, but also is a corollary of the key aim of Chapter 11 of the Code, that of avoidance of liquidation. The drafters of the Code announced this goal, declaring that reorganization is more efficient than liquidation because "assets that are used for production in the industry for which they were designed are more valuable than those same assets sold for scrap." Moreover, reorganization also fosters the goals of preservation of jobs in the threatened entity.

In the instant case, not only would liquidation be wasteful and inefficient in destroying the utility of valuable assets of the companies as well as jobs, but, more importantly, liquidation would preclude just compensation of some present asbestos victims and all future asbestos claimants. This unassailable reality represents all the more reason for this Court to adhere to this . . . liquidation avoidance aim of Chapter 11 and deny the motions to dismiss. Manville must not be required to wait until its economic picture has deteriorated beyond salvation to file for reorganization. . . . All of the motions to dismiss the Manville petition are denied in their entirety.

ADJUSTMENT OF DEBTS

Chapter 13 of the 1978 Code, "Adjustment of Debts of an Individual with Regular Income," provides a method by which an individual can pay his or her debts from future income over an extended period of time. It is intended for use by an individual whose primary income is from salary, wages, or commissions (that is, an employee). There is, however, nothing to prevent a self-employed individual, such as the owner of a business, from using this chapter of the bankruptcy law. But the debtor must be an *individual*; partnerships and corporations cannot institute this type of proceeding. The most important aspects of an **adjustment case** are summarized below.

1. There is no such thing as an involuntary adjustment case; only the debtor can file the petition. As in the other types of proceedings, an *automatic stay* exists upon filing. To be eligible to file an adjustment case, the debtor must have (a) "regular income," (b) less than $100,000 in noncontingent, undisputed debts which are *unsecured,* and (c) less than $350,000 in noncontingent, undisputed debts which are *secured.*

2. The Bankruptcy Court will always appoint a trustee in an adjustment case. The primary function of the trustee in this type of proceeding is to receive and distribute the debtor's income on a periodic basis.

3. The debtor prepares and files an *adjustment plan* with the court. Neither the trustee, creditors, nor anyone else can file the plan. The essential functions of the plan are to designate the portion of the debtor's future income that will be turned over to the trustee for distribution to creditors, to describe how creditors are to be paid, and to indicate the period of time during which payment will be accomplished. If the plan segregates creditors into classes, each creditor within a class must be treated equally. As a general rule, the plan cannot extend the period for payment of debts more than three years. It can provide for less than full payment of many types of claims, but must call for full payment of the types of claims which are given priority in a liquidation case.

4. The court will confirm (approve) the plan if (a) the debtor proposed it in *good faith,* and (b) if all secured creditors have accepted it. It is not necessary for unsecured creditors to accept the plan; they are bound by it if the court confirms it, even if it modifies their claims. Furthermore, even if a secured creditor objects to the plan, the court may approve it if special provision is made to insure that the secured creditor is either fully paid or permitted to retain the lien or security interest protecting the claim.

5. At any time before or after confirmation of the plan, the debtor has the privilege of converting the adjustment proceeding to a liquidation case. The bankruptcy court may convert the adjustment proceeding to a liquidation case, or dismiss the case altogether, if the debtor fails to perform according to the plan. On the other hand, if the debtor does perform, he or she will ordinarily be granted a discharge upon completion of the payments provided for in the plan. There is no discharge, however, from the types of claims that cannot be discharged in a liquidation case. A discharge may be revoked within one year if it is discovered that the discharge was obtained through fraud.

SUMMARY

When a debtor encounters difficulty in making repayment to creditors, many alternatives for attempting to resolve the problem exist under state statutory and common-law principles. Although bankruptcy under federal law traditionally has been viewed as a last resort, thousands of federal bankruptcy cases are filed each year. The 1978 Bankruptcy Code, as amended in 1984, provides for three basic types of proceedings: liquidation, business reorganization, and adjustment of debts. Liquidation or reorganization proceedings can be either voluntary or involuntary, and can be instituted by or against either individuals, corporations, or partnerships. An adjustment proceeding can only be filed voluntarily by an individual.

The commencement of any type of proceeding causes an automatic stay of most other proceedings against the debtor. Contrary to prior law, under the 1978 Code a debtor does not have to be insolvent to file a voluntary petition, although insolvency is a requirement for the commencement of an involuntary case by creditors.

In a liquidation proceeding, a trustee is appointed by the bankruptcy court to administer the debtor's estate. The debtor's estate consists of practically all property interests of the debtor except for designated exempt items and is ultimately used to pay the claims of creditors according to a list of priorities contained in the Code. A debtor may select the property exemptions allowed by the law of the state where he or she resides, or the exemptions permitted by the Code; a particular state may, however, require debtors in that state to use only the state exemptions in a bankruptcy proceeding. The powers of the trustee include taking legal action to cancel (1) preferential transfers of property by the debtor to certain creditors and (2) other voidable transfers from the debtor. The trustee may also take legal action to collect claims owed to the debtor.

At the conclusion of a liquidation proceeding, a debtor is normally discharged from the unpaid portion of his or her obligations. Certain types of debts are not dischargeable, however. Moreover, proof of certain facts, such as concealment of assets or other fraudulent conduct by the debtor, may cause the court to deny the debtor a discharge.

A reorganization proceeding is intended to permit a financially overextended business to continue operating and work out a fair plan with creditors for repayment of its debts. A trustee may or may not be appointed in a reorganization proceeding; if one is not appointed, the debtor is called a debtor-in-possession and continues to control the business with all the powers of a trustee. An adjustment case is intended primarily to permit *employees* to work out repayment plans with creditors under court protection and supervision, but it can be used by self-employed individuals.

KEY TERMS

Foreclosure
Artisan's lien
Mechanic's lien
Writ of execution
Garnishment
Receivership
Fraud in fact
Fraud implied in law
Composition of creditors
Assignment for the benefit of creditors
Creditors' committee
Liquidation proceeding
Voluntary case
Involuntary case
Automatic stay
Interim trustee
Permanent trustee
Debtor's estate
Exemptions
Voidable transfers
Preference
Insider
Secured creditors
General creditors
Discharge
Nondischargeable debts
Reaffirmation
Reorganization case
Debtor-in-possession
Adjustment case

QUESTIONS AND PROBLEMS

1. Monroe, owner of a stereo equipment dealership, was several months behind on his obligations to an office supply store, a janitorial service, an advertising agency, and an accountant. After being unable to work out settlements with Monroe, these creditors joined in filing a petition for involuntary bankruptcy. Their claims totalled $6,200, all of which were unsecured. Monroe contested the petition, claiming that he was merely having "cash flow problems" and that his business was actually solvent. He said that lately all his cash receipts had been required to pay his landlord and inventory suppliers. Audited financial statements showed Monroe's total liabilities to be $184,000 and the fair value of his assets $202,000. Can these creditors force Monroe into bankruptcy? Discuss.

2. Moore a former law professor, filed a voluntary bankruptcy petition in June 1976. A few days later he filed a separate lawsuit against Slonim, president of the school at which Moore had been a faculty member. In this suit, Moore claimed that, as a result of Slonim's fraudulent misrepresentations, Moore had been induced to sign a contract deferring payment of certain back wages for a period of five years. Slonim sought to have the suit dismissed on the ground that only Moore's trustee in bankruptcy had authority to file such a lawsuit. Should Moore's suit have been dismissed? Explain. (*Moore v. Slonim,* 426 F.Supp. 524, 1977.)

3. Gay, an attorney, had performed legal services for Browy prior to Browy's bankruptcy. Because he had not been paid for these services, Gay exercised his legal right to keep those papers and records belonging to Browy which remained in Gay's possession. During Browy's bankruptcy proceeding, the trustee, Brannon, requested that the judge order Gay to turn over these records. These records contained information relevant to the trustee's investigation of Browy's financial affairs. Gay argued that, since he was merely asserting a lawful "retaining lien" which existed only if he retained possession, the trustee had no right to take the records from him. What resulted? (*Browy v. Brannon,* 527 F.2d 799, 1976.)

4. Several affiliated companies, including Ron San Realty Co., Allvend Industries, Inc., and La Staiti Associates, Inc., were the subject of a single bankruptcy proceeding. Suval was employed by Allvend Industries as its bookkeeper. Although not officially employed by La Staiti, a subsidiary of Allvend, he performed most managerial functions at the subsidiary. In investigating the affairs of La Staiti, the Bankruptcy Court ordered Suval to appear at a hearing and be examined under oath. Suval claimed that he could not be required to testify for La Staiti since he had no formal relationship with that company. Was Suval bound to perform the debtor's duties in the bankruptcy proceeding? Explain. (*In the Matter of Ron San Realty Co., Inc.*, 457 F.Supp. 994, 1978.)

5. Which of the following items of property would *not* be part of a debtor's estate in a bankruptcy case? Explain.
   a. A one-half interest in a patent on a machine the debtor had helped invent
   b. A fifty-acre tract of ranch land, used by the debtor to pasture cattle
   c. An easement which permitted the debtor to drive his pickup and run his cattle over another person's land to get to the public road
   d. The debtor's residence in the city
   e. One hundred head of cattle
   f. A diamond ring, as an inheritance from his father, which the debtor became entitled to receive thirty days after the petition filing date but which he actually received more than seven months later
   g. The debtor's salary earned within 180 days after the petition filing date
   h. Future payments under a veteran's pension, to which the debtor has a vested right
   i. A claim by the debtor against a third party for breach of contract, whose claim could be worth anything from zero to $100,000

6. In her bankruptcy case, Levin claimed a 1972 Volkswagen as exempt property under applicable Massachusetts law. The pertinent part of this statute provided an exemption for "an automobile necessary for personal transportation or to secure or maintain employment, not exceeding seven hundred dollars in value." The car had a fair market value of $1,000, subject to a $350 security interest, leaving Levin with an equity of $650. It was established that she needed the car for her job and for personal transportation. The trustee, Mauro, challenged the exemption. Was the automobile exempt? Discuss. (*Levin v. Mauro,* 425 F.Supp. 205, 1977.)

7. Ferris Enterprises, Inc., built and began operating a theater and restaurant on land leased from Atkinson for a 25-year term. Seven years later Ferris Enterprises became insolvent and was approximately one year behind on rental payments to Atkinson. In accordance with the lease agreement and applicable state law, Atkinson terminated the lease and reclaimed the premises. One month after the termination, Ferris became subject to an involuntary bankruptcy proceeding. At this time, the value of the buildings and equipment which Ferris had added to the premises was at least $343,000. Ferris still owed $214,000 on the loan which had been taken out to construct the buildings and purchase the equipment. Thus, Ferris's interest was worth at least $129,000. By terminating the lease, Atkinson received this value, plus the right to income from the property. Atkinson lost about $6,000 in rent that Ferris had not paid, as well as the right to receive rental payments from Ferris for the remainder of the lease term. However, it was established that Atkinson could relet the premises to someone else for over twice the rental he was to get from Ferris. Ferris's trustee in bankruptcy sued to cancel the termination and reclaim the property for the unexpired portion of the lease, alleging that Atkinson had been the recipient of a fraudulent transfer. What was the result? Discuss. (*In re Ferris,* 415 F.Supp. 33, 1976.)

8. Mr. and Mrs. Scanlon received a payment of $25,000 from Multipane, Inc., in settlement of the Scanlons' claim against Multipane for alleged securities law violations. Multipane was a subsidiary of Gluckin & Co. Two months after the payment, Gluckin & Co. went into bankruptcy. Gluckin's trustee, Mandel, sued the Scanlons, alleging that they had received a voidable preference. Was the trustee successful? Discuss. (*Mandel v. Scanlon,* 426 F.Supp. 519, 1977.)

9. During Martin's bankruptcy case, he sent his books and records to the trustee. When the trustee examined them, however, he discovered that check stubs covering a recent two-year period were missing. Martin claimed that he had sent the stubs and that they must have been lost in transit. He also asserted that the transactions covered by the missing check stubs could be documented by other records. The bankruptcy judge gave Martin no opportunity to prove these allegations, and denied his discharge on the basis of inadequate records. Martin appealed. What was the result on appeal? Discuss. (*In the Matter of Martin,* 554 F.2d 55, 1977.)

10. It is often said that the Bankruptcy Code aids the *honest* debtor. List and explain those provisions of the Code which indicate that this is true.

Part VI

Business Organizations

Business firms vary greatly in product line, size, and management philosophy. Regardless of their differences, however, all businesses must have an organizational structure of some type. The organizational structures of various firms differ, of course, but they also have many elements in common. Their fundamental purpose is to provide a means for implementing business decisions as efficiently as possible. As the implementation of decisions almost always involves a number of individuals working in the firm, the company's organizational framework serves primarily as a vehicle for delegating authority.

In the following chapters we examine the various types of business organization. In Chap-ter 31 we briefly look at the different kinds of business organization, and the major advantages and disadvantages of each. Then, in Chapters 32 through 34, we discuss business partnerships in detail. Chapter 35 examines a special type of partnership—the limited partnership. Chapters 36 through 39 provide thorough coverage of corporations as a business organizational format. Finally, Chapter 40 deals with the legal responsi-bilities of the certified public accountant (CPA). This subject is discussed here because most of a CPA's legal responsibilities arise from his or her relationship with business organizations.

Chapter 31

FORMS OF BUSINESS ORGANIZATION

A business can operate in any of several different organizational forms, the most common of which are the sole proprietorship, the partnership, the limited partnership, and the corporation. Certain other types of organization are of limited usefulness and are therefore not frequently employed. These include the joint stock company, the business trust, the joint venture, and the syndicate.

In this chapter we will outline the basic structure of each form and indicate the factors one should consider in selecting the appropriate form. Later chapters explore in much greater detail the predominant types of organizations in use today: the partnership, the limited partnership, and the corporation.

STRUCTURE OF THE VARIOUS FORMS

Sole Proprietorship

A person who does business for himself or herself is engaged in the operation of a **sole proprietorship.** In reality, anyone who does business without creating an organization is a sole proprietor. The sole proprietorship is obviously the most elementary organizational form: the owner *is* the business. No legal formalities are necessary to create this form, and any business affairs not handled personally by the owner are handled through his or her agents. A sole proprietor is personally liable for all obligations of the business. The sole proprietorship is usually associated with small, local enterprises, but there is no legal or theoretical limit to the scope or complexity of its operations.

Partnership

A **partnership** is an association of two or more persons who carry on a business. The partners are co-owners of the business, and as such they have joint control over its operation and the right to share in its profits. Each partner is personally liable for the partnership's obligations. A partnership is created by agreement of the parties. Although the agreement need not be formal, it is usually desirable that a formal partnership agreement be executed. The Uniform Partnership Act (UPA), adopted in most states, sets out rules to govern the operation of a partnership in the absence of a formal agreement or if certain areas are not covered in the formal agreement. Thus the parties can vary many of the rules set forth in this statute. They cannot, however, vary the rules relating to their liability to a third party (a nonpartner, such as a creditor) unless the third party agrees.

The partnership is suitable for almost any type of business and is very widely used. It is discussed in much greater detail in Chapters 32 to 34.

Limited Partnership

A **limited partnership** is a partnership composed of at least one general partner and at least one limited partner. The general partner is treated by the law the same as a partner in an ordinary partnership. The limited partner, on the other hand, is only an investor. He or she merely contributes capital and does not exercise any powers of management. This form of organization was created for the purpose of allowing a person to invest in a partnership and share in its profits without becoming personally liable to partnership creditors. *Limited liability* is the key characteristic of the limited partnership. In almost all states, either the Uniform Limited Partnership Act (ULPA) or the Revised Uniform Limited Partnership Act (RULPA) governs the organization and operation of such partnerships. Limited partnerships are discussed in Chapter 35.

Corporation

The **corporation** is perhaps the most important form of business organization, not only because it is so widely employed but also because most large businesses operate as corporations. Like the limited partnership, the corporation is entirely a creature of statute. It simply cannot exist unless provided for by an applicable statute and unless the requirements of that statute are met. Every state does, in fact, have statutes governing the formation and operation of corporations.

Essentially, a corporation consists of its *shareholders* (the owners of the business) and its *board of directors* (those people elected by the shareholders to manage the business). The directors commonly employ agents (such as *officers* and other subordinate employees) to oversee the daily operation of the business.

An outstanding characteristic of the corporation is that its shareholders are not personally liable for business obligations beyond the amount of their respective investments. The reason is that the corporation is recognized as a *legal entity* separate and apart from its owners. Corporations will be extensively dealt with in Chapters 36 to 39.

Other Organizational Forms

Joint Stock Company: A **joint stock company** is an unincorporated association that closely resembles a corporation but for most purposes is treated as a partnership. It can exist even where there is no governing statute. Management of the enterprise is usually delegated to one or a few persons. Ownership of the business is evidenced by shares of transferable stock, and each of the shareholders is as liable for business obligations as a partner in a partnership. However, the shareholders are not generally treated as agents of one another (as is true of partners). This form of organization is not widely used today.

Business Trust: The **business trust** (sometimes called the "Massachusetts trust," after the state of its origin) is another organization created by agreement. Legal ownership and management of business property rest with one or more "trustees," and the profits are distributed to "beneficiaries." The business trust originated as an attempt to obtain certain advantages of corporate status, such as limited liability, without incorporation. It was a fairly popular ar-

rangement for a few years during the early 1900s, but it is seldom used today, for two primary reasons:

1. A number of states enacted statutes subjecting the business trust to many of the same burdens placed upon corporations, such as payment of certain corporate taxes.

2. In many states, the beneficiaries were treated as partners by being held personally liable to business creditors.

Joint Venture: A **joint venture** (sometimes called a *joint adventure* or a *joint enterprise*) is essentially a partnership created for a limited purpose or duration. It is treated virtually the same as a partnership.[1] The implied authority of one participant to obligate the enterprise to third parties under the rules of agency law is more limited than in most partnerships because of the restricted scope of the organization's operation. (An example is the association formed a number of years ago by Pennsalt Chemicals Corporation and Olin Mathieson Chemical Corporation. The two companies formed Penn-Olin Chemical Company, a joint venture, solely for the purpose of producing and selling sodium chlorate in the southeastern United States.)

Syndicate or Investment Group: The terms **syndicate** and **investment group** are often used to describe a group of investors in a particular enterprise (such as financing a professional football team or a real estate development). The precise nature of the organization depends entirely on the terms of the parties' agreement and the actual operation of the enter-

---

[1] Technically speaking, there must be a *business purpose* rather than a *social purpose* for a joint venture to exist. In many cases, however, courts have used the terms *joint venture* or *joint enterprise* to describe a situation in which persons are engaged in some common pursuit even if the transaction is not for a business purpose. The most common example is a car pool, where passengers in an automobile share expenses of and control over a trip for a common purpose. The courts have applied the *joint venture* concept to impose joint liability for the negligent driving of one of the participants.

prise. The parties can be partners, members of some other type of association, or simply joint owners of a property interest with no legally recognized business relationship. One pitfall in such arrangements is that the investors may find themselves liable to third parties as partners without having realized the possibility of that occurrence.

SELECTING THE APPROPRIATE FORM

Choosing the appropriate form from among the suitable alternatives is a necessary and important step in the organization of a business enterprise. This choice should be made only after careful analysis of the needs and desires of the owner or owners of the business—and with the aid of legal counsel. Several of the available alternatives may be suitable; there usually will not be one form that *must* be used. Since the organizational form is only a vehicle, the owners should choose the one that enables them to reach their objectives in the easiest, most direct, and most inexpensive way.

Following are some of the factors that should be considered in choosing the most appropriate organizational form. The discussion is devoted primarily to the most frequently used forms: sole proprietorship, partnership, and corporation.

Liability of Owners

The significance of the owners' potential liability for business debts varies with the circumstances. In a given case, its importance depends not only on the degree of probability that substantial claims will arise against the business but also on the practical likelihood of owners having to meet these claims from personal assets not devoted to the business and on the proportion of their wealth that they intend to risk in the business. More specifically:

1. The potential liability (in proportion to capital) is much heavier in some businesses than in others.

2. Those who expect to risk their total accumulated wealth in an enterprise are less in need of limited liability than those who possess substantial assets not being committed to the business.

3. The practicability of obtaining agreements from business creditors to look only to business assets in satisfying their claims varies greatly from one situation to another.

4. The practicability of obtaining liability insurance covering tort claims varies significantly among different types of businesses.

As mentioned earlier, freedom from personal liability for business obligations ordinarily is enjoyed by shareholders of a corporation and by limited partners in a limited partnership. Owners are not usually shielded from liability by any other organizational forms.[2]

By itself, though, the *form* of the organization does not always determine the issue of owners' liability. It is sometimes more dependent on simple bargaining power, particularly in smaller businesses. For example, a corporation with relatively few shareholders and limited assets may be unable to obtain credit solely on the basis of its own credit standing. A creditor in such a case will frequently require as a condition of granting credit that the shareholders personally obligate themselves to satisfy the claim in the event of default by the corporation. On the other hand, a sole proprietorship, partnership, or other organization with ample business assets and financial strength might be able to obtain the agreement of a creditor to look only to business assets for satisfaction of its claim.

Control

The power to make business decisions is of interest to almost anyone undertaking to organize a business. As a purely legal matter, the sole proprietor exercises the most control over the en-

---

[2] However, beneficiaries of a *business trust*, assuming that they refrain from exercising control over the business, are shielded from liability in a few jurisdictions.

terprise, for he or she *is* the business. The individual degree of control naturally decreases as other owners enter the picture. Thus a partner must share control with other partners. When an organizational form that employs centralized management (such as a corporation) is used, the owners surrender even more control. Business decisions in a corporation are delegated to the board of directors, who may or may not be shareholders. Of course, in the small corporation, where shares of stock are held by only a few persons and are not publicly sold (called a **close corporation**), most or all of the shareholders might be on the board of directors. The owners of a close corporation usually do not relinquish as much direct control as do the owners of a corporation with widely distributed shares. (Close corporations are further explored in the chapters on corporations.)

Control, like limited liability, is not necessarily determined only by legal structure. Control of the enterprise often is shaped by other practical matters such as finances and personality. For example, even in a large enterprise, a shareholder who owns a substantial percentage of a corporation's stock frequently can exercise a great deal of indirect control even if not a member of the board. (Of course, such a person probably can win election to the board if he or she so desires.) At the other end of the continuum, the sole proprietor, who theoretically possesses total control over a business, often surrenders some of that control in borrowing substantial sums of money. Few lenders will allow their capital to be used in a business without retaining a certain amount of control over how it is used. Thus a creditor may impose various conditions in the loan agreement and will almost certainly acquire a lien on business assets that will limit or exhaust the credit of the enterprise.

Sometimes a partner, a shareholder, or other business associate exerts a degree of control much greater than his or her actual financial interest. This can occur because the person possesses either experience or a persuasive personality.

Continuity

Most business owners are concerned about the extent to which their business interests will be passed on to their heirs when they die. The entire interest of a sole proprietor passes to his or her heirs. However, if several heirs exist, disputes will probably occur about the continued operation of the business and the heirs will end up selling it and dividing the proceeds. A sole proprietor who wants the business to continue in the family after his or her death will have to plan very carefully (and even then continuity is often impossible).

As we will see later, the partnership is a fragile structure that dissolves on the death or withdrawal of a partner. However, a carefully planned and drafted agreement can strengthen the partnership as a continuing enterprise by providing, for example, that remaining partners have the right to purchase the interest of a retiring or deceased partner.

A corporation, because its shares of stock are transferable, possesses the continuity usually lacking in a partnership.[3] Neither a shareholder's sale of stock nor his or her death terminates the corporation. The purchaser or heir simply becomes the owner of the interest in the business represented by those shares. In most cases a corporation continues until the shareholders vote to dissolve it; theoretically, it can continue forever.

While continuity is usually desirable, under some circumstances it may be undesirable. For example, suppose that a small business is organized as a close corporation. All the shareholders know one another personally, and each plays a significant part in the everyday operation of the business. One shareholder transfers all his stock to a third party, and the other shareholders find themselves forced to share control with someone they don't know and never contemplated dealing with. For this reason, it is advisa-

---

[3] Usually the interests of limited partners in a limited partnership, as well as the owners' interests in joint stock companies and business trusts, also are freely transferable.

ble to include certain restrictions on the transfer of shares in close corporations, particularly in family-owned corporations. (Restrictions on transferability are discussed in Chapter 38.)

Capital Requirements

Expansion of the business and the resulting need for additional capital is perhaps the most common reason for changing the organizational form from a sole proprietorship or partnership to a corporation.

If an interest in a sole proprietorship is sold to raise capital, the owner is no longer a "sole" proprietor. Therefore, a sole proprietor wanting to remain one can raise capital only by borrowing. But borrowing as a method of satisfying capital requirements has limitations that are quickly reached. They include not only the exhaustion of one's credit but also the onerous burden of fixed interest charges.

A partnership presents more possibilities for raising capital:

1. The existing partners themselves are possible sources of additional funds.

2. New partners who will bring more capital into the enterprise can be admitted.

3. In most (but not all) cases, a partnership can secure more funds through borrowing, because the cumulative value of all the partners' assets usually exceeds that of a sole proprietor, thereby improving the business's credit standing.

Definite limitations exist, however, on the capital-raising ability of a partnership. Existing partners provide sources of new funds only insofar as they are willing and financially able to further invest in the business. Bringing in new partners results in a smaller share of profits for each partner. But, perhaps most important, the point may quickly be reached at which there are simply *too many partners* to operate efficiently. The larger the number of owners, the greater the need for centralized management. Ultimately, the same limitations on borrowing to satisfy

capital requirements exist in a partnership as in a sole proprietorship, although the limits may not be reached so quickly.

In most cases, the corporation is the most suitable form of organization if large amounts of capital are required. As with any other organization, the amount of capital that can be raised by borrowing depends on the financial strength and credit standing of the business. Almost limitless possibilities for capital procurement exist, however, in the issuance of *capital stock* (see Chapter 36)—assuming, of course, that the business has been profitable and it appears that financial success will continue, thus making new issues of stock attractive to investors.

Cost and Convenience of Doing Business

Because of the tremendous demands from many different directions, it would be naive to state that doing business in any organizational form is simple or convenient. We can observe, however, that the sole proprietorship involves fewer organizational costs and formalities than other available forms. Even though a partnership can be organized without formalities, it usually is not as simple or as convenient to operate as a sole proprietorship. In a partnership, the rights of other owners must always be considered, as well as their voices in the decision-making process. For all its advantages, the corporation involves more formalities and organizational costs than any other form. This is true not only because the required statutory formalities must be strictly adhered to but also because the corporation is subject to a wider variety of government regulation than the other forms. Greater fees to the government are usually required, and greater attorneys' fees are usually the rule because of the necessity of legal counsel to insure that all formalities are met.

The question of cost and convenience of doing business is not ordinarily the determining factor in the choice of an organizational form. If the objectives of the organizers are best achieved by incorporation, the inconveniences to be encountered will probably not change the decision. But the organizers will have to decide whether the advantages of the corporate form are worth the additional cost and inconvenience. However, in several states today some formalities of operating a *close corporation* have been substantially relaxed. This is considered in further detail in Chapter 37.

Taxation

The subject of business taxation is one of such complexity that only a few of the most basic principles can be given in a text of this nature.

Any business, regardless of its form, is subject to certain types of taxation (for example, property taxes and sales taxes). However, corporations encounter certain types of taxation not dealt with by other organizations (such as franchise taxes).

By far the most important type of taxation to consider is the federal income tax. However, the form of organization offering the most income tax advantages differs from case to case. Under the Internal Revenue Code, federal income taxation of businesses depends on how the enterprise actually operates rather than on what it is called. For this purpose, all business organizations are classified as either sole proprietorships, partnerships, or corporations. Other types of associations are taxed as either partnerships or corporations, depending on their characteristics. Thus an organization will be taxed as a corporation if it has a *majority* of the following corporate characteristics:

1. *Continuity of life.* The death, bankruptcy, or resignation of a member does not dissolve or otherwise interrupt its continuity.

2. *Centralization of management.* Management is centralized in one or more persons who act in a representative capacity.

3. *Limited liability.* No member is liable beyond his or her investment for the firm's debts.

4. *Free transferability of interests.* A member can freely transfer his or her interest without obtaining the consent of other members.

Because of this approach, joint stock companies and business trusts are usually taxed as corporations. Limited partnerships, however, are usually taxed as partnerships.

The income tax treatment of sole proprietorships and partnerships differs significantly from that of corporations. Since the sole proprietor *is* the business, the net income of the business is taxed as personal income. Similarly, the net income of a partnership is taxed as personal income to the partners, each being responsible for the tax on his or her share.

In ordinary circumstances, the income of a corporation is taxed in a substantially different manner. Initially, the net income of the corporation itself is subject to taxation. When any of this income is subsequently distributed to shareholders as dividends, the amount received by each shareholder is taxed as personal income. The result is a form of **double taxation.**

In an effort to diminish the importance of the income tax as a factor in choosing a form of business organization, Congress amended the Internal Revenue Code in 1958 to permit formation of a so-called **S corporation** (until 1982, called a "Subchapter S corporation"). Under this provision, certain small business corporations can elect to be taxed in a manner similar to that of partnerships. In other words, the corporation itself pays no income tax, but each shareholder's portion is taxed as personal income to that person, thus eliminating double taxation.[4] Several requirements must be met for qualification as an S corporation, the most important of which are:

1. There must be 35 or fewer shareholders (although there is no limit on the amount of capital or assets).

---

[4]Each shareholder pays federal income tax on his or her proportionate share of the income regardless of whether it is actually received.

2. All shareholders must be individuals, estates of deceased individuals, or trusts. Thus a partnership or another corporation cannot be a shareholder in an S corporation.

3. There must be only one class of stock.[5]

4. The corporation must be independent, not part of an affiliated group of corporations.

5. All shareholders must file with the Internal Revenue Service a written statement indicating their consent to S corporation status.

SUMMARY

The most important forms of business organization are the sole proprietorship, partnership, limited partnership, and corporation. A sole proprietorship exists when the owner does not form any other type of organization. In such a case, the owner is the business, with the only limitations on his or her control of the business being those imposed by creditors and the exigencies of raising capital. The partnership permits greater capital-raising opportunities, but each partner has less control than if he or she were a sole proprietor. Both sole proprietorships and partnerships are rather fragile organizational forms, although careful drafting of the partnership agreement can increase its continuity. In each of these forms, the owners of the business are personally liable for all business debts.

A limited partnership resembles a partnership in many ways, except that compliance with certain statutory requirements is necessary in addition to the partnership agreement. The reason for these additional requirements is that the limited partners are only investors; they do not manage the business, and usually are not personally liable for business debts. Limited liability can be created only by statute. The limited liability characteristic of a limited partnership makes it somewhat similar to a corporation; thus, a limited partnership is something of a hybrid organization.

A corporation presents much greater capital-raising opportunities than other organizational forms, and is characterized by centralized management in a board of directors, owners who are merely investors, and a theoretically perpetual existence.

The best organizational form for a given business depends on many factors, including the nature of the business, the importance of limited liability and continuity, the capital requirements of the business, and the desires of particular individuals regarding control over the business.

KEY TERMS

Sole proprietorship
Partnership
Limited partnership
Corporation
Joint stock company
Business trust
Joint venture
Syndicate
Investment group
Close corporation
Double taxation
S corporation

QUESTIONS AND PROBLEMS

1. Must a partnership strictly follow all the provisions of the Uniform Partnership Act? Discuss.

2. Are there any similarities between a limited partnership and a corporation? Discuss.

3. What are the similarities between a partnership and a limited partnership? Discuss.

4. What are the characteristics of a joint stock company?

---

[5] Classes of stock are discussed in Chapter 38.

5. A, B, C, D, and E organized a syndicate for the operation of an apartment building. From this statement alone do we know anything about the rights and liabilities of A, B, C, D, and E? Discuss.

6. Why is the personal liability of the owners of a business not always dependent solely on the form of their organization?

7. What part do capital requirements play in selecting a form of business organization?

8. What is meant by the term *double taxation?*

Chapter 32

PARTNERSHIPS
Nature, Formation, and Property

THE NATURE AND HISTORY OF PARTNERSHIPS

Historical Background

The precise origin of the partnership form of business organization is unknown. It has been stated that "some form of partnership is probably as old as the first exhibition of the gregarious instinct of man."[1] We do know that the basic partnership concept of two or more persons combining their skills and property for mutual reward has existed in every organized society.

The English common law of partnership, from which the American law has developed, traces its derivations back to the Roman law and to the law merchant.[2] For several hundred years the rules of law regarding partnerships in England and America were developed almost solely by the courts. Shortly after the turn of the century, in 1914, work was completed on the Uniform Partnership Act (UPA). The UPA codified most of the common-law rules relating to partnerships and significantly altered a few of them. It has been adopted by forty-eight states, the exceptions being Louisiana and Georgia.[3]

Defining a Partnership

Section 6 of the UPA defines a *partnership* as "an association of two or more persons to carry on as co-owners a business for profit." This definition can be broken into elements as follows.

Association: The term *association* indicates that a partnership is a voluntary arrangement formed by agreement.

---

[1] Walter Jaeger, "Partnership or Joint Adventure," *Notre Dame Lawyer* 37 (1961): 138.

[2] The law merchant, discussed earlier, was the body of rules created by English merchants that ultimately was absorbed into the English common law.

[3] The UPA, which appears in its entirety in Appendix B, and other "uniform" laws were created by the American Law Institute and the National Conference of Commissioners on Uniform State Laws. Since these groups possessed no legislative power, the laws were proposed to each of the state legislatures.

Person: Under the UPA the term *person* includes not only individuals but also corporations, other partnerships, and other types of associations. Problems traditionally have occurred over the question of whether a *corporation* can be a partner. Although the UPA attempts to solve these problems by including corporations within its definition of a person, it is not the controlling authority on the point. To determine whether a corporation has the power to enter a partnership, one must look to the corporation laws of each individual jurisdiction. Until recent years, the general rule was that a corporation could not be a partner. The Model Business Corporation Act has taken the contrary view, however, and the legislatures in about half the states have passed corporation laws based on that act, thereby allowing corporations to be partners.[4] With regard to minors and insane persons, the same basic rules apply to partnership agreements as to other types of contracts. Thus a minor can treat the partnership agreement with the other partners as voidable. The minor usually can also repudiate personal liabilities to creditors beyond the amount of his or her investment in the business. But this investment *is* subject to the claims of partnership creditors, although it is the maximum liability that the minor ordinarily can incur.

Co-owners: The partners are defined as co-owners of the business, which distinguishes them from those who are merely agents, servants, or other subordinates. Each partner has a voice in the management of the enterprise and a right to share in the profits.

To carry on a business: The term *business* has been defined in Section 2 of the UPA as including "every trade, occupation, or profession."

---

[4] The Model Business Corporation Act, drafted by the American Bar Association, serves as a model for state legislatures that are revising their corporation laws.

For Profit: An association cannot be a partnership unless the purpose of forming it is to make profits directly through its business activities. Associations for other purposes (including religious, patriotic, or public improvement purposes, or furtherance of the *separate* economic interests of members) are not partnerships, even if they engage in business transactions. Thus the local chapter of a fraternal lodge cannot be a partnership, and the rights and duties of partners cannot attach to its members. For example, individual members are not personally liable for debts incurred for the lodge by its officers unless an agency relationship has been expressly created.

The Entity Theory versus the Aggregate Theory

Don't need to read

For centuries there have been two theories of the nature of the partnership association. One theory, the **entity theory,** is that the partnership is a separate *legal entity*—in other words, a "legal person." Traditionally the viewpoint of those in the commercial world, it was the approach taken by the Roman civil law. A legal person can own and dispose of property, make contracts, commit wrongs, sue, and be sued. In our legal system most adults are considered legal persons. The English courts, however, found difficulty with the concept of a partnership as a legal person. They evidently felt that no one but the Crown could create a legal entity. Corporations, being creations of the Crown, were deemed to be separate legal entities. This remains true today; corporations are created by authority of the government, not simply by agreement, and are regarded as legal persons.

Partnerships, on the other hand, are formed simply by the express or implied agreement of the partners. And since the English courts would not allow private parties to create a legal person separate from their own identities, the traditional approach of the common law in both England and the United States was to treat the partnership as an aggregation of individuals. Under this approach, commonly called the **aggregate theory,** a partnership was not recognized as a separate legal entity. That is:

1. The partnership could not own property; the property of the business had to be owned individually by one partner or by two or more partners as co-owners.

2. The partnership could not sue or be sued in its own name, and a court could not render judgment separately against the partnership; such actions had to be in the name of one or more individual partners.

3. One partnership could not sue another where the two had a member in common, because a party cannot be both plaintiff and defendant in the same legal proceeding.

Although most American courts followed the aggregate theory, a few contrary decisions were rendered. In reality, the courts sometimes employed the different theories as rationalizations of results reached on other grounds. Professor Judson Crane, a leading authority on partnership law, has observed that "the entity may be recognized or disregarded according to the demands of justice in the particular situation."[5]

The UPA does not expressly adopt either the entity theory or the aggregate theory. In a sense it has retained the aggregate theory by defining a partnership as "an *association of two or more persons* to carry on a business for profit." (Emphasis added.) On the other hand, it has used the entity approach for selected purposes. For example, the UPA recognizes the concept of *partnership property* and allows a partnership to own and convey property in the partnership name. Also, it places liability for acts of the partners in conducting partnership business primarily on the partnership itself and the partnership property and only secondarily on individual

---

[5] Judson Crane, *Handbook on the Law of Partnership,* 2d ed. (St. Paul, Minn.: West Publishing Co., 1952), Sec. 3.

partners and their individual property. The UPA says nothing of procedural matters such as lawsuits in the partnership name, but most states have enacted other statutes allowing suit to be brought by or against the partnership in the partnership name. In many instances, the procedural rules in federal courts also allow suits in the partnership name.

Many legal problems, such as those involving taxation, are not governed by the UPA. Depending on the particular problem presented, courts and certain other statutes sometimes treat the partnership as a separate legal entity, and sometimes as an aggregation of individuals.

FORMATION OF A PARTNERSHIP

The Partnership Agreement

As previously mentioned, the partnership is formed by agreement, either express or implied. It is not created by statute, as is a corporation. Few, if any, statutory requirements must be met in order to *form* a partnership. While the UPA governs many aspects of the *operation* of a partnership, it is intended primarily to fill in the gaps of the partnership agreement. Many UPA rules are applicable only if the partners do not agree otherwise.

The agreement obviously must have a *legal object,* but a partnership can be formed even if one or more of the other elements of a valid contract is absent. A valid contract usually does exist as a practical matter, but it is not required. A partnership can be created without a written document, although any part of the agreement falling within the statute of frauds does require a writing for enforceability.

Despite the fact that a written partnership agreement is usually not required, it is highly desirable. Formation of a business is a substantial undertaking and should not be left to the oral declarations of the parties—for several reasons:

1. There are many inherent problems in proving the exact terms of an oral agreement.

2. Numerous problems (such as those relating to taxation) can be satisfactorily resolved only by a carefully drafted written instrument.

3. If the parties go through the process of drafting a formal document with the aid of an attorney, they are much more likely to foresee many problems they otherwise would not have thought about. For example, matters such as procedures for expulsion of a partner or for settlement of disputes between partners are easily overlooked because they seem so remote when the partnership is first formed.

Desirable Elements of a Partnership Agreement

The formal partnership agreement, often referred to as the **articles of partnership,** should clearly reflect the intent of the partners as to the rights and obligations they wish to assume in the business. What is contained in these articles will depend on the nature of the business and the desires of the partners, but ordinarily the written instrument should include such items as the following:

1. Name of the firm. The partnership is not required to have a firm name, but it is usually a good idea to have one. The name can be that of one or more of the partners, or it can be fictitious. (But it cannot be deceptively similar to that of another business for the purpose of attracting its customers.) If the name is fictitious, it usually must be registered. Most states have **assumed name statutes** (sometimes called **fictitious name statutes**) that require any firm, including a partnership, to register with a state official the fictitious name under which the firm is doing business. The purpose of such statutes is to enable creditors of the firm to learn the identities of those responsible.

2. Nature and location of the business.

3. Date of commencement and duration of the partnership.

4. Amount of contributions in money or property each partner is to make (in other words, the amount of their investments in the business).

5. Time within which the contribution of each partner is to be made.

6. Salaries and drawing accounts of each partner, if such are desired.

7. Division of work and duties of each partner, including rights in management.

8. Admission requirements for new partners.

9. Each partner's proportionate share of net profits while the business is continuing to operate and upon dissolution.

10. Any proposed restrictions on the power of individual members to bind the firm.

11. Clear delineation of partnership assets as distinguished from individual partners' assets.

12. Bookkeeping and accounting methods to be used and location of and access to books.

13. Procedures for withdrawal or exclusion of a partner.

14. Indication of whether withdrawal or exclusion causes dissolution, and if not, rules for continuing the business after such an event.

15. Method for determining the value of a withdrawing or excluded partner's interest.

16. Requirements and procedures for notice to partners and partnership creditors in case of dissolution.

17. Which partner or partners will be in charge of winding up the business upon dissolution.

18. Procedures for settling disputes between partners, such as submitting them to arbitration.

The following case illustrates the value of a carefully planned and drafted partnership agreement. In this case a partnership of physicians was able to terminate an unsatisfactory relationship with one of their group who simply could not get along with the others. This would have been much more difficult had it not been for their well-planned partnership agreement.

Gelder Medical Group v. Webber
Court of Appeals of New York, 363 N.E.2d 573 (1977)

The Gelder Medical Group, a partnership engaged in practicing medicine and surgery in Sidney, New York, was first formed in 1956. Some 17 years later, defendant Dr. Webber, then 61 years old and a newcomer to Sidney, was admitted to the partnership following a one-year trial period in which he was employed by the group as a surgeon.

Like the other members of the group who had joined since its inception, Dr. Webber agreed that he "will not for five years after any voluntary or involuntary termination of his association with said Gelder Medical Group, practice his profession within a radius of 30 miles of the Village of Sidney, as a physician or surgeon . . . without the consent, in writing, of said Gelder Medical Group." The partnership agreement also provided a procedure for the involuntary withdrawal of partners. It stated that "In the event that any member is requested to resign or withdraw from the group by a majority vote of the other members of the group, such notice shall be effective immediately and his share of the profits to the date of termination shall be computed and he shall be paid in full to the date of termination of his employment pursuant to his agreement with the association."

Dr. Webber's association turned out to be unsatisfactory to his partners. His conduct, both professional and personal, became abrasive and objectionable to his partners and their patients, a cause of "intolerable" embarrassment to the group. A psychiatrist who examined Dr. Webber a number of times on the referral of the partnership stated that Dr. Webber had "what would be termed an adjustment reaction of adult life with anxiety and depression." While the psychiatrist concluded that the adjustment reaction soon cleared, he summed up his description of Dr. Webber as a perfectionist who was a "rather idealistic, sincere, direct, frank individual who quite possibly could be perceived at times as being somewhat blunt."

Although the difficulties were from time to time discussed with Dr. Webber, the unhappy relationship persisted. In October, 1973, the discord culminated with the group's unanimous decision to terminate Dr. Webber's association with the partnership. After Dr. Webber refused to withdraw voluntarily, the group, in writing, formally notified him of the termination. It was effective immediately, and, on the basis of an accounting, Webber was paid $18,568.41 in full compliance with the partnership agreement.

In about two months, Dr. Webber, disregarding the restrictive covenant, resumed his surgical practice as a single practitioner in Sidney. The group, to protect its practice, promptly sued to enjoin Dr. Webber's violation of the restrictive covenant. Dr. Webber instituted his own lawsuit for damages resulting from his expulsion. The two lawsuits were consolidated. The trial court and the intermediate level appellate court both ruled in favor of the partnership, granting an injunction prohibiting Dr. Webber from violating the noncompetition clause and dismissing his claim for damages. Dr. Webber appealed.

Breitel, Chief Justice:

The applicable law is straightforward. Covenants restricting a professional, and in particular a physician, from competing with a former employer or associate are common and generally acceptable. As with all restrictive covenants, if they are reasonable as to time and area, necessary to protect legitimate interests, not harmful to the public, and not unduly burdensome, they will be enforced.

Similarly common and acceptable are provisions in a partnership agreement to provide for the withdrawal or expulsion of a partner. While there is no common-law or statutory right to expel a member of a partnership, partners may provide, in their agreement, for the involuntary dismissal, with or without cause, of one of their number.

Turning to the Gelder Group agreement, no acceptable reason is offered for limiting the plainly stated provisions for expulsion, freely subscribed to by Dr. Webber when he joined the group, and none is perceived. When, as here, the agreement provides for dismissal of one of their number on the majority vote of the partners, the court may not frustrate the intention of the parties at least so long as the provisions for dismissal work no undue penalty or unjust forfeiture, overreaching, or other violation of public policy. . . .

[The court then held that the covenant not to compete was reasonably limited as to time and area, and was not unduly burdensome.] . . .

Hence, Dr. Webber's attempts to free himself from the covenant not to compete . . . must be rejected. It is true, as the group stated in its letter of termination to Dr. Webber, that the termination was a tragedy which it regretted. But the expulsion clause was designed to function when the conflict between the group and one of its members was insoluble, and the necessity for its use must always be unfortunate. . . .

Affirmed.

Determining the Existence of a Partnership

When the parties have clearly expressed their intentions in a written instrument, there is ordinarily no difficulty in determining whether a partnership exists. But when the parties have not been explicit in declaring their intentions, problems frequently arise. The most fundamental, of course, is whether a partnership has even been *created.* This issue arises with surprising frequency, because of its importance in regard to the rights and obligations of the "partners" and third parties as well. For example, a creditor may seek to hold several persons liable for the transactions of one of them on the ground that they are partners. Or one party might claim that he and another are partners and that the other party has violated a resulting fiduciary duty by having a conflicting business interest.

When the existence of a partnership is disputed by an interested party, such existence becomes a question of fact to be decided on the basis of all the circumstances. No single factor usually is controlling, and the court's ultimate decision commonly is based on several considerations, the most important of which are (1) sharing of profits, (2) joint control of the business, and (3) joint ownership and control of capital or property.

Sharing of Profits: A distinction should be made between gross revenues and net profits. It has been consistently held by the courts, and reiterated in the UPA, that an agreement to share the *gross revenues* from a particular enterprise does not in itself indicate the existence of a partnership. Sharing of *net profits,* however, usually creates a very strong inference that the parties have formed a partnership. Indeed, where there has been no sharing of profits or agreement to share them, the court is very likely to find that no partnership exists.

In certain situations, profits are shared by persons who obviously never intended to become partners. Under such circumstances the fact that profits are shared or that the parties have agreed to share them will not by itself create a presumption that a partnership was intended. These situations are described below.

Where the Profits Are Received by a Creditor in Payment of a Debt: For example, O, the owner of a business in financial difficulty, owes debts to X, Y, and Z. In settlement of these debts, X, Y, and Z agree to accept a certain percentage of O's profits for a period of time. No inference of partnership is created by the sharing of profits, and no partnership exists between O, X, Y, and Z (unless, perhaps, X, Y, and Z take title to a portion of the business property and take part in managing the business).

Where the Profits Are Received as Wages by an Employee: Suppose that X is the owner of a business and A, B, and C are her employees. As an incentive to the employees, X establishes a plan whereby they share in the profits of the business. There is no presumption of a partnership so long as the evidence as a whole indicates an *employment* relationship; that is, X withholds federal taxes from the employees' salaries, exercises control over them, and does not allow them any management powers or co-ownership of business property.

Where the Profits Are Received as Rent by a Landlord: If the probable returns of a business being undertaken by a party are uncertain, that party may wish to avoid the burden of fixed charges as much as possible by leasing necessary equipment or real estate at a variable price. It is not uncommon, if the owner of the equipment or real estate is willing, for a rental agreement in such a case to provide that the rent will be based in whole or in part on the profitability of the business. Such an arrangement does not of itself make the owner a partner with the person carrying on the business. However, if the owner of the property also takes part in managing the business, this might be enough for a court to rule that a partnership has been formed.

Where the Profits Are Received as an Annuity by the Spouse or Representative of a Deceased Partner: If a successful partnership is dissolved by the death of a partner, it is often desirable to continue (rather than liquidate) the business because of the value of the goodwill it possesses as a going concern. Thus, it may be agreed, either in the original articles of partnership or by contract after a partner's death between the spouse, executor, or administrator and the surviving partners, that the dead partner's interest will not be liquidated. In consideration for allowing this interest to remain in the business, the spouse or representative might receive a share of the profits. Such facts do not by themselves make that person a partner. If, however, such a party exercises powers of control and management, a court might find that a partnership has been created.

Where the Profits Are Received as Interest on a Loan: If a creditor who has lent money to a person or persons carrying on a business agrees to receive a share of profits in lieu of interest, the courts generally have held that the lender has not become a partner unless he or she also participates in management. In a number of cases the courts also have held that no partnership exists even where the lender has been given a degree of control in the business, so long as the control is of a limited nature for the sole purpose of protecting the loan.

Where the Profits Are Received as Consideration for the Sale of Property: When an item of property having an uncertain value is sold to someone who expects to use it in carrying on a business, it is sometimes agreed that the price payable to the seller will include a share of the profits made from use of the property. Two common examples are *goodwill* and *trademarks.* The seller usually retains no ownership of the property or control over its use;[6] nor is he or she usually expected to share any losses

---

[6] However, if there is no sale of the trademark but only a *license* (a permission to *use* the trademark), the licensor does retain ownership and, usually, a measure of control over how it is used. But the receipt of profits by the licensor as consideration for the license does not by itself make that person a partner in this case either.

incurred by the buyer. In many instances this is simply the best way of computing the value of a particular property right. No partnership is created by such an arrangement.

Joint Control and Management: Although sharing of profits is a cardinal element of the partnership, another factor often felt to be important by the courts is whether the parties have *joint control* over the operation of the business. For instance, where sharing of profits by itself is not sufficient to indicate existence of a partnership, the addition of the factor of joint control might well cause a court to hold that a partnership has been created. *Exercise of management powers* is obviously very strong evidence of control. But the fact that management powers have been expressly delegated to one or more of the partners does not mean that those who do not manage are not true partners if the other facts indicate that they are. In a sense, agreeing to relinquish control is itself an exercise of the right of control.

Joint Ownership of Property: Another factor that frequently finds its way into court opinions is *joint ownership of assets.* Of the three basic tests for existence of a partnership, this is the least important, although it certainly is taken into account by the court, along with all the other evidence. The UPA takes the position that co-ownership of property does not, of itself, establish a partnership. An inference of partnership is also not necessarily created by the fact that the co-owners share any profits made by the use of the property. This seems at first to be inconsistent with our earlier discussion of the presumption of partnership that is usually engendered by profit sharing. But there is no real inconsistency. In the case of co-owners of property, the sharing of profits made from the property is a basic part of co-ownership. In most cases the owner of property wishes to receive whatever income it generates; thus it is reasonable to assume that co-owners will want to share the income from their jointly owned property. A partnership should not be presumed simply because the owners act in a way totally consistent with simple co-ownership.

On the other hand, if the property and its use are only part of a larger enterprise, and the parties share profits from the whole enterprise, an inference of partnership is justified. For instance, co-ownership of a commercial building and sharing of its rental income by A and B does not necessarily make them partners. If, however, they use part of the building as premises for the operation of a going business of some type, sharing not only the rental income from the remainder of the building but also the profits and management of the business, they are quite likely to be considered partners.

The two cases below illustrate the type of evidence considered by courts in determining whether a partnership has been formed where no formal agreement has been made. In the first case there was no express agreement at all. In the second there was an express oral agreement to be partners, but the nature of the business venture changed over a period of time, thus prompting a question whether the original partnership agreement extended to the transformed enterprise.

Lupien v. Malsbenden
Supreme Judicial Court of Maine, 477 A.2d 746 (1984)

York Motor Mart was in the business of assembling Bradley automobiles. The Bradley was a "kit car"; when a customer placed an order, York purchased from the manufacturer a kit that was used to build an automobile on a Volkswagen chassis. York Motor Mart was

run by Stephen Cragin and Frederick Malsbenden, although they had no formal agreement as to the nature of their business relationship. As part of York Motor Mart, Cragin also operated a general automotive repair business. The repair shop was conducted on the same premises and under the same name as the Bradley business, but Malsbenden and Cragin apparently treated the two operations as separate and Malsbenden played no part in the repair business.

Robert Lupien placed an order with Cragin for a Bradley. The written contract was signed by Cragin but identified the seller as "York Motor Mart." Lupien made a deposit of $500 toward the purchase price of $8,020, and one week later made a further payment of $3,950. Lupien then made visits to York Motor Mart on the average of once or twice a week to check on the progress being made on his Bradley. During those visits Lupien generally dealt with Malsbenden, because Cragin was seldom present. On one such visit, Malsbenden told Lupien that he would have to transfer ownership of his pickup truck to York Motor Mart. It was agreed that this transfer would constitute the balance of Lupien's consideration under the contract and that York Motor Mart would sell the pickup and use the proceeds to complete construction of the Bradley. When Lupien complied, Malsbenden supplied him with a rental car, and later supplied him with a demonstrator model ("demo") of the Bradley for his use pending completion of the car he had ordered. When it was discovered that the "demo" actually belonged to a third party who had entrusted it to York Motor Mart for resale, Malsbenden purchased it for Lupien's use.

Lupien never received the Bradley he had ordered, and Cragin disappeared. Lupien filed suit against Malsbenden, claiming that Cragin and Malsbenden were partners in the operation of York Motor Mart and that Malsbenden was personally liable for the partnership's obligations. Malsbenden claimed that his interest in York Motor Mart was basically that of a "banker" rather than a partner. He testified that he had loaned $85,000 to Cragin, without interest, to finance the Bradley portion of York Motor Mart's business. The loan was to be repaid from the proceeds of each car sold. Malsbenden admitted that Bradley kits were purchased with his personal checks and that he had also purchased equipment for York Motor Mart. Malsbenden also admitted that after Cragin disappeared in May 1980, he had physical control of the York Motor Mart premises and that he continued to dispose of assets there even to the time of trial in 1983. The trial court held in favor of Lupien and Malsbenden appealed.

McKusick, Chief Justice:

The Uniform Partnership Act, adopted in Maine, defines a partnership as "an association of two or more persons . . . to carry on as co-owners a business for profit." Whether a partnership exists is an inference of law based on established facts. A finding that the relationship between two persons constitutes a partnership may be based upon evidence of an agreement, either express or implied, to place their money, effects, labor, and skill, or some or all of them, in lawful commerce or business with the understanding that a community of profits will be shared. . . . No one factor is alone determinative of the existence of a partnership. . . . If the arrangement between the parties otherwise qualifies as a partnership, it is of no matter that the parties did not expressly agree to form a partnership or did not even intend to form one: It is possible for parties to intend no partnership and yet to form one. If they agree upon an arrangement which is a partnership in fact, it is of no importance that they call it something else, or that they even expressly declare that they are not to be partners. The law must declare what is the legal import of their agreements, and names go for nothing when the substance of the arrangement shows them to be inapplicable.

Here the trial justice concluded that, notwithstanding Malsbenden's assertion that he was only a "banker," his "total involvement" in the Bradley operation was that of a partner. The testimony at trial, both respecting Malsbenden's financial interest in the enterprise and his involvement in day-to-day business operations, amply supported the trial court's conclusion. Malsbenden had a financial interest of $85,000 in the Bradley portion of York Motor Mart's operations. Although Malsbenden termed the investment a loan, significantly he conceded that the "loan" carried no interest. His "loan" was not made in the form of a fixed payment or payments, but was made to the business, at least in substantial part, in the form of day-to-day purchases of Bradley kits, other parts and equipment, and in the payment of wages. Furthermore, the "loan" was not to be repaid in fixed amounts or at fixed times, but rather only upon the sale of Bradley automobiles.

The evidence also showed that, unlike a banker, Malsbenden had the right to participate in control of the business and in fact did so on a day-to-day basis. [The court then noted that the facts of this case were clearly distinguishable from a previous one in which no partnership was found to exist. In the earlier case, the defendant had advanced money for the purchase of automobiles and the money was to be repaid upon the sale of each car, but the defendant exercised no control over the business.] According to Urbin Savaria, who worked at York Motor Mart from late April through June 1980, Malsbenden during that time opened the business establishment each morning, remained present through part of every day, had final say on the ordering of parts, paid for parts and equipment, and paid Savaria's salary. On plaintiff's frequent visits to York Motor Mart, he generally dealt with Malsbenden because Cragin was not present. It was Malsbenden who insisted that plaintiff trade in his truck prior to the completion of the Bradley because the proceeds from the sale of the truck were needed to complete the Bradley. When it was discovered that the "demo" Bradley had given to plaintiff while he awaited completion of his car actually belonged to a third party, it was Malsbenden who bought the car for plaintiff's use. As of three years after the making of the contract now in litigation, Malsbenden was still doing business at York Motor Mart, "just disposing of property." Malsbenden and Cragin may well have viewed their relationship to be that of creditor-borrower, rather than a partnership. At trial Malsbenden so asserts, and Cragin's departure from the scene in the spring of 1980 deprives us of the benefit of his view of his business arrangement with Malsbenden. In any event, whatever the intent of these two men as to their respective involvements in the business of making and selling Bradley cars, there is no clear error in the trial court's finding that the Bradley car operation represented a pooling of Malsbenden's capital and Cragin's automotive skills, with joint control over the business and intent to share the fruits of the enterprise. As a matter of law, that arrangement amounted to a partnership.

Judgment affirmed.

Shawn v. England
Court of Appeals of Oklahoma, 570 P.2d 628 (1977)

In the summer of 1973 Gary England was a weathercaster for television station KWTV Channel 9, Oklahoma City, and Bill Shawn—a stock broker with E. F. Hutton and Company—was a stock market reporter and commentator for the same station.

For some time England had made occasional reference to what he called a "thunder lizard" while telecasting the weather. Usually he did so during thunderstorms as an interest provoker, particularly during his early morning reports. The make-believe creature engaged Shawn's imagination and eventually it occurred to him that it might be profitable to design and promote the sale of a stuffed thunder lizard which the kids could hold during thunderstorms as a sleep-inducing comforter.

One day Shawn broached the idea to his friend England, who immediately thought he saw merit in it. After some discussion the parties decided they needed a commercial artist to help design the mythical animal. To Shawn's mind came a longtime friend and artist, Larry May, with whom he had attended grade, junior high, and high school. Shawn contacted May, told him of the idea, and upon inquiry learned that the commercial artist was not only interested but willing to help "poor boy" the project by contributing the art work.

The three individuals staged their initial meeting at May's office and at that time discussed ways to achieve maximum publicity for the fictional lizard. They accepted England's proposal that the three consider themselves equal partners in their venture and divide any profits realized three ways. During the next several months the threesome met nearly every week for a so-called "brainstorming session." At one early meeting they decided to have a drawing contest wherein they would ask the youngsters and adults alike to send in drawings of what they envisioned the thunder lizard to be with the promise of a prize to the winner. The contest met with a good response and May, as judge, picked a nine-year-old boy's drawing for the prize. A little later while continuing pursuit of still better promotional ideas the trio hit upon the idea of a weather fact cartoon book featuring thunder lizard drawings, which after further thought was transformed into a coloring book for the kiddies.

Gary England began gathering material for the coloring book and after accumulating considerable weather data the three men concluded that the publication of a regular weather booklet about the weather in Oklahoma would have even more profit potential than a coloring book in that it would have broader appeal. And so they turned their joint efforts to the development of a weather book.

By January of 1974 England had not only gathered considerable data for the booklet but had written the manuscript. Shawn was given the responsibility of having it typed and edited and he accomplished the assignment promptly. England made additional changes in the text and added pictures here and there in an effort to finalize it for publication.

In the meantime, England met with the management of KWTV and discussed the possibility of the station's underwriting and helping to promote the booklet. England reported back that the station agreed to "bankroll" the project by buying enough copies to pay for the initial production of the work—estimated to be about 13,000 copies—and proceeds from sales exceeding this were to be the profit of the three-man partnership.

Then it happened. In April of 1974, at one of their regular Saturday morning meetings, Shawn was abruptly informed he was no longer needed and the partnership was ended. He tried to get the other two to reconsider, but they insisted on terminating his relationship with them. England and May said that there were too many people in the deal and that the partnership arrangement only applied to the "thunder lizard" idea.

Shawn, plaintiff, sued England and May, defendants, claiming that their original partnership agreement extended to the weather book. He sought to recover a one-third share of all profits to be made from the book. In the trial court a jury found that there was a partnership and that plaintiff should receive one-third of the profits, but the judge granted defendants' motion for judgment notwithstanding the verdict. Plaintiff appealed.

Brightmire, Presiding Judge:

. . . In arguing that there was no partnership, defendants acknowledge that "all parties to this controversy concede that a partnership existed for the specific purpose of marketing a 'thunder lizard' doll" but this partnership, they insist, was terminated with the "abandonment of that plan." The crux of their argument is that profit sharing was restricted to the thunder lizard doll and perished with the toy and since there was no new agreement made with regard to later projects, namely, the thunder lizard color book or the weather book, Shawn failed to prove any factual foundation for recovery. It makes no difference legally, goes defendants' argument, that Shawn thought the initial partnership continued because the fact of the matter is that it could not have continued since it was never discussed after the first meeting. Defendants' conclusion is, therefore, that the only way plaintiff could have succeeded in this lawsuit was to have presented proof that the disputants specifically articulated an express agreement to participate as partners in the marketing of the weather book—an event which never occurred. . . .

In our opinion plaintiff was justified in thinking the partnership status established in the summer of 1973 continued until the day defendants terminated it. The fact that the particular creation at the partnership's inception was abandoned did not prevent it from serving as the metamorphic progenitor of the genre's ultimate yield—namely, the weather booklet. It was a weather related idea that brought the parties together; it was a weather related idea that became the focal point of their first discussions; and it was the same weather related theme which one finds threading through all nine months of weekly meetings.

If in advance of this lawsuit defendants considered the partnership ended with the abandoned lizard plaything they took care to conceal it. Not only did they fail to disclose their thoughts about this but conducted themselves in a manner that demonstrated the very opposite. They continued to welcome plaintiff to their meetings and accept the benefit of his knowledge, experience and thinking. They assigned him a task to perform with reference to the weather booklet as though he was still partner in the enterprise. And when at last it began to look like success of the venture was near at hand two members of the triumphant trinity decide to tell the third, "We don't need you anymore!" This act, we think, is comparable to that of a pilot at the end of a transoceanic flight who, as soon as he sees the runway and commences his final approach, ejects his navigator from the aircraft with the declaration, "I don't need you anymore!"

Moreover, there is another circumstance which we think undermines defendants' position and that is that each admitted he considered himself a partner with regard to the weather booklet venture both before the ouster of Shawn and afterwards, notwithstanding the absence of further definitive discussion of their status after the initial partnership agreement was made. Certainly if between themselves defendants had reason to believe the original partnership status continued throughout the course of their meetings then why would not plaintiff be entitled to entertain the same belief? Neither defendant testified to any circumstance or fact that would have led the plaintiff to believe that the original arrangement did not obtain as to all results of the "brainstorming" sessions particularly with reference to figuring out weather related projects to promote for profit production purposes. No evidence does the record contain justifying defendants' conclusion that the thunder lizard doll project was an isolated endeavor disconnected from what went on afterwards. On the contrary, a fair evaluation of the evidence leads comfortably to the conclusion that the weather booklet was a natural end product of a creative ideological evolution that began with the thunder lizard.

Under the facts, it seems to us, and certainly it must have seemed to twelve jurors, as though defendants used the efforts and the mental ability of the plaintiff for as long as they thought they needed him and then, when they got their book about ready to publish and thought they had marketing arrangements made, arbitrarily decided to eliminate his interest in joint venture assets by terminating it. This they could not do. If a partner decides to dissolve a partnership and appropriate the business to himself, he must first fully compensate his copartner for his share of the gain to be realized from the fulfillment of a prospective business undertaking the consummation of which is imminent. . . .

[Reversed, and judgment rendered for plaintiff for one-third of the profits, in accordance with the jury's verdict.]

Partnership can hold property & be in partnership name

PARTNERSHIP PROPERTY

A partnership commonly requires various types of property for the operation of its business, including, for example, real estate, equipment, inventory, or intangibles such as cash or securities. The prevailing rule at common law was that a partnership, not being a separate legal entity, could not own real estate. Somewhat inconsistently, it was also generally held that a partnership *could own* other types of property. Under the UPA, a partnership is recognized as an entity insofar as property ownership is concerned and can own either real estate or other types of property. The UPA uses the phrase **tenants in partnership** to describe the status of individual partners with respect to the partnership property. (The rights that individual partners have regarding partnership property will be discussed in the next chapter.)

Although today a partnership can (and quite often does) own such property itself, it is not essential that it own *any property at all.* The partners themselves may wish to *individually* own the property needed for the operation of the business.

For a number of reasons it is sometimes important to determine whether an item of property belongs to the partnership or to an individual partner. Among them:

1. Creditors of the partnership must resort to partnership property for satisfaction of their claims before they can take property of individual partners.

2. The right of a partner to use partnership property is usually limited to purposes of furthering the partnership business.

3. The question of ownership can also be important with regard to taxation, distribution of assets upon dissolution of the partnership, and other matters.

Factors in Determining Ownership

Agreement: The ownership of property is determined by *agreement* of the partners. Sound business practices dictate that the partners should explicitly agree on the matter and keep accurate records of their dealings with property. Unfortunately, partners often fail to indicate clearly their intentions as to whether ownership of particular items of property rests with the partnership or with one or more individual partners. In such cases, the courts consider all pertinent facts in an attempt to discover the partners' *intent*. Where it appears that the matter of property ownership never occurred to the partners, so that they actually had no definite intention, the court determines which of the possible alternatives—partnership or individual ownership—more closely accords with their general intentions and objectives for the business as a whole and which is fairer both to partners and to third parties.

Legal Title: In the absence of a clear agreement as to ownership, the strongest evidence of property ownership is the name in which the property is held, often referred to as the **legal title.** If an item of property is held in the name of the partnership, courts will hold it to be partnership property in almost every case. This principle most often plays a part where *real estate* is involved, because a deed has been executed in the name of some party and usually has been "recorded" (made part of official county records). Such formal evidence of ownership is frequently not available for property other than real estate, but if it is available, it will play the same important role. For example, this principle applies to motor vehicles, for which there is usually a state-issued certificate of title.

Problems regarding ownership seldom arise if title to the property in question is held in the partnership name. Those that do arise usually occur in either of two situations: (1) where the property is of a type for which there is no deed, certificate, or other formal evidence of ownership; or (2) where title is held in the name of one or more individual partners, but there is a claim that it is actually partnership property. In the first instance, evidence must be presented to establish just where ownership actually rests. In the second, evidence must be introduced to overcome the presumption of individual ownership and prove that the property actually belongs to the partnership. No single factor is controlling;

the court's determination ordinarily is based on the cumulative weight of several factors. Discussion of some of the more important ones follows.

Purchase with Partnership Funds: The funds generated by the business operations of a partnership are partnership property. Additionally, the funds paid into the partnership by individual partners and used by the partnership as working capital are *presumed* to be partnership property. The courts will hold such funds to be individual property only if very strong evidence is produced to show that the payment was intended as a *loan* to the partnership by a partner, rather than a contribution to capital.

An item of property *purchased with partnership funds* is also presumed to be partnership property. The use of partnership funds in making a purchase often plays an important part in a court's decision that ownership resides in the partnership. Indeed, proof that partnership funds were used to buy the property is sufficient to establish the partnership as owner *even if this is the only evidence presented*. Moreover, the presumption created by use of partnership funds is very difficult to overcome. If property has been purchased with such funds, it will take a great deal of contrary evidence to establish that the property does not actually belong to the partnership—even if it is held in the name of an individual partner or other person.[7]

The Way the Property Is Used: Evidence indicating that the property has been used in the

---

[7]On the other hand, if the fact that the property is held in the name of an individual has *misled an innocent third party*, such as a creditor, a different result may be reached. To illustrate: A tract of land was purchased with funds belonging to the B Company, a partnership; but title is held in the name of X, one of the partners. When X applies to C for credit, C innocently relies upon the fact that title to the land appears to rest with X, and C grants credit to X and obtains a lien on the land. If X defaults, C can reach the land for satisfaction of his claim. Even though it is really partnership property, it will be treated as X's individual property insofar as C is concerned. Of course, X will be held responsible to the partnership for the loss of its property.

business of the partnership is considered by the courts, but by itself it is not sufficient to enable a court to hold that the property belongs to the partnership. For example, if the property is held in the name of an individual partner, the fact that it has been used for partnership purposes is not enough to make the partnership the owner. Courts realize that it is not uncommon for an individual partner to allow his or her property to be used in the partnership business without intending to surrender ownership of it.

Treatment in the Partnership Records: If the property is carried in the partnership books as an asset of the firm, this strongly tends to indicate that it is partnership property. The inference is even stronger if an unpaid balance on the property is carried in the records as a partnership liability.

Other Factors: Any number of other factors might influence a court's decision that an item is partnership property:

1. If property had been purchased with funds of an individual partner, the fact that partnership funds were later used to improve, repair, or maintain the property *tends* to show that it now belongs to the partnership. (But additional evidence usually is required, because most courts have been unwilling to infer that the property is owned by the partnership *solely* on the basis that partnership funds were later used to maintain it.)

2. The fact that *taxes* on the property have been paid by the partnership can be important.

3. The receipt by the partnership of *income* generated by the property is evidence that the partnership is the owner.

4. Any other conduct of those involved is considered if it tends to indicate their intent regarding property ownership.

In the case below the court was concerned with two questions: (1) whether a particular parcel of real estate was partnership property, and (2) if so, whether the contract to sell the property, signed by only one partner, was binding on the partnership.

Kay v. Gitomer
Court of Appeals of Maryland, 251 A.2d 853 (1969)

Albert J. Kay and Benjamin F. Eckles, brothers-in-law, decided to go into the plumbing and contracting business as partners but never entered into a formal partnership agreement. Mr. and Mrs. Kay and Mr. and Mrs. Eckles pooled their resources and purchased real estate consisting of "lot 5," on which was located a small shed, and the rear fifty feet of "lots 1 to 4," on which was located a frame bungalow. Lots 1 to 4 adjoined lot 5. Title to the property was not taken in the name of the partnership, but rather was in the names of Kay and Eckles, individually, as co-owners. The partnership of "Kay and Eckles, Building Contractors," established its office in the bungalow on lots 1 to 4. It is not clear whether lot 5 was ever actually used in the partnership business, but Kay and Eckles did rent it out as a parking lot.

The partnership was financially unsuccessful during the first few years of its operation, and Eckles and Kay decided to sell lot 5 to raise cash. Kay by himself signed a contract to sell lot 5 to Gitomer. A dispute then arose as to the terms of the sale, and Kay and Eckles refused to sell. Gitomer, as plaintiff, sued for a decree of specific performance, which would require Kay and Eckles, defendants, to convey the lot 5 title to him. The trial court held for plaintiff, and defendants appealed. The first question to be decided by the appellate court was whether lot 5 was actually partnership property.

Singley, Justice

. . . The resolution of the questions presented can be accomplished by equating the facts of this case to the pertinent provisions of the Uniform [Partnership] Act. . . . §8(1) provides:

All property originally brought into the partnership stock or subsequently acquired, by purchase or otherwise on account of the partnership is partnership property.

In *Williams v. Dovell,* 96 A.2d 484 (1953), we held that the Uniform [Partnership] Act does not prevent a partnership from acquiring real estate by having the partners take title as co-tenants [that is, co-owners], and in *Vlamis v. De Weese,* 140 A.2d 665 (1958), that where record title to real estate was in the name of the partners [individually] as [co-owners] ". . . The criterion of whether property not held in the partnership name is partnership property is the intention of the parties to devote it to partnership purposes, to be found from the facts and circumstances surrounding the transaction considered in connection with the conduct of the parties in relation to the property."

The testimony of Mr. Kay, taken at a pretrial deposition, was read into the record below without objection:

Q. Now, Mr. Kay, what was the intention in your mind when you purchased Lot 5 in Block H in Easley's subdivision on Fenton Street in connection with the ownership of the real estate and the partnership that you had formed or were forming with your brother-in-law, B. F. Eckles?

A. We figured it would be a fairly good place to work out of in the business that we sort of hoped to develop and let's say a likely spot for maybe the appreciation of the property rather than a depreciation in its value.

Q. Well, was it your intention that the partnership of you and Mr. Eckles would have the beneficial ownership of this property?

A. We had the use of it.

Q. Was that your intention?

A. Oh, yes.

It was stipulated that the capital account of the partnership consisted principally of land at a cost of $38,583.62 and improvements at a cost of $15,000, which were equally reflected on the accounts of the two partners. The United States income tax return filed by the partnership for the calendar year 1960, which was an exhibit in the case, disclosed that the *partnership had recognized as income $55.00 received as rent from lot 5, then used as a parking lot, and had taken as deductions* $750.00 in depreciation on the frame building on lots 1 to 4, *$704.66 in real estate taxes which included the taxes* *on lot 5,* and $690.00 in interest on the mortgage on lots 1 to 4. *It was stipulated that of taxes paid by the partnership in 1961, $524.99 related to lots 1 to 4 and lot 5.* [Emphasis added.]

This is the evidence on which the lower court relied in finding that when Kay and Eckles took title to lots 1 to 4 and lot 5 on 18 June 1959, they intended the real estate to be the property of the partnership which they had formed. There was no necessity for it to have been purchased with partnership funds. It constituted Kay's and Eckles' contribution to partnership capital, for, in the language of the Uniform [Partnership] Act, it was "originally brought into the partnership stock."

[The court thus held that the evidence in the record was sufficient to support the trial court's conclusion that lot 5 was partnership property and not owned by Kay and Eckles as individuals. The court then held that the contract signed only by Kay did bind the partnership in this case and that Gitomer was entitled to specific performance.]

Decree affirmed.

SUMMARY

A partnership is defined as "an association of two or more persons to carry on as co-owners a business for profit." In some respects, a partnership is treated as a separate legal entity. For example, it is legally capable of owning property and making contracts, and partnership property is primarily liable for partnership debts. In other respects, however, the law treats a partnership as an aggregation of individuals rather than an entity. For example, individual partners are personally responsible for partnership debts after partnership assets are exhausted.

The partnership is created by agreement. Although this agreement does not have to be a formal written one, it ought to be. Partners should devote great care to the creation of a formal written partnership agreement, a document often called the articles of partnership.

Courts may examine a variety of factors to determine whether a partnership exists when there is no formal partnership agreement. The sharing of profits is an important indicator of partnership status, but there are several situations in which profit sharing does not mean that the parties intended to be partners. Showing that the parties each exercised control and management over the business is another important way of establishing the existence of a partnership. Joint ownership of property is a relevant factor, but it is not weighed as heavily in determining whether a partnership exists.

A partnership is legally capable of owning property, although it is not necessary that a partnership own property in order to operate its business. A partnership can use property that is owned by individual partners. It can be important to determine whether a particular item of property is owned by the partnership or by one or more individual partners, for several reasons. For example, partnership creditors must look first to partnership property for satisfaction of their claims, and an individual partner's right to use partnership property is restricted. The articles of partnership should specify which property is to be owned by the partnership. When a question of property ownership is not resolved by the articles of partnership, courts consider such things as the name in which legal title is held, whether the property was purchased with partnership funds, the way the property is used, and its treatment in the partnership records.

KEY TERMS

Entity theory
Aggregate theory
Articles of partnership
Assumed name statute (or fictitious name statute)
Tenants in partnership
Legal title

QUESTIONS AND PROBLEMS

1. Discuss whether the UPA adopts the *entity* or *aggregate* theory of the nature of a partnership.

2. Wishing to invest their money, Johnson and Watkins combined funds in equal portions and purchased a substantial amount of corporate stock as well as corporate and government bonds. They owned these securities jointly, shared equally in all dividends and other investment income, and jointly made all decisions relating to the management of their investments. Are they partners? Discuss.

3. Nelson was employed by Cox as an accountant for Cox's large chicken-raising business. Nelson contributed no capital to the business and followed Cox's orders in performing his duties. Nelson's pay, however, was to be one-third of each month's profits from the business. Does a partnership exist between Nelson and Cox? Explain.

4. X, Y, and Z were partners in an automobile dealership. Their partnership agreement provided for continuation of the business in the event of the death of any partner. X died, and Y and Z agreed with X's widow that she would receive a lump sum payment of $50,000 and a 25 percent share of the business's profits as compensation for X's share in the partnership. It was agreed, however, that she would not be required to perform any duties for the business and would take no part in management. Is X's widow a partner of Y and Z? Explain.

5. Shaw was the owner of a shopping center. He rented a store in the center to Winn and agreed to accept, as rent, 20 percent of the net profits of the business. Did this agreement make him a partner? Explain.

6. Wyman and Harvey, college students, each contributed $500 for the purchase of a refreshment stand near the beach of a summer resort. They spent the summer operating the stand and, at the end of the summer, divided the approximately $5,000 profit they had made. They had not entered into a written agreement at any time, and nothing had ever been said about their being partners. Did a partnership between them exist during the summer? Discuss.

7. Corley and Foster were partners in a grain brokerage business, Southwest Grain Brokers. They invested $10,000 of the profits from the business in the stock of Zeron Corp. The Zeron stock certificates were issued jointly to Corley and Foster in their individual names. Corley died, and his widow, as the sole heir of his estate, claimed a one-half interest in the Zeron stock. Will her claim be upheld? Discuss.

8. What is an *assumed name statute?*

9. Discuss why anyone wishing to form a partnership should obtain legal advice and prepare a written partnership agreement.

10. Give three reasons for the importance of determining whether a particular item of property belongs to the partnership or to one or more partners as individuals.

Chapter 33

PARTNERSHIPS
Operating
the Business

RELATIONS AMONG PARTNERS

Management Rights

One of the basic rights of a partner is to participate in the management of the enterprise. Unless the partnership agreement provides otherwise, all partners have equal rights in the conduct and management of the partnership business. This is true regardless of the amount of their capital contributions or services to the business.

Many partnership agreements expressly provide that a particular partner will be the "managing partner," exercising control over the daily operations of the business. Such agreements can also be implied from the conduct of the partners. For example: Ajax Co. is a partnership composed of partners A, B, C, D, and E. Over a substantial period of time, C, D, and E have left the management of the business to A and B, who possess recognized ability and experience as managers. If C, D, and E suddenly complain about a management decision made by A and B, the court probably will find that there was an implied agreement to give management powers completely to A and B and that they were therefore justified in acting without first consulting C, D, and E.

Unless it has been expressly or impliedly agreed otherwise, differences among the partners regarding management are usually settled by a *majority vote.* A few matters, however, such as admission of a new partner or amendment of the articles of partnership, require the consent of *all* the partners unless they have previously agreed that a less-than-unanimous vote will suffice.

Individual Rights in Partnership Property

Although a partner does not actually *own,* as an individual, any part of the partnership property (the partnership is the owner), he or she does have *rights* in specific partnership assets. However, the interests of the partnership as a business entity are of greater importance than the rights of any of the individual partners. Let us assume that a partnership owns a piece of equipment and that this ownership is undisputed. If one of the partners wishes to make use of the property or otherwise control it, he or she is subject to a number of limitations.

Limitations by Agreement: The first limitation is that of the *partnership agreement.* If the agreement among the partners stipulates the rights each is to have with respect to partnership property, then the individual who wants to use or control the property is bound by the agreement. For example, the agreement might provide that one of the other partners has the exclusive right to possess or deal with the property.

Equal Right to Possession: Where there has been no agreement regarding partnership property, certain limitations are imposed by law on individual partners. Under the UPA, each partner has an *equal right to possess partnership property for partnership purposes.* Without the consent of all the other partners, an individual is not entitled to exclusive possession or control of partnership assets. Furthermore, the equal right of possession enjoyed by each partner is limited to purposes that further the partnership business, unless the other partners consent to a use for some different purpose.

Nontransferability: A partner's right to possess and control partnership property for partnership purposes *cannot be transferred by that person to a third party outside the partnership.* The reason is simple. In this situation the third party would be exercising a right that for all practical purposes would make him or her a new partner, and a new partner can be brought into the partnership only by the agreement of all the partners. For similar reasons, this right cannot be reached by a partner's personal creditors. Additionally, it does not pass to the executor or administrator of a partner's estate when he or she dies; instead it passes to the surviving partner or partners.

A partner's rights with respect to specific partnership property should not be confused with his or her interest in the partnership. The **interest in the partnership** is each partner's· share of the profits and surplus, and it is subject to different rules than the right to use partnership property. (This concept is more fully developed later in the chapter.)

The next case discusses and illustrates the principle that a partner does not actually own specific items of partnership property.

Putnam v. Shoaf
Court of Appeals of Tennessee, 620 S.W.2d 510 (1981)

The Frog Jump Gin Company was a partnership in the business of running a cotton gin operation. Originally, the gin was operated as an equal partnership between E. C. Charlton, Louise Charlton, Lyle Putnam, and Carolyn Putnam. In 1974 Mr. Putnam died and his widow, Carolyn Putnam, received his interest. In 1976 Carolyn Putnam wished to sever her relationship with the other partners, and another couple, John and Maurine Shoaf, wanted to acquire Mrs. Putnam's one-half interest. The gin was heavily indebted to the Bank of Trenton, and had a $90,000 excess of liabilities over assets. The Shoafs agreed to take over Mrs. Putnam's interest if she and the Charltons would each pay $21,000 into the partnership account. The Shoafs agreed to assume personal liability for all partnership debts, including Putnam's share of any partnership debts made prior to their coming into the partnership. (It should be noted that if the Shoafs had not expressly agreed to assume liability for prior partnership debts, under the Uniform Partnership Act they would have been personally responsible only for debts incurred after their entry into the partnership.) In addition, Mrs. Putnam executed a deed purporting to convey to the Shoafs Mrs. Putnam's interest in specific assets of the partnership. These assets consisted of the cotton gin, its equipment, and the land on which it was located.

When the Shoafs assumed their positions as partners, the company's old bookkeeper was terminated and a new bookkeeper hired. Two months later, with the assistance of the new bookkeeper, it was learned that the old bookkeeper had engaged in a scheme of systematic embezzlement from the Frog Jump Gin Company from the time of Mr. Putnam's death until the bookkeeper's employment was terminated. The partnership filed suit against the old bookkeeper and the banks that had honored checks forged by the bookkeeper. The court allowed Mrs. Putnam to intervene and become a party to the lawsuit, as well. Judgment was rendered against the defendants, and $68,000 in damages was paid into court. By agreement, one-half of this amount was paid to the Charltons as owners of a one-half interest in the partnership. Ownership of the rest of the money was disputed by the Shoafs and Mrs. Putnam. The Shoafs asserted that the claim against the bookkeeper and banks was a partnership asset, Mrs. Putnam had transferred her interest in the partnership to the Shoafs, and, therefore, Mrs. Putnam had no right to any of the money. Mrs. Putnam asserted that she had only executed a deed transferring title to specific partnership assets, the claim against the bookkeeper and banks was unknown and unmentioned at the time of that transfer, and, therefore, Mrs. Putnam retained a one-half interest in the claim. The trial court agreed with the Shoafs and held that Mrs. Putnam had no right to any of the money.

Nearn, Judge:

First, we must discover the nature of the ownership interest of Mrs. Putnam in that which she conveyed. Under the Uniform Partnership Act, her partnership property rights consisted of her (1) rights in specific partnership property, (2) interest in the partnership, and (3) right to participate in management. The right in "specific partnership property" is the . . . right of equal use or possession by partners for partnership purposes. This possessory *right* is incident to the partnership, [and it] does not exist absent the partnership. The possessory right is not the partner's "*interest*" in the assets of the partnership. The real interest of a partner, as opposed to that incidental possessory right just discussed, is the partner's interest in the partnership which is defined as "his share of the profits and surplus. . . ." Therefore, a partner owns no personal specific *interest* in any specific property or asset of the partnership. The *partnership* owns the property or the asset. The partner's interest is . . . the partner's pro rata share of the net value or deficit of the partnership. For this reason a conveyance of partnership property . . . is not a conveyance of the individual interests of the partners.

This being true, all Mrs. Putnam had to convey was her interest in the partnership. Accordingly, she had no specific interest in the admittedly unknown [claim] to separately convey or retain. Therefore, the determinative question is: Did Mrs. Putnam intend to convey her interest in the partnership to the Shoafs? There can be no doubt that such was the intent of Mrs. Putnam, as she had no other interest to convey. To give any other intent to the actions of Mrs. Putnam would require a fraudulent intent on her part, which intent certainly did not exist. Therefore, the intent of Mrs. Putnam was to convey the interest she owned, which was "her share of the profits and surplus." . . . It is abundantly evident that the last thing Mrs. Putnam wanted was to remain a partner. She wanted out, and out she got.

Since neither the Shoafs nor Mrs. Putnam knew of the embezzlement by accountant Bennie Johnston, there can be no doubt that neither the Shoafs nor Mrs. Putnam knew of the valuable asset that the partnership possessed in its claim against the banks. However, it was the partnership's asset and not her personal asset. Just as she could not have retained it, had she known of it, and at the same time conveyed her partnership interest, we cannot now say she conveyed her partnership interest in 1976, but is still entitled to a share in it.

This situation is no different from a hypothetical oil discovery on the partnership real property after transfer of a partnership interest with neither party believing oil to be present at the time of the conveyance. The interest in the real property always was and remained in the partnership. . . .

It is inescapable to us that the interest in the [claim against the banks] remained in the partnership at all times regardless of the composition of the partners; and, it is equally inescapable that Mrs. Putnam intended to convey her partnership interest.

This is not a case of mutual mistake but one of mutual ignorance. They are not necessarily the same thing. . . . In this case Mrs. Putnam had to intend to convey her interest in the partnership. Hindsight now shows that it had more value than either party thought. But, hindsight is not a basis for a money judgment. . . . We wonder what would be the position of Mrs. Putnam . . . had the Frog Jump Gin failed, leaving a sizeable deficit, even after the influx of the bank's refund. Would she accept a partner's share of the Frog Jump Gin's liabilities for a share of the bank's refund? The question answers itself and we pose it only to show that she did not have a specific interest in any specific assets of the Frog Jump Gin, either to retain or convey. All she had was a partner's interest in a "share of the profits" (and losses) which she certainly intended to convey. . . .

[The judgment of the trial court is affirmed.]

Profits, Losses, and Other Compensation

As previously mentioned, a partner's *interest in the partnership* is his or her share in the profits of the business as well as a share of what the excess would be at a given time if all the partnership's debts were paid and all the accounts were tallied up and settled. The proportion of partnership profits to be received by each partner is ordinarily determined by an express provision in the articles of partnership. This proportion can be determined on the basis of each partner's contribution of capital, property, or services or by any other method the partners wish to use. If the agreement makes no provision for distributing profits, they will be divided *equally*. The rule requiring equal division in the absence of contrary agreement applies without regard to the amount of capital, property, or service contributed by each partner.

The agreement may also provide for the sharing of losses, although it is often silent on the matter, since few people enter a business expecting to lose money. If the agreement says nothing about losses, they are shared *in the same proportion as profits.* Thus, if nothing is agreed as to either profits or losses, both are shared equally.

The articles of partnership may provide for salaries or other compensation to be paid an individual partner or partners for services rendered in behalf of the partnership. If, however, the agreement does not so provide, a partner is *not entitled to any compensation for such services.* The law presumes in such cases that the parties' intent was that a share of the profits be each partner's only compensation. The sole exception to this rule occurs after the partnership has been dissolved. A partner who is in charge of winding up the affairs of the dissolved partnership is entitled to reasonable compensation for these services.

Unless otherwise agreed, a partner is *not entitled to interest on his or her contribution of capital* to the partnership (the partner's investment). But if the partners originally agreed upon a date for repayment to individual partners of their capital contributions, a partner has a right to receive interest on his or her contribution from that date if it remains unpaid. As we saw in the previous chapter, a partner's payment of money to the partnership is presumed to be a capital contribution rather than a *loan.* However, if a payment is clearly a loan, then the partner is entitled to receive interest computed from the date of the loan.

If an individual partner, acting reasonably in the ordinary and proper conduct of partnership business, makes a payment or incurs personal liability to a third party, the partner is entitled to be *reimbursed* or *indemnified* by the partnership. For example, suppose that the partnership has contracted to sell goods to a buyer. The buyer breaches the contract and refuses to accept the goods. While attempting to find another buyer, it is necessary for the partner handling the transaction to store the goods or to ship them elsewhere. If that partner personally pays such expenses, he or she is entitled to be reimbursed by the partnership.

Basic Fiduciary Duties

Each partner maintains a *fiduciary* relationship with the partnership and with every other partner in matters pertaining to the partnership. This relationship is much the same as the one existing between principal and agent. (The analogy is particularly appropriate because each partner is an agent of the partnership.) Since such a relationship requires the highest standards of loyalty, good faith, and integrity, a partner who acts in his or her own self-interest and to the detriment of the partnership is accountable to it for any profits made from the endeavor. The seriousness with which courts view this fiduciary relationship is very well described in the following statement by Judge Benjamin Cardozo (who later became a member of the U.S. Supreme Court):

[Partners] owe to one another, while the enterprise continues, the duty of the finest loyalty. Many forms of conduct permissible in a workaday world for those acting at arm's length, are forbidden to those bound by fiduciary ties. A [partner] is held to something stricter than the morals of the marketplace. Not honesty alone, but the punctilio of an honor the most sensitive, is then the standard of behavior. As to this there has developed a tradition that is unbending and inveterate. Uncompromising rigidity has been the attitude of courts of equity when petitioned to undermine the rule of undivided loyalty by the "disintegrating erosion" of particular exceptions. . . . Only thus has the level of conduct for fiduciaries been kept at a level higher than that trodden by the crowd. It will not consciously be lowered by any judgment of this court.[1]

A partner may engage in his or her own enterprises outside the partnership, so long as the articles of partnership do not prohibit such activity and so long as the outside involvement does not cause the partner to neglect partnership affairs. But a partner cannot *compete* with the partnership. (For example, a partner in a grocery business obviously cannot legally run a competing store in the neighborhood.) Going one step farther, a partner cannot even *acquire* a business interest adverse to the interests of the partnership. Thus it has been held that a partner cannot acquire a partnership asset without the consent of the other partners. To illustrate: A lease on real estate held by the partnership is about to expire. One of the partners, acting on his own and for his own benefit, cannot secretly secure from the owner a renewal of the lease for himself. In a similar vein, if a partner in a partnership whose business is purchasing and selling real estate purchases and resells in his or her

---

[1] *Meinhard v. Salmon,* 164 N.E. 545 (1928).

own name (or in the name of a relative) a lot that he or she should have purchased for the partnership, the partner is accountable to the partnership for the profit.

The fiduciary relationship also demands that each partner be utterly scrupulous when transacting business on his or her own behalf with the partnership or with another partner in matters pertaining to the partnership. To illustrate: If the partners decide to sell an item of partnership property to one of the partners, the purchasing partner is under a duty to disclose all material facts relevant to the transaction. If this partner has any information relating to the present or prospective value of the property, he or she must reveal it to the other partners. The same holds true where one partner is selling his or her interest in the partnership to another partner. Such transactions are not of an "arm's-length" nature, with each party looking after its own interests. They are, to the contrary, transactions in which individual self-interest must take a back seat to the requirements of complete disclosure and rigid fairness.

A partner can also be held responsible to the partnership for losses resulting from negligence. The partner is not liable simply because of bad judgment but is liable if the business is harmed because of carelessness or neglect.

Partnership Books

All matters relating to record keeping should be dealt with in the articles of partnership. If the agreement is silent in this regard, the partnership books are required to be kept at the partnership's *principal place of business*. Every partner must at all times have access to the books and the opportunity to inspect or copy any of them.

If the partners have named one of themselves to be the managing partner or if they have given record-keeping duties to a particular partner, that partner must keep complete and accurate accounts and can be held liable for the failure to do so. He or she also has the burden of proving that the records are correct; and if an accurate account is not kept, any doubts that may arise when partnership affairs are being closed will usually be resolved against the responsible partner.

If in a particular situation the partnership agreement does not expressly resolve a question concerning the adequacy of partnership records, a court will consider the nature of the business, the experience and education of the partners, and other relevant circumstantial evidence when determining whether a partner has fulfilled his or her record-keeping responsibilities.

Right to an Account

Under certain circumstances a partner can institute a legal proceeding called an **account** (or an **accounting**). In such a suit, all records of the partnership must formally be produced and all balances computed under court supervision. Since each partner ordinarily has free access to the books, this kind of lawsuit usually is filed only when the partnership has been dissolved.

There are circumstances, however, in which a partner may demand a formal account from his or her copartners without seeking the dissolution of the partnership. Then, if the copartners refuse or if the partner making the demand is dissatisfied with the accounting, he or she may institute legal action. Under Sec. 22 of the UPA, a partner has the right to a formal account as to partnership affairs under any of the following circumstances:

1. He or she has been *wrongfully excluded* by the other partners from the partnership business or from possession of partnership property.

2. The right to a formal account has been provided for in an *agreement* between the partners.

3. One of the other partners has, without consent, derived a *personal benefit* from a transaction related to partnership business.

4. Other circumstances render it "just and reasonable" (for example, if he or she has been traveling for a long period of time on partnership business and the other partners are in possession of the company's records).

The following case provides a practical example of the rule that partners owe fiduciary duties to each other, and that a partner who assumes responsibility for partnership records also assumes a correspondingly higher duty.

Couri v. Couri
Supreme Court of Illinois, 447 N.E.2d 334 (1983)

In 1941, Joseph, Anthony, and Peter Couri orally agreed to operate as equal partners the "Couri Brothers Supermarket," a business which their father began in 1928. The brothers agreed that they would have equal control of the partnership, share equally in profits and losses, and have equal rights in the partnership property. The agreement was of indefinite duration. Later, Peter Couri withdrew from the partnership and his interest was purchased by Joseph and Anthony, who orally agreed that they would be equal partners. Over the years, Joseph had essentially worked in the supermarket at all times, as a clerk, butcher, and general supervisor of daily operations. Anthony worked full-time in the supermarket during World War II when Joseph was in the Army. After the war Anthony usually did not work at the supermarket itself, but had responsibility for the partnership's books, records, and investments. At times, Anthony also maintained other business interests separate from the partnership.

In September, 1973, Joseph claimed that Anthony would not let him participate fully in the management of the business, and when the brothers were not able to reconcile their differences Joseph left the store permanently. Anthony claimed that Joseph unjustifiably abandoned the business and refused to participate. In November Joseph visited Anthony at his home and requested and received some of the partnership records for the previous two years. They still were unable to resolve their dispute, and Joseph demanded that Anthony wind up the partnership's affairs. Instead, in July, 1974, Anthony changed the locks on the store, closed out the partnership checking account, opened a new account which was in his exclusive control, and changed the name of the grocery store from "Couri Brothers Supermarket" to "Couri's Supermarket." Anthony continued to operate the store until Joseph, plaintiff, filed a lawsuit seeking an accounting and court-supervised winding up of the partnership's affairs.

The trial court ordered Anthony, the defendant, not to destroy, alter, or otherwise modify any of the partnership's records, and to render a complete accounting of revenues and expenses since 1957 (plaintiff and defendant agreed not to go back any further than

1957) and its current assets and liabilities. The records and tax returns of the partnership had been prepared and maintained by defendant since 1941. The records consisted of daily reports and monthly and yearly summaries. Tax returns were prepared from the summaries. Although the daily reports were theoretically restated in the monthly and yearly summaries, Anthony admitted that in several of the years of operation the summaries and tax returns did not accurately reflect actual income because the partnership's income was substantially understated. The daily reports themselves would provide the most accurate reflection of actual income, although these reports were often confusing and contradictory because defendant's bookkeeping practices were not in accord with generally accepted accounting principles. However, most of the daily reports were not available: some time after the plaintiff filed suit, the defendant's son cleaned his parents' attic while they were on vacation and destroyed several boxes of the partnership's daily reports. In court, the son testified that he was instructed to clean the garage and attic by his mother, who testified that she had acted without consulting the defendant.

Consequently, the evidence presented to the trial court was extremely incomplete. Both parties submitted sworn statements indicating how they thought the partnership's income should be computed from the available evidence. Defendant's computations produced a total net income figure for the period 1957–1980 ranging from $433,000 to $487,000, while plaintiff's computations produced a figure of over $1 million. The income that had actually been reported to the Internal Revenue Service during the period was $424,000. The trial court held that defendant's accounting did not accurately reflect income, and that the partnership's total net income for the period was approximately $750,000. Based on this total income, the trial court computed plaintiff's share of the remaining surplus as $122,000 and rendered a judgment for plaintiff in that amount. Both parties appealed to the intermediate appellate court, which reversed the trial court's decision and dismissed plaintiff's suit on the ground that plaintiff had not proved any specific amount to which he was entitled. Plaintiff then appealed to the Illinois Supreme Court.

Underwood, Justice:

In our judgment the basic flaw in the appellate court's reasoning is its mischaracterization of the consequences of the breaches of defendant's fiduciary duties and the destruction of the daily records which the court had ordered him to preserve. Those records were in defendant's sole possession and control, and while the defendant's proof indicates he did not know they were being destroyed, it is clear that he had not informed his family of their importance and the necessity of their preservation. Plaintiff's inability to be more specific in his proof is the direct result of the breach of defendant's obligations under the court order as well as his failure to adequately discharge his fiduciary duties.

The basic partnership principles involved here are well settled. A fiduciary relationship existed between the partners and embraced all matters relating to the partnership business; each was bound to exercise the utmost good faith and honesty in all dealings and transactions relating to the partnership. As the managing partner who was admittedly responsible for virtually all of the financial aspects of the partnership, defendant had a duty, as trustee, to maintain regular and accurate records and to account for partnership transactions. All doubts and obscurities created by his own negligent failure to keep adequate records were properly resolved against him by the trial court.

Despite the imprecise nature of some of plaintiff's proof, there was sufficient evidence from which the trial court could fashion an equitable decree, and we do not believe, as the appellate court apparently did, that in these circumstances the trial court was required to detail the nature or method of its calculations. . . .

Defendant's argument here that "right or wrong" the only concrete evidence available shows that net income was approximately $546,143 ignores the record and the applicable fiduciary principles. Based upon the available books and records, the testimony and reports of two accountants, the testimony of the parties, and the reasonable inferences from the evidence, the trial court could have reasonably concluded that income was substantially greater than defendant contended. Indeed, it was evident that the tax returns were not accurate. . . . The trial court had evidence from which it could determine the approximate amount of the understatement for the years 1971–74. Further, the court could well have rejected much of defendant's evidence and testimony concerning the period from 1974–80, given the absence of any daily reports (which he no longer prepared) or other supporting documents to verify actual income, and the obvious disparity between the profits defendant claimed and the known profits for the period in which he admitted the understatements. Too, the probative value of defendant's explanation concerning his change of accounting methods and his testimony concerning the accrual method upon which he had previously operated was not great. Even assuming that he had attempted to follow that method in previous years—which an accountant commissioned by the court was unable to verify from records which seemed to indicate the contrary—his methods were inconsistent with accepted accounting principles. Thus, had the court, based upon this evidence, determined that defendant continued to understate income during the years 1974–80, albeit in a somewhat lesser amount, it could have reasonably concluded that the net income of the partnership over the period in question was $750,000. While we express no opinion on defendant's testimony concerning his blamelessness in the destruction of the daily reports, we do point out that had defendant preserved those records as he was ordered to do, he might have been able to overcome or rebut some of the presumptions which were resolved against him. His inability to do so is the result of his own handling of the partnership's affairs. . . .

As we have indicated, the trial court had sufficient evidence from which it could determine the approximate net income of the partnership, and its finding in the amount of $750,000 is not against the manifest weight of the evidence. Given the difficulties of proof, which were largely of defendant's making, the court's finding is not an unreasonable resolution of the parties' conflicting claims. . . .

For the reasons stated, the appellate court's judgment is reversed. [The Illinois Supreme Court then reinstated the trial court's judgment, with one exception: the trial court had also ruled that defendant was entitled to $65,000 compensation for the period since plaintiff had withdrawn from the business. The Supreme Court held that defendant was not entitled to any such compensation, and that this $65,000 should be included as part of the partnership surplus. Thus, the court's final judgment awarded plaintiff the $122,000 as found by the trial court plus $32,500 (one-half of $65,000).]

RELATIONS WITH THIRD PARTIES
3rd parties (usually creditors)

General Application of Agency Rules

In partnership transactions with third parties, the law of agency governs the liabilities of the partnership, the partners, and the third party. Technically, *the partnership is the principal and each partner an agent* with respect to partnership affairs. Statements are also found in many cases to the effect that each partner is an agent for the other partners (who are principals), as well as for the partnership as an entity. Of course, this is often the practical result anyway, since the other partners can be held personally liable if partnership assets are insufficient to satisfy the partnership liability.

The partnership is liable to third parties for a partner's transactions that are contractual in nature if the partner had actual or apparent authority. (Actual authority can, of course, be express or implied.) Partnership liability can also exist if the partnership, acting through the other partners, ratifies an unauthorized transaction of a partner. (More will be said later about partnership liability for a partner's contracts.)

As in agency law generally, the partnership is liable to third parties harmed by the tort or other wrongful act of a partner only if the tort was committed while the partner was acting in the ordinary course (or scope) of the partnership business. However, even if a partner's tort did not involve partnership business, any other partner participating in, directing, or authorizing the wrongful act is personally liable along with the one actually committing it.

The courts are somewhat more reluctant to impose *criminal liability* on a partnership or on the other partners for the act of one of them. Such liability is, of course, placed on any partner who participated in, directed, or expressly authorized the act of the other. However, the partnership as an entity (and other partners who did *not* participate in, direct, or expressly authorize the wrongful act) will be liable for the crime of a partner only if (1) it was committed in the ordinary course of the partnership business *and* (2) proof of criminal intent is *not* required for conviction. Examples include illegal liquor sales, mislabeling of goods, and unsafe transporting of explosives.

Examples of a Partner's Implied Authority

Most questions concerning partnership liability for acts of individual partners stem from commercial dealings and other transactions of a contractual nature. The partnership, as principal, is usually liable for a partner's transaction only if it is *authorized.* Such authority can be expressly granted in the partnership agreement or by the other partners at a later time.

Even where no express authority has been given, under the UPA a partner can bind the partnership in transactions that are for the purpose of "carrying on the partnership business in the usual way." This *implied authority* exists with regard to those types of transactions that are *customary* in conducting the kind of business in which the partnership is engaged. In the articles of partnership or by other agreement the partners can expressly limit the authority of a partner to act for the partnership. If such a limitation restricts a partner's implied authority by prohibiting transactions that would otherwise be normal and customary, third parties are bound by the limitation only if they know of it. For example, suppose that a partnership is in the business of buying and selling real estate. It is customary in such a business for a partner to have authority to sell for the partnership real estate that is held for resale. Suppose, however, that the articles of partnership provide that such sales can be made only by two or more partners acting together. A third party who does not know of this restriction and who buys from a single partner is not affected by the limitation, and the partnership is bound by the transaction under the doctrine of *apparent authority.*

The following transactions are of such a usual and customary nature that a partner *ordinarily* is impliedly authorized to undertake them. These are only examples; other instances of implied authority exist, but they depend more on particular circumstances. Furthermore, these transactions might not be impliedly authorized in certain situations, particularly where the nature of the business is such that they are not usual and customary. Ultimately, the type of business conducted by the partnership and all the surrounding circumstances determine the extent of a partner's implied authority.

Borrowing Money: In determining whether a partner has implied authority to borrow money

in behalf of the partnership, most courts have traditionally distinguished between *trading* and *nontrading* partnerships. Implied borrowing authority has been held to exist in trading partnerships but not in nontrading ones. A partner in a nontrading partnership usually has been held to have authority to borrow money only if this authority has been expressly granted by a majority of the other partners.

Essentially, a **trading partnership** is one that engages in the business of buying and selling goods. All others, ranging from professional partnerships such as those of lawyers and physicians to partnerships for the purpose of carrying on a real estate, insurance, or loan business, are classified as **nontrading partnerships.** In view of the increasing complexity of the business world, the simple division into trading and nontrading categories is of doubtful usefulness. Today many types of partnership require working capital, even though their business is not limited to merchandising.

The courts, perhaps sensing the inadequacies of the simple dichotomy between trading and nontrading partnerships, have expanded the trading category to include businesses such as those of tailors, plumbing and construction contractors, manufacturers, and dairy farmers. The courts will probably continue to use the terms *trading* and *nontrading,* but their importance will diminish. If a court holds a business to be a trading partnership, the authority of a partner to borrow money is automatically present unless the other partners expressly limit this authority and make such limitation known to third parties. In other types of partnerships, the courts will probably look at all the surrounding circumstances. If it is usual and customary for a partner in this particular partnership, or perhaps even in similar partnerships, to have borrowing authority, then such authority will probably be found to exist by many courts.

What has been said about implied authority to borrow money applies also to the execution of promissory notes and other types of instruments purporting to obligate the partnership to make a future payment of money. In fact, many of the cases decided on this point have involved such instruments.

Selling Partnership Property: A partner has implied authority to sell goods, real estate, or other property belonging to the partnership if sales of such items are within the ordinary course of the partnership's business. For example, suppose that a partnership engages in the wholesale grocery business and also owns real estate for investment purposes. In this case a partner has implied authority to sell groceries held for resale but usually does not have implied authority to sell the real estate. The latter authority will have to be expressly granted by a majority of the other partners. On the other hand, if the business of the partnership consists of buying and selling real estate, a partner *does have* implied authority to sell partnership real estate.

The addition of other facts might change the above example. For instance, if the other partners had in the past always allowed one partner to make all investment decisions individually, that partner might have implied authority to sell the grocery partnership's real estate.

Even if the sale of a certain type of property, such as goods, is part of the ordinary business of the partnership, a partner generally does not have implied authority to sell most or all of the

items held in inventory if this will result in a suspension of the business.

Hiring Employees: A partner ordinarily has implied authority to hire employees whose services are necessary for carrying on the business of the partnership, to make reasonable agreements for their compensation, and to discharge them.

Making Purchases: A partner usually has implied authority to purchase items that are reasonably necessary to the operation of the partnership's business.

Receiving and Enforcing Performance of Obligations: If the partnership is entitled to some type of performance, such as a payment of money or delivery of goods, a partner ordinarily has implied authority to accept performance of the obligation in behalf of the partnership. In addition, a partner has implied authority to take legal action for the partnership if the other party defaults on the obligation.

In the first case below, the court applies basic agency concepts contained in the UPA to the plaintiff's claim against a partnership on a real estate sale contract signed by a single partner. In the second case, a partner's improper motive transformed several authorized transactions into a breach of his fiduciary duties.

Owens v. Palos Verdes Monaco
Court of Appeal of California, 191 Cal. Rptr. 381 (1983)

Seymour Owens, Albert Fink, and Manny Borinstein were in the business of acquiring, holding, and developing real estate on the Palos Verdes peninsula in California. They bought 250 acres, divided it into four tracts, and formed four separate partnerships to own and develop the tracts. Borinstein died, and the surviving partners agreed that Borinstein's widow, Pearl, would become a partner, but would hold the interests in the four partnerships in trust for her daughter Joan. Several years later, Kajima International, Inc., became interested in buying one of these tracts of land. The tract in question, 57 acres, was held by a partnership called Monaco Land Holders (MLH).

A representative of Kajima contacted a real estate brokerage firm in the Palos Verdes area. The brokerage firm contacted Owens, one of the three partners in MLH and the other partnerships. Owens told the broker to show the 57-acre tract to the Kajima representative, to "pursue the sale," and "keep him [Owens] informed." After Kajima's representative had seen the land and conferred with his superiors, Kajima made a written offer to buy. This offer was delivered by the broker to both Owens and Fink. They rejected the offer and Owens told the broker that "Al Fink will be handling this from now on; just keep me apprised of what's going on." A second offer was made and was again delivered to both Owens and Fink. Fink met with Owens and they decided to reject this offer, as well. At this time, and later, Pearl Borinstein was kept informed about the negotiations and indicated that she would go along with any proposal that met with Owens' approval.

Over the next several months, the broker tried to put together a deal that would be agreeable to both sides. Three different meetings were held to negotiate the sale. Present at all three meetings were the broker and several representatives of Kajima, including a vice-president and another high-ranking officer. At the first two meetings, MLH was represented by Fink and Joan Borinstein (Pearl's daughter). Owens was informed about each of the meetings in advance, but each time he indicated that if Fink was going to be present, there was no need for him (Owens) to be there. At the third meeting, when the sale was finally concluded and the written contract was signed, only Fink was present in behalf of MLH, although Owens, Pearl, and Joan had all been notified of the meeting. Thus, Fink was the only partner signing the contract for the partnership. At this meeting, a question was raised about the fact that only one partner was signing, and Fink assured the buyers that he had authority to act for the partnership.

About two weeks after this third meeting, Owens indicated that he was unhappy with the terms of the sale contract and did not want the sale to go forward. The buyer insisted on completing the sale, and Owens filed suit against both the partnership and Kajima. In the suit, Owens sought a declaratory judgment that the contract was invalid and an injunction prohibiting the partnership from transferring title to the 57-acre tract to Kajima. Kajima filed a counterclaim against the partnership, Owens, and the other partners, seeking a decree of specific performance that would require the contract to be carried out by transferring title to Kajima. (Because initially there was some confusion as to whether the 57-acre tract was owned by MLH or by one of the other partnerships, Palos Verdes Monaco, both partnerships were named as parties to the lawsuit. Consequently, the name of Palos Verdes Monaco appears in the title of the case. After the suit was filed, it was determined that MLH owned this particular tract.) The trial court ruled that the contract was valid because Fink had authority to sign in behalf of the partnership, denied Owens' request for an

injunction, and granted Kajima's request for specific performance of the contract. Owens, the partnership, and the other partners appealed.

Feinerman, Presiding Justice:

The seminal issue in this appeal is whether Fink's signature alone was sufficient to bind MLH to the terms of the April 1 agreement. The resolution of that question depends upon the conclusion we reach regarding Fink's authority to act for the partnership. . . .

In our view of the matter, the provisions of [the Uniform Partnership Act, §9] are dispositive of the issue of Fink's authority to bind the partnership. . . .

Section 9 provides in pertinent part as follows:

(1) Every partner is an agent of the partnership for the purpose of its business, and the act of every partner, including the execution in the partnership name of any instrument, for apparently carrying on in the usual way the business of the partnership of which he is a member binds the partnership, *unless the partner so acting has in fact no authority to act for the partnership in the particular matter, and the person with whom he is dealing has knowledge of the fact that he has no such authority.* [Emphasis added by the court.]

(2) An act of a partner which is not apparently for carrying on the business of the partnership in the usual way does not bind the partnership unless authorized by the other partners. . . .

The Supreme Court in analyzing section 9 in *Ellis v. Mihelis* (1963) 384 P.2d 7, stated: "These provisions distinguish between acts of a partner which bind the partnership because of his status as a partner without any express authority being required and acts binding on the partnership only after express authorization by all partners. Under the express terms of subdivision (1) of the section all acts of a partner which are apparently within the usual course of the particular business bind the partnership. The effect of the provision is that the status of a partner, without more, serves as a complete authority with respect to such acts, obviating the necessity of any express authority, either oral or written, from the other members of the firm. It necessarily follows that insofar as a partner limits his conduct to matters apparently within the partnership business, he can bind the other partners without obtaining their written consent. Subdivision (2), however, provides that there must be express authority for acts of a partner which do not appear to be in the usual course of the business. . . ."

In the case before us, Fink's signature alone was sufficient to bind the partnership if the sale of the subject property was an act "for apparently carrying on in the usual way the business of the partnership." The apparent scope of the partnership business depends primarily on the conduct of the partnership and its partners and what they cause third persons to believe about the authority of the partners. . . .

The trial court found that "[t]he sale of the land to Kajima was apparently in the ordinary course of the selling partnership's business. . . . Fink was the only partner who ever attended meetings with representatives of Kajima regarding this transaction up to and including April 1, 1977. Fink conducted the negotiations on behalf of the sellers. In the context of the negotiations for the sale of the land, Fink's role as sale negotiator for the sellers, and Owens' statements [to the broker] that Fink would handle the deal on behalf of the sellers, statements which were reported to Kajima, [reasonably led] Kajima to believe that Fink had authority to sell the land."

The conduct of the partnership and its partners in this case was sufficient to sustain the findings that the partnership was in the business of selling property and that Fink, a partner, was authorized to act for the partnership.

[The partners also] argue that sale of the subject property cannot be considered to be within the apparent scope of the partnership business because sale of said property would make it impossible to carry on the partnership business. Section 9, subdivision (3) specifies certain acts which are not within the scope of the usual course of business. It provides: "Unless authorized by the other partners or unless they have abandoned the business, one or more but less than all the partners have no authority to: . . . (c) Do any other act which would make it impossible to carry on the ordinary business of a partnership." . . .

A number of reported decisions, including *Petrikis v. Hanges* (1952) 245 P.2d 39, hold that the sale of a partnership's only asset is beyond the scope of usual partnership business and thus cannot be effected by a single partner. In *Petrikis*, the seller of real property, Mr. Petrikis, sold the partnership's only asset, a cocktail lounge, without written authority from his partners. The Court of Appeal held that Petrikis had not bound the partnership because he had acted beyond the scope of usual business in selling the partnership's only asset. *Petrikis* is distinguishable from the present case in that. . . . Petrikis' partnership was in the business of running a bar, not the business of holding a bar in anticipation of its eventual sale. In the present case, MLH had a singular purpose. It existed solely to hold and sell a piece of real property. The business of MLH was selling its land. Thus, the sale was in the ordinary course of MLH's business. . . .

[The judgment of the trial court that the contract was valid and ordering its enforcement is affirmed.]

Oswald v. Leckey
Supreme Court of Oregon, 572 P.2d 1316 (1977)

Early in 1966 Oswald and Leckey, certified public accountants, executed a partnership agreement to conduct an accounting practice. After forming the partnership each partner continued to bill the clients that he personally served. The relationship between Oswald and Leckey was not harmonious and the partnership was dissolved in June 1968. Oswald, plaintiff, filed suit for an accounting to determine each partner's share of a partnership bank account. In the lawsuit,

Oswald claimed that Leckey, defendant, had improperly "written down" several accounts while they were partners. An account is "written down" when the amount actually billed is less than the amount due as shown on the books. The trial court ruled that defendant had not acted properly in writing down the accounts and that he was responsible to the partnership for the amount of the write-downs. Defendant appealed.

Bryson, Justice:

. . . The first item in contention is defendant's "write-down" of several accounts he serviced. Defendant collected $4,610.85 less on these accounts than the books showed was due. The partnership agreement does not specify the responsibility of partners in collecting partnership debts. Thus, this issue must be decided by the general principles of partnership law.

Partners have authority to make compromises with partnership debtors, even after dissolution. This power to compromise claims is stated briefly as follows: "A partner may receive payment of obligations due to the partnership, may compromise with firm debtors, and release them. . . ." Crane & Bromberg, Law of Partnership 456, §80 (1968).

So defendant had the power to compromise claims, but in exercising this power he had to follow the fiduciary duty imposed on him as a partner, "to act with the utmost candor and good faith." Although defendant testified that his "write-downs" were consistent with his past practices and with good practice, he also testified:

> *Q. And in your opinion, knowing these clients, what would have happened if you had billed it out at the amounts that you had written off?*
>
> *A. Well, these are clients that were under my responsibility and that came with me when I left the partnership. And I would have been out a substantial number of clients and future work, future income.*

In other words, in adjusting downwards the amounts due for work in progress, defendant was partly motivated by a desire to retain certain clients. This falls far short of the duty of good faith imposed on partners. We conclude, as did the trial court, that defendant ought to pay the partnership the difference between the amount stated on the books and the amount actually collected by defendant on these accounts. . . .

Affirmed.

Examples of Authority Not Usually Implied

The following actions are those for which implied authority usually does not exist. Again, these are only examples, and other actions also might not be impliedly authorized, depending on the nature of the business and the surrounding circumstances. Furthermore, the activities below might be impliedly authorized if the circumstances are such that the activity is usual and customary in the particular business involved. Remember, too, that any of these acts may be *expressly* authorized by the other partners if they so desire.

Assumption of Debts: In most cases, a partner does *not* have implied authority to assume, in the name of the partnership, liability for the debt of another. Such authority *may* exist, however, if the nature of the business includes this type of transaction. For instance, it might be customary for a partnership that sells stocks, bonds, and other securities to guarantee the securities it sells. This is, in effect, an assumption of the obligation of the company that originally issued the securities, but a partner can nevertheless have implied authority to make such a guarantee where it is a normal part of the partnership's business.

Purchases of Corporate Stock: The courts have generally held that a partner does not have implied authority to purchase or agree to purchase, for the partnership, stock in a corporation. Of course, such authority may exist if this type of transaction is within the usual scope of the business (for example, if the partnership's business is the sale of corporate stocks).

Gratuitous Activities: Since partnerships are formed for the purpose of operating a profit-making enterprise, a partner usually does not have implied authority to involve the partnership in a charitable undertaking or to give away partnership property. Such authority ordinarily has to be expressly given by the other partners. Exceptions might exist where it is customary for a business to provide certain free goods or services to customers in an effort to generate goodwill and enhance future business. Thus it might be customary for a brokerage firm to furnish free market information to prospective customers.

Actions Expressly Disallowed by the UPA

In Sec. 9, the UPA specifically designates several types of actions that are completely unauthorized. In other words, a partner cannot bind the partnership by these acts regardless of the nature of the business or what is customary. Furthermore, even a *majority* of the partners do not have the power to bind the partnership by these acts; there must be express agreement by *all* the partners.[2]

Confession of Judgment: Action by all partners is required to confess judgment. A *confession of judgment* is the agreement of a debtor that allows the creditor to obtain a court judgment for a specified sum against the debtor without the necessity of legal proceedings. Agreement of all the partners is required because of the unusual and severe nature of a confession of judgment.[3]

Arbitration: Unanimous consent is also required to submit a claim by or against the partnership to *arbitration.* Although arbitration is now a common and accepted method of settling commercial disputes, this has not always been the case. Courts were not particularly receptive to the idea of arbitration at an earlier time, an antagonism reflected in the UPA when it was drafted in 1914.

Acts Restricting Partnership Business: The UPA also requires unanimous agreement by the partners to perform certain types of acts that restrict the operation of the partnership business. For example, consent of all partners is required before the partnership property can be placed in trust for the partnership's creditors. Such a transaction is commonly referred to as an *assignment for the benefit of creditors,* and it represents one way an insolvent business can settle with its creditors without formal bankruptcy proceedings.

---

[2] One exception exists. The consent of a partner who has abandoned the business need not be obtained.

[3] In some states a confession of judgment is not permitted at all. Also, a rule passed by the Federal Trade Commission in 1985 prohibits a creditor from including a confession of judgment clause in any *consumer credit transaction.*

Agreement of all partners is also necessary to dispose of the goodwill of the partnership. The courts have construed this provision as requiring unanimous consent to a covenant not to compete. For example, the partnership might sell part of its business and agree not to compete with the buyer. Such an agreement would bind the partnership only if it was made by all the partners.

The UPA also states that consent of all partners is required to "do any other act which would make it impossible to carry on the ordinary business" of the partnership. An example is an agreement to cancel the lease of the premises where the partnership conducts its business.

Satisfaction of Creditors' Claims

One of the cardinal characteristics of the partnership form of business is that the individual partners are *personally liable* for the obligations of the partnership. This liability is secondary. A creditor having a claim against a partnership must first look to *partnership property* for satisfaction of the claim. The creditor can reach the assets of individual partners only after partnership assets are exhausted. Moreover, the assets of an individual partner must first be used to satisfy claims of his or her personal creditors before partnership creditors can assert their claims.

Quite naturally, then, creditors of an individual partner must first look to the personal assets of that partner for satisfaction of their claims. In fact, such creditors *cannot* reach specific items of partnership property. If some debt remains after a partner's personal assets have been exhausted, the creditor's only recourse with regard to the partnership is to obtain a **charging order** against the partner's *interest in the partnership* (that is, the partner's right to share in the profits and surplus of the partnership). A charging order issued by a court will order that partner's share of the profits to be paid to his or her creditor until the debt is fully discharged. If the debt has not been completely paid when the partnership is dissolved, the charging order will require payment to the creditor of that partner's share in the surplus, if any remains when all partnership affairs are settled.

Special Rules Regarding Liability to Third Parties

The Incoming Partner: When a new partner is admitted into an existing partnership, he or she naturally becomes responsible along with the other partners for all partnership obligations that arise *after* the admittance. The new partner is also responsible for partnership obligations that arose *before* he or she became a partner, but this liability does not extend beyond his or her interest in the partnership. Partnership creditors whose claims against the partnership arose prior to admission of the new partner cannot reach his or her individual assets for satisfaction of the claims.

Partner by Estoppel: Even if a person is not a member of a particular partnership, under certain circumstances there may be personal liability to third parties as if the individual were a partner. If someone has represented himself or herself as a partner to a third party (or allowed such a representation to be made), that person is liable as a partner if the third party grants credit to the partnership because of the representation. This liability results because the individual is "estopped" (prohibited) from denying that he or she is a partner in a suit brought by the third party.

To illustrate: Regency Co., a partnership, wished to obtain credit. Fearful of being unable to do so, the partners in Regency Co., X and Y, appealed to Jones, a businessman whose name and financial capabilities were well known in the business community. Out of friendship, Jones agreed that X and Y could tell prospective creditors that he was a member of the partnership in order to obtain credit. Subsequently, X and Y represented to the First National Bank that Jones was a partner. Relying on the representation, the bank granted the loan to the partnership. Even though Jones is not actually a partner, he is liable to the bank as if he were one. However, he is not treated as a partner for any other purpose. No partnership relations have been created between Jones and X and Y, and he is not liable as a partner to third parties who have not relied on the representation.

Assignment of a Partner's Interest

As previously discussed, a partner's right to possess and control partnership property cannot be assigned to a third party. However, a partner's interest in the partnership *can* be assigned to a third party without the consent of the other partners.

The assignee of a partner's interest is merely entitled to receive the profits to which the assigning partner would otherwise be entitled. If the partnership is subsequently dissolved, the assignee is entitled to receive whatever share of the surplus the assigning partner would have been entitled to receive. But the assignee acquires *nothing else.* He or she does not become a partner unless all the partners consent to the admission. Therefore, the assignee acquires no management powers, does not become an agent of the partnership, and, while the partnership exists, is not entitled to inspect the partnership books or to receive a formal account of partnership transactions.

Before enactment of the UPA, the assignment by a partner to a third party of his or her interest in the partnership was generally deemed to automatically *dissolve* the partnership, unless the partnership agreement provided otherwise. Under the UPA, this is not the case. The UPA recognizes that a partner may wish to assign the interest with absolutely no intention of bringing an end to the partnership. For example, a partner may wish to assign this interest to an individual creditor as security for a loan. On the other hand, in some circumstances a partner's assignment can be considered evidence of an intent to dissolve the partnership. For example, if, after the assignment, the assigning partner neglects partnership affairs and acts as if there is no longer any business relationship with the other partners, a court will be justified in holding the partnership to be dissolved. But the mere act of assignment, with nothing more, does not bring about dissolution. (The subject of dissolution will be treated more fully in the next chapter.)

SUMMARY

One of the basic rights of a partner is to participate in the management of the business. It is possible, however, for partners to alter their management rights by agreement. If there is no agreement otherwise, most management decisions in a partnership are made by majority vote of the partners. A few unusual matters require consent of all the partners unless they had previously agreed to let such decisions be made by less-than-unanimous vote.

Unless the articles of partnership provide otherwise, an individual partner's right in partnership property is limited to the equal right (with other partners) to possess such property for partnership purposes. This right is not transferable. When the agreement does not provide otherwise, all partners share equally in profits and losses, regardless of the relative amounts of capital they contributed. A partner normally is not entitled to compensation other than a share of profits, unless the partnership agreement states otherwise.

Partners owe fiduciary duties to each other and must act with reasonable care and with the utmost good faith. Each partner has a right to have complete access to partnership records. Under certain circumstances, a partner has the right to an account, which is a court-supervised audit of all partnership records.

The partnership's relations with third parties are governed by the basic rules of the law of agency. Each partner is an agent of the partnership for the purposes of its business, and the partnership is bound by a partner's actions when they have the apparent purpose of operating the partnership's business in the usual manner.

KEY TERMS

Interest in the partnership
Account (or accounting)
Trading partnership
Nontrading partnership
Charging order

QUESTIONS AND PROBLEMS

1. X, Y, and Z were partners in Snappy Delivery Service Co. The partnership owned three delivery trucks. X borrowed one of the trucks to haul some of his personal belongings and never returned it to the business. Y and Z demanded the return of the truck, but X refused. X said that he owned a third of the partnership; and since the partnership owned three trucks, one of them naturally belonged to him personally. Is X correct? Explain.

2. Anderson, Richards, and Williams formed a partnership for the purpose of producing rock music concerts. The three partners initially contributed $2,000, $4,000, and $3,000, respectively, to the partnership for use as working capital. The partnership agreement made no provision for the division of profits. At the end of the first year, the partnership had made a profit of $4,500. What is each partner's share of the profits? Explain.

3. Suppose that in Question 2 the partnership agreement had provided that profits were to be divided equally but had made no provision for the division of losses. If the partnership loses $3,000 the first year, what proportion of this loss must each partner bear? Explain.

4. Wilkes, Watkins, and Weston formed a partnership for the express purpose, as provided in the partnership agreement, of engaging in the retail shoe business. Even though the business was relatively successful, Wilkes and Watkins wanted to change the nature of their business from a shoe store to a men's clothing store. Weston objected. Can Wilkes and Watkins take such action over Weston's objection? Discuss.

5. In Question 4, suppose that Wilkes and Watkins had merely wanted to expand their business to include athletic shoes as well as dress and casual shoes. Could they do so over Weston's objection? Discuss.

6. What is the distinction between a trading and a nontrading partnership? What is the significance of this distinction?

7. A, B, C, and D owned a used car business as partners. D sold a car to Johnson, guaranteeing in writing that any defects in the car would be repaired free of charge during the 90-day period following the sale. Johnson brought the car back a month later, claiming that the transmission was not operating properly. A, B, and C stated that the warranty was no good because D had not been given express authority to make warranties. Must the partnership honor the warranty made by D? Discuss.

8. Suppose that in Question 7 the partnership agreement had expressly provided that a partner does not have authority to make warranties in connection with the sale of cars. Would this fact make any difference? Would Johnson's knowledge of the provision be of any importance? Explain.

9. Jurgenson and Taylor were partners in an automobile repair business. Driver brought his car to Jurgenson and Taylor's garage to have the brakes repaired. Jurgenson repaired the brakes. Two days later Driver had a collision caused by failure of the brakes. The brake failure was due to Jurgenson's negligence in doing the repair work, so Driver sued the partnership. Is the partnership liable? Explain.

10. Suppose that in Question 9 Driver's suit against the partnership was successful. The assets of the partnership, however, were not sufficient to satisfy the judgment awarded to Driver by the court. Driver then sought to hold the individual partners personally liable for the unpaid portion of the judgment. Could he hold them personally responsible? Explain. Suppose that Jurgenson and Taylor had admitted Leonard as a new partner in the business. If Driver also tries to hold Leonard personally liable, what will be the importance of the time of Leonard's admission as a new partner? Discuss.

Chapter 34

PARTNERSHIPS
Termination

Complete termination of the partnership as a business organization is composed of two elements: *dissolution* and *winding up.* Dissolution does not of itself bring the partnership business to a close; it is, rather, the "beginning of the end." Essentially, the word **dissolution** designates that point in time when the object of the partners changes from continuing the organization in its present form to discontinuing it.[1] The partnership is not terminated at that time, but its object has become termination.

The second element of termination, commonly referred to as **winding up,** involves the actual process of settling partnership affairs after dissolution. After both dissolution and winding up have occurred, the partnership as an organization will have terminated.

DISSOLUTION

Causes of Dissolution

The events that cause dissolution can be divided into four categories: (1) act of one or more partners not in violation of their agreement, (2) act of one or more partners in violation of their agreement, (3) operation of law, and (4) court decree.

Act of One or More Partners Not in Violation of Their Agreement: As we have seen in the discussion of partnership formation and operation, the partnership is created by agreement. Thus, when the question becomes one of dissolution, the partnership agreement (articles of partnership) should be the first place to look for guidance.

The partnership agreement may provide, for example, that the partnership will exist for only a specified period of time. Upon expiration of this period, the partnership dissolves in accordance with the original agreement, unless all the partners agree to amend the articles of partnership and extend the prescribed duration.[2] The partnership agreement similarly could provide for automatic dissolution of the partnership upon the occurrence of some particular event. When this event takes place, the partnership dissolves unless the partners unanimously amend the agreement.

Where the partnership agreement makes no provision for a definite duration and places no other limitations on a partner's right to withdraw, a **partnership at will** exists. This means that any partner can withdraw at any time without violating the agreement and, therefore, without incurring contractual liability to the other partners. Such a withdrawal automatically dissolves the partnership unless the partnership agreement provides that withdrawal will not result in dissolution.

Similarly, as seen in Chapter 32 in *Gelder Medical Group v. Webber,* the partnership agreement may allow for exclusion of a partner by the other partners. Such a provision might permit exclusion of a partner only for specified reasons, or it might even permit exclusion without cause by vote of a specified number of the other partners. In any event, the partners relying on the exclusion clause are not in violation of the agreement if they act in accordance with its terms. Moreover, an exclusion clause in the partnership agreement usually is interpreted by a court as an agreement among the partners that

---

[1] Later in the chapter we will discuss the situation where certain of the partners wish to continue the *business,* even though the partnership as an organization is dissolved. It might be continued as a new partnership or in some other organizational form. In such a case, the termination of the partnership consists primarily of bookkeeping entries and purchase of the interests of noncontinuing partners.

[2] Continuance of the business by the partners after expiration of the agreed term constitutes an implied partnership agreement even in the absence of an express amendment of the articles of partnership. The partnership will then be one "at will," which means that the individual partners are legally free to withdraw at any time thereafter. So long as they actually continue, however, the partnership exists and the terms of the implied partnership agreement are those of the original agreement, insofar as they are applicable.

dissolution will not occur when a partner is excluded according to the clause.

Since a partnership is created by agreement, it can be dissolved by agreement. Regardless of the terms of the original partnership agreement, a partnership can be dissolved at any time without violating that agreement if all the partners consent to dissolution. A unanimous dissolution agreement overrides the original articles of partnership. A dissolution agreement that is not unanimous, however, constitutes a violation of the original partnership agreement by those causing dissolution unless their action is in accordance with a provision in the original agreement expressly permitting dissolution by a less-than-unanimous vote.[3]

The following case more fully explains the overriding nature of the partnership agreement in resolving questions relating to dissolution.

---

[3] However, if a partner has assigned his or her interest in the partnership to a third party, or if a partner's personal creditor has subjected the partner's interest in the partnership to a "charging order," the consent of that partner is not required for dissolution.

Osborne v. Workman
Supreme Court of Arkansas, 621 S.W.2d 478 (1981)

In 1966 Merrill Osborne, a physician, joined with five other physicians in a partnership to operate a medical clinic. Their written partnership agreement specified no definite term, but only that it would continue "until said partnership is dissolved mutually or by law." The agreement also provided that if a doctor withdrew from the partnership he was to be paid his percentage share of the clinic's asset value at the time of withdrawal, *excluding* accounts receivable. When the partnership was formed, the clinic's accounts receivable were $105,000 and were treated as a partnership asset. The accounts gradually increased, and by 1979 totaled $513,000. Estimates of actual collectability of these accounts in 1979 varied from $100,000 to $400,000. Between 1966 and 1979 a number of new physicians were admitted to the partnership, and a total of seven withdrew. In six of the seven withdrawals, the withdrawing physicians received nothing from accounts receivable; one had received a portion of the accounts by unanimous vote of the remaining partners in 1968.

In 1978 Osborne announced his intention to withdraw from the partnership, and by 1979 he had relocated to a private medical practice. The remaining partners offered to pay him his percentage share of the partnership's present asset value, excluding accounts receivable, but Osborne insisted on receiving a share of those accounts. When the remaining partners refused, he filed suit seeking dissolution of the partnership and a winding up that would include liquidation of its assets. The trial court held for the partnership and remaining partners, and Osborne, appellant, appealed to the Supreme Court of Arkansas.

Hays, Associate Justice:

Appellant contends that dissolution should have been ordered under [§31 of the UPA], entitled "Causes of Dissolution," which provides some nine instances of dissolution by operation of law, including the express will of any partner where no definite term is specified in the agreement. The agreement here did not provide for a specific term; hence it is urged that any partner could dissolve the partnership at will. But the argument fails in two respects: It ignores the precondition clearly stated in §31, that the section applies "without violation of the agreement between the parties;" and it fails to consider what was intended by the partnership agreement itself. Moreover, §29 defines dissolution:

The dissolution of a partnership is the change in the relation of the partners caused by any partner ceasing to be associated in the carrying on as distinguished from the winding up of the business; provided that this change in the relation of the partners shall not effect a dissolution of the partnership in contravention or violation of the agreement between the partners. *[Emphasis added by the court.]*

Self-limiting language appears throughout the UPA which renders it "subject to any agreement to the contrary." Even the section for the settling of accounts after dissolution and winding up, which provides the method of distribution among the partners, is "subject to any agreement to the contrary." The clear intent of the UPA [is] to defer to any existing partnership agreement. . . .

Turning to the agreement itself, we note that in construing the agreement we are governed by what the parties intended. Appellant contends that the wording "until said partnership is dissolved mutually or by law" triggers that provision in UPA Section 31 giving any partner the right to dissolve at will. Certainly any partner can withdraw at will and to the extent that withdrawal is a dissolution he is correct. But appellant seeks . . . the termination of the partnership by liquidation, and we cannot agree these partners intended such a result. We think the clear intent was that [actual] termination would occur only by mutual agreement and not by the unilateral act of a single partner. Appellant's contention cannot be reconciled with the words "mutually dissolved," [because according to his argument] the dissolution could be achieved by a single partner—the reverse of mutual. It is undisputed that seven doctors withdrew over the years and [with only one unanimously voted exception] the partnership retained all of the accounts receivable and in determining what the parties intended, reference is made to what they did. It is inconceivable that six doctors would form a partnership, enter into an elaborate agreement intended to promote longevity, set up a common practice, pool their equipment, records and resources, [but to have] intended that any one of them could end it at any time by demanding dissolution and liquidation. . . .

Persons with professional qualifications commonly associate in business partnerships. The practice of continuing the operation of the partnership business, even though there are some changes in partnership personnel, is also common. The reasons for an agreement that a medical partnership should continue without disruption of the services rendered are self-evident. If the partnership agreement provides for continuation, sets forth a method of paying the withdrawing partner his agreed share, and does not jeopardize the rights of creditors, the agreement is enforceable. . . .

In conclusion, where competent parties knowingly enter into an agreement suited to their purposes, keep that agreement in effect over many years to their mutual benefit, it is not for the courts to nullify such agreement. . . .

The decree is affirmed. [Dr. Osborne is bound by the express terms of the partnership agreement, cannot force liquidation, and is not entitled to a share of the accounts receivable.]

Act of One or More Partners in Violation of Their Agreement: Regardless of the terms of the partnership agreement, one or more partners can withdraw from the partnership at any time. Although the power to withdraw from a partnership always exists, any partner whose withdrawal violates the partnership agreement is liable to the nonwithdrawing partners for damages caused by the withdrawal. Such withdrawal causes a dissolution of the partnership unless the partnership agreement provided that dissolution would not result in these circumstances. Although withdrawal can cause dissolution without any formal court action, one or more of the withdrawing or nonwithdrawing partners often will seek a court decree of dissolution if there is any disagreement about whether the withdrawal actually violated the partnership agreement or about the amount of damages.

By Operation of Law: The partnership automatically dissolves if an event occurs that makes it illegal to carry on the business. The *business itself* may become illegal, as where a partnership for the purpose of selling liquor loses its liquor license. Or it may become illegal for *these particular partners* to carry on the business together, as where an individual partner in a medical practice has his or her license revoked.

Unless otherwise agreed, dissolution also occurs automatically on the *death* of a partner or on the *bankruptcy* of either a partner or the partnership itself. The articles of partnership may, of course, provide that the death or bankruptcy of an individual partner will not cause a dissolution.

By Court Decree: Section 32 of the UPA specifically enumerates several situations in which dissolution of a partnership can be accomplished by seeking and obtaining a formal court decree. They can be divided into two broad categories: (1) situations in which a *partner* can obtain a decree of dissolution and (2) situations in which a *third party* can obtain such a decree.

Decree Obtained by a Partner: When a partner has become *insane,* either that person or another partner can obtain a court decree dissolving the partnership. In such a case dissolution does not occur automatically (as it does in the case of death or bankruptcy). A formal court decree is required in the instance of insanity because a person's mental competency is inherently subject to doubt and dispute, whereas death and bankruptcy are more certain events. The decree can be sought (1) when a partner has already been declared insane by a court in a sanity hearing or (2) when such a formal adjudication has not yet occurred. In the latter case, the court asked to dissolve the partnership will itself determine whether the partner is insane. The court will not dissolve the partnership in either case, however, unless it appears probable that the insanity will continue for a substantial part of the partnership's duration.

Dissolution also can be obtained by court decree if a partner becomes in any other way *incapable of performing his or her part of the partnership agreement.* This provision is usually applied to disabilities other than insanity (such as prolonged illness, a paralytic stroke, or a serious accident) when it appears that the disability will continue for a substantial period of time and will materially obstruct or negatively affect the objectives of the partnership. The court decree in this case can be sought by either the partner suffering the disability or any other partner.

A partner can obtain a decree of dissolution when one of the other partners has been guilty of *serious misconduct.* Breach of the partnership agreement is, of course, one example of such misconduct. Even if the partnership agreement has not been breached, under the UPA a decree of dissolution can be obtained if another partner has been "guilty of such conduct as tends to affect prejudicially the carrying on of the business" or if the other partner "so conducts himself in matters relating to the partnership business that it is not reasonably practicable to carry on the business in partnership with him." Examples of such conduct are fraud in dealing with partnership property or funds, substantial overdraft of a drawing account by a partner who has been temporarily left in charge of the business, and serious neglect of partnership affairs.

Where misconduct has occurred, the guilty partner cannot obtain dissolution by court decree; this right belongs solely to one or more of the other partners. Furthermore, if the other partner or partners so desire, they can simply withdraw and cause dissolution. A court decree is not essential, and the guilty partner cannot sue them for damages even if their withdrawal is contrary to the partnership agreement. Although formal court action is not essential in cases of misconduct, it is often desirable where any doubt exists as to whether the misconduct is serious enough to warrant dissolution or where disagreement exists regarding damages or the value of partners' interests.

Finally, any partner can obtain a decree of dissolution when it becomes evident that the business is *unprofitable* and will probably not be profitable in the future.

Decree Obtained by a Third Party: Two types of third parties are considered to have a sufficient interest in partnership affairs to obtain a decree of dissolution in certain circumstances: (1) an *assignee* of a partner's interest in the partnership and (2) a partner's *personal creditor* who has subjected that partner's interest to a charging order. Either of these third parties, however, can obtain a decree of dissolution in only two situations: (1) after expiration of the period of time or accomplishment of the purpose specified in the articles of partnership, in cases where the articles include such a provision, or (2) at any time, if the partnership is a partnership "at will" when the third party acquires his or her interest.

In the next case, a partner sought dissolution by court decree on the basis of a claim that one of the other partners had breached the partnership agreement. The question also arose whether the partner who violated the agreement forfeited all of his rights as a partner, or whether he was just liable for whatever monetary damage his breach caused to the other partners.

Staszak v. Romanik
U.S. Court of Appeals for the Sixth Circuit, 690 F.2d 578 (1982)

Joseph Staszak and his cousin, Walter Romanik, formed a partnership in 1959 under the name North Star Tree Company for the purpose of growing and selling Christmas trees. Walter lived in Michigan, and Joseph in Maryland; both owned land in Michigan where the trees were to be grown. They made an oral agreement that Walter's 20 acres and Joseph's 80 acres both would be used in the business: Walter would supply labor and manage the operation, Joseph would supply the working capital, and profits and losses would be shared equally. In 1968 Walter and Joseph agreed that Walter should begin receiving a salary for his management services. Between 1959 and 1969 the partnership purchased and leased substantial additional land, so that by 1969 trees were being grown on 1,573 acres. Also by 1969, 94 full-time and part-time employees worked for the partnership.

In early 1969 Walter and Joseph purchased another Christmas tree business in Michigan, Sno Kist Tree Corporation, using as a down payment $134,000 that Joseph had personally borrowed and contributed to the partnership. The purchase included the Sno Kist trademark, a long-term lease on Sno Kist's land and equipment, and assignments of leases held by Sno Kist on several other tracts of land used for growing and harvesting trees. All of these leases included tree harvesting rights. Walter and Joseph agreed at the same time to admit Joseph's son Richard Staszak as an equal partner in the larger enterprise. Essentially, a new partnership was formed at this time, and the purchase of Sno Kist Tree Company was made in the names of all three partners. Thereafter, North Star and Sno Kist were operated as a single business, and in 1970 the three partners executed a written partnership agreement that formally adopted the Sno Kist name for the entire operation, and provided that the capital contributions of the partners were to be their interests in partnership real estate and other assets. The written agreement also stated that profits were to be shared equally, but that these profits were to be distributed in such a way as to eventually equalize the partners' capital contributions.

During the first year's harvest after formation of the three-way partnership, Richard Staszak went from Maryland to Michigan and stayed throughout the harvest season, overseeing the work on a portion of the operation. Richard spent part of each succeeding year, during the harvesting season, in Michigan. Beginning in 1972, Walter began complaining that Richard was not doing what was required by their agreement, because they had an unwritten understanding that Richard was to move to Michigan and work full time in the business. By 1975 relations between Walter and the Staszaks had completely

deteriorated, and Joseph and Richard tried to buy out Walter's interest in the partnership. Walter refused to sell and filed suit claiming
that the partnership should be dissolved because of Richard's breach
of the partnership agreement. The trial court concluded that, even
though the partnership agreement did not so state, there was an
implied agreement that Richard Staszak would move to Michigan and
work full time in the business, and that Richard had breached this
agreement. Because the agreement had required Richard initially to
contribute only services, and no capital, to the partnership, the trial
court found that there was a complete failure of consideration on
Richard's part. Consequently, the trial court held that Richard had
never become a partner and had to return to the partnership over
$80,000 in profit distributions he had received since 1969. Joseph and
Richard appealed.

Lively, Circuit Judge:

The [trial court] found that Richard Staszak was a partner at the inception of
the Sno Kist partnership. This finding was correct. . . .

Since the UPA is intended to be comprehensive, whenever its provisions
cover a situation involving a partnership those provisions should be applied.
Only when presented with a case not provided for in the Act should a court
be governed by general rules of law and equity. The Act provides [that] when
dissolution is caused by the wrongful act of a partner, that partner is entitled
to his share of partnership [surplus] subject to the right of partners who have
not breached the agreement to recover from him any damages caused by his
breach.

Instead of applying the foregoing provisions of the UPA the trial court
determined that Richard Staszak should, in effect, be removed retroactively as
a partner, should be denied all equity in partnership assets and should be
required to refund to the partnership all profits previously distributed to
him. . . .

It is clear that at least part of the consideration for formation of the Sno Kist
partnership was the agreement of each partner to contribute his interest in
real and personal property transferred to the partnership as capital and to
permit distributions of profit in such a manner as to equalize the capital
contribution of each. . . .

The partnership agreement described the capital of the partnership as the
real estate described in Schedule A and the personal property described in
Schedule B. . . . Both schedules were attached. . . . The [next] paragraph of
the agreement provided that the contribution of each partner consisted of his
interest in the property described in Schedules A and B and any other property or money "conveyed" to the partnership. Richard Staszak had a one-third
interest in the assets purchased from the . . . Sno Kist Tree Corporation which
became the property of the Sno Kist partnership. Yet the trial court found that
Richard's only contribution was to consist of personal services to the partnership. Further, Richard Staszak's share of the profits of the partnership between

1970 and 1977 was substantially in excess of the approximately $80,000 which he withdrew. Paragraph XIV of the agreement provided that the undistributed profits of the partners were to be applied to equalize their capital contributions. The finding that Richard Staszak made no contribution to the capital of the partnership was clearly erroneous. Thus, even though Richard Staszak failed to perform services as promised, there was not a total failure of consideration.

Richard Staszak has not appealed from the finding that there was an implied agreement that he would move to Michigan and work full time for the partnership or from the conclusion that his breach of this agreement was sufficient to require dissolution of the partnership. He contends, however, that the proper remedy for this breach is that provided in [the Uniform Partnership Act]. We agree. . . .

In this case the trial court found that a partnership was formed. It is clear that Richard Staszak made some contribution to capital—his share of the assets purchased by the three partners in equal shares from the . . . Sno Kist Tree Corporation. The partners were equally liable for payment of the balance of the purchase price above the down payment of $100,000. Richard Staszak made further contributions of capital by withdrawing less than his total share of partnership profits. Finally, he performed services for the corporation each year until 1976. His breach of partnership duties consisted only of his failure to move to Michigan and work full time for the partnership. The other partners are entitled to recover any damages which this breach caused the partnership. But forfeiture of Richard's interest was not a permitted sanction for the breach.

The judgment of the district court is reversed insofar as it holds that Richard Staszak was not entitled to a partner's share in the assets of the partnership and insofar as it directs Richard Staszak to repay to the partnership the amounts which he has previously withdrawn as distributions of partnership profits. Upon remand the district court will determine the amount of damages, if any, sustained by the partnership as the result of Richard Staszak's breach and award such damages equally to the other partners.

Effect of Dissolution on Partners' Authority

Despite the fact that dissolution does not sound the instantaneous death knell of the partnership, it is frequently important to ascertain the precise moment when it occurs. The reason is simple. When dissolution takes place, certain significant changes occur in the nature of the partners' relationships with one another and with outsiders. Of paramount significance is the effect dissolution has on the *authority of partners to bind the partnership*. In most cases, of course, a partner acting without authority must personally shoulder the burden of any liability resulting from such action.

Upon dissolution, the authority of individual partners to act in behalf of the partnership usually ceases, *except for acts necessary to complete unfinished transactions or those appropriate for winding up partnership affairs.* For example, suppose that a partnership, before dissolution, had made a contract to sell goods. After dissolution, a partner would have authority to arrange for shipping those goods in accordance with the existing contract. However, he or she would not have authority to make new contracts without the consent of the other partners, unless these contracts were in furtherance of liquidating the business. Thus the partner probably would be authorized to make contracts for the sale of existing inventory. Similarly, he or she usually would be able to do such things as hire an accountant to take inventory and perform an audit, pay partnership debts and receive payment of obligations owing to the partnership, and make reasonable compromise agreements with debtors and creditors. Obviously a partner's authority to borrow money would be severely restricted after dissolution. Borrowing in order to pay existing obligations would probably be authorized in many situations, but borrowing for any other reason probably would not.

If, instead of liquidating the business, some of the partners intend to continue it as a new partnership or other type of organization, these limitations on authority may cause short-term difficulties. During the changeover period, certain transactions not within the scope of this limited authority may be necessary to keep the business going. In such a case, the consent of *all* partners must be obtained to authorize this kind of transaction.

In the absence of a contrary agreement among the partners, the type of authority still existing after dissolution can be exercised by *any* of the partners. If they choose, however, they can agree that such authority rests only with a certain partner. The person delegated this type of responsibility is sometimes referred to as the **liquidating partner** (or **winding-up partner**). Then, if third parties are so notified, they can hold the partnership liable only if they deal with the designated partner.

Special Situations: Regarding the effect of dissolution, three exceptional situations must be mentioned.

Partner's Knowledge: Under some circumstances it is important to determine whether the partner transacting business for the partnership after dissolution has *knowledge* of certain facts. If dissolution is caused either by the *act* of any partner (whether in violation of the partnership agreement or not), the *death* of any partner, or the *bankruptcy* of any partner, the partnership will be bound by any transaction made by a partner who *did not know* the facts that caused dissolution.[4] This liability exists even if the transaction was not merely a completion of unfinished business and was not otherwise appropriate for winding up partnership affairs. (Of course, the transaction must be of a type that would have been binding upon the partnership if dissolution had *not* occurred.)

Notice to Third Parties: In some situations the *absence of notice to third parties* may result in partnership liability for unauthorized transactions entered into after dissolution. If the transaction is of a type that would have bound the partnership if dissolution had *not* taken place, the firm will be liable for it *after* dissolution if the third party being dealt with has not been properly notified of the dissolution. If, before dissolution, the third party has extended credit to the partnership, a transaction with this person after dissolution will bind the partnership unless he or she is proven to have had knowledge of the dissolution. The best way to prevent such a possibility is to directly notify all the partnership's creditors that dissolution has occurred. Since their names and addresses will almost certainly be in the partnership records, no undue inconvenience will result. If the third party had not extended credit to the partnership in the past but did know of its existence prior to dissolution, *the partnership is not liable for transactions with that party* made after dissolution if he

---

[4]Section 3 of the UPA makes a distinction between *knowledge* and *notice.* This distinction makes no difference in the majority of cases and its technicality is of too refined a nature for our discussion.

or she either knows of the dissolution or if the fact of dissolution has been advertised in a newspaper of general circulation in those places where the partnership has regularly done business.[5] These rules regarding notice to third parties are simply an application of the principle of *apparent authority.*

The Bankrupt Partner: Under the UPA, the partnership is not bound in any circumstances where the postdissolution transaction is made by a partner who is personally *bankrupt.* In such a case it does not matter whether the third party knows of the partner's bankruptcy or of the resulting dissolution; the UPA's view is that one should know the status of the person with whom one is dealing.

Effect of Dissolution on Existing Liabilities

A cardinal rule of partnership law is that dissolution in and of itself does not alter the existing liabilities of the partnership or of individual partners. In some circumstances the event causing dissolution may also cause a discharge from certain liabilities, but it is not the dissolution itself that causes the discharge. Contracts in force at the time of the event that causes dissolution may or may not be discharged, depending upon the rules of contract law. For instance, the death of a partner might terminate an existing partnership contract if the contract had called for some type of personal service by the deceased partner. And bankruptcy of the partnership will not only result in dissolution but also will discharge partnership liabilities that are in excess of the combined assets of the partnership and all the partners. Whether existing liabilities in other situations will be discharged depends entirely on the circumstances.

WINDING UP PARTNERSHIP AFFAIRS

Winding up is the second and final step after dissolution in the termination of a partnership.

The Right to Wind Up

The question of which partners have the right to wind up partnership affairs can be determined by agreement of the partners.[6] In the absence of an agreement, all partners have an equal right to settle partnership affairs, with two notable exceptions. A partner who has *wrongfully caused dissolution* and a partner who is *personally bankrupt* do not have the right to exercise any control over the winding up process.

Distribution of Assets

When dissolution has occurred and the business is to be terminated, the winding up process entails such activities as liquidating partnership property (turning it into cash), collecting outstanding accounts, paying outstanding debts, and any other actions required to bring partnership affairs to a close.

After all partnership assets have been liquidated, they are distributed to those having claims against the partnership. The order in which they are distributed is of little importance if the partnership has been profitable and all claims can be paid in full. Where partnership assets are insufficient to completely satisfy all claims, however, the issue obviously becomes quite significant.

As previously noted, when partnership assets are insufficient to pay partnership debts, assets of individual partners can be used insofar as necessary. Before this can happen, however, any claims of that partner's individual creditors must be satisfied.

---

[5] Before enactment of the UPA, some courts had recognized other methods of publicizing the dissolution, but the UPA speaks only of advertisement by newspaper.

[6] If the partners disagree as to who shall wind up, a court may appoint a qualified disinterested third party as a *receiver* to handle the winding up process.

Claims against the partnership are paid in the following order:

1. First to be paid are claims of outside creditors of the partnership.

2. Next are claims of individual partners for repayment of loans they have made to the partnership. Interest is ordinarily payable unless it had been agreed that the loan would be interest-free.

3. Claims of individual partners for return of contributions they have made to the partnership's working capital are third in line. Interest is not payable on contributions to capital unless the partners had agreed otherwise.

4. If any partnership assets remain after satisfying the other claims, these are distributed as profits to the partners in the proportion in which profits were to be shared.

To illustrate: Jones and Smith are partners in the retail clothing business. The partnership has not been profitable and is dissolved. The financial position of the partnership after all assets have been reduced to cash is summarized as follows (assuming no interest payable on partners' loans or capital contributions):

Assets		Liabilities and Partner's Equity		
Cash	$200,000	*Liabilities*		
	$200,000	Accounts payable	$225,000	
		Loans from partners		
		Jones	25,000	
		Smith	10,000	$260,000
		Partners' equity		
		Jones (contribution to capital)	$50,000	
		Smith (contribution to capital)	50,000	100,000
				$360,000

As we can see, the operations of the partnership have resulted in an overall loss of $160,000. As-

suming that losses are to be divided equally, Jones and Smith will each have to personally bear an $80,000 loss. The following summary indicates the personal financial positions of Jones and Smith:

	Jones	Smith
Assets	$150,000	$200,000
Liabilities	−75,000	−250,000
	$75,000	($50,000)

Here we see that Smith is insolvent. Since his individual assets must first be used to pay his individual debts, he is financially unable to pay partnership obligations. As a result, Jones must use his personal assets to pay the remaining partnership debts to partnership creditors. This obligation amounts to $25,000, since partnership accounts payable were $225,000 and partnership assets were $200,000. The losses actually borne by each partner are summarized as follows:

	Jones	Smith
Loans to partnership (unrepaid)	$ 25,000	$10,000
Contributions to partnership capital (unreturned)	50,000	50,000
Use of individual's assets to pay partnership creditors	25,000	—
	$100,000	$60,000

Since each partner should have borne a loss of $80,000, Jones now has a claim against Smith for $20,000. Whether this claim will be collectible, as a practical matter, is a problem Jones must face.

Continuing the Business

The business of a partnership is not always terminated after dissolution, even though the partnership as an organization comes to an end. Where the operations of the partnership have been profitable and customer goodwill has been built up, the business will be more valuable as a going concern than it will if it is liquidated. Thus some of the partners may wish to continue the business—and they can do so unless continuation would be illegal for some reason. If they decide to continue, the winding up process will consist primarily of bookkeeping entries and the purchase by continuing partners of the interests of withdrawing partners. Customers may never know there has been any change, unless some change is made in the firm name. And creditors of the dissolved partnership will continue to be creditors of the reorganized partnership.[7]

According to Agreement: If the articles of partnership provide for continuing the business after dissolution, these provisions dictate the procedures to be followed. For instance, the articles of partnership might specify procedures for continuing the business after the withdrawal, expulsion, or death of a partner, including methods for valuing that partner's interest and settling accounts between the continuing and noncontinuing partners. It also is possible for the partners to make a binding agreement concerning the continuation of the business at the time of dissolution.

Without Agreement: When there is no agreement for continuing the business, either in the articles of partnership or in a separate agreement made at the time of dissolution, the procedures for continuation are guided by the UPA. In this regard, the UPA makes a distinction between two situations: (1) where dissolution has occurred *without* a wrongful act by any partner,

and (2) where it *has been caused* by such a wrongful act.

Where Dissolution Occurred without a Wrongful Act: The most common situations of no wrongful act are dissolution caused by death of a partner or by the withdrawal of a partner in a situation where he or she had the right to do so. In such a case, the continuing partners must immediately settle with the withdrawing partner or the estate of the deceased partner (the term *withdrawing partner* hereafter will also include the estate of a deceased partner) if the latter so desires. If settlement is made *immediately,* it consists only of a payment to the withdrawing partner of an amount equal to the value of that partner's interest in the partnership at the time of dissolution. This, of course, will be his or her share of any existing surplus of partnership asset value (including goodwill) over partnership liabilities. If settlement is *postponed,* the withdrawing partner receives not only the value of his or her interest in the partnership (computed as of the moment of dissolution) but also an additional amount to compensate for the delay. The additional amount is computed in one of two ways, depending on the choice of the withdrawing partner—either as *interest* on the amount due since dissolution or as an amount equal to that partner's proportionate share of partnership *profits* earned since dissolution.

Where Dissolution Was Caused by a Partner's Wrongful Act: In the second situation, where dissolution has been caused by a partner's wrongful act, somewhat different rules are applied. The wrongfully withdrawing partner is still entitled to receive the value of his or her interest in the partnership, but the value of partnership *goodwill* is not included in computing this value. Further, the damages caused by the wrongful dissolution are deducted from the total amount. If settlement is not made immediately, the rules for compensating the with-

---

[7] The situation may be different if the business is reorganized and continued in some form other than a partnership, such as a corporation. In such a case, all those who were partners in the dissolved partnership will be liable for debts incurred by the partnership before dissolution, unless the creditors release them. This is true for those persons continuing the business (who may now be officers, directors, and/or stockholders in the new corporation) and for those who have left it. The corporation itself is a separate legal entity not liable for these old debts unless it assumes them. This frequently occurs, however, because the new corporation ordinarily is controlled by at least some of the former partners, and it will often assume the old debts in return for a release by creditors of the former partners.

drawing partner for the delay are the same as in the first situation.

Notice to Third Parties: Notice of dissolution to third parties is as important when the business is continued as when it is terminated. Those continuing the business must take it upon themselves to provide proper notification (as explained earlier). If they do not, they may be bound by certain later acts of a former partner who has left the business. Also, if those continuing the business reorganize it as a *corporation* rather than as another partnership, they will need to notify their business creditors of the change in status. If this is not done, and new obligations to these creditors are incurred (the creditors still thinking they are dealing with a partnership), the former partners might find themselves personally liable for the new obligations as if they were still partners. If proper notice is given, of course, they will be able to claim the limited liability that is enjoyed by those who are officers, directors, or stockholders in a corporation.

As we observed earlier, it is always best to deal thoroughly with the question of dissolu-

tion, continuation of the business, valuation of partners' interests, and similar matters in the original partnership agreement. In the first case that follows, the partners had done so in a comprehensive fashion. Later, several of the partners pulled out of the partnership and tried to get around some of the terms of the partnership agreement relating to dissolution.

If the original partnership agreement does not deal with dissolution and its many implications, or if the partners wish to modify the original agreement's dissolution provisions, they can make a separate agreement at the time of dissolution. This can be a risky proposition, however, because at such a time the partners are less likely to be in an agreeable frame of mind than they were when the partnership was formed. But if an agreement can be reached at this later time, it can resolve the various issues arising from dissolution. The second case below illustrates an agreement made by the partners when one of them withdrew from the partnership. When the withdrawing partner later had second thoughts about the agreement, he found out that courts take such agreements quite seriously, as they do all contracts.

Curtin v. Glazier
Supreme Court of New York, Appellate
Division, 464 N.Y.S.2d 899 (1983)

In 1968 Louis Glazier and Joseph Jackler formed a partnership, Glazier, Jackler & Company, for the practice of accounting. In 1972 Robert Nelkin was admitted as a partner with a 10 percent interest in the partnership. At that time, Articles of Partnership (the basic partnership agreement) and a Partnership Continuation Agreement were executed by the three partners. Thereafter, these agreements were executed in basically the same form each time a new partner was admitted. Paragraph 15 of the Articles of Partnership provided for removal of a partner without cause by the affirmative vote of partners representing a majority interest. In the event of such removal, the Articles also provided for the purchase by remaining partners of the removed partner's interest in accordance with the terms of the Part-

nership Continuation Agreement. The Partnership Continuation Agreement contained "Buy-Sell" provisions specifying the remaining partners' right to buy the removed partner's interest at a price to be computed according to a stated formula. The formula attempted to value the partnership's total value as a going concern, with the removed partner receiving his or her pro rata share of that value. Under the agreed formula in the buy-sell provisions, this value was to be based on the net service receipts of the prior calendar year adjusted to account for future income from accounts receivable and work in progress, as well as for future expenses and accounts payable.

In the event of a dissolution of the partnership and actual termination of the business, the buy-sell provisions of the Continuation Agreement obviously would not apply. Instead, the dissolution provisions of the Articles would apply, which provided for payment to each partner of his or her share of the partnership's surplus. The going concern value of the partnership could not be taken into account in such a case, and a partner's share necessarily would be less than if the going concern value were included. Basically, these two methods of computing the values of partners' interests dealt with fundamentally different situations. However, the Articles also contemplated that the partners might remove one of the group and then attempt to circumvent the buy-sell provisions by dissolving the partnership and forming a new partnership to assume the business. In other words, the remaining partners might try to disguise a removal and continuation as a dissolution and liquidation, thus depriving the removed partner of his part of the going concern value computed under the buy-sell provisions. To prevent such a result, paragraph 10 of the Articles stated:

The parties hereto are further in accord in their desire that under no circumstances are the obligations of the remaining partners who continue the business of this partnership to be circumvented by said remaining partners upon legal dissolution of the partnership caused by the termination of any partner by the formation of a "different" partnership, which would nevertheless take over the business of the present partnership without satisfying its obligations.

The same idea was also expressed in paragraph 16, in which the partners had agreed that, in the case of a removal, if the remaining partners chose not to continue the partnership they should not attempt to accomplish a continuation in an indirect manner without giving the removed partner the benefit of the buy-sell provisions.

In May 1982 all of the partners except Thomas Curtin signed a written agreement to dissolve the partnership and distribute their shares of partnership surplus in accordance with the dissolution provisions of the original Articles of Partnership. The buy-sell provisions of the original Continuation Agreement were not used. These partners, minus Curtin, then split into two groups and formed two new

partnerships. One of the new partnerships continued to do business at the offices previously used by Glazier, Jackler & Co., and served the same clients. Curtin, plaintiff, filed suit against the other partners, defendants, claiming that there had actually been a continuation of the business, and the buy-sell provisions of the Continuation Agreement should be enforced. The trial court granted summary judgment in favor of Curtin, and the other partners appealed.

Denman, Judge:

Plaintiff contends that defendants' action in dissolving the partnership and forming two different partnerships from which he has been excluded is precisely the situation which the parties sought to avoid by incorporating paragraphs 10 and 16 in the articles. He argues that defendants "constructively removed" him from the partnership and that he is entitled to be compensated for the value of his interest based on the formula governing involuntary removal in the Buy-Sell Provisions. The applicability of that formula is of substantial financial consequence to plaintiff: the value of his interest under the Buy-Sell Provisions is $100,638.78 as opposed to only $26,057.65 under the dissolution agreement.

Defendants [argued] that there was a true dissolution of Glazier, Jackler & Company, CPAs, occasioned by unresolved differences of opinion between defendants Glazier and Jackler; that the partnership was in the process of complete liquidation; and that under the dissolution provision of the articles of partnership, plaintiff was entitled only to the value of his respective share of partnership assets. . . .

Defendants claim that [disputed] issues of fact exist with respect to whether there was a true dissolution of the partnership or whether there has been a continuation of the partnership by the remaining partners, albeit in a different form. [The trial court] treated the issue as one of contract interpretation and construed paragraphs 10 and 16 of the articles of partnership as precluding defendants from continuing to practice accounting under the arrangement described without purchasing plaintiff's interest for the amount determined under the Buy-Sell Provisions. We agree that the issue turns on interpretation of the partnership agreements and that it was properly determined as a matter of law.

It has long been settled that partnership rights and obligations may be fixed by agreement. Where, as here, there is a writing intended to be a complete expression of the parties' intention, the language of the agreement controls. It is not open to speculation and cannot be rewritten. Intention plainly expressed in clear, unambiguous terms raises no question of fact and summary judgment is appropriate. . . . Additionally, the facts upon which [the trial court] relied were undisputed. The dissolution agreement provided for defendants to purchase all of the outstanding accounts receivable and permitted them to purchase assets of the partnership including its computer, Xerox machine and word processor. Defendants did not controvert the fact that the "new" partnership formed by defendants Jackler, Nelkin, Liberman and Ewanyk would continue to maintain its office at the location previously occupied by Glazier, Jackler & Company. Although defendants dispute the fact that partnership debts have been canceled with respect to some of the defendants by offsetting their obligations against their interests in the new partnership, one is hard-pressed to find another explanation as to why defendants Gerber, Jackler, Liberman and Ewanyk, [whose shares of existing partnership debts were] $44,000, $56,000, $56,000 and $97,000, respectively, would agree to dissolution under which their respective distributive shares are estimated to be $21,520, $17,520, $17,520 and $7,720. In any event, the worksheet attached to plaintiff's affidavit . . . clearly provides for cancellation of partnership debts, which is an indirect method of offsetting those obligations against defendants' interests in the newly formed partnerships. Once plaintiff alleged the offsetting of these partnership debts, it was incumbent upon defendant to come forward with [evidence to rebut] that allegation. Inasmuch as defendants failed to do so, interpreting the partnership agreement in light of the undisputed facts and uncontroverted allegations before it, [the trial court] properly found a constructive removal as a matter of law and granted summary judgment. We also agree that an accounting is unnecessary as the figures used to calculate the value of plaintiff's interest under the Buy-Sell Provisions were undisputed.

[The judgment is affirmed. Plaintiff is entitled to receive an interest under the buy-sell provisions that takes into account the going concern value of the business.]

Dixon, Odom & Company v. Sledge
Court of Appeals of North Carolina, 296 S.E.2d 512 (1982)

In 1974 David Sledge signed a partnership agreement with the accounting firm of Dixon, Odom & Company. In 1977 Sledge withdrew from the partnership, and he and the other partners signed an agreement defining Sledge's and the partnership's rights and duties in connection with his withdrawal.

In the agreement, the partnership agreed to pay Sledge a salary through April 1977 and to cancel all debts due to the partnership from Sledge. The partnership also promised to pay Sledge a total of $12,000 by yearly payments of $1,200 through 1986, with 6 percent interest. The partnership also had the right at any time to prepay the balance due in whole or in part. Sledge agreed to provide the partnership with a list of clients anticipated to discontinue using the partnership's services and become Sledge's clients. As for Sledge's obligations, the agreement contained the following:

The Withdrawing Partner agrees to pay to the Partnership fifty percent (50%) of all fees earned by him, either directly or indirectly as a partner or employee, from clients who were formerly clients of the Partnership at any time after January 17, 1975, subject to the following terms and conditions:

(a) The Withdrawing Partner shall not pay to the Partnership any part of fees earned by him after January 17, 1987, and

(b) With respect to each client served by the Withdrawing Partner, the Withdrawing Partner shall not pay any part of fees earned by him from that client after he has paid to the Partnership fifty percent (50%) of fees earned by him from that client for a period of three (3) years, and

(c) With respect to each client served by the Withdrawing Partner in a bookkeeping capacity, the Withdrawing Partner shall not pay any part of fees earned by him from that client after he has paid one hundred fifty percent (150%) of the amount of fees earned by the Partnership from that client during its last year of service to that client, and

(d) The Withdrawing Partner shall give to the Partnership on November 15, 1977 and annually thereafter until November 15, 1987 a list of former clients of the Partnership which he has served directly or indirectly since he ceased to be a partner of the Partnership and since his last similar report, together with a list of the amount of fees earned by him from each such client and the amount of fees received by him from each client, excluding any clients which sub-parts (a), (b) or (c) of this provision shall eliminate from the list, together with his payment of 50% of the fees received by him directly or indirectly, and. . . .

(g) The Withdrawing Partner shall maintain records adequate to provide the information required by this provision and shall allow his records to be examined by a representative of the Partnership for purposes of verification at any reasonable time and place.

In 1980 Sledge completely repudiated the agreement, and the partnership, plaintiff, filed suit against Sledge and the new partnership he had formed with another accountant, defendants, seeking an accounting for the 1977–80 period and a decree of specific performance requiring Sledge to carry out the terms of the contract. The trial court granted summary judgment for the plaintiff, and defendants appealed.

Hedrick, Judge:

Even though Sledge denies having complied with this agreement during 1977, he did supply a list of clients to the plaintiff and pay $12,466.30 to the plaintiff. Also during 1977, plaintiff paid, and defendant Sledge accepted, $9,791.67 in salary and $1,823.00 under the provision to pay $12,000 in yearly payments. Plaintiff also cancelled defendant Sledge's debt instruments. Again in 1978, Sledge supplied the plaintiff with a list of clients and paid $7,341.39 to plaintiff and the plaintiff made its annual payment to Sledge. In 1979, Sledge failed to provide a list of clients, but paid $6,478 to plaintiff and the plaintiff fulfilled its financial obligation to Sledge. During 1980, Sledge refused to give plaintiff a list of clients and did not pay any money to plaintiff. . . .

Defendants first contend that summary judgment was improperly granted for the plaintiff because a genuine issue of material fact exists as to what constitutes a "former client" under the agreement. Defendants argue the term "former client" is ambiguous and does not describe the intentions of the contracting parties. One interpretation of "former clients" given by the defendants is that one of plaintiff's clients could change to a third, unrelated accounting firm and later change to defendant Sledge's firm. This, argues the defendants, was not a situation contemplated by the contracting parties when they entered into the agreement. Yet, a likely occurrence would come about where defendants advised potential clients, who were also former clients of the plaintiff, to use a third firm before moving their business to defendants in order to circumvent the agreement between plaintiff and defendants.

Nonetheless, this court need not entertain all the possible interpretations of "former clients" in order to decide this case. Where the provisions of a contract are plainly set out, the court is not free to disregard them and a party may not contend for a different interpretation on the ground that it does not truly express the intent of the parties. We find the language of this agreement, made between professional men, who are deemed capable of guarding their own interests and remaining free from compulsion, is clear and unambiguous on its face. This finding obviates defendants' argument that "former clients" is not what the parties meant at the time of contracting. We note that the agreement contains seven subparagraphs below the provision setting out the obligations concerning "former clients." Furthermore, plaintiff's "Exhibit F" shows that defendant Sledge suggested that "fees be paid to cover present or future clients who become my client during a ten year period to end January 10, 1987." Plaintiff's affidavits and exhibits further demonstrate that the original partnership agreement signed by defendant Sledge in 1974 contained certain covenants not to compete and that the agreement in dispute here was adopted in lieu of the original partnership agreement limiting a withdrawing partner's right to compete with the plaintiff partnership. . . .

Summary judgment for the plaintiff is affirmed.

SUMMARY

Termination of a partnership involves dissolution and winding up. Dissolution is the point when the object of the partners changes from continuing the organization in its present form to discontinuing it. Winding up is the actual process of settling partnership affairs after dissolution. The partnership agreement may specify the events that will or will not cause dissolution. In the absence of agreement to the contrary, withdrawal of a partner causes dissolution. Whether such withdrawal also amounts to a breach of the partnership agreement depends on the terms of that agreement.

Dissolution occurs by operation of law in the case of the death of a partner or the bankruptcy of either the partnership or an individual partner. Dissolution can be obtained by court decree when a partner becomes insane or otherwise incapable of performing his or her part of the partnership agreement. Dissolution by court decree also can be obtained when the partnership is unprofitable, or when a partner is found guilty of serious misconduct. Dissolution substantially restricts the authority of a partner to act as an agent for the partnership, but dissolution in and of itself has no effect on existing partnership liabilities.

In the winding up process, claims against the partnership by outside creditors are paid first, followed by repayment of loans from partners and repayment of partners' capital contributions; any remainder is distributed to partners as profits. When the business itself is continued after dissolution, winding up does not involve an asset liquidation but consists primarily of bookkeeping changes and payment to a withdrawing or excluded partner or to the estate of a deceased partner.

KEY TERMS

Dissolution
Winding up
Partnership at will
Liquidating partner (or winding-up partner)

QUESTIONS AND PROBLEMS

1. Discuss the difference between the terms *dissolution* and *winding up.*

2. Henderson and Alden were partners in a partnership that owned and operated a chain of movie theaters. Alden died, and his widow, who was his sole heir, informed Henderson that she would take her husband's place as a partner in the business. Henderson would not agree to this. Mrs. Alden stated that, as an alternative to becoming a partner, she would simply take half of the theaters in the chain, since her husband had owned a one-half interest in the partnership. Henderson refused to agree to this proposal and insisted on buying her interest even though the partnership agreement between Henderson and Alden had said nothing about the purchase of a deceased partner's interest. What is the effect of Alden's death on the partnership? Discuss.

3. In Question 2, what rights does Henderson have after Alden's death? Explain.

4. In Question 2, what rights does Alden's widow have regarding the partnership? Discuss.

5. What is the nature of a partner's authority to bind the partnership after dissolution? Give three examples of actions that might fall within the scope of this authority.

6. Does the fact that a partnership is dissolved necessarily mean that the business itself will cease to operate? Explain.

7. Parsons and Raymond were partners in the construction business. The business was not successful and the partnership was dissolved. After all the partnership's assets were liquidated, the partnership had a cash balance of $400,000 and accounts payable of $500,000. A $60,000 loan from Parsons to the partnership remained unpaid, and the unreturned capital contributions of Parsons and Raymond to the partnership were $75,000 and $50,000, respectively. Parsons had personal assets of $800,000 and liabilities of $400,000. Raymond had personal assets of $300,000 and liabilities of $200,000. Assuming that losses are to be divided equally, how much of each partner's assets should be used to pay partnership creditors? Explain.

8. In Question 7, how would your answer change if Raymond's liabilities were $250,000 instead of $200,000? Explain.

9. A partnership was created by Atkins, Benson, and Collier, who agreed to share profits equally. Nothing was agreed as to the sharing of losses. The partners decided to dissolve the partnership after a year of operation, at which time the partnership's books revealed the following: Atkins had loaned the partnership $10,000 and had made a capital contribution of $20,000; Benson had made a $10,000 capital contribution; Collier had made no capital contribution; the partnership had assets of $80,000 and owed outside creditors $55,000. Explain how distribution of assets should be made to the partnership's creditors and to the partners.

10. What is the proper basis for valuation of partnership assets after dissolution? Discuss.

Chapter 35

LIMITED PARTNERSHIPS

[handwritten: filing a Certificate as opposed to the regular partnership of Partnership]

THE NATURE AND HISTORY OF LIMITED PARTNERSHIPS

The Nature of the Limited Partnership

The amount of capital required in a business often is greater than an individual is able to obtain or willing to risk. Meeting these capital requirements is one of the most important reasons for the formation of partnerships. In an ordinary partnership, however, each partner is personally liable for the partnership's obligations. The prospect of unlimited personal liability in the case of a partnership may create a major obstacle to capital raising efforts because many potential investors will be unwilling to accept such a risk.

As we will see in subsequent chapters, the creation of a corporation may provide the necessary means for meeting a firm's capital requirements. In many situations, however, the *limited partnership* is an attractive alternative for this purpose. A limited partnership is a partnership formed by two or more persons *and having at least one general partner and at least one limited partner.* The **general partners** essentially run the business as they would an ordinary partnership. The **limited partners,** on the other hand, are merely investors. Limited partners have little voice in the basic operation of the business, and their liability usually is limited to the amount of their investment in the enterprise.

Historical Background

The type of organization we now call a limited partnership has existed since the Middle Ages. Legislation in France gave legal status to the limited partnership in the early eighteenth century. In the United States several states passed statutes governing limited partnerships in the nineteenth century. The need for uniformity and consistency in the way limited partnerships were treated in the various states led to the drafting of the Uniform Limited Partnership Act (ULPA) in 1916. The ULPA eventually was adopted in 49 states.

Because of several problems with the ULPA, the National Conference of Commissioners on Uniform State Laws drafted the Revised Uniform Limited Partnership Act (RULPA). The RULPA was completed in 1976 and made available to state legislatures for adoption in 1977.

Although the RULPA generally was hailed as a much-needed improvement, the position initially taken by the Internal Revenue Service toward taxation of limited partnerships under the RULPA caused most states to defer action. Traditionally, the IRS had treated most limited partnerships as partnerships for taxation purposes. When the RULPA was first proposed, however, the IRS indicated that limited partnerships under the new law might be taxed as corporations.

The tax treatment of these business organizations is important for several reasons. In a partnership, the income of the business passes directly to the partners and is treated as personal income to them. Perhaps more important, however, partnership losses are passed directly to the individual partners, who may offset these losses against personal income. Taxation of limited partnerships as partnerships is an especially attractive feature in businesses commonly showing low profits or "paper" losses despite positive cash flows. Such a phenomenon occurs frequently in enterprises having large depreciation or depletion deductions, substantial investment tax credits, and so forth. In addition, taxation as a partnership permits individual partners to take advantage of any tax exempt earnings the firm may have. If the firm is taxed as a corporation, these benefits do not pass directly to the investors, but go to the corporation as a separate entity.

The IRS ultimately decided to continue treating limited partnerships as partnerships in most situations, even in states adopting the RULPA. Since then, 30 states have passed the RULPA. Although 19 states still use the original ULPA, it is anticipated that most of them will adopt the RULPA in the near future.

FORMING THE LIMITED PARTNERSHIP

The limited partnership is something of a hybrid between an ordinary partnership and a corporation. Like a partnership, the agreement of the

existence of 50 yrs.
as opposed to the partnership agreement
10 yrs.

partners determines the amount of capital contributions, the proportions in which profits and losses are shared, procedures for admitting new partners, procedures for the voluntary or involuntary withdrawal of partners, and many other matters concerning the operation of the business. However, the partners cannot confer limited liability on their members simply by agreeing to do so, because outsiders (creditors) are affected. Thus, like a corporation, the limited partnership can exist only if permitted by statute and the procedural requirements of the statute are met.

Filing the Certificate

The agreement among the general and limited partners is embodied in the **certificate of limited partnership.** This certificate must be filed with the designated state official in order for the limited partnership to have legal status. Under the ULPA, designation of the official with whom the certificate must be filed was left up to the individual states. Although a few states permitted centralized filing with the secretary of state, many states required the certificate to be filed in the county where the firm was organized. This led to uncertainty as to whether the limited partnership would be legally recognized in other counties in which it might do business. As a result, many attorneys advised limited partnership clients to file a certificate in every county in which business was transacted. Under the RULPA, however, a limited partnership needs only to file one certificate with the secretary of state in the state where it operates.

Under both the ULPA and RULPA, technical defects in the certificate do not affect the status of a limited partnership. There simply must be "substantial compliance" with statutory requirements.

The ULPA and RULPA require essentially the same types of information to be included in the certificate. Section 201 of the RULPA requires the certificate to set forth:

1. The name of the limited partnership

2. The general character of its business

3. The address of the office of the firm's agent who is authorized to receive summonses or other legal notices

4. The name and business address of each partner, specifying which ones are general partners and which are limited partners

5. The amount of cash contributions actually made, and agreed to be made in the future, by each partner

6. A description and statement of value of noncash contributions made or to be made by each partner

7. The times at which additional contributions are to be made by any of the partners

8. Whether and under what conditions a limited partner has the right to grant limited partner status to an assignee of his or her interest in the partnership

9. If agreed upon, the time or the circumstances when a partner may withdraw from the firm

10. If agreed upon, the amount of, or the method for determining, the funds to be received by a withdrawing partner

11. Any right of a partner to receive distributions of cash or other property from the firm, and the times and circumstances for such distributions

12. The time or circumstances when the limited partnership is to be dissolved

13. The rights of the remaining general partners to continue the business after withdrawal of a general partner

14. Any other matters the partners wish to include.

The Name of the Business

Both the ULPA and RULPA require that the surname of a limited partner *not* appear in the name of the business unless (1) that name is also the name of a general partner, or (2) the business had been carried on under this name before the limited partnership was formed. The purpose of this restriction is to prevent outsiders from thinking that a limited partner has managerial control or personal liability.

The RULPA imposes some restrictions, however, that the ULPA does not. Specifically, the RULPA provides that the name of the business (1) must contain, without abbreviation, the words "limited partnership," (2) may not contain any word or phrase indicating or implying that the firm is organized for any purpose other than that stated in its certificate, and (3) may not be the same as or deceptively similar to the name of any corporation or limited partnership already formed or registered in the state.

Doing Business in Other States

The ULPA makes no provision for the conduct of business by a limited partnership in states other than that in which it was formed. Several states passed special legislation dealing with this situation, but many did not. In the absence of such legislation, a limited partnership formed in state X would have to re-form in state Y (and probably file the certificate in various counties in state Y) in order to do business there.

The RULPA resolves the problem by permitting a limited partnership formed in one state simply to *register* with the secretary of state in another state in which it wishes to do business. Registration is much simpler, and requires disclosure of less information, than the original certificate filing.

FINANCING THE LIMITED PARTNERSHIP

Partners' Contributions

The capital requirements of limited partnerships are met in the same way as those of ordinary partnerships—primarily by contributions from partners to the firm's capital. In addition to the investments of partners, borrowing may also be used to raise needed funds, although the availability of borrowed funds will depend on the amount and nature of the partnership's assets, its past and projected performance, and other factors.

For several reasons, the limited partnership usually provides greater capital raising opportunities than ordinary partnerships. First, a larger number of investors and larger amounts of individual investment may be attracted because prospective limited partners know they normally are shielded from personal liability. Second, the number of limited partners has no practical bounds because they do not participate in management. As we observed in Chapter 31, a large number of partners sometimes proves to be unwieldy in the case of an ordinary partnership.

The contributions of general partners can take any form—cash, property, or services. Under the ULPA the investments of limited partners are restricted to cash or property. A limited partner can provide services to the business, whether for compensation or not. But services of a limited partner cannot be considered as part of the initial contribution to the firm. Violation of this principle makes the limited partner liable as a general partner. The RULPA makes a major change in this regard by permitting the partners to place a value on services performed or promised by a limited partner and count that value as a contribution to capital.

Securities Laws

Obtaining investments from limited partners is viewed as a sale of securities under state and federal securities regulation laws.[1] In most circumstances limited partnership interests are not advertised and sold publicly. As a result, the so-called "private placement" exemption for nonpublic offerings of securities is usually available. This exemption frees the general partners from having to comply with burdensome securities registration requirements. Care must be taken, however, to structure the capital raising effort to insure the availability of this or some other ex-

---

[1] Securities laws are discussed at several points in the chapters on corporations, and explored in depth in Chapter 50, "Securities Regulation."

emption. Even if the sale of limited partnership interests is exempt from registration, the antifraud provisions of state and federal securities laws will still apply.

RIGHTS AND DUTIES OF GENERAL PARTNERS

With very few exceptions, the general partners in a limited partnership have the same rights and duties as partners in an ordinary partnership. For example, they have the right and authority to manage the business, use partnership property for partnership purposes, act as agents for the partnership in carrying on its normal business activities, and share profits. They also are personally liable for the obligations of the partnership. The rights and types of authority possessed by general partners can be modified by their agreement, as reflected in the certificate of limited partnership, but they obviously may not modify their liability to outsiders.

On unusual occasions, when one or more general partners are considering actions which will have a fundamental effect on the business, they must obtain the written consent of all general and limited partners. Such consent is required, for example, before one or more general partners may (1) admit a new general partner, (2) do any act which would make it impossible for the partnership to carry on its normal business, or (3) use partnership property for nonpartnership purposes. Several other kinds of action require *either* written consent of all general and limited partners *or* express authorization in the certificate. These actions include (1) admission of a new limited partner and (2) continuation of the business after the death, retirement, or insanity of a general partner.

RIGHTS AND DUTIES OF LIMITED PARTNERS

Limited partners are essentially *investors.* They have no right to manage the business. They also have no right to use partnership property or conduct business in behalf of the partnership unless expressly authorized by the general partners or the certificate.

Limited partners do, however, have certain rights which are necessary to protect their investments. Thus, they are entitled to inspect and copy partnership records and to receive full disclosure of any information affecting the partnership. Limited partners are entitled to a share of profits only as agreed upon and specified in the certificate.

As we have seen, a limited partner ordinarily can be held liable for partnership obligations only to the extent of his or her investment in the business. Thus, if the partnership's assets are insufficient to pay its debts, limited partners are not liable for the deficiency.

Restrictions on Participation in Management

Limited partners lose their limited liability, and consequently are personally liable for partnership debts, if they participate in control of the business. Limited partners clearly must take part in some business decisions which may have a fundamental effect on their investments. Moreover, the general partners would be quite foolish in some cases not to take advantage of a limited partner's expertise. What limited partners must not do, however, is participate in the decisionmaking process on a continuing basis.

The ULPA simply provides that a limited partner becomes liable as a general partner if he or she "takes part in the control of the business." For decades, courts have had difficulty interpreting this provision. Almost all courts have held that limited partners may provide services or advice to the partnership, with or without compensation, and still retain their limited liability. The line between permissible and impermissible activities is often blurred, however.

A question of particular difficulty has been whether a specific creditor must have *relied* on the limited partner's apparent managerial status before the limited partner can be held personally liable to that creditor.

One group of courts has employed the **control test.** These courts have held the limited partner liable whenever control of the business has been exercised, regardless of whether the particular creditor has relied on the limited partner's actions. Another group of courts, however, has applied the **reliance test,** and has held the limited partner liable only where the evidence shows that the limited partner's conduct probably caused the third party to view the limited partner as a general partner.

In the following case the court is faced with a perplexing question. If a corporation is a general partner and it acts through one of its officers who also serves as a limited partner, is the limited partner personally liable for participating in the control of the limited partnership? An important part of the court's decision involves the question whether control by itself is enough to make the limited partner liable or whether the outsider must have been misled by the situation.

Western Camps, Inc. v. Riverway Ranch Enterprises
Court of Appeal of California, 138 Cal. Rptr. 918 (1977)

In 1965, Constructors Research Corporation (CRC) leased 40 acres of land in Tulare County, California, from the owners. At the same time, CRC received several options to purchase other pieces of real estate from the same people. These options permitted CRC to buy the leased property and additional land each year from 1967 to 1973. The lease agreement between CRC and the owners provided that the lease would terminate if CRC failed to exercise any one of the options.

Later in 1965, Riverway Ranch Enterprises (Riverway) was formed. Riverway was a limited partnership, with CRC as its only general partner. There were several limited partners, including McCoy, who also was an officer, director, and shareholder of CRC. Shortly thereafter, CRC assigned all of its rights under the lease and option agreements to Riverway. Thus, Riverway then stood in CRC's place as tenant and holder of the options.

In 1966 Riverway executed a ten-year sublease of the 40 acres to Western Camps, Inc. (Western). Western already conducted a summer children's camp on the property, and obtained the sublease for the purpose of continuing the camp operation. The sublease was negotiated by Stanford Oken and Leonard Mann in behalf of Western, and by McCoy in behalf of Riverway. In order to get the sublease, Western had to put up a $5,000 deposit and spend $25,000 for improvements on the property. Riverway promised that it would exercise the purchase options necessary to keep the original lease alive. Riverway also promised that if it caused the lease (and consequently the sublease) to be terminated, it would pay Western $60,000 plus the depreciated value of the improvements Western had made on the land, and return the $5,000 deposit. The purpose of the $60,000 payment was to provide Western with the means to exercise the options if Riverway failed to do so.

In 1970 Riverway decided not to exercise any more options. This caused the original lease to terminate. Riverway made no payments to Western and Western was not able to exercise the options itself. Western had to cease its camp operation on the 40-acre site, and it then filed suit against Riverway and McCoy for breach of contract. The trial court found in favor of Western and awarded it $117,000 in damages, interest, and attorneys' fees. Defendants Riverway and McCoy appealed on several grounds. One of the main grounds for McCoy's appeal was that he was a limited partner of Riverway and was not liable for its obligations.

Dunn, Associate Justice:

. . . A limited partner is not bound by the obligations of the limited partnership, and is not liable as a general partner, unless he takes part in the control of the partnership business. The trial court found that at the time the sublease was negotiated McCoy, in addition to being a limited partner, also was one of the three officers, directors and shareholders of CRC, the corporate general partner. The court further found that McCoy exercised complete management and control in the negotiations for the sublease and in its termination, and acted without the advice or guidance of the other officers and directors of CRC. Pointing out that a corporation may be a general partner in a limited partnership, and that a corporation may act only through its agents, McCoy argues that he is not liable as general partner because, in the transactions regarding the sublease, he was acting in his capacity as agent of the corporate general partner, not in his capacity as a limited partner. The question thus presented is whether a limited partner in a limited partnership becomes liable as a general partner if he takes part in the control of the partnership business while acting as an agent of the corporation which is the sole general partner of the limited partnership.

This question apparently has not been considered in California. In two other jurisdictions, conflicting conclusions have been reached on the point. In *Delaney v. Fidelity Lease Limited,* 526 S.W.2d 543, 545 (Tex. 1975), it was held that "the personal liability, which attaches to a limited partner when 'he takes part in the control and management of the business,' cannot be evaded merely by acting through a corporation." The court rejected the argument that, for the purpose of fixing personal liability upon a limited partner, the "control" test should be coupled with a determination of whether the limited partner held himself out as being a general partner having personal liability to the extent that the third party (i.e., plaintiff) relied upon the limited partner's general liability. In this regard, the opinion pointed out that section 7 of the Uniform Limited Partnership Act simply provides that a limited partner who takes part in the control of the business subjects himself to personal liability as a general partner, and does not mention any requirement of reliance on the part of the party attempting to hold the limited partner personally liable. The court further expressed concern that the statutory requirement of at least one general partner with general liability in a limited partnership could be circumvented by limited partners operating the partnership through a corporation with minimum capitalization and, therefore, with limited liability.

In *Frigidaire Sales Corp. v. Union Properties, Inc.*, 14 Wash. App. 634, 544 P.2d 781 (1976), the court rejected the reasoning of the *Delaney* case and concluded that the dominant consideration in determining the personal liability of a limited partner is reliance by the third party, not control by the limited partner. It was there stated: "If a corporate general partner in a limited partnership is organized without sufficient capitalization so that it was foreseeable that it would not have sufficient assets to meet its obligations, the corporate entity could be disregarded to avoid injustice. We find no substantive difference between the creditor who does business with a corporation that is the general partner in a limited partnership and a creditor who simply does business with a corporation. In the absence of fraud or other inequitable conduct, the corporate entity should be respected. . . . Here, there was an overt intention to regard the corporate entity and no showing of the violation of any duty owing to the creditor. The creditor dealt with the corporate general partner in full awareness of the corporate status of the general partner. There is no showing of any fraud, wrong or injustice perpetrated upon the creditor, merely that [section 7 of the Uniform Limited Partnership Act] provides that a limited partner becomes liable as a general partner if he takes part in the control of the business. When these are the circumstances, we hold that the corporate entity should be upheld rather than the statute applied blindly with no inquiry as to the purpose it seeks to achieve. . . . A limited partner is made liable as a general partner when he participates in the 'control' of the business in order to protect third parties from dealing with the partnership under the mistaken assumption that the limited partner is a general partner with general liability. . . . A third party dealing with a corporation must reasonably rely on the solvency of the corporate entity. It makes little difference if the corporation is or is not the general partner in a limited partnership. In either instance, the third party cannot justifiably rely on the solvency of the individuals who own the corporation."

We agree with the views expressed in the *Frigidaire* case, and accordingly apply the principles there stated to the facts in the instant case. Such facts are: before the sublease was negotiated, Oken was aware of the corporate capacity of CRC, the general partner, and he knew that McCoy was one of its "principals." In June or July 1970 Oken asked Dick Browne, then the president of CRC, who would be representing CRC in its negotiations with plaintiff regarding the sublease. Browne replied that McCoy would be "making the decisions." McCoy signed the sublease on behalf of Riverway, adding after his signature the words "for CRC." Moreover, the trial court found, as a fact, that "CRC was organized in good faith and had an adequate capitalization necessary to liquidate its indebtedness." Under these circumstances, no fraud or injustice to plaintiff results from respecting the corporate entity of the general partner. We hold, therefore, that CRC, the corporate general partner, is solely liable for the obligations of the limited partnership under the sublease, and that McCoy, a limited partner, has no personal liability for such obligations. . . .

The judgment against defendant Riverway is affirmed. The judgment against defendant McCoy is reversed. [Note: CRC, the general partner of Riverway, was also liable, but it was not clear whether CRC was also a defendant in this case.]

(Comes under the state statutes)

"Safe Harbor" Provisions of the RULPA ✓

Providing clearer guidelines for determining the permissible extent of limited partners' participation in the business was one of the main goals of the RULPA.

The RULPA has achieved this increased clarity primarily by specifying certain "safe harbors" for limited partners. Section 303(b) states that limited partners do not become personally liable for partnership debts solely by doing one or more of the following:

1. Being a contractor for or an agent or employee of the limited partnership or of a general partner

2. Consulting with and advising a general partner regarding partnership business

3. Acting as a surety for the limited partnership

4. Approving or disapproving an amendment to the partnership agreement

5. Voting on one or more of the following matters:

  a. The dissolution and winding up of the limited partnership

  b. The sale, exchange, lease, mortgage, pledge, or other transfer of all or substantially all of the limited partnership's assets when such transfer is not in the ordinary course of business

  c. The incurrence of indebtedness by the limited partnership when it is not in the ordinary course of business

  d. A change in the nature of the business

  e. The removal of a general partner.

Thus, in the case of actions enumerated in Section 303(b), other evidence of managerial control must be present before a limited partner becomes liable.

When a limited partner participates in the business in some way that is not specifically protected by these safe harbor provisions, the RULPA's guidelines are less clear. Section 303(a) of the RULPA uses language identical to that of Section 7 of the ULPA and states that a limited partner is personally liable if he or she "takes part in the control of the business." Section 303(a) then continues, however, by providing that the limited partner is liable only to those creditors who had actual knowledge of the limited partner's participation in control, unless that participation was "substantially the same as the exercise of the powers of a general partner."

Thus the RULPA, like the ULPA, does not specifically define the phrase "takes part in the control of the business." The control concept cannot be defined with precision because of the almost infinite variety of circumstances in which the issue may arise. On the question of whether reliance by the outsider is a necessary element, the RULPA identifies two levels of participation by the limited partner. First, when the limited partner's participation in control is essentially the same as that of a general partner (i.e., on a continuing, not a sporadic, basis), the limited partner is personally liable regardless of an outsider's reliance. Second, when the limited partner's participation does not reach the level of a general partner's participation, the limited partner is personally liable only to those creditors who actually knew of his or her participation. In this second situation, the outsider's reliance on the limited partner's apparent managerial status does not have to be proved—it is conclusively presumed from the outsider's knowledge of the limited partner's participation in control.

Other Situations in which a Limited Partner May Be Liable

A limited partner may be liable for partnership debts in a few other unusual situations.

1. If the name of the limited partnership contains the name of a limited partner, that limited partner is liable unless (a) the name is also the name of a general partner or (b) the business had been conducted under that name prior to becoming a limited partnership.

2. A limited partner who *knows* of a false statement in the certificate is liable to anyone who is harmed by relying on the false statement.[2]

Being a General Partner and a Limited Partner at the Same Time

It is possible for a person to be both a general partner and a limited partner at the same time. Such a person is liable to outsiders as a general partner. His or her additional status as a limited partner is important only with respect to the dealings among the partners themselves. Thus, that portion of the person's investment designated as a limited partner contribution is treated as such for assignment, distribution, or other purposes.

ASSIGNMENT OF AN INTEREST IN A LIMITED PARTNERSHIP

The rules regarding assignment of a partner's interests in a limited partnership are basically the same as for an ordinary partnership. The in-

terests of both general and limited partners can be assigned, totally or partially, to third parties. An assignment by either a general or limited partner does not terminate the limited partnership.

Such an assignment also does not cause the assignee to become a partner—the assignee merely becomes entitled to receive the assigning partner's share of profits or other asset distributions.

The assignee of a *general partner's* interest can be admitted as a new general partner only by written consent of all the general and limited partners (other than the assigning partner), followed by formal amendment of the certificate. The assignee of a *limited partner's* interest can be admitted as a new limited partner by written consent of all general and limited partners (other than the assigning partner), *or* by a provision in the certificate permitting the assigning limited partner to designate an assignee as a new limited partner. In either case, the certificate must be amended formally to reflect admission of the new limited partner.

The provisions of the RULPA relating to assignments are substantially the same as those of the ULPA. There are two differences, however: (1) under the RULPA, the partnership agreement may specifically make the interests of general or limited partners *nonassignable;* and (2) the RULPA states that a general or limited partner ceases to be a partner upon assignment of *all* of his or her interest, unless the partnership agreement provides for a different result.

DISSOLUTION AND WINDING UP OF THE LIMITED PARTNERSHIP

Dissolution

A limited partnership dissolves at the time or under the circumstances specified in the certificate. It also can be dissolved at any time by written agreement of all the general and limited partners, followed by formal cancellation of the certificate.

---

[2] A general partner obviously would be liable under the same circumstances.

Under both the ULPA and the RULPA, the death, insanity, or withdrawal[3] of a *general partner* causes dissolution of the limited partnership *unless* continuation of the business is provided for (1) in the certificate or (2) by written consent of all remaining general and limited partners. To continue the business as a limited partnership in any event, there must remain at least one general partner and one limited partner. To meet this requirement, new partners may be admitted.

Under the ULPA, a general partner's bankruptcy or involvement in some other insolvency proceeding is not treated as an automatic withdrawal from the limited partnership. The RULPA does, however, treat such an event as a withdrawal unless the certificate or unanimous written agreement of the partners provides otherwise.

The death, insanity, withdrawal, or bankruptcy of a *limited partner* does not cause dissolution of the limited partnership. (This statement assumes, of course, that at least one limited partner remains.) When a limited partner dies, the executor or administrator of the person's estate exercises control over the interest in the limited partnership. In the case of insanity, such control is exercised by the limited partner's guardian. The interest of a bankrupt limited partner is controlled by the trustee in bankruptcy.

Winding Up.   As is true of an ordinary partnership, a limited partnership continues to exist after dissolution for so long as necessary to wind up its affairs. Control of the winding up process is in the hands of the general partners. Their authority to act in behalf of the partnership is restricted to those activities necessary to bring the business to an end. Limited partners may supervise the process, however, if no general partners remain. Moreover, any general or limited partner, as well as the representative or assignee of any general or limited partner, may obtain court supervision of the winding up process.

After winding up, the assets of the limited partnership are liquidated and distributed. Under both the ULPA and RULPA, the claims of creditors must be satisfied first. The claims of *outside* creditors obviously are included in this priority group. The ULPA also includes the claims of limited partners who are creditors, but the claims of general partners who have lent money to the business are given a lower priority. The RULPA includes in the top priority the claims of both general and limited partners who are creditors of the partnership.

The certificate may specify the order in which the partners receive a return of their capital contributions and an allocation of any surplus. If not so specified, Section 23 of the ULPA or Section 804 of the RULPA governs the distribution. The most important difference between the asset distribution rules of the two statutes is that the ULPA gives priority to limited partners while the RULPA treats general and limited partners essentially the same.

SUMMARY

A limited partnership is a partnership consisting of one or more general partners and one or more limited partners. The general partners have the same authority and liability as partners in an ordinary partnership. Limited partners, on the other hand, are merely investors who have little voice in the basic operation of the business and whose liability is limited to their investment in the partnership. Today, the law of limited partnerships is found primarily in the Revised Uniform Limited Partnership Act (RULPA) and in the original Uniform Limited Partnership Act (ULPA).

Because limited liability can be created only by statute, creation of a limited partnership involves compliance with statutory requirements

---

[3] Aside from the question of dissolution, the withdrawal of either a general or limited partner may subject him or her to liability for damages to the other partners if the withdrawal violates their partnership agreement.

in addition to a partnership agreement. The most important statutory requirement is the filing of a certificate of limited partnership. The capital requirements of a limited partnership are met in basically the same way as in an ordinary partnership, by contributions from partners. Although the general partners normally have the power to manage the partnership, they must have the written consent of all general and limited partners, or express authorization in the certificate, to perform certain actions that fundamentally affect the business. Limited partners lose their limited liability if they participate in the control of the business. Some courts have found the limited partner liable if such control has been exercised, regardless of whether the particular creditor has relied on the limited partner's actions. Other courts, however, have found the limited partner liable only if the evidence indicates that the limited partner's conduct probably caused the creditor to view the limited partner as a general partner. The RULPA does not specifically resolve this conflict, but does specify certain "safe harbors" in which particular types of conduct by a limited partner definitely will not cause a limited partner to be personally liable for partnership debts.

A limited partnership is dissolved by the death, insanity, or withdrawal of a general partner unless continuation is provided for by the certificate or written consent of all general and limited partners. The winding up of a limited partnership is very similar to that of an ordinary partnership. Outside creditors have first priority in the distribution of partnership assets. Remaining partnership assets are distributed as specified in the certificate of limited partnership; if the certificate does not so specify, the ULPA gives limited partners priority over general partners but the RULPA treats general and limited partners essentially the same.

KEY TERMS

General partner
Limited partner
Certificate of limited partnership
Control test
Reliance test

QUESTIONS AND PROBLEMS

1. An agreement for the creation of a limited partnership was signed in November. It named Dimentia Corporation and its president, Wilson, as general partners. Franklin and several others were named as limited partners. In December the limited partnership, acting through Wilson and Dimentia Corp., contracted to buy land from Rigg. The next April the limited partnership defaulted on the contractual obligation. It was not until shortly after this default that a certificate was filed to bring the limited partnership legally into existence. The limited partners then formally renounced (disclaimed) their interests in the limited partnership. Rigg sued and obtained a judgment against Dimentia Corp. and Wilson. Almost two years later, after discovering that the certificate had been filed late, Rigg also sued Franklin and the other limited partners to hold them personally liable. Should the limited partners be personally liable in this situation? Discuss. (*Franklin v. Rigg,* 237 S.E.2d 526, Ga. Ct. App. 1977.)

2. McRea owned an automobile dealership, and Rowlett operated an automobile repair business. The manufacturer for whom McRea was a dealer insisted that McRea have a repair shop as part of the dealership. As a result, McRea and Rowlett agreed to form a limited partnership with McRea as sole general partner and Rowlett as sole limited partner. Rowlett moved his equipment to the dealership premises, and also contributed cash to the limited partnership's capital. Rowlett served as foreman of the repair shop, while McRea continued to run the dealership as a whole. Although Rowlett supervised the repair shop, he was under the ultimate direction and control of McRea. McRea had to approve all extensions of credit in the repair shop, except in the case of customers personally known by Rowlett. If a credit customer known and approved by Rowlett did not pay, however, Rowlett had to make up the loss. The partnership's bank account was under the complete control of McRea, and he was the only person authorized to draw checks on the account. Some time later, the business ran into financial difficulties. Silvola, a creditor of the dealership, was unable to collect his claim from McRea or the partnership. Consequently, Silvola sued Rowlett on the debt, claiming that Rowlett's activities had made him liable as a general partner. Should Rowlett be held liable? Discuss. (*Silvola v. Rowlett,* 272 P.2d 287, Colo. Sup. Ct. 1954.)

3. Diversified Properties was a limited partnership engaged in buying, selling, and managing real estate. The limited partnership consisted of Weil as the sole general partner and a group of limited partners. About a year after its formation the business ran into severe cash flow problems and was on the verge of collapse. The limited partners had several meetings and hired two new employees to take over management of the business from Weil. During this time all of the limited partners also were personally involved in negotiations with creditors concerning the refinancing of Diversified's obligations. Weil was still formally the sole general partner, and creditors still recognized him as such. However, he no longer received a salary or occupied the partnership office, and exercised little authority. He subsequently went to work for another real estate firm. Weil then filed a lawsuit in which he sought a declaratory judgment that the limited partners had become liable as general partners because of their activities. Is Weil's contention correct? Discuss. (*Weil v. Diversified Properties,* 319 F.Supp. 778, D.D.C. 1970.)

4. Hacienda Farms, Limited, was organized as a limited partnership to engage in vegetable farming, with de Escamilla as the general partner and Russell and Andrews as limited partners. Most of Hacienda's vegetable crops were marketed through a separate produce company controlled by Andrews. Decisions as to which crops to plant were always made jointly by the three partners. Sometimes de Escamilla disagreed with Russell and Andrews on planting decisions;

when this happened, de Escamilla was overruled by the limited partners. Checks could be drawn on the partnership account only with the signatures of at least two partners. Most of the checks were actually signed by Russell and Andrews, although a few were signed by de Escamilla and one of the limited partners. The firm went bankrupt, and Holzman, the trustee in bankruptcy, filed suit for the purpose of determining whether Russell and Andrews had become personally liable for partnership debts. Were the limited partners liable as general partners? Discuss. (*Holzman v. de Escamilla,* 195 P.2d 833, Cal. Dist. Ct. App. 1948.)

5. Westwood Place, Ltd., was a limited partnership with Dobbs Industries, Inc., and Oliver Dobbs as general partners. The partnership's only limited partner withdrew and transferred his interest to Leventhal, who then was formally admitted as the limited partner. One of the provisions in the limited partnership agreement stated that a limited partner would be liable for a proportionate share of any indebtedness secured by a mortgage "that may at any time or times in the future be placed on partnership property." The proportionate liability was stated as being the same as the limited partner's share of profits. Leventhal's specified share of profits was 30 percent. Leventhal became a limited partner on October 1. About three weeks prior to that time, on September 12, the limited partnership had borrowed money from a pension trust fund, and signed a promissory note for the indebtedness. The loan was secured by a fourth mortgage on partnership property. The loan was not paid when due, and Green, trustee for the pension trust fund, filed suit against the limited partnership, the two general partners, and Leventhal. After suit was filed, the two general partners withdrew from the partnership, and Leventhal became general partner. The limited partnership and the two former general partners were held liable for the debt. Should Leventhal also be liable for all or any part of the obligation? Discuss. (*Leventhal v. Green,* 271 S.E.2d 194, Ga. Sup. Ct. 1980.)

Chapter 36

CORPORATIONS
Nature and Formation

THE NATURE AND HISTORY OF CORPORATIONS

The Nature of the Corporation

Suppose for a moment that you have been given the authority to create a new organizational form for conducting a business enterprise. You probably would want to create an artificial being with a legally recognized identity of its own, so that it could make contracts, own property, sue and be sued, and do all the other things necessary for running a business. This artificial being, having existence only on paper but nevertheless recognized by law as a "person," could have perpetual existence. It would be completely unfettered by the limitations of a flesh-and-blood existence. There would be no worries about death and its effect upon the continuing vitality of the business. True, it would have to act through human agents, but these agents could be replaced with no effect on the artificial being.

You probably would want the ownership of this new organizational form to rest in the hands of investors who would have no management responsibilities. In this way, an investor's interest in the business could be sold to another investor with no effect on the operation of the enterprise. And management would be centralized, thus improving the efficiency of the business.

Investors could be attracted by making their ownership interests freely transferable and by shielding them from liability for business debts. The possibilities for raising capital would be practically endless. New shares in the ownership of the business could be issued as needed for capital requirements, and if the business had been successful, investors would buy them.

But despite the worthiness of your creation, it possesses one flaw: it is not new. It has already been conceived of and put into practice. *It is called a corporation.*

Historical Background of Corporations

Early History: The concept of granting legal recognition to a group of individuals was developed to a very limited degree in Babylonian law

as early as the twenty-first century B.C. More formal acceptance of the idea is found in ancient Roman law, although its application to commercial ventures was yet to come. At this time, the organizations acknowledged by the sovereign were formed primarily for religious, educational, governmental, and other noncommercial purposes.

Under canon law (the law of the Roman Catholic church), the corporation was employed by the church as a convenient vehicle for property ownership. Indeed, canon law made an extremely important theoretical contribution in the thirteenth century when Pope Innocent IV developed the concept of the corporation as an artificial person legally separate from the natural persons composing it.

Recognition of the corporation in English common law had become fairly sophisticated by the fourteenth century. However, the corporation had not yet been substantially utilized for commercial purposes; its use as an instrument of commerce did not become commonplace in England until the sixteenth century. Shortly thereafter, in the seventeenth century, the "concession theory" appeared in English law, treating the corporation as a concession of the government and thus justifying increased regulation and taxation.

The famous overseas trading companies of the sixteenth and seventeenth centuries, such as Hudson's Bay Company and the British East India Company, were chartered by the English government for purposes of exploration, colonization, and foreign trading. These companies, which were given substantial governmental powers and many trading privileges, became the models for our present-day business corporations.

Sources of American Corporation Law: During the first few decades after the Revolutionary War, corporations in the United States were formed only by special acts of state legislatures. In the nineteenth century, however, states began to enact "general incorporation" laws, under which persons could form corporations by following specified procedures and without special legislative action. By the end of that century general incorporation was the established rule.

The federal government can also charter corporations—insofar as it is "necessary and proper" for carrying out other express federal powers. Examples of federally chartered corporations are the national banks, the Tennessee Valley Authority, and the American Red Cross. Additionally, many of the federal regulatory statutes, such as the securities, antitrust, and labor laws, weigh heavily upon the operations of corporations.

However, despite increasing involvement by the federal government in the affairs of corporations, their organization and operation are still largely a matter of state law. Each state has its own corporation statutes, and they are not entirely uniform. The Model Business Corporation Act (the Model Act), drafted by the American Bar Association (ABA) in 1969, has provided a basic guideline for the modern corporation statutes of over half the states. In 1984 the ABA drafted the Revised Model Business Corporation Act (the Revised Model Act), which substantially changes many provisions of the Model Act. The Revised Model Act has not yet had an effect on state corporation statutes, and will not be mentioned further in these chapters.

The state of Delaware enacted an extremely flexible corporation statute at the end of the nineteenth century, when most state corporation laws were quite inflexible. Because the Delaware law permitted corporate management more alternatives in structuring and operating the business, and also because Delaware courts developed a relatively well-settled body of judicial precedent at an early time, many companies incorporated in Delaware even though their principal places of business were to be elsewhere. This trend has continued to the present, with many of the nation's largest companies being incorporated in Delaware. In recent years, several states have modeled their corporation statutes after those of Delaware.

Classification of Corporations

Domestic and Foreign Corporations: A corporation that has been incorporated in a particular state is referred to as a **domestic corporation** in that particular state. One that has been incorporated in some other state or in another nation is called a **foreign corporation.**

Private and Government Corporations: A corporation formed by private parties is a **private corporation.** Almost all corporations, including those formed for business and nonprofit purposes, fall within this category. The **government corporation,** on the other hand, is one formed by the state or federal government. Incorporated cities and towns are examples of government corporations at the state level; the Tennessee Valley Authority and the United States Postal Service are examples at the federal level. (Government corporations are sometimes referred to as *public* corporations, but it is best to avoid this term because it tends to be confused with the *publicly held* corporation, discussed below.)

Business and Nonprofit Corporations: Private corporations are either of the business or the nonprofit variety. A **business corporation** is simply one that is formed to engage in a business activity for profit. A **nonprofit corporation** (sometimes called a *not-for-profit* corporation) is one formed for social, charitable, religious, or other nonprofit purposes.

Publicly Held and Close Corporations: A **publicly held corporation** is one whose shares of stock are offered for sale to the public. (Sometimes such a corporation is called a *public* corporation, a term that should be avoided because of potential confusion with the government corporation.) A **close corporation** is one whose shares of stock are not offered for sale to the public, but instead are owned by either a single shareholder or a small, closely knit group of shareholders. The shareholders themselves are usually active in managing the business of a close corporation. (The close corporation is sometimes referred to by a variety of other names, such as a *closed, closely held, one-person,* or *family corporation.*)

Professional Corporations: Until the early 1960s, state corporation laws usually did not allow persons to form corporations for the purpose of engaging in the practice of a profession such as medicine or law. Since that time, however, most states have enacted statutes permitting one or a group of professionals to form a **professional corporation.** Probably the most important result of these statutes is that physicians, attorneys, and members of other professions can now receive several federal tax advantages (such as tax-deductible insurance or pension plans) as "employees" of the corporation that they could not receive as sole proprietors or as members of a partnership.

THE CORPORATION AS A LEGAL ENTITY

Consequences

Perhaps the most important characteristic of the corporation is its recognition as a legal entity—an artificial being or person. This has many consequences, the most important of which are discussed below.

Normal Business Operations: The corporation can own property, make contracts, sue and be sued in court, and generally perform all legal functions that an individual can perform.

Liability for Debts: The individuals who own the corporation (the shareholders or stockholders) and those who manage it (the officers and members of the board of directors) generally are not personally liable for its debts. Con-

versely, the corporation is not liable for the personal debts of those who own and manage it. The legal identity of the corporation is thus distinct from the identities of its owners and managers. (Of course, these individuals can assume personal liability for corporate obligations if they so choose.)

Income Taxation: The income of the corporation is taxed under the federal income tax laws. And because the corporation and its shareholders have separate identities, the distribution of this income to shareholders as "dividends" is again taxed, this time as personal income to the individuals receiving it. As discussed in Chapter 31, a form of double taxation can result from the separate identities of the corporation and its owners. On the other hand, as also mentioned earlier, certain small corporations may elect to be taxed as partnerships in some circumstances. Those corporations making such a choice are referred to as "S corporations."

Constitutional Rights: As a "person," the corporation enjoys many of the same rights and privileges under the Constitution that are granted to individuals. For example, it has the right to be secure from "unreasonable searches and seizures"; the right to freedom of speech; the right not to be deprived of life, liberty, or property without "due process of law"; the right not to be tried twice for the same offense ("double jeopardy"); and the right not to be denied "equal protection of the laws." On the other hand, the corporation does *not* enjoy the privilege against "self-incrimination."

In the following case concerning the applicability to corporations of the Constitution's double jeopardy clause, the court discusses the rationale for recognizing the corporation as a "person" in the realm of constitutional protections.

United States v. Hospital Monteflores
U.S. Court of Appeals for the First Circuit, 575 F.2d 332 (1978)

A corporation engaged in the business of operating a hospital, Hospital Monteflores, together with the director of the hospital, was charged with making false statements on Medicare reimbursement forms in violation of a federal criminal statute. The defendants were acquitted in federal district court, and the U.S. government, as prosecutor, sought to appeal the judgment of acquittal to a U.S. Court of Appeals. The double jeopardy clause of the Fifth Amendment to the U.S. Constitution prohibits a person from being tried twice for the same criminal offense. If a defendant in a criminal case is acquitted, the double jeopardy clause usually prevents the government from being able to appeal the acquittal to a higher court. In this case, the government did not attempt to appeal with regard to the hospital director because such an appeal clearly would not be permitted. However, the government claimed that the double jeopardy clause did not apply to corporations, and that it should be able to appeal the trial court's judgment of acquittal with respect to the corporation.

Coffin, Chief Judge:

The government's principal argument is that the corporation's interests are adequately protected by the principles of res judicata and collateral estoppel. [Authors' note: The doctrine of res judicata prohibits a party from raising a claim that has already been litigated—in other words, someone can't "sue again" on the basis of the same or a closely related legal theory; the doctrine of collateral estoppel, which is similar to res judicata, prevents a specific issue from being relitigated when that issue has previously been resolved in some other lawsuit between the parties.] This argument ignores practicalities. These principles protect individuals as well, but the Double Jeopardy Clause still applies. The government responds that, unlike individuals, corporations cannot be put in jail and do not "experience the intense human emotions" that justify special protection. The fact is, of course, that double jeopardy protection focuses on the potential or risk of trial rather than of punishment. Moreover, the clause applies more generally than just to "jeopardy of life or limb," so long as the proceeding is "essentially criminal." Even misdemeanors are within the sweep of this principle.

It is true that corporations do not have human emotions, but that does not mean that they do not "suffer" during criminal trials in the sense of experiencing harm to a legitimate, protectible interest. We can take judicial notice of the fact that corporate well-being is heavily dependent on that elusive quality known as "good will." A corporation that falls out of favor with society will suffer. Its suffering may be of a different character than an individual's, but that does not make those sufferings any the less real or hazardous. Corporations can lose money, sometimes substantial amounts, as the result of criminal prosecutions. Corporations can be made very insecure by prolonged periods of bad publicity. This insecurity may not be emotional, but it is very real and may affect the corporation's ability to do business with the public or to raise capital on public markets, among other possible ill effects.

Part of the penal sanction is the criminal stigma that attaches to those who are convicted of crimes. Whether the penalty is imprisonment or a fine, the stigma still attaches, and it will attach whether the accused is an individual or a corporation. "No corporation, large or small, can escape the 'incalculable effect' which a conviction may have on the public attitude toward the company." *United States v. Security National Bank,* 546 F.2d 492, 494 (2d Cir. 1976).

To argue that res judicata and collateral estoppel are adequate protections is to argue that the Double Jeopardy Clause is superfluous. We do not agree, but, of course, even if we did we could not write it out of the Constitution. Just as individuals will suffer from repeated exposure to criminal sanction, so will corporations. To this it is no answer to respond that we can trust the government to use its power responsibly. We are sure that normally governmental power is not abused, but the guarantees in the Bill of Rights exist precisely to protect the relatively rare victims who suffer when there are abuses. We prefer not to guess how much greater the danger of abuse would be if we were to eliminate constitutional protections. It is enough that such abuses can exist.

For the reasons stated above, we rule that a corporation is entitled to protection against double jeopardy. Since we rule that the Constitution would bar further prosecution of the corporate defendant in this case, this appeal is barred. . . .

Appeal dismissed.

Disregarding the Corporate Entity

The general rule that a corporation possesses an identity separate from its owners and managers is almost always applied. For example, suppose that Beta Corporation becomes insolvent and goes into bankruptcy proceedings. Under most circumstances, the shareholders of Beta are not personally liable to Beta's creditors for its debts. These shareholders, whether they are individuals or other corporations, will lose their investments in Beta because their stock will be worthless, but Beta's creditors normally can reach only Beta's corporate assets to satisfy their claims.

In unusual situations, however, courts may ignore the separate status of the corporation and its owners. This disregard of the corporate identity is often referred to as **piercing the corporate veil.** Sometimes courts use different terminology for the concept; for instance, occasionally a court that disregards the separateness of the corporation and its owners will say that the corporation is the "alter ego" or the "mere instrumentality" of its owners. A court is most likely to pierce the corporate veil in the following circumstances:

1. When the corporation is used as a mere tool for accomplishing a fraud or some other illegal act, a court will disregard the separate identities of the corporation and its owners. For example, suppose that the sole or principal shareholder of the corporation sets fire to corporate property, and the corporation then sues to recover on its fire insurance policy. The court will disregard the separateness of the corporation and the shareholder and will not allow the corporation to recover from the insurance company.

2. When the corporation has been formed with insufficient capital to meet reasonably expectable business obligations *and* the shareholders themselves have intermingled and confused their personal identities with the corporation's identity, a court is likely to disregard the separateness of the corporation and its owners. This confusion of identities might, for instance, take the form of intermingling corporate and personal funds, failing to maintain corporate records separate from personal records, or failing to keep shareholder and corporate identities separate in dealings with outsiders. In such a case, an unpaid corporate creditor who is harmed by the inadequacy of corporate assets may be able to reach the personal assets of shareholders to satisfy its claims.

Corporations are sometimes formed by a single individual or by two or three persons (often family members) who own all the stock. This fact by itself will not cause a court to ignore the separateness of the corporation from its owners; one-person, family-owned, and similar close corporations are entirely permissible. However, those situations in which courts disregard the separateness of the corporation are much more likely to occur when a one-person, family-owned, or similar close corporation is involved. The reason is that the factors leading a court to pierce the corporate veil, such as undercapitalization and confusion of identities, are much more likely to exist in such a corporation.

Subsidiary and Affiliated Corporations: Often a corporation, as the "parent," forms or acquires another corporation as a "subsidiary" for some particular purpose. In such a case, the **parent corporation** owns all or a controlling portion of the stock of the **subsidiary corporation.** In the same manner as an individual shareholder, the parent corporation usually is treated as a separate entity from the subsidiary corporation. This is true even if some or all of the same people serve on the boards of directors of the two corporations. However, just as in the case of individual shareholders, in unusual situations a court will pierce the corporate veil and hold the parent liable for its subsidiary's debts or wrongful acts. The circumstances in which a court will take such action are essentially the same as in the case of an individual shareholder, although courts sometimes use different terminology to describe the concept in the parent-subsidiary context. For example, courts frequently say that a parent corporation is liable for the debts or wrongful acts of its subsidiary if the parent "dominates" or "controls" the subsidiary. However, the factors leading a court to reach such a conclusion are usually the same ones leading to this conclusion in the case of an individual shareholder, namely, (1) use of the subsidiary as a mere tool to accomplish a fraud or other illegal act, or (2) undercapitalization plus confusion of the parent's and subsidiary's identities.

Even if the two corporations technically do not have a parent-subsidiary relationship, a court may still disregard their separate identities if they are otherwise closely affiliated and one dominates the other. Such a situation might occur, for instance, where one person owns a controlling stock interest in two corporations, and one of these corporations dominates the other. The legal principles applied to determine whether the separate identities of the corporations should be disregarded are the same as in a situation where a plaintiff seeks to hold either a parent corporation or an individual shareholder liable for the debts or wrongful acts of the allegedly dominated corporation.

The following case involves two corporations affiliated through the stock ownership of a single individual, and provides an excellent illustration of the type of facts that will cause a court to pierce the corporate veil.

Glenn v. Wagner
Supreme Court of North Carolina, 329 S.E.2d 326 (1985)

Salem Manor, an apartment complex in Winston-Salem, North Carolina, was owned by B-Bom, Inc. David Wagner and George Hill each owned 50 percent of B-Bom's stock, and David Wagner served as the corporation's president. David Wagner also formed another corporation, D&S Enterprises, Inc., in which he was the sole stockholder. B-Bom executed a lease on Salem Manor to D&S, and D&S managed the apartment complex through its agent Smilie Wagner, who was David Wagner's cousin.

Richard Glenn and other members of his family rented an apartment at Salem Manor. Under circumstances in which he had no legal right to take such action, Smilie Wagner evicted Glenn and his family from the apartment, padlocked it, removed and damaged Glenn's personal belongings, and had Glenn's mail returned to the post office. Glenn sued Smilie Wagner, D&S Enterprises, and B-Bom, Inc., claiming that Smilie had committed a trespass. D&S clearly was liable for Smilie's actions because he was acting within the scope of his employment for D&S. Because D&S had no assets, Glenn also attempted to hold B-Bom liable on the theory that B-Bom had completely dominated D&S and, therefore, that D&S was the "alter ego" or "instrumentality" of B-Bom.

In the trial, the evidence indicated that David Wagner had set up D&S mainly to benefit his cousin Smilie and to give the latter a source of income. The management of Salem Manor was D&S's only business. David Wagner testified that he and Smilie each owned 50 percent of D&S (although the articles of incorporation of D&S showed David to be the only stockholder). He stated that he "thought" that he was the president and treasurer of D&S and that Smilie "must be" the vice-president and secretary. He could not recall whether there had been an organizational meeting, when the by-laws were adopted, who was on the initial board of directors, or how many board meetings had been held. Although he and Smilie met regularly to deal with business matters, David could not recall having a formal shareholder meeting. According to David Wagner, Smilie managed Salem Manor for D&S on a daily basis, and David's own involvement in the operation of the apartment complex was "more of an advisory nature because that business was operated exclusively by Smilie . . . as a general rule he operated the business pretty much as he saw fit."

The only formal instrument executed on behalf of D&S was the agreement under which D&S leased Salem Manor from B-Bom. B-Bom established the amount of rent to be charged for each of the Salem Manor units, and most of D&S's rents and profits went to B-Bom as payment on the lease. David Wagner's office, from which he directed several business enterprises, served as the corporate office of both B-Bom and D&S. A few months after Smilie's wrongful eviction of Glenn, Smilie left D&S and went into business for himself, and Wagner terminated the lease between B-Bom and D&S. B-Bom then directly collected rent from Salem Manor for three months until an employee of another one of David Wagner's corporations, also located in the Salem Manor premises, was authorized to collect rent from the premises. D&S was never formally dissolved, but had no assets.

Based on this evidence, the trial court submitted to the jury the question whether B-Bom had so completely dominated D&S as to be its alter ego and to be liable for the trespass committed by D&S. The jury found that B-Bom was liable, and the court rendered judgment for Glenn for damages of approximately $10,000. The intermediate appellate court reversed, holding that there was insufficient evidence of B-Bom's control over D&S. Glenn appealed to the North Carolina Supreme Court.

Branch, Chief Justice:

In North Carolina, what has been commonly referred to as the "instrumentality rule," forms the basis for disregarding the corporate entity or "piercing the corporate veil." The decisions of this Court have stated the rule as follows: "[A] corporation which exercises actual control over another, operating the latter as a mere instrumentality or tool, is liable for the torts of the corporation thus controlled. In such instances, the separate identities of parent and subsidiary or affiliated corporations may be disregarded." . . .

[The separate identities of corporations will be disregarded under the "instrumentality" rule only if the evidence demonstrates] control, not mere majority or complete stock control, but complete domination, not only of finances, but of policy and business practice in respect to the transaction attacked so that the corporate entity as to this transaction had at the time no separate mind, will or existence of its own. [Two of the factors that are relevant to the question of whether one corporation has completely dominated another are inadequate capitalization of the allegedly dominated corporation and the failure to observe corporate formalities.]

Domination sufficient to pierce the corporate veil need not be limited to the particular transaction attacked. . . . It is sufficient where, as here, one affiliated corporation is dominated by another to the extent that the dominated corporation has no separate mind, will or identity of its own. In this case there was [ample] evidence that from its inception D&S had no separate identity and was never anything other than a tool of B-Bom.

In finding the disregard of corporate entity permissible in this case, we note that the evidence showed that the primary function of D&S was to collect rent for B-Bom and that it was the manner in which D&S, through its agent Smilie Wagner, went about that function that gave rise to the wrong alleged. David Wagner, the president and one of two directors for both B-Bom and D&S, frequently discussed business affairs with Smilie. Indeed, his control over D&S, of which he was the sole subscribing shareholder, was sufficient to allow him unilaterally to dissolve the lease agreement between B-Bom and D&S. In David Wagner's words, "that's like me informing me" that the lease, the only significant asset of D&S, was dissolved. D&S was formed without adherence to corporate formalities, and without adequate capitalization. . . .

Where an affiliated corporation is without a separate and distinct corporate identity and is operated as a mere shell, created to perform a function for an affiliated corporation or its common shareholders, we do not believe an analysis of domination need be narrowly limited to control over the particular transaction attacked—here the padlocking of the rooms at Salem Manor. . . . David Wagner exercised such control over the existence and functioning of D&S that if, as he contended, he were not aware of the actual [wrongful act being challenged], under the instrumentality rule we hold that he, and through him B-Bom, is deemed to have had notice of the transaction. . . .

It should be remembered that the theory of liability under the instrumentality rule is an equitable doctrine. Its purpose is to place the burden of the loss upon the party who should be responsible. Focus is upon reality, not form, upon the operation of the corporation, and upon the defendant's relationship to that operation. It is not the presence or absence of any particular factor that is determinative. Rather, it is a combination of factors which, when taken together with an element of injustice or abuse of corporate privilege, suggest that the corporate entity attacked had "no separate mind, will or existence of its own" and was therefore the "mere instrumentality or tool" of the dominant corporation [or of the dominant shareholder]. . . .

Our rule with regard to piercing the corporate veil is broad enough to encompass both those situations where there is direct stock ownership of a subsidiary corporation by a parent corporation, and stock control as exercised through a mutual shareholder as in the present case. Thus, when there is evidence of common ownership and actual working control, as in the case of affiliated corporations, taken together with other factors suggesting domination of finances, policy or business practice (including, but not limited to undercapitalization, disregard of corporate formalities, and insolvency), [there is enough evidence to support a verdict that the corporate veil should be pierced].

[The decision of the Court of Appeals is reversed, and the trial court's judgment for plaintiff against B-Bom, Inc., is reinstated.]

FORMATION OF THE CORPORATION

Promoters' Activities

For various reasons the word *promoter* sometimes elicits unfavorable reactions from people. The negative connotations of the word are generally unwarranted, though, because promoters usually serve a legitimate and socially useful function. In essence, a **promoter** is the motivating force behind the creation of the corporation. He or she recognizes the business opportunity, analyzes it to determine its economic feasibility, and brings together the necessary resources and personnel.

In planning for the proposed corporation, the promoter often finds it necessary to employ the services of attorneys, accountants, architects, or other professionals. He or she may also have to borrow money or contract for the purchase of real estate, equipment, patent rights, or other property. And in some circumstances the promoter may find it desirable prior to incorporation to contract with persons to serve as officers and employees upon formation of the corporation. Several legal questions can arise in connection with such transactions. For example: Is the promoter personally liable on these contracts? Is the corporation liable once it is formed? What if the corporation is never actually formed? The approach taken by the courts is summarized as follows.

Where Corporation Is Formed and Contract Adopted: If the proposed corporation *is* later formed, it can adopt the promoter's contract and become a party to it. The corporation is not bound unless it adopts the transaction. Assuming that the corporation is formed and does adopt the contract, the question remains whether the promoter is still liable on the contract. If the promoter made the contract in his or her own name, with no reference to the proposed corporation, the promoter obviously continues to be liable unless released by the third party. On the other hand, if the promoter made the contract in the name of, or with reference to, the proposed corporation, there is a split of opinion among the various states: courts in several states have held that the promoter is automatically discharged from responsibility under the contract when the corporation adopts it, but in a majority of states courts have ruled that the promoter continues to be liable unless released by the third party.

Where Corporation Is Not Formed or Contract Not Adopted: If the proposed corporation is not ever formed, or if it is formed but does not adopt the contract, the promoter usually is personally liable on the contract. Under basic principles of contract law, however, the promoter is not liable if (1) the contract expressly provided that the promoter would be discharged from responsibility if the corporation was not formed or did not adopt the contract; (2) the third party later releases the promoter from liability; or (3) the court concludes that the promoter and the third party had originally intended only an informal agreement and that neither of them had intended to be bound unless the corporation ultimately was formed and became a party to the agreement.

Many times two or more promoters are involved. Prior to the actual creation of the corporation these promoters are viewed by the law as being engaged in a *joint venture.* As a result, they maintain the same kind of fiduciary relationship that exists among partners. In their dealings with one another they must exercise the highest standards of honesty and openness.

Once the corporation is formed, the promoters also owe the same type of fiduciary responsibility to the corporation itself and to all interested parties. Complete disclosure must be made, for example, to the board of directors and to all investors (shareholders). Promoters are not allowed to make secret profits on the promotional scheme.

In the two cases that follow, the courts deal with two difficult questions arising from the activities of corporate promoters. In the first case, the issue is whether a promoter is personally liable on a contract made prior to formation of the corporation. In the second, the issue is whether the promoters violated their fiduciary responsibilities to the other shareholders, and if so, whether the promoters' bank had participated in the wrongful conduct so as also to be liable.

Goodman v. Darden, Doman, & Stafford Associates
Supreme Court of Washington, 670 P.2d 648 (1983)

John Goodman sold an apartment building to a partnership, Darden, Doman, & Stafford Associates (DDS) during August of 1979. The apartments needed extensive renovation, and Goodman contracted to perform the renovation for DDS, the work to be completed by October 15. While the renovation contract was being negotiated, Goodman told Don Doman, managing partner of DDS, that Goodman was going to form a corporation to limit his liability. Goodman signed the contract as "Building Design & Development, Inc. (In Formation), John A. Goodman, President." Between August and December 1979, DDS made five progress payments on the contract. The first payment was made to "Building Design & Development Inc.—John Goodman." Goodman struck out his name on the face of the check and endorsed it on the back "Bldg. Design & Dev. Inc., John A. Goodman, Pres." Goodman instructed DDS to make all further payments to the corporation only, which was done. Although Goodman had represented to Doman that Goodman was qualified to do the renovation, immediately after making the contract Goodman got a third party to do the work. On October 15, the work was not completed, and much of what had been done was allegedly of poor quality. On November 1 Goodman filed the articles of incorporation, and on November 2 the certificate bringing the corporation into existence was issued.

DDS then began arbitration proceedings in accordance with a clause in their contract providing that any disputes would be submitted to binding arbitration, and sought to hold Goodman personally liable for breach of the renovation agreement. Goodman filed suit, claiming that he should not be a party to the proceedings, because only the corporation was liable under the contract. The trial court agreed with Goodman that only the corporation was responsible, but the court of appeals reversed. Goodman appealed to the Washington Supreme Court.

Dimmick, Justice:

As a general rule where a corporation is contemplated but has not yet been organized at the time when a promoter makes a contract for the benefit of the contemplated corporation, the promoter is personally liable on it, even though the contract will also benefit the future corporation. There is a strong inference that a person intends to make a present contract with an existing person.

An exception to the general rule is that if the contracting party knew that the corporation was not in existence at the time of contracting but nevertheless agreed to look solely to the corporation for performance, the promoter is not a party to the contract.

As the proponent of the alleged agreement to look solely to the corporation, Goodman has the burden of proving the agreement. As with any agreement, release of the promoter depends on the intent of the parties. The parties did not manifest their intentions in the contract. Goodman argues that the language indicating that the corporation was "in formation" was an expression by the parties of their intent to make the corporation alone a party to the contract. Some courts do look to such language in the contract and contemporaneous documents to determine intent to release the promoter. Those cases and others cited by Goodman do not analyze the agreements in light of a "strong inference" that one intends to contract with an existing party—an inference we must keep in mind. The mere signing of a contract with a corporation "in formation" does not suffice to show an agreement to look solely to the corporation. It simply begs the question to say that such language in a contract with a promoter in and of itself constitutes an agreement to release the promoter from the contract. Rather, the language raises the question of the parties' intent. Given the "strong inference" that DDS intended to contract with an existing party, the "in formation" language drafted by Goodman is at best ambiguous as to the parties' intentions. . . .

We do not believe the agreement to release a promoter from liability must say in so many words, "I agree to release." Where the promoter cannot show an express agreement, existence of the agreement to release him from liability may be shown by circumstances. Of course, where circumstantial evidence is relied on, the circumstances must be such as to make it reasonably certain that the parties intended to and did enter into the agreement.

Goodman cites [two other cases] as similar to this one. The courts in those cases found that the promoter had been released from liability. Among the circumstances considered by those courts was the fact that the parties seeking personal liability on the part of the promoter actually urged that the contract be made in the name of the proposed corporation. DDS did not so urge Goodman or even suggest incorporation to him. . . .

[In the present case,] the trial court relied on three considerations in holding that the parties agreed to release Goodman from the contract: (1) DDS knew of the corporation's nonexistence; (2) Goodman told Doman that he was forming a corporation to limit his personal liability; and (3) the progress payments were made to the corporation.

The fact that DDS knew of the corporation's nonexistence is not dispositive in any way of its intent. . . . The fact that a contracting party knows that the corporation is nonexistent does not indicate any agreement to release the promoter. To the contrary, such knowledge alone would seem to indicate that the members of DDS intended to make Goodman a party to the contract. They could not hold the corporation, a nonexistent entity, responsible and of course they would expect to have recourse against someone (Goodman) if default occurred. This consideration also relates to another factor the trial court apparently had in mind—that the members of DDS were all educated people. Goodman argues that as such they should have expressly requested that he be personally liable. This was unnecessary because under the law as set out above, Goodman was liable until the partners of DDS agreed otherwise. Thus, they were not required to specify personal liability.

The fact that Goodman expressed a desire to form the corporation to limit his liability also is not dispositive of the intentions of the members of DDS. No one from DDS objected to his incorporating, but this failure to object does not indicate an affirmative assent to limit Goodman's personal liability. Apparently Goodman believed that incorporation would automatically limit his liability, thus misunderstanding the rules regarding promoter liability. The Court of Appeals correctly held in this regard: "Even if the expression of desire constituted an offer to make release a term of the contract, silence is acceptance only when there is a duty to speak. DDS had no duty to correct, or even perceive, Goodman's mistaken interpretation of the promoter liability rules."

The only other evidence of the parties' intent to make the corporation the sole party to the contract is that the progress payments were made payable to the corporation. However, they were so written only at the instruction of Goodman and in fact the first check written by DDS after the signing of the contract was written to the corporation and Goodman as an individual. This evidence does not show by reasonable certainty that DDS intended to contract only with the corporation.

[The trial court's finding that DDS had manifested an intent to release Goodman and to hold only the corporation responsible is not supported by the evidence. The judgment of the Court of Appeals is affirmed; the decision of the trial court is reversed.]

First National Bank of Council Bluffs v. One Craig Place, Ltd.
Supreme Court of Iowa, 303 N.W.2d 688 (1981)

Midlands Corporation, a wholly-owned subsidiary of First National Bank of Council Bluffs (the Bank), was in the process of constructing a shopping mall and desired to lease space to tenants. Guy and Diane Craig, husband and wife, decided to open a clothing store in the mall and signed a lease with Midlands for this purpose. Each store premises in the mall was leased in an unfinished condition, and Midlands provided the tenant with an allowance to finish the interior to suit the particular type of store to be operated. Midlands agreed to furnish $57,600 for finishing the premises leased by the Craigs.

The Craigs calculated that a store such as they planned would require about $100,000 capital. They had only $3,000 cash, and a total net worth of about $31,000. They contacted Robert Emerine, senior vice-president of the Bank, who began to serve as their financial

advisor. He helped them complete and file a loan application to the Small Business Administration, but the application was not approved. Realizing that they would not be able to borrow the necessary funds, the Craigs decided to form a corporation with a capitalization of $100,000. The corporation, One Craig Place, Ltd., was formed with the Craigs serving as promoters, officers, and directors. They persuaded four friends, Melvin Kvasnicka, Marvin Seibold, Carmen Craig, and John Williams, to invest $12,000 each—a total of $48,000 for 48,000 shares of stock.

Robert Erskine, who continued to advise the Craigs, then helped them put together a plan for raising the remaining $52,000. The plan consisted of two transactions: (1) In the first transaction, the Craigs paid their $3,000 to the corporation toward the purchase of 52,000 shares of stock. As part of this transaction, the Craigs then assigned their lease to the corporation, so that the $57,600 to be provided by Midlands for finishing the interior of the store was payable to the corporation. In behalf of the corporation, the Craigs agreed that $49,000 out of the $57,600 to be received from Midlands would be treated as payment by the Craigs for the remainder of their 52,000 shares of stock. (2) In the second transaction, the Bank (through Emerine) lent $49,000 *to the corporation* (not to the Craigs personally). In return for this loan, the Bank received a promissory note from the corporation, a security interest in all of the corporation's assets, an assignment from the corporation of the lease on the store premises, and a personal guaranty from the Craigs coupled with a security interest in all of the Craigs' personal assets.

As a result of these transactions, $100,000 ostensibly was paid to the corporation for 100,000 shares of stock, and the four minority shareholders thought that this was the case. In actuality, however, only the minority shareholders' $48,000 and the Craigs' $3,000 was paid to the corporation, because the remainder was offset by the corporation's secured $49,000 note to the bank.

During its first three months of operation the store did very little business, and was not able to meet its heavy rental obligation to Midlands or its other expenses. The four minority shareholders and Guy Craig each lent $5,000 to the corporation in return for the corporation's unsecured promissory notes, and the Craigs used this money to make back rental payments to Midlands. During the next two months the business fell further into debt, and the Craigs again called on the four minority shareholders. One of them, Williams, dropped out. The Bank lent the corporation an additional $36,000, the corporation gave the Bank another promissory note for $36,000, and the three remaining minority shareholders signed written guaranties of the note in the amount of $12,000 each. These three shareholders were not aware of the corporation's $49,000 obligation to the Bank and, consequently, thought the store's inventory and other assets were sufficient to justify the extension of further credit.

The store continued to lose money, the notes to the bank became due, and the three minority shareholders learned for the first time about the way the Craigs had financed their purchase of 52,000 shares of stock. Without the knowledge of the three minority shareholders, the Craigs, the Bank, and Midlands executed an agreement to close the business and liquidate its assets. The proceeds from the sale of the corporation's assets, and from foreclosure of a second mortgage on the Craigs' home, were paid to Midlands for back rent and to the Bank in partial satisfaction of the $49,000 note. The Bank then attempted to enforce the guaranties that had been executed by the three minority shareholders on the $36,000 note. They refused to pay, and the Bank filed suit against them, the Craigs, and the corporation. The trial court gave judgment for the Bank against the minority shareholders enforcing their guaranties and ordering them to pay the Bank $12,000 each plus interest. They appealed to the Iowa Supreme Court.

Uhlenhopp, Justice:

If the Bank's instruments are taken at face value, the judgment must be affirmed. The notes for $49,000 and $36,000 are signed for the corporation by its officers; and the guaranties of the three remaining minority stockholders, guaranteeing the corporation's $36,000 note and its other debts to the Bank to a limit of $12,000 each, are signed by those stockholders. . . . But the case goes deeper than that. It is the not uncommon case of corporation promoters who are long on hope but short on funds.

The Craigs were the promoters of this corporation. They obtained 52,000 shares of its stock. In obtaining that stock, what was their duty as promoters toward the other prospective stockholders? . . . As promoters [the Craigs] stood in a fiduciary relation to the company to be organized, and to those who should subscribe for its stock. As such they were bound to act in good faith and to deal with them in perfect candor. . . . The promoter of a company, like its directors, is bound to disclose to them fully all material facts touching his relation to them. . . . The corporate entity and the stockholders, in particular, may presume that these promoters will perform their duties with the diligence, honesty and the utmost good faith, inherent and implicit in their functions. They are not required to be ever on their guard and watchful lest those trustees misapply, destroy, steal the corporate assets, or defraud them. . . .

The understanding of the Craigs and the minority stockholders was that the corporation would have $100,000 capital, of which the minority stockholders would provide $48,000 and the Craigs would provide $52,000, and that the Craigs would borrow if necessary to obtain their shares.

In addition, a statute intervenes at this point. The corporation was formed under Chapter 496A of the Iowa Code. Section 496A.22 provides in part: "No certificate shall be issued for any share until such share is fully paid." . . . The Craigs did not comply with the parties' understanding or with the statute. They paid the corporation only $3,000 in money. They purported to pay the remaining $49,000 in two ways. One was by assigning the lease to the corporation [and treating the payment for finishing as a capital contribution]. But the lease is not shown to have had any value in excess of the rent reserved, even considering the clause for finishing the building. No attempt was made to show that the amount of rent to be paid was a bargain for the tenant. Actually, the substantial rent was one of the factors that drove the business to the wall. . . .

A sound argument cannot be constructed that the landlord's commitment to finish the store building for occupancy by the tenant, by the device of paying the contractor through the tenant, constituted a contribution of equity capital to the corporation. Landlords frequently remodel or complete [leased] premises for tenants. This is not a gift to the tenant or a payment for stock issued by a corporate tenant. The expectation is that the landlord will recover its investment in rent, or perhaps partially in the improvements themselves on termination of the lease, plus a return on its money. The landlord's funds to remodel or finish a building for a tenant do not provide a corporate tenant with uncommitted funds for capital. . . . The landlord here invested in its own property, not in the corporation. . . . The landlord's finishing of its own building for occupancy did not fulfill the Craigs' obligation to provide the corporation with capital of $49,000.

Neither did the second way the Craigs purported to pay for their stock actually accomplish that end—the Bank's loan to the corporation of $49,000. Had that loan been to the Craigs, and had the Craigs then paid the corporation $49,000, they would have paid for their stock. But the corporation actually paid for its own stock it issued to the Craigs. The corporation was the primary obligor which would repay the note; the Craigs' guaranty of the note did not mean that they paid $49,000. . . .

What are the consequences of the Craigs' breach of fiduciary duty? The minority stockholders assert that they are not liable on the Bank's $49,000 note and that the proceeds of liquidation must be applied on the note for $36,000, relieving them of liability. . . .

As between the corporation and minority stockholders, on the one hand, and the Craigs, on the other, the note for $49,000 to the Bank is a nullity because it was made in violation of the Craigs' fiduciary obligation and is contrary to public policy.

What then is the situation as between the corporation and minority stockholders, on the one hand, and the Bank, on the other? If the Bank participated in the Craigs' breach of trust, it likewise stands responsible for the consequences. . . . We are convinced from the record that Emerine himself, senior vice president of the Bank and of long experience in banking, knew that the loan of $49,000 to the corporation was for the Craigs' stock. In addition to the testimony to this effect, the evidence shows that Emerine knew the background and development of this financing running back to the SBA loan application. He knew that the Craigs had only $3,000 in money. The loan he made of $49,000 was the exact amount the Craigs needed above their own $3,000 to acquire their 52,000 shares. Emerine verified that the other stockholders' money had actually been paid in before he made the loan. He made the loan to the corporation, not to the Craigs as principals, and participated with his eyes open in the Craigs' breach of trust. As between the corporation and minority stockholders on the one side, and the Bank, on the other, the note for $49,000 is a nullity.

The note of $49,000 resulted from a breach of trust in which the Bank took part. The court will not enforce the note, and the Bank can have nothing on account of it. The entire fund which the Bank received from the liquidation, the second-mortgage foreclosure, and checking account, together with interest . . . is to be applied, first, upon the note of $36,000. . . . Second, any surplus is to be applied pro rata upon the corporation's other indebtedness excluding the note for $49,000. . . . The minority stockholders are discharged from any liability. . . .

Reversed and remanded.

Incorporation

The word **incorporation** refers to the procedural mechanics of forming a corporation. Although the details of these procedures differ from state to state, substantial similarity exists with respect to their basic outline.

Articles of Incorporation: The first step in the formative process is preparation of **articles of incorporation,** a legal document that should be prepared by an attorney and that must be signed by the **incorporators.** A few states require the signature of only one incorporator, but most states follow the traditional requirement of three signatures. The incorporators are those individuals who *technically* apply to the state for incorporation. They must be adults, but they need not have any interest in the business enterprise itself. Often they are the persons actually forming the corporation, but they can be completely disinterested parties (such as secretaries in the office of the attorney who is preparing the articles).

The following is a summary of those matters which generally should be included in the articles of incorporation.

1. *The name of the corporation:* This name cannot be the same as, or deceptively similar to, that of any other corporation legally doing business within the state.

2. *The duration of the corporation:* In most states this can be perpetual. And in the few states that do place limitations on the number of years a corporation can exist, it is usually only a formality to renew the corporation's existence on expiration of the stated time period.

3. *The purpose or purposes for which the corporation is organized:* While most states allow the formation of a business corporation for any lawful purpose, a few still prohibit corporations from practicing medicine, law, or other professions. Also, many states do not allow banks, loan companies, insurance companies, public utilities, or railroads to be formed under the general incorporation statutes. These types of businesses are often required to incorporate under other, specialized statutes.

4. *The financial structure of the corporation:* Detailed information must usually be included about the methods by which the corporation will raise capital needed for its operations.

5. *Provisions for regulating the internal affairs of the corporation:* Examples of such provisions are the location of shareholders' meetings, quorum and voting requirements at shareholders' and board of directors' meetings, removal of directors, and filling director vacancies.

6. *The address of the corporation's registered office and the name of its registered agent at this address:* The registered office is simply the corporation's official office in the state, and the registered agent is its official representative. The purpose of requiring a corporation to have a registered office and registered agent is to insure that there will be an easily identifiable place and person for the receipt by the corporation of summonses, subpoenas, and other legal documents.

7. *Information relating to the first board of directors of the corporation:* The board of directors is the group of individuals who manage the affairs of the corporation. The number of directors constituting the initial board must be indicated in the articles. Additionally, the articles usually must include the names and addresses of those individuals who will serve as directors until the first annual shareholders' meeting or until another board of directors is otherwise selected.

8. *The name and address of each incorporator.*

Certificate of Incorporation: The articles of incorporation must be filed with the designated state official (usually the secretary of state). If they are in conformance with all legal requirements and if all required fees are paid, the state official will issue a **certificate of incorporation** (sometimes called a **charter**). This certificate represents the permission given by the state to conduct business in the corporate form. The corporation comes into existence when the certificate of incorporation is issued. After issuance, the certificate and an attached copy of the articles of incorporation are returned to the incorporators or their representatives.

Initial Organization: Under the laws of most states, the incorporators must hold an *organizational meeting* after issuance of the charter. In states where the first board of directors is not named in the articles of incorporation, the incorporators elect the directors at this meeting. In all states, authorization will usually be given to the board of directors to issue shares of stock. Perhaps the most important purpose of the meeting, however, is to adopt bylaws.[1]

Bylaws are the rules or "private laws" that regulate and govern the actions and affairs of the corporation. Although they ordinarily are *not* filed with a state official, the bylaws must not conflict in any way with the provisions of the articles of incorporation. The relationship between the articles and the bylaws is analogous to the relationship between the constitution and the statutes of a state. A corporation's bylaws sometimes amount to only a brief statement of rules for internal management of the corporation. Often, however, the bylaws are extremely detailed, sometimes even including a restatement of applicable statutes as well as provisions from the articles of incorporation. As an example of the type of details frequently included in the bylaws, many provisions relate to the specifics of conducting directors' and shareholders' meetings.

The board of directors also holds an organizational meeting, at which time it transacts whatever business is necessary to launch the operations of the enterprise. In some states the incorporators do *not* hold an organizational meeting, and in these states the board of directors adopts bylaws and performs the other tasks described earlier as functions of the incorporators. In the states in which incorporators *do* meet, the directors at their initial meeting usually approve all actions taken by the incorporators. In addition, the agenda of the first directors' meeting includes such matters as approval of the corporate seal, election of corporate officers, adoption of preincorporation agreements made by the promoters, selection of a bank for depositing corporate funds, and other pertinent items of business. Figure 36.1 outlines the steps in forming the corporation.

---

[1] In some states, however, formulation of the initial bylaws is a function of the shareholders, and in others it is a function of the board of directors.

Figure 36.1   Basic Steps in Forming a Corporation

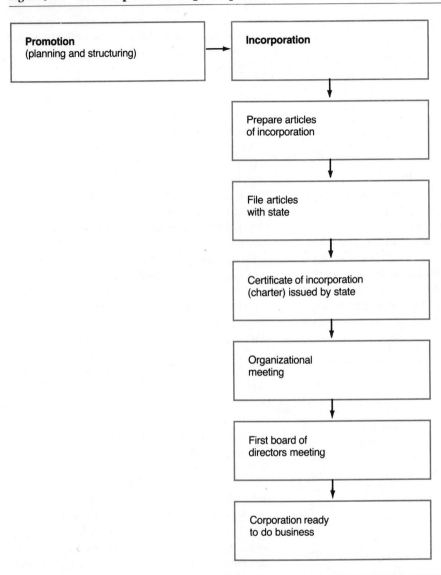

Effect of Improper Incorporation Procedures

If all requirements for incorporation have been followed to the letter, it is said that a *de jure* corporation exists. The existence of such a cor-

poration cannot be challenged by either the state or any other party so long as the corporation acts lawfully in the conduct of its business.

Occasionally there occurs some deviation from the procedures required for incorporation.

can file suit in state

If the deviation is relatively insignificant (in other words, if there is "substantial compliance" with procedures) and if no harm to the public interest results, the corporation still has *de jure* status. (An example of such an inconsequential procedural defect is a mistake in the address of one of the incorporators in the articles of incorporation.)

On the other hand, the defect may be sufficiently important that there is not substantial compliance with mandatory incorporation procedures. In such a case, there will not be a *de jure* corporation. There might, however, be what is commonly referred to as a **de facto corporation.** If the corporation has *de facto* status, the *state* can challenge the validity of its existence, but no other party can do so. (If it has neither *de jure* nor *de facto* status, the validity of its existence can be challenged by the state or by any other interested party, such as a creditor seeking to hold a shareholder personally liable for a corporate debt.) The requirements for the existence of a *de facto* corporation are:

[handwritten margin note: illegal Corp. can't file suit in state]

1. There must be a state statute under which the corporation could have been validly incorporated.

2. There must have been a genuine, good-faith attempt by the incorporators to follow statutory requirements.

3. There must have been some type of business transacted by the enterprise *as a corporation.*

Historically, issues relating to *de facto* corporations have not arisen very frequently, and the importance of the concept in actual practice appears to be further diminishing.

Even if a corporation has neither *de jure* nor *de facto* status, particular situations exist where a party can be estopped (prohibited) from denying the validity of its existence. If, for example, the individuals operating a business represent their enterprise as being a corporation, they can be estopped from denying the corporate status in a particular lawsuit. (This concept is often denoted by the phrase *corporation by estoppel.*)

Doing Business in Other States

A corporation that has been incorporated in one state may wish to do business in other states as well. Before doing so, the corporation must apply for and receive a **certificate of authority** in each state where it plans to do business. The process of obtaining the certificate is largely a formality, and the initial steps in applying for it often are taken at the organizational meeting of the board of directors. However, the corporation is also usually required to maintain a registered office and registered agent in each state where it does business.

The penalties levied by various states against foreign corporations that have not obtained a certificate of authority include fines, denial of the privilege of filing lawsuits in the courts of that state, and placement of personal liability for corporate obligations incurred in that state on the directors, officers, or agents involved.

Financing the Corporation

After incorporation, the corporation must obtain the funds necessary to launch and initially operate the business. When the business has been in operation for a substantial period of time, a wider range of financing alternatives are available, including retained earnings, short-term borrowing, and accounts receivable financing. At the beginning, however, fewer alternatives exist.

The principal method of initially financing a corporation is by the issuance of **securities,** which are sold to investors. The board of directors usually authorizes their issuance during its initial organizational meeting. The most common types are equity securities and debt securities.

Equity securities are usually referred to as **shares of capital stock,** or simply as *shares.* Each share represents an interest in the ownership of the corporation. Therefore, the investors who purchase them (the **shareholders** or **stockholders**) are the owners of the corporation. (More is said about the various types of shares in Chapter 38.)

Debt securities are usually referred to as **bonds.** Corporate bonds do not represent ownership interests in the corporation, but are loans to the corporation from the investors who purchase them. The relationship between the investor who purchases bonds and the corporation which issues them is that of creditor and debtor.

Registration of Securities

When a corporation issues securities to meet either its initial capital requirements or its later financial needs, it usually must comply with the securities laws of those states in which they are offered for sale.[2] The laws of some states simply prohibit fraud in the sale of securities. In many states, however, the issue of securities must be *registered* with the state agency empowered to administer the law. To register, the corporation must supply extremely detailed financial and other information about itself. These state agencies commonly have broad discretionary powers to pass judgment on the merits of a particular issue of securities—even to forbid such issuance—and penalties for failing to register with them can be quite severe.[3]

Many issues of securities, such as those sold in interstate commerce or through the mails, must also be registered under the **Securities Act of 1933,** a federal law. Here again, detailed financial and other information must be supplied. This information must be given both to the appropriate federal agency—the **Securities and Exchange Commission (SEC)**—and to the persons to whom the securities are offered for sale. The SEC does not pass judgment on the merits of a particular issue of securities but attempts only

to insure full and complete disclosure of relevant information. The underlying rationale is that the light of publicity will serve to deter misconduct in the sale of securities. Under the Securities Act of 1933, failing to register or willfully making false statements in the registration is punishable by a fine of up to $10,000 and/or imprisonment of up to five years. Civil actions for damages can also be brought by injured private parties.

The purpose of both state and federal securities laws is protection of the investing public. Although compliance with these laws is costly and time-consuming, failure to comply can be even more costly. What is more, the protection afforded by these laws benefits not only the investors but also the corporations themselves by encouraging investment in corporate enterprises.

Securities laws are discussed in depth in Chapter 50, "Securities Regulation."

SUMMARY

The concept of the corporation is of ancient origin, dating to the twenty-first century B.C. in Babylonian law. The famous overseas trading companies of the sixteenth and seventeenth century became the models for modern corporations. American corporation law today is found primarily in state statutes and the judicial interpretations of those statutes, although federal securities regulation law also plays an important role.

The most important characteristic of the corporation is its status as a legal entity with an identity separate from that of its owners and managers. In most situations the separateness of the corporate identity is recognized, but in unusual circumstances courts will disregard the corporate entity, or "pierce the corporate veil," in order to prevent the separateness of the corporation from being used as a mere tool to perpetrate fraud.

The promoter serves as the motivating force for the identification of a business opportunity, the marshalling of resources to exploit the op-

---

[2] These state laws are often referred to as *blue-sky laws,* because they are largely antifraud statutes intended to prevent the sale of worthless securities ("pieces of the blue sky").

[3] For example, the sale of unregistered securities in the state of Texas is a felony punishable by a fine of up to $10,000 and/or imprisonment for up to ten years.

portunity, and the formation of the corporation as an operating format. The corporation, once formed, is liable for the promoter's preincorporation contracts only if the corporation adopts them. The promoter usually is liable on such contracts even if the corporation is later formed and adopts them. When two or more promoters act together, they are viewed prior to formation of the corporation as participants in a joint venture, and owe fiduciary duties to each other. A promoter also owes fiduciary duties to the corporation and its shareholders when the corporation is formed.

The actual procedure of forming a corporation is referred to as *incorporation*, and must strictly follow the statutory requirements of the state in which it is registered. The most important means for obtaining a corporation's necessary financing is the issuance of securities. The two most important types of securities are equity securities and debt securities. Equity securities are commonly called shares of capital stock. The purchasers of these securities, shareholders, are the owners of the corporation. Debt securities are commonly called bonds. The purchasers of these securities are creditors rather than owners of the corporation. New issues of securities usually must be registered with federal and state government agencies.

KEY TERMS

Domestic corporation
Foreign corporation
Private corporation
Government corporation
Business corporation
Nonprofit corporation
Publicly held corporation
Close corporation
Professional corporation
Piercing the corporate veil
Parent corporation
Subsidiary corporation
Promoter
Incorporation

Articles of incorporation
Incorporators
Certificate of incorporation (charter)
Bylaws
De jure **corporation**
De facto **corporation**
Certificate of authority
Securities
Equity securities
Shares of capital stock
Shareholders (stockholders)
Debt securities
Bonds
Securities Act of 1933
Securities and Exchange Commission (SEC)

QUESTIONS AND PROBLEMS

1. Progress Tailoring Co. advertised that it manufactured garments, although these garments actually were manufactured by its wholly owned subsidiary. The Federal Trade Commission instituted proceedings in which it sought to stop such advertising on the ground that it was deceptive. Did the FTC prevail? Discuss. (*Progress Tailoring Co. v. FTC*, 153 F.2d 103, 1946.)

2. A federal statute prohibited railroads from giving rebates to those using the railroad for shipping goods. X Corp. shipped substantial quantities of goods by rail. The officers and principal shareholders of X Corp. formed a separate corporation for the purpose of obtaining what were, in actuality, rebates. Did X Corp. violate the antirebate law by receiving rebates through the separate corporation? Explain.

3. Discuss why a nonprofit organization such as a church, fraternal club, or hospital might want to incorporate.

4. Boss, a promoter, signed a contract for architectural services as "agent for a Minnesota corporation to be formed which will be the obligor." The architectural drawings were prepared, but the proposed corporation was never formed, and the architects sued Boss for their fee. Will the architects recover from Boss? Discuss. (*Stanley J. How & Associates v. Boss,* 222 F.Supp. 936, 1963.)

5. Acting in his own behalf and not in behalf of any proposed corporation, Caparella purchased equipment subject to a debt, used it, then turned it over to a subsequently created corporation, of which he became president. The creditor sent bills to the corporation, but the corporation never responded. The creditor then sued the corporation. Will the creditor prevail? Explain.

6. Under what types of circumstances might it be useful to use "dummy" incorporators (those having no real interest in the corporation to be formed)?

7. Baum Holding Co. was formed in Nebraska in 1922, when there was no state statute authorizing the formation of holding companies (corporations whose operations consist only of the ownership of interests in other corporations). In 1941, a holding companies statute was enacted, but the company made no attempt to comply with its provisions. Sometime thereafter, several shareholders who were dissatisfied with the way the company was being run filed suit challenging the validity of the corporation's existence. Should they prevail? Discuss. (*Baum v. Baum Holding Co.*, 62 N.W.2d 864, 1954.)

8. Plaintiff entered the "corporation's" building on business and fell into an unlit, unguarded elevator shaft. Although the organizers of the "corporation" had filed its articles before the accident, no arrangements had been made for the issuance of shares of stock, no meeting of shareholders had been held, officers had not been elected, and the corporation had not done any business as a corporation. The plaintiff sued the individual organizers for his injuries. Should he recover? Explain.

9. What is a major difference between the authority of the SEC and the authority of many state securities agencies?

Chapter 37

CORPORATIONS
Corporate Powers
and Management

CORPORATE POWERS

As an "artificial person," a corporation possesses the power to do most of the things an individual can do in the operation of a business enterprise, such as own property, make contracts, borrow money, and hire employees. Corporate powers derive from several sources, traditionally classified as statutory, express, and implied powers. State corporation laws ordinarily contain a list of **statutory powers**—those activities in which corporations are permitted to engage. **Express powers** are those set forth in the articles of incorporation. The articles frequently restate the powers granted by the statutes of their jurisdiction and then enumerate other powers specifically related to the corporation's business. Of course, the powers stated in the articles must not conflict with the statutory powers, but this rarely happens, because most of the statutes are drafted in a rather broad fashion. With some exceptions, a corporation also has **implied powers** to do any other things reasonably necessary for carrying on its business. These powers simply serve to fill in gaps that exist in the statutory and express powers.

Problem Areas

Rather than discuss in detail all the various powers possessed by corporations, we will begin with the general notion that a corporation can do just about everything an individual can do in operating a business, and we will proceed to examine a few of the problem areas with respect to these powers.

Lending Corporate Funds: A corporation generally has implied power to make use of idle funds by lending them and charging interest. It also has the power to lend funds or extend credit (with or without interest) to customers or to other corporations in which it owns shares or with which it has contractual relations. But when no such relationship exists, the corporation does *not* have the implied power to cosign or guarantee the obligations of others merely as an *accommodation* to them (that is, with no value received in return)—although this power can be expressly provided for in the articles of incorporation. Additionally, the statutes of a significant number of states prohibit corporations from making loans to their directors or officers.

Charitable Contributions: In early cases, courts generally held that corporations did not have implied power to make contributions to charity. Their reasoning was that since the primary purpose of business corporations is to make profits, gifts could be made only if expressly authorized by the corporation's articles. This older view has undergone radical change, however, both by statute and by more recent court decisions. As a result, the general rule today is that corporations do possess implied power to make charitable contributions.

Joining a Partnership: Traditionally, a corporation did not have the power to become a member of a partnership. It was felt by the courts that allowing a corporation to become a partner would effectively delegate to the other partners a degree of control over corporate affairs that should be exercised only by duly elected directors. The courts not only refused to recognize the joining of a partnership as an implied power, but in many cases (though not all) they refused to recognize such power even if it was expressly granted in the articles of incorporation. Curiously (and illogically) the courts usually did permit a corporation to become a member of a joint venture. The modern trend, however, is to empower corporations to join partnerships. This trend is observable in numerous recent changes in state corporation statutes.

Torts and Crimes: A corporation obviously has power to act only through human agents and servants. Like any other employer, it is liable for the torts of its servants committed in the scope of their employment. In some situations, corporations also are responsible for the *criminal acts* of their subordinates.[1] Corporate criminal liability may exist, for example, in the following situations:

1. The illegal act is committed by an officer or other high-ranking managerial employee.

2. The illegal act is authorized or ratified by the board of directors or by vote of the stockholders.

3. The particular crime does not require proof of criminal intent, such as engaging in an activity without a required license.

4. The statute defining the criminal offense provides specifically for corporate responsibility or for responsibility by employers in general. For example, the federal antitrust laws provide expressly for the imposition of criminal penalties on corporations.

The *Ultra Vires* Doctrine ✓

A corporation is organized for particular purposes. An important principle in the area of corporate powers is that *a corporation is empowered to act only insofar as is necessary to further the purposes for which it was organized.* All that has been said regarding corporate powers must be qualified by this principle. Thus even such ordinary powers as making contracts and owning property can be exercised only within the limits of a corporation's expressed purposes.

Any act by a corporation that is beyond the scope of its business as defined in the articles of incorporation is said to be *ultra vires*.[2] Many of the cases in which the *ultra vires* doctrine has been at issue have involved corporate contracts made for unauthorized purposes. The treatment

② goes beyond its authorized purposes

---

[1] A corporation obviously cannot be imprisoned, but it can be fined or dissolved. And, of course, those *individuals* who actually commit the crime are also subject to criminal penalties, including imprisonment when appropriate.

[2] *Ultra vires* acts should not be confused with illegal ones. All illegal corporate acts are inherently *ultra vires;* but not all *ultra vires* acts are illegal. In fact, most are not illegal but are merely beyond the scope of corporate powers.

accorded *ultra vires* contracts by the courts is summarized below.

1. In past years, some courts treated *ultra vires* contracts as absolutely void, with no rights or duties created on either side.

2. Most courts, however, did not apply an absolute rule of invalidity to *ultra vires* contracts unless they were illegal as well. Where the contracts were merely *ultra vires* but not otherwise illegal, these courts varied their treatment according to how far performance had progressed. For example, a fully executed *ultra vires* contract, where both parties had completely performed, was treated as valid and left undisturbed. On the other hand, where the contract was entirely executory, neither party having performed, the *ultra vires* nature of the agreement could be raised by either party; and this defense would prevent enforcement of the contract. Where the contract was partially executed, it would be enforceable under some circumstances. (For example, where one party had received benefits under the contract, that party would be estopped from asserting the defense of *ultra vires.*)

3. Although some courts still take the approach discussed in item 2, a majority of states have passed statutes in recent years greatly diminishing the significance of the *ultra vires* doctrine. Most of these statutes follow the lead of the Model Act, which abolishes *ultra vires* as a contractual defense. In other words, in these states the *ultra vires* nature of the contract does not affect its validity as far as the parties themselves are concerned. However, other legal consequences continue to ensue from an *ultra vires* contract, including (a) a suit by shareholders for an injunction to prevent performance where it has not yet taken place, (b) a suit by the corporation itself or by shareholders acting in its behalf to recover damages from the directors and officers responsible for the action, and (c) a suit by the state either for an injunction or for dissolution of the corporation.

The diminishing importance of the *ultra vires* doctrine can be observed in other ways as well. For example, corporate attorneys have become increasingly adept at including within the statement of purpose in the articles of incorporation all remotely conceivable activities. This ordinarily is more convenient than amending the articles at a later time. In addition, several states have changed their corporation laws so as to permit incorporation for "any lawful purpose," with no requirement that the articles state specific purposes.

CORPORATE MANAGEMENT

When one speaks of corporate "management" one is usually referring to the board of directors, officers, and managerial employees who oversee the details of corporate operation. Although shareholders generally do not take part in the daily running of the corporation, they do, as owners, have ultimate control over its policies.

The structure of corporate control can be viewed as pyramidal in nature, the shareholders forming the broad base of the pyramid. The shareholders exercise their control, for the most part, by selecting the individuals who serve on the board of directors. The board, in turn, usually selects corporate officers and other managerial employees at the top of the pyramid.

Shareholders' Functions ✓

The power to control the details of daily corporate operation resides with the board of directors, which often delegates much of the responsibility to officers and other employees. In most situations, the remedy for shareholder dissatisfaction with the manner in which corporate affairs are being handled is to elect a new board of directors. The most important shareholder functions are (1) election and removal of directors, (2) amendment of articles and bylaws, and (3) approval of certain extraordinary corporate matters.

✓Election and Removal of Directors: ✓ Although the initial board of directors is either named in the articles of incorporation or selected by the incorporators, its term ordinarily extends only until the first meeting of shareholders. The selection of directors then becomes a shareholder function.

Except for death or resignation, a director usually serves until the expiration of his or her term of office, and frequently is reelected to one or more subsequent terms. However, shareholders have always had the inherent power to remove directors at any time *for cause* (fraud, misconduct, neglect of duties, and so on)—subject, of course, to court review. On the other hand, the traditional common-law rule was that a director could not be removed *without cause* during his or her term unless the shareholders had expressly reserved that right at the time of election. Today, however, this rule has been changed by statute in a majority of states to permit shareholders to remove directors at any time *with or without cause.* Removal of a director in either case is accomplished by majority vote. However, if "cumulative voting" was used to elect the director, removing him or her may be somewhat more difficult. The concept of cumulative voting and its effects will be discussed shortly.

Amendment of Articles and Bylaws: Shareholders have the power to amend the articles of incorporation. Of course, since the corporation's articles must be filed with the secretary of state, any later amendments must also be filed.

In different states the bylaws are initially adopted by either the incorporators, the directors, or the shareholders. But regardless of which body possesses the power of original adoption, the shareholders are empowered to amend or even repeal them subsequently.

In many jurisdictions the directors have the power to amend or repeal the bylaws, but this power is really subordinate in nature. In other words, even when the directors are given such authority by statute, by the articles, or by the bylaws themselves, the ultimate power rests with the shareholders. Because they possess an inherent power with respect to bylaws, they can override the directors' actions even if such actions were authorized.

Approval of Extraordinary Corporate Matters: Although the authority to conduct most corporate affairs is held by the directors, certain matters are of such an unusual nature as to require shareholder approval. This approval is ordinarily given in the form of a "resolution" voted on at a shareholders' meeting. Extraordinary matters requiring shareholder approval include (1) sale or lease of corporate assets *not* in the regular course of the corporation's business, and (2) merger, consolidation, or dissolution of the corporation.[3]

Exercise of Shareholders' Functions ✓

Shareholders as such are not agents of the corporation and therefore cannot bind the corporation by acting *individually;* their powers must be exercised *collectively.* The most common vehicle for the exercise of shareholder functions is the *shareholders' meeting.* In recent years, however, most states have amended their corporation laws to allow shareholders to take action by *written consent.* This consent must ordinarily be signed by all shareholders entitled to vote on the matter.[4] But the shareholders' meeting still remains the most common forum for shareholder action.

Types of Meetings: Shareholders' meetings are either *annual* or *special.* Corporations are usually required by state law to hold annual meetings; the most important item of business at these meetings is usually the election of some or all of the directors. Between annual meetings, special meetings may be called to transact business that cannot or should not wait until the next annual meeting.

Time and Place of Meetings: The time of annual meetings and the place for annual and special meetings may be set forth in the articles, but they are more commonly found in the bylaws. Most annual meetings are held in the spring. Older statutes often required shareholders' meetings to be held in the state of incorporation, but this generally is no longer a requirement.

Notice of Meetings: State laws usually require written notice of any shareholders' meeting to be sent to each shareholder a reasonable time prior to the meeting, although shareholders can waive this requirement by signing a waiver before or after the meeting. In some instances a shareholder's *conduct* may constitute a waiver of notice. For example, where a shareholder receives no formal notice but knows of the meeting and attends without protesting the lack of notice, he or she waives the requirement of notice.

The notice generally must state the place, day, and hour of the meeting; and in the case of a special meeting, the notice must state the purpose or purposes for which the meeting is being called. The business transacted at a special meeting must be limited to the purposes set forth in the notice.

✓**Quorum:** Before action can validly be taken at a shareholders' meeting, a **quorum** must be present. Quorum requirements are expressed in terms of either a specific portion of outstanding shares or a specific portion of shares entitled to vote. These requirements are usually set forth in the articles or the bylaws within limits defined by state statute. As an example, the Model Act allows the articles of incorporation to set the quorum requirement so long as it is not less than one-third of all outstanding shares. The Model

---

[3] Mergers, consolidations, and dissolutions are discussed in Chapter 39.

[4] A few states allow shareholder action by a less-than-unanimous written consent.

Act further provides that, if the articles are silent on the matter, a majority of outstanding shares constitutes a quorum.

√ **Voting:**   Action at a shareholders' meeting is taken by voting. The number of votes a shareholder has is determined by the number of shares he or she owns. Assuming that a quorum is present, the majority vote of the *shares represented at the meeting* (not the shares outstanding or entitled to vote) is usually sufficient for ordinary matters. More than a majority is sometimes required by state law or by the articles or bylaws for certain unusual matters such as mergers or consolidations. When a greater-than-majority vote is required, it is usually expressed in terms of all shares entitled to vote, not just those represented at the meeting.

State laws frequently require that a corporation keep a record of all its shareholders, listing their names and addresses as well as the number and type of shares held by each. Usually corporations are also required to prepare a *voting list* (a list of shareholders who can vote and the number of votes each is entitled to) prior to each shareholders' meeting. The record of shareholders and the voting list must be kept at a designated place (such as the principal corporate office) and must be available for inspection by shareholders.

Impartial individuals referred to as *tellers* (or sometimes as *judges* or *inspectors*) are usually present to supervise elections at shareholders' meetings. Although tellers are not generally required by law, many state statutes do require them if a shareholder so requests or if they are called for in the bylaws.

√ **Methods for Concentrating Voting Power:** Several methods exist by which a shareholder who owns a relatively small portion of the corporation's shares can increase his or her voting power.

√ *Cumulative Voting:*   Practically every state provides for **cumulative voting** by shareholders. A few states *require* it, but most merely *permit* it if the articles of incorporation provide for it. Cumulative voting applies only to the *election of directors,* and it is designed to increase the likelihood of minority representation on the board. (*Minority* refers to the owner[s] of a less-than-controlling number of shares, not to an ethnic minority.) The following example illustrates the mechanics of cumulative voting: J is the owner of a hundred shares of stock in Gemini Corp. At the annual shareholders' meeting, three directors are to be elected. The slate of candidates includes A, B, C, D, E, and F. J wants to elect A, B, and C, or at least one of them. If "straight" voting is used, J can cast a hundred votes each for A, B, and C (that is, one vote per share for each directorship to be filled). But if cumulative voting is allowed, J can take the total three hundred votes that he is entitled to cast at the election and cast them *all* in favor of A or divide them in any manner he wishes.

We previously mentioned that a director may be removed from office by majority vote. This is true if the director is being removed *for cause,* even though he may have been elected by minority interests through cumulative voting. However, if a corporation uses cumulative voting and if the attempted removal is *without cause,* a director cannot be removed from office if the vote *against removal* would be sufficient to elect that director by cumulative voting.

Shareholder Agreements: Agreements in which a group of shareholders decide prior to a meeting to cast their votes in certain ways are sometimes employed to concentrate voting power. These agreements are usually valid and enforceable.

√ *Voting Trusts:*   Another method of concentrating voting power is the **voting trust.** This is formed by an agreement in which the "record ownership" of shares is transferred to trustees whose sole function is to vote the shares. "Voting trust certificates" are given by the trustees to the original shareholders, entitling them to all rights of share ownership other than voting rights.

Proxies: Shareholders can vote their shares at a meeting either in person or by proxy. A **proxy** is simply a signed, written document authorizing a person present at the meeting to vote the shares of a shareholder. Proxies (which create an agency relationship) are useful both to alleviate problems of distance between a shareholder's residence and the site of a meeting and to concentrate voting power. For example, one person might solicit and accumulate proxies au-

thorizing him or her to vote in behalf of a number of shareholders. Proxies are usually solicited by corporate managers prior to each shareholder's meeting. (More is said later, particularly in Chapter 38, about the duties of one who solicits proxies.)

The two following cases involve challenges to the procedures followed in connection with shareholders' meetings. In the first case the challenge was raised *before* the meeting took place. In the second case the challenge was raised *after* the meeting, and the court scrutinized the action that had been taken at the meeting.

Campbell v. Loew's, Inc.
Court of Chancery of Delaware, 134 A.2d 852 (1957)

Two factions were fighting for control of Loew's. One faction was headed by Joseph Tomlinson (the "Tomlinson faction"), the other by the president of Loew's, Joseph Vogel (the "Vogel faction"). At the annual shareholders' meeting in February 1957 a compromise was reached by which each faction nominated six directors, who in turn nominated a thirteenth, neutral director. But the battle had only begun. After several more months of controversy, on July 17 and 18, two of the six Vogel directors and the neutral director resigned.

On July 19 the Tomlinson faction asked that a directors' meeting be called for July 30 to consider the problem of filling director vacancies. On the eve of this meeting one of the Tomlinson directors resigned. This left five Tomlinson directors and four Vogel directors in office. A quorum was seven. Only the five Tomlinson directors attended the July 30 meeting. They purported to fill two of the director vacancies and to take other action. (In a separate case, this court had ruled that for want of a quorum the two directors were not validly elected and the subsequent action taken at that meeting was invalid.)

On July 29, the day before the directors' meeting, Vogel, as president, sent out a notice calling a shareholders' meeting for September 12 for the purposes of (1) filling director vacancies, (2) amending the bylaws to increase the number of directors from thirteen to nineteen and the quorum requirement from seven to ten, (3) electing six additional directors, and (4) removing Stanley Meyer and Joseph Tomlinson as directors and filling the resulting vacancies.

In August, Vogel sent out another notice for the September 12 shareholders' meeting, along with a "proxy statement" (essentially a request sent to shareholders asking that they grant proxies to the sender, authorizing him or her to cast their votes in a particular way). The notice and proxy statement were accompanied by a letter from Vogel soliciting shareholder support for the matters stated in the notice and particularly seeking to fill the vacancies and newly created directorships with "his" nominees.

Campbell, a shareholder, promptly filed this suit. He requested an injunction either to prevent the holding of the shareholders' meeting or to prevent the meeting from considering certain matters. The trial court ordered that the meeting be postponed until October 15 to allow time to decide the case. It ultimately rendered the following decision.

Seitz, Chancellor:

[The court first ruled that Vogel did have the power to call the shareholders' meeting for the purposes of filling director vacancies and amending the bylaws. It then turned to the question of whether the meeting could be called for the purpose of removing Meyer and Tomlinson from the board.] . . .

Plaintiff next argues that the shareholders of a Delaware corporation have no power to remove directors from office even for cause and thus the call for that purpose is invalid. . . .

While there are some cases suggesting the contrary, I believe that the stockholders have the power to remove a director for cause. This power must be implied when we consider that otherwise a director who is guilty of the worst sort of violation of his duty could nevertheless remain on the board. It is hardly to be believed that a director who is disclosing the corporation's trade secrets to a competitor would be immune from removal by the stockholders. Other examples, such as embezzlement of corporate funds, etc., come readily to mind. . . .

Plaintiff next argues that the removal of Tomlinson and Meyer as directors would violate the right of minority shareholders to representation on the board and would be contrary to the policy of the Delaware law regarding cumulative voting. Plaintiff contends that where there is cumulative voting, as provided by the Loew's certificate, a director cannot be removed by the stockholders even for cause.

. . . [I]t is certainly evident that if not carefully supervised the existence of a power in the stockholders to remove a director even for cause could be abused and used to defeat cumulative voting.

Does this mean that there can be no removal of a director by the stockholders for cause in any case where cumulative voting exists? The conflicting considerations involved make the answer to this question far from easy. Some states have passed statutes dealing with this problem but Delaware has not. The possibility of stockholder removal action designed to circumvent the effect of cumulative voting is evident. This is particularly true where the removal vote is, as here, by mere majority vote. On the other hand, if we assume a case where a director's presence or action is clearly damaging the corporation and its stockholders in a substantial way, it is difficult to see why that director should be free to continue such damage merely because he was elected under a cumulative voting provision.

On balance, I conclude that the stockholders have the power to remove a director for cause even where there is a provision for cumulative voting. I think adequate protection is afforded . . . by the existence of a remedy to test the validity of any such action, if taken.

. . . [Thus,] the meeting was validly called by the president. . . .

I next consider plaintiff's contention that the charges against the two directors do not constitute "cause" as a matter of law. It would take too much space to narrate in detail the contents of the president's letter. I must therefore give my summary of its charges. First of all, it charges that the two directors (Tomlinson and Meyer) failed to cooperate with Vogel in his announced program for rebuilding the company; that their purpose has been to put themselves in control; that they made baseless accusations against him and other management personnel and attempted to divert him from his normal duties as president by bombarding him with correspondence containing unfounded charges and other similar acts; that they moved into the company's building, accompanied by lawyers and accountants, and immediately proceeded upon a planned scheme of harassment. They called for many records, some going back twenty years, and were rude to the personnel. Tomlinson sent daily letters to the directors making serious charges directly and by means of innuendos and misinterpretations.

Are the foregoing charges, if proved, legally sufficient to justify the ouster of the two directors by the stockholders? I am satisfied that a charge that the directors desired to take over control of the corporation is not a reason for their ouster. Standing alone, it is a perfectly legitimate objective which is a part of the very fabric of corporate existence. Nor is a charge of lack of cooperation a legally sufficient basis for removal for cause.

The next charge is that these directors, in effect, engaged in a calculated plan of harassment to the detriment of the corporation. Certainly a director may examine books, ask questions, etc., in the discharge of his duty, but a point can be reached when his actions exceed the call of duty and become deliberately obstructive. In such a situation, if his actions constitute a real burden on the corporation then the stockholders are entitled to relief. The charges in this area made by the Vogel letter are legally sufficient to justify the stockholders in voting to remove such directors. In so concluding I of course express no opinion as to the truth of the charges. . . .

[Thus, the court held that the meeting had been validly called and the shareholders could vote on the removal of Meyer and Tomlinson from the board.]

Comment: At the October 15 shareholders' meeting, the Vogel group prevailed by a large margin, but the Tomlinson faction was able to obtain some representation on the board through cumulative voting. However, at the urging of the Vogel group, shareholders eliminated cumulative voting the next year. (For a fascinating account of the struggle for control of Loew's, read the chapter "Proxy Battle" in *My Life in Court* by Louis Nizer, who served as attorney for the Vogel faction.)

Valerino v. Little
Court of Special Appeals of Maryland, 490 A.2d 756 (1985)

As of April 1, 1979, Frederick Valerino, Theresa Valerino, Gregory Hays, and Ann Hays owned, as a group, 195 shares of Electra-Mechanical of America, Inc. (EMA). Charles Little and Anna Little together owned 195 shares. The board of directors consisted of Charles Little, Anna Little, and Frederick Valerino. No shareholders meeting was held in 1980, and so this board was held over. On April 1, 1981, the shareholders were unable to elect a board of directors because a dispute over the operation of the company had resulted in a stalemate. At a board of directors meeting that same day, attended by all three directors, Charles and Anna Little voted to remove Frederick Valerino as vice-president of EMA. In addition the three agreed, as reflected in the minutes of the meeting, that Frederick Valerino would prepare a proposal offering to sell the Valerino/Hays block of shares to the corporation.

On April 10, 1981, a letter was sent to Frederick Valerino notifying him that a special meeting of the board of directors was called for April 17, "for the sale and purchase of the capital stock of EMA, Inc. No proposal will be considered unless it is reduced to writing, signed, witnessed, and notarized." Frederick Valerino responded with a telegram stating that the Valerino/Hays group was not yet prepared to make a proposal for the sale of their stock. Charles Little acknowledged receipt of the telegram by a letter dated April 13, and requested that Valerino "let us know when you have prepared proposals and we will have a special board of directors meeting at that time." Nevertheless, the special board meeting called for April 17 was held, with Frederick Valerino absent. At this meeting, the other two board members (the Littles) voted to issue an additional 520 shares of stock, 490 shares to be distributed to the Littles, and 10 shares each to be distributed to three other persons who previously had not been shareholders. As a result of this issuance of stock, the 50 percent interest of the Valerino/Hays group was reduced to less than 25 percent.

The Valerinos and the Hays then filed a lawsuit claiming that the notice of the April 17 meeting was insufficient because it spoke only of the sale and purchase of stock and not its issuance. Consequently, they argued, the action of the board at that meeting was void and they still owned 50 percent of EMA's stock. A Maryland statutory provision permitted the owners of at least 50 percent of the shares of a corporation to obtain a court-ordered dissolution on the grounds that the shareholders had failed to elect a board of directors for two consecutive years. On this basis, the plaintiffs sought dissolution of the corporation. (The subject of dissolution is discussed in Chapter 39.) The trial court ruled that the notice and the board's action were valid, and dismissed plaintiff's petition for dissolution. The plaintiffs appealed.

Alpert, Judge:

Where the sufficiency of notice is complained of, courts have acknowledged that notice must be given to all directors so that the corporation may benefit from the counsel and advice of all. In the absence of proper notice, any action of the Board is invalid unless later ratified by the absent directors and thus waived by them.

. . . [N]otice of a special meeting . . . "should state fully the object of the meeting, so that each director may be informed in advance and fully appreciate the importance of his personal attendance." *Wall v. Utah Copper Co.*, 62 A. 533 (N.J. 1905). In *Wall* the notice provided that a purpose of the meeting was "to consider the advisability of, and, if deemed advisable, to authorize an issue and sale of $3,000,000 in par value *bonds.* . . ." [Emphasis added.] The objection to the notice was that it did not advise the directors of a $1,500,000 *stock* issue. [Emphasis added.] . . . The court indicated that the directors should have been advised of an increase in capital stock.

In *Bourne v. Stanford*, 41 N.W.2d 515 (Mich. 1950) notice of a special meeting was sent to the directors indicating that the purpose of the meeting was to "discuss . . . and analyze . . . financial and legal problems which faced the corporation and for the purpose of authorizing . . . any action which might be necessary for the solution of such financial and legal problems. . . ." At the meeting, however, it was decided that a petition for dissolution of the corporation should be filed. . . . The court . . . found the notice given inadequate in that it should have advised the directors that "dissolution was the contemplated matter for consideration."

The adequacy of the notice . . . was also addressed in *In re Wm. Faehndrich, Inc.*, 141 N.E.2d 597 (N.Y. 1957). In *Faehndrich* the notice advised that the meeting was "for the purpose of electing directors of the corporation for the ensuing year, or for such action on further business, as may arise at said meeting." At the meeting the director who was not in attendance was ousted by his son and daughter-in-law who elected themselves directors and terminated the absent director's employment. The court, in upholding the action taken at the meeting, held that:

The notice of the stockholders' meeting . . . fairly and adequately apprised the petitioner of the purpose of the meeting; in so many words, it recited that the meeting was called "for the purpose of electing directors." It is quite likely that the father did not fully realize the significance of such an election or the consequences to himself that would flow therefrom, but it may not be said that the notice of the meeting was insufficient or misleading in any way. If the purpose of the meeting be clearly stated

. . . there generally is no duty to explain the consequences that will follow from the action they plan to take. [Authors' note: In the Faehndrich *case, the meeting in question actually was a special* shareholder's *meeting, rather than a director's meeting; however, the principles regarding adequacy of notice are the same, especially in view of the fact that all of the shareholders in* Faehndrich *were also directors.]*

[In the present case the question is] whether notice of sale and purchase of stock may reasonably be interpreted to include the issuance of stock. . . . The word "issue" in this context . . . refers to putting stock into circulation. . . . The ambiguity in the notice in the [present case] is found in the word "sale." If the "sale" of stock means the issuance of stock, notice was adequate; if, on the other hand, "sale" refers only to outstanding stock which the corporation has redeemed [i.e., treasury stock, or stock that has been repurchased from shareholders] but not yet retired, then the notice received by Mr. Valerino was inadequate. . . .

When stock is issued, it is issued to an individual shareholder in exchange for consideration. . . . Logically, this process necessarily contemplates a two-step transaction. First the stock is issued, then it is sold. The two steps necessarily occur contemporaneously. . . . It is impossible to issue stock without the concomitant sale; it is, however, possible for a corporation to sell stock without the contemporaneous issuance of it. A corporation may sell stock which has already been issued and is being held by it as treasury stock. Treasury stock is stock which is authorized and issued but not outstanding.

In the instant case this ambiguity raised by the notice which states that stock will be purchased and sold can only be resolved by a consideration of the circumstances under which the notice was received. The notice was received after the Valerino/Hays group indicated a willingness to have the corporation buy them out. They, apparently, were to prepare a proposal to be submitted to the Board. When the notice was received, Mr. Valerino advised the Board, through Mr. Little, that he was not yet prepared to make a proposal. Mr. Little's response was to advise Mr. Valerino that when the proposal was prepared, the meeting would be held. At that time Mr. Valerino was unaware of any other proposals pending before the Board. Given these circumstances, it was reasonable to conclude that the "purchase and sale" referred to in the notice concerned the corporation's purchase of and the Valerino/Hays group's sale of EMA stock. Had the notice advised of the possible issuance of stock, Mr. Valerino would have been alerted of the attempt to defeat his ability to petition for involuntary dissolution. We hold the notice was invalid.

Because we have determined that the notice to Mr. Valerino was invalid, appellants remain 50% shareholders in EMA, Inc. . . . The trial court must conduct further proceedings [concerning] appellants' petition for involuntary dissolution.

Judgment reversed; case remanded for further proceedings consistent with this opinion.

Board of Directors: √
Choice and Functions

Number: State statutes have traditionally required that there be at least *three* directors. In recent years, however, the laws in a majority of states have been changed to permit fewer directors in corporations that have fewer than three shareholders. Subject to these statutory limitations, the number of directors is usually set forth in either the articles or the bylaws.

Qualifications: In most states directors no longer have to meet minimum age requirements, although in a few states they do. Requirements that directors be residents of the state of incorporation, still found in a few states, are also becoming much less common. In the past, most states required that directors be shareholders. This requirement also is vanishing; statutes in a majority of states now provide that directors need not be shareholders unless they are so required by the articles or bylaws. In actual practice, most directors *are* shareholders; however, there is a growing trend toward obtaining the services of disinterested outsiders as "watchdogs" on the board of directors. Also, it is permissible for an individual to be both a director and a corporate officer, and this frequently occurs.

Election and Term: The initial board ordinarily serves until the first annual shareholders' meeting, when new directors are elected by majority vote of the shareholders.

The term of office for corporate directors is one year (that is, until the next annual shareholders' meeting) unless the board is "classified" (divided into classes, with only one class elected each year, the result being that the directors serve "staggered" terms). Today, most states permit a **classified board.** When this system is used, the most common practice is to have *three* classes, with one-third of the directors being elected each year for a three-year term. Classification prevents replacement of the entire board

at the same time, thereby providing greater management continuity.

We mentioned earlier that removal of a director during his or her term is a shareholder function. The power to remove a director *for cause* can also be given, in the articles or bylaws, to the board of directors itself, although the shareholders have inherent power to review the action. But the board cannot be empowered to remove a director *without cause.*

When vacancies occur on the board (through death, resignation, or removal) or when an amendment to the articles or bylaws creates a new place on the board, filling of the opening generally is also a shareholder function. But several states now allow such openings to be filled by the board itself if it is so authorized by the articles or bylaws.

√**Management Functions:** Even though the corporation generally is bound by the actions of the board, the directors are not agents of the corporation or of the shareholders who elect them. There are two reasons for this. First, their powers are conferred by the *state* rather than by the shareholders. And second, they do not have *individual* power to bind the corporation, as agents do; instead, they can only act *as a body.* Directors thus occupy a position unique in our legal system.

With the exception of certain extraordinary matters mentioned earlier, the board of directors is empowered to manage all the affairs of the corporation. It not only determines corporate policies but also supervises their execution. The management powers of the board of directors usually include the following:

1. Setting of basic corporation policy in such areas as product lines, services, prices, wages, and labor-management relations

2. Decisions relating to financing the corporation, such as the issuance of shares or bonds

3. Determination of whether (and how large) a dividend is to be paid to shareholders at a particular time

4. Selection, supervision, and removal of corporate officers and other managerial employees[5]

5. Decisions relating to compensation of managerial employees, pension plans, and similar matters.

√Exercise of Board's Functions

As we previously mentioned, most states now allow *shareholders* to act by unanimous written consent in addition to annual and special meetings. A majority of states (but not as many as allow shareholder action by written consent) also now allow the *board of directors* to act by unanimous written consent. The traditional, and still most uncommon, method for board action, however, is the board of directors' meeting.

√**Time and Place of Board Meetings:** Board meetings are of two types—regular and special. The time and place of *regular meetings* is ordinarily established by the bylaws, by a standing resolution of the board, or simply by custom. Unless expressly required, notice of such meetings does not have to be given to directors. If the need arises, *special meetings* can be called between regular meetings. Prior notice is required in most cases, since special meetings by their very nature are not regularly scheduled.[6]

---

[5] Several states now permit the shareholders to select corporate officers if so provided in the articles or bylaws.

[6] State laws usually provide, however, that a director waives any notice requirement if he or she actually attends the meeting, unless such attendance is limited to the express purpose of objecting that the meeting was not lawfully called.

√**Quorum:** Before action can validly be taken at a board of directors' meeting, a quorum must be present. Most state statutes are flexible on the matter of what constitutes a quorum. They usually provide that a quorum will be a majority of the authorized number of directors unless the articles or bylaws say otherwise. Some state statutes also place a maximum and a minimum on the quorum requirement.

√**Voting:** As is true at shareholders' meetings, action at a board meeting is taken by voting. But a director's voting power is not determined by the size or nature of any financial interest he or she has in the corporation. Instead, each director has *only one vote.* Board action usually requires only a *majority vote,* although some states permit the articles or bylaws to require a greater-than-majority vote for certain actions. (The "majority" referred to here is a majority of the directors actually attending a meeting at which a quorum is present.) Unlike shareholders, directors cannot vote by proxy. However, a small number of states have recently changed their laws to permit a director to fully participate in a meeting by telephone. In such cases, a "conference call" must be used, so that the absent director and those present at the meeting can all speak and listen as a group.

In the next chapter, the fiduciary duties of directors are discussed in connection with their responsibilities and resulting liabilities to the corporation. Although a director's conflict of interest can cause the director to be liable for resulting harm to the corporation, such a conflict also can affect the fundamental power of the board to manage the corporation. The next case illustrates such an effect.

Also - Proxy

Weiss Medical Complex, Ltd. v. Kim
Appellate Court of Illinois, 408 N.E.2d 959 (1980)

Weiss Medical Complex, Ltd., a professional corporation, operated a medical clinic in Harvey, Illinois. Sun Kim and Chusak Ladpli, licensed physicians, entered into employment contracts with the cor-

poration in 1972 and 1973, respectively. The contracts were for a term of one year, to be automatically renewed unless either party gave written notice of termination at least 90 days prior to the end of the year. Each contract contained a restrictive covenant in which the employee agreed not to practice medicine within a ten-mile radius of the corporation for a period of one year after termination of the employment.

In early 1977 the board of directors voted to cancel the restrictive covenants in physicians' contracts. At this time the corporation's by-laws provided for thirteen directors, but only seven directors had been elected. All seven directors attended the board meeting at which this action was taken. The minutes of this meeting were subsequently reviewed by the corporation's attorney, who indicated that the board's action was questionable because four of the directors had restrictive covenants in their own contracts, thus creating a possible conflict of interest. The attorney advised that the board should attempt to get shareholder approval of the action. At the shareholders' meeting that was held subsequently, the board's action was not ratified, mainly because the majority shareholder, Dr. Weiss, opposed the action.

In 1979 Dr. Kim and Dr. Ladpli terminated their employment with the corporation and opened their own medical practices within a ten-mile radius of the Weiss facility. At the insistence of Dr. Weiss, the corporation filed suit seeking an injunction enforcing the restrictive covenants in its former employees' contracts. The trial court held that the board's action had been valid, and dismissed the suit. The corporation appealed.

McNamara, Justice:

Plaintiff urges that it was legal error to allow four personally interested directors having restrictive covenants in their employment contracts to be counted toward the quorum and majority vote of plaintiff's board of directors.

A quorum is composed of a majority of the number of directors fixed by the corporation's bylaws. The act of a majority of the directors at a meeting at which a quorum is present is the act of the board of directors. At the time of the resolution in issue, plaintiff's bylaws provided for 13 directors; thus seven directors constituted a quorum.

Duties imposed upon a director of the corporation as a fiduciary require him to manage the corporation with undivided and unqualified loyalty, and prohibit him from profiting personally at corporate expense or permitting his private interests to clash with those of his corporation. In Illinois, a director who has a personal interest in a subject under consideration is disqualified to vote on the matter and may not be counted for the purpose of making a quorum. The only exception is that a director, irrespective of any personal interest, may vote to establish reasonable compensation to all directors for service to the corporation. Whether a director is personally interested in a matter is a question of fact. Where there is no quorum because of the disqualification of directors, a contract executed pursuant to a resolution of the board is voidable and may be rendered valid by shareholder ratification.

Four of the seven directors who voted affirmatively to delete the restrictive covenant from all existing contracts had a restrictive covenant in their own employment contracts with plaintiff. The trial court did not make a determination whether these four directors had a personal interest in the matter under consideration by the board, although it did note that they benefited from the action.

We believe that the evidence conclusively demonstrated that these four directors had a personal interest in the matter under consideration by the board. They were among the intended beneficiaries of the board's resolution. Removal of the restrictive covenant would enable a director to leave the clinic and yet continue to render services to patients previously treated at the clinic. This access to plaintiff's patients would provide clientele and a source of income to physicians leaving the clinic. Consequently, a director who was restrained from such ongoing patient contact by the restrictive covenant in issue stood to benefit from a favorable outcome on the vote to delete the provision from all existing contracts. . . . We conclude, therefore, that the directors with restrictive covenants in their contracts were clearly disqualified to vote this benefit of removal to themselves.

In view of the personal interest of four board members, when the matter of restrictive covenants was considered, there were only three directors whose lack of personal interest entitled them to be counted towards a quorum. Consequently, no affirmative action on restrictive covenants was taken by a qualified majority of the board of directors.

Under such circumstances, the board's action was voidable. Although the action could have been ratified by the shareholders, the shareholders expressed objections at a meeting on June 6, 1977, and ratification was not achieved. . . .

In view of the personal interest of four directors, there was no quorum present at the board meeting on February 3, 1977. And since shareholder ratification was refused, the resolution to remove restrictive covenants from all existing employment contracts was not binding on the corporation. Consequently, the trial court erred in finding that the board's action cancelled the restrictive covenant in [the] employment contracts. . . .

For the reasons stated, the order of the circuit court of Cook County . . . denying plaintiff's motion for a preliminary injunction . . . is reversed, and the cause is remanded for further proceedings not inconsistent with this opinion.

Delegation of Board Powers to Officers and Employees: We said earlier that all functions of the board of directors must be exercised by the board as a whole, usually by majority vote. This does not mean, however, that the board itself must carry out all the details of corporate management; it can, and quite often does, *delegate authority* to carry out its decisions. The most common instance of such delegation is the authority given by the board to corporate officers and other managerial employees. Not only is authority usually given to carry out board decisions, but managerial personnel also are generally given authority to make management decisions. The delegation of decision-making authority is usually a practical necessity, because daily business activities require too many decisions for each one to be made by the board. The powers delegated by the board, however, must not exceed two boundaries:

1. They must relate only to ordinary corporate affairs, not to matters of an unusual nature.

2. They must not be so broad as to give an officer or employee complete managerial discretion. In other words, the delegated authority must be either relatively limited in scope or accompanied by adequate guidelines.

Thus, even though certain management functions are often delegated to officers and other employees, the ultimate power to manage the corporation still rests with the board. And the authority delegated to managerial personnel is, of course, subject to board supervision.[7] The duties owed by the board of directors to the corporation and its shareholders are discussed in the next chapter, but we must emphasize here that a delegation of authority by the board·does not relieve it of the responsibility to fulfill these duties.

Other Delegations of Board Powers: Most state corporation laws permit the board of directors to select a certain number of its members (usually two or more) to serve as the "executive committee." The rules governing delegation of authority to an executive committee are somewhat similar to those governing delegation to managerial personnel:

1. An executive committee is usually authorized to make management decisions relating

only to ordinary business affairs. Power to make decisions on unusual matters generally cannot be delegated to the committee. Examples of unusual matters include: (a) amending corporate bylaws, (b) filling vacancies on the board, and (c) submitting to shareholders matters that require their approval.

2. The delegation of authority to an executive committee cannot be too broad in scope.

3. The committee can usually exercise its delegated powers only during the intervals between meetings of the whole board of directors.

✓ Officers and Other Managerial Employees

Officers: The officers of the corporation are usually selected by the board of directors, although in a few states they can be chosen by the shareholders. Most commonly, the corporate officers are the president, one or more vice-presidents, secretary, and treasurer. Some corporations also have other officers, such as chief executive officer, chairman of the board, general manager, comptroller (sometimes called "controller"), and general counsel.

✓ *Qualifications:* In the past, many state laws required the president also to be a director. This requirement no longer exists in most states. In actual practice, however, the president almost always is a director as well. And when a corporation has a chairman of the board, he or she obviously must be a director. Other qualifications for the various officers can be included in the articles or bylaws if desired. In most states the same individual can hold more than one office. For example, it is not unusual for the offices of secretary and treasurer to be occupied by the same person. Limitations are frequently placed, however, on certain types of dual office holding. Most states, for instance, prohibit the same person from serving simultaneously as *president and secretary,* or as *president and vice-president.*

---

[7] This is a statement of the *law.* However, in actual practice, because of personalities or financial interests, the boards of some corporations serve primarily as a "rubber stamp" for decisions initiated by high-ranking managerial employees.

√ Term of Office: In a few states the term of office is limited by statute to a specific duration, such as one year. But in most states the only limitations are those expressed in the articles or bylaws. For the most part, officers hold their positions at the pleasure of the board and can be removed by the board either with or without cause and regardless of any enforceable employment contract. Of course, if the termination of an officer constitutes a breach of contract, the corporation can be held liable for damages to the discharged officer.

Other Managerial Employees: A corporation of almost any size requires the services of many employees to conduct its daily affairs. Some of these employees occupy supervisory positions and exercise certain managerial functions even though they are not officers. Selection of a few of the higher-ranking supervisory personnel is often done by the board of directors, but the task of hiring employees is generally delegated to the officers or even to other employees.

Applicability of the Law of Agency: Officers and other employees are agents of the corporation, and all the rules of agency law apply to the relationships created. Thus the corporation is bound by the actions of its officers and employees if they are acting within the scope of their authority—whether it is express, implied, or apparent. The express authority of *officers* comes only rarely from state laws or the articles of incorporation. It most frequently emanates from the corporate bylaws or from a resolution of the board of directors. The express authority of *other employees* most commonly comes from the officers or from higher-ranking employees. Implied and apparent authority are created in essentially the same way as in any other principal-agent relationship.

√ Figure 37.1   **Relationship of Shareholders, Directors, and Officers in a Corporation**

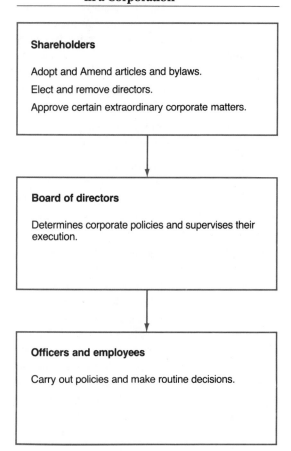

Figure 37.1 illustrates the relationship of shareholders, directors, and officers.

In the following case, the court deals with several important issues regarding the role of both shareholders and directors in the management of a corporation.

Rowland v. Rowland
Supreme Court of Idaho, 633 P.2d 599 (1981)

Rowland's, Inc., was a corporation engaged primarily in the dairy business in Power County, Idaho. The corporation's bylaws specified that the board of directors would consist of nine members, the presence of seven members would be necessary for a quorum at any board meeting, and a vote of three-fourths of the directors present at a meeting would be required for action by the board. At an annual shareholder meeting a proposal was introduced to amend the bylaws so that the presence of only five members would be required for a quorum at any board meeting, and a vote of only a majority of the directors present would be required for board action. Two shareholders, V. C. Rowland and Tom Rowland, strenuously objected to the consideration of this proposal because the notice of the shareholder meeting had not mentioned the matter. (At that time, Idaho law required notice of all shareholder meetings, including annual meetings; later, Idaho adopted a new corporation law based on the Model Business Corporation Act, which required notice of only special shareholder meetings. The prior law applied to this case.) Despite these objections, the proposal was passed by votes representing 60 percent of the corporation's outstanding shares. V. C. and Tom Rowland abstained from voting their shares on this proposal, but then participated along with the other shareholders in acting upon several other items of business at the meeting.

The annual board of directors meeting was held one week later and was attended by eight of the nine directors. By majority vote (but not three-fourths) the board elected officers of the corporation; V. C. and Tom Rowland were not reelected to officer positions. Later, V. C. and Tom Rowland filed suit claiming that the amendment of the bylaws at the shareholder meeting was void because it had not been mentioned in the notice of the meeting, and that the subsequent election of officers by the board was also void because this action was based on the amended bylaw. They also claimed that a series of management actions taken during the next year-and-a-half were void because the actions were accomplished without approval of the board of directors acting as a body. The trial court ruled against V. C. and Tom Rowland on all their claims, and they appealed.

McFadden, Justice:

Appellants [i.e., V. C. and Tom Rowland] contend that consideration of the proposed amendment to . . . the by-laws was an improper order of business at the annual meeting of the shareholders. . . . The contention is predicated on the undisputed fact that the notice of the annual meeting of the shareholders failed to indicate that the proposed amendment would be considered at the meeting. . . .

Appellants . . . attended the annual meeting of the shareholders . . . [and] voiced an objection to consideration of the proposed amendment on the basis that it was an improper order of business since the notice of the meeting failed to indicate it would be considered at the meeting. Neither V. C. Rowland nor Tom Rowland cast any votes on the motion to amend the by-laws. The next item of business was taken up in the meeting at the request of V. C. Rowland. The record of the meeting indicates that both appellants continued to discuss with the other shareholders the remaining items of business considered at the meeting. Under these circumstances appellants cannot complain of the propriety of the meeting insofar as it related to consideration of the proposed amendment to the by-laws and at the same time participate therein as to other matters coming before the meeting. [In other words, they waived their objection by continuing to participate.] . . .

[Next, the appellants challenge the legality of certain corporate transactions entered into without formal approval of the board of directors.] Specifically . . . [they] challenged the following series of transactions which were consummated by the corporation without formal approval of the board of directors: (1) the purchase of Eastern Idaho Dairy; (2) the borrowing of funds from First Security Bank of Idaho and Idaho First National Bank; (3) the purchase of a computer; (4) the entering into a contract with the employee's union; and (5) increases in corporate officers' salaries.

Ordinarily, the authority of a corporation's board of directors to make a particular corporate decision may be exercised by the directors only when meeting together as a body with proper notice to all. On the basis of this well-accepted proposition of corporate law, appellants challenge numerous transactions undertaken by the corporation which were consummated without formal approval of the board of directors acting as a body.

Appellants' argument overlooks the fact that the courts have frequently upheld informal action of a board of directors. For example, where a corporate decision is made informally by a majority of the directors, and the participating directors own a majority of the shares of stock in the corporation, the courts have been willing to hold that the action so taken is legal and binding on the corporation. Moreover, the courts have consistently held that the directors of a close corporation may transact the corporation's business affairs informally, especially where informality has become customary. Underlying these decisions is the view that the general rule against informal corporate action exists solely for the protection of the shareholders; if they do not want or need the protection, a waiver may be inferred from their acquiescence in or knowing silence to a corporate decision arrived at through an informal procedure.

In the instant case the record discloses that since incorporation the board of directors meetings have been used merely as a vehicle for the election of corporate officers and the hearing of management reports concerning corporate activities for the past year. The standard practice of Rowland's Inc. has been that a management team, consisting of the corporate officers, would discuss, review and determine the corporation's course of action in its conduct of major as well as routine business decisions and practices. While neither V. C. Rowland nor Tom Rowland were members of the management team during the period when the challenged transactions were entered into, the record discloses that the management team invited both appellants to attend and participate in the management team's meetings and decisions. The record further discloses that there has never been any attempt by appellants to alter or change this informal procedure of corporate decision-making utilized by Rowland's Inc. Under these circumstances, it was neither illegal nor improper for this close corporation's business affairs to be transacted without formal approval of the board of directors acting as a body. .

Judgment affirmed.

MANAGEMENT OF CLOSE CORPORATIONS

As indicated in the previous chapter, a close corporation is one whose shares of stock are held by either a single shareholder or a small, closely knit group of shareholders. Since all these shareholders usually hold positions as directors and officers, the management of a close corporation in practice more closely resembles a sole proprietorship or partnership than a corporation. In fact, close corporations with more than one shareholder are frequently referred to as "incorporated partnerships."

However, the nature of a close corporation should not be misconstrued. In the eyes of the law, *it is still a corporation* and must meet the same legal requirements as other corporations. While this has sometimes caused practical problems for close corporations, the problems have usually been overcome by the exercise of organizational ingenuity. For example, the law traditionally required at least *three* directors. But what if only *two* individuals own shares of stock and are interested in the operation of the corporation? One method of resolving the problem has been to set the number of directors at three in the articles of incorporation but then to operate with a permanent vacancy on the board. Another method has been to persuade a disin-

terested party to serve as a director in name only, with authority delegated to an executive committee composed of the two interested directors. And if the delegation of powers is too broad, there is really no one to complain.

Given that the law recognizes the validity of close corporations, one might wonder why the parties are forced to resort to these clever devices. Modern corporation laws are beginning to recognize this dilemma. As indicated earlier, for example, a majority of states now require only one or two directors where there are only one or two shareholders. Furthermore, in recent years a few states have enacted special laws to deal with the unique nature of close corporations. The most striking of these is a provision found in a handful of states permitting the shareholders of a close corporation (as defined in the particular statute) to manage the enterprise *without a board of directors.* The primary purpose of these recent statutory innovations is to allow more internal flexibility in the management of a close corporation, thereby enabling the enterprise to operate with approximately the same degree of freedom and owner control that is found in partnerships while retaining the advantages of doing business as a corporation (such as limited shareholder liability for business debts).

Several of the cases in these chapters on corporations involve the application of the general rules of corporation law to close corporations. In most situations, the same basic principles apply to the close corporation as apply to those whose stock is publicly traded. Sometimes, however, the rules are modified somewhat to recognize the particular nature of a close corporation. For example, in the last case, *Rowland v. Rowland,* the court recognized that informal board action is more likely to be valid in a close corporation because there is a much greater likelihood that the directors involved have a majority stock interest and that informal board action has become customary. Moreover, as just mentioned, in recent years a substantial number of states have passed special legislation modifying some of the rules applicable to close corporations.

The following two cases each involve claims that majority shareholders violated fiduciary duties to a minority shareholder in a close corporation. The fiduciary responsibilities of those who manage and control a corporation are discussed in greater detail in the next chapter; at this point, however, we present these two cases because they illustrate some of the problems for managers and investors that are somewhat more likely to occur in the context of a close corporation. In each case, the court expressly discusses the special nature of the close corporation and the recognition given to it by courts and legislatures.

Goode v. Ryan
Supreme Judicial Court of Massachusetts,
489 N.E.2d 1001 (1986)

Alice Marr owned 800 shares out of a total of 11,340 outstanding shares of the common stock of Gloucester Ice & Cold Storage Co. Gloucester engaged in the manufacture and sale of ice to fishing industry customers. Until 1980, Gloucester also operated a separate fish cold storage business. When Alice Marr died, the administrator of her estate, Thomas Goode, demanded that Gloucester purchase Marr's 800 shares. The demand was refused, and Goode filed suit against the officers, directors, and a controlling shareholder of Gloucester, seeking an order of the court requiring the corporation to purchase the 800 shares. The trial court granted the defendants' motion for summary judgment, and plaintiff appealed.

Hennessey, Chief Justice:

Gloucester is a close corporation. . . . The number of shareholders is small, no ready market exists for the Gloucester stock, and majority shareholder participation in the management of the corporation is substantial. The parties agree that no provisions restricting the transfer of stock or requiring the corporation or remaining shareholders to redeem its stock on the death of a shareholder appear in the corporation's articles of organization or by-laws, or in any agreement among the shareholders.

In *Donahue v. Rodd Electrotype Co.*, 367 Mass. 578 (1975), we [held] that shareholders in a close corporation owe one another substantially the same fiduciary duty of utmost good faith and loyalty in operation of the enterprise that partners owe one another. Applying that rule, we held in *Donahue* that a controlling shareholder selling a close corporation its own shares must cause the corporation to offer to purchase shares ratably from all other shareholders. Subsequently [in another case], we applied the rule to provide relief to a minority shareholder in a close corporation whose employment and income from the corporation were terminated without cause by the majority shareholders. The plaintiff in the instant case asks us to apply the fiduciary principles established in those cases to hold that, on the death of a minority shareholder, majority shareholders are obligated to purchase, or to cause the corporation to purchase, the shares owned by the minority shareholder.

As we stated in the *Donahue* case, one identifying characteristic of a close corporation is the absence of a ready market for corporate stock. A shareholder wishing to convert an investment in a close corporation to cash for personal financial reasons or because of unhappiness with the management of the enterprise will have only a limited number of opportunities for disposing of the asset. Similarly, the executor or administrator of the estate of a deceased shareholder in a close corporation will be confronted with an illiquid asset that may have a high value in the estate, but have little, if any, dividend value for the beneficiaries. In both situations, the only prospective purchasers for the stock may be the remaining shareholders in the corporation or the corporation itself.

Investors in other types of firms have easier mechanisms available for disposing of their interests. A shareholder in a large, public-issue corporation can sell the stock on the financial markets at no price disadvantage relative to other sellers of that stock. A member of a partnership can convert the investment to cash by exercising the right to dissolve the partnership.

The shareholder who owns less than a majority interest in a close corporation does not have any of these options. In the absence of an agreement among shareholders or between the corporation and the shareholder, or a provision in the corporation's articles of organization or by-laws, neither the corporation nor a majority of shareholders is under any obligation to purchase the shares of minority shareholders when minority shareholders wish to dispose of their interest in the corporation.

The minority shareholder in a close corporation is susceptible to oppression by the majority or controlling shareholders. In the instant case, there is no evidence of any oppressive conduct on the part of defendants directed at excluding the shares Goode represented from participation in the affairs of the corporation. In fact, the deceased shareholder, Alice Marr, never held corporate office, or served on the board of directors, or received any salary from Gloucester, and there is no indication that she or her estate was aggrieved by the absence of involvement in corporate management. The majority shareholders made no effort to curtail, or interfere with, any benefits to which Marr or her estate was entitled as a minority shareholder in Gloucester. The majority shareholders simply refused to purchase the Marr estate stock. This refusal violated no agreement or corporate governance provision and did not violate any fiduciary obligation they owed to the plaintiff. Nor are any facts present to permit us to conclude that the majority used assets of the corporation to enrich themselves at the expense of minority shareholders.

While the plaintiff's predicament in not being able to dispose of the Gloucester stock to facilitate prompt settlement of the Marr estate is unfortunate, the situation was not caused by the defendants but is merely one of the risks of ownership of stock in a close corporation. It is not the proper function of this court to reallocate the risks inherent in the ownership of corporate stock in the absence of corporate or majority shareholder misconduct. . . .

Judgment affirmed.

Estate of Schroer v. Stamco Supply, Inc.
Court of Appeals of Ohio, 482 N.E.2d 975 (1984)

Since 1973, a controlling stock interest (approximately 84 percent of the voting power) in Stamco Supply, Inc., had been owned by Ralph Grimme and several members of his family. Ralph Grimme also was chief executive officer of the corporation. In 1974 the corporation repurchased all of the shares of Stamco stock owned by Ralph Grimme's mother for $208 per share. In 1976 the corporation repurchased all of the shares owned by Ralph Grimme's brother for $259 per share. The minority shareholders were not informed of either transaction. One of these minority shareholders, Dorothy Schroer, later learned of the stock repurchases, and in 1980 demanded that the corporation repurchase her shares "on terms as favorable as those given to members of the controlling family group." The corporation refused, and she filed suit claiming that the controlling shareholders had breached their fiduciary duties to her and other minority shareholders. (The duties and liabilities of controlling shareholders to minority shareholders, as well as the duties and liabilities of officers and directors to the corporation and to all shareholders, are discussed in more detail in the next chapter.) The trial court ruled for Dorothy Schroer and granted her request for an order requiring the corporation to repurchase her shares on terms at least as favorable as those given to members of the Grimme family. The corporation and the controlling shareholder group appealed. During the litigation, Dorothy Schroer died, and the executor of her estate continued the lawsuit in her place.

Palmer, Judge:

[The court first observed that there was nothing in the relevant statutory provisions, prior court decisions, or in the corporation's articles or bylaws creating any *general* obligation on the part of the corporation or its majority shareholders to repurchase the stock of a minority shareholder. The court then continued:] Stamco is . . . a "close corporation," a phrase which by now may be said to have assumed status as a phrase of art, replacing less inclusive and perhaps misleading alternates like "closed corporations" or "closely held corporations." A close corporation is characterized, perhaps always, by at least two indicia: first, a relatively small number of shareholders as compared to a publicly held corporation, and, second, one whose shares are not traded on a national securities exchange or regularly quoted on an over-the-counter market, and are only rarely bought and sold. In addition to these universals, it is frequently characterized by an identity of management and ownership, by restrictions on the free alienability [i.e., transferability] of shares, and, of most immediate relevance, by its unmistakable resemblance to the partnership form. It has, indeed, been referred to at times as a "chartered partnership," "incorporated partnership," and as "a corporation de jure and a partnership de facto," and other terms descriptive of the participants' usual and customary intention to consider themselves as partners [among themselves] while obtaining the advantages of the corporate form.

Various [statutory enactments] of these indicia have been attempted in a number of states. . . . [A statute enacted in Ohio in 1981 basically accepts] the foregoing definitional expressions. Thus, for example, a close corporation [in Ohio] . . . may restrict or eliminate the board of directors and delegate director authority to a shareholder, and, in general, comport itself as though it were in fact a partnership. As [a section of the Ohio statute] provides: "No close corporation agreement is invalid among the parties on any of the following grounds: (1) The agreement is an attempt to treat the corporation as if it were a partnership or to arrange their relationships in a manner that would be appropriate only among partners. . . ."

It seems fair to say that by this enactment Ohio has signalled its recognition of the eclectic tendencies of the close corporation in blending features of the corporate and the partnership form, and given compliance with the statutory safeguards, has approved the hybridization. It is also doubtless a tacit recognition of the flexibility inherent in the form, the realization of which, over the past twenty years, has helped to make the close corporation a ubiquitous and indispensable factor in our economic life.

Given the nature of the close corporation, which, while it shares many of the advantages of the publicly held corporation such as limited liability, indefinite life, tax benefits, and so on, may more closely resemble a partnership or individual proprietorship in actual operation, it is not surprising that courts have been called upon to step outside the traditional rules of law that have long governed corporate operation and to borrow from allied disciplines those principles and rules which seem best to comport with the mixed nature of the close corporation form. . . .

One such interdisciplinary borrowing is of particular relevance in the instant case. Because of the relatively small number of shareholders involved and the usual intimate relationship between majority shareholders and the actual operation and direction of the close corporation, the form is peculiarly susceptible to a particular form of misuse or abuse by the majority or control-ling shareholders. Commonly known as a "squeeze-out" or "freeze-out," it refers to manipulative use of corporate control to eliminate minority share-holders, or to reduce their share of voting power or percentage of ownership of assets, or otherwise unfairly deprive them of advantages or opportunities to which they are entitled. Instances and methods of squeeze-outs, as re-ported in the decisions dealing with the problem, are many and varied, and appear limited only by human ingenuity motivated by greed or hope of advantage.

The judicial response provided by these episodes of abuse was to borrow from the law of partnerships the concept that where several owners carry on a business together in the close corporation form, their relationship should be considered a fiduciary one. Notwithstanding corporate statutes and common-law doctrines conferring authority to manage on directors, and authority in defined percentages of assenting shareholders to effect fundamental changes, "this does not mean that the directors or the majority shareholders should be permitted to exercise their powers arbitrarily or without regard to the legiti-mate expectations of the minority shareholders; and many of the older deci-sions and practically all of the recent ones indicate that controlling share-holders . . . owe fiduciary duties to minority shareholders, and that the courts will require them (whether they act in their capacity as shareholders or through directors or officers whom they control) to observe accepted standards of business ethics in transactions affecting rights of minority shareholders."

We conclude, therefore, that under the facts stipulated in this case, the Grimme controlling shareholder group owed a fiduciary duty to the minority shareholders, including [Dorothy Schroer], substantially akin to that fiduciary duty owed by one partner to another, to deal in the utmost good faith, which duty was breached by the refusal of the majority shareholders to cause the corporation to extend to Mrs. Schroer, as a minority shareholder, the same right to have her stock purchased by the corporation at a price and on terms similar to the offer extended to members of the controlling family group. . . .

The judgment of the trial court is affirmed.

SUMMARY

In modern times a corporation has the power to perform almost any legal act that an individual can perform. Under the *ultra vires* doctrine, a corporation has the power to engage only in those activities that are in furtherance of the stated purposes for which it is organized. In re-cent years, however, most state corporation stat-utes have been changed so as to (1) permit very broad statements of purpose in the articles of incorporation and (2) make *ultra vires* contracts legally enforceable; consequently, this doctrine does not limit a corporation's activities nearly as much as in earlier times.

In managing a modern corporation, the share-holders have ultimate control because they are the owners of the company. The power to make most business decisions, however, rests with the board of directors, and the shareholders usually exercise their ultimate control only through their election of directors. Shareholders do, however, have the right to act directly in the case of certain fundamental corporate changes such as amendment of the articles and bylaws and the approval of mergers.

Shareholders usually elect directors and take other action by voting at an annual shareholder meeting. Voting power corresponds to the number of shares owned; shareholders may, however, concentrate their voting power by a number of methods such as cumulative voting, shareholder agreements, voting trusts, and proxies. Special shareholder meetings may also be called by the board of directors upon the giving of adequate notice of the time, place, and purpose of the meeting.

The board of directors sets basic corporate policy and makes important business decisions; often it delegates to officers and other corporate employees the authority to make daily operational decisions. Directors take formal action only as a body; such action is usually taken at meetings, although some states permit board action by written consent or conference call in some situations. Each director has one vote, regardless of whether he or she owns shares in the corporation and regardless of the number of shares owned. Directors usually have regularly scheduled meetings, but special meetings may also be called upon the giving of adequate notice of the time, place, and purpose of the meeting.

Close corporations involve some special management problems because all or most of the shareholders themselves are usually intimately involved in managing the business; in actual operation, a close corporation resembles a partnership.

KEY TERMS

Statutory powers
Express powers
Implied powers
Ultra vires
Quorum

Cumulative voting
Voting trust
Proxy
Classified board

QUESTIONS AND PROBLEMS

1. Can a corporation be a partner? Explain.

2. Explain how the *ultra vires* doctrine has diminished in importance in recent years.

3. Charlestown Co. was dissolved, and its shareholders elected a committee to work with the board of directors in winding up the business. The laws of New Hampshire, where the case arose, provided that "the business of every such corporation shall be managed by the directors thereof, subject to the bylaws and votes of the corporation, and under their direction by such officers and agents as shall be duly appointed by the directors or by the corporation." The board ignored the committee. A shareholder filed suit challenging the board's failure to recognize the committee. Did the board act properly? Discuss. (*Charlestown Boot and Shoe Co. v. Dunsmore,* 60 N.H. 85, 1880.)

4. The directors of Omega Corp. proposed an amendment to the bylaws that would create a new class of shares with rights equal to an existing class. A special meeting was called to consider the amendment. The notice of the special meeting gave a brief statement about the amendment but did not mention the new class. The amendment was adopted at the meeting, but its validity was then challenged by a shareholder. Is the amendment valid? Discuss.

5. The bylaws of Thompson Co. set the quorum requirement for directors' meetings as a "majority of the directors." The number of directors provided for in the articles was eleven, but because of one death and one resignation, the board actually had only nine directors in office when it held a meeting in January 1976. Five directors attended. The action taken at the meeting was challenged by a shareholder on the ground that there had not been a quorum. Is the shareholder correct? Discuss.

6. Prince Co. owns a manufacturing plant, several trucks, and other items of equipment; it also owns two tracts of land of about 500 acres each, which it holds as an investment. Prince Co. was in need of cash, so Girard, who is both president and treasurer, sought to obtain a loan for the company from City National Bank. As security for the loan, the bank wanted a mortgage on one of the tracts of land. Can Girard execute the mortgage without express authority from the board of directors? Discuss.

7. The president of Hessler, Inc., made a contract with an employee, Farrell, in which retirement benefits were promised to him. In the past, the president had been allowed to manage the company's affairs more or less independently of the board; he also owned approximately 80 percent of the corporation's stock. When Farrell retired, the corporation refused to pay the benefits, and Farrell sued. The corporation claimed that the agreement made with Farrell by the president was invalid because it had not been approved by the board of directors. Is the corporation correct? Discuss. (*Hessler, Inc. v. Farrell,* 226 A.2d 708, 1967.)

8. Acting for the company, the executive committee of Ace Corp.'s board of directors made a contract with Henson, who was to perform services for Ace. The corporation's bylaws provided that all contracts must be approved "by the board of directors," but elsewhere in the bylaws it was stated that "the executive committee shall conduct the corporation's business." Is the contract valid? Discuss.

9. Plymouth Co. made an agreement with United National Bank in which Plymouth was to receive a substantial loan. In consideration of the loan, it was agreed that Plymouth's shareholders would elect two directors designated by United, one of whom would be comptroller and have complete charge of all the corporation's finances. Is the agreement valid? Explain.

10. Should a corporation's board of directors be permitted to hire an employee under a contract guaranteeing lifetime employment? Discuss.

Chapter 38

CORPORATIONS
Rights and Liabilities
of Shareholders
and Managers

Successful operation of the corporate enterprise involves the concerted efforts of many people. Although success demands that their efforts be focused on essentially the same goals and objectives, their own *individual* interests inevitably come into play on some occasions. For this reason, we will now discuss the rights and liabilities of the parties to the corporate venture, with respect to one another, and with respect to the corporation as an entity.

RIGHTS OF SHAREHOLDERS

Voting Rights

As indicated in the previous chapter, shareholders exercise their ultimate control by voting. Unless otherwise provided in the articles of incorporation, a shareholder has one vote for each share. The right to vote does not have to be expressed in the articles; it is inherent in the ownership of shares. Of course, the articles can expressly exclude or limit the right to vote—for example, by providing for the issuance of a certain number of special shares without voting rights.

Treasury stock is made up of shares that have been issued and later repurchased by the corporation. They carry no voting rights, since a corporation cannot logically act as a shareholder of itself. If these shares are subsequently resold, however, they once again carry voting rights.

Dividends

A person who purchases corporate shares is making an investment from which he or she obviously intends to receive a profit. Depending on the nature of the business and the type of shares purchased, the shareholder may expect such profit to arise either from increases in the market value of the shares, or from dividends, or perhaps from both.

Dividends are simply payments made by the corporation to its shareholders, representing income or profit on their investment. The payment is usually in the form of money, but it can consist of some type of property, such as the securities of another company that the corporation has been holding as an asset.

Sometimes the corporation pays a **stock dividend,** which is the issuance to shareholders of additional shares of the corporation's own stock. Such a distribution is *technically not a dividend,* because it does not represent a transfer of any property from the corporation to its shareholders. Instead, each shareholder simply becomes the owner of a larger number of shares. Although shareholders may not benefit immediately from a stock dividend, because the value of the preexisting shares is diluted, they usually do benefit in the long run because of the tendency of such shares to later increase in value.

The laws of the various states differ substantially with respect to the circumstances in which dividends can legally be paid. Generally, however, the following limitations are imposed:

1. Dividends cannot be paid if the corporation is insolvent or if the payment itself will cause the corporation to become insolvent. Depending on the particular state statute involved, *insolvency* is defined either as (a) the inability of the corporation to pay its debts as they become due, or (b) the possession of insufficient assets to meet all outstanding liabilities.

2. Dividends ordinarily can be paid only from a particular source. For example, some states allow dividends to be paid only from "current net earnings." This means that the source of funds for the payment must be the net profits of the corporation for the current year or the year just ended. Many states, however, permit dividends to be paid from any existing "surplus." In effect, this means that the payment must not be made out of the original capital investment in the corporation.

Shareholders do not have an absolute "right" to receive dividends. It is true that many corporations actually have long-established policies regarding payment of dividends. But whether a dividend is to be paid ("declared") in a given situation, and how large it is to be, are largely left to the discretion of the board of directors and usually cannot be challenged. A challenge to their decision ordinarily can be made only if (1) funds were not legally available for the dividend, (2) the division among shareholders was not fair and uniform, or (3) the special rights of any particular class of stock were not observed.

Preferences ✓

We have referred several times to different "classes" of corporate stock. The rights enjoyed by individual shareholders sometimes depend on the class of shares they own. In a given situation, a corporation might issue only one class of stock or it might issue several, depending upon the needs of the business.

Corporate stock is generally classified either as common or preferred. **Common stock,** the *(no-par stock - no value)* most basic and frequently issued type, enjoys no special privileges or preferences. **Preferred stock,** on the other hand, guarantees to its owner some type of special privilege or "preference" over the owners of common stock. The most frequently granted preferences relate to *dividends* and to *distribution of assets upon liquidation.*

Dividend Preferences: A preference as to dividends does not mean that the owners of the preferred shares are guaranteed the right to receive dividends. What it does mean is that, *if a dividend is declared,* owners of preferred stock have a priority over owners of common stock. For example: Zeta Corp. has issued one class of common stock and one class of preferred stock (the preferred stock being "$3 preferred"). In any given year, the owners of the common stock cannot be paid a dividend until the owners of the preferred stock have received a dividend of $3 per share. The preference can also be expressed as a percentage, such as "4 percent preferred." If this is the case, the owners of common stock cannot be paid a dividend until the preferred shareholders have received a dividend equal to 4 percent of the par value of their shares.

Shares that are preferred as to dividends may or may not be cumulative. The effect of a **cumulative dividend preference** is that if dividends are not paid in any year in the amount of the preference, they accumulate and must be paid in a future year before any dividend is paid to common shareholders. A majority of courts have held that preferred stock *is* cumulative unless there is an express statement in the articles of incorporation that it is not.

Furthermore, shares that are preferred as to dividends may or may not be participating. Holders of **participating preferred stock** are not only entitled to the original dividend, but, after the common shareholders receive a specified amount, they also share with the owners of common stock any additional dividends. Most of the time there is an express statement in the articles of incorporation that preferred stock is nonparticipating. But even without such a provision, a majority of courts have held preferred stock to be nonparticipating—in most states the only way for preferred stock to be participating is for the articles of incorporation to say that it is.

Liquidation Preferences: Owners of preferred stock sometimes are given a preference as to the distribution of corporate assets in the event that the corporation is dissolved. It is customary to limit this preference to the par value of the preferred shares plus any unpaid dividends. And, of course, a liquidation preference gives preferred shareholders a priority only over common shareholders, not over creditors of the corporation.

Preemptive Rights ✓ *as stockholder you have the rights to add more stock as*

Common Law Treatment: Suppose that Jupiter Corp. has a capitalization of $100,000 consisting of 1,000 shares of $100 par value common stock. X owns 100 shares of this stock. The corporation is in need of additional capital funds, so the shareholders authorize the issuance of another 1,000 shares. (This authorization is accomplished by a vote of the shareholders to amend the articles of incorporation.) If X is not given an opportunity to purchase shares of the new issue of stock, her proportionate interest in the corporation obviously will be reduced, and this will decrease her voting power and may result in her receiving a smaller amount of income from dividends.

For these reasons, the courts traditionally have recognized a concept known as the **preemptive right.** When a corporation issues new stock, the common-law preemptive right gives each shareholder an opportunity to purchase the number of new shares that will maintain his or her proportionate interest in the corporation. A shareholder possessing a preemptive right must be given notice and a reasonable amount of time to exercise the right by purchasing new shares. Anyone who fails to exercise this right within a reasonable time loses the right with respect to that particular issue of stock. A thirty-day period for exercising the right has been frequently used and is generally deemed reasonable.

Preemptive rights are of vital importance in a *close corporation,* where each shareholder possesses a substantial interest in the enterprise and usually takes an active role in management. But the significance of preemptive rights diminishes when the corporation's stock is *publicly sold and traded* (i.e., when the company is a so-called "publicly held" corporation). In the latter case, the number of shareholders is often quite large and each shareholder usually owns a relatively small portion of the total outstanding shares.

Courts have not recognized preemptive rights in all circumstances. Following are two of the most important situations in which such rights have been held not to exist.

Treasury Stock: If a corporation sells shares that it has been holding as treasury stock, it is obvious that this is not a "new issue" of shares and that there is no reduction in the proportionate interests of existing shareholders. Therefore, shareholders do not have preemptive rights with respect to sales of treasury stock.

Shares Issued for Consideration Other than Money: A corporation may sometimes have a good reason for accepting something other than cash as the consideration for shares that it issues. This occurs very frequently in connection with a *merger.* As we will see in Chapter 39, the merger of two corporations can be achieved by various means. In some cases the acquiring corporation may issue new shares of its stock, which will then be exchanged for the assets or the shares of the acquired corporation. In other situations not involving a merger, a corporation might issue shares to be used in the purchase of patent rights, real estate, equipment, or other property. Or shares may be issued and used as part of a compensation package to recruit a top executive. In these examples and in other instances of noncash share issuances, the corporation is ordinarily pursuing legitimate objectives that may be hindered, if not completely defeated, by the exercise of preemptive rights on the part of existing shareholders. For this reason, courts have generally held that preemptive rights do not apply to noncash issuances.

Statutory Treatment: In the earlier mentioned example of Jupiter Corp., the recognition of X's preemptive right was an easy matter. But the financial structure of many modern corporations is much more complex than that of Jupiter. This is particularly true of publicly held corporations, which often have several different classes of stock, each carrying different rights and preferences. This diversity of classes, coupled with the large number of shareholders, often makes it impractical to give complete recognition to preemptive rights. Furthermore, as previously mentioned, preemptive rights are often not of vital importance in publicly held corporations. For these reasons, most state statutes today permit the articles of incorporation to determine the matter of preemptive rights. The articles can limit the circumstances in which these rights exist or can abolish them altogether. In actual practice, most publicly held corporations have abolished preemptive rights in their articles.

Transferability of Shares

Shares of corporate stock are recognized by the law as items of property. As is true of other kinds of property, shares ordinarily can be sold or otherwise transferred as the owner wishes. Thus a shareholder has the right to transfer his or her shares to someone else unless a valid restriction has been placed on such transferability.

Restrictions: In some circumstances, it may be desirable for the corporation to restrict the shareholder's right to transfer his or her shares. Such restrictions are commonly employed by *close corporations,* because the shareholders themselves, who are few in number, actively manage the corporation and deal personally with one another on a daily basis. For example, assume that A, B, and C are the only shareholders of Prestige Corp. A and B will not want to wake up one morning and find that C has transferred his interest to D, a complete stranger with whom they will then have to share the management of the business.

Most restrictions on transferability take the form of *options to purchase,* which provide that a shareholder who wishes to sell his or her shares must first offer them to the corporation or to the other shareholders. Such restrictions are generally valid if a *reasonable time limit* is set for the exercise of the option. Provisions aimed at restricting transferability can be included in the articles or bylaws, but they are more often established by agreements among all the shareholders.

The existence of a transferability restriction should always be indicated explicitly on the **stock certificate.** The stock certificate is the formal document that provides evidence of the ownership of particular shares. It also provides evidence of the *agreement between the corporation and the shareholder* as to preferences, voting rights, and other terms. If the certificate does not include a notice of transfer restrictions, a purchaser of the shares is not bound by the restriction unless it can be proved that he or she knew of it.

Method of Transfer: An agreement for the sale of stock in a close corporation normally is reached by individualized negotiation between the seller and buyer. (The other shareholders must also be involved in many cases, because contractual restrictions on transfer frequently exist in close corporations.) When shares of a publicly held corporation are traded, however, the sale is usually accomplished through a stock broker. The broker has access to the public market for corporate stock in two ways. First, with respect to the shares of a corporation that is listed on one of the national or regional stock exchanges, the broker has access through membership in the exchange where the company's stock is listed or through contact with another broker who is a member of that exchange. Second, with respect to the shares of a corporation whose shares are publicly traded but that is not listed on an exchange, the broker has access through his or her knowledge of the so-called *over-the-counter market.*

Performance of an agreement to sell shares is accomplished by the owner's endorsement and delivery of the stock certificate in return for payment.[1] Although the transfer of ownership technically requires no other formalities, as a practical matter it is extremely important that the buyer properly notify the corporation of the change in ownership so that the corporation's shareholder list can be changed. The corporation's records do not actually determine ownership, but they do determine who receives various information from the corporation, such as proxy materials, notice of shareholder meetings, and financial and operational reports. Corporate records of share ownership also determine where dividend checks are sent and who is permitted to vote at the shareholders' meeting.

---

[1]Under Sec. 8-319 of the UCC, an unperformed agreement for the sale of securities usually must be in writing to be legally enforceable.

Inspection Rights

Unless limited by statute, every shareholder possesses the basic right of *access to corporate records.* This includes not only the right to inspect and copy corporate records personally but also the right to employ accountants, attorneys, stenographers, or other assistants as may reasonably be required to get the necessary information.

The right of inspection is one that possesses a definite potential for abuse. It could be used, for example, merely for harassment during a struggle for control of the corporation. Or a competitor could purchase a few shares and use the right to obtain trade secrets or other confidential information. Furthermore, even if the purposes for the inspection are legitimate, the existence of a large number of shareholders might cause unrestricted inspection rights to be impractical.

For these reasons, limitations are often placed on the inspection right. An illustration of the types of limitations that are frequently imposed is found in Sec. 52 of the Model Act:

Any person who shall have been a holder of record of shares . . . at least six months immediately preceding his demand or shall be the holder of record of . . . at least five percent of all the outstanding shares of the corporation, upon written demand stating the purpose thereof, shall have the right to examine, in person, or by agent or attorney, at any reasonable time or times, for any proper purpose its relevant books and records of accounts, minutes, and record of shareholders and to make extracts therefrom.

The following case presents an excellent illustration of a corporation's response to a rather wide-ranging request by a shareholder for inspection of corporate records, and of the court's review of both the request and the company's response.

Riser v. Genuine Parts Co.
Court of Appeals of Georgia, 258 S.E.2d 184 (1979)

Riser, a shareholder and a former employee of Genuine Parts Co., made demand upon the corporation for copies of a lengthy list of corporate documents. The corporation responded by providing a variety of papers, including (1) shareholder lists; (2) minute books of directors' meetings; (3) minute books of the stock option committee's meetings; (4) corporate bylaws; (5) audited annual reports; (6) unaudited quarterly reports; (7) statements of attorneys' fees for 1974–76; and (8) the securities registration statements, prospectuses, and proxy statements filed by the corporation with the SEC.

On the other hand, the corporation refused to provide the following information: (1) Monthly profit and loss statements for the past five years of the corporation's 286 company-owned jobbing stores, 39 auto parts centers, and a wide range of other divisions and subsidiaries were not disclosed to Riser on the grounds that they were irrelevant and misleading because all intra-company sales reflected on such reports would be eliminated before preparation of the corpo-

ration's overall profit and loss statements. (2) Earnings projections for all divisions and subsidiaries were not given to Riser because, according to the corporation, the quarterly and annual financial reports furnish all the necessary information of this type. (3) Attorneys' work papers and other files relating to the investigation of the corporation by the Federal Trade Commission, were refused on the grounds that such information is legally privileged. (4) Records of investments of pension and retirement funds of the corporation, its divisions and its subsidiaries, were refused on the grounds that such information is confidential and not relevant to any proper purpose of Riser. (5) All data relating to a merger between the corporation and Motion Industries, including the statements and opinions of the attorneys, were refused on the grounds that such information is confidential. (6) All corporate tax returns and all reports submitted to the board of directors by the auditors were refused on the grounds that this information was already provided in the annual profit and loss statements. (7) All records relating to aircraft purchase and maintenance, plus the flight logs for such aircraft, were refused because, according to the corporation, it owns only one airplane and does not maintain a separate category for the airplane in its records of costs and maintenance.

Riser filed suit against the corporation asserting his rights under the Georgia statute permitting shareholder inspection of "books and records of account, minutes, and record of shareholders," and demanding disclosure of those documents that had been refused by the corporation. The trial court held that the corporation did not have to disclose any of the material that had been refused, and Riser, the plaintiff, appealed.

Deen, Chief Judge:

The trial judge . . . found that [Genuine Parts Co.] is a publicly held corporation regulated by the Securities & Exchange Commission, with over 18,000,000 outstanding shares divided among over 6,000 shareholders and a wide diversity of operations, and that the plaintiff and other shareholders regularly receive or have available a wide range of published information including summaries of operations, SEC quarterly and annual filings, audited financial statements, statements of changes in financial position and notes on the consolidated financial statements, among other material. The documents [in this case] are sought [by the plaintiff] in order to determine whether proper records are being kept, the performance of management and the condition of the company. There has been no suggestion of mismanagement, impropriety or unstable financial condition. Plaintiff agrees that the company has "an excellent record."

We agree with the parties and the trial court that this constitutes a proper purpose . . . for seeking the "books and records of account, minutes and record of shareholders" which may be available to shareholders on demand,

and that the only question is whether those documents which have been refused . . . should also be forthcoming. This boils down to a definition of the words "books and records of account," the shareholder and minutes information having been furnished. . . . The plaintiff relies on language in *Meyer v. Ford Industries, Inc.*, 538 P.2d 353, for the proposition that the words, as used in this and similar statutes founded basically on the Model Business Corporations Act, are subject to a broad and liberal construction so as to extend to all records, contracts, paper and correspondence to which the common-law right of inspection of a stockholder might properly apply. One of the listed items was records relating to the investment of the amount which the defendant contributed to its employee pension plan. We agree with [the court in the *Meyer* case] that this is a proper demand. It would be relevant to the plaintiff's interest in the corporation as a stockholder and former employee, and the defendant has shown no reason why the information would be a breach of confidentiality. It was error to deny this item of the requested documents.

Work sheets, particularly those of attorneys, have been held confidential and unavailable. In *Goldstein v. Lees,* 120 Cal. Rptr. 253, it was held: "Moreover, it is apparent that although shareholders have some rights to corporate information not available to the general public, shareholder status does not in and of itself entitle an individual to unfettered access to corporate confidences and secrets . . . shareholders have less right to acquire corporate information than do directors. This proposition is also supported by the interpretations governing the scope of attorney-client privilege." And the right does not, at least in the absence of other considerations, extend automatically to income tax returns, [or to] general demands which are overly broad in their scope. The term "books and records of account" has been held not to apply to a file on a proposed merger.

It is also recognized that requests for certain documents are to be granted as a matter of course, while more peripheral documents may be produced or not dependent on circumstances. The "law looks more favorably upon requests for access to the stock register than for access to other company records."

As to these more peripheral requests, the Georgia statute has structured a summary decision-making process leaving much to the discretion of the trial judge. [The statute] provides that when documents called for by a shareholder who has demonstrated a proper purpose are refused and he establishes that he is qualified and entitled to an inspection, it shall be ordered "subject to any limitations which the court may prescribe."

The common law right of a shareholder to inspect the books and records of the company has long been recognized in Georgia. While the statutory language is frequently enlarged over that of its common law ancestry it also places much discretion in the trial judge to determine whether the purpose named is a proper one, whether the request is vexatious or arising from idle curiosity, whether the documents called for are relevant, material, and not overly burdensome, whether granting the requests would violate principles of confidentiality, lead to legal difficulties with federal agencies, or give an unfair advantage to the petitioning stockholders—in all such matters the unbridled right which attaches to stockholders lists does not apply. As the trial judge stated, the burden of showing a proper purpose as to specific materials is on the plaintiff and "this burden should become somewhat heavier as the information sought becomes increasingly remote from the statutory objects of 'books and records of account, minutes and record of shareholders.'" The language cannot be enlarged to include "every document generated by or received by Genuine Parts, even including confidential management data, confidential legal opinions and personnel evaluation" in the absence of a more compelling reason than the plaintiff has shown.

With the exception of [the material relating to the corporation's investment of plaintiff's retirement plan contributions], the trial court did not err in denying the additional corporate information sought.

Judgment affirmed in part and reversed in part.

LIABILITIES OF SHAREHOLDERS ✓

As we saw earlier, one of the basic attributes of the corporate form of doing business is the limited liability of the owners. That is, shareholders are usually not personally liable for the debts of the corporation; they may lose their investment in the corporation if it is a failure, but usually their liability ends there. We also saw that in a few exceptional circumstances the separate identity of the corporation can be disregarded and liability imposed on the shareholders. We will now examine a few other situations in which the personal liability of shareholders can become an issue.

Liability on Stock Subscriptions

A **stock subscription** is an offer by a prospective investor (a "subscriber") to buy shares of stock in a corporation. The ordinary rules of contract law apply to such offers, and they can thus be revoked prior to acceptance by the corporation—with two important exceptions:

1. Stock subscriptions are frequently made by the promoters before formation of the corporation. It is not uncommon for several promoters

to agree that their subscriptions cannot be revoked for some period of time. In such a case, the subscriptions are irrevocable for the agreed time.

2. The statutes of a majority of states provide that a subscription is irrevocable for a certain time period, unless the subscription itself expressly provides that it can be revoked. For example, the Model Act provides for a six-month period of irrevocability.

A stock subscription can be made either before or after incorporation. Where it is made prior to formation of the corporation, some states hold that acceptance of the offer occurs automatically when the corporation comes into existence. In other states, the subscription must be formally accepted by the board after incorporation. Where the subscription is made for shares in an existing corporation, there obviously must be a formal acceptance by the board. (Of course, the sale of shares by an existing corporation often does not involve stock subscriptions at all. Instead, the corporation itself is frequently the offeror.)

In any event, an accepted stock subscription is a contract, and the subscriber is liable for damages to the corporation if he or she breaches that contract by refusing to pay the agreed price.

Liability for Watered Stock

Corporate stock can be issued either as par value or no-par value stock. If the articles of incorporation assign a specific value to each share of stock, it is known as **par value stock.** The par value is a completely arbitrary figure and may be only nominal. It may or may not have any relation to the actual value of the stock as reflected by the financial condition of the corporation. If the articles do not state a value, the stock is called **no-par value stock.** In such a case, the board of directors normally places a value (called the "stated value") on the shares after they have been authorized but before they are actually issued.

Par value shares cannot lawfully be issued unless the corporation receives consideration at least equal to the par value. In the case of no-par value shares, the consideration must be at least equal to the stated value.

The consideration can be in the form of money, property, or services actually rendered (not just promised) to the corporation.[2] The board of directors generally determines the value of property or services received in return for shares, and this determination ordinarily will not be reviewed by a court so long as it appears to have been made in good faith.

Shares issued for less than the par or stated value are referred to as watered stock. A shareholder is personally liable for the deficiency (the "water"). This liability is usually to the corporation itself, but in some states an owner of watered stock is liable directly to the corporation's creditors when their claims cannot be satisfied out of corporate assets. Thus a shareholder can incur liability even if he or she has paid the agreed price for the shares, if that agreed price was less than the par or stated value. Of course, this rule applies only to the initial purchase of shares from the corporation upon their issuance,

not to later purchases from the shareholder ("on the market") or to purchases of treasury shares.

Liability for Illegal Dividends

Shareholders usually are liable for the return of any dividend that was improperly paid, as indicated below:

1. If the dividend is paid while the corporation is *insolvent,* shareholders are *always* liable for its return.

2. In the case of any other illegal dividend, a shareholder usually is required to account for its return only if he or she *knew* of the illegality when receiving payment. Examples of such illegal dividends are those that cause the corporation to become insolvent (as opposed to those made when the corporation is already insolvent) and those paid from an unauthorized source.

The liability of a shareholder for the return of an illegal dividend ordinarily is to the corporation itself. If the corporation is insolvent, however, the shareholder's liability often is to the corporation's creditors instead. Of course, those directors responsible for paying the illegal dividend also incur liability. When directors are subjected to such liability, however, they generally are allowed to recoup their loss from those shareholders who *knew* the dividend was illegal when they received it.

RIGHTS OF CORPORATE MANAGERS

In the following discussion, the rights of directors will be dealt with separately from the rights of officers and other managerial employees. The reason for this is that some of the rights possessed by directors are unique to their position.

Directors

Recognition and Participation: A director who has been properly elected possesses several rights of a very basic nature—for instance, the

---

[2] In some states, the preincorporation services rendered by promoters or others can be treated as consideration for shares.

right to be recognized as a director by his or her associates, the right to receive notice of board meetings, and the right to attend and participate in them. A duly elected director who is excluded from recognition or participation by his or her associates can obtain a court order enforcing these rights.

Inspection: The right of directors to inspect all corporate records is somewhat similar to the inspection right possessed by shareholders. However, the reasons for allowing inspection by directors are even stronger than those for allowing shareholder inspection. Directors *must* have complete access to corporate records in order to fully discharge their decision-making responsibilities. It obviously would be unfair to hold them responsible for paying an illegal dividend, for example, if corporate financial records had not been completely at their disposal.

Because of this compelling need for access to corporate books, most states hold that a director's right of inspection is *absolute and unqualified* (that is, not subject to the various limitations that are often placed on a shareholder's inspection right). Of course, a director's abuse of this right can provide a basis for his or her removal from the board, as illustrated in *Campbell v. Loew's, Inc.*, in the previous chapter. And a director is liable for any damage to the corporation resulting from abuse of the right (such as its use for an improper purpose). But in the majority of states where the director's inspection right is absolute, *neither the other directors, the officers, nor the shareholders can restrict his or her examination of corporate records.*[3]

Compensation: The traditional rule was that directors were not entitled to compensation for their services to the corporation. This rule was predicated on the assumption that directors were usually shareholders and would receive their compensation in the form of dividends. It also took into account the fact that some directors also served as corporate officers and received compensation for their services in those positions.

The basis for this rule is not applicable to many modern corporations, however. It is not uncommon today for individuals having little or no stock ownership to serve as directors. Furthermore, a great many directors serve only as directors and do not hold other positions with the corporation.

For these reasons, there is a growing trend in modern corporations toward compensation of directors as such. The traditional rule provides no real obstacle to this trend, because it simply holds that directors have no inherent *right* to be compensated. They can in fact be paid if there is a valid authorization for such payment in the articles or bylaws. Indeed, the statutes of some states today go even farther, providing, for example, that the board of directors can fix the compensation of its own members unless the articles or bylaws state otherwise. Directors are, of course, responsible for any abuse of this power.

Indemnification: The performance of their management responsibilities sometimes causes directors to become involved in legal proceedings. For example, the directors may be sued by a shareholder who claims that they acted negligently in managing the corporation. Or they may be charged by the government in a civil or criminal suit with a violation of the antitrust laws.

The costs of such lawsuits to the individual director, in terms of both expenses and potential liability for damages or fines, may be quite substantial. Under the common-law rule a director had no right to be indemnified (reimbursed) by the corporation for expenses or other losses. Today, however, the statutes of most states do permit indemnification of corporate directors in some circumstances. An excellent illustration of the modern statutory trend is found in Sec. 5 of the Model Act. Under this provision, a corpora-

---

[3] The courts in a *few* states, however, have held that a director's inspection right can be denied where his or her motive is obviously hostile or otherwise improper.

tion generally is authorized (but not required) to indemnify a director regardless of whether he or she actually committed a wrongful act, "if he acted in good faith and in a manner he reasonably believed to be in . . . the best interests of the corporation." On the other hand, the Model Act applies special rules to a "shareholders derivative suit," which is discussed in detail later in this chapter. In such a suit, which is brought by a shareholder in behalf of the corporation (rather than in the shareholder's own behalf), indemnification usually is not permitted if the director is actually found guilty of negligence or misconduct in the performance of his or her duties.

Officers and Other Managerial Employees

Corporate officers and other individuals who have managerial responsibilities are simply *employees* of the corporation.[4] It naturally follows, therefore, that the rights they have with respect to compensation and other matters are determined by their employment contracts.

Since their positions involve them in corporate decision making, officers and other managerial employees are subject to many of the same risks of litigation as are directors. Thus the rules regarding indemnification are the same for directors, officers, and managerial employees. That is, everything we have said about indemnification of directors applies with equal force to all others occupying management positions.

√ LIABILITIES OF CORPORATE MANAGERS

Those who manage the corporate enterprise owe to the corporation and its shareholders a number of basic duties that can be classified

under the headings of *obedience, due care,* and *loyalty.* A corporate manager incurs personal liability for the failure to fulfill any of these duties. In addition to these fundamental duties, certain special liabilities are imposed by federal securities laws. Unlike the previous section on the *rights* of corporate managers, our discussion of *liabilities* make no distinction between directors and other types of managers. The duties and liabilities of all who manage the corporation are essentially the same.

√ Obedience - Fiduciary Duty

Corporate managers have a duty to see that the corporation obeys the law and confines its operations to those activities that are within the limits of its corporate powers. If they knowingly or carelessly involve the corporation in either an illegal or *ultra vires* act, they are personally liable for any resulting damage to the corporation.[5]

√ Due Care and the Business Judgment Rule

The duty of due care is sometimes referred to as the duty of "diligence." It is, in effect, a duty "not to be negligent." In applying this standard, courts normally require a director, officer, or other manager to exercise the kind of care that an ordinarily prudent person would exercise in a similar position and under similar circumstances.

Although held to a standard of reasonable care, a manager is not liable for honest mistakes of judgment. Under normal circumstances, courts are extremely reluctant to interfere with the business decisions of a corporation's managers, and will not second-guess the wisdom of those decisions. Courts feel that if bad decisions are made, the proper remedy is for shareholders to exercise their voting power to bring in new management, and not to subject business deci-

---

[4] The word *employee* is used in a nontechnical sense. Managers and supervisors are not considered "employees" under some other specialized laws, such as those governing labor-management relations. But such laws are not our concern here.

[5] Of course, any manager who participates in the commission of an illegal act also may be personally subject to fines or other penalties imposed by the particular law.

sions to judicial review. Under this so-called **business judgment rule**, a court will not hold a manager liable for the consequences of a decision, even if harm resulted to the corporation, so long as the manager made a reasonably informed decision and apparently acted in a good faith belief at the time that the decision was in the best interests of the corporation. The term "business judgment rule" is simply another way of referring to the manager's basic duty of due care.

Examples of those relatively unusual situations in which a manager might be liable despite the business judgment rule would include (1) the failure to review corporate records or to carefully consider other relevant evidence before making an important decision; (2) the failure to seek expert advice (such as that of an attorney, accountant, or engineer) about a technical matter that clearly called for input from such an expert; and (3) the complete reliance on someone else's opinion without making a reasonable inquiry, where the person giving the opinion clearly had a selfish interest in the matter, or where the opinion itself obviously was erroneous or baseless (such as relying totally on the opinion of another director who had a personal interest in the matter, or relying on the advice of an attorney that bid rigging or bribery was perfectly legitimate).

Although the business judgment rule, or duty of due care, is applied to all aspects of the manager's decision-making role, in recent years courts have been called upon with increasing frequency to apply the standard to managers' actions when the corporation is the target of an attempted takeover by another company. For this reason, in the discussion of mergers in the next chapter, a separate section deals with the responsibilities of corporate managers when responding to a takeover attempt.

In a non-takeover context, the next two cases each involve claims that corporate directors violated the duty of due care in their management of the business.

Shlensky v. Wrigley
Appellate Court of Illinois, 237 N.E.2d 776 (1968)

 Shlensky, the plaintiff, was a minority shareholder in Chicago National League Ball Club, Inc. The corporation owned and operated the major league professional baseball team known as the Chicago Cubs. The individual defendants were directors of the Cubs. Defendant Philip K. Wrigley was also president of the corporation and owner of approximately 80 percent of the corporation's shares.

Shlensky filed suit in behalf of the corporation (a derivative suit), claiming that it had been damaged by the failure of the directors to have lights installed in Wrigley Field, the Cubs' home park. No trial was held, however, because the trial court dismissed his complaint on the ground that it did not set forth a claim that the law would recognize even if his version of the facts were correct. Shlensky appealed.

Sullivan, Justice:

. . . Plaintiff alleges that since night baseball was first played in 1935 nineteen of the twenty major league teams have scheduled night games. In 1966, out of a total of 1620 games in the major leagues, 932 were played at night. Plaintiff alleges that every member of the major leagues, other than the Cubs, scheduled substantially all of its home games in 1966 at night, exclusive of opening days, Saturdays, Sundays, holidays and days prohibited by league rules. Allegedly this has been done for the specific purpose of maximizing attendance and thereby maximizing revenue and income.

The Cubs, in the years 1961–65, sustained operating losses from its direct baseball operations. Plaintiff attributes these losses to inadequate attendance at Cubs' home games. He concludes that if the directors continue to refuse to install lights at Wrigley Field and schedule night baseball games, the Cubs will continue to sustain comparable losses and its financial condition will continue to deteriorate.

Plaintiff alleges that, except for the year 1963, attendance at Cubs' home games has been substantially below that at their road games, many of which were played at night.

Plaintiff compares attendance at Cubs' games with that of the Chicago White Sox, an American League club, whose weekday games were generally played at night. The weekend attendance figures for the two teams was similar; however, the White Sox week-night games drew many more patrons than did the Cubs' weekday games. . . .

Plaintiff further alleges that defendant Wrigley has refused to install lights, not because of interest in the welfare of the corporation but because of his personal opinions "that baseball is a 'daytime sport' and that the installation of lights and night baseball games will have a deteriorating effect upon the surrounding neighborhood." It is alleged that he has admitted that he is not interested in whether the Cubs would benefit financially from such action because of his concern for the neighborhood, and that he would be willing for the team to play night games if a new stadium were built in Chicago. . . .

Plaintiff . . . argues that the directors are acting for reasons unrelated to the financial interest and welfare of the Cubs. However, we are not satisfied that the motives assigned to Philip K. Wrigley, and through him to the other directors, are contrary to the best interests of the corporation and the stockholders. For example, it appears to us that the effect on the surrounding neighborhood might well be considered by a director who was considering patrons who would or would not attend the games if the park were in a poor neighborhood. Furthermore, the long run interest of the corporation in its property value at Wrigley Field might demand all efforts to keep the neighborhood from deteriorating. By these thoughts we do not mean to say that we have decided that the decision of the directors was a correct one. That is beyond our jurisdiction and ability. We are merely saying that the decision is one [for the] directors [to make]. . . .

Finally, we do not agree with plaintiff's contention that failure to follow the example of the other major league clubs in scheduling night games constituted negligence. Plaintiff made no allegation that these teams' night schedules were profitable or that the purpose for which night baseball had been undertaken was fulfilled. Furthermore, it cannot be said that directors, even those of corporations that are losing money, must follow the lead of the other corporations in the field. Directors are elected for their business capabilities and judgment and the courts cannot require them to forego their judgment because of the decisions of directors of other companies. Courts may not decide these questions in the absence of a clear showing of dereliction of duty on the part of the specific directors and mere failure to "follow the crowd" is not such a dereliction.

For the foregoing reasons the order of dismissal entered by the trial court is affirmed.

Francis v. United Jersey Bank
Superior Court of New Jersey, 392 A.2d 1233 (1978)

Pritchard & Baird Intermediaries Corp. ("Pritchard & Baird") was engaged in the business of being a "reinsurance broker." (If an insurance company has a very large individual risk or a number of similar risks on which it has given coverage, it often protects itself from too heavy a loss by shifting the risk to another large insurer or group of insurers. It does this by "reinsuring," that is, by purchasing insurance on all or part of the underlying risk from one or more other insurers. A reinsurance broker brings the parties together in a reinsurance arrangement.) Charles Pritchard, Sr., the founder of the company, was for many years its principal shareholder and controlling force. In 1970 he took his sons, Charles, Jr. and William, into the business. Because of the father's advancing age, the two sons played an increasingly dominant role in the affairs of the corporation. After the father's death in 1973, the sons took complete control.

Pritchard & Baird had been a successful company under the control of Charles, Sr., even though he engaged in various questionable business practices. He commingled the funds of different clients, commingled the company's funds with his own personal funds, and kept incredibly poor records. However, his clients were always taken care of and his creditors were always paid. After his sons took over, they continued his sloppy business practices but did not continue taking care of clients and paying creditors. In essence, they "looted" the company of millions of dollars and by the end of 1975 had plunged it into bankruptcy.

Francis was appointed as trustee in bankruptcy for Pritchard & Baird. In this capacity he sought to recover for Pritchard & Baird's creditors several million dollars which had been wrongfully taken from the company. He brought suit against two defendants: (1) the father's estate, of which United Jersey Bank was administrator; and (2) the estate of Lillian Pritchard. Lillian Pritchard was the wife of Charles, Sr., and had served as a director of the corporation from its creation until its bankruptcy. She died after the bankruptcy proceedings began. **Apparently because of the size of Lillian Pritchard's personal estate, the primary question in the case was whether she had acted negligently in her role as a director by not discovering and stopping the illegal actions of her sons. If so, her estate would be liable for that negligence. The trial court's opinion follows. (Note: There was no mention of the whereabouts of the two sons.)**

Stanton, Judge:

. . . Directors are responsible for the general management of the affairs of a corporation. They have particular responsibility with respect to distributions of assets to shareholders and with respect to loans to officers and directors. It is true that in this case the directors were never asked to take explicit and formal action with respect to any of the unlawful payments made to members of the Pritchard family. I am satisfied that, in terms of her actual knowledge, Mrs. Pritchard did not know what her sons were doing to the corporation and she did not know that it was unlawful. She did not intend to cheat anyone or to defraud creditors of the corporation. However, if Mrs. Pritchard had paid the slightest attention to her duties as a director, and if she had paid the slightest attention to the affairs of the corporation, she would have known what was happening.

Financial statements were prepared for Pritchard & Baird every year. They were simple statements, typically no longer than three or four pages. The annual financial statements accurately and clearly reflected the payments to members of the Pritchard family, and they clearly reflected the desperate financial condition of the corporation. For example, a brief glance at the statement for the fiscal year ending on January 31, 1970 would have revealed that Charles, Jr. had withdrawn from the corporation $230,932 to which he was not entitled, and William had improperly withdrawn $207,329. A brief glance at the statement for the year ending January 31, 1973 would have shown Charles, Jr. owing the corporation $1,899,288 and William owing it $1,752,318. The same statement showed a working capital deficit of $3,506,460. The statement for the fiscal year ending January 31, 1975, a simple four-page document, showed Charles, Jr. owing the corporation $4,373,928, William owing $5,417,388, and a working capital deficit of $10,176,419. All statements reflected the fact that the corporation had virtually no assets and that liabilities vastly exceeded assets. In short, anyone who took a brief glance at the annual statements at any time after January 31, 1970 and who had the slightest knowledge of the corporation's business activities would know that Charles, Jr. and William were, in simple and blunt terms, stealing money which should have been paid to the corporation's customers.

. . . [T]he inherent nature of a corporate director's job necessarily implies that he must have a basic idea of the corporation's activities. He should know what business the corporation is in, and he should have some broad idea of the scope and range of the corporation's affairs. In terms of our case, Mrs. Pritchard should have known that Pritchard & Baird was in the reinsurance business as a broker and that it annually handled millions of dollars belonging to, or owing to various clients. Charged with that knowledge, it seems to me that a director in Mrs. Pritchard's position had, at the bare minimum, an obligation to ask for and read the annual financial statements of the corporation. She would then have the obligation to react appropriately to what a reading of the statements revealed.

It has been urged in this case that Mrs. Pritchard should not be held responsible for what happened while she was a director of Pritchard & Baird because she was a simple housewife who served as a director as an accommodation to her husband and sons. Let me start by saying that I reject the sexism which is unintended but which is implicit in such an argument. There is no reason why the average housewife could not adequately discharge the functions of a director of a corporation such as Pritchard & Baird, despite a lack of business career experience, if she gave some reasonable attention to what she was supposed to be doing. The problem is not that Mrs. Pritchard was a simple housewife. The problem is that she was a person who took a job which necessarily entailed certain responsibilities and she then failed to make any effort whatever to discharge those responsibilities. The ultimate insult to the fundamental dignity and equality of women would be to treat a grown woman as though she were a child not responsible for her acts and omissions.

It has been argued that allowance should be made for the fact that during the last years in question Mrs. Pritchard was old, was grief-stricken at the loss of her husband, sometimes consumed too much alcohol and was psychologically overborne by her sons. I was not impressed by the testimony supporting that argument. There is no proof whatever that Mrs. Pritchard ever ceased to be fully competent. There is no proof that she ever made any effort as a director to question or stop the unlawful activities of Charles, Jr. and William. The actions of the sons were so blatantly wrongful that it is hard to see how they could have resisted any moderately firm objection to what they were doing. The fact is that Mrs. Pritchard never knew what they were doing because she never made the slightest effort to discharge any of her responsibilities as a director of Pritchard & Baird.

Defense counsel have argued that Mrs. Pritchard should not be held liable because she was a mere "figurehead director." . . . In legal contemplation there is no such thing as a "figurehead" director. This has been clearly recognized for many years so far as banking corporations are concerned. 3A *Fletcher, Cyclopedia of the Law of Private Corporations*, §1090, has this to say:

> *It frequently happens that persons become directors of banking houses for the purpose of capitalizing the position in the community where the bank does business, without any intention of watching or participating in the conduct of its affairs. It is a dangerous practice for the director, since such figureheads and rubber stamps are universally held liable on the ground that they have not discharged their duty nor exercised the required amount of diligence exacted of them.*

There is no reason why the rule stated by *Fletcher* should be limited to banks. Certainly, there is no reason why the rule should not be extended to a corporation such as Pritchard & Baird which routinely handled millions of dollars belonging to, or owing to, other persons. . . .

I hold that Mrs. Pritchard was negligent in performing her duties as a director of Pritchard & Baird. Had she performed her duties with due care, she would readily have discovered the wrongdoing of Charles, Jr. and William shortly after the close of the fiscal year ending on January 31, 1970, and she could easily have taken effective steps to stop the wrongdoing. Her negligence caused customers and creditors of Pritchard & Baird to suffer losses amounting to $10,355,736.91. There will be a judgment against her estate in that amount.

Loyalty

Directors, officers, and other corporate managers are deemed to be *fiduciaries* of the corporation they serve. Their relationship to the corporation and its shareholders is one of trust. They must act in good faith and with the highest regard for the corporation's interests as opposed to their personal interests. Several problems that commonly arise in the context of the duty of loyalty are discussed below.

Use of Corporate Funds: Obviously, a director or other party who occupies a fiduciary position with respect to the corporation must not use corporate funds for his or her own purposes.

Confidential Information: A director or other manager sometimes possesses confidential information that is valuable to the corporation, such as secret formulas, product designs, marketing strategies, or customer lists. The manager is not allowed to appropriate such information for his or her own use.

Contracts with the Corporation: A corporate manager who enters into a contract with the corporation should realize that it is not an "arm's-length" transaction. That is, the manager must make a full disclosure of all material information he or she possesses regarding the transaction. Furthermore, if the contract is at all unfair to the corporation, it is *voidable* at the corporation's option.

For obvious reasons, courts have not looked kindly upon contracts in which a *director* has a personal interest. (The contract might be with the director personally or with another company in which he or she has a financial stake.) If a contract of this nature was authorized at a board meeting where the presence of the interested director was necessary for a quorum or where this director's vote was required for a majority, most states hold the contract to be voidable at the corporation's option *regardless of its fairness.*

Corporate Opportunity: The **corporate opportunity rule** prohibits corporate managers from personally taking advantage of business opportunities that, in all fairness, should belong to the corporation. An obvious violation of this rule occurs when a manager has been authorized to purchase land or other property for the corporation but instead purchases it for himself.

Application of the corporate opportunity rule is sometimes not so clear-cut, however. A much more difficult problem is presented, for instance, when a director or other manager is confronted with a business opportunity arising from an *outside source* rather than from direct corporate authorization. For example: C is a director of Ace Air Freight, a corporation engaged in the business of transporting freight by air. C learns that M, a third party, has a used airplane in excellent condition that he is offering for sale at a low price. Can C purchase the airplane for himself? If the plane is of a type suitable for the corporation's freight business, the answer probably is no. He is obligated to inform the corporation of the opportunity.

This example illustrates the so-called "line of business" test employed by most courts in resolving such problems. Under this approach, a corporate manager cannot take personal advantage of a business opportunity that is *closely associated with the corporation's line of business.* Furthermore, the rule includes opportunities not only in the area of current corporate business but also in areas where the corporation might naturally expand.

Of course, if the corporation is actually offered the opportunity and *rejects* it, an individual manager can then exploit it. Some courts also

have held that if the corporation is financially *unable* to take a business opportunity, a manager can lawfully take personal advantage of it without first disclosing it to the corporation. Other courts, however, have held that the manager always must first disclose the opportunity and give the corporation a reasonable time to decide whether it is able and willing to exploit the opportunity before the manager can personally seize it.

The following case illustrates the type of double-dealing that the corporate opportunity doctrine is designed to prevent. In addition, the case involves the question whether a corporation's financial inability to take a business opportunity excuses a manager's failure to disclose the opportunity to the corporation.

Klinicki v. Lundgren
Supreme Court of Oregon, 695 P.2d 906 (1985)

In January 1977 Klinicki conceived the idea of engaging in the air transportation business in Berlin, West Germany. He discussed the idea with his friend Lundgren. At that time, both men were furloughed Pan American Airlines pilots stationed in West Germany. They decided to enter the air transportation business, planning to begin operations with an air taxi service and later to expand into other service, such as regularly scheduled or charter flights. In April 1977 they incorporated Berlinair, Inc., as an Oregon corporation. Lundgren was the corporation's president and a director; Klinicki was vice-president and a director. Each owned 33 percent of the corporation's stock. Lelco, Inc., a corporation owned by Lundgren and members of his family, also owned 33 percent, and the corporation's attorney owned the remaining 1 percent. Berlinair obtained the necessary government licenses, purchased an aircraft, and in November 1977 began passenger service.

As president, Lundgren was primarily responsible for developing and promoting Berlinair's transportation business. Klinicki was in charge of operations and maintenance. In November 1977 Klinicki and Lundgren, as representatives of Berlinair, met with representatives of the Berliner Flug Ring (BFR), a consortium of Berlin travel agents that contracts for charter flights to take German tourists to various vacation resorts. The BFR contract was considered a lucrative business opportunity by those familiar with the air transportation business, and Klinicki and Lundgren had contemplated pursuing the contract when they formed Berlinair. After the initial meeting, all subsequent contacts with BFR were made by Lundgren or other Berlinair employees acting under his direction.

During the early stages of negotiations, Lundgren believed that Berlinair could not obtain the contract because BFR was then satisfied with its existing carrier. In early June 1978, however, Lundgren learned that there was a good chance that the BFR contract might be available. He informed a BFR representative that he would make a proposal on behalf of a new company. On July 7, 1978, he incorporated Air Berlin Charter Co. (ABC) and was its sole owner. On August 20, 1978, ABC presented BFR with a contract proposal, and after a series of discussions it was awarded the contract on September 1, 1978. Lundgren effectively concealed from Klinicki his negotiations with BFR and his diversion of the BFR contract.

Klinicki, as a minority stockholder in Berlinair, filed suit against ABC and Lundgren for usurping a corporate opportunity of Berlinair. The trial court ruled in Klinicki's favor and imposed a constructive trust on ABC, which required ABC's profits to be turned over to Berlinair. The court of appeals affirmed, and Lundgren and ABC appealed.

Jones, Justice:

ABC . . . contend[s] that the concealment and diversion of the BFR contract was not a usurpation of a corporate opportunity, because Berlinair did not have the financial ability to undertake that contract. ABC argues that proof of financial ability is a necessary part of a corporate opportunity case. . . .

There is no dispute that the corporate opportunity doctrine precludes corporate fiduciaries from diverting to themselves business opportunities in which the corporation has an expectancy, property interest or right, or which in fairness should otherwise belong to the corporation. The doctrine follows from a corporate fiduciary's duty of undivided loyalty to the corporation. . . . If there is presented to [a director or officer] a business opportunity which is within the scope of the [corporation's] activities and of present or potential advantage to it, the law will not permit him to seize the opportunity for himself; if he does so, the corporation may elect to claim all of the benefits of the transaction. . . .

We first address the issue . . . of the relevance of a corporation's financial ability to undertake a business opportunity. . . . This is an issue of first impression in Oregon. . . .

A rigid rule was applied in *Irving Trust Co. v. Deutsch,* 73 F.2d 121 (2nd Cir. 1934). In that case a syndicate made up of directors of Acoustic Products Co. purchased for themselves . . . the rights to manufacture under certain radio patents which were essential to Acoustic. They justified this on the ground that Acoustic was not financially able to purchase the patents on which the defendants later made very substantial profits. The court refused to inquire whether the conclusion of financial inability was justified. Referring to the facts which raised a question whether Acoustic actually did lack the funds or credit necessary to make the acquisition, the court said:

> *Nevertheless, [the facts in the case concerning whether Acoustic lacked funds to carry out the contract] tend to show the wisdom of a rigid rule forbidding directors of a solvent corporation to take over for their own profit a corporate contract on the plea of the corporation's financial inability to perform. If the directors are uncertain whether the corporation can make the necessary outlays, they need not embark upon the venture; if they do, they may not substitute themselves for the corporation any place along the line and divert possible benefits into their own pockets.*

On the other end of the legal spectrum from *Irving Trust Co. v. Deutsch* [is a] Minnesota case, *Miller v. Miller,* 222 N.W.2d 71 (1974). . . . In *Miller,* the Minnesota Supreme Court . . . found that [the corporation's] financial ability [to pursue the business opportunity] is a prerequisite to establishing a corporate opportunity. . . . Defendant, relying on *Miller,* contends [that the plaintiff must prove that the corporation was financially able to obtain the BFR contract]. We reject this argument. . . .

Where a director or [officer] wishes to take personal advantage of a "corporate opportunity," the director or [officer] must . . . promptly offer the opportunity and disclose all material facts known regarding the opportunity to the disinterested directors or, if there is no disinterested director, to the disinterested shareholders. . . . The director or [officer] may take advantage of the corporate opportunity only after full disclosure and only if the opportunity is rejected by a majority of the disinterested directors or, if there are no disinterested directors, by a majority of the disinterested shareholders. If, after full disclosure, the disinterested directors or shareholders unreasonably fail to reject the offer, the interested director or [officer] may proceed to take the opportunity if he can prove the taking was otherwise "fair" to the corporation. Full disclosure to the appropriate corporate body is, however, an absolute condition precedent to the validity of any forthcoming rejection as well as to the availability to the director or [officer] of the defense of fairness. . . .

The BFR contract was a "corporate opportunity" of Berlinair. . . . Lundgren did not offer Berlinair the BFR contract . . . and did not attempt to obtain the consent of Berlinair to his taking of the BFR corporate opportunity. . . . Berlinair never rejected the opportunity presented by the BFR contract . . . [and did not subsequently ratify] the appropriation of the BFR contract. . . .

Because of the above, the defendant may not now contend that Berlinair did not have the financial ability to successfully pursue the BFR contract.

The Court of Appeals is affirmed. [ABC holds the BFR contract in trust for Berlinair, and all profits from the contract must be paid to Berlinair.]

Controlling Shareholders: In some situations, **controlling shareholders** are placed under fiduciary duties similar to those owed by directors, officers, and other managers. If a single shareholder, or a group of shareholders acting in concert, owns a sufficient number of shares to control the direction of corporate affairs, the possibility exists that they will try to exercise this control so as to further their own personal interests at the expense of the corporation and the other shareholders. Corporate control must not be abused, however, and the controlling shareholders are required to act in the best interests of the corporation as a whole and with complete fairness to minority shareholders.

√ Liability under Federal Securities Laws

The **Securities Act of 1933** and the **Securities Exchange Act of 1934** place a number of specific duties and liabilities upon corporate managers and others. In many cases, an activity that violates one of these federal regulatory provisions also amounts to a breach of duty under the state common-law rules previously discussed. Even in such instances, however, these federal statutes are of extreme importance because they (1) define some types of duties with greater precision than existed at common law, (2) provide for penalties that may not have existed under state law, and (3) provide for enforcement by a federal agency, the **Securities and Exchange Commission (SEC).** Several of the more important federal statutory provisions relating to duties and liabilities are discussed below. (These and other provisions of the securities laws are dealt with in much greater detail in Chapter 50, "Securities Regulation.")

Registration Statements: As indicated in Chapter 36, the 1933 Act requires corporations to file a registration statement with the SEC when nonexempt issues of securities are offered for sale in interstate commerce or through the mails. Under Secs. 5 and 11, if a violation occurs, either by filing a misleading registration statement or by failing to file one at all, the corporate managers involved in the securities issuance can be held personally responsible. Others involved, such as accountants, attorneys, and underwriters, may also be liable.

Use of Inside Information: Section 10b of the 1934 Act essentially prohibits *fraud* in the

sale or purchase of securities.[6] Pursuant to this section, the SEC has promulgated Rule 10b-5, which makes the 10b prohibition more specific.

One of the most important features of Rule 10b-5 is that it effectively prohibits the use of **material inside information** in the sale or purchase of securities. The purpose of this rule is to prevent an "insider" from using inside information to take advantage of the other party to the transaction. In most cases, insiders are directors, officers, or holders of large amounts of stock. It is not required, however, that any such position be held in order for a person to be liable under Rule 10b-5. Others employed by the corporation, as well as friends, relatives, or business associates of true insiders, can also incur liability. The key is whether the person has actually acquired material information about the corporation that is not available to the other party to the transaction. If so, he or she must either reveal the information or refrain from selling or buying the corporation's securities until the information becomes generally available to investors.

We have said that the duty of disclosure with respect to inside information applies only if the information is "material." By its nature, the word *material* is rather difficult to define with precision. A determination must be made on the basis of all the circumstances of the particular case. Broadly speaking, however, material information has been judicially defined as "information which, if generally known, would probably affect the market price of the corporation's securities." It has been defined by other courts as "information which would probably affect the decision of a reasonable investor as to whether to sell or buy the securities." An example of the type of information likely to be considered material is knowledge that the corporation is planning to merge with another company. Other examples of material information include knowl-

---

[6] This provision applies to fraud in the sale or purchase of securities *after* their initial issuance. Another provision, Sec. 17 of the 1933 Act, prohibits fraudulent practices with respect to the original issuance.

edge that the corporation has just discovered a major mineral deposit or that it is about to be sued by the Department of Justice for an alleged violation of the antitrust laws.

Short-Swing Profits: Under Sec. 16b of the 1934 Act, **short-swing profits** are defined as any profits made on either the sale and subsequent purchase or purchase and subsequent sale of equity securities where both purchase and sale take place within a six-month period. This section does not actually prohibit short-swing profits; it does, however, prevent certain insiders from keeping any short-swing profits made on transactions in the shares of their own corporation. Such profits made by these insiders must be turned over to the corporation. The **insiders** who are required to turn over their short-swing profits to the corporation are (1) directors, (2) officers, and (3) owners of 10 percent or more of any type of shares issued by the corporation.[7]

Section 16b is essentially a preventive measure designed to discourage the misuse of inside information. It applies, however, without regard to whether the particular insider actually possessed material inside information. But it applies only to the types of insiders who are specifically listed. Short-swing profits made by others are not subject to the statute.

Proxy Solicitation: In the previous chapter we saw that corporate managers often solicit proxies from shareholders prior to a shareholders' meeting. In the "proxy statement" sent to shareholders, the managers request authority to cast votes in behalf of the shareholders for particular board candidates and for particular proposals the managers have made. The shareholders are, of course, under no obligation to grant this request; they can attend the meeting themselves or choose not to vote at all.

Section 14a of the 1934 Act prohibits making any false or misleading statements in the proxy material sent to shareholders. Furthermore, the proxy statement must disclose all material facts relating to the matters to be voted on. In other words, when corporate managers solicit proxies, they must reveal to the shareholders, in a clear and truthful manner, all facts that will probably affect the voting decision. Violation of this section subjects the responsible managers to personal liability.

Shareholder Derivative Suits

As we saw in the previous chapter, the basic power to manage a corporation rests with the board of directors. Ordinarily, if a shareholder disagrees with a decision of the board to act or not act in a particular way, the shareholder's only recourse is to use his or her voting power, alone or in combination with the voting power of other shareholders, in an attempt to elect different directors at the next annual shareholders' meeting. Unless the shareholder can prove that directors have violated the duties of obedience, due care, or loyalty, the shareholder can obtain no assistance through the courts.

This fundamental principle of board control also applies to any decision regarding the filing of a lawsuit in behalf of the corporation. The board of directors has the power and the responsibility to determine whether the corporation's legal rights have been violated, and if so, whether it is in the best interests of the corporation to initiate legal action. Thus, if one or more shareholders feels that a wrong has been committed against the corporation and files a lawsuit *in behalf of the corporation,* the shareholder may find the courts less than totally receptive. Such a suit, called a **shareholder derivative suit** (or "stockholder" derivative suit) will be heard by the court only after the shareholder has fulfilled one of the following conditions.

Demand and Refusal: The shareholder must have formally demanded that the board of directors initiate legal action in behalf of the corpora-

---

[7]Under Sec. 16a, these types of insiders are also required to make periodic reports to the SEC of *any* personal transaction in the shares of their corporation.

tion but the board refused to do so. After the demand and refusal, the shareholder then files a derivative suit. When deciding whether to permit the shareholder to maintain the derivative suit, the court reviews the directors' decision not to take legal action under the same standards that are applied to other decisions by directors. Thus, the shareholder must prove that the directors' refusal violated the duties of obedience, due care, or loyalty to the corporation. The court's interpretation of the duty of due care is, of course, governed by the business judgment rule. As a result, courts are very reluctant to permit derivative suits when the shareholder claims that the corporation has been harmed by a person or firm totally unconnected with the corporation (such as a supplier, customer, or government agency). Whether to take legal action against such a party is a fundamental matter of business judgment within the directors' discretion, and the court will not second-guess that judgment so long as the directors apparently examined the facts and did not act in their own self-interest.

If the shareholder has demanded that the board take legal action against one or more of its own members, and the board refuses, the court applies the same standards in reviewing the board's refusal as it applies when an alleged wrong was committed by an outsider. If a majority of the board was not implicated in the alleged wrongdoing, there is no evidence that any members of this majority otherwise acted in their own self-interest, and the members of this majority apparently gave careful consideration to the charges and the relevant evidence, the decision not to take legal action usually will be upheld under the business judgment rule and the court will dismiss the shareholder derivative suit. On the other hand, if a majority of the board was implicated in the alleged wrongdoing, the vote of a member with a personal interest in the decision was necessary for there to be a quorum or a majority decision not to take legal action, *or* the majority apparently did not give careful consideration to the charges and relevant evidence, the court probably will permit the derivative

suit to continue. Once the derivative suit is allowed, the court then will fully review the merits of the charges to determine whether any of the directors violated their duties to the corporation.

When deciding whether to file a lawsuit, either on its own initiative or in response to a shareholder demand, the board may act as a whole or it may delegate the responsibility to a **special litigation committee** composed of several of the directors. Appointment of a special litigation committee is particularly desirable when improper action by one or more of the directors themselves has been alleged. In fact, in such a situation it is highly desirable that the committee consist of the board's *outside directors* (i.e., those not owning substantial amounts of shares or holding high management positions in the corporation). The decision of a special litigation committee that it would not be in the corporation's best interests to take legal action against one or more of the directors is far more likely to be upheld by a court when the committee consists of disinterested outside directors.

Futility of Demand: If the shareholder filing a derivative suit has not made a formal demand to the board that it take legal action, the court will permit the derivative suit to continue only if the shareholder convinces the court that such a demand would be futile. For example, if a shareholder produces plausible evidence that a majority of the board was guilty of wrongdoing or otherwise was acting in its own self-interest, the shareholder will be permitted to maintain the derivative suit without having first made a formal demand to the board. The court then will examine the merits of the charges against the directors.

It should be noted that a shareholder's lawsuit is characterized as a derivative one only if it asserts that harm has been done to the corporation as an entity or to shareholders as a group. If the shareholder has a plausible claim that action by directors or officers caused harm that is personal or unique to this particular shareholder, and not to the corporation as an entity or to its shareholders in general, the lawsuit is not a derivative one and the shareholder can pursue it as any other claim. Such a claim, that is not derivative in nature, is much more likely to arise in the context of a close corporation.

SUMMARY

Although the various people involved in a corporation have many common objectives, their own individual interests can also be important. A substantial body of legal rules has been developed to achieve a workable balance among these interests. These rules, for example, provide shareholders with certain rights. Among the most important of these rights are those concerning voting, dividends, preferences, preemptive rights, transferability of shares, and inspection of corporate records. All of these rights are subject to limitations. Shareholders also are subject to liabilities in several situations, including contractual liability on stock subscriptions and liability for watered stock and illegal dividends.

A corporate director is given a number of rights necessary to the effective performance of his or her functions, including the right to be recognized as a director by associates, the right to receive notice of board meetings, and the right to attend and participate in those meetings. A director also has the right of inspection. Although there is no inherent right to compensation, the law normally permits corporations to compensate directors, and the trend is clearly toward the granting of substantial compensation. A director also has no inherent right to be indemnified for liabilities incurred while acting on corporate matters, but today the law usually does permit such indemnification. The rights of other managers, such as officers, are normally determined by their employment contracts with the corporation.

Directors, officers, and other corporate managers owe to the corporation and its shareholders the duties of obedience, due care, and loyalty. The business judgment rule is used by courts when interpreting and applying the duty of due care. Corporate managers may be held liable under federal securities laws in several situations, including those in which they either fail to file required registration statements or file statements that are misleading, buy or sell the company's securities on the basis of material inside information, make short-swing profits on the company's securities, and fail to reveal in a clear and truthful manner all relevant material information in a proxy solicitation. The general rule that the directors are charged with managing the corporation includes the filing of lawsuits in behalf of the corporation, and attempts by shareholders to sue in behalf of the corporation (shareholder derivative suits) are subject to very substantial limitations.

KEY TERMS

Treasury stock
Dividend
Stock dividend
Common stock
Preferred stock
Cumulative dividend preference
Participating preferred stock
Preemptive right
Stock certificate
Stock subscription
Par value stock
No-par value stock
Watered stock
Business judgment rule
Corporate opportunity rule
Controlling shareholders
Securities Act of 1933
Securities Exchange Act of 1934
Securities and Exchange Commission (SEC)
Material inside information
Short-swing profits
Insiders
Shareholder derivative suit
Special litigation committee

QUESTIONS AND PROBLEMS

1. Hanrahan, a shareholder of Puget Sound Corp., demanded the right to inspect corporate records prior to a shareholders' meeting. His purpose was to obtain the names and addresses of other shareholders so that he could urge them to elect directors who would seek a merger of Puget Sound with another corporation. Puget Sound refused the demand, and Hanrahan sued to enforce his right of inspection. Will Hanrahan win? Explain. (*Hanrahan v. Puget Sound Power & Light Co.*, 126 N.E.2d 499, 1955.)

2. Pioneer Savings & Loan Co. issued an additional 100,000 shares of common stock. The circumstances were such that Pioneer's existing shareholders should have been accorded preemptive rights. Because of a mistake, however, several of these shareholders had not been given an opportunity to exercise those rights. Upon discovering the situation, Pioneer sought to cancel the entire issue of stock. Can it do so? Discuss. (*Barsan v. Pioneer Savings & Loan Co.*, 121 N.E.2d 76, 1954.)

3. Explain the difference in the relative importance of preemptive rights in a close corporation and in a publicly held corporation.

4. An amendment to the articles of Constantin & Co. stated that "the holders of the preferred stock shall be entitled to receive, and the company shall be bound to pay thereon, but only out of the net profits of the company, a fixed yearly dividend of Fifty Cents (50¢) per share." The dividend was not paid in a particular year, and a preferred shareholder sued to compel its payment. Assuming that the company actually made a net profit that year, will the shareholder prevail? Discuss.

5. The articles of Apex Co. provide that, if preferred shareholders fail to receive a dividend in any given year, they "shall be entitled to the same voting power as the holders of the common stock." Except for this situation, the preferred shares of Apex carry no voting rights. One

year the preferred shareholders did not receive a dividend. At the next shareholders' meeting, where the preferred shareholders were to exercise their newly acquired voting power, an issue arose as to the extent of this power. The preferred shareholders contended that the meaning of the quoted provision was that they *as a class* should have the same voting power as that possessed by the common shareholders *as a class.* Under this interpretation, each share of the preferred would be worth eighty-nine votes, rather than the ordinary one vote per share to which the common shareholders would be entitled. Are the preferred shareholders correct? Discuss.

6. The directors of Southwest State Bank were warned by the bank examiner that the bank was in a precarious condition. After the warning, the directors made no audit of the bank's affairs for the next year, did not check the cashier's statement as to loans made, and thus did not discover that the cashier was frequently using forged notes in the names of third parties to cover his embezzlements. The bank's directors were sued for negligence by a shareholder. What is the result? Explain.

7. Reese, a director of Lafleer, Inc., was seventy-five years old and in failing health. He was suspicious of the activities of the company's vice-president, but because of his poor health he no longer attended board meetings and did nothing about the matter. It was later discovered that the vice-president had involved the company in a number of prohibited activities, including illegal campaign contributions. The company was damaged by these activities, and a shareholder sued not only the vice-president but also Reese. Is Reese liable? Discuss.

8. Johnson, the president of Continental Co., badly mismanaged its affairs and caused the company to sustain heavy losses. The board of directors had allowed Johnson a free hand in running the company. A shareholder filed a derivative suit against Johnson and all the directors for negligence. One of the directors, Wembley, claimed that he should not be held responsible. His defense was that, because of the great distance between his home and Continental's headquarters (2,500 miles), he had not attended a board meeting in almost a year. Should Wembley's defense shield him from liability? Discuss.

9. Explain the rationale behind the corporate opportunity rule.

10. Carlton owned 1 percent of the shares of Zepco, Inc. He was not an officer or director. He sought to buy a piece of equipment worth $30,000 from Zepco for $25,000. Zepco's board of directors voted 9–2 to sell the equipment to him for $25,000. After the sale, another Zepco shareholder sued Carlton to force him either to return the equipment or to pay an additional $5,000. What was the result? Discuss.

Chapter 39

CORPORATIONS
Merger, Consolidation, and Termination

In the preceding chapters we examined the nature and formation of the corporation, its basic operation, and the rights and liabilities of its individual participants. This final chapter focuses on more unusual aspects of corporate operation. Initially, we discuss changes in the fundamental structure of the corporation brought about by mergers and consolidations. Then we deal with the various circumstances in which the corporate existence can be terminated.

MERGERS AND ✓
CONSOLIDATIONS

The terms *merger* and *consolidation* are often used interchangeably to describe any situation in which two or more independent businesses are combined under a single ownership. Technically, however, there is a difference in meaning between the two terms. A **merger** is the absorption of one existing corporation by another; the absorbing corporation continues to exist while the one being absorbed ceases to exist. A **consolidation,** on the other hand, is a union resulting in the creation of an entirely new corporation and the termination of the existing ones. Symbolically, a merger can be illustrated by the equation A + B = A, while a consolidation is represented by A + B = C.

The distinction between mergers and consolidations has very little practical significance. Whether a particular combination is a merger or consolidation, the rights and liabilities of the corporations and their shareholders and creditors are the same. For this reason, the popular term *merger* is sometimes used in the following discussion to describe both combinations.

Reasons for Merging

The reasons for merging two corporations vary greatly, depending on the particular circumstances. The most common reasons are discussed below.

General Advantages of Size: In many cases the motive for a merger is the acquisition of some or all of the benefits that result from an increase in size. An ability to buy and produce in larger amounts, for example, may bring about greater efficiency and lower overhead costs.

Because the combination possesses greater resources than its constituent companies had possessed separately, it may be able to obtain capital more easily and to engage in more extensive advertising and research. Furthermore, the larger organization sometimes finds it easier to attract the best managers, technical advisers, and other personnel.

These advantages of size are usually legitimate. Occasionally, however, the motives of corporate managers in pursuing mergers may be less valid. Sometimes growth is sought merely for its own sake, without any resulting increase in efficiency. For instance, a merger might produce a much more impressive set of financial statements for the acquiring company, not through any improvement in its performance but simply because of the "larger numbers" brought about by the acquisition. And, of course, the personal rewards of the corporate managers may increase accordingly.

Eliminating Competition: Some mergers are motivated by the desire to lessen the rigors of competition. The most obvious example, of course, is the acquisition of a direct competitor for the purpose of suppressing competition between the two.[1] Mergers brought about solely for this purpose are somewhat less common than in the past, however, because of the enforcement of the antitrust laws.

Acquisition of Know-how: A large corporation might acquire a much smaller one in the same or a related line of business for the purpose of obtaining patents or other technological know-how owned by the smaller company. In addition, some of that company's employees might possess useful capabilities.

---

[1] A merger between two competitors is called a *horizontal merger.*

Guaranteed Supplies or Outlets: A company might seek to assure itself of an adequate supply of an essential item by acquiring a producer of that item. Conversely, a guaranteed outlet might be the motivating factor behind the acquisition of a company that purchases a product supplied by the acquiring firm.[2]

Diversification: One corporation sometimes wishes to acquire another in a totally unrelated line of business solely for the purpose of diversifying. Doing business in several diversified lines removes some of the economic risks that exist when a corporation commits all its resources to a single industry.[3]

Defensive Mergers: Occasionally a corporation actually seeks to be acquired by another. For example, suppose that X Corporation is attempting to acquire Y Corporation. However, the managers and shareholders of Y Corporation are opposed to the takeover because of differing business philosophies. Y Corporation thus arranges a merger with Z Corporation to avoid the takeover attempt by X. Such a merger is often called a **defensive merger.**

Another merger that might be classified as defensive is illustrated as follows. Jones, the founder of General Steel Corp. and its primary manager throughout its existence, now wishes to retire. Jones is afraid that "his" company will not be managed properly in his absence, so he arranges for General Steel to be acquired by a larger company whose management capabilities he trusts.[4]

Tax Savings: Although tax considerations are beyond the scope of this discussion, the lessening of federal income tax liability sometimes is

an important reason for undertaking a particular merger.

Unused Capital: Sometimes a merger may simply be an investment outlet for unused capital. For example, a corporation may have accumulated profits that it does not choose to pay out as dividends. The acquisition of another corporation may be an attractive investment opportunity for these funds.

Procedures

The procedure for a merger or consolidation is governed by statute. Every state has a statute that authorizes the combination of two or more *domestic* corporations. In almost every state, the statutory procedures also allow the combination of a domestic and a *foreign* corporation. The procedures vary somewhat from state to state, but they can be outlined generally as follows:

1. The board of directors of each corporation must adopt a resolution approving the merger or consolidation. This resolution should set forth:
   a. The names of the combining corporations and the name of the corporation that will result from the combination.
   b. The terms and conditions of the proposed combination.
   c. The method and basis to be used in converting the securities of each corporation into securities of the resulting corporation.
   d. In the case of a merger, any changes caused thereby in the articles of incorporation of the surviving corporation. In the case of a consolidation, the resolutions of the respective boards should include the entire articles of incorporation for the resulting new corporation.

2. The plan must then be approved by the shareholders of each corporation, at either an annual or a special meeting. The vote required for approval varies among the states from a simple majority to four-fifths of the outstanding shares; a *two-thirds* vote is the most common requirement.

---

[2] A merger between firms in a supplier-customer relationship is called a *vertical merger.*

[3] A merger between firms in unrelated lines of business is called a *conglomerate merger.*

[4] In this case Jones is probably a controlling shareholder in General Steel Corp. and thus has the power to carry out his wish.

3. After shareholder approval, the plan for the combination must be submitted to the appropriate state official (usually the secretary of state) in a document referred to as the **articles of merger or consolidation.**

4. If all documents are in the proper form, the state official issues a **certificate of merger or consolidation** to the surviving or new corporation.

Merger with a Subsidiary

In a majority of states, the procedures have been greatly simplified for the merger of a subsidiary corporation into its parent. These streamlined procedures allow such a merger to be consummated *without shareholder approval.*

If the parent owns *all* the subsidiary's shares, the only requirements are that (1) the parent's board of directors adopt a resolution setting forth the plan for the merger, (2) articles of merger be filed, and (3) a certificate of merger be issued. If some of the subsidiary's shares are owned by others, there is an additional requirement that these minority shareholders be given prior notice of the merger. These simplified procedures can be used, however, only if the parent owns a *very large portion* of the subsidiary's shares (90 or 95 percent in most states).

Effects of Merger or Consolidation

The effects of a merger or consolidation can be summarized as follows:

1. The corporations who are parties to the merger become a single corporation.

2. All of the corporate parties to the merger, other than the surviving or new corporation, cease to exist.

3. The surviving or new corporation possesses all the rights, privileges, and powers of the combining corporations.

4. The surviving or new corporation acquires all the property of the combining corporations without the necessity of a deed or other formal transfer.

5. The surviving or new corporation is liable for all the debts and obligations of the combining corporations.

6. In the case of a merger, the articles of incorporation of the surviving corporation are deemed to be amended to the extent, if any, that changes in these articles are stated in the articles of merger. In the case of a consolidation, the articles of consolidation serve as the articles of incorporation for the new corporation.

The Appraisal Right ✓

At common law a merger, consolidation, or other combination required the *unanimous* approval of the shareholders of each corporation. In an effort to lessen the severity of this restriction on corporate action, all the states at a fairly early time passed statutes providing for approval by less than unanimous vote.

One result of this change, however, was that any shareholders who disapproved of a merger might find themselves unwilling investors in a corporation different from the one whose shares they originally had purchased. Out of concern for fairness to these shareholders, provisions were included in the state laws giving them the right to sell their shares back to the corporation for cash. This right has generally become known as the **appraisal right.**

A dissenting shareholder must strictly follow the required procedures, or this appraisal right will be lost. The most important requirement is that the dissenting shareholder *object to the merger and demand payment within the designated time period.* For example, the Model Act provides that a dissenting shareholder must give the corporation written notice of objection to the proposed combination either prior to or at the meeting where the matter is voted upon. If the merger is approved at the meeting, the Model Act requires that the dissenting shareholder make written demand for payment from the corporation within the next ten days.

When the merger or consolidation takes place, the surviving or new corporation must make a written offer to each dissenting shareholder regarding the purchase of his or her shares. Under the Model Act, this offer must be made within ten days after the effective date of the combination and must be accompanied by the most recent balance sheet and income statement of the corporation whose stock is owned by the dissenting shareholder.

The overriding concern of the dissenting shareholder is, of course, the price to be paid for his or her shares. The requirement found in most state statutes is that the corporation pay the "fair value" of the shares, computed as of the date of the merger. If the dissenting shareholder feels that the offer does not reflect the fair value of the shares and refuses to accept it, the corporation can institute a court action to have the value determined. The shareholder can personally file such a suit only if the corporation fails to do so within a specified period of time (under the Model Act, 60 days after the merger). In the court proceeding, the judge sometimes appoints an official "appraiser" to hear evidence and recommend a fair value.

Figure 39.1 illustrates the steps in a typical merger or consolidation.

Asset and Stock Acquisitions

Thus far our discussion has been limited to "statutory" mergers and consolidations, in which all of the requisite formalities have been carried out. However, corporations can achieve the same practical results by less formal means, particularly through *asset acquisition* and *stock acquisition.* In legal circles these transactions are sometimes called *de facto* **mergers,** as contrasted with "statutory" mergers and consolidations. In everyday usage they are more frequently referred to simply as "mergers," or "takeovers."

Asset Acquisitions: Suppose that X Co. wishes to acquire all or most of the assets of Y Co. It may purchase these assets with cash or with a combination of cash and promissory notes. Or it may make the purchase by issuing shares of its stock to Y in return for Y's assets.

Although the practical effect of such an asset acquisition is to merge one company into the other, the *acquiring company* usually does not have to obtain shareholder approval. Ordinarily, the only situation in which the approval of the acquiring company's shareholders must be obtained is when the assets are to be bought with shares and there are not enough authorized but unissued shares to make the purchase. In such a case the shareholders will have to amend the articles of incorporation to authorize the issuance of additional shares.

The rules are substantially different, however, with respect to the *acquired company.* The sale of all or most of its assets puts its shareholders into a position very different from the one they previously occupied. Therefore, they must approve the sale. Indeed, in the past, the common-law rule required unanimous approval. This strict requirement was relaxed, however, along with the relaxation of the approval requirement for formal mergers and acquisitions. Today, the general rule is that the shareholders of the acquired company must approve the sale by the same vote required for a merger or consolidation. And the dissenting shareholders of the acquired company possess an appraisal right just as in a formal merger or consolidation.

After the sale, the corporation that has sold its assets may simply choose to dissolve. It may, however, decide to start its operations anew (either in the same or some other line of business). A third alternative is for the corporation to continue in existence as a **holding company** (or **investment company**). In the latter case, its sole (or at least primary) function will be to own and receive income from securities, such as those it may have received as the purchase price for its assets.

Stock Acquisitions: A frequently employed method for achieving a combination between two corporations is the purchase by one corporation of the shares of another. This generally is accomplished by action of the acquiring company's board of directors, without any need for approval by its shareholders. Unless the pur-

Figure 39.1 Steps in Merger or Consolidation

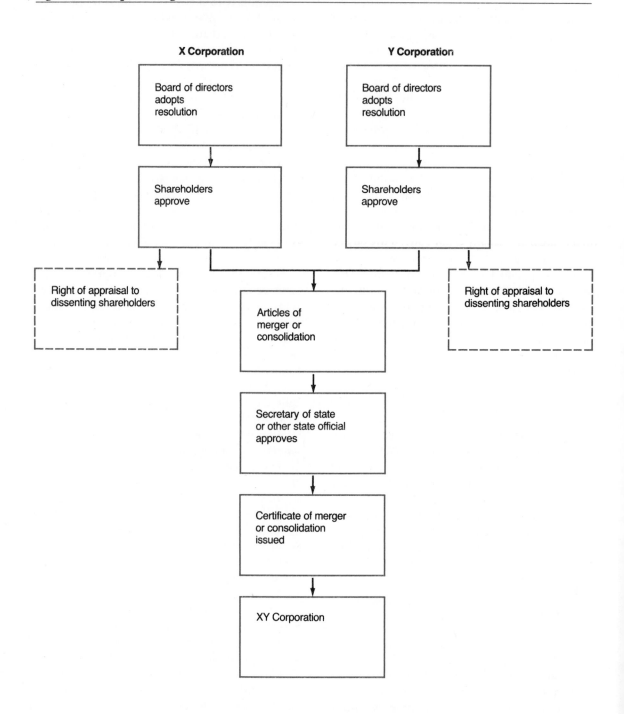

chase is being made merely for investment purposes, the aim of the purchaser obviously is to obtain a sufficient number of shares so that it *controls* the company whose shares are acquired. Control usually requires ownership of over 50 percent of a corporation's voting shares. (Although the present discussion involves acquisition by one *corporation* of a controlling stock interest in another corporation, the same principles apply to such an acquisition by an *individual.*)[5]

Open Market Purchases: Although it is theoretically possible for the acquiring company to negotiate individually with the target company's shareholders for the purchase of their shares, this usually is not done. If the target company's shares are publicly traded, the large number of shareholders involved makes individual negotiation practically impossible; if the target company is a close corporation, transfer of the shares is usually restricted by a shareholder agreement that can be changed only by the shareholders as a group. Instead of individual negotiation, if the target company's shares are publicly traded the acquiring company can purchase the shares on the open market. Even if a sufficient number of shares can be obtained on

the market, however, this method of acquiring control may be too slow if the target company's board opposes the change of control. Although the formal approval of the target company's board of directors is not a legal requirement for acquisition of the company's shares, the board is in a position to make acquisition of a controlling interest much more difficult. As we will see in a separate section on directors' responsibilities in a takeover situation, the target company's board often will take various steps either to persuade its shareholders not to sell their shares or to make the acquisition less attractive to the acquiring company. The slowness of open market purchases for the purpose of acquiring control gives the target company's board ample time to devise various strategies to defeat the attempted takeover.

✓***Tender Offers:*** Because fast action is often necessary, it has become common for the acquiring company to make a **tender offer** for the target company's shares. A tender offer is a publicly advertised offer to the target company's shareholders to buy at a specified price those shares that are "tendered" (i.e., made available) to the acquiring company. The main advantage of a tender offer is speed—the acquiring company is more likely to obtain enough shares for control before the target company's board can erect effective barriers to the acquisition.

The price specified in a tender offer usually is substantially above the prevailing market price for the shares, because the market price does not reflect the value of having control over the corporation. Although this price often is in cash, it may consist of a stated number of the acquiring company's shares per share of the target company, or a combination of cash and a stated number of the acquiring company's shares. The specified price can even take the form of bonds or other property owned by the acquiring company, or a combination of such property with cash.

If the acquiring company's objective is to obtain control over the target company, the acquiring company may not want to purchase any

---

[5]As noted in previous chapters, control of a corporation can change without an actual change in stock ownership when two or more shareholders agree to vote in the same way. Even though a single shareholder does not own enough shares to control the company, a group of shareholders may do so if the group as a whole owns a sufficient number of shares to exercise control. In a publicly held corporation, acquiring proxies from a large number of shareholders is the most common method of concentrating voting power to gain control. Current managers often perpetuate their control by acquiring proxies giving them the power to vote for themselves or others of their choosing as directors. Occasionally, one or more shareholders desiring a change in control may challenge existing management by attempting to persuade owners of a majority of the outstanding shares to grant proxies to the challenger giving him or her the power to elect different directors. Control acquired by the use of proxies is far less secure than control accomplished by purchasing shares, because the control gained in a proxy battle can be lost in another such contest at the next shareholder meeting. On the other hand, if shareholder approval of a *formal merger* is obtained through the use of proxies, the change in control is structural and is as permanent as in any other merger.

shares unless it is assured of gaining control. Thus, the tender offer may provide that it will be valid only if accepted by the holders of a stated number of shares. On the other hand, the acquiring company may not want to buy any more shares than are necessary to achieve control. Thus, the tender offer may expressly limit the number of shares to be purchased and may provide that if more than this number are tendered, they will be purchased on a proportionate basis from all tendering shareholders.

The **Williams Act,** passed by Congress in 1968, amended the Securities Exchange Act of 1934 to regulate tender offers. One of the primary aspects of this law is the requirement that the individual or corporation making a tender offer supply a wide variety of detailed information to the target company's shareholders so that those shareholders can make a completely informed decision whether to tender their shares. (The Williams Act is discussed in more detail in Chapter 50, Securities Regulation.)

Management Responsibilities in a Takeover Attempt

In modern times, many of the court cases applying corporation law principles arise in the takeover context, and much of this litigation focuses on the response of the target company's board to a tender offer. When one corporation attempts to acquire a controlling stock interest in another corporation, the target company's board of directors occupies a central role, for two reasons. First, the board's recommendation to accept or reject a tender offer often will strongly influence the decision of the target company's shareholders. Second, as mentioned previously, the board has the ability to erect a number of obstacles to the takeover.

Sometimes the target company's board will view a tender offer favorably and will recommend to the shareholders that they sell their shares. It must be realized, however, that a formal merger probably would have been negotiated and presented to the target company's shareholders if that company's board had been

favorably disposed toward the takeover. Consequently, in most situations the target company's board will resist the takeover attempt. A tender offer that is resisted by the target company's board is referred to as a "hostile" or "unfriendly" tender offer.

When responding to a tender offer, directors owe to the corporation and its shareholders the same fundamental duties of obedience, due care, and loyalty as they owe in other circumstances. Fulfilling these duties becomes especially demanding in the takeover setting, however, because the future ownership, control, and direction of the company are suddenly at stake, and tender offers do not permit a great deal of time for study and reflection.

The Duty of Loyalty in the Takeover Setting: Directors are fiduciaries of the corporation and its shareholders, and the duty of loyalty requires that directors act in the best interests of the shareholders. Inside directors, who also hold office or own significant numbers of shares, must be especially vigilant to fulfill the duty of loyalty because the takeover attempt presents them with an inherent conflict. Their position as directors requires them always to serve the interests of shareholders as a group, and sometimes a takeover by another company actually is in the best interests of those shareholders. On the other hand, inside directors face the probable loss of their management jobs if the takeover is successful. A court will conclude that directors have violated the duty of loyalty if it finds that they acted primarily for the purpose of maintaining their positions and control, or if they did not properly disclose relevant facts to shareholders. Directors must fully assess the tender offer and make a good faith decision whether the shareholders will receive the greatest benefit by accepting or rejecting it. If the directors make any recommendation to shareholders concerning a tender offer or other takeover attempt, they must fully disclose all material information relevant to that recommendation.

Weinberger v. UOP, Inc., 457 A.2d 701 (Del. 1983), provides a good example of inadequate disclosure to shareholders during a takeover. In 1974 Signal Company acquired 50.5 percent of UOP's shares. Some of this stock was bought directly from UOP in the form of authorized but unissued shares, but most of it was acquired through a tender offer. In 1978 Signal sought to acquire the remainder of UOP's stock at $21 per share. This offer was presented to UOP's board, which included four members who also served on Signal's board. Two of these directors serving on both boards conducted a study and concluded that buying the remainder of UOP's stock would be a good investment for Signal at a price of up to $24 per share. However, the president of UOP, who was a former Signal officer, then commissioned another study by the Lehman Brothers investment banking firm. In commissioning this other study, UOP's president dealt with a partner of the Lehman Brothers firm who also served on UOP's board of directors. The study was performed very quickly and resulted in a conclusion that the $21 per share offer represented a fair price. UOP's board approved the offer from Signal to purchase UOP's remaining stock at $21 per share and formally recommended the sale to UOP's shareholders, who also approved it. Some of UOP's shareholders filed suit challenging the fairness of the transaction, however, primarily on the grounds that a complete disclosure of relevant information had not been made to the UOP shareholders. The Supreme Court of Delaware agreed with the plaintiffs and awarded damages to the UOP shareholders. The court's holding was based on its conclusion that UOP's board and Signal (as a controlling shareholder) had violated the fiduciary duty of loyalty to UOP's shareholders by failing to disclose the initial study indicating that any price up to $24 would be a good investment for Signal.

Due Care and the Business Judgment Rule in the Takeover Setting: Courts apply the business judgment rule when determining whether directors have fulfilled their duty of due care in responding to a takeover attempt. Directors are expected to give the matter the type of concentrated attention warranted by its great importance, but courts do take into account the fact that tender offers frequently do not give the target company's board a substantial amount of time for study. Essentially, the business judgment rule requires directors to make a decision that is as fully informed as the circumstances permit.

Shark Repellants: The boards of target companies have many methods at their disposal for resisting a takeover attempt. These methods sometimes are referred to generally as "shark repellants." Although some of these methods can be implemented without any change in the corporation's articles or bylaws, a few of them do require that the articles or bylaws be amended. It is increasingly common for boards of publicly held companies to anticipate possible future takeover attempts by persuading the shareholders to amend the articles or bylaws in advance. In addition, in some states directors have power to amend the bylaws themselves; this power sometimes is sufficient to enable the board to quickly adopt effective takeover defenses. Two of the more common shark repellants are described below.

The Poison Pill: This maneuver involves granting existing shareholders special rights that are contingent upon the occurrence of a takeover. For instance, shareholders might be given the contingent right to purchase at a very low price shares in the new company that would result from a takeover. The exercise of this right after a takeover would greatly dilute the value of the new corporation, and thus makes the target company much less attractive to a prospective acquirer. Poison pills are usually upheld by the courts so long as the target company's board fully and completely disclosed to its shareholders all material information relating to the effect of the measure before it was adopted.

Finding a White Knight: Sometimes the target company's board may resist a hostile tender offer by negotiating a merger with a third company (a "white knight"). Presumably, the white knight has a management philosophy more closely resembling that of the target company, or will permit the target company to continue operating independently after the merger. The target company's directors usually do not violate their duties to shareholders when negotiating a merger with a white knight, so long as (1) their recommendation that shareholders approve the merger is accompanied by complete factual disclosure, and (2) it does not deprive shareholders of a fair price for their shares by prematurely taking the company off the market. An example of the second situation is found in *Revlon v. MacAndrews & Forbes Holdings,* 506 A.2d 173 (Del. 1986). In that case, the target company's board resisted a hostile takeover attempt by negotiating a "lock-up option" with a third corporation. In this arrangement, the board of the target company (Revlon) gave the white knight (1) an option to acquire two valuable divisions of Revlon at a bargain price if another acquirer obtained as much as 40 percent of Revlon's shares, (2) a commitment that Revlon's board would not deal with any other prospective acquirer, (3) a promise to pay the white knight a $25 million cancellation fee if another acquirer obtained as much as 20 percent of Rev-

lon's shares, and (4) access to Revlon's private financial data that was not available to any other potential acquirer. The Delaware Supreme Court held that Revlon's board violated its duty of due care to its shareholders by prematurely taking the company completely off the market and ending any possibility that the price of Revlon's shares might be "bid up" by a takeover contest between competing acquirers.[6]

The Self-Tender and the Standstill Agreement: In the following two cases, the duty of due care is applied to two other types of shark repellants: a "self-tender" and a "standstill" agreement.

---

[6] The white knight itself must also be careful not to intervene after an agreement between the initial acquirer and the target has already been made. For example, Pennzoil Corporation attempted to acquire Getty Oil Company. Getty then entered a formal merger agreement with Texaco, the white knight. After Getty and Texaco merged, Pennzoil sued Texaco. Pennzoil claimed that it had a contract of merger with Getty before Texaco entered the picture, and that Texaco had committed the tort of wrongful interference with a contractual relationship. The jury and trial judge agreed with Pennzoil and rendered a $10.5 billion judgment against Texaco. As this text went to press, an intermediate level appellate court had just affirmed the trial court's decision but reduced the damages to $9 billion.

Unocal Corporation v. Mesa Petroleum Co.
Supreme Court of Delaware, 493 A.2d 946 (1985)

Unocal and Mesa are oil companies incorporated in Delaware. Mesa had previously acquired 13 percent of Unocal's stock, and in 1985 commenced a "two-tiered, front loaded" tender offer for the remainder. This type of tender offer consists of two stages, the first being much more attractive than the second. In this instance, the first tier of the offer was $54 cash per share for 64 million shares, or about 37 percent of Unocal's stock. The second tier, or back end, offered other securities, claimed to be worth $54 per share, in exchange for the rest of Unocal's stock. The securities offered in the second tier were highly subordinated bonds, often referred to as "junk bonds." Such bonds may have relatively high returns, but also carry a very high risk because the assets securing them are subject to substantial secured claims of other creditors that are superior to the claims of the bondholders.

Unocal's board, which consisted of eight independent outside directors and six inside directors, met five days after the tender offer was made to consider it. All of the outside directors and five of the six inside directors were present, and the meeting lasted nine and one-half hours. Detailed presentations were given by legal counsel regarding the board's obligations under both Delaware corporate law and the federal securities laws. The board then received a presentation from an expert financial advisor who discussed the basis for the opinions of two large investment banking firms that the Mesa proposal was wholly inadequate. The advisor stated that the minimum cash value that could be expected from a sale or orderly liquidation of 100 percent of Unocal's stock was in excess of $60 per share. He also showed slides outlining the valuation techniques used by the two investment firms and others, depicting recent business combinations in the oil and gas industry. Finally, the financial advisor presented various defensive strategies available to the board if it concluded that Mesa's tender offer was inadequate and should be opposed. One of these devices was a self-tender by Unocal for its own stock with a reasonable price range of $70 to $75 per share. The cost of such a proposal would cause the company to incur $6.1–$6.5 billion of additional debt, and a part of the presentation discussed Unocal's ability to handle this debt. The directors were told that the primary effect of this debt would be to reduce exploratory drilling, but that the company would remain a viable entity.

The eight outside directors, constituting a clear majority of the thirteen members present, then met separately with Unocal's financial advisors and attorneys. Thereafter, they unanimously agreed to advise the board that it should reject Mesa's tender offer as inadequate, and that Unocal should pursue a self-tender to provide the shareholders with a fairly priced alternative. The board then reconvened and voted unanimously to reject the tender offer as inadequate. Two days later the same thirteen directors met again, with four directors participating by telephone as permitted by Delaware law, and heard a detailed presentation from Unocal's top financial officer and its assistant general counsel regarding the proposed terms of the self-tender. They ultimately voted unanimously to make the self-tender in the form of secured, unsubordinated Unocal bonds worth an aggregate of $72 per share. The self-tender was to become effective if the first tier of Mesa's tender offer was successful, provided for the purchase of the remaining 49 percent of Unocal's shares, and expressly excluded Mesa from being able to accept Unocal's self-tender for the shares Mesa owned.

Mesa filed suit in Delaware seeking an injunction prohibiting Unocal's self-tender. Mesa claimed that Unocal's board owed a fiduciary

duty to act in the best interest of all shareholders, including Mesa, and that treating shareholders selectively (i.e., excluding Mesa from the self-tender) was a violation of this duty. Mesa also claimed that Unocal's board had violated its duty of due care. The trial court ruled in favor of Mesa and granted a preliminary injunction against Unocal and its directors. Unocal appealed to the Delaware Supreme Court.

Moore, Justice:

The issues we address involve these fundamental questions: Did the Unocal board have the power and duty to oppose a takeover threat it reasonably perceived to be harmful to the corporate enterprise, and if so, is its action here entitled to the protection of the business judgment rule?

Mesa contends that the discriminatory exchange offer [i.e., the self-tender offer] violates the fiduciary duties Unocal owes it. Mesa argues that because of the Mesa exclusion the business judgment rule is inapplicable. . . . Unocal answers that it does not owe a duty of "fairness" to Mesa, given the facts here. Specifically, Unocal contends that its board of directors reasonably and in good faith concluded that Mesa's $54 two-tier tender offer was coercive and inadequate, and that Mesa sought selective treatment for itself. Furthermore, Unocal argues that the board's approval of the exchange offer was made in good faith, on an informed basis, and in the exercise of due care. Under these circumstances, Unocal contends that its directors properly employed this device to protect the company and its stockholders from Mesa's harmful tactics. . . .

In the acquisition of its shares a Delaware corporation may deal selectively with its stockholders, provided the directors have not acted out of a sole or primary purpose to entrench themselves in office. . . . [Also,] the board's power to act derives from its fundamental duty and obligation to protect the corporate enterprise, which includes stockholders, from harm reasonably perceived, irrespective of its source. Thus, we are satisfied that in the broad context of corporate governance, including issues of fundamental corporate change, a board of directors is not a passive instrumentality. . . .

We turn to the standards by which director action is to be measured. . . . The business judgment rule . . . is applicable in the context of a takeover. The business judgment rule is a "presumption that in making a business decision the directors of a corporation acted on an informed basis, in good faith and in the honest belief that the action taken was in the best interests of the company." . . .

When a board addresses a pending takeover bid it has an obligation to determine whether the offer is in the best interest of the corporation and its shareholders. In that respect a board's duty is no different from any other responsibility it shoulders, and its decisions should be no less entitled to the respect they otherwise would be accorded in the realm of business judgment. There are, however, certain caveats to a proper exercise of this function. Because of the omnipresent specter that a board may be acting primarily in its own interests, rather than those of the corporation and its shareholders, there is an enhanced duty which calls for judicial examination at the threshold before the protections of the business judgment rule may be conferred.

This Court has long recognized that:

We must bear in mind the inherent danger in the purchase of shares with corporate funds to remove a threat to corporate policy when a threat to control is involved. The directors are of necessity confronted with a conflict of interest, and an objective decision is difficult.

In the face of this inherent conflict directors must show that they had reasonable grounds for believing that a danger to corporate policy and effectiveness existed because of another person's stock ownership. However, they satisfy that burden "by showing good faith and reasonable investigation. . . ." Furthermore, such proof is materially enhanced, as here, by the approval of a board comprised of a majority of outside independent directors who have acted in accordance with the foregoing standards. . . .

A further aspect is the element of balance. If a defensive measure is to come within the ambit of the business judgment rule, it must be reasonable in relation to the threat posed. This entails an analysis by the directors of the nature of the takeover bid and its effect on the corporate enterprise. Examples of such concerns may include: inadequacy of the price offered, nature and timing of the offer, questions of illegality, the impact on "constituencies" other than shareholders (i.e., creditors, customers, employees, and perhaps even the community generally), the risk of nonconsummation, and the quality of securities being offered in the exchange. While not a controlling factor, it also seems to us that a board may reasonably consider the basic stockholder interests at stake, including those of short term speculators, whose actions may have fueled the coercive aspect of the offer at the expense of the long term investor. Here, the threat posed was viewed by the Unocal board as a grossly inadequate two-tier coercive tender offer coupled with the threat of "greenmail." . . . [Authors' note: The term "greenmail" refers to the situation in which the corporation attempting a takeover has already acquired a substantial number of the target company's shares when it moves to obtain control, and in return for abandonment of the takeover attempt the target company purchases these shares from the acquiring company at a premium price (i.e., the "greenmail") that is not available to other shareholders. Mesa had made huge profits by this method in several "unsuccessful" takeover attempts in recent years.]

Specifically, the Unocal directors had concluded that the value of Unocal was substantially above the $54 per share offered in cash at the front end. Furthermore, they determined that the subordinated securities to be exchanged in Mesa's announced squeeze out of the remaining shareholders in the "back-end" merger were "junk bonds" worth far less than $54. It is now well recognized that such offers are a classic coercive measure designed to stampede shareholders into tendering at the first tier, even if the price is inadequate, out of fear of what they will receive at the back end of the transaction. Wholly beyond the coercive aspect of an inadequate two-tier tender offer, the threat was posed by a corporate raider with a national reputation as a "greenmailer."

In adopting the selective exchange offer, the board stated that its objective was either to defeat the inadequate Mesa offer or, should the offer still succeed, provide the 49% of its stockholders, who would otherwise be forced to accept "junk bonds," with $72 worth of senior debt. We find that both purposes are valid.

However, such efforts would have been thwarted by Mesa's participation in the exchange offer. First, if Mesa could tender its shares, Unocal would effectively be subsidizing the former's continuing effort to buy Unocal stock at $54 per share. Second, Mesa could not, by definition, fit within the class of shareholders being protected from its own coercive and inadequate tender offer. . . .

[The decision of the trial court for Mesa is therefore reversed, and the preliminary injunction against Unocal is vacated.]

Comment: After the *Unocal* case was decided, the federal Securities and Exchange Commission (SEC) adopted an "all holders rule," which prohibits the making of a tender offer that excludes any shareholders. The rule applies to all tender offers, including a self-tender. Thus, this rule will now prevent a target company from using a discriminatory self-tender as Unocal did to defeat an attempted takeover. Although the precise result in the case would be different today, the court's excellent discussion of the business judgment rule in the takeover setting continues to be completely valid. In addition, the new SEC rule will not prevent a target company from using a self-tender, so long as it is not discriminatory. A self-tender sometimes can be an effective defensive measure even if it is not discriminatory.

Enterra Corporation v. SGS Associates
U.S. District Court for the Eastern District of
Pennsylvania, 600 F.Supp. 678 (1985)

Enterra is a publicly held corporation that was incorporated and has its principal place of business in Pennsylvania. Its board consisted of five outside and three inside directors. In 1982 SGS acquired 5 percent of Enterra's stock in a relatively short time. These purchases generated significant market interest in the stock, as well as rumors of a takeover of Enterra, and caused the price of Enterra's stock to climb substantially. This price rise made acquisition of additional shares by SGS much more costly, and the company did not then have the desire to acquire control over Enterra. SGS and Enterra's board then negotiated and signed a ten-year "standstill agreement," under which SGS promised not to acquire more than 15 percent of Enterra's stock and not to undertake a tender offer, and Enterra promised not to oppose SGS's acquisition of Enterra stock up to the 15 percent limit. Enterra disclosed the detailed terms of the agreement in a press release and in a direct mailing to its shareholders. During the next two years, SGS acquired more Enterra stock and began to approach the 15 percent limit. It apparently also acquired the financial backing to acquire a much larger amount of Enterra stock, and decided to seek a controlling interest in Enterra. SGS wanted to make a tender offer for all of Enterra's stock at $21 per share, but Enterra's financial advisors informed its board that $21 per share was inadequate and the board refused to amend or cancel the standstill agreement. SGS then asked Enterra's board to convey the offer to Enterra's shareholders, and the board again refused.

SGS filed documents with the Securities and Exchange Commission indicating its intent to pursue a tender offer for all of Enterra's stock, and Enterra immediately filed suit in federal court alleging, among other things, that SGS's tender offer constituted a breach of the standstill agreement. SGS claimed, in response, that Enterra's board had violated its fiduciary duties of due care and loyalty by not informing its shareholders of SGS's tender offer, and sought an injunction requiring the board to convey the $21 offer to its shareholders.

Broderick, Judge:

In Pennsylvania, as in most jurisdictions, officers and directors of a corporation stand in a fiduciary relation to the corporation, and must discharge the duties of their positions in good faith and with the diligence, care, and skill which ordinarily prudent persons would exercise under similar circumstances. . . .

It is an axiomatic principle of corporate law that "[c]ourts are reluctant to interfere in the internal management of a corporation" at the behest of a shareholder, and that "[shareholders] cannot secure the aid of a court to correct . . . mistakes of judgment on the part of the [directors]." . . . It has been held that the presumption of good faith and sound judgment afforded by the business judgment rule is heightened where the majority of the board consists of independent, outside directors and where the directors have obtained and considered expert legal and business advice. . . . In order to overcome the presumption of the business judgment rule, "the plaintiff must make a showing that the sole or primary motive of [the directors] was to retain control." . . .

A "target" corporation's decision to accept or resist a takeover bid (generally manifested as a tender offer) necessarily rests with the board of directors, since it is the directors, and not the shareholders, who are best able to evaluate the numerous and often complex financial factors which must be considered in determining whether the takeover proposal serves the best interests of the corporation. The wave of corporate takeover attempts in recent years has spawned sufficient litigation to establish that the fiduciary duty of corporate directors "to act in the best interests of the corporation's shareholders . . . requires the directors to attempt to block takeovers that would [in their judgment] be harmful to the target company."

Courts applying the business judgment rule have upheld a wide variety of sometimes drastic defensive tactics undertaken by a target company to prevent a takeover bid, including the sale of large blocks of treasury stock to "friendly" purchasers; acquisitions designed to make the target less attractive or create antitrust obstacles for the offeror; and the institution of antitrust or securities litigation by the target company against the offeror in an effort to block the takeover. It is well-established that such "[d]efensive tactics are illegitimate only if a target's management fails to exercise its business judgment and engages in such tactics for the primary purpose of entrenchment." . . .

The use of standstill agreements is a relatively recent corporate development. . . . The standstill agreement is "in essence, a corporate peace treaty, designed to inject a degree of stability, certainty, and cooperation into the relationship between an issuer and a major investor." The typical standstill agreement serves to relieve the antagonism, suspicion, and hostility which, in this era of corporate takeover bids, often exists between a corporation and a substantial shareholder. The essential provision of a standstill agreement is a limitation, usually expressed as a percentage figure, on the shareholder's holding of the corporation's stock, and generally prohibits the shareholder from making any tender offers for the corporation's stock during the terms of the agreement. Such agreements may also restrict the shareholders' ability to transfer the corporation's shares by affording the corporation a right of first refusal. By entering into such agreements, the directors ensure that the relationship between the corporation and an investor who has been purchasing significant blocks of stock will be clearly governed and defined. Such agreements also serve to avoid the unsettling impact on the corporation's business and workforce which could result from anticipation on the part of customers, shareholders, and employees that a takeover bid may be imminent. The corporation may seek to avert a costly control fight with the contracting shareholder by arriving at a negotiated understanding in advance of an anticipated bid for control. . . .

The contracting shareholder, in return, receives assurance that the corporation will not oppose its acquisitions up to the specified limit. Often an investor's substantial purchases of the corporation's stock initially will cause the market price of the stock to rise, and it becomes more costly for the investor to acquire additional stock. The investor may therefore seek to clearly set forth its "investment-only" intentions in order to dispel any anticipation of a tender offer and reduce the market price for the corporation's stock. . . .

The application of the business judgment rule discussed above leads one to conclude that where "a valid corporate purpose [for executing a standstill agreement] exists and if management has consulted appropriate legal and business advisors before concluding the agreement," courts should not "second-guess management's judgment that the corporation would benefit from an extended period of corporate peace." . . . Although this Court would be inclined to challenge the validity of any provision in a standstill agreement requiring the shareholder to vote with management on any material matter, in this case the Agreement's voting provisions are not at issue. . . .

[SGS] contends that, notwithstanding the provisions of the standstill agreement there exists a common law fiduciary duty to (1) consider the adequacy of SGS' offer to buy all of Enterra's shares; (2) communicate that offer to Enterra's shareholders, together with the Board's decision to approve or disapprove the offer and its reasons therefore; and (3) provide some means by which each shareholder actually may accept SGS' offer and sell their shares to SGS. . . .

Assuming that the Board had a fiduciary obligation to the corporation and shareholders to consider in good faith the adequacy of the SGS proposal, it is clear that the Board fulfilled that responsibility. . . . [SGS also claims] that after deciding to reject the SGS proposal, the Board had a fiduciary responsibility to inform all shareholders of the terms of the SGS offer and the reasons for the Board's decision not to approve the offer. Ordinarily, of course, an offeror which has been rejected by the board of directors in its efforts to acquire control of the corporation is free to communicate its offer to any and all shareholders by tender offer or otherwise. Thus, ordinarily, there is no need for the directors to disclose the terms of any rejected offer or the substance of any negotiations because the offeror has unfettered access to the shareholders. However, since SGS is restrained by the terms of its agreement with the Board from approaching the shareholders with an offer to purchase their shares, [SGS] contends that the Board is under a fiduciary obligation to disclose the terms of the offer (and the Board's decision) to the shareholders. . . .

A corporate board of directors must submit a proposal to merge or consolidate to the shareholders for approval only if the board has approved the proposal. . . . The Board was under no duty imposed by any federal, state, or common law standard to communicate the terms of the SGS proposal (and the Board's decision to reject it) to Enterra's shareholders. . . .

[The standstill agreement is valid, and Enterra's board did not violate the fiduciary duties of due care or loyalty by making the agreement and subsequently refusing to communicate SGS's offer to Enterra's shareholders. SGS's request for an injunction is denied.]

As we have seen, the duty of due care requires that directors make an "informed" decision. Thus, despite the business judgment rule, directors violate the duty of due care if they do not give appropriate attention to an important matter and do not seek expert advice when it is clearly needed. In the case that follows, the target company actually initiated a "friendly" takeover by another company. After the resulting merger, several of the target company's shareholders challenged the action of the target company's board as having been "uninformed."

Smith v. Van Gorkom
Supreme Court of Delaware, 488 A.2d 858 (1985)

Trans Union was a widely diversified company, with its most substantial earnings coming from its railcar leasing business. Federal tax laws gave Trans Union a tremendous amount of investment tax credits (ITCs) to offset against income, but accelerated depreciation deductions were decreasing its taxable income to such an extent that it was unable to use all of its ITCs. By not using its ITCs, Trans Union was losing millions of dollars in tax benefits. Van Gorkom had been an officer of Trans Union for 24 years, its Chief Executive Officer for 17 years, and Chairman of the Board for two years. He was nearing retirement, and personally owned 75,000 shares of Trans Union stock. Trans Union's board consisted of five outside and five inside directors. In late August, 1980, the board, strongly led by Van Gorkom, concluded that it should seek a merger with a company having large amounts of taxable income so that the ITCs could be used. The type of merger they wished to pursue was a "leveraged buyout," in which the acquirer would borrow the funds necessary to purchase Trans Union's stock and then use the cash flow from Trans Union's operations to service the debt. Van Gorkom and two other Trans Union officers and directors, Romans and Chelberg, performed calculations indicating that such a leveraged buyout would be "easy" at $50 per share and "very difficult" at $60 per share. No independent financial advisors were consulted, and no study was done to determine what actually would be a fair price for Trans Union's shares. The only studies were aimed at determining what price would make a leveraged buyout feasible.

Van Gorkom then arranged meetings on September 13 and 15 with Jay Pritzker, a social acquaintance and well-known takeover specialist. At the first meeting, Van Gorkom proposed that Pritzker accomplish a leveraged buyout of Trans Union at $55 per share, and at the second meeting Pritzker indicated a definite interest in the proposal. Two other Van Gorkom–Pritzker meetings were held on the 16th and 17th, which were also attended by two other Trans Union officers (Chelberg and Peterson) and a paid consultant. At a final private meeting between Van Gorkom and Pritzker on September 18, Pritzker stated definitely that a corporation completely owned by Pritzker would offer to buy all of Trans Union's stock for $55 per share, that Trans Union's board would have only three days to act on the proposal, and that Trans Union would have to arrange the financing needed by Pritzker to make the acquisition.

Pritzker then had his attorney draft a formal merger agreement. In the meantime, Van Gorkom arranged for Trans Union's banks to finance Pritzker's purchase. On Friday, September 19, Van Gorkom called a special meeting of the Trans Union board for the next day. The directors were not given an agenda or told of the purpose of the meeting. At the meeting on September 20, which lasted two hours, presentations were made only by Van Gorkom and his personal attorney. Romans, one of the inside directors who had earlier performed the calculations concerning an appropriate price per share, told the board that his calculations did not deal with the question of a fair price but only with the question of a price that would make a leveraged buyout feasible. Copies of the formal merger agreement did not arrive until the end of the meeting, and were not examined by the directors. The board then voted to approve the merger and submit it to shareholders. That night at a social event hosted by Van Gorkom for the opening of the Chicago Lyric Opera, Van Gorkom and Pritzker signed the formal merger agreement. Neither Van Gorkom nor any other Trans Union board member read the agreement before it was executed.

The proposed merger between Trans Union and Pritzker's company was submitted to Trans Union's shareholders, and they voted to approve it. They were not informed about the basis for the $55 per share figure, however. Several shareholders then discovered how the transaction came about, and filed a class action in behalf of all Trans Union shareholders. The plaintiffs claimed that Trans Union's directors violated their duty of due care to the shareholders. The trial court ruled in favor of Trans Union's directors, and the shareholders appealed.

Horsey, Justice:

Under the business judgment rule there is no protection for directors who have made "an unintelligent or unadvised judgment." A director's duty to inform himself in preparation for a decision derives from the fiduciary capacity in which he serves the corporation and its stockholders. . . . Representation of the financial interests of others imposes on a director an affirmative duty to protect those interests and to proceed with a critical eye in assessing information of the type and under the circumstances present here. . . .

The standard of care applicable to a director's duty of care has been recently restated by this Court. In *Aronson v. Lewis,* we stated:

While the Delaware cases use a variety of terms to describe the applicable standard of care, our analysis satisfies us that under the business judgment rule director liability is predicated upon concepts of gross negligence.

We again confirm that view. We think the concept of gross negligence is the proper standard for determining whether a business judgment reached by a board of directors was an informed one. . . .

On the record before us, we must conclude that the Board of Directors did not reach an informed business judgment on September 20, 1980 in voting to "sell" the Company for $55 per share pursuant to the Pritzker merger proposal. Our reasons, in summary, are as follows:

The directors (1) did not adequately inform themselves as to Van Gorkom's role in forcing the "sale" of the Company and in establishing the per share purchase price; (2) were uninformed as to the intrinsic value of the Company; and (3) given these circumstances, at a minimum, were grossly negligent in approving the "sale" of the Company upon two hours' consideration, without prior notice, and without the exigency of a crisis or emergency. . . .

Without any documents before them concerning the proposed transaction, the members of the Board were required to rely entirely upon Van Gorkom's 20-minute oral presentation of the proposal. No written summary of the terms of the merger was presented; the directors were given no documentation to support the adequacy of $55 price per share for sale of the company; and the Board had before it nothing more than Van Gorkom's statement of his understanding of the substance of an agreement which he admittedly had never read, nor which any member of the Board had ever seen.

Considering all of the surrounding circumstances—hastily calling the meeting without any prior notice of its subject matter, the proposed sale of the Company without any prior consideration of the issue or necessity therefor, the urgent time contraints imposed by Pritzker, and the total absence of any documentation whatsoever—the directors were duty bound to make reasonable inquiry of Van Gorkom and Romans, and if they had done so, the inadequacy of that upon which they now claim to have relied would have been apparent.

[The judgment of the trial court for the directors is reversed, and the case is remanded to the trial court for a determination of the fair value of Trans Union's stock and calculation of damages to the shareholders.]

√ TERMINATION

As we saw earlier, a primary characteristic of the corporation is that it can have a perpetual existence. (While a few states do place time limits on the duration of the certificate of incorporation, this is of no real consequence because renewal is usually only a formality.) This is not to say, however, that a corporation *must* exist forever. A number of different circumstances can bring about an end to its existence.

In discussing the termination of a corporation, a distinction must be made between liquidation and dissolution. **Liquidation** is the conversion of the corporation's assets to cash and the distribution of these funds to creditors and shareholders. **Dissolution** is the actual termination of the corporation's existence as an artificial person—its "legal death." A liquidation can occur without an actual dissolution, as where the corporation sells its assets to another company. The shareholders might then choose to dissolve the corporation, but it would not be required. On the other hand, dissolution sometimes takes place before liquidation. The remainder of our discussion is devoted primarily to the various circumstances that bring about dissolution, with a final mention of the process of winding up corporate affairs after dissolution.

Voluntary Dissolution

A corporation can voluntarily terminate its own existence. Dissolution can be accomplished by the incorporators in some unusual circumstances, but the shareholders are ordinarily the only ones with such power. The board of directors does *not* have the power to dissolve the corporation.

By Incorporators:

If the corporation has never gotten off the ground, it can be voluntarily dissolved by the incorporators. This can occur where the corporation has not done any business and no shares have been issued. In such a situation, the incorporators dissolve the corporation by filing "articles of dissolution" with the appropriate state official, who then issues a "certificate of dissolution."

By Shareholders:

If the shareholders wish to discontinue the corporation's existence for any reason, they can do so. The most common reason for voluntary dissolution is that the enterprise has proved unprofitable.

The procedures for voluntary dissolution vary somewhat from state to state, but their general outline is basically the same. The process is usually initiated by resolution of the board of directors. A meeting of the shareholders is then called, at which time the matter is voted on. The vote required for approval varies among the states in the same manner as for mergers and consolidations, from a simple majority to four-fifths, with a *two-thirds* vote being the most common requirement. After shareholder approval, articles of dissolution are filed and the certificate of dissolution is issued.

Dissenting shareholders can challenge the dissolution in court. However, a court will issue an injunction prohibiting dissolution only if these shareholders are able to prove that the controlling shareholders dissolved the corporation in *bad faith,* with the intent of defrauding the minority.

Involuntary Dissolution

In some circumstances, a court action can be instituted for the purpose of dissolving the corporation. A legal proceeding of this nature can be brought by a shareholder or by the state. Dissolution ordered by a court in such a proceeding is often referred to as an "involuntary" dissolution.

By Shareholders:

The laws of the various states generally provide that one or more shareholders can file a lawsuit requesting that the court dissolve the corporation. Those situations in which a shareholder can obtain dissolution by court order are listed below.

Oppression of Minority Shareholders:

In most states, oppression of minority shareholders by those in control is a ground for judicial dissolution. Oppressive conduct generally includes any act by which controlling shareholders seek to take unfair advantage of the minority. One example is the purchase of corporate assets by controlling shareholders, who then lease them back to the corporation for exorbitant rental fees.

Deadlock:

Most states authorize dissolution by the court if it is proved that the corporation is unable to function because of a management deadlock. This is not a common occurrence and ordinarily could only happen in a closely held corporation. In order for there to be an unbreakable management deadlock, of course, there would have to be equal ownership interests by two separate factions and a board of directors with an even number of members split into equal, opposing groups.

Mismanagement:

Courts are generally reluctant to interfere with decisions made by corporate managers. However, a court may order dissolution of the corporation if it is being so grossly mismanaged that its assets are actually being wasted.

The following case illustrates the difficulty a shareholder may encounter in seeking to have the corporation involuntarily dissolved because of alleged mismanagement.

Gruenberg v. Goldmine Plantation, Inc.
Court of Appeal of Louisiana, 360 So.2d 884 (1978)

Goldmine Corp's. principal asset was a 900-acre tract of land fronting on the Mississippi River in Louisiana. Acquired in 1941 for $65,000, the property was appraised at $3,000 per acre in 1975, giving it a value at that time of $2,700,000. Since its acquisition the land had been used solely for growing sugar cane, a business which in recent years had not been very profitable. However, since 1966 various industrial interests had expressed a desire to buy the land, the latest proposed price being $3,600 per acre.

Without even investigating the merits of these offers, Goldmine's directors voted to reject them. The directors apparently were motivated by a feeling that the land would probably continue to increase in value, but they made no effort to obtain information that would enable them to intelligently weigh the proposals and determine the best interests of the shareholders.

Ten of Goldmine's shareholders, who collectively owned 40 percent of its stock, filed suit seeking to have the corporation dissolved by court order. They were opposed by four shareholders who collectively owned the remaining 60 percent. These four also served as the company's directors. Louisiana law provided several grounds for involuntary dissolution, the following two of which were asserted by plaintiffs as applying to Goldmine's situation: (1) "The objects of the corporation have wholly failed, or are entirely abandoned, or their accomplishment is impracticable"; or (2) "It is beneficial to the interests of the shareholders that the corporation should be liquidated and dissolved."

The trial court dismissed the suit, and plaintiffs appealed.

Stoulig, Judge:

. . . Meanwhile, back at the farm, the sugar cane crop was yielding dismal dividends which, over the past 10 years, averaged a net profit of less than one-half of 1 percent and the only reason the operation did not result in a loss for most of these years was that no charge for the use of the land was included in the operating expenses. . . .

From the minority standpoint, approximately $1,080,000 of their collective funds are tied up in a farming operation that has no future and from which they realize sparse returns. Aware of the tax consequences of liquidating, they nonetheless reason that 50 percent plus of something they can use is better than 100 percent of a paper asset beyond their reach.

In the light of this situation, we consider whether plaintiffs have sustained the proof to support their demands for involuntary dissolution. . . . First we hold the evidence does not support our concluding the objects of incorporation have "wholly failed" or "been abandoned" or that "their accomplishment is impracticable." Sugar cane has been grown continuously on this property since 1941. . . . Although the future of sugar cane farming on plantations the size of Goldmine is at best speculative and the record leaves no doubt that the highest and best use of this land at present is for industrial purposes, we cannot conclude that the accomplishment of sugar farming is impracticable.

Low profits per se do not render the accomplishment of the objects of the corporation impracticable. . . . To us "impracticability" connotes an element of obsolescence as well as a low return operation. Therefore relief is not available [on this ground].

We next consider whether the record supports the view that dissolution would be more beneficial to the shareholders. It can be urged validly in this case that the low returns of the past have been more than offset by the appreciation of the corporate assets. With the completion of the river bridge at Luling within the next few years, the land value, according to [an expert appraiser], should increase tremendously. Thus the proof required [for this ground] is lacking.

. . . We appreciate the frustrations of the minority who are locked into a financial situation in which they have a substantial interest but no control. They suggest the shareholders be equated to partners and be permitted to disengage from the corporation as they could were Goldmine operated as a partnership. Our substantive law provides for involuntary dissolution but offers no remedy for the minority shareholder with substantial holdings who is out of control and trapped in a closed corporation. We will not arrogate the legislative function to provide relief. . . .

Affirmed.

By the State: Since a corporation derives its right to exist from the state where it is incorporated, it seems natural that the state should also be able to take away that right. This power can be exercised, however, only in certain circumstances. The grounds for dissolution by the state (which are remarkably similar in the various jurisdictions) are discussed below.

Failure to Comply with Administrative Requirements: All states insist that corporations comply with various administrative requirements. With respect to some of these duties, noncompliance may be cause for dissolution at the instance of the state. The most common examples are (1) failure to file required annual reports with the secretary of state, (2) failure to pay franchise fees or other state taxes, and (3)

failure to appoint or maintain a registered agent. Many states acknowledge the relative insignificance of such omissions by providing for easy reinstatement upon compliance and payment of any penalties owed.

Ultra Vires Acts: The performance of acts that are beyond the corporation's powers constitutes a reason for dissolution. This principle is of little practical importance today, however, because most articles of incorporation now grant such broad powers that *ultra vires* acts are rather infrequent.

Dormancy: If a corporation never commences business after it is formed or if it becomes dormant by abandoning its operations, the state can seek its dissolution in court. But the absence of corporate activity does not automatically bring about dissolution; it simply gives the state a basis for obtaining court-ordered dissolution.

Antitrust Violations: In many jurisdictions, a corporation's violation of the state (not federal) antitrust laws is a cause for dissolution.

Fraudulent Formation: Several states provide for dissolution where the corporation obtained its certificate of incorporation by misrepresenting material facts.

The attorney general of a state usually acts as its representative when a court action seeking dissolution is filed. But where the basis for dissolution is merely the failure to comply with an administrative requirement, some states authorize the secretary of state or other official to cancel the certificate of incorporation without court action.

Winding Up

Where Dissolution Is Voluntary: When voluntary dissolution occurs, the corporation's directors become *trustees* who hold corporate assets for the benefit of creditors and shareholders. They usually are allowed to wind up corporate affairs without court supervision. The directors in this situation have four duties:

1. They must not undertake any new business. Their authority is limited to the fulfillment of existing corporate obligations.

2. They must make a reasonable attempt to collect debts owed to the corporation.

3. After liquidation of corporate assets, they must pay creditors insofar as these assets are sufficient to do so.

4. When the claims of corporate creditors have been satisfied, they must distribute any remaining funds to shareholders. This distribution is required to be in the proportion of shareholders' respective interests and in accordance with any special rights enjoyed by preferred shareholders.

The directors can be held personally responsible for the breach of any of these winding-up duties. However, if they are unwilling to serve as trustees in liquidating the corporation, a *receiver* will be appointed and supervised by a court for the purpose of winding up corporate affairs. The court can also take such action if a creditor or shareholder shows cause why the directors should not be allowed to perform this function.

Where Dissolution Is Involuntary: In any case where dissolution is involuntary, the liquidation of corporate assets and other winding-up activities are always performed by a court-appointed receiver.

SUMMARY

Although there are technical differences between a merger and a consolidation, there really are no practical differences, and the two terms are often used interchangeably to describe a combination of independent corporations under common ownership. The term merger is usually used to describe both types of combinations, as well as a number of other variations.

The reasons for a merger between two corporations are many and varied. A merger begins with approval by the board of each company, and then must also be approved by a vote of each company's shareholders, usually by an extraordinary majority such as two-thirds. A dissenting shareholder, one who voted against an approved merger, usually has the right of appraisal. This right permits the shareholder to have his or her shares appraised and bought by the corporation at their fair value.

In addition to formal mergers and consolidations, corporations may be combined under common ownership by other means, such as asset or stock acquisitions. These variations often are also referred to as mergers in everyday usage. Stock acquisitions may be accomplished in different ways, including open market purchases and tender offers. When the target company's board resists an attempted takeover by stock acquisition, the acquiring company is likely to use a tender offer because it is faster and allows the target company's board less time to raise obstacles to the takeover. In responding to a takeover attempt, however, the target company's board must continue to fulfill its basic duties of obedience, due care, and loyalty. In the takeover setting, these duties require the board to act in good faith, make decisions that are as completely informed as possible under the circumstances, and seek the best interests of their company's shareholders.

A corporation can be dissolved in several different ways: there may be a voluntary dissolution by vote of an extraordinary majority (such as two-thirds) of the shareholders, or there may be an involuntary dissolution for prescribed reasons in a court action instituted by a shareholder or by the state.

KEY TERMS

Merger
Consolidation
Defensive merger
Articles of merger or consolidation
Certificate of merger or consolidation
Appraisal right
De facto **merger**
Holding company (or investment company)
Tender offer
Williams Act
Liquidation
Dissolution

QUESTIONS AND PROBLEMS

1. X Co. manufactures casual and dress shoes of all types. It wishes to expand its product line by getting into the athletic shoe business. What factors should its board of directors consider in deciding whether to get into the new line by internal expansion or by acquiring an existing maker of athletic shoes?

2. Discuss the rationale behind the appraisal right.

3. Pierce Co. was merged into Rayex Co. One of Pierce's creditors was not paid before the merger took place. The creditor demanded payment from Rayex, but its directors refused, saying that Pierce no longer existed and Rayex had not agreed to take over Pierce's obligations. Is the position taken by Rayex correct? Explain.

4. Chemco, Inc., was merged into Atlas Industries according to a merger plan adopted by the controlling shareholders of both companies. Under the plan, Chemco's controlling shareholders received cash in return for their Chemco shares. Chemco's minority shareholders, on the other hand, were given Atlas shares in return for their Chemco shares. Although the amount of cash received by the controlling shareholders was reasonable and fair, several members of the minority filed suit, challenging the plan because of its different treatment of controlling and minority shareholders. Will their suit be successful? Discuss.

5. Tandem Corp. purchased all the assets of Kilmer Company for cash. After the sale, a creditor of Kilmer demanded payment from Tandem. The creditor asserted that by buying Kilmer's assets Tandem had automatically assumed Kilmer's obligations. Is the creditor correct? Discuss.

6. Portsmouth, Inc., had two classes of shares outstanding: common shares and nonvoting preferred shares. At the annual meeting, Portsmouth's shareholders voted to merge the company into International Conglomerate, Inc. Only the common shareholders, whose shares carried voting rights, were allowed to vote. As had been the case at past meetings, the preferred shareholders, who did not have voting rights, were not allowed to vote. The preferred shareholders challenged the validity of the merger, claiming that this situation was "different" than earlier ones and that they should have been allowed to vote. Will their challenge be successful? Explain.

7. What are the advantages of the tender offer as

a method for obtaining control over another corporation?

8. What type of corporation seems the most susceptible to a deadlock? Explain.

9. National Equipment Rental Co. was dissolved, its assets liquidated, and all its liabilities paid. Remaining for distribution to shareholders was $5,000,000. Two classes of shares were outstanding: 150,000 shares of $35 par value common and 100,000 shares of $35 par value 8 percent preferred. National's articles of incorporation were silent on the matter of a preference as to assets on liquidation. What division will be made of the $5,000,000?

Chapter 40

LEGAL LIABILITY OF ACCOUNTANTS

Modern economies are critically dependent on accurate, reliable financial information, which provides the basis by which investors and businesspersons value assets and enterprises. As accumulations of capital grow larger and economic transactions become more complex, the importance of this information grows ever greater.

Accountants provide much of this financial information. An accountant who audits a corporation's books is relied on not just by the corporation but also by investors, creditors, government agencies, and others to provide an accurate financial picture. Because the role of the accountant is so critical to our economy and the potential damage if the accountant errs is so great, all states regulate use of the title *certified public accountant* (*CPA*). All states require examinations for qualification, and many require additional experience and continuing education for CPAs. An extensive code of ethics promulgated by the American Institute of Certified Public Accountants (AICPA) sets out rules of conduct.

Despite a generally exemplary record, the accounting profession occasionally stubs its collective toe. A vast network of statutes and rules provides an arsenal of legal weapons for those who may be injured by the accountant's errors. Furthermore, when a company fails, its independent auditor may be one of the few potential defendants that is solvent. The auditor's assets and liability insurance policies present an attractive target for suit. Indeed, there have been more suits against accounting firms in the past 15 years than in the entire previous history of the profession. Between 1980 and mid-1986 the "Big Eight" accounting firms paid out $180 million in audit-related litigation, and still had $2 billion worth of damage claims pending against them. It is no wonder liability insurance rates have skyrocketed for accountants in recent years.

It is important to be familiar with the legal obligations of accountants. This chapter surveys the many potential sources of an accountant's legal liability. Of the three major accounting functions—auditing, tax practice, and manage-ment advisory services—auditing is emphasized because it generates the most accounting revenue and gives rise to most of the lawsuits filed against accountants.

COMMON LAW LIABILITY TO CLIENTS

Contractual Liability

An accountant hired to audit a company's books is an independent contractor who must perform the auditing responsibilities properly and with due care. Though not a guarantor of the accuracy of the client's financial records, the auditor must act diligently, independently, and honestly. The auditor's responsibilities are established by the contract with the client.

An audit is an independent critique of a business entity's financial statements in order to determine their accuracy and reliability. The audit consists of three phases: (1) collection of data, (2) analysis of data, and (3) report of data and conclusions in an appropriate form. The goal of the audit is an opinion by the auditor regarding the quality of the client's financial statements.

An auditor who is unable to form a valid opinion as to the accuracy of the company's records—perhaps because the company has allowed only a limited review, or the underlying financial records are incomplete, or the accuracy is dependent upon an event that has not yet transpired, such as the closing of a pending sale—uses a **disclaimer.** A disclaimer informs the reader that the auditor has had to qualify the opinion and is therefore not vouching for the total accuracy of the company's financial statements. In one case an auditor was able to avoid legal liability by clearly noting that the auditors did not confirm the accounts receivable or review their collectability and that the balance sheet had not been adjusted for uncollectable receivables.[1] However, if the disclaimer is not

---

[1] *Stephens Industries, Inc. v. Haskins & Sells,* 438 F.2d 357 (10th Cir. 1971).

sufficiently clear and definite to qualify a general impression of accuracy in the financial statements, the auditor may still be liable.[2]

The defensibility of the auditor's opinion is frequently the subject of litigation. Any number of auditing errors can produce an inaccurate opinion and constitute a breach of the auditing contract. The auditor may be inadequately trained or supervised or not sufficiently familiar with the client's business. Lapses in examination, such as the failure to verify inventory, or to discover that accounts receivable are uncollectable, may occur. Poor judgment in analyzing the data or a misleading manner of reporting conclusions are other errors. Such mistakes constitute a breach of the auditing contract and may result in liability on a breach of contract claim.

Negligence Liability

The same auditing mistakes that constitute a breach of contract will normally also constitute a breach of the auditor's duty of due care and therefore provide a basis for a tort claim of negligence. An auditor who fails to observe professional standards is liable just like a doctor or lawyer who commits malpractice.

Standard of Care in Auditing: The duty of an auditor is to exercise the special care and skill that the typical professional auditor would exercise in the same circumstances. At trial, expert testimony will help establish that standard of care.

Where does the standard of care come from? The auditor may be guided by **Generally Accepted Accounting Standards (GAAS),** which establish the objectives to be obtained by an audit and set the quality of performance in terms of skill, independence, and care. **Generally Accepted Accounting Principles (GAAP)** address the theoretical aspects of how various transactions should be carried on the books.

GAAS and GAAP are derived from such sources as (1) pronouncements of the AICPA, (2) pronouncements of the Financial Accounting Standards Board (FASB), (3) Securities and Exchange Commission accounting rules and releases, (4) rules of state boards of accounting and societies of CPAs, and (5) Internal Revenue Service rules of practice. These standards can be raised in a specific instance if more is promised by the auditor in a particular engagement contract.

A thorny question regarding the appropriate standard of care relates to the auditor's duty to discover fraud by the client's employees. Auditors have been described as "watchdogs, not bloodhounds"; they are not guarantors of their client's honesty. Nonetheless, the SEC and many courts demand that auditors keep a watchful eye out for fraudulent conduct. A predominant view, expressed in a recent opinion, is that "general accounting standards . . . require the auditor to use his professional skill to follow up any signs of fraud that he discovers in the audit. . . . Auditors are not detectives hired to ferret out fraud, but if they chance on signs of fraud they may not avert their eyes—they must investigate."[3]

A violation of GAAP or GAAS will be considered *prima facie* evidence of negligence by the auditor. On the other hand, compliance with GAAP and GAAS does not ensure an auditor of nonliability. Even if proper procedures and standards are used, poor judgment in analyzing the data collected can lead to liability. Furthermore, some courts demand more of auditors than mere mechanical application of GAAP and GAAS. For example, in *United States v. Simon,* defendant auditors were convicted of conspiring to commit criminal fraud by knowingly certifying a false and misleading financial statement, despite their calling eight expert independent accountants who testified that defendants had complied with GAAP and GAAS.[4] The court held such ex-

---

[2] An example is shown in *Herzfeld v. Laventhol, Krekstein, Horwath & Horwath,* 540 F.2d 27 (2d Cir. 1976).

[3] *Cenco, Inc. v. Seidman & Seidman,* 686 F.2d 449 (7th Cir. 1982).

[4] *United States v. Simon,* 425 F.2d 796 (2d Cir. 1969), *cert. denied,* 397 U.S. 1006 (1970).

pert testimony to be "persuasive" but not "conclusive" and left to the jury the ultimate decision as to whether the financial statements as a whole did not fairly present the client's financial position. In most recent cases, however, courts have held that auditors fulfill their duty of due care by complying with GAAP and GAAS in good faith.[5]

Standard of Care in Nonauditing Situations: Sometimes accountants are hired to do less exacting work than a full audit. Traditionally, if the accountant did an unaudited financial statement or bookkeeping, he or she could avoid liability by marking each page as unaudited and accompanying all documents with a disclaimer to clearly indicate the auditor expressed no opinion on accuracy.

However, cases decided in the 1970s held accountants civilly and even criminally liable for their "unauditor" activities. The courts clearly expected the auditors to take a more active role in detecting fraud and misstatements than did the accounting profession in these situations.

Because there was a lack of guidance as to what was expected of an accountant doing "unauditor" work, the AICPA issued Statements on Standards for Accounting and Review Services No. 1 (SSARS No. 1), which provides the heretofore missing standards. SSARS No. 1 divides nonaudit work into **compilation** (assembly and preparation of financial statements from records of the client) and **review** (limited review of financial statements prepared by the client), and provides specific guidelines as to what is expected of the accountant in both activities.

Independence

Because the client pays the auditor's fees, it is not always easy for the auditor to remain independent. In 1984, for example, approximately 450 public corporations changed auditors. Though most switches were supposedly motivated by an opportunity for lower fees, 20 percent of the changes followed issuance of a qualified opinion. This development has led both Congress and the SEC to scrutinize possible "opinion shopping"—a corporation's scouting about until it can find an accounting firm willing to support a favorable accounting treatment. As the SEC has stated: "If the manner in which the issuer changes its auditors restricts the independence of the new auditors or calls into question their objectivity, such conduct erodes the public's belief in the integrity of both the financial markets and the independent audit function."[6]

The following guidelines serve to preserve the auditor's independence.

1. Accountants must not have any direct or material indirect financial interest in the client.

2. Auditors should not loan money to or accept loans from the client.

3. Auditors should not be officers or directors of the client.

4. Auditors should not work for a contingent fee.

5. Auditors should not allow clients to indemnify them for their professional liability exposure.

If independence is lacking, any issued reports should indicate it in an accompanying disclosure.

Defenses

Lack of Reliance: Plaintiffs cannot recover on account of an auditor's careless mistake if they knew the true facts and therefore did not rely on the erroneous opinion of the auditor.

Contributory Negligence: Contributory negligence by the client has been asserted successfully as a defense by careless auditors, but the courts disagree as to the scope of the defense. If the client's contributory negligence consists of disregarding the auditor's recommendations or

[5]*SEC v. Arthur Young & Co.*, 590 F.2d 785 (9th Cir. 1979).

[6]*In re Broadview Financial Corp.*, Securities Exchange Act Release No. 21949.

of activity which prevented the auditor from effectively performing his or her duties, most courts would either bar recovery or reduce it.

If, on the other hand, the auditor's negligence lies in failure to detect fraud by the client's employees, the courts are split. Some hold that careless supervision by client management con-tributing to the success of the fraud constitutes contributory negligence. Other courts hold that careless supervision is not the type of conduct which should block or reduce recovery.

The following case illustrates one school of thought.

Lincoln Grain, Inc. v. Coopers & Lybrand
Nebraska Supreme Court, 345 N.W.2d 300 (1984)

Plaintiff Lincoln Grain, Inc., hired defendant Coopers & Lybrand to audit its financial statements. As part of that audit, defendant investigated the accuracy of the valuation placed upon the inventory of plaintiff's Iowa division. Its inventory consisted only of contracts to sell or purchase commodities. On June 30, 1975, Lincoln Grain valued the inventory of its Iowa division at nearly $2 million. Defendant certified that plaintiff's financial statements containing this figure fairly presented plaintiff's financial picture. In fact, because of embezzlement by the manager of the Iowa division, its inventory was worth only $143,000.

Lincoln Grain filed this suit contending that if the audit had been conducted in accordance with GAAS, the fraudulent activities of its employee would have been discovered earlier and that it was damaged by the delay. Plaintiff appeals from a jury verdict for defendant, raising several issues.

Caporale, Justice:

[Lincoln Grain claims the trial court erred in instructing] the jury, in essence, that if Lincoln Grain knew and appreciated the danger of employee fraud, voluntarily or deliberately exposed itself to that danger, and was proximately damaged as a result, then and in that event the verdict must be for Coopers & Lybrand.

The assumption of risk doctrine is predicated upon an implied consent to be treated negligently. Restatement (Second) of Torts §496A at 560 (1965) states the general principle as follows: "A plaintiff who voluntarily assumes a risk of harm arising from the negligent or reckless conduct *of the defendant* cannot recover for such harm." (Emphasis supplied.) Lincoln Grain's employee is not the defendant. The defendant in this case is an independent, professional contractor engaged to conduct an independent audit; certainly it cannot be said that one who engages such an accountant assumes the risk that the accountant will fail to adhere to proper professional standards in performing the contractual duties of the engagement.

The [next] assignment of error presents a more complicated problem. In substance, the trial court instructed the jury that if it found Coopers & Lybrand to have been negligent, then it must consider whether Lincoln Grain had been contributorily negligent—that is—whether Lincoln Grain had failed to properly monitor and review the Iowa division's financial data; failed to properly supervise that division; failed to take notice of information in its possession which should have put it on notice of the falsifications of the Iowa division's manager; and whether Lincoln Grain furnished to Coopers & Lybrand incorrect data relating to the Iowa division. If so, and if such negligence on the part of Lincoln Grain was the proximate or a proximately contributing cause of Lincoln Grain's damage, then the jury should compare the negligence of both Lincoln Grain and Coopers & Lybrand.

. . . [A]ccountants are not to be rendered immune from the consequences of their own negligence merely because those who employ them may have conducted their own business negligently. Allowing such a defense would render illusory the notion that an accountant is liable for the negligent performance of his duties. We hereby adopt the rule enunciated [in *National Surety Corp. v. Lybrand,* 9 N.Y.S.2d 554 (1939) and *Shapiro v. Glekel,* 380 F.Supp. 1053 (S.D.N.Y. 1974)] that the contributory negligence of the client is a defense only where it has contributed to the accountant's failure to perform the contract and to report the truth. The evidence here is such that whether Lincoln Grain was contributorily negligent in its dealings with the auditors and whether such negligence contributed to Coopers & Lybrand's failure to perform its contract in accordance with generally accepted auditing standards are questions for the jury under an instruction in accordance with the foregoing rule.

[Because of these and other erroneous instructions, the case is] reversed and remanded for a new trial.

COMMON LAW LIABILITY TO THIRD PARTIES

In recent years auditors have increasingly found themselves subject to suit by nonclient plaintiffs. As the defense of lack of privity has slowly eroded in many other areas of the law, so it has diminished as a shield for auditors. Increasing reliance by client creditors, investors, and others on the work of the auditors has led to their increasing liability.

Fraud

An auditor is guilty of fraud whenever he or she intentionally assists a client in deceiving others with false financial statements. If an auditor makes a false statement which he or she does not know is false but does not have reasonable grounds to believe is true, the act is deemed constructive fraud or gross negligence and the result is the same—liability to injured parties. Many years ago, a court said:

A representation certified as true to the knowledge of the accountants when knowledge there is none, reckless misstatement, or an opinion based on grounds so flimsy as to lead to the conclusion that there was no genuine belief in its truth, are all sufficient upon which to base liability. A refusal to see the obvious, a failure to investigate the doubtful, if sufficiently gross, may furnish evidence leading to an inference of fraud so as to impose liability for losses suffered by those who rely on the balance sheet. In other words, heedlessness and reckless disregard of consequence may take the place of deliberate intention.[7]

An auditor's liability to third parties in fraud cases was firmly established many years ago in *Ultramares Corp. v. Touche* wherein the defendants certified a firm's accounts knowing that banks and other lenders were relying on the audit. The certified balance sheet showed a net worth of a million dollars when, in reality, the company's capital had been wiped out. Justice Cardozo held that "To creditors and investors to whom the [auditor's] employer exhibited the certificate, the defendants owed a . . . duty to make it without fraud, since there was notice in the circumstances of its making that the employer did not intend to keep it to himself." Regarding fraud, constructive fraud, or gross negligence, Justice Cardozo's statement remains the rule today.[8]

Negligence

In the *Ultramares* opinion, Justice Cardozo drew a sharp distinction between fraudulent conduct and negligent conduct, holding that the auditor would not be liable to third parties for the latter:

> If liability for negligence exists, a thoughtless slip or blunder, the failure to detect a theft or forgery beneath the cover of deceptive entries, may expose accountants to a liability in an indeterminate amount for an indeterminate time to an indeterminate class. The hazards of a business conducted on these terms are so extreme as to enkindle doubt whether a flaw may not exist in the implication of a duty that exposes to these consequences.

Although the force of Justice Cardozo's reasoning protected auditors from negligent liability to third parties for many years, the modern trend is toward breaking down the privity barrier to recovery in negligence cases. The following case discusses the possible approaches.

---

[7] *State St. Trust Co. v. Ernst,* 15 N.E.2d 416 (N.Y. 1938).

[8] *Ultramares Corp. v. Touche,* 174 N.E. 441 (N.Y. 1931).

H. Rosenblum, Inc. v. Adler
New Jersey Supreme Court, 461 A.2d 138 (1983)

Defendant Touche Ross & Co. (Touche) audited the financial statements of Giant Stores Corp. (Giant). Relying on the correctness of these statements, plaintiffs Harry and Barry Rosenblum sold their businesses in New Jersey to Giant in exchange for Giant stock. The stock turned out to be worthless because Touche had carelessly failed to discover that Giant had manipulated its books by listing assets it did not have and omitting substantial debts it owed. Plaintiffs sued Touche and its partners, including Adler, on a number of theories, including negligence. The trial court granted defendant's summary judgment motion. Plaintiff appealed.

Schreiber, Justice:

This case focuses upon the issue of whether accountants should be responsible for their negligence in auditing financial statements. If so, we must decide whether a duty is owed to those with whom the auditor is in privity, to third persons known and intended by the auditor to be the recipients of the audit, and to those who foreseeably might rely on the audit. . . .

An independent auditor is engaged to review and examine a company's financial statements and then to issue an opinion with respect to the fairness of that presentation. That report is customarily attached to the financial statements and then distributed by the company for various purposes. Recipients may be stockholders, potential investors, creditors and potential creditors. When these parties rely upon a negligently prepared auditor's report and suffer damages as a result, the question arises whether they may look to the auditor for compensation. In other words, to whom does the auditor owe a duty? The traditional rule is that the auditor's duty is owed only to those with whom he is in privity or to those who are known beneficiaries at the time of the auditor's undertaking. This rule is commonly attributed to an opinion of Chief Judge Cardozo in *Ultramares v. Touche,* 255 N.Y. 170, 174 N.E. 441 (1931). A second rule has been expressed in Section 552 of the *Restatement (Second) of Torts.* Under the *Restatement,* liability is extended to a known and intended class of beneficiaries. For example, if the auditor knows that the report is to be prepared for bank borrowing, then his duty would run to the bank to whom the company delivered the opinion. A third rule is that the auditor's duty is owed to those whom the auditor should reasonably foresee as recipients from the company of the financial statements for authorized business purposes. . . .

Both *Ultramares* and the *Restatement* demand a relationship between the relying third party and the auditor. Unless some policy considerations warrant otherwise, privity should not be, and is not, a salutary predicate to prevent recovery. Generally, within the outer limits fixed by the court as a matter of law, the reasonably foreseeable consequences of the negligent act define the duty and should be actionable.

We long ago discarded the requirement of privity in a products liability case based on negligence. . . . Why should a claim of negligent misrepresentation be barred in the absence of privity when no such limit is imposed where the plaintiff's claim also sounds in tort, but is based on liability for defects in products arising out of a negligent misrepresentation? If recovery for defective products may include economic loss, why should such loss not be compensable if caused by negligent misrepresentation? The maker of the product and the person making a written representation with intent that it be relied upon are, respectively, impliedly holding out that the product is reasonably fit, suitable and safe and that the representation is reasonably sufficient, suitable and accurate. . . .

At one time the audit was made primarily to inform management of irregularities and inefficiencies in the business. . . . It is now well recognized that the audited statements are made for the use of third parties who have no contractual relationship with the auditor. Moreover, it is common knowledge that companies use audits for many proper business purposes, such as submission to banks and other lending institutions that might advance funds and to suppliers of services and goods that might advance credit. The SEC twenty-five years ago stated: "The responsibility of a public accountant is not only to the client who pays his fee, but also to investors, creditors and others who may rely on the financial statements which he certifies." *In re Touche, Niven, Bailey & Smart,* 37 S.E.C. 629, 670 (1957). . . .

Independent auditors have apparently been able to obtain liability insurance covering these risks or otherwise to satisfy their financial obligations. We have no reason to believe that they may not purchase malpractice insurance policies that cover their negligent acts leading to misstatements relied upon by persons who receive the audit from the company pursuant to a proper business purpose.

The imposition of a duty to foreseeable users may cause accounting firms to engage in more thorough reviews. This might entail setting up stricter standards and applying closer supervision, which should tend to reduce the number of instances in which liability would ensue. Much of the additional costs incurred either because of more thorough auditing review or increased insurance premiums would be borne by the business entity and its stockholders or customers.

The extent of financial exposure has certain built-in limits. The plaintiffs would have to establish that they received the audited statements from the company pursuant to a proper company purpose, that they, in accordance with that purpose, relied on the statements and that the misstatements therein were due to the auditor's negligence and were a proximate cause of the plaintiff's damage. The injured party would be limited to recovery of actual losses due to reliance on the misstatement. Negligence of the injured party could bar or limit the amount of recovery under the Comparative Negligence Act. The accounting firm could seek indemnification or contribution from the company and those blameworthy officers or employees. The auditors could in some circumstances, such as when auditing a privately owned company, expressly limit in their certificates the persons or class of persons who would be entitled to rely upon the audit. . . . In the final analysis the injured party should recover damages due to an independent auditor's negligence from that auditor. This would shift the loss from the innocent creditor or investor to the one responsible for the loss. Accountants will also be encouraged to exercise greater care leading to greater diligence in conducting audits. . . .

[Reversed and remanded.]

The liberal approach to third-party recovery adopted in *Adler* is a minority view at present, but it and the Restatement approach are becoming increasingly popular.[9]

MANAGEMENT ADVISORY SERVICES

A second basic function of accountants is to perform management advisory services (MAS). More and more accountants are expanding into management consulting, giving general advice on such matters as choosing types of computers, methods of inventory control, and tax shelters.

Because the AICPA has promulgated few concrete standards to govern MAS and there have been few litigated cases, the accountant venturing into MAS has little guidance. Many predict litigation in this area will increase, especially because accountants are starting to give advice as to matters outside their traditional competence.

Potential liability in this area is high. In a case involving the band Creedence Clearwater Revival, a jury rendered an $8.6 million verdict against an accounting firm which placed $5 million of the band's money in a Bahamian bank which the firm should have known was in financial trouble.[10]

In another case which has ramifications for accountants, a computer firm which installed an inventory control system which failed was held liable to the purchaser for executive salaries for supervision, increased clerical and office supplies, and the cost of renting related equip-

ment.[11] The court allowed recovery despite a disclaimer of warranties, which was held contrary to Minnesota law. Other cases, however, have sustained such disclaimers where they were clear and not the product of one-sided bargaining power.

In the past the SEC has discouraged accounting firms from expanding into MAS for fear it might create situations which would dilute the effectiveness of the auditing function. The SEC presently seems to be reducing its resistance to MAS activities.

TAX PRACTICE

The tax practice in which many accountants engage is an increasingly big business.[12] Heavy government regulation of the area exposes the accountant to a variety of legal constraints.

For example, the Tax Reform Act of 1976 requires a preparer of tax returns to furnish a complete copy of each return to the taxpayer at the time or before the taxpayer signs the return, and to retain copies of the returns for three years or retain lists of client names and taxpayer identification numbers for IRS inspection. All returns prepared by CPAs must be signed by them even if no fee is charged (however, they should be signed only if the accountant is satisfied that all relevant information has been provided and all questions answered).

The Internal Revenue Code penalizes accountants who prepare returns yet do not (1) furnish copies to the taxpayer; (2) retain copies of returns or lists of names and taxpayer identification numbers; or (3) correct incorrectly prepared returns. The law also imposes civil liability on accountants who aid and abet taxpayers in substantial underpayment of taxes, and criminal liability for aiding, abetting, or counseling the

---

[9] California recently adopted the *Adler* "foreseeability" test in *International Mortgage Co. v. John P. Butler Accountancy Corp.*, 177 Cal. App.3d 806 (1986). However, New York recently reaffirmed its allegiance to the *Ultramares* rule, though modifying it slightly to allow liability to third parties relying on inaccurate financial reports only where: (1) the accountant was aware that the financial reports were to be used for a particular purpose; (2) in the furtherance of which a known party was intended to rely; and (3) some conduct on the part of the accountants *linking* them to that party evinced the accountants' understanding of that party's reliance. *Credit Alliance Corp. v. Arthur Andersen & Co.*, 493 N.Y.S.2d 435 (1985).

[10] *Clifford v. Kanter*, #778142 (San Francisco Superior Court, 1983).

[11] *Clements Auto Co. v. Service Bureau*, 444 F.2d 169 (8th Cir. 1971).

[12] In 1986, Congress passed a dramatic reform of the nation's tax laws. The new law may alter the tax work of accountants, but it is unlikely to drastically reduce it.

preparation of false tax returns. Penalties for violation are not insubstantial.

An accountant who carelessly advises a client on tax matters, miscalculates a client's tax liability, forgets to file a client's return on time, or loses a client's papers can be held liable for negligence. Liability can extend to fees and penalties incurred by the client in correcting the mistake, occasional punitive damages, and even loss on prospective transactions. In one case, for example, defendant accountants advised plaintiff she could sell certain stock at a loss to reduce her income tax liability by offsetting an earlier gain in selling North American Company stock. Unfortunately, defendants had erroneously calculated the North American sale which really resulted in a loss. Because there was no reason to sell the additional stock at a loss, plaintiff was entitled to recover the difference between the sale price and the cost of replacement after she learned of the mistake.[13]

The IRS has substantial powers to obtain the papers of an accountant in investigating the tax liability of the accountant's client. Failure to comply with IRS subpoenas can lead to a contempt citation.

ACCOUNTANTS AND THE FEDERAL SECURITIES LAWS

In the wake of the great stock market crash of 1929, Congress passed several laws to regulate the sale of securities in this country. These acts protect the investing public by requiring companies to fully disclose information about themselves, by punishing fraudulent activity, and by promoting fair dealing.

The impact of these laws upon the accounting profession has been profound. Both Congress and the Securities Exchange Commission rely on auditors to play a major role in producing accurate financial information. Recently the SEC noted:

During the past several years, public and Congressional attention has been focused to an unprecedented degree on the accounting profession and on its role in promoting public confidence in the integrity of financial reporting. The Federal securities laws, since their enactment in the aftermath of the economic crisis of the early 1930's, have authorized the Commission to require that independent accountants audit the financial statements of publicly-held corporations. Thus, those laws have placed upon the accountant unique and important responsibilities in facilitating the proper functioning of this nation's capital formation processes and, more broadly, of our economic system as a whole.[14]

Recognizing the importance of reliable accounting and auditing to the effectiveness of the securities law, Congress gave the SEC substantial powers to make and enforce rules for accounting. Although the SEC has let the accounting profession lead the way, it has retained final authority and issues several types of rules and pronouncements governing the accounting practices of companies and the proper form for information in financial statements which must be filed with the SEC. Any accountant who audits for a public company is vitally concerned with the rules that the SEC promulgates, and with those of the Financial Accounting Standards Board (FASB), which the SEC recognizes as the private sector's primary standard-setting entity. Although the SEC's express authority to regulate accounting practices extends only to those public companies which must file statements with it on a regular basis, its influence on the actions of the FASB and AICPA ultimately affects the work of all independent auditors no matter how small the client company.

---

[13] *Rassieur v. Charles,* 188 S.W.2d 817 (Mo. 1945).

[14] Report of the Securities and Exchange Commission on the Accounting Profession and the Commission's Oversight Role (1978). The Supreme Court's statements in *United States v. Arthur Young & Co.*, the last major case in this chapter, clearly indicate that the Supreme Court also believes in the public responsibilities of the accounting profession.

SEC Rule 2(e) provides for discipline of those who "practice" before the commission. An accountant who prepares any statement, opinion, or other paper filed with the SEC with the preparer's consent is deemed to be "practicing" before the commission. Under Rule 2(e), the SEC can punish those who are unqualified, unethical, or in violation of its rules, or who have lost their state license or been convicted of various crimes.

Though the audit failure rate among public corporations is less than 1 percent, SEC enforcement actions against accountants directly and against public corporations for their accounting activities have greatly increased in recent years. In 1983 and 1984 there were 23 SEC enforcement actions brought against accounting firms. Fifteen of these led to suspensions of one or more accountants. The suspensions ranged from thirty days to over five years. Typically, a suspended accountant may reapply for the right to practice before the SEC after taking additional coursework and joining the AICPA's SEC Practice Section (a peer review group).

Any accountant who undertakes to audit for a public corporation must also face the possibility of substantial liability in *civil lawsuits* filed under various provisions of the securities laws.[15]

Securities Act of 1933

The Securities Act of 1933 regulates the initial sale of new stock by corporations to the public. It is frequently called the "truth in securities" law because its major goal is full disclosure to the investing public. If the financial statements required by the Securities Act of 1933 are inaccurate and investors are injured, lawsuits frequently follow. Accountants are often defendants in such lawsuits because of their role in preparing and auditing these statements.

Section 11: Section 11 of the Securities Act of 1933 expressly provides that if any part of a registration statement when it became effective

contained an untrue statement of a material fact (or omitted a fact necessary to insure that the statements made were not misleading), any person who acquired such a security may sue for injuries sustained. Section 11 then expressly lists as among potential defendants the issuing company, directors, the underwriter who sold the stock, and "every accountant" who helped prepare any part of the registration statement or any financial statement used in it.

A plaintiff making a Section 11 claim need prove only that a false statement was made in the registration statement and that a loss was sustained. Section 11 plaintiffs need not prove that they relied on the false statements or that the false statements caused their loss; these are presumed. Significantly, plaintiffs need not prove that defendants acted fraudulently, nor do they have the burden of proving mere negligence. Negligence, which is a sufficient basis for liability, is presumed from the fact of the misleading statement.

An issuing company has virtually no defense under Section 11 if there has been a false statement and a loss. Individual defendants, such as accountants, can defend by proving (1) the false statements had no causal connection to plaintiff's loss; (2) plaintiff knew of the falsity of the statement at the time of the stock purchase; or (3) the defendant acted with "due diligence." The harsh negligence standard of Section 11 is made even more stringent by placing the burden of proof on defendants to prove they were not negligent, but subsection (b)(3)(B) provides that accountants may carry that burden by showing that both at the time of registration and at the time the statement became effective (after SEC review and approval) they "had after reasonable investigation, reasonable grounds to believe and did believe . . . that the statements were true and that there was no omission to state a material fact required to be stated therein or necessary to make the statements therein not misleading."

In a leading Section 11 case, *Escott v. Barchris Construction Corp.*, a company (Barchris) which constructed bowling alleys became insolvent

---

[15] A lengthier discussion of the substance of the U.S. securities laws is contained in Chapter 50. Here we only highlight those provisions most directly pertaining to accountants.

soon after selling stock to the public pursuant to a registration statement. Among the many defendants in a Section 11 suit by investors was Peat, Marwick, the company's auditor. The registration statement contained reference to Peat, Marwick's 1960 audit of the company, which had several defects. The court noted that the accountant whom Peat, Marwick assigned to the task (Berardi) had little experience, was unfamiliar with the bowling industry, asked questions but did nothing to verify the answers, did not discover Barchris was listing sales that had not occurred, did not discover Barchris was holding up checks in substantial amounts because there was no money to pay them, and did not learn about some major problems Barchris was having with delinquent notes. In summary, the court held:

> Accountants should not be held to a standard higher than that recognized in their profession. I do not do so here. Berardi's review did not come up to that standard. He did not take some of the steps which Peat, Marwick's written program prescribed. He did not spend an adequate amount of time on a task of this magnitude. Most important of all, he was too easily satisfied with glib answers to his inquiries.
> . . . [T]here were enough danger signals in the materials which he did examine to require some further investigation on his part. Generally accepted accounting principles required such further investigation under these circumstances. It is not always sufficient merely to ask questions. . . . I conclude that Peat, Marwick has not established its due diligence defense.[16]

Section 12(2): Accountants are sometimes sued under Section 12(2) of the Securities Act of 1933, which provides that any person who offers or sells a security by means of a prospectus or oral statements that contain an untrue state-

---

[16]*Escott v. Barchris Construction Corp.*, 283 F.Supp. 643 (S.D.N.Y. 1968).

ment or misleading omission, and who does not sustain the burden of proving he or she did not know, and in the exercise of reasonable care could not have known of the untrue statement or omission, shall be liable to the purchaser for damages sustained.

Section 12(2) liability is patterned after Section 11. However, many courts hold that accountants are not liable under Section 12(2) because only those who "offer or sell" a security are listed in the section as liable. These courts hold that only the issuing company can be liable under Section 12(2). Other courts, however, take a broader view by holding accountants liable for **aiding and abetting** Section 12(2) violations if they substantially assisted or substantially participated in the sale. Such assistance might consist of providing a false financial statement upon which the buyer relied in making the purchase. In any event, good faith and due diligence appear to be affirmative defenses for the accountant sued under Section 12(2).

Securities Exchange Act of 1934

The Securities Exchange Act of 1934 complements the Securities Act of 1933 by regulating the trading of securities after their initial issuance. The 1934 Act regulates such diverse matters as proxy solicitation, tender offers to purchase shares of other companies, and the activities of brokers and dealers who sell stock at the "retail" level. It contains numerous antifraud provisions and allows the SEC to keep tabs on major public companies by requiring them to file a registration statement with the Commission and to update that statement with annual reports, quarterly reports, and interim reports whenever material changes occur in the company's financial situation. The work of accountants in preparing and auditing the financial statements that go into the registration documents and supplemental reports is critical to the success of the Securities Exchange Act of 1934. If the accountant errs, liability may ensue.

Section 10(b): Perhaps the most litigated of all securities provisions are Section 10(b) of the

1934 Act and Rule 10b-5 which supplements it. The elements of a Section 10(b) violation are a manipulative or deceptive practice in connection with a purchase or sale of stock which results in a loss to plaintiff. Additionally, in most instances plaintiff must prove reliance on the deceptive statements or acts. Unlike in Section 11 of the Securities Act of 1933, the plaintiff carries the burden of proof under Section 10(b).

For many years it was unclear whether a defendant under Section 10(b) could be liable if guilty only of negligence in making a deceptive statement, or if plaintiff would have to prove fraudulent *intent* on defendant's part. The Supreme Court clarified the matter in the following case, which involved an accountant defendant.

Ernst & Ernst v. Hochfelder
U.S. Supreme Court, 476 U.S. 185 (1976)

Defendant-petitioner Ernst & Ernst is an accounting firm which from 1946 through 1967 periodically audited the books of First Securities Company of Chicago, a small brokerage firm. Plaintiffs-respondents, including Hochfelder, were induced by Nay, president of First Securities, to invest in "escrow" accounts which he said would yield a high return. In fact, there were no such accounts; Nay immediately converted these funds to his personal use. The accounts were not carried on First Securities' books, and were not discovered until after Nay committed suicide in 1968, leaving behind a note that described the escrow accounts as "spurious" and First Securities as bankrupt. Plaintiffs sued Ernst & Ernst under Section 10(b) and Rule 10b-5. Plaintiffs did not claim Ernst & Ernst knew of Nay's scheme or intentionally committed any wrong. Rather, plaintiffs claimed defendant's audits were negligently performed in that they failed to detect Nay's "mail rule"—that he was the only person in the office who could open mail. Had Ernst & Ernst discovered this unusual practice, it would have had to have been reported in the audit reports, leading to discovery of the fraud.

The trial court dismissed the action, and on appeal the Seventh Circuit held that negligence could be a proper basis for Section 10(b) liability. Ernst & Ernst petitioned for Supreme Court review.

Powell, Justice:

. . . We granted certiorari to resolve the question whether a private cause of action for damages will lie under §10(b) and Rule 10b-5 in the absence of any allegation of "scienter"—intent to deceive, manipulate, or defraud. We conclude that it will not and therefore we reverse. . . . In addressing this question, we turn first to the language of §10(b), for "[t]he starting point in every case involving construction of a statute is the language itself." *Blue Chip Stamps* [*v. Manor Drug Stores*, 421 U.S. 723, 756 (1975)].

Section 10(b) makes unlawful the use or employment of "any manipulative or deceptive device or contrivance" in contravention of Commission rules. The words "manipulative or deceptive" used in conjunction with "device or contrivance" strongly suggest that §10(b) was intended to proscribe knowing or intentional misconduct.

In its *amicus curiae* ["friend of the court"] brief, however, the Commission contends that nothing in the language "manipulative or deceptive device or contrivance" limits its operation to knowing or intentional practices. In support of its view, the Commission cites the overall congressional purpose in the 1933 and 1934 Acts to protect investors against false and deceptive practices that might injure them. The Commission then reasons that since the "effect" upon investors of given conduct is the same regardless of whether the conduct is negligent or intentional, Congress must have intended to bar all such practices and not just those done knowingly or intentionally. The logic of this effect-oriented approach would impose liability for wholly faultless conduct where such conduct results in harm to investors, a result the Commission would be unlikely to support. But apart from where its logic might lead, the Commission would add a gloss to the operative language of the statute quite different from its commonly accepted meaning. The argument simply ignores the use of the words "manipulative," "device," and "contrivance"—terms that make unmistakable a congressional intent to proscribe a type of conduct quite different from negligence. Use of the word "manipulative" is especially significant. It is and was virtually a term of art when used in connection with securities markets. It connotes intentional or willful conduct designed to deceive or defraud investors by controlling or artificially affecting the price of securities.

In addition to relying upon the Commission's argument with respect to the operative language of the statute, respondents contend that since we are dealing with "remedial legislation," it must be construed "'not technically and restrictively, but flexibly to effectuate its remedial purposes.'" *Affiliated Ute Citizens v. United States,* 405 U.S. 128, 151 (1972). They argue that the "remedial purposes" of the Acts demand a construction of §10(b) that embraces negligence as a standard of liability. But in seeking to accomplish its broad remedial goals, Congress did not adopt uniformly a negligence standard even as to express civil remedies. In some circumstances and with respect to certain classes of defendants, Congress did create express liability predicated upon a failure to exercise reasonable care. E.g., 1933 Act §11(b)(3)(B) (liability of "experts," such as accountants, for misleading statements in portions of registration statements for which they are responsible). But in other situations good faith is an absolute defense. 1934 Act §18 (misleading statements in any document filed pursuant to the 1934 Act). And in still other circumstances, Congress created express liability regardless of the defendant's fault, 1933 Act §11(a) (issuer liability for misleading statements in the registration statement).

It is thus evident that Congress fashioned standards of fault in the express civil remedies in the 1933 and 1934 Acts on a particularized basis. Ascertainment of congressional intent with respect to the standard of liability created by a particular section of the Acts must rest primarily on the language of that section. Where, as here, we deal with a judicially implied liability, the statutory language is no less important. In view of the language of §10(b), which so clearly connotes intentional misconduct, and mindful that the language of a statute controls when sufficiently clear in its context, further inquiry may be unnecessary. We turn now, nevertheless, to the legislative history of the 1934 Act to ascertain whether there is support for the meaning attributed to §10(b) by the Commission and respondents. . . .

Neither the intended scope of §10(b) nor the reasons for the changes in its operative language are revealed explicitly in the legislative history of the 1934 Act, which deals primarily with other aspects of the legislation. There is no indication, however, that §10(b) was intended to proscribe conduct not involving scienter. The extensive hearings that preceded passage of the 1934 Act touched only briefly on §10, and most of the discussion was devoted to the enumerated devices that the Commission is empowered to proscribe under §10(a). The most relevant exposition of the provision that was to become §10(b) was by Thomas G. Corcoran, a spokesman for the drafters. Corcoran indicated:

"Subsection (c) [§10(b)] says, 'Thou shalt not devise any other cunning devices'. . . . Of course subsection (c) is a catch-all clause to prevent manipulative devices. I do not think there is any objection to that kind of clause. The Commission should have the authority to deal with new manipulative devices."

This brief explanation of §10(b) by a spokesman for its drafters is significant. The section was described rightly as a "catchall" clause to enable the Commission "to deal with new manipulative [or cunning] devices." It is difficult to believe that any lawyer, legislative draftsmen, or legislator would use these words if the intent was to create liability for merely negligent acts or omissions. . . .

When a statute speaks so specifically in terms of manipulation and deception, and of implementing devices and contrivances—the commonly understood terminology of intentional wrongdoing—and when its history reflects no more expansive intent, we are quite unwilling to extend the scope of the statute to negligent conduct.

[Reversed.]

Comment: Following the *Hochfelder* decision, which involved a private cause of action by injured investors, the Supreme Court held the SEC itself would also have to prove scienter in order to obtain an injunction under Section 10(b). Also, although the Supreme Court has not spoken on the issue, a majority of lower courts have held that "recklessness" by a defendant is sufficient to satisfy the scienter requirement of Section 10(b), though mere negligence is not.

Section 14: Section 14 of the 1934 Act sets forth a comprehensive scheme governing solicitation of proxies. The SEC requires management to include an annual statement when it mails proxy solicitations to shareholders. The annual statement contains much useful information about the company, including financial statements which accountants helped compile and audit. If a group of shareholders (called insurgents) would like to oust incumbent management and gain control of the board of directors, a proxy fight may result in which insurgents and incumbents vie for shareholders' proxies to vote at the annual meeting. Proxy fights may also revolve around policy decisions which must be made by shareholders, such as whether to approve a merger. These elections frequently turn on the financial performance of the company, so the accuracy of the accountants' work is of vital importance.

Rule 14a-9, promulgated by the SEC, outlaws proxy solicitation by use of false statements or misleading omissions.

Individual causes of action are permitted under Section 14, and, although the courts are in disagreement, accountants have been held liable for both primary violations of Section 14 and for aiding and abetting violations by others. In one influential but controversial case, *Adams v. Standard Knitting Mills, Inc.*, Standard shareholders such as Adams were solicited to cast their proxies in favor of a merger with Chadbourn, Inc. The proxy statement was accompanied by Chadbourn's financial statements which had been prepared by its accountants, Peat, Marwick. Although Standard shareholders were convinced to approve the merger and exchange their Standard shares for Chadbourn shares of equal value and supposedly higher dividends, when Chadbourn's sales declined the following year it was unable to pay the promised dividends because of certain restrictions in its loan agreements with banks. These restrictions were not disclosed in the proxy statement, and the court held Peat, Marwick was negligent, but not guilty of scienter, in omitting them.[17]

Although it recognized other courts had held corporations liable for mere negligence under

Section 14, the *Adams* court declined to do so, stating "we are influenced by the fact that the accountant here, unlike the corporate issuer, does not directly benefit from the proxy vote and is not in privity with the stockholder. Unlike the corporate issuer, the preparation of financial statements to be appended to proxies and other reports is the daily fare of accountants, and the accountant's potential liability for mistakes would be enormous under a negligence standard." Although Peat, Marwick, guilty only of negligence, was held not liable in this case, accountants guilty of scienter or recklessness may be held civilly liable for Section 14 violations. Even criminal liability may attach to intentional violations.

Foreign Corrupt Practices Act of 1977

In the wake of Watergate and other political scandals of the 1970s, hundreds of American corporations were found to have been paying bribes to foreign political officials to obtain or keep business in foreign countries. Congress responded by passing the Foreign Corrupt Practices Act of 1977 (FCPA), which has broad implications for accountants.

The first part of the FCPA, which applies to all U.S. companies, officers, directors, employees, agents, or shareholders, outlaws bribes to foreign officials where the purpose of the payment is to obtain or retain business. (There are exceptions for "grease payments" to lower level clerical employees.)

The second part of the FCPA more directly involves accountants. Because bribes had been concealed by doctoring corporate records, Congress decided all public companies must (1) keep detailed records which "accurately and fairly" reflect the company's financial activities, and (2) devise a system of internal accounting controls sufficient to provide "reasonable assurance" that all transactions are authorized and accounted for. Though designed primarily to aid detection of foreign bribes, these accounting provisions are not limited to that function.

---

[17] 623 F.2d 422 (6th Cir. 1980), *cert. denied,* 449 U.S. 1067 (1980).

The FCPA has strengthened financial accounting of public corporations. The requirement of record-keeping and internal accounting controls are more stringent than the previous financial materiality standard that accountants had used.

Rule 13b2-1 prohibits any person from falsifying any book, record, or account subject to the FCPA. Rule 13b2-2 prohibits officers and directors of companies from making false statements to accountants. Penalties for violation of FCPA provisions are substantial and may include jail terms.

Because the accounting provisions of the FCPA do not give accountants much concrete guidance as to when records "accurately and fairly" reflect a company's financial picture, or when an internal accounting control system allows "reasonable assurance" of accuracy, many accountants have been deeply concerned that the FCPA would lead to unfair imposition of large liabilities. This is particularly so because the FCPA has no scienter requirement; negligence could suffice to impose liability. Fortunately, the SEC has generally refused to take any action against perceived violations of the accounting provisions of the FCPA unless those violations were linked to breaches of other securities laws. Nonetheless Congress has often considered amending the FCPA to clarify (and some would say weaken) its accounting provisions.

RICO

The Racketeering Influenced and Corrupt Organizations Act (RICO) was passed in an attempt to blunt organized crime's infiltration into legitimate business. Perhaps unfortunately, Congress drafted the law in such broad terms that it has led to a plethora of suits against businesses having no connection to real mobsters. The elements of RICO civil liability are (1) the conduct, (2) of an enterprise, (3) through a pattern, (4) of racketeering activity. Because "racketeering activity" is defined to include several "garden varieties" of fraud (such as mail fraud and securities

fraud), virtually all traditional securities cases can now include a RICO count.

The incentive to include a RICO count is simple—RICO provides for recovery of treble damages and attorneys' fees. Furthermore, RICO can provide a powerful bargaining chip—no mild-mannered accountant wants the neighbors reading in the morning paper that the accountant has been named in a "racketeering" lawsuit. Along with the nation's most respected corporations, banks, and insurance companies, virtually every major accounting firm has been sued in one or more RICO suits.

Because many people believe RICO has gotten out of hand, as this chapter is written, the AICPA has joined many other groups in lobbying Congress to amend RICO to end the flood of lawsuits against "legitimate" businesses.[18]

CRIMINAL LIABILITY OF ACCOUNTANTS

Accountants face a number of criminal provisions which constrain their activities. Some accountants have gone to jail for violating these provisions.

Federal Securities Acts

The two most important criminal provisions for accountants are those of the Securities Act of 1933 and the Securities Exchange Act of 1934. Section 24 of the 1933 Act makes it a crime to willfully violate any section or rule of the Act or to willfully make a false statement in any registration statement. Section 32 of the 1934 Act similarly makes it a crime to willfully violate any section or rule of the 1934 Act or to willfully make a false statement in any document filed with the SEC. Because the accounting provisions of the FCPA amended the 1934 Act, willful violation of these provisions is also a crime.

Section 24 of the 1933 Act carries a potential penalty of up to five years in jail and/or a $10,000

---

[18] For more detail on RICO, consult Chapter 50 and see *Sedima v. Imrex* in Chapter 4.

fine. Section 32 of the 1934 Act is similar, except that the fine can be as high as $100,000.

Because both provisions require violations be "willful" before they constitute crimes, scienter is an element of a criminal violation. Courts have held that negligence or mistake is insufficient for liability, but recklessness may be sufficient. For example, in *U.S. v. Natelli,* defendant auditors helped a company cover up the fact that previously reported sales had not really occurred by hiding a discrepancy in a footnote.[19] The appellate court approved the trial judge's instruction that "good faith, an honest belief in the truth of the data set forth in the footnote and entries in the proxy statement would constitute a complete defense here." On the other hand, the court quoted a holding that "Congress equally could not have intended that men holding themselves out as members of these ancient professions [law and accounting] should be able to escape criminal liability on a plea of ignorance when they shut their eyes to what was plainly to be seen or have represented a knowledge they knew they did not possess."

Other Criminal Provisions

The most important additional criminal provision for accountants is the Federal Mail Fraud Statute, which outlaws use of the federal mails to carry out fraudulent schemes. The penalty for violation is a fine up to $1,000, imprisonment of not more than five years, or both. Scienter is required for violation. In *U.S. v. Glick,* Chisolm, a con man with some flair, induced people to pay him nonrefundable front end fees to obtain loans for them. He represented himself as a man of great wealth who would guarantee the loans. Chisolm would show his victims financial statements prepared by his accountant, Glick. Glick knew the financial statements contained blatant violations of GAAP and that no lending institution would furnish a loan to Chisolm based on them. Glick also knew of Chisolm's use of the

statements. Although Glick professed his good faith belief that Chisolm really did possess substantial wealth, the appellate court affirmed his conviction under the mail fraud law, holding he could not deliberately close his eyes to what was obvious to him.[20]

Accountants must also be wary of the Federal False Filing Statement Statute, which attaches criminal penalties to the filing of knowingly false statements with any federal agency, including the SEC.

Furthermore, most state securities statutes, called "blue sky" laws, contain criminal provisions comparable to those of the 1933 and 1934 Acts.

As noted earlier, intentionally filing false income tax returns on behalf of a taxpayer-client is also a crime.

Finally, accountants must be aware of federal statutes which outlaw **conspiracy** (agreement) to violate, or aiding and abetting (taking action) violations of other federal laws, such as securities statutes. Again, these provisions require intentional wrongdoing. For example, the required elements of aiding and abetting a securities violation are "that [defendant-auditor] knew of the [securities law] violations and of its role in the scheme, and, with this knowledge, substantially assisted in the violation."[21]

ACCOUNTANTS' PRIVILEGE AND CONFIDENTIALITY

Just as lawyers and doctors receive confidential, sensitive information from their clients and patients, so do accountants frequently receive extremely sensitive financial information from their clients. Indeed, AICPA ethics standards provide that accountants should not disclose confidential client information unless (1) the client consents; (2) it is necessary to avoid violation of GAAP or GAAS; (3) disclosure is in re-

---

[19] *U.S. v. Natelli,* 527 F.2d 311 (2d Cir. 1975), *cert. denied,* 425 U.S. 934 (1976).

[20] 710 F.2d 639 (10th Cir. 1983).

[21] *Seiffer v. Topsy's Int'l, Inc.,* 487 F.Supp. 653 (D.Kan. 1980).

sponse to an enforceable subpoena; or (4) disclosure is necessitated by an inquiry made by the ethics division or trial board of the AICPA or a state CPA regulatory body.

To the chagrin of most accountants, the common law does not recognize an accountant-client privilege similar to that afforded to lawyers, doctors, or members of the clergy. A part of the rationale for this is that much of what the accountant does is aimed at preparing forms and documents which will be disclosed publicly anyway.

The Federal Rules of Evidence do not provide for an accountant-client privilege, and traditionally there has been none at the federal level. Recently the Supreme Court confirmed the traditional federal approach by reversing a lower court decision which had created a limited confidential accountant-client privilege for tax accrual papers.[22] The next case is a summary of that proceeding. (Note the opinion's emphasis on the *public* nature of an accountant's responsibilities.)

_____

[22] *United States v. Arthur Young & Co.*, 465 U.S. 805 (1984).

United States v. Arthur Young & Co.
U.S. Supreme Court, 465 U.S. 805 (1984)

Respondent Arthur Young was the independent auditor of respondent Amerada Hess Corp., and therefore responsible for reviewing the corporation's financial statements as required by the federal securities laws. In so doing it verified Amerada's statement of contingent tax liabilities, preparing tax accrual workpapers relating to the evaluation of the corporation's reserves for such liabilities. In an IRS criminal investigation of Amerada's tax returns, the auditor's workpapers were summoned under §7602 of the IRS Code. Amerada instructed Arthur Young not to comply with the summons, so the IRS commenced an enforcement action in federal district court.

The district court ordered enforcement of the summons. On appeal, the Court of Appeals, while concluding that the papers were relevant to the IRS investigation, created a work-product immunity for independent auditors' work for public corporations. It found that the IRS had not made a sufficient showing to overcome the immunity and refused to enforce the summons. The government appealed.

Burger, Chief Justice:

. . . Based upon its evaluation of the competing policies of the federal tax and securities laws, the Court of Appeals found it necessary to create a so-called privilege for the independent auditor's workpapers.

Congress has endowed the IRS with expansive information-gathering authority; §7602 is the centerpiece of that congressional design. . . . [C]ourts should be chary in recognizing exceptions to the broad summons authority of the IRS or in fashioning new privileges that would curtail disclosure under §7602.

The Court of Appeals nevertheless concluded that "substantial countervailing policies" required the fashioning of a work-product immunity for an independent auditor's tax accrual workpapers. To the extent that the Court of Appeals, in its concern for the "chilling effect" of the disclosure of tax accrual workpapers, sought to facilitate communication between independent auditors and their clients, its remedy more closely resembles a testimonial accountant-client privilege than a work-product immunity for accountants' workpapers. But as this Court stated in Couch v. United States, 409 U.S. 322 (1973), "no confidential accountant-client privilege exists under federal law, and no state-created privilege has been recognized in federal cases."

Nor do we find persuasive the argument that a work-product immunity for accountants' tax accrual workpapers is a fitting analogue to the attorney work-product doctrine established in Hickman v. Taylor, 329 U.S. 495 (1947). The Hickman work-product doctrine was founded upon the private attorney's role as the client's confidential adviser and advocate, a loyal representative whose duty it is to present the client's case in the most favorable possible light. An independent certified public accountant performs a different role. By certifying the public reports that collectively depict a corporation's financial status, the independent auditor assumes a *public* responsibility transcending any employment relationship with the client. The independent public accountant performing this special function owes ultimate allegiance to the corporation's creditors and stockholders, as well as to the investing public. This "public watchdog" function demands that the accountant maintain total independence from the client at all times and requires complete fidelity to the public trust. To insulate from disclosure a certified public accountant's interpretations of the client's financial statements would be to ignore the significance of the accountant's role as a disinterested analyst charged with public obligations.

We cannot accept the view that the integrity of the securities markets will suffer absent some protection for accountants' tax accrual workpapers. The Court of Appeals apparently feared that, were the IRS to have access to tax accrual workpapers, a corporation might be tempted to withhold from its auditor certain information relevant and material to a proper evaluation of its financial statements. But the independent certified public accountant cannot be content with the corporation's representations that its tax accrual reserves are adequate; the auditor is ethically and professionally obligated to ascertain for himself as far as possible whether the corporation's contingent tax liabilities have been accurately stated. Responsible corporate management would not risk a qualified evaluation of a corporate taxpayer's financial posture to afford cover for questionable positions reflected in a prior tax return. Thus, the independent auditor's obligation to serve the public interest assures that the integrity of the securities markets will be preserved without the need for a work-product immunity for accountants' tax accrual workpapers.

[Reversed.]

At the state level, almost twenty jurisdictions have statutorily recognized an accountant-client privilege; the scope of the privilege varies from state to state. Most of the statutes have exceptions for criminal actions, bankruptcy proceedings, and the like.

The privilege, where it exists, belongs to the client, not to the accountant. The client waives the privilege by relying on the accountant's audits or opinions in litigation. Obviously clients cannot rely on the auditor's opinion and then prevent the opposing litigant from examining the procedures that the accountant used to reach the opinion.

SUMMARY

Plaintiffs are reaching into the "deep pocket" of accountants with growing frequency. On a variety of fronts, litigation, the size of judgments, and liability insurance rates are all increasing.

Accountants can be held liable to their clients for both breach of contract and negligence when they fail to carefully and reasonably perform their agreed-upon services. At the same time, they must maintain independence from their clients, or the auditing function will be thwarted. If the client is also negligent, the courts are divided on how that fact should influence the liability of a negligent accountant.

There is also a trend to hold accountants liable to foreseeable third parties, such as creditors or investors, who rely on prepared financial statements for business decisions.

Accountants do extensive tax work and are expanding into management advisory services. There is likely to be an increase in litigation against them in these areas.

Numerous provisions in both the 1933 and 1934 securities acts give rise to potential liability for accountants. The standard of care imposed on the auditor varies from section to section; thus, each rule must be analyzed independently. In recent years the Foreign Corrupt Practices Act, and especially RICO, have expanded accountants' liability extensively.

In addition to being subject to civil penalties, accountants may have criminal penalties imposed on them if they are found to have intentionally violated any of a number of federal rules.

Unlike attorneys, at the federal level at least accountants have been denied an accountant-client privilege.

KEY TERMS

Disclaimer
Generally Accepted Accounting Standards (GAAS)
Generally Accepted Accounting Principles (GAAP)
Compilation
Review
Aiding and abetting
Conspiracy

QUESTIONS AND PROBLEMS

1. The Professional Rodeo Cowboys Association (PRCA) hired the accounting firm of Wilch, Smith & Brock (WSB) to verify the prize money winnings of professional rodeo cowboys so that it could crown the World's Champion All-Around Cowboy on the basis of who had won the most prize money in sanctioned rodeos during the season. WSB determined that Camarillo was the top money winner, so he was crowned champion. Unfortunately, WSB had made two errors in its calculations; Ferguson was actually entitled to be champion. This led to a dispute which was settled by PRCA declaring the cowboys co-champions and awarding prizes and money to Ferguson equal to what had been awarded Camarillo. PRCA then sued the accountants, WSB. Are the accountants liable? Discuss. (*Professional Rodeo Cowboys Assoc. v. Wilch, Smith & Brock,* 589 P.2d 510, Colo. App. 1978.)

2. Shortly before a large corporation declared bankruptcy, three checks totaling $315,000 were drawn on the corporation's account and paid to the corporation's sole shareholder and to a corporate officer, to the detriment of corporate creditors. Birnie, who worked for Wilkes & Co., which had long been the corporation's outside auditor, helped conceal the transfers. Birnie then told the bankruptcy trustee that the corporate records were not complete, so the trustee hired Wilkes to compile complete records. Wilkes did so, and included false entries intended to conceal the fraudulent transfers. Later the fraud was discovered, and the trustee sued Wilkes for breach of contract. Wilkes argued the fraud occurred before the trustee had hired him. Is this a good defense? Discuss. (*In re F. W. Koenecke & Sons, Inc.*, 605 F.2d 310, 7th Cir. 1979.)

3. Timm, Schmidt & Co. (Timm) audited the financial statements of CFA, Inc., from 1973 to 1976. In November 1975, CFA obtained a $300,000 loan from Citizens State Bank (Citizens), which relied on the financial statements prepared by Timm. In early 1977, Timm discovered material errors totaling over $400,000 in the 1974 and 1975 statements of CFA. When Citizens learned of these errors, it called CFA's loan due, and CFA went into receivership. Citizens lost $150,000 on its loans and sued Timm for negligence. All Timm employees swore they did not know the financial statements would be used by CFA to obtain loans, but the senior partner stated "as a certified public accountant, I know that audited statements are used for many purposes and that it is common for them to be supplied to lenders and creditors, and other persons." Timm claimed its contract was with CFA and it had no liability to Citizens. Is Timm correct? Discuss. (*Citizens State Bank v. Timm, Schmidt & Co.*, 335 N.W.2d 361, Wis. 1983.)

4. Alexander Grant & Co. (AGC) was engaged by GHP Corp. to prepare an unaudited financial statement based on information provided by GHP. GHP submitted copies of the statement to Spherex, Inc., to obtain credit. Later Spherex sustained losses in its dealings with GHP, it appearing that the information in the unaudited statements was inaccurate. Spherex sued AGC, which argued that it should not be liable in negligence to a third party with whom it had no con-

tract, especially on an *unaudited* statement. Does it matter that the statement was unaudited? Discuss. (*Spherex, Inc. v. Alexander Grant & Co.*, 451 A.2d 1308, N.H. 1982.)

5. Reid, a fashion designer, turned $1.4 million over to her accountant, Silver, who in effect became her business manager. Over the course of his employment, Silver paid himself $90,000 for services rendered and $72,500 for accounting fees, frequently made interest-free loans to himself from Reid's funds, and was reluctant to make full and fair disclosure to Reid about the details of his activities. Reid sued for an accounting. Will Reid prevail? Discuss. (*Reid v. Silver*, 354 F.2d 600, 7th Cir. 1965.)

6. Beck Industries' trustee in bankruptcy sued Beck's auditors, Ernst & Ernst, alleging the auditors were guilty of negligence and breach of contract in failing to detect that Beck's earnings and overall financial condition had been much worse than publicly reported. The trustee alleged that the false statements caused Beck's board of directors to embark on an ill-advised acquisition program which led to ruin. Two of Beck's directors, including its president, knew of the overstatements; the other directors did not. Ernst & Ernst raised a contributory negligence defense. Is this defense valid? Discuss. (*Shapiro v. Glekel*, 380 F.Supp. 1053, S.D.N.Y. 1974.)

7. Early in 1964, PMM acted as independent auditor for Yale Express System. Later PMM was hired to do some "special studies" of Yale's past and current income and expenses. While engaged in these studies sometime in 1964, PMM discovered that the earlier financial statements it had audited were substantially misleading. PMM did not disclose this fact to the stock exchanges on which Yale stock was traded until May 1965. Investors who had traded in Yale stock during the interim sued PMM for common-law fraud and for a Section 10(b) violation. PMM claimed it had no duty to disclose the information since the original error was not its fault. Is PMM liable under Section 10(b)? Discuss. (*Fischer v. Kletz*, 266 F.Supp. 180, S.D.N.Y. 1967.)

8. Bunge, a merchandiser of grain, extended credit to county elevators throughout the northern Plains states. From 1963 until 1970, Bunge extended large sums to R. F. Gunkelman and Sons, Inc., in Fargo, North Dakota. In fact, the sums lent Gunkelman were much larger and less extensively secured than any other loans made by Bunge in the region. When Gunkelman went bankrupt in 1970, causing a $1.5 million loss to Bunge, Bunge sued Gunkelman's accountant. Bunge claimed the accountant's audit reports from 1963 to 1968 valued Gunkelman's sunflower seeds in the closing inventory as something more than cost in violation of AICPA guidelines, and sued for negligence. Is Bunge's negligence claim valid? Discuss. (*Bunge Corp. v. Eide,* 372 F.Supp. 1058, D.N.D. 1974.)

9. Al had Aberrant Fund, Inc. (AF), which he controlled, purchase substantial amounts of Dilly Modest Systems (DMS) shares. These purchases kept the market price of DMS stock high, allowing Al to sell his personal DMS stock holdings at a big profit. AF later sold at a big loss because, *inter alia,* DMS's registration statement had stated that DMS had over $12 million in back orders when in reality it had much less, and had not disclosed that the primary back order customer was in financial trouble, could not pay its debts, and was controlled by DMS. AF sued Etan

& Etan (E&E), accountants who helped prepare the registration statement. E&E showed that although it knew of the overstatement of back orders, GAAP did not require that the back orders be audited or that the overreporting be noted in the audit. Does compliance with GAAP insulate E&E from liability? Discuss. (*Admiralty Fund v. Hugh Johnson & Co.*, 677 F.2d 1301, 9th Cir. 1982.)

10. Accountants Arthur Young & Co. (AY) prepared the financial information contained in the June 1971 prospectus of Land & Leisure, Inc. Several times during the next 18 months, Summer bought Land & Leisure stock, relying on the prospectus. Summer later sued AY for fraud under Sections 17(a) and 10(b) of the Securities Exchange Act of 1934, challenging the "clean" opinion which AY had given. The financial statements did not disclose that AY was to receive $50,000 in past due accounting fees from Land & Leisure out of the proceeds of the sale of stock under the prospectus. Summer claimed AY breached its duty of independence and committed fraud by not disclosing this fact. AY defended by claiming, among other things, that Summer could not rely on a prospectus which had become "stale" after 18 months. Should AY be liable? Discuss. (*Summer v. Land & Leisure, Inc.*, 571 F.Supp. 380, S.D. Fla. 1983.)

Part VII

PROPERTY: OWNERSHIP, CONTROL, AND PROTECTION

All of the world's material wealth consists of *property* of one type or another. The acquisition of property has been and continues to be one of the primary goals of a major portion of the world's population. What is more, a substantial percentage of all the civil lawsuits ever commenced have arisen out of disputes over some sort of property. For these reasons, the rules of law governing the ownership of property are among the most fundamental in our legal system.

In a society without a system of laws, "ownership" of property would consist merely of physical possession plus the strength and wits to keep it. In an organized society, however, with rights and duties determined by law, the concept of ownership is considerably more sophisticated, in terms of both its complexity and the orderliness of its protection. In the modern sense, then, ownership comprises a group of rights (such as possession, use, enjoyment, and transfer) that

are *protected and guaranteed by governmental authority.*

All property is divided into two basic categories: real property and personal property. Essentially, *real property* (often called "real estate" or "realty") is land and most things affixed to it. *Personal property,* on the other hand, consists of every item of tangible or intangible property not included within the definition of real property. Items of tangible personal property are usually called *goods.*

In Part VII we explore various legal aspects of owning, controlling, and protecting real and personal property. Chapter 41 surveys the law of real property. In Chapter 42 we examine the landlord-tenant relationship, which is created when real property is leased. Chapter 43 surveys the law of personal property, and then discusses the bailment relationship, which is created when the owner of an item of personal property transfers possession, but not title, to another. In Chapter 44, we deal with (1) the disposition of both real and personal property upon the death of the owner and (2) the transfer of real and personal property through the establishment of a trust. Finally, Chapter 45 discusses insurance—one of the most important means of protecting the value of all types of property. The chapter also examines other kinds of insurance, such as life insurance.

Chapter 41

REAL PROPERTY

In this chapter we survey the principles of law relating to the ownership and control of real property. After exploring the fundamental nature of real property, we examine the various types of ownership interests and the process of transferring these interests.

THE NATURE OF REAL PROPERTY

The most important element of real property is, of course, the land itself. Things affixed to the land take the form of either vegetation or fixtures.

Land

The definition of *land* includes not only the surface of the earth but also everything above and beneath it. Thus the ownership of a tract of land theoretically includes both the air space above it and the soil from its surface to the center of the earth.

Air Rights: A landowner's rights with respect to the air space above the surface are called **air rights.** In recent years, air rights have become an important part of land ownership in some areas. In densely populated metropolitan areas, for instance, air space is often quite valuable from a commercial standpoint. Thus the owner of an office building might sell a portion of its air space to a party who wishes to build and operate a restaurant or group of apartments atop the building. And railroad companies with tracks running through downtown areas, where building space is at a premium, sometimes sell the space above their tracks for office building construction.

For practical reasons, modern courts have held that a landowner's air rights are not violated by airplanes flying at reasonable heights. If, however, a flight is low enough to actually interfere with the owner's use of the land (such as when the plane is taking off or landing), there is a violation of these air rights.

Subsurface Rights: The most practical result of the rule extending a landowner's property rights to the center of the earth is that he or she owns the *minerals* beneath the surface. When the land is sold, the buyer acquires any existing minerals, such as coal, even if they are not expressly mentioned. These minerals in the ground can also be owned *separately.* Thus a landowner might sell only the minerals or sell the rest of the land and expressly retain the minerals.

In some states (such as Texas and Pennsylvania) oil and natural gas are treated like other minerals with respect to ownership. That is, they can be owned while they are still in the ground.[1] The courts in a few states (such as California) take a contrary view, holding that oil and gas are not owned by anyone until pumped out of the ground. Of course, regardless of the type of mineral or the particular jurisdiction, an owner who *first removes* the minerals and *then sells* them is making a sale of personal property (i.e., goods), not real property.

Vegetation

Both natural vegetation, such as trees, and cultivated vegetation, such as corn, wheat, or other growing crops, are considered to be real property. Thus, in a land-sale transaction, the vegetation passes to the buyer along with the land unless expressly excluded from the sale.

When growing vegetation is sold by itself, and not with the land, the general rule today is that the transaction is a sale of personal property (goods). This rule holds true almost universally for growing crops.[2] The same rule is followed for growing timber in a majority of states, but several states treat a sale of growing timber as a sale of real property.

---

[1] Ownership of oil, gas, or other minerals while still in the ground is referred to as *ownership in place.*

[2] See UCC Sec. 2-107.

Fixtures

A **fixture** is an item that was originally personal property but that has been attached to the land (or to another fixture) in a relatively permanent fashion. Fixtures are viewed by the law as *real property*. Thus title to them passes to the buyer of real property unless the seller expressly excludes them from the transaction. In other words, even if the documents employed in the transaction describe only the land and are silent with respect to fixtures, title to them nevertheless passes to the buyer. Items that are not fixtures, however, do not pass along with a sale of land unless they are expressly included in the terms of the transaction.

To illustrate: Jones contracts to sell his farm to Williams, and the contract describes only the boundaries of the land. Located on the farm are a house and a barn. These buildings are fixtures and will pass to Williams as part of the real property, as will the fence around the land. Inside the house, Jones's clothing and furniture are not fixtures, but the built-in cabinets and plumbing are. The hay stored in the barn is not a fixture, but the built-in feeding troughs are.

As is true of minerals, when a landowner removes a fixture from the soil or from the building to which it was attached and then sells the item *by itself*, it is considered a sale of *personal property* rather than real property. In fact, if a landowner removes a fixture with the intention that removal will be permanent, the item reverts back to its original status as personal property regardless of whether it is sold.

Determining Whether an Item Is a Fixture: Although the decision on whether a particular article is a fixture is often obvious (as in the case of a house), many items are difficult to classify. In general, a court will hold that an item is a fixture if there was *an intent that it become a permanent part of the real property*. When the owner or occupier of land has not clearly expressed his or her intent, it must be determined from all the circumstances of the case. Following are three factors that are often considered in determining whether an item was intended to be a fixture.

Attachment: An item is usually classified as a fixture if it is attached to a building in such a manner that it cannot be removed without damage to the building. Examples include shingles on the roof, built-in cabinets or appliances, a floor furnace, or a floor covering that is cemented in place.

Specialized Use: An item is usually considered a fixture if it was specially made or altered for installation in a particular building. Examples include specially fitted window screens, drapes custom-made for an odd-sized window, and a neon sign created for particular business premises.

Custom: Sometimes local custom dictates whether an item is a fixture. For example, in some parts of the country it is customary for houses to be sold with refrigerators. Where this custom exists a landowner's intent when installing the refrigerator is probably that it be a permanent addition. Thus it is a fixture. (The same principle applies, of course, to any other "customary" item.)

The following case illustrates the analytical approach employed by courts when determining whether an item was intended to be a fixture.

Johnson v. Hicks
Court of Appeals of Oregon, 626 P.2d 938 (1981)

Margaret and Hoy Johnson owned a tract of land in Klamath County, Oregon. Neil and Maxine Hicks (Hoy Johnson's sister) lived on an adjoining tract. In 1964, Hoy Johnson and Neil Hicks installed an irrigation system to serve both pieces of land. They shared both the labor and costs of installation. After installation, they also shared equally the maintenance and electricity costs for the system. The irrigation system contained approximately 700 feet of two-inch pipe that crossed the Johnson land and ran along the edge of the Hicks land. In addition, the system included 1,500 feet of aluminum pipe used to irrigate the pasture on the Johnson land, and a pump, motor, and pump house not located on the Johnson or Hicks land. About three-fourths of the system was underground. Later, in this lawsuit, Hoy Johnson testified that his purpose in installing the system was to irrigate the pastureland, on which he raised cattle and horses. He also testified that the installation was to be permanent and that when he sold the pastureland he "let the sprinkler system go with it." Neil Hicks wanted the system primarily to irrigate his yard.

In April 1967, when Margaret and Hoy Johnson were experiencing marital problems, Hoy Johnson and Neil Hicks entered into an agreement declaring the irrigation system to be their joint property and "upon the death or incapacity of either of the parties hereto the property shall be in the ownership and control of the surviving party." Hicks later testified in this lawsuit that their intent in drawing up the agreement was as follows:

Well, at the time we made it up Hoy was the one—I told Hoy we were going to have trouble because—if something happened to him and she was involved in it. You know, we can't get along with her to begin with and he said that he can see our point and that we'll go to a lawyer and have him write this paper up, you know, in case something happened to him or to myself and there wouldn't be no women involved into it.

In 1969 Margaret and Hoy Johnson were divorced. The divorce decree awarded to Margaret the family home and the one-third of an acre on which it was located, her personal property, and all furniture and fixtures in the home. Hoy was awarded two other parcels of land and all other personal property. The irrigation system was not mentioned in the decree. From 1969 until April 1979 a portion of the irrigation pipe remained on Margaret's land, and she continued to use the water from the system for watering her yard and trees. During this time she neither offered nor was asked to contribute to the expense of operating the system; Hoy Johnson and Neil Hicks continued to split all costs for the system. Margaret did, however, pay an annual assessment to the Klamath Basin Improvement District for the right to use the irrigation water.

In 1979 Neil suggested to Hoy that they "cut her off," but Hoy refused because the amount of water Margaret used was very small and he had no objection to it. On April 1, 1979, however, Neil moved 140 feet of irrigation pipe from Margaret's land and placed it on his land and on adjoining land owned by a brother of Hoy's. Margaret, plaintiff, filed suit against Neil Hicks, defendant, alleging that the irrigation system was a fixture and that the part of the system on her property passed to her in the divorce decree as part of the real estate. She sought an injunction requiring Neil to restore the pipe to its original position on her land and prohibiting him from further interference with it. Margaret also sought damages caused by the loss of water, and Neil asserted a counterclaim for the expenses of maintaining and operating the system. The trial court held that the part of the system on Margaret's property was not a fixture, and dismissed all claims. Margaret appealed.

Roberts, Judge:

In deciding whether an article used in connection with real property should be considered as a fixture and a part of the land . . . the usual tests are: (1) real or constructive annexation of the article to the realty; (2) appropriation or adaptation to the use or purposes of the realty with which it is connected; (3) the intention to make the annexation permanent.

The intention of making the article permanently accessory to the real property is to be inferred from the nature of the article, the relation of the party making or maintaining the annexation, the policy of the law in relation thereto, the structure and mode of annexation, and the purpose and use for which it is made. . . . It is the trend of judicial opinion to regard all of those things as fixtures which have been attached, whether physically or constructively to the realty with a view to the purposes for which the real property is held or employed, however slight or temporary the connection between the articles and the land. The important element to be considered is the intention of the party making the annexation. . . . The controlling intention is that which the law deduces from all of the circumstances of the installation of the article upon the land. [Many courts] have emphasized intent at the time of the attachment of the item to the real property as the controlling factor.

In this case we have the intent of both defendant Neil Hicks and plantiff's former husband to consider, as well as their April 1, 1967, agreement, which purports to formalize their intent. A written agreement that a chattel [i.e., an item of personal property] already annexed to the soil shall [revert to its original status as personal property], however, is binding only upon the parties to the agreement and those having notice. Plaintiff had no knowledge of the 1967 agreement. We therefore have to determine the intent of plaintiff's former husband and Neil Hicks with respect to the permanency of the pipe at the time of its installation in 1964. . . .

It is apparent that [Hoy Johnson and Neil Hicks] installed the irrigation system on the farm with a view to enhancing the production of the [land]. Irrigation in a semiarid region, like parts of Klamath County, is the very life of the land. It is beyond comprehension that the system was installed for any temporary purpose. . . . We infer Mr. Hicks' intent to be that the system they installed would be used to provide water for the two properties for so long as the Johnsons remained in possession of their parcel. We think it obvious that if Hoy Johnson had remained in possession of the entire three-acre parcel, he would have viewed the irrigation system as a permanent accessory, increasing the value and use of the property. That the parcel of land was later, in effect, subdivided, makes no difference as to his intention at the time of installation or in the status of the pipe at the present time. Further, Mr. Johnson said he had always been content to let plaintiff use the water and had resisted attempts to remove her supply.

It is important to note that we are not here determining water rights of any kind, but only plaintiff's right to continued possession of the irrigation pipe which had been on her property for 15 years and for 10 years in her exclusive possession. We find the pipe installed on plaintiff's property was a fixture and that defendants' removal of the pipe and subsequent possession wrongfully interfered with her rights. The trial court's order denying the mandatory injunction is therefore reversed. The injunction should be issued on remand.

We remand to the trial court on the issue of damages. The only evidence in the record is that by the time of trial plaintiff had suffered some $870 in damages to trees, shrubs and lawn on her property due to lack of water after the removal of the irrigation pipe. There is also evidence, however, that there was city water available to her but that she had this hookup removed. We therefore remand to the trial court to ascertain the actual damage to plaintiff's property, and whether she could have mitigated these damages. We express no opinion on defendant Hicks' right to recover for contribution to the repair and maintenance of the system, since, because of the disposition of the case, no evidence was taken on this issue.

Reversed and remanded for further proceedings consistent with this opinion.

INTERESTS IN REAL PROPERTY

Ownership of real property is not an "all or nothing" proposition. The total group of legal rights constituting complete ownership can be divided among several individuals. The particular set of rights owned in a given situation is referred to as an *estate* or an *interest* in real property. The common law developed a complex system of classifying and defining these various interests, a system which is described here in simplified form. Much of the terminology used to classify real property interests is of ancient origin. At the outset, the law distinguishes those interests that include the right of possession from those that do not. The so-called **pos-**

sessory interests are further subdivided into **freehold estates** and **nonfreehold estates.** The following discussion examines these types of possessory interests, and then outlines the different **nonpossessory interests.** It concludes by describing another classification, the so-called **future interests** in real property.

Freehold Estates

A freehold estate is one that can legally exist for an indefinite period of time.

Fee Simple: When a person has complete ownership of real property, his or her interest is described as a **fee simple estate.**[3] This is the most important type of freehold estate. In everyday usage, when someone is spoken of as the "owner" or as "having title," it generally means that the individual owns a fee simple interest. The characteristics of a fee simple interest are: (1) ownership is of unlimited duration and (2) so long as the owner abides by the law and does not interfere with the rights of adjoining landowners, the owner is free to do whatever he or she chooses with the property.

If O, the owner of a fee simple interest in real property, conveys (transfers) the property to B, it is presumed that the entire fee simple is being conveyed. B will acquire a lesser interest only if the terms of the conveyance clearly so indicate. Thus a conveyance of the property "from O to B," with nothing said about the type of interest being conveyed, is deemed to transfer the entire fee simple interest to B.

Fee Simple Defeasible: Some interests in real property are classified as fee simple interests despite the fact that ownership is not absolute. Suppose, for example, that O conveys a fee simple interest to B, subject to the limitation that B's interest will cease upon the occurrence

of a specified event. B's interest in this case is called a **fee simple defeasible.** It is a fee simple in every respect except that it is subject to the possibility of termination.

One of the most common limitations of this type relates to the *use* that is to be made of the land. For instance, the terms of the conveyance from O to B may state that B's ownership will continue only if the land is used for recreational purposes. The person entitled to the property if and when B's interest terminates is said to own a *future interest.* Future interests are discussed later in the chapter.

Life Estate: A **life estate** is an interest in real property, the duration of which is measured by the life of some designated person. For example, O, the fee simple owner, might convey the property to B "for B's lifetime." During his lifetime B would own a life estate. Similarly, if O's conveyance to B was "for the life of X," B would still own a life estate. (The latter is a much less common situation.) The person entitled to ownership after termination of a life estate owns a future interest.

Owning a life estate is not the equivalent of owning a fee simple for one's lifetime. It is true that the owner of the life estate (called the "life tenant") has the right to *normal use* of the property. For example, the life tenant can use it as a residence, farm it, conduct a business on it, allow another to use it in return for the payment of rent, or make any other reasonable use of it. However, the life tenant cannot do anything that will permanently damage the property and thus harm the owner of the future interest.

As an example of the limitations on a life tenant's use of the property, the right to cut timber on the land is somewhat restricted. The timber can be cut if it is required for fuel, fencing, or agricultural operations. But it cannot be cut for the purpose of *sale* unless (1) the life estate was conveyed to the life tenant specifically for that purpose, or (2) selling timber is the only profitable use that can be made of the land, or (3) the land was used for that purpose at the time the

---

[3]Various other phrases are also employed. It is sometimes said that the person is the *fee owner* or that he or she owns the land *in fee, in fee simple,* or *in fee simple absolute.*

person became a life tenant, or (4) the owner of the future interest expressly permits the cutting.

Similarly, a life tenant can take oil and gas from existing wells and other minerals from existing mines if subsurface rights were not expressly excluded from the life estate. But this party cannot drill *new* wells or open *new* mines without authorization either in the document creating the life estate or at a later time from the owner of the future interest.

Although a life tenant is responsible to the owner of the future interest for any permanent damage he or she personally causes to the land, there is no such responsibility for damage caused by accidents, by third parties, or otherwise without the life tenant's fault.

A life tenant is also under a duty to pay taxes on the property. If this duty is neglected and the land is taken by the taxing authority, the life tenant is liable to the owner of the future interest.

Nonfreehold Estates

The nonfreehold estates, sometimes called **leasehold estates,** are created by a *lease* of real property in which the owner grants to another the temporary right to possess the property in return for the payment of rent.[4] In such a case, the owner is called the *lessor,* or *landlord,* and the occupier is called the *lessee,* or *tenant.*[5] Several different types of nonfreehold, or leasehold, estates may be created, depending on the terms of the lease agreement. The next chapter discusses the landlord-tenant relationship in detail.

Nonpossessory Interests

Easements: Essentially, an **easement** is the right to make some limited use of another's real property without taking possession of it. Stated

---

[4] Although the granting of a *right to drill* for oil and gas is often called a *lease* in popular usage, it is not truly a lease because it does not convey a possessory interest in real property.

[5] The "owner" in this situation might be the owner of a fee simple, of a fee simple defeasible, of a life estate, or even of a leasehold.

another way, it is the right to do a specific thing on another's land. Sometimes an easement is referred to informally as a *right-of-way.* Examples of easements include the right to run a driveway or road across another's land, to run a power or telephone line above it, or to run a pipeline under it.

Types of Easements: Easements are either *appurtenant* or *in gross.* An **easement appurtenant** is one created specifically for use in connection with another tract of land. For example: A and B own adjoining tracts. A grants to B an easement to cross A's land to get to and from a highway. Here the easement on A's land is appurtenant, because it was created for use in connection with B's land. In this situation, A's land is called the **servient estate** and B's the **dominant estate.**

An **easement in gross,** on the other hand, is one *not* used in connection with another tract of land. For example, a telephone company has an easement in gross when it acquires the right to run poles and wires across A's land.

Whenever a tract of land subject to either type of easement is sold, the purchaser must continue to recognize the easement if he or she knew or should have known of its existence at the time of purchase. Even without such knowledge, the purchaser's ownership is subject to the easement if a document creating the interest was *recorded* (filed with the appropriate county official) prior to the purchase.

An easement appurtenant is said to "run with the land." This means that if the land being benefited by the easement (the dominant estate) is sold, the easement goes along with it. However, the owner of an easement appurtenant cannot sell or otherwise transfer it *by itself,* apart from the dominant estate. On the other hand, the owner of an easement in gross today is generally allowed to transfer it to another party.

Creation of Easements: An easement can be created in several ways. Creation of an **easement by express grant or reservation** is the most common method. An express grant occurs when a landowner expresses an intent to convey an easement to another party. An express reservation occurs when a landowner sells the land itself but expressly reserves, or keeps, an easement on the land being sold. Because an easement is an interest in real property, the expression of an intent to grant or reserve such an interest must be made in a written document containing a legally sufficient description of both the land and the scope of the easement. The document also must contain the names of the parties, the duration of the interest, and the signature of at least the party making the grant or reservation. The document could be either a *deed,* discussed later in the chapter, or a *will,* discussed in Chapter 44.

An **easement by implication** also can be created where surrounding circumstances reasonably indicate that the parties probably intended to create such an interest. An easement exists by implication only if the following facts are proved:

1. An easement will be implied only when land is subdivided into two or more segments. This would occur, for example, when A, who owns twenty acres of land, sells ten acres out of the tract to B.

2. Prior to the subdivision, the owner of the entire tract must have been making a particular use of the property, and continuance of this use after the subdivision would require recognition of an easement. Thus, suppose that prior to A's sale of ten acres to B, A had constructed and used a ditch to improve the drainage of one part of the property. The ditch went through the portion that A kept, but it benefited the part sold to B by improving the drainage of that portion.

3. The use that A was making of the property before the subdivision must have been apparent; in other words, it must have been observable to anyone conducting a reasonable inspection of the property.

4. Continuation of the use must be reasonably necessary to B's use of his ten acres. In this case,

because the drainage improvement benefited the land purchased by B, the ditch across A's ten acres probably would be viewed as reasonably necessary.

In the circumstances just described, B would have an easement across A's land giving B the right to continue using the ditch to drain water from B's land.

An **easement by necessity** also can be created in some circumstances. In contrast with an easement by implication, neither a subdivision of land nor a particular prior use is a prerequisite for the existence of an easement by necessity. However, the easement must be an absolute necessity, not just a reasonably necessary use. For example, a person leasing space in an office building has an easement by necessity that permits use of the stairs, elevators, hallways, and other common areas. Another example could be found in a situation similar to the one in which A sold a portion of his land to B. If B's ten acres had been at the back of the original tract, with no means of access to a public road other than by crossing A's ten acres, B would have an easement by necessity to cross A's land when going to and from B's land.

An **easement by prescription** (or **prescriptive easement**) may be created when someone actually does something on another's land for a period of time. Creation of an easement by prescription is similar to the acquisition of title by adverse possession, which is discussed later in the chapter. Such an easement is created if one party has actually exercised an easement (such as a driveway) on someone else's land continuously for a period of time specified by state statute, the use was made without the express consent of the landowner, and the use was an apparent one. The required period of time for creation of a prescriptive easement in a particular state is usually the same as for acquisition of title by adverse possession.

Profits: A **profit,** technically called a *profit à prendre,* is the right to go upon land and take something from it. Examples include the right to mine minerals, drill for oil, or take wild game or fish. A *right to take* minerals, which is a profit, must be distinguished from an actual *sale* of the fee simple interest in the minerals in the ground. The form the transaction takes depends on the intent of the parties, as evidenced primarily by the language used. Of course, in those states where oil and gas are not deemed capable of being owned while in the ground, any transaction in which the buyer is to drill for oil and gas is a profit.

The legal principles applicable to the creation, classification, transfer, and enforceability of profits are exactly the same as in the case of easements.

Licenses: In essence, a **license** is simply the landowner's permission for someone else to come upon his or her land. It does not create an interest in real property, because the landowner can revoke it at any time. But even though the grantee of the license does not have a legally enforceable *right* to go upon the land, the license (prior to its revocation) does keep the grantee from being considered a trespasser. Two examples of situations where licenses exist are:

1. The purchaser of a ticket to a movie or other amusement or sporting event has a license to enter the premises.

2. Sometimes a license is created when there is an ineffective attempt to create an easement or profit. For example, since these are required to be in writing, an oral easement or profit is merely a license.

Mortgages and Liens: A person who borrows money frequently has to grant the lender an interest in some item of property to secure payment of the debt. When the property to be used as security is real property, the landowner grants the lender an interest by executing a **mortgage.** The landowner-debtor is called the *mortgagor,* and the lender is called the *mortgagee.* In most states, the interest created by the mortgage is a

lien.[6] If the mortgagor defaults on the obligation, the mortgagee has a right to *foreclose* the mortgage. This means that the real property can be seized and sold, usually at a public sale (auction), and the proceeds used to pay off the debt. The most common situation in which a mortgage is executed occurs when a buyer of real property borrows a portion of the purchase price and signs a mortgage giving the lender an interest in the property being purchased. Because a mortgage conveys an interest in real property, it must be expressed in a written document that is sufficient to satisfy the statute of frauds.

In some situations, real property may be subjected to a creditor's interest without the landowner's consent. Such an interest is referred to very generally as an **involuntary lien,** to contrast it with the voluntary lien created by a mortgage. Statutes or constitutional provisions in most states provide for the involuntary creation of a **mechanic's lien** to secure payment for work done on or materials added to real property. For example, the contractor who builds a house on the land or adds a new room to an existing house usually has a mechanic's lien on the real estate that can be foreclosed if payment is not made. Many states require that, before any work is done or materials provided, the person claiming the lien give the landowner written notice that a mechanic's lien will be asserted. In addition, most states require that a written document in which the mechanic's lien is claimed be filed with the county clerk, recorder of deeds, or other designated county official.

Other types of involuntary liens also exist. When a plaintiff in a civil lawsuit receives a judgment for money damages against the defendant, and the defendant does not pay, in some states

---

[6]In several states, however, a mortgage actually transfers *legal title* to the property to the mortgagee. In such a state, the mortgage normally provides that the mortgagee does not have the right of possession unless the mortgagor defaults on the underlying obligation; but the mortgagor does not actually own the property until the debt is paid and the mortgage released.

the plaintiff may create a **judgment lien** against the defendant's real property by filing a copy of the judgment with the appropriate county official.

It is important to note that, in the case of mechanic's liens, judgment liens, and other involuntary liens, the act of filing the written document with a public official actually *creates* the lien. As we will discuss later in the chapter, deeds, mortgages, and other documents creating *voluntary* interests in real property can be recorded to give greater protection to the person holding the interest, but the act of recording does not create the interest in such situations.

Future Interests

A final category of real property interest is the **future interest,** which consists of the residue remaining when the owner of a fee simple estate transfers less than a fee simple to someone else. Despite its name, a future interest does have a present existence and can be transferred, mortgaged, and so on. It is the actual use and enjoyment of the interest that is unavailable until a future time.

The subject of future interests is quite complex, with its own system of classification. Very generally, there are two basic types of future interest: the reversion and the remainder. A **reversion** exists when the owner of a fee simple transfers a lesser interest and retains the residue. For example, suppose that O, the owner of a fee simple estate, conveys a fee simple defeasible or life estate to B. If no provision is made for ownership of the future interest, it is owned by O and is called a reversion. O can separately transfer the reversion to someone else, or let it pass to his or her heirs. Upon expiration of B's interest, the reversion becomes a present fee simple estate. On the other hand, a **remainder** exists when the owner of a fee simple transfers a lesser interest and expressly provides that ownership will pass to a third party upon expiration of the lesser interest. Suppose that when O conveys the fee simple defeasible or life estate to B, O expressly

provides that ownership will pass to C upon expiration of B's interest. In this case, C's future interest is called a remainder. C can separately transfer the future interest or let it pass to his or her heirs. When B's interest terminates, the remainder becomes a fee simple estate.

CONCURRENT OWNERSHIP

Any interest in real property that can be owned by one person can also be owned jointly by two or more persons. We will examine some of the more important types of concurrent ownership.

Tenancy in Common and Joint Tenancy

Characteristics: The most frequently encountered types of concurrent ownership are the **tenancy in common** and the **joint tenancy.** In a tenancy in common, the co-owners are called *tenants in common* or *cotenants.* In a joint tenancy they are called *joint tenants.*

The most important distinction between these two types of concurrent ownership has to do with disposition of a co-owner's interest when he or she dies. The interest of a tenant in common passes to that person's heirs according to his or her will, or according to state statute if there was no will. The heirs and the surviving co-owner(s) then become tenants in common. The joint tenancy, on the other hand, is characterized by a *right of survivorship,* which means that the interest of a deceased joint tenant passes to the surviving joint tenant(s).

Creation: A tenancy in common can be created in several ways. For example, if O conveys a fee simple estate "to A and B," the real property will be owned by A and B as tenants in common. Similarly, if O dies and his land passes to his heirs, A and B, the property will be owned by A and B as tenants in common. Or if O conveys a fractional interest (such as one-half or one-third) to A, the property will be owned by O and A as tenants in common.

A joint tenancy is more difficult to create and, consequently, is not as frequently used or as important as a tenancy in common. In most states, concurrent ownership of real property is presumed to be a tenancy in common, and will be a joint tenancy only if explicitly created. Even the use of the terms "joint tenancy" or "joint tenants" is not a clear enough expression to create a joint tenancy in most states, because people often use such terms in a nontechnical sense to refer to a tenancy in common. Thus, if O wishes to create a joint tenancy between A and B, in most states O would have to refer expressly to the *right of survivorship* in addition to using the terms joint tenancy or joint tenants. Moreover, a joint tenancy traditionally could be created only if the joint tenants received their interests at the same time and in the same document, and only if their fractional interests were *equal.* In recent years, statutes in a few states have removed the requirement that a joint tenancy must be created at the same time by a single document. These requirements have never existed for the creation of a tenancy in common.

Partition: In either a tenancy in common or a joint tenancy, none of the co-owners owns any segregated portion of the land. Instead, each owns an undivided fractional interest in the entire tract of land. The tenants in common or joint tenants can agree in writing to *partition* the land; but if they do so, their relationship as co-owners ends, and each becomes the owner of a specifically designated section of the property. If one or more of the co-owners wants to partition the land but the parties are unable to reach unanimous agreement on the division, any one of them can initiate a lawsuit to have the land partitioned. In their decisions, courts commonly express a preference for a partition *in kind,* which is a physical division of the property into sections of equal value. As a practical matter, however, it is extremely difficult for a court to accomplish a physical division that gives each former co-owner a section of clearly equal value. Consequently, most court-ordered partitions ulti-mately involve a sale of the property and an equal division of the proceeds.

Condominiums and Cooperatives

Although the **condominium** form of ownership was used in some European cities before and during the Middle Ages, only in recent years has it become popular in this country. Most buildings subject to condominium ownership today are physically similar to apartments, and may contain only a few units or as many as several hundred. Ordinarily, a person owns a fee simple estate in the living space of a particular unit, but not in the land on which the unit rests. The fee simple interest in the living space may be owned solely by an individual, or it may be subject to any of the various forms of concurrent ownership such as a tenancy in common. In addition, a tenancy in common among the owners of the living space units exists with respect to other areas such as common roofs and walls, parking lots, and recreation areas.

Although a building subject to **cooperative** ownership may also physically resemble an apartment building, this form of ownership is quite different than a condominium. A *cooperative corporation* is formed under special state statutory provisions, and the corporation owns the building. Each occupier of a living unit owns a share of stock in the corporation and leases the unit from the corporation. Because the corporate entity itself owns the real property, a cooperative is not technically a form of concurrent ownership.

Marital Property

Tenancy by the Entireties: Under the English Common law, a conveyance of real property to husband and wife created a **tenancy by the entireties.** A tenancy by the entireties is essentially the same as a joint tenancy with right of survivorship, the surviving spouse taking complete ownership on the death of the other. Unlike a joint tenancy, a tenancy by the entireties cannot be severed by one party. A tenancy by the entireties also cannot be transferred by one spouse without the consent of the other, and the creditors of one spouse cannot reach the property without consent of the other.

The tenancy by the entireties has been abolished in several states and modified in others during recent years. Today, the tenancy by the entireties exists in about 20 states. In those states abolishing this form of ownership, a conveyance of real property to husband and wife will create either a joint tenancy or tenancy in common, depending on the language of conveyance.

Traditionally, the husband had the exclusive right to control and possession of property held in a tenancy by the entireties. Today, in those states still recognizing the tenancy by the entireties, statutory changes have given the spouses equal rights of control and possession.

Community Property: Another system of marital property ownership in this country is referred to as **community property.** The origin of the community property system can be traced directly to Spanish marital property law, which had borrowed the concept from medieval Germanic tribes in Europe. Nine American states presently employ the community property system. In five of these—Arizona, California, Louisiana, New Mexico, and Texas—the community property system was simply a continuation of Spanish law that had been in effect before statehood. Idaho, Nevada, and Washington voluntarily adopted the system early in their settlement, and Wisconsin adopted it in 1986.

The community property system recognizes two types of property: community property and separate property. Each spouse owns an undivided one-half interest in all community property, an interest which passes to his or her heirs upon death. Each has complete ownership of his or her separate property.

Because the community property system is based on the concept that the marital relationship itself is an entity, and that this entity benefits materially from the time and effort of both spouses, most property acquired by the husband or wife during marriage is community property. This includes the salary, wages, or other income earned by either spouse, income earned from community property, and property bought with the proceeds or income from community property. Money or property is the separate property of one of the spouses only if it was acquired by that person before marriage, or acquired after marriage by gift or inheritance. The income generated by one spouse's separate property is his or her separate property in a majority of the community property states. In any situation in which there is a question whether an item of property is community or separate, there is a strong legal presumption that it is community. The various community property states have their own specific rules for determining which spouse has management rights over particular types of community property.

Other Marital Property Rights: Various other property rights are created by marriage. The English common law gave the wife a right called **dower,** consisting of a life estate in one-third of her husband's real property after his death. The husband had a right called **curtesy,** consisting of a life estate in all of his wife's real property after her death. Almost all states have abolished or greatly altered these common-law rights in recent years. Most states, however, do provide a surviving spouse with some type of interest after the death of the other spouse to insure that the survivor will at least be able to continue living in their shared residence (i.e., the **homestead**).

SALES OF REAL PROPERTY

Next to leases, sales are the most commonly occurring real estate transactions. Whether such sales involve a residential house and lot, a farm, or other real property, they are the most monetarily significant transactions many people ever experience.

Most real estate sales involve the transfer of a fee simple interest in the surface, minerals, or both. Transfer of other types of interests may be accomplished in much the same way, but the procedures are often modified to fit the particular circumstances. Leasehold interests are usually created simply by the signing of a lease contract. Throughout the following discussion we will assume that the transaction is of the most common type—the sale of a fee simple interest.

Brokers

When a landowner wishes to sell property, the first step usually is to contact and employ a real estate broker (or "agent"). Although this is not required (the landowner can, of course, sell the land without help), it is usually desirable unless the owner already has a buyer lined up.

The function of the broker is to find a buyer. This is usually the extent of the broker's authority; he or she ordinarily is not given authority to actually sell or even to make a contract to sell. In return for finding a buyer the broker is entitled to be compensated by receiving an agreed-upon *commission,* which is usually a percentage of the selling price.

A formal employment contract setting out the terms of the arrangement should be made with the broker. Indeed, in many states a broker has no legally enforceable right to a commission unless the agreement to pay it is in writing.

The arrangement with the broker can be of several types, including an open listing, exclusive agency, or exclusive right to sell. In an **open listing,** the broker is entitled to a commission only if he or she is the *first one* to procure a buyer who is "ready, willing, and able" to buy at the stated selling price. The owner is free to sell the land personally or through another broker without incurring liability to the employed broker. Open listings are not extremely common today.

A second type, the **exclusive agency,** arises when the owner gives assurance that no other broker will be hired during the term of the agreement. If the owner does employ another broker who procures a buyer, the sale is valid but the original broker is still entitled to the agreed commission. However, the owner is entitled to sell the land *personally,* without the aid of the employed broker or any other broker. If the owner makes the sale without assistance, the employed broker is not entitled to a commission.

The type of arrangement most advantageous to the broker is an **exclusive right to sell,** in which the employed broker is entitled to the agreed commission if the property is sold during the agreement's duration by anyone, whether done with the aid of the employed broker or some other broker or by the owner acting alone.

Multiple Listing Services: In many localities today, real estate brokers have formed multiple listing services. A **multiple listing service (MLS)** is an arrangement whereby brokers in the area pool their listings, each member having access to the pool. A participating broker ordinarily obtains either an exclusive agency or exclusive right to sell agreement from the landowner, and then places that listing in the local MLS. If another broker who also is a member of the MLS finds a buyer for the property, the commission is split between the listing and selling brokers under the terms of the MLS membership agreement signed by each participating broker.

The Contract

When a buyer is found, a contract for sale will ordinarily be made. When making an offer to buy, or when entering the contract itself, the buyer often makes a deposit referred to as **earnest money.** The real estate sale contract sometimes is called an *earnest money contract,* and normally provides that the buyer will forfeit the earnest money if he or she breaches the contract.

To be enforceable, a contract for the sale of land has to be in writing in almost all circumstances. Although the contract usually is evidenced by a detailed formal document signed by both seller and buyer, the requirement of written documentation can be satisfied by informal instruments such as letters or telegrams. The writing, whether formal or not, must contain *all the essential terms* of the agreement and must be signed by the party against whom enforcement is sought.[7] If any of the essential terms are missing, the writing is considered insufficient; oral testimony will not be allowed to fill in the gaps, and the contract is unenforceable.

Specifically, the terms that must be included in the written contract for sale are (1) the *names* of the seller and buyer and an indication of their intent to be bound, (2) a *description* of the property sufficient to identify it, and (3) the *price.*

More is said about the required description in the discussion of deeds later in this chapter. (Incidentally, if the seller does ultimately convey title by giving a deed, it is immaterial whether there was an enforceable contract. The contract simply prevents one party from reneging prior to transfer of title.)

Title Examination, Insurance, and Survey

One of the main reasons for initially making a sale contract rather than immediately transferring ownership is to give the buyer an opportunity to investigate the seller's title (often called a **title examination**). This essentially involves an examination of all officially recorded documents concerning the property. The examination is usually made by an attorney employed either by the purchaser, by the lending institution from which the purchase price is being borrowed, or by a title insurance company.

The attorney may personally search the public records and on the basis of this investigation issue a "certificate of title" giving his or her opinion as to the validity of the seller's title. Or the attorney may examine an **abstract,** which is a compilation of the official records relating to a particular parcel of land. Privately owned *abstract companies* or *abstracters* produce such abstracts and keep them current.

The sale contract often requires the seller to provide evidence of a good title. The certificate of title is used as such evidence in some parts of the country, while in other areas the abstract and the attorney's opinion based thereon provide the required evidence. It is also becoming more frequent for the contract to require the seller to provide the buyer with "title insurance." This may be used as the sole evidence of title, or it may be required in addition to other evidence. Title insurance, which is purchased from a company engaged in the business of selling such insurance (often called a *title company*), simply provides that the issuing company will compensate the buyer for any loss if the title ultimately proves defective. Of course, the title company will issue such a policy only if its own attorneys feel, after making a title examination, that the title is good.

Unless a survey has been made very recently, the seller is often required under the contract to have a new survey made. A licensed surveyor will be employed to make sure that the described boundaries are correct and that no buildings or other encroachments lie on the boundary line.

Financing and Closing the Sale

Many times the buyer does not have sufficient funds available to pay the agreed price. In such cases, after the contract is made but before the transfer of title, the buyer must obtain the necessary financing. Savings and loan associations are one of the most frequently used sources of such funds, especially for the purchase of residential property. As we mentioned earlier, the buyer (mortgagor) normally executes a mortgage to the lender (mortgagee) as security for the loan.

Sometimes the seller provides the financing by permitting the buyer to pay the purchase price in installments. In such a case, the seller may immediately transfer title to the buyer and take a mortgage to secure payment, or the seller and buyer may agree that title will not be transferred to the buyer until the purchase price is

---

[7] The signature can be that of the party's authorized agent. However, in most states, a contract for the sale of real estate signed by an agent is enforceable only if the agent's authorization is also in writing. (The same is true for the signing of a deed, discussed later in this chapter.)

completely paid. The latter type of arrangement is often called a **contract for deed.**

The actual transfer of ownership usually takes place at the **closing** (or **settlement**)—the meeting attended by the seller and buyer as well as other interested parties such as their attorneys, the broker, and a representative of the mortgagee. At the meeting the seller signs and delivers to the buyer a *deed* that transfers the ownership; and the buyer pays the purchase price. (As a practical matter, however, the representative of the mortgagee may actually pay the seller.) It is also common for the mortgage to be executed at the closing and for other incidental financial matters to be settled (such as apportionment of property taxes and insurance that the seller may have prepaid).

Sometimes a closing occurs in a different manner, by the use of an "escrow agent." The **escrow agent** is a disinterested third party to whom the seller has delivered the deed and to whom the buyer has made payment. It is fairly common for an institution such as a title insurance company to serve as escrow agent. This party's instructions generally are to close the deal by delivering the deed to the buyer and the payment to the seller on receipt of the required evidence of good title.

The Deed

Types of Deeds: As we stated earlier, title to real property is conveyed by means of a written deed. Several types of deeds exist, each involving particular legal consequences.

General Warranty Deed: From the buyer's point of view, the **general warranty deed** is by far the most desirable kind to obtain, because it carries certain warranties, or covenants, that the title is good. These warranties may be expressed in the deed, but even if not expressed they are *implied* if the document is actually a general warranty deed. Whether a particular deed is one of general warranty depends on the language used in it. The wording necessary to create such a deed varies from state to state. In Illinois and

Michigan, for example, the verb phrase *convey and warrant* makes it a general warranty deed. The warranties, which overlap somewhat, usually consist of the following: (1) **Covenant of seisin.** The seller (called *grantor* in the deed) guarantees that he or she has good title to the land conveyed. (2) **Covenant against encumbrances.** The grantor guarantees that there are no encumbrances on the land except as stated in the deed. (An *encumbrance* includes any type of lien or easement held by a third party.) The existence of such an encumbrance causes a breach of this warranty by the grantor, even if the grantee (the buyer) knows about it when receiving the deed, unless the deed states that the title is "subject to" the particular encumbrance. (3) **Covenant for quiet enjoyment.** The grantor guarantees that the grantee (or those to whom the grantee later conveys the property) will not be evicted or disturbed by a person having a better title or a lien.

Special Warranty Deed: In a **special warranty deed,** there is a warranty only that the title has not been diminished in any way by a personal act of the grantor. For example, suppose the grantor had previously executed a mortgage on the land that the deed does not mention. If the grantee later has to pay off the mortgage or if it is foreclosed and the grantee loses the property, the grantor will be liable to the grantee for damages. On the other hand, if the grantor has not personally encumbered the title but an outstanding title or interest in the land is later asserted by some third person, the grantor incurs no liability. This situation might arise, for instance, if the land is encumbered by a valid lien created by someone who owned the land prior to the grantor. The special warranty deed is a sufficient performance of the seller's obligations under the sale contract unless that contract specifically required a general warranty deed.

Quitclaim Deed: In a **quitclaim deed,** the grantor does not really purport to convey any title at all to the grantee. The deed says, in essence, "If I have any present interest in this land, I hereby convey it to you." This deed is not a sufficient performance of the grantor's obligations under the sale contract unless the contract so provides. Quitclaim deeds are often used as a form of *release.* For example: A owns the land, but X arguably has some type of interest in it, and A negotiates with X for a release of X's claim. One way of accomplishing the release is for A to obtain a quitclaim deed from X. Quitclaim deeds are also frequently employed by government entities (such as cities and counties) when they sell land.

Deed of Bargain and Sale:

The **deed of bargain and sale** purports to convey title but does not contain any warranties. Even though differing in form, this deed conveys the same type of title as a quitclaim deed. It also is not a sufficient performance of the grantor's obligations under the sale contract unless the contract so provides.

Requirements of a Valid Deed:

Because a deed accomplishes a present transfer of a property interest, *consideration* is not required. The owner can give away the property if he or she wishes. Of course, a *sale contract* must be supported by consideration, as must any other executory contract. A promise to make a gift of land or of anything else is generally not enforceable; but a completed gift by delivery of a deed is perfectly valid, assuming that there is no intent to defraud the grantor's creditors. Even though there is no requirement that a grantee give consideration for a deed or that consideration be stated in the deed, it is customary for the deed to contain a *recital of consideration*—a statement of what consideration is being given by the grantee. It is also customary for the recital to state merely a nominal consideration (such as $10) rather than the price actually paid.

There are several requirements that a deed must meet in order to transfer a real property interest. Although these requirements vary slightly among the states, they may be summarized as follows.

Grantor and Grantee:

The deed must name a grantor and grantee. The grantor must have legal capacity. If the grantor is married, it is generally desirable to have the grantor's spouse named as a grantor as well, for several reasons. In most states, if the property is occupied by husband and wife as their residence, or homestead, both must join in a conveyance of the property even if only one of them owns it. And as previously mentioned, the laws of many states give one spouse certain types of rights with respect to the property of the other regardless of whether the property is their homestead, and these rights are extinguished only if the grantor's spouse joins in the deed.

Words of Conveyance:

The deed must contain words of conveyance—words indicating a present intent to transfer ownership to the grantee, such as "I, Ruth Smith, do hereby grant, sell, and convey. . . ."

Description:

The deed must contain an adequate description of the land being conveyed.

Signature:

The deed must be signed by the grantor. For the reasons already discussed, it is also usually desirable to obtain the signature of a married grantor's spouse.

Delivery:

The deed must be delivered to the grantee.

Methods of Describing Land:

As previously mentioned, a valid deed must contain an adequate description of the property being conveyed. Although this description should be (and usually is) stated in the deed, it is permissible for the deed to refer to a sufficient description contained in another document.

Land can be adequately described in several ways, but regardless of the method employed the property must be identified in such a way that there can be no mistake about exactly which parcel of land is being conveyed. There is a general tendency for the courts to require a greater degree of precision in a deed than in a sale contract. For example, in the case of residential property, a sale contract usually is enforceable if the description is merely a street name and number in a particular city and state. In many states, however, such a description is not sufficient for a deed to be a valid conveyance of title to the property.

Government Survey: In those states west of the Mississippi River (except Texas) and in Alabama, Mississippi, Florida, Illinois, Indiana, Ohio, and Michigan, land can be described by reference to the **United States Government Survey.** This survey was adopted by Congress in 1785 for the purpose of describing government-owned land that was to be transferred to states, railroads, and settlers. It uses meridians and parallels to divide the surveyed areas into quadrangles that are approximately 24 miles on each side. Each quadrangle is further divided into 16 tracts called **townships** that are approximately 6 miles on each side.

Metes and Bounds: In those states not using the U.S. Government Survey (the eastern states and Texas), it is common for land to be described by **metes and bounds.** *Metes* means measures of length; *bounds* refers to the bounda-

ries of the property. A metes and bounds description essentially just delineates the exterior lines of the land being conveyed. It may make use of a *monument* (a natural or artificial landmark such as a river or street) to constitute a boundary or to mark a corner of the tract. A metes and bounds description begins at a well-identified point and runs stated distances at stated angles, tracing the boundary until it returns to the starting point.

Plat: The two methods just discussed, reference to the government survey and metes and bounds, are normally used to describe land in rural and semirural areas that have not been formally subdivided and platted. Most land in urban areas has been surveyed by private developers and subdivided into numbered blocks and lots on a **plat** (map) that is recorded (filed) with a designated county official. In almost all parts of the country, it is common to describe urban land by reference to the lot and block number in the recorded plat.

In the following case, we will see how problems can arise from "homemade" deeds. The case also illustrates that a court will, where it is possible to do so, attempt to make sense out of an imprecisely drafted deed.

Baker v. Zingelman
Superior Court of Pennsylvania, 393 A.2d 908 (1978)

Margaret and Carl DeBow owned a tract of land known as the Lakeland Allotment. There was a plat subdividing the land into lots, but no actual subdivision had occurred. The property was mostly farmland, and the DeBows lived in the farm house and operated an antique shop in the barn behind the house. There also were several other sheds and garages on their property. In 1968 they built and moved into a new home west of the land in question. They then asked Marie Baker (Margaret's sister) and her husband George to leave their home in Cleveland, Ohio, move to the farmhouse on the Lakeland Allotment, and operate the antique shop. They agreed to do so, and Margaret prepared a deed conveying the property to the Bakers.

Before preparing the deed, Margaret had "walked off" (measured) the land to be transferred, and asked the Bakers if they thought it was sufficient footage to include the buildings located on the land. Margaret stated that if the land she measured off was not sufficient to include the buildings, "we can clear it up later." The deed prepared by Margaret began "at a point where the east line of the proposed Michigan Avenue intersects the south line of West Erie Street" and then followed the directional and distance description matching a lot on the Lakeland Allotment plat. Michigan Avenue was an unopened street, and Margaret admitted that she did not know exactly where it began when she prepared the deed.

The Bakers moved into the farmhouse and reopened and operated the antique shop in 1971. During the same year Carl DeBow died. In 1973 Margaret married Zingelman, her present husband. It appears that this remarriage contributed in some way to the problems that later arose. Sometime in 1973 George Baker became upset with Margaret because she parked her truck in the garage which the Bakers claim is located on their property. There was a falling out between the families about this time. Margaret informed the Bakers that part of the barn, the garage, and sheds located on the land extended onto her adjacent land. By early 1975, Margaret's attorney informed the Bakers that the part of the barn which projected onto Margaret's property would be forcibly removed unless the Bakers chose to purchase for $10,000 the strip of property which would clear up the location problem of the buildings. The Bakers, plaintiffs, then sued to enjoin Margaret from parking her truck in the garage and from cutting off part of the barn.

At the trial, the testimony of two surveyors disclosed that all of one shed and garage and a portion of another shed and 13 feet of the barn extended onto Margaret's property. The lower court, however, enjoined Margaret from any further trespass and ordered her to convey to the Bakers the strip of land which would then place the buildings on the Baker property, in order to effectuate the original intent of the parties in their conveyance of 1971. Margaret, the defendant, appealed.

Cercone, Judge:

. . . Defendant's argument stems from the legal principles and cases stating that when the language of a deed is clear and unambiguous, the intent of the parties must be gleaned solely from the instrument. Where a portion of a building is not included in the description of the deed and it is not clear from the deed that the parties meant for the entire building to pass, only that portion of the building passes that is covered in the description. In the case before us, defendant argues that the description in the deed was clear, . . . [and] that since there was no mention of any of the buildings in the deed, the judge should not have allowed parol evidence concerning the alleged inducement by Margaret for her sister to move to Pennsylvania.

Although this is a correct statement of the law, we must remember the lower court sat in equity. It is a general proposition of equity that when a person grants a thing, he intends to grant also that without which the thing cannot be enjoyed. We must assume the parties intended a reasonable result. The description in the deed before us was not prepared by a professional, but by defendant, who admitted she did not know exactly where Michigan Avenue began at the time of the deed preparation. There very easily could have been a mistake or ambiguity in the deed concerning the description, regardless of the omission of the word "building." Where such an ambiguity exists, the surrounding circumstances may be considered to determine the intent of the parties, and the subsequent acts of the parties are important to manifest their intentions. The actions of the parties subsequent to the deed were that the Bakers moved into the farmhouse and operated the antique shop in the barn. They obviously relied on the deed as having conveyed to them their interest in the property and in the buildings. It was only after the sisters' "falling out" that the boundary dispute arose. The proposed sale of the strip of land which would clear the building at a price of $10,000 seems extremely unreasonable in light of the fact that the deed of 1971 conveyed the majority of the land without any consideration passing.

Even if the language of the deed can be construed as being precise and clear on its face, the cases do make exceptions where encroachments are minor and where it would be illogical and unreasonable for the grantor to have conveyed only part of buildings. Here, plaintiffs were living in the house and operating the antique shop in the barn unhindered until the argument occurred. It is extremely unlikely that 13 feet of the barn, one garage, and part of two other sheds were deliberately excluded from the conveyance.

Taking all these facts into consideration, we must agree with the lower court that the defendant intended to convey sufficient footage to cover the house, barn, and related buildings to her sister and her husband at the time of the original deed in 1971.

[Judgment for plaintiffs, the Bakers, is affirmed.]

Acknowledgment: An **acknowledgment** is a formal declaration before a designated public official, such as a notary public, by a person who has signed a document, that he or she executed the document as a voluntary act. The public official places his or her signature and seal after the declaration and the declarant's signature. The resulting instrument, referred to as a *certificate of acknowledgment*, is attached to the document to which it relates.

In most states an acknowledgment is not required for a deed to be valid, but it is required as a prerequisite to "recording."

Recording: **Recording** is the act of filing the deed with a public official, referred to in different states as the "recorder of deeds," "register of deeds," or any of several other titles. The official copies the deed into the record books, indexes it, and returns the original to the person who filed it.

As between the grantor and grantee, an otherwise valid deed is perfectly good even if it is not recorded. The purpose of recording procedures, which exist in every state, is to give notice to the world at large that the transfer of title has taken place. Frequently referred to as "constructive notice," this means that third parties are treated as having notice regardless of whether they actually do.

State recording statutes generally provide that an unrecorded deed, though valid between grantor and grantee, is void with respect to any subsequent bona fide purchaser. A **bona fide purchaser (BFP)** is a good faith purchaser for value. For example, suppose that O sells a tract of land to B, and B does not record her deed. O then sells the same land to C by executing another deed. If C pays for the land rather than receiving it as a gift, he is giving *value.* If C does not know of the earlier conveyance to B when he purchases, he is acting in *good faith.* Thus C qualifies as a BFP and has good title. In this situation B has no title. But if B has recorded her deed prior to C's purchase, B would have title even if C later gave value and acted in good faith. The reasoning is that C could have discovered B's interest if he had checked the records.

Although there is some conflict on the point, the courts in a majority of states hold that C qualifies as a BFP even if he does not record his own deed. (Of course, if he does not do so, he runs the risk of having the same thing happen to him that happened to B. If there was a "C," there could later be a "D.")

Regarding the status of C as a BFP, another point must be made. If B, the first grantee from O, is actually *in possession of the land* when C acquires his interest, this possession serves as notice to C. Thus, even if B did not record and C did not have actual knowledge of B's interest, C nevertheless is not a BFP.

Recording statutes apply not only to the sale of a fee simple interest but also to the conveyance of any other type of interest in land. For example, if O executes a mortgage to B, giving her a lien on the property, B should record her mortgage. If she does not, she risks losing her interest to a subsequent BFP.

Furthermore, the word *purchaser* actually means a grantee of any type of interest in the land, even such interests as liens or easements. Suppose, for instance, that O sells to B, who does not record her deed. O later borrows money from C and executes a mortgage purporting to give C a lien on the land. By making the loan to O, C is giving value. If C receives the mortgage without knowledge of the earlier conveyance to B, he is acting in good faith and is treated as a BFP. Thus C's mortgage is valid, and B's ownership is subject to it. If B had been a mortgagee herself instead of an actual grantee of the title, the same rules would apply to the conflict between B and C, the two mortgagees.

ADVERSE POSSESSION

Under some circumstances, a party can acquire ownership of land by taking possession of it and staying in possession for a certain number of years. The required time period is established by statute and varies from state to state, ranging from five years in California to thirty years in Louisiana.

Ownership acquired in this manner is frequently referred to as **title by adverse possession** or **title by limitation.**[8] Since it is not acquired by deed, there is nothing to record. Thus the recording statutes do not apply, and title by adverse possession, once acquired, cannot be lost to a subsequent BFP. Of course, even though such title is not *acquired* by deed, it can be *conveyed* by deed to someone else. Such a deed would be subject to all the rules applicable to deeds in general, including the recording statutes.

---

[8]The latter phrase is explained by the fact that the prescribed time periods are, in essence, statutes of limitations setting forth the maximum length of time an owner has to sue someone who is wrongfully in possession of the owner's land.

Requirements for Title by Adverse Possession

Not all types of possession will ripen into ownership. The possession must be "adverse," which means, in effect, that it must be actual, hostile, open and notorious, and continuous.[9]

Actual Possession: The requirement that possession be *actual* simply means that the possessor must have exercised some type of *physical control* over the land that indicates a claim of ownership. The person need not actually live on the property, although this certainly constitutes actual possession. What is required is that the possessor act toward the land as an average owner probably would act, taking into account the nature of the land. For example, if it is farmland, the farming of it constitutes actual possession. Erecting buildings or other improvements may also be sufficient.

Construction of a fence or building that extends over the true boundary line and onto the land of an adjoining property owner generally constitutes actual possession of that part of the land encompassed by the fence or located under the building. Thus, if the other requirements of adverse possession are met, the party erecting the fence or building will become the owner of the area in question after the prescribed period of time.

Hostile Possession: The requirement that the possession be *hostile* does not mean that it must be accompanied by ill feelings. What it means is that possession must be *nonconsensual*; it is not adverse if it occurs with the consent of the true owner. Thus a tenant's possession of the landlord's property under a lease agreement is not hostile unless the tenant clearly

communicated to the landlord that the tenant was claiming ownership.

Similarly, if two parties are co-owners of a tract of land, each of them has a right to possession. Therefore, possession by one co-owner is not hostile as to the other unless the possessor notifies the other that he or she is claiming sole ownership.

Open and Notorious Possession: The possession must be *open and notorious* rather than secretive. In other words, it must be a type of possession that will be easily noticeable by the true owner if a reasonable inspection is made.

Continuous Possession: In order for adverse possession to ultimately ripen into ownership, it must be *reasonably continuous* for the required period of time. The possessor does not have to be in possession every single day of the period. For instance, he or she could leave temporarily with an intent to return, and the law would treat the possession as not having been interrupted.

In answering the question of whether possession has been continuous, a court will take into account the nature of the land and the type of use being made of it. Thus farming the land only during the growing season each year constitutes continuous possession.

Also, the uninterrupted possession by two or more successive possessors can sometimes be added together, or "tacked," to satisfy the statutory time requirement. For "tacking" to be permitted, there must have been *privity* between the successive possessors. This simply means that the possessions by different persons must not have been independent of each other; rather, there must have been a transaction between them which purported to transfer the property. To illustrate: In State X the required period for adverse possession is ten years. O is the true owner. B meets all the requirements for adverse possession except that he stays on the land only six years. B then purports to sell or otherwise

---

[9]Some courts have also said that the possession must be "exclusive" and "under claim of right." These requirements will not be discussed because they overlap with the four listed here and really add nothing to what is required for adverse possession to exist.

transfer the land to C. If C stays in possession for four more years, continuing to meet all the requirements for obtaining title by adverse possession, C becomes the owner of the land.

The following case illustrates the applicability of the adverse possession doctrine to a common problem—a boundary dispute between "unneighborly" neighbors.

Kline v. Kramer
Court of Appeals of Indiana, 386 N.E.2d 982 (1979)

The Klines and the Kramers were adjoining landowners who both claimed ownership of a strip of land 1 to 4 feet wide and 309 feet long. The disputed strip formed the northern boundary of the Kramer property and the southern boundary of the Kline property. Both claimed ownership through previous owners. The Klines, who acquired their property in 1972, based their claim to the strip on the legal description contained in their deed. The Kramers, who purchased their property in 1968, claimed the strip on the theory of adverse possession. The position of the Kramers was that the ten-year period of possession necessary to establish adverse possession had been satisfied by the previous owners of the Kramer property, Harry and Hazel Britt.

The Kramers, plaintiffs, filed suit against the Klines, defendants, seeking to establish ownership of the boundary strip. The trial court granted the plaintiffs' motion for summary judgment, ruling that they had title by adverse possession, and the defendants appealed.

Staton, Judge:

. . . Harry Britt testified at the hearing on Kramer's motion for summary judgment that when he purchased the present-day Kramer property in 1947, a fence existed along the northern boundary of the land. Britt maintained the fence during his period of ownership. Photographs of the fence-line were introduced into evidence at the hearing in which Britt identified old fence posts he had set in maintaining the existing fence and familiar trees which had grown in the fence-line during his tenure on the land. While Britt testified that he never contemplated that he was claiming land that belonged to his neighbor, the fence in fact described a line which ran roughly one to four feet north of and parallel to the legally-described northern boundary of his property.

Britt testified that he felt that he owned the property up to the fence line and that he used it to plant crops and pasture cattle. It was his belief that he had bought "what was inside the fence." Similarly, Britt stated that when he sold the land to the Kramers in 1968 he intended to convey to them all the land enclosed by the fence.

F. Richard Kramer testified that he believed that he had purchased the property up to the fence that ran along the northern edge of his acreage. In 1972, Kramer inadvertently allowed his tractor to roll through the fence, tearing out a middle portion of it. Kramer repaired the break in the fence by stretching new fencing between the remaining old fence and fence posts to the east and west of the break. The new portion of the fence was set in the exact location of the old fence, according to Kramer, who noted that the new section followed a trail which cattle had worn along the old section.

Kramer concluded his testimony by stating that he had made improvements which encroached on the disputed stretch of land, that he had no knowledge of the true boundary line until Kline had conducted a survey of the land, and that he had paid taxes on his property according to the tax receipts sent to him by the County Treasurer.

. . . The trial court's entry of summary judgment was predicated on its conclusion that the Kramers had acquired title to the property through adverse possession. The ten year possessory period necessary to acquire title on that basis is a statute of limitations which runs against the titleholder. If the titleholder fails to oust the intruder within the ten year period, title to the property vests in the intruder, assuming all other elements of adverse possession are satisfied.

. . . The Klines contend that summary judgment was improper because the undisputed evidence reveals the absence of the elements necessary to acquire title by adverse possession. Specifically, the Klines maintain that the Kramers' predecessors-in-interest, the Britts, whose possessory period provides the foundation for the Kramers' claim, lacked the necessary adverseness, hostility, and intention to claim title to the strip. This argument is premised largely on the testimony of both Harry and Hazel Britt that they never intended to lay claim to any land that belonged to their neighbor to the north. Accordingly, the Klines argue, the Britts held the land by mistake and lacked the adverse intent or hostility which is requisite to establishing a claim of adverse possession.

We note that in the law of adverse possession, "adverse" is synonymous with "hostile." So long as an occupant of another's land does not disavow his or her right to possession of the property nor acknowledge that the possession is subservient to the title held by the true owner, the possession is adverse or hostile.

. . . While it is true that the Britts did not intend to claim the land of their neighbors, the record clearly reveals that they intended to claim all the land within the parameters of the fence which ran along the northern boundary of their property. They did not recognize that their ownership was subservient to their neighbor's title, nor did they acknowledge that they had no legal right to possession of the property. In all respects they acted as the sole owner of the property, maintaining the fence and using the land in a manner consistent with its normal purposes. This evidence clearly establishes that the Britts intended to claim title to the disputed strip of land. The only mistake involved in the Britts' possession was their belief that they were merely acting in a manner consistent with their ownership rights, a fact which does not negate the conclusion that their possession was adverse.

This uncontroverted evidence also establishes the Britts' "intent to claim title" to the contiguous strip of land, as the Klines have characterized the element of adverse possession. This element is more aptly defined as "a claim of ownership." The element is satisfied by entering upon and occupying the land with the intent to hold the land as one's own. The trial court was thus justified in finding that the Britts' possession was both hostile and under a claim of ownership. . . .

[Affirmed. The Kramers, plaintiffs, own the boundary strip because of adverse possession.]

REGULATION OF REAL PROPERTY OWNERSHIP, USE, AND SALE

Eminent Domain

The power of the government to take private property for public purposes (such as a highway) is referred to as the power of **eminent domain.** The federal government derives the power of eminent domain from the Fifth Amendment to the U.S. Constitution. Individual states draw the power from their own constitutions. In addition, states have delegated the power of eminent domain by statute to local governments (such as counties, cities, and school districts) and to railroads and public utilities.

The power can be exercised without the owner's consent, but the government must pay *just compensation* (i.e., the fair value of the property) to the owner. In many cases, a governmental body seeking to acquire property for a public purpose will negotiate a purchase from the owner. If the owner does not consent, or if there is disagreement as to the fair value of the property, the government exercises the power of eminent domain by instituting a court action called **condemnation.** In a condemnation proceeding the court will set a fair value for the property based on the evidence of that value.

In some situations, a property owner may claim that an activity by a governmental body has so deprived the owner of the use of the property that a "taking" of the property has actually occurred. The property owner can institute a legal action known as **inverse condemnation,** in which a court will determine whether there has been a taking of the property and, if so, the fair value to be paid the owner. The mere fact that a governmental activity has diminished the use or value of property does not establish that there has been a "taking"; the evidence must demonstrate that the owner has been effectively deprived of any reasonable use of the land. For example, the taking off and landing of airplanes at a city-owned airport could constitute a taking of an adjoining property owner's land if the land was so close to the airport that the planes flew over it at extremely low altitude.

Land Use Control

Restrictive Covenants: A deed may contain significant restrictions on the use of the property. For example, it might provide that only a single-family dwelling can be built on the land. Such **restrictive covenants** are usually valid and can be enforced by surrounding landowners. It also is common for a real estate developer to place restrictive covenants on all the residential lots in a subdivision and to specify those restrictions in the recorded plat. Such restrictions, such as those relating to the type and appearance of structures that can be built on the lots, are intended to preserve property values and can also be enforced by surrounding landowners in the subdivision.

Zoning: Pursuant to their constitutional police power, all states have passed legislation giving cities the power to enact zoning ordinances. In some states, similar powers have been given to counties. A **zoning ordinance** is essentially a law specifying the permissible uses of land in designated areas. Such an ordinance might specify zones for single-family dwellings, several categories of multiple-family dwellings, office buildings, various classifications of commercial structures, industrial facilities, and so on. Moreover, a zoning ordinance may impose even more detailed restrictions on use, such as minimum distances of structures from streets, lot sizes, and minimum parking accommodations for commercial buildings. The purposes of zoning laws are to permit the orderly planning of growth, protect against deterioration of surrounding property values by obnoxious uses, maintain the residential character of neighborhoods, and further other public purposes such as the prevention of overcrowding.

To prevent zoning from constituting a "taking" of property, zoning ordinances usually permit the continuance of a preexisting use even though it does not conform to the zoning restrictions for that area. In addition, a landowner may obtain a **variance**—permission from the city to make a use of the property that does not conform to the zoning ordinance—if he or she proves the following: (1) The zoning ordinance makes it impossible for the owner to receive a reasonable return on his or her investment in the land. (2) The negative effect of the zoning ordinance is unique to this owner's property; it is not an effect that is common to other landowners in the zone. (3) Granting the variance will not substantially alter the basic character of the surrounding neighborhood.

The Implied Warranty of Habitability

In recent years courts in a majority of states have recognized an **implied warranty of habitability** in the sale of new residential housing. The warranty exists separately from, and in addition to, any express warranties made by the seller. The warranty of habitability does not apply to minor defects, but only to major defects that substantially interfere with the buyer's use of the property as a residence. Examples of defects that probably would be a breach of the warranty include a defective foundation, leaking roof, malfunctioning heating or cooling system, and unsafe electrical wiring. Breach of the warranty entitles the buyer to receive damages from the seller based on the cost of repairing defects that are reasonably correctable, or the amount by which the home's market value has been reduced in the case of noncorrectable defects.

The implied warranty of habitability generally has been applied only to sales by a builder or other seller who is in the housing business. Real estate brokers and agents normally have not been held responsible under this warranty. Although some courts have extended the builder's liability under the implied warranty of habitability to the subsequent sale of used homes, a majority of courts have restricted it to the first sale of new homes. In recent years most states also have imposed an implied warranty of habitability on the landlord who leases residential property; a detailed discussion of the warranty in that setting is included in the next chapter.

SUMMARY

Real property includes (1) land, consisting of the surface, air rights, and subsurface rights, and (2) things affixed to the land, consisting of vegetation and fixtures. A fixture is an item that formerly was personal property and that has been attached to the land with an intent that it become a permanent part of the land.

The complete ownership of land can be divided in a number of ways. The particular set of rights owned in a given situation is an estate, or interest, in real property. These interests can be classified as freehold, nonfreehold, nonpossessory, and future. Any interest in real property that can be owned by one individual can also be owned concurrently by two or more individuals. There are several forms of co-ownership of real property.

Sales of real property commonly involve a transfer of complete ownership—the fee simple estate—but similar procedures may be employed to transfer lesser interests. In the typical sale of real property, the owner obtains the services of a broker, a buyer is found, a sale contract is executed, the buyer procures the necessary financing, various steps are taken to insure that the seller has a good title, and the closing or settlement occurs. The seller transfers title by executing and delivering a written deed. Although there are several types of deed, the general warranty deed is the best from the buyer's perspective. The deed must meet several requirements in order to transfer ownership effectively. Deeds should be acknowledged and recorded for the buyer's protection.

Title to real property can also be acquired by adverse possession, in which the taking of land must be actual, hostile, open and notorious, and the taking party must have continuous possession for a period of time specified by state statute. The ownership, use, and sale of real property is subject to several types of regulation, including the government's power of eminent domain, restrictive covenants, zoning ordinances, and the implied warranty of habitability.

KEY TERMS

Air rights
Fixture
Possessory interests
Freehold estates
Nonfreehold estates
Nonpossessory interests
Fee simple estate
Fee simple defeasible
Life estate
Leasehold estates
Easement
Easement appurtenant
Servient estate
Dominant estate
Easement in gross
Easement by express grant or reservation
Easement by implication
Easement by necessity
Easement by prescription (or prescriptive easement)
Profit
License
Mortgage
Lien
Involuntary lien
Mechanic's lien
Judgment lien
Future interest
Reversion
Remainder
Tenancy in common
Joint tenancy
Condominium
Cooperative
Tenancy by the entireties
Community property
Dower
Curtesy
Homestead
Open listing
Exclusive agency
Exclusive right to sell
Multiple listing service
Earnest money
Title examination
Abstract
Contract for deed
Closing (or settlement)
Escrow agent
General warranty deed
Covenant of seisin

Covenant against encumbrances
Covenant for quiet enjoyment
Special warranty deed
Quitclaim deed
Deed of bargain and sale
United States Government Survey
Townships
Metes and bounds
Plat
Acknowledgment
Recording
Bona fide purchaser (BFP)
Title by adverse possession (or title by
    limitation)
Eminent domain
Condemnation
Inverse condemnation
Restrictive covenants
Zoning ordinance
Variance
Implied warranty of habitability

QUESTIONS AND PROBLEMS

1. Talley and Warren were adjoining landowners. Talley drilled a producing oil well on his land close to the boundary line between his and Warren's property. Warren sued Talley for trespass. Although the entire well was on Talley's property, Warren proved that the well was drawing oil not only from beneath Talley's land but also from beneath Warren's. Will Warren prevail? Discuss.

2. In the above situation, suppose that Talley had drilled a "slant well," which began on his land but ended beneath Warren's land because it had been drilled at an angle. What will be the result if Warren sues for trespass in this case? Discuss.

3. Jenkins sold a 10-acre tract of land to Watkins. In the past, Jenkins had engaged in the business of raising rabbits, and at the time of the sale a number of rabbit hutches were still on the land. They were not attached to the soil but merely rested upon it. Each hutch had a wire-covered wooden frame and a tin roof; each measured approximately 4 feet by 4 feet by 4 feet. These hutches were never mentioned in the transaction. When Jenkins moved from the premises after the sale, he claimed that the rabbit hutches were still his and that he was entitled to take them. Watkins disagreed. Who is correct? Discuss.

4. Discuss whether wall-to-wall carpeting should be considered a fixture.

5. What are some probable reasons for the rule that the owner of a fee simple interest is presumed to be selling the entire interest unless the terms of the conveyance clearly indicate transference of a lesser interest? Explain.

6. Kempin was the owner of a life estate in a 60-acre parcel of land. A valuable stand of growing timber was situated on the property, and substantial deposits of lignite were located beneath it. Kempin began cutting the timber, both for firewood and for the purpose of sale. He also undertook to mine the lignite, some of which he intended to use for fuel and some of which he intended to sell. Moskovitz, who was to become the fee simple owner on Kempin's death, sued Kempin to enjoin him from all of the above activities. Who will prevail? Explain.

7. Explain the difference between easements, profits, and licenses.

8. In connection with the employment of a real estate broker, what is the difference between an open listing, an exclusive agency, and an exclusive right to sell?

9. Poindexter sold his farm to Samuelson, who did not record his deed. Several weeks later, before Samuelson had taken possession of the land, Poindexter sold the same property to Rosser, who made a large down payment and knew nothing of the earlier sale to Samuelson. Does Samuelson or Rosser have title to the land? Explain. Would it matter whether Rosser recorded his deed? Explain. Would it make any difference if Samuelson had already taken possession of the land when Rosser bought it? Explain.

10. Arnold and Ross were adjoining landowners. The opening of a cave was located on Arnold's land, but the cave ran beneath Ross's land. Ross did not know of the cave's existence. For a continuous period of 25 years, Arnold used the entire cave for various purposes, including storage. On a number of occasions, doing business as the Marengo Cave Co., he also guided visitors through the cave for a fee. Ross finally learned of the cave and of the use Arnold had been making of it. He demanded that Arnold cease his use of the part of the cave beneath Ross's land. Arnold refused, claiming that he had acquired title to the cave by adverse possession. The pertinent state statute provided for acquisition of such title after 20 years. Ross filed suit to establish ownership of the cave. Who owned the portion of the cave located beneath Ross's land? Discuss. (*Marengo Cave Co. v. Ross,* 10 N.E.2d 917, 1937.)

Chapter 42

LANDLORD AND TENANT

THE NATURE OF THE LANDLORD-TENANT RELATIONSHIP

The landlord-tenant relationship is created when the owner of real estate transfers temporary possession of the property to another person in return for the payment of rent.[1] The agreement providing for this transfer of possession and payment of rent is a **lease,** or *rental agreement.* The owner is referred to as the *landlord,* or *lessor,* and the one taking possession is the *tenant,* or *lessee.*

The identifying characteristic of a lease is the tenant's temporary acquisition of *exclusive possession* and *control* of the premises or the particular portion of it which he or she occupies. The tenant is distinguished from a *purchaser* because no title passes. On the other hand, the tenant is distinguished from a mere *licensee* who receives the temporary right to park a car in a space, occupy a seat in a theater, or make some other nonexclusive, revocable use of the premises. The tenant also is different from a *lodger* who occupies a room in a hotel but does not have legal control over the occupied area.

The law governing the landlord-tenant relationship consisted almost solely of common-law principles until recent times. Today many states have specific statutes concerning the rights and duties of landlords and tenants. A Uniform Residential Landlord and Tenant Act was proposed in 1972 by the National Conference of Commissioners on Uniform State Laws and, with some variations, has been adopted in 17 states. Common-law principles still control, however, in many situations not covered by specific statutes. This area of law is thus a mixture of statutory provisions and case precedents.

Landlord-tenant law developed in a basically agrarian economy when the focal point of the lease was the land itself. As a result, the transaction was viewed primarily as one for the transfer of an interest in real estate, and the principles of real estate law governed most aspects of the arrangement. In the great majority of leases today, however, the focal point of the transaction is the house, apartment, office, or other structure on the land. Consequently, the law has gradually changed so as to view the arrangement primarily as a contract, with the rules of contract law governing more and more aspects of the relationship. The movement in recent years toward greater legal protection for the consumer also has had a substantial impact on landlord-tenant law.

CREATION AND TERMINATION OF THE LANDLORD-TENANT RELATIONSHIP

The Lease

The Importance of the Lease:　The landlord-tenant relationship is created by agreement. Therefore, the lease and its particular terms determine the rights and duties of the parties. Most of the relevant legal principles serve only to specify rights and duties when the lease is silent on a disputed matter. There are a few legal principles, however, which do take precedence over a conflicting lease term.

Because the specific terms of the lease are of such great importance, it is critical that the parties draft their agreement carefully to clearly reflect their intent and to provide for various contingencies that might arise. It is also important for one party to closely examine any lease form proposed by the other. There is no standard form that must be used. Some groups, such as landlord associations, have developed their own standard form, but there is no law requiring it to be followed or preventing it from being changed.

Form of the Lease:　A lease may be oral unless a state statute requires it to be written. Most states have statutes requiring a written document for any lease extending beyond a stated time period. In some states, leases for a term

---

[1] The "owner" might own a fee simple interest, life estate, or other type of possessory interest. See Chapter 41 for details.

greater than one year must be written; in other states the period is three years.

Whether oral or written, a valid lease agreement must (1) indicate an intent to create the landlord-tenant relationship; (2) identify the parties, each of whom must have contractual capacity; (3) clearly identify the premises; and (4) state the amount of the rent and when it is to be paid.

Covenants and Conditions: A lease provision in which the landlord or the tenant promises to do something or not to do something is either a **covenant** or a **condition.** The difference lies in the consequences resulting from the breach of a promise. If one party fails to perform a *covenant,* the other party's recourse normally is to file suit for money damages. The innocent party is not relieved from his or her obligations, and the breaching party does not forfeit his or her rights under the lease.

On the other hand, the failure to perform a *condition* does cause a forfeiture of the lease and relieves the innocent party from further obligations. Because of the drastic nature of forfeiture, most lease provisions traditionally have been viewed as covenants unless the lease expressly provides for forfeiture as a consequence of breach.

For example, suppose that the tenant fails to make a rent payment within the agreed time. If the lease does not expressly provide for forfeiture of the lease as a result of nonpayment, the landlord's only remedy under the common-law rule is to sue for the unpaid rent. However, if the lease had expressly made rent payment a condition by providing for forfeiture in the event of nonpayment, the landlord could declare the lease terminated and evict the tenant. Today it is common for many lease clauses to provide for forfeiture as the penalty for breach of the clause. This is especially true of clauses spelling out tenants' duties in standard form leases prepared by landlords.

In recent years, statutes have been enacted in most states which make forfeiture the penalty for a tenant's failure to pay rent, even without an express lease clause to that effect.

Types of Tenancies

The interest acquired by a tenant is called a **tenancy,** or **leasehold.** Several types of tenancies exist.

Tenancy for Years: The most common tenancy is one that is technically called a **tenancy for years.** The name of this tenancy is rather misleading because it actually is created whenever a lease provides for a specific duration, such as thirty days, six months, one year, or fifty years. Such a tenancy terminates automatically when the term expires.

Periodic Tenancy: A **periodic tenancy** exists when the parties have not agreed on a specific duration, but have agreed that rent is to be paid at particular intervals (such as monthly or yearly). In such a case, the tenancy exists from period to period and can be terminated by one party giving notice to the other. The parties may expressly agree on the form and timing of the notice. If the lease is silent on the question, the common-law rule required that such notice be given at least one full rental period prior to termination. An exception was made for leases having rental periods of one year or more—in such cases six months' notice was required. Most states now have statutes which modify the common-law rule. Many of these statutes shorten the notice requirement to thirty days for periodic tenancies having rental periods longer than one month.

Tenancy at Will: A **tenancy at will** is a landlord-tenant relationship which may be terminated at any time by either party without advance notice. It exists when the parties have not agreed on either an express duration or a particular interval for rental payment. A tenancy at will is an uncommon occurrence.

Tenancy at Sufferance: When a valid tenancy is terminated, but the tenant continues to occupy the premises after he or she no longer has the right to do so, a **tenancy at sufferance** is created. The landlord can choose to make another lease or force the tenant to leave. The phrase tenancy at sufferance merely distinguishes the tenant from a complete trespasser who never had permission to be on the premises in the first place.

Termination for Reasons Other than Expiration of the Lease

We already have seen some of the ways in which tenancies can terminate: expiration of the term in a tenancy for years, advance notice in a periodic tenancy, and breach of a condition in the lease.

Although leases usually are *not* terminated by the death or disability of either party, there are several other ways in which leases may come to an end.[2] The parties may, for example, terminate the lease by mutual agreement. This is sometimes called **surrender and acceptance**—the tenant surrenders the lease, and the landlord accepts the surrender.

If the primary subject matter of a lease is a structure, such as a house or apartment, most courts hold that destruction of the structure through no fault of either party (such as fire or flood) will terminate the lease. As with other contracts, leases can also be terminated because of fraud, mistake, duress, undue influence, or minority.

Sale of the Leased Property

The landlord continues to own an interest in the premises during the term of the lease. This interest is called a **reversion** and consists of the landlord's future right to possession after termination of the lease.

A landlord may sell the leased property during the term of the lease, but such a sale does not terminate the lease. In actuality, the landlord merely sells what he has—the reversion. The purchaser buys the property subject to the rights of the tenant.

There are a few limited exceptions to this principle. In some ways a modern-day lease is still considered to be a transfer of an interest in real estate, rather than a mere contract, and to be subject to some of the rules of real estate law. For example, real estate *recording statutes* (discussed in Chapter 41) generally do apply to leases. Therefore, a purchaser from the landlord does not have to honor the preexisting lease if (1) the lease had not been recorded prior to the sale, *and* (2) the tenant was not in possession of the premises at the time of the sale. Either the recording or the tenant's possession will put the purchaser on notice of the tenant's rights, and the purchaser must honor the lease.

POSSESSION OF THE PREMISES

Landlord's Obligation to Turn Over Possession

One of the most important obligations of the landlord is to give the tenant possession. However, the laws of the various states are in conflict as to the extent of this obligation. One group of states follows the so-called "English rule," which requires the landlord to give the tenant actual physical possession. Under this rule, for example, if a holdover tenant from a previous lease is still in possession when the new tenant becomes entitled to possession, the landlord breaches the obligation to the new tenant.

Another group of states follows the "American rule," which requires only that the landlord transfer the *legal right to possession* to the tenant. Under this rule, the presence of a holdover tenant who has no legal right to be there is really the new tenant's problem, not the landlord's.

---

[2] In the event of death, the rights and duties under the lease are part of the estate of the deceased under the control of the executor or administrator. In the event of insanity, the insane person's guardian exercises the rights and duties existing under the lease.

The new tenant must take the necessary steps to remove the holdover.

Covenant of Quiet Enjoyment

During the term of the lease, the landlord owes to the tenant an obligation not to interfere with the tenant's lawful possession and use of the premises. This obligation, the **covenant of quiet enjoyment,** is expressly stated in most leases, but in most states is implied by law even if not stated in the lease. The covenant may be breached by the conduct of the landlord, someone acting under the landlord's authority, or someone having better title to the premises than the landlord has. It ordinarily may not be breached by other third parties—for example, in a majority of states the independent conduct of another tenant does not make the landlord liable for breach of this obligation. Therefore, if tenant X interferes with tenant Y's lawful possession and use, Y's remedy is against X and not against the landlord.

The most common actions of the landlord that breach this covenant are *eviction* and *constructive eviction.*

Eviction: An **eviction** occurs if the landlord padlocks the premises, changes the door lock and refuses to give the tenant a new key, or in some other way physically bars the tenant from entering the premises. A tenant who has a legal right to possession has a choice. He or she may (1) sue for damages or (2) treat the eviction as a breach of *condition* and be relieved from further obligations under the lease.

Constructive Eviction: Even without physically barring the tenant from entry, the landlord's action or inaction may cause the property to be unsuitable for the purpose for which it was leased. An example would be the failure to provide heat in the winter as promised in the lease. In such a case, the tenant may remain on the premises and sue for damages. If the tenant remains, he or she usually continues to be liable for rent. The tenant may, however, choose to abandon the property and treat the landlord's conduct as a **constructive eviction.** The tenant then is under no further obligation to pay rent.

USE OF THE PREMISES BY THE TENANT

Restrictions on Use

The uses that can be made of the property by the tenant usually are specified by agreement. In fact, clauses detailing permissible and impermissible uses are among the most common and important parts of leases. Such provisions frequently concern matters such as number of occupants, whether pets are permitted, and so forth.

In the absence of a lease provision prohibiting a particular use, the tenant is entitled to make any use of the premises that is (1) legal and (2) reasonably in line with the basic purpose for which the property was leased.

Damaging the Landlord's Reversionary Interest: The tenant has no right to use the property in such a way as to cause permanent damage to it. The duty of a tenant not to damage the landlord's reversionary interest is sometimes referred to as the duty not to commit **waste.** For example, a tenant cannot take timber or minerals from the land unless the right to do so was (1) expressly permitted by the lease or by later agreement or (2) clearly implied from surrounding circumstances. The right may be implied, for instance, when the primary value of the leased property is its timber or minerals, so that the parties probably would not have executed the lease if these materials had not been there.[3]

---

[3] A point that was made in Chapter 41 must be reiterated. What is ordinarily called an oil and gas "lease" is not really a lease at all. It is either the sale of a fee simple interest in the minerals in the ground or it is the sale of a right to take the minerals from the ground (a so-called "profit").

A tenant can be held liable for either intentionally or negligently damaging the leased property. When determining whether a tenant was negligent, the courts apply general principles of tort law. Many cases of this type involve claims by landlords that fire damage was caused by the tenant's negligence. For the landlord to prevail in such a case, there must be evidence that the tenant failed to act with reasonable care, such as by smoking in bed or leaving the premises to go shopping while food was left cooking on the kitchen range. Many cases also involve assertions by the tenant that the provisions of the lease excused him or her from liability for negligent damage to the leased premises. The language of the lease itself is the starting point for resolving most disputes arising from the landlord-tenant relationship, including this type of dispute. In the following case, the question for the court is whether the provisions of the lease should be interpreted so as to excuse the tenant from liability for fire damage caused by the tenant's negligence.

Acquisto v. Joe R. Hahn Enterprises, Inc.
Supreme Court of New Mexico, 619 P.2d 1237 (1980)

The defendant, Acquisto, leased a building from the plaintiff, Hahn Enterprises. During the term of the lease a fire broke out in the building, and the landlord sued Acquisto for damages caused by the fire. The landlord claimed that Acquisto had negligently caused the fire. Based upon a jury verdict, the trial court found that Acquisto had been guilty of negligence, and that there was no provision in the lease excusing Acquisto from responsibility for his negligence. The court of appeals reversed, holding that the lease did excuse Acquisto from such liability, and the landlord appealed to the New Mexico Supreme Court.

Sosa, Chief Justice:

The relevant provisions of the lease pertinent to the disposition of this case are as follows:

IV. USE OF PREMISES. Lessee . . . hereby agrees and covenants with Lessor . . . not to use . . . said premises in any manner . . . so as to tend to increase the existing rate of fire insurance for the said demised premises.

V. CONDITION OF PREMISES AND REPAIRS. Lessee . . . hereby agrees . . . that . . . at the expiration of the term of this Lease, or any renewal or extension thereof, Lessee will yield up peaceably the said premises to Lessor in as good order and condition as when the same were entered upon by Lessee, loss by fire or inevitable accident, damage by the elements, and reasonable use and wear excepted. . . . [Emphasis added by court.]

XII. TAXES, OTHER ASSESSMENTS, AND INSURANCE. . . . Fire and extended coverage insurance upon all buildings . . . upon the said premises shall be provided for as follows: [blank]   and fire and extended coverage insurance upon all of the

contents . . . situated upon the said premises shall be provided for as follows:
__[blank]__ . . . .

XV. DESTRUCTION. Lessee . . . agrees and covenants with Lessor that if at any time during the term of this Lease . . . the said demised premises shall be totally or partially destroyed by fire, earthquake, or other calamity, then Lessor shall have the option to rebuild or repair the same. . . .

The tenant contends that the lease provisions operate to relieve him of liability for all fires, including those he negligently causes. Whether express language must be used to exculpate [i.e., excuse] a party to the lease is a question of first impression in New Mexico. The courts in other jurisdictions are divided on the issue. One line of cases hold that no specific exculpatory language is required and that the intent to relieve one of the parties from liability for negligence must be determined from the lease as a whole. These cases hold that the parties' intent must be determined from the lease as a whole, in light of the subject matter, surrounding circumstances and the natural meaning of the language used. In all of these cases, the court found that the parties had intended that the landlord provide fire insurance for the benefit of both parties; this finding, coupled with the clause excepting loss by fire or other casualty, was sufficient to show an intent not to hold the tenant liable for his negligence. This is the line of cases upon which the Court of Appeals based its opinion. The second line of cases, rejected by the Court of Appeals, hold that the lease must state explicitly that the tenant is released from liability for a fire resulting from his own negligence. We hold that leases are to be construed as a whole to determine the parties' intent. In the absence of an agreement between the parties specifying which of them will carry fire insurance for the benefit of both parties, or an express clause in the lease relieving a party from his negligence, each party must bear the risk of loss for his own negligence.

A lease is subject to the basic rules of contract construction. It must be read as a whole to effectuate the intent of the parties. We will not look beyond the four corners of the document unless the lease is ambiguous. The Court of Appeals found that the lease was patently ambiguous because Paragraph XII, which would have provided which party would carry fire insurance, was left blank. We disagree that this constitutes an ambiguity; rather it is a clear indication that the parties failed to agree which of them would provide the insurance. This conclusion is supported by the fact that the other blanks in the same paragraph providing for the payment of taxes were completed. We conclude that the parties were aware of the blanks relative to fire insurance and chose not to fill them in. Since we hold that the lease is complete, plain and unambiguous, parol evidence may not be introduced to vary the terms of the agreement. The trial court properly excluded extrinsic evidence of the parties' intent with respect to fire insurance.

The tenant contends that the use of "fire" in Paragraph V of the lease operates to exculpate him from his negligence because it refers to all fires, including those caused by his negligence. We disagree. The word "fire" must be construed in the context of the other words in the clause, which provide that the tenant is to surrender the premises to the landlord in the same condition they were in at the beginning of the lease term, "loss by fire or inevitable accident, damage by the elements . . . excepted." The plain meaning of this language is that only fire caused by unavoidable consequences or acts of God were to be exempt, but not fire caused by negligence. The use of such phrases as "inevitable accident" and "damage by the elements" support this construction. These are all non-negligent occurrences and we must construe "fire" to fall within the same type of occurrence.

The arguments that Paragraph IV, which prohibits the tenant from doing anything which would increase the insurance rates, or Paragraph XV, which gives the landlord the option of rebuilding the premises when loss by "fire, earthquake or other calamity" occurs, indicate an intent by the parties that the landlord provide fire insurance thereby relieving tenant from liability, are rejected. First, the type of "fire" referred to in Paragraph XV is that which can be classified as purely accidental and non-negligent. This is clear from the use of "other calamity" in the same clause, indicating a use of "fire" in the context of a calamity rather than in the context of negligence. Secondly, Paragraph IV is a clause found in many leases without regard to which party is responsible for providing insurance. It does not follow from the language therein that the landlord agreed to provide insurance. This is especially so when read in conjunction with Paragraph XII which is specifically designed to establish which party will carry the insurance. Since Paragraph XII is blank, the only logical conclusion to be drawn is that the parties did not agree that either of them would carry insurance.

Having decided that the lease is not ambiguous, that the landlord did not agree to provide fire insurance, and that the use of "fire" does not include negligently caused fire, it follows that the responsibility for loss of the premises due to negligence must be borne by the negligent party. This is merely a restatement of the common law rule of tort liability. While the law allows one to exculpate himself by contract, it will do so only if the exculpation is set forth with such clarity that the intent to negate the usual consequences of tortious conduct is made plain. In this case, where the parties failed to agree that one, or both, of them would carry fire insurance, and where there is no specific exculpatory language relieving the tenant from liability for negligence, each party will be responsible for damages caused by his negligence. This is more equitable than requiring the innocent landlord to pay for a fire he did not cause.

For the foregoing reasons we reverse the decision of the Court of Appeals and affirm the decision of the trial court. [Thus, although the court held that an express exculpatory clause was not required to excuse the tenant from liability for negligent damage to the premises, in this case the lease as a whole did not indicate that the parties intended to excuse the tenant.]

Altering the Premises

Suppose that a tenant in an apartment or house wants to add some built-in bookshelves or paint the interior walls. Or suppose that a business tenant wishes to build an additional storage area for inventory. Does the tenant have a right to alter the property?

Many leases expressly forbid the tenant from making alterations to the premises without specific consent of the landlord. Even if the lease contains no such clause, however, the tenant generally has no right to make alterations without consent.

In many states the law imposes an absolute requirement that the tenant return the premises to the landlord at the end of the lease in exactly the same condition they were in at the beginning, except for normal wear and tear. If the tenant has made any changes without the landlord's consent, the tenant is liable for the cost of putting the property back into the condition it was in at the beginning of the lease.

In a growing number of states, however, the tenant is not liable for the cost of "undoing" such alterations if (1) the alteration was consistent with and necessary for the tenant's reasonable use of the premises, and (2) the alteration did not diminish the value of the property.

Fixtures: We saw in Chapter 41 that an item of personal property becomes a *fixture* when it is affixed to real property. Even if not actually attached, the item is a fixture if circumstances indicate that it was intended to be part of the real estate.

If a tenant affixes an item to the leased property, the same basic rules are applied to determine whether the item is a fixture as are applied in other situations. Thus, a tenant who installs built-in bookshelves, new cabinets, or other such items probably has added fixtures to the property and cannot remove them when the lease expires.

However, many courts traditionally have drawn a distinction between fixtures added by a residential tenant and those added by a tenant who conducts a business on the leased property. Fixtures added by a business tenant are called **trade fixtures.** Courts generally have held that a business tenant probably did not intend for a trade fixture to become part of the real estate. Thus if an item such as a gasoline pump or neon sign can be removed without substantial damage to the real estate, the business tenant usually can remove it at the end of the lease.

This distinction between residential and business tenants has been frequently criticized as illogical.

THE DUTY TO MAINTAIN THE PREMISES

The traditional common-law view was that the landlord was not responsible for the condition of the premises at the beginning of the lease or for making repairs during the lease. The tenant leased the premises "as is," and was responsible for making later repairs so that the premises were substantially in the same condition at the end of the lease as at the beginning.

The tenant's duty to repair has always been subject to certain important limits. The duty does not apply to major structural components such as the foundation and framework, but only to relatively minor items like windows, venetian blinds, and so forth. However, whether classified as major or minor, the tenant is responsible for making emergency repairs to protect the premises from the elements and thus prevent further damage. This responsibility is part of the tenant's overall duty not to commit waste by negligently or intentionally damaging the property.

The general rule that a landlord has no duty to maintain the premises still exists *in theory.* However, over the years the courts have recognized many exceptions to the rule. Today the exceptions are practically as broad as the general rule. We will examine the most important situations in which the landlord does have a duty to make repairs.

Express Covenant

As with most other matters, the obligation to make repairs may be dealt with in a specific lease clause. If the landlord expressly promises to keep the premises in good repair, he or she is legally responsible for complying with the promise.[4] The extent of the obligation is determined by the language used.

A lease may sometimes place certain repair duties on the tenant. In such a situation, the language of the clause again determines the scope of the obligation.

Common Areas

When a landlord leases several units of a multi-unit property to different tenants, the landlord is responsible for maintaining common areas in a reasonably safe condition. The most common example of a multi-unit property is an apartment complex. Common areas include swimming pools, stairs, halls, and similar places over which the landlord retains control. The duty of repair extends to defects that the landlord actually knows about and to those that he or she reasonably *should* know about. Thus, the landlord is obligated to make reasonable, periodic inspections of common areas.

Like any other individual or company, a landlord is responsible for the actions of its agents and employees when they are acting within the scope of their authority or employment. Thus, when an apartment manager is notified of an unsafe condition in a common area, the landlord is treated legally as knowing about the condition. Similarly, the manager or other agent's failure to inspect common areas is treated as the landlord's failure.

Building Codes

Many state statutes and city ordinances specify certain standards for both the construction and maintenance of buildings. In the case of leased premises, the landlord, as owner, is ordinarily responsible for compliance with these codes. Provisions dealing with electrical wiring, heating, and other structural concerns usually apply to both commercial and residential structures. Some codes, however, impose a greater duty on the landlord in leases of residential property by requiring that the owner keep the premises in overall good repair. A few state legislatures have even adopted separate "housing codes" dealing especially with residential property.

Implied Warranty of Habitability

Perhaps the most important development in landlord-tenant law in recent years has been the recognition of an **implied warranty of habitability** in leases of residential property.[5] Most courts that have considered the question recently have adopted the warranty. A few have based their decisions on particular language in state housing codes placing certain duties of repair on residential landlords. Most of them, however, have recognized the warranty as a matter of public policy regardless of the existence or wording of a housing code. In addition, several states have adopted the implied warranty of habitability by express legislative enactment.

The warranty of habitability requires landlords to maintain residential property, such as a house, apartment, or duplex, in a "habitable" or livable condition. Although this warranty is most commonly applied to physical defects in the property, it has also been applied to the provision of essential services such as garbage collection. The obligation of the landlord exists at the time the property is leased and throughout the term of the lease. Defects in the premises constitute a breach of the warranty only when the landlord knows or should know about them and has had a reasonable time to make repairs.

---

[4]When such a promise is separately made *after* the lease has been agreed to, the new promise must be supported by new consideration.

[5]Judicial recognition of the implied warranty of habitability has also been a major development in the law relating to the *sale of new homes,* as was mentioned in the previous chapter.

A dwelling can be habitable even though it has minor defects. Therefore, the warranty of habitability only applies to major deficiencies. Of course, in some cases a whole host of minor problems existing at the same time may render a dwelling unlivable even though each defect alone is not major.

Some defects, such as a large hole in the ceiling or the lack of heat in a cold climate, obviously cause a dwelling to be unhabitable. Others, such as an occasional drip from the kitchen faucet, just as obviously do not cause the premises to be unhabitable. In many cases, however, the question is much closer. The courts in such situations must determine whether the particular defect involves an item which is truly essential or merely an amenity. One court observed:

> [I]n a modern society one cannot be expected to live in a multi-storied apartment building without heat, hot water, garbage disposal, or elevator service. Failure to supply such things is a breach of the implied covenant of habitability. Malfunction of venetian blinds, water leaks, wall cracks, lack of painting, at least of the magnitude presented here, go to what may be called

"amenities." Living with lack of painting, water leaks and defective venetian blinds may be unpleasant, aesthetically unsatisfying, but does not come within the category of unhabitability.[6]

When determining whether defects are substantial enough to violate the warranty of habitability, the courts consider a variety of factors, including the following: (1) the impact of the defect on basic life functions—sleeping, eating, relaxing, and so on; (2) the actual or possible effect of the defect on the safety and health of tenants; (3) the length of time the defect has existed; (4) the age of the building—the newer the building, the higher are the tenant's reasonable expectations regarding its condition; and (5) whether the defect violates a building or housing code.

The next case discusses the public policy considerations underlying the implied warranty of habitability, and illustrates the standards used by courts in applying the warranty.

---

[6] *Academy Spires, Inc. v. Brown,* 111 N.J. 477, 268 A.2d 556, 559 (1970).

Park West Management Corp. v. Mitchell
Court of Appeals of New York, 391 N.E.2d 1288 (1979)

Park West owned an apartment complex consisting of seven highrise buildings on the Upper West Side of Manhattan in New York City. Because of a strike by Employees' Union Local 32-B, the landlord's entire maintenance and janitorial staff did not report to work for a 17-day period. All of the incinerators were wired shut, thus requiring the tenants to dispose of garbage at the curbs in paper bags. Because employees of the New York Sanitation Department refused to cross the striking employees' picket lines, uncollected trash piled up to the height of the first floor windows. The garbage and the stench it produced led the Health Department to declare a health emergency at the complex.

Also during this period, regular exterminating service was not performed, which, together with the accumulated trash, created condi-

tions in which rats, roaches, and vermin flourished. Routine maintenance and other service was not performed, and common areas were not cleaned.

A group of tenants withheld their rent payments during the period, and the landlord sued for the rent. About 400 tenants ultimately joined in the legal proceeding. The tenants defended against the landlord's suit by claiming a breach of the implied warranty of habitability. The trial court and intermediate appellate courts ruled that the warranty had been breached, and granted a 10 percent reduction in the tenants' June rent bill. The landlord appealed to the highest court in New York.

Cooke, Chief Judge:

Under the traditional common-law principles governing the landlord-tenant relationship, a lease was regarded as a conveyance of an estate for a specified term and thus as a transfer of real property. Consequently, the duty the law imposed upon the lessor was satisfied when the legal right of possession was delivered to the lessee. The lessor impliedly warranted only the continued quiet enjoyment of the premises by the lessee. This covenant of quiet enjoyment was the only obligation imposed upon the landlord which was interdependent with the lessee's covenant to pay rent. As long as the undisturbed right to possession of the premises remained in the tenant, regardless of the condition of the premises, the duty to pay rent remained unaffected.

Because the common law of leasehold interests developed in rural, agrarian England, the right to possession of the land itself was considered the essential part of the bargain; structures upon the land were deemed incidental. . . .

As society slowly moved away from an agrarian economy, the needs and expectations of tenants underwent a marked change. No longer was the right of bare possession the vital part of the parties' bargain. The urban tenant seeks shelter and the services necessarily appurtenant thereto—heat, light, water, sanitation and maintenance. . . .

A number of factors mandated departure from the antiquated common-law rules governing the modern landlord-tenant relationship. The modern-day tenant, unlike his medieval counterpart, is primarily interested in shelter and shelter-related services. He is usually not competent to perform maintenance chores, even assuming ability to gain access to the necessary equipment and to areas within the exclusive control of the landlord. . . .

The transformation of the nature of the housing market occasioned by rapid urbanization and population growth was further impetus for the change. Well-documented shortages of low- and middle-income housing in many of our urban centers has placed landlords in a vastly superior bargaining position, leaving tenants virtually powerless to compel the performance of essential services. . . . While it is true that many municipalities have enacted housing codes setting minimum safety and sanitation standards, historically those codes could be enforced only by municipal authorities.

In short, until development of the warranty of habitability in residential leases, the contemporary tenant possessed few private remedies and little real power, under either the common law or modern housing codes, to compel his landlord to make necessary repairs or provide essential services. . . . A residential lease is now effectively deemed a sale of shelter and services by the landlord who impliedly warrants: first, that the premises are fit for human habitation; second, that the condition of the premises is in accord with the uses reasonably intended by the parties; and, third, that the tenants are not subjected to any conditions endangering or detrimental to their life, health or safety. . . . The obligation of the tenant to pay rent is dependent upon the landlord's satisfactory maintenance of the premises in habitable condition.

Naturally, it is [an] impossibility to attempt to document every instance in which the warranty of habitability could be breached. Each case must, of course, turn on its own peculiar facts. However, the standards of habitability set forth in local housing codes will often be of help in resolution of this question. . . . However, a simple finding that conditions on the leased premises are in violation of an applicable housing code does not necessarily constitute automatic breach of the warranty. In some instances, it may be that the code violation is *de minimis* or has no impact upon habitability. . . .

But, while certainly a factor in the measurement of the landlord's obligation, violation of a housing code or sanitary regulation is not the exclusive determinant of whether there has been a breach. Housing codes do not provide a complete delineation of the landlord's obligation, but rather serve as a starting point in that determination by establishing minimal standards that all housing must meet. In some localities, comprehensive housing, building or sanitation codes may not have been enacted; in others, their provisions may not address the particular condition claimed to render the premises uninhabitable. Threats to the health and safety of the tenant—not merely violations of the codes—determine the reach of the warranty of habitability. . . .

To be sure, absent an express agreement to the contrary, a landlord is not required to ensure that the premises are in perfect or even aesthetically pleasing condition; he does warrant, however, that there are no conditions that materially affect the health and safety of tenants. For example, no one will dispute that health and safety are adversely affected by insect or rodent infestation, insufficient heat and plumbing facilities, significantly dangerous electrical outlets or wiring, inadequate sanitation facilities or similar services which constitute the essence of the modern dwelling unit. If, in the eyes of a reasonable person, defects in the dwelling deprive the tenant of those essential functions which a residence is expected to provide, a breach of the implied warranty of habitability has occurred.

Under the facts presented here, respondents [tenants] have proven that petitioner [landlord] breached its implied warranty of habitability. As a result of the strike, essential services bearing directly on the health and safety of the tenants were curtailed, if not eliminated. Not only were there numerous violations of housing and sanitation codes, but conditions of the premises were serious enough to necessitate the declaration of a health emergency. In light of these factors, it ill behooves petitioner to maintain that the tenants suffered only a trifling inconvenience. . . .

Problematical in these cases is the method of ascertaining damages occasioned by the landlord's breach. That damages are not susceptible to precise determination does not insulate the landlord from liability. Inasmuch as the duty of the tenant to pay rent is coextensive with the landlord's duty to maintain the premises in habitable condition, the proper measure of damages for breach of the warranty is the difference between the fair market value of the premises if they had been as warranted, as measured by the rent reserved under the lease, and the value of the premises during the period of the breach. . . . In ascertaining damages, the finder of fact must weigh the severity of the violation and duration of the conditions giving rise to the breach as well as the effectiveness of steps taken by the landlord to abate those conditions. . . . The record here amply supports the 10% reduction in rent ordered by Civil Court.

[Affirmed.]

Tenant's Remedies for Landlord's Failure to Maintain the Premises

The instances in which a landlord has the duty to maintain the premises have been increasing in recent times. Along with the expansion of the landlord's obligation to maintain the premises, there has also been a general expansion of the tenant's remedies for breach of the obligation. The remedies available to the tenant will depend on the circumstances and on the law of the particular state.

Suit for Damages: Any time the landlord breaches a duty to repair, the tenant may sue for the damages caused by the landlord's failure. Damages in the case of relatively minor defects are based on the cost of repairing them. For major defects, damages usually are calculated as the difference between the rental value of the premises in unrepaired and repaired conditions. Because of the time and expense of pursuing a damage suit, it is a feasible remedy only for major defects. Even in the case of major defects, a damage lawsuit usually makes economic sense

only if (1) the lease is a long-term one or (2) the tenant uses the premises for business purposes so that the attorney fees and other expenses of pursuing the claim can be treated as a business expense for tax purposes.

Repair and Deduct: In the past several years many states have enacted so-called **repair and deduct** statutes. This type of legislation permits the tenant to make repairs and then deduct the cost of such repairs from the rent. Courts in several states have recognized the right to repair and deduct even without a specific statute. The right of tenants to use this remedy is subject to several important limitations: (1) the defect must have been one that the landlord was legally obligated to repair; (2) the landlord must have been notified of the defect and failed to repair it within a prescribed period of time; (3) the amount that can be deducted by the tenant usually is limited—in some states the limitation is expressed as a specific maximum amount, such as $200; in other states it is based on a set formula, such as one month's rent; and (4) in several states, the tenant's right to repair and deduct applies only to defects that relate to essential services such as water and electricity.

The repair and deduct remedy has been applied most commonly to situations in which a landlord breached the implied warranty of habitability.

Rent Withholding: By statute or court decision, many states in recent years have authorized a reduction in the tenant's rent until the landlord makes required repairs. The amount of the reduction is computed in various ways, but generally must be proportionate to the diminishment of rental value caused by the defect. When the **rent withholding** right is created by statute, the statute usually requires the tenant to deposit the amount withheld with a court or other designated agency until the dispute is resolved.

Regardless of whether the right to reduce and withhold rent has been created by statute or judicial decision in a particular state, a tenant exercising the right always runs the risk of withholding too much. If a court ultimately determines that a tenant has withheld more than the law permits, the tenant is liable to the landlord for the amount that was impermissibly withheld.

Like the repair and deduct remedy, the rent withholding remedy also has usually been connected with the implied warranty of habitability. The *Park West* case provides an illustration of this remedy.

Lease Cancellation: The landlord's breach of a duty to repair ordinarily does not give the tenant a right to cancel the lease. However, when the defects are so major that the implied warranty of habitability is breached, most courts permit the tenant to cancel the lease, abandon the premises, and be relieved of any further rent payment obligation. When the tenant chooses this alternative, the implied warranty of habitability is essentially the same as the older principle of constructive eviction.

INJURIES ON THE PREMISES

Suppose that a defect in the leased premises causes injury to the tenant, a member of the tenant's family, or someone else who is lawfully on the premises. Who is legally responsible for the damages caused by these injuries? Liability commonly depends upon whether the landlord or tenant has control over the particular area where the injury occurred. In a few situations, however, the existence of a duty to repair may create such liability regardless of control.

Liability of the Tenant

The tenant has a general duty to maintain in a reasonably safe condition that part of the leased premises which is under his or her control. Thus, if a visitor on residential property or a customer on business property is injured by an unsafe condition, the tenant usually is responsible. Clearly, however, the tenant's responsibility does not extend to injuries occurring in those common areas controlled by the landlord.

The tenant's duty to maintain the premises in a safe condition exists even in situations where the landlord has a duty to make repairs. Consequently, in some situations both landlord and tenant may be legally responsible for injuries to a third party. Making both of them responsible increases the likelihood that the premises will be kept in a safe condition. Such a policy takes into account the fact that outsiders are less familiar with the property and less likely to be aware of potentially dangerous conditions than the landlord or tenant.

Liability of the Landlord

The landlord's liability for injuries may be based on control, on an affirmative duty to make repairs, or on both factors.

Public Purpose: Ordinarily, the circumstances in which a landlord is liable for injuries are the same whether the injured person is a tenant or anyone else lawfully on the premises. There is, however, one major exception to this principle. When premises are leased for a purpose that involves admission of the public, such as a retail store, the landlord owes a continuing duty to the public to maintain the premises in a safe condition. This duty makes the landlord liable for injuries to members of the public even when there would have been no basis for landlord liability if the *tenant* had been the injured party.

When premises are leased for a public purpose, and a member of the public is injured by a defect in the property, the tenant also is respon-

sible. The injured party could thus take action against both landlord and tenant.

Common Areas: The landlord is liable for injuries caused by defects in common areas over which the landlord has control. This liability to tenants or others lawfully on the premises is co-extensive with the landlord's general duty to make repairs in common areas.

The following case presents a situation in which the landlord was held liable for injuries caused by defects in an outside porch.

Cruz v. Drezek
Supreme Court of Connecticut, 397 A.2d 1335 (1978)

The Cruz family rented a third-floor apartment in a three-family house in New Britain, Connecticut, from the owners, Edward and Jeanette Drezek. Outside the third-floor apartment was a porch. The evidence did not indicate whether other tenants also had access to the porch. Regardless of whether it was a true "common" area, the evidence did clearly show that the landlord retained control over this exterior porch.

Fourteen-year-old Hector Cruz was helping his family move in. A small mattress was being raised by ropes from the ground to the third-floor porch. Hector was on the porch pulling the mattress up. As he leaned on the railing surrounding the porch, it gave way and he fell to the ground. The Cruzes sued the Drezeks for damages resulting from Hector's injuries. Based on a jury verdict, the trial court awarded judgment in favor of Hector for $20,000 and Hector's parents for $1,952.40 to cover the medical bills they had paid. The Drezeks, defendants, appealed on the grounds that there was not enough evidence of negligence on their part to even create a jury question, and that the trial court should have ruled in their favor as a matter of law.

Healey, Justice:

. . . The defendants were under the duty to use reasonable care to keep those portions of the premises, and specifically the third-floor porch, together with its railings, over which they had control, in a reasonably safe condition. . . . There could be no breach of the duty resting upon the defendants unless they knew of the defective condition or were chargeable with notice of it because, had they exercised a reasonable inspection of their premises, they would have discovered it; and it was the defendants' duty to make a reasonable inspection of premises in their control to discover possible defects therein.

Turning to the question of the specific defective condition, the evidence, while contradictory, furnished a reasonable basis for the jury's conclusion that the plaintiffs had proven that there did exist at the time of this accident a specific defective condition pertaining to the front porch railing, that the specific defective condition in fact caused Hector's fall and that that specific condition had existed for a sufficient length of time so as to have afforded the defendants an opportunity on a reasonable inspection to discover and remedy it. . . .

The following evidence was also before the jury: Detective Walsh of the New Britain Police Department, who had been a policeman for twenty-three years and a detective for sixteen years, arrived at the scene of this accident within two or three minutes after receiving a radio call. He learned that two men had fallen from the third-floor porch and had been injured. He testified, with respect to the railing, that the railing, where it pulled away, looked "rotted"; that there were nails sticking out and that the wood "looked rotted; it looked old"; that "the railing had carried away from its anchor, from the nails which anchored it to the side of the building, of the posts"; that when he found the railing, the nails were still in it and that he recalled that some nails were left in the posts upstairs and some stayed with the railing which fell below; and that, with respect to both the railing and posts, the exterior wood was "badly weathered," and that "the paint was chipped away, and where the paint was chipped away the wood was gray from weathering." Mrs. Ehritz, a witness called by the defendants, had lived two houses away for about fifteen years. She testified that the "railing was old and the nails were rusty." . . .

The defendants had purchased this house about ten weeks or two months before this accident. While admitting the house needed a paint job, Edward Drezek claimed it did not need new porches. He applied, however, in November, 1970, for a building permit to repair and enclose three front porches on this house. Before buying this property Edward Drezek personally inspected it. With reference to the third-floor porch, he visually inspected it and specifically checked that porch's railings and banisters, all of which he claimed were fine.

Frank Costanzo is a foreman for a moving company for which he has worked for fifty years and he has spent at least forty years working on the trucks, helping people to move. He has had "plenty of occasions" to move mattresses and, in the course of his work, ropes have been used many times to pull up mattresses. According to him, this was a customary and common way of handling them because they are otherwise too hard to handle. . . .

This was a third-floor porch, and the greater the likelihood of danger, the greater the amount of care required in making an inspection of the premises to meet the standard of due care. The controlling question in deciding whether the defendants had constructive notice of the defective condition is whether the condition existed for such a length of time that the defendants should, in the exercise of reasonable care, have discovered it in time to remedy it. Given the evidence before the jury, they could reasonably have found that this specific defective condition existed for a reasonable length of time within which the defendants should have learned of it, especially because of Edward Drezek's having been on that porch approximately two months before, just before he bought this property, at which time he looked at the railings, and that a reasonable length of time had passed for remedying the condition of which he should have known. . . .

A permissible and reasonable view of the evidence by the jury permitted them to find for the plaintiffs.

[Affirmed.]

Latent Defects: A **latent defect** is one that is hidden to such an extent that the tenant is not likely to discover it during a normal initial inspection. If such a defect exists at the time a lease is made, and the landlord either knows or reasonably should know about it, the landlord has a duty to disclose the defect to the tenant. Failure to disclose makes the landlord liable for injuries subsequently caused by the defect. It is important to note that the landlord fulfills his or her duty by disclosing the existence of the defect—the landlord is not required to actually fix it unless there is some other legal basis for imposing a duty of repair.

The landlord's nondisclosure of hidden defects may bring about other consequences as well, such as giving the tenant a legal basis for cancelling the lease.

Negligent Repairs: Regardless of whether the landlord has a duty to make repairs, if he or she makes them and does so in a *negligent* manner, the landlord is liable for any injuries caused by the negligent repairs.

Express Agreement, Statutory Duty, and Implied Warranty: In the previous section we saw that, in modern times, the landlord has increasingly been placed under a duty to make repairs. This duty may exist because the landlord has agreed in an express lease provision to make repairs, or the duty may be imposed by a building or housing code or the implied warranty of habitability. In these situations, the landlord may have the duty to make repairs even with respect to those parts of the premises under the tenant's control.

Suppose that Thompson has leased an apartment from Leonard. Assume that, because of an express lease clause, an applicable code provision, or an implied warranty, Leonard has a duty to repair and maintain the apartment. Leonard then breaches this duty by failing to make certain repairs. If either Thompson or someone else lawfully on the premises is injured because of the defect, is Leonard liable for the injury?

The court decisions in the various states are somewhat evenly split on this issue. Some of them focus on the repair duty itself and conclude that liability for injuries is a logical component of the duty. Others focus on the factor of control and conclude that the landlord's liability for injuries should not extend to areas over which the landlord has very little daily control, even when the landlord has a duty to repair those areas.

Of course, when the injured person is an outsider who does not live on the leased premises, the tenant generally is liable for the injuries even though the landlord may also be liable.

Exculpatory and Indemnification Clauses

Leases often contain **exculpatory clauses,** which state that the landlord is not liable for injuries on the premises. Such a clause cannot excuse the landlord from liability to outsiders who are not parties to the lease. However, it is also common for an **indemnification clause** to accompany the exculpatory clause. The indemnification clause states that the tenant must indemnify, or reimburse, the landlord for damages the landlord has to pay to outsiders.

The courts have reached different conclusions on the question of whether exculpatory and indemnification clauses are effective to shield the landlord. Some of these different results are based upon the language of the particular clause or the existence of a specific statute in the particular state. However, many of the decisions are simply in conflict with one another.

As a general proposition, courts are much more likely to throw out such clauses in residential leases than in commercial ones. Moreover, regardless of the type of lease, there is a gradual trend in the courts toward invalidating these clauses.

It should be emphasized that here we are speaking of exculpatory clauses that seek to excuse the *landlord* from liability. If the lease contains a clause purporting to excuse the *tenant* from liability, such a clause is normally valid. The question whether a lease expresses an intent to excuse the tenant was dealt with earlier in the chapter.

LANDLORD'S RESPONSIBILITY TO PROTECT TENANTS FROM CRIMES

The landlord does not have an absolute duty to protect tenants from the criminal acts of outsiders. As part of the general expansion of the landlord's duties in recent years, however, several courts have found landlords responsible for providing such protection in certain circumstances. The situations in which the landlord has been found liable for crimes committed against tenants usually involve evidence that (1) the area around the leased premises has a high crime rate, (2) the landlord knew or should have known of the danger caused by criminal activity in the area, and (3) the landlord did not take precautions that were reasonably necessary to protect tenants under the circumstances.

When these facts are proved, the landlord is held responsible for criminal conduct occurring both in common areas and in the leased premises itself. The landlord's responsibility can take several forms. First, he or she may be held liable to a tenant for damages caused by the crime. Courts have based this liability on either the tort of negligence or the implied warranty of habitability. Second, a landlord's inadequate precautions in the face of known criminal activity could constitute a breach of the implied warranty of habitability or the covenant for quiet enjoyment even if the particular tenant making the claim has not actually been injured by a crime. In this situation, the tenant would be entitled to the normal remedies for breach of those obligations, including rent reduction, cancellation of the lease, and so on. The following case provides an illustration of the latter type of situation.

Highview Associates v. Koferl
District Court of Suffolk County, 477 N.Y.S.2d 585 (1984)

Jeanne Koferl, a single woman with an eight-year-old son, was a tenant in a large garden apartment complex owned by Highview in Selden, New York. Burglaries and robberies had become fairly common in the complex, and the landlord had done nothing to improve security. On one occasion, Koferl discovered a "peeping tom" looking through her window on the first floor, and she notified the apartment manager of the incident. Somewhat later, toward the end of January 1983, two unknown men attempted to burglarize Koferl's apartment at 3:00 a.m. She was awakened when one of the burglars started to rip the screen from the sliding glass door. She was able to ward off the criminals, and in terror she then grabbed her son and fled to her mother's home, never to return to the apartment. The lease did not expire until May 26, and the landlord was not able to rerent the apartment to another tenant until April 1.

The landlord sued Koferl, claiming that she breached the lease by moving out and paying no further rent. The landlord sought damages of $588, consisting of unpaid rent, painting and repairs, expenses involved in finding another tenant, and attorney fees, minus Koferl's $930 security deposit that the landlord had kept. Koferl defended by asserting that the landlord had breached the implied warranty of habitability and the covenant for quiet enjoyment by failing to provide adequate protection against criminals, thus relieving her of any responsibility under the lease. She did not seek damages or the return of her security deposit.

Colaneri, Judge:

The issue posed by the defendant is . . .: Should the landlord of a large garden apartment complex in a rural or suburban community furnish protection to its tenants . . . against the depredations of burglars, thieves and other criminals?

This court is mindful of the cases of *Brownstein v. Edison,* 425 N.Y.S.2d 773 and *Sherman v. Concourse Realty Corp.*, 365 N.Y.S.2d 239. The fact situations in these cases differ from the facts in the instant case in that the landlords in both cases had provided special locks and buzzer systems on the front doors to prevent criminal types from intruding into high-rise apartment buildings in New York City.

In both cases the landlord had raised the rent to include the cost of the special locks and protective systems. In both cases the locks and protective devices were broken and inoperable. The tenant in the *Brownstein* case was murdered in the apartment lobby, and the tenant in the *Sherman* case was severely assaulted—again in the apartment lobby.

The courts in both cases held that the landlord had assumed the duty to provide some degree of protection to the tenants by providing these protective devices, and the landlords in both cases were to render an essential service affecting habitability. Thus, when the locks and devices became inoperable, the landlords breached the implied warranty of habitability.

In [*Park West Management Corp. v. Mitchell,*] Chief Judge Cooke discussed the transition of landlord-tenant law from the common-law concept of a tenant's estate in land to the modern day theory that a lease is not an estate in land, but is a contract between the owner of real property and the occupier of real property. It was held in that case that the landlord "is not a guarantor of every amenity customarily rendered in the landlord-tenant relationship," and that the warranty of habitability was not [created] for the purpose of rendering landlords absolute insurers of services which do not affect habitability. The [New York statute adopting this warranty] was designed to give rise to an implied promise on the part of the landlord that both the leased premises and areas within the landlord's control are fit for human occupation at the inception of the tenancy, and the premises will remain so throughout the lease term.

In the present case, there was no initial obligation on the part of the landlord to supply security devices for the protection of the tenants. After a number of years, however, this apartment complex has become the object of burglars and thieves, so that break-ins and thefts have become frequent. Mr. David Orenstein, the manager of the plaintiff's complex, testified that there were approximately 5 to 10 burglaries each year in the entire complex. Mr. Orenstein, however, was quite evasive and vague about the actual number of burglaries.

If this court accepts the figure of (only) 10 burglaries per year as the number of burglaries committed in the subject premises, this amounts to one burglary in every 36.6 apartments. Thus, if we use this one statistic, and, if we extend this ratio over a period of years, almost 10% of the tenants in the plaintiff's garden apartment complex will be victims of burglaries, thefts and worse over a three-year period.

Relying upon the reasoning of Chief Judge Cooke [in the *Park West* case], this court shall extend the concept of the implied warranty of habitability and make it applicable to the present case. This court finds that living conditions in the plaintiff's garden apartment complex had become dangerous and that the landlord had become obligated to take steps to protect its tenants by whatever means available to it.

Despite many notices to the plaintiff of thefts and burglaries committed in the plaintiff's garden apartment complex, the landlord had not (and has not) taken any steps to protect its tenants. The plaintiff has thus breached the implied warranty of habitability, as well as the [covenant] of use and quiet enjoyment.

The defendant acted reasonably and properly when she fled the premises, since it became apparent to her that it was not safe to live in the apartment any longer.

Accordingly, judgment is rendered for the defendant dismissing the plaintiff's complaint, with costs awarded to the defendant.

RENT AND OTHER FINANCIAL OBLIGATIONS OF THE TENANT

Rent

Rent is the compensation paid to the landlord for the tenant's possession and use of the leased premises. Leases almost always contain provisions expressly setting the rent. If this is omitted, the law of most states obligates the tenant to pay the reasonable rental value of the property. The right to receive rent can be *assigned,* or transferred, to a third party.

The time, method, and place for rent payment usually are specified in the lease. Most leases expressly require advance payment at the *beginning* of each rental period. If the parties do not agree on the time for payment, however, the general rule is that rent is due at the *end* of each rental period.

When the lease expressly requires payment of rent on or before a stated date, payment by this date usually is an absolute requirement. The tenant breaches his or her obligation by late payment. In a few states, however, statutes have been passed which provide a short "grace period" beyond the due date, such as five days. Until expiration of this grace period, the landlord may not terminate the lease for nonpayment. Also, if the landlord has customarily accepted late rental payments, he or she may have *waived* the right to prompt payment. In such a case, the landlord must continue to accept similarly late payments unless he or she expressly announces that late payments will not be accepted in the future.

Rent normally is not considered "paid" until actually received by the landlord or the landlord's agent. However, most courts do not permit lease termination because of relatively short, unexpected delays in mail delivery.

Rent is payable in money unless the parties agree on some other form of consideration. Payment by check is sufficient unless the landlord expressly requires cash.

The lease usually specifies the place for payment. If it does not, the leased property itself is the place where the rent is payable. In such a case, before the landlord can legally terminate the lease for nonpayment he or she must come onto the leased premises and demand the rent.

Security Deposits

A **security deposit** of cash or property by the tenant is required only if the lease provides for it. Most leases do provide for security deposits. The purpose of a security deposit is to provide the landlord with a quick and sure remedy when the tenant damages the property, fails to pay rent, or breaks the lease.

Some landlords attempt to keep security deposits regardless of whether there is any justification for doing so. Legally, the landlord is entitled to keep only so much of the deposit as is necessary to compensate him or her for damages that actually can be proved. Today, many states have statutes specifically regulating the landlord's handling of the security deposit when a lease is terminated.

Typically, these statutes require that the landlord return the tenant's security deposit within a certain period of time, such as 30 days, and prohibit any deduction from the deposit that is not explained on an accompanying itemized list of damages and repairs.

Other Payments

Unless the lease provides otherwise, the landlord is obligated to pay taxes on the leased property and the tenant is required to pay utility bills.

THE LANDLORD'S REMEDIES

Detainer

A lease legally may be terminated for several reasons, as we saw earlier in the chapter. For instance, expiration of the agreed duration terminates the lease. Also, in most states today, the landlord may terminate the lease for nonpayment of rent.

If the tenant wrongfully remains in possession after termination, the landlord may file a court action to have the tenant removed. This action, usually called **unlawful detainer, forcible entry and detainer,** or some similar name, is given special expedited treatment by the court and decided very quickly. If the landlord proves a right to possession, the sheriff or other officer removes the tenant from the property.[7]

---

[7]An older type of remedy, *ejectment*, still exists in many states. It is a much slower procedure for evicting tenants and has not often been used by landlords since statutes have created the quicker detainer procedure.

Landlord's Lien

At common law, the landlord had the right to seize, and hold or sell, the tenant's personal property for nonpayment of rent. The **landlord's lien** extended only to items actually located on the leased premises. Today in most states this remedy is regulated by statute. In some states the landlord must file a court action to exercise his or her lien. In these states, items of the tenant's property located on the leased premises are seized by a sheriff or other officer. Other states permit the landlord to seize the tenant's belongings, but a court proceeding normally is required before they can be sold.

Many leases, particularly residential ones, expressly grant the landlord a lien on the tenant's belongings located on the leased premises. The extent of the lien and method of enforcement are governed primarily by the language of the lease.

Damages

When the tenant fails to pay rent or harms the property, the landlord is entitled to receive money damages to compensate for the loss. If the security deposit is inadequate to pay these damages, the landlord may file suit to collect the remainder.

Duty to Mitigate Damages: Suppose that T, the tenant, and L, the landlord, have agreed to the lease of a house for eighteen months at a monthly rental of $500. After six months T stops paying rent, and two months later she leaves (either voluntarily or involuntarily). T certainly is liable to L for $1,000—two months' unpaid rent. But is T also responsible for the $5,000 rent for the remaining ten months of the lease?

Traditionally, L could recover the $5,000 and was not obligated to *mitigate,* or lessen, his damages by seeking another tenant. He could simply leave the premises vacant. If L actually does find another tenant, the damages L can recover from T are reduced by the rent L receives from the substitute tenant during the remainder of the original lease term.

In a substantial minority of states, L is under a duty to mitigate his damages by making reasonable efforts to find a new tenant. Suppose that L finds a new tenant six months after T leaves (that is, with four months remaining in the original lease term). Obviously, L still could recover the $1,000 unpaid rent from T. But what about L's claim for $3,000 rent for the six months during which the house was vacant? In one of those states requiring L to mitigate his damages, the court will determine whether L had made a reasonable effort to find a new tenant after T left. If the court concludes that such an effort was made, and that the period of vacancy was not due to any lack of diligence on L's part, L can recover $3,000 in addition to the $1,000. On the other hand, if the court concludes that L did not make a reasonable effort and probably could have found a new tenant in *three months* had such an effort been made, L's recovery from T will be limited to $1,000 plus $1,500.

The requirement that L mitigate damages is being adopted by more and more courts and legislatures as they have an opportunity to consider the question, and probably will become the majority rule in the next few years.

ASSIGNMENTS AND SUBLEASES

A tenant sometimes may want to transfer his or her rights and obligations under the lease to a third party. Such a transfer is either an assignment or a sublease.

Distinction between Assignment and Sublease

An **assignment** of the lease occurs when the tenant transfers the entire remaining portion of the lease to a third party. A **sublease** occurs when the tenant transfers the lease for only part of its remaining duration. Suppose, for example, that two years remain on what was originally a three-year lease. If the tenant transfers the lease to another party for the remaining two years, the transfer is an assignment. If the tenant executes a transfer for less than two years, such as twelve or eighteen months, the transfer is a sublease.

When an assignment occurs, the third party (assignee) essentially takes the place of the original tenant. The landlord-tenant relationship, with all of its rights and responsibilities, then exists between the landlord and the assignee. The landlord and assignee each have the right to legally enforce the lease obligations of the other. However, the original tenant is not excused from his or her obligations unless expressly released by the landlord. Thus, if the assignee fails to pay rent, the landlord can proceed against the assignee, the original tenant, or both. If the original tenant has to pay, he or she is entitled to recoup the loss from the assignee.

In the case of a sublease, no legal relationship is created between the landlord and the third party (sublessee). Neither the landlord nor the sublessee has legally enforceable obligations to or rights against the other. The landlord-tenant relationship, with all its rights and duties, continues to exist between the landlord and the original tenant. Another landlord-tenant relationship is created between the original tenant and the sublessee.

The Tenant's Right to Transfer

As a general rule, a tenant has the right to execute an assignment or sublease unless (1) the lease places express limitations on the right, or (2) a specific state statute modifies the right in some way. Today, most leases expressly prohibit assignments or subleases unless the landlord consents. Moreover, several states have statutes which regulate the execution of assignments and subleases. In some states, the transfer must be in writing to have any effect, and in some states recording statutes must be complied with to protect the interest of the assignee or sublessee.

SUMMARY

The landlord-tenant relationship is created by an agreement commonly called a lease, which provides for the transfer of exclusive possession and control of real property in return for the payment of rent. The interest acquired by the tenant, or lessee, is called a tenancy, or leasehold, and takes different forms depending on the terms of the lease. The landlord, or lessor, is the owner of the reversionary fee simple interest, and owes the tenant the duty to allow possession and not to interfere with the lawful possession and use of the premises. The tenant, on the other hand, has a duty not to intentionally or negligently damage the premises, and usually has no right to add fixtures or otherwise alter the premises without the landlord's consent.

Although the traditional rule that a landlord has no duty to maintain the premises still exists theoretically, in modern times it has become subject to a great many important exceptions, including the duty to keep common areas in a reasonably safe condition and to observe the maintenance obligations imposed by building codes and the implied warranty of habitability. Both the tenant and the landlord can be held liable in some circumstances for injuries occurring on the premises. The tenant's liability is based on the duty to maintain in a reasonably safe condition that part of the premises under his or her control. The landlord can be held liable for injuries on premises that were leased for a purpose involving admission of the public and for those occurring in common areas, as well as for injuries resulting from latent defects or negligent repairs. In some states the landlord is liable for injuries caused by breach of an express lease provision, statutory duty, or implied warranty.

There is a modern trend for landlords to be held responsible for taking reasonable precautions to protect tenants from criminal activities. The landlord has a basic right to receive rent from the tenant, and may require the tenant to post a security deposit to cover possible damage to the property. The landlord has several remedies for the tenant's breach of the lease agreement, including detainer, exercise of the landlord's lien, and a suit for damages. As a general rule, a tenant has the right to transfer the right to possession by assignment or sublease unless such right is restricted by the lease or by statutory provision.

KEY TERMS

Lease
Covenant
Condition
Tenancy (or leasehold)
Tenancy for years
Periodic tenancy
Tenancy at will
Tenancy at sufferance
Surrender and acceptance
Reversion
Covenant of quiet enjoyment
Eviction
Constructive eviction
Waste
Trade fixtures
Implied warranty of habitability
Repair and deduct
Rent withholding
Latent defect
Exculpatory clause
Indemnification clause
Rent
Security deposit
Unlawful detainer (or forcible entry and detainer)
Landlord's lien
Assignment
Sublease

QUESTIONS AND PROBLEMS

1. Kolea rented a building from Greenfield for the purpose of storing automobiles. Approximately one year later, while the lease was still in effect, the building was destroyed by fire. The lease agreement was silent as to the effect of such an occurrence on the rental obligation. Thereafter, Kolea refused to continue paying rent, claiming that the destruction of the building excused him from any further obligation to pay rent. Greenfield sued for the unpaid rent under the remaining portion of the lease. Will Greenfield be successful? Discuss. (*Albert M. Greenfield & Co. v. Kolea,* 380 A.2d 758, Pa. 1977.)

2. Kilbourne rented an apartment from Forester for one year, beginning in June 1966. A provision in the lease stated that it was "renewable at the end of the year period." Kilbourne renewed the lease for an additional year in June 1967. Toward the end of the second year Kilbourne gave notice to Forester that she wished to renew the lease for a third one-year term. Forester refused to execute another lease, Kilbourne refused to leave, and Forester filed suit to have Kilbourne removed from the apartment. Who will prevail? Discuss. (*Kilbourne v. Forester,* 464 S.W.2d 770, Mo. Ct. App. 1971.)

3. Applegate and Turnquist leased an apartment from Inland for a one-year term. Before signing the lease agreement, Applegate inspected the apartment with the building manager. The apartment was very dirty and a couple of dead roaches could be seen. The manager said "it would be fixed" before Applegate moved in. At the time the lease was being signed, Applegate asked the manager if the apartment had any problem with roaches, because she didn't want to move in if it did. The manager replied that she hadn't heard anything about roaches. The next day, Applegate and Turnquist moved into the apartment and immediately saw roaches everywhere. They attempted for two days to exterminate the roaches, but were unsuccessful. The two tenants then moved out and refused to pay rent. Inland kept the security deposit. Applegate filed suit in which she sought to recover the security deposit, claiming that Inland had committed a constructive eviction. Inland asserted a counterclaim for damages, claiming that Applegate breached the lease agreement. Discuss whether a constructive eviction had occurred. (*Applegate v. Inland Real Estate Corporation,* 441 N.E.2d 379, Ill. App. Ct. 1982.)

4. The Norwoods rented a second-floor apartment from Lazarus. There were seven other apartments on the second floor, and a common hallway served all eight units. Children of various tenants, including the Norwoods' two-year-old daughter, regularly played in the hallway. Lazarus periodically inspected the building and saw the children playing. The paint on the walls and baseboards of the hallway was cracked and flaking. Flakes of paint were on the hall floor. On several occasions the Norwoods saw their daughter put paint flakes in her mouth. Each time they spanked her and told her to stop. Later she became ill and was diagnosed as having chronic lead poisoning. The paint in the hallway was tested by the Lead Poison Control Unit of the City of St. Louis, and was found to contain high levels of lead in violation of a city ordinance. The Norwoods sued Lazarus for damages, claiming that he was negligent in permitting an unsafe condition to exist. Are the Norwoods correct? Discuss. (*Norwood v. Lazarus,* 634 S.W.2d 584, Mo. Ct. App. 1982.)

5. Winslar rented an apartment from Bartlett. The police came to the apartment to arrest Winslar. When they knocked on the door, Winslar shot through the door with a gun, wounding one of the police officers. The police then threw tear gas canisters into the apartment and subsequently arrested Winslar. The tear gas caused substantial damage to the apartment, and Bartlett filed suit against Winslar. Should Winslar be held responsible to Bartlett for the damages to the apartment? Why or why not? (*Winslar v. Bartlett,* 573 S.W.2d 608, Tex. Ct. Civ. App. 1978.)

6. Williams worked for a company which conducted its business in offices leased from Koplin. To get to and from work, it was necessary for Williams to use an outside stairway. One day when Williams was leaving the building after

work, she slipped on snow and ice which had accumulated on the stairs. She was injured in the resulting fall, and filed suit against Koplin, the owner of the building, and Hinsdale, who managed the building for Koplin. Should Williams win? Discuss. (*Williams v. Alfred N. Koplin & Co.,* 448 N.E.2d 1042, Ill. App. Ct. 1983.)

7. Crowell leased an apartment from the City of Dallas Housing Authority, a city government agency serving the purpose of providing safe and sanitary dwellings to persons of low income. In the standard lease agreement provided by the Housing Authority, a clause stipulated that the Authority would not be liable for any damages caused by the condition of the premises. A heater in Crowell's apartment was defective and caused the apartment to fill with carbon monoxide, killing Crowell. Crowell's son, in behalf of his father's estate, sued for damages resulting from medical expenses and his father's pain and suffering. The Housing Authority defended on the grounds that it was excused from liability by the clause in the lease. Is the Housing Authority's defense a good one? Discuss. (*Crowell v. Housing Authority of the City of Dallas,* 495 S.W.2d 887, Tex. 1973.)

8. In anticipation of his upcoming marriage, Kridel leased an apartment from Sommer for a two-year period. Shortly before the wedding, however, Kridel's fiancée broke the engagement. Kridel notified Sommer that he was breaking the lease. Sommer made no effort to rent the apartment to anyone else. In fact, another person wanted to rent it shortly thereafter, but Sommer refused, stating that the apartment was already leased to Kridel. Sommer finally put the apartment up for rent fifteen months later and immediately leased it to another tenant. Sommer sued Kridel for the unpaid rent during the time the apartment was vacant. Was Kridel responsible for the rent during this period? (*Sommer v. Kridel,* 378 A.2d 767, N.J. 1977.)

9. Trentacost was a 61-year-old widow who had rented an apartment from Brussel for more than ten years. The apartment was located in a building containing a total of eight units located over street-level stores. Access was provided by front and rear entrances. A padlock secured the back entrance, but there was no lock on the front entrance. One afternoon Trentacost was returning to her apartment from a shopping trip. After she had entered the building from the front and reached the top of a flight of stairs leading to her apartment, an assailant grabbed her ankles from behind and dragged her down the stairs. Her purse was stolen and she suffered severe injuries. She later filed suit against Brussel, claiming that he was negligent in not providing a lock or other adequate security for the front entrance.

The evidence showed that during the past three years, police had investigated from 75 to 100 crimes in the neighborhood, mostly burglaries and street muggings. Two months before the attack, Trentacost herself had reported to Brussel an attempt by someone to break into the building's cellar. At other times she had notified him of the presence of unauthorized persons in the hallways. She claimed that Brussel had promised to put a lock on the front door, but he denied ever discussing the subject. Should the court hold Brussel liable for Trentacost's damages? Discuss. (*Trentacost v. Brussel,* 412 A.2d 436, N.J. 1980.)

Chapter 43

PERSONAL PROPERTY AND BAILMENTS

OWNERSHIP OF PERSONAL PROPERTY

As we saw in the introduction to Part VII, all property is classified as either real or personal property. In some ways, the legal framework for personal property ownership is similar to that for real property. For example, personal property can be subject to many of the same categories of concurrent ownership as real property, including tenancy in common and joint tenancy, as well as marital co-ownership categories such as tenancy by the entireties and community property. The rules for creating and regulating these types of co-ownership are essentially the same for personal property as for real property.

In addition, a creditor can acquire a voluntary security interest in an item of personal property that is similar to the interest created by a real property mortgage. The debtor retains title to the property, but the creditor with such a security interest owns an interest that serves as security until the debt is paid. The creation, protection, and enforcement of security interests in personal property are governed by Article 9 of the Uniform Commercial Code, and are discussed separately in Chapter 29, "Secured Transactions."

In many ways, however, ownership of personal property is legally quite different than ownership of real property. Ownership of personal property is usually a simpler matter than ownership of real property, primarily because the law does not formally recognize the numerous types of interests that it does for real property. Ordinarily, a person either is the owner of an item of personal property or is not. There sometimes can be a difficult question regarding *who* is the owner of an item of personal property, but once that question is resolved, ownership usually is an all-or-nothing proposition. One example of this fact is found in the use of leases. As we saw in the previous chapter, a lease of real property actually creates another type of ownership interest. A lease of personal property, however, merely creates a *bailment;* the lessee has temporary possession but no ownership interest in the item of personal property.

This chapter deals with several basic topics concerning the ownership, possession, and use of personal property. It first discusses gifts of personal property, and then examines several other methods by which ownership of personal property can change. The chapter then provides a detailed discussion of bailments, an important form of personal property transaction in which possession but not ownership is transferred. It should be pointed out that several other topics related to personal property are sufficiently specialized and complex that they are dealt with in separate chapters. The subject of *sales of goods,* for instance, is thoroughly explored in Chapters 20 through 23. As already mentioned, the topic of secured transactions is covered in Chapter 29. In addition, transfers of both real and personal property by *will* are discussed in Chapter 44.

GIFTS OF PERSONAL PROPERTY

A gift occurs when an owner of property (the **donor**) voluntarily transfers ownership of the property to another (the **donee**) without receiving any consideration in return. In order for the donor to accomplish a transfer of ownership by gift, two fundamental requirements must be met: (1) the donor must have a *present intent* to transfer ownership and (2) the donor must *deliver possession* to the donee.[1]

Present Intent to Transfer Ownership

The language and conduct of the donor, considered in the light of all the surrounding circumstances, must indicate a present intent to transfer ownership. Thus, a promise or expression of intent to transfer ownership in the future is not sufficient. A promise to make a gift is not the same thing as an actual gift. By its very nature, such a promise is not made in return for consideration, as required by contract law. Accord-

---

[1] There is also a requirement that the donee accept the gift, but acceptance is presumed unless the donee expressly rejects the gift. This issue arises only on rare occasions.

ingly, it usually confers no rights on the promisee and cannot be enforced.

It also is critical that the expression of present intent relate to *ownership*. If the evidence indicates that the current owner merely intends to transfer present custody or the right to use the property, there is no gift.

Delivery of Possession

The donor also must actually carry out the expression of intent by delivering possession of the property to the donee. Once there has been an expression of present intent to transfer ownership coupled with actual delivery, the absence of consideration from the donee becomes irrelevant. Title to the property has passed. Many of the disputes involving gifts of personal property have centered on the question of whether there was delivery of possession to the donee. The most common problems relating to the question of delivery are outlined below.

Retention of Control: If the donor attempts to retain a degree of control over the property, there usually is not a legally effective gift. As one court stated, there must be "a complete stripping of the donor of dominion or control over the thing given."[2] To illustrate: X indicates he wants to give a diamond ring to Y. If X then places the ring in a safe-deposit box to which both X and Y have access, there is not a sufficient delivery. Another example is found in the case of *Lee v. Lee*, 5 F.2d 767 (1925): The widow of a grandson of General Robert E. Lee prepared a written document stating that she was giving to her two sons a trunk containing several items which had belonged to the general. She deposited the trunk with a storage company, with instructions to the company obligating it to deliver the trunk to either her or her sons. In holding that there had not been an adequate delivery, the court said, "[T]here was not that quality of completeness present in the trans-

action which distinguishes a mere intention to give from the completed act, and where this element is lacking the gift fails."

Delivery to an Agent: If delivery of the property is made to the donor's *own agent,* with instructions to deliver to the donee, there is not a completed gift until the donee actually receives the item. The reason, again, is that the donor does not part with sufficient control until the donee takes possession. If the donor delivers possession to the *donee's agent,* however, a valid gift has been made.

Property Already in Possession of the Donee: If the donee already possesses the property when the donor indicates an intent to presently make a gift, the gift is immediately effective. There is no need to make a formal delivery in this situation.

Constructive Delivery: In most cases, delivery of actual physical possession is required. In two types of circumstances, however, a **constructive delivery** (or **symbolic delivery**) will suffice.

Impracticality: If it is *impractical or inconvenient* to deliver actual physical possession because the item is too large or because it is located at too great a distance from the parties, constructive delivery is allowed. In such cases it ordinarily takes the form of a delivery of something that gives the donee *control* over the property. For example, if the item being given is a car, delivery of the car's key to the donee is sufficient. Similarly, delivery to the donee of a key to a building, room, or container in which an item is located constitutes a valid delivery if physical delivery of the property itself is impractical or inconvenient.

Intangibles: Constructive delivery is permissible for a gift of *intangible* personal property, for the obvious reason that there is nothing physical to deliver. Some types of intangible

---

[2]*Allen v. Hendrick,* 206 Pac. 733 (1922).

property rights are evidenced by written documents that by either law or business custom are accepted as representing the intangible right itself. Examples are bonds, promissory notes, corporate stock certificates, insurance policies, and savings account books. For these types of property rights, delivery of the written instrument evidencing the right is treated as delivery of the right itself. If the property right is an ordinary contract right not represented by any commercially recognized document, most courts allow constructive delivery of it by delivery of a writing setting forth the *present intent* to assign the right to the donee.

Grounds for Invalidating Gifts: Of course, a gift will not be valid if the donor's action was induced by fraud, duress, mistake, or undue influence. In addition, the courts always examine very carefully any gift occurring between persons in a "fiduciary" relationship. Thus, if X owes a higher degree of trust to Y because of a fiduciary relationship, and X receives a gift from Y, the law places the burden upon X to prove that all was fair. The following case illustrates this important principle.

Gordon v. Bialystoker Center & Bikur Cholim, Inc.
Court of Appeals of New York, 385 N.E.2d 285 (1978)

Ida Gorodetsky, who was 85 years old at the time, suffered a stroke and was admitted to Brookland-Cumberland Hospital in August 1972. Her closest relatives, two brothers and a niece, had not seen her for several years, and she had lived alone since 1962. From the time of her stroke until her death four months later, Ida remained partially paralyzed, confused, and sometimes semicomatose.

At the suggestion of one of Ida's acquaintances, the Bialystoker nursing home sent one of its social workers to visit the elderly lady in the hospital in October 1972. After learning that Ida had funds of her own, the director of the nursing home sent the social worker back to visit Ida on November 3 for the purpose of having her sign a withdrawal slip. A request had already been made for her admittance to the home, and the purpose of the withdrawal slip was to obtain funds for her care at the home. Using her withdrawal slip, the home obtained a $15,000 check from Ida's account payable to the home "for the benefit of Ida Gorodetsky."

On November 13 Ida was moved to the infirmary of the nursing home. That same day, within an hour and a half of admission, she was visited by a group consisting of the home's executive director, its fund raiser, one of its social workers, and a notary public. She was presented with a collection of instruments on each of which she placed her mark. These instruments included an application for admission to the home, an admission agreement, a withdrawal slip for the $12,864.46 remaining in her bank account, an assignment of that amount to the home, and a letter making a donation to the home of

**any part of the $27,864.46 remaining after paying expenses for her
lifetime care.**

**Ida died on December 5 while still a resident of the nursing home.
Her brother, Sam Gordon, administrator of her estate, filed suit
against the nursing home to recover these funds, less the amount
necessary to pay her expenses. The trial court ruled for the defendant
nursing home on the ground that a valid gift had been made. The
intermediate level appellate court reversed, ruling in favor of plaintiff
administrator, and defendant appealed to New York's highest court.**

Jones, Justice:

. . . It is indisputable that on November 13, 1972, when the gift on which
defendant predicates its claim to the funds in dispute was made, there existed
between the donor and donee a fiduciary relationship arising from the nursing home's assumption of complete control, care and responsibility of and for
its resident. As the executive director of that institution testified at some
length, the residents of the nursing home are dependent on the home "to take
care in effect of their very livelihood, their existence;" they "rely upon the
people in the home to take care of them . . . ; they have no means of taking
care of themselves;" and ask and receive help from the staff of the home.
According to the witness, "every one of the residents' particular needs . . . is
administered to them by the help, the nurses or the doctors" of the home and
in many instances—as was the case with the decedent—"they have no other
source of getting that kind of help and don't get any help other than from the
institution." The acceptance of such responsibility with respect to the aged
and infirm who, for substantial consideration availed themselves of the
custodial care offered by the institution, resulted in the creation of a fiduciary
relationship and the applicability of the law of constructive fraud. Under that
doctrine, where a fiduciary relationship exists between parties, transactions
between them are scrutinized with extreme vigilance, and clear evidence is
required that the transaction was understood, and that there was no fraud,
mistake, or undue influence. Where those relations exist there must be clear
proof of the integrity and fairness of the transaction, or any instrument thus
obtained will be set aside, or held as invalid between the parties. As was said
long ago, in articulating the concept of constructive fraud: "It may be stated
as universally true that fraud vitiates all contracts, but as a general thing it is
not presumed but must be proved by the party seeking to relieve himself
from an obligation on that ground. Whenever, however, the relations between the contracting parties appear to be of such a character as to render it
certain that they do not deal on terms of equality but that either on the one
side from superior knowledge of the matter derived from a fiduciary relation,
or from an overmastering influence, or on the other from weakness, dependence, or trust justifiably reposed, unfair advantage in a transaction is
rendered probable, there the burden is shifted, the transaction is presumed
void, and it is incumbent upon the stronger party to show affirmatively that

no deception was practiced, no undue influence was used, and that all was fair, open, voluntary and well understood. This doctrine is well settled." (*Cowee v. Cornell*, 75 N.Y. 91, 99–100). So here, the defendant, rather than plaintiff, bore the burden of proof on the issue whether Ida's gift of funds was freely, voluntarily and understandingly made. *Examination of the record demonstrates that that burden had not been met.* [Emphasis added.]

. . . The home was aware of the patient's mental and physical infirmities and weakness. Nothing to that point had remotely suggested that the patient might be disposed to make a gift to the home, or indeed that she even knew of its existence. The parties were brought together only in contemplation of the patient's transfer to the home; the transaction between them had no other meaning. That the patient was inescapably reposing confidence in the home from the moment of their first encounter was implicit in the circumstances.

We reject out of hand defendant's contention that, as a charitable organization, it should not be made subject to the same evidentiary burden that would be imposed on a profitmaking institution. However worthy may be the objectives to which its funds are dedicated, no justification exists for relieving it of the obligation, when circumstances suggest a substantial risk of overreaching, of affirmatively demonstrating that assets it has acquired have come to it from a willing and informed donor, untainted by impermissible initiative on the part of the donee.

. . . [T]he testimony offered, in conjunction with the other evidence in the case, was insufficient as a matter of law to sustain the burden of proof resting on the nursing home.

[The judgment of the intermediate level appellant court is affirmed; defendant nursing home must return to Ida's estate all funds beyond what was necessary to pay her expenses.]

Special Treatment of Joint Bank Accounts

It is rather common for a bank account to be in the names of two persons, such as husband and wife. The phrase *joint account* is often used in a nontechnical sense to describe any bank account in the names of two people. These accounts are either a tenancy in common or a joint tenancy with survivorship rights, depending on the terms of the agreement with the bank.

In connection with the law of gifts, the requirement that the donor part with all control over the property is frequently an issue in cases involving a bank account jointly owned by the donor and the donee. For example, suppose that

X deposits money belonging to him in a bank account that is in the name of X and Y. Both X and Y have the right to withdraw funds from the account. Obviously there is a completed gift from X to Y of all money actually taken from the account by Y. But because of the retention of control by X, money that is not withdrawn from the account by Y is not considered a gift.

Suppose, however, that the agreement between X and the bank provides that on the death of X or Y, the funds remaining in the account will go to the *survivor* (that is, a "joint tenancy" is created). If X dies first, the question will arise whether a valid gift of the remaining funds has been made by X to Y. A few courts have held that in such a situation there is not a sufficient relinquishment of control by X to create a gift. However, they also have usually held that Y is nevertheless entitled to the money as a *third party beneficiary* of an enforceable contract between X and the bank. On the other hand, a majority of courts have simply relaxed the delivery requirement in this type of case and have held that there is a valid gift to Y despite the retention of some control by X.

Of course, as is true of any other gift, X must have *intended* to make a gift to Y. In the case of a joint tenancy bank account (one with a right of survivorship), there is a *presumption* of intent on the part of X to make a gift to Y, and this presumption can be rebutted only by evidence clearly showing that X did *not* intend to make a gift. For instance, the evidence might show that the joint account was established solely to give Y access to X's funds so as to enable Y to help X handle his financial affairs.

Gifts *Inter Vivos* and *Causa Mortis*

Gifts are classified as either *inter vivos* or *causa mortis*. A **gift *inter vivos*** is simply an ordinary gift between two living persons. A **gift *causa mortis*** is also between living persons, but it is made by the donor in contemplation of his or her death from some existing affliction or impending peril.

Although a gift *causa mortis* resembles a *will*, because both involve gifts in contemplation of death, it is important to emphasize their differences. As we will see in Chapter 44, a will must meet several formal statutory requirements such as written documentation and the signed attestation of a specified number of witnesses. A gift *causa mortis*, on the other hand, must meet the same requirements as a regular gift, intent and delivery. Execution of a formal will is the only way to make a gift conditional on the donor's death without an immediate transfer of possession.

Two special rules apply to the gift *causa mortis*, distinguishing it slightly from a regular gift: (1) The gift is revoked automatically if the do-

nee dies before the donor, with the result that ownership reverts back to the donor. (2) The gift is also revoked automatically if the donor does not die from the current illness or peril.

OTHER METHODS OF ACQUIRING OWNERSHIP

Ownership of Wild Game

As a general rule, the law views wild animals, fish, and birds as being *unowned* property. The first person who takes possession with an intent to become an owner usually acquires legal ownership. The technical name for such acquisition is **occupation.** The one taking possession does not become the owner, however, if that person is a *trespasser* or is acting in violation of state or federal game and fish laws. A trespasser is one who is on land without the express or implied consent of the owner or tenant who has legal control of the land. Wild game taken by a trespasser belongs to the owner or the tenant of the land. In addition, no title is acquired to wild game taken in violation of state or federal laws.

Abandoned, Lost, and Mislaid Property

The common law made a distinction between abandoned, lost, and mislaid property. An item was deemed to be **abandoned property** if found under circumstances indicating either that it was left by someone who did not want it anymore, or was left so long ago that the former owner almost certainly was no longer living. The nature of the property, its location, and other relevant factors can be taken into account in determining whether the property should be classified as abandoned. The common law characterized an item as **lost property** if it was discovered under circumstances indicating that it was *not* placed there voluntarily by the owner (such as a purse, billfold, or ring found on a street or sidewalk or on the floor of a hotel or theater lobby). **Mislaid property,** on the other hand, was property discovered under circumstances indicating that it was placed there voluntarily by the owner and then forgotten (such as a suitcase under the seat of an airplane or bus or a purse on a table in a restaurant).

The common law treated abandoned property in the same manner as wild game, the first person taking possession becoming the owner. If the acquirer was a trespasser on the land where the game was taken, however, the landowner or tenant became the owner. The finding of lost or mislaid property, on the other hand, did not change ownership of the item. Either the finder or the landowner (or tenant, if leased) acquired only a right to possession that was superior to the rights of everyone but the true owner. The finder or landowner taking possession was required to take reasonable steps to preserve the property and locate its owner. If the owner appeared to claim the property, he or she was obligated to pay the reasonable costs of storing and preserving it, but was not legally required to pay a reward. All of this assumes, of course, that the identity of the true owner was unknown; if known, the finder or landowner voluntarily taking possession had an absolute duty to deliver the property to its owner and was guilty of a crime for not doing so.

The distinction between lost and mislaid property was used to determine who was entitled to possession in the situation where the item was found by someone who did not own or control the premises. The owner or tenant of the land was entitled to possession if the item was characterized as mislaid property, because of the possibility that the true owner might remember where it was left and return to reclaim it. In the case of lost property, however, the finder was entitled to possession unless he or she was a trespasser, in which case the landowner or tenant had the possessory right.

Finding Statutes: In modern times, almost all jurisdictions have enacted legislation regulating the possession and ownership of found property. These laws are referred to as **finding statutes** (or **estray statutes**), and vary substantially from state to state. Several of these statutes, as interpreted by the courts, have retained the common-law distinctions between abandoned, lost, and mislaid property. Some of them apply only to lost property, not to mislaid or abandoned property. However, the courts in some of these states have applied a strong presumption that found property is lost and therefore subject to the statute. In other states, the finding statutes have completely preempted the common-law rules and apply to any found property regardless of its characterization as abandoned, mislaid, or lost.

State finding statutes typically require that the finder of an item of personal property turn it over to a designated governmental authority within a certain period of time, such as ten days. Some statutes designate a local authority for receipt and custody of the item, such as the city police, county sheriff, or county clerk. Others designate a state authority such as the state police. Depending on the provisions of the statute, either the finder or the custodial authority must then take specified steps to locate the true owner, such as by publishing newspaper notices a certain number of times during a particular time period. If the prior owner does not appear and establish ownership within a stated period of time, such as one year, most statutes provide that the finder acquires ownership (not just possession) of the property. A finder who does not comply with the finding statute in a particular state does not acquire ownership or a right to possession, and usually is guilty of a crime. Finding statutes normally place obligations and give rights to the *finder*, regardless of who owns or controls the land where the property is found. Some of these statutes, however, have been interpreted as incorporating the common-law rule that a finder who is a willful trespasser acquires no rights in found property; in such a case, the owner or tenant of the land where the item was found acquires the rights granted by the statute.

Escheat Statutes: All states also have enacted **escheat statutes,** which normally provide that intangible property such as money, corporate stock, or bonds is presumed abandoned if it has remained in the possession of a custodian, such as a bank or securities dealer, for a specified time period without any deposits, withdrawals, or other contact by the owner. The time period provided by these statutes is usually lengthy, seven years being a common term. After passage of this time period, a state governmental authority ordinarily is required to publish notices identifying the property; if the property still re-

mains unclaimed for a shorter period, such as six months, the state becomes the owner. Escheat statutes generally apply also to unclaimed stolen property recovered by police, and to the unclaimed property of a person who dies without heirs or a will. Some escheat statutes include other abandoned property as well.

The following case illustrates the application of a finding statute to a hunter's unexpected discovery.

Willsmore v. Township of Oceola
Michigan Court of Appeals, 308 N.W.2d 796 (1981)

While hunting on unposted (i.e., there were no signs prohibiting entry) and unoccupied land, Duane Willsmore's attention was drawn to a place on the ground where branches were arranged in a criss-cross pattern. When he kicked aside the branches and some loose dirt, he found a watertight suitcase in a freshly dug hole. Inside the suitcase he found $383,400, which he immediately turned over to the state police. The police noted that some of the money had teller bands around it, indicating that it recently had been in a bank, but they were not able to trace the money to any particular source. The police placed the money in an interest-bearing account, and shortly thereafter Willsmore complied with the Michigan Lost Goods Act by notifying the clerk of the township where the money was found and properly publicizing the find. The statute provided that, one year after the required public notice, a finder who had complied with the law became owner of one-half of the property and the township in which it was found became owner of the other half.

After expiration of the one year, Willsmore filed suit against the township to determine ownership. The state of Michigan also asserted ownership of the money as abandoned property under the Code of Escheats—the Michigan escheat statute. The land on which the money was found was the subject of a sale contract at the time of the finding, although the landowner rightfully cancelled the transaction before the trial of this case because the buyer had breached the contract. The landowner expressly refused to assert any claim to the money. However, the person who had been the buyer under the contract, Powell, alleged that he was the true owner of the money and asserted a claim in the lawsuit. At the trial, Powell offered his deposition into evidence, but it was not admitted because he was available to testify and he had refused to answer any questions on cross-examination at the taking of the deposition. Powell refused to testify

at the trial, asserting his constitutional right to remain silent on the grounds that his statements might tend to incriminate him. The trial court granted a directed verdict awarding Willsmore and the township one half of the money each according to the Lost Goods Act. Powell and the state of Michigan appealed.

Corsiglia, Judge:

The Lost Goods Act of Michigan . . . provides that the finder shall give notice to potential owners, post notice in two places within the township of the find, publish notice in a newspaper if the goods are of a value of $10 or more and give notice in writing to the township clerk. The statute requires that these things be done within very short time periods. Willsmore did not comply with the strict language of the statute. This lapse is understandable in light of the advice he received from the police. After the State Police took custody of the suitcase, they told the finder and his wife to keep silent about the money, informed them that their lives might be in danger, suggested that leaving town for a time might be a good idea and even transported them in a state vehicle at speeds reaching up to 100 m.p.h. accompanied by officers armed with rifles. There is no indication on the record that the delay in complying with the provisions of the Lost Goods Act was a willful refusal to comply, or that it caused it to be more difficult for the true owner of the money to be located. Indeed, Willsmore's initial action upon finding the property was to notify a governmental authority, not attempt to keep it himself. It is understandable that after receiving instructions from the State Police to keep quiet, Willsmore did not act within the time limits set in the statute. [We hold] that Willsmore substantially complied with the notice provisions of the Lost Goods Act. . . .

[Regarding Powell's claim of ownership,] it is required that a party claiming as true owner prove his ownership. When faced with questions about how he obtained the money and hid it, Powell had the right to assert his constitutional privilege to remain silent. However, the court not only had the right, but also the duty, to conclude from such silence that Powell did not carry his burden of proof. . . . Powell's claim as true owner fails as a matter of law. . . . Because of his continued assertion of the right to remain silent at his deposition, relevant cross-examination was impossible. Powell, by choice, did not testify at the trial. Other evidence bearing on his alleged ownership of the money was not admissible because of its nature as hearsay. . . .

The brief period of time that the money was buried also effectively eliminates the Code of Escheats from application to this case. . . . The state carries the burden of establishing its right to escheatable property. The Attorney General has the power to intervene to claim property as escheatable upon one of three grounds:

(1) Death of an owner intestate (without a will) with no known heirs;
(2) Owner's disappearance or absence from last known place of residence for a continuous period of seven years leaving no known heirs; or
(3) Owner's abandonment of the property.

It is the third basis of standing which might appear to apply in this case. However, the Code of Escheats establishes a clear, narrow definition of "abandonment" which could not apply to the money based on undisputed facts before the trial court. Under the Code of Escheats, "abandoned property" is defined as "property against which a full period of dormancy has run." A "period of dormancy" is defined to mean a full and continuous period of seven years during which an owner has ceased, failed, or neglected to exercise dominion or control over his property or to assert a right of ownership or possession. . . .

Clearly, money in the ground for only a few months does not fall within the plain language of the Code of Escheats. Nor does it fall within the policy and historical derivation of the Code. The Law of Escheats developed out of the need for a sovereign to take title when tenure failed because of the absence of heirs. The statute has always been strictly construed, and the burden is on the state to prove that the property is escheatable. Initially, the Code of Escheats involved only real property. It was later expanded to cover personal property in certain narrow instances. In general, it covers personal property in situations where the property has been left with holders who would not be considered "finders" in the usual sense. For example, it is commonly applied to banks and similar institutions. It is generally not applied to individual holders of funds. . . . The Code of Escheats is not applicable to the present case. . . .

This Court finds that the Lost Goods Act is applicable to this property. It could be argued that applying the Lost Goods Act to a suitcase buried on another's land will encourage inappropriate behavior on the part of people in order that they might become "finders" under the provisions of the act. However, upon reflection, this argument is of limited merit. In the type of case where such a "find" would be inappropriate, the publicity given under the provisions of the Lost Goods Act would bring forward the true owner of the property, very possibly the property owner upon whose land it was found. Notice provisions would require notice to this potential true owner. In addition, in a different factual context, the remedy of trespass would be appropriate to discourage such "finds." The facts of this case do not support a trespass argument against the finder. The testimony indicated that the land was unposted and unoccupied, and that it had been hunted upon for many years by claimant Willsmore without objection.

The Lost Goods Act encourages the goals which this Court considers important in such cases. It provides certainty of title to property by eventually vesting clear title after a set period of time. It encourages honesty in finders by providing penalties for not turning in property in accord with its provisions and providing incentives for compliance. The act provides notice to potential true owners and publication to seek them out. It provides for registration of the find in a central location where an owner could locate the goods with ease. The Lost Goods Act provides for appraisal of the goods. There is a reasonable time limit before title to goods is cut off from the former owner or holder. The public obtains a portion of the benefit of a find through receipt of one half of the value by the township. The finder receives an award for his honesty by receiving one half of the value of the property plus costs. . . .

Parties to this suit urge this Court to draw a distinction between categories of found property [which] are derived from the common law. . . . "Lost property," as used in the [Lost Goods Act], is a broad generic category. . . . The statute is in effect a "finder's statute."

The provisions of the act are an eminently reasonable solution to a troublesome problem. Obviously there is a potential for a true owner to turn up in a year and a day to discover that his title has been cut off. However, a line must be drawn to establish clear title to goods at some point. . . .

The trial court correctly . . . [granted] motions for a directed verdict in favor of the finder, Duane Willsmore, and the Township of Oceola.

Affirmed.

Accession

An **accession** is a change in or an addition to an item of personal property. If the change or addition occurs with the owner's knowledge or consent, there is no effect on ownership of the item of property, and the question of compensation to the one making the addition or change depends entirely on the express or implied contract between the parties.

If the change or addition occurs without the owner's knowledge or consent, however, it is possible for ownership to be affected. The person causing the change or addition might have acted with knowledge that the action was wrongful (in bad faith), or with the honestly mistaken belief that he or she owned the item or otherwise had the right to make the change or addition (in good faith). Good faith accessions frequently occur when someone buys an item such as a boat or automobile, makes substantial changes or additions, and then finds out that the title to the purchased item was void because the seller had stolen it. The rules regarding accessions are outlined below.

Change in Personal Property by Labor: If a change in an item of personal property is brought about entirely or almost entirely by a nonowner's *labor,* ownership passes to the person performing the labor only if (1) the *identity* of the property has been changed, or (2) the value of the property is *many times greater* than

it was prior to the change. An example of a change in identity is shown in the situation where A makes B's grapes into wine without B's consent. An example of a sufficiently great increase in value is found in the case where A takes a piece of stone belonging to B and carves a statue from it without B's consent. There is a definite tendency on the part of courts to deal more harshly with someone who caused the accession while knowing that it was wrong. A greater magnitude of change is often required to pass title to such a party than to someone who acted in good faith.

Addition of Other Property: When one person permanently attaches something to another's personal property without the latter's consent, ownership of the resulting product goes to the owner of the "principal" item. For example, if A puts a new engine in a car owned by B, the car and the new engine belong to B. On the other hand, if A puts an engine owned by B in A's car, the car and engine are owned by A.

Compensation to Owner: In either of these situations, where an item is changed by a nonowner's labor or where other property has been added to the item, the party who caused the accession (the improver) is responsible for any loss to the other party. Thus, if the circumstances are such that the improver acquired title to the item as a result of the accession, that person must compensate the original owner. If the improver acted in good faith, he or she is required to pay the original owner only for the value of the property in its original condition. But if the improver acted in bad faith, he or she is required to pay to the original owner the value of the property in its improved state.

Where the accession itself does not cause title to pass to the improver, but the original owner simply chooses not to reclaim the property, the situation is treated the same as if the accession *had* caused title to pass. Where the accession does not cause title to pass to the improver, and the original owner *reclaims* the improved property, the improver usually is not entitled to any compensation at all, regardless of whether he or she acted in good faith.

Confusion of Goods

A **confusion of goods** occurs where there has been an intermingling of the goods of different persons. It usually occurs in connection with **fungible goods** (i.e., each unit is identical), such as the same grade of grain, oil, or chemicals. It can, however, occur with nonfungible goods, such as cattle or quantities of packaged merchandise.

If the goods of A and B have been confused (1) by agreement between A and B, (2) by an honest mistake or accident, or (3) by the act of some third party, a tenancy in common is created. Here, A and B each owns an undivided interest in the mass according to the particular proportions they contributed to it.

Suppose, however, that A caused the confusion by deliberately wrongful or negligent conduct. In this case, if the goods of A and B are fungible, A can get his portion back if he proves with reasonable certainty how much that portion is. On the other hand, if the goods are not fungible, A must prove which specific items are his or else he gets nothing.

After there has been a confusion, the quantity of goods might be diminished by fire, theft, or other cause so that not enough is left to give each owner a complete share. If one owner caused the confusion by deliberately wrongful or negligent conduct, that person must bear the entire burden of the decrease. If the confusion came about by agreement, by accident or honest mistake, or by an act of a third party, the burden of the decrease is borne proportionately by both owners.

BAILMENTS OF PERSONAL PROPERTY

The term *bailment* initially evokes a feeling of puzzlement in most people. Once it is described, however, it is immediately recognized as a simple and commonplace occurrence in everyday life. The taking of a dress to a dry cleaner, the lending of a car to a friend, and the delivering of goods to a railroad for shipment are all actions that result in the creation of bailments. A **bailment** can be defined as the delivery of possession of personal property from one person to another under an agreement by which the latter is obligated to return the property to the former or to deliver it to a third party. The person transferring possession is the **bailor,** and the one receiving it is the **bailee.**

Elements of a Bailment

By definition, the creation of a bailment requires that (1) one party must deliver possession (but not title) to the other, (2) the property delivered must be classified as personal property, and (3) the parties must agree that the recipient of the property will later return it, deliver it to a third party, or otherwise dispose of it in some specified manner.

Delivery of Possession: The requirement that possession of the property be delivered normally means that (1) the property must be transferred to the bailee, (2) the bailee must acquire control over the item, and (3) the bailee must knowingly accept the property.

Although actual physical possession of the bailed property is almost always transferred to the bailee, it is possible for a bailment to be created by delivery of something that gives the bailee effective control over the item, such as the keys or certificate of title to a boat or car.[3]

In addition to a transfer of the property, the circumstances must indicate that the recipient acquired control over it. For example, when a customer hangs his or her coat on a coatrack at a restaurant, and can get it back without notifying the restaurant's management or employees, there is no bailment of the coat because the restaurant did not acquire control over it. Similarly, if a waiter or other restaurant employee takes the coat and hangs it on a rack that is freely accessible to the customer, who may retrieve it without notice or assistance, there still is no bailment. On the other hand, if the coat is left with a coatroom attendant or other restaurant employee, who puts it in a place that is not accessible to the customer without assistance, a bailment has been created because the restaurant has control over the coat.

For the same reason, leaving a car at a parking lot or parking garage is generally held to constitute a bailment only if the car owner is required to leave the keys with an attendant. Otherwise, the parking lot company does not have sufficient control over the car. In a situation in which the car owner is permitted to lock the car and keep the keys, the transaction usually is not a bailment, but is merely a *license*—a contractual permission to use the parking space. The owner of the parking lot is a *licensor* and the car owner is a *licensee*.

Although the bailor normally is the owner of the bailed property, this is not always the case. What is required is that the bailor have a "superior right of possession" with regard to the bailee. Thus, if Joe lends his lawn mower to Robert for the summer and Robert takes it to a repair shop in September before returning it to Joe, a bailment exists between Robert and the repair shop while the mower is being repaired.

As we have seen, a physical delivery of property by one person to another does not create a

bailment unless the recipient knowingly accepts the property. For example, suppose that Joan has several packages of merchandise in the trunk of her car when she leaves it at a parking lot under circumstances in which a bailment exists as to the car. There is no bailment of the packages unless Joan notifies the parking lot attendant of their presence.

Personal Property: As we previously observed, all property is either *real* or *personal.* By definition, bailments involve only transfers of personal property. Although owners of real property frequently transfer possession of it to others for limited periods of time, such transactions are not bailments.

Most bailments involve items of tangible personal property, such as automobiles or jewelry. It is possible, however, for intangible personal property to be the subject of a bailment. This occurs, for example, when a stock certificate representing ownership of corporate stock is delivered by a debtor to a creditor as security for the debt.

The Agreement to Return: A bailment necessarily involves an agreement that the property ultimately is to be returned by the bailee to the bailor or delivered to a designated third party. The bailment contract can be either express or implied, and in most cases is not legally required to be in writing. Obviously, however, it is advisable to have the bailment contract in writing if the value of the bailed property is substantial and particularly if a commercial bailor or bailee is involved. Most commercial bailors, such as car rental agencies, and commercial bailees, such as a company that is in the business of storing the property of others, customarily use detailed written contracts.[4]

---

[3]This is another example of the concept of *constructive delivery,* which was discussed earlier in the chapter with regard to gifts of personal property.

[4]A federal law, the Consumer Leasing Act, applies to many leases of personal property in or affecting interstate commerce. Such leases create bailments. The statute is an effort by Congress to require lessors to make a full disclosure of contract terms to their lessees and to explain adequately the lessees' rights under such contracts. In general, the law applies to all types of leased personal property if the lease period is at least four months and the value of the property does not exceed $25,000.

As a general rule, the bailee is required to return or deliver the *identical* goods at the end of the bailment. Thus, if a Buick dealer delivers a car to Joyce under a contract providing that in return she will deliver her used motor home to the dealer within a month, the transaction is a sale rather than a bailment. The arrangement also would be a sale if the contract gives Joyce the option of returning the car or delivering the motor home in a month.

The rule requiring delivery of the identical property is subject to two well-established exceptions, which are outlined below.

Fungible Goods: If the subject matter of the transaction is *fungible goods,* each unit of which is interchangeable, with the contract obligating the recipient merely to later redeliver the same quantity of goods of the same description to the owner or to a third party, the transaction is still a bailment. This rule is especially important in grain storage situations, with the result that grain elevators taking in grain for storage are bailees even though the grain they later return to their customers or deliver to third parties is not the same grain they originally received.

Options to Purchase: The second exception arises in a situation where the one receiving possession of the property has a specified period of time within which to decide whether to purchase or return it. This type of transaction, sometimes called a *bailment with the option to purchase,* is a bailment despite the fact that the bailee has the choice of turning it into a sale by giving the bailor the agreed price rather than the property itself. Bailments of this type can take several forms, e.g., a *lease with the option to purchase.* Another example is the *sale on approval,* which was discussed in Chapter 21 concerning sale transactions.

Constructive Bailments: There are a few cases in which the courts treat transactions as if they are bailments even though one of the ordinarily required elements is missing. One example of such a **constructive bailment** is

found in the use of a bank safe-deposit box. When a customer places property in a safe-deposit box, the bank does not acquire *exclusive* control because access to the box requires both the customer's and the bank's key. In addition, the bank usually does not have actual knowledge of the contents of the box. Despite these differences from a traditional bailment, a majority of courts treat the arrangement as a bailment and hold the bank to the responsibilities of a bailee. In a few states, however, legislation has been passed declaring the use of a safe-deposit box to be only a rental of the space—that is, a *license* rather than a bailment.

The courts also usually treat a finder of personal property as a bailee even though the owner did not deliver the item to the finder. The bailment continues until the finder surrenders possession to a governmental authority or becomes the owner of the property by complying with a state finding statute.

Types of Bailments

Bailments can be broadly classified as *ordinary bailments* and *special bailments.* As the name implies, ordinary bailments comprise the vast majority of bailment transactions. Special bailments are discussed briefly at the end of the chapter. Ordinary bailments may be further subdivided into (1) bailments for the sole benefit of the bailee, (2) bailments for the sole benefit of the bailor, and (3) mutual benefit bailments.

Sole Benefit of the Bailee: A bailment for the sole benefit of the bailee exists when the owner of an item permits another to use it without compensation or any other benefit. Examples include the loan of a car to a friend or a lawn mower to a neighbor.

Sole Benefit of the Bailor: A bailment for the sole benefit of the bailor exists when a person stores or takes care of someone else's property as a favor, without receiving any compensation or other benefit. Such a bailment would arise, for example, where Ruth permits George to store his furniture in her garage while he is away for the summer, with no benefit at all to Ruth.

Mutual Benefit Bailments: Because people ordinarily do not enter into bailments unless they receive some sort of gain from the transaction, mutual benefit bailments are by far the most common kind. Most mutual bailments involve a bailor or bailee who receives direct compensation, as in the case of an equipment rental firm or a company that is in the business of storing the property of others.

It is possible, however, for the benefit to be an indirect one. Suppose, for example, that an employer prohibits its employees from keeping their coats or other personal belongings in the immediate working area, and maintains a separate coatroom or other area where such items are left under the control of an attendant. Even though no direct compensation is paid, there is a mutual benefit bailment. The employees benefit by having a secure place to keep their property during working hours. The employer, on the other hand, benefits in several ways, including having an uncluttered working area with fewer distractions for employees, and with less potential for problems arising from theft among employees.

The example of the restaurant's provision of a coatroom where it takes control of customers' coats and hats, presented earlier in the discussion of bailments, also illustrates a mutual benefit bailment involving indirect compensation.

Rights of the Bailee

The bailee's rights in a bailment transaction depend almost entirely on the express or implied terms of the parties' contract. These rights normally involve *possession, use,* and *compensation.*

If the contract provides that the bailee is to have possession for a specified period of time and if the bailor is receiving consideration in return, the bailee ordinarily has the right to retain possession for the entire time. And if the bailor wrongfully retakes possession before the

agreed time has expired, the bailee is entitled to damages for breach of contract. The bailee also can enforce this possessory right against a third party who wrongly interferes with it. Thus, if the bailed property is stolen, destroyed, or damaged by a third party, the bailee has the right to initiate legal action to recover the property or receive money damages from the third party.

Whether the bailee has the right to use the bailed property depends on the express terms of the contract or, if there are no such terms, on the general purposes of the bailment. If the contract is for *storage,* for example, the bailee usually has no right to use the property while it is in his or her possession. On the other hand, if the bailee is *renting* the property, he or she obviously has the right to use it in a normal manner.

Except for bailments in which the bailee is renting property for the purpose of using it, or in situations where there is a clear understanding that he or she is not to receive any payment, the bailee normally has the right to some form of compensation for the safekeeping of the property. In the case of a bailee who is in the business of storing the property of others, the compensation is almost always spelled out in the contract. Where the amount of the compensation is not expressly agreed upon, the bailee is entitled to the reasonable value of his or her services. If the purpose of the bailment is to have the bailee perform a service, such as automobile repairs, the amount of the compensation again depends on the express or implied terms of the contract.

Duties of the Bailee

A bailee has the fundamental duties of using and returning the bailed property in accordance with the bailment contract and exercising due care (or reasonable care) in handling the property.

Use and Return: If the bailee uses it in a way that is beyond the consent granted in the agreement, such use constitutes a breach of contract and the bailee is liable for any damages resulting from the unauthorized use regardless of whether he or she committed negligence or any other tort. For instance, Vance, a resident of Sacramento, California, borrows a pickup truck from his neighbor, Perez, to move some furniture from Stockton to Sacramento. After Vance reaches Stockton and loads the furniture, he decides to go on to Modesto, about 25 miles farther, to visit his brother. If the truck is damaged in an accident while Vance is in Modesto, he is fully liable to Perez for the damage even if the accident was not his fault in any respect.

A bailee who intentionally does not return the bailed property at the end of the bailment commits both a breach of contract and the tort of conversion, and is liable to the bailor for the value of the property.

Due Care and the Presumption of Negligence: When the bailed property is damaged, lost, stolen, or destroyed because the bailee has failed to exercise due care in handling the item, he or she is guilty of the torts of negligence and conversion and is responsible to the bailor for the amount of the damage or loss.

A variety of circumstances are taken into account to determine whether the bailee exercised due care, including the value of the bailed property, the susceptibility of this particular type of bailed property to damage or theft, and the amount of experience the bailee has had in dealing with similar types of property in the past. Thus, a bailee is expected to exercise greater care in handling a $2,000 diamond ring than a $100 chair. A bailee also would be expected to exercise more care in handling extremely flammable chemicals or a thoroughbred horse than a truckload of bricks.

Until recent years, most courts applied different degrees of care to the different categories of bailment. The bailee was required to exercise great care in a bailment for the sole benefit of the bailee, and only slight care in a bailment for the sole benefit of the bailor. In a mutual benefit bailment the bailee was required to exercise reasonable care, which was defined as the amount of care a reasonable person would exercise in protecting his or her own property. Although the courts in some states still make this rigid distinction, many of them have abandoned it as a strict basis for determining the bailee's required degree of care. These courts apply the general standard of reasonable care to all types of bailments, and simply treat the amount of benefit the bailee was receiving from the bailment as another one of the factors relevant to the question of whether he or she exercised such care.

Courts often emphasize that the bailee is ordinarily not an absolute insurer of the safety of the property, however, and is not liable unless the damage or loss results from his or her intentional or negligent act. Although true, this statement is somewhat misleading. The reason is that when a bailee fails to return the property in its former condition, there is a **presumption of negligence.** In other words, when the bailor proves that the property was not returned at all, or was returned in a damaged condition, the burden then shifts to the bailee to explain exactly what happened and to demonstrate how the loss occurred without his or her fault. Sometimes the courts use different terminology to refer to this presumption and say that the bailor's proof of damage or loss establishes a *prima facie* case of negligence. However it is stated, the rule makes it very difficult for a bailee to avoid liability once it is established that a bailment existed and the property was damaged or not returned.

The presumption of negligence greatly increases the importance of determining whether a bailment actually existed. A person who causes damage to or loss of another's property by failing to exercise due care is ordinarily liable for that damage or loss regardless of whether a bailment or any other particular relationship existed between the parties. In most situations, however, the property owner must prove specific acts on the part of the defendant that constituted negligence. In some cases, as where the item was stolen or destroyed by fire while on the defendant's premises, it can be almost impossible for the plaintiff to produce any specific evidence of what happened. Therefore, the question of whether a bailment existed frequently determines the outcome of such a case.

Exculpatory Clauses: Bailees frequently attempt to contractually excuse themselves from liability for harm to the bailed property. It is common, for example, for parking lots, automotive repair shops, or dry cleaners to post signs or give tickets or documents to bailors containing statements such as "The owner assumes all risk for damage to or loss of the property, and the proprietor is not responsible for such damage or loss resulting from fire, theft, flood, or negligence." Statements of this nature are referred to as **exculpatory clauses.**

In most situations exculpatory clauses are not effective to free the bailee from liability, for two reasons. First, as discussed in Chapter 11 regarding the formation of contracts, courts normally hold that such provisions are *not legally communicated* to the bailor unless specifically called to the bailor's attention. Second, even if the exculpatory clause is legally communicated and thus becomes part of the bailment contract, courts usually conclude that the clause *violates public policy* and is unenforceable on the grounds of illegality. This conclusion is almost always reached when the bailee is in the business of handling the property of others and the terms of the bailment contract are presented by the bailee to the bailor on a nonnegotiated "take it or leave it" basis. (In other words, the agreement is a *contract of adhesion,* a concept that was discussed at several points in the chapters on contracts.)

The following two cases illustrate the approach taken by courts to determine whether a bailment exists, and emphasize the critical importance of that question in situations where no one really knows exactly what happened to the bailed property. In addition, the second case provides an example of the courts' usual attitude toward exculpatory clauses in bailment contracts.

Pinto v. Bridgeport Mack Trucks, Inc.
Superior Court of Connecticut, Appellate Session, 458 A.2d 696 (1983)

Alfred Pinto had worked as a diesel mechanic for Bridgeport Mack Trucks for nine years. As was the custom in the industry, the employer supplied all the larger tools and employees furnished their own hand tools. It also was customary for employees to leave their tools in the work area of the employer's premises after finishing a day's work. Pinto was hired with the understanding that he would provide his own hand tools, and he maintained a two-piece tool chest in the employer's work area. The top section of the chest loaded with his tools weighed approximately 500 pounds. There were about 25 other tool boxes scattered around the work area. This work area consisted of a 39,000 square foot space in the rear of the employer's building; a showroom area was in the front.

As often was the case, on the occasion in question the employer's volume of work required the services of two shifts of mechanics. The first shift worked from 8:00 a.m. to 4:30 p.m., and the second shift from 3:00 p.m. to 11:30 p.m. The employer was open for business until 11:00 p.m., but at the end of the first shift a chain link fence surrounding the sides and rear of the building was locked, leaving a

front door leading into the showroom area as the only means of access to the work area. After finishing his work on the first shift, Pinto locked his tools in his box and left it beside the truck he was repairing. The second shift reported for work as usual and, as was their custom, the employees on the second shift took a meal break between 7:00 and 7:30 p.m. Some of the employees left the building during their break, while others ate in a lunchroom at the rear of the work area. During this half hour, McDonald, the foreman of the second shift, went back and forth between the lunchroom and work area answering the telephone and attending to other business matters. He was out of the work area a total of ten minutes during the entire break.

Upon returning from the break, an employee noticed that a battery charger was missing. The next morning Pinto discovered that the top section of his tool chest was also missing. The foreman had locked the building after the second shift the previous evening, and an investigation disclosed no signs of forced entry during the night. The employer refused to pay for Pinto's tools, so he filed suit against the employer seeking damages for their value. At the trial, evidence was presented showing that during the preceding year there had been discussions among employees and managers about storing the employees' tools to avoid their damaging or being damaged by the large trucks moving about the area. The employer's managers offered to provide a separate area where tool boxes could be wheeled and stored, and to obtain chains to secure them, but this action was never taken. The evidence also showed that, prior to the loss of the battery charger and Pinto's tools, there had been no thefts from the employer's building in nine years.

The trial court found that there was not a bailment of Pinto's tools, but held the employer liable because there was independent evidence of the employer's negligence. The employer appealed.

Covello, Judge:

A bailment is a consensual relation and it includes, in its broadest sense, any delivery of personal property in trust for a lawful purpose. Assumption of control is the determinative factor. A bailee is one who receives personal property from another in trust for a specific purpose, with a contract, express or implied, that the trust shall be faithfully executed and the property returned or duly accounted for when the special purpose is accomplished.

Here there was no delivery of the plaintiff's tools to the defendant nor receipt of them in a sense that could serve as a basis for concluding that the defendant had assumed control over them. Delivery connotes a handing over or surrender of possession to another. Locking the tools in a box and leaving the box wherever one chooses in the work area of the employer's premises, pursuant to a trade custom, is not consistent with a handing over or surrender of possession of either the tools or the box to the employer within the meaning of a bailment.

A conclusion that there was no bailment is not necessarily dispositive of the ultimate issue, as the existence of a bailment does nothing more than create a presumption of negligence. The failure of a bailee to return goods delivered to him raises a presumption that their nonproduction is due to his negligence. This presumption prevails unless and until the bailee proves the actual circumstances involved in the damaging of the property. If those circumstances are proved, then the burden is upon the bailor to satisfy the court that the bailee's conduct in the matter constituted negligence. If negligence may be independently demonstrated, the absence of the benefit of a presumption is not necessarily fatal to the plaintiff's cause of action.

In this connection, the trial court concluded that "[b]y not following up on the offer to set aside a caged or protected area or in supplying chains and insisting that the tool boxes be made secure each night, the defendant could be easily aware of the harm that was eventually suffered." The court further concluded that "[t]he employer controlled the work area and also set general policies to be followed by the employees. That control and management imposed an affirmative duty upon the employer that it failed to meet. If the adequate protection of the caged or locked area had been provided and a general policy of seeing that the employees used the protection had been enforced by the employer, then the duty would have been met."

[We disagree with the trial court's conclusion.] Negligence is a breach of duty. That duty is to exercise due care. The ultimate test of the existence of a duty to use care is found in the foreseeability that harm may result if it is not exercised. By that is not meant that one charged with negligence must be found actually to have foreseen the . . . particular injury which resulted . . . but the test is, would the ordinary person in the defendant's position, knowing what he knew or should have known, anticipate that harm of the general nature of that suffered was likely to result?

On the facts, the defendant could not be charged with that reasonable anticipation of harm which would be the basis of liability in negligence. Reasonable care does not require that one must guard against eventualities which, at best, are too remote to be reasonably foreseeable. The defendant did not know, nor did its employees have any knowledge of facts which would charge it with knowledge that thieves might steal an employee's 500 pound tool chest. There was no evidence of prior thefts. On the contrary, there was evidence that there had been no thefts in the preceding nine years. A chain link fence surrounding the sides and rear of this commercial building was secured by the day shift. The sole night access to the 39,000 square foot building was through a single door leading into the showroom. The tool chests, meanwhile, were in a maintenance area in the rear of the building. Employees were in and out of this area constantly. The totality of the facts and the circumstances militating against such a thing occurring remove the theft from the realm of what was reasonably foreseeable. . . .

There is error. The judgment is set aside and the case is remanded with direction to render judgment for the defendant.

Employers Insurance of Wausau v. Chemical Bank
Civil Court of New York, 459 N.Y.S.2d 238 (1983)

Suncrest Pharmacal Corp. claimed that Chemical Bank failed to credit one of Suncrest's deposits, resulting in a loss of over $11,000. Suncrest received $3,000 from its insurer, Employers Insurance of Wausau, and both Suncrest and the insurance company then filed suit against the bank to recover damages for the loss.

At the trial, Weintraub, president of Suncrest, testified that on a Friday evening about 7:00 p.m. he placed a paper bag containing two of the bank's cloth deposit bags in a night depository. Before leaving, he checked to see that the paper bag did in fact go down the chute. One of the deposit bags contained 850 one dollar bills, and the other contained cash and checks totalling $19,191.52. The deposit slip for both bags was in the one that contained $850. The following Monday the bank notified Weintraub that it had received only the bag containing the deposit slip and $850. Suncrest was able to have payment stopped on all of the checks in the missing bag on which it was the payee, but was unable to do so on any of the checks payable to others and endorsed over to Suncrest, because there was no record of the names of the makers of those checks. The lost cash and checks totalled $11,084.50.

An officer of the bank described the procedure used by the bank in opening the night deposit vault, and Suncrest conceded that it was unable to prove any specific acts of negligence relating to the bank's procedure in handling night deposits. Suncrest asserted, however, that the deposit had created a bailment, and that the bank had the burden of explaining exactly what happened to the lost bag. The bank claimed that there was no bailment, and that its liability was limited by the written deposit agreement between it and Suncrest, which provided that permission to use the night depository was a "privilege" and "gratuitous," and that "the exercise of that privilege [was] at the sole risk" of Suncrest. The following is the opinion of the trial court.

Lehner, Judge:

Until a deposit bag is opened and the contents credited to the depositor's account, the relationship between the bank and its night depository customer is that of bailor and bailee and only ordinary care is required of the bank in operating the facility. . . . [Authors' note: After the deposit is credited, a debtor-creditor relationship is created between the bank and its customer, and the bank is absolutely liable for the amount of the deposit.]

However, plaintiff must first establish that a bailment was in fact created by a proper deposit. For the trier of fact to determine whether a bailment was created many factors should be taken into account, such as the depositor's prior deposit history, method of depositing, his over-all character, and corroboration. Suncrest has been a long-time customer of the bank, a frequent user of its night depository service, and has never registered any complaints about the facility until now. Its method of depositing was as precautionary and circumspect as possible. Mr. Weintraub's testimony was, in part, corroborated by the foreman of Suncrest, who accompanied him to the bank and saw him place a paper bag in the night depository, but was unable to testify with respect to its contents.

Observing Mr. Weintraub from the witness stand leads the court to find him a rather credible witness. The bank acknowledged that many customers will place the bank's cloth deposit bag in a paper bag for security purposes in order to conceal possession. The bank officer testified that after the cloth bags are removed from the vault each morning, any paper bags used are thrown on the floor and discarded. The bank's supposition that Mr. Weintraub may not have checked to see that the deposit went down the chute is not a viable contention if the court believes (which it does) that both cloth bags were contained in the one paper bag, [because] the bank did receive one of the cloth bags. Finally, the fact that so many checks that had to be stopped were contained in the missing bag tends to lessen any concern that the claim is fraudulent.

In light of the above, the court finds that the aforesaid second bag containing cash and checks totaling $19,191.52 was in fact properly placed in the night depository vault in the paper bag with the other bag containing $850. When the paper bag entered the chute, a bailment was created. Although in the typical bailment there is personal delivery from the bailor to the bailee, here the bailment occurred upon delivery into a device under the exclusive care and control of the bank.

The finding of the creation of a bailment brings the court to the question of where the loss shall lie when neither plaintiffs nor defendant alleged any wrongdoing by the other. It is difficult to impose a burden upon either party to demonstrate fault, as the bank is never aware of a night deposit until the next morning when the vault is opened, and the depositor is never present when the vault is opened.

The general rule is that when a bailee is unable to advance an adequate explanation for the failure to return property subject to a bailment, it is liable for the loss, but that if the bailee provides a sufficient explanation for the loss so as to raise an issue of fact, the bailor must then prove negligence. . . .

In *Gramore Stores v. Bankers Trust Co.*, 402 N.Y.S.2d 326, the court held that a bank "may not contract away its liability for negligence" and struck an affirmative defense based on an exculpatory provision similar to that executed herein. . . .

Chemical Bank is not claiming exemption from liability for negligence, but rather is arguing that unless negligence or a conversion is established, the contract prohibits a recovery. In its brief it states: "The bank has merely defined its liability to protect itself against fraudulent claims." . . . It is hard to see where the contract provision would apply unless defendant is seeking to distinguish between negligence established by conduct as opposed to a presumption thereof that might ensue from application of the rules of bailment. If this is defendant's argument, the court cannot accept it. First, the court agrees with the holding in *Gramore Stores* that public policy [does not look favorably on an attempt by] a public institution such as a bank [to contract] away its liability for negligence. Second, [in any kind of transaction an attempt to contract away one's liability for negligence is not effective] unless it is absolutely clear that this was the understanding. Such an interpretation could not be garnered from an examination of the agreement herein. . . .

In *Vilner v. Crocker National Bank,* 152 Cal. Rptr. 850, a similar set of facts to those herein was presented with the bank arguing that proof that it exercised ordinary care met its conceded burden of explaining the failure to return the depositor's bag. The court disagreed, stating: "A simple showing of the exercise of ordinary care is not a sufficient explanation. Something has gone terribly awry. There is no evidence that explains it but, as Thoreau reminds us, 'Some circumstantial evidence is very strong, as when you find a trout in the milk.' A general showing of prudence and caution will not do absent an explanation of the cause of the disappearance." . . .

The court is acutely aware of the possibility of opening the floodgates to numerous fraudulent claims. But each and every claimant must first overcome the not insignificant threshold of demonstrating that a deposit was in fact made. Thereafter, the burden shifts to the bank to offer an explanation of how the loss occurred. Needless to say, requiring a bank to prove that it was not negligent in handling a particular deposit it claims it did not receive is rather difficult. But in the present case, with a court finding that the deposit was made, the court can only presume that the loss thereafter occurred as a result of the negligence of or conversion by the bank's employees. Possibly the second cloth bag was left in the paper bag that was thrown away, was dropped or even stolen. In any event, the exculpatory provision, which defendant concedes would not preclude a recovery for negligence or conversion, cannot therefore prohibit the imposition of liability.

Between the bank, that can offer no evidence with respect to how the deposit was made, and the depositor, who is in a similar position with respect to the opening of the bags, the loss should fall on the bank if it cannot explain what happened to the bag. . . . The excuse that the deposit was not received can consequently be analogized to the position of the warehouse in *I.C.C. Metals v. Municipal Warehouse Co.*, 50 N.Y.2d 657, which when it was unable to return stored goods merely offered the supposition that they were stolen. The Court of Appeals held that such explanation was insufficient to shift the burden back to the bailor to establish the bailee's fault and therefore allowed a recovery based on conversion to stand.

The defendant having failed to offer any explanation as to how the loss occurred is liable to the plaintiff Suncrest in the sum of $8,084.50, with interest from the date of the loss, and to plaintiff Employers Insurance Company of Wausau for $3,000, with interest from the date it paid Suncrest.

Rights of the Bailor

Essentially, the rights of the bailor arise from the duties of the bailee. Thus, the bailor's most important rights are to have the bailed property returned at the end of the bailment period, to have the bailee use due care in protecting the property, and to have the bailee use the property (if use is contemplated at all) in conformity with the express or implied terms of the bailment contract. Additionally, if the bailor is having work performed on the property by the bailee, the bailor is entitled to have it done in a workmanlike fashion. If the purpose of the bailment is use of the property by the bailee, the bailor has the right to compensation under the express or implied terms of the contract.

Duties of the Bailor

Liability for Defects in the Bailed Property: Obviously, the bailor has duties corresponding to the rights of the bailee discussed previously. In addition, the bailor has certain basic duties with respect to the condition of the bailed property.

Negligence: The bailor must not knowingly deliver property containing a hidden defect that is likely to cause injury. In either a mutual benefit bailment or one for the sole benefit of the bailee, the bailor is legally required to notify the bailee of any dangerous defect about which the bailor has *actual knowledge.* In a mutual benefit bailment, the bailor's duty regarding the condition of the bailed property is somewhat greater, and he or she can be held responsible for injury caused by hidden defects about which the bailor *either knew or should have known.*[5] Thus, in a mutual benefit bailment, the bailor's duty includes reasonably inspecting the prop-

erty and maintaining it in a safe condition before delivery to a bailee.

In either of these situations, a violation of the bailor's duty constitutes negligence, and the bailor is liable for resulting harm to the bailee and to others coming into contact with the defective property in a reasonably foreseeable manner. For example, a bailor's liability for delivering a defective automobile to the bailee would include injuries to the bailee and his or her immediate family, as well as to innocent third parties such as the driver of another automobile involved in an accident because of the defect.

Warranty and Strict Liability: In addition to imposing liability for the bailor's negligence, most courts in recent years have placed additional liability on commercial bailors. In the case of bailors who are in the business of renting property, such as automobiles, construction equipment, and so on, a majority of courts have held the bailor responsible for dangerous defects in the bailed property on basis of the *implied warranty* and *strict products liability* theories. These courts have drawn an analogy from the liability imposed on merchants in *sales* transactions. The importance of this development, as we saw in Chapter 22, "Warranties and Products Liability," is that the supplier of a defective item can be held liable without any proof that the supplier knew or should have known of the defect. Moreover, the supplier's defenses are much more limited under the warranty and strict liability theories.

Bailor's Disclaimers: We saw previously that commercial *bailees* frequently attempt to limit their liability contractually. It also is very common for commercial *bailors* to make similar attempts. This type of provision, whether it is called an exculpatory clause, disclaimer, or liability limitation, is given essentially the same treatment by the courts as bailees' exculpatory clauses. In fact, in the majority of states that have drawn an analogy between the bailor who is in the business of renting personal property and

---

[5] Questions concerning the condition of the bailed property almost never arise in a bailment for the sole benefit of the bailor, because the bailee does not *use* the property. If the bailed property was defective and harmed the bailee in such a case, however, the bailor's duty presumably would be the same as in a mutual benefit bailment.

the merchant who is in the business of selling goods, a disclaimer by the bailor is given even harsher treatment by the courts. Such a provision violates public policy and thus is not allowed to shield a commercial bailor from liability for negligence, breach of warranty, or strict liability when a defect in the bailed property causes personal injury or property damage to either the bailee or someone else whose contact with the item was reasonably foreseeable.

SPECIAL BAILMENTS

Special bailments are those involving common carriers, warehouse companies, and innkeepers (or hotelkeepers). Although bailments involving these types of bailees have most of the characteristics of ordinary bailments and are subject to most of the same rules, they are singled out because of certain unique aspects.

Common Carriers

A **common carrier** is a company that is licensed by the state or federal government to provide transportation services to the general public. Most airlines, trucking companies, and railroad companies are common carriers. A company doing business as a common carrier must make its services available to the public on a nondiscriminatory basis. A common carrier can be contrasted with a **contract carrier,** which does not hold itself out as providing transportation services to the public and is not licensed to do so. A contract carrier provides service under contract only to a few selected customers.

Suppose that a furniture manufacturer in Pittsburgh, Pennsylvania, delivers a large quantity of furniture to a railroad company for shipment to a wholesale furniture distributor in St. Louis, Missouri. When the manufacturer, called the *shipper,* turns over possession of the furniture to the railroad company, called the *carrier,* a type of mutual benefit bailment has been created.

Bailments of this type are different from ordinary bailments in several important respects.

Obligation to Transport: Unlike most bailees, the carrier has a contractual obligation to transport the bailed property.

Bills of Lading: Also unlike other bailees, the carrier issues a **bill of lading** to the shipper. The bill of lading, the rules for which are set forth in Article 7 of the Uniform Commercial Code, serves as both a *contract of bailment* and a *document of title.* In other words, it sets forth the terms of the agreement between shipper and carrier and also serves as evidence of title to the goods.

As was discussed in Chapter 20 dealing with sales of goods, a bill of lading or other document of title can be either *negotiable* or *nonnegotiable.* A bill of lading ordering the carrier to "deliver to X" is a nonnegotiable document of title. The carrier's obligation in such a case is to deliver the goods only to X, and the nonnegotiable document does not confer the right to receive the goods to anyone else who might come into possession of the document.

On the other hand, a bill of lading ordering the carrier to "deliver to the order of X," or to "deliver to bearer," is a negotiable document of title. Lawful possession of a negotiable document is tantamount to ownership of the goods, and the carrier is obligated to deliver them to anyone having such possession. In the case of a bill of lading ordering the carrier to "deliver to the order of X," the carrier is required to surrender the goods to Y if X has endorsed and delivered the document to Y and Y presents it to the carrier. In the case of a bill of lading ordering the carrier to "deliver to bearer," the carrier is required to surrender the goods to anyone to whom the document has been delivered, even without the presence of an endorsement.

Bills of lading, especially negotiable ones, are often used to facilitate sales transactions by providing the seller (shipper) a document that can be sent to the buyer and then used by the buyer to take possession of the goods when they reach their destination. This document may be sent directly from the seller to the buyer, or it may be sent through banking channels with the seller's and buyer's banks acting as agents for delivery of the document and receipt of payment.

Strict Liability: Contrary to ordinary bailments, the carrier is absolutely liable to the shipper for damage to or loss of the goods. In other words, the carrier's liability is not based upon negligence or other fault.[6] There are, however, several narrow categories of circumstances in which the carrier is not liable. If the goods are damaged, stolen, lost, or destroyed during shipment, the carrier has the burden of proving that the situation falls within one of these categories. The categories are as follows.

Act of God: The carrier is not liable if it can show that the loss was caused by an unexpected force of nature that was of such magnitude that damage to the goods could not have been prevented. The term Act of God is interpreted very strictly; evidence that the goods were damaged or destroyed by a flood, for example, will not suffice to excuse the carrier unless the flood was of such an unprecedented nature that no reasonable precautions could have forestalled the loss.

Act of a Public Enemy: This term is also interpreted very narrowly, and is usually applied only to a situation in which the goods were damaged, destroyed, or seized by a foreign nation at war with the United States.

Act of a Public Authority: The term public authority is much broader, and applies to actions by various local, state, or federal government officials. Examples would include the seizure of an illegal drug shipment by law enforcement officers, or the seizure of goods by a sheriff acting under a *writ of execution.* A writ of execution is a court order requiring an officer to seize property and sell it for the purpose of paying off a judgment against the owner.

Act of the Shipper: The carrier is not responsible if the shipper's own actions are shown to have caused the loss. For example, the carrier is not liable for the death of the shipper's chickens if proved to have been caused by the shipper's improperly ventilated crates.

The Inherent Nature of the Goods: The carrier is not liable if the loss is caused by an inherent characteristic of the goods themselves that the carrier had no control over. This category also is construed very strictly. For example, it would not be sufficient for the carrier to show that a shipment of fruit spoiled and that fruit is prone to spoilage. To escape liability, the carrier would have to prove that the fruit spoiled for a very specific reason, such as the fact that it was overripe at the time of shipment, and that the carrier could not have prevented the spoilage.

Liability Limitations: Despite the fact that carriers are liable for harm to the bailed property even without being at fault, they are permitted to limit their liability contractually to a greater extent than ordinary bailees. Under federal and state regulations, common carriers may obtain the shipper's agreement to place a dollar limit on the carrier's liability, and the limitation is valid if the shipper was given a choice of paying a higher transportation fee for a higher dollar limitation.

Warehouse Companies

A **warehouse company** is in the business of storing other people's property for compensation. A *public* warehouse company is obligated to serve the general public without discrimina-

---

[6]Frequently, one carrier will transport the goods for only part of the total trip, and other carriers will provide transportation for other portions of the journey. In such a situation, involving *connecting carriers,* the last carrier to have the goods is presumed to have received them in good condition, and is liable to the shipper for damage to the goods. If this carrier claims that the goods were damaged while in the hands of an earlier carrier, it must initiate legal action against the other carrier to recoup its loss.

tion. Most of the principles applicable to warehouse companies are exactly the same as those for ordinary bailees. In fact, some of the illustrations presented in the discussion of ordinary bailments involved warehouses.

The most important characteristic that warehouse operators have in common with other bailees is the nature of the bailee's liability. A warehouse company is not absolutely liable like a common carrier, but is liable for damage to or loss of the bailed property only in those circumstances in which an ordinary bailee is liable, namely, where the damage or loss is caused by the bailee's negligence, conversion, or breach of contract. Warehouse companies, however, are also subject to the same presumption of negligence as ordinary bailees.

Thus, for most purposes a warehouse company is an ordinary bailee. It is often singled out as a special bailee, however, for three reasons: (1) Like a common carrier, and unlike other bailees, a warehouse operator may obtain the bailor's agreement to limit the warehouse's liability, and the limitation is valid if the bailor was given a choice of a higher dollar limitation in return for a higher fee. (2) Also like a common carrier, a warehouse company issues documents of title for the goods it receives. The document of title issued by a warehouse company is called a **warehouse receipt,** and is governed by the same rules as bills of lading under Article 7 of the UCC. (3) A warehouse company is subject to more extensive regulation by the state than most other bailees. For example, warehouses are usually subject to special building standards and fire prevention measures.

Innkeepers

The taking of articles of personal property to a hotel or motel room by a guest does not create a bailment, for two reasons. First, the **innkeeper** (i.e., the hotel owner) normally does not have knowledge of the specific items that are brought into the room. Second, because the guest is free to remove the items from the room without no-

tice to the innkeeper, the latter does not have exclusive possession of the items.

Despite the absence of a true bailment relationship, under common-law principles the innkeeper had exactly the same absolute liability as a common carrier for damage to or loss of guest's personal property. In modern times, however, all states have passed statutes diminishing the innkeeper's liability. The typical statute requires innkeepers to maintain a safe or other appropriate facility for the safekeeping of its guests' valuables. If a guest deposits property with the innkeeper, a bailment is created. Under most statutes, if the property then is damaged or lost, the innkeeper has the same absolute liability as a common carrier. Some statutes, however, place dollar limits on the innkeeper's liability.

With regard to property that is *not* turned over to the innkeeper for safekeeping, the statutes vary. Many provide that the innkeeper's common-law liability is reduced to that of an ordinary bailee. Other statutes do not remove the innkeeper's absolute responsibility, but place a dollar limit such as $50 on that liability.

SUMMARY

Although the legal framework for personal property ownership bears a number of similarities to that for real property, there are also many differences. Primary among the differences is that ownership of personal property usually is an all-or-nothing proposition, and is not subdivided into the wide variety of interests that characterize real property ownership. Ownership of personal property can be acquired in a sale transaction or by will, subjects that are dealt with elsewhere in this book. Personal property ownership can be transferred by gift, which requires expression of a present intent to transfer ownership and delivery of possession. Other methods by which title to an article of personal property can be affected are occupation, finding, accession, and confusion.

A bailment of personal property arises when one party transfers temporary possession (but not title) to another under an agreement in which the recipient is required to return the property later or to deliver it to a designated third person. Bailments can be ordinary or special. Ordinary bailments can be further subdivided into those for the sole benefit of the bailee, sole benefit of the bailor, and mutual benefit of the parties. The most important duties of the bailee in an ordinary bailment are to use and return the property only in accordance with the bailment contract, and to exercise due care in protecting the property. When bailed property is not returned or is returned in a damaged condition, there is a presumption of negligence.

The most important duties of the bailor are to conform to the terms of the contract regarding the bailee's use and possession of the property, and not to deliver bailed property having a known dangerous defect. This duty is somewhat greater in a mutual benefit bailment than in one for the sole benefit of the bailee. In addition to this liability for negligence, in recent years liability under warranty and strict products liability theories has been imposed on commercial bailors.

Special bailments are those involving common carriers, warehouse companies, and innkeepers. A common carrier is absolutely liable for damage to or loss of the goods unless the carrier can prove that the damage or loss was caused by one of five narrowly interpreted events. A warehouse company has the liability of an ordinary bailee, but is different in that it issues warehouse receipts and is subject to greater regulation. An innkeeper, though not technically a bailee of the property its guests keep in their rooms, had the same absolute liability as a common carrier under common-law rules. All states have passed statutes modifying this liability in certain ways.

KEY TERMS

Donor
Donee
Constructive delivery (or symbolic delivery)
Gift *inter vivos*
Gift *causa mortis*
Occupation
Abandoned property
Lost property
Mislaid property
Finding statute (or estray statute)
Escheat statute
Accession
Confusion of goods
Fungible goods
Bailment
Bailor
Bailee
Constructive bailment
Presumption of negligence
Exculpatory clause
Special bailments
Common carrier
Contract carrier
Bill of lading
Warehouse company
Warehouse receipt
Innkeeper

QUESTIONS AND PROBLEMS

1. Closter was despondent and had decided to commit suicide. Before doing so, he inserted into an envelope a promissory note that he owned. On the note he wrote that he was giving it to Schutz. Closter then shot and killed himself. Schutz, who occupied another room in the same boardinghouse, heard the shot, rushed to his friend's room and found his body there. Schutz saw the envelope lying on the desk where Closter had placed it. Thinking that it might be a suicide note, Schutz opened it and found the promissory note containing Closter's expression of donative intent. Schutz pocketed the envelope and note. The existence of the note later came to light, and Liebe, the administrator of Closter's estate, filed suit to collect on the note from Battman, who had originally executed it. Schutz claimed that *he* was the owner of the note and was entitled to collect on it from Battman. Who won? Discuss. (*Liebe v. Battman,* 54 Pac. 179, 1898.)

2. Walters suffered a heart attack. Fearful of impending death, he gave his diamond ring to his sister while he was still in the hospital. Walters' condition improved, and he was discharged from the hospital two months later. He asked his sister to return the ring, but she refused. Not wanting to cause a family quarrel, he said nothing more. Five years later he died from heart disease. Does the ring belong to his sister? Explain. Would it make any difference if he had never asked for the return of the ring? Discuss.

3. Hillebrant indicated to Brewer that he was making a gift to Brewer of a herd of cattle. Hillebrant then obtained Brewer's branding iron and branded the cattle with Brewer's registered brand. Before the cattle were delivered to Brewer, however, Hillebrant changed his mind. Brewer sued, claiming that a completed gift of the cattle had been made. Was Brewer correct? Discuss. (*Hillebrant v. Brewer,* 6 Tex. 45, 1851.)

4. Harkness was elderly and bedridden. So that his close friend Kuntz could pay his bills for him a joint account was established with money belonging to Harkness. The account was a joint tenancy with right of survivorship. It was used for its intended purpose until Harkness died two years later (that is, Kuntz never used the funds for any purpose other than to pay bills for Harkness). When Harkness died, Kuntz claimed the money remaining in the account, asserting that it was his as a gift. Harkness' heirs disagreed. What is the result? Explain.

5. X and Y consented to the mixing of their wheat in a grain storage elevator owned by Z. What is the status of the ownership of the wheat? Explain. Would the answer be different if Z had caused the confusion accidently? Explain. Would the answer be different if X had intentionally caused the confusion with knowledge that he had no right to do so? Explain.

6. Hanson agreed to loan $1,000 to Kristofferson only after Kristofferson agreed to *pledge* a

ring valued at $3,000 with Hanson. A pledge involves transfer of possession of personal property to a creditor as security for the debt. Soon after the loan was made, the ring was stolen while in Hanson's possession. In subsequent litigation between the parties, Hanson contended that he was not a bailee in this situation because his obligation to return the ring was not absolute—he would not have to return it if Kristofferson defaulted on his loan. Is Hanson's contention correct? Why or why not?

7. X left her expensive leather handbag in a medical clinic waiting room when she was called into her doctor's office for her appointment. When she returned to the waiting room 45 minutes later, the handbag was gone. She later brought suit against the clinic to recover its value. At the trial the clinic receptionist and X's doctor testified that they did not see the handbag at any time during the day of her appointment. Assuming the receptionist and the doctor were telling the truth, would this testimony necessarily rule out a bailment relationship? Explain. If the receptionist had testified that she had noticed X placing the handbag in a corner of a couch before entering the doctor's office, would this fact clearly establish a bailment? Discuss.

8. Scarlet, a Ford dealer, delivered a new Taurus automobile to his neighbor, Gray, for ten days; the understanding between the two men was that at the end of that period Gray would have the option of (a) giving his 1913 Ford Model T to Scarlet in payment for the Taurus, or (b) paying Scarlet $15,000 in cash for the Taurus. During the ten-day period while Gray is in possession of the Taurus, is he a bailee of the car? Discuss. Would your answer be any different if the agreement had simply given Gray, at the end of the ten-day period, the option of either returning the Taurus or paying $15,000 cash for it? Explain.

9. X leaves his car at the Y Company's parking lot and returns an hour later to find that it has been badly damaged while in the Y Company's possession. In this situation, X's right to recover damages from the parking lot company might be seriously jeopardized if the legal relationship between X and the Y Company was merely that of licensee and licensor rather than bailor and bailee. Explain why this is so.

10. David Crystal, Inc., delivered goods to a trucking company for transportation. While in the trucking company's possession, the goods were lost when the truck carrying them was hijacked in New York City. In a legal action by David Crystal against the trucking firm, a common carrier, the trucking firm defended on the ground that truck hijackers are "public enemies," and that it thus was not liable for the loss. Is this contention correct? Why or why not? (*David Crystal, Inc. v. Ehrlich-Newmark Truck Co.*, 314 N.Y.S.2d 559, 1970.)

Chapter 44

WILLS, TRUSTS, AND ESTATE PLANNING

Although few people amass large fortunes in their lifetimes, most will not die penniless. Many people are surprised at the actual value of what they may have considered to be modest holdings. Real estate acquired early in life may appreciate dramatically; life insurance, both individual and group, may be owned in substantial amounts, and investment in the stock market through mutual funds is commonplace. One's personal property, slowly acquired over a period of years, may constitute a sizable asset. Some knowledge of wills, trusts, and other estate planning devices is essential to make informed decisions about one's personal situation.

The case of Pablo Picasso is a good example of what can happen when a person with a substantial estate fails to provide for its orderly disposition. When the famous artist died in 1973 he left a tremendous fortune—millions of dollars in assets. To whom did he leave it? As a matter of fact, Picasso died **intestate;** that is, at the time of his death he had not prepared a document—a will—to provide specific and detailed instructions about what to do with his property. A properly planned, drafted, and executed will might have eliminated most of the bitter controversy that arose among those close to him over the disposition of his wealth.

Picasso apparently felt that making a will was an act in contemplation of death and therefore an unpleasant subject to be avoided. He resisted all efforts by those who anticipated protracted legal proceedings to persuade him to make a will to provide for an orderly disposition of his property. When any person of considerable means refuses to provide for his or her estate's distribution on death, controversy is almost as certain as death itself.

WILLS

A will transforms a person's wishes about the disposition of his or her property into a valid, legal instrument. This section covers formal, written wills in detail and mentions other types briefly. Following are some commonly used terms with which the student may be unfamiliar. A man who makes a will is a **testator,** a woman is a **testatrix.** A person who dies is a *decedent.* A decedent leaving a valid will is said to die *testate.* It is customary for a testator to designate a personal representative to carry out the provisions of the will. This person is an **executor** if male and an **executrix** if female. If there is no will, the court will appoint an **administrator** (or *administratrix*) to handle the decedent's estate. With regard to the testator's property, disposition of real estate is called a **devise,** money passing under a will is a **legacy,** and other property is disposed of by **bequest.**[1]

Testamentary Capacity

A will is valid only if the testator had **testamentary capacity** at the time of its making. In most states the testator must have attained a specific minimum age, usually 18. In all states the testator must possess the mental capacity to dispose of the property intelligently. Testamentary capacity is not identical to capacity to contract. In general, testators have the capacity to make wills if they have attained the statutory age, if they know what property they own, and if they reasonably understand how and to whom they want to leave their property. The following case illustrates this principle.

---

[1] The Uniform Probate Code, which has been largely adopted in about 15 states and partially in a dozen more, uses the term "devise" to refer to any sort of testamentary gift whether of land, money, or personal property.

Holladay v. Holladay
Court of Appeals of Kentucky, 172 S.W.2d 36 (1943)

This action was a will contest involving the will of Lewis Holladay. A college graduate, Holladay made his home on his mother's farm with her and a sister until his mother's death in 1929. He remained on the farm until he died in 1940 at age 66. He was survived by a brother, Joe, and three sisters. Joe was the sole beneficiary under Lewis's will. When he submitted the will for probate, the sisters opposed the proceeding on a number of grounds. The primary basis for the contest was the allegation by the sisters, the contestants, that Lewis did not possess sufficient mental capacity to execute a will.

Upon a verdict rendered in the Clark Circuit Court a judgment was entered adjudging that a paper executed by Lewis Holladay was his last will and testament. This appeal is prosecuted from that judgment.

Sims, Justice:

. . . Lewis Holladay had a college education and made his home on his mother's farm with her and a maiden sister, Miss Denia, until his mother's death in 1929. His mother was quite old and her death greatly upset him. The testimony for contestants is that Lewis was far from normal mentally years before his mother died, but was much more unstable afterwards. It was testified he shot and killed his pet dog without reason in 1917 or 1918. During electrical storms he would take his seat under a tree, saying it was safer there than in the house. He was afflicted with stomach ulcers and could not sleep at nights and would roam over the premises and farm, and on occasion would stand like a statue in the county road even at midnight, requiring travelers to drive around him. At times he would go to the barn during the night and throw down hay for his stock when it was not in the barn but was out on pasture. He would bathe at night in a pond which was little more than a hog wallow, saying it gave him relief. It was testified that if the least thing went wrong, such as some meat falling down or the spilling of some lard from a bucket, he became so upset that it was necessary to put him to bed to quiet him. Pages could be consumed in reciting the testimony relative to his queer, weird and unnatural actions. There were many suicides and much insanity on both sides of his family, and it appears in the evidence that he threatened to destroy himself.

Opposing such testimony, twenty-six of his neighbors, friends, business acquaintances and associates testified he was perfectly sane and normal; that he was a good farmer and a successful business man. These twenty-six witnesses made up a cross section of the community and included people from all walks of life: doctors, bankers, veterinarians, livestock buyers, farmers and shop keepers, practically all of whom had business or social contacts with him. Upon the written request of his sisters, he and his brother, Joe, were named administrators of his mother's $23,000 estate, which testator wound up practically without assistance from Joe. In 1930, the year he wrote his will, Lewis contracted with his sisters that he would bid $137.50 per acre for his mother's farm of 146 acres if it were sold at public auction; and he carried out his contract and purchased the farm. He raised and sold registered sheep; was the moving spirit in some important and successful litigation in 1929 involving damages to farm lands in the community when a water dam broke. From 1929 to 1933 he served twice on the petit jury and twice on the grand jury; and in the interim between 1927 and 1940 he wrote more than 2,000 checks aggregating $29,000.

. . . The court did not err in refusing to give contestants' proffered instruction on the alleged insane delusions Lewis had against his sisters. His feelings toward them were unkind and even bitter, but they were based upon facts and not delusions. His sisters had objected to the fee allowed him as administrator of his mother's estate, although it was slightly less than the statutory limit of 5 percent. They had insinuated that when he and Joe, the morning after the death of their brother Felix, went through the deceased's personal effects they were looking for his will with the sinister motive of destroying it if they found one in favor of the sisters. Miss Denia had intimated that Lewis had sensual plans in bringing in a housekeeper after his mother's death. Then after Lewis had agreed to bid $137.50 per acre on his mother's farm, his three sisters attempted to raise the price. This combination of incidents had turned Lewis against his sisters, but it cannot be said his feelings were insane delusions, which are ideas or beliefs springing spontaneously from a diseased or perverted mind without reason or foundation in fact. A belief which is based upon reason and evidence, be it ever so slight, cannot be an insane delusion. . . .

The judgment is affirmed.

Undue Influence

Even if a testator or testatrix has the legal capacity to make a will, that will should not be admitted to probate if it is the product of fraud, duress, or, more typically, undue influence. Many courts use a four-factor test to determine the existence of undue influence. That test is applied in the following case.

Casper v. McDowell
Wisconsin Supreme Court, 205 N.W. 2d 753 (1973)

On April 2, 1970, 78-year-old Joseph Casper died. His will, drafted ten months before his death by a local attorney, provided for payment of debts and funeral expenses, bequeathed $1,500 to each of Casper's two sons (Alger and Richard), and left the residue and remainder of the estate to Wilma Jean McDowell, who had lived with Casper as housekeeper and friend from October 1964 to his death. Nothing was left to Joseph's brother, John. The will specified Wilma Jean's father or her brother as executor.

After the will was submitted for admission to probate, objections were filed by Alger and Richard. Later they also challenged, on undue influence grounds, transactions in which Joseph had named Wilma Jean a joint tenant on a bank account and two deposit certificates. A jury found no undue influence in the transactions, and the trial court admitted the will to probate. Alger and Richard appealed.

Wilkie, Justice:

This court has often reiterated the elements necessary to establish undue influence. In Will of Freitag [101 N.W.2d 108 (Wis. 1960)] they were capsulized as follows:

> . . . *Susceptibility, opportunity to influence, disposition to influence, and coveted result; stated more completely: 1. A person who is susceptible of being unduly influenced by the person charged with exercising undue influence; 2. the opportunity of the person charged to exercise such influence on the susceptible person to procure the improper favor; 3. a disposition on the part of the party charged, to influence unduly such susceptible person for the purpose of procuring an improper favor either for himself or another; 4. a result caused by, or the effect of such undue influence.*

Joseph Casper's first marriage ended in divorce in the early 1930s. After the divorce the sons [Alger and Richard] lived with their mother but continued to see their father. Both sons eventually moved to California in the 1950s. Joseph Casper remarried but . . . his second wife died in 1958. In October 1964, the testator placed an advertisement in the Kenosha newspaper for a housekeeper. Wilma Jean McDowell, then twenty-two years old, answered the ad . . . and continuously resided in the testator's home until his death in 1970. Although Jean McDowell testified that she had not had sexual relations with the testator, several witnesses testified the two were intimate. There was very little contact [between testator and his sons] after 1965. The testator's brother, John, testified that after 1965 he did not see his brother very often.

A. *Susceptibility.* As evidence of Joseph Casper's susceptibility to undue influence, appellants cite his deteriorating physical condition, his dissociation from family members, former friends and associates, and his inordinate attraction to this young girl. Testimony from various witnesses regarding Casper's odd conduct included his failure to recognize a grandchild and an old friend; his cutting off the top of several of his trees and one of his neighbor's trees; the severe cutting of his hand by placing it in his lawnmower. Appellants also cite as conclusive proof of susceptibility a boast made by Jean McDowell to a neighbor that she could get anything she wanted from Casper.

The prevailing evidence, however, is that Joseph Casper was a strong willed and independent person. A neighbor, Frank Novelen, stated: "Well, he had a mind of his own. . . . Yeah, I'd say if he wanted to do something, he'd do it." Casper's stockbroker, Harry Myers, testified he had talked with Casper a couple of days before his death. According to Myers the two men had a conversation for fifteen minutes concerning the stock market. Myers stated the only difference he perceived in Casper was that his hair was a "shade grayer than the time I'd seen him before."

His personal physician testified that, in his opinion, Casper was "orientated" during the fourteen years they were acquainted. We conclude from this evidence that Casper, during the last half dozen years of his life, did not lose his characteristic independence. He was not susceptible to undue influence as claimed by appellants. While his health declined with age, his mental condition did not deteriorate severely.

B. *Disposition.* The disposition to influence is shown by "a willingness to do something wrong or unfair, and grasping or overreaching characteristics." [Estate of Brehmer, 164 N.W.2d 318 (Wis. 1969).] Not every act of kindness may be considered as indicating a disposition to influence a testator. In Estate of McGonigal [174 N.W.2d 205 (Wis. 1970)] we noted "There is nothing wrong with aiding and comforting a failing testator; indeed, such activity should be encouraged."

While Jean McDowell's aid and comfort to Joseph Casper may have exceeded that which is normally expected of a nurse or housekeeper, this fact, standing alone, does not require the inference of a disposition to unduly influence.

While Casper's diminished contacts with his friends and family may give rise to the suspicion that Jean McDowell was "poisoning" the testator's mind, such inference or suspicion is not necessarily true. Casper's friend, John Schanock, stated that he felt Casper's interests simply turned to love. Quite natural is Casper's diminished need to depend upon friends and family after Jean McDowell's arrival. The two, despite several spats, were quite close.

[Also] on June 2, 1964, [testator] designated Linda Corn as beneficiary of [a savings] account. This indicates that Casper, although maintaining contact with friends and family, did not regard them as potential recipients of his bounty even before he and Jean McDowell met.

C. *Coveted result.* At first blush, the will and [property] transfers in the instant case appear unnatural. Indeed, as stated in Estate of Culver [126 N.W.2d 536 (Wis. 1964)], they raise a "red flag of warning." It does not automatically follow, however, that Joseph Casper's giving the majority of his wealth to nonkin is unnatural. The naturalness of a will depends upon the circumstances of each case.

Here, the testator's closest kin, his two sons, lived in California and had for many years. It appears that Casper's closest friend was Jean McDowell.

Although there is a claim that Casper deviated from socially acceptable behavior for a man of his age in hiring Jean McDowell, fifty years his junior, as a resident housekeeper and in considering her as his closest friend through his last years, this does not necessarily lead to but one inference that his giving the majority of his estate to her was an unnatural testamentary result obtained by undue influence.

D. *Opportunity.* The only element of the four essential to a finding of undue influence that is present here is the "opportunity" to influence the testator.

[Affirmed.]

The Formal Will

The term *formal* indicates that the will has been prepared and executed in compliance with the state's law of wills ("probate code"). Although the right to make a will generally exists independent of statute, the procedures for drafting, executing, and witnessing the formal written document are governed by statute. Such statutory requirements, although basically similar, vary from state to state. Therefore the drafter must be thoroughly acquainted with the law of the state in which the testator's will is to be effective and must be sure to comply with its provisions. Noncompliance usually means that the will is declared invalid. If this happens, the decedent's property passes in accordance with the state's law of descent and distribution. (Such statutes and their application are discussed later in another section.)

General Requirements: A will must be written; it must be signed by the testator or testatrix or at his or her direction. In most states, the signing must be witnessed by two competent persons who themselves must sign as witnesses in the presence of each other and of the testator or testatrix.[2] Most states require an **attestation clause,** a paragraph beneath the testator's signature to the effect that the will was *published*— that is, declared by the testator to be the last will and testament, and signed in the presence of the witnesses, who themselves signed as attesting witnesses. These are the formalities required by statute, and they must be strictly observed. The witnesses do not need to read or know the contents of the will. The testator or testatrix simply announces to them that the document is the will and that he or she is going to sign it. The function of the attestation clause is to serve as a self-proving affidavit to relieve the witnesses of the burden of testifying when the will is submitted for admission to probate after the death of the testator or testatrix.

Specific Provisions: The main function of a will is to provide for the disposal of property. However, it can appoint an executor and cancel all previous wills if it so states. It can also provide for an alternative disposition of property in the event the primary beneficiary predeceases the testator. If the testator or testatrix is married, the surviving spouse is usually appointed as the executor or executrix; if unmarried, a close relative or friend may be designated.

A will can also cover the disposition of property in the event that husband and wife die nearly simultaneously. It is essential for the will to state that it revokes any and all prior wills. The existence of two or more wills can create insurmountable problems. Sometimes none are admitted to probate (the court proceedings whereby a will is proved and the estate of the decedent is disposed of), in which event the state's statutory provisions for the division of an estate are followed.

The will can also name a guardian for minor children. If both husband and wife die, the guardian they have appointed in their wills can be confirmed by the court if he or she is qualified and willing to serve in that capacity. This will obviate the necessity for a court-appointed guardian and a possible controversy between the two competing, though well-meaning, sides of the family.

---

[2] A few states require three witnesses.

Modification: While it is possible in some states to change one's will by erasure, by striking out portions, or by interlineation, such procedures are risky undertakings at best. The proper method is to modify by means of a **codicil.** This is an addition to the will and must be executed with the same formalities as the original document. Consequently, if extensive modification is necessary, the testator would be well-advised to consider making a new will.

Revocation: A will becomes effective only at the death of the testator. The testator can revoke or amend the will at any time until death. Revocation can be accomplished in several ways, but usually must be done in strict compliance with statute by means evincing a clear intent to revoke. Executing a new will with a clause expressly revoking all prior wills and codicils is a customary method of revoking a will. The necessity for strict statutory compliance is illustrated in the following case.

In re Estate of Haugk
Wisconsin Supreme Court, 280 N.W.2d 684 (1979)

On January 6, 1965, Marie Haugk executed a will naming the Lutheran Children's Friend Society and the Easter Seal Society of Milwaukee County ("appellants") as residual beneficiaries. On September 2, 1976, Marie's husband, Horst Haugk, burned the 1965 will in the family basement, while Marie, who was suffering from a heart condition and was thus unable to descend the stairs into the basement, stayed upstairs in the kitchen. Soon thereafter, Marie spoke to her attorney about execution of a new will which would have eliminated appellants as beneficiaries, purportedly because she had wearied of their repeated requests for funds. However, Marie died before the new will could be executed.

Haugk filed a petition with the probate court claiming his wife died intestate, leaving him as sole beneficiary of her $130,000 estate. Appellants then petitioned the court for admission of the 1965 will. The trial court found that the 1965 will was properly revoked and ruled for Haugk. Appellants challenge this ruling on appeal.

Coffey, Justice:

The common law requirements for revocation of a will by physical act have been codified in sec. 853.11(1)(b), Stats., which recites:

> *853.11 Revocation (1) subsequent writing or physical act. A will is revoked in whole or in part by:*
>
> . . .
>
> *(b) Burning, tearing, canceling or obliterating the will or part, with the intent to revoke, by the testator or by some person in the testator's presence and by his direction.*

Thus the revocation statute clearly delineates that, in order for the revocation of Marie's will to be effective, Haugk had to burn the will: (1) in Marie's presence, and (2) at her direction.

The record discloses that Marie was in the kitchen of her apartment while Haugk was in the basement burning the will in the incinerator. He explained that Marie's heart condition prevented her from going to the basement because of the strain of climbing the stairs. Contrary to the strict wording of sec. 853.11(1)(b), Stats., the trial court found that Marie, being in near proximity in the same house, 13 steps away, was in Haugk's "constructive presence" at the time the will was destroyed.

In *Estate of Murphy,* 259 N.W. 430 (1935), this court discussed the necessity of the testator's presence during the destruction of a will.

> *Inasmuch as revocation involves intention, the inference arises that the physical act must be performed by the testatory himself or under his sanction and direction. . . . Both presence and direction of the testator being usually essential where the act is performed by another, a will is not legally revoked though destroyed by the testator's own order, if burned or torn where he did not or could not see or take cognizance of the deed done, as statutes commonly require the revocation by physical act to be by testator himself or in his presence and in such states cancellation by a third party out of the presence of testator is of no effect.*

In the present case, a valid revocation could have been achieved if Haugk had torn up and destroyed the will in Marie's presence; thus she would not have had to endanger her health by climbing the basement stairs. It makes even more sense and eliminates all suggestion of fraud if the testator personally revoked the will, defacing each page of the document and placing her initials thereon.

The requirement that a will must be destroyed in the "testator's presence" must be strictly construed. This strict construction is necessary so as to prevent the inadvertent or more importantly the fraudulent destruction of a will contrary to the testator's intentions. Each element must be established by adequate evidence as this court will not adopt a position that will promote either intestacy or the fraudulent destruction of an individual's last will and testament.

[Reversed.]

Revocation can also be caused by operation of law. Marriage, divorce, or the birth of a child subsequent to making a will may affect its validity by revoking it completely or partially. State laws on wills are not uniform—the birth of a child may revoke a will completely in one state but only partially in another. Marriage and divorce also affect wills differently from state to state.

Limitations: There are a few limitations on a person's right to dispose of property through a will. For example, if a married person's will leaves no provision for inheritance by the spouse, many states allow the spouse to claim a share of the estate, typically one-third, under what is called a "forced share," "widow's share," or "elective share." If the spouse is left less than the statutory "forced share," the spouse has the right to renounce the actual devise and take the larger "forced share." In addition, many states provide the spouse a "homestead right" to a specific amount of land (for example, 1 acre in town or 160 acres in the country).

In community property states, each spouse owns one-half of the community property. In most of these states, the surviving spouse receives title to half the community property and the deceased spouse's share passes by will, if one exists, or by intestacy if no will exists. In no event can either spouse dispose of more than one-half the community property by will.

Holographic Wills

Almost half the states allow testators to execute their own wills without formal attestation. These **holographic wills** must be entirely in the testator's own handwriting, including the signature. These wills differ from formal wills in that no attestation clause or witnesses are required. However, most states allowing holographic wills require that the testator's handwriting and signature be proved by two witnesses familiar with them during probate of the will. Competent witnesses would include persons who had received correspondence from the testator. A holographic will is purely statutory—that is, it must be made in accordance with the appropriate state's law and is subject to prescribed conditions and limitations. The principal requirement is that it be entirely in the testator's own handwriting. In *Estate of Thorn*, a testator in a holographic will used a rubber stamp to insert "Cragthorn" in the phrase "my country place Cragthorn." The will was held to be invalid since it was not entirely in the testator's handwriting.[3] In some jurisdictions the holographic will must be dated in the testator's handwriting. The requirements of testamentary capacity and intent are the same as those for formal wills, but a holographic will is otherwise informal and may even take the form of a letter if it conveys testamentary intent (the mental determination or intention of the testator that the document constitute the person's will).

Nuncupative Wills

About half the states permit **nuncupative wills,** or *oral wills.* In general, statutes impose strict limitations on the disposal of property through a nuncupative will. Most states require that it be made during the testator's "last sickness"; that it be written down within a short period; that it be proved by two witnesses who were present at its making; and that the value of the estate bequeathed not exceed a certain amount, usually quite small. Some states also require that the decedent have been a soldier in the field or a sailor at sea in actual contemplation or fear of death.[4] Nuncupative wills, where recognized, usually effect distribution of personal property only, not real property.

Nuncupative wills are difficult to establish, and the restrictions placed on them are intended to discourage their use. There is always the possibility of mistake or fraud and, except on rare occasions, a testator can easily plan sufficiently ahead to use the more traditional and acceptable type of will.

INTESTACY—STATUTES OF DESCENT AND DISTRIBUTION

State laws govern the disposition of a decedent's estate when the decedent has died without a will—intestate. Such laws are called statutes of descent and distribution. They provide for disposition of the decedent's property, both real and personal, in accordance with a prescribed statutory scheme. Real property descends; personal property is distributed. Consequently, the law of the state where the decedent's real estate is located will determine the heirs, by class, to whom it will descend. The decedent's personal property will be distributed in accordance with the law of the state in which he or she is domiciled. In addition to prescribing the persons who will inherit a decedent's property, statutes of descent and distribution also prescribe the order and proportions in which they will take. The effect of this is that intestate dece-

---

[3] 183 Cal. 512, 192 P. 19 (1920).

[4] These are commonly known as soldiers' and sailors' wills.

dents permit the state to select their heirs by default.

The Surviving Spouse

Without exception, statutes of descent and distribution specify the portion of a decedent's estate that will be taken by his or her lawful, surviving spouse. Variation in this area is significant from state to state. Formerly, under common law, the surviving spouse was entitled only to a life estate (ownership for life) or *dower* (to the widow) or *curtesy* (to the widower) in the real property owned by the decedent. Personal property was divided among the surviving spouse and any children of the marriage. Today, the law of dower and curtesy has been either abolished or altered significantly by statute in all jurisdictions. Typically, if a husband or wife dies intestate, the statutes provide that the surviving spouse takes one-half or one-third of the estate if there are children or grandchildren. If there are no children or grandchildren, in most jurisdictions the surviving spouse takes the entire estate. However, the states vary considerably in their treatment of this matter. In one jurisdiction, for example, children of the decedent take the real estate, to the exclusion of a surviving spouse, with the spouse taking one-third of the personal property. If there are no children or descendants of children the spouse takes the entire estate. In another, if there are children or representatives of deceased children, the surviving wife takes a child's share but not less than one-fifth of the estate.

In general, if there are children the surviving spouse must share the estate with them. The number of children or grandchildren will determine the share which is to pass to the surviving spouse. If there are no children or grandchildren, or none have survived the decedent, the surviving spouse takes everything.

As noted earlier, in a community property state, one-half of the community property is owned by the surviving spouse. The remaining half is subject to intestacy rules if no will exists.

Descendants of the Decedent

There is little disparity in the statutes that govern the shares of an intestate's children or other lineal descendants (those in a direct line from the decedent—children and grandchildren). It is generally the case that, subject to the statutory share of a surviving spouse, children of the decedent share and share alike, with the children of a deceased child taking that child's share. This latter provision is known as a **per stirpes** distribution. For example, the decedent dies leaving two children, A and B, each of whom has two children. If both A and B survive the decedent, each will take half the estate. However, if A predeceases the decedent, the grandchildren of the decedent will take their parents' share, each of them taking one-fourth of the estate with B taking the other one-half. The estate considered here is what remains after the surviving spouse, if any, has taken his or her share. If the descendants are all of one class, that is, children or grandchildren, they will take **per capita,** each getting an equal share. Thus, if the intestate had five children all of whom survive him, each will take one-fifth of what is left after the surviving spouse's share has been provided for. Adopted children are generally treated the same as natural children; illegitimate children generally inherit only from their mother unless their father's paternity has been either acknowledged or established through legal proceedings.

The Surviving Ascendants

There is general agreement that children of the decedent and subsequent generations of lineal descendants will take to the exclusion of other blood relatives such as parents or brothers and sisters. With regard to the ascendants of the intestate (parents and grandparents), there is much less uniformity in state law. In most states, where decedents leave no descendants, their parents will take the estate, with brothers and sisters (known as collaterals) taking if the parents are not living. In other jurisdictions, brothers and sisters share with the parents. Nephews and nieces may take the share of a predeceased parent if other brothers and sisters of the decedent are still living. If not, the nephews and nieces, as sole survivors, share and share alike in a *per capita* distribution. In any event, a distribution to ascendants and collaterals is made only if there are no surviving descendants or spouse.

Other than the surviving spouse, relatives by marriage have no claim on the decedent's estate. If the intestate has died leaving no heirs or next-of-kin whatsoever—no spouse, children, grandchildren, ascendants, or collaterals—the estate will pass to the state by a process known as **escheat.** This rarely happens, but it is provided for by law.

ADMINISTRATION OF THE ESTATE

Administration of decedents' estates is accomplished by a proceeding in **probate** if they die leaving a will. The word derives from the Latin *probatio,* proof. In the law of wills it means the proof or establishment of a document as the valid last will and testament of the deceased. In most states, the court having jurisdiction is called the probate court, and the principal question to be decided by judicial determination is the validity or invalidity of the will. Once the will has been admitted to probate—that is, determined to be valid—the probate court insures efficient distribution of the estate. Funeral expenses, debts to creditors and taxes are paid first. Then homestead rights and forced shares must be taken into account. Finally, the remaining assets are distributed impartially to heirs, devisees, legatees, and others, in accordance with the testator's wishes.

The *personal representative* of the decedent (called the executor if appointed by will and the administrator if appointed by the court) administers the estate under the supervision of the court—to collect decedent's assets, to pay or settle any lawful claims against the estate, and to distribute the remainder to those who will take under the will. If there is no will, the state's law of descent and distribution will determine how the estate is to be distributed.

Probate and the administration of decedents' estates are strictly regulated by statute and can be complex procedures when the estate is substantial and the interest in property of the deceased is not clear. Many parties may be affected by the administration process, so attention to detail and compliance with the state's probate law or code are essential. A personal representative who has effectively handled the estate and wound up its affairs may petition the court and be discharged from any further responsibilities.

Avoiding Administration

Quite frequently, the formal administration of decedents' estates can be wholly or partially avoided. In fact, it is safe to say that fewer than half the deaths in this country result in administration proceedings. Obviously, if the decedent died with no assets or a very small estate, there is no need for an involved administration. Most jurisdictions permit the handling of decedents' affairs without official administration in such cases.

There are, however, still other situations in which probate or formal administration can be avoided, at least for a portion of the decedent's assets. For example, if some or all of the property was co-owned with others as a "joint tenancy" with a right of survivorship, it passes to the surviving owners and not to the estate.[5] Joint tenancy bank accounts or securities or a residence owned as a joint tenancy or as a tenancy by the entirety all pass to the surviving owner. This method of owning property is sometimes referred to as the "poor man's will." It should be noted, however, that even though the decedent's interest in such property bypasses the estate, it can still be subject to an estate or inheritance tax.

If the decedent owned one or more life insurance policies, they will not be subject to admin-

---

[5]See Chapter 41 for a discussion of concurrent ownership and the right of survivorship.

istration if a beneficiary has been named. If one has not been named or if the one named has predeceased the decedent, the proceeds pass to the estate.

CONTINUING A BUSINESS BY WILL

A testator who is the sole proprietor of a successful business or a partner in an ongoing partnership can insure that the individual business is continued or that the interest and membership in the partnership pass to a chosen successor. This can be done by will if thorough advance planning has taken place. Sole proprietors seldom are meticulous about keeping business assets separate from personal assets. Upon death it might be difficult to differentiate between them. To pass on a partnership interest, care must be exercised to insure compliance with the preexisting formal partnership agreement. Certain problems are inherent in bequeathing a business interest. Nevertheless, it is something a person in business might wish to consider. Anticipation, planning, and competent advice are essential.

TRUSTS

The trust is a versatile legal concept that is typically used to conserve family wealth from generation to generation, to provide for the support and education of children, and to minimize the tax burden on substantial estates. Trust law recognizes two types of property ownership, legal and equitable. One person can hold legal title to property while another can have the equitable title.

To establish a trust, the party intending to create a trust, called a **settlor** or *trustor,* transfers legal ownership of property to a *trustee* for the benefit of a third party, the **beneficiary.** The trustee is the legal owner of the property, called the *res* or *corpus,* but it is owned in trust to be used and managed solely for the benefit of others, who own the equitable title. A trust es-

tablished and effective during the life of the settlor is known as an ***inter vivos*** or "living" **trust.** If it is created by the settlor's will, to be effective on that person's death, it is a **testamentary trust.** Trusts are also classified as *express, implied, private,* or *charitable,* depending on the purpose they serve and how they are created.

The Express Private Trust

An express private trust is created when a settlor, with clear intent to do so, and observing certain formalities, sets up a fiduciary relationship involving a trustee, the beneficiaries, and management of the trust *res* for a lawful purpose. There is little uniformity in the statutes that govern trusts and their creation. It is a general requirement, however, that trusts be established by a writing or, if oral, subsequently proved by a writing. The writing need not be formal so long as it clearly identifies the trust property and the beneficiary and states the purpose for which the trust is created. The intent of the settlor to create a trust must be clear from the circumstances and the action taken. No particular language is required, but the settlor's instructions should be direct and unambiguous. If the purpose of the trust is to put children through college, this should be stated clearly. Language that "requests," or "hopes," or "desires" that the trustee do certain things is considered to be precatory in nature (a mere request and not an order or command) and may not be binding on the trustee. Further, words or phrases that fall short of appointing a trustee or imposing positive responsibilities should be avoided. For example, when a husband left his estate to his wife, stating in the will that it was his "request" that upon her death his wife "shall give my interest to each of my brothers," the language was viewed as purely **precatory.** The brothers had no legal right to object when the wife gave the land to her nephew instead.[6]

---

[6] *Comford v. Cantrell,* 151 S.W.2d 1076 (Tenn. 1941).

The Trust Property

The subject matter of a trust may be any property of value. Money, interests in real estate, securities, and insurance are commonly used. However, settlors must own the property at the time they create the trust. They cannot transfer in trust property they expect to acquire and own at a later date. When the property is transferred to the trustee it becomes his or hers to manage for the benefit of the beneficiaries and in accordance with the terms of the trust. If the essential elements of a valid trust are missing or if the trust fails, the property will revert to the settlor, if living, or to that person's estate, if deceased.

The Trustee

A **trustee** is, of course, essential; a trust without one cannot be effective. However, the courts will not let an otherwise valid trust fail for want of a trustee. If the named trustee dies or declines to serve or is removed for cause, the court will appoint a replacement. The court will also appoint a trustee when the settlor fails to name one in the trust. No special qualifications are necessary. Since trustees take title to property and manage it, they must be capable of owning property. Minors and incompetents can own property, but they are under a disability in regard to contractual capacity. Consequently, since their contracts are voidable, they cannot function as trustees. Settlors can appoint themselves trustees and, in fact, designate themselves as beneficiaries. The settlor cannot, however, be the sole trustee and the sole beneficiary of a single trust. This relationship would merge both legal and equitable titles to the trust property in the trustee, and he or she would hold it free of any trust.

If a corporation (an artificial person) is not prohibited by its charter from doing so, it can act as a trustee. Trust companies and banks, for example, frequently serve as trustees for both large and small trusts. They typically charge fees amounting to 1 percent of the value of the **res** per year.

Beneficiaries

The express private trust is ordinarily created for the benefit of identified, or identifiable, beneficiaries. A father can establish a trust for the care and education of his minor children—and can name them in the trust instrument. However, a settlor can also simply specify as the beneficiaries a class of persons, such as "my minor children" or "my brothers and sisters." In either case, the persons who are to benefit are readily identifiable. Trusts have also been held to be valid when established for domestic animals, household pets, and even inanimate objects. Such trusts present problems, since nonhuman and inanimate beneficiaries are incapable of holding title to property. Additionally, there will be no beneficiary with the capacity to enforce the provisions of the trust against the trustee. This is not to say that a charitable trust for animals in general or a trust for humane purposes will fail. (The charitable trust is discussed in a following section.)

The beneficiary does not have to agree to accept the benefits of the trust. It is presumed that beneficiaries accept the trust unless they make a specific rejection. Their interest in the trust can, in general, be reached by creditors, and they can sell or otherwise dispose of their interests. However, beneficiaries can transfer only the interests they hold—the equitable title. If a beneficiary holds more than a life estate, and the trust does not make other provisions, this interest can be disposed of in a will or can pass to the beneficiary's estate after death.

Managing the Trust

The administration of a trust is highly regulated by statute. Trustees must know the law of their jurisdictions. In general, they must make every effort to carry out the purpose of the trust. They must act with care and prudence and use their best judgment, and at all times they must exercise an extraordinary degree of loyalty to the beneficiary—the degree of loyalty required of those in a fiduciary position.

In carrying out the purposes of a trust, the trustees ordinarily have broad powers that are usually described in the trust instrument. In addition, they may have implied powers that are necessary to carry out their express duties. For example, trustees can have express authority to invest the trust property and pay the beneficiary the income from such investments. They can also have the implied power to incur reasonable expenses in administering the trust.

Insofar as it is possible trustees should exercise the care and skill of a "prudent person" in managing the trust. Ordinarily this will not require that they possess special skills or a high degree of expertise, or that they be financial wizards. A reasonable goal for a trustee is to exercise the diligence necessary to preserve the corpus and realize a reasonable return on income from "prudent" investments at the same time. State laws often specify the types of investments a trustee can make. In Georgia, for example, trust law authorizes investment in bonds or securities issued by the state and by the U.S. government and certain of its agencies and in certain banks or trust companies insured by the Federal Deposit Insurance Corporation. With certain exceptions, any other investment of trust funds must be under an order of the superior court or at the risk of the trustee. If the trust instrument gives the trustee wide discretion to invest in "other" securities, many jurisdictions allow this. However, the trustee can still be held accountable for a failure to exercise prudence and care. In other words, the law discourages bad investments.

The relationship between the trustee and the beneficiary is fiduciary in nature. Consequently, in managing trusts, trustees must act solely for the benefit of the beneficiaries. The fiduciary duty of loyalty requires that trustees always act in the best interests of the beneficiaries. For example, trustees cannot borrow any portion of the trust funds or sell their own property to the trust. Neither can they purchase trust property for themselves. Even though the trustee's personal dealings with the trust may prove to be advantageous to the beneficiary, the duty of loyalty is breached and the trustee can be charged with such breach. The rules in this matter may seem harsh, but they are designed to prevent a trustee from making a personal profit at the expense of the trust.

The duties of a trustee are highlighted in the following case.

Witmer v. Blair
Missouri Court of Appeals, 588 S.W.2d 222 (1979)

At his death in 1960, Henry Nussbaum's will created a trust for the education of his grandchildren. Defendant Jane Ann Blair, Nussbaum's niece, was named trustee. Nussbaum's daughter, Dorothy Janice Witmer (defendant's cousin) was given a reversionary interest in the residue of the trust should none of the grandchildren survive to inherit the estate. Marguerite Janice Witmer (Dorothy's daughter) became the only beneficiary of the trust.

Defendant Blair received the trust estate in 1961. It consisted of $1,905 in checking and savings accounts, $5,700 in certificates of deposit, and a house valued at $6,000. The house was sold in 1962, netting $4,467 to the trust estate, which amount was deposited in a trust checking account. For the next several years, the trustee kept funds in checking and savings accounts and in certificates of deposit.

As of December 31, 1975, the trust assets consisted of $2,741 checking account, $5,474 savings, and $8,200 certificates of deposit.

Marguerite was 23 years old at the time of trial. She had not attended college, but various sums of money had been expended from the trust for her benefit, including a typewriter, clothes, glasses, modeling school tuition and expenses, and a tonsillectomy, all totalling some $1,250. The trust also spent $350 for dentures for Dorothy.

Marguerite and Dorothy brought this suit against Blair for breach of trust for failure to properly invest the funds of the trust. The trial judge removed the trustee and surcharged her account for $309 in unexplained expenditures, but refused to assess actual or punitive damages for breach of trust. Plaintiffs appealed.

Welborn, Special Judge:

The trust was handled by appellant rather informally. She kept no books for the trust. The expenditures were in most cases advanced by her from her personal account and she reimbursed herself from the trust income. In 1965, the bank erroneously credited the trust account with $560 which should have gone to the trustee's personal account. The mistake was not corrected and that amount remained in the trust account. The trustee received no compensation for her services. Asked at the trial whether she had ever been a trustee before, she responded negatively, adding "And never again." She explained the large checking account balances in the trust account by the fact that college for Janice "was talked about all the way through high school. . . . [I]n my opinion, it was the sensible way to keep the money where I could get it to her without any problems at all in case she needed it quickly."

An accountant testified that had $800 been kept in the checking and savings accounts (the $800 was based upon the maximum disbursement in any year) and the balance of the trust placed in one-year certificates of deposit, $9,138 more interest would have been earned as of September 30, 1976.

A concise summary of the law applicable to the situation appears in 76 Am. Jur.2d *Trusts* §379 (1975):

> *It is a general power and duty of a trustee, implied if not expressed, at least in the case of an ordinary trust, to keep trust funds properly invested. Having uninvested funds in his hands, it is his duty to make investments of them, where at least they are not soon to be applied to the purposes and objects or turned over to the beneficiaries of the trust. Generally, he cannot permit trust funds to lie dormant or on deposit for a prolonged period, but he may keep on hand a fund sufficient to meet expenses, including contingent expenses, and he need not invest a sum too small to be prudently invested. A trustee ordinarily may not say in excuse of a failure to invest that he kept the funds on hand to pay the beneficiaries on demand.*
>
> *The trustee is under a duty to the beneficiary to use reasonable care and skill to make the trust property productive. Restatement (Second) of Trusts §181 (1959).*
>
> *A breach of trust is a violation by the trustee of any duty which as trustee he owes to the beneficiary. Restatement (Second) of Trusts §201 (1959).*

Comment b to this section states:

> Mistake of law as to existence of duties and powers. *A trustee commits a breach of trust not only where he violates a duty in bad faith, or intentionally although in good faith, or negligently, but also where he violates a duty because of a mistake as to the extent of his duties and powers. This is true not only where his mistake is in regard to a rule of law, whether a statutory or common-law rule, but also where he interprets the trust instrument as authorizing him to do acts which the court determines he is not authorized by the instrument to do. In such a case, he is not protected from liability merely because he acts in good faith, nor is he protected merely because he relies upon the advice of counsel.*

> Under the above rules, there has been a breach of trust by the trustee in this case and her good faith is not a defense to appellants' claim. In 1962, appellant Marguerite was some nine years of age. Obviously there was no prospect of the beneficiary's attending college for a number of years. However, when Marguerite became of college age [around 1971] and was considering a college education, the respondent should not be faulted for keeping readily available a sum of money which would permit the use of the trust fund for such purpose.

> Reversed, and remanded with directions [to enter judgment for plaintiffs for $2,840].

The Spendthrift Trust

Settlors may be concerned that beneficiaries may be incapable of managing their own affairs either because of inexperience and immaturity or simply because they are "spendthrifts." Settlors can therefore determine that beneficiaries will not sell, mortgage, or otherwise transfer their rights to receive principal and income and that the beneficiaries' creditors will not reach the income or principal while it is in the hands of the trustee. Such a provision no longer applies after the income or principal has been paid over to the beneficiary. Further, modern statutes limit the **spendthrift trust.** They either limit the income that is protected from creditors or they permit creditors to reach amounts in excess of what the beneficiary is considered to need.

Trust Termination

In most states, settlors can revoke a trust at any time if they have reserved that power. However, most trusts are terminated when the stated period has elapsed or when the trust purpose has been served. In a trust for the care of minor children, it logically ends when the beneficiaries have reached their majority. In a trust for the college education of the beneficiary, it will terminate when that goal has been attained. In any event, upon termination of a trust, any balance of funds remaining reverts to the settlor or is disposed of in accordance with the instructions contained in the trust.

Charitable Trusts

The purpose of a charitable trust is the general benefit of humanity. Its beneficiaries can be education, science, religion, hospitals, homes for the aged or handicapped, and a host of other charitable or public entities. Charitable trusts are much like private trusts. Furthermore, the courts of most jurisdictions will find another suitable purpose for a charitable trust when the settlor's stated purpose is impossible or difficult to achieve. The courts do so under the doctrine of *cy pres,* meaning so near or as near. The doctrine is used to prevent a charitable trust from failing for want of a beneficiary. To illustrate: a testator establishes a testamentary trust for the support and maintenance of orphans in a specified orphanage. If the specified orphanage ceased to exist before the testator's death, the court could use the *cy pres* doctrine, find that the trustor's intent was to benefit orphans generally, and apply the trust to some other orphanage in the area. The *cy pres* doctrine applies only where there is definite charitable intent, never to private trusts.

Implied Trusts

An implied trust, constructive or resulting, is created by law. While the distinction is not always clear, a **constructive trust** is usually imposed upon property by the courts to correct or rectify fraud or to prevent one party from being unjustly enriched at the expense of another. In reality, it is a fiction or remedy to which a court of equity will resort to prevent injustice. Suppose that A and B have agreed to purchase a tract of land jointly with the deed to list both of them as grantees. If, despite the agreement, A secretly buys the land alone, and the deed fails to list B as grantee, the court will impose a constructive trust on the property to the extent of the half interest B should have. This procedure assumes that B is ready and willing to pay half the purchase price. In another case, directors of corporations who take advantage of their positions to make secret profits from corporate opportunities will be constructive trustees for the corporations to the extent of the profits they make. Constructive trusts commonly arise out of the breach of a fiduciary relationship where no trust intent is present or required.

The **resulting trust** arises out of, or is created by, the conduct of the parties. It is imposed in order to carry out the apparent intentions of the parties at the time they entered into the transaction that gave rise to the trust. The most frequent use of the resulting trust occurs when one party purchases property but records the title in the name of another. For example, A wants to purchase a tract of real estate but does not want it subjected to the hazards of his busi-

ness ventures. He therefore buys the land but has the deed made out in the name of a friend, B. There is no problem if B conveys the real estate to A on demand in accordance with their understanding of the nature of the transaction. However, if B refuses to convey the land, the courts can impose a resulting trust on B for A's benefit. Some difficulty can arise if, in the situation above, A has title taken in the name of his wife or a close relative, because it could be valid to presume that A intended the land as a gift. And if A had purchased in the name of another to defraud his creditors, it is likely that the courts would refuse to impose the resulting trust, being reluctant to afford relief to a wrongdoer.

ESTATE PLANNING

"*Estate Planning* is applying the law of property, trusts, wills, future interests, insurance, and taxation to the ordering of one's affairs, keeping in mind the possibility of retirement and the certainty of death."[7] Wills and trusts are the most commonly used estate planning devices. This final section briefly explores other aspects of the estate planning process, touching first on the philosophy that has previously guided or misguided many in the disposition of their property—a disposition that usually occurs after death, with dire results for the surviving heirs. The general public equates estate planning with death; lifetime planning is more important than death planning. The aim is not merely to dispose of one's estate at death but to organize resources during life in order to provide for the present and future well-being of one's family.

The major consideration in preserving estate integrity today is the impact taxes may have if little thought is given to methods for reducing estate shrinkage. In fact, it is quite likely for the decedent's survivors to find on settling the estate that the principal heir is the government. It is, of

[7] R. J. Lynn, *An Introduction to Estate Planning* (St. Paul, Minn.: West Publishing, 1975), 1.

course, unlawful to evade taxes, but there is nothing illegal about doing everything possible to avoid paying unnecessary taxes. Various planning devices can keep unwanted heirs, in the form of estate and inheritance taxes, and the expense of probate and administration to a minimum.

Gifts

One of the keys to cutting estate taxes is to give away some assets before death. The gifts shift income to children or perhaps retired parents who may be in lower tax brackets. Giving, as an estate planning device, may be hard to accept for the donor who has spent a lifetime slowly accumulating an estate. Nevertheless, it is something to consider, keeping in mind one's personal situation. Amateur philanthropy, however, can be dangerous. Property given outright to a poor manager can be wasted away; a gift with too many strings attached can be something less than useful to the donee. Gift taxes must also be considered.

Life Insurance

Life insurance, in its various forms, can serve many purposes in estate planning. Ownership can be so arranged that the proceeds will not become part of the insured's estate to be taxed. It is a good means of providing liquid funds so that forced sales of other property to pay estate charges or debts can be avoided. In general, life insurance is not subject to probate and administration expenses and is a good way to make *inter vivos* (during lifetime) gifts to children, to grandchildren, or, if the donor is so inclined, to charity. Many kinds of policies are available— term, whole life, and endowment, for example— and there may be a place for one or more types in an estate plan. For the average wage earner life insurance is the major, perhaps the only, means of providing security for the family. Indeed, it may be all that is necessary, other than a valid will. With regard to business ventures, the members of a partnership often enter into buy and sell agreements with a view to continuing the partnership after the death of a partner. The partnership agreement sometimes provides that the estates of deceased partners will sell their interests to surviving partners and that the partners will buy such interests. Insurance is frequently used by the partnership to fund the agreement.

The Marital Deduction

For federal estate tax purposes the **marital deduction** is a useful device in estate planning involving substantial assets. It reflects the social concept that property accumulated during marriage should be treated as community property, disregarding the fact that differing amounts could have been contributed by the husband and wife. The marital deduction was designed to more nearly equate tax treatment between residents of states that have community property laws and those of states which do not. No matter what amount a decedent spouse passes to a surviving spouse, that amount will not be taxed in the decedent spouse's estate. This allows the surviving spouse to continue to have the use of up to all of the "community" assets for the rest of his or her life. The amount passing to the surviving spouse is included in his or her estate and will be taxed at the surviving spouse's death. The amount passing to the surviving spouse under the marital deduction must be determined through careful planning to maximize tax savings and meet the objectives of a particular family. Competent legal counsel and financial advice should be sought early in the estate planning process.

SUMMARY

The inevitability of death makes proper estate planning a very wise idea. A basic method of distributing property upon death is through an instrument known as a will. A testator must have testamentary capacity, that is, the mental ability to understand the property owned and the persons to whom he or she would like to give it, and not be under the undue influence of any particular person. A formal will must meet several statutory requirements, including being signed in the presence of witnesses. Modifications and even revocations must similarly follow a proper statutory pattern; for example, a will burned at the direction of a testatrix may not be effectively revoked if the destruction does not take place in her presence.

Many states allow handwritten wills, and even oral wills may be effective in limited circumstances. Should no valid will exist, a decedent's possessions will pass to relatives under state laws of descent and distribution, which impose a standardized division of the property.

Use of a trust is another method of estate planning. The settlor of a trust places property in the control of a trustee who administers the property for the advantage of beneficiaries. There are several types of trusts, and tax laws have traditionally had a significant impact on their numbers and use. The trustee owes a fiduciary duty to the beneficiaries, and may be liable in damages for wrongful or negligent administration of the assets.

Intelligent estate planning frequently uses gifts and life insurance in addition to wills and, where appropriate, trusts.

KEY TERMS

Intestate
Testator
Testatrix
Executor
Administrator
Devise
Legacy
Bequest
Testamentary capacity
Attestation clause
Codicil
Holographic will
Nuncupative will
Per stirpes
Per capita

Escheat
Probate
Settlor
Beneficiary
Inter vivos **trust**
Testamentary trust
Precatory
Trustee
Res
Spendthrift trust
Cy pres
Constructive trust
Resulting trust
Marital deduction

QUESTIONS AND PROBLEMS

1. Decedent, Matilda Manchester, prepared the following document, wholly in her own handwriting:

I, Matilda Manchester, leave and bequeath all my estate and effects, after payment of legal, funeral and certain foreign shipment expenses (as directed) to the following legatees, viz.

Then followed a statement of devises and bequests to divers persons. It ended as follows:

Whereunto I hereby set my hand this fourteenth day of January, 1914.

Decedent did not sign the document, her name appearing only in the opening clause as shown above. The paper was folded and sealed in an envelope which was endorsed by the decedent: "My Will, Ida Matilda Manchester." Should the document be admitted to probate as a valid holographic will? (*Estate of Manchester,* 163 P. 358, Cal. 1917.)

2. A father purchased 100 shares of stock for each of his two children, using money he had withdrawn from their savings accounts. The shares of stock were issued to the mother and registered in her name. When the mother died, a question arose as to ownership of the stock. What are the children's rights in this matter? (*Markert v. Bosley,* 207 N.E.2d 414, 1965.)

3. A state's law required that all formal wills must be "subscribed at the end thereof by the testator" and that attesting witnesses must "sign the instrument as a witness, at the end of the will." The will in question consisted of three pages. The first page was a printed form entitled "Last Will and Testament." Typed on the form were two testamentary provisions and the appointment of executors. On the same form, in the spaces provided, appeared the signature of the testatrix and an attestation clause signed by three witnesses. There were two additional typewritten pages containing testamentary clauses, each of the two pages being signed at the bottom by only the testatrix. The attesting witnesses had not signed the additional pages, their signatures appearing only on the first, "form" page. Does the document qualify as a will? (*Estate of Howell,* 324 P.2d 578, Cal. 1958.)

4. A testator wanted to revoke his will by having his wife burn it. In his presence she burned an envelope which she fraudulently represented to him to contain his will. (*Brazil v. Silva,* 185 P. 174, 1919.)
   a. If she was the sole legatee under his will, is she likely to take his estate?
   b. If the testator had two children, are they, in effect, disinherited?

5. A widow died intestate. There had been four children; but one, who had two children, predeceased his mother. How will the estate be divided among the widow's descendants?

6. A trustee sold to herself, at an advantageous price, property belonging to the trust. She then resold the property and deposited a substantial profit in her personal bank account. Discuss the propriety of this transaction.

7. The will of Lauren M. Townsend, after a statement of several specific bequests, provided: ". . . that the remainder be made into a fund, the interest of which shall be used to help defray the expense of educating some girl or boy in music or art. I appoint Paul Gill to have charge of selecting the recipient of this last bequest." Is the quoted language sufficiently specific to create a charitable trust? (*Estate of Huebner,* 15 P.2d 758, Cal. 1932.)

8. When the testatrix died, her will consisted of four pages—dated, signed by her, and properly attested by two witnesses. However, a fifth page was attached on which was typed: "CODICIL— Having forgotten my nephew James, I hereby give and bequeath to him the sum of $1,000." It was signed by the testatrix but had no attestation clause; nor had any witnesses signed it. What is the effect of this fifth page?

9. A testator provided in his will: "To my brother, John, I leave my house in Jackson County and the sum of $5,000. I do this trusting that he will provide a place for our older sister, Mary, for so long as she lives; and I request that he use this legacy to improve her lot in life." Upon the testator's death, Mary claimed that the house and money were conveyed to John in trust and must be used for her benefit. Do you agree? Explain.

10. A man died intestate, leaving a widow and the following property:
   a. His residence, which he held as a joint tenant with his surviving spouse.
   b. A thousand-acre farm of which he was the sole owner.
   c. A savings account of $5,000, which was jointly owned by him and his wife.
   d. Two automobiles—he was the sole owner of one and joint owner, with his wife, of the other.
   e. A life insurance policy in the amount of $10,000 on which his son was listed as the beneficiary and on which he had reserved the right to change the beneficiary.

Which of the above assets are subject to administration as a part of his estate? Explain.

Chapter 45

INSURANCE AND RISK MANAGEMENT

NATURE AND FUNCTIONS OF INSURANCE

Almost every type of endeavor or venture, individual or business, involves risk or uncertainty concerning financial loss. Insurance is a means of transferring or shifting risk from the individual or business to a group whose members agree to share losses on some equitable basis. Suppose that a manufacturer produces and markets a line of products the use of which poses considerable risk, such as bicycles, swings and slides, and power lawnmowers. An injury or death caused by such products may result in a lawsuit and a substantial damages award to the injured user or, if the product has caused death, to his or her surviving family. Such awards may be in the millions of dollars, causing extreme economic hardship to an individual manufacturer. The design, manufacture, and marketing of a potentially dangerous product may pose a risk too great for a single business to assume.

Manufacturers can collectively share products liability losses by transferring the risk to a professional risk bearer, the insurer, through the purchase of an insurance contract. The group of manufacturers share the cost of losses as they occur so that no one of them will be forced to bear the entire cost of a substantial judgment awarded as the result of a products liability lawsuit.

The exact cost of insurance is established statistically based upon the loss costs and expenses of insurers writing the coverage involved. The premium paid by the insured is an expense of doing business.

This chapter examines briefly the general types of insurance, placing major emphasis on the coverages that are relevant for business: *life, health, property,* and *liability.* In addition, the concept of risk management is presented.

The Insurance Contract

An insurance contract is often called a *policy.* The person or company purchasing insurance coverage is called the *insured,* or the *policy-holder.* The company issuing the insurance policy is called the *insurer,* or the *insurance company.* To be an enforceable agreement, a contract of insurance must contain the essential elements of contract: *offer and acceptance, consideration, legal purpose, competent parties,* and *legal form.*

Offer and Acceptance: The offer is customarily made by the prospective insured when he or she makes application for the desired coverage. The acceptance occurs when the agent or broker issues a **binder** (a temporary contract) or when the policy itself is issued by the insurance company. A binder can be either written or oral and is used to bind the company immediately prior to the receipt of the application and issuance of the policy.

Consideration: The considerations exchanged in an insurance transaction are the payment of the **premium** by the insured or other responsible party (such as the parents of an insured minor), and the promise of the insurer to pay if the covered contingency occurs.

Legal Purpose: A contract made for an illegal purpose, or containing an illegal provision, is usually void and cannot be enforced by either party. This general principle is equally applicable to contracts of insurance. If the insurance company violates state law by failing to include a required provision that was intended to protect policyholders, however, the policyholder can still enforce the contract under a well-established exception to the illegality doctrine. The most important application of the requirement of a legal purpose is the *insurable interest* rule, which is discussed separately in the following section.

Insurable Interest: A fundamental requirement of a legally valid insurance contract is that an insured must have an **insurable interest** in the subject matter of the insurance, that is, a benefit to be derived from the continued existence of the person or property insured. Without the existence of an insurable interest, the policyholder is simply wagering on the occurrence of death, in the case of life insurance, or property damage, in the case of property insurance. Because gambling contracts are void, an insurance policy issued to an insured not having an insurable interest is unenforceable. In addition to furthering the general prohibition against gambling agreements, the requirement of insurable interest also helps protect against murder or property destruction for the purpose of collecting insurance proceeds. The rationale for the insurable interest requirement in the life insurance context was expressed as follows by the court in *New England Mutual Life Insurance Co. v. Null*, 605 F.2d 421 (1979):

> It is contrary to sound public policy to permit one, having no interest in the continuance of the life of another, to speculate upon that other's life—and it should be added that to permit the same might tend to incite the crime of murder—and the rule is enforced, and the defense permitted, not in the interest of the defendant insurer, but solely for the sake of the law, and in the interest of a sound public policy.

The absence of an insurable interest causes the contract to be void, and no benefits are payable under the policy. In such a case the insured is entitled to a refund of premiums paid, however. Other legal consequences can also result from the issuance of a policy to someone without an insurable interest. For instance, if an insurance company issues a life insurance policy to someone who does not have an insurable interest, and the insured then murders the subject of the life insurance, the insurance company can be held liable for negligence to the estate of the murder victim. Similarly, if an insurance company issues a policy covering property to someone not having an insurable interest, and the insured then intentionally destroys the property, the insurance company can be held liable for negligence to the owner of the property.

Insurable Interest Distinguished from Other Concepts: It is important to distinguish the insurable interest requirement from other related concepts. For example, life insurance policies normally contain a provision expressly excluding liability if the person whose life is insured commits suicide. This provision applies even if the person taking out the policy had an insurable interest. Also, courts do not permit a beneficiary named in a life insurance policy to recover under the policy if the beneficiary murders the person whose life is insured. Again, this rule applies even if the person taking out the insurance had an insurable interest in the life being insured, and the policy itself is valid. In such a case, since the policy is valid, the proceeds are payable either to a secondary beneficiary specified in the policy or to the estate of the deceased if there is no secondary beneficiary. Similarly, a person who intentionally damages or destroys property is not permitted to collect under an insurance policy covering the property, even if the insured had an insurable interest.

Insurable Interest in Life: A person obviously may obtain a policy of insurance on his or her own life. If one person takes out life insurance on someone else's life, however, it is required that the policyholder have an insurable interest in the life of the person who is the subject of the insurance. In the case of life insurance, the insurable interest must exist at the time the policy is issued, but does not have to exist at the time of death. Thus, if a wife takes out life insurance on her husband, there is an insurable interest at the time the policy is issued; the policy remains valid even after divorce unless a specific provision calls for termination upon divorce.

As a general rule, an insurable interest exists when the policyholder and the person whose life is being insured have a relationship such that the policyholder will benefit from the continuance of the person's life or suffer financial loss from the person's death. State laws usually specify the types of relationships that create insurable interests, and these laws vary somewhat. In all states, husband and wife have an insurable interest in each other's life. In some states, other relationships within the immediate family, such as parent-child or brother-sister, also create an insurable interest. The relationship between a nephew or niece and an aunt or uncle usually does not create an insurable interest. Except for husband and wife, relationships through marriage do not create insurable interests. For example, a person does not have an insurable interest in the life of his or her mother-in-law.

An employer has an insurable interest in the life of a *key employee,* that is, an employee whose death would cause substantial hardship to the employer. An employee with significant managerial or supervisory responsibilities, or especially valuable knowledge or skills would, for example, be a key employee. In addition, an unsecured creditor usually has an insurable interest in the life of the debtor up to the amount of the indebtedness. The following case presents an illustration and discussion of the insurable interest requirement in life insurance.

New York Life Insurance Co. v. Baum
U.S. Court of Appeals for the Fifth Circuit, 700 F.2d 928 (1983)

Baum and Cook made preliminary plans for the formation of a media advertising business in Louisiana. It was agreed that Baum would provide capital and Cook would furnish the experience necessary to launch the venture. Their understanding was that a corporation would be formed to carry on the business. Over the next several months, Baum lent Cook $16,500 for getting the business started. Shortly after Baum and Cook had made their agreement, however, Cook made a separate agreement with Cutler to form a partnership in Texas under the name of Media Sales. The Cook-Cutler partnership, also engaged in the media advertising business, was unknown to Baum.

After Baum had lent money to Cook, Baum decided to obtain "key man" life insurance coverage on Cook to protect Baum's investment, and a policy was purchased from New York Life Insurance Company. At first, Baum listed himself as the beneficiary; upon the insistence of the insurance company, however, the named beneficiary was changed to Media Sales & Marketing, Inc., the planned name of the corporation Baum and Cook were to form. The name of the prospective corporation was used because Baum was an agent of New York Life, and the insurance company would not permit one of its agents to be named as a beneficiary except in a policy issued on the life of one of the agent's family members. A few days after Baum obtained this policy, Cook and Cutler incorporated their business in Texas as Media Sales Corporation, and totally excluded Baum. Baum paid premiums on the life insurance policy until Cook died one year later. After Cook's death, Baum filed suit in federal district court asserting a claim to the life insurance proceeds because his money had provided the primary capital for the business and he was actually the intended

beneficiary. Media Sales Corporation also asserted a claim because it claimed to be the same corporation as the one that was expressly named as beneficiary. (Presumably, Cutler was behind the assertion of a claim by Media Sales.)

The trial court held that neither Baum nor Media Sales Corporation had an insurable interest in Cook's life, and that the policy was completely void. Both parties appealed to the U.S. Court of Appeals.

Thornberry, Circuit Judge:

[The court initially concluded that New York law applied to the case because the life insurance contract was formed in New York and most of its performance was to take place in that state.] Section 146 [of the New York Insurance Law] defines an insurable interest in the case of persons not related by blood or by law as follows:

[I]n the case of other persons, a lawful and substantial economic interest in having the life, health or bodily safety of the person insured continue, as distinguished from an interest which would arise only by, or would be enhanced in value by, the death, disablement or injury, as the case may be, of the person insured.

[In one New York case, the court said:] "It may be generally stated that the reasoning behind legislation requiring an insurable interest . . . is in furtherance of the public policy against wagering or gambling on human lives. This policy has been adopted in most jurisdictions to prevent speculation in human life, since the incentive to shorten the life of the insured would be increased." While discussing the subject of insurable interest between creditors and their debtors another New York court held as follows: "It is now well settled that the bank had an insurable interest in the life of [the deceased debtor] at the time it made the loan to him and under such circumstances the bank had the right to enter into any agreement with the insurance company so that it would receive a sum of money as indemnity in case its interest in the subject matter should suffer diminution of value by reason of certain specified causes or contingencies. The bank with such an insurable interest in the borrower clearly had the right to secure itself against the death of the borrower." . . .

Applying these principles to our case, we hold that . . . Baum had an insurable interest in the life of Cook, his debtor, as a matter of law. A creditor-debtor relationship existed between Baum and Cook at the time the policy was executed and Baum loaned the majority of the funds to Cook after the policy went into effect. The facts fail to show that the policy was taken as a wager. As creditor, Baum had a reasonable ground to expect some benefit or advantage from the continuation of Cook's life, namely, repayment of the loan. Furthermore, there are compelling arguments against allowing the insurer to escape its obligation.

It is surely not a sound policy to permit insurers to contract to insure the lives of persons, receive premiums therefor as long as the . . . beneficiary . . . will continue to pay, and then, when the time comes for the insurers to pay what they agreed to pay, allow them to escape their contract on the ground of want of insurable interest in the life insured, unless it clearly appears that such contracts are pernicious and dangerous to society.

Regarding Media Texas, the situation is less clear. While it is true that, as a general rule, a corporation has an insurable interest in the life of its key employees, the district court found that "the record clearly demonstrates that Media Sales (Texas) was nothing more than a nonfunctioning corporate shell." Indeed, no stock was apparently ever issued by Media Texas. The district court also found that "the creation of a Texas corporation was never contemplated by the parties, as evidenced by the representations made by Baum in the application for the life insurance policy." . . .

For the reasons stated above, the judgment of the district court is reversed. [Baum did have an insurable interest in the life of Cook. In a rehearing of this case, the court of appeals ordered that the case be remanded to the district court for resolution of several remaining factual issues, including the question whether it was possible under the facts for Media Sales Corp. also to have an insurable interest. The appeals court's directions to the lower court made it highly likely that Baum would ultimately receive all of the insurance proceeds.]

Insurable Interest in Property: The underlying rationale for the requirement of an insurable interest in property is essentially the same as the requirement of an insurable interest in life: one should be permitted to obtain insurance coverage on property only if that person would suffer a financial loss as a result of damage to or destruction of the property. While an insurable interest in life must be present when the policy is issued, the rule is different for property. An insurable interest in property must exist at the time the loss occurs, and is not required to have existed when the policy was issued. An owner of property obviously has an insurable interest in it, but others also may have such an interest. Thus, the mortgagee has an insurable interest in the mortgaged real estate, and a secured creditor has an insurable interest in the specific item of personal property (such as an automobile) that serves as collateral to secure the debt. In cases in which a nonowner has an insurable interest in property, the owner continues to have such an interest as well. Both parties may obtain insurance coverage on the value of their respective interests in the property.

The next case provides a further example of one of the many types of situations in which a person may have an insurable interest in property.

Motorists Mutual Insurance Co. v. Richmond
Court of Appeals of Kentucky, 676 S.W.2d 478 (1984)

After thirteen years of marriage and two children, Linda Richmond and Eddie Durham were divorced in 1977. The divorce decree called for their house to be sold within six months, but no sale ever took place. Instead, the couple attempted to reconcile their differences

until March 1981 when Richmond and the two children moved out. During this four-year period between the divorce and Richmond's departure, the couple made extensive improvements in the house, including interior remodeling and the addition of exterior walkways and a porch. Each of them contributed equally to the labor and expense of the improvements. In February 1980, while they were still living together, Richmond executed a deed transferring her interest in the house and lot to Durham. In March 1980, Durham executed a second mortgage on the property to secure a loan of almost $5,000. In June 1981, three months after Richmond moved out, Durham died of chronic heart disease.

Richmond immediately moved back into the house with her two children and made it their residence. She assumed liability on the second mortgage and made the payments. In January 1982 Richmond took out a fire insurance policy on the home and its contents from Motorists Mutual Insurance Co. When making application for the insurance policy, Richmond was asked by the insurance company's agent whether there was a lien on the property. She replied that there was, and stated that the lien was in her name. Although this statement was technically in error because the mortgage was still in Durham's name, Richmond's reply was based on a good faith belief that her assumption of liability on the mortgage meant that the lien was in her name. Nothing was said about legal title to the property, but the agent checked a box on the application form indicating that Richmond was the sole owner of the property. In actuality, her two children owned legal title as the only heirs of Durham, who died without a will.

In October 1982 the property was totally destroyed by fire. In response to Richmond's claim under the policy, the insurance company paid her $11,740 for the value of the contents, but refused to pay anything for the value of the house on the grounds that she had no insurable interest in the real estate. Richmond, her two children, and her mortgagee, Farmers National Bank (which was entitled to a portion of the insurance proceeds to satisfy the mortgage), sued the insurance company to recover the policy amount for the house. The trial court held that she had an insurable interest, and awarded her and the mortgagee a judgment of $29,000. The insurance company appealed.

Clayton, Judge:

Seeking to avoid payment under the contract, Motorists would now cast Richmond as nothing more than a trespassing squatter who "surreptitiously" returned to the residence and thereafter fraudulently represented her true lack of ownership interest. . . . We cannot accept these characterizations.

Linda Richmond, both before and after the death of her late former husband, made substantial monetary contribution to the maintenance and improvement of the destroyed residence. As natural guardian for her minor children, and later as administratrix of the Durham estate, she was obligated to provide for the care and custody of their offspring, including the duty to protect their home, of which the children became sole owners in fee simple by statute of descent upon the death of their father. Thus, when Richmond returned to the property following Durham's death she was not a surreptitious trespasser. Her offspring and she as their guardian were fully entitled to use and dominion over the premises. While not possessed of title, Richmond certainly possessed an insurable interest in the residence; first, by her status as natural guardian for the protection of her minor children's interest; and second, by her extensive investment in the residence. . . . In general, it is well-settled law that a person has an insurable interest in the subject matter insured where he has such a relation or connection with, or concern in, such subject matter that he will derive pecuniary benefit or advantage from its preservation, or will suffer pecuniary loss or damage from its destruction, termination, or injury by the happening of the event insured against.

Nor does the present record contain any suggestion of fraud or unwitting assumption of risk by Motorists. Richmond made no claim of ownership to the residence. Her only direct action with regard to the [application] was to place her signature upon it. Motorists' own agent was responsible for completing the remainder of the document including the portion indicating Richmond's ownership. Had he so chosen, he could have easily verified his assumptions concerning Richmond's ownership simply by calling Farmers State Bank. It is a well settled principle of law in this state that an insurer as principal is bound by the acts of his agent within the scope of his apparent authority. . . .

Motorists is further obligated to make payment by the definition provisions of its policy. Under that policy "insured" is defined as:

You and the following representatives of your household:
a. your relatives; b. any other person under the age of 21 who is in the care of any person named above.

At the time of issuance of the policy, Linda's children, Melody and James, were each, by statute of descent, fee simple owners of an indivisible one-half interest in the residence. As minors under the age of 15, neither child was legally capable of contracting for insurance in his or her own behalf. Therefore, absent Linda's efforts in securing insurance, neither Melody nor James could have directly protected his or her ownership interest in the home. By defining the terms of its policy so as to include the ownership interest of the children, Motorists undertook exactly the risk it bargained for. . . . The contract speaks for itself.

[After] having determined that both Richmond and her children possessed an insurable interest in the residence throughout the life of the policy, [the court then concluded that the mortgagee also had such an interest because it would benefit by the continuing existence of the home as security for its loan.]

The judgment [against the insurance company] is affirmed.

Competent Parties: As is the case with other contracts, the parties to an insurance contract must have contractual capacity. Certain persons (minors and mental incompetents, for example) lack capacity or are under a disability. Minors, defined by statute in most states as anyone under the age of eighteen, may disaffirm a contract. In the absence of a statute regulating insurance for minors, a minor could purchase insurance, pay premiums until nearly eighteen, and then disaffirm and demand the refund of premiums paid. However, most states have conferred capacity on minors to contract for annuities, endowments, life insurance, accident and health insurance, and other forms of insurance in which the minor has an insurable interest. The minor may cancel the policy, as may an adult, but he or she may not demand return of the premiums paid. The age at which a minor may contract for insurance varies from state to state.

Legal Form: The form and content of insurance contracts are highly regulated by state law. Certain standard provisions relating to the specific type of insurance must be included in the policy and are spelled out in detail by statute in most states. Consequently, the proper form of insurance contracts is prescribed by law.

An agreement as complex as an insurance policy obviously should be in writing. Some states require that all insurance contracts be in writing, but several states merely prohibit oral agreements for certain types of insurance. Even in those states that do not prohibit all oral insurance contracts, it is exceedingly rare for an insurance agreement to be oral because of its inherently complex nature.

Other Aspects of the Insurance Contract

Unilateral in Nature: Most commercial contracts are *bilateral:* each of the parties makes a legally enforceable promise and each is therefore obligated to perform as promised. An insurance contract, however, is *unilateral.* Only one party, the insurer, makes an enforceable promise.

After the insurance is in effect, the insured having paid the first premium, he or she is under no obligation to pay further premiums or to comply with other policy provisions. Payment must be made to continue the coverage, but only the insurer is legally required to perform.

Contract of Adhesion: Even though state laws prescribe the form and provisions of insurance contracts, the insurer prepares the contract, and it can be accepted or rejected by the other party, the insured. There is little negotiation as to terms; if the insured wishes to accept the contract it must be taken "as is" (this type of contract is called a **contract of adhesion**). Because the insurer prepares the contract, questions of construction or interpretation are construed most strictly against the insurer. Ambiguity in the wording of the contract is interpreted by the courts in favor of the insured.

Aleatory in Nature: The ultimate discharge of the parties to an insurance contract is governed by chance. The profit and loss involved usually depend upon an uncertain event or contingency; the values exchanged by the contracting parties will quite likely be unequal. For example, a motorist may pay automobile insurance premiums for years and never have reason to make a claim against the insurance company. In this case, the insured pays a substantial sum and the insurer pays nothing to that particular insured.

TYPES OF INSURANCE

Life Insurance

A contract of life insurance typically provides that the insurer will pay a specified sum of money—the face amount of the policy—upon the death of the insured if the premiums have been paid in accordance with the terms of the contract. There are basically three types of life insurance policies, *whole life, term insurance,* and *endowment insurance.*

Whole Life: The key characteristic of **whole life insurance** is that it provides protection for the whole of life (or to age 100, the end of the mortality table on which premiums are based). There are two primary types of whole life coverage: ordinary life and limited payment whole life. Under ordinary life contracts, premiums are payable for the entire lifetime of the insured or until he or she reaches age 100. Under limited payment whole life policies (examples are twenty payment, thirty payment, or paid-up at age sixty-five), premiums are payable until death or until the end of the predetermined premium paying period, whichever occurs first. Under both ordinary and limited payment whole life policies, payment of the specified sum of money is made upon the death of the insured to a named beneficiary or to the estate of the deceased. Payment to a named beneficiary may be a lump sum or periodic payments, as elected by the insured or the beneficiary. After the policy has been in effect for a specified number of years, the insured can discontinue paying premiums and receive a paid-up policy to the extent that his or her premiums have purchased such coverage.

During the life of the policy the insured has a right to borrow from the insurer an amount approximately equal to the cash surrender value of the policy. Should the insured die with all or part of such a loan unpaid the unpaid loan or balance would be deducted from the proceeds paid to the beneficiary.

Term Insurance: **Term insurance** is written for a specified period of time. It is relatively inexpensive but provides protection for death occurring only during the period of the policy. Term insurance can be written for any number of years. The insured may, in most cases, renew the policy for additional terms at increased premiums as age increases, and may have the option to convert the policy to some form of permanent insurance without a medical examination.

Because it is temporary protection, term insurance does not build cash values, nor may the insured borrow on the policy. Because of its low cost for younger ages, it is useful for those who cannot afford the higher cost of whole life. This might be the case for a young person with a family who wants to provide protection but is not yet in a position to purchase insurance as part of his or her estate plan.

Endowment Insurance: **Endowment insurance** provides that the insurer will pay the policy face amount to the insured when he or she reaches the end of the policy period (such as at age 65) or, should the insured die before the end of the period, to a designated beneficiary. Since maturity of the policy is ordinarily prior to the death of the insured, the cost of the endowment policy is substantially higher than that of whole life or term insurance.

State Regulation of Life Insurance: The states exercise extensive regulatory control over the insurance industry within their jurisdictions. State insurance laws require that certain provisions be included in each policy delivered or issued within the state. Examples of typical required provisions include:

1. *Grace period:* A period of not less than 30 days within which the payment of any premium after the first may be made without the policy lapsing.

2. *Incontestability:* After a policy has been in force for a period of two years from its date of issue, the policy shall become incontestable during the lifetime of the insured.

3. *Misstatement of age:* Where the age of the insured has been misstated, the benefit accruing under the policy shall be that which the premium would have purchased at the correct age.

Health Insurance

Many types of health insurance are available both to individuals and to employees as a group under a company-sponsored health plan. Health insurance can be divided into two basic types, *income replacement* and *medical expense* insurance.

Income Replacement: Income replacement policies provide for the payment of a stated periodic sum in the event the insured becomes disabled through sickness or injury and is unable to work. Eligibility for benefits is usually based on the fact that the insured is so sick or severely injured that he or she is unable to pursue the usual line of work.

The benefit period purchased under income replacement policies can be either short-term or long-term. A period longer than two years is considered long-term; the majority of policies are short-term.

Medical Expense: Medical expense insurance pays the cost of medical care required as a result of injury or sickness. Included are payments for physicians, hospital, nursing, and medicines and medical supplies. The insured is reimbursed for medical expenses within certain limits; the payments may be made either to the facility providing the medical service or to the insured.

The Health Maintenance Organization: A **health maintenance organization (HMO)** is a formal organization of physicians who provide medical care to their subscriber patients on an as-needed basis. HMOs provide benefits that are in many respects broader than those offered by other plans. For example, the typical HMO stresses prevention of sickness by offering preventive medical care. The Health Maintenance Organization Act of 1973 requires employers of more than twenty-five employees to offer enrollment in an HMO as an option to existing health care plans.

An HMO subscriber pays a fixed fee in exchange for all the medical care that may be required. In addition to the fee, the subscriber may pay a nominal fee, $1 or $2, for each visit to the facility, but the charge is the same regardless of the nature of the service or treatment rendered by the physician.

Social Insurance

While the normal expectation is that individuals and families should be able to care for themselves, economic security is beyond the reach of part of society. The concept of **social insurance** involves the notion that a certain segment of society is unable to fully care for itself and is thus subject to the risk of existing without an adequate standard of living. Social insurance, as defined by the Committee on Social Insurance of the Commission on Insurance Terminology of the American Risk and Insurance Association, is a device for pooling risks by transfer to a governmental service organization.

Various governmental programs have been enacted into law to assure each member of society at least a minimum standard of living. These include far-reaching social insurance programs.

Old-Age, Survivors', Disability, and Health Insurance: Known as Social Security, old-age, survivors', disability, and health insurance is an extremely comprehensive social insurance program that affects almost every individual in the country. As enacted in 1935 and extensively amended over the years, it provides a measure of security for eligible workers and their families against the risks associated with old age and the loss of ability to provide for themselves (although the benefits were never intended to provide full financial support). Its chief features are *old-age benefits, survivors' benefits, disability benefits,* and *medicare benefits.* Many claims may be controversial with regard to eligibility. An administrative hearing is frequently required to resolve a disputed claim for benefits. To illustrate the scope of the problem, there are approximately 1,100 administrative law judges assigned to federal agencies to conduct administrative hearings. Of that number, about 700 are assigned to the Social Security Administration alone.

Unemployment Compensation: Unemployment compensation is intended for workers who have been laid off and are unable to find other work through no fault of their own. Individual states operate the system, with each state levying a tax on employers to finance benefits. Each state has its own rules for determining eligibility. Benefit amounts are usually based on a fraction of average wages during a recent period, subject to minimum and maximum amounts, and are paid for a prescribed period. (When the general level of unemployment reaches a certain level, benefits may be paid for an additional period, usually 13 weeks. One-half of the benefits paid during this extended period are financed by the federal government.)

State Workers' Compensation Laws: As discussed in Chapter 49, Employment Law, the basic thrust of **workers' compensation** legislation is to provide medical care expense, income replacement, and rehabilitation benefits to employees suffering from work-related injury or occupational disease. The costs of these benefits, or the premiums for insurance to pay them, are borne by the employer and reflected in the cost of producing the employer's product or service. Although most employment is covered by workers' compensation, many states exclude farm laborers, domestic servants, and casual employees because their work is often of a sporadic or multi-employer nature. Workers' compensation is a no-fault system. If the agency (or the court) decides that the injury was job-related, compensation is awarded regardless of whether the employer, employee, or anyone else was at fault in causing the injury.

Property Insurance

Property insurance protects against financial loss because of damage to or destruction of the covered property. It is available in many forms and can be written to protect against a variety of perils. The basic kinds of coverage and a few of the important principles that apply are examined here.

Standard Fire Policy: Fire is the most common type of peril to which buildings and other structures are susceptible. Consequently, insurance coverage to protect against the risk of fire loss is the oldest, and still the most important, form of property insurance. A standard fire insurance policy was adopted by the state of New York in 1943 and has served as a model for standard fire policies in most states. Even though the standard fire policies in most states still retain the basic provisions of the New York Standard Fire Policy, much of the language has been changed by many states in recent years in an effort to make policies more easily understood by policyholders.

Homeowner's Policy: The **homeowner's policy** is a package agreement covering (1) damage to the dwelling, (2) damage to or loss of the policyholder's personal property located either on or off the premises, and (3) legal liability of the homeowner for injury to others. Each type of coverage is subject to dollar limitations specified in the policy. Because of its broad coverage, the homeowner's policy has become very popular in modern times.

The typical homeowner's policy covers damage to the home, its contents, and many other items of personal property caused by fire, lightning, wind, hail, vandalism, and other specified perils. Coverage against theft of items of personal property is also frequently included. The coverage for personal property normally excludes motor vehicles, farm equipment, and airplanes, as well as boats while they are in the water. Such items are the subject of separate insurance policies. In addition, coverage is often excluded or limited for several other types of personal property, such as money, securities, and jewelry unless additional coverage is obtained in return for a higher premium.

One of the most attractive features of the typical homeowner's policy is its provision of coverage on a **replacement cost basis.** In other words, subject to the policy's dollar limits, and sometimes subject to other restrictions, the insurance company pays the amount required to repair or replace the structure without deduction for depreciation or obsolescence.

Interpretation of Fire Coverage: Most property insurance policies cover fire losses only from so-called *hostile* fires, and do not cover losses from *friendly* fires. If a fire is characterized as hostile, covered losses include those from fire and smoke as well as from water or other efforts to save the property. A hostile fire is one that begins in a place that was not intended or escapes from its originally intended place; a friendly fire is one that is confined to the place where it should be. The lighted burner of a gas cooking stove is a friendly fire, as is the fire in a fireplace or a backyard incinerator, because these fires are confined to their intended places. Consequently, damage caused by smoke from the fireplace or incinerator is normally not covered by insurance. Similarly, the loss is not covered when someone accidently throws a ring or other valuable property into the incinerator. On the other hand, a fire started by an electrical short in the attic is a hostile fire, as is a fire started when furniture or clothing catches fire from a fireplace or heater. In addition, if the flame from a cooking stove flares up because of spilled or overheated grease and spreads to the kitchen window curtains, the fire has become a hostile one within the meaning of fire insurance coverage.

Coinsurance Requirement: Today, most property insurance policies include a **coinsurance clause.** The basic purpose of such a clause is to encourage policyholders to insure their property for an amount that is at least close to its full value. If a policyholder does not insure the property for an amount that is sufficiently close to its full replacement cost, the policyholder must bear a proportionate part of any loss from fire or other covered peril. The coinsurance requirement applies only to partial losses. Coinsurance clauses do not apply to cases of total destruction.

In most policies, the coinsurance clause requires that the amount of the coverage be at least 80 percent of the property's replacement cost. If the coverage amount is less than 80 percent, the insurance company pays a fraction of the replacement cost, the fraction derived by dividing the policy amount by the amount that would have satisfied the coinsurance clause. Suppose, for example, that Otto owns a home with a current replacement cost of $100,000. To satisfy the usual coinsurance clause, he must obtain and pay for insurance in an amount of at least $80,000. If he insures the home for $80,000 or more and it is damaged by fire or other covered peril, he will receive the replacement cost for the damage. Thus, if it will cost $15,000 to repair the damage, he will receive the full $15,000 (minus, of course, any deductible the parties have agreed upon and specified in the policy). If he insures the home for only $60,000, however, the insurance company will pay only $12,000 (again, minus any agreed deductible). This amount is calculated as follows: Otto's policy amount ($60,000) divided by the amount of coverage that would have been necessary to satisfy the coinsurance clause ($80,000) is 3/4. The $15,000 replacement cost multiplied by this fraction equals $12,000.

In times of inflation, it is particularly important for the policyholder to review the amount of coverage periodically and increase it as necessary to continue meeting the coinsurance requirement. Today, many insurance companies offer an *inflation guard endorsement,* an optional provision in homeowner's policies that periodically increases the coverage automatically by predetermined amounts.

Prorata Coverage: An owner who obtains two or more policies from different insurance companies covering the same property could potentially profit by receiving more than the replacement cost. Today, most property insurance policies (as well as other types of insurance, such as health insurance) contain a **prorata clause,** which specifies that each insurance company is responsible only for a proportionate share of the loss. Thus, if Ruth obtains two homeowner's policies on her house, one from X insurance company for $100,000 and the other from Y insurance company for $50,000, the prorata clauses in the policies would result in X being responsible for 2/3 and Y for 1/3 of any covered loss.

Liability Insurance

Liability insurance provides protection against the risk of a legal action for damages that may be brought against the policyholder. Liability insurance may be written to meet a variety of needs.

Each year individuals and businesses are exposed to legal liability resulting in the payment of millions of dollars to compensate plaintiffs for injury to their persons or property. A homeowner may fail to remove ice from a sidewalk, and a caller falls and is injured. A bottle of cooking oil has been broken on the floor of a supermarket, and a patron is injured. A manufacturer produces and markets a consumer product that proves to be dangerously defective, and a user is injured. Lawsuits by injured parties against the property owner or manufacturer are being filed with increasing frequency as our society has become more consumer-protection oriented. And the judgments awarded by juries, both of actual damages, to compensate the plaintiff, and punitive damages, to punish the defendant, are sometimes staggering. The possibility that accidents will occur on residential or commercial premises presents another form of risk that can be transferred to an insurer. General liability exposure can be classified as *personal liability, business liability,* and *professional liability.*

Personal Liability—Coverage by the Homeowner's Policy: Personal liability coverage is an integral part of the homeowner's policy. In essence, it protects the policyholder against the financial risk of injuries or property damage to others. This coverage usually applies to damage caused to others by the unsafe condition of the policyholder's premises, or by the negligence of the policyholder. As in other types of insurance, the coverage limits are specified in the policy. A typical homeowner's policy might limit personal liability coverage, for example, to $100,000, with higher limits available upon payment of a higher premium.

Liability coverage in the homeowner's policy normally applies only to personal activities, not to business or professional activities. In addition, liability resulting from the operation of a motor vehicle or airplane usually is not covered. The risks associated with these excluded activities are the subject of separate insurance policies.

The basic thrust of liability coverage is to insure against the policyholder's *negligence* or carelessness. Consequently, most liability insurance provisions do not cover damage claims against the policyholder resulting from his or her *intentionally wrongful acts.* As is true of most other issues, the question whether someone has been harmed by the policyholder's negligence, or by his or her intentional conduct, is not always easy to resolve. In the following case, these principles are applied to a situation in which harm certainly was intended, but the policyholder made a mistake in his choice of a target.

Peters v. Trousclair
District Court of Appeal of Florida, 431 So.2d 296 (1983)

James Trousclair was a riverboat pilot whose occupation required extended absences from his wife and home. During one of those absences, Peters, Mrs. Trousclair's cousin, had been residing at Trousclair's home for several days. The record reflects that although Trousclair had extended the invitation, he had only met Peters on two prior occasions, was not familiar with him, and was unaware that Peters had begun residing in the home. In the meantime, one Humphreys, not at Trousclair's invitation, was also residing at the home, having become amorously involved with Mrs. Trousclair. On the occasion that led to this lawsuit, Trousclair returned home without forewarning to find his wife and the two men lounging in the living room in the early morning hours. In a fit of jealous rage, Trousclair burst into the room, grabbed Peters, whom he did not recognize, and repeatedly stabbed him, causing serious injury. He then pursued Humphreys.

Upon venting the remainder of his frustration on Humphreys, Trousclair suddenly realized that Peters was his wife's cousin and promptly took him to a hospital. Peters initiated a civil lawsuit alleging that Trousclair had committed the tort of either assault and battery or negligence, in the alternative. Trousclair held a homeowner's insurance policy with American Liberty Insurance Company that included personal liability coverage. His request that the company defend him was denied. Judgment was rendered for Peters against Trousclair for compensatory and punitive damages totalling $105,606.55. Peters then sought to have the court hold the insurance company responsible for this amount under the personal liability provision of Trousclair's policy. The trial court found no coverage because the insurance policy expressly excluded liability for intentional harm, and Peters appealed.

Wigginton, Judge:

[The insurance company claimed, and the trial court concluded, that] Trousclair's act was intentional and excluded from the policy, the exclusion reading:

1. Coverage E—Personal Liability and Coverage F—Medical Payments to Others do not apply to bodily injury or property damage:
a. which is expected or intended by the insured. . . .

The record supports the trial court's finding. It reveals that although Trousclair was unaware at the time of the stabbing of the identity of Peters as being his wife's cousin, knowledge which might have otherwise stayed his hand, the act was nonetheless intentionally, specifically directed toward the person of Peters. This feature serves to distinguish the instant case from *Grange Mutual Casualty Co. v. Thomas,* 301 So.2d 158 (Fla. Dist. Ct. App. 1974), which [held that liability coverage applied to a case involving] the shooting of a nonparticipant observer of a family quarrel who was the unfortunate recipient of an errant bullet intended for another. Compare also *Phoenix Insurance Co. v. Helton,* 298 So.2d 177 (Fla. Dist. Ct. App. 1974), and *Cloud v. Shelby Mutual Insurance Co.*, So.2d 217 (Fla. Dist. Ct. App. 1971), in which it was ruled that coverage was not excluded as a matter of law where there was an "intentional act" but not an "intentionally caused" injury. However, as pointed out in *Hartford Fire Insurance Co. v. Spreen,* 343 So.2d 649 (Fla. Dist. Ct. App. 1977): "Running through all of these cases is an act of negligence by the insured, sometimes gross or even culpable negligence. But never has coverage been found under such policies where the insured's act was deliberately designed to cause harm to the injured party."

Here, it is evident from Trousclair's own statements in the record that Peters was the immediate and intended object of his wrath. There is no doubt that Trousclair's act was "deliberately designed to cause harm" to Peters at the moment he committed the act. . . .

[The judgment of the trial court is affirmed. The insurance company is not liable.]

Business Liability Coverage: Businesses that need broad, all-risk coverage against the perils of doing business may obtain what is known as the comprehensive general liability form of insurance. This form covers a variety of risks and, with appropriate endorsements, can be tailored to fit specific business needs. The broad form comprehensive general liability endorsement adds coverage for a wide range of liability exposures that are otherwise excluded from the basic coverage. Included are such items as blanket contractual liability, personal injury and advertising injury, premises medical payments, host liquor liability (this covers the selling or serving of liquor at social events), and other coverages that a business may need but has overlooked.

There are special policies to cover storekeepers, the owners and operators of small shops, and so-called dram shop (bar or saloon) owners or operators. In some states owners of dram shops may be liable for injury or damage caused by their patrons to third parties. For example, a saloon keeper who permits a patron to overimbibe may be guilty of negligence and therefore liable for the injury or damage caused by the patron who, while driving, is involved in an auto accident.

Products Liability Coverage: Manufacturers of consumer and other products face special risks. In the Federal District Courts, there were over 10,000 products liability cases commenced between July 1, 1984, and June 30,

1985. This number, of course, does not include the many products liability suits filed in *state* courts. Products liability and the risks faced by the manufacturer whose product may injure a user are discussed in the risk management section of this chapter.

Professional Malpractice Liability Coverage: The term *malpractice* is often used to refer to negligence by a professional. The proliferation of lawsuits alleging malpractice against physicians and hospitals in recent years has generated a heavy demand for medical **malpractice insurance.** Moreover, the number and size of damage awards and settlements against insurance companies providing malpractice coverage have increased dramatically. As a result, premium rates for such insurance have skyrocketed.

While malpractice insurance is generally thought of as needed only by physicians and hospitals, others who render specialized services to the public also find themselves increasingly liable for malpractice. Attorneys, engineers, pharmacists, and architects, for example, have experienced greater exposure to damage claims and much higher liability insurance premiums in the last few years. Similarly, the demand and the premiums for liability insurance covering the activities of corporate managers have grown. Today, so-called "D & O" (directors and officers) insurance is frequently demanded by executives as part of their compensation packages, although it is becoming extremely expensive and much more difficult to obtain.

Automobile Insurance

Ownership of an automobile poses risks that are too great for most individuals to assume on their own. Consequently, the automobile owner must transfer the risk to a professional risk bearer by purchasing automobile insurance of the various kinds and in the amounts of coverage that fit his or her needs. These needs may be dictated by statute.

Types of Coverage: The typical automobile insurance policy includes several types of coverage which are discussed below.

Liability Coverage: The liability coverage in the automobile policy protects the insured, the insured's family members, and certain others against loss that may arise as a result of legal liability when the insured's auto is involved in an accident and causes personal injury or property damage. The policy is written subject to limits and is expressed in terms such as $25/$50/$5. In this example, coverage is provided for up to $50,000 for all persons injured in a single accident, with a limit of $25,000 for any one individual; the $5 figure indicates that up to $5,000 will be paid for property damage resulting from a single accident. Larger amounts can be pur-

chased and, as the limits are increased, the cost is proportionately greater.

Most states have enacted **financial responsibility laws** that, in effect, require a driver to have at least a specified amount of coverage or risk the imposition of some form of state sanction. State requirements vary, ranging from $5/$10/$1 to $25/$50/$10 (numbers expressed in thousands). And more than half the states have "compulsory" insurance laws requiring some form of state-approved security.

Under the automobile insurance policy the insurer is obligated to pay for injuries "arising out of the ownership, maintenance, or use" of the insured vehicle. In litigation involving the insurer's obligation to pay, the issue is frequently "use," that is, was there a causal relationship or connection between the injury and the use of the vehicle. Obviously, if the vehicle is being driven for some legitimate purpose it is being "used" and resulting injuries would be covered. But suppose that a plaintiff slips and falls while pushing an insured auto, with a dead battery, on an icy driveway. Did the injury from the fall arise out of the use of the vehicle? The court in *Union Mutual Fires Ins. Co. v. King,* 300 A.2d 335 (N.H. 1973), said yes and the insurer paid. The following case also confronts the "use" question.

McNeill v. Maryland Insurance Guaranty Association
Court of Special Appeals of Maryland, 427 A.2d 1056 (1981)

When Charlie McNeill could not start his car, he asked his friend, Evelyn Watkins, to bring her car to where McNeill's was located so that he could use her car's battery to "jump start" his own. Watkins got a third person, Edwin Hill, to drive her car and keep it running during the operation. McNeill correctly attached the jumper cables to the battery posts of both cars while the engine of the Watkins car was running, and removed one or more of the caps from his battery to check its fluid level. (These caps were removable for the addition of water to the battery; at the time of these events, car batteries were not of the sealed, maintenance-free variety.) While Hill was operating Watkins' car, Hill lit a match, presumably to light a cigarette, and tossed it out the window. The match evidently landed close to the battery, and the flame caused McNeill's battery to explode. McNeill, who was standing beside and leaning over his battery, was seriously injured.

Watkins had an insurance policy covering her car, and it included provisions making the insurance company liable for any bodily injury or property damage to others that Watkins would be responsible for. These provisions expressly applied, however, only to such injuries or damages "arising out of the ownership, maintenance, or use" of Watkins' car. McNeill filed suit against the insurance company that had issued the policy on Watkins' car. Attorneys for both parties stipulated that the accident was caused by the negligence of Hill, acting as Watkins' agent, and that McNeill was not contributorily negligent. The trial court ruled that McNeill's injuries did not arise out of the ownership, maintenance, or use of Watkins' car, and held that the insurance company was not liable. McNeill appealed.

Liss, Judge:

The Watkins vehicle was covered by the . . . policy which provided in pertinent part:

Coverage A—Bodily Injury Liability . . . To pay on behalf of the insured all sums which the insured shall become legally obligated to pay as damages because of:
A. bodily injury . . . arising out of the ownership, maintenance or use of the owned automobile. . . .

The standard adopted by the Court of Appeals [i.e., Maryland's highest court] in the interpretation of provisions of an insurance policy where the disputed provision is susceptible to more than one construction is that the provision must be "literally construed in order to promote . . . recovery for innocent victims of motor vehicle accidents." "Ownership, maintenance or use clauses" do not limit recovery solely to injuries that are caused by direct physical contact with the insured vehicle; nor is it necessary that the damages be directly sustained or inflicted by the operation of the motor vehicle. . . .

[The insurance company] relies heavily upon *Plaxco v. United States Fidelity & Guaranty Co.*, 166 S.E.2d 799 (S.C. 1969). . . . The issue in *Plaxco* was whether the use by an insured of his automobile battery to crank the engines of his airplane by connecting the batteries with jumper cables constituted a use of an automobile within the meaning of the automobile liability insurance policy providing coverage arising out of the ownership, maintenance or use of any automobile. In *Plaxco,* the plaintiff drove his automobile to the airport for the purpose of making a trip in his airplane. The plane battery was either dead or too weak to start the engine so he drove his automobile to the left wing and connected the batteries of the plane to the auto by use of a jumper cable. When this was done he entered the plane, started the engine and engaged the brakes and alighted to disconnect the jumper cables, leaving the airplane engine running. After the plaintiff disconnected one of the cables from the automobile battery, and while attempting to disconnect the other, the airplane brakes failed to hold and struck another aircraft. The court held that the accident did not result from the use of plaintiff's automobile, when it stated:

The accident in question did not result from the use of plaintiff's automobile. The only connection between the automobile and the airplane was the use of the automobile battery to start the airplane engine. This purpose had been completed when the airplane moved forward, after the brakes failed to hold. We find nothing in the facts or circumstances to show a causal connection between the use of the automobile battery as a source of power to start the airplane engine and the subsequent forward movement of the airplane. . . . The facts show that the accident resulted from the use of the airplane and not the insured automobile.

We conclude that the facts in *Plaxco* are distinguishable from the present case. The use of the Watkins vehicle was clearly a use which was or should have been contemplated and anticipated by the insurance carrier and the owner of the vehicle. It is not unusual that an insured might on occasion be required to use his vehicle to charge the battery of another vehicle. At the time the explosion took place, the Watkins vehicle was still being used in an activity permitted by her policy. . . . The Watkins vehicle was still attached by the jumper cables to McNeill's vehicle at the time Watkins' driver negligently threw the match. McNeill's activity in unscrewing the battery caps was entirely consistent with an effort to determine whether the battery had sufficient fluid and charge to permit McNeill's car to operate without being attached to the jumper cables. The lighting of the cigarette by Watkins' driver was not an intervening or independent cause, as was the failure of the airplane brakes in *Plaxco.*

Our conclusion, under a policy such as is here before us, is that where a dangerous situation causing injury is one which arose out of or had its source in, the use or operation of the automobile, the chain of responsibility must be deemed to [continue] until broken by the intervention of some event which has no direct or substantial relation to the use or operation. . . . [In other words,] the event which breaks the chain, and which, therefore, would exclude liability under the automobile policy, must be an event which bears no direct or substantial relation to the use or operation; and until an event of the latter nature transpires the liability under the policy exists. . . .

Under the facts in this case we conclude that there was a causal relationship between the use of the Watkins vehicle to start McNeill's automobile and . . . the explosion. . . . We find that at the time [the negligently caused explosion] occurred, the Watkins vehicle was being "used" as contemplated by the Watkins liability insurance policy.

Judgment reversed. [Watkins' insurance company is liable.]

Medical Payments Coverage: The medical payments coverage provides that the insurer will pay reasonable expenses for necessary medical and funeral services rendered because of bodily injury or death caused by an accident and suffered by a person covered by the policy. Included would be any occupant of the insured's automobile. There are limitations on the medical payments, usually ranging from $500 to $5,000 per person per accident.

Uninsured Motorist Coverage: Another part of the automobile policy covers the driver and passengers in the event of bodily injury caused by a hit-and-run driver or by a negligent driver who is financially irresponsible (unable to pay). Under the coverage the insurer will pay up to a specified amount to compensate for the insured's being unable to collect from the negligent driver. Uninsured motorist coverage usually has the same limits as the bodily injury limits of the liability coverage.

Additionally, if an insured purchases increased uninsured motorist coverage he or she may also purchase *underinsured* motorist coverage. This endorsement to the policy covers the situation in which the other driver, at fault, has some insurance but the limits of his or her policy are less than those of the insured's uninsured motorist coverage.

Physical Damage—Collision and Comprehensive Coverage: Physical damage coverage protects the insured against the loss of or damage to his or her automobile. There are two basic forms, *collision* and *comprehensive* (other than collision). As the term implies, collision coverage protects the insured against the perils of upset of the covered automobile or its impact with some object. Many perils are not covered by the collision insurance. These include damage or loss caused by thrown or falling objects, explosion, windstorm, earthquake, hail, flood, vandalism, and glass breakage. For example, suppose that the insured's car is severely pitted by large hailstones or dented by a tree limb blown down in a storm. There has been impact, but the collision insurance would not cover the damage.

To protect against the perils not covered by collision insurance the insured can purchase

comprehensive coverage. The items noted above as being excluded would thus be covered.

Both types of physical damage coverage are less costly if there is a deductible provision. That is, the insured agrees to pay for any damages that do not exceed the amount of the deductible, perhaps $100 or $200. If the insured with $200 deductible collision coverage suffers collision damage of $500, the insurer would pay $300 and the balance, $200, would be paid by the insured.

Duties after an Accident or Loss: An insured involved in an auto accident is under a contractual agreement to promptly notify his or her insurer of all the details of the accident together with the names and addresses of any injured persons and any witnesses. The policy further provides for the insured to cooperate fully with the insurance company in its conduct of an investigation, settlement, or defense of a claim or suit. In its handling of a claim or lawsuit, the insurer will settle, or defend the insured, as it deems appropriate and will pay all defense costs. However, the insurer's duty to settle or defend ends when the limits of its liability have been reached.

Subrogation: *Subrogation* may be defined as the substitution of one person in another's place, allowing the party substituted the same rights and claims as the party being substituted. The subrogation clause in the automobile policy provides:

> A. If we make a payment under this policy and the person to or for whom payment was made has a right to recover damages from another we shall be subrogated to that right. That person shall do:
>
> 1. Whatever is necessary to enable us to exercise our rights; and
>
> 2. Nothing after loss to prejudice them.

To illustrate, suppose that the insured's car is totally demolished in an accident, the other driver being at fault. The insurance company would pay the insured in accordance with the terms of the policy. However, the insured has the right to proceed against the negligent driver but, having been paid by his or her own insurance company, relinquishes that right to the company. The insurer may now proceed against the negligent driver to recover the amount it had paid the insured. In other words, the insurer is subrogated to the rights of the insured.

Cancellation of the Automobile Policy: By state law, after the insured has had the policy for a specified number of days, from 30 to 90 depending upon the state, it may be terminated by the insurer only for certain reasons. Typical of these reasons are:

1. Nonpayment of required premiums.

2. Material misrepresentations by the insured in the policy application.

3. Making of a fraudulent claim by the insured.

4. Suspension or revocation of the insured's driver's license.

5. The insured's addiction to drugs.

6. The insured or other customary operator has been convicted or forfeited bail during the 36 months preceding cancellation for any felony, criminal negligence while operating a motor vehicle, driving under the influence, leaving the scene of an accident, theft of a motor vehicle, or making false statements in an application for a driver's license.

No-Fault Insurance: Under traditional tort law a party who drives negligently and causes personal injury or property damage may be held liable and forced to pay damages. Traditionally, it must be determined which insured is at fault with his or her insurer then paying the damages. Under certain states' *no-fault* systems the determination of fault is unnecessary; each insured collects for injuries and damages from his or her own insurer. Both negligent and nonnegligent parties are covered.

A strict **no-fault insurance** system would do away with tort actions for bodily injuries caused by automobile accidents. There would be no recovery for damages other than bodily injury, and recovery for "pain and suffering" would not be allowed. However, in most of the 23 states having no-fault laws, modification of the pure no-fault concept permits tort suits subject to specific restrictions and limitations on the right to sue. There is considerable variation from state to state, with no state having a pure no-fault law.

Since the first no-fault insurance law, enacted by Massachusetts in 1970, considerable dissatisfaction with the concept has been expressed by those with a vested interest in automobile insurance. American trial lawyers and certain segments of the insurance industry have voiced objections on grounds ranging from unconstitutionality to claims that under no-fault the allocation of the costs of accidents will be unfair and incentives for careful driving will be reduced.

On the other hand, proponents of the system argue that the long-run effect will be to cut costs and reduce premiums for motorists. Whether or not this will happen remains to be seen. The many factors to be taken into account in determining costs in those states having no-fault systems have made it difficult to ascertain how much is being saved if indeed lower premiums are being realized.

Proposals for Federal No-Fault Legislation: Because there is little or no uniformity among the states in their approach to no-fault laws, many proponents of the concept feel that federal regulation is a necessity. Several no-fault proposals have been introduced in Congress but none have been received with much enthusiasm. They have been opposed by a large segment of the insurance industry, the American Bar Association, and the American Trial Lawyers Association. Consequently, passage of a federal no-fault bill, at least for the immediate future, seems a remote possibility. A more likely solution may be federal legislation that prescribes standards for the states to follow in developing their own no-fault laws. There has been some movement in this direction.

RISK MANAGEMENT

The possibility that some undesirable event will occur and cause loss, either minor or catastrophic, is ever present, both for the individual and for businesses of all types. The possibility that something unfavorable will happen—theft, vandalism, arson, or accident, for example—is the essence of risk and cannot be overlooked as a major consideration for the individual in the conduct of his or her private or business affairs.

Risk and the Family

Every family is exposed to the risk that income may be affected, expenses increased, or assets destroyed or reduced by the occurrence of some unforeseen event. Death of the head of the family, a disabling injury or sickness, loss of or damage to the family home by fire, and negligence on the part of a family member resulting in a substantial judgment for damages are examples of the kinds of generally unexpected events that put the family fortune at risk. (The single person, of course, faces the same problems, being spared only the responsibility for dependents.)

Steps can be taken to avoid or minimize risk by exercising accepted measures of prevention and control. For instance, smoke detectors, fire extinguishers, sprinkler systems, conspicuous posting of the telephone number of the local fire department, and carefully planned escape routes will help to reduce a loss by fire. However, there can never be a guarantee that a fire will not occur. Consequently, the family must carefully develop its risk management plan based on its needs for protection in the areas of not only property risk but personal and liability risks as well. Risk transferral through the use of insurance is the most widely used means of coping with risk.

Business Risks and Their Management

The risks confronting businesses are, while perhaps more impersonal than those faced by the family, so broad in scope and various in nature that successful management can be a difficult and involved process. As is the case at the family level, risk avoidance is generally an integral part of any risk management plan. Business managers are primarily concerned with preserving the company's assets and in using those assets to produce income. Property and liability insurance are the primary tools of risk management and effectively transfer the risk of loss to an underwriter. However, risk management in today's complex business environment requires concerted efforts on the part of all levels of management and embraces much more than insurance.

The approach taken will vary from firm to firm depending upon the nature and scope of the business. These factors often determine the perils that confront the business and how best to cope with them. One firm may have an individual whose primary responsibility is risk management. Another firm may have a formal department that is concerned with the problem. Increasingly, however, industry is turning for guidance to the professional risk management specialist.

Liability for defective products provides an example. A manufacturer must be concerned about the risks inherent in producing and marketing a product that may prove to be defective and cause personal injury to a consumer. Attention to detail in design, production, and quality control are essential parts of the manufacturer's risk management plan and will help to minimize the risk. This is necessary because the dollar cost to recall and make adjustments to defective products can be high. Other costs, such as the effect on the reputation of the manufacturer, can be catastrophic, particularly if the product involved has caused serious injury or death. The manufacturer must therefore constantly seek to minimize the risk and, where possible and affordable, shift it to an underwriter.

More and more corporations are looking to corporate risk management specialists for solutions to their product liability problems. As an illustration of this phenomenon, in recent years there has been a tremendous increase in the membership of the Risk and Insurance Management Society, the leading trade association of corporate risk managers. The corporate risk manager asks, "What if . . . ?" and then plans for the answer. And, since no product can be made absolutely accident-proof, consideration must be given to products liability insurance.

Products hazard coverage can be tailored to fit the risks posed by specific products. For example, products recall insurance can be obtained to cover such items as media announcements, destruction or disposal of the recalled product, and wages and salaries for any additional employees hired to handle the activities required for disposition or correction of the recalled item. Although coverage can be through a comprehensive general liability policy, coverage for a specific product can also be obtained. Whether or not such coverage is affordable will depend primarily upon the hazards presented by the product. A pillow presents few hazards; a power lawn mower presents great hazard. In the area of toys, bodily injury coverage for chemistry sets and fuel-powered toys, such as rockets and planes, is more than triple the cost of the same coverage for such items as wooden blocks and balls.

Risk management is a complex subject for which expert guidance is advisable in the development of comprehensive plans to minimize risks and prevent losses. Without such plans, the manufacturer may find that the risks of continuing a particular product line or even staying in business are too great to assume.

accepted either by the agent's issuance of a binder or the insurance company's issuance of the policy itself. One of the most important elements in the case of insurance is that the insured, or policyholder, must possess an insurable interest in the subject matter of the policy. Insurance issued to one without an insurable interest amounts to an illegal gambling contract, and is void. The policyholder also must be of sufficient age, and most insurance contracts are required by state law to be in writing.

Insurance contracts are usually contracts of adhesion and are therefore construed in the insured's favor when an ambiguity arises. They also are unilateral and aleatory in nature.

The major types of insurance are life, health, social, property, liability, and automobile. Several subcategories exist within each type, and many aspects of the different types are overlapping. Homeowner's insurance, for example, includes both property and liability coverage. Automobile insurance is a specialized type of property and liability insurance. The typical property insurance policy includes a coinsurance clause that encourages the owner to insure his or her property for at least close to its full value by requiring the owner to bear a proportionate part of any loss if coverage is not maintained for a specified percentage of the property's replacement cost.

Most types of liability insurance cover the policyholder's liability only for negligence, and not for intentionally wrongful acts. With rapidly increasing product-related damage claims against businesses, and malpractice claims against those who offer professional services, liability insurance is becoming very expensive. As a result, the role of the corporate risk manager is becoming more important.

SUMMARY

An insurance contract, or policy, must possess the same essential elements as other contracts. The person purchasing the insurance makes an offer by submitting the application; the offer is

KEY TERMS

Binder
Premium
Insurable interest
Contract of adhesion

Whole life insurance
Term insurance
Endowment insurance
Health maintenance organization (HMO)
Social insurance
Unemployment compensation
Workers' compensation
Homeowner's policy
Replacement cost basis
Coinsurance clause
Prorata clause
Liability insurance
Malpractice insurance
Financial responsibility laws
No-fault insurance

QUESTIONS AND PROBLEMS

1. Kludt and his family live on a farm that is entirely owned by his wife. The deed to the farm names only his wife as the owner. However Kludt operates the farm and applies any profit he makes to improvements and the support of himself and his family. He has insured the property naming himself as the insured. When the farm was damaged by fire the insurance company refused to pay Kludt's claim, alleging that the policy was void because Kludt has no insurable interest in the property. Is the insurer correct? (*Kludt v. German Mutual Fire Ins. Co.*, 140 N.W. 321, Wis. 1913.)

2. John Smith and Jane Doe have been close to each other since childhood and made plans to marry in June 1984. With this in mind, and to take advantage of the lower premiums for younger persons, in February 1984 Jane purchased a policy of life insurance on John naming herself as beneficiary. Should John die after they are married will Jane be paid the proceeds of the policy?

3. The X, Y, Z partnership has been in business for twenty years and has been profitable. It is estimated that each partner's interest in the firm amounts to approximately $120,000. Partner X died suddenly, and his surviving spouse wants to

be paid her deceased husband's share of partnership assets as soon as the amount has been determined. What problems might this pose for the surviving partners if they want to continue the business? How could these problems have been avoided?

4. Plaintiff was the insured under an accidental death and dismemberment policy that provided full coverage for, among other things, the "total and irrecoverable loss of entire sight of an eye." After a cataract operation on his right eye the plaintiff was fitted with a contact lens that permitted him very limited vision in the eye. However, he could not tolerate the contact lens and without it the eye was practically sightless with no medical assurance that it would ever be any better. When the insurer denied coverage plaintiff filed an action against it claiming the total and irrecoverable loss of entire sight of an eye. A major issue in the case was the meaning of the phrase "irrecoverable loss of sight." In deciding this case what rule of construction will the court apply? (*Roy v. Allstate Ins. Co.*, 383 A.2d 637, Conn. 1978.)

5. A bakery oven was badly damaged in the amount of $2,160 when its thermostatic control failed and caused it to overheat to 650° and become red hot on the outside. This charred the wooden floor, which was damaged to the extent of $800. On what grounds might the insurer attempt to deny coverage? Will it be successful? (*L. L. Freeberg Pie Co. v. St. Paul Mut. Ins. Co.*, 100 N.W.2d 753, Minn. 1960.)

6. A home has a market value of $80,000. To replace the home in the event of total destruction would cost $120,000. The owner has a homeowner's policy with $90,000 of coverage. If a fire damages the house in the amount of $20,000, at replacement cost, how much will the insurer pay?

7. A woman operates a beauty salon in a building she owns that in 1980 was valued at $85,000. She has a policy of fire insurance for $85,000 with a 90 percent coinsurance clause. In 1982 a hair dryer overheated and resulted in a fire that caused $25,000 in damages. After the fire it was determined that the building, in its pre-fire state, was worth $130,000. How much will the owner collect from her insurer?

8. The phrase "arising out of the . . . use" of the insured automobile frequently raises questions as to the kinds of things that constitute "use" so that the injured insured, or others, are covered by the insured's policy. A truckdriver, while fueling the truck for a trip, is injured when the fuel tank explodes. The driver was not in the truck at the time of the explosion. Did this accident result from "use" of the truck so that there was coverage? (*Red Ball Motor Freight, Inc. v. Employers Mut. Liab. Ins. Co.*, 189 F.2d 374, 1951.)

Part VIII

GOVERNMENT REGULATION OF BUSINESS

Today, for better or for worse, the major business activities that are carried on in this country are subject to a substantial amount of federal and state regulation. This fact of life was mentioned in Chapter 6 (Lawmaking by Administrative Agencies), because much of the regulation is, in fact, carried on by government boards and commissions.

In that chapter, however, our primary mission was to see how administrative agencies—whether regulatory or not—actually "make law." We did not attempt to cover the entire subject of government regulation itself. In these final chapters we will make several excursions into this highly complex area of law. It is important to note, also that several state and federal regulatory laws have been examined elsewhere in the text. For example, in Chapter 22, Warranties and Products Liability, the Magnusson-Moss and Consumer Product Safety Acts are discussed along with other aspects of products liability law.

The subject of government regulation of business is so broad, far-reaching, and varied that a balanced treatment of it, in any degree of depth, would require a work of several volumes. Obviously, that is not our purpose here.

Instead, our goals will be more modest. In Chapter 46 we take a rather cursory look at the most important kinds of government regulation and identify the underlying factors that gave rise to such regulation. Then, in Chapters 47 and 48 we focus on the antitrust statutes, with particular attention to (1) the most common problems of interpretation that arise thereunder, and (2) consideration of the various factors—including questions of public policy—that affect the interpretive processes, as illustrated by selected "landmark" cases decided over the years by the U.S. Supreme Court. Chapter 49 examines government regulation of the employment relationship, and Chapter 50 discusses the important subject of securities regulation. Finally, Chapter

51 is devoted to a survey of federal and state regulatory provisions aimed at protecting the consumer.

Throughout Part VIII, our primary goal is a presentation of the nature of the problems that arise in this area of law rather than a comprehensive examination of the regulatory statutes themselves.

Chapter 46

GOVERNMENT REGULATION: AN OVERVIEW

As mentioned in the introduction to Part VIII, the basic purpose of this first chapter is to explore the background and underlying rationale for government regulation of business activities, and to provide a brief overview of the most important federal regulatory laws and agencies.

HISTORICAL BACKGROUND

While this nation's founders may not have been in complete agreement as to the structure and powers that the federal government ought to have, they did share several fundamental tenets. Chief among these, certainly, were the ideas that the right of private ownership of property should be fully protected, that the concept of free competition should be given the fullest possible recognition, and that government regulation of the individual should be kept to a minimum.

Accordingly, there were virtually no attempts by the federal government or the states to impose restrictions on business enterprises prior to the middle of the nineteenth century. The basic concept prevailing at that time (frequently referred to as the **laissez-faire doctrine**) was that free competition could best thrive—and the interests of the consumer best be served—by freeing economic enterprises from virtually all state direction and control.

In the early years of this country, the laissez-faire doctrine brought about generally satisfactory results. By about 1870, however, two factors caused both the federal and state governments to embark on a policy of limited regulation. The first of these was the recognition that the inherent nature of some industries "so affected the public interest" that the control of companies in such industries could not be left totally in the hands of private owners.[1] The banking, transportation, and utility industries were prime examples of these.

Second, at about the same time, other companies engaged in more general types of commerce were taking advantage of the absence of regulation to engage in *anticompetitive* practices that had serious consequences to their competitors and customers alike. For example, large firms—particularly those in the oil and sugar industries—increasingly entered price-fixing agreements and agreements not to compete with one another in specified areas. This second factor was the impetus for enactment of the federal antitrust laws over the next several decades, beginning with the Sherman Act in 1890.

THE REGULATED INDUSTRIES

Railroads and Motor Carriers

The railroad industry was the first industry subjected to specific regulatory statutes at both the state and federal levels—for two important reasons:

1. It had an obvious relationship to the public interest; literally thousands of business firms and millions of individuals relied upon the railroad companies' services in carrying on their daily activities.

2. The heavy financial investments that were inherently necessary to the construction and maintenance of railroad operations were such as to make it economically impossible for competing lines to be built in any but the most heavily populated areas. This condition (also true for the public utility industry) is what the economists refer to as a **natural monopoly**—a situation in which the expected revenues along given routes are sufficient to maintain profitable operation of one company but not two or more.

Some of the first railroads to be built took advantage of these conditions and began, soon after the Civil War, to fix shipping rates that many of their users felt were unreasonably high. Additionally, some lines engaged in rate discrimination that brought about widespread discontent. Early state laws, called "Granger laws" because the impetus for their enactment came

---

[1] For simplicity, such companies hereafter are referred to as the "regulated companies."

from farm groups, were meant to eliminate these rate abuses; in general, however, they were ineffective.

Federal Legislation: In response to these problems and in recognition of the fact that unlimited regulation of the railroads simply could not, as a practical matter, be left to the states, Congress passed the Interstate Commerce Act in 1887. This statute expressly vested the primary control of interstate rail carriers in the federal government, required that the rates of such companies be "just and reasonable," and prohibited the charging of discriminatory rates. Additionally, it created the Interstate Commerce Commission for the purpose of enforcing the law's provisions.

Over the next few years, largely as the result of certain court decisions, various weaknesses in the law appeared. As a result of these inadequacies, Congress passed several more laws, beginning with the Elkins Act of 1903. This act expressly granted the commission power to fix maximum rates and gave the courts jurisdiction to set aside rates found to be in excess of those permitted. The Elkins Act was followed by the Hepburn Act in 1906, which broadened the authority of the Interstate Commerce Commission, allowing it to cover many railroad activities that had been outside its jurisdiction.

These acts were followed by the Motor Carrier Act of 1935, which extended the jurisdiction of the Interstate Commerce Commission to motor carriers; the Transportation Act of 1940, which extended federal regulation to water carriers; and the Transportation Act of 1958. The latter provided, among other things, that the commission could not keep the rates of carriers in one industry artificially high for the purpose of "protecting the traffic of any other mode of transportation, giving due consideration to the objectives of the national transportation policy declared in this Act."

Congress gave substantially greater economic freedom to railroads in 1980 with the passage of the Staggers Act. This legislation permits a railroad company great latitude in determining whether to abandon unprofitable routes. Route abandonments were severely restricted prior to the Staggers Act.

Air Transportation

The regulation of air transport is essentially in the hands of two federal agencies. The Federal Aviation Administration (FAA), an agency within the U.S. Department of Transportation, is charged primarily with the safety aspects of air travel. Under its jurisdiction is the air control system, which regulates such matters as the establishment of the many airways (routes ten miles in width) across the country. It also has responsibility for the several thousand traffic controllers at approximately 300 airports. Another agency, the National Transportation Safety Board (NTSB), is responsible for investigating air crashes.

Until recently, a third agency, the Civil Aeronautics Board (CAB), was perhaps the most important federal agency involved in airline regulation. It controlled the entry of airlines into the industry, approved airline schedules, set subsidies, and regulated air fares. As a result of the movement toward airline industry deregulation, which is discussed later in the chapter, the CAB lost most of its authority, and was abolished in 1985. The few remaining regulatory functions of the CAB, such as approval of airline mergers, were transferred to the Department of Transportation.

Public Utilities

The same general factors that gave rise to the regulation of railroads also existed in the area of public utilities. The economic considerations are much the same in the two industries, with public utility firms (such as light and power, natural gas, and telephone and telegraph companies) almost always existing as natural monopolies. The result is that particular companies in these fields are generally granted the exclusive right to operate in given areas. In return for this privilege the regulating government reserves the right to control rates and to prescribe the types of services that must be made available.

There is one major difference between the regulation of the two industries, however: whereas the transportation companies are essentially regulated by the federal government, the regulation of public utility companies is largely left in the hands of the states. Today all states have public utility or public service commissions with similar regulatory authority over the various utility companies that operate within their jurisdictions.

The Electric Companies:　State regulation of electric companies roughly parallels federal regulation of the railroads and other forms of transportation. That is, most of the work of the state commissions involves fixing rates and promulgating procedures designed to insure adequate availability of consumer services.

While the commissions of some states are strong, in the sense that they are well staffed by experts and exert impartial control, the commissions of other states frequently lack these qualities. In the latter states, the financial and political powers of the "regulated" companies are such that the protection afforded to consumers is often only nominal.

Other Utilities:　In addition to regulating electric companies, most of the state commissions also have jurisdiction over gas and water companies, intrastate motor carriers, and telephone companies. The regulation of public utilities is not, however, entirely in the states' hands. The Federal Energy Regulatory Commission, for example, has regulatory authority—including rate-making powers—over the *interstate* transmission of natural gas and electricity; thus it is sometimes said that rate-fixing at the "wholesale" level is in the hands of the federal government, while at the consumer level it is left to the states. The Federal Energy Regulatory Commission also has jurisdiction of power company projects built on navigable rivers. Additionally, the Federal Communications Commission regulates interstate telephone and telegraph services, along with those of television and radio.

Banking

Banks are so inherently involved with the public interest that they have been subject to strict government regulation from the very beginning. In general, national banks are governed by the Comptroller of the Currency and the Federal Reserve Board, while state banks are regulated by the banking department of the state governments. Additionally, all national banks are subject to the voluminous regulations of the Federal Deposit Insurance Corporation, as are the state banks that have elected to join that corporation.

THE MOVEMENT TOWARD DEREGULATION

Beginning in the late 1970s rather broad support developed for the limited "deregulation" of a few of the industries which had been tightly regulated for decades. The transportation business was a primary object of this movement. In recent years Congress enacted legislation loosening the reins on the airline, trucking, and railroad industries. Firms in these three industries now have much more freedom in deciding which markets to serve and what prices to charge. The consensus in Congress was that these industries had changed sufficiently over the years that competition could play a much more important role than it had in the past.

Deregulation has recently occurred to a lesser extent in the banking and communications fields. It is possible that limited degrees of deregulation could occur in a few other regulated industries.

Regardless of this new trend, however, the so-called regulated industries will continue to be subject to substantial government regulation. Even in the transportation business, where deregulation has been the most pronounced, a great deal of regulation will almost certainly remain in the future.

OTHER IMPORTANT REGULATORY LAWS

Securities Laws

In order to insure a degree of protection for the nation's investors, Congress passed the Securities Act of 1933 and the Securities Exchange Act of 1934, which are briefly discussed at several points in the chapters on corporations and explored more thoroughly in Chapter 50, "Securities Regulation." The Securities Act of 1933 regulates the issuance of stocks, bonds, and other securities in interstate commerce primarily by requiring the issuing company to file a registration statement containing detailed financial information. The Securities Exchange Act of 1934 (1) created the Securities and Exchange Commission to enforce federal securities laws; (2) prohibits fraud in the sale and purchase of securities after their initial issuance; (3) prohibits the sale or purchase of securities by anyone with "inside" information of a material nature unless the information is disclosed to the other party to the transaction; (4) prohibits various practices designed to artificially manipulate securities prices; (5) requires full disclosure of material information in materials accompanying proxy solicitations and tender offers; (6) requires corporate insiders to file periodic financial reports and to give back to the company any short-swing profits (selling and buying or buying and selling within six months) made on their company's securities; and (7) regulates securities brokers, dealers, underwriters, and exchanges.

Most states also have securities regulation laws.

Employment Laws

Many federal and state laws have been enacted to regulate various aspects of the employment relationship. These regulatory laws are discussed in greater detail in Chapter 49, Employment Law. Among the most important of these laws are state workers' compensation statutes, which provide employee benefits for on-the-job injuries and occupational diseases and the employment discrimination laws, which protect workers from discrimination based on race, sex, religion, age, or handicap.

The National Labor Relations Act of 1935 (called the NLRA or Wagner Act), coupled with later amendments by the Taft-Hartley Act of 1947 and the Landrum-Griffin Act of 1959, closely regulates relations between companies and labor unions. Employers are required to recognize and bargain with unions having majority employee support. Employers and unions are prohibited from engaging in various unfair labor practices, such as discriminating against employees on the basis of their union membership, nonmembership, or union-related activities. The NLRA, as amended, is enforced by the National Labor Relations Board, an independent federal administrative agency.

The Fair Labor Standards Act (FLSA) was passed by Congress in 1938 for the primary purposes of (1) establishing a nationwide minimum wage, (2) requiring time-and-a-half pay for all hours over forty per week, and (3) regulating the employment of children. FLSA is enforced by the Wage and Hour Division of the U.S. Department of Labor. Most states also have minimum wage, overtime, and child labor laws which apply in situations where federal laws do not.

In 1970, Congress enacted the Occupational Safety and Health Act in an effort to improve the safety and promote healthful environments of workplaces across the nation. The Act is enforced by the Occupational Safety and Health Administration, which is also part of the U.S. Department of Labor. This agency prescribes detailed standards for employee exposure to toxic substances and dangerous conditions on the employer's premises. Enforcement is accomplished by unannounced inspections and monetary penalties.

Trademark Laws

Trademarks used to be names or symbols that indicated the origin of particular goods. Beginning in 1888, Congress has enacted laws that permit the registration of trademarks and grant to their holders the exclusive right to their use.

The basic trademark statute today is the Trademark Act of 1946, commonly referred to as the Lanham Act. This statute permits the registration of any mark that has become "distinctive," regardless of whether it indicates the source or origin of particular goods. The act defines a trademark as "any word, name, symbol, or device, or any combination thereof adopted and used by a manufacturer or merchant to identify his goods and distinguish them from those manufactured or sold by others." Additionally, the law permits registration of "service marks"—distinctive marks adopted by firms in service businesses.

One of the most vexatious legal problems arising under the trademark laws has to do with the measure of protection that should be afforded the trademark owner and the extent to which that protection should depend on efforts of the owner to police the rights after acquiring them. The problem, essentially, is that once a mark is registered, if it is not adequately protected by the holder, it may become a generic term for the goods themselves rather than an indicator of a particular producer or distributor. The terms *cellophane, linoleum,* and *aspirin* were all registered trademarks at one time, but because of careless use (or their strong appeal to the public) they became accepted as the names of the goods themselves, and trademark rights were thereby lost.[2]

Patent and Copyright Laws

To encourage innovation and creative effort, Congress has enacted patent and copyright laws. These statutes provide for exceptions to the general rule of open competition by giving inventors, authors, composers, and artists the exclusive legal rights to use and market their inventions and creative works for limited time periods.

To be patentable, an invention, formula, or process must be "new, useful, and nonobvious." The period of patent protection is 17 years.

Creative works are protected under federal copyright law for the life of the author plus 50 years. If the work was done *for hire* (such as a book written under contract for a publishing company, which then owns the copyright), the period of protection is seventy-five years from publication or one hundred years from creation, whichever expires first.

Consumer Protection Laws

Several of the most important laws aimed at protecting the consumer, such as the Consumer Credit Protection Act, are discussed in depth in Chapter 51.

THE ANTITRUST LAWS

As noted earlier, certain statutes applicable to businesses were being enacted by Congress during the same period that control over the regulated industries was developing. Since these more general laws, which apply to virtually all businesses in interstate commerce, are examined in some detail in the following chapters, only their basic import will be described here.

The Sherman Act

Passed in 1890, the Sherman Act was the first of the antitrust laws at the federal level. Prior to this time, a number of large firms were engaging in flagrant anticompetitive practices that had very serious consequences both to their smaller competitors and to the public at large. The increased use of the corporate form of organization, the concentration of industrial power in the hands of a few firms, and the development of

---

[2] As one manifestation of this danger, the larger firms have people on their staffs whose sole duty, it seems, is to write letters to advertisers, newspapers, and writers who have used terms such as *Coca Cola* or *Xerox* in lower case form. Such letters politely point out that these terms are registered and should therefore always be capitalized in print.

markets on a national scale all provided a climate in which agreements to fix prices and to divide markets could be made with abandon.

While it is true that the common law outlawed monopolies, it proved to be completely inadequate in dealing with these practices. In the first place, the common-law principles usually prohibited only the end result—monopolies—rather than the *means* by which monopoly positions were attained. Second, even where monopolies did exist, action could be taken against them only when they were challenged by private parties in court. And third, the common-law principles were only statewide in scope; thus the possibility of action by the federal government under such principles was virtually nil.

It was in this situation that Congress passed the Sherman Act. As we will see more fully in the next chapter, the Act basically declared that contracts in restraint of trade and monopolies were illegal. Additionally, the act contained certain penalty provisions and provided procedures for criminal and civil enforcement actions.

Because the Sherman Act addressed only the twin evils of restraints of trade and monopolization, many other restrictive business practices remained perfectly lawful. For example, discriminatory pricing—the selling of goods to favored buyers at prices lower than those charged other buyers—did not, in and of itself, violate the act. For this reason Congress enacted the Clayton Act and the Robinson-Patman Act in subsequent years.[3]

---

[3] The use of the term *antitrust* to describe the Sherman Act and other related statutes grew out of the fact that many of the firms engaging in the anticompetitive practices described above used the "trust" device to attain their ends. Under this method, the owners of the controlling shares of stock in two or more competing corporations transferred title of these shares to a small number of specified individuals, called trustees. By virtue of such ownership, the trustees were able to control the policies of the affected companies with a single voice. In this sense, then, the Sherman Act is "antitrust." However, because the Act prohibits monopolistic practices regardless of whether the trust device is used (and today it is used rarely), the term *anti-monopoly* is a much more accurate label for this kind of legislation, although only infrequently used.

The Clayton Act

In 1914 Congress passed the Clayton Act to prohibit certain restrictive practices even if they did not result in the unreasonable restraint of trade or in the creation of a monopoly. Since this act will be considered further in Chapter 48, suffice it to say that the statute generally forbade sellers of goods in interstate commerce "to discriminate in price between different purchasers of commodities" (with certain stated exceptions), prohibited the sale of products on condition that the buyer not handle the goods of a competitor, and generally forbade any corporation in interstate commerce to acquire the stock of a competitor.

The Federal Trade Commission Act

In order to strengthen enforcement of the Clayton Act, and to provide a means for more continuous surveillance of business activities, Congress also passed the Federal Trade Commission Act (FTC Act) in 1914. This legislation created the Federal Trade Commission (FTC), an independent federal regulatory agency, and gave it the power to enforce and monitor compliance with the provisions of the Clayton Act.

In addition to giving the FTC authority to enforce the Clayton Act, the FTC Act separately declared "unfair methods of competition" to be unlawful. This provision, which is found in Section 5 of the Act, gives the FTC extremely broad antitrust enforcement power. Any type of conduct that would violate any of the provisions of the Sherman or Clayton Acts also constitutes an "unfair method of competition" in violation of Section 5 of the FTC Act. Moreover, some practices that harm competition may violate Section 5 even if they would not constitute violations of either the Sherman or Clayton Acts.

In 1938, Congress passed the Wheeler-Lea Act, which amended Section 5 of the FTC Act by adding a prohibition against "unfair or deceptive acts or practices" in interstate commerce. Thus, after this 1938 amendment, Section 5 of the FTC Act consists of two separate prohibitions. Although Section 5 is technically not an antitrust statute, the first prohibition against unfair methods of competition is aimed at the same basic type of conduct that is prohibited by the antitrust laws (i.e., the Sherman and Clayton Acts). The provision added to Section 5 in 1938, however, aims at an entirely different type of conduct. It is, in essence, a consumer protection measure, and has been used by the FTC to take action against false advertising and other deceptive commercial practices. This latter portion of Section 5 is dealt with at length in Chapter 51, Consumer Transactions and the Law.

The Robinson-Patman Act

The Robinson-Patman Act, a lengthy amendment to the Clayton Act, was enacted in 1936 to prohibit certain practices used by sellers to escape the price discrimination provisions of the Clayton Act. Essentially, it further narrowed the situations in which price discrimination was permissible and forbade payment of commissions to brokers except where brokerage services were actually rendered. This Act is also considered further in Chapter 48.

Exemptions from the Antitrust Laws

Three major types of organizations have full or partial statutory exemption from the antitrust laws: agricultural organizations, labor unions, and export associations. Additionally, companies in the regulated industries are subject to such extensive special regulation that the government has seldom seen fit to challenge the activities of these firms under the antitrust laws. However, such firms are not exempt from these laws; and recently, in special circumstances, successful antitrust actions have been brought against companies in the regulated industries. For example, in the case of *United States v. Philadelphia National Bank,* 374 U.S. 321 (1963), a proposed merger was found to be prohibited by Section 7 of the Clayton Act; and in *Otter Tail Power Company v. United States,* 410 U.S. 366 (1973), the utility was found to have monopolized its relevant market in violation of Section 2 of the Sherman Act.

Enforcement of the Antitrust Laws

The federal antitrust laws are enforced in several ways. Violations of the Sherman Act are felonies and may be prosecuted in a federal district court by the Antitrust Division of the U.S. Department of Justice. The Department of Justice operates under the U.S. Attorney General and is the prosecutorial arm of the federal government. Criminal prosecutions usually are instituted against only the most blatant Sherman Act violations, such as price fixing among competitors. In a criminal antitrust case, the maximum penalties that may be assessed by the federal district court are as follows: (1) in the case of *individuals,* a fine of up to $250,000, a prison term of up to three years, or both; and (2) in the case of *corporations,* a fine of up to $1,000,000.

The Department of Justice also is authorized to file civil cases in federal court for violations of the Sherman Act and the other antitrust laws. This is, in fact, the course of action usually taken by the Department of Justice. If an antitrust law violation is proved by the department in a civil case, the remedy granted by the federal court is an injunction. The injunction prohibits further activities in violation of the antitrust laws, and more important, frequently requires substantial alterations of a company's business practices. Failure to comply with the injunction amounts to contempt of court and may result in a fine or jail term. Sometimes the terms of an injunction are the result of an out-of-court settlement between the department and the defendants. In such a situation, the injunction often is referred to as a **consent decree.**

The Federal Trade Commission (FTC) also has authority to enforce the Clayton Act, Robinson-Patman Act, and Federal Trade Commission Act. Even though the FTC does not have authority to enforce the Sherman Act, any business practice which violates the Sherman Act will also violate the Federal Trade Commission Act and can be subjected to FTC enforcement under the latter statute. Enforcement by the FTC takes the form of civil administrative hearings and issuance of **cease and desist orders.** Noncompliance with an FTC order can result in penalties of up to $10,000 per day.

Private parties can also file civil lawsuits in a federal district court against alleged violators of the antitrust laws. The plaintiffs in such suits usually are customers, suppliers, or competitors of the defendants. The law permits successful plaintiffs in private antitrust cases to recover **treble damages.** This means that a plaintiff who proves that its business has been damaged by defendant's violation of the antitrust laws is entitled to an amount equal to *three times the damages.* The plaintiff in a private antitrust suit may also receive an injunction against the defendant. Lawsuits by private parties are an extremely important part of antitrust enforcement—in fact, over 90 percent of all antitrust cases are instituted by private plaintiffs.

SUMMARY

During the late nineteenth and early twentieth centuries, the prevailing laissez-faire attitude toward the U.S. economy changed substantially. In its place there developed an attitude on the part of many state and federal policy makers that a degree of government intervention in business activities was necessary to protect the public interest.

The railroad industry was the first to be subjected to major economic regulation by the federal government. The motor carrier and airline industries were later regulated in a similar fashion. Other major businesses subjected to close government regulation include public utilities, communications firms, and financial institutions. In recent years, however, there has been a general movement away from rigid government regulation of economic activity in the transportation industries, and railroads, motor carriers,

and airlines have been permitted substantially more freedom to set rates and decide which markets to serve. Regulation of banks and other financial institutions also has been relaxed somewhat in recent years, although these and other so-called regulated industries will continue to operate under significant state and federal government supervision.

Other important regulatory laws include those applying to the issuance and trading of securities, the employment relationship, trademarks, patents and copyrights, and protection of consumers. Of an even more fundamental nature are the antitrust laws, which attempt to remove artificial obstacles from the operation of markets and to let the forces of competition work freely.

KEY TERMS

Laissez-faire doctrine
Natural monopoly
Consent decree
Cease and desist order
Treble damages

QUESTIONS AND PROBLEMS

1. Several problems during the laissez-faire era caused Congress to pass the Sherman Act. What kinds of problems were they?

2. What difficulties led Congress to pass the Interstate Commerce Act of 1887?

3. Is the Interstate Commerce Commission charged with the regulation of interstate commerce generally, or only with certain aspects of such commerce? Explain.

4. Companies that produce and transmit natural gas and electricity are subject to both state and federal regulation. As a rule of thumb, which of these companies' activities are governed by the state, and which by the federal government?

5. Some companies, because of their inherent nature, were regulated by the federal or state governments at a much earlier time than companies in more general types of commerce. Explain why this happened.

6. What factors are responsible for the fact that utility firms are characterized as "natural monopolies"?

7. What was a basic shortcoming in the Sherman Act that led to the passage of additional regulatory legislation by Congress?

8. Is it correct to say that companies in the regulated industries are exempt from operation of the antitrust laws? Why or why not?

Chapter 47

ANTITRUST LAW
The Sherman Act

The basic provisions of the Sherman Act are so short that they can be easily quoted almost in their entirety.

Section 1 reads as follows: "Every contract, combination in the form of trust or otherwise, or conspiracy, in restraint of trade or commerce among the several states, or with foreign nations is hereby declared to be illegal. . . ."

Section 2 provides: "Every person who shall monopolize, or attempt to monopolize, or combine or conspire with any other person or persons, to monopolize any part of the trade or commerce among the several states, or with foreign nations, shall be guilty of a felony. . . ."

Because of their general nature these provisions have required a great deal of judicial interpretation in the complex cases that have arisen under them. In this chapter we will look at some of the most common problems presented by cases arising under Sections 1 and 2 of the Sherman Act. We will also discuss the somewhat narrower questions regarding the status of horizontal and vertical price-fixing agreements under these sections.

GENERAL OBSERVATIONS ABOUT THE SHERMAN ACT

The cases appearing in this chapter are typical of those arising under the Sherman Act. Before turning to their specific problems, however, we will make several general observations about the Act:

1. The language of Sections 1 and 2 is so general that it is obvious Congress meant to give the courts considerable latitude in interpreting the prohibitions that each contains. Thus it is left to the courts to decide whether a particular contract is "in restraint of trade" and what the criteria are for determining whether a company has "monopolized" part of the trade or commerce among the states.

2. While some types of conduct may violate both Sections 1 and 2 of the Sherman Act, these sections prohibit essentially different kinds of conduct. Section 1 is aimed at joint conduct between *two or more* firms that limits competition, whereas Section 2 targets *single-firm* monopolization or attempted monopolization of a market.

3. Since the federal antitrust laws are all based on the commerce clause of the Constitution, their provisions apply only to conduct that occurs in the course of interstate or foreign commerce, or in situations that "substantially affect" interstate or foreign commerce.

SELECTED SECTION 1 PROBLEMS

Proving the Existence of an Agreement

As noted earlier, Section 1 provides that contracts, combinations, and conspiracies in restraint of trade or commerce are illegal. Since each requires two or more parties, there will always be at least two defendants in any action. The plaintiff in such cases has the burden of proving that the defendants acted in concert—that is, as a result of some type of *agreement*—to bring about the restraint. If direct proof of agreement is weak or lacking, judgment will ordinarily be in favor of the defendants.

In some actions where direct proof is lacking, the plaintiff will fall back on the doctrine of **conscious parallelism.** In such cases the plaintiff (either the government or a private party) contends that evidence proving that the actions of each defendant closely paralleled those of the others should also be accepted as proof that such actions *resulted from prior agreement.* The usual view in this area is that parallel action in and of itself is not proof of agreement; however, proof of parallel action accompanied by almost any independent evidence tending to show agreement is usually enough to sustain a conviction.

The Rule of Reason

Section 1 provides that "every" contract and combination in restraint of trade is illegal. However, in the landmark case of *Standard Oil of*

New Jersey v. United States, 221 U.S. 1 (1911), the U.S. Supreme Court ruled that it was the intent of Congress, in enacting Section 1, to prohibit only those contracts and combinations that *unreasonably* restrained trade.[1] Under this **rule of reason,** the plaintiff not only had to prove that one or more restrictive agreements were entered into between the defendants but, additionally, that the agreements covered rather substantial quantities of goods or services. Thus if two small companies in the same industry entered into a restrictive contract (for example, that neither would act in a particular way without the consent of the other), this agreement would not violate Section 1. On the other hand, the same agreement between two or more major companies in the same industry *would* violate it.

Per Se Violations

Under the rule of reason, where the legality of a particular contract in restraint of trade is involved, an examination of the facts of the case is required to determine whether the effect of the restraint was actually unreasonable—that is, of such a magnitude as to adversely affect competition to a significant degree.

While this rule or test is still applied to many kinds of contracts in Section 1 cases, since the Standard Oil case the U.S. Supreme Court has taken the view in an increasing number of cases that certain kinds of restrictive contracts are so inherently anticompetitive that they restrain trade unreasonably *as a matter of law.* Thus, under the so-called **per se rule,** some types of conduct automatically violate Section 1, and there is no need to look at other facts to measure their impact or the scope of their use. Further-

more, in regard to such contracts, *no defenses* on the part of the defendant companies are accepted by the courts.

Four major types of agreements or other joint actions in interstate commerce that are ordinarily held by the courts to constitute per se violations are (1) horizontal price fixing, (2) vertical price fixing, (3) horizontal market divisions, and (4) joint refusals to deal.

Horizontal Price Fixing: An agreement involving **horizontal price fixing** is one where competitors at the same level—such as two wholesalers—expressly or impliedly agree to charge the same prices for their competing products (or, perhaps, agree that their price changes will be made in parallel fashion). Since these agreements automatically remove the possibility of price competition between the two companies, they are inherently anticompetitive and thus a violation of Section 1 without resort to further facts.[2] Additionally, it is no defense to such an action that the prices actually fixed were reasonable—that is, no higher than those of their competitors—or that an insignificant amount of commerce was involved.

Vertical Price Fixing: An agreement involving **vertical price fixing** (or resale price maintenance) is one in which a seller at one level—usually a manufacturer—sells goods to a buyer at a different level—usually a retailer—on condition that the buyer will, upon resale, not sell the goods below a certain price stated in the contract. Under U.S. Supreme Court decisions, such contracts today are per se violations of the Sherman Act. (Between 1937 and 1976 resale price maintenance contracts were lawful because another act of Congress, the Miller-Tydings Act, generally exempted them from the operation of the Sherman Act. This exemption ended in 1976, however, when Miller-Tydings was repealed.)

---

[1] In this case, the court found that the agreements in question clearly *did* restrain trade unreasonably, in view of the fact that they involved 34 of the nation's largest corporations in the oil and transportation industries. As a result of this violation of Section 1, the court ordered the Standard Oil of New Jersey holding company to be split up into a number of independent oil companies (such as Standard Oil of California, Standard Oil of Ohio, and Atlantic Richfield).

[2] Leading cases on this point are *United States v. Trenton Potteries,* 273 U.S. 392 (1927), and *United States v. Socony-Vacuum Oil Co.,* 310 U.S. 150 (1940).

Horizontal Market Divisions: When two competitors at the same level agree, expressly or impliedly, that one will not sell its products in a given geographical area and that the other, in return, will not sell its products in another area, a **horizontal market division** has occurred. Because this type of agreement eliminates virtually all competition between the parties, it is considered essentially anticompetitive and therefore a per se violation of Section 1. The case of *United States v. Topco Associates, Inc.* 405 U.S. 596 (1972), is one example of the strictness with which this view is applied. In that decision, the court held that such a contract violated Section 1 *as a matter of law* even though the defendant firms produced evidence that the arrangement affected only small portions of the relevant markets.

Joint Refusals to Deal (Group Boycotts): As a general rule, any seller of goods or services has the right to select the customers with whom he or she will do business (subject to the qualification that a refusal to deal cannot be made on the basis of the customer's race, color, or place of national origin). This principle is recognized under the antitrust laws, with the result that a refusal by a single manufacturer or a single wholesaler to sell goods to a potential buyer or group of buyers does not, in most circumstances, violate the Sherman Act.

However, when two or more sellers act *in concert* in refusing to sell to a particular buyer or class of buyers, a much different situation is presented. Because the motive underlying the vast majority of such refusals is inherently anticompetitive in nature—i.e., the elimination of a competitor by the conspirators—a so-called **group boycott** is almost always found by the courts to violate Section 1 of the Sherman Act.

The following case is described by the U.S. Supreme Court as a "classic example" of a group boycott.

United States v. General Motors Corp. et al.
U.S. Supreme Court, 384 U.S. 127 (1966)

In the 1950s, when automobile production was very high, twelve Chevrolet dealers in southern California (referred to as the "participating dealers") frequently disposed of their excess inventory by selling new cars slightly above cost to "discounters" in the area. These discounters offered stiff competition to other local Chevrolet dealers, who complained to General Motors (and the Chevrolet Division) about the conduct of the participating dealers.

As a result, General Motors pressured all of its southern California Chevrolet dealers and three dealers' associations to sign agreements promising never to sell cars to the discounters. Soon thereafter G.M. learned that several of the dealers had broken this agreement. When G.M. moved to punish these dealers for breach of contract, the dealers contended that all of the agreements violated Section 1 of the Sherman Act, and were thus illegal and unenforceable.

When the United States learned of the controversy it agreed with the dealers' position, and brought this action against G.M. and the dealers' associations asking that they be enjoined from enforcing the promises made by the dealers not to do business with the discounters. The trial court ruled that the agreements (the promises) did *not* violate the Sherman Act, on the ground that they were merely a valid implementation of the "location clause" that was contained in all of the dealers' basic franchise contracts with G.M. and dismissed the action. (The location clause essentially provided that a franchised dealer would not move to a new location, or establish a branch sales office at a new location, without approval of Chevrolet.) The government appealed to the U.S. Supreme Court.

Fortas, Justice:

. . . The appellee-defendants argue that . . . [the trial court was correct in ruling that the participating dealers' arrangements with the discounters] constitute the establishment of additional sales outlets in violation of the location clause, and that the [conduct of General Motors in making all Chevrolet dealers promise not to deal with discounters was therefore lawful.]

[The court then conceded that the sale of the cars to discounters could be viewed as a breach of the location clause, in which case G.M. could proceed against any dealer violating the clause *if* the only agreements between G.M. and its dealers were the separate franchise agreements. In such a situation no antitrust violation would exist. But the court said that in this case the agreement between G.M. on the one hand and all of its southern California dealers on the other was of a much different character. The court elaborated as follows:]

Here we have a classic conspiracy in restraint of trade [because of] joint, collaborative action by dealers, dealers' associations, and General Motors to eliminate a class of competitors by terminating business dealings between them and a minority of Chevrolet dealers and to deprive franchised dealers of their freedom to deal through discounters if they so choose. Against this fact of unlawful combination [under the antitrust laws], the "location clause" is of no avail. . . .

Neither individual dealers nor the associations acted independently or separately. The dealers collaborated, through the associations and otherwise, among themselves and with General Motors, both to enlist the aid of General Motors and to enforce dealers' promises to forsake the discounters. The associations explicitly entered into a joint venture to assist General Motors in policing the dealers' promises, and their joint proffer of aid was accepted and utilized by General Motors. . . . What resulted was a fabric interwoven by many strands of joint action to eliminate the discounters from participation in the market, to inhibit the free choice of franchised dealers to select their own methods of trade. . . .

There can be no doubt that the effect of the combination or conspiracy here was to restrain trade and commerce within the meaning of the Sherman Act. *Elimination, by joint collaborative action, of discounters from access to the market is a per se violation of the act.* [Emphasis added.] . . .

Accordingly, we reverse [the judgment of the lower court] and remand the case to [it] in order that it may fashion appropriate equitable relief [in favor of the United States and those dealers wishing to continue to sell cars to the discounters.]

Vertical Customer and Territorial Restrictions

Manufacturers often sell their products to wholesalers or retailers under contracts that prohibit such purchasers from reselling the products to certain classes of buyers or to buyers whose businesses or residences are outside a designated geographical area. (The latter has been used especially when the wholesaler or retailer is an exclusive dealer—one who has been granted a certain territory within which the manufacturer-seller has promised not to install a competing dealer.) Restrictions of the first type are called **vertical customer restrictions** and those of the second type **vertical territorial restrictions.**

The U.S. Supreme Court once ruled that such provisions in sales contracts under which title passed directly to the purchaser (as distinguished from sales on consignment, where title was retained by the seller) violated Section 1 of the Sherman Act as a matter of law. *United States v. Arnold, Schwinn and Co.*, 388 U.S. 365 (1967). After the decision this restriction became a fifth type of per se violation. However, in a later case involving a closely related issue, the Supreme Court expressly overruled that portion of *Schwinn* referred to above—*Continental T.V., Inc. v. GTE Sylvania,* 433 U.S. 36 (1977). As a result of this case, customer and territorial limitation clauses are lawful—even when title passes to the buyer—unless it is shown that their use actually restrains trade *unreasonably* under the circumstances.

MONOPOLIZATION UNDER SECTION 2

Having provided that it shall be unlawful to "monopolize" or to "attempt to monopolize" any part of trade or commerce, Congress left it up to the courts to interpret these terms on a case-by-case basis. As noted peripherally in the decision of the next case, *United States v. Du Pont,* the U.S. Supreme Court has adopted the general rule that a **monopolization** of commerce exists only when the evidence establishes that the defendant firm has reached such a size that it "has the power to control price" of the specified commodity or possesses the power "to exclude competitors from the market." (When either or both conditions are met, it is frequently said that the defendant possesses "overwhelming market power.")

Factors to Be Considered

To examine all the factors that the courts consider in determining whether or not monopoly power exists, it would be necessary to summarize the fact-patterns and decisions of the leading cases in this area of the law—an impossible task in a text of this sort. Nevertheless, we can say that the single most important factor is the *size of the market share* held by the defendant. Thus, if the market share of a manufacturer is shown to be less than 50 percent of the total relevant market, it is unlikely that additional facts would support a finding that the defendant-manufacturer possessed monopoly powers, and the action against it would probably fail. On the other hand, if the market share of a manufacturer approaches 75 percent or more of the relevant market, the courts are likely to rule that this fact alone would support a finding of monopoly power.

The great majority of cases, of course, present situations in which the market shares of the defendant companies fall within the extremes mentioned above. In these cases, then, the courts have to look to additional factors in order to determine whether or not the power to control prices or to exclude competitors really exists. Additional factors increasing the chances that a court will conclude that such a firm is actually a monopolist include the following: (1) the remainder of the market consists of very small firms, rather than one or two firms large enough to compete effectively against the dominant firm; (2) the dominant firm's exercise of market power is insulated by high **entry barriers,** such as very large capital requirements, critical patents[3] or trade secrets, complex distribution channels, and other conditions making it much more difficult and costly for other firms to enter the market; (3) the market is *not* characterized by rapidly changing technology that would make it more difficult for the dominant firm to maintain its dominance; (4) there are no large, powerful buyers in the market to counter the dominant firm's exercise of power; and

(5) the dominant firm's share of the market has been stable or increasing over a substantial period of time.

Determining the Relevant Market

In any action brought under Section 2 of the Sherman Act (and indeed in many actions brought under the other antitrust laws as well) one of the most critical questions likely to face the courts is that of determining the "relevant product market" within which the extent of the defendant company's production is to be measured. Obviously, a particular market has to be defined before one can go about the determination of market shares.

The following landmark case brought against Du Pont graphically illustrates this fact. Because Du Pont produced 75 percent of the nation's cellophane, it probably would have possessed monopoly power if the relevant product market consisted of cellophane alone. On the other hand, if the relevant product market should properly be defined as consisting of all flexible wrapping materials, its market share would be much less significant.

---

[3] As we will see in the next section, however, if a monopoly exists solely because of one or more legal patents, the monopoly does not violate Section 2.

United States v. Du Pont de Nemours and Company
U.S. Supreme Court, 351 U.S. 377 (1956)

The United States initiated this civil action against Du Pont in 1947, charging it with monopolizing, attempting to monopolize, and conspiring to monopolize interstate commerce in cellophane in violation of Section 2 of the Sherman Act. Relief by injunction was sought against the defendant company and its officers, forbidding "monopolizing or attempting to monopolize interstate trade in cellophane."

The government introduced evidence tending to show that the characteristics of cellophane were so different from other packaging materials that the relevant product market should be defined as consisting of cellophane alone. Du Pont, by contrast, introduced substantial evidence tending to prove that cellophane did, in fact, receive heavy competition from other flexible packaging materials, such as

pliofilm and aluminum foil. **The trial court, after making over 3,000 findings of fact, agreed with Du Pont's position and ruled that the relevant product market consisted of *all flexible wrapping materials*. On this basis the court ruled that Du Pont's share of this larger market fell far short of constituting a monopoly, and dismissed the action. The government appealed to the U.S. Supreme Court.**

Reed, Justice:

. . . During the period that is relevant to this action Du Pont produced almost 75 percent of the cellophane sold in the United States, [but cellophane alone] constituted less than 20 percent of all "flexible packaging material" sales. . . .

If cellophane is the "market" that Du Pont is found to dominate, it may be assumed it does have monopoly power over that "market." Monopoly power is the power to control prices or exclude competition. . . . [It may be true that it is] practically impossible for anyone to commence manufacturing cellophane without full access to Du Pont's technique. However, Du Pont has no power to prevent competition from other wrapping materials. *The trial court consequently had to determine whether competition from the other wrappings prevented Du Pont from possessing monopoly power in violation of Section 2.* [Emphasis added.] . . .

When a product is controlled by one interest, without substitutes available in the market, there is monopoly power. . . . But where there are market alternatives that buyers may readily use for their purposes, illegal monopoly does not exist merely because the product said to be monopolized differs from others. . . .

But despite cellophane's advantages, it has to meet competition from other materials in every one of its uses. [The court here summarized a number of the trial court's findings as follows:] Food products are the chief outlet, with cigarettes next. . . . [But] cellophane furnishes less than 7 percent of wrappings for bakery products, 25 percent for candy, 32 percent for snacks, 35 percent for meats and poultry, 27 percent for crackers and biscuits, 47 percent for fresh produce and 34 percent for frozen foods. . . . The result is that cellophane shares the packaging market with others, [and thus it can be said that] a very considerable degree of functional interchangeability exists between these products. . . .

An element for consideration . . . is the responsiveness of the sales of one product to price changes of the other. If a slight decrease in the price of cellophane causes a considerable number of customers of other flexible wrappings to switch to cellophane, it would be an indication that a high cross-elasticity of demand exists between them; that the products compete in the same market. The court below held that the "great sensitivity of customers in the flexible packaging markets to price or quality changes" prevented Du Pont from possessing monopoly control over price. The record sustains these findings [and also the finding that Du Pont never possessed power to exclude any other producers] from the rapidly expanding packaging market. . . .

> *It seems to us that Du Pont should not be found to monopolize cel-*
> *lophane when that product has the competition and interchangeability*
> *with other wrappings that this record shows.* [Emphasis added.]
> On the findings of the District Court, this judgment is affirmed.

Intent to Monopolize

A company that has been found to possess monopoly power violates Section 2 only if it is also proved that the company intended to acquire or maintain its monopoly position. Thus, a monopolist does not violate the statute if the evidence demonstrates that it achieved its overwhelming market power through the natural functioning of the market rather than through intentional means. For example, a monopoly is legal if it resulted solely from superior efficiency or skill or if it occurred solely because of lawful patents. In a similar vein, a monopoly is not illegal if the evidence shows that this particular market can really support only one profitable firm, a so-called **natural monopoly.** Although very unusual, a natural monopoly can occur when capital expenditures are so high in relation to demand that other firms could not earn a sufficient rate of return on the enormous investment. Public utilities are usually viewed as natural monopolies, and also are usually regulated directly by a specific government agency because of recognition that competition cannot effectively regulate the firm's behavior.

Examples of conduct that often will be sufficient to support a conclusion that a monopolist intended to monopolize include the following: (1) systematically and persistently discriminating in prices charged to different categories of customers (discussed as a separate violation in the next chapter); (2) refusing to sell equipment but instead requiring customers to enter long-term leases, thus greatly reducing the opportunities for other manufacturers to get into this market; (3) intentionally creating large excess production capacity, which also may deter other firms from entering the market; (4) systematically selling below marginal cost, thus incurring

short-term losses that can only be recovered by charging monopoly prices at a later time when competition has been eliminated; and (5) intentionally increasing the costs of smaller rivals, as by falsely disparaging their products, stealing their trade secrets, and so on.

Oligopolistic Industries

In general terms, an **oligopolistic industry** is one in which a small number of firms control most of the industry's total output. (The automobile and cereal industries are two of the best examples.)

While oligopolistic situations are frequently referred to as "shared monopolies," companies in such industries do not violate Section 2 of the Sherman Act merely because of their size (assuming they have achieved such size through normal growth processes). Thus the mere fact that a handful of companies sell most of the the new cars sold in the United States does not cause them to be in violation of Section 2.

On the other hand, if two or more companies in oligopolistic industries act *in concert* in any material way, their chance of having violated Section 2 (as well as Section 1) is very high. An action brought by the United States against the American Tobacco Co., Liggett and Myers Tobacco Co., and R. J. Reynolds Tobacco Co. was a leading case of this kind. *American Tobacco Co. v. United States,* 328 U.S. 781 (1946). The defendant companies, which historically produced from 70 to 80 percent of the nation's cigarettes, were found guilty both of attempting to monopolize and of monopolizing the cigarette industry. Substantial evidence was presented that the companies had, among other activities, systematically and concertedly purchased quantities of tobacco whenever this was necessary to keep it out of the hands of smaller competitors.

SUMMARY

The first of the federal antitrust statutes was the Sherman Act, and it continues to be the most fundamental law aimed at preserving competition in the marketplace. The Sherman Act consists of two substantive sections. Section 1 prohibits "contracts, combinations, and conspiracies in restraint of trade." It can be violated only by two or more separate entities acting together. One of the most frequently litigated issues under Section 1 is whether there has actually been agreement, or collusion, between two or more independent entities.

The basic standard for interpreting Section 1 is the Rule of Reason, under which particular joint conduct is illegal only if proved to have had the purpose or effect of unreasonably limiting competition. Several types of conduct, however, have been declared per se illegal under Section 1. In other words, such conduct is illegal without proof of an unreasonably anticompetitive purpose or effect. The types of conduct that have been held per se illegal are horizontal price fixing, vertical price fixing, horizontal market divisions, and group boycotts. Vertical customer and territorial restraints were within the Per Se Rule for a time; today, however, these arrangements are judged under the Rule of Reason.

Section 2 of the Sherman Act prohibits monopolization, which essentially consists of a single firm's exercise of overwhelming market power to control prices or exclude competition. Defining the relevant market is usually an important first step when a court is trying to determine whether a firm has violated Section 2. Even if a firm has a monopoly, however, there is no violation of Section 2 unless it is shown that the firm intended to acquire or maintain monopoly powers. In other words, if the monopoly was the inevitable consequence of inherent market conditions or superior efficiency, there is no violation of Section 2.

KEY TERMS

Conscious parallelism
Rule of reason
Per se rule
Horizontal price fixing
Vertical price fixing
Horizontal market division
Group boycott
Vertical customer restriction
Vertical territorial restriction
Monopolization
Entry barrier
Natural monopoly
Oligopolistic industry

QUESTIONS AND PROBLEMS

1. Certain types of business conduct might violate Section 1 of the Sherman Act without violating Section 2, and other kinds of conduct might violate Section 2 without violating Section 1. Given an example of each type of violation.

2. Members of the Chicago Board of Trade, consisting of 1600 grain traders, held daily "sessions" at which all offers to buy grain, and all sales of grain, were made public. All selling prices were thus known to members. After each session was over, which was usually 2 p.m., members were generally free to buy grain from country grain elevators at prices mutually agreed upon. To limit this activity, the Board of Trade adopted a rule that provided that such post-session purchases of grain could not be made at prices other than those in effect at the end of each regular session. Thus if the "to arrive" price of wheat at the end of the session was $1.50 per bushel, members could not buy wheat from grain elevators the rest of the day at prices higher or lower than that figure. This Board of Trade rule was promptly challenged in court as being a violation of Section 1 of the Sherman Act. If the legality of the rule were tested by the "rule of reason," do you think it might be found to be lawful under the Sherman Act? Explain. (*Chicago Board of Trade v. United States*, 246 U.S. 231, 1918.)

3. Klor's, Inc., was a San Francisco retailer who sold radios, TVs, and refrigerators in competition with a department store next door. (The store next door was part of a large California retail chain.) Klors alleged that the chain, in order to injure Klor's business, pressured such manufacturers as General Electric, RCA, and Zenith to agree amongst themselves not to sell any of their products to Klor's. When Klor's charged that this agreement between the chain and the manufacturers was a contract that unreasonably restrained trade in violation of Section 1 of the Sherman Act, the chain's basic defense was that the agreement did *not* unreasonably restrain trade in view of the fact that there were a number of retailers in the immediate vicinity who continued to offer General Electric, RCA, and Zenith products, and thus consumers who wished to buy these products from someone other than the chain could easily buy from these other retailers. Do you think the chain's argument is a valid one? Why or why not? (*Klor's, Inc. v. Broadway-Hale Stores, Inc.,* 359 U.S. 207, 1959.)

4. Explain the concept of "intent to monopolize" and how it can be proved.

5. What is the explanation for the fact that some business practices are per se violations of the Sherman Act (i.e., violations regardless of the intent of the particular parties involved or the significance of the effects on the market)?

6. When a charge of "monopolization" under Section 2 of the Sherman Act is made against a company, why does the defendant's guilt or innocence sometimes turn upon the court's definition of the *relevant market?*

7. What is meant by the statement that in some situations there exists a "high degree of cross-elasticity of demand" between two or more somewhat similar products?

8. What is an oligopolistic industry, and under what circumstances might firms in such an industry violate Section 2 of the Sherman Act?

Chapter 48

ANTITRUST LAW
The Clayton and
Robinson-Patman Acts

As noted earlier, following the Sherman Act, Congress passed several statutes designed to prohibit certain practices in interstate commerce if their effect was substantially anticompetitive. In this chapter we examine the salient provisions of such acts and the judicial interpretation given them by the courts, with particular emphasis on the Clayton Act and the Robinson-Patman Act (which amended the Clayton Act).

ORIGINAL PROVISIONS OF THE CLAYTON ACT

In the years following its enactment, the courts interpreted the Sherman Act rather strictly. While a number of cases were successfully prosecuted under it, others were dismissed because the restrictive agreements complained of by the government were found not to have unreasonably restrained trade under Section 1 or not to have constituted monopolizations of or attempts to monopolize commerce under Section 2.

Thus, as a result of judicial interpretation, many anticompetitive agreements and practices continued to be lawful in particular situations. As one example, sellers remained free to discriminate in the prices they charged different customers as long as the discrimination was not part of a conspiracy to restrain trade and was not done to obtain or exploit a monopoly position. In this situation Congress passed the Clayton Act in 1914, the primary purpose of which was to prohibit certain *specific* practices that were felt to be harmful to free competition. The Act contained three particularly important sections, which we will summarize briefly. Then we will consider selected problems arising under each section, as subsequently amended.

Section 2

Section 2 deals with **price discrimination.** It generally prohibited sellers of goods from discriminating in the prices charged different pur-

chasers "where the effect of such discrimination may be to substantially lessen competition or tend to create a monopoly in any line of commerce." Certain exceptions were recognized, however. For example, quantity discounts could be granted under certain circumstances, as will be discussed in more detail later. Additionally, while sellers generally could not discriminate in prices charged to different buyers, they could refuse to make sales to any buyer at their discretion, as long as such refusal did not constitute an attempt to create a monopoly or unreasonably restrain trade. This right was guaranteed in a clause providing that "nothing herein contained shall prevent persons engaged in selling goods . . . from selecting their own customers in bona fide transactions and not in restraint of trade."

Section 3

Section 3 prohibited "exclusive dealing" agreements (and, by judicial interpretation, "tying" agreements) where the effect of these "may be to substantially lessen competition or tend to create a monopoly in any line of commerce." **Exclusive dealing agreements** are those in which the seller of goods, usually a manufacturer, requires the buyer to promise not to handle the products of a competitor of the seller. **Tying agreements** are those in which a seller of a commodity (or a lessor of equipment) agrees to sell or lease it only on condition that the buyer (or lessee) purchase other commodities or articles produced or distributed by the seller. (We will discuss both kinds of agreements later in the chapter.)

Section 7

Section 7 prohibited any corporation from acquiring "the whole or any part of the stock of another corporation where the effect . . . may be to substantially lessen competition between the corporation whose stock is so acquired and the corporation making the acquisition, or to restrain . . . commerce in any section or community, or tend to create a monopoly in any line of commerce. . . ." Acquisition of stock solely for investment purposes or for the purpose of forming lawful subsidiaries of the acquiring corporation was, however, expressly permitted. This section, as amended by the Celler-Kefauver Act, is the primary law under which the legality of corporate mergers is tested today. It too will be discussed later in the chapter.

PRICE DISCRIMINATION UNDER THE CLAYTON ACT

The basic purpose of Section 2 of the Clayton Act was to prohibit those types of price discrimination that were being used by sellers as a means of achieving monopoly positions in their industries, especially the reduction of prices in certain areas for the purpose of keeping out competitors. While Section 2 was generally successful in this regard, it was found in practice to contain several shortcomings:

1. The clause that forbade price discrimination where the effect of such discrimination "may be to substantially lessen competition" was interpreted by the courts as meaning the lessening of competition only *between the seller and one or more competitors of the seller;* any other price discrimination continued to be lawful. Thus, if S sold goods to buyer A at lower prices than those charged buyer B, the mere fact that the discrimination lessened competition *between A and B* did not constitute a violation of this section.

2. Congress found by 1936 that many sellers were being pressured by large-scale buyers to grant them price reductions much larger than could be justified on economic grounds alone. That is, sellers were granting buyers discounts greatly in excess of the actual cost savings attributable to production and handling efficiencies resulting from the quantities being sold, and the courts were permitting this practice under the "quantity discount" exception.

3. It was also apparent by this time that many sellers were circumventing Section 2 by granting rebates to favored buyers and that some sellers were taking advantage of the exception permitting price reductions "to meet competition" by lowering their prices in certain areas far below those of their competitors for the purpose of driving them out of business.

THE ROBINSON-PATMAN ACT

To remedy these problems, Congress passed the Robinson-Patman Act in 1936. By this amendment to the Clayton Act, Section 2 was completely rewritten and considerably lengthened. The section now has six subsections, the first two of which merit particular attention.

Subsection A makes it unlawful for a seller "to discriminate in price between different purchasers of goods of like grade and quality" where the effect of such discrimination "may be to substantially lessen competition or tend to create a monopoly in any line of commerce, or to injure, destroy or prevent competition *with any person who either grants or knowingly receives the benefit of such discrimination, or with customers of either of them. . . .*" (Emphasis added.)

This section further provides, however, that price differences based on actual "differences in the cost of manufacture, sale or delivery resulting from the differing methods or quantities in which such commodities are . . . sold or delivered" are lawful. In other words, if a manufacturer makes a large production run to fill a particular order with the result that the per-unit cost of production is less than what it normally would be, this saving may be passed along to the large-scale buyer. Additionally, subsection A permits "price changes from time to time in response to changing conditions affecting the market for or the marketability of the goods concerned. . . ." Subsection B contains an additional exception by providing that a seller may charge lower prices to some customers than it charges others if such reductions are made solely to meet prices of its competitors.

A Cautionary Note:

While the Robinson-Patman Act brought about certain clarifications to the law, it can by no means be said that price discrimination problems have been eliminated. In the first place, considerable discriminatory pricing continues to exist in the real world of business because the act is enforced only sporadically (as the Federal Trade Commission occasionally admits). Second, as the following case indicates, difficult problems of statutory interpretation under Section 2 still arise—particularly on the question of whether proven price discrimination in a given case may result in a substantial lessening of competition.

Federal Trade Commission v. Morton Salt Company
U.S. Supreme Court, 334 U.S. 37 (1948)

The Morton Salt Company manufactured and sold different brands of table salt to wholesalers (jobbers) and to large retail grocery chains. Morton sold its finest brand of salt, Blue Label, on a "standard quantity discount system" which was purportedly available to all of its customers.

The Federal Trade Commission, after a hearing, concluded that Morton's sales of salt under the system resulted in price discrimination in violation of Section 2 of the Robinson-Patman Act. Accordingly, the FTC issued a cease and desist order prohibiting further sales of salt under this system. A U.S. Court of Appeals set aside this order, finding no violation of Section 2. The FTC appealed this judgment to the U.S. Supreme Court.

In this appeal, there were two primary issues: (1) whether the discount system resulted in price discrimination within the meaning of Section 2; and (2) if so, whether the discrimination caused an injury to competition. (In the decision of the U.S. Supreme Court, Morton is referred to as "the respondent" throughout.)

Black, Justice:

. . . Under [respondent's] system the purchasers pay a delivered price, and the cost to both wholesale and retail purchasers of this brand differs according to the quantities bought. These prices are as follows, after making allowances for rebates and discounts:

	Per Case
Less-than-carload purchases	$1.60
Carload purchases	1.50
5,000-case purchases in any consecutive 12 months	1.40
50,000-case purchases in any consecutive 12 months	1.35

Only five companies have ever bought sufficient quantities of respondent's salt to obtain the $1.35 per case price. These companies could buy in such quantities because they operate large chains of retail stores in various parts of the country. As a result of this low price these five companies have been able to sell Blue Label salt at retail cheaper than wholesale purchasers from respondent could reasonably sell the same brand of salt to independently operated retail stores, many of whom competed with the local outlets of the five chain stores. . . .

In addition to these standard quantity discounts, special allowances were granted certain favored customers who competed with other customers to whom [the allowances] were denied.

Respondent's basic contention, which it argues this case hinges upon, is that its "standard quantity discounts, available to all on equal terms, as contrasted, for example, to hidden or special rebates, allowances, prices or discounts, are not discriminatory, within the meaning of the Robinson-Patman Act." Theoretically, these discounts are equally available to all, but functionally they are not. For as the record indicates (if reference to it on this point were necessary) no single independent retail grocery store, and probably no single wholesaler, bought as many as 50,000 cases or as much as $50,000 worth of table salt in one year. Furthermore, the record shows that, while certain purchasers were enjoying one or more of respondent's standard quantity discounts, some of their competitors made purchases in such small quantities that they could not qualify for any of respondent's discounts, even those based on carload shipments. The legislative history of the Robinson-Patman Act makes it abundantly clear that Congress considered it to be an evil that a large buyer could secure a competitive advantage over a small buyer solely because of the large buyer's quantity purchasing ability. The Robinson-Patman Act was passed to deprive a large buyer of such advantages except to the extent that a lower price *could be justified* by reason of a seller's diminished costs due to quantity manufacture, delivery, or sale, or by reason of the seller's good faith effort to meet a competitor's equally low price. [Emphasis added.] . . .

[The court then agreed with the FTC that Morton's evidence failed to justify its price differential—i.e., that Morton was unable to show that the discounts that it gave its very large customers were based on actual cost savings alone. The court then turned to the second question, the magnitude of the effect of the discrimination.]

It is argued [by respondent] that the findings fail to show that [its] discriminatory discounts had in fact caused injury to competition. There are specific findings that such injuries had resulted from respondent's discounts, although the statute does not require the Commission to find that injury has actually resulted. The statute requires no more than that the effect of the prohibited price discriminations "may be substantially to lessen competition . . . or to injure, destroy or prevent competition." After a careful consideration of this provision of the Robinson-Patman Act, we have said that "the statute does not require that the discrimination must in fact have harmed competition, *but only that there is a reasonable possibility that they 'may' have such an effect.*" [Emphasis added.] *Corn Products Co. v. Federal Trade*

Comm'n, 324 U.S. 726. Here the Commission found what would appear to be obvious, that the competitive opportunities of certain merchants were injured when they had to pay respondent substantially more for their goods than their competitors had to pay. The findings are adequate. . . . Judgment [of the Court of Appeals] reversed, [and order of the FTC reinstated]. . . .

EXCLUSIVE DEALING AND TYING AGREEMENTS UNDER THE CLAYTON ACT

Exclusive Dealing Contracts

As noted earlier, an exclusive dealing agreement is one in which a seller of goods requires the buyer (usually a retailer) to promise *not to handle the products of any competitor of the seller.* The controlling provision of the Clayton Act—Section 3—provides:

> that it shall be unlawful for any person engaged in [interstate commerce] . . . to lease or make a sale . . . of goods, wares, merchandise, machinery, supplies or other commodities . . . on the condition, agreement, or understanding that the lessee or purchaser thereof shall not use or deal in the goods, wares, merchandise, machinery, supplies, or other commodities of a competitor . . . of the lessor or seller, where the effect of such lease, sale, or . . . such condition, agreement, or understanding may be to substantially lessen competition or tend to create a monopoly in any line of commerce.

As one might expect, the typical case brought under Section 3 turns upon the question of whether the seller's contracts (within the particular fact-pattern presented) were likely to result in a substantial lessening of competition. In order to follow the thinking of the courts over the years on this point, we will refer briefly to several cases.

The "Dominant Seller" View: In several early cases, the Supreme Court ruled that exclusive dealing contracts substantially lessened competition (and thus were illegal) only when the seller "dominated" the relevant market. If such dominance was lacking, the seller's contracts were lawful even if such contracts were entered into with a number of buyers.

The "Substantial Share of Commerce" View: In somewhat more recent years, the U.S. Supreme Court has seemingly adopted a "harder" line in regard to exclusive dealing contracts. Beginning with the case of *Standard Oil of California v. United States,* 337 U.S. 293 (1949), the court has held that such contracts violate Section 3 if they affect a substantial portion of commerce, even if the seller does not occupy a dominant position in the industry. In that case, Standard Oil had exclusive dealing contracts with the operators of nearly 6,000 independent stations in the western states (16 percent of the total independent gas stations in the area). Through these stations Standard sold $57 million worth of gasoline in 1947, which was about 7 percent of total retail gasoline sales in the western states. The U.S. Supreme Court ruled that such widespread use of exclusive dealing contracts constituted just such a "clog on competition" which Congress meant to eliminate by enacting Section 3. Thus the court found a violation of that section, even though it conceded that Standard was not the dominant seller of gasoline in the affected area.

Requirements Contracts: In most exclusive dealing contracts, such as those discussed so far, the buyer of goods is purchasing them for resale. Another form of exclusive dealing arrangement, however, is the **requirements contract**—one in which the buyer of a commodity, such as coal or oil, agrees to purchase all of the commodity he or she will *need or use in his or her business* for a specified period from that seller and no one else. Such contracts do restrain trade in that the buyer is prevented from buying his or her requirements from any other seller (and the seller is not able to sell this quantity of goods— whatever the buyer's requirements turn out to be—to any other buyer). The contracts do not, however, necessarily violate Section 3; like others challenged under this section, their legality depends on whether they may result in a substantial lessening of competition. Under this test, there is little doubt that most requirements contracts *do not violate* the act, because the quantities of goods involved are normally rather small when compared to the quantities of similar goods produced by other sellers that remain available to other buyers in the affected market.

The leading case in point is *Tampa Electric Co. v. Nashville Coal Co.,* 365 U.S. 320 (1961). There Tampa Electric had contracted to purchase all the coal that it would need over a 20 year period from Nashville Coal, at specified prices per ton. A dispute subsequently arose, and in resulting litigation the primary question was whether the contract violated Section 3 of the Clayton Act.

The trial court ruled that the contract *did* substantially lessen competition in violation of Section 3, in view of the fact that the quantities of coal that were involved greatly exceeded the total quantity of coal purchased by all other purchasers in southern Florida. The U.S. Supreme Court disagreed with this conclusion, noting that there were still 700 coal producers in addition to Nashville Coal who were able to fill these other buyers' needs, and that their total production was over 359 million tons of coal a year, of which 290 million tons were sold by them on the open market annually. Thus the contract was found to be lawful.

Tying Agreements

A contract in which a supplier of a product or service makes it available only on the condition that the customer purchase other products or services usually is in violation of one or more of the antitrust laws. If it is shown that the contract unreasonably restrains trade or constitutes an attempt to create a monopoly, it is illegal under the Sherman Act. (There are a number of cases where such a showing has been made.) And even if the tying agreement does not have this effect, it still violates Section 3 of the Clayton Act if its effect "may be to substantially lessen competition or tend to create a monopoly in any line of commerce." (Literally, Section 3 applies only to exclusive dealing contracts. However, it has been extended by judicial interpretation to cover tying contracts on the theory that in regard to the unwanted goods or services involved, the buyer is foreclosed from purchasing such goods or services from any competitor of the seller.)

The following case is one of the best known cases involving tying contracts that have reached the U.S. Supreme Court.

Northern Pacific Railway Co. v. United States
U.S. Supreme Court, 356 U.S. 1 (1958)

In the 1860s Congress granted the Northern Pacific Railway Company 40 million acres of land in several northwestern states and territories to facilitate its construction of a railroad line from Lake Superior to Puget Sound. This grant consisted of every alternate section of land in a belt 20 miles wide on each side of track through the states and 40 miles wide through the territories.

Some of the lands contained great stands of timber, some contained valuable minerals, and others were useful for agriculture, grazing, or industry. By 1949 the railroad had sold or leased almost all of these lands to farmers and corporations. Most of the sale and lease contracts contained "preferential routing" clauses, which compelled the buyer or lessee to ship over Northern Pacific lines all commodities produced or manufactured on the land (with minor exceptions).

In 1949 the government filed suit against the railroad, contending that the preferential clauses unreasonably restrained trade, and thus violated Section 1 of the Sherman Act. The trial court ruled that these contracts were per se violations of the act, and issued an order restraining the railroad from enforcing its preferential routing clauses. Northern Pacific appealed this order directly to the U.S. Supreme Court.

Black, Justice:

. . . Although [the Sherman Act's prohibition against restraints of trade] is literally all-encompassing, the courts have construed it as precluding only those contracts or combinations which "unreasonably" restrain competition. . . . However, there are certain agreements or practices which because of their pernicious effect on competition and lack of any redeeming virtue are conclusively presumed to be unreasonable, and therefore illegal, without elaborate inquiry as to the precise harm they have caused. . . . This is known as the principle of per se unreasonableness. . . .

For our purposes a tying arrangement may be defined as an agreement by a party to sell one product but only on condition that the buyer also purchases a different [or tied] product, or at least agrees that he will not purchase that product from any other supplier.

[The court then noted that, as a general rule, tying contracts were not illegal unless there was proof that their use actually restrained trade unreasonably. However, the court also noted that in some circumstances tying contracts had been held to be per se violations of the Sherman Act, as follows:] *Tying contracts are unreasonable in and of themselves whenever a party has sufficient economic power with respect to the tying product to appreciably restrain free competition in the market for the tied product and a "not insubstantial" amount of interstate commerce is affected.* [Emphasis added.] *International Salt Co. v. United States,* 332 U.S. 392. . . .

In this case, we believe the district judge was clearly correct in entering summary judgment declaring the defendant's "preferential routing" clauses unlawful restraints of trade. We wholly agree that the undisputed facts established beyond any genuine question that *the defendant possessed substantial economic power by virtue of its extensive landholdings which it used as leverage to induce large numbers of purchasers and lessees to give it preference, to the exclusion of its competitors, in carrying goods or produce from the land transferred to them. Nor can there be any real doubt that a "not insubstantial" amount of interstate commerce was and is affected by these restrictive provisions.* [Emphasis added.] . . .

Judgment affirmed.

MERGERS UNDER THE CLAYTON ACT

A **merger** between two companies clearly is a "combination," and if the merger has a substantial anticompetitive effect it could be invalidated under Section 1 of the Sherman Act. Early judicial interpretation of this statute, however, made it a relatively ineffective weapon against mergers. The courts held that it could only be applied to mergers between competitors, and not to other types of mergers. Moreover, the language of the statute itself permitted its use only against mergers that had actually caused a substantial restraint of trade and not to those having a probable future anticompetitive effect.[1]

As a result, Section 7 of the Clayton Act was passed in 1914. Even though this statute prohibited mergers that were demonstrated to have probable future anticompetitive effects, it nevertheless was not very effective for two reasons. First, it applied only to those mergers accomplished through stock acquisitions, and many firms circumvented the law by using asset acquisitions. Second, like Section 1 of the Sherman Act, it was interpreted as applying only to mergers between competitors.

In 1950, Congress passed the Celler-Kefauver Act, which amended Section 7 so as to close these two loopholes. In essence, modern antimerger law was born in 1950. Today, Section 7 essentially prohibits a firm from acquiring all or part of the stock or assets of another firm, "where in any line of commerce in any section of the

country, the effect of such acquisition may be substantially to lessen competition. . . ."

What Is a Merger?

Combinations between firms can take many forms. There may be a formal corporate merger or consolidation under state corporation statutes. In many cases there is merely an acquisition of all or a substantial part of the stock or assets of another company without a formal merger. Sometimes the shareholders of the acquired company may exchange their shares of stock for shares of the acquiring company. A merger may involve a single transaction negotiated between the two firms' managers and approved by the acquired company's shareholders. On the other hand, the acquiring company's managers may go directly to the target company's shareholders through a publicly advertised "tender offer" because of opposition by the target company's managers. After the merger, there may be a total or partial integration of the two firms, or they may operate separately.

The term "merger" is used to describe a variety of combinations. Under Section 7 of the Clayton Act the form of the transaction is relatively unimportant—in fact, the statute itself does not even use the word "merger." Regardless of the form, a combination that involves a stock or asset acquisition is covered by Section 7.

Market Definition

One of the initial steps in most merger cases is definition of the relevant market. There are two reasons for the necessity of market definition. First, Section 7 clearly mandates it when refer-

---

[1] It should be noted that in later years, in nonmerger cases, the courts frequently did interpret Section 1 of the Sherman Act in such a way as to prohibit contracts, combinations, and conspiracies having only *probable* anticompetitive effects.

ring to acquisitions which may have the effect of substantially lessening competition *in any line of commerce in any section of the country.* Second, even without the clear requirement in Section 7, market definition would still be required because anticompetitive effects do not exist in the abstract—they must occur *somewhere.*

The methods employed by courts to define markets in merger cases are essentially the same as in monopoly cases. A good illustration of this methodology at work in merger analysis is found in *United States v. Philadelphia National Bank,* 374 U.S. 321 (1963). In that case, the Supreme Court struck down a merger between Philadelphia National Bank and Girard Bank, the second and third largest banks with head offices in the Philadelphia metropolitan area. The Court held that the relevant product market was commercial banking, and did not include services offered by the various other types of nonbank financial institutions. The justices recognized that some types of credit and other services offered by savings and loan companies, credit unions, and other institutions competed with certain bank services. However, they ruled that commercial banking was unique and there was not substantial cross-elasticity between it and the services of other institutions because (1) no other type of institution could legally offer checking accounts, and (2) no other type of institution actually offered the same "package" or "cluster" of services as banks did. The market share affected by the merger obviously was much larger than if other institutions had been included in the market definition. (Today, savings and loan companies, credit unions, and other financial institutions may offer checking accounts, and the total package of services offered by banks is not as unique as it once was. Thus, "commercial banking" may no longer be a separate product market but part of a larger financial services market. Regardless of this fact, the Court's *methodology* continues to be completely valid.)

The Court defined the relevant geographic market as the four-county Philadelphia metropolitan area. In the Court's analysis, it acknowl-edged that the large Philadelphia banks, such as the merging ones, had some customers outside this area. Also, a few banks ouside the area, such as the large New York banks, did some business in Philadelphia. On the other end of the spectrum, some very small customers would not even consider searching for a bank over an area as large as four counties. However, the four-county region was chosen because this was the area in which (1) most of the customers, who were neither extremely large nor extremely small, found it practical to do their banking business, and (2) state law permitted the operation of branches by Philadelphia banks.

Trends toward Concentration

The Court in the *Philadelphia National Bank* case also took note of the historical **trend toward concentration** in the Philadelphia banking market. The importance of such a trend results from the underlying purpose of Section 7 of the Clayton Act. Section 7, particularly as amended in 1950, was intended to be a *preventive measure.* Congress was concerned with what it perceived as a disturbing trend toward concentration of economic power into fewer and fewer firms, and sought to discourage the movement toward oligopolistic markets.[2]

As a result, when a merger is challenged and the evidence shows a definite historical trend toward concentration in the relevant market, courts generally are more likely to invalidate the merger. Evidence of such a trend does not automatically make the merger illegal, but may tip the scales in favor of illegality when the question is a close one. Of course, a historical trend toward concentration in a given market will not weigh heavily against the challenged merger if the trend apparently was the result of natural market forces driving out less efficient firms.

---

[2]There is debate as to whether Congress was correct in its assessment that the American economy was coming under the control of fewer and fewer companies. Evidence can be found to support both sides of the issue.

Types of Mergers

Mergers traditionally have been classified as horizontal, vertical, or conglomerate. A **horizontal merger** occurs if the two firms are competitors and a **vertical merger** exists if one of the firms sells something that the other firm buys. Any other merger is classified as a **conglomerate merger.** A merger may sometimes fit more than one category. For instance, in *Brown Shoe Co. v. United States,* 370 U.S. 294 (1962), the challenged merger involved both horizontal and vertical aspects. The reason was that each of the merging firms, Brown Shoe Co. and Kinney Shoe Co., was both a manufacturer *and* a retailer of shoes.

These classifications are important to very broadly describe the different types of fact situations, but two cautionary statements are in order.

1. How a merger is labeled does not determine whether it is legal or illegal.

2. The same basic test, whether substantial anti-competitive effects have resulted or are likely to result in the foreseeable future, is applied to all types of mergers.

Horizontal Mergers: A merger between competitors poses the greatest danger to competition: after the merger, the firms are not likely to compete. This does not mean, however, that every horizontal merger will be illegal. The following factors usually are the most important in a case involving such a merger.

1. The relative size of the firms usually is the most significant factor. At opposite ends of the spectrum, for example, a merger between two firms each having one to three percent of the market would almost never be illegal, while a merger between two firms each having 20 percent would almost always be illegal. More will be said about this factor.

2. The overall level of concentration in the market also is extremely important. As a general rule, the more concentrated a market is at the time of the merger, the more likely it is that a questionable merger will be ruled illegal.

3. As we have seen, a definite historical trend toward concentration in the market in recent years can affect the court's decision even if the market has not yet become highly concentrated.

4. If the market is characterized by high **entry barriers,** a questionable merger is more likely to be ruled illegal. As discussed in the previous chapter, an entry barrier is any market condition, such as extremely high capital requirements or difficult-to-obtain technology, that makes it much more difficult for a new firm to enter a market on its own.

5. A variety of other factors can be important. For example, a firm with 15 or 20 percent of a market ordinarily could legally acquire a company with a two or three percent share. Suppose, however, that the smaller firm traditionally had been an innovator or had recently obtained a patent of major significance. Or suppose that the smaller firm traditionally had been a "maverick" and frequently had led the way in vigorous price competition. In these scenarios, the merger might very well be found to violate Section 7.

As noted above, the relative size of the merging firms themselves usually is the most important factor. In the Philadelphia National Bank case, the Supreme Court ruled that a horizontal merger should be *presumed* illegal when the merger causes or threatens to cause "undue" concentration of the market. In that case, the Court said that a horizontal merger between firms having a combined market share of 30 percent or more certainly is one that threatens to cause "undue" concentration. In other cases, a combined market share as low as 20 percent has led courts to engage in a presumption of illegality.

This concept of "presumptive illegality" does not mean that a merger producing a lower level of concentration is automatically legal or that one producing a higher level is automatically illegal. What it means is that, wherever the line is to be drawn, a merger above this line is illegal unless the defendants come forward with evidence showing that the merger is not likely to harm competition. In essence, the presumption shifts the burden of persuading the court from plaintiff to defendants. The *General Dynamics* case which follows provides a good example of the type of evidence that defendants might use to rebut this presumption successfully. (This case is extremely important for another reason.

During the 1950s and 1960s the Supreme Court usually decided merger cases solely on the basis of market share statistics and data showing whether the number of firms in the market had been decreasing. The *General Dynamics* case marked a turning point. Beginning with this decision, and continuing since that time, the Court has engaged in a more in-depth economic analysis of challenged mergers and has considered a wider variety of factors.)

United States v. General Dynamics Corp.
U.S. Supreme Court, 415 U.S. 486 (1974)

Material Service Corp. owned Freeman Coal Mining Co. In 1954 Material Service began purchasing the stock of United Electric Coal Co., and by 1959 had acquired effective control of United. General Dynamics Corp. then acquired Material Service Corp. Subsequently, the government sued General Dynamics, claiming that the merger of Freeman and United violated Section 7 of the Clayton Act.

Freeman and United together accounted for about 23 percent of total coal production in the state of Illinois. If the geographic market was defined more broadly as the Eastern Interior Coal Province, one of the country's four major coal producing areas, the combined share would have been about 12 percent. The district court found that the merger did not violate Section 7, and the government appealed to the Supreme Court. The Supreme Court pointed out that such market share figures likely would lead to a ruling of illegality except for the existence of other important factors. These other economic factors caused the court to approve the merger regardless of the market shares.

Stewart, Justice:

. . . Much of the District Court's opinion was devoted to a description of the changes that have affected the coal industry since World War II. . . . To a growing extent since 1954, the electric utility industry has become the mainstay of coal consumption. While electric utilities consumed only 15.76% of the coal produced nationally in 1947, their share of total consumption increased every year thereafter, and in 1968 amounted to more than 59% of all the coal consumed throughout the Nation.

To an increasing degree, nearly all coal sold to utilities is transferred under long-term requirements contracts, under which coal producers promise to meet utilities' coal consumption requirements for a fixed period of time, and at predetermined prices. . . .

Because of these fundamental changes in the structure of the market for coal, the District Court was justified in viewing the statistics relied on by the Government as insufficient to sustain its case. Evidence of past production does not, as a matter of logic, necessarily give a proper picture of a company's future ability to compete. In most situations, of course, the unstated assumption is that a company that has maintained a certain share of a market in the recent past will be in a position to do so in the immediate future. . . .

In the coal market, however, statistical evidence of coal *production* was of considerably less significance. The bulk of the coal produced is delivered under long-term requirements contracts, and such sales thus do not represent the exercise of competitive power but rather the obligation to fulfill previously negotiated contracts at a previously fixed price. The focus of competition in a given time-frame is not on the disposition of coal already produced but on the procurement of new long-term supply contracts. In this situation, a company's past ability to produce is of limited significance, since it is in a position to offer for sale neither its past production nor the bulk of the coal it is presently capable of producing, which is typically already committed under a long-term supply contract. A more significant indicator of a company's power effectively to compete with other companies lies in the state of a company's uncommitted reserves of recoverable coal. . . .

The testimony and exhibits in the District Court revealed that United Electric's coal reserve prospects were "unpromising." United's relative position of strength in reserves was considerably weaker than its past and current ability to produce. While United ranked fifth among Illinois coal producers in terms of annual production, it was 10th in reserve holdings, and controlled less than 1% of the reserves held by coal producers in Illinois, Indiana, and western Kentucky. Many of the reserves held by United had already been depleted, at the time of trial, forcing the closing of some of United's midwest mines. Even more significantly, the District Court found that of the 52,033,304 tons of currently mineable reserves in Illinois, Indiana, and Kentucky controlled by United, only four million tons had not already been committed under long-term contracts. United was found to be facing the future with relatively depleted resources at its disposal, and with the vast majority of those resources already committed under contracts allowing no further adjustment in price. In addition, the District Court found that "United Electric has neither the possibility of acquiring more [reserves] nor the ability to develop deep coal reserves," and thus was not in a position to increase its reserves to replace those already depleted or committed.

Viewed in terms of present and future reserve prospects—and thus in terms of probable future ability to compete—rather than in terms of past production, the District Court held that United Electric was a far less significant factor in the coal market than the Government contended or the production statistics seemed to indicate. While the company had been and remained a "highly profitable" and efficient producer of relatively large amounts of coal, its current and future power to compete for subsequent long-term contracts was severely limited by its scarce uncommitted resources. Irrespective of the company's size when viewed as a producer, its weakness as a competitor was properly analyzed by the District Court and fully substantiated that court's conclusion that [the merger] would not "substantially . . . lessen competition. . ."

Affirmed.

Vertical Mergers: Although less likely to harm competition than a horizontal merger, a vertical merger in some circumstances can create dangers to the competitive process. These dangers can be summarized as follows.

Supply Foreclosure: Such a merger has the potential for creating a **supply foreclosure.** Suppose, for example, that S Company acquires B Corporation. S is a leading producer of a key component or ingredient used by B in manufacturing an end product. S probably will prefer B as a customer over B's competitors. This may or may not cause problems, depending on the circumstances. If S accounts for a large portion of the supply and if this item periodically is in short supply, B's competitors can be hurt by the merger regardless of their level of efficiency. A violation of Section 7 can exist when the evidence shows that a substantial degree of supply foreclosure is very likely.

Market Foreclosure: A vertical merger also can sometimes cause foreclosure of a portion of the market. If the portion foreclosed is viewed as substantial, the merger violates Section 7. This **market foreclosure** is just the other side of the coin from supply foreclosure. In the case of supply foreclosure above we were concerned with injuring competition at B's level. In the case of market foreclosure we are concerned with injuring competition at S's level. B probably will prefer S as a supplier, and if B is a major purchaser of the item in question, S's competitors could be blocked from a substantial part of the market. The competitive advantage acquired by S is not attributable to its own improved production efficiency.

In two important vertical merger cases, market foreclosure was the Supreme Court's pri-

mary concern. *United States v. du Pont,* 353 U.S. 586 (1957), a completely different case from the *du Pont* case involving cellophane, concerned du Pont's acquisition of a 23 percent stock interest in General Motors Corporation (GM). At that time, GM accounted for 40 to 50 percent of U.S. automobile sales. Du Pont supplied about two-thirds of GM's requirements of "automotive finishes" (paint and lacquer, for instance) and about one-half of GM's requirements of "automotive fabrics" (upholstery, for example). The Court invalidated the acquisition mainly because of its fear that du Pont's competitors were being foreclosed from almost half of the total market for auto finishes and fabrics. In *Brown Shoe Co. v. United States,* 370 U.S. 294 (1962), one of the Court's major reasons for striking down the Brown-Kinney merger was the concern that Brown's competitors in shoe manufacturing would be at least partly blocked from selling their shoes through Kinney's retail outlets. Kinney was the largest family-oriented shoe store chain in America.

At the present time it is difficult to determine the amount of supply or market foreclosure that will be viewed by the courts as "substantial." The evidence probably will have to demonstrate supply or market foreclosure of at least 20 percent.

Raising Entry Barriers: A vertical merger may contribute to increased *entry barriers* resulting from vertical integration. Vertical integration occurs when a firm operates at more than one level in the chain of production and distribution. Vertical integration resulting from independent expansion into another level does not raise any questions under Section 7 of the Clayton Act. If it occurs through a vertical merger, however, Section 7 does apply. Sometimes vertical integration can actually reduce costs by making distribution from seller to buyer more efficient. For instance, when seller and buyer (S and B) are owned by the same firm, selling expenses can be less, paperwork can be reduced, and supplies and requirements can be better coordinated and planned. Distribution efficiencies clearly are to be encouraged, but these cost savings can have other effects. If a substantial part of the relevant market is controlled by vertically integrated firms, a new entrant into the market will also have to enter as a vertically integrated firm in order to compete effectively. Entering a market at two levels simultaneously requires much greater capital outlays and thus makes new market entry less likely.

In the end, there are two opposing considerations. Distribution efficiencies are a positive effect in the short run; increased entry barriers are a negative effect in the long run. If competition at the lower level (B's level) is vigorous, these cost savings will be substantially passed on to ultimate consumers, and the increased entry barriers alone should not cause the merger to be illegal. On the other hand, if competition at B's level is rather stagnant, the cost savings probably will not be passed on to consumers, and the potential for increased entry barriers may lead a court to strike down the merger.

Conglomerate Mergers: Conglomerate mergers usually are not illegal. The courts have identified certain situations, however, in which Section 7 may be violated.

Perceived Potential Entrant: Suppose that X Company enters the widget market by acquiring Y Company, a producer of widgets. The merger can be illegal under the **perceived potential entrant** theory if the following factors are present.

1. For a significant period of time before the merger, X was a uniquely situated potential entrant into the widget market. In other words, the evidence shows that X had a special incentive to enter the market and the ability to do so. Entry

barriers in the widget market were high, so that there were not many firms like X who were willing and able to enter. But the entry barriers were not insurmountable for a firm like X with a special incentive and substantial resources. The circumstances creating this "special incentive" vary, but often involve "product extension" or "market extension" acquisitions. A product extension merger is one in which X buys into a market that involves a product closely related to one or more of X's present products and thus represents a logical extension of X's product line. A market extension merger is one in which X buys into a market involving a product that X already sells, but in a different geographic area.[3]

2. The market for widgets was already quite concentrated, with only a handful of firms dominating. Thus, the market probably was not as competitive as it should have been.

3. The evidence shows that, prior to the merger, the major firms in the widget market perceived the existence of X as a likely future entrant into the market.

Under these circumstances, X's position "on the edge" of the widget market was probably having a beneficial effect on that market prior to the merger by causing widget makers to keep prices lower in the hope of discouraging X from actually entering. When X acquired Y, this beneficial "edge effect" disappeared. If X had entered the market on its own by building a widget plant (de novo entry), this in itself would have been beneficial. Or if X had entered the market by acquiring a very small, inconsequential firm (a "toehold" acquisition) the beneficial effect of the merger would counteract the removal of the edge effect. But if X entered by acquiring a firm that was a significant competitor in the widget market, there is nothing beneficial to counteract

---

[3] Labels like "vertical" and "conglomerate" can be deceiving if not fully understood. The supplier-customer relationship may sometimes create this "special incentive." Thus a vertical merger in some cases may also be challenged under the potential entrant theory.

the removal of the edge effect. In this case the merger usually will violate Section 7.

Entrenchment: Suppose that Magnum Co. is already dominant in the market for electric motors. Giant Corp., which operates in other markets, has great financial resources and is much larger than Magnum or any other firm in the electric motor market. Giant acquires Magnum. In this situation, because of access to Giant's resources, there is a very real danger that Magnum will become even more firmly entrenched in its position of dominance in the electric motor market. In addition, other firms in that market are likely to be more timid about competing vigorously against Giant-Magnum than against Magnum alone. A third danger is that entry barriers will be raised—new firms are less likely to want to face Giant-Magnum than Magnum alone. Thus, under the so-called **entrenchment theory** (or "deep pockets" theory, so named because of the acquiring firm's formidable resources), the merger may be illegal.

Tending to Cause Reciprocity: Reciprocity essentially is "I'll buy from you if you'll buy from me." Systematic reciprocity on a fairly large scale can distort markets by foreclosing other firms without regard to their efficiency. The Supreme Court held, in *FTC v. Consolidated Foods Corp.,* 380 U.S. 598 (1965), that a merger violates Section 7 when it creates a high likelihood of reciprocity. In that case, Consolidated was a large customer of food processing firms. Consolidated acquired Gentry, which produced dehydrated onion and garlic used in food processing. The Court invalidated the merger. Despite this case, indications are that this theory will not be used against mergers to any appreciable extent in the foreseeable future.

Failing Company Defense

Suppose that M Company and P Company undertake a merger that probably would be illegal under ordinary circumstances. However, suppose further that P was in danger of failure prior to the merger. The so-called **failing company defense** can be used, and the merger will be legal, if the following facts are proved: (1) P probably will not be able to meet its financial obligations in the near future; (2) P will not be able to reorganize successfully and continue in business under the protection of Chapter 11 of the Bankruptcy Code; and (3) P has made a good faith, but unsuccessful, effort to obtain a reasonable merger offer from another firm that would pose less danger to competition than does the merger between M and P.

Merger Guidelines

The Justice Department's Antitrust Division first issued **Merger Guidelines** in 1968. These guidelines, which also were followed by the FTC, indicated the circumstances in which one of these agencies could ordinarily be expected to challenge a merger. The guidelines were not law, but did provide business with a valuable planning tool.

New, substantially revised guidelines were issued by the Justice Department in 1982 and revised slightly in 1984. The FTC concurred with most, but not all, of the statements in the new guidelines. Two reasons brought about the revision: (1) developing case law during the 1970s resulted in the original guidelines being somewhat stricter than the law actually being applied by the courts; and (2) political conservatives made tremendous gains in the 1980 elections, ultimately resulting in the appointment of Justice Department officials who favored more lenient treatment of mergers.

The fundamental principles of merger law discussed in this chapter continue to be the law, and basically are still reflected in the new guidelines. The guidelines indicate, however, that the Justice Department and the FTC will be more reluctant than in past years to challenge vertical and conglomerate mergers. Another switch in the political climate, however, could cause this reluctance to disappear.

One of the key innovations of the new guidelines is the use of the Herfindahl-Hirschman Index (HHI) for deciding whether to challenge horizontal mergers. This index involves the squaring of the market share of each firm in the market and then adding the squares. If, after the merger in question, the HHI is under 1,000, the merger will almost never be challenged. If the postmerger HHI is between 1,000 and 1,800, whether the merger is challenged will depend on other factors such as those discussed earlier in this chapter. In this 1,000 to 1,800 range, the Justice Department usually will take legal action only if the merging firms are large enough so that the merger adds at least 100 points to the HHI. When the postmerger HHI is above 1,800, the Justice Department usually will take legal action if the merger adds as much as 50 points. Thus, the merging firms must be very small for the merger to go unchallenged when the HHI is this high.

Premerger Notification

In 1976 Congress amended Section 7 of the Clayton Act by adding a requirement that certain large firms give advance notice and detailed information to the Justice Department and FTC of proposed mergers. The purpose of this provision is to enable these agencies to have adequate information about the transaction in advance so they can assess its probable effects and, if necessary, challenge it *before* the merger is actually consummated. This is much easier than trying to "unscramble the eggs" after the merger has already been completed.

In situations where notification is required, the firms cannot complete the merger for at least 30 days after the agencies receive notice. The waiting period is only 15 days in the case of a merger to be accomplished through a public tender offer. If either agency requests additional information, the waiting period is extended 20 days (10 days for tender offers) from receipt of the additional information.

Premerger notification is required when (1) either firm engages in or affects interstate commerce; *and* (2) one firm has sales or assets of at least $100 million and the other firm has

sales or assets of at least $10 million; *and* (3) after the proposed acquisition the acquiring firm will own at least 15 percent or $15 million worth of the stock or assets of the acquired firm.

SUMMARY

The Clayton Act was passed by Congress in 1914 to identify certain anticompetitive practices and to provide a basis for challenging such practices before they resulted in actual monopolies or restraints of trade. Section 2 of the Clayton Act prohibited price discrimination. This provision was substantially amended in 1936 by the Robinson-Patman Act. Section 3 prohibits exclusive dealing and tying agreements in particular circumstances. Section 7 of the Clayton Act, as amended in 1950 by the Celler-Kefauver Act, prohibits mergers that threaten to lessen competition substantially.

Market definition is usually an important first step in determining whether a merger violates Section 7. The methodology for defining the relevant market is the same under Section 7 as it is under Section 2 of the Sherman Act. Evidence of a recent trend toward substantially greater economic concentration in the relevant market has been an important factor in a number of merger cases.

The three categories of mergers are horizontal, vertical, and conglomerate. A merger is horizontal if it involves competing firms, and vertical if one of the merging firms sells something that the other firm buys. Mergers without horizontal or vertical characteristics are called conglomerate mergers. Of the different types, horizontal mergers are the most likely to limit competition and, therefore, are the most likely to violate Section 7. Whether a vertical merger poses any significant danger to competition primarily depends on the portion of the relevant supply source or market that will be foreclosed by the merger. Conglomerate mergers are the least likely to harm competition and usually do not violate Section 7. Even if a merger appears likely to limit competition substantially, there is no violation of Section 7 if the elements of the failing company defense are proved. The Department of Justice has issued Merger Guidelines to provide the business community with a clearer idea of the circumstances in which a particular merger is likely to be challenged under Section 7. Because it is so difficult to "undo" a merger after it has been completed, in 1976 Congress passed a premerger notification statute requiring the participants in certain large mergers to notify the Justice Department and the FTC at least 30 days before carrying out the merger. This provision gives the two agencies time to study the merger and act while it is still feasible to do so.

KEY TERMS

Price discrimination
Exclusive dealing agreement
Tying agreement
Requirements contract
Merger
Trend toward concentration
Horizontal merger
Vertical merger
Conglomerate merger
Entry barrier
Supply foreclosure
Market foreclosure
Perceived potential entrant
Entrenchment theory
Failing company defense
Merger Guidelines

QUESTIONS AND PROBLEMS

1. Utah Pie had its bakery in Salt Lake City, and for some years had been the sole seller of frozen pies in the area. In 1960 another distributor of pies, Pet Milk, started selling pies in Salt Lake City in competition with Utah. A price war broke out and continued for several years with the result that (a) Pet sold its pies to groceries in Salt Lake City from time to time at prices lower than

it was charging grocers located in other parts of the state in order to undercut Utah's prices, and (b) Utah suffered financial losses during the years that the war continued. Utah then sued Pet, charging Pet with price discrimination in violation of Section 2 of the Clayton Act. In regard to this charge, which of the facts stated above (if any) would support Utah's claim that Pet had engaged in discriminatory pricing? Discuss. (*Utah Pie Co. v. Continental Baking Co.,* 386 U.S. 685, 1967.)

2. Referring to the *Utah* case, above, Utah had to prove—in addition to discriminatory pricing on Pet's part—an "injury" as a result of the pricing. On this aspect of the case, Utah proved not only that it had suffered occasional losses at specific times, but also introduced evidence of "predatory" pricing policies on the part of Pet—evidence that many of Pet's price cuts were so large as to be made only with the intent to drive Utah out of business. Do you think this kind of evidence is relevant in determining whether there was an injury, and, if so, the size of the injury? Explain.

3. Sun Oil sold gasoline to many independent retail dealers in Florida, including McLean's in Jacksonville. When a competitor of McLean's located just across the street started selling "Super Test" at prices lower than McLean was charging for Sunoco, Sun lowered its prices to McLean but did not lower them to other buyers of its gas in the area. The Federal Trade Commission then charged Sun with price discrimination in violation of the Clayton Act, and Sun defended on the ground that it had lowered its price simply to meet the price of a competitor as permitted by Clayton. The FTC replied that Sun had not lowered its price to meet that of a competitor, but rather to permit a customer to meet the price of one of the *customer's* competitors. Is the FTC argument valid? Why or why not? (*Federal Trade Commission v. Sun Oil,* 371 U.S. 505, 1963.)

4. On the subject of *requirements contracts,* (a) define such contracts, and (b) explain whether such contracts are usually lawful or usually unlawful under Section 3 of the Clayton Act.

5. Chicken Delight licensed several hundred franchisees to operate neighborhood fast food stores. It did not charge the franchisees any fees or royalties for use of its name, but it did require them to purchase certain packaging supplies and mixes exclusively from Chicken Delight, and also designated quantities of cookers and fryers. The prices charged the franchisees for these items were higher than those charged by competing suppliers. Several franchisees brought an action against Chicken Delight, claiming that the clauses in the franchises requiring them to buy these items from Chicken Delight alone were a form of tying agreement, and that these requirements therefore violated Section 1 of the Sherman Act. (a) Do you think these clauses do create tying contracts, and (b) if so, do you think that they unreasonably restrain trade in violation of the Sherman Act? Explain. (*Siegel v. Chicken Delight, Inc.,* 448 F.2d 43, 1971.)

6. The nation's second largest can producer acquired the nation's third largest producer of glass containers. Cans and bottles did not compete for all end uses, but for some uses they did compete. For example, there was clear rivalry between cans and bottles for the business of soft drink and beer producers. Both industries were relatively concentrated: the top two can manufacturers had 70 percent of can sales; the top three bottle manufacturers had 55 percent of bottle sales. If cans and bottles were viewed as a single market, the two firms would have, respectively, 22 percent and 3 percent of that market. Discuss whether this merger would violate Section 7 of the Clayton Act. (*United States v. Continental Can Co.,* 378 U.S. 441, 1964.)

7. Von's Grocery Co. acquired Shopping Bag Food Stores. Von's was the third largest retail grocery in the Los Angeles area; Shopping Bag was the sixth largest. Together, they accounted for 7.5 percent of retail grocery sales in the Los Angeles area. After the merger, the Von's-Shopping Bag combination was the second largest grocery chain in the area. Each firm had been very successful and had grown very rapidly during the ten years prior to the merger. The evidence also showed that, during the previous thirteen years, the number of grocery store owners operating a single store in the area dropped from 5,365 to 3,590. During the same period, the number of chains with two or more stores increased from 96 to 150. During approximately the same period, 9 of the top 20 chains had acquired 126 of their smaller competitors. Discuss whether this merger would violate Section 7 of the Clayton Act. (*United States v. Von's Grocery Co.,* 384 U.S. 270, 1966.)

8. General Motors, Ford, and Chrysler, in that order, were the largest automobile producers in America. Together they accounted for 90 percent of domestic production. The domestic spark plug market was dominated by Champion (40 percent), AC (30 percent—wholly owned by General Motors), and Autolite (15 percent). The remainder of the spark plug market was accounted for by very small producers.

The independent spark plug makers (primarily Champion and Autolite) sold spark plugs to the automakers (primarily Ford and Chrysler) at cost or below. These original equipment (OE) plugs were sold so cheaply because auto mechanics almost always replace worn out plugs with the same brand that had been original equipment (called the OE tie). Thus, it was essential to get into the OE market in order to get into the market for replacement plugs—the aftermarket. Large profits were made in this aftermarket.

Ford, whose purchases of OE plugs from the independent spark plug makers amounted to 10 percent of all the spark plugs produced domestically, wanted to gain entry into the profitable spark plug aftermarket. It did so by purchasing Autolite's only spark plug factory, as well as its trademark and distribution facilities. Discuss whether this merger might violate Section 7 of the Clayton Act. (*Ford Motor Co. v. United States,* 405 U.S. 562, 1972.)

Chapter 49

EMPLOYMENT LAW

The law of employment relations has undergone a fundamental transformation within recent years and change continues even today. For much of our nation's history, the legal relationship between employer and employee was governed by general traditional principles of common law, which in practice typically tilted in the direction of the employer's authority. For example, employers lawfully could discharge their workers for any (or no) reason, including the individual employee's race, union membership, or job-related injury.

The growth of unions was the working person's first response to this legal regime, which seemingly favored employers to an inordinate degree. Unionization was frustrated at first by a series of judicial decisions, but once Congress provided statutory protection in the 1930s, the new labor organizations were able to thrive and provided considerable benefits to member workers.

Notwithstanding the advantages provided the majority of employees, unions had some serious shortcomings, especially when it came to protecting small groups of employees and dealing with noneconomic issues. In the 1960s Congress once again intervened to expand the protection of workers in areas where unions had contributed little. A number of antidiscrimination laws were enacted, the most significant being the Civil Rights Act of 1964. The Occupational Safety and Health Act of 1968 established a new agency and granted it considerable power to guard against workplace hazards. Legislation expanded worker rights in other areas as well. Perhaps prodded by this congressional activity, the courts also began to reexamine old precedents and initiate new common-law protections for employees. This chapter explores these developments in the law of employment relations and the complications the changes create for employers.

LABOR RELATIONS LAW

In the early nineteenth century, attempts to unionize were stymied by the doctrine that they represented unlawful criminal conspiracies at common law. This theory gradually fell into disfavor and by the end of the century unions began to achieve some success, especially with the advent of industrialization and a rise in perceived employer abuse of power. Even in the early twentieth century, however, the courts continued to frustrate union development by enjoining critical functions of such organizations, such as striking and picketing. This was an era of much labor strife and periodic outbreaks of violence associated with labor/management disputes.

Recognizing the existence of a serious national problem, Congress passed several laws in an attempt to resolve labor/management difficulties, including the Railway Labor Act and the Norris–La Guardia Act, which prohibited, among other provisions, the use of injunctions against many union activities. Although these statutes eased the situation somewhat, it soon became clear that more extensive legislation was necessary. In 1935 Congress created a comprehensive framework for labor relations law by passing the National Labor Relations Act (NLRA). While this act has been amended, the basic rules established by the original NLRA survive today as the foundation of current law.

The NLRA unambiguously recognized an employee's right to organize by forming unions and authorized these labor organizations to bargain collectively with employers. Certain practices were declared to be **unfair labor practices,** and these were prohibited. Unfair labor practices were defined to include employer domination of unions, interference with employee organizing, discrimination against union members, and refusal to bargain collectively.

In order to enforce these requirements, the NLRA established a new agency, the National Labor Relations Board (NLRB). The NLRB consists of the General Counsel and the Board itself. The

General Counsel investigates charges of unfair labor practices and, if they are found merit-worthy, initiates an action against the responsible party. These actions are heard by an administrative law judge and may be appealed to the entire Board. If the Board finds a violation, it can seek enforcement of a number of sanctions, including cease-and-desist orders and back pay awards. Board decisions may be appealed to the U.S. Courts of Appeals.

Coverage

The NLRA applies generally to all employers involved in or affecting interstate commerce. As discussed in Chapter 5 (Constitutional Law), this language is quite broad in scope. The act is limited to protection of employees, however, and does not cover independent contractors, a distinction explained in Chapter 19. In addition, some categories of employees are specifically excluded from the act's coverage. Government employees, as well as workers for railways and airlines (protected under a different statute) are outside the NLRA's coverage. Significantly, managerial and supervisory employees are not covered by the act, as they are considered to be part of "management" rather than "labor."

Right to Organize

Central to the NLRA is its guarantee of a right to form unions. Once a group of employees determines that it desires to form an organization for collective bargaining, the group seeks out other workers for support. Once 30 percent of the eligible employees in an appropriate job category sign authorization cards, the employee group may petition for an election to certify a union as the employees' bargaining representative. Conduct of such elections is carefully scrutinized by the NLRB to ensure "laboratory conditions" of fairness. Employers opposing unionization must take special care in their actions and statements lest they be found to have committed an unfair labor practice, in which case the union may be automatically certified by the Board, regardless of the election's outcome. The following case illustrates the care that an employer must take to avoid disturbing the laboratory conditions required for a unionization election.

NLRB v. Exchange Parts Co.
U.S. Supreme Court, 375 U.S. 405 (1964)

Exchange Parts Co. is in the automobile parts rebuilding business. On November 9, 1959, the International Brotherhood of Boilermakers, Iron Shipbuilders, Blacksmiths, Forgers and Helpers informed the company that a majority of workers favored unionization and on February 19 the Board granted an election petition.

On February 25, the company held a dinner for employees, at which a vice-president announced that a previously granted extra vacation day could be either a floating holiday or could be taken on the individual employee's birthday. The workers chose the latter. The vice-president also mentioned the upcoming election as an opportunity for employees to "determine whether they wished to hand over their right to speak and act for themselves."

On March 4, the company sent its employees a letter that spoke of the "Empty Promises of the Union" and "the fact that it is the Company that puts things in your envelope. . . ." After mentioning a number of benefits, the letter stated: "The Union can't put any of those things in your envelope—only the Company can do that." The letter also went on to state that "it didn't take a Union to get any of those things and . . . it won't take a Union to get additional improvements in the future." Past company benefits were summarized and new benefits were announced, including the new birthday holiday, a new system for computing overtime that had the effect of increasing wages, and a new vacation schedule that enabled employees to take more time off per year.

The election was held on March 18, and the union lost. The union promptly filed a charge with the Board, which held that the company actions had the intent to induce employees to vote against the union, thereby disrupting laboratory conditions and amounting to an unfair labor practice. The Board sought enforcement of its ruling in the Court of Appeals, which held against the Board. The Board then appealed this decision to the Supreme Court.

Harlan, Justice:

. . . [The NLRA] makes it an unfair labor practice for an employer "to interfere with, restrain, or coerce employees in the exercise of [their rights to form labor unions]." . . . We think the Court of Appeals was mistaken in concluding that the conferral of employee benefits while a representation election is pending, for the purpose of inducing employees to vote against the union does not "interfere with" the protected right to organize. . . .

In *Medo Photo Supply Corp. v. N.L.R.B.*, 321 U.S. 678, 686, this Court said: "The action of employees with respect to the choice of their bargaining agents may be induced by favors bestowed by the employer as well as by his threats or domination." . . . The danger inherent in well-timed increases in employee benefits is the suggestion of a fist inside the velvet glove. Employees are not likely to miss the inference that the source of benefits now conferred is also the source from which future benefits must flow and which may dry up if it is not obliged. . . .

We cannot agree with the Court of Appeals that enforcement of the Board's order will have the "ironic" result of "discouraging benefits for labor." The beneficence of an employer is likely to be ephemeral if prompted by a threat of unionization which is subsequently removed. Insulating the right of collective organization from calculated good will of this sort deprives employees of little that has lasting value.

Reversed. [The Board's order shall be enforced.]

In addition to benefits, employers must be careful not to say anything that may be interpreted as a "threat." An employer's statement that a plant shutdown was possible because the union would make company survival impossible was held to be unlawful.

Collective Bargaining

Collective bargaining is the term for negotiations between an employer and the union representative. Once a union has been certified as an official bargaining representative of a category of employees, the NLRA imposes a duty to bargain in good faith on both employer and union. Mandatory subjects of bargaining include wages and most working conditions. The good faith provision requires the parties to make a sincere effort to reach agreement. Approaches such as "take it or leave it" proposals may support an inference of bad faith and hence an unfair labor practice finding. An employer also must be willing to furnish certain information to the union and cannot delay unduly in doing so.

Strikes

The most powerful device possessed by unions under the NLRA is the right to strike. This right is available when collective bargaining has reached an impasse. For a strike to be legal it must be supported by a majority of members and cannot be a "wildcat" strike by a disgruntled minority. The NLRA also restricts strikes to those against the primary employer and prohibits strikes against third parties in an attempt to coerce that third party to pressure the primary employer. Even primary strikes are unlawful if they are violent or designed to compel "featherbedding" (the hiring of unnecessary employees) or other illegal contract terms.

The NLRA imposes other conditions on the conduct of strikes. For example, if workers are on strike against one employer at a multi-employer location (such as a construction site), the employees may not picket the entire site, as this applies unlawful secondary pressure against the other employers. Workers may picket a portion of the site that is used largely by their primary employer. If a strike is legal, the employer may be restricted in dealing with his striking employees. If the workers are engaged in an authorized strike protesting the employer's unfair labor practices, the strikers are automatically entitled to reinstatement after the strike is resolved. In the more traditional economic wage strike, the employer need not necessarily rehire strikers but never can discriminate against strikers, who have a right to seek reemployment on terms equal to those offered other prospective employees.

Nonunion Employees

Although the NLRA was designed primarily to protect unionization, it extends certain rights to nonunion workers as well. Where nonunion employees engage in concerted activity, such as a walkout in response to perceived unsafe working conditions, they are protected much like strikers on behalf of a union. In general, however, employers have a relatively free hand in dealing with nonunion workers. This situation gives rise to one potentially serious pitfall, however. If an employer sets up "employee committees" or other groups to address grievances in the absence of a union, the committee's independence from management must be carefully ensured. Otherwise, the employer may be found to have created a company-dominated labor organization, which is an unfair labor practice under the NLRA.

The above discussion represents an exceedingly brief review of labor relations law. There is a huge body of precedent under the NLRA elaborating on the above principles. Many of the legal rules in this field have become quite picayune. Consequently, employers must take special care in any controversy involving an organization of employees.

EMPLOYMENT DISCRIMINATION LAW

For much of America's history, employers had the legal right to discriminate among employees on any basis other than union membership. Recently, however, antidiscrimination laws have been enacted that affect all phases of the employment process and that prohibit discrimination based on race, color, religion, sex, age, national origin, or perceived handicap. Worker use of these laws has grown to the point where they may exceed the NLRA as a source of litigation and potential employer liability.

Title VII

The Civil Rights Act of 1964 initiated antidiscrimination protection throughout society, and Title VII of the Act applied to employers. While Title VII was among the first antidiscrimination provisions in employment law, it remains probably the most significant.

Coverage: Title VII covers "employers," defined broadly to include individuals, corporations, partnerships, and virtually any other entity with employees. To be covered an employer must be engaged in or affecting interstate commerce and have 15 or more employees. Except for some very small businesses and religious organizations protected by the First Amendment, coverage of employers is universal. Title VII's prohibitions also apply to employment agencies involved in hiring and to labor organizations.

Protected Classes: Title VII protects certain defined groups against employment discrimination. Race and color discrimination is proscribed, although a controversy persists regarding the degree to which the majority of whites are protected. Blacks, Hispanics, American Indians, and Orientals are the major groups covered by Title VII. It also protects individuals from discrimination based on interracial associations. For example, a white may not be punished for being married to a black. Closely related is a provision prohibiting discrimination based on national origin, though it is still lawful to prefer U.S. citizens. Much current litigation has been instigated by Title VII's proscription against discrimination based on sex. Both sexual harassment and sex as a factor in employer decisions are now illegal. Congress has more recently amended the Act to protect women from discrimination against pregnancy and childbirth. The final protected class is religion, and an employer must make "reasonable accommodation" of his employees' religious beliefs. "Religion" encompasses a belief in a Supreme Being, rituals, or ethical principles for life.

Prohibited Acts: If an employee from a protected class is involved, Title VII prohibits any discrimination with respect to hiring or "compensation, terms, conditions, or privileges of employment." In the early years of the Act, discrimination against blacks was often intentional and blatant. As prejudice became more subtly practiced, the courts created an inference of discrimination when an employee alleged "disparate individual treatment" and proved:

1. that he or she was a member of a protected class;

2. that he or she applied for a job and was qualified to hold the job;

3. that he or she was rejected by the employer; and

4. that the employer continued to seek applicants.

Once these facts have been proved, the individual has made a *prima facie* case of Title VII violation and the burden shifts to the employer to show a legitimate reason for not hiring the person. Analogous requirements apply if a worker is alleging unlawful discharge or on-the-job discrimination.

A second category of Title VII suits is known as disparate statistical impact. In some circumstances, an apparently neutral practice may have a discriminatory effect on a protected class. Certain tests prerequisite to hiring, for example, may exclude a disproportionately large number of minority applicants or women. To maintain such a case, a plaintiff must demonstrate that an employer's percentage of minority employees, for example, is much smaller than would be expected by comparison to the number of minorities within the geographical area. The plaintiff must then link this disparity to some definable employer practice that *could* be considered discriminatory. If proved, this represents a *prima facie* case and the burden shifts to the employer to justify its past practice.

Defenses: Once the plaintiff in a Title VII action has met the requirements of the *prima facie* case, the defendant has the opportunity to offer defenses to justify the challenged practice. Title VII itself exempts "bona fide seniority systems" from its prohibitions. Although such systems may have the effect of perpetuating past patterns of discrimination, Congress chose to protect the seniority benefits of existing workers.

A second statutory defense is where the alleged discrimination is the consequence of a **bona fide occupational qualification (BFOQ).** While race may never be a BFOQ under Title VII, this defense is common in sex discrimination actions. To maintain a BFOQ defense, an employer must demonstrate a nexus between the protected classification and job performance and must also prove that the performance affected is of the "essence" of the job and not merely tangential to the fundamental job functions. The Supreme Court grappled with the contours of the BFOQ defense in the following case that, though criticized, represents the leading decision on the defense.

Dothard v. Rawlinson
U.S. Supreme Court, 433 U.S. 321 (1977)

Dianne Rawlinson applied for employment as a prison guard ("corrections counselor") in Alabama and was rejected. She challenged the decision not to hire her and alleged three bases for a Title VII violation: (1) the requirement that prison employees weigh at least 120 pounds; (2) the requirement that such employees be at least 5 feet 2 inches tall; and (3) a policy (Regulation 204) explicitly restricting the employment of women in maximum security prisons in the state. In the past, quite a few women met the height and weight requirements but none were employed at maximum security prisons. The state attempted to prove that all these challenged rules were essential to security in its prison system. The district court ruled for Ms. Rawlinson on all three issues, and Alabama appealed to the Supreme Court.

Stewart, Justice:

The gist of the claim that the height and weight requirements discriminate against women does not involve an assertion of purposeful discriminatory motive. It is asserted, rather, that these facially neutral qualification standards work in fact disproportionately to exclude women from eligibility for employment. To establish a prima facie case of discrimination, a plaintiff need only show that the facially neutral standards select applicants for hire in a significantly discriminatory pattern. Once it is thus shown that the employment standards are discriminatory in effect, the employer must show that any given requirement has a manifest relation to the employment in question. If the employer proves that the challenged requirements are job-related, the plaintiff may show that other selection devices without a similar discriminatory effect would also serve the employer's legitimate interests.

Although women 14 years or older comprise 52.75 percent of the Alabama population and 36.89 percent of its labor force, they hold only 12.9 percent of its correctional counselor positions. . . . When the height and weight restrictions are combined, Alabama's statutory standards would exclude 41.13 percent of the female population while excluding less than 1 percent of the male population.

We turn to the state's argument that it rebutted the prima facie case of discrimination by showing that the height and weight requirements are job-related. These requirements, they say, are related to strength, a sufficient but unspecified amount of which is essential to effective performance as a correctional counselor. However, the state produced no evidence correlating the requirements with the requisite amount of strength thought essential to good job performance. If the job-related quality that the state identifies is bona fide, its purpose could be achieved by adopting and validating a test that measures strength directly. Such a test, fairly administered, would satisfy Title VII because it would measure the person for the job and not the person in the abstract.

Thus, Title VII prohibits application of the height and weight requirements. Unlike the height and weight requirements, Regulation 204 explicitly discriminates on the basis of sex. In defense of this overt discrimination, the state relies on [the BFOQ defense]. The BFOQ exception was meant to be an extremely narrow exception to the general prohibition of discrimination on the basis of sex. In the particular factual circumstances of this case, however, we conclude that the District Court erred in rejecting the BFOQ exception.

The environment of Alabama's penitentiaries is a peculiarly inhospitable one for human beings of whatever sex. Because of inadequate staff and facilities, no attempt is made to classify or segregate inmates according to their offense or level of dangerousness. Consequently, the estimated 20 percent of the male prisoners who are sex offenders are scattered throughout the penitentiaries' dormitory facilities. In this environment of violence and disorganization, it would be an oversimplification to characterize Regulation 204 as an exercise in romantic paternalism. In the usual case, the argument that a job is too dangerous for women may be met by the rejoinder that it is the purpose of Title VII to allow the individual woman to make that choice for herself. More is at stake in this case, however.

The essence of a correctional counselor's job is to maintain prison security. A woman's relative ability to maintain order in a male, maximum security, unclassified penitentiary of the type Alabama now runs could be directly reduced by her womanhood. There is a basis for expecting that sex offenders who have criminally assaulted women in the past would be moved to do so again if access to women were established within the prison. There would also be a real risk that other inmates, deprived of a normal heterosexual environment, would assault women guards because they are women. The likelihood that inmates would assault a woman because she was a woman would pose a real threat not only to the victim of the assault but also to the basic control of the penitentiary and protection of its inmates and other security personnel.

[Affirmed in part and reversed in part.]

In instances when the plaintiff alleges discrimination by virtue of disparate statistical impact, defendants have the benefit of yet another important defense—business necessity. To succeed with this defense, an employer must show that its business purpose is sufficiently compelling to override any demonstrated racial impact, that the practice challenged effectively carries out the business purpose, and that there are no available alternative policies that would better accomplish the business purpose without adverse impact on racial workforce representation.

This defense generally enables employers to require experience, even though such a test often may have an adverse impact on women or minority applicants. Educational requirements have been held a business necessity for some jobs (such as where safety is involved or specific knowledge is required) but not for other, relatively uncomplicated positions. As discussed in *Dothard*, physical requirements must be closely correlated to actual work tasks. Any subjective business necessity criteria are especially suspect.

Procedures and Remedies: Title VII establishes special procedures for enforcing its dictates. An individual who believes him- or herself to be the victim of unlawful discrimination cannot simply take an employer to court. Rather, the Civil Rights Act created the Equal Employment Opportunity Commission (EEOC) to receive complaints of violations. The EEOC investigates these complaints and, when they are adequately supported by facts, the Commission attempts conciliation measures between the employer and employees. If conciliation efforts fail, EEOC may file suit in federal district court. Individuals may sue to enforce Title VII only after EEOC and state equal employment opportunity organizations have had the opportunity to take action.

Once a court finds that Title VII has been violated, the court is empowered to grant an injunction prohibiting future violations and correcting past actions. Retroactive back pay or seniority may be ordered for employees who have suffered from unlawful discrimination. In addition, a court may compel an offending company to implement an "affirmative action" program to recruit and retain minority employees.

The Affirmative Action Controversy

Among the most divisive and intensely felt political controversies of recent years is the concept of **affirmative action.** Known by its critics as "reverse discrimination," affirmative action entails the granting of preferences based on race to minority employees. In some cases an affirmative action program may include goals and timetables for increasing the percentage of minorities or women in an organization's workforce. Such programs may be compelled by government action but commonly are voluntarily undertaken by companies fearful of being sued or simply concerned over their past unfair practices.

Opponents of affirmative action contend that these programs are tantamount to racial quotas and undermine the "color-blind" principle on which the Civil Rights Act is based. The advocates of affirmative action counter that the programs represent a measured response to correct past discrimination and are essential to racial progress. The Supreme Court has yet to resolve this controversy. As the following cases indicate, some but not all forms of affirmative action are lawful.

United Steelworkers of America v. Weber
U.S. Supreme Court, 443 U.S. 193 (1979)

The Kaiser Aluminum and Chemical Corporation was operating a craft workforce with only 1.83 percent blacks, even though the surrounding area workforce was 39 percent black. Apparently this was primarily due to past discrimination by the union representing Kaiser's employees. Kaiser and the United Steelworkers reached a collective bargaining agreement that established a new on-the-job craft training program designed to increase the number of blacks in the company's workforce. At least 50 percent of new trainees were to be black until the time that the percentage of black membership in Kaiser's craft workforce approximated the percentage of blacks in the local labor force.

A rejected white applicant for the training program, Brian Weber, sued the union, arguing that the program violated Title VII's ban on racial discrimination in employment. Both the district court and the court of appeals ruled for Weber, and Kaiser and the union appealed to the U.S. Supreme Court.

Brennan, Justice:

Weber argues that Congress intended in Title VII to prohibit all race-conscious affirmative action plans. His argument rests upon a literal interpretation of sections 703(a) and (d) of the Act. Those sections make it unlawful to "discriminate . . . because of . . . race" in hiring and in the selection of apprentices for training programs. Since, the argument runs, Title VII forbids discrimination against whites as well as blacks, and since the plan operates to discriminate against white employees solely because they are white, the plan violates Title VII.

Weber's argument is not without force. But it overlooks the fact that the Kaiser-USWA plan is voluntarily adopted by private parties to eliminate traditional patterns of racial segregation. In this context, Weber's reliance upon a literal construction of sections 703(a) and (d) is misplaced. It is a familiar rule that a thing may be within the letter of the statute and yet not within the statute, because not within its spirit, nor within the intention of its makers. The prohibition against racial discrimination in Title VII must therefore be read against the background of the legislative history of Title VII and the historical context from which the Act arose. Examination of those sources makes clear that an interpretation of the sections that forbade all race-conscious affirmative action would bring about an end completely at variance with the purpose of the statute and must be rejected.

Congress's primary concern in enacting the prohibition against racial discrimination in Title VII was the plight of the Negro in our economy. Before 1964, blacks were largely relegated to unskilled and semi-skilled jobs. Because of automation the number of such jobs was rapidly decreasing. As a consequence, the relative position of the Negro was steadily worsening. Congress feared that the goals of the Civil Rights Act—the integration of blacks into American society—could not be achieved unless this trend were reversed. Accordingly, it was clear to Congress that the crux of the problem was to open employment opportunities for Negroes in occupations traditionally closed to them. It was to this problem that Title VII's prohibition against racial discrimination in employment was primarily addressed.

We need not define in detail the line between permissible and impermissible affirmative action plans. It suffices to hold that the Kaiser-USWA plan falls on the permissible side of the line. The purposes of the plan mirror those of the statute. Both were designed to break down old patterns of racial segregation and hierarchy. The plan does not unnecessarily trammel the interests of the white employees [or] require the discharge of white workers and their replacement with new black hires. Nor does the plan create an absolute bar to the advancement of white employees; half of those trained in the program will be white. Moreover, the plan is a temporary measure; it is not intended to maintain racial balance, but simply to eliminate a manifest racial imbalance. Preferential selection of craft trainees will end as soon as the percentage of black skilled craft workers approximates the percentage of blacks in the local labor force.

[Reversed.]

Firefighters Local Union No. 1784 v. Stotts
U.S. Supreme Court, 104 S.Ct. 2576 (1984)

In 1977, Carl Stotts brought a Title VII action alleging that the Memphis Fire Department was engaged in unlawful racial discrimination. In 1980, the case was settled by consent decree between the parties. To increase black participation in the department, the consent decree established the goal of 50 percent black hiring and 20 percent black promotions for a designated time. In 1981, budget constraints in Memphis necessitated the layoff of numerous firefighters. Under the "last hired, first fired" protection of the Fire Department's seniority system, the laid off workers were predominantly blacks hired under the terms of the consent decree.

Mr. Stotts went back to court seeking an injunction that would prevent layoffs from obstructing the goal of the consent decree to

increase the number of black firefighters. The union intervened to oppose this request and protect the terms of their seniority system. The district court held for Stotts and entered an injunction that effectively required the department to fire white firefighters with seniority protection rather than the more recently hired black firefighters. This injunction was upheld on appeal, and the union appealed to the U.S. Supreme Court.

White, Justice:

Section 703(h) of Title VII provides that it is not an unlawful employment practice to apply different terms, conditions, or privileges of employment pursuant to a bona fide seniority system, provided that such differences are not the result of an intention to discriminate because of race. It is clear that the city had a seniority system, that its proposed layoff plan conformed to that system, and that in making the settlement the city had not agreed to award competitive seniority to any minority member whom the city later proposed to lay off. The District Court held that the city could not follow its seniority system in making its proposed layoffs because its proposal was discriminatory in effect. Section 703(h), permits the routine application of a seniority system absent proof of an intention to discriminate. Here, the layoff proposal was not adopted with the purpose or intent to discriminate on the basis of race.

[The injunction to implement the consent decree] overstates the authority of the trial court to disregard a seniority system in fashioning a remedy after an employer has followed a pattern or practice having a discriminatory effect on black applicants or employees. If individual members of a plaintiff class demonstrate that they have been actual victims of the discriminatory practice, they may be given their rightful place on the seniority roster. However, mere membership in the disadvantaged class is insufficient to warrant a seniority award; each individual must prove that the discriminatory practice had an impact on him. Here, there was no finding that any of the blacks protected from layoff had been a victim of discrimination and no award of competitive seniority to any of them.

[The Court went on to quote Senator Hubert Humphrey during the debate on Title VII, to the effect that "there is nothing in it that will give any power to any court to require firing of employees in order to meet a racial quota or to achieve a certain racial balance."]

[Reversed.]

The results in *Weber* and *Stotts* can be reconciled by the presence of a seniority system in the latter case. The status of affirmative action is in some flux. Some preferential affirmative action treatment for new hires clearly is permissible, but when such a program conflicts with the rights or interests of a company's preexisting workers, the lawfulness of affirmative action is somewhat unclear. The importance of this distinction was reemphasized in *Wygant v. State*

Board of Education, 106 S.Ct. 1842 (1986), which ruled against a plan that protected minority teachers from layoffs at the expense of white teachers with greater seniority. Interestingly, in *Johnson v. Transportation Agency,* 55 U.S.L.W. 4379 (1987), the Supreme Court approved a public employer's voluntary affirmative action plan that favored *women.*

Sexual Harassment

Sexual harassment on the job is disturbingly commonplace. Recent interpretations of Title VII protect against sexual harassment, under the theory that the harassment is based at least in part on the sex of the employee. While the employer *per se* is often not the responsible party in instances of sexual harassment, EEOC guidelines make the employer strictly liable for the acts of supervisory employees and also liable for some instances of harassment by co-workers and clients of the company.

The traditional form of sexual harassment is the *quid pro quo* situation, where sexual favors are demanded in exchange for job advancement. This is clearly prohibited under Title VII and is treated as a disparate individual treatment case. A second, and probably more common, form of abuse is the harassing work environment that interferes with the employee's work performance. This may amount to a series of sexual inquiries, comments, jokes, and inappropriate touchings by co-workers. When this harassment becomes commonplace and the supervisory employees know or should know of its existence, yet do nothing, the employer is liable under Title VII.

Equal Pay Act

The first antidiscrimination in employment act, predating even Title VII, is the Equal Pay Act. This statute prohibits an employer from paying an employee of one sex less than an employee of the opposite sex, when the two are performing jobs that require "equal skill, effort, and responsibility" and "under similar working conditions." Proof that the pay differential is due to the work-

ers' varying merit or pursuant to a legitimate seniority system are available defenses under the Act. The Equal Pay Act is limited to sex discrimination in the form of wages and overlaps considerably with Title VII. There are slight differences in employers covered by the two Acts, however, and the Equal Pay Act may be a worker's only recourse for wage discrimination in some companies with fewer than 15 employees.

The Comparable Worth Controversy

Traditionally, the Equal Pay Act was limited to closely comparable positions, such as tailor and seamstress. Advocates of women's rights have noted, however, that a disparity exists between pay for jobs traditionally held by women and those traditionally held by men. For example, a male custodial employee may be paid more than a female nurse. Viewing this disparity as a serious structural form of wage discrimination based on sex, women's rights advocates have attacked these differences under the theory of **comparable worth.** Critics of comparable worth have argued that the concept seriously distorts economic efficiency by displacing the free market's evaluation of job worth.

The Equal Pay Act's definition of "equal work" is too constricted to invoke the comparable worth theory, but Title VII may provide a basis for equalizing pay among jobs. In general, however, courts have been reluctant to embrace the comparable worth theory, which seems to go well beyond Congress's original intent in adopting the Civil Rights Act. Comparable worth has made much greater headway in state legislatures, with many such bodies passing statutes to study or correct this perceived problem.

Age Discrimination in Employment Act

Title VII expanded the scope of employment discrimination protection in 1967, when it passed the Age Discrimination in Employment Act (ADEA). The coverage of this Act is quite similar to Title VII, except that it applies only to situations where there is a minimum of 20 employees. The ADEA prohibits discrimination based on age against anyone over age 40. Prohibited discrimination may take the form of disparate individual treatment, when an individual is penalized for being part of the protected age range, or disparate impact, when an employer's general policy needlessly discriminates against those aged 40 and over. Only the age of the victim of discrimination is relevant. Thus, an employer automatically favoring a 45-year-old over a 60-year-old, or vice versa, has violated the ADEA just as surely as if the employer had favored a 25-year-old.

The ADEA provides several statutory defenses for employers. An employee may always be discharged or otherwise penalized for good cause other than age. A bona fide occupational qualification defense also exists and closely resembles that under Title VII. Bona fide seniority systems or employee benefit plans are also exempted from ADEA violation. Courts have interpreted these defenses somewhat more expansively, in the employer's favor, than in most cases decided under Title VII.

Rehabilitation Act

The Rehabilitation Act of 1973 was enacted to protect handicapped individuals from employment discrimination. This legislation has narrower focus than the previous acts, and is limited to federal agencies, employers having contracts with the federal government in excess of $2,500, and employers receiving any form of federal financial assistance. Given the federal government's prevalence in many aspects of our economy, the Rehabilitation Act has relatively broad reach.

The Rehabilitation Act protects individuals who have "a physical or mental impairment, which substantially limits one or more of such person's major life activities." Also protected are individuals "regarded as having such an impairment." "Major life activities" are defined broadly and the Act encompasses virtually any disease or disability that might be the subject of discrimination.

To be protected, an individual must be "qualified" for the job. While this is somewhat difficult to define, the Act requires employers to make reasonable accommodations for a handicap, where an individual is otherwise qualified. Thus an employer may be required to provide, for example, wheelchair access or telephone amplifiers, so long as the expense of accommodation is not unreasonable. The Rehabilitation Act prohibits discrimination against the protected class, and government contractors must undertake affirmative action programs to encourage the hiring of the handicapped.

PROTECTION OF SAFETY AND WELFARE

Although unions undoubtedly have improved the safety and welfare of individual employees, they have failed to provide full protection, at least in the judgment of Congress and the states. Numerous laws have been passed to protect workers from on-the-job injuries and the financial consequences of such injuries. Congress also has legislated to preserve the financial welfare of workers, especially in the context of pension and other employee benefit plans.

Workers' Compensation

In the 19th century, workers were frequently injured on the job and often without legal recourse to compensate them for their injuries. In response, state legislatures passed workers' compensation statutes. All fifty states have such laws and while they vary somewhat, the laws all share certain common features. Workers' compensation is paid without regard to employer negligence and workers receive a predetermined amount, based on the injury suffered. Benefits payable include medical costs, income replacement, death benefits, and rehabilitation costs. Levels of compensation are typically lower than a worker might receive in a lawsuit, but the statutory system avoids much of the attorney and other costs of litigation, while eliminating most employer defenses to payment of the lesser sum.

The main restriction on recovery under workers' compensation statutes is the requirement that the injury must have arisen "out of and in the course of employment." Although the majority of injuries are clearly job-related, a large number of cases lie on the disputed borderline of work. For example, an employee whose job requires travel will ordinarily be able to receive benefits for injuries incurred in the course of such travel. By contrast, a mere commuter will not be compensated if injured on the way to work.

Employees typically are also covered while engaging in activities reasonably incidental to job duties. Thus, an employee on a lunch break who slips and falls in the employer's cafeteria would be covered. State laws also cover diseases arising out of employment, but proof of the source of disease is much more complicated to obtain than is proof of work injuries, and such cases are more often disputed.

Occupational Safety and Health Act

In 1970, Congress passed the Occupational Safety and Health Act to help prevent workplace disease and injuries. The Act creates the Occupational Safety and Health Administration (OSHA), part of the U.S. Department of Labor, to administer its provisions. This statute applies to virtually every United States employer.

Central to OSHA's powers is its standard-setting authority. The agency promulgates regulations compelling employers to make their workplaces safer in a variety of ways. Most of the early standards were intended to prevent job injuries, and OSHA suffered considerable ridicule because of the highly detailed nature of its rules. For example, the agency devoted considerable effort to regulating the number of toilets to be available and the allowable design of such facilities. As the agency has gained experience, its standards have allowed more flexibility for employers, and the regulatory focus has shifted toward prevention of occupational diseases.

Unlike some agencies that have been largely co-opted by the industries they regulate, OSHA has maintained standards that are often quite strict. These rules have given rise to litigation that has helped define the extent of the agency's powers. In an attempt to prevent a cancer associated with the inhalation of benzene, a petroleum byproduct, OSHA promulgated a stringent standard without attempting to specify the magnitude of the harm created by existing levels. The agency believed that it was simply fulfilling its mandate to create the healthiest workplace feasible, but the Supreme Court overturned the regulation in *Industrial Union Department v. American Petroleum Institute*, 448 U.S. 607 (1980). The Court held that OSHA could regulate only "significant risks" and generally should quantitatively measure a risk before promulgating rules. Shortly after this decision, industry challenged an OSHA regulation limiting exposure to cotton dust, which causes several lung diseases. Industry contended that OSHA had to base regulation on a cost/benefit analysis, but the Supreme Court upheld the agency's regulation in *American Textile Manufacturers Inst. v. Donovan*, 452 U.S. 490 (1981). This decision held that OSHA possessed authority to require any health protection "feasible" for industry and was not required to weigh the costs of a rule against its benefits before acting.

While OSHA has broad standard-setting authority, the task of establishing rules against all workplace hazards is beyond the capabilities of any agency. In recognition of this limit, Congress created a "general duty clause" in the Safety Act. This provision requires all employers to provide a place of employment free from recognized hazards of death or serious harm, regardless of whether a federal standard applies to the particular situation. As an example of the application of this clause, one employer was found in violation for permitting untrained employees to attempt electrical repairs on a wet floor without any protective equipment.

Beyond standards development, OSHA is also responsible for enforcing the Act, and considerable controversy has circulated around these enforcement powers. The agency's compliance officers make unannounced inspections. While search warrants are required for the inspections, they are liberally granted. When violations are found, OSHA may issue citations to an employer that include penalties of up to $1,000 per violation. An employer may contest these penalties before a separate, independent organization known as the Occupational Safety and Health Review Commission.

Fair Labor Standards Act

The Fair Labor Standards Act (FLSA) was among the federal government's first employment law statutes. Passed in response to the Great Depression, the FLSA regulates the hours that employees may be required to work and the wages they must be paid. As was the case in the statutes discussed above, the coverage of the FLSA is extremely broad. An employer involved in any way in interstate commerce falls under the Act's purview. An exception is made for managerial employees, as well as those employed in the professions, such as lawyers and accountants.

Among the most controversial provisions of FLSA immediately after its passage was the Act's prohibition of certain forms of child labor. Employees under 18 years of age are excluded from occupations designated as hazardous, such as mining, logging, and excavation work. Hours are strictly regulated for employees who are less than 16 years old.

The FLSA is also the source of the federal minimum wage requirements. This wage level is currently set at $3.35 per hour for each of the first 40 hours worked in a week. Any work in excess of 40 hours per week must be paid at a "time-and-a-half" rate, 50 percent greater than the employee's normal wage. If employees are not paid on an hourly basis, the FLSA requires at least as much compensation as a per hour minimum wage rate would require for the hours they actually worked. Employers must maintain complete employment and payroll records for review by the Department of Labor. Substantial

penalties are imposed for violations. With the exception of the above provisions, the Act imposes no other requirements on the employment relationship, such as mandatory vacations or rest periods.

ERISA

With the rise of unions in the twentieth century, employees began to receive a variety of new benefits. One of the most significant of these benefits was the commonplace adoption of pension plans by major employers. Frequently, both employees and employer contribute to a plan that provides benefits upon retirement. Other similar programs, known as welfare plans, provide benefits in the event of accident, injury, or unemployment of participating workers. Although many pension plans have been created by a single employer for its employees, other plans have resulted from collective bargaining agreements between a union and a group of employers, known as multi-employer pension plans.

While some of these pension plans worked out well, many others did not. Some were mismanaged and others suffered from corruption. In more instances, the plans were insufficiently funded and unable to pay the promised pension level to retirees. To correct these and other problems, Congress in 1974 passed the Employee Retirement Income Security Act, usually referred to as ERISA. This Act is among the most complex and byzantine of all federal employment laws and may have serious consequences for employers.

ERISA's provisions cover both welfare and pension plans, but the statute's focus is on the latter. The Act does not require employers to establish plans for the protection of its workers but regulates such plans as do exist. ERISA is administered jointly by the Department of Labor and the Internal Revenue Service.

Vesting Rights: Perhaps the most important feature of ERISA is the creation of a vesting right. A right is said to "vest" when a participating employee acquires a legally enforceable right to benefits, usually to be paid out at some future date. Prior to ERISA, employers often postponed the vesting date until late into the life of employment and thereby avoided paying benefits to workers who were fired or switched jobs prior to that date. Under ERISA, any pension benefits based on the employee's own contribution, such as through wage deductions, vest immediately. For employer contributions, several different vesting approaches are permitted under the Act, but all these approaches must provide for full vesting within 15 years service or less.

Other Provisions: ERISA creates other pension protections as well. In the past, an employee who required a break in service, such as a pregnancy or disability leave, could lose all pension rights accrued up to that time. ERISA's complex rules on this subject essentially prevent short breaks in service from substantially diminishing an employee's right to benefits. ERISA also provided for rules to prevent the mismanagement of pension funds, setting up standards for the funds' managers and limiting the transactions in which such funds may be invested. Other provisions of the Act include rules for fair allocation of benefits among employees; recordkeeping and disclosure requirements; and insurance against the possibility that termination of a pension plan will cause workers to lose vested benefits.

New Problems: Although ERISA undeniably has solved serious past pension plan abuses, the statute has created some new problems of its own. The Act has some provisions to finance pension plans but has done little to make up for serious underfunding of preexisting plans. As a result, many workers have a "vested right" to receive revenues that simply do not exist in a plan's assets. This has meant that some small employers have found themselves owing huge amounts of back pension accumulations that may exceed the value of all the companies' assets.

A second problem derives from ERISA's complexity. The reporting and record-keeping provi-

sions, accompanied by much uncertainty regarding the precise requirements of the Act, have been quite onerous for some employers. One unintended consequence has been the relative demise of the pension plan as an institution. Many preexisting plans have terminated and few new private pension plans have been created. Some future amendments to ERISA are probable, in response to these difficulties. For the time being, however, employers must live with the current complex provisions and must take special care in managing employee benefit plans covered by the Act.

EMPLOYER'S RIGHT TO DISCHARGE EMPLOYEES

Traditionally, employment law was governed by the common-law doctrine of **employment at will.** Employers often hired workers for an indefinite period of time. In such a contract, either party could terminate the employment contract at any time, without any reason being given. Although apparently evenhanded, the effect of this doctrine was to enable employers to discharge employees for reasons that might be considered improper.

Public Policy Exception

The traditional doctrine of employment at will, once firmly entrenched, is being changed by the courts in many states. Different states have overturned the doctrine under a variety of theories. The most common exception to the doctrine is the "public policy" exception. In the states that recognize the public policy exception, an employer is prohibited from discharging an employee for reasons that contravene fundamental public policy objectives of the state. Thus, employers may not fire employees who refuse to commit perjury or otherwise break the law at the behest of the employer. Other unlawful reasons for dismissal have included filing a workers' compensation claim and participating in jury service. It should be noted at this point that federal statutes also prohibit discharging an employee for union membership or for seeking redress for discrimination that is in violation of Title VII. Some states have used the public policy exception to prohibit dismissals based on "whistle-blowing," where an employee turns in an employer for a suspected violation of the law. The public policy exception does not protect employees who refuse to work on projects for their own personal ethical reasons, when no law has been violated.

Implied Covenant of Good Faith Exception

The second exception to the employment at will doctrine is the "implied covenant of good faith" exception, which is potentially broader than the public policy exception. Most contracts have been interpreted to contain an implied promise of good faith dealing by both parties. Applying this implied promise in employment contracts would all but eliminate the at will doctrine, by requiring a party to demonstrate a good faith reason for terminating the contract. Relatively fewer courts have recognized this principle than have recognized the public policy exception, but it holds the potential for undermining the entire at will doctrine. The following case illustrates a set of circumstances in which the good faith exception was used by a court to invalidate the discharge of an employee.

Monge v. Beebe Rubber Co.
Supreme Court of New Hampshire, 316 A.2d 549 (1974)

Olga Monge, a married woman with three children, was hired by Beebe in 1968 to work on a conversion machine in a factory. After working without incident for three months, she applied for a promotion. She received the raise and was then asked out on a date by her foreman but declined. Shortly thereafter, she was reassigned to a lower paying job. Ms. Monge claimed that the foreman continued to bother her in 1969 through ridicule and by refusing to cooperate with her work requirements. The foreman went on to fire her, but she was reinstated after her union complained. Ms. Monge became ill and after calling in sick for a disputed number of days, attempted to go back to work. She collapsed in the ladies' room and was taken to the hospital. After several days, the foreman alleged that Ms. Monge did not notify him of the reason for her absence and fired her. She claims that she did in fact call the company during the time she was at the hospital.

Lampron, Justice:

. . . The law governing the relations between employer and employee has similarly evolved over the years to reflect changing legal, social and economic conditions. . . . In this area "[w]e are in the midst of a period in which the pot boils the hardest and in the process of change the fastest." Although many of these changes have resulted from the activity and influence of labor unions, the courts cannot ignore the new climate prevailing generally in the relationship of employer and employee.

In all employment contracts, whether at will or for a definite term, the employer's interest in running his business as he sees fit must be balanced against the interest of the employee in maintaining his employment, and the public's interest in maintaining a proper balance between the two. . . . We hold that a termination by the employer of a contract of employment at will which is motivated by bad faith or malice or based on retaliation is not the best interest of the economic system or the public good and constitutes a breach of the employment contract. . . . Such a rule affords the employee a certain stability of employment and does not interfere with the employer's normal exercise of his right to discharge, which is necessary to permit him to operate his business efficiently and profitably.

[Remanded for rehearing on damages.]

Violation of the Employment Contract

A third exception, found by some courts, is when dismissal would violate express or implied terms of the employment contract. For example, where a company's personnel handbook stated that an employee would be dismissed only for sufficient cause and after conciliation efforts, that company was legally precluded from firing an employee for no reason under the at will doctrine. Hence, if employers make promises in hiring interviews or other contexts regarding the conditions of dismissal, those promises may effectively become part of the employment contract and impose limits on subsequent efforts to discharge the employee for other reasons, when the employee can demonstrate reliance on the promises.

Wrongful Discharge

The above discussion applies to cases where a worker is suing under a contract cause of action for job reinstatement. In a few states, courts have also recognized that such a worker may have a claim in tort for abusive or wrongful discharge. Even where this tort is recognized, the worker usually will have to prove malice on the part of the employer, who has a possible good faith defense. Employees may also be able to sue a com-

pany for intentional infliction of emotional distress, defamation, or fraud as a consequence of discharges that satisfy the requirements of those torts.

In sum, the courts seem to be following the lead of the legislature in extending additional protections to employees and eroding the doctrine of employment at will. Contributing to the erosion of this doctrine is the tendency of courts to award punitive damages to employees who were fired for inappropriate and abusive reasons. No longer can employers hire and fire employees at their whim. Now, in order to be safe from court challenges, an employer should have documented good cause reasons for the discharge of his or her employees.

SUMMARY

The law of employment relationships has undergone a series of fundamental changes in recent decades. For much of our nation's history, employment was governed by traditional common-law rules of contracts, with little government involvement. Today's employer, however, must be cognizant of numerous government requirements in the areas of health and safety, discrimination, wages, employee benefits, and labor organization.

The first inroads in the common law came in the National Labor Relations Act. This legislation facilitated unionization of the workplace by protecting organizing campaigns, compelling collective bargaining between management and lawfully recognized employee representatives, prohibiting discrimination against union members, and guaranteeing the right to strike, among other provisions. A long list of employer activities may be considered unfair labor practices, for which the employer may be penalized. This labor law also provides some benefits to employers in terms of prohibiting certain types of actions by union and nonunion employees.

The most significant recent labor laws are those against employment discrimination. Under Title VII of the Civil Rights Act, employers are prohibited from discriminating against employees because of their race, sex, color, religion, or national origin. Even seemingly neutral employment practices may be found illegal if they have the effect of discriminating against one or more of the protected classes. This statute has given rise to the controversial social issue of affirmative action, in which protected classes are granted special benefits, often at the expense of other workers. While some forms of affirmative action are legal, courts have placed limits on many programs. Other related legislation proscribes discrimination against the handicapped and compels equal pay for equal work.

Another significant area of employment law regulation deals with worker safety and welfare. The Occupational Safety and Health Act enables the federal government to set standards for workplace safety. When accidents do occur, state workers' compensation statutes ensure that employees are compensated for their injuries. The Fair Labor Standards Act regulates pay levels for workers, and the Employee Retirement Income Security Act establishes rules for pension and other benefit plans to grant some measure of income security to covered employees.

A final employment law issue involves standards for firing workers. Recent court decisions are placing important limits upon an employer's discretion in discharging employees. Such a decision may be unlawful if it violates public policy principles or is taken in bad faith. In some cases, a discharged worker may even be able to recover damages in tort for unlawful discharge.

In sum, the employment relationship is laden with legislative and administrative requirements, of which an employer should be aware. Legal requirements now govern virtually every substantial action that employers may take regarding their workers. The employer who ignores them may find him- or herself subject to serious damages.

KEY TERMS

Unfair labor practice
Collective bargaining
Bona fide occupational qualification (BFOQ)
Affirmative action
Comparable worth
Employment at will

QUESTIONS AND PROBLEMS

1. Republic Aviation Corp. operated a large military aircraft manufacturing plant that was not unionized. Republic had a rule against soliciting union membership within the plant. A worker ignored the rule and passed out application cards on his own time during lunch periods. Republic fired the worker for violating company rules, and the worker filed a complaint with the NLRB. Has the company committed an unfair labor practice? (*Republic Aviation Corp. v. NLRB,* 324 U.S. 793, 1945.)

2. A building stone supplier and its union were involved in a labor dispute and a strike was called. The company's customers at construction sites rented independent trucking companies to deliver the company's stones during the strike and deducted the rental cost from their payments to the supplier. The stone supplier's union picketed the construction site customers and the rental trucking companies. Has the union committed an unfair labor practice?

(*Laborers Local 859 v. NLRB (Thomas S. Byrne, Inc.*), 446 F.2d 1319, D.C. Cir. 1971.)

3. As a protest against the Russian invasion of Afghanistan, members of the International Longshoremen's Association refused to handle cargoes arriving from or departing to the Soviet Union. An American company that imports Russian wood products for sale in the United States complained to the NLRB that the union action was illegal. Has the union committed an unfair labor practice? (*Int'l Longshoremen's Assn. v. Allied Int'l Inc.,* 102 S.Ct. 1656, 1982.)

4. The Los Angeles Dept. of Water & Power provided retirement and death benefits for its employees. Because, statistically speaking, the women employees would outlive the male employees by a number of years, the total retirement benefits paid out would be greater. Consequently, the Department required female employees to pay more toward the retirement fund. A female employee claimed that this was unlawful sex discrimination and sued. Should she win? (*L.A. Dept. of Water & Power v. Manhart,* 435 U.S. 702, 1978.)

5. A male airline pilot decided that he would be more comfortable as a woman and underwent a sex change operation. The pilot's employment record as a man was very good. After the operation, however, the airline fired the pilot, expressing a variety of medical and psychological concerns for safety. The pilot claimed that she was discriminated against as a transsexual in a way "based on sex" and that her firing therefore constituted illegal discrimination. Should she win?

6. Employee X has been exposed to the AIDS virus. After admitting this fact on a questionnaire, he was fired by the employer. Assume that the employer receives federal funds. Can the employee successfully sue for unlawful discrimination under the Rehabilitation Act?

7. A railroad had an absolute policy of refusing consideration for employment to any person convicted of a crime other than a minor traffic offense. Green, a prospective employee, had been convicted for refusing military induction

in 1967. Statistics showed that in urban areas between 37 and 78 percent of all blacks would be excluded by this policy, while 11 to 17 percent of whites would be so excluded. Green, refused employment as a consequence of the policy, sued the railroad under Title VII of the Civil Rights Act. Should Green win? (*Green v. Missouri Pacific Railroad Co.,* 523 F.2d 1290, 8th Cir. 1975.)

8. McKeever worked as an attorney of New Jersey Bell Telephone Co. While driving home from work one day he was killed in an auto accident. His family claimed for workers' compensation death benefits, noting that at-home work was a regular part of McKeever's job, that the employer encouraged and benefited from this at-home work, and that he had work in his briefcase in the car at the time he was killed. Is this a valid workers' compensation claim? (*McKeever v. New Jersey Bell Telephone Co.,* Workmen's Comp. Law Rep. (CCH) Sec. 2566, N.J. Super. Ct. App. Div. 1981.)

9. An employee of Sanders Roofing Co. fell from the flat roof where he was working. Because there was no catch platform around the roof the Labor Department issued a citation to Sanders for violating the "general duty" clause of OSHA. Sanders argued in defense that OSHA had a specific standard requiring catch platforms around sloped roofs but not flat ones. Should Sanders be found guilty of violating OSHA? (*R. L. Sanders Roofing Co. v. OSHRC,* 620 F.2d 97, 5th Cir. 1980.)

10. Cleary worked for American Airlines for 20 years as a payroll clerk and an airport operations agent. American fired Cleary for being absent from his work area and threatening another employee, but provided him no hearing to answer these charges. Cleary alleged that the real reason for his firing was his union activities and sued American Airlines for unlawful discharge, claiming that the company violated an implied covenant of good faith. Should Cleary prevail? (*Cleary v. American Airlines, Inc.,* 168 Cal. Rptr. 722, 2nd Ct. App. 1980.)

Chapter 50

SECURITIES REGULATION

The great stock market crash of 1929 was one of the most dramatic turning points in American economic history. That event not only ushered in the Great Depression but also heralded the creation of modern securities regulation. Securities regulation is one of the most complicated areas of the law; attorneys who practice in the securities field are among the most specialized and well-paid of all lawyers. Although this vast, everchanging subject may be intimidating to the novice, few persons in business can remain ignorant of its effects on the way business is done in this country.

Many aspects of securities regulation are highly visible. Most Americans are familiar with the hustle and bustle of the New York Stock Exchange. Over 30 million Americans own stock, many in major corporations such as General Motors and IBM. Through securities regulation the federal government, and to a lesser degree the states, regulate trading on the stock exchanges, protect the interests of shareholders, and attempt to insure that the collapse of 1929 is never repeated.

In this chapter, some of the more important aspects of the law of securities regulation are surveyed.

INTRODUCTION TO SECURITIES REGULATION

As explained in Chapter 31, there are various forms of business organizations including partnerships and corporations. There are sufficient advantages to incorporating, especially for very large businesses, that almost three million corporations exist in the United States. The corporate form allows for accumulation of capital investment from many shareholders. These investors do not directly own the assets of the business; rather, they own part of the corporate entity, as evidenced by shares of stock. Shares of stock constitute the most familiar type of security regulated by federal and state governments.

A security such as a stock or a bond has no intrinsic value—its value lies in the ownership interest which it represents. The value of that ownership interest may be difficult to discover and easy to misrepresent. Securities may be produced in nearly limitless supply at virtually no cost by anyone with access to a printing press. For all these reasons, fraud, manipulation, and deceit have been frequent companions of the security. Government regulation of securities dates back to at least 1285, when King Edward I of England attempted to gain some control over the capital markets by licensing brokers located in London.

Securities regulation in the United States was almost nonexistent until 1911, when Kansas enacted securities laws. Other states soon followed suit, but without federal laws, companies could evade regulation by operating across state lines.

The 1920s were an especially active time for the issuance and trading of securities. The securities business was then characterized by price manipulation, deceitful practices, selling on excessive credit, and the abuse of secret information by corporate insiders. Of the $50 billion of new securities offered for sale in the United States in the 1920s, about one-half were worthless. The public and the national economy were devastated when stock market prices fell 89 percent between 1929 and 1933, a situation which finally produced federal action.

Federal Legislation

The first federal securities law was the *Securities Act of 1933* (the 1933 Act), which regulated the initial issuance of securities by companies. Fraudulent and deceptive practices were outlawed, and registration was required before a new security could be offered or sold, unless that security was entitled to an exemption from registration.

A year later, Congress passed the *Securities Exchange Act of 1934* (the 1934 Act), which extended federal regulation to trading in securities already issued and outstanding, required registration of securities brokers and dealers, and created the Securities and Exchange Commission (SEC), the federal agency which enforces the federal securities laws through its extensive powers.

In 1935, Congress passed the *Public Utility Holding Company Act* in response to manipulative and monopolistic practices in the public utilities industry. The SEC in its early years was largely concerned with correcting abuses in the financing and operating of large public utilities. Because the commission has been very successful in this area, separate enforcement of the Public Utility Holding Company Act is no longer a major SEC priority.

The next securities law passed by Congress was the *Trust Indenture Act of 1939,* which helped protect persons investing in bonds, debentures, notes, and other debt securities by imposing qualification requirements on trustees of such instruments. A year later, the *Investment Company Act of 1940* imposed additional requirements on companies engaged primarily in the business of investing, reinvesting, and trading securities. For example, that Act prohibits anyone found guilty of securities fraud from being associated with investment companies and bans transactions between such companies and their officers without prior SEC approval. The *Investment Advisers Act of 1940* required persons or firms who engage in the business of advising others about investments for compensation to register with the SEC, as brokers and dealers are required to register under the 1934 Act.

The *Securities Investor Protection Act of 1970* amended the 1934 Act in response to a rash of failures in the late 1960s in the broker-dealer business. The Act creates the Securities Investor Protection Corporation (SIPC), which manages a fund to protect investors from the failure of broker-dealers in the same manner as the Federal Deposit Insurance Corporation protects the customers of banks.

In 1977 Congress passed the *Foreign Corrupt Practices Act* (FCPA) in response to questionable foreign political payments by U.S. companies, disclosed in the wake of the Watergate scandal. This act bans bribery of high foreign political officials and establishes certain accounting requirements for corporations so that such illegal activities cannot be easily concealed. Substantial criminal penalties are provided for violation.

The Racketeering Influenced and Corrupt Organizations Act of 1970 (RICO) though not a securities act in any strict sense, must also be noted. Congress passed RICO to attack organized crime, especially its infiltration into legitimate business. However, RICO neither includes a definition of "organized crime" nor expressly requires a link between a defendant's activities and organized crime. Therefore, about nine-tenths of the suits brought under RICO have had no connection with professional criminals. A RICO plaintiff need prove only: (1) a pattern of racketeering activity by the defendant; (2) the existence of an enterprise affecting interstate commerce; (3) a nexus between the pattern of racketeering activity and the enterprise; and (4) an injury to the plaintiff's business or property by reason of the racketeering activity. Because racketeering activity is defined by means of a long "laundry list" of offenses, including mail fraud, wire fraud, and securities fraud, and a pattern is proved (according to some courts) by showing that the defendant has committed two or more such acts within a ten-year period, RICO claims have become popular in securities litigation. An important reason is that RICO's civil remedies include treble damages and attorneys' fees.

A very important RICO case, *Sedima v. Imrex, Inc.*, was excerpted in Chapter 4.

Of these acts, the 1933 Act and the 1934 Act remain the most important.

What Is a Security?

Securities are commonly thought of as the stock issued by corporations. The shares of common and preferred stock issued by corporations constitute a major type of security. These are *equity securities* which evidence an ownership interest in the corporation. Holders of equity securities are normally entitled to vote on important corporate matters and to receive dividends as their share of the corporate profits. The other major type of security is the *debt security,* such as the bond, note, or debenture. Holders of debt securities are creditors rather than owners. They have no voice in corporate affairs but are entitled to receive regular interest payments according to the terms of the bond or note.

Because the inventive mind of man has devised an inordinate variety of investment interests, securities regulation goes beyond items that are clearly labeled "stocks" or "bonds." Section 2(1) of the 1933 Act broadly defines security to include

> any note, stock, treasury stock, bond, debenture, evidence of indebtedness, certificate of interest or participation in any profit-sharing agreement, . . . investment

contract, voting-trust certificate, fractional undivided interest in oil, gas or other mineral rights, or, in general, any interest or instrument commonly known as a 'security.' . . .

This broad definition has, of necessity, been liberally construed by the courts. Interest in limited partnerships, condominiums, farm animals with accompanying agreements for their care, franchises, whiskey warehouse receipts, and many other varied items have been deemed to be securities.

The inclusion of the term "investment contract" in the 1933 Act's definition of security has produced much litigation. Some very interesting investment opportunities have been held to constitute investment contracts, as the following case illustrates.

Smith v. Gross
U.S. Ninth Circuit Court of Appeals, 604 F.2d 292 (1979)

Gross used a promotional newsletter to solicit buyer-investors to raise earthworms in order to help him reach his quota of selling earthworms to fishermen. Buyers were promised that the seller's instructions would enable them to have a profitable worm farm, that the time required was similar to that of a garden, that the worms doubled in quantity every 60 days, and that Gross would buy back all bait-size worms produced by buyers at $2.25 per pound.

The Smiths invested, but later sued claiming that contrary to Gross's representations, the worms multiplied at a maximum of eight rather than sixty-four times per year, and that the promised profits could be achieved only if the multiplication rate were as fast as represented and Gross repurchased the Smiths' production at $2.25 per pound, which was much higher than the true market value. Gross could pay that amount only by selling the worms to new worm farmers at inflated prices.

The Smiths claimed that Gross made false representations which violated the federal securities laws. The federal district court dismissed the action for want of subject matter jurisdiction after concluding that no "security" was involved in the case. The Smiths appealed.

Per Curiam:

. . . The Smiths contend that the transactions between the parties involved an investment contract type of security. In *SEC v. W. J. Howey Co.*, 328 U.S. 293, 301 (1946), the Supreme Court set out the conditions for an investment contract: "[t]he test is whether the scheme involves [1] an investment of money [2] in a common enterprise [3] with profits to come solely from the efforts of others." This court in *SEC v. Glenn W. Turner Enterprises, Inc.*, 474 F.2d 476, 482 (9th Cir.), *cert. denied*, 414 U.S. 821 (1973), held that, despite the Supreme Court's use of the word "solely," the third element of the *Howey* test is "whether the efforts made by those other than the investor are the undeniably significant ones, those essential managerial efforts which affect the failure or success of the enterprise." The *Turner* court defined a common enterprise as "one in which the fortunes of the investor are interwoven with and dependent upon the efforts and success of those seeking the investment or of third parties."

We find this case virtually identical with *Miller v. Central Chinchilla Group, Inc.*, 494 F.2d 414 (8th Cir. 1974). In *Miller* the defendants entered into contracts under which they sold chinchillas to the plaintiffs with the promise to repurchase the offspring. The plaintiffs were told that it was simple to breed chinchillas according to the defendants' instructions and that the venture would be highly profitable. The plaintiffs alleged that the chinchillas were difficult to raise and had a high mortality rate, and that the defendants could return the promised profits only if they repurchased the offspring and sold them to other prospective chinchilla raisers at an inflated price.

The *Miller* court focused on two features in holding there was an investment contract: (1) the defendants persuaded the plaintiffs to invest by representing that the efforts required of them would be very minimal; and (2) that if the plaintiffs diligently exerted themselves, they still would not gain the promised profits because those profits could be achieved only if the defendants secured additional investors at the inflated prices. Both of these features are present in the instant case. We find *Miller* to be persuasive and consistent with *Turner*. . . .

There was a common enterprise as required by *Turner*. The Smiths alleged that, although they were free under the terms of the contract to sell their production anywhere they wished, they could have received the promised profits only if the defendants repurchased above the market price, and that the defendants could have repurchased above the market price only if the defendants secured additional investors at inflated prices. Thus, the fortune of the Smiths was interwoven with and dependent upon the efforts and success of the defendants.

We also find that here, as in *Miller,* the third element of an investment contract set forth in *Turner*—that the efforts of those other than the investor are the undeniably significant ones—was present here. The *Miller* court noted that the plaintiffs there had been assured by the sellers that the effort needed to raise chinchillas was minimal. The significant effort necessary for success in the endeavor was that of the seller in procuring new investors who would purchase the chinchillas at inflated prices. Here, the Smiths alleged that they were promised that the effort necessary to raise worms was minimal and they alleged that they could not receive the promised income unless the defendants purchased their harvest.

We find the analysis in *Miller* persuasive and hold that the Smiths alleged facts that, if true, were sufficient to establish an investment contract. . . .

The judgment of the district court is reversed.

1933 ACT: REGULATING THE ISSUANCE OF SECURITIES

A major portion of federal securities regulation concerns the issuance of securities by companies. Congressional investigations following the 1929 stock market crash disclosed that enthusiasm for investment opportunities in the 1920s was often so great that large offerings of stock would be gobbled up by an investing public that knew virtually nothing about the selling company.

The goal of the 1933 Act is to protect the investing public. The 1933 Act is a disclosure statute which is frequently called the "Truth in Securities" law. The Act requires full disclosure by companies wishing to issue and sell stock to the public. By requiring such companies to file a registration statement with the SEC and to use an offering circular called a **prospectus** when attempting to sell securities, the law attempts to enable the investor to make an informed decision. The SEC, which is charged with enforcement of the law, does not attempt to pass on the value of the securities offered nor to advise investors to purchase or not purchase the securities of particular companies.

The 1933 Act also protects investors by prohibiting fraud and deceit in the distribution of shares, even those which the law does not require to be registered.

The Registration Process

Elements of the Process: Securities are distributed much like any product. The corporation selling securities to raise capital, the *issuer,*

is analogous to the manufacturer of goods. *Underwriters* act as wholesalers, *dealers* act as retailers, and the *investor* is a consumer. By regulating the activities of the issuer, underwriter, and dealer, the 1933 Act seeks to insure that the investor has access to adequate information before purchasing a particular security.

The keystones to the disclosure process are the registration statement and the prospectus, the contents of which are discussed presently. Section 5(a) of the 1933 Act makes it unlawful to sell or deliver any security without first filing with the SEC a registration statement which has become effective. Section 5(b)(1) makes it unlawful to sell a security by means of a prospectus which does not meet statutory standards. Section 5(b)(2) makes it unlawful to sell securities which are not accompanied or preceded by a prospectus.

SEC Approval: The registration statement filed with the SEC is not automatically effective. Rather, the staff of the SEC may review the statement for omissions and inaccuracies. Some reviews may be more thorough than others. Because of budgetary cutbacks and staff reductions, the SEC in recent years has had to give cursory reviews to many registration statements, reserving the full review process primarily for statements filed by new issuers selling to the public for the first time. Indeed, today most registration statements are not reviewed at all.

Section 8(a) of the 1933 Act provides that if the SEC is silent, the registration statement automatically becomes effective on the twentieth day after its filing. Whenever the SEC requires changes in the statement because insufficient or inaccurate information has been disclosed, each amendment that must be filed restarts the twenty-day period. Because the SEC has substantial powers to delay or even to block issuance of shares pursuant to a defective registration statement, most issuers strive to satisfy quickly any SEC objections to the form or content of the registration statement. The review process is aimed at insuring that full information in the proper form is contained in the registration statement.

When a prospective issuer has satisfied any SEC objections to the registration statement, the issuer must usually file a final amendment to set the price of the shares to reflect market conditions which have changed since the statement was first filed. If certain conditions pertaining to distribution of the prospectus are met, the SEC has the power (under SEC Rule 460) to accelerate the effective date by allowing the registration statement to become effective immediately after the price amendment, without the twenty-day waiting period.

The registration process may be analyzed in terms of its three major time periods. The first stage of the process is the period before the registration statement is filed (the "pre-filing" period). The second stage lasts from the filing of the statement until it becomes effective (the "waiting" period). The final stage is, of course, after the statement becomes effective (the "post-effective" period).

The Pre-Filing Period:

To prevent circumvention of the provisions of Section 5, an issuer is strictly limited during the pre-filing period. The issuer may not sell or even offer to sell a security before the registration statement is filed. The term "offer" is broadly construed and encompasses not only formal sales campaigns, but any type of activity meant to "precondition" the market. A simple speech by a corporate executive or a press release about how well the company is doing may be improper if it "just happens" to be soon followed by the filing of a registration statement.

The only activities permitted during the pre-filing period, other than normal advertising and communications with shareholders by an issuer, are preliminary negotiations between the issuer and underwriters. This is necessary because a large distribution of securities may require that an entire syndicate of underwriters be assembled.

The Waiting Period:

The purpose of the waiting period is to slow the distribution process so that the dealers and the public have time to familiarize themselves with the information disclosed in the registration process. Though no sales may be consummated during this period, certain types of offers are allowed, and underwriters may now make arrangements with dealers for their assistance in distribution.

In addition to oral offers, certain types of written offers are permissible during the waiting period. For example, an issuer may place in *The Wall Street Journal* a short announcement known as a tombstone ad because it is usually surrounded by a black border. Under SEC Rule 134, the announcement may state only a few limited items, such as (1) the kind of security, (2) the amount, (3) by whom purchase orders will be executed, and (4) the location at which a prospectus may be obtained. The announcement must state that no offer to purchase can actually be accepted during the waiting period, and that an indication of interest is not binding on a prospective investor.

Offers may also be made by use of a preliminary prospectus, which contains information from the registration statement then under review. These are called "red herring" prospectuses, because SEC Rule 430 requires that a special legend be printed in red ink on each one labeling it a preliminary prospectus, stating that a registration statement has been filed but is not yet effective, that no final sale can be made during the waiting period, and that it does not constitute an offer to sell.

Allowing offers to be made by use of the preliminary prospectus encourages the dissemination of information about the issuer. So does the

SEC practice under Rule 460 of conditioning acceleration upon a prior distribution of "red herring" prospectuses to all underwriters and dealers who might participate in the distribution. Furthermore, Rule 15c2-8 of the 1934 Act makes it an illegally deceptive practice for a managing underwriter to fail to take reasonable steps to insure that dealers receive sufficient copies of the preliminary prospectus, for dealers to fail to provide sufficient copies to their sales force, and for dealers to fail to provide copies to investors desiring them.

Post-Effective Period: Once the registration statement becomes effective, sales of securities may be completed. However, the law still imposes requirements aimed at encouraging dissemination of information. With some exceptions, the issuer, underwriter, and dealer must provide a copy of the final prospectus with every written offer, supplemental sales literature, written confirmation of sale, or delivery of securities. The prospectus must be used as long as the distribution is taking place; if this period extends beyond nine months, Section 10(a)(3) requires that the prospectus be updated to reflect more recent information on the status of the issuer. In addition, the issuer must update the prospectus whenever important new developments occur; otherwise the information can become stale and misleading, resulting in liability for fraud under Section 17(a) of the 1933 Act.

Shelf Registration: Traditionally, an issuer has been required to file a new registration statement every time it sought to initiate a new distribution of stock. However, the new Rule 415 establishes a system known as **shelf registration.** Under this system a company is allowed to file one registration statement announcing its long-term plans for sales of securities. Then, whenever the company thinks market conditions and its own financial needs require the sale of securities, it can issue the additional securities without going through the registration process described above to achieve SEC approval because it already has a registration statement and

a prospectus "on the shelf." If periodically updated, the registration statement will remain continuously effective. Rule 415 enhances the ability of corporations to raise capital on short notice, but its use has been restricted primarily to the larger, more reliable corporations.

Disclosure Requirements

The information disclosure requirements of the 1933 Act and the 1934 Act were for a long time separate, often overlapping, and sometimes conflicting. In recent years, the SEC has made an effort to coordinate the requirements for information disclosure contained in the two acts. The filing requirements of the 1934 Act must be mentioned here because they now bear significantly on the disclosure requirements of the 1933 Act regarding the registration statement and prospectus.

Registration and Reporting: Section 12 of the 1934 Act requires all companies whose securities are traded on the national stock exchanges (such as the New York Stock Exchange) and any other companies with more than $5 million in assets and more than 500 shareholders to register their securities with the SEC. These companies are referred to as registered or reporting companies. There are about 10,000 such companies. The required registration statement must contain extensive information about such areas as the organization, financial structure, and nature of the business, the structure of present classes of stock, the directors and officers and their remuneration, important contracts, balance sheets, and profit-and-loss statements for the three preceding fiscal years.

Section 13 requires that the registration statement be continually updated with annual reports (called 10-Ks) and quarterly reports (10-Qs). In addition, if important facts change between quarterly reports, the company should amend the registration statement by use of an 8-K report.

Integration of Registration Requirements: Despite all the information made public under the 1934 Act, even reporting companies have traditionally had to go through the expensive registration process under the 1933 Act, which required disclosure of information already made public in the 1934 Act reports. Complaints about the expense of filing a full 1933 Act registration statement—estimated at $100,000 to $200,000 per statement—prompted the SEC to attempt to streamline the requirements. The shelf registration procedure is one such attempt. Another step to integrate the disclosure requirements of the two Acts was taken in early 1982 when the SEC reduced the disclosure requirements under the 1933 Act for some companies.

Until the 1982 changes, there were approximately 14 different forms for registration under the 1933 Act, each tailored to a different type of offering. The main form applicable to most full-blown registration statements, Form S-1, required extensive disclosures regarding such matters as the plan of distribution; the intended use of proceeds; the company's capital structure; a summary of earnings; description of the registrant's organization, business, and property; a listing of directors and executive officers; and financial statements.

The new amendments sought to make disclosure requirements uniform under the 1933 and 1934 Acts and to utilize the periodic reports of the 1934 Act to satisfy many of the disclosure requirements of the 1933 Act registration statements by a process of incorporation by reference. The core of the new procedure is a three-tiered registration structure which creates three distinct categories of registration statement, depending upon the issuer's financial size and prior reporting history. Form S-3, applicable to the larger and more reliable corporations, maximizes incorporation by reference of 1934 Act disclosures, and has minimal prospectus disclosure requirements. Form S-2 is used by other reporting companies which have been filing 1934 Act reports for at least three years. Some incorporation by reference is allowed. Form S-1, designed primarily for companies going public for the first time, resembles the former Form S-1

by requiring full disclosure in the prospectus and registration statement and allowing no incorporation by reference to the 1934 Act reports.

Section 10 of the 1933 Act, as supplemented by various rules issued by the SEC, controls the content of the prospectus. The most important information in the registration statement regarding the financial structure, organization, operations, and officers and directors of the issuer must be summarized in the prospectus (unless incorporation by reference is allowed under the new system).

Materiality: Exactly which details must be included in the registration statement and prospectus is a matter governed not only by statutes and rules, but also by the concept of **materiality.** The most important element in the disclosure provisions of both the 1933 and 1934 Acts is that all matters that are important or material to an investor's decision should be disclosed. Materiality is an elusive concept, but the Supreme Court has described information as material "if there is a substantial likelihood that a reasonable shareholder would consider it important" in making an investment decision.[1] This is usually limited to matters having a significant bearing on the economic and financial performance of the company.

Examples of material facts include an erratic pattern of earnings, an intention to enter into a new line of business, adverse competitive conditions, litigation with the government which might lead to imposition of a financially damaging fine, and a substantial disparity between the price at which the shares are being offered to the public and the cost of the shares owned by officers, directors, and promoters. The following case illustrates one application of the concept of materiality in the context of the 1933 Act disclosure requirements.

---

[1] *TSC Industries, Inc. v. Northway, Inc.,* 426 U.S. 438, 449 (1976).

In re Doman Helicopters, Inc.
Securities and Exchange Commission, 41 S.E.C. 431 (1963)

Doman Helicopters, Inc., was formed in 1945, but never was able to do business on a profitable basis. Except for one experimental model sold in 1950, two prototypes delivered to the Army in 1956 and 1957 (both subsequently repurchased by Doman) and one helicopter on loan to its Italian licensee, by 1962 Doman had never manufactured or sold any helicopters. Instead, it had continually flirted with bankruptcy. By September 30, 1961, its accumulated losses totalled over $5.7 million. On January 31, 1962, Doman's current liabilities were $292,446 while its assets were only $13,178.

On April 19, 1962, Doman filed a Form S-1 registration statement proposing to offer publicly 681,971 shares, some to current shareholders, some to creditors, and some to the public. The contemplated price was $1.50 per share. Doman's future plans were predicated on development of a proposed helicopter, the D-10B.

The SEC commenced a proceeding under Section 8(d) of the 1933 Act to determine whether a stop order should issue suspending the effectiveness of Doman's registration statement. The focus of the investigation was on deficiencies in the prospectus.

By the Commission:

. . . 1. Status and Prospectus of the Model D-10B. The prospectus describes the D-10B as though it were an existing and operational helicopter possessing superiority in specified respects [economy of operation, range, payload per dollar invested] over other helicopters offered on the market. . . . There is no adequate factual foundation for the[se] statements, and they were false and misleading.

The D-10B has never been flown or tested or even assembled in prototype form, crucial facts which are nowhere disclosed in the registration statement.

2. The Doman Hingeless Rotor System. The prospectus makes the following claims for the so-called "Doman Hingeless Rotor System": "In comparison with other devices, this system provides greater inherent stability in forward flight, less vibration in any flight attitude or maneuver, long life for the rotor and blade assembly, relatively low initial and maintenance costs and exceptional permissible range of the center of gravity of the fuselage and its cargo." . . .

These representations present in their totality a misleading picture of uniqueness and substantiated superiority of the Doman rotor system. That system has been used only on a few converted or prototype models. No production model using the Doman rotor system has ever been subjected to normal day to day usage by a user or customer. In such circumstances the unqualified claims as to superior durability and lower maintenance costs were not warranted, and it was deceptive to describe the system as "fully developed and proven." . . .

3. Efforts to Secure Defense Contracts. The prospectus makes only a passing reference to the fact that registrant unsuccessfully attempted to secure a military market for its helicopters. It does not disclose the nature of those attempts or of the action of the Department of Defense with respect to them. Registrant had from 1951 to 1962 made strenuous and persistent efforts to interest that Department in its proposals and devices. The Department made a number of tests with the two prototype helicopters that it purchased from the registrant and made an extensive study of the Doman rotor system. It found "no significant advantages in the Doman rotor system over other types," and those findings were reaffirmed upon successive reviews following objections raised by registrant. . . . Irrespective of the correctness of the Department's conclusions, they constitute a determination by the technical staff and responsible authorities of the largest single purchaser of helicopters that for their purposes registrant's rotor system had no special merit. Such determination was a significant adverse factor, and the failure to disclose it rendered the prospectus misleading.

4. Application of Proceeds. The prospectus stated that the proceeds of the offering would be used to develop the D-10B, but failed to state the order of priority in which the proceeds would be applied as required by Instruction 2 to Item 3 of Form S-1. The prospectus did not adequately disclose that except to the extent that the creditors to whom part of the offering is to be made elected to take stock in exchange for their debt claims, $292,466 of the proceeds from the public offering would first have to be applied to the liquidation of registrant's outstanding indebtedness, thereby reducing and perhaps exhausting the funds that the prospectus stated would be allocated to the D-10B. It also failed to disclose that approximately $13,000 of the estimated proceeds would have to be used to pay the accrued salaries of certain officers and directors, and that a large portion of the proceeds would have to be used to meet current expenses, which were being incurred at the rate of $11,000 per month, and would be used for that purpose even if the proceeds of the offering were insufficient to permit registrant to go forward with its D-10B program.

5. Dilution Aspects of Offering. The prospectus fails to disclose the dilution aspects of the offering. As of January 31, 1962, registrant's shares had a book value of minus 30 cents per share. If all the shares that the registrant proposes to offer to its existing stockholders and to its creditors were in fact sold at the proposed offering prices, that book value would increase to 55 cents per share. Purchasers paying $1.50 per share would therefore suffer an immediate dilution of 95 cents per share, the benefit of which will inure entirely to the present stockholders. It was pertinent to an informed appraisal by the persons to whom the securities being offered may be sold that this dilution be described in the prospectus. . . .

A stop order will issue.

Exemptions

In certain situations where there is less need for regulation, Sections 3 and 4 of the 1933 Act provide exemptions from Section 5's registration requirements (though not from the anti-fraud provisions of the 1933 and 1934 Acts).

Perhaps the most important exemption is that for "transactions by any person other than an issuer, underwriter, or dealer" provided by Section 4(1). This simply means that once the issue is sold to the investing public, the public may trade, and the dealers may handle most transactions, without any worry about registration or prospectus delivery requirements. Thus, the 1933 Act does not apply to so-called "secondary trading," which is regulated by the 1934 Act.

Section 3(a) exempts from registration the securities of governments (state and federal), charitable organizations, banks, savings and loans, and common carriers, which are regulated under other federal laws.

Small Issues: There are also exemptions for small issues and small issuers. Section 4(2) exempts "transactions by an issuer not involving any public offering," an exemption used primarily in connection with (1) bank loans, (2) privately negotiated sales of securities to large institutional investors (private placements), and (3) the promotion of business ventures by a few closely related persons. Section 3(b) authorizes the SEC to exempt securities if it finds that registration "is not necessary in the public interest and for the protection of investors by reason of the small amount involved [a five-million-dollar ceiling] or the limited character of the public offering."

Regulation D: Specific SEC rules flesh out the 4(2) and 3(b) exemptions, and all were renumbered and revamped in early 1982 with the promulgation of Regulation D. A key concept in Regulation D is that of the "accredited investor" which, by its nature, is not likely to need government protection in its investment decisions. **Accredited investors** include (1) institutional investors, such as pension funds and banks, (2) the seller's "insiders," such as directors and officers, (3) an individual with a net worth of over $1 million, (4) an individual with an annual income of over $200,000 for three consecutive years, and (5) a person who buys $150,000 of securities at one time (so long as the total purchase does not exceed 20 percent of the investor's net worth).

Regulation D's Rule 504 exempts from registration any offering in a 12-month period totalling less than $500,000 (reduced by amounts sold in reliance on other exemptions). This exemption is aimed at smaller businesses and is not available to 1934 Act reporting companies.

Rule 505 allows a company, including reporting companies, to sell up to five million dollars (reduced by amounts sold in reliance on other exemptions) in securities in any 12-month period without registering, provided the sales are to no more than 35 unaccredited investors. The number of sales to accredited investors is not limited. However, no general advertising or soliciting is allowed.

Rule 506 clarifies Section 4(2)'s exemption by allowing companies, including reporting companies, to sell an unlimited amount of securities in an issuance if sales are limited to 35 unaccredited investors and an unlimited number of accredited investors. There is an obligation on the part of the issuer to make a determination that all purchasers are "sophisticated" and therefore capable of protecting themselves without the assistance of a registration statement and prospectus. Accredited investors are assumed to be sophisticated, and an unsophisticated purchaser may act through a sophisticated purchaser representative. No general advertising or soliciting is allowed, or the distribution would lose its nonpublic nature.

Rule 502 provides that if any sales are made to unaccredited investors pursuant to Rules 505 and 506, all purchasers must be given certain specified information about the issuer. The required information is less comprehensive than the normal prospectus.

Local Offerings: A final important exemption is Section 3(a)(11)'s exemption for intrastate offerings, which applies where a selling company doing business in a state offers and sells securities only to residents of the same state and intends to use the proceeds there. An issuer, according to Rule 147, is doing business within a state if (1) it derives 80 percent or more of its revenue from operations within the state, (2) at least 80 pecent of its assets are located within the state, (3) at least 80 percent of the net proceeds of the issuance will be used within the state, and (4) the issuer's principal office is located there. Offer of the shares for sale to a single nonresident will void the exemption. Federal regulation is deemed unnecessary because of the availability of state regulation and the close proximity of purchaser to seller.

Enforcement and Civil Liabilities

Government Action: The SEC has numerous powers to enforce compliance with the provisions of the 1933 Act. For example, if the SEC believes that a registration statement is incomplete or inaccurate, Section 8(b) authorizes issuance of a "refusal order" which prevents the statement from becoming effective until SEC objections are satisfied. If inaccuracies are discovered after the effective date, the SEC may issue a "stop order" pursuant to Section 8(d), as was done in the *Doman Helicopters* case, to suspend the effectiveness of the statement. Section 8(e) authorizes the SEC to conduct an "examination" to fully investigate whether a stop order should issue.

More generally, Section 19(b) gives the SEC power of subpoena to aid investigations of any potential violation of the 1933 Act. Section 20(b) allows the SEC to go into federal district court to seek an injunction whenever it appears that any person is violating the 1933 Act.

The 1933 Act even contains criminal provisions. Section 24 provides that any person who willfully violates any provision of the Act or any SEC rule, or any person who willfully makes an untrue statement or omits a material fact in a registration statement, is subject to a fine of not more than $10,000, imprisonment of not more than five years, or both.

Private Suit: The 1933 Act provides remedies for violation of its provisions in the form of lawsuits that may be brought by injured investors.

Section 11:   An investor who is injured after buying securities with reliance on a rosy picture falsely painted in a prospectus will probably not be satisfied with the SEC's injunction remedy or even criminal prosecution. The investor will desire to recoup losses through a civil action for damages, and the 1933 Act has express provision for such lawsuits. Section 11 states that if "any part of the registration statement, when such part became effective, contained an untrue statement of a material fact or omitted to state a material fact required to be stated therein or necessary to make the statements therein not misleading, any person acquiring such security" may file a civil action. Potential defendants in such an action include every person who signed the registration statement (which includes the issuer, its principal executive officers, chief financial officer, principal accounting officers, and a majority of the board of directors), every person who was a director or identified as about to become a director, every accountant, every appraiser or other expert who is named as having helped prepare it, and every underwriter.

The Section 11 cause of action is loosely patterned after a common-law fraud action, but is modified so as to greatly ease a plaintiff's burdens in seeking recovery. For example, the common-law fraud elements of privity of contract and reliance are not necessary in a Section 11 claim so long as plaintiff can trace the purchased shares back to the defective offering and show they were not previously issued shares of the same company being publicly traded at the same time.

If plaintiff proves the registration statement contained misstatements or omissions of material facts, the law presumes that these caused plaintiff's damages, and the burden of proof shifts to defendants to prove that other factors were the true cause of plaintiff's losses.

Furthermore, Section 11 does not require proof of fraudulent intent. Proof of misstatement or omission shifts the burden of proof to defendants to establish that they were guilty of neither fraudulent intent nor negligence in preparing the registration statement. Individual defendants must establish that they used "due diligence" in preparing the registration statement. The amount of diligence that is due from a defendant depends on his or her position as an "insider" (with full access to key information) or an "outsider," and a defendant is generally allowed to rely on "expertised" portions of the statement—those portions prepared by experts such as independent auditors. The due diligence defense is not available to the issuing company, which is strictly liable for inaccuracies in the registration statement.

Section 12:   Section 12(1) allows an investor to recover when offers or sales are made in violation of Section 5—that is, without the filing of a registration statement, by use of a defective prospectus, or where securities are delivered without an accompanying prospectus. The elements of a Section 12(1) claim are similar to those of a Section 11 claim, except that lack of privity of contract is a valid defense under Section 12(1). Thus, if an issuer sold to an underwriter, who sold to a dealer, who sold to the plaintiff, plaintiff could recover only from the dealer, even though the issuer and underwriter violated Section 5.

Section 12(2) renders civilly liable any person who sells securities by use of a misstatement or omission of material fact who "shall not sustain the burden of proof that he did not know, and in the exercise of reasonable care could not have known, of such untruth or omission." This section applies even to sales of securities which were exempt from registration. Due diligence is an affirmative defense. Lack of privity is also a defense, although many courts have limited its use-

fulness by rendering liable not only the person who actually conveyed the title to the buyer, but also any person, such as a stockbroker, who substantially facilitated or participated in the sale.

1934 ACT: REGULATING THE TRADING OF SECURITIES

While the 1933 Act regulates primarily the initial issuance of securities, the 1934 Act regulates the subsequent trading of those securities. An array of complex problems comes within the purview of the 1934 Act. The general registration and reporting requirements of the 1934 Act have already been discussed. Attention is now turned to several other major concerns of the Act.

Insider Trading

Knowledge of the inner workings of a corporation would be very valuable in making investment decisions. For example, if a corporate vice-president learned that his company's scientists had just been granted an important patent which will open up a new sales field, he would have a distinct and arguably unfair trading advantage over the general investing public. Insider trading was a widespread phenomenon in the 1920s, yet the common law provided little protection from such abusive practices.

Section 16(b):   One response to the insider trading problem is Section 16 of the 1934 Act. Subsection (a) is a reporting requirement which applies to three categories of persons: officers, directors, and owners of more than 10 percent of the shares of any one class of stock of a 1934 Act reporting company. These three categories of persons are deemed the corporation's "insiders." Section 16(a) requires that they file two types of reports with the stock exchanges and the SEC: an initial report revealing the holdings when a director or officer takes office or when a stockholder first obtains a 10 percent holding, and an additional report each month thereafter in which a change in holdings occurs.

Subsection (b) of Section 16 provides that any profits realized by such an insider in connection with a purchase and sale or sale and purchase within a six-month period is an illegal "short-swing" profit. Any such profit may be recaptured by the issuer.

The striking aspect of Section 16(b) liability is its near absolute nature. Because of the difficulty of proving that someone has improperly used inside information for personal gain, Congress elected to omit such actual use as a requirement for Section 16(b) liability. Instead, if someone fitting the definition of an insider does have a purchase and sale or sale and purchase within a six-month period which results in a profit, liability is automatic. There are no defenses. Even proof that inside information was not used is no defense in a standard transaction.

Calculation of Profit: Another extraordinary feature of Section 16(b) is the manner in which the profit realized is calculated. A first-in, first-out matching of shares might seem a sensible approach to calculating profits. However, in order to discourage insider trading, the courts have held that all purchases and sales or sales and purchases within a six-month period should be matched on a lowest in, highest out basis in order to maximize the profits that may be recaptured. Furthermore, transactions which resulted in a loss will not be deducted from those which were profitable. For example, assume that an insider engaged in the following transactions involving a company's securities:

January 1, bought 1000 shares at $5 per share

February 1, bought 1000 shares at $8 per share

March 1, sold 1000 shares at $4 per share

April 1, sold 1000 shares at $7 per share.

All transactions occurred within a six-month period, so all could be matched for Section 16(b) purposes. It seems apparent the insider spent $13,000 in buying the shares, but received only $11,000 when they were sold, resulting in an actual loss of $2,000. But for Section 16(b) purposes, the January 1 purchase (lowest in) will be matched with the April 1 sale (highest out), to show a $2,000 profit. When the remaining February 1 purchase is matched with the remaining March 1 sale, a $4,000 loss is produced, but such losses are disregarded in Section 16(b) calculations. Therefore, although the insider has sustained an actual loss of $2,000, according to Section 16(b) an illegal profit of $2,000 is calculated, which may not be kept.

Incentive to Sue: The SEC has no enforcement powers for Section 16(b) violations. Nor does the person who bought from or sold to the insider have a right to sue. Rather, the right to recoup the insider's profit belongs to the corporation itself. Because the corporation's decision to sue must be made by some of the very people at which the statute is aimed—the officers and directors—Section 16(b) provides that if the corporation refuses a request to file suit, any shareholder may file a derivative action on the corporation's behalf.

In order to encourage enforcement of Section 16(b), the courts have liberally construed its enforcement provisions, holding that a plaintiff need be a shareholder only at the time suit is brought, not necessarily at the time of the violation. Because the recovery goes into the corporate till and any shareholder would profit only indirectly and usually in a miniscule amount, it would seem that there is little incentive to bring such an action. The courts have added incentive by liberally granting attorney's fees to prevailing plaintiffs. Because of the near absolute liability under Section 16(b), some attorneys have found it lucrative to search the Section 16(a) reports on insider holdings for transactions resulting in a profit, to purchase a single share of the subject corporation's stock, and then to sue when the corporation refuses to do so. Attorney's fee awards well into six figures are unusual but not unknown in Section 16(b) litigation.

Section 10(b): Another provision of the 1934 Act which regulates insider trading, as well as many other facets of securities trading, is Section 10(b). This provision makes it unlawful to "use or employ, in connection with the purchase or sale of any security, . . . any manipulative or deceptive device or contrivance in contravention of such rules and regulations as the Commission may prescribe. . . ."

Pursuant to Section 10(b), the SEC has issued the most important of all its rules, Rule 10b-5, quoted in full:

It shall be unlawful for any person, directly or indirectly, by the use of any means or instrumentality of interstate commerce, or of the mails, or of any facility of any national securities exchange,

(1) to employ any device, scheme or artifice to defraud,

(2) to make any untrue statement of a material fact or to omit to state a material fact necessary in order to make the statements made, in the light of the circumstances under which they were made, not misleading, or

(3) to engage in any act, practice, or course of business which operates or would operate as a fraud or deceit upon any person, in connection with the purchase or sale of any security.

General Provisions: One important category of Rule 10b-5 cases involves insider trading. Although a Section 10(b) case is more difficult to prove, its coverage is broader than Section 16(b)'s. The broad purpose of Section 10(b) and Rule 10b-5 is to protect the investing public by preventing fraud and equalizing access to material information. Section 10(b) applies to any purchase or sale by any person of any security—there are no exceptions. Thus, small close corporations (the shares of which are not offered to the public for sale but are typically held by just a few, perhaps members of a single family) are covered as well as the largest public corporations. Transactions covered include those occurring on the stock exchanges, in over-the-counter sales through stockbrokers, or even

in privately negotiated sales. Any person connected with the transaction is regulated, not only insiders as in Section 16(b).

Unlike Section 16(b), Section 10(b) requires proof of actual use of inside information to establish a violation. There is no automatic presumption. Furthermore, the information must be material and it must be nonpublic.

Disclose or Abstain: The key to insider trading liability is the "disclose or abstain" rule. A leading case, *SEC v. Texas Gulf Sulphur,*[2] which involved the purchase of securities of the Texas Gulf Sulphur Company by its employees and their tippees who possessed nonpublic information about a massive ore strike by the company in Canada, laid down the basic disclose or abstain rule in these words: "Anyone in possession of material inside information must either disclose it to the investing public, or, if he is disabled from disclosing it in order to protect a corporate confidence, or he chooses not to do so, must abstain from trading in or recommending the securities concerned while such inside information remains undisclosed."

The disclose or abstain rule promotes fairness in securities trading by attempting to equalize *access* to important information affecting the value of securities. Equal information is not the goal; equal *access* is. Although the goal cannot be perfectly achieved, small investors will likely have more confidence in the market if they know the SEC is actively promoting equal access.

Enforcement: If abuse of nonpublic information is proved, the SEC can hold disciplinary proceedings if a regulated broker, dealer, or underwriter is involved. It can also go to court to obtain an injunction halting the illegal practices and perhaps an order rescinding the fraudulent sale. Sometimes the SEC obtains an order forcing defendants to disgorge their illicit profits.

A willful violation of Section 10(b), or of any provision of the 1934 Act, subjects the violator

[2] 401 F.2d 833 (2d Cir. 1968).

to the criminal provisions of Section 32, which carry penalties of imprisonment up to five years, a fine or both. To discourage insider trading, Congress passed the Insider Trading Sanctions Act of 1984 (ITSA), which increased the maximum fine for a criminal violation of any 1934 Act provision from $10,000 to $100,000 and authorized the SEC in insider trading cases to seek relief in the form of disgorgement of illicit profits and assessment of a civil money penalty of up to three times the profit gained or the loss avoided.

These ITSA provisions were invoked many times when a major insider trading scandal rocked Wall Street in late 1986 and into 1987. Among the key figures in the scandal, Ivan Boesky agreed to disgorge $50 million in illicit profits and to pay a fine of $100 million, and Dennis Levine was sentenced to 2 years in jail and fined $362,000.

In addition to government civil and criminal actions, perhaps the most important remedy for a Section 10(b) violation is the private civil lawsuit which may be brought by victims of fraud, such as insider trading, against the perpetrators. Although the 1934 Act does not explicitly provide for such a private right of action, the courts have implied one since 1946.[3] Private lawsuits brought under Section 10(b) and Rule 10b-5 in the1960s and 1970s dramatically altered the law of securities regulation in the United States.

Potential Defendants: Those barred from insider trading have always included corporate "insiders," a term defined more broadly than in the §16(b) provisions, including any corporate

---

[3] *Kardon v. National Gypsum Co.,* 69 F.Supp. 512 (E.D.Pa. 1946).

employee with access to material inside information, not just officers and directors. Also barred are the "tippees" of these insiders. Unless tippees are covered, a corporate president could tip his or her spouse and then enjoy indirectly the fruits of the spouse's trading. The Supreme Court made it clear in *Dirks v. SEC,* 436 U.S. 646 (1983), that a tippee could not be liable for insider trading unless the tipping insider had breached a duty to the corporation in passing along the information. Such a breach would occur if the information was passed for a personal benefit (whether monetary or otherwise).

A third major category of potential insider trading defendant are "temporary insiders." These are persons who receive confidential corporate information for a corporate purpose and with the expectation that it will be kept confidential, but then use it in insider trading. Classic examples are attorneys, accountants, and investment bankers hired temporarily by a corporation. For example, if an attorney is hired to help Corporation A merge with Corporation B, and the attorney realizes that this will be a very favorable arrangement for Corporation A, he may be tempted to trade in its stock. That would be illegal so long as the information is nonpublic.

A final category of potential insider trading defendant consists of "misappropriators"—noninsiders who steal confidential inside information. The "disclose or abstain" obligation must rest on a *duty* to someone. Insiders, their tippees, and temporary insiders all owe a duty to the corporation in whose shares they trade. It can be a little more elusive to determine the duty owed by a misappropriator. There have been many such cases brought recently, and the following case is a leading one.

SEC v. Materia
U.S. Second Circuit Court of Appeals, 745 F.2d 197 (1984)

Materia was a proofreader for Bowne of New York City, Inc. (Bowne), a firm specializing in the printing of financial documents. Because even a hint of an upcoming tender offer may send the price of the target company's stock soaring, information regarding the target's identity is zealously guarded. The law firms which draft tender offer documents for Bowne to print omit identifying information until the last minute and use code names. Bowne scrupulously attempts to keep all such information confidential to serve its clients.

Nonetheless, Materia was able to divine the identities of at least four tender offer targets. Within hours of each discovery he purchased stock in the target and within days—after the offer had been made public—he sold all his holdings at substantial gains. The SEC filed a civil enforcement action against Materia, alleging that he was guilty of insider trading in violation of §10(b) and Rule 10b-5 because he had misappropriated information from his employer and its clients. The trial judge issued an order restraining Materia from further violations and ordering him to disgorge illegally obtained profits of $99,862.50. Materia appealed.

Kaufman, Circuit Judge:

Our era aptly has been styled, and well may be remembered as, the "age of information." Francis Bacon recognized nearly 400 years ago that "knowledge is power," but only in the last generation has it risen to the equivalent of the coin of the realm. Nowhere is this commodity more valuable or volatile than in the world of high finance, where facts worth fortunes while secret may be rendered worthless once revealed.

Materia does not contest the district court's finding that he misappropriated confidential information and traded on it to his advantage. His sole argument is that such activity does not contravene Section 10(b) and Rule 10b-5. In light of this court's holding in *United States v. Newman*, 664 F.2d 12 (2d Cir. 1981), we hold that such actions do, indeed, lie within the proscriptive purview of the antifraud provisions of the securities laws.

Newman addressed the criminal liability under Section 10(b) and Rule 10b-5 of an individual defendant charged with participating in a scheme to misappropriate confidential information regarding upcoming tender offers. Along with his co-conspirators, employees of two investment banking firms, Newman surreptitiously gathered and traded on this nonpublic data. The court held that Newman's "conduct . . . could be found to constitute criminal violation of Section 10(b) and Rule 10b-5." The facts in the instant appeal are sufficiently similar to those in *Newman* for us to affirm on the authority of that precedent alone.

Rule 10b-5, promulgated in 1942 pursuant to the Commission's rulemaking power under Section 10(b), makes it "unlawful for any person . . . [t]o engage in any act . . . which operates . . . as a fraud or deceit upon any person, in connection with the purchase or sale of securities." As in *Newman,* "we need spend little time on the issue of fraud and deceit." Materia "misappropriated—stole to put it bluntly—valuable nonpublic information entrusted to him in utmost confidence." *United States v. Chiarella,* 445 U.S. 222, 245 (1980) (Burger, C.J., dissenting). We hold that such activity falls squarely within the "fraud or deceit" language of the Rule. Legislative history to the Securities Exchange Act of 1934 makes clear that the antifraud provision was intended to be broad in scope, encompassing all "manipulative and deceptive practices which have been demonstrated to fulfill no useful function." S.Rep. No. 792, 73d Cong., 2d Sess., 6 (1934). This language negates the suggestion that the provision was aimed solely at the eradication of fraudulent trading by corporate insiders. Against this expansive construction of "fraud or deceit," Materia's theft of information was indeed as fraudulent as if he had converted corporate funds for his personal benefit.

In an effort to circumvent this conclusion, Materia attempts to argue that he could not have defrauded his employer, since he was unaware of the confidential nature of the information he handled in the course of his work. [The trial judge] explicitly found that Bowne's diligent efforts to communicate the need for secrecy vitiated this claim, and the record contains ample support for such a finding. We find similarly unavailing Materia's argument that Bowne was not injured as a result of his misappropriation of client information. Among a financial printer's most valuable assets is its reputation as a safe repository for client secrets. By purloining and trading on confidences entrusted to Bowne, it cannot be gainsaid that Materia undermined his employer's integrity. Accordingly, we are driven to the conclusion that, by his misappropriation of material nonpublic information, Materia perpetrated a fraud upon Bowne.

We announced [in *Newman*] and reiterate now, that one who misappropriates nonpublic information in breach of a fiduciary duty and trades on that information to his own advantage violates Section 10(b) and Rule 10b-5. We do not believe that the drafters of the Securities Exchange Act of 1934—envisaging as they did an open and honest market—would have countenanced the activities engaged in by Anthony Materia.

[Affirmed.]

Potential Civil Plaintiffs: The SEC or Department of Justice may bring civil or criminal actions against any violator of Section 10(b)'s ban against insider trading. However, plaintiffs in civil suits under Section 10(b) for damages may sue only those defendants who breached a duty *to the plaintiffs.* Thus, shareholders who sold their shares in M Corporation not knowing of secret material information that induced insiders, tippees, and temporary insiders of M Corporation to buy at the same time, may sue those traders, because they breached a duty to M Corporation and therefore to plaintiff shareholders. On the other hand, misappropriators may be a little more difficult to sue. Materia, for example, traded in the shares of target corporations. However, the duty he was held to have breached ran to his employer and its client, the potential acquiror in a tender offer. Because Materia breached no duty to the target or its shareholders, those shareholders may not sue him for civil damages, though he was open to SEC injunctive and criminal action.

A defendant who is properly sued may be liable to *all* persons who traded during the time he exploited inside information. Thus, in *Shapiro v. Merrill Lynch,* 495 F.2d 228 (2d Cir. 1974), tippers and tippees who sold Douglas Aircraft stock upon nonpublic information that its earnings projections had dived, were held liable for damages "not only to the purchasers of the actual shares sold by defendants (in the unlikely event they can be identified) but to all persons who during the same period purchased Douglas stock in the open market without knowledge of the material inside information which was in the possession of defendants." Although defendants sold only about one-half of the total Douglas shares sold during the relevant five-day period, they were held liable to all investors who bought Douglas shares during that time period only to see their value tumble upon public disclosure of the information.

Measure of Damages: The *Shapiro* case's method of measuring liability in a civil damage suit can be draconian. Therefore, the trend is to limit recovery to disgorgement of the amount of illicit profits gained by the traders.[4] If plaintiffs' losses exceed the disgorged profits, they share recovery on a *pro rata* basis. The "disgorgement" measure of damages has been analogized to punishing bank robbers merely by making them give back the loot. It leaves the fines and treble damages which the SEC can secure under ITSA as the major civil deterrents to insider trading.

False or Inadequate Corporate Disclosures

A second major category of Section 10(b) cases relates to disclosures of information about corporations. Already noted are the registration and reporting requirements of the 1934 Act. The registration forms—the 10-Ks, 10-Qs, and 8-Ks—are all designed to promote full disclosure of information important to the investing public. When a corporation or some person fraudulently misstates or fails to disclose material information, a Section 10(b) violation may occur.[5]

An investor who is injured because he or she bought or sold shares on the basis of inaccurate or incomplete corporate information may bring a private cause of action under the antifraud provisions of Section 10(b). The requirements of a valid claim in such a lawsuit are patterned after those of common-law fraud: (1) a misrepresentation of material fact, (2) made by defendant with knowledge of the falsity, (3) an intent to induce plaintiff to rely, (4) actual reliance by the plaintiff, (5) privity of contract between plaintiff and defendant, and (6) damage sustained. Modification of some of these common-law elements has been a source of controversy in this type of Section 10(b) case.

Privity: Privity of contract has been largely eliminated as a requirement of a Section 10(b) cause of action in the corporate disclosure setting. An injured shareholder is normally allowed to sue those persons responsible for false statements whether or not the stockholder purchased shares from or sold shares to the defendants.

---

[4] *Elkind v. Liggett & Myers, Inc.,* 635 F.2d 156 (2d Cir. 1980).

[5] False or misleading statements in documents filed with the SEC may also lead to liability under Section 18(a) of the 1934 Act.

Intent: Actual intent to defraud arising from knowledge of the falsity of a statement is a traditional element of common-law fraud. In order to advance the remedial purposes of the 1934 Act, many lower courts formerly interpreted Section 10(b) so as to virtually eliminate the requirement of intent by holding defendants liable though they were guilty of nothing more than simple negligence.

The Supreme Court overruled these cases, however, in *Ernst & Ernst v. Hochfelder,* a case excerpted in Chapter 40. There the Court held that the defendant accounting firm was not liable for a Section 10(b) violation "in the absence of any allegation of **scienter**—intent to deceive, manipulate, or defraud."

The question has subsequently arisen as to whether a defendant should be liable if guilty of "recklessness," which means being highly negligent or so careless as to exhibit a complete disregard for possible damage to others. Most lower courts have concluded that reckless conduct is sufficient for imposition of liability, although the Supreme Court has not spoken on the issue.

Reliance: In a common-law fraud case, plaintiff must normally prove that the defendant's fraudulent statement was relied on in making the sale or purchase. In order to advance the broadly remedial purposes of the 1934 Act, some adjustments have been made to the traditional reliance requirement.

A misleading corporate disclosure can occur either when a material fact is concealed or when it is misrepresented. Because it is impractical to require an investor to prove reliance on a fact that was concealed from him or her, the Supreme Court has eliminated the reliance requirement in concealment cases. In *Affiliated Ute Citizens v. United States,* 406 U.S. 128 (1972), plaintiffs, mixed-blood Ute Indians, sold shares in the Ute Development Corporation through defendants, bank officials. Defendants failed to disclose to plaintiffs their own interest in the transactions or the fact that shares were trading at higher prices among whites. The Court held:

> Under the circumstances of this case, involving primarily a failure to disclose, positive proof of reliance is not a prerequisite to recovery. All that is necessary is that the facts withheld be material in the sense that a reasonable investor might have considered them important in the making of this decision. This obligation to disclose and this withholding of a material fact establish the requisite element of causation in fact.

In cases of active misrepresentation, proof of reliance is practicable; nonetheless, there have been some important modifications of the reliance requirements even in misrepresentation cases, due partly to the impersonal nature of transactions which occur through the stock exchanges. A leading case follows.

Blackie v. Barrack
U.S. Ninth Circuit Court of Appeals, 524 F.2d 892 (1975)

In fiscal 1970, Ampex Corporation reported a $12 million profit. Soon losses began to occur, but their full extent was not revealed until over two years later, when Ampex reported a $90 million loss for fiscal 1972. The company's independent auditors withdrew certification of 1971 financial statements and refused to certify those of 1972 because of suspicions that much of the loss had been sustained earlier but

concealed. A class action was filed by Ampex shareholders who purchased during the two-year period in which Ampex was issuing annual reports, interim reports, SEC filings, and press releases which inaccurately stated the company's financial condition. Defendants included Ampex, its officers, and its independent auditors.

The trial judge certified a class action, rejecting the contention of defendants that a class action was inappropriate because each and every class member (purchasers of 21 million shares in 120,000 transactions) would have to separately prove reliance on a particular misstatement. Defendants appealed the class certification on this and other grounds.

Koelsch, Judge:

. . . Individual questions of reliance are . . . not an impediment [to class certification]—subjective reliance is not a distinct element of proof of 10b-5 claims of the type involved in this case.

The class members' substantive claims either are, or can be, cast in omission or non-disclosure terms—the company's financial reporting failed to disclose the need for reserves, conditions reflecting on the value of the inventory, or other facts necessary to make the reported figures not misleading. [The court then quoted the above passage from the *Affiliated Ute* case holding that reliance is not an element of proof in a concealment case.]

Moreover, proof of subjective reliance on particular misrepresentations is unnecessary to establish a 10b-5 claim for a deception inflating the price of stock traded in the open market. Proof of reliance is adduced to demonstrate the causal connection between the defendant's wrongdoing and the plaintiff's loss. We think causation is adequately established in the impersonal stock exchange context by proof of reliance. Materiality circumstantially establishes the reliance of some market traders and hence the inflation in the stock price—when the purchase is made the causal chain between defendant's conduct and plaintiff's loss is sufficiently established to make out a prima facie case. . . .

That the prima facie case each class member must establish differs from the traditional fraud action, and may, unlike the fraud action, be established by common proof, is irrelevant; although derived from it, the 10b-5 action is not coterminous with a common law fraud action.

Here, we eliminate the requirement that plaintiffs prove reliance directly in this context because the requirement imposes an unreasonable and irrelevant evidentiary burden. A purchaser on the stock exchanges may be either unaware of a specific fact representation, or may not directly rely on it; he may purchase because of a favorable price trend, price earnings ratio, or some other factor. Nevertheless, he relies generally on the supposition that the market price is validly set and that no unsuspected manipulation has artificially inflated the price, and thus indirectly on the truth of the representations underlying the stock price—whether he is aware of it or not, the price he pays reflects material representations. Requiring direct proof from each purchaser that he relied on a particular representation when purchasing would defeat recovery by those whose reliance was indirect, despite the fact that the causational chain is broken only if the purchaser would have purchased the stock even had he known of the misrepresentation. We decline to leave such open market purchasers unprotected. The statute and rule are designed to foster an expectation that securities markets are free from fraud—an expectation on which purchasers should be able to rely. . . .

Affirmed.

Although the outer limit of permissible 10b-5 actions is not completely settled, the Supreme Court has attempted to confine the actions to situations involving deceit and manipulation. Simple corporate mismanagement or breaches of fiduciary duty by corporate officials, not involving deceit, are not actionable under Rule 10b-5.[6]

Proxy Regulation

Although most corporate decisions are made by the officers and directors, shareholders do occasionally vote on matters of importance. At the annual shareholders meeting, which state incorporation laws require be held, the shareholders elect directors to the board of directors. Their approval may also be required for certain extraordinary matters, such as amendments to corporate bylaws or articles of incorporation, mergers, or sales of major assets.

Valid shareholder approval requires at least a majority vote (and sometimes a two-thirds or three-fourths approval) of a quorum of shares eligible to vote. However, in a large corporation with thousands of shareholders, it is very unusual for more than a small percentage of shareholders to appear at the annual meeting. In order to obtain a quorum, corporate management is usually required to solicit *proxies* from the shareholders. A **proxy** is an authorization to vote shares owned by someone else. At a typical corporation's annual meeting, incumbent man-

agement will solicit and receive proxies from a sufficient number of shareholders to vote itself into control for another year.

Section 14(a) of the 1934 Act prohibits solicitation of proxies for any shares registered under the Act in contravention of rules promulgated by the SEC. The rules which the SEC has issued have three broad goals: full disclosure, fraud prevention, and increased shareholder participation.

Full Disclosure: State laws have not always required corporate management to be responsive to the informational needs and desires of shareholders. The SEC, knowing that most major corporations solicit proxies at least annually, requires in Rule 14a-3 that no soliciting occur unless each person solicited is furnished with a written proxy statement containing the information specified in Schedule 14A.

Schedule 14A contains over 20 items, some of which are applicable only if specified matters, such as merger approval, are involved. In the typical solicitation by management relating to election of directors, the proxy statement must be accompanied by an annual report to contain, *inter alia,* comparative financial statements for the last two fiscal years, a summary of operations, a brief description of the business done by the issuer and its subsidiaries, and identification of the issuer's directors and executive officers and their principal occupations. This information must be clearly presented.

Rule 14a-6 requires that preliminary proxy soliciting material be submitted to the SEC for review at least ten days before actual solicita-

---

[6] *Santa Fe Industries v. Green,* 430 U.S. 462 (1977).

tion. The SEC can require changes before the material is mailed. Copies of the final statement are to be provided the SEC and any exchange where the issuer's shares are registered.

Proxy Contests: Normally, incumbent management will face no organized opposition in the election of directors at the annual meeting. But if the corporation is floundering financially, perhaps a group of "insurgent" shareholders will attempt to elect its own slate of candidates to the board of directors. Or perhaps the insurgents have lined up a merger with or tendered their shares to another corporation, which intends to fire incumbent management, and incumbent management has negotiated a proposed defensive merger with yet another company, which would be willing to retain the incumbents in their present positions. In these and other situations, proxy contests arise over the control of the corporation. Incumbent management and insurgent shareholders vie for sufficient proxies to prevail in the shareholders' vote. Federal regulations specify the procedure for such contests and punish any fraud which may occur.

Prior to solicitation, Rule 14a-11 requires insurgents to file an informational statement with the SEC and exchanges disclosing the participants in the insurgent group—those persons soliciting the proxies, financing the effort, or serving as attorneys and accountants for the group. Schedule 14B sets out the information which must be disclosed about the participants, including their employment history, past criminal violations, and stock holdings. At the time of solicitation, the insurgents must provide the shareholders with their own proxy statement similar to that which management is required to provide.

Insurgents' Rights: One of the most important tools in a proxy fight is the shareholder list. It is essential for the proxy solicitor to know who the corporation's shareholders are, where they can be contacted, and the extent of their holdings. Incumbent management will have such a list, but it is not readily available to insurgents under most states' laws.

In order to even the odds, Rule 14a-7 provides that upon the insurgents' request, incumbent management must either mail the insurgents' proxy solicitation materials for them (at the insurgents' expense) or provide the insurgents with a shareholder list. If the former option is chosen, incumbent management is under no obligation to mail the insurgents' materials until the earlier of either the date incumbent management sends out its own materials or the date incumbent management began to solicit proxies the preceding year.

Anti-Fraud: Proxy contests sometimes become quite heated. To prevent fraud, Rule 14a-9 prohibits the use of false or misleading statements to solicit proxies. The term "solicitation" is broadly defined to cover both statements seeking proxies and communications urging shareholders to refuse to give proxies. Thus, if incumbent management falsely states or omits to state a material fact in urging shareholders not to grant proxies to an insurgent group, a violation of Rule 14a-9 and Section 14(a) occurs. A private cause of action is available to remedy such a violation.

Shareholder Proposals: The **shareholder proposal** is a method by which the shareholders can attempt to influence the course set by the officers and directors of a corporation. In a shareholder proposal, a shareholder suggests a matter to be placed on the agenda of the annual meeting (or a special shareholder meeting) for a vote by shareholders.

Procedures: Rule 14a-8 regulates such proposals. Subsection (a) lists the requirements for such a proposal. The proponent, who must own shares worth at least $1,000 or constituting 1 percent of the shares to be voted, must give management notice of an intent to appear at the meeting with a proposal. The notice must be written and given at least 120 days before the date management sent out notice of the prior annual meeting. A shareholder can offer only one proposal which, when combined with a supporting statement, does not exceed 500 words. A proper shareholder proposal must be printed by management in its proxy solicitation materials and placed on the agenda of the annual meeting.

To protect management from burdens caused by "crackpots," subsection (c) of Rule 14a-8 provides several grounds upon which management can refuse to include a proposal in its proxy materials. For example, a proposal may be omitted if it would require violation of state or federal law, relates to a personal claim or grievance, is not a proper subject for shareholder concern under state law, is not significantly related to the issuer's business, or relates to the ordinary business operations of the corporation (the day-to-day matters delegated to corporate officers). Management may also omit proposals which have been submitted recently but which received virtually no shareholder support.

Should management decide to omit the proposal, under subsection (d) it must so inform the proponent and submit all relevant materials to the SEC for possible review. Management should express the reasons for its decision, supported by an opinion of legal counsel.

Proper Proposals: Matters which are clearly of proper shareholder concern include proposals for selection of an independent auditing firm by shareholder vote, proposals to amend the bylaws, and proposals to adopt cumulative voting (a method of voting which increases the voice of minority shareholders). In recent years, many shareholder proposals have dealt with social and political issues. Proposals have called for corporations to stop manufacturing napalm, to cease doing business in South Africa, to cease trading with the Soviet Union and other communist nations, and to invest in solar rather than nuclear energy. So long as the proposal has some connection with a shareholder's economic interests as an owner and is not a purely social or political statement, it usually is a proper matter for shareholder consideration.

Shareholder proposals seldom receive more than 2 to 3 percent of the vote at a major corpo-

ration's shareholder meeting when opposed by management. Some question exists whether the shareholder proposal mechanism is worth the burden. Proponents note that such proposals attract publicity and indirectly place pressure on management. Supporters also point to several instances where corporations appear to have been influenced by the proposals to stop doing business in South Africa, to publish equal employment opportunity statistics, to place minorities and women on the board of directors, to cease illegal campaign contributions abroad, and the like.

Tender Offers

A final important area of federal securities law regulates a method of taking control of a corporation, called a **tender offer.** In a typical tender offer, one corporation (the "offeror") will publicly offer to purchase a controlling interest (over 50 percent of the shares) in another corporation (the "target"). The target's shareholders are invited to tender their shares to the offeror in return for cash or the offeror's equity or debt securities (or a combination) in an amount usually well above the prior market price of the target's stock. Two examples of large tender offers occurred in 1981—the Du Pont takeover of Conoco and the U.S. Steel Corporation's purchase of Marathon Oil Company. Both purchases involved sums exceeding $6 billion.

Because of the easy availability of credit then and lack of government regulation, the tender offer gained widespread usage in the 1960s. One variety, termed the "Saturday Night Special," featured a "take-it-or-leave-it" offer to the target's shareholders with a very short time for them to make up their minds. Afraid of losing an opportunity to sell their shares at above the market price, shareholders frequently would tender their shares without time to learn anything about the offeror or to evaluate the possibility of a higher offer from a different source.

Federal Legislation: Comprehensive federal regulation of tender offers began with the passage of the Williams Act in 1968. That act amended Sections 13 and 14 of the 1934 Act with the basic purpose of increasing both the amount of information flowing to target shareholders and the time available to utilize that information.

Filing Requirements:

Section 13(d) of the 1934 Act requires that any person or group acquiring more than 5 percent of the shares of any corporation must file a Schedule 13D within ten days with the SEC. That schedule requires disclosure of the background of the person or group, their source of funds, their purpose, the number of shares owned, relevant contracts or other arrangements with the target, and any plans for change of the target's affairs.

Procedural Rules:

Section 14(d) and Rule 14d-2 provide that a tender offer is commenced on the date of public announcement of the offer. On that date, Rule 14d-3 requires the offeror to file with the SEC a Schedule 14D-1, which requires informational disclosures similar to those of Schedule 13D.

The target's management may support a tender offer; perhaps the management even negotiated it. But tender offers frequently are "hostile," and the offeror intends to replace the target's management with its own people. Even if the target's management opposes the offer, Section 14(d) and Rule 14d-5 require the target's management to mail the tender offer to the target's shareholders or to promptly provide the offeror with a shareholder list so it can do the mailing itself.

Target management must file with the SEC a Schedule 14D-9. This document (1) discloses whether the officers and directors intend to hold their shares or to tender, (2) describes any contractual arrangements management may have with the offeror (for instance, the offeror sometimes can obtain management's support through monetary incentives), and (3) discloses any concrete negotiations with a "white knight"—a company willing to make a competing tender offer that is more advantageous to incumbent management.

Substantive Rules:

Substantively, Section 14(d) and Rule 14e-1 provide that a tender offer must be held open for a minimum of 20 business days, so the target's shareholders will have an opportunity to fully evaluate the offer. No more Saturday Night Specials will occur. If more shares are tendered than the offeror wishes to purchase, the offeror must purchase from each shareholder on a *pro rata* basis. This requirement promotes equal treatment of shareholders.

What if an offeror initiates the tender offer at $40 per share, seeking to purchase 51 percent of the target's shares, but only 25 percent are tendered? The offeror may choose to extend the offering period and amend the offer to $50 per share. This higher price must be given to all tendering shareholders, including those who were willing to sell at the lower price.

The final important provision of the Williams Act is Section 14(e), the prohibition of fraud or manipulation in either supporting or opposing a tender offer.

Remedies:

Violations of Sections 13(d), 14(d), and 14(e) may be remedied by civil actions for injunctive relief. Injured shareholders who, relying on fraudulent statements, either tendered when they would not have done so had they known the truth or failed to tender when they would have had they not been defrauded, also can sue for damages under Section 14(e). Defeated tender offerors and target companies probably cannot sue for such damages, because the Williams Act was not meant to protect them. However, they can seek injunctive relief, because an injunction blocking illegal activity will inure to the benefit of the shareholders.

Defensive Tactics:

A recent controversy has focused on the latitude that should be accorded target management in opposing hostile tender offers. Normally, a court is hesitant to review the business judgments of a corporation's management. However, in recent years target managements have often taken extreme measures to fend off tender offers. For example, they have taken out large loans which are payable in full immediately upon a change in control of the corporation. They have moved the corporation to states with laws which tend to make tender offers more difficult to consummate successfully. They have acquired competitors of the offeror to create an antitrust impediment to the tender offer. They have even sold the corporation's "crown jewel" (the subsidiary which attracted the offer in the first place) and threatened "corporate suicide" (liquidation and dissolution).

There have been several types of legal challenges to defensive tactics used by target managements to fend off hostile tender offers. One basis for attack is the argument that target managements are breaching their fiduciary duties to shareholders by using defensive tactics to save their jobs at the expense of the shareholders' opportunity to sell at a profit. Until recently, these attacks had been almost universally rejected by the courts on the basis of the "business judgment rule"—the courts' determination to defer to the business expertise of the board of directors. For example, in *Panter v. Marshall*

Field & Co., 646 F.2d 271 (7th Cir. 1981), the board of Marshall Field & Co. prevented a contemplated tender offer from ever being made by creating antitrust problems for the potential acquiror. Marshall Field stock had been trading at $20 and fell below $15 after the offer plan was scrapped. The contemplated offering price had been $42, a price many Marshall Field shareholders would gladly have accepted. Many disappointed shareholders sued Marshall Field, but the defensive tactics were upheld under the business judgment rule.

Recently, however, courts have become more cognizant of the conflict of interest in which target management sometimes finds itself. The courts are subjecting such decisions to increasing scrutiny, as some of the cases discussed in Chapter 39 indicate.[7]

Another basis for attacking defensive tactics is that they are "manipulative" in violation of §14(e) of the Williams Act. The Supreme Court dealt a serious blow to this argument in the following case.

---

[7] E.g., *Smith v. Van Gorkom* and *Revlon, Inc. v. McAndrews & Forbes Holdings, Inc.*

Schreiber v. Burlington Northern, Inc.
U.S. Supreme Court, 105 S.Ct. 2458 (1985)

On December 21, 1982, Burlington Northern, Inc. made a hostile tender offer for 25 million shares of El Paso Gas Co. at $24 per share. Though El Paso's management initially opposed the offer, its shareholders fully subscribed it. Burlington did not accept the tendered shares, however. Instead, after negotiations with El Paso's management, Burlington rescinded the December tender offer, purchased 4 million shares from El Paso, substituted a new tender offer for only 21 million shares at $24 each, and recognized certain contractual arrangements between El Paso and its management which guaranteed the managers substantial compensation upon a change of control ("golden parachutes"). Over 40 million shares were tendered in response to the second tender offer.

Rescission of the first offer diminished payment to those shareholders who had tendered during the first offer. Not only were fewer shares purchased, but the shareholders who retendered were subjected to substantial proration. Petitioner Schreiber sued on behalf of similarly situated shareholders, alleging that Burlington, El Paso, and members of El Paso's board violated §14(e). She claimed that withdrawal of the first tender offer coupled with substitution of the second was a "manipulative" distortion of the market for El Paso stock.

The trial court dismissed the suit for failure to state a claim. The U.S. Court of Appeals for the Third Circuit affirmed. Schreiber petitioned to the Supreme Court.

Burger, Chief Justice:

We are asked in this case to interpret §14(e) of the Securities Exchange Act. The starting point is the language of the statute. Section 14(e) provides:

"It shall be unlawful for any person to make any untrue statement of a material fact or omit to state any material fact necessary in order to make the statements made, in the light of the circumstances under which they are made, not misleading, or to engage in any fraudulent, deceptive or manipulative acts or practices, in connection with any tender offer or request or invitation for tenders, or any solicitation of security holders in opposition to or in favor of any such offer, request, or invitation. The Commission shall, for the purposes of this subsection, by rules and regulations define, and prescribe means reasonably designed to prevent, such acts and practices as are fraudulent, deceptive, or manipulative."

Petitioner reads the phrase "fraudulent, deceptive or manipulative acts or practices" to include acts which, although fully disclosed, "artificially" affect the price of the takeover target's stock. Petitioner's interpretation relies on the belief that §14(e) is directed at purposes broader than providing full and true information to investors.

Petitioner's reading of the term "manipulative" conflicts with the normal meaning of the term. We have held in the context of an alleged violation of §10(b) of the Securities Exchange Act:

"Use of the word 'manipulative' is especially significant. It is and was virtually a term of art when used in connection with the securities markets. It connotes intentional or willful conduct designed to deceive or defraud *investors by controlling or artificially affecting the price of securities."* Ernst & Ernst v. Hochfelder, *425 U.S. 185, 199 (1976) (emphasis added).*

The meaning the Court has given the term "manipulative" is consistent with the use of the term at common law, and with its traditional dictionary definition.

Our conclusion that "manipulative" acts under §14(e) require misrepresentation or nondisclosure is buttressed by the purpose and legislative history of the provision. "The purpose of the Williams Act is to insure that public shareholders who are confronted by a cash tender offer for their stock will not be required to respond without adequate information." Rondeau v. Mosinee Paper Corp., *422 U.S. 49, 58 (1975).*

The expressed legislative intent was to preserve a neutral setting in which the contenders could fully present their arguments. The Senate sponsor [said]:

"We have taken extreme care to avoid tipping the scales either in favor of management or in favor of the person making the takeover bids. S. 510 is designed solely to require full and fair disclosure for the benefit of investors. The bill will at the same time provide the offeror and management equal opportunity to present their case."

To implement this objective, the Williams Act added §§13(d), 13(e), 14(d), 14(e), and 14(f) to the Securities Exchange Act. Some relate to disclosure; §§13(d), 14(d) and 14(f) all add specific registration and disclosure provisions. Others—§§13(e) and 14(d)—require or prohibit certain acts so that investors will possess additional time within which to take advantage of the disclosed information.

Section 14(e) adds a "broad antifraud prohibition," *Piper v. Chris Craft Industries,* 430 U.S. 1, 24 (1977), modeled on the antifraud provisions of §10(b) of the Act and Rule 10b-5. Nowhere in the legislative history is there the slightest suggestion that §14(e) serves any purpose other than disclosure, or that the term "manipulative" should be read as an invitation to the courts to oversee the substantive fairness of tender offers; the quality of any offer is a matter for the marketplace.

To adopt the reading of the term "manipulative" urged by petitioner would not only be unwarranted in light of the legislative purpose but would be at odds with it. Inviting judges to read the term "manipulative" with their own sense of what constitutes "unfair" or "artificial" conduct would inject uncertainty into the tender offer process. An essential piece of information— whether the court would deem the fully disclosed actions of one side or the other to be "manipulative"—would not be available until after the tender offer had closed. This uncertainty would directly contradict the expressed Congressional desire to give investors full information.

Congress' consistent emphasis on disclosure persuades us that it intended takeover contests to be addressed to shareholders. In pursuit of this goal, Congress, consistent with the core mechanism of the Securities Exchange Act, created sweeping disclosure requirements and narrow substantive safeguards. The same Congress that placed such emphasis on shareholder choice would not at the same time have required judges to oversee tender offers for substantive fairness. It is even less likely that a Congress implementing that intention would express it only through the use of a single word placed in the middle of a provision otherwise devoted to disclosure.

We hold that the term "manipulative" as used in §14(e) requires misrepresentation or nondisclosure. Without misrepresentation or nondisclosure, §14(e) has not been violated.

Applying that definition to this case, we hold that the actions of respondents were not manipulative. The amended complaint fails to allege that the cancellation of the first tender offer was accompanied by any misrepresentation, nondisclosure or deception. The District Court correctly found, "All activity of the defendants that could have conceivably affected the price of El Paso shares was done openly."

Petitioner also alleges that El Paso management and Burlington entered into certain undisclosed and deceptive agreements during the making of the second tender offer. The substance of the allegations is that, in return for certain undisclosed benefits, El Paso managers agreed to support the second tender offer. But both courts noted that petitioner's complaint seeks redress only for injuries related to the cancellation of the first tender offer. Since the deceptive and misleading acts alleged by the petitioner all occurred with reference to the making of the second tender offer—when the injuries suffered by petitioner had already been sustained—these acts bear no possible causal relationship to petitioner's alleged injuries.

Affirmed.

STATE REGULATION

Because every state has its own system of securities regulation, corporations must always be cognizant of these rules also. The Commissioners on Uniform State Laws have produced the Uniform Securities Act, which has been used as a pattern for many states' laws. Still, because many large states have not followed this act and many have amended it to varying degrees, there is a lack of uniformity which complicates the marketing of securities. Perhaps the Revised Uniform Securities Act, promulgated in late 1985, will lead to more uniformity. It will likely change some of the present state practices described below.

Registration

Most states have laws which, like the 1933 Securities Act, regulate the original distribution of securities. A corporation which intends to market its shares nationwide must comply with not only the 1933 Act but also approximately 40 separate state registration laws. There are three basic systems of state registration. Some states use *registration by notification,* which requires the filing of certain material and then a waiting period before the securities may be sold, similar to the procedure under the 1933 Act.

Registration by qualification is used by some states. This process goes beyond the simple disclosure philosophy of the 1933 Act and actually involves merit review of the securities by state officials. Typically, states using merit review refuse to allow sales of securities which do not meet a "fair, just and equitable" standard. The standard may not be met, for example, if the organizers and promoters of the corporation intend to sell to the public at per share prices much greater than they themselves paid.

The third type is *registration by coordination,* which results in automatic state approval whenever a security's registration has become effective under the 1933 Act at the federal level.

Some states allow registration by more than one method.

Exemptions

State registration laws contain exemptions, as does the 1933 Act. There is an ongoing effort to coordinate state and federal exemptions to produce uniformity. A uniform system of exemptions would greatly simplify matters for a corporation planning a widespread distribution of securities, but the chances of achieving complete uniformity appear slim.

Other Provisions

Many state securities laws also contain antifraud provisions similar to those in the 1933 and 1934 federal laws. In states without such laws, the courts have extended the common law of fraud to prohibit deceitful securities practices.

Some states also have qualification and registration provisions governing the activities of securities brokers and dealers, which are usually similar to federal registration provisions in the 1934 Act.

Many states also regulate tender offers. The constitutionality of one such state act was upheld recently in *CTS Corp. v. Dynamics Corp.,* 55 U.S.L.W. 4478 (S.Ct. 1987).

SUMMARY

Securities law is enmeshed in federal and state regulation. Securities, whether debt or equity, must upon initial issuance be registered with the SEC, unless an exemption is available. The goal of registration is to force disclosure of material facts regarding the issuing company so that potential investors can make an informed decision.

The registration process is burdensome and expensive. Companies are severely limited in terms of the publicity in which they can engage before and immediately after registration. To reduce the paperwork burden, the SEC has done its best in recent years to integrate the requirements of the 1933 Act, which govern the one-time registration of shares about to be issued, with those of the 1934 Act, which govern the continuous disclosures which larger corporations must make.

If errors of omission or misrepresentation appear in a registration statement, a battery of government and private actions are available to punish the wrongdoers.

The 1934 Act governs a number of important areas of trading in securities. Insider trading is an unfair practice of particular concern to the SEC these days. Both §16(b) which provides a form of strict liability for trading by officers, directors and 10 percent owners, and §10(b) which ranges more broadly but requires proof of actual use of material, nonpublic information, are available to punish such trading.

Section 10(b) is also available to remedy false or inadequate corporate disclosures in press releases, SEC filings, annual reports and the like. Private litigation under §10(b) for damages has reshaped securities law in the United States.

Two methods of gaining control of a corporation, proxy fights and tender offers, involve particularly high stakes. The opportunities for profit and abuse of shareholder interests are great. Both processes are subject to a web of federal regulation designed to protect shareholder interests. In the proxy realm, the key is full disclosure. In tender offers, it is disclosure plus fair treatment of all shareholders.

Finally, though federal regulation tends to dominate the scene, no securities attorney may safely ignore the securities rules that most states have enacted to cover issuance of shares, fraud, tender offers, and other related matters.

KEY TERMS

Securities
Prospectus
Shelf registration
Materiality
Accredited investor
Scienter
Proxy
Shareholder proposal
Tender offer

QUESTIONS AND PROBLEMS

1. Co-op City was a massive, government-subsidized housing complex, operated as a non-profit corporation. To acquire an apartment, eligible prospective tenants had to buy 18 shares of Co-op stock for each room at $25 per share. The purchase was in effect a recoverable deposit. The shares could not be transferred to a nontenant, did not carry votes as to management of the co-op, and had to be offered to the co-op for sale at the initial selling price whenever the tenant moved out. When rental rates went up, some tenants sued claiming inadequate disclosure under the federal securities law. Discuss whether these "shares of stock," as they were labeled, constituted securities under federal law. (*United Housing Foundation, Inc. v. Forman,* 421 U.S. 837, 1975.)

2. Holiday Inns' profits for the first quarter of 1975 were 20 cents per share. In the spring of 1976, Holiday Inns made a public offering. Straus purchased Holiday Inns stock on March 23, 1976, but its value declined soon thereafter when it was disclosed that Holiday Inns' profits for the first quarter of 1976 were only 7 cents per share. Plaintiff sued under Section 11 of the 1933 Act because the prospectus had not disclosed the drop in profits. Holiday Inns claimed that of the 13 cent decline, 12 cents occurred in March, and that could not have been known at the time Straus purchased. Discuss Holiday Inns' disclosure responsibilities in light of the concept of materiality. (*Straus v. Holiday Inns, Inc.,* 460 F.Supp. 729, S.D.N.Y. 1978.)

3. The SEC sued seeking to enjoin Schlitz Brewing Co. from further violations of the antifraud provisions of the 1933 and 1934 Acts. The suit was predicated on Schlitz's failure to disclose in its registration statements, prospectuses, and periodic reports that (1) it was involved in a nationwide scheme to induce retailers to purchase Schlitz's products by making kickback payments, and (2) it had violated Spanish tax and exchange laws. Schlitz claimed the omissions were nonmaterial, especially considering that the alleged kickbacks amounted to $3 million compared to Schlitz's annual sales of $1 billion. The SEC claimed they were material because they reflected on the integrity of management. Discuss. (*SEC v. Jos. Schlitz Brewing Co.*, 452 F.Supp. 824, E.D.Wis. 1978.)

4. Plaintiffs were worried about tax liability, so they consulted defendant, a tax adviser. Defendant recommended that plaintiffs look into a particular real estate deal which he described as the "best investment so far as tax shelter is concerned" he had ever seen. Plaintiffs invested in the deal, but did not get the tax break they wanted. Plaintiffs sued defendant under Section 12(2) of the 1933 Act because of alleged misrepresentations the sellers made regarding the property's taxable basis. Defendant was not a seller, so he raised the defense of lack of privity. Discuss. (*Croy v. Campbell,* 624 F.2d 709, 5th Cir. 1980.)

5. Claiming the intrastate exemption of Section 3(a)(11) of the 1933 Act, McDonald Investment Company did not register its offering of shares with the SEC. McDonald is a Minnesota corporation with its only offices in that state. It sold shares only to Minnesota residents. However, the funds were raised to lend to real estate developers in Arizona. Discuss the availability of the exemption. (*SEC v. McDonald Investment Co.,* 343 F.Supp. 343, D.Minn. 1972.)

6. Moore, a psychiatrist, was treating the wife of an officer of Posi-Seal. Another company was planning to acquire Posi-Seal. At a treatment session with the wife which the Posi-Seal officer attended in order to facilitate the treatment process, Moore learned of the planned acquisition. Before public announcement of the acquisition, Moore bought 9,000 shares of Posi-Seal stock. He sold them after the acquisition at a profit of $26,933.74. Discuss whether Moore has violated §10(b)'s ban on insider trading. *SEC v. Morgan F. Moore,* No. N-86-88-PCD (D.Conn. 1986).

7. A registered broker-dealer's sales force repeatedly made false and misleading statements in an effort to sell Lawn-A-Mat common stock. After several complaints were ignored, the SEC sought an injunction to halt the illicit practices. One respondent was the sales supervisor, who was informed of the misdeeds but did not take affirmative steps to prevent a recurrence of the deceit. One issue which arose was whether the SEC would have to prove scienter in order to obtain an injunction against practices which allegedly violated Rule 10b-5. Discuss. (*Aaron v. SEC,* 446 U.S. 680, 1980.)

8. Plaintiff purchased some industrial revenue bonds which turned out to be largely worthless. Later he sued under Rule 10b-5, claiming that the bonds' offering circular contained such fraudulent statements that the bonds could never have been placed on the market without the misrepresentations. However, plaintiff admitted that he had not read the circular before purchasing. Should this admission bar recovery? Discuss. (*Shores v. Sklar,* 647 F.2d 462, 5th Cir. 1981.)

9. The management of IBM decided to omit from its proxy solicitation materials a shareholder proposal calling for an end to all the company's business dealings with Communist countries. This decision was submitted to the SEC for review in accordance with Rule 14a-8. Discuss. (*International Business Machines Corp.,* 1979

Federal Securities Law Reporter, CCH, §82,009, 1979.)

10. Pantry Pride made a hostile tender offer for Revlon at $47.50. Revlon engaged in certain defensive tactics, leading Pantry Pride to raise its bid to $53 per share. Revlon's board then approved a deal to sell to Forstmann at $56. Pantry Pride raised its offer to $56.25. Forstmann responded by raising its bid to $57.25, contingent upon Revlon (a) giving it an option to buy two Revlon divisions for $100–175 million below value if another acquiror such as Pantry Pride bought 40 percent of Revlon, (b) agreeing not to seek out a competing bidder, and (c) paying a $25 million cancellation fee if another acquiror got more than 19.9 percent of Revlon's stock. Revlon's board consented. Pantry Pride raised its offer to $58, conditioned on cancellation of the favorable provisions to Forstmann. Pantry Pride then went to court challenging the legality of the arrangements with Forstmann as a breach of the Revlon board's fiduciary duty to its shareholders. Discuss. *Revlon, Inc. v. McAndrews & Forbes Holdings, Inc.,* 506 A.2d 173 (Del. 1986).

Chapter 51

CONSUMER TRANSACTIONS AND THE LAW

During recent years the creditor-debtor relationship has undergone a significant shift in emphasis from protection of the creditor to protection of the debtor in the **consumer transaction,** in which a consumer borrows to purchase a product or purchases on credit. Consumer protection law is designed to protect the buyer-debtor from such things as **usury** (lending money at interest rates higher than the law allows), excessive **garnishments,** and hidden costs in credit transactions. This is not to say that the creditor, or seller, is completely at the mercy of the buyer, or debtor. However, the rights of the seller-creditor are defined by the numerous laws on the subject. Therefore, a knowledge of the basic provisions of consumer protection statutes is essential to the businessperson of today to operate a commercially successful venture and, at the same time, conduct consumer transactions within the law.

The law of consumer transactions is primarily statutory. Consumers derive their rights and incur their obligations from the many state and federal statutes available for their benefit. Some laws protect consumers from false advertising and other deceptive practices. A number of statutes protect consumers in the financial dealings associated with borrowing or buying. Others afford protection in the purchasing process and set guidelines for the degree of performance and satisfaction it is reasonable to expect from a purchase. Finally, some statutes and a large body of case law relate to product safety. They provide a measure of protection against unsafe products and allow recovery for damages or injury caused by such products. Table 51.1 is a guide to some of the more important statutes.

DECEPTIVE TRADE PRACTICES

A consumer who is misled by false advertising or other deceptive practices may have the right to sue under a common-law fraud theory, or perhaps a breach of express warranty theory if the advertising involved a product. These theories have been discussed in earlier chapters.[1] However, two federal statutes help protect consumers from such deceptive practices without involving the consumers as plaintiffs. These are §5 of the Federal Trade Commission Act and §43(a) of the Lanham Act.

Federal Trade Commission Act

Section 5(a)(1) of the FTC Act declares invalid (1) unfair methods of competition, and (2) unfair or deceptive acts or practices. Both must at least "affect" interstate commerce for federal jurisdiction to exist. Unfair methods of competition substantially duplicate the antitrust violations that were covered earlier in Part VIII.[2] Our major concern in this chapter on consumer protection relates to the prohibition against "unfair or deceptive acts or practices."

Illicit Acts: Deceptive advertising is the main target of FTC concern in the realm of "unfair or deceptive acts or practices." With assistance from the courts, the FTC has prohibited and often punished: (1) deceptive price advertising (e.g., advertising a sale as 20 percent off a "suggested retail price" when in fact the goods are hardly ever sold at that price); (2) affirmative product claims which cannot be substantiated (e.g., claiming without evidence that a mouthwash helps fight the common cold); (3) deceptive advertising demonstrations (e.g., claiming that a shaving cream moisturizes so well that sandpaper can easily be shaved, yet demonstrating this by passing a razor through loose sand scattered on plexiglass); (4) product endorsements by celebrities who do not really use the product; (5) failure to indicate the origin of foreign goods; (6) misleading product comparisons (e.g., claiming that a cigarette contains only 1 mg. of tar, when the mechanical device nor-

---

[1] Fraud is covered in Chapter 7; products liability warranty claims are discussed in Chapter 22.

[2] Antitrust law is discussed in Chapters 47 and 48.

Table 51.1 **Current Consumer Protection Statutes**

Popular Name	Purpose	References
Child Protection and Toy Safety	Requires special labeling and child-proof devices	15 U.S.C.A. §§1261 *et seq*
Cigarette Labeling and Ad	Surgeon general's warning of possible health hazard	15 U.S.C.A. §§1331 *et seq*
Consumer Credit Protection	Comprehensive protection, all phases of credit transactions	15 U.S.C.A. §§1601 *et seq*
Consumer Leasing Act	Improves disclosure of true costs in leasing transactions	15 U.S.C.A. §§1667
Consumer Product Safety	Protects consumer against defective or dangerous products	15 U.S.C.A. §§2051 *et seq*
Equal Credit Opportunity	Prohibits discrimination in extending credit	15 U.S.C.A. §1691
Fair Credit Reporting	Protects consumer's credit reputation	15 U.S.C.A. §1681
Fair Debt Collection Practices	Prohibits abuses by debt collectors	15 U.S.C.A. §1692
Fair Packaging and Labeling	Requires accurate name, weight, quantity	15 U.S.C.A. §§1451 *et seq*
Federal Trade Commission	Prohibits unfair or deceptive trade practices	15 U.S.C.A. §45
Flammable Fabrics	Eliminates or controls manufacture and marketing of dangerous fabrics	15 U.S.C.A. §§1191 *et seq*
Food, Drug, and Cosmetic	Prohibits marketing of impure, adulterated products	21 U.S.C.A. §§301 *et seq*
Fur Products Labeling	Prohibits misbranding of fur products	15 U.S.C.A. §69
Interstate Land Sales Act	Protects against land sale abuses	15 U.S.C.A. §1701
Lanham Act	Prohibits deceptive acts or practices in product sales	15 U.S.C.A. §43(a)
Magnuson-Moss Warranty	Governs content of warranties	15 U.S.C.A. §§2301 *et seq*
National Traffic and Motor Vehicle Safety	Promotes traffic and auto safety	15 U.S.C.A. §§1381 *et seq*
Real Estate Settlement Procedures	Requires disclosure of home buying costs	HUD Reg. X
Truth in Lending	Requires complete disclosure of credit terms	15 U.S.C.A. §§1601 *et seq*
Uniform Commercial Code	Law of sales—unconscionable contracts	§2-302
Uniform Consumer Credit Code	Similar to federal Truth in Lending	9 states have adopted[a]
Wholesome Meat	Controls meat processing	21 U.S.C.A. §§601 *et seq*
Wholesome Poultry Products	Controls processing of poultry and poultry products	21 U.S.C.A. §§451 *et seq*
Wool Products Labeling	Requires accurate labeling of wool products	15 U.S.C.A. §68

[a] Colorado, Idaho, Indiana, Iowa, Kansas, Maine, Oklahoma, Utah, and Wyoming have adopted substantial parts of some version of the UCCC.

mally used to establish the tar content of cigarettes did not accurately measure the impact of the advertiser's special filter which allowed humans to receive 3–7 mg. of tar, a higher amount than contained in many competitors' "low-tar" cigarettes); and (7) product claims which "tend to deceive" (e.g., selling a facial cream under the name "Rejuvenescence," although it did not truly rejuvenate the skin).

The FTC's reach under §5 extends beyond deceptive advertising to other deceptive practices, including: (1) "bait and switch" tactics (e.g., advertising a low-quality good at a low price to induce consumers to come to the store and then pressuring them to buy a higher-priced model); (2) deceptive debt collection practices (e.g., sending letters to delinquent creditors which promised that a suit would be filed if no payments were made when, in fact, a determination to sue had not been made); and (3) unfair door-to-door selling—the FTC has promulgated a rule allowing consumers three days to rescind purchases made in their homes from door-to-door salesmen.[3]

Enforcement: The FTC issues various rules, regulations and guidelines regarding deceptive or unfair acts and practices. If the FTC discovers a potential violation, it can institute proceedings by filing a formal administrative complaint against the offender. The charge is normally heard before an FTC administrative law judge (ALJ) whose decision is reviewed by the FTC. The FTC's decisions may be reviewed by the courts.

Normally the FTC issues a "cease and desist" order to recalcitrant violators, ordering them to stop the deceptive acts or practices. Violation of such an order can precipitate fines of up to $10,000 per day. If the FTC has a strong case, an offender may agree to a "consent" order in which the FTC promises no further prosecution if the offender agrees to "go and sin no more."

In addition to obtaining injunctive orders from courts to support its cease and desist orders, the FTC is empowered to seek redress for consumers, perhaps in the form of refunds or cancellation of unfair contracts.

In the advertising cases, the FTC has occasionally ordered "corrective advertising" by a company which has long deceived the public. In such a case, the company must spend its own money to inform the public that its prior claims were untrue. "Multiproduct orders" are more frequently issued. Such an order is typically used for a company that has flagrantly engaged in falsely advertising a few of its products, and is aimed at *all* of the company's products. The rationale for such an order is that a company that has engaged flagrantly in the false advertising of some of its products is likely to do the same with others of its products.

The Lanham Act

Section 43(a) of the Lanham Act outlaws "any false description or representation" in connection with goods or services. While this section is frequently used to allow trademark owners to sue competitors for trademark infringement, a topic we discussed in Chapter 8, it has also created a general federal law of unfair competition which is frequently applied to deceptive advertising. Designed in large part to protect consumers from being misled, the cause of action is given to the competitors of the deceptive advertiser.

Illicit Acts: Section 43(a) of the Lanham Act has supported suits against companies which: (1) used pictures of the plaintiff's product to advertise their own inferior brand; (2) used a confusingly similar color and shape of drug capsule which could mislead consumers into thinking they were buying plaintiff's nontrademarked brand; (3) advertised "$2.99 as advertised on TV" when only the plaintiff had run such ads; (4) claimed that their pain-relieving product

---

[3]A similar provision under the Uniform Consumer Credit Code is discussed later in this chapter. The subject was earlier addressed near the end of Chapter 14.

worked faster than the plaintiff's when it did not; and (5) displayed a rock star's picture on an album creating the impression that he was a featured performer when, in fact, he was not.

As in all advertising, some "puffing" is permitted by the Lanham Act. For example, when a computerized chess game was advertised as "like having Karpov as your opponent," mere puffing was found.[4]

---

[4]*Data Cash Systems, Inc. v. JS&A Group, Inc.*, 223 U.S.P.Q. 865 (N.D.Ill. 1984).

Enforcement: Most courts do not allow deceived consumers to bring a §43(a) claim. Instead, suit is brought by competitors who, while redressing their own injuries, seek the end of false advertising that injures consumers. These competitors have been termed "vicarious avengers" of the consumer interest. A competitor's motive for bringing such a suit is easily seen in this recent case.

U-Haul International, Inc. v. Jartran, Inc.
U.S. District Court for Arizona, 601 F.Supp. 1140 (1984)

In 1979 plaintiff U-Haul International rented almost all of the "self-move" household goods trailers in the United States, and 60 percent of the "self-move" trucks. In that year defendant James A. Ryder entered the market by forming defendant Jartran, Inc. Jartran had limited financing, but bought a fleet of trucks and trailers with financing packages of 110 percent (i.e., equipment plus cash). However, these trucks and trailers were mostly in Detroit where they were manufactured, and it would cost $8,000,000 to move them to rental outlets.

Jartran decided to incorporate the distribution effort into an advertising campaign so that persons would rent the equipment at Detroit and move it throughout the United States. A massive advertising campaign had an immediate impact. Jartran's gross revenues rose from $3,000,000 in 1979 to $58,000,000 in 1980, and $95,000,000 in 1981. At the same time, U-Haul's gross revenue for 1981 was $49,000,000 less than it had predicted before it knew Jartran would be a competitor.

Jartran's ad campaign, on which it spent $6,000,000, featured comparisons of the one-way rental rates charged by U-Haul and Jartran. Most stated "U-Haul It to (City) . . . Jartran It to (City) . . ." with rates for U-Haul and Jartran stated after the name of the city. Jartran's advertised price to the advertised destination was a special promotional price relating to the nationwide distribution of the equipment, but was not advertised as such. It was meant to be perceived, and was perceived by the consuming public, as the price Jartran would normally charge.

Jartran's ads frequently included in the U-Haul price a basic rate and a distribution fee, without disclosing that the distribution fee was included. The self-move industry imposes distribution fees as a temporary device to regulate rentals to areas in which there is a build-up of equipment. Such fees are usually quoted separately to indicate their temporary nature. Distribution fees apply to less than 5 percent of U-Haul's yearly transactions.

Jartran's advertised prices were lower than rates reflected on Jartran's own rate sheet, and lower than the rates Jartran actually charged in most transactions. Jartran's company policy was to price above its competition; its rate structure was the same or slightly higher than U-Haul's. Jartran published an ad showing a Jartran truck and a U-Haul truck with the comparative sizes of the vehicles adjusted to make the U-Haul truck appear smaller and less attractive.

After spending $13 million in advertising to combat Jartran's advertising campaign, U-Haul brought this §43(a) suit under the Lanham Act. The following are some of the trial judge's conclusions of law.

Carroll, Judge:

Under the Lanham Act, a false representation of fact may be an actual false statement; an affirmatively misleading statement; a partially correct statement; a statement which is untrue as a result of a failure to disclose information; or a statement which is literally true but conveys a false impression through innuendo, indirect intimation or ambiguous suggestion which has a tendency to mislead or deceive the consumer.

A false representation must be about Jartran's equipment, either standing alone or in comparison to U-Haul's equipment. . . . [Surveys submitted into evidence] demonstrate significant levels of actual consumer deception and reliance on the Jartran advertisements at issue. [The number of deceived consumers] was sufficiently substantial to conclude that the claims were material for purposes of plaintiff's Section 43(a) claim.

Publication of deliberately false comparative claims gives rise to a presumption of actual deception and reliance. Defendants have not rebutted this presumption.

Jartran is liable to plaintiff under Section 43(a) of the Lanham Act because the advertisements at issue (1) contain false, misleading, deceptive and incomplete statements of fact; (2) which statements are likely to deceive and actually did deceive a substantial segment of the buying public; (3) and which are material in that they are likely to and did influence the customer's choice of a self-move company; (4) because Jartran's goods and services travel in interstate commerce; and (5) the disputed advertisements actually injured U-Haul.

The First Amendment does not protect commercial speech which exceeds the bounds of truthful advertising.

[On the basis of expert testimony, the judge then calculated U-Haul's actual damages in lost revenues to be $20,000,000.] Under the Lanham Act claim, a Court may award additional damages, up to three times the amount awarded for actual damages "according to the circumstances of the case." The circumstances of this case make such an award proper. U-Haul has sustained damages above and beyond those actually awarded. Additional damages are appropriate in the amount of $20,000,000.

[Judgment entered against Jartran, Inc. and James A. Ryder in the amount of $40,000,000.]

THE CONSUMER CREDIT PROTECTION ACT

It is a fairly easy matter for the average householder to obtain and use any number of credit cards. The cash purchase of major appliances and automobiles is now a rare occurrence. Even the smallest supermarket purchases are paid for by check. The proliferation of credit has required legislation to define the rights and obligations of those who deal in it.

Congress enacted the Consumer Credit Protection Act (CCPA) in 1968 in response to unscrupulous and predatory practices on the part of creditors extending credit in consumer transactions. Congress was concerned with consumer credit disclosure methods, credit advertising, garnishment methods, questionable procedures used by some credit reporting agencies, and certain debt collection practices (a problem recognized in a 1977 amendment to the act).

Truth in Lending

Before the **truth-in-lending** portion of the CCPA was passed in 1969, it was very difficult for consumers to understand what they were being charged for borrowing money or buying on time. Some lenders or sellers on credit would quote a "discount," others would refer to an "add on," and still others to various fees plus "simple interest." Some would quote monthly rates, while others quoted annual rates. The purpose of the Truth in Lending Act (TILA) is not to limit interest rates but to mandate disclosure of the true cost of credit so consumers borrowing money or buying on time can comparison shop.

Unfortunately, TILA, as originally passed, was quite complicated and burdensome. Indeed, it was virtually impossible for creditors to comply with. Over 14,000 lawsuits were filed by consumers under TILA in federal courts alone in the ten years following its passage. There were thousands more of these suits in state courts. This led to passage of the Truth in Lending Simplification and Reform Act of 1980 which simplified disclosure requirements, and limited the creditor liability in civil suits by debtors.[5]

Coverage: TILA now applies to credit transactions involving personal, family, or household purposes. Loans for commercial or agricultural purposes are not covered. And, because Congress assumed that borrowers of large sums can protect themselves, TILA only applies to consumer loans not exceeding $25,000. Unlike many other consumer protection statutes, however, TILA also applies to credit secured by real property or a dwelling, such as a mortgage loan. There is no ceiling amount for this type of transaction; TILA applies even if the amount involved exceeds $25,000.

Only natural persons are protected by TILA's provisions. Debtors such as corporations or other organizations are not protected. All creditors who in the ordinary course of business lend money or sell on credit must comply with TILA provisions. TILA would not, however, apply to one consumer's loan to another.

Disclosure: TILA is primarily a disclosure act. It is clarified by Regulation Z, a set of rules promulgated by the Federal Reserve Board. TILA's two key disclosure requirements relate

---

[5] The impact of the 1980 Act is illustrated in *King v. State of California*, which is excerpted later in this chapter.

to the **annualized percentage rate (APR)**, which is the yearly cost of credit calculated on a uniform basis, and the *finance charge,* which is any additional amount the consumer pays as a result of buying on credit instead of paying cash. Examples of a finance charge would include application and processing charges such as a loan origination fee charged by mortgage lenders, investigation or credit reporting fees, and premiums for required credit insurance.

All disclosures must be written, clear, and conspicuous. The APR and finance charge must be more conspicuous than the other required disclosures.

Specific disclosure requirements are keyed to the type of transaction. On the one hand is an *open-end* (revolving) transaction, such as a gasoline credit card or VISA and MasterCard. On the other hand are all transactions other than open-end, usually characterized as closed-end (installment) sales or loans with a fixed number of payments. If repeated transactions are reasonably expected by the creditor, the open-end requirements apply.

In an open-end transaction, there are two types of required disclosure—an initial disclosure and periodic supplementary disclosures. The initial disclosure, which should be made prior to the first transaction, is general in nature, covering important terms of the credit plan rather than specific transactions. Required initial disclosures include: (1) a statement of when finance charges begin to accrue, including any "free ride" period; (2) the APR; (3) in a variable rate plan, conditions under which the interest rate may increase; (4) an explanation of the method used to determine the balance on which the finance charge may be computed and of how the amount of finance charge will be determined; (5) conditions under which the creditor may acquire a security interest in the debtor's property; and (6) a statement of the debtor's billing rights.

Creditors in open-end transactions must also make periodic disclosures at the end of each billing cycle. These disclosures are geared to the specific transactions which have occurred, and include such things as: (1) the account balance at the beginning of the cycle; (2) identification of each transaction with descriptions of date, amount, and creditor; (3) the periodic rates that may be used to compute the finance charge and corresponding APR; (4) amounts of other charges; (5) account balance as of the closing date of the cycle; (6) any free ride period; and (7) an address to be used for notice of billing errors. These disclosures are contained in the monthly statements credit card holders receive.

Disclosures in a closed-end transaction are somewhat different. They must be made before consummation of the transaction in question. An important concept is the "federal box." The written disclosures should, by use of lines, a separate sheet of paper, boldface type or the like call attention to the required TILA disclosures. If the creditor puts too much information in the "federal box", thus detracting from attention given the required federal disclosures, a TILA violation occurs just the same as if insufficient information is disclosed.

Among the required disclosures in a closed-end transaction are: (1) the creditor's identity; (2) the amount financed and how it is computed; (3) the finance charge and APR (and circumstances under which it may be increased); (4) number, amounts, and timing of payments; (5) total dollar value of all payments; and (6) effect of prepayment.

Substantive Provisions: Although TILA is primarily a disclosure statute, it does shape some credit practices through substantive provisions. For example, it provides a three-day right of rescission for consumers who use their residence to secure credit in a nonpurchase money transaction. The rule does not apply to the first mortgage, issued when a house is purchased. But assume a homeowner contracts to buy a new air conditioner on credit. If the credit purchase is secured by the retailer's receiving a second mortgage on the residence, the right of rescission would apply. Absent an emergency, the seller should not deliver goods or perform services during that three-day period.

TILA also contains certain rules regarding how credit may be advertised. Again, the purpose is to create uniform, clear statements that will allow for comparison shopping. Furthermore, TILA contains numerous provisions regarding use of credit cards, even where no finance charge exists. One such provision is the $50 maximum ceiling for credit card holder liability which is discussed later in this chapter.

Enforcement: Various federal agencies, most importantly the FTC, enforce the civil provisions of TILA, and the Department of Justice can bring criminal charges for TILA violations. The maximum criminal penalty is one year in jail and/or a $5,000 fine for *each* violation.

Consumers are accorded a private right of action under TILA, and may recover their actual damages *plus* two times the finance charge (not to be less than $100 nor more than $1,000) and attorneys' fees. Suit should be brought within one year of a disclosure violation. The statute of limitations in a case involving a house being used as collateral is three years from the date of violation. The statute of limitations figures prominently in the following case, which also illustrates the easing of disclosure requirements which occurred in 1980.

King v. State of California
U.S. Ninth Circuit Court of Appeals, 784 F.2d 910 (1986)

Defendant Integrity Home Loan served as a loan broker on behalf of third party lenders in a series of three loans to plaintiff King. Each loan was secured by a deed of trust (mortgage) on King's home. The first loan occurred in June 1979, the second in March 1981, and the third (which simply refinanced the second) in November 1981. The identity of the third party lenders was not disclosed.

On May 23, 1983, Integrity disclosed to King the identity of the lenders in each of the disputed transactions. On May 26, King tried to rescind the contracts under TILA's provisions regarding faulty disclosure. Integrity then sought to foreclose on the security interest in King's home. In September, King filed a class action against Integrity on behalf of herself and other borrowers, and named the State of California and various of its officials as defendants in an attempt to prevent a foreclosure sale of her home.

The trial court dismissed King's suit, and she appealed. The following portion of the appellate court's opinion deals with King's TILA claim for rescission.

Farris, Circuit Judge:

If a lender fails to make the required material disclosures, TILA gives an obligor the right to rescind any credit transaction in which a security interest is created in the obligor's home. King's claim for rescission of the June 1979 loan is barred by the three-year absolute limitation on rescission actions set out in 15 U.S.C. §1635(f). The three years begin at the "consummation of the transaction or upon the sale of the property, whichever occurs first;" the period applicable to King began in June 1979 and expired in June 1982, more than a year before she filed suit.

The loan of March 1981 cannot be rescinded, because there is nothing to rescind. King refinanced that loan in November 1981, and the deed of trust underlying the March 1981 loan has been superseded.

As for the November 1981 loan, King's claim for rescission fails, because Congress amended the TILA and Regulation Z [in the TILA Simplification and Reform Act of 1980], effective April 1, 1981, in such a way as to eliminate her cause of action for material nondisclosure. King contends that failure to disclose all third-party lenders was material nondisclosure. The amended Regulation Z did not include a general disclosure provision, but classified the disclosure requirement according to whether the credit transaction was "open-end" or "closed-end." The transaction here would qualify as closed-end, because it does not fit any of the definitions of an open-end credit transaction. In closed-end transactions when there are multiple creditors, only the creditor making the disclosures need be identified on the disclosure statement. In addition, the new Regulation Z defines the term "material disclosures" as "the required disclosures of annual percentage rate, the finance charge, the amount financed, the total of payments and the payment schedule." Under the new regulations, therefore, the identity of each creditor in a multiple creditor transaction is not a "material disclosure." Integrity's November 1981 loan did not violate the new Regulation Z, and King cannot rescind.

[Affirmed as to this issue.]

Restrictions on Garnishment

Garnishment can be defined as the legal proceedings of a judgment creditor to require a third person owing money to the debtor or holding property belonging to the debtor to turn over to the court or sheriff the property or money for the satisfaction of the judgment.[6] Congressional hearings leading to the enactment of the CCPA revealed that the unrestricted garnishment of wages encouraged predatory extension of credit, that employers were often quick to discharge an employee whose wages were garnished, and that the laws of the states on the subject were so different they effectively de-

stroyed the uniformity of the bankruptcy laws and defeated their purpose. Consequently, the CCPA section on garnishment set limits on the extent to which the wages of an individual could be garnished. In general, wages cannot be garnished in any workweek in excess of 25 percent of the individual's disposable (after-tax) earnings or the amount by which the disposable earnings for that workweek exceed 30 times the federal minimum hourly wage, whichever is less. Such restrictions do not apply in the case of a court order for the support of any person (wife or child, for example), any order of a court of bankruptcy under Chapter 13, Adjustment of Debts of an Individual with Regular Income, of the Federal Bankruptcy Act, or any debt due for state or federal taxes.

---

[6]See the discussion on garnishment in Chapter 30.

The Fair Credit Reporting Act

The section of the CCPA known as the Fair Credit Reporting Act is directed at consumer reporting agencies. It is an effort by Congress to ensure that the elaborate mechanism developed for investigating and evaluating the credit-worthiness, credit standing, credit capacity, character, and general reputation of consumers is fair with respect to the confidentiality, accuracy, relevance, and proper utilization of the reported information. Too often in the past, the consumer was denied credit because of misleading or inaccurate information supplied to a prospective creditor by a consumer reporting agency.[7] The effect could be devastating, particularly as it affected the consumer's credit standing and general reputation in the business community.

The information on individual consumers is derived from many sources, including creditors, court and other official records, and, in many cases, from facts consumers supply themselves. Information accumulated in a **consumer report** and disseminated to users can and often does include such items as judgments, liens, bankruptcies, arrest records, and employment history. In addition, the Fair Credit Reporting Act covers the **investigative reports** made by credit reporting agencies. Often used by prospective employers or by insurance companies, investigative reports are more personal in nature than consumer reports and can contain information on the subject's personal habits, marital status (past and present), education, political affiliation, and so on.

With regard to both consumer reports and investigative reports, the law requires that, upon request and proper identification, consumers are entitled to know the nature and substance of all information about them (except medical information) in the agency's file, the sources of the

information, and the identity of those who have received the report from the credit reporting agency. Those entitled to receive consumer reports include businesses that may want to extend credit to the consumer, prospective employers or insurers, and government licensing agencies that may be concerned with the financial responsibility of the consumer. Access to the information can also be gained by court order. In addition, an investigative report cannot be prepared on an individual consumer unless that person is first notified and given the right to request information on the nature and scope of the pending investigation.

An important provision of the act requires that all information in consumer reports be current and that consumer reporting agencies maintain reasonable procedures designed to avoid violations of certain other provisions. This is an obvious effort to reduce the incidence of carelessly prepared reports having inaccurate information.

Finally, civil penalties for a *negligent* violation of the act include the actual damages to the consumer and, in a successful action, court costs and reasonable attorneys' fees. In case of *willful* noncompliance, punitive damages may also be awarded to the successful plaintiff-consumer. It is interesting to note that administrative enforcement of the act and compliance with its provisions is a function of the Federal Trade Commission because violations are considered unfair or deceptive acts or practices.

Credit Cards

The widespread use of credit cards, issued by all manner of companies, created much legal controversy when a card fell into the wrong hands through loss or theft. Many companies provided their credit cards indiscriminately to any person who might want one and to many who had not requested them. It became a major problem to determine who was to assume the liability for unauthorized credit card purchases: the person to whom the card was issued, the unauthorized

---

[7] This is not an agency of the government. Such agencies are persons or businesses that regularly assemble credit information and provide it to others for a fee.

user, the merchant who made the sale, or the credit card issuer. Congress addressed the problem in CCPA provisions that prohibit the issuance of credit cards except in response to a request or application and that place limits on the liability of a cardholder for its unauthorized use. In general, if a cardholder loses a credit card and it is used by someone without authority to do so, the cardholder is liable if: (1) the liability does not exceed $50; (2) the card is an accepted card; (3) the issuer has given notice to the cardholder as to the potential liability; (4) the issuer has provided the cardholder with a self-addressed, prestamped notification to be mailed by the cardholder in the event of loss or theft; (5) the

unauthorized use occurs before the cardholder has notified the issuer that an unauthorized use of the card has occurred; and (6) the card issuer has provided a method whereby the user of the card can be identified by the merchant, either by photograph or signature, as the authorized user.

The above provisions are for the protection of a lawful cardholder. Unauthorized use of a credit card can result in severe penalties. If the unauthorized transaction involves goods or services, or both, having a retail value of $5,000 or more, the penalty can be a fine of up to $10,000 or imprisonment for up to five years, or both. These provisions are at issue in the following case.

Transamerica Insurance Co. v. Standard Oil Co.
North Dakota Supreme Court, 325 N.W.2d 210 (1982)

Smith was office manager of MBS. In March 1967 he obtained Amoco credit cards for employees; charges were paid by MBS. In May 1975, Smith made a written request to Amoco for a Torch Club credit card which can be used to purchase consumer goods. The application contained Smith's signature as office manager, and Switzer's signature as general manager of MBS. However, Smith had forged Switzer's signature. Amoco issued the card after checking MBS's payment record, without contacting credit references or inquiring into Smith's authority.

Between May 1975 and July 1978, Smith fraudulently used the Torch Club card to obtain goods and services worth $26,376.53. Smith again used forgery to cause MBS to pay these bills. Neither MBS nor its auditors detected the fraud until July 1978 when Smith was fired. Plaintiff Transamerica, MBS's fidelity-bond carrier, paid MBS its claim in full for the loss. Transamerica now sues defendant, which does business as Amoco, as a subrogee under MBS's claim, alleging that it was not liable for the charges under TILA provisions dealing with credit card liability.

The trial court entered judgment for Transamerica in the amount of $26,376.53. Amoco appealed.

Vande Walle, Justice:

. . . In 15 U.S.C. §1643(a), a cardholder is liable for a limited amount [$50] if certain conditions are met and if the use of the credit card was unauthorized. Accordingly, the initial determination is whether or not the use of the credit card in the case at hand was unauthorized. [15 U.S.C. §1602(o) defines "unauthorized use" as:] "a use of a credit card by a person other than the cardholder who does not have actual, implied, or apparent authority for such use and from which the cardholder receives no benefit." The test for determining unauthorized use is agency, and State agency law must be used to resolve this issue.

Smith did not have actual or implied actual authority to request an Amoco Torch Club credit card. . . . "Ostensible authority" is also called "apparent authority" and it "is such as the principal [MBS] intentionally or by want of ordinary care causes or allows a third person [Amoco] to believe the agent [Smith] to possess." Sec. 3-02-02, N.D.C.C. MBS is bound by Smith's acts under ostensible authority only to third persons who have incurred a liability in good faith and without ordinary negligence. The trial court determined that Amoco acted negligently by issuing MBS a Torch Club credit card without independently verifying Smith's authority. [This finding] was not clearly erroneous. Credit-card issuers should make the necessary investigation prior to issuing a credit card. Amoco did not use the requisite reasonable diligence to ascertain whether or not Smith was acting within the scope of his authority. Therefore, Amoco is unable to rely on the doctrine of ostensible authority. Smith's request for a Torch Club credit card was "unauthorized."

A second requirement for imposing limited cardholder liability under Federal law is that the card must be an accepted card. An "accepted credit card" is any credit card which the cardholder has requested, signed, used, or authorized another to use. . . . In the case at hand, MBS did not sign, use or authorize Smith to use the credit card. . . . [W]hen all the statutory requirements for limited liability are not met, the cardholder incurs no liability based upon the unauthorized use of any credit card. [Therefore,] MBS and its subrogee, Transamerica, are not liable for the initial fraudulent charges made by Smith.

However, the trial court erred in not looking beyond Amoco's negligence in issuing Smith the card. After receiving the first statement from Amoco containing the fraudulent charges, MBS was negligent in not finding and reporting the fraud. If the person to whom a credit card is issued is careless, he may be held liable. For example, in *Martin v. American Express, Inc.*, 361 So.2d 597 (Ala.Civ.App. 1978), a cardholder voluntarily permitted another who was involved in a business venture with him to use his credit card. The court held that the limit on liability in 15 U.S.C. §1643(a) was inapplicable to these facts for policy reasons. Otherwise, an unscrupulous cardholder could allow another to charge hundreds of dollars in goods and services and then attempt to limit his liability to 50 dollars.

We believe that MBS's negligence in not examining its monthly statements from Amoco removes this case from the statutory limit on cardholder liability.

A bank customer has a duty to examine his bank statement promptly, using reasonable care to discover unauthorized signatures or alterations. Sec. 41-04-33(1), N.D.C.C. . . . If someone at MBS other than Smith had examined its statements from Amoco, he would have discovered Smith's fraud. It was the responsibility of MBS to institute internal procedures for the examination of the statements from Amoco which would have disclosed Smith's defalcation. It was solely within MBS's power to do so. . . .

Because of MBS's negligence, we will reexamine whether or not Smith acquired ostensible authority in his use of the Torch Club card after MBS became negligent. . . . [D]uring Smith's fraudulent use of the card, Amoco was not negligent. Rather, MBS was negligent. We conclude that Amoco is liable for Smith's fraudulent purchases from the time the credit card was issued until MBS received the first statement from Amoco containing Smith's fraudulent charges plus a reasonable time to examine that statement. After that time, MBS's subrogee, Transamerica, is liable for the remaining fraudulent charges.

[Reverse and remand for a determination of when MBS should have examined its statements and discovered Smith's fraud.]

The Fair Debt Collection Practices Act

A 1977 amendment to the CCPA, the Fair Debt Collection Practices Act, became effective March 20, 1978. It has as its purpose the elimination of abusive debt collection practices by debt collectors and the protection of individual debtors against debt collection abuses. The act was brought about by the unscrupulous methods used by some debt collectors in pursuing debtors. Instances of harassment in the form of threats of violence, the use of obscene or profane language, publication of lists of consumers who allegedly refused to pay their debts, and annoyance by repeated use of the telephone were commonplace before the act was passed. The following excerpt from *Duty v. General Finance Co.*, 273 S.W.2d 64 (Tex. 1954), illustrates some of the tactics employed by an overzealous debt collector. It is important to note that each and every tactic employed by the General Finance Company debt collector is now prohibited by the Fair Debt Collection Practices Act.

The harassment alleged may be summarized as follows: Daily telephone calls to both Mr. & Mrs. Duty which extended to great length; threatening to blacklist them with the Merchants' Retail Credit Association; accusing them of being deadbeats; talking to them in a harsh, insinuating, loud voice; stating to their neighbors and employers that they were deadbeats; asking Mrs. Duty what she was doing with her money; accusing her of spending money in other ways than in payments on the loan transaction; threatening to cause both plaintiffs to lose their jobs unless they made the payments demanded; calling each of the plaintiffs at the respective places of their employment several times daily; threatening to garnish their wages; berating plaintiffs to their fellow employees; requesting their employers to require them to pay; calling on them at their work; flooding them with a barrage of demand letters, dun cards, special delivery letters, and telegrams both at their homes and their places of work; sending them cards bearing this opening statement: "Dear Customer: We made you a loan because we thought that you were honest."; sending telegrams and special delivery letters to them at approximately midnight, causing them to be awakened from their sleep; calling a neighbor in the disguise of a sick brother of one of the plaintiffs, and on another occasion as a stepson; calling Mr. Duty's mother at her place of employment in Wichita Falls long distance, collect; leaving red cards in their door, with insulting notes on the back and thinly-veiled threats; calling Mr. Duty's brother long distance, collect, in Albuquerque, New Mexico, at his residence at a cost to him in excess of $11, and haranguing him about the alleged balance owed by plaintiffs.

The debt collector's communications with others and with the debtor in an effort to locate the debtor are governed by a provision of the act. The debt collector is prohibited from making false representations or misleading the debtor about the nature of the collection process. The collector cannot solicit or take from any person a check postdated by more than five days without notice of the intent to deposit the check. On occasion, debt collectors have encouraged the debtor to write a postdated check for the amount of the debt knowing that the debtor had insufficient funds to cover the check. A threat to deposit the postdated check was often enough to compel the debtor to seek the funds necessary to pay the collector and thereby avoid criminal prosecution for issuing a bad check. The act further provides that written notice of the amount of the debt and the name of the creditor be sent to the consumer together with a statement that, unless the consumer disputes the validity of the debt within 30 days, the debt collector can assume it is a valid obligation. If the consumer owes multiple debts and makes a single payment, the debt collector cannot apply the payment to any debt that is disputed by the consumer.[8]

The Fair Debt Collection Practices Act protects the consumer-debtor and places significant burdens on the debt collector. Compliance with the act is enforced by the Federal Trade Commission, since violations are considered to be unfair or deceptive trade practices. A debt collector who fails to comply with the provisions of the act may incur civil liability to the extent of actual damages sustained by the plaintiff, additional punitive damages not to exceed $1,000, and court costs and reasonable attorneys' fees.

Fair Credit Billing

Prior to the Fair Credit Billing Act, the burden of resolving a billing dispute rested mainly on the customer-debtor. This is no longer true. The Fair Credit Billing Act requires that creditors maintain procedures whereby consumers can complain about billing errors and obtain satisfaction within a specified period, not later than two billing cycles or ninety days. The consumer must give the creditor notice of the billing error with a statement explaining the reasons for questioning the item or items felt to be in error. The creditor must then either make appropriate corrections in the consumer's account or conduct an investigation into the matter. If, after the investigation, the creditor feels that the statement is accurate, it must so notify the debtor and explain why it believes the original statement of account to be correct. The act also requires that payments be credited promptly and that any overpayment be refunded (on request by the debtor) or credited to the debtor's account.

Equal Credit Opportunity

The Equal Credit Opportunity Act (ECOA), as amended, quite simply prohibits discrimination based on race, color, religion, national origin, sex, marital status, or age in connection with extensions of credit. The applicant must, however, have contractual capacity; minors, for example, cannot insist on credit under the act. The enactment is the result of complaints by married persons that credit frequently was denied unless both parties to the marriage obligated themselves. Each party can now separately and voluntarily apply for and obtain credit accounts, and

---

[8]This provision may be contrary to a commonly accepted principle of contract law: Where a debtor owes multiple debts and fails to specify to which debt the payment is to be applied, the creditor can make the choice.

state laws prohibiting separate credit no longer apply. The act also directs the Board of Governors of the Federal Reserve System to establish a Consumer Advisory Council to provide advice and consultation on consumer credit and other matters. The following case offers an interesting application of the ECOA.

United States v. American Future Systems, Inc.
U.S. Third Circuit Court of Appeals, 743 F.2d 169 (1984)

American Future Systems, Inc. (AFS), sells china, cookware, crystal, and tableware, 95 percent of the time on credit. AFS markets its wares through three separate programs. Its summer program targets as preferred customers single white females between the ages of 18 and 21 who live at home. AFS hopes parents will co-sign the order, but will extend credit and automatically ship goods to the buyer even without a co-signature. Nonpreferred customers, almost always young black females, are extended credit only after a satisfactory credit check. If the buyer does not pass the check, goods will not be shipped. AFS sales employees are urged to sell only in areas believed to be all or predominantly white, and work under commission arrangements which encourage sales to whites.

AFS's winter program has two aspects. Its preferred sales targets are single white females in their final three years of college. They are given immediate credit and the ordered goods are shipped to them immediately, regardless of age, prior credit histories, or any other normal indicia of creditworthiness. Nonpreferred customers for the winter program include all minorities, males, married persons, and freshmen in college. AFS will not ship goods to these customers until they have made three successive monthly payments. Although these customers are led to believe they are being treated the same as other AFS customers, AFS has made a marketing judgment to prefer white females.

The Department of Justice sued AFS, its president and an affiliated company, claiming violation of the ECOA. AFS defended, claiming that minority customers are, as a group, less creditworthy than their white counterparts. AFS could produce no reliable evidence to support this position, so the trial court found both the winter and summer programs to violate the ECOA. AFS appealed as to the winter program only.

Higginbotham, Circuit Judge:

The Equal Credit Opportunity Act proscribes discrimination in the extension of credit. Section 1691(a) of the ECOA states that *[i]t shall be unlawful for any creditor to discriminate against any applicant, with respect to any aspect of a credit transaction—(1) on the basis of race, color, religion, national origin, sex or marital status, or age (provided the applicant has the capacity to contract).*

The ECOA does provide, however, for special purpose credit programs responsible to special social needs of a class of persons. Section 1691(c)(3) carves out this exception:

It is not a violation of this section for a creditor to refuse to extend credit offered pursuant to . . . any special purpose credit program offered by a profit-making organization to meet special social needs which meets standards prescribed in regulations by the [Federal Reserve] Board.

The district court made a finding which shows that the class of persons between the ages of 18 and 21 are in special need of credit assistance. [The court then found that AFS's program met the three conditions for this exception in that (a) there was a "special social need" for credit for this age group, (b) the program was in writing, and (c) the preferred class "probably would not receive such credit or probably would receive it on less favorable terms" absent the program.]

Notwithstanding a credit program having satisfied these three requirements, a program once established cannot discriminate on prohibited bases such as race, sex or marital status.

Congressman Annunzio, who recommended key amendments which broadened the types of discrimination prohibited by the ECOA, elaborated on the purpose of the ECOA:

The essential concept of nondiscrimination in the extension of credit is that each individual has a right when he applies for credit to be evaluated as an individual: to be evaluated on his individual creditworthiness, rather than based on some generalization or stereotype about people who are similar to him in race, color, national origin, religion, age, sex, or marital status. Bias is not creditworthiness. Impression is not creditworthiness. An individual's ability and willingness to repay an extension of credit is creditworthiness.

Thus the specific issue before us is whether the ECOA permits [preferred treatment to single white females] where the district court expressly found that each person in the group of individuals between the ages of 18 and 21 shares the same credit disability. . . .

There is a particular irony in AFS's approach where it singles out white women as a "disadvantaged" group and gives them a special advantage that it unhesitatingly denies to black and other minority women.

Despite all of the disadvantages that women have had, historically and at present, the significant disadvantages suffered by white women have been far less than those disadvantages black women, Native American women (Indians), Hispanic and other minority American women have had to endure for centuries. Yet, the paradox of AFS's plan is that it perpetuates the past disparities between white and minority women and rather than helping all women it aids only white women and slams the door of equal credit opportunity in the faces of minority women.

> We do not believe that it was the intention of Congress to accentuate the disparities among disadvantaged groups by helping those women who have been the *least* deprived while denying equal opportunity to those women who have been the most deprived.
>
> [Affirmed.]

THE UNIFORM CONSUMER CREDIT CODE

Federal legislation does not necessarily preclude similar state legislation. For example, Sec. 1610 of the Consumer Credit Protection Act provides:

> This subchapter does not annul, alter, or affect, or exempt any creditor from complying with the laws of any State relating to the disclosure of information in connection with credit transactions, except to the extent that those laws are inconsistent with the provisions of this subchapter or regulations thereunder, and then only to the extent of the inconsistency.

Federal statutes frequently exempt state-regulated credit transactions if, for example, the state law is more stringent to creditors than it is to the credit consumer.[9] This principle—that state laws are enforceable even though they may regulate an area already covered by federal statutes—is illustrated by the Uniform Consumer Credit Code (UCCC).

The Uniform Consumer Credit Code has been promulgated by the National Conference of Commissioners on Uniform State Laws in two versions—one in 1968 and one in 1974. Nine states have adopted substantial parts of one form or another of the UCCC. Many other states have similar provisions. However, there is great variation from state to state, even among the UCCC adopters. Therefore, our discussion of the UCCC's features must be somewhat general.

The UCCC is much like the Federal Consumer Credit Protection Act. It covers consumer credit sales, loans, garnishment, and insurance provided in relation to a consumer credit sale. Its truth-in-lending provisions require full disclosure to the consumer of all aspects of the credit transaction and further require that charges to the consumer be computed and disclosed as an annual percentage rate. The code does not prescribe any specific rates for credit service charges, but it sets maximums based on unpaid balances—36 percent per year on $300 or less in non-open-end accounts, 21 percent per year for balances of $300 to $1,000, and 15 percent for unpaid balances in excess of $1,000. Since the law permits higher charges for smaller transactions, it forbids creditors from breaking large transactions down into smaller ones to take advantage of higher credit charges.

Home Solicitation Sales

The UCCC covers door-to-door solicitation in some detail, since this is a troublesome area for consumers. Consumers tend to be more vulnerable to high-pressure selling tactics in their homes; after signing an agreement to purchase, they often regret the decision. The UCCC therefore permits the rescission of a credit sale solicited and finalized in the customer's home if the customer gives written notice to the seller within 72 hours after signing the agreement to

---

[9] For example, state laws that prohibit garnishments or provide for more limited garnishments than are allowed under the federal statute are effective and enforceable despite the federal regulations on the same subject.

purchase.[10] The cancellation notice is effective when deposited in a mailbox and can take any form so long as it clearly expresses the buyer's intention to void the home solicitation sale. Sellers are required to provide a statement informing buyers of their right to cancel, including the mailing address for the written cancellation notice.

Debtor Default

Generally, if a consumer defaults on payments, creditors can repossess the property the consumer has purchased and sell it to satisfy the unpaid debt. If the sale earns too little to discharge the debt, the creditor can normally sue the debtor and obtain a deficiency judgment. However, the 1968 UCCC distinguishes between debts incurred in the purchase of goods for $1,000 or less and debts exceeding $1,000. If the goods purchased were worth $1,000 or less, the creditor must *either* repossess the goods *or* sue the debtor for the unpaid balance. If the creditor chooses to repossess, the debtor is not personally liable for the unpaid balance. Only if the original sale exceeded $1,000 can the creditor repossess *and* seek a deficiency judgment if repossession fails to cover the unpaid balance.

With regard to garnishment, the UCCC prevents any prejudgment attachment of the debtor's unpaid earnings and limits the garnishment to 25 percent of net income or to that portion of the income in excess of 40 times the federal minimum hourly wage. The UCCC also prohibits an employer from discharging an employee whose wages are garnished to pay a judgment arising from a consumer credit sale, lease, or loan.

Although the UCCC has been adopted by nine states, the law as adopted can vary considerably

from state to state. It is generally true of the so-called uniform laws that a state can make significant changes so the law reflects local attitudes or conforms to local policy in the particular matter covered.

THE REAL ESTATE SETTLEMENT PROCEDURES ACT

The purchase of a residence is the largest single transaction most consumers ever make. It can be a traumatic experience for the novice who finds that, in addition to the down payment, substantial sums of money will be required on settlement, or closing day. Items to be paid for may include attorney's fees; title insurance; various inspections, surveys, and appraisals; agent's or broker's services; taxes and insurance; and many other miscellaneous items. Congress found that because of the variation in the kinds of items included in the settlement costs and the amount charged for each, significant reforms were needed in the real estate settlement process. The purpose of the Real Estate Settlement Procedures Act (RESPA), enacted in 1974 and amended in 1976, is to insure that buyers of residential property are given timely information on the nature and costs of the settlement process and that they are protected against obvious abuses. The Act requires that effective advance disclosure be made to home buyers and sellers. It prohibits kickbacks or referral fees and, in general, affords considerable protection by letting the home buyer know what it is going to cost to buy a given home.

RESPA applies to all federally related mortgage loans and is administered and enforced by the Secretary of Housing and Urban Development.[11] The secretary has issued comprehensive

---

[10] Many of the states that have not adopted the UCCC do have statutes governing door-to-door solicitation, and many municipalities have ordinances regulating solicitors, peddlers, and transient merchants. The latter regulations are known as Green River ordinances. See *Green River v. Fuller Brush Co.*, 65 F.2d 112 (1933).

[11] Most, if not all, mortgage loans on residential property are federally related. The deposits or accounts of the lending institution may be insured by an agency of the federal government or the lender may be regulated by a federal agency.

regulations, known as Regulation X, to prescribe procedures for curbing questionable practices in real estate transactions. Various forms have been devised and are in use, and a special information booklet has been developed for the lender to distribute to the borrower at the time a loan application is made. The lender is also required to provide the borrower with "good faith estimates" of the dollar amount or range of each settlement service charge that the borrower is likely to incur. Generally speaking, RESPA places the burden on the lender to provide the borrower good advance information about the costs of purchasing a home—the basic cost and the substantial sums needed on settlement day.

ADDITIONAL CONSUMER PROTECTION MEASURES

Federal legislation primarily insures fair treatment for consumers seeking credit, borrowing money, or contemplating the purchase of a residence or automobile. For the most part, the statutes examined in this chapter have been remedial in nature. Their purpose is to correct what Congress has determined to be persistent abuses. Many other statutes, however, are designed to protect the consumer's safety and well-being. These laws concern general health and welfare and alert the consumer to the possibility of harm from the use or misuse of certain products.

Packaging and Labeling

The controversial Public Health Cigarette Smoking Act of 1969, popularly known as the Cigarette Labeling and Advertising Act, establishes a comprehensive federal program to deal with labeling and advertising the ill effects of smoking on health. The act requires that the statement "Warning: The Surgeon General Has Determined That Cigarette Smoking Is Dangerous to Your Health" appear on cigarette and little cigar packages. Additionally, beginning in 1971, it became

unlawful to advertise cigarettes and little cigars on any medium of electronic communication subject to the jurisdiction of the Federal Communications Commission.

The Wholesome Poultry Products Act and the Wholesome Meat Act are also examples of the protective statute. Each establishes procedures to insure that only wholesome products are distributed to consumers and that they are properly labeled and packaged.

The Federal Food, Drug, and Cosmetic Act establishes extensive controls over various products and regulates their development, premarketing testing, labeling, and packaging.

In the Fair Packaging and Labeling Act, effective July 1, 1967, Congress has stated that informed consumers are essential to the fair and efficient functioning of a free market economy and that packages and labels should enable consumers to obtain accurate information about the quantity of the contents and should facilitate value comparisons. The act therefore establishes comprehensive requirements for the identification of commodities and provides that net quantities must be conspicuously displayed in a uniform location on the principal panel of the product. The main purpose of the act, set forth in some detail, is the prevention of unfair or deceptive packaging and labeling and general misbranding of consumer commodities.

An important amendment, the Poison Prevention Packaging Act of 1970, resulted in the mandatory development and use of child-proof devices on household substances that could harm young children if mishandled or ingested. Other statutes for children are the Flammable Fabrics Act and the Child Protection and Toy Safety Act. The Consumer Product Safety Commission is responsible for administering many of the statutes relating to product safety.

In Chapter 22 we also discussed the work of the CPSC and the Magnuson-Moss Act which help assure that consumers receive what they bargain for when they purchase products.

Motor Vehicles

With the increased emphasis on consumer product safety, cost disclosure requirements, energy, and environmental quality, the automobile has been singled out for special treatment in the Motor Vehicle Information and Cost Savings Act, amended in 1975 and 1976. The purpose of the law is to help consumers make more reasoned judgments in their choice of automobiles by requiring the auto industry to effect measures to reduce the cost of repairs, to provide consumers with the means to compare the safety and repairability of the many available models, to prevent tampering with the odometer readings of autos for sale, and to improve automobile fuel economy.

The act authorized the Secretary of Transportation to develop and promulgate bumper standards applicable to passenger vehicles. It also encouraged the states to conduct diagnostic inspection demonstration projects through periodic safety inspections of motor vehicles. The goal was to promote development of diagnostic equipment for use by inspection facilities designed to evaluate the safety, noise, emissions, and fuel efficiency of motor vehicles.

A major criterion in purchasing a "used" car is its mileage. The act forbids dealers and others from turning back odometers or tampering with their accuracy. Criminal and civil penalties are imposed for violations.

Finally, the act deals with automotive fuel economy by authorizing the Secretary of Transportation to establish average fuel economy standards to be met by the auto industry. This program, though its goals have not always been precisely met, has led to improved fuel economy in American automobiles.

SUMMARY

Many state and federal consumer protection laws now create an atmosphere in which many believe *caveat venditor* ("let the seller be-

ware") has replaced the traditional *caveat emptor.*

Consumers are protected from deceptive practices, including deceptive advertising, by §5 of the Federal Trade Commission Act and §43(a) of the Lanham Act. These laws authorize the FTC, as well as competitors of the misleading advertiser, to bring suit to correct deceptive ads.

The Consumer Credit Protection Act creates an arsenal of weapons which protect the borrower or purchaser on credit. The Truth in Lending Act mandates extensive disclosures whenever a consumer borrows money or buys on credit. The purpose is to ensure that the consumer knows the true cost of the borrowing and can comparison shop. The Fair Credit Reporting Act protects consumers from the serious damage that misleading credit reports can have on consumers' economic status. The Fair Debt Collection Practices Act protects debtors from abusive collection practices by professional collection agencies. Also, in this nonexclusive listing of protective statutes, the Equal Credit Opportunity Act promotes equality in the extension of credit by outlawing discrimination on the basis of sex, age, race, and other grounds.

The Uniform Consumer Credit Code, which has been adopted by nine states, and copied in many others, also contains credit disclosure requirements and home solicitation provisions protecting vulnerable consumers from unfair practices by door-to-door salesmen.

Packaging and labeling laws, motor vehicle disclosure laws, and the Real Estate Settlement Procedures Act are just a few more of an extensive battery of proconsumer statutes which every businessperson must understand and comply with.

KEY TERMS

Consumer transaction
Usury
Garnishment
Truth in lending

Annual percentage rate (APR)
Consumer report
Investigative report

QUESTIONS AND PROBLEMS

1. Bristol ran an ad with high-fashion model Cristina Ferrare stating: "In shampoo tests with over 900 women like me, Body on Tap got higher ratings than Prell for body. Higher than Flex for conditioning. Higher than Sassoon for strong, healthy looking hair." Sassoon brought suit under the Lanham Act's §43(a), showing: (a) none of the 900 women tried more than one shampoo; (b) each tried a single shampoo and rated it on a qualitative scale; (c) when the ratings "very good," "good," "outstanding," and "excellent" were combined, there was only a 1 percent difference between the ratings of Body on Tap and Sassoon respecting "strong, healthy looking hair"; and (d) one-third of the "women" were ages 13–18. Discuss Sassoon's likelihood of success. (*Vidal Sassoon, Inc. v. Bristol-Myers Co.,* 661 F.2d 272, 2d Cir. 1981.)

2. A husband and wife signed an agreement to subscribe to several magazines with a door-to-door salesperson who had called on them one evening during the dinner hour. What are the rights of both seller and buyer if the husband and wife decide the next morning that they have been high-pressured and want to void the transaction?

3. Litton Industries advertised that a survey of "independent microwave oven service technicians" indicated that 76 percent of the surveyed population "recommend Litton." Evidence showed that in conducting its survey, Litton used only its own service agency lists, though it had lists of its competitors; Litton knew at least 100 agencies were excluded from the survey; Litton surveyed only one technician at each agency; Litton knew its list contained some dealers who sold Litton microwaves and therefore had reason to favor them and certainly were not "independent"; Litton knew many of

those surveyed had insufficient experience with other brands to respond accurately. In a §5 action, the FTC entered a "multiproducts" order, prohibiting Litton from misusing survey information with all of its products, not just microwaves. Should the court uphold this order? (*Litton Industries, Inc. v. FTC,* 676 F.2d 364, 9th Cir. 1982.)

4. An ambulance company charges its customers an additional $5.00 when they do not pay by cash or check at the time services are rendered. Does this arrangement constitute a "finance charge" that must be disclosed under the Truth in Lending Act? Discuss. (*Hahn v. Hank's Ambulance Service, Inc.,* 787 F.2d 543, 11th Cir. 1986.)

5. Maurice had an American Express card. Later, his wife Virginia was granted a supplementary card. When Maurice died, Virginia's card was cancelled under American Express's general policy of automatically terminating supplemental cards upon the death of the basic cardholder. The cancellation had nothing to do with Virginia's creditworthiness or ability to pay. Virginia did reapply for a card and was granted it. Still, she sued American Express for violation of the ECOA. Discuss. (*Miller v. American Express Co.,* 688 F.2d 1235, 9th Cir. 1982.)

6. John Smith is the sole proprietor of a small restaurant. Desiring to renovate and extend his premises he borrowed $30,000 from a local bank. Does the Truth in Lending Act have any applicability to this transaction?

7. The odometer of a motorcycle purchased by plaintiff indicated that it had been driven 875 miles. The actual mileage was 14,000. Plaintiff sought damages claiming that defendant failed to disclose the actual mileage or that the true mileage was unknown; that defendant altered the odometer intending to defraud; or that defendant repaired the odometer, failed to adjust it to zero, and failed to so notify the purchaser of the repair. Such allegations, if proven, would constitute violations of the Motor Vehicle Information and Cost Savings Act. Defendant moved to dismiss claiming that the act did not apply to motorcycles, and if it did, it was unconstitutionally vague. The act provided that notice of any alteration in mileage must be attached to the left door frame of the vehicle. Motorcycles, claimed defendant, do not have door frames. Is this a good defense? Discuss. (*Grambo v. Loomis Cycle Sales, Inc.,* 404 F.Supp. 1073, N.D.Ind. 1975.)

8. In October 1974, Sheehan purchased a Ford automobile which was financed by Ford Credit on a retail installment contract. Later Sheehan moved to various locations and became delinquent on his account. When Ford Credit was unable to locate Sheehan it assigned the delinquent account to a central recovery office for collection or repossession. A short time later Sheehan's mother, who resided in Rhode Island, received a phone call from a woman who identified herself as an employee of the Mercy Hospital in San Francisco. (The call actually emanated from Ford Credit's office in Dearborn, Michigan.) She advised Sheehan's mother that one or both of Sheehan's children had been involved in a serious automobile accident and that she, the caller, was attempting to locate Sheehan. The mother supplied the caller with Sheehan's home and business addresses and phone numbers. The following day Sheehan's car was repossessed and subsequent inquiry revealed that the call referred to above was a ruse and that Sheehan's

children had not been injured. Are consumers protected against such practices? (*Ford Motor Credit Company v. Frances C. Sheehan,* 373 So.2d 956, Fla. 1979.)

9. A consumer who tried to obtain information from a credit reporting agency on the nature and substance of items in his file was denied such information and forced to return to the credit reporting agency's office several times. The consumer was finally given some of the information held by the agency, but several items were withheld. Discuss this situation with regard to the Fair Credit Reporting Act. (*Millstone v. O'Hanlon Reports, Inc.*, 383 F.Supp. 269, 1974.)

10. Betty Jones had a VISA and Master Charge account with defendant Bank. Upon her request, the Bank issued cards on those accounts to her husband also. On November 11, 1977, Jones informed the Bank by two separate letters that she would no longer honor charges made by her husband on the two accounts, whereupon the Bank immediately revoked both accounts and requested the return of the cards. Despite numerous notices and requests for surrender of the cards, both Jones and her husband retained the cards and continued to make charges against the accounts. Not until March 9, 1978 did Jones relinquish her credit cards. Is Jones responsible for the balance owing on the account, which includes sums charged by her husband after November 11, 1977? Discuss. (*Walker Bank & Trust Co. v. Jones,* 672 P.2d 73, Utah 1983.)

Appendix A

THE UNIFORM COMMERCIAL CODE

ARTICLE 1/General Provisions

PART 1/Short Title, Construction, Application and Subject Matter of the Act

§ 1—101
Short Title

This Act shall be known and may be cited as Uniform Commercial Code.

§ 1—102
Purposes; Rules of Construction; Variation by Agreement

(1) This Act shall be liberally construed and applied to promote its underlying purposes and policies.

(2) Underlying purposes and policies of this Act are

(a) to simplify, clarify and modernize the law governing commercial transactions;

(b) to permit the continued expansion of commercial practices through custom, usage and agreement of the parties;

(c) to make uniform the law among the various jurisdictions.

(3) The effect of provisions of this Act may be varied by agreement, except as otherwise provided in this Act and except that the obligations of good faith, diligence, reasonableness and care prescribed by this Act may not be disclaimed by agreement but the parties may by agreement determine the standards by which the performance of such obligations is to be measured if such standards are not manifestly unreasonable.

(4) The presence in certain provisions of this Act of the words "unless otherwise agreed" or words of similar import does not imply that the effect of other provisions may not be varied by agreement under subsection (3).

(5) In this Act unless the context otherwise requires

(a) words in the singular number include the plural, and in the plural include the singular;

(b) words of the masculine gender include the feminine and the neuter, and when the sense so indicates words of the neuter gender may refer to any gender.

§ 1—103
Supplementary General Principles of Law Applicable

Unless displaced by the particular provisions of this Act, the principles of law and equity, including the law merchant and the law relative to capacity to contract, principal and agent, estoppel, fraud, misrepresentation, duress, coercion, mistake, bankruptcy, or other validating or invalidating cause shall supplement its provisions.

§ 1—104
Construction Against Implicit Repeal

This Act being a general act intended as a unified coverage of its subject matter, no part of it shall be deemed to be impliedly repealed by subsequent legislation if such construction can reasonably be avoided.

§ 1—105
Territorial Application of the Act; Parties' Power to Choose Applicable Law

(1) Except as provided hereafter in this section, when a transaction bears a reasonable relation to this state and also to another state or nation the parties may agree that the law either of this state or of such other state or nation shall govern their rights and duties. Failing such agreement this Act applies to transactions bearing an appropriate relation to this state.

(2) Where one of the following provisions of this Act specifies the applicable law, that provision governs and a contrary agreement is effective only to the extent permitted by the law (including the conflict of laws rules) so specified:

Rights of creditors against sold goods. Section 2—402.

Applicability of the Article on Bank Deposits and Collections. Section 4—102.

Bulk transfers subject to the Article on Bulk Transfers. Section 6—102.

Applicability of the Article on Investment Securities. Section 8—106.

Perfection provisions of the Article on Secured Transactions. Section 9—103.

§ 1—106
Remedies to Be Liberally Administered

(1) The remedies provided by this Act shall be liberally administered to the end that the aggrieved party may be put in as good a position as if the other party had fully performed but neither consequential or special nor penal damages may be had except as specifically provided in this Act or by other rule of law.

(2) Any right or obligation declared by this Act is enforceable by action unless the provision declaring it specifies a different and limited effect.

§ 1—107
Waiver or Renunciation of Claim or Right After Breach

Any claim or right arising out of an alleged breach can be discharged in whole or in part without consideration by a written waiver or renunciation signed and delivered by the aggrieved party.

§ 1—108
Severability

If any provision or clause of this Act or application thereof to any person or circumstances is held invalid, such invalidity shall not affect other provisions or applications of the Act which can be given effect without the invalid provision or

application, and to this end the provisions of this Act are declared to be severable.

§ 1—109
Section Captions

Section captions are parts of this Act.

PART 2/General Definitions and Principles of Interpretation

§ 1—201
General Definitions

Subject to additional definitions contained in the subsequent Articles of this Act which are applicable to specific Articles or Parts thereof, and unless the context otherwise requires, in this Act:

(1) "Action" in the sense of a judicial proceeding includes recoupment, counterclaim, set-off, suit in equity and any other proceedings in which rights are determined.

(2) "Aggrieved party" means a party entitled to resort to a remedy.

(3) "Agreement" means the bargain of the parties in fact as found in their language or by implication from other circumstances including course of dealing or usage of trade or course of performance as provided in this Act (Sections 1—205 and 2—208). Whether an agreement has legal consequences is determined by the provisions of this Act, if applicable; otherwise by the law of contracts (Section 1—103). (Compare "Contract".)

(4) "Bank" means any person engaged in the business of banking.

(5) "Bearer" means the person in possession of an instrument, document of title, or certified security payable to bearer or indorsed in blank.

(6) "Bill of lading" means a document evidencing the receipt of goods for shipment issued by a person engaged in the business of transporting or forwarding goods, and includes an airbill. "Airbill" means a document serving for air transportation as a bill of lading does for marine or rail transportation, and includes an air consignment note or air waybill.

(7) "Branch" includes a separately incorporated foreign branch of a bank.

(8) "Burden of establishing" a fact means the burden of persuading the triers of fact that the existence of the fact is more probable than its non-existence.

(9) "Buyer in ordinary course of business" means a person who in good faith and without knowledge that the sale to him is in violation of the ownership rights or security interest of a third party in the goods buys in ordinary course from a person in the business of selling goods of that kind but does not include a pawnbroker. All persons who sell minerals or the like (including oil and gas) at wellhead or minehead shall be deemed to be persons in the business of selling goods of that kind. "Buying" may be for cash or by exchange of other property or on secured or unsecured credit and includes receiving goods or documents of title under a pre-existing contract for sale but does not include a transfer in bulk or as security for or in total or partial satisfaction of a money debt.

(10) "Conspicuous": A term or clause is conspicuous when it is so written that a reasonable person against whom it is to operate ought to have noticed it. A printed heading in capitals (as: NON-NEGOTIABLE BILL OF LADING) is conspicuous. Language in the body of a form is "conspicuous" if it is in larger or other contrasting type or color. But in a telegram any stated term is "conspicuous". Whether a term or clause is "conspicuous" or not is for decision by the court.

(11) "Contract" means the total legal obligation which results from the parties' agreement as affected by this Act and any other applicable rules of law. (Compare "Agreement".)

(12) "Creditor" includes a general creditor, a secured creditor, a lien creditor and any representative of creditors, including an assignee for the benefit of creditors, a trustee in bankruptcy, a receiver in equity and an executor or administrator of an insolvent debtor's or assignor's estate.

(13) "Defendant" includes a person in the position of defendant in a cross-action or counterclaim.

(14) "Delivery" with respect to instruments, documents of title, chattel paper or securities means voluntary transfer of possession.

(15) "Document of title" includes bill of lading, dock warrant, dock receipt, warehouse receipt or order for the delivery of goods, and also any other document which in the regular course of business or financing is treated as adequately evidencing that the person in possession of it is entitled to receive, hold and dispose of the document and the goods it covers. To be a document of title a document must purport to be issued by or addressed to a bailee and purport to cover goods in the bailee's possession which are either identified or are fungible portions of an identified mass.

(16) "Fault" means wrongful act, omission or breach.

(17) "Fungible" with respect to goods or securities means goods or securities of which any unit is, by nature or usage of trade, the equivalent of any other like unit. Goods which are not fungible shall be deemed fungible for the purposes of this Act to the extent that under a particular agreement or document unlike units are treated as equivalents.

(18) "Genuine" means free of forgery or counterfeiting.

(19) "Good faith" means honesty in fact in the conduct or transaction concerned.

(20) "Holder" means a person who is in possession of a document of title or an instrument or a certificated investment security drawn, issued or indorsed to him or to his order or to bearer or in blank.

(21) To "honor" is to pay or to accept and pay, or where a credit so engages to purchase or discount a draft complying with the terms of the credit.

(22) "Insolvency proceedings" includes any assignment for the benefit of creditors or other proceedings intended to liquidate or rehabilitate the estate of the person involved.

(23) A person is "insolvent" who either has ceased to pay his debts in the ordinary course of business or cannot pay his debts as they become due or is insolvent within the meaning of the federal bankruptcy law.

(24) "Money" means a medium of exchange authorized or adopted by a domestic or foreign government as a part of its currency.

(25) A person has "notice" of a fact when

(a) he has actual knowledge of it; or

(b) he has received a notice or notification of it; or

(c) from all the facts and circumstances known to him at the time in question he has reason to know that it exists.

A person "knows" or has "knowledge" of a fact when he has actual knowledge of it. "Discover" or "learn" or a word or phrase of similar import refers to knowledge rather than to reason to know. The time and circumstances under which a notice or notification may cease to be effective are not determined by this Act.

(26) A person "notifies" or "gives" a notice or notification to another by taking such steps as may be reasonably required to inform the other in ordinary course whether or not such other actually comes to know of it. A person "receives" a notice or notification when

(a) it comes to his attention; or

(b) it is duly delivered at the place of business through which the contract was made or at any other place held out by him as the place for receipt of such communications.

(27) Notice, knowledge or a notice or notification received by an organization is effective for a particular transaction from the time when it is brought to the attention of the individual conducting that transaction, and in any event from the time when it would have been brought to his attention if the organization had exercised due diligence. An organization exercises due diligence if it maintains reasonable routines for communicating significant information to the person conducting the transaction and there is reasonable compliance with the routines. Due diligence does not require an individual acting for the organization to communicate information unless such communication is part of his regular duties or unless he has reason to know of the transaction and that the transaction would be materially affected by the information.

(28) "Organization" includes a corporation, government or governmental subdivision or agency, business trust, estate, trust, partnership or association, two or more persons having a joint or common interest, or any other legal or commercial entity.

(29) "Party," as distinct from "third party", means a person who has engaged in a transaction or made an agreement within this Act.

(30) "Person" includes an individual or an organization (See Section 1—102).

(31) "Presumption" or "presumed" means that the trier of fact must find the existence of the fact presumed unless and until evidence is introduced which would support a finding of its non-existence.

(32) "Purchase" includes taking by sale, discount, negotiation, mortgage, pledge, lien, issue or re-issue, gift or any other voluntary transaction creating an interest in property.

(33) "Purchaser" means a person who takes by purchase.

(34) "Remedy" means any remedial right to which an aggrieved party is entitled with or without resort to a tribunal.

(35) "Representative" includes an agent, an officer of a corporation or association, and a trustee, executor or administrator of an estate, or any other person empowered to act for another.

(36) "Rights" includes remedies.

(37) "Security interest" means an interest in personal property or fixtures which secures payment or performance of an obligation. The retention or reservation of title by a seller of goods notwithstanding shipment or delivery to the buyer (Section 2—401) is limited in effect to a reservation of a "security interest". The term also includes any interest of a buyer of accounts or chattel paper which is subject to Article 9. The special property interest of a buyer of goods on identification of such goods to a contract for sale under Section 2—401 is not a "security interest", but a buyer may also acquire a "security interest" by complying with Article 9. Unless a lease or consignment is intended as security, reservation of title thereunder is not a "security interest" but a consignment is in any event subject to the provisions on consignment sales (Section 2—326). Whether a lease is intended as security is to be determined by the facts of each case; however, (a) the inclusion of an option to purchase does not of itself make the lease one intended for security, and (b) an agreement that upon compliance with the terms of the lease the lessee shall become or has the option to become the owner of the property for no additional consideration or for a nominal consideration does make the lease one intended for security.

(38) "Send" in connection with any writing or notice means to deposit in the mail or deliver for transmission by any other usual means of communication with postage or cost of transmission provided for and properly addressed and in the case of an instrument to an address specified thereon or otherwise agreed, or if there be none to any address reasonable under the circumstances. The receipt of any writing or notice within the time at which it would have arrived if properly sent has the effect of a proper sending.

(39) "Signed" includes any symbol executed or adopted by a party with present intention to authenticate a writing.

(40) "Surety" includes guarantor.

(41) "Telegram" includes a message transmitted by radio,

teletype, cable, any mechanical method of transmission, or the like.

(42) "Term" means that portion of an agreement which relates to a particular matter.

(43) "Unauthorized" signature or indorsement means one made without actual, implied or apparent authority and includes a forgery.

(44) "Value". Except as otherwise provided with respect to negotiable instruments and bank collections (Sections 3—303, 4—208 and 4—209) a person gives "value" for rights if he acquires them

(a) in return for a binding commitment to extend credit or for the extension of immediately available credit whether or not drawn upon and whether or not a chargeback is provided for in the event of difficulties in collection; or

(b) as security for or in total or partial satisfaction of a pre-existing claim; or

(c) by accepting delivery pursuant to a pre-existing contract for purchase; or

(d) generally, in return for any consideration sufficient to support a simple contract.

(45) "Warehouse receipt" means a receipt issued by a person engaged in the business of storing goods for hire.

(46) "Written" or "writing" includes printing, typewriting or any other intentional reduction to tangible form.

Amended in 1962, 1972 and 1977.

§ 1—202
Prima Facie Evidence by Third Party Documents

A document in due form purporting to be a bill of lading, policy or certificate of insurance, official weigher's or inspector's certificate, consular invoice, or any other document authorized or required by the contract to be issued by a third party shall be prima facie evidence of its own authenticity and genuineness and of the facts stated in the document by the third party.

§ 1—203
Obligation of Good Faith

Every contract or duty within this Act imposes an obligation of good faith in its performance or enforcement.

§ 1—204
Time; Reasonable Time; "Seasonably"

(1) Whenever this Act requires any action to be taken within a reasonable time, any time which is not manifestly unreasonable may be fixed by agreement.

(2) What is a reasonable time for taking any action depends on the nature, purpose and circumstances of such action.

(3) An action is taken "seasonably" when it is taken at or

within the time agreed or if no time is agreed at or within a reasonable time.

§ 1—205
Course of Dealing and Usage of Trade

(1) A course of dealing is a sequence of previous conduct between the parties to a particular transaction which is fairly to be regarded as establishing a common basis of understanding for interpreting their expressions and other conduct.

(2) A usage of trade is any practice or method of dealing having such regularity of observance in a place, vocation or trade as to justify an expectation that it will be observed with respect to the transaction in question. The existence and scope of such a usage are to be proved as facts. If it is established that such a usage is embodied in a written trade code or similar writing the interpretation of the writing is for the court.

(3) A course of dealing between parties and any usage of trade in the vocation or trade in which they are engaged or of which they are or should be aware give particular meaning to and supplement or qualify terms of an agreement.

(4) The express terms of an agreement and an applicable course of dealing or usage of trade shall be construed wherever reasonable as consistent with each other; but when such construction is unreasonable express terms control both course of dealing and usage of trade and course of dealing controls usage trade.

(5) An applicable usage of trade in the place where any part of performance is to occur shall be used in interpreting the agreement as to that part of the performance.

(6) Evidence of a relevant usage of trade offered by one party is not admissible unless and until he has given the other party such notice as the court finds sufficient to prevent unfair surprise to the latter.

§ 1—206
Statute of Frauds for Kinds of Personal Property Not Otherwise Covered

(1) Except in the cases described in subsection (2) of this section a contract for the sale of personal property is not enforceable by way of action or defense beyond five thousand dollars in amount or value of remedy unless there is some writing which indicates that a contract for sale has been made between the parties at a defined or stated price, reasonably identifies the subject matter, and is signed by the party against whom enforcement is sought or by his authorized agent.

(2) Subsection (1) of this section does not apply to contracts for the sale of goods (Section 2—201) nor of securities (Section 8—319) nor to security agreements (Section 9—203).

§ 1—207
Performance or Acceptance Under Reservation of Rights

A party who with explicit reservation of rights performs or promises performance or assents to performance in the manner demanded or offered by the other party does not thereby prejudice the rights reserved. Such words as "without prejudice", "under protest" or the like are sufficient.

§ 1—208
Option to Accelerate at Will

A term providing that one party or his successor in interest may accelerate payment or performance or require collateral or additional collateral "at will" or "when he deems himself insecure" or in words of similar import shall be construed to mean that he shall have power to do so only if he in good faith believes that the prospect of payment or performance is impaired. The burden of establishing lack of good faith is on the party against whom the power has been exercised.

§ 1—209
Subordinated Obligations

An obligation may be issued as subordinated to payment of another obligation of the person obligated, or a creditor may subordinate his right to payment of an obligation by agreement with either the person obligated or another creditor of the person obligated. Such a subordination does not create a security interest as against either the common debtor or a subordinated creditor. This section shall be construed as declaring the law as it existed prior to the enactment of this section and not as modifying it. Added 1966.

Note: *This new section is proposed as an optional provision to make it clear that a subordination agreement does not create a security interest unless so intended.*

ARTICLE 2/Sales

PART 1/Short Title, General Construction and Subject Matter

§ 2—101
Short Title

This Article shall be known and may be cited as Uniform Commercial Code—Sales.

§ 2—102
Scope; Certain Security and Other Transactions Excluded From This Article

Unless the context otherwise requires, this Article applies to transactions in goods; it does not apply to any transaction which although in the form of an unconditional contract to sell or present sale is intended to operate only as a security transaction nor does this Article impair or repeal any statute regulating sales to consumers, farmers or other specified classes of buyers.

§ 2—103
Definitions and Index of Definitions

(1) In this Article unless the context otherwise requires

(a) "Buyer" means a person who buys or contracts to buy goods.

(b) "Good faith" in the case of a merchant means honesty in fact and the observance of reasonable commercial standards of fair dealing in the trade.

(c) "Receipt" of goods means taking physical possession of them.

(d) "Seller" means a person who sells or contracts to sell goods.

(2) Other definitions applying to this Article or to specified Parts thereof, and the sections in which they appear are:

"Acceptance". Section 2—606.

"Banker's credit". Section 2—325.

"Between merchants". Section 2—104.

"Cancellation". Section 2—106(4).

"Commercial unit". Section 2—105.

"Confirmed credit". Section 2—325.

"Conforming to contract". Section 2—106.

"Contract for sale". Section 2—106.

"Cover". Section 2—712.

"Entrusting". Section 2—403.

"Financing agency". Section 2—104.

"Future goods". Section 2—105.

"Goods". Section 2—105.

"Identification". Section 2—501.

"Installment contract". Section 2—612.

"Letter of Credit". Section 2—325.

"Lot". Section 2—105.

"Merchant". Section 2—104.

"Overseas". Section 2—323.

"Person in position of seller". Section 2—707.

"Present sale". Section 2—106.

"Sale". Section 2—106.

"Sale on approval". Section 2—326.

"Sale or return". Section 2—326.

"Termination". Section 2—106.

(3) The following definitions in other Articles apply to this Article:

"Check". Section 3—104.

"Consignee". Section 7—102.

"Consignor". Section 7—102.

"Consumer goods". Section 9—109.

"Dishonor". Section 3—507.

"Draft". Section 3—104.

(4) In addition Article 1 contains general definitions and principles of construction and interpretation applicable throughout this Article.

§ 2—104
Definitions: "Merchant"; "Between Merchants"; "Financing Agency"

(1) "Merchant" means a person who deals in goods of the kind or otherwise by his occupation holds himself out as having knowledge or skill peculiar to the practices or goods involved in the transaction or to whom such knowledge or skill may be attributed by his employment of an agent or broker or other intermediary who by his occupation holds himself out as having such knowledge or skill.

(2) "Financing agency" means a bank, finance company or other person who in the ordinary course of business makes advances against goods or documents of title or who by arrangement with either the seller or the buyer intervenes in ordinary course to make or collect payment due or claimed under the contract for sale, as by purchasing or paying the seller's draft or making advances against it or by merely taking it for collection whether or not documents of title accompany the draft. "Financing agency" includes also a bank or other person who similarly intervenes between persons who are in the position of seller and buyer in respect to the goods (Section 2—707).

(3) "Between merchants" means in any transaction with respect to which both parties are chargeable with the knowledge or skill of merchants.

§ 2—105
Definitions: Transferability; "Goods"; "Future" Goods; "Lot"; "Commercial Unit"

(1) "Goods" means all things (including specially manufactured goods) which are movable at the time of identification to the contract for sale other than the money in which the price is to be paid, investment securities (Article 8) and things in action. "Goods" also includes the unborn young of animals and growing crops and other identified things attached to realty as described in the section on goods to be severed from realty (Section 2—107).

(2) Goods must be both existing and identified before any interest in them can pass. Goods which are not both existing and identified are "future" goods. A purported present sale of future goods or of any interest therein operates as a contract to sell.

(3) There may be a sale of a part interest in existing identified goods.

(4) An undivided share in an identified bulk of fungible goods is sufficiently identified to be sold although the quantity of the bulk is not determined. Any agreed proportion of such a bulk or any quantity thereof agreed upon by number, weight or other measure may to the extent of the seller's interest in the bulk be sold to the buyer who then becomes an owner in common.

(5) "Lot" means a parcel or a single article which is the subject matter of a separate sale or delivery, whether or not it is sufficient to perform the contract.

(6) "Commercial unit" means such a unit of goods as by commercial usage is a single whole for purposes of sale and division of which materially impairs its character or value on the market or in use. A commercial unit may be a single article (as a machine) or a set of articles (as a suite of furniture or an assortment of sizes) or a quantity (as a bale, gross, or carload) or any other unit treated in use or in the relevant market as a single whole.

§ 2—106
Definitions: "Contract"; "Agreement"; "Contract for Sale"; "Sale"; "Present Sale"; "Conforming" to Contract; "Termination"; "Cancellation"

(1) In this Article unless the context otherwise requires "contract" and "agreement" are limited to those relating to the present or future sale of goods. "Contract for sale" includes both a present sale of goods and a contract to sell goods at a future time. A "sale" consists in the passing of title from the seller to the buyer for a price (Section 2—401). A "present sale" means a sale which is accomplished by the making of the contract.

(2) Goods or conduct including any part of a performance are "conforming" or conform to the contract when they are in accordance with the obligations under the contract.

(3) "Termination" occurs when either party pursuant to a power created by agreement or law puts an end to the contract otherwise than for its breach. On "termination" all obligations which are still executory on both sides are discharged but any right based on prior breach or performance survives.

(4) "Cancellation" occurs when either party puts an end to the contract for breach by the other and its effect is the same as that of "termination" except that the cancelling party also retains any remedy for breach of the whole contract or any unperformed balance.

§ 2—107
Goods to Be Severed From Realty: Recording

(1) A contract for the sale of minerals or the like (including oil and gas) or a structure or its materials to be removed from realty is a contract for the sale of goods within this Article if they are to be severed by the seller but until severance a purported present sale thereof which is not effective as a transfer of an interest in land is effective only as a contract to sell.

(2) A contract for the sale apart from the land of growing crops or other things attached to realty and capable of severance without material harm thereto but not described in subsection (1) or of timber to be cut is a contract for the sale of goods within this Article whether the subject matter is to be severed by the buyer or by the seller even though it forms part of the realty at the time of contracting, and the parties can by identification effect a present sale before severance.

(3) The provisions of this section are subject to any third party rights provided by the law relating to realty records, and the contract for sale may be executed and recorded as a document transferring an interest in land and shall then constitute notice to third parties of the buyer's rights under the contract for sale.

PART 2/Form, Formation and Readjustment of Contract

§ 2—201
Formal Requirements; Statute of Frauds

(1) Except as otherwise provided in this section a contract for the sale of goods for the price of $500 or more is not enforceable by way of action or defense unless there is some writing sufficient to indicate that a contract for sale has been made between the parties and signed by the party against whom enforcement is sought or by his authorized agent or broker. A writing is not insufficient because it omits or incorrectly states a term agreed upon but the contract is not enforceable under this paragraph beyond the quantity of goods shown in such writing.

(2) Between merchants if within a reasonable time a writing in confirmation of the contract and sufficient against the sender is received and the party receiving it has reason to know its contents, it satisfies the requirements of subsection (1) against such party unless written notice of objection to its contents is given within ten days after it is received.

(3) A contract which does not satisfy the requirements of subsection (1) but which is valid in other respects is enforceable

   (a) if the goods are to be specially manufactured for the buyer and are not suitable for sale to others in the ordinary course of the seller's business and the seller, before notice of repudiation is received and under circumstances which reasonably indicate that the goods are for the buyer, has made either a substantial beginning of their manufacture or commitments for their procurement; or

   (b) if the party against whom enforcement is sought admits in his pleading, testimony or otherwise in court that a contract for sale was made, but the contract is not enforceable under this provision beyond the quantity of goods admitted; or

(c) with respect to goods for which payment has been made and accepted or which have been received and accepted (Sec. 2—606).

§ 2—202
Final Written Expression: Parol or Extrinsic Evidence

Terms with respect to which the confirmatory memoranda of the parties agree or which are otherwise set forth in a writing intended by the parties as a final expression of their agreement with respect to such terms as are included therein may not be contradicted by evidence of any prior agreement or of a contemporaneous oral agreement but may be explained or supplemented

(a) by course of dealing or usage of trade (Section 1—205) or by course of performance (Section 2—208); and

(b) by evidence of consistent additional terms unless the court finds the writing to have been intended also as a complete and exclusive statement of the terms of the agreement.

§ 2—203
Seals Inoperative

The affixing of a seal to a writing evidencing a contract for sale or an offer to buy or sell goods does not constitute the writing a sealed instrument and the law with respect to sealed instruments does not apply to such a contract or offer.

§ 2—204
Formation in General

(1) A contract for sale of goods may be made in any manner sufficient to show agreement, including conduct by both parties which recognizes the existence of such a contract.

(2) An agreement sufficient to constitute a contract for sale may be found even though the moment of its making is undetermined.

(3) Even though one or more terms are left open a contract for sale does not fail for indefiniteness if the parties have intended to make a contract and there is a reasonably certain basis for giving an appropriate remedy.

§ 2—205
Firm Offers

An offer by a merchant to buy or sell goods in a signed writing which by its terms gives assurance that it will be held open is not revocable, for lack of consideration, during the time stated or if no time is stated for a reasonable time, but in no event may such period of irrevocability exceed three months; but any such term of assurance on a form supplied by the offeree must be separately signed by the offeror.

§ 2—206
Offer and Acceptance Formation of Contract

(1) Unless otherwise unambiguously indicated by the language or circumstances

(a) an offer to make a contract shall be construed as inviting acceptance in any manner and by any medium reasonable in the circumstances;

(b) an order or other offer to buy goods for prompt or current shipment shall be construed as inviting acceptance either by a prompt promise to ship or by the prompt or current shipment of conforming or nonconforming goods, but such a shipment of nonconforming goods does not constitute an acceptance if the seller seasonably notifies the buyer that the shipment is offered only as an accommodation to the buyer.

(2) Where the beginning of a requested performance is a reasonable mode of acceptance an offeror who is not notified of acceptance within a reasonable time may treat the offer as having lapsed before acceptance.

§ 2—207
Additional Terms in Acceptance or Confirmation

(1) A definite and seasonable expression of acceptance or a written confirmation which is sent within a reasonable time operates as an acceptance even though it states terms additional to or different from those offered or agreed upon, unless acceptance is expressly made conditional on assent to the additional or different terms.

(2) The additional terms are to be construed as proposals for addition to the contract. Between merchants such terms become part of the contract unless:

(a) the offer expressly limits acceptance to the terms of the offer;

(b) they materially alter it; or

(c) notification of objection to them has already been given or is given within a reasonable time after notice of them is received.

(3) Conduct by both parties which recognizes the existence of a contract is sufficient to establish a contract for sale although the writings of the parties do not otherwise establish a contract. In such case the terms of the particular contract consist of those terms on which the writings of the parties agree, together with any supplementary terms incorporated under any other provisions of this Act.

§ 2—208
Course of Performance or Practical Construction

(1) Where the contract for sale involves repeated occasions for performance by either party with knowledge of the nature of the performance and opportunity for objection to it

by the other, any course of performance accepted or acquiesced in without objection shall be relevant to determine the meaning of the agreement.

(2) The express terms of the agreement and any such course of performance, as well as any course of dealing and usage of trade, shall be construed whenever reasonable as consistent with each other; but when such construction is unreasonable, express terms shall control course of performance and course of performance shall control both course of dealing and usage of trade (Section 1—205).

(3) Subject to the provisions of the next section on modification and waiver, such course of performance shall be relevant to show a waiver or modification of any term inconsistent with such course of performance.

§ 2—209
Modification, Rescission and Waiver

(1) An agreement modifying a contract within this Article needs no consideration to be binding.

(2) A signed agreement which excludes modification or rescission except by a signed writing cannot be otherwise modified or rescinded, but except as between merchants such a requirement on a form supplied by the merchant must be separately signed by the other party.

(3) The requirements of the statute of frauds section of this Article (Section 2—201) must be satisfied if the contract as modified is within its provisions.

(4) Although an attempt at modification or rescission does not satisfy the requirements of subsection (2) or (3) it can operate as a waiver.

(5) A party who has made a waiver affecting an executory portion of the contract may retract the waiver by reasonable notification received by the other party that strict performance will be required of any term waived, unless the retraction would be unjust in view of a material change of position in reliance on the waiver.

§ 2—210
Delegation of Performance; Assignment of Rights

(1) A party may perform his duty through a delegate unless otherwise agreed or unless the other party has a substantial interest in having his original promisor perform or control the acts required by the contract. No delegation of performance relieves the party delegating of any duty to perform or any liability for breach.

(2) Unless otherwise agreed all rights of either seller or buyer can be assigned except where the assignment would materially change the duty of the other party, or increase materially the burden or risk imposed on him by his contract, or impair materially his chance of obtaining return performance. A right to damages for breach of the whole contract or a right arising out of the assignor's due performance of

his entire obligation can be assigned despite agreement otherwise.

(3) Unless the circumstances indicate the contrary a prohibition of assignment of "the contract" is to be construed as barring only the delegation to the assignee of the assignor's performance.

(4) An assignment of "the contract" or of "all my rights under the contract" or an assignment in similar general terms is an assignment of rights and unless the language or the circumstances (as in an assignment for security) indicate the contrary, it is a delegation of performance of the duties of the assignor and its acceptance by the assignee constitutes a promise by him to perform those duties. This promise is enforceable by either the assignor or the other party to the original contract.

(5) The other party may treat any assignment which delegates performance as creating reasonable grounds for insecurity and may without prejudice to his rights against the assignor demand assurances from the assignee (Section 2—609).

PART 3/General Obligation and Construction of Contract

§ 2—301
General Obligations of Parties

The obligation of the seller is to transfer and deliver and that of the buyer is to accept and pay in accordance with the contract.

§ 2—302
Unconscionable Contract or Clause

(1) If the court as a matter of law finds the contract or any clause of the contract to have been unconscionable at the time it was made the court may refuse to enforce the contract, or it may enforce the remainder of the contract without the unconscionable clause, or it may so limit the application of any unconscionable clause as to avoid any unconscionable result.

(2) When it is claimed or appears to the court that the contract or any clause thereof may be unconscionable the parties shall be afforded a reasonable opportunity to present evidence as to its commercial setting, purpose and effect to aid the court in making the determination.

§ 2—303
Allocations or Division of Risks

Where this Article allocates a risk or a burden as between the parties "unless otherwise agreed," the agreement may not only shift the allocation but may also divide the risk or burden.

§ 2—304
Price Payable in Money, Goods, Realty, or Otherwise

(1) The price can be made payable in money or otherwise. If it is payable in whole or in part in goods each party is a seller of the goods which he is to transfer.

(2) Even though all or part of the price is payable in an interest in realty the transfer of the goods and the seller's obligations with reference to them are subject to this Article, but not the transfer of the interest in realty or the transferor's obligations in connection therewith.

§ 2—305
Open Price Term

(1) The parties if they so intend can conclude a contract for sale even though the price is not settled. In such a case the price is a reasonable price at the time for delivery if

(a) nothing is said as to price; or

(b) the price is left to be agreed by the parties and they fail to agree; or

(c) the price is to be fixed in terms of some agreed market or other standard as set or recorded by a third person or agency and it is not so set or recorded.

(2) A price to be fixed by the seller or by the buyer means a price for him to fix in good faith.

(3) When a price left to be fixed otherwise than by agreement of the parties fails to be fixed through fault of one party the other may at his option treat the contract as cancelled or himself fix a reasonable price.

(4) Where, however, the parties intend not to be bound unless the price be fixed or agreed and it is not fixed or agreed there is no contract. In such a case the buyer must return any goods already received or if unable so to do must pay their reasonable value at the time of delivery and the seller must return any portion of the price paid on account.

§ 2—306
Output, Requirements and Exclusive Dealings

(1) A term which measures the quantity by the output of the seller or the requirements of the buyer means such actual output or requirements as may occur in good faith, except that no quantity unreasonably disproportionate to any stated estimate or in the absence of a stated estimate to any normal or otherwise comparable prior output or requirements may be tendered or demanded.

(2) A lawful agreement by either the seller or the buyer for exclusive dealing in the kind of goods concerned imposes unless otherwise agreed an obligation by the seller to use best efforts to supply the goods and by the buyer to use best efforts to promote their sale.

§ 2—307
Delivery in Single Lot or Several Lots

Unless otherwise agreed all goods called for by a contract for sale must be tendered in a single delivery and payment is due only on such tender but where the circumstances give either party the right to make or demand delivery in lots the price if it can be apportioned may be demanded for each lot.

§ 2—308
Absence of Specified Place for Delivery

Unless otherwise agreed

(a) the place for delivery of goods is the seller's place of business or if he has none his residence; but

(b) in a contract for sale of identified goods which to the knowledge of the parties at the time of contracting are in some other place, that place is the place for their delivery; and

(c) documents of title may be delivered through customary banking channels.

§ 2—309
Absence of Specific Time Provisions; Notice of Termination

(1) The time for shipment or delivery or any other action under a contract if not provided in this Article or agreed upon shall be a reasonable time.

(2) Where the contract provides for successive performances but is indefinite in duration it is valid for a reasonable time but unless otherwise agreed may be terminated at any time by either party.

(3) Termination of a contract by one party except on the happening of an agreed event requires that reasonable notification be received by the other party and an agreement dispensing with notification is invalid if its operation would be unconscionable.

§ 2—310
Open Time for Payment or Running of Credit; Authority to Ship Under Reservation

Unless otherwise agreed

(a) payment is due at the time and place at which the buyer is to receive the goods even though the place of shipment is the place of delivery; and

(b) if the seller is authorized to send the goods he may ship them under reservation, and may tender the documents of title, but the buyer may inspect the goods after their arrival before payment is due unless such inspection is inconsistent with the terms of the contract (Section 2—513); and

(c) if delivery is authorized and made by way of documents of title otherwise than by subsection (b) then payment is due at the time and place at which the buyer is to receive the documents regardless of where the goods are to be received; and

(d) where the seller is required or authorized to ship the goods on credit the credit period runs from the time of shipment but post-dating the invoice or delaying its dispatch will correspondingly delay the starting of the credit period.

§ 2—311
Options and Cooperation Respecting Performance

(1) An agreement for sale which is otherwise sufficiently definite (subsection (3) of Section 2—204) to be a contract is not made invalid by the fact that it leaves particulars of performance to be specified by one of the parties. Any such specification must be made in good faith and within limits set by commercial reasonableness.

(2) Unless otherwise agreed specifications relating to assortment of the goods are at the buyer's option and except as otherwise provided in subsections (1)(c) and (3) of Section 2—319 specifications or arrangements relating to shipment are at the seller's option.

(3) Where such specification would materially affect the other party's performance but is not seasonably made or where one party's cooperation is necessary to the agreed performance of the other but is not seasonably forthcoming, the other party in addition to all other remedies

(a) is excused for any resulting delay in his own performance; and

(b) may also either proceed to perform in any reasonable manner or after the time for a material part of his own performance treat the failure to specify or to cooperate as a breach by failure to deliver or accept the goods.

§ 2—312
Warranty of Title and Against Infringement; Buyer's Obligation Against Infringement

(1) Subject to subsection (2) there is in a contract for sale a warranty by the seller that

(a) the title conveyed shall be good, and its transfer rightful; and

(b) the goods shall be delivered free from any security interest or other lien or encumbrance of which the buyer at the time of contracting has no knowledge.

(2) A warranty under subsection (1) will be excluded or modified only by specific language or by circumstances which give the buyer reason to know that the person selling does not claim title in himself or that he is purporting to sell only such right or title as he or a third person may have.

(3) Unless otherwise agreed a seller who is a merchant regularly dealing in goods of the kind warrants that the goods

shall be delivered free of the rightful claim of any third person by way of infringement or the like but a buyer who furnishes specifications to the seller must hold the seller harmless against any such claim which arises out of compliance with the specifications.

§ 2—313
Express Warranties by Affirmation, Promise, Description, Sample

(1) Express warranties by the seller are created as follows:

(a) Any affirmation of fact or promise made by the seller to the buyer which relates to the goods and becomes part of the basis of the bargain creates an express warranty that the goods shall conform to the affirmation or promise.

(b) Any description of the goods which is made part of the basis of the bargain creates an express warranty that the goods shall conform to the description.

(c) Any sample or model which is made part of the basis of the bargain creates an express warranty that the whole of the goods shall conform to the sample or model.

(2) It is not necessary to the creation of an express warranty that the seller use formal words such as "warrant" or "guarantee" or that he have a specific intention to make a warranty, but an affirmation merely of the value of the goods or a statement purporting to be merely the seller's opinion or commendation of the goods does not create a warranty.

§ 2—314
Implied Warranty: Merchantability; Usage of Trade

(1) Unless excluded or modified (Section 2—316), a warranty that the goods shall be merchantable is implied in a contract for their sale if the seller is a merchant with respect to goods of that kind. Under this section the serving for value of food or drink to be consumed either on the premises or elsewhere is a sale.

(2) Goods to be merchantable must be at least such as

(a) pass without objection in the trade under the contract description; and

(b) in the case of fungible goods, are of fair average quality within the description; and

(c) are fit for the ordinary purposes for which such goods are used; and

(d) run, within the variations permitted by the agreement, of even kind, quality and quantity within each unit and among all units involved; and

(e) are adequately contained, packaged, and labeled as the agreement may require; and

(f) conform to the promises or affirmations of fact made on the container or label if any.

(3) Unless excluded or modified (Section 2—316) other implied warranties may arise from course of dealing or usage of trade.

§ 2—315
Implied Warranty: Fitness for Particular Purpose

Where the seller at the time of contracting has reason to know any particular purpose for which the goods are required and that the buyer is relying on the seller's skill or judgment to select or furnish suitable goods, there is unless excluded or modified under the next section an implied warranty that the goods shall be fit for such purpose.

§ 2—316
Exclusion or Modification of Warranties

(1) Words or conduct relevant to the creation of an express warranty and words or conduct tending to negate or limit warranty shall be construed wherever reasonable as consistent with each other; but subject to the provisions of this Article on parol or extrinsic evidence (Section 2—202) negation or limitation is inoperative to the extent that such construction is unreasonable.

(2) Subject to subsection (3), to exclude or modify the implied warranty of merchantability or any part of it the language must mention merchantability and in case of a writing must be conspicuous, and to exclude or modify any implied warranty of fitness the exclusion must be by a writing and conspicuous. Language to exclude all implied warranties of fitness is sufficient if it states, for example, that "There are no warranties which extend beyond the description on the face hereof."

(3) Notwithstanding subsection (2)

(a) unless the circumstances indicate otherwise, all implied warranties are excluded by expressions like "as is", "with all faults" or other language which in common understanding calls the buyer's attention to the exclusion of warranties and makes plain that there is no implied warranty; and

(b) when the buyer before entering into the contract has examined the goods or the sample or model as fully as he desired or has refused to examine the goods there is no implied warranty with regard to defects which an examination ought in the circumstances to have revealed to him; and

(c) an implied warranty can also be excluded or modified by course of dealing or course of performance or usage of trade.

(4) Remedies for breach of warranty can be limited in accordance with the provisions of this Article on liquidation or limitation of damages and on contractual modification of remedy (Sections 2—718 and 2—719).

§ 2—317
Cumulation and Conflict of Warranties Express or Implied

Warranties whether express or implied shall be construed as consistent with each other and as cumulative, but if such construction is unreasonable the intention of the parties shall determine which warranty is dominant. In ascertaining that intention the following rules apply:

(a) Exact or technical specifications displace an inconsistent sample or model or general language of description.

(b) A sample from an existing bulk displaces inconsistent general language of description.

(c) Express warranties displace inconsistent implied warranties other than an implied warranty of fitness for a particular purpose.

§ 2—318
Third Party Beneficiaries of Warranties Express or Implied

Note: *If this Act is introduced in the Congress of the United States this section should be omitted. (States to select one alternative.)*

Alternative A

A seller's warranty whether express or implied extends to any natural person who is in the family or household of his buyer or who is a guest in his home if it is reasonable to expect that such person may use, consume or be affected by the goods and who is injured in person by breach of the warranty. A seller may not exclude or limit the operation of this section.

Alternative B

A seller's warranty whether express or implied extends to any natural person who may reasonably be expected to use, consume or be affected by the goods and who is injured in person by breach of the warranty. A seller may not exclude or limit the operation of this section.

Alternative C

A seller's warranty whether express or implied extends to any person who may reasonably be expected to use, consume or be affected by the goods and who is injured by breach of the warranty. A seller may not exclude or limit the operation of this section with respect to injury to the person of an individual to whom the warranty extends. As amended 1966.

§ 2—319
F.O.B. and F.A.S. Terms

(1) Unless otherwise agreed the term F.O.B. (which means "free on board") at a named place, even though used only in

connection with the stated price, is a delivery term under which

(a) when the term is F.O.B. the place of shipment, the seller must at that place ship the goods in the manner provided in this Article (Section 2—504) and bear the expense and risk of putting them into the possession of the carrier; or

(b) when the term is F.O.B. the place of destination, the seller must at his own expense and risk transport the goods to that place and there tender delivery of them in the manner provided in this Article (Section 2—503);

(c) when under either (a) or (b) the term is also F.O.B. vessel, car or other vehicle, the seller must in addition at his own expense and risk load the goods on board. If the term is F.O.B. vessel the buyer must name the vessel and in an appropriate case the seller must comply with the provisions of this Article on the form of bill of lading (Section 2—323).

(2) Unless otherwise agreed the term F.A.S. vessel (which means "free alongside") at a named port, even though used only in connection with the stated price, is a delivery term under which the seller must

(a) at his own expense and risk deliver the goods alongside the vessel in the manner usual in that port or on a dock designated and provided by the buyer; and

(b) obtain and tender a receipt for the goods in exchange for which the carrier is under a duty to issue a bill of lading.

(3) Unless otherwise agreed in any case falling within subsection (1)(a) or (c) or subsection (2) the buyer must seasonably give any needed instructions for making delivery, including when the term is F.A.S. or F.O.B. the loading berth of the vessel and in an appropriate case its name and sailing date. The seller may treat the failure of needed instructions as a failure of cooperation under this Article (Section 2—311). He may also at his option move the goods in any reasonable manner preparatory to delivery or shipment.

(4) Under the term F.O.B. vessel or F.A.S. unless otherwise agreed the buyer must make payment against tender of the required documents and the seller may not tender nor the buyer demand delivery of the goods in substitution for the documents.

§ 2—320
C.I.F. and C. & F. Terms

(1) The term C.I.F. means that the price includes in a lump sum the cost of the goods and the insurance and freight to the named destination. The term C. & F. or C.F. means that the price so includes cost and freight to the named destination.

(2) Unless otherwise agreed and even though used only in connection with the stated price and destination, the term C.I.F. destination or its equivalent requires the seller at his own expense and risk to

(a) put the goods into the possession of a carrier at the port for shipment and obtain a negotiable bill or bills of lading covering the entire transportation to the named destination; and

(b) load the goods and obtain a receipt from the carrier (which may be contained in the bill of lading) showing that the freight has been paid or provided for; and

(c) obtain a policy or certificate of insurance, including any war risk insurance, of a kind and on terms then current at the port of shipment in the usual amount, in the currency of the contract, shown to cover the same goods covered by the bill of lading and providing for payment of loss to the order of the buyer or for the account of whom it may concern; but the seller may add to the price the amount of the premium for any such war risk insurance; and

(d) prepare an invoice of the goods and procure any other documents required to effect shipment or to comply with the contract; and

(e) forward and tender with commercial promptness all the documents in due form and with any indorsement necessary to perfect the buyer's rights.

(3) Unless otherwise agreed the term C. & F. or its equivalent has the same effect and imposes upon the seller the same obligations and risks as a C.I.F. term except the obligation as to insurance.

(4) Under the term C.I.F. or C. & F. unless otherwise agreed the buyer must make payment against tender of the required documents and the seller may not tender nor the buyer demand delivery of the goods in substitution for the documents.

§ 2—321
C.I.F. or C. & F.: "Net Landed Weights"; "Payment on Arrival"; Warranty of Condition on Arrival

Under a contract containing a term C.I.F. or C. & F.

(1) Where the price is based on or is to be adjusted according to "net landed weights", "delivered weights", "out turn" quantity or quality or the like, unless otherwise agreed the seller must reasonably estimate the price. The payment due on tender of the documents called for by the contract is the amount so estimated, but after final adjustment of the price a settlement must be made with commercial promptness.

(2) An agreement described in subsection (1) or any warranty of quality or condition of the goods on arrival places upon the seller the risk of ordinary deterioration, shrinkage and the like in transportation but has no effect on the place or time of identification to the contract for sale or delivery or on the passing of the risk of loss.

(3) Unless otherwise agreed where the contract provides for payment on or after arrival of the goods the seller must before payment allow such preliminary inspection as is fea-

sible; but if the goods are lost delivery of the documents and payment are due when the goods should have arrived.

§ 2—322
Delivery "Ex-Ship"

(1) Unless otherwise agreed a term for delivery of goods "ex-ship" (which means from the carrying vessel) or in equivalent language is not restricted to a particular ship and requires delivery from a ship which has reached a place at the named port of destination where goods of the kind are usually discharged.

(2) Under such a term unless otherwise agreed

(a) the seller must discharge all liens arising out of the carriage and furnish the buyer with a direction which puts the carrier under a duty to deliver the goods; and

(b) the risk of loss does not pass to the buyer until the goods leave the ship's tackle or are otherwise properly unloaded.

§ 2—323
Form of Bill of Lading Required in Overseas Shipment; "Overseas"

(1) Where the contract contemplates overseas shipment and contains a term C.I.F. or C. & F. or F.O.B. vessel, the seller unless otherwise agreed must obtain a negotiable bill of lading stating that the goods have been loaded on board or, in the case of a term C.I.F. or C. & F., received for shipment.

(2) Where in a case within subsection (1) a bill of lading has been issued in a set of parts, unless otherwise agreed if the documents are not to be sent from abroad the buyer may demand tender of the full set; otherwise only one part of the bill of lading need be tendered. Even if the agreement expressly requires a full set

(a) due tender of a single part is acceptable within the provisions of this Article on cure of improper delivery (subsection (1) of Section 2—508); and

(b) even though the full set is demanded, if the documents are sent from abroad the person tendering an incomplete set may nevertheless require payment upon furnishing an indemnity which the buyer in good faith deems adequate.

(3) A shipment by water or by air or a contract contemplating such shipment is "overseas" insofar as by usage of trade or agreement it is subject to the commercial, financing or shipping practices characteristic of international deep water commerce.

§ 2—324
"No Arrival, No Sale" Term

Under a term "no arrival, no sale" or terms of like meaning, unless otherwise agreed,

(a) the seller must properly ship conforming goods and if they arrive by any means he must tender them on

arrival but he assumes no obligation that the goods will arrive unless he has caused the non-arrival; and

(b) where without fault of the seller the goods are in part lost or have so deteriorated as no longer to conform to the contract or arrive after the contract time, the buyer may proceed as if there had been casualty to identified goods (Section 2—613).

§ 2—325
"Letter of Credit" Term; "Confirmed Credit"

(1) Failure of the buyer seasonably to furnish an agreed letter of credit is a breach of the contract for sale.

(2) The delivery to seller of a proper letter of credit suspends the buyer's obligation to pay. If the letter of credit is dishonored, the seller may on seasonable notification to the buyer require payment directly from him.

(3) Unless otherwise agreed the term "letter of credit" or "banker's credit" in a contract for sale means an irrevocable credit issued by a financing agency of good repute and, where the shipment is overseas, of good international repute. The term "confirmed credit" means that the credit must also carry the direct obligation of such an agency which does business in the seller's financial market.

§ 2—326
Sale on Approval and Sale or Return; Consignment Sales and Rights of Creditors

(1) Unless otherwise agreed, if delivered goods may be returned by the buyer even though they conform to the contract, the transaction is

(a) a "sale on approval" if the goods are delivered primarily for use, and

(b) a "sale or return" if the goods are delivered primarily for resale.

(2) Except as provided in subsection (3), goods held on approval are not subject to the claims of the buyer's creditors until acceptance; goods held on sale or return are subject to such claims while in the buyer's possession.

(3) Where goods are delivered to a person for sale and such person maintains a place of business at which he deals in goods of the kind involved, under a name other than the name of the person making delivery, then with respect to claims of creditors of the person conducting the business the goods are deemed to be on sale or return. The provisions of this subsection are applicable even though an agreement purports to reserve title to the person making delivery until payment or resale or uses such words as "on consignment" or "on memorandum". However, this subsection is not applicable if the person making delivery

(a) complies with an applicable law providing for a consignor's interest or the like to be evidenced by a sign, or

(b) establishes that the person conducting the business

is generally known by his creditors to be substantially engaged in selling the goods of others, or

(c) complies with the filing provisions of the Article on Secured Transactions (Article 9).

(4) Any "or return" term of a contract for sale is to be treated as a separate contract for sale within the statute of frauds section of this Article (Section 2—201) and as contradicting the sale aspect of the contract within the provisions of this Article on parol or extrinsic evidence (Section 2—202).

§ 2—327
Special Incidents of Sale on Approval and Sale or Return

(1) Under a sale on approval unless otherwise agreed

(a) although the goods are identified to the contract the risk of loss and the title do not pass to the buyer until acceptance; and

(b) use of the goods consistent with the purpose of trial is not acceptance but failure seasonably to notify the seller of election to return the goods is acceptance, and if the goods conform to the contract acceptance of any part is acceptance of the whole; and

(c) after due notification of election to return, the return is at the seller's risk and expense but a merchant buyer must follow any reasonable instructions.

(2) Under a sale or return unless otherwise agreed

(a) the option to return extends to the whole or any commercial unit of the goods while in substantially their original condition, but must be exercised seasonably; and

(b) the return is at the buyer's risk and expense.

§ 2—328
Sale by Auction

(1) In a sale by auction if goods are put up in lots each lot is the subject of a separate sale.

(2) A sale by auction is complete when the auctioneer so announces by the fall of the hammer or in other customary manner. Where a bid is made while the hammer is falling in acceptance of a prior bid the auctioneer may in his discretion reopen the bidding or declare the goods sold under the bid on which the hammer was falling.

(3) Such a sale is with reserve unless the goods are in explicit terms put up without reserve. In an auction with reserve the auctioneer may withdraw the goods at any time until he announces completion of the sale. In an auction without reserve, after the auctioneer calls for bids on an article or lot, that article or lot cannot be withdrawn unless no bid is made within a reasonable time. In either case a bidder may retract his bid until the auctioneer's announcement of completion of the sale, but a bidder's retraction does not revive any previous bid.

(4) If the auctioneer knowingly receives a bid on the seller's behalf or the seller makes or procures such a bid, and notice has not been given that liberty for such bidding is reserved, the buyer may at his option avoid the sale or take the goods at the price of the last good faith bid prior to the completion of the sale. This subsection shall not apply to any bid at a forced sale.

PART 4/Title, Creditors and Good Faith Purchasers

§ 2—401
Passing of Title; Reservation for Security; Limited Application of This Section

Each provision of this Article with regard to the rights, obligations and remedies of the seller, the buyer, purchasers or other third parties applies irrespective of title to the goods except where the provision refers to such title. Insofar as situations are not covered by the other provisions of this Article and matters concerning title become material the following rules apply:

(1) Title to goods cannot pass under a contract for sale prior to their identification to the contract (Section 2—501), and unless otherwise explicitly agreed the buyer acquires by their identification a special property as limited by this Act. Any retention or reservation by the seller of the title (property) in goods shipped or delivered to the buyer is limited in effect to a reservation of a security interest. Subject to these provisions and to the provisions of the Article on Secured Transactions (Article 9), title to goods passes from the seller to the buyer in any manner and on any conditions explicitly agreed on by the parties.

(2) Unless otherwise explicitly agreed title passes to the buyer at the time and place at which the seller completes his performance with reference to the physical delivery of the goods, despite any reservation of a security interest and even though a document of title is to be delivered at a different time or place; and in particular and despite any reservation of a security interest by the bill of lading

(a) if the contract requires or authorizes the seller to send the goods to the buyer but does not require him to deliver them at destination, title passes to the buyer at the time and place of shipment; but

(b) if the contract requires delivery at destination, title passes on tender there.

(3) Unless otherwise explicitly agreed where delivery is to be made without moving the goods,

(a) if the seller is to deliver a document of title, title passes at the time when and the place where he delivers such documents; or

(b) if the goods are at the time of contracting already identified and no documents are to be delivered, title passes at the time and place of contracting.

(4) A rejection or other refusal by the buyer to receive or retain the goods, whether or not justified, or a justified revocation of acceptance revests title to the goods in the seller. Such revesting occurs by operation of law and is not a "sale".

§ 2—402
Rights of Seller's Creditors Against Sold Goods

(1) Except as provided in subsections (2) and (3), rights of unsecured creditors of the seller with respect to goods which have been identified to a contract for sale are subject to the buyer's rights to recover the goods under this Article (Sections 2—502 and 2—716).

(2) A creditor of the seller may treat a sale or an identification of goods to a contract for sale as void if as against him a retention of possession by the seller is fraudulent under any rule of law of the state where the goods are situated, except that retention of possession in good faith and current course of trade by a merchant-seller for a commercially reasonable time after a sale or identification is not fraudulent.

(3) Nothing in this Article shall be deemed to impair the rights of creditors of the seller

    (a) under the provisions of the Article on Secured Transactions (Article 9); or

    (b) where identification to the contract or delivery is made not in current course of trade but in satisfaction of or as security for a pre-existing claim for money, security or the like and is made under circumstances which under any rule of law of the state where the goods are situated would apart from this Article constitute the transaction a fraudulent transfer or voidable preference.

§ 2—403
Power to Transfer; Good Faith Purchase of Goods; "Entrusting"

(1) A purchaser of goods acquires all title which his transferor had or had power to transfer except that a purchaser of a limited interest acquires rights only to the extent of the interest purchased. A person with voidable title has power to transfer a good title to a good faith purchaser for value. When goods have been delivered under a transaction of purchase the purchaser has such power even though

    (a) the transferor was deceived as to the identity of the purchaser, or

    (b) the delivery was in exchange for a check which is later dishonored, or

    (c) it was agreed that the transaction was to be a "cash sale", or

    (d) the delivery was procured through fraud punishable as larcenous under the criminal law.

(2) Any entrusting of possession of goods to a merchant who deals in goods of that kind gives him power to transfer all rights of the entruster to a buyer in ordinary course of business.

(3) "Entrusting" includes any delivery and any acquiescence in retention of possession regardless of any condition expressed between the parties to the delivery or acquiescence and regardless of whether the procurement of the entrusting or the possessor's disposition of the goods have been such as to be larcenous under the criminal law.

(4) The rights of other purchasers of goods and of lien creditors are governed by the Articles on Secured Transactions (Article 9), Bulk Transfers (Article 6) and Documents of Title (Article 7).

PART 5/Performance

§ 2—501
Insurable Interest in Goods; Manner of Identification of Goods

(1) The buyer obtains a special property and an insurable interest in goods by identification of existing goods as goods to which the contract refers even though the goods so identified are nonconforming and he has an option to return or reject them. Such identification can be made at any time and in any manner explicitly agreed to by the parties. In the absence of explicit agreement identification occurs

    (a) when the contract is made if it is for the sale of goods already existing and identified;

    (b) if the contract is for the sale of future goods other than those described in paragraph (c), when goods are shipped, marked or otherwise designated by the seller as goods to which the contract refers;

    (c) when the crops are planted or otherwise become growing crops or the young are conceived if the contract is for the sale of unborn young to be born within twelve months after contracting or for the sale of crops to be harvested within twelve months or the next normal harvest season after contracting whichever is longer.

(2) The seller retains an insurable interest in goods so long as title to or any security interest in the goods remains in him and where the identification is by the seller alone he may until default or insolvency or notification to the buyer that the identification is final substitute other goods for those identified.

(3) Nothing in this section impairs any insurable interest recognized under any other statute or rule of law.

§ 2—502
Buyer's Right to Goods on Seller's Insolvency

(1) Subject to subsection (2) and even though the goods have not been shipped a buyer who has paid a part or all of the price of goods in which he has a special property under the provisions of the immediately preceding section may on making and keeping good a tender of any unpaid portion of their price recover them from the seller if the seller becomes insolvent within ten days after receipt of the first installment on their price.

(2) If the identification creating his special property has been made by the buyer he acquires the right to recover the goods only if they conform to the contract for sale.

§ 2—503
Manner of Seller's Tender of Delivery

(1) Tender of delivery requires that the seller put and hold conforming goods at the buyer's disposition and give the buyer any notification reasonably necessary to enable him to take delivery. The manner, time and place for tender are determined by the agreement and this Article, and in particular

(a) tender must be at a reasonable hour, and if it is of goods they must be kept available for the period reasonably necessary to enable the buyer to take possession; but

(b) unless otherwise agreed the buyer must furnish facilities reasonably suited to the receipt of the goods.

(2) Where the case is within the next section respecting shipment tender requires that the seller comply with its provisions.

(3) Where the seller is required to deliver at a particular destination tender requires that he comply with subsection (1) and also in any appropriate case tender documents as described in subsections (4) and (5) of this section.

(4) Where goods are in the possession of a bailee and are to be delivered without being moved

(a) tender requires that the seller either tender a negotiable document of title covering such goods or procure acknowledgment by the bailee of the buyer's right to possession of the goods; but

(b) tender to the buyer of a non-negotiable document of title or of a written direction to the bailee to deliver is sufficient tender unless the buyer seasonably objects, and receipt by the bailee of notification of the buyer's rights fixes those rights as against the bailee and all third persons; but risk of loss of the goods and of any failure by the bailee to honor the non-negotiable document of title or to obey the direction remains on the seller until the buyer has had a reasonable time to present the document or direction, and a refusal by the bailee to honor the document or to obey the direction defeats the tender.

(5) Where the contract requires the seller to deliver documents

(a) he must tender all such documents in correct form, except as provided in this Article with respect to bills of lading in a set (subsection (2) of Section 2—323); and

(b) tender through customary banking channels is sufficient and dishonor of a draft accompanying the documents constitutes non-acceptance or rejection.

§ 2—504
Shipment by Seller

Where the seller is required or authorized to send the goods to the buyer and the contract does not require him to deliver them at a particular destination, then unless otherwise agreed he must

(a) put the goods in the possession of such a carrier and make such a contract for their transportation as may be reasonable having regard to the nature of the goods and other circumstances of the case; and

(b) obtain and promptly deliver or tender in due form any document necessary to enable the buyer to obtain possession of the goods or otherwise required by the agreement or by usage of trade; and

(c) promptly notify the buyer of the shipment.

Failure to notify the buyer under paragraph (c) or to make a proper contract under paragraph (a) is a ground for rejection only if material delay or loss ensues.

§ 2—505
Seller's Shipment Under Reservation

(1) Where the seller has identified goods to the contract by or before shipment:

(a) his procurement of a negotiable bill of lading to his own order or otherwise reserves in him a security interest in the goods. His procurement of the bill to the order of a financing agency or of the buyer indicates in addition only the seller's expectation of transferring that interest to the person named.

(b) a non-negotiable bill of lading to himself or his nominee reserves possession of the goods as security but except in a case of conditional delivery (subsection (2) of Section 2—507) a non-negotiable bill of lading naming the buyer as consignee reserves no security interest even though the seller retains possession of the bill of lading.

(2) When shipment by the seller with reservation of a security interest is in violation of the contract for sale it constitutes an improper contract for transportation within the preceding section but impairs neither the rights given to the buyer by shipment and identification of the goods to the contract nor the seller's powers as a holder of a negotiable document.

§ 2—506
Rights of Financing Agency

(1) A financing agency by paying or purchasing for value a draft which relates to a shipment of goods acquires to the extent of the payment or purchase and in addition to its own rights under the draft and any document of title securing it any rights of the shipper in the goods including the right to stop delivery and the shipper's right to have the draft honored by the buyer.

(2) The right to reimbursement of a financing agency which has in good faith honored or purchased the draft under commitment to or authority from the buyer is not impaired by subsequent discovery of defects with reference to any relevant document which was apparently regular on its face.

§ 2—507
Effect of Seller's Tender; Delivery on Condition

(1) Tender of delivery is a condition to the buyer's duty to accept the goods and, unless otherwise agreed, to his duty to pay for them. Tender entitles the seller to acceptance of the goods and to payment according to the contract.

(2) Where payment is due and demanded on the delivery to the buyer of goods or documents of title, his right as against the seller to retain or dispose of them is conditional upon his making the payment due.

§ 2—508
Cure by Seller of Improper Tender or Delivery; Replacement

(1) Where any tender or delivery by the seller is rejected because non-conforming and the time for performance has not yet expired, the seller may seasonably notify the buyer of his intention to cure and may then within the contract time make a conforming delivery.

(2) Where the buyer rejects a non-conforming tender which the seller had reasonable grounds to believe would be acceptable with or without money allowance the seller may if he seasonably notifies the buyer have a further reasonable time to substitute a conforming tender.

§ 2—509
Risk of Loss in the Absence of Breach

(1) Where the contract requires or authorizes the seller to ship the goods by carrier

  (a) if it does not require him to deliver them at a particular destination, the risk of loss passes to the buyer when the goods are duly delivered to the carrier even though the shipment is under reservation (Section 2—505); but

  (b) if it does require him to deliver them at a particular destination and the goods are there duly tendered while in the possession of the carrier, the risk of loss passes to the buyer when the goods are there duly so tendered as to enable the buyer to take delivery.

(2) Where the goods are held by a bailee to be delivered without being moved, the risk of loss passes to the buyer

  (a) on his receipt of a negotiable document of title covering the goods; or

  (b) on acknowledgment by the bailee of the buyer's right to possession of the goods; or

  (c) after his receipt of a non-negotiable document of title or other written direction to deliver, as provided in subsection (4)(b) of Section 2—503.

(3) In any case not within subsection (1) or (2), the risk of loss passes to the buyer on his receipt of the goods if the seller is a merchant; otherwise the risk passes to the buyer on tender of delivery.

(4) The provisions of this section are subject to contrary agreement of the parties and to the provisions of this Article on sale on approval (Section 2—327) and on effect of breach on risk of loss (Section 2—510).

§ 2—510
Effect of Breach on Risk of Loss

(1) Where a tender or delivery of goods so fails to conform to the contract as to give a right of rejection the risk of their loss remains on the seller until cure or acceptance.

(2) Where the buyer rightfully revokes acceptance he may to the extent of any deficiency in his effective insurance coverage treat the risk of loss as having rested on the seller from the beginning.

(3) Where the buyer as to conforming goods already identified to the contract for sale repudiates or is otherwise in breach before risk of their loss has passed to him, the seller may to the extent of any deficiency in his effective insurance coverage treat the risk of loss as resting on the buyer for a commercially reasonable time.

§ 2—511
Tender of Payment by Buyer; Payment by Check

(1) Unless otherwise agreed tender of payment is a condition to the seller's duty to tender and complete any delivery.

(2) Tender of payment is sufficient when made by any means or in any manner current in the ordinary course of business unless the seller demands payment in legal tender and gives any extension of time reasonably necessary to procure it.

(3) Subject to the provisions of this Act on the effect of an instrument on an obligation (Section 3—802), payment by check is conditional and is defeated as between the parties by dishonor of the check on due presentment.

§ 2—512
Payment by Buyer Before Inspection

(1) Where the contract requires payment before inspection non-conformity of the goods does not excuse the buyer from so making payment unless

  (a) the non-conformity appears without inspection; or

  (b) despite tender of the required documents the circumstances would justify injunction against honor under the provisions of this Act (Section 5—114).

(2) Payment pursuant to subsection (1) does not constitute an acceptance of goods or impair the buyer's right to inspect or any of his remedies.

§ 2—513
Buyer's Right to Inspection of Goods

(1) Unless otherwise agreed and subject to subsection (3), where goods are tendered or delivered or identified to the contract for sale, the buyer has a right before payment or

acceptance to inspect them at any reasonable place and time and in any reasonable manner. When the seller is required or authorized to send the goods to the buyer, the inspection may be after their arrival.

(2) Expenses of inspection must be borne by the buyer but may be recovered from the seller if the goods do not conform and are rejected.

(3) Unless otherwise agreed and subject to the provisions of this Article on C.I.F. contracts (subsection (3) of Section 2—321), the buyer is not entitled to inspect the goods before payment of the price when the contract provides

(a) for delivery "C.O.D." or on other like terms; or

(b) for payment against documents of title, except where such payment is due only after the goods are to become available for inspection.

(4) A place or method of inspection fixed by the parties is presumed to be exclusive but unless otherwise expressly agreed it does not postpone identification or shift the place for delivery or for passing the risk of loss. If compliance becomes impossible, inspection shall be as provided in this section unless the place or method fixed was clearly intended as an indispensable condition failure of which voids the contract.

§ 2—514
When Documents Deliverable on Acceptance; When on Payment

Unless otherwise agreed documents against which a draft is drawn are to be delivered to the drawee on acceptance of the draft if it is payable more than three days after presentment; otherwise, only on payment.

§ 2—515
Preserving Evidence of Goods in Dispute

In furtherance of the adjustment of any claim or dispute

(a) either party on reasonable notification to the other and for the purpose of ascertaining the facts and preserving evidence has the right to inspect, test and sample the goods including such of them as may be in the possession or control of the other; and

(b) the parties may agree to a third party inspection or survey to determine the conformity or condition of the goods and may agree that the findings shall be binding upon them in any subsequent litigation or adjustment.

PART 6/Breach, Repudiation and Excuse

§ 2—601
Buyer's Rights on Improper Delivery

Subject to the provisions of this Article on breach in installment contracts (Section 2—612) and unless otherwise agreed under the sections on contractual limitations of remedy (Sections 2—718 and 2—719), if the goods or the tender of delivery fail in any respect to conform to the contract, the buyer may

(a) reject the whole; or

(b) accept the whole; or

(c) accept any commercial unit or units and reject the rest.

§ 2—602
Manner and Effect of Rightful Rejection

(1) Rejection of goods must be within a reasonable time after their delivery or tender. It is ineffective unless the buyer seasonably notifies the seller.

(2) Subject to the provisions of the two following sections on rejected goods (Sections 2—603 and 2—604),

(a) after rejection any exercise of ownership by the buyer with respect to any commercial unit is wrongful as against the seller; and

(b) if the buyer has before rejection taken physical possession of goods in which he does not have a security interest under the provisions of this Article (subsection (3) of Section 2—711), he is under a duty after rejection to hold them with reasonable care at the seller's disposition for a time sufficient to permit the seller to remove them; but

(c) the buyer has no further obligations with regard to goods rightfully rejected.

(3) The seller's rights with respect to goods wrongfully rejected are governed by the provisions of this Article on seller's remedies in general (Section 2—703).

§ 2—603
Merchant Buyer's Duties as to Rightfully Rejected Goods

(1) Subject to any security interest in the buyer (subsection (3) of Section 2—711), when the seller has no agent or place of business at the market of rejection a merchant buyer is under a duty after rejection of goods in his possession or control to follow any reasonable instructions received from the seller with respect to the goods and in the absence of such instructions to make reasonable efforts to sell them for the seller's account if they are perishable or threaten to decline in value speedily. Instructions are not reasonable if on demand indemnity for expenses is not forthcoming.

(2) When the buyer sells goods under subsection (1), he is entitled to reimbursement from the seller or out of the proceeds for reasonable expenses of caring for and selling them, and if the expenses include no selling commission then to such commission as is usual in the trade or if there is none to a reasonable sum not exceeding ten per cent on the gross proceeds.

(3) In complying with this section the buyer is held only to good faith and good faith conduct hereunder is neither ac-

ceptance nor conversion nor the basis of an action for damages.

§ 2—604
Buyer's Options as to Salvage of Rightfully Rejected Goods

Subject to the provisions of the immediately preceding section on perishables if the seller gives no instructions within a reasonable time after notification of rejection the buyer may store the rejected goods for the seller's account or reship them to him or resell them for the seller's account with reimbursement as provided in the preceding section. Such action is not acceptance or conversion.

§ 2—605
Waiver of Buyer's Objections by Failure to Particularize

(1) The buyer's failure to state in connection with rejection a particular defect which is ascertainable by reasonable inspection precludes him from relying on the unstated defect to justify rejection or to establish breach

(a) where the seller could have cured it if stated seasonably; or

(b) between merchants when the seller has after rejection made a request in writing for a full and final written statement of all defects on which the buyer proposes to rely.

(2) Payment against documents made without reservation of rights precludes recovery of the payment for defects apparent on the face of the documents.

§ 2—606
What Constitutes Acceptance of Goods

(1) Acceptance of goods occurs when the buyer

(a) after a reasonable opportunity to inspect the goods signifies to the seller that the goods are conforming or that he will take or retain them in spite of their non-conformity; or

(b) fails to make an effective rejection (subsection (1) of Section 2—602), but such acceptance does not occur until the buyer has had a reasonable opportunity to inspect them; or

(c) does any act inconsistent with the seller's ownership; but if such act is wrongful as against the seller it is an acceptance only if ratified by him.

(2) Acceptance of a part of any commercial unit is acceptance of that entire unit.

§ 2—607
Effect of Acceptance; Notice of Breach; Burden of Establishing Breach After Acceptance; Notice of Claim or Litigation to Person Answerable Over

(1) The buyer must pay at the contract rate for any goods accepted.

(2) Acceptance of goods by the buyer precludes rejection of the goods accepted and if made with knowledge of a non-conformity cannot be revoked because of it unless the acceptance was on the reasonable assumption that the non-conformity would be seasonably cured but acceptance does not of itself impair any other remedy provided by this Article for non-conformity.

(3) Where a tender has been accepted

(a) the buyer must within a reasonable time after he discovers or should have discovered any breach notify the seller of breach or be barred from any remedy; and

(b) if the claim is one for infringement or the like (subsection (3) of Section 2—312) and the buyer is sued as a result of such a breach he must so notify the seller within a reasonable time after he receives notice of the litigation or be barred from any remedy over for liability established by the litigation.

(4) The burden is on the buyer to establish any breach with respect to the goods accepted.

(5) Where the buyer is sued for breach of a warranty or other obligation for which the seller is answerable over

(a) he may give his seller written notice of the litigation. If the notice states that the seller may come in and defend and that if the seller does not do so he will be bound in any action against him by his buyer by any determination of fact common to the two litigations, then unless the seller after seasonable receipt of the notice does come in and defend he is so bound.

(b) if the claim is one for infringement or the like (subsection (3) of Section 2—312) the original seller may demand in writing that his buyer turn over to him control of the litigation including settlement or else be barred from any remedy over and if he also agrees to bear all expense and to satisfy any adverse judgment, then unless the buyer after seasonable receipt of the demand does turn over control the buyer is so barred.

(6) The provisions of subsections (3), (4) and (5) apply to any obligation of a buyer to hold the seller harmless against infringement or the like (subsection (3) of Section 2—312).

§ 2—608
Revocation of Acceptance in Whole or in Part

(1) The buyer may revoke his acceptance of a lot or commercial unit whose non-conformity substantially impairs its value to him if he has accepted it

(a) on the reasonable assumption that its non-conformity would be cured and it has not been seasonably cured; or

(b) without discovery of such non-conformity if his acceptance was reasonably induced either by the difficulty of discovery before acceptance or by the seller's assurances.

(2) Revocation of acceptance must occur within a reasonable time after the buyer discovers or should have discovered the ground for it and before any substantial change in condition of the goods which is not caused by their own defects. It is not effective until the buyer notifies the seller of it.

(3) A buyer who so revokes has the same rights and duties with regard to the goods involved as if he had rejected them.

§ 2—609
Right to Adequate Assurance of Performance

(1) A contract for sale imposes an obligation on each party that the other's expectation of receiving due performance will not be impaired. When reasonable grounds for insecurity arise with respect to the performance of either party the other may in writing demand adequate assurance of due performance and until he receives such assurance may if commercially reasonable suspend any performance for which he has not already received the agreed return.

(2) Between merchants the reasonableness of grounds for insecurity and the adequacy of any assurance offered shall be determined according to commercial standards.

(3) Acceptance of any improper delivery or payment does not prejudice the aggrieved party's right to demand adequate assurance of future performance.

(4) After receipt of a justified demand failure to provide within a reasonable time not exceeding thirty days such assurance of due performance as is adequate under the circumstances of the particular case is a repudiation of the contract.

§ 2—610
Anticipatory Repudiation

When either party repudiates the contract with respect to a performance not yet due the loss of which will substantially impair the value of the contract to the other, the aggrieved party may

(a) for a commercially reasonable time await performance by the repudiating party; or

(b) resort to any remedy for breach (Section 2—703 or Section 2—711), even though he has notified the repudiating party that he would await the latter's performance and has urged retraction; and

(c) in either case suspend his own performance or proceed in accordance with the provisions of this Article on the seller's right to identify goods to the contract notwithstanding breach or to salvage unfinished goods (Section 2—704).

§ 2—611
Retraction of Anticipatory Repudiation

(1) Until the repudiating party's next performance is due he can retract his repudiation unless the aggrieved party has since the repudiation cancelled or materially changed his position or otherwise indicated that he considers the repudiation final.

(2) Retraction may be by any method which clearly indicates to the aggrieved party that the repudiating party intends to perform, but must include any assurance justifiably demanded under the provisions of this Article (Section 2—609).

(3) Retraction reinstates the repudiating party's rights under the contract with due excuse and allowance to the aggrieved party for any delay occasioned by the repudiation.

§ 2—612
"Installment Contract"; Breach

(1) An "installment contract" is one which requires or authorizes the delivery of goods in separate lots to be separately accepted, even though the contract contains a clause "each delivery is a separate contract" or its equivalent.

(2) The buyer may reject any installment which is non-conforming if the non-conformity substantially impairs the value of that installment and cannot be cured or if the non-conformity is a defect in the required documents; but if the non-conformity does not fall within subsection (3) and the seller gives adequate assurance of its cure the buyer must accept that installment.

(3) Whenever non-conformity or default with respect to one or more installments substantially impairs the value of the whole contract there is a breach of the whole. But the aggrieved party reinstates the contract if he accepts a non-conforming installment without seasonably notifying of cancellation or if he brings an action with respect only to past installments or demands performance as to future installments.

§ 2—613
Casualty to Identified Goods

Where the contract requires for its performance goods identified when the contract is made, and the goods suffer casualty without fault of either party before the risk of loss passes to the buyer, or in a proper case under a "no arrival, no sale" term (Section 2—324) then

(a) if the loss is total the contract is voided; and

(b) if the loss is partial or the goods have so deteriorated as no longer to conform to the contract the buyer may nevertheless demand inspection and at his option either treat the contract as voided or accept the goods with due allowance from the contract price for the deterioration or the deficiency in quantity but without further right against the seller.

§ 2—614
Substituted Performance

(1) Where without fault of either party the agreed berthing, loading, or unloading facilities fail or an agreed type of carrier becomes unavailable or the agreed manner of delivery otherwise becomes commercially impracticable but a commercially reasonable substitute is available, such substitute performance must be tendered and accepted.

(2) If the agreed means or manner of payment fails because of domestic or foreign governmental regulation, the seller may withhold or stop delivery unless the buyer provides a means or manner of payment which is commercially a substantial equivalent. If delivery has already been taken, payment by the means or in the manner provided by the regulation discharges the buyer's obligation unless the regulation is discriminatory, oppressive or predatory.

§ 2—615
Excuse by Failure of Presupposed Conditions

Except so far as a seller may have assumed a greater obligation and subject to the preceding section on substituted performance:

(a) Delay in delivery or non-delivery in whole or in part by a seller who complies with paragraphs (b) and (c) is not a breach of his duty under a contract for sale if performance as agreed has been made impracticable by the occurrence of a contingency the non-occurrence of which was a basic assumption on which the contract was made or by compliance in good faith with any applicable foreign or domestic governmental regulation or order whether or not it later proves to be invalid.

(b) Where the causes mentioned in paragraph (a) affect only a part of the seller's capacity to perform, he must allocate production and deliveries among his customers but may at his option include regular customers not then under contract as well as his own requirements for further manufacture. He may so allocate in any manner which is fair and reasonable.

(c) The seller must notify the buyer seasonably that there will be delay or non-delivery and, when allocation is required under paragraph (b), of the estimated quota thus made available for the buyer.

§ 2—616
Procedure on Notice Claiming Excuse

(1) Where the buyer receives notification of a material or indefinite delay or an allocation justified under the preceding section he may by written notification to the seller as to any delivery concerned, and where the prospective deficiency substantially impairs the value of the whole contract under the provisions of this Article relating to breach of installment contracts (Section 2—612), then also as to the whole,

(a) terminate and thereby discharge any unexecuted portion of the contract; or

(b) modify the contract by agreeing to take his available quota in substitution.

(2) If after receipt of such notification from the seller the buyer fails so to modify the contract within a reasonable time not exceeding thirty days the contract lapses with respect to any deliveries affected.

(3) The provisions of this section may not be negated by agreement except in so far as the seller has assumed a greater obligation under the preceding section.

PART 7/Remedies

§ 2—701
Remedies for Breach of Collateral Contracts Not Impaired

Remedies for breach of any obligation or promise collateral or ancillary to a contract for sale are not impaired by the provisions of this Article.

§ 2—702
Seller's Remedies on Discovery of Buyer's Insolvency

(1) Where the seller discovers the buyer to be insolvent he may refuse delivery except for cash including payment for all goods theretofore delivered under the contract, and stop delivery under this Article (Section 2—705).

(2) Where the seller discovers that the buyer has received goods on credit while insolvent he may reclaim the goods upon demand made within ten days after the receipt, but if misrepresentation of solvency has been made to the particular seller in writing within three months before delivery the ten day limitation does not apply. Except as provided in this subsection the seller may not base a right to reclaim goods on the buyer's fraudulent or innocent misrepresentation of solvency or of intent to pay.

(3) The seller's right to reclaim under subsection (2) is subject to the rights of a buyer in ordinary course or other good faith purchaser under this Article (Section 2—403). Successful reclamation of goods excludes all other remedies with respect to them.

§ 2—703
Seller's Remedies in General

Where the buyer wrongfully rejects or revokes acceptance of goods or fails to make a payment due on or before delivery or repudiates with respect to a part or the whole, then with respect to any goods directly affected and, if the breach is of the whole contract (Section 2—612), then also with respect to the whole undelivered balance, the aggrieved seller may

(a) withhold delivery of such goods;

(b) stop delivery by any bailee as hereafter provided (Section 2—705);

(c) proceed under the next section respecting goods still unidentified to the contract;

(d) resell and recover damages as hereafter provided (Section 2—706);

(e) recover damages for non-acceptance (Section 2—708) or in a proper case the price (Section 2—709);

(f) cancel.

§ 2—704
Seller's Right to Identify Goods to the Contract Notwithstanding Breach or to Salvage Unfinished Goods

(1) An aggrieved seller under the preceding section may

(a) identify to the contract conforming goods not already identified if at the time he learned of the breach they are in his possession or control;

(b) treat as the subject of resale goods which have demonstrably been intended for the particular contract even though those goods are unfinished.

(2) Where the goods are unfinished an aggrieved seller may in the exercise of reasonable commercial judgment for the purposes of avoiding loss and of effective realization either complete the manufacture and wholly identify the goods to the contract or cease manufacture and resell for scrap or salvage value or proceed in any other reasonable manner.

§ 2—705
Seller's Stoppage of Delivery in Transit or Otherwise

(1) The seller may stop delivery of goods in the possession of a carrier or other bailee when he discovers the buyer to be insolvent (Section 2—702) and may stop delivery of carload, truckload, planeload or larger shipments of express or freight when the buyer repudiates or fails to make a payment due before delivery or if for any other reason the seller has a right to withhold or reclaim the goods.

(2) As against such buyer the seller may stop delivery until

(a) receipt of the goods by the buyer; or

(b) acknowledgment to the buyer by any bailee of the goods except a carrier that the bailee holds the goods for the buyer; or

(c) such acknowledgment to the buyer by a carrier by reshipment or as warehouseman; or

(d) negotiation to the buyer of any negotiable document of title covering the goods.

(3)(a) To stop delivery the seller must so notify as to enable the bailee by reasonable diligence to prevent delivery of the goods.

(b) After such notification the bailee must hold and deliver the goods according to the directions of the seller but the seller is liable to the bailee for any ensuing charges or damages.

(c) If a negotiable document of title has been issued for goods the bailee is not obliged to obey a notification to stop until surrender of the document.

(d) A carrier who has issued a non-negotiable bill of lading is not obliged to obey a notification to stop received from a person other than the consignor.

§ 2—706
Seller's Resale Including Contract for Resale

(1) Under the conditions stated in Section 2—703 on seller's remedies, the seller may resell the goods concerned or the undelivered balance thereof. Where the resale is made in good faith and in a commercially reasonable manner the seller may recover the difference between the resale price and the contract price together with any incidental damages allowed under the provisions of this Article (Section 2—710), but less expenses saved in consequence of the buyer's breach.

(2) Except as otherwise provided in subsection (3) or unless otherwise agreed resale may be at public or private sale including sale by way of one or more contracts to sell or of identification to an existing contract of the seller. Sale may be as a unit or in parcels and at any time and place and on any terms but every aspect of the sale including the method, manner, time, place and terms must be commercially reasonable. The resale must be reasonably identified as referring to the broken contract, but it is not necessary that the goods be in existence or that any or all of them have been identified to the contract before the breach.

(3) Where the resale is at private sale the seller must give the buyer reasonable notification of his intention to resell.

(4) Where the resale is at public sale

(a) only identified goods can be sold except where there is a recognized market for a public sale of futures in goods of the kind; and

(b) it must be made at a usual place or market for public sale if one is reasonably available and except in the case of goods which are perishable or threaten to decline in value speedily the seller must give the buyer reasonable notice of the time and place of the resale; and

(c) if the goods are not to be within the view of those attending the sale the notification of sale must state the place where the goods are located and provide for their reasonable inspection by prospective bidders; and

(d) the seller may buy.

(5) A purchaser who buys in good faith at a resale takes the goods free of any rights of the original buyer even though the seller fails to comply with one or more of the requirements of this section.

(6) The seller is not accountable to the buyer for any profit made on any resale. A person in the position of a seller (Section 2—707) or a buyer who has rightfully rejected or justifiably revoked acceptance must account for any excess over the amount of his security interest, as hereinafter defined (subsection (3) of Section 2—711).

§ 2—707
"Person in the Position of a Seller"

(1) A "person in the position of a seller" includes as against a principal an agent who has paid or become responsible for the price of goods on behalf of his principal or anyone who otherwise holds a security interest or other right in goods similar to that of a seller.

(2) A person in the position of a seller may as provided in this Article withhold or stop delivery (Section 2—705) and resell (Section 2—706) and recover incidental damages (Section 2—710).

§ 2—708
Seller's Damages for Non-Acceptance or Repudiation

(1) Subject to subsection (2) and to the provisions of this Article with respect to proof of market price (Section 2—723), the measure of damages for non-acceptance or repudiation by the buyer is the difference between the market price at the time and place for tender and the unpaid contract price together with any incidental damages provided in this Article (Section 2—710), but less expenses saved in consequence of the buyer's breach.

(2) If the measure of damages provided in subsection (1) is inadequate to put the seller in as good a position as performance would have done then the measure of damages is the profit (including reasonable overhead) which the seller would have made from full performance by the buyer, together with any incidental damages provided in this Article (Section 2—710), due allowance for costs reasonably incurred and due credit for payments or proceeds of resale.

§ 2—709
Action for the Price

(1) When the buyer fails to pay the price as it becomes due the seller may recover, together with any incidental damages under the next section, the price

(a) of goods accepted or of conforming goods lost or damaged within a commercially reasonable time after risk of their loss has passed to the buyer; and

(b) of goods identified to the contract if the seller is unable after reasonable effort to resell them at a reasonable price or the circumstances reasonably indicate that such effort will be unavailing.

(2) Where the seller sues for the price he must hold for the buyer any goods which have been identified to the contract and are still in his control except that if resale becomes possible he may resell them at any time prior to the collection of the judgment. The net proceeds of any such resale must be credited to the buyer and payment of the judgment entitles him to any goods not resold.

(3) After the buyer has wrongfully rejected or revoked acceptance of the goods or has failed to make a payment due or has repudiated (Section 2—610), a seller who is held not entitled to the price under this section shall nevertheless be awarded damages for non-acceptance under the preceding section.

§ 2—710
Seller's Incidental Damages

Incidental damages to an aggrieved seller include any commercially reasonable charges, expenses or commissions incurred in stopping delivery, in the transportation, care and custody of goods after the buyer's breach, in connection with return or resale of the goods or otherwise resulting from the breach.

§ 2—711
Buyer's Remedies in General; Buyer's Security Interest in Rejected Goods

(1) Where the seller fails to make delivery or repudiates or the buyer rightfully rejects or justifiably revokes acceptance then with respect to any goods involved, and with respect to the whole if the breach goes to the whole contract (Section 2—612), the buyer may cancel and whether or not he has done so may in addition to recovering so much of the price as has been paid

(a) "cover" and have damages under the next section as to all the goods affected whether or not they have been identified to the contract; or

(b) recover damages for non-delivery as provided in this Article (Section 2—713).

(2) Where the seller fails to deliver or repudiates the buyer may also

(a) if the goods have been identified recover them as provided in this Article (Section 2—502); or

(b) in a proper case obtain specific performance or replevy the goods as provided in this Article (Section 2—716).

(3) On rightful rejection or justifiable revocation of acceptance a buyer has a security interest in goods in his possession or control for any payments made on their price and any expenses reasonably incurred in their inspection, receipt, transportation, care and custody and may hold such goods and resell them in like manner as an aggrieved seller (Section 2—706).

§ 2—712
"Cover"; Buyer's Procurement of Substitute Goods

(1) After a breach within the preceding section the buyer may "cover" by making in good faith and without unreasonable delay any reasonable purchase of or contract to purchase goods in substitution for those due from the seller.

(2) The buyer may recover from the seller as damages the difference between the cost of cover and the contract price together with any incidental or consequential damages as hereinafter defined (Section 2—715), but less expenses saved in consequence of the seller's breach.

(3) Failure of the buyer to effect cover within this section does not bar him from any other remedy.

§ 2—713
Buyer's Damages for Non-Delivery or Repudiation

(1) Subject to the provisions of this Article with respect to proof of market price (Section 2—723), the measure of damages for non-delivery or repudiation by the seller is the difference between the market price at the time when the buyer learned of the breach and the contract price together with any incidental and consequential damages provided in this Article (Section 2—715), but less expenses saved in consequence of the seller's breach.

(2) Market price is to be determined as of the place for tender or, in cases of rejection after arrival or revocation of acceptance, as of the place of arrival.

§ 2—714
Buyer's Damages for Breach in Regard to Accepted Goods

(1) Where the buyer has accepted goods and given notification (subsection (3) of Section 2—607) he may recover as damages for any non-conformity of tender the loss resulting in the ordinary course of events from the seller's breach as determined in any manner which is reasonable.

(2) The measure of damages for breach of warranty is the difference at the time and place of acceptance between the value of the goods accepted and the value they would have had if they had been as warranted, unless special circumstances show proximate damages of a different amount.

(3) In a proper case any incidental and consequential damages under the next section may also be recovered.

§ 2—715
Buyer's Incidental and Consequential Damages

(1) Incidental damages resulting from the seller's breach include expenses reasonably incurred in inspection, receipt, transportation and care and custody of goods rightfully re-

jected, any commercially reasonable charges, expenses or commissions in connection with effecting cover and any other reasonable expense incident to the delay or other breach.

(2) Consequential damages resulting from the seller's breach include

(a) any loss resulting from general or particular requirements and needs of which the seller at the time of contracting had reason to know and which could not reasonably be prevented by cover or otherwise; and

(b) injury to person or property proximately resulting from any breach of warranty.

§ 2—716
Buyer's Right to Specific Performance or Replevin

(1) Specific performance may be decreed where the goods are unique or in other proper circumstances.

(2) The decree for specific performance may include such terms and conditions as to payment of the price, damages, or other relief as the court may deem just.

(3) The buyer has a right of replevin for goods identified to the contract if after reasonable effort he is unable to effect cover for such goods or the circumstances reasonably indicate that such effort will be unavailing or if the goods have been shipped under reservation and satisfaction of the security interest in them has been made or tendered.

§ 2—717
Deduction of Damages From the Price

The buyer on notifying the seller of his intention to do so may deduct all or any part of the damages resulting from any breach of the contract from any part of the price still due under the same contract.

§ 2—718
Liquidation or Limitation of Damages; Deposits

(1) Damages for breach by either party may be liquidated in the agreement but only at an amount which is reasonable in the light of the anticipated or actual harm caused by the breach, the difficulties of proof of loss, and the inconvenience or nonfeasibility of otherwise obtaining an adequate remedy. A term fixing unreasonably large liquidated damages is void as a penalty.

(2) Where the seller justifiably withholds delivery of goods because of the buyer's breach, the buyer is entitled to restitution of any amount by which the sum of his payments exceeds

(a) the amount to which the seller is entitled by virtue of terms liquidating the seller's damages in accordance with subsection (1), or

(b) in the absence of such terms, twenty per cent of the value of the total performance for which the buyer is obligated under the contract or $500, whichever is smaller.

(3) The buyer's right to restitution under subsection (2) is subject to offset to the extent that the seller establishes

(a) a right to recover damages under the provisions of this Article other than subsection (1), and

(b) the amount or value of any benefits received by the buyer directly or indirectly by reason of the contract.

(4) Where a seller has received payment in goods their reasonable value or the proceeds of their resale shall be treated as payments for the purposes of subsection (2); but if the seller has notice of the buyer's breach before reselling goods received in part performance, his resale is subject to the conditions laid down in this Article on resale by an aggrieved seller (Section 2—706).

§ 2—719
Contractual Modification or Limitation of Remedy

(1) Subject to the provisions of subsections (2) and (3) of this section and of the preceding section on liquidation and limitation of damages,

(a) the agreement may provide for remedies in addition to or in substitution for those provided in this Article and may limit or alter the measure of damages recoverable under this Article, as by limiting the buyer's remedies to return of the goods and repayment of the price or to repair and replacement of non-conforming goods or parts; and

(b) resort to a remedy as provided is optional unless the remedy is expressly agreed to be exclusive, in which case it is the sole remedy.

(2) Where circumstances cause an exclusive or limited remedy to fail of its essential purpose, remedy may be had as provided in this Act.

(3) Consequential damages may be limited or excluded unless the limitation or exclusion is unconscionable. Limitation of consequential damages for injury to the person in the case of consumer goods is prima facie unconscionable but limitation of damages where the loss is commercial is not.

§ 2—720
Effect of "Cancellation" or "Rescission" on Claims for Antecedent Breach

Unless the contrary intention clearly appears, expressions of "cancellation" or "rescission" of the contract or the like shall not be construed as a renunciation or discharge of any claim in damages for an antecedent breach.

§ 2—721
Remedies for Fraud

Remedies for material misrepresentation or fraud include all remedies available under this Article for non-fraudulent breach. Neither rescission or a claim for rescission of the contract for sale nor rejection or return of the goods shall bar or be deemed inconsistent with a claim for damages or other remedy.

§ 2—722
Who Can Sue Third Parties for Injury to Goods

Where a third party so deals with goods which have been identified to a contract for sale as to cause actionable injury to a party to that contract

(a) a right of action against the third party is in either party to the contract for sale who has title to or a security interest or a special property or an insurable interest in the goods; and if the goods have been destroyed or converted a right of action is also in the party who either bore the risk of loss under the contract for sale or has since the injury assumed that risk as against the other;

(b) if at the time of the injury the party plaintiff did not bear the risk of loss as against the other party to the contract for sale and there is no arrangement between them for disposition of the recovery, his suit or settlement is, subject to his own interest, as a fiduciary for the other party to the contract;

(c) either party may with the consent of the other sue for the benefit of whom it may concern.

§ 2—723
Proof of Market Price: Time and Place

(1) If an action based on anticipatory repudiation comes to trial before the time for performance with respect to some or all of the goods, any damages based on market price (Section 2—708 or Section 2—713) shall be determined according to the price of such goods prevailing at the time when the aggrieved party learned of the repudiation.

(2) If evidence of a price prevailing at the times or places described in this Article is not readily available the price prevailing within any reasonable time before or after the time described or at any other place which in commercial judgment or under usage of trade would serve as a reasonable substitute for the one described may be used, making any proper allowance for the cost of transporting the goods to or from such other place.

(3) Evidence of a relevant price prevailing at a time or place other than the one described in this Article offered by one party is not admissible unless and until he has given the other party such notice as the court finds sufficient to prevent unfair surprise.

§ 2—724
Admissibility of Market Quotations

Whenever the prevailing price or value of any goods regularly bought and sold in any established commodity market is in issue, reports in official publications or trade journals or in newspapers or periodicals of general circulation published as the reports of such market shall be admissible in evidence. The circumstances of the preparation of such a report may be shown to affect its weight but not its admissibility.

§ 2—725
Statute of Limitations in Contracts for Sale

(1) An action for breach of any contract for sale must be commenced within four years after the cause of action has accrued. By the original agreement the parties may reduce the period of limitation to not less than one year but may not extend it.

(2) A cause of action accrues when the breach occurs, regardless of the aggrieved party's lack of knowledge of the breach. A breach of warranty occurs when tender of delivery is made, except that where a warranty explicitly extends to future performance of the goods and discovery of the breach must await the time of such performance the cause of action accrues when the breach is or should have been discovered.

(3) Where an action commenced within the time limited by subsection (1) is so terminated as to leave available a remedy by another action for the same breach such other action may be commenced after the expiration of the time limited and within six months after the termination of the first action unless the termination resulted from voluntary discontinuance or from dismissal for failure or neglect to prosecute.

(4) This section does not alter the law on tolling of the statute of limitations nor does it apply to causes of action which have accrued before this Act becomes effective.

ARTICLE 3/Commercial Paper

PART 1/Short Title, Form and Interpretation

§ 3—101
Short Title

This Article shall be known and may be cited as Uniform Commercial Code—Commercial Paper.

§ 3—102
Definitions and Index of Definitions

(1) In this Article unless the context otherwise requires

(a) "Issue" means the first delivery of an instrument to a holder or a remitter.

(b) An "order" is a direction to pay and must be more than an authorization or request. It must identify the person to pay with reasonable certainty. It may be addressed to one or more such persons jointly or in the alternative but not in succession.

(c) A "promise" is an undertaking to pay and must be more than an acknowledgment of an obligation.

(d) "Secondary party" means a drawer or endorser.

(e) "Instrument" means a negotiable instrument.

(2) Other definitions applying to this Article and the sections in which they appear are:

"Acceptance". Section 3—410.

"Accommodation party". Section 3—415.

"Alteration". Section 3—407.

"Certificate of deposit". Section 3—104.

"Certification". Section 3—411.

"Check". Section 3—104.

"Definite time". Section 3—109.

"Dishonor". Section 3—507.

"Draft". Section 3—104.

"Holder in due course". Section 3—302.

"Negotiation". Section 3—202.

"Note". Section 3—104.

"Notice of dishonor". Section 3—508.

"On demand". Section 3—108.

"Presentment". Section 3—504.

"Protest". Section 3—509.

"Restrictive Indorsement". Section 3—205.

"Signature". Section 3—401.

(3) The following definitions in other Articles apply to this Article:

"Account". Section 4—104.

"Banking Day". Section 4—104.

"Clearing House". Section 4—104.

"Collecting Bank". Section 4—105.

"Customer". Section 4—104.

"Depositary Bank". Section 4—105.

"Documentary Draft". Section 4—104.

"Intermediary Bank". Section 4—105.

"Item". Section 4—104.

"Midnight deadline". Section 4—104.

"Payor Bank". Section 4—105.

(4) In addition Article 1 contains general definitions and principles of construction and interpretation applicable throughout this Article.

§ 3—103
Limitations on Scope of Article

(1) This Article does not apply to money, documents of title or investment securities.

(2) The provisions of this Article are subject to the provisions of the Article on Bank Deposits and Collections (Article 4) and Secured Transactions (Article 9).

§ 3—104
Form of Negotiable Instruments; "Draft"; "Check"; "Certificate of Deposit"; "Note"

(1) Any writing to be a negotiable instrument within this Article must

(a) be signed by the maker or drawer; and

(b) contain an unconditional promise or order to pay a sum certain in money and no other promise, order, obligation or power given by the maker or drawer except as authorized by this Article; and

(c) be payable on demand or at a definite time; and

(d) be payable to order or to bearer.

(2) A writing which complies with the requirements of this section is

(a) a "draft" ("bill of exchange") if it is an order;

(b) a "check" if it is a draft drawn on a bank and payable on demand;

(c) a "certificate of deposit" if it is an acknowledgment by a bank of receipt of money with an engagement to repay it;

(d) a "note" if it is a promise other than a certificate of deposit.

(3) As used in other Articles of this Act, and as the context may require, the terms "draft", "check", "certificate of deposit" and "note" may refer to instruments which are not negotiable within this Article as well as to instruments which are so negotiable.

§ 3—105
When Promise or Order Unconditional

(1) A promise or order otherwise unconditional is not made conditional by the fact that the instrument

(a) is subject to implied or constructive conditions; or

(b) states its consideration, whether performed or promised, or the transaction which gave rise to the instrument, or that the promise or order is made or the instrument matures in accordance with or "as per" such transaction; or

(c) refers to or states that it arises out of a separate agreement or refers to a separate agreement for rights as to prepayment or acceleration; or

(d) states that it is drawn under a letter of credit; or

(e) states that it is secured, whether by mortgage, reservation of title or otherwise; or

(f) indicates a particular account to be debited or any other fund or source from which reimbursement is expected; or

(g) is limited to payment out of a particular fund or the proceeds of a particular source, if the instrument is issued by a government or governmental agency or unit; or

(h) is limited to payment out of the entire assets of a partnership, unincorporated association, trust or estate by or on behalf of which the instrument is issued.

(2) A promise or order is not unconditional if the instrument

(a) states that it is subject to or governed by any other agreement; or

(b) states that it is to be paid only out of a particular fund or source except as provided in this section.

§ 3—106
Sum Certain

(1) The sum payable is a sum certain even though it is to be paid

(a) with stated interest or by stated installments; or

(b) with stated different rates of interest before and after default or a specified date; or

(c) with a stated discount or addition if paid before or after the date fixed for payment; or

(d) with exchange or less exchange, whether at a fixed rate or at the current rate; or

(e) with costs of collection or an attorney's fee or both upon default.

(2) Nothing in this section shall validate any term which is otherwise illegal.

§ 3—107
Money

(1) An instrument is payable in money if the medium of exchange in which it is payable is money at the time the instrument is made. An instrument payable in "currency" or "current funds" is payable in money.

(2) A promise or order to pay a sum stated in a foreign currency is for a sum certain in money and, unless a different medium of payment is specified in the instrument, may be satisfied by payment of that number of dollars which the stated foreign currency will purchase at the buying sight rate for that currency on the day on which the instrument is payable or, if payable on demand, on the day of demand. If such an instrument specifies a foreign currency as the medium of payment the instrument is payable in that currency.

§ 3—108
Payable on Demand

Instruments payable on demand include those payable at sight or on presentation and those in which no time for payment is stated.

§ 3—109
Definite Time

(1) An instrument is payable at a definite time if by its terms it is payable

(a) on or before a stated date or at a fixed period after a stated date; or

(b) at a fixed period after sight; or

(c) at a definite time subject to any acceleration; or

(d) at a definite time subject to extension at the option of the holder, or to extension to a further definite time at the option of the maker or acceptor or automatically upon or after a specified act or event.

(2) An instrument which by its terms is otherwise payable only upon an act or event uncertain as to time of occurrence is not payable at a definite time even though the act or event has occurred.

§ 3—110
Payable to Order

(1) An instrument is payable to order when by its terms it is payable to the order or assigns of any person therein specified with reasonable certainty, or to him or his order, or when it is conspicuously designated on its face as "exchange" or the like and names a payee. It may be payable to the order of

(a) the maker or drawer; or

(b) the drawee; or

(c) a payee who is not maker, drawer or drawee; or

(d) two or more payees together or in the alternative; or

(e) an estate, trust or fund, in which case it is payable to the order of the representative of such estate, trust or fund or his successors; or

(f) an office, or an officer by his title as such in which case it is payable to the principal but the incumbent of the office or his successors may act as if he or they were the holder; or

(g) a partnership or unincorporated association, in which case it is payable to the partnership or association and may be indorsed or transferred by any person thereto authorized.

(2) An instrument not payable to order is not made so payable by such words as "payable upon return of this instrument properly indorsed."

(3) An instrument made payable both to order and to bearer is payable to order unless the bearer words are handwritten or typewritten.

§ 3—111
Payable to Bearer

An instrument is payable to bearer when by its terms it is payable to

(a) bearer or the order of bearer; or

(b) a specified person or bearer; or

(c) "cash" or the order of "cash", or any other indication which does not purport to designate a specific payee.

§ 3—112
Terms and Omissions Not Affecting Negotiability

(1) The negotiability of an instrument is not affected by

(a) the omission of a statement of any consideration or of the place where the instrument is drawn or payable; or

(b) a statement that collateral has been given to secure obligations either on the instrument or otherwise of an obligor on the instrument or that in case of default on those obligations the holder may realize on or dispose of the collateral; or

(c) a promise or power to maintain or protect collateral or to give additional collateral; or

(d) a term authorizing a confession of judgment on the instrument if it is not paid when due; or

(e) a term purporting to waive the benefit of any law intended for the advantage or protection of any obligor; or

(f) a term in a draft providing that the payee by indorsing or cashing it acknowledges full satisfaction of an obligation of the drawer; or

(g) a statement in a draft drawn in a set of parts (Section 3—801) to the effect that the order is effective only if no other part has been honored.

(2) Nothing in this section shall validate any term which is otherwise illegal.

§ 3—113
Seal

An instrument otherwise negotiable is within this Article even though it is under a seal.

§ 3—114
Date, Antedating, Postdating

(1) The negotiability of an instrument is not affected by the fact that it is undated, antedated or postdated.

(2) Where an instrument is antedated or postdated the time when it is payable is determined by the stated date if the instrument is payable on demand or at a fixed period after date.

(3) Where the instrument or any signature thereon is dated, the date is presumed to be correct.

§ 3—115
Incomplete Instruments

(1) When a paper whose contents at the time of signing show that it is intended to become an instrument is signed while still incomplete in any necessary respect it cannot be

enforced until completed, but when it is completed in accordance with authority given it is effective as completed.

(2) If the completion is unauthorized the rules as to material alteration apply (Section 3—407), even though the paper was not delivered by the maker or drawer; but the burden of establishing that any completion is unauthorized is on the party so asserting.

§ 3—116
Instruments Payable to
Two or More Persons

An instrument payable to the order of two or more persons

(a) if in the alternative is payable to any one of them and may be negotiated, discharged or enforced by any of them who has possession of it;

(b) if not in the alternative is payable to all of them and may be negotiated, discharged or enforced only by all of them.

§ 3—117
Instruments Payable With
Words of Description

An instrument made payable to a named person with the addition of words describing him

(a) as agent or officer of a specified person is payable to his principal but the agent or officer may act as if he were the holder;

(b) as any other fiduciary for a specified person or purpose is payable to the payee and may be negotiated, discharged or enforced by him;

(c) in any other manner is payable to the payee unconditionally and the additional words are without effect on subsequent parties.

§ 3—118
Ambiguous Terms and
Rules of Construction

The following rules apply to every instrument:

(a) Where there is doubt whether the instrument is a draft or a note the holder may treat it as either. A draft drawn on the drawer is effective as a note.

(b) Handwritten terms control typewritten and printed terms, and typewritten control printed.

(c) Words control figures except that if the words are ambiguous figures control.

(d) Unless otherwise specified a provision for interest means interest at the judgment rate at the place of payment from the date of the instrument, or if it is undated from the date of issue.

(e) Unless the instrument otherwise specifies two or more persons who sign as maker, acceptor or drawer or indorser and as a part of the same transaction are jointly

and severally liable even though the instrument contains such words as "I promise to pay."

(f) Unless otherwise specified consent to extension authorizes a single extension for not longer than the original period. A consent to extension, expressed in the instrument, is binding on secondary parties and accommodation makers. A holder may not exercise his option to extend an instrument over the objection of a maker or acceptor or other party who in accordance with Section 3—604 tenders full payment when the instrument is due.

§ 3—119
Other Writings Affecting Instrument

(1) As between the obligor and his immediate obligee or any transferee the terms of an instrument may be modified or affected by any other written agreement executed as a part of the same transaction, except that a holder in due course is not affected by any limitation of his rights arising out of the separate written agreement if he had no notice of the limitation when he took the instrument.

(2) A separate agreement does not affect the negotiability of an instrument.

§ 3—120
Instruments "Payable Through" Bank

An instrument which states that it is "payable through" a bank or the like designates that bank as a collecting bank to make presentment but does not of itself authorize the bank to pay the instrument.

§ 3—121
Instruments Payable at Bank

Note: *If this Act is introduced in the Congress of the United States this section should be omitted.*

(States to select either alternative)

Alternative A

A note or acceptance which states that it is payable at a bank is the equivalent of a draft drawn on the bank payable when it falls due out of any funds of the maker or acceptor in current account or otherwise available for such payment.

Alternative B

A note or acceptance which states that it is payable at a bank is not of itself an order or authorization to the bank to pay it.

§ 3—122
Accrual of Cause of Action

(1) A cause of action against a maker or an acceptor accrues

(a) in the case of a time instrument on the day after maturity;

(b) in the case of a demand instrument upon its date or, if no date is stated, on the date of issue.

(2) A cause of action against the obligor of a demand or time certificate of deposit accrues upon demand, but demand on a time certificate may not be made until on or after the date of maturity.

(3) A cause of action against a drawer of a draft or an indorser of any instrument accrues upon demand following dishonor of the instrument. Notice of dishonor is a demand.

(4) Unless an instrument provides otherwise, interest runs at the rate provided by law for a judgment

> (a) in the case of a maker, acceptor or other primary obligor of a demand instrument, from the date of demand;

> (b) in all other cases from the date of accrual of the cause of action.

PART 2/Transfer and Negotiation

§ 3—201
Transfer: Right to Indorsement

(1) Transfer of an instrument vests in the transferee such rights as the transferor has therein, except that a transferee who has himself been a party to any fraud or illegality affecting the instrument or who as a prior holder had notice of a defense or claim against it cannot improve his position by taking from a later holder in due course.

(2) A transfer of a security interest in an instrument vests the foregoing rights in the transferee to the extent of the interest transferred.

(3) Unless otherwise agreed any transfer for value of an instrument not then payable to bearer gives the transferee the specifically enforceable right to have the unqualified indorsement of the transferor. Negotiation takes effect only when the indorsement is made and until that time there is no presumption that the transferee is the owner.

§ 3—202
Negotiation

(1) Negotiation is the transfer of an instrument in such form that the transferee becomes a holder. If the instrument is payable to order it is negotiated by delivery with any necessary indorsement; if payable to bearer it is negotiated by delivery.

(2) An indorsement must be written by or on behalf of the holder and on the instrument or on a paper so firmly affixed thereto as to become a part thereof.

(3) An indorsement is effective for negotiation only when it conveys the entire instrument or any unpaid residue. If it purports to be of less it operates only as a partial assignment.

(4) Words of assignment, condition, waiver, guaranty, limitation or disclaimer of liability and the like accompanying an indorsement do not affect its character as an indorsement.

§ 3—203
Wrong or Misspelled Name

Where an instrument is made payable to a person under a misspelled name or one other than his own he may indorse in that name or his own or both; but signature in both names may be required by a person paying or giving value for the instrument.

§ 3—204
Special Indorsement; Blank Indorsement

(1) A special indorsement specifies the person to whom or to whose order it makes the instrument payable. Any instrument specially indorsed becomes payable to the order of the special indorsee and may be further negotiated only by his indorsement.

(2) An indorsement in blank specifies no particular indorsee and may consist of a mere signature. An instrument payable to order and indorsed in blank becomes payable to bearer and may be negotiated by delivery alone until specially indorsed.

(3) The holder may convert a blank indorsement into a special indorsement by writing over the signature of the indorser in blank any contract consistent with the character of the indorsement.

§ 3—205
Restrictive Indorsements

An indorsement is restrictive which either

> (a) is conditional; or

> (b) purports to prohibit further transfer of the instrument; or

> (c) includes the words "for collection", "for deposit", "pay any bank", or like terms signifying a purpose of deposit or collection; or

> (d) otherwise states that it is for the benefit or use of the indorser or of another person.

§ 3—206
Effect of Restrictive Indorsement

(1) No restrictive indorsement prevents further transfer or negotiation of the instrument.

(2) An intermediary bank, or a payor bank which is not the depositary bank, is neither given notice nor otherwise affected by a restrictive indorsement of any person except the bank's immediate transferor or the person presenting for payment.

(3) Except for an intermediary bank, any transferee under an indorsement which is conditional or includes the words "for collection", "for deposit", "pay any bank", or like terms (subparagraphs (a) and (c) of Section 3—205) must pay or apply any value given by him for or on the security of the instrument consistently with the indorsement and to the

extent that he does so he becomes a holder for value. In addition such transferee is a holder in due course if he otherwise complies with the requirements of Section 3—302 on what constitutes a holder in due course.

(4) The first taker under an indorsement for the benefit of the indorser or another person (subparagraph (d) of Section 3—205) must pay or apply any value given by him for or on the security of the instrument consistently with the indorsement and to the extent that he does so he becomes a holder for value. In addition such taker is a holder in due course if he otherwise complies with the requirements of Section 3—302 on what constitutes a holder in due course. A later holder for value is neither given notice nor otherwise affected by such restrictive indorsement unless he has knowledge that a fiduciary or other person has negotiated the instrument in any transaction for his own benefit or otherwise in breach of duty (subsection (2) of Section 3—304).

§ 3—207
Negotiation Effective Although It May Be Rescinded

(1) Negotiation is effective to transfer the instrument although the negotiation is

(a) made by an infant, a corporation exceeding its powers, or any other person without capacity; or

(b) obtained by fraud, duress or mistake of any kind; or

(c) part of an illegal transaction; or

(d) made in breach of duty.

(2) Except as against a subsequent holder in due course such negotiation is in an appropriate case subject to rescission, the declaration of a constructive trust or any other remedy permitted by law.

§ 3—208
Reacquisition

Where an instrument is returned to or reacquired by a prior party he may cancel any indorsement which is not necessary to his title and reissue or further negotiate the instrument, but any intervening party is discharged as against the reacquiring party and subsequent holders not in due course and if his indorsement has been cancelled is discharged as against subsequent holders in due course as well.

PART 3/Rights of a Holder

§ 3—301
Rights of a Holder

The holder of an instrument whether or not he is the owner may transfer or negotiate it and, except as otherwise provided in Section 3—603 on payment or satisfaction, discharge it or enforce payment in his own name.

§ 3—302
Holder in Due Course

(1) A holder in due course is a holder who takes the instrument

(a) for value; and

(b) in good faith; and

(c) without notice that it is overdue or has been dishonored or of any defense against or claim to it on the part of any person.

(2) A payee may be a holder in due course.

(3) A holder does not become a holder in due course of an instrument:

(a) by purchase of it at judicial sale or by taking it under legal process; or

(b) by acquiring it in taking over an estate; or

(c) by purchasing it as part of a bulk transaction not in regular course of business of the transferor.

(4) A purchase of a limited interest can be a holder in due course only to the extent of the interest purchased.

§ 3—303
Taking for Value

A holder takes the instrument for value

(a) to the extent that the agreed consideration has been performed or that he acquires a security interest in or a lien on the instrument otherwise than by legal process; or

(b) when he takes the instrument in payment of or as security for an antecedent claim against any person whether or not the claim is due; or

(c) when he gives a negotiable instrument for it or makes an irrevocable commitment to a third person.

§ 3—304
Notice to Purchaser

(1) The purchaser has notice of a claim or defense if

(a) the instrument is so incomplete, bears such visible evidence of forgery or alteration, or is otherwise so irregular as to call into question its validity, terms or ownership or to create an ambiguity as to the party to pay; or

(b) the purchaser has notice that the obligation of any party is voidable in whole or in part, or that all parties have been discharged.

(2) The purchaser has notice of a claim against the instrument when he has knowledge that a fiduciary has negotiated the instrument in payment of or as security for his own debt or in any transaction for his own benefit or otherwise in breach of duty.

(3) The purchaser has notice that an instrument is overdue if he has reason to know

(a) that any part of the principal amount is overdue or that there is an uncured default in payment of another instrument of the same series; or

(b) that acceleration of the instrument has been made; or

(c) that he is taking a demand instrument after demand has been made or more than a reasonable length of time after its issue. A reasonable time for a check drawn and payable within the states and territories of the United States and the District of Columbia is presumed to be thirty days.

(4) Knowledge of the following facts does not of itself give the purchaser notice of a defense or claim

(a) that the instrument is antedated or postdated;

(b) that it was issued or negotiated in return for an executory promise or accompanied by a separate agreement, unless the purchaser has notice that a defense or claim has arisen from the terms thereof;

(c) that any party has signed for accommodation;

(d) that an incomplete instrument has been completed, unless the purchaser has notice of any improper completion;

(e) that any person negotiating the instrument is or was a fiduciary;

(f) that there has been default in payment of interest on the instrument or in payment of any other instrument, except one of the same series.

(5) The filing or recording of a document does not of itself constitute notice within the provisions of this Article to a person who would otherwise be a holder in due course.

(6) To be effective notice must be received at such time and in such manner as to give a reasonable opportunity to act on it.

§ 3—305
Rights of a Holder in Due Course

To the extent that a holder is a holder in due course he takes the instrument free from

(1) all claims to it on the part of any person; and

(2) all defenses of any party to the instrument with whom the holder has not dealt except

(a) infancy, to the extent that it is a defense to a simple contract; and

(b) such other incapacity, or duress, or illegality of the transaction, as renders the obligation of the party a nullity; and

(c) such misrepresentation as has induced the party to sign the instrument with neither knowledge nor reasonable opportunity to obtain knowledge of its character or its essential terms; and

(d) discharge in insolvency proceedings; and

(e) any other discharge of which the holder has notice when he takes the instrument.

§ 3—306
Rights of One Not Holder in Due Course

Unless he has the rights of a holder in due course any person takes the instrument subject to

(a) all valid claims to it on the part of any person; and

(b) all defenses of any party which would be available in an action on a simple contract; and

(c) the defenses of want or failure of consideration, nonperformance of any condition precedent, non-delivery, or delivery for a special purpose (Section 3—408); and

(d) the defense that he or a person through whom he holds the instrument acquired it by theft, or that payment or satisfaction to such holder would be inconsistent with the terms of a restrictive indorsement. The claim of any third person to the instrument is not otherwise available as a defense to any party liable thereon unless the third person himself defends the action for such party.

§ 3—307
Burden of Establishing Signatures, Defenses and Due Course

(1) Unless specifically denied in the pleadings each signature on an instrument is admitted. When the effectiveness of a signature is put in issue

(a) the burden of establishing it is on the party claiming under the signature; but

(b) the signature is presumed to be genuine or authorized except where the action is to enforce the obligation of a purported signer who has died or become incompetent before proof is required.

(2) When signatures are admitted or established, production of the instrument entitles a holder to recover on it unless the defendant establishes a defense.

(3) After it is shown that a defense exists a person claiming the rights of a holder in due course has the burden of establishing that he or some person under whom he claims is in all respects a holder in due course.

PART 4/Liability of Parties

§ 3—401
Signature

(1) No person is liable on an instrument unless his signature appears thereon.

(2) A signature is made by use of any name, including any trade or assumed name, upon an instrument, or by any word or mark used in lieu of a written signature.

§ 3—402
Signature in Ambiguous Capacity

Unless the instrument clearly indicates that a signature is made in some other capacity it is an indorsement.

§ 3—403
Signature by Authorized Representative

(1) A signature may be made by an agent or other representative, and his authority to make it may be established as in other cases of representation. No particular form of appointment is necessary to establish such authority.

(2) An authorized representative who signs his own name to an instrument

(a) is personally obligated if the instrument neither names the person represented nor shows that the representative signed in a representative capacity;

(b) except as otherwise established between the immediate parties, is personally obligated if the instrument names the person represented but does not show that the representative signed in a representative capacity, or if the instrument does not name the person represented but does show that the representative signed in a representative capacity.

(3) Except as otherwise established the name of an organization preceded or followed by the name and office of an authorized individual is a signature made in a representative capacity.

§ 3—404
Unauthorized Signatures

(1) Any unauthorized signature is wholly inoperative as that of the person whose name is signed unless he ratifies it or is precluded from denying it; but it operates as the signature of the unauthorized signer in favor of any person who in good faith pays the instrument or takes it for value.

(2) Any unauthorized signature may be ratified for all purposes of this Article. Such ratification does not of itself affect any rights of the person ratifying against the actual signer.

§ 3—405
Impostors; Signature in Name of Payee

(1) An indorsement by any person in the name of a named payee is effective if

(a) an impostor by use of the mails or otherwise has induced the maker or drawer to issue the instrument to him or his confederate in the name of the payee; or

(b) a person signing as or on behalf of a maker or drawer intends the payee to have no interest in the instrument; or

(c) an agent or employee of the maker or drawer has supplied him with the name of the payee intending the latter to have no such interest.

(2) Nothing in this section shall affect the criminal or civil liability of the person so indorsing.

§ 3—406
Negligence Contributing to Alteration or Unauthorized Signature

Any person who by his negligence substantially contributes to a material alteration of the instrument or to the making of an unauthorized signature is precluded from asserting the alteration or lack of authority against a holder in due course or against a drawee or other payor who pays the instrument in good faith and in accordance with the reasonable commercial standards of the drawee's or payor's business.

§ 3—407
Alteration

(1) Any alteration of an instrument is material which changes the contract of any party thereto in any respect, including any such change in

(a) the number or relations of the parties; or

(b) an incomplete instrument, by completing it otherwise than as authorized; or

(c) the writing as signed, by adding to it or by removing any part of it.

(2) As against any person other than a subsequent holder in due course

(a) alteration by the holder which is both fraudulent and material discharges any party whose contract is thereby changed unless that party assents or is precluded from asserting the defense;

(b) no other alteration discharges any party and the instrument may be enforced according to its original tenor, or as to incomplete instruments according to the authority given.

(3) A subsequent holder in due course may in all cases enforce the instrument according to its original tenor, and when an incomplete instrument has been completed, he may enforce it as completed.

§ 3—408
Consideration

Want or failure of consideration is a defense as against any person not having the rights of a holder in due course (Section 3—305), except that no consideration is necessary for an instrument or obligation thereon given in payment of or as security for an antecedent obligation of any kind. Nothing in this section shall be taken to displace any statute outside this Act under which a promise is enforceable notwithstanding lack or failure of consideration. Partial failure of consideration is a defense pro tanto whether or not the failure is in an ascertained or liquidated amount.

§ 3—409
Draft Not an Assignment

(1) A check or other draft does not of itself operate as an assignment of any funds in the hands of the drawee available for its payment, and the drawee is not liable on the instrument until he accepts it.

(2) Nothing in this section shall affect any liability in contract, tort, or otherwise arising from any letter of credit or other obligation or representation which is not an acceptance.

§ 3—410
Definition and Operation of Acceptance

(1) Acceptance is the drawee's signed engagement to honor the draft as presented. It must be written on the draft, and may consist of his signature alone. It becomes operative when completed by delivery or notification.

(2) A draft may be accepted although it has not been signed by the drawer or is otherwise incomplete or is overdue or has been dishonored.

(3) Where the draft is payable at a fixed period after sight and the acceptor fails to date his acceptance the holder may complete it by supplying a date in good faith.

§ 3—411
Certification of a Check

(1) Certification of a check is acceptance. Where a holder procures certification the drawer and all prior indorsers are discharged.

(2) Unless otherwise agreed a bank has no obligation to certify a check.

(3) A bank may certify a check before returning it for lack of proper indorsement. If it does so the drawer is discharged.

§ 3—412
Acceptance Varying Draft

(1) Where the drawee's proffered acceptance in any manner varies the draft as presented the holder may refuse the acceptance and treat the draft as dishonored in which case the drawee is entitled to have his acceptance cancelled.

(2) The terms of the draft are not varied by an acceptance to pay at any particular bank or place in the United States, unless the acceptance states that the draft is to be paid only at such bank or place.

(3) Where the holder assents to an acceptance varying the terms of the draft each drawer and indorser who does not affirmatively assent is discharged.

§ 3—413
Contract of Maker, Drawer and Acceptor

(1) The maker or acceptor engages that he will pay the instrument according to its tenor at the time of his engage-ment or as completed pursuant to Section 3—115 on incomplete instruments.

(2) The drawer engages that upon dishonor of the draft and any necessary notice of dishonor or protest he will pay the amount of the draft to the holder or to any indorser who takes it up. The drawer may disclaim this liability by drawing without recourse.

(3) By making, drawing or accepting the party admits as against all subsequent parties including the drawee the existence of the payee and his then capacity to indorse.

§ 3—414
Contract of Indorser; Order of Liability

(1) Unless the indorsement otherwise specifies (as by such words as "without recourse") every indorser engages that upon dishonor and any necessary notice of dishonor and protest he will pay the instrument according to its tenor at the time of his indorsement to the holder or to any subsequent indorser who takes it up, even though the indorser who takes it up was not obligated to do so.

(2) Unless they otherwise agree indorsers are liable to one another in the order in which they indorse, which is presumed to be the order in which their signatures appear on the instrument.

§ 3—415
Contract of Accommodation Party

(1) An accommodation party is one who signs the instrument in any capacity for the purpose of lending his name to another party to it.

(2) When the instrument has been taken for value before it is due the accommodation party is liable in the capacity in which he has signed even though the taker knows of the accommodation.

(3) As against a holder in due course and without notice of the accommodation oral proof of the accommodation is not admissible to give the accommodation party the benefit of discharges dependent on his character as such. In other cases the accommodation character may be shown by oral proof.

(4) An indorsement which shows that it is not in the chain of title is notice of its accommodation character.

(5) An accommodation party is not liable to the party accommodated, and if he pays the instrument has a right of recourse on the instrument against such party.

§ 3—416
Contract of Guarantor

(1) "Payment guaranteed" or equivalent words added to a signature mean that the signer engages that if the instrument is not paid when due he will pay it according to its tenor without resort by the holder to any other party.

(2) "Collection guaranteed" or equivalent words added to a signature mean that the signer engages that if the instrument

is not paid when due he will pay it according to its tenor, but only after the holder has reduced his claim against the maker or acceptor to judgment and execution has been returned unsatisfied, or after the maker or acceptor has become insolvent or it is otherwise apparent that it is useless to proceed against him.

(3) Words of guaranty which do not otherwise specify guarantee payment.

(4) No words of guaranty added to the signature of a sole maker or acceptor affect his liability on the instrument. Such words added to the signature of one or two or more makers or acceptors create a presumption that the signature is for the accommodation of the others.

(5) When words of guaranty are used presentment, notice of dishonor and protest are not necessary to charge the user.

(6) Any guaranty written on the instrument is enforceable notwithstanding any statute of frauds.

§ 3—417
Warranties on Presentment and Transfer

(1) Any person who obtains payment or acceptance and any prior transferor warrants to a person who in good faith pays or accepts that

    (a) he has a good title to the instrument or is authorized to obtain payment or acceptance on behalf of one who has a good title; and

    (b) he has no knowledge that the signature of the maker or drawer is unauthorized, except that this warranty is not given by a holder in due course acting in good faith

        (i) to a maker with respect to the maker's own signature; or

        (ii) to a drawer with respect to the drawer's own signature, whether or not the drawer is also the drawee; or

        (iii) to an acceptor of a draft if the holder in due course took the draft after the acceptance or obtained the acceptance without knowledge that the drawer's signature was unauthorized; and

    (c) the instrument has not been materially altered, except that this warranty is not given by a holder in due course acting in good faith

        (i) to the maker of a note; or

        (ii) to the drawer of a draft whether or not the drawer is also the drawee; or

        (iii) to the acceptor of a draft with respect to an alteration made prior to the acceptance if the holder in due course took the draft after the acceptance, even though the acceptance provided "payable as originally drawn" or equivalent terms; or

        (iv) to the acceptor of a draft with respect to an alteration made after the acceptance.

(2) Any person who transfers an instrument and receives consideration warrants to his transferee and if the transfer is by indorsement to any subsequent holder who takes the instrument in good faith that

    (a) he has a good title to the instrument or is authorized to obtain payment or acceptance on behalf of one who has a good title and the transfer is otherwise rightful; and

    (b) all signatures are genuine or authorized; and

    (c) the instrument has not been materially altered; and

    (d) no defense of any party is good against him; and

    (e) he has no knowledge of any insolvency proceeding instituted with respect to the maker or acceptor or the drawer of an unaccepted instrument.

(3) By transferring "without recourse" the transferor limits the obligation stated in subsection (2)(d) to a warranty that he has no knowledge of such a defense.

(4) A selling agent or broker who does not disclose the fact that he is acting only as such gives the warranties provided in this section, but if he makes such disclosure warrants only his good faith and authority.

§ 3—418
Finality of Payment or Acceptance

Except for recovery of bank payments as provided in the Article on Bank Deposits and Collections (Article 4) and except for liability for breach of warranty on presentment under the preceding section, payment or acceptance of any instrument is final in favor of a holder in due course, or a person who has in good faith changed his position in reliance on the payment.

§ 3—419
Conversion of Instrument; Innocent Representative

(1) An instrument is converted when

    (a) a drawee to whom it is delivered for acceptance refuses to return it on demand; or

    (b) any person to whom it is delivered for payment refuses on demand either to pay or to return it; or

    (c) it is paid on a forged indorsement.

(2) In an action against a drawee under subsection (1) the measure of the drawee's liability is the face amount of the instrument. In any other action under subsection (1) the measure of liability is presumed to be the face amount of the instrument.

(3) Subject to the provisions of this Act concerning restrictive indorsements a representative, including a depositary or collecting bank, who has in good faith and in accordance with the reasonable commercial standards applicable to the business of such representative dealt with an instrument or its proceeds on behalf of one who was not the true owner is

not liable in conversion or otherwise to the true owner beyond the amount of any proceeds remaining in his hands.

(4) An intermediary bank or payor bank which is not a depositary bank is not liable in conversion solely by reason of the fact that proceeds of an item indorsed restrictively (Sections 3—205 and 3—206) are not paid or applied consistently with the restrictive indorsement of an indorser other than its immediate transferor.

PART 5/Presentment, Notice of Dishonor and Protest

§ 3—501
When Presentment, Notice of Dishonor, and Protest Necessary or Permissible

(1) Unless excused (Section 3—511) presentment is necessary to charge secondary parties as follows:

(a) presentment for acceptance is necessary to charge the drawer and indorsers of a draft where the draft so provides, or is payable elsewhere than at the residence or place of business of the drawee, or its date of payment depends upon such presentment. The holder may at his option present for acceptance any other draft payable at a stated date;

(b) presentment for payment is necessary to charge any indorser;

(c) in the case of any drawer, the acceptor of a draft payable at a bank or the maker of a note payable at a bank, presentment for payment is necessary, but failure to make presentment discharges such drawer, acceptor or maker only as stated in Section 3—502(1)(b).

(2) Unless excused (Section 3—511)

(a) notice of any dishonor is necessary to charge any indorser;

(b) in the case of any drawer, the acceptor of a draft payable at a bank or the maker of a note payable at a bank, notice of any dishonor is necessary, but failure to give such notice discharges such drawer, acceptor or maker only as stated in Section 3—502(1)(b)

(3) Unless excused (Section 3—511) protest of any dishonor is necessary to charge the drawer and indorsers of any draft which on its face appears to be drawn or payable outside of the states, territories, dependencies and possessions of the United States, the District of Columbia and the Commonwealth of Puerto Rico. The holder may at his option make protest of any dishonor of any other instrument and in the case of a foreign draft may on insolvency of the acceptor before maturity make protest for better security.

(4) Notwithstanding any provision of this section, neither presentment nor notice of dishonor nor protest is necessary to charge an indorser who has indorsed an instrument after maturity.

§ 3—502
Unexcused Delay; Discharge

(1) Where without excuse any necessary presentment or notice of dishonor is delayed beyond the time when it is due

(a) any indorser is discharged; and

(b) any drawer or the acceptor of a draft payable at a bank or the maker of a note payable at a bank who because the drawee or payor bank becomes insolvent during the delay is deprived of funds maintained with the drawee or payor bank to cover the instrument may discharge his liability by written assignment to the holder of his rights against the drawee or payor bank in respect of such funds, but such drawer, acceptor or maker is not otherwise discharged.

(2) Where without excuse a necessary protest is delayed beyond the time when it is due any drawer or indorser is discharged.

§ 3—503
Time of Presentment

(1) Unless a different time is expressed in the instrument the time for any presentment is determined as follows:

(a) where an instrument is payable at or a fixed period after a stated date any presentment for acceptance must be made on or before the date it is payable;

(b) where an instrument is payable after sight it must either be presented for acceptance or negotiated within a reasonable time after date or issue whichever is later;

(c) where an instrument shows the date on which it is payable presentment for payment is due on that date;

(d) where an instrument is accelerated presentment for payment is due within a reasonable time after the acceleration;

(e) with respect to the liability of any secondary party presentment for acceptance or payment of any other instrument is due within a reasonable time after such party becomes liable thereon.

(2) A reasonable time for presentment is determined by the nature of the instrument, any usage of banking or trade and the facts of the particular case. In the case of an uncertified check which is drawn and payable within the United States and which is not a draft drawn by a bank the following are presumed to be reasonable periods within which to present for payment or to initiate bank collection:

(a) with respect to the liability of the drawer, thirty days after date or issue whichever is later; and

(b) with respect to the liability of an indorser, seven days after his indorsement.

(3) Where any presentment is due on a day which is not a full business day for either the person making presentment or the party to pay or accept, presentment is due on the next following day which is a full business day for both parties.

(4) Presentment to be sufficient must be made at a reasonable hour, and if at a bank during its banking day.

§ 3—504
How Presentment Made

(1) Presentment is a demand for acceptance or payment made upon the maker, acceptor, drawee or other payor by or on behalf of the holder.

(2) Presentment may be made

(a) by mail, in which event the time of presentment is determined by the time of receipt of the mail; or

(b) through a clearing house; or

(c) at the place of acceptance or payment specified in the instrument or if there be none at the place of business or residence of the party to accept or pay. If neither the party to accept or pay nor anyone authorized to act for him is present or accessible at such place presentment is excused.

(3) It may be made

(a) to any one of two or more makers, acceptors, drawees or other payors; or

(b) to any person who has authority to make or refuse the acceptance or payment.

(4) A draft accepted or a note made payable at a bank in the United States must be presented at such bank.

(5) In the cases described in Section 4—210 presentment may be made in the manner and with the result stated in that section.

§ 3—505
Rights of Party to Whom
Presentment Is Made

(1) The party to whom presentment is made may without dishonor require

(a) exhibition of the instrument; and

(b) reasonable identification of the person making presentment and evidence of his authority to make it if made for another; and

(c) that the instrument be produced for acceptance or payment at a place specified in it, or if there be none at any place reasonable in the circumstances; and

(d) a signed receipt on the instrument for any partial or full payment and its surrender upon full payment.

(2) Failure to comply with any such requirement invalidates the presentment but the person presenting has a reasonable time in which to comply and the time for acceptance or payment runs from the time of compliance.

§ 3—506
Time Allowed for Acceptance or Payment

(1) Acceptance may be deferred without dishonor until the close of the next business day following presentment. The holder may also in a good faith effort to obtain acceptance and without either dishonor of the instrument or discharge of secondary parties allow postponement of acceptance for an additional business day.

(2) Except as a longer time is allowed in the case of documentary drafts drawn under a letter of credit, and unless an earlier time is agreed to by the party to pay, payment of an instrument may be deferred without dishonor pending reasonable examination to determine whether it is properly payable, but payment must be made in any event before the close of business on the day of presentment.

§ 3—507
Dishonor; Holder's Right of Recourse;
Term Allowing Re-Presentment

(1) An instrument is dishonored when

(a) a necessary or optional presentment is duly made and due acceptance or payment is refused or cannot be obtained within the prescribed time or in case of bank collections the instrument is seasonably returned by the midnight deadline (Section 4—301); or

(b) presentment is excused and the instrument is not duly accepted or paid.

(2) Subject to any necessary notice of dishonor and protest, the holder has upon dishonor an immediate right of recourse against the drawers and indorsers.

(3) Return of an instrument for lack of proper indorsement is not dishonor.

(4) A term in a draft or an indorsement thereof allowing a stated time for re-presentment in the event of any dishonor of the draft by nonacceptance if a time draft or by nonpayment if a sight draft gives the holder as against any secondary party bound by the term an option to waive the dishonor without affecting the liability of the secondary party and he may present again up to the end of the stated time.

§ 3—508
Notice of Dishonor

(1) Notice of dishonor may be given to any person who may be liable on the instrument by or on behalf of the holder or any party who has himself received notice, or any other party who can be compelled to pay the instrument. In addition an agent or bank in whose hands the instrument is dishonored may give notice to his principal or customer or to another agent or bank from which the instrument was received.

(2) Any necessary notice must be given by a bank before its midnight deadline and by any other person before midnight of the third business day after dishonor or receipt of notice of dishonor.

(3) Notice may be given in any reasonable manner. It may be oral or written and in any terms which identify the instrument and state that it has been dishonored. A misdescription which does not mislead the party notified does not vitiate the notice. Sending the instrument bearing a stamp, ticket or writing stating that acceptance or payment has been refused or sending a notice of debit with respect to the instrument is sufficient.

(4) Written notice is given when sent although it is not received.

(5) Notice to one partner is notice to each although the firm has been dissolved.

(6) When any party is in insolvency proceedings instituted after the issue of the instrument notice may be given either to the party or to the representative of his estate.

(7) When any party is dead or incompetent notice may be sent to his last known address or given to his personal representative.

(8) Notice operates for the benefit of all parties who have rights on the instrument against the party notified.

§ 3—509
Protest; Noting for Protest

(1) A protest is a certificate of dishonor made under the hand and seal of a United States consul or vice consul or a notary public or other person authorized to certify dishonor by the law of the place where dishonor occurs. It may be made upon information satisfactory to such person.

(2) The protest must identify the instrument and certify either that due presentment has been made or the reason why it is excused and that the instrument has been dishonored by non-acceptance or nonpayment.

(3) The protest may also certify that notice of dishonor has been given to all parties or to specified parties.

(4) Subject to subsection (5) any necessary protest is due by the time that notice of dishonor is due.

(5) If, before protest is due, an instrument has been noted for protest by the officer to make protest, the protest may be made at any time thereafter as of the date of the noting.

§ 3—510
Evidence of Dishonor and Notice of Dishonor

The following are admissible as evidence and create a presumption of dishonor and of any notice of dishonor therein shown:

(a) a document regular in form as provided in the preceding section which purports to be a protest;

(b) the purported stamp or writing of the drawee, payor bank or presenting bank on the instrument or accompanying it stating that acceptance or payment has been refused for reasons consistent with dishonor.

(c) any book or record of the drawee, payor bank, or any collecting bank kept in the usual course of business which shows dishonor, even though there is no evidence of who made the entry.

§ 3—511
Waived or Excused Presentment, Protest or Notice of Dishonor or Delay Therein

(1) Delay in presentment, protest or notice of dishonor is excused when the party is without notice that it is due or when the delay is caused by circumstances beyond his control and he exercises reasonable diligence after the cause of the delay ceases to operate.

(2) Presentment or notice or protest as the case may be is entirely excused when

(a) the party to be charged has waived it expressly or by implication either before or after it is due; or

(b) such party has himself dishonored the instrument or has countermanded payment or otherwise has no reason to expect or right to require that the instrument be accepted or paid; or

(c) by reasonable diligence the presentment or protest cannot be made or the notice given.

(3) Presentment is also entirely excused when

(a) the maker, acceptor or drawee of any instrument except a documentary draft is dead or in insolvency proceedings instituted after the issue of the instrument; or

(b) acceptance or payment is refused but not for want of proper presentment.

(4) Where a draft has been dishonored by nonacceptance a later presentment for payment and any notice of dishonor and protest for nonpayment are excused unless in the meantime the instrument has been accepted.

(5) A waiver of protest is also a waiver of presentment and of notice of dishonor even though protest is not required.

(6) Where a waiver of presentment or notice or protest is embodied in the instrument itself it is binding upon all parties; but where it is written above the signature of an indorser it binds him only.

PART 6/Discharge

§ 3—601
Discharge of Parties

(1) The extent of the discharge of any party from liability on an instrument is governed by the sections on

(a) payment or satisfaction (Section 3—603); or

(b) tender of payment (Section 3—604); or

(c) cancellation or renunciation (Section 3—605); or

(d) impairment of right of recourse or of collateral (Section 3—606); or

(e) reacquisition of the instrument by a prior party (Section 3—208); or

(f) fraudulent and material alteration (Section 3—407); or

(g) certification of a check (Section 3—411); or

(h) acceptance varying a draft (Section 3—412); or

(i) unexcused delay in presentment or notice of dishonor or protest (Section 3—502).

(2) Any party is also discharged from his liability on an instrument to another party by any other act or agreement with such party which would discharge his simple contract for the payment of money.

(3) The liability of all parties is discharged when any party who has himself no right of action or recourse on the instrument

(a) reacquires the instrument in his own right; or

(b) is discharged under any provision of this Article, except as otherwise provided with respect to discharge for impairment of recourse or of collateral (Section 3—606).

§ 3—602
Effect of Discharge Against Holder in Due Course

No discharge of any party provided by this Article is effective against a subsequent holder in due course unless he has notice thereof when he takes the instrument.

§ 3—603
Payment or Satisfaction

(1) The liability of any party is discharged to the extent of his payment or satisfaction to the holder even though it is made with knowledge of a claim of another person to the instrument unless prior to such payment or satisfaction the person making the claim either supplies indemnity deemed adequate by the party seeking the discharge or enjoins payment or satisfaction by order of a court of competent jurisdiction in an action in which the adverse claimant and the holder are parties. This subsection does not, however, result in the discharge of the liability

(a) of a party who in bad faith pays or satisfies a holder who acquired the instrument by theft or who (unless having the rights of a holder in due course) holds through one who so acquired it; or

(b) of a party (other than an intermediary bank or a payor bank which is not a depositary bank) who pays or satisfies the holder of an instrument which has been restrictively indorsed in a manner not consistent with the terms of such restrictive indorsement.

(2) Payment or satisfaction may be made with the consent of the holder by any person including a stranger to the instrument. Surrender of the instrument to such a person gives him the rights of a transferee (Section 3—201).

§ 3—604
Tender of Payment

(1) Any party making tender of full payment to a holder when or after it is due is discharged to the extent of all subsequent liability for interest, costs and attorney's fees.

(2) The holder's refusal of such tender wholly discharges any party who has a right of recourse against the party making the tender.

(3) Where the maker or acceptor of an instrument payable otherwise than on demand is able and ready to pay at every place of payment specified in the instrument when it is due, it is equivalent to tender.

§ 3—605
Cancellation and Renunciation

(1) The holder of an instrument may even without consideration discharge any party

(a) in any manner apparent on the face of the instrument or the indorsement, as by intentionally cancelling the instrument or the party's signature by destruction or mutilation, or by striking out the party's signature; or

(b) by renouncing his rights by a writing signed and delivered or by surrender of the instrument to the party to be discharged.

(2) Neither cancellation nor renunciation without surrender of the instrument affects the title thereto.

§ 3—606
Impairment of Recourse or of Collateral

(1) The holder discharges any party to the instrument to the extent that without such party's consent the holder

(a) without express reservation of rights releases or agrees not to sue any person against whom the party has to the knowledge of the holder a right of recourse or agrees to suspend the right to enforce against such person the instrument or collateral or otherwise discharges such person, except that failure or delay in effecting any required presentment, protest or notice of dishonor with respect to any such person does not discharge any party as to whom presentment, protest or notice of dishonor is effective or unnecessary; or

(b) unjustifiably impairs any collateral for the instrument given by or on behalf of the party or any person against whom he has a right of recourse.

(2) By express reservation of rights against a party with a right of recourse the holder preserves

(a) all his rights against such party as of the time when the instrument was originally due; and

(b) the right of the party to pay the instrument as of that time; and

(c) all rights of such party to recourse against others.

PART 7/Advice of International Sight Draft

§ 3—701
Letter of Advice of International Sight Draft

(1) A "letter of advice" is a drawer's communication to the drawee that a described draft has been drawn.

(2) Unless otherwise agreed when a bank receives from another bank a letter of advice of an international sight draft the drawee bank may immediately debit the drawer's account and stop the running of interest pro tanto. Such a debit and any resulting credit to any account covering outstanding drafts leaves in the drawer full power to stop payment or otherwise dispose of the amount and creates no trust or interest in favor of the holder.

(3) Unless otherwise agreed and except where a draft is drawn under a credit issued by the drawee, the drawee of an international sight draft owes the drawer no duty to pay an unadvised draft but if it does so and the draft is genuine, may appropriately debit the drawer's account.

PART 8/Miscellaneous

§ 3—801
Drafts in a Set

(1) Where a draft is drawn in a set of parts, each of which is numbered and expressed to be an order only if no other part has been honored, the whole of the parts constitutes one draft but a taker of any part may become a holder in due course of the draft.

(2) Any person who negotiates, indorses or accepts a single part of a draft drawn in a set thereby becomes liable to any holder in due course of that part as if it were the whole set, but as between different holders in due course to whom different parts have been negotiated the holder whose title first accrues has all rights to the draft and its proceeds.

(3) As against the drawee the first presented part of a draft drawn in a set is the part entitled to payment, or if a time draft to acceptance and payment. Acceptance of any subsequently presented part renders the drawee liable thereon under subsection (2). With respect both to a holder and to the drawer payment of a subsequently presented part of a draft payable at sight has the same effect as payment of a check notwithstanding an effective stop order (Section 4—407).

(4) Except as otherwise provided in this section, where any part of a draft in a set is discharged by payment or otherwise the whole draft is discharged.

§ 3—802
Effect of Instrument on Obligation for Which It Is Given

(1) Unless otherwise agreed where an instrument is taken for an underlying obligation

(a) the obligation is pro tanto discharged if a bank is drawer, maker or acceptor of the instrument and there is no recourse on the instrument against the underlying obligor; and

(b) in any other case the obligation is suspended pro tanto until the instrument is due or if it is payable on demand until its presentment. If the instrument is dishonored action may be maintained on either the instrument or the obligation; discharge of the underlying obligor on the instrument also discharges him on the obligation.

(2) The taking in good faith of a check which is not postdated does not of itself so extend the time on the original obligation as to discharge a surety.

§ 3—803
Notice to Third Party

Where a defendant is sued for breach of an obligation for which a third person is answerable over under this Article he may give the third person written notice of the litigation, and the person notified may then give similar notice to any other person who is answerable over to him under this Article. If the notice states that the person notified may come in and defend and that if the person notified does not do so he will in any action against him by the person giving the notice be bound by any determination of fact common to the two litigations, then unless after seasonable receipt of the notice the person notified does come in and defend he is so bound.

§ 3—804
Lost, Destroyed or Stolen Instruments

The owner of an instrument which is lost, whether by destruction, theft or otherwise, may maintain an action in his own name and recover from any party liable thereon upon due proof of his ownership, the facts which prevent his production of the instrument and its terms. The court may require security indemnifying the defendant against loss by reason of further claims on the instrument.

§ 3—805
Instruments Not Payable to Order or to Bearer

This Article applies to any instrument whose terms do not preclude transfer and which is otherwise negotiable within this Article but which is not payable to order or to bearer, except that there can be no holder in due course of such an instrument.

ARTICLE 4/Bank Deposits and Collections

PART 1/General Provisions and Definitions

§ 4—101
Short Title

This Article shall be known and may be cited as Uniform Commercial Code—Bank Deposits and Collections.

§ 4—102
Applicability

(1) To the extent that items within this Article are also within the scope of Articles 3 and 8, they are subject to the provisions of those Articles. In the event of conflict the provisions of this Article govern those of Article 3 but the provisions of Article 8 govern those of this Article.

(2) The liability of a bank for action or non-action with respect to any item handled by it for purposes of present-ment, payment or collection is governed by the law of the place where the bank is located. In the case of action or non-action by or at a branch or separate office of a bank, its liability is governed by the law of the place where the branch or separate office is located.

§ 4—103
Variation by Agreement; Measure of Damages; Certain Action Constituting Ordinary Care

(1) The effect of the provisions of this Article may be varied by agreement except that no agreement can disclaim a bank's responsibility for its own lack of good faith or failure to exercise ordinary care or can limit the measure of dam-ages for such lack or failure; but the parties may by agree-ment determine the standards by which such responsibility is to be measured if such standards are not manifestly unreasonable.

(2) Federal Reserve regulations and operating letters, clear-ing house rules, and the like, have the effect of agreements under subsection (1), whether or not specifically assented to by all parties interested in items handled.

(3) Action or non-action approved by this Article or pur-suant to Federal Reserve regulations or operating letters con-stitutes the exercise of ordinary care and, in the absence of special instructions, action or non-action consistent with clearing house rules and the like or with a general banking usage not disapproved by this Article, prima facie constitutes the exercise of ordinary care.

(4) The specification or approval of certain procedures by this Article does not constitute disapproval of other proce-dures which may be reasonable under the circumstances.

(5) The measure of damages for failure to exercise ordinary care in handling an item is the amount of the item reduced by an amount which could not have been realized by the use of ordinary care, and where there is bad faith it includes other damages, if any, suffered by the party as a proximate consequence.

§ 4—104
Definitions and Index of Definitions

(1) In this Article unless the context otherwise requires

   (a) "Account" means any account with a bank and in-cludes a checking, time, interest or savings account;

   (b) "Afternoon" means the period of a day between noon and midnight;

   (c) "Banking day" means that part of any day on which a bank is open to the public for carrying on substantially all of its banking functions;

   (d) "Clearing house" means any association of banks or other payors regularly clearing items;

   (e) "Customer" means any person having an account with a bank or for whom a bank has agreed to collect items and includes a bank carrying an account with an-other bank;

   (f) "Documentary draft" means any negotiable or non-negotiable draft with accompanying documents, se-curities or other papers to be delivered against honor of the draft;

   (g) "Item" means any instrument for the payment of money even though it is not negotiable but does not include money;

   (h) "Midnight deadline" with respect to a bank is mid-night on its next banking day following the banking day on which it receives the relevant item or notice or from which the time for taking action commences to run, whichever is later;

   (i) "Properly payable" includes the availability of funds for payment at the time of decision to pay or dishonor;

   (j) "Settle" means to pay in cash, by clearing house settlement, in a charge or credit or by remittance, or otherwise as instructed. A settlement may be either pro-visional or final;

   (k) "Suspends payments" with respect to a bank means that it has been closed by order of the supervisory authorities, that a public officer has been appointed to take it over or that it ceases or refuses to make payments in the ordinary course of business.

(2) Other definitions applying to this Article and the sec-tions in which they appear are:

   "Collecting bank" Section 4—105.

   "Depositary bank" Section 4—105.

   "Intermediary bank" Section 4—105.

"Payor bank" Section 4—105.

"Presenting bank" Section 4—105.

"Remitting bank" Section 4—105.

(3) The following definitions in other Articles apply to this Article:

"Acceptance" Section 3—410.

"Certificate of deposit" Section 3—104.

"Certification" Section 3—411.

"Check" Section 3—104.

"Draft" Section 3—104.

"Holder in due course" Section 3—302.

"Notice of dishonor" Section 3—508.

"Presentment" Section 3—504.

"Protest" Section 3—509.

"Secondary party" Section 3—102.

(4) In addition Article 1 contains general definitions and principles of construction and interpretation applicable throughout this Article.

§ 4—105
"Depositary Bank"; "Intermediary Bank"; "Collecting Bank"; "Payor Bank"; "Presenting Bank"; "Remitting Bank"

In this Article unless the context otherwise requires:

(a) "Depositary bank" means the first bank to which an item is transferred for collection even though it is also the payor bank

(b) "Payor bank" means a bank by which an item is payable as drawn or accepted;

(c) "Intermediary bank" means any bank to which an item is transferred in course of collection except the depositary or payor bank;

(d) "Collecting bank" means any bank handling the item for collection except the payor bank;

(e) "Presenting bank" means any bank presenting an item except a payor bank;

(f) "Remitting bank" means any payor or intermediary bank remitting for an item.

§ 4—106
Separate Office of a Bank

A branch or separate office of a bank [maintaining its own deposit ledgers] is a separate bank for the purpose of computing the time within which and determining the place at or to which action may be taken or notices or orders shall be given under this Article and under Article 3.

Note: *The brackets are to make it optional with the several states whether to require a branch to maintain its own deposit ledgers in order to be considered to be a separate*

bank for certain purposes under Article 4. In some states "maintaining its own deposit ledgers" is a satisfactory test. In others branch banking practices are such that this test would not be suitable.

§ 4—107
Time of Receipt of Items

(1) For the purpose of allowing time to process items, prove balances and make the necessary entries on its books to determine its position for the day, a bank may fix an afternoon hour of two P.M. or later as a cut-off hour for the handling of money and items and the making of entries on its books.

(2) Any item or deposit of money received on any day after a cut-off hour so fixed or after the close of the banking day may be treated as being received at the opening of the next banking day.

§ 4—108
Delays

(1) Unless otherwise instructed, a collecting bank in a good faith effort to secure payment may, in the case of specific items and with or without the approval of any person involved, waive, modify or extend time limits imposed or permitted by this Act for a period not in excess of an additional banking day without discharge of secondary parties and without liability to its transferor or any prior party.

(2) Delay by a collecting bank or payor bank beyond time limits prescribed or permitted by this Act or by instructions is excused if caused by interruption of communication facilities, suspension of payments by another bank, war, emergency conditions or other circumstances beyond the control of the bank provided it exercises such diligence as the circumstances require.

§ 4—109
Process of Posting

The "process of posting" means the usual procedure followed by a payor bank in determining to pay an item and in recording the payment including one or more of the following or other steps as determined by the bank:

(a) verification of any signature;

(b) ascertaining that sufficient funds are available;

(c) affixing a "paid" or other stamp;

(d) entering a charge or entry to a customer's account;

(e) correcting or reversing an entry or erroneous action with respect to the item.

PART 2/Collection of Items: Depositary and Collecting Banks

§ 4—201
Presumption and Duration of Agency Status of Collecting Banks and Provisional Status of Credits; Applicability of Article; Item Indorsed "Pay Any Bank"

(1) Unless a contrary intent clearly appears and prior to the time that a settlement given by a collecting bank for an item is or becomes final (subsection (3) of Section 4—211 and Sections 4—212 and 4—213) the bank is an agent or sub-agent of the owner of the item and any settlement given for the item is provisional. This provision applies regardless of the form of indorsement or lack of indorsement and even though credit given for the item is subject to immediate withdrawal as of right or is in fact withdrawn; but the conti-nuance of ownership of an item by its owner and any rights of the owner to proceeds of the item are subject to rights of a collecting bank such as those resulting from outstanding advances on the item and valid rights of setoff. When an item is handled by banks for purposes of presentment, payment and collection, the relevant provisions of this Article apply even though action of parties clearly establishes that a par-ticular bank has purchased the item and is the owner of it.

(2) After an item has been indorsed with the words "pay any bank" or the like, only a bank may acquire the rights of a holder

(a) until the item has been returned to the customer initiating collection; or

(b) until the item has been specially indorsed by a bank to a person who is not a bank.

§ 4—202
Responsibility for Collection; When Action Seasonable

(1) A collecting bank must use ordinary care in

(a) presenting an item or sending it for presentment; and

(b) sending notice of dishonor or non-payment or re-turning an item other than a documentary draft to the bank's transferor [or directly to the depositary bank under subsection (2) of Section 4—212] (*see note to Section 4—212*) after learning that the item has not been paid or accepted, as the case may be; and

(c) settling for an item when the bank receives final settlement; and

(d) making or providing for any necessary protest; and

(e) notifying its transferor of any loss or delay in transit within a reasonable time after discovery thereof.

(2) A collecting bank taking proper action before its mid-night deadline following receipt of an item, notice or pay-ment acts seasonably; taking proper action within a reason-ably longer time may be seasonable but the bank has the burden of so establishing.

(3) Subject to subsection (1)(a), a bank is not liable for the insolvency, neglect, misconduct, mistake or default of an-other bank or person or for loss or destruction of an item in transit or in the possession of others.

§ 4—203
Effect of Instructions

Subject to the provisions of Article 3 concerning conversion of instruments (Section 3—419) and the provisions of both Article 3 and this Article concerning restrictive indorse-ments only a collecting bank's transferor can give instruc-tions which affect the bank or constitute notice to it and a collecting bank is not liable to prior parties for any action taken pursuant to such instructions or in accordance with any agreement with its transferor.

§ 4—204
Methods of Sending and Presenting; Sending Direct to Payor Bank

(1) A collecting bank must send items by reasonably prompt method taking into consideration any relevant in-structions, the nature of the item, the number of such items on hand, and the cost of collection involved and the method generally used by it or others to present such items.

(2) A collecting bank may send

(a) any item direct to the payor bank;

(b) any item to any non-bank payor if authorized by its transferor; and

(c) any item other than documentary drafts to any non-bank payor, if authorized by Federal Reserve regulation or operating letter, clearing house rule or the like.

(3) Presentment may be made by a presenting bank at a place where the payor bank has requested that presentment be made.

§ 4—205
Supplying Missing Indorsement; No Notice from Prior Indorsement

(1) A depositary bank which has taken an item for collection may supply any indorsement of the customer which is neces-sary to title unless the item contains the words "payee's indorsement required" or the like. In the absence of such a requirement a statement placed on the item by the deposi-tary bank to the effect that the item was deposited by a customer or credited to his account is effective as the cus-tomer's indorsement.

(2) An intermediary bank, or payor bank which is not a depositary bank, is neither given notice nor otherwise affected by a restrictive indorsement of any person except the bank's immediate transferor.

§ 4—206
Transfer Between Banks

Any agreed method which identifies the transferor bank is sufficient for the item's further transfer to another bank.

§ 4—207
Warranties of Customer and Collecting Bank on Transfer or Presentment of Items; Time for Claims

(1) Each customer or collecting bank who obtains payment or acceptance of an item and each prior customer and collecting bank warrants to the payor bank or other payor who in good faith pays or accepts the item that

(a) he has a good title to the item or is authorized to obtain payment or acceptance on behalf of one who has a good title; and

(b) he has no knowledge that the signature of the maker or drawer is unauthorized, except that this warranty is not given by any customer or collecting bank that is a holder in due course and acts in good faith

(i) to a maker with respect to the maker's own signature; or

(ii) to a drawer with respect to the drawer's own signature, whether or not the drawer is also the drawee; or

(iii) to an acceptor of an item if the holder in due course took the item after the acceptance or obtained the acceptance without knowledge that the drawer's signature was unauthorized; and

(c) the item has not been materially altered, except that this warranty is not given by any customer or collecting bank that is a holder in due course and acts in good faith

(i) to the maker of a note; or

(ii) to the drawer of a draft whether or not the drawer is also the drawee; or

(iii) to the acceptor of an item with respect to an alteration made prior to the acceptance if the holder in due course took the item after the acceptance, even though the acceptance provided "payable as originally drawn" or equivalent terms; or

(iv) to the acceptor of an item with respect to an alteration made after the acceptance.

(2) Each customer and collecting bank who transfers an item and receives a settlement or other consideration for it warrants to his transferee and to any subsequent collecting bank who takes the item in good faith that

(a) he has a good title to the item or is authorized to obtain payment or acceptance on behalf of one who has a good title and the transfer is otherwise rightful; and

(b) all signatures are genuine or authorized; and

(c) the item has not been materially altered; and

(d) no defense of any party is good against him; and

(e) he has no knowledge of any insolvency proceeding instituted with respect to the maker or acceptor or the drawer of an unaccepted item.

In addition each customer and collecting bank so transferring an item and receiving a settlement or other consideration engages that upon dishonor and any necessary notice of dishonor and protest he will take up the item.

(3) The warranties and the engagement to honor set forth in the two preceding subsections arise notwithstanding the absence of indorsement or words of guaranty or warranty in the transfer or presentment and a collecting bank remains liable for their breach despite remittance to its transferor. Damages for breach of such warranties or engagement to honor shall not exceed the consideration received by the customer or collecting bank responsible plus finance charges and expenses related to the item, if any.

(4) Unless a claim for breach of warranty under this section is made within a reasonable time after the person claiming learns of the breach, the person liable is discharged to the extent of any loss caused by the delay in making claim.

§ 4—208
Security Interest of Collecting Bank in Items, Accompanying Documents and Proceeds

(1) A bank has a security interest in an item and any accompanying documents or the proceeds of either

(a) in case of an item deposited in an account to the extent to which credit given for the item has been withdrawn or applied;

(b) in case of an item for which it has given credit available for withdrawal as of right, to the extent of the credit given whether or not the credit is drawn upon and whether or not there is a right of charge-back; or

(c) if it makes an advance on or against the item.

(2) When credit which has been given for several items received at one time or pursuant to a single agreement is withdrawn or applied in part the security interest remains upon all the items, any accompanying documents or the proceeds of either. For the purpose of this section, credits first given are first withdrawn.

(3) Receipt by a collecting bank of a final settlement for an item is a realization on its security interest in the item, accompanying documents and proceeds. To the extent and so long as the bank does not receive final settlement for the item or give up possession of the item or accompanying documents for purposes other than collection, the security interest continues and is subject to the provisions of Article 9 except that

(a) no security agreement is necessary to make the security interest enforceable (subsection (1)(b) of Section 9—203); and

(b) no filing is required to perfect the security interest; and

(c) the security interest has priority over conflicting perfected security interests in the item, accompanying documents or proceeds.

§ 4—209
When Bank Gives Value for Purposes of Holder in Due Course

For purposes of determining its status as a holder in due course, the bank has given value to the extent that it has a security interest in an item provided that the bank otherwise complies with the requirements of Section 3—302 on what constitutes a holder in due course.

§ 4—210
Presentment by Notice of Item Not Payable by, Through or at a Bank; Liability of Secondary Parties

(1) Unless otherwise instructed, a collecting bank may present an item not payable by, through or at a bank by sending to the party to accept or pay a written notice that the bank holds the item for acceptance or payment. The notice must be sent in time to be received on or before the day when presentment is due and the bank must meet any requirement of the party to accept or pay under Section 3—505 by the close of the bank's next banking day after it knows of the requirement.

(2) Where presentment is made by notice and neither honor nor request for compliance with a requirement under Section 3—505 is received by the close of business on the day after maturity or in the case of demand items by the close of business on the third banking day after notice was sent, the presenting bank may treat the item as dishonored and charge any secondary party by sending him notice of the facts.

§ 4—211
Media of Remittance; Provisional and Final Settlement in Remittance Cases

(1) A collecting bank may take in settlement of an item

(a) a check of the remitting bank or of another bank on any bank except the remitting bank; or

(b) a cashier's check or similar primary obligation of a remitting bank which is a member of or clears through a member of the same clearing house or group as the collecting bank; or

(c) appropriate authority to charge an account of the remitting bank or of another bank with the collecting bank; or

(d) if the item is drawn upon or payable by a person other than a bank, a cashier's check, certified check or other bank check or obligation.

(2) If before its midnight deadline the collecting bank properly dishonors a remittance check or authorization to charge on itself or presents or forwards for collection a remittance instrument of or on another bank which is of a kind approved by subsection (1) or has not been authorized by it, the collecting bank is not liable to prior parties in the event of the dishonor of such check, instrument or authorization.

(3) A settlement for an item by means of a remittance instrument or authorization to charge is or becomes a final settlement as to both the person making and the person receiving the settlement

(a) if the remittance instrument or authorization to charge is of a kind approved by subsection (1) or has not been authorized by the person receiving the settlement and in either case the person receiving the settlement acts seasonably before its midnight deadline in presenting, forwarding for collection or paying the instrument or authorization,—at the time the remittance instrument or authorization is finally paid by the payor by which it is payable;

(b) if the person receiving the settlement has authorized remittance by a non-bank check or obligation or by a cashier's check or similar primary obligation of or a check upon the payor or other remitting bank which is not of a kind approved by subsection (1)(b),—at the time of the receipt of such remittance check or obligation; or

(c) if in a case not covered by sub-paragraphs (a) or (b) the person receiving the settlement fails to seasonably present, forward for collection, pay or return a remittance instrument or authorization to it to charge before its midnight deadline,—at such midnight deadline.

§ 4—212
Right of Charge-Back or Refund

(1) If a collecting bank has made provisional settlement with its customer for an item and itself fails by reason of dishonor, suspension of payments by a bank or otherwise to receive a settlement for the item which is or becomes final, the bank may revoke the settlement given by it, charge back the amount of any credit given for the item to its customer's account or obtain refund from its customer whether or not it is able to return the items if by its midnight deadline or within a longer reasonable time after it learns the facts it returns the item or sends notification of the facts. These rights to revoke, charge-back and obtain refund terminate if and when a settlement for the item received by the bank is or becomes final (subsection (3) of Section 4—211 and subsections (2) and (3) of Section 4—213).

[(2) Within the time and manner prescribed by this section and Section 4—301, an intermediary or payor bank, as the case may be, may return an unpaid item directly to the depositary bank and may send for collection a draft on the depositary bank and obtain reimbursement. In such case, if the depositary bank has received provisional settlement for the item, it must reimburse the bank drawing the draft and any provisional credits for the item between banks shall become and remain final.]

Note: *Direct returns are recognized as an innovation that is not yet established bank practice, and therefore, Paragraph 2 has been bracketed. Some lawyers have doubts whether it should be included in legislation or left to development by agreement.*

(3) A depositary bank which is also the payor may charge-back the amount of an item to its customer's account or obtain refund in accordance with the section governing return of an item received by a payor bank for credit on its books (Section 4—301).

(4) The right to charge-back is not affected by

(a) prior use of the credit given for the item; or

(b) failure by any bank to exercise ordinary care with respect to the item but any bank so failing remains liable.

(5) A failure to charge-back or claim refund does not affect other rights of the bank against the customer or any other party.

(6) If credit is given in dollars as the equivalent of the value of an item payable in a foreign currency the dollar amount of any charge-back or refund shall be calculated on the basis of the buying sight rate for the foreign currency prevailing on the day when the person entitled to the charge-back or refund learns that it will not receive payment in ordinary course.

§ 4—213
Final Payment of Item by Payor Bank; When Provisional Debits and Credits Become Final; When Certain Credits Become Available for Withdrawal

(1) An item is finally paid by a payor bank when the bank has done any of the following, whichever happens first:

(a) paid the item in cash; or

(b) settled for the item without reserving a right to revoke the settlement and without having such right under statute, clearing house rule or agreement; or

(c) completed the process of posting the item to the indicated account of the drawer, maker or other person to be charged therewith; or

(d) made a provisional settlement for the item and failed to revoke the settlement in the time and manner permitted by statute, clearing house rule or agreement.

Upon a final payment under subparagraphs (b), (c) or (d) the payor bank shall be accountable for the amount of the item.

(2) If provisional settlement for an item between the presenting and payor banks is made through a clearing house or by debits or credits in an account between them, then to the extent that provisional debits or credits for the item are entered in accounts between the presenting and payor banks or between the presenting and successive prior collecting banks seriatim, they become final upon final payment of the item by the payor bank.

(3) If a collecting bank receives a settlement for an item which is or becomes final (subsection (3) of Section 4—211, subsection (2) of Section 4—213) the bank is accountable to its customer for the amount of the item and any provisional credit given for the item in an account with its customer becomes final.

(4) Subject to any right of the bank to apply the credit to an obligation of the customer, credit given by a bank for an item in an account with its customer becomes available for withdrawal as of right

(a) in any case where the bank has received a provisional settlement for the item,—when such settlement becomes final and the bank has had a reasonable time to learn that the settlement is final;

(b) in any case where the bank is both a depositary bank and a payor bank and the item is finally paid,—at the opening of the bank's second banking day following receipt of the item.

(5) A deposit of money in a bank is final when made but, subject to any right of the bank to apply the deposit to an obligation of the customer, the deposit becomes available for withdrawal as of right at the opening of the bank's next banking day following receipt of the deposit.

§ 4—214
Insolvency and Preference

(1) Any item in or coming into the possession of a payor or collecting bank which suspends payment and which item is not finally paid shall be returned by the receiver, trustee or agent in charge of the closed bank to the presenting bank or the closed bank's customer.

(2) If a payor bank finally pays an item and suspends payments without making a settlement for the item with its customer or the presenting bank which settlement is or becomes final, the owner of the item has a preferred claim against the payor bank.

(3) If a payor bank gives or a collecting bank gives or receives a provisional settlement for an item and thereafter suspends payments, the suspension does not prevent or interfere with the settlement becoming final if such finality occurs automatically upon the lapse of certain time or the happening of certain events (subsection (3) of Section 4—211, subsections (1)(d), (2) and (3) of Section 4—213).

(4) If a collecting bank receives from subsequent parties settlement for an item which settlement is or becomes final and suspends payments without making a settlement for the item with its customer which is or becomes final, the owner

of the item has a preferred claim against such collecting bank.

PART 3/Collection of Items: Payor Banks

§ 4—301
Deferred Posting; Recovery of Payment by Return of Items; Time of Dishonor

(1) Where an authorized settlement for a demand item (other than a documentary draft) received by a payor bank otherwise than for immediate payment over the counter has been made before midnight of the banking day of receipt the payor bank may revoke the settlement and recover any payment if before it has made final payment (subsection (1) of Section 4—213) and before its midnight deadline it

    (a) returns the item; or

    (b) sends written notice of dishonor or nonpayment if the item is held for protest or is otherwise unavailable for return.

(2) If a demand item is received by a payor bank for credit on its books it may return such item or send notice of dishonor and may revoke any credit given or recover the amount thereof withdrawn by its customer, if it acts within the time limit and in the manner specified in the preceding subsection.

(3) Unless previous notice of dishonor has been sent an item is dishonored at the time when for purposes of dishonor it is returned or notice sent in accordance with this section.

(4) An item is returned:

    (a) as to an item received through a clearing house, when it is delivered to the presenting or last collecting bank or to the clearing house or is sent or delivered in accordance with its rules; or

    (b) in all other cases, when it is sent or delivered to the bank's customer or transferor or pursuant to his instructions.

§ 4—302
Payor Bank's Responsibility for Late Return of Item

In the absence of a valid defense such as breach of a presentment warranty (subsection (1) of Section 4—207), settlement effected or the like, if an item is presented on and received by a payor bank the bank is accountable for the amount of

    (a) a demand item other than a documentary draft whether properly payable or not if the bank, in any case where it is not also the depositary bank, retains the item beyond midnight of the banking day of receipt without settling for it or, regardless of whether it is also the depositary bank, does not pay or return the item or send notice of dishonor until after its midnight deadline; or

    (b) any other properly payable item unless within the time allowed for acceptance or payment of that item the bank either accepts or pays the item or returns it and accompanying documents.

§ 4—303
When Items Subject to Notice, Stop-Order, Legal Process or Setoff; Order in Which Items May Be Charged or Certified

(1) Any knowledge, notice or stop-order received by, legal process served upon or setoff exercised by a payor bank, whether or not effective under other rules of law to terminate, suspend or modify the bank's right or duty to pay an item or to charge its customer's account for the item, comes too late to so terminate, suspend or modify such right or duty if the knowledge, notice, stop-order or legal process is received or served and a reasonable time for the bank to act thereon expires or the setoff is exercised after the bank has done any of the following:

    (a) accepted or certified the item;

    (b) paid the item in cash;

    (c) settled for the item without reserving a right to revoke the settlement and without having such right under statute, clearing house rule or agreement;

    (d) completed the process of posting the item to the indicated account of the drawer, maker or other person to be charged therewith or otherwise has evidenced by examination of such indicated account and by action its decision to pay the item; or

    (e) become accountable for the amount of the item under subsection (1)(d) of Section 4—213 and Section 4—302 dealing with the payor bank's responsibility for late return of items.

(2) Subject to the provisions of subsection (1) items may be accepted, paid, certified or charged to the indicated account of its customer in any order convenient to the bank.

PART 4/Relationship Between Payor Bank and Its Customer

§ 4—401
When Bank May Charge Customer's Account

(1) As against its customer, a bank may charge against his account any item which is otherwise properly payable from that account even though the charge creates an overdraft.

(2) A bank which in good faith makes payment to a holder may charge the indicated account of its customer according to

    (a) the original tenor of his altered item; or

    (b) the tenor of his completed item, even though the bank knows the item has been completed unless the bank has notice that the completion was improper.

§ 4—402
Bank's Liability to Customer for Wrongful Dishonor

A payor bank is liable to its customer for damages proximately caused by the wrongful dishonor of an item. When the dishonor occurs through mistake liability is limited to actual damages proved. If so proximately caused and proved damages may include damages for an arrest or prosecution of the customer or other consequential damages. Whether any consequential damages are proximately caused by the wrongful dishonor is a question of fact to be determined in each case.

§ 4—403
Customer's Right to Stop Payment; Burden of Proof of Loss

(1) A customer may by order to his bank stop payment of any item payable for his account but the order must be received at such time and in such manner as to afford the bank a reasonable opportunity to act on it prior to any action by the bank with respect to the item described in Section 4—303.

(2) An oral order is binding upon the bank only for fourteen calendar days unless confirmed in writing within that period. A written order is effective for only six months unless renewed in writing.

(3) The burden of establishing the fact and amount of loss resulting from the payment of an item contrary to a binding stop payment order is on the customer.

§ 4—404
Bank Not Obligated to Pay Check More Than Six Months Old

A bank is under no obligation to a customer having a checking account to pay a check, other than a certified check, which is presented more than six months after its date, but it may charge its customer's account for a payment made thereafter in good faith.

§ 4—405
Death or Incompetence of Customer

(1) A payor or collecting bank's authority to accept, pay or collect an item or to account for proceeds of its collection if otherwise effective is not rendered ineffective by incompetence of a customer of either bank existing at the time the item is issued or its collection is undertaken if the bank does not know of an adjudication of incompetence. Neither death nor incompetence of a customer revokes such authority to accept, pay, collect or account until the bank knows of the fact of death or of an adjudication of incompetence and has reasonable opportunity to act on it.

(2) Even with knowledge a bank may for ten days after the date of death pay or certify checks drawn on or prior to that date unless ordered to stop payment by a person claiming an interest in the account.

§ 4—406
Customer's Duty to Discover and Report Unauthorized Signature or Alteration

(1) When a bank sends to its customer a statement of account accompanied by items paid in good faith in support of the debit entries or holds the statement and items pursuant to a request or instructions of its customer or otherwise in a reasonable manner makes the statement and items available to the customer, the customer must exercise reasonable care and promptness to examine the statement and items to discover his unauthorized signature or any alteration on an item and must notify the bank promptly after discovery thereof.

(2) If the bank establishes that the customer failed with respect to an item to comply with the duties imposed on the customer by subsection (1) the customer is precluded from asserting against the bank

  (a) his unauthorized signature or any alteration on the item if the bank also establishes that it suffered a loss by reason of such failure; and

  (b) an unauthorized signature or alteration by the same wrongdoer on any other item paid in good faith by the bank after the first item and statement was available to the customer for a reasonable period not exceeding fourteen calendar days and before the bank receives notification from the customer of any such unauthorized signature or alteration.

(3) The preclusion under subsection (2) does not apply if the customer establishes lack of ordinary care on the part of the bank in paying the item(s).

(4) Without regard to care or lack of care of either the customer or the bank a customer who does not within one year from the time the statement and items are made available to the customer (subsection (1)) discover and report his unauthorized signature or any alteration on the face or back of the item or does not within three years from that time discover and report any unauthorized indorsement is precluded from asserting against the bank such unauthorized signature or indorsement or such alteration.

(5) If under this section a payor bank has a valid defense against a claim of a customer upon or resulting from payment of an item and waives or fails upon request to assert the defense the bank may not assert against any collecting bank or other prior party presenting or transferring the item a claim based upon the unauthorized signature or alteration giving rise to the customer's claim.

§ 4—407
Payor Bank's Right to Subrogation on Improper Payment

If a payor bank has paid an item over the stop payment order of the drawer or maker or otherwise under circumstances giving a basis for objection by the drawer or maker, to prevent unjust enrichment and only to the extent necessary to prevent loss to the bank by reason of its payment of the item, the payor bank shall be subrogated to the rights

(a) of any holder in due course on the item against the drawer or maker; and

(b) of the payee or any other holder of the item against the drawer or maker either on the item or under the transaction out of which the item arose; and

(c) of the drawer or maker against the payee or any other holder of the item with respect to the transaction out of which the item arose.

PART 5/Collection of Documentary Drafts

§ 4—501
Handling of Documentary Drafts; Duty to Send for Presentment and to Notify Customer of Dishonor

A bank which takes a documentary draft for collection must present or send the draft and accompanying documents for presentment and upon learning that the draft has not been paid or accepted in due course must seasonably notify its customer of such fact even though it may have discounted or bought the draft or extended credit available for withdrawal as of right.

§ 4—502
Presentment of "On Arrival" Drafts

When a draft or the relevant instructions require presentment "on arrival", "when goods arrive" or the like, the collecting bank need not present until in its judgment a reasonable time for arrival of the goods has expired. Refusal to pay or accept because the goods have not arrived is not dishonor; the bank must notify its transferor of such refusal but need not present the draft again until it is instructed to do so or learns of the arrival of the goods.

§ 4—503
Responsibility of Presenting Bank for Documents and Goods; Report of Reasons for Dishonor; Referee in Case of Need

Unless otherwise instructed and except as provided in Article 5 a bank presenting a documentary draft

(a) must deliver the documents to the drawee on acceptance of the draft if it is payable more than three days after presentment; otherwise, only on payment; and

(b) upon dishonor, either in the case of presentment for acceptance or presentment for payment, may seek and follow instructions from any referee in case of need designated in the draft or if the presenting bank does not choose to utilize his services it must use diligence and good faith to ascertain the reason for dishonor, must notify its transferor of the dishonor and of the results of its

effort to ascertain the reasons therefor and must request instructions.

But the presenting bank is under no obligation with respect to goods represented by the documents except to follow any reasonable instructions seasonably received; it has a right to reimbursement for any expense incurred in following instructions and to prepayment of or indemnity for such expenses.

§ 4—504
Privilege of Presenting Bank to Deal With Goods; Security Interest for Expenses

(1) A presenting bank which, following the dishonor of a documentary draft, has seasonably requested instructions but does not receive them within a reasonable time may store, sell, or otherwise deal with the goods in any reasonable manner.

(2) For its reasonable expenses incurred by action under subsection (1) the presenting bank has a lien upon the goods or their proceeds, which may be foreclosed in the same manner as an unpaid seller's lien.

ARTICLE 5/Letters of Credit

§ 5—101
Short Title

This Article shall be known and may be cited as Uniform Commercial Code—Letters of Credit.

§ 5—102
Scope

(1) This Article applies

(a) to a credit issued by a bank if the credit requires a documentary draft or a documentary demand for payment; and

(b) to a credit issued by a person other than a bank if the credit requires that the draft or demand for payment be accompanied by a document of title; and

(c) to a credit issued by a bank or other person if the credit is not within subparagraphs (a) or (b) but conspicuously states that it is a letter of credit or is conspicuously so entitled.

(2) Unless the engagement meets the requirements of subsection (1), this Article does not apply to engagements to make advances or to honor drafts or demands for payment, to authorities to pay or purchase, to guarantees or to general agreements.

(3) This Article deals with some but not all of the rules and concepts of letters of credit as such rules or concepts have developed prior to this act or may hereafter develop. The fact that this Article states a rule does not by itself require, imply or negate application of the same or a converse rule to

a situation not provided for or to a person not specified by this Article.

§ 5—103
Definitions

(1) In this Article unless the context otherwise requires

(a) "Credit" or "letter of credit" means an engagement by a bank or other person made at the request of a customer and of a kind within the scope of this Article (Section 5—102) that the issuer will honor drafts or other demands for payment upon compliance with the conditions specified in the credit. A credit may be either revocable or irrevocable. The engagement may be either an agreement to honor or a statement that the bank or other person is authorized to honor.

(b) A "documentary draft" or a "documentary demand for payment" is one honor of which is conditioned upon the presentation of a document or documents. "Document" means any paper including document of title, security, invoice, certificate, notice of default and the like.

(c) An "issuer" is a bank or other person issuing a credit.

(d) A "beneficiary" of a credit is a person who is entitled under its terms to draw or demand payment.

(e) An "advising bank" is a bank which gives notification of the issuance of a credit by another bank.

(f) A "conforming bank" is a bank which engages either that it will itself honor a credit already issued by another bank or that such a credit will be honored by the issuer or a third bank.

(g) A "customer" is a buyer or other person who causes an issuer to issue a credit. The term also includes a bank which procures issuance or confirmation on behalf of that bank's customer.

(2) Other definitions applying to this Article and the sections in which they appear are:

"Notation of Credit". Section 5—108.

"Presenter". Section 5—112(3).

(3) Definitions in other Articles applying to this Article and the sections in which they appear are:

"Accept" or "Acceptance". Section 3—410.

"Contract for sale". Section 2—106.

"Draft". Section 3—104.

"Holder in due course". Section 3—302.

"Midnight deadline". Section 4—104.

"Security". Section 8—102.

(4) In addition, Article 1 contains general definitions and principles of construction and interpretation applicable throughout this Article.

§ 5—104
Formal Requirements; Signing

(1) Except as otherwise required in subsection (1)(c) of Section 5—102 on scope, no particular form of phrasing is required for a credit. A credit must be in writing and signed by the issuer and a confirmation must be in writing and signed by the confirming bank. A modification of the terms of a credit or confirmation must be signed by the issuer or confirming bank.

(2) A telegram may be a sufficient signed writing if it identifies its sender by an authorized authentication. The authentication may be in code and the authorized naming of the issuer in an advice of credit is a sufficient signing.

§ 5—105
Consideration

No consideration is necessary to establish a credit or to enlarge or otherwise modify its terms.

§ 5—106
Time and Effect of Establishment of Credit

(1) Unless otherwise agreed a credit is established

(a) as regards the customer as soon as a letter of credit is sent to him or the letter of credit or an authorized written advice of its issuance is sent to the beneficiary; and

(b) as regards the beneficiary when he receives a letter of credit or an authorized written advice of its issuance.

(2) Unless otherwise agreed once an irrevocable credit is established as regards the customer it can be modified or revoked only with the consent of the customer and once it is established as regards the beneficiary it can be modified or revoked only with his consent.

(3) Unless otherwise agreed after a revocable credit is established it may be modified or revoked by the issuer without notice to or consent from the customer or beneficiary.

(4) Notwithstanding any modification or revocation of a revocable credit any person authorized to honor or negotiate under the terms of the original credit is entitled to reimbursement for or honor of any draft or demand for payment duly honored or negotiated before receipt of notice of the modification or revocation and the issuer in turn is entitled to reimbursement from its customer.

§ 5—107
Advice of Credit; Confirmation; Error in Statement of Terms

(1) Unless otherwise specified an advising bank by advising a credit issued by another bank does not assume any obligation to honor drafts drawn or demands for payment made under the credit but it does assume obligation for the accuracy of its own statement.

(2) A confirming bank by confirming a credit becomes di-

rectly obligated on the credit to the extent of its confirmation as though it were its issuer and acquires the rights of an issuer.

(3) Even though an advising bank incorrectly advises the terms of a credit it has been authorized to advise the credit is established as against the issuer to the extent of its original terms.

(4) Unless otherwise specified the customer bears as against the issuer all risk of transmission and reasonable translation or interpretation of any message relating to a credit.

§ 5—108
"Notation Credit"; Exhaustion of Credit

(1) A credit which specifies that any person purchasing or paying drafts drawn or demands for payment made under it must note the amount of the draft or demand on the letter or advice of credit is a "notation credit".

(2) Under a notation credit

(a) a person paying the beneficiary or purchasing a draft or demand for payment from him acquires a right to honor only if the appropriate notation is made and by transferring or forwarding for honor the documents under the credit such a person warrants to the issuer that the notation has been made; and

(b) unless the credit or a signed statement that an appropriate notation has been made accompanies the draft or demand for payment the issuer may delay honor until evidence of notation has been procured which is satisfactory to it but its obligation and that of its customer continue for a reasonable time not exceeding thirty days to obtain such evidence.

(3) If the credit is not a notation credit

(a) the issuer may honor complying drafts or demands for payment presented to it in the order in which they are presented and is discharged pro tanto by honor of any such draft or demand;

(b) as between competing good faith purchasers of complying drafts or demands the person first purchasing has priority over a subsequent purchaser even though the later purchased draft or demand has been first honored.

§ 5—109
Issuer's Obligation to Its Customer

(1) An issuer's obligation to its customer includes good faith and observance of any general banking usage but unless otherwise agreed does not include liability or responsibility

(a) for performance of the underlying contract for sale or other transaction between the customer and the beneficiary; or

(b) for any act or omission of any person other than itself or its own branch or for loss or destruction of a draft, demand or document in transit or in the possession of others; or

(c) based on knowledge or lack of knowledge of any usage of any particular trade.

(2) An issuer must examine documents with care so as to ascertain that on their face they appear to comply with the terms of the credit but unless otherwise agreed assumes no liability or responsibility for the genuineness, falsification or effect of any document which appears on such examination to be regular on its face.

(3) A non-bank issuer is not bound by any banking usage of which it has no knowledge.

§ 5—110
Availability of Credit in Portions; Presenter's Reservation of Lien or Claim

(1) Unless otherwise specified a credit may be used in portions in the discretion of the beneficiary.

(2) Unless otherwise specified a person by presenting a documentary draft or demand for payment under a credit relinquishes upon its honor all claims to the documents and a person by transferring such draft or demand or causing such presentment authorizes such relinquishment. An explicit reservation of claim makes the draft or demand non-complying.

§ 5—111
Warranties on Transfer and Presentment

(1) Unless otherwise agreed the beneficiary by transferring or presenting a documentary draft or demand for payment warrants to all interested parties that the necessary conditions of the credit have been complied with. This is in addition to any warranties arising under Articles 3, 4, 7 and 8.

(2) Unless otherwise agreed a negotiating, advising, confirming, collecting or issuing bank presenting or transferring a draft or demand for payment under a credit warrants only the matters warranted by a collecting bank under Article 4 and any such bank transferring a document warrants only the matters warranted by an intermediary under Articles 7 and 8.

§ 5—112
Time Allowed for Honor or Rejection; Withholding Honor or Rejection by Consent; "Presenter"

(1) A bank to which a documentary draft or demand for payment is presented under a credit may without dishonor of the draft, demand or credit

(a) defer honor until the close of the third banking day following receipt of the documents; and

(b) further defer honor if the presenter has expressly or impliedly consented thereto.

Failure to honor within the time here specified constitutes dishonor of the draft or demand and of the credit [except as otherwise provided in subsection (4) of Section 5—114 on conditional payment].

Note: *The bracketed language in the last sentence of subsection (1) should be included only if the optional provisions of Section 5—114(4) and (5) are included.*

(2) Upon dishonor the bank may unless otherwise instructed fulfill its duty to return the draft or demand and the documents by holding them at the disposal of the presenter and sending him an advice to that effect.

(3) "Presenter" means any person presenting a draft or demand for payment for honor under a credit even though that person is a confirming bank or other correspondent which is acting under an issuer's authorization.

§ 5—113
Indemnities

(1) A bank seeking to obtain (whether for itself or another) honor, negotiation or reimbursement under a credit may give an indemnity to induce such honor, negotiation or reimbursement.

(2) An indemnity agreement inducing honor, negotiation or reimbursement

    (a) unless otherwise explicitly agreed applies to defects in the documents but not in the goods; and

    (b) unless a longer time is explicitly agreed expires at the end of ten business days following receipt of the documents by the ultimate customer unless notice of objection is sent before such expiration date. The ultimate customer may send notice of objection to the person from whom he received the documents and any bank receiving such notice is under a duty to send notice to its transferor before its midnight deadline.

§ 5—114
Issuer's Duty and Privilege to Honor;
Right to Reimbursement

(1) An issuer must honor a draft or demand for payment which complies with the terms of the relevant credit regardless of whether the goods or documents conform to the underlying contract for sale or other contract between the customer and the beneficiary. The issuer is not excused from honor of such a draft or demand by reason of an additional general term that all documents must be satisfactory to the issuer, but an issuer may require that specified documents must be satisfactory to it.

(2) Unless otherwise agreed when documents appear on their face to comply with the terms of a credit but a required document does not in fact conform to the warranties made on negotiation or transfer of a document of title (Section 7—507) or of a certificated security (Section 8—306) or is forged or fraudulent or there is fraud in the transaction:

    (a) the issuer must honor the draft or demand for payment if honor is demanded by a negotiating bank or other holder of the draft or demand which has taken the draft or demand under the credit and under circumstances which would make it a holder in due course (Section 3—302) and in an appropriate case would make it a person to whom a document of title has been duly negotiated (Section 7—502) or a bona fide purchaser of a certificated security (Section 8—302); and

    (b) in all other cases as against its customer, an issuer acting in good faith may honor the draft or demand for payment despite notification from the customer of fraud, forgery or other defect not apparent on the face of the documents but a court of appropriate jurisdiction may enjoin such honor.

(3) Unless otherwise agreed an issuer which has duly honored a draft or demand for payment is entitled to immediate reimbursement of any payment made under the credit and to be put in effectively available funds not later than the day before maturity of any acceptance made under the credit.

[(4) When a credit provides for payment by the issuer on receipt of notice that the required documents are in the possession of a correspondent or other agent of the issuer

    (a) any payment made on receipt of such notice is conditional; and

    (b) the issuer may reject documents which do not comply with the credit if it does so within three banking days following its receipt of the documents; and

    (c) in the event of such rejection, the issuer is entitled by charge back or otherwise to return of the payment made.]

[(5) In the case covered by subsection (4) failure to reject documents within the time specified in subparagraph (b) constitutes acceptance of the documents and makes the payment final in favor of the beneficiary.]

Amended in 1977.

Note: *Subsections (4) and (5) are bracketed as optional. If they are included the bracketed language in the last sentence of Section 5—112(1) should also be included.*

§ 5—115
Remedy for Improper Dishonor
or Anticipatory Repudiation

(1) When an issuer wrongfully dishonors a draft or demand for payment presented under a credit the person entitled to honor has with respect to any documents the rights of a person in the position of a seller (Section 2—707) and may recover from the issuer the face amount of the draft or demand together with incidental damages under Section 2—710 on seller's incidental damages and interest but less any amount realized by resale or other use or disposition of the subject matter of the transaction. In the event no resale or other utilization is made the documents, goods or other subject matter involved in the transaction must be turned over to the issuer on payment of judgment.

(2) When an issuer wrongfully cancels or otherwise repudiates a credit before presentment of a draft or demand for

payment drawn under it the beneficiary has the rights of a seller after anticipatory repudiation by the buyer under Section 2—610 if he learns of the repudiation in time reasonably to avoid procurement of the required documents. Otherwise the beneficiary has an immediate right of action for wrongful dishonor.

§ 5—116
Transfer and Assignment

(1) The right to draw under a credit can be transferred or assigned only when the credit is expressly designated as transferable or assignable.

(2) Even though the credit specifically states that it is non-transferable or nonassignable the beneficiary may before performance of the conditions of the credit assign his right to proceeds. Such an assignment is an assignment of an account under Article 9 on Secured Transactions and is governed by that Article except that

    (a) the assignment is ineffective until the letter of credit or advice of credit is delivered to the assignee which delivery constitutes perfection of the security interest under Article 9; and

    (b) the issuer may honor drafts or demands for payment drawn under the credit until it receives a notification of the assignment signed by the beneficiary which reasonably identifies the credit involved in the assignment and contains a request to pay the assignee; and

    (c) after what reasonably appears to be such a notification has been received the issuer may without dishonor refuse to accept or pay even to a person otherwise entitled to honor until the letter of credit or advice of credit is exhibited to the issuer.

(3) Except where the beneficiary has effectively assigned his right to draw or his right to proceeds, nothing in this section limits his right to transfer or negotiate drafts or demands drawn under the credit.

5—117
Insolvency of Bank Holding Funds for Documentary Credit

(1) Where an issuer or an advising or confirming bank or a bank which has for a customer procured issuance of a credit by another bank becomes insolvent before final payment under the credit and the credit is one to which this Article is made applicable by paragraphs (a) or (b) of Section 5—102 (1) on scope, the receipt or allocation of funds or collateral to secure or meet obligations under the credit shall have the following results:

    (a) to the extent of any funds or collateral turned over after or before the insolvency as indemnity against or specifically for the purpose of payment of drafts or demands for payment drawn under the designated credit, the drafts or demands are entitled to payment in prefer-

ence over depositors or other general creditors of the issuer or bank; and

    (b) on expiration of the credit or surrender of the beneficiary's rights under it unused any person who has given such funds or collateral is similarly entitled to return thereof; and

    (c) a charge to a general or current account with a bank if specifically consented to for the purpose of indemnity against or payment of drafts or demands for payment drawn under the designated credit falls under the same rules as if the funds had been drawn out in cash and then turned over with specific instructions.

(2) After honor or reimbursement under this section the customer or other person for whose account the insolvent bank has acted is entitled to receive the documents involved.

ARTICLE 6/Bulk Transfers

§ 6—101
Short Title

This Article shall be known and may be cited as Uniform Commercial Code—Bulk Transfers.

§ 6—102
"Bulk Transfers"; Transfers of Equipment; Enterprises Subject to This Article; Bulk Transfers Subject to This Article

(1) A "bulk transfer" is any transfer in bulk and not in the ordinary course of the transferor's business of a major part of the materials, supplies, merchandise or other inventory (Section 9—109) of an enterprise subject to this Article.

(2) A transfer of a substantial part of the equipment (Section 9—109) of such an enterprise is a bulk transfer if it is made in connection with a bulk transfer of inventory, but not otherwise.

(3) The enterprises subject to this Article are all those whose principal business is the sale of merchandise from stock, including those who manufacture what they sell.

(4) Except as limited by the following section all bulk transfers of goods located within this state are subject to this Article.

§ 6—103
Transfers Excepted From This Article

The following transfers are not subject to this Article:

(1) Those made to give security for the performance of an obligation;

(2) General assignments for the benefit of all the creditors of the transferor, and subsequent transfers by the assignee thereunder;

(3) Transfers in settlement or realization of a lien or other security interest;

(4) Sales by executors, administrators, receivers, trustees in bankruptcy, or any public officer under judicial process;

(5) Sales made in the course of judicial or administrative proceedings for the dissolution or reorganization of a corporation and of which notice is sent to the creditors of the corporation pursuant to order of the court or administrative agency;

(6) Transfers to a person maintaining a known place of business in this State who becomes bound to pay the debts of the transferor in full and gives public notice of that fact, and who is solvent after becoming so bound;

(7) A transfer to a new business enterprise organized to take over and continue the business, if public notice of the transaction is given and the new enterprise assumes the debts of the transferor and he receives nothing from the transaction except an interest in the new enterprise junior to the claims of creditors;

(8) Transfers of property which is exempt from execution.

Public notice under subsection (6) or subsection (7) may be given by publishing once a week for two consecutive weeks in a newspaper of general circulation where the transferor had its principal place of business in this state an advertisement including the names and addresses of the transferor and transferee and the effective date of the transfer.

§ 6—104
Schedule of Property; List of Creditors

(1) Except as provided with respect to auction sales (Section 6—108), a bulk transfer subject to this Article is ineffective against any creditor of the transferor unless:

(a) the transferee requires the transferor to furnish a list of his existing creditors prepared as stated in this section; and

(b) the parties prepare a schedule of the property transferred sufficient to identify it; and

(c) the transferee preserves the list and schedule for six months next following the transfer and permits inspection of either or both and copying therefrom at all reasonable hours by any creditor of the transferor, or files the list and schedule in (*a public office to be here identified*).

(2) The list of creditors must be signed and sworn to or affirmed by the transferor or his agent. It must contain the names and business addresses of all creditors of the transferor, with the amounts when known, and also the names of all persons who are known to the transferor to assert claims against him even though such claims are disputed. If the transferor is the obligor of an outstanding issue of bonds, debentures or the like as to which there is an indenture trustee, the list of creditors need include only the name and address of the indenture trustee and the aggregate outstanding principal amount of the issue.

(3) Responsibility for the completeness and accuracy of the list of creditors rests on the transferor, and the transfer is not rendered ineffective by errors or omissions therein unless the transferee is shown to have had knowledge.

§ 6—105
Notice to Creditors

In addition to the requirements of the preceding section, any bulk transfer subject to this Article except one made by auction sale (Section 6—108) is ineffective against any creditor of the transferor unless at least ten days before he takes possession of the goods or pays for them, whichever happens first, the transferee gives notice of the transfer in the manner and to the persons hereafter provided (Section 6—107).

[§ 6—106
Application of the Proceeds

In addition to the requirements of the two preceding sections:

(1) Upon every bulk transfer subject to this Article for which new consideration becomes payable except those made by sale at auction it is the duty of the transferee to assure that such consideration is applied so far as necessary to pay those debts of the transferor which are either shown on the list furnished by the transferor (Section 6—104) or filed in writing in the place stated in the notice (Section 6—107) within thirty days after the mailing of such notice. This duty of the transferee runs to all the holders of such debts, and may be enforced by any of them for the benefit of all.

(2) If any of said debts are in dispute the necessary sum may be withheld from distribution until the dispute is settled or adjudicated.

(3) If the consideration payable is not enough to pay all of the said debts in full distribution shall be made pro rata.]

Note: *This section is bracketed to indicate division of opinion as to whether or not it is a wise provision, and to suggest that this is a point on which State enactments may differ without serious damage to the principle of uniformity. In any State where this section is omitted, the following parts of sections, also bracketed in the text, should also be omitted, namely:*

Section 6—107(2)(c).
6—108(3)(c).
6—109(2).

In any State where this section is enacted, these other provisions should be also.

Optional Subsection (4)

[(4) The transferee may within ten days after he takes possession of the goods pay the consideration into the (specify court) in the county where the transferor had its principal place of business in this state and thereafter may discharge his duty under this section by giving notice by registered or certified mail to all the persons to whom the duty runs that the consideration has been paid into that court and that they should file their claims there. On motion of any interested party, the court may order the distribution of the consideration to the persons entitled to it.]

Note: *Optional subsection (4) is recommended for those states which do not have a general statute providing for payment of money into court.*

§ 6—107
The Notice

(1) The notice to creditors (Section 6—105) shall state:

  (a) that a bulk transfer is about to be made; and

  (b) the names and business addresses of the transferor and transferee, and all other business names and addresses used by the transferor within three years last past so far as known to the transferee; and

  (c) whether or not all the debts of the transferor are to be paid in full as they fall due as a result of the transaction, and if so, the address to which creditors should send their bills.

(2) If the debts of the transferor are not to be paid in full as they fall due or if the transferee is in doubt on that point then the notice shall state further:

  (a) the location and general description of the property to be transferred and the estimated total of the transferor's debts;

  (b) the address where the schedule of property and list of creditors (Section 6—104) may be inspected;

  (c) whether the transfer is to pay existing debts and if so the amount of such debts and to whom owing;

  (d) whether the transfer is for new consideration and if so the amount of such consideration and the time and place of payment; [and]

  [(e) if for new consideration the time and place where creditors of the transferor are to file their claims.]

(3) The notice in any case shall be delivered personally or sent by registered or certified mail to all the persons shown on the list of creditors furnished by the transferor (Section 6—104) and to all other persons who are known to the transferee to hold or assert claims against the transferor.

§ 6—108
Auction Sales; "Auctioneer"

(1) A bulk transfer is subject to this Article even though it is by sale at auction, but only in the manner and with the results stated in this section.

(2) The transferor shall furnish a list of his creditors and assist in the preparation of a schedule of the property to be sold, both prepared as before stated (Section 6—104).

(3) The person or persons other than the transferor who direct, control or are responsible for the auction are collectively called the "auctioneer". The auctioneer shall:

  (a) receive and retain the list of creditors and prepare and retain the schedule of property for the period stated in this Article (Section 6—104);

  (b) give notice of the auction personally or by registered or certified mail at least ten days before it occurs to all persons shown on the list of creditors and to all other persons who are known to him to hold or assert claims against the transferor; [and]

  [(c) assure that the net proceeds of the auction are applied as provided in this Article (Section 6—106).]

(4) Failure of the auctioneer to perform any of these duties does not affect the validity of the sale or the title of the purchasers, but if the auctioneer knows that the auction constitutes a bulk transfer such failure renders the auctioneer liable to the creditors of the transferor as a class for the sums owing to them from the transferor up to but not exceeding the net proceeds of the auction. If the auctioneer consists of several persons their liability is joint and several.

§ 6—109
What Creditors Protected; [Credit for Payment to Particular Creditors]

(1) The creditors of the transferor mentioned in this Article are those holding claims based on transactions or events occurring before the bulk transfer, but creditors who become such after notice to creditors is given (Sections 6—105 and 6—107) are not entitled to notice.

[(2) Against the aggregate obligation imposed by the provisions of this Article concerning the application of the proceeds (Section 6—106 and subsection (3)(c) of 6—108) the transferee or auctioneer is entitled to credit for sums paid to particular creditors of the transferor, not exceeding the sums believed in good faith at the time of the payment to be properly payable to such creditors.]

§ 6—110
Subsequent Transfers

When the title of a transferee to property is subject to a defect by reason of his non-compliance with the requirements of this Article, then:

(1) a purchaser of any of such property from such transferee who pays no value or who takes with notice of such non-compliance takes subject to such defect, but

(2) a purchaser for value in good faith and without such notice takes free of such defect.

§ 6—111
Limitation of Actions and Levies

No action under this Article shall be brought nor levy made more than six months after the date on which the transferee took possession of the goods unless the transfer has been concealed. If the transfer has been concealed, actions may be brought or levies made within six months after its discovery.

Note to Article 6: *Section 6—106 is bracketed to indicate division of opinion as to whether or not it is a wise provision, and to suggest that this is a point on which State enactments may differ without serious damage to the principle of uniformity. In any State where Section 6—106 is not enacted, the following parts of sections, also bracketed in the text, should also be omitted, namely:*

Sec. 6—107(2)(e).
6—108(3)(c).
6—109(2).

In any State where Section 6—106 is enacted, these other provisions should be also.

ARTICLE 7/Warehouse Receipts, Bills of Lading and Other Documents of Title

PART 1/General

§ 7—101
Short Title

This Article shall be known and may be cited as Uniform Commercial Code—Documents of Title.

§ 7—102
Definitions and Index of Definitions

(1) In this Article, unless the context otherwise requires:

(a) "Bailee" means the person who by a warehouse receipt, bill of lading or other document of title acknowledges possession of goods and contracts to deliver them.

(b) "Consignee" means the person named in a bill to whom or to whose order the bill promises delivery.

(c) "Consignor" means the person named in a bill as the person from whom the goods have been received for shipment.

(d) "Delivery order" means a written order to deliver goods directed to a warehouseman, carrier or other person who in the ordinary course of business issues warehouse receipts or bills of lading.

(e) "Document" means document of title as defined in the general definitions in Article 1 (Section 1—201).

(f) "Goods" means all things which are treated as movable for the purposes of a contract of storage or transportation.

(g) "Issuer" means a bailee who issues a document except that in relation to an unaccepted delivery order it means the person who orders the possessor of goods to deliver. Issuer includes any person for whom an agent or employee purports to act in issuing a document if the agent or employee has real or apparent authority to issue documents, notwithstanding that the issuer received no goods or that the goods were misdescribed or that in any other respect the agent or employee violated his instructions.

(h) "Warehouseman" is a person engaged in the business of storing goods for hire.

(2) Other definitions applying to this Article or to specified Parts thereof, and the sections in which they appear are:

"Duly negotiate". Section 7—501.

"Person entitled under the document". Section 7—403(4).

(3) Definitions in other Articles applying to this Article and the sections in which they appear are:

"Contract for sale". Section 2—106.

"Overseas". Section 2—323.

"Receipt" of goods. Section 2—103.

(4) In addition Article 1 contains general definitions and principles of construction and interpretation applicable throughout this Article.

§ 7—103
Relation of Article to Treaty, Statute, Tariff, Classification or Regulation

To the extent that any treaty or statute of the United States, regulatory statute of this State or tariff, classification or regulation filed or issued pursuant thereto is applicable, the provisions of this Article are subject thereto.

§ 7—104
Negotiable and Non-Negotiable Warehouse Receipt, Bill of Lading or Other Document of Title

(1) A warehouse receipt, bill of lading or other document of title is negotiable

(a) if by its terms the goods are to be delivered to bearer or to the order of a named person; or

(b) where recognized in overseas trade, if it runs to a named person or assigns.

(2) Any other document is non-negotiable. A bill of lading in which it is stated that the goods are consigned to a named person is not made negotiable by a provision that the goods are to be delivered only against a written order signed by the same or another named person.

§ 7—105
Construction Against Negative Implication

The omission from either Part 2 or Part 3 of this Article of a provision corresponding to a provision made in the other Part does not imply that a corresponding rule of law is not applicable.

PART 2/Warehouse Receipts: Special Provisions

§ 7—201
Who May Issue a Warehouse Receipt; Storage Under Government Bond

(1) A warehouse receipt may be issued by any warehouseman.

(2) Where goods including distilled spirits and agricultural commodities are stored under a statute requiring a bond against withdrawal or a license for the issuance of receipts in the nature of warehouse receipts, a receipt issued for the goods has like effect as a warehouse receipt even though issued by a person who is the owner of the goods and is not a warehouseman.

§ 7—202
Form of Warehouse Receipt; Essential Terms; Optional Terms

(1) A warehouse receipt need not be in any particular form.

(2) Unless a warehouse receipt embodies within its written or printed terms each of the following, the warehouseman is liable for damages caused by the omission to a person injured thereby:

(a) the location of the warehouse where the goods are stored;

(b) the date of issue of the receipt;

(c) the consecutive number of the receipt;

(d) a statement whether the goods received will be delivered to the bearer, to a specified person, or to a specified person or his order;

(e) the rate of storage and handling charges, except that where goods are stored under a field warehousing arrangement a statement of that fact is sufficient on a non-negotiable receipt;

(f) a description of the goods or of the packages containing them;

(g) the signature of the warehouseman, which may be made by his authorized agent;

(h) if the receipt is issued for goods of which the warehouseman is owner, either solely or jointly or in common with others, the fact of such ownership; and

(i) a statement of the amount of advances made and of liabilities incurred for which the warehouseman claims a lien or security interest (Section 7—209). If the precise amount of such advances made or of such liabilities incurred is, at the time of the issue of the receipt, unknown to the warehouseman or to his agent who issues it, a statement of the fact that advances have been made or liabilities incurred and the purpose thereof is sufficient.

(3) A warehouseman may insert in his receipt any other terms which are not contrary to the provisions of this Act and do not impair his obligation of delivery (Section 7—403) or his duty of care (Section 7—204). Any contrary provisions shall be ineffective.

§ 7—203
Liability for Non-Receipt or Misdescription

A party to or purchaser for value in good faith of a document of title other than a bill of lading relying in either case upon the description therein of the goods may recover from the issuer damages caused by the non-receipt or misdescription of the goods, except to the extent that the document conspicuously indicates that the issuer does not know whether any part or all of the goods in fact were received or conform to the description, as where the description is in terms of marks or labels or kind, quantity or condition, or the receipt or description is qualified by "contents, condition and quality unknown", "said to contain" or the like, if such indication be true, or the party or purchaser otherwise has notice.

§ 7—204
Duty of Care; Contractual Limitation of Warehouseman's Liability

(1) A warehouseman is liable for damages for loss of or injury to the goods caused by his failure to exercise such care in regard to them as a reasonably careful man would exercise under like circumstances but unless otherwise agreed he is not liable for damages which could not have been avoided by the exercise of such care.

(2) Damages may be limited by a term in the warehouse receipt or storage agreement limiting the amount of liability in case of loss or damage, and setting forth a specific liability per article or item, or value per unit of weight, beyond which the warehouseman shall not be liable; provided, however, that such liability may on written request of the bailor at the time of signing such storage agreement or within a reasonable time after receipt of the warehouse receipt be increased on part or all of the goods thereunder, in which event increased rates may be charged based on such increased valuation, but that no such increase shall be permitted contrary to a lawful limitation of liability contained in the warehouseman's tariff, if any. No such limitation is effective with respect to the warehouseman's liability for conversion to his own use.

(3) Reasonable provisions as to the time and manner of presenting claims and instituting actions based on the bailment may be included in the warehouse receipt or tariff.

(4) This section does not impair or repeal . . .

Note: *Insert in subsection (4) a reference to any statute which imposes a higher responsibility upon the warehouseman or invalidates contractual limitations which would be permissible under this Article.*

§ 7—205
Title Under Warehouse Receipt Defeated in Certain Cases

A buyer in the ordinary course of business of fungible goods sold and delivered by a warehouseman who is also in the business of buying and selling such goods takes free of any claim under a warehouse receipt even though it has been duly negotiated.

§ 7—206
Termination of Storage at Warehouseman's Option

(1) A warehouseman may on notifying the person on whose account the goods are held and any other person known to claim an interest in the goods require payment of any charges and removal of the goods from the warehouse at the termination of the period of storage fixed by the document, or, if no period is fixed, within a stated period not less than thirty days after the notification. If the goods are not removed before the date specified in the notification, the warehouseman may sell them in accordance with the provisions of the section on enforcement of a warehouseman's lien (Section 7—210).

(2) If a warehouseman in good faith believes that the goods are about to deteriorate or decline in value to less than the amount of his lien within the time prescribed in subsection (1) for notification, advertisement and sale, the warehouseman may specify in the notification any reasonable shorter time for removal of the goods and in case the goods are not removed, may sell them at public sale held not less than one week after a single advertisement or posting.

(3) If as a result of a quality or condition of the goods of which the warehouseman had no notice at the time of deposit the goods are a hazard to other property or to the warehouse or to persons, the warehouseman may sell the goods at public or private sale without advertisement on reasonable notification to all persons known to claim an interest in the goods. If the warehouseman after a reasonable effort is unable to sell the goods he may dispose of them in any lawful manner and shall incur no liability by reason of such disposition.

(4) The warehouseman must deliver the goods to any person entitled to them under this Article upon due demand made at any time prior to sale or other disposition under this section.

(5) The warehouseman may satisfy his lien from the proceeds of any sale or disposition under this section but must hold the balance for delivery on the demand of any person to whom he would have been bound to deliver the goods.

§ 7—207
Goods Must Be Kept Separate; Fungible Goods

(1) Unless the warehouse receipt otherwise provides, a warehouseman must keep separate the goods covered by each receipt so as to permit at all times identification and delivery of those goods except that different lots of fungible goods may be commingled.

(2) Fungible goods so commingled are owned in common by the persons entitled thereto and the warehouseman is severally liable to each owner for that owner's share. Where because of overissue a mass of fungible goods is insufficient to meet all the receipts which the warehouseman has issued against it, the persons entitled include all holders to whom overissued receipts have been duly negotiated.

§ 7—208
Altered Warehouse Receipts

Where a blank in a negotiable warehouse receipt has been filled in without authority, a purchaser for value and without notice of the want of authority may treat the insertion as authorized. Any other unauthorized alteration leaves any receipt enforceable against the issuer according to its original tenor.

§ 7—209
Lien of Warehouseman

(1) A warehouseman has a lien against the bailor on the goods covered by a warehouse receipt or on the proceeds thereof in his possession for charges for storage or transportation (including demurrage and terminal charges), insurance, labor, or charges present or future in relation to the goods, and for expenses necessary for preservation of the goods or reasonably incurred in their sale pursuant to law. If the person on whose account the goods are held is liable for like charges or expenses in relation to other goods whenever deposited and it is stated in the receipt that a lien is claimed for charges and expenses in relation to other goods, the warehouseman also has a lien against him for such charges and expenses whether or not the other goods have been delivered by the warehouseman. But against a person to whom a negotiable warehouse receipt is duly negotiated a warehouseman's lien is limited to charges in an amount or at a rate specified on the receipt or if no charges are so specified then to a reasonable charge for storage of the goods covered by the receipt subsequent to the date of the receipt.

(2) The warehouseman may also reserve a security interest against the bailor for a maximum amount specified on the receipt for charges other than those specified in subsection (1), such as for money advanced and interest. Such a security interest is governed by the Article on Secured Transactions (Article 9).

(3) (a) A warehouseman's lien for charges and expenses under subsection (1) or a security interest under subsection (2) is also effective against any person who so entrusted the bailor with possession of the goods that a pledge of them by him to a good faith purchaser for value would have been valid but is not effective against a person as to whom the document confers no right in the goods covered by it under Section 7—503.

(b) A warehouseman's lien on household goods for charges and expenses in relation to the goods under subsection (1) is also effective against all persons if the depositor was the legal possessor of the goods at the time of deposit. "Household goods" means furniture, furnishings and personal effects used by the depositor in a dwelling.

(4) A warehouseman loses his lien on any goods which he voluntarily delivers or which he unjustifiably refuses to deliver.

§ 7—210
Enforcement of Warehouseman's Lien

(1) Except as provided in subsection (2), a warehouseman's lien may be enforced by public or private sale of the goods in block or in parcels, at any time or place and on any terms which are commercially reasonable, after notifying all persons known to claim an interest in the goods. Such notification must include a statement of the amount due, the nature of the proposed sale and the time and place of any public sale. The fact that a better price could have been obtained by a sale at a different time or in a different method from that selected by the warehouseman is not of itself sufficient to establish that the sale was not made in a commercially reasonable manner. If the warehouseman either sells the goods in the usual manner in any recognized market therefor, or if he sells at the price current in such market at the time of his sale, or if he has otherwise sold in conformity with commercially reasonable practices among dealers in the type of goods sold, he has sold in a commercially reasonable manner. A sale of more goods than apparently necessary to be offered to insure satisfaction of the obligation is not commercially reasonable except in cases covered by the preceding sentence.

(2) A warehouseman's lien on goods other than goods stored by a merchant in the course of his business may be enforced only as follows:

(a) All persons known to claim an interest in the goods must be notified.

(b) The notification must be delivered in person or sent by registered or certified letter to the last known address of any person to be notified.

(c) The notification must include an itemized statement of the claim, a description of the goods subject to the lien, a demand for payment within a specified time not less than ten days after receipt of the notification, and a conspicuous statement that unless the claim is paid within the time the goods will be advertised for sale and sold by auction at a specified time and place.

(d) The sale must conform to the terms of the notification.

(e) The sale must be held at the nearest suitable place to that where the goods are held or stored.

(f) After the expiration of the time given in the notification, an advertisement of the sale must be published once a week for two weeks consecutively in a newspaper of general circulation where the sale is to be held. The advertisement must include a description of the goods, the name of the person on whose account they are being held, and the time and place of the sale. The sale must take place at least fifteen days after the first publication. If there is no newspaper of general circulation where the sale is to be held, the advertisement must be posted at least ten days before the sale in not less than six conspicuous places in the neighborhood of the proposed sale.

(3) Before any sale pursuant to this section any person claiming a right in the goods may pay the amount necessary to satisfy the lien and the reasonable expenses incurred under this section. In that event the goods must not be sold, but must be retained by the warehouseman subject to the terms of the receipt and this Article.

(4) The warehouseman may buy at any public sale pursuant to this section.

(5) A purchaser in good faith of goods sold to enforce a warehouseman's lien takes the goods free of any rights of persons against whom the lien was valid, despite noncompliance by the warehouseman with the requirements of this section.

(6) The warehouseman may satisfy his lien from the proceeds of any sale pursuant to this section but must hold the balance, if any, for delivery on demand to any person to whom he would have been bound to deliver the goods.

(7) The rights provided by this section shall be in addition to all other rights allowed by law to a creditor against his debtor.

(8) Where a lien is on goods stored by a merchant in the course of his business the lien may be enforced in accordance with either subsection (1) or (2).

(9) The warehouseman is liable for damages caused by failure to comply with the requirements for sale under this section and in case of willful violation is liable for conversion.

PART 3/Bills of Lading: Special Provisions

§ 7—301
Liability for Non-Receipt or Misdescription; "Said to Contain"; "Shipper's Load and Count"; Improper Handling

(1) A consignee of a non-negotiable bill who has given value in good faith or a holder to whom a negotiable bill has been duly negotiated relying in either case upon the description

therein of the goods, or upon the date therein shown, may recover from the issuer damages caused by the misdating of the bill or the non-receipt or misdescription of the goods, except to the extent that the document indicates that the issuer does not know whether any part or all of the goods in fact were received or conform to the description, as where the description is in terms of marks or labels or kind, quantity, or condition or the receipt or description is qualified by "contents or condition of contents of packages unknown", "said to contain", "shipper's weight, load and count" or the like, if such indication be true.

(2) When goods are loaded by an issuer who is a common carrier, the issuer must count the packages of goods if package freight and ascertain the kind and quantity if bulk freight. In such cases "shipper's weight, load and count" or other words indicating that the description was made by the shipper are ineffective except as to freight concealed by packages.

(3) When bulk freight is loaded by a shipper who makes available to the issuer adequate facilities for weighing such freight, an issuer who is a common carrier must ascertain the kind and quantity within a reasonable time after receiving the written request of the shipper to do so. In such cases "shipper's weight" or other words of like purport are ineffective.

(4) The issuer may by inserting in the bill the words "shipper's weight, load and count" or other words of like purport indicate that the goods were loaded by the shipper; and if such statement be true the issuer shall not be liable for damages caused by the improper loading. But their omission does not imply liability for such damages.

(5) The shipper shall be deemed to have guaranteed to the issuer the accuracy at the time of shipment of the description, marks, labels, number, kind, quantity, condition and weight, as furnished by him; and the shipper shall indemnify the issuer against damage caused by inaccuracies in such particulars. The right of the issuer to such indemnity shall in no way limit his responsibility and liability under the contract of carriage to any person other than the shipper.

§ 7—302
Through Bills of Lading and Similar Documents

(1) The issuer of a through bill of lading or other document embodying an undertaking to be performed in part by persons acting as its agents or by connecting carriers is liable to anyone entitled to recover on the document for any breach by such other persons or by a connecting carrier of its obligation under the document but to the extent that the bill covers an undertaking to be performed overseas or in territory not contiguous to the continental United States or an undertaking including matters other than transportation this liability may be varied by agreement of the parties.

(2) Where goods covered by a through bill of lading or other document embodying an undertaking to be performed

in part by persons other than the issuer are received by any such person, he is subject with respect to his own performance while the goods are in his possession to the obligation of the issuer. His obligation is discharged by delivery of the goods to another such person pursuant to the document and does not include liability for breach by any other such persons or by the issuer.

(3) The issuer of such through bill of lading or other document shall be entitled to recover from the connecting carrier or such other person in possession of the goods when the breach of the obligation under the document occurred, the amount it may be required to pay to anyone entitled to recover on the document therefor, as may be evidenced by any receipt, judgment, or transcript thereof, and the amount of any expense reasonably incurred by it in defending any action brought by anyone entitled to recover on the document therefor.

§ 7—303
Diversion; Reconsignment; Change of Instructions

(1) Unless the bill of lading otherwise provides, the carrier may deliver the goods to a person or destination other than that stated in the bill or may otherwise dispose of the goods on instructions from

    (a) the holder of a negotiable bill; or

    (b) the consignor on a non-negotiable bill notwithstanding contrary instructions from the consignee; or

    (c) the consignee on a non-negotiable bill in the absence of contrary instructions from the consignor, if the goods have arrived at the billed destination or if the consignee is in possession of the bill; or

    (d) the consignee on a non-negotiable bill if he is entitled as against the consignor to dispose of them.

(2) Unless such instructions are noted on a negotiable bill of lading, a person to whom the bill is duly negotiated can hold the bailee according to the original terms.

§ 7—304
Bills of Lading in a Set

(1) Except where customary in overseas transportation, a bill of lading must not be issued in a set of parts. The issuer is liable for damages caused by violation of this subsection.

(2) Where a bill of lading is lawfully drawn in a set of parts, each of which is numbered and expressed to be valid only if the goods have not been delivered against any other part, the whole of the parts constitute one bill.

(3) Where a bill of lading is lawfully issued in a set of parts and different parts are negotiated to different persons, the title of the holder to whom the first due negotiation is made prevails as to both the document and the goods even though any later holder may have received the goods from the carrier in good faith and discharged the carrier's obligation by surrender of his part.

(4) Any person who negotiates or transfers a single part of a bill of lading drawn in a set is liable to holders of that part as if it were the whole set.

(5) The bailee is obliged to deliver in accordance with Part 4 of this Article against the first presented part of a bill of lading lawfully drawn in a set. Such delivery discharges the bailee's obligation on the whole bill.

§ 7—305
Destination Bills

(1) Instead of issuing a bill of lading to the consignor at the place of shipment a carrier may at the request of the consignor procure the bill to be issued at destination or at any other place designated in the request.

(2) Upon request of anyone entitled as against the carrier to control the goods while in transit and on surrender of any outstanding bill of lading or other receipt covering such goods, the issuer may procure a substitute bill to be issued at any place designated in the request.

§ 7—306
Altered Bills of Lading

An unauthorized alteration or filling in of a blank in a bill of lading leaves the bill enforceable according to its original tenor.

§ 7—307
Lien of Carrier

(1) A carrier has a lien on the goods covered by a bill of lading for charges subsequent to the date of its receipt of the goods for storage or transportation (including demurrage and terminal charges) and for expenses necessary for preservation of the goods incident to their transportation or reasonably incurred in their sale pursuant to law. But against a purchaser for value of a negotiable bill of lading a carrier's lien is limited to charges stated in the bill or the applicable tariffs, or if no charges are stated then to a reasonable charge.

(2) A lien for charges and expenses under subsection (1) on goods which the carrier was required by law to receive for transportation is effective against the consignor or any person entitled to the goods unless the carrier had notice that the consignor lacked authority to subject the goods to such charges and expenses. Any other lien under subsection (1) is effective against the consignor and any person who permitted the bailor to have control or possession of the goods unless the carrier had notice that the bailor lacked such authority.

(3) A carrier loses his lien on any goods which he voluntarily delivers or which he unjustifiably refuses to deliver.

§ 7—308
Enforcement of Carrier's Lien

(1) A carrier's lien may be enforced by public or private sale of the goods, in block or in parcels, at any time or place and on any terms which are commercially reasonable, after noti-

fying all persons known to claim an interest in the goods. Such notification must include a statement of the amount due, the nature of the proposed sale and the time and place of any public sale. The fact that a better price could have been obtained by a sale at a different time or in a different method from that selected by the carrier is not of itself sufficient to establish that the sale was not made in a commercially reasonable manner. If the carrier either sells the goods in the usual manner in any recognized market therefor or if he sells at the price current in such market at the time of his sale or if he has otherwise sold in conformity with commercially reasonable practices among dealers in the type of goods sold he has sold in a commercially reasonable manner. A sale of more goods than apparently necessary to be offered to ensure satisfaction of the obligation is not commercially reasonable except in cases covered by the preceding sentence.

(2) Before any sale pursuant to this section any person claiming a right in the goods may pay the amount necessary to satisfy the lien and the reasonable expenses incurred under this section. In that event the goods must not be sold, but must be retained by the carrier subject to the terms of the bill and this Article.

(3) The carrier may buy at any public sale pursuant to this section.

(4) A purchaser in good faith of goods sold to enforce a carrier's lien takes the goods free of any rights of persons against whom the lien was valid, despite noncompliance by the carrier with the requirements of this section.

(5) The carrier may satisfy his lien from the proceeds of any sale pursuant to this section but must hold the balance, if any, for delivery on demand to any person to whom he would have been bound to deliver the goods.

(6) The rights provided by this section shall be in addition to all other rights allowed by law to a creditor against his debtor.

(7) A carrier's lien may be enforced in accordance with either subsection (1) or the procedure set forth in subsection (2) of Section 7—210.

(8) The carrier is liable for damages caused by failure to comply with the requirements for sale under this section and in case of willful violation is liable for conversion.

§ 7—309
Duty of Care; Contractual Limitation of Carrier's Liability

(1) A carrier who issues a bill of lading whether negotiable or non-negotiable must exercise the degree of care in relation to the goods which a reasonably careful man would exercise under like circumstances. This subsection does not repeal or change any law or rule of law which imposes liability upon a common carrier for damages not caused by its negligence.

(2) Damages may be limited by a provision that the carrier's liability shall not exceed a value stated in the document if the

carrier's rates are dependent upon value and the consignor by the carrier's tariff is afforded an opportunity to declare a higher value or a value as lawfully provided in the tariff, or where no tariff is filed he is otherwise advised of such opportunity; but no such limitation is effective with respect to the carrier's liability for conversion to its own use.

(3) Reasonable provisions as to the time and manner of presenting claims and instituting actions based on the shipment may be included in a bill of lading or tariff.

PART 4/Warehouse Receipts and Bills of Lading: General Obligations

§ 7—401
Irregularities in Issue of Receipt or Bill or Conduct of Issuer

The obligations imposed by this Article on an issuer apply to a document of title regardless of the fact that

(a) the document may not comply with the requirements of this Article or of any other law or regulation regarding its issue, form or content; or

(b) the issuer may have violated laws regulating the conduct of his business; or

(c) the goods covered by the document were owned by the bailee at the time the document was issued; or

(d) the person issuing the document does not come within the definition of warehouseman if it purports to be a warehouse receipt.

§ 7—402
Duplicate Receipt or Bill; Overissue

Neither a duplicate nor any other document of title purporting to cover goods already represented by an outstanding document of the same issuer confers any right in the goods, except as provided in the case of bills in a set, overissue of documents for fungible goods and substitutes for lost, stolen or destroyed documents. But the issuer is liable for damages caused by his overissue or failure to identify a duplicate document as such by conspicuous notation on its face.

§ 7—403
Obligation of Warehouseman or Carrier to Deliver; Excuse

(1) The bailee must deliver the goods to a person entitled under the document who complies with subsections (2) and (3), unless and to the extent that the bailee establishes any of the following:

(a) delivery of the goods to a person whose receipt was rightful as against the claimant;

(b) damage to or to delay, loss or destruction of the goods for which the bailee is not liable [but the burden of establishing negligence in such cases is on the person entitled under the document];

Note: *The brackets in (1)(b) indicate that State enactments may differ on this point without serious damage to the principle of uniformity.*

(c) previous sale or other disposition of the goods in lawful enforcement of a lien or on warehouseman's lawful termination of storage;

(d) the exercise by a seller of his right to stop delivery pursuant to the provisions of the Article on Sales (Section 2—705);

(e) a diversion, reconsignment or other disposition pursuant to the provisions of this Article (Section 7—303) or tariff regulating such right;

(f) release, satisfaction or any other fact affording a personal defense against the claimant;

(g) any other lawful excuse.

(2) A person claiming goods covered by a document of title must satisfy the bailee's lien where the bailee so requests or where the bailee is prohibited by law from delivering the goods until the charges are paid.

(3) Unless the person claiming is one against whom the document confers no right under Section 7—503(1), he must surrender for cancellation or notation of partial deliveries any outstanding negotiable document covering the goods, and the bailee must cancel the document or conspicuously note the partial delivery thereon or be liable to any person to whom the document is duly negotiated.

(4) "Person entitled under the document" means holder in the case of a negotiable document, or the person to whom delivery is to be made by the terms of or pursuant to written instructions under a non-negotiable document.

§ 7—404
No Liability for Good Faith Delivery Pursuant to Receipt or Bill

A bailee who in good faith including observance of reasonable commercial standards has received goods and delivered or otherwise disposed of them according to the terms of the document of title or pursuant to this Article is not liable therefor. This rule applies even though the person from whom he received the goods had no authority to procure the document or to dispose of the goods and even though the person to whom he delivered the goods had no authority to receive them.

PART 5/Warehouse Receipts and Bills of Lading: Negotiation and Transfer

§ 7—501
Form of Negotiation and Requirements of "Due Negotiation"

(1) A negotiable document of title running to the order of a named person is negotiated by his indorsement and delivery. After his indorsement in blank or to bearer any person can negotiate it by delivery alone.

(2) (a) A negotiable document of title is also negotiated by delivery alone when by its original terms it runs to bearer.

(b) When a document running to the order of a named person is delivered to him the effect is the same as if the document had been negotiated.

(3) Negotiation of a negotiable document of title after it has been indorsed to a specified person requires indorsement by the special indorsee as well as delivery.

(4) A negotiable document of title is "duly negotiated" when it is negotiated in the manner stated in this section to a holder who purchases it in good faith without notice of any defense against or claim to it on the part of any person and for value, unless it is established that the negotiation is not in the regular course of business or financing or involves receiving the document in settlement or payment of a money obligation.

(5) Indorsement of a non-negotiable document neither makes it negotiable nor adds to the transferee's rights.

(6) The naming in a negotiable bill of a person to be notified of the arrival of the goods does not limit the negotiability of the bill nor constitute notice to a purchaser thereof of any interest of such person in the goods.

§ 7—502
Rights Acquired by Due Negotiation

(1) Subject to the following section and to the provisions of Section 7—205 on fungible goods, a holder to whom a negotiable document of title has been duly negotiated acquires thereby:

(a) title to the document;

(b) title to the goods;

(c) all rights accruing under the law of agency or estoppel, including rights to goods delivered to the bailee after the document was issued; and

(d) the direct obligation of the issuer to hold or deliver the goods according to the terms of the document free of any defense or claim by him except those arising under the terms of the document or under this Article. In the case of a delivery order the bailee's obligation accrues only upon acceptance and the obligation acquired by the holder is that the issuer and any indorser will procure the acceptance of the bailee.

(2) Subject to the following section, title and rights so acquired are not defeated by any stoppage of the goods represented by the document or by surrender of such goods by the bailee, and are not impaired even though the negotiation or any prior negotiation constituted a breach of duty or even though any person has been deprived of possession of the document by misrepresentation, fraud, accident, mistake, duress, loss, theft, or conversion, or even though a previous sale or other transfer of the goods or document has been made to a third person.

§ 7—503
Document of Title to Goods Defeated in Certain Cases

(1) A document of title confers no right in goods against a person who before issuance of the document had a legal interest or a perfected security interest in them and who neither

(a) delivered or entrusted them or any document of title covering them to the bailor or his nominee with actual or apparent authority to ship, store or sell or with power to obtain delivery under this Article (Section 7—403) or with power of disposition under this Act (Sections 2—403 and 9—307) or other statute or rule of law; nor

(b) acquiesced in the procurement by the bailor or his nominee of any document of title.

(2) Title to goods based upon an unaccepted delivery order is subject to the rights of anyone to whom a negotiable warehouse receipt or bill of lading covering the goods has been duly negotiated. Such a title may be defeated under the next section to the same extent as the rights of the issuer or a transferee from the issuer.

(3) Title to goods based upon a bill of lading issued to a freight forwarder is subject to the rights of anyone to whom a bill issued by the freight forwarder is duly negotiated; but delivery by the carrier in accordance with Part 4 of this Article pursuant to its own bill of lading discharges the carrier's obligation to deliver.

§ 7—504
Rights Acquired in the Absence of Due Negotiation; Effect of Diversion; Seller's Stoppage of Delivery

(1) A transferee of a document, whether negotiable or non-negotiable, to whom the document has been delivered but not duly negotiated, acquires the title and rights which his transferor had or had actual authority to convey.

(2) In the case of a non-negotiable document, until but not after the bailee receives notification of the transfer, the rights of the transferee may be defeated

(a) by those creditors of the transferor who could treat the sale as void under Section 2—402; or

(b) by a buyer from the transferor in ordinary course of business if the bailee has delivered the goods to the buyer or received notification of his rights; or

(c) as against the bailee by good faith dealings of the bailee with the transferor.

(3) A diversion or other change of shipping instructions by the consignor in a non-negotiable bill of lading which causes the bailee not to deliver to the consignee defeats the consignee's title to the goods if they have been delivered to a buyer in ordinary course of business and in any event defeats the consignee's rights against the bailee.

(4) Delivery pursuant to a non-negotiable document may be stopped by a seller under Section 2—705, and subject to the requirement of due notification there provided. A bailee honoring the seller's instructions is entitled to be indemnified by the seller against any resulting loss or expense.

§ 7—505
Indorser Not a Guarantor for Other Parties

The indorsement of a document of title issued by a bailee does not make the indorser liable for any default by the bailee or by previous indorsers.

§ 7—506
Delivery Without Indorsement: Right to Compel Indorsement

The transferee of a negotiable document of title has a specifically enforceable right to have his transferor supply any necessary indorsement but the transfer becomes a negotiation only as of the time the indorsement is supplied.

§ 7—507
Warranties on Negotiation or Transfer of Receipt or Bill

Where a person negotiates or transfers a document of title for value otherwise than as a mere intermediary under the next following section, then unless otherwise agreed he warrants to his immediate purchaser only in addition to any warranty made in selling the goods

(a) that the document is genuine; and

(b) that he has no knowledge of any fact which would impair its validity or worth; and

(c) that his negotiation or transfer is rightful and fully effective with respect to the title to the document and the goods it represents.

§ 7—508
Warranties of Collecting Bank as to Documents

A collecting bank or other intermediary known to be entrusted with documents on behalf of another or with collection of a draft or other claim against delivery of documents warrants by such delivery of the documents only its own good faith and authority. This rule applies even though the intermediary has purchased or made advances against the claim or draft to be collected.

§ 7—509
Receipt or Bill: When Adequate Compliance With Commercial Contract

The question whether a document is adequate to fulfill the obligations of a contract for sale or the conditions of a credit is governed by the Articles on Sales (Article 2) and on Letters of Credit (Article 5).

PART 6/Warehouse Receipts and Bills of Lading: Miscellaneous Provisions

§ 7—601
Lost and Missing Documents

(1) If a document has been lost, stolen or destroyed, a court may order delivery of the goods or issuance of a substitute document and the bailee may without liability to any person comply with such order. If the document was negotiable the claimant must post security approved by the court to indemnify any person who may suffer loss as a result of non-surrender of the document. If the document was not negotiable, such security may be required at the discretion of the court. The court may also in its discretion order payment of the bailee's reasonable costs and counsel fees.

(2) A bailee who without court order delivers goods to a person claiming under a missing negotiable document is liable to any person injured thereby, and if the delivery is not in good faith becomes liable for conversion. Delivery in good faith is not conversion if made in accordance with a filed classification or tariff or, where no classification or tariff is filed, if the claimant posts security with the bailee in an amount at least double the value of the goods at the time of posting to indemnify any person injured by the delivery who files a notice of claim within one year after the delivery.

§ 7—602
Attachment of Goods Covered by a Negotiable Document

Except where the document was originally issued upon delivery of the goods by a person who had no power to dispose of them, no lien attaches by virtue of any judicial process to goods in the possession of a bailee for which a negotiable document of title is outstanding unless the document be first surrendered to the bailee or its negotiation enjoined, and the bailee shall not be compelled to deliver the goods pursuant to process until the document is surrendered to him or impounded by the court. One who purchases the document for value without notice of the process or injunction takes free of the lien imposed by judicial process.

§ 7—603
Conflicting Claims; Interpleader

If more than one person claims title or possession of the goods, the bailee is excused from delivery until he has had a reasonable time to ascertain the validity of the adverse claims or to bring an action to compel all claimants to interplead and may compel such interpleader, either in defending an action for non-delivery of the goods, or by original action, whichever is appropriate.

ARTICLE 8
Investment Securities

PART 1/Short Title and General Matters

§ 8—101
Short Title

This Article shall be known and may be cited as Uniform Commercial Code—Investment Securities.

§ 8—102
Definitions and Index of Definitions

(1) In this Article unless the context otherwise requires

(a) A "certificated security" is a share, participation, or other interest in property of or an enterprise of the issuer or an obligation of the issuer which is

(i) represented by an instrument issued in bearer or registered form;

(ii) of a type commonly dealt in on securities exchanges or markets or commonly recognized in any area in which it is issued or dealt in as a medium for investment; and

(iii) either one of a class or series or by its terms divisible into a class or series of shares, participations, interests, or obligations.

(b) An "uncertificated security" is a share, participation, or other interest in property or an enterprise of the issuer or an obligation of the issuer which is

(i) not represented by an instrument and the transfer of which is registered upon books maintained for that purpose by or on behalf of the issuer;

(ii) of a type commonly dealt in on securities exchanges or markets; and

(iii) either one of a class or series or by its terms divisible into a class or series of shares, participations, interests, or obligations.

(c) A "security" is either a certificated or an uncertificated security. If a security is certificated, the terms "security" and "certificated security" may mean either the intangible interest, the instrument representing that interest, or both, as the context requires. A writing that is a certificated security is governed by this Article and not by Article 3, even though it also meets the requirements of that Article. This Article does not apply to money. If a certificated security has been retained by or surrendered to the issuer or its transfer agent for reasons other than registration of transfer, other temporary purpose, payment, exchange, or acquisition by the issuer, that security shall be treated as an uncertificated security for purposes of this Article.

(d) A certificated security is in "registered form" if

(i) it specifies a person entitled to the security or the rights it represents; and

(ii) its transfer may be registered upon books maintained for that purpose by or on behalf of the issuer, or the security so states.

(e) A certificated security is in "bearer form" if it runs to bearer according to its terms and not by reason of any indorsement.

(2) A "subsequent purchaser" is a person who takes other than by original issue.

(3) A "clearing corporation" is a corporation registered as a "clearing agency" under the federal securities laws or a corporation:

(a) at least 90 percent of whose capital stock is held by or for one or more organizations, none of which, other than a national securities exchange or association, holds in excess of 20 percent of the capital stock of the corporation, and each of which is

(i) subject to supervision or regulation pursuant to the provisions of federal or state banking laws or state insurance laws,

(ii) a broker or dealer or investment company registered under the federal securities laws, or

(iii) a national securities exchange or association registered under the federal securities laws; and

(b) any remaining capital stock of which is held by individuals who have purchased it at or prior to the time of their taking office as directors of the corporation and who have purchased only so much of the capital stock as is necessary to permit them to qualify as directors.

(4) A "custodian bank" is a bank or trust company that is supervised and examined by state or federal authority having supervision over banks and is acting as custodian for a clearing corporation.

(5) Other definitions applying to this Article or to specified Parts thereof and the sections in which they appear are:

"Adverse claim". Section 8—302.
"Bona fide purchaser". Section 8—302.
"Broker". Section 8—303.
"Debtor". Section 9—105.
"Financial intermediary". Section 8—313.
"Guarantee of the signature". Section 8—402.
"Initial transaction statement". Section 8—408.
"Instruction". Section 8—308.
"Intermediary bank". Section 4—105.
"Issuer". Section 8—201.
"Overissue". Section 8—104.
"Secured Party". Section 9—105.
"Security Agreement". Section 9—105.

(6) In addition, Article 1 contains general definitions and principles of construction and interpretation applicable throughout this Article.

Amended in 1962, 1973 and 1977.

§ 8—103
Issuer's Lien

A lien upon a security in favor of an issuer thereof is valid against a purchaser only if:

(a) the security is certificated and the right of the issuer to the lien is noted conspicuously thereon; or

(b) the security is uncertificated and a notation of the right of the issuer to the lien is contained in the initial transaction statement sent to the purchaser or, if his interest is transferred to him other than by registration of transfer, pledge, or release, the initial transaction statement sent to the registered owner or the registered pledgee.

Amended in 1977.

§ 8—104
Effect of Overissue; "Overissue"

(1) The provisions of this Article which validate a security or compel its issue or reissue do not apply to the extent that validation, issue, or reissue would result in overissue; but if:

(a) an identical security which does not constitute an overissue is reasonably available for purchase, the person entitled to issue or validation may compel the issuer to purchase the security for him and either to deliver a certificated security or to register the transfer of an uncertificated security to him, against surrender of any certificated security he holds; or

(b) a security is not so available for purchase, the person entitled to issue or validation may recover from the issuer the price he or the last purchaser for value paid for it with interest from the date of his demand.

(2) "Overissue" means the issue of securities in excess of the amount the issuer has corporate power to issue.

Amended in 1977.

§ 8—105
Certificated Securities Negotiable; Statements and Instructions Not Negotiable; Presumptions

(1) Certificated securities governed by this Article are negotiable instruments.

(2) Statements (Section 8—408), notices, or the like, sent by the issuer of uncertificated securities and instructions (Section 8—308) are neither negotiable instruments nor certificated securities.

(3) In any action on a security:

(a) unless specifically denied in the pleadings, each signature on a certificated security, in a necessary indorsement, on an initial transaction statement, or on an instruction, is admitted;

(b) If the effectiveness of a signature is put in issue, the burden of establishing it is on the party claiming under

the signature, but the signature is presumed to be genuine or authorized;

(c) if signatures on a certificated security are admitted or established, production of the security entitles a holder to recover on it unless the defendant establishes a defense or a defect going to the validity of the security;

(d) if signatures on an initial transaction statement are admitted or established, the facts stated in the statement are presumed to be true as of the time of its issuance; and

(e) after it is shown that a defense or defect exists, the plaintiff has the burden of establishing that he or some person under whom he claims is a person against whom the defense or defect is ineffective (Section 8—202).

Amended in 1977.

§ 8—106
Applicability

The law (including the conflict of laws rules) of the jurisdiction of organization of the issuer governs the validity of a security, the effectiveness of registration by the issuer, and the rights and duties of the issuer with respect to:

(a) registration of transfer of a certificated security;

(b) registration of transfer, pledge, or release of an uncertificated security; and

(c) sending of statements of uncertificated securities.

Amended in 1977.

§ 8—107
Securities Transferable; Action for Price

(1) Unless otherwise agreed and subject to any applicable law or regulation respecting short sales, a person obligated to transfer securities may transfer any certificated security of the specified issue in bearer form or registered in the name of the transferee, or indorsed to him or in blank, or he may transfer an equivalent uncertificated security to the transferee or a person designated by the transferee.

(2) If the buyer fails to pay the price as it comes due under a contract of sale, the seller may recover the price of:

(a) certificated securities accepted by the buyer;

(b) uncertificated securities that have been transferred to the buyer or a person designated by the buyer; and

(c) other securities if efforts at their resale would be unduly burdensome or if there is no readily available market for their resale.

Amended in 1977.

§ 8—108
Registration of Pledge and Release of Uncertificated Securities

A security interest in an uncertificated security may be evidenced by the registration of pledge to the secured party or a person designated by him. There can be no more than one registered pledge of an uncertificated security at any time. The registered owner of an uncertificated security is the person in whose name the security is registered, even if the security is subject to a registered pledge. The rights of a registered pledgee of an uncertificated security under this Article are terminated by the registration of release.

Added in 1977.

PART 2/Issue—Issuer

§ 8—201
"Issuer"

(1) With respect to obligations on or defenses to a security, "issuer" includes a person who:

(a) places or authorizes the placing of his name on a certificated security (otherwise than as authenticating trustee, registrar, transfer agent, or the like) to evidence that it represents a share, participation, or other interest in his property or in an enterprise, or to evidence his duty to perform an obligation represented by the certificated security;

(b) creates shares, participations, or other interests in his property or in an enterprise or undertakes obligations, which shares, participations, interests, or obligations are uncertificated securities;

(c) directly or indirectly creates fractional interests in his rights or property, which fractional interests are represented by certificated securities; or

(d) becomes responsible for or in place of any other person described as an issuer in this section.

(2) With respect to obligations on or defenses to a security, a guarantor is an issuer to the extent of his guaranty, whether or not his obligation is noted on a certificated security or on statements of uncertificated securities sent pursuant to Section 8—408.

(3) With respect to registration of transfer, pledge, or release (Part 4 of this Article), "issuer" means a person on whose behalf transfer books are maintained.

Amended in 1977.

§ 8—202
Issuer's Responsibility and Defenses; Notice of Defect or Defense

(1) Even against a purchaser for value and without notice, the terms of a security include:

(a) if the security is certificated, those stated on the security;

(b) if the security is uncertificated, those contained in the initial transaction statement sent to such purchaser or, if his interest is transferred to him other than by registration of transfer, pledge, or release, the initial transaction statement sent to the registered owner or registered pledgee; and

(c) those made part of the security by reference, on the certificated security or in the initial transaction statement, to another instrument, indenture, or document or to a constitution, statute, ordinance, rule, regulation, order or the like, to the extent that the terms referred to do not conflict with the terms stated on the certificated security or contained in the statement. A reference under this paragraph does not of itself charge a purchaser for value with notice of a defect going to the validity of the security, even though the certificated security or statement expressly states that a person accepting it admits notice.

(2) A certificated security in the hands of a purchaser for value or an uncertificated security as to which an initial transaction statement has been sent to a purchaser for value, other than a security issued by a government or governmental agency or unit, even though issued with a defect going to its validity, is valid with respect to the purchaser if he is without notice of the particular defect unless the defect involves a violation of constitutional provisions, in which case the security is valid with respect to a subsequent purchaser for value and without notice of the defect. This subsection applies to an issuer that is a government or governmental agency or unit only if either there has been substantial compliance with the legal requirements governing the issue or the issuer has received a substantial consideration for the issue as a whole or for the particular security and a stated purpose of the issue is one for which the issuer has power to borrow money or issue the security.

(3) Except as provided in the case of certain unauthorized signatures (Section 8—205), lack of genuineness of a certificated security or an initial transaction statement is a complete defense, even against a purchaser for value and without notice.

(4) All other defenses of the issuer of a certificated or uncertificated security, including nondelivery and conditional delivery of a certificated security, are ineffective against a purchaser for value who has taken without notice of the particular defense.

(5) Nothing in this section shall be construed to affect the right of a party to a "when, as and if issued" or a "when distributed" contract to cancel the contract in the event of a material change in the character of the security that is the subject of the contract or in the plan or arrangement pursuant to which the security is to be issued or distributed.

Amended in 1977.

§ 8—203
Staleness as Notice of Defects or Defenses

(1) After an act or event creating a right to immediate performance of the principal obligation represented by a certificated security or that sets a date on or after which the security is to be presented or surrendered for redemption or

exchange, a purchaser is charged with notice of any defect in its issue or defense of the issuer if:

(a) the act or event is one requiring the payment of money, the delivery of certificated securities, the registration of transfer of uncertificated securities, or any of these on presentation or surrender of the certificated security, the funds or securities are available on the date set for payment or exchange, and he takes the security more than one year after that date; and

(b) the act or event is not covered by paragraph (a) and he takes the security more than 2 years after the date set for surrender or presentation or the date on which performance became due.

(2) A call that has been revoked is not within subsection (1).

Amended in 1977.

§ 8—204
Effect of Issuer's Restrictions on Transfer

A restriction on transfer of a security imposed by the issuer, even if otherwise lawful, is ineffective against any person without actual knowledge of it unless:

(a) the security is certificated and the restriction is noted conspicuously thereon; or

(b) the security is uncertificated and a notation of the restriction is contained in the initial transaction statement sent to the person or, if his interest is transferred to him other than by registration of transfer, pledge, or release, the initial transaction statement sent to the registered owner or the registered pledgee.

Amended in 1977.

§ 8—205
Effect of Unauthorized Signature on Certificated Security or Initial Transaction Statement

An unauthorized signature placed on a certificated security prior to or in the course of issue or placed on an initial transaction statement is ineffective, but the signature is effective in favor of a purchaser for value of the certificated security or a purchaser for value of an uncertificated security to whom the initial transaction statement has been sent, if the purchaser is without notice of the lack of authority and the signing has been done by:

(a) an authenticating trustee, registrar, transfer agent, or other person entrusted by the issuer with the signing of the security, of similar securities, or of initial transaction statements or the immediate preparation for signing of any of them; or

(b) an employee of the issuer, or of any of the foregoing, entrusted with responsible handling of the security or initial transaction statement.

Amended in 1977.

§ 8—206
Completion or Alteration of Certificated Security or Initial Transaction Statement

(1) If a certificated security contains the signatures necessary to its issue or transfer but is incomplete in any other respect:

(a) any person may complete it by filling in the blanks as authorized; and

(b) even though the blanks are incorrectly filled in, the security as completed is enforceable by a purchaser who took it for value and without notice of the incorrectness.

(2) A complete certificated security that has been improperly altered, even though fraudulently, remains enforceable, but only according to its original terms.

(3) If an initial transaction statement contains the signatures necessary to its validity, but is incomplete in any other respect:

(a) any person may complete it by filling in the blanks as authorized; and

(b) even though the blanks are incorrectly filled in, the statement as completed is effective in favor of the person to whom it is sent if he purchased the security referred to therein for value and without notice of the incorrectness.

(4) A complete initial transaction statement that has been improperly altered, even though fraudulently, is effective in favor of a purchaser to whom it has been sent, but only according to its original terms.

Amended in 1977.

§ 8—207
Rights and Duties of Issuer With Respect to Registered Owners and Registered Pledgees

(1) Prior to due presentment for registration of transfer of a certificated security in registered form, the issuer or indenture trustee may treat the registered owner as the person exclusively entitled to vote, to receive notifications, and otherwise to exercise all the rights and powers of an owner.

(2) Subject to the provisions of subsections (3), (4), and (6), the issuer or indenture trustee may treat the registered owner of an uncertificated security as the person exclusively entitled to vote, to receive notifications, and otherwise to exercise all the rights and powers of an owner.

(3) The registered owner of an uncertificated security that is subject to a registered pledge is not entitled to registration of transfer prior to the due presentment to the issuer of a release instruction. The exercise of conversion rights with respect to a convertible uncertificated security is a transfer within the meaning of this section.

(4) Upon due presentment of a transfer instruction from the registered pledgee of an uncertificated security, the issuer shall:

(a) register the transfer of the security to the new owner free of pledge, if the instruction specifies a new owner (who may be the registered pledgee) and does not specify a pledgee;

(b) register the transfer of the security to the new owner subject to the interest of the existing pledgee, if the instruction specifies a new owner and the existing pledgee; or

(c) register the release of the security from the existing pledge and register the pledge of the security to the other pledgee, if the instruction specifies the existing owner and another pledgee.

(5) Continuity of perfection of a security interest is not broken by registration of transfer under subsection (4)(b) or by registration of release and pledge under subsection (4)(c), if the security interest is assigned.

(6) If an uncertificated security is subject to a registered pledge:

(a) any uncertificated securities issued in exchange for or distributed with respect to the pledged security shall be registered subject to the pledge;

(b) any certificated securities issued in exchange for or distributed with respect to the pledged security shall be delivered to the registered pledgee; and

(c) any money paid in exchange for or in redemption of part or all of the security shall be paid to the registered pledgee.

(7) Nothing in this Article shall be construed to affect the liability of the registered owner of a security for calls, assessments, or the like.

Amended in 1977.

§ 8—208
Effect of Signature of Authenticating Trustee, Registrar, or Transfer Agent

(1) A person placing his signature upon a certificated security or an initial transaction statement as authenticating trustee, registrar, transfer agent, or the like, warrants to a purchaser for value of the certificated security or a purchaser for value of an uncertificated security to whom the initial transaction statement has been sent, if the purchaser is without notice of the particular defect, that:

(a) the certificated security or initial transaction statement is genuine;

(b) his own participation in the issue or registration of the transfer, pledge, or release of the security is within his capacity and within the scope of the authority received by him from the issuer; and

(c) he has reasonable grounds to believe the security is in the form and within the amount the issuer is authorized to issue.

(2) Unless otherwise agreed, a person by so placing his signature does not assume responsibility for the validity of the security in other respects.

Amended in 1962 and 1977.

PART 3/Transfer

§ 8—301
Rights Acquired by Purchaser

(1) Upon transfer of a security to a purchaser (Section 8—313), the purchaser acquires the rights in the security which his transferor had or had actual authority to convey unless the purchaser's rights are limited by Section 8—302(4).

(2) A transferee of a limited interest acquires rights only to the extent of the interest transferred. The creation or release of a security interest in a security is the transfer of a limited interest in that security.

Amended in 1977.

§ 8—302
"Bona Fide Purchaser"; "Adverse Claim"; Title Acquired by Bona Fide Purchaser

(1) A "bona fide purchaser" is a purchaser for value in good faith and without notice of any adverse claim:

(a) who takes delivery of a certificated security in bearer form or in registered form, issued or indorsed to him or in blank;

(b) to whom the transfer, pledge, or release of an uncertificated security is registered on the books of the issuer; or

(c) to whom a security is transferred under the provisions of paragraph (c), (d)(i), or (g) of Section 8—313(1).

(2) "Adverse claim" includes a claim that a transfer was or would be wrongful or that a particular adverse person is the owner of or has an interest in the security.

(3) A bona fide purchaser in addition to acquiring the rights of a purchaser (Section 8—301) also acquires his interest in the security free of any adverse claim.

(4) Notwithstanding Section 8—301(1), the transferee of a particular certificated security who has been a party to any fraud or illegality affecting the security, or who as a prior holder of that certificated security had notice of an adverse claim, cannot improve his position by taking from a bona fide purchaser.

Amended in 1977.

§ 8—303
"Broker"

"Broker" means a person engaged for all or part of his time in the business of buying and selling securities, who in the transaction concerned acts for, buys a security from, or sells a security to, a customer. Nothing in this Article determines the capacity in which a person acts for purposes of any other statute or rule to which the person is subject.

§ 8—304
Notice to Purchaser of Adverse Claims

(1) A purchaser (including a broker for the seller or buyer, but excluding an intermediary bank) of a certificated security is charged with notice of adverse claims if:

(a) the security, whether in bearer or registered form, has been indorsed "for collection" or "for surrender" or for some other purpose not involving transfer; or

(b) the security is in bearer form and has on it an unambiguous statement that it is the property of a person other than the transferor. The mere writing of a name on a security is not such a statement.

(2) A purchaser (including a broker for the seller or buyer, but excluding an intermediary bank) to whom the transfer, pledge, or release of an uncertificated security is registered is charged with notice of adverse claims as to which the issuer has a duty under Section 8—403(4) at the time of registration and which are noted in the initial transaction statement sent to the purchaser or, if his interest is transferred to him other than by registration of transfer, pledge, or release, the initial transaction statement sent to the registered owner or the registered pledgee.

(3) The fact that the purchaser (including a broker for the seller or buyer) of a certificated or uncertificated security has notice that the security is held for a third person or is registered in the name of or indorsed by a fiduciary does not create a duty of inquiry into the rightfulness of the transfer or constitute constructive notice of adverse claims. However, if the purchaser (excluding an intermediary bank) has knowledge that the proceeds are being used or the transaction is for the individual benefit of the fiduciary or otherwise in breach of duty, the purchaser is charged with notice of adverse claims.

Amended in 1977.

§ 8—305
Staleness as Notice of Adverse Claims

An act or event that creates a right to immediate performance of the principal obligation represented by a certificated security or sets a date on or after which a certificated security is to be presented or surrendered for redemption or exchange does not itself constitute any notice of adverse claims except in the case of a transfer:

(a) after one year from any date set for presentment or surrender for redemption or exchange; or

(b) after 6 months from any date set for payment of money against presentation or surrender of the security if funds are available for payment on that date.

Amended in 1977.

§ 8—306
Warranties on Presentment and Transfer of Certificated Securities; Warranties of Originators of Instructions

(1) A person who presents a certificated security for registration of transfer or for payment or exchange warrants to the issuer that he is entitled to the registration, payment, or exchange. But, a purchaser for value and without notice of adverse claims who receives a new, reissued, or re-registered certificated security on registration of transfer or receives an initial transaction statement confirming the registration of transfer of an equivalent uncertificated security to him warrants only that he has no knowledge of any unauthorized signature (Section 8—311) in a necessary indorsement.

(2) A person by transferring a certificated security to a purchaser for value warrants only that:

(a) his transfer is effective and rightful;

(b) the security is genuine and has not been materially altered; and

(c) he knows of no fact which might impair the validity of the security.

(3) If a certificated security is delivered by an intermediary known to be entrusted with delivery of the security on behalf of another or with collection of a draft or other claim against delivery, the intermediary by delivery warrants only his own good faith and authority, even though he has purchased or made advances against the claim to be collected against the delivery.

(4) A pledgee or other holder for security who redelivers a certificated security received, or after payment and on order of the debtor delivers that security to a third person, makes only the warranties of an intermediary under subsection (3).

(5) A person who originates an instruction warrants to the issuer that:

(a) he is an appropriate person to originate the instruction; and

(b) at the time the instruction is presented to the issuer he will be entitled to the registration of transfer, pledge, or release.

(6) A person who originates an instruction warrants to any person specially guaranteeing his signature (subsection 8—312(3)) that:

(a) he is an appropriate person to originate the instruction; and

(b) at the time the instruction is presented to the issuer

(i) he will be entitled to the registration of transfer, pledge, or release; and

(ii) the transfer, pledge, or release requested in the instruction will be registered by the issuer free from all liens, security interests, restrictions, and claims other than those specified in the instruction.

(7) A person who originates an instruction warrants to a purchaser for value and to any person guaranteeing the instruction (Section 8—312(6)) that:

(a) he is an appropriate person to originate the instruction;

(b) the uncertificated security referred to therein is valid; and

(c) at the time the instruction is presented to the issuer

(i) the transferor will be entitled to the registration of transfer, pledge, or release;

(ii) the transfer, pledge, or release requested in the instruction will be registered by the issuer free from all liens, security interests, restrictions, and claims other than those specified in the instruction; and

(iii) the requested transfer, pledge, or release will be rightful.

(8) If a secured party is the registered pledgee or the registered owner of an uncertificated security, a person who originates an instruction of release or transfer to the debtor or, after payment and on order of the debtor, a transfer instruction to a third person, warrants to the debtor or the third person only that he is an appropriate person to originate the instruction and, at the time the instruction is presented to the issuer, the transferor will be entitled to the registration of release or transfer. If a transfer instruction to a third person who is a purchaser for value is originated on order of the debtor, the debtor makes to the purchaser the warranties of paragraphs (b), (c)(ii) and (c)(iii) of subsection (7).

(9) A person who transfers an uncertificated security to a purchaser for value and does not originate an instruction in connection with the transfer warrants only that:

(a) his transfer is effective and rightful; and

(b) the uncertificated security is valid.

(10) A broker gives to his customer and to the issuer and a purchaser the applicable warranties provided in this section and has the rights and privileges of a purchaser under this section. The warranties of and in favor of the broker, acting as an agent are in addition to applicable warranties given by and in favor of his customer.

Amended in 1962 and 1977.

§ 8—307
Effect of Delivery Without Indorsement; Right to Compel Indorsement

If a certificated security in registered form has been delivered to a purchaser without a necessary indorsement he may become a bona fide purchaser only as of the time the indorsement is supplied; but against the transferor, the transfer is complete upon delivery and the purchaser has a specifically enforceable right to have any necessary indorsement supplied.

Amended in 1977.

§ 8—308
Indorsements; Instructions

(1) An indorsement of a certificated security in registered form is made when an appropriate person signs on it or on a separate document an assignment or transfer of the security or a power to assign or transfer it or his signature is written without more upon the back of the security.

(2) An indorsement may be in blank or special. An indorsement in blank includes an indorsement to bearer. A special indorsement specifies to whom the security is to be transferred, or who has power to transfer it. A holder may convert a blank indorsement into a special indorsement.

(3) An indorsement purporting to be only of part of a certificated security representing units intended by the issuer to be separately transferable is effective to the extent of the indorsement.

(4) An "instruction" is an order to the issuer of an uncertificated security requesting that the transfer, pledge, or release from pledge of the uncertificated security specified therein be registered.

(5) An instruction originated by an appropriate person is:

(a) a writing signed by an appropriate person; or

(b) a communication to the issuer in any form agreed upon in a writing signed by the issuer and an appropriate person.

If an instruction has been originated by an appropriate person but is incomplete in any other respect, any person may complete it as authorized and the issuer may rely on it as completed even though it has been completed incorrectly.

(6) "An appropriate person" in subsection (1) means the person specified by the certificated security or by special indorsement to be entitled to the security.

(7) "An appropriate person" in subsection (5) means:

(a) for an instruction to transfer or pledge an uncertificated security which is then not subject to a registered pledge, the registered owner; or

(b) for an instruction to transfer or release an uncertificated security which is then subject to a registered pledge, the registered pledgee.

(8) In addition to the persons designated in subsections (6) and (7), "an appropriate person" in subsections (1) and (5) includes:

(a) if the person designated is described as a fiduciary but is no longer serving in the described capacity, either that person or his successor;

(b) if the persons designated are described as more than one person as fiduciaries and one or more are no longer serving in the described capacity, the remaining fiduciary or fiduciaries, whether or not a successor has been appointed or qualified;

(c) if the person designated is an individual and is without capacity to act by virtue of death, incompetence, infancy, or otherwise, his executor, administrator, guardian, or like fiduciary;

(d) if the persons designated are described as more than one person as tenants by the entirety or with right of survivorship and by reason of death all cannot sign, the survivor or survivors;

(e) a person having power to sign under applicable law or controlling instrument; and

(f) to the extent that the person designated or any of the foregoing persons may act through an agent, his authorized agent.

(9) Unless otherwise agreed, the indorser of a certificated security by his indorsement or the originator of an instruction by his origination assumes no obligation that the security will be honored by the issuer but only the obligations provided in Section 8—306.

(10) Whether the person signing is appropriate is determined as of the date of signing and an indorsement made by or an instruction originated by him does not become unauthorized for the purposes of this Article by virtue of any subsequent change of circumstances.

(11) Failure of a fiduciary to comply with a controlling instrument or with the law of the state having jurisdiction of the fiduciary relationship, including any law requiring the fiduciary to obtain court approval of the transfer, pledge, or release, does not render his indorsement or an instruction originated by him unauthorized for the purposes of this Article.

Amended in 1962 and 1977.

§ 8—309
Effect of Indorsement Without Delivery

An indorsement of a certificated security, whether special or in blank, does not constitute a transfer until delivery of the certificated security on which it appears or, if the indorsement is on a separate document, until delivery of both the document and the certificated security.

Amended in 1977.

§ 8—310
Indorsement of Certificated Security in Bearer Form

An indorsement of a certificated security in bearer form may give notice of adverse claims (Section 8—304) but does not otherwise affect any right to registration the holder possesses.

Amended in 1977.

§ 8—311
Effect of Unauthorized Indorsement or Instruction

Unless the owner or pledgee has ratified an unauthorized indorsement or instruction or is otherwise precluded from asserting its ineffectiveness:

(a) he may assert its ineffectiveness against the issuer or any purchaser, other than a purchaser for value and without notice of adverse claims, who has in good faith received a new, reissued, or re-registered certificated security on registration of transfer or received an initial transaction statement confirming the registration of transfer, pledge, or release of an equivalent uncertificated security to him; and

(b) an issuer who registers the transfer of a certificated security upon the unauthorized indorsement or who registers the transfer, pledge, or release of an uncertificated security upon the unauthorized instruction is subject to liability for improper registration (Section 8—404).

Amended in 1977.

§ 8—312
Effect of Guaranteeing Signature, Indorsement or Instruction

(1) Any person guaranteeing a signature of an indorser of a certificated security warrants that at the time of signing:

(a) the signature was genuine;

(b) the signer was an appropriate person to indorse (Section 8—308); and

(c) the signer had legal capacity to sign.

(2) Any person guaranteeing a signature of the originator of an instruction warrants that at the time of signing:

(a) the signature was genuine;

(b) the signer was an appropriate person to originate the instruction (Section 8—308) if the person specified in the instruction as the registered owner or registered pledgee of the uncertificated security was, in fact, the registered owner or registered pledgee of the security, as to which fact the signature guarantor makes no warranty;

(c) the signer had legal capacity to sign; and

(d) the taxpayer identification number, if any, appearing on the instruction as that of the registered owner or registered pledgee was the taxpayer identification number of the signer or of the owner or pledgee for whom the signer was acting.

(3) Any person specially guaranteeing the signature of the originator of an instruction makes not only the warranties of a signature guarantor (subsection (2)) but also warrants that at the time the instruction is presented to the issuer:

(a) the person specified in the instruction as the registered owner or registered pledgee of the uncertificated security will be the registered owner or registered pledgee; and

(b) the transfer, pledge, or release of the uncertificated security requested in the instruction will be registered by the issuer free from all liens, security interests, restrictions, and claims other than those specified in the instruction.

(4) The guarantor under subsections (1) and (2) or the

special guarantor under subsection (3) does not otherwise warrant the rightfulness of the particular transfer, pledge, or release.

(5) Any person guaranteeing an indorsement of a certificated security makes not only the warranties of a signature guarantor under subsection (1) but also warrants the rightfulness of the particular transfer in all respects.

(6) Any person guaranteeing an instruction requesting the transfer, pledge, or release of an uncertificated security makes not only the warranties of a special signature guarantor under subsection (3) but also warrants the rightfulness of the particular transfer, pledge, or release in all respects.

(7) No issuer may require a special guarantee of signature (subsection (3)), a guarantee of indorsement (subsection (5)), or a guarantee of instruction (subsection (6)) as a condition to registration of transfer, pledge, or release.

(8) The foregoing warranties are made to any person taking or dealing with the security in reliance on the guarantee, and the guarantor is liable to the person for any loss resulting from breach of the warranties.

Amended in 1977.

§8—313
When Transfer to Purchaser Occurs; Financial Intermediary as Bona Fide Purchaser; "Financial Intermediary"

(1) Transfer of a security or a limited interest (including a security interest) therein to a purchaser occurs only:

    (a) at the time he or a person designated by him acquires possession of a certificated security;

    (b) at the time the transfer, pledge, or release of an uncertificated security is registered to him or a person designated by him;

    (c) at the time his financial intermediary acquires possession of a certificated security specially indorsed to or issued in the name of the purchaser;

    (d) at the time a financial intermediary, not a clearing corporation, sends him confirmation of the purchase and also by book entry or otherwise identifies as belonging to the purchaser

        (i) a specific certificated security in the financial intermediary's possession;

        (ii) a quantity of securities that constitute or are part of a fungible bulk of certificated securities in the financial intermediary's possession or of uncertificated securities registered in the name of the financial intermediary; or

        (iii) a quantity of securities that constitute or are part of a fungible bulk of securities shown on the account of the financial intermediary on the books of another financial intermediary;

    (e) with respect to an identified certificated security to be delivered while still in the possession of a third person, not a financial intermediary, at the time that person acknowledges that he holds for the purchaser;

    (f) with respect to a specific uncertificated security the pledge or transfer of which has been registered to a third person, not a financial intermediary, at the time that person acknowledges that he holds for the purchaser;

    (g) at the time appropriate entries to the account of the purchaser or a person designated by him on the books of a clearing corporation are made under Section 8—320;

    (h) with respect to the transfer of a security interest where the debtor has signed a security agreement containing a description of the security, at the time a written notification, which, in the case of the creation of the security interest, is signed by the debtor (which may be a copy of the security agreement) or which, in the case of the release or assignment of the security interest created pursuant to this paragraph, is signed by the secured party, is received by

        (i) a financial intermediary on whose books the interest of the transferor in the security appears;

        (ii) a third person, not a financial intermediary, in possession of the security, if it is certificated;

        (iii) a third person, not a financial intermediary, who is the registered owner of the security, if it is uncertificated and not subject to a registered pledge; or

        (iv) a third person, not a financial intermediary, who is the registered pledgee of the security, if it is uncertificated and subject to a registered pledge;

    (i) with respect to the transfer of a security interest where the transferor has signed a security agreement containing a description of the security, at the time new value is given by the secured party; or

    (j) with respect to the transfer of a security interest where the secured party is a financial intermediary and the security has already been transferred to the financial intermediary under paragraphs (a), (b), (c), (d), or (g), at the time the transferor has signed a security agreement containing a description of the security and value is given by the secured party.

(2) The purchaser is the owner of a security held for him by a financial intermediary, but cannot be a bona fide purchaser of a security so held except in the circumstances specified in paragraphs (c), (d)(i), and (g) of subsection (1). If a security so held is part of a fungible bulk, as in the circumstances specified in paragraphs (d)(ii) and (d)(iii) of subsection (1), the purchaser is the owner of a proportionate property interest in the fungible bulk.

(3) Notice of an adverse claim received by the financial intermediary or by the purchaser after the financial intermediary takes delivery of a certificated security as a holder for value or after the transfer, pledge, or release of an uncertificated security has been registered free of the claim to a financial intermediary who has given value is not effective

either as to the financial intermediary or as to the purchaser. However, as between the financial intermediary and the purchaser the purchaser may demand transfer of an equivalent security as to which no notice of adverse claim has been received.

(4) A "financial intermediary" is a bank, broker, clearing corporation, or other person (or the nominee of any of them) which in the ordinary course of its business maintains security accounts for its customers and is acting in that capacity. A financial intermediary may have a security interest in securities held in account for its customer.

Amended in 1962 and 1977.

§8—314
Duty to Transfer, When Completed

(1) Unless otherwise agreed, if a sale of a security is made on an exchange or otherwise through brokers:

(a) the selling customer fulfills his duty to transfer at the time he:

(i) places a certificated security in the possession of the selling broker or a person designated by the broker;

(ii) causes an uncertificated security to be registered in the name of the selling broker or a person designated by the broker;

(iii) if requested, causes an acknowledgment to be made to the selling broker that a certificated or uncertificated security is held for the broker; or

(iv) places in the possession of the selling broker or of a person designated by the broker a transfer instruction for an uncertificated security, providing the issuer does not refuse to register the requested transfer if the instruction is presented to the issuer for registration within 30 days thereafter; and

(b) the selling broker, including a correspondent broker acting for a selling customer, fulfills his duty to transfer at the time he:

(i) places a certificated security in the possession of the buying broker or a person designated by the buying broker;

(ii) causes an uncertificated security to be registered in the name of the buying broker or a person designated by the buying broker;

(iii) places in the possession of the buying broker or of a person designated by the buying broker a transfer instruction for an uncertificated security, providing the issuer does not refuse to register the requested transfer if the instruction is presented to the issuer for registration within 30 days thereafter; or

(iv) effects clearance of the sale in accordance with the rules of the exchange on which the transaction took place.

(2) Except as provided in this section or unless otherwise agreed, a transferor's duty to transfer a security under a contract of purchase is not fulfilled until he:

(a) places a certificated security in form to be negotiated by the purchaser in the possession of the purchaser or of a person designated by the purchaser;

(b) causes an uncertificated security to be registered in the name of the purchaser or a person designated by the purchaser; or

(c) if the purchaser requests, causes an acknowledgment to be made to the purchaser that a certificated or uncertificated security is held for the purchaser.

(3) Unless made on an exchange, a sale to a broker purchasing for his own account is within subsection (2) and not within subsection (1).

Amended in 1977.

§8—315
Action Against Transferee Based Upon Wrongful Transfer

(1) Any person against whom the transfer of a security is wrongful for any reason, including his incapacity, as against anyone except a bona fide purchaser, may:

(a) reclaim possession of the certificated security wrongfully transferred;

(b) obtain possession of any new certificated security representing all or part of the same rights;

(c) compel the origination of an instruction to transfer to him or a person designated by him an uncertificated security constituting all or part of the same rights; or

(d) have damages.

(2) If the transfer is wrongful because of an unauthorized indorsement of a certificated security, the owner may also reclaim or obtain possession of the security or a new certificated security, even from a bona fide purchaser, if the ineffectiveness of the purported indorsement can be asserted against him under the provisions of this Article on unauthorized indorsements (Section 8—311).

(3) The right to obtain or reclaim possession of a certificated security or to compel the origination of a transfer instruction may be specifically enforced and the transfer of a certificated or uncertificated security enjoined and a certificated security impounded pending the litigation.

Amended in 1977.

§8—316
Purchaser's Right to Requisites for Registration of Transfer, Pledge, or Release on Books

Unless otherwise agreed, the transferor of a certificated security or the transferor, pledgor, or pledgee of an uncertificated security on due demand must supply his purchaser with any proof of his authority to transfer, pledge, or release or with any other requisite necessary to obtain registration of the transfer, pledge, or release of the security; but if the transfer, pledge, or release is not for value, a transferor, pledgor, or pledgee need not do so unless the purchaser furnishes the necessary expenses. Failure within a reasonable time to comply with a demand made gives the purchaser the right to reject or rescind the transfer, pledge, or release.

Amended in 1977.

§8—317
Creditors' Rights

(1) Subject to the exceptions in subsections (3) and (4), no attachment or levy upon a certificated security or any share or other interest represented thereby which is outstanding is valid until the security is actually seized by the officer making the attachment or levy, but a certificated security which has been surrendered to the issuer may be reached by a creditor by legal process at the issuer's chief executive office in the United States.

(2) An uncertificated security registered in the name of the debtor may not be reached by a creditor except by legal process at the issuer's chief executive office in the United States.

(3) The interest of a debtor in a certificated security that is in the possession of a secured party not a financial intermediary or in an uncertificated security registered in the name of a secured party not a financial intermediary (or in the name of a nominee of the secured party) may be reached by a creditor by legal process upon the secured party.

(4) The interest of a debtor in a certificated security that is in the possession of or registered in the name of a financial intermediary or in an uncertificated security registered in the name of a financial intermediary may be reached by a creditor by legal process upon the financial intermediary on whose books the interest of the debtor appears.

(5) Unless otherwise provided by law, a creditor's lien upon the interest of a debtor in a security obtained pursuant to subsection (3) or (4) is not a restraint on the transfer of the security, free of the lien, to a third party for new value; but in the event of a transfer, the lien applies to the proceeds of the transfer in the hands of the secured party or financial intermediary, subject to any claims having priority.

(6) A creditor whose debtor is the owner of a security is entitled to aid from courts of appropriate jurisdiction, by injunction or otherwise, in reaching the security or in satisfying the claim by means allowed at law or in equity in regard to property that cannot readily be reached by ordinary legal process.

Amended in 1977.

§8—318
No Conversion by Good Faith Conduct

An agent or bailee who in good faith (including observance of reasonable commercial standards if he is in the business of buying, selling, or otherwise dealing with securities) has received certificated securities and sold, pledged, or delivered them or has sold or caused the transfer or pledge of uncertificated securities over which he had control according to the instructions of his principal, is not liable for conversion or for participation in breach of fiduciary duty although the principal had no right so to deal with the securities.

Amended in 1977.

§8—319
Statute of Frauds

A contract for the sale of securities is not enforceable by way of action or defense unless:

(a) there is some writing signed by the party against whom enforcement is sought or by his authorized agent or broker, sufficient to indicate that a contract has been made for sale of a stated quantity of described securities at a defined or stated price;

(b) delivery of a certificated security or transfer instruction has been accepted, or transfer of an uncertificated security has been registered and the transferee has failed to send written objection to the issuer within 10 days after receipt of the initial transaction statement confirming the registration, or payment has been made, but the contract is enforceable under this provision only to the extent of the delivery, registration, or payment;

(c) within a reasonable time a writing in confirmation of the sale or purchase and sufficient against the sender under paragraph (a) has been received by the party against whom enforcement is sought and he has failed to send written objection to its contents within 10 days after its receipt; or

(d) the party against whom enforcement is sought admits in his pleading, testimony, or otherwise in court that a contract was made for the sale of a stated quantity of described securities at a defined or stated price.

Amended in 1977.

§8—320
Transfer or Pledge Within Central Depository System

(1) In addition to other methods, a transfer, pledge, or release of a security or any interest therein may be effected by the making of appropriate entries on the books of a clearing corporation reducing the account of the transferor, pledgor, or pledgee and increasing the account of the transferee, pledgee, or pledgor by the amount of the obligation or the

number of shares or rights transferred, pledged, or released, if the security is shown on the account of a transferor, pledgor, or pledgee on the books of the clearing corporation; is subject to the control of the clearing corporation; and

   (a) if certificated,

        (i) is in the custody of the clearing corporation, another clearing corporation, a custodian bank, or a nominee of any of them; and

        (ii) is in bearer form or indorsed in blank by an appropriate person or registered in the name of the clearing corporation, a custodian bank, or a nominee of any of them; or

   (b) if uncertificated, is registered in the name of the clearing corporation, another clearing corporation, a custodian bank, or a nominee of any of them.

(2) Under this section entries may be made with respect to like securities or interests therein as a part of a fungible bulk and may refer merely to a quantity of a particular security without reference to the name of the registered owner, certificate or bond number, or the like, and, in appropriate cases, may be on a net basis taking into account other transfers, pledges, or releases of the same security.

(3) A transfer under this section is effective (Section 8—313) and the purchaser acquires the rights of the transferor (Section 8—301). A pledge or release under this section is the transfer of a limited interest. If a pledge or the creation of a security interest is intended, the security interest is perfected at the time when both value is given by the pledgee and the appropriate entries are made (Section 8—321). A transferee or pledgee under this section may be a bona fide purchaser (Section 8—302).

(4) A transfer or pledge under this section is not a registration of transfer under Part 4.

(5) That entries made on the books of the clearing corporation as provided in subsection (1) are not appropriate does not affect the validity or effect of the entries or the liabilities or obligations of the clearing corporation to any person adversely affected thereby.

Added in 1962; amended in 1977.

§8—321
Enforceability, Attachment, Perfection and Termination of Security Interests

(1) A security interest in a security is enforceable and can attach only if it is transferred to the secured party or a person designated by him pursuant to a provision of Section 8—313(1).

(2) A security interest so transferred pursuant to agreement by a transferor who has rights in the security to a transferee who has given value is a perfected security interest, but a security interest that has been transferred solely under paragraph (i) of Section 8—313(1) becomes unperfected after

21 days unless, within that time, the requirements for transfer under any other provision of Section 8—313(1) are satisfied.

(3) A security interest in a security is subject to the provisions of Article 9, but:

   (a) no filing is required to perfect the security interest; and

   (b) no written security agreement signed by the debtor is necessary to make the security interest enforceable, except as provided in paragraph (h), (i), or (j) of Section 8—313(1). The secured party has the rights and duties provided under Section 9—207, to the extent they are applicable, whether or not the security is certificated, and, if certificated, whether or not it is in his possession.

(4) Unless otherwise agreed, a security interest in a security is terminated by transfer to the debtor or a person designated by him pursuant to a provision of Section 8—313(1). If a security is thus transferred, the security interest, if not terminated, becomes unperfected unless the security is certificated and is delivered to the debtor for the purpose of ultimate sale or exchange or presentation, collection, renewal, or registration of transfer. In that case, the security interest becomes unperfected after 21 days unless, within that time, the security (or securities for which it has been exchanged) is transferred to the secured party or a person designated by him pursuant to a provision of Section 8—313(1).

Added in 1977.

PART 4/Registration

§8—401
Duty of Issuer to Register Transfer, Pledge, or Release

(1) If a certificated security in registered form is presented to the issuer with a request to register transfer or an instruction is presented to the issuer with a request to register transfer, pledge, or release, the issuer shall register the transfer, pledge, or release as requested if:

   (a) the security is indorsed or the instruction was originated by the appropriate person or persons (Section 8—308);

   (b) reasonable assurance is given that those indorsements or instructions are genuine and effective (Section 8—402);

   (c) the issuer has no duty as to adverse claims or has discharged the duty (Section 8—403);

   (d) any applicable law related to the collection of taxes has been complied with; and

   (e) the transfer, pledge, or release is in fact rightful or is to a bona fide purchaser.

(2) If an issuer is under a duty to register a transfer, pledge, or release of a security, the issuer is also liable to the person

presenting a certificated security or an instruction for registration or his principal for loss resulting from any unreasonable delay in registration or from failure or refusal to register the transfer, pledge, or release.

Amended in 1977.

§ 8—402
Assurance that Indorsements and Instructions Are Effective

(1) The issuer may require the following assurance that each necessary indorsement of a certificated security or each instruction (Section 8—308) is genuine and effective:

(a) in all cases, a guarantee of the signature (Section 8—312(1) or (2)) of the person indorsing a certificated security or originating an instruction including, in the case of an instruction, a warranty of the taxpayer identification number or, in the absence thereof, other reasonable assurance of identity;

(b) if the indorsement is made or the instruction is originated by an agent, appropriate assurance of authority to sign;

(c) if the indorsement is made or the instruction is originated by a fiduciary, appropriate evidence of appointment or incumbency;

(d) if there is more than one fiduciary, reasonable assurance that all who are required to sign have done so; and

(e) if the indorsement is made or the instruction is originated by a person not covered by any of the foregoing, assurance appropriate to the case corresponding as nearly as may be to the foregoing.

(2) A "guarantee of the signature" in subsection (1) means a guarantee signed by or on behalf of a person reasonably believed by the issuer to be responsible. The issuer may adopt standards with respect to responsibility if they are not manifestly unreasonable.

(3) "Appropriate evidence of appointment or incumbency" in subsection (1) means:

(a) in the case of a fiduciary appointed or qualified by a court, a certificate issued by or under the direction or supervision of that court or an officer thereof and dated within 60 days before the date of presentation for transfer, pledge, or release; or

(b) in any other case, a copy of a document showing the appointment or a certificate issued by or on behalf of a person reasonably believed by the issuer to be responsible or, in the absence of that document or certificate, other evidence reasonably deemed by the issuer to be appropriate. The issuer may adopt standards with respect to the evidence if they are not manifestly unreasonable. The issuer is not charged with notice of the contents of any document obtained pursuant to this paragraph

(b) except to the extent that the contents relate directly to the appointment or incumbency.

(4) The issuer may elect to require reasonable assurance beyond that specified in this section, but if it does so and, for a purpose other than that specified in subsection (3)(b), both requires and obtains a copy of a will, trust, indenture, articles of co-partnership, bylaws, or other controlling instrument, it is charged with notice of all matters contained therein affecting the transfer, pledge, or release.

Amended in 1977.

§ 8—403
Issuer's Duty as to Adverse Claims

(1) An issuer to whom a certificated security is presented for registration shall inquire into adverse claims if:

(a) a written notification of an adverse claim is received at a time and in a manner affording the issuer a reasonable opportunity to act on it prior to the issuance of a new, reissued, or re-registered certificated security, and the notification identifies the claimant, the registered owner, and the issue of which the security is a part, and provides an address for communications directed to the claimant; or

(b) the issuer is charged with notice of an adverse claim from a controlling instrument it has elected to require under Section 8—402(4).

(2) The issuer may discharge any duty of inquiry by any reasonable means, including notifying an adverse claimant by registered or certified mail at the address furnished by him or, if there be no such address, at his residence or regular place of business that the certificated security has been presented for registration of transfer by a named person, and that the transfer will be registered unless within 30 days from the date of mailing the notification, either:

(a) an appropriate restraining order, injunction, or other process issues from a court of competent jurisdiction; or

(b) there is filed with the issuer an indemnity bond, sufficient in the issuer's judgment to protect the issuer and any transfer agent, registrar, or other agent of the issuer involved from any loss it or they may suffer by complying with the adverse claim.

(3) Unless an issuer is charged with notice of an adverse claim from a controlling instrument which it has elected to require under Section 8—402(4) or receives notification of an adverse claim under subsection (1), if a certificated security presented for registration is indorsed by the appropriate person or persons the issuer is under no duty to inquire into adverse claims. In particular:

(a) an issuer registering a certificated security in the name of a person who is a fiduciary or who is described as a fiduciary is not bound to inquire into the existence, extent, or correct description of the fiduciary relationship; and thereafter the issuer may assume without inquiry that the newly registered owner continues to be the fiduciary until the issuer receives written notice that the fiduciary is no longer acting as such with respect to the particular security;

(b) an issuer registering transfer on an indorsement by a fiduciary is not bound to inquire whether the transfer is made in compliance with a controlling instrument or with the law of the state having jurisdiction of the fiduciary relationship, including any law requiring the fiduciary to obtain court approval of the transfer; and

(c) the issuer is not charged with notice of the contents of any court record or file or other recorded or unrecorded document even though the document is in its possession and even though the transfer is made on the indorsement of a fiduciary to the fiduciary himself or to his nominee.

(4) An issuer is under no duty as to adverse claims with respect to an uncertificated security except:

(a) claims embodied in a restraining order, injunction, or other legal process served upon the issuer if the process was served at a time and in a manner affording the issuer a reasonable opportunity to act on it in accordance with the requirements of subsection (5);

(b) claims of which the issuer has received a written notification from the registered owner or the registered pledgee if the notification was received at a time and in a manner affording the issuer a reasonable opportunity to act on it in accordance with the requirements of subsection (5);

(c) claims (including restrictions on transfer not imposed by the issuer) to which the registration of transfer to the present registered owner was subject and were so noted in the initial transaction statement sent to him; and

(d) claims as to which an issuer is charged with notice from a controlling instrument it has elected to require under Section 8—402(4).

(5) If the issuer of an uncertificated security is under a duty as to an adverse claim, he discharges that duty by:

(a) including a notation of the claim in any statements sent with respect to the security under Sections 8—408(3), (6), and (7); and

(b) refusing to register the transfer or pledge of the security unless the nature of the claim does not preclude transfer or pledge subject thereto.

(6) If the transfer or pledge of the security is registered subject to an adverse claim, a notation of the claim must be included in the initial transaction statement and all subsequent statements sent to the transferee and pledgee under Section 8—408.

(7) Notwithstanding subsections (4) and (5), if an uncertificated security was subject to a registered pledge at the time the issuer first came under a duty as to a particular adverse claim, the issuer has no duty as to that claim if transfer of the security is requested by the registered pledgee or an appropriate person acting for the registered pledgee unless:

(a) the claim was embodied in legal process which expressly provides otherwise;

(b) the claim was asserted in a written notification from the registered pledgee;

(c) the claim was one as to which the issuer was charged with notice from a controlling instrument it required under Section 8—402(4) in connection with the pledgee's request for transfer; or

(d) the transfer requested is to the registered owner.

Amended in 1977.

§ 8—404
Liability and Non-Liability for Registration

(1) Except as provided in any law relating to the collection of taxes, the issuer is not liable to the owner, pledgee, or any other person suffering loss as a result of the registration of a transfer, pledge, or release of a security if:

(a) there were on or with a certificated security the necessary indorsements or the issuer had received an instruction originated by an appropriate person (Section 8—308); and

(b) the issuer had no duty as to adverse claims or has discharged the duty (Section 8—403).

(2) If an issuer has registered a transfer of a certificated security to a person not entitled to it, the issuer on demand shall deliver a like security to the true owner unless:

(a) the registration was pursuant to subsection (1);

(b) the owner is precluded from asserting any claim for registering the transfer under Section 8—405(1); or

(c) the delivery would result in overissue, in which case the issuer's liability is governed by Section 8—104.

(3) If an issuer has improperly registered a transfer, pledge, or release of an uncertificated security, the issuer on demand from the injured party shall restore the records as to the injured party to the condition that would have obtained if the improper registration had not been made unless:

(a) the registration was pursuant to subsection (1); or

(b) the registration would result in overissue, in which case the issuer's liability is governed by Section 8—104.

Amended in 1977.

§ 8—405
Lost, Destroyed, and Stolen Certificated Securities

(1) If a certificated security has been lost, apparently destroyed, or wrongfully taken, and the owner fails to notify the issuer of that fact within a reasonable time after he has notice

of it and the issuer registers a transfer of the security before receiving notification, the owner is precluded from asserting against the issuer any claim for registering the transfer under Section 8—404 or any claim to a new security under this section.

(2) If the owner of a certificated security claims that the security has been lost, destroyed, or wrongfully taken, the issuer shall issue a new certificated security or, at the option of the issuer, an equivalent uncertificated security in place of the original security if the owner:

(a) so requests before the issuer has notice that the security has been acquired by a bona fide purchaser;

(b) files with the issuer a sufficient indemnity bond; and

(c) satisfies any other reasonable requirements imposed by the issuer.

(3) If, after the issue of a new certificated or uncertificated security, a bona fide purchaser of the original certificated security presents it for registration of transfer, the issuer shall register the transfer unless registration would result in over-issue, in which event the issuer's liability is governed by Section 8—104. In addition to any rights on the indemnity bond, the issuer may recover the new certificated security from the person to whom it was issued or any person taking under him except a bona fide purchaser or may cancel the uncertificated security unless a bona fide purchaser or any person taking under a bona fide purchaser is then the registered owner or registered pledgee thereof.

Amended in 1977.

§ 8—406
Duty of Authenticating Trustee, Transfer Agent, or Registrar

(1) If a person acts as authenticating trustee, transfer agent, registrar, or other agent for an issuer in the registration of transfers of its certificated securities or in the registration of transfers, pledges, and releases of its uncertificated securities, in the issue of new securities, or in the cancellation of surrendered securities:

(a) he is under a duty to the issuer to exercise good faith and due diligence in performing his functions; and

(b) with regard to the particular functions he performs, he has the same obligation to the holder or owner of a certificated security or to the owner or pledgee of an uncertificated security and has the same rights and privileges as the issuer has in regard to those functions.

(2) Notice to an authenticating trustee, transfer agent, registrar or other agent is notice to the issuer with respect to the functions performed by the agent.

Amended in 1977.

§ 8—407
Exchangeability of Securities

(1) No issuer is subject to the requirements of this section unless it regularly maintains a system for issuing the class of securities involved under which both certificated and uncertificated securities are regularly issued to the category of owners, which includes the person in whose name the new security is to be registered.

(2) Upon surrender of a certificated security with all necessary indorsements and presentation of a written request by the person surrendering the security, the issuer, if he has no duty as to adverse claims or has discharged the duty (Section 8—403), shall issue to the person or a person designated by him an equivalent uncertificated security subject to all liens, restrictions, and claims that were noted on the certificated security.

(3) Upon receipt of a transfer instruction originated by an appropriate person who so requests, the issuer of an uncertificated security shall cancel the uncertificated security and issue an equivalent certificated security on which must be noted conspicuously any liens and restrictions of the issuer and any adverse claims (as to which the issuer has a duty under Section 8—403(4)) to which the uncertificated security was subject. The certificated security shall be registered in the name of and delivered to:

(a) the registered owner, if the uncertificated security was not subject to a registered pledge; or

(b) the registered pledgee, if the uncertificated security was subject to a registered pledge.

Added in 1977.

§ 8—408
Statements of Uncertificated Securities

(1) Within 2 business days after the transfer of an uncertificated security has been registered, the issuer shall send to the new registered owner and, if the security has been transferred subject to a registered pledge, to the registered pledgee a written statement containing:

(a) a description of the issue of which the uncertificated security is a part;

(b) the number of shares or units transferred;

(c) the name and address and any taxpayer identification number of the new registered owner and, if the security has been transferred subject to a registered pledge, the name and address and any taxpayer identification number of the registered pledgee;

(d) a notation of any liens and restrictions of the issuer and any adverse claims (as to which the issuer has a duty under Section 8—403(4)) to which the uncertificated security is or may be subject at the time of registration or a statement that there are none of those liens, restrictions, or adverse claims; and

(e) the date the transfer was registered.

(2) Within 2 business days after the pledge of an uncertificated security has been registered, the issuer shall send to the registered owner and the registered pledgee a written statement containing:

(a) a description of the issue of which the uncertificated security is a part;

(b) the number of shares or units pledged;

(c) the name and address and any taxpayer identification number of the registered owner and the registered pledgee;

(d) a notation of any liens and restrictions of the issuer and any adverse claims (as to which the issuer has a duty under Section 8—403(4)) to which the uncertificated security is or may be subject at the time of registration or a statement that there are none of those liens, restrictions, or adverse claims; and

(e) the date the pledge was registered.

(3) Within 2 business days after the release from pledge of an uncertificated security has been registered, the issuer shall send to the registered owner and the pledgee whose interest was released a written statement containing:

(a) a description of the issue of which the uncertificated security is a part;

(b) the number of shares or units released from pledge;

(c) the name and address and any taxpayer identification number of the registered owner and the pledgee whose interest was released;

(d) a notation of any liens and restrictions of the issuer and any adverse claims (as to which the issuer has a duty under Section 8—403(4)) to which the uncertificated security is or may be subject at the time of registration or a statement that there are none of those liens, restrictions, or adverse claims; and

(e) the date the release was registered.

(4) An "initial transaction statement" is the statement sent to:

(a) the new registered owner and, if applicable, to the registered pledgee pursuant to subsection (1);

(b) the registered pledgee pursuant to subsection (2); or

(c) the registered owner pursuant to subsection (3).

Each initial transaction statement shall be signed by or on behalf of the issuer and must be identified as "Initial Transaction Statement."

(5) Within 2 business days after the transfer of an uncertificated security has been registered, the issuer shall send to the former registered owner and the former registered pledgee, if any, a written statement containing:

(a) a description of the issue of which the uncertificated security is a part;

(b) the number of shares or units transferred;

(c) the name and address and any taxpayer identification number of the former registered owner and of any former registered pledgee; and

(d) the date the transfer was registered.

(6) At periodic intervals, no less frequent than annually and at any time upon the reasonable written request of the registered owner, the issuer shall send to the registered owner of each uncertificated security a dated written statement containing:

(a) a description of the issue of which the uncertificated security is a part;

(b) the name and address and any taxpayer identification number of the registered owner;

(c) the number of shares or units of the uncertificated security registered in the name of the registered owner on the date of the statement;

(d) the name and address and any taxpayer identification number of any registered pledgee and the number of shares or units subject to the pledge; and

(e) a notation of any liens and restrictions of the issuer and any adverse claims (as to which the issuer has a duty under Section 8—403(4)) to which the uncertificated security is or may be subject or a statement that there are none of those liens, restrictions, or adverse claims.

(7) At periodic intervals no less frequent than annually and at any time upon the reasonable written request of the registered pledgee, the issuer shall send to the registered pledgee of each uncertificated security a dated written statement containing:

(a) a description of the issue of which the uncertificated security is a part;

(b) the name and address and any taxpayer identification number of the registered owner;

(c) the name and address and any taxpayer identification number of the registered pledgee;

(d) the number of shares or units subject to the pledge; and

(e) a notation of any liens and restrictions of the issuer and any adverse claims (as to which the issuer has a duty under Section 8—403(4)) to which the uncertificated security is or may be subject or a statement that there are none of those liens, restrictions, or adverse claims.

(8) If the issuer sends the statements described in subsections (6) and (7) at periodic intervals no less frequent than quarterly, the issuer is not obligated to send additional statements upon request unless the owner or pledgee requesting them pays to the issuer the reasonable cost of furnishing them.

(9) Each statement sent pursuant to this section must bear a conspicuous legend reading substantially as follows: "This statement is merely a record of the rights of the addressee as of the time of its issuance. Delivery of this statement, of itself,

confers no rights on the recipient. This statement is neither a negotiable instrument nor a security."

Added in 1977.

ARTICLE 9/Secured Transactions; Sales of Accounts and Chattel Paper

Note: *The adoption of this Article should be accompanied by the repeal of existing statutes dealing with conditional sales, trust receipts, factor's liens where the factor is given a non-possessory lien, chattel mortgages, crop mortgages, mortgages on railroad equipment, assignment of accounts and generally statutes regulating security interests in personal property.*

Where the state has a retail installment selling act or small loan act, that legislation should be carefully examined to determine what changes in those acts are needed to conform them to this Article. This Article primarily sets out rules defining rights of a secured party against persons dealing with the debtor; it does not prescribe regulations and controls which may be necessary to curb abuses arising in the small loan business or in the financing of consumer purchases on credit. Accordingly there is no intention to repeal existing regulatory acts in those fields by enactment or re-enactment of Article 9. See Section 9—203(4) and the Note thereto.

PART 1/Short Title, Applicability and Definitions

§ 9—101
Short Title

This Article shall be known and may be cited as Uniform Commercial Code—Secured Transactions.

§ 9—102
Policy and Subject Matter of Article

(1) Except as otherwise provided in Section 9—104 on excluded transactions, this Article applies

(a) to any transaction (regardless of its form) which is intended to create a security interest in personal property or fixtures including goods, documents, instruments, general intangibles, chattel paper or accounts; and also

(b) to any sale of accounts or chattel paper.

(2) This Article applies to security interests created by contract including pledge, assignment, chattel mortgage, chattel trust, trust deed, factor's lien, equipment trust, conditional sale, trust receipt, other lien or title retention contract and lease or consignment intended as security. This Article does not apply to statutory liens except as provided in Section 9—310.

(3) The application of this Article to a security interest in a secured obligation is not affected by the fact that the obligation is itself secured by a transaction or interest to which this Article does not apply. Amended in 1972.

§ 9—103
Perfection of Security Interest in Multiple State Transactions

(1) Documents, instruments and ordinary goods.

(a) This subsection applies to documents and instruments and to goods other than those covered by a certificate of title described in subsection (2), mobile goods described in subsection (3), and minerals described in subsection (5).

(b) Except as otherwise provided in this subsection, perfection and the effect of perfection or non-perfection of a security interest in collateral are governed by the law of the jurisdiction where the collateral is when the last event occurs on which is based the assertion that the security interest is perfected or unperfected.

(c) If the parties to a transaction creating a purchase money security interest in goods in one jurisdiction understand at the time that the security interest attaches that the goods will be kept in another jurisdiction, then the law of the other jurisdiction governs the perfection and the effect of perfection or non-perfection of the security interest from the time it attaches until thirty days after the debtor receives possession of the goods and thereafter if the goods are taken to the other jurisdiction before the end of the thirty-day period.

(d) When collateral is brought into and kept in this state while subject to a security interest perfected under the law of the jurisdiction from which the collateral was removed, the security interest remains perfected, but if action is required by Part 3 of this Article to perfect the security interest,

(i) if the action is not taken before the expiration of the period of perfection in the other jurisdiction or the end of four months after the collateral is brought into this state, whichever period first expires, the security interest becomes unperfected at the end of that period and is thereafter deemed to have been unperfected as against a person who became a purchaser after removal;

(ii) if the action is taken before the expiration of the period specified in subparagraph (i), the security interest continues perfected thereafter;

(iii) for the purpose of priority over a buyer of consumer goods (subsection (2) of Section 9—307), the period of the effectiveness of a filing in the jurisdiction from which the collateral is removed is governed by the rules with respect to perfection in subparagraphs (i) and (ii).

(2) Certificate of title.

(a) This subsection applies to goods covered by a certificate of title issued under a statute of this state or of another jurisdiction under the law of which indication of a security interest on the certificate is required as a condition of perfection.

(b) Except as otherwise provided in this subsection, perfection and the effect of perfection or non-perfection of the security interest are governed by the law (including the conflict of laws rules) of the jurisdiction issuing the certificate until four months after the goods are removed from that jurisdiction and thereafter until the goods are registered in another jurisdiction, but in any event not beyond surrender of the certificate. After the expiration of that period, the goods are not covered by the certificate of title within the meaning of this section.

(c) Except with respect to the rights of a buyer described in the next paragraph, a security interest, perfected in another jurisdiction otherwise than by notation on a certificate of title, in goods brought into this state and thereafter covered by a certificate of title issued by this state is subject to the rules stated in paragraph (d) of subsection (1).

(d) If goods are brought into this state while a security interest therein is perfected in any manner under the law of the jurisdiction from which the goods are removed and a certificate of title is issued by this state and the certificate does not show that the goods are subject to the security interest or that they may be subject to security interests not shown on the certificate, the security interest is subordinate to the rights of a buyer of the goods who is not in the business of selling goods of that kind to the extent that he gives value and receives delivery of the goods after issuance of the certificate and without knowledge of the security interest.

(3) Accounts, general intangibles and mobile goods.

(a) This subsection applies to accounts (other than an account described in subsection (5) on minerals) and general intangibles (other than uncertificated securities) and to goods which are mobile and which are of a type normally used in more than one jurisdiction, such as motor vehicles, trailers, rolling stock, airplanes, shipping containers, road building and construction machinery and commercial harvesting machinery and the like, if the goods are equipment or are inventory leased or held for lease by the debtor to others, and are not covered by a certificate of title described in subsection (2).

(b) The law (including the conflict of laws rules) of the jurisdiction in which the debtor is located governs the perfection and the effect of perfection or non-perfection of the security interest.

(c) If, however, the debtor is located in a jurisdiction which is not a part of the United States, and which does not provide for perfection of the security interest by filing or recording in that jurisdiction, the law of the jurisdiction in the United States in which the debtor has its major executive office in the United States governs the perfection and the effect of perfection or non-perfection of the security interest through filing. In the alternative, if the debtor is located in a jurisdiction which is not a part of the United States or Canada and the collateral is accounts or general intangibles for money due or to become due, the security interest may be perfected by notification to the account debtor. As used in this paragraph, "United States" includes its territories and possessions and the Commonwealth of Puerto Rico.

(d) A debtor shall be deemed located at his place of business if he has one, at his chief executive office if he has more than one place of business, otherwise at his residence. If, however, the debtor is a foreign air carrier under the Federal Aviation Act of 1958, as amended, it shall be deemed located at the designated office of the agent upon whom service of process may be made on behalf of the foreign air carrier.

(e) A security interest perfected under the law of the jurisdiction of the location of the debtor is perfected until the expiration of four months after a change of the debtor's location to another jurisdiction, or until perfection would have ceased by the law of the first jurisdiction, whichever period first expires. Unless perfected in the new jurisdiction before the end of that period, it becomes unperfected thereafter and is deemed to have been unperfected as against a person who became a purchaser after the change.

(4) Chattel paper.

The rules stated for goods in subsection (1) apply to a possessory security interest in chattel paper. The rules stated for accounts in subsection (3) apply to a non-possessory security interest in chattel paper, but the security interest may not be perfected by notification to the account debtor.

(5) Minerals.

Perfection and the effect of perfection or non-perfection of a security interest which is created by a debtor who has an interest in minerals or the like (including oil and gas) before extraction and which attaches thereto as extracted, or which attaches to an account resulting from the sale thereof at the wellhead or minehead are governed by the law (including the conflict of laws rules) of the jurisdiction wherein the wellhead or minehead is located.

(6) Uncertificated securities.

The law (including the conflict of laws rules) of the jurisdiction of organization of the issuer governs the perfection and the effect of perfection or non-perfection of a security interest in uncertificated securities.

Amended in 1972 and 1977.

§ 9—104
Transactions Excluded From Article

This Article does not apply

(a) to a security interest subject to any statute of the United States, to the extent that such statute governs the rights of parties to and third parties affected by transactions in particular types of property; or

(b) to a landlord's lien; or

(c) to a lien given by statute or other rule of law for services or materials except as provided in Section 9—310 on priority of such liens; or

(d) to a transfer of a claim for wages, salary or other compensation of an employee; or

(e) to a transfer by a government or governmental subdivision or agency; or

(f) to a sale of accounts or chattel paper as part of a sale of the business out of which they arose, or an assignment of accounts or chattel paper which is for the purpose of collection only, or a transfer of a right to payment under a contract to an assignee who is also to do the performance under the contract or a transfer of a single account to an assignee in whole or partial satisfaction of a preexisting indebtedness; or

(g) to a transfer of an interest in or claim in or under any policy of insurance, except as provided with respect to proceeds (Section 9—306) and priorities in proceeds (Section 9—312); or

(h) to a right represented by a judgment (other than a judgment taken on a right to payment which was collateral); or

(i) to any right of set-off; or

(j) except to the extent that provision is made for fixtures in Section 9—313, to the creation or transfer of an interest in or lien on real estate, including a lease or rents thereunder; or

(k) to a transfer in whole or in part of any claim arising out of tort; or

(l) to a transfer of an interest in any deposit account (sub-section (1) of Section 9—105) except as provided with respect to proceeds (Section 9—306) and priorities in proceeds (Section 9—312).

Amended in 1972.

§ 9—105
Definitions and Index of Definitions

(1) In this Article unless the context otherwise requires:

(a) "Account debtor" means the person who is obligated on an account, chattel paper or general intangible;

(b) "Chattel paper" means a writing or writings which evidence both a monetary obligation and a security interest in or a lease of specific goods, but a charter or other contract involving the use or hire of a vessel is not chattel paper. When a transaction is evidenced both by such a security agreement or a lease and by an instrument or a series of instruments, the group of writings taken together constitutes chattel paper;

(c) "Collateral" means the property subject to a security interest, and includes accounts and chattel paper which have been sold;

(d) "Debtor" means the person who owes payment or other performance of the obligation secured, whether or not he owns or has rights in the collateral, and includes the seller of accounts or chattel paper. Where the debtor and the owner of the collateral are not the same person, the term "debtor" means the owner of the collateral in any provision of the Article dealing with the obligation, and may include both where the context so requires;

(e) "Deposit account" means a demand, time, savings, passbook or like account maintained with a bank, savings and loan association, credit union or like organization, other than an account evidenced by a certificate of deposit;

(f) "Document" means document of title as defined in the general definitions of Article 1 (Section 1—201), and a receipt of the kind described in subsection (2) of Section 7—201;

(g) "Encumbrance" includes real estate mortgages and other liens on real estate and all other rights in real estate that are not ownership interests;

(h) "Goods" includes all things which are movable at the time the security interest attaches or which are fixtures (Section 9—313), but does not include money, documents, instruments, accounts, chattel paper, general intangibles, or minerals or the like (including oil and gas) before extraction. "Goods" also includes standing timber which is to be cut and removed under a conveyance or contract for sale, the unborn young of animals, and growing crops;

(i) "Instrument" means a negotiable instrument (defined in Section 3—104), or a security (defined in Section 8—102) or any other writing which evidences a right to the payment of money and is not itself a security agreement or lease and is of a type which is in ordinary course of business transferred by delivery with any necessary indorsement or assignment;

(j) "Mortgage" means a consensual interest created by a real estate mortgage, a trust deed on real estate, or the like;

(k) An advance is made "pursuant to commitment" if the secured party has bound himslf to make it, whether or not a subsequent event of default or other event not within his control has relieved or may relieve him from his obligation;

(l) "Security agreement" means an agreement which creates or provides for a security interest;

(m) "Secured party" means a lender, seller or other person in whose favor there is a security interest, including a person to whom accounts or chattel paper have been sold. When the holders of obligations issued under an indenture of trust, equipment trust agreement or the like are represented by a trustee or other person, the representative is the secured party;

(n) "Transmitting utility" means any person primarily engaged in the railroad, street railway or trolley bus business, the electric or electronics communications transmission business, the transmission of goods by pipeline, or the transmission or the production and transmission of electricity, steam, gas or water, or the provision of sewer service.

(2) Other definitions applying to this Article and the sections in which they appear are:

"Account". Section 9—106.

"Attach". Section 9—203.

"Construction mortgage". Section 9—313(1).

"Consumer goods". Section 9—109(1).

"Equipment". Section 9—109(2).

"Farm products". Section 9—109(3).

"Fixture". Section 9—313(1).

"Fixture filing". Section 9—313(1).

"General intangibles". Section 9—106.

"Inventory". Section 9—109(4).

"Lien creditor". Section 9—301(3).

"Proceeds". Section 9—306(1).

"Purchase money security interest". Section 9—107.

"United States". Section 9—103.

(3) The following definitions in other Articles apply to this Article:

"Check". Section 3—104.

"Contract for sale". Section 2—106.

"Holder in due course". Section 3—302.

"Note". Section 3—104.

"Sale". Section 2—106.

(4) In addition Article 1 contains general definitions and principles of construction and interpretation applicable throughout this Article.

Amended in 1966, 1972, and 1977.

§ 9—106
Definitions: "Account"; "General Intangibles"

"Account" means any right to payment for goods sold or leased or for services rendered which is not evidenced by an instrument or chattel paper, whether or not it has been earned by performance. "General intangibles" means any personal property (including things in action) other than goods, accounts, chattel paper, documents, instruments, and money. All rights to payment earned or unearned under a charter or other contract involving the use or hire of a vessel and all rights incident to the charter or contract are accounts.

Amended in 1966, 1972.

§ 9—107
Definitions: "Purchase Money Security Interest"

A security interest is a "purchase money security interest" to the extent that it is

(a) taken or retained by the seller of the collateral to secure all or part of its price; or

(b) taken by a person who by making advances or incurring an obligation gives value to enable the debtor to acquire rights in or the use of collateral if such value is in fact so used.

§ 9—108
When After-Acquired Collateral Not Security for Antecedent Debt

Where a secured party makes an advance, incurs an obligation, releases a perfected security interest, or otherwise gives new value which is to be secured in whole or in part by after-acquired property his security interest in the after-acquired collateral shall be deemed to be taken for new value and not as security for an antecedent debt if the debtor acquires his rights in such collateral either in the ordinary course of his business or under a contract of purchase made pursuant to the security agreement within a reasonable time after new value is given.

§ 9—109
Classification of Goods; "Consumer Goods"; "Equipment"; "Farm Products"; "Inventory"

Goods are

(1) "consumer goods" if they are used or bought for use primarily for personal, family or household purposes;

(2) "equipment" if they are used or bought for use primarily in business (including farming or a profession) or by a debtor who is a non-profit organization or a governmental subdivision or agency or if the goods are not included in the definitions of inventory, farm products or consumer goods;

(3) "farm products" if they are crops or livestock or supplies used or produced in farming operations or if they are products of crops or livestock in their unmanufactured states (such as ginned cotton, woolclip, maple syrup, milk and eggs), and if they are in the possession of a debtor engaged in raising, fattening, grazing or other farming operations. If

goods are farm products they are neither equipment nor inventory;

(4) "inventory" if they are held by a person who holds them for sale or lease or to be furnished under contracts of service or if he has so furnished them, or if they are raw materials, work in process or materials used or consumed in a business. Inventory of a person is not to be classified as his equipment.

§ 9—110
Sufficiency of Description

For the purposes of this Article any description of personal property or real estate is sufficient whether or not it is specific if it reasonably identifies what is described.

§ 9—111
Applicability of Bulk Transfer Laws

The creation of a security interest is not a bulk transfer under Article 6 (see Section 6—103).

§ 9—112
Where Collateral Is Not Owned by Debtor

Unless otherwise agreed, when a secured party knows that collateral is owned by a person who is not the debtor, the owner of the collateral is entitled to receive from the secured party any surplus under Section 9—502(2) or under Section 9—504(1), and is not liable for the debt or for any deficiency after resale, and he has the same right as the debtor

(a) to receive statements under Section 9—208;

(b) to receive notice of and to object to a secured party's proposal to retain the collateral in satisfaction of the indebtedness under Section 9—505;

(c) to redeem the collateral under Section 9—506;

(d) to obtain injunctive or other relief under Section 9—507(1); and

(e) to recover losses caused to him under Section 9—208(2).

§ 9—113
Security Interests Arising Under Article on Sales

A security interest arising solely under the Article on Sales (Article 2) is subject to the provisions of this Article except that to the extent that and so long as the debtor does not have or does not lawfully obtain possession of the goods

(a) no security agreement is necessary to make the security interest enforceable; and

(b) no filing is required to perfect the security interest; and

(c) the rights of the secured party on default by the debtor are governed by the Article on Sales (Article 2).

§ 9—114
Consignment

(1) A person who delivers goods under a consignment which is not a security interest and who would be required to file under this Article by paragraph (3)(c) of Section 2—326 has priority over a secured party who is or becomes a creditor of the consignee and who would have a perfected security interest in the goods if they were the property of the consignee, and also has priority with respect to identifiable cash proceeds received on or before delivery of the goods to a buyer, if

(a) the consignor complies with the filing provision of the Article on Sales with respect to consignments (paragraph (3)(c) of Section 2—326) before the consignee receives possession of the goods; and

(b) the consignor gives notification in writing to the holder of the security interest if the holder has filed a financing statement covering the same types of goods before the date of the filing made by the consignor; and

(c) the holder of the security interest receives the notification within five years before the consignee receives possession of the goods; and

(d) the notification states that the consignor expects to deliver goods on consignment to the consignee, describing the goods by item or type.

(2) In the case of a consignment which is not a security interest and in which the requirements of the preceding subsection have not been met, a person who delivers goods to another is subordinate to a person who would have a perfected security interest in the goods if they were the property of the debtor.

Added in 1972.

PART 2/Validity of Security Agreement and Rights of Parties Thereto

§ 9—201
General Validity of Security Agreement

Except as otherwise provided by this Act a security agreement is effective according to its terms between the parties, against purchasers of the collateral and against creditors. Nothing in this Article validates any charge or practice illegal under any statute or regulation thereunder governing usury, small loans, retail installment sales, or the like, or extends the application of any such statute or regulation to any transaction not otherwise subject thereto.

§ 9—202
Title to Collateral Immaterial

Each provision of this Article with regard to rights, obligations and remedies applies whether title to collateral is in the secured party or in the debtor.

§ 9—203
Attachment and Enforceability of Security Interest; Proceeds; Formal Requisites

(1) Subject to the provisions of Section 4—208 on the security interest of a collecting bank, Section 8—321 on security interests in securities and Section 9—113 on a security interest arising under the Article on Sales, a security interest is not enforceable against the debtor or third parties with respect to the collateral and does not attach unless:

  (a) the collateral is in the possession of the secured party pursuant to agreement, or the debtor has signed a security agreement which contains a description of the collateral and in addition, when the security interest covers crops growing or to be grown or timber to be cut, a description of the land concerned;

  (b) value has been given; and

  (c) the debtor has rights in the collateral.

(2) A security interest attaches when it becomes enforceable against the debtor with respect to the collateral. Attachment occurs as soon as all of the events specified in subsection (1) have taken place unless explicit agreement postpones the time of attaching.

(3) Unless otherwise agreed a security agreement gives the secured party the rights to proceeds provided by Section 9—306.

(4) A transaction, although subject to this Article, is also subject to . . . .*, and in the case of conflict between the provisions of this Article and any such statute, the provisions of such statute control. Failure to comply with any applicable statute has only the effect which is specified therein.

Amended in 1972 and 1977.

Note: *At * in subsection (4) insert reference to any local statute regulating small loans, retail installment sales and the like.*

The foregoing subsection (4) is designed to make it clear that certain transactions, although subject to this Article, must also comply with other applicable legislation.

This Article is designed to regulate all the "security" aspects of transactions within its scope. There is, however, much regulatory legislation, particularly in the consumer field, which supplements this Article and should not be repealed by its enactment. Examples are small loan acts, retail installment selling acts and the like. Such acts may provide for licensing and rate regulation and may prescribe particular forms of contract. Such provisions should remain in force despite the enactment of this Article. On the other hand if a retail installment selling act contains provisions on filing, rights on default, etc., such provisions should be repealed as inconsistent with this Article except that inconsistent provisions as to deficiencies, penalties, etc., in the Uniform Consumer Credit Code and other recent related legislation should remain because those statutes were drafted after the substantial enactment of the Article and with the intention of modifying certain provisions of this Article as to consumer credit.

§ 9—204
After-Acquired Property; Future Advances

(1) Except as provided in subsection (2), a security agreement may provide that any or all obligations covered by the security agreement are to be secured by after-acquired collateral.

(2) No security interest attaches under an after-acquired property clause to consumer goods other than accessions (Section 9—314) when given as additional security unless the debtor acquires rights in them within ten days after the secured party gives value.

(3) Obligations covered by a security agreement may include future advances or other value whether or not the advances or value are given pursuant to commitment (subsection (1) of Section 9—105).

Amended in 1972.

§ 9—205
Use or Disposition of Collateral Without Accounting Permissible

A security interest is not invalid or fraudulent against creditors by reason of liberty in the debtor to use, commingle or dispose of all or part of the collateral (including returned or repossessed goods) or to collect or compromise accounts or chattel paper, or to accept the return of goods or make repossessions, or to use, commingle or dispose of proceeds, or by reason of the failure of the secured party to require the debtor to account for proceeds or replace collateral. This section does not relax the requirements of possession where perfection of a security interest depends upon possession of the collateral by the secured party or by a bailee.

Amended in 1972.

§ 9—206
Agreement Not to Assert Defenses Against Assignee; Modification of Sales Warranties Where Security Agreement Exists

(1) Subject to any statute or decision which establishes a different rule for buyers or lessees of consumer goods, an agreement by a buyer or lessee that he will not assert against an assignee any claim or defense which he may have against the seller or lessor is enforceable by an assignee who takes his assignment for value, in good faith and without notice of a claim or defense, except as to defenses of a type which may be asserted against a holder in due course of a negotiable instrument under the Article on Commercial Paper (Article 3). A buyer who as part of one transaction signs both a negotiable instrument and a security agreement makes such an agreement.

(2) When a seller retains a purchase money security interest in goods the Article on Sales (Article 2) governs the sale and any disclaimer, limitation or modification of the seller's warranties.

Amended in 1962.

§ 9—207
Rights and Duties When Collateral is in Secured Party's Possession

(1) A secured party must use reasonable care in the custody and preservation of collateral in his possession. In the case of an instrument or chattel paper reasonable care includes taking necessary steps to preserve rights against prior parties unless otherwise agreed.

(2) Unless otherwise agreed, when collateral is in the secured party's possession

(a) reasonable expenses (including the cost of any insurance and payment of taxes or other charges) incurred in the custody, preservation, use or operation of the collateral are chargeable to the debtor and are secured by the collateral;

(b) the risk of accidental loss or damage is on the debtor to the extent of any deficiency in any effective insurance coverage;

(c) the secured party may hold as additional security any increase or profits (except money) received from the collateral, but money so received, unless remitted to the debtor, shall be applied in reduction of the secured obligation;

(d) the secured party must keep the collateral identifiable but fungible collateral may be commingled;

(e) the secured party may repledge the collateral upon terms which do not impair the debtor's right to redeem it.

(3) A secured party is liable for any loss caused by his failure to meet any obligation imposed by the preceding subsections but does not lose his security interest.

(4) A secured party may use or operate the collateral for the purpose of preserving the collateral or its value or pursuant to the order of a court of appropriate jurisdiction or, except in the case of consumer goods, in the manner and to the extent provided in the security agreement.

§ 9—208
Request for Statement of Account or List of Collateral

(1) A debtor may sign a statement indicating what he believes to be the aggregate amount of unpaid indebtedness as of a specified date and may send it to the secured party with a request that the statement be approved or corrected and returned to the debtor. When the security agreement or any other record kept by the secured party identifies the collat-

eral a debtor may similarly request the secured party to approve or correct a list of the collateral.

(2) The secured party must comply with such a request within two weeks after receipt by sending a written correction or approval. If the secured party claims a security interest in all of a particular type of collateral owned by the debtor he may indicate that fact in his reply and need not approve or correct an itemized list of such collateral. If the secured party without reasonable excuse fails to comply he is liable for any loss caused to the debtor thereby; and if the debtor has properly included in his request a good faith statement of the obligation or a list of the collateral or both the secured party may claim a security interest only as shown in the statement against persons misled by his failure to comply. If he no longer has an interest in the obligation or collateral at the time the request is received he must disclose the name and address of any successor in interest known to him and he is liable for any loss caused to the debtor as a result of failure to disclose. A successor in interest is not subject to this section until a request is received by him.

(3) A debtor is entitled to such a statement once every six months without charge. The secured party may require payment of a charge not exceeding $10 for each additional statement furnished.

PART 3/Rights of Third Parties; Perfected and Unperfected Security Interests; Rules of Priority

§ 9—301
Persons Who Take Priority Over Unperfected Security Interests; Rights of "Lien Creditor"

(1) Except as otherwise provided in subsection (2), an unperfected security interest is subordinate to the rights of

(a) persons entitled to priority under Section 9—312;

(b) a person who becomes a lien creditor before the security interest is perfected;

(c) in the case of goods, instruments, documents, and chattel paper, a person who is not a secured party and who is a transferee in bulk or other buyer not in ordinary course of business or is a buyer of farm products in ordinary course of business, to the extent that he gives value and receives delivery of the collateral without knowledge of the security interest and before it is perfected;

(d) in the case of accounts and general intangibles, a person who is not a secured party and who is a transferee to the extent that he gives value without knowledge of the security interest and before it is perfected.

(2) If the secured party files with respect to a purchase money security interest before or within ten days after the debtor receives possession of the collateral, he takes priority over the rights of a transferee in bulk or of a lien creditor

which arise between the time the security interest attaches and the time of filing.

(3) A "lien creditor" means a creditor who has acquired a lien on the property involved by attachment, levy or the like and includes an assignee for benefit of creditors from the time of assignment, and a trustee in bankruptcy from the date of the filing of the petition or a receiver in equity from the time of appointment.

(4) A person who becomes a lien creditor while a security interest is perfected takes subject to the security interest only to the extent that it secures advances made before he becomes a lien credit or within 45 days thereafter or made without knowledge of the lien or pursuant to a commitment entered into without knowledge of the lien.

Amended in 1972.

§ 9—302
When Filing Is Required to Perfect Security Interest; Security Interests to Which Filing Provisions of This Article Do Not Apply

(1) A financing statement must be filed to perfect all security interests except the following:

(a) a security interest in collateral in possession of the secured party under Section 9—305;

(b) a security interest temporarily perfected in instruments or documents without delivery under Section 9—304 or in proceeds for a 10 day period under Section 9—306;

(c) a security interest created by an assignment of a beneficial interest in a trust or a decedent's estate;

(d) a purchase money security interest in consumer goods; but filing is required for a motor vehicle required to be registered; and fixture filing is required for priority over conflicting interests in fixtures to the extent provided in Section 9—313;

(e) an assignment of accounts which does not alone or in conjunction with other assignments to the same assignee transfer a significant part of the outstanding accounts of the assignor;

(f) a security interest of a collecting bank (Section 4—208) or in securities (Section 8—321) or arising under the Article on Sales (see Section 9—113) or covered in subsection (3) of this section;

(g) an assignment for the benefit of all the creditors of the transferor, and subsequent transfers by the assignee thereunder.

(2) If a secured party assigns a perfected security interest, no filing under this Article is required in order to continue the perfected status of the security interest against creditors of and transferees from the original debtor.

(3) The filing of a financing statement otherwise required by this Article is not necessary or effective to perfect a security interest in property subject to

(a) a statute or treaty of the United States which provides for a national or international registration or a national or international certificate of title or which specifies a place of filing different from that specified in this Article for filing of the security interest; or

(b) the following statutes of this state; [list any certificate of title statute covering automobiles, trailers, mobile homes, boats, farm tractors, or the like, and any central filing statute]; but during any period in which collateral is inventory held for sale by a person who is in the business of selling goods of that kind, the filing provisions of this Article (Part 4) apply to a security interest in that collateral created by him as debtor; or

(c) a certificate of title statute of another jurisdiction under the law of which indication of a security interest on the certificate is required as a condition of perfection (subsection (2) of Section 9—103).

(4) Compliance with a statute or treaty described in subsection (3) is equivalent to the filing of a financing statement under this Article, and a security interest in property subject to the statute or treaty can be perfected only by compliance therewith except as provided in Section 9—103 on multiple state transactions. Duration and renewal of perfection of a security interest perfected by compliance with the statute or treaty are governed by the provisions of the statute or treaty; in other respects the security interest is subject to this Article.

Amended in 1972 and 1977.

§ 9—303
When Security Interest Is Perfected; Continuity of Perfection

(1) A security interest is perfected when it has attached and when all of the applicable steps required for perfection have been taken. Such steps are specified in Sections 9—302, 9—304, 9—305 and 9—306. If such steps are taken before the security interest attaches, it is perfected at the time when it attaches.

(2) If a security interest is originally perfected in any way permitted under this Article and is subsequently perfected in some other way under this Article, without an intermediate period when it was unperfected, the security interest shall be deemed to be perfected continuously for the purposes of this Article.

§ 9—304
Perfection of Security Interest in Instruments, Documents, and Goods Covered by Documents; Perfection by Permissive Filing; Temporary Perfection Without Filing or Transfer of Possession

(1) A security interest in chattel paper or negotiable documents may be perfected by filing. A security interest in money or instruments (other than certificated securities or

instruments which constitute part of chattel paper) can be perfected only by the secured party's taking possession, except as provided in subsections (4) and (5) of this section and subsections (2) and (3) of Section 9—306 on proceeds.

(2) During the period that goods are in the possession of the issuer of a negotiable document therefor, a security interest in the goods is perfected by perfecting a security interest in the document, and any security interest in the goods otherwise perfected during such period is subject thereto.

(3) A security interest in goods in the possession of a bailee other than one who has issued a negotiable document therefor is perfected by issuance of a document in the name of the secured party or by the bailee's receipt of notification of the secured party's interest or by filing as to the goods.

(4) A security interest in instruments (other than certificated securities) or negotiable documents is perfected without filing or the taking of possession for a period of 21 days from the time it attaches to the extent that it arises for new value given under a written security agreement.

(5) A security interest remains perfected for a period of 21 days without filing where a secured party having a perfected security interest in an instrument (other than a certificated security), a negotiable document or goods in possession of a bailee other than one who has issued a negotiable document therefor

(a) makes available to the debtor the goods or documents representing the goods for the purpose of ultimate sale or exchange or for the purpose of loading, unloading, storing, shipping, transshipping, manufacturing, processing or otherwise dealing with them in a manner preliminary to their sale or exchange, but priority between conflicting security interests in the goods is subject to subsection (3) of Section 9—312; or

(b) delivers the instrument to the debtor for the purpose of ultimate sale or exchange or of presentation, collection, renewal or registration of transfer.

(6) After the 21 day period in subsections (4) and (5) perfection depends upon compliance with applicable provisions of this Article.

Amended in 1972 and 1977.

§ 9—305
When Possession by Secured Party Perfects Security Interest Without Filing

A security interest in letters of credit and advices of credit (subsection (2)(a) of Section 5—116), goods, instruments (other than certificated securities), money, negotiable documents or chattel paper may be perfected by the secured party's taking possession of the collateral. If such collateral other than goods covered by a negotiable document is held by a bailee, the secured party is deemed to have possession from the time the bailee receives notification of the secured party's interest. A security interest is perfected by possession from the time possession is taken without a relation back and continues only so long as possession is retained, unless otherwise specified in this Article. The security interest may be otherwise perfected as provided in this Article before or after the period of possession by the secured party.

Amended in 1972.

§ 9—306
"Proceeds"; Secured Party's Rights on Disposition of Collateral

(1) "Proceeds" includes whatever is received upon the sale, exchange, collection or other disposition of collateral or proceeds. Insurance payable by reason of loss or damage to the collateral is proceeds, except to the extent that it is payable to a person other than a party to the security agreement. Money, checks, deposit accounts, and the like are "cash proceeds". All other proceeds are "non-cash proceeds".

(2) Except where this Article otherwise provides, a security interest continues in collateral notwithstanding sale, exchange or other disposition thereof unless the disposition was authorized by the secured party in the security agreement or otherwise, and also continues in any identifiable proceeds including collections received by the debtor.

(3) The security interest in proceeds is a continuously perfected security interest if the interest in the original collateral was perfected but it ceases to be a perfected security interest and becomes unperfected ten days after receipt of the proceeds by the debtor unless

(a) a filed financing statement covers the original collateral and the proceeds are collateral in which a security interest may be perfected by filing in the office or offices where the financing statement has been filed and, if the proceeds are acquired with cash proceeds, the description of collateral in the financing statement indicates the types of property constituting the proceeds; or

(b) a filed financing statement covers the original collateral and the proceeds are identifiable cash proceeds; or

(c) the security interest in the proceeds is perfected before the expiration of the ten day period.

Except as provided in this section, a security interest in proceeds can be perfected only by the methods or under the circumstances permitted in this Article for original collateral of the same type.

(4) In the event of insolvency proceedings instituted by or against a debtor, a secured party with a perfected security interest in proceeds has a perfected security interest only in the following proceeds:

(a) in identifiable non-cash proceeds and in separate deposit accounts containing only proceeds;

(b) in identifiable cash proceeds in the form of money which is neither commingled with other money nor deposited in a deposit account prior to the insolvency proceedings;

(c) in identifiable cash proceeds in the form of checks and the like which are not deposited in a deposit account prior to the insolvency proceedings; and

(d) in all cash and deposit accounts of the debtor in which proceeds have been commingled with other funds, but the perfected security interest under this paragraph (d) is

(i) subject to any right to set-off; and

(ii) limited to an amount not greater than the amount of any cash proceeds received by the debtor within ten days before the institution of the insolvency proceedings less the sum of (I) the payments to the secured party on account of cash proceeds received by the debtor during such period and (II) the cash proceeds received by the debtor during such period to which the secured party is entitled under paragraphs (a) through (c) of this subsection (4).

(5) If a sale of goods results in an account or chattel paper which is transferred by the seller to a secured party, and if the goods are returned to or are repossessed by the seller or the secured party, the following rules determine priorities:

(a) If the goods were collateral at the time of sale, for an indebtedness of the seller which is still unpaid, the original security interest attaches again to the goods and continues as a perfected security interest if it was perfected at the time when the goods were sold. If the security interest was originally perfected by a filing which is still effective, nothing further is required to continue the perfected status; in any other case, the secured party must take possession of the returned or repossessed goods or must file.

(b) An unpaid transferee of the chattel paper has a security interest in the goods against the transferor. Such security interest is prior to a security interest asserted under paragraph (a) to the extent that the transferee of the chattel paper was entitled to priority under Section 9—308.

(c) An unpaid transferee of the account has a security interest in the goods against the transferor. Such security interest is subordinate to a security interest asserted under paragraph (a).

(d) A security interest of an unpaid transferee asserted under paragraph (b) or (c) must be perfected for protection against creditors of the transferor and purchasers of the returned or repossessed goods.

Amended in 1972.

§ 9—307
Protection of Buyers of Goods

(1) A buyer in ordinary course of business (subsection (9) of Section 1—201) other than a person buying farm products from a person engaged in farming operations takes free of a security interest created by his seller even though the security interest is perfected and even though the buyer knows of its existence.

(2) In the case of consumer goods, a buyer takes free of a security interest even though perfected if he buys without knowledge of the security interest, for value and for his own personal, family or household purposes unless prior to the purchase the secured party has filed a financing statement covering such goods.

(3) A buyer other than a buyer in ordinary course of business (subsection (1) of this section) takes free of a security interest to the extent that it secures future advances made after the secured party acquires knowledge of the purchase, or more than 45 days after the purchase, whichever first occurs, unless made pursuant to a commitment entered into without knowledge of the purchase and before the expiration of the 45 day period.

Amended in 1972.

§ 9—308
Purchase of Chattel Paper and Instruments

A purchaser of chattel paper or an instrument who gives new value and takes possession of it in the ordinary course of his business has priority over a security interest in the chattel paper or instrument

(a) which is perfected under Section 9—304 (permissive filing and temporary perfection) or under Section 9—306 (perfection as to proceeds) if he acts without knowledge that the specific paper or instrument is subject to a security interest; or

(b) which is claimed merely as proceeds of inventory subject to a security interest (Section 9—306) even though he knows that the specific paper or instrument is subject to the security interest.

Amended in 1972.

§ 9—309
Protection of Purchasers of Instruments, Documents and Securities

Nothing in this Article limits the rights of a holder in due course of a negotiable instrument (Section 3—302) or a holder to whom a negotiable document of title has been duly negotiated (Section 7—501) or a bona fide purchaser of a security (Section 8—302) and the holders or purchasers take priority over an earlier security interest even though perfected. Filing under this Article does not constitute notice of the security interest to such holders or purchasers.

Amended in 1977.

§ 9—310
Priority of Certain Liens Arising by Operation of Law

When a person in the ordinary course of his business furnishes services or materials with respect to goods subject to a security interest, a lien upon goods in the possession of such person given by statute or rule of law for such materials or services takes priority over a perfected security interest unless the lien is statutory and the statute expressly provides otherwise.

§ 9—311
Alienability of Debtor's Rights: Judicial Process

The debtor's rights in collateral may be voluntarily or involuntarily transferred (by way of sale, creation of a security interest, attachment, levy, garnishment or other judicial process) notwithstanding a provision in the security agreement prohibiting any transfer or making the transfer constitute a default.

§ 9—312
Priorities Among Conflicting Security Interests in the Same Collateral

(1) The rules of priority stated in other sections of this Part and in the following sections shall govern when applicable: Section 4—208 with respect to the security interests of collecting banks in items being collected, accompanying documents and proceeds; Section 9—103 on security interests related to other jurisdictions; Section 9—114 on consignments.

(2) A perfected security interest in crops for new value given to enable the debtor to produce the crops during the production season and given not more than three months before the crops become growing crops by planting or otherwise takes priority over an earlier perfected security interest to the extent that such earlier interest secures obligations due more than six months before the crops become growing crops by planting or otherwise, even though the person giving new value had knowledge of the earlier security interest.

(3) A perfected purchase money security interest in inventory has priority over a conflicting security interest in the same inventory and also has priority in identifiable cash proceeds received on or before the delivery of the inventory to a buyer if

(a) the purchase money security interest is perfected at the time the debtor receives possession of the inventory; and

(b) the purchase money secured party gives notification in writing to the holder of the conflicting security interest if the holder had filed a financing statement covering the same types of inventory (i) before the date of the filing made by the purchase money secured party, or (ii) before the beginning of the 21 day period where the purchase money security interest is temporarily perfected without filing or possession (subsection (5) of Section 9—304); and

(c) the holder of the conflicting security interest receives the notification within five years before the debtor receives possession of the inventory; and

(d) the notification states that the person giving the notice has or expects to acquire a purchase money security interest in inventory of the debtor, describing such inventory by item or type.

(4) A purchase money security interest in collateral other than inventory has priority over a conflicting security interest in the same collateral or its proceeds if the purchase money security interest is perfected at the time the debtor receives possession of the collateral or within ten days thereafter.

(5) In all cases not governed by other rules stated in this section (including cases of purchase money security interests which do not qualify for the special priorities set forth in subsections (3) and (4) of this section), priority between conflicting security interests in the same collateral shall be determined according to the following rules:

(a) Conflicting security interests rank according to priority in time of filing or perfection. Priority dates from the time a filing is first made covering the collateral or the time the security interest is first perfected, whichever is earlier, provided that there is no period thereafter when there is neither filing nor perfection.

(b) So long as conflicting security interests are unperfected, the first to attach has priority.

(6) For the purposes of subsection (5) a date of filing or perfection as to collateral is also a date of filing or perfection as to proceeds.

(7) If future advances are made while a security interest is perfected by filing, the taking of possession, or under Section 8—321 on securities, the security interest has the same priority for the purposes of subsection (5) with respect to the future advances as it does with respect to the first advance. If a commitment is made before or while the security interest is so perfected, the security interest has the same priority with respect to advances made pursuant thereto. In other cases a perfected security interest has priority from the date the advance is made.

Amended in 1972 and 1977.

§ 9—313
Priority of Security Interests in Fixtures

(1) In this section and in the provisions of Part 4 of this Article referring to fixture filing, unless the context otherwise requires

(a) goods are "fixtures" when they become so related to particular real estate that an interest in them arises under real estate law

(b) a "fixture filing" is the filing in the office where a mortgage on the real estate would be filed or recorded of a financing statement covering goods which are or are to become fixtures and conforming to the requirements of subsection (5) of Section 9—402

(c) a mortgage is a "construction mortgage" to the extent that it secures an obligation incurred for the construction of an improvement on land including the acquisition cost of the land, if the recorded writing so indicates.

(2) A security interest under this Article may be created in goods which are fixtures or may continue in goods which become fixtures, but no security interest exists under this Article in ordinary building materials incorporated into an improvement on land.

(3) This Article does not prevent creation of an encumbrance upon fixtures pursuant to real estate law.

(4) A perfected security interest in fixtures has priority over the conflicting interest of an encumbrancer or owner of the real estate where

(a) the security interest is a purchase money security interest, the interest of the encumbrancer or owner arises before the goods become fixtures, the security interest is perfected by a fixture filing before the goods become fixtures or within ten days thereafter, and the debtor has an interest of record in the real estate or is in possession of the real estate; or

(b) the security interest is perfected by a fixture filing before the interest of the encumbrancer or owner is of record, the security interest has priority over any conflicting interest of a predecessor in title of the encumbrancer or owner, and the debtor has an interest of record in the real estate or is in possession of the real estate; or

(c) the fixtures are readily removable factory or office machines or readily removable replacements of domestic appliances which are consumer goods, and before the goods become fixtures the security interest is perfected by any method permitted by this Article; or

(d) the conflicting interest is a lien on the real estate obtained by legal or equitable proceedings after the security interest was perfected by any method permitted by this Article.

(5) A security interest in fixtures, whether or not perfected, has priority over the conflicting interest of an encumbrancer or owner of the real estate where

(a) the encumbrancer or owner has consented in writing to the security interest or has disclaimed an interest in the goods as fixtures; or

(b) the debtor has a right to remove the goods as against the encumbrancer or owner. If the debtor's right terminates, the priority of the security interest continues for a reasonable time.

(6) Notwithstanding paragraph (a) of subsection (4) but otherwise subject to subsections (4) and (5), a security interest in fixtures is subordinate to a construction mortgage recorded before the goods become fixtures if the goods become fixtures before the completion of the construction. To the extent that it is given to refinance a construction mortgage, a mortgage has this priority to the same extent as the construction mortgage.

(7) In cases not within the preceding subsections, a security interest in fixtures is subordinate to the conflicting interest of an encumbrancer or owner of the related real estate who is not the debtor.

(8) When the secured party has priority over all owners and encumbrancers of the real estate, he may, on default, subject to the provisions of Part 5, remove his collateral from the real estate but he must reimburse any encumbrancer or owner of the real estate who is not the debtor and who has not otherwise agreed for the cost of repair of any physical injury, but not for any diminution in value of the real estate caused by the absence of the goods removed or by any necessity of replacing them. A person entitled to reimbursement may refuse permission to remove until the secured party gives adequate security for the performance of this obligation.

Amended in 1972.

§ 9—314
Accessions

(1) A security interest in goods which attaches before they are installed in or affixed to other goods takes priority as to the goods installed or affixed (called in this section "accessions") over the claims of all persons to the whole except as stated in subsection (3) and subject to Section 9—315(1).

(2) A security interest which attaches to goods after they become part of a whole is valid against all persons subsequently acquiring interests in the whole except as stated in subsection (3) but is invalid against any person with an interest in the whole at the time the security interest attaches to the goods who has not in writing consented to the security interest or disclaimed an interest in the goods as part of the whole.

(3) The security interests described in subsections (1) and (2) do not take priority over

(a) a subsequent purchaser for value of any interest in the whole; or

(b) a creditor with a lien on the whole subsequently obtained by judicial proceedings; or

(c) a creditor with a prior perfected security interest in the whole to the extent that he makes subsequent advances.

If the subsequent purchase is made, the lien by judicial proceedings obtained or the subsequent advance under the prior perfected security interest is made or contracted for without knowledge of the security interest and before it is perfected. A purchaser of the whole at a foreclosure sale other than the holder of a perfected security interest purchasing at his own foreclosure sale is a subsequent purchaser within this section.

(4) When under subsections (1) or (2) and (3) a secured party has an interest in accessions which has priority over the claims of all persons who have interests in the whole, he may on default subject to the provisions of Part 5 remove his collateral from the whole but he must reimburse any en-

cumbrancer or owner of the whole who is not the debtor and who has not otherwise agreed for the cost of repair of any physical injury but not for any diminution in value of the whole caused by the absence of the goods removed or by any necessity for replacing them. A person entitled to reimbursement may refuse permission to remove until the secured party gives adequate security for the performance of this obligation.

§ 9—315
Priority When Goods Are Commingled or Processed

(1) If a security interest in goods was perfected and subsequently the goods or a part thereof have become part of a product or mass, the security interest continues in the product or mass if

(a) the goods are so manufactured, processed, assembled or commingled that their identity is lost in the product or mass; or

(b) a financing statement covering the original goods also covers the product into which the goods have been manufactured, processed or assembled.

In a case to which paragraph (b) applies, no separate security interest in that part of the original goods which has been manufactured, processed or assembled into the product may be claimed under Section 9—314.

(2) When under subsection (1) more than one security interest attaches to the product or mass, they rank equally according to the ratio that the cost of the goods to which each interest originally attached bears to the cost of the total product or mass.

§ 9—316
Priority Subject to Subordination

Nothing in this Article prevents subordination by agreement by any person entitled to priority.

§ 9—317
Secured Party Not Obligated on Contract of Debtor

The mere existence of a security interest or authority given to the debtor to dispose of or use collateral does not impose contract or tort liability upon the secured party for the debtor's acts or omissions.

§ 9—318
Defenses Against Assignee; Modification of Contract After Notification of Assignment; Term Prohibiting Assignment Ineffective; Identification and Proof of Assignment

(1) Unless an account debtor has made an enforceable agreement not to assert defenses or claims arising out of a sale as provided in Section 9—206 the rights of an assignee are subject to

(a) all the terms of the contract between the account debtor and assignor and any defense or claim arising therefrom; and

(b) any other defense or claim of the account debtor against the assignor which accrues before the account debtor receives notification of the assignment.

(2) So far as the right to payment or a part thereof under an assigned contract has not been fully earned by performance, and notwithstanding notification of the assignment, any modification of or substitution for the contract made in good faith and in accordance with reasonable commercial standards is effective against an assignee unless the account debtor has otherwise agreed but the assignee acquires corresponding rights under the modified or substituted contract. The assignment may provide that such modification or substitution is a breach by the assignor.

(3) The account debtor is authorized to pay the assignor until the account debtor receives notification that the amount due or to become due has been assigned and that payment is to be made to the assignee. A notification which does not reasonably identify the rights assigned is ineffective. If requested by the account debtor, the assignee must seasonably furnish reasonable proof that the assignment has been made and unless he does so the account debtor may pay the assignor.

(4) A term in any contract between an account debtor and an assignor is ineffective if it prohibits assignment of an account or prohibits creation of a security interest in a general intangible for money due or to become due or requires the account debtor's consent to such assignment or security interest.

Amended in 1972.

PART 4/Filing

§ 9—401
Place of Filing; Erroneous Filing; Removal of Collateral

First Alternative Subsection (1)

(1) The proper place to file in order to perfect a security interest is as follows:

(a) when the collateral is timber to be cut or is minerals or the like (including oil and gas) or accounts subject to subsection (5) of Section 9—103, or when the financing statement is filed as a fixture filing (Section 9—313) and the collateral is goods which are or are to become fixtures, then in the office where a mortgage on the real estate would be filed or recorded;

(b) in all other cases, in the office of the [Secretary of State].

Second Alternative Subsection (1)

(1) The proper place to file in order to perfect a security interest is as follows:

(a) when the collateral is equipment used in farming operations, or farm products, or accounts or general intangibles arising from or relating to the sale of farm products by a farmer, or consumer goods, then in the office of the . . . . in the county of the debtor's residence or if the debtor is not a resident of this state then in the office of the . . . . in the county where the goods are kept, and in addition when the collateral is crops growing or to be grown in the office of the . . . . in the county where the land is located;

(b) when the collateral is timber to be cut or is minerals or the like (including oil and gas) or accounts subject to subsection (5) of Section 9—103, or when the financing statement is filed as a fixture filing (Section 9—313) and the collateral is goods which are or are to become fixtures, then in the office where a mortgage on the real estate would be filed or recorded;

(c) in all other cases, in the office of the [Secretary of State].

Third Alternative Subsection (1)

(1) The proper place to file in order to perfect a security interest is as follows:

(a) when the collateral is equipment used in farming operations, or farm products, or accounts or general intangibles arising from or relating to the sale of farm products by a farmer, or consumer goods, then in the office of the . . . . in the county of the debtor's residence or if the debtor is not a resident of this state then in the office of the . . . . in the county where the goods are kept, and in addition when the collateral is crops growing or to be grown in the office of the . . . . in the county where the land is located;

(b) when the collateral is timber to be cut or is minerals or the like (including oil and gas) or accounts subject to subsection (5) of Section 9—103, or when the financing statement is filed as a fixture filing (Section 9—313) and the collateral is goods which are or are to become fixtures, then in the office where a mortgage on the real estate would be filed or recorded;

(c) in all other cases, in the office of the [Secretary of State] and in addition, if the debtor has a place of business in only one county of this state, also in the office of . . . . of such county, or, if the debtor has no place of business in this state, but resides in the state, also in the office of . . . . of the county in which he resides.

Note: *One of the three alternatives should be selected as subsection (1).*

(2) A filing which is made in good faith in an improper place or not in all of the places required by this section is nevertheless effective with regard to any collateral as to which the filing complied with the requirements of this Article and is also effective with regard to collateral covered by the financing statement against any person who has knowledge of the contents of such financing statement.

(3) A filing which is made in the proper place in this state continues effective even though the debtor's residence or place of business or the location of the collateral or its use, whichever controlled the original filing, is thereafter changed.

Alternative Subsection (3)

[(3) A filing which is made in the proper county continues effective for four months after a change to another county of the debtor's residence or place of business or the location of the collateral, whichever controlled the original filing. It becomes ineffective thereafter unless a copy of the financing statement signed by the secured party is filed in the new county within said period. The security interest may also be perfected in the new county after the expiration of the four-month period; in such case perfection dates from the time of perfection in the new county. A change in the use of the collateral does not impair the effectiveness of the original filing.]

(4) The rules stated in Section 9—103 determine whether filing is necessary in this state.

(5) Notwithstanding the preceding subsections, and subject to subsection (3) of Section 9—302, the proper place to file in order to perfect a security interest in collateral, including fixtures, of a transmitting utility is the office of the [Secretary of State]. This filing constitutes a fixture filing (Section 9—313) as to the collateral described therein which is or is to become fixtures.

(6) For the purposes of this section, the residence of an organization is its place of business if it has one or its chief executive office if it has more than one place of business.

Amended in 1962 and 1972.

Note: *Subsection (6) should be used only if the state chooses the Second or Third Alternative Subsection (1).*

§ 9—402
Formal Requisites of Financing Statement; Amendments; Mortgage as Financing Statement

(1) A financing statement is sufficient if it gives the names of the debtor and the secured party, is signed by the debtor, gives an address of the secured party from which information concerning the security interest may be obtained, gives a mailing address of the debtor and contains a statement indicating the types, or describing the items, of collateral. A financing statement may be filed before a security agreement is made or a security interest otherwise attaches. When the financing statement covers crops growing or to be grown, the statement must also contain a description of the real estate concerned. When the financing statement covers timber to be cut or covers minerals or the like (including oil and gas) or accounts subject to subsection (5) of Section 9—

103, or when the financing statement is filed as a fixture filing (Section 9—313) and the collateral is goods which are or are to become fixtures, the statement must also comply with subsection (5). A copy of the security agreement is sufficient as a financing statement if it contains the above information and is signed by the debtor. A carbon, photographic or other reproduction of a security agreement or a financing statement is sufficient as a financing statement if the security agreement so provides or if the original has been filed in this state.

(2) A financing statement which otherwise complies with subsection (1) is sufficient when it is signed by the secured party instead of the debtor if it is filed to perfect a security interest in

(a) collateral already subject to a security interest in another jurisdiction when it is brought into this state, or when the debtor's location is changed to this state. Such a financing statement must state that the collateral was brought into this state or that the debtor's location was changed to this state under such circumstances; or

(b) proceeds under Section 9—306 if the security interest in the original collateral was perfected. Such a financing statement must describe the original collateral; or

(c) collateral as to which the filing has lapsed; or

(d) collateral acquired after a change of name, identity or corporate structure of the debtor (subsection (7)).

(3) A form substantially as follows is sufficient to comply with subsection (1):

Name of debtor (or assignor) ....
Address ....
Name of secured party (or assignee) ....
Address ....
1. This financing statement covers the following types (or items) of property:
   (Describe).................................
2. (If collateral is crops) The above described crops are growing or are to be grown on:
   (Describe Real Estate) ....
3. (If applicable) The above goods are to become fixtures on *

* Where appropriate substitute either "The above timber is standing on . . . ." or "The above minerals or the like (including oil and gas) or accounts will be financed at the wellhead or minehead of the well or mine located on . . . ."

   (Describe Real Estate) ....
and this financing statement is to be filed [for record] in the real estate records. (If the debtor does not have an interest of record) The name of a record owner is .....
4. (If products of collateral are claimed) Products of the collateral are also covered.

        (use whichever signature is applicable)
. . . .
        Signature of Debtor (or Assignor)

. . . .
        Signature of Secured Party (or Assignee)

(4) A financing statement may be amended by filing a writing signed by both the debtor and the secured party. An amendment does not extend the period of effectiveness of a financing statement. If any amendment adds collateral, it is effective as to the added collateral only from the filing date of the amendment. In this Article, unless the context otherwise requires, the term "financing statement" means the original financing statement and any amendments.

(5) A financing statement covering timber to be cut or covering minerals or the like (including oil and gas) or accounts subject to subsection (5) of Section 9—103, or a financing statement filed as a future filing (Section 9—313) where the debtor is not a transmitting utility, must show that it covers this type of collateral, must recite that it is to be filed [for record] in the real estate records, and the financing statement must contain a description of the real estate [sufficient if it were contained in a mortgage of the real estate to give constructive notice of the mortgage under the law of this state]. If the debtor does not have an interest of record in the real estate, the financing statement must show the name of a record owner.

(6) A mortgage is effective as a financing statement filed as a fixture filing from the date of its recording if

(a) the goods are described in the mortgage by item or type; and

(b) the goods are or are to become fixtures related to the real estate described in the mortgage; and

(c) the mortgage complies with the requirements for a financing statement in this section other than a recital that it is to be filed in the real estate records; and

(d) the mortgage is duly recorded.

No fee with reference to the financing statement is required other than the regular recording and satisfaction fees with respect to the mortgage.

(7) A financing statement sufficiently shows the name of the debtor if it gives the individual, partnership or corporate name of the debtor, whether or not it adds other trade names or names of partners. Where the debtor so changes his name or in the case of an organization its name, identity or corporate structure that a filed financing statement becomes seriously misleading, the filing is not effective to perfect a security interest in collateral acquired by the debtor more than four months after the change, unless a new appropriate financing statement is filed before the expiration of that time. A filed financing statement remains effective with respect to collateral transferred by the debtor even though the secured party knows of or consents to the transfer.

(8) A financing statement substantially complying with the requirements of this section is effective even though it contains minor errors which are not seriously misleading.

Amended in 1972.

Note: *Language in brackets is optional.*

Note: *Where the state has any special recording system for real estate other than the usual grantor-grantee index (as, for instance, a tract system or a title registration or Torrens system) local adaptations of subsection (5) and Section 9—403(7) may be necessary. See Mass.Gen.Laws Chapter 106, Section 9—409.*

§ 9—403
What Constitutes Filing; Duration of Filing; Effect of Lapsed Filing; Duties of Filing Officer

(1) Presentation for filing of a financing statement and tender of the filing fee or acceptance of the statement by the filing officer constitutes filing under this Article.

(2) Except as provided in subsection (6) a filed financing statement is effective for a period of five years from the date of filing. The effectiveness of a filed financing statement lapses on the expiration of the five year period unless a continuation statement is filed prior to the lapse. If a security interest perfected by filing exists at the time insolvency proceedings are commenced by or against the debtor, the security interest remains perfected until termination of the insolvency proceedings and thereafter for a period of sixty days or until expiration of the five year period, whichever occurs later. Upon lapse the security interest becomes unperfected, unless it is perfected without filing. If the security interest becomes unperfected upon lapse, it is deemed to have been unperfected as against a person who became a purchaser or lien creditor before lapse.

(3) A continuation statement may be filed by the secured party within six months prior to the expiration of the five year period specified in subsection (2). Any such continuation statement must be signed by the secured party, identify the original statement by file number and state that the original statement is still effective. A continuation statement signed by a person other than the secured party of record must be accompanied by a separate written statement of assignment signed by the secured party of record and complying with subsection (2) of Section 9—405, including payment of the required fee. Upon timely filing of the continuation statement, the effectiveness of the original statement is continued for five years after the last date to which the filing was effective whereupon it lapses in the same manner as provided in subsection (2) unless another continuation statement is filed prior to such lapse. Succeeding continuation statements may be filed in the same manner to continue the effectiveness of the original statement. Unless a statute on disposition of public records provides otherwise, the filing officer may remove a lapsed statement from the files and destroy it immediately if he has retained a microfilm or other photographic record, or in other cases after one year after the lapse. The filing officer shall so arrange matters by physical annexation of financing statements to continuation statements or other related filings, or by other means, that if

he physically destroys the financing statements of a period more than five years past, those which have been continued by a continuation statement or which are still effective under subsection (6) shall be retained.

(4) Except as provided in subsection (7) a filing officer shall mark each statement with a file number and with the date and hour of filing and shall hold the statement or a microfilm or other photographic copy thereof for public inspection. In addition the filing officer shall index the statement according to the name of the debtor and shall note in the index the file number and the address of the debtor given in the statement.

(5) The uniform fee for filing and indexing and for stamping a copy furnished by the secured party to show the date and place of filing for an original financing statement or for a continuation statement shall be $ . . . . if the statement is in the standard form prescribed by the [Secretary of State] and otherwise shall be $ . . . . , plus in each case, if the financing statement is subject to subsection (5) of Section 9—402, $ . . . . The uniform fee for each name more than one required to be indexed shall be $ . . . . The secured party may at his option show a trade name for any person and an extra uniform indexing fee of $ . . . . shall be paid with respect thereto.

(6) If the debtor is a transmitting utility (subsection (5) of Section 9—401) and a filed financing statement so states, it is effective until a termination statement is filed. A real estate mortgage which is effective as a fixture filing under subsection (6) of Section 9—402 remains effective as a fixture filing until the mortgage is released or satisfied of record or its effectiveness otherwise terminates as to the real estate.

(7) When a financing statement covers timber to be cut or covers minerals or the like (including oil and gas) or accounts subject to subsection (5) of Section 9—103, or is filed as a fixture filing, [it shall be filed for record and] the filing officer shall index it under the names of the debtor and any owner of record shown on the financing statement in the same fashion as if they were the mortgagors in a mortgage of the real estate described, and, to the extent that the law of this state provides for indexing of mortgages under the name of the mortgagee, under the name of the secured party as if he were the mortgagee thereunder, or where indexing is by description in the same fashion as if the financing statement were a mortgage of the real estate described.

Amended in 1972.

Note: *In states in which writings will not appear in the real estate records and indices unless actually recorded the bracketed language in subsection (7) should be used.*

§ 9—404
Termination Statement

(1) If a financing statement covering consumer goods is filed on or after . . . . , then within one month or within ten days following written demand by the debtor after there is no outstanding secured obligation and no commit-

ment to make advances, incur obligations or otherwise give value, the secured party must file with each filing officer with whom the financing statement was filed, a termination statement to the effect that he no longer claims a security interest under the financing statement, which shall be identified by file number. In other cases whenever there is no outstanding secured obligation and no commitment to make advances, incur obligations or otherwise give value, the secured party must on written demand by the debtor send the debtor, for each filing officer with whom the financing statement was filed, a termination statement to the effect that he no longer claims a security interest under the financing statement, which shall be identified by file number. A termination statement signed by a person other than the secured party of record must be accompanied by a separate written statement of assignment signed by the secured party of record complying with subsection (2) of Section 9—405, including payment of the required fee. If the affected secured party fails to file such a termination statement as required by this subsection, or to send such a termination statement within ten days after proper demand therefor, he shall be liable to the debtor for one hundred dollars, and in addition for any loss caused to the debtor by such failure.

(2) On presentation to the filing officer of such a termination statement he must note it in the index. If he has received the termination statement in duplicate, he shall return one copy of the termination statement to the secured party stamped to show the time of receipt thereof. If the filing officer has a microfilm or other photographic record of the financing statement, and of any related continuation statement, statement of assignment and statement of release, he may remove the originals from the files at any time after receipt of the termination statement, or if he has no such record, he may remove them from the files at any time after one year after receipt of the termination statement.

(3) If the termination statement is in the standard form prescribed by the [Secretary of State], the uniform fee for filing and indexing the termination statement shall be $ . . . . , and otherwise shall be $ . . . . , plus in each case an additional fee of $ . . . . for each name more than one against which the termination statement is required to be indexed.

Amended in 1972.

Note: *The date to be inserted should be the effective date of the revised Article 9.*

§ 9—405
Assignment of Security Interest; Duties of Filing Officer; Fees

(1) A financing statement may disclose an assignment of a security interest in the collateral described in the financing statement by indication in the financing statement of the name and address of the assignee or by an assignment itself or a copy thereof on the face or back of the statement. On presentation to the filing officer of such a financing statement the filing officer shall mark the same as provided in Section 9—403(4). The uniform fee for filing, indexing and furnishing filing data for a financing statement so indicating an assignment shall be $ . . . . if the statement is in the standard form prescribed by the [Secretary of State] and otherwise shall be $ . . . . , plus in each case an additional fee of $ . . . . for each name more than one against which the financing statement is required to be indexed.

(2) A secured party may assign of record all or part of his rights under a financing statement by the filing in the place where the original financing statement was filed of a separate written statement of assignment signed by the secured party of record and setting forth the name of the secured party of record and the debtor, the file number and the date of filing of the financing statement and the name and address of the assignee and containing a description of the collateral assigned. A copy of the assignment is sufficient as a separate statement if it complies with the preceding sentence. On presentation to the filing officer of such a separate statement, the filing officer shall mark such separate statement with the date and hour of the filing. He shall note the assignment on the index of the financing statement, or in the case of a fixture filing, or a filing covering timber to be cut, or covering minerals or the like (including oil and gas) or accounts subject to subsection (5) of Section 9—103, he shall index the assignment under the name of the assignor as grantor and, to the extent that the law of this state provides for indexing the assignment of a mortgage under the name of the assignee, he shall index the assignment of the financing statement under the name of the assignee. The uniform fee for filing, indexing and furnishing filing data about such a separate statement of assignment shall be $ . . . . if the statement is in the standard form prescribed by the [Secretary of State] and otherwise shall be $ . . . . , plus in each case an additional fee of $ . . . . for each name more than one against which the statement of assignment is required to be indexed. Notwithstanding the provisions of this subsection, an assignment of record of a security interest in a fixture contained in a mortgage effective as a fixture filing (subsection (6) of Section 9—402) may be made only by an assignment of the mortgage in the manner provided by the law of this state other than this Act.

(3) After the disclosure or filing of an assignment under this section, the assignee is the secured party of record.

Amended in 1972.

§ 9—406
Release of Collateral; Duties of Filing Officer; Fees

A secured party of record may by his signed statement release all or a part of any collateral described in a filed financing statement. The statement of release is sufficient if it contains a description of the collateral being released, the name and address of the debtor, the name and address of the secured party, and the file number of the financing statement. A statement of release signed by a person other than the secured party of record must be accompanied by a separate written statement of assignment signed by the secured party of record and complying with subsection (2) of Section 9—405, including payment of the required fee. Upon presentation of such a statement of release to the filing officer he shall mark the statement with the hour and date of filing and shall note the same upon the margin of the index of the filing of the financing statement. The uniform fee for filing and noting such a statement of release shall be $ . . . . if the statement is in the standard form prescribed by the [Secretary of State] and otherwise shall be $ . . . . , plus in each case an additional fee of $ . . . . for each name more than one against which the statement of release is required to be indexed.

Amended in 1972.

[§ 9—407
Information From Filing Officer

[(1) If the person filing any financing statement, termination statement, statement of assignment, or statement of release, furnishes the filing officer a copy thereof, the filing officer shall upon request note upon the copy the file number and date and hour of the filing of the original and deliver or send the copy to such person.]

[(2) Upon request of any person, the filing officer shall issue his certificate showing whether there is on file on the date and hour stated therein, any presently effective financing statement naming a particular debtor and any statement of assignment thereof and if there is, giving the date and hour of filing of each such statement and the names and addresses of each secured party therein. The uniform fee for such a certificate shall be $ . . . . if the request for the certificate is in the standard form prescribed by the [Secretary of State] and otherwise shall be $ . . . . Upon request the filing officer shall furnish a copy of any filed financing statement or statement of assignment for a uniform fee of $ . . . . per page.]

Amended in 1972.

Note: *This section is proposed as an optional provision to require filing officers to furnish certificates. Local law and practices should be consulted with regard to the advisability of adoption.*

§ 9—408
Financing Statements Covering Consigned or Leased Goods

A consignor or lessor of goods may file a financing statement using the terms "consignor," "consignee," "lessor," "lessee" or the like instead of the terms specified in Section 9—402. The provisions of this Part shall apply as appropriate to such a financing statement but its filing shall not of itself be a factor in determining whether or not the consignment or lease is intended as security (Section 1—201(37)). However, if it is determined for other reasons that the consignment or lease is so intended, a security interest of the consignor or lessor which attaches to the consigned or leased goods is perfected by such filing.

Added in 1972.

PART 5/Default

§ 9—501
Default; Procedure When Security Agreement Covers Both Real and Personal Property

(1) When a debtor is in default under a security agreement, a secured party has the rights and remedies provided in this Part and except as limited by subsection (3) those provided in the security agreement. He may reduce his claim to judgment, foreclose or otherwise enforce the security interest by any available judicial procedure. If the collateral is documents the secured party may proceed either as to the documents or as to the goods covered thereby. A secured party in possession has the rights, remedies and duties provided in Section 9—207. The rights and remedies referred to in this subsection are cumulative.

(2) After default, the debtor has the rights and remedies provided in this Part, those provided in the security agreement and those provided in Section 9—207.

(3) To the extent that they give rights to the debtor and impose duties on the secured party, the rules stated in the subsections referred to below may not be waived or varied except as provided with respect to compulsory disposition of collateral (subsection (3) of Section 9—504 and Section 9—505) and with respect to redemption of collateral (Section 9—506) but the parties may by agreement determine the standards by which the fulfillment of these rights and duties is to be measured if such standards are not manifestly unreasonable:

> (a) subsection (2) of Section 9—502 and subsection (2) of Section 9—504 insofar as they require accounting for surplus proceeds of collateral;

> (b) subsection (3) of Section 9—504 with subsection (1) of Section 9—505 which deal with disposition of collateral;

> (c) subsection (2) of Section 9—505 which deals with acceptance of collateral as discharge of obligation;

> (d) Section 9—506 which deals with redemption of collateral; and

> (e) subsection (1) of Section 9—507 which deals with the secured party's liability for failure to comply with this Part.

(4) If the security agreement covers both real and personal property, the secured party may proceed under this Part as to the personal property or he may proceed as to both the real

and the personal property in accordance with his rights and remedies in respect of the real property in which case the provisions of this Part do not apply.

(5) When a secured party has reduced his claim to judgment the lien of any levy which may be made upon his collateral by virtue of any execution based upon the judgment shall relate back to the date of the perfection of the security interest in such collateral. A judicial sale, pursuant to such execution, is a foreclosure of the security interest by judicial procedure within the meaning of this section, and the secured party may purchase at the sale and thereafter hold the collateral free of any other requirements of this Article.

Amended in 1972.

§ 9—502
Collection Rights of Secured Party

(1) When so agreed and in any event on default the secured party is entitled to notify an account debtor or the obligor on an instrument to make payment to him whether or not the assignor was theretofore making collections on the collateral, and also to take control of any proceeds to which he is entitled under Section 9—306.

(2) A secured party who by agreement is entitled to charge back uncollected collateral or otherwise to full or limited recourse against the debtor and who undertakes to collect from the account debtors or obligors must proceed in a commercially reasonable manner and may deduct his reasonable expenses of realization from the collections. If the security agreement secures an indebtedness, the secured party must account to the debtor for any surplus, and unless otherwise agreed, the debtor is liable for any deficiency. But, if the underlying transaction was a sale of accounts or chattel paper, the debtor is entitled to any surplus or is liable for any deficiency only if the security agreement so provides.

Amended in 1972.

§ 9—503
Secured Party's Right to Take Possession After Default

Unless otherwise agreed a secured party has on default the right to take possession of the collateral. In taking possession a secured party may proceed without judicial process if this can be done without breach of the peace or may proceed by action. If the security agreement so provides the secured party may require the debtor to assemble the collateral and make it available to the secured party at a place to be designated by the secured party which is reasonably convenient to both parties. Without removal a secured party may render equipment unusable, and may dispose of collateral on the debtor's premises under Section 9—504.

§ 9—504
Secured Party's Right to Dispose of Collateral After Default; Effect of Disposition

(1) A secured party after default may sell, lease or otherwise dispose of any or all of the collateral in its then condition or following any commercially reasonable preparation or processing. Any sale of goods is subject to the Article on Sales (Article 2). The proceeds of disposition shall be applied in the order following to

(a) the reasonable expenses of retaking, holding, preparing for sale or lease, selling, leasing and the like and, to the extent provided for in the agreement and not prohibited by law, the reasonable attorneys' fees and legal expenses incurred by the secured party;

(b) the satisfaction of indebtedness secured by the security interest under which the disposition is made;

(c) the satisfaction of indebtedness secured by any subordinate security interest in the collateral if written notification of demand therefor is received before distribution of the proceeds is completed. If requested by the secured party, the holder of a subordinate security interest must seasonably furnish reasonable proof of his interest, and unless he does so, the secured party need not comply with his demand.

(2) If the security interest secures an indebtedness, the secured party must account to the debtor for any surplus, and, unless otherwise agreed, the debtor is liable for any deficiency. But if the underlying transaction was a sale of accounts or chattel paper, the debtor is entitled to any surplus or is liable for any deficiency only if the security agreement so provides.

(3) Disposition of the collateral may be by public or private proceedings and may be made by way of one or more contracts. Sale or other disposition may be as a unit or in parcels and at any time and place and on any terms but every aspect of the disposition including the method, manner, time, place and terms must be commercially reasonable. Unless collateral is perishable or threatens to decline speedily in value or is of a type customarily sold on a recognized market, reasonable notification of the time and place of any public sale or reasonable notification of the time after which any private sale or other intended disposition is to be made shall be sent by the secured party to the debtor, if he has not signed after default a statement renouncing or modifying his right to notification of sale. In the case of consumer goods no other notification need be sent. In other cases notification shall be sent to any other secured party from whom the secured party has received (before sending his notification to the debtor or before the debtor's renunciation of his rights) written notice of a claim of an interest in the collateral. The secured party may buy at any public sale and if the collateral is of a type customarily sold in a recognized market or is of a

type which is the subject of widely distributed standard price quotations he may buy at private sale.

(4) When collateral is disposed of by a secured party after default, the disposition transfers to a purchaser for value all of the debtor's rights therein, discharges the security interest under which it is made and any security interest or lien subordinate thereto. The purchaser takes free of all such rights and interests even though the secured party fails to comply with the requirements of this Part or of any judicial proceedings

(a) in the case of a public sale, if the purchaser has no knowledge of any defects in the sale and if he does not buy in collusion with the secured party, other bidders or the person conducting the sale; or

(b) in any other case, if the purchaser acts in good faith.

(5) A person who is liable to a secured party under a guaranty, indorsement, repurchase agreement or the like and who receives a transfer of collateral from the secured party or is subrogated to his rights has thereafter the rights and duties of the secured party. Such a transfer of collateral is not a sale or disposition of the collateral under this Article.

Amended in 1972.

§ 9—505
Compulsory Disposition of Collateral; Acceptance of the Collateral as Discharge of Obligation

(1) If the debtor has paid sixty per cent of the cash price in the case of a purchase money security interest in consumer goods or sixty per cent of the loan in the case of another security interest in consumer goods, and has not signed after default a statement renouncing or modifying his rights under this Part a secured party who has taken possession of collateral must dispose of it under Section 9—504 and if he fails to do so within ninety days after he takes possession the debtor at his option may recover in conversion or under Section 9—507(1) on secured party's liability.

(2) In any other case involving consumer goods or any other collateral a secured party in possession may, after default, propose to retain the collateral in satisfaction of the obligation. Written notice of such proposal shall be sent to the debtor if he has not signed after default a statement renouncing or modifying his rights under this subsection. In the case of consumer goods no other notice need be given. In other cases notice shall be sent to any other secured party from whom the secured party has received (before sending his notice to the debtor or before the debtor's renunciation of his rights) written notice of a claim of an interest in the collateral. If the secured party receives objection in writing from a person entitled to receive notification within twenty-one days after the notice was sent, the secured party must dispose of the collateral under Section 9—504. In the absence of such written objection the secured party may retain the collateral in satisfaction of the debtor's obligation.

Amended in 1972.

§ 9—506
Debtor's Right to Redeem Collateral

At any time before the secured party has disposed of collateral or entered into a contract for its disposition under Section 9—504 or before the obligation has been discharged under Section 9—505(2) the debtor or any other secured party may unless otherwise agreed in writing after default redeem the collateral by tendering fulfillment of all obligations secured by the collateral as well as the expenses reasonably incurred by the secured party in retaking, holding and preparing the collateral for disposition, in arranging for the sale, and to the extent provided in the agreement and not prohibited by law, his reasonable attorneys' fees and legal expenses.

§ 9—507
Secured Party's Liability for Failure to Comply With This Part

(1) If it is established that the secured party is not proceeding in accordance with the provisions of this Part disposition may be ordered or restrained on appropriate terms and conditions. If the disposition has occurred the debtor or any person entitled to notification or whose security interest has been made known to the secured party prior to the disposition has a right to recover from the secured party any loss caused by a failure to comply with the provisions of this Part. If the collateral is consumer goods, the debtor has a right to recover in any event an amount not less than the credit service charge plus ten per cent of the principal amount of the debt or the time price differential plus 10 percent of the cash price.

(2) The fact that a better price could have been obtained by a sale at a different time or in a different method from that selected by the secured party is not of itself sufficient to establish that the sale was not made in a commercially reasonable manner. If the secured party either sells the collateral in the usual manner in any recognized market therefor or if he sells at the price current in such market at the time of his sale or if he has otherwise sold in conformity with reasonable commercial practices among dealers in the type of property sold he has sold in a commercially reasonable manner. The principles stated in the two preceding sentences with respect to sales also apply as may be appropriate to other types of disposition. A disposition which has been approved in any judicial proceeding or by any bona fide creditors' committee or representative of creditors shall conclusively be deemed to be commercially reasonable, but this sentence does not indicate that any such approval must be obtained in any case nor does it indicate that any disposition not so approved is not commercially reasonable.

ARTICLE 10/Effective Date and Repealer

§ 10—101
Effective Date

This Act shall become effective at midnight on December 31st following its enactment. It applies to transactions entered into and events occurring after that date.

§ 10—102
Specific Repealer; Provision for Transition

(1) The following acts and all other acts and parts of acts inconsistent herewith are hereby repealed:
(Here should follow the acts to be specifically repealed including the following:

> Uniform Negotiable Instruments Act
>
> Uniform Warehouse Receipts Act
>
> Uniform Sales Act
>
> Uniform Bills of Lading Act
>
> Uniform Stock Transfer Act
>
> Uniform Conditional Sales Act
>
> Uniform Trust Receipts Act

Also any acts regulating:

> Bank collections
>
> Bulk sales
>
> Chattel mortgages
>
> Conditional sales
>
> Factor's lien acts
>
> Farm storage of grain and similar acts
>
> Assignment of accounts receivable)

(2) Transactions validly entered into before the effective date specified in Section 10—101 and the rights, duties and interests flowing from them remain valid thereafter and may be terminated, completed, consummated or enforced as required or permitted by any statute or other law amended or repealed by this Act as though such repeal or amendment had not occurred.

Note: *Subsection (1) should be separately prepared for each state. The foregoing is a list of statutes to be checked.*

§ 10—103
General Repealer

Except as provided in the following section, all acts and parts of acts inconsistent with this Act are hereby repealed.

§ 10—104
Laws Not Repealed

(1) The Article on Documents of Title (Article 7) does not repeal or modify any laws prescribing the form or contents of documents of title or the services or facilities to be afforded by bailees, or otherwise regulating bailees' businesses in respects not specifically dealt with herein; but the fact that such laws are violated does not affect the status of a document of title which otherwise complies with the definition of a document of title (Section 1—201).

[(2) This Act does not repeal . . . .*, cited as the Uniform Act for the Simplification of Fiduciary Security Transfers, and if in any respect there is any inconsistency between that Act and the Article of this Act on investment securities (Article B) the provisions of the former Act shall control.]

Note: *At * in subsection (2) insert the statutory reference to the Uniform Act for the Simplification of Fiduciary Security Transfers if such Act has previously been enacted. If it has not been enacted, omit subsection (2).*

Appendix B

THE UNIFORM PARTNERSHIP ACT

PART I/Preliminary Provisions

§ 1
Name of Act

This act may be cited as Uniform Partnership Act.

§ 2
Definition of Terms

In this act, "Court" includes every court and judge having jurisdiction in the case.

"Business" includes every trade, occupation, or profession.

"Person" includes individuals, partnerships, corporations, and other associations.

"Bankrupt" includes bankrupt under the Federal Bankruptcy Act or insolvent under any state insolvent act.

"Conveyance" includes every assignment, lease, mortgage, or encumbrance.

"Real property" includes land and any interest or estate in land.

§ 3
Interpretation of Knowledge and Notice

(1) A person has "knowledge" of a fact within the meaning of this act not only when he has actual knowledge thereof, but also when he has knowledge of such other facts as in the circumstances shows bad faith.

(2) A person has "notice" of a fact within the meaning of this act when the person who claims the benefit of the notice:

(a) States the fact to such person, or

(b) Delivers through the mail, or by other means of communication, a written statement of the fact to such person or to a proper person at his place of business or residence.

§ 4
Rules of Construction

(1) The rule that statutes in derogation of the common law are to be strictly construed shall have no application to this act.

(2) The law of estoppel shall apply under this act.

(3) The law of agency shall apply under this act.

(4) This act shall be so interpreted and construed as to effect its general purpose to make uniform the law of those states which enact it.

(5) This act shall not be construed so as to impair the obligations of any contract existing when the act goes into effect, nor to affect any action or proceedings begun or right accrued before this act takes effect.

§ 5
Rules for Cases Not Provided for in This Act

In any case not provided for in this act the rules of law and equity, including the law merchant, shall govern.

PART II/Nature of Partnership

§ 6
Partnership Defined

(1) A partnership is an association of two or more persons to carry on as co-owners a business for profit.

(2) But any associaton formed under any other statute of this state, or any statute adopted by authority, other than the authority of this state, is not a partnership under this act, unless such association would have been a partnership in this state prior to the adoption of this act; but this act shall apply to limited partnerships except in so far as the statutes relating to such partnerships are inconsistent herewith.

§ 7
Rules for Determining the Existence of a Partnership

In determining whether a partnership exists, these rules shall apply:

(1) Except as provided by section 16 persons who are not partners as to each other are not partners as to third persons.

(2) Joint tenancy, tenancy in common, tenancy by the entireties, joint property, common property, or part ownership does not of itself establish a partnership, whether such co-owners do or do not share any profits made by the use of the property.

(3) The sharing of gross returns does not of itself establish a partnership, whether or not the persons sharing them have a joint or common right or interest in any property from which the returns are derived.

(4) The receipt by a person of a share of the profits of a business is prima facie evidence that he is a partner in the business, but no such inference shall be drawn if such profits were received in payment:

(a) As a debt by installments or otherwise,

(b) As wages of an employee or rent to a landlord,

(c) As an annuity to a widow or representative of a deceased partner,

(d) As interest on a loan, though the amount of payment vary with the profits of the business,

(e) As the consideration for the sale of a good-will of a business or other property by installments or otherwise.

§ 8
Partnership Property

(1) All property originally brought into the partnership stock or subsequently acquired by purchase or otherwise, on account of the partnership, is partnership property.

(2) Unless the contrary intention appears, property acquired with partnership funds is partnership property.

(3) Any estate in real property may be acquired in the partnership name. Title so acquired can be conveyed only in the partnership name.

(4) A conveyance to a partnership in the partnership name, though without words of inheritance, passes the entire estate of the grantor unless a contrary intent appears.

PART III/Relations of Partners to Persons Dealing with the Partnership

§ 9
Partner Agent of Partnership as to Partnership Business

(1) Every partner is an agent of the partnership for the purpose of its business, and the act of every partner, including the execution in the partnership name of any instrument, for apparently carrying on in the usual way the business of the partnership of which he is a member binds the partnership, unless the partner so acting has in fact no authority to act for the partnership in the particular matter, and the person with whom he is dealing has knowledge of the fact that he has no such authority.

(2) An act of a partner which is not apparently for the carrying on of the business of the partnership in the usual way does not bind the partnership unless authorized by the other partners.

(3) Unless authorized by the other partners or unless they have abandoned the business, one or more but less than all the partners have no authority to:

(a) Assign the partnership property in trust for creditors or on the assignee's promise to pay the debts of the partnership,

(b) Dispose of the good-will of the business,

(c) Do any other act which would make it impossible to carry on the ordinary business of a partnership,

(d) Confess a judgment,

(e) Submit a partnership claim or liability to arbitration or reference.

(4) No act of a partner in contravention of a restriction on authority shall bind the partnership to persons having knowledge of the restriction.

§ 10
Conveyance of Real Property of the Partnership

(1) Where title to real property is in the partnership name, any partner may convey title to such property by a conveyance executed in the partnership name; but the partnership may recover such property unless the partner's act binds the partnership under the provisions of paragraph (1) of section 9, or unless such property has been conveyed by the grantee or a person claiming through such grantee to a holder for value without knowledge that the partner, in making the conveyance, has exceeded his authority.

(2) Where title to real property is in the name of the partnership, a conveyance executed by a partner, in his own name, passes the equitable interest of the partnership, pro-

vided the act is one within the authority of the partner under the provisions of paragraph (1) of section 9.

(3) Where title to real property is in the name of one or more but not all the partners, and the record does not disclose the right of the partnership, the partners in whose name the title stands may convey title to such property, but the partnership may recover such property if the partners' act does not bind the partnership under the provisions of paragraph (1) of section 9, unless the purchaser or his assignee, is a holder for value, without knowledge.

(4) Where the title to real property is in the name of one or more or all the partners, or in a third person in trust for the partnership, a conveyance executed by a partner in the partnership name, or in his own name, passes the equitable interest of the partnership, provided the act is one within the authority of the partner under the provisions of paragraph (1) of section 9.

(5) Where the title to real property is in the names of all the partners a conveyance executed by all the partners passes all their rights in such property.

§ 11
Partnership Bound by Admission of Partner

An admission or representation made by any partner concerning partnership affairs within the scope of his authority as conferred by this act is evidence against the partnership.

§ 12
Partnership Charged with Knowledge of or Notice to Partner

Notice to any partner of any matter relating to partnership affairs, and the knowledge of the partner acting in the particular matter, acquired while a partner or then present to his mind, and the knowledge of any other partner who reasonably could and should have communicated it to the acting partner, operate as notice to or knowledge of the partnership, except in the case of a fraud on the partnership committed by or with the consent of that partner.

§ 13
Partnership Bound by Partner's Wrongful Act

Where, by any wrongful act or omission of any partner acting in the ordinary course of the business of the partnership or with the authority of his co-partners, loss or injury is caused to any person, not being a partner in the partnership, or any penalty is incurred, the partnership is liable therefor to the same extent as the partner so acting or omitting to act.

§ 14
Partnership Bound by Partner's Breach of Trust

The partnership is bound to make good the loss:

(a) Where one partner acting within the scope of his apparent authority receives money or property of a third person and misapplies it; and

(b) Where the partnership in the course of its business receives money or property of a third person and the money or property so received is misapplied by any partner while it is in the custody of the partnership.

§ 15
Nature of Partner's Liability

All partners are liable

(a) Jointly and severally for everything chargeable to the partnership under sections 13 and 14.

(b) Jointly for all other debts and obligations of the partnership; but any partner may enter into a separate obligation to perform a partnership contract.

§ 16
Partner by Estoppel

(1) When a person, by words spoken or written or by conduct, represents himself, or consents to another representing him to any one, as a partner in an existing partnership or with one or more persons not actual partners, he is liable to any such person to whom such representation has been made, who has, on the faith of such representation, given credit to the actual or apparent partnership, and if he has made such representation or consented to its being made in a public manner he is liable to such person, whether the representation has or has not been made or communicated to such person so giving credit by or with the knowledge of the apparent partner making the representation or consenting to its being made.

(a) When a partnership liability results, he is liable as though he were an actual member of the partnership.

(b) When no partnership liability results, he is liable jointly with the other persons, if any, so consenting to the contract or representation as to incur liability, otherwise separately.

(2) When a person has been thus represented to be a partner in an existing partnership, or with one or more persons not actual partners, he is an agent of the persons consenting to such representation to bind them to the same extent and in the same manner as though he were a partner in fact, with respect to persons who rely upon the representation. Where all the members of the existing partnership consent to the representation, a partnership act or obligation results; but in all other cases it is the joint act or obligation of the person acting and the persons consenting to the representation.

§ 17
Liability of Incoming Partner

A person admitted as a partner into an existing partnership is liable for all the obligations of the partnership arising before his admission as though he had been a partner when such obligations were incurred, except that this liability shall be satisfied only out of partnership property.

PART IV/Relations of Partners to One Another

§ 18
Rules Determining Rights and Duties of Partners

The rights and duties of the partners in relation to the partnership shall be determined, subject to any agreement between them, by the following rules:

(a) Each partner shall be repaid his contributions, whether by way of capital or advances to the partnership property and share equally in the profits and surplus remaining after all liabilities, including those to partners, are satisfied; and must contribute towards the losses, whether of capital or otherwise, sustained by the partnership according to his share in the profits.

(b) The partnership must indemnify every partner in respect of payments made and personal liabilities reasonably incurred by him in the ordinary and proper conduct of its business, or for the preservation of its business or property.

(c) A partner, who in aid of the partnership makes any payment or advance beyond the amount of capital which he agreed to contribute, shall be paid interest from the date of the payment or advance.

(d) A partner shall receive interest on the capital contributed by him only from the date when repayment should be made.

(e) All partners have equal rights in the management and conduct of the partnership business.

(f) No partner is entitled to remuneration for acting in the partnership business, except that a surviving partner is entitled to reasonable compensation for his services in winding up the partnership affairs.

(g) No person can become a member of a partnership without the consent of all the partners.

(h) Any difference arising as to ordinary matters connected with the partnership business may be decided by a majority of the partners; but no act in contravention of any agreement between the partners may be done rightfully without the consent of all the partners.

§ 19
Partnership Books

The partnership books shall be kept, subject to any agreement between the partners, at the principal place of business of the partnership, and every partner shall at all times have access to and may inspect and copy any of them.

§ 20
Duty of Partners to Render Information

Partners shall render on demand true and full information of all things affecting the partnership to any partner or the legal representative of any deceased partner or partner under legal disability.

§ 21
Partner Accountable as a Fiduciary

(1) Every partner must account to the partnership for any benefit, and hold as trustee for it any profits derived by him without the consent of the other partners from any transaction connected with the formation, conduct, or liquidation of the partnership or from any use by him of its property.

(2) This section applies also to the representatives of a deceased partner engaged in the liquidation of the affairs of the partnership as the personal representatives of the last surviving partner.

§ 22
Right to an Account

Any partner shall have the right to a formal account as to partnership affairs:

(a) If he is wrongfully excluded from the partnership business or possession of its property by his co-partners,

(b) If the right exists under the terms of any agreement,

(c) As provided by section 21,

(d) Whenever other circumstances render it just and reasonable.

§ 23
Continuation of Partnership Beyond Fixed Term

(1) When a partnership for a fixed term or particular undertaking is continued after the termination of such term or particular undertaking without any express agreement, the rights and duties of the partners remain the same as they were at such termination, so far as is consistent with a partnership at will.

(2) A continuation of the business by the partners or such of them as habitually acted therein during the term, without any settlement or liquidation of the partnership affairs, is prima facie evidence of a continuation of the partnership.

PART V / Property Rights of a Partner

§ 24
Extent of Property Rights of a Partner

The property rights of a partner are (1) his rights in specific partnership property, (2) his interest in the partnership, and (3) his right to participate in the management.

§ 25
Nature of a Partner's Right in Specific Partnership Property

(1) A partner is co-owner with his partners of specific partnership property holding as a tenant in partnership.

(2) The incidents of this tenancy are such that:

(a) A partner, subject to the provisions of this act and to any agreement between the partners, has an equal right with his partners to possess specific partnership property for partnership purposes; but he has no right to possess such property for any other purpose without the consent of his partners.

(b) A partner's right in specific partnership property is not assignable except in connection with the assignment of rights of all the partners in the same property.

(c) A partner's right in specific partnership property is not subject to attachment or execution, except on a claim against the partnership. When partnership property is attached for a partnership debt the partners, or any of them, or the representatives of a deceased partner, cannot claim any right under the homestead or exemption laws.

(d) On the death of a partner his right in specific partnership property vests in the surviving partner or partners, except where the deceased was the last surviving partner, when his right in such property vests in his legal representative. Such surviving partner or partners, or the legal representative of the last surviving partner, has no right to possess the partnership property for any but a partnership purpose.

(e) A partner's right in specific partnership property is not subject to dower, curtesy, or allowances to widows, heirs, or next of kin.

§ 26
Nature of Partner's Interest in the Partnership

A partner's interest in the partnership is his share of the profits and surplus, and the same is personal property.

§ 27
Assignment of Partner's Interest

(1) A conveyance by a partner of his interest in the partnership does not of itself dissolve the partnership, nor, as against the other partners in the absence of agreement, entitle the assignee, during the continuance of the partnership, to interfere in the management or administration of the partnership business or affairs, or to require any information or account of partnership transactions, or to inspect the partnership books; but it merely entitles the assignee to receive in accordance with his contract the profits to which the assigning partner would otherwise be entitled.

(2) In case of a dissolution of the partnership, the assignee is entitled to receive his assignor's interest and may require an account from the date only of the last account agreed to by all the partners.

§ 28
Partner's Interest Subject to Charging Order

(1) On due application to a competent court by any judgment creditor of a partner, the court which entered the judgment, order, or decree, or any other court, may charge the interest of the debtor partner with payment of the unsatisfied amount of such judgment debt with interest thereon; and may then or later appoint a receiver of his share of the profits, and of any other money due or to fall due to him in respect of the partnership, and make all other orders, directions, accounts and inquiries which the debtor partner might have made, or which the circumstances of the case may require.

(2) The interest charged may be redeemed at any time before foreclosure, or in case of a sale being directed by the court may be purchased without thereby causing a dissolution:

(a) With separate property, by any one or more of the partners, or

(b) With partnership property, by any one or more of the partners with the consent of all the partners whose interests are not so charged or sold.

(3) Nothing in this act shall be held to deprive a partner of his right, if any, under the exemption laws, as regards his interest in the partnership.

PART VI / Dissolution and Winding Up

§ 29
Dissolution Defined

The dissolution of a partnership is the change in the relation of the partners caused by any partner ceasing to be associated in the carrying on as distinguished from the winding up of the business.

§ 30
Partnership not Terminated by Dissolution

On dissolution the partnership is not terminated, but continues until the winding up of partnership affairs is completed.

§ 31
Causes of Dissolution

Dissolution is caused:

(1) Without violation of the agreement between the partners,

(a) By the termination of the definite term or particular undertaking specified in the agreement,

(b) By the express will of any partner when no definite term or particular undertaking is specified,

(c) By the express will of all the partners who have not assigned their interests or suffered them to be charged for their separate debts, either before or after the termination of any specified term or particular undertaking,

(d) By the expulsion of any partner from the business bona fide in accordance with such a power conferred by the agreement between the partners;

(2) In contravention of the agreement between the partners, where the circumstances do not permit a dissolution under any other provision of this section, by the express will of any partner at any time;

(3) By any event which makes it unlawful for the business of the partnership to be carried on or for the members to carry it on in partnership;

(4) By the death of any partner;

(5) By the bankruptcy of any partner or the partnership;

(6) By decree of court under section 32.

§ 32
Dissolution by Decree of Court

(1) On application by or for a partner the court shall decree a dissolution whenever:

(a) A partner has been declared a lunatic in any judicial proceeding or is shown to be of unsound mind,

(b) A partner becomes in any other way incapable of performing his part of the partnership contract,

(c) A partner has been guilty of such conduct as tends to affect prejudicially the carrying on of the business,

(d) A partner wilfully or persistently commits a breach of the partnership agreement, or otherwise so conducts himself in matters relating to the partnership business that it is not reasonably practicable to carry on the business in partnership with him,

(e) The business of the partnership can only be carried on at a loss,

(f) Other circumstances render a dissolution equitable.

(2) On the application of the purchaser of a partner's interest under sections 28 or 29:

(a) After the termination of the specified term or particular undertaking,

(b) At any time if the partnership was a partnership at will when the interest was assigned or when the charging order was issued.

§ 33
General Effect of Dissolution on Authority of Partner

Except so far as may be necessary to wind up partnership affairs or to complete transactions begun but not then finished, dissolution terminates all authority of any partner to act for the partnership,

(1) With respect to the partners,

(a) When the dissolution is not by the act, bankruptcy or death of a partner; or

(b) When the dissolution is by such act, bankruptcy or death of a partner, in cases where section 34 so requires.

(2) With respect to persons not partners, as declared in section 35.

§ 34
Right of Partner to Contribution from Co-partners after Dissolution

Where the dissolution is caused by the act, death or bankruptcy of a partner, each partner is liable to his co-partners for his share of any liability created by any partner acting for the partnership as if the partnership had not been dissolved unless

(a) The dissolution being by act of any partner, the partner acting for the partnership had knowledge of the dissolution, or

(b) The dissolution being by the death or bankruptcy of a partner, the partner acting for the partnership had knowledge or notice of the death or bankruptcy.

§ 35
Power of Partner to Bind Partnership to Third Persons after Dissolution

(1) After dissolution a partner can bind the partnership except as provided in Paragraph (3)

(a) By any act appropriate for winding up partnership affairs or completing transactions unfinished at dissolution;

(b) By any transaction which would bind the partnership if dissolution had not taken place, provided the other party to the transaction

(I) Had extended credit to the partnership prior to dissolution and had no knowledge or notice of the dissolution; or

(II) Though he had not so extended credit, had nevertheless known of the partnership prior to dissolution, and, having no knowledge or notice of dissolution, the fact of dissolution had not been advertised in a newspaper of general circulation in the place (or in each place if more than one) at which the partnership business was regularly carried on.

(2) The liability of a partner under Paragraph (1b) shall be

satisfied out of partnership assets alone when such partner had been prior to dissolution

(a) Unknown as a partner to the person with whom the contract is made; and

(b) So far unknown and inactive in partnership affairs that the business reputation of the partnership could not be said to have been in any degree due to his connection with it.

(3) The partnership is in no case bound by any act of a partner after dissolution

(a) Where the partnership is dissolved because it is unlawful to carry on the business, unless the act is appropriate for winding up partnership affairs; or

(b) Where the partner has become bankrupt; or

(c) Where the partner has no authority to wind up partnership affairs; except by a transaction with one who

(I) Had extended credit to the partnership prior to dissolution and had no knowledge or notice of his want of authority; or

(II) Had not extended credit to the partnership prior to dissolution, and, having no knowledge or notice of his want of authority, the fact of his want of authority has not been advertised in the manner provided for advertising the fact of dissolution in Paragraph (1bII).

(4) Nothing in this section shall affect the liability under Section 16 of any person who after dissolution represents himself or consents to another representing him as a partner in a partnership engaged in carrying on business.

§ 36
Effect of Dissolution on Partner's Existing Liability

(1) The dissolution of the partnership does not of itself discharge the existing liability of any partner.

(2) A partner is discharged from any existing liability upon dissolution of the partnership by an agreement to that effect between himself, the partnership creditor and the person or partnership continuing the business; and such agreement may be inferred from the course of dealing between the creditor having knowledge of the dissolution and the person or partnership continuing the business.

(3) Where a person agrees to assume the existing obligations of a dissolved partnership, the partners whose obligations have been assumed shall be discharged from any liability to any creditor of the partnership who, knowing of the agreement, consents to a material alteration in the nature or time of payment of such obligations.

(4) The individual property of a deceased partner shall be liable for all obligations of the partnership incurred while he was a partner but subject to the prior payment of his separate debts.

§ 37
Right to Wind Up

Unless otherwise agreed the partners who have not wrongfully dissolved the partnership or the legal representative of the last surviving partner, not bankrupt, has the right to wind up the partnership affairs; provided, however, that any partner, his legal representative or his assignee, upon cause shown, may obtain winding up by the court.

§ 38
Rights of Partners to Application of Partnership Property

(1) When dissolution is caused in any way, except in contravention of the partnership agreement, each partner, as against his co-partners and all persons claiming through them in respect of their interests in the partnership, unless otherwise agreed, may have the partnership property applied to discharge its liabilities, and the surplus applied to pay in cash the net amount owing to the respective partners. But if dissolution is caused by expulsion of a partner, bona fide under the partnership agreement and if the expelled partner is discharged from all partnership liabilities, either by payment or agreement under section 36(2), he shall receive in cash only the net amount due him from the partnership.

(2) When dissolution is caused in contravention of the partnership agreement the rights of the partners shall be as follows:

(a) Each partner who has not caused dissolution wrongfully shall have,

(I) All the rights specified in paragraph (1) of this section, and

(II) The right, as against each partner who has caused the dissolution wrongfully, to damages for breach of the agreement.

(b) The partners who have not caused the dissolution wrongfully, if they all desire to continue the business in the same name, either by themselves or jointly with others, may do so, during the agreed term for the partnership and for that purpose may possess the partnership property, provided they secure the payment by bond approved by the court, or pay to any partner who has caused the dissolution wrongfully, the value of his interest in the partnership at the dissolution, less any damages recoverable under clause (2aII) of this section, and in like manner indemnify him against all present or future partnership liabilities.

(c) A partner who has caused the dissolution wrongfully shall have:

(I) If the business is not continued under the provisions of paragraph (2b) all the rights of a partner under paragraph (1), subject to clause (2aII), of this section,

(II) If the business is continued under paragraph (2b) of this section the right as against his co-partners and all claiming through them in respect of their interests in the partnership, to have the value of his interest in the partnership, less any damages caused to his co-partners by the dissolution, ascertained and paid to him in cash, or the payment secured by bond approved by the court, and to be released from all existing liabilities of the partnership; but in ascertaining the value of the partner's interest the value of the good-will of the business shall not be considered.

§ 39
Rights Where Partnership Is Dissolved for Fraud or Misrepresentation

Where a partnership contract is rescinded on the ground of the fraud or misrepresentation of one of the parties thereto, the party entitled to rescind is, without prejudice to any other right, entitled,

(a) To a lien on, or a right of retention of, the surplus of the partnership property after satisfying the partnership liabilities to third persons for any sum of money paid by him for the purchase of an interest in the partnership and for any capital or advances contributed by him; and

(b) To stand, after all liabilities to third persons have been satisfied, in the place of the creditors of the partnership for any payments made by him in respect of the partnership liabilities; and

(c) To be indemnified by the person guilty of the fraud or making the representation against all debts and liabilities of the partnership.

§ 40
Rules for Distribution

In settling accounts between the partners after dissolution, the following rules shall be observed, subject to any agreement to the contrary:

(a) The assets of the partnership are:

(I) The partnership property,

(II) The contributions of the partners necessary for the payment of all the liabilities specified in clause (b) of this paragraph.

(b) The liabilities of the partnership shall rank in order of payment, as follows:

(I) Those owing to creditors other than partners,

(II) Those owing to partners other than for capital and profits,

(III) Those owing to partners in respect of capital,

(IV) Those owing to partners in respect of profits.

(c) The assets shall be applied in order of their declaration in clause (a) of this paragraph to the satisfaction of the liabilities.

(d) The partners shall contribute, as provided by section 18 (a) the amount necessary to satisfy the liabilities; but if any, but not all, of the partners are insolvent, or, not being subject to process, refuse to contribute, the other partners shall contribute their share of the liabilities, and, in the relative proportions in which they share the profits, the additional amount necessary to pay the liabilities.

(e) An assignee for the benefit of creditors or any person appointed by the court shall have the right to enforce the contributions specified in clause (d) of this paragraph.

(f) Any partner or his legal representative shall have the right to enforce the contributions specified in clause (d) of this paragraph, to the extent of the amount which he has paid in excess of his share of the liability.

(g) The individual property of a deceased partner shall be liable for the contributions specified in clause (d) of this paragraph.

(h) When partnership property and the individual properties of the partners are in possession of a court for distribution, partnership creditors shall have priority on partnership property and separate creditors on individual property, saving the rights of lien or secured creditors as heretofore.

(i) Where a partner has become bankrupt or his estate is insolvent the claims against his separate property shall rank in the following order:

(I) Those owing to separate creditors,

(II) Those owing to partnership creditors,

(III) Those owing to partners by way of contribution.

§ 41
Liability of Persons Continuing the Business in Certain Cases

(1) When any new partner is admitted into an existing partnership, or when any partner retires and assigns (or the representative of the deceased partner assigns) his rights in partnership property to two or more of the partners, or to one or more of the partners and one or more third persons, if the business is continued without liquidation of the partnership affairs, creditors of the first or dissolved partnership are also creditors of the partnership so continuing the business.

(2) When all but one partner retire and assign (or the representative of a deceased partner assigns) their rights in partnership property to the remaining partner, who continues the business without liquidation of partnership affairs, either alone or with others, creditors of the dissolved partnership are also creditors of the person or partnership so continuing the business.

(3) When any partner retires or dies and the business of the dissolved partnership is continued as set forth in paragraphs (1) and (2) of this section, with the consent of the retired partners or the representative of the deceased partner, but without any assignment of his right in partnership property,

rights of creditors of the dissolved partnership and of the creditors of the person or partnership continuing the business shall be as if such assignment had been made.

(4) When all the partners or their representatives assign their rights in partnership property to one or more third persons who promise to pay the debts and who continue the business of the dissolved partnership, creditors of the dissolved partnership are also creditors of the person or partnership continuing the business.

(5) When any partner wrongfully causes a dissolution and the remaining partners continue the business under the provisions of section 38(2b), either alone or with others, and without liquidation of the partnership affairs, creditors of the dissolved partnership are also creditors of the person or partnership continuing the business.

(6) When a partner is expelled and the remaining partners continue the business either alone or with others, without liquidation of the partnership affairs, creditors of the dissolved partnership are also creditors of the person or partnership continuing the business.

(7) The liability of a third person becoming a partner in the partnership continuing the business, under this section, to the creditors of the dissolved partnership shall be satisfied out of partnership property only.

(8) When the business of a partnership after dissolution is continued under any conditions set forth in this section the creditors of the dissolved partnership, as against the separate creditors of the retiring or deceased partner or the representative of the deceased partner, have a prior right to any claim of the retired partner or the representative of the deceased partner against the person or partnership continuing the business, on account of the retired or deceased partner's interest in the dissolved partnership or on account of any consideration promised for such interest or for his right in partnership property.

(9) Nothing in this section shall be held to modify any right of creditors to set aside any assignment on the ground of fraud.

(10) The use by the person or partnership continuing the business of the partnership name, or the name of a deceased partner as part thereof, shall not of itself make the individual property of the deceased partner liable for any debts contracted by such person or partnership.

§ 42
Rights of Retiring or Estate of Deceased Partner When the Business Is Continued

When any partner retires or dies, and the business is continued under any of the conditions set forth in section 41(1, 2, 3, 5, 6), or section 38(2b) without any settlement of accounts as between him or his estate and the person or partnership continuing the business, unless otherwise agreed, he or his legal representative as against such persons or partnership may have the value of his interest at the date of dissolution ascertained, and shall receive as an ordinary creditor an amount equal to the value of his interest in the dissolved partnership with interest, or, at his option or at the option of his legal representative, in lieu of interest, the profits attributable to the use of his right in the property of the dissolved partnership; provided that the creditors of the dissolved partnership as against the separate creditors, or the representative of the retired or deceased partner, shall have priority on any claim arising under this section, as provided by section 41(8) of this act.

§ 43
Accrual of Actions

The right to an account of his interest shall accrue to any partner, or his legal representative, as against the winding up partners or the surviving partners or the person or partnership continuing the business, at the date of dissolution, in the absence of any agreement to the contrary.

PART VII / Miscellaneous Provisions

§ 44
When Act Takes Effect

This act shall take effect on the . . . . day of . . . . one thousand nine-hundred and . . . .

§ 45
Legislation Repealed

All acts or parts of acts inconsistent with this act are hereby repealed.

Appendix C

UNIFORM LIMITED PARTNERSHIP ACT

§ 1
Limited Partnership Defined

A limited partnership is a partnership formed by two or more persons under the provisions of Section 2, having as members one or more general partners and one or more limited partners. The limited partners as such shall not be bound by the obligations of the partnership.

§ 2
Formation

(1) Two or more persons desiring to form a limited partnership shall

    (a) Sign and swear to a certificate, which shall state

      I. The name of the partnership,

      II. The character of the business,

      III. The location of the principal place of business,

      IV. The name and place of residence of each member; general and limited partners being respectively designated,

      V. The term for which the partnership is to exist,

      VI. The amount of cash and a description of and the agreed value of the other property contributed by each limited partner,

      VII. The additional contributions, if any, agreed to be made by each limited partner and the times at which or events on the happening of which they shall be made,

      VIII. The time, if agreed upon, when the contribution of each limited partner is to be returned,

      IX. The share of the profits or the other compensation by way of income which each limited partner shall receive by reason of his contribution,

      X. The right, if given, of a limited partner to substitute an assignee as contributor in his place, and the terms and conditions of the substitution,

      XI. The right, if given, of the partners to admit additional limited partners,

      XII. The right, if given, of one or more of the limited partners to priority over other limited partners, as to contributions or as to compensation by way of income, and the nature of such priority,

      XIII. The right, if given, of the remaining general partner or partners to continue the business on the death, retirement or insanity of a general partner, and

      XIV. The right, if given, of a limited partner to demand and receive property other than cash in return for his contribution.

    (b) File for record the certificate in the office of [here designate the proper office].

(2) A limited partnership is formed if there has been substantial compliance in good faith with the requirements of paragraph (1).

§3
Business Which May Be Carried On

A limited partnership may carry on any business which a partnership without limited partners may carry on, except [here designate the business to be prohibited].

§4
Character of Limited Partner's Contribution

The contributions of a limited partner may be cash or other property, but not services.

§5
A Name Not to Contain Surname of Limited Partner; Exceptions

(1) The surname of a limited partner shall not appear in the partnership name, unless

(a) It is also the surname of a general partner, or

(b) Prior to the time when the limited partner became such the business had been carried on under a name in which his surname appeared.

(2) A limited partner whose name appears in a partnership name contrary to the provisions of paragraph (1) is liable as a general partner to partnership creditors who extend credit to the partnership without actual knowledge that he is not a general partner.

§6
Liability for False Statements in Certificate

If the certificate contains a false statement, one who suffers loss by reliance on such statement may hold liable any party to the certificate who knew the statement to be false.

(a) At the time he signed the certificate, or

(b) Subsequently, but within a sufficient time before the statement was relied upon to enable him to cancel or amend the certificate, or to file a petition for its cancellation or amendment as provided in Section 25(3).

§7
Limited Partner Not Liable to Creditors

A limited partner shall not become liable as a general partner unless, in addition to the exercise of his rights and powers as a limited partner, he takes part in the control of the business.

§8
Admission of Additional Limited Partners

After the formation of a limited partnership, additional limited partners may be admitted upon filing an amendment to the original certificate in accordance with the requirements of Section 25.

§9
Rights, Powers and Liabilities of a General Partner

(1) A general partner shall have all the rights and powers and be subject to all the restrictions and liabilities of a partner in a partnership without limited partners, except that without the written consent or ratification of the specific act by all the limited partners, a general partner or all of the general partners have no authority to

(a) Do any act in contravention of the certificate,

(b) Do any act which would make it impossible to carry on the ordinary business of the partnership,

(c) Confess a judgment against the partnership,

(d) Possess partnership property, or assign their rights in specific partnership property, for other than a partnership purpose.

(e) Admit a person as a general partner,

(f) Admit a person as a limited partner, unless the right so to do is given in the certificate,

(g) Continue the business with partnership property on the death, retirement or insanity of a general partner, unless the right so to do is given in the certificate.

§10
Rights of a Limited Partner

(1) A limited partner shall have the same rights as a general partner to

(a) Have the partnership books kept at the principal place of business of the partnership, and at all times to inspect and copy any of them

(b) Have on demand true and full information of all things affecting the partnership, and a formal account of partnership affairs whenever circumstances render it just and reasonable, and

(c) Have dissolution and winding up by decree of court.

(2) A limited partner shall have the right to receive a share of the profits or other compensation by way of income, and to the return of his contribution as provided in Sections 15 and 16.

§11
Status of Person Erroneously Believing Himself a Limited Partner

A person who has contributed to the capital of a business conducted by a person or partnership erroneously believing that he has become a limited partner in a limited partnership, is not, by reason of his exercise of the rights of a limited partner, a general partner with the person or in the partnership carrying on the business, or bound by the obligations of such person or partnership; provided that on ascertaining the mistake he promptly renounces his interest in the profits of the business, or other compensation by way of income.

§ 12
One Person Both General and Limited Partner

(1) A person may be a general partner and a limited partner in the same partnership at the same time.

(2) A person who is a general, and also at the same time a limited partner, shall have all the rights and powers and be subject to all the restrictions of a general partner; except that, in respect to his contribution, he shall have the rights against the other members which he would have had if he were not also a general partner.

§ 13
Loans and Other Business Transactions with Limited Partner

(1) A limited partner also may loan money to and transact other business with the partnership, and, unless he is also a general partner, receive on account of resulting claims against the partnership, with general creditors, a pro rata share of the assets. No limited partner shall in respect to any such claim

(a) Receive or hold as collateral security any partnership property, or

(b) Receive from a general partner of the partnership any payment, conveyance, or release from liability, if at the time the assets of the partnership are not sufficient to discharge partnership liabilities to persons not claiming as general or limited partners,

(2) The receiving of collateral security, or a payment, conveyance, or release in violation of the provisions of paragraph (1) is a fraud on the creditors of the partnership.

§ 14
Relation of Limited Partners Inter Se

Where there are several limited partners the members may agree that one or more of the limited partners shall have a priority over other limited partners as to the return of their contributions, as to their compensation by way of income, or as to any other matter. If such an agreement is made it shall be stated in the certificate, and in the absence of such a statement all the limited partners shall stand upon equal footing.

§ 15
Compensation of Limited Partner

A limited partner may receive from the partnership the share of the profits or the compensation by way of income stipulated for in the certificate; provided, that after such payment is made, whether from the property of the partnership or that of a general partner, the partnership assets are in excess of all liabilities of the partnership except liabilities to limited partners on account of their contributions and to general partners.

§ 16
Withdrawal or Reduction of Limited Partner's Contribution

(1) A limited partner shall not receive from a general partner or out of partnership property any part of his contribution until

(a) All liabilities of the partnership, except liabilities to general partners and to limited partners on account of their contributions, have been paid or there remains property of the partnership sufficient to pay them,

(b) The consent of all members is had, unless the return of the contribution may be rightfully demanded under the provisions of paragraph (2), and

(c) The certificate is cancelled or so amended as to set forth the withdrawal or reduction.

(2) Subject to the provisions of paragraph (1) a limited partner may rightfully demand the return of his contribution

(a) On the dissolution of a partnership, or

(b) When the date specified in the certificate for its return has arrived, or

(c) After he has given six months' notice in writing to all other members, if no time is specified in the certificate either for the return of the contribution or for the dissolution of the partnership,

(3) In the absence of any statement in the certificate to the contrary or the consent of all members, a limited partner, irrespective of the nature of his contribution, has only the right to demand and receive cash in return for his contribution.

(4) A limited partner may have the partnership dissolved and its affairs wound up when

(a) He rightfully but unsuccessfully demands the return of his contribution, or

(b) The other liabilities of the partnership have not been paid, or the partnership property is insufficient for their payment as required by paragraph (1a) and the limited partner would otherwise be entitled to the return of his contribution.

§ 17
Liability of Limited Partner to Partnership

(1) A limited partner is liable to the partnership

(a) For the difference between his contribution as actually made and that stated in the certificate as having been made, and

(b) For any unpaid contribution which he agreed in the certificate to make in the future at the time and on the conditions stated in the certificate.

(2) A limited partner holds as trustee for the partnership

(a) Specific property stated in the certificate as contributed by him, but which was not contributed or which has been wrongfully returned, and

(b) Money or other property wrongfully paid or conveyed to him on account of his contribution.

(3) The liabilities of a limited partner as set forth in this section can be waived or compromised only by the consent of all members; but a waiver or compromise shall not affect the right of a creditor of a partnership who extended credit or whose claim arose after the filing and before a cancellation or amendment of the certificate, to enforce such liabilities.

(4) When a contributor has rightfully received the return in whole or in part of the capital of his contribution, he is nevertheless liable to the partnership for any sum, not in excess of such return with interest, necessary to discharge its liabilities to all creditors who extended credit or whose claims arose before such return.

§ 18
Nature of Limited Partner's Interest in Partnership

A limited partner's interest in the partnership is personal property.

§ 19
Assignment of Limited Partner's Interest

(1) A limited partner's interest is assignable.

(2) A substituted limited partner is a person admitted to all the rights of a limited partner who has died or has assigned his interest in a partnership.

(3) An assignee, who does not become a substituted limited partner, has no right to require any information or account of the partnership transactions or to inspect the partnership books; he is only entitled to receive the share of the profits or other compensation by way of income, or the return of his contribution, to which his assignor would otherwise be entitled.

(4) An assignee shall have the right to become a substituted limited partner if all the members (except the assignor) consent thereto or if the assignor, being thereunto empowered by the certificate, gives the assignee that right.

(5) An assignee becomes a substituted limited partner when the certificate is appropriately amended in accordance with Section 25.

(6) The substituted limited partner has all the rights and powers, and is subject to all the restrictions and liabilities of his assignor, except those liabilities of which he was ignorant at the time he became a limited partner and which could not be ascertained from the certificate.

(7) The substitution of the assignee as a limited partner does not release the assignor from liability to the partnership under Sections 6 and 17.

§ 20
Effect of Retirement, Death or Insanity of a General Partner

The retirement, death or insanity of a general partner dissolves the partnership, unless the business is continued by the remaining general partners

(a) Under a right so to do stated in the certificate, or

(b) With the consent of all members.

§ 21
Death of Limited Partner

(1) On the death of a limited partner his executor or administrator shall have all the rights of a limited partner for the purpose of settling his estate, and such power as the deceased had to constitute his assignee a substituted limited partner.

(2) The estate of a deceased limited partner shall be liable for all his liabilities as a limited partner.

§ 22
Rights of Creditors of Limited Partner

(1) On due application to a court of competent jurisdiction by any judgment creditor of a limited partner, the court may charge the interest of the indebted limited partner with payment of the unsatisfied amount of the judgment debt; and may appoint a receiver, and make all other orders, directions, and inquiries which the circumstances of the case may require.

In those states where a creditor on beginning an action can attach debts due the defendant before he has obtained a judgment against the defendant it is recommended that paragraph (1) of this section read as follows:

On due application to a court of competent jurisdiction by any creditor of a limited partner, the court may charge the interest of the indebted limited partner with payment of the unsatisfied amount of such claim; and may appoint a receiver, and make all other orders, directions, and inquiries which the circumstances of the case may require.

(2) The interest may be redeemed with the separate property of any general partner, but may not be redeemed with partnership property.

(3) The remedies conferred by paragraph (1) shall not be deemed exclusive of others which may exist.

(4) Nothing in this act shall be held to deprive a limited partner of his statutory exemption.

§ 23
Distribution of Assets

(1) In settling accounts after dissolution the liabilities of the partnership shall be entitled to payment in the following order:

(a) Those to creditors, in the order of priority as provided by law, except those to limited partners on account of their contributions, and to general partners,

(b) Those to limited partners in respect to their share of the profits and other compensation by way of income on their contributions,

(c) Those to limited partners in respect to the capital of their contributions,

(d) Those to general partners other than for capital and profits.

(e) Those to general partners in respect to profits,

(f) Those to general partners in respect to capital.

(2) Subject to any statement in the certificate or to subsequent agreement, limited partners share in the partnership assets in respect to their claims for capital, and in respect to their claims for profits or for compensation by way of income on their contributions respectively, in proportion to the respective amounts of such claims.

§ 24
When Certificate Shall Be Cancelled or Amended

(1) The certificate shall be cancelled when the partnership is dissolved or all limited partners cease to be such.

(2) A certificate shall be amended when

(a) There is a change in the name of the partnership or in the amount or character of the contribution of any limited partner,

(b) A person is substituted as a limited partner,

(c) An additional limited partner is admitted,

(d) A person is admitted as a general partner,

(e) A general partner retires, dies or becomes insane, and the business is continued under Section 20,

(f) There is a change in the character of the business of the partnership,

(g) There is a false or erroneous statement in the certificate,

(h) There is a change in the time as stated in the certificate for the dissolution of the partnership or for the return of a contribution,

(i) A time is fixed for the dissolution of the partnership, or the return of a contribution, no time having been specified in the certificate, or

(j) The members desire to make a change in any other statement in the certificate in order that it shall accurately represent the agreement between them.

§ 25
Requirements for Amendment and for Cancellation of Certificate

(1) The writing to amend a certificate shall

(a) Conform to the requirements of Section 2(1a) as far as necessary to set forth clearly the change in the certificate which it is desired to make, and

(b) Be signed and sworn to by all members, and an amendment substituting a limited partner or adding a limited or general partner shall be signed also by the member to be substituted or added, and when a limited partner is to be substituted, the amendment shall also be signed by the assigning limited partner.

(2) The writing to cancel a certificate shall be signed by all members.

(3) A person desiring the cancellation or amendment of a certificate, if any person designated in paragraphs (1) and (2) as a person who must execute the writing refuses to do so, may petition the [here designate the proper court] to direct a cancellation or amendment thereof.

(4) If the court finds that the petitioner has a right to have the writing executed by a person who refuses to do so, it shall order the [here designate the responsible official in the office designated in Section 2] in the office where the certificate is recorded to record the cancellation or amendment of the certificate; and where the certificate is to be amended, the court shall also cause to be filed for record in said office a certified copy of its decree setting forth the amendment.

(5) A certificate is amended or cancelled when there is filed for record in the office [here designate the office designated in Section 2] where the certificate is recorded

(a) A writing in accordance with the provisions of paragraph (1), or (2) or

(b) A certified copy of the order of court in accordance with the provisions of paragraph (4).

(6) After the certificate is duly amended in accordance with this section, the amended certificate shall thereafter be for all purposes the certificate provided for by this act.

§ 26
Parties to Actions

A contributor, unless he is a general partner, is not a proper party to proceedings by or against a partnership, except where the object is to enforce a limited partner's right against or liability to the partnership.

§ 27
Name of Act

This act may be cited as The Uniform Limited Partnership Act.

§ 28
Rules of Construction

(1) The rule that statutes in derogation of the common law are to be strictly construed shall have no application to this act.

(2) This act shall be so interpreted and construed as to effect its general purpose to make uniform the law of those states which enact it.

(3) This act shall not be so construed as to impair the obligations of any contract existing when the act goes into effect, nor to affect any action or proceedings begun or right accrued before this act takes effect.

§ 29
Rules for Cases Not Provided for in This Act

In any case not provided for in this act the rules of law and equity, including the law merchant, shall govern.

§ 30
Provisions for Existing Limited Partnerships

(1) A limited partnership formed under any statute of this state prior to the adoption of this act, may become a limited partnership under this act by complying with the provisions of Section 2; provided the certificate sets forth

(a) The amount of the original contribution of each limited partner, and the time when the contribution was made, and

(b) That the property of the partnership exceeds the amount sufficient to discharge its liabilities to persons not claiming as general or limited partners by an amount greater than the sum of the contributions of its limited partners.

(2) A limited partnership formed under any statute of this state prior to the adoption of this act, until or unless it becomes a limited partnership under this act, shall continue to be governed by the provisions of [here insert proper reference to the existing limited partnership act or acts], except that such partnership shall not be renewed unless so provided in the original agreement.

§ 31
Act [Acts] Repealed

Except as affecting limited partnerships to the extent set forth in Section 30, the act (acts) of [here designate the existing limited partnership act or acts] is (are) hereby repealed.

Appendix D

REVISED UNIFORM LIMITED PARTNERSHIP ACT

The Act consists of 11 Articles as follows:

ARTICLE 1/General Provisions

§ 101
Definitions

As used in this Act, unless the context otherwise requires:

(1) "Certificate of limited partnership" means the certificate referred to in Section 201, as that certificate is amended from time to time.

(2) "Contribution" means any cash, property, or services rendered, or a promissory note or other binding obligation to contribute cash or property or to perform services, which a partner contributes to a limited partnership in his capacity as a partner.

(3) "Event of withdrawal of a general partner" means an event that causes a person to cease to be a general partner as provided in Section 402.

(4) "Foreign limited partnership" means a partnership formed under the laws of any State other than this State and having as partners one or more general partners and one or more limited partners.

(5) "General partner" means a person who has been admitted to a limited partnership as a general partner in accordance with the partnership agreement and named in the certificate of limited partnership as a general partner.

(6) "Limited partner" means a person who has been admitted to a limited partnership as a limited partner in accordance with the partnership agreement and named in the certificate of limited partnership as a limited partner.

(7) "Limited partnership" and "domestic limited partnership" mean a partnership formed by 2 or more persons under the laws of this State and having one or more general partners and one or more limited partners.

(8) "Partner" means any limited partner or general partner.

(9) "Partnership agreement" means any valid agreement, written or oral, of the partners as to the affairs of a limited partnership and the conduct of its business.

(10) "Partnership interest" means a partner's share of the profits and losses of a limited partnership and the right to receive distributions of partnership assets.

(11) "Person" means a natural person, partnership, limited partnership (domestic or foreign), trust, estate, association, or corporation.

(12) "State" means a state, territory, or possession of the United States, the District of Columbia, or the Commonwealth of Puerto Rico.

§ 102
Name

The name of each limited partnership as set forth in its certificate of limited partnership:

(1) shall contain without abbreviation the words "limited partnership";

(2) may not contain the name of a limited partner unless (i) it is also the name of a general partner or the corporate name of a corporate general partner, or (ii) the business of the limited partnership had been carried on under that name before the admission of that limited partner;

(3) may not contain any word or phrase indicating or implying that it is organized other than for a purpose stated in its certificate of limited partnership;

(4) may not be the same as, or deceptively similar to, the name of any corporation or limited partnership organized under the laws of this State or licensed or registered as a foreign corporation or limited partnership in this State; and

(5) may not contain the following words [here insert prohibited words].

§ 103
Reservation of Name

(a) The exclusive right to the use of a name may be reserved by:

(1) any person intending to organize a limited partnership under this Act and to adopt that name;

(2) any domestic limited partnership or any foreign limited partnership registered in this State which, in either case, intends to adopt that name;

(3) any foreign limited partnership intending to register in this State and to adopt that name; and

(4) any person intending to organize a foreign limited partnership and intending to have it registered in this State and to adopt that name.

(b) The reservation shall be made by filing with the Secretary of State an application, executed by the applicant, to reserve a specified name. If the Secretary of State finds that the name is available for use by a domestic or foreign limited partnership, he shall reserve the name for the exclusive use of the applicant for a period of 120 days. Once having reserved a name, the same applicant may not again reserve the same name until more than 60 days after the expiration of the last 120-day period for which that applicant reserved that name. The right to the exclusive use of a reserved name may be transferred to any other person by filing in the office of the Secretary of State a notice of the transfer, executed by the applicant for whom the name was reserved and specifying the name and address of the transferee.

§ 104
Specified Office and Agent

Each limited partnership shall continuously maintain in this State:

(1) an office, which may but need not be a place of its business in this State, at which shall be kept the records required by Section 105 to be maintained; and

(2) an agent for service of process on the limited partnership, which agent must be an individual resident of this State, a domestic corporation, or a foreign corporation authorized to do business in this State.

§ 105
Records to be Kept

Each limited partnership shall keep at the office referred to in Section 104(1) the following: (1) a current list of the full name and last known business address of each partner set forth in alphabetical order, (2) a copy of the certificate of limited partnership and all certificates of amendment thereto, together with executed copies of any powers of attorney pursuant to which any certificate has been executed, (3) copies of the limited partnership's federal, state, and local income tax returns and reports, if any, for the 3 most recent years, and (4) copies of any then effective written partnership agreements and of any financial statements of the limited partnership for the 3 most recent years. These records are subject to inspection and copying at the reasonable request, and at the expense, of any partner during ordinary business hours.

§ 106
Nature of Business

A limited partnership may carry on any business that a partnership without limited partners may carry on except [here designate prohibited activities].

§ 107
Business Transactions of Partner
With the Partnership

Except as provided in the partnership agreement, a partner may lend money to and transact other business with the limited partnership and, subject to other applicable law, has the same rights and obligations with respect thereto as a person who is not a partner.

ARTICLE 2/Formation; Certificate of Limited Partnership

§ 201
Certificate of Limited Partnership

(a) In order to form a limited partnership two or more persons must execute a certificate of limited partnership. The certificate shall be filed in the office of the Secretary of State and set forth:

(1) the name of the limited partnership;

(2) the general character of its business;

(3) the address of the office and the name and address of the agent for service of process required to be maintained by Section 104;

(4) the name and the business address of each partner (specifying separately the general partners and limited partners);

(5) the amount of cash and a description and statement of the agreed value of the other property or services contributed by each partner and which each partner has agreed to contribute in the future;

(6) the times at which or events on the happening of which any additional contributions agreed to be made by each partner are to be made;

(7) any power of a limited partner to grant the right to become a limited partner to an assignee of any part of his partnership interest and the terms and conditions of the power;

(8) if agreed upon, the time at which or the events on the happening of which a partner may terminate his membership in the limited partnership and the amount of, or the method of determining, the distribution to which he may be entitled respecting his partnership interest, and the terms and conditions of the termination and distribution;

(9) any right of a partner to receive distributions of property, including cash from the limited partnership;

(10) any right of a partner to receive, or of a general partner to make, distributions to a partner which include a return of all or any part of the partner's contribution;

(11) any time at which or events upon the happening of which the limited partnership is to be dissolved and its affairs wound up;

(12) any right of the remaining general partners to continue the business on the happening of an event of withdrawal of a general partner; and

(13) any other matters the partners determine to include therein.

(b) A limited partnership is formed at the time of the filing of the certificate of limited partnership in the office of the Secretary of State or at any later time specified in the certificate of limited partnership if, in each case, there has been substantial compliance with the requirements of this section.

§ 202
Amendment to Certificate

(a) A certificate of limited partnership is amended by filing a certificate of amendment thereto in the office of the Secretary of State. The certificate shall set forth:

(1) the name of the limited partnership;

(2) the date of filing of the certificate; and

(3) the amendments to the certificate.

(b) Within 30 days after the happening of any of the following events an amendment to a certificate of limited partnership reflecting the occurrence of the event or events shall be filed:

(1) a change in the amount or character of the contribution of any partner, or in any partner's obligation to make a contribution;

(2) the admission of a new partner;

(3) the withdrawal of a partner; or

(4) the continuation of the business under Section 801 after an event of withdrawal of a general partner.

(c) A general partner who becomes aware that any statement in a certificate of limited partnership was false when made or that any arrangements or other facts described have changed, making the certificate inaccurate in any respect, shall promptly amend the certificate, but an amendment to show a change of address of a limited partner need be filed only once every 12 months.

(d) A certificate of limited partnership may be amended at any time for any other proper purpose the general partners may determine.

(e) No person has any liability because an amendment to a certificate of limited partnership has not been filed to reflect the occurrence of any event referred to in subsection (b) of this Section if the amendment is filed within the 30-day period specified in subsection (b).

§ 203
Cancellation of Certificate

A certificate of limited partnership shall be cancelled upon the dissolution and the commencement of winding up of the partnership and at any other time there are no remaining limited partners. A certificate of cancellation shall be filed in the office of the Secretary of State and shall set forth:

(1) the name of the limited partnership;

(2) the date of filing of its certificate of limited partnership;

(3) the reason for filing the certificate of cancellation;

(4) the effective date (which shall be a date certain) of cancellation if it is not to be effective upon the filing of the certificate; and

(5) any other information the general partners filing the certificate may determine.

§ 204
Execution of Certificates

(a) Each certificate required by this Article to be filed in the office of the Secretary of State shall be executed in the following manner:

(1) each original certificate of limited partnership must be signed by each partner named therein;

(2) each certificate of amendment must be signed by at least one general partner and by each other partner designated in the certificate as a new partner or whose contribution is described as having been increased; and

(3) each certificate of cancellation must be signed by all general partners.

(b) Any person may sign a certificate by an attorney-in-fact, but a power of attorney to sign a certificate relating to the admission, or increased contribution, of a partner must specifically describe the admission or increase.

(c) The execution of a certificate by a general partner constitutes an affirmation under the penalties of perjury that the facts stated therein are true.

§ 205
Amendment or Cancellation by Judicial Act

If a person required by Section 204 to execute a certificate of amendment or cancellation fail or refuse to do so, any other partner, and any assignee of a partnership interest, who is adversely affected by the failure or refusal, may petition the [here designate the proper court] to direct the amendment or cancellation. If the court finds that the amendment or cancellation is proper and that the person so designated has failed or refused to execute the certificate, it shall order the Secretary of State to record an appropriate certificate of amendment or cancellation.

§ 206
Filing in the Office of the Secretary of State

(a) Two signed copies of the certificate of limited partnership and of any certificates of amendment or cancellation (or of any judicial decree of amendment or cancellation) shall be delivered to the Secretary of State. A person who executes a certificate as an agent or fiduciary need not exhibit evidence of his authority as a prerequisite to filing. Unless the Secretary of State finds that any certificate does not conform to law, upon receipt of all filing fees required by law he shall:

(1) endorse on each duplicate original the word "Filed" and the day, month, and year of the filing thereof;

(2) file one duplicate original in his office; and

(3) return the other duplicate original to the person who filed it or his representative.

(b) Upon the filing of a certificate of amendment (or judicial decree of amendment) in the office of the Secretary of State, the certificate of limited partnership shall be amended as set forth therein, and upon the effective date of a certificate of cancellation (or a judicial decree thereof), the certificate of limited partnership is cancelled.

§ 207
Liability for False Statement in Certificate

If any certificate of limited partnership or certificate of amendment or cancellation contains a false statement, one who suffers loss by reliance on the statement may recover damages for the loss from:

(1) any person who executes the certificate, or causes another to execute it on his behalf, and knew, and any general partner who knew or should have known, the statement to be false at the time the certificate was executed; and

(2) any general partner who thereafter knows or should have known that any arrangement or other fact described in the certificate have changed, making the statement inaccurate in any respect within a sufficient time before the statement was relied upon reasonably to have enabled that general partner to cancel or amend the certificate, or to file a petition for its cancellation or amendment under Section 205.

§ 208
Notice

The fact that a certificate of limited partnership is on file in the office of the Secretary of State is notice that the partnership is a limited partnership and the persons designated therein as limited partners are limited partners, but is not notice of any other fact.

§ 209
Delivery of Certificates to Limited Partners

Upon the return by the Secretary of State pursuant to Section 206 of a certificate marked "Filed," the general partners shall promptly deliver or mail a copy of the certificate of limited partnership and each certificate to each limited partner unless the partnership agreement provides otherwise.

ARTICLE 3/Limited Partners

§ 301
Admission of Additional Limited Partners

(a) After the filing of a limited partnership's original certificate of limited partnership, a person may be admitted as a new limited partner:

(1) in the case of a person acquiring a partnership interest directly from the limited partnership, upon the compliance with the partnership agreement or, if the partnership agreement does not so provide, upon the written consent of all partners; and

(2) in the case of an assignee of a partnership interest of a partner who has the power, as provided in Section 704, to grant the assignee the right to become a limited partner, upon the exercise of that power and compliance with any conditions limiting the grant or exercise of the power.

(b) In each case under subsection (a), the person acquiring the partnership interest becomes a limited partner only upon amendment of the certificate of limited partnership reflecting that fact.

§ 302
Voting

Subject to Section 303, the partnership agreement may grant to all or a specified group of the limited partners the right to vote (on a per capita or any other basis) upon any matter.

§ 303
Liability to Third Parties

(a) Except as provided in subsection (d), a limited partner is not liable for the obligations of a limited partnership unless he is also a general partner or, in addition to the exercise of his rights and powers as a limited partner, he takes part in the control of the business. However, if the limited partner's participation in the control of the business is not substantially the same as the exercise of the powers of a general partner, he is liable only to persons who transact business with the limited partnership with actual knowledge of his participation in control.

(b) A limited partner does not participate in the control of the business within the meaning of subsection (a) solely by doing one or more of the following:

(1) being a contractor for or an agent or employee of the limited partnership or of a general partner;

(2) consulting with and advising a general partner with respect to the business of the limited partnership;

(3) acting as surety for the limited partnership;

(4) approving or disapproving an amendment to the partnership agreement; or

(5) voting on one or more of the following matters:

(i) the dissolution and winding up of the limited partnership;

(ii) the sale, exchange, lease, mortgage, pledge, or other transfer of all or substantially all of the assets of the limited partnership other than in the ordinary course of its business;

(iii) the incurrence of indebtedness by the limited partnership other than in the ordinary course of its business;

(iv) a change in the nature of the business; or

(v) the removal of a general partner.

(c) The enumeration in subsection (b) does not mean that the possession or exercise of any other powers by a limited partner constitutes participation by him in the business of the limited partnership.

(d) A limited partner who knowingly permits his name to be used in the name of the limited partnership, except under circumstances permitted by Section 102(2)(i), is liable to

creditors who extend credit to the limited partnership without actual knowledge that the limited partner is not a general partner.

§ 304
Person Erroneously Believing Himself a Limited Partner

(a) Except as provided in subsection (b), a person who makes a contribution to a business enterprise and erroneously but in good faith believes that he has become a limited partner in the enterprise is not a general partner in the enterprise and is not bound by its obligations by reason of making the contribution, receiving distributions from the enterprise, or exercising any rights of a limited partner, if, on ascertaining the mistake; he:

(1) causes an appropriate certificate of limited partnership or a certificate of amendment to be executed and filed; or

(2) withdraws from future equity participation in the enterprise.

(b) Any person who makes a contribution of the kind described in subsection (a) is liable as a general partner to any third party who transacts business with the enterprise (i) before the person withdraws and an appropriate certificate is filed to show withdrawal, or (ii) before an appropriate certificate is filed to show his status as a limited partner and, in the case of an amendment, after expiration of the 30-day period for filing an amendment relating to the person as a limited partner under Section 202, but in either case only if the third party actually believed in good faith that the person was a general partner at the time of the transaction.

§ 305
Information

Each limited partner has the right to:

(1) inspect and copy any of the partnership records required to be maintained by Section 105; and

(2) obtain from the general partners from time to time upon reasonable demand (i) true and full information regarding the state of the business and financial condition of the limited partnership, (ii) promptly after becoming available, a copy of the limited partnership's federal, state, and local income tax returns for each year, and (iii) other information regarding the affairs of the limited partnership as is just and reasonable.

ARTICLE 4/General Partners

§ 401
Admission of Additional General Partners

After the filing of a limited partnership's original certificate of limited partnership, additional general partners may be admitted only with the specific written consent of each partner.

§402
Events of Withdrawal

Except as approved by the specific written consent of all partners at the time, a person ceases to be a general partner of a limited partnership upon the happening of any of the following events:

(1) the general partner withdraws from the limited partnership as provided in Section 602;

(2) the general partner ceases to be a member of the limited partnership as provided in Section 702;

(3) the general partner is removed as a general partner in accordance with the partnership agreement;

(4) unless otherwise provided in the certificate of limited partnership, the general partner: (i) makes an assignment for the benefit of creditors; (ii) files a voluntary petition in bankruptcy; (iii) is adjudicated a bankrupt or insolvent; (iv) files a petition or answer seeking for himself any reorganization, arrangement, composition, readjustment, liquidation, dissolution, or similar relief under any statute, law, or regulation; (v) files an answer or other pleading admitting or failing to contest the material allegations of a petition filed against him in any proceeding of this nature; or (vi) seeks, consents to, or acquiesces in the appointment of a trustee, receiver, or liquidator of the general partner or of all or any substantial part of his properties;

(5) unless otherwise provided in the certificate of limited partnership, [120] days after the commencement of any proceeding against the general partner seeking any reorganization, arrangement, composition, readjustment, liquidation, dissolution, or similar relief under any statute, law, or regulation, the proceeding has not been dismissed, or if within [90] days after the appointment without his consent or acquiescence of any trustee, receiver, or liquidator of the general partner or of all or any substantial part of his properties, the appointment is not vacated or stayed, or within [90] days after the expiration of any such stay, the appointment is not vacated;

(6) in the case of a general partner who is a natural person

(i) his death; or

(ii) the entry by a court of competent jurisdiction adjudicating him incompetent to manage his person or his property;

(7) in the case of a general partner who is acting as a general partner by virtue of being a trustee of a trust, the termination of the trust (but not merely the substitution of a new trustee);

(8) in the case of a general partner that is a separate partnership, the dissolution and commencement of winding up of the partnership;

(9) in the case of a general partner that is a corporation, the filing of a certificate of dissolution, or its equivalent, for the corporation or the revocation of its charter; and

(10) in the case of an estate, the distribution by the fiduciary of all the estate's entire interest in the partnership.

§403
General Powers and Liabilities

Except as otherwise provided in this Act and in the partnership agreement, a general partner of a limited partnership has the rights and powers and is subject to the restrictions and liabilities of a partner in a partnership without limited partners.

§404
Contributions by a General Partner

A general partner of a limited partnership may make contribution to the partnership and share in the profits and losses of, and in distributions from, the limited partnership as a general partner. A general partner also may make contributions to and share in profits, losses, and distributions as a limited partner. A person who is both a general partner and a limited partner has the rights and powers, and is subject to the restrictions and liabilities, of a general partner and, except as provided in the partnership agreement, also has the powers, and is subject to the restrictions, of a limited partner to the extent of his participation in the partnership as a limited partner.

§405
Voting

The partnership agreement may grant to all or certain identified general partners the right to vote (on a per capita or any other basis), separately or with all or any class of the limited partners, on any matter.

ARTICLE 5/Finance

§501
Form of Contributions

The contribution of a partner may be in cash, property, or services rendered, or a promissory note or other obligation to contribute cash or property or to perform services.

§502
Liability for Contributions

(a) Except as otherwise provided in the certificate of limited partnership, a partner is obligated to the limited partnership to perform any promise to contribute cash or property or to perform services even if he is unable to perform because of death, disability or any other reason. If a partner does not make the required contribution of property or services, he is obligated at the option of the limited partnership to contribute cash equal to that portion of the value (as stated in the certificate of limited partnership) of the stated contribution that has not been made.

(b) Unless otherwise provided in the partnership agreement, the obligation of a partner to make a contribution or return money or other property paid or distributed in violation of this Act may be compromised only by consent of all of the partners. Notwithstanding the compromise, a creditor of a limited partnership who extends credit, or whose claim arises, after the filing of the certificate of limited partnership or an amendment thereto which, in either case, reflects the obligation and before the amendment or cancellation thereof to reflect the compromise, may enforce the obligation.

§ 503
Sharing of Profits and Losses

The profits and losses of a limited partnership shall be allocated among the partners, and among classes of partners, in the manner provided in the partnership agreement. If the partnership agreement does not so provide, profits and losses shall be allocated on the basis of the value (as stated in the certificate of limited partnership) of the contributions made by each partner to the extent they have been received by the partnership and have not been returned.

§ 504
Sharing of Distributions

Distributions of cash or other assets of a limited partnership shall be allocated among the partners, and among classes of partners, in the manner provided in the partnership agreement. If the partnership agreement does not so provide, distributions shall be made on the basis of the value (as stated in the certificate of limited partnership) of the contributions made by each partner to the extent they have not been received by the partnership and have not been returned.

ARTICLE 6/Distributions and Withdrawal

§ 601
Interim Distributions

Except as provided in this Article, a partner is entitled to receive distributions from a limited partnership before his withdrawal from the limited partnership and before the dissolution and winding up thereof:

(1) to the extent and at the times or upon the happening of the events specified in the partnership agreement; and

(2) if any distribution constitutes a return of any part of his contribution under Section 608(c), to the extent and at the times or upon the happening of the events specified in the certificate of limited partnership.

§ 602
Withdrawal of General Partner

A general partner may withdraw from a limited partnership at any time by giving written notice to the other partners, but if the withdrawal violates the partnership agreement, the limited partnership may recover from the withdrawing general partner damages for breach of the partnership agreement and offset the damages against the amount otherwise distributable to him.

§ 603
Withdrawal of Limited Partner

A limited partner may withdraw from a limited partnership at the time or upon the happening of the events specified in the certificate of limited partnership and in accordance with the partnership agreement. If the certificate does not specify the time or the events upon the happening of which a limited partner may withdraw or a definite time for the dissolution and winding up of the limited partnership, a limited partner may withdraw upon not less than 6 months' prior written notice to each general partner at his address on the books of the limited partnership at its office in this State.

§ 604
Distribution Upon Withdrawal

Except as provided in this Article, upon withdrawal any withdrawing partner is entitled to receive any distribution to which he is entitled under the partnership agreement and, if not otherwise provided in the agreement, he is entitled to receive, within a reasonable time after withdrawal, the fair value of his interest in the limited partnership as of the date of withdrawal based upon his right to share in distributions from the limited partnership.

§ 605
Distribution in Kind

Except as provided in the certificate of limited partnership, a partner, regardless of the nature of his contribution, has no right to demand and receive any distribution from a limited partnership in any form other than cash. Except as provided in the partnership agreement, a partner may not be compelled to accept a distribution of any asset in kind from a limited partnership to the extent that the percentage of the asset distributed to him exceeds a percentage of that asset which is equal to the percentage in which he shares in distributions from the limited partnership.

§ 606
Right to Distribution

At the time a partner becomes entitled to receive a distribution, he has the status of, and is entitled to all remedies available to, a creditor of the limited partnership with respect to the distribution.

§607
Limitations on Distribution

A partner may not receive a distribution from a limited partnership to the extent that, after giving effect to the distribution, all liabilities of the limited partnership, other than liabilities to partners on account of their partnership interests, exceed the fair value of the partnership assets.

§608
Liability Upon Return of Contributions

(a) If a partner has received the return of any part of his contribution without violation of the partnership agreement or this Act, he is liable to the limited partnership for a period of one year thereafter for the amount of the returned contribution, but only to the extent necessary to discharge the limited partnership's liabilities to creditors who extended credit to the limited partnership during the period the contribution was held by the partnership.

(b) If a partner has received the return of any part of his contribution in violation of the partnership agreement or this Act, he is liable to the limited partnership for a period of 6 years thereafter for the amount of the contribution wrongfully returned.

(c) A partner receives a return of his contribution to the extent that a distribution to him reduces his share of the fair value of the net assets of the limited partnership below the value (as set forth in the certificate of limited partnership) of his contributions which has not been distributed to him.

ARTICLE 7/Assignment of Partnership Interests

§701
Nature of Partnership Interest

A partnership interest is personal property.

§702
Assignment of Partnership Interest

Except as provided in the partnership agreement, a partnership interest is assignable in whole or in part. An assignment of a partnership interest does not dissolve a limited partnership or entitle the assignee to become or to exercise any rights of a partner. An assignment entitles the assignee to receive, to the extent assigned, only the distribution to which the assignor would be entitled. Except as provided in the partnership agreement, a partner ceases to be a partner upon assignment of all his partnership interest.

§703
Rights of Creditor

On application to a court of competent jurisdiction by any judgment creditor of a partner, the court may charge the partnership interest of the partner with payment of the un-

satisfied amount of the judgment with interest. To the extent so charged, the judgment creditor has only the rights of an assignee of the partnership interest. This Act does not deprive any partner of the benefit of any exemption laws applicable to his partnership interest.

§704
Right of Assignee to Become Limited Partner

(a) An assignee of a partnership interest, including an assignee of a general partner, may become a limited partner if and to the extent that (1) the assignor gives the assignee that right in accordance with authority described in the certificate of limited partnership, or (2) all other partners consent.

(b) An assignee who has become a limited partner has, to the extent assigned, the rights and powers, and is subject to the restrictions and liabilities, of a limited partner under the partnership agreement and this Act. An assignee who becomes a limited partner also is liable for the obligations of his assignor to make and return contributions as provided in Article 6. However, the assignee is not obligated for liabilities unknown to the assignee at the time he became a limited partner and which could not be ascertained from the certificate of limited partnership.

(c) If an assignee of a partnership interest becomes a limited partner, the assignor is not released from his liability to the limited partnership under Sections 207 and 502.

§705
Power of Estate of Deceased or Incompetent Partner

If a partner who is an individual dies or a court of competent jurisdiction adjudges him to be incompetent to manage his person or his property, the partner's executor, administrator, guardian, conservator, or other legal representative may exercise all of the partner's rights for the purpose of settling his estate or administering his property, including any power the partner had to give an assignee the right to become a limited partner. If a partner is a corporation, trust, or other entity and is dissolved or terminated, the powers of that partner may be exercised by its legal representative or successor.

ARTICLE 8/Dissolution

§801
Nonjudicial Dissolution

A limited partnership is dissolved and its affairs shall be wound up upon the happening of the first to occur of the following:

(1) at the time or upon the happening of events specified in the certificate of limited partnership;

(2) written consent of all partners;

(3) an event of withdrawal of a general partner unless at the

time there is at least one other general partner and the certificate of limited partnership permits the business of the limited partnership to be carried on by the remaining general partner and that partner does so, but the limited partnership is not dissolved and is not required to be wound up by reason of any event of withdrawal if, within 90 days after the withdrawal, all partners agree in writing to continue the business of the limited partnership and to the appointment of one or more additional general partners if necessary or desired; or

(4) entry of a decree of judicial dissolution under Section 802.

§802
Judicial Dissolution

On application by or for a partner the [here designate the proper court] court may decree a dissolution of a limited partnership whenever it is not reasonably practicable to carry on the business in conformity with the partnership agreement.

§803
Winding Up

Except as provided in the partnership agreement, the general partners who have not wrongfully dissolved a limited partnership or, if none, the limited partners, may wind up the limited partnership's affairs; but the [here designate the proper court] court may wind up the limited partnership's affairs upon application of any partner, his legal representative, or assignee.

§804
Distribution of Assets

Upon the winding up of a limited partnership, the assets shall be distributed as follows:

(1) to creditors, including partners who are creditors, to the extent otherwise permitted by law, in satisfaction of liabilities of the limited partnership other than liabilities for distributions to partners under Section 601 or 604:

(2) except as provided in the partnership agreement, to partners and former partners in satisfaction of liabilities for distributions under Section 601 or 604; and

(3) except as provided in the partnership agreement, to partners *first* for the return of their contributions and *secondly* respecting their partnership interests, in the proportions in which the partners share in distributions.

ARTICLE 9/Foreign Limited Partnerships

§901
Law Governing

Subject to the Constitution of this State, (1) the laws of the state under which a foreign limited partnership is organized govern its organization and internal affairs and the liability of its limited partners, and (2) a foreign limited partnership may not be denied registration by reason of any difference between those laws and the laws of this State.

§902
Registration

Before transacting business in this State, a foreign limited partnership shall register with the Secretary of State. In order to register, a foreign limited partnership shall submit to the Secretary of State, in duplicate, an application for registration as a foreign limited partnership, signed and sworn to by a general partner and setting forth:

(1) the name of the foreign limited partnership and, if different, the name under which it proposes to register and transact business in this State;

(2) the state and date of its formation;

(3) the general character of the business it proposes to transact in this State;

(4) the name and address of any agent for service of process on the foreign limited partnership whom the foreign limited partnership elects to appoint, the agent must be an individual resident of this State, a domestic corporation, or a foreign corporation having a place of business in, and authorized to do business in this State;

(5) a statement that the Secretary of State is appointed the agent of the foreign limited partnership for service of process if no agent has been appointed under paragraph (4) or, if appointed, the agent's authority has been revoked or if the agent cannot be found or served with the exercise of reasonable diligence;

(6) the address of the office required to be maintained in the State of its organization by the laws of that State or, if not so required, of the principal office of the foreign limited partnership; and

(7) If the certificate of limited partnership filed in the foreign limited partnership's state of organization is not required to include the names and business addresses of the partners, a list of the names and addresses.

§903
Issuance of Registration

(a) If the Secretary of State finds that an application for registration conforms to law and all requisite fees have been paid, he shall:

(1) endorse on the application the word "Filed," and the month, day, and year of the filing thereof;

(2) file in his office a duplicate original of the application; and

(3) issue a certificate of registration to transact business in this State.

(b) The certificate of registration, together with a duplicate original of the application, shall be returned to the person who filed the application or his representative.

§904
Name

A foreign limited partnership may register with the Secretary of State under any name (whether or not it is the name under which it is registered in its state of organization) that includes without abbreviation the words "limited partnership" and that could be registered by a domestic limited partnership.

§905
Changes and Amendments

If any statement in a foreign limited partnership's application for registration was false when made or any arrangements or other facts described have changed, making the application inaccurate in any respect, the foreign limited partnership shall promptly file in the office of the Secretary of State a certificate, signed and sworn to by a general partner, correcting the statement.

§906
Cancellation of Registration

A foreign limited partnership may cancel its registration by filing with the Secretary of State a certificate of cancellation signed and sworn to by a general partner. A cancellation does not terminate the authority of the Secretary of State to accept service of process on the foreign limited partnership with respect to [claims for relief] [causes of action] arising out of the transaction of business in this State.

§907
Transaction of Business
Without Registration

(a) A foreign limited partnership transacting business in this State may not maintain any action, suit, or proceeding in any court of this State until it has registered in this State.

(b) The failure of a foreign limited partnership to register in this State does not impair the validity of any contract or act of the foreign limited partnership or prevent the foreign limited partnership from defending any action, suit, or proceeding in any court of this State.

(c) A limited partner of a foreign limited partnership is not liable as a general partner of the foreign limited partnership solely by reason of having transacted business in this State without registration.

(d) A foreign limited partnership, by transacting business in this State without registration, appoints the Secretary of State as its agent for service of process with respect to [claims for relief] [causes of action] arising out of the transaction of business in this State.

§908
Action by [Appropriate Official]

The [appropriate official] may bring an action to restrain a foreign limited partnership from transacting business in this State in violation of this Article.

ARTICLE 10/Derivative Actions

§1001
Right of Action

A limited partner may bring an action in the right of a limited partnership to recover a judgment in its favor if general partners with authority to do so have refused to bring the action or if an effort to cause those general partners to bring the action is not likely to succeed.

§1002
Proper Plaintiff

In a derivative action, the plaintiff must be a partner at the time of bringing the action and (1) at the time of the transaction of which he complains or (2) his status as a partner had devolved upon him by operation of law or pursuant to the terms of the partnership agreement from a person who was a partner at the time of the transaction.

§1003
Pleading

In any derivative action, the complaint shall set forth with particularity the effort of the plaintiff to secure initiation of the action by a general partner or the reasons for not making the effort.

§1004
Expenses

If a derivative action is successful, in whole or in part, or if anything is received by the plaintiff as a result of a judgment, compromise, or settlement of an action or claim, the court may award the plaintiff reasonable expenses, including reasonable attorney's fees, and shall direct him to remit to the limited partnership the remainder of those proceeds received by him.

ARTICLE 11/Miscellaneous

§ 1101
Construction and Application

This Act shall be so applied and construed to effectuate its general purpose to make uniform the law with respect to the subject of this Act among states enacting it.

§ 1102
Short Title

This Act may be cited as the Uniform Limited Partnership Act.

§ 1103
Severability

If any provision of this Act or its application to any person or circumstance is held invalid, the invalidity does not affect other provisions or applications of the Act which can be given effect without the invalid provision or application, and to this end the provisions of this Act are severable.

§ 1104
Effective Date, Extended Effective Date and Repeal

Except as set forth below, the effective date of this Act is _____ and the following Acts [list prior limited partnership acts] are hereby repealed:

(1) The existing provisions for execution and filing of certificates of limited partnerships and amendments thereunder and cancellations thereof continue in effect until [specify time required to create central filing system], the extended effective date, and Sections 102, 103, 104, 105, 201, 202, 203, 204 and 206 are not effective until the extended effective date.

(2) Section 402, specifying the conditions under which a general partner ceases to be a member of a limited partnership, is not effective until the extended effective date, and the applicable provisions of existing law continue to govern until the extended effective date.

(3) Sections 501, 502 and 608 apply only to contributions and distributions made after the effective date of this Act.

(4) Section 704 applies only to assignments made after the effective date of this Act.

(5) Article 9, dealing with registration of foreign limited partnerships, is not effective until the extended effective date.

§ 1105
Rules for Cases Not Provided for in This Act

In any case not provided for in this Act the provisions of the Uniform Partnership Act govern.

Appendix E

THE MODEL BUSINESS
CORPORATION ACT

§ 1.
Short Title

This Act shall be known and may be cited as the
".......... *Business Corporation Act."

§ 2.
Definitions

As used in this Act, unless the context otherwise requires,
the term:

(a) "Corporation" or "domestic corporation" means a corporation for profit subject to the provisions of this Act, except a foreign corporation.

(b) "Foreign corporation" means a corporation for profit
organized under laws other than the laws of this State for a
purpose or purposes for which a corporation may be organized under this Act.

(c) "Articles of incorporation" means the original or restated articles of incorporation or articles of consolidation
and all amendments thereto including articles of merger.

(d) "Shares" means the units into which the proprietary
interests in a corporation are divided.

(e) "Subscriber" means one who subscribes for shares in a
corporation, whether before or after incorporation.

(f) "Shareholder" means one who is a holder of record of
shares in a corporation. If the articles of incorporation or the

by-laws so provide, the board of directors may adopt by
resolution a procedure whereby a shareholder of the corporation may certify in writing to the corporation that all or a
portion of the shares registered in the name of such shareholder are held for the account of a specified person or
persons. The resolution shall set forth (1) the classification of
shareholder who may certify, (2) the purpose or purposes
for which the certification may be made, (3) the form of
certification and information to be contained therein, (4) if
the certification is with respect to a record date or closing of
the stock transfer books within which the certification must
be received by the corporation and (5) such other provisions with respect to the procedure as are deemed necessary
or desirable. Upon receipt by the corporation of a certification complying with the procedure, the persons specified in
the certification shall be deemed, for the purpose or purposes set forth in the certification, to be the holders of record
of the number of shares specified in place of the shareholder
making the certification.

(g) "Authorized shares" means the shares of all classes
which the corporation is authorized to issue.

(h) "Employee" includes officers but not directors. A director may accept duties which make him also an employee.

(i) "Distribution" means a direct or indirect transfer of
money or other property (except its own shares) or incurrence of indebtedness, by a corporation to or for the benefit
of any of its shareholders in respect of any of its shares,
whether by dividend or by purchase, redemption or other
acquisition of its shares, or otherwise.

§ 3.
Purposes

Corporations may be organized under this Act for any lawful purpose or purposes, except for the purpose of banking or insurance.

§ 4.
General Powers

Each corporation shall have power:

(a) To have perpetual succession by its corporate name unless a limited period of duration is stated in its articles of incorporation.

(b) To sue and be sued, complain and defend, in its corporate name.

(c) To have a corporate seal which may be altered at pleasure, and to use the same by causing it, or a facsimile thereof, to be impressed or affixed or in any other manner reproduced.

(d) To purchase, take, receive, lease, or otherwise acquire, own, hold, improve, use and otherwise deal in and with, real or personal property, or any interest therein wherever situated.

(e) To sell, convey, mortgage, pledge, lease, exchange, tranfer and otherwise dispose of all or any part of its property and assets.

(f) To lend money and use its credit to assist its employees.

(g) To purchase, take, receive, subscribe for, or otherwise acquire, own, hold, vote, use, employ, sell, mortgage, lend, pledge, or otherwise dispose of, and otherwise use and deal in and with, shares or other interests in, or obligations of, other domestic or foreign corporations, associations, partnerships or individuals, or direct or indirect obligations of the United States or of any other government, state, territory, governmental district or municipality or of any instrumentality thereof.

(h) To make contracts and guarantees and incur liabilities, borrow money at such rates of interest as the corporation may determine, issue its notes, bonds, and other obligations, and secure any of its obligations by mortgage or pledge of all or any of its property, franchises and income.

(i) To lend money for its corporate purposes, invest and reinvest its funds, and take and hold real and personal property as security for the payment of funds so loaned or invested.

(j) To conduct its business, carry on its operations and have offices and exercise the powers granted by this Act, within or without this State.

(k) To elect or appoint officers and agents of the corporation, and define their duties and fix their compensation.

(l) To make and alter by-laws, not inconsistent with its articles of incorporation or with the laws of this State, for the administration and regulation of the affairs of the corporation.

(m) To make donations for the public welfare or for charitable, scientific or educational purposes.

(n) To transact any lawful business which the board of directors shall find will be in aid of governmental policy.

(o) To pay pensions and establish pension plans, pension trusts, profit sharing plans, stock bonus plans, stock option plans and other incentive plans for any or all of its directors, officers and employees.

(p) To be a promoter, partner, member, associate, or manager of any partnership, joint venture, trust or other enterprise.

(q) To have and exercise all powers necessary or convenient to effect its purposes.

§ 5.
Indemnification of Directors and Officers

(a) As used in this section:

(1) "Director" means any person who is or was a director of the corporation and any person who, while a director of the corporation, is or was serving at the request of the corporation as a director, officer, partner, trustee, employee or agent of another foreign or domestic corporation, partnership, joint venture, trust, other enterprise or employee benefit plan.

(2) "Corporation" includes any domestic or foreign predecessor entity of the corporation in a merger, consolidation or other transaction in which the predecessor's existence ceased upon consummation of such transaction.

(3) "Expenses" include attorneys' fees.

(4) "Official capacity" means

    (A) when used with respect to a director, the office of director in the corporation, and

    (B) when used with respect to a person other than a director, as contemplated in subsection (i), the elective or appointive office in the corporation held by the officer or the employment or agency relationship undertaken by the employee or agent in behalf of the corporation.

but in each case does not include service for any other foreign or domestic corporation or any partnership, joint venture, trust, other enterprise, or employee benefit plan.

(5) "Party" includes a person who was, is, or is threatened to be made, a named defendant or respondent in a proceeding.

(6) "Proceeding" means any threatened, pending or completed action, suit or proceeding, whether civil, criminal, administrative or investigative.

(b) A corporation shall have power to indemnify any person made a party to any proceeding by reason of the fact that he is or was a director if

(1) he conducted himself in good faith; and

(2) he reasonably believed

    (A) in the case of conduct in his official capacity with the corporation, that his conduct was in its best interests, and

(B) in all other cases, that his conduct was at least not opposed to its best interests; and

(3) in the case of any criminal proceeding, he had no reasonable cause to believe his conduct was unlawful.

Indemnification may be made against judgments, penalties, fines, settlements and reasonable expenses, actually incurred by the person in connection with the proceeding; except that if the proceeding was by or in the right of the corporation, indemnification may be made only against such reasonable expenses and shall not be made in respect of any proceeding in which the person shall have been adjudged to be liable to the corporation. The termination of any proceeding by judgment, order, settlement, conviction, or upon a plea of nolo contendere or its equivalent, shall not, of itself, be determinative that the person did not meet the requisite standard of conduct set forth in this subsection (b).

(c) A director shall not be indemnified under subsection (b) in respect of any proceeding charging improper personal benefit to him, whether or not involving action in his official capacity, in which he shall have been adjudged to be liable on the basis that personal benefit was improperly received by him.

(d) Unless limited by the articles of incorporation,

(1) a director who has been wholly successful, on the merits or otherwise, in the defense of any proceeding referred to in subsection (b) shall be indemnified against reasonable expenses incurred by him in connection with the proceeding; and

(2) a court of appropriate jurisdiction, upon application of a director and such notice as the court shall require, shall have authority to order indemnification in the following circumstances:

(A) if it determines a director is entitled to reimbursement under clause (1), the court shall order indemnification, in which case the director shall also be entitled to recover the expenses of securing such reimbursement; or

(B) if it determines that the director is fairly and reasonably entitled to indemnification in view of all the relevant circumstances, whether or not he has met the standard of conduct set forth in subsection (b) or has been adjudged liable in the circumstances described in subsection (c), the court may order such indemnification as the court shall deem proper, except that indemnification with respect to any proceeding by or in the right of the corporation or in which liability shall have been adjudged in the circumstances described in subsection (c) shall be limited to expenses.

A court of appropriate jurisdiction may be the same court in which the proceeding involving the director's liability took place.

(e) No indemnification under subsection (b) shall be made by the corporation unless authorized in the specific case after a determination has been made that indemnification of the director is permissible in the circumstances because he has met the standard of conduct set forth in subsection (b). Such determination shall be made:

(1) by the board of directors by a majority vote of a quorum consisting of directors not at the time parties to the proceeding; or

(2) if such a quorum cannot be obtained, then by a majority vote of a committee of the board, duly designated to act in the matter by a majority vote of the full board (in which designation directors who are parties may participate), consisting solely of two or more directors not at the time parties to the proceeding; or

(3) by special legal counsel, selected by the board of directors or a committee thereof by vote as set forth in clauses (1) or (2) of this subsection (e), or, if the requisite quorum of the full board cannot be obtained therefor and such committee cannot be established, by a majority vote of the full board (in which selection directors who are parties may participate); or

(4) by the shareholders.

Authorization of indemnification and determination as to reasonableness of expenses shall be made in the same manner as the determination that indemnification is permissible, except that if the determination that indemnification is permissible is made by special legal counsel, authorization of indemnification and determination as to reasonableness of expenses shall be made in a manner specified in clause (3) in the preceding sentence for the selection of such counsel. Shares held by directors who are parties to the proceeding shall not be voted on the subject matter under this subsection (e).

(f) Reasonable expenses incurred by a director who is a party to a proceeding may be paid or reimbursed by the corporation in advance of the final disposition of such proceeding upon receipt by the corporation of

(1) a written affirmation by the director of his good faith belief that he has met the standard of conduct necessary for indemnification by the corporation as authorized in this section, and

(2) a written undertaking by or on behalf of the director to repay such amount if it shall ultimately be determined that he has not met such standard of conduct, and after a determination that the facts then known to those making the determination would not preclude indemnification under this section. The undertaking required by clause (2) shall be an unlimited general obligation of the director but need not be secured and may be accepted without reference to financial ability to make repayment. Determinations and authorizations of payments under this subsection (f) shall be made in the manner specified in subsection (e).

(g) No provision for the corporation to indemnify or to advance expenses to a director who is made a party to a proceeding, whether contained in the articles of incorporation, the by-laws, a resolution of shareholders or directors, an agreement or otherwise (except as contemplated by subsection (j)), shall be valid unless consistent with this section or, to the extent that indemnity hereunder is limited by the articles of incorporation, consistent therewith. Nothing contained in this section shall limit the corporation's power to pay or reimburse expenses incurred by a director in connection with his appearance as a witness in a proceeding at a time when he has not been made a named defendant or respondent in the proceeding.

(h) For purposes of this section, the corporation shall be deemed to have requested a director to serve an employee benefit plan whenever the performance by him of his duties to the corporation also imposes duties on, or otherwise involves services by, him to the plan or participants or beneficiaries of the plan; excise taxes assessed on a director with respect to an employee benefit plan pursuant to applicable law shall be deemed "fines"; and action taken or omitted by him with respect to an employee benefit plan in the performance of his duties for a purpose reasonably believed by him to be in the interest of the participants and beneficiaries of the plan shall be deemed to be for a purpose which is not opposed to the best interests of the corporation.

(i) Unless limited by the articles of incorporation,

(1) an officer of the corporation shall be indemnified as and to the same extent provided in subsection (d) for a director and shall be entitled to the same extent as a director to seek indemnification pursuant to the provisions of subsection (d);

(2) a corporation shall have the power to indemnify and to advance expenses to an officer, employee or agent of the corporation to the same extent that it may indemnify and advance expenses to directors pursuant to this section; and

(3) a corporation, in addition, shall have the power to indemnify and to advance expenses to an officer, employee or agent who is not a director to such further extent, consistent with law, as may be provided by its articles of incorporation, by-laws, general or specific action of its board of directors, or contract.

(j) A corporation shall have power to purchase and maintain insurance on behalf of any person who is or was a director, officer, employee or agent of the corporation, or who, while a director, officer, employee or agent of the corporation, is or was serving at the request of the corporation as a director, officer, partner, trustee, employee or agent of another foreign or domestic corporation, partnership, joint venture, trust, other enterprise or employee benefit plan, against any liability asserted against him and incurred by him in any such capacity or arising out of his status as such, whether or not the corporation would have the power to indemnify him against such liability under the provisions of this section.

(k) Any indemnification of, or advance of expenses to, a director in accordance with this section, if arising out of a proceeding by or in the right of the corporation, shall be reported in writing to the shareholders with or before the notice of the next shareholders' meeting.

§ 6.
Power of Corporation to Acquire Its Own Shares

A corporation shall have the power to acquire its own shares. All of its own shares acquired by a corporation shall, upon acquisition, constitute authorized but unissued shares, unless the articles of incorporation provide that they shall not be reissued, in which case the authorized shares shall be reduced by the number of shares acquired.

If the number of authorized shares is reduced by an acquisition, the corporation shall, not later than the time it files its next annual report under this Act with the Secretary of State, file a statement of cancellation showing the reduction in the authorized shares. The statement of cancellation shall be executed in duplicate by the corporation by its president or a vice president and by its secretary or an assistant secretary, and verified by one of the officers signing such statement, and shall set forth:

(a) The name of the corporation.

(b) The number of acquired shares cancelled, itemized by classes and series.

(c) The aggregate number of authorized shares, itemized by classes and series, after giving effect to such cancellation.

Duplicate originals of such statement shall be delivered to the Secretary of State. If the Secretary of State finds that such statement conforms to law, he shall, when all fees and franchise taxes have been paid as in this Act prescribed:

(1) Endorse on each of such duplicate originals the word "Filed," and the month, day, and year of the filing thereof.

(2) File one of such duplicate originals in his office.

(3) Return the other duplicate original to the corporation or its representative.

§ 7.
Defense of Ultra Vires

No act of a corporation and no conveyance or transfer of real or personal property to or by a corporation shall be invalid by reason of the fact that the corporation was without capacity or power to do such act or to make or receive such conveyance or transfer, but such lack of capacity or power may be asserted:

(a) In a proceeding by a shareholder against the corporation to enjoin the doing of any act or the transfer of real or personal property by or to the corporation. If the unauthorized act or transfer sought to be enjoined is being, or is to be, performed or made pursuant to a contract to which the corporation is a party, the court may, if all of the parties to the contract are parties to the proceeding and if it deems the same to be equitable, set aside and enjoin the performance of such contract, and in so doing may allow to the corporation or to the other parties to the contract, as the case may be, compensation for the loss or damage sustained by either of them which may result from the action of the court in setting aside and enjoining the performance of such contract, but anticipated profits to be derived from the performance of the contract shall not be awarded by the court as a loss or damage sustained.

(b) In a proceeding by the corporation, whether acting directly or through a receiver, trustee, or other legal representative, or through shareholders in a representative suit, against the incumbent or former officers or directors of the corporation.

(c) In a proceeding by the Attorney General, as provided in this Act, to dissolve the corporation, or in a proceeding by the Attorney General to enjoin the corporation from the transaction of unauthorized business.

§ 8.
Corporate Name

The corporate name:

(a) Shall contain the word "corporation," "company," "incorporated" or "limited," or shall contain an abbreviation of one of such words.

(b) Shall not contain any word or phrase which indicates or implies that it is organized for any purpose other than one or more of the purposes contained in its articles of incorporation.

(C) Shall not be the same as, or deceptively similar to, the name of any domestic corporation existing under the laws of this State or any foreign corporation authorized to transact business in this State, or a name the exclusive right to which is, at the time, reserved in the manner provided in this Act, or the name of a corporation which has in effect a registration of its corporate name as provided in this Act, except that this provision shall not apply if the applicant files with the Secretary of State either of the following: (1) the written consent of such other corporation or holder of a reserved or registered name to use the same or deceptively similar name and one or more words are added to make such name distinguishable from such other name, or (2) a certified copy of a final decree of a court of competent jurisdiction establishing the prior right of the applicant to the use of such name in this State.

A corporation with which another corporation, domestic or foreign, is merged, or which is formed by the reorganization or consolidation of one or more domestic or foreign corporations or upon a sale, lease or other disposition to or exchange with, a domestic corporation of all or substantially all the assets of another corporation, domestic or foreign, including its name, may have the same name as that used in this State by any of such corporations if such other corporation was organized under the laws of, or is authorized to transact business in, this State.

§ 9.
Reserved Name

The exclusive right to the use of a corporate name may be reserved by:

(a) Any person intending to organize a corporation under this Act.

(b) Any domestic corporation intending to change its name.

(c) Any foreign corporation intending to make application for a certificate of authority to transact business in this State.

(d) Any foreign corporation authorized to transact business in this State and intending to change its name.

(e) Any person intending to organize a foreign corporation and intending to have such corporation make application for a certificate of authority to transact business in this State.

The reservation shall be made by filing with the Secretary of State an application to reserve a specified corporate name, executed by the applicant. If the Secretary of State finds that the name is available for corporate use, he shall reserve the same for the exclusive use of the applicant for a period of one hundred and twenty days.

The right to the exclusive use of a specified corporate name so reserved may be transferred to any other person or corporation by filing in the office of the Secretary of State a notice of such transfer, executed by the applicant for whom the name was reserved, and specifying the name and address of the transferee.

§ 10.
Registered Name

Any corporation organized and existing under the laws of any state or territory of the United States may register its corporate name under this Act, provided its corporate name is not the same as, or deceptively similar to, the name of any domestic corporation existing under the laws of this State, or the name of any foreign corporation authorized to transact business in this State, or any corporate name reserved or registered under this Act.

Such registration shall be made by:

(a) Filing with the Secretary of State (1) an application for registration executed by the corporation by an officer thereof, setting forth the name of the corporation, the state or territory under the laws of which it is incorporated, the date of its incorporation, a statement that it is carrying on or doing business, and a brief statement of the business in which it is engaged, and (2) a certificate setting forth that such corporation is in good standing under the laws of the state or territory wherein it is organized, executed by the Secretary of State of such state or territory or by such other official as may have custody of the records pertaining to corporations, and

(b) Paying to the Secretary of State a registration fee in the amount of . . . . for each month, or fraction thereof, between the date of filing such application and December 31st of the calendar year in which such application is filed.

Such registration shall be effective until the close of the calendar year in which the application for registration is filed.

§ 11.
Renewal of Registered Name

A corporation which has in effect a registration of its corporate name, may renew such registration from year to year by annually filing an application for renewal setting forth the facts required to be set forth in an original application for registration and a certificate of good standing as required for the original registration and by paying a fee of . . . .
A renewal application may be filed between the first day of October and the thirty-first day of December in each year, and shall extend the registration for the following calendar year.

§ 12.
Registered Office and Registered Agent

Each corporation shall have and continuously maintain in this State:

(a) A registered office which may be, but need not be, the same as its place of business.

(b) A registered agent, which agent may be either an individual resident in this State whose business office is identical with such registered office, or a domestic corporation, or a foreign corporation authorized to transact business in this State, having a business office identical with such registered office.

§ 13.
Change of Registered Office or Registered Agent

A corporation may change its registered office or change its registered agent, or both, upon filing in the office of the Secretary of State a statement setting forth:

(a) The name of the corporation.

(b) The address of its then registered office.

(c) If the address of its registered office is to be changed, the address to which the registered office is to be changed.

(d) The name of its then registered agent.

(e) If its registered agent is to be changed, the name of its successor registered agent.

(f) That the address of its registered office and the address of the business office of its registered agent, as changed, will be identical.

(g) That such change was authorized by resolution duly adopted by its board of directors.

Such statement shall be executed by the corporation by its president, or a vice president, and verified by him, and delivered to the Secretary of State. If the Secretary of State finds that such statement conforms to the provisions of this Act, he shall file such statement in his office, and upon such filing the change of address of the registered office, or the appointment of a new registered agent, or both, as the case may be, shall become effective.

Any registered agent of a corporation may resign as such agent upon filing a written notice thereof, executed in duplicate, with the Secretary of State, who shall forthwith mail a copy thereof to the corporation at its registered office. The appointment of such agent shall terminate upon the expiration of thirty days after receipt of such notice by the Secretary of State.

If a registered agent changes his or its business address to another place within the same . . . . ,* he or it may change such address and the address of the registered office of any corporation of which he or it is registered agent by filing a statement as required above except that it need be signed only by the registered agent and need not be responsive to (e) or (g) and must recite that a copy of the statement has been mailed to the corporation.

§ 14.
Service of Process on Corporation

The registered agent so appointed by a corporation shall be an agent of such corporation upon whom any process, notice or demand required or permitted by law to be served upon the corporation may be served.

Whenever a corporation shall fail to appoint or maintain a registered agent in this State, or whenever its registered agent cannot with reasonable diligence be found at the registered office, then the Secretary of State shall be an agent of such corporation upon whom any such process, notice, or demand may be served. Service on the Secretary of State of any such process, notice, or demand shall be made by delivering to and leaving with him, or with any clerk having charge of the corporation department of his office, duplicate copies of such process, notice or demand. In the event any such process, notice or demand is served on the Secretary of State, he shall immediately cause one of the copies thereof to be forwarded by registered mail, addressed to the corporation at its registered office. Any service so had on the Secretary of State shall be returnable in not less than thirty days.

The Secretary of State shall keep a record of all processes, notices and demands served upon him under this section, and shall record therein the time of such service and his action with reference thereto.

Nothing herein contained shall limit or affect the right to serve any process, notice or demand required or permitted by law to be served upon a corporation in any other manner now or hereafter permitted by law.

§ 15.
Authorized Shares

Each corporation shall have power to create and issue the number of shares stated in its articles of incorporation. Such shares may be divided into one or more classes with such designations, preferences, limitations, and relative rights as

---

* Supply designation of jurisdiction, such as county, etc., in accordance with local practice.

shall be stated in the articles of incorporation. The articles of incorporation may limit or deny the voting rights of or provide special voting rights for the shares of any class to the extent not inconsistent with the provisions of this Act.

Without limiting the authority herein contained, a corporation, when so provided in its articles of incorporation, may issue shares of preferred or special classes:

(a) Subject to the right of the corporation to redeem any of such shares at the price fixed by the articles of incorporation for the redemption thereof.

(b) Entitling the holders thereof to cumulative, noncumulative or partially cumulative dividends.

(c) Having preference over any other class or classes of shares as to the payment of dividends.

(d) Having preference in the assets of the corporation over any other class or classes of shares upon the voluntary or involuntary liquidation of the corporation.

(e) Convertible into shares of any other class or into shares of any series of the same or any other class, except a class having prior or superior rights and preferences as to dividends or distribution of assets upon liquidation.

§ 16.
Issuance of Shares of Preferred or Special Classes in Series

If the articles of incorporation so provide, the shares of any preferred or special class may be divided into and issued in series. If the shares of any such class are to be issued in series, then each series shall be so designated as to distinguish the shares thereof from the shares of all other series and classes. Any or all of the series of any such class and the variations in the relative rights and preferences as between different series may be fixed and determined by the articles of incorporation, but all shares of the same class shall be identical except as to the following relative rights and preferences, as to which there may be variations between different series:

(a) The rate of dividend.

(b) Whether shares may be redeemed and, if so, the redemption price and the terms and conditions of redemption.

(c) The amount payable upon shares in the event of voluntary and involuntary liquidation.

(d) Sinking fund provisions, if any, for the redemption or purchase of shares.

(e) The terms and conditions, if any, on which shares may be converted.

(f) Voting rights, if any.

If the articles of incorporation shall expressly vest authority in the board of directors, then, to the extent that the articles of incorporation shall not have established series and fixed and determined the variations in the relative rights and preferences as between series, the board of directors shall have authority to divide any or all of such classes into series and, within the limitations set forth in this section and in the articles of incorporation, fix and determine the relative rights and preferences of the shares of any series so established.

In order for the board of directors to establish a series, where authority so to do is contained in the articles of incorporation, the board of directors shall adopt a resolution setting forth the designation of the series and fixing and determining the relative rights and preferences thereof, or so much thereof as shall not be fixed and determined by the articles of incorporation.

Prior to the issue of any shares of a series established by resolution adopted by the board of directors, the corporation shall file in the office of the Secretary of State a statement setting forth:

(1) The name of the corporation.

(2) A copy of the resolution establishing and designating the series, and fixing and determining the relative rights and preferences thereof.

(3) The date of adoption of such resolution.

(4) That such resolution was duly adopted by the board of directors.

Such statement shall be executed in duplicate by the corporation by its president or a vice president and by its secretary or an assistant secretary, and verified by one of the officers signing such statement, and shall be delivered to the Secretary of State. If the Secretary of State finds that such statement conforms to law, he shall, when all franchise taxes and fees have been paid as in this Act prescribed:

(A) Endorse on each of such duplicate originals the word "Filed," and the month, day, and year of the filing thereof.

(B) File one of such duplicate originals in his office.

(C) Return the other duplicate original to the corporation or its representative.

Upon the filing of such statement by the Secretary of State, the resolution establishing and designating the series and fixing and determining the relative rights and preferences thereof shall become effective and shall constitute an amendment of the articles of incorporation.

§ 17.
Subscriptions for Shares

A subscription for shares of a corporation to be organized shall be irrevocable for a period of six months, unless otherwise provided by the terms of the subscription agreement or unless all of the subscribers consent to the revocation of such subscription.

Unless otherwise provided in the subscription agreement, subscriptions for shares, whether made before or after the organization of a corporation, shall be paid in full at such time, or in such installments and at such times, as shall be determined by the board of directors. Any call made by the board of directors for payment on subscriptions shall be uniform as to all shares of the same class or as to all shares of the same series, as the case may be. In case of default in the payment of any installment or call when such payment is due, the corporation may proceed to collect the amount due in the same manner as any debt due the corporation. The by-laws may prescribe other penalties for failure to pay install-ments or calls that may become due, but no penalty working a forfeiture of a subscription, or of the amounts paid thereon, shall be declared as against any subscriber unless the amount due thereon shall remain unpaid for a period of twenty days after written demand has been made therefor. If mailed, such written demand shall be deemed to be made when deposited in the United States mail in a sealed envelope addressed to the subscriber at his last post-office address known to the corporation, with postage thereon prepaid. In the event of the sale of any shares by reason of any forfeiture, the excess of proceeds realized over the amount due and unpaid on such shares shall be paid to the delinquent subscriber or to his legal representative.

§ 18.
Issuance of Shares

Subject to any restrictions in the articles of incorporation:

(a) Shares may be issued for such consideration as shall be authorized by the board of directors establishing a price (in money or other consideration) or a minimum price or gen-eral formula or method by which the price will be deter-mined; and

(b) Upon authorization by the board of directors, the corpo-ration may issue its own shares in exchange for or in conver-sion of its outstanding shares, or distribute its own shares, pro rata to its shareholders or the shareholders of one or more classes or series, to effectuate stock dividends or splits, and any such transaction shall not require consideration; provided, that no such issuance of shares of any class or series shall be made to the holders of shares of any other class or series unless it is either expressly provided for in the articles of incorporation, or is authorized by an affirmative vote or the written consent of the holders of at least a major-ity of the outstanding shares of the class or series in which the distribution is to be made.

§ 19.
Payment for Shares

The consideration for the issuance of shares may be paid, in whole or in part, in money, in other property, tangible or intangible, or in labor or services actually performed for the corporation. When payment of the consideration for which shares are to be issued shall have been received by the corpo-ration, such shares shall be nonassessable.

Neither promissory notes nor future services shall consti-tute payment or part payment for the issuance of shares of a corporation.

In the absence of fraud in the transaction, the judgment of the board of directors or the shareholders, as the case may be, as to the value of the consideration received for shares shall be conclusive.

§ 20.
Stock Rights and Options

Subject to any provisions in respect thereof set forth in its articles of incorporation, a corporation may create and issue, whether or not in connection with the issuance and sale of any of its shares or other securities, rights or options entitling the holders thereof to purchase from the corporation shares of any class or classes. Such rights or options shall be evi-denced in such manner as the board of directors shall ap-prove and, subject to the provisions of the articles of incor-poration, shall set forth the terms upon which, the time or times within which and the price or prices at which such shares may be purchased from the corporation upon the exercise of any such right or option. If such rights or options are to be issued to directors, officers or employees as such of the corporation or of any subsidiary thereof, and not to the shareholders generally, their issuance shall be approved by the affirmative vote of the holders of a majority of the shares entitled to vote thereon or shall be authorized by and consis-tent with a plan approved or ratified by such a vote of share-holders. In the absence of fraud in the transaction, the judg-ment of the board of directors as to the adequacy of the consideration received for such rights or options shall be conclusive.

§ 21.
Determination of Amount of Stated Capital

[Repealed in 1979.]

§ 22.
Expenses of Organization, Reorganization and Financing

The reasonable charges and expenses of organization or re-organization of a corporation, and the reasonable expenses of and compensation for the sale or underwriting of its shares, may be paid or allowed by such corporation out of the consideration received by it in payment for its shares without thereby rendering such shares assessable.

§ 23.
Shares Represented by Certificates and Uncertified Shares

The shares of a corporation shall be represented by certifi-cates or shall be uncertificated shares. Certificates shall be signed by the chairman or vice-chairman of the board of directors or the president or a vice president and by the treasurer or an assistant treasurer or the secretary or an assistant secretary of the corporation, and may be sealed with the seal of the corporation or a facsimile thereof. Any of or all the signatures upon a certificate may be a facsimile. In case any officer, transfer agent or registrar who has signed or whose facsimile signature has been placed upon such certifi-cate shall have ceased to be such officer, transfer agent or registrar before such certificate is issued, it may be issued by the corporation with the same effect as if he were such officer, transfer agent or registrar at the date of its issue.

Every certificate representing shares issued by a corporation which is authorized to issue shares of more than one class shall set forth upon the face or back of the certificate, or shall state that the corporation will furnish to any shareholder upon request and without charge, a full statement of the designations, preferences, limitations, and relative rights of the shares of each class authorized to be issued, and if the corporation is authorized to issue any preferred or special class in series, the variations in the relative rights and preferences between the shares of each such series so far as the same have been fixed and determined and the authority of the board of directors to fix and determine the relative rights and preferences of subsequent series.

Each certificate representing shares shall state upon the face thereof:

(a) That the corporation is organized under the laws of this State.

(b) The name of the person to whom issued.

(c) The number and class of shares, and the designation of the series, if any, which such certificate represents.

(d) The par value of each share represented by such certificate, or a statement that the shares are without par value.

No certificate shall be issued for any share until such share is fully paid.

Unless otherwise provided by the articles of incorporation or by-laws, the board of directors of a corporation may provide by resolution that some or all of any or all classes and series of its shares shall be uncertificated shares, provided that such resolution shall not apply to shares represented by a certificate until such certificate is surrendered to the corporation. Within a reasonable time after the issuance or transfer of uncertificated shares, the corporation shall send to the registered owner thereof a written notice containing the information required to be set forth or stated on certificates pursuant to the second and third paragraphs of this section. Except as otherwise expressly provided by law, the rights and obligations of the holders of uncertificated shares and the rights and obligations of the holders of certificates representing shares of the same class and series shall be identical.

§ 24.
Fractional Shares

A corporation may (1) issue fractions of a share, either represented by a certificate or uncertificated, (2) arrange for the disposition of fractional interests by those entitled thereto, (3) pay in money the fair value of fractions of a share as of a time when those entitled to receive such fractions are determined, or (4) issue scrip in registered or bearer form which shall entitle the holder to receive a certificate for a full share or an uncertificated full share upon the surrender of such scrip aggregating a full share. A certificate for a fractional share or an uncertificated fractional share shall, but scrip shall not unless otherwise provided therein, entitle the holder to exercise voting rights, to receive dividends thereon, and to participate in any of the assets of the corporation in the event of liquidation. The board of directors may cause scrip to be issued subject to the condition that it shall become void if not exchanged for certificates representing full shares or uncertificated full shares before a specified date, or subject to the condition that the shares for which scrip is exchangeable may be sold by the corporation and the proceeds thereof distributed to the holders of scrip, or subject to any other conditions which the board of directors may deem advisable.

§ 25.
Liability of Subscribers and Shareholders

A holder of or subscriber to shares of a corporation shall be under no obligation to the corporation or its creditors with respect to such shares other than the obligation to pay to the corporation the full consideration for which such shares were issued or to be issued.

Any person becoming an assignee or transferee of shares or of a subscription for shares in good faith and without knowledge or notice that the full consideration therefor has not been paid shall not be personally liable to the corporation or its creditors for any unpaid portion of such consideration.

An executor, administrator, conservator, guardian, trustee, assignee for the benefit of creditors, or receiver shall not be personally liable to the corporation as a holder of or subscriber to shares of a corporation but the estate and funds in his hands shall be so liable.

No pledgee or other holder of shares as collateral security shall be personally liable as a shareholder.

§ 26.
Shareholders' Preemptive Rights

The shareholders of a corporation shall have no preemptive right to acquire unissued shares of the corporation, or securities of the corporation convertible into or carrying a right to subscribe to or acquire shares, except to the extent, if any, that such right is provided in the articles of incorporation.

§ 26A.
Shareholders' Preemptive Rights
[Alternative]

Except to the extent limited or denied by this section or by the articles of incorporation, shareholders shall have a preemptive right to acquire unissued shares or securities convertible into such shares or carrying a right to subscribe to or acquire shares.

Unless otherwise provided in the articles of incorporation,

(a) No preemptive right shall exist

(1) to acquire any shares issued to directors, officers

or employees pursuant to approval by the affirmative vote of the holders of a majority of the shares entitled to vote thereon or when authorized by and consistent with a plan theretofore approved by such a vote of shareholders; or

(2) to acquire any shares sold otherwise than for money.

(b) Holders of shares of any class that is preferred or limited as to dividends or assets shall not be entitled to any preemptive right.

(c) Holders of shares of common stock shall not be entitled to any preemptive right to shares of any class that is preferred or limited as to dividends or assets or to any obligations, unless convertible into shares of common stock or carrying a right to subscribe to or acquire shares of common stock.

(d) Holders of common stock without voting power shall have no preemptive right to shares of common stock with voting power.

(e) The preemptive right shall be only an opportunity to acquire shares or other securities under such terms and conditions as the board of directors may fix for the purpose of providing a fair and reasonable opportunity for the exercise of such right.

§ 27.
By-Laws

The initial by-laws of a corporation shall be adopted by its board of directors. The power to alter, amend or repeal the by-laws or adopt new by-laws, subject to repeal or change by action of the shareholders, shall be vested in the board of directors unless reserved to the shareholders by the articles of incorporation. The by-laws may contain any provisions for the regulation and management of the affairs of the corporation not inconsistent with law or the articles of incorporation.

§ 27A.
By-Laws and Other Powers in Emergency [Optional]

The board of directors of any corporation may adopt emergency by-laws, subject to repeal or change by action of the shareholders, which shall, notwithstanding any different provision elsewhere in this Act or in the articles of incorporation or by-laws, be operative during any emergency in the conduct of the business of the corporation resulting from an attack on the United States or any nuclear or atomic disaster. The emergency by-laws may make any provision that may be practical and necessary for the circumstances of the emergency, including provisions that:

(a) A meeting of the board of directors may be called by any officer or director in such manner and under such conditions as shall be prescribed in the emergency by-laws;

(b) The director or directors in attendance at the meeting,

or any greater number fixed by the emergency by-laws, shall constitute a quorum; and

(c) The officers or other persons designated on a list approved by the board of directors before the emergency, all in such order of priority and subject to such conditions, and for such period of time (not longer than reasonably necessary after the termination of the emergency) as may be provided in the emergency by-laws or in the resolution approving the list shall, to the extent required to provide a quorum at any meeting of the board of directors, be deemed directors for such meeting.

The board of directors, either before or during any such emergency, may provide, and from time to time modify, lines of succession in the event that during such an emergency any or all officers or agents of the corporation shall for any reason be rendered incapable of discharging their duties.

The board of directors, either before or during any such emergency, may, effective in the emergency, change the head office or designate several alternative head offices or regional offices, or authorize the officers so to do.

To the extent not inconsistent with any emergency by-laws so adopted, the by-laws of the corporation shall remain in effect during any such emergency and upon its termination the emergency by-laws shall cease to be operative.

Unless otherwise provided in emergency by-laws, notice of any meeting of the board of directors during any such emergency may be given only to such of the directors as it may be feasible to reach at the time and by such means as may be feasible at the time, including publication or radio.

To the extent required to constitute a quorum at any meeting of the board of directors during any such emergency, the officers of the corporation who are present shall, unless otherwise provided in emergency by-laws, be deemed, in order of rank and within the same rank in order of seniority, directors for such meeting.

No officer, director or employee acting in accordance with any emergency by-laws shall be liable except for willful misconduct. No officer, director or employee shall be liable for any action taken by him in good faith in such an emergency in furtherance of the ordinary business affairs of the corporation even though not authorized by the by-laws then in effect.

§ 28.
Meetings of Shareholders

Meetings of shareholders may be held at such place within or without this State as may be stated in or fixed in accordance with the by-laws. If no other place is stated or so fixed, meetings shall be held at the registered office of the corporation.

An annual meeting of the shareholders shall be held at such time as may be stated in or fixed in accordance with the by-laws. If the annual meeting is not held within any thirteen-month period the Court of . . . . may, on the application of any shareholder, summarily order a meeting to be held.

Special meetings of the shareholders may be called by the board of directors, the holders of not less than one-tenth of all the shares entitled to vote at the meeting, or such other persons as may be authorized in the articles of incorporation or the by-laws.

§ 29.
Notice of Shareholders' Meetings

Written notice stating the place, day, and hour of the meeting and, in case of a special meeting, the purpose or purposes for which the meeeting is called, shall be delivered not less than ten nor more than fifty days before the date of the meeting, either personally or by mail, by or at the direction of the president, the secretary, or the officer or persons calling the meeting, to each shareholder of record entitled to vote at such meeting. If mailed, such notice shall be deemed to be delivered when deposited in the United States mail addressed to the shareholder at his address as it appears on the stock transfer books of the corporation, with postage thereon prepaid.

§ 30.
Closing of Transfer Books and Fixing Record Date

For the purpose of determining shareholders entitled to notice of or to vote at any meeting of shareholders or any adjournment thereof, or entitled to receive payment of any dividend, or in order to make a determination of shareholders for any other proper purpose, the board of directors of a corporation may provide that the stock transfer books shall be closed for a stated period but not to exceed, in any case, fifty days. If the stock transfer books shall be closed for the purpose of determining shareholders entitled to notice of or to vote at a meeting of shareholders, such books shall be closed for at least ten days immediately preceding such meeting. In lieu of closing the stock transfer books, the by-laws, or in the absence of an applicable by-law the board of directors, may fix in advance a date as the record date for any such determination of shareholders, such date in any case to be not more than fifty days and, in case of a meeting of shareholders, not less than ten days prior to the date on which the particular action, requiring such determination of shareholders, is to be taken. If the stock transfer books are not closed and no record date is fixed for the determination of shareholders entitled to notice of or to vote at a meeting of shareholders, or shareholders entitled to receive payment of a dividend, the date on which notice of the meeting is mailed or the date on which the resolution of the board of directors declaring such dividend is adopted, as the case may be, shall be the record date for such determination of shareholders. When a determination of shareholders entitled to vote at any

meeting of shareholders has been made as provided in this section, such determination shall apply to any adjournment thereof.

§ 31.
Voting Record

The officer or agent having charge of the stock transfer books for shares of a corporation shall make a complete record of the shareholders entitled to vote at such meeting or any adjournment thereof, arranged in alphabetical order, with the address of and the number of shares held by each. Such record shall be produced and kept open at the time and place of the meeting and shall be subject to the inspection of any shareholder during the whole time of the meeting for the purposes thereof.

Failure to comply with the requirements of this section shall not affect the validity of any action taken at such meeting.

An officer or agent having charge of the stock transfer books who shall fail to prepare the record of shareholders, or produce and keep it open for inspection at the meeting, as provided in this section, shall be liable to any shareholder suffering damage on account of such failure, to the extent of such damage.

§ 32.
Quorum of Shareholders

Unless otherwise provided in the articles of incorporation, a majority of the shares entitled to vote, represented in person or by proxy, shall constitute a quorum at a meeting of share-holders, but in no event shall a quorum consist of less than one-third of the shares entitled to vote at the meeting. If a quorum is present, the affirmative vote of the majority of the shares represented at the meeting and entitled to vote on the subject matter shall be the act of the shareholders, unless the vote of a greater number or voting by classes is required by this Act or the articles of incorporation or by-laws.

§ 33.
Voting of Shares

Each outstanding share, regardless of class, shall be entitled to one vote on each matter submitted to a vote at a meeting of shareholders, except as may be otherwise provided in the articles of incorporation. If the articles of incorporation provide for more or less than one vote for any share, on any matter, every reference in this Act to a majority or other proportion of shares shall refer to such a majority or other proportion of votes entitled to be cast.

Shares held by another corporation if a majority of the shares entitled to vote for the election of directors of such other corporation is held by the corporation, shall not be voted at any meeting or counted in determining the total number of outstanding shares at any given time.

A shareholder may vote either in person or by proxy executed in writing by the shareholder or by his duly authorized attorney-in-fact. No proxy shall be valid after eleven months from the date of its execution, unless otherwise provided in the proxy.

[Either of the following prefatory phrases may be inserted here: "The articles of incorporation may provide that" or "Unless the articles of incorporation otherwise provide"] at each election for directors every shareholder entitled to vote at such election shall have the right to vote, in person or by proxy, the number of shares owned by him for as many persons as there are directors to be elected and for whose election he has a right to vote, or to cumulate his votes by giving one candidate as many votes as the number of such directors multiplied by the number of his shares shall equal, or by distributing such votes on the same principle among any number of such candidates.

Shares standing in the name of another corporation, domestic or foreign, may be voted by such officer, agent or proxy as the by-laws of such other corporation may prescribe, or, in the absence of such provision, as the board of directors of such other corporation may determine.

Shares held by an administrator, executor, guardian or conservator may be voted by him, either in person or by proxy, without a transfer of such shares into his name. Shares standing in the name of a trustee may be voted by him, either in person or by proxy, but no trustee shall be entitled to vote shares held by him without a transfer of such shares into his name.

Shares standing in the name of a receiver may be voted by such receiver, and shares held by or under the control of a receiver may be voted by such receiver without the transfer thereof into his name if authority so to do be contained in an appropriate order of the court by which such receiver was appointed.

A shareholder whose shares are pledged shall be entitled to vote such shares until the shares have been transferred into the name of the pledgee, and thereafter the pledgee shall be entitled to vote the shares so transferred.

On and after the date on which written notice of redemption of redeemable shares has been mailed to the holders thereof and a sum sufficient to redeem such shares has been deposited with a bank or trust company with irrevocable instruction and authority to pay the redemption price to the holders thereof upon surrender of certificates therefor, such shares shall not be entitled to vote on any matter and shall not be deemed to be outstanding shares.

§ 34.
Voting Trusts and Agreements Among Shareholders

Any number of shareholders of a corporation may create a voting trust for the purpose of conferring upon a trustee or trustees the right to vote or otherwise represent their shares, for a period of not to exceed ten years, by entering into a written voting trust agreement specifying the terms and conditions of the voting trust, by depositing a counterpart of the agreement with the corporation at its registered office, and by transferring their shares to such trustee or trustees for the purposes of the agreement. Such trustee or trustees shall keep a record of the holders of voting trust certificates evidencing a beneficial interest in the voting trust, giving the names and addresses of all such holders and the number and class of the shares in respect of which the voting trust certificates held by each are issued, and shall deposit a copy of such record with the corporation at its registered office. The counterpart of the voting trust agreement and the copy of such record so deposited with the corporation shall be subject to the same right of examination by a shareholder of the corporation, in person or by agent or attorney, as are the books and records of the corporation, and such counterpart and such copy of such record shall be subject to examination by any holder of record of voting trust certificates, either in person or by agent or attorney, at any reasonable time for any proper purpose.

Agreements among shareholders regarding the voting of their shares shall be valid and enforceable in accordance with their terms. Such agreements shall not be subject to the provisions of this section regarding voting trusts.

§ 35.
Board of Directors

All corporate powers shall be exercised by or under authority of, and the business and affairs of a corporation shall be managed under the direction of, a board of directors except as may be otherwise provided in this Act or the articles of incorporation. If any such provision is made in the articles of incorporation, the powers and duties conferred or imposed upon the board of directors by this Act shall be exercised or performed to such extent and by such person or persons as shall be provided in the articles of incorporation. Directors need not be residents of this State or shareholders of the corporation unless the articles of incorporation or by-laws so require. The articles of incorporation or by-laws may prescribe other qualifications for directors. The board of directors shall have authority to fix the compensation of directors unless otherwise provided in the articles of incorporation.

A director shall perform his duties as a director, including his duties as a member of any committee of the board upon which he may serve, in good faith, in a manner he reasonably believes to be in the best interests of the corporation, and with such care as an ordinarily prudent person in a like position would use under similar circumstances. In performing his duties, a director shall be entitled to rely on information, opinions, reports or statements, including financial statements and other financial data, in each case prepared or presented by:

(a) one or more officers or employees of the corporation

whom the director reasonably believes to be reliable and competent in the matters presented;

(b) counsel, public accountants or other persons as to matters which the director reasonably believes to be within such person's professional or expert competence; or

(c) a committee of the board upon which he does not serve, duly designated in accordance with a provision of the articles of incorporation or the by-laws, as to matters within its designated authority, which committee the director reasonably believes to merit confidence;

but he shall not be considered to be acting in good faith if he has knowledge concerning the matter in question that would cause such reliance to be unwarranted. A person who so performs his duties shall have no liability by reason of being or having been a director of the corporation.

A director of a corporation who is present at a meeting of its board of directors at which action on any corporate matter is taken shall be presumed to have assented to the action taken unless his dissent shall be entered in the minutes of the meeting or unless he shall file his written dissent to such action with the secretary of the meeting before the adjournment thereof or shall forward such dissent by registered mail to the secretary of the corporation immediately after the adjournment of the meeting. Such right to dissent shall not apply to a director who voted in favor of such action.

§ 36.
Number and Election of Directors

The board of directors of a corporation shall consist of one or more members. The number of directors shall be fixed by, or in the manner provided in, the articles of incorporation or the by-laws, except as to the number constituting the initial board of directors, which number shall be fixed by the articles of incorporation. The number of directors may be increased or decreased from time to time by amendment to, or in the manner provided in, the articles of incorporation or the by-laws, but no decrease shall have the effect of shortening the term of any incumbent director. In the absence of a by-law providing for the number of directors, the number shall be the same as that provided for in the articles of incorporation. The names and addresses of the members of the first board of directors shall be stated in the articles of incorporation. Such persons shall hold office until the first annual meeting of shareholders, and until their successors shall have been elected and qualified. At the first annual meeting of shareholders and at each annual meeting thereafter the shareholders shall elect directors to hold office until the next succeeding annual meeting, except in case of the classification of directors as permitted by this Act. Each director shall hold office for the term for which he is elected and until his successor shall have been elected and qualified.

§ 37.
Classification of Directors

When the board of directors shall consist of nine or more members, in lieu of electing the whole number of directors annually, the articles of incorporation may provide that the directors be divided into either two or three classes, each class to be as nearly equal in number as possible, the term of office of directors of the first class to expire at the first annual meeting of shareholders after their election, that of the second class to expire at the second annual meeting after their election, and that of the third class, if any, to expire at the third annual meeting after their election. At each annual meeting after such classification the number of directors equal to the number of the class whose term expires at the time of such meeting shall be elected to hold office until the second succeeding annual meeting, if there be two classes, or until the third succeeding annual meeting, if there be three classes. No classification of directors shall be effective prior to the first annual meeting of shareholders.

§ 38.
Vacancies

Any vacancy occurring in the board of directors may be filled by the affirmative vote of a majority of the remaining directors though less than a quorum of the board of directors. A director elected to fill a vacancy shall be elected for the unexpired term of his predecessor in office. Any directorship to be filled by reason of an increase in the number of directors may be filled by the board of directors for a term of office continuing only until the next election of directors by the shareholders.

§ 39.
Removal of Directors

At a meeting of shareholders called expressly for that purpose, directors may be removed in the manner provided in this section. Any director or the entire board of directors may be removed, with or without cause, by a vote of the holders of a majority of the shares then entitled to vote at an election of directors.

In the case of a corporation having cumulative voting, if less than the entire board is to be removed, no one of the directors may be removed if the votes cast against his removal would be sufficient to elect him if then cumulatively voted at an election of the entire board of directors, or, if there be classes of directors, at an election of the class of directors of which he is a part.

Whenever the holders of the shares of any class are entitled to elect one or more directors by the provisions of the articles of incorporation, the provisions of this section shall apply, in respect to the removal of a director or directors so elected, to the vote of the holders of the outstanding shares of that class and not to the vote of the outstanding shares as a whole.

§ 40.
Quorum of Directors

A majority of the number of directors fixed by or in the manner provided in the by-laws or in the absence of a by-law fixing or providing for the number of directors, then of the number stated in the articles of incorporation, shall constitute a quorum for the transaction of business unless a greater number is required by the articles of incorporation or the by-laws. The act of the majority of the directors present at a meeting at which a quorum is present shall be the act of the board of directors, unless the act of a greater number is required by the articles of incorporation or the by-laws.

§ 41.
Director Conflicts of Interest

No contract or other transaction between a corporation and one or more of its directors or any other corporation, firm, association or entity in which one or more of its directors are directors or officers or are financially interested, shall be either void or voidable because of such relationship or interest or because such director or directors are present at the meeting of the board of directors or a committee thereof which authorizes, approves or ratifies such contract or transaction or because his or their votes are counted for such purpose, if:

(a) the fact of such relationship or interest is disclosed or known to the board of directors or committee which authorizes, approves or ratifies the contract or transaction by a vote or consent sufficient for the purpose without counting the votes or consents of such interested directors; or

(b) the fact of such relationship or interest is disclosed or known to the shareholders entitled to vote and they authorize, approve or ratify such contract or transaction by vote or written consent; or

(c) the contract or transaction is fair and reasonable to the corporation.

Common or interested directors may be counted in determining the presence of a quorum at a meeting of the board of directors or a committee thereof which authorizes, approves or ratifies such contract or transaction.

§ 42.
Executive and Other Committees

If the articles of incorporation or the by-laws so provide, the board of directors, by resolution adopted by a majority of the full board of directors, may designate from among its members an executive committee and one or more other committees each of which, to the extent provided in such resolution or in the articles of incorporation or the by-laws of the corporation, shall have and may exercise all the authority of the board of directors, except that no such committee shall have authority to (1) authorize distributions, (2) approve or recommend to shareholders actions or proposals required

by this Act to be approved by shareholders, (3) designate candidates for the office of director, for purposes of proxy solicitation or otherwise, or fill vacancies on the board of directors or any committee thereof, (4) amend the by-laws, (5) approve a plan of merger not requiring shareholder approval, (6) authorize or approve the reacquisition of shares unless pursuant to a general formula or method specified by the board of directors, or (7) authorize or approve the issuance or sale of, or any contract to issue or sell, shares or designate the terms of a series of a class of shares, provided that the board of directors, having acted regarding general authorization for the issuance or sale of shares, or any contract therefor, and, in the case of a series, the designation thereof, may, pursuant to a general formula or method specified by the board by resolution or by adoption of a stock option or other plan, authorize a committee to fix the terms of any contract for the sale of the shares and to fix the terms upon which such shares may be issued or sold, including, without limitation, the price, the dividend rate, provisions for redemption, sinking fund, conversion, voting or preferential rights, and provisions for other features of a class of shares, or a series of a class of shares, with full power in such committee to adopt any final resolution setting forth all the terms thereof and to authorize the statement of the terms of a series for filing with the Secretary of State under this Act.

Neither the designation of any such committee, the delegation thereto of authority, nor action by such committee pursuant to such authority shall alone constitute compliance by any member of the board of directors, not a member of the committee in question, with his responsibility to act in good faith, in a manner he reasonably believes to be in the best interests of the corporation, and with such care as an ordinarily prudent person in a like position would use under similar circumstances.

§ 43.
Place and Notice of Directors' Meetings; Committee Meetings

Meetings of the board of directors, regular or special, may be held either within or without this State.

Regular meetings of the board of directors or any committee designated thereby may be held with or without notice as prescribed in the by-laws. Special meetings of the board of directors or any committee designated thereby shall be held upon such notice as is prescribed in the by-laws. Attendance of a director at a meeting shall constitute a waiver of notice of such meeting, except where a director attends a meeting for the express purpose of objecting to the transaction of any business because the meeting is not lawfully called or convened. Neither the business to be transacted at, nor the purpose of, any regular or special meeting of the board of directors or any committee designated thereby need be specified in the notice or waiver of notice of such meeting unless required by the by-laws.

Except as may be otherwise restricted by the articles of incorporation or by-laws, members of the board of directors or any committee designated thereby may participate in a meeting of such board or committee by means of a conference telephone or similar communications equipment by means of which all persons participating in the meeting can hear each other at the same time and participation by such means shall constitute presence in person at a meeting.

§ 44.
Action by Directors Without a Meeting

Unless otherwise provided by the articles of incorporation or by-laws, any action required by this Act to be taken at a meeting of the directors of a corporation, or any action which may be taken at a meeting of the directors or of a committee, may be taken without a meeting if a consent in writing, setting forth the action so taken, shall be signed by all of the directors, or all of the members of the committee, as the case may be. Such consent shall have the same effect as a unanimous vote.

§ 45.
Distributions to Shareholders

Subject to any restrictions in the articles of incorporation, the board of directors may authorize and the corporation may make distributions, except that no distribution may be made if, after giving effect thereto, either:

(a) the corporation would be unable to pay its debts as they become due in the usual course of its business; or

(b) the corporation's total assets would be less than the sum of its total liabilities and (unless the articles of incorporation otherwise permit) the maximum amount that then would be payable, in any liquidation, in respect of all outstanding shares having preferential rights in liquidation.

Determinations under subparagraph (b) may be based upon (1) financial statements prepared on the basis of accounting practices and principles that are reasonable in the circumstances, or (2) a fair valuation or other method that is reasonable in the circumstances.

In the case of a purchase, redemption or other acquisition of a corporation's shares, the effect of a distribution shall be measured as of the date money or other property is tranferred or debt is incurred by the corporation, or as of the date the shareholder ceases to be a shareholder of the corporation with respect to such shares, whichever is earlier. In all other cases, the effect of a distribution shall be measured as of the date of its authorization if payment occurs 120 days or less following the date of authorization, or as of the date of payment if payment occurs more than 120 days following the date of authorization.

Indebtedness of a corporation incurred or issued to a shareholder in a distribution in accordance with this Section shall be on a parity with the indebtedness of the corporation to its general unsecured creditors except to the extent subordinated by agreement.

§ 46.
Distributions from Capital Surplus

[Repealed in 1979.]

§ 47.
Loans to Employees and Directors

A corporation shall not lend money to or use its credit to assist its directors without authorization in the particular case by its shareholders, but may lend money to and use its credit to assist any employee of the corporation or of a subsidiary, including any such employee who is a director of the corporation, if the board of directors decides that such loan or assistance may benefit the corporation.

§ 48.
Liability of Directors in Certain Cases

In addition to any other liabilities, a director who votes for or assents to any distribution contrary to the provisions of this Act or contrary to any restrictions contained in the articles of incorporation, shall, unless he complies with the standard provided in this Act for the performance of the duties of directors, be liable to the corporation, jointly and severally with all other directors so voting or assenting, for the amount of such dividend which is paid or the value of such distribution in excess of the amount of such distribution which could have been made without a violation of the provisions of this Act or the restrictions in the articles of incorporation.

Any director against whom a claim shall be asserted under or pursuant to this section for the making of a distribution and who shall be held liable thereon, shall be entitled to contribution from the shareholders who accepted or received any such distribution, knowing such distribution to have been made in violation of this Act, in proportion to the amounts received by them.

Any director against whom a claim shall be asserted under or pursuant to this section shall be entitled to contribution from any other director who voted for or assented to the action upon which the claim is asserted and who did not comply with the standard provided in this Act for the performance of the duties of directors.

§49.
Provisions Relating to Actions by Shareholders

No action shall be brought in this State by a shareholder in the right of a domestic or foreign corporation unless the plaintiff was a holder of record of shares or of voting trust certificates therefor at the time of the transaction of which he complains, or his shares or voting trust certificates thereafter devolved upon him by operation of law from a person who was a holder of record at such time.

In any action hereafter instituted in the right of any domestic or foreign corporation by the holder or holders of record of shares of such corporation or of voting trust certificates therefor, the court having jurisdiction, upon final judgment and a finding that the action was brought without reasonable cause, may require the plaintiff or plaintiffs to pay to the parties named as defendant the reasonable expenses, including fees of attorneys, incurred by them in the defense of such action.

In any action now pending or hereafter instituted or maintained in the right of any domestic or foreign corporation by the holder or holders of record of less than five per cent of the outstanding shares of any class of such corporation or of voting trust certificates therefor, unless the shares or voting trust certificates so held have a market value in excess of twenty-five thousand dollars, the corporation in whose right such action is brought shall be entitled at any time before final judgment to require the plaintiff or plaintiffs to give security for the reasonable expenses, including fees of attorneys, that may be incurred by it in connection with such action or may be incurred by other parties named as defendant for which it may become legally liable. Market value shall be determined as of the date that the plaintiff institutes the action or, in the case of an intervenor, as of the date that he becomes a party to the action. The amount of such security may from time to time be increased or decreased, in the discretion of the court, upon showing that the security provided has or may become inadequate or is excessive. The corporation shall have recourse to such security in such amount as the court having jurisdiction shall determine upon the termination of such action, whether or not the court finds the action was brought without reasonable cause.

§ 50.
Officers

The officers of a corporation shall consist of a president, one or more vice presidents as may be prescribed by the by-laws, a secretary, and a treasurer, each of whom shall be elected by the board of directors at such time and in such manner as may be prescribed by the by-laws. Such other officers and assistant officers and agents as may be deemed necessary may be elected or appointed by the board of directors or chosen in such other manner as may be prescribed by the by-laws. Any two or more offices may be held by the same person, except the offices of president and secretary.

All officers and agents of the corporation, as between themselves and the corporation, shall have such authority and perform such duties in the management of the corporation as may be provided in the by-laws, or as may be determined by resolution of the board of directors not inconsistent with the by-laws.

§ 51.
Removal of Officers

Any officer or agent may be removed by the board of directors whenever in its judgment the best interests of the corporation will be served thereby, but such removal shall be without prejudice to the contract rights, if any, of the person so removed. Election or appointment of an officer or agent shall not of itself create contract rights.

§ 52.
Books and Records: Financial Reports to Shareholders, Examination of Records

Each corporation shall keep correct and complete books and records of account and shall keep minutes of the proceedings of its shareholders and board of directors and shall keep at its registered office or principal place of business, or at the office of its transfer agent or registrar, a record of its shareholders, giving the names and addresses of all shareholders and the number and class of the shares held by each. Any books, records and minutes may be in written form or in any other form capable of being converted into written form within a reasonable time.

Any person who shall have been a holder of record of shares or of voting trust certificates therefor at least six months immediately preceding his demand or shall be the holder of record of, or the holder of record of voting trust certificates for, at least five percent of all the outstanding shares of the corporation, upon written demand stating the purpose thereof, shall have the right to examine, in person, or by agent or attorney, at any reasonable time or times, for any proper purpose its relevant books and records of account, minutes, and record of shareholders and to make extracts therefrom.

Any officer or agent who, or a corporation which, shall refuse to allow any such shareholder or holder of voting trust certificates, or his agent or attorney, so to examine and make extracts from its books and records of account, minutes, and record of shareholders, for any proper purpose, shall be liable to such shareholder or holder of voting trust certificates in a penalty of ten percent of the value of the shares owned by such shareholder, or in respect of which such voting trust certificates are issued, in addition to any other damages or remedy afforded him by law. It shall be a defense to any action for penalties under this section that the person suing therefor has within two years sold or offered for sale any list of shareholders or of holders of voting trust certificates for shares of such corporation or any other corporation or has aided or abetted any person in procuring any list of shareholders or of holders of voting trust certificates for any such purpose, or has improperly used any information secured through any prior examination of the books and records of account, or minutes, or record of shareholders or of holders of voting trust certificates for shares of such corporation or any other corporation, or was not acting in good faith or for a proper purpose in making his demand.

Nothing herein contained shall impair the power of any court of competent jurisdiction, upon proof by a shareholder or holder of voting trust certificates of proper purpose, irrespective of the period of time during which such shareholder or holder of voting trust certificates shall have been a shareholder of record or a holder of record of voting trust certificates, and irrespective of the number of shares held by him or represented by voting trust certificates held by him, to compel the production for examination by such shareholder or holder of voting trust certificates of the books and records of account, minutes and record of shareholders of a corporation.

Each corporation shall furnish to its shareholders annual financial statements, including at least a balance sheet as of the end of each fiscal year and a statement of income for such fiscal year, which shall be prepared on the basis of generally accepted accounting principles, if the corporation prepares financial statements for such fiscal year on that basis for any purpose, and may be consolidated statements of the corporation and one or more of its subsidiaries. The financial statements shall be mailed by the corporation to each of its shareholders within 120 days after the close of each fiscal year and, after such mailing and upon written request, shall be mailed by the corporation to any shareholder (or holder of a voting trust certificate for its shares) to whom a copy of the most recent annual financial statements has not previously been mailed. In the case of statements audited by a public accountant, each copy shall be accompanied by a report setting forth his opinion thereon; in other cases, each copy shall be accompanied by a statement of the president or the person in charge of the corporation's financial accounting records (1) stating his reasonable belief as to whether or not the financial statements were prepared in accordance with generally accepted accounting principles and, if not, describing the basis of presentation, and (2) describing any respects in which the financial statements were not prepared on a basis consistent with those prepared for the previous year.

§ 53.
Incorporators

One or more persons, or a domestic or foreign corporation, may act as incorporator or incorporators of a corporation by signing and delivering in duplicate to the Secretary of State articles of incorporation for such corporation.

§ 54.
Articles of Incorporation

The articles of incorporation shall set forth:

(a) The name of the corporation.

(b) The period of duration, which may be perpetual.

(c) The purpose or purposes for which the corporation is organized which may be stated to be, or to include, the transaction of any or all lawful business for which corporations may be incorporated under this Act.

(d) The aggregate number of shares which the corporation shall have authority to issue and, if such shares are to be divided into classes, the number of shares of each class.

(e) If the shares are to be divided into classes, the designation of each class and a statement of the preferences, limitations and relative rights in respect of the shares of each class.

(f) If the corporation is to issue the shares of any preferred or special class in series, then the designation of each series and a statement of the variations in the relative rights and preferences as between series insofar as the same are to be fixed in the articles of incorporation, and a statement of any authority to be vested in the board of directors to establish series and fix and determine the variations in the relative rights and preferences as between series.

(g) If any preemptive right is to be granted to shareholders, the provisions therefor.

(h) The address of its initial registered office, and the name of its initial registered agent at such address.

(i) The number of directors constituting the initial board of directors and the names and addresses of the persons who are to serve as directors until the first annual meeting of shareholders or until their successors be elected and qualify.

(j) The name and address of each incorporator.

In addition to provisions required therein, the articles of incorporation may also contain provisions not inconsistent with law regarding:

(1) the direction of the management of the business and the regulation of the affairs of the corporation;

(2) the definition, limitation and regulation of the powers of the corporation, the directors, and the shareholders, or any class of the shareholders, including restrictions on the transfer of shares;

(3) the par value of any authorized shares or class of shares;

(4) any provision which under this Act is required or permitted to be set forth in the by-laws.

It shall not be necessary to set forth in the articles of incorporation any of the corporate powers enumerated in this Act.

§ 55.
Filing of Articles of Incorporation

Duplicate originals of the articles of incorporation shall be delivered to the Secretary of State. If the Secretary of State finds that the articles of incorporation conform to law, he shall, when all fees have been paid as in this Act prescribed:

(a) Endorse on each of such duplicate originals the word "Filed," and the month, day and year of the filing thereof.

(b) File one of such duplicate originals in his office.

(c) Issue a certificate of incorporation to which he shall affix the other duplicate original.

The certificate of incorporation, together with the duplicate original of the articles of incorporation affixed thereto by the

Secretary of State, shall be returned to the incorporators or their representative.

§ 56.
Effect of Issuance of Certificate of Incorporation

Upon the issuance of the certificate of incorporation, the corporate existence shall begin, and such certificate of incorporation shall be conclusive evidence that all conditions precedent required to be performed by the incorporators have been complied with and that the corporation has been incorporated under this Act, except as against this State in a proceeding to cancel or revoke the certificate of incorporation or for involuntary dissolution of the corporation.

§ 57.
Organization Meeting of Directors

After the issuance of the certificate of incorporation an organization meeting of the board of directors named in the articles of incorporation shall be held, either within or without this State, at the call of a majority of the directors named in the articles of incorporation, for the purpose of adopting by-laws, electing officers and transacting such other business as may come before the meeting. The directors calling the meeting shall give at least three days' notice thereof by mail to each director so named, stating the time and place of the meeting.

§ 58.
Right to Amend Articles of Incorporation

A corporation may amend its articles of incorporation, from time to time, in any and as many respects as may be desired, so long as its articles of incorporation as amended contain only such provisions as might be lawfully contained in original articles of incorporation at the time of making such amendment, and, if a change in shares or the rights of shareholders, or an exchange, reclassification or cancellation of shares or rights of shareholders is to be made, such provisions as may be necessary to effect such change, exchange, reclassification or cancellation.

In particular, and without limitation upon such general power of amendment, a corporation may amend its articles of incorporation, from time to time, so as:

(a) To change its corporate name.

(b) To change its period of duration.

(c) To change, enlarge or diminish its corporate purposes.

(d) To increase or decrease the aggregate number of shares, or shares of any class, which the corporation has authority to issue.

(e) To provide, change or eliminate any provision with respect to the par value of any shares or class of shares.

(f) To exchange, classify, reclassify or cancel all or any part of its shares, whether issued or unissued.

(g) To change the designation of all or any part of its shares, whether issued or unissued, and to change the preferences, limitations, and the relative rights in respect of all or any part of its shares, whether issued or unissued.

(h) To change the shares of any class, whether issued or unissued, into a different number of shares of the same class or into the same or a different number of shares of other classes.

(i) To create new classes of shares having rights and preferences either prior and superior or subordinate and inferior to the shares of any class then authorized, whether issued or unissued.

(j) To cancel or otherwise affect the right of the holders of the shares of any class to receive dividends which have accrued but have not been declared.

(k) To divide any preferred or special class of shares, whether issued or unissued, into series and fix and determine the designations of such series and the variations in the relative rights and preferences as between the shares of such series.

(l) To authorize the board of directors to establish, out of authorized but unissued shares, series of any preferred or special class of shares and fix and determine the relative rights and preferences of the shares of any series so established.

(m) To authorize the board of directors to fix and determine the relative rights and preferences of the authorized but unissued shares of series theretofore established in respect of which either the relative rights and preferences have not been fixed and determined or the relative rights and preferences theretofore fixed and determined are to be changed.

(n) To revoke, diminish, or enlarge the authority of the board of directors to establish series out of authorized but unissued shares of any preferred or special class and fix and determine the relative rights and preferences of the shares of any series so established.

(o) To limit, deny or grant to shareholders of any class the preemptive right to acquire additional shares of the corporation, whether then or thereafter authorized.

§ 59.
Procedure to Amend Articles of Incorporation

Amendments to the articles of incorporation shall be made in the following manner:

(a) The board of directors shall adopt a resolution setting forth the proposed amendment and, if shares have been issued, directing that it be submitted to a vote at a meeting of shareholders, which may be either the annual or a special meeting. If no shares have been issued, the amendment shall be adopted by resolution of the board of directors and the provisions for adoption by shareholders shall not apply. If the corporation has only one class of shares outstanding, an amendment solely to change the number of authorized shares to effectuate a split of, or stock dividend in, the corporation's own shares, or solely to do so and to change the number of authorized shares in proportion thereto, may be adopted by the board of directors; and the provisions for adoption by shareholders shall not apply, unless otherwise provided by the articles of incorporation. The resolution may incorporate the proposed amendment in restated articles of incorporation which contain a statement that except for the designated amendment the restated articles of incorporation correctly set forth without change the corresponding provisions of the articles of incorporation as theretofore amended, and that the restated articles of incorporation together with the designated amendment supersede the original articles of incorporation and all amendments thereto.

(b) Written notice setting forth the proposed amendment or a summary of the changes to be effected thereby shall be given to each shareholder of record entitled to vote thereon within the time and in the manner provided in this Act for the giving of notice of meetings of shareholders. If the meeting be an annual meeting, the proposed amendment of such summary may be included in the notice of such annual meeting.

(c) At such meeting a vote of the shareholders entitled to vote thereon shall be taken on the proposed amendment. The proposed amendment shall be adopted upon receiving the affirmative vote of the holders of a majority of the shares entitled to vote thereon, unless any class of shares is entitled to vote thereon as a class, in which event the proposed amendment shall be adopted upon receiving the affirmative vote of the holders of a majority of the shares of each class of shares entitled to vote thereon as a class and of the total shares entitled to vote thereon.

Any number of amendments may be submitted to the shareholders, and voted upon by them, at one meeting.

§ 60.
Class Voting on Amendments

The holders of the outstanding shares of a class shall be entitled to vote as a class upon a proposed amendment, whether or not entitled to vote thereon by the provisions of the articles of incorporation, if the amendment would:

(a) Increase or decrease the aggregate number of authorized shares of such class.

(b) Effect an exchange, reclassification or cancellation of all or part of the shares of such class.

(c) Effect an exchange, or create a right of exchange, of all or any part of the shares of another class into the shares of such class.

(d) Change the designations, preferences, limitations or relative rights of the shares of such class.

(e) Change the shares of such class into the same or a differ-

ent number of shares of the same class or another class or classes.

(f) Create a new class of shares having rights and preferences prior and superior to the shares of such class, or increase the rights and preferences or the number of authorized shares, of any class having rights and preferences prior or superior to the shares of such class.

(g) In the case of a preferred or special class of shares, divide the shares of such class into series and fix and determine the designation of such series and the variations in the relative rights and preferences between the shares of such series, or authorize the board of directors to do so.

(h) Limit or deny any existing preemptive rights of the shares of such class.

(i) Cancel or otherwise affect dividends on the shares of such class which have accrued but have not been declared.

§ 61.
Articles of Amendment

The articles of amendment shall be executed in duplicate by the corporation by its president or a vice president and by its secretary or an assistant secretary, and verified by one of the officers signing such articles, and shall set forth:

(a) The name of the corporation.

(b) The amendments so adopted.

(c) The date of the adoption of the amendment by the shareholders, or by the board of directors where no shares have been issued.

(d) The number of shares outstanding, and the number of shares entitled to vote thereon, and if the shares of any class are entitled to vote thereon as a class, the designation and number of outstanding shares entitled to vote thereon of each such class.

(e) The number of shares voted for and against such amendment, respectively, and, if the shares of any class are entitled to vote thereon as a class, the number of shares of each such class voted for and against such amendment, respectively, or if no shares have been issued, a statement to that effect.

(f) If such amendment provides for an exchange, reclassification or cancellation of issued shares, and if the manner in which the same shall be effected is not set forth in the amendment, then a statement of the manner in which the same shall be effected.

§ 62.
Filing of Articles of Amendment

Duplicate originals of the articles of amendment shall be delivered to the Secretary of State. If the Secretary of State finds that the articles of amendment conform to law, he shall, when all fees and franchise taxes have been paid as in this Act prescribed:

(a) Endorse on each of such duplicate originals the word "Filed," and the month, day and year of the filing thereof.

(b) File one of such duplicate originals in his office.

(c) Issue a certificate of amendment to which he shall affix the other duplicate original.

The certificate of amendment, together with the duplicate original of the articles of amendment affixed thereto by the Secretary of State, shall be returned to the corporation or its representative.

§ 63.
Effect of Certificate of Amendment

Upon the issuance of the certificate of amendment by the Secretary of State, the amendment shall become effective and the articles of incorporation shall be deemed to be amended accordingly.

No amendment shall affect any existing cause of action in favor of or against such corporation, or any pending suit to which such corporation shall be a party, or the existing rights of persons other than shareholders; and, in the event the corporate name shall be changed by amendment, no suit brought by or against such corporation under its former name shall abate for that reason.

§ 64.
Restated Articles of Incorporation

A domestic corporation may at any time restate its articles of incorporation as theretofore amended, by a resolution adopted by the board of directors.

Upon the adoption of such resolution, restated articles of incorporation shall be executed in duplicate by the corporation by its president or a vice president and by its secretary or assistant secretary and verified by one of the officers signing such articles and shall set forth all of the operative provisions of the articles of incorporation as theretofore amended together with a statement that the restated articles of incorporation correctly set forth without change the corresponding provisions of the articles of incorporation as theretofore amended and that the restated articles of incorporation supersede the original articles of incorporation and all amendments thereto.

Duplicate originals of the restated articles of incorporation shall be delivered to the Secretary of State. If the Secretary of State finds that such restated articles of incorporation conform to law, he shall, when all fees and franchise taxes have been paid as in this Act prescribed:

(1) Endorse on each of such duplicate originals the word "Filed," and the month, day and year of the filing thereof.

(2) File one of such duplicate originals in his office.

(3) Issue a restated certificate of incorporation, to which he shall affix the other duplicate original.

The restated certificate of incorporation, together with the duplicate original of the restated articles of incorporation affixed thereto by the Secretary of State, shall be returned to the corporation or its representative.

Upon the issuance of the restated certificate of incorporation by the Secretary of State, the restated articles of incorporation shall become effective and shall supersede the original articles of incorporation and all amendments thereto.

§ 65.
Amendment of Articles of Incorporation in Reorganization Proceedings

Whenever a plan of reorganization of a corporation has been confirmed by decree or order of a court of competent jurisdiction in proceedings for the reorganization of such corporation, pursuant to the provisions of any applicable statute of the United States relating to reorganizations of corporations, the articles of incorporation of the corporation may be amended, in the manner provided in this section, in as many respects as may be necessary to carry out the plan and put it into effect, so long as the articles of incorporation as amended contain only such provisions as might be lawfully contained in original articles of incorporation at the time of making such amendment.

In particular and without limitation upon such general power of amendment, the articles of incorporation may be amended for such purpose so as to:

(a) Change the corporate name, period of duration or corporate purposes of the corporation;

(b) Repeal, alter or amend the by-laws of the corporation;

(c) Change the aggregate number of shares or shares of any class, which the corporation has authority to issue;

(d) Change the preferences, limitations and relative rights in respect of all or any part of the shares of the corporation, and classify, reclassify or cancel all or any part thereof, whether issued or unissued;

(e) Authorize the issuance of bonds, debentures or other obligations of the corporation, whether or not convertible into shares of any class or bearing warrants or other evidences of optional rights to purchase or subscribe for shares of any class, and fix the terms and conditions thereof; and

(f) Constitute or reconstitute and classify or reclassify the board of directors of the corporation, and appoint directors and officers in place of or in addition to all or any of the directors or officers then in office.

Amendments to the articles of incorporation pursuant to this section shall be made in the following manner:

(1) Articles of amendment approved by decree or order of such court shall be executed and verified in duplicate by such person or persons as the court shall designate or appoint for the purpose, and shall set forth the name of the corporation, the amendments of the articles of incorporation approved by the court, the date of the decree or order approving the articles of amendment, the title of the proceedings in which the decree or order was entered, and a statement that such decree or order was entered by a court

having jurisdiction of the proceedings for the reorganization of the corporation pursuant to the provisions of an applicable statute of the United States.

(2) Duplicate originals of the articles of amendment shall be delivered to the Secretary of State. If the Secretary of State finds that the articles of amendment conform to law, he shall, when all fees and franchise taxes have been paid as in this Act prescribed:

(A) Endorse on each of such duplicate originals the word "Filed," and the month, day and year of the filing thereof.

(B) File one of such duplicate originals in his office.

(C) Issue a certificate of amendment to which he shall affix the other duplicate original.

The certificate of amendment, together with the duplicate original of the articles of amendment affixed thereto by the Secretary of State, shall be returned to the corporation or its representative.

Upon the issuance of the certificate of amendment by the Secretary of State, the amendment shall become effective and the articles of incorporation shall be deemed to be amended accordingly, without any action thereon by the directors or shareholders of the corporation and with the same effect as if the amendments had been adopted by unanimous action of the directors and shareholders of the corporation.

§ 66.
Restriction on Redemption or Purchase of Redeemable Shares

[Repealed in 1979.]

§ 67.
Cancellation of Redeemable Shares by Redemption or Purchase

[Repealed in 1979.]

§ 68.
Cancellation of Other Reacquired Shares

[Repealed in 1979.]

§ 69.
Reduction of Stated Capital in Certain Cases

[Repealed in 1979.]

§ 70.
Special Provisions Relating to Surplus and Reserves

[Repealed in 1979.]

§ 71.
Procedure for Merger

Any two or more domestic corporations may merge into one of such corporations pursuant to a plan of merger approved in the manner provided in this Act.

The board of directors of each corporation shall, by resolution adopted by each such board, approve a plan of merger setting forth:

(a) The names of the corporations proposing to merge, and the name of the corporation into which they propose to merge, which is hereinafter designated as the surviving corporation.

(b) The terms and conditions of the proposed merger.

(c) The manner and basis of converting the shares of each corporation into shares, obligations or other securities of the surviving corporation or of any other corporation or, in whole or in part, into cash or other property.

(d) A statement of any changes in the articles of incorporation of the surviving corporation to be effected by such merger.

(e) Such other provisions with respect to the proposed merger as are deemed necessary or desirable.

§ 72.
Procedure for Consolidation

Any two or more domestic corporations may consolidate into a new corporation pursuant to a plan of consolidation approved in the manner provided in this Act.

The board of directors of each corporation shall, by a resolution adopted by each such board, approve a plan of consolidation setting forth:

(a) The names of the corporations proposing to consolidate, and the name of the new corporation into which they propose to consolidate, which is hereinafter designated as the new corporation.

(b) The terms and conditions of the proposed consolidation.

(c) The manner and basis of converting the shares of each corporation into shares, obligations or other securities of the new corporation or of any other corporation or, in whole or in part, into cash or other property.

(d) With respect to the new corporation, all of the statements required to be set forth in articles of incorporation for corporations organized under this Act.

(e) Such other provisions with respect to the proposed consolidation as are deemed necessary or desirable.

§ 72A.
Procedure for Share Exchange

All the issued or all the outstanding shares of one or more classes of any domestic corporation may be acquired through the exchange of all such shares of such class or classes by another domestic or foreign corporation pursuant to a plan of exchange approved in the manner provided in this Act.

The board of directors of each corporation shall, by resolution adopted by each such board, approve a plan of exchange setting forth:

(a) The name of the corporation the shares of which are proposed to be acquired by exchange and the name of the corporation to acquire the shares of such corporation in the exchange, which is hereinafter designated as the acquiring corporation.

(b) The terms and conditions of the proposed exchange.

(c) The manner and basis of exchanging the shares to be acquired for shares, obligations or other securities of the acquiring corporation or any other corporation, or, in whole or in part, for cash or other property.

(d) Such other provisions with respect to the proposed exchange as are deemed necessary or desirable.

The procedure authorized by this section shall not be deemed to limit the power of a corporation to acquire all or part of the shares of any class or classes of a corporation through a voluntary exchange or otherwise by agreement with the shareholders.

§ 73.
Approval by Shareholders

(a) The board of directors of each corporation in the case of a merger or consolidation, and the board of directors of the corporation the shares of which are to be acquired in the case of an exchange, upon approving such plan of merger, consolidation or exchange, shall, by resolution, direct that the plan be submitted to a vote at a meeting of its shareholders, which may be either an annual or a special meeting. Written notice shall be given to each shareholder of record, whether or not entitled to vote at such meeting, not less than twenty days before such meeting, in the manner provided in this Act for the giving of notice of meetings of shareholders, and, whether the meeting be an annual or a special meeting, shall state that the purpose or one of the purposes is to consider the proposed plan of merger, consolidation or exchange. A copy or a summary of the plan of merger, consolidation or exchange, as the case may be, shall be included in or enclosed with such notice.

(b) At each such meeting, a vote of the shareholders shall be taken on the proposed plan. The plan shall be approved upon receiving the affirmative vote of the holders of a majority of the shares entitled to vote thereon of each such corporation, unless any class of shares of any such corporation is entitled to vote thereon as a class, in which event, as to such corporation, the plan shall be approved upon receiving the affirmative vote of the holders of a majority of the shares of each class of shares entitled to vote thereon as a class and of the total shares entitled to vote thereon. Any class of shares of any such corporation shall be entitled to vote as a class if any such plan contains any provision which, if contained in a proposed amendment to articles of incorporation, would entitle such class of shares to vote as a class and, in the case of an exchange, if the class is included in the exchange.

(c) After such approval by a vote of the shareholders of each such corporation, and at any time prior to the filing of the articles of merger, consolidation or exchange, the merger, consolidation or exchange may be abandoned pursuant to provisions therefor, if any, set forth in the plan.

(d) (1) Notwithstanding the provisions of subsections (a) and (b), submission of a plan of merger to a vote at a meeting of shareholders of a surviving corporation shall not be required if:

(A) the articles of incorporation of the surviving corporation do not differ except in name from those of the corporation before the merger,

(B) each holder of shares of the surviving corporation which were outstanding immediately before the effective date of the merger is to hold the same number of shares with identical rights immediately after,

(C) the number of voting shares outstanding immediately after the merger, plus the number of voting shares issuable on conversion of other securities issued by virtue of the terms of the merger and on exercise of rights and warrants so issued, will not exceed by more than twenty percent the number of voting shares outstanding immediately before the merger, and

(D) the number of participating shares outstanding immediately after the merger, plus the number of participating shares issuable on conversion of other securities issued by virtue of the terms of the merger and on exercise of rights and warrants so issued, will not exceed by more than twenty percent the number of participating shares outstanding immediately before the merger.

(2) As used in this subsection:

(A) "voting shares" means shares which entitle their holders to vote unconditionally in elections of directors;

(B) "participating shares" means shares which entitle their holders to participate without limitation in distribution of earnings or surplus.

§ 74.
Articles of Merger, Consolidation or Exchange

(a) Upon receiving the approvals required by Sections 71, 72 and 73, articles of merger or articles of consolidation shall be executed in duplicate by each corporation by its president or a vice president and by its secretary or an assistant secretary, and verified by one of the officers of each corporation signing such articles, and shall set forth:

(1) The plan of merger or the plan of consolidation;

(2) As to each corporation, either (A) the number of shares outstanding, and, if the shares of any class are entitled to vote as a class, the designation and number of outstanding shares of each such class, or (B) a statement that the vote of shareholders is not required by virtue of subsection 73(d);

(3) As to each corporation the approval of whose shareholders is required, the number of shares voted for and against such plan, respectively, and, if the shares of any class are entitled to vote as a class, the number of shares of each such class voted for and against such plan, respectively.

(b) Duplicate originals of the articles of merger, consolidation or exchange shall be delivered to the Secretary of State. If the Secretary of State finds that such articles conform to law, he shall, when all fees and franchise taxes have been paid as in this Act prescribed:

(1) Endorse on each of such duplicate originals the word "Filed," and the month, day and year of the filing thereof.

(2) File one of such duplicate originals in his office.

(3) Issue a certificate of merger, consolidation or exchange to which he shall affix the other duplicate original.

(c) The certificate of merger, consolidation or exchange together with the duplicate original of the articles affixed thereto by the Secretary of State, shall be returned to the surviving, new or acquiring corporation, as the case may be, or its representative.

§ 75.
Merger of Subsidiary Corporation

Any corporation owning at least ninety per cent of the outstanding shares of each class of another corporation may merge such other corporation into itself without approval by a vote of the shareholders of either corporation. Its board of directors shall, by resolution, approve a plan of merger setting forth:

(a) The name of the subsidiary corporation and the name of the corporation owning at least ninety per cent of its shares, which is hereinafter designated as the surviving corporation.

(b) The manner and basis of converting the shares of the subsidiary corporation into shares, obligations or other securities of the surviving corporation or of any other corporation or, in whole or in part, into cash or other property.

A copy of such plan of merger shall be mailed to each shareholder of record of the subsidiary corporation.

Articles of merger shall be executed in duplicate by the surviving corporation by its president or a vice president and by its secretary or an assistant secretary, and verified by one of its officers signing such articles, and shall set forth:

(1) The plan of merger;

(2) The number of outstanding shares of each class of the subsidiary corporation and the number of such shares of each class owned by the surviving corporation; and

(3) The date of the mailing to shareholders of the subsidiary corporation of a copy of the plan of merger.

On and after the thirtieth day after the mailing of a copy of the plan of merger to shareholders of the subsidiary corporation or upon the waiver thereof by the holders of all outstanding shares duplicate originals of the articles of merger shall be delivered to the Secretary of State. If the Secretary of

State finds that such articles conform to law, he shall, when all fees and franchise taxes have been paid as in this Act prescribed:

(A) Endorse on each of such duplicate originals the word "Filed," and the month, day and year of the filing thereof,

(B) File one of such duplicate originals in his office, and

(C) Issue a certificate of merger to which he shall affix the other duplicate original.

The certificate of merger, together with the duplicate original of the articles of merger affixed thereto by the Secretary of State, shall be returned to the surviving corporation or its representative.

§ 76.
Effect of Merger, Consolidation or Exchange

Upon the issuance of the certificate of merger or the certificate of consolidation by the Secretary of State, the merger or consolidation shall be effected.

When such merger or consolidation has been effective:

(a) The several corporations parties to the plan of merger or consolidation shall be a single corporation, which, in the case of a merger, shall be that corporation designated in the plan of merger as the surviving corporation, and, in the case of a consolidation, shall be the new corporation provided for in the plan of consolidation.

(b) The separate existence of all corporations parties to the plan of merger or consolidation, except the surviving or new corporation, shall cease.

(c) Such surviving or new corporation shall have all the rights, privileges, immunities and powers and shall be subject to all the duties and liabilities of a corporation organized under this Act.

(d) Such surviving or new corporation shall thereupon and thereafter possess all the rights, privileges, immunities, and franchises, of a public as well as of a private nature, of each of the merging or consolidating corporations; and all property, real, personal and mixed, and all debts due on whatever account, including subscriptions to shares, and all other choses in action, and all and every other interest of or belonging to or due to each of the corporations so merged or consolidated, shall be taken and deemed to be transferred to and vested in such single corporation without further act or deed; and the title to any real estate, or any interest therein, vested in any of such corporations shall not revert or be in any way impaired by reason of such merger or consolidation.

(e) Such surviving or new corporation shall thenceforth be responsible and liable for all the liabilities and obligations of each of the corporations so merged or consolidated; and any claim existing or action or proceeding pending by or against any of such corporations may be prosecuted as if such merger or consolidation had not taken place, or such surviving or new corporation may be substituted in its place. Neither the rights of creditors nor any liens upon the property of any such corporation shall be impaired by such merger or consolidation.

(f) In the case of a merger, the articles of incorporation of the surviving corporation shall be deemed to be amended to the extent, if any, that changes in its articles of incorporation are stated in the plan of merger; and, in the case of a consolidation, the statements set forth in the articles of consolidation and which are required or permitted to be set forth in the articles of incorporation of corporations organized under this Act shall be deemed to be the original articles of incorporation of the new corporation.

§ 77.
Merger, Consolidation or Exchange of Shares Between Domestic and Foreign Corporations

One or more foreign corporations and one or more domestic corporations may be merged or consolidated in the following manner, if such merger or consolidation is permitted by the laws of the state under which each such foreign corporation is organized:

(a) Each domestic corporation shall comply with the provisions of this Act with respect to the merger or consolidation, as the case may be, of domestic corporations and each foreign corporation shall comply with the applicable provisions of the laws of the state under which it is organized.

(b) If the surviving or new corporation, as the case may be, is to be governed by the laws of any state other than this State, it shall comply with the provisions of this Act with respect to foreign corporations if it is to transact business in this State, and in every case it shall file with the Secretary of State of this State:

   (1) An agreement that it may be served with process in this State in any proceeding for the enforcement of any obligation of any domestic corporation which is a party to such merger or consolidation and in any proceeding for the enforcement of the rights of a dissenting shareholder of any such domestic corporation against the surviving or new corporation;

   (2) An irrevocable appointment of the Secretary of State of this State as its agent to accept service of process in any such proceeding; and

   (3) An agreement that it will promptly pay to the dissenting shareholders of any such domestic corporation the amount, if any, to which they shall be entitled under the provisions of this Act with respect to the rights of dissenting shareholders.

The effect of such merger or consolidation shall be the same as in the case of the merger or consolidation of domestic corporations, if the surviving or new corporation is to be governed by the laws of this State. If the surviving or new corporation is to be governed by the laws of any state other than this State, the effect of such merger or consolidation shall be the same as in the case of the merger or consolidation of domestic corporations except insofar as the laws of such other state provide otherwise.

At any time prior to the filing of the articles of merger or consolidation, the merger or consolidation may be abandoned pursuant to provisions therefor, if any, set forth in the plan of merger or consolidation.

§ 78.
Sale of Assets in Regular Course of Business and Mortgage or Pledge of Assets

The sale, lease, exchange, or other disposition of all, or substantially all, the property and assets of a corporation in the usual and regular course of its business and the mortgage or pledge of any or all property and assets of a corporation whether or not in the usual and regular course of business may be made upon such terms and conditions and for such consideration, which may consist in whole or in part of cash or other property, including shares, obligations or other securities of any other corporation, domestic or foreign, as shall be authorized by its board of directors; and in any such case no authorization or consent of the shareholders shall be required.

§ 79.
Sale of Assets Other Than in Regular Course of Business

A sale, lease, exchange, or other disposition of all, or substantially all, the property and assets, with or without the good will, of a corporation, if not in the usual and regular course of its business, may be made upon such terms and conditions and for such consideration, which may consist in whole or in part of cash or other property, including shares, obligations or other securities of any other corporation, domestic or foreign, as may be authorized in the following manner:

(a) The board of directors shall adopt a resolution recommending such sale, lease, exchange, or other disposition and directing the submission thereof to a vote at a meeting of shareholders, which may be either an annual or a special meeting.

(b) Written notice shall be given to each shareholder of record, whether or not entitled to vote at such meeting, not less than twenty days before such meeting, in the manner provided in this Act for the giving of notice of meetings of shareholders, and, whether the meeting be an annual or a special meeting, shall state that the purpose, or one of the purposes is to consider the proposed sale, lease, exchange, or other disposition.

(c) At such meeting the shareholders may authorize such sale, lease, exchange, or other disposition and may fix, or may authorize the board of directors to fix, any or all of the terms and conditions thereof and the consideration to be received by the corporation therefor. Such authorization shall require the affirmative vote of the holders of a majority of the shares of the corporation entitled to vote thereon, unless any class of shares is entitled to vote thereon as a class, in which event such authorization shall require the affirmative vote of the holders of a majority of the shares of each class of shares entitled to vote as a class thereon and of the total shares entitled to vote thereon.

(d) After such authorization by a vote of shareholders, the board of directors nevertheless, in its discretion, may abandon such sale, lease, exchange, or other disposition of assets, subject to the rights of third parties under any contracts relating thereto, without further action or approval by shareholders.

§ 80.
Right of Shareholders to Dissent and Obtain Payment for Shares

(a) Any shareholder of a corporation shall have the right to dissent from, and to obtain payment for his shares in the event of, any of the following corporate actions:

(1) Any plan of merger or consolidation to which the corporation is a party, except as provided in subsection (c);

(2) Any sale or exchange of all or substantially all of the property and assets of the corporation not made in the usual or regular course of its business, including a sale in dissolution, but not including a sale pursuant to an order of a court having jurisdiction in the premises or a sale for cash on terms requiring that all or substantially all of the net proceeds of sale be distributed to the shareholders in accordance with their respective interests within one year after the date of sale;

(3) Any plan of exchange to which the corporation is a party as the corporation the shares of which are to be acquired;

(4) Any amendment of the articles of incorporation which materially and adversely affects the rights appurtenant to the shares of the dissenting shareholder in that it:

(A) alters or abolishes a preferential right of such shares;

(B) creates, alters or abolishes a right in respect of the redemption of such shares, including a provision respecting a sinking fund for the redemption or repurchase of such shares;

(C) alters or abolishes a preemptive right of the holder of such shares to acquire shares or other securities;

(D) excludes or limits the right of the holder of such shares to vote on any matter, or to cumulate his votes, except as such right may be limited by dilution through the issuance of shares or other securities with similar voting rights; or

(5) Any other corporate action taken pursuant to a shareholder vote with respect to which the articles of incorporation, the bylaws, or a resolution of the board of directors directs that dissenting shareholders shall have a right to obtain payment for their shares.

(b) (1) A record holder of shares may assert dissenters' rights as to less than all of the shares registered in his name only if he dissents with respect to all the shares beneficially owned by any one person, and discloses the name and address of the person or persons on whose behalf he dissents. In that event, his rights shall be determined as if the shares as to which he has dissented and his other shares were registered in the names of different shareholders.

(2) A beneficial owner of shares who is not the record holder may assert dissenters' rights with respect to shares held on his behalf, and shall be treated as a dissenting shareholder under the terms of this section and section 81 if he submits to the corporation at the time of or before the assertion of these rights a written consent of the record holder.

(c) The right to obtain payment under this section shall not apply to the shareholders of the surviving corporation in a merger if a vote of the shareholders of such corporation is not necessary to authorize such merger.

(d) A shareholder of a corporation who has a right under this section to obtain payment for his shares shall have no right at law or in equity to attack the validity of the corporate action that gives rise to his right to obtain payment, nor to have the action set aside or rescinded, except when the corporate action is unlawful or fraudulent with regard to the complaining shareholder or to the corporation.

§ 81.
Procedures for Protection of Dissenters' Rights

(a) As used in this section:

(1) "Dissenter" means a shareholder or beneficial owner who is entitled to and does assert dissenters' rights under section 80, and who has performed every act required up to the time involved for the assertion of such rights.

(2) "Corporation" means the issuer of the shares held by the dissenter before the corporate action, or the successor by merger or consolidation of that issuer.

(3) "Fair value" of shares means their value immediately before the effectuation of the corporate action to which the dissenter objects, excluding any appreciation or depreciation in anticipation of such corporate action unless such exclusion would be inequitable.

(4) "Interest" means interest from the effective date of the corporate action until the date of payment, at the average rate currently paid by the corporation on its principal bank loans, or, if none, at such rate as is fair and equitable under all the circumstances.

(b) If a proposed corporate action which would give rise to dissenters' rights under section 80(a) is submitted to a vote at a meeting of shareholders, the notice of meeting shall notify all shareholders that they have or may have a right to dissent and obtain payment for their shares by complying with the terms of this section, and shall be accompanied by a copy of sections 80 and 81 of this Act.

(c) If the proposed corporate action is submitted to a vote at a meeting of shareholders, any shareholder who wishes to dissent and obtain payment for his shares must file with the corporation, prior to the vote, a written notice of intention to demand that he be paid fair compensation for his shares if the proposed action is effectuated, and shall refrain from voting his shares in approval of such action. A shareholder who fails in either respect shall acquire no right to payment for his shares under this section or section 80.

(d) If the proposed corporate action is approved by the required vote at a meeting of shareholders, the corporation shall mail a further notice to all shareholders who gave due notice of intention to demand payment and who refrained from voting in favor of the proposed action. If the proposed corporate action is to be taken without a vote of shareholders, the corporation shall send to all shareholders who are entitled to dissent and demand payment for their shares a notice of the adoption of the plan of corporate action. The notice shall (1) state where and when a demand for payment must be sent and certificates of certificated shares must be deposited in order to obtain payment, (2) inform holders of uncertificated shares to what extent transfer of shares will be restricted from the time that demand for payment is received, (3) supply a form for demanding payment which includes a request for certification of the date on which the shareholder, or the person on whose behalf the shareholder dissents, acquired beneficial ownership of the shares, and (4) be accompanied by a copy of sections 80 and 81 of this Act. The time set for the demand and deposit shall be not less than 30 days from the mailing of the notice.

(e) A shareholder who fails to demand payment, or fails (in the case of certificated shares) to deposit certificates, as required by a notice pursuant to subsection (d) shall have no right under this section or section 80 to receive payment for his shares. If the shares are not represented by certificates, the corporation may restrict their transfer from the time of receipt of demand for payment until effectuation of the proposed corporate action, or the release of restrictions under the terms of subsection (f). The dissenter shall retain all other rights of a shareholder until these rights are modified by effectuation of the proposed corporate action.

(f) (1) Within 60 days after the date set for demanding payment and depositing certificates, if the corporation has not effectuated the proposed corporate action and remitted payment for shares pursuant to paragraph (3), it shall return any certificates that have been deposited, and release uncertificated shares from any transfer restrictions imposed by reason of the demand for payment.

(2) When uncertificated shares have been released from transfer restrictions, and deposited certificates have been returned, the corporation may at any later time send a new notice conforming to the requirements of subsection (d), with like effect.

(3) Immediately upon effectuation of the proposed corporate action, or upon receipt of demand for payment if the corporate action has already been effectuated, the corporation shall remit to dissenters who have made demand and (if their shares are certificated) have deposited their certificates the amount which the corporation estimates to be the fair value of the shares, with interest if any has accrued. The remittance shall be accompanied by:

(A) the corporation's closing balance sheet and statement of income for a fiscal year ending not more than 16 months before the date of remittance, together with the latest available interim financial statements;

(B) a statement of the corporation's estimate of fair value of the shares; and

(C) a notice of the dissenter's right to demand supplemental payment, accompanied by a copy of sections 80 and 81 of this Act.

(g) (1) If the corporation fails to remit as required by subsection (f), or if the dissenter believes that the amount remitted is less than the fair value of his shares, or that the interest is not correctly determined, he may send the corporation his own estimate of the value of the shares or of the interest, and demand payment of the deficiency.

(2) If the dissenter does not file such an estimate within thirty days after the corporation's mailing of its remittance, he shall be entitled to no more than the amount remitted.

(h) (1) Within sixty days after receiving a demand for payment pursuant to subsection (g), if any such demands for payment remain unsettled, the corporation shall file in an appropriate court a petition requesting that the fair value of the shares and interest thereon be determined by the court.

(2) An appropriate court shall be a court of competent jurisdiction in the county of this state where the registered office of the corporation is located. If, in the case of a merger or consolidation or exchange of shares, the corporation is a foreign corporation without a registered office in this state, the petition shall be filed in the county where the registered office of the domestic corporation was last located.

(3) All dissenters, wherever residing, whose demands have not been settled shall be made parties to the proceeding as in an action against their shares. A copy of the petition shall be served on each such dissenter; if a dissenter is a nonresident, the copy may be served on him by registered or certified mail or by publication as provided by law.

(4) The jurisdiction of the court shall be plenary and exclusive. The court may appoint one or more persons as appraisers to receive evidence and recommend a decision on the question of fair value. The appraisers shall have such power and authority as shall be specified in the order of their appointment or in any amendment thereof. The dissenters shall be entitled to discovery in the same manner as parties in other civil suits.

(5) All dissenters who are made parties shall be entitled to judgment for the amount by which the fair value of their

shares is found to exceed the amount previously remitted, with interest.

(6) If the corporation fails to file a petition as provided in paragraph (1) of this subsection, each dissenter who made a demand and who has not already settled his claim against the corporation shall be paid by the corporation the amount demanded by him, with interest, and may sue therefor in an appropriate court.

(i) (1) The costs and expenses of any proceeding under subsection (h), including the reasonable compensation and expenses of appraisers appointed by the court, shall be determined by the court and assessed against the corporation, except that any part of the costs and expenses may be apportioned and assessed as the court may deem equitable against all or some of the dissenters who are parties and whose action in demanding supplemental payment the court finds to be arbitrary, vexatious, or not in good faith.

(2) Fees and expenses of counsel and of experts for the respective parties may be assessed as the court may deem equitable against the corporation and in favor of any or all dissenters if the corporation failed to comply substantially with the requirements of this section, and may be assessed against either the corporation or a dissenter, in favor of any other party, if the court finds that the party against whom the fees and expenses are assessed acted arbitrarily, vexatiously, or not in good faith in respect to the rights provided by this Section and Section 80.

(3) If the court finds that the services of counsel for any dissenter were of substantial benefit to other dissenters similarly situated, and should not be assessed against the corporation, it may award to these counsel reasonable fees to be paid out of the amounts awarded to the dissenters who were benefitted.

(j) (1) Notwithstanding the foregoing provisions of this section, the corporation may elect to withhold the remittance required by subsection (f) from any dissenter with respect to shares of which the dissenter (or the person on whose behalf the dissenter acts) was not the beneficial owner on the date of the first announcement to news media or to shareholders of the terms of the proposed corporate action. With respect to such shares, the corporation shall, upon effectuating the corporate action, state to each dissenter its estimate of the fair value of the shares, state the rate of interest to be used (explaining the basis thereof), and offer to pay the resulting amounts on receiving the dissenter's agreement to accept them in full satisfaction.

(2) If the dissenter believes that the amount offered is less than the fair value of the shares and interest determined according to this section, he may within thirty days after the date of mailing of the corporation's offer, mail the corporation his own estimate of fair value and interest, and demand their payment. If the dissenter fails to do so, he shall be entitled to no more than the corporation's offer.

. . . .

§ 82.
Voluntary Dissolution by Incorporators

A corporation which has not commenced business and which has not issued any shares, may be voluntarily dissolved by its incorporators at any time in the following manner:

(a) Articles of dissolution shall be executed in duplicate by a majority of the incorporators, and verified by them, and shall set forth:

(1) The name of the corporation.

(2) The date of issuance of its certificate of incorporation.

(3) That none of its shares has been issued.

(4) That the corporation has not commenced business.

(5) That the amount, if any, actually paid in on subscriptions for its shares, less any part thereof disbursed for necessary expenses, has been returned to those entitled thereto.

(6) That no debts of the corporation remain unpaid.

(7) That a majority of the incorporators elect that the corporation be dissolved.

(b) Duplicate originals of the articles of dissolution shall be delivered to the Secretary of State. If the Secretary of State finds that the articles of dissolution conform to law, he shall, when all fees and franchise taxes have been paid as in this Act prescribed:

(1) Endorse on each of such duplicate originals the word "Filed," and the month, day and year of the filing thereof.

(2) File one of such duplicate originals in his office.

(3) Issue a certificate of dissolution to which he shall affix the other duplicate original.

The certificate of dissolution, together with the duplicate original of the articles of dissolution affixed thereto by the Secretary of State, shall be returned to the incorporators or their representative. Upon the issuance of such certificate of dissolution by the Secretary of State, the existence of the corporation shall cease.

§ 83.
Voluntary Dissolution by Consent of Shareholders

A corporation may be voluntarily dissolved by the written consent of all of its shareholders.

Upon the execution of such written consent, a statement of intent to dissolve shall be executed in duplicate by the corporation by its president or a vice president and by its secretary or an assistant secretary, and verified by one of the officers signing such statement, which statement shall set forth:

(a) The name of the corporation.

(b) The names and respective addresses of its officers.

(c) The names and respective addresses of its directors.

(d) A copy of the written consent signed by all shareholders of the corporation.

(e) A statement that such written consent has been signed by all shareholders of the corporation or signed in their names by their attorneys thereunto duly authorized.

§ 84.
Voluntary Dissolution by Act of Corporation

A corporation may be dissolved by the act of the corporation, when authorized in the following manner:

(a) The board of directors shall adopt a resolution recommending that the corporation be dissolved, and directing that the question of such dissolution be submitted to a vote at a meeting of shareholders, which may be either an annual or a special meeting.

(b) Written notice shall be given to each shareholder of record entitled to vote at such meeting within the time and in the manner provided in this Act for the giving of notice of meetings of shareholders, and, whether the meeting be an annual or special meeting, shall state that the purpose, or one of the purposes, of such meeting is to consider the advisability of dissolving the corporation.

(c) At such meeting a vote of shareholders entitled to vote thereat shall be taken on a resolution to dissolve the corporation. Such resolution shall be adopted upon receiving the affirmative vote of the holders of a majority of the shares of the corporation entitled to vote thereon, unless any class of shares is entitled to vote theron as a class, in which event the resolution shall be adopted upon receiving the affirmative vote of the holders of a majority of the shares of each class of shares entitled to vote thereon as a class and of the total shares entitled to vote thereon.

(d) Upon the adoption of such resolution, a statement of intent to dissolve shall be executed in duplicate by the corporation by its president or a vice president and by its secretary or an assistsant secretary, and verified by one of the officers signing such statement, which statement shall set forth:

(1) The name of the corporation.

(2) The names and respective addresses of its officers.

(3) The names and respective addresses of its directors.

(4) A copy of the resolution adopted by the shareholders authorizing the dissolution of the corporation.

(5) The number of shares outstanding, and, if the shares of any class are entitled to vote as a class, the designation and number of outstanding shares of each such class.

(6) The number of shares voted for and against the resolution, respectively, and, if the shares of any class are entitled to vote as a class, the number of shares of each such class voted for and against the resolution, respectively.

§ 85.
Filing of Statement of Intent to Dissolve

Duplicate originals of the statement of intent to dissolve, whether by consent of shareholders or by act of the corporation, shall be delivered to the Secretary of State. . . .

§ 86.
Effect of Statement of Intent to Dissolve

Upon the filing by the Secretary of State of a statement of intent to dissolve, whether by consent of shareholders or by act of the corporation, the corporation shall cease to carry on its business, except insofar as may be necessary for the winding up thereof, but its corporate existence shall continue until a certificate of dissolution has been issued by the Secretary of State or until a decree dissolving the corporation has been entered by a court of competent jurisdiction as in this Act provided.

§ 87.
Procedure after Filing of Statement of Intent to Dissolve

After the filing by the Secretary of State of a statement of intent to dissolve:

(a) The corporation shall immediately cause notice thereof to be mailed to each known creditor of the corporation.

(b) The corporation shall proceed to collect its assets, convey and dispose of such of its properties as are not to be distributed in kind to its shareholders, pay, satisfy and discharge its liabilities and obligations and do all other acts required to liquidate its business and affairs, and, after paying or adequately providing for the payment of all its obligations, distribute the remainder of its assets, either in cash or in kind, among its shareholders according to their respective rights and interests.

(c) The corporation, at any time during the liquidation of its business and affairs, may make application to a court of competent jurisdiction with the state and judicial subdivision in which the registered office or principal place of business of the corporation is situated, to have the liquidation continued under the supervision of the court as provided in this Act.

§ 88.
Revocation of Voluntary Dissolution Proceedings by Consent of Shareholders

. . . .

§ 89.
Revocation of Voluntary Dissolution Proceedings by Act of Corporation

. . . .

(d) Upon the adoption of such resolution, a statement of revocation of voluntary dissolution proceedings shall be executed in duplicate by the corporation by its president or a vice president and by its secretary or an assistant secretary, and verified by one of the officers signing such statement, which statement shall set forth:

(1) The name of the corporation.

(2) The names and respective addresses of its officers.

(3) The names and respective addresses of its directors.

(4) A copy of the resolution adopted by the shareholders revoking the voluntary dissolution proceedings.

(5) The number of shares outstanding.

(6) The number of shares voted for and against the resolution, respectively.

§ 90.
Filing of Statement of Revocation of Voluntary Dissolution Proceedings

. . . .

§ 91.
Effect of Statement of Revocation of Voluntary Dissolution Proceedings

. . . .

§ 92.
Articles of Dissolution

If voluntary dissolution proceedings have not been revoked, then when all debts, liabilities and obligations of the corporation have been paid and discharged, or adequate provision has been made therefor, and all of the remaining property and assets of the corporation have been distributed to its shareholders, articles of dissolution shall be executed in duplicate by the corporation by its president or a vice president and by its secretary or an assistant secretary, and verified by one of the officers signing such statement, which statement shall set forth:

(a) The name of the corporation.

(b) That the Secretary of State has theretofore filed a statement of intent to dissolve the corporation, and the date on which such statement was filed.

(c) That all debts, obligations and liabilities of the corporation have been paid and discharged or that adequate provision has been made therefor.

(d) That all the remaining property and assets of the corporation have been distributed among its shareholders in accordance with their respective rights and interests.

(e) That there are no suits pending against the corporation in any court, or that adequate provision has been made for the satisfaction of any judgment, order or decree which may be entered against it in any pending suit.

§ 93.
Filing of Articles of Dissolution

Duplicate originals of such articles of dissolution shall be delivered to the Secretary of State. If the Secretary of State finds that such articles of dissolution conform to law, he shall, when all fees and franchise taxes have been paid as in this Act prescribed: . . .

(c) Issue a certificate of dissolution to which he shall affix the other duplicate original. . . .

§ 94.
Involuntary Dissolution

A corporation may be dissolved involuntarily by a decree of the . . . . court in an action filed by the Attorney General when it is established that:

(a) The corporation has failed to file its annual report within the time required by this Act, or has failed to pay its franchise tax on or before the first day of August of the year in which such franchise tax becomes due and payable; or

(b) The corporation procured its articles of incorporation through fraud; or

(c) The corporation has continued to exceed or abuse the authority conferred upon it by law; or

(d) The corporation has failed for thirty days to appoint and maintain a registered agent in this State; or

(e) The corporation has failed for thirty days after change of its registered office or registered agent to file in the office of the Secretary of State a statement of such change.

§ 95.
Notification to Attorney General

The Secretary of State, on or before the last day of December of each year, shall certify to the Attorney General the names of all corporations which have failed to file their annual reports or to pay franchise taxes in accordance with the provisions of this Act, together with the facts pertinent thereto. He shall also certify, from time to time, the names of all corporations which have given other cause for dissolution as provided in this Act, together with the facts pertinent thereto. Whenever the Secretary of State shall certify the name of a corporation to the Attorney General as having given any cause for dissolution, the Secretary of State shall concurrently mail to the corporation at its registered office a notice that such certification has been made. Upon the receipt of such certification, the Attorney General shall file an action in the name of the State against such corporation for its dissolution. . . .

§ 96.
Venue and Process

. . . .

§ 97.
Jurisdiction of Court to Liquidate Assets and Business of Corporation

The . . . . courts shall have full power to liquidate the assets and business of a corporation:

(a) In an action by a shareholder when it is established:

(1) That the directors are deadlocked on the management of the corporate affairs and the shareholders are unable to break the deadlock, and that irreparable injury to the corporation is being suffered or is threatened by reason thereof; or

(2) That the acts of the directors or those in control of the corporation are illegal, oppressive or fraudulent; or

(3) That the shareholders are deadlocked in voting power, and have failed, for a period which includes at least two consecutive annual meeting dates, to elect successors to directors whose terms have expired or would have expired upon the election of their successors; or

(4) That the corporate assets are being misapplied or wasted.

(b) In an action by a creditor:

(1) When the claim of the creditor has been reduced to judgment and an execution thereon returned unsatisfied and it is established that the corporation is insolvent; or

(2) When the corporation has admitted in writing that the claim of the creditor is due and owing and it is established that the corporation is insolvent.

(c) Upon application by a corporation which has filed a statement of intent to dissolve, as provided in this Act, to have its liquidation continued under the supervision of the court.

(d) When an action has been filed by the Attorney General to dissolve a corporation and it is established that liquidation of its business and affairs should precede the entry of a decree of dissolution.

Proceedings under clause (a), (b) or (c) of this section shall be brought in the county in which the registered office or the principal office of the corporation is situated.

It shall not be necessary to make shareholders parties to any such action or proceeding unless relief is sought against them personally.

§ 98.
Procedure in Liquidation of Corporation by Court

In proceedings to liquidate the assets and business of a corporation the court shall have the power to issue injunctions, to appoint a receiver or receivers pendente lite, with such powers and duties as the court, from time to time, may direct, and to take such other proceedings as may be requisite to preserve the corporate assets wherever situated, and carry on the business of the corporation until a full hearing can be had.

After a hearing had upon such notice as the court may direct to be given to all parties to the proceedings and to any other parties in interest designated by the court, the court may appoint a liquidating receiver or receivers with authority to collect the assets of the corporation, including all amounts owing to the corporation by subscribers on account of any unpaid portion of the consideration for the issuance of shares. Such liquidating receiver or receivers shall have authority, subject to the order of the court, to sell, convey and dispose of all or any part of the assets of the corporation wherever situated, either at public or private sale. The assets of the corporation or the proceeds resulting from a sale, conveyance or other disposition thereof shall be applied to the expenses of such liquidation and to the payment of the liabilities and obligations of the corporation, and any remaining assets or proceeds shall be distributed among its shareholders according to their respective rights and interests. The order appointing such liquidating receiver or receivers shall state their powers and duties. Such powers and duties may be increased or diminished at any time during the proceedings.

The court shall have power to allow from time to time as expenses of the liquidation compensation to the receiver or receivers and to attorneys in the proceeding, and to direct the payment thereof out of the assets of the corporation or the proceeds of any sale or disposition of such assets.

A receiver of a corporation appointed under the provisions of this section shall have authority to sue and defend in all courts in his own name as receiver of such corporation. The court appointing such receiver shall have exclusive jurisdiction of the corporation and its property, wherever situated.

§ 99.
Qualifications of Receivers

. . . .

§ 100.
Filing of Claims in Liquidation Proceedings

. . . .

§ 101.
Discontinuance of Liquidation Proceedings

. . . .

§ 102.
Decree of Involuntary Dissolution

In proceedings to liquidate the assets and business of a corporation, when the costs and expenses of such proceedings and all debts, obligations and liabilities of the corporation shall have been paid and discharged and all of its remaining property and assets distributed to its shareholders, or in case its property and assets are not sufficient to satisfy and discharge such costs, expenses, debts, and obligations, all the property and assets have been applied so far as they will go to their payment, the court shall enter a decree dissolving the corporation, whereupon the existence of the corporation shall cease.

§ 103.
Filing of Decree of Dissolution

. . . .

§ 104.
Deposit with State Treasurer of Amount Due Certain Shareholders

Upon the voluntary or involuntary dissolution of a corporation, the portion of the assets distributable to a creditor or shareholder who is unknown or cannot be found, or who is under disability and there is no person legally competent to receive such distributive portion, shall be reduced to cash and deposited with the State Treasurer and shall be paid over to such creditor or shareholder or to his legal representative upon proof satisfactory to the State Treasurer of his right thereto.

§ 105.
Survival of Remedy after Dissolution

The dissolution of a corporation either (1) by the issuance of a certificate of dissolution by the Seretary of State, or (2) by a decree of court when the court has not liquidated the assets and business of the corporation as provided in this Act, or (3) by expiration of its period of duration, shall not take away or impair any remedy available to or against such corporation, its directors, officers, or shareholders, for any right or claim existing, or any liability incurred, prior to such dissolution if action or other proceeding thereon is commenced within two years after the date of such dissolution. Any such action or proceeding by or against the corporation may be prosecuted or defended by the corporation in its corporate name. The shareholders, directors and officers shall have power to take such corporate or other action as shall be appropriate to protect such remedy, right or claim. If such corporation was dissolved by the expiration of its period of duration, such corporation may amend its articles of incorporation at any time during such period of two years so as to extend its period of duration.

§ 106.
Admission of Foreign Corporation

No foreign corporation shall have the right to transact business in this State until it shall have procured a certificate of authority so to do from the Secretary of State. No foreign corporation shall be entitled to procure a certificate of authority under this Act to transact in this State any business which a corporation organized under this Act is not permitted to transact. A foreign corporation shall not be denied a certificate of authority by reason of the fact that the laws of the state or county under which such corporation is orga-

nized governing its organization and internal affairs differ from the laws of this State, and nothing in this Act contained shall be construed to authorize this State to regulate the organization or the internal affairs of such corporation.

Without excluding other activities which may not constitute transacting business in this State, a foreign corporation shall not be considered to be transacting business in this State, for the purposes of this Act, by reason of carrying on in this State any one or more of the following activities:

(a) Maintaining or defending any action or suit or any administrative or arbitration proceeding, or effecting the settlement thereof or the settlement of claims or disputes.

(b) Holding meetings of its directors or shareholders or carrying on other activities concerning its internal affairs.

(c) Maintaining bank accounts.

(d) Maintaining offices or agencies for the transfer, exchange and registration of its securities, or appointing and maintaining trustees or depositaries with relation to its securities.

(e) Effecting sales through independent contractors.

(f) Soliciting or procuring orders, whether by mail or through employees or agents or otherwise, where such orders require acceptance without this State before becoming binding contracts.

(g) Creating as borrower or lender, or acquiring, indebtedness or mortgages or other security interests in real or personal property.

(h) Securing or collecting debts or enforcing any rights in property securing the same.

(i) Transacting any business in interstate commerce.

(j) Conducting an isolated transaction completed within a period of thirty days and not in the course of a number of repeated transactions of like nature.

§ 107.
Powers of Foreign Corporation

A foreign corporation which shall have received a certificate of authority under this Act shall, until a certificate of revocation or of withdrawal shall have been issued as provided in this Act, enjoy the same, but no greater, rights and privileges as a domestic corporation organized for the purposes set forth in the application pursuant to which such certificate of authority is issued; and, except as in this Act otherwise provided, shall be subject to the same duties, restrictions, penalties and liabilities now or hereafter imposed upon a domestic corporation of like character.

§ 108.
Corporate Name of Foreign Corporation

No certificate of authority shall be issued to a foreign corporation unless the corporate name of such corporation:

(a) Shall contain the word "corporation," "company," "incorporated," or "limited," or shall contain an abbreviation of one of such words, or such corporation shall, for use in this State, add at the end of its name one of such words or an abbreviation thereof.

(b) Shall not contain any word or phrase which indicates or implies that it is organized for any purpose other than one or more of the purposes contained in its articles of incorporation or that it is authorized or empowered to conduct the business of banking or insurance.

(c) Shall not be the same as, or deceptively similar to, the name of any domestic corporation existing under the laws of this State or any foreign corporation authorized to transact business in this State, or a name the exclusive right to which is, at the time, reserved in the manner provided in this Act, or the name of a corporation which has in effect a registration of its name as provided in this Act except that this provision shall not apply if the foreign corporation applying for a certificate of authority files with the Secretary of State any one of the following:

(1) a resolution of its board of directors adopting a fictitious name for use in transacting business in this State which fictitious name is not deceptively similar to the name of any domestic corporation or of any foreign corporation authorized to transact business in this State or to any name reserved or registered as provided in this Act, or

(2) the written consent of such other corporation or holder of a reserved or registered name to use the same or deceptively similar name and one or more words are added to make such name distinguishable from such other name, or

(3) a certified copy of a final decree of a court of competent jurisdiction establishing the prior right of such foreign corporation to the use of such name in this State.

§ 109.
Change of Name by Foreign Corporation

Whenever a foreign corporation which is authorized to transact business in this State shall change its name to one under which a certificate of authority would not be granted to it on application therefor, the certificate of authority of such corporation shall be suspended and it shall not thereafter transact any business in this State until it has changed its name to a name which is available to it under the laws of this State or has otherwise complied with the provisions of this Act.

§ 110.
Application for Certificate of Authority

A foreign corporation, in order to procure a certificate of authority to transact business in this State, shall make application therefor to the Secretary of State, which application shall set forth:

(a) The name of the corporation and the state or county under the laws of which it is incorporated.

(b) If the name of the corporation does not contain the word "corporation," "company," "incorporated," or "lim-

ited," or does not contain an abbreviation of one of such words, then the name of the corporation with the word or abbreviation which it elects to add thereto for use in this State.

(c) The date of incorporation and the period of duration of the corporation.

(d) The address of the principal office of the corporation in the state or country under the laws of which it is incorporated.

(e) The address of the proposed registered office of the corporation in this State, and the name of its proposed registered agent in this State at such address.

(f) The purpose or purposes of the corporation which it proposes to pursue in the transaction of business in this State.

(g) The names and respective addresses of the directors and officers of the corporation.

(h) A statement of the aggregate number of shares which the corporation has authority to issue, itemized by classes and series, if any, within a class.

(i) A statement of the aggregate number of issued shares, itemized by class and by series, if any, within each class.

(j) An estimate, expressed in dollars, of the value of all property to be owned by the corporation for the folowing year, wherever located, and an estimate of the value of the property of the corporation to be located within this State during such year, and an estimate, expressed in dollars of the gross amount of business which will be transacted by the corporation during such year, and an estimate of the gross amount thereof which will be transacted by the corporation at or from places of business in this State during such year.

(k) Such additional information as may be necessary or appropriate in order to enable the Secretary of State to determine whether such corporation is entitled to a certificate of authority to transact business in this State and to determine and assess the fees and franchise taxes payable as in this Act prescribed.

Such application shall be made on forms prescribed and furnished by the Secretary of State and shall be executed in duplicate by the corporation by its president or a vice president and by its secretary or an assistant secretary, and verified by one of the officers signing such application.

§ 111:
Filing of Application for Certificate of Authority

Duplicate originals of the application of the corporation for a certificate of authority shall be delivered to the Secretary of State, together with a copy of its articles of incorporation and all amendments thereto, duly authenticated by the proper officer of the state or country under the laws of which it is incorporated.

If the Secretary of State finds that such application conforms to law, he shall, when all fees and franchise taxes have been paid as in this Act prescribed: . . .

(c) Issue a certificate of authority to transact business in this State to which he shall affix the other duplicate original application. . . .

§ 112.
Effect of Certificate of Authority

Upon the issuance of a certificate of authority by the Secretary of State, the corporation shall be authorized to transact business in this State for those purposes set forth in its application, subject, however, to the right of this State to suspend or to revoke such authority as provided in this Act.

§ 113.
Registered Office and Registered Agent of Foreign Corporation

Each foreign corporation authorized to transact business in this State shall have and continuously maintain in this State:

(a) A registered office which may be, but need not be, the same as its place of business in this State.

(b) A registered agent, which agent may be either an individual resident in this State whose business office is identical with such registered office, or a domestic corporation, or a foreign corporation authorized to transact business in this State, having a business office identical with such registered office.

§ 114.
Change of Registered Office or Registered Agent of Foreign Corporation

A foreign corporation authorized to transact business in this State may change its registered office or change its registered agent, or both, upon filing in the office of the Secretary of State a statement setting forth:

(a) The name of the corporation.

(b) The address of its then registered office.

(c) If the address of its registered office be changed, the address to which the registered office is to be changed.

(d) The name of its then registered agent.

(e) If its registered agent be changed, the name of its successor registered agent.

(f) That the address of its registered office and the address of the business office of its registered agent, as changed, will be identical.

(g) That such change was authorized by resolution duly adopted by its board of directors.

Such statement shall be executed by the corporation by its president or a vice president, and verified by him, and delivered to the Secretary of State. If the Secretary of State finds that such statement conforms to the provisions of this Act, he shall file such statement in his office, and upon such filing the change of address of the registered office, or the appointment of a new registered agent, or both, as the case may be, shall become effective.

Any registered agent of a foreign corporation may resign as such agent upon filing a written notice thereof, executed in duplicate, with the Secretary of State, who shall forthwith mail a copy thereof to the corporation at its principal office in the state or country under the laws of which it is incorporated. The appointment of such agent shall terminate upon the expiration of thirty days after receipt of such notice by the Secretary of State.

If a registered agent changes his or its business address to another place within the same . . . . ,* he or it may change such address and the address of the registered office of any corporation of which he or it is registered agent by filing a statement as required above except that it need be signed only by the registered agent and need not be responsive to (e) or (g) and must recite that a copy of the statement has been mailed to the corporation.

§ 115.
Service of Process on Foreign Corporation

The registered agent so appointed by a foreign corporation authorized to transact business in this State shall be an agent of such corporation upon whom any process, notice or demand required or permitted by law to be served upon the corporation may be served.

Whenever a foreign corporation authorized to transact business in this State shall fail to appoint or maintain a registered agent in this State, or whenever any such registered agent cannot with reasonable diligence be found at the registered office, or whenever the certificate of authority of a foreign corporation shall be suspended or revoked, then the Secretary of State shall be an agent of such corporation upon whom any such process, notice, or demand may be served. Service on the Secretary of State of any such process, notice or demand shall be made by delivering to and leaving with him, or with any clerk having charge of the corporation department of his office, duplicate copies of such process, notice or demand. In the event any such process, notice or demand is served on the Secretary of State, he shall immediately cause one of such copies thereof to be forwarded by registered mail, addressed to the corporation at its principal office in the state or country under the laws of which it is incorporated. Any service so had on the Secretary of State shall be returnable in not less than thirty days.

The Secretary of State shall keep a record of all processes, notices and demands served upon him under this section, and shall record therein the time of such service and his action with reference thereto.

Nothing herein contained shall limit or affect the right to serve any process, notice or demand, required or permitted by law to be served upon a foreign corporation in any other manner now or hereafter permitted by law.

---

*Supply designation of jurisdiction, such as county, etc., in accordance with local practice.

§ 116.
Amendment to Articles of Incorporation of Foreign Corporation

Whenever the articles of incorporation of a foreign corporation authorized to transact business in this State are amended, such foreign corporation shall, within thirty days after such amendment becomes effective, file in the office of the Secretary of State a copy of such amendment duly authenticated by the proper officer of the state or country under the laws of which it is incorporated; but the filing thereof shall not of itself enlarge or alter the purpose or purposes which such corporation is authorized to pursue in the transaction of business in this State, nor authorize such corporation to transact business in this State under any other name than the name set forth in its certificate of authority.

§ 117.
Merger of Foreign Corporation Authorized to Transact Business in This State

Whenever a foreign corporation authorized to transact business in this State shall be a party to a statutory merger permitted by the laws of the state or country under the laws of which it is incorporated, and such corporation shall be the surviving corporation, it shall, within thirty days after such merger becomes effective, file with the Secretary of State a copy of the articles of merger duly authenticated by the proper officer of the state or country under the laws of which such statutory merger was effected; and it shall not be necessary for such corporation to procure either a new or amended certificate of authority to transact business in this State unless the name of such corporation be changed thereby or unless the corporation desires to pursue in this State other or additional purposes than those which it is then authorized to transact in this State.

§ 118.
Amended Certificate of Authority

A foreign corporation authorized to transact business in this State shall procure an amended certificate of authority in the event it changes its corporate name, or desires to pursue in this State other or additional purposes than those set forth in its prior application for a certificate of authority, by making application therefor to the Secretary of State.

The requirements in respect to the form and contents of such application, the manner of its execution, the filing of duplicate originals thereof with the Secretary of State, the issuance of an amended certificate of authority and the effect thereof, shall be the same as in the case of an original application for a certificate of authority.

§ 119.
Withdrawal of Foreign Corporation

A foreign corporation authorized to transact business in this State may withdraw from this State upon procuring from the Secretary of State a certificate of withdrawal. In order to procure such certificate of withdrawal, such foreign corporation shall deliver to the Secretary of State an application for withdrawal, which shall set forth:

(a) The name of the corporation and the state or country under the laws of which it is incorporated.

(b) That the corporation is not transacting business in this State.

(c) That the corporation surrenders its authority to transact business in this State.

(d) That the corporation revokes the authority of its registered agent in this State to accept service of process and consents that service of process in any action, suit or proceeding based upon any cause of action arising in this State during the time the corporation was authorized to transact business in this State may thereafter be made on such corporation by service thereof on the Secretary of State.

(e) A post-office address to which the Secretary of State may mail a copy of any process against the corporation that may be served on him.

(f) A statement of the aggregate number of shares which the corporation has authority to issue, itemized by class and series, if any, within each class, as of the date of such application.

(g) A statement of the aggregate number of issued shares, itemized by class and series, if any, within each class, as of the date of such application.

(h) Such additional information as may be necessary or appropriate in order to enable the Secretary of State to determine and assess any unpaid fees or franchise taxes payable by such foreign corporation as in this Act prescribed.

The application for withdrawal shall be made on forms prescribed and furnished by the Secretary of State and shall be executed by the corporation by its president or a vice president and by its secretary or an assistant secretary, and verified by one of the officers signing the application, or, if the corporation is in the hands of a receiver or trustee, shall be executed on behalf of the corporation by such receiver or trustee and verified by him.

§ 120.
Filing of Application for Withdrawal

. . . .

§ 121.
Revocation of Certificate of Authority

The certificate of authority of a foreign corporation to transact business in this State may be revoked by the Secretary of State upon the conditions prescribed in this section when:

(a) The corporation has failed to file its annual report within the time required by this Act, or has failed to pay any fees, franchise taxes or penalties prescribed by this Act when they have become due and payable; or

(b) The corporation has failed to appoint and maintain a registered agent in this State as required by this Act; or

(c) The corporation has failed, after change of its registered office or registered agent, to file in the office of the Secretary of State a statement of such change as required by this Act; or

(d) The corporation has failed to file in the office of the Secretary of State any amendment to its articles of incorporation or any articles of merger within the time prescribed by this Act; or

(e) A misrepresentation has been made of any material matter in any application, report, affidavit, or other document submitted by such corporation pursuant to this Act.

No certificate of authority of a foreign corporation shall be revoked by the Secretary of State unless (1) he shall have given the corporation not less than sixty days' notice thereof by mail addressed to its registered office in this State, and (2) the corporation shall fail prior to revocation to file such annual report, or pay such fees, franchise taxes or penalties, or file the required statement of change of registered agent or registered office, or file such articles of amendment or articles of merger, or correct such misrepresentation.

§ 122.
Issuance of Certificate of Revocation

. . . .

§ 123.
Application to Corporations Heretofore Authorized to Transact Business in This State

. . . .

§ 124.
Transacting Business Without Certificate of Authority

No foreign corporation transacting business in this State without a certificate of authority shall be permitted to maintain any action, suit or proceeding in any court of this State, until such corporation shall have obtained a certificate of authority. Nor shall any action, suit or proceeding be maintained in any court of this State by any successor or assignee of such corporation on any right, claim or demand arising out of the transaction of business by such corporation in this State, until a certificate of authority shall have been obtained by such corporation or by a corporation which has acquired all or substantially all of its assets.

The failure of a foreign corporation to obtain a certificate of authority to transact business in this State shall not impair the validity of any contract or act of such corporation, and shall not prevent such corporation from defending any action, suit or proceeding in any court of this State.

A foreign corporation which transacts business in this State without a certificate of authority shall be liable to this State, for the years or parts thereof during which it transacted business in this State without a certificate of authority, in an amount equal to all fees and franchise taxes which would have been imposed by this Act upon such corporation had it

duly applied for and received a certificate of authority to transact business in this State as required by this Act and thereafter filed all reports required by this Act, plus all penalties imposed by this Act for failure to pay such fees and franchise taxes. The Attorney General shall bring proceedings to recover all amounts due this State under the provisions of this Section.

§ 125.
Annual Report of Domestic and Foreign Corporations

Each domestic corporation, and each foreign corporation authorized to transact business in this State, shall file, within the time prescribed by this Act, an annual report setting forth:

(a) The name of the corporation and the state or country under the laws of which it is incorporated.

(b) The address of the registered office of the corporation in this State, and the name of its registered agent in this State at such address, and, in case of a foreign corporation, the address of its principal office in the state or country under the laws of which it is incorporated.

(c) A brief statement of the character of the business in which the corporation is actually engaged in this State.

(d) The names and respective addresses of the directors and officers of the corporation.

(e) A statement of the aggregate number of shares which the corporation has authority to issue, itemized by class and series, if any, within each class.

(f) A statement of the aggregate number of issued shares, itemized by class and series, if any, within each class.

(g) A statement, expressed in dollars, of the value of all the property owned by the corporation, wherever located, and the value of the property of the corporation located within this State, and a statement, expressed in dollars, of the gross amount of business transacted by the corporation for the twelve months ended on the thirty-first day of December preceding the date herein provided for the filing of such report and the gross amount thereof transacted by the corporation at or from places of business in this State. If, on the thirty-first day of December preceding the time herein provided for the filing of such report, the corporation had not been in existence for a period of twelve months, or in the case of a foreign corporation had not been authorized to transact business in this State for a period of twelve months, the statement with respect to business transacted shall be furnished for the period between the date of incorporation or the date of its authorization to transact business in this State, as the case may be, and such thirty-first day of December. If all the property of the corporation is located in this State and all of its business is transacted at or from places of business in this State, then the information required by this subparagraph need not be set forth in such report.

(h) Such additional information as may be necessary or appropriate in order to enable the Secretary of State to determine and assess the proper amount of franchise taxes payable by such corporation.

Such annual report shall be made on forms prescribed and furnished by the Secretary of State, and the information therein contained shall be given as of the date of the execution of the report, except as to the information required by subparagraphs (g) and (h) which shall be given as of the close of business on the thirty-first day of December next preceding the date herein provided for the filing of such report. It shall be executed by the corporation by its president, a vice president, secretary, an assistant secretary, or treasurer, and verified by the officer executing the report, or, if the corporation is in the hands of a receiver or trustee, it shall be executed on behalf of the corporation and verified by such receiver or trustee.

§ 126.
Filing of Annual Report of Domestic and Foreign Corporations

. . . .

§ 127.
Fees, Franchise Taxes and Charges to be Collected by Secretary of State

. . . .

§ 128.
Fees for Filing Documents and Issuing Certificates

. . . .

§ 129.
Miscellaneous Charges

. . . .

§ 130.
License Fees Payable by Domestic Corporations

. . . .

§ 131.
License Fees Payable by Foreign Corporations

. . . .

§ 132.
Franchise Taxes Payable by Domestic Corporations

. . . .

§ 133.
Franchise Taxes Payable by Foreign Corporations

. . . .

§ 134.
Assessment and Collection of Annual Franchise Taxes

. . . .

§ 135.
Penalties Imposed Upon Corporations

Each corporation, domestic or foreign, that fails or refuses to file its annual report for any year within the time prescribed by this Act shall be subject to a penalty of ten percent of the amount of the franchise tax assessed against it for the period beginning July 1 of the year in which such report should have been filed. Such penalty shall be assessed by the Secretary of State at the time of the assessment of the franchise tax. If the amount of the franchise tax as originally assessed against such corporation be thereafter adjusted in accordance with the provisions of this Act, the amount of the penalty shall be likewise adjusted to ten percent of the amount of the adjusted franchise tax. The amount of the franchise tax and the amount of the penalty shall be separately stated in any notice to the corporation with respect thereto.

If the franchise tax assessed in accordance with the provisions of this Act shall not be paid on or before the thirty-first day of July, it shall be deemed to be delinquent, and there shall be added a penalty of one percent for each month or part of month that the same is delinquent, commencing with the month of August.

Each corporation, domestic or foreign, that fails or refuses to answer truthfully and fully within the time prescribed by this Act interrogatories propounded by the Secretary of State in accordance with the provisions of this Act, shall be deemed to be guilty of a misdemeanor and upon conviction thereof may be fined in any amount not exceeding five hundred dollars.

§ 136.
Penalties Imposed Upon Officers and Directors

Each officer and director of a corporation, domestic or foreign, who fails or refuses within the time prescribed by this Act to answer truthfully and fully interrogatories propounded to him by the Secretary of State in accordance with the provisions of this Act, or who signs any articles, statement, report, application or other document filed with the Secretary of State which is known to such officer or director to be false in any material respect, shall be deemed to be guilty of a misdemeanor, and upon conviction thereof may be fined in any amount not exceeding . . . . dollars.

§ 137.
Interrogatories by Secretary of State

The Secretary of State may propound to any corporation, domestic or foreign, subject to the provisions of this Act, and to any officer or director thereof, such interrogatories as may be reasonably necessary and proper to enable him to ascertain whether such corporation has complied with all the provisions of this Act applicable to such corporation. Such interrogatories shall be answered within thirty days after the mailing thereof, or within such additional time as shall be fixed by the Secretary of State, and the answers thereto shall be full and complete and shall be made in writing and under oath. If such interrogatories be directed to an individual they shall be answered by him, and if directed to a corporation they shall be answered by the president, vice president, secretary or assistant secretary thereof. The Secretary of State need not file any document to which such interrogatories relate until such interrogatories be answered as herein provided, and not then if the answers thereto disclose that such document is not in conformity with the provisions of this Act. The Secretary of State shall certify to the Attorney General, for such action as the Attorney General may deem appropriate, all interrogatories and answers thereto which disclose a violation of any of the provisions of this Act.

§ 138.
Information Disclosed by Interrogatories

. . . .

§ 139.
Powers of Secretary of State

. . . .

§ 140.
Appeal from Secretary of State

If the Secretary of State shall fail to approve any articles of incorporation, amendment, merger, consolidation or dissolution, or any other document required by this Act to be approved by the Secretary of State before the same shall be filed in his office, he shall, within ten days after the delivery thereof to him, give written notice of his disapproval to the person or corporation, domestic or foreign, delivering the same, specifying the reasons therefor. From such disapproval such person or corporation may appeal to the . . . . court of the county in which the registered office of such corporation is, or is proposed to be, situated by filing with the clerk of such court a petition setting forth a copy of the articles or other document sought to be filed and a copy of the written disapproval thereof by the Secretary of State; whereupon the matter shall be tried de novo by the court, and the court shall either sustain the action of the Secretary of State or direct him to take such action as the court may deem proper.

If the Secretary of State shall revoke the certificate of authority to transact business in this State of any foreign corporation, pursuant to the provisions of this Act, such foreign corporation may likewise appeal to the . . . . court of the county where the registered office of such corporation in this State is situated, by filing with the clerk of such court a petition setting forth a copy of its certificate of authority to transact business in this State and a copy of the notice of revocation given by the Secretary of State; whereupon the matter shall be tried de novo by the court, and the court shall either sustain the action of the Secretary of State or direct him to take such action as the court may deem proper.

Appeals from all final orders and judgments entered by the . . . . court under this section in review of any ruling or decision of the Secretary of State may be taken as in other civil actions.

§ 141.
Certificates and Certified Copies to be Received in Evidence

All certificates issued by the Secretary of State in accordance with the provisions of this Act, and all copies of documents filed in his office in accordance with the provisions of this Act when certified by him, shall be taken and received in all courts, public offices, and official bodies as prima facie evidence of the facts therein stated. A certificate by the Secretary of State under the great seal of this State, as to the existence or nonexistence of the facts relating to corporations shall be taken and received in all courts, public offices, and official bodies as prima facie evidence of the existence or nonexistence of the facts therein stated.

§ 142.
Forms to be Furnished by Secretary of State

. . . .

§ 143.
Greater Voting Requirements

Whenever, with respect to any action to be taken by the shareholders of a corporation, the articles of incorporation require the vote or concurrence of the holders of a greater proportion of the shares, or of any class or series thereof, than required by this Act with respect to such action, the provisions of the articles of incorporation shall control.

§ 144.
Waiver of Notice

Whenever any notice is required to be given to any shareholder or director of a corporation under the provisions of this Act or under the provisions of the articles of incorporation or by-laws of the corporation, a waiver thereof in writing signed by the person or persons entitled to such notice, whether before or after the time stated therein, shall be equivalent to the giving of such notice.

§ 145.
Action by Shareholders Without a Meeting

Any action required by this Act to be taken at a meeting of the shareholders of a corporation, or any action which may be taken at a meeting of the shareholders, may be taken without a meeting if a consent in writing, setting forth the action so taken, shall be signed by all of the shareholders entitled to vote with respect to the subject matter thereof.

Such consent shall have the same effect as a unanimous vote of shareholders, and may be stated as such in any articles or document filed with the Secretary of State under this Act.

§ 146.
Unauthorized Assumption of Corporate Powers

All persons who assume to act as a corporation without authority so to do shall be jointly and severally liable for all debts and liabilities incurred or arising as a result thereof.

§ 147.
Application to Existing Corporations

. . . .

Appendix F

THE CONSTITUTION OF
THE UNITED STATES OF AMERICA

We the People of the United States, in Order to form a more perfect Union, establish Justice, insure domestic Tranquility, provide for the common defence, promote the general Welfare, and secure the Blessings of Liberty to ourselves and our Posterity, do ordain and establish this Constitution for the United States of America.

ARTICLE I

Section 1

All legislative Powers herein granted shall be vested in a Congress of the United States, which shall consist of a Senate and House of Representatives.

Section 2

The House of Representatives shall be composed of Members chosen every second Year by the People of the several States, and the Electors in each State shall have the Qualifications requisite for Electors of the most numerous Branch of the State Legislature.

No Person shall be a Representative who shall not have attained to the Age of twenty five Years, and been seven Years a Citizen of the United States, and who shall not, when elected, be an Inhabitant of that State in which he shall be chosen.

Representatives and direct Taxes shall be apportioned among the several States which may be included within this Union, according to their respective Numbers, which shall be determined by adding to the whole Number of free Persons, including those bound to Service for a Term of Years, and excluding Indians not taxed, three fifths of all other Persons. The actual Enumeration shall be made within three Years after the first Meeting of the Congress of the United States, and within every subsequent Term of ten Years, in such Manner as they shall by Law direct. The number of Representatives shall not exceed one for every thirty Thousand, but each State shall have at Least one Representative; and until such enumeration shall be made, the State of New Hampshire shall be entitled to chuse three, Massachusetts eight, Rhode Island and Providence Plantations one, Connecticut five, New-York six, New Jersey four, Pennsylvania eight, Delaware one, Maryland six, Virginia ten, North Carolina five, South Carolina five, and Georgia three.

When vacancies happen in the Representation from any State, the Executive Authority thereof shall issue Writs of Election to fill such vacancies.

The House of Representatives shall chuse their Speaker and other Officers; and shall have the sole Power of Impeachment.

Section 3

The Senate of the United States shall be composed of two Senators from each State, chosen by the Legislature thereof, for six Years; and each Senator shall have one Vote.

Immediately after they shall be assembled in Consequence of the first Election, they shall be divided as equally as may be into three Classes. The Seats of the Senators of the first Class shall be vacated at the Expiration of the second Year, of the second Class at the Expiration of the fourth Year, and of the third Class at the Expiration of the sixth Year, so that one third may be chosen every second Year; and if Vacancies happen by Resignation, or otherwise, during the Recess of the Legislature of any State, the Executive thereof may make temporary Appointments until the next Meeting of the Legislature, which shall then fill such Vacancies.

No Person shall be a Senator who shall not have attained to the Age of thirty Years, and been nine Years a Citizen of the United States, and who shall not, when elected, be an Inhabitant of that State for which he shall be chosen.

The Vice President of the United States shall be President of the Senate, but shall have no Vote, unless they be equally divided.

The Senate shall chuse their other Officers, and also a President pro tempore, in the Absence of the Vice President, or when he shall exercise the Office of President of the United States.

The Senate shall have the sole power to try all Impeachments. When sitting for that Purpose, they shall be on Oath or Affirmation. When the President of the United States is tried, the Chief Justice shall preside: And no Person shall be convicted without the Concurrence of two thirds of the Members present.

Judgment in Cases of Impeachment shall not extend further than to removal from Office, and disqualification to hold and enjoy any Office of honor, Trust or Profit under the United States: but the Party convicted shall nevertheless be liable and subject to Indictment, Trial, Judgment and Punishment, according to Law.

Section 4

The Times, Places and Manner of holding Elections for Senators and Representatives, shall be prescribed in each State by the Legislature thereof: but the Congress may at any time by Law make or alter such Regulations, except as to the Places of chusing Senators.

The Congress shall assemble at least once in every Year, and such Meeting shall be on the first Monday in December, unless they shall by Law appoint a different Day.

Section 5

Each House shall be the Judge of the Elections, Returns and Qualifications of its own Members, and a Majority of each shall constitute a Quorum to do Business; but a smaller Number may adjourn from day to day, and may be authorized to compel the Attendance of absent Members, in such Manner, and under such Penalties as each House may provide.

Each House may determine the Rules of its Proceedings, punish its Members for disorderly Behaviour, and, with the Concurrence of two thirds, expel a Member.

Each House shall keep a Journal of its Proceedings, and from time to time publish the same, excepting such Parts as may in their Judgment require Secrecy; and the Yeas and Nays of the Members of either House on any question shall,

at the Desire of one fifth of those Present, be entered on the Journal.

Neither House, during the Session of Congress, shall, without the Consent of the other, adjourn for more than three days, nor to any other Place than that in which the two Houses shall be sitting.

Section 6

The Senators and Representatives shall receive a Compensation for their Services, to be ascertained by Law, and paid out of the Treasury of the United States. They shall in all Cases, except Treason, Felony and Breach of the Peace, be privileged from Arrest during their Attendance at the Session of their respective Houses, and in going to and returning from the same; and for any Speech or Debate in either House, they shall not be questioned in any other Place.

No Senator or Representative shall, during the Time for which he was elected, be appointed to any civil Office under the Authority of the United States, which shall have been created, or the Emoluments whereof shall have been encreased during such time; and no Person holding any Office under the United States, shall be a Member of either House during his Continuance in Office.

Section 7

All Bills for raising Revenue shall originate in the House of Representatives; but the Senate may propose or concur with Amendments as on other Bills.

Every Bill which shall have passed the House of Representatives and the Senate, shall, before it become a Law, be presented to the President of the United States; If he approve he shall sign it, but if not he shall return it, with his Objections to that House in which it shall have originated, who shall enter the Objections at large on their Journal, and proceed to reconsider it. If after such Reconsideration two thirds of that House shall agree to pass the Bill, it shall be sent, together with the Objections, to the other House, by which it shall likewise be reconsidered, and if approved by two thirds of that House, it shall become a Law. But in all such Cases the Votes of both Houses shall be determined by Yeas and Nays, and the Names of the Persons voting for and against the Bill shall be entered on the Journal of each House respectively. If any Bill shall not be returned by the President within ten Days (Sundays excepted) after it shall have been presented to him, the Same shall be a Law, in like Manner as if he had signed it, unless the Congress by their Adjournment prevent its Return, in which Case it shall not be a Law.

Every Order, Resolution, or Vote to which the Concurrence of the Senate and House of Representatives may be necessary (except on a question of Adjournment) shall be presented to the President of the United States; and before the Same shall take Effect, shall be approved by him, or being disapproved by him, shall be repassed by two thirds of the

Senate and House of Representatives, according to the Rules and Limitations prescribed in the Case of a Bill.

Section 8

The Congress shall have Power to lay and collect Taxes, Duties, Imposts and Excises, to pay the Debts and provide for the common Defence and general Welfare of the United States; but all Duties, Imposts and Excises shall be uniform throughout the United States;

To borrow Money on the credit of the United States;

To regulate Commerce with foreign Nations, and among the several States, and with the Indian Tribes;

To establish an uniform Rule of Naturalization, and uniform Laws on the subject of Bankruptcies throughout the United States;

To coin Money, regulate the Value thereof, and of foreign Coin, and fix the Standard of Weights and Measures;

To provide for the Punishment of counterfeiting the Securities and current Coin of the United States;

To establish Post Offices and post Roads;

To promote the Progress of Science and useful Arts, by securing for limited Times to Authors and Inventors the exclusive Right to their respective Writings and Discoveries;

To constitute Tribunals inferior to the supreme Court;

To define and punish Piracies and Felonies committed on the high Seas, and Offenses against the Law of Nations;

To declare War, grant Letters of Marque and Reprisal, and make Rules concerning Captures on Land and Water;

To raise and support Armies, but no Appropriation of Money to that Use shall be for a longer Term than two Years;

To provide and maintain a Navy;

To make Rules for the Government and Regulation of the land and naval Forces;

To provide for calling forth the Militia to execute the Laws of the Union, suppress Insurrections and repel Invasions;

To provide for organizing, arming, and disciplining, the Militia, and for governing such Part of them as may be employed in the Service of the United States, reserving to the States respectively, the Appointment of the Officers, and the Authority of training the Militia according to the discipline prescribed by Congress;

To exercise exclusive Legislation in all Cases whatsoever, over such District (not exceeding ten Miles square) as may, by Cession of particular States, and the Acceptance of Congress, become the Seat of the Government of the United States, and to exercise like Authority over all Places purchased by the Consent of the Legislature of the State in which the Same shall be, for the Erection of Forts, Magazines, Arsenals, dock-Yards, and other needful Buildings;—And

To make all Laws which shall be necessary and proper for carrying into Execution the foregoing Powers, and all other Powers vested by this Constitution in the Government of the United States, or in any Department or Officer thereof.

Section 9

The Migration or Importation of such Persons as any of the States now existing shall think proper to admit, shall not be prohibited by the Congress prior to the Year one thousand eight hundred and eight, but a Tax or Duty may be imposed on such Importation, not exceeding ten dollars for each Person.

The Privilege of the Writ of Habeas Corpus shall not be suspended, unless when in Cases of Rebellion or Invasion the public Safety may require it.

No Bill of Attainder or ex post facto Law shall be passed.

No Capitation, or other direct, Tax shall be laid, unless in Proportion to the Census or Enumeration herein before directed to be taken.

No Tax or Duty shall be laid on Articles exported from any State.

No Preference shall be given by any Regulation of Commerce or Revenue to the Ports of one State over those of another: nor shall Vessels bound to, or from, one State, be obliged to enter, clear, or pay Duties in another.

No Money shall be drawn from the Treasury, but in Consequence of Appropriations made by Laws; and a regular Statement and Account of the Receipts and Expenditures of all public Money shall be published from time to time.

No Title of Nobility shall be granted by the United States: And no Person holding any Office of Profit or Trust under them, shall, without the Consent of the Congress, accept of any present, Emolument, Office, or Title, of any kind whatever, from any King, Prince, or foreign State.

Section 10

No State shall enter into any Treaty, Alliance, or Confederation; grant Letters of Marque and Reprisal; coin Money; emit Bills of Credit; make any Thing but gold and silver Coin a Tender in Payment of Debts; pass any Bill of Attainder, ex post facto Law, or Law impairing the Obligation of Contracts, or grant any Title of Nobility.

No State shall, without the Consent of the Congress, lay any Imposts or Duties on Imports or Exports, except what may be absolutely necessary for executing its inspection Laws: and the net Produce of all Duties and Imposts, laid by any State on Imports or Exports, shall be for the Use of the Treasury of the United States; and all such Laws shall be subject to the Revision and Controul of the Congress.

No State shall, without the Consent of Congress, lay any Duty of Tonnage, keep Troops, or Ships of War in time of Peace, enter into any Agreement or Compact with another State, or with a foreign Power, or engage in War, unless actually invaded, or in such imminent Danger as will not admit of delay.

ARTICLE II

Section 1

The executive Power shall be vested in a President of the United States of America. He shall hold his Office during the Term of four Years, and, together with the Vice President, chosen for the same Term, be elected, as follows:

Each State shall appoint, in such Manner as the Legislature thereof may direct, a Number of Electors, equal to the whole Number of Senators and Representatives to which the State may be entitled in the Congress: but no Senator or Representative, or Person holding an Office of Trust or Profit under the United States, shall be appointed an Elector.

The Electors shall meet in their respective States, and vote by Ballot for two Persons, of whom one at least shall not be an Inhabitant of the same State with themselves. And they shall make a List of all the Persons voted for, and of the Number of Votes for each; which List they shall sign and certify, and transmit sealed to the Seat of the Government of the United States, directed to the President of the Senate. The President of the Senate shall, in the Presence of the Senate and House of Representatives, open all the Certificates, and the Votes shall then be counted. The Person having the greatest Number of Votes shall be the President, if such Number be a Majority of the whole Number of Electors appointed; and if there be more than one who have such Majority, and have an equal Number of Votes, then the House of Representatives shall immediately chuse by Ballot one of them for President; and if no Person have a Majority, then from the five highest on the List the said House shall in like Manner chuse the President. But in chusing the President, the Votes shall be taken by States, the Representation from each State having one Vote; A quorum for this Purpose shall consist of a Member or Members from two thirds of the States, and a Majority of all the States shall be necessary to a Choice. In every Case, after the Choice of the President, the Person having the greatest Number of Votes of the Electors shall be the Vice President. But if there should remain two or more who have equal Votes, the Senate shall chuse from them by Ballot the Vice President.

The Congress may determine the Time of chusing the Electors, and the Day on which they shall give their Votes; which Day shall be the same throughout the United States.

No Person except a natural born Citizen, or a Citizen of the United States, at the time of the Adoption of this Constitution, shall be eligible to the Office of President; neither shall any Person be eligible to that Office who shall not have attained to the Age of thirty five Years, and been fourteen Years a Resident within the United States.

In Case of the Removal of the President from Office, or of his Death, Resignation, or Inability to discharge the Powers and Duties of the said Office, the Same shall devolve on the Vice President, and the Congress may by Law provide for the Case of Removal, Death, Resignation or Inability, both of the President and Vice President, declaring what Officer shall then act as President, and such Officer shall act accordingly, until the Disability be removed, or a President shall be elected.

The President shall, at stated Times, receive for his Services, a Compensation, which shall neither be encreased nor diminished during the Period for which he shall have been elected, and he shall not receive within that Period any other Emolument from the United States, or any of them.

Before he enter on the Execution of his Office, he shall take the following Oath or Affirmation:—"I do solemnly swear (or affirm) that I will faithfully execute the Office of President of the United States, and will to the best of my Ability, preserve, protect and defend the Constitution of the United States."

Section 2

The President shall be Commander in Chief of the Army and Navy of the United States, and of the Militia of the several States, when called into the actual Service of the United States; he may require the Opinion, in writing, of the principal Officer in each of the executive Departments, upon any Subject relating to the Duties of their respective Offices, and he shall have Power to grant Reprieves and Pardons for Offences against the United States, except in Cases of Impeachment.

He shall have Power, by and with the Advice and Consent of the Senate, to make Treaties, providing two thirds of the Senators present concur; and he shall nominate, and by and with the Advice and Consent of the Senate, shall appoint Ambassadors, other public Ministers and Consuls, Judges of the supreme Court, and all other Officers of the United States, whose Appointments are not herein otherwise provided for, and which shall be established by Law: but the Congress may by Law vest the Appointment of such inferior Officers, as they think proper, in the President alone, in the Courts of Law, or in the Heads of Departments.

The President shall have Power to fill up all Vacancies that may happen during the Recess of the Senate, by granting Commissions which shall expire at the End of their next Session.

Section 3

He shall from time to time give to the Congress Information of the State of the Union, and recommend to their Consideration such Measures as he shall judge necessary and expedient; he may, on extraordinary Occasions, convene both Houses, or either of them, and in Case of Disagreement between them, with Respect to the Time of Adjournment, he may adjourn them to such Time as he shall think proper, he shall receive Ambassadors and other public Ministers; he shall take Care that the Laws be faithfully executed, and shall Commission all the Officers of the United States.

Section 4

The President, Vice President and all civil Officers of the United States, shall be removed from Office on Impeachment for, and Conviction of, Treason, Bribery, or other high Crimes and Misdemeanors.

ARTICLE III

Section 1

The judicial Power of the United States, shall be vested in one supreme Court, and in such inferior Courts as the Congress may from time to time ordain and establish. The Judges, both of the supreme and inferior Courts, shall hold their Offices during good Behaviour, and shall, at stated Times, receive for their Services, a Compensation, which shall not be diminished during their Continuance in Office.

Section 2

The judicial Power shall extend to all Cases, in Law and Equity, arising under this Constitution, the Laws of the United States, and Treaties made, or which shall be made, under their Authority;—to all Cases affecting Ambassadors, other public Ministers and Consuls;—to all Cases of admirality and maritime Jurisdiction;—to Controversies to which the United States shall be a Party;—to Controversies between two or more States;—between a State and Citizens of another State;—between Citizens of different States;—between Citizens of the same State claiming Lands under Grants of different States, and between a State, or the Citizens thereof, and foreign States, Citizens or Subjects.

In all Cases affecting Ambassadors, other public Ministers and Consuls, and those in which a State shall be Party, the supreme Court shall have original Jurisdiction. In all the other Cases before mentioned, the supreme Court shall have appellate Jurisdiction, both as to Law and Fact, with such Exceptions, and under such Regulations as the Congress shall make.

The Trial of all Crimes, except in Cases of Impeachment, shall be by Jury; and such Trial shall be held in the State where the said Crimes shall have been committed; but when not committed within any State, the Trial shall be at such Place or Places as the Congress may by Law have directed.

Section 3

Treason against the United States, shall consist only in levying War against them, or in adhering to their Enemies, giving them Aid and Comfort. No Person shall be convicted of Treason unless on the Testimony of two Witnesses to the same overt Act, or on Confession in open Court.

The Congress shall have Power to declare the Punishment of Treason, but no Attainder of Treason shall work Corruption of Blood, or Forfeiture except during the Life of the Person attainted.

ARTICLE IV

Section 1

Full Faith and Credit shall be given in each State to the public Acts, Records, and judicial Proceedings of every other State. And the Congress may by general Laws prescribe the Manner in which such Acts, Records and Proceedings shall be proved, and the Effect thereof.

Section 2

The Citizens of each State shall be entitled to all Privileges and Immunities of Citizens in the several States.

A Person charged in any State with Treason, Felony, or other Crime, who shall flee from Justice, and be found in another State, shall on Demand of the executive Authority of the State from which he fled, be delivered up, to be removed to the State having Jurisdiction of the Crime.

No Person held to Service or Labour in one State, under the Laws thereof, escaping into another, shall, in Consequence of any Law or Regulation therein, be discharged from such Service or Labour, but shall be delivered up on Claim of the Party to whom such Service or Labour may be due.

Section 3

New States may be admitted by the Congress into this Union; but no new State shall be formed or erected within the Jurisdiction of any other State; nor any State be formed by the Junction of two or more States, or Parts of States, without the Consent of the Legislatures of the States concerned as well as of the Congress.

The Congress shall have Power to dispose of and make all needful Rules and Regulations respecting the Territory or other Property belonging to the United States; and nothing in this Constitution shall be so construed as to Prejudice any Claims of the United States, or of any particular State.

Section 4

The United States shall guarantee to every State in this Union a Republican Form of Government, and shall protect each of them against Invasion; and on Application of the Legislature, or of the Executive (when the Legislature cannot be convened) against domestic Violence.

ARTICLE V

The Congress, whenever two thirds of both Houses shall deem it necessary, shall propose Amendments to this Constitution, or, on the Application of the Legislatures of two thirds of the several States, shall call a Convention for proposing Amendments, which, in either Case, shall be valid to all Intents and Purposes, as Part of this Constitution, when ratified by the Legislatures of three fourths of the several States, or by Conventions in three fourths thereof, as the one or the other Mode of Ratification may be proposed by the Congress; Provided that no Amendment which may be made prior to the Year One thousand eight hundred and eight shall in any Manner affect the first and fourth Clauses in the Ninth Section of the first Article; and that no State, without its Consent, shall be deprived of its equal Suffrage in the Senate.

ARTICLE VI

All Debts contracted and Engagements entered into, before the Adoption of this Constitution, shall be as valid against the United States under this Constitution, as under the Confederation.

This Constitution, and the Laws of the United States which shall be made in Pursuance thereof; and all Treaties made, or which shall be made, under the Authority of the United States, shall be the supreme Law of the Land; and the Judges in every State shall be bound thereby, any Thing in the Constitution or Laws of any State to the Contrary notwithstanding.

The Senators and Representatives before mentioned, and the Members of the several State Legislatures, and all executive and judicial Officers, both of the United States and of the several States, shall be bound by Oath or Affirmation, to support this Constitution; but no religious Test shall ever be required as a Qualification to any Office or public Trust under the United States.

ARTICLE VII

The Ratification of the Conventions of nine States, shall be sufficient for the Establishment of this Constitution between the States so ratifying the Same.

AMENDMENT I [1791]

Congress shall make no law respecting an establishment of religion, or prohibiting the free exercise thereof; or abridging the freedom of speech, or of the press; or the right of the people peaceably to assemble, and to petition the Government for a redress of grievances.

AMENDMENT II [1791]

A well regulated Militia, being necessary to the security for a free State, the right of the people to keep and bear Arms, shall not be infringed.

AMENDMENT III [1791]

No Soldier shall, in time of peace be quartered in any house, without the consent of the Owner, nor in time of war, but in a manner to be prescribed by law.

AMENDMENT IV [1791]

The right of the people to be secure in their persons, houses, papers, and effects, against unreasonable searches and seizures, shall not be violated, and no Warrants shall issue, but upon probable cause, supported by Oath or affirmation, and particularly describing the place to be searched, and the persons or things to be seized.

AMENDMENT V [1791]

No person shall be held to answer for a capital, or otherwise infamous crime, unless on a presentment or indictment of a Grand Jury, except in cases arising in the land or naval forces, or in the Militia, when in actual service in time of War or public danger; nor shall any person be subject for the same offense to be twice put in jeopardy of life or limb; nor shall be compelled in any criminal case to be a witness against himself, nor be deprived of life, liberty, or property, without due process of law; nor shall private property be taken for public use, without just compensation.

AMENDMENT VI [1791]

In all criminal prosecutions, the accused shall enjoy the right to a speedy and public trial, by an impartial jury of the State and district wherein the crime shall have been committed, which district shall have been previously ascertained by law, and to be informed of the nature and cause of the accusation; to be confronted with the Witnesses against him; to have compulsory process for obtaining witnesses in his favor, and to have the Assistance of counsel for his defence.

AMENDMENT VII [1791]

In Suits at common law, where the value in controversy shall exceed twenty dollars, the right of trial by jury shall be preserved, and no fact tried by a jury, shall be otherwise reexamined in any Court of the United States, than according to the rules of the common law.

AMENDMENT VIII [1791]

Excessive bail shall not be required, no excessive fines imposed, nor cruel and unusual punishments inflicted.

AMENDMENT IX [1791]

The enumeration in the Constitution, of certain rights, shall not be construed to deny or disparage others retained by the people.

AMENDMENT X [1791]

The powers not delegated to the United States by the Constitution, nor prohibited by it to the States, are reserved to the States respectively, or to the people.

AMENDMENT XI [1798]

The Judicial power of the United States shall not be construed to extend to any suit in law or equity, commenced or prosecuted against one of the United States by Citizens of another State, or by Citizens or Subjects of any Foreign State.

AMENDMENT XII [1804]

The Electors shall meet in their respective states and vote by ballot for President and Vice-President, one of whom, at least, shall not be an inhabitant of the same state with themselves; they shall name in their ballots the person voted for as President, and in distinct ballots the person voted for as Vice-President, and they shall make distinct lists of all persons voted for as President, and of all persons voted for as Vice-President, and of the number of votes for each, which lists they shall sign and certify, and transmit sealed to the seat of the government of the United States, directed to the President of the Senate;—The President of the Senate shall, in the presence of the Senate and House of Representatives, open all the certificates and the votes shall then be counted;—The person having the greatest number of votes for President, shall be the President, if such number be a majority of the whole number of Electors appointed; and if no person have such majority, then from the persons having the highest numbers not exceeding three on the list of those voted for as President, the House of Representatives shall choose immediately, by ballot, the President. But in choosing the President, the votes shall be taken by states, the representation from each state having one vote; a quorum for this purpose shall consist of a member or members from two-thirds of the states, and a majority of all the states shall be necessary to a choice. And if the House of Representatives shall not choose a President whenever the right of choice shall devolve upon them, before the fourth day of March next following, then the Vice-President shall act as President, as in the case of the death or other constitutional disability of the President. The person having the greatest number of votes as Vice-President, shall be the Vice-President, if such number be a majority of the whole number of Electors appointed, and if

no person have a majority, then from the two highest numbers on the list, the Senate shall choose the Vice-President; a quorum for the purpose shall consist of two-thirds of the whole number of Senators, and a majority of the whole number shall be necessary to a choice. But no person constitutionally ineligible to the office of President shall be eligible to that of the Vice-President of the United States.

AMENDMENT XIII [1865]

Section 1

Neither slavery nor involuntary servitude, except as a punishment for crime whereof the party shall have been duly convicted, shall exist within the United States, or any place subject to their jurisdiction.

Section 2

Congress shall have power to enforce this article by appropriate legislation.

AMENDMENT XIV [1868]

Section 1

All persons born or naturalized in the United States, and subject to the jurisdiction thereof, are citizens of the United States and of the State wherein they reside. No State shall make or enforce any law which shall abridge the privileges or immunities of citizens of the United States; nor shall any State deprive any person of life, liberty, or property, without due process of law; nor deny to any person within its jurisdiction the equal protection of the laws.

Section 2

Representatives shall be appointed among the several States according to their respective numbers, counting the whole number of persons in each State, excluding Indians not taxed. But when the right to vote at any election for the choice of electors for President and Vice President of the United States, Representatives in Congress, the Executive and Judicial officers of a State, or the members of the Legislature thereof, is denied to any of the male inhabitants of such State, being twenty-one years of age, and citizens of the United States, or in any way abridged, except for participation in rebellion, or other crime, the basis of representation therein shall be reduced in the proportion which the number of such male citizens shall bear to the whole number of male citizens twenty-one years of age in such State.

Section 3

No person shall be a Senator or Representative in Congress, or elector of President and Vice President, or hold any office, civil or military, under the United States, or under any State, who, having previously taken an oath, as a member of Congress, or as an officer of the United States, or as a member of any State legislature, or as an executive or judicial officer of any State, to support the Constitution of the United States, shall have engaged in insurrection or rebellion against the same, or given aid or comfort to the enemies thereof. But Congress may by a vote of two-thirds of each House, remove such disability.

Section 4

The validity of the public debt of the United States, authorized by law, including debts incurred for payment of pensions and bounties for services in suppressing insurrection or rebellion, shall not be questioned. But neither the United States nor any State shall assume or pay any debt or obligation incurred in aid of insurrection or rebellion against the United States, or any claim for the loss or emancipation of any slave; but all such debts, obligations and claims shall be held illegal and void.

Section 5

The Congress shall have power to enforce, by appropriate legislation, the provisions of this article.

AMENDMENT XV [1870]

Section 1

The right of citizens of the United States to vote shall not be denied or abridged by the United States or by any State on account of race, color, or previous condition of servitude.

Section 2

The Congress shall have power to enforce this article by appropriate legislation.

AMENDMENT XVI [1913]

The Congress shall have power to lay and collect taxes on incomes, from whatever source derived, without apportionment among the several States, and without regard to any census or enumeration.

AMENDMENT XVII [1913]

The Senate of the United States shall be composed of two Senators from each State, elected by the people thereof, for six years; and each Senator shall have one vote. The electors in each State shall have the qualifications requisite for electors of the most numerous branch of the State legislatures.

When vacancies happen in the representation of any State in the Senate, the executive authority of each State shall issue writs of election to fill such vacancies; *Provided*, That the legislature of any State may empower the executive thereof to make temporary appointments until the people fill the vacancies by election as the legislature may direct.

This amendment shall not be so construed as to affect the election or term of any Senator chosen before it becomes valid as part of the Constitution.

AMENDMENT XVIII [1919]

Section 1

After one year from the ratification of this article the manufacture, sale, or transportation of intoxicating liquors within, the importation thereof into, or the exportation thereof from the United States and all territory subject to the jurisdiction thereof for beverage purposes is hereby prohibited.

Section 2

The Congress and the several States shall have concurrent power to enforce this article by appropriate legislation.

Section 3

This article shall be inoperative unless it shall have been ratified as an amendment to the Constitution by the legislatures of the several States, as provided in the Constitution, within seven years from the date of the submission hereof to the States by the Congress.

AMENDMENT XIX [1920]

The right of citizens of the United States to vote shall not be denied or abridged by the United States or by any State on account of sex.

Congress shall have power to enforce this article by appropriate legislation.

AMENDMENT XX [1933]

Section 1

The terms of the President and Vice President shall end at noon on the 20th day of January, and the terms of Senators and Representatives at noon on the 3d day of January, of the years in which such terms would have ended if this article had not been ratified; and the terms of their successors shall then begin.

Section 2

The Congress shall assemble at least once in every year, and such meeting shall begin at noon on the 3d day of January, unless they shall by law appoint a different day.

Section 3

If, at the time fixed for the beginning of the term of the President, the President elect shall have died, the Vice President elect shall become President. If a President shall not have been chosen before the time fixed for the beginning of his term, or if the President elect shall have failed to qualify, then the Vice President elect shall act as President until a President shall have qualified; and the Congress may by law provide for the case wherein neither a President elect nor a Vice President elect shall have qualified, declaring who shall then act as President, or the manner in which one who is to act shall be selected, and such person shall act accordingly until a President or Vice President shall have qualified.

Section 4

The Congress may by law provide for the case of the death of any of the persons from whom the House of Representatives may choose a President whenever the right of choice shall have devolved upon them, and for the case of the death of any of the persons from whom the Senate may choose a Vice President whenever the right of choice shall have devolved upon them.

Section 5

Sections 1 and 2 shall take effect on the 15th day of October following the ratification of this article.

Section 6

This article shall be inoperative unless it shall have been ratified as an amendment to the Constitution by the legislatures of three-fourths of the several States within seven years from the date of its submission.

AMENDMENT XXI [1933]

Section 1

The eighteenth article of amendment to the Constitution of the United States is hereby repealed.

Section 2

The transportation or importation into any State, Territory, or possession of the United States for delivery or use therein of intoxicating liquors, in violation of the laws thereof, is hereby prohibited.

Section 3

This article shall be inoperative unless it shall have been ratified as an amendment to the Constitution by conventions in the several States, as provided in the Constitution, within seven years from the date of the submission hereof to the States by the Congress.

AMENDMENT XXII [1951]

Section 1

No person shall be elected to the office of the President more than twice, and no person who has held the office of President, or acted as President, for more than two years of a term to which some other person was elected President shall be elected to the office of the President more than once. But this Article shall not apply to any person holding the office of President when this Article was proposed by the Congress, and shall not prevent any person who may be holding the office of President, or acting as President, during the term within which this Article becomes operative from holding the office of President or acting as President during the remainder of such term.

Section 2

This article shall be inoperative unless it shall have been ratified as an amendment to the Constitution by the legislatures of three-fourths of the several States within seven years from the date of its submission to the States by the Congress.

AMENDMENT XXIII [1961]

Section 1

The District constituting the seat of Government of the United States shall appoint in such manner as the Congress may direct:

A number of electors of President and Vice President equal to the whole number of Senators and Representatives in Congress to which the District would be entitled if it were a State, but in no event more than the least populous State; they shall be in addition to those appointed by the States, but they shall be considered, for the purposes of the election of President and Vice President, to be electors appointed by a State; and they shall meet in the District and perform such duties as provided by the twelfth article of amendment.

Section 2

The Congress shall have power to enforce this article by appropriate legislation.

AMENDMENT XXIV [1964]

Section 1

The right of citizens of the United States to vote in any primary or other election for President or Vice President, for electors for President or Vice President, or for Senator or Representative in Congress, shall not be denied or abridged by the United States or any State by reason of failure to pay any poll tax or other tax.

Section 2

The Congress shall have power to enforce this article by appropriate legislation.

AMENDMENT XXV [1967]

Section 1

In case of the removal of the President from office or of his death or resignation, the Vice President shall become President.

Section 2

Whenever there is a vacancy in the office of the Vice President, the President shall nominate a Vice President who shall take office upon confirmation by a majority vote of both Houses of Congress.

Section 3

Whenever the President transmits to the President pro tempore of the Senate and the Speaker of the House of Representatives his written declaration that he is unable to discharge the powers and duties of his office, and until he transmits to them a written declaration to the contrary, such powers and duties shall be discharged by the Vice President as Acting President.

Section 4

Whenever the Vice President and a majority of either the principal officers of the executive departments or of such other body as Congress may by law provide, transmit to the President pro tempore of the Senate and the Speaker of the House of Representatives their written declaration that the President is unable to discharge the powers and duties of his office, the Vice President shall immediately assume the powers and duties of the office as Acting President.

Thereafter, when the President transmits to the President pro tempore of the Senate and the Speaker of the House of Representatives his written declaration that no inability exists, he shall resume the powers and duties of his office unless the Vice President and a majority of either the principal officers of the executive department or of such other body as Congress may by law provide, transmit within four days to the President pro tempore of the Senate and the Speaker of the House of Representatives their written declaration that the President is unable to discharge the powers and duties of his office. Thereupon Congress shall decide the issue, assembling within forty-eight hours for that purpose if not in session. If the Congress, within twenty-one days after receipt of the latter written declaration, or, if Congress is not in session, within twenty-one days after Congress is required to assemble, determines by two-thirds vote of both Houses that the President is unable to discharge the powers and duties of his office, the Vice President shall continue to discharge the same as Acting President; otherwise, the President shall resume the powers and duties of his office.

AMENDMENT XXVI [1971]

Section 1

The right of citizens of the United States, who are eighteen years of age or older, to vote shall not be denied or abridged by the United States or by any State on account of age.

Section 2

The Congress shall have power to enforce this article by appropriate legislation.

GLOSSARY

abandoned property Property that is unowned because the owner has given up dominion and control with the intent to relinquish all claim or rights to it.

ab initio From the very beginning (Latin).

abstract In real property law, a summary compilation of the official records relating to a particular parcel of land.

abuse of discretion The failure of a judge or administrator to use sound or reasonable judgment in arriving at a decision.

acceleration clause In commercial paper, a statement in a time instrument (where payment is to be made at a prescribed time or times) that permits the entire debt to become due immediately upon the occurrence of some event, such as failure to pay one installment when due.

acceptance In contract law, the agreement of the offeree to the proposal or offer of the offeror.

acceptor In commercial paper, a drawee who agrees by his or her signature to honor a draft as presented.

accession An addition to, product of, or change in personal property; depending on the circumstances, either the owner of the original property or another

person responsible for the accession might be the owner of the altered property.

accommodated party The person who benefits by having another party lend his or her name (credit) on an instrument.

accommodation party A person who signs an instrument for the purpose of lending his or her name (credit) to another party on that instrument.

accord and satisfaction A form of discharge in contract law by which an agreement between the parties of a contract permits a substituted performance in lieu of the required obligation under the existing contract. The contract can be effectively terminated (satisfied) by performance as originally agreed upon or by the substitute performance.

account receivable A record of a debt owed to a person but not yet paid.

accredited investor An investor who is deemed not to need protection and, thus, can be sold securities exempt from SEC regulation.

accretion The gradual adding of land by natural causes, such as a deposit of soil by the action of a river.

acknowledgment A formal declaration or admission before a designated public official, such as a notary public, that something is genuine or that a particular act has taken place.

action at law A suit in which the plaintiff is seeking a legal remedy (such as damages), as distinguished from an equitable remedy (such as an injunction).

action in equity A civil suit in which the plaintiff is seeking an equitable remedy, such as an injunction or decree of specific performance.

action *in personam* A suit to hold a defendant personally liable for a wrong committed.

action *in rem* A suit to enforce a right against property of the defendant.

actual authority The express and implied authority of an agent.

adjudication The legal process of resolving a dispute.

adjudicatory power In administrative agency law, the right of an administrative agency to initiate actions as both prosecutor and judge against those thought to be in violation of the law (including agency rules and regulations) under the jurisdiction of the administrative agency—referred to as the quasi-judicial function of an agency.

adjustment case A procedure under Chapter 13 of the Bankruptcy Act which allows an individual to pay his or her debts from future income over an extended period of time.

administrative agency A board, commission, agency, or service authorized by a legislative enactment to implement specific laws on either the local, state, or national level.

administrative law Public law administered and/or formulated by a government unit such as a board, agency, or commission to govern the conduct of an individual, association, or corporation.

administrator In probate law, a person appointed by a probate court to supervise the distribution of a deceased person's property. This title is usually given when there is no will or when the person named as executor or executrix in the will cannot serve.

adverse possession The acquisition of title to real property by actually taking possession of the land without the owner's consent and retaining such possession openly for a prescribed statutory period.

affidavit A written sworn statement made before a person officially authorized to administer an oath.

affirmative action The granting of preferences based on race to minority employees.

affirmative defense A defendant's claim to dissolve himself or herself of liability even if the plaintiff's claim is true.

after-acquired property Property received or added after a specific event has taken place. For example, in secured transactions law, an after-acquired property clause in a security agreement means that property received by the debtor after the security agreement is made will be subject to the same security interest as the existing property referred to therein.

agency A relationship created by contract, agreement, or law between a principal and an agent whereby the principal is bound by the authorized actions of the agent.

agency coupled with an interest A relationship in which an agent, with consideration, has the right to exercise authority or is given an interest in the property of the principal subject to the agency.

agent One who is authorized to act for another, called a principal, whose acts bind the principal to his or her actions.

aggregate theory An approach under which associations or organizations are treated as a collection of persons, each with individual rights and liabilities.

agreement A meeting of the minds between two or more parties, which may or may not constitute a contract.

air rights A landowner's rights to the air space above his or her real property.

alien corporation A corporation chartered or incorporated in another country but doing business in the United States.

alteration (material) In commercial paper, the modification of the terms of an instrument that results in a change of the contract of any party on that instrument.

amendment The changing of a law, right, or interest that usually becomes binding upon fulfillment of a required act or action.

ancillary covenant   A covenant that is a subsidiary or auxiliary part of a larger agreement; to be valid, a covenant not to compete must be ancillary as well as reasonably limited in time and area.

annual percentage rate   The total of the items making up the finance charge, or cost of borrowing money or buying on credit, expressed as a yearly percentage rate that the consumer can use to "shop around" for the best credit terms.

answer   In pleadings, the defendant's response to the plaintiff's complaint or petition.

anticipatory breach   The repudiation of a contract by a party before the time of performance has arrived, allowing the nonbreaching party the opportunity to seek a remedy.

anticipatory repudiation   Breaching a contract by refusing to perform before it is actually time to perform.

apparent authority   Authority created by the words or conduct of the principal that leads a third person to believe the agent has such authority.

apparent intent   The establishment of a person's motive from his or her actions and/or words as interpreted by a reasonable person.

appellant   The party who appeals a decision of a lower court, usually that of a trial court.

appellee   The party against whom an appeal is made (sometimes referred to as a respondent—a person who defends on an appeal).

appraisal right   The right of a dissenting shareholder to sell back his or her shares to the corporation for cash.

arbitration   The submission of a dispute to a third party or parties for settlement.

articles of incorporation   A legal document, meeting the legal requirements of a given state, filed with a designated state official as an application for a certificate of incorporation.

articles of partnership   The agreement of the partners that forms and governs the operation of the partnership.

artisan's lien   A possessory lien held by one who has expended labor upon or added value to another's personal property as security for the work performed (labor and/or value added).

ascendants   The heirs of a decedent in the ascending line—parents or grandparents.

assault   The intentional movement or exhibition of force that would place a reasonable person in fear of physical attack or harm.

assault and battery   Any intentional physical contact by a person on another without consent or privilege.

assignee   The one to whom an assignment has been made.

assignment   The transfer of rights or a property interest to a third person, who can receive no greater rights than those possessed by the transferor.

assignment for the benefit of creditors   The voluntary transfer by a debtor of some or all of his or her property to an assignee or trustee, who sells or liquidates the debtor's assets and tenders to the creditors (on a pro rata basis) payment in satisfaction of the debt.

assignor   The one who makes an assignment.

association   The voluntary act or agreement by which two or more persons unite together for some special purpose or business.

assumed name statute   A law in most states which requires any firm, including a partnership, to register with a state official the fictitious name under which the firm is doing business; also called fictitious name statute.

attachment   (1) A legal proceeding provided by statute that permits a plaintiff in an existing court action to have nonexempt property of the defendant seized and a lien placed on the property as security of a judgment that may be rendered in the plaintiff's favor (this action being independent of plaintiff's suit and exercisable only on grounds provided by statute). (2) In secured transactions law, a method of perfecting a security interest without the secured party taking possession of the collateral or making a proper filing (which in most states applies only to a purchase money security interest in consumer goods).

attestation   The act of witnessing a document, such as a will, and signing to that effect.

attorney-at-law A lawyer.

attorney-in-fact An agent.

auction with reserve An auction in which the auctioneer, as agent for the owner of the goods, has the right to withdraw the goods from sale at any time prior to accepting a particular bid (such acceptance usually being signified by the fall of the hammer).

auction without reserve An auction where once the goods are placed on the auction block (for sale) they must be sold to the highest bidder.

award In arbitration proceedings, the decision or determination rendered by an arbitrator on a controversy submitted for settlement. For example, the arbitrator's **award** was unfair. In general usage, to grant some type of remedy. For example, the court **awards** an injunction.

bailee The person to whom a bailor has entrusted or transferred personal property without transferring title.

bailee's lien Usually a possessory lien held by a bailee on bailed property for which the bailee is entitled to compensation or reimbursement.

bailment The creation of a legal relationship through delivery or transfer of personal property (but not title) by one person, called the bailor, to another person, called the bailee, usually for a specific purpose as directed by the bailor.

bailor A person who entrusts or transfers personal property (but not title) to another, called the bailee, usually for the accomplishment of a specific purpose.

bank draft A draft by one bank on funds held by another bank.

bankruptcy A court procedure by which a person who is unable to pay his or her debts may be declared bankrupt, have nonexempt assets distributed to his or her creditors, and thereupon be given a release from any further payment of the balance due on most of these debts.

battery The wrongful intentional physical contact by a person (or object under control of that person) on another.

bearer In commercial paper, the person possessing an instrument either payable to anyone without specific designation or one indorsed in blank.

bearer instrument An instrument either payable to anyone without specific designation or one indorsed in blank.

beneficiary A person for whose benefit a will, trust, insurance policy, or contract is made.

benefit test A test through which the law determines whether a promise has consideration by seeing if the promisor has received an advantage, profit, or privilege in return for his or her promise.

bequest In a will a gift by the testator of specific personal property other than money.

bilateral contract A contract formed by the mutual exchange of promises of the offeror and the offeree.

bilateral mistake A mistake in which both parties to a contract are in error as to the terms of or performance expected under the contract. Also called mutual mistake.

bill of lading A negotiable or nonnegotiable document of title evidencing the receipt of goods for shipment, with shipping instructions to the carrier. A negotiable bill of lading is both a receipt and evidence of title to the goods shipped.

binder A temporary insurance contract formed when the insurance agent or broker accepts a prospective policyholder's application.

blank indorsement An indorsement that specifies no particular indorsee and that usually consists of a mere signature of the indorser.

blue laws Statutes and ordinances that limit or prohibit the carrying on of specified business activities on Sundays.

blue sky laws Laws enacted for the protection of investors that regulate the sales of stocks and bonds, and that also regulate other activities of investment companies related to such sales.

board of directors A body composed of persons elected by the corporation's shareholders and entrusted with the responsibility of managing the corporation.

bona fide occupational qualification (BFOQ) A defense in Title VII discrimination suits in which an employer must demonstrate a connection between the protected classification and job performance, and must prove that the performance affected is of the "essence" of the job and not merely tangential to the fundamental job function.

bona fide purchaser   A purchaser who acts in good faith and gives something of value for the goods received.

bonds   In corporate financing, secured or unsecured debt obligations of a corporation in the form of securities (instruments).

boycott   In antitrust law, an agreement between two or more parties to not deal with a third party. When the purpose is to exclude a firm or firms from a market, such an agreement is per se illegal under Section 1 of the Sherman Act. In labor law, action by a union to prevent others from doing business with the employer. A primary boycott, directed at the employer with whom the union has a labor dispute, is usually legal. A secondary boycott, aimed at an employer with whom the union does not have a labor dispute, is usually an unfair labor practice.

breach of duty   Failure to fulfill a legal obligation.

broker   In real property law, an agent employed by a landowner to find an acceptable buyer for his or her real property or employed by a prospective buyer to find a landowner willing to sell such property.

bulk transfer   A transfer of goods—such as materials, supplies, merchandise, or inventory (including equipment)—in such quantity or under such circumstances that the transfer is considered not to be in the ordinary course of the transferor's business.

burden of proof   The duty of a party to prove or disprove certain facts.

business judgment rule   A rule which protects corporate managers from responsibility for honest errors of judgment.

business trust   A business association created by agreement in which legal ownership and management of property is transferred, in return for trust certificates, to trustees who have the power to operate the business for the benefit of the original owners or certificate holders. It is usually treated in the same manner as a corporation if certificate holders do not control the management activities of the trustees.

bylaws   The internal rules made to regulate and govern the actions and affairs of a corporation.

capacity   The legal ability to perform an act—especially an act from which legal consequences flow, such as the making of a contract.

case law   Essentially synonymous with "common law."

cashier's check   A check drawn by a bank on itself.

cause of action   A person's right to seek a remedy when his or her rights have been breached or violated.

caveat emptor   In sales law, "let the buyer beware."

Celler-Kefauver Act   A 1950 congressional enactment amending Section 7 of the Clayton Act. The act prohibits a firm from acquiring all or part of the stock or assets of another firm where, in any line of commerce in any section of the country, the effect of such acquisition may be substantially to lessen competition.

certificate of authority   A foreign corporation's permission to do business in the state of issuance.

certificate of deposit   An instrument (essentially a note) that is an acknowledgment by a bank that it has received money and promises to repay the amount upon presentment when due.

certificate of incorporation   A document of a state that grants permission to do business in that state in the corporate form—sometimes called a charter.

certificate of title   A written opinion by an attorney as to the validity of a title.

certified check   A bank's guaranty (acceptance) by an appropriate signature that it will pay the check upon presentment.

challenge for cause   In jury selection, an objection to a prospective juror hearing a particular case, stating a reason that questions the impartiality of the juror.

charging order   An action by a creditor which requires that a partner's share of partnership profits be paid to the creditor until the debt is fully discharged.

chattel   Any property or interest therein other than real property.

chattel mortgage   A security document whereby the owner of personal property either transfers title to the lender or gives the lender a lien on the property as security for the performance of an obligation owed by the owner. Called a security interest under the UCC.

chattel paper Any writing or writings that evidence both a monetary obligation for and a security interest in (or a lease of) specific goods.

check A draft drawn on a bank (drawee) payable on demand.

CIF Cost, insurance, and freight; that is, the price charged by the seller includes not only the cost of the goods but also the cost of freight and insurance charges on the goods to the named destination.

circumstantial context In the process of statutory interpretation, a court's examination of the problem or problems that caused the enactment of the statute.

civil law As compared to criminal law, rules for establishing rights and duties between individuals whereby an individual can seek personal redress for a wrong committed by another individual. As compared to common law, codified rules reduced to formal written propositions as the law of a state or country. The written code serves as the basis of all decisions.

Civil Rights Act A comprehensive 1964 congressional enactment that prohibits discrimination in housing, public accommodations, education, and employment.

civil rights law The body of statutory and constitutional law defining and enforcing the privileges and freedoms belonging to every person in the United States. The objective of civil rights law is to secure equality of opportunity for all persons.

class action A legal proceeding initiated by one or more members of a similarly situated group or class of persons on behalf of themselves and other group members.

classified board A board of directors divided into classes with only one class elected each year; the result is directors who serve staggered terms.

Clayton Act A 1914 congressional enactment to generally prohibit price discrimination by a seller of goods, exclusive dealing and tying of a seller's products, mergers and consolidations of corporations that result in a substantial lessening of competition or tend to create a monopoly, and certain interlocking directorates. The act also provides an exemption from the antitrust laws for the organization and normal activities of labor unions.

close corporation A corporation that has a limited number of outstanding shares of stock, usually held by a single person or small group of persons, with restrictions on the right to transfer those shares to others.

closing In real property law, a meeting between the seller and buyer and any other interested parties at which passage of title and matters relating thereto are executed.

COD Collect on delivery; that is, the buyer must pay for the goods before he or she can inspect or receive possession of them.

codicil An addition to or change in a will executed with the same formalities as the will itself.

coinsurance clause A provision in a property insurance policy specifying that the property owner must bear a proportionate part of a casualty loss if he or she does not insure the property in an amount equal to a stated percentage of the property's value.

collateral In secured transactions law, the property subject to a security interest.

collateral note A note secured by personal property.

collective bargaining The term for negotiations between an employer and the union representative.

co-makers Two or more persons who create or execute a note or certificate of deposit.

commerce clause A clause contained in Article I, Section 8, of the U.S. Constitution, which permits Congress to control trade among the several states (and with foreign nations).

commercial contract A contract between two or more persons (merchants) engaged in trade or commerce.

commercial impracticability A legal doctrine which excuses a seller of goods from performance because an unforeseen occurrence has caused performance to be extremely burdensome.

commercial paper Instruments that are written promises or obligations to pay sums of money (called drafts, checks, certificates of deposit, or notes). When used in Article 3 of the UCC, the term refers only to negotiable instruments; when used elsewhere, to negotiable and nonnegotiable instruments.

commercial speech Expressions that primarily

convey a commercial message (i.e., advertising); recently recognized by the Supreme Court as being protected by the first amendment to the U.S. Constitution.

commingle   To blend or mix together.

common carrier   A carrier that holds itself out for hire to the general public to transport goods.

common law   Rules that have been developed from custom or judicial decisions without the aid of written legislation, and subsequently used as a basis for later decisions by a court—also referred to as judge-made or case law.

common stock   A class of stock that carries no rights or priorities over other classes of stock as to payment of dividends or distribution of corporate assets upon dissolution.

community property   A system of marital property ownership recognized in eight states under which property acquired after marriage (except by gift or inheritance) is co-owned by the husband and wife, regardless of which person acquired it.

comparable worth   The theory that jobs having comparable worth should receive comparable pay.

comparative negligence   The rule used in negligence cases in many states that provides for computing both the plaintiff's and the defendant's negligence, with the plaintiff's damages being reduced by a percentage representing the degree of his or her contributing fault. If the plaintiff's negligence is found to be greater than the defendant's, the plaintiff will receive nothing and will be subject to a counterclaim by the defendant.

compensatory damages   A monetary sum awarded for the actual loss a person has sustained for a wrong committed by another person.

complaint   In an action at law, the initial pleading filed by the plaintiff in a court with proper jurisdiction. In an action in equity, it is frequently referred to as a *petition*.

composition of creditors   An agreement between a debtor and his or her creditors that each creditor will accept a lesser amount than the debt owed as full satisfaction of that debt.

conclusions of law   Answers derived by applying law to facts.

concurrent jurisdiction   Where more than one court of a different name or classification has the right to hear a particular controversy.

condemnation   The process by which the government either exercises its power of eminent domain to take private property or officially declares property unfit for use.

condition   In contract law, a provision or clause in a contract which, upon the occurrence or nonoccurrence of a specified event, either creates, suspends, or terminates the rights and duties of the contracting parties.

condition concurrent   A condition in a contract that both parties' performances are to take place at the same time.

condition precedent   A condition that must take place before the parties are bound to their contractual obligations.

condition subsequent   A condition that terminates the rights and obligations of the parties under an existing contract.

conditional indorsement   An indorsement whereby the indorser agrees to be liable on the instrument only if a specified event takes place.

conditional sale contract   Usually a contract for the sale of goods wherein the seller reserves title (though possession is with the buyer) until the purchase price is paid in full (used as a security device). Called a security interest under the UCC.

confession of judgment   An agreement whereby a debtor allows a creditor to obtain a court judgment without legal proceedings in the event of nonpayment or other breach by the debtor. Usually not permissible today.

conflict of laws   The body of rules specifying the circumstances in which a state or federal court sitting in one state shall, in deciding a case before it, apply the rules of another state (rather than the rules of the state in which the court is sitting).

confusion   In personal property law, property of two or more persons intermingled so that the property of each can no longer be distinguished.

confusion of goods   An intermingling of the goods of different persons such that the property of each can no longer be distinguished.

conglomerate merger A merger between two companies which are not competitors and do not occupy a supplier-customer relationship.

conscious parallelism Uniformity of action by firms who apparently know their actions are uniform. Does not prove conspiracy under Section 1 of the Sherman Act, but is an extremely important factor in determining whether a conspiracy existed.

consent A defense in an assault and battery action where it is alleged that the plaintiff expressly or implicitly agreed to expose himself to certain physical dangers.

consent decree A court injunction, the terms of which are arrived at by agreement of the parties.

consent order An administrative agency order, the terms of which are arrived at by agreement between the agency and the charged party.

consideration In contract law, a detriment to the promisee or benefit to the promisor, bargained for and given in exchange for a promise.

consolidation A transaction in which two corporations combine to form an entirely new corporation, thereby losing their former identities.

constructive annexation The situation existing when personal property not physically attached to real property is adapted to the use to which the realty is designed so that the law considers it a fixture.

constructive bailment A bailment created when a bailee comes into possession of personal property without the consent of the owner. (An example is lost property found by a person—a bailee.)

constructive delivery A legal substitute for actual delivery of property which is the subject of a gift; consists of delivery of something which represents an item of intangible property or which gives control over an item of tangible property; also called symbolic delivery.

constructive eviction Legally justified abandonment of leased property by a tenant because of a landlord's action which has caused the property to be unsuitable for the purpose for which it was leased.

constructive trust A trust imposed by law to correct or rectify a fraud or to prevent one party from being unjustly enriched at the expense of another.

consumer goods Goods that are used or bought primarily for personal, family, or household purposes.

Consumer Product Safety Act A congressional enactment that created the Consumer Product Safety Commission, which has the responsibility of establishing and enforcing rules and standards to insure that products covered under the Act are safe for consumers' use.

continuation statement In secured transactions law, a document filed with a proper public official to continue public notice of the priority of an existing security interest in collateral upon the expiration of a previous filing.

contract An agreement that establishes enforceable legal relationships between two or more persons.

contract carrier A carrier who transports goods only for those under individual contract.

contract, combination, or conspiracy Express or tacit agreement required for a violation of the Sherman Act.

contributory negligence The fault (negligence) of a plaintiff, the result of which contributed to or added to his or her injury (used as a defense by a defendant against whom the plaintiff has filed a negligence action).

controlling shareholders Usually the majority shareholders or those with sufficient voting power to elect a majority of the directors, pass motions, or make binding decisions.

conversion An action which unlawfully injures the personal property of another or unlawfully interferes with the owner's right to possess and enjoy such property.

conveyance A transfer of an interest in property.

corporate opportunity A doctrine that prohibits directors, officers, or any other corporate managers from personally taking advantage of business situations that belong solely to or should be given to the corporation.

corporate stock Shares of stock, each representing an ownership interest in the business, issued by a corporation for the purpose of raising capital.

corporation An association of persons created by

statute as a legal entity (artificial person) with authority to act and to have liability separate and apart from its owners.

counterclaim   A pleading by the defendant in a civil suit against the plaintiff, the purpose being to defeat or sue the plaintiff so as to gain a judgment favorable to the defendant.

counteroffer   A proposal made by an offeree in response to the offer extended him or her, the terms varying appreciably from the terms of the offer. Such a proposal by the offeree usually constitutes a rejection of the offer.

course of dealing   The situation in which past conduct between two parties in performing a prior contract is used as a basis for interpreting their present conduct or agreement.

course of performance   When a contract for the sale of goods involves repeated occasions for performance known by both parties and not objected to by either, the performance is considered interpretive of the remaining obligations of the contract.

covenant against encumbrances   A guaranty by a grantor that there are no outstanding liens, easements, or liabilities held by a third party on the real property he or she is conveying, except as stated in the deed.

covenant of quiet enjoyment   A guaranty by a grantor of real property that the grantee or those who hold the property in the future will not be evicted or disturbed by a person having a better title or a right of foreclosure of a lien. Also, a guaranty by a landlord to a tenant that the tenant's right to possession will not be disturbed substantially.

covenant not to compete   A clause within a contract legally permitting a restraint of trade where such is a legitimate protection of a property interest and the restraint as to area and time is reasonable under the circumstances. An example is a clause in a sale of business contract where the seller agrees not to start up a competing business within a reasonable time and within the area where the said business has been operating.

covenant of seisin   A guaranty by a grantor that he or she has good title to the real property being conveyed.

covenants of title   The guarantees given by the grantor in a warranty deed.

cover   In response to a seller's failure to deliver goods, the buyer's purchase of the goods from someone else in a commercially reasonable manner; the buyer's basic measure of damages for breach of contract in such a case is the difference between the contract price and the cover price.

creditor beneficiary   A creditor who has rights in a contract (of which he or she is not a party) made by the debtor and a third person, where the terms of said contract expressly benefit the creditor.

creditors' committee   A committee composed of a debtor's creditors, which manages the debtor's business and financial affairs until his or her debts are paid off. The committee's formation is by agreement between the debtor and creditors and is usually part of an agreed-upon payment plan of the debtor.

crime   Any wrongful action by an individual or persons for which a statute prescribes redress in the form of a death penalty, imprisonment, fine, or removal from an office of public trust.

cross-elasticity of demand   The extent to which the quantity of a commodity demanded responds to changes in price of a related commodity. Used to help courts define the relevant market.

cumulative dividend preference   A characteristic of most preferred stock whereby all dividends in arrears must be paid to the preferred shareholders before any dividends can be paid to owners of common stock.

cumulative preferred stock   A type of preferred stock on which dividends not paid in any given year are accumulated to the next succeeding year. The total amount accumulated must be paid before common shareholders can receive a dividend.

cumulative voting   Where permitted, the procedure by which a shareholder is entitled to take his or her total number of shares, multiply that total by the number of directers to be elected, and cast the multiplied total for any director or directors to be elected.

curtesy   The common-law right of a surviving husband to a life estate in a portion of his deceased wife's real property.

cy pres   So near or as near. The doctrine by which the courts will find a substitute purpose when the stated purpose of a charitable trust is not possible to accomplish.

damages   The monetary loss suffered by a party as a result of a wrong.

deadlock   A situation in a corporation where two equally divided factions exist in opposition to each other, thus bringing the affairs of the corporation to a virtual standstill.

debenture   In securities regulation law, a debt security; a written promise by a corporation to repay borrowed money. Usually refers to a corporate bond or promissory note that is not secured by specific assets of the firm (i.e., is not secured by a mortgage on corporate assets).

debit   A charge of indebtedness to an account (for example, a charge against a bank deposit account).

debt securities   Instruments representing the bonded indebtedness of a corporation (they may be secured by corporate property or simply by a general obligation debt of the corporation).

debtor   A person who owes payment of a debt and/or performance on an obligation.

decedent   A person who has died.

deceit   A false statement, usually intentional, that causes another person harm.

deed   The document representing ownership of real property.

deed of bargain and sale   A deed without warranties.

de facto corporation   A corporation not formed in substantial compliance with the laws of a given state but which has sufficiently complied to be a corporation in fact, not right. Only the state can challenge the corporation's existence.

de facto merger   A less formal means of merger where the results are achieved through asset or stock acquisition. Also called a practical merger.

defamation   Injury of a person's character or reputation, usually by publication of a false statement about that person.

default   The failure to perform a legal obligation.

defendant   The party who defends the initial action brought against him or her by the plaintiff.

defense   Any matter which is advanced or put forth by a defendant as a reason in law or fact why the plaintiff is not entitled to recover the relief he seeks.

defensive merger   A merger sought by management in order to avoid consequences it does not feel will be in its best interests.

deficiency judgment   A personal judgment given by a court against a debtor in default where the value of the property placed as security for the debt is less than the debt owed.

de jure corporation   A corporation formed in substantial compliance with the laws of a given state; a corporation by right.

delegated powers   The constitutional right of the federal government to pass laws concerning certain subjects and fields, thereby keeping the states from passing laws in these areas (sometimes referred to as enumerated powers).

delegation   In contract law, the transfer of the power or right to represent or act for another; usually referred to as the delegation of duties to a third party, as compared to the assignment of rights to a third party.

delegation of authority   In administrative law, a grant of authority from a legislative body to an administrative agency.

demand instrument   An instrument which is payable immediately when the holder decides to present it.

demurrer   A pleading by a defendant in the form of a motion denying that plaintiff's complaint or petition states a cause of action.

de novo   To start completely new. A trial *de novo* is a completely new trial requiring the same degree of proof as if the case were being heard for the first time.

depositary bank   The first bank to which an instrument is transferred for collection.

deposition   Testimony of a witness, under oath and subject to cross examination, which is taken outside of court; an important discovery procedure.

descendants   The lineal heirs of a decedent in a descending line—children and grandchildren.

destination contract In sales law, a contract whereby the seller is required to tender goods to the buyer at a place designated by the buyer.

detriment test A test to determine whether a promise is supported by consideration. The law requires the promisee to have done something not otherwise legally required or to have refrained from doing something he or she had a right to do.

devise A term of conveyance in real estate transactions. In a will, a gift of real estate by the testator is a devise.

direct collection The collection by the assignee (of an assignor-creditor) of a debt originally owed the creditor.

directed verdict A verdict that is directed by the court because reasonable persons could not differ as to the result.

disaffirmance The legal avoidance, or setting aside, of an obligation.

discharge in bankruptcy A release granted by a bankruptcy court to a debtor who has gone through proper bankruptcy proceedings; the release frees the person from any further liability on provable claims filed during the proceedings.

disclaimer A provision in a sales contract which attempts to prevent the creation of a warranty.

discovery Full disclosure of the evidence in a particular case before it comes to trial; various procedures are available to accomplish this disclosure.

discretionary powers The right of an administrative agency to exercise judgment and discretion in carrying out the law, as opposed to ministerial powers (the routine day-to-day duty to enforce the law).

dishonor In commercial paper, a refusal to pay or accept an instrument upon proper presentment.

disparagement of goods Making malicious and false statements of fact as to the quality or performance of another's goods.

dissolution The termination of a partnership's or corporation's right to exist as a going concern.

diversity of citizenship An action in which the plaintiff and defendant are citizens of different states.

dividend A payment made by a corporation in cash or property from the income or profit of the corporation to a shareholder on the basis of his or her investment.

documents of title Bills of lading, dock warrants, dock receipts, warehouse receipts, and any other paper that, in the regular course of business or financing, is evidence of the holder's right to obtain possession of the goods covered.

domestic corporation A corporation chartered or incorporated in the state in which the corporation is doing business.

dominant estate The land that benefits from an easement appurtenant.

donee The person to whom a gift is made or a power is given.

donee beneficiary A person who has rights in a contract (to which he or she is not a party) made between two or more parties for his or her express benefit.

donor The person making a gift or giving another the power to do something.

dower The common-law right of a widow to a life estate in a specific portion of her deceased husband's real property.

draft An instrument created by a party (the drawer) that orders another (the drawee) to pay the instrument to a third party (the payee); also called a bill of exchange.

drawee The person on whom a draft or check is drawn and who is requested (ordered) to pay the instrument.

drawee bank A bank on which a draft or check is drawn, such bank being ordered to pay the instrument when it is duly presented.

drawer The person creating (drafting) a draft or check.

due process The right of every person not to be deprived of life, liberty, or property without a fair hearing and/or just compensation.

duress The overcoming of a person's free will through the use of threat, force, or actions whereby the person is forced to do something he or she otherwise would not do.

earnest money A deposit paid by a buyer to hold a seller to a contractual obligation. Frequently this amount also serves as liquidated damages in the event of the buyer's breach. Historically, the deposit was said to show the buyer's good faith in entering into the contract with the seller.

easement A nonpossessory interest in real property that gives the holder the right to use another's land in a particular way.

easement appurtenant An easement created specifically for use in connection with an adjoining tract of land.

easement in gross An easement that is not used in connection with another tract of land.

economic duress The overcoming of a person's free will by means of a threat or other action involving the wrongful use of economic pressure, whereby the person is forced to do something he or she otherwise would not do.

election A principle of law whereby a third person who learns of the identity of the undisclosed principal prior to receiving a judgment must choose to receive the judgment against either the agent or the undisclosed principal. Election of one releases the other from liability to the third party.

eminent domain The power of the government to take private property for public use by paying just compensation.

employment at will A common-law doctrine under which workers are hired for an indefinite period of time. Either party can terminate the employment contract at any time, with no reason being given.

endowment insurance Life insurance which is payable either to the insured when he or she reaches a specified age or to the named beneficiary if the insured dies before reaching the specified age.

entity theory The view that a partnership is a legal entity separate from the individual partners.

environmental impact statement The statement required by federal law that describes the effect of proposed major federal action on the quality of the human environment.

Environmental Protection Agency The federal agency charged with the responsibility for establishing and enforcing environmental standards and for continuing research on pollution and measures to eliminate or control it.

equal protection clause A provision in the fourteenth amendment to the U.S. Constitution that prohibits states from making distinctions among persons or firms without a reasonable, rational basis.

equipment Goods that are used or bought for use primarily in business.

equitable action An action brought in a court seeking an equitable remedy, such as an injunction or decree of specific performance.

equity securities Shares of capital stock representing an ownership interest in the corporation.

escheat The process by which a decedent's property passes to the state when he or she did not leave a valid will and there are no legal heirs.

escrow agent An agent who, by agreement, holds property, documents, or money of one party with the authority to transfer such property to a designated person upon the occurrence of a specified event.

establishment of religion clause The clause in the first amendment to the U.S. Constitution which prohibits the federal government from "establishing" a religion. This restriction has also been applied to the states under the due process clause.

ethics The study and application of moral principles.

ethos The character of our society as a whole.

eviction Action by the landlord which physically bars the tenant from entering the leased premises.

exclusive agency In real property law, the arrangement by a seller of real property with a broker whereby only that broker is entitled to a commission if a sale of the real property is made through the efforts of anyone other than the seller.

exclusive dealing agreement An agreement which commits a buyer to purchase a certain product only from one seller. These agreements, often called requirements contracts, can foreclose markets to competitors. Section 1 of the Sherman Act and Section 3 of the Clayton Act are applied in analyzing these actions.

exclusive right to sell In real property law, the arrangement by a seller of real property with a broker whereby the broker is entitled to his or her commission if a sale of the real property is made through the effort of anyone, including the seller.

exculpatory clause A contract clause providing that one party agrees to free the other of all liability in the event he or she suffers a physical or monetary injury in a particular situation, even if the loss is caused by the negligence of the other party to the contract.

excusing conditions Reasons which are sufficient to justify *prima facie* wrong conduct.

executed contract A contract wholly performed by both parties to the contract, as opposed to an executory contract, which is wholly unperformed by both parties.

execution of a judgment The process by which a judgment creditor obtains a writ directing the sheriff or other officer to seize nonexempt property of the debtor and sell it to satisfy the judgment.

executive committee In a corporation, a certain number of the members of the board of directors appointed by the board as a committee with the delegated authority to make decisions concerning ordinary business matters that come up during intervals between regular board meetings.

executive order An order by the president of the United States or governor of a state that has the force of law.

executor (female, executrix) The personal representative in a testator's will to dispose of an estate as the will has directed.

executory contract A contract wholly unperformed by both parties to the contract, as opposed to an executed contract, where both parties have fully performed their obligations under the contract.

executory interest A future interest held by a third party.

exempt property Real or personal property of a debtor that cannot by law be seized to satisfy a debt owed to an unsecured creditor.

ex parte On one side only. For example, an *ex parte* proceeding is held on the application of one party only, without notice to the other party; and an *ex parte* order is made at the request of one party when the other party fails to show up in court, when the other party's presence is not needed, or when there is no other party.

express authority Authority specifically given by the principal to the agent.

express contract A contract formed from the words (oral and/or in writing) of the parties, as opposed to an implied contract, which is formed from the conduct of the parties.

express warranty In sales law, a guarantee or assurance as to the quality or performance of goods that arises from the words or conduct of the seller.

ex-ship From the carrying vessel; a delivery term indicating that the seller's risk and expense for shipment of goods by vessel extends until the goods are unloaded at the port of destination.

extension clause A clause in a time instrument providing that under certain circumstances the maturity date can be extended.

extraordinary bailment A bailment in which the bailee is given by law greater duties and liabilities than an ordinary bailee. Common carriers and innkeepers are the most common examples of extraordinary bailees.

fair courts Courts established by early merchants to settle disputes and obligations among themselves. These were not recognized as law courts.

Fair Labor Standards Act (FLSA) A 1938 congressional enactment regulating minimum wages, overtime, and child labor.

false imprisonment The wrongful detention or restraint of one person by another.

family purpose doctrine The doctrine under which (in a few states) the head of a household is liable for the negligent acts of any members of his or her family that occur while they are driving the family car.

farm products Goods that are crops, livestock, or supplies used or produced in farming operations, or goods that are products or livestock in their unmanufactured state (such as ginned cotton, maple syrup, milk, and eggs). For secured transactions law these goods must be in the possession of a debtor engaged in raising, fattening, grazing, or other farm operations.

FAS   Free alongside ship; a delivery term indicating that the seller must deliver goods to the designated dock alongside the vessel on which the goods are to be loaded and must bear the expenses of delivery to the dock site.

fault   Breach of a legal duty.

Federal Communications Commission (FCC)   A seven-member commission established in 1934 by congressional enactment of the Federal Communications Act. The commission is empowered to regulate all interstate communication by telephone, telegraph, radio, and television.

federal preemption   A legal principle which grants the Congress, the federal courts, and federal agencies exclusive authority in certain matters of law where the need for a uniform national body of law is great. Labor relations law, for example, is almost exclusively the domain of the federal government.

federal question   A question presented by a case in which one party, usually the plaintiff, is asserting a right (or counterclaim, in the case of the defendant) which is based upon a federal rule of law—e.g., a provision of the U.S. Constitution, an act of Congress, or a U.S. treaty.

Federal Trade Commission (FTC)   A five-member commission established in 1914 by congressional enactment of the Federal Trade Commission Act. The commission enforces prohibitions against unfair methods of competition and unfair or deceptive acts or practices in commerce; it also enforces numerous federal laws (particularly federal consumer protection acts, such as "Truth in Lending" and "Fair Packaging and Labeling").

fee simple   The absolute ownership of real property.

fee simple defeasible   An ownership interest in real property subject to termination by the occurrence of a specific event.

felony   A serious crime resulting in either punishment by death or imprisonment in a state or federal penitentiary, or where a given statute declares a wrong to be a felony without regard to a specific punishment.

fictitious payee   A payee on an instrument who is either nonexistent or an actual person not entitled to payment. (Usually the fraud is perpetrated by a dis-

honest employee in charge of payroll or payment of accounts who drafts an instrument with intent to defraud his or her employer.)

fiduciary   A position of trust in relation to another person or his or her property.

financing statement   An instrument filed with a proper public official that gives notice of an outstanding security interest in collateral.

finding of fact   The process whereby from testimony and evidence a judge, agency, or examiner determines that certain matters, events, or acts took place upon which conclusions of law can be based.

firm offer   In sales law, an irrevocable offer dealing with the sale of goods made by a merchant offeror in a signed writing and giving assurance to the offeree that the offer will remain open. This offer is irrevocable without consideration for the stated period of time or, if no period is stated, for a reasonable period, neither period to exceed three months.

fixture   A piece of personal property that is attached to real property in such a manner that the law deems the item to be part of the real property.

floating lien concept   In secured transactions law, the concept whereby a security interest is permitted to be retained in collateral even though the collateral changes in character and classification. For example, a security interest in raw materials is retained even if the raw materials change character in the manufacturing process and end up as inventory.

FOB   Free on board; a delivery term indicating that the seller must ship the goods and bear the expenses of shipment to the FOB point of designation (which can be either the seller's or the buyer's place of business).

forebearance   The refraining from doing something that a person has a legal right to do.

foreclosure   The procedure or action taken by a mortgagee, upon default of the mortgagor, whereby the mortgagee satisfies his or her claim by some action (usually by selling off the mortgaged property).

foreign corporation   A corporation chartered or incorporated in one state but doing business in a different state.

forgery   A fraudulent, fake instrument or document, or a signature of another without authorization.

formal contract   A contract that derives its validity only from compliance with a specific form or format required by law. Examples are contracts under seal (where a seal is required), negotiable instruments, and recognizances (formal acknowledgments of indebtedness made in a court of law).

franchise   (1) A business conducted under someone else's trademark or tradename. The owner of the business, which may be a sole proprietorship, partnership, corporation, or other form of organization, is usually referred to as the *franchisee*. The owner of the trademark or tradename, who contractually permits use of the mark or name, in return for a fee and usually subject to various restrictions, is ordinarily referred to as the *franchisor*. The permission to use the mark or name, which is part of the franchising agreement, is called a *trademark license*. (2) The term can also be used to refer to a privilege granted by a governmental body, such as the exclusive right granted to someone by a city to provide cable TV service in that city.

fraud   An intentional or reckless misrepresentation of a material fact that causes anyone relying on it injury or damage.

fraud implied in law   A presumption of fraud which exists when a debtor transfers property without receiving fair consideration in return and the debtor has insufficient assets remaining to satisfy creditors; burden of proof falls to debtor to show absence of fraud.

fraud in the execution   In commercial paper, inducing a person to sign an instrument, the party signing being deceived as to the nature or essential terms of the instrument.

fraud in fact   An action by a debtor in which he transfers property with the specific intent of defrauding creditors.

fraud in the inducement   In commercial paper, the use of deceit in inducing a person to sign an instrument, although the deceived party knows what he or she is signing and the essential terms of the instrument. This knowledge is what distinguishes fraud in inducement from fraud in the execution.

fraudulent conveyance   The transfer of property in such a manner that the conveyance is deemed either in fact or by law to defraud creditors.

free speech clause   The clause in the first amendment to the U.S. Constitution which prohibits the federal government from abridging the freedom of speech. This restriction has also been applied to the states under the due process clause.

frustration of purpose doctrine   A legal doctrine followed in many states which excuses a party from a contract because of an occurrence which undermines the basic purpose of the contract.

FTC holder in due course rule   An FTC rule which states that it is illegal for a seller to execute a sales contract or arrange a direct loan unless the contract includes a clause which informs the holder of the contract that he or she is subject to all claims and defenses against such contract.

full faith and credit clause   The provision in the U.S. Constitution which requires the courts of one state to recognize judgments and other public actions of its sister states.

fungible   In sales or securities law, goods or securities of which any unit is, by nature or usage of trade, the equivalent of any other like unit.

future advance   In secured transactions law, the concept whereby an outstanding security interest applies to future loans made by the secured party. If the security interest is properly perfected, the future loan, for priority purposes, dates back to the time the original security interest was created.

future interest   An interest in real property, the use or enjoyment of which is postponed until a later date or the occurrence of a designated event.

futures contract   A contract to buy or sell standard commodities (such as rice, coffee, or wheat) at a future date and a specified price. (The seller is agreeing to sell goods he or she does not own at the time of making the contract.)

garnishee   A person who holds money owed to or property of a debtor subject to a garnishment action.

garnishment   The legal proceeding of a judgment creditor to require a third person owing money to the debtor or holding property belonging to the debtor to turn over to the court or sheriff the property or money owed for the satisfaction of the judgment. State and federal laws generally permit only a limited amount of a debtor's wages to be garnished.

general warranty deed   A deed to real property which guarantees that the title is a good, marketable one.

gift   A voluntary transfer of property to another without consideration.

gift *causa mortis*   A gift made by a donor in contemplation of his or her death from some existing affliction or impending peril.

gift *inter vivos*   A gift made during the lifetime of a donor and not in contemplation of his or her death.

Golden Rule, The   A rule of ethical conduct stating that one should do to others as he would have others do to him.

good faith   Honesty in fact on the part of a person in negotiating a contract, or in the carrying on of some other transaction.

goods   Tangible and movable personal property except for money used as medium of exchange.

grantee   The person to whom an interest in real property is conveyed by deed.

grantor   The person conveying an interest in real property by deed.

Green River ordinances   State and municipal laws that regulate door-to-door sales on private premises. So called after the Green River, Wyoming, case in which such laws were held to be valid and enforceable.

group boycott   In antitrust law, the express or implied agreement of two or more persons or firms to refuse to deal (buy, sell, etc.) with a third party. Such an agreement is usually illegal.

guaranty   A promise to pay an obligation of a debtor if the debtor is in default.

holder   Any person in possession of a document, security, or instrument that is drawn, issued, or indorsed to him or her.

holder in due course (HDC)   A holder who takes an instrument for value, in good faith, and without notice that the instrument is overdue or has been dishonored or that any defense or claim by any person exists against it.

holder through a holder in due course   A holder who fails to qualify as a holder in due course but has the rights of one (by law of assignment) if he or she can show that a prior holder of the instrument qualified as a holder in due course. This is referred to as the "shelter provision."

holding company   A company whose main function is to own other companies through control of their stock. Also called an investment company.

holographic will   A will entirely in the handwriting of the testator. Witnesses are not required for its execution but are necessary at probate to prove the handwriting of the testator.

horizontal merger   A merger of two competing firms at the same level in the production or distribution of a product.

horizontal price fixing   Price fixing among competitors. *Per se* illegal under Section 1 of the Sherman Act.

illusory contract   An agreement of the parties that, on examination, lacks mutuality of obligation—i.e., one in which consideration is found to be lacking on the part of one party. The result is that neither party is bound by the agreement.

implied authority   Authority inferred for an agent to carry out his or her express authority and/or authority inferred from the position held by the agent to fulfill his or her agency duties.

implied contract   A contract in which the parties' manifestation of assent or agreement is inferred, in whole or in part, from their conduct, as opposed to an express contract formed by the parties' words.

implied warranties   Assurances or guarantees of certain standards or actions imposed by law.

implied warranty of habitability   An obligation imposed on the landlord to keep residential property in a liveable condition.

incidental beneficiary   One who benefits from a contract between others but who cannot legally enforce the contract because his or her benefit is a secondary effect, not an intended result of the contract.

incorporated partnership   A close corporation with more than one shareholder.

incorporation   The act or process of forming or creating a corporation.

indemnification   Where allowed, the right to reimbursement for expenses, losses, or costs incurred.

independent contractor   One who is hired by another to perform a given task in a manner and method independent from the control of employer.

indirect collection The creditor's collection of payment(s) of a debt, even though the debt has been assigned by the creditor to an assignee.

indorsee The person who receives an indorsed instrument.

indorsement The signature of the indorser (usually on the back of an instrument) for the purpose of transferring an instrument and establishing the limits of his or her liability.

indorsement for deposit A type of restrictive indorsement that requires the depositary bank to place into the account of the restrictive indorser the amount of the instrument.

indorsement in trust A type of restrictive indorsement whereby the amount on the instrument is to be paid to the indorsee, who in turn is to use or hold the funds for the benefit of the indorser or a third party.

indorser The person who indorses an instrument, usually for the purpose of transferring it to a third person.

informal contract Any contract that does not depend on a specified form or formality for its validity.

injunction A decree issued by a court hearing an equity action either prohibiting a person from performing a certain act or acts or requiring the person to perform a certain act or acts.

innkeeper An operator of a hotel, motel, or any place of business offering living accommodations for transient guests.

innocent misrepresentation A false statement of fact, not known to be false, that causes another harm or damage.

insider trading The buying or selling of corporate securities of a particular firm by persons having business knowledge about such firm that is not available to the general public, with the expectation of making a personal profit in such transactions.

insolvency In bankruptcy law, the financial condition of a debtor when his or her assets at fair market value are less than his or her debts and liabilities.

installment contract In sales law, a contract that authorizes or requires the delivery and acceptance of goods in separate lots.

installment note An instrument (note) in which the principal (plus interest usually) is payable in specified partial amounts at specified times until the full amount is paid.

insurable interest The rights of a person who will be directly or financially affected by the death of a person or the loss of property. Only these rights can be protected by an insurance policy.

intermediary bank Any bank to which an instrument is transferred in the course of collection and which is not the depositary or payor bank.

interrogatories In a lawsuit, a discovery procedure involving the submission of written questions by one party to the other, which the other party must answer under oath.

interstate commerce The carrying on of commercial activities or the commercial transportation of persons or property between points lying in different states.

Interstate Commerce Commission (ICC) An administrative agency established in 1887 by congressional enactment of the Interstate Commerce Act regulating the licensing and rates of common carriers in interstate commerce.

inter vivos "Between the living," as an *inter vivos* gift (one made during the life of the donor) or an *inter vivos* trust.

***inter vivos* trust** A trust established and effective during the life of the settlor.

intestate The situation in which a person dies without leaving a valid will.

inventory Goods held by a person or firm for sale or lease in the ordinary course of business; also refers to raw materials (and work in process on them) where held by a manufacturing company.

investigative power In administrative agency law, the right of an administrative agency by statute to hold hearings, subpoena witnesses, examine persons under oath, and require that records be submitted to it in order to determine violations and to do research for future rule making.

investment company Any corporation organized

for the purpose of owning and holding the stock of other corporations.

involuntary case In bankruptcy, a liquidation proceeding that is brought about by the unpaid creditors.

irrevocable offer An offer or proposal that by law cannot be withdrawn by an offeror without liability.

issue The first delivery of an instrument to a holder.

joint stock company An unincorporated association that closely resembles a corporation but for most purposes is treated as a partnership.

joint tenancy A co-ownership of property by two or more parties in which each owns an undivided interest that passes to the other co-owners on his or her death (known as the "right of survivorship").

joint tortfeasors Two or more persons who in concert commit a tort; also two or more persons whose independent torts are so linked to an injury that a court will hold either or both liable.

judgment note An instrument (note) in which the maker authorizes, on default, immediate confession and entry of judgment against him or her by a court without due process of service or trial. Most states have abolished or restricted confession of judgment notes.

judgment notwithstanding the verdict (judgment n.o.v.) The entry of a judgment by a trial judge in favor of one party even though the jury returned a verdict in favor of the other party.

judicial review The process by which the courts oversee and determine the legitimacy or validity of executive, legislative, or administrative agency action.

judicial self-restraint The philosophy that controversies must be settled, insofar as possible, in conformity with previously established principles and decisions.

junior security interest A security interest or right that is subordinate to another security interest or right.

jurisdiction of a court The power of a court to hear and decide a particular dispute and to issue a judgment that is legally binding on the parties in the dispute.

justice The application of rules to arrive at what is recognized as a fair and reasonable result; also a title given to a judge.

laissez-faire doctrine The doctrine whereby business is permitted to operate without interference by government.

landlord's lien The right held by the landlord to seize, hold, or sell a tenant's personal property for nonpayment of rent.

Landrum-Griffin Act A 1959 congressional amendment of the 1935 NLRA which established a bill of rights for union members, required public financial disclosures by unions and union leaders, and regulated election procedures for union officials by union members.

latent defect In sales law, an imperfection in a good that cannot be discovered by ordinary observation or inspection.

law Enforceable rules governing the relationship of individuals and persons, their relationship to one another, and their relationship to an organized society.

law merchant Rules and regulations developed by merchants and traders that governed their transactions before being absorbed by common law. These rules and regulations were developed and enforced by "fair courts" established by the merchants themselves.

lease A conveyance to another of the right to possess property in return for a payment called rent.

leasehold The interest acquired by the lessee under a lease.

leasehold estate The real property held by the lessee who has been given temporary possession in return for payment of rent.

legacy In a will, a specific gift of money.

legal detriment A required element of contractual consideration; exists when the promisee does or promises to do something he or she is not legally obligated to do, or refrains or promises to refrain from doing something he or she has a legal right to do.

legal entity An association recognized by law as having the legal rights and duties of a person.

legal environment A broad, imprecise term referring generally to those judicial, legislative, and administrative processes and rules that have particular application to the business world.

legal impossibility of performance An event that takes place after a contract is made, rendering performance under the contract, in the eyes of the law, something that cannot be done. Also referred to as objective impossibility, it legally discharges a party's obligation; it can be compared to subjective impossibility, which makes the contractual obligation more difficult to perform but does not discharge it.

legal rate of interest The rate of interest applied by statute where there is an agreement for interest to be paid but none is stated, or where the law implies a duty to pay interest irrespective of agreement. In the latter case, this may be referred to as a *judgment rate*, a rate of interest applied to judgments until paid by the defendant.

legal tender Any currency recognized by law as the medium of exchange that must be accepted by a creditor in satisfaction of a debtor's debt.

legal title That which represents ownership of property.

legislative history The history of the legislative enactment used by the court as a means of interpreting the terms of a statute. It consists primarily of legislative committee reports and the transcripts of committee hearings and floor debates.

lessee The person who leases or rents property from a lessor. If the lease involves an interest in real property, the lessee is frequently referred to as the tenant.

lessor The person who leases property to the lessee. If the lease involves an interest in real property, the lessor is frequently referred to as the landlord.

libel Written defamation of one's character or reputation.

license In real property law, the landowner's permission for another to come upon his or her land.

lien An interest held by a creditor in property of the debtor for the purpose of securing payment of the debt.

lien creditor In secured transactions law, any creditor who is able to legally attach the property of

the debtor. This includes an assignee for the benefit of creditors, a trustee in bankruptcy, or an appointed receiver in equity.

life estate An interest in real property for the duration of the life of some designated person, who may be the life tenant or a third person.

life tenant The person holding (owning) a life estate in designated property.

limitation of remedies A provision in a sales contract which attempts to limit the remedies available to a party; usually employed by a seller to limit a buyer's remedies for breach of warranty.

limited defense See *personal defense*.

limited partnership A partnership created under statute with at least one limited and one general partner. The limited partner's liability to third persons is restricted to his or her capital contributions.

liquidated damages An amount of, or a method for computing, breach of contract damages that is agreed upon by the parties to a contract before a dispute actually arises.

liquidated debt An undisputed debt; that is, a debt about which there is no reasonable basis for dispute as to its existence or amount.

liquidating partner After an act of dissolution of the partnership, any partner who has authority to wind up the partnership, thereby terminating it.

liquidation Conversion of the assets of a corporation to cash and the subsequent distribution of the cash to creditors and shareholders.

liquidation preference Preferred shareholders' priority over common shareholders to the distribution of corporate assets upon the corporation's dissolution.

liquidation proceeding Under the Bankruptcy Act, a proceeding in which the debtor's assets are sold to pay off creditors insofar as it is possible to do so and the debtor is discharged from further responsibility.

lobbying contract A contract made by one person with another under the terms of which the former agrees to represent the latter's interest before legislative or administrative bodies by attempting to influence their votes or decisions on legislative, quasi-legislative, or related proceedings.

long-arm statutes Laws that permit a plaintiff to bring a certain action and recover a judgment in a court in his or her home state against a defendant who resides in another state.

lost property Property located at a place where it was not put by its owner, which place is unknown by the owner.

Magnuson-Moss Warranty Act A congressional enactment designed to prevent deceptive warranty practices, make warranties easier to understand, and create procedures for consumer enforcement of warranties. The act applies only to written warranties given in a consumer sales transaction and can be enforced by the Federal Trade Commission, Attorney General, or an aggrieved party.

maker The person who creates or executes a promissory note or certificate of deposit.

marital deduction An estate planning device that can be used by the surviving husband or wife to effect substantial estate tax savings.

market (1) An area over which buyers and sellers negotiate the exchange of a well-defined commodity. (2) From the point of view of the consumer, the firms from which he or she can buy a well-defined product. (3) From the point of view of a producer, the buyers to whom it can sell a well-defined product. Market definition is crucial in determining the market shares of firms under antitrust scrutiny.

market division arrangements Any concerted action among actual or potential competitors to divide *geographic* markets, to assign particular *customers*, or to market particular *products* among themselves so as to avoid or limit competition. Such market divisions are treated as *per se* violations of Section 1 of the Sherman Act.

master In employment law, one who appoints or designates another to perform physical tasks or activities for him or her and under his or her control as to the manner of performance (sometimes designated employer).

maturity In commercial paper, the time when a debt or obligation is due.

maximum rate of interest A statutory limit on the amount of interest that can be charged on a given transaction.

mechanic's lien A statutory lien against real property for labor, services, or materials used in improving the real property.

merchant In sales law, a person who customarily deals in goods of the kind that are involved in a transaction, or who otherwise by occupation holds himself or herself out as having knowledge or skill peculiar to the goods involved in the transaction.

merger The purchase of either the physical assets or the controlling share ownership of one company by another. As a business combination, a merger can come under antitrust review if the Justice Department or the FTC have reason to believe it might lessen competition.

metes and bounds A term used to describe the exterior lines of a parcel of land where metes means measure of length and bounds refers to the boundaries of the property.

ministerial power In administrative agency law, the routine day-to-day administration of the law, as opposed to discretionary powers, which involve the power to exercise judgment in the rendering of decisions.

minor Any person under the age of majority. In most states the age of majority is eighteen years; in some it is twenty-one.

minority shareholders Those shareholders whose voting power is not sufficient to elect a majority of the directors, pass motions, or make binding decisions.

mirror image rule A principle used in contract law where the acceptance must adhere exactly to the offer in order for it to be valid.

misdemeanor Any crime less serious than a felony, resulting in a fine and/or confinement in a jail other than a state or federal penitentiary.

mislaid property Property located at a place where it was put by the owner, who has now forgotten the location.

mistake An unintentional error.

Model Business Corporation Act Uniform rules governing the incorporation and operation of corporations for profit recommended by the American Bar Association for enactment by the various states.

money In commercial paper, any medium of exchange authorized or adopted by a domestic or foreign government as part of its currency.

monopoly According to the economic model, a market having only one seller, high barriers to entry, and no close substitutes for the product being sold. The courts generally define a monopolist as a firm possessing such an overwhelming degree of market power that it is able to control prices or exclude competition.

moral dilemmas Situations involving two distinct obligations that are mutually exclusive.

moral minimum The minimum obligations of moral responsibility.

moral responsibility of corporations The obligation of corporate entities to observe fundamental moral duties.

morality Conformity to ideals of right conduct.

morals Rules of conduct established by a given community and enforced by voluntary compliance of those within the community. If the rule is a law, it is also enforceable by judicial process.

mortgage The agreement by which a lien on a debtor's property is conveyed to a creditor.

mortgagee The creditor in a mortgage agreement.

mortgagor The debtor in a mortgage agreement.

motion to dismiss Motion filed by the defendant in which he alleges that the complaint does not state a cause of action, in other words, that the complaint fails to state a legally recognizable claim.

mutual-benefit bailment A nongratuitous bailment frequently formed by contract through which both parties benefit.

mutuality of obligation The principle in contract law that both parties must obligate themselves in order for either to be obligated.

National Labor Relations Act (NLRA) A 1935 congressional enactment regulating labor-management relations. This act (1) established methods for selecting a labor union that would represent a particular group of employees, (2) required the employer to bargain with that union, (3) prescribed certain fundamental employee rights, (4) prohibited several "unfair labor practices" by employers, and (5) created the National Labor Relations Board to administer and enforce the NLRA. Also known as the Wagner Act.

natural monopoly Unusual market structure resulting from unique characteristics of the product or service offered. Some goods (e.g., electricity) or services (e.g., local telephone system) require large capital outlays and/or require uniformity in delivery systems so that only one firm can efficiently provide them at a profit.

necessaries In contract law, items contracted for which the law deems essential to a person's life or health (usually such items as food, clothing, shelter, medical services, and primary and secondary education).

negligence The failure to exercise reasonable care required under the circumstances, which failure is the proximate or direct cause of damage or injury to another.

negotiability The status of an instrument that meets the requirements under the UCC for an instrument to be negotiable.

negotiable document of title A document of title in which the terms state the goods are to be delivered to "bearer" or to the "order" of a named person. The person who is in legal possession of the document is entitled to the goods described therein.

negotiable instrument A signed written document that contains an unconditional promise or order to pay a sum certain in money on demand or at a definite time to the order of a specific person or to bearer. The document can be either a draft, a check, a certificate of deposit, or a note.

negotiation The transfer of an instrument in such form that the transferee becomes a holder.

nominal damages A monetary award by a court where there is a breach of duty or contract but where no financial loss has occurred or been proven.

nonexempt property The property of a debtor subject to the claims of unsecured creditors.

nonexistent principal A principal not recognized by law.

nonnegotiable document of title A document of title which states that the goods are to be delivered to a specific person or entity. Legal possession of this document is not tantamount to ownership of the goods.

nonnegotiable instrument An instrument that does not meet the requirements of negotiability under the UCC.

nonprofit corporation A private corporation formed to perform a religious, charitable, educational, or benevolent purpose without a profit-oriented goal.

nonstock corporation A corporation in which capital stock is not issued; usually occurs only in the case of a nonprofit corporation.

nontrading partnership A partnership formed primarily for the production (but not sale) of commodities or for the providing of services.

no-par value stock Stock issued by a corporation with no amount stated in the certificate. The amount a subscriber pays is determined by the board of directors.

note In commercial paper, an instrument whereby one party (the maker) promises to pay another (the payee or bearer) a sum of money on demand or at a stated date.

notice A fact that a person actually knows, or one he or she should know exists based on all facts and circumstances.

novation The substitution, by agreement, of a new contract for an existing one, thereby terminating the old contract. This is usually accomplished by a three-sided agreement of the parties that a third person's performance be substituted for that of one of the original parties to the contract.

nuisance Action by a defendant that impinges upon or interferes with the rights of others. The remedy for plaintiff is an injunction compelling abatement.

nuncupative will An oral will permitted by some states but on which significant restrictions and conditions are imposed by statute.

obligee The person to whom a duty is owed.

obligor A person who owes a duty to another.

occupation In personal property law, the acquisition of unowned property by the first person to take possession with an intent to become the owner.

Occupational Safety and Health Act (OSHA) A 1970 congressional enactment creating the Occupational Safety and Health Administration as part of the Labor Department, and requiring that agency to develop and enforce occupational safety and health standards for American industries.

offer In contract law, a proposal made by an offeror which manifests a present intent to be legally bound and expresses the proposed terms with reasonable definiteness.

offeree The person to whom an offer is made.

offeror A person who makes a proposal to another, with the view in mind that if it is accepted, it will create a legally enforceable agreement between the parties.

oligopoly A market structure in which a small number of firms dominate the industry.

open listing The arrangement by a seller of real property whereby the seller's obligation to pay a commission to a broker arises only if he or she is the first broker to procure an acceptable buyer (a buyer who is ready, willing, and able to buy at the stated price).

option An irrevocable offer formed by contract and supported by consideration.

option contract A contract in which consideration is given to the offeror from the offeree in return for the promise to keep the offer open.

order instrument An instrument payable to a designated payee or payees, or whomever they so direct, and requiring for its negotiation the indorsement of those persons.

ordinary bailment Any bailment not classified as an extraordinary bailment.

output contract An enforceable agreement for the sale of all the goods produced by a seller (the exact amount of which is not set or known at the time of the agreement) or all those produced at a given plant of the seller during the term of the contract; a contract in which the seller agrees to sell and the buyer agrees to buy all or up to a stated amount that the seller produces.

owner-consent statute A legislative enactment in a few states whereby the owner is liable for the negligence of any person driving the owner's car with his or her permission.

ownership in place The rights to oil, gas, and other minerals while they are still in the ground.

pari delicto Parties equally at fault.

parol evidence rule A rule that in some instances prohibits the introduction of evidence, oral or written, that would, if admitted, vary, change, alter, or modify any terms or provisions of a complete and unambiguous written contract.

partially-disclosed principal In agency law, a principal who is known to exist but whose identity is unknown by third persons dealing with the agent.

participating preferred stock A type of preferred stock giving its holders the right to share with common shareholders in any dividends remaining after the preferred shareholders have received their preferred dividend and common shareholders have received their specified dividend.

partition The dividing of land co-owned by several persons into specific designated pieces (sections) of property.

partnership An association of two or more persons who by agreement as co-owners carry on a business for profit.

par value stock Stock that has been assigned a specific value by the board of directors; the amount is stated in the certificate, and the subscriber to the corporation must pay at least this amount.

payee The person to whom an instrument is made payable.

payment against documents A term in a contract that requires payment for goods upon receipt of their documents of title, even though the goods have not as yet arrived.

payor bank The bank (drawee) on which an instrument is drawn (payable).

per capita "By heads," in descent and distribution of a decedent's estate where the heirs are of one class (such as children) and take equal shares.

peremptory challenge The right to exclude a prospective juror without having to state a reason or cause.

perfection In secured transactions law, the concept whereby a secured party obtains a priority claim on the collateral of his or her debtor as against other interested parties by giving some form of notice of his or her outstanding security interest.

perfect tender rule In sales law, a rule of law providing that it is a seller's obligation to deliver or tender delivery of goods that are in strict conformance with the terms of the sales contract.

performance Carrying out of an obligation or promise according to the terms agreed to or specified. In contract law, complete performance by both parties discharges the contract.

periodic tenancy The interest created by a lease for an indefinite duration where rent is paid at specified intervals and a prescribed time for giving notice of termination is required.

***per se* rule** Antitrust doctrine wherein certain types of group business behavior are inherently anti-competitive and are therefore automatically illegal. Horizontal price fixing and boycotts are examples of *per se* illegal activities.

personal defense In commercial paper, any defense by a party that cannot be asserted against a holder in due course or against a holder through a holder in due course. A personal defense (often referred to as a limited defense) is effective only against ordinary holders.

personal property All property not classified as real property; "movables." May be tangible (e.g., cars and gasoline) or intangible (e.g., shares of corporate stock and other contractual rights).

per stirpes "By roots or stocks," in descent and distribution of a decedent's estate, where a class of heirs take the share their predeceased ancestor would have taken.

piercing the corporate veil The action of a court in disregarding the separate legal entity (identity) of the corporation, thereby subjecting the owners to possible personal liability.

plain meaning rule The rule under which a court applies a particular statute literally, where it feels the wording of the statute is so clear as to require no interpretation (that is, no resort to outside factors).

plaintiff The party who initiates an action at law and who seeks a specified remedy.

plat A map showing how pieces of real property are subdivided.

pledge In secured transactions law, a transfer of personal property from the debtor to the creditor, as security for a debt owed.

pledgee A person to whom personal property is pledged by a pledgor.

pledgor A person who makes a pledge of personal property to a pledgee.

police power The inherent power of a government to regulate matters affecting the health, safety, morals, and general welfare of its citizens; usually used to refer to such power possessed by the state governments, as distinguished from the federal police power.

possibility of reverter A future interest retained by the grantor when he or she conveys real property subject to a condition that upon the occurrence of a designated event the title will automatically be returned to the grantor or his or her heirs.

power of attorney An instrument or document authorizing one person to act as an agent for another (the principal), who is issuing the instrument or document. The agent does not have to be an attorney-at-law.

precatory Expressive of a wish or desire, as in a devise by a testator of real estate expressing the "hope" that the devisee will pass it on to another named party. Such language may not be legally binding.

precedent A rule of a previously decided case that serves as authority for a decision in a current controversy—the basis of the principle of *stare decisis*.

preemption The federal regulation of an area of law which is so complete that any state statutes or other regulations affecting that area are, as to such area, completely void.

preemptive right The right of a shareholder to purchase shares of new stock issues of a corporation equal in number to enable the shareholder to

maintain his or her proportionate interest in the corporation.

preexisting obligation A legal duty for performance previously contracted or imposed by statute. A later promise to perform an existing contractual obligation or a promise to perform a duty imposed by law is a promise without consideration and therefore unenforceable.

preference The transfer of property or payment of money by a debtor to one or more creditors in a manner that results in favoring those creditors over others. This is an act of bankruptcy, and the trustee can set aside the transfer if the creditors knew or had reason to know that the debtor was insolvent and if the transfer took place within four months of filing the petition in bankruptcy.

preferred stock A class of stock that has a priority or right over common stock as to payment of dividends and/or distribution of corporate assets upon dissolution.

preliminary negotiations In contract law, usually an invitation to a party to make an offer—not the offer itself but only an inquiry.

preponderance of the evidence The greater weight and degree of the credible evidence; this is the burden of proof in most civil lawsuits.

prescriptive easement An easement acquired without consent of the owner by continuous and open use for a prescribed statutory period.

presentment In commercial paper, the demand by a holder for payment or acceptance of an instrument.

presumption Upon introduction of certain proof, a fact that is assumed even though direct proof is lacking. Presumptions of fact usually are rebuttable while presumptions of law usually are not.

price discrimination Under the Robinson-Patman Act, the practice of charging different prices to different buyers for goods of like grade and quality.

price fixing Any action or agreement which tampers with the free market pricing mechanism of a product or service.

prima facie At first sight (Latin); on the face of it; a fact that will be considered as true unless disproved.

primary party The maker of a note or the acceptor of a draft or check.

principal One who agrees with another (called an *agent*) that that person will act on his or her behalf.

prior restraint Government action which prevents a rally, assembly, or expressive activity from taking place because of the probability of violence or other unlawful conduct. A prior restraint usually is unconstitutional.

private corporation A corporation formed by individuals, as compared to one formed by the government.

private law Rules of laws that determine rights and duties between private parties, that is, between individuals, associations, and corporations.

privilege An advantage or right granted by law. Using it as a defense, a person is permitted to perform an act that is not ordinarily permitted to others without liability. In some cases the defense of privilege is absolute, resulting in complete immunity from liability, while in other cases it is qualified, resulting in immunity only if certain factors are proven.

privileges and immunities clause A provision in the U.S. Constitution which usually prohibits a state from discriminating against the citizens of another state because of their out-of-state residency.

privity of contract Relationship of contract; a relationship that exists between two parties by virtue of their having entered into a contract.

probate The legal procedure by which a deceased person's property is inventoried and appraised, claims against the estate are paid, and remaining property is distributed to the heirs under the will or according to state law if there is no will.

procedural due process The constitutional requirement that government action be preceded by fair procedures, including notice and an opportunity to be heard.

procedural law The rules for carrying on a lawsuit (pleading, evidence, jurisdiction), as opposed to substantive law.

proceeds The money or property received from a sale.

professional corporation Where permitted, the formation of a corporation by persons engaged in a particular profession, such as medicine, law, or architecture.

profit Under real property law, a nonpossessory right to go upon the land of another and take something from it—sometimes referred to as "profit à prendre" (French), particularly when the interest involves the right to take growing crops from another's land.

promise In commercial paper, an undertaking to pay an instrument. The promise must be more than a mere acknowledgment of an obligation, such as an IOU.

promisee The person who has the legal right to demand performance of the promisor's obligation. In a bilateral contract both the offeror and the offeree are promisees. In a unilateral contract only the offeree is the promisee.

promisor The person who obligates himself or herself to do something. In a bilateral contract both offeror and offeree are promisors. In a unilateral contract only the offeror is the promisor.

promissory estoppel A doctrine whereby a promise made by a promisor will be enforced, although not supported by consideration, if such promise would reasonably induce the promisee to rely on that promise and thereby so change his or her position that injustice can be avoided only by enforcement of the promise.

promissory note A note containing the promise of the maker to pay the instrument upon presentment when due.

promoter A person who makes necessary arrangements and/or contracts for the formation of a corporation. Promoters are the planners for the creation of a corporation.

prospectus A document provided by a corporation that sets forth the nature and purposes of an issue of stock, bonds, or other securities being offered for sale, usually including additional financial data about the issuing corporation.

protest A formal certification of an instrument's notice of dishonor, under the seal of an authorized person or a notary public (required only for notice of dishonor of foreign drafts).

proximate cause   The foreseeable or direct connection between the breach of duty and an injury resulting from that breach.

proxy   An authorization by one person to act for another; usually refers to the exercise of a shareholder's voting rights by another person or group.

public corporation   A corporation formed by the government, as distinguished from one formed by private parties.

public law   Rules that deal with either the opinion of government or the relationship between a government and its people.

public policy   Any conduct, act, or objective that the law recognizes as being in the best interest of society at a given time. Any act or conduct contrary to the recognized standard is illegal, even if there is no statute expressly governing such act or conduct.

punitive damages   A monetary sum awarded as a punishment for certain wrongs committed by one person against another. The plaintiff must prove his or her actual out-of-pocket losses directly flowing from the wrong before punitive damages will be awarded.

purchase money security interest   A security interest taken or retained by a seller to secure all or part of the price of the collateral; also a security interest taken by a secured party who lends money specifically to allow the debtor to acquire the collateral (where the acquisition does subsequently take place).

qualified indorsement   An indorsement whereby the indorser does not guarantee payment but does extend warranties to subsequent holders; usually a blank or special indorsement accompanied by the words *without recourse.*

qualified indorser   An indorser who only guarantees that he or she has no knowledge of any defense against him or her.

quasi-contract   A contract imposed upon the parties by law to prevent unjust enrichment, even though the parties did not intend to enter into a contract (sometimes referred to as an *implied-in-law contract*).

quasi-judicial   The case-hearing function of an administrative agency.

quasi-legislative   The rule-making power of an administrative agency.

quid pro quo   Something given or received for something else.

quitclaim deed   A deed by a grantor that passes to the grantee only those rights and interests (if any) the grantor has in the real property. This deed does not purport to convey any particular interest.

quorum   The number of qualified persons whose presence is required at a meeting for any action taken at the meeting to be valid. Unless otherwise specified, a majority.

ratification   The affirmance of a previous act.

rational basis test   The usual test applied by the courts in determining the constitutionality of a statute that is challenged on the ground that it violates the equal protection clause; under this test, if the classification of subject-matter in the statute is found to be reasonably related to the purposes of the statute, the statute is not a violation of the equal protection clause.

real defenses   In commercial paper, certain defenses listed in the UCC that can be asserted against any holder, including a holder in due course (sometimes referred to as universal defenses).

real estate mortgage note   A note secured by a parcel or parcels of the maker's real property.

real property   Land and most things attached to the land, such as buildings and vegetation.

reasonable definiteness   In contract law, the requirement that a contract possess sufficient certainty to enable a court to determine the rights and obligations of the parties (especially to determine whether a breach has occurred).

receiver   A person appointed and supervised by the court to temporarily manage a business or other assets for the benefit of creditors or others who ultimately may be entitled to the assets. The business or other property is said to be placed in *receivership.*

recording   The filing of a document with a proper public official, which serves as notice to the public of a person's interest.

redemption   The exercise of the right to buy back or reclaim property upon the performance of a specified act.

registration statement   A document setting forth

certain corporate financial and ownership data, including a prospectus, that is generally required by the SEC to be filed with it before the corporation can offer its securities for sale.

regulatory law Essentially, the state and federal rules emanating from Congress, state legislatures, and administrative bodies that impose duties and restrictions upon business firms.

rejection In contract law, a refusal by the offeree of proposal or offer of the offeror, such refusal being known to the offeror.

release The voluntary relinquishing of a right, lien, interest, or any other obligation.

relevant market In antitrust law, the geographic area and/or product or products determined by a court or government agency to measure whether an antitrust violation has taken place.

remand To send back a case from an appellate court to the lower court with instructions (usually to hold a new trial).

remedy Generally, the means by which a right is enforced or a wrong is prevented; in a narrower sense, a court order addressed to the defendant, in proper circumstances, requiring the defendant to do a particular act requested by plaintiff (e.g., payment of damages) or to refrain from a particular act (e.g., prohibition of specified conduct on the part of defendant by the issuance of an injunction).

renunciation In commercial paper, the action of a holder who gives up his or her rights against a party to an instrument either by giving a signed writing or by surrendering the instrument to that party.

reorganization case A procedure under Chapter 11 of the Bankruptcy Act which reorganizes a company and restructures its debt in order to allow for the continuance of a business.

replevin A legal remedy that permits recovery of possession of chattels (personal property).

repossession The taking back or regaining of possession of property, usually on the default of a debtor. Repossession can take place peaceably (without breach of the peace) or by judicial process.

requirements contract An enforceable agreement for a supply of goods, the exact amount of which is not set or known at the time of the agreement but which is intended to satisfy the needs of a buyer during the term of the contract; a contract in which the seller agrees to sell and the buyer agrees to buy all (or up to a stated amount) of the goods that the buyer needs.

res In law a thing or things; property (corpus) made subject to a trust.

rescission In contract law, the cancellation of a contract by a court, the effect being as if the contract had never been made.

reserved powers The constitutional rights of states to pass laws under powers that are not specifically delegated to the federal government.

respondeat superior The doctrine under which a master or employer can be held liable for the actions of his or her subordinate.

restraint of trade Any contract, agreement, or combination which eliminates or restricts competition (usually held to be against public policy and therefore illegal).

restrictive indorsement An indorsement that either is conditional or purports to prohibit the further transfer of an instrument, or an indorsement that states a particular purpose to be fulfilled before the restrictive indorser can be held liable on the instrument.

resulting trust A trust created by law, when none was intended, to carry out the intentions of the parties to a transaction where one of the parties is guilty of wrongdoing.

reversion A future right to possession kept by a person who has transferred land; an example is the landlord's right to possession after termination of a lease.

revocation In contract law, the withdrawing of an offer by the offeror.

risk of loss The financial burden for damage or destruction of property.

Robinson-Patman Act A 1936 congressional enactment that substantially amended Section 2 of the Clayton Act, basically making it illegal for a seller in interstate commerce to so discriminate in price that the likely result would be competitive injury.

rule-making power The statutory right of an administrative agency to issue rules and regulations governing both the conduct and the activities of those within the agency's jurisdiction (referred to as an agency's *quasi-legislative function*).

sale Passage of a title from a seller to a buyer for a price.

sale of control A transfer by sale of a sufficient number of a corporation's shares of stock to allow the purchaser to control the corporation.

sale on approval A bailment of goods coupled with an offer to sell the goods to the bailee.

sale or return A sale of goods with possession and title passing to the buyer but with the buyer given the right, by agreement, to retransfer both possession and title to the seller without liability for doing so.

sanction A penalty used as a means of coercing obedience with the law or with rules and regulations.

scienter The intent to deceive, manipulate, or defraud.

scope of employment The range of activities of a servant for which the master is liable to third persons. These actions may be expressly directed by the master or incidental to or foreseeable in the performance of employment duties.

secondary party The drawer or indorser of an instrument.

secured party The lender, seller, or other person in whose favor there is a security interest.

securities In securities regulation law, primarily stocks and bonds; also includes such items as debentures, investment contracts, and certificates of interest or participation in profit-sharing agreements.

Securities Act of 1933 A federal statute establishing requirements for the registration of securities sold in interstate commerce or through the mails (prior to sale). The statute basically requires that pertinent financial information be disclosed to both the Securities and Exchange Commission and to the prospective purchaser. A misleading failure to make such disclosure renders directors, officers, accountants, and underwriters severally and jointly liable.

Securities and Exchange Commission A federal agency given the responsibility to administer and enforce federal securities laws.

Securities Exchange Act of 1934 A federal statute designed to strengthen the Securities Act of 1933 and expand regulation in the securities business. This act deals with regulation of national stock exchanges and over-the-counter markets. Numerous provisions were enacted to prevent unfair practices in trading of stock, to control bank credit used for speculation, to compel publicity as to the affairs of corporations listed on these exchanges, and to prohibit the use of inside information. This act created the Securities and Exchange Commission (SEC).

security agreement The contractual arrangement made between a debtor and a secured party.

security interest The right or interest in property held by a secured party to guarantee the payment or performance of an obligation.

separation of powers The result of the U.S. Constitution, which created and balanced the powers of three branches of government (executive, legislative, and judicial) by giving each separate duties and jurisdictions.

servant In employment law, one who performs physical tasks or activities for and under the control of a master (sometimes designated an *employee* of the master).

servient estate The land that gives up or is subject to an easement.

settlor The party who establishes a trust by transferring property to a trustee to be managed for the benefit of another.

severable In contract law, the portion of a contract that, in the eyes of the law, is capable of possessing an independent legal existence separate from other parts of the same contract. Thus certain obligations of a severable contract may be construed as legally valid even though a clause or part of the contract purporting to create other obligations is declared illegal.

shareholder The owner of one or more shares of capital stock in a corporation.

shareholder agreement A binding agreement made prior to a meeting by a group of shareholders as to the manner in which they will cast their votes on certain issues.

shares of capital stock Instruments in the form of equity securities representing an ownership interest in a corporation.

shelf registration   A SEC rule which allows a company to file one registration statement for the future sale of securities and, thus, enables the company to react quickly to favorable market conditions and raise capital on short notice.

Sherman Antitrust Act   An 1890 congressional enactment that (1) made illegal every contract, combination in the form of trust or otherwise, or conspiracy in restraint of trade or commerce among the several states, and (2) made it illegal for any person to monopolize, or attempt to monopolize, or combine or conspire with any other person or persons to monopolize any part of the trade or commerce among the several states.

shipment contract   In sales law, a contract whereby the seller is authorized or required to ship goods to the buyer by delivery to a carrier.

short-swing profits   In securities law, any profits made on a sale and purchase or purchase and sale of securities where both took place within a six-month period.

sight draft   A draft payable on demand; that is, upon presentment to the drawee.

slander   Oral defamation of one's character or reputation.

sole proprietorship   A person engaged in business for himself or herself without creating any form of business organization.

sovereign immunity   The doctrine that bars a person from suing a government body without its consent.

special indorsement   An indorsement that specifies the person to whom or to whose order the instrument is payable and that requires a proper indorsement of the indorsee for further negotiation.

special warranty deed   A deed containing a warranty by the grantor that the title being conveyed has not been impaired by the grantor's own act; in other words, the grantor's liability is limited to his or her own actions.

specific performance   A decree issued by a court of equity that compels a person to perform his or her part of the contract where damages are inadequate as a remedy and the subject matter of the contract is unique.

spendthrift trust   A provision in a private, express trust to prevent the beneficiary from squandering the principal or income of the trust.

stale check   Any noncertified check which is over six months old.

standing   The right to sue.

stare decisis   Literally "stand by the decision"—a principle by which once a decision has been made by a court, it serves as a precedent or a basis for future decisions of similar cases.

statute of frauds   The requirement that certain types of contracts be in writing (or that there be written evidence of the existence of the oral contract) in order for the contract to be enforceable in a lawsuit.

statute of limitations   A law that sets forth a maximum time period, from the happening of an event, for a legal action to be properly filed in or taken to court. The statute bars the use of the courts for recovery if such action is not filed during the specified time.

statutes of descent and distribution   State laws that specify to whom and in what proportions the estate of an intestate decedent will be distributed.

statutory law   Enforceable rules enacted by a legislative body.

stock   Equity securities that evidence an ownership interest in a corporation; shares of ownership in a corporation.

stock certificate   A formal document that provides evidence of the ownership of particular shares of stock.

stock dividend   A dividend which consists of the issuance of additional shares of the corporation's own stock to be given to the current shareholders.

stock subscription   An offer by a prospective investor to buy shares in a corporation.

stop payment order   A bank customer's direction (order) to his or her bank to refuse to honor (pay) a check drawn by him or her upon presentment.

strict liability   A legal theory under which a person can be held liable for damage or injury even if not at fault or negligent. Basically, any seller of a defective product that is unreasonably dangerous is liable for any damage or injury caused by the product, provided that the seller is a merchant and the product has not been modified or substantially changed since leaving the seller's possession. This rule applies even if there is no sale of the product and even if the seller exercised due care.

strike A cessation of work by employees for the purpose of coercing their employer to accede to some demand. A strike is legal only if it consists of a complete work stoppage by a participating majority of employees for a legally recognized labor objective.

Subchapter S corporation A corporation with only one class of stock held by thirty-five or fewer individual stockholders who all agree in writing that the corporation will be taxed in the same manner as a partnership.

sublease The transfer by the lessee (tenant) of a portion of the leasehold to a third party, as compared to an assignment of a lease, where the lessee transfers the entire unexpired term of the leasehold to a third party.

subrogation The substitution of one person in another's place, allowing the party substituted the same rights and claims as the party being substituted.

subsidiary corporation A corporation that is controlled by another corporation (called a *parent corporation*) through the ownership of a controlling amount of voting stock.

substantial performance The doctrine that a person who performs his or her contract in all major respects and in good faith, with only slight deviation, has adequately performed the contract and can therefore recover the contract price less any damages resulting from the slight deviation.

substantive due process The constitutional requirement that government action must be fair and reasonable in substance.

substantive law The basic rights and duties of parties as provided for in any field of law, as opposed to procedural law, under which these rights and duties are determined in a lawsuit.

subsurface rights The right of a landowner to use or own minerals, oil, gas, and the like beneath the land's surface.

summary judgment A court's judgment for one party in a lawsuit, before trial, on the ground that there are no disputed issues of fact which would nec-

essitate a trial. The court's conclusion is based upon the motion of that party, the pleadings, affidavits, depositions, and other documentary evidence.

summons A writ by a court that is served on the defendant, notifying that person of the cause of action claimed by the plaintiff and of the requirement to answer.

surety A person or business entity that insures or guarantees the debt of another by becoming legally liable for the debt upon default.

symbolic delivery The delivery of something that represents ownership of or control over an item of property in a case where actual physical delivery of the property itself is not feasible because of its bulk or because it is intangible (often referred to as constructive delivery).

syndicate An association or combination of individual investors formed primarily for a particular financial transaction.

Taft-Hartley Act A 1947 congressional amendment of the 1935 NLRA which (1) prohibited certain "unfair labor practices" by unions, (2) outlawed closed shop agreements, (3) established the Federal Mediation and Conciliation Service for the purpose of assisting employers and unions in reaching compromises, (4) granted employers and unions the power to file lawsuits to enforce collective bargaining agreements, and (5) gave the president authority to intervene in industry-wide disputes when, in the president's opinion, the occurrence or continuance of the dispute would "imperil the national health or safety." This act is also known as the Labor-Management Relations Act.

tellers Impartial individuals used to supervise an election (sometimes referred to as judges or inspectors).

tenancy at sufferance The interest held by a tenant who remains on the land beyond the period of his or her rightful tenancy and without permission of the landlord.

tenancy at will The interest created by a lease for an indefinite duration that either party can terminate at any time.

tenancy by the entirety A joint tenancy between husband and wife. In some states neither of the spouses can convey their interest without the consent of the other.

tenancy for years The interest created by a lease for a specific period of time.

tenancy in common A co-ownership of property by two or more parties in which each owns an undivided interest that passes to his or her heirs at death.

tenants in partnership The legal interest of partners in partnership property.

tender An offer by a contracting party to pay money, or deliver goods, or perform any other act required of him or her under the contract.

tender of delivery In sales law, where the seller places or holds conforming goods at the buyer's disposition and gives the buyer notification sufficient to enable that person to take possession of the goods.

tender offer In securities regulation law, an offer to buy a certain amount of a corporation's stock at a specified price per share; usually made with the intention of obtaining the controlling interest in the corporation.

tenor In commercial paper, the exact copy of an instrument. If the amount of an instrument has been altered, the holder in due course can recover only the original amount on the instrument, called the original tenor.

termination The ending of an offer, contract, or legal relationship (usually an ending without liability).

term insurance Life insurance which is effective only for a specified period of time, and which does not build up a cash surrender value or include a borrowing privilege.

testamentary capacity The state of mind of a testator in knowing what property is owned and how he or she wants to dispose of it.

testamentary trust A trust created by the settlor's will, to be effective on his or her death.

testate The situation in which a person dies leaving a valid will.

testator (female, testatrix) A person who makes a will.

textual context The court's reading of a statute in its entirety rather than a single section or part; a principle of statutory interpretation.

time instrument An instrument which is payable at a specific future date.

time is of the essence In contract law, a phrase in a contract that requires performance within a specified time as a condition precedent to liability.

title A person's right of ownership in property. The extent of this right is dependent on the type of title held.

title examination The buyer's investigation of a seller's title to real property.

title insurance A policy issued by an insurance company to compensate a buyer of real property for any loss he or she will suffer if the title proves to be defective.

title warranty In sales law, an assurance or guarantee given by the seller, expressly or impliedly, to the buyer that he or she has good title and the right to transfer that title, and that the goods are free from undisclosed security interests.

tort A noncontractual wrong committed by one against another. To be considered a tort, the wrong must be a breach of a legal duty directly resulting in harm.

tortfeasor A person who commits a noncontractual wrong (sometimes referred to as a *wrongdoer*).

tort of conversion One's unlawful interference with the right of another to possess or use his or her personal property.

trade acceptance A draft or bill of exchange drawn by a seller of goods on the purchaser and obligating the purchaser to pay the instrument upon acceptance.

trade fixture A piece of personal property affixed by a tenant to the real property that is necessary for carrying on the tenant's business.

trademark A distinctive mark, sign, or motto that a business can reserve by law for its exclusive use in identifying itself or its product.

trade secret Valuable, confidential data or know-how developed and possessed by a business firm; can be legally protected.

trading partnership A partnership formed primarily for the purpose of buying and selling commodities.

transferee   A person to whom a transfer is made.

transferor   A person who makes a transfer.

treasury stock   Shares of stock that were originally issued by a corporation and that subsequently were reacquired by it.

trespass   In realty and personalty, the wrongful invasion of the property rights of another.

trust   Two or more companies that have a monopoly. In the law of property, a relationship whereby a settlor transfers legal ownership of property to a trustee to be held and managed for a beneficiary who has equitable title to the property.

trustee   One who administers a trust.

trustee in bankruptcy   A person elected or appointed to administer the estate of the bankrupt person.

trust indorsement   A restrictive indorsement that by its terms shows an intent to benefit the indorser or some third party.

tying agreement   Any arrangement in which one party agrees to supply a product or service only on the condition that the customer also take another product or service. Such activity is scrutinized under Section 1 of the Sherman Act and Section 3 of the Clayton Act.

ultra vires   Any acts or actions of a corporation that are held to be unauthorized and beyond the scope of the corporate business as determined by law or by the articles of incorporation.

unconscionable contract   A contract or a clause within a contract which is so grossly unfair that a court will refuse to enforce it.

underwriter   The person or entity who markets a security offering from the issuer to dealers; analogous to a wholesaler.

undisclosed principal   In agency law, a principal whose identity and existence are unknown by third parties, leading them to believe that the agent is acting solely for himself or herself.

undue influence   The overcoming of a person's free will by misusing a position of confidence or relationship, thereby taking advantage of that person to affect his or her decisions or actions.

unenforceable contract   Generally a valid contract that cannot be enforced in a court of law because of a special rule of law or a failure to meet an additional legal requirement (such as a writing).

unfair labor practices   Certain practices, including employer domination of unions, interference with employee organizing, discrimination against union members, and refusal to bargain collectively, which were prohibited by the National Labor Relations Act (NLRA).

Uniform Commercial Code (UCC)   Uniform rules dealing with the sale of goods, commercial paper, secured transactions in personal property, and certain aspects of banking, documents of title, and investment securities. Recommended by the National Conference of Commissioners on Uniform State Laws for enactment by the various states, it has been adopted by forty-nine states (and Louisiana has adopted parts of it).

Uniform Limited Partnership Act (ULPA)   Uniform rules governing the organization and operation of limited partnerships recommended by the National Conference of Commissioners on Uniform State Laws for enactment by the various states. The ULPA was substantially modified in 1976 by the Revised Uniform Limited Partnership Act (RULPA).

Uniform Partnership Act (UPA)   Uniform rules governing the partnership operation, particularly in the absence of an agreement, recommended by the National Conference of Commissioners on Uniform State Laws for enactment by the various states.

unilateral contract   An offer or promise of the offeror which can become binding only by the completed performance of the offeree; an act for a promise, whereby the offeree's act is not only his or her acceptance but also the completed performance under the contract.

unilateral mistake   A mistake in which only one party to a contract is in error as to the terms or performance expected under the contract.

universal defenses   See *real defenses*.

unliquidated debt   A disputed debt; a debt about which there is a reasonable basis for dispute as to its existence or amount.

unqualified indorsement   A special or blank indorsement that guarantees payment upon proper presentment, dishonor, and notice of dishonor.

unqualified indorser   An indorser who guarantees that no defense of any party is good against him or her.

usage of trade   Any practice or method repeated with such regularity in a vocation or business that it becomes the legal basis for expected performance in future events within that vocation or business.

usury   An interest charge exceeding the maximum amount permitted by statute.

U.S. Code   The full and complete compilation of all federal statutes.

Utilitarianism   An ethical theory that is committed solely to the purpose of promoting "the greatest good for the greatest number."

valid contract   A contract that meets the four basic requirements for enforceability by the parties to it.

venue   A designation of the right of the defendant to be tried in a proper court within a specific geographic area.

vertical merger   A merger of two firms, one of which is a supplier or customer of the other.

vertical price fixing   Price fixing between supplier and customer, relating to the price at which the customer will resell. *Per se* illegal under Section 1 of the Sherman Act.

vicarious liability   The liability of a person, not himself or herself at fault, for the actions of others.

voidable contract   A contract from which one or both parties can, if they choose, legally withdraw without liability.

voidable transfer   In bankruptcy law, a transfer by a bankrupt debtor that can be set aside by a trustee in bankruptcy.

void contract   A contract without legal effect.

voir dire   The examination of prospective jurors by lawyers in a particular case to determine their fitness (i.e., to discover whether they have an interest in the outcome of the suit, a bias or prejudice against a party, or are otherwise unlikely to exercise the objectivity necessary in jury deliberations).

voluntary case   Under the Bankruptcy Act, a proceeding that is instituted by the debtor, not the creditors.

voting trust   A trust whereby shareholders transfer their shares of stock to a trustee for the sole purpose of voting those shares. The shareholders, through trust certificates, retain all other rights as they pertain to the transferred shares.

wagering agreement   Any agreement, bet, or lottery arrangement the performance of which is dependent primarily upon chance, such agreement usually being prohibited by statute. These agreements are in contrast to risk-shifting (insurance) contracts and speculative bargaining (commodity market) transactions, which are usually legal by statute.

waiver   The voluntary giving up of a legal right.

warehouseman   A person engaged in the business of storing the property of others for compensation.

warehouse receipt   A document of title issued by a person engaged in the business of storing goods for hire and containing the terms of the storage agreement. A negotiable warehouse receipt acts as both receipt and evidence of title to the goods stored.

warranty   An assurance or guaranty, expressly or impliedly made, that certain actions or rights can take place, that information given is correct, or that performance will conform to certain standards.

warranty deed   A deed with covenants, express or implied, that the title to real property is good and complete.

warranty of fitness for a particular purpose   In sales law, an implied warranty imposed by law on a seller, who has reason to know of the buyer's intended use of the goods (where the buyer relies on the seller's skill and judgment), that the goods are suitable for the buyer's intended use.

warranty of merchantability   In sales law, an implied warranty imposed by law upon a merchant seller of goods that the goods are fit for the ordinary purposes for which goods of that kind are used.

waste   A term used to describe a tenant's duty not to damage a landlord's reversionary interest.

watered stock   Shares of stock issued by a corporation for a consideration less than the par value or stated value of the stock.

whole life insurance   Life insurance which continues in effect during the entire life of the insured; this type of life insurance also builds up a cash surrender value over time, and often includes the privilege of borrowing money from the insurance company.

will A document by which a person directs the disposition of his or her property (estate) upon his or her death.

winding up The actual process of settling the affairs of a partnership or corporation after dissolution.

workers' compensation laws State statutory provisions calling for payments to employees for accidental injuries or diseases arising out of and in the course of employment. These payments, for medical expenses and lost income, are made regardless of whether anyone is at fault.

writ of certiorari What the appellant seeks by application to a higher court. An order issued by an appellate court directing a lower court to remit to it the record and proceedings of a particular case so that the actions of the lower court may be reviewed.

writ of execution In a civil lawsuit in which the plaintiff has won, a court order directing an enforcement agent to sell the defendant's nonexempt property in order to pay the judgment against him or her.

Case Index*

*Cases appearing in boldface are excerpted in the text.

Subject Index